NCAA BASKETBALL

THE OFFICIAL 1997 MEN'S COLLEGE BASKETBALL RECORDS BOOK

NATIONAL COLLEGIATE ATHLETIC ASSOCIATION

THE NATIONAL COLLEGIATE ATHLETIC ASSOCIATION
6201 College Boulevard, Overland Park, Kansas 66211-2422
913/339-1906
http://www.ncaa.org

November 1996

Compiled By:
Gary K. Johnson, *Statistics Coordinator.*
Richard M. Campbell, *Statistics Coordinator.*
John D. Painter, *Statistics Coordinator.*
Sean W. Straziscar, *Statistics Coordinator.*
James F. Wright, *Director of Statistics.*

Edited By:
Laurie Bollig, *Publications Editor.*

Production By:
Lee Newman, *Publishing Production Manager.*

Design By:
Teri Wolfgang, *Graphic Designer.*

Cover Design By:
Wayne Davis, *Graphic Designer.*

Cover Photograph By:
Hank Young/Young Company.

Distributed to sports information directors and conference publicity directors.

Contents

NAME CHANGE KEY

The following players changed their names after their collegiate careers ended. They are listed throughout the book by the names they played under in college (those listed at the left). Their current names are listed below. In addition, various schools have experienced name changes during their histories and the current school name is listed along with other names by which the schools have been referred.

PLAYER name changes

Name as a collegian:	Changed to:
Lew Alcindor (UCLA)	Kareem Abdul-Jabbar
Walt Hazzard (UCLA)	Mahdi Abdul-Rahman
Chris Jackson (LSU)	Mahmoud Abdul-Rauf
Akeem Olajuwon (Houston)	Hakeem Olajuwon
Keith Wilkes (UCLA)	Jamaal Wilkes

SCHOOL name changes

Current school name:	Changed from:
UAB	Ala.-Birmingham
Alcorn St.	Alcorn A&M
Ark.-Pine Bluff	Arkansas AM&N
Armstrong Atlantic	Armstrong St.
Auburn	Alabama Poly
Augusta St.	Augusta
Bemidji St.	Bemidji Teachers
Benedictine (Ill.)	Ill. Benedictine
Central Fla.	Florida Tech
Central Okla.	Central St. (Okla.)
Charleston So.	Baptist (S.C.)
Charleston (W.Va.)	Morris Harvey
Colorado St.	Colorado A&M
Columbus St.	Columbus
Concordia (Ill.)	Concordia Teachers
Detroit	Detroit Mercy; Detroit Tech
Dist. of Columbia	D.C. Teachers; Federal City
Drexel	Drexel Tech
Fresno St.	Fresno Pacific
Hawthorne	Nathaniel Hawthorne
Ill.-Chicago	Ill.-Chicago Circle
Illinois St.	Illinois St. Normal
Indianapolis	Indiana Central
James Madison	Madison
Kent	Kent St.
Lamar	Lamar Tech
Lyon	Arkansas College
Mankato St.	Mankato Teachers
Maritime (N.Y.)	N.Y. Maritime
Martin Luther	Northwestern (Wis.)
Mass.-Dartmouth	Southeastern Mass.
Mass.-Lowell	Lowell; Lowell St.; Lowell Tech
Memphis	Memphis St.
Merchant Marine	King's Point
Metro St.	Metropolitan St.
Mont. St.-Billings	Eastern Montana
Moorhead St.	Moorhead Teachers
Murray St.	Murray Teachers
Neb.-Kearney	Kearney St.
UNLV	Nevada Southern
New England U.	St. Francis (Me.)
Col. of New Jersey	Trenton St.
New Jersey Tech	Newark Engineering
New Mexico St.	New Mexico A&M
New Orleans	Louisiana St. (N.O.)
N.C.-Pembroke	Pembroke St.
North Texas	North Tex. St.
Northern Ariz.	Arizona St.-Flagstaff; Flagstaff Teachers
Northern Colo.	Colorado St. College
Oklahoma St.	Oklahoma A&M
Old Dominion	William & Mary (Norfolk)
Polytechnic (N.Y.)	New York Poly; Brooklyn Poly
Rhodes	Southwestern (Tenn.)
Rice	Rice Institute
Richard Stockton	Stockton St.
Rowan	Glassboro St.
Southern U.	Southern-B.R.
Southern Ind.	Indiana St.-Evansville
Southern Me.	Maine Portland-Gorham; Gorham St. (Me.)
Tennessee St.	Tennessee A&I
Tex. A&M-Commerce	East Tex. St.
Tex. A&M-Kingsville	Texas A&I
Tex.-Pan American	Pan American
Truman St.	Northeast Mo. St.
UTEP	Texas Western
VMI	Va. Military
West Ala.	Livingston
West Texas A&M	West Texas St.
Western Ore.	Oregon Tech
Western St.	Colo. Western
Widener	Pennsylvania Military College
Wm. Paterson	Paterson St.
Wis.-Eau Claire	Eau Claire Teachers
Wis.-La Crosse	La Crosse Teachers
Wis.-River Falls	River Falls Teachers

SCHOOLS also known as

Current school name:	Also known as:
Baruch	Bernard M. Baruch
Lehman	Herbert H. Lehman
Merchant Marine	King's Point

Division I Records

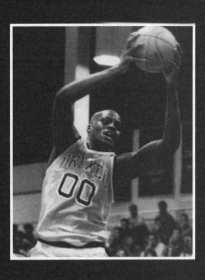

Individual Records

Basketball records are confined to the "modern era," which began with the 1937-38 season, the first without the center jump after each goal scored. Except for the school's all-time won-lost record or coaches' records, only statistics achieved while an institution was an active member of the NCAA are included in team or individual categories. Official weekly statistics rankings in scoring and shooting began with the 1947-48 season; individual rebounds were added for the 1950-51 season, although team rebounds were not added until 1954-55. Assists were added in 1983-84, blocked shots and steals were added in 1985-86 and three-point field goals were added in 1986-87. Scoring, rebounding, assists, blocked shots and steals are ranked on total number and on per-game average; shooting, on percentage. In statistical rankings, the rounding of percentages and/or averages may indicate ties where none exist. In these cases, the numerical order of the rankings is accurate. In 1973, freshmen became eligible to compete on the varsity level.

Scoring

POINTS
Game
100—Frank Selvy, Furman vs. Newberry, Feb. 13, 1954 (41 FGs, 18 FTs)
Season
1,381—Pete Maravich, LSU, 1970 (522 FGs, 337 FTs, 31 games)
Career
3,667—Pete Maravich, LSU, 1968-70 (1,387 FGs, 893 FTs, 83 games)

POINTS VS. DIVISION I OPPONENT
Game
72—Kevin Bradshaw, U.S. Int'l vs. Loyola Marymount, Jan. 5, 1991

AVERAGE PER GAME
Season
44.5—Pete Maravich, LSU, 1970 (1,381 in 31)
Career
44.2—Pete Maravich, LSU, 1968-70 (3,667 in 83)

MOST COMBINED POINTS, TWO TEAMMATES
Game
125—Frank Selvy (100) and Darrell Floyd (25), Furman vs. Newberry, Feb. 13, 1954

MOST COMBINED POINTS, TWO TEAMMATES VS. DIVISION I OPPONENT
Game
92—Kevin Bradshaw (72) and Isaac Brown (20), U.S. Int'l vs. Loyola Marymount, Jan. 5, 1991

MOST COMBINED POINTS, TWO OPPOSING PLAYERS ON DIVISION I TEAMS
Game
115—Pete Maravich (64), LSU and Dan Issel (51), Kentucky, Feb. 21, 1970

GAMES SCORING AT LEAST 50 POINTS
Season
10—Pete Maravich, LSU, 1970
Season—Consecutive Games
3—Pete Maravich, LSU, Feb. 10 to Feb. 15, 1969
Career
28—Pete Maravich, LSU, 1968-70

MOST GAMES SCORING AT LEAST 40 POINTS
Career
56—Pete Maravich, LSU, 1968-70

MOST GAMES SCORING IN DOUBLE FIGURES
Career
132—Danny Manning, Kansas, 1985-88

CONSECUTIVE GAMES SCORING IN DOUBLE FIGURES
Career
115—Lionel Simmons, La Salle, 1987-90

Field Goals

FIELD GOALS
Game
41—Frank Selvy, Furman vs. Newberry, Feb. 13, 1954 (66 attempts)
Season
522—Pete Maravich, LSU, 1970 (1,168 attempts)
Career
1,387—Pete Maravich, LSU, 1968-70 (3,166 attempts)

CONSECUTIVE FIELD GOALS
Game
16—Doug Grayson, Kent vs. North Caro., Dec. 6, 1967 (18 of 19)
Season
25—Ray Voelkel, American, 1978 (during nine games, Nov. 24-Dec. 16)

FIELD-GOAL ATTEMPTS
Game
71—Jay Handlan, Wash. & Lee vs. Furman, Feb. 17, 1951 (30 made)
Season
1,168—Pete Maravich, LSU, 1970 (522 made)
Career
3,166—Pete Maravich, LSU, 1968-70 (1,387 made)

FIELD-GOAL PERCENTAGE
Game
(Min. 15 made) 100%—Clifford Rozier, Louisville vs. Eastern Ky., Dec. 11, 1993 (15 of 15)
(Min. 20 made) 95.5%—Bill Walton, UCLA vs. Memphis, March 26, 1973 (21 of 22)
*Season
74.6%—Steve Johnson, Oregon St., 1981 (235 of 315)
*Based on qualifiers for national championship.
Career
(Min. 400 made) 69.0%—Ricky Nedd, Appalachian St., 1991-94 (412 of 597)
(Min. 600 made) 67.8%—Steve Johnson, Oregon St., 1976-81 (828 of 1,222)

Three-Point Field Goals

THREE-POINT FIELD GOALS
Game
14—Dave Jamerson, Ohio vs. Charleston (S.C.), Dec. 21, 1989 (17 attempts); Askia Jones, Kansas St. vs. Fresno St., March 24, 1994 (18)
Season
158—Darrin Fitzgerald, Butler, 1987 (362 attempts)
Career
401—Doug Day, Radford, 1990-93 (1,068 attempts)

THREE-POINT FIELD GOALS MADE PER GAME
Season
5.6—Darrin Fitzgerald, Butler, 1987 (158 in 28)
Career
(Min. 200 made) 4.6—Timothy Pollard, Mississippi Val., 1988-89 (256 in 56)

CONSECUTIVE THREE-POINT FIELD GOALS
Game
11—Gary Bossert, Niagara vs. Siena, Jan. 7, 1987
Season
15—Todd Leslie, Northwestern, 1990 (during four games, Dec. 15-28)

CONSECUTIVE GAMES MAKING A THREE-POINT FIELD GOAL
Season
38—Steve Kerr, Arizona, Nov. 27, 1987, to April 2, 1988
Career
73—Wally Lancaster, Virginia Tech, Dec. 30, 1986, to March 4, 1989

THREE-POINT FIELD-GOAL ATTEMPTS
Game
26—Lindsey Hunter, Jackson St. vs. Kansas, Dec. 27, 1992 (11 made)
Season
362—Darrin Fitzgerald, Butler, 1987 (158 made)
Career
1,068—Doug Day, Radford, 1990-93 (401 made)

THREE-POINT FIELD-GOAL ATTEMPTS PER GAME
Season
12.9—Darrin Fitzgerald, Butler, 1987 (362 in 28)
Career
7.8—Wally Lancaster, Virginia Tech, 1987-89 (694 in 89)

THREE-POINT FIELD-GOAL PERCENTAGE
Game
(Min. 8 made) 100%—Tomas Thompson, San Francisco vs. Loyola Marymount, March 7, 1992 (8 of 8); Shawn Haughn, Dayton vs. St. Louis, Feb. 13, 1994 (8 of 8)
(Min. 12 made) 85.7%—Gary Bossert, Niagara vs. Siena, Jan. 7, 1987 (12 of 14)
Season
(Min. 50 made) 63.4%—Glenn Tropf, Holy Cross, 1988 (52 of 82)
(Min. 100 made) 57.3%—Steve Kerr, Arizona, 1988 (114 of 199)
Career
(Min. 200 made) 49.7%—Tony Bennett, Wis.-Green Bay, 1989-92 (290 of 584)
(Min. 300 made) 45.5%—Shawn Respert, Michigan St., 1992-95 (331 of 728)

Free Throws

FREE THROWS
Game
30—Pete Maravich, LSU vs. Oregon St., Dec. 22, 1969 (31 attempts)
Season
355—Frank Selvy, Furman, 1954 (444 attempts)
Career
(3 yrs.) 893—Pete Maravich, LSU, 1968-70 (1,152 attempts)
(4 yrs.) 905—Dickie Hemric, Wake Forest, 1952-55 (1,359 attempts)

CONSECUTIVE FREE THROWS
Game
24—Arlen Clark, Oklahoma St. vs. Colorado, March 7, 1959 (24 of 24)
Season
64—Joe Dykstra, Western Ill., 1981-82 (during eight games, Dec. 1-Jan. 4)
Career
64—Joe Dykstra, Western Ill., 1981-82 (during eight games, Dec. 1-Jan. 4)

FREE-THROW ATTEMPTS
Game
36—Ed Tooley, Brown vs. Amherst, Dec. 4, 1954 (23 made)
Season
444—Frank Selvy, Furman, 1954 (355 made)
Career
(3 yrs.) 1,152—Pete Maravich, LSU, 1968-70 (893 made)
(4 yrs.) 1,359—Dickie Hemric, Wake Forest, 1952-55 (905 made)

FREE-THROW PERCENTAGE
Game
(Min. 24 made) 100%—Arlen Clark, Oklahoma St. vs. Colorado, March 7, 1959 (24 of 24)
*Season
95.9%—Craig Collins, Penn St., 1985 (94 of 98)
*Based on qualifiers for national championship.
Career
(Min. 300 made) 90.9%—Greg Starrick, Kentucky and Southern Ill., 1969, 1970-72 (341 of 375)
(Min. 600 made) 88.5%—Ron Perry, Holy Cross, 1976-80 (680 of 768)
(Min. 2.5 made per game) 92.3%—Dave Hildahl, Portland St., 1979-81 (131 of 142)

Rebounds

REBOUNDS
Game
51—Bill Chambers, William & Mary vs. Virginia, Feb. 14, 1953
Season
734—Walt Dukes, Seton Hall, 1953 (33 games)
(Since 1973) 597—Marvin Barnes, Providence, 1974 (32 games)
Career
(3 yrs.) 1,751—Paul Silas, Creighton, 1962-64 (81 games)
(4 yrs.) 2,201—Tom Gola, La Salle, 1952-55 (118 games)
(Since 1973) 1,537—Derrick Coleman, Syracuse, 1987-90 (143 games)

AVERAGE PER GAME
Season
25.6—Charlie Slack, Marshall, 1955 (538 in 21)
(Since 1973) 20.4—Kermit Washington, American, 1973 (511 in 25)
Career
(Min. 800) 22.7—Artis Gilmore, Jacksonville, 1970-71 (1,224 in 54)
(Since 1973) 15.2—Glenn Mosley, Seton Hall, 1974-77 (1,263 in 83)

Assists

ASSISTS
Game
22—Tony Fairley, Charleston So. vs. Armstrong Atlantic, Feb. 9, 1987; Avery Johnson, Southern U. vs. Texas Southern, Jan. 25, 1988; Sherman Douglas, Syracuse vs. Providence, Jan. 28, 1989
Season
406—Mark Wade, UNLV, 1987 (38 games)
Career
1,076—Bobby Hurley, Duke, 1990-93 (140 games)

AVERAGE PER GAME
Season
13.3—Avery Johnson, Southern U., 1988 (399 in 30)
Career
8.9—Avery Johnson, Cameron and Southern U., 1985 and 1987-88 (838 in 94)

Blocked Shots

BLOCKED SHOTS
Game
14—David Robinson, Navy vs. N.C.-Wilmington, Jan. 4, 1986; Shawn Bradley, Brigham Young vs. Eastern Ky., Dec. 7, 1990; Roy Rogers, Alabama vs. Georgia, Feb. 10, 1996
Season
207—David Robinson, Navy, 1986 (35 games)
Career
453—Alonzo Mourning, Georgetown, 1989-92 (120 games)

AVERAGE PER GAME
Season
6.4—Keith Closs, Central Conn. St., 1996 (178 in 28)
Career
(Min. 225) 5.2—David Robinson, Navy, 1986-87 (351 in 67)

Steals

STEALS
Game
13—Mookie Blaylock, Oklahoma vs. Centenary (La.), Dec. 12, 1987; and vs. Loyola Marymount, Dec. 17, 1988
Season
150—Mookie Blaylock, Oklahoma, 1988 (39 games)

Career
376—Eric Murdock, Providence, 1988-91 (117 games)

AVERAGE PER GAME
Season
5.0—Darron Brittman, Chicago St., 1986 (139 in 28)
Career
(Min. 225) 3.8—Mookie Blaylock, Oklahoma, 1988-89 (281 in 74)
(Min. 300) 3.2—Eric Murdock, Providence, 1988-91 (376 in 117)

Fouls

SHORTEST PLAYING TIME BEFORE BEING DISQUALIFIED
Game
1:38—Mike Pflugner, Butler vs. Ill.-Chicago, March 2, 1996

Games

GAMES PLAYED (Since 1947-48)
Season
40—Mark Alarie, Tommy Amaker, Johnny Dawkins, Danny Ferry and Billy King, Duke, 1986; Larry Johnson, UNLV, 1990
Career
148—Christian Laettner, Duke, 1989-92

General

AVERAGING 20 POINTS AND 20 REBOUNDS
Career
Walt Dukes, Seton Hall, 1952-53 (23.5 points and 21.1 rebounds)
Bill Russell, San Francisco, 1954-56 (20.7 points and 20.3 rebounds)
Paul Silas, Creighton, 1962-64 (20.5 points and 21.6 rebounds)
Julius Erving, Massachusetts, 1970-71 (26.3 points and 20.2 rebounds)
Artis Gilmore, Jacksonville, 1970-71 (24.3 points and 22.7 rebounds)
Kermit Washington, American, 1971-73 (20.1 points and 20.2 rebounds)

Team Records

Note: Where records involve both teams, each team must be an NCAA Division I member institution.

SINGLE-GAME RECORDS

Scoring

MOST POINTS
186—Loyola Marymount vs. U.S. Int'l (140), Jan. 5, 1991

MOST POINTS BY LOSING TEAM
150—U.S. Int'l vs. Loyola Marymount (181), Jan. 31, 1989

MOST POINTS, BOTH TEAMS
331—Loyola Marymount (181) vs. U.S. Int'l (150), Jan. 31, 1989

MOST POINTS IN A HALF
97—Oklahoma vs. U.S. Int'l, Nov. 29, 1989 (1st)

Photo from Alabama sports information

Alabama's Roy Rogers equaled the Division I record for most blocked shots in a game when he knocked away 14 field-goal attempts against Georgia on February 10, 1996.

MOST POINTS IN A HALF, BOTH TEAMS
172—Loyola Marymount (86) vs. Gonzaga (86), Feb. 18, 1989 (2nd)

LARGEST LEAD BEFORE THE OPPONENT SCORES AT THE START OF A GAME
32-0—Connecticut vs. New Hampshire, Dec. 12, 1990

LARGEST DEFICIT OVERCOME TO WIN GAME
32—Duke (74) vs. Tulane (72), Dec. 30, 1950 (trailed 22-54 with 2:00 left in the first half)

LARGEST SECOND-HALF DEFICIT OVERCOME TO WIN GAME
31—Duke (74) vs. Tulane (72), Dec. 30, 1950 (trailed 27-58 with 19:00 left in the second half); Kentucky (99) vs. LSU (95), Feb. 15, 1994 (trailed 37-68 with 15:34 left in the second half)

LARGEST HALF-TIME DEFICIT OVERCOME TO WIN GAME
29—Duke (74) vs. Tulane (72), Dec. 30, 1950 (trailed 27-56 at half time)

LARGEST DEFICIT BEFORE SCORING OVERCOME TO WIN GAME
28—New Mexico St. (117) vs. Bradley (109), Jan. 27, 1977 (trailed 0-28 with 13:49 left in first half)

FEWEST POINTS ALLOWED (Since 1938)
6—Tennessee (11) vs. Temple, Dec. 15, 1973; Kentucky (75) vs. Arkansas St., Jan. 8, 1945

FEWEST POINTS, BOTH TEAMS (Since 1938)
17—Tennessee (11) vs. Temple (6), Dec. 15, 1973

WIDEST MARGIN OF VICTORY
97—Southern U. (154) vs. Patten (57), Nov. 26, 1993

Field Goals

MOST FIELD GOALS
74—Houston vs. Valparaiso, Feb. 24, 1968 (112 attempts)

MOST FIELD GOALS, BOTH TEAMS
130—Loyola Marymount (67) vs. U.S. Int'l (63), Jan. 31, 1989

MOST FIELD GOALS IN A HALF
42—Oklahoma vs. U.S. Int'l, Nov. 29, 1989 (90 attempts) (1st)

MOST FIELD-GOAL ATTEMPTS
147—Oklahoma vs. U.S. Int'l, Nov. 29, 1989 (70 made)

MOST FIELD-GOAL ATTEMPTS, BOTH TEAMS
245—Loyola Marymount (124) vs. U.S. Int'l (121), Jan. 7, 1989

MOST FIELD-GOAL ATTEMPTS IN A HALF
90—Oklahoma vs. U.S. Int'l, Nov. 29, 1989 (42 made) (1st)

FEWEST FIELD GOALS (Since 1938)
2—Duke vs. North Caro. St., March 8, 1968 (11 attempts); Arkansas St. vs. Kentucky, Jan. 8, 1945

FEWEST FIELD-GOAL ATTEMPTS (Since 1938)
9—Pittsburgh vs. Penn St., March 1, 1952 (3 made)

HIGHEST FIELD-GOAL PERCENTAGE
(Min. 15 made) 83.3%—Maryland vs. South Caro., Jan. 9, 1971 (15 of 18)
(Min. 30 made) 81.4%—New Mexico vs. Oregon St., Nov. 30, 1985 (35 of 43)

HIGHEST FIELD-GOAL PERCENTAGE, HALF
94.1%—North Caro. vs. Virginia, Jan. 7, 1978 (16 of 17) (2nd)

Three-Point Field Goals

MOST THREE-POINT FIELD GOALS
28—Troy St. vs. George Mason, Dec. 10, 1994 (74 attempts)

MOST THREE-POINT FIELD GOALS, BOTH TEAMS
44—Troy St. (28) vs. George Mason (16), Dec. 10, 1994

CONSECUTIVE THREE-POINT FIELD GOALS MADE WITHOUT A MISS
11—Niagara vs. Siena, Jan. 7, 1987; Eastern Ky. vs. N.C.-Asheville, Jan. 14, 1987

MOST THREE-POINT FIELD-GOAL ATTEMPTS WITHOUT MAKING ONE
22—Canisius vs. St. Bonaventure, Jan. 21, 1995

HIGHEST NUMBER OF DIFFERENT PLAYERS TO SCORE A THREE-POINT FIELD GOAL, ONE TEAM
9—Dartmouth vs. Boston College, Nov. 30, 1993

MOST THREE-POINT FIELD-GOAL ATTEMPTS
74—Troy St. vs. George Mason, Dec. 10, 1994 (28 made)

MOST THREE-POINT FIELD-GOAL ATTEMPTS, BOTH TEAMS
108—Troy St. (74) vs. George Mason (34), Dec. 10, 1994

HIGHEST THREE-POINT FIELD-GOAL PERCENTAGE
(Min. 10 made) 90.9%—Duke vs. Clemson, Feb. 1, 1988 (10 of 11); Hofstra vs. Rhode Island, Jan. 16, 1993 (10 of 11)
(Min. 15 made) 83.3%—Eastern Ky. vs. N.C.-Asheville, Jan. 14, 1987 (15 of 18)

HIGHEST THREE-POINT FIELD-GOAL PERCENTAGE, BOTH TEAMS
(Min. 10 made) 83.3%—Lafayette (7 of 8) vs. Marist (3 of 4), Dec. 6, 1986 (10 of 12)
(Min. 15 made) 76.2%—Florida (10 of 14) vs. California (6 of 7), Dec. 27, 1986 (16 of 21)
(Min. 20 made) 72.4%—Princeton (12 of 15) vs. Brown (9 of 14), Feb. 20, 1988 (21 of 29)

Free Throws

MOST FREE THROWS
53—Morehead St. vs. Cincinnati, Feb. 11, 1956 (65 attempts); Miami (Ohio) vs. Central Mich., Jan. 29, 1992 (64 attempts)

MOST FREE THROWS, BOTH TEAMS
88—Morehead St. (53) vs. Cincinnati (35), Feb. 11, 1956 (111 attempts)

MOST FREE-THROW ATTEMPTS
79—Northern Ariz. vs. Arizona, Jan. 26, 1953 (46 made)

MOST FREE-THROW ATTEMPTS, BOTH TEAMS
130—Northern Ariz. (79) vs. Arizona (51), Jan. 26, 1953 (78 made)

FEWEST FREE THROWS
0—Many teams

FEWEST FREE-THROW ATTEMPTS
0—Many teams

HIGHEST FREE-THROW PERCENTAGE
(Min. 30 made) 100.0%—UC Irvine vs. Pacific (Cal.), Feb. 21, 1981 (34 of 34); Samford vs. Central Fla., Dec. 20, 1990 (34 of 34)
(Min. 35 made) 97.2%—Vanderbilt vs. Mississippi St., Feb. 26, 1986 (35 of 36); Butler vs. Dayton, Feb. 21, 1991 (35 of 36); Marquette vs. Memphis, Jan. 23, 1993 (35 of 36)
(Min. 40 made) 95.5%—UNLV vs. San Diego St., Dec. 11, 1976 (42 of 44)

HIGHEST FREE-THROW PERCENTAGE, BOTH TEAMS
100%—Purdue (25 of 25) vs. Wisconsin (22 of 22), Feb. 7, 1976 (47 of 47)

Rebounds

MOST REBOUNDS
108—Kentucky vs. Mississippi, Feb. 8, 1964

MOST REBOUNDS, BOTH TEAMS
152—Indiana (95) vs. Michigan (57), March 11, 1961

HIGHEST REBOUND MARGIN
84—Arizona (102) vs. Northern Ariz. (18), Jan. 6, 1951

Assists

MOST ASSISTS (INCLUDING OVERTIMES)
44—Colorado vs. George Mason, Dec. 2, 1995 (ot)

MOST ASSISTS (REGULATION)
41—North Caro. vs. Manhattan, Dec. 27, 1985; Weber St. vs. Northern Ariz., March 2, 1991

MOST ASSISTS, BOTH TEAMS (INCLUDING OVERTIMES)
67—Colorado (44) vs. George Mason (23), Dec. 2, 1995 (ot)

MOST ASSISTS, BOTH TEAMS (REGULATION)
65—Dayton (34) vs. Central Fla. (31), Dec. 3, 1988

Blocked Shots

MOST BLOCKED SHOTS
21—Georgetown vs. Southern (N.O.), Dec. 1, 1993

MOST BLOCKED SHOTS, BOTH TEAMS
29—Rider (17) vs. Fairleigh Dickinson (12), Jan. 9, 1989

Steals

MOST STEALS
34—Oklahoma vs. Centenary (La.), Dec. 12, 1987; Northwestern St. vs. LeTourneau, Jan. 20, 1992

MOST STEALS, BOTH TEAMS
44—Oklahoma (34) vs. Centenary (La.) (10), Dec. 12, 1987

Fouls

MOST FOULS
50—Arizona vs. Northern Ariz., Jan. 26, 1953

MOST FOULS, BOTH TEAMS
84—Arizona (50) vs. Northern Ariz. (34), Jan. 26, 1953

MOST PLAYERS DISQUALIFIED
8—St. Joseph's (Pa.) vs. Xavier (Ohio), Jan. 10, 1976

MOST PLAYERS DISQUALIFIED, BOTH TEAMS
12—UNLV (6) vs. Hawaii (6), Jan. 19, 1979 (ot); Arizona (7) vs. West Tex. A&M (5), Feb. 14, 1952

Overtimes

MOST OVERTIME PERIODS
7—Cincinnati (75) vs. Bradley (73), Dec. 21, 1981

MOST POINTS IN ONE OVERTIME PERIOD
25—Texas A&M vs. North Caro., March 9, 1980; Wis.-Green Bay vs. Cleveland St., Feb. 27, 1988; Old Dominion vs. William & Mary, Feb. 1, 1992

MOST POINTS IN ONE OVERTIME PERIOD, BOTH TEAMS
40—Old Dominion (25) vs. William & Mary (15), Feb. 1, 1992

MOST POINTS IN OVERTIME PERIODS
39—Cleveland St. vs. Kent, Dec. 23, 1993 (4 ot)

MOST POINTS IN OVERTIME PERIODS, BOTH TEAMS
75—Cleveland St. (39) vs. Kent (36), Dec. 23, 1993 (4 ot)

LARGEST WINNING MARGIN IN OVERTIME GAME
18—Nebraska (85) vs. Iowa St. (67), Dec. 30, 1949

SEASON RECORDS

Scoring

MOST POINTS
4,012—Oklahoma, 1988 (39 games)

HIGHEST AVERAGE PER GAME
122.4—Loyola Marymount, 1990 (3,918 in 32)

HIGHEST AVERAGE SCORING MARGIN
30.3—UCLA, 1972 (94.6 offense, 64.3 defense)

MOST GAMES AT LEAST 100 POINTS
28—Loyola Marymount, 1990

MOST CONSECUTIVE GAMES AT LEAST 100 POINTS
12—UNLV, 1977; Loyola Marymount, 1990

Field Goals

MOST FIELD GOALS
1,533—Oklahoma, 1988 (3,094 attempts)

MOST FIELD GOALS PER GAME
46.3—UNLV, 1976 (1,436 in 31)

MOST FIELD-GOAL ATTEMPTS
3,094—Oklahoma, 1988 (1,533 made)

MOST FIELD-GOAL ATTEMPTS PER GAME
98.5—Oral Roberts, 1973 (2,659 in 27)

HIGHEST FIELD-GOAL PERCENTAGE
57.2%—Missouri, 1980 (936 of 1,635)

Three-Point Field Goals

MOST THREE-POINT FIELD GOALS
361—Arkansas, 1995 (917 attempts)

MOST THREE-POINT FIELD GOALS PER GAME
11.1—Troy St., 1996 (300 in 27)

MOST THREE-POINT FIELD-GOAL ATTEMPTS
917—Arkansas, 1995 (361 made)

MOST THREE-POINT FIELD-GOAL ATTEMPTS PER GAME
32.7—Troy St., 1996 (884 in 27)

HIGHEST THREE-POINT FIELD-GOAL PERCENTAGE
(Min. 100 made) 50.8%—Indiana, 1987 (130 of 256)
(Min. 150 made) 50.0%—Mississippi Val., 1987 (161 of 322)
(Min. 200 made) 49.2%—Princeton, 1988 (211 of 429)

CONSECUTIVE GAMES SCORING A THREE-POINT FIELD GOAL (Multiple Seasons)
324—UNLV, Nov. 26, 1986, to present

Free Throws

MOST FREE THROWS
865—Bradley, 1954 (1,263 attempts)

MOST FREE THROWS PER GAME
28.9—Morehead St., 1956 (838 in 29)

MOST CONSECUTIVE FREE THROWS
49—Indiana St., 1991 (during two games, Feb. 13-18)

MOST FREE-THROW ATTEMPTS
1,263—Bradley, 1954 (865 made)

MOST FREE-THROW ATTEMPTS PER GAME
41.0—Bradley, 1953 (1,107 in 27)

HIGHEST FREE-THROW PERCENTAGE
82.2%—Harvard, 1984 (535 of 651)

Rebounds

MOST REBOUNDS
2,074—Houston, 1968 (33 games)

HIGHEST AVERAGE PER GAME
70.0—Connecticut, 1955 (1,751 in 25)

HIGHEST AVERAGE REBOUND MARGIN
25.0—Morehead St., 1957 (64.3 offense, 39.3 defense)

Assists

MOST ASSISTS
926—UNLV, 1990 (40 games)

HIGHEST AVERAGE PER GAME
24.7—UNLV, 1991 (863 in 35)

Blocked Shots

MOST BLOCKED SHOTS
309—Georgetown, 1989 (34 games)

HIGHEST AVERAGE PER GAME
9.1—Georgetown, 1989 (309 in 34)

Steals

MOST STEALS
486—Oklahoma, 1988 (39 games)

HIGHEST AVERAGE PER GAME
14.8—Texas-San Antonio, 1991 (430 in 29)

Fouls

MOST FOULS
966—Providence, 1987 (34 games)

MOST FOULS PER GAME
29.3—Indiana, 1952 (644 in 22)

FEWEST FOULS
253—Air Force, 1962 (23 games)

FEWEST FOULS PER GAME
11.0—Air Force, 1962 (253 in 23)

Defense

LOWEST SCORING AVERAGE PER GAME ALLOWED
(Since 1938) 25.7—Oklahoma St., 1939 (693 in 27)
(Since 1948) 32.5—Oklahoma St., 1948 (1,006 in 31)
(Since 1965) 47.1—Fresno St., 1982 (1,412 in 30)

LOWEST FIELD-GOAL PERCENTAGE ALLOWED (Since 1978)
35.8—Marquette, 1994 (750 of 2,097)

Overtimes

MOST OVERTIME GAMES
8—Western Ky., 1978 (won 5, lost 3); Portland, 1984 (won 4, lost 4); Valparaiso, 1993 (won 4, lost 4)

MOST CONSECUTIVE OVERTIME GAMES
4—Jacksonville, 1982 (won 3, lost 1); Illinois St., 1985 (won 3, lost 1); Dayton, 1988 (won 1, lost 3)

MOST OVERTIME WINS
6—Tenn.-Chatt., 1989 (6-0); Wake Forest, 1984 (6-1)

MOST OVERTIME HOME WINS
5—Cincinnati, 1967 (5-0)

MOST OVERTIME ROAD WINS
4—Delaware, 1973 (4-0); Arizona St., 1981 (4-0); Cal St. Fullerton, 1989 (4-0); New Mexico St., 1994 (4-0)

MOST OVERTIME PERIODS
14—Bradley, 1982 (3-3)

MOST CONSECUTIVE OVERTIME WINS—ALL-TIME
11—Louisville, Feb. 10, 1968-March 29, 1975; Massachusetts, March 21, 1991-present; Virginia, Dec. 5, 1991-present

General Records

MOST GAMES IN A SEASON (Since 1947-48)
40—Duke, 1986 (37-3); UNLV, 1990 (35-5)

MOST VICTORIES IN A SEASON
37—Duke, 1986 (37-3); UNLV, 1987 (37-2)

MOST VICTORIES IN A PERFECT SEASON
32—North Caro., 1957; Indiana, 1976

MOST CONSECUTIVE VICTORIES
88—UCLA, from Jan. 30, 1971, through Jan. 17, 1974 (ended Jan. 19, 1974, at Notre Dame, 71-70; last UCLA defeat before streak also came at Notre Dame, 89-82)

MOST CONSECUTIVE HOME-COURT VICTORIES
129—Kentucky, from Jan. 4, 1943, to Jan. 8, 1955 (ended by Georgia Tech, 59-58)

MOST CONSECUTIVE REGULAR-SEASON VICTORIES (National Post-Season Tournaments Not Included)
76—UCLA, 1971-74

MOST DEFEATS IN A SEASON
28—Prairie View, 1992 (0-28)

MOST CONSECUTIVE DEFEATS IN A SEASON
28—Prairie View, 1992 (0-28)

MOST CONSECUTIVE DEFEATS
37—Citadel, from Jan. 16, 1954, to Dec. 12, 1955

MOST CONSECUTIVE HOME-COURT DEFEATS
32—New Hampshire, from Feb. 9, 1988, to Feb. 2, 1991 (ended vs. Holy Cross, 72-56)

MOST CONSECUTIVE ROAD DEFEATS
55—Cal St. Sacramento, from Nov. 22, 1991, to Jan. 5, 1995 [ended at Loyola (Ill.), 68-56]

MOST CONSECUTIVE 20-WIN SEASONS
26—North Caro., 1971-96

MOST CONSECUTIVE WINNING SEASONS
48—UCLA, 1949-96

MOST CONSECUTIVE NON-LOSING SEASONS (Includes .500 Record)
60—Kentucky, 1928-52, 54-88# (2 .500 seasons)

#*Kentucky did not play basketball during the 1953 season.*

MOST CONSECUTIVE NON-LOSING SEASONS (Includes .500 Record)-CURRENT
48—UCLA, 1949-96

UNBEATEN TEAMS (Since 1938; Number Of Victories In Parentheses)
1939 LIU-Brooklyn (24)†
1940 Seton Hall (19)††
1944 Army (15)††
1954 Kentucky (25)††
1956 San Francisco (29)*
1957 North Caro. (32)*
1964 UCLA (30)*
1967 UCLA (30)*
1972 UCLA (30)*
1973 UCLA (30)*
1973 North Caro. St. (27)††
1976 Indiana (32)*

*NCAA champion. †NIT champion. ††Not in either tourney.

UNBEATEN IN REGULAR SEASON BUT LOST IN NCAA (*) OR NIT (†)
1939 Loyola (Ill.) (20; 21-1)†
1941 Seton Hall (19; 20-2)†
1951 Columbia (21; 21-1)*
1961 Ohio St. (24; 27-1)*
1968 Houston (28; 31-2)*
1968 St. Bonaventure (22; 23-2)*
1971 Marquette (26; 28-1)*
1971 Pennsylvania (26; 28-1)*
1975 Indiana (29; 31-1)*
1976 Rutgers (28; 31-2)*
1979 Indiana St. (27; 33-1)*
1979 Alcorn St. (25; 28-1)†
1991 UNLV (30; 34-1)*

30-GAME WINNERS (Since 1938)
37—Duke, 1986; UNLV, 1987.
36—Kentucky, 1948.
35—Arizona, 1988; Georgetown, 1985; Kansas, 1986; Massachusetts, 1996; UNLV, 1990; Oklahoma, 1988.
34—Arkansas, 1991; Duke, 1992; Georgetown, 1984; Kentucky, 1947 & 1996; UNLV, 1991; North Caro., 1993.
33—Indiana St., 1979; Louisville, 1980; UNLV, 1986.
32—Arkansas, 1978 & 1995; Bradley, 1950, 1951 & 1986; Connecticut, 1996; Duke, 1991; Houston, 1984; Indiana, 1976; Kentucky, 1949, 1951 & 1986; Louisville, 1983 & 1986; Marshall, 1947; North Caro., 1957, 1982 & 1987; Temple, 1987 & 1988.
31—Arkansas, 1994; Connecticut, 1990; Houston, 1968 & 1983; Illinois, 1989; Indiana, 1975 & 1993; LSU, 1981; Memphis, 1985; Michigan, 1993; Oklahoma, 1985; Oklahoma St., 1946; Rutgers, 1976; St. John's (N.Y.), 1985 & 1986; Seton Hall, 1953 & 1989; Syracuse, 1987; UCLA, 1995; Wyoming, 1943.
30—Arkansas, 1990; Georgetown, 1982; Indiana, 1987; Iowa, 1987; Kansas, 1990; Kentucky, 1978 & 1993; La Salle, 1990; Massachusetts, 1992; Michigan, 1989; Navy, 1986; North Caro., 1946; North Caro. St., 1951 & 1974; Oklahoma, 1989; Oregon, 1946; Syracuse, 1989; Texas Tech, 1996; UCLA, 1964, 1967, 1972 & 1973; Utah, 1991; Virginia, 1982; Western Ky., 1938.

All-Time Individual Leaders

Single-Game Records

SCORING HIGHS VS. DIVISION I OPPONENT

Pts.	Player, Team vs. Opponent	Date
72	Kevin Bradshaw, U.S. Int'l vs. Loyola Marymount	Jan. 5, 1991
69	Pete Maravich, LSU vs. Alabama	Feb. 7, 1970
68	Calvin Murphy, Niagara vs. Syracuse	Dec. 7, 1968
66	Jay Handlan, Wash. & Lee vs. Furman	Feb. 17, 1951
66	Pete Maravich, LSU vs. Tulane	Feb. 10, 1969
66	Anthony Roberts, Oral Roberts vs. North Caro. A&T	Feb. 19, 1977
65	Anthony Roberts, Oral Roberts vs. Oregon	Mar. 9, 1977
65	Scott Haffner, Evansville vs. Dayton	Feb. 18, 1989
64	Pete Maravich, LSU vs. Kentucky	Feb. 21, 1970
63	Johnny Neumann, Mississippi vs. LSU	Jan. 30, 1971
63	Hersey Hawkins, Bradley vs. Detroit	Feb. 22, 1988
62	Darrell Floyd, Furman vs. Citadel	Jan. 14, 1956
62	Oscar Robertson, Cincinnati vs. North Texas	Feb. 6, 1960
62	Askia Jones, Kansas St. vs. Fresno St.	Mar. 24, 1994
61	Lew Alcindor, UCLA vs. Washington St.	Feb. 25, 1967
61	Pete Maravich, LSU vs. Vanderbilt	Dec. 11, 1969
61	Rick Mount, Purdue vs. Iowa	Feb. 28, 1970
61	Austin Carr, Notre Dame vs. Ohio	Mar. 7, 1970
61	Wayman Tisdale, Oklahoma vs. Texas-San Antonio	Dec. 28, 1983
60	Elgin Baylor, Seattle vs. Portland	1958
60	Billy McGill, Utah vs. Brigham Young	1962
60	John Mengelt, Auburn vs. Alabama	Feb. 14, 1970
60	Johnny Neumann, Mississippi vs. Baylor	Dec. 29, 1970
59	Pete Maravich, LSU vs. Alabama	Feb. 17, 1968
59	Ernie Fleming, Jacksonville vs. St. Peter's	Jan. 29, 1972
59	Kevin Bradshaw, U.S. Int'l vs. Florida Int'l	Jan. 14, 1991

SCORING HIGHS VS. NON-DIVISION I OPPONENT

Pts.	Player, Team vs. Opponent	Date
100	Frank Selvy, Furman vs. Newberry	Feb. 13, 1954
85	Paul Arizin, Villanova vs. Philadelphia NAMC	Feb. 12, 1949
81	Freeman Williams, Portland St. vs. Rocky Mountain	Feb. 3, 1978
73	Bill Mlkvy, Temple vs. Wilkes	Mar. 3, 1951
71	Freeman Williams, Portland St. vs. Southern Ore.	Feb. 9, 1977
67	Darrell Floyd, Furman vs. Morehead St.	Jan. 22, 1955
66	Freeman Williams, Portland St. vs. George Fox	Jan. 13, 1978
65	Bob Zawoluk, St. John's (N.Y.) vs. St. Peter's	Mar. 30, 1950
63	Sherman White, LIU-Brooklyn vs. John Marshall	Feb. 1950
63	Frank Selvy, Furman vs. Mercer	Feb. 11, 1953
62	Elvin Hayes, Houston vs. Valparaiso	Feb. 24, 1968
61	Matt Teahan, Denver vs. Neb. Wesleyan	Feb. 26, 1979
60	Bob Pettit, LSU vs. Louisiana College	Dec. 7, 1953
60	Harry Kelly, Texas Southern vs. Jarvis Christian	Feb. 23, 1983

David McMahan of Winthrop connected on 12 three-point field-goal attempts against Coastal Carolina on January 15, 1996. McMahan's performance ranks tied for third all-time in Division I.

Pts.	Player, Team vs. Opponent	Date
60	Dave Jamerson, Ohio vs. Charleston (S.C.)	Dec. 21, 1989
59	Rick Barry, Miami (Fla.) vs. Rollins	1965
58	Frank Selvy, Furman vs. Wofford	Feb. 23, 1954
57	David Thompson, North Caro. St. vs. Buffalo St.	Dec. 5, 1974
57	Calvin Murphy, Niagara vs. Villa Madonna	Dec. 6, 1967
56	Stan Davis, Appalachian St. vs. Carson-Newman	Jan. 24, 1974
56	Tim Roberts, Southern U. vs. Faith Baptist	Dec. 12, 1994
55	Rick Barry, Miami (Fla.) vs. Tampa	1965
55	Elvin Hayes, Houston vs. Southwest Tex. St.	Feb. 12, 1966
55	Wayman Tisdale, Oklahoma vs. Southwest Tex. St.	Dec. 10, 1984
54	Rick Barry, Miami (Fla.) vs. Florida Southern	1965

FIELD-GOAL PERCENTAGE
(Minimum 12 field goals made)

Pct.	Player, Team vs. Opponent (FG-FGA)	Date
100	Clifford Rozier, Louisville vs. Eastern Ky. (15 of 15)	Dec. 11, 1993
100	Dan Henderson, Arkansas St. vs. Ga. Southern (14 of 14)	Feb. 26, 1976
100	Cornelius Holden, Louisville vs. Southern Miss. (14 of 14)	Mar. 3, 1990
100	Dana Jones, Pepperdine vs. Boise St. (14 of 14)	Nov. 30, 1991
100	Ted Guzek, Butler vs. Michigan (13 of 13)	Dec. 15, 1956
100	Rick Dean, Syracuse vs. Colgate (13 of 13)	Feb. 14, 1966
100	Gary Lechman, Gonzaga vs. Portland St. (13 of 13)	Jan. 21, 1967
100	Kevin King, N.C.-Charlotte vs. South Ala. (13 of 13)	Feb. 20, 1978
100	Vernon Smith, Texas A&M vs. Alas. Anchorage (13 of 13)	Nov. 26, 1978
100	Steve Johnson, Oregon St. vs. Hawaii-Hilo (13 of 13)	Dec. 5, 1979
100	Antoine Carr, Wichita St. vs. Abilene Christian (13 of 13)	Nov. 28, 1980
100	Doug Hashley, Montana St. vs. Idaho St. (13 of 13)	Feb. 5, 1982
100	Brad Daugherty, North Caro. vs. UCLA (13 of 13)	Nov. 24, 1985
100	Ricky Butler, UC Irvine vs. Cal St. Fullerton (13 of 13)	Feb. 21, 1991
100	Rafael Solis, Brooklyn vs. Wagner (13 of 13)	Dec. 11, 1991
100	George Faerber, Purdue vs. Iowa (12 of 12)	Mar. 13, 1971
100	Jeff Tropf, Central Mich. vs. Northern Ill. (12 of 12)	Jan. 4, 1978
100	Durand Macklin, LSU vs. Mississippi St. (12 of 12)	Jan. 5, 1980
100	Ron Charles, Michigan vs. Michigan (12 of 12)	Jan. 24, 1980
100	Ricky Frazier, Missouri vs. Oklahoma St. (12 of 12)	Feb. 26, 1980
100	Bryan Warrick, St. Joseph's (Pa.) vs. N.C.-Charlotte (12 of 12)	Jan. 16, 1982
100	David Robinson, Navy vs. East Caro. (12 of 12)	Mar. 7, 1985
100	Michael Ansley, Alabama vs. New Mexico St. (12 of 12)	Nov. 27, 1987
100	Mike Doktorczyk, UC Irvine vs. Pacific (Cal.) (12 of 12)	Jan. 21, 1989
100	Brian Parker, Chicago St. vs. Eastern Ill. (12 of 12)	Jan. 30, 1989
100	Alan Ogg, UAB vs. Mo. Western St. (12 of 12)	Dec. 30, 1989
100	Samuel Hines, South Ala. vs. Auburn (12 of 12)	Dec. 21, 1991
100	Jarrell Evans, Mississippi vs. Abilene Christian (12 of 12)	Nov. 29, 1993
100	Ben Handlogten, Western Mich. vs. Toledo (12 of 12)	Jan. 27, 1996

THREE-POINT FIELD GOALS MADE

3FG	Player, Team vs. Opponent	Date
14	Dave Jamerson, Ohio vs. Charleston (S.C.)	Dec. 21, 1989
14	Askia Jones, Kansas St. vs. Fresno St.	Mar. 24, 1994
12	Gary Bossert, Niagara vs. Siena	Jan. 7, 1987
12	Darrin Fitzgerald, Butler vs. Detroit	Feb. 9, 1987
12	Alex Dillard, Arkansas St. vs. Delaware St.	Dec. 11, 1993
12	Mitch Taylor, Southern U. vs. La. Christian	Dec. 1, 1994
12	David McMahan, Winthrop vs. Coastal Caro.	Jan. 15, 1996
11	Jeff Hodson, Augusta St. vs. Armstrong Atlantic	Jan. 28, 1986
11	Dennis Scott, Georgia Tech vs. Houston	Dec. 28, 1988
11	Scott Haffner, Evansville vs. Dayton	Feb. 18, 1989
11	Bobby Phills, Southern U. vs. Alcorn St.	Feb. 3, 1990
11	Dave Jamerson, Ohio vs. Kent	Feb. 24, 1990
11	Jeff Fryer, Loyola Marymount vs. Michigan	Mar. 18, 1990
11	Doug Day, Radford vs. Central Conn. St.	Dec. 12, 1990
11	Brent Price, Oklahoma vs. Loyola Marymount	Dec. 15, 1990
11	Bobby Phills, Southern U. vs. Manhattan	Dec. 28, 1990
11	Terry Brown, Kansas vs. North Caro. St.	Jan. 5, 1991
11	Marc Rybczyk, Central Conn. St. vs. LIU-Brooklyn	Nov. 26, 1991
11	Mark Alberts, Akron vs. Wright St.	Feb. 8, 1992
11	Mike Alcorn, Youngstown St. vs. Pitt.-Bradford	Feb. 24, 1992
11	Doug Day, Radford vs. Morgan St.	Dec. 9, 1992
11	Lindsey Hunter, Jackson St. vs. Kansas	Dec. 27, 1992
11	Keith Veney, Lamar vs. Prairie View	Feb. 2, 1993
11	Keith Veney, Lamar vs. Ark.-Little Rock	Feb. 11, 1993
11	Scott Neely, Campbell vs. Coastal Caro.	Jan. 29, 1994
11	Chris Brown, UC Irvine vs. New Mexico St.	Mar. 13, 1994
11	Randy Rutherford, Oklahoma St. vs. Kansas	Mar. 5, 1995
11	Troy Hudson, Southern Ill. vs. Hawaii-Hilo	Dec. 29, 1995

FREE-THROW PERCENTAGE
(Minimum 12 free throws made)

Pct.	Player, Team vs. Opponent (FT-FTA)	Date
100	Arlen Clark, Oklahoma St. vs. Colorado (24 of 24)	Mar. 7, 1959
100	York Larese, North Caro. vs. Duke (21 of 21)	Dec. 29, 1959
100	Roger Webb, South Ala. vs. Florida Tech (21 of 21)	Feb. 8, 1969
100	Steve Nash, Santa Clara vs. St. Mary's (Cal.) (21 of 21)	Jan. 7, 1995

Pct.	Player, Team vs. Opponent (FT-FTA)	Date
100	Paul Renfro, Texas-Arlington vs. Lafayette (20 of 20)	Feb. 11, 1979
100	Anthony Peeler, Missouri vs. Iowa St. (20 of 20)	Jan. 31, 1990
100	Donyell Marshall, Connecticut vs. St. John's (N.Y.)	Jan 15, 1994
100	Skip Chappelle, Maine vs. Massachusetts (19 of 19)	1961
100	Gene Phillips, Southern Methodist vs. Texas A&M (19 of 19)	Feb. 2, 1971
100	Jim Kennedy, Missouri vs. Hawaii (19 of 19)	Dec. 22, 1975
100	Kevin Smith, Michigan St. vs. Indiana (19 of 19)	Jan. 7, 1982
100	Sidney Goodman, Coppin St. vs. North Caro. A&T (19 of 19)	Feb. 18, 1995
100	Ted Kitchel, Indiana vs. Illinois (18 of 18)	Jan. 10, 1981
100	Eric Rhodes, Stephen F. Austin vs. Southwest Tex. St. (18 of 18)	Feb. 21, 1987
100	Todd Lichti, Stanford vs. UC Santa Barb. (18 of 18)	Dec. 28, 1987
100	Lionel Simmons, La Salle vs. American (18 of 18)	Feb. 2, 1988
100	Jeff Webster, Oklahoma vs. Southern Methodist (18 of 18)	Jan. 2, 1994
100	Anquell McCollum, Western Caro. vs. Marshall (18 of 18)	Feb. 5, 1996
100	16 tied (17 of 17)	

REBOUNDS

Reb.	Player, Team vs. Opponent	Date
51	Bill Chambers, William & Mary vs. Virginia	Feb. 14, 1953
43	Charlie Slack, Marshall vs. Morris Harvey	Jan. 12, 1954
42	Tom Heinsohn, Holy Cross vs. Boston College	Mar. 1, 1955
40	Art Quimby, Connecticut vs. Boston U.	Jan. 11, 1955
39	Maurice Stokes, St. Francis (Pa.) vs. John Carroll	Jan. 28, 1955
39	Dave DeBusschere, Detroit vs. Central Mich.	Jan. 30, 1960
39	Keith Swagerty, Pacific (Cal.) vs. UC Santa Barb.	Mar. 5, 1965
38	Jerry Koch, St. Louis vs. Bradley	Mar. 5, 1954
38	Charlie Tyra, Louisville vs. Canisius	Dec. 10, 1955
38	Steve Hamilton, Morehead St. vs. Florida St.	Jan. 2, 1957
38	Paul Silas, Creighton vs. Centenary (La.)	Feb. 19, 1962
38	Tommy Woods, East Tenn. St. vs. Middle Tenn. St.	Mar. 1, 1965
36	Herb Neff, Tennessee vs. Georgia Tech	Jan. 26, 1952
36	Dickie Hemric, Wake Forest vs. Clemson	Feb. 4, 1955
36	Swede Halbrook, Oregon St. vs. Idaho	Feb. 15, 1955
36	Wilt Chamberlain, Kansas vs. Iowa St.	1958
35	Ronnie Shavlik, North Caro. St. vs. Villanova	Jan. 29, 1955
35	Bill Ebben, Detroit vs. Brigham Young	Dec. 28, 1955
34	Bob Burrow, Kentucky vs. Temple	Dec. 10, 1955
34	Ronnie Shavlik, North Caro. St. vs. South Caro.	Feb. 11, 1955
34	Fred Cohen, Temple vs. Connecticut	Mar. 16, 1956
34	Bailey Howell, Mississippi St. vs LSU	Feb. 1, 1957
34	David Vaughn, Oral Roberts vs. Brandeis	Jan. 8, 1973
33	Jerry Harper, Alabama vs. Louisiana College	Jan. 21, 1956
33	Walt Bellamy, Indiana vs. Michigan	Mar. 11, 1961

(Since 1973)

Reb.	Player, Team vs. Opponent	Date
34	David Vaughn, Oral Roberts vs. Brandeis	Jan. 8, 1973
32	Durand Macklin, LSU vs. Tulane	Nov. 26, 1976
32	Jervaughn Scales, Southern U. vs. Grambling	Feb. 7, 1994
31	Jim Bradley, Northern Ill. vs. Wis.-Milwaukee	Feb. 19, 1973
31	Calvin Natt, Northeast La. vs. Ga. Southern	Dec. 29, 1976
30	Marvin Barnes, Providence vs. Assumption	Feb. 3, 1973
30	Brad Robinson, Kent vs. Central Mich.	Feb. 9, 1974
30	Monti Davis, Tennessee St. vs. Alabama St.	Feb. 8, 1979
29	Lionel Garrett, Southern U. vs. Bishop	Feb. 16, 1979
29	Donald Newman, Ark.-Little Rock vs. Centenary (La.)	Jan. 24, 1984
29	Hank Gathers, Loyola Marymount vs. U.S. Int'l	Jan. 31, 1989
28	Alvan Adams, Oklahoma vs. Indiana St.	Nov. 27, 1972
28	Cliff Robinson, Southern Cal vs. Portland St.	Jan. 20, 1978
28	Eric McArthur, UC Santa Barb. vs. New Mexico St.	Jan. 11, 1990
28	Marcus Mann, Mississippi Val. vs. Jackson St.	Mar. 9, 1996
27	Andy Hopson, Oklahoma St. vs. Missouri	Jan. 30, 1973
27	Henry Ray, McNeese St. vs. Texas-Arlington	1974
27	Bill Walton, UCLA vs. Loyola (Ill.)	Jan. 25, 1973
27	Bill Walton, UCLA vs. Maryland	Dec. 1, 1973
27	Rick Kelley, Stanford vs. Kentucky	Dec. 22, 1974
27	Kerry Davis, Cal St. Fullerton vs. Central Mich.	Dec. 15, 1975
27	Hank Gathers, Loyola Marymount vs. U.S. Int'l	Dec. 7, 1989
27	Dikembe Mutombo, Georgetown vs. Connecticut	Mar. 8, 1991
27	Reginald Slater, Wyoming vs. Troy St.	Dec. 14, 1991
27	Ervin Johnson, New Orleans vs. Lamar	Feb. 18, 1973
27	Willie Fisher, Jacksonville vs. Louisiana Tech	Dec. 4, 1993
27	Kareem Carpenter, Eastern Mich. vs. Western Mich.	Feb. 8, 1995

ASSISTS

Ast.	Player, Team vs. Opponent	Date
22	Tony Fairley, Charleston So. vs. Armstrong Atlantic	Feb. 9, 1987
22	Avery Johnson, Southern U. vs. Texas Southern	Jan. 25, 1988
22	Sherman Douglas, Syracuse vs. Providence	Jan. 28, 1989
21	Mark Wade, UNLV vs. Navy	Dec. 29, 1986
21	Kelvin Scarborough, New Mexico vs. Hawaii	Feb. 13, 1987
21	Anthony Manuel, Bradley vs. UC Irvine	Dec. 19, 1987
21	Avery Johnson, Southern U. vs. Alabama St.	Jan 16, 1988
20	Grayson Marshall, Clemson vs. Md.-East. Shore	Nov. 25, 1985

Ast.	Player, Team vs. Opponent	Date
20	James Johnson, Middle Tenn. St. vs. Freed-Hardeman	Jan. 2, 1986
20	Avery Johnson, Southern U. vs. Texas Southern	Mar. 6, 1987
20	Avery Johnson, Southern U. vs. Mississippi Val.	Feb. 8, 1988
20	Howard Evans, Temple vs. Villanova	Feb. 10, 1988
20	Jasper Walker, St. Peter's vs. Holy Cross	Feb. 11, 1989
20	Chris Corchiani, North Caro. St. vs. Maryland	Feb. 27, 1991
20	Drew Henderson, Fairfield vs. Loyola (Md.)	Jan. 25, 1992
20	Dana Harris, Md.-Balt. County vs. St. Mary's (Md.)	Dec. 12, 1992
20	Sam Crawford, New Mexico St. vs. Sam Houston St.	Dec. 21, 1992
20	Ray Washington, Nicholls St. vs. McNeese St.	Jan. 28, 1995
19	Frank Nardi, Wis.-Green Bay vs. Northern Iowa	Feb. 24, 1986
19	Avery Johnson, Southern U. vs. Tex. A&M-Kingsville	Dec. 6, 1986
19	Avery Johnson, Southern U. vs. Jackson St.	Jan. 16, 1987
19	Andre Van Drost, Wagner vs. LIU-Brooklyn	Feb. 25, 1987
19	Todd Lehmann, Drexel vs. Liberty	Feb. 5, 1990
19	Greg Anthony, UNLV vs. Pacific (Cal.)	Dec. 29, 1990
19	Keith Jennings, East Tenn. St. vs. Appalachian St.	Feb. 2, 1991
19	Nelson Haggerty, Baylor vs. Oral Roberts	Feb. 27, 1993

BLOCKED SHOTS

Blk.	Player, Team vs. Opponent	Date
14	David Robinson, Navy vs. N.C.-Wilmington	Jan. 4, 1986
14	Shawn Bradley, Brigham Young vs. Eastern Ky.	Dec. 7, 1990
14	Roy Rogers, Alabama vs. Georgia	Feb. 10, 1996
13	Kevin Roberson, Vermont vs. New Hampshire	Jan. 9, 1992
13	Jim McIlvaine, Marquette vs. Northeastern Ill.	Dec. 9, 1992
13	Keith Closs, Central Conn. St. vs. St. Francis (Pa.)	Dec. 21, 1994
12	David Robinson, Navy vs. James Madison	Jan. 9, 1986
12	Derrick Lewis, Maryland vs. James Madison	Jan. 28, 1987
12	Rodney Blake, St. Joseph's (Pa.) vs. Cleveland St.	Dec. 2, 1987
12	Walter Palmer, Dartmouth vs. Harvard	Jan. 9, 1988
12	Alan Ogg, UAB vs. Florida A&M	Dec. 16, 1988
12	Dikembe Mutombo, Georgetown vs. St. John's (N.Y.)	Jan. 23, 1989
12	Shaquille O'Neal, LSU vs. Loyola Marymount	Feb. 3, 1990
12	Cedric Lewis, Maryland vs. South Fla.	Jan. 19, 1991
12	Ervin Johnson, New Orleans vs. Texas A&M	Dec. 29, 1992
12	Kurt Thomas, Texas Christian vs. Texas A&M	Feb. 25, 1995
12	Keith Closs, Central Conn. St. vs. Troy St.	Jan. 20, 1996
11	17 tied	

STEALS

Stl.	Player, Team vs. Opponent	Date
13	Mookie Blaylock, Oklahoma vs. Centenary (La.)	Dec. 12, 1987
13	Mookie Blaylock, Oklahoma vs. Loyola Marymount	Dec. 17, 1988
12	Kenny Robertson, Cleveland St. vs. Wagner	Dec. 3, 1988
12	Terry Evans, Oklahoma vs. Florida A&M	Jan. 27, 1993
11	Darron Brittman, Chicago St. vs. McKendree	Jan. 24, 1986
11	Darron Brittman, Chicago St. vs. St. Xavier	Feb. 8, 1986
11	Marty Johnson, Towson St. vs. Bucknell	Feb. 17, 1988
11	Aldwin Ware, Florida A&M vs. Tuskegee	Feb. 24, 1988
11	Mark Macon, Temple vs. Notre Dame	Jan. 29, 1989
11	Carl Thomas, Eastern Mich. vs. Chicago St.	Feb. 20, 1991
11	Ron Arnold, St. Francis (N.Y.) vs. Mt. St. Mary's (Md.)	Feb. 4, 1993
11	Tyus Edney, UCLA vs. George Mason	Dec. 22, 1995
10	Tom Gormley, Loyola (Md.) vs. Towson St.	Dec. 21, 1985
10	Michael Boswell, Colgate vs. Niagara	Jan. 10, 1987
10	Tony Fairley, Charleston So. vs. N.C.-Asheville	Jan. 29, 1987
10	Tim Keyes, Sam Houston St. vs. Texas	Dec. 1, 1988
10	Lorenzo Neely, Eastern Mich. vs. Cleveland St.	Dec. 14, 1988
10	Kenny Robertson, Cleveland St. vs. Northern Iowa	Feb. 16, 1989
10	Delvon Anderson, Montana vs. Simon Fraser	Nov. 15, 1990
10	Shawn Griggs, LSU vs. Tennessee	Feb. 23, 1991
10	Michael Finley, Wisconsin vs. Purdue	Feb. 13, 1993
10	Brandon Born, Tenn.-Chatt. vs. South Caro.-Aiken	Nov. 26, 1994
10	Mario Miller, Bethune-Cookman vs. Warner Southern	Dec. 3, 1994
10	Tick Rogers, Louisville vs. Western Caro.	Dec. 5, 1994
10	Bonzi Wells, Ball St. vs. Ohio	Jan. 3, 1996
10	Allen Iverson, Georgetown vs. Miami (Fla.)	Jan. 13, 1996

Season Records

POINTS

Player, Team	Season	G	FG	3FG	FT	Pts.
Pete Maravich, LSU	†1970	31	522	—	337	1,381
Elvin Hayes, Houston	†1968	33	519	—	176	1,214
Frank Selvy, Furman	†1954	29	427	—	355	1,209
Pete Maravich, LSU	†1969	26	433	—	282	1,148
Pete Maravich, LSU	1968	26	432	—	274	1,138
Bo Kimble, Loyola Marymount	†1990	32	404	92	231	1,131
Hersey Hawkins, Bradley	†1988	31	377	87	284	1,125
Austin Carr, Notre Dame	1970	29	444		218	1,106

Player, Team	Season	G	FG	3FG	FT	Pts.
Austin Carr, Notre Dame	†1971	29	430	—	241	1,101
Otis Birdsong, Houston	†1977	36	452	—	186	1,090
Dwight Lamar, Southwestern La.	†1972	29	429	—	196	1,054
Kevin Bradshaw, U.S. Int'l	1991	28	358	60	278	1,054
Glenn Robinson, Purdue	1994	34	368	79	215	1,030
Hank Gathers, Loyola Marymount	†1989	31	419	0	177	1,015
Oscar Robertson, Cincinnati	†1960	30	369	—	273	1,011
Freeman Williams, Portland St.	1977	26	417	—	176	1,010
Billy McGill, Utah	1962	26	394	—	221	1,009
Rich Fuqua, Oral Roberts	1972	28	423	—	160	1,006
Oscar Robertson, Cincinnati	1958	28	352	—	280	984
Oscar Robertson, Cincinnati	†1959	30	331	—	316	978
Rick Barry, Miami (Fla.)	1965	26	340	—	293	973
Larry Bird, Indiana St.	1979	34	376	—	221	973
Dennis Scott, Georgia Tech	1990	35	336	137	161	970
Freeman Williams, Portland St.	†1978	27	410	—	149	969
Chris Jackson, LSU	1989	32	359	84	163	965

†National champion.

SCORING AVERAGE

Player, Team	Season	G	FG	3FG	FT	Pts.	Avg.
Pete Maravich, LSU	†1970	31	522	—	337	1,381	44.5
Pete Maravich, LSU	†1969	26	433	—	282	1,148	44.2
Pete Maravich, LSU	†1968	26	432	—	274	1,138	43.8
Frank Selvy, Furman	†1954	29	427	—	355	1,209	41.7
Johnny Neumann, Mississippi	†1971	23	366	—	191	923	40.1
Freeman Williams, Portland St.	†1977	26	417	—	176	1,010	38.8
Billy McGill, Utah	†1962	26	394	—	221	1,009	38.8
Calvin Murphy, Niagara	1968	24	337	—	242	916	38.2
Austin Carr, Notre Dame	1970	29	444	—	218	1,106	38.2
Austin Carr, Notre Dame	1971	29	430	—	241	1,101	38.0
Kevin Bradshaw, U.S. Int'l	1991	28	358	60	278	1,054	37.6
Rick Barry, Miami (Fla.)	1965	26	340	—	293	973	37.4
Elvin Hayes, Houston	1968	33	519	—	176	1,214	36.8
Marshall Rogers, Tex.-Pan American	†1976	25	361	—	197	919	36.8
Howard Komives, Bowling Green	†1964	23	292	—	260	844	36.7
Dwight Lamar, Southwestern La.	†1972	29	429	—	196	1,054	36.3
Hersey Hawkins, Bradley	†1988	31	377	87	284	1,125	36.3
Darrell Floyd, Furman	†1955	25	344	—	209	897	35.9
Rich Fuqua, Oral Roberts	1972	28	423	—	160	1,006	35.9
Freeman Williams, Portland St.	†1978	27	410	—	149	969	35.9
Rick Mount, Purdue	1970	20	285	—	138	708	35.4
Bo Kimble, Loyola Marymount	†1990	32	404	92	231	1,131	35.3
Oscar Robertson, Cincinnati	†1958	28	352	—	280	984	35.1
Anthony Roberts, Oral Roberts	1977	28	402	—	147	951	34.0
Dan Issel, Kentucky	1970	28	369	—	210	948	33.9
William Averitt, Pepperdine	†1973	25	352	—	144	848	33.9

†National champion.

FIELD-GOAL PERCENTAGE
(Based on qualifiers for annual championship)

Player, Team	Season	G	FG	FGA	Pct.
Steve Johnson, Oregon St.	†1981	28	235	315	74.6
Dwayne Davis, Florida	†1989	33	179	248	72.2
Keith Walker, Utica	†1985	27	154	216	71.3
Steve Johnson, Oregon St.	†1980	30	211	297	71.0
Oliver Miller, Arkansas	†1991	38	254	361	70.4
Alan Williams, Princeton	†1987	25	163	232	70.3
Mark McNamara, California	†1982	27	231	329	70.2
Warren Kidd, Middle Tenn. St.	1991	30	173	247	70.0
Pete Freeman, Akron	1991	28	175	250	70.0
Joe Senser, West Chester	†1977	25	130	186	69.9
Lee Campbell, Southwest Mo. St.	†1990	29	192	275	69.8
Stephen Scheffler, Purdue	1990	30	173	248	69.8
Mike Atkinson, Long Beach St.	†1994	26	141	203	69.5
Lester James, St. Francis (N.Y.)	1991	29	149	215	69.3
Murray Brown, Florida St.	†1979	29	237	343	69.1
Joe Senser, West Chester	†1978	25	135	197	68.5
Charles Outlaw, Houston	†1992	31	156	228	68.4
Shane Kline-Ruminski, Bowling Green	†1995	26	181	265	68.3
Marcus Kennedy, Eastern Mich.	1991	33	240	352	68.2
Felton Spencer, Louisville	1990	35	188	276	68.1
Tyrone Howard, Eastern Ky.	1987	30	156	230	67.8
Ron Charles, Michigan St.	1980	27	169	250	67.6
Quadre Lollis, Montana St.	1996	30	212	314	67.5
Akeem Olajuwon, Houston	†1984	37	249	369	67.5
Troy Lee Mikell, East Tenn. St.	†1983	29	197	292	67.5

†National champion.

THREE-POINT FIELD GOALS MADE

Player, Team	Season	G	3FG
Darrin Fitzgerald, Butler	†1987	28	158

Player, Team	Season	G	3FG
Freddie Banks, UNLV	1987	39	152
Randy Rutherford, Oklahoma St.	†1995	37	146
Dennis Scott, Georgia Tech	†1990	35	137
Timothy Pollard, Mississippi Val.	†1988	28	132
Dave Jamerson, Ohio	1990	28	131
Sydney Grider, Southwestern La.	1990	29	131
Lazelle Durden, Cincinnati	1995	34	127
Jeff Fryer, Loyola Marymount	†1989	31	126
Timothy Pollard, Mississippi Val.	1989	28	124
Bobby Phills, Southern U.	†1991	28	123
Sydney Grider, Southwestern La.	1989	29	122
Andy Kennedy, UAB	1989	34	122
Mark Alberts, Akron	1990	28	122
Chris Brown UC Irvine	†1994	26	122
Darren McLinton, James Madison	†1996	30	122
Jeff Fryer, Loyola Marymount	1990	28	121
Randy Woods, La Salle	†1992	31	121
Dominick Young, Fresno St.	1996	29	120
Shawn Respert, Michigan St.	1995	28	119
Gerald Paddio, UNLV	1988	34	118
Doug Day, Iowa	1992	29	117
Chris Kingsbury, Iowa	1995	33	117
Dennis Scott, Georgia Tech	1989	32	116
Ronnie Schmitz, Mo.-Kansas City	1991	29	116
Doug Day, Radford	1993	31	116

†National champion.

THREE-POINT FIELD GOALS MADE PER GAME
(Based on qualifiers for annual championship)

Player, Team	Season	G	3FG	Avg.
Darrin Fitzgerald, Butler	†1987	28	158	5.64
Timothy Pollard, Mississippi Val.	†1988	28	132	4.71
Chris Brown, UC Irvine	†1994	26	122	4.69
Dave Jamerson, Ohio	1990	28	131	4.68
Sydney Grider, Southwestern La.	1990	29	131	4.52
Timothy Pollard, Mississippi Val.	†1989	28	124	4.43
Keke Hicks, Coastal Caro.	1994	26	115	4.42
Bobby Phills, Southern U.	†1991	28	123	4.39
Mitch Taylor, Southern U.	†1995	25	109	4.36
Mark Alberts, Akron	1990	28	122	4.36
Jeff Fryer, Loyola Marymount	1990	28	121	4.32
Shawn Respert, Michigan St.	1995	28	119	4.25
Sydney Grider, Southwestern La.	1989	29	122	4.21
Bernard Haslett, Southern Miss.	†1993	26	109	4.19
Stevin Smith, Arizona St.	1993	27	113	4.19
Tim Roberts, Southern U.	1995	26	108	4.15
Dominick Young, Fresno St.	†1996	29	120	4.14
Mark Alberts, Akron	1993	26	107	4.12
Lazelle Durden, Cincinnati	1994	25	102	4.08
Darren McLinton, James Madison	1996	30	122	4.07
Jeff Fryer, Loyola Marymount	1989	31	126	4.06
Doug Day, Radford	†1992	29	117	4.03
Ronnie Schmitz, Mo.-Kansas City	1991	29	116	4.00
Scott Brooks, UC Irvine	1987	28	111	3.96
Keith Veney, Marshall	1996	28	111	3.96
Darryl Brooks, Tennessee St.	1990	24	95	3.96

†National champion.

THREE-POINT FIELD-GOAL PERCENTAGE
(Based on qualifiers for annual championship)

Player, Team	Season	G	3FG	3FGA	Pct.
Glenn Tropf, Holy Cross	†1988	29	52	82	63.4
Sean Wightman, Western Mich.	†1992	30	48	76	63.2
Keith Jennings, East Tenn. St.	†1991	33	84	142	59.2
Dave Calloway, Monmouth (N.J.)	†1989	28	48	82	58.5
Steve Kerr, Arizona	1988	38	114	199	57.3
Reginald Jones, Prairie View	†1987	28	64	112	57.1
Joel Tribelhorn, Colorado St.	1989	33	76	135	56.3
Mike Joseph, Bucknell	1988	28	65	116	56.0
Brian Jackson, Evansville	†1995	27	53	95	55.8
Christian Laettner, Duke	1992	35	54	97	55.7
Reginald Jones, Prairie View	1988	27	85	155	54.8
Eric Rhodes, Stephen F. Austin	1987	30	58	106	54.7
Dave Orlandini, Princeton	1988	26	60	110	54.5
Mike Joseph, Bucknell	1989	31	62	115	53.9
John Bays, Towson St.	1989	29	71	132	53.8
Jeff Anderson, Kent	†1993	26	44	82	53.7
Jay Edwards, Indiana	1988	23	59	110	53.6
Anthony Davis, George Mason	1987	27	45	84	53.6
Mark Anglavar, Marquette	1989	28	53	99	53.5
Scot Dimak, Stephen F. Austin	1987	30	46	86	53.5
Matt Lapin, Princeton	†1990	27	71	133	53.4

Player, Team	Season	G	3FG	3FGA	Pct.
Michael Charles, UAB	1988	28	63	118	53.4
Tony Bennett, Wis.-Green Bay	1991	31	80	150	53.3
Roosevelt Moore, Sam Houston St.	1993	25	73	137	53.3
Eric Longino, Southern Methodist	1989	29	50	94	53.2
Paul Maley, Yale	1988	26	41	77	53.2

†National champion.

FREE-THROW PERCENTAGE
(Based on qualifiers for annual championship)

Player, Team	Season	G	FT	FTA	Pct.
Craig Collins, Penn St.	†1985	27	94	98	95.9
Rod Foster, UCLA	†1982	27	95	100	95.0
Carlos Gibson, Marshall	†1978	28	84	89	94.4
Danny Basile, Marist	†1994	27	84	89	94.4
Jim Barton, Dartmouth	†1986	26	65	69	94.2
Jack Moore, Nebraska	1982	27	123	131	93.9
Rob Robbins, New Mexico	†1990	34	101	108	93.5
Dandrea Evans, Troy St.	1994	27	72	77	93.5
Tommy Boyer, Arkansas	†1962	23	125	134	93.3
Damon Goodwin, Dayton	1986	30	95	102	93.1
Brian Magid, Geo. Washington	†1980	26	79	85	92.9
Mike Joseph, Bucknell	1990	29	144	155	92.9
Steve Kaplan, Rutgers	†1970	23	102	110	92.7
Dave Hildahl, Portland St.	†1981	21	76	82	92.7
Mike Dillard, Sam Houston St.	†1996	25	63	68	92.6
Casey Schmidt, Valparaiso	1994	25	75	81	92.6
Greg Starrick, Southern Ill.	†1972	26	148	160	92.5
Steve Henson, Kansas St.	†1988	34	111	120	92.5
Randy Nesbit, Citadel	1980	27	74	80	92.5
Robert Smith, UNLV	†1977	32	98	106	92.5
Matthew Hildebrand, Liberty	1994	30	149	161	92.5
Michael Smith, Brigham Young	†1989	29	160	173	92.5
Kevin Kelly, Vermont	1977	25	171	77	92.2
Jack Moore, Nebraska	1981	27	118	128	92.2
Kent Culuko, James Madison	1994	30	117	127	92.1
Don MacLean, UCLA	†1992	32	197	214	92.1
Steve Alford, Indiana	1985	32	116	126	92.1
Bob Lloyd, Rutgers	†1967	29	255	277	92.1

†National champion.

REBOUNDS

Player, Team	Ht.	Season	G	Reb.
Walt Dukes, Seton Hall	6-10	†1953	33	734
Leroy Wright, Pacific (Cal.)	6-8	†1959	26	652
Tom Gola, La Salle	6-6	†1954	30	652
Charlie Tyra, Louisville	6-8	†1956	29	645
Paul Silas, Creighton	6-7	†1964	29	631
Elvin Hayes, Houston	6-8	†1968	33	624
Artis Gilmore, Jacksonville	7-2	†1970	28	621
Tom Gola, La Salle	6-6	†1955	31	618
Ed Conlin, Fordham	6-5	1953	26	612
Art Quimby, Connecticut	6-5	1955	25	611
Bill Russell, San Francisco	6-9	1956	29	609
Jim Ware, Oklahoma City	6-8	†1966	29	607
Joe Holup, Geo. Washington	6-6	1956	26	604
Artis Gilmore, Jacksonville	7-2	†1971	26	603
Elton Tuttle, Creighton	6-5	1954	30	601
Marvin Barnes, Providence	6-9	†1974	32	597
Bill Russell, San Francisco	6-9	1955	29	594
Art Quimby, Connecticut	6-5	1954	26	588
Ed Conlin, Fordham	6-5	1955	27	578
Marvin Barnes, Providence	6-9	†1973	30	571
Bill Spivey, Kentucky	7-0	†1951	33	567
Bob Pelkington, Xavier (Ohio)	6-7	1964	26	567
Paul Silas, Creighton	6-7	†1962	25	563
Elgin Baylor, Seattle	6-6	†1959	29	559
Paul Silas, Creighton	6-7	†1963	27	557

†National champion.

(Since 1973)

Player, Team	Ht.	Season	G	Reb.
Marvin Barnes, Providence	6-9	†1974	32	597
Marvin Barnes, Providence	6-9	†1973	30	571
Kermit Washington, American	6-8	1973	25	511
Bill Walton, UCLA	6-11	1973	30	506
Larry Bird, Indiana St.	6-9	†1979	34	505
Larry Kenon, Memphis	6-9	†1973	30	501
Akeem Olajuwon, Houston	7-0	†1984	37	500
Glenn Mosley, Seton Hall	6-8	†1977	29	473
Popeye Jones, Murray St.	6-8	†1991	33	469
Pete Padgett, Nevada	6-8	†1973	26	462
Xavier McDaniel, Wichita St.	6-8	†1985	31	460
Larry Johnson, UNLV	6-7	†1990	40	457

Player, Team	Ht.	Season	G	Reb.
Anthony Bonner, St. Louis	6-8	1990	33	456
Bill Cartwright, San Francisco	7-1	1979	29	455
David Robinson, Navy	6-11	†1986	35	455
Benoit Benjamin, Creighton	7-0	1985	32	451
Jerome Lane, Pittsburgh	6-6	†1987	33	444
Robert Elmore, Wichita St.	6-10	1977	28	441
John Irving, Hofstra	6-9	1977	27	440
Lionel Garrett, Southern U.	6-9	1979	28	433
Popeye Jones, Murray St.	6-8	†1992	30	431
Jim Bradley, Northern Ill.	6-10	1973	24	426
Hank Gathers, Loyola Marymount	6-7	†1989	31	426
Jimmie Baker, UNLV	6-9	1973	28	424
Brad Robinson, Kent	6-7	1974	26	423
John Irving, Hofstra	6-9	†1976	29	423
Gary Trent, Ohio	6-8	†1995	33	423

†National champion.

REBOUND AVERAGE

Player, Team	Ht.	Season	G	Reb.	Avg.
Charlie Slack, Marshall	6-5	†1955	21	538	25.6
Leroy Wright, Pacific (Cal.)	6-8	†1959	26	652	25.1
Art Quimby, Connecticut	6-5	1955	25	611	24.4
Charlie Slack, Marshall	6-5	1956	22	520	23.6
Ed Conlin, Fordham	6-5	†1953	26	612	23.5
Joe Holup, Geo. Washington	6-6	††1956	26	604	23.2
Artis Gilmore, Jacksonville	7-2	†1971	26	603	23.2
Art Quimby, Connecticut	6-5	†1954	26	588	22.6
Paul Silas, Creighton	6-7	1962	25	563	22.5
Leroy Wright, Pacific (Cal.)	6-8	†1960	17	380	22.4
Walt Dukes, Seton Hall	6-10	1953	33	734	22.2
Charlie Tyra, Louisville	6-8	1956	29	645	22.2
Charlie Slack, Marshall	6-5	1954	21	466	22.2
Artis Gilmore, Jacksonville	7-2	†1970	28	621	22.2
Bill Chambers, William & Mary	6-4	1953	22	480	21.8
Bob Pelkington, Xavier (Ohio)	6-7	†1964	26	567	21.8
Dick Cunningham, Murray St.	6-10	†1967	22	479	21.8
Paul Silas, Creighton	6-7	1964	29	631	21.8
Tom Gola, La Salle	6-6	1954	30	652	21.7
Jerry Harper, Alabama	6-8	1956	24	517	21.5
Spencer Haywood, Detroit	6-8	†1969	22	472	21.5
Ed Conlin, Fordham	6-5	1955	27	578	21.4
Tom Heinsohn, Holy Cross	6-7	1956	26	549	21.1
Bill Russell, San Francisco	6-9	1956	29	609	21.0
Toby Kimball, Connecticut	6-8	†1965	23	483	21.0

†National champion. ††From 1956 through 1962, individual champions were determined by percentage of all recoveries; Holup led in percentage of recoveries and Slack led in average in 1956.

(Since 1973)

Player, Team	Ht.	Season	G	Reb.	Avg.
Kermit Washington, American	6-8	†1973	25	511	20.4
Marvin Barnes, Providence	6-9	1973	30	571	19.0
Marvin Barnes, Providence	6-9	†1974	32	597	18.7
Pete Padgett, Nevada	6-8	1973	26	462	17.8
Jim Bradley, Northern Ill.	6-10	1973	24	426	17.8
Bill Walton, UCLA	6-11	1973	30	506	16.9
Larry Kenon, Memphis	6-9	1973	30	501	16.7
Glenn Mosley, Seton Hall	6-8	†1977	29	473	16.3
John Irving, Hofstra	6-9	1977	27	440	16.3
Carlos McCullough, Tex.-Pan American	6-7	1974	22	358	16.3
Brad Robinson, Kent	6-7	1974	26	423	16.3
Monti Davis, Tennessee St.	6-7	†1979	26	421	16.2
Sam Pellom, Buffalo	6-8	†1976	26	420	16.2
Robert Elmore, Wichita St.	6-10	1977	28	441	15.8
Bill Cartwright, San Francisco	7-1	1979	29	455	15.7
Bill Champion, Manhattan	6-10	1973	26	402	15.5
Bill Champion, Manhattan	6-10	1974	27	419	15.5
Lionel Garrett, Southern U.	6-9	1979	28	433	15.5
Dwayne Barnett, Samford	6-6	1976	23	354	15.4
John Irving, Hofstra	6-9	†1975	21	323	15.4
Cornelius Cash, Bowling Green	6-8	1973	26	396	15.2
Pete Padgett, Nevada	6-8	1974	26	395	15.2
Jimmie Baker, UNLV	6-9	1973	28	424	15.1
Larry Smith, Alcorn St.	6-8	†1980	26	392	15.1
Charles McKinney, Baylor	6-6	1974	25	375	15.0
Lewis Lloyd, Drake	6-6	1980	27	406	15.0

†National champion.

ASSISTS

Player, Team	Season	G	Ast.
Mark Wade, UNLV	†1987	38	406
Avery Johnson, Southern U.	†1988	30	399
Anthony Manuel, Bradley	1988	31	373

Georgetown's Allen Iverson led the nation in steals in 1996, registering 124 thefts, including a season-best 10 vs. Miami (Florida) on January 13, 1996.

Photo by David Hobson

Player, Team	Season	G	Ast.
Avery Johnson, Southern U.	1987	31	333
Mark Jackson, St. John's (N.Y.)	†1986	32	328
Sherman Douglas, Syracuse	†1989	38	326
Greg Anthony, UNLV	†1991	35	310
Sam Crawford, New Mexico St.	†1993	34	310
Reid Gettys, Houston	†1984	37	309
Carl Golston, Loyola (Ill.)	†1985	33	305
Craig Neal, Georgia Tech	1988	32	303
Keith Jennings, East Tenn. St.	1991	33	301
Chris Corchiani, North Caro. St.	1991	31	299
Keith Jennings, East Tenn. St.	†1990	34	297
Howard Evans, Temple	1988	34	294
Danny Tarkanian, UNLV	1984	34	289
Sherman Douglas, Syracuse	1987	38	289
Bobby Hurley, Duke	1991	39	289
Greg Anthony, UNLV	1990	39	289
Sherman Douglas, Syracuse	1988	35	288
Bobby Hurley, Duke	1990	38	288
Kenny Anderson, Georgia Tech	1990	35	285
Nelson Haggerty, Baylor	†1995	28	284
Mark Wade, UNLV	1986	38	283
Terrell Lowery, Loyola Marymount	1991	31	283

†National champion.

ASSIST AVERAGE

Player, Team	Season	G	Ast.	Avg.
Avery Johnson, Southern U.	†1988	30	399	13.30
Anthony Manuel, Bradley	1988	31	373	12.03
Avery Johnson, Southern U.	†1987	31	333	10.74
Mark Wade, UNLV	1987	38	406	10.68
Nelson Haggerty, Baylor	†1995	28	284	10.14
Glenn Williams, Holy Cross	†1989	28	278	9.92
Chris Corchiani, North Caro. St.	†1991	31	299	9.65
Tony Fairley, Charleston So.	1987	28	270	9.64
Tyrone Bogues, Wake Forest	1987	29	276	9.52
Ron Weingard, Hofstra	†1985	24	228	9.50
Craig Neal, Georgia Tech	1988	32	303	9.47
Craig Lathan, Ill.-Chicago	†1984	29	274	9.45
Curtis McCants, George Mason	1995	27	251	9.30
Andre Van Drost, Wagner	1987	28	260	9.29
Todd Lehmann, Drexel	†1990	28	260	9.29
Danny Tirado, Jacksonville	1991	28	259	9.25
Carl Golston, Loyola (Ill.)	1985	33	305	9.24
Terrell Lowery, Loyola Marymount	1991	31	283	9.13
Keith Jennings, East Tenn. St.	1991	33	301	9.12
Sam Crawford, New Mexico St.	†1993	34	310	9.12
Mark Jackson, St. John's (N.Y.)	†1986	36	328	9.11
Aaron Mitchell, Southwestern La.	1990	29	264	9.10

Player, Team	Season	G	Ast.	Avg.
Jason Kidd, California	†1994	30	272	9.07
Greg Anthony, UNLV	1991	35	310	8.86
David Edwards, Texas A&M	1994	30	265	8.83

†National champion.

BLOCKED SHOTS

Player, Team	Season	G	Blk.
David Robinson, Navy	†1986	35	207
Keith Closs, Central Conn. St.	†1996	28	178
Shawn Bradley, Brigham Young	†1991	34	177
Alonzo Mourning, Georgetown	†1989	34	169
Adonal Foyle, Colgate	1996	29	165
Alonzo Mourning, Georgetown	†1992	32	160
Shaquille O'Neal, LSU	1992	30	157
Roy Rogers, Alabama	1996	32	156
Dikembe Mutombo, Georgetown	1991	32	151
Adonal Foyle, Colgate	†1995	30	147
Theo Ratliff, Wyoming	1995	28	144
David Robinson, Navy	†1987	32	144
Cedric Lewis, Maryland	1991	28	143
Jim McIlvaine, Marquette	†1994	33	142
Shaquille O'Neal, LSU	1991	28	140
Keith Closs, Central Conn. St.	1995	26	139
Kevin Roberson, Vermont	1992	28	139
Tim Duncan, Wake Forest	1995	32	135
Alan Ogg, UAB	1989	34	129
Dikembe Mutombo, Georgetown	†1990	31	128
Marcus Camby, Massachusetts	1996	33	128
Derrick Coleman, Syracuse	1989	37	127
Duane Causwell, Temple	1989	30	124
Kenny Green, Rhode Island	1990	26	124
Theo Ratliff, Wyoming	†1993	28	124
Sharone Wright, Clemson	†1993	30	124
Tim Duncan, Wake Forest	1994	33	124
Pascal Fleury, Md.-Balt. County	1995	27	124

†National champion.

BLOCKED-SHOT AVERAGE

Player, Team	Season	G	Blk.	Avg.
Keith Closs, Central Conn St.	†1996	28	178	6.36
David Robinson, Navy	†1986	35	207	5.91
Adonal Foyle, Colgate	1996	29	165	5.69
Keith Closs, Central Conn. St.	†1995	26	139	5.35
Shaquille O'Neal, LSU	†1992	30	157	5.23
Shawn Bradley, Brigham Young	†1991	34	177	5.21
Theo Ratliff, Wyoming	1995	28	144	5.14
Cedric Lewis, Maryland	1991	28	143	5.11
Shaquille O'Neal, LSU	1991	28	140	5.00
Alonzo Mourning, Georgetown	1992	32	160	5.00
Alonzo Mourning, Georgetown	†1989	34	169	4.97
Kevin Roberson, Vermont	1992	28	139	4.96
Adonal Foyle, Colgate	1995	30	147	4.90
Roy Rogers, Alabama	1996	32	156	4.88
Kenny Green, Rhode Island	†1990	26	124	4.77
Dikembe Mutombo, Georgetown	1991	32	151	4.72
Pascal Fleury, Md.-Balt. County	1995	27	124	4.59
Lorenzo Coleman, Tennessee Tech	1995	27	122	4.52
David Robinson, Navy	†1987	32	144	4.50
Theo Ratliff, Wyoming	†1993	28	124	4.43
Grady Livingston, Howard	†1994	26	115	4.42
Jerome James, Florida A&M	1996	27	119	4.41
Derrick Lewis, Maryland	1987	26	114	4.38
Jim McIlvaine, Marquette	1994	33	142	4.30
Tim Duncan, Wake Forest	1995	32	135	4.22

†National champion.

STEALS

Player, Team	Season	G	Stl.
Mookie Blaylock, Oklahoma	†1988	39	150
Aldwin Ware, Florida A&M	1988	29	142
Darron Brittman, Chicago St.	†1986	28	139
Nadav Henefeld, Connecticut	†1990	37	138
Mookie Blaylock, Oklahoma	†1989	35	131
Ronn McMahon, Eastern Wash.	1990	29	130
Marty Johnson, Towson St.	1988	29	124
Allen Iverson, Georgetown	†1996	37	124
Jim Paguaga, St. Francis (N.Y.)	1986	28	120
Shawn Griggs, Southwestern La.	†1994	30	120
Pointer Williams, McNeese St.	1996	27	118
Tony Fairley, Charleston So.	†1987	28	114
Scott Burrell, Connecticut	†1991	31	112
Kenny Robertson, Cleveland St.	1989	28	111
Lance Blanks, Texas	1989	34	111

Player, Team	Season	G	Stl.
Eric Murdock, Providence	1991	32	111
Jason Kidd, California	†1993	29	110
Johnny Rhodes, Maryland	1996	30	110
Robert Dowdell, Coastal Caro.	1990	29	109
Keith Jennings, East Tenn. St.	1991	33	109
Mark Woods, Wright St.	1993	30	109
Gerald Walker, San Francisco	1994	28	109
Edgar Padilla, Massachusetts	1996	37	108
Avery Johnson, Southern U.	1988	30	106
Greg Anthony, UNLV	1990	39	106
Roderick Taylor, Jackson St.	1996	29	106

†National champion.

STEAL AVERAGE

Player, Team	Season	G	Stl.	Avg.
Darron Brittman, Chicago St.	†1986	28	139	4.96
Aldwin Ware, Florida A&M	†1988	29	142	4.90
Ronn McMahon, Eastern Wash.	†1990	29	130	4.48
Pointer Williams, McNeese St.	†1996	27	118	4.37
Jim Paguaga, St. Francis (N.Y.)	1986	28	120	4.29
Marty Johnson, Towson St.	1988	30	124	4.13
Tony Fairley, Charleston So.	†1987	28	114	4.07
Shawn Griggs, Southwestern La.	†1994	30	120	4.00
Kenny Robertson, Cleveland St.	†1989	28	111	3.96
Gerald Walker, San Francisco	1994	28	109	3.89
Mookie Blaylock, Oklahoma	1988	39	150	3.85
Jason Kidd, California	†1993	29	110	3.79
Jay Goodman, Utah St.	1993	27	102	3.78
Andre Cradle, LIU-Brooklyn	1994	21	79	3.76
Robert Dowdell, Coastal Caro.	1990	29	109	3.76
Mookie Blaylock, Oklahoma	1989	35	131	3.74
Johnny Rhodes, Maryland	1996	30	110	3.67
Roderick Taylor, Jackson St.	1996	29	106	3.66
Mark Woods, Wright St.	1993	30	109	3.63
Scott Burrell, Connecticut	1991	31	112	3.61
Rasul Salahuddin, Long Beach St.	1996	28	101	3.61
Andrell Hoard, Northeastern Ill.	1996	27	97	3.59
Leroy Allen, Hofstra	1986	28	100	3.57
Haywoode Workman, Oral Roberts	1988	29	103	3.55
Avery Johnson, Southern U.	1988	30	106	3.53

†National champion.

Top Season Performances By Class

SCORING AVERAGE

Class	Player, Team	Season	G	FG	3FG	FT	Pts.	Avg.
Senior	Pete Maravich, LSU	1970	31	522	—	337	1,381	44.5
Junior	Pete Maravich, LSU	1969	26	433	—	282	1,148	44.2
Sophomore	Pete Maravich, LSU	1968	26	432	—	274	1,138	43.8
Freshman	Chris Jackson, LSU	1989	32	359	84	163	965	30.2

FIELD-GOAL PERCENTAGE

Class	Player, Team	Season	G	FG	FGA	Pct.
Senior	Steve Johnson, Oregon St.	1981	28	235	315	74.6
Junior	Steve Johnson, Oregon St.	1980	30	211	297	71.0
Sophomore	Dwayne Davis, Florida	1989	33	179	248	72.2
Freshman	Sidney Moncrief, Arkansas	1976	28	149	224	66.5

THREE-POINT FIELD GOALS MADE PER GAME

Class	Player, Team	Season	G	3FG	Avg.
Senior	Darrin Fitzgerald, Butler	1987	28	158	5.64
Junior	Timothy Pollard, Mississippi Val.	1988	28	132	4.71
Sophomore	Mark Alberts, Akron	1990	28	122	4.36
Freshman	Keith Veney, Lamar	1993	27	106	3.93

THREE-POINT FIELD-GOAL PERCENTAGE

Class	Player, Team	Season	G	3FG	3FGA	Pct.
Senior	Keith Jennings, East Tenn. St.	1991	33	84	142	59.2
Junior	Glenn Tropf, Holy Cross	1988	29	52	82	63.4
Sophomore	Dave Calloway, Monmouth (N.J.)	1989	28	48	82	58.5
Freshman	Jay Edwards, Indiana	1988	23	59	110	53.6

FREE-THROW PERCENTAGE

Class	Player, Team	Season	G	FT	FTA	Pct.
Senior	Craig Collins, Penn St.	1985	27	94	98	95.9
Junior	Rod Foster, UCLA	1982	27	95	100	95.0
Sophomore	Danny Basile, Marist	1994	27	84	89	94.4
Freshman	Jim Barton, Dartmouth	1986	26	65	69	94.2

REBOUND AVERAGE

Class	Player, Team	Season	G	Reb.	Avg.
Senior	Art Quimby, Connecticut	1955	25	611	24.4
Junior	Charlie Slack, Marshall	1955	21	538	25.6
Sophomore	Ed Conlin, Fordham	1953	26	612	23.5
Freshman	Pete Padgett, Nevada	1973	26	462	17.8

ASSIST AVERAGE

Class	Player, Team	Season	G	Ast.	Avg.
Senior	Avery Johnson, Southern U.	1988	30	399	13.30
Junior	Anthony Manuel, Bradley	1988	31	373	12.03
Sophomore	Curtis McCants, George Mason	1995	27	251	9.30
Freshman	Orlando Smart, San Francisco	1991	29	237	8.17

BLOCKED-SHOT AVERAGE

Class	Player, Team	Season	G	Blk.	Avg.
Senior	Theo Ratliff, Wyoming	1995	28	144	5.14
Junior	David Robinson, Navy	1986	35	207	5.91
Sophomore	Keith Closs, Central Conn. St.	1996	28	178	6.36
Freshman	Keith Closs, Central Conn. St.	1995	26	139	5.35

STEAL AVERAGE

Class	Player, Team	Season	G	Stl.	Avg.
Senior	Darron Brittman, Chicago St.	1986	28	139	4.96
Junior	Kenny Robertson, Cleveland St.	1989	28	111	3.96
Sophomore	Gerald Walker, San Francisco	1994	28	109	3.89
Freshman	Jason Kidd, California	1993	29	110	3.79

Top Season Performances By A Freshman

POINTS

Player, Team	Season	G	FG	3FG	FT	Pts.
Chris Jackson, LSU	1989	32	359	84	163	965
James Williams, Austin Peay	1973	29	360	—	134	854
Wayman Tisdale, Oklahoma	1983	33	338	—	134	810
Alphonso Ford, Mississippi Val.	1990	27	289	104	126	808
Mark Aguirre, DePaul	1979	32	302	—	163	767

SCORING AVERAGE

Player, Team	Season	G	FG	3FG	FT	Pts.	Avg.
Chris Jackson, LSU	1989	32	359	84	163	965	30.2
Alphonso Ford, Mississippi Val.	1990	27	289	104	126	808	29.9
James Williams, Austin Peay	1973	29	360	—	134	854	29.4
Harry Kelly, Texas Southern	1980	26	313	—	127	753	29.0
Bernard King, Tennessee	1975	25	273	—	115	661	26.4

FIELD-GOAL PERCENTAGE

Player, Team	Season	G	FG	FGA	Pct.
Sidney Moncrief, Arkansas	1976	28	149	224	66.5
Gary Trent, Ohio	1993	27	194	298	65.1
Ed Pinckney, Villanova	1982	32	169	264	64.0
Jimmy Lunsford, Alabama St.	1993	22	142	223	63.7
Alexander Koul, Geo. Washington	1995	32	160	253	63.2
Cedric Robinson, Nicholls St.	1983	24	146	231	63.2

THREE-POINT FIELD GOALS MADE

Player, Team	Season	G	3FG	Avg.
Keith Veney, Lamar	1993	27	106	3.93
Alphonso Ford, Mississippi Val.	1990	27	104	3.85
Tony Ross, San Diego St.	1987	28	104	3.71
Troy Green, Southeastern La.	1996	27	98	3.63
Ben Larson, Cal Poly SLO	1996	29	94	3.24

THREE-POINT FIELD-GOAL PERCENTAGE

Player, Team	Season	G	3FG	3FGA	Pct.
Jay Edwards, Indiana	1988	23	59	110	53.6
Ross Richardson, Loyola Marymount	1991	25	61	116	52.6
Lance Barker, Valparaiso	1992	26	61	117	52.1
Ed Peterson, Yale	1989	28	53	104	51.0
Willie Brand, Texas-Arlington	1988	29	65	128	50.8

FREE-THROW PERCENTAGE

Player, Team	Season	G	FT	FTA	Pct.
Jim Barton, Dartmouth	1986	26	65	69	94.2
Steve Alford, Indiana	1984	31	137	150	91.3
Jay Edwards, Indiana	1988	23	69	76	90.8
LaBradford Smith, Louisville	1988	35	143	158	90.5
Geoff Billet, Rutgers	1996	26	72	80	90.0

REBOUNDS

Player, Team	Season	G	Reb.
Pete Padgett, Nevada	1973	26	462
Kenny Miller, Loyola (Ill.)	1988	29	395
Shaquille O'Neal, LSU	1990	32	385
Ralph Sampson, Virginia	1980	34	381
Adonal Foyle, Colgate	1995	30	371

REBOUND AVERAGE

Player, Team	Season	G	Reb.	Avg.
Pete Padgett, Nevada	1973	26	462	17.8
Glenn Mosley, Seton Hall	1974	21	299	14.2
Ira Terrell, Southern Methodist	1973	25	352	14.1
Kenny Miller, Loyola (Ill.)	1988	29	395	13.6
Bob Stephens, Drexel	1976	23	307	13.3

ASSISTS

Player, Team	Season	G	Ast.
Bobby Hurley, Duke	1990	38	288
Kenny Anderson, Georgia Tech	1990	35	285
Andre LaFleur, Northeastern	1984	32	252
Orlando Smart, San Francisco	1991	29	237
Chris Corchiani, North Caro. St.	1988	32	235

ASSIST AVERAGE

Player, Team	Season	G	Ast.	Avg.
Orlando Smart, San Francisco	1991	29	237	8.17
Kenny Anderson, Georgia Tech	1990	35	285	8.14
Taurence Chisholm, Delaware	1985	28	224	8.00
Andre LaFleur, Northeastern	1984	32	252	7.88
Marc Brown, Siena	1988	29	222	7.66
Jason Kidd, California	1993	29	222	7.66

BLOCKED SHOTS

Player, Team	Season	G	Blk.
Shawn Bradley, Brigham Young	1991	34	177
Alonzo Mourning, Georgetown	1989	34	169
Adonal Foyle, Colgate	1995	30	147
Keith Closs, Central Conn. St.	1995	26	139
Tim Duncan, Wake Forest	1994	33	124

BLOCKED-SHOT AVERAGE

Player, Team	Season	G	Blk.	Avg.
Keith Closs, Central Conn. St.	1995	26	139	5.35
Shawn Bradley, Brigham Young	1991	34	177	5.21
Alonzo Mourning, Georgetown	1989	34	169	4.97
Adonal Foyle, Colgate	1995	30	147	4.90
Tim Duncan, Wake Forest	1994	33	124	3.76

STEALS

Player, Team	Season	G	Stl.
Nadav Henefeld, Connecticut	1990	37	138
Jason Kidd, California	1993	29	110
Ben Larson, Cal Poly SLO	1996	29	100
Eric Murdock, Providence	1988	28	90
Pat Baldwin, Northwestern	1991	28	90
Clarence Ceasar, LSU	1992	31	90

STEAL AVERAGE

Player, Team	Season	G	Stl.	Avg.
Jason Kidd, California	1993	29	110	3.79
Nadav Henefeld, Connecticut	1990	37	138	3.73
Ben Larson, Cal Poly SLO	1996	29	100	3.45
Eric Murdock, Providence	1988	28	90	3.21
Pat Baldwin, Northwestern	1991	28	90	3.21

Career Records

POINTS

Player, Team	Ht.	Last Season	Yrs.	G	FG	3FG#	FT	Pts.
Pete Maravich, LSU	6-5	1970	3	83	1,387	—	893	3,667
Freeman Williams, Portland St.	6-4	1978	4	106	1,369	—	511	3,249
Lionel Simmons, La Salle	6-7	1990	4	131	1,244	56	673	3,217
Alphonso Ford, Mississippi Val.	6-2	1993	4	109	1,121	333	590	3,165
Harry Kelly, Texas Southern	6-7	1983	4	110	1,234	—	598	3,066
Hersey Hawkins, Bradley	6-3	1988	4	125	1,100	118	690	3,008
Oscar Robertson, Cincinnati	6-5	1960	3	88	1,052	—	869	2,973
Danny Manning, Kansas	6-10	1988	4	147	1,216	10	509	2,951
Alfredrick Hughes, Loyola (Ill.)	6-5	1985	4	120	1,226	—	462	2,914
Elvin Hayes, Houston	6-8	1968	3	93	1,215	—	454	2,884
Larry Bird, Indiana St.	6-9	1979	3	94	1,154	—	542	2,850
Otis Birdsong, Houston	6-4	1977	4	116	1,176	—	480	2,832

Player, Team	Ht.	Last Season	Yrs.	G	FG	3FG#	FT	Pts.
Kevin Bradshaw, Bethune-Cookman & U.S. Int'l	6-6	1991	4	111	1,027	132	618	2,804
Allan Houston, Tennessee	6-5	1993	4	128	902	346	651	2,801
Hank Gathers, Southern Cal & Loyola Marymount	6-7	1990	4	117	1,127	0	469	2,723
Reggie Lewis, Northeastern	6-7	1987	4	122	1,043	30(1)	592	2,708
Daren Queenan, Lehigh	6-5	1988	4	118	1,024	29	626	2,703
Byron Larkin, Xavier (Ohio)	6-3	1988	4	121	1,022	51	601	2,696
David Robinson, Navy	7-1	1987	4	127	1,032	1	604	2,669
Wayman Tisdale, Oklahoma	6-9	1985	3	104	1,077	—	507	2,661
Michael Brooks, La Salle	6-7	1980	4	114	1,064	—	500	2,628
Calbert Cheaney, Indiana	6-6	1993	4	132	1,018	148	429	2,613
Mark Macon, Temple	6-5	1991	4	126	980	246	403	2,609
Don MacLean, UCLA	6-10	1992	4	127	943	11	711	2,608
Joe Dumars, McNeese St.	6-3	1985	4	116	941	(5)	723	2,605
Terrance Bailey, Wagner	6-2	1987	4	110	985	42	579	2,591
Dickie Hemric, Wake Forest	6-6	1955	4	104	841	—	905	2,587
Calvin Natt, Northeast La.	6-5	1979	4	108	1,017	—	547	2,581
Derrick Chievous, Missouri	6-7	1988	4	130	893	30	764	2,580
Skip Henderson, Marshall	6-2	1988	4	125	1,000	133	441	2,574
Austin Carr, Notre Dame	6-3	1971	3	74	1,017	—	526	2,560
Sean Elliott, Arizona	6-8	1989	4	133	896	140	623	2,555
Rodney Monroe, North Caro. St.	6-3	1991	4	124	885	322	459	2,551
Calvin Murphy, Niagara	5-10	1970	3	77	947	—	654	2,548
Frank Selvy, Furman	6-3	1954	3	78	922	—	694	2,538
Johnny Dawkins, Duke	6-2	1986	4	133	1,026	(19)	485	2,537
Willie Jackson, Centenary (La.)	6-6	1984	4	114	995	(18)	545	2,535
Steve Rogers, Alabama St.	6-5	1992	4	113	817	187	713	2,534
Steve Burtt, Iona	6-2	1984	4	121	1,003	—	528	2,534
Shawn Respert, Michigan St.	6-3	1995	4	118	866	331	468	2,531
Joe Jakubick, Akron	6-5	1984	4	108	973	(53)	584	2,530
Andrew Toney, Southwestern La.	6-3	1980	4	107	996	—	534	2,526
Ron Perry, Holy Cross	6-2	1980	4	109	922	—	680	2,524
Mike Olliver, Lamar	6-1	1981	4	122	1,130	—	258	2,518
Bryant Stith, Virginia	6-5	1992	4	131	856	114	690	2,516
Bill Bradley, Princeton	6-5	1965	3	83	856	—	791	2,503
Jeff Grayer, Iowa St.	6-5	1988	4	125	974	27	527	2,502
Elgin Baylor, Col. Idaho & Seattle	6-6	1958	3	80	956	—	588	2,500

#Listed is the number of three-pointers scored since it became the national rule in 1987; the number in the parenthesis is number scored before 1987—these counted as three points in the game but counted as two-pointers in the national rankings. The three-pointers in the parenthesis are not included in total points.

2,000-POINT SCORERS

A total of 342 players in Division I history have scored at least 2,000 points over their careers. The first was Jim Lacy, Loyola (Md.), with 2,154 over four seasons ending in 1949. The first to reach 2,000 in a three-season career was Furman's Frank Selvy, 2,538 through 1954. The 342 come from 188 different colleges. Duke leads with seven 2,000-pointers: Jim Spanarkel (last season was 1979), Mike Gminski (1980), Gene Banks (1981), Mark Alarie (1986), Johnny Dawkins (1986), Danny Ferry (1989) and Christian Laettner (1992). Georgia Tech, North Carolina, Oklahoma, Tennessee and Villanova are next with five apiece.

SCORING AVERAGE

Player, Team	Last Season	Yrs.	G	FG	3FG	FT	Pts.	Avg.
Pete Maravich, LSU	1968	3	83	1,387	—	893	3,667	44.2
Austin Carr, Notre Dame	1971	3	74	1,017	—	526	2,560	34.6
Oscar Robertson, Cincinnati	1960	3	88	1,052	—	869	2,973	33.8
Calvin Murphy, Niagara	1970	3	77	947	—	654	2,548	33.1
Dwight Lamar, Southwestern La.	†1973	2	57	768	—	326	1,862	32.7
Frank Selvy, Furman	1954	3	78	922	—	694	2,538	32.5
Rick Mount, Purdue	1970	3	72	910	—	503	2,323	32.3
Darrell Floyd, Furman	1956	3	71	868	—	545	2,281	32.1
Nick Werkman, Seton Hall	1964	3	71	812	—	649	2,273	32.0
Willie Humes, Idaho St.	1971	2	48	565	—	380	1,510	31.5
William Averitt, Pepperdine	1973	2	49	615	—	311	1,541	31.4
Elgin Baylor, Col. Idaho & Seattle	1958	3	80	956	—	588	2,500	31.3
Elvin Hayes, Houston	1968	3	93	1,215	—	454	2,884	31.0
Freeman Williams, Portland St.	1978	4	106	1,369	—	511	3,249	30.7
Larry Bird, Indiana St.	1979	3	94	1,154	—	542	2,850	30.3
Bill Bradley, Princeton	1965	3	83	856	—	791	2,503	30.2
Rich Fuqua, Oral Roberts	†1973	2	54	692	—	233	1,617	29.9
Wilt Chamberlain, Kansas	1958	2	48	503	—	427	1,433	29.9
Rick Barry, Miami (Fla.)	1965	3	77	816	—	666	2,298	29.8
Doug Collins, Illinois St.	1973	3	77	894	—	452	2,240	29.1
Alphonso Ford, Mississippi Val.	1993	4	109	1,121	333	590	3,165	29.0
Chris Jackson, LSU	1990	2	64	664	172	354	1,854	29.0
Dave Schellhase, Purdue	1966	3	74	746	—	582	2,074	28.8
Dick Wilkinson, Virginia	1955	3	78	783	—	665	2,233	28.6
James Williams, Austin Peay	1974	2	54	632	—	277	1,541	28.5

†Each played two years of non-Division I competition (Lamar—four years, 3,493 points and 31.2 average; Fuqua—four years, 3,004 points and 27.1 average).

DIVISION I

FIELD-GOAL PERCENTAGE
(Minimum 400 field goals made)

Player, Team	Ht.	Last Season	Yrs.	G	FG	FGA	Pct.
Ricky Nedd, Appalachian St.	6-7	1994	4	113	412	597	69.0
Stephen Scheffler, Purdue	6-9	1990	4	110	408	596	68.5
Steve Johnson, Oregon St.	6-10	1981	4	116	828	1,222	67.8
Murray Brown, Florida St.	6-8	1980	4	106	566	847	66.8
Lee Campbell, Middle Tenn. St. & Southwest Mo. St.	6-7	1990	3	88	411	618	66.5
Warren Kidd, Middle Tenn. St.	6-9	1993	3	83	496	747	66.4
Joe Senser, West Chester	6-5	1979	4	96	476	719	66.2
Kevin Magee, UC Irvine	6-8	1982	2	56	552	841	65.6
Orlando Phillips, Pepperdine	6-7	1983	2	58	404	618	65.4
Bill Walton, UCLA	6-11	1974	3	87	747	1,147	65.1
William Herndon, Massachusetts	6-3	1992	4	100	472	728	64.8
Larry Stewart, Coppin St.	6-8	1991	3	91	676	1,046	64.6
Larry Johnson, UNLV	6-7	1991	2	75	612	952	64.3
Dwayne Davis, Florida	6-7	1991	4	124	572	892	64.1
Lew Alcindor, UCLA	7-2	1969	3	88	943	1,476	63.9
Akeem Olajuwon, Houston	7-0	1984	3	100	532	833	63.9
Oliver Miller, Arkansas	6-9	1992	4	137	680	1,069	63.6
Mike Coleman, Liberty	6-7	1992	4	105	421	663	63.5
Jeff Ruland, Iona	6-10	1980	4	89	717	1,130	63.5
Mark McNamara, California	6-10	1982	4	107	709	1,119	63.4
Marro Hawkins, Centenary (La.)	6-7	1990	4	115	459	725	63.3
Cherokee Rhone, Centenary (La.)	6-8	1982	3	63	421	667	63.1
Brian Hill, Evansville	6-7	1990	4	120	424	672	63.1
Bobby Lee Hurt, Alabama	6-9	1985	4	126	646	1,024	63.1
Keith Walker, Utica	6-5	1985	4	99	429	681	63.0

THREE-POINT FIELD GOALS MADE

Player, Team	Ht.	Last Season	Yrs.	G	3FG
Doug Day, Radford	6-1	1993	4	117	401
Ronnie Schmitz, Mo.-Kansas City	6-3	1993	4	112	378
Mark Alberts, Akron	6-1	1993	4	107	375
Jeff Fryer, Loyola Marymount	6-2	1990	4	112	363
Dennis Scott, Georgia Tech	6-8	1990	3	99	351
Allan Houston, Tennessee	6-5	1993	4	128	346
Alphonso Ford, Mississippi Val.	6-2	1993	4	109	333
Shawn Respert, Michigan St.	6-3	1995	4	118	331
Andy Kennedy, North Caro. St. & UAB	6-8	1991	4	121	330
Randolph Childress, Wake Forest	6-2	1995	4	120	329
Stevin Smith, Arizona St.	6-2	1994	4	115	323
Tim Roberts, Southern U.	6-5	1996	4	113	323
Rodney Monroe, North Caro. St.	6-3	1991	4	124	322
Kent Culuko, James Madison	6-4	1995	4	119	320
Bernard Haslett, Southern Miss.	6-3	1994	4	113	316
Terry Dehere, Seton Hall	6-3	1993	4	128	315
Scott Hartzell, N.C.-Greensboro	6-0	1996	4	113	309
Henry Williams, N.C.-Charlotte	6-2	1992	4	118	308
Dewayne Powell, Tenn.-Martin	6-2	1996	4	107	302
Kareem Townes, La Salle	6-3	1995	3	81	300
Mark Lueking, Army	5-10	1996	4	104	300
Chris McGuthrie, Mt. St. Mary's (Md.)	5-9	1996	4	115	300
Lindsey Hunter, Jackson St.	6-2	1993	4	120	297
Ronnie McMahan, Vanderbilt	6-5	1995	4	124	296
Josh Kohn, N.C.-Asheville	5-10	1996	4	109	296

THREE-POINT FIELD GOALS MADE PER GAME
(Minimum 200 three-point field goals made)

Player, Team	Ht.	Last Season	Yrs.	G	3FG	Avg.
Timothy Pollard, Mississippi Val.	6-3	1989	2	56	256	4.57
Sydney Grider, Southwestern La.	6-3	1990	2	58	253	4.36
Kareem Townes, La Salle	6-3	1995	3	81	300	3.70
Dave Mooney, Coastal Caro.	6-4	1988	2	56	202	3.61
Dennis Scott, Georgia Tech	6-8	1990	3	99	351	3.55
Mark Alberts, Akron	6-1	1993	4	107	375	3.50
Doug Day, Radford	6-1	1993	4	117	401	3.43
Ronnie Schmitz, Mo.-Kansas City	6-3	1993	4	112	378	3.38
Jeff Fryer, Loyola Marymount	6-2	1990	4	112	363	3.24
Dana Barros, Boston College	5-11	1989	3	91	291	3.20
Tony Ross, San Diego St.	6-3	1989	3	85	270	3.18
Randy Woods, La Salle	6-0	1992	3	88	278	3.16
Wally Lancaster, Virginia Tech	6-5	1989	3	82	257	3.13
Jim Barton, Dartmouth	6-4	1989	3	78	242	3.10
Alphonso Ford, Mississippi Val.	6-2	1993	4	109	333	3.06
Keke Hicks, Coastal Caro.	6-4	1995	4	93	282	3.03
Lazelle Durden, Cincinnati	6-2	1995	3	90	260	2.89
Mark Lueking, Army	5-10	1996	4	104	300	2.88
Tim Roberts, Southern U.	6-5	1996	4	113	323	2.86
Terry Brown, Kansas	6-2	1991	2	70	200	2.86
Tucker Neale, Colgate	6-3	1995	3	87	248	2.85
Dewayne Powell, Tenn.-Martin	6-2	1996	4	107	302	2.82
Randy Rutherford, Oklahoma St.	6-3	1995	3	99	279	2.82

Player, Team	Ht.	Last Season	Yrs.	G	3FG	Avg.
Scott Haffner, Evansville	6-4	1989	3	87	245	2.82
Stevin Smith, Arizona St.	6-2	1994	4	115	323	2.81
Gerald Paddio, UNLV	6-7	1988	2	73	205	2.81
Shawn Respert, Michigan St.	6-3	1995	4	118	331	2.81

THREE-POINT FIELD-GOAL PERCENTAGE
(Minimum 200 three-point field goals made)

Player, Team	Ht.	Last Season	Yrs.	G	3FG	3FGA	Pct.
Tony Bennett, Wis.-Green Bay	6-0	1992	4	118	290	584	49.7
Keith Jennings, East Tenn. St.	5-7	1991	4	127	223	452	49.3
Kirk Manns, Michigan St.	6-1	1990	4	120	212	446	47.5
Tim Locum, Wisconsin	6-4	1991	4	118	227	446	47.2
David Olson, Eastern Ill.	6-4	1992	4	111	262	562	46.6
Sean Jackson, Ohio & Princeton	5-11	1992	4	104	243	528	46.0
Barry Booker, Vanderbilt	6-3	1989	3	98	246	535	46.0
Kevin Booth, Mt. St. Mary's (Md.)	6-0	1993	5	110	265	577	45.9
Dave Calloway, Monmouth (N.J.)	6-3	1991	4	115	260	567	45.9
Tony Ross, San Diego St.	6-3	1992	3	85	270	589	45.8
Jason Matthews, Pittsburgh	6-3	1991	4	123	259	567	45.7
Jim Barton, Dartmouth	6-4	1989	3	78	242	532	45.5
Shawn Respert, Michigan St.	6-3	1995	4	118	331	728	45.5
Carlton Becton, North Caro. A&T	6-6	1989	3	84	209	462	45.2
Ray Allen, Connecticut	6-5	1996	3	101	233	520	44.8
Curtis Shelton, Southeast Mo. St.	5-9	1994	4	107	215	480	44.8
Steve Henson, Kansas St.	6-1	1990	4	127	240	537	44.7
Jeff McCool, New Mexico St.	6-5	1989	3	92	201	450	44.7
Todd Leslie, Northwestern	6-5	1994	4	113	203	455	44.6
Ben Berlowski, Wis.-Green Bay	6-3	1996	4	120	218	491	44.4
Scott Neely, Campbell	6-3	1996	4	115	244	553	44.1
Wesley Person, Auburn	6-6	1994	4	108	262	594	44.1
Mark Alberts, Akron	6-1	1993	4	107	375	853	44.0
John Rillie, Gonzaga	6-5	1995	3	88	230	524	43.9
Scott Hartzell, N.C.-Greensboro	6-0	1996	4	113	309	704	43.9
Andy Kennedy, North Caro. St. & UAB	6-8	1991	4	121	330	752	43.9

FREE-THROW PERCENTAGE
(Minimum 300 free throws made)

Player, Team	Last Season	Yrs.	G	FT	FTA	Pct.
Greg Starrick, Kentucky & Southern Ill.	1972	4	72	341	375	90.9
Jack Moore, Nebraska	1982	4	105	446	495	90.1
Steve Henson, Kansas St.	1990	4	127	361	401	90.0
Steve Alford, Indiana	1987	4	125	535	596	89.8
Bob Lloyd, Rutgers	1967	3	77	543	605	89.8
Jim Barton, Dartmouth	1989	4	104	394	440	89.5
Tommy Boyer, Arkansas	1963	3	70	315	353	89.2
Rob Robbins, New Mexico	1991	4	133	309	348	88.8
Sean Miller, Pittsburgh	1992	4	128	317	358	88.5
Ron Perry, Holy Cross	1980	4	109	680	768	88.5
Joe Dykstra, Western Ill.	1983	4	117	587	663	88.5
Mike Joseph, Bucknell	1990	4	115	397	449	88.4
Kyle Macy, Purdue & Kentucky	1980	5	125	416	471	88.3
Matt Hildebrand, Liberty	1994	4	117	398	451	88.2
Jimmy England, Tennessee	1971	3	81	319	362	88.1
Rod Foster, UCLA	1983	4	113	309	351	88.0
Michael Smith, Brigham Young	1989	4	122	431	491	87.8
Jason Matthews, Pittsburgh	1991	4	123	481	548	87.8
Mike Iuzzolino, Penn St. & St. Francis (Pa.)	1991	4	112	402	458	87.8
Rick Suder, Duquesne	1986	4	105	342	390	87.7
Bill Bradley, Princeton	1965	3	83	791	903	87.6
William Lewis, Monmouth (N.J.)	1992	4	112	317	362	87.6
Charlie Davis, Wake Forest	1971	3	79	578	662	87.3
Scott Haffner, Illinois & Evansville	1989	4	116	306	351	87.2
Andy Kennedy, North Caro. St. & UAB	1991	4	121	415	477	87.0

REBOUNDS

Player, Team	Ht.	Last Season	Yrs.	G	Reb.
Tom Gola, La Salle	6-6	1955	4	118	2,201
Joe Holup, Geo. Washington	6-6	1956	4	104	2,030
Charlie Slack, Marshall	6-5	1956	4	88	1,916
Ed Conlin, Fordham	6-5	1955	4	102	1,884
Dickie Hemric, Wake Forest	6-6	1955	4	104	1,802
Paul Silas, Creighton	6-7	1964	3	81	1,751
Art Quimby, Connecticut	6-5	1955	4	80	1,716
Jerry Harper, Alabama	6-8	1956	4	93	1,688
Jeff Cohen, William & Mary	6-7	1961	4	103	1,679
Steve Hamilton, Morehead St.	6-7	1958	4	102	1,675
Charlie Tyra, Louisville	6-8	1957	4	95	1,617
Bill Russell, San Francisco	6-9	1956	3	79	1,606
Elvin Hayes, Houston	6-8	1968	3	93	1,602
Ron Shavlik, North Caro. St.	6-8	1956	3	95	1,598

Malik Rose established himself as one of the most prolific rebounders in Division I history, hauling down 1,514 missed field-goal attempts in four years at Drexel. Rose averaged 12.6 rebounds per game over his career.

Player, Team	Ht.	Last Season	Yrs.	G	Reb.
Marvin Barnes, Providence	6-9	1974	3	89	1,592
Elgin Baylor, Col. Idaho & Seattle	6-6	1958	3	80	1,559
Ernie Beck, Pennsylvania	6-4	1953	3	82	1,557
Dave DeBusschere, Detroit	6-5	1962	3	80	1,552
Wes Unseld, Louisville	6-8	1968	3	82	1,551
Derrick Coleman, Syracuse	6-9	1990	4	143	1,537
Malik Rose, Drexel	6-7	1996	4	120	1,514
Ralph Sampson, Virginia	7-4	1983	4	132	1,511
Chris Smith, Virginia Tech	6-6	1961	4	88	1,508
Keith Swagerty, Pacific (Cal.)	6-7	1967	3	82	1,505
Kermit Washington, American	6-8	1973	3	73	1,478

(For careers beginning in 1973 or after)

Player, Team	Ht.	Last Season	Yrs.	G	Reb.
Derrick Coleman, Syracuse	6-9	1990	4	143	1,537
Malik Rose, Drexel	6-7	1996	4	120	1,514
Ralph Sampson, Virginia	7-4	1983	4	132	1,511
Pete Padgett, Nevada	6-8	1976	4	104	1,464
Lionel Simmons, La Salle	6-7	1990	4	131	1,429
Anthony Bonner, St. Louis	6-7	1990	4	133	1,424
Tyrone Hill, Xavier (Ohio)	6-9	1990	4	126	1,380
Popeye Jones, Murray St.	6-8	1992	4	123	1,374
Michael Brooks, La Salle	6-7	1980	4	114	1,372
Xavier McDaniel, Wichita St.	6-7	1985	4	117	1,359
John Irving, Arizona & Hofstra	6-9	1977	4	103	1,348
Sam Clancy, Pittsburgh	6-6	1981	4	116	1,342
Keith Lee, Memphis	6-10	1985	4	128	1,336
Larry Smith, Alcorn St.	6-8	1980	4	111	1,334
Clarence Weatherspoon, Southern Miss.	6-7	1992	4	117	1,320
Michael Cage, San Diego St.	6-9	1984	4	112	1,317
Bob Stephens, Drexel	6-7	1979	4	99	1,316
Patrick Ewing, Georgetown	7-0	1985	4	143	1,316
David Robinson, Navy	7-1	1987	4	127	1,314
Wayne Rollins, Clemson	7-1	1977	4	110	1,311
Bob Warner, Maine	6-6	1976	4	96	1,304
Ervin Johnson, New Orleans	6-11	1993	4	123	1,287
Calvin Natt, Northeast La.	6-5	1979	4	108	1,285
Leon Douglas, Alabama	6-10	1976	4	111	1,279
Reggie King, Alabama	6-6	1979	4	118	1,279
Durand Macklin, LSU	6-7	1981	5	123	1,276
Sidney Green, UNLV	6-9	1983	4	119	1,276

REBOUND AVERAGE
(Minimum 800 rebounds)

Player, Team	Ht.	Last Season	Yrs.	G	Reb.	Avg.
Artis Gilmore, Jacksonville	7-2	1971	2	54	1,224	22.7
Charlie Slack, Marshall	6-5	1956	4	88	1,916	21.8
Paul Silas, Creighton	6-7	1964	3	81	1,751	21.6
Leroy Wright, Pacific (Cal.)	6-8	1960	3	67	1,442	21.5
Art Quimby, Connecticut	6-5	1955	4	80	1,716	21.5
Walt Dukes, Seton Hall	6-10	1953	2	59	1,247	21.1
Bill Russell, San Francisco	6-9	1956	3	79	1,606	20.3
Kermit Washington, American	6-8	1973	3	73	1,478	20.2
Julius Erving, Massachusetts	6-6	1971	2	52	1,049	20.2
Joe Holup, Geo. Washington	6-6	1956	4	104	2,030	19.5
Elgin Baylor, Col. Idaho & Seattle	6-6	1958	3	80	1,559	19.5
Dave DeBusschere, Detroit	6-5	1962	3	80	1,552	19.4
Ernie Beck, Pennsylvania	6-4	1953	3	82	1,557	19.0
Wes Unseld, Louisville	6-8	1968	3	82	1,551	18.9
Tom Gola, La Salle	6-6	1955	4	118	2,201	18.7
Ed Conlin, Fordham	6-5	1955	4	102	1,884	18.5
Keith Swagerty, Pacific (Cal.)	6-7	1967	3	82	1,505	18.4
Wilt Chamberlain, Kansas	7-0	1958	2	48	877	18.3
Jerry Harper, Alabama	6-8	1956	4	93	1,688	18.2
Dick Cunningham, Murray St.	6-10	1968	3	71	1,292	18.2
Marvin Barnes, Providence	6-9	1974	3	89	1,592	17.9
Alex Ellis, Niagara	6-5	1958	3	77	1,376	17.9
Dickie Hemric, Wake Forest	6-6	1955	4	104	1,802	17.3
Elvin Hayes, Houston	6-8	1968	3	93	1,602	17.2
Chris Smith, Virginia Tech	6-6	1961	4	88	1,508	17.1

(For careers beginning in 1973 or after; minimum 800 rebounds)

Player, Team	Ht.	Last Season	Yrs.	G	Reb.	Avg.
Glenn Mosley, Seton Hall	6-8	1977	4	83	1,263	15.2
Bill Campion, Manhattan	6-10	1975	3	74	1,070	14.6
Pete Padgett, Nevada	6-8	1976	4	104	1,464	14.1
Bob Warner, Maine	6-6	1976	4	96	1,304	13.6
Shaquille O'Neal, LSU	7-1	1992	3	90	1,217	13.5
Cornelius Cash, Bowling Green	6-8	1975	3	79	1,068	13.5
Ira Terrell, Southern Methodist	6-8	1976	3	80	1,077	13.5
Bob Stephens, Drexel	6-7	1979	4	99	1,316	13.3
Larry Bird, Indiana St.	6-9	1979	3	94	1,247	13.3
Bernard King, Tennessee	6-7	1977	3	76	1,004	13.2
John Irving, Arizona & Hofstra	6-9	1977	4	103	1,348	13.1
Carey Scurry, LIU-Brooklyn	6-9	1985	3	79	1,013	12.8
Warren Kidd, Middle Tenn. St.	6-6	1993	3	83	1,048	12.6
Malik Rose, Drexel	6-7	1996	4	120	1,514	12.6
Jervaughn Scales, Southern U.	6-6	1994	3	88	1,099	12.5
Michael Brooks, La Salle	6-7	1980	4	114	1,372	12.0
Larry Smith, Alcorn St.	6-8	1980	4	111	1,334	12.0
Wayne Rollins, Clemson	7-1	1977	4	110	1,311	11.9
Calvin Natt, Northeast La.	6-5	1979	4	108	1,285	11.9
Ed Lawrence, McNeese St.	7-0	1976	4	102	1,212	11.9
Michael Cage, San Diego St.	6-9	1984	4	112	1,317	11.8
Xavier McDaniel, Wichita St.	6-7	1985	4	117	1,359	11.6
John Rudd, McNeese St.	6-6	1978	4	102	1,181	11.6
Sam Clancy, Pittsburgh	6-6	1981	4	116	1,342	11.6
Larry Stewart, Coppin St.	6-6	1991	3	91	1,052	11.6
Reggie Jackson, Nicholls St.	6-6	1995	4	110	1,271	11.6

ASSISTS

Player, Team	Ht.	Last Season	Yrs.	G	Ast.
Bobby Hurley, Duke	6-0	1993	4	140	1,076
Chris Corchiani, North Caro. St.	6-1	1991	4	124	1,038
Keith Jennings, East Tenn. St.	5-7	1991	4	127	983
Sherman Douglas, Syracuse	6-0	1989	4	138	960
Tony Miller, Marquette	6-0	1995	4	123	956
Greg Anthony, Portland & UNLV	6-1	1991	4	138	950
Gary Payton, Oregon St.	6-2	1990	4	120	939
Orlando Smart, San Francisco	6-0	1994	4	116	902
Andre LaFleur, Northeastern	6-3	1987	4	128	894
Jim Les, Bradley	5-11	1986	4	118	884
Frank Smith, Old Dominion	6-0	1988	4	120	883
Taurence Chisholm, Delaware	5-7	1988	4	110	877
Grayson Marshall, Clemson	6-2	1988	4	122	857
Anthony Manuel, Bradley	5-11	1989	4	108	855
Pooh Richardson, UCLA	6-1	1989	4	122	833
Butch Moore, Southern Methodist	5-10	1986	4	125	828
Drafton Davis, Marist	6-0	1988	4	115	804
Marc Brown, Siena	5-11	1991	4	123	796
Tyrone Bogues, Wake Forest	5-3	1987	4	119	781
Jeff Timberlake, Boston U.	6-2	1989	4	121	778
Kenny Smith, North Caro.	6-3	1987	4	127	768
Bruce Douglas, Illinois	6-3	1986	4	130	765
Andre Turner, Memphis	5-10	1986	4	132	763
David Edwards Georgetown & Texas A&M	5-9	1994	4	116	752
Howard Evans, Temple	6-1	1988	4	132	748

ASSIST AVERAGE
(Minimum 550 assists)

Player, Team	Ht.	Last Season	Yrs.	G	Ast.	Avg.
Avery Johnson, Cameron & Southern U.	5-11	1988	3	94	838	8.91
Sam Crawford, New Mexico St.	5-8	1993	2	67	592	8.84
Mark Wade, Oklahoma & UNLV	6-0	1987	3	79	693	8.77
Chris Corchiani, North Caro. St.	6-1	1991	4	124	1,038	8.37
Taurence Chisholm, Delaware	5-7	1988	4	110	877	7.97
Van Usher, Tennessee Tech	6-0	1992	3	85	676	7.95
Anthony Manuel, Bradley	5-11	1989	4	108	855	7.92
Gary Payton, Oregon St.	6-2	1990	4	120	938	7.82
Orlando Smart, San Francisco	6-0	1994	4	116	902	7.78
Tony Miller, Marquette	6-0	1995	4	123	956	7.77
Keith Jennings, East Tenn. St.	5-7	1991	4	127	983	7.74
Bobby Hurley, Duke	6-0	1993	4	140	1,076	7.69
Chuck Evans, Old Dominion & Mississippi St.	5-11	1993	3	85	648	7.62
Jim Les, Bradley	5-11	1986	4	118	884	7.49
Frank Smith, Old Dominion	6-0	1988	4	120	883	7.36
Doug Wojcik, Navy	6-1	1987	3	99	714	7.21
Mark Woods, Wright St.	6-1	1993	4	113	811	7.18
Nelson Haggerty, Baylor	6-0	1995	4	98	699	7.13
Grayson Marshall, Clemson	6-2	1988	4	122	857	7.02
Drafton Davis, Marist	6-0	1988	4	115	804	6.99
Andre LaFleur, Northeastern	6-3	1987	4	128	894	6.98
Sherman Douglas, Syracuse	6-0	1989	4	138	960	6.96
Greg Anthony, Portland & UNLV	6-1	1991	4	138	950	6.88
Pooh Richardson, UCLA	6-1	1989	4	122	833	6.83
Dan Pogue, Campbell	6-1	1996	4	104	701	6.74

BLOCKED SHOTS

Player, Team	Ht.	Last Season	Yrs.	G	Blk.
Alonzo Mourning, Georgetown	6-10	1992	4	120	453
Theo Ratliff, Wyoming	6-10	1995	4	111	425
Rodney Blake, St. Joseph's (Pa.)	6-8	1988	4	116	419
Shaquille O'Neal, LSU	7-1	1992	3	90	412
Kevin Roberson, Vermont	6-7	1992	4	112	409
Jim McIlvaine, Marquette	7-1	1994	4	118	399
Tim Perry, Temple	6-9	1988	4	130	392
#Tim Duncan, Wake Forest	6-10	1996	3	97	379
Pervis Ellison, Louisville	6-9	1989	4	136	374
Acie Earl, Iowa	6-10	1993	4	116	365
Dikembe Mutombo, Georgetown	7-2	1991	3	96	354
David Robinson, Navy	6-11	1987	2	67	351
Charles Smith, Pittsburgh	6-10	1988	4	122	346
Rik Smits, Marist	7-4	1988	4	107	345
Oliver Miller, Arkansas	6-9	1992	4	137	345
Derrick Lewis, Maryland	6-7	1988	4	127	339
Luc Longley, New Mexico	7-2	1991	4	132	336
David Van Dyke, UTEP	6-8	1992	4	127	336
Marcus Camby, Massachusetts	6-11	1996	3	92	336
Kenny Green, Rhode Island	6-8	1990	4	122	335
Elden Campbell, Clemson	6-10	1990	4	123	334
Rony Seikaly, Syracuse	6-10	1988	4	136	319
Derrick Coleman, Syracuse	6-9	1990	4	143	318
#Keith Closs, Central Conn. St.	7-2	1996	2	54	317
#Adonal Foyle, Colgate	6-10	1996	2	59	312

#Active player.

BLOCKED-SHOT AVERAGE
(Minimum 225 blocked shots)

Player, Team	Ht.	Last Season	Yrs.	G	Blk.	Avg.
David Robinson, Navy	6-11	1987	2	67	351	5.24
Shaquille O'Neal, LSU	7-1	1992	3	90	412	4.58
Theo Ratliff, Wyoming	6-10	1995	4	111	425	3.83
Alonzo Mourning, Georgetown	6-10	1992	4	120	453	3.78
Lorenzo Williams, Stetson	6-9	1991	2	63	234	3.71
Dikembe Mutombo, Georgetown	7-2	1991	3	96	354	3.69
Marcus Camby, Massachusetts	6-11	1996	3	92	336	3.65
Kevin Roberson, Vermont	6-7	1992	4	112	409	3.65
Rodney Blake, St. Joseph's (Pa.)	6-8	1988	4	116	419	3.61
Jim McIlvaine, Marquette	7-1	1994	4	118	399	3.38
Rik Smits, Marist	7-4	1988	4	107	345	3.22
Acie Earl, Iowa	6-10	1993	4	116	365	3.15
Sharone Wright, Clemson	6-11	1994	3	92	286	3.11
Tim Perry, Temple	6-9	1988	4	130	392	3.02
Charles Smith, Pittsburgh	6-10	1988	4	122	346	2.84
Theron Wilson, Eastern Mich.	6-9	1996	4	92	257	2.79
Damon Lopez, Fordham	6-9	1991	3	93	258	2.77
Pervis Ellison, Louisville	6-9	1989	4	136	374	2.75
Kenny Green, Rhode Island	6-8	1990	4	122	335	2.75
Elden Campbell, Clemson	6-10	1990	4	123	334	2.72
Donyell Marshall, Connecticut	6-8	1994	3	91	245	2.69
Erick Dampier, Mississippi St.	6-11	1996	3	93	249	2.68
Derrick Lewis, Maryland	6-7	1988	4	127	339	2.67
David Cully, William & Mary	6-8	1996	4	93	248	2.67
David Van Dyke, UTEP	6-8	1992	4	127	336	2.65

STEALS

Player, Team	Ht.	Last Season	Yrs.	G	Stl.
Eric Murdock, Providence	6-2	1991	4	117	376
Gerald Walker, San Francisco	6-1	1996	4	111	344
Johnny Rhodes, Maryland	6-6	1996	4	122	344
Michael Anderson, Drexel	5-11	1988	4	115	341
Kenny Robertson, Cleveland St.	6-0	1990	4	119	341
Keith Jennings, East Tenn. St.	5-7	1991	4	127	334
Greg Anthony, Portland & UNLV	6-1	1991	4	138	329
Chris Corchiani, North Caro. St.	6-1	1991	4	124	328
Gary Payton, Oregon St.	6-2	1990	4	120	321
Mark Woods, Wright St.	6-1	1993	4	113	314
Pointer Williams, Tulane & McNeese St.	6-0	1996	4	115	314
Scott Burrell, Connecticut	6-7	1993	4	119	310
Clarence Ceasar, LSU	6-7	1995	4	112	310
Elliot Perry, Memphis	6-1	1991	4	126	304
Aldwin Ware, Florida A&M	6-2	1988	4	110	301
Drafton Davis, Marist	6-0	1988	4	115	301
Gary Grant, Michigan	6-3	1988	4	129	300
Taurence Chisholm, Delaware	5-7	1988	4	110	298
Frank Smith, Old Dominion	6-0	1988	4	120	295
D'Wayne Tanner, Rice	5-9	1990	4	109	291
Lee Mayberry, Arkansas	6-2	1992	4	139	291
Mike Bright, Bucknell	6-6	1993	4	117	286
Michael Williams, Baylor	6-2	1988	4	115	282
Orlando Smart, San Francisco	6-0	1994	4	116	282
Mookie Blaylock, Oklahoma	6-0	1989	2	74	281
Mark Macon, Temple	6-5	1991	4	126	281

STEAL AVERAGE
(Minimum 225 steals)

Player, Team	Ht.	Last Season	Yrs.	G	Stl.	Avg.
Mookie Blaylock, Oklahoma	6-0	1989	2	74	281	3.80
Ronn McMahon, Eastern Wash.	5-9	1990	3	64	225	3.52
Eric Murdock, Providence	6-2	1991	4	117	376	3.21
Van Usher, Tennessee Tech	6-0	1992	3	85	270	3.18
Gerald Walker, San Francisco	6-1	1996	4	111	344	3.10
Michael Anderson, Drexel	5-11	1988	4	115	341	2.97
Haywoode Workman, Oral Roberts	6-3	1989	3	85	250	2.94
Shawn Griggs, LSU & Southwestern La.	6-6	1994	3	89	260	2.92

Gerald Walker accumulated 344 steals in four years at San Francisco, the second-highest total ever in Division I. Walker averaged 3.10 steals per game during his career to rank fifth all-time among Division I competitors.

Player, Team	Ht.	Last Season	Yrs.	G	Stl.	Avg.
Kenny Robertson, Cleveland St.	6-0	1990	4	119	341	2.87
Darnell Mee, Western Ky.	6-3	1993	3	91	259	2.85
Pat Baldwin, Northwestern	6-1	1994	4	96	272	2.83
Johnny Rhodes, Maryland	6-6	1996	4	122	344	2.82
Mark Woods, Wright St.	6-1	1993	4	113	314	2.78
Clarence Ceasar, LSU	6-7	1995	4	112	310	2.77
Aldwin Ware, Florida A&M	6-2	1988	4	110	301	2.74
Pointer Williams, Tulane & McNeese St.	6-0	1996	4	115	314	2.73
Taurence Chisholm, Delaware	5-7	1988	4	110	298	2.71
Chuck Evans, Mississippi St.	5-11	1993	3	85	229	2.69
Gary Payton, Oregon St.	6-2	1990	4	120	321	2.68
D'Wayne Tanner, Rice	5-9	1990	4	109	291	2.67
Marcus Walton, Nevada	6-2	1995	4	103	273	2.65
Chris Corchiani, North Caro. St.	6-1	1991	4	124	328	2.65
Keith Jennings, East Tenn. St.	5-7	1991	4	127	334	2.63
Drafton Davis, Marist	6-0	1988	4	115	301	2.62
Charlie Ward, Florida St.	6-1	1994	4	91	238	2.62

GAMES PLAYED

Player, Team	Last Season	Yrs.	G
Christian Laettner, Duke	1992	4	148
Danny Manning, Kansas	1988	4	147
Stacey Augmon, UNLV	1991	4	145
Patrick Ewing, Georgetown	1985	4	143
Danny Ferry, Duke	1989	4	143
Derrick Coleman, Syracuse	1990	4	143
Brian Davis, Duke	1992	4	141
Ralph Beard, Kentucky	1949	4	139
Lee Mayberry, Arkansas	1992	4	139
Reggie Williams, Georgetown	1987	4	138
Sherman Douglas, Syracuse	1989	4	138
Doug West, Villanova	1989	4	138
Greg Anthony, Portland & UNLV	1991	4	138
Darryl Kennedy, Oklahoma	1987	4	137
Gene Melchiorre, Bradley	1951	4	137
Oliver Miller, Arkansas	1992	4	137
Hubert Davis, North Caro.	1992	4	137
Tim McCalister, Oklahoma	1987	4	136
Rony Seikaly, Syracuse	1988	4	136
Pervis Ellison, Louisville	1989	4	136
Paul Unruh, Bradley	1950	4	135
Sam Perkins, North Caro.	1984	4	135
Brad Daugherty, North Caro.	1986	4	135
Dante Calabria, North Caro.	1996	4	135
Michael Young, Houston	1984	4	134
Roy Marble, Iowa	1989	4	134
Glen Rice, Michigan	1989	4	134
Felton Spencer, Louisville	1990	4	134
Lou Roe, Massachusetts	1995	4	134

2,000 POINTS & 1,000 REBOUNDS

Player, Team	Ht.	Last Season	Yrs.	G	Pts.	Reb.
Lionel Simmons, La Salle	6-7	1990	4	131	3,217	1,429
Harry Kelly, Texas Southern	6-7	1983	4	110	3,066	1,085
Oscar Robertson, Cincinnati	6-5	1960	3	88	2,973	1,338
Danny Manning, Kansas	6-10	1988	4	147	2,951	1,187
Elvin Hayes, Houston	6-8	1968	3	93	2,884	1,602
Larry Bird, Indiana St.	6-9	1979	3	94	2,850	1,247
Hank Gathers, Southern Cal & Loyola Marymount	6-7	1990	4	117	2,723	1,128
Daren Queenan, Lehigh	6-5	1988	4	118	2,703	1,013
David Robinson, Navy	7-1	1987	4	127	2,669	1,314
Wayman Tisdale, Oklahoma	6-9	1985	3	104	2,661	1,048
Michael Brooks, La Salle	6-7	1980	4	114	2,628	1,372
Dickie Hemric, Wake Forest	6-6	1955	4	104	2,587	1,802
Calvin Natt, Northeast La.	6-5	1979	4	108	2,581	1,285
Willie Jackson, Centenary (La.)	6-6	1984	4	114	2,535	1,013
Bill Bradley, Princeton	6-5	1965	3	83	2,503	1,008
Elgin Baylor, Col. Idaho & Seattle	6-6	1958	3	80	2,500	1,559
Tom Gola, La Salle	6-6	1955	4	118	2,462	2,201
Christian Laettner, Duke	6-11	1992	4	148	2,460	1,149
Keith Lee, Memphis	6-11	1985	4	128	2,408	1,336
Phil Sellers, Rutgers	6-5	1976	4	114	2,399	1,115
Byron Houston, Oklahoma St.	6-7	1992	4	127	2,379	1,190
Ron Harper, Miami (Ohio)	6-6	1986	4	120	2,377	1,119
Bryant Reeves, Oklahoma St.	7-0	1995	4	136	2,367	1,152
Lew Alcindor, UCLA	7-2	1969	3	88	2,325	1,367
Mike Gminski, Duke	6-11	1980	4	122	2,323	1,242
Billy McGill, Utah	6-9	1962	3	86	2,321	1,106
Adam Keefe, Stanford	6-9	1992	4	125	2,319	1,119
Jerry West, West Va.	6-3	1960	3	93	2,309	1,240
Jonathan Moore, Furman	6-8	1980	4	117	2,299	1,242

Player, Team	Ht.	Last Season	Yrs.	G	Pts.	Reb.
Rick Barry, Miami (Fla.)	6-7	1965	3	77	2,298	1,274
Gary Winton, Army	6-5	1978	4	105	2,296	1,168
Kenneth Lyons, North Texas	6-7	1983	4	111	2,291	1,020
Tom Davis, Delaware St.	6-6	1991	4	95	2,274	1,013
Nick Werkman, Seton Hall	6-3	1964	3	71	2,273	1,036
Jim McDaniels, Western Ky.	7-0	1971	3	81	2,238	1,118
Joe Holup, Geo. Washington	6-6	1956	4	104	2,226	2,030
Ralph Sampson, Virginia	7-4	1983	4	132	2,225	1,511
Patrick Ewing, Georgetown	7-0	1985	4	143	2,184	1,316
Doug Smith, Missouri	6-10	1991	4	128	2,184	1,054
Kenny Sanders, George Mason	6-5	1989	4	107	2,177	1,026
Joe Barry Carroll, Purdue	7-1	1980	4	123	2,175	1,148
Reggie King, Alabama	6-6	1979	4	118	2,168	1,279
Len Chappell, Wake Forest	6-8	1962	3	87	2,165	1,213
Danny Ferry, Duke	6-10	1989	4	143	2,155	1,003
Xavier McDaniel, Wichita St.	6-7	1985	4	117	2,152	1,359
Derrick Coleman, Syracuse	6-9	1990	4	143	2,143	1,537
Joe Binion, North Caro. A&T	6-8	1984	4	116	2,143	1,194
Pervis Ellison, Louisville	6-9	1989	4	136	2,143	1,149
Dan Issel, Kentucky	6-9	1970	3	83	2,138	1,078
Jesse Arnelle, Penn St.	6-5	1955	4	102	2,138	1,238
Sam Perkins, North Caro.	6-10	1984	4	135	2,133	1,167
Bob Elliott, Arizona	6-10	1977	4	114	2,131	1,083
Clarence Weatherspoon, Southern Miss.	6-7	1992	4	117	2,130	1,320
Reggie Jackson, Nicholls St.	6-6	1995	4	120	2,124	1,271
Greg Grant, Utah St.	6-7	1986	4	115	2,124	1,003
John Wallace, Syracuse	6-8	1996	4	127	2,119	1,065
Bill Cartwright, San Francisco	6-11	1979	4	111	2,116	1,137
Bob Harstad, Creighton	6-6	1991	4	128	2,110	1,126
Gary Trent, Ohio	6-8	1995	3	93	2,108	1,050
B. B. Davis, Lamar	6-8	1981	4	119	2,084	1,122
Durand Macklin, LSU	6-7	1981	5	123	2,080	1,276
Ralph Crosthwaite, Western Ky.	6-9	1959	4	103	2,076	1,309
Sidney Green, UNLV	6-9	1983	4	119	2,069	1,276
Bob Lanier, St. Bonaventure	6-11	1970	3	75	2,067	1,180
Fred West, Texas Southern	6-9	1990	4	118	2,066	1,136
Sidney Moncrief, Arkansas	6-4	1979	4	122	2,066	1,015
Popeye Jones, Murray St.	6-8	1992	4	123	2,057	1,374
Mark Acres, Oral Roberts	6-11	1985	4	110	2,038	1,051
Fred Hetzel, Davidson	6-8	1965	3	79	2,032	1,094
Bailey Howell, Mississippi St.	6-7	1959	3	75	2,030	1,277
Malik Rose, Drexel	6-7	1996	4	120	2,024	1,514
Larry Krystkowiak, Montana	6-9	1986	4	120	2,017	1,105
Greg Kelser, Michigan St.	6-7	1979	4	115	2,014	1,092
Herb Williams, Ohio St.	6-10	1981	4	114	2,011	1,111
Stacey Augmon, UNLV	6-8	1991	4	145	2,011	1,005
Jeff Cohen, William & Mary	6-7	1961	4	103	2,003	1,679
Tyrone Hill, Xavier (Ohio)	6-9	1990	4	126	2,003	1,380
Alonzo Mourning, Georgetown	6-10	1992	4	120	2,001	1,032
Josh Grant, Utah	6-9	1993	5	131	2,000	1,066

Annual Individual Champions

Scoring Average

Season	Player, Team	Ht.	Cl.	G	FG	FT	Pts.	Avg.
1948	Murray Wier, Iowa	5-9	Sr.	19	152	95	399	21.0
1949	Tony Lavelli, Yale	6-3	Sr.	30	228	215	671	22.4
1950	Paul Arizin, Villanova	6-3	Sr.	29	260	215	735	25.3
1951	Bill Mlkvy, Temple	6-4	Sr.	25	303	125	731	29.2
1952	Clyde Lovellette, Kansas	6-9	Sr.	28	315	165	795	28.4
1953	Frank Selvy, Furman	6-3	Jr.	25	272	194	738	29.5
1954	Frank Selvy, Furman	6-3	Sr.	29	427	*355	1,209	41.7
1955	Darrell Floyd, Furman	6-1	Sr.	25	344	209	897	35.9
1956	Darrell Floyd, Furman	6-1	Sr.	28	339	268	946	33.8
1957	Grady Wallace, South Caro.	6-4	Sr.	29	336	234	906	31.2
1958	Oscar Robertson, Cincinnati	6-5	So.	28	352	280	984	35.1
1959	Oscar Robertson, Cincinnati	6-5	Jr.	30	331	316	978	32.6
1960	Oscar Robertson, Cincinnati	6-5	Sr.	30	369	273	1,011	33.7
1961	Frank Burgess, Gonzaga	6-1	Sr.	26	304	234	842	32.4
1962	Billy McGill, Utah	6-9	Sr.	26	394	221	1,009	38.8
1963	Nick Werkman, Seton Hall	6-3	Jr.	22	221	208	650	29.5
1964	Howard Komives, Bowling Green	6-1	Sr.	23	292	260	844	36.7
1965	Rick Barry, Miami (Fla.)	6-7	Sr.	26	340	293	973	37.4
1966	Dave Schellhase, Purdue	6-4	Sr.	24	284	213	781	32.5
1967	Jim Walker, Providence	6-3	Sr.	28	323	205	851	30.4

DIVISION I

Season	Player, Team	Ht.	Cl.	G	FG	FT	Pts.	Avg.
1968	Pete Maravich, LSU	6-5	So.	26	432	274	1,138	43.8
1969	Pete Maravich, LSU	6-5	Jr.	26	433	282	1,148	44.2
1970	Pete Maravich, LSU	6-5	Sr.	31	*522	337	*1,381	*44.5
1971	Johnny Neumann, Mississippi	6-6	So.	23	366	191	923	40.1
1972	Dwight Lamar, Southwestern La.	6-1	Jr.	29	429	196	1,054	36.3
1973	William Averitt, Pepperdine	6-1	Sr.	25	352	144	848	33.9
1974	Larry Fogle, Canisius	6-5	So.	25	326	183	835	33.4
1975	Bob McCurdy, Richmond	6-7	Sr.	26	321	213	855	32.9
1976	Marshall Rodgers, Tex.-Pan American	6-2	Sr.	25	361	197	919	36.8
1977	Freeman Williams, Portland St.	6-4	Jr.	26	417	176	1,010	38.8
1978	Freeman Williams, Portland St.	6-4	Sr.	27	410	149	969	35.9
1979	Lawrence Butler, Idaho St.	6-3	Sr.	27	310	192	812	30.1
1980	Tony Murphy, Southern U.	6-3	Sr.	29	377	178	932	32.1
1981	Zam Fredrick, South Caro.	6-2	Sr.	27	300	181	781	28.9
1982	Harry Kelly, Texas Southern	6-7	Jr.	29	336	190	862	29.7
1983	Harry Kelly, Texas Southern	6-7	Sr.	29	333	169	835	28.8
1984	Joe Jakubick, Akron	6-5	Sr.	27	304	206	814	30.1
1985	Xavier McDaniel, Wichita St.	6-8	Sr.	31	351	142	844	27.2
1986	Terrance Bailey, Wagner	6-2	Jr.	29	321	212	854	29.4

Season	Player, Team	Ht.	Cl.	G	FG	3FG	FT	Pts.	Avg.
1987	Kevin Houston, Army	5-11	Sr.	29	311	63	268	953	32.9
1988	Hersey Hawkins, Bradley	6-3	Sr.	31	377	87	284	1,125	36.3
1989	Hank Gathers, Loyola Marymount	6-7	Jr.	31	419	0	177	1,015	32.7
1990	Bo Kimble, Loyola Marymount	6-5	Sr.	32	404	92	231	1,131	35.3
1991	Kevin Bradshaw, U.S. Int'l	6-6	Sr.	28	358	60	278	1,054	37.6
1992	Brett Roberts, Morehead St.	6-8	Sr.	29	278	66	193	815	28.1
1993	Greg Guy, Tex.-Pan American	6-1	Jr.	19	189	67	111	556	29.3
1994	Glenn Robinson, Purdue	6-8	Jr.	34	368	79	215	1,030	30.3
1995	Kurt Thomas, Texas Christian	6-9	Sr.	27	288	3	202	781	28.9
1996	Kevin Granger, Texas Southern	6-3	Sr.	24	194	30	230	648	27.0

*Record.

Field-Goal Percentage

Season	Player, Team	Cl.	G	FG	FGA	Pct.
1948	Alex Peterson, Oregon St.	Jr.	27	89	187	47.6
1949	Ed Macauley, St. Louis	Sr.	26	144	275	52.4
1950	Jim Moran, Niagara	Jr.	27	98	185	53.0
1951	Don Meineke, Dayton	Jr.	32	240	469	51.2
1952	Art Spoelstra, Western Ky.	So.	31	178	345	51.6
1953	Vernon Stokes, St. Francis (N.Y)	Sr.	24	147	247	59.5
1954	Joe Holup, Geo. Washington	So.	26	179	313	57.2
1955	Ed O'Connor, Manhattan	Sr.	23	147	243	60.5
1956	Joe Holup, Geo. Washington	Sr.	26	200	309	64.7
1957	Bailey Howell, Mississippi St.	So.	25	217	382	56.8
1958	Ralph Crosthwaite, Western Ky.	Jr.	25	202	331	61.0
1959	Ralph Crosthwaite, Western Ky.	Sr.	26	191	296	64.5
1960	Jerry Lucas, Ohio St.	So.	27	283	444	63.7
1961	Jerry Lucas, Ohio St.	Jr.	27	256	411	62.3
1962	Jerry Lucas, Ohio St.	Sr.	28	237	388	61.1
1963	Lyle Harger, Houston	Sr.	26	193	294	65.6
1964	Terry Holland, Davidson	Sr.	26	135	214	63.1
1965	Tim Kehoe, St. Peter's	Sr.	19	138	209	66.0
1966	Julian Hammond, Tulsa	Sr.	29	172	261	65.9
1967	Lew Alcindor, UCLA	So.	30	346	519	66.7
1968	Joe Allen, Bradley	Sr.	28	258	394	65.5
1969	Lew Alcindor, UCLA	Sr.	30	303	477	63.5
1970	Willie Williams, Florida St.	Sr.	26	185	291	63.6
1971	John Belcher, Arkansas St.	Jr.	24	174	275	63.3
1972	Kent Martens, Abilene Christian	Sr.	21	136	204	66.7
1973	Elton Hayes, Lamar	Sr.	24	146	222	65.8
1974	Al Fleming, Arizona	So.	26	136	204	66.7
1975	Bernard King, Tennessee	Fr.	25	273	439	62.2
1976	Sidney Moncrief, Arkansas	Fr.	28	149	224	66.5
1977	Joe Senser, West Chester	So.	25	130	186	69.9
1978	Joe Senser, West Chester	Jr.	25	135	197	68.5
1979	Murray Brown, Florida St.	Jr.	29	237	343	69.1
1980	Steve Johnson, Oregon St.	Jr.	30	211	297	71.0
1981	Steve Johnson, Oregon St.	Sr.	28	235	315	*74.6
1982	Mark McNamara, California	Sr.	27	231	329	70.2
1983	Troy Lee Mikel, East Tenn. St.	Sr.	29	197	292	67.5
1984	Akeem Olajuwon, Houston	Jr.	37	249	369	67.5
1985	Keith Walker, Utica	Sr.	27	154	216	71.3
1986	Brad Daugherty, North Caro.	Sr.	34	284	438	64.8
1987	Alan Williams, Princeton	Sr.	25	163	232	70.3
1988	Arnell Jones, Boise St.	Sr.	30	187	283	66.1
1989	Dwayne Davis, Florida	So.	33	179	248	72.2
1990	Lee Campbell, Southwest Mo. St.	Sr.	29	192	275	69.8
1991	Oliver Miller, Arkansas	Jr.	30	254	361	70.4

Season	Player, Team	Cl.	G	FG	FGA	Pct.
1992	Charles Outlaw, Houston	Jr.	31	156	228	68.4
1993	Charles Outlaw, Houston	Sr.	30	196	298	65.8
1994	Mike Atkinson, Long Beach St.	Jr.	26	141	203	69.5
1995	Shane Kline-Ruminski, Bowling Green	Sr.	26	181	265	68.3
1996	Quadre Lollis, Montana St.	Sr.	30	212	314	67.5

*Record.

Three-Point Field Goals Made Per Game

Season	Player, Team	Cl.	G	3FG	Avg.
1987	Darrin Fitzgerald, Butler	Sr.	28	158	*5.64
1988	Timothy Pollard, Mississippi Val.	Jr.	28	132	4.71
1989	Timothy Pollard, Mississippi Val.	Sr.	28	124	4.43
1990	Dave Jamerson, Ohio	Sr.	28	131	4.68
1991	Bobby Phills, Southern U.	Sr.	28	123	4.39
1992	Doug Day, Radford	Jr.	29	117	4.03
1993	Bernard Haslett, Southern Miss.	Jr.	26	109	4.19
1994	Chris Brown, UC Irvine	Jr.	26	122	4.69
1995	Mitch Taylor, Southern U.	Sr.	25	109	4.36
1996	Dominick Young, Fresno St.	Jr.	29	120	4.14

*Record.

Three-Point Field-Goal Percentage

Season	Player, Team	Cl.	G	3FG	3FGA	Pct.
1987	Reginald Jones, Prairie View	Jr.	28	64	112	57.1
1988	Glenn Tropf, Holy Cross	Jr.	29	52	82	*63.4
1989	Dave Calloway, Monmouth (N.J.)	So.	28	48	82	58.5
1990	Matt Lapin, Princeton	Sr.	27	71	133	53.4
1991	Keith Jennings, East Tenn. St.	Sr.	33	84	142	59.2
1992	Sean Wightman, Western Mich.	Jr.	30	48	76	63.2
1993	Jeff Anderson, Kent	Jr.	26	44	82	53.7
1994	Brent Kell, Evansville	So.	29	62	123	50.4
1995	Brian Jackson, Evansville	Jr.	27	53	95	55.8
1996	Joe Stafford, Western Caro.	Jr.	30	58	110	52.7

*Record.

Free-Throw Percentage

Season	Player, Team	Cl.	G	FT	FTA	Pct.
1948	Sam Urzetta, St. Bonaventure	So.	22	59	64	92.2
1949	Bill Schroer, Valparaiso	So.	24	59	68	86.8
1950	Sam Urzetta, St. Bonaventure	Sr.	22	54	61	88.5
1951	Jay Handlan, Wash. & Lee	Jr.	22	148	172	86.0
1952	Sy Chadroff, Miami (Fla.)	Sr.	22	99	123	80.5
1953	John Weber, Yale	Sr.	24	117	141	83.0
1954	Dick Daugherty, Arizona St.	Sr.	23	75	86	87.2
1955	Jim Scott, West Tex. A&M	Sr.	23	153	171	89.5
1956	Bill Von Weyhe, Rhode Island	Jr.	25	180	208	86.5
1957	Ernie Wiggins, Wake Forest	Sr.	28	93	106	87.7
1958	Semi Mintz, Davidson	Sr.	24	105	119	88.2
1959	Arlen Clark, Oklahoma St.	Sr.	25	201	236	85.2
1960	Jack Waters, Mississippi	Sr.	24	103	118	87.3
1961	Stew Sherard, Army	Sr.	24	135	154	87.7
1962	Tommy Boyer, Arkansas	Jr.	23	125	134	93.3
1963	Tommy Boyer, Arkansas	Sr.	24	147	161	91.3
1964	Rick Park, Tulsa	Jr.	25	121	134	90.3
1965	Bill Bradley, Princeton	Sr.	29	273	308	88.6
1966	Bill Blair, Providence	Sr.	27	101	112	90.2
1967	Bob Lloyd, Rutgers	Sr.	29	255	277	92.1
1968	Joe Heiser, Princeton	Sr.	26	117	130	90.0
1969	Bill Justus, Tennessee	Sr.	28	133	147	90.5
1970	Steve Kaplan, Rutgers	So.	23	102	110	92.7
1971	Greg Starrick, Southern Ill.	Jr.	23	119	132	90.2
1972	Greg Starrick, Southern Ill.	Sr.	26	148	160	92.5
1973	Don Smith, Dayton	Sr.	26	111	122	91.0
1974	Rickey Medlock, Arkansas	Sr.	26	87	95	91.6
1975	Frank Oleynick, Seattle	Sr.	26	135	152	88.8
1976	Tad Dufelmeier, Loyola (Ill.)	Jr.	25	71	80	88.8
1977	Robert Smith, UNLV	Sr.	32	98	106	92.5
1978	Carlos Gibson, Marshall	Sr.	28	84	89	94.4
1979	Darrell Mauldin, Campbell	Jr.	26	70	76	92.1
1980	Brian Magid, Geo. Washington	Sr.	26	79	85	92.9
1981	Dave Hildahl, Portland St.	Sr.	21	76	82	92.7
1982	Rod Foster, UCLA	Jr.	27	95	100	95.0
1983	Rob Gonzalez, Colorado	Sr.	28	75	82	91.5
1984	Steve Alford, Indiana	Fr.	31	137	150	91.3
1985	Craig Collins, Penn St.	Sr.	27	94	98	*95.9
1986	Jim Barton, Dartmouth	Fr.	26	65	69	94.2

Season	Player, Team	Cl.	G	FT	FTA	Pct.
1987	Kevin Houston, Army	Sr.	29	268	294	91.2
1988	Steve Henson, Kansas St.	So.	34	111	120	92.5
1989	Michael Smith, Brigham Young	Sr.	29	160	173	92.5
1990	Rob Robbins, New Mexico	Jr.	34	101	108	93.5
1991	Darin Archbold, Butler	Jr.	29	187	205	91.2
1992	Don MacLean, UCLA	Sr.	32	197	214	92.1
1993	Josh Grant, Utah	Sr.	31	104	113	92.0
1994	Danny Basile, Marist	So.	27	84	89	94.4
1995	Greg Bibb, Tennessee Tech	Jr.	27	106	117	90.6
1996	Mike Dillard, Sam Houston St.	Jr.	25	63	68	92.6

*Record.

Rebound Average

Season	Player, Team	Ht.	Cl.	G	Reb.	Avg.
1951	Ernie Beck, Pennsylvania	6-4	So.	27	556	20.6
1952	Bill Hannon, Army	6-3	So.	17	355	20.9
1953	Ed Conlin, Fordham	6-5	So.	26	612	23.5
1954	Art Quimby, Connecticut	6-5	Jr.	26	588	22.6
1955	Charlie Slack, Marshall	6-5	Jr.	21	538	*25.6
1956	Joe Holup, Geo. Washington	6-6	Sr.	26	604	†.256
1957	Elgin Baylor, Seattle	6-6	Jr.	25	508	†.235
1958	Alex Ellis, Niagara	6-5	Sr.	25	536	†.262
1959	Leroy Wright, Pacific (Cal.)	6-8	Jr.	26	652	†.238
1960	Leroy Wright, Pacific (Cal.)	6-8	Sr.	17	380	†.234
1961	Jerry Lucas, Ohio St.	6-8	Jr.	27	470	†.198
1962	Jerry Lucas, Ohio St.	6-8	Sr.	28	499	†.211
1963	Paul Silas, Creighton	6-7	Sr.	27	557	20.6
1964	Bob Pelkington, Xavier (Ohio)	6-7	Sr.	26	567	21.8
1965	Toby Kimball, Connecticut	6-8	Sr.	23	483	21.0
1966	Jim Ware, Oklahoma City	6-8	Sr.	29	607	20.9
1967	Dick Cunningham, Murray St.	6-10	Jr.	22	479	21.8
1968	Neal Walk, Florida	6-10	Jr.	25	494	19.8
1969	Spencer Haywood, Detroit	6-8	So.	22	472	21.5
1970	Artis Gilmore, Jacksonville	7-2	Jr.	28	621	22.2
1971	Artis Gilmore, Jacksonville	7-2	Sr.	26	603	23.2
1972	Kermit Washington, American	6-8	Jr.	23	455	19.8
1973	Kermit Washington, American	6-8	Sr.	22	439	20.0
1974	Marvin Barnes, Providence	6-9	Sr.	32	597	18.7
1975	John Irving, Hofstra	6-9	So.	21	323	15.4
1976	Sam Pellom, Buffalo	6-8	So.	26	420	16.2
1977	Glenn Mosley, Seton Hall	6-8	Sr.	29	473	16.3
1978	Ken Williams, North Texas	6-7	Sr.	28	411	14.7
1979	Monti Davis, Tennessee St.	6-7	Jr.	26	421	16.2
1980	Larry Smith, Alcorn St.	6-8	Sr.	26	392	15.1
1981	Darryl Watson, Mississippi Val.	6-7	Sr.	27	379	14.0
1982	LaSalle Thompson, Texas	6-10	Jr.	27	365	13.5
1983	Xavier McDaniel, Wichita St.	6-7	So.	28	403	14.4
1984	Akeem Olajuwon, Houston	7-0	Jr.	37	500	13.5
1985	Xavier McDaniel, Wichita St.	6-8	Sr.	31	460	14.8
1986	David Robinson, Navy	6-11	Jr.	35	455	13.0
1987	Jerome Lane, Pittsburgh	6-6	So.	33	444	13.5
1988	Kenny Miller, Loyola (Ill.)	6-9	Fr.	29	395	13.6
1989	Hank Gathers, Loyola Marymount	6-7	Jr.	31	426	13.7
1990	Anthony Bonner, St. Louis	6-8	Sr.	33	456	13.8
1991	Shaquille O'Neal, LSU	7-1	So.	28	411	14.7
1992	Popeye Jones, Murray St.	6-8	Sr.	30	431	14.4
1993	Warren Kidd, Middle Tenn. St.	6-9	Sr.	26	386	14.8
1994	Jerome Lambert, Baylor	6-8	Jr.	24	355	14.8
1995	Kurt Thomas, Texas Christian	6-9	Sr.	27	393	14.6
1996	Marcus Mann, Mississippi Val.	6-8	Sr.	29	394	13.6

*Record. †From 1956 through 1962, championship was determined on highest individual recoveries out of total by both teams in all games.

Assist Average

Season	Player, Team	Cl.	G	Ast.	Avg.
1984	Craig Lathen, Ill.-Chicago	Jr.	29	274	9.45
1985	Rob Weingard, Hofstra	Sr.	24	228	9.50
1986	Mark Jackson, St. John's (N.Y.)	Jr.	36	328	9.11
1987	Avery Johnson, Southern U.	Jr.	31	333	10.74
1988	Avery Johnson, Southern U.	Sr.	30	399	*13.30
1989	Glenn Williams, Holy Cross	Sr.	28	278	9.93
1990	Todd Lehmann, Drexel	Sr.	28	260	9.29
1991	Chris Corchiani, North Caro. St.	Sr.	31	299	9.65
1992	Van Usher, Tennessee Tech	Sr.	29	254	8.76
1993	Sam Crawford, New Mexico St.	Sr.	34	310	9.12
1994	Jason Kidd, California	So.	30	272	9.07
1995	Nelson Haggerty, Baylor	Sr.	28	284	10.14
1996	Raimonds Miglinieks, UC Irvine	Sr.	27	230	8.52

*Record.

Blocked-Shot Average

Season	Player, Team	Cl.	G	Blk.	Avg.
1986	David Robinson, Navy	Jr.	35	207	5.91
1987	David Robinson, Navy	Sr.	32	144	4.50
1988	Rodney Blake, St. Joseph's (Pa.)	Sr.	29	116	4.00
1989	Alonzo Mourning, Georgetown	Fr.	34	169	4.97
1990	Kenny Green, Rhode Island	Sr.	26	124	4.77
1991	Shawn Bradley, Brigham Young	Fr.	34	177	5.21
1992	Shaquille O'Neal, LSU	Jr.	30	157	5.23
1993	Theo Ratliff, Wyoming	Jr.	28	124	4.43
1994	Grady Livingston, Howard	Jr.	26	115	4.42
1995	Keith Closs, Central Conn. St.	Fr.	26	139	5.35
1996	Keith Closs, Central Conn. St.	So.	28	178	*6.36

*Record.

Steal Average

Season	Player, Team	Cl.	G	Stl.	Avg.
1986	Darron Brittman, Chicago St.	Sr.	28	139	*4.96
1987	Tony Fairley, Charleston So.	Sr.	28	114	4.07
1988	Aldwin Ware, Florida A&M	Sr.	29	142	4.90
1989	Kenny Robertson, Cleveland St.	Jr.	28	111	3.96
1990	Ronn McMahon, Eastern Wash.	Sr.	29	130	4.48
1991	Van Usher, Tennessee Tech	Jr.	28	104	3.71
1992	Victor Snipes, Northeastern Ill.	So.	25	86	3.44
1993	Jason Kidd, California	Fr.	29	110	3.79
1994	Shawn Griggs, Southwestern La.	Sr.	30	120	4.00
1995	Roderick Anderson, Texas	Sr.	30	101	3.37
1996	Pointer Williams, McNeese St.	Sr.	27	118	4.37

*Record.

All-Time Team Leaders

Single-Game Records

SCORING HIGHS

Pts.	Team vs. Opponent (Opp. Pts.)	Date
186	Loyola Marymount vs. U.S. Int'l (140)	Jan. 5, 1991
181	Loyola Marymount vs. U.S. Int'l (150)	Jan. 31, 1989
173	Oklahoma vs. U.S. Int'l (101)	Nov. 29, 1989
172	Oklahoma vs. Loyola Marymount (112)	Dec. 15, 1990
166	Arkansas vs. U.S. Int'l (101)	Dec. 9, 1989
164	UNLV vs. Hawaii-Hilo (111)	Feb. 19, 1976
164	Loyola Marymount vs. Azusa-Pacific (138)	Nov. 28, 1988
162	Loyola Marymount vs. U.S. Int'l (144)	Jan. 7, 1989
162	Loyola Marymount vs. Chaminade (129)	Nov. 25, 1990
162	Oklahoma vs. Angelo St. (99)	Dec. 1, 1990
159	Southern U. vs. Texas College (65)	Dec. 6, 1990
159	LSU vs. Northern Ariz. (86)	Dec. 28, 1991
157	Loyola Marymount vs. San Francisco (115)	Feb. 5, 1990
156	Southern U. vs. Baptist Christian (91)	Dec. 14, 1992
156	South Ala. vs. Prairie View (114)	Dec. 2, 1994
155	Oral Roberts vs. Union (Tenn.) (113)	Feb. 24, 1972
155	Southern U. vs. Prairie View (91)	Feb. 22, 1993
154	Texas-Arlington vs. Huston-Tillotson (85)	Nov. 29, 1990
154	Southern U. vs. Patten (57)	Nov. 26, 1993
152	Jacksonville vs. St. Peter's (106)	Dec. 3, 1970
152	Oklahoma vs. Centenary (La.) (84)	Dec. 12, 1987
152	Oklahoma vs. Oral Roberts (122)	Dec. 10, 1988
152	Loyola Marymount vs. U.S. Int'l (137)	Dec. 7, 1989
152	Northeastern vs. Loyola Marymount (123)	Nov. 24, 1990
151	Loyola Marymount vs. U.S. Int'l (107)	Jan. 11, 1986
151	Oklahoma vs. Dayton (99)	Dec. 24, 1987
151	Alabama St. vs. Grambling (97)	Jan. 21, 1991

SCORING HIGHS BY LOSING TEAM

Pts.	Team vs. Opponent (Opp. Pts.)	Date
150	U.S. Int'l vs. Loyola Marymount (181)	Jan. 31, 1989
144	U.S. Int'l vs. Loyola Marymount (162)	Jan. 7, 1989
141	Loyola Marymount vs. Oklahoma (136)	Dec. 23, 1989
141	Loyola Marymount vs. LSU (148) (ot)	Feb. 3, 1990
140	Utah St. vs. UNLV (142) (3 ot)	Jan. 2, 1985
140	U.S. Int'l vs. Loyola Marymount (186)	Jan. 5, 1991
137	U.S. Int'l vs. Loyola Marymount (152)	Dec. 7, 1989

Pts.	Team vs. Opponent (Opp. Pts.)	Date
136	Gonzaga vs. Loyola Marymount (147)	Feb. 18, 1989
132	Troy St. vs. George Mason (148)	Dec. 10, 1994
127	Pepperdine vs. Loyola Marymount (142)	Feb. 20, 1988
127	Troy St. vs. George Mason (142)	Nov. 28, 1995
125	Nevada vs. Loyola Marymount (130)	Dec. 30, 1988
123	San Francisco vs. Loyola Marymount (137)	Feb. 9, 1990
123	Loyola Marymount vs. Pepperdine (148)	Feb. 17, 1990
123	Loyola Marymount vs. Northeastern (152)	Nov. 24, 1990
122	Oral Roberts vs. Oklahoma (152)	Dec. 10, 1988
121	Loyola Marymount vs. LSU (148) (ot)	Feb. 3, 1990
121	Loyola Marymount vs. Oklahoma (136)	Dec. 23, 1989

SCORING HIGHS BOTH TEAMS COMBINED

Pts.	Team (Pts.) vs. Team (Pts.)	Date
331	Loyola Marymount (181) vs. U.S. Int'l (150)	Jan. 31, 1989
326	Loyola Marymount (186) vs. U.S. Int'l (140)	Jan. 5, 1991
306	Loyola Marymount (162) vs. U.S. Int'l (144)	Jan. 7, 1989
289	Loyola Marymount (152) vs. U.S. Int'l (137)	Dec. 7, 1989
289	LSU (148) vs. Loyola Marymount (141) (ot)	Feb. 3, 1990
284	Oklahoma (172) vs. Loyola Marymount (112)	Dec. 15, 1990
283	Loyola Marymount (147) vs. Gonzaga (136)	Feb. 18, 1989
282	UNLV (142) vs. Utah St. (140) (3 ot)	Jan. 2, 1985
280	George Mason (148) vs. Troy St. (132)	Dec. 10, 1994
275	Northeastern (152) vs. Loyola Marymount (123)	Nov. 24, 1990
274	Oklahoma (152) vs. Oral Roberts (122)	Dec. 10, 1988
274	Oklahoma (173) vs. U.S. Int'l (101)	Nov. 29, 1989
272	Loyola Marymount (157) vs. San Francisco (115)	Feb. 4, 1990
269	Loyola Marymount (142) vs. Pepperdine (127)	Feb. 20, 1988
269	Loyola Marymount (150) vs. St. Mary's (Cal.) (119)	Feb. 1, 1990
269	George Mason (142) vs. Troy St. (127)	Nov. 28, 1995

SCORING HIGHS IN A HALF

Pts.	Team vs. Opponent (Half)	Date
97	Oklahoma vs. U.S. Int'l (1st)	Nov. 29, 1989
96	Southern U. vs. Texas College (2nd)	Dec. 6, 1990
94	Loyola Marymount vs. U.S. Int'l (1st)	Jan. 31, 1989
94	Oklahoma vs. Northeastern Ill. (2nd)	Dec. 2, 1989
94	Loyola Marymount vs. U.S. Int'l (1st)	Jan. 5, 1991
93	Loyola Marymount vs. U.S. Int'l (1st)	Jan. 7, 1989
93	Oklahoma vs. Loyola Marymount (2nd)	Dec. 15, 1990
92	Loyola Marymount vs. U.S. Int'l (2nd)	Jan. 5, 1991
92	Alabama St. vs. Grambling (2nd)	Jan. 21, 1991
91	Oklahoma vs. Angelo St. (2nd)	Dec. 1, 1990
87	Oklahoma vs. Oral Roberts (2nd)	Dec. 10, 1988
87	Loyola Marymount vs. U.S. Int'l (2nd)	Jan. 31, 1989
86	Jacksonville vs. St. Peter's (2nd)	Dec. 3, 1970
86	Lamar vs. Portland St. (2nd)	Jan. 12, 1980
86	Loyola Marymount vs. Gonzaga (2nd)	Feb. 18, 1989
86	Gonzaga vs. Loyola Marymount (2nd)	Feb. 18, 1989
86	Kentucky vs. LSU (1st)	Jan. 16, 1996

SCORING HIGHS IN A HALF BOTH TEAMS COMBINED

Pts.	Team (Pts.) vs. Team (Pts.) (Half)	Date
172	Loyola Marymount (86) vs. Gonzaga (86) (2nd)	Feb. 18, 1989
170	Loyola Marymount (94) vs. U.S. Int'l (76) (1st)	Jan. 31, 1989
164	Loyola Marymount (94) vs. U.S. Int'l (70) (1st)	Jan. 5, 1991
162	Loyola Marymount (92) vs. U.S. Int'l (70) (2nd)	Jan. 5, 1991
161	Loyola Marymount (93) vs. U.S. Int'l (68) (1st)	Jan. 7, 1989
161	Loyola Marymount (87) vs. U.S. Int'l (74) (2nd)	Jan. 31, 1989
160	Oklahoma (87) vs. Oral Roberts (73) (2nd)	Dec. 10, 1988

FIELD-GOAL PERCENTAGE

Pct.	Team (FG-FGA) vs. Opponent	Date
83.3	Maryland (15-18) vs. South Caro.	Jan. 9, 1971
81.4	New Mexico (35-43) vs. Oregon St.	Nov. 30, 1985
81.0	Fresno St. (34-42) vs. Portland St.	Dec. 3, 1977
81.0	St. Peter's (34-42) vs. Utica	Dec. 4, 1984
80.5	Fordham (33-41) vs. Fairfield	Feb. 27, 1984
80.0	Holy Cross (32-40) vs. Vermont	Nov. 30, 1981
80.0	Oklahoma St. (28-35) vs. Tulane	Mar. 22, 1992
79.4	Arkansas (27-34) vs. Texas Tech	Feb. 20, 1979
79.4	Columbia (27-34) vs. Dartmouth	Mar. 2, 1984
79.0	North Caro. (49-62) vs. Loyola Marymount	Mar. 19, 1988
78.6	Villanova (22-28) vs. Georgetown	Apr. 1, 1985
78.6	St. Peter's (22-28) vs. Army	Jan. 9, 1982
78.4	Western Ky. (29-37) vs. Dayton	Jan. 24, 1979
78.1	Army (25-32) vs. Manhattan	Jan. 20, 1979
77.8	Samford (35-45) vs. Loyola (La.)	Dec. 12, 1992
77.5	Nicholls St. (31-40) vs. Samford	Dec. 30, 1983
77.4	Richmond (24-31) vs. Citadel	Feb. 8, 1976

THREE-POINT FIELD GOALS MADE

3FG	Team vs. Opponent	Date
28	Troy St. vs. George Mason	Dec. 10, 1994
23	Lamar vs. Louisiana Tech	Feb. 28, 1993
23	Kansas St. vs. Fresno St.	Mar. 24, 1994
23	Troy St. vs. George Mason	Nov. 28, 1995
22	Gonzaga vs. San Francisco	Feb. 23, 1995
21	Kentucky vs. North Caro.	Dec. 27, 1989
21	Loyola Marymount vs. Michigan	Mar. 18, 1990
21	UNLV vs. Nevada	Dec. 8, 1990
20	Navy vs. Mt. St. Mary's (Md.)	Nov. 26, 1990
20	Lamar vs. Prairie View	Feb. 3, 1993
20	Arkansas vs. Texas Southern	Dec. 29, 1993
20	Baylor vs. Texas Christian	Feb. 14, 1995
19	Valparaiso vs. Butler	Feb. 6, 1989
19	St. Francis (Pa.) vs. LIU-Brooklyn	Feb. 25, 1989
19	Kentucky vs. Furman	Dec. 19, 1989
19	Loyola Marymount vs. Chaminade	Nov. 25, 1990
19	New Mexico St. vs. Morgan St.	Dec. 29, 1990
19	Southern U. vs. Southeastern La.	Feb. 14, 1991
19	Temple vs. Geo. Washington	Mar. 4, 1992
19	Arkansas vs. Montevallo	Feb. 1, 1994
19	Southern U. vs. Louisiana College	Jan. 5, 1995
18	18 tied	

THREE-POINT FIELD GOALS ATTEMPTED

3FGA	Team vs. Opponent	Date
74	Troy St. vs. George Mason	Dec. 10, 1994
53	Kentucky vs. Southwestern La.	Dec. 23, 1989
51	Texas-Arlington vs. New Mexico	Nov. 23, 1990
51	Arizona St. vs. Brigham Young	Dec. 1, 1992
48	Kentucky vs. North Caro.	Dec. 27, 1989
47	Kentucky vs. Furman	Dec. 19, 1989
47	Charleston So. vs. Clemson	Dec. 1, 1993
47	Centenary (La.) vs. Central Fla.	Jan. 11, 1993
46	UNLV vs. Nevada	Dec. 8, 1990
46	Georgetown vs. Boston College	Feb. 26, 1994
45	Loyola Marymount vs. LSU	Feb. 3, 1990
45	Houston vs. St. Louis	Dec. 15, 1990
45	Drake vs. Iowa	Nov. 29, 1994
44	Cal St. Northridge vs. Colorado	Nov. 23, 1990
44	Central Conn. St. vs. Colorado	Dec. 8, 1990
44	Kentucky vs. LSU	Feb. 2, 1992
44	North Texas vs. Texas-Arlington	Jan. 9, 1993
44	Kentucky vs. LSU	Mar. 14, 1993
44	Samford vs. Mercer	Feb. 18, 1995
43	Tennessee St. vs. Mo.-Kansas City	Jan. 8, 1990
43	Fairfield vs. Rice	Dec. 30, 1991
43	La Salle vs. St. Joseph's (Pa.)	Feb. 11, 1992
43	South Ala. vs. Jacksonville	Jan. 16, 1993
43	Baylor vs. Texas Christian	Feb. 14, 1995

THREE-POINT FIELD-GOAL PERCENTAGE

Pct.	Team (3FG-3FGA) vs. Opponent	Date
90.9	Duke (10-11) vs. Clemson	Feb. 1, 1988
90.9	Hofstra (10-11) vs. Rhode Island	Jan. 16, 1993
87.5	Stetson (14-16) vs. Centenary (La.)	Jan. 13, 1996
85.7	Western Ill. (12-14) vs. Valparaiso	Jan. 13, 1992
84.6	Murray St. (11-13) vs. Southeast Mo. St.	Jan. 16, 1993
83.3	Eastern Ky. (15-18) vs. N.C.-Asheville	Jan. 14, 1987
83.3	Princeton (10-12) vs. Pennsylvania	Jan. 6, 1990
83.3	Evansville (10-12) vs. Butler	Feb. 9, 1991
83.3	Southern Utah (10-12) vs. Cal St. Northridge	Mar. 1, 1991
83.3	Wis.-Milwaukee (10-12) vs. Eastern Mich.	Feb. 19, 1992
83.3	Purdue (10-12) vs. Michigan	Feb. 7, 1993
83.3	UNLV (10-12) vs. William & Mary	Feb. 11, 1995
83.3	Evansville (10-12) vs. Southern Ill.	Feb. 24, 1996
81.3	Niagara (13-16) vs. Siena	Jan. 7, 1987
80.0	Marshall (12-15) vs. Wyoming	Dec. 7, 1991
80.0	Washington St. (12-15) vs. Princeton	Dec. 29, 1992
80.0	Princeton (12-15) vs. Columbia	Feb. 13, 1993
80.0	Niagara (12-15) vs. Iona	Feb. 17, 1995
78.9	Ohio (15-19) vs. Charleston (S.C.)	Dec. 21, 1989
78.6	Toledo (11-14) vs. Akron	Jan. 20, 1993
78.6	Md.-Balt. County (11-14) vs. Charleston So.	Jan. 23, 1993
78.6	Ohio (11-14) vs. Youngstown St.	Dec. 20, 1993
78.2	South Caro. (18-28) vs. North Caro. A&T	Mar. 5, 1994

FREE-THROW PERCENTAGE
(Minimum 30 free throws made)

Pct.	Team (FG-FGA) vs. Opponent	Date
100	UC Irvine (34 of 34) vs. Pacific (Cal.)	Feb. 21, 1981
100	Samford (34 of 34) vs. Central Fla.	Dec. 20, 1990

Pct.	Team (FG-FGA) vs. Opponent	Date
100	Marshall (31 of 31) vs. Davidson	Dec. 17, 1979
100	Indiana St. (31 of 31) vs. Wichita St.	Feb. 18, 1991
97.2	Vanderbilt (35 of 36) vs. Mississippi St.	Feb. 26, 1986
97.2	Butler (35 of 36) vs. Dayton	Feb. 21, 1991
97.0	Toledo (32 of 33) vs. Old Dominion	Dec. 9, 1995
97.0	Hawaii (32 of 33) vs. New Mexico	Feb. 24, 1996
95.5	UNLV (42 of 44) vs. San Diego St.	Dec. 11, 1976

REBOUNDS

Reb.	Team vs. Opponent	Date
108	Kentucky vs. Mississippi	Feb. 8, 1964
103	Holy Cross vs. Boston College	Mar. 1, 1956
102	Arizona vs. Northern Ariz.	Jan. 6, 1951
101	Weber St. vs. Idaho St.	Jan. 22, 1966
100	William & Mary vs. Virginia	Feb. 14, 1954
95	Indiana vs. Michigan	Mar. 11, 1961
95	Murray St. vs. MacMurray	Jan. 2, 1967
92	Santa Clara vs. St. Mary's (Cal.)	Feb. 15, 1971
92	Oral Roberts vs. Brandeis	Jan. 8, 1973
91	Notre Dame vs. St. Norbert	Dec. 7, 1965
91	Southern Miss. vs. Tex.-Pan American	Feb. 9, 1970
91	Houston vs. Rice	Mar. 7, 1974
90	Vanderbilt vs. Sewanee	Dec. 4, 1954

ASSISTS

Ast.	Team vs. Opponent	Date
44	Colorado vs. George Mason (ot)	Dec. 2, 1995
41	North Caro. vs. Manhattan	Dec. 27, 1985
41	Weber St. vs. Northern Ariz.	Mar. 2, 1991
40	New Mexico vs. Texas-Arlington	Nov. 23, 1990
40	Loyola Marymount vs. U.S. Int'l	Jan. 5, 1991
40	Southern Utah vs. Texas Wesleyan	Jan. 25, 1992
40	Lamar vs. Prairie View	Feb. 2, 1993
39	Southern Miss. vs. Virginia Tech	Jan. 16, 1988
39	UNLV vs. Pacific (Cal.)	Feb. 8, 1990
39	UNLV vs. Rutgers	Feb. 3, 1991
39	Davidson vs. Warren Wilson	Dec. 9, 1991
39	Texas Christian vs. Midwestern St.	Nov. 30, 1994
38	New Mexico vs. U.S. Int'l	Dec. 3, 1985
38	Pepperdine vs. U.S. Int'l	Jan. 7, 1986
38	UCLA vs. Loyola Marymount	Dec. 2, 1990
38	Arizona vs. Northern Ariz.	Dec. 18, 1991
38	Tex.-Pan American vs. Concordia Lutheran	Dec. 4, 1993
38	LSU vs. George Mason	Dec. 3, 1994
37	10 tied	

BLOCKED SHOTS

Blk.	Team vs. Opponent	Date
21	Georgetown vs. Southern (N.O.)	Dec. 1, 1993
20	Iona vs. Northern Ill.	Jan. 7, 1989
20	Georgia vs. Bethune-Cookman	Dec. 7, 1993
20	Massachusetts vs. West Va.	Jan. 3, 1995
18	North Caro. vs. Stanford	Dec. 20, 1985
17	Maryland vs. Md.-East. Shore	Feb. 27, 1987
17	Rider vs. Fairleigh Dickinson	Jan. 9, 1989
17	Georgetown vs. Providence	Feb. 22, 1989
17	Georgetown vs. Hawaii-Loa	Nov. 23, 1990
17	Brigham Young vs. Eastern Ky.	Dec. 7, 1990
17	Northwestern St. vs. Oauchita Baptist	Nov. 30, 1991
17	New Orleans vs. Texas A&M	Dec. 29, 1992
17	Massachusetts vs. Hartford	Dec. 28, 1994
17	Louisville vs. Kentucky	Jan. 1, 1995
17	William & Mary vs. George Mason	Feb. 26, 1996
16	UTEP vs. Fort Lewis	Nov. 26, 1988
16	Maryland vs. Md.-East. Shore	Dec. 1, 1988
16	Oklahoma St. vs. Oklahoma	Feb. 11, 1989
16	Clemson vs. Radford	Dec. 9, 1989
16	Villanova vs. Drexel	Dec. 16, 1989
16	LSU vs. Texas	Jan. 2, 1990
16	UCLA vs. UC Irvine	Nov. 23, 1990
16	Kentucky vs. Georgia	Feb. 3, 1991
16	Rutgers vs. St. Bonaventure	Jan. 16, 1992
16	William & Mary vs. Marymount (Va.)	Nov. 29, 1995
16	Kentucky vs. Morehead St.	Dec. 16, 1995

STEALS

Stl.	Team vs. Opponent	Date
34	Oklahoma vs. Centenary (La.)	Dec. 12, 1987
34	Northwestern St. vs. LeTourneau	Jan. 20, 1992
33	Connecticut vs. Pittsburgh	Jan. 6, 1990
32	Manhattan vs. Lehman	Dec. 14, 1987
32	Oklahoma vs. Angelo St.	Dec. 1, 1990

Stl.	Team vs. Opponent	Date
32	LIU-Brooklyn vs. Medgar Evers	Nov. 29, 1994
32	Southwestern La. vs. Baptist Christian	Nov. 25, 1995
30	Southern U. vs. Baptist Christian	Dec. 14, 1992
30	Cal Poly SLO vs. Notre Dame (Cal.)	Nov. 25, 1995
29	Cleveland St. vs. Canisius	Dec. 28, 1986
29	Oklahoma vs. U.S. Int'l	Nov. 19, 1989
29	Centenary (La.) vs. East Texas Baptist	Dec. 12, 1992
28	Oklahoma vs. Morgan St.	Dec. 21, 1991
28	Memphis vs. Southeastern La.	Jan. 11, 1993
28	Oklahoma vs. Florida A&M	Jan. 27, 1993
27	Oregon St. vs. Hawaii-Loa	Dec. 22, 1985
27	Cal St. Fullerton vs. Lamar	Nov. 24, 1989
27	Texas-San Antonio vs. Samford	Jan. 19, 1991
27	Iowa St. vs. Bethune-Cookman	Dec. 31, 1992
27	San Francisco vs. Delaware St.	Nov. 27, 1993
27	Charleston So. vs. Warner Southern	Dec. 11, 1993

Season Records

WON-LOST PERCENTAGE

Team	Season	Won	Lost	Pct.
North Caro.	†1957	32	0	1.000
Indiana	†1976	32	0	1.000
UCLA	†1964	30	0	1.000
UCLA	†1967	30	0	1.000
UCLA	†1972	30	0	1.000
UCLA	†1973	30	0	1.000
San Francisco	†1956	29	0	1.000
North Caro. St.	1973	27	0	1.000
Kentucky	†1954	25	0	1.000
LIU-Brooklyn	†1939	24	0	1.000
Seton Hall	†1940	19	0	1.000
Army	†1944	15	0	1.000
UNLV	†1991	34	1	.971
Indiana St.	†1979	33	1	.971
Indiana	†1975	31	1	.969
North Caro. St.	†1974	30	1	.968
UCLA	†1968	29	1	.967
UCLA	†1969	29	1	.967
UCLA	†1971	29	1	.967
San Francisco	†1955	28	1	.966
UTEP	†1966	28	1	.966
Marquette	1971	28	1	.966
Pennsylvania	1971	28	1	.966
Alcorn St.	1979	28	1	.966
Ohio St.	†1961	27	1	.964

†National leader.

MOST IMPROVED TEAMS
(Since 1974)

Team	Season	W-L Record	Previous Yr. W-L	Games Up
North Caro. A&T	†1978	20-8	3-24	16½
Murray St.	†1980	23-8	4-22	16½
Liberty	†1992	22-7	5-23	16½
North Texas	†1976	22-4	6-20	16
Radford	†1991	22-7	7-22	15
Tulsa	†1981	26-7	8-19	15
Utah St.	†1983	20-9	4-23	15
Western Mich.	1992	21-9	5-22	14½
Tennessee St.	†1993	19-10	4-24	14½
Fresno St.	1978	21-6	7-20	14
James Madison	†1987	20-10	5-23	14
Loyola Marymount	†1988	28-4	12-16	14
Cal Poly SLO	†1996	16-13	1-26	14
Michigan St.	1978	25-5	10-17	13½
Loyola (Md.)	†1994	17-13	2-25	13½
Kansas	†1974	23-7	8-18	13
Wagner	†1979	21-7	7-19	13
Xavier (Ohio)	1983	22-8	8-20	13
Arizona	1988	35-3	18-12	13
Ball St.	†1989	29-3	14-14	13
Nebraska	1991	26-8	10-18	13
Wagner	1992	16-12	4-26	13
Southwestern La.	†1977	21-8	7-19	12½
Cincinnati	†1985	17-14	3-25	12½
Bradley	†1986	32-3	17-13	12½
Hawaii	1989	17-13	4-25	12½
Illinois St.	1992	18-11	5-23	12½
Western Ill.	†1995	20-8	7-20	12½

†National leader.

POINTS

Team	Season	G	Pts.
Oklahoma	†1988	39	4,012
Loyola Marymount	†1990	32	3,918
Arkansas	†1991	38	3,783
UNLV	1990	40	3,739
Oklahoma	†1989	36	3,680
UNLV	†1987	39	3,612
Loyola Marymount	1988	32	3,528
Loyola Marymount	1989	31	3,486
Houston	†1977	37	3,482
UNLV	†1976	31	3,426
UNLV	1977	32	3,426
Duke	1991	39	3,421
UNLV	1991	35	3,420
Arkansas	†1995	39	3,416
Syracuse	1989	38	3,410
Michigan	1989	37	3,393
Duke	1990	38	3,386
Oklahoma	1991	35	3,363
Arkansas	1990	35	3,345
North Caro.	1989	37	3,331
Oklahoma	†1985	37	3,328
Kentucky	†1996	36	3,292
North Caro.	1987	36	3,285
North Caro.	†1993	38	3,272
Missouri	1989	37	3,256

†National leader.

SCORING OFFENSE

Team	Season	G	Pts.	Avg.
Loyola Marymount	†1990	32	3,918	122.4
Loyola Marymount	†1989	31	3,486	112.5
UNLV	†1976	31	3,426	110.5
Loyola Marymount	†1988	32	3,528	110.3
UNLV	†1977	32	3,426	107.1
Oral Roberts	†1972	28	2,943	105.1
Southern U.	†1991	28	2,924	104.4
Loyola Marymount	1991	31	3,211	103.6
Oklahoma	1988	39	4,012	102.9
Oklahoma	1989	36	3,680	102.2
Oklahoma	1990	32	3,243	101.3
Southern U.	†1994	27	2,727	101.0
Jacksonville	†1970	28	2,809	100.3
Jacksonville	†1971	26	2,598	99.9
Arkansas	1991	38	3,783	99.6
Southern U.	1990	31	3,078	99.3
Syracuse	†1966	28	2,773	99.0
Iowa	1970	25	2,467	98.7
Miami (Fla.)	†1965	26	2,558	98.4
Houston	1966	29	2,845	98.1
Southwestern La.	1972	29	2,840	97.9
U.S. Int'l	1990	28	2,738	97.8
Houston	†1968	33	3,226	97.8
UNLV	1991	35	3,420	97.7
Md.-Eastern Shore	†1974	29	2,831	97.6
Troy St.	1994	27	2,634	97.6
Oklahoma City	1966	29	2,829	97.6

†National leader.

SCORING DEFENSE

Team	Season	G	Pts.	Avg.
Oklahoma St.	†1948	31	1,006	32.5
Oklahoma St.	†1949	28	985	35.2
Oklahoma St.	†1950	27	1,059	39.2
Alabama	1948	27	1,070	39.6
Creighton	1948	23	925	40.2
Wyoming	1948	27	1,101	40.8
Wyoming	1950	36	1,491	41.4
Siena	1948	28	1,161	41.5
St. Bonaventure	1948	22	921	41.9
Siena	1949	29	1,215	41.9
Tulane	1948	26	1,102	42.4
Wyoming	1949	35	1,509	43.1
Texas	1948	25	1,079	43.2
Utah	1948	20	868	43.4
Minnesota	1949	21	912	43.4
Washington (Mo.)	1948	21	915	43.6
St. Bonaventure	1949	26	1,137	43.7
St. Louis	1948	27	1,183	43.8
Kentucky	1949	34	1,492	43.9
Washington St.	1949	30	1,317	43.9
Texas A&M	†1951	29	1,275	44.0

Team	Season	G	Pts.	Avg.
Kentucky	1948	39	1,730	44.4
Baylor	1949	24	1,068	44.5
Tulsa	1950	23	1,027	44.7
Hamline	1948	31	1,389	44.8

†National leader.

(Since 1965)

Team	Season	G	Pts.	Avg.
Fresno St.	†1982	30	1,412	47.1
Princeton	†1992	28	1,349	48.2
Princeton	†1991	27	1,320	48.9
North Caro. St.	1982	32	1,570	49.1
Princeton	1982	26	1,277	49.1
Princeton	†1984	28	1,403	50.1
St. Peter's	†1980	31	1,563	50.4
Fresno St.	†1981	29	1,470	50.7
Princeton	†1990	27	1,378	51.0
Princeton	1981	28	1,438	51.4
St. Peter's	1981	26	1,338	51.5
Wyoming	1982	30	1,545	51.5
Princeton	†1977	26	1,343	51.7
Princeton	†1996	29	1,498	51.7
Princeton	†1983	29	1,507	52.0
James Madison	1982	30	1,559	52.0
Fresno St.	†1978	27	1,417	52.5
Princeton	†1976	27	1,427	52.9
Columbia	1982	26	1,375	52.9
Princeton	†1989	27	1,430	53.0
Fresno St.	†1985	32	1,696	53.0
UTEP	1982	28	1,497	53.5
Georgetown	1982	37	1,979	53.5
Army	†1969	28	1,498	53.5
Fresno St.	1983	35	1,880	53.7
Fairleigh Dickinson	†1971	23	1,236	53.7

†National leader.

SCORING MARGIN

Team	Season	Off.	Def.	Mar.
UCLA	†1972	94.6	64.3	30.3
North Caro. St.	†1948	75.3	47.2	28.1
Kentucky	†1954	87.5	60.3	27.2
Kentucky	†1952	82.3	55.4	26.9
UNLV	1991	97.7	71.0	26.7
UCLA	†1968	93.4	67.2	26.2
UCLA	†1967	89.6	63.7	25.9
Houston	1968	97.8	72.5	25.3
Kentucky	1948	69.0	44.4	24.6
Kentucky	†1949	68.2	43.9	24.3
Bowling Green	1948	70.5	46.7	23.8
Loyola (Ill.)	†1963	91.8	68.1	23.7
N.C.-Charlotte	†1975	88.9	65.2	23.7
Arizona St.	†1962	90.1	67.6	22.5
St. Bonaventure	†1970	88.4	65.9	22.5
Kentucky	†1951	74.7	52.5	22.2
Indiana	1975	88.0	65.9	22.1
Kentucky	†1996	91.4	69.4	22.1
Cincinnati	†1960	86.7	64.7	22.0
Oklahoma	†1988	102.9	81.0	21.9
North Caro. St.	†1973	92.9	71.1	21.8
Jacksonville	1970	100.3	78.5	21.8
UNLV	†1976	110.5	89.0	21.5
UCLA	1973	81.3	60.1	21.2
Oklahoma	†1990	101.3	80.4	21.0

†National leader.

FIELD-GOAL PERCENTAGE

Team	Season	FG	FGA	Pct.
Missouri	†1980	936	1,635	57.2
Michigan	†1989	1,325	2,341	56.6
Oregon St.	†1981	862	1,528	56.4
UC Irvine	†1982	920	1,639	56.1
Michigan St.	†1986	1,043	1,860	56.1
North Caro.	1986	1,197	2,140	55.9
Kansas	1986	1,260	2,266	55.6
Kentucky	†1983	869	1,564	55.6
Notre Dame	1981	824	1,492	55.2
Houston Baptist	†1984	797	1,445	55.2
Maryland	1980	985	1,789	55.1
Idaho	1981	816	1,484	55.0
UC Irvine	1981	934	1,703	54.8
Navy	†1985	946	1,726	54.8
Stanford	1983	752	1,373	54.8
Maryland	†1975	1,049	1,918	54.7

Team	Season	FG	FGA	Pct.
New Orleans	1983	937	1,714	54.7
Georgia Tech	1986	1,008	1,846	54.6
Arkansas	†1978	1,060	1,943	54.6
Michigan	†1988	1,198	2,196	54.6
New Mexico	1989	992	1,819	54.5
Southern U.	1978	1,107	2,031	54.5
Arkansas	†1977	849	1,558	54.5
Arizona	1988	1,147	2,106	54.5
Pepperdine	1983	900	1,653	54.4
Oregon St.	1980	943	1,732	54.4
Ohio St.	†1970	831	1,527	54.4
N.C.-Wilmington	1977	816	1,500	54.4
Davidson	†1964	894	1,644	54.4

†National leader.

FIELD-GOAL PERCENTAGE DEFENSE
(Since 1978)

Team	Season	FG	FGA	Pct.
Marquette	†1994	750	2,097	35.8
UNLV	†1992	628	1,723	36.5
Georgetown	†1991	680	1,847	36.8
Temple	1994	621	1,686	36.8
Wis.-Green Bay	1994	664	1,777	37.4
Alabama	†1995	771	2,048	37.6
Kansas	1995	768	2,032	37.8
Princeton	1992	445	1,169	38.1
Marquette	1995	747	1,957	38.2
Mississippi St.	1995	698	1,821	38.3
Kansas	1994	823	2,147	38.3
Manhattan	1995	670	1,747	38.4
UAB	1994	661	1,718	38.5
Temple	†1996	670	1,741	38.5
Marquette	1996	682	1,772	38.5
Mississippi St.	1996	803	2,084	38.5
Massachusetts	1995	799	2,072	38.6
Connecticut	1996	840	2,175	38.6
Temple	1995	628	1,623	38.7
Kansas	1996	777	2,008	38.7
Manhattan	1994	671	1,734	38.7
Wake Forest	1995	736	1,898	38.8
Geo. Washington	1994	685	1,766	38.8
Northern Ill.	1991	616	1,587	38.8
Drexel	1994	713	1,835	38.9

†National leader.

THREE-POINT FIELD GOALS MADE

Team	Season	G	3FG
Arkansas	†1995	39	361
Kentucky	†1993	34	340
Kentucky	†1992	36	317
UNLV	†1987	39	309
East Tenn. St.	†1991	33	301
Arkansas	†1994	34	301
Kentucky	1994	34	301
New Mexico	1994	31	300
Troy St.	†1996	27	300
Loyola Marymount	†1990	32	298
Georgia Tech	1996	36	296
La Salle	1992	31	294
North Caro. St.	1996	31	292
Loyola Marymount	†1989	31	287
Troy St.	1995	27	287
Auburn	1996	32	287
East Tenn. St.	1990	34	285
St. Louis	1995	31	284
Marshall	1996	28	284
Kentucky	1990	28	281
Samford	1995	27	279
Fresno St.	1996	33	279
Lamar	1993	27	271
Vermont	1995	27	268
Southern Ill.	1996	29	268

†National leader.

THREE-POINT FIELD GOALS MADE PER GAME

Team	Season	G	3FG	Avg.
Troy St.	†1996	27	300	11.11
Troy St.	†1995	27	287	10.63
Samford	1995	27	279	10.33
Marshall	1996	28	284	10.14
Lamar	†1993	27	271	10.04
Kentucky	†1990	28	281	10.04
Kentucky	1993	34	340	10.00

Team	Season	G	3FG	Avg.
Vermont	1995	27	268	9.93
Troy St.	†1994	27	262	9.70
New Mexico	1994	31	300	9.68
La Salle	†1992	31	294	9.48
Baylor	1995	28	265	9.46
North Caro. St.	1996	31	292	9.42
Arizona St.	1993	28	263	9.39
Marshall	1995	27	253	9.37
Loyola Marymount	1990	32	298	9.31
Loyola Marymount	†1989	31	287	9.26
Arkansas	1995	39	361	9.26
Northwestern St.	1992	28	259	9.25
Southern Ill.	1996	29	268	9.24
Southern U.	1995	26	239	9.19
St. Louis	1995	31	284	9.16
VMI	1995	27	247	9.15
Texas-Arlington	†1991	29	265	9.14
East Tenn. St.	1991	33	301	9.12

†National leader.

THREE-POINT FIELD-GOAL PERCENTAGE
(Minimum 100 three-point field goals made)

Team	Season	G	3FG	3FGA	Pct.
Indiana	†1987	34	130	256	50.8
Mississippi Val.	1987	28	161	322	50.0
Stephen F. Austin	1987	30	120	241	49.8
Princeton	†1988	26	211	429	49.2
Prairie View	1988	27	129	266	48.5
Kansas St.	1988	34	179	370	48.4
Arizona	1988	38	254	526	48.3
Indiana	†1989	35	121	256	47.3
Bucknell	1988	28	154	328	47.0
Holy Cross	1988	29	158	337	46.9
Michigan	1989	37	196	419	46.8
Wis.-Green Bay	†1992	30	204	437	46.7
Citadel	1989	28	153	328	46.6
Niagara	1987	31	128	275	46.5
Eastern Mich.	1987	29	144	310	46.5
Wis.-Green Bay	†1991	31	189	407	46.4
Colorado St.	1989	33	141	305	46.2
Bucknell	1989	31	160	347	46.1
Illinois	1987	31	112	243	46.1
Illinois St.	1987	32	110	240	45.8
Jacksonville	1987	30	188	412	45.6
Rider	1987	28	151	331	45.6
Davidson	1987	30	138	303	45.5
New Mexico St.	1988	32	143	314	45.5
Gonzaga	1989	28	119	262	45.4
Indiana	†1994	30	182	401	45.4

†National leader.

FREE-THROW PERCENTAGE

Team	Season	FT	FTA	Pct.
Harvard	†1984	535	651	82.2
Brigham Young	†1989	527	647	81.5
Harvard	†1985	450	555	81.1
Ohio St.	†1970	452	559	80.9
Vanderbilt	†1974	477	595	80.2
Michigan St.	†1986	490	613	79.9
Butler	†1988	413	517	79.9
Miami (Fla.)	†1975	642	807	79.6
Tulane	†1963	390	492	79.3
Tennessee	†1971	538	679	79.2
Auburn	1966	476	601	79.2
Oklahoma St.	1958	488	617	79.1
Duke	†1978	665	841	79.1
Utah	†1993	476	602	79.1
Gonzaga	1989	485	614	79.0
Oral Roberts	†1980	481	610	78.9
Marshall	1958	479	608	78.8
Bucknell	1989	590	749	78.8
Alabama	†1987	521	662	78.7
Butler	†1991	725	922	78.6
Western Ill.	†1982	447	569	78.6
Morehead St.	1965	487	620	78.5
Princeton	1974	332	423	78.5
Duke	†1973	496	632	78.5
St. Francis (Pa.)	†1979	350	446	78.5

†National leader.

REBOUND MARGIN
(Since 1973)

Team	Season	Off.	Def.	Mar.
Manhattan	†1973	56.5	38.0	18.5
American	1973	56.7	40.3	16.4
Alcorn St.	†1978	52.3	36.0	16.3
Oral Roberts	1973	66.9	50.3	15.6
Alcorn St.	†1980	49.2	33.8	15.4
UCLA	1973	49.0	33.9	15.1
Houston	1973	54.7	40.8	13.9
Massachusetts	†1974	44.5	30.7	13.8
Alcorn St.	†1979	50.1	36.3	13.8
Minnesota	1973	49.0	36.0	13.0
Va. Commonwealth	1974	55.1	42.1	13.0
Northeastern	†1981	44.9	32.0	12.9
Stetson	1975	47.1	34.7	12.4
Notre Dame	†1976	46.3	34.1	12.2
Harvard	1973	53.5	41.3	12.2
Tennessee St.	1980	46.5	34.3	12.2
Tennessee St.	1979	49.7	37.9	11.8
Buffalo	1976	51.5	39.7	11.8
Southern U.	1978	43.1	31.4	11.7
Wyoming	1981	42.0	30.3	11.7
Alabama	1973	50.9	39.3	11.6
Mississippi Val.	†1996	48.3	36.8	11.6
Iowa	†1987	43.1	31.5	11.5
Long Beach St.	1973	55.5	44.3	11.2
Massachusetts	†1993	43.9	32.8	11.2

†National leader.

ASSISTS

Team	Season	G	Ast.
UNLV	†1990	40	926
UNLV	†1991	35	863
Oklahoma	†1988	39	862
UNLV	†1987	39	853
Oklahoma	†1985	37	828
Arkansas	1991	38	819
Kansas	†1986	39	814
North Caro.	1986	34	800
North Caro.	†1989	37	788
Southern Methodist	1988	35	786
Kentucky	†1996	36	783
North Caro.	1987	36	782
Loyola Marymount	1990	32	763
Kansas	1990	35	762
Oklahoma	1989	36	743
Arkansas	†1995	39	721
North Caro.	1991	35	699
North Caro.	†1993	38	698
Kansas	1993	36	687
Arkansas	†1994	34	687
Oklahoma St.	1994	34	677
Arkansas	†1992	34	674
Kentucky	1993	34	665
Georgia Tech	1992	35	662
Kentucky	1992	36	661

†National leader.

ASSISTS PER GAME

Team	Season	G	Ast.	Avg.
UNLV	†1991	35	863	24.7
Loyola Marymount	†1990	32	762	23.8
North Caro.	†1986	34	800	23.5
UNLV	1990	40	926	23.2
Southern Methodist	†1987	29	655	22.6
Southern Methodist	†1988	35	786	22.5
Oklahoma	†1985	37	828	22.4
Oklahoma	1988	39	862	22.1
Northwestern St.	†1993	26	570	21.9
UNLV	1987	39	853	21.9
Kansas	1990	35	763	21.8
Kentucky	†1996	36	783	21.8
North Caro.	1987	36	782	21.7
Iowa St.	1988	32	694	21.7
Arkansas	1991	38	819	21.6
North Caro.	†1989	37	788	21.3
Georgia Tech	1988	32	680	21.3
Montana St.	1996	30	627	20.9
Montana St.	†1995	29	606	20.9
Arkansas	†1994	34	687	20.2
Oklahoma St.	1994	34	677	19.9
Arkansas	†1992	34	674	19.8

Team	Season	G	Ast.	Avg.
UCLA	1995	33	653	19.8
Loyola Marymount	1992	28	552	19.7
Nicholls St.	1995	30	590	19.7

†National leader.

BLOCKED SHOTS

Team	Season	G	Blk.
Georgetown	†1989	34	309
Massachusetts	†1995	34	273
UNLV	†1991	35	266
Brigham Young	1991	34	246
Clemson	†1990	35	235
Georgetown	1991	32	235
Central Conn. St.	†1996	28	235
Navy	†1986	35	233
Georgetown	1990	31	233
Massachusetts	1996	37	232
Arkansas	1991	38	229
LSU	1990	32	225
Alabama	†1992	35	223
North Caro.	†1994	35	219
Connecticut	1994	34	218
Memphis	1995	34	218
UTEP	1992	34	217
Louisville	1986	39	216
Jackson St.	†1993	34	215
Massachusetts	1994	35	214
Florida St.	1993	35	210
Oklahoma	1989	36	209
LSU	1992	31	206
Georgetown	1992	32	204
Duke	1994	34	204
Kansas	1996	34	204

†National leader.

BLOCKED SHOTS PER GAME

Team	Season	G	Blk.	Avg.
Georgetown	†1989	34	309	9.09
Central Conn. St.	†1996	28	235	8.39
Massachusetts	†1995	34	273	8.03
UNLV	†1991	35	266	7.60
Georgetown	†1990	31	233	7.52
Central Conn. St.	1995	26	194	7.46
Georgetown	1991	32	235	7.34
Florida A&M	1996	27	198	7.33
Brigham Young	1991	34	246	7.24
LSU	1990	32	225	7.03
Vermont	†1992	29	198	6.83
Clemson	1990	35	235	6.71
Tennessee Tech	1995	27	181	6.70
Navy	†1986	35	233	6.66
Siena	†1988	29	193	6.66
LSU	1992	31	206	6.65
Howard	†1994	27	179	6.63
Maryland	1991	28	185	6.61
LSU	1991	30	198	6.60
Wyoming	†1993	28	184	6.57
Memphis	1994	29	189	6.52
Colgate	1996	30	195	6.50
Connecticut	1994	34	218	6.41
Memphis	1995	34	218	6.41
UTEP	1992	34	217	6.38
Georgetown	1992	32	204	6.38

†National leader.

STEALS

Team	Season	G	Stl.
Oklahoma	†1988	39	486
Connecticut	†1990	37	484
Cleveland St.	†1987	33	473
Arkansas	1991	38	467
Texas	†1994	34	453
Loyola Marymount	1990	32	450
Arkansas	†1995	39	445
Cleveland St.	†1986	33	436
Kentucky	†1996	36	435
Georgetown	1996	37	431
Texas-San Antonio	1991	29	430
Oklahoma	†1993	32	405
UNLV	1991	35	399
Florida A&M	1988	30	395
Kentucky	1994	34	394

Team	Season	G	Stl.
Tulane	†1992	31	388
Southern U.	1993	31	387
Iowa St.	1992	34	381
Centenary (La.)	1993	27	380
Cleveland St.	1988	30	376
Nicholls St.	1995	30	376
Arkansas	†1989	32	372
Oklahoma	1990	32	371
Oklahoma	1991	35	370
Kentucky	1992	36	368
Tulane	1993	31	368
New Mexico St.	1995	35	368

†National leader.

STEALS PER GAME

Team	Season	G	Stl.	Avg.
Texas-San Antonio	†1991	29	430	14.83
Cleveland St.	†1987	33	473	14.33
Centenary (La.)	†1993	27	380	14.07
Loyola Marymount	†1990	32	450	14.06
Texas	†1994	34	453	13.32
Cleveland St.	†1986	33	436	13.21
Florida A&M	†1988	30	395	13.17
Connecticut	1990	37	484	13.08
N.C.-Charlotte	1991	28	363	12.96
Northeastern Ill.	†1992	28	358	12.79
Oklahoma	1993	32	405	12.66
Southern U.	1991	28	352	12.57
Cleveland St.	1988	30	376	12.53
Nicholls St.	†1995	30	376	12.53
Tulane	1992	31	388	12.52
Southern U.	1993	31	387	12.48
Drake	1994	27	337	12.48
McNeese St.	†1996	27	330	12.22
Kentucky	1996	36	435	12.08
Arizona St.	1993	28	337	12.04
Cal Poly SLO	1996	29	349	12.03
St. Francis (N.Y.)	1993	27	324	12.00
LIU-Brooklyn	1994	27	322	11.93
Troy St.	1994	27	321	11.89
Tulane	1993	31	368	11.87

†National leader.

Annual Team Champions

Won-Lost Percentage

Season	Team	Won	Lost	Pct.
1948	Western Ky.	28	2	.933
1949	Kentucky	32	2	.941
1950	Holy Cross	27	4	.871
1951	Columbia	21	1	.956
1952	Kansas	26	2	.929
1953	Seton Hall	31	2	.939
1954	Kentucky	25	0	1.000
1955	San Francisco	28	1	.966
1956	San Francisco	29	0	1.000
1957	North Caro.	32	0	1.000
1958	West Va.	26	2	.929
1959	Mississippi St.	24	1	.960
1960	California	28	2	.933
	Cincinnati	28	2	.933
1961	Ohio St.	27	1	.964
1962	Mississippi St.	24	1	.960
1963	Loyola (Ill.)	29	2	.935
1964	UCLA	30	0	1.000
1965	UCLA	28	2	.933
1966	UTEP	28	1	.966
1967	UCLA	30	0	1.000
1968	UCLA	29	1	.967
1969	UCLA	29	1	.967
1970	UCLA	28	2	.933
1971	UCLA	29	1	.967
1972	UCLA	30	0	1.000
1973	UCLA	30	0	1.000
	North Caro. St.	27	0	1.000
1974	North Caro. St.	30	1	.968
1975	Indiana	31	1	.969

Season	Team	Won	Lost	Pct.
1976	Indiana	32	0	1.000
1977	San Francisco	29	2	.935
1978	Kentucky	30	2	.938
1979	Indiana St.	33	1	.971
1980	Alcorn St.	28	2	.933
1981	DePaul	27	2	.931
1982	North Caro.	32	2	.941
1983	Houston	31	3	.912
1984	Georgetown	34	3	.919
1985	Georgetown	35	3	.921
1986	Duke	37	3	.925
1987	UNLV	37	2	.949
1988	Temple	32	2	.941
1989	Ball St.	29	3	.906
1990	La Salle	30	2	.938
1991	UNLV	34	1	.971
1992	Duke	34	2	.944
1993	North Caro.	34	4	.895
1994	Arkansas	31	3	.912
1995	UCLA	31	2	.939
1996	Massachusetts	35	2	.946

Most Improved Teams

Season	Team	W-L Record	Previous Yr. W-L	Games Up
1974	Kansas	23-7	8-18	13
1975	Holy Cross	20-8	8-18	11
1976	North Texas	22-4	6-20	16
1977	Southwestern La.	21-8	7-19	12½
1978	North Caro. A&T	20-8	3-24	16½
1979	Wagner	21-7	7-19	13
1980	Murray St.	23-8	4-22	16½
1981	Tulsa	26-7	8-19	15
1982	Cal St. Fullerton	18-14	4-23	11½
1983	Utah St.	20-9	4-23	15
1984	Northeastern	27-5	13-15	12
	Loyola (Md.)	16-12	4-24	12
1985	Cincinnati	17-14	3-25	12½
1986	Bradley	32-3	17-13	12½
1987	James Madison	20-10	5-23	14
1988	Loyola Marymount	28-4	12-16	14
1989	Ball St.	29-3	14-14	13
1990	South Fla.	20-11	7-21	11½
	Geo. Washington	14-17	1-27	11½
1991	Radford	22-7	7-22	15
1992	Liberty	22-7	5-23	16½
1993	Tennessee St.	19-10	4-24	14½
1994	Loyola (Md.)	17-13	2-25	13½
1995	Western Ill.	20-8	7-20	12½
1996	Cal Poly SLO	16-13	1-26	14

Scoring Offense

Season	Team	G	W-L	Pts.	Avg.
1948	Rhode Island	23	17-6	1,755	76.3
1949	Rhode Island	22	16-6	1,575	71.6
1950	Villanova	29	25-4	2,111	72.8
1951	Cincinnati	22	18-4	1,694	77.0
1952	Kentucky	32	29-3	2,635	82.3
1953	Furman	27	21-6	2,435	90.2
1954	Furman	29	20-9	2,658	91.7
1955	Furman	27	17-10	2,572	95.3
1956	Morehead St.	29	19-10	2,782	95.9
1957	Connecticut	25	17-8	2,183	87.3
1958	Marshall	24	17-7	2,113	88.0
1959	Miami (Fla.)	25	18-7	2,190	87.6
1960	Ohio St.	28	25-3	2,532	90.4
1961	St. Bonaventure	28	24-4	2,479	88.5
1962	Loyola (Ill.)	27	23-4	2,436	90.2
1963	Loyola (Ill.)	31	29-2	2,847	91.8
1964	Detroit	25	14-11	2,402	96.1
1965	Miami (Fla.)	26	22-4	2,558	98.4
1966	Syracuse	28	22-6	2,773	99.0
1967	Oklahoma City	26	16-10	2,496	96.0
1968	Houston	33	31-2	3,226	97.8
1969	Purdue	28	23-5	2,605	93.0
1970	Jacksonville	28	26-2	2,809	100.3
1971	Jacksonville	26	22-4	2,598	99.9
1972	Oral Roberts	28	26-2	2,943	105.1
1973	Oral Roberts	27	21-6	2,626	97.3

Season	Team	G	W-L	Pts.	Avg.
1974	Md.-East. Shore	29	27-2	2,831	97.6
1975	South Ala.	26	19-7	2,412	92.8
1976	UNLV	31	29-2	3,426	110.5
1977	UNLV	32	29-3	3,426	107.1
1978	New Mexico	28	24-4	2,731	97.5
1979	UNLV	29	21-9	2,700	93.1
1980	Alcorn St.	30	28-2	2,729	92.0
1981	UC Irvine	27	17-10	2,332	86.4
1982	LIU-Brooklyn	30	20-10	2,605	86.8
1983	Boston College	32	25-7	2,697	84.3
1984	Tulsa	31	27-4	2,816	90.8
1985	Oklahoma	37	31-6	3,328	89.9
1986	U.S. Int'l	28	8-20	2,542	90.8
1987	UNLV	39	37-2	3,612	92.6
1988	Loyola Marymount	32	28-4	3,528	110.3
1989	Loyola Marymount	31	20-11	3,486	112.5
1990	Loyola Marymount	32	26-6	3,918	*122.4
1991	Southern U.	28	19-9	2,924	104.4
1992	Northwestern St.	28	15-13	2,660	95.0
1993	Southern U.	31	21-10	3,011	97.1
1994	Southern U.	27	16-11	2,727	101.0
1995	Texas Christian	27	16-11	2,529	93.7
1996	Troy St.	27	11-16	2,551	94.5

*Record.

Scoring Defense

Season	Team	G	W-L	Pts.	Avg.
1948	Oklahoma St.	31	27-4	1,006	*32.5
1949	Oklahoma St.	28	23-5	985	35.2
1950	Oklahoma St.	27	18-9	1,059	39.2
1951	Texas A&M	29	17-12	1,275	44.0
1952	Oklahoma St.	27	19-8	1,228	45.5
1953	Oklahoma St.	30	23-7	1,614	53.8
1954	Oklahoma St.	29	24-5	1,539	53.1
1955	San Francisco	29	28-1	1,511	52.1
1956	San Francisco	29	29-0	1,514	52.2
1957	Oklahoma St.	26	17-9	1,420	54.6
1958	San Francisco	27	25-2	1,363	50.5
1959	California	29	25-4	1,480	51.0
1960	California	30	28-2	1,486	49.5
1961	Santa Clara	27	18-9	1,314	48.7
1962	Santa Clara	25	19-6	1,302	52.1
1963	Cincinnati	28	26-2	1,480	52.9
1964	San Jose St.	24	14-10	1,307	54.5
1965	Tennessee	25	20-5	1,391	55.6
1966	Oregon St.	28	21-7	1,527	54.5
1967	Tennessee	28	21-7	1,511	54.0
1968	Army	25	20-5	1,448	57.9
1969	Army	28	18-10	1,498	53.5
1970	Army	28	22-6	1,515	54.1
1971	Fairleigh Dickinson	23	16-7	1,236	53.7
1972	Minnesota	25	18-7	1,451	58.0
1973	UTEP	26	16-10	1,460	56.2
1974	UTEP	25	18-7	1,413	56.5
1975	UTEP	26	20-6	1,491	57.3
1976	Princeton	27	22-5	1,427	52.9
1977	Princeton	26	21-5	1,343	51.7
1978	Fresno St.	27	21-6	1,417	52.5
1979	Princeton	26	14-12	1,452	55.8
1980	St. Peter's	31	22-9	1,563	50.4
1981	Fresno St.	29	25-4	1,470	50.7
1982	Fresno St.	30	27-3	1,412	47.1
1983	Princeton	29	20-9	1,507	52.0
1984	Princeton	28	18-10	1,403	50.1
1985	Fresno St.	32	23-9	1,696	53.0
1986	Princeton	26	13-13	1,429	55.0
1987	Southwest Mo. St.	34	28-6	1,958	57.6
1988	Ga. Southern	31	24-7	1,725	55.6
1989	Princeton	27	19-8	1,430	53.0
1990	Princeton	27	20-7	1,378	51.0
1991	Princeton	27	24-3	1,320	48.9
1992	Princeton	28	22-6	1,349	48.2
1993	Princeton	26	15-11	1,421	54.7
1994	Princeton	26	18-8	1,361	52.3
1995	Princeton	26	16-10	1,501	57.7
1996	Princeton	29	22-7	1,498	51.7

*Record.

Photo from Princeton sports information

Aggressive defense, as displayed by Sydney Johnson, once again helped Princeton lead Division I in scoring defense. The Tigers limited opponents to 51.7 points per game, marking the eighth consecutive year Princeton has ranked No. 1 in the category.

Scoring Margin

Season	Team	Off.	Def.	Mar.
1949	Kentucky	68.2	43.9	24.3
1950	Holy Cross	72.6	55.4	17.2
1951	Kentucky	74.7	52.5	22.2
1952	Kentucky	82.3	55.4	26.9
1953	La Salle	80.1	61.8	18.3
1954	Kentucky	87.5	60.3	27.2
1955	Utah	79.0	59.9	19.1
1956	San Francisco	72.2	52.2	20.0
1957	Kentucky	84.2	69.4	14.8
1958	Cincinnati	86.5	65.9	20.6
1959	Idaho St.	74.2	53.7	20.5
1960	Cincinnati	86.7	64.7	22.0
1961	Memphis	85.0	64.2	20.8
1962	Arizona St.	90.1	67.6	22.5
1963	Loyola (Ill.)	91.8	68.1	23.7
1964	Davidson	89.3	70.5	18.8
1965	Connecticut	85.1	66.5	18.6
1966	Loyola (Ill.)	97.5	76.6	20.9
1967	UCLA	89.6	63.7	25.9
1968	UCLA	93.4	67.2	26.2
1969	UCLA	84.7	63.8	20.9
1970	St. Bonaventure	88.4	65.9	22.5
1971	Jacksonville	99.9	79.0	20.9
1972	UCLA	94.6	64.3	*30.3
1973	North Caro. St.	92.9	71.1	21.8
1974	N.C.-Charlotte	90.2	69.4	20.8
1975	N.C.-Charlotte	88.9	65.2	23.7
1976	UNLV	110.5	89.0	21.5
1977	UNLV	107.1	87.7	19.4
1978	UCLA	85.3	67.4	17.9
1979	Syracuse	88.7	71.5	17.2
1980	Alcorn St.	91.0	73.6	17.4
1981	Wyoming	73.6	57.5	16.1
1982	Oregon St.	69.6	55.0	14.6
1983	Houston	82.4	64.9	17.4
1984	Georgetown	74.3	57.9	16.4
1985	Georgetown	74.3	57.3	17.1
1986	Cleveland St.	88.9	69.6	19.3
1987	UNLV	92.6	75.5	17.1
1988	Oklahoma	102.9	81.0	21.9
1989	St. Mary's (Cal.)	76.1	57.6	18.5
1990	Oklahoma	101.3	80.4	21.0
1991	UNLV	97.7	71.0	26.7
1992	Indiana	83.4	65.8	17.6

Season	Team	Off.	Def.	Mar.
1993	North Caro.	86.1	68.3	17.8
1994	Arkansas	93.4	75.6	17.9
1995	Kentucky	87.4	69.0	18.4
1996	Kentucky	91.4	69.4	22.1

*Record.

Field-Goal Percentage

Season	Team	FG	FGA	Pct.
1948	Oregon St.	668	1,818	36.7
1949	Muhlenberg	593	1,512	39.2
1950	Texas Christian	476	1,191	40.0
1951	Maryland	481	1,210	39.8
1952	Boston College	787	1,893	41.6
1953	Furman	936	2,106	44.4
1954	Geo. Washington	744	1,632	45.6
1955	Geo. Washington	867	1,822	47.6
1956	Geo. Washington	725	1,451	50.0
1957	Manhattan	679	1,489	45.6
1958	Fordham	693	1,440	48.1
1959	Auburn	593	1,216	48.8
1960	Auburn	532	1,022	52.1
1961	Ohio St.	939	1,886	49.8
1962	Florida St.	709	1,386	51.2
1963	Duke	984	1,926	51.1
1964	Davidson	894	1,644	54.4
1965	St. Peter's	579	1,089	53.2
1966	North Caro.	838	1,620	51.7
1967	UCLA	1,082	2,081	52.0
1968	Bradley	927	1,768	52.4
1969	UCLA	1,027	1,999	51.4
1970	Ohio St.	831	1,527	54.4
1971	Jacksonville	1,077	2,008	53.6
1972	North Caro.	1,031	1,954	52.8
1973	North Caro.	1,150	2,181	52.7
1974	Notre Dame	1,056	1,992	53.0
1975	Maryland	1,049	1,918	54.7
1976	Maryland	996	1,854	53.7
1977	Arkansas	849	1,558	54.5
1978	Arkansas	1,060	1,943	54.6
1979	UCLA	1,053	1,897	55.5
1980	Missouri	936	1,635	*57.2
1981	Oregon St.	862	1,528	56.4
1982	UC Irvine	920	1,639	56.1
1983	Kentucky	869	1,564	55.6
1984	Houston Baptist	797	1,445	55.2
1985	Navy	946	1,726	54.8
1986	Michigan St.	1,043	1,860	56.1
1987	Princeton	601	1,111	54.1
1988	Michigan	1,198	2,196	54.6
1989	Michigan	1,325	2,341	56.6
1990	Kansas	1,204	2,258	53.3
1991	UNLV	1,305	2,441	53.5
1992	Duke	1,108	2,069	53.6
1993	Indiana	1,076	2,062	52.2
1994	Auburn	854	1,689	50.6
1995	Washington St.	902	1,743	51.7
1996	UCLA	897	1,698	52.8

*Record.

Field-Goal Percentage Defense

Season	Team	FG	FGA	Pct.
1977	Minnesota	766	1,886	40.6
1978	Delaware St.	733	1,802	40.7
1979	Illinois	738	1,828	40.4
1980	Penn St.	543	1,309	41.5
1981	Wyoming	637	1,589	40.1
1982	Wyoming	584	1,470	39.7
1983	Wyoming	599	1,441	41.6
1984	Georgetown	799	2,025	39.5
1985	Georgetown	833	2,064	40.4
1986	St. Peter's	574	1,395	41.1
1987	San Diego	660	1,645	40.1
1988	Temple	777	1,981	39.2
1989	Georgetown	795	1,993	39.9
1990	Georgetown	713	1,929	37.0
1991	Georgetown	680	1,847	36.8
1992	UNLV	628	1,723	36.4
1993	Marquette	634	1,613	39.3
1994	Marquette	750	2,097	*35.8

Season	Team	FG	FGA	Pct.
1995	Alabama	771	2,048	37.6
1996	Temple	670	1,741	38.5

*Record.

Three-Point Field Goals Made Per Game

Season	Team	G	3FG	Avg.
1987	Providence	34	280	8.24
1988	Princeton	26	211	8.12
1989	Loyola Marymount	31	287	9.26
1990	Kentucky	28	281	10.04
1991	Texas-Arlington	29	265	9.14
1992	La Salle	31	294	9.48
1993	Lamar	27	271	10.04
1994	Troy St.	27	262	9.70
1995	Troy St.	27	287	10.63
1996	Troy St.	27	300	*11.11

*Record.

Three-Point Field-Goal Percentage

Season	Team	G	3FG	3FGA	Pct.
1987	Indiana	34	130	256	*50.8
1988	Princeton	26	211	429	49.2
1989	Indiana	35	121	256	47.3
1990	Princeton	27	208	460	45.2
1991	Wis.-Green Bay	31	189	407	46.4
1992	Wis.-Green Bay	30	204	437	46.7
1993	Valparaiso	28	214	500	42.8
1994	Indiana	30	182	401	45.4
1995	Southern Utah	28	244	571	42.7
1996	Weber St.	30	245	577	42.5

*Record.

Free-Throw Percentage

Season	Team	FT	FTA	Pct.
1948	Texas	351	481	73.0
1949	Davidson	347	489	71.0
1950	Temple	342	483	70.8
1951	Minnesota	287	401	71.6
1952	Kansas	491	707	69.4
1953	Geo. Washington	502	696	72.1
1954	Wake Forest	734	1,010	72.7
1955	Wake Forest	709	938	75.6
1956	Southern Methodist	701	917	76.4
1957	Oklahoma St.	569	752	75.7
1958	Oklahoma St.	488	617	79.1
1959	Tulsa	446	586	76.1
1960	Auburn	424	549	77.2
1961	Tulane	459	604	76.0
1962	Southern Methodist	552	718	76.9
1963	Tulane	390	492	79.3
1964	Miami (Fla.)	593	780	76.0
1965	Miami (Fla.)	642	807	79.6
1966	Auburn	476	601	79.2
1967	West Tex. A&M	400	518	77.2
1968	Vanderbilt	527	684	77.0
1969	Jacksonville	574	733	78.3
1970	Ohio St.	452	559	80.9
1971	Tennessee	538	679	79.2
1972	Lafayette	656	844	77.7
1973	Duke	496	632	78.5
1974	Vanderbilt	477	595	80.2
1975	Vanderbilt	530	692	76.6
1976	Morehead St.	452	577	78.3
1977	Utah	499	638	78.2
1978	Duke	665	841	79.1
1979	St. Francis (Pa.)	350	446	78.5
1980	Oral Roberts	481	610	78.9
1981	Connecticut	487	623	78.2
1982	Western Ill.	447	569	78.6
1983	Western Ill.	526	679	77.5
1984	Harvard	535	651	*82.2
1985	Harvard	450	555	81.1
1986	Michigan St.	490	613	79.9
1987	Alabama	521	662	78.7
1988	Butler	413	517	79.9
1989	Brigham Young	527	647	81.5

Season	Team	FT	FTA	Pct.
1990	Lafayette	461	588	78.4
1991	Butler	725	922	78.6
1992	Northwestern	497	651	76.3
1993	Utah	476	602	79.1
1994	Colgate	511	665	76.8
1995	Brigham Young	617	798	77.3
1996	Utah	649	828	78.4

*Record.

Rebounding

Season	Team	G	Reb.	Pct.
1955	Niagara	26	1,507	.624
1956	Geo. Washington	26	1,451	.616
1957	Morehead St.	27	1,735	.621
1958	Manhattan	26	1,437	.591
1959	Mississippi St.	25	1,012	.589
1960	Iona	18	1,054	.607
1961	Bradley	26	1,330	.592
1962	Cornell	25	1,463	.590
1963	UTEP	26	1,167	.591
1964	Iona	20	1,071	.640
1965	Iona	23	1,191	.628
1966	UTEP	29	1,430	.577
1967	Florida	25	1,275	.600

Season	Team	G	Reb.	Avg.
1968	Houston	33	2,074	62.8
1969	Middle Tenn. St.	26	1,685	64.8
1970	Florida St.	26	1,451	55.8
1971	Pacific (Cal.)	28	1,643	58.7
1972	Oral Roberts	28	1,686	60.2

Season	Team	Off.	Def.	Mar.
1973	Manhattan	56.5	38.0	*18.5
1974	Massachusetts	44.5	30.7	13.8
1975	Stetson	47.1	34.7	12.4
1976	Notre Dame	46.3	34.1	12.2
1977	Notre Dame	42.4	31.6	10.8
1978	Alcorn St.	52.3	36.0	16.3
1979	Alcorn St.	50.1	36.3	13.8
1980	Alcorn St.	49.2	33.8	15.4
1981	Northeastern	44.9	32.0	12.9
1982	Northeastern	41.2	30.8	10.4
1983	Wichita St.	42.4	33.6	8.8
1984	Northeastern	40.1	30.3	9.8
1985	Georgetown	39.6	30.5	9.1
1986	Notre Dame	36.4	27.8	8.6
1987	Iowa	43.1	31.5	11.5
1988	Notre Dame	36.0	26.2	9.9
1989	Iowa	41.4	31.8	9.6
1990	Georgetown	44.8	34.0	10.8
1991	New Orleans	41.7	32.4	9.3
1992	Delaware	42.1	33.8	8.3
1993	Massachusetts	43.9	32.8	11.2
1994	Utah St.	38.4	29.8	8.6
1995	Navy	40.6	29.6	11.0
1996	Mississippi Val.	48.3	36.8	11.6

Note: From 1955 through 1967, the rebounding champion was determined on the basis of highest team recoveries out of the total by both teams in all games. From 1968 through 1972, the champion was determined on the basis of rebound average per game. Beginning with the 1973 season, the champion has been determined on the basis of rebounding margin.

*Record.

Assists

Season	Team	G	Ast.	Avg.
1984	Clemson	28	571	20.4
1985	Oklahoma	37	828	22.4
1986	North Caro.	34	800	23.5
1987	Southern Methodist	29	655	22.6
1988	Southern Methodist	35	786	22.5
1989	North Caro.	37	788	21.3
1990	Loyola Marymount	32	762	23.8
1991	UNLV	35	863	*24.7
1992	Arkansas	34	674	19.8
1993	Northwestern St.	26	570	21.9
1994	Arkansas	34	687	20.2
1995	Montana St.	29	606	20.9
1996	Kentucky	36	783	21.8

*Record.

Blocked Shots

Season	Team	G	Blk.	Avg.
1986	Navy	35	233	6.66
1987	Siena	29	188	6.48
1988	Siena	29	193	6.66
1989	Georgetown	34	309	*9.09
1990	Georgetown	31	233	7.52
1991	UNLV	35	266	7.60
1992	Vermont	29	198	6.83
1993	Wyoming	28	184	6.57
1994	Howard	27	179	6.63
1995	Massachusetts	34	273	8.03
1996	Central Conn. St.	28	235	8.39

*Record.

Steals

Season	Team	G	Stl.	Avg.
1986	Cleveland St.	33	436	13.2
1987	Cleveland St.	33	473	14.3
1988	Florida A&M	30	395	13.2
1989	Arkansas	32	372	11.6
1990	Loyola Marymount	32	450	14.1
1991	Texas-San Antonio	29	430	*14.8
1992	Northeastern Ill.	28	358	12.8
1993	Centenary (La.)	27	380	14.1
1994	Texas	34	453	13.3
1995	Nicholls St.	30	376	12.5
1996	McNeese St.	27	330	12.2

*Record.

Anthony Epps and his Kentucky teammates passed their way to the top of the Division I assists chart in 1996, averaging 21.8 assists per contest. Epps, a junior guard, led the way for the Wildcats amassing 175 assists in 36 games—a 4.9 per game average.

Photo by Rich Clarkson/NCAA photos

32   STATISTICAL TRENDS

Statistical Trends

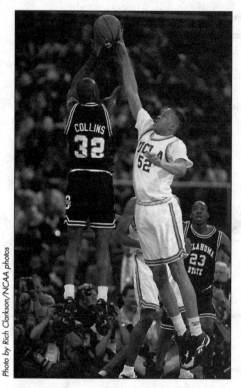

Photo by Rich Clarkson/NCAA photos

UCLA, backed by the play of J. R. Henderson, posted a .741 winning percentage (23-8) in 1996. The Bruins rank fourth all-time in won-lost percentage.

Season	Games	FG Made	FG Att.	Pct.	FT Made	FT Att.	Pct.	PF	Pts.
1948	3,945	40.6	138.7	29.3	25.3	42.2	59.8	36.9	106.5
1949	3,737	41.4	134.7	30.8	26.7	43.3	61.6	38.7	109.5
1950	3,659	43.2	136.8	31.6	28.7	46.5	61.8	39.0	115.1
1951	3,974	45.6	137.8	33.1	30.2	48.1	62.8	42.7	121.4
1952	4,009	47.5	*140.6	33.7	31.6	50.5	62.6	*44.9	126.6
1953	3,754	48.0	138.1	34.7	42.1	*65.8	64.0	42.5	138.1
1954	3,933	48.8	135.5	35.4	41.9	64.3	65.2	42.0	137.9
1955	3,829	51.1	138.6	36.9	*43.1	64.7	66.5	37.9	145.3
1956	4,098	52.1	139.0	37.5	42.3	63.3	66.8	37.7	146.5
1957	4,113	51.6	135.1	38.2	40.8	60.6	67.3	36.5	144.0
1958	4,153	51.6	134.2	38.4	33.6	50.5	66.4	36.4	136.8
1959	4,234	51.7	132.3	39.1	34.0	50.7	67.1	36.3	137.4
1960	4,295	52.6	132.3	39.8	34.7	51.5	67.4	36.7	139.9
1961	4,238	53.3	131.1	40.7	34.7	50.9	68.2	36.4	141.3
1962	4,341	54.0	134.5	40.2	33.0	48.6	67.9	36.1	141.0
1963	4,180	53.2	127.6	41.7	32.6	47.8	68.2	36.4	139.0
1964	4,347	57.3	134.7	42.5	34.2	50.1	68.3	38.1	148.8
1965	4,520	58.3	135.4	43.1	34.7	50.3	69.0	38.5	151.4
1966	3,986	60.0	137.6	43.6	35.0	50.5	69.2	38.4	154.9
1967	4,602	57.7	131.9	43.8	34.4	49.8	69.0	38.3	149.8
1968	4,739	58.1	133.1	43.7	34.7	50.2	69.1	38.0	150.9
1969	4,883	58.2	132.8	43.8	34.8	50.8	68.4	37.9	151.2
1970	4,979	59.9	135.5	44.2	35.3	51.4	68.7	38.6	155.1
1971	5,232	60.2	135.6	44.4	35.0	51.3	68.1	38.5	*155.4
1972	5,404	60.2	134.3	44.8	35.0	51.1	68.6	38.4	155.3
1973	5,582	62.3	139.2	44.8	26.2	38.3	68.4	38.4	150.9
1974	6,060	62.0	136.5	45.4	25.6	37.4	68.4	38.4	149.5
1975	6,147	*62.9	136.7	46.0	27.4	39.7	69.0	40.3	153.1
1976	6,240	61.9	132.5	46.7	27.6	39.8	69.2	40.4	151.3
1977	6,676	60.7	129.8	46.7	28.4	41.0	69.4	40.2	149.7
1978	6,901	60.2	127.2	47.3	28.6	41.4	69.2	40.4	148.9
1979	7,131	59.2	124.1	47.7	29.5	42.2	*69.7	41.1	147.9
1980	7,304	57.2	119.3	47.9	29.7	42.6	69.6	40.3	144.0
1981	7,407	55.6	115.9	48.0	29.0	42.1	68.9	40.2	140.1
1982	7,646	53.3	111.2	47.9	28.5	41.6	68.6	38.7	135.1
1983	7,957	54.3	114.0	47.7	29.0	42.3	68.5	39.7	138.6
1984	8,029	53.4	111.1	*48.1	29.5	42.8	68.9	39.9	136.3
1985	8,269	54.5	113.9	47.9	29.3	42.5	68.9	39.3	138.3
1986	8,360	54.7	114.6	47.7	29.4	42.5	69.1	39.1	138.7

Season	Games	FG Made	FG Att.	Pct.	3FG Made	3FG Att.	Pct.	FT Made	FT Att.	Pct.	PF	Pts.
1987	8,580	54.4	117.3	46.4	7.0	18.3	*38.4	29.7	43.0	69.1	39.3	145.5
1988	8,587	54.8	116.6	47.0	8.0	20.8	38.2	30.2	43.8	68.9	39.4	147.8
1989	8,677	55.7	118.5	47.0	8.9	23.6	37.6	31.1	45.0	69.1	40.2	151.4
1990	8,646	54.7	118.9	46.0	9.4	25.7	36.7	31.1	45.1	68.9	39.6	149.8
1991	8,720	55.6	121.3	45.8	10.0	27.6	36.1	31.7	46.3	68.5	39.2	152.9
1992	*8,803	53.0	116.6	45.5	9.9	28.0	35.5	31.6	46.4	68.1	40.0	147.6
1993	8,528	52.9	117.2	45.2	10.5	29.8	35.4	30.8	45.5	67.7	39.1	147.2
1994	8,630	53.7	121.1	44.3	11.4	33.0	34.5	31.2	46.4	67.1	39.7	150.0
1995	8,662	52.7	119.1	44.2	*11.8	*34.3	34.5	30.4	45.0	67.6	39.4	147.6
1996	8,741	51.3	116.8	43.9	11.7	34.2	34.2	30.0	44.5	67.4	38.9	144.2

*All-time high.

Note: Averages and percentages are for both teams, per game.

All-Time Winningest Teams

Percentage

(Minimum 25 years in Division I)

No.	Team	First Season	Yrs.	Won	Lost	Tied	Pct.
1.	Kentucky	1903	93	1,650	520	1	.760
2.	North Caro.	1911	86	1,647	588	0	.737
3.	UNLV	1959	38	789	284	0	.735
4.	UCLA	1920	77	1,374	596	0	.697
5.	Kansas	1899	98	1,596	708	0	.693
6.	St. John's (N.Y.)	1908	89	1,519	682	0	.690
7.	Syracuse	1901	95	1,432	670	0	.681
8.	Western Ky.	1915	77	1,344	635	0	.679
9.	Duke	1906	91	1,492	740	0	.668
10.	DePaul	1924	73	1,171	596	0	.663
11.	Arkansas	1924	73	1,250	648	0	.659
12.	Louisville	1912	82	1,299	687	0	.654
13.	Notre Dame	1898	91	1,398	748	1	.651
14.	Indiana	1901	96	1,388	744	0	.651
15.	Weber St.	1963	34	625	338	0	.649
16.	Temple	1895	100	1,455	793	0	.647
17.	Utah	1909	88	1,317	724	0	.645
18.	Purdue	1897	98	1,337	738	0	.644
19.	Illinois	1906	91	1,299	726	0	.641
20.	Villanova	1921	76	1,232	695	0	.639
21.	Pennsylvania	1897	96	1,425	806	2	.639
22.	La Salle	1931	66	1,075	613	0	.637
23.	Houston	1946	51	901	515	0	.636
24.	North Caro. St.	1913	84	1,292	748	0	.633
25.	Arizona	1905	91	1,252	741	0	.628
26.	Alabama	1913	83	1,234	731	1	.628
27.	UTEP	1947	50	843	504	0	.626
28.	Murray St.	1926	71	1,122	678	0	.623
29.	Illinois St.	1972	25	453	274	0	.623
30.	Holy Cross	1901	77	1,065	652	0	.620
31.	West Va.	1904	87	1,304	802	0	.619
32.	Bradley	1903	92	1,306	805	0	.619
33.	Providence	1927	69	1,058	653	0	.618
34.	Cincinnati	1902	95	1,257	786	0	.615
35.	Princeton	1901	96	1,335	837	0	.615

No.	Team	First Season	Yrs.	Won	Lost	Tied	Pct.
36.	Duquesne	1914	80	1,124	705	0	.615
37.	Connecticut	1901	93	1,164	733	0	.614
38.	Georgetown	1907	88	1,214	768	0	.613
39.	Texas	1906	90	1,264	802	0	.612
40.	Brigham Young	1918	79	1,209	772	0	.610
41.	San Francisco	1924	69	1,030	658	0	.610
42.	Marquette	1917	79	1,151	738	0	.609
43.	Akron	1902	95	1,163	746	0	.609
44.	Memphis	1921	75	1,056	678	0	.609
45.	Navy	1907	90	1,079	693	0	.609
46.	Washington	1896	94	1,348	873	0	.607
47.	Michigan	1909	80	1,141	740	0	.607
48.	LIU-Brooklyn	1929	62	935	609	2	.605
49.	Tennessee	1909	87	1,184	773	2	.605
50.	Oregon St.	1902	95	1,434	950	0	.602

Victories

(Minimum 25 years in Division I)

No.	Team	First Season	Yrs.	Won	Lost	Tied	Pct.
1.	Kentucky	1903	93	1,650	520	1	.760
2.	North Caro.	1911	86	1,647	588	0	.737
3.	Kansas	1899	98	1,596	708	0	.693
4.	St. John's (N.Y.)	1908	89	1,519	682	0	.690
5.	Duke	1906	91	1,492	740	0	.668
6.	Temple	1895	100	1,455	793	0	.647
7.	Oregon St.	1902	95	1,434	950	0	.602
8.	Syracuse	1901	95	1,432	670	0	.681
9.	Pennsylvania	1897	96	1,425	806	2	.639
10.	Notre Dame	1898	91	1,398	748	1	.651
11.	Indiana	1901	96	1,388	744	0	.651
12.	UCLA	1920	77	1,374	596	0	.697
13.	Washington	1896	94	1,348	873	0	.607
14.	Western Ky.	1915	77	1,344	635	0	.679
15.	Purdue	1897	98	1,337	738	0	.644
16.	Princeton	1901	96	1,335	837	0	.615
17.	Utah	1909	88	1,317	724	0	.645
18.	Fordham	1903	93	1,307	947	0	.580
19.	Bradley	1903	92	1,306	805	0	.619
20.	West Va.	1904	87	1,304	802	0	.619
21.	Louisville	1912	82	1,299	687	0	.654
21.	Illinois	1906	91	1,299	726	0	.641
23.	North Caro. St.	1913	84	1,292	748	0	.633
24.	Washington St.	1902	95	1,287	1,126	0	.533
25.	Texas	1906	90	1,264	802	0	.612
26.	Cincinnati	1902	95	1,257	786	0	.615
27.	Arizona	1905	91	1,252	741	0	.628
28.	Montana St.	1902	94	1,250	955	0	.567
28.	Arkansas	1924	73	1,250	648	0	.659
30.	Ohio St.	1899	97	1,246	863	0	.591
31.	Alabama	1913	83	1,234	731	1	.628
32.	Villanova	1921	76	1,232	695	0	.639
33.	Southern Cal	1907	90	1,229	870	0	.586
34.	Kansas St.	1903	92	1,224	849	0	.590
35.	St. Joseph's (Pa.)	1910	87	1,223	813	0	.601
35.	Iowa	1902	95	1,223	834	0	.595
37.	Georgetown	1907	88	1,214	768	0	.613
38.	Missouri	1907	90	1,210	846	0	.589
39.	Brigham Young	1918	79	1,209	772	0	.610
40.	Oklahoma	1908	89	1,190	821	0	.592
41.	Minnesota	1896	101	1,188	918	4	.564
42.	Oklahoma St.	1908	87	1,185	893	0	.570
43.	Tennessee	1909	87	1,184	773	2	.605
44.	Vanderbilt	1901	94	1,181	847	0	.582
45.	Oregon	1903	91	1,180	1,081	0	.522
45.	California	1908	87	1,180	867	0	.576
47.	DePaul	1924	73	1,171	596	0	.663
48.	Virginia	1906	91	1,168	894	1	.566
49.	Dayton	1904	91	1,166	850	0	.578
50.	Connecticut	1901	93	1,164	733	0	.614

All-Time Won-Lost Records

(No Minimum Seasons of Competition)

Team	First Season	Yrs.	Won	Lost	Tied	Pct.
Air Force	1957	40	439	586	0	.428
Akron	1902	95	1,163	746	0	.609
Alabama	1913	83	1,234	731	1	.628
UAB	1979	18	365	204	0	.641

Team	First Season	Yrs.	Won	Lost	Tied	Pct.
Alabama St.	1983	14	204	190	0	.518
Alcorn St.	1978	19	274	272	0	.502
American	1927	70	878	766	0	.534
Appalachian St.	1920	71	879	778	0	.530
Arizona	1905	91	1,252	741	0	.628
Arizona St.	1912	80	969	852	0	.532
Arkansas	1924	73	1,250	648	0	.659
Arkansas St.	1971	26	381	340	0	.528
Ark.-Little Rock	1979	18	319	211	0	.602
Army	1903	94	983	832	0	.542
Auburn	1906	88	957	848	1	.530
Austin Peay	1930	65	820	746	0	.524
Ball St.	1972	25	400	308	0	.565
Baylor	1907	90	933	1,058	0	.469
Bethune-Cookman	1962	34	430	476	0	.475
Boise St.	1972	25	369	322	0	.534
Boston College	1905	63	813	654	0	.554
Boston U.	1902	87	789	816	0	.492
Bowling Green	1916	81	1,021	836	0	.550
Bradley	1903	92	1,306	805	0	.619
Brigham Young	1918	79	1,209	772	0	.610
Brown	1901	89	764	1,132	0	.403
Bucknell	1896	101	1,021	936	0	.522
Buffalo	1915	77	825	758	0	.521
Butler	1897	98	1,056	901	0	.540
California	1908	87	1,180	867	0	.576
UC Irvine	1966	31	424	438	0	.492
UC Santa Barb.	1938	56	768	696	0	.525
Cal Poly SLO	1995	2	17	39	0	.304
Cal St. Fullerton	1961	36	459	514	0	.472
Cal St. Northridge	1959	38	471	535	0	.468
Cal St. Sacramento	1949	48	562	694	0	.447
Campbell	1978	19	236	289	0	.450
Canisius	1904	92	991	875	0	.531
Centenary (La.)	1946	46	607	648	0	.484
Central Conn. St.	1935	60	794	579	0	.578
Central Fla.	1971	26	396	305	0	.565
Central Mich.	1974	23	291	337	0	.463
Charleston (S.C.)	1979	18	424	125	0	.772
Charleston So.	1966	31	360	461	0	.438
Chicago St.	1985	12	102	228	0	.309
Cincinnati	1902	95	1,257	786	0	.615
Citadel	1913	83	748	925	0	.447
Clemson	1912	85	911	979	2	.482
Cleveland St.	1973	24	354	307	0	.536
Coastal Caro.	1975	22	323	304	0	.515
Colgate	1901	96	982	1,012	0	.492
Colorado	1902	93	912	880	0	.509
Colorado St.	1902	93	882	936	0	.485
Columbia	1901	96	1,010	946	0	.516
Connecticut	1901	93	1,164	733	0	.614
Coppin St.	1986	11	193	128	0	.601
Cornell	1899	98	977	1,076	0	.476
Creighton	1917	78	1,061	791	0	.573
Dartmouth	1901	95	1,077	1,090	0	.497
Davidson	1909	87	984	967	0	.504
Dayton	1904	91	1,166	850	0	.578
Delaware	1906	91	842	943	2	.472
Delaware St.	1974	23	250	379	0	.397
DePaul	1924	73	1,171	596	0	.663
Detroit	1906	89	1,046	880	0	.543
Drake	1907	90	943	1,074	0	.468
Drexel	1895	97	910	800	0	.532
Duke	1906	91	1,492	740	0	.668
Duquesne	1914	80	1,124	705	0	.615
East Caro.	1932	64	790	752	0	.512
East Tenn. St.	1928	66	854	704	0	.548
Eastern Ill.	1982	15	218	217	0	.501
Eastern Ky.	1926	70	865	747	1	.537
Eastern Mich.	1974	23	323	332	0	.493
Eastern Wash.	1984	13	110	243	0	.312
Evansville	1978	19	315	211	0	.599
Fairfield	1949	47	594	585	0	.504
Fairleigh Dickinson	1968	28	400	344	0	.538
Florida	1916	76	864	869	0	.499
Florida A&M	1979	18	220	288	0	.433
Fla. Atlantic	1989	8	85	136	0	.385
Florida Int'l	1982	15	180	233	0	.436
Florida St.	1948	49	779	540	0	.591
Fordham	1903	93	1,307	947	0	.580
Fresno St.	1922	74	978	815	0	.545
Furman	1946	51	690	682	0	.503

Team	First Season	Yrs.	Won	Lost	Tied	Pct.
George Mason	1979	18	250	258	0	.492
Geo. Washington	1907	79	952	816	0	.538
Georgetown	1907	88	1,214	768	0	.613
Georgia	1906	91	1,016	957	0	.515
Ga. Southern	1974	23	339	304	0	.527
Georgia St.	1964	33	242	609	0	.492
Georgia Tech	1906	80	1,005	872	0	.538
Gonzaga	1908	89	1,037	962	0	.519
Grambling	1978	19	231	301	0	.434
Hampton	1953	44	615	513	0	.545
Hartford	1958	39	477	500	0	.488
Harvard	1901	85	787	1,040	0	.431
Hawaii	1971	26	354	378	0	.484
Hofstra	1937	58	844	640	0	.569
Holy Cross	1901	77	1,065	652	0	.620
Houston	1946	51	901	515	0	.636
Howard	1974	23	325	317	0	.506
Idaho	1906	91	1,049	1,098	0	.489
Idaho St.	1927	69	928	795	0	.539
Illinois	1906	91	1,299	726	0	.641
Illinois St.	1972	25	453	274	0	.623
Ill.-Chicago	1948	49	538	590	0	.477
Indiana	1901	96	1,388	744	0	.651
Indiana St.	1924	73	1,009	773	0	.566
Iona	1941	53	758	560	0	.575
Iowa	1902	95	1,223	834	0	.595
Iowa St.	1908	89	928	1,020	0	.476
Jackson St.	1978	19	275	269	0	.506
Jacksonville	1958	39	553	491	0	.530
Jacksonville St.	1926	65	985	454	0	.685
James Madison	1970	27	452	291	0	.608
Kansas	1899	98	1,596	708	0	.693
Kansas St.	1903	92	1,224	849	0	.590
Kent	1914	80	747	973	0	.434
Kentucky	1903	93	1,650	520	1	.760
La Salle	1931	66	1,075	613	0	.637
Lafayette	1901	86	1,017	895	0	.532
Lamar	1952	45	668	536	0	.555
Lehigh	1902	95	765	1,063	0	.418
Liberty	1973	24	349	339	0	.507
Long Beach St.	1951	46	671	558	0	.546
LIU-Brooklyn	1929	62	935	609	2	.605
LSU	1909	88	1,152	864	0	.571
Louisiana Tech	1974	23	377	277	0	.576
Louisville	1912	82	1,299	687	0	.654
Loyola Marymount	1907	73	794	849	0	.483
Loyola (Ill.)	1914	78	993	800	1	.554
Loyola (Md.)	1909	85	1,003	903	0	.571
Maine	1905	76	704	797	0	.469
Manhattan	1905	90	1,034	888	1	.538
Marist	1982	15	227	202	0	.529
Marquette	1917	79	1,151	738	0	.609
Marshall	1907	85	1,132	781	2	.592
Maryland	1924	73	1,033	759	0	.576
Md.-Balt. County	1969	28	295	435	0	.404
Md.-East. Shore	1982	15	111	301	0	.269
Massachusetts	1902	86	918	814	0	.404
McNeese St.	1974	23	328	317	0	.509
Memphis	1921	75	1,056	678	0	.609
Mercer	1974	23	306	331	0	.480
Miami (Fla.)	1927	46	596	474	0	.557
Miami (Ohio)	1906	91	1,025	842	0	.549
Michigan	1909	80	1,141	740	0	.607
Michigan St.	1899	97	1,129	874	0	.564
Middle Tenn. St.	1914	73	817	768	0	.515
Minnesota	1896	101	1,188	918	4	.564
Mississippi	1909	86	863	1,016	0	.459
Mississippi St.	1909	84	990	883	0	.529
Mississippi Val.	1980	17	211	268	0	.441
Missouri	1907	90	1,210	846	0	.589
Mo.-Kansas City	1970	26	386	344	0	.529
Monmouth (N.J.)	1984	13	184	183	0	.501
Montana	1906	88	1,077	956	0	.530
Montana St.	1902	94	1,250	955	0	.567
Morehead St.	1930	67	830	750	0	.529
Morgan St.	1985	12	96	241	0	.285
Mt. St. Mary's (Md.)	1909	87	1,232	719	0	.631
Murray St.	1926	71	1,122	678	0	.623
Navy	1907	90	1,079	693	0	.609
Nebraska	1897	100	1,133	1,006	0	.530
Nevada	1913	83	901	900	0	.500
UNLV	1959	38	789	284	0	.735
New Hampshire	1903	92	693	1,046	0	.399

Team	First Season	Yrs.	Won	Lost	Tied	Pct.
New Mexico	1900	93	1,050	853	0	.552
New Mexico St.	1905	89	1,094	845	2	.564
New Orleans	1970	27	493	275	0	.642
Niagara	1906	90	1,116	888	1	.557
Nicholls St.	1981	16	187	248	0	.430
North Caro.	1911	86	1,647	588	0	.737
North Caro. A&T	1974	23	392	253	0	.608
North Caro. St.	1913	84	1,292	748	0	.633
N.C.-Asheville	1965	32	460	455	0	.503
N.C.-Charlotte	1966	31	464	393	0	.541
N.C.-Greensboro	1968	29	321	386	0	.454
N.C.-Wilmington	1977	20	294	264	0	.527
North Texas	1917	78	843	944	0	.472
Northeast La.	1952	45	704	496	0	.587
Northeastern	1921	75	859	764	0	.529
Northeastern Ill.	1966	31	350	525	0	.400
Northern Ariz.	1910	79	802	899	0	.471
Northern Ill.	1968	29	389	392	0	.498
Northern Iowa	1904	88	889	825	0	.519
Northwestern	1905	91	758	1,135	1	.400
Northwestern St.	1977	20	217	329	0	.397
Notre Dame	1898	91	1,398	748	1	.651
Ohio	1908	89	1,117	839	0	.571
Ohio St.	1899	97	1,246	863	0	.591
Oklahoma	1908	89	1,190	821	0	.592
Oklahoma St.	1908	87	1,185	893	0	.570
Old Dominion	1966	31	563	338	0	.625
Oral Roberts	1972	30	522	355	0	.595
Oregon	1903	91	1,180	1,081	0	.522
Oregon St.	1902	95	1,434	950	0	.602
Pacific (Cal.)	1911	86	887	952	0	.482
Penn St.	1897	100	1,139	795	1	.589
Pennsylvania	1897	96	1,425	806	2	.639
Pepperdine	1939	58	917	701	0	.567
Pittsburgh	1906	89	1,116	901	0	.553
Portland	1923	72	903	913	0	.497
Prairie View	1981	16	71	360	0	.165
Princeton	1901	96	1,335	837	0	.615
Providence	1927	69	1,058	653	0	.618
Purdue	1897	98	1,337	738	0	.644
Radford	1985	12	187	157	0	.544
Rhode Island	1907	88	1,111	789	0	.585
Rice	1917	80	781	996	0	.440
Richmond	1913	84	961	886	0	.520
Rider	1968	29	398	405	0	.496
Robert Morris	1977	20	254	306	0	.454
Rutgers	1907	84	930	827	0	.529
St. Bonaventure	1920	76	1,015	689	0	.596
St. Francis (N.Y.)	1902	77	893	915	0	.494
St. Francis (Pa.)	1946	51	681	619	1	.524
St. John's (N.Y.)	1908	89	1,519	682	0	.690
St. Joseph's (Pa.)	1910	87	1,223	813	0	.601
St. Louis	1916	80	1,028	871	0	.541
St. Mary's (Cal.)	1926	69	809	912	0	.470
St. Peter's	1931	63	818	664	0	.552
Samford	1973	24	247	405	0	.379
Sam Houston St.	1932	61	770	749	0	.507
San Diego	1956	41	554	542	0	.505
San Diego St.	1922	75	1,004	830	0	.547
San Francisco	1924	69	1,030	658	0	.610
San Jose St.	1910	82	929	917	0	.503
Santa Clara	1918	77	1,061	706	0	.600
Seton Hall	1904	84	1,113	754	2	.596
Siena	1939	55	730	619	0	.541
South Ala.	1969	28	445	332	0	.573
South Caro.	1909	88	1,024	913	1	.529
South Caro. St.	1958	39	609	435	0	.583
South Fla.	1972	25	342	355	0	.491
Southeast Mo. St.	1982	15	294	153	0	.658
Southeastern La.	1981	15	171	244	0	.412
Southern Cal	1907	90	1,229	870	0	.586
Southern Ill.	1968	29	446	366	0	.549
Southern Methodist	1917	80	941	903	0	.510
Southern Miss.	1913	77	879	738	1	.544
Southern Utah	1969	28	437	306	0	.588
Southern U.	1978	19	339	208	0	.620
Southwest Mo. St.	1909	84	1,258	662	0	.655
Southwest Tex. St.	1985	12	139	197	0	.414
Southwestern La.	1912	80	1,054	780	0	.575
Stanford	1914	81	1,033	901	0	.534
Stephen F. Austin	1925	70	1,069	659	0	.619
Stetson	1972	25	367	326	0	.530

Team	First Season	Yrs.	Won	Lost	Tied	Pct.
Syracuse	1901	95	1,432	670	0	.681
Temple	1895	100	1,455	793	0	.647
Tennessee	1909	87	1,184	773	2	.605
Tennessee St.	1978	19	242	275	0	.468
Tennessee Tech	1926	71	766	769	1	.499
Tenn.-Chatt.	1978	19	384	181	0	.680
Tenn.-Martin	1952	45	510	574	0	.470
Texas	1906	90	1,264	802	0	.612
Texas A&M	1913	84	1,030	943	0	.522
Texas Christian	1914	83	846	1,012	0	.455
Texas Southern	1978	19	286	244	0	.540
Texas Tech	1926	71	1,033	764	0	.575
Texas-Arlington	1960	37	371	614	0	.377
UTEP	1947	50	843	504	0	.626
Tex.-Pan American	1969	28	368	376	0	.495
Texas-San Antonio	1982	15	233	194	0	.546
Toledo	1917	79	1,079	737	0	.594
Towson St.	1980	17	232	253	0	.478
Troy St.	1951	46	724	518	0	.583
Tulane	1913	77	864	854	0	.503
Tulsa	1908	85	989	868	0	.533
UCLA	1920	77	1,374	596	0	.697
Utah	1909	88	1,317	724	0	.645
Utah St.	1909	83	1,056	852	0	.553
Valparaiso	1918	79	901	943	0	.489
Vanderbilt	1901	94	1,181	847	0	.582
Vermont	1901	82	788	871	0	.475
Villanova	1921	76	1,232	695	0	.639
Virginia	1906	91	1,168	894	1	.566
Va. Commonwealth	1969	28	487	286	0	.630
VMI	1911	86	619	1,117	0	.357
Virginia Tech	1909	88	1,089	869	0	.556
Wagner	1977	20	230	322	0	.417
Wake Forest	1906	90	1,125	901	0	.555
Washington	1896	94	1,348	873	0	.607
Washington St.	1902	95	1,287	1,126	0	.533
Weber St.	1963	34	625	338	0	.649
West Va.	1904	87	1,304	802	0	.619
Western Caro.	1977	20	254	300	0	.458
Western Ill.	1982	15	204	219	0	.482
Western Ky.	1915	77	1,344	635	0	.679
Western Mich.	1914	83	956	870	0	.524
Wichita St.	1906	89	1,095	938	0	.539
William & Mary	1906	91	924	1,021	0	.475
Winthrop	1979	18	266	276	0	.491
Wisconsin	1899	98	1,079	971	0	.526
Wis.-Green Bay	1974	23	417	253	0	.622
Wis.-Milwaukee	1897	99	1,003	913	0	.523
Wofford	1952	45	651	615	0	.514
Wright St.	1971	26	466	253	0	.648
Wyoming	1905	91	1,150	846	0	.576
Xavier (Ohio)	1920	75	948	774	0	.551
Yale	1896	101	1,140	1,153	0	.497
Youngstown St.	1928	66	831	739	0	.529

Winningest Teams By Decade

The 1930s

Rk.	Team	Won	Lost	Pct.
1.	LIU-Brooklyn	198	38	.839
2.	Kentucky	162	34	.827
3.	St. John's (N.Y.)	181	40	.819
4.	Kansas	153	37	.805
5.	Syracuse	143	37	.794
6.	Purdue	148	39	.791
7.	Western Ky.	197	52	.791
8.	Rhode Island	142	39	.785
9.	Notre Dame	170	49	.776
10.	CCNY	120	35	.774
11.	Washington	206	63	.766
12.	DePaul	142	44	.763
13.	Arkansas	167	57	.746
14.	Duquesne	143	50	.741
15.	Wyoming	147	52	.739
16.	Navy	108	40	.730

Rk.	Team	Won	Lost	Pct.
17.	North Caro.	163	61	.728
18.	Geo. Washington	129	50	.721
19.	New York U.	124	49	.717
20.	Western Mich.	123	50	.711

The 1940s

Rk.	Team	Won	Lost	Pct.
1.	Kentucky	239	42	.851
2.	Oklahoma St.	237	55	.812
3.	Rhode Island	178	44	.802
4.	Eastern Ky.	145	40	.784
5.	Western Ky.	222	66	.771
6.	Tennessee	152	46	.768
7.	Bowling Green	204	66	.756
8.	Notre Dame	162	55	.747
9.	Toledo	176	65	.730
10.	St. John's (N.Y.)	162	60	.730
11.	North Caro.	196	75	.723
12.	West Va.	157	59	.727
13.	Illinois	150	57	.725
14.	DePaul	180	69	.723
15.	Bradley	144	56	.720
16.	New York U.	150	60	.714
17.	Utah	159	68	.700
18.	Wyoming	163	70	.700
19.	Texas	168	73	.697
20.	CCNY	133	62	.682

Only played seven seasons:

	Team	Won	Lost	Pct.
	Seton Hall	128	22	.853
	Duquesne	118	32	.787
	Geo. Washington	117	47	.713

The 1950s

Rk.	Team	Won	Lost	Pct.
1.	Kentucky	224	33	.872
2.	North Caro. St.	240	65	.787
3.	Seattle	233	69	.772
4.	La Salle	209	65	.763
5.	Dayton	228	71	.763
6.	Holy Cross	199	65	.754
7.	Kansas St.	179	63	.740
8.	Connecticut	187	67	.736
9.	West Va.	205	74	.735
10.	Louisville	202	77	.724
11.	Illinois	165	64	.721
12.	Western Ky.	205	82	.714
13.	UCLA	193	78	.712
14.	Duquesne	187	76	.711
15.	Kansas	171	74	.698
16.	St. John's (N.Y.)	176	77	.696
17.	Cincinnati	175	80	.686
18.	Oklahoma St.	192	88	.686
19.	Lafayette	171	81	.679
20.	St. Louis	185	88	.678

The 1960s

Rk.	Team	Won	Lost	Pct.
1.	UCLA	234	52	.818
2.	Cincinnati	214	63	.773
3.	Providence	204	64	.761
4.	Duke	213	67	.761
5.	Kentucky	197	69	.741
6.	Ohio St.	188	69	.732
7.	St. Joseph's (Pa.)	201	74	.731
8.	Dayton	207	77	.729
9.	Bradley	197	74	.727
10.	Princeton	188	71	.726
11.	Vanderbilt	182	69	.725
12.	North Caro.	184	72	.719
13.	St. Bonaventure	172	69	.714
14.	Villanova	193	79	.710
15.	Houston	198	82	.707
16.	St. John's (N.Y.)	185	79	.701
17.	Miami (Fla.)	183	82	.691
18.	West Va.	197	89	.689
19.	Temple	183	83	.688
20.	UTEP	177	81	.686

Only played seven seasons:

	Team	Won	Lost	Pct.
	Weber St.	147	36	.803

The 1970s

Rk.	Team	Won	Lost	Pct.
1.	UCLA	273	27	.910
2.	Marquette	251	41	.860
3.	Pennsylvania	223	56	.799
4.	North Caro.	239	65	.786
5.	Kentucky	223	69	.764
6.	Louisville	224	70	.762
7.	Syracuse	213	69	.755
8.	Long Beach St.	209	71	.746
9.	Indiana	208	75	.735
10.	Florida St.	201	74	.731
11.	UNLV	203	78	.722
12.	North Caro. St.	208	80	.722
13.	San Francisco	202	79	.719
14.	Houston	210	84	.714
15.	Providence	209	84	.713
16.	South Caro.	198	80	.712
17.	St. John's (N.Y.)	205	85	.707
18.	Maryland	199	85	.701
19.	Rutgers	193	84	.697
20.	Notre Dame	202	89	.694

Only played eight seasons:

	Oral Roberts	161	59	.732

The 1980s

Rk.	Team	Won	Lost	Pct.
1.	North Caro.	281	63	.817
2.	UNLV	271	65	.807
3.	Georgetown	269	69	.796
4.	DePaul	235	67	.778
5.	Temple	225	78	.743
6.	Syracuse	243	87	.736
7.	UTEP	227	82	.735
8.	Oklahoma	245	90	.731
9.	Kentucky	233	86	.730
10.	St. John's (N.Y.)	228	85	.728
11.	Indiana	228	86	.726
12.	Oregon St.	212	80	.726
13.	Louisville	250	96	.723
14.	Illinois	233	90	.721
15.	Memphis	225	89	.717
16.	Northeastern	213	86	.712
17.	Tenn.-Chatt.	215	89	.707
18.	Arkansas	218	92	.703
19.	Missouri	227	99	.696
20.	West Va.	217	95	.696

The 1990s

Rk.	Team	Won	Lost	Pct.
1.	Kansas	194	44	.815
2.	Kentucky	184	45	.803
3.	Arkansas	195	49	.799
4.	Arizona	179	46	.796
5.	Massachusetts	183	53	.775
6.	Connecticut	175	53	.768
7.	North Caro.	184	57	.763
8.	UCLA	170	53	.762
9.	Wis.-Green Bay	160	53	.751
10.	Syracuse	166	58	.741

Rk.	Team	Won	Lost	Pct.
11.	Duke	178	63	.739
12.	Indiana	164	60	.732
13.	New Mexico St.	159	60	.726
14.	Cincinnati	166	63	.725
15.	Princeton	137	52	.725
16.	Utah	163	63	.721
17.	UNLV	153	61	.715
18.	Purdue	155	63	.711
19.	Montana	145	60	.707
20.	Xavier (Ohio)	147	61	.707

Winning Streaks

Full Season

Wins	Team	Seasons	Ended By	Score
88	UCLA	1971-74	Notre Dame	71-70
60	San Francisco	1955-57	Illinois	62-33
47	UCLA	1966-68	Houston	71-69
45	UNLV	1990-91	Duke	79-77
44	Texas	1913-17	Rice	24-18
43	Seton Hall	1939-41	LIU-Brooklyn	49-26
43	LIU-Brooklyn	1935-37	Stanford	45-31
41	UCLA	1968-69	Southern Cal	46-44
39	Marquette	1970-71	Ohio St.	60-59
37	Cincinnati	1962-63	Wichita St.	65-64
37	North Caro.	1957-58	West Va.	75-64
36	North Caro. St.	1974-75	Wake Forest	83-78
35	Arkansas	1927-29	Texas	26-25

Regular Season

(Does not include national postseason tournaments)

Wins	Team	Seasons	Ended By	Score
76	UCLA	1971-74	Notre Dame	71-70
57	Indiana	1975-77	Toledo	59-57
56	Marquette	1970-72	Detroit	70-49
54	Kentucky	1952-55	Georgia Tech	59-58
51	San Francisco	1955-57	Illinois	62-33
48	Pennsylvania	1970-72	Temple	57-52
47	Ohio St.	1960-62	Wisconsin	86-67
44	Texas	1913-17	Rice	24-18
43	UCLA	1966-68	Houston	71-69
43	LIU-Brooklyn	1935-37	Stanford	45-31
42	Seton Hall	1939-41	LIU-Brooklyn	49-26

Home Court

Wins	Team	Start	End
129	Kentucky	1943	1955
99	St. Bonaventure	1948	1961
98	UCLA	1970	1976
86	Cincinnati	1957	1964
81	Arizona	1945	1951
81	Marquette	1967	1973
80	Lamar	1978	1984
75	Long Beach St.	1968	1974
72	UNLV	1974	1978
71	Arizona	1987	1992

National Polls

Final Regular-Season Polls

The Helms Foundation of Los Angeles selected the national college men's basketball champions from 1942-82 and researched retroactive picks from 1901-41. The Helms winners are listed in this section up to the time The Associated Press (AP) poll started in 1949. The AP is the writers' poll, while the UPI and USA Today/CNN and USA Today/NABC polls are the coaches' polls.

HELMS

1901 Yale	1925 Princeton
1902 Minnesota	1926 Syracuse
1903 Yale	1927 Notre Dame
1904 Columbia	1928 Pittsburgh
1905 Columbia	1929 Montana St.
1906 Dartmouth	1930 Pittsburgh
1907 Chicago	1931 Northwestern
1908 Chicago	1932 Purdue
1909 Chicago	1933 Kentucky
1910 Columbia	1934 Wyoming
1911 St. John's (N.Y.)	1935 New York U.
1912 Wisconsin	1936 Notre Dame
1913 Navy	1937 Stanford
1914 Wisconsin	1938 Temple
1915 Illinois	1939 LIU-Brooklyn
1916 Wisconsin	1940 Southern Cal
1917 Washington St.	1941 Wisconsin
1918 Syracuse	1942 Stanford
1919 Minnesota	1943 Wyoming
1920 Pennsylvania	1944 Army
1921 Pennsylvania	1945 Oklahoma St.
1922 Kansas	1946 Oklahoma St.
1923 Kansas	1947 Holy Cross
1924 North Caro.	1948 Kentucky

1949

AP
1. Kentucky
2. Oklahoma St.
3. St. Louis
4. Illinois
5. Western Ky.
6. Minnesota
7. Bradley
8. San Francisco
9. Tulane
10. Bowling Green
11. Yale
12. Utah
13. North Caro. St.
14. Villanova
15. UCLA
16. Loyola (Ill.)
17. Wyoming
18. Butler
19. Hamline
20. Ohio St.

1950

AP
1. Bradley
2. Ohio St.
3. Kentucky
4. Holy Cross
5. North Caro. St.
6. Duquesne
7. UCLA
8. Western Ky.
9. St. John's (N.Y.)
10. La Salle
11. Villanova
12. San Francisco
13. LIU-Brooklyn
14. Kansas St.
15. Arizona
16. Wisconsin
17. San Jose St.
18. Washington St.
19. Kansas
20. Indiana

1951

AP
1. Kentucky
2. Oklahoma St.
3. Columbia
4. Kansas St.
5. Illinois
6. Bradley
7. Indiana
8. North Caro. St.
9. St. John's (N.Y.)
10. St. Louis
11. Brigham Young
12. Arizona
13. Dayton
14. Toledo
15. Washington
16. Murray St.
17. Cincinnati
18. Siena
19. Southern Cal
20. Villanova

UPI
1. Kentucky
2. Oklahoma St.
3. Kansas St.
4. Illinois
5. Columbia
6. Bradley
7. North Caro. St.
8. Indiana
9. St. John's (N.Y.)
10. Brigham Young
11. St. Louis
12. Arizona
13. Washington
14. Beloit
14. Villanova
16. UCLA
17. Cincinnati
18. Dayton
18. St. Bonaventure
18. Seton Hall
18. Texas A&M

1952

AP
1. Kentucky
2. Illinois
3. Kansas St.
4. Duquesne
5. St. Louis
6. Washington
7. Iowa
8. Kansas
9. West Va.
10. St. John's (N.Y.)
11. Dayton
12. Duke
13. Holy Cross
14. Seton Hall
15. St. Bonaventure
16. Wyoming
17. Louisville
18. Seattle
19. UCLA
20. Southwest Tex. St.

UPI
1. Kentucky
2. Illinois
3. Kansas
4. Duquesne
5. Washington
6. Kansas St.
7. St. Louis
8. Iowa
9. St. John's (N.Y.)
10. Wyoming
11. St. Bonaventure
12. Seton Hall
13. Texas Christian
14. West Va.
15. Holy Cross
16. Western Ky.
17. La Salle
18. Dayton
19. Louisville
20. UCLA
20. Indiana

1953

AP
1. Indiana
2. Seton Hall
3. Kansas
4. Washington
5. LSU
6. La Salle
7. St. John's (N.Y.)
8. Oklahoma St.
9. Duquesne
10. Notre Dame
11. Illinois
12. Kansas St.
13. Holy Cross
14. Seattle
15. Wake Forest
16. Santa Clara
17. Western Ky.
18. North Caro. St.
19. DePaul
20. Southwest Mo. St.

UPI
1. Indiana
2. Seton Hall
3. Washington
4. La Salle
5. Kansas
6. LSU
7. Oklahoma St.
8. North Caro. St.
9. Kansas St.
10. Illinois
11. Western Ky.
12. California
13. Notre Dame
14. DePaul
14. Wyoming
16. St. Louis
17. Holy Cross
18. Oklahoma City
19. Brigham Young
20. Duquesne

1954

AP
1. Kentucky
2. La Salle
3. Holy Cross
4. Indiana
5. Duquesne
6. Notre Dame
7. Bradley
8. Western Ky.
9. Penn St.
10. Oklahoma St.
11. Southern Cal
12. Geo. Washington
13. Iowa
14. LSU
15. Duke
16. Niagara
17. Seattle
18. Kansas
19. Illinois
20. Maryland

UPI
1. Indiana
2. Kentucky
3. Duquesne
4. Oklahoma St.
5. Notre Dame
6. Western Ky.
7. Kansas
8. LSU
9. Holy Cross
10. Iowa
11. La Salle
12. Illinois
13. Colorado St.
14. North Caro. St.
14. Southern Cal
16. Oregon St.
17. Seattle
17. Dayton
19. Rice
20. Duke

1955

AP
1. San Francisco
2. Kentucky
3. La Salle
4. North Caro. St.
5. Iowa
6. Duquesne
7. Utah
8. Marquette
9. Dayton
10. Oregon St.
11. Minnesota
12. Alabama
13. UCLA
14. Geo. Washington
15. Colorado
16. Tulsa
17. Vanderbilt
18. Illinois
19. West Va.
20. St. Louis

UPI
1. San Francisco
2. Kentucky
3. La Salle
4. Utah
5. Iowa
6. North Caro. St.
7. Duquesne
8. Oregon St.
9. Marquette
10. Dayton
11. Colorado
12. UCLA
13. Minnesota
14. Tulsa
15. Geo. Washington
16. Illinois
17. Niagara
18. St. Louis
19. Holy Cross
20. Cincinnati

1956

AP
1. San Francisco
2. North Caro. St.
3. Dayton
4. Iowa
5. Alabama
6. Louisville
7. Southern Methodist
8. UCLA
9. Kentucky
10. Illinois
11. Oklahoma City
12. Vanderbilt
13. North Caro.
14. Holy Cross
15. Temple
16. Wake Forest
17. Duke
18. Utah
19. Oklahoma St.
20. West Va.

UPI
1. San Francisco
2. North Caro. St.
3. Dayton
4. Iowa
5. Alabama
6. Southern Methodist
7. Louisville
8. Illinois
9. UCLA
10. Vanderbilt
11. North Caro.
12. Kentucky
13. Utah
14. Temple
15. Holy Cross
16. Oklahoma St.
16. St. Louis
18. Seattle
18. Duke
18. Canisius

1957

AP
1. North Caro.
2. Kansas
3. Kentucky
4. Southern Methodist
5. Seattle
6. Louisville
7. West Va.
8. Vanderbilt
9. Oklahoma City
10. St. Louis
11. Michigan St.
12. Memphis
13. California
14. UCLA
15. Mississippi St.
16. Idaho St.
17. Notre Dame
18. Wake Forest
19. Canisius
19. Oklahoma St.

UPI
1. North Caro.
2. Kansas
3. Kentucky
4. Southern Methodist
5. Seattle
6. California
7. Michigan St.
8. Louisville
9. UCLA
10. St. Louis
11. West Va.
12. Dayton
13. Bradley
14. Brigham Young
15. Indiana
16. Vanderbilt
16. Xavier (Ohio)
18. Oklahoma City
19. Notre Dame
20. Kansas St.

1958

AP
1. West Va.
2. Cincinnati
3. Kansas St.
4. San Francisco
5. Temple
6. Maryland
7. Kansas
8. Notre Dame
9. Kentucky
10. Duke
11. Dayton
12. Indiana
13. North Caro.
14. Bradley
15. Mississippi St.
16. Auburn
17. Michigan St.
18. Seattle
19. Oklahoma St.
20. North Caro. St.

UPI
1. West Va.
2. Cincinnati
3. San Francisco
4. Kansas St.
5. Temple
6. Maryland
7. Notre Dame
8. Kansas
9. Dayton
10. Indiana
11. Bradley
12. North Caro.
13. Duke
14. Kentucky
15. Oklahoma St.
16. Oregon St.
16. North Caro. St.
18. St. Bonaventure
19. Michigan St.
19. Wyoming
19. Seattle

1959

AP
1. Kansas St.
2. Kentucky
3. Mississippi St.
4. Bradley
5. Cincinnati
6. North Caro. St.
7. Michigan St.
8. Auburn
9. North Caro.
10. West Va.
11. California
12. St. Louis
13. Seattle
14. St. Joseph's (Pa.)
15. St. Mary's (Cal.)
16. Texas Christian
17. Oklahoma City
18. Utah
19. St. Bonaventure
20. Marquette

UPI
1. Kansas St.
2. Kentucky
3. Michigan St.
4. Cincinnati
5. North Caro. St.
6. North Caro.
7. Mississippi St.
8. Bradley
9. California
10. Auburn
11. West Va.
12. Texas Christian
13. St. Louis
14. Utah
15. Marquette
16. Tennessee Tech
17. St. John's (N.Y.)
18. Navy
18. St. Mary's (Cal.)
20. St. Joseph's (Pa.)

1960

AP
1. Cincinnati
2. California
3. Ohio St.
4. Bradley
5. West Va.
6. Utah
7. Indiana
8. Utah St.
9. St. Bonaventure
10. Miami (Fla.)
11. Auburn
12. New York U.
13. Georgia Tech
14. Providence
15. St. Louis
16. Holy Cross
17. Villanova
18. Duke
19. Wake Forest
20. St. John's (N.Y.)

UPI
1. California
2. Cincinnati
3. Ohio St.
4. Bradley
5. Utah
6. West Va.
7. Utah St.
8. Georgia Tech
9. Villanova
10. Indiana
11. St. Bonaventure
12. New York U.
13. Texas
14. North Caro.
15. Duke
16. Kansas St.
17. Auburn
18. Providence
19. St. Louis
20. Dayton

1961

AP
1. Ohio St.
2. Cincinnati
3. St. Bonaventure
4. Kansas St.
5. North Caro.
6. Bradley
7. Southern Cal
8. Iowa
9. West Va.
10. Duke
11. Utah
12. Texas Tech
13. Niagara
14. Memphis
15. Wake Forest
16. St. John's (N.Y.)
17. St. Joseph's (Pa.)
18. Drake
19. Holy Cross
20. Kentucky

UPI
1. Ohio St.
2. Cincinnati
3. St. Bonaventure
4. Kansas St.
5. Southern Cal
6. North Caro.
7. Bradley
8. St. John's (N.Y.)
9. Duke
10. Wake Forest
11. Iowa
12. West Va.
13. Utah
14. St. Louis
15. Louisville
16. St. Joseph's (Pa.)
17. Dayton
18. Kentucky
18. Texas Tech
20. Memphis

1962

AP
1. Ohio St.
2. Cincinnati
3. Kentucky
4. Mississippi St.
5. Bradley
6. Kansas St.
7. Utah
8. Bowling Green
9. Colorado
10. Duke
11. Loyola (Ill.)
12. St. John's (N.Y.)
13. Wake Forest
14. Oregon St.
15. West Va.
16. Arizona St.
17. Duquesne
18. Utah St.
19. UCLA
20. Villanova

UPI
1. Ohio St.
2. Cincinnati
3. Kentucky
4. Mississippi St.
5. Kansas St.
6. Bradley
7. Wake Forest
8. Colorado
9. Bowling Green
10. Utah
11. Oregon St.
12. St. John's (N.Y.)
13. Duke
14. Loyola (Ill.)
15. Arizona St.
16. West Va.
17. UCLA
18. Duquesne
19. Utah St.
20. Villanova

1963

AP
1. Cincinnati
2. Duke
3. Loyola (Ill.)
4. Arizona St.
5. Wichita St.
6. Mississippi St.
7. Ohio St.
8. Illinois
9. New York U.
10. Colorado

UPI
1. Cincinnati
2. Duke
3. Arizona St.
4. Loyola (Ill.)
5. Illinois
6. Wichita St.
7. Mississippi St.
8. Ohio St.
9. Colorado
10. Stanford
11. New York U.
12. Texas
13. Providence
14. Oregon St.
15. UCLA
16. St. Joseph's (Pa.)
16. West Va.
18. Bowling Green
19. Kansas St.
19. Seattle

1964

AP
1. UCLA
2. Michigan
3. Duke
4. Kentucky
5. Wichita St.
6. Oregon St.
7. Villanova
8. Loyola (Ill.)
9. DePaul
10. Davidson

UPI
1. UCLA
2. Michigan
3. Kentucky
4. Duke
5. Oregon St.
6. Wichita St.
7. Villanova
8. Loyola (Ill.)
9. UTEP
10. Davidson
11. DePaul
12. Kansas St.
13. Drake
13. San Francisco
15. Utah St.
16. Ohio St.
16. New Mexico
18. Texas A&M
19. Arizona St.
19. Providence

1965

AP
1. Michigan
2. UCLA
3. St. Joseph's (Pa.)
4. Providence
5. Vanderbilt
6. Davidson
7. Minnesota
8. Villanova
9. Brigham Young
10. Duke

UPI
1. Michigan
2. UCLA
3. St. Joseph's (Pa.)
4. Providence
5. Vanderbilt
6. Brigham Young
7. Davidson
8. Minnesota
9. Duke
10. San Francisco
11. Villanova
12. North Caro. St.
13. Oklahoma St.
14. Wichita St.
15. Connecticut
16. Illinois
17. Tennessee
18. Indiana
19. Miami (Fla.)
20. Dayton

1966

AP
1. Kentucky
2. Duke
3. UTEP
4. Kansas
5. St. Joseph's (Pa.)
6. Loyola (Ill.)
7. Cincinnati
8. Vanderbilt
9. Michigan
10. Western Ky.

UPI
1. Kentucky
2. Duke
3. UTEP
4. Kansas
5. Loyola (Ill.)
6. St. Joseph's (Pa.)
7. Michigan
8. Vanderbilt
9. Cincinnati
10. Providence
11. Nebraska
12. Utah
13. Oklahoma City
14. Houston
15. Oregon St.
16. Syracuse
17. Pacific (Cal.)
18. Davidson
19. Brigham Young
19. Dayton

1967

AP
1. UCLA
2. Louisville
3. Kansas
4. North Caro.
5. Princeton
6. Western Ky.
7. Houston
8. Tennessee
9. Boston College
10. UTEP

UPI
1. UCLA
2. Louisville
3. North Caro.
4. Kansas
5. Princeton
6. Houston
7. Western Ky.
8. UTEP
9. Tennessee
10. Boston College
11. Toledo
12. St. John's (N.Y.)
13. Tulsa
14. Vanderbilt
14. Utah St.
16. Pacific (Cal.)
17. Providence
18. New Mexico
19. Duke
20. Florida

1968

AP
1. Houston
2. UCLA
3. St. Bonaventure
4. North Caro.
5. Kentucky
6. New Mexico
7. Columbia
8. Davidson
9. Louisville
10. Duke

UPI
1. Houston
2. UCLA
3. St. Bonaventure
4. North Caro.
5. Kentucky
6. Columbia
7. New Mexico
8. Louisville
9. Davidson
10. Marquette
11. Duke
12. New Mexico St.
13. Vanderbilt
14. Kansas St.
15. Princeton
16. Army
17. Santa Clara
18. Utah
19. Bradley
20. Iowa

1969

AP
1. UCLA
2. La Salle
3. Santa Clara
4. North Caro.
5. Davidson
6. Purdue
7. Kentucky
8. St. John's (N.Y.)
9. Duquesne
10. Villanova
11. Drake
12. New Mexico St.
13. South Caro.
14. Marquette
15. Louisville
16. Boston College
17. Notre Dame
18. Colorado
19. Kansas
20. Illinois

UPI
1. UCLA
2. North Caro.
3. Davidson
4. Santa Clara
5. Kentucky
6. La Salle
7. Purdue
8. St. John's (N.Y.)
9. New Mexico St.
10. Duquesne
11. Drake
12. Colorado
13. Louisville
14. Marquette
15. Villanova
15. Boston College
17. Weber St.
17. Wyoming
19. Colorado St.
20. South Caro.
20. Kansas

1970

AP
1. Kentucky
2. UCLA
3. St. Bonaventure
4. Jacksonville
5. New Mexico St.
6. South Caro.
7. Iowa
8. Marquette
9. Notre Dame
10. North Caro. St.
11. Florida St.
12. Houston
13. Pennsylvania
14. Drake
15. Davidson
16. Utah St.
17. Niagara
18. Western Ky.
19. Long Beach St.
20. Southern Cal

UPI
1. Kentucky
2. UCLA
3. St. Bonaventure
4. New Mexico St.
5. Jacksonville
6. South Caro.
7. Iowa
8. Notre Dame
9. Drake
10. Marquette
11. Houston
12. North Caro. St.
13. Pennsylvania
14. Florida St.
15. Long Beach St.
17. Western Ky.
17. Utah St.
17. Niagara
20. Cincinnati
20. UTEP

1971

AP
1. UCLA
2. Marquette
3. Pennsylvania
4. Kansas
5. Southern Cal
6. South Caro.
7. Western Ky.
8. Kentucky
9. Fordham
10. Ohio St.
11. Jacksonville
12. Notre Dame
13. North Caro.
14. Houston
15. Duquesne
16. Long Beach St.
17. Tennessee
18. Villanova
19. Drake
20. Brigham Young

UPI
1. UCLA
2. Marquette
3. Pennsylvania
4. Kansas
5. Southern Cal
6. South Caro.
7. Western Ky.
8. Kentucky
9. Fordham
10. Ohio St.
11. Jacksonville
11. Brigham Young
13. North Caro.
14. Notre Dame
14. Long Beach St.
16. Drake
17. Villanova
18. Duquesne
18. Houston
20. Weber St.

1972

AP
1. UCLA
2. North Caro.
3. Pennsylvania
4. Louisville
5. Long Beach St.
6. South Caro.
7. Marquette
8. Southwestern La.
9. Brigham Young
10. Florida St.
11. Minnesota
12. Marshall
13. Memphis
14. Maryland
15. Villanova
16. Oral Roberts
17. Indiana
18. Kentucky
19. Ohio St.
20. Virginia

UPI
1. UCLA
2. North Caro.
3. Pennsylvania
4. Louisville
5. South Caro.
6. Long Beach St.
7. Marquette
8. Southwestern La.
9. Brigham Young
10. Florida St.
11. Maryland
12. Minnesota
13. Memphis
14. Kentucky
15. Villanova
16. Kansas St.
17. UTEP
18. Marshall
19. Missouri
19. Weber St.

1973

AP
1. UCLA
2. North Caro. St.
3. Long Beach St.
4. Providence
5. Marquette
6. Indiana
7. Southwestern La.
8. Maryland
9. Kansas St.
10. Minnesota
11. North Caro.
12. Memphis
13. Houston
14. Syracuse
15. Missouri
16. Arizona St.
17. Kentucky
18. Pennsylvania
19. Austin Peay
20. San Francisco

UPI
1. UCLA
2. North Caro. St.
3. Long Beach St.
4. Marquette
5. Providence
6. Indiana
7. Southwestern La.
7. Kansas St.
9. Minnesota
10. Maryland
11. Memphis
12. North Caro.
13. Arizona St.
14. Syracuse
15. Kentucky
16. South Caro.
17. Missouri
18. Weber St.
18. Houston
20. Pennsylvania

1974

AP
1. North Caro. St.
2. UCLA
3. Marquette
4. Maryland
5. Notre Dame
6. Michigan
7. Kansas
8. Providence
9. Indiana
10. Long Beach St.
11. Purdue
12. North Caro.
13. Vanderbilt
14. Alabama
15. Utah
16. Pittsburgh
17. Southern Cal
18. Oral Roberts
19. South Caro.
20. Dayton

UPI
1. North Caro. St.
2. UCLA
3. Notre Dame
4. Maryland
5. Marquette
6. Providence
7. Vanderbilt
8. North Caro.
9. Indiana
10. Kansas
11. Long Beach St.
12. Michigan
13. Southern Cal
14. Pittsburgh
15. Louisville
16. South Caro.
17. Creighton
18. New Mexico
19. Alabama
19. Dayton

1975

AP
1. UCLA
2. Kentucky
3. Indiana
4. Louisville
5. Maryland
6. Syracuse
7. North Caro. St.
8. Arizona St.
9. North Caro.
10. Alabama
11. Marquette
12. Princeton
13. Cincinnati
14. Notre Dame
15. Kansas St.
16. Drake
17. UNLV
18. Oregon St.
19. Michigan
20. Pennsylvania

UPI
1. Indiana
2. UCLA
3. Louisville
4. Kentucky
5. Maryland
6. Marquette
7. Arizona St.
8. Alabama
9. North Caro. St.
10. North Caro.
11. Pennsylvania
12. Southern Cal
13. Utah St.
14. UNLV
14. Notre Dame
16. Creighton
17. Arizona
18. New Mexico St.
19. Clemson
20. UTEP

1976

AP
1. Indiana
2. Marquette
3. UNLV
4. Rutgers
5. UCLA
6. Alabama
7. Notre Dame
8. North Caro.
9. Michigan
10. Western Mich.
11. Maryland
12. Cincinnati
13. Tennessee
14. Missouri
15. Arizona
16. Texas Tech
17. DePaul
18. Virginia
19. Centenary (La.)
20. Pepperdine

UPI
1. Indiana
2. Marquette
3. Rutgers
4. UNLV
5. UCLA
6. North Caro.
7. Alabama
8. Notre Dame
9. Michigan
10. Washington
11. Missouri
12. Arizona
13. Maryland
14. Tennessee
15. Virginia
16. Cincinnati
16. Florida St.
18. St. John's (N.Y.)
19. Western Mich.
19. Princeton

1977

AP
1. Michigan
2. UCLA
3. Kentucky
4. UNLV
5. North Caro.
6. Syracuse
7. Marquette
8. San Francisco
9. Wake Forest
10. Notre Dame
11. Alabama
12. Detroit
13. Minnesota
14. Utah
15. Tennessee
16. Kansas St.
17. N.C.-Charlotte
18. Arkansas
19. Louisville
20. VMI

UPI
1. Michigan
2. San Francisco
3. North Caro.
4. UCLA
5. Kentucky
6. UNLV
7. Arkansas
8. Tennessee
9. Syracuse
10. Utah
11. Kansas St.
12. Cincinnati
13. Louisville
14. Marquette
15. Providence
16. Indiana St.
17. Minnesota
18. Alabama
19. Detroit
20. Purdue

1978

AP
1. Kentucky
2. UCLA
3. DePaul
4. Michigan St.
5. Arkansas
6. Notre Dame
7. Duke
8. Marquette
9. Louisville
10. Kansas
11. San Francisco
12. New Mexico
13. Indiana
14. Utah
15. Florida St.
16. North Caro.
17. Texas
18. Detroit
19. Miami (Ohio)
20. Pennsylvania

UPI
1. Kentucky
2. UCLA
3. Marquette
4. New Mexico
5. Michigan St.
6. Arkansas
7. DePaul
8. Kansas
9. Duke
10. North Caro.
11. Notre Dame
12. Florida St.
13. San Francisco
14. Louisville
15. Indiana
16. Houston
17. Utah St.
18. Utah
19. Texas
20. Georgetown

1979

AP
1. Indiana St.
2. UCLA
3. Michigan St.
4. Notre Dame
5. Arkansas
6. DePaul
7. LSU
8. Syracuse
9. North Caro.
10. Marquette
11. Duke
12. San Francisco
13. Louisville
14. Pennsylvania
15. Purdue
16. Oklahoma
17. St. John's (N.Y.)
18. Rutgers
19. Toledo
20. Iowa

UPI
1. Indiana St.
2. UCLA
3. North Caro.
4. Michigan St.
5. Notre Dame
6. Arkansas
7. Duke
8. DePaul
9. LSU
10. Syracuse
11. Iowa
12. Georgetown
13. Marquette
14. Purdue
15. Texas
16. Temple
17. San Francisco
18. Tennessee
19. Louisville
20. Detroit

1980

AP
1. DePaul
2. Louisville
3. LSU
4. Kentucky
5. Oregon St.
6. Syracuse
7. Indiana
8. Maryland
9. Notre Dame
10. Ohio St.
11. Georgetown
12. Brigham Young
13. St. John's (N.Y.)
14. Duke
15. North Caro.
16. Missouri
17. Weber St.
18. Arizona St.
19. Iona
20. Purdue

UPI
1. DePaul
2. LSU
3. Kentucky
4. Louisville
5. Oregon St.
6. Syracuse
7. Indiana
8. Maryland
9. Ohio St.
10. Georgetown
11. Notre Dame
12. Brigham Young
13. St. John's (N.Y.)
14. Missouri
15. North Caro.
16. Duke
17. Weber St.
18. Texas A&M
19. Arizona St.
20. Kansas St.

1981

AP
1. DePaul
2. Oregon St.
3. Arizona St.
4. LSU
5. Virginia
6. North Caro.
7. Notre Dame
8. Kentucky
9. Indiana
10. UCLA
11. Wake Forest
12. Louisville
13. Iowa
14. Utah
15. Tennessee
16. Brigham Young
17. Wyoming
18. Maryland
19. Illinois
20. Arkansas

UPI
1. DePaul
2. Oregon St.
3. Virginia
4. LSU
5. Arizona St.
6. North Caro.
7. Indiana
8. Kentucky
9. Notre Dame
10. Utah
11. UCLA
12. Iowa
13. Louisville
14. Wake Forest
15. Tennessee
16. Wyoming
17. Brigham Young
18. Illinois
19. Kansas
20. Maryland

1982

AP
1. North Caro.
2. DePaul
3. Virginia
4. Oregon St.
5. Missouri
6. Georgetown
7. Minnesota
8. Idaho
9. Memphis
10. Tulsa
11. Fresno St.
12. Arkansas
13. Alabama
14. West Va.
15. Kentucky
16. Iowa
17. UAB
18. Wake Forest
19. UCLA
20. Louisville

UPI
1. North Caro.
2. DePaul
3. Virginia
4. Oregon St.
5. Missouri
6. Minnesota
7. Georgetown
8. Idaho
9. Memphis
10. Fresno St.
11. Tulsa
12. Alabama
13. Arkansas
14. Kentucky
15. Wyoming
16. Iowa
17. West Va.
18. Kansas St.
19. Wake Forest
20. Louisville

1983

AP
1. Houston
2. Louisville
3. St. John's (N.Y.)
4. Virginia
5. Indiana
6. UNLV
7. UCLA
8. North Caro.
9. Arkansas
10. Missouri
11. Boston College
12. Kentucky
13. Villanova
14. Wichita St.
15. Tenn.-Chatt.
16. North Caro. St.
17. Memphis
18. Georgia
19. Oklahoma St.
20. Georgetown

UPI
1. Houston
2. Louisville
3. St. John's (N.Y.)
4. Virginia
5. Indiana
6. UNLV
7. UCLA
8. North Caro.
9. Arkansas
10. Kentucky
11. Villanova
12. Missouri
13. Boston College
14. North Caro. St.
15. Georgia
16. Tenn.-Chatt.
17. Memphis
18. Illinois St.
19. Oklahoma St.
20. Georgetown

1984

AP
1. North Caro.
2. Georgetown
3. Kentucky
4. DePaul
5. Houston
6. Illinois
7. Oklahoma
8. Arkansas
9. UTEP
10. Purdue
11. Maryland
12. Tulsa
13. UNLV
14. Duke
15. Washington
16. Memphis
17. Oregon St.
18. Syracuse
19. Wake Forest
20. Temple

UPI
1. North Caro.
2. Georgetown
3. Kentucky
4. DePaul
5. Houston
6. Illinois
7. Arkansas
8. Oklahoma
9. UTEP
10. Maryland
11. Purdue
12. Tulsa
13. UNLV
14. Duke
15. Washington
16. Memphis
16. Syracuse
18. Indiana
19. Auburn
20. Oregon St.

1985

AP
1. Georgetown
2. Michigan
3. St. John's (N.Y.)
4. Oklahoma
5. Memphis
6. Georgia Tech
7. North Caro.
8. Louisiana Tech
9. UNLV
10. Duke
11. Va. Commonwealth
12. Illinois
13. Kansas
14. Loyola (Ill.)
15. Syracuse
16. North Caro. St.
17. Texas Tech
18. Tulsa
19. Georgia
20. LSU

UPI
1. Georgetown
2. Michigan
3. St. John's (N.Y.)
4. Memphis
5. Oklahoma
6. Georgia Tech
7. North Caro.
8. Louisiana Tech
9. UNLV
10. Illinois
11. Va. Commonwealth
12. Duke
13. Kansas
14. Tulsa
15. Syracuse
16. Texas Tech
17. Loyola (Ill.)
18. North Caro. St.
19. LSU
20. Michigan St.

1986

AP
1. Duke
2. Kansas
3. Kentucky
4. St. John's (N.Y.)
5. Michigan
6. Georgia Tech
7. Louisville
8. North Caro.
9. Syracuse
10. Notre Dame
11. UNLV
12. Memphis
13. Georgetown
14. Bradley
15. Oklahoma
16. Indiana
17. Navy
18. Michigan St.
19. Illinois
20. UTEP

UPI
1. Duke
2. Kansas
3. St. John's (N.Y.)
4. Kentucky
5. Michigan
6. Georgia Tech
7. Louisville
8. North Caro.
9. Syracuse
10. UNLV
11. Notre Dame
12. Memphis
13. Bradley
14. Indiana
15. Georgetown
16. UTEP
17. Oklahoma
18. Michigan St.
19. Alabama
20. Illinois

1987

AP
1. UNLV
2. North Caro.
3. Indiana
4. Georgetown
5. DePaul
6. Iowa
7. Purdue
8. Temple
9. Alabama
10. Syracuse
11. Illinois
12. Pittsburgh
13. Clemson
14. Missouri
15. UCLA
16. New Orleans
17. Duke
18. Notre Dame
19. Texas Christian
20. Kansas

UPI
1. UNLV
2. Indiana
3. North Caro.
4. Georgetown
5. DePaul
6. Purdue
7. Iowa
8. Temple
9. Alabama
10. Syracuse
11. Illinois
12. Pittsburgh
13. UCLA
14. Missouri
15. Clemson
16. Texas Christian
17. Wyoming
18. Notre Dame
19. New Orleans
19. Oklahoma
19. UTEP

1988

AP
1. Temple
2. Arizona
3. Purdue
4. Oklahoma
5. Duke
6. Kentucky
7. North Caro.
8. Pittsburgh
9. Syracuse
10. Michigan
11. Bradley
12. UNLV
13. Wyoming
14. North Caro. St.
15. Loyola Marymount
16. Illinois
17. Iowa
18. Xavier (Ohio)
19. Brigham Young
20. Kansas St.

UPI
1. Temple
2. Arizona
3. Purdue
4. Oklahoma
5. Duke
6. Kentucky
7. Pittsburgh
8. North Caro.
9. Syracuse
10. Michigan
11. UNLV
12. Bradley
13. North Caro. St.
14. Wyoming
15. Illinois
16. Loyola Marymount
17. Brigham Young
18. Iowa
19. Indiana
20. Kansas St.

1989

AP
1. Arizona
2. Georgetown
3. Illinois
4. Oklahoma
5. North Caro.
6. Missouri
7. Syracuse
8. Indiana
9. Duke
10. Michigan
11. Seton Hall
12. Louisville
13. Stanford
14. Iowa
15. UNLV
16. Florida St.
17. West Va.
18. Ball St.
19. North Caro. St.
20. Alabama

UPI
1. Arizona
2. Georgetown
3. Illinois
4. North Caro.
5. Oklahoma
6. Indiana
7. Duke
8. Missouri
9. Syracuse
10. Michigan
11. Seton Hall
12. Stanford
13. Louisville
14. UNLV
15. Iowa
16. Florida St.
17. Arkansas
18. North Caro. St.
19. West Va.
20. Alabama

1990

AP
1. Oklahoma
2. UNLV
3. Connecticut
4. Michigan St.
5. Kansas
6. Syracuse
7. Arkansas
8. Georgetown
9. Georgia Tech
10. Purdue
11. Missouri
12. La Salle
13. Michigan
14. Arizona
15. Duke
16. Louisville
17. Clemson
18. Illinois
19. LSU
20. Minnesota
21. Loyola Marymount
22. Oregon St.
23. Alabama
24. New Mexico St.
25. Xavier (Ohio)

UPI
1. Oklahoma
2. UNLV
3. Connecticut
4. Michigan St.
5. Kansas
6. Syracuse
7. Georgia Tech
8. Arkansas
9. Georgetown
10. Purdue
11. Missouri
12. Arizona
13. La Salle
14. Duke
15. Michigan
16. Louisville
17. Clemson
18. Illinois
19. Alabama
20. New Mexico St.

1991

AP
1. UNLV
2. Arkansas
3. Indiana
4. North Caro.
5. Ohio St.
6. Duke
7. Syracuse
8. Arizona
9. Kentucky
10. Utah
11. Nebraska
12. Kansas
13. Seton Hall
14. Oklahoma St.
15. New Mexico St.
16. UCLA
17. East Tenn. St.
18. Princeton
19. Alabama
20. St. John's (N.Y.)
21. Mississippi St.
22. LSU
23. Texas
24. DePaul
25. Southern Miss.

UPI
1. UNLV
2. Arkansas
3. Indiana
4. North Caro.
5. Ohio St.
6. Duke
7. Arizona
8. Syracuse
9. Nebraska
10. Utah
11. Seton Hall
12. Kansas
13. Oklahoma St.
14. UCLA
15. East Tenn. St.
16. Alabama
17. New Mexico St.
18. Mississippi St.
19. St. John's (N.Y.)
20. Princeton
21. LSU
22. Michigan St.
23. Georgetown
24. North Caro. St.
25. Texas

1992

AP
1. Duke
2. Kansas
3. Ohio St.
4. UCLA
5. Indiana
6. Kentucky
7. UNLV
8. Southern Cal
9. Arkansas
10. Arizona
11. Oklahoma St.
12. Cincinnati
13. Alabama
14. Michigan St.
15. Michigan
16. Missouri
17. Massachusetts
18. North Caro.
19. Seton Hall
20. Florida St.
21. Syracuse
22. Georgetown
23. Oklahoma
24. DePaul
25. LSU

UPI
1. Duke
2. Kansas
3. UCLA
4. Ohio St.
5. Arizona
6. Indiana
7. Southern Cal
8. Arkansas
9. Kentucky
10. Oklahoma St.
11. Michigan St.
12. Missouri
13. Alabama
14. Cincinnati
15. North Caro.
16. Florida St.
17. Michigan
18. Seton Hall
19. Georgetown
20. Syracuse
21. Massachusetts
22. Oklahoma
23. DePaul
24. St. John's (N.Y.)
25. Tulane

1993
AP
1. Indiana
2. Kentucky
3. Michigan
4. North Caro.
5. Arizona
6. Seton Hall
7. Cincinnati
8. Vanderbilt
9. Kansas
10. Duke
11. Florida St.
12. Arkansas
13. Iowa
14. Massachusetts
15. Louisville
16. Wake Forest
17. New Orleans
18. Georgia Tech
19. Utah
20. Western Ky.
21. New Mexico
22. Purdue
23. Oklahoma St.
24. New Mexico St.
25. UNLV

USA TODAY/CNN
1. Indiana
2. North Caro.
3. Kentucky
4. Michigan
5. Arizona
6. Seton Hall
7. Cincinnati
8. Kansas
9. Vanderbilt
10. Duke
11. Florida St.
12. Arkansas
13. Iowa
14. Louisville
15. Wake Forest
16. Utah
17. Massachusetts
18. New Orleans
19. UNLV
20. Georgia Tech
21. Purdue
22. Virginia
23. Oklahoma St.
24. New Mexico St.
25. Western Ky.

1994
AP
1. North Caro.
2. Arkansas
3. Purdue
4. Connecticut
5. Missouri
6. Duke
7. Kentucky
8. Massachusetts
9. Arizona
10. Louisville
11. Michigan
12. Temple
13. Kansas
14. Florida
15. Syracuse
16. California
17. UCLA
18. Indiana
19. Oklahoma St.
20. Texas
21. Marquette
22. Nebraska
23. Minnesota
24. St. Louis
25. Cincinnati

USA TODAY/CNN
1. Arkansas
2. North Caro.
3. Connecticut
4. Purdue
5. Missouri
6. Duke
7. Massachusetts
8. Kentucky
9. Louisville
10. Arizona
11. Michigan
12. Temple
13. Kansas
14. Syracuse
15. Florida
16. UCLA
17. California
18. Indiana
19. Oklahoma St.
20. Minnesota
21. St. Louis
22. Marquette
23. UAB
24. Texas
25. Cincinnati

1995
AP
1. UCLA
2. Kentucky
3. Wake Forest
4. North Caro.
5. Kansas
6. Arkansas
7. Massachusetts
8. Connecticut
9. Villanova
10. Maryland
11. Michigan St.
12. Purdue
13. Virginia
14. Oklahoma St.
15. Arizona
16. Arizona St.
17. Oklahoma
18. Mississippi St.
19. Utah
20. Alabama
21. Western Ky.
22. Georgetown
23. Missouri
24. Iowa St.
25. Syracuse

USA TODAY/NABC
1. UCLA
2. Kentucky
3. Wake Forest
4. Kansas
5. North Caro.
6. Arkansas
7. Massachusetts
8. Connecticut
9. Michigan St.
10. Maryland
11. Purdue
12. Villanova
13. Arizona
14. Oklahoma St.
15. Virginia
16. Arizona St.
17. Utah
18. Iowa St.
19. Mississippi St.
20. Oklahoma
21. Alabama
22. Syracuse
23. Missouri
24. Oregon
25. Stanford

1996
AP
1. Massachusetts
2. Kentucky
3. Connecticut
4. Georgetown
5. Kansas
6. Purdue
7. Cincinnati
8. Texas Tech
9. Wake Forest
10. Villanova
11. Arizona
12. Utah
13. Georgia Tech
14. UCLA
15. Syracuse
16. Memphis
17. Iowa St.
18. Penn St.
19. Mississippi St.
20. Marquette
21. Iowa
22. Virginia Tech
23. New Mexico
24. Louisville
25. North Caro.

USA TODAY/NABC
1. Massachusetts
2. Kentucky
3. Connecticut
4. Purdue
5. Georgetown
6. Cincinnati
7. Texas Tech
8. Kansas
9. Wake Forest
10. Utah
11. Arizona
12. Villanova
13. UCLA
14. Syracuse
15. Georgia Tech
16. Iowa St.
17. Memphis
18. Penn St.
19. Iowa
20. Mississippi St.
21. Virginia Tech
22. Marquette
23. Louisville
24. North Caro.
25. Stanford

Final Post-Tournament Polls

1994
USA TODAY/CNN
1. Arkansas
2. Duke
3. Arizona
4. Florida
5. Purdue
6. Missouri
7. Connecticut
8. Michigan
9. North Caro.
10. Louisville
11. Boston College
12. Kansas
13. Kentucky
14. Syracuse
15. Massachusetts
16. Indiana
17. Marquette
18. Temple
19. Tulsa
20. Maryland
21. Oklahoma St.
22. UCLA
23. Minnesota
24. Texas
25. Pennsylvania

1995
USA TODAY/NABC
1. UCLA
2. Arkansas
3. North Caro.
4. Oklahoma St.
5. Kentucky
6. Connecticut
7. Massachusetts
8. Virginia
9. Wake Forest
10. Kansas
11. Maryland
12. Mississippi St.
13. Arizona St.
14. Memphis
15. Tulsa
16. Georgetown
17. Syracuse
18. Missouri
19. Purdue
20. Michigan St.
21. Alabama
22. Utah
23. Villanova
24. Texas
25. Arizona

1996
USA TODAY/NABC
1. Kentucky
2. Massachusetts
3. Syracuse
4. Mississippi St.
5. Kansas
6. Cincinnati
7. Georgetown
8. Connecticut
9. Wake Forest
10. Texas Tech
11. Arizona
12. Utah
13. Georgia Tech
14. Louisville
15. Purdue
16. Georgia
17. Villanova
18. Arkansas
19. UCLA
20. Iowa St.
21. Virginia Tech
22. Iowa
23. Marquette
24. North Caro.
25. New Mexico

American Sports Wire Poll

The following poll ranks the top historically black institutions of the NCAA as selected by American Sports Wire and compiled by Dick Simpson.

Year	Team	Won	Lost
1992	Howard	17	14
1993	Jackson St.	25	9
1994	Texas Southern	19	11
1995	Texas Southern	22	7
1996	South Caro. St.	22	8

No. 1 vs. No. 2 (Since 1980)

Date	No. 1, Score	W-L	No. 2, Score	Site
Dec. 26, 1981	North Caro. 82	W	Kentucky 69	East Rutherford, N.J.
Jan. 9, 1982	North Caro. 65	W	Virginia 60	Chapel Hill, N.C.
April 2, 1983	Houston 94	W	Louisville 81	Albuquerque, N.M.
Dec. 15, 1984	Georgetown 77	W	DePaul 57	Landover, Md.
Feb. 27, 1985	St. John's (N.Y.) 69	L	Georgetown 85	New York, N.Y.
Mar. 9, 1985	Georgetown 92	W	St. John's (N.Y.) 80	New York, N.Y.
Feb. 4, 1986	North Caro. 78	W (ot)	Georgia Tech 77	Atlanta, Ga.
Mar. 29, 1986	Duke 71	W	Kansas 67	Dallas, Tex.
Feb. 13, 1990	Kansas 71	L	Missouri 77	Lawrence, Kan.
Mar. 10, 1990	Oklahoma 95	W	Kansas 77	Kansas City, Mo.
Feb. 10, 1991	UNLV 112	W	Arkansas 105	Fayetteville, Ark.
Feb. 3, 1994	Duke 78	L	North Caro. 89	Chapel Hill, N.C.
Mar. 30, 1996	Massachusetts 74	L	Kentucky 81	East Rutherford, N.J.

Division II Records

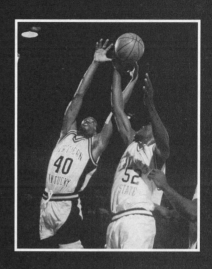

Individual Records

Basketball records are confined to the "modern era," which began with the 1937-38 season, the first without the center jump after each goal scored. Official weekly statistics rankings in scoring and shooting began with the 1947-48 season. Individual rebounds were added for the 1950-51 season, while team rebounds were added for the 1959-60 season. Assists were added for the 1988-89 season. Blocked shots and steals were added for the 1992-93 season. Scoring and rebounding are ranked on per-game average; shooting, on percentage. Beginning with the 1967-68 season, Division II rankings were limited only to NCAA members. The 1973-74 season was the first under a three-division reorganization plan adopted by the special NCAA Convention of August 1973. In statistical rankings, the rounding of percentages and/or averages may indicate ties where none exist. In these cases, the numerical order of the rankings is accurate.

Scoring

POINTS
Game
113—Clarence "Bevo" Francis, Rio Grande vs. Hillsdale, Feb. 2, 1954
Season
1,329—Earl Monroe, Winston-Salem, 1967 (31 games)
Career
4,045—Travis Grant, Kentucky St., 1969-72 (121 games)

AVERAGE PER GAME
Season
†46.5—Clarence "Bevo" Francis, Rio Grande, 1954 (1,255 in 27)
Career
(Min. 1,400) 33.4—Travis Grant, Kentucky St., 1969-72 (4,045 in 121)

†Season and career figures for Francis limited only to his 39 games (27 in 1954) against four-year colleges.

GAMES SCORING AT LEAST 50 POINTS
Season
†8—Clarence "Bevo" Francis, Rio Grande, 1954
Career
†14—Clarence "Bevo" Francis, Rio Grande, 1953-54

†Season and career figures for Francis limited only to his 39 games (27 in 1954) against four-year colleges.

MOST GAMES SCORING IN DOUBLE FIGURES
Career
130—Lambert Shell, Bridgeport, 1989-92

Field Goals

FIELD GOALS
Game
38—Clarence "Bevo" Francis, Rio Grande vs. Alliance, Jan. 16, 1954 (71 attempts) and vs. Hillsdale, Feb. 2, 1954 (70 attempts)
Season
539—Travis Grant, Kentucky St., 1972 (869 attempts)
Career
1,760—Travis Grant, Kentucky St., 1969-72 (2,759 attempts)

CONSECUTIVE FIELD GOALS
Game
20—Lance Berwald, North Dak. St. vs. Augustana (S.D.), Feb. 17, 1984
Season
28—Don McAllister, Hartwick, 1980 (during six games, Jan. 26-Feb. 9); Lance Berwald, North Dak. St., 1984 (during three games, Feb. 13-18)

FIELD-GOAL ATTEMPTS
Game
71—Clarence "Bevo" Francis, Rio Grande vs. Alliance, Jan. 16, 1954 (38 made)
Season
925—Jim Toombs, Stillman, 1965 (388 made)
Career
3,309—Bob Hopkins, Grambling, 1953-56 (1,403 made)

FIELD-GOAL PERCENTAGE
Game
(Min. 20 made) 100%—Lance Berwald, North Dak. St. vs. Augustana (S.D.), Feb. 17, 1984 (20 of 20)
*Season
75.2%—Todd Linder, Tampa, 1987 (282 of 375)
*Based on qualifiers for annual championship.
Career
(Min. 400 made) 70.8%—Todd Linder, Tampa, 1984-87 (909 of 1,284)

Three-Point Field Goals

THREE-POINT FIELD GOALS
Game
14—Andy Schmidtmann, Wis.-Parkside vs. Lakeland, Feb. 14, 1989 (32 attempts)
Season
167—Alex Williams, Cal St. Sacramento, 1988 (369 attempts)
Career
431—Tony Smith, Pfeiffer, 1989-92 (1,047 attempts)

THREE-POINT FIELD GOALS MADE PER GAME
Season
5.6—Alex Williams, Cal St. Sacramento, 1988 (167 in 30)
Career
4.3—Alex Williams, Cal St. Sacramento, 1987-88 (247 in 58)

CONSECUTIVE THREE-POINT FIELD GOALS
Game
10—Duane Huddleston, Mo.-Rolla vs. Truman St., Jan. 23, 1988
Season
18—Dan Drews, Le Moyne (during 11 games, Dec. 11, 1993 to Feb. 2, 1994)

CONSECUTIVE GAMES MAKING A THREE-POINT FIELD GOAL
Season
32—Reggie Evans, Central Okla., Nov. 23, 1991, to March 26, 1992
Career
79—Bryan Williams, Tampa, Jan. 11, 1989, to March 9, 1991

THREE-POINT FIELD-GOAL ATTEMPTS
Game
32—Andy Schmidtmann, Wis.-Parkside vs. Lakeland, Feb. 14, 1989 (14 made)
Season
369—Alex Williams, Cal St. Sacramento, 1988 (167 made)
Career
1,047—Tony Smith, Pfeiffer, 1989-92 (431 made)

THREE-POINT FIELD-GOAL ATTEMPTS PER GAME
Season
12.3—Alex Williams, Cal St. Sacramento, 1988 (369 in 30)
Career
9.3—Kwame Morton, Clarion, 1991-94 (980 in 105)

THREE-POINT FIELD-GOAL PERCENTAGE
Game
(Min. 9 made) 100%—Steve Divine, Ky. Wesleyan vs. Wayne St. (Mich.), March 14, 1992 (9 of 9)
*Season
(Min. 35 made) 65.0%—Ray Lee, Hampton, 1988 (39 of 60)
(Min. 50 made) 60.3%—Aaron Fehler, Oakland City, 1995 (73 of 121)

(Min. 100 made) 56.7%—Scott Martin, Rollins, 1991 (114 of 201)
(Min. 150 made) 45.3%—Alex Williams, Cal St. Sacramento, 1988 (167 of 369)
*Based on qualifiers for annual championship.
Career
(Min. 200 made) 51.3%—Scott Martin, Rollins, 1988-91 (236 of 460)

Free Throws

FREE THROWS
Game
37—Clarence "Bevo" Francis, Rio Grande vs. Hillsdale, Feb. 2, 1954 (45 attempts)
Season
401—Joe Miller, Alderson-Broaddus, 1957 (496 attempts)
Career
1,130—Joe Miller, Alderson-Broaddus, 1954-57 (1,460 attempts)

CONSECUTIVE FREE THROWS
Game
23—Carl Hartman, Alderson-Broaddus vs. Salem, Dec. 6, 1954
Season
74—Mike Hall, Adams St., 1992 (during 13 games, Jan. 11-Feb. 15)

FREE-THROW ATTEMPTS
Game
45—Clarence "Bevo" Francis, Rio Grande vs. Hillsdale, Feb. 2, 1954 (37 made)
Season
†510—Clarence "Bevo" Francis, Rio Grande, 1954 (367 made)
Career
1,460—Joe Miller, Alderson-Broaddus, 1954-57 (1,130 made)

†Season figure for Francis limited to 27 games against four-year colleges.

FREE-THROW PERCENTAGE
Game
(Min. 20 made) 100%—Forrest "Butch" Meyeraan, Mankato St. vs. Wis.-River Falls, Feb. 21, 1961 (20 of 20)
*Season
94.4%—Kent Andrews, McNeese St., 1968 (85 of 90); Billy Newton, Morgan St., 1976 (85 of 90)
*Based on qualifiers for annual championship.
Career
(Min. 250 made) 91.6%—Kent Andrews, McNeese St., 1967-69 (252 of 275)
(Min. 500 made) 87.9%—Steve Nisenson, Hofstra, 1963-65 (602 of 685)

Rebounds

REBOUNDS
Game
46—Tom Hart, Middlebury vs. Trinity (Conn.), Feb. 5, 1955, and vs. Clarkson, Feb. 12, 1955
Season
799—Elmore Smith, Kentucky St., 1971 (33 games)
Career
2,334—Jim Smith, Steubenville, 1955-58 (112 games)

AVERAGE PER GAME
Season
29.5—Tom Hart, Middlebury, 1956 (620 in 21)
Career
(Min. 900) 27.6—Tom Hart, Middlebury, 1953, 55-56 (1,738 in 63)

Assists

ASSISTS
Game
25—Ali Baaqar, Morris Brown vs. Albany St. (Ga.),

Jan. 26, 1991; Adrian Hutt, Metro St. vs. Cal St. Sacramento, Feb. 9, 1991

Season
400—Steve Ray, Bridgeport, 1989 (32 games)
Career
1,044—Demetri Beekman, Assumption, 1990-93 (119 games)

AVERAGE PER GAME
Season
12.5—Steve Ray, Bridgeport, 1989 (400 in 32)
Career
(Min. 550) 12.1—Steve Ray, Bridgeport, 1989-90 (785 in 65)

Blocked Shots

BLOCKED SHOTS
Game
15—Mark Hensel, Pitt.-Johnstown vs. Slippery Rock, Jan. 22, 1994
Season
155—Antonio Harvey, Pfeiffer, 1993 (29 games)
Career
305—Kino Outlaw, Mount Olive, 1994-96 (81 games)

AVERAGE PER GAME
Season
5.3—Antonio Harvey, Pfeiffer, 1993 (155 in 29)
Career
3.80—John Burke, LIU-Southampton, 1995-96 (205 in 54)

Steals

STEALS
Game
11—Ken Francis, Molloy vs. Concordia (N.Y.), Jan. 29, 1994; Aaron Johnson, LIU-C.W. Post vs. Concordia (N.Y.), Jan. 22, 1994; Steve Maryin, Bowie St. vs. Shaw, Nov. 29, 1993
Season
118—David Clark, Bluefield St., 1996 (31 games)
Career
278—David Clark, Bluefield St., 1994-96 (83 games)

AVERAGE PER GAME
Season
4.5—John Morris, Bluefield St., 1994 (104 in 23)
Career
3.70—John Morris, Bluefield St., 1994-95 (185 in 50)

Games

GAMES PLAYED
Season
36—Bill Reigel, Frank Glenn, Jesse Perry and Ruble Scarborough, McNeese St., 1956
Career
133—Pat Morris, Bridgeport, 1989-92

Team Records

Note: Where records involve both teams, each team must be an NCAA Division II member institution.

SINGLE-GAME RECORDS

Scoring

MOST POINTS
258—Troy St. vs. DeVry (Ga.) (141), Jan. 12, 1992

MOST POINTS VS. DIVISION II TEAM
169—Stillman vs. Miles (123), Feb. 17, 1966

MOST POINTS BY LOSING TEAM
146—Mississippi Col. vs. West Ala. (160), Dec. 2, 1969

MOST POINTS, BOTH TEAMS
306—West Ala. (160) and Mississippi Col. (146), Dec. 2, 1969

MOST POINTS IN A HALF
135—Troy St. vs. DeVry (Ga.), Jan. 12, 1992

FEWEST POINTS ALLOWED (Since 1938)
4—Albion (76) vs. Adrian, Dec. 12, 1938; Tennessee St. (7) vs. Oglethorpe, Feb. 16, 1971

FEWEST POINTS, BOTH TEAMS (Since 1938)
11—Tennessee St. (7) and Oglethorpe (4), Feb. 16, 1971

WIDEST MARGIN OF VICTORY
118—Mississippi Col. (168) vs. Dallas Bible (50), Dec. 9, 1971

Field Goals

MOST FIELD GOALS
102—Troy St. vs. DeVry (Ga.), Jan. 12, 1992 (190 attempts)

MOST FIELD-GOAL ATTEMPTS
190—Troy St. vs. DeVry (Ga.), Jan. 12, 1992 (102 made)

FEWEST FIELD GOALS (Since 1938)
0—Adrian vs. Albion, Dec. 12, 1938 (28 attempts)

FEWEST FIELD-GOAL ATTEMPTS
7—Mansfield vs. West Chester, Dec. 8, 1984 (4 made)

HIGHEST FIELD-GOAL PERCENTAGE
81.6%—Youngstown St. vs. Northern Iowa, Jan. 26, 1980 (31 of 38)

HIGHEST FIELD-GOAL PERCENTAGE, HALF
95.0%—Abilene Christian vs. Cameron, Jan. 21, 1989 (19 of 20)

Three-Point Field Goals

MOST THREE-POINT FIELD GOALS
51—Troy St. vs. DeVry (Ga.), Jan. 12, 1992 (109 attempts)

MOST THREE-POINT FIELD GOALS, BOTH TEAMS
39—Columbus St. (22) vs. Troy St. (17), Feb. 14, 1991

CONSECUTIVE THREE-POINT FIELD GOALS MADE WITHOUT A MISS
12—Pace vs. Medgar Evers, Nov. 27, 1991

HIGHEST NUMBER OF DIFFERENT PLAYERS TO SCORE A THREE-POINT FIELD GOAL, ONE TEAM
10—Troy St. vs. DeVry (Ga.), Jan. 12, 1992

MOST THREE-POINT FIELD-GOAL ATTEMPTS
109—Troy St. vs. DeVry (Ga.), Jan. 12, 1992 (51 made)

MOST THREE-POINT FIELD-GOAL ATTEMPTS, BOTH TEAMS
95—Columbus St. (52) vs. Troy St. (43), Feb. 14, 1991

HIGHEST THREE-POINT FIELD-GOAL PERCENTAGE
(Min. 10 made) 90.9%—Phila. Textile vs. Spring Garden, Nov. 24, 1987 (10 of 11); Armstrong Atlantic vs. Columbus St., Feb. 24, 1990 (10 of 11); Norfolk St. vs. Clark Atlanta, Dec. 26, 1992 (10 of 11)

HIGHEST THREE-POINT FIELD-GOAL PERCENTAGE, BOTH TEAMS
(Min. 10 made) 83.3%—Tampa (9 of 10) vs. St. Leo (1 of 2), Jan. 21, 1987 (10 of 12)

(Min. 20 made) 75.9%—Indiana (Pa.) (11 of 15) vs. Cheyney (11 of 14), Jan. 26, 1987 (22 of 29)

Free Throws

MOST FREE THROWS
64—Wayne St. (Mich.) vs. Grand Valley St., Feb. 13, 1993 (79 attempts); Baltimore vs. Washington (Md.), Feb. 9, 1955 (84 attempts)

MOST FREE THROWS, BOTH TEAMS
89—Baltimore (64) and Washington (Md.) (25), Feb. 9, 1955

MOST FREE-THROW ATTEMPTS
84—Baltimore vs. Washington (Md.), Feb. 9, 1955 (64 made)

MOST FREE-THROW ATTEMPTS, BOTH TEAMS
121—Illinois Tech (70) and Illinois Col. (51), Dec. 13, 1952 (66 made)

FEWEST FREE THROWS
0—Many teams

FEWEST FREE-THROW ATTEMPTS
0—Many teams

HIGHEST FREE-THROW PERCENTAGE
(Min. 31 made) 100%—Dowling vs. LIU-Southampton, Feb. 6, 1985 (31 of 31)

HIGHEST FREE-THROW PERCENTAGE, BOTH TEAMS
(Min. 30 made) 97.0%—Hartford (17 of 17) vs. Bentley (15 of 16), Feb. 22, 1983 (32 of 33)

Rebounds

MOST REBOUNDS
111—Central Mich. vs. Alma, Dec. 7, 1963

MOST REBOUNDS, BOTH TEAMS
141—Loyola (Md.) (75) vs. Western Md. (66), Dec. 6, 1961; Concordia (Ill.) (72) vs. Concordia (Neb.) (69), Feb. 26, 1965

HIGHEST REBOUND MARGIN
65—Moravian (100) vs. Drew (35), Feb. 18, 1969

Assists

MOST ASSISTS
65—Troy St. vs. DeVry (Ga.), Jan. 12, 1992

MOST ASSISTS, BOTH TEAMS
65—Central Okla. (34) vs. Stonehill (31), Dec. 29, 1990

Personal Fouls

MOST PERSONAL FOULS
50—Steubenville vs. West Liberty, 1952

MOST PERSONAL FOULS, BOTH TEAMS (Including Overtimes)
75—Edinboro (47) vs. Calif. (Pa.) (28) (5 ot), Feb. 4, 1989

MOST PERSONAL FOULS, BOTH TEAMS (Regulation Time)
74—Bentley (36) vs. Mass.-Boston (38), Jan. 23, 1971

MOST PLAYERS DISQUALIFIED
7—Illinois Col. vs. Illinois Tech, Dec. 13, 1952; Steubenville vs. West Liberty, 1952; Washington (Md.) vs. Baltimore, Feb. 9, 1955; Southern Colo. vs. Air Force, Jan. 12, 1972; Edinboro vs. Calif. (Pa.) (5 ot), Feb. 4, 1989

MOST PLAYERS DISQUALIFIED, BOTH TEAMS
12—Alfred (6) and Rensselaer (6), Jan. 9, 1971

DIVISION II

Overtimes

MOST OVERTIME PERIODS
7—Yankton (79) vs. Black Hills (80), Feb. 18, 1956

MOST POINTS IN ONE OVERTIME PERIOD
27—Southern Ind. vs. Central Mo. St., Jan. 5, 1985

MOST POINTS IN ONE OVERTIME PERIOD, BOTH TEAMS
42—Southern Ind. (27) vs. Central Mo. St. (15), Jan. 5, 1985

MOST POINTS IN OVERTIME PERIODS
60—Calif. (Pa.) vs. Edinboro (5 ot), Feb. 4, 1989

MOST POINTS IN OVERTIME PERIODS, BOTH TEAMS
114—Calif. (Pa.) (60) vs. Edinboro (54) (5 ot), Feb. 4, 1989

LARGEST WINNING MARGIN IN OVERTIME GAME
22—Pfeiffer (72) vs. Belmont Abbey (50), Dec. 8, 1960

SEASON RECORDS

Scoring

MOST POINTS
3,566—Troy St., 1993 (32 games); Central Okla., 1992 (32 games)

HIGHEST AVERAGE PER GAME
121.1—Troy St., 1992 (3,513 in 29)

HIGHEST AVERAGE SCORING MARGIN
31.4—Bryan, 1961 (93.8 offense, 62.4 defense)

MOST GAMES AT LEAST 100 POINTS
25—Troy St., 1993 (32-game season)

MOST CONSECUTIVE GAMES AT LEAST 100 POINTS
17—Norfolk St., 1970

Field Goals

MOST FIELD GOALS
1,455—Kentucky St., 1971 (2,605 attempts)

MOST FIELD GOALS PER GAME
46.9—Lincoln (Mo.), 1967 (1,267 in 27)

MOST FIELD-GOAL ATTEMPTS
2,853—Ark.-Pine Bluff, 1967 (1,306 made)

MOST FIELD-GOAL ATTEMPTS PER GAME
108.2—Stillman, 1968 (2,814 in 26)

HIGHEST FIELD-GOAL PERCENTAGE
62.4%—Kentucky St., 1976 (1,093 of 1,753)

Three-Point Field Goals

MOST THREE-POINT FIELD GOALS
444—Troy St., 1992 (1,303 attempts)

MOST THREE-POINT FIELD GOALS PER GAME
15.3—Troy St., 1992 (444 in 29)

MOST THREE-POINT FIELD-GOAL ATTEMPTS
1,303—Troy St., 1992 (444 made)

MOST THREE-POINT FIELD-GOAL ATTEMPTS PER GAME
44.9—Troy St., 1992 (1,303 in 29)

HIGHEST THREE-POINT FIELD-GOAL PERCENTAGE
(Min. 90 made) 53.8%—Winston-Salem, 1988 (98 of 182)
(Min. 200 made) 50.2%—Oakland City, 1992 (244 of 486)

Free Throws

MOST FREE THROWS
896—Ouachita, 1965 (1,226 attempts)

MOST FREE THROWS PER GAME
36.1—Baltimore, 1955 (686 in 19)

MOST FREE-THROW ATTEMPTS
1,226—Ouachita, 1965 (896 made)

MOST FREE-THROW ATTEMPTS PER GAME
49.6—Baltimore, 1955 (943 in 19)

HIGHEST FREE-THROW PERCENTAGE
81.5%—South Ala., 1971 (422 of 518)

Rebounds

MOST REBOUNDS
1,667—Norfolk St., 1973 (31 games)

HIGHEST AVERAGE PER GAME
65.8—Bentley, 1964 (1,513 in 23)

HIGHEST AVERAGE REBOUND MARGIN
24.4—Mississippi Val., 1976 (63.9 offense, 39.5 defense)

Assists

MOST ASSISTS
736—New Hamp. Col., 1993 (33 games)

HIGHEST AVERAGE PER GAME
25.6—Quincy, 1994 (716 in 28)

Personal Fouls

MOST PERSONAL FOULS
947—Seattle, 1952 (37 games)

MOST PERSONAL FOULS PER GAME
29.9—Shaw, 1987 (748 in 25)

FEWEST PERSONAL FOULS
184—Sewanee, 1962 (17 games)

FEWEST PERSONAL FOULS PER GAME
10.0—Ashland, 1969 (301 in 30)

Defense

LOWEST POINTS PER GAME ALLOWED
20.2—Alcorn St., 1941 (323 in 16)

LOWEST POINTS PER GAME ALLOWED (Since 1948)
29.1—Miss. Industrial, 1948 (436 in 15)

LOWEST FIELD-GOAL PERCENTAGE ALLOWED (Since 1978)
35.9—Virginia Union, 1994 (705 of 1,966)

Overtimes

MOST OVERTIME GAMES
8—Belmont Abbey, 1983 (won 4, lost 4)

MOST CONSECUTIVE OVERTIME GAMES
3—Nine times, most recent: Cal St. Dom. Hills, 1994 (won 1, lost 2)

MOST MULTIPLE-OVERTIME GAMES
5—Cal St. Dom. Hills, 1987 (four 2 ot, one 3 ot; won 2, lost 3)

General Records

MOST GAMES IN A SEASON
39—Regis (Colo.), 1949 (36-3)

MOST VICTORIES IN A SEASON
36—Regis (Colo.), 1949 (36-3)

MOST VICTORIES IN A PERFECT SEASON
34—Fort Hays St., 1996

MOST CONSECUTIVE VICTORIES
52—Langston (from 1943-44 opener through fifth game of 1945-46 season)

MOST CONSECUTIVE HOME-COURT VICTORIES
79—Denver (from Feb. 12, 1980, to Jan. 8, 1985)

MOST CONSECUTIVE REGULAR-SEASON VICTORIES (Postseason Tournaments Not Included)
52—Langston (from 1943-44 opener through fifth game of 1945-46 season)

MOST DEFEATS IN A SEASON
27—Colorado Mines, 1992 (0-27); Bowie St., 1985 (1-27)

MOST CONSECUTIVE DEFEATS IN A SEASON
27—Colorado Mines, 1992 (0-27)

MOST CONSECUTIVE DEFEATS
46—Olivet, Feb. 21, 1959, to Dec. 4, 1961; Southwest St. (Minn.), Dec. 11, 1971, to Dec. 1, 1973

MOST CONSECUTIVE WINNING SEASONS
34—Norfolk St., 1963-96

MOST CONSECUTIVE NON-LOSING SEASONS
34—Norfolk St., 1963-96

††UNBEATEN TEAMS (Since 1938; Number Of Victories In Parentheses)
1938 Glenville St. (28)
1941 Milwaukee St. (16)
1942 Indianapolis (16)
1942 Rochester (16)
1944 Langston (23)
1945 Langston (24)
1948 West Va. St. (23)
1949 Tennessee St. (24)
1956 Rochester Inst. (17)
1959 Grand Canyon (20)
1961 Calvin (20)
1964 Bethany (W. Va.) (18)
1965 Central St. (Ohio) (30)
1965 Evansville (29)#
1993 Cal St. Bakersfield (33)#
1996 Fort Hays St. (34)#

††At least 15 victories. #NCAA Division II champion.

All-Time Individual Leaders

Single-Game Records

SCORING HIGHS

Pts.	Player, Team vs. Opponent	Season
113	Clarence "Bevo" Francis, Rio Grande vs. Hillsdale	1954
84	Clarence "Bevo" Francis, Rio Grande vs. Alliance	1954
82	Clarence "Bevo" Francis, Rio Grande vs. Bluffton	1954
80	Paul Crissman, Southern Cal. Col. vs. Pacific Christian	1966
77	William English, Winston-Salem vs. Fayetteville St.	1968
75	Travis Grant, Kentucky St. vs. Northwood	1970
72	Nate DeLong, Wis.-River Falls vs. Winona St.	1948
72	Lloyd Brown, Aquinas vs. Cleary	1953
72	Clarence "Bevo" Francis, Rio Grande vs. Calif. (Pa.)	1953
72	John McElroy, Youngstown St. vs. Wayne St. (Mich.)	1969
71	Clayborn Jones, L. A. Pacific vs. L. A. Baptist	1965
70	Paul Wilcox, Davis & Elkins vs. Glenville St.	1959
70	Bo Clark, Central Fla. vs. Fla. Memorial	1977

Season Records

SCORING AVERAGE

Player, Team	Season	G	FG	FT	Pts.	Avg.
Clarence "Bevo" Francis, Rio Grande	†1954	27	444	367	1,255	*46.5
Earl Glass, Miss. Industrial	†1963	19	322	171	815	42.9
Earl Monroe, Winston-Salem	†1967	32	509	311	*1,329	41.5
John Rinka, Kenyon	†1970	23	354	234	942	41.0
Willie Shaw, Lane	†1964	18	303	121	727	40.4
Travis Grant, Kentucky St.	†1972	33	*539	226	1,304	39.5
Thales McReynolds, Miles	†1965	18	294	118	706	39.2
Bob Johnson, Fitchburg St.	1963	18	213	277	703	39.1
Roger Kuss, Wis.-River Falls	†1953	21	291	235	817	38.9
Florindo Vieira, Quinnipiac	1954	14	191	138	520	37.1

†National champion. *Record.

FIELD-GOAL PERCENTAGE
(Based on qualifiers for annual championship)

Player, Team	Season	G	FG	FGA	Pct.
Todd Linder, Tampa	†1987	32	282	375	*75.2
Maurice Stafford, North Ala.	†1984	34	198	264	75.0
Matthew Cornegay, Tuskegee	†1982	29	208	278	74.8
Brian Moten, West Ga.	†1992	26	141	192	73.4
Ed Phillips, Alabama A&M	†1968	22	154	210	73.3
Ray Strozier, Central Mo. St.	†1980	28	142	195	72.8
Harold Booker, Cheyney	†1965	24	144	198	72.7
Chad Scott, Calif. (Pa.)	†1994	30	178	245	72.7
Tom Schurfranz, Bellarmine	†1991	30	245	339	72.3
Marv Lewis, LIU-Southampton	†1969	24	271	375	72.3
Louis Newsome, North Ala.	†1988	29	192	266	72.2
Ed Phillips, Alabama A&M	†1971	24	159	221	71.9
Gregg Northington, Alabama St.	1971	26	324	451	71.8

†National champion. *Record.

THREE-POINT FIELD GOALS MADE

Player, Team	Season	G	3FG
Alex Williams, Cal St. Sacramento	1988	30	167
Eric Kline, Northern St.	1995	30	148
Eric Kline, Northern St.	1994	33	148
Ray Gutierrez, Calif. (Pa.)	1993	27	135
Jason Garrow, Augustana (S.D.)	1992	27	135
Shawn Williams, Central Okla.	1991	29	129
Robert Martin, Cal St. Sacramento	1988	30	128
Tommie Spearman, Columbus	1995	29	126
Kwame Morton, Clarion	1994	26	126
Damien Blair, West Chester	1994	28	125
John Boyd, LeMoyne-Owen	1992	26	123
Stephen Hamrick, Eastern N.M.	1994	27	120
Duane Huddleston, Mo.-Rolla	1988	25	118
Robert Martin, Cal St. Sacramento	1989	28	118
Bill Harris, Northern Mich.	1987	27	117
Eric Carpenter, Cal St. San B'dino	1994	26	116
Mike Sinclair, Bowie St.	1988	28	115

THREE-POINT FIELD GOALS MADE PER GAME

Player, Team	Season	G	3FG	Avg.
Alex Williams, Cal St. Sacramento	†1988	30	*167	*5.6
Jason Garrow, Augustana (S.D.)	†1992	27	135	5.0
Eric Kline, Northern St.	†1995	30	148	4.9
Ray Gutierrez, Calif. (Pa.)	†1993	29	142	4.9
Kwame Morton, Clarion	†1994	26	126	4.8
John Boyd, LeMoyne-Owen	1992	26	123	4.7
Duane Huddleston, Mo.-Rolla	1988	25	118	4.7
Eric Kline, Northern St.	1994	33	148	4.5
Damien Blair, West Chester	1994	28	125	4.5
Eric Carpenter, Cal St. San B'dino	1994	26	116	4.5
Shawn Williams, Central Okla.	†1991	29	129	4.4
Stephen Hamrick, Eastern N.M.	1994	27	120	4.4
Tommie Spearman, Columbus St.	1995	29	126	4.3
Robert Martin, Cal St. Sacramento	1988	30	128	4.3
Bill Harris, Northern Mich.	†1987	27	117	4.3
Robert Martin, Cal St. Sacramento	†1989	28	118	4.2
Louis Smart, Tuskegee	1989	25	103	4.1
Kwame Morton, Clarion	1993	26	107	4.1
Mike Sinclair, Bowie St.	1988	28	115	4.1
Daren Alix, Merrimack	†1996	28	114	4.1
Andy Schmidtmann, Wis.-Parkside	1989	28	114	4.1
Scott Martin, Rollins	1991	28	114	4.1

†National champion. *Record.

THREE-POINT FIELD-GOAL PERCENTAGE
(Based on qualifiers for annual championship)

Player, Team	Season	G	3FG	3FGA	Pct.
Ray Lee, Hampton	†1988	24	39	60	*65.0
Steve Hood, Winston-Salem	1988	28	42	67	62.7
Mark Willey, Fort Hays St.	†1990	29	49	81	60.5
Aaron Fehler, Oakland City	†1995	26	73	121	60.3
Aaron Baker, Mississippi Col.	†1989	27	69	117	59.0
Walter Hurd, Johnson Smith	1989	27	49	84	58.3
Matt Hopson, Oakland City	†1996	31	84	145	57.9
Jon Bryant, St. Cloud St.	1996	27	54	94	57.4
Scott Martin, Rollins	†1991	28	114	201	56.7
Charles Byrd, West Tex. A&M	†1987	31	95	168	56.5
Jay Nolan, Bowie St.	1987	27	70	124	56.5
Kris Kidwell, Oakland City	1996	28	44	78	56.4
Tony Harris, Dist. Columbia	1987	30	79	141	56.0
Rickey Barrett, Ala.-Huntsville	1987	26	63	113	55.8
Quinn Murphy, Drury	1995	27	45	81	55.6
Erik Fisher, San Fran. St.	1991	28	80	144	55.6
Mike Doyle, Phila. Textile	1988	30	82	149	55.0

†National champion. *Record.

FREE-THROW PERCENTAGE
(Based on qualifiers for annual championship)

Player, Team	Season	G	FT	FTA	Pct.
Billy Newton, Morgan St.	†1976	28	85	90	*94.4
Kent Andrews, McNeese St.	†1968	24	85	90	*94.4
Mike Sanders, Northern Colo.	†1987	28	82	87	94.3
Jay Harrie, Mont. St.-Billings	†1994	26	86	92	93.5
Joe Cullen, Hartwick	†1969	18	96	103	93.2
Charles Byrd, West Tex. A&M	†1988	29	92	99	92.9
Brian Koephick, Mankato St.	1988	28	104	112	92.9
Jon Hagen, Mankato St.	1963	25	76	82	92.7
Paul Cluxton, Northern Ky.	†1996	32	100	108	92.6
Jim Borodawka, Mass.-Lowell	†1995	27	74	80	92.5
Carl Gonder, Augustana (S.D.)	†1982	27	86	93	92.5
Hal McManus, Lander	†1992	28	110	119	92.4
Terry Gill, New Orleans	†1974	30	97	105	92.4
Emery Sammons, Phila. Textile	†1977	28	145	157	92.4

†National champion. *Record.

REBOUND AVERAGE

Player, Team	Season	G	Reb.	Avg.
Tom Hart, Middlebury	†1956	21	620	*29.5
Tom Hart, Middlebury	†1955	22	649	29.5
Frank Stronczek, American Int'l	†1966	26	717	27.6
R. C. Owens, College of Idaho	†1954	25	677	27.1
Maurice Stokes, St. Francis (Pa.)	1954	26	689	26.5
Roman Turmon, Clark Atlanta	1954	23	602	26.2
Pat Callahan, Lewis	1955	20	523	26.2
Hank Brown, Lowell Tech	1966	19	496	26.1
Maurice Stokes, St. Francis (Pa.)	1955	28	726	25.9

†National champion. *Record.

ASSISTS

Player, Team	Season	G	Ast.
Steve Ray, Bridgeport	†1989	32	*400
Steve Ray, Bridgeport	†1990	33	385

Player, Team	Season	G	Ast.
Tony Smith, Pfeiffer	†1992	35	349
Rob Paternostro, New Hamp. Col.	1995	33	309
Jim Ferrer, Bentley	1989	31	309
Brian Gregory, Oakland	1989	28	300
Charles Jordan, Erskine	1992	34	298
Ernest Jenkins, N.M. Highlands	†1995	27	291
Pat Chambers, Phila. Textile	1994	30	290
Craig Lottie, Alabama A&M	1995	32	287
Adrian Hutt, Metro St.	†1991	28	285
Patrick Boen, Stonehill	1989	32	278
Ernest Jenkins, N.M. Highlands	†1994	27	277
Darnell White, Calif. (Pa.)	1994	30	273
Demetri Beekman, Assumption	1992	32	271
Tyrone Tate, Southern Ind.	1994	32	270
Gallagher Driscoll, St. Rose	1991	29	267

†National champion. *Record.

ASSIST AVERAGE

Player, Team	Season	G	Ast.	Avg.
Steve Ray, Bridgeport	†1989	32	*400	*12.5
Steve Ray, Bridgeport	†1990	33	385	11.7
Demetri Beekman, Assumption	†1993	23	264	11.5
Ernest Jenkins, N.M. Highlands	†1995	27	291	10.8
Brian Gregory, Oakland	1989	28	300	10.7
Brent Schremp, Slippery Rock	1995	25	259	10.4
Ernest Jenkins, N.M. Highlands	†1994	27	277	10.3
Adrian Hutt, Metro St.	†1991	28	285	10.2
Tony Smith, Pfeiffer	†1992	35	349	10.0
Jim Ferrer, Bentley	1989	31	309	10.0
Pat Chambers, Phila. Textile	1994	30	290	9.7
Marcus Talbert, Colo. Christian	1994	27	261	9.7
Paul Beaty, Miles	1992	26	248	9.5
Lawrence Jordan, IU/PU-Ft. Wayne	1990	28	266	9.5
Hal Chambers, Columbus St.	1993	24	227	9.5
Rob Paternostro, New Hamp. Col.	1995	33	309	9.4
Gallagher Driscoll, St. Rose	1991	29	267	9.2
David Daniels, Colo. Christian	1993	29	264	9.1
Darnell White, Calif. (Pa.)	1994	30	273	9.1

†National champion. *Record.

BLOCKED SHOTS

Player, Team	Season	G	Blk.
Antonio Harvey, Pfeiffer	†1993	29	*155
John Burke, LIU-Southampton	†1996	28	142
Vonzell McGrew, Mo. Western St.	†1995	31	132
Corey Johnson, Pace	1995	30	130
Johnny Tyson, Central Okla.	†1994	27	126
Kino Outlaw, Mount Olive	1995	28	124
Kino Outlaw, Mount Olive	1996	27	117
Ben Wallace, Virginia Union	1996	31	114
Mark Hensel, Pitt.-Johnstown	1994	27	113
Ben Wallace, Virginia Union	1995	31	111
Elwood Vines, Bloomsburg	1993	27	107
Horacio Llamas, Grand Canyon	1996	29	106
Coata Malone, Alabama A&M	1995	32	106
Eugene Haith, Phila. Textile	1993	31	105

†National champion. *Record.

BLOCKED-SHOT AVERAGE

Player, Team	Season	G	Blk.	Avg.
Antonio Harvey, Pfeiffer	†1993	29	*155	*5.34
John Burke, LIU-Southampton	†1996	28	142	5.07
Johnny Tyson, Central Okla.	†1994	27	126	4.66
Kino Outlaw, Mount Olive	†1995	28	124	4.43
Kino Outlaw, Mount Olive	1996	27	117	4.33
Corey Johnson, Pace	1995	30	130	4.33
Vonzell McGrew, Mo. Western St.	1995	31	132	4.26
Mark Hensel, Pitt.-Johnstown	1994	27	113	4.19
Victorius Payne, Lane	1996	25	101	4.04
Elwood Vines, Bloomsburg	1993	27	107	3.96
Lawrence Williams, San Fran. St.	1995	27	103	3.81
Derek Moore, S.C.-Aiken	1996	26	97	3.73
Ben Wallace, Virginia Union	1996	31	114	3.68
Horacio Llamas, Grand Canyon	1996	29	106	3.66
Marcellus Stiede, Emporia St.	1993	27	97	3.59

†National champion. *Record.

STEALS

Player, Team	Season	G	Stl.
David Clark, Bluefield St.	†1996	31	*118
Tyrone McDaniel, Lenoir-Rhyne	†1993	32	116

Player, Team	Season	G	Stl.
Ken Francis, Molloy	†1994	27	116
Darnell White, Calif. (Pa.)	1994	30	115
Marcus Stubblefield, Queens (N.C.)	1993	28	110
Shannon Holmes, New York Tech	†1995	30	110
Craig Ferguson, Columbus St.	1996	32	107
John Morris, Bluefield St.	1994	23	104
Kevin Nichols, Bemidji St.	1994	26	104
Rudy Berry, Cal St. Stanislaus	1993	28	100
Alex Wright, Central Okla.	1993	28	100
Jesse White, Fla. Southern	1993	32	99

†National champion. *Record.

STEAL AVERAGE

Player, Team	Season	G	Stl.	Avg.
John Morris, Bluefield St.	1994	23	104	*4.52
Ken Francis, Molloy	†1994	27	116	4.29
Kevin Nichols, Bemidji St.	1994	26	104	4.00
Marcus Stubblefield, Queens (N.C.)	1993	28	110	3.93
Demetri Beekman, Assumption	1993	23	89	3.87
Darnell White, Calif. (Pa.)	1994	30	115	3.83
David Clark, Bluefield St.	†1996	31	*118	3.81
Shannon Holmes, New York Tech	†1995	30	110	3.66
Tyrone McDaniel, Lenoir-Rhyne	†1993	32	116	3.63
Patrick Herron, Winston-Salem	1994	27	97	3.59
Rudy Berry, Cal St. Stanislaus	1993	28	100	3.57
Alex Wright, Central Okla.	1993	28	100	3.57

†National champion. *Record.

Career Records

POINTS

Player, Team	Seasons	Pts.
Travis Grant, Kentucky St.	1969-72	*4,045
Bob Hopkins, Grambling	1953-56	3,759
Tony Smith, Pfeiffer	1989-92	3,350
Earnest Lee, Clark Atlanta	1984-87	3,298
Joe Miller, Alderson-Broaddus	1954-57	3,294
Henry Logan, Western Caro.	1965-68	3,290
John Rinka, Kenyon	1967-70	3,251
Dick Barnett, Tennessee St.	1956-59	3,209
Willie Scott, Alabama St.	1966-69	3,155
Johnnie Allen, Bethune-Cookman	1966-69	3,058
Bennie Swain, Texas Southern	1955-58	3,008
Lambert Shell, Bridgeport	1989-92	3,001
Carl Hartman, Alderson-Broaddus	1952-55	2,959
Earl Monroe, Winston-Salem	1964-67	2,935

*Record.

SCORING AVERAGE
(Minimum 1,400 points)

Player, Team	Seasons	G	FG	3FG	FT	Pts.	Avg.
Travis Grant, Kentucky St.	1969-72	121	*1,760	—	525	*4,045	*33.4
John Rinka, Kenyon	1967-70	99	1,261	—	729	3,251	32.8
Florindo Vieira, Quinnipiac	1954-57	69	761	—	741	2,263	32.8
Willie Shaw, Lane	1961-64	76	960	—	459	2,379	31.3
Mike Davis, Virginia Union	1966-69	89	1,014	—	730	2,758	31.0
Henry Logan, Western Caro.	1965-68	107	1,263	—	764	3,290	30.7
Willie Scott, Alabama St.	1966-69	103	1,277	—	601	3,155	30.6
George Gilmore, Chaminade	1991-92	51	485	174	387	1,531	30.0
Brett Beeson, Moorhead St.	1995-96	54	551	92	421	1,615	29.9
Bob Hopkins, Grambling	1953-56	126	1,403	—	953	3,759	29.8
Rod Butler, Western New Eng.	1968-70	59	697	—	331	1,725	29.2
Gregg Northington, Alabama St.	1970-72	75	894	—	403	2,191	29.2
Isaiah Wilson, Baltimore	1969-71	67	731	—	471	1,933	28.9

*Record.

FIELD-GOAL PERCENTAGE
(Minimum 400 field goals made)

Player, Team	Seasons	G	FG	FGA	Pct.
Todd Linder, Tampa	1984-87	122	909	1,284	*70.8
Tom Schurfranz, Bellarmine	1987-88, 91-92	112	742	1,057	70.2
Chad Scott, Calif. (Pa.)	1991-94	115	465	664	70.0
Ed Phillips, Alabama A&M	1968-71	95	610	885	68.9
Ulysses Hackett, S.C.-Spartanburg	1990-92	90	824	1,213	67.9
Larry Tucker, Lewis	1981-83	84	677	999	67.8
Otis Evans, Wayne St. (Mich.)	1989-92	106	472	697	67.7
Matthew Cornegay, Tuskegee	1979-82	105	524	783	66.9
Ray Strozier, Central Mo. St.	1978-81	110	563	843	66.8
Dennis Edwards, Fort Hays St.	1994-95	59	666	998	66.7

Player, Team	Seasons	G	FG	FGA	Pct.
James Morris, Central Okla.	1990-93	76	532	798	66.7
Lance Berwald, North Dak. St.	1983-84	58	475	717	66.2
Harold Booker, Cheyney	1965-67, 69	108	662	1,002	66.1

*Record.

THREE-POINT FIELD GOALS MADE

Player, Team	Seasons	G	3FG
Tony Smith, Pfeiffer	1989-92	126	*431
Kwame Morton, Clarion	1991-94	105	411
Gary Duda, Merrimack	1989-92	122	389
Columbus Parker, Johnson Smith	1990-93	115	354
Gary Paul, Indianapolis	1987-90	111	354
Mike Ziegler, Colorado Mines	1987-90	118	344
Chris Brown, Tuskegee	1993-96	104	339
Stephen Hamrick, Eastern N.M.	1993-96	107	339
Brent Kincaid, Calif. (Pa.)	1993-96	115	325
Jon Cronin, Stonehill	1989-92	117	308
Wil Pierce, Western St.	1993-96	114	307
Bryan Williams, Tampa	1988-91	123	303
Brendan McCarthy, St. Anselm	1993-96	120	300
Steve Schieppe, Truman St.	1988-91	105	300
Mike Sinclair, Bowie St.	1987-89	82	299
Kevin McCarthy, New Hamp. Col.	1989-92	117	297
Mike Lake, Hillsdale	1992-95	106	294
Robert Martin, Cal St. Sacramento	1987-89	85	294

*Record.

THREE-POINT FIELD GOALS MADE PER GAME
(Minimum 200 three-point field goals made)

Player, Team	Seasons	G	3FG	Avg.
Alex Williams, Cal St. Sacramento	1987-88	58	247	*4.26
Tommie Spearman, Columbus St.	1994-95	56	233	4.16
Kwame Morton, Clarion	1991-94	105	411	3.91
Zoderick Green, Central Okla.	1993-95	57	212	3.72
Shawn Williams, Central Okla.	1989-91	57	212	3.72
Mike Sinclair, Bowie St.	1987-89	82	299	3.65
Robert Martin, Cal St. Sacramento	1987-89	85	294	3.46
Tony Smith, Pfeiffer	1989-92	126	*431	3.42
Chris Brown, Tuskegee	1993-96	104	339	3.26
Gary Paul, Indianapolis	1987-90	111	354	3.19
Gary Duda, Merrimack	1989-92	122	389	3.19
Stephen Hamrick, Eastern N.M.	1993-96	107	339	3.17
Rod Harris, LIU-Southampton	1987-89	78	241	3.09
Columbus Parker, Johnson Smith	1990-93	115	354	3.08

*Record.

THREE-POINT FIELD-GOAL PERCENTAGE
(Minimum 200 three-point field goals made)

Player, Team	Seasons	G	3FG	3FGA	Pct.
Scott Martin, Rollins	1988-91	104	236	460	*51.3
Matt Markle, Shippensburg	1989-92	101	202	408	49.5
Lance Gelnett, Millersville	1989-92	109	266	547	48.6
Mark Willey, Fort Hays St.	1989-92	117	224	478	46.9
Todd Bowden, Randolph-Macon	1987-89	84	229	491	46.6
Gary Paul, Indianapolis	1987-90	111	354	768	46.1
Matt Ripaldi, New Hamp. Col.	1993-96	123	277	604	45.9
Alex Williams, Cal St. Sacramento	1987-88	58	247	541	45.7
Jason Bullock, Indiana (Pa.)	1993-96	119	287	637	45.1
Boyd Printy, Truman St.	1990-92	77	201	447	45.0
Lance Luitjens, Northern St.	1994-96	95	275	614	44.8
Buck Williams, North Ala.	1987-89	84	238	535	44.5

*Record.

FREE-THROW PERCENTAGE
(Minimum 250 free throws made)

Player, Team	Seasons	G	FT	FTA	Pct.
Kent Andrews, McNeese St.	1967-69	67	252	275	*91.6
Jon Hagen, Mankato St.	1963-65	73	252	280	90.0
Dave Reynolds, Davis & Elkins	1986-89	107	383	429	89.3
Tony Budzik, Mansfield	1989-92	107	367	416	88.2
Terry Gill, New Orleans	1972-74	79	261	296	88.2
Bryan Vacca, Randolph-Macon	1980-83	94	262	298	87.9
Steve Nisenson, Hofstra	1963-65	83	602	685	87.9
Jeff Gore, St. Rose	1991-93	91	333	379	87.9
Jack Sparks, Bentley	1976-80	99	253	288	87.8
Wayne Profitt, Lynchburg	1965-67	57	482	551	87.5
Clyde Briley, McNeese St.	1962-65	101	561	642	87.4
Foy Ballance, Armstrong Atlantic	1978-81	108	351	402	87.3
Jehu Brabham, Mississippi Col.	1969-71	72	452	518	87.3
Pete Chambers, West Chester	1966-68	67	267	306	87.3

*Record.

REBOUND AVERAGE
(Minimum 900 rebounds)

Player, Team	Seasons	G	Reb.	Avg.
Tom Hart, Middlebury	1953, 55-56	63	1,738	*27.6
Maurice Stokes, St. Francis (Pa.)	1953-55	72	1,812	25.2
Frank Stronczek, American Int'l	1965-67	62	1,549	25.0
Bill Thieben, Hofstra	1954-56	76	1,837	24.2
Hank Brown, Lowell Tech	1965-67	49	1,129	23.0
Elmore Smith, Kentucky St.	1969-71	85	1,917	22.6
Charles Wrinn, Trinity (Conn.)	1951-53	53	1,176	22.2
Roman Turmon, Clark Atlanta	1952-54	60	1,312	21.9
Tony Missere, Pratt	1966-68	62	1,348	21.7
Ron Horton, Delaware St.	1966-68	64	1,384	21.6

*Record.

ASSISTS

Player, Team	Seasons	G	Ast.
Demetri Beekman, Assumption	1990-93	119	*1,044
Rob Paternostro, New Hamp. Col.	1992-95	129	919
Gallagher Driscoll, St. Rose	1989-92	121	878
Tony Smith, Pfeiffer	1989-92	126	828
Steve Ray, Bridgeport	1989-90	65	785
Dan Ward, St. Cloud St.	1992-95	100	774
Charles Jordan, Erskine	1989-92	119	727
Patrick Chambers, Phila. Textile	1991-94	123	709
Lamont Jones, Bridgeport	1992-95	119	708
Ernest Jenkins, N.M. Highlands	1992-95	84	699
Pat Madden, Jacksonville St.	1989-91	88	688
Candice Pickens, Calif. (Pa.)	1993-96	121	675
Mark Benson, Tex. A&M-Kingsville	1989-91	86	674
Craig Lottie, Alabama A&M	1992-95	93	673
Warren Burgess, St. Anselm	1991-94	117	662
Willis Cheaney, Ky. Wesleyan	1992-95	114	635
Tom Quinlan, Bentley	1991-94	112	633
Mike Buscetto, Quinnipiac	1990-93	99	624
Patrick Herron, Winston-Salem	1992-95	97	604
Orlando Vandross, American Int'l	1989-92	111	597

*Record.

ASSIST AVERAGE
(Minimum 550 assists)

Player, Team	Seasons	G	Ast.	Avg.
Steve Ray, Bridgeport	1989-90	65	785	*12.1
Demetri Beekman, Assumption	1990-93	119	1,044	8.8
Ernest Jenkins, N.M. Highlands	1992-95	84	699	8.3
Mark Benson, Tex. A&M-Kingsville	1989-91	86	674	7.8
Pat Madden, Jacksonville St.	1989-91	88	688	7.8
Dan Ward, St. Cloud St.	1992-95	100	774	7.7
Gallagher Driscoll, St. Rose	1989-92	121	*878	7.3
Craig Lottie, Alabama A&M	1992-95	93	673	7.2
Rob Paternostro, New Hamp. Col.	1992-95	129	919	7.1
Tony Smith, Pfeiffer	1989-92	126	828	6.6
Mike Buscetto, Quinnipiac	1990-93	99	624	6.3
Patrick Herron, Winston-Salem	1992-95	97	604	6.2
Charles Jordan, Erskine	1989-92	119	727	6.1

*Record.

BLOCKED SHOTS

Player, Team	Seasons	G	Blk.
Kino Outlaw, Mount Olive	1994-96	81	305
Kerwin Thompson, Eckerd	1993-96	116	284
Eugene Haith, Phila. Textile	1993-95	86	267
Coata Malone, Alabama A&M	1994-96	90	243
Ben Wallace, Virginia Union	1995-96	62	225
Vonzell McGrew, Mo. Western St.	1993-95	57	211
Corey Johnson, Pace	1993-95	58	210
John Burke, LIU-Southampton	1995-96	54	205
Adrian Machado, Stonehill	1993-96	108	196
Tihomir Juric, Wis.-Parkside	1993-94	53	193
John Skokan, Neb.-Omaha	1993-96	106	185
Mark Hensel, Pitt.-Johnstown	1993-94	53	180
Garth Joseph, St. Rose#	1995-96	55	176
Lawrence Williams, San Fran. St.	1993-95	79	176
Yogi Leo, Queens (N.C.)	1994-96	83	175
Horacio Llamas, Grand Canyon	1995-96	57	172
James Doyle, Concord#	1995-96	59	166
Alonzo Goldston, Fort Hays St.#	1995-96	65	161
Antonio Harvey, Pfeiffer	1993	29	155

#Active player.

DIVISION II

BLOCKED-SHOT AVERAGE
(Minimum 175 blocked shots)

Player, Team	Seasons	G	Blk.	Avg.
John Burke, LIU-Southampton	1995-96	54	205	3.80
Kino Outlaw, Mount Olive	1994-96	81	305	3.77
Vonzell McGrew, Mo. Western St.	1993-95	57	211	3.70
Tihomir Juric, Wis.-Parkside	1993-94	53	193	3.64
Ben Wallace, Virginia Union	1995-96	62	225	3.63
Corey Johnson, Pace	1993-95	58	210	3.62
Mark Hensel, Pitt.-Johnstown	1993-94	53	180	3.40
Eugene Haith, Phila. Textile	1993-95	86	267	3.10
Coata Malone, Alabama A&M	1994-96	90	243	2.70
Kerwin Thompson, Eckerd	1993-96	116	284	2.45
Lawrence Williams, San Fran. St.	1993-95	79	176	2.23

STEALS

Player, Team	Seasons	G	Stl.
David Clark, Bluefield St.	1994-96	83	278
Patrick Herron, Winston-Salem	1993-95	78	263
Ken Francis, Molloy	1993-95	81	260
Lamont Jones, Bridgeport	1993-95	84	256
Deartrus Goodmon, Alabama A&M	1993-96	126	255
Orron Brown, Clarion#	1994-96	77	241
Marlon Lindsey, New York Tech	1993-96	109	237
Craig Lottie, Alabama A&M	1993-95	93	226
Candice Pickens, Calif. (Pa.)	1993-96	121	216
Shannon Holmes, New York Tech	1994-96	78	203
Spencer Staggs, Mass.-Lowell	1993-95	83	200
Steve Alston, Phila. Textile	1993-96	106	195
Darnell White, Calif. (Pa.)	1993-94	59	192
Craig Fergeson, Columbus St.	1995-96	61	191
Hassan Robinson, Springfield	1993-95	77	188
Willis Cheaney, Ky. Wesleyan	1993-95	83	187
John Morris, Bluefield St.	1994-95	50	185

#Active player.

STEAL AVERAGE
(Minimum 150 steals)

Player, Team	Seasons	G	Stl.	Avg.
John Morris, Bluefield St.	1994-95	50	185	3.70
Patrick Herron, Winston-Salem	1993-95	78	263	3.37
David Clark, Bluefield St.	1994-96	83	278	3.35
Darnell White, Calif. (Pa.)	1993-94	59	192	3.25
Rudy Berry, Cal St. Stanislaus	1993-94	51	164	3.21
Ken Francis, Molloy	1993-95	81	260	3.21
Bob Cunningham, New York Tech	1995-96	55	175	3.18
Craig Fergeson, Columbus St.	1995-96	61	191	3.13

Brett Beeson became the first player from Moorhead State to lead Division II in scoring average as he registered 33.3 points per contest in 1996. Beeson, who compiled 900 points in 27 games, posted the highest-scoring average in Division II since 1989 when A. J. English of Virginia Union averaged 33.4 points per game.

Photo from Moorhead State sports information

Player, Team	Seasons	G	Stl.	Avg.
Bryan Heaps, Abilene Christian	1993-94	56	171	3.05
Lamont Jones, Bridgeport	1993-95	84	256	3.05
Malcolm Turner, Sonoma St.	1995-96	52	152	2.92
Tullius Pate, Coker	1994-95	55	158	2.87
Aaron Johnson, LIU-C. W. Post	1993-94	56	160	2.86
Shannon Holmes, New York Tech	1994-96	78	203	2.60
Hassan Robinson, Springfield	1993-95	77	188	2.44
Craig Lottie, Alabama A&M	1993-95	93	226	2.43

Annual Individual Champions

Scoring Average

Season	Player, Team	G	FG	FT	Pts.	Avg.
1948	Nate DeLong, Wis.-River Falls	22	206	206	618	28.1
1949	George King, Charleston (W.Va.)	26	289	179	757	29.1
1950	George King, Charleston (W.Va.)	31	354	259	967	31.2
1951	Scott Seagall, Millikin	31	314	260	888	28.6
1952	Harold Wolfe, Findlay	22	285	101	671	30.5
1953	Roger Kuss, Wis.-River Falls	21	291	235	817	38.9
1954	Clarence "Bevo" Francis, Rio Grande	27	444	367	1,255	*46.5
1955	Bill Warden, North Central	13	162	127	451	34.7
1956	Bill Reigel, McNeese St.	36	425	370	1,220	33.9
1957	Ken Hammond, West Va. Tech	27	334	274	942	34.9
1958	John Lee Butcher, Pikeville	27	330	210	870	32.2
1959	Paul Wilcox, Davis & Elkins	23	289	195	773	33.6
1960	Don Perrelli, Southern Conn. St.	22	263	168	694	31.5
1961	Lebron Bell, Bryan	14	174	114	462	33.0
1962	Willie Shaw, Lane	18	239	115	593	32.9
1963	Earl Glass, Miss. Industrial	19	322	171	815	42.9
1964	Willie Shaw, Lane	18	303	121	727	40.4
1965	Thales McReynolds, Miles	18	294	118	706	39.2
1966	Paul Crissman, Southern Cal College	23	373	90	836	36.3
1967	Earl Monroe, Winston-Salem	32	509	311	*1,329	41.5
1968	Mike Davis, Virginia Union	25	351	206	908	36.3
1969	John Rinka, Kenyon	26	340	202	882	33.9
1970	John Rinka, Kenyon	23	354	234	942	41.0
1971	Bo Lamar, Southwestern La.	29	424	196	1,044	36.0
1972	Travis Grant, Kentucky St.	33	*539	226	1,304	39.5
1973	Claude White, Elmhurst	18	248	101	597	33.2
1974	Aaron James, Grambling	27	366	137	869	32.2
1975	Ron Barrow, Southern U.	23	296	115	707	30.7
1976	Ron Barrow, Southern U.	27	318	136	772	28.6
1977	Ed Murphy, Merrimack	28	369	158	896	32.0
1978	Harold Robertson, Lincoln (Mo.)	28	408	149	965	34.5
1979	Bo Clark, Central Fla.	23	315	97	727	31.6
1980	Bill Fennelly, Central Mo. St.	28	337	189	863	30.8
1981	Gregory Jackson, St. Paul's	26	267	183	717	27.6
1982	John Ebeling, Fla. Southern	32	286	284	856	26.8
1983	Danny Dixon, Alabama A&M	27	379	152	910	33.7
1984	Earl Jones, Dist. Columbia	22	215	200	630	28.6
1985	Earnest Lee, Clark Atlanta	29	380	230	990	34.1
1986	Earnest Lee, Clark Atlanta	28	314	191	819	29.3

Season	Player, Team	G	FG	3FG	FT	Pts.	Avg.
1987	Earnest Lee, Clark Atlanta	29	326	35	174	861	29.7
1988	Daryl Cambrelen, LIU-Southampton	25	242	32	170	686	27.4
1989	Steve deLaveaga, Cal Lutheran	28	278	79	151	786	28.1
1990	A. J. English, Virginia Union	30	333	65	270	1,001	33.4
1991	Gary Mattison, St. Augustine's	26	277	53	159	766	29.5
1992	George Gilmore, Chaminade	28	280	82	238	880	31.4
1993	Darrin Robinson, Sacred Heart	26	313	75	130	831	32.0
1994	Kwame Mortin, Clarion	26	264	126	191	845	32.5
1995	Carlos Knox, IU/PU-Indianapolis	29	284	39	218	825	28.4
1996	Brett Beeson, Moorhead St.	27	305	58	232	900	33.3

*Record.

Field-Goal Percentage

Season	Player, Team	G	FG	FGA	Pct.
1949	Vern Mikkelson, Hamline	30	203	377	53.8
1950	Nate DeLong, Wis.-River Falls	29	287	492	58.3
1951	Johnny O'Brien, Seattle	33	248	434	57.1
1952	Forrest Hamilton, Southwest Mo. St.	30	147	246	59.8
1953	Bob Buis, Carleton	21	149	246	60.6
1954	Paul Lauritzen, Augustana (Ill.)	19	158	251	62.9

Season	Player, Team	G	FG	FGA	Pct.
1955	Jim O'Hara, UC Santa Barb.	24	140	214	65.4
1956	Logan Gipe, Ky. Wesleyan	22	134	224	59.8
1957	John Wilfred, Winston-Salem	30	229	381	60.1
1958	Bennie Swain, Texas Southern	35	363	587	61.8
1959	Dick O'Meara, Babson	18	144	225	64.0
1960	Edwin Cox, Howard Payne	26	126	194	64.9
1961	Tony Solomon, St. Paul's	20	94	149	63.1
1962	Tom Morris, St. Paul's	17	108	168	64.3
1963	Howard Trice, Howard Payne	26	168	237	70.9
1964	Robert Springer, Howard Payne	24	119	174	68.4
1965	Harold Booker, Cheyney	24	144	198	72.7
1966	Harold Booker, Cheyney	27	170	240	70.8
1967	John Dickson, Arkansas St.	24	214	308	69.5
1968	Edward Phillips, Alabama A&M	22	154	210	73.3
1969	Marvin Lewis, LIU-Southampton	24	271	375	72.3
1970	Travis Grant, Kentucky St.	31	482	688	70.1
1971	Edward Phillips, Alabama A&M	24	159	221	71.9
1972	Don Manley, Otterbein	23	146	207	70.5
1973	Glynn Berry, LIU-Southampton	26	191	302	63.2
1974	Kirby Thurston, Western Caro.	25	242	367	65.9
1975	Gerald Cunningham, Kentucky St.	29	280	411	68.1
1976	Thomas Blue, Elizabeth City St.	24	270	388	69.6
1977	Kelvin Hicks, New York Tech	24	161	232	69.4
1978	Ron Ripley, Wis.-Green Bay	32	162	239	67.8
1979	Carl Bailey, Tuskegee	27	210	307	68.4
1980	Ray Strozier, Central Mo. St.	28	142	195	72.8
1981	Matthew Cornegay, Tuskegee	26	177	247	71.7
1982	Matthew Cornegay, Tuskegee	29	208	278	74.8
1983	Rudy Burton, Elizabeth City St.	24	142	201	70.6
1984	Maurice Stafford, North Ala.	34	198	264	75.0
1985	Todd Linder, Tampa	31	219	306	71.6
1986	Todd Linder, Tampa	28	204	291	70.1
1987	Todd Linder, Tampa	32	282	375	*75.2
1988	Louis Newsome, North Ala.	29	192	266	72.2
1989	Tom Schurfranz, Bellarmine	28	164	240	68.2
1990	Ulysses Hackett, S.C.-Spartanburg	32	301	426	70.7
1991	Tom Schurfranz, Bellarmine	30	245	339	72.3
1992	Brian Moten, West Ga.	26	141	192	73.4
1993	Chad Scott, Calif. (Pa.)	28	173	245	70.6
1994	Chad Scott, Calif. (Pa.)	30	178	245	72.7
1995	John Pruett, SIU-Edwardsville	26	138	193	71.5
1996	Kyle Kirby, IU/PU-Ft. Wayne	26	133	195	68.2

*Record.

Three-Point Field Goals Made Per Game

Season	Player, Team	G	3FG	Avg.
1987	Bill Harris, Northern Mich.	27	117	4.3
1988	Alex Williams, Cal St. Sacramento	30	*167	*5.6
1989	Robert Martin, Cal St. Sacramento	28	118	4.2
1990	Gary Paul, Indianapolis	28	110	3.9
1991	Shawn Williams, Central Okla.	29	129	4.4
1992	Jason Garrow, Augustana (S.D.)	27	135	5.0
1993	Ray Gutierrez, Calif. (Pa.)	29	142	4.9
1994	Kwame Morton, Clarion	26	126	4.8
1995	Eric Kline, Northern St.	30	148	4.9
1996	Daren Alix, Merrimack	28	114	4.1

*Record.

Three-Point Field-Goal Percentage

Season	Player, Team	G	3FG	3FGA	Pct.
1987	Charles Byrd, West Tex. A&M	31	95	168	56.5
1988	Ray Lee, Hampton	24	39	60	*65.0
1989	Aaron Baker, Mississippi Col.	27	69	117	59.0
1990	Mark Willey, Fort Hays St.	29	49	81	60.5
1991	Scott Martin, Rollins	28	114	201	56.7
1992	Jeff Duvall, Oakland City	30	49	91	53.8
1993	Greg Wilkinson, Oakland City	32	82	152	53.9
1994	Todd Jones, Southern Ind.	29	56	105	53.3
1995	Aaron Fehler, Oakland City	26	73	121	60.3
1996	Matt Hopson, Oakland City	31	84	145	57.9

*Record.

Free-Throw Percentage

Season	Player, Team	G	FT	FTA	Pct.
1948	Frank Cochran, Delta St.	22	36	43	83.7
1949	Jim Walsh, Spring Hill	25	62	75	82.7
1950	Dean Ehlers, Central Methodist	33	186	213	87.3
1951	Jim Hoverder, Central Mo. St.	23	75	85	88.2
1952	Jim Fenton, Akron	24	104	121	86.0
1953	Dick Parfitt, Central Mich.	22	93	105	88.6
1954	Bill Parrott, David Lipscomb	24	174	198	87.9
1955	Pete Kovacs, Monmouth (Ill.)	20	175	199	87.9
1956	Fred May, Loras	22	127	146	87.0
1957	Jim Sutton, South Dak. St.	22	127	138	92.0
1958	Arnold Smith, Allen	22	103	113	91.2
1959	Bill Reece, Lenoir-Rhyne	27	84	92	91.3
1960	Ron Slaymaker, Emporia St.	20	80	88	90.9
1961	Harvey Rosen, Wilkes	22	105	115	91.3
1962	Wayne Mahone, Stephen F. Austin	26	76	84	90.5
1963	Jon Hagen, Mankato St.	25	76	82	92.7
1964	Steve Nisenson, Hofstra	28	230	252	91.3
1965	Jon Hagen, Mankato St.	23	103	112	92.0
1966	Jack Cryan, Rider	25	182	198	91.9
1967	Kent Andrews, McNeese St.	22	101	110	91.8
1968	Kent Andrews, McNeese St.	24	85	90	*94.4
1969	Joe Cullen, Hartwick	18	96	103	93.2
1970	John Rinka, Kenyon	23	234	263	89.0
1971	Ed Roeth, Defiance	26	138	152	90.8
1972	Jeff Kuntz, St. Norbert	25	142	155	91.6
1973	Bob Kronisch, Brooklyn	30	93	105	88.6
1974	Terry Gill, New Orleans	30	97	105	92.4
1975	Clarence Rand, Alabama St.	29	91	101	90.1
1976	Billy Newton, Morgan St.	28	85	90	*94.4
1977	Emery Sammons, Phila. Textile	28	145	157	92.4
1978	Dana Skinner, Merrimack	28	142	154	92.2
1979	Jack Sparks, Bentley	28	76	84	90.5
1980	Grey Giovanine, Central Mo. St.	28	75	83	90.4
1981	Ted Smith, SIU-Edwardsville	26	67	73	91.8
1982	Carl Gonder, Augustana (S.D.)	27	86	93	92.5
1983	Joe Sclafani, New Haven	28	86	98	87.8
1984	Darrell Johnston, New Hamp. Col.	29	74	81	91.4
1985	Tom McDonald, South Dak. St.	33	88	97	90.7
1986	Todd Mezzulo, Alas. Fairbanks	27	114	125	91.2
1987	Mike Sanders, Northern Colo.	28	82	87	94.3
1988	Charles Byrd, West Tex. A&M	29	92	99	92.8
1989	Mike Boschee, North Dak.	28	71	77	92.2
1990	Mike Morris, Ala.-Huntsville	28	114	125	91.2
1991	Ryun Williams, South Dak.	30	114	125	91.2
1992	Hal McManus, Lander	28	110	119	92.4
1993	Jason Williams, New Haven	27	115	125	92.0
1994	Jay Harrie, Mont. St.-Billings	26	86	92	93.5
1995	Jim Borodawka, Mass.-Lowell	27	74	80	92.5
1996	Paul Cluxton, Northern Ky.	32	100	108	92.6

*Record.

Rebound Average

Season	Player, Team	G	Reb.	Avg.
1951	Walter Lenz, Frank. & Marsh.	17	338	19.9
1952	Charley Wrinn, Trinity (Conn.)	19	486	25.6
1953	Ellerbe Neal, Wofford	23	609	26.5
1954	R. C. Owens, College of Idaho	25	677	27.1
1955	Tom Hart, Middlebury	22	649	29.5
1956	Tom Hart, Middlebury	21	620	*29.5
1957	Jim Smith, Steubenville	26	651	25.0
1958	Marv Becker, Widener	18	450	25.0
1959	Jim Davis, King's (Pa.)	17	384	22.6
1960	Jackie Jackson, Virginia Union	19	424	†.241
1961	Jackie Jackson, Virginia Union	26	641	24.7
1962	Jim Ahrens, Buena Vista	28	682	24.4
1963	Gerry Govan, St. Mary's (Kan.)	18	445	24.7
1964	Ernie Brock, Virginia St.	24	597	24.9
1965	Dean Sandifer, Lakeland	23	592	25.7
1966	Frank Stronczek, American Int'l	26	717	27.6
1967	Frank Stronczek, American Int'l	25	602	24.1
1968	Ron Horton, Delaware St.	23	543	23.6
1969	Wilbert Jones, Albany St. (Ga.)	28	670	23.9
1970	Russell Jackson, Southern U.	22	544	24.7
1971	Tony Williams, St. Francis (Me.)	24	599	25.0
1972	No rankings			
1973	No rankings			
1974	Larry Johnson, Prairie View	23	519	22.6
1975	Major Jones, Albany St. (Ga.)	27	608	22.5
1976	Major Jones, Albany St. (Ga.)	24	475	19.8
1977	Andre Means, Sacred Heart	32	516	16.1
1978	Scott Mountz, Calif. (Pa.)	24	431	18.0
1979	Keith Smith, Shaw	20	329	16.5
1980	Ricky Mahorn, Hampton	31	490	15.8

Season	Player, Team	G	Reb.	Avg.
1981	Earl Jones, Dist. Columbia	25	333	13.3
1982	Donnie Carter, Tuskegee	29	372	12.8
1983	David Binion, N.C. Central	25	400	16.0
1984	Jerome Kersey, Longwood	27	383	14.2
1985	Charles Oakley, Virginia Union	31	535	17.3
1986	Raheem Muhammad, Wayne St. (Mich.)	31	428	13.8
1987	Andre Porter, LIU-Southampton	23	309	13.4
1988	Anthony Ikeobi, Clark Atlanta	27	380	14.1
1989	Toby Barber, Winston-Salem	24	327	13.6
1990	Leroy Gasque, Morris Brown	24	375	15.6
1991	Sheldon Owens, Shaw	27	325	12.0
1992	David Allen, Wayne St. (Neb.)	28	362	12.9
1993	James Hector, American Int'l	28	389	13.9
1994	Pat Armour, Jacksonville St.	25	363	14.5
1995	Lorenzo Poole, Albany St. (Ga.)	26	417	16.0
1996	J. J. Sims, West Ga.	28	374	13.4

Record. †Championship determined by highest individual recoveries out of total by both teams in all games.

Assist Average

Season	Player, Team	G	Ast.	Avg.
1989	Steve Ray, Bridgeport	32	*400	*12.5
1990	Steve Ray, Bridgeport	33	385	11.7
1991	Adrian Hutt, Metro St.	28	285	10.2
1992	Tony Smith, Pfeiffer	35	349	10.0
1993	Demetri Beekman, Assumption	23	264	11.5
1994	Ernest Jenkins, N.M. Highlands	27	277	10.3
1995	Ernest Jenkins, N.M. Highlands	27	291	10.8
1996	Bobby Banks, Metro St.	27	244	9.0

*Record.

Blocked-Shot Average

Season	Player, Team	G	Blk.	Avg.
1993	Antonio Harvey, Pfeiffer	29	*155	*5.3
1994	Johnny Tyson, Central Okla.	27	126	4.7
1995	Kino Outlaw, Mount Olive	28	124	4.4
1996	John Burke, LIU-Southampton	28	142	5.1

*Record.

Steal Average

Season	Player, Team	G	Stl.	Avg.
1993	Marcus Stubblefield, Queens (N.C.)	28	110	3.9
1994	Ken Francis, Molloy	27	116	*4.3
1995	Shannon Holmes, New York Tech	30	110	3.7
1996	David Clark, Bluefield St.	31	*118	3.8

*Record.

Annual Team Champions

Won-Lost Percentage

Season	Team	Won	Lost	Pct.
1968	Monmouth (N.J.)	27	2	.931
1969	Alcorn St.	26	1	.963
1970	Central Wash.	31	2	.939
1971	Kentucky St.	31	2	.939
1972	Olivet	22	1	.957
1973	Coe	24	1	.960
1974	West Ga.	29	4	.879
1975	Bentley	23	2	.920
1976	Phila. Textile	25	3	.893
1977	Clarion	27	3	.900
	Kentucky St.	27	3	.900
	Towson St.	27	3	.900
1978	Wis.-Green Bay	30	2	.938
1979	Roanoke	25	3	.893
1980	Alabama St.	32	2	.941
1981	Mt. St. Mary's (Md.)	28	3	.903
1982	Cheyney	28	3	.903

Season	Team	Won	Lost	Pct.
1983	Dist. Columbia	29	3	.906
1984	Norfolk St.	29	2	.935
1985	Jacksonville St.	31	1	.969
	Virginia Union	31	1	.969
1986	Wright St.	28	3	.903
1987	Norfolk St.	28	3	.903
1988	Fla. Southern	31	3	.912
1989	UC Riverside	30	4	.882
1990	Ky. Wesleyan	31	2	.939
1991	Southwest Baptist	29	3	.906
1992	Calif. (Pa.)	31	2	.939
1993	Cal St. Bakersfield	33	0	1.000
1994	Phila. Textile	29	2	.935
1995	Jacksonville St.	24	1	.960
1996	Fort Hays St.	34	0	1.000

Scoring Offense

Season	Team	G	W-L	Pts.	Avg.
1948	St. Anselm	19	12-7	1,329	69.9
1949	Charleston (W.Va.)	26	18-8	2,023	77.8
1950	Charleston (W.Va.)	31	22-9	2,477	79.9
1951	Beloit	23	18-5	1,961	85.3
1952	Lambuth	22	17-5	1,985	90.2
1953	Arkansas Tech	21	20-1	1,976	94.1
1954	Montclair St.	22	18-4	2,128	96.7
1955	West Va. Tech	20	15-5	2,150	107.5
1956	West Va. Tech	22	16-6	2,210	100.5
1957	West Va. Tech	29	26-3	2,976	102.6
1958	West Va. Tech	29	24-5	2,941	101.4
1959	Grambling	29	28-1	2,764	95.3
1960	Mississippi Col.	19	15-4	2,169	114.2
1961	Lawrence Tech	25	19-6	2,409	96.4
1962	Troy St.	25	20-5	2,402	96.1
1963	Miles	21	17-4	2,011	95.8
1964	Benedict	27	19-8	2,730	101.1
1965	Ark.-Pine Bluff	26	22-4	2,655	102.1
1966	Southern Cal College	23	15-8	2,480	107.8
1967	Lincoln (Mo.)	27	24-3	2,925	108.3
1968	Stillman	26	17-9	2,898	111.5
1969	Norfolk St.	25	21-4	2,653	106.1
1970	Norfolk St.	26	19-7	2,796	107.5
1971	Savannah St.	29	18-11	3,051	105.2
1972	Florida A&M	28	18-10	2,869	102.5
1973	Md.-East. Shore	31	26-5	2,974	95.9
1974	Texas Southern	28	15-13	2,884	103.0
1975	Prairie View	26	16-10	2,774	106.7
1976	Southern U.	27	13-14	2,637	97.7
1977	Virginia Union	30	25-5	2,966	98.9
1978	Merrimack	28	22-6	2,606	93.1
1979	Armstrong Atlantic	27	21-6	2,626	97.3
1980	Ashland	27	11-16	2,514	93.1
1981	Virginia St.	31	20-11	2,761	89.1
1982	Alabama St.	28	22-6	2,429	86.8
1983	Virginia St.	29	19-10	2,802	96.6
1984	New Hamp. Col.	29	18-11	2,564	88.4
1985	Alabama A&M	31	21-10	2,881	92.9
1986	Alabama A&M	32	23-9	2,897	90.5
1987	Alabama A&M	30	23-7	2,826	94.2
1988	Oakland	28	19-9	2,685	95.9
1989	Stonehill	32	23-9	3,244	101.4
1990	Jacksonville St.	29	24-5	2,872	99.0
1991	Troy St.	30	22-8	3,259	108.6
1992	Troy St.	29	23-6	3,513	*121.1
1993	Central Okla.	29	23-6	3,293	113.6
1994	Central Okla.	27	17-10	2,782	103.0
1995	Central Okla.	30	23-7	3,219	107.3
1996	Central Okla.	29	19-10	2,933	101.1

*Record.

Scoring Defense

Season	Team	G	W-L	Pts.	Avg.
1948	Miss. Industrial	15	13-2	436	‡29.1
1949	Gordon	20	16-4	655	32.8
1950	Corpus Christi	26	25-1	1,030	39.6
1951	St. Martin's	24	11-13	1,137	47.4
1952	Truman St.	19	12-7	876	46.1
1953	Cal St. Sacramento	26	18-8	1,381	53.1
1954	Cal St. Sacramento	18	9-9	883	49.1
1955	Amherst	22	16-6	1,233	56.0

Season	Team	G	W-L	Pts.	Avg.
1956	Amherst	22	16-6	1,277	58.0
1957	Stephen F. Austin	26	23-3	1,337	51.4
1958	McNeese St.	23	19-4	1,068	46.4
1959	Humboldt St.	23	14-9	1,166	50.7
1960	Wittenberg	24	22-2	1,122	46.8
1961	Wittenberg	29	25-4	1,270	43.8
1962	Wittenberg	26	21-5	1,089	41.9
1963	Wittenberg	28	26-2	1,285	45.9
1964	Wittenberg	23	18-5	1,186	51.6
1965	Cheyney	25	24-1	1,393	55.7
1966	Chicago	16	12-4	894	55.9
1967	Ashland	24	21-3	1,025	42.7
1968	Ashland	30	23-7	1,164	38.8
1969	Ashland	30	26-4	1,017	33.9
1970	Ashland	27	23-4	1,118	41.4
1971	Ashland	28	25-3	1,523	54.4
1972	Chicago	20	16-4	1,132	56.6
1973	Steubenville	29	22-7	1,271	43.8
1974	Steubenville	26	14-12	1,336	51.4
1975	Cal Poly SLO	26	15-11	1,590	61.2
1976	Wis.-Green Bay	29	21-8	1,768	61.0
1977	Wis.-Green Bay	29	26-3	1,682	58.0
1978	Wis.-Green Bay	32	30-2	1,682	52.6
1979	Wis.-Green Bay	32	24-8	1,612	50.4
1980	Wis.-Green Bay	27	15-12	1,577	58.4
1981	San Fran. St.	26	17-9	1,463	56.3
1982	Cal Poly SLO	29	23-6	1,537	53.0
1983	Cal Poly SLO	28	18-10	1,553	55.5
1984	Cal Poly SLO	28	20-8	1,458	52.1
1985	Cal Poly SLO	27	16-11	1,430	53.0
1986	Lewis	30	24-6	1,702	56.7
1987	Denver	29	20-9	1,844	63.6
1988	N.C. Central	29	26-3	1,683	58.0
1989	N.C. Central	32	28-4	1,791	56.0
1990	Humboldt St.	31	20-11	1,831	59.1
1991	Minn.-Duluth	32	27-5	1,899	59.3
1992	Pace	30	23-7	1,517	50.6
1993	Phila. Textile	32	30-2	1,898	59.3
1994	Pace	29	19-10	1,715	59.1
1995	Armstrong Atlantic	31	20-11	1,929	62.2
1996	Coker	26	16-10	1,592	61.2

‡ Record since 1948.

Scoring Margin

Season	Team	Off.	Def.	Mar.
1950	Montana	77.4	57.7	19.7
1951	Eastern Ill.	84.7	57.9	26.8
1952	Southwest Tex. St.	77.4	48.9	28.5
1953	Arkansas Tech	94.7	74.3	20.4
1954	Texas Southern	89.2	63.3	25.9
1955	Mt. St. Mary's (Md.)	95.2	73.3	21.9
1956	Western Ill.	92.5	72.1	20.4
1957	West Va. Tech.	102.6	77.2	25.4
1958	Tennessee St.	88.7	64.1	24.6
1959	Grambling	95.3	73.3	22.0
1960	Mississippi Col.	114.2	92.9	21.3
1961	Bryan	93.8	62.4	*31.4
1962	Mansfield	87.6	64.7	22.9
1963	Gorham St.	94.7	69.7	25.0
1964	Central Conn. St.	94.5	67.7	26.8
1965	Cheyney	80.7	55.7	25.0
1966	Cheyney	90.0	64.4	25.6
1967	Lincoln (Mo.)	108.3	82.2	26.1
1968	Western New Eng.	104.7	76.8	27.9
1969	Indiana (Pa.)	88.6	64.5	24.1
1970	Husson	106.1	79.0	27.1
1971	Kentucky St.	103.5	78.2	25.3
1972	Brockport St.	93.8	70.3	23.5
1973	Wis.-Green Bay	71.2	52.1	19.1
1974	Alcorn St.	96.9	79.8	17.1
1975	Bentley	95.2	78.7	16.5
1976	Central Fla.	94.8	78.4	16.4
1977	Texas Southern	88.4	71.9	16.5
1978	Wis.-Green Bay	68.8	52.6	16.2
1979	Roanoke	77.8	60.8	17.0
1980	Central Fla.	91.7	72.1	19.6
1981	West Ga.	88.5	70.2	18.3
1982	Minn.-Duluth	81.7	64.8	16.9
1983	Minn.-Duluth	84.8	69.8	15.0
1984	Chicago St.	85.9	70.2	15.7
1985	Virginia Union	87.6	67.8	19.8

Alonzo Goldston (52) and his Fort Hays State teammates posted a perfect 34-0 mark in 1996 to join Evansville (1965) and Cal State Bakersfield (1993) as the only teams in Division II history to finish the season undefeated and win the national championship.

Photo by Chris Hall/NCAA photos

DIVISION II

Season	Team	Off.	Def.	Mar.
1986	Mt. St. Mary's (Md.)	80.0	65.7	14.3
1987	Ky. Wesleyan	92.4	72.9	19.8
1988	Fla. Southern	89.6	70.5	19.1
1989	Virginia Union	88.2	69.6	18.6
1990	Ky. Wesleyan	97.3	76.8	20.5
1991	Ashland	99.8	78.2	21.6
1992	Oakland City	99.5	77.1	22.4
1993	Phila. Textile	78.8	59.3	19.4
1994	Oakland City	87.8	65.5	22.3
1995	Jacksonville St.	101.2	77.6	23.6
1996	Fort Hays St.	92.1	70.2	21.9

*Record.

Field-Goal Percentage

Season	Team	FG	FGA	Pct.
1948	Tex. A&M-Commerce	445	1,119	39.8
1949	Southwest Mo. St.	482	1,106	43.6
1950	Corpus Christi	555	1,290	43.0
1951	Beloit	773	1,734	44.6
1952	Southwest Mo. St.	890	1,903	46.8
1953	Lebanon Valley	637	1,349	47.2
1954	San Diego St.	675	1,502	44.9
1955	UC Santa Barb.	672	1,383	48.6
1956	UC Santa Barb.	552	1,142	48.3
1957	Alderson-Broaddus	1,006	2,094	48.0
1958	North Caro. A&T	552	1,072	51.5
1959	Grambling	1,048	2,048	51.2
1960	William Carey	708	1,372	51.6
1961	Virginia Union	908	1,735	52.3
1962	West Va. Tech	871	1,575	55.3
1963	Lenoir-Rhyne	869	1,647	52.8
1964	LeMoyne-Owen	844	1,520	55.5
1965	Southern U.	1,036	1,915	54.1
1966	Howard Payne	932	1,710	54.5
1967	Alabama St.	874	1,555	56.2
1968	South Caro. St.	588	1,010	58.2
1969	LIU-Southampton	846	1,588	58.3
1970	Savannah St.	1,145	1,969	58.2
1971	Alabama St.	1,196	2,100	57.0
1972	Florida A&M	1,194	2,143	55.7
1973	Wis.-Green Bay	929	1,700	54.6

Season	Team	FG	FGA	Pct.
1974	Kentucky St.	1,252	2,266	55.3
1975	Kentucky St.	1,121	1,979	56.6
1976	Kentucky St.	1,093	1,753	*62.4
1977	Merrimack	1,120	2,008	55.8
1978	Wis.-Green Bay	840	1,509	55.7
1979	Morris Brown	980	1,763	55.6
1980	N.C.-Pembroke	849	1,544	55.0
1981	Bellarmine	851	1,561	54.5
1982	Fla. Southern	943	1,644	57.4
1983	Lewis	807	1,448	55.7
1984	Lewis	851	1,494	57.0
1985	Virginia Union	1,132	1,967	57.5
1986	Tampa	856	1,546	55.4
1987	Johnson Smith	995	1,817	54.8
1988	Fla. Southern	1,118	2,026	55.2
1989	Millersville	1,119	2,079	53.8
1990	S.C.-Spartanburg	954	1,745	54.7
1991	S.C.-Spartanburg	923	1,631	56.6
1992	S.C.-Spartanburg	898	1,664	54.0
1993	Cal St. Bakersfield	1,002	1,849	54.2
1994	Southern Ind.	1,171	2,142	54.7
1995	High Point	862	1,603	53.8
1996	Fort Hays St.	1,158	2,145	54.0

*Record.

Field-Goal Percentage Defense

Season	Team	FG	FGA	Pct.
1978	Wis.-Green Bay	681	1,830	37.2
1979	Wis.-Green Bay	639	1,709	37.4
1980	Wis.-Parkside	688	1,666	41.3
1981	Central St. (Ohio)	675	1,724	39.2
1982	Mankato St.	699	1,735	40.3
1983	Central Mo. St.	746	1,838	40.6
1984	Norfolk St.	812	1,910	42.5
1985	Central Mo. St.	683	1,660	41.1
1986	Norfolk St.	782	1,925	40.6
1987	Denver	691	1,709	40.4
1988	Minn.-Duluth	702	1,691	41.5
1989	N.C. Central	633	1,642	38.6
1990	Central Mo. St.	696	1,757	39.6
1991	Southwest Baptist	758	1,942	39.0
1992	Virginia Union	766	2,069	37.0
1993	Pfeiffer	767	2,028	37.8
1994	Virginia Union	705	1,966	*35.9
1995	Virginia Union	723	1,973	36.6
1996	Virginia Union	718	1,944	36.9

*Record.

Three-Point Field Goals Made Per Game

Season	Team	G	3FG	Avg.
1987	Northern Mich.	27	187	6.9
1988	Cal St. Sacramento	30	303	10.1
1989	Central Okla.	27	280	10.4
1990	Stonehill	27	259	9.6
1991	Hillsdale	27	318	11.8
1992	Troy St.	29	*444	*15.3
1993	Hillsdale	28	366	13.1
1994	Hillsdale	25	315	12.6
1995	Hillsdale	29	330	11.4
1996	Mont. St.-Billings	28	304	10.9

*Record.

Three-Point Field-Goal Percentage

Season	Team	G	3FG	3FGA	Pct.
1987	St. Anselm	30	97	189	51.3
1988	Winston-Salem	28	98	182	*53.8
1989	Mississippi Col.	27	144	276	52.2
1990	Shaw	27	74	143	51.7
1991	Rollins	28	278	585	47.5
1992	Oakland City	30	244	486	50.2
1993	Oakland City	32	215	465	46.2
1994	Oakland City	28	225	495	45.5
1995	Oakland City	30	256	561	45.6
1996	Oakland City	31	260	537	48.4

*Record.

Free-Throw Percentage

Season	Team	FT	FTA	Pct.
1948	Charleston (W.Va.)	446	659	67.7
1949	Linfield	276	402	68.7
1950	Jacksonville St.	452	613	73.7
1951	Millikin	603	846	71.3
1952	Eastern Ill.	521	688	75.7
1953	Upsala	513	69	74.0
1954	Central Mich.	376	509	73.9
1955	Mississippi Col.	559	733	76.3
1956	Wheaton (Ill.)	625	842	74.2
1957	Wheaton (Ill.)	689	936	73.6
1958	Wheaton (Ill.)	517	689	75.0
1959	Wabash	418	545	76.7
1960	Allen	225	297	75.8
1961	Southwest Mo. St.	453	605	74.9
1962	Lenoir-Rhyne	477	599	79.6
1963	Hampden-Sydney	442	559	79.1
1964	Western Caro.	492	621	79.2
1965	Mississippi Col.	529	663	79.8
1966	Athens St.	631	802	78.7
1967	Northwestern St.	528	678	77.9
1968	Kenyon	684	858	79.7
1969	Kenyon	583	727	80.2
1970	Wooster	571	714	80.0
1971	South Ala.	422	518	*81.5
1972	Clark Atlanta	409	520	78.7
1973	Rockford (Ill.)	367	481	76.3
1974	New Orleans	537	701	76.6
1975	Alabama St.	456	565	80.7
1976	Alabama St.	451	576	78.3
1977	Puget Sound	495	637	77.7
1978	Merrimack	508	636	79.9
1979	Bentley	506	652	77.6
1980	Phila. Textile	436	549	79.4
1981	Coppin St.	401	514	78.0
1982	Fla. Southern	726	936	77.6
1983	Transylvania	463	606	76.4
1984	Transylvania	491	639	76.8
1985	Mankato St.	349	445	78.4
1986	New Hamp. Col.	507	672	75.4
1987	Columbus St.	339	433	78.3
1988	Rollins	631	795	79.4
1989	Rollins	477	607	78.6
1990	Rollins	449	582	77.1
1991	Lenoir-Rhyne	441	564	78.2
1992	Adams St.	397	512	77.5
1993	Phila. Textile	491	630	77.9
1994	West Liberty St.	473	602	78.6
1995	Western St.	469	603	77.8
1996	South Dak.	501	648	77.3

*Record.

Rebound Margin

Season	Team	Off.	Def.	Mar.
1976	Mississippi Val.	63.9	39.5	*24.4
1977	Phila. Textile	38.7	24.1	14.6
1978	Mass.-Lowell	49.0	37.5	11.5
1979	Dowling	48.2	32.6	15.6
1980	Ark.-Pine Bluff	40.3	25.9	14.4
1981	Wis.-Green Bay	40.6	26.5	14.1
1982	Central St. (Ohio)	48.0	37.2	10.8
1983	Hampton	50.2	38.5	11.8
1984	Calif. (Pa.)	46.4	33.1	13.3
1985	Virginia Union	44.1	32.0	12.1
1986	Tampa	39.9	28.0	11.8
1987	Millersville	44.7	33.8	10.9
1988	Clark Atlanta	44.7	32.5	12.1
1989	Hampton	46.7	36.3	10.3
1990	Fla. Atlantic	41.0	29.4	11.6
1991	Calif. (Pa.)	44.6	32.0	12.6
1992	Oakland City	43.4	31.8	11.6
1993	Metro St.	45.5	32.0	13.5
1994	Oakland City	44.0	33.7	10.3
1995	Jacksonville St.	47.7	35.2	12.5
1996	Virginia Union	48.0	36.1	11.9

*Record.

All-Time Winningest Teams

Includes records as a senior college only; minimum 10 seasons of competition. Postseason games are included.

Percentage

Team	Yrs.	Won	Lost	Pct.
1. Norfolk St.	43	884	309	.741
2. Cheyney	33	661	264	.715
3. Phila. Textile	72	981	407	.707
4. Cal St. Bakersfield	25	499	223	.691
5. LeMoyne-Owen	37	699	324	.683
6. New Hamp. Col.	33	631	299	.678
7. Virginia Union	71	1,118	531	.678
8. Gardner-Webb	27	515	261	.664
9. Ky. Wesleyan	85	*1,165	597	.661
10. Sacred Heart	31	576	312	.649
11. Fla. Southern	40	718	391	.647
12. Fort Hays St.	78	1,075	591	.645
13. Grand Canyon	48	808	446	.644
14. Carson-Newman	38	750	415	.644
15. Central Ark.	74	1,219	677	.643
16. LIU-C. W. Post	40	639	365	.636
17. Gannon	52	844	487	.634
18. Bentley	33	546	318	.632
19. Fairmont St.	73	1,139	686	.624
20. Bloomsburg	93	1,049	632	.624
21. North Dak.	91	1,228	740	.624
22. Central Mo. St.	91	1,246	756	.622
23. Millersville	66	907	551	.622
24. St. Rose	22	382	238	.616
25. Lincoln Memorial	16	300	187	.616

*Includes one tie.

Victories

Team	Yrs.	Won	Lost	Pct.
1. Central Mo. St.	91	1,246	756	.622
2. North Dak.	91	1,228	740	.624
3. Central Ark.	74	1,219	677	.643
4. North Dak. St.	98	1,204	863	.582
5. Washburn	90	1,182	902	.567
6. Ky. Wesleyan	85	*1,165	597	.661
7. Drury	87	1,164	728	.615
8. Fairmont St.	73	1,139	686	.624
9. Virginia Union	71	1,118	531	.678
10. Elon	87	1,115	914	.550
11. West Tex. A&M	75	1,111	713	.609
12. Emporia St.	90	1,097	858	.561
13. Fort Hays St.	78	1,075	591	.645
14. Cal St. Chico	83	1,058	890	.543
15. South Dak. St.	88	1,056	763	.581
16. Bloomsburg	93	1,049	632	.624
17. Lenoir-Rhyne	75	1,033	784	.569
18. Pittsburg St.	80	1,010	863	.539
19. Denver	93	995	953	.511
20. Indianapolis	71	991	690	.590
21. Phila. Textile	72	981	407	.707
22. Neb.-Kearney	88	980	748	.567
23. Tex A&M-Commerce	81	971	810	.545
24. Northern Mich.	90	969	664	.593
25. Northwest Mo. St.	80	956	768	.555

*Includes one tie.

All-Time Won-Lost Records

(No Minimum Seasons of Competition)

Team	First Season	Yrs.	Won	Lost	Pct.
Abilene Christian	1920	73	887	795	.527
Adelphi	1946	49	680	598	.532
Ala.-Huntsville	1974	23	252	365	.408
Alas. Anchorage	1972	25	393	289	.576
Alas. Fairbanks	1953	40	401	482	.454
Albany (N.Y.)	1910	83	915	597	.605
Alderson-Broaddus	1936	58	835	779	.517
American Int'l	1934	62	709	711	.499
Angelo St.	1966	31	423	419	.502

Team	First Season	Yrs.	Won	Lost	Pct.
Armstrong Atlantic	1967	30	436	394	.525
Ashland	1922	75	856	760	.530
Assumption	1924	67	838	655	.561
Augusta St.	1966	31	457	396	.536
Augustana (S.D.)	1928	66	701	792	.470
Barry	1985	12	137	188	.422
Bellarmine	1952	46	367	310	.542
Bemidji St.	1922	70	699	754	.481
Bentley	1964	33	546	318	.632
Bloomsburg	1902	93	1049	632	.624
Bryant	1963	34	450	445	.503
Cal Poly Pomona	1948	49	639	673	.487
Cal St. Bakersfield	1972	25	499	223	.691
Cal St. Chico	1914	83	1058	890	.543
Cal St. Dom. Hills	1978	19	287	223	.563
Cal St. Hayward	1962	35	340	587	.367
Cal St. Los Angeles	1949	48	591	642	.479
Cal St. San B'dino	1985	12	155	153	.503
Cal St. Stanislaus	1967	30	326	380	.462
Carson-Newman	1959	38	750	415	.644
Catawba	1927	71	948	857	.525
Central Ark.	1921	74	1219	677	.643
Central Mo. St.	1906	91	1246	756	.622
Central Okla.	1921	69	905	754	.546
Chadron St.	1922	71	847	791	.517
Chaminade	1977	20	330	246	.573
Cheyney	1964	33	661	264	.715
Columbus St.	1967	29	423	340	.554
Delta St.	1928	66	878	626	.584
Denver	1904	93	995	953	.511
Drury	1909	87	1164	728	.615
East Stroudsburg	1927	69	747	739	.503
Eckerd	1964	33	433	366	.542
Edinboro	1929	66	780	577	.575
Elon	1908	87	1115	914	.550
Emporia St.	1902	90	1097	858	.561
Erskine	1914	71	880	718	.551
Fairmont St.	1917	73	1139	686	.624
Ferris St.	1926	67	793	686	.536
Fla. Southern	1957	40	718	391	.647
Florida Tech	1965	32	326	490	.400
Fort Hays St.	1917	78	1075	591	.645
Fort Lewis	1963	34	395	476	.454
Francis Marion	1970	26	367	360	.505
Franklin Pierce	1964	33	522	327	.615
Gannon	1945	52	844	487	.634
Gardner-Webb	1969	27	515	261	.664
Grand Canyon	1949	48	808	446	.644
Grand Valley St.	1967	30	477	343	.582
Hawaii-Hilo	1977	20	379	243	.609
Humboldt St.	1924	73	521	741	.413
Indiana (Pa.)	1927	68	872	563	.608
Indianapolis	1923	71	991	690	.590
IU/PU-Indianapolis	1973	24	340	368	.480
Johnson Smith	1929	56	780	579	.574
Keene St.	1926	68	539	728	.425
Kennesaw St.	1986	11	166	156	.516
Ky. Wesleyan	1908	85	*1165	597	.661
Lake Superior St.	1947	49	698	500	.583
Lander	1969	28	476	367	.565
Le Moyne	1949	48	681	481	.586
LeMoyne-Owen	1960	37	699	324	.683
Lenoir-Rhyne	1920	75	1033	784	.569
Lewis	1949	47	730	512	.588
Lincoln Memorial	1981	16	300	187	.616
LIU-C. W. Post	1956	40	639	365	.636
Longwood	1977	20	307	226	.576
Lynn	1994	3	59	28	.678
Mankato St.	1921	71	858	654	.567
Mansfield	1918	69	719	598	.546
Mass.-Lowell	1976	21	267	307	.465
Merrimack	1950	47	576	576	.500
Metro St.	1985	12	198	137	.591
Michigan Tech	1920	74	555	795	.411
Millersville	1929	66	907	551	.622
Minn.-Duluth	1930	65	919	589	.609
Mo.-Rolla	1910	84	629	906	.410
Mo. Southern St.	1969	28	428	384	.527
Mo. Western St.	1970	27	463	336	.579
Mo.-St. Louis	1967	30	404	375	.519
Mont. St.-Billings	1927	67	757	676	.528
Morehouse	1911	85	875	823	.515

Marc Hostetter and the Screaming Eagles of Southern Indiana have enjoyed great success in the 1990s, registering a .732 winning percentage. Southern Indiana has advanced to the Elite Eight on two occasions, including 1995 when the Screaming Eagles defeated UC Riverside to win their first Division II title.

Photo by Chris Hall/NCAA photos

Team	First Season	Yrs.	Won	Lost	Pct.
St. Francis (Ill.)	1973	24	402	321	.556
St. Joseph's (Ind.)	1906	84	849	747	.532
St. Leo	1966	31	314	470	.401
St. Michael's	1921	76	824	778	.514
St. Rose	1974	22	382	238	.616
Seattle Pacific	1943	52	736	604	.549
Shepherd	1950	47	626	564	.526
SIU-Edwardsville	1968	29	376	354	.515
Slippery Rock	1926	66	742	680	.522
Sonoma St.	1964	27	262	407	.392
S.C.-Spartanburg	1975	22	390	245	.614
South Dak. St.	1906	88	1056	763	.581
Southern Colo.	1964	33	553	355	.609
Southern Ind.	1970	27	434	298	.593
Southwest Baptist	1966	31	468	371	.558
Stonehill	1949	47	680	500	.576
Stony Brook	1960	36	473	373	.559
Tampa	1950	34	501	419	.545
Tex. A&M-Commerce	1916	81	971	810	.545
Truman St.	1920	77	888	752	.541
Valdosta St.	1955	46	577	423	.577
Virginia Union	1926	71	1118	531	.678
Washburn	1905	90	1182	902	.567
Wayne St. (Neb.)	1912	81	923	810	.533
West Ala.	1957	39	450	529	.460
West Fla.	1968	12	168	148	.532
West Ga.	1957	39	544	448	.548
West Tex. A&M	1921	75	1111	713	.609
Wheeling Jesuit	1958	40	482	525	.479
Winona St.	1916	79	647	931	.410

*Includes one tie.

Team	First Season	Yrs.	Won	Lost	Pct.
Morningside	1902	95	703	796	.469
Neb.-Kearney	1906	88	980	748	.567
Neb.-Omaha	1911	81	798	870	.478
New Hamp. Col.	1964	33	631	299	.678
New Haven	1962	33	519	358	.592
N.M. Highlands	1924	70	739	779	.487
Norfolk St.	1954	43	884	309	.741
North Ala.	1932	63	760	604	.557
N.C. Central	1928	62	858	643	.572
N.C.-Pembroke	1940	57	758	624	.548
North Dak.	1905	91	1228	740	.624
North Dak. St.	1898	98	1204	863	.582
North Fla.	1993	4	46	65	.414
Northern Colo.	1902	95	870	878	.498
Northern Ky.	1972	25	369	316	.539
Northern Mich.	1906	90	969	664	.593
Northwest Mo. St.	1917	80	956	768	.555
Oakland	1968	29	398	385	.508
Oakland City	1923	55	651	589	.525
Pace	1948	48	577	593	.493
Phila. Textile	1920	72	981	407	.707
Pittsburg St.	1916	80	1010	863	.539
Presbyterian	1969	28	438	370	.542
Quincy	1940	57	851	607	.584
Quinnipiac	1952	45	647	513	.558
Regis (Colo.)	1945	49	696	589	.542
Sacred Heart	1966	31	576	312	.649
Saginaw Valley	1970	27	407	347	.540
St. Anselm	1935	62	740	592	.556
St. Cloud St.	1923	72	920	627	.595

Winningest Teams of the 1990s

	Team	Won	Lost	Pct.	EE	Highest '90s Finish
1.	Virginia Union	191	26	.880	3	CH (1992)
2.	Cal St. Bakersfield	186	38	.830	6	CH (1993 & 1994)
3.	Phila. Textile	178	38	.824	2	—
4.	Calif. (Pa.)	168	43	.796	2	3rd (1992 & 1996)
5.	New Hamp. Col.	174	48	.784	3	3rd (1993 & 1994)
5.	Pfeiffer	174	48	.784	—	—
7.	Ky. Wesleyan	160	47	.773	2	CH (1990)
8.	Northern St.	177	52	.773	—	—
9.	Fla. Southern	161	49	.767	—	—
10.	S.C.-Spartanburg	155	48	.764	—	—
11.	St. Rose	139	44	.760	1	—
12.	Alabama A&M	161	52	.756	3	—
13.	Norfolk St.	160	53	.751	1	3rd (1995)
14.	UC Riverside	153	53	.743	1	2nd (1995)
15.	North Ala.	152	53	.741	2	CH (1991)
16.	Tampa	154	54	.740	—	—
17.	South Dak.	150	54	.735	2	—
18.	North Dak.	160	58	.734	2	3rd (1990)
19.	Mo. Western St.	153	56	.732	—	—
19.	Southern Ind.	153	56	.732	2	CH (1995)
21.	Washburn	157	58	.730	2	3rd (1994)
22.	Millersville	145	55	.725	—	—
23.	Indiana (Pa.)	142	58	.710	2	3rd (1995)
24.	Central Mo. St.	150	63	.704	1	—
25.	Minn.-Duluth	142	62	.696	—	—
25.	West Tex. A&M	142	62	.696	—	—
27.	Mississippi Col.	134	59	.694	—	—
28.	Central Okla.	143	63	.694	1	—
29.	Fort Hays St.	144	67	.682	1	CH (1996)
30.	Franklin Pierce	140	66	.680	—	—

EE - Elite Eight Appearances

Division III Records

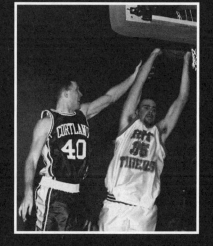

Individual Records

Division III men's basketball records are based on the performances of Division III teams since the three-division reorganization plan was adopted by the special NCAA Convention in August 1973. Assists were added for the 1988-89 season. In statistical rankings, the rounding of percentages and/or averages may indicate ties where none exist. In these cases, the numerical order of the rankings is accurate.

Scoring

POINTS
Game
69—Steve Diekmann, Grinnell vs. Simpson, Nov. 19, 1994
Season
1,044—Greg Grant, Col. of New Jersey, 1989 (32 games)
Career
2,940—Andre Foreman, Salisbury St., 1988-89, 91-92 (109 games)

AVERAGE PER GAME
Season
37.3—Steve Diekmann, Grinnell, 1995 (745 in 20)
Career
(Min. 1,400) 32.8—Dwain Govan, Bishop, 1974-75 (1,805 in 55)

MOST POINTS SCORED WITH NO TIME ELAPSING OFF OF THE CLOCK
Game
24—Rob Rittgers, UC San Diego vs. Menlo, Jan. 16, 1988 (made 24 consecutive free throws due to 12 bench technical fouls)

GAMES SCORING AT LEAST 50 POINTS
Season
2—Ed Brands, Grinnell, 1996; Steve Diekmann, Grinnell, 1995; Dana Wilson, Husson, 1974

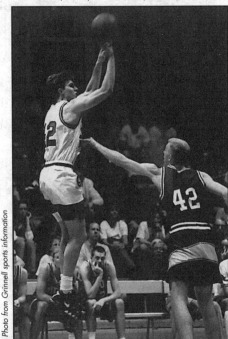
Photo from Grinnell sports information

Grinnell's Ed Brands enjoyed a record-setting season in 1996, shattering and tying numerous Division III game and season records, including most games in a season scoring at least 50 points (2), and most three-point field goals in a game (14) and season (158).

Career
4—Steve Diekmann, Grinnell, 1993-95

MOST GAMES SCORING IN DOUBLE FIGURES
Career
116—Lamont Strothers, Chris. Newport, 1988-91

CONSECUTIVE GAMES SCORING IN DOUBLE FIGURES
Career
116—Lamont Strothers, Chris. Newport, from Nov. 20, 1987, to March 8, 1991

Field Goals

FIELD GOALS
Game
29—Shannon Lilly, Bishop vs. Southwest Assembly of God, Jan. 31, 1983 (36 attempts)
Season
394—Dave Russell, Shepherd, 1975 (687 attempts)
Career
1,140—Andre Foreman, Salisbury St., 1988-89, 91-92 (2,125 attempts)

CONSECUTIVE FIELD GOALS
Game
18—Jason Light, Emory & Henry vs. King (Tenn.), Dec. 2, 1995
Season
21—Tod Hart, Ithaca, 1982 (during three games, Feb. 20-24); Mark Jones, Binghamton, 1986 (during three games, Jan. 29-Feb. 4)

FIELD-GOAL ATTEMPTS
Game
42—Steve Diekmann, Grinnell vs. Illinois Col., Feb. 18, 1994 (19 made)
Season
742—Greg Grant, Col. of New Jersey, 1989 (387 made)
Career
2,149—Lamont Strothers, Chris. Newport, 1988-91 (1,016 made)

FIELD-GOAL PERCENTAGE
Game
(Min. 18 made) 100%—Jason Light, Emory & Henry vs. King (Tenn.), Dec. 2, 1995 (18 of 18)
***Season**
76.6—Travis Weiss, St. John's (Minn.), 1994 (160 of 209)

Based on qualifiers for annual championship.
Career
(Min. 400 made) 73.6—Tony Rychlec, Mass. Maritime, 1981-83 (509 of 692)

Three-Point Field Goals

THREE-POINT FIELD GOALS
Game
14—Ed Brands, Grinnell vs. Ripon, Feb. 24, 1996; Steve Diekmann, Grinnell vs. Simpson, Nov. 19, 1994; Steve Diekmann, Grinnell vs. Coe, Feb. 11, 1994
Season
158—Ed Brands, Grinnell, 1996 (394 attempts)
Career
402—Chris Carideo, Widener, 1992-95 (1,033 attempts)

THREE-POINT FIELD GOALS MADE PER GAME
Season
6.9—Steve Diekmann, Grinnell, 1995 (137 in 20)
Career
4.4—Ed Brands, Grinnell, 1993-96 (347 in 78)

CONSECUTIVE THREE-POINT FIELD GOALS
Game
10—Brad Block, Aurora vs. Rockford, Feb. 20, 1988; Jim Berrigan, Framingham St. vs. Western New Eng., Feb. 27, 1988
Season
16—John Richards, Sewanee (during five games, Feb. 10 to Feb. 25, 1990)

CONSECUTIVE GAMES MAKING A THREE-POINT FIELD GOAL
Season
31—Troy Greenlee, DePauw, Nov. 17, 1989, to March 17, 1990
Career
75—Chris Carideo, Widener, 1992-95

THREE-POINT FIELD-GOAL ATTEMPTS
Game
30—Steve Diekmann, Grinnell vs. Simpson, Nov. 19, 1994 (14 made)
Season
394—Ed Brands, Grinnell, 1996 (158 made)
Career
1,033—Chris Carideo, Widener, 1992-95 (402 made)

THREE-POINT FIELD-GOAL ATTEMPTS PER GAME
Season
17.5—Steve Diekmann, Grinnell, 1995 (350 in 20)
Career
11.1—Ed Brands, Grinnell, 1993-96 (865 in 78)

THREE-POINT FIELD-GOAL PERCENTAGE
Game
(Min. 9 made) 100%—Jim Durrell, Colby-Sawyer vs. Southern Vt., Jan. 15, 1991 (9 of 9)
Season
(Min. 40 made) 67.0%—Reggie James, N.J. Inst. of Tech., 1989 (59 of 88)
(Min. 90 made) 56.9%—Eric Harris, Bishop, 1987 (91 of 160)
Career
(Min. 200 made) 51.3%—Jeff Seifriz, Wis.-Whitewater, 1987-89 (217 of 432)

Free Throws

FREE THROWS
Game
30—Rob Rittgers, UC San Diego vs. Menlo, Jan. 16, 1988 (30 attempts)
Season
249—Dave Russell, Shepherd, 1975 (293 attempts)
Career
792—Matt Hancock, Colby, 1987-90 (928 attempts)

CONSECUTIVE FREE THROWS
Game
30—Rob Rittgers, UC San Diego vs. Menlo, Jan. 16, 1988
Season
59—Mike Michelson, Coast Guard (during 13 games, Jan. 16 to Feb. 27, 1990)

FREE-THROW ATTEMPTS
Game
30—Rob Rittgers, UC San Diego vs. Menlo, Jan. 16, 1988 (30 made)
Season
326—Moses Jean-Pierre, Plymouth St., 1994 (243 made)
Career
928—Matt Hancock, Colby, 1987-90 (792 made)

FREE-THROW PERCENTAGE
Game
(Min. 30 made) 100%—Rob Rittgers, UC San Diego vs. Menlo, Jan. 16, 1988 (30 of 30)
***Season**
95.3%—Andy Enfield, Johns Hopkins, 1991 (123 of 129)

Based on qualifiers for annual championship.
Career
(Min. 250 made) 92.5%—Andy Enfield, Johns Hopkins, 1988-91 (431 of 466)
(Min. 500 made) 85.9%—Kevin Brown, Emory & Henry, 1984-87 (507 of 590)

Rebounds

REBOUNDS
Game
36—Mark Veenstra, Calvin vs. Southern Colo., Feb. 3,

1976; Clinton Montford, Methodist vs. Warren Wilson, Jan. 21, 1989

Season
579—Joe Manley, Bowie St., 1976 (29 games)

Career
1,628—Michael Smith, Hamilton, 1989-92 (107 games)

AVERAGE PER GAME

Season
20.0—Joe Manley, Bowie St., 1976 (579 in 29)

Career
(Min. 900) 17.4—Larry Parker, Plattsburgh St., 1975-78 (1,482 in 85)

Assists

ASSISTS
Game
26—Robert James, Kean vs. N.J. Inst. of Tech., March 11, 1989

Season
391—Robert James, Kean, 1989 (29 games)

Career
909—Steve Artis, Chris. Newport, 1990-93 (112 games)

AVERAGE PER GAME

Season
13.5—Robert James, Kean, 1989 (391 in 29)

Career
(Min. 550) 8.6—Phil Dixon, Shenandoah, 1993-96 (889 in 103)

Blocked Shots

BLOCKED SHOTS
Game
15—Antoine Hyman, Keuka vs. Hobart, Feb. 21, 1996; Roy Woods, Fontbonne vs. MacMurray, Jan. 26, 1995; Ira Nicholson, Mt. St. Vincent vs. Stevens Tech, Nov. 27, 1994; Erick Lidecis, Maritime (N.Y.) vs. Stevens Tech, Nov. 30, 1993

Season
188—Ira Nicholson, Mt. St. Vincent, 1995 (28 games)

Career
425—Ira Nicholson, Mt. St. Vincent, 1994-96 (76 games)

AVERAGE PER GAME

Season
6.7—Ira Nicholson, Mt. St. Vincent, 1995 (188 in 28)

Career
4.3—Andrew South, N.J. Inst. of Tech., 1993-95 (344 in 80)

Steals

STEALS
Game
17—Matt Newton, Principia vs. Harris-Stowe, Jan. 4, 1994

Season
189—Moses Jean-Pierre, Plymouth St., 1994 (30 games)

Career
355—Eric Bell, New Paltz St., 1993-96 (94 games)

AVERAGE PER GAME

Season
6.3—Moses Jean-Pierre, Plymouth St., 1994 (189 in 30)

Career
5.5—Moses Jean-Pierre, Plymouth St., 1993-94 (303 in 55 games)

Games

GAMES PLAYED
Season
34—Thane Anderson, Matt Benedict, Tim Blair, Lanse

Carter, Mike Johnson, Todd Oehrlein, Mike Prasher and Derrick Shelton, Wis.-Eau Claire, 1990

Career
119—Steve Honderd, Calvin, 1990-93; Chris Finch, Frank. & Marsh., 1989-92; Chris Fite, Rochester, 1989-92; Jim Clausen, North Park, 1978-81

Team Records

Note: Where records involve both teams, each team must be an NCAA Division III member institution.

SINGLE-GAME RECORDS

Scoring

MOST POINTS
168—Bishop vs. Southwest Assembly of God (76), Jan. 31, 1983

MOST POINTS BY LOSING TEAM
149—Grinnell vs. Illinois Col. (157), Feb. 18, 1994

MOST POINTS, BOTH TEAMS
315—Simpson (167) vs. Grinnell (148), Nov. 19, 1994

MOST POINTS IN A HALF
92—Wis.-Platteville vs. Mt. St. Clare, Dec. 14, 1989 (first)

MOST POINTS SCORED WITH NO TIME ELAPSING OFF OF THE CLOCK
24—UC San Diego vs. Menlo, Jan. 16, 1988 (made 24 consecutive free throws due to 12 bench technical fouls)

FEWEST POINTS ALLOWED
6—Dickinson (15) vs. Muhlenberg, Feb. 3, 1982

FEWEST POINTS ALLOWED IN A HALF
0—Dickinson (2) vs. Muhlenberg (first), Feb. 3, 1982

FEWEST POINTS, BOTH TEAMS
21—Dickinson (15) vs. Muhlenberg (6), Feb. 3, 1982

FEWEST POINTS, HALF, BOTH TEAMS
2—Dickinson (2) vs. Muhlenberg (0) (first), Feb. 3, 1982

WIDEST MARGIN OF VICTORY
112—Eureka (149) vs. Barat (37), Nov. 29, 1989

Field Goals

MOST FIELD GOALS
78—Bishop vs. Southwest Assembly of God, Jan. 31, 1983 (103 attempts)

MOST FIELD-GOAL ATTEMPTS
135—Grinnell vs. Simpson, Nov. 25, 1995 (52 made)

FEWEST FIELD GOALS
3—Muhlenberg vs. Dickinson, Feb. 3, 1982 (11 attempts)

FEWEST FIELD-GOAL ATTEMPTS
11—Muhlenberg vs. Dickinson, Feb. 3, 1982 (3 made)

HIGHEST FIELD-GOAL PERCENTAGE
83.8%—Wabash vs. Anderson, Feb. 10, 1990 (31 of 37)

HIGHEST FIELD-GOAL PERCENTAGE, HALF
91.3%—Wis.-Stevens Point vs. Wis.-La Crosse, Feb. 12, 1980 (21 of 23)

Three-Point Field Goals

MOST THREE-POINT FIELD GOALS
30—Grinnell vs. Colorado Col., Nov. 17, 1995 (79 attempts)

MOST THREE-POINT FIELD GOALS, BOTH TEAMS
35—Grinnell (30) vs. Colorado Col. (5), Nov. 17, 1995; Manhattanville (25) vs. St. Joseph's (N.Y.) (10), Dec. 10, 1994; Beloit (21) vs. Carthage (14), Nov. 23, 1993

CONSECUTIVE THREE-POINT FIELD GOALS MADE WITHOUT A MISS
11—Willamette vs. Western Baptist, Jan. 8, 1987

HIGHEST NUMBER OF DIFFERENT PLAYERS TO SCORE A THREE-POINT FIELD GOAL, ONE TEAM
11—St. Mary's (Md.) vs. Bard, Jan. 21, 1994

MOST THREE-POINT FIELD-GOAL ATTEMPTS
79—Grinnell vs. Colorado Col., Nov. 17, 1995 (30 made)

MOST THREE-POINT FIELD-GOAL ATTEMPTS, BOTH TEAMS
97—Grinnell (79) vs. Colorado Col. (18), Nov. 17, 1995

HIGHEST THREE-POINT FIELD-GOAL PERCENTAGE
(Min. 10 made) 100%—Willamette vs. Western Baptist, Jan. 8, 1987 (11 of 11); Kean vs. Ramapo, Feb. 11, 1987 (10 of 10)
(Min. 15 made) 83.3%—Rockford vs. Trinity (Ill.), Jan. 21, 1989 (15 of 18)

HIGHEST THREE-POINT FIELD-GOAL PERCENTAGE, BOTH TEAMS
(Min. 10 made) 92.9%—Luther (8 of 8) vs. Wartburg (5 of 6), Feb. 14, 1987 (13 of 14)
(Min. 15 made) 75.0%—Anna Maria (4 of 6) vs. Nichols (11 of 14), Feb. 10, 1987 (15 of 20)
(Min. 20 made) 62.2%—Beloit (13 of 23) vs. Rockford (10 of 14), Jan. 18, 1988 (23 of 37)

Free Throws

MOST FREE THROWS
53—UC San Diego vs. Menlo, Jan. 16, 1988 (59 attempts)

MOST FREE THROWS, BOTH TEAMS
77—Waynesburg (41) vs. Thiel (36), Feb. 3, 1993

MOST FREE-THROW ATTEMPTS
71—Earlham vs. Oberlin, Dec. 5, 1992 (46 made)

MOST FREE-THROW ATTEMPTS, BOTH TEAMS
105—Earlham (71) vs. Oberlin (34), Dec. 5, 1992

FEWEST FREE THROWS
0—Many teams

FEWEST FREE-THROW ATTEMPTS
0—Many teams

HIGHEST FREE-THROW PERCENTAGE
(Min. 28 made) 100.0%—Albany (N.Y.) vs. Potsdam St., Feb. 19, 1994 (28 of 28)
(Min. 30 made) 97.1%—Rochester Inst. vs. Rensselaer, Feb. 16, 1980 (34 of 35)
(Min. 45 made) 89.8%—UC San Diego vs. Menlo, Jan. 16, 1988 (53 of 59)

HIGHEST FREE-THROW PERCENTAGE, BOTH TEAMS
(Min. 20 made) 95.5%—Baldwin-Wallace (13 of 13) vs. Muskingum (8 of 9), Dec. 29, 1977 (21 of 22)
(Min. 30 made) 94.9%—Muskingum (30 of 31) vs. Ohio Wesleyan (7 of 8), Jan. 10, 1981 (37 of 39)

Rebounds

MOST REBOUNDS
98—Alma vs. Marion, Dec. 28, 1973

MOST REBOUNDS, BOTH TEAMS
124—Ill. Wesleyan (62) vs. North Central (62), Feb. 8, 1977; Rochester Inst. (72) vs. Thiel (52), Nov. 18, 1988

DIVISION III

HIGHEST REBOUND MARGIN
56—MIT (74) vs. Emerson-MCA (18), Feb. 21, 1990

Assists

MOST ASSISTS
53—Simpson vs. Grinnell, Nov. 25, 1995

MOST ASSISTS, BOTH TEAMS
79—Simpson (53) vs. Grinnell (26), Nov. 25, 1995

Personal Fouls

MOST PERSONAL FOULS
47—Concordia (Ill.) vs. Trinity Christian, Feb. 26, 1988

MOST PERSONAL FOULS, BOTH TEAMS
76—Bates (42) vs. Norwich (34), Feb. 14, 1988

MOST PLAYERS DISQUALIFIED
6—Union (N.Y.) vs. Rochester, Feb. 15, 1985; Haverford vs. Drew, Jan. 10, 1990; Manhattanville vs. Drew, Jan. 11, 1992; Roger Williams vs Curry, Jan. 14, 1995

MOST PLAYERS DISQUALIFIED, BOTH TEAMS
11—Union (N.Y.) (6) vs. Rochester (5), Feb. 15, 1985

Overtimes

MOST OVERTIME PERIODS
5—Capital (86) vs. Muskingum (89), Jan. 5, 1980; Carnegie Mellon (81) vs. Allegheny (76), Feb. 12, 1983; Rochester (99) vs. Union (N.Y.) (98), Feb. 15, 1985

MOST POINTS IN ONE OVERTIME PERIOD
28—Wash. & Lee vs. Mary Washington, Jan. 9, 1995

MOST POINTS IN ONE OVERTIME PERIOD, BOTH TEAMS
51—Wash. & Lee (28) vs. Mary Washington (23), Jan. 9, 1995

MOST POINTS IN OVERTIME PERIODS
48—Hampden-Sydney vs. Guilford (4 ot), Feb. 2, 1994

MOST POINTS IN OVERTIME PERIODS, BOTH TEAMS
89—Hampden-Sydney (48) vs. Guilford (41) (4 ot), Feb. 2, 1994

SEASON RECORDS

Scoring

MOST POINTS
3,073—Franklin Pierce, 1980 (31 games)

HIGHEST AVERAGE PER GAME
115.3—Grinnell, 1995 (2,422 in 21)

HIGHEST AVERAGE SCORING MARGIN
31.1—Husson, 1976 (98.7 offense, 67.6 defense)

MOST GAMES AT LEAST 100 POINTS
17—Grinnell, 1995 (21-game season); Me.-Farmington, 1991 (24-game season)

MOST CONSECUTIVE GAMES AT LEAST 100 POINTS
11—Grinnell, from Nov. 18, 1994, to Jan. 13, 1995

MOST CONSECUTIVE GAMES AT LEAST 100 POINTS (Multiple Seasons)
15—Grinnell, from Feb. 11, 1994, to Jan. 13, 1995

Field Goals

MOST FIELD GOALS
1,323—Shepherd, 1975 (2,644 attempts)

MOST FIELD GOALS PER GAME
42.5—Mercy, 1977 (1,062 in 25)

MOST FIELD-GOAL ATTEMPTS
2,644—Shepherd, 1975 (1,323 made)

MOST FIELD-GOAL ATTEMPTS PER GAME
90.1—Stillman, 1975 (2,342 in 26)

HIGHEST FIELD-GOAL PERCENTAGE
60.0—Stony Brook, 1978 (1,033 of 1,721)

Three-Point Field Goals

MOST THREE-POINT FIELD GOALS
415—Grinnell, 1996 (1,218 attempts)

MOST THREE-POINT FIELD GOALS PER GAME
17.5—Grinnell, 1995 (368 in 21)

MOST THREE-POINT FIELD-GOAL ATTEMPTS
1,218—Grinnell, 1996 (415 made)

MOST THREE-POINT FIELD-GOAL ATTEMPTS PER GAME
48.7—Grinnell, 1996 (1,218 in 25)

HIGHEST THREE-POINT FIELD-GOAL PERCENTAGE
(Min. 100 made) 62.0%—N.J. Inst. of Tech., 1989 (124 of 200)
(Min. 150 made) 49.1%—Eureka, 1994 (317 of 646)

Free Throws

MOST FREE THROWS
698—Ohio Wesleyan, 1988 (888 attempts)

MOST FREE THROWS PER GAME
23.7—Grinnell, 1995 (498 in 21)

MOST FREE-THROW ATTEMPTS
930—Queens (N.Y.), 1981 (636 made)

MOST FREE-THROW ATTEMPTS PER GAME
33.2—Grinnell, 1995 (698 in 21)

HIGHEST FREE-THROW PERCENTAGE
80.2%—Colby, 1990 (485 of 605)

Rebounds

MOST REBOUNDS
1,616—Keene St., 1976 (29 games)

HIGHEST AVERAGE PER GAME
56.3—Mercy, 1977 (1,408 in 25)

HIGHEST AVERAGE REBOUND MARGIN
17.0—Hamilton, 1991 (49.6 offense, 32.5 defense)

Assists

MOST ASSISTS
861—Salisbury St., 1991 (29 games)

HIGHEST AVERAGE PER GAME
31.2—Me.-Farmington, 1991 (748 in 24)

Fouls

MOST FOULS
737—Jersey City St., 1986 (32 games)

MOST FOULS PER GAME
27.8—Western New Eng., 1994 (696 in 25)

FEWEST FOULS
239—Yeshiva, 1990 (22 games)

FEWEST FOULS PER GAME
10.9—Yeshiva, 1990 (239 in 22)

Defense

FEWEST POINTS PER GAME ALLOWED
47.7—Fredonia St., 1974 (1,049 in 22)

LOWEST FIELD-GOAL PERCENTAGE ALLOWED (Since 1978)
36.5—Scranton, 1993 (659 of 1,806)

Overtimes

MOST OVERTIME GAMES
7—Albany (N.Y.), 1981 (won 5, lost 2); Col. of New Jersey, 1982 (won 6, lost 1); St. John's (Minn.), 1983 (won 4, lost 3); Jersey City St., 1994 (won 4, lost 3)

MOST CONSECUTIVE OVERTIME GAMES
3—Ithaca, 1987 (won 3, lost 0); Cortland St., 1989 (won 1, lost 2); Oberlin, 1989 (won 1, lost 2); Susquehanna, 1989 (won 3, lost 0)

General Records

MOST GAMES IN A SEASON
34—LeMoyne-Owen, 1980 (26-8); Wis.-Eau Claire, 1990 (30-4)

MOST VICTORIES IN A SEASON
32—Potsdam St., 1986 (32-0)

MOST CONSECUTIVE VICTORIES
60—Potsdam St. (from first game of 1985-86 season to March 14, 1987)

MOST CONSECUTIVE HOME-COURT VICTORIES
62—North Park (from Feb. 8, 1984, to Feb. 3, 1988)

MOST CONSECUTIVE REGULAR SEASON VICTORIES
59—Potsdam St. (from Nov. 22, 1985, to Dec. 12, 1987)

MOST DEFEATS IN A SEASON
26—Otterbein, 1988 (1-26); Maryville (Mo.), 1991 (0-26)

MOST CONSECUTIVE DEFEATS IN A SEASON
26—Maryville (Mo.), 1991 (0-26)

MOST CONSECUTIVE DEFEATS
108—Rutgers-Camden (from Jan. 22, 1992, to present)

MOST CONSECUTIVE WINNING SEASONS
31—Albany (N.Y.), 1965-1995

MOST CONSECUTIVE NON-LOSING SEASONS
40—Albany (N.Y.), 1956-1995

UNBEATEN TEAMS (NUMBER OF VICTORIES IN PARENTHESES)
1986 Potsdam St. (32); 1995 Wis.-Platteville (31)

All-Time Individual Leaders

Single-Game Records

SCORING HIGHS

Pts.	Player, Team vs. Opponent	Season
69	Steve Diekmann, Grinnell vs. Simpson	1995
63	Joe DeRoche, Thomas vs. St. Joseph's (Me.)	1988
62	Shannon Lilly, Bishop vs. Southwest Assembly of God	1983
61	Steve Honderd, Calvin vs. Kalamazoo	1993
61	Dana Wilson, Husson vs. Ricker	1974
60	Ed Brands, Grinnell vs. Ripon	1996
60	Steve Diekmann, Grinnell vs. Coe	1994
59	Ed Brands, Grinnell vs. Chicago	1996
59	Steve Diekmann, Grinnell vs. Monmouth (Ill.)	1995
57	David Otte, Simpson vs. Grinnell	1995
56	Steve Diekmann, Grinnell vs. Illinois Col.	1994
56	Kyle Price, Illinois Col. vs. Grinnell	1994
56	Shay DeLaney, Coe vs. Grinnell	1994
56	Mark Veenstra, Calvin vs. Adrian	1976
55	Eric Ochel, Sewanee vs. Emory	1995
55	Dwain Govan, Bishop vs. Texas Southern	1975
54	Jack Ecker, North Park vs. Carthage	1995
54	Bill Simpson, Elmhurst vs. Wheaton (Ill.)	1975
54	Victor Harp, Thiel vs. Penn St.-Behrend	1985
54	David Peach, Framingham St. vs. Westfield St.	1986

Season Records

SCORING AVERAGE

Player, Team	Season	G	FG	3FG	FT	Pts.	Avg.
Steve Diekmann, Grinnell	†1995	20	223	137	162	745	*37.3
Rickey Sutton, Lyndon St.	†1976	14	207	—	93	507	36.2
Shannon Lilly, Bishop	†1983	26	345	—	218	908	34.9
Dana Wilson, Husson	†1974	20	288	—	122	698	34.9
Rickey Sutton, Lyndon St.	†1977	16	223	—	112	558	34.9
Steve Diekmann, Grinnell	†1994	21	250	117	106	723	34.4
Ed Brands, Grinnell	†1996	24	260	*158	136	814	33.9
Dwain Govan, Bishop	†1975	29	392	—	179	963	33.2
Clarence Caldwell, Greensboro	1976	22	306	—	111	723	32.8
Greg Grant, Col. of New Jersey	†1989	32	387	76	194	*1,044	32.6
Dave Russell, Shepherd	1975	32	*394	—	*249	1,037	32.4
Dwain Govan, Bishop	1974	26	358	—	126	842	32.4
Ron Stewart, Otterbein	1983	24	297	—	166	760	31.7

†National champion. *Record.

FIELD-GOAL PERCENTAGE
(Based on qualifiers for annual championship)

Player, Team	Season	G	FG	FGA	Pct.
Travis Weiss, St. John's (Minn.)	†1994	26	160	209	*76.6
Pete Metzelaars, Wabash	†1982	28	271	360	75.3
Tony Rychlec, Mass. Maritime	†1981	25	233	311	74.9
Tony Rychlec, Mass. Maritime	1982	20	193	264	73.1
Russ Newnan, Menlo	1991	26	130	178	73.0
Ed Owens, Hampden-Sydney	†1979	24	140	192	72.9
Scott Baxter, Capital	†1991	26	164	226	72.6
Maurice Woods, Potsdam St.	1982	30	203	280	72.5
Earl Keith, Stony Brook	1979	24	164	227	72.2
Pete Metzelaars, Wabash	1981	25	204	283	72.1
Jon Rosner, Yeshiva	1991	22	141	196	71.9
Pete Metzelaars, Wabash	1979	24	122	170	71.8
Anthony Farley, Miles	1982	26	168	235	71.5

†National champion. *Record.

THREE-POINT FIELD GOALS MADE

Player, Team	Season	G	3FG
Ed Brands, Grinnell	1996	24	*158
Chris Peterson, Eureka	1994	31	145
Steve Diekmann, Grinnell	1995	20	137
Chris Jans, Loras	1991	25	133
Eric Burdette, Wis.-Whitewater	1996	28	130
Ed Brands, Grinnell	1995	20	129
Tommy Doyle, Salem St.	1996	28	124
Everett Foxx, Ferrum	1992	29	124
Kirk Anderson, Augustana (Ill.)	1993	30	123
Jeff deLaveaga, Cal Lutheran	1992	28	122
David Bailey, Concordia (Ill.)	1994	24	120
Steve Diekmann, Grinnell	1994	21	117
Jeff Seifriz, Wis.-Whitewater	1989	31	114
Chris Carideo, Widener	1995	27	113
Brad Block, Aurora	1989	26	112
Chris Geruschat, Bethany (W.Va.)	1991	24	111
Mike Connelly, Catholic	1993	27	111
Chris Carideo, Widener	1994	24	110
Patrick Miller, Wis.-Whitewater	1989	31	107
John Hebert, Colby	1996	27	106
Moses Jean-Pierre, Plymouth St.	1994	30	106

*Record.

THREE-POINT FIELD GOALS MADE PER GAME

Player, Team	Season	G	3FG	Avg.
Steve Diekmann, Grinnell	†1995	20	137	*6.9
Ed Brands, Grinnell	†1996	24	*158	6.6
Ed Brands, Grinnell	1995	29	129	6.5
Steve Diekmann, Grinnell	1994	21	117	5.6
Chris Jans, Loras	†1991	25	133	5.3
David Bailey, Concordia (Ill.)	1994	24	120	5.0
Chris Peterson, Eureka	1994	31	145	4.7
Eric Burdette, Wis.-Whitewater	1996	28	130	4.6
Chris Geruschat, Bethany (W.Va.)	1991	24	111	4.6
Chris Carideo, Widener	1994	24	110	4.6
Luke Madsen, Wis.-River Falls	1996	22	98	4.5
Tommy Doyle, Salem St.	1996	28	124	4.4
Ernie Bray, UC Santa Cruz	1994	24	105	4.4
Jeff deLaveaga, Cal Lutheran	†1992	28	122	4.4
Brad Block, Aurora	†1989	26	112	4.3
Mike Miller, Beloit	1989	24	103	4.3
Everett Foxx, Ferrum	1992	29	124	4.3
Matt Garvey, Bates	1995	23	98	4.3
Jeff Jones, Lycoming	†1988	23	97	4.2
Chris Payne, Elmhurst	1996	25	105	4.2
Chris Carideo, Widener	1995	27	113	4.2
Joe Trent, Stevens Tech	1991	23	96	4.2

†National champion. *Record.

THREE-POINT FIELD-GOAL PERCENTAGE
(Based on qualifiers for annual championship)

Player, Team	Season	G	3FG	3FGA	Pct.
Reggie James, N.J. Inst. of Tech.	†1989	29	59	88	*67.0
Chris Miles, N.J. Inst. of Tech.	†1987	26	41	65	63.1
Chris Miles, N.J. Inst. of Tech.	1989	29	46	75	61.3
Matt Miota, Lawrence	†1990	22	33	54	61.1
Mike Bachman, Alma	†1991	26	46	76	60.5
Ray Magee, Richard Stockton	†1988	26	41	71	57.7
Keith Orchard, Whitman	1988	26	42	73	57.5
Brian O'Donnell, Rutgers-Camden	1988	24	65	114	57.0
Eric Harris, Bishop	1987	26	91	160	56.9
Rick Brown, Muskingum	1988	30	71	125	56.8
Jamie Eichel, Fredonia St.	1989	24	51	90	56.7

†National champion. *Record.

FREE-THROW PERCENTAGE
(Based on qualifiers for annual championship)

Player, Team	Season	G	FT	FTA	Pct.
Andy Enfield, Johns Hopkins	†1991	29	123	129	*95.3
Chris Carideo, Widener	†1992	26	80	84	95.2
Yudi Teichman, Yeshiva	†1989	21	119	125	95.2
Mike Scheib, Susquehanna	†1977	22	80	85	94.1
Jason Prenevost, Middlebury	†1994	22	60	64	93.8
Jerry Prestier, Baldwin-Wallace	†1978	25	125	134	93.3
Charlie Nanick, Scranton	1996	25	96	103	93.2
Jeff Bowers, Southern Me.	†1988	29	95	102	93.1
Eric Jacobs, Scranton	1986	29	81	87	93.1
Jim Durrell, Colby-Sawyer	†1993	25	67	72	93.1
Joe Purcell, King's (Pa.)	†1979	26	66	71	93.0
Todd Reinhardt, Wartburg	†1990	26	91	98	92.9
Reiner Kolodinski, Occidental	1979	24	65	70	92.9
Shannon Lilly, Bishop	†1982	22	142	153	92.8
Matt Freesemann, Wartburg	†1995	24	128	138	92.8
Dan Trippler, Wis.-Superior	1996	25	63	68	92.6
Andy Enfield, Johns Hopkins	1990	28	137	148	92.6
Tim Mieure, Hamline	†1976	25	88	95	92.6
Scott Anderson, Wis.-Stevens Point	1990	28	86	93	92.5

†National champion. *Record.

REBOUND AVERAGE

Player, Team	Season	G	Reb.	Avg.
Joe Manley, Bowie St.	†1976	29	*579	*20.0
Fred Petty, New Hamp. Col.	†1974	22	436	19.8

DIVISION III

Photo from Shenandoah sports information

Phil Dixon of Shenandoah (3) amassed 258 assists in 27 games, a 9.6 per game average, in 1996. Dixon led all Division III players in assists and assists per game in 1994.

Player, Team	Season	G	Reb.	Avg.
Larry Williams, Pratt	†1977	24	457	19.0
Charles Greer, Thomas	1977	17	318	18.7
Larry Parker, Plattsburgh St.	†1975	23	430	18.7
John Jordan, Southern Me.	1978	29	536	18.5
Keith Woolfolk, Upper Iowa	1978	26	479	18.4
Michael Stubbs, Trinity (Conn.)	†1990	22	398	18.1
Mike Taylor, Pratt	1978	23	414	18.0
Walt Edwards, Husson	1976	26	467	18.0
Dave Kufeld, Yeshiva	†1979	20	355	17.8

†National champion. *Record.

ASSISTS

Player, Team	Season	G	Ast.
Robert James, Kean	†1989	29	*391
Ricky Spicer, Wis.-Whitewater	1989	31	295
Joe Marcotte, N.J. Inst. of Tech	†1995	30	292
Andre Bolton, Chris. Newport	†1996	30	289
Ron Torgalski, Hamilton	1989	26	275
Albert Kirchner, Mt. St. Vincent	†1990	24	267
Steve Artis, Chris. Newport	1991	29	262
Phil Dixon, Shenandoah	1996	27	258
Phil Dixon, Shenandoah	†1994	26	253
Steve Artis, Chris. Newport	1990	28	251
David Genovese, Mt. St. Vincent	1994	27	248
Russell Springman, Salisbury St.	1990	27	246
Tom Genco, Manhattanville	1990	26	244
Andre Bolton, Chris. Newport	1995	28	243
Mark Cottom, Ferrum	1991	25	242
Tim Lawrence, Maryville (Tenn.)	1992	29	241

†National champion. *Record.

ASSIST AVERAGE

Player, Team	Season	G	Ast.	Avg.
Robert James, Kean	†1989	29	*391	*13.5
Albert Kirchner, Mt. St. Vincent	†1990	24	267	11.1
Ron Torgalski, Hamilton	1989	26	275	10.6
Louis Adams, Rust	1989	22	227	10.3
Eric Johnson, Coe	†1991	24	238	9.9
Joe Marcotte, N.J. Inst. of Tech	†1995	30	292	9.7
Phil Dixon, Shenandoah	†1994	26	253	9.7
Mark Cottom, Ferrum	1991	25	242	9.7
Andre Bolton, Chris. Newport	†1996	30	289	9.6
Phil Dixon, Shenandoah	1996	27	258	9.6
Ricky Spicer, Wis.-Whitewater	1989	31	295	9.5
Pat Heldman, Maryville (Tenn.)	1989	25	236	9.4
Tom Genco, Manhattanville	1990	26	244	9.4
Justin Culhane, Suffolk	1992	24	225	9.4

†National champion. *Record.

BLOCKED SHOTS

Player, Team	Season	G	Blk.
Ira Nicholson, Mt. St. Vincent	†1995	28	*188
Ira Nicholson, Mt. St. Vincent	†1996	27	163
Matt Cusano, Scranton	†1993	29	145
Antoine Hyman, Keuka	1996	25	131
Andrew South, N.J. Inst. of Tech	†1994	27	128
Mike Mientus, Allentown	1995	27	118
Roy Woods, Fontbonne	1995	25	117
Eric Lidecis, Maritime (N.Y.)	1994	26	116
Andrew South, N.J. Inst. of Tech	1993	26	111
Jeremy Putman, Dubuque	1995	25	110
Robert Clyburn, Kean	1995	27	108
Damon Avinger, CCNY	1996	25	106
Andrew South, N.J. Inst. of Tech	1995	27	105

†National champion. *Record.

BLOCKED-SHOT AVERAGE

Player, Team	Season	G	Blk.	Avg.
Ira Nicholson, Mt. St. Vincent	†1995	28	*188	*6.71
Ira Nicholson, Mt. St. Vincent	†1996	27	163	6.04
Antoine Hyman, Keuka	1996	25	131	5.24
Matt Cusano, Scranton	†1993	29	145	5.00
Andrew South, N.J. Inst. of Tech	†1994	27	128	4.74
Roy Woods, Fontbonne	1995	25	117	4.68
Erik Lidecis, Maritime (N.Y.)	1994	26	116	4.46
Jeremy Putman, Dubuque	1995	25	110	4.40
Mike Mientus, Allentown	1995	27	118	4.37
Andrew South, N.J. Inst. of Tech	1993	26	111	4.26
Damon Avinger, CCNY	1996	25	106	4.24
Nick Brown, Carleton	1994	25	102	4.08
Robert Clyburn, Kean	1995	27	108	4.00

†National champion. *Record.

STEALS

Player, Team	Season	G	Stl.
Moses Jean-Pierre, Plymouth St.	†1994	30	*189
Purvis Presha, Stillman	†1996	25	144
Matt Newton, Principia	1994	25	138
Scott Clarke, Utica	†1995	24	126
Deron Black, Allegheny	1996	27	123
David Brown, Westfield St.	1994	25	122
Barry Aranoff, Yeshiva	1995	22	121
Brian Meehan, Salve Regina	1995	28	120
Scott Clarke, Utica	1996	26	118
Moses Jean-Pierre, Plymouth St.	†1993	25	114
Shawn McCartney, Hunter	1995	28	111
Gerald Garlic, Goucher	1995	29	111
Greg Dean, Concordia-M'head	1996	27	108
Andre Self, Col. of New Jersey	1993	27	107

†National champion. *Record.

STEAL AVERAGE

Player, Team	Season	G	Stl.	Avg.
Moses Jean-Pierre, Plymouth St.	†1994	30	*189	*6.30
Purvis Presha, Stillman	†1996	25	144	5.76
Matt Newton, Principia	1994	25	138	5.52
Barry Aranoff, Yeshiva	†1995	22	121	5.50
Scott Clarke, Utica	1995	24	126	5.25
Joel Heckendorf, Martin Luther	1996	17	84	4.94
David Brown, Westfield St.	1994	25	122	4.88
Ivo Moyano, Polytechnic (N.Y.)	1994	19	91	4.78
Moses Jean-Pierre, Plymouth St.	†1993	25	114	4.56
Deron Black, Allegheny	1996	27	123	4.55
Scott Clarke, Utica	1996	26	118	4.54
Carl Small, Cornell College	1995	22	96	4.36
Brian Meehan, Salve Regina	1995	28	120	4.29
Ivo Moyano, Polytechnic (N.Y.)	1995	23	97	4.22

†National champion. *Record.

Career Records

POINTS

Player, Team	Seasons	Pts.
Andre Foreman, Salisbury St.	1988-89, 91-92	*2,940
Lamont Strothers, Chris. Newport	1988-91	2,709
Matt Hancock, Colby	1987-90	2,678
Scott Fitch, Geneseo St.	1990-91, 93-94	2,634
Greg Grant, Col. of New Jersey	1987-89	2,611

Player, Team	Seasons	Pts.
Rick Hughes, Thomas More	1993-96	2,605
Wil Peterson, St. Andrews	1980-83	2,553
Ron Stewart, Otterbein	1980-83	2,549
Scott Tedder, Ohio Wesleyan	1985-88	2,501
Moses Jean-Pierre, Plymouth St.	1991-94	2,483
Steve Honderd, Calvin	1990-93	2,469
Herman Alston, Kean	1988-91	2,457
Dick Hempy, Otterbein	1984-87	2,439
Kevin Moran, Curry	1983-86	2,415
Rickey Sutton, Lyndon St.	1976-79	2,379
Frank Wachlarowicz, St. John's (Minn.)	1975-79	2,357
Cedric Oliver, Hamilton	1976-79	2,349
Dana Janssen, Neb. Wesleyan	1983-86	2,333
Kevin Brown, Emory & Henry	1984-87	2,322

*Record.

SCORING AVERAGE
(Minimum 1,400 points)

Player, Team	Seasons	G	FG	3FG	FT	Pts.	Avg.
Dwain Govan, Bishop	1974-75	55	750	—	305	1,805	*32.8
Dave Russell, Shepherd	1974-75	60	710	—	413	1,833	30.6
Rickey Sutton, Lyndon St.	1976-79	80	960	—	459	2,379	29.7
John Atkins, Knoxville	1976-78	70	845	—	322	2,012	28.7
Steve Peknik, Windham	1974-77	76	816	—	467	2,099	27.6
Andre Foreman, Salisbury St.	1988-89, 91-94	109	1,140	68	592	*2,940	27.0
Matt Hancock, Colby	1987-90	102	844	198	*792	2,678	26.3
Terrence Dupree, Polytechnic (N.Y.)	1990-92	70	700	22	407	1,829	26.1
Steve Diekmann, Grinnell	1992-95	85	741	371	365	2,218	26.1
Rick Hughes, Thomas More	1993-96	101	1,039	13	514	2,605	25.8
Mark Veenstra, Calvin	1974-77	89	960	—	341	2,261	25.4
Ron Swartz, Hiram	1984-87	90	883	78	408	2,252	25.0
Clarence Caldwell, Greensboro.	1974-77	93	971	—	363	2,309	24.8
James Rehnquist, Amherst	1975-77	61	614	—	284	1,512	24.8

*Record.

FIELD-GOAL PERCENTAGE
(Minimum 400 field goals made)

Player, Team	Seasons	G	FG	FGA	Pct.
Tony Rychlec, Mass. Maritime	1981-83	55	509	692	*73.6
Pete Metzelaars, Wabash	1979-82	103	784	1,083	72.4
Maurice Woods, Potsdam St.	1980-82	93	559	829	67.4
Earl Keith, Stony Brook	1975-76, 78-79	94	777	1,161	66.9
Dan Rush, Bridgewater (Va.)	1992-95	102	712	1,069	66.6
Wade Gugino, Hope	1989-92	97	664	1,010	65.7
David Otte, Simpson	1992-95	76	549	840	65.4
Rick Batt, UC San Diego	1989-92	106	558	855	65.2
Kevin Ryan, Col. of New Jersey	1987-90	102	619	955	64.8
Greg Kemp, Aurora	1991-94	102	680	1,051	64.7
Scott Baxter, Capital	1988-91	104	505	782	64.6
Paul Rich, Geneseo St.	1978-81	88	452	700	64.6
Tod Hart, Ithaca	1980-83	97	726	1,133	64.1
Tony Seay, Averett	1989-90	55	465	726	64.0
Dick Hempy, Otterbein	1984-87	112	923	1,447	63.8
John Wassenbergh, St. Joseph's (Me.)	1993-96	108	815	1,281	63.6
Mike Johnson, Wis.-Eau Claire	1989-91	89	402	636	63.2
Damon Forney, Greensboro	1978-81	92	586	928	63.1
Kevin Folkl, Washington (Mo.)	1993-96	97	543	860	63.1
Bob Richardson, Hamline	1975-77	83	560	887	63.1

*Record.

THREE-POINT FIELD GOALS MADE

Player, Team	Seasons	G	3FG
Chris Carideo, Widener	1992-95	103	*402
Steve Diekmann, Grinnell	1992-95	85	371
Ray Wilson, UC Santa Cruz	1989-92	100	354
Ed Brands, Grinnell	1993-96	78	347
Chris Hamilton, Blackburn	1988-91	101	334
Scott Fitch, Geneseo St.	1990-91, 93-94	109	332
Billy Collins, Nichols	1992-95	92	331
Jason Valant, Colorado Col.	1990-93	103	315
Everett Foxx, Ferrum	1989-92	104	315
Aaron Lee, Mass.-Dartmouth	1992-95	115	313
Jim Durrell, Colby-Sawyer	1991-94	100	308
Chris Geruschat, Bethany (W.Va.)	1989-92	89	307
Tommy Doyle, Salem St.	1993-96	110	304
Gene Nolan, Washington (Mo.)	1993-96	106	296
Anthony Jones, Gallaudet	1991-94	101	295
Mike Connelly, Catholic	1990-93	103	292
Scott Lamond, Gettysburg	1988-91	98	284
Greg Bonczkowski, Hartwick	1993-96	105	282

Player, Team	Seasons	G	3FG
Brad Alberts, Ripon	1989-92	95	277
Jamie Harless, Kenyon	1992-95	110	276
Dan Lenert, Benedictine (Ill.)	1990-93	104	276

*Record.

THREE-POINT FIELD GOALS MADE PER GAME
(Minimum 200 three-point field goals made)

Player, Team	Seasons	G	3FG	Avg.
Ed Brands, Grinnell	1993-96	78	347	*4.45
Steve Diekmann, Grinnell	1992-95	85	371	4.36
Chris Carideo, Widener	1992-95	103	*402	3.90
Billy Collins, Nichols	1992-95	92	331	3.60
Ray Wilson, UC Santa Cruz	1989-92	100	354	3.54
Chris Geruschat, Bethany (W.Va.)	1989-92	89	307	3.45
Chris Hamilton, Blackburn	1988-91	101	334	3.31
Jeff Jones, Lycoming	1987-89	71	232	3.27
Jim Durrell, Colby-Sawyer	1991-94	100	308	3.08
Jason Valant, Colorado Col.	1990-93	103	315	3.06
Scott Fitch, Geneseo St.	1990-91, 93-94	109	332	3.05
Everett Foxx, Ferrum	1989-92	104	315	3.03
Perry Junius, Allegheny	1988-91	93	275	2.96
Anthony Jones, Gallaudet	1991-94	101	295	2.92
Eric Ochel, Sewanee	1992-95	86	251	2.92
Brad Alberts, Ripon	1989-92	95	277	2.92
Scott Lamond, Gettysburg	1988-91	98	284	2.90
Dameon Ross, Salisbury St.	1991-94	77	222	2.88
Kelvin Richardson, Maryville (Tenn.)	1990-93	82	236	2.88
Mike Connelly, Catholic	1990-93	103	292	2.83

*Record.

THREE-POINT FIELD-GOAL PERCENTAGE
(Minimum 200 three-point field goals made)

Player, Team	Seasons	G	3FG	3FGA	Pct.
Jeff Seifriz, Wis.-Whitewater	1987-89	85	217	423	*51.3
Chris Peterson, Eureka	1991-94	78	215	421	51.1
Everett Foxx, Ferrum	1989-92	104	315	630	50.0
Brad Alberts, Ripon	1989-92	95	277	563	49.2
Jeff Jones, Lycoming	1987-89	71	232	472	49.2
Troy Greenlee, DePauw	1988-91	106	232	473	49.0
David Todd, Pomona-Pitzer	1987-90	84	212	439	48.3

*Record.

FREE-THROW PERCENTAGE
(Minimum 250 free throws made)

Player, Team	Seasons	G	FT	FTA	Pct.
Andy Enfield, Johns Hopkins	1988-91	108	431	466	*92.5
Doug Brown, Elizabethtown	1976-80	96	252	279	90.3
Tim McGraw, Hartwick	1985-88	107	330	371	88.9
Eric Jacobs, Wilkes & Scranton	1984-87	106	303	343	88.3
Todd Reinhardt, Wartburg	1988-91	105	283	322	87.9
Jeff Thomas, King's (Pa.)	1989-92	110	466	532	87.6
Brian Andrews, Alfred	1984-87	101	306	350	87.4
Matt Freesemann, Wartburg	1994-96	73	297	340	87.4
Eric Elliott, Hope	1988-91	103	350	403	86.8
Chad Onofrio, Tufts	1993-96	100	329	379	86.8
Pat Pruitt, Albright	1989-92	87	261	301	86.7
Mike Johnson, Wis.-Eau Claire	1989-91	89	421	486	86.6
Ron Barczak, Kalamazoo	1988-91	98	360	416	86.5
Scott Smith, Salisbury St.	1981-85	106	290	336	86.3
Roy Mosser, Millikin	1973-77	105	274	318	86.2

*Record.

REBOUND AVERAGE
(Minimum 900 rebounds)

Player, Team	Seasons	G	Reb.	Avg.
Larry Parker, Plattsburgh St.	1975-78	85	1,482	*17.4
Charles Greer, Thomas	1975-77	58	926	16.0
Willie Parr, LeMoyne-Owen	1974-76	76	1,182	15.6
Michael Smith, Hamilton	1989-92	107	*1,628	15.2
Dave Kufeld, Yeshiva	1977-80	81	1,222	15.1
Ed Owens, Hampden-Sydney	1977-80	77	1,160	15.1
Kevin Clark, Clark (Mass.)	1978-81	101	1,450	14.4
Mark Veenstra, Calvin	1974-77	89	1,260	14.2

*Record.

ASSISTS

Player, Team	Seasons	G	Ast.
Steve Artis, Chris. Newport	1990-93	112	*909
Phil Dixon, Shenandoah	1993-96	103	889
David Genovese, Mt. St. Vincent	1992-95	107	800

DIVISION III

Player, Team	Seasons	G	Ast.
Andre Bolton, Chris. Newport	1993-96	109	737
Moses Jean-Pierre, Plymouth St.	1991-94	109	669
Lance Andrews, N.J. Inst. of Tech.	1990-93	113	664
Dennis Jacobi, Bowdoin	1989-92	93	662
Tim Lawrence, Maryville (Tenn.)	1989-92	106	660
Pat Skerry, Tufts	1989-92	95	650
Eric Johnson, Coe	1989-92	90	637
John Snyder, King's (Pa.)	1989-92	107	631
Anthony Robinson, Wittenberg	1993-96	117	618
Jerry Dennis, Otterbein	1989-92	118	613
Kevin Beard, Greensboro	1992-95	107	607
Paul Ferrell, Guilford	1991-94	99	607
Tony Wyzzard, Emerson-MCA	1992-95	90	604
Kevin Alexander, Emory & Henry	1993-96	105	601
Jeremy Greenberg, Binghamton	1991-94	109	588
James Braxton, Averett	1989-92	106	583
Kevin Root, Eureka	1989-91	81	579

*Record.

ASSIST AVERAGE
(Minimum 550 assists)

Player, Team	Seasons	G	Ast.	Avg.
Phil Dixon, Shenandoah	1993-96	103	889	*8.6
Steve Artis, Chris. Newport	1990-93	112	909	8.1
David Genovese, Mt. St. Vincent	1992-95	107	800	7.5
Kevin Root, Eureka	1989-91	81	579	7.1
Dennis Jacobi, Bowdoin	1989-92	93	662	7.1
Eric Johnson, Coe	1989-92	90	637	7.1
Pat Skerry, Tufts	1989-92	95	650	6.8
Andre Bolton, Chris. Newport	1993-96	109	737	6.8
Tony Wyzzard, Emerson-MCA	1992-95	90	604	6.7
Tim Lawrence, Maryville (Tenn.)	1989-92	106	660	6.2
Moses Jean-Pierre, Plymouth St.	1991-94	109	669	6.1
Paul Ferrell, Guilford	1991-94	99	607	6.1
John Snyder, King's (Pa.)	1989-92	107	631	5.9
Lance Andrews, N.J. Inst. of Tech.	1990-93	113	664	5.9
Keith Newman, Bethel (Minn.)	1989-92	96	560	5.8
Kevin Alexander, Emory & Henry	1993-96	105	601	5.7
Kelley McClure, Otterbein	1993-96	99	566	5.7
Kevin Beard, Greensboro	1992-95	107	607	5.7
James Braxton, Averett	1989-92	106	583	5.5
Jeremy Greenberg, Binghamton	1991-94	109	588	5.4

*Record.

BLOCKED SHOTS

Player, Team	Seasons	G	Blk.
Ira Nicholson, Mt. St. Vincent#	1994-96	76	*425
Andrew South, N.J. Inst. of Tech	1993-95	80	344
Jeremy Putman, Dubuque	1993-96	99	274
Terry Thomas, Chris. Newport	1993-96	113	271
Mike Mientus, Allentown#	1994-96	61	212
David Stephens, Colby	1993-96	102	201
Robert Clyburn, Kean	1993-95	77	201
Jason White, Westminster (Mo.)	1993-96	103	194
John Garber, Millsaps#	1994-96	77	189
John Karalis, Emerson-MCA	1993-96	96	188
Jeff Manning, Curry	1993-95	74	184

*Record. #Active player.

BLOCKED-SHOT AVERAGE
(Minimum 175 blocked shots)

Player, Team	Seasons	G	Blk.	Avg.
Andrew South, N.J. Inst. of Tech	1993-95	80	344	*4.30
Jeremy Putman, Dubuque	1993-96	99	274	2.77
Robert Clyburn, Kean	1993-95	77	201	2.61
Jeff Manning, Curry	1993-95	74	184	2.49
Terry Thomas, Chris. Newport	1993-96	113	271	2.40

*Record.

STEALS

Player, Team	Seasons	G	Stl.
Eric Bell, New Paltz St.	1993-96	94	*355
Scott Clarke, Utica	1993-96	96	346
Moses Jean-Pierre, Plymouth St.	1993-94	55	303
Keith Poppor, Amherst	1993-96	98	283
Ivo Moyano, Polytechnic (N.Y.)#	1994-96	65	281
Terrence Stewart, Rowan	1993-96	113	277
Clarence Pierce, N.J. Inst. of Tech.	1993-96	102	273
Ernie Peavy, Wis.-Platteville	1993-95	87	264
Shawn McCarthy, Hunter	1993-95	81	261
Gerald Garlic, Goucher	1993-95	70	244

Player, Team	Seasons	G	Stl.
Jeff Landis, York (Pa.)	1993-95	82	243
Deron Black, Allegheny	1993-96	78	240
Stefan Pagios, Mass.-Dartmouth	1993-95	87	240
Richie Cole, Mt. St. Vincent	1993-96	99	235
Dave Ulloa, Cal Lutheran	1993-96	94	234
Jamal Elliott, Haverford	1993-96	93	227
Reuben Reyes, Salve Regina	1993-95	74	226
Carl Small, Cornell College	1993-95	69	222
Tee Jennings, Hampden-Sydney	1993-95	83	221
Kelley McClure, Otterbein	1993-96	99	220

*Record. #Active player.

STEAL AVERAGE
(Minimum 175 steals)

Player, Team	Seasons	G	Stl.	Avg.
Moses Jean-Pierre, Plymouth St.	1993-94	55	303	5.51
Rodney Lusain , UC San Diego	1993-94	50	193	3.86
Eric Bell, New Paltz St.	1993-96	94	*355	3.78
David Brown, Westfield St.	1993-95	53	193	3.64
Scott Clarke, Utica	1993-96	96	346	3.60
Gerald Garlic, Goucher	1993-95	70	244	3.49
Shawn McCarthy, Hunter	1993-95	81	261	3.22
Carl Small, Cornell College	1993-95	69	222	3.22
Deron Black, Allegheny	1993-96	78	240	3.08
Reuben Reyes, Salve Regina	1993-95	74	226	3.05
Ernie Peavy, Wis.-Platteville	1993-95	87	264	3.03
Jeff Landis, York (Pa.)	1993-95	82	243	2.96
Keith Poppor, Amherst	1993-96	98	283	2.89
Brian Meehan, Salve Regina	1993-95	75	214	2.85

Annual Individual Champions

Scoring Average

Season	Player, Team	G	FG	FT	Pts.	Avg.
1974	Dana Wilson, Husson	20	288	122	698	34.9
1975	Dwain Govan, Bishop	29	392	179	963	33.2
1976	Rickey Sutton, Lyndon St.	14	207	93	507	36.2
1977	Rickey Sutton, Lyndon St.	16	223	112	558	34.9
1978	John Atkins, Knoxville	25	340	103	783	31.3
1979	Scott Rogers, Kenyon	24	289	109	687	28.6
1980	Ray Buckland, Mass.-Boston	25	271	153	695	27.8
1981	Gerald Reece, William Penn	27	306	145	757	28.0
1982	Ashley Cooper, Ripon	22	256	89	601	27.3
1983	Shannon Lilly, Bishop	26	345	218	908	34.9
1984	Mark Van Valkenburg, Framingham St.	25	312	133	757	30.3
1985	Adam St. John, Maine Maritime	18	193	135	521	28.9
1986	John Saintignon, UC Santa Cruz	22	291	104	686	31.2

Season	Player, Team	G	FG	3FG	FT	Pts.	Avg.
1987	Rod Swartz, Hiram	23	232	78	133	675	29.3
1988	Matt Hancock, Colby	27	275	56	247	853	31.6
1989	Greg Grant, Col. of New Jersey	32	387	76	194	*1,044	32.6
1990	Grant Glover, Rust	23	235	1	164	635	27.6
1991	Andre Foreman, Salisbury St.	29	350	39	175	914	31.5
1992	Jeff deLaveaga, Cal Lutheran	28	258	122	187	825	29.5
1993	Dave Shaw, Drew	23	210	74	169	663	28.8
1994	Steve Diekmann, Grinnell	21	250	117	106	723	34.4
1995	Steve Diekmann, Grinnell	20	223	137	162	745	*37.3
1996	Ed Brands, Grinnell	24	260	*158	136	814	33.9

*Record.

Field-Goal Percentage

Season	Player, Team	G	FG	FGA	Pct.
1974	Fred Waldstein, Wartburg	28	163	248	65.7
1975	Dan Woodard, Elizabethtown	23	190	299	63.5
1976	Paul Merlis, Yeshiva	21	145	217	66.8
1977	Brent Cawelti, Trinity (Conn.)	20	107	164	65.2
1978	Earl Keith, Stony Brook	29	228	322	70.8
1979	Ed Owens, Hampden-Sydney	24	140	192	72.9
1980	E. D. Schechterley, Lynchburg	25	184	259	71.0
1981	Tony Rychlec, Mass. Maritime	25	233	311	74.9
1982	Pete Metzelaars, Wabash	28	271	360	75.3

Season	Player, Team	G	FG	FGA	Pct.
1983	Mike Johnson, Drew	23	138	205	67.3
1984	Mark Van Valkenburg, Framingham St.	25	312	467	66.8
1985	Reinout Brugman, Muhlenberg	26	176	266	66.2
1986	Oliver Kyler, Frostburg St.	28	183	266	68.8
1987	Tim Ervin, Albion	21	127	194	65.5
1988	Matt Strong, Hope	27	163	232	70.3
1989	Kevin Ryan, Col. of New Jersey	32	246	345	71.3
1990	Bill Triplett, N.J. Inst. of Tech.	28	169	237	71.3
1991	Scott Baxter, Capital	26	164	226	72.6
1992	Brett Grebing, Redlands	23	125	176	71.0
1993	Jim Leibel, St. Thomas (Minn.)	28	141	202	69.8
1994	Travis Weiss, St. John's (Minn.)	26	160	209	*76.6
1995	Justin Wilkins, Neb. Wesleyan	28	163	237	68.8
1996	Jason Light, Emory & Henry	25	207	294	70.4

*Record.

Three-Point Field Goals Made Per Game

Season	Player, Team	G	3FG	Avg.
1987	Scott Fearrin, MacMurray	25	96	3.8
1988	Jeff Jones, Lycoming	23	97	4.2
1989	Brad Block, Aurora	26	112	4.3
1990	Chris Hamilton, Blackburn	24	109	4.5
1991	Chris Jans, Loras	25	133	5.3
1992	Jeff deLaveaga, Cal Lutheran	28	122	4.4
1993	Mike Connelly, Catholic	27	111	4.1
1994	Steve Diekmann, Grinnell	21	117	5.6
1995	Steve Diekmann, Grinnell	20	137	*6.8
1996	Ed Brands, Grinnell	24	158	6.6

*Record.

Three-Point Field-Goal Percentage

Season	Player, Team	G	3FG	3FGA	Pct.
1987	Chris Miles, N.J. Inst. of Tech.	26	41	65	63.1
1988	Ray Magee, Richard Stockton	26	41	71	57.7
1989	Reggie James, N.J. Inst. of Tech.	29	59	88	*67.0
1990	Matt Miota, Lawrence	22	33	54	61.1
1991	Mike Bachman, Alma	26	46	76	60.5
1992	John Kmack, Plattsburgh St.	26	44	84	52.4
1993	Brad Apple, Greensboro	26	49	91	53.8
1994	Trever George, Coast Guard	23	38	72	52.8
1995	Tony Frieden, Manchester	32	58	107	54.2
1996	Joey Bigler, John Carroll	27	54	111	48.6

*Record.

Free-Throw Percentage

Season	Player, Team	G	FT	FTA	Pct.
1974	Bruce Johnson, Plymouth St.	17	73	81	90.1
1975	Harold Howard, Austin	24	83	92	90.2
1976	Tim Mieure, Hamline	25	88	95	92.6
1977	Mike Scheib, Susquehanna	22	80	85	94.1
1978	Jerry Prestier, Baldwin-Wallace	25	125	134	93.3
1979	Joe Purcell, King's (Pa.)	26	66	71	93.0
1980	David Whiteside, N.C.-Greensboro	28	120	132	90.9
1981	Jim Cooney, Elmhurst	26	65	72	90.3
1982	Shannon Lilly, Bishop	22	142	153	92.8
1983	Mike Sain, Eureka	26	66	72	91.7
1984	Chris Genian, Redlands	24	71	78	91.0
1985	Bob Possehl, Coe	22	59	65	90.8
1986	Eric Jacobs, Scranton	29	81	87	93.1
1987	Chris Miles, N.J. Inst. of Tech.	26	70	76	92.1
1988	Jeff Bowers, Southern Me.	29	95	102	93.1
1989	Yudi Teichman, Yeshiva	21	119	125	95.2
1990	Todd Reinhardt, Wartburg	26	91	98	92.9
1991	Andy Enfield, Johns Hopkins	29	123	129	*95.3
1992	Chris Carideo, Widener	26	80	84	95.2
1993	Jim Durrell, Colby-Sawyer	25	67	72	93.1
1994	Jason Prenevost, Middlebury	22	60	64	93.8
1995	Matt Freesemann, Wartburg	24	128	138	92.8
1996	Charlie Nanick, Scranton	25	96	103	93.2

*Record.

Photo from Rochester Inst. sports information

Craig Jones of the Rochester Institute of Technology (35) was at his best underneath the basket in 1996. Jones hauled down a Division III-best 14.0 rebounds per game.

Rebound Average

Season	Player, Team	G	Reb.	Avg.
1974	Fred Petty, New Hamp. Col.	22	436	19.8
1975	Larry Parker, Plattsburgh St.	23	430	18.7
1976	Joe Manley, Bowie St.	29	*579	*20.0
1977	Larry Williams, Pratt	24	457	19.0
1978	John Jordan, Southern Me.	29	536	18.5
1979	Dave Kufeld, Yeshiva	20	355	17.8
1980	Dave Kufeld, Yeshiva	20	353	17.7
1981	Kevin Clark, Clark (Mass.)	27	465	17.2
1982	Len Washington, Mass.-Boston	23	361	15.7
1983	Luis Frias, Anna Maria	23	320	13.9
1984	Joe Weber, Aurora	27	370	13.7
1985	Albert Wells, Rust	22	326	14.8
1986	Russell Thompson, Westfield St.	22	338	15.4
1987	Randy Gorniak, Penn St.-Behrend	25	410	16.4
1988	Mike Nelson, Hamilton	26	349	13.4
1989	Clinton Montford, Methodist	27	459	17.0
1990	Michael Stubbs, Trinity (Conn.)	22	398	18.1
1991	Mike Smith, Hamilton	27	435	16.1
1992	Jeff Black, Fitchburg St.	22	363	16.5
1993	Steve Lemmer, Hamilton	27	404	15.0
1994	Chris Sullivan, St. John Fisher	23	319	13.9
1995	Scott Suhr, Milwaukee Engr.	25	349	14.0
1996	Craig Jones, Rochester Inst.	26	363	14.0

*Record.

Assist Average

Season	Player, Team	G	Ast.	Avg.
1989	Robert James, Kean	27	*391	*13.5
1990	Albert Kirchner, Mt. St. Vincent	24	267	11.1
1991	Eric Johnson, Coe	24	238	9.9
1992	Edgar Loera, La Verne	23	202	8.8
1993	David Genovese, Mt. St. Vincent	27	237	8.8
1994	Phil Dixon, Shenandoah	26	253	9.7
1995	Joe Marcotte, N.J. Inst. of Tech	30	292	9.7
1996	Andre Bolton, Chris. Newport	30	289	9.6

*Record.

DIVISION III

Blocked-Shot Average

Season	Player, Team	G	Blk.	Avg.
1993	Matt Cusano, Scranton	29	145	5.0
1994	Andrew South, N.J. Inst. of Tech.	27	128	4.7
1995	Ira Nicholson, Mt. St. Vincent	28	188	6.7
1996	Ira Nicholson, Mt. St. Vincent	27	163	6.0

Steal Average

Season	Player, Team	G	Stl.	Avg.
1993	Moses Jean-Pierre, Plymouth St.	25	114	4.6
1994	Moses Jean-Pierre, Plymouth St.	30	*189	*6.3
1995	Barry Aranoff, Yeshiva	22	121	5.5
1996	Purvis Presha, Stillman	25	144	5.8

*Record.

Annual Team Champions

Won-Lost Percentage

Season	Team	Won	Lost	Pct.
1974	Calvin	21	2	.913
1975	Calvin	22	1	.957
1976	Husson	25	1	.961
1977	Mass.-Boston	25	3	.893
1978	North Park	29	2	.935
1979	Stony Brook	24	3	.889
1980	Franklin Pierce	29	2	.935
1981	Potsdam St.	30	2	.938
1982	St. Andrews	27	3	.900
1983	Roanoke	31	2	.939
1984	Roanoke	27	2	.931
1985	Colby	22	3	.880
1986	Potsdam St.	32	0	1.000
1987	Potsdam St.	28	1	.966
1988	Scranton	29	3	.906
1989	Col. of New Jersey	30	2	.938
1990	Colby	26	1	.963
1991	Hamilton	26	1	.963
1992	Calvin	31	1	.969
1993	Rowan	29	2	.935
1994	Wittenberg	30	2	.938
1995	Wis.-Platteville	31	0	1.000
1996	Wilkes	28	2	.933

Scoring Offense

Season	Team	G	W-L	Pts.	Avg.
1974	Bishop	26	14-12	2,527	97.2
1975	Bishop	29	25-4	2,932	101.1
1976	Husson	26	25-1	2,567	98.7
1977	Mercy	25	16-9	2,587	103.5
1978	Mercy	26	16-10	2,602	100.1
1979	Ashland	25	14-11	2,375	95.0
1980	Franklin Pierce	31	29-2	*3,073	99.1
1981	Husson	23	20-3	2,173	94.5
1982	Husson	26	19-7	2,279	87.7
1983	Bishop	26	18-8	2,529	97.3
1984	St. Joseph's (Me.)	29	24-5	2,666	91.9
1985	St. Joseph's (Me.)	30	22-8	2,752	91.7
1986	St. Joseph's (Me.)	30	26-4	2,837	94.6
1987	Bishop	26	13-13	2,534	97.5
1988	St. Joseph's (Me.)	29	20-9	2,785	96.0
1989	Redlands	25	15-10	2,507	100.3
1990	Salisbury St.	27	14-13	2,822	104.5
1991	Redlands	26	15-11	2,726	104.8
1992	Redlands	25	18-7	2,510	100.4
1993	Salisbury St.	26	18-8	2,551	98.1
1994	Grinnell	21	13-8	2,297	109.4
1995	Grinnell	21	14-7	2,422	*115.3
1996	Grinnell	25	17-8	2,587	103.5

*Record.

Scoring Defense

Season	Team	G	W-L	Pts.	Avg.
1974	Fredonia St.	22	13-9	1,049	*47.7
1975	Chicago	15	9-6	790	52.7
1976	Fredonia St.	23	10-13	1,223	53.2
1977	Hamline	30	22-8	1,560	52.0
1978	Widener	31	26-5	1,693	54.6
1979	Coast Guard	24	21-3	1,160	48.3
1980	John Jay	27	10-17	1,411	52.3
1981	Wis.-Stevens Point	26	19-7	1,394	53.6
1982	Wis.-Stevens Point	28	22-6	1,491	53.3
1983	Ohio Northern	26	18-8	1,379	53.0
1984	Wis.-Stevens Point	32	28-4	1,559	48.7
1985	Wis.-Stevens Point	30	25-3	1,438	47.9
1986	Widener	27	15-12	1,356	50.2
1987	Muskingum	27	16-11	1,454	53.9
1988	Ohio Northern	30	21-9	1,734	57.8
1989	Wooster	28	21-7	1,600	57.1
1990	Randolph-Macon	29	24-5	1,646	56.8
1991	Ohio Northern	27	14-13	1,508	55.9
1992	Wittenberg	29	23-6	1,651	56.9
1993	St. Thomas (Minn.)	28	19-9	1,599	57.1
1994	Yeshiva	22	12-10	1,308	59.5
1995	Johnson St.	26	15-11	1,559	60.0
1996	Upper Iowa	26	21-5	1,500	57.7

*Record.

Scoring Margin

Season	Team	Off.	Def.	Mar.
1974	Fisk	83.3	65.7	17.6
1975	Monmouth (Ill.)	83.9	66.0	17.9
1976	Husson	98.7	67.6	*31.1
1977	Husson	101.2	78.6	22.6
1978	Stony Brook	86.6	68.7	17.9
1979	North Park	84.4	67.3	17.1
1980	Franklin Pierce	99.1	76.5	22.6
1981	Husson	94.5	70.1	24.4
1982	Hope	83.9	70.0	13.8
1983	Trinity (Conn.)	79.8	61.4	18.4
1984	Wis.-Stevens Point	68.4	48.7	19.7
1985	Hope	85.4	66.0	19.4
1986	Potsdam St.	81.5	57.3	24.2
1987	N.J. Inst. of Tech.	90.8	63.9	26.9
1988	Cal St. San B'dino	89.4	69.4	20.0
1989	Col. of New Jersey	92.3	68.5	23.8
1990	Colby	94.7	71.9	22.8
1991	Hamilton	89.8	66.2	23.6
1992	N.J. Inst. of Tech.	95.0	73.4	21.6
1993	N.J. Inst. of Tech.	90.4	65.7	24.7
1994	Rowan	89.6	64.4	25.3
1995	Colby-Sawyer	94.4	71.7	22.6
1996	Cabrini	89.4	67.6	21.8

*Record.

Field-Goal Percentage

Season	Team	FG	FGA	Pct.
1974	Muskingum	560	1,056	53.0
1975	Savannah St.	1,072	1,978	54.2
1976	Stony Brook	778	1,401	55.5
1977	Stony Brook	842	1,455	57.9
1978	Stony Brook	1,033	1,721	*60.0
1979	Stony Brook	980	1,651	59.4
1980	Framingham St.	924	1,613	57.3
1981	Averett	845	1,447	58.4
1982	Lebanon Valley	608	1,098	55.4
1983	Bishop	1,037	1,775	58.4
1984	Framingham St.	849	1,446	58.7
1985	Me.-Farmington	751	1,347	55.8
1986	Frostburg St.	971	1,747	55.6
1987	N.J. Inst. of Tech.	969	1,799	53.9
1988	Rust	878	1,493	58.8
1989	Bridgewater (Va.)	650	1,181	55.0
1990	Wartburg	792	1,474	53.7
1991	Otterbein	1,104	2,050	53.9
1992	Bridgewater (Va.)	706	1,315	53.7
1993	St. John's (Minn.)	744	1,415	52.6

Season	Team	FG	FGA	Pct.
1994	Oglethorpe	774	1,491	51.9
1995	Simpson	892	1,627	54.8
1996	Simpson	946	1,749	54.1

*Record.

Field-Goal Percentage Defense

Season	Team	FG	FGA	Pct.
1978	Grove City	589	1,477	39.9
1979	Coast Guard	464	1,172	39.6
1980	Calvin	552	1,364	40.5
1981	Wittenberg	670	1,651	40.6
1982	Tufts	622	1,505	41.3
1983	Trinity (Conn.)	580	1,408	41.2
1984	Widener	617	1,557	39.6
1985	Colby	679	1,712	39.7
1986	Widener	531	1,344	39.5
1987	Widener	608	1,636	37.2
1988	Rust	603	1,499	40.2
1989	Wooster	595	1,563	38.1
1990	Rochester	760	1,990	38.2
1991	Hamilton	679	1,771	38.3
1992	Scranton	589	1,547	38.1
1993	Scranton	659	1,806	*36.5
1994	Lebanon Valley	708	1,925	36.8
1995	Jersey City St.	702	1,897	37.0
1996	Bowdoin	569	1,482	38.4

*Record.

Three-Point Field Goals Made Per Game

Season	Team	G	3FG	Avg.
1987	Grinnell	22	166	7.5
1988	Southern Me.	29	233	8.0
1989	Redlands	25	261	10.4
1990	Augsburg	25	266	10.6
1991	Redlands	26	307	11.8
1992	Catholic	26	335	12.9
1993	Anna Maria	27	302	11.2
1994	Grinnell	21	297	14.1
1995	Grinnell	21	368	*17.5
1996	Grinnell	25	*415	16.6

*Record.

Three-Point Field-Goal Percentage

Season	Team	G	3FG	3FGA	Pct.
1987	Mass.-Dartmouth	28	102	198	51.5
1988	Richard Stockton	26	122	211	57.8
1989	N.J. Inst. of Tech.	29	124	200	*62.0
1990	Western New Eng.	26	85	167	50.9
1991	Ripon	26	154	331	46.5
1992	Dickinson	27	126	267	47.2
1993	DePauw	26	191	419	45.6
1994	Eureka	31	317	646	49.1
1995	Manchester	32	222	487	45.6
1996	John Carroll	27	169	388	43.6

*Record.

Free-Throw Percentage

Season	Team	FT	FTA	Pct.
1974	Lake Superior St.	369	461	80.0
1975	Muskingum	298	379	78.6
1976	Case Reserve	266	343	77.6
1977	Hamilton	491	640	76.7
1978	Case Reserve	278	351	79.2
1979	Marietta	364	460	79.1
1980	Denison	377	478	78.9
1981	Ripon	378	494	76.5
1982	Otterbein	458	589	77.8
1983	DePauw	368	475	77.5
1984	Redlands	426	534	79.8
1985	Wis.-Stevens Point	363	455	79.8
1986	Heidelberg	375	489	76.7
1987	Denison	442	560	78.9
1988	Capital	377	473	79.7

Season	Team	FT	FTA	Pct.
1989	Colby	464	585	79.3
1990	Colby	485	605	*80.2
1991	Wartburg	565	711	79.5
1992	Thiel	393	491	80.0
1993	Colby	391	506	77.3
1994	Wheaton (Ill.)	455	572	79.5
1995	Baldwin-Wallace	454	582	78.0
1996	Anderson	454	592	76.7

*Record.

Rebound Margin

Season	Team	Off.	Def.	Mar.
1976	Bowie St.	54.0	37.5	16.5
1977	Husson	51.6	35.0	16.7
1978	Gallaudet	46.3	33.0	13.3
1979	St. Lawrence	43.2	28.7	14.5
1980	Elmira	41.4	28.7	12.7
1981	Clark (Mass.)	40.0	25.0	15.0
1982	Maryville (Mo.)	41.0	26.7	14.4
1983	Framingham St.	38.0	22.2	15.8
1984	New England Col.	43.3	29.3	14.0
1985	Bethel (Minn.)	45.0	32.2	12.8
1986	St. Joseph's (Me.)	43.7	29.5	14.2
1987	Elmira	40.6	29.3	11.3
1988	Cal St. San B'dino	46.6	29.7	16.9
1989	Yeshiva	49.8	34.6	15.2
1990	Bethel (Minn.)	42.2	30.3	12.0
1991	Hamilton	49.6	32.5	*17.0
1992	Bethel (Minn.)	42.3	31.0	11.3
1993	Eureka	33.9	22.2	11.7
1994	Maritime (N.Y.)	46.3	32.3	14.1
1995	Wittenberg	43.1	29.2	13.9
1996	Cabrini	47.9	34.7	13.1

*Record.

All-Time Winningest Teams

Includes records as a senior college only; minimum 10 seasons of competition. Postseason games are included.

Percentage

Team	Yrs.	Won	Lost	Pct.
1. Cabrini	16	323	133	.708
2. Wittenberg	85	1,309	558	.701
3. Jersey City St.	61	625	300	.676
4. Defiance	49	826	406	.670
5. Calvin	76	981	502	.661
6. St. Joseph's (Me.)	25	432	223	.660
7. Hope	90	1,138	595	.657
8. Wis.-Eau Claire	80	1,101	*577	.656
9. Staten Island	19	343	185	.650
10. Richard Stockton	24	407	222	.647
11. Hartwick	66	879	492	.641
12. Roanoke	83	1,068	613	.635
13. North Park	38	607	355	.631
14. Beloit	89	1,041	613	.629
15. Wooster	96	1,169	693	.628
16. St. Thomas (Minn.)	79	1,147	681	.627
17. Williams	95	1,038	617	.627
18. Ill. Wesleyan	86	1,210	721	.627
19. New York U.	78	959	573	.626
20. Mt. St. Vincent	16	239	143	.626
21. Wartburg	60	870	548	.614
22. Chris. Newport	29	460	291	.613
23. Augsburg	37	573	366	.610
24. Colby	57	794	516	.606
25. Augustana (Ill.)	91	1,093	723	.602

*Includes one tie.

DIVISION III

Victories

Team	Yrs.	Won	Lost	Pct.
1. Wittenberg	85	1,309	558	.701
2. Ill. Wesleyan	86	1,210	721	.627
3. Wooster	96	1,169	693	.628
4. St. Thomas (Minn.)	79	1,147	681	.627
5. Hope	90	1,138	595	.657
5. Neb. Wesleyan	91	1,138	791	.590
7. Springfield	87	1,116	744	.600
8. Wis.-Eau Claire	80	1,101	*577	.656
9. Augustana (Ill.)	91	1,093	723	.602
10. Hamline	86	1,092	728	.600
11. Scranton	79	1,090	744	.594
12. Randolph-Macon	83	1,074	755	.587
13. Roanoke	83	1,068	613	.635
14. Wheaton (Ill.)	95	1,065	*878	.548
15. Gust. Adolphus	85	1,049	812	.564
16. Loras	88	1,045	800	.566
17. Beloit	89	1,041	613	.629
18. Muskingum	92	1,038	758	.578
18. Williams	95	1,038	617	.627
20. Ohio Wesleyan	91	1,027	879	.539
20. Wis.-Stevens Point	97	1,027	703	.594
22. Millikin	89	1,013	823	.552
23. Monmouth (Ill.)	96	1,010	738	.578
24. Capital	90	1,007	671	.600
25. Mount Union	99	1,002	864	.537

*Includes one tie.

All-Time Won-Lost Records

(No Minimum Seasons of Competition)

Team	First Season	Yrs.	Won	Lost	Pct.
Albion	1898	85	825	770	.517
Albright	1911	84	968	855	.531
Alfred	1921	74	618	827	.428
Allegheny	1896	101	914	771	.542
Allentown	1969	28	284	388	.423
Amherst	1902	95	804	630	.561
Anderson	1931	65	772	774	.499
Augsburg	1960	37	573	366	.610
Augustana (Ill.)	1901	91	1,093	723	.602
Aurora	1928	66	635	751	.458
Beloit	1906	89	1,041	613	.629
Benedictine (Ill.)	1966	30	395	364	.520
Bethel (Minn.)	1947	50	537	602	.471
Binghamton	1947	50	421	613	.407
Bluffton	1915	81	661	953	.410
Bridgewater (Va.)	1903	75	649	837	.437
Bri'water (Mass.)	1907	91	657	701	.484
Brockport St.	1929	64	654	617	.515
Cabrini	1981	16	323	133	.708
Cal Lutheran	1962	35	394	561	.413
UC San Diego	1966	21	408	380	.518
Calvin	1920	76	981	502	.661
Capital	1907	90	1,007	671	.600
Carroll (Wis.)	1956	41	382	595	.391
Carthage	1907	88	766	967	.442
Case Reserve	1902	95	983	761	.564
Catholic	1912	82	864	**911	.487
Central (Iowa)	1924	73	783	720	.521
Chicago	1903	92	943	949	.498
Chris. Newport	1968	29	460	291	.613
CCNY	1905	91	895	800	.528
Clarkson	1930	67	501	805	.384
Coast Guard	1926	71	572	762	.429
Colby	1938	57	794	516	.606
Colorado Col.	1915	82	683	839	.449
Cornell College	1910	87	809	784	.508
Cortland St.	1926	71	691	649	.516
Curry	1967	31	237	479	.331
Defiance	1948	49	826	406	.670
Delaware Valley	1949	47	318	695	.314
DePauw	1904	90	989	**801	.552
Dickinson	1900	86	725	*828	.467
Dubuque	1915	82	779	775	.501
Edgewood	1972	21	288	224	.563
Elmira	1971	26	344	303	.532
Emory	1987	10	111	140	.442
Emory & Henry	1927	65	678	729	.482

Team	First Season	Yrs.	Won	Lost	Pct.
Eureka	1920	75	872	693	.557
FDU-Madison	1959	38	412	437	.485
Franklin	1907	90	913	847	.519
Frank. & Marsh.	1900	92	985	746	.569
Frostburg St.	1937	53	580	621	.483
Gallaudet	1904	93	488	*1,123	.303
Gettysburg	1901	93	956	884	.520
Goucher	1991	6	71	81	.467
Guilford	1906	82	742	839	.469
Gust. Adolphus	1904	85	1,049	812	.564
Hamilton	1921	70	733	553	.570
Hamline	1910	86	1,092	728	.600
Hampden-Sydney	1909	85	928	809	.534
Hartwick	1928	66	879	492	.641
Heidelberg	1903	90	767	888	.463
Hope	1901	90	1,138	595	.657
Hunter	1953	42	518	457	.531
Ill. Wesleyan	1910	86	1,210	721	.627
Ithaca	1930	66	796	567	.584
Jersey City St.	1935	61	625	300	.676
John Carroll	1920	75	699	782	.472
Johns Hopkins	1920	71	583	798	.422
Juniata	1905	92	683	971	.413
Kalamazoo	1907	89	945	778	.548
King's (Pa.)	1947	50	651	540	.547
Knox	1909	87	784	748	.512
Lakeland	1934	63	950	683	.582
Lebanon Valley	1904	93	786	815	.491
Loras	1909	88	1,045	800	.566
Luther	1905	92	491	349	.585
Lycoming	1949	48	481	577	.455
Lynchburg	1957	40	438	554	.442
Manhattanville	1974	23	281	307	.478
Marietta	1902	92	824	919	.473
Mary Washington	1975	22	205	343	.374
Marymount (Va.)	1988	9	98	133	.424
Mass.-Boston	1981	16	162	244	.399
Mass.-Dartmouth	1967	30	465	308	.602
Menlo	1987	10	144	113	.560
Merchant Marine	1946	51	459	704	.395
Messiah	1962	35	376	417	.474
Millikin	1904	89	1,013	823	.552
Monmouth (Ill.)	1900	96	1,010	738	.578
Montclair St.	1931	67	834	658	.559
Moravian	1936	55	650	618	.513
Mt. St. Vincent	1981	16	239	143	.626
Mount Union	1896	99	1,002	864	.537
Muhlenberg	1901	89	967	873	.526
Muskingum	1903	92	1,038	758	.578
Nazareth	1978	19	288	195	.596
Neb. Wesleyan	1906	91	1,138	791	.590
N.J. Inst. of Tech.	1954	43	549	408	.574
New York U.	1906	78	959	573	.626
N.C. Wesleyan	1964	33	345	420	.451
North Central	1948	49	468	702	.400
North Park	1959	38	607	355	.631
Oberlin	1903	93	682	883	.436
Occidental	1981	16	191	219	.466
Ohio Northern	1911	84	935	769	.549
Ohio Wesleyan	1906	91	1,027	879	.539
Otterbein	1903	93	947	787	.546
Plymouth St.	1948	49	581	484	.546
Ramapo	1972	25	207	385	.350
Randolph-Macon	1910	83	1,074	755	.587
Redlands	1917	79	857	697	.551
Richard Stockton	1973	24	407	222	.647
Ripon	1898	98	910	739	.552
Roanoke	1911	83	1,068	613	.635
Rochester	1902	95	984	760	.564
Rochester Inst.	1916	76	769	719	.517
Rose-Hulman	1901	74	724	709	.505
Rowan	1923	54	695	540	.563
St. John Fisher	1964	33	471	321	.595
St. John's (Minn.)	1903	94	870	**902	.491
St. Joseph's (Me.)	1972	25	432	223	.660
St. Mary's (Md.)	1967	30	322	434	.426
St. Norbert	1917	78	736	685	.518
St. Thomas (Minn.)	1917	79	1,147	681	.627
Salisbury St.	1963	34	403	426	.486
Salve Regina	1975	22	174	276	.387
Scranton	1917	79	1,090	744	.594
Sewanee	1927	70	572	749	.433
Southern Me.	1923	79	714	534	.572

Team	First Season	Yrs.	Won	Lost	Pct.
Springfield	1906	87	1,116	744	.600
Staten Island	1978	19	343	185	.650
Stevens Tech	1917	80	596	634	.485
Susquehanna	1902	94	752	*922	.449
Swarthmore	1902	95	693	951	.422
Thiel	1920	75	412	976	.297
Trinity (Conn.)	1914	83	796	654	.549
Tufts	1912	85	839	792	.514
Upper Iowa	1916	81	700	787	.471
Upsala	1925	64	761	650	.539
Wabash	1897	100	937	*871	.518
Wartburg	1936	60	870	548	.614
Washington (Md.)	1914	84	866	*794	.522
Washington (Mo.)	1905	90	835	796	.512
Wash. & Jeff.	1913	84	801	685	.539
Wash. & Lee	1907	78	964	*848	.532
Wesleyan (Conn.)	1902	95	853	758	.529
Western Conn. St.	1947	50	512	555	.480
Western New Eng.	1966	28	355	381	.482
Westminster (Mo.)	1906	81	792	*846	.484
Wheaton (Ill.)	1902	95	1,065	*878	.548
Widener	1906	89	915	701	.566
Wilkes	1947	50	529	612	.464
Wm. Paterson	1939	55	648	654	.498
William Penn	1906	91	706	724	.494
Williams	1901	95	1,038	617	.627
Wis.-Eau Claire	1917	80	1,101	*577	.656
Wis.-Platteville	1905	85	929	685	.576
Wis.-Stevens Point	1897	97	1,027	703	.594
Wis.-Whitewater	1903	87	855	739	.536
Wittenberg	1912	85	1,309	558	.701
Wooster	1901	96	1,169	693	.628
Worcester St.	1950	45	490	543	.474
Worcester Tech	1910	87	721	797	.475
Yeshiva	1936	61	509	680	.428

*Includes one tie. **Includes two ties.*

Winningest Teams of the 1990s

(Minimum 3 seasons as an NCAA member)

Team	Won	Lost	Pct.	QTR	Highest '90s Finish
1. Frank. & Marsh.	184	22	.893	3	2nd (1991)
2. Wis.-Platteville	182	22	.892	4	CH (1991 & 1995)
3. Wittenberg	174	33	.841	3	3rd (1994)
4. N.J. Inst. of Tech.	163	34	.827	1	—
5. Colby	150	32	.824	—	—
6. Williams	148	32	.822	—	—
7. Rowan	168	38	.816	3	CH (1996)
8. Hope	156	36	.813	1	2nd (1996)
9. Calvin	162	38	.810	4	CH (1992)
10. Salem St.	155	40	.795	—	—
11. Buffalo St.	155	41	.791	—	—
12. Wooster	153	41	.789	—	—
13. Western Conn. St.	152	42	.784	1	—
14. Ripon	134	38	.779	—	—
15. Hamilton	143	43	.769	—	—
16. Mass.-Dartmouth	152	46	.768	1	4th (1993)
17. Wis.-Eau Claire	149	46	.764	—	—
18. Maryville (Tenn.)	139	44	.760	1	—
19. Ill. Wesleyan	149	48	.756	3	3rd (1996)
20. St. Joseph's (Me.)	151	49	.755	—	—
21. New York U.	143	47	.753	1	2nd (1994)
22. St. Thomas (Minn.)	146	49	.749	1	4th (1994)
23. Chris. Newport	147	50	.746	—	—
24. Eureka	142	52	.732	—	—
25. Richard Stockton	140	52	.729	1	—
26. Hampden-Sydney	139	54	.720	1	—
27. Rhodes	127	50	.718	—	—
28. Scranton	133	53	.715	1	—
29. Babson	131	54	.708	—	—
30. Geneseo St.	133	55	.707	—	—

QTR - Quarterfinal Appearances

DIVISION III

Individual
Collegiate Records

Individual Collegiate Records

Individual collegiate leaders are determined by comparing the best records in all three divisions in equivalent categories. Included are players whose careers were split between two divisions (e.g., Dwight Lamar of Southwestern Louisiana or Howard Shockley of Salisbury State).

Single-Game Records

POINTS

Pts.	Div.	Player, Team vs. Opponent	Date
113	II	Clarence "Bevo" Francis, Rio Grande vs. Hillsdale	Feb. 2, 1954
100	I	Frank Selvy, Furman vs. Newberry	Feb. 13, 1954
85	I	Paul Arizin, Villanova vs. Philadelphia NAMC	Feb. 12, 1949
84	II	Clarence "Bevo" Francis, Rio Grande vs. Alliance	1954
82	II	Clarence "Bevo" Francis, Rio Grande vs. Bluffton	1954
81	I	Freeman Williams, Portland St. vs. Rocky Mountain	Feb. 3, 1978
80	II	Paul Crissman, Southern Cal. Col. vs. Pacific Christian	Feb. 18, 1966
77	II	William English, Winston-Salem vs. Fayetteville St.	Feb. 19, 1968
75	II	Travis Grant, Kentucky St. vs. Northwood	1970
73	I	Bill Mlkvy, Temple vs. Wilkes	Mar. 3, 1951
72	II	Nate DeLong, Wis.-River Falls vs. Winona St.	Feb. 24, 1948
72	II	Lloyd Brown, Aquinas vs. Cleary	1953
72	II	Clarence "Bevo" Francis, Rio Grande vs. Calif. (Pa.)	1953
72	II	John McElroy, Youngstown St. vs. Wayne St. (Mich.)	Feb. 26, 1969
72	I	Kevin Bradshaw, U.S. Int'l vs. Loyola Marymount	Jan. 5, 1991
71	II	Clayborn Jones, L.A. Pacific vs. L.A. Baptist	Jan. 30, 1965
71	I	Freeman Williams, Portland St. vs. Southern Ore.	Feb. 9, 1977
70	II	Paul Wilcox, Davis & Elkins vs. Glenville St.	1959
70	II	Bo Clark, Central Fla. vs. Fla. Memorial	Jan. 31, 1977
69	II	Clarence "Bevo" Francis, Rio Grande vs. Wilberforce	1953
69	II	Clarence Burks, St. Augustine's vs. St. Paul's	1955
69	I	Pete Maravich, LSU vs. Alabama	Feb. 7, 1970
69	II	John Rinka, Kenyon vs. Wooster	Dec. 9, 1969
69	III	Steve Diekmann, Grinnell vs. Simpson	Nov. 19, 1994
68	II	Florindo Vieira, Quinnipiac vs. Brooklyn Poly	Feb. 13, 1957
68	II	Wayne Proffitt, Lynchburg vs. N.C.-Charlotte	Feb. 5, 1966
68	II	Earl Monroe, Winston-Salem vs. Fayetteville St.	Jan. 6, 1967
68	I	Calvin Murphy, Niagara vs. Syracuse	Dec. 7, 1968

FIELD-GOAL PERCENTAGE

(Minimum 13 field goals made)

Pct.	Div.	Player, Team vs. Opponent (FG-FGA)	Date
100	II	Lance Berwald, North Dak. St. vs. Augustana (S.D.) (20 of 20)	Feb. 17, 1984

Ben Handlogten of Western Michigan etched his name in the records book on January 27, 1996, when he made 13 of 13 field-goal attempts against Toledo.

Pct.	Div.	Player, Team vs. Opponent (FG-FGA)	Date
100	III	Jason Light, Emory & Henry vs. King (Tenn.) (18 of 18)	Dec. 2, 1995
100	I	Clifford Rozier, Louisville vs. Eastern Ky. (15 of 15)	Dec. 11, 1993
100	II	Derrick Scott, Calif. (Pa.) vs. Columbia Union (14 of 14)	Dec. 6, 1995
100	I	Dan Henderson, Arkansas St. vs. Ga. Southern (14 of 14)	Feb. 26, 1976
100	I	Cornelius Holden, Louisville vs. Southern Miss. (14 of 14)	Mar. 3, 1990
100	I	Dana Jones, Pepperdine vs. Boise St. (14 of 14)	Nov. 30, 1991
100	III	Waverly Yates, Clark (Mass.) vs. Suffolk (14 of 14)	Feb. 10, 1993
100	II	Derrick Freeman, Indiana (Pa.) vs. Clarion (13 of 13)	Feb. 17, 1996
100	I	Ben Handlogten, Western Mich. vs. Toledo (13 of 13)	Jan. 27, 1996
100	I	Ralfs Jansons, St. Rose vs. Concordia (N.Y.) (13 of 13)	Jan. 13, 1996
100	I	Ted Guzek, Butler vs. Michigan (13 of 13)	Dec. 15, 1956
100	I	Rick Dean, Syracuse vs. Colgate (13 of 13)	Feb. 14, 1966
100	I	Gary Lechman, Gonzaga vs. Portland St. (13 of 13)	Jan. 21, 1967
100	I	Kevin King, N.C.-Charlotte vs. South Ala. (13 of 13)	Feb. 20, 1978
100	I	Vernon Smith, Texas A&M vs. Alas. Anchorage (13 of 13)	Nov. 26, 1978
100	I	Steve Johnson, Oregon St. vs. Hawaii-Hilo (13 of 13)	Dec. 5, 1979
100	I	Antoine Carr, Wichita St. vs. Abilene Christian (13 of 13)	Nov. 28, 1980
100	III	Rich Lengieza, Nichols vs. Mass.-Dartmouth (13 of 13)	Feb. 22, 1981
100	I	Doug Hashley, Montana St. vs. Idaho St. (13 of 13)	Feb. 5, 1982
100	I	Brad Daugherty, North Caro. vs. UCLA (13 of 13)	Nov. 24, 1985
100	III	Bruce Merklinger, Susquehanna vs. Drew (13 of 13)	Jan. 22, 1986
100	III	Antonio Randolph, Averett vs. Methodist (13 of 13)	Jan. 26, 1991
100	III	Pat Holland, Randolph-Macon vs. East. Mennonite (13 of 13)	Feb. 9, 1991
100	I	Ricky Butler, UC Irvine vs. Cal St. Fullerton (13 of 13)	Feb. 21, 1991
100	I	Rafael Solis, Brooklyn vs. Wagner (13 of 13)	Dec. 11, 1991
100	III	Todd Seifferlein, DePauw vs. Franklin (13 of 13)	Jan. 18, 1992

THREE-POINT FIELD GOALS MADE

3FG	Div.	Player, Team vs. Opponent	Date
14	III	Ed Brands, Grinnell vs. Ripon	Feb. 24, 1996
14	I	Dave Jamerson, Ohio vs. Charleston (S.C.)	Dec. 21, 1989
14	I	Askia Jones, Kansas St. vs. Fresno St.	Mar. 24, 1994
14	II	Andy Schmidtmann, Wis.-Parkside vs. Lakeland	Feb. 14, 1989
14	III	Steve Diekmann, Grinnell vs. Illinois Col.	Feb. 18, 1994
14	III	Steve Diekmann, Grinnell vs. Simpson	Nov. 19, 1994
13	II	Danny Lewis, Wayne St. (Mich.) vs. Michigan Tech	Feb. 20, 1993
13	III	Eric Ochel, Sewanee vs. Emory	Feb. 22, 1995
12	III	Eric Burdette, Wis.-Whitewater vs. Wis.-Eau Claire	Feb. 24, 1996
12	II	Tony Sanders, Cal St. San B'dino vs. Grand Canyon	Feb. 22, 1996
12	I	David McMahan, Winthrop vs. Coastal Caro.	Jan. 15, 1996
12	III	Mike Webster, Rose-Hulman vs. Eureka	Dec. 13, 1986
12	I	Gary Bossert, Niagara vs. Siena	Jan. 7, 1987
12	I	Darrin Fitzgerald, Butler vs. Detroit	Feb. 9, 1987
12	II	Thomas Jones, Ala.-Huntsville vs. Cumberland	Dec. 14, 1989
12	III	Todd Hennink, Calvin vs. Malone	Nov. 24, 1990
12	III	Craig Studer, Grinnell vs. Knox	Dec. 7, 1990
12	II	Phil Clark, Armstrong Atlantic vs. West Ga.	Dec. 28, 1991
12	II	Mike Morrison, Keene St. vs. New Hamp. Col.	Nov. 21, 1992
12	III	Brett Hefner, Illinois Col. vs. Maryville (Mo.)	Nov. 25, 1992
12	II	Russ Crafton, Chadron St. vs. Adams St.	Feb. 5, 1993
12	II	Eric Carpenter, Cal St. San B'dino vs. Metro St.	Feb. 19, 1993
12	III	Kirk Anderson, Augustana (Ill.) vs. Wis.-Platteville	Mar. 13, 1993
12	I	Alex Dillard, Arkansas vs. Delaware St.	Dec. 11, 1993
12	I	Mitch Taylor, Southern U. vs. La. Christian	Dec. 1, 1994
12	III	Steve Diekmann, Grinnell vs. Monmouth (Ill.)	Dec. 7, 1994
12	II	Rick Barry, Quinnipiac vs. Bentley	Feb. 1, 1995
12	II	Brent Kincaid, Calif. (Pa.) vs. Slippery Rock	Feb. 8, 1995
12	II	Damien Blair, West Chester vs. Cheyney	Feb. 11, 1995

REBOUNDS

Reb.	Div.	Player, Team vs. Opponent	Date
51	I	Bill Chambers, William & Mary vs. Virginia	Feb. 14, 1953
46	II	Tom Hart, Middlebury vs. Trinity (Conn.)	Feb. 5, 1955
46	II	Tom Hart, Middlebury vs. Clarkson	Feb. 12, 1955
45	II	William Henrikson, Windham vs. New England Col.	Feb. 4, 1970
44	II	Charles McCullough, Loyola (Md.) vs. Western Md.	Feb. 17, 1955
44	II	Norman Rokeach, LIU-Brooklyn vs. Brooklyn Poly	Dec. 28, 1963
43	I	Charlie Slack, Marshall vs. Morris Harvey	Jan. 12, 1954
43	II	Bob Bessoir, Scranton vs. King's (Pa.)	Mar. 5, 1955
42	I	Tom Heinsohn, Holy Cross vs. Boston College	Mar. 1, 1955
42	II	Larry Gooding, St. Augustine's vs. Shaw	Jan. 12, 1974
41	II	Richard Kross, American Int'l vs. Springfield	Feb. 19, 1958
40	II	Ellerbe Neal, Wofford vs. Presbyterian	Jan. 3, 1953
40	I	Art Quimby, Connecticut vs. Boston U.	Jan. 11, 1955
40	II	Donnie Fowler, Wofford vs. Mercer	Jan. 22, 1955
40	II	Charlie Harrison, North Caro. A&T vs. Johnson Smith	Feb. 8, 1958
40	II	Anthony Romano, Willimantic St. vs. Fitchburg St.	Jan. 5, 1963
40	II	Ed Halicki, Monmouth (N.J.) vs. Southeastern	Dec. 4, 1970

Reb.	Div.	Player, Team vs. Opponent	Date
39	II	Maurice Stokes, St. Francis (Pa.) vs. John Carroll	Jan. 28, 1955
39	II	Roger Lotchin, Millikin vs. Lake Forest	Feb. 11, 1956
39	II	Joe Cole, Southwest Tex. St. vs. Tex. Lutheran	Dec. 10, 1956
39	I	Dave DeBusschere, Detroit vs. Central Mich.	Jan. 30, 1960
39	I	Keith Swagerty, Pacific (Cal.) vs. UC Santa Barb.	Mar. 5, 1965
39	II	Curtis Pritchett, St. Augustine vs. St. Paul's	Jan. 24, 1970
38		14 tied	

(Since 1973)

Reb.	Div.	Player, Team vs. Opponent	Date
42	II	Larry Gooding, St. Augustine's vs. Shaw	Jan. 12, 1974
36	III	Mark Veenstra, Calvin vs. Southern Colo.	Feb. 3, 1976
36	III	Clinton Montford, Methodist vs. Warren Wilson	Jan. 21, 1989
35	III	Ayal Hod, Yeshiva vs. Vassar	Feb. 22, 1989
34	I	David Vaughn, Oral Roberts vs. Brandeis	Jan. 8, 1973
34	II	Major Jones, Albany St. (Ga.) vs. Valdosta St.	Jan. 23, 1975
34	II	Herman Harris, Mississippi Val. vs. Texas Southern	Jan. 12, 1976
34	III	Walt Edwards, Husson vs. Me.-Farmington	Feb. 24, 1976
33	II	Joe Dombrowski, St. Anselm vs. New Hampshire	Dec. 8, 1974
33	II	Lee Roy Williams, Cal Poly Pomona vs. Wheaton	Dec. 15, 1973
33	III	Willie Parr, LeMoyne Owen vs. Southern U.	Jan. 10, 1976
33	III	Larry Williams, Pratt vs. Mercy	Jan. 22, 1977
32	II	Marvin Webster, Morgan St. vs. South Caro. St.	Dec. 8, 1973
32	II	Earl Williams, Winston-Salem vs. N.C. Central	Dec. 13, 1973
32	III	Fred Petty, New Hamp. College vs. Curry	Jan. 28, 1974
32	II	George Wilson, Union (Ky.) vs. Southwestern	1974
32	II	Tony DuCros, Regis vs. Neb. Wesleyan	Feb. 28, 1975
32	I	Durand Macklin, LSU vs. Tulane	Nov. 26, 1976
32	II	Robert Clements, Jacksonville vs. Shorter	Jan. 12, 1977
32	I	Jervaughn Scales, Southern U. vs. Grambling St.	Feb. 7, 1994
31	II	Pete Harris, Stephen F. Austin vs. Texas A&M	Jan. 22, 1973
31	I	Jim Bradley, Northern Ill. vs. Wis.-Milwaukee	Feb. 19, 1973
31	III	John Humphrie, Swarthmore vs. Ursinus	Dec. 8, 1973
31	II	Roy Smith, Kentucky St. vs. Union (Ky.)	Feb. 10, 1975
31	III	Larry Parker, Plattsburgh St. vs. Clarkson	Jan. 19, 1976
31	I	Calvin Natt, Northeast La. vs. Ga. Southern	Dec. 29, 1976
31	II	Charles Wode, Mississippi Val. vs. Miss. Industrial	Dec. 10, 1977
31	III	Jon Ford, Norwich vs. Johnson St.	Feb. 16, 1982

ASSISTS

Ast.	Div.	Player, Team vs. Opponent	Date
26	III	Robert James, Kean vs. N.J. Inst. of Tech	Mar. 11, 1989
25	II	Ali Baaqar, Morris Brown vs. Albany St. (Ga.)	Jan. 26, 1991
25	II	Adrian Hutt, Metro St. vs. Cal St. Sacramento	Feb. 9, 1991
24	II	Steve Ray, Bridgeport vs. Sacred Heart	Jan. 25, 1989
24	II	Steve Ray, Bridgeport vs. New Haven	Feb. 8, 1989
24	III	Adam Dzierzynski, Chapman vs. Amer. Indian Bible	Feb. 9, 1995
23	II	Steve Ray, Bridgeport vs. St. Anselm	Nov. 26, 1989
23	II	Jeff Duvall, Oakland City vs. St. Meinrad	Dec. 3, 1991
22	I	Tony Fairley, Charleston So. vs. Armstrong Atlantic	Feb. 9, 1987
22	I	Avery Johnson, Southern U. vs. Texas Southern	Jan. 25, 1988
22	I	Sherman Douglas, Syracuse vs. Providence	Jan. 28, 1989
22	II	Antonio Whitley, St. Augustine's vs. Shaw	Feb. 1, 1992
22	II	Ernest Jenkins, N.M. Highlands vs. Panhandle St.	Jan. 29, 1994
21	I	Mark Wade, UNLV vs. Navy	Dec. 29, 1986
21	I	Kelvin Scarborough, New Mexico vs. Hawaii	Feb. 13, 1987
21	I	Anthony Manuel, Bradley vs. UC Irvine	Dec. 19, 1987
21	I	Avery Johnson, Southern U. vs. Alabama St.	Jan. 16, 1988
21	III	Ron Torgalski, Hamilton vs. Vassar	Jan. 28, 1989
21	III	Mark Cottom, Ferrum vs. Concord	Dec. 15, 1990
21	II	Candice Pickens, Calif. (Pa.) vs. Slippery Rock	Feb. 8, 1995
20		21 tied	

BLOCKED SHOTS

Blk.	Div.	Player, Team vs. Opponent	Date
15	III	Antoine Hyman, Keuka vs. Hobart	Feb. 21, 1996
15	III	Erick Lidecis, Maritime (N.Y.) vs. Stevens Tech	Nov. 30, 1993
15	II	Mark Hensel, Pitt.-Johnstown vs. Slippery Rock	Jan. 22, 1994
15	III	Roy Woods, Fontbonne vs. MacMurray	Jan. 26, 1995
15	III	Ira Nicholson, Mt. St. Vincent vs. Stevens Tech	Nov. 27, 1994
14	I	Roy Rogers, Alabama vs. Georgia	Feb. 10, 1996
14	II	Victorlus Payne, Lane vs. Talladega	Jan. 26, 1996
14	I	David Robinson, Navy vs. N.C.-Wilmington	Jan. 4, 1986
14	I	Shawn Bradley, Brigham Young vs. Eastern Ky.	Dec. 7, 1990
14	II	Maurice Barnett, Elizabeth City St. vs. Bowie St.	Feb. 3, 1994
14	III	Andrew South, N.J. Inst. of Tech vs. Stevens Tech	Feb. 14, 1994
13	III	Damon Avinger, CCNY vs. St. Joseph's (N.Y.)	Jan. 7, 1996
13	I	Kevin Roberson, Vermont vs. New Hampshire	Jan. 9, 1992
13	I	Jim McIlvaine, Marquette vs. Northeastern Ill.	Dec. 9, 1992
13	II	Mark Hensel, Pitt.-Johnstown vs. Wheeling Jesuit	Jan. 31, 1994
13	I	Keith Closs, Central Conn. St. vs. St. Francis (Pa.)	Dec. 21, 1994
12		15 tied	

STEALS

Stl.	Div.	Player, Team vs. Opponent	Date
17	III	Matt Newton, Principia vs. Harris-Stowe	Jan. 4, 1994
14	III	Moses Jean-Pierre, Plymouth St. vs. Rivier	Dec. 7, 1993
13	I	Mookie Blaylock, Oklahoma vs. Centenary (La.)	Dec. 12, 1987
13	I	Mookie Blaylock, Oklahoma vs. Loyola Marymount	Dec. 17, 1988
12	III	Deron Black, Allegheny vs. Case Reserve	Jan. 17, 1996
12	III	Jamal Elliott, Haverford vs. Gwynedd Mercy	Jan. 15, 1996
12	I	Kenny Robertson, Cleveland St. vs. Wagner	Dec. 3, 1988
12	III	Moses Jean-Pierre, Plymouth St. vs. Rhode Island Col.	Jan. 23, 1993
12	I	Terry Evans, Oklahoma vs. Florida A&M	Jan. 27, 1993
12	III	David Brown, Westfield St. vs. Albertus Magnus	Jan. 8, 1994
12	III	Barry Aranoff, Yeshiva vs. Purchase St.	Feb. 13, 1995
11		24 tied	

Season Records

(Based on qualifiers for annual championship)

POINTS

Player, Team (Division)	Season	G	FG	3FG	FT	Pts.
Pete Maravich, LSU (I)	1970	31	522	—	337	1,381
Earl Monroe, Winston-Salem (II)	1967	32	509	—	311	1,329
Travis Grant, Kentucky St. (II)	1972	33	539	—	226	1,304
Clarence "Bevo" Francis, Rio Grande (II)	1954	27	444	—	367	1,255
Bill Reigel, McNeese St. (II)	1956	36	425	—	370	1,220
Elvin Hayes, Houston (I)	1968	33	519	—	176	1,214
Frank Selvy, Furman (I)	1954	29	427	—	355	1,209
Pete Maravich, LSU (I)	1969	26	433	—	282	1,148
Pete Maravich, LSU (I)	1968	26	432	—	274	1,138
Bo Kimble, Loyola Marymount (I)	1990	32	404	92	231	1,131
Hersey Hawkins, Bradley (I)	1988	31	377	87	284	1,125
Austin Carr, Notre Dame (I)	1970	29	444	—	218	1,106
Austin Carr, Notre Dame (I)	1971	29	430	—	241	1,101
Otis Birdsong, Houston (I)	1977	36	452	—	186	1,090
Dwight Lamar, Southwestern La. (I)	1972	29	429	—	196	1,054
Kevin Bradshaw, U.S. Int'l (I)	1991	28	358	60	278	1,054
Dwight Lamar, Southwestern La. (II)	1971	29	424	—	196	1,044
Greg Grant, Trenton St. (III)	1989	32	387	76	194	1,044
Dave Russell, Shepherd (III)	1975	32	394	—	249	1,037
Glenn Robinson, Purdue (I)	1994	34	368	79	215	1,030
Oscar Robertson, Cincinnati (I)	1958	28	352	—	280	984
Oscar Robertson, Cincinnati (I)	1959	30	331	—	316	978
Rick Barry, Miami (Fla.) (I)	1965	26	340	—	221	973
Larry Bird, Indiana St. (I)	1979	34	376	—	221	973
Dennis Scott, Georgia Tech (I)	1990	35	336	137	161	970

SCORING AVERAGE

Player, Team (Division)	Season	G	FG	3FG	FT	Pts.	Avg.
Clarence "Bevo" Francis, Rio Grande (II)	1954	27	444	—	367	1,255	46.5
Pete Maravich, LSU (I)	1970	31	522	—	337	1,381	44.5
Pete Maravich, LSU (I)	1969	26	433	—	282	1,148	44.2
Pete Maravich, LSU (I)	1968	26	432	—	274	1,138	43.8
Earl Glass, Miss. Industrial (II)	1963	19	322	—	171	815	42.9
Frank Selvy, Furman (I)	1954	29	427	—	355	1,209	41.7
Earl Monroe, Winston-Salem (II)	1967	32	509	—	311	1,329	41.5
John Rinka, Kenyon (II)	1970	23	354	—	234	942	41.0
Willie Shaw, Lane (II)	1964	18	303	—	121	727	40.4
Johnny Neumann, Mississippi (I)	1971	23	366	—	191	923	40.1
Travis Grant, Kentucky St. (II)	1972	33	539	—	226	1,304	39.5
Thales McReynolds, Miles (II)	1965	18	294	—	118	706	39.2
Bob Johnson, Fitchburg St. (II)	1963	18	213	—	277	703	39.1
Roger Kuss, Wis.-River Falls (II)	1953	21	291	—	235	817	38.9
Freeman Williams, Portland St. (I)	1977	26	417	—	176	1,010	38.8
Billy McGill, Utah (I)	1962	26	394	—	221	1,009	38.8
Calvin Murphy, Niagara (I)	1968	24	337	—	242	916	38.2
Austin Carr, Notre Dame (I)	1970	29	444	—	218	1,106	38.1
Austin Carr, Notre Dame (I)	1971	29	430	—	241	1,101	38.0
Kevin Bradshaw, U.S. Int'l (I)	1991	28	358	60	278	1,054	37.6
Rick Barry, Miami (Fla.) (I)	1965	26	340	—	221	973	37.4
Steve Diekmann, Grinnell (III)	1995	20	223	137	162	745	37.3
Florindo Vieira, Quinnipiac (II)	1954	14	191	—	138	520	37.1
Elvin Hayes, Houston (I)	1968	33	519	—	176	1,214	36.8
Marshall Rogers, Tex.-Pan American (I)	1976	25	361	—	197	919	36.8

FIELD-GOAL PERCENTAGE

Player, Team (Division)	Season	G	FG	FGA	Pct.
Travis Weiss, St. John's (Minn.) (III)	1994	26	160	209	76.6
Pete Metzelaars, Wabash (III)	1982	28	271	360	75.3
Todd Linder, Tampa (II)	1987	32	282	375	75.2
Maurice Stafford, North Ala. (II)	1984	34	198	264	75.0

Player, Team (Division)	Season	G	FG	FGA	Pct.
Tony Rychlec, Mass. Maritime (III)	1981	25	233	311	74.9
Matthew Cornegay, Tuskegee (II)	1982	29	208	278	74.8
Steve Johnson, Oregon St. (I)	1981	28	235	315	74.6
Brian Moten, West Ga. (II)	1992	26	141	192	73.4
Ed Phillips, Alabama A&M (II)	1968	22	154	210	73.3
Tony Rychlec, Mass. Maritime (III)	1982	20	193	264	73.1
Russ Newman, Menlo (III)	1991	26	130	178	73.0
Ed Owens, Hampden-Sydney (III)	1979	24	140	192	72.9
Ray Strozier, Central Mo. St. (II)	1980	28	142	195	72.8
Harold Booker, Cheyney (II)	1965	24	144	198	72.7
Chad Scott, Calif. (Pa.) (II)	1994	30	178	245	72.7
Scott Baxter, Capital (III)	1991	26	164	226	72.6
Maurice Woods, Potsdam St. (III)	1982	30	203	280	72.5
Tom Schurfranz, Bellarmine (II)	1991	30	245	339	72.3
Marv Lewis, LIU-Southampton (II)	1969	24	271	375	72.3
Earl Keith, Stony Brook (III)	1979	24	164	227	72.2
Louis Newsome, North Ala. (II)	1988	29	192	266	72.2
Pete Metzelaars, Wabash (III)	1981	25	204	283	72.1
Ed Phillips, Alabama A&M (II)	1971	24	159	221	71.9
Jon Rosner, Yeshiva (III)	1991	22	141	196	71.9
Gregg Northington, Alabama St. (II)	1971	26	324	451	71.8
Pete Metzelaars, Wabash (III)	1979	24	122	170	71.8

THREE-POINT FIELD GOALS MADE

Player, Team (Division)	Season	G	3FG
Alex Williams, Cal St. Sacramento (II)	1988	30	167
Ed Brands, Grinnell (III)	1996	24	158
Darrin Fitzgerald, Butler (I)	1987	28	158
Freddie Banks, UNLV (I)	1987	39	152
Eric Kline, Northern St. (II)	1994	33	148
Eric Kline, Northern St. (II)	1995	30	148
Randy Rutherford, Oklahoma St. (I)	1995	37	146
Chris Peterson, Eureka (III)	1994	31	145
Dennis Scott, Georgia Tech (I)	1990	35	137
Steve Diekmann, Grinnell (III)	1995	20	137
Ray Gutierrez, Calif. (Pa.) (II)	1993	27	135
Jason Garrow, Augustana (S.D.) (II)	1992	27	135
Chris Jans, Loras (III)	1991	25	133
Timothy Pollard, Mississippi Val. (I)	1988	28	132
Dave Jamerson, Ohio (I)	1990	28	131
Sydney Grider, Southwestern La. (I)	1990	29	131
Eric Burdette, Wis.-Whitewater (III)	1996	28	130
Shawn Williams, Central Okla. (II)	1991	29	129
Ed Brands, Grinnell (III)	1995	20	129
Robert Martin, Cal St. Sacramento (II)	1988	30	128
Lazelle Durden, Cincinnati (I)	1995	34	127
Jeff Fryer, Loyola Marymount (I)	1989	31	126
Kwame Morton, Clarion (II)	1994	26	126
Tommie Spearman, Columbus St. (II)	1995	29	126
Damien Blair, West Chester (II)	1994	28	125

THREE-POINT FIELD GOALS MADE PER GAME

Player, Team (Division)	Season	G	3FG	Avg.
Steve Diekmann, Grinnell (III)	1995	20	137	6.85
Ed Brands, Grinnell (III)	1996	24	158	6.58
Ed Brands, Grinnell (III)	1995	20	129	6.45
Darrin Fitzgerald, Butler (I)	1987	28	158	5.64
Steve Diekmann, Grinnell (III)	1994	21	117	5.57
Alex Williams, Cal St. Sacramento (II)	1988	30	167	5.57
Chris Jans, Loras (III)	1991	25	133	5.32
Jason Garrow, Augustana (S.D.) (II)	1992	27	135	5.00
David Bailey, Concordia (Ill.) (III)	1994	24	120	5.00
Eric Kline, Northern St. (II)	1995	30	148	4.93
Ray Gutierrez, Calif. (Pa.) (II)	1993	29	142	4.90
Kwame Morton, Clarion (II)	1994	26	126	4.85
John Boyd, LeMoyne-Owen (II)	1992	26	123	4.73
Duane Huddleston, Mo.-Rolla (II)	1988	25	118	4.72
Timothy Pollard, Mississippi Val. (I)	1988	28	132	4.71
Chris Brown, UC Irvine (I)	1994	26	122	4.69
Dave Jamerson, Ohio (I)	1990	28	131	4.68
Chris Peterson, Eureka (III)	1994	31	145	4.68
Eric Burdette, Wis.-Whitewater (III)	1996	28	130	4.64
Chris Geruschat, Bethany (W.Va.) (III)	1991	24	111	4.63
Chris Carideo, Widener (III)	1994	24	110	4.58
Sydney Grider, Southwestern La. (I)	1990	29	131	4.52
Eric Kline, Northern St. (II)	1994	33	148	4.48
Damien Blair, West Chester (II)	1994	28	125	4.46
Eric Carpenter, Cal St. San B'dino (II)	1994	26	116	4.46

THREE-POINT FIELD-GOAL PERCENTAGE

Player, Team (Division)	Season	G	3FG	3FGA	Pct.
Reggie James, N.J. Inst. of Tech (III)	1989	29	59	88	67.0
Ray Lee, Hampton (II)	1988	24	39	60	65.0
Glenn Tropf, Holy Cross (I)	1988	29	52	82	63.4
Sean Wightman, Western Mich. (I)	1992	30	48	76	63.2
Chris Miles, N.J. Inst. of Tech (III)	1987	26	41	65	63.1
Steve Hood, Winston-Salem (II)	1988	28	42	67	62.7
Chris Miles, N.J. Inst. of Tech (III)	1989	29	46	75	61.3
Matt Miota, Lawrence (III)	1990	22	33	54	61.1
Mike Bachman, Alma (III)	1991	26	46	76	60.5
Mark Wiley, Fort Hays St. (II)	1990	29	49	81	60.5
Aaron Fehler, Oakland City (II)	1995	26	73	121	60.3
Keith Jennings, East Tenn. St. (I)	1991	33	84	142	59.2
Aaron Baker, Mississippi Col. (II)	1989	27	69	117	59.0
Dave Calloway, Monmouth (N.J.) (I)	1989	28	48	82	58.5
Walter Hurd, Johnson Smith (II)	1989	27	49	84	58.3
Matt Hopson, Oakland City (II)	1996	31	84	145	57.9
Ray Magee, Richard Stockton (III)	1988	26	41	71	57.7
Keith Orchard, Whitman (III)	1988	26	42	73	57.5
Jon Bryant, St. Cloud St. (II)	1996	27	54	94	57.4
Steve Kerr, Arizona (I)	1988	38	114	199	57.3
Reginald Jones, Prairie View (I)	1987	28	64	112	57.1
Brian O'Donnell, Rutgers-Camden (III)	1988	24	65	114	57.0
Eric Harris, Bishop (III)	1987	26	91	160	56.9
Rick Brown, Muskingum (III)	1988	30	71	125	56.8
Scott Martin, Rollins (II)	1991	28	114	201	56.7
Jamie Eichel, Fredonia St. (III)	1989	24	51	90	56.7

FREE-THROW PERCENTAGE

Player, Team (Division)	Season	G	FT	FTA	Pct.
Craig Collins, Penn St. (I)	1985	27	94	98	95.9
Andy Enfield, Johns Hopkins (III)	1991	29	123	129	95.3
Chris Carideo, Eureka (III)	1992	26	80	84	95.2
Yudi Teichman, Yeshiva (III)	1989	21	119	125	95.2
Rod Foster, UCLA (I)	1982	27	95	100	95.0
Kent Andrews, McNeese St. (II)	1968	24	85	90	94.4
Billy Newton, Morgan St. (II)	1976	28	85	90	94.4
Carlos Gibson, Marshall (I)	1978	28	84	89	94.4
Danny Basile, Marist (I)	1994	27	84	89	94.4
Mike Sanders, Northern Colo. (II)	1987	28	82	87	94.3
Jim Barton, Dartmouth (I)	1986	26	65	69	94.2
Mike Scheib, Susquehanna (III)	1977	22	80	85	94.1
Jack Moore, Nebraska (I)	1982	27	123	131	93.9
Jason Prenevost, Middlebury (III)	1994	22	60	64	93.8
Rob Robbins, New Mexico (I)	1990	34	101	108	93.5
Dandrea Evans, Troy St. (I)	1994	27	72	77	93.5
Jay Harrie, Mont. St.-Billings (II)	1994	26	86	92	93.5
Tommy Boyer, Arkansas (I)	1962	23	125	134	93.3
Jerry Prestier, Baldwin-Wallace (III)	1978	25	125	134	93.3
Charlie Nanick, Scranton (III)	1996	25	96	103	93.2
Joe Cullen, Hartwick (II)	1969	18	96	103	93.2
Damon Goodwin, Dayton (I)	1986	30	95	102	93.1
Jeff Bowers, Southern Me. (III)	1988	29	95	102	93.1
Eric Jacobs, Scranton (III)	1986	29	81	87	93.1
Jim Durrell, Colby-Sawyer (III)	1993	25	67	72	93.1

REBOUNDS

Player, Team (Division)	Season	G	Reb.
Elmore Smith, Kentucky St. (II)	1972	33	799
Marvin Webster, Morgan St. (II)	1974	33	740
Walt Dukes, Seton Hall (I)	1953	33	734
Maurice Stokes, St. Francis (Pa.) (II)	1955	28	726
Frank Stronczek, American Int'l (II)	1966	26	717
Maurice Stokes, St. Francis (Pa.) (II)	1954	26	689
Jim Ahrens, Buena Vista (II)	1962	28	682
Elmore Smith, Kentucky St. (II)	1970	30	682
R. C. Owens, Col. Idaho (II)	1954	25	677
Wilbert Jones, Albany St. (Ga.) (II)	1969	28	670
Leroy Wright, Pacific (Cal.) (I)	1959	26	652
Tom Gola, La Salle (I)	1954	30	652
Jim Smith, Steubenville (II)	1957	26	651
Marvin Webster, Morgan St. (II)	1973	28	650
Tom Hart, Middlebury (II)	1955	22	649
Charlie Tyra, Louisville (I)	1956	29	645
Jackie Jackson, Virginia Union (II)	1961	26	641
Vincent White, Savannah St. (II)	1972	29	633
Paul Silas, Creighton (I)	1964	29	631
Bill Thieben, Hofstra (II)	1955	26	627
Lucious Jackson, Tex.-Pan American (II)	1963	32	626
Elvin Hayes, Houston (I)	1968	33	624
Vincent White, Savannah St. (II)	1970	27	624
Artis Gilmore, Jacksonville (I)	1970	28	621
Bill Thieben, Hofstra (II)	1954	24	620
Tom Hart, Middlebury (II)	1956	21	620

(Since 1973)

Player, Team (Division)	Season	G	Reb.
Marvin Webster, Morgan St. (II)	1974	33	740
Marvin Webster, Morgan St. (II)	1973	28	650
Major Jones, Albany St. (Ga.) (II)	1975	27	608
Marvin Barnes, Providence (I)	1974	32	597
Joe Manley, Bowie St. (III)	1976	29	579
Marvin Barnes, Providence (I)	1973	30	571
Earl Williams, Winston-Salem (II)	1974	26	553
John Jordan, Southern Me. (III)	1978	29	536
Charles Oakley, Virginia Union (III)	1985	31	535
Lawrence Johnson, Prairie View (II)	1974	23	519
Andre Means, Sacred Heart (II)	1977	32	516
Major Jones, Albany St. (Ga.) (II)	1975	25	513
Kermit Washington, American (I)	1973	25	511
Bill Walton, UCLA (I)	1973	30	506
Larry Bird, Indiana St. (I)	1979	34	505
Harvey Jones, Alabama St. (II)	1974	28	503
Larry Kenon, Memphis (I)	1973	30	501
Akeem Olajuwon, Houston (I)	1984	37	500
Andre Means, Sacred Heart (II)	1978	30	493
Ricky Mahorn, Hampton (II)	1980	31	490
Rob Roesch, Staten Island (II)	1989	31	482
Howard Shockley, Salisbury St. (III)	1974	27	482
Keith Woolfolk, Upper Iowa (III)	1978	26	479
Leonard Robinson, Tennesee St. (I)	1974	28	478
Major Jones, Albany St. (Ga.) (II)	1976	24	475

REBOUND AVERAGE

Player, Team (Division)	Season	G	Reb.	Avg.
Tom Hart, Middlebury (II)	1956	21	620	29.5
Tom Hart, Middlebury (II)	1955	22	649	29.5
Frank Stronczek, American Int'l (II)	1966	26	717	27.6
R. C. Owens, Col. Idaho (II)	1954	25	677	27.1
Maurice Stokes, St. Francis (Pa.) (II)	1954	26	689	26.5
Ellerbe Neal, Wofford (II)	1953	23	609	26.5
Roman Turmon, Clark Atlanta (II)	1954	23	602	26.2
Pat Callahan, Lewis (II)	1955	20	523	26.2
Hank Brown, Lowell Tech (II)	1966	19	496	26.1
Maurice Stokes, St. Francis (Pa.) (II)	1955	28	726	25.9
Bill Thieben, Hofstra (II)	1954	24	620	25.8
Dean Sandifer, Lakeland (II)	1965	23	592	25.7
Charlie Slack, Marshall (II)	1955	21	538	25.6
Charles Wrinn, Trinity (Conn.) (II)	1952	19	486	25.6
Leroy Wright, Pacific (Cal.) (I)	1959	26	652	25.1
Jim Smith, Steubenville (II)	1957	26	651	25.0
Marv Becker, Widener (II)	1958	18	450	25.0
Tony Williams, St. Francis (Me.) (II)	1971	24	599	25.0
Ernie Brock, Virginia St. (II)	1964	24	597	24.9
Russell Jackson, Southern U. (II)	1970	22	544	24.7
Gerry Govan, St. Mary's (Kan.) (II)	1963	18	445	24.7
Merv Shorr, CCNY (II)	1954	18	444	24.7
Art Quimby, Connecticut (I)	1955	25	611	24.4
Charlie Slack, Marshall (I)	1956	22	520	23.6
Ed Conlin, Fordham (I)	1953	26	612	23.5

(Since 1973)

Player, Team (Division)	Season	G	Reb.	Avg.
Marvin Webster, Morgan St. (II)	1973	28	650	23.2
Lawrence Johnson, Prairie View (II)	1974	23	519	22.6
Major Jones, Albany St. (Ga.) (II)	1975	27	608	22.5
Marvin Webster, Morgan St. (II)	1974	33	740	22.4
Earl Williams, Winston-Salem (II)	1974	26	553	21.3
Major Jones, Albany St. (Ga.) (II)	1975	25	513	20.5
Kermit Washington, American (I)	1973	25	511	20.4
Larry Gooding, St. Augustine's (II)	1974	22	443	20.1
Joe Manley, Bowie St. (III)	1976	29	579	20.0
Fred Petty, New Hamp. Col. (III)	1974	22	436	19.8
Major Jones, Albany St. (Ga.) (II)	1976	24	475	19.8
Larry Williams, Pratt (III)	1977	24	457	19.0
Marvin Barnes, Providence (I)	1973	30	571	19.0
Calvin Robinson, Mississippi Val. (II)	1976	23	432	18.8
Larry Williams, Pratt (III)	1977	17	318	18.7
Larry Parker, Plattsburgh St. (III)	1975	23	430	18.7
Marvin Barnes, Providence (I)	1974	32	597	18.7
Charles Greer, Thomas (III)	1977	17	318	18.7
John Jordan, Southern Me. (III)	1978	29	536	18.5
Keith Woolfolk, Upper Iowa (III)	1978	26	479	18.4
Michael Stubbs, Trinity (Conn.) (III)	1990	22	398	18.1
Mike Taylor, Pratt (III)	1978	23	414	18.0
Harvey Jones, Alabama St. (II)	1974	28	503	18.0
Walt Edwards, Husson (III)	1976	26	467	18.0
Scott Mountz, Calif. (Pa.) (II)	1978	24	431	18.0

ASSISTS

Player, Team (Division)	Season	G	Ast.
Mark Wade, UNLV (I)	1987	38	406
Steve Ray, Bridgeport (II)	1989	32	400
Avery Johnson, Southern U. (I)	1988	30	399
Robert James, Kean (III)	1989	29	391
Steve Ray, Bridgeport (II)	1990	33	385
Anthony Manuel, Bradley (I)	1988	31	373
Tony Smith, Pfeiffer (II)	1992	35	349
Avery Johnson, Southern U. (I)	1987	31	333
Mark Jackson, St. John's (N.Y.) (I)	1986	32	328
Sherman Douglas, Syracuse (I)	1989	38	326
Greg Anthony, UNLV (I)	1991	35	310
Sam Crawford, New Mexico St. (I)	1993	34	310
Reid Gettys, Houston (I)	1984	37	309
Jim Ferrer, Bentley (II)	1989	31	309
Rob Paternostro, New Hamp. Col. (II)	1995	33	309
Carl Golson, Loyola (Ill.) (I)	1985	33	305
Craig Neal, Georgia Tech (I)	1988	32	303
Keith Jennings, East Tenn. St. (I)	1991	33	301
Brian Gregory, Oakland (II)	1989	28	300
Chris Corchiani, North Caro. St. (I)	1991	31	299
Charles Jordan, Erskine (II)	1992	34	298
Keith Jennings, East Tenn. St. (I)	1990	34	297
Ricky Spicer, Wis.-Whitewater (III)	1989	31	295
Howard Evans, Temple (I)	1988	34	294
Joe Marcotte, N.J. Inst. of Tech (III)	1995	30	292

ASSIST AVERAGE

Player, Team (Division)	Season	G	Ast.	Avg.
Robert James, Kean (III)	1989	29	391	13.48
Avery Johnson, Southern U. (I)	1988	30	399	13.30
Steve Ray, Bridgeport (II)	1989	32	400	12.50
Anthony Manuel, Bradley (I)	1988	31	373	12.03
Steve Ray, Bridgeport (II)	1990	33	385	11.66
Demetri Beekman, Assumption (II)	1993	23	264	11.47
Albert Kirchner, Mt. St. Vincent (III)	1990	24	267	11.12
Ernest Jenkins, N.M. Highlands (II)	1995	27	291	10.78
Avery Johnson, Southern U. (I)	1987	31	333	10.74
Brian Gregory, Oakland (II)	1989	28	300	10.71
Mark Wade, UNLV (I)	1987	38	406	10.68
Ron Torgalski, Hamilton (III)	1989	26	275	10.57
Brent Schremp, Slippery Rock (II)	1995	25	259	10.36
Louis Adams, Rust (III)	1989	22	227	10.31
Ernest Jenkins, N.M. Highlands (II)	1994	27	277	10.31
Adrian Hutt, Metro St. (II)	1991	28	285	10.17
Nelson Haggerty, Baylor (I)	1995	28	284	10.14
Tony Smith, Pfeiffer (II)	1992	35	349	9.97
Jim Ferrer, Bentley (II)	1989	31	309	9.96
Glenn Williams, Holy Cross (I)	1989	28	278	9.92
Eric Johnson, Coe (III)	1991	24	238	9.91
Joe Marcotte, N.J. Inst. of Tech (III)	1995	30	292	9.73
Phil Dixon, Shenandoah (III)	1994	26	253	9.73
Mark Cottom, Ferrum (III)	1991	25	242	9.68
Pat Chambers, Phila. Textile (II)	1994	30	290	9.67
Marcus Talbert, Colo. Christian (II)	1994	27	261	9.67

BLOCKED SHOTS

Player, Team (Division)	Season	G	Blk.
David Robinson, Navy (I)	1986	35	207
Ira Nicholson, Mt. St. Vincent (III)	1995	28	188
Keith Closs, Central Conn. St. (I)	1996	28	178
Shawn Bradley, Brigham Young (I)	1991	34	177
Alonzo Mourning, Georgetown (I)	1989	34	169
Adonal Foyle, Colgate (I)	1996	29	165
Ira Nicholson, Mt. St. Vincent (III)	1996	27	163
Alonzo Mourning, Georgetown (I)	1992	32	160
Shaquille O'Neal, LSU (I)	1992	30	157
Roy Rogers, Alabama (I)	1996	32	156
Antonio Harvey, Pfeiffer (II)	1993	29	155
Dikembe Mutombo, Georgetown (I)	1991	32	151
Adonal Foyle, Colgate (I)	1995	30	147
Matt Cusano, Scranton (III)	1993	29	145
David Robinson, Navy (I)	1987	32	144
Theo Ratliff, Wyoming (I)	1995	28	144
Cedric Lewis, Maryland (I)	1991	28	143
John Burke, LIU-Southampton (II)	1996	28	142
Jim McIlvaine, Marquette (I)	1994	33	142
Shaquille O'Neal, LSU (I)	1991	28	140
Kevin Roberson, Vermont (I)	1992	28	139
Keith Closs, Central Conn. St. (I)	1995	26	139
Tim Duncan, Wake Forest (I)	1995	32	135
Vonzell McGrew, Mo. Western St. (II)	1995	31	132
Antoine Hyman, Keuka (III)	1996	25	131

BLOCKED-SHOT AVERAGE

Player, Team (Division)	Season	G	Blk.	Avg.
Ira Nicholson, Mt. St. Vincent (III)	1995	28	188	6.71
Keith Closs, Central Conn. St. (I)	1996	28	178	6.36
Ira Nicholson, Mt. St. Vincent (III)	1996	27	163	6.04
David Robinson, Navy (I)	1986	35	207	5.91
Adonal Foyle, Colgate (I)	1996	29	165	5.69
Keith Closs, Central Conn. St. (I)	1995	26	139	5.35
Antonio Harvey, Pfeiffer (II)	1993	29	155	5.34
Antoine Hyman, Keuka (III)	1996	25	131	5.24
Shaquille O'Neal, LSU (I)	1992	30	157	5.23
Shawn Bradley, Brigham Young (I)	1991	34	177	5.21
Theo Ratliff, Wyoming (I)	1995	28	144	5.14
Cedric Lewis, Maryland (I)	1991	28	143	5.11
John Burke, LIU-Southampton (II)	1996	28	142	5.07
Shaquille O'Neal, LSU (I)	1991	28	140	5.00
Alonzo Mourning, Georgetown (I)	1992	32	160	5.00
Matt Cusano, Scranton (III)	1993	29	145	5.00
Alonzo Mourning, Georgetown (I)	1989	34	169	4.97
Kevin Roberson, Vermont (I)	1992	28	139	4.96
Roy Rogers, Alabama (I)	1996	32	156	4.88
Kenny Green, Rhode Island (I)	1990	26	124	4.77
Andrew South, N.J. Inst. of Tech (III)	1994	27	128	4.74
Dikembe Mutombo, Georgetown (I)	1991	32	151	4.72
Roy Woods, Fontbonne (III)	1995	25	117	4.68
Johnny Tyson, Central Okla. (II)	1994	27	126	4.66
Pascal Fleury, Md.-Balt. County (I)	1995	27	124	4.59

STEALS

Player, Team (Division)	Season	G	Stl.
Moses Jean-Pierre, Plymouth St. (III)	1994	30	189
Mookie Blaylock, Oklahoma (I)	1988	39	150
Purvis Presha, Stillman (III)	1996	25	144
Aldwin Ware, Florida A&M (I)	1988	29	142
Darron Brittman, Chicago St. (I)	1986	28	139
Nadav Henefeld, Connecticut (I)	1990	37	138
Matt Newton, Principia (III)	1994	25	138
Mookie Blaylock, Oklahoma (I)	1989	35	131
Ronn McMahon, Eastern Wash. (I)	1990	29	130
Scott Clarke, Utica (III)	1995	24	126
Allen Iverson, Georgetown (I)	1996	37	124
Marty Johnson, Towson St. (I)	1988	30	124
Deron Black, Allegheny (III)	1996	27	123
David Brown, Westfield St. (III)	1994	25	122
Barry Aranoff, Yeshiva (III)	1995	22	121
Jim Paguaga, St. Francis (N.Y.) (I)	1986	28	120
Shawn Griggs, Southwestern La. (I)	1994	30	120
Brian Meehan, Salve Regina (III)	1995	28	120
Scott Clarke, Utica (III)	1996	26	118
Pointer Williams, McNeese St. (I)	1996	27	118
David Clark, Bluefield St. (II)	1996	31	118
Tyrone McDaniel, Lenoir-Rhyne (II)	1993	32	116
Ken Francis, Molloy (II)	1994	27	116
Darnell White, Calif. (Pa.) (II)	1994	30	115
Tony Fairley, Charleston So. (I)	1987	28	114
Moses Jean-Pierre, Plymouth St. (III)	1993	25	114

STEAL AVERAGE

Player, Team (Division)	Season	G	Stl.	Avg.
Moses Jean-Pierre, Plymouth St. (III)	1994	30	189	6.30
Purvis Presha, Stillman (III)	1996	25	144	5.76
Matt Newton, Principia (III)	1994	25	138	5.52
Barry Aranoff, Yeshiva (III)	1995	22	121	5.50
Scott Clarke, Utica (III)	1995	24	126	5.25
Darron Brittman, Chicago St. (I)	1986	28	139	4.96
Joel Heckendorf, Martin Luther (III)	1996	17	84	4.94
Aldwin Ware, Florida A&M (I)	1988	29	142	4.90
David Brown, Westfield St. (III)	1994	25	122	4.88
Ivo Moyano, Polytechnic (N.Y.) (III)	1994	19	91	4.78
Moses Jean-Pierre, Plymouth St. (III)	1993	25	114	4.56
Deron Black, Allegheny (III)	1996	27	123	4.56
Scott Clark, Utica (III)	1996	26	118	4.54
John Morris, Bluefield St. (II)	1994	23	104	4.52
Ronn McMahon, Eastern Wash. (I)	1990	29	130	4.48
Pointer Williams, McNeese St. (I)	1996	27	118	4.37
Carl Small, Cornell College (III)	1995	22	96	4.36
Ken Francis, Molloy (II)	1994	27	116	4.29
Brian Meehan, Salve Regina (III)	1995	28	120	4.29
Jim Paguaga, St. Francis (N.Y.) (I)	1986	28	120	4.29
Ivo Moyano, Polytechnic (N.Y.) (III)	1996	22	93	4.23
Ivo Moyano, Polytechnic (N.Y.) (III)	1995	23	97	4.22
Don Walls, Buena Vista (III)	1994	25	105	4.20
Reuben Reyes, Salve Regina (III)	1993	25	104	4.16
Marty Johnson, Towson St. (I)	1988	30	124	4.13

Career Records

POINTS

Player, Team (Division)	Last Season	Yrs.	G	FG	3FG	FT	Pts.
Travis Grant, Kentucky St. (II)	1972	4	121	1,760	—	525	4,045
Bob Hopkins, Grambling (II)	1956	4	126	1,403	—	953	3,759
Pete Maravich, LSU (I)	1970	3	83	1,387	—	893	3,667
Dwight Lamar, Southwestern La. (II & I)	1973	4	112	1,445	—	603	3,493
Tony Smith, Pfeiffer (II)	1992	4	126	1,150	431	619	3,350
Earnest Lee, Clark Atlanta (II)	1987	4	115	1,270	35	723	3,298
Joe Miller, Alderson-Broaddus (II)	1957	4	129	1,082	—	1,130	3,294
Henry Logan, Western Caro. (II)	1968	4	107	1,263	—	764	3,290
John Rinka, Kenyon (II)	1970	4	99	1,261	—	729	3,251
Freeman Williams, Portland St. (I)	1978	4	106	1,369	—	511	3,249
Lionel Simmons, La Salle (I)	1990	4	131	1,244	56	673	3,217
Dick Barnett, Tennessee St. (II)	1959	4	136	1,312	—	585	3,209
Alphonso Ford, Mississippi Val. (I)	1993	4	109	1,121	333	590	3,165
Willie Scott, Alabama St. (II)	1969	4	103	1,277	—	601	3,155
Harry Kelly, Texas Southern (I)	1983	4	110	1,234	—	598	3,066
Johnnie Allen, Bethune-Cookman (II)	1969	4	111	1,306	—	446	3,058
Bennie Swain, Texas Southern (II)	1958	4	137	1,157	—	694	3,008
Hersey Hawkins, Bradley (I)	1988	4	125	1,100	118	690	3,008
Rich Fuqua, Oral Roberts (II & I)	1973	4	111	1,273	—	458	3,004
Lambert Shell, Bridgeport (II)	1992	4	132	1,102	22	775	3,001
Oscar Robertson, Cincinnati (I)	1960	3	88	1,052	—	869	2,973
Carl Hartman, Alderson-Broaddus (II)	1955	4	118	1,124	—	711	2,959
Danny Manning, Kansas (I)	1988	4	147	1,216	10	509	2,951
Andre Foreman, Salisbury St. (III)	1992	5	109	1,141	68	592	2,940
Earl Monroe, Winston-Salem (II)	1967	4	110	1,158	—	619	2,935

SCORING AVERAGE
(Minimum 1,500 points)

Player, Team (Division)	Last Season	Yrs.	G	FG	3FG	FT	Pts.	Avg.
Pete Maravich, LSU (I)	1970	3	83	1,387	—	893	3,667	44.2
Austin Carr, Notre Dame (I)	1971	3	74	1,017	—	526	2,560	34.6
Oscar Robertson, Cincinnati (I)	1960	3	88	1,052	—	869	2,973	33.8
Travis Grant, Kentucky St. (II)	1972	4	121	1,760	—	525	4,045	33.4
Calvin Murphy, Niagara (I)	1970	3	77	947	—	654	2,548	33.1
John Rinka, Kenyon (II)	1970	4	99	1,261	—	729	3,251	32.8
Dwain Govan, Bishop (III)	1975	2	55	750	—	305	1,805	32.8
Florindo Vieira, Quinnipiac (II)	1957	4	69	761	—	741	2,263	32.8
Dwight Lamar, Southwestern La. (I)	1973	2	57	768	—	326	1,862	32.7
Frank Selvy, Furman (I)	1954	3	78	922	—	694	2,538	32.5
Rick Mount, Purdue (I)	1970	3	72	910	—	503	2,323	32.3
Darrell Floyd, Furman (I)	1956	3	71	868	—	545	2,281	32.1
Nick Werkman, Seton Hall (I)	1964	3	71	812	—	649	2,273	32.0
Willie Humes, Idaho St. (I)	1971	2	48	565	—	380	1,510	31.5
William Averitt, Pepperdine (I)	1973	2	48	615	—	311	1,541	31.4
Elgin Baylor, Col. Idaho & Seattle (I)	1958	3	80	956	—	588	2,500	31.3
Willie Shaw, Lane (II)	1964	4	76	960	—	459	2,379	31.3
Mike Davis, Virginia Union (II)	1969	4	89	1,014	—	730	2,758	31.0
Elvin Hayes, Houston (I)	1968	3	93	1,215	—	454	2,884	31.0
Freeman Williams, Portland St. (I)	1978	4	106	1,369	—	511	3,249	30.7
Henry Logan, Western Caro. (II)	1968	4	107	1,263	—	764	3,290	30.7
Willie Scott, Alabama St. (II)	1969	4	103	1,277	—	601	3,155	30.6
Dave Russell, Shepherd (III)	1975	2	60	710	—	413	1,833	30.6
Larry Bird, Indiana St. (I)	1979	3	94	1,154	—	542	2,850	30.3
George Gilmore, Chaminade (II)	1992	2	51	485	174	387	1,531	30.0

FIELD-GOAL PERCENTAGE
(Minimum 400 field goals made)

Player, Team (Division)	Last Season	Yrs.	G	FG	FGA	Pct.
Tony Rychlec, Mass. Maritime (III)	1983	3	55	509	692	73.6
Pete Metzelaars, Wabash (III)	1982	4	103	784	1,083	72.4
Todd Linder, Tampa (II)	1987	4	122	909	1,284	70.8
Tom Schurfranz, Bellarmine (II)	1992	4	112	742	1,057	70.2
Chad Scott, Calif. (Pa.) (II)	1994	4	115	465	664	70.0
Ricky Nedd, Appalachian St. (I)	1994	4	113	412	597	69.0
Ed Phillips, Alabama A&M (II)	1971	4	95	610	885	68.9
Stephen Scheffler, Purdue (I)	1990	4	110	408	596	68.5
Ulysses Hackett, S.C.-Spartanburg (II)	1992	3	90	824	1,213	67.9
Larry Tucker, Lewis (II)	1983	3	84	677	994	68.1
Steve Johnson, Oregon St. (I)	1981	4	116	828	1,222	67.8
Otis Evans, Wayne St. (Mich.) (III)	1992	4	106	472	697	67.7
Maurice Woods, Potsdam St. (III)	1982	3	93	559	829	67.4
Matthew Cornegay, Tuskegee (II)	1982	4	105	524	783	66.9
Earl Keith, Stony Brook (III)	1979	4	94	777	1,161	66.9
Murray Brown, Florida St. (I)	1980	4	106	566	847	66.8
Ray Strozier, Central Mo. St. (II)	1981	4	110	563	843	66.8
Dennis Edwards, Fort Hays St. (II)	1995	2	59	666	998	66.7

Player, Team (Division)	Last Season	Yrs.	G	FG	FGA	Pct.
James Morris, Central Okla. (II)	1993	4	76	532	798	66.7
Dan Rush, Bridgewater (Va.) (III)	1995	4	102	712	1,069	66.6
Lee Campbell, Middle Tenn. St. & Southwest Mo. St. (I)	1990	3	88	411	618	66.5
Warren Kidd, Middle Tenn. St. (I)	1993	3	83	496	747	66.4
Joe Senser, West Chester (I)	1979	4	96	476	719	66.2
Lance Berwald, North Dak. St. (II)	1984	2	58	475	717	66.2
Harold Booker, Cheyney (II)	1969	4	108	662	1,002	66.1

THREE-POINT FIELD GOALS MADE

Player, Team (Division)	Last Season	Yrs.	G	3FG
Tony Smith, Pfeiffer (II)	1992	4	126	431
Kwame Morton, Clarion (II)	1994	4	105	411
Chris Carideo, Widener (III)	1995	4	103	402
Doug Day, Radford (I)	1993	4	117	401
Gary Duda, Merrimack (II)	1992	4	122	389
Ronnie Schmitz, Mo.-Kansas City (I)	1993	4	112	378
Mark Alberts, Akron (I)	1993	4	107	375
Steve Diekmann, Grinnell (III)	1995	4	85	371
Jeff Fryer, Loyola Marymount (I)	1990	4	112	363
Columbus Parker, Johnson Smith (II)	1993	4	115	354
Gary Paul, Indianapolis (II)	1990	4	111	354
Ray Wilson, UC Santa Cruz (III)	1992	4	100	354
Dennis Scott, Georgia Tech (I)	1990	3	99	351
Ed Brands, Grinnell (III)	1996	4	78	347
Allan Houston, Tennessee (I)	1993	4	128	346
Mike Ziegler, Colorado Mines (II)	1990	4	118	344
Chris Brown, Tuskegee (II)	1996	4	104	339
Stephen Hamrick, Eastern N.M. (II)	1996	4	107	339
Chris Hamilton, Blackburn (III)	1991	4	101	334
Alphonso Ford, Mississippi Val. (I)	1993	4	109	333
Scott Fitch, Geneseo St. (III)	1994	4	109	332
Shawn Respert, Michigan St. (I)	1995	4	118	331
Billy Collins, Nichols (III)	1995	4	92	331
Andy Kennedy, North Caro. St. & UAB (I)	1991	4	121	330
Randolph Childress, Wake Forest (I)	1995	4	120	329

THREE-POINT FIELD GOALS MADE PER GAME
(Minimum 200 three-point field goals made)

Player, Team (Division)	Last Season	Yrs.	G	3FG	Avg.
Timothy Pollard, Mississippi Val. (I)	1989	2	56	256	4.57
Ed Brands, Grinnell (III)	1996	4	78	347	4.45
Steve Diekmann, Grinnell (III)	1995	4	85	371	4.36
Sydney Grider, Southwestern La. (I)	1990	2	58	253	4.36
Alex Williams, Cal St. Sacramento (I)	1988	2	58	247	4.26
Tommie Spearman, Columbus St. (II)	1995	2	56	233	4.16
Kwame Morton, Clarion (II)	1994	4	105	411	3.91
Chris Carideo, Widener (III)	1995	4	103	402	3.90
Shawn Williams, Central Okla. (II)	1991	3	57	212	3.72
Zoderick Green, Central Okla. (II)	1995	3	57	212	3.72
Kareem Townes, La Salle (I)	1995	3	81	300	3.70
Mike Sinclair, Bowie St. (II)	1989	3	82	299	3.65
Dave Mooney, Coastal Caro. (I)	1988	2	56	202	3.61
Billy Collins, Nichols (III)	1995	4	92	331	3.60
Dennis Scott, Georgia Tech (I)	1990	3	99	351	3.55
Ray Wilson, UC Santa Cruz (III)	1992	4	100	354	3.54
Mark Alberts, Akron (I)	1993	4	107	375	3.50
Robert Martin, Cal St. Sacramento (II)	1989	3	85	294	3.46
Chris Geruschat, Bethany (W.Va.) (III)	1992	4	89	307	3.45
Doug Day, Radford (I)	1993	4	117	401	3.43
Tony Smith, Pfeiffer (II)	1992	4	126	431	3.42
Ronnie Schmitz, Mo.-Kansas City (I)	1993	4	112	378	3.38
Chris Hamilton, Blackburn (III)	1991	4	101	334	3.31
Jeff Jones, Lycoming (III)	1989	3	91	232	3.27
Chris Brown, Tuskegee (II)	1996	4	104	339	3.26

THREE-POINT FIELD-GOAL PERCENTAGE
(Minimum 200 three-point field goals made)

Player, Team (Division)	Last Season	Yrs.	G	3FG	3FGA	Pct.
Scott Martin, Rollins (II)	1991	4	104	236	460	51.3
Jeff Seifriz, Wis.-Whitewater (III)	1989	3	85	217	423	51.3
Chris Peterson, Eureka (III)	1994	4	78	215	421	51.1
Everett Foxx, Ferrum (III)	1992	4	104	315	630	50.0
Tony Bennett, Wis.-Green Bay (I)	1992	4	118	290	584	49.7
Matt Markle, Shippensburg (II)	1992	4	101	202	408	49.5
Keith Jennings, East Tenn. St. (I)	1991	4	127	223	452	49.3
Brad Stewart, Ripon (III)	1992	4	95	277	563	49.2
Jeff Jones, Lycoming (III)	1989	3	71	232	472	49.2
Troy Greenlee, DePauw (III)	1991	4	106	232	473	49.0

Colgate's Adonal Foyle averaged 5.69 blocks per game in 1996. Foyle turned back 165 opponents' field-goal attempts, the sixth-highest total ever.

Player, Team (Division)	Last Season	Yrs.	G	3FG	3FGA	Pct.
Lance Gelnett, Millersville (II)	1992	4	109	266	547	48.6
David Todd, Pomona-Pitzer (III)	1990	4	84	212	439	48.3
Jason Bullock, Indiana (Pa.) (II)	1995	4	88	235	491	47.9
Matt Ripaldi, New Hamp. Col. (II)	1995	4	95	205	431	47.6
Kirk Manns, Michigan St. (I)	1990	4	120	212	446	47.5
Tim Locum, Wisconsin (I)	1991	4	118	227	481	47.2
Mark Willey, Fort Hays St. (II)	1992	4	117	224	478	46.9
David Olson, Eastern Ill. (I)	1992	4	111	262	562	46.6
Todd Bowden, Randolph-Macon (II)	1989	3	84	229	491	46.6
Gary Paul, Indianapolis (II)	1990	4	111	354	768	46.1
Sean Jackson, Ohio & Princeton (I)	1992	4	104	243	528	46.0
Barry Booker, Vanderbilt (I)	1989	3	98	246	535	46.0
Kevin Booth, Mt. St. Mary's (Md.) (I)	1993	5	110	265	577	45.9
Matt Ripaldi, New Hamp. Col. (II)	1996	4	123	277	604	45.9
Dave Calloway, Monmouth (N.J.) (I)	1991	4	115	260	567	45.9

FREE-THROW PERCENTAGE
(Minimum 300 free throws made)

Player, Team (Division)	Last Season	Yrs.	G	FT	FTA	Pct.
Andy Enfield, Johns Hopkins (III)	1991	4	108	431	466	92.5
Greg Starrick, Kentucky & Southern Ill. (I)	1972	4	72	341	375	90.9
Jack Moore, Nebraska (I)	1982	4	105	446	495	90.1
Steve Henson, Kansas St. (I)	1990	4	127	361	401	90.0
Steve Alford, Indiana (I)	1987	4	125	535	596	89.8
Bob Lloyd, Rutgers (I)	1967	3	77	543	605	89.8
Jim Barton, Dartmouth (I)	1989	4	104	394	440	89.5
Dave Reynolds, Davis & Elkins (II)	1989	4	107	383	429	89.3
Tommy Boyer, Arkansas (I)	1963	3	70	315	353	89.2
Tim McGraw, Hartwick (III)	1988	4	107	330	371	88.9
Rob Robbins, New Mexico (I)	1991	4	133	309	348	88.8
Sean Miller, Pittsburgh (I)	1992	4	128	317	358	88.5
Ron Perry, Holy Cross (I)	1980	4	109	680	768	88.5
Joe Dykstra, Western Illinois (I)	1983	4	117	587	663	88.5
Mike Joseph, Bucknell (I)	1990	4	115	397	449	88.4
Kyle Macy, Purdue & Kentucky (I)	1980	5	125	416	471	88.3
Eric Jacobs, Wilkes & Scranton (III)	1987	4	106	303	343	88.3
Matt Hildebrand, Liberty (I)	1994	4	117	398	451	88.2
Tony Budzik, Mansfield (II)	1992	4	107	367	416	88.2
Jimmy England, Tennessee (I)	1971	3	81	319	362	88.1
Rod Foster, UCLA (I)	1983	4	113	309	351	88.0
Steve Nisenson, Hofstra (II)	1965	3	83	602	685	87.9
Michael Smith, Brigham Young (I)	1989	4	122	431	491	87.8
Jason Mathews, Pittsburgh (I)	1991	4	123	481	548	87.8
Mike Iuzzolino, Penn St. & St. Francis (Pa.) (I)	1991	4	112	402	458	87.8

REBOUNDS

Player, Team (Division)	Last Season	Yrs.	G	Reb.
Jim Smith, Steubenville (II)	1958	4	112	2,334
Marvin Webster, Morgan St. (II)	1975	4	114	2,267
Tom Gola, La Salle (I)	1955	4	118	2,201
Major Jones, Albany St. (Ga.) (II)	1976	4	105	2,052
Joe Holup, George Washington (I)	1956	4	104	2,030
Charles Hardnett, Grambling (II)	1962	4	117	1,983
Jim Ahrens, Buena Vista (II)	1962	4	95	1,977
Elmore Smith, Kentucky St. (II)	1971	3	85	1,917
Charlie Slack, Marshall (I)	1956	4	88	1,916
Zelmo Beaty, Prairie View (II)	1962	4	97	1,916
Ed Conlin, Fordham (I)	1955	4	102	1,884
Hal Booker, Cheyney (II)	1969	4	103	1,882
Bill Thieben, Hofstra (II)	1956	3	76	1,837
Maurice Stokes, St. Francis (Pa.) (II)	1955	3	72	1,812
Dickie Hemric, Wake Forest (I)	1955	4	104	1,802
Paul Silas, Creighton (I)	1964	3	81	1,751
James Morgan, Md.-Eastern Shore (II)	1970	4	95	1,747
Tom Hart, Middlebury (II)	1956	3	63	1,738
Joe Casey, Boston St. (II)	1969	4	102	1,733
Art Quimby, Connecticut (I)	1955	4	80	1,716
Jerry Harper, Alabama (I)	1956	4	93	1,688
Jeff Cohen, William & Mary (I)	1961	4	103	1,679
Steve Hamilton, Morehead St. (I)	1958	4	102	1,675
Herb Lake, Youngstown St. (II)	1959	4	95	1,638
Jim Fay, St. Ambrose (II)	1953	4	95	1,633

(For careers beginning in 1973 or after)

Player, Team (Division)	Last Season	Yrs.	G	Reb.
Major Jones, Albany St. (Ga.) (II)	1976	4	105	2,052
Michael Smith, Hamilton (III)	1992	4	107	1,628
Derrick Coleman, Syracuse (I)	1990	4	143	1,537
Malik Rose, Drexel (I)	1996	4	120	1,514
Ralph Sampson, Virginia (I)	1983	4	132	1,511
John Jordan, Southern Me. (III)	1981	4	105	1,504
Clemon Johnson, Florida A&M (II)	1978	4	109	1,494
Larry Parker, Plattsburgh St. (III)	1978	4	85	1,482
Carlos Terry, Winston-Salem (II)	1978	4	117	1,467
Pete Padgett, Nevada (I)	1976	4	104	1,464
Kevin Clark, Clark (Mass.) (III)	1981	4	101	1,450
Lionel Simmons, La Salle (I)	1990	4	131	1,429
Anthony Bonner, St. Louis (I)	1990	4	133	1,424
E. D. Schecterly, Lynchburg (III)	1980	4	104	1,404
Jeff Covington, Youngstown St. (II)	1978	4	106	1,381
Tyrone Hill, Xavier (Ohio) (I)	1990	4	126	1,380
Larry Sheets, East. Mennonite (III)	1983	4	105	1,378
Popeye Jones, Murray St. (I)	1992	4	123	1,374
Michael Brooks, La Salle (I)	1980	4	114	1,372
Xavier McDaniel, Wichita St. (I)	1985	4	117	1,359
John Irving, Arizona & Hofstra (I)	1977	4	103	1,348
Sam Clancy, Pittsburgh (I)	1981	4	116	1,342
Keith Lee, Memphis (I)	1985	4	128	1,336
Larry Smith, Alcorn St. (I)	1980	4	111	1,334
Clarence Weatherspoon, Southern Miss. (I)	1992	4	117	1,320

REBOUND AVERAGE
(Minimum 800 rebounds)

Player, Team (Division)	Last Season	Yrs.	G	Reb.	Avg.
Tom Hart, Middlebury (II)	1956	3	63	1,738	27.6
Maurice Stokes, St. Francis (Pa.) (II)	1955	3	72	1,812	25.2
Frank Stronczek, American Int'l (II)	1967	3	62	1,549	25.0
Bill Thieben, Hofstra (II)	1956	3	76	1,837	24.2
Hank Brown, Lowell Tech (II)	1967	3	49	1,129	23.0
Artis Gilmore, Jacksonville (I)	1970	2	54	1,224	22.7
Elmore Smith, Kentucky St. (II)	1971	3	85	1,917	22.6
Charles Wrinn, Trinity (Conn.) (II)	1953	3	53	1,176	22.2
Roman Turmon, Clark Atlanta (II)	1954	3	60	1,312	21.9
Charlie Slack, Marshall (I)	1956	4	88	1,916	21.8
Tony Missere, Pratt (II)	1968	3	62	1,348	21.7
Ron Horton, Delaware St. (II)	1968	3	64	1,384	21.6
Paul Silas, Creighton (I)	1964	3	81	1,751	21.6
Leroy Wright, Pacific (Cal.) (I)	1960	3	67	1,442	21.5
Art Quimby, Connecticut (I)	1955	4	80	1,716	21.5
Walt Dukes, Seton Hall (I)	1953	2	59	1,247	21.1
Jim Smith, Steubenville (II)	1958	4	112	2,334	20.8
Jim Ahrens, Buena Vista (II)	1962	4	95	1,977	20.8
Bob Brandes, Upsala (II)	1962	3	74	1,520	20.5
Jackie Jackson, Virginia Union (II)	1961	3	66	1,351	20.5
Bill Russell, San Francisco (I)	1956	3	79	1,606	20.3
Kermit Washington, American (I)	1973	3	73	1,478	20.2
Julius Erving, Massachusetts (I)	1971	2	52	1,049	20.2
Frank Hunter, Northland (II)	1962	4	79	1,581	20.0
Marvin Webster, Morgan St. (II)	1975	4	114	2,267	19.9

(For careers beginning in 1973 or after)

Player, Team (Division)	Last Season	Yrs.	G	Reb.	Avg.
Major Jones, Albany St. (Ga.) (II)	1976	4	105	2,052	19.5
Larry Parker, Plattsburgh St. (III)	1978	4	85	1,482	17.4
Howard Shockley, Salisbury St. (III & II)	1976	3	76	1,299	17.1
Andre Means, Sacred Heart (II)	1978	2	62	1,009	16.3
Charles Greer, Thomas (II)	1977	3	58	926	16.0
Willie Parr, LeMoyne-Owen (III)	1976	3	76	1,182	15.6
Glenn Mosley, Seton Hall (I)	1977	4	83	1,263	15.2
Michael Smith, Hamilton (III)	1992	4	107	1,628	15.2
Dave Kufeld, Yeshiva (III)	1980	4	81	1,222	15.1
Ed Owens, Hampden-Sydney (III)	1980	4	77	1,160	15.1
Tony Rychlec, Mass. Maritime (III)	1983	3	55	812	14.8
Bill Campion, Manhattan (I)	1975	3	74	1,070	14.5
John Jordan, Southern Me. (III)	1981	4	105	1,504	14.4
Kevin Clark, Clark (Mass.) (III)	1981	4	101	1,450	14.4
Mark Veenstra, Calvin (III)	1977	4	89	1,260	14.2
Pete Padgett, Nevada (I)	1976	4	104	1,464	14.1
Rob Roesch, Staten Island (III)	1989	2	61	850	13.9
Clemon Johnson, Florida A&M (II)	1978	4	109	1,494	13.7
Larry Johnson, Ark.-Little Rock (II)	1978	3	69	944	13.7
Carlo DeTommaso, Rhode Island Col. (III)	1976	3	72	984	13.7
Bob Warner, Maine (I)	1976	4	96	1,304	13.6
Shaquille O'Neal, LSU (I)	1992	3	90	1,217	13.5
Cornelius Cash, Bowling Green (I)	1975	3	79	1,068	13.5
E. D. Schecterly, Lynchburg (III)	1980	4	104	1,404	13.5
Ira Terrell, Southern Methodist (I)	1976	3	80	1,077	13.5

ASSISTS

Player, Team (Division)	Last Season	Yrs.	G	Ast.
Bobby Hurley, Duke (I)	1993	4	140	1,076
Demetri Beekman, Assumption (II)	1993	4	119	1,044
Chris Corchiani, North Caro. St. (I)	1991	4	124	1,038
Keith Jennings, East Tenn. St. (I)	1991	4	127	983
Sherman Douglas, Syracuse (I)	1989	4	138	960
Tony Miller, Marquette (I)	1995	4	123	956
Greg Anthony, Portland & UNLV (I)	1991	4	138	950
Gary Payton, Oregon St. (I)	1990	4	120	938
Rob Paternostro, New Hamp. Col. (II)	1995	4	129	919
Steve Artis, Chris. Newport (III)	1993	4	112	909
Orlando Smart, San Francisco (I)	1994	4	116	902
Andre LaFleur, Northeastern (I)	1987	4	128	894
Phil Dixon, Shenandoah (III)	1996	4	103	889
Jim Les, Bradley (I)	1986	4	118	884
Frank Smith, Old Dominion (I)	1988	4	120	883
Gallagher Driscoll, St. Rose (II)	1992	4	121	878
Taurence Chisholm, Delaware (I)	1988	4	110	877
Grayson Marshall, Clemson (I)	1988	4	122	857
Anthony Manuel, Bradley (I)	1989	4	108	855
Pooh Richardson, UCLA (I)	1989	4	122	833
Butch Moore, Southern Methodist (I)	1986	4	125	828
Tony Smith, Pfeiffer (II)	1992	4	126	828
Drafton Davis, Marist (I)	1988	4	115	804
David Genovese, Mt. St. Vincent (III)	1995	4	107	800
Marc Brown, Siena (I)	1991	4	123	796

ASSIST AVERAGE
(Minimum 550 assists)

Player, Team (Division)	Last Season	Yrs.	G	Ast.	Avg.
Steve Ray, Bridgeport (II)	1990	2	65	785	12.08
Avery Johnson, Southern U. (I)	1988	2	61	732	12.00
Sam Crawford, New Mexico St. (I)	1993	2	67	592	8.84
Mark Wade, Oklahoma & UNLV (I)	1987	3	79	693	8.77
Demetri Beekman, Assumption (II)	1993	4	119	1,044	8.77
Phil Dixon, Shenandoah (III)	1996	4	103	889	8.63
Chris Corchiani, North Caro. St. (I)	1991	4	124	1,038	8.37
Ernest Jenkins, N.M. Highlands (II)	1995	4	84	699	8.32
Steve Artis, Chris. Newport (III)	1993	4	112	909	8.12
Taurence Chisholm, Delaware (I)	1988	4	110	877	7.97
Van Usher, Tennessee Tech (I)	1992	3	85	676	7.95
Anthony Manuel, Bradley (I)	1989	4	108	855	7.92
Mark Benson, Tex. A&M-Kingsville (II)	1991	3	86	674	7.84
Pat Madden, Jacksonville St. (II)	1991	3	88	688	7.82
Gary Payton, Oregon St. (I)	1990	4	120	938	7.82
Orlando Smart, San Francisco (I)	1994	4	116	902	7.78
Tony Miller, Marquette (I)	1995	4	123	956	7.77
Keith Jennings, East Tenn. St. (I)	1991	4	127	983	7.74
Dan Ward, St. Cloud St. (II)	1995	4	100	774	7.74
Bobby Hurley, Duke (I)	1993	4	140	1,076	7.69
Chuck Evans, Old Dominion & Mississippi St. (I)	1993	3	85	648	7.62
Jim Les, Bradley (I)	1986	4	118	884	7.49
David Genovese, Mt. St. Vincent (III)	1995	4	107	800	7.48

Player, Team (Division)	Last Season	Yrs.	G	Ast.	Avg.
Frank Smith, Old Dominion (I)	1988	4	120	883	7.36
Gallagher Driscoll, St. Rose (II)	1992	4	121	878	7.26

BLOCKED SHOTS

Player, Team (Division)	Last Season	Yrs.	G	Blk.
Alonzo Mourning, Georgetown (I)	1992	4	120	453
Ira Nicholson, Mt. St. Vincent (III)	#1996	3	76	425
Theo Ratliff, Wyoming (I)	1995	4	111	425
Rodney Blake, St. Joseph's (Pa.) (I)	1988	4	116	419
Shaquille O'Neal, LSU (I)	1992	3	90	412
Kevin Roberson, Vermont (I)	1992	4	112	409
Jim McIlvaine, Marquette (I)	1994	4	118	399
Tim Perry, Temple (I)	1988	4	130	392
Tim Duncan, Wake Forest (I)	#1996	3	97	379
Pervis Ellison, Louisville (I)	1989	4	136	374
Acie Earl, Iowa (I)	1993	3	116	365
Dikembe Mutombo, Georgetown (I)	1991	2	96	354
David Robinson, Navy (I)	1987	4	67	351
Charles Smith, Pittsburgh (I)	1988	4	122	346
Rik Smits, Marist (I)	1988	4	107	345
Oliver Miller, Arkansas (I)	1992	4	137	345
Andrew South, N.J. Inst. of Tech (III)	1995	3	80	344
Derrick Lewis, Maryland (I)	1988	4	127	339
Marcus Camby, Massachusetts (I)	1996	3	92	336
Luc Longley, New Mexico (I)	1991	4	132	336
David Van Dyke, UTEP (I)	1992	4	127	336
Kenny Green, Rhode Island (I)	1990	4	122	335
Elden Campbell, Clemson (I)	1990	4	123	334
Rony Seikaly, Syracuse (I)	1988	4	136	319
Derrick Coleman, Syracuse (I)	1990	4	143	318

#Active player.

BLOCKED-SHOT AVERAGE
(Minimum 200 blocked shots)

Player, Team (Division)	Last Season	Yrs.	G	Blk.	Avg.
David Robinson, Navy (I)	1987	2	67	351	5.24
Shaquille O'Neal, LSU (I)	1992	3	90	412	4.58
Andrew South, N.J. Inst. of Tech (III)	1995	3	80	344	4.30
Theo Ratliff, Wyoming (I)	1995	4	111	425	3.83
John Burke, LIU-Southampton (II)	1996	2	54	205	3.80
Alonzo Mourning, Georgetown (I)	1992	4	120	453	3.78
Kino Outlaw, Mount Olive (II)	1996	3	81	305	3.77
Lorenzo Williams, Stetson (I)	1991	2	63	234	3.71
Vonzell McGrew, Mo. Western St. (II)	1995	3	57	211	3.70
Dikembe Mutombo, Georgetown (I)	1991	2	96	354	3.69
Marcus Camby, Massachusetts (I)	1996	3	92	336	3.65
Kevin Roberson, Vermont (I)	1992	4	112	409	3.65
Ben Wallace, Virginia Union (II)	1996	2	62	225	3.63
Corey Johnson, Pace (II)	1995	3	58	210	3.62
Rodney Blake, St. Joseph's (Pa.) (I)	1988	4	116	419	3.61
Jim McIlvaine, Marquette (I)	1994	4	118	399	3.38
Rik Smits, Marist (I)	1988	4	107	345	3.22
Acie Earl, Iowa (I)	1993	4	116	365	3.15
Sharone Wright, Clemson (I)	1994	3	92	286	3.11
Eugene Haith, Phila. Textile (II)	1995	3	86	267	3.10
Tim Perry, Temple (I)	1988	4	130	392	3.02
Charles Smith, Pittsburgh (I)	1988	4	122	346	2.84
Theron Wilson, Eastern Mich. (I)	1996	4	92	257	2.79
Damon Lopez, Fordham (I)	1991	3	93	258	2.77
Jeremy Putman, Dubuque (III)	1996	4	99	274	2.77

STEALS

Player, Team (Division)	Last Season	Yrs.	G	Stl.
Eric Murdock, Providence (I)	1991	4	117	376
Eric Bell, New Paltz St. (III)	1996	4	94	355
Scott Clarke, Utica (III)	1996	4	96	346
Gerald Walker, San Francisco (I)	1996	4	111	344
Johnny Rhodes, Maryland (I)	1996	4	122	344
Michael Anderson, Drexel (I)	1988	4	115	341
Kenny Robertson, Cleveland St. (I)	1990	4	119	341
Keith Jennings, East Tenn. St. (I)	1991	4	127	334
Greg Anthony, Portland & UNLV (I)	1991	4	138	329
Chris Corchiani, North Caro. St. (I)	1991	4	124	328
Gary Payton, Oregon St. (I)	1990	4	120	321
Pointer Williams, Tulane & McNeese St. (I)	1996	4	115	314
Mark Woods, Wright St. (I)	1993	4	113	314

Player, Team (Division)	Last Season	Yrs.	G	Stl.
Scott Burrell, Connecticut (I)	1993	4	119	310
Clarence Ceasar, LSU (I)	1995	4	112	310
Elliot Perry, Memphis (I)	1991	4	126	304
Moses Jean-Pierre, Plymouth St. (III)	1994	2	55	303
Aldwin Ware, Florida A&M (I)	1988	4	110	301
Drafton Davis, Marist (I)	1988	4	115	301
Gary Grant, Michigan (I)	1988	4	129	300
Taurence Chisholm, Delaware (I)	1988	4	110	298
Frank Smith, Old Dominion (I)	1988	4	120	295
D'Wayne Tanner, Rice (I)	1990	4	109	291
Lee Mayberry, Arkansas (I)	1992	4	139	291
Mike Bright, Bucknell (I)	1993	4	117	286

STEAL AVERAGE
(Minimum 200 steals)

Player, Team (Division)	Last Season	Yrs.	G	Stl.	Avg.
Moses Jean-Pierre, Plymouth St. (III)	1994	2	55	303	5.51
Rodney Lusain, UC San Diego (III)	1994	2	50	193	3.86
Mookie Blaylock, Oklahoma (I)	1989	2	74	281	3.80
Eric Bell, New Paltz St. (III)	1996	4	94	355	3.78
David Brown, Westfield St. (III)	1994	2	53	193	3.64
Scott Clarke, Utica (III)	1996	4	96	346	3.60
Ronn McMahon, Eastern Wash. (I)	1990	3	64	225	3.52
Gerald Garlic, Goucher (III)	1995	3	70	244	3.49
Patrick Herron, Winston-Salem (II)	1995	3	78	263	3.37
David Clark, Bluefield St. (II)	1996	3	83	278	3.35
Shawn McCartney, Hunter (III)	1995	3	81	261	3.22
Carl Small, Cornell College (III)	1995	3	69	222	3.22
Eric Murdock, Providence (I)	1991	4	117	376	3.21
Ken Francis, Molloy (II)	1995	3	81	260	3.21
Van Usher, Tennessee Tech (I)	1992	3	85	270	3.18
Gerald Walker, San Francisco (I)	1996	4	111	344	3.10
Deron Black, Allegheny (III)	1996	4	78	240	3.08
Reuben Reyes, Salve Regina (III)	1995	3	74	226	3.05
Lamont Jones, Bridgeport (II)	1995	3	84	256	3.05
Ernie Peavy, Wis.-Platteville (III)	1995	3	87	264	3.03
Micheal Anderson, Drexel (I)	1988	4	115	341	2.97
Jeff Landis, York (Pa.) (III)	1995	3	82	243	2.96
Haywoode Workman, Oral Roberts (I)	1989	3	85	250	2.94
Shawn Griggs, LSU & Southwestern La. (I)	1994	3	89	260	2.92
Kenny Robertson, Cleveland St. (I)	1990	4	119	341	2.87

Eric Bell of New Paltz State secured his place among the all-time collegiate steal leaders, compiling 355 steals in four years. Bell, who averaged 3.78 steals per game during his career, ranks second all-time in steals.

INDIVIDUAL COLLEGIATE

Award Winners

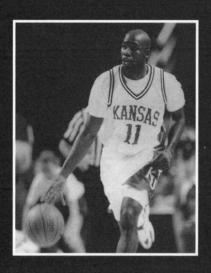

Division I Consensus All-American Selections

By Season

1929
Charley Hyatt, Pittsburgh; Joe Schaaf, Pennsylvania; Charles Murphy, Purdue; Vern Corbin, California; Thomas Churchill, Oklahoma; John Thompson, Montana St.

1930
Charley Hyatt, Pittsburgh; Charles Murphy, Purdue; Branch McCracken, Indiana; John Thompson, Montana St.; Frank Ward, Montana St.; John Wooden, Purdue.

1931
John Wooden, Purdue; Joe Reiff, Northwestern; George Gregory, Columbia; Wes Fesler, Ohio St.; Elwood Romney, Brigham Young.

1932
Forest Sale, Kentucky; Ed Krause, Notre Dame; John Wooden, Purdue; Louis Berger, Maryland; Les Witte, Wyoming.

1933
Forest Sale, Kentucky; Don Smith, Pittsburgh; Elliott Loughlin, Navy; Joe Reiff, Northwestern; Ed Krause, Notre Dame; Jerry Nemer, Southern Cal.

1934
Claire Cribbs, Pittsburgh; Ed Krause, Notre Dame; Les Witte, Wyoming; Hal Lee, Washington; Norman Cottom, Purdue.

1935
Jack Gray, Texas; Lee Guttero, Southern Cal; Claire Cribbs, Pittsburgh; Bud Browning, Oklahoma; Leroy Edwards, Kentucky.

1936
Bob Kessler, Purdue; Paul Nowak, Notre Dame; Hank Luisetti, Stanford; Vern Huffman, Indiana; John Moir, Notre Dame; Ike Poole, Arkansas; Bill Kinner, Utah.

1937
Hank Luisetti, Stanford; Paul Nowak, Notre Dame; Jules Bender, LIU-Brooklyn; John Moir, Notre Dame; Jewell Young, Purdue.

1938
Hank Luisetti, Stanford; John Moir, Notre Dame; Fred Pralle, Kansas; Jewell Young, Purdue; Paul Nowak, Notre Dame; Meyer Bloom, Temple.

1939
First Team—Irving Torgoff, LIU-Brooklyn; Urgel Wintermute, Oregon; Chet Jaworski, Rhode Island; Ernie Andres, Indiana; Jimmy Hull, Ohio St.

Second Team—Bob Calihan, Detroit; Michael Novak, Loyola (Ill.); Bernard Opper, Kentucky; Robert Anet, Oregon; Bob Hassmiller, Fordham.

1940
First Team—Ralph Vaughn, Southern Cal; John Dick, Oregon; Bill Hapac, Illinois; George Glamack, North Caro.; Gus Broberg, Dartmouth.

Second Team—Jack Harvey, Colorado; Marvin Huffman, Indiana; James McNatt, Oklahoma; Jesse Renick, Oklahoma St.

1941
First Team—Gus Broberg, Dartmouth; John Adams, Arkansas; Howard Engleman, Kansas; George Glamack, North Caro.; Gene Englund, Wisconsin.

Second Team—Frank Baumholtz, Ohio; Paul Lindeman, Washington St.; Oscar Schechtman, LIU-Brooklyn; Robert Kinney, Rice; Stan Modzelewski, Rhode Island.

1942
First Team—John Kotz, Wisconsin; Price Brookfield, West Tex. A&M; Bob Kinney, Rice; Andrew Phillip, Illinois; Robert Davies, Seton Hall.

Second Team—Robert Doll, Colorado; Wilfred Doerner, Evansville; Donald Burness, Stanford; George Munroe, Dartmouth; Stan Modzelewski, Rhode Island; John Mandic, Oregon St.

1943
First Team—Andrew Phillip, Illinois; George Senesky, St. Joseph's (Pa.); Ken Sailors, Wyoming; Harry Boykoff, St. John's (N.Y.); Charles Black, Kansas; Ed Beisser, Creighton; William Closs, Rice.

Second Team—Gerald Tucker, Oklahoma; Bob Rensberger, Notre Dame; Gene Rock, Southern Cal; John Kotz, Wisconsin; Otto Graham, Northwestern; Gale Bishop, Washington St.

1944
First Team—George Mikan, DePaul; Audley Brindley, Dartmouth; Otto Graham, Northwestern; Robert Brannum, Kentucky; Alva Paine, Oklahoma; Robert Kurland, Oklahoma St.; Leo Klier, Notre Dame.

Second Team—Arnold Ferrin, Utah; Dale Hall, Army; Don Grate, Ohio St.; Bob Dille, Valparaiso; William Henry, Rice; Dick Triptow, DePaul.

1945
First Team—George Mikan, DePaul; Robert Kurland, Oklahoma St.; Arnold Ferrin, Utah; Walton Kirk, Illinois; William Hassett, Notre Dame; William Henry, Rice; Howard Dallmar, Pennsylvania; Wyndol Gray, Bowling Green.

Second Team—Richard Ives, Iowa; Vince Hanson, Washington St.; Dale Hall, Army; Max Norris, Northwestern; Don Grate, Ohio St.; Herb Wilkinson, Iowa.

1946
First Team—George Mikan, DePaul; Robert Kurland, Oklahoma St.; Leo Klier, Notre Dame; Max Norris, Northwestern; Sid Tanenbaum, New York U.

Second Team—Jack Parkinson, Kentucky; John Dillon, North Caro.; Ken Sailors, Wyoming; Charles Black, Kansas; Tony Lavelli, Yale; William Hassett, Notre Dame.

1947
First Team—Ralph Beard, Kentucky; Gerald Tucker, Oklahoma; Alex Groza, Kentucky; Sid Tanenbaum, New York U.; Ralph Hamilton, Indiana.

Second Team—George Kaftan, Holy Cross; John Hargis, Texas; Don Barksdale, UCLA; Arnold Ferrin, Utah; Andrew Phillip, Illinois; Ed Koffenberger, Duke; Vern Gardner, Utah.

1948
First Team—Murray Wier, Iowa, 5-9, Muscatine, Iowa; Ed Macauley, St. Louis, 6-8, St. Louis; Jim McIntyre, Minnesota, 6-10, Minneapolis; Kevin O'Shea, Notre Dame, 6-1, San Francisco; Ralph Beard, Kentucky, 5-10, Louisville, Ky.

Second Team—Dick Dickey, North Caro. St.; Arnold Ferrin, Utah; Alex Groza, Kentucky; Harold Haskins, Hamline; George Kaftan, Holy Cross; Duane Klueh, Indiana St.; Tony Lavelli, Yale; Jack Nichols, Washington; Andy Wolfe, California.

1949
First Team—Tony Lavelli, Yale, 6-3, Somerville, Mass.; Vince Boryla, Denver, 6-5, East Chicago, Ind.; Ed Macauley, St. Louis, 6-8, St. Louis; Alex Groza, Kentucky, 6-7, Martin's Ferry, Ohio; Ralph Beard, Kentucky, 5-10, Louisville, Ky.

Second Team—Bill Erickson, Illinois; Vern Gardner, Utah; Wallace Jones, Kentucky; Jim McIntyre, Minnesota; Ernie Vandeweghe, Colgate.

1950
First Team—Dick Schnittker, Ohio St., 6-5, Sandusky, Ohio; Bob Cousy, Holy Cross, 6-1, St. Albans, N.Y.; Paul Arizin, Villanova, 6-3, Philadelphia; Paul Unruh, Bradley, 6-4, Toulon, Ill.; Bill Sharman, Southern Cal, 6-2, Porterville, Calif.

Second Team—Charles Cooper, Duquesne; Don Lofgran, San Francisco; Kevin O'Shea, Notre Dame; Don Rehfeldt, Wisconsin; Sherman White, LIU-Brooklyn.

1951
First Team—Bill Mlkvy, Temple, 6-4, Palmerton, Pa.; Sam Ranzino, North Caro. St., 6-1, Gary, Ind.; Bill Spivey, Kentucky, 7-0, Macon, Ga.; Clyde Lovellette, Kansas, 6-9, Terre Haute, Ind.; Gene Melchiorre, Bradley, 5-8, Highland Park, Ill.

Second Team—Ernie Barrett, Kansas St.; Bill Garrett, Indiana; Dick Groat, Duke; Mel Hutchins, Brigham Young; Gale McArthur, Oklahoma St.

1952
First Team—Cliff Hagan, Kentucky, 6-4, Owensboro, Ky.; Rod Fletcher, Illinois, 6-4, Champaign, Ill.; Chuck Darling, Iowa, 6-8, Denver; Clyde Lovellette, Kansas, 6-9, Terre Haute, Ind.; Dick Groat, Duke, 6-0, Swissvale, Pa.

Second Team—Bob Houbregs, Washington; Don Meineke, Dayton; Johnny O'Brien, Seattle; Mark Workman, West Va.; Bob Zawoluk, St. John's (N.Y.).

1953
First Team—Ernie Beck, Pennsylvania, 6-4, Philadelphia; Bob Houbregs, Washington, 6-7, Seattle; Walt Dukes, Seton Hall, 6-11, Rochester, N.Y.; Tom Gola, La Salle, 6-6, Philadelphia; Johnny O'Brien, Seattle, 5-8, South Amboy, N.J.

Second Team—Dick Knostman, Kansas St.; Bob Pettit, LSU; Joe Richey, Brigham Young; Don Schlundt, Indiana; Frank Selvy, Furman.

1954
First Team—Frank Selvy, Furman, 6-3, Corbin, Ky.; Tom Gola, La Salle, 6-6, Philadelphia; Don Schlundt, Indiana, 6-10, South Bend, Ind.; Bob Pettit, LSU, 6-9, Baton Rouge, La.; Cliff Hagan, Kentucky, 6-4, Owensboro, Ky.

Second Team—Bob Leonard, Indiana; Tom Marshall, Western Ky.; Bob Mattick, Oklahoma St.; Frank Ramsey, Kentucky; Dick Ricketts, Duquesne.

1955
First Team—Tom Gola, La Salle, 6-6, Philadelphia; Dick Ricketts, Duquesne, 6-8, Pottstown, Pa.; Bill Russell, San Francisco, 6-9, Oakland, Calif.; Si Green, Duquesne, 6-3, Brooklyn, N.Y.; Dick Garmaker, Minnesota, 6-3, Hibbing, Minn.

Second Team—Darrell Floyd, Furman; Robin Freeman, Ohio St.; Dickie Hemric, Wake Forest; Don Schlundt, Indiana; Ron Shavlik, North Caro. St.

1956
First Team—Tom Heinsohn, Holy Cross, 6-7, Union City, N.J.; Ron Shavlik, North Caro. St., 6-9, Denver; Bill Russell, San Francisco, 6-9, Oakland, Calif.; Si Green, Duquesne, 6-3, Brooklyn, N.Y.; Robin Freeman, Ohio St., 5-11, Cincinnati.

Second Team—Bob Burrow, Kentucky; Darrell Floyd, Furman; Rod Hundley, West Va.; K. C. Jones, San Francisco; Willie Naulls, UCLA; Bill Uhl, Dayton.

1957

First Team—Rod Hundley, West Va., 6-4, Charleston, W.Va.; Lenny Rosenbluth, North Caro., 6-5, New York; Jim Krebs, Southern Methodist, 6-8, Webster Groves, Mo.; Wilt Chamberlain, Kansas, 7-0, Philadelphia; Charlie Tyra, Louisville, 6-8, Louisville, Ky.; Chet Forte, Columbia, 5-9, Hackensack, N.J.

Second Team—Elgin Baylor, Seattle; Frank Howard, Ohio St.; Guy Rodgers, Temple; Gary Thompson, Iowa St.; Grady Wallace, South Caro.

1958

First Team—Bob Boozer, Kansas St., 6-8, Omaha, Neb.; Elgin Baylor, Seattle, 6-6, Washington, D.C.; Wilt Chamberlain, Kansas, 7-0, Philadelphia; Oscar Robertson, Cincinnati, 6-5, Indianapolis; Guy Rodgers, Temple, 6-0, Philadelphia; Don Hennon, Pittsburgh, 5-9, Wampum, Pa.

Second Team—Pete Brennan, North Caro.; Archie Dees, Indiana; Dave Gambee, Oregon St.; Mike Farmer, San Francisco; Bailey Howell, Mississippi St.

1959

First Team—Bailey Howell, Mississippi St., 6-7, Middleton, Tenn.; Bob Boozer, Kansas St., 6-8, Omaha, Neb.; Oscar Robertson, Cincinnati, 6-5, Indianapolis; Jerry West, West Va., 6-3, Cabin Creek, W.Va.; Johnny Cox, Kentucky, 6-4, Hazard, Ky.

Second Team—Leo Byrd, Marshall; Johnny Green, Michigan St.; Tom Hawkins, Notre Dame; Don Hennon, Pittsburgh; Alan Seiden, St. John's (N.Y.).

1960

First Team—Oscar Robertson, Cincinnati, 6-5, Indianapolis; Jerry West, West Va., 6-3, Cabin Creek, W.va.; Jerry Lucas, Ohio St., 6-8, Middletown, Ohio; Darrall Imhoff, California, 6-10; Alhambra, Calif.; Tom Stith, St. Bonaventure, 6-5, Brooklyn, N.Y.

Second Team—Terry Dischinger, Purdue; Tony Jackson, St. John's (N.Y.); Roger Kaiser, Georgia Tech; Lee Shaffer, North Caro.; Len Wilkens, Providence.

1961

First Team—Jerry Lucas, Ohio St., 6-8, Middletown, Ohio; Tom Stith, St. Bonaventure, 6-5, Brooklyn, N.Y.; Terry Dischinger, Purdue, 6-7, Terre Haute, Ind.; Roger Kaiser, Georgia Tech, 6-1, Dale, Ind.; Chet Walker, Bradley, 6-6, Benton Harbor, Mich.

Second Team—Walt Bellamy, Indiana; Frank Burgess, Gonzaga; Tony Jackson, St. John's (N.Y.); Billy McGill, Utah; Larry Siegfried, Ohio St.

1962

First Team—Jerry Lucas, Ohio St., 6-8, Middletown, Ohio; Len Chappell, Wake Forest, 6-8, Portage Area, Pa.; Billy McGill, Utah, 6-9, Los Angeles; Terry Dischinger, Purdue, 6-7, Terre Haute, Ind.; Chet Walker, Bradley, 6-6, Benton Harbor, Mich.

Second Team—Jack Foley, Holy Cross; John Havlicek, Ohio St.; Art Heyman, Duke; Cotton Nash, Kentucky; John Rudometkin, Southern Cal; Rod Thorn, West Va.

1963

First Team—Art Heyman, Duke, 6-5, Rockville Center, N.Y.; Ron Bonham, Cincinnati, 6-5, Muncie, Ind.; Barry Kramer, New York U., 6-4, Schenectady, N.Y.; Jerry Harkness, Loyola (Ill.), 6-3, New York; Tom Thacker, Cincinnati, 6-2, Covington, Ky.

Second Team—Gary Bradds, Ohio St.; Bill Green, Colorado St.; Cotton Nash, Kentucky; Rod Thorn, West Va.; Nate Thurmond, Bowling Green.

1964

First Team—Bill Bradley, Princeton, 6-5, Crystal City, Mo.; Dave Stallworth, Wichita St., 6-7, Dallas; Gary Bradds, Ohio St., 6-8, Jamestown, Ohio; Walt Hazzard, UCLA, 6-2, Philadelphia; Cotton Nash, Kentucky, 6-5, Leominster, Mass.

Second Team—Ron Bonham, Cincinnati; Mel Counts, Oregon St.; Fred Hetzel, Davidson; Jeff Mullins, Duke; Cazzie Russell, Michigan.

1965

First Team—Bill Bradley, Princeton, 6-5, Crystal City, Mo.; Rick Barry, Miami (Fla.), 6-7, Roselle Park, N.J.; Fred Hetzel, Davidson, 6-8, Washington, D.C.; Cazzie Russell, Michigan, 6-5, Chicago; Gail Goodrich, UCLA, 6-1, North Hollywood, Calif.

Second Team—Bill Buntin, Michigan; Wayne Estes, Utah St.; Clyde Lee, Vanderbilt; Dave Schellhase, Purdue; Dave Stallworth, Wichita St.

1966

First Team—Dave Bing, Syracuse, 6-3, Washington, D.C.; Dave Schellhase, Purdue, 6-4, Evansville, Ind.; Clyde Lee, Vanderbilt, 6-9, Nashville, Tenn.; Cazzie Russell, Michigan, 6-5, Chicago; Jim Walker, Providence, 6-3, Boston.

Second Team—Lou Dampier, Kentucky; Matt Guokas, St. Joseph's (Pa.); Jack Marin, Duke; Dick Snyder, Davidson; Bob Verga, Duke; Walt Wesley, Kansas.

1967

First Team—Lew Alcindor, UCLA, 7-2, New York; Elvin Hayes, Houston, 6-8, Rayville, La.; Wes Unseld, Louisville, 6-8, Louisville, Ky.; Jim Walker, Providence, 6-3, Boston; Clem Haskins, Western Ky., 6-3, Campbellsville, Ky.; Bob Lloyd, Rutgers, 6-1, Upper Darby, Pa.; Bob Verga, Duke, 6-0, Sea Girt, N.J.

Second Team—Mel Daniels, New Mexico; Sonny Dove, St. John's (N.Y.); Larry Miller, North Caro.; Don May, Dayton; Lou Dampier, Kentucky.

1968

First Team—Wes Unseld, Louisville, 6-8, Louisville, Ky.; Elvin Hayes, Houston, 6-8, Rayville, La.; Lew Alcindor, UCLA, 7-2, New York; Pete Maravich, LSU, 6-5, Raleigh, N.C.; Larry Miller, North Caro., 6-4, Catasauga, Pa.

Second Team—Lucius Allen, UCLA; Bob Lanier, St. Bonaventure; Don May, Dayton; Calvin Murphy, Niagara; Jo Jo White, Kansas.

1969

First Team—Lew Alcindor, UCLA, 7-2, New York; Spencer Haywood, Detroit, 6-8, Detroit, Mich.; Pete Maravich, LSU, 6-5, Raleigh, N.C.; Rick Mount, Purdue, 6-4, Lebanon, Ind.; Calvin Murphy, Niagara, 5-10, Norwalk, Conn.

Second Team—Dan Issel, Kentucky; Mike Maloy, Davidson; Bud Ogden, Santa Clara; Charlie Scott, North Caro.; Jo Jo White, Kansas.

1970

First Team—Pete Maravich, LSU, 6-5, Raleigh, N.C.; Rick Mount, Purdue, 6-4, Lebanon, Ind.; Bob Lanier, St. Bonaventure, 6-11, Buffalo, N.Y.; Dan Issel, Kentucky, 6-9, Batavia, Ill.; Calvin Murphy, Niagara, 5-10, Norwalk, Conn.

Second Team—Austin Carr, Notre Dame; Jim Collins, New Mexico St.; John Roche, South Caro.; Charlie Scott, North Caro.; Sidney Wicks, UCLA.

1971

First Team—Austin Carr, Notre Dame, 6-3, Washington, D.C.; Sidney Wicks, UCLA, 6-8, Los Angeles; Artis Gilmore, Jacksonville, 7-2, Dothan, Ala.; Dean Meminger, Marquette, 6-1, New York; Jim McDaniels, Western Ky., 7-0, Scottsville, Ky.

Second Team—John Roche, South Caro.; Johnny Neumann, Mississippi; Ken Durrett, La Salle; Howard Porter, Villanova; Curtis Rowe, UCLA.

1972

First Team—Bill Walton, UCLA, 6-11, La Mesa, Calif.; Dwight Lamar, Southwestern La., 6-1, Columbus, Ohio; Ed Ratleff, Long Beach St., 6-6, Columbus, Ohio; Bob McAdoo, North Caro., 6-8, Greensboro, N.C.; Tom Riker, South Caro., 6-10, Oyster Bay, N.Y.; Jim Chones, Marquette, 6-11, Racine, Wis.; Henry Bibby, UCLA, 6-1, Franklinton, N.C.

Second Team—Barry Parkhill, Virginia; Jim Price, Louisville; Bud Stallworth, Kansas; Henry Willmore, Michigan; Rich Fuqua, Oral Roberts.

1973

First Team—Doug Collins, Illinois St., 6-6, Benton, Ill.; Ed Ratleff, Long Beach St., 6-6, Columbus, Ohio; Dwight Lamar, Southwestern La., 6-1, Columbus, Ohio; Bill Walton, UCLA, 6-11, La Mesa, Calif.; Ernie DiGregorio, Providence, 6-0, North Providence, R.I.; David Thompson, North Caro. St., 6-4, Shelby, N.C.; Keith Wilkes, UCLA, 6-6, Santa Barbara, Calif.

Second Team—Jim Brewer, Minnesota; Kevin Joyce, South Caro.; Kermit Washington, American; Tom Burleson, North Caro. St.; Larry Finch, Memphis; Tom McMillen, Maryland.

1974

First Team—Keith Wilkes, UCLA, 6-6, Santa Barbara, Calif.; John Shumate, Notre Dame, 6-9, Elizabeth, N.J.; Bill Walton, UCLA, 6-11, La Mesa, Calif.; David Thompson, North Caro. St., 6-4, Shelby, N.C.; Marvin Barnes, Providence, 6-9, Providence, R.I.

Second Team—Len Elmore, Maryland; Bobby Jones, North Caro.; Bill Knight, Pittsburgh; Larry Fogle, Canisius; Campy Russell, Michigan.

1975

First Team—David Thompson, North Caro. St., 6-4, Shelby, N.C.; Adrian Dantley, Notre Dame, 6-5, Washington, D.C.; Scott May, Indiana, 6-7, Sandusky, Ohio; John Lucas, Maryland, 6-4, Durham, N.C.; Dave Meyers, UCLA, 6-8, La Habra, Calif.

Second Team—Luther Burden, Utah; Kevin Grevey, Kentucky; Leon Douglas, Alabama; Gus Williams, Southern Cal; Ron Lee, Oregon.

1976

First Team—Scott May, Indiana, 6-7, Sandusky, Ohio; Richard Washington, UCLA, 6-10, Portland, Ore.; John Lucas, Maryland, 6-4, Durham, N.C.; Kent Benson, Indiana, 6-11, New Castle, Ind.; Adrian Dantley, Notre Dame, 6-5, Washington, D.C.

Second Team—Mitch Kupchak, North Caro.; Phil Sellers, Rutgers; Phil Ford, North Caro.; Earl Tatum, Marquette; Bernard King, Tennessee.

1977

First Team—Otis Birdsong, Houston, 6-4, Winter Haven, Fla.; Marques Johnson, UCLA, 6-7, Los Angeles; Kent Benson, Indiana, 6-11, New Castle, Ind.; Rickey Green, Michigan, 6-2, Chicago; Phil Ford, North Caro., 6-2, Rocky Mount, N.C.; Bernard King, Tennessee, 6-7, Brooklyn, N.Y.

Second Team—Phil Hubbard, Michigan; Mychal Thompson, Minnesota; Ernie Grunfield, Tennessee; Greg Ballard, Oregon; Rod Griffin, Wake Forest; Butch Lee, Marquette; Bill Cartwright, San Francisco.

1978

First Team—Phil Ford, North Caro., 6-2, Rocky Mount, N.C.; Butch Lee, Marquette, 6-2, Bronx, N.Y.; David Greenwood, UCLA, 6-9, Los Angeles; Mychal Thompson, Minnesota, 6-10, Nassau, Bahamas; Larry Bird, Indiana St., 6-9, French Lick, Ind.

Second Team—Jack Givens, Kentucky; Freeman Williams, Portland St.; Rick Robey, Kentucky; Ron Brewer, Arkansas; Rod Griffin, Wake Forest.

1979

First Team—Larry Bird, Indiana St., 6-9, French Lick, Ind.; David Greenwood, UCLA, 6-9, Los Angeles; Earvin Johnson, Michigan St., 6-8, Lansing, Mich.; Sidney Moncrief, Arkansas, 6-4, Little Rock, Ark.; Mike Gminski, Duke, 6-11, Monroe, Conn.

Second Team—Bill Cartwright, San Francisco; Calvin Natt, Northeast La.; Kelly Tripucka, Notre Dame; Mike O'Koren, North Caro.; Jim Spanarkel, Duke; Jim Paxson, Dayton; Sly Williams, Rhode Island.

1980

First Team—Mark Aguirre, DePaul, 6-7, Chicago; Michael Brooks, La Salle, 6-7, Philadelphia; Joe Barry Carroll, Purdue, 7-1, Denver; Kyle Macy, Kentucky, 6-3, Peru, Ind.; Darrell Griffith, Louisville, 6-4, Louisville, Ky.

Second Team—Albert King, Maryland; Mike Gminski, Duke; Mike O'Koren, North Caro.; Sam Worthen, Marquette; Kelvin Ransey, Ohio St.

1981

First Team—Mark Aguirre, DePaul, 6-7, Chicago; Danny Ainge, Brigham Young, 6-5, Eugene, Ore.; Steve Johnson, Oregon St., 6-11, San Bernardino, Calif.; Ralph Sampson, Virginia, 7-4, Harrisonburg, Va.; Isiah Thomas, Indiana, 6-1, Chicago.

Second Team—Sam Bowie, Kentucky; Jeff Lamp, Virginia; Durand Macklin, LSU; Kelly Tripucka, Notre Dame; Danny Vranes, Utah; Al Wood, North Caro.

1982

First Team—Terry Cummings, DePaul, 6-9, Chicago; Quintin Dailey, San Francisco, 6-4, Baltimore, Md.; Eric Floyd, Georgetown, 6-3, Gastonia, N.C.; Ralph Sampson, Virginia, 7-4, Harrisonburg, Va.; James Worthy, North Caro., 6-9, Gastonia, N.C.

Second Team—Dale Ellis, Tennessee; Kevin Magee, UC Irvine; John Paxson, Notre Dame; Sam Perkins, North Caro.; Paul Pressey, Tulsa.

1983

First Team—Dale Ellis, Tennessee, 6-7, Marietta, Ga.; Patrick Ewing, Georgetown, 7-0, Cambridge, Mass.; Michael Jordan, North Caro., 6-6, Wilmington, N.C.; Sam Perkins, North Caro., 6-9, Latham, N.Y.; Ralph Sampson, Virginia, 7-4, Harrisonburg, Va.; Wayman Tisdale, Oklahoma, 6-9, Tulsa, Okla.; Keith Lee, Memphis, 6-9, West Memphis, Ark.

Second Team—Clyde Drexler, Houston; John Paxson, Notre Dame; Steve Stipanovich, Missouri; Jon Sundvold, Missouri; Darrell Walker, Arkansas; Sidney Green, UNLV; Randy Wittman, Indiana.

1984

First Team—Wayman Tisdale, Oklahoma, 6-9, Tulsa, Okla.; Sam Perkins, North Caro., 6-10, Latham, N.Y.; Patrick Ewing, Georgetown, 7-0, Cambridge, Mass.; Akeem Olajuwon, Houston, 7-0, Lagos, Nigeria; Michael Jordan, North Caro., 6-5, Wilmington, N.C.

Second Team—Chris Mullin, St. John's (N.Y.); Devin Durrant, Brigham Young; Leon Wood, Cal St. Fullerton; Keith Lee, Memphis; Melvin Turpin, Kentucky; Michael Cage, San Diego St.

1985

First Team—Wayman Tisdale, Oklahoma, 6-9, Tulsa, Okla.; Patrick Ewing, Georgetown, 7-0, Cambridge, Mass.; Keith Lee, Memphis, 6-10, West Memphis, Ark.; Chris Mullin, St. John's (N.Y.), 6-6, Brooklyn, N.Y.; Xavier McDaniel, Wichita St., 6-7, Columbia, S.C.; Johnny Dawkins, Duke, 6-2, Washington, D.C.

Second Team—Kenny Walker, Kentucky; Jon Koncak, Southern Methodist; Len Bias, Maryland; Mark Price, Georgia Tech; Dwayne Washington, Syracuse.

1986

First Team—Len Bias, Maryland, 6-8, Landover, Md.; Kenny Walker, Kentucky, 6-8, Roberta, Ga.; Walter Berry, St. John's (N.Y.), 6-8, Bronx, N.Y.; Johnny Dawkins, Duke, 6-2, Washington, D.C.; Steve Alford, Indiana, 6-2, New Castle, Ind.

Second Team—Dell Curry, Virginia Tech; Brad Daugherty, North Caro.; Danny Manning, Kansas; Ron Harper, Miami (Ohio); Scott Skiles, Michigan St.; David Robinson, Navy.

1987

First Team—David Robinson, Navy, 7-1, Woodbridge, Va.; Danny Manning, Kansas, 6-11, Lawrence, Kan.; Reggie Williams, Georgetown, 6-7, Baltimore, Md.; Steve Alford, Indiana, 6-2, New Castle, Ind.; Kenny Smith, North Caro., 6-3, Queens, N.Y.

Second Team—Armon Gilliam, UNLV; Dennis Hopson, Ohio St.; Mark Jackson, St. John's (N.Y.); Ken Norman, Illinois; Horace Grant, Clemson.

1988

First Team—Gary Grant, Michigan, 6-3, Canton, Ohio; Hersey Hawkins, Bradley, 6-3, Chicago; J. R. Reid, North Caro., 6-9, Virginia Beach, Va.; Sean Elliott, Arizona, 6-8, Tucson, Ariz.; Danny Manning, Kansas, 6-11, Lawrence, Kan.

Second Team—Mark Macon, Temple; Rony Seikaly, Syracuse; Danny Ferry, Duke; Jerome Lane, Pittsburgh; Mitch Richmond, Kansas St.; Michael Smith, Brigham Young.

1989

First Team—Sean Elliott, Arizona, 6-8, Sr., Tucson, Ariz.; Pervis Ellison, Louisville, 6-9, Sr., Savannah, Ga.; Danny Ferry, Duke, 6-10, Sr., Bowie, Md.; Chris Jackson, LSU, 6-1, Fr., Gulfport, Miss.; Stacey King, Oklahoma, 6-11, Sr., Lawton, Okla.

Second Team—Mookie Blaylock, Oklahoma, 6-1, Sr.; Sherman Douglas, Syracuse, 6-0, Sr.; Jay Edwards, Indiana, 6-4, So.; Todd Lichti, Stanford, 6-4, Sr.; Glen Rice, Michigan, 6-7, Sr.; Lionel Simmons, La Salle, 6-6, Jr.

1990

First Team—Derrick Coleman, Syracuse, 6-10, Sr., Detroit, Mich.; Chris Jackson, LSU, 6-1, So., Gulfport, Miss.; Larry Johnson, UNLV, 6-7, Jr., Dallas; Gary Payton, Oregon St., 6-3, Sr., Oakland, Calif.; Lionel Simmons, La Salle, 6-6, Sr., Philadelphia.

Second Team—Hank Gathers, Loyola Marymount, 6-7, Sr.; Kendall Gill, Illinois, 6-5, Sr.; Bo Kimble, Loyola Marymount, 6-5, Sr.; Alonzo Mourning, Georgetown, 6-10, So.; Rumeal Robinson, Michigan, 6-2, Sr.; Dennis Scott, Georgia Tech, 6-8, Jr.; Doug Smith, Missouri, 6-10, Jr.

1991

First Team—Kenny Anderson, Georgia Tech, 6-2, So., Rego Park, N.Y.; Jim Jackson, Ohio St., 6-6, So., Toledo, Ohio; Larry Johnson, UNLV, 6-7, Sr., Dallas; Shaquille O'Neal, LSU, 7-1, So., San Antonio, Texas; Billy Owens, Syracuse, 6-9, Jr., Carlisle, Pa.

Second Team—Stacey Augmon, UNLV, 6-8, Sr.; Keith Jennings, East Tenn. St., 5-7, Sr.; Christian Laettner, Duke, 6-11, Jr.; Eric Murdock, Providence, 6-2, Sr.; Steve Smith, Michigan St., 6-6, Sr.

1992

First Team—Jim Jackson, Ohio St., 6-6, Jr., Toledo, Ohio; Christian Laettner, Duke, 6-11, Sr., Angola, N.Y.; Harold Miner, Southern Cal, 6-5, Jr., Inglewood, Calif.; Alonzo Mourning, Georgetown, 6-10, Sr., Chesapeake, Va.; Shaquille O'Neal, LSU, 7-1, Jr., San Antonio, Texas.

Second Team—Byron Houston, Oklahoma St., 6-7, Sr.; Don MacLean, UCLA, 6-10, Sr.; Anthony Peeler, Missouri, 6-4, Sr.; Malik Sealy, St. John's (N.Y.), 6-7, Sr.; Walt Williams, Maryland, 6-8, Sr.

1993

First Team—Calbert Cheaney, Indiana, 6-7, Sr., Evansville, Ind.; Anfernee Hardaway, Memphis, 6-7, Jr., Memphis, Tenn.; Bobby Hurley, Duke, 6-0, Sr., Jersey City, N.J.; Jamal Mashburn, Kentucky, 6-8, Jr., New York; Chris Webber, Michigan, 6-9, So., Detroit, Mich.

Second Team—Terry Dehere, Seton Hall, 6-3, Sr.; Grant Hill, Duke, 6-7, Jr.; Billy McCaffrey, Vanderbilt, 6-3, Jr.; Eric Montross, North Caro., 7-0, Jr.; J. R. Rider, UNLV, 6-7, Sr.; Glenn Robinson, Purdue, 6-9, So.; Rodney Rogers, Wake Forest, 6-8, Jr.

1994

First Team—Grant Hill, Duke, 6-8, Sr., Reston, Va.; Jason Kidd, California, 6-4, So., Oakland, Calif.; Donyell Marshall, Connecticut, 6-9, Jr., Reading, Pa.; Glenn Robinson, Purdue, 6-8, Jr., Gary, Ind.; Clifford Rozier, Louisville, 6-9, Jr., Bradenton, Fla.

Second Team—Melvin Booker, Missouri, 6-2, Sr.; Eric Montross, North Caro., 7-0, Sr.; Lamond Murray, California, 6-7, Jr.; Khalid Reeves, Arizona, 6-2, Sr.; Jalen Rose, Michigan, 6-8, Jr.; Corliss Williamson, Arkansas, 6-7, So.

1995

First Team—Ed O'Bannon, UCLA, 6-8, Sr., Lakewood, Calif.; Shawn Respert, Michigan St., 6-3, Sr., Detroit, Mich.; Joe Smith, Maryland, 6-10, So., Norfolk, Va.; Jerry Stackhouse, North Caro., 6-6, So., Kingston, N.C.; Damon Stoudamire, Arizona, 6-10, Sr., Portland, Ore.

Second Team—Randolph Childress, Wake Forest, 6-2, Sr.; Kerry Kittles, Villanova, 6-5, Jr.; Lou Roe, Massachusetts, 6-7, Sr.; Rasheed Wallace, North Caro., 6-10, So.; Corliss Williamson, Arkansas, 6-7, Jr.

1996

First Team—Ray Allen, Connecticut, 6-5, Jr., Dalzell, S.C.; Marcus Camby, Massachusetts, 6-11, Jr., Hartford, Conn.; Tony Delk, Kentucky, 6-1, Sr., Brownsville, Tenn.; Tim Duncan, Wake Forest, 6-10, Jr., St. Croix, Virgin Islands; Allen Iverson, Georgetown, 6-1, So., Hampton, Va.; Kerry Kittles, Villanova, 6-5, Sr., New Orleans.

Second Team—Danny Fortson, Cincinnati, 6-7, So.; Keith Van Horn, Utah, 6-9, Jr.; Jacque Vaughn, Kansas, 6-1, Jr.; John Wallace, Syracuse, 6-8, Sr.; Lorenzen Wright, Memphis, 6-11, So.

Teams used for consensus selections:
Helms Foundation—1929-48
Converse Yearbook—1932-48
College Humor Magazine—1929-33, 1936
Christy Walsh Syndicate—1929-30
Literary Digest Magazine—1934
Madison Square Garden—1937-42
Omaha World Newspaper—1937
Newspaper Enterprises Assn.—1938, 1953-63
Colliers (Basketball Coaches)—1939, 1949-56
Pic Magazine—1942-44
Sporting News—1943-46
Argosy Magazine—1945
True Magazine—1946-47
International News Service—1950-58
Look Magazine—1949-63
The Associated Press—1948-96
United Press International—1949-96
National Association of Basketball Coaches—1957-96
U.S. Basketball Writers Association—1960-96

Consensus All-Americans By Team

ARIZONA
88—Sean Elliott
89—Sean Elliott
95—Damon Stoudamire

ARKANSAS
36—Ike Poole
41—John Adams
79—Sidney Moncrief

BOWLING GREEN
45—Wyndol Gray

BRADLEY
50—Paul Unruh
51—Gene Melchiorre
61—Chet Walker
62—Chet Walker
88—Hersey Hawkins

BRIGHAM YOUNG
31—Elwood Romney
81—Danny Ainge

CALIFORNIA
29—Vern Corbin
60—Darrall Imhoff
94—Jason Kidd

CINCINNATI
58—Oscar Robertson
59—Oscar Robertson
60—Oscar Robertson
63—Ron Bonham
  Tom Thacker

COLUMBIA
31—George Gregory
57—Chet Forte

CONNECTICUT
94—Donyell Marshall
96—Ray Allen

CREIGHTON
43—Ed Beisser

DARTMOUTH
40—Gus Broberg
41—Gus Broberg
44—Audley Brindley

DAVIDSON
65—Fred Hetzel

DENVER
49—Vince Boryla

DEPAUL
44—George Mikan
45—George Mikan
46—George Mikan
80—Mark Aguirre
81—Mark Aguirre
82—Terry Cummings

DETROIT
69—Spencer Haywood

DUKE
52—Dick Groat
63—Art Heyman
67—Bob Verga
79—Mike Gminski
85—Johnny Dawkins
86—Johnny Dawkins
89—Danny Ferry
92—Christian Laettner
93—Bobby Hurley
94—Grant Hill

DUQUESNE
55—Dick Ricketts
  Si Green
56—Si Green

FURMAN
54—Frank Selvy

GEORGETOWN
82—Eric Floyd
83—Patrick Ewing
84—Patrick Ewing
85—Patrick Ewing
87—Reggie Williams
92—Alonzo Mourning
96—Allen Iverson

GEORGIA TECH
61—Roger Kaiser
91—Kenny Anderson

HOLY CROSS
50—Bob Cousy
56—Tom Heinsohn

HOUSTON
67—Elvin Hayes
68—Elvin Hayes
77—Otis Birdsong
84—Akeem Olajuwon

ILLINOIS
40—Bill Hapac
42—Andrew Phillip
43—Andrew Phillip
45—Walton Kirk
52—Rod Fletcher

ILLINOIS ST.
73—Doug Collins

INDIANA
30—Branch McCracken
36—Vern Huffman
39—Ernie Andres
47—Ralph Hamilton
54—Don Schlundt
75—Scott May
76—Scott May
  Kent Benson
77—Kent Benson
81—Isiah Thomas
86—Steve Alford
87—Steve Alford
93—Calbert Cheaney

INDIANA ST.
78—Larry Bird
79—Larry Bird

IOWA
48—Murray Wier
52—Chuck Darling

JACKSONVILLE
71—Artis Gilmore

KANSAS
38—Fred Pralle
41—Howard Engleman
43—Charles Black
51—Clyde Lovellette
52—Clyde Lovellette
57—Wilt Chamberlain
58—Wilt Chamberlain
87—Danny Manning
88—Danny Manning

KANSAS ST.
58—Bob Boozer
59—Bob Boozer

KENTUCKY
32—Forest Sale
33—Forest Sale
35—Leroy Edwards
44—Robert Brannum
47—Ralph Beard
  Alex Groza
48—Ralph Beard
49—Ralph Beard
  Alex Groza
51—Bill Spivey
52—Cliff Hagan
54—Cliff Hagan
59—Johnny Cox
64—Cotton Nash
70—Dan Issel
80—Kyle Macy

86—Kenny Walker
93—Jamal Mashburn
96—Tony Delk

LA SALLE
53—Tom Gola
54—Tom Gola
55—Tom Gola
80—Michael Brooks
90—Lionel Simmons

LONG BEACH ST.
72—Ed Ratleff
73—Ed Ratleff

LIU-BROOKLYN
37—Jules Bender
39—Irving Torgoff

LSU
54—Bob Pettit
68—Pete Maravich
69—Pete Maravich
70—Pete Maravich
89—Chris Jackson
90—Chris Jackson
91—Shaquille O'Neal
92—Shaquille O'Neal

LOUISVILLE
57—Charlie Tyra
67—Wes Unseld
68—Wes Unseld
80—Darrell Griffith
89—Pervis Ellison
94—Clifford Rozier

LOYOLA (ILL.)
63—Jerry Harkness

MARQUETTE
71—Dean Meminger
72—Jim Chones
78—Butch Lee

MARYLAND
32—Louis Berger
75—John Lucas
76—John Lucas
86—Len Bias

95—Joe Smith

MASSACHUSETTS
96—Marcus Camby

MEMPHIS
83—Keith Lee
85—Keith Lee
93—Anfernee Hardaway

MIAMI (FLA.)
65—Rick Barry

MICHIGAN
65—Cazzie Russell
66—Cazzie Russell
77—Rickey Green
88—Gary Grant
93—Chris Webber

MICHIGAN ST.
79—Earvin Johnson
95—Shawn Respert

MINNESOTA
48—Jim McIntyre
55—Dick Garmaker
78—Mychal Thompson

MISSISSIPPI ST.
59—Bailey Howell

MONTANA ST.
29—John Thompson
30—John Thompson
  Frank Ward

NAVY
33—Elliott Loughlin
87—David Robinson

UNLV
90—Larry Johnson
91—Larry Johnson

NEW YORK U.
46—Sid Tanenbaum
47—Sid Tanenbaum
63—Barry Kramer

NIAGARA
69—Calvin Murphy

Tony Delk, who helped Kentucky to a 34-2 record and its sixth Division I national championship, became the 14th Wildcats player to earn consensus all-America honors. Kentucky has amassed a Division I-record 19 honors.

70—Calvin Murphy

NORTH CARO.
40—George Glamack
41—George Glamack
57—Lenny Rosenbluth
68—Larry Miller
72—Bob McAdoo
77—Phil Ford
78—Phil Ford
82—James Worthy
83—Michael Jordan
    Sam Perkins
84—Michael Jordan
    Sam Perkins
87—Kenny Smith
88—J. R. Reid
95—Jerry Stackhouse

NORTH CARO. ST.
51—Sam Ranzino
56—Ron Shavlik
73—David Thompson
74—David Thompson
75—David Thompson

NORTHWESTERN
31—Joe Reiff
33—Joe Reiff
44—Otto Graham
46—Max Norris

NOTRE DAME
32—Ed Krause
33—Ed Krause
34—Ed Krause
36—Paul Nowak
    John Moir
37—Paul Nowak
    John Moir
38—Paul Nowak
    John Moir
44—Leo Klier
45—William Hassett
46—Leo Klier
48—Kevin O'Shea
71—Austin Carr
74—John Shumate
75—Adrian Dantley
76—Adrian Dantley

OHIO ST.
31—Wes Fesler
39—Jimmy Hull
50—Dick Schnittker
56—Robin Freeman
60—Jerry Lucas
61—Jerry Lucas
62—Jerry Lucas
64—Gary Bradds
91—Jim Jackson
92—Jim Jackson

OKLAHOMA
29—Thomas Churchill
35—Bud Browning
44—Alva Paine
47—Gerald Tucker
83—Wayman Tisdale
84—Wayman Tisdale
85—Wayman Tisdale
89—Stacey King

OKLAHOMA ST.
44—Robert Kurland
45—Robert Kurland
46—Robert Kurland

OREGON
39—Urgel Wintermute
40—John Dick

OREGON ST.
81—Steve Johnson
90—Gary Payton

PENNSYLVANIA
29—Joe Schaaf
45—Howard Dallmar
53—Ernie Beck

PITTSBURGH
29—Charley Hyatt
30—Charley Hyatt
33—Don Smith
34—Claire Cribbs
35—Claire Cribbs
58—Don Hennon

PRINCETON
64—Bill Bradley
65—Bill Bradley

PROVIDENCE
66—Jim Walker
67—Jim Walker
73—Ernie DiGregorio
74—Marvin Barnes

PURDUE
29—Charles Murphy
30—Charles Murphy
    John Wooden
31—John Wooden
32—John Wooden
34—Norman Cottom
36—Bob Kessler
37—Jewell Young
38—Jewell Young
61—Terry Dischinger
62—Terry Dischinger
66—Dave Schellhase
69—Rick Mount
70—Rick Mount
80—Joe Barry Carroll
94—Glenn Robinson

RHODE ISLAND
39—Chet Jaworski

RICE
42—Bob Kinney
43—William Closs
45—William Henry

RUTGERS
67—Bob Lloyd

ST. BONAVENTURE
60—Tom Stith
61—Tom Stith
70—Bob Lanier

ST. JOHN'S (N.Y.)
43—Harry Boykoff
85—Chris Mullin
86—Walter Berry

ST. JOSEPH'S (PA.)
43—George Senesky

ST. LOUIS
48—Ed Macauley
49—Ed Macauley

SAN FRANCISCO
55—Bill Russell
56—Bill Russell
82—Quintin Dailey

SEATTLE
53—Johnny O'Brien
58—Elgin Baylor

SETON HALL
42—Robert Davies
53—Walt Dukes

SOUTH CARO.
72—Tom Riker

SOUTHERN CAL
33—Jerry Nemer
35—Lee Guttero
40—Ralph Vaughn
50—Bill Sharman
92—Harold Miner

SOUTHERN METHODIST
57—Jim Krebs

SOUTHWESTERN LA.
72—Dwight Lamar
73—Dwight Lamar

STANFORD
36—Hank Luisetti

37—Hank Luisetti
38—Hank Luisetti

SYRACUSE
66—Dave Bing
90—Derrick Coleman
91—Billy Owens

TEMPLE
38—Meyer Bloom
51—Bill Mlkvy
58—Guy Rodgers

TENNESSEE
77—Bernard King
83—Dale Ellis

TEXAS
35—Jack Gray

UCLA
64—Walt Hazzard
65—Gail Goodrich
67—Lew Alcindor
68—Lew Alcindor
69—Lew Alcindor
71—Sidney Wicks
72—Bill Walton
    Henry Bibby
73—Bill Walton
    Keith Wilkes
74—Bill Walton
    Keith Wilkes
75—Dave Meyers
76—Richard Washington
77—Marques Johnson
78—David Greenwood
79—David Greenwood
95—Ed O'Bannon

UTAH
36—Bill Kinner
45—Arnold Ferrin
62—Billy McGill

VANDERBILT
66—Clyde Lee

VILLANOVA
50—Paul Arizin
96—Kerry Kittles

VIRGINIA
81—Ralph Sampson
82—Ralph Sampson
83—Ralph Sampson

WAKE FOREST
62—Len Chappell
96—Tim Duncan

WASHINGTON
34—Hal Lee
53—Bob Houbregs

WEST TEX. A&M
42—Price Brookfield

WEST VA.
57—Rod Hundley
59—Jerry West
60—Jerry West

WESTERN KY.
67—Clem Haskins
71—Jim McDaniels

WICHITA ST.
64—Dave Stallworth
85—Xavier McDaniel

WISCONSIN
41—Gene Englund
42—John Kotz

WYOMING
32—Les Witte
34—Les Witte
43—Ken Sailors

YALE
49—Tony Lavelli

Team Leaders In Consensus All-Americans

(Ranked on total number of selections)

Team	No.	Players
Kentucky	19	14
UCLA	18	12
Notre Dame	17	9
Purdue	16	10
North Caro.	15	11
Indiana	13	10
Duke	10	9
Ohio St.	10	7
Kansas	9	6
Oklahoma	8	6
LSU	8	4
Georgetown	7	5
Louisville	6	5
Pittsburgh	6	4
DePaul	6	3
Southern Cal	5	5
Bradley	5	4
Illinois	5	4
Maryland	5	4
Cincinnati	5	3
La Salle	5	3
Michigan	5	3
North Caro. St.	5	3

Division I Academic All-Americans By Team

AIR FORCE
68—Cliff Parsons
70—Jim Cooper
78—Tom Schneeberger

AMERICAN
72—Kermit Washington
73—Kermit Washington
87—Patrick Witting

ARIZONA
76—Bob Elliott
77—Bob Elliott

ARIZONA ST.
64—Art Becker

ARKANSAS
78—Jim Counce

ARMY
64—Mike Silliman

BAYLOR
96—Doug Brandt

BOSTON COLLEGE
68—Terry Driscoll

BRIGHAM YOUNG
80—Danny Ainge
81—Danny Ainge
83—Devin Durrant
84—Devin Durrant
87—Michael Smith
88—Michael Smith
89—Michael Smith
90—Andy Toolson

BROWN
86—Jim Turner

CALIFORNIA
87—David Butler

CENTRAL MICH.
93—Sander Scott

CINCINNATI
67—Mike Rolf

CLEVELAND ST.
73—Pat Lyons

CONNECTICUT
67—Wes Bialosuknia

CREIGHTON
64—Paul Silas
78—Rick Apke

DARTMOUTH
84—Paul Anderson
96—Seamus Lonergan

DAVIDSON
88—Derek Rucker

DAYTON
79—Jim Paxson
81—Mike Kanieski
82—Mike Kanieski

DEPAUL
91—Stephen Howard
92—Stephen Howard

DUKE
63—Jay Buckley
64—Jay Buckley
71—Dick DeVenzio
72—Gary Melchionni
75—Bob Fleischer
78—Mike Gminski
   Jim Spanarkel
79—Mike Gminski
   Jim Spanarkel
80—Mike Gminski

DUQUESNE
69—Bill Zopf
70—Bill Zopf

EVANSVILLE
89—Scott Haffner

FAIRLEIGH DICKINSON
78—John Jorgensen

FORDHAM
75—Darryl Brown

GEO. WASHINGTON
76—Pat Tallent
86—Steve Frick

GEORGIA
88—Alec Kessler
89—Alec Kessler
90—Alec Kessler

GEORGIA TECH
64—Jim Caldwell
69—Rich Yunkus
70—Rich Yunkus
71—Rich Yunkus

GONZAGA
84—Bryce McPhee
   John Stockton
85—Bryce McPhee
92—Jarrod Davis
93—Jeff Brown
94—Jeff Brown

HARVARD
85—Joe Carrabino
87—Arne Duncan

HOLY CROSS
69—Ed Siudut
78—Ronnie Perry
79—Ronnie Perry
80—Ronnie Perry
91—Jim Nairus

ILLINOIS
68—Dave Scholz
69—Dave Scholz
71—Rich Howatt

74—Rick Schmidt
75—Rick Schmidt

ILLINOIS ST.
73—Doug Collins

INDIANA
64—Dick Van Arsdale
65—Dick Van Arsdale
65—Tom Van Arsdale
73—John Ritter
74—Steve Green
75—Steve Green
76—Kent Benson
77—Kent Benson
78—Wayne Radford
82—Randy Wittman
83—Randy Wittman
85—Uwe Blab
89—Joe Hillman

IOWA ST.
95—Fred Hoiberg

JACKSONVILLE
71—Vaughan Wedeking
83—Maurice Roulhac

KANSAS
71—Bud Stallworth
74—Tom Kivisto
77—Ken Koenigs
   Chris Barnthouse
78—Ken Koenigs
79—Darnell Valentine
80—Darnell Valentine
81—Darnell Valentine
82—David Magley
96—Jacque Vaughn

KANSAS ST.
68—Earl Seyfert
82—Tim Jankovich
   Ed Nealy

KENTUCKY
66—Lou Dampier
67—Lou Dampier
69—Larry Conley
70—Dan Issel
   Mike Pratt
71—Mike Casey
75—Bob Guyette
   Jimmy Dan Conner
79—Kyle Macy

LA SALLE
77—Tony DiLeo
88—Tim Legler
92—Jack Hurd

LEWIS
89—Jamie Martin

LOUISVILLE
76—Phil Bond

LOYOLA MARYMOUNT
73—Steve Smith

MARQUETTE
82—Marc Marotta
83—Marc Marotta
84—Marc Marotta

MARSHALL
72—Mike D'Antoni
73—Mike D'Antoni

MARYLAND
72—Tom McMillen
73—Tom McMillen
74—Tom McMillen
91—Matt Roe

MIAMI (OHIO)
93—Craig Michaelis

MICHIGAN
76—Steve Grote
81—Marty Bodnar

MICHIGAN ST.
70—Ralph Simpson
79—Greg Kelser

Kansas' Jacque Vaughn, the Jayhawks' team leader on the court, also led the way in the classroom in 1996, earning academic all-America honors. Vaughn is the first Kansas player since David Magley in 1982 to be so recognized.

MISSISSIPPI
75—Dave Shepherd

MISSOURI
83—Steve Stipanovich

MONTANA
81—Craig Zanon
85—Larry Krystkowiak
86—Larry Krystkowiak

MURRAY ST.
85—Mike Lahm

NEBRASKA
84—John Matzke

UNLV
83—Danny Tarkanian
84—Danny Tarkanian

NEW MEXICO
69—Ron Becker
70—Ron Becker

NORTH CARO.
65—Billy Cunningham
70—Charlie Scott
72—Dennis Wuycik
   Steve Previs
76—Tommy LaGarde
86—Steve Hale
94—Eric Montross

NORTH CARO. ST.
84—Terry Gannon
85—Terry Gannon
95—Todd Fuller
96—Todd Fuller

NORTHEASTERN
77—David Caligaris
78—David Caligaris

NORTHERN ILL.
84—Tim Dillion

NORTHERN IOWA
84—Randy Kraayenbrink

NORTHWESTERN
67—Jim Burns
80—Mike Campbell
87—Shon Morris
88—Shon Morris

NOTRE DAME
67—Bob Arnzen
68—Bob Arnzen
69—Bob Arnzen
74—Gary Novak
79—Kelly Tripucka
80—Rich Branning
82—John Paxson
83—John Paxson

OHIO
71—Craig Love
77—Steve Skaggs
90—Dave Jamerson

OHIO ST.
68—Bill Hosket

OKLAHOMA
74—Alvin Adams
75—Alvin Adams
80—Terry Stotts

OKLAHOMA ST.
64—Gary Hassmann
69—Joe Smith

PACIFIC (CAL.)
67—Keith Swagerty

PENNSYLVANIA
72—Robert Morse

PENN ST.
94—John Amaechi
95—John Amaechi

PRINCETON
65—Bill Bradley
91—Kit Mueller

PURDUE
65—Dave Schellhase

66—Dave Schellhase
72—Robert Ford
81—Brian Walker
82—Keith Edmonson
83—Steve Reid
85—Steve Reid

RICE
94—Adam Peakes

ST. FRANCIS (PA.)
90—Michael Iuzzolino
91—Michael Iuzzolino

ST. LOUIS
68—Rich Niemann
94—Scott Highmark
95—Scott Highmark

SAN DIEGO ST.
76—Steve Copp

SANTA CLARA
68—Dennis Awtrey
69—Dennis Awtrey
70—Dennis Awtrey

SIENA
85—Doug Peotzch
92—Bruce Schroeder

SOUTH CARO.
70—John Roche

71—John Roche

SOUTHERN ILL.
76—Mike Glenn
77—Mike Glenn

SOUTHERN METHODIST
77—Pete Lodwick

SYRACUSE
81—Dan Schayes

TENNESSEE
68—Bill Justus
93—Lang Wiseman

TEXAS
79—Jim Krivacs

TEXAS A&M
64—Bill Robinette

UCLA
67—Mike Warren
69—Kenny Heitz
71—Sidney Wicks
72—Bill Walton
　　Keith Wilkes
　　Greg Lee
73—Bill Walton
　　Keith Wilkes
　　Greg Lee
74—Bill Walton

　　Keith Wilkes
　　Greg Lee
75—Ralph Drollinger
77—Marques Johnson
79—Kiki Vandeweghe
80—Kiki Vandeweghe
95—George Zidek

UTAH
70—Mike Newlin
71—Mike Newlin
77—Jeff Jonas

UTAH ST.
64—Gary Watts
80—Dean Hunger
82—Larry Bergeson
96—Eric Franson

VANDERBILT
75—Jeff Fosnes
76—Jeff Fosnes
93—Bruce Elder

VILLANOVA
73—Tom Inglesby
82—John Pinone
83—John Pinone
86—Harold Jensen
87—Harold Jensen

VIRGINIA
76—Wally Walker
81—Jeff Lamp
　　Lee Raker

VMI
80—Andy Kolesar
81—Andy Kolesar

WASHINGTON
82—Dave Henley

WASHINGTON ST.
89—Brian Quinnett

WEBER ST.
85—Randy Worster

WICHITA ST.
67—Jamie Thompson
69—Ron Mendell

WILLIAM & MARY
85—Keith Cieplicki

WISCONSIN
74—Dan Anderson

WIS.-GREEN BAY
92—Tony Bennett

Division I Player Of The Year

Season	United Press International	The Associated Press	U.S. Basketball Writers Assn.	Wooden Award	Nat'l Assn. of Basketball Coaches	Naismith Award	Frances Pomeroy Naismith Award
1955	Tom Gola La Salle						
1956	Bill Russell San Francisco						
1957	Chet Forte Columbia						
1958	Oscar Robertson Cincinnati						
1959	Oscar Robertson Cincinnati		Oscar Robertson Cincinnati				
1960	Oscar Robertson Cincinnati		Oscar Robertson Cincinnati				
1961	Jerry Lucas Ohio St.	Jerry Lucas Ohio St.	Jerry Lucas Ohio St.				
1962	Jerry Lucas Ohio St.	Jerry Lucas Ohio St.	Jerry Lucas Ohio St.				
1963	Art Heyman Duke	Art Heyman Duke	Art Heyman Duke				
1964	Gary Bradds Ohio St.	Gary Bradds Ohio St.	Walt Hazzard UCLA				
1965	Bill Bradley Princeton	Bill Bradley Princeton	Bill Bradley Princeton				
1966	Cazzie Russell Michigan	Cazzie Russell Michigan	Cazzie Russell Michigan				
1967	Lew Alcindor UCLA	Lew Alcindor UCLA	Lew Alcindor UCLA				
1968	Elvin Hayes Houston	Elvin Hayes Houston	Elvin Hayes Houston				
1969	Lew Alcindor UCLA	Lew Alcindor UCLA	Lew Alcindor UCLA			Lew Alcindor UCLA	Billy Keller Purdue
1970	Pete Maravich LSU	Pete Maravich LSU	Pete Maravich LSU			Pete Maravich LSU	John Rinka Kenyon
1971	Austin Carr Notre Dame	Austin Carr Notre Dame	Sidney Wicks UCLA			Austin Carr Notre Dame	Charlie Johnson California
1972	Bill Walton UCLA	Bill Walton UCLA	Bill Walton UCLA			Bill Walton UCLA	Scott Martin Oklahoma
1973	Bill Walton UCLA	Bill Walton UCLA	Bill Walton UCLA			Bill Walton UCLA	Bobby Sherwin Army
1974	Bill Walton UCLA	David Thompson North Caro. St.	Bill Walton UCLA			Bill Walton UCLA	Mike Robinson Michigan St.

Season	United Press International	The Associated Press	U.S. Basketball Writers Assn.	Wooden Award	Nat'l Assn. of Basketball Coaches	Naismith Award	Frances Pomeroy Naismith Award
1975	David Thompson North Caro. St.	David Thompson North Caro. St.	David Thompson North Caro. St.		David Thompson North Caro. St.	David Thompson North Caro. St.	Monty Towe North Caro. St.
1976	Scott May Indiana	Scott May Indiana	Adrian Dantley Notre Dame		Scott May Indiana	Scott May Indiana	Frank Algia St. John's (N.Y.)
1977	Marques Johnson UCLA	Marques Johnson UCLA	Marques Johnson UCLA	Marques Johnson UCLA	Marques Johnson UCLA	Marques Johnson UCLA	Jeff Jonas Utah
1978	Butch Lee Marquette	Butch Lee Marquette	Phil Ford North Caro.	Phil Ford North Caro.	Phil Ford North Caro.	Butch Lee Marquette	Mike Schib Susquehanna
1979	Larry Bird Indiana St.	Larry Bird Indiana St.	Larry Bird Indiana St.	Larry Bird Indiana St.	Larry Bird Indiana St.	Larry Bird Indiana St.	Alton Byrd Columbia
1980	Mark Aguirre DePaul	Mark Aguirre DePaul	Mark Aguirre DePaul	Darrell Griffith Louisville	Michael Brooks La Salle	Mark Aguirre DePaul	Jim Sweeney Boston College
1981	Ralph Sampson Virginia	Ralph Sampson Virginia	Ralph Sampson Virginia	Danny Ainge Brigham Young	Danny Ainge Brigham Young	Ralph Sampson Virginia	Terry Adolph West Tex. A&M
1982	Ralph Sampson Virginia	Ralph Sampson Virginia	Ralph Sampson Virginia	Ralph Sampson Virginia	Ralph Sampson Virginia	Ralph Sampson Virginia	Jack Moore Nebraska
1983	Ralph Sampson Virginia	Ralph Sampson Virginia	Ralph Sampson Virginia	Ralph Sampson Virginia	Ralph Sampson Virginia	Ralph Sampson Virginia	Ray McCallum Ball St.
1984	Michael Jordan North Caro.	Michael Jordan North Caro.	Michael Jordan North Caro.	Michael Jordan North Caro.	Michael Jordan North Caro.	Michael Jordan North Caro.	Ricky Stokes Virginia
1985	Chris Mullin St. John's (N.Y.)	Patrick Ewing Georgetown	Chris Mullin St. John's (N.Y.)	Chris Mullin St. John's (N.Y.)	Patrick Ewing Georgetown	Patrick Ewing Georgetown	Bubba Jennings Texas Tech
1986	Walter Berry St. John's (N.Y.)	Walter Berry St. John's (N.Y.)	Walter Berry St. John's (N.Y.)	Walter Berry St. John's (N.Y.)	Walter Berry St. John's (N.Y.)	Johnny Dawkins Duke	Jim Les Bradley
1987	David Robinson Navy	David Robinson Navy	David Robinson Navy	David Robinson Navy	David Robinson Navy	David Robinson Navy	Tyrone Bogues Wake Forest
1988	Hersey Hawkins Bradley	Hersey Hawkins Bradley	Hersey Hawkins Bradley	Danny Manning Kansas	Danny Manning Kansas	Danny Manning Kansas	Jerry Johnson Fla. Southern
1989	Danny Ferry Duke	Sean Elliott Arizona	Danny Ferry Duke	Sean Elliott Arizona	Sean Elliott Arizona	Danny Ferry Duke	Tim Hardaway UTEP
1990	Lionel Simmons La Salle	Lionel Simmons La Salle	Lionel Simmons La Salle	Lionel Simmons La Salle	Lionel Simmons La Salle	Lionel Simmons La Salle	Boo Harvey St. John's (N.Y.)
1991	Shaquille O'Neal LSU	Shaquille O'Neal LSU	Larry Johnson UNLV	Larry Johnson UNLV	Larry Johnson UNLV	Larry Johnson UNLV	Keith Jennings East Tenn. St.
1992	Jim Jackson Ohio St.	Christian Laettner Duke	Christian Laettner Duke	Christian Laettner Duke	Christian Laettner Duke	Christian Laettner Duke	Tony Bennett Wis.-Green Bay
1993	Calbert Cheaney Indiana	Calbert Cheaney Indiana	Calbert Cheaney Indiana	Calbert Cheaney Indiana	Calbert Cheaney Indiana	Calbert Cheaney Indiana	Sam Crawford New Mexico S.
1994	Glenn Robinson Purdue	Glenn Robinson Purdue	Glenn Robinson Purdue	Glenn Robinson Purdue	Glenn Robinson Purdue	Glenn Robinson Purdue	Greg Brown Evansville
1995	Joe Smith Maryland	Joe Smith Maryland	Ed O'Bannon UCLA	Ed O'Bannon UCLA	Shawn Respert Michigan St.	Joe Smith Maryland	Tyus Edney UCLA
1996	Marcus Camby Massachusetts	Marcus Camby Massachusetts	Marcus Camby Massachusetts	Marcus Camby Massachusetts	Marcus Camby Massachusetts	Marcus Camby Massachusetts	Eddie Benton Vermont

Divisions II and III First-Team All-Americans By Team

Current Division I member denoted by (*). Non-NCAA member denoted by (†).

ABILENE CHRISTIAN
68—John Godfrey

AKRON*
67—Bill Turner
72—Len Paul

ALA.-HUNTSVILLE
78—Tony Vann

ALAS. ANCHORAGE
87—Jesse Jackson
87—Hansi Gnad

89—Michael Johnson
90—Todd Fisher

ALBANY ST. (GA.)
75—Major Jones

ALCORN ST.*
76—John McGill

AMERICAN*
60—Willie Jones

AMERICAN INT'L
69—Greg Hill
70—Greg Hill

AMHERST
70—Dave Auten
71—James Rehnquist

ARKANSAS ST.*
65—Jerry Rook

ARMSTRONG ATLANTIC
75—Ike Williams

ASSUMPTION
70—Jake Jones
71—Jake Jones
73—Mike Boylan
74—John Grochowalski
75—John Grochowalski
76—Bill Wurm

AUGUSTANA (ILL.)
73—John Laing

BABSON
92—Jim Pierrakos

BENTLEY
74—Brian Hammel
75—Brian Hammel

BISHOP
83—Shannon Lilly

BRIDGEPORT
69—Gary Baum
76—Lee Hollerbach
85—Manute Bol
91—Lambert Shell
92—Lambert Shell
95—Lamont Jones

BRIDGEWATER (VA.)
95—Dan Rush

BRYANT
81—Ernie DeWitt

CALIF. (PA.)
93—Ray Gutierrez

UC RIVERSIDE
89—Maurice Pullum

CAL ST. BAKERSFIELD
96—Kebu Stewart

CALVIN
93—Steve Honderd

CAMERON
74—Jerry Davenport

CARLETON
93—Gerrick Monroe

CENTENARY (LA.)*
57—Milt Williams

CENTRAL CONN. ST.*
69—Howie Dickenman

CENTRAL FLA.*
79—Bo Clark
80—Bo Clark

CENTRAL MO. ST.
81—Bill Fennelly
85—Ron Nunnelly
91—Armando Becker

CENTRAL OKLA.
93—Alex Wright

CENTRAL WASHINGTON
67—Mel Cox

CHEYNEY
79—Andrew Fields
81—George Melton
82—George Melton

CHRIS. NEWPORT
91—Lamont Strothers

CLAREMONT-M-S
92—Chris Greene

CLARION
94—Kwame Morton

CLARK (MASS.)
80—Kevin Clark
81—Kevin Clark
88—Kermit Sharp

COLBY
77—Paul Harvey
78—Paul Harvey
89—Matt Hancock
90—Matt Hancock

DAVID LIPSCOMB†
88—Phillip Hutcheson
89—Phillip Hutcheson
90—Phillip Hutcheson
92—John Pierce

DAVIS & ELKINS
59—Paul Wilcox

DELTA ST.
69—Sammy Little

DEPAUW
87—David Galle

DIST. COLUMBIA
82—Earl Jones
83—Earl Jones
        Michael Britt
84—Earl Jones

EASTERN MICH.*
71—Ken McIntosh
72—George Gervin

EDINBORO
96—Tyrone Mason

EMORY
90—Tim Garrett

EVANSVILLE*
59—Hugh Ahlering
60—Ed Smallwood
65—Jerry Sloan
        Larry Humes
66—Larry Humes

FLA. SOUTHERN
81—John Ebeling
82—John Ebeling
88—Jerry Johnson
        Kris Kearney
89—Kris Kearney
90—Donolly Tyrell

FRAMINGHAM ST.
84—Mark Van Valkenburg

FRANK. & MARSH.
92—Will Lasky
96—Jeremiah Henry

GANNON
85—Butch Warner

GENESEO ST.
94—Scott Fitch

GEORGETOWN (KY.)†
64—Cecil Tuttle

GRAMBLING*
61—Charles Hardnett
62—Charles Hardnett
64—Willis Reed
66—Johnny Comeaux
76—Larry Wright

GRAND CANYON
76—Bayard Forest

GUILFORD
68—Bob Kauffman
75—Lloyd Free

HAMILTON
77—Cedric Oliver
78—Cedric Oliver
79—Cedric Oliver
87—John Cavanaugh

HAMPDEN-SYDNEY
92—Russell Turner

HANOVER
96—David Benter

HARTFORD*
79—Mark Noon

HARTWICK
77—Dana Gahres
83—Tim O'Brien

HAVERFORD
77—Dick Vioth

HOPE
84—Chip Henry

ILLINOIS ST.*
68—Jerry McGreal

ILL. WESLEYAN
77—Jack Sikma
89—Jeff Kuehl
95—Chris Simich

INDIANA (PA.)
95—Derrick Freeman

IU/PU-INDIANAPOLIS
96—Carlos Knox

INDIANA ST.*
68—Jerry Newsome

JACKSON ST.*
74—Eugene Short
75—Eugene Short
77—Purvis Short

JACKSONVILLE*
62—Roger Strickland
63—Roger Strickland

JERSEY CITY ST.
79—Brett Wyatt

KEAN
93—Fred Drains

KENTUCKY ST.
71—Travis Grant
        Elmore Smith
72—Travis Grant
75—Gerald Cunningham
77—Gerald Cunningham

KY. WESLEYAN
57—Mason Cope
67—Sam Smith
68—Dallas Thornton
69—George Tinsley
84—Rod Drake
        Dwight Higgs
88—J. B. Brown
90—Corey Crowder
91—Corey Crowder
95—Willis Cheaney

KENYON
69—John Rinka
70—John Rinka
79—Scott Rogers
80—Scott Rogers

LEBANON VALLEY
95—Mike Rhodes

LEWIS & CLARK†
63—Jim Boutin
64—Jim Boutin

LINCOLN (MO.)
78—Harold Robertson

LIU-BROOKLYN*
68—Luther Green
        Larry Newbold

LONGWOOD
84—Jerome Kersey

LOUISIANA COLLEGE†
79—Paul Poe

LOUISIANA TECH*
73—Mike Green

MAINE*
61—Tom Chappelle

MASS.-DARTMOUTH
93—Steve Haynes

MASS.-LOWELL
89—Leo Parent

MERCHANT MARINE
90—Kevin D'Arcy

MERRIMACK
77—Ed Murphy
78—Ed Murphy
        Dana Skinner
83—Joe Dickson

MO.-ST. LOUIS
77—Bob Bone

MORGAN ST.
74—Marvin Webster
75—Marvin Webster

MT. ST. MARY'S (MD.)*
57—Jack Sullivan

MUSKINGUM
92—Andy Moore

NEB.-OMAHA
92—Phil Cartwright

NEB. WESLEYAN
86—Dana Janssen

NEW HAVEN
88—Herb Watkins

N.J. INST. OF TECH.
96—Clarence Pierce

NEW ORLEANS*
71—Xavier Webster

NEW YORK TECH
80—Kelvin Hicks

NICHOLLS ST.*
78—Larry Wilson

NORFOLK ST.
79—Ken Evans
84—David Pope
87—Ralph Talley
95—Corey Williams

NORTH ALA.
80—Otis Boddie

NORTH DAK.
66—Phil Jackson
67—Phil Jackson
91—Dave Vonesh
93—Scott Guldseth

NORTH DAK. ST.
60—Marvin Bachmeier

NORTH PARK
79—Mike Harper
80—Mike Harper
81—Mike Thomas

NORTHERN MICH.
87—Bill Harris

NORTHWOOD
73—Fred Smile

OHIO NORTHERN
82—Stan Mories
95—D'Artis Jones

OHIO WESLEYAN
87—Scott Tedder
88—Scott Tedder

OKLAHOMA CITY†
92—Eric Manuel

OLD DOMINION*
72—Dave Twardzik
74—Joel Copeland
76—Wilson Washington

OTTERBEIN
66—Don Carlos
82—Ron Stewart

83—Ron Stewart
85—Dick Hempy
86—Dick Hempy
87—Dick Hempy
91—James Bradley
94—Nick Gutman

PACIFIC LUTHERAN†
59—Chuck Curtis

PFEIFFER
92—Tony Smith

PHILA. TEXTILE
76—Emory Sammons
77—Emory Sammons

PLYMOUTH ST.
94—Moses Jean-Pierre

POTSDAM ST.
80—Derrick Rowland
81—Derrick Rowland
82—Maurice Woods
83—Leroy Witherspoon
84—Leroy Witherspoon
86—Roosevelt Bullock
86—Brendan Mitchell
87—Brendan Mitchell
88—Steve Babiarz
89—Steve Babiarz

PRAIRIE VIEW*
62—Zelmo Beaty

PUGET SOUND
79—Joe Leonard

RANDOLPH-MACON
83—Bryan Vacca

ROANOKE
72—Hal Johnston
73—Jay Piccola
74—Jay Piccola
83—Gerald Holmes
84—Reggie Thomas
85—Reggie Thomas
94—Hilliary Scott

ROCHESTER
91—Chris Fite
92—Chris Fite

ROCHESTER INST.
96—Craig Jones

SACRED HEART
72—Ed Czernota
78—Hector Olivencia
        Andre Means
82—Keith Bennett
83—Keith Bennett
86—Roger Younger
93—Darrin Robinson

ST. CLOUD ST.
57—Vern Baggenstoss
86—Kevin Catron

ST. JOSEPH'S (IND.)
60—Bobby Williams

ST. MICHAEL'S
65—Richie Tarrant

ST. NORBERT
63—Mike Wisneski

SALEM (W.VA.)†
76—Archie Talley

SALISBURY ST.
91—Andre Foreman
92—Andre Foreman

SAM HOUSTON ST.
73—James Lister

SCRANTON
63—Bill Witaconis
77—Irvin Johnson
78—Irvin Johnson
84—Bill Bessoir
85—Bill Bessoir
93—Matt Cusano

SHENANDOAH
96—Phil Dixon

SLIPPERY ROCK
91—Myron Brown
SOUTH DAK.
58—Jim Daniels
SOUTH DAK. ST.
61—Don Jacobsen
64—Tom Black
SE OKLAHOMA†
57—Jim Spivey
SOUTHERN ILL.*
66—George McNeil
67—Walt Frazier
SOUTHERN IND.
95—Stan Gouard
96—Stan Gouard
SOUTHWEST TEX. ST.*
59—Charles Sharp
60—Charles Sharp
SOUTHWESTERN LA.*
65—Dean Church
70—Marvin Winkler
71—Dwight Lamar
SPRINGFIELD
70—Dennis Clark
86—Ivan Olivares
STEPHEN F. AUSTIN*
70—Surry Oliver
STETSON*
70—Ernie Killum
STEUBENVILLE†
58—Jim Smith
STONEHILL
79—Bill Zolga
80—Bill Zolga
82—Bob Reitz
STONY BROOK
79—Earl Keith
SUSQUEHANNA
86—Dan Harnum
TAMPA
85—Todd Linder
86—Todd Linder
87—Todd Linder
94—DeCarlo Deveaux
TENN.-CHATT.*
77—Wayne Golden
TENNESSEE ST.*
58—Dick Barnett
59—Dick Barnett
71—Ted McClain
72—Lloyd Neal
74—Leonard Robinson
TEX.-PAN AMERICAN*
64—Lucious Jackson
68—Otto Moore
TEXAS SOUTHERN*
58—Bennie Swain
77—Alonzo Bradley
THOMAS MORE
96—Rick Hughes
TRENTON ST.
88—Greg Grant
89—Greg Grant
TRINITY (TEX.)
68—Larry Jeffries
69—Larry Jeffries
TROY ST.*
93—Terry McCord
TUFTS
95—Chris McMahon
UPSALA
81—Steve Keenan

82—Steve Keenan
VIRGINIA UNION
85—Charles Oakley
90—A. J. English
94—Derrick Johnson
    Warren Peebles
96—Ben Wallace
WABASH
82—Pete Metzelaars
WASHBURN
94—Clarence Tyson
WASH. & LEE
78—Pat Dennis
WEST GA.
74—Clarence Walker
WESTERN CARO.*
68—Henry Logan
WESTMINSTER (PA.)†
62—Ron Galbreath
WESTMINSTER (UTAH)†
69—Ken Hall
WHEATON (ILL.)
58—Mel Peterson
WIDENER
78—Dennis James
88—Lou Stevens
WILLIAMS
61—Bob Mahland
62—Bob Mahland
96—Mike Nogelo
WINSTON-SALEM
67—Earl Monroe
80—Reginald Gaines
WIS.-EAU CLAIRE
72—Mike Ratliff
WIS.-GREEN BAY*
78—Tom Anderson
79—Ron Ripley
WIS.-OSHKOSH
96—Dennis Ruedinger
WIS.-PARKSIDE
76—Gary Cole
WIS.-PLATTEVILLE
92—T. J. Van Wie
WIS.-STEVENS POINT
85—Terry Porter
WIS.-WHITEWATER
90—Ricky Spicer
94—Ty Evans
WITTENBERG
61—George Fisher
63—Al Thrasher
80—Brian Agler
81—Tyrone Curtis
85—Tim Casey
89—Steve Allison
90—Brad Baldridge
91—Brad Baldridge
WRIGHT ST.
81—Rodney Benson
86—Mark Vest
XAVIER (LA.)†
73—Bruce Seals
YOUNGSTOWN ST.*
77—Jeff Covington
78—Jeff Covington

Teams used for selections:
AP Little All-America—1957-79
NABC College Division—1967-76
NABC Divisions II, III—1977-96

Divisions II and III Academic All-Americans By Team

AKRON
72—Wil Schwarzinger
ALBANY (N.Y.)
88—John Carmello
ALBION
79—John Nibert
ARKANSAS TECH
90—Gray Townsend
94—David Bevis
95—David Bevis
ASHLAND
67—Jim Basista
70—Jay Franson
ASSUMPTION
67—George Ridick
AUGUSTANA (ILL.)
73—Bruce Hamming
74—Bruce Hamming
75—Bruce Hamming
79—Glen Heiden
AUGUSTANA (S.D.)
74—John Ritterbusch
75—John Ritterbusch
BALDWIN-WALLACE
85—Bob Scelza
BARRINGTON
82—Shawn Smith
BATES
83—Herb Taylor
84—Herb Taylor
BEMIDJI ST.
76—Steve Vogel
77—Steve Vogel
78—Steve Vogel
BENTLEY
80—Joe Betley
BETHEL (MINN.)
94—Jason Mekelburg
BLOOMSBURG
78—Steve Bright
BRANDEIS
78—John Martin
BRIAR CLIFF
89—Chad Neubrand
BRIDGEWATER (VA.)
85—Sean O'Connell
BRYAN
81—Dean Ropp
CALIF. (PA.)
93—Raymond Guttierez
CAL LUTHERAN
83—Bill Burgess
UC DAVIS
70—Tom Cupps
83—Preston Neumayr
UC RIVERSIDE
71—Kirby Gordon
CALVIN
92—Steve Honderd
93—Steve Honderd

94—Chris Knoester
CAPITAL
73—Charles Gashill
CARNEGIE MELLON
73—Mike Wegener
79—Larry Hufnagel
80—Larry Hufnagel
CASE RESERVE
96—Jim Fox
CASTLETON ST.
85—Bryan DeLoatch
CENTRAL FLA.
82—Jimmie Farrell
CENTRAL MICH.
67—John Berends
71—Mike Hackett
CENTRAL ST. (OHIO)
71—Sterling Quant
CHADRON ST.
92—Josh Robinson
COAST GUARD
71—Ken Bicknell
COLORADO MINES
91—Daniel McKeon
91—Hank Prey
CORNELL COLLEGE
74—Randy Kuhlman
77—Dick Grant
78—Robert Wisco
79—Robert Wisco
87—Jeff Fleming
DAVID LIPSCOMB
89—Phil Hutcheson
90—Phil Hutcheson
92—Jerry Meyer
DELTA ST.
72—Larry MaGee
DENISON
67—Bill Druckemiller
70—Charles Claggett
87—Kevin Locke
88—Kevin Locke
DENVER
87—Joe Fisher
DEPAUW
70—Richard Tharp
73—Gordon Pittenger
87—David Galle
DICKINSON
71—Lloyd Bonner
81—David Freysinger
82—David Freysinger
DREXEL
67—Joe Hertrich
ELON
88—Brian Branson
88—Steve Page
FORT HAYS ST.
78—Mike Pauls
GETTYSBURG
75—Jeffrey Clark
GRINNELL
76—John Haigh
94—Steve Diekmann
95—Steve Diekmann
96—Ed Brands
GROVE CITY
79—Mike Donahoe
84—Curt Silverling
85—Curt Silverling
GUST. ADOLPHUS
83—Mark Hanson

Photo from Trinity (Connecticut) sports information

Keith Wolff of Trinity (Connecticut) was recognized by the college sports information directors for his performance on and off the court in 1996 as he was awarded academic all-America honors.

HAMILTON
78—John Klauberg

HAMLINE
86—Paul Westling
89—John Banovetz

HAMPDEN-SYDNEY
92—Russell Turner

HARDING
85—Kenneth Collins
86—Kenneth Collins

HOWARD PAYNE
73—Garland Bullock
74—Garland Bullock

ILL. WESLEYAN
72—Dean Gravlin
73—Dean Gravlin
75—Jack Sikma
     Bob Spear
76—Jack Sikma
     Bob Spear
77—Jack Sikma
     Bob Spear
79—Al Black
81—Greg Yess
82—Greg Yess
87—Brian Coderre

INCARNATE WORD
93—Randy Henderson

JAMES MADISON
76—Sherman Dillard

JAMESTOWN
80—Pete Anderson
81—Pete Anderson

JOHNS HOPKINS
91—Andy Enfield

KENYON
70—John Rinka
77—Tim Appleton
85—Chris Coe Russell

LAGRANGE
80—Todd Whitsitt

LIBERTY
80—Karl Hess

LIU-C. W. POST
73—Ed Fields

LUTHER
81—Doug Kintzinger
82—Doug Kintzinger

MACMURRAY
70—Tom Peters

MANHATTAN
90—Peter Runge

MARIETTA
82—Rick Clark
83—Rick Clark

MASS.-LOWELL
70—Alfred Spinell
84—John Paganetti

MIT
80—Ray Nagem
91—David Tomlinson

MCGILL
83—Willie Hinz

MCNEESE ST.
72—David Wallace

MERRIMACK
83—Joseph Dickson
84—Joseph Dickson

MICHIGAN TECH
81—Russ VanDuine
85—Wayne Helmila

MILLIKIN
77—Roy Mosser
     Dale Wills
78—Gregg Finigan
79—Rich Rames
     Gary Jackson

80—Gary Jackson
81—Gary Jackson
89—Brian Horst

MILWAUKEE ENGR.
83—Jeffrey Brezovar

MO.-ROLLA
84—Todd Wentz

MO.-ST. LOUIS
75—Bobby Bone
76—Bobby Bone
77—Bobby Bone

MONMOUTH (ILL.)
90—S. Juan Mitchell

MOORHEAD ST.
96—Brett Beeson

MOUNT UNION
71—Jim Howell

MUHLENBERG
79—Greg Campisi
81—Dan Barletta

NEB.-KEARNEY
74—Tom Kropp
75—Tom Kropp

NEB.-OMAHA
81—Jim Gregory

NEB. WESLEYAN
84—Kevin Cook
86—Kevin Cook
95—Justin Wilkins

N.C.-ASHEVILLE
74—Randy Pallas

NORTHERN COLO.
67—Dennis Colson

OBERLIN
71—Vic Guerrieri
72—Vic Guerrieri

OHIO WESLEYAN
90—Mark Slayman

OLD DOMINION
74—Gray Eubank
75—Gray Eubank

OTTERBEIN
80—Mike Cochran

PACIFIC LUTHERAN
67—Doug Leeland

POINT PARK
86—Richard Condo

ROCHESTER
84—Joe Augustine

ROCKFORD
76—John Morrissey
77—John Morrissey

ST. JOHN'S (MINN.)
95—Joe Deignan

ST. JOSEPH'S (IND.)
75—James Thordsen

ST. LEO
77—Ralph Nelson

ST. THOMAS (FLA.)
76—Arthur Collins
77—Mike LaPrete

ST. THOMAS (MINN.)
67—Dan Hansard
78—Terry Fleming

SCRANTON
83—Michael Banas
84—Michael Banas
85—Dan Polacheck
93—Matt Cusano

SHIPPENSBURG
79—John Whitmer

81—Brian Cozzens
82—Brian Cozzens

SLIPPERY ROCK
71—Robert Wiegand
79—Mike Hardy
83—John Samsa
95—Mark Metzka

SOUTH DAK.
70—Bill Hamer
75—Rick Nissen
76—Rick Nissen
78—Jeff Nannen
80—Jeff Nannen
85—Rob Swanhorst

SOUTH DAK. ST.
71—Jim Higgins
72—Jim Higgins

SOUTHERN COLO.
72—Jim Von Loh

SUSQUEHANNA
86—Donald Harnum
94—Tres Wolf

TENNESSEE TEMPLE
77—Dan Smith
78—Dan Smith

TRINITY (CONN.)
96—Keith Wolff

TRUMAN ST.
84—Mark Campbell

UNION (N.Y.)
70—Jim Tedisco

VIRGINIA TECH
68—Ted Ware

WABASH
73—Joe Haklin

WARTBURG
71—Dave Platte
72—Dave Platte
74—Fred Waldstein
90—Dan Nettleton
91—Dan Nettleton

WASHINGTON (MO.)
88—Paul Jackson

WASH. & JEFF.
80—David Damico

WESLEYAN (CONN.)
72—James Akin
74—Rich Fairbrother
82—Steven Maizes

WESTERN MD.
83—Douglas Pinto
85—David Malin

WESTERN ST. (COLO.)
70—Michael Adams
73—Rod Smith

WESTMINSTER (PA.)
67—John Fontanella

WIS.-EAU CLAIRE
72—Steven Johnson
75—Ken Kaiser
76—Ken Kaiser

WIS.-GREEN BAY
74—Tom Jones

WIS.-PLATTEVILLE
92—T. J. Van Wie
93—T. J. Van Wie

WITTENBERG
67—Jim Appleby

WORCESTER TECH
96—James Naughton

NCAA Postgraduate Scholarship Winners By Team

AIR FORCE
70—James Cooper
73—Thomas Blase
74—Richard Nickelson
78—Thomas Schneeberger
92—Brent Roberts
93—Brad Boyer

ALBANY (N.Y.)
88—John Carmello

ALLEGHENY
76—Robert Del Greco

ALLENTOWN
85—George Bilicic Jr.

ALMA
76—Stuart TenHoor

AMERICAN
73—Kermit Washington

ARIZONA
88—Steve Kerr
91—Matt Muehlebach

ARIZONA ST.
65—Dennis Dairman

ARKANSAS ST.
75—J. H. Williams

ARMY
65—John Ritch III
72—Edward Mueller
73—Robert Sherwin Jr.
85—Randall Cozzens
94—David Ardayfio

ASSUMPTION
75—Paul Brennan
77—William Wurm

AUBURN
76—Gary Redding

AUGUSTANA (ILL.)
75—Bruce Hamming

AUGUSTANA (S.D.)
75—Neil Klutman
92—Jason Garrow

BALL ST.
89—Richard Hall

BATES
84—Herbert Taylor

BELLARMINE
92—Tom Schurfranz

BENTLEY
80—Joseph Betley

BOSTON COLLEGE
67—William Wolters
70—Thomas Veronneau
72—James Phelan
80—James Sweeney
95—Marc Molinsky

BOWDOIN
66—Howard Pease

BOWLING GREEN
65—Robert Dwors

BRANDEIS
72—Donald Fishman
78—John Martin

BRIDGEWATER (VA.)
70—Frederick Wampler

BRIGHAM YOUNG
66—Richard Nemelka
83—Gregory Kite
84—Devin Durrant
87—Brent Stephenson
89—Michael Smith
90—Andy Toolson
91—Steve Schreiner

BROWN
72—Arnold Berman

BUTLER
77—Wayne Burris
91—John Karaffa

CALIFORNIA
87—David Butler

UC DAVIS
70—Thomas Cupps
77—Mark Ford
83—Preston Neumayr
91—Matt Cordova

UC IRVINE
75—Carl Baker

UC RIVERSIDE
75—Randy Burnett

UC SANTA BARB.
73—Robert Schachter
93—Michael Meyer

CALIF. (PA.)
84—William Belko

CAL POLY POMONA
78—Thomas Ispas

CAL ST. DOM. HILLS
87—John Nojima

CAL ST. STANISLAUS
83—Richard Thompson

CAL TECH
66—Alden Holford
67—James Pearson
68—James Stanley
71—Thomas Heinz

CALVIN
77—Mark Veenstra
93—Steve Honderd

CARLETON
69—Thomas Weaver
82—James Tolf

CARNEGIE MELLON
80—Lawrence Hufnagel

CASE RESERVE
71—Mark Estes

CATHOLIC
72—Joseph Good

CENTRAL (IOWA)
73—Dana Snoap
80—Jeffrey Verhoef

CENTRAL MICH.
93—Sander Scott

CENTRE
85—Thomas Cowens

CHAPMAN
70—Anthony Mason

CHICAGO
69—Dennis Waldon
74—Gerald Clark
85—Keith Libert

CINCINNATI
77—Gary Yoder

CLAREMONT-M-S
72—Jeffrey Naslund

CLARION
73—Joseph Sebestyen

CLEMSON
67—James Sutherland
80—Robert Conrad Jr.

COE
65—Gary Schlarbaum

COLBY
72—Matthew Zweig

COLORADO
66—Charles Gardner
85—Alex Stivrins

COLORADO MINES
91—Hank Prey
94—Todd Kenyon

COLORADO ST.
86—Richard Strong Jr.

COLUMBIA
68—William Ames

CORNELL COLLEGE
67—David Crow
79—Robert Wisco
81—Eric Reitan
87—Jefferson Fleming
94—Abram Tubbs

CREIGHTON
71—Dennis Bresnahan Jr.
78—Richard Apke

DARTMOUTH
68—Joseph Colgan
76—William Healey
84—Paul Anderson

DAVIDSON
69—Wayne Huckel
83—Clifford Tribus

DAYTON
79—Jim Paxson
85—Larry Schellenberg

DELAWARE
78—Brian Downie

DENISON
68—William Druckemiller Jr.
88—Kevin Locke
93—Kevin Frye

DENVER
68—Richard Callahan

DEPAUL
92—Stephen Howard

DEPAUW
69—Thomas McCormick
70—Richard Tharp
73—Gordon Pittenger
86—Phillip Wendel

DICKINSON
82—David Freysinger
87—Michael Erdos

DREW
89—Joe Novak

DUKE
75—Robert Fleischer

EMORY
93—Kevin Felner

EVANSVILLE
89—Scott Haffner

FAIRLEIGH DICKINSON
78—John Jorgensen
93—Kevin Conway

FLORIDA
70—Andrew Owens Jr.
73—Anthony Miller

FLA. SOUTHERN
69—Richard Lewis
79—Larry Tucker
89—Kris Kearney

FRANKLIN
94—David Dunkle

GEO. WASHINGTON
76—Pat Tallent
87—Steve Frick

GEORGETOWN
68—Bruce Stinebrickner

GEORGIA
65—McCarthy Crenshaw Jr.
87—Chad Kessler
90—Alec Kessler

GONZAGA
92—Jarrod Davis
94—Jeff Brown
96—Jon Kinloch

GRAMBLING
83—William Hobdy

GRINNELL
68—James Schwartz
76—John Haigh

HAMILTON
69—Brooks McCuen
78—John Klauberg

HAMLINE
89—John Banovetz

HAMPDEN-SYDNEY
83—Christopher Kelly

HARVARD
79—Glenn Fine

HAVERFORD
66—Hunter Rawlings III
67—Michael Bratman
77—Richard Voith

HIRAM
77—Edwin Niehaus

HOLY CROSS
69—Edward Siudut
77—William Doran Jr.
79—John O'Connor
80—Ronnie Perry

HOUSTON BAPTIST
85—Albert Almanza

IDAHO
67—Michael Wicks

IDAHO ST.
93—Corey Bruce

ILLINOIS
71—Rich Howat

ILLINOIS ST.
88—Jeffrey Harris

ILLINOIS TECH
69—Eric Wilson

ILL. WESLEYAN
88—Brian Coderre

INDIANA
75—Steven Green
82—Randy Wittman
85—Uwe Blab

INDIANA ST.
72—Danny Bush
81—Steven Reed

IOWA
66—Dennis Pauling
76—G. Scott Thompson
81—Steven Waite

IOWA ST.
89—Marc Urquhart

ITHACA
73—David Hollowell

JACKSONVILLE
71—Vaughn Wedeking
83—Maurice Roulhac
86—Thomas Terrell

JAMES MADISON
78—Sherman Dillard

JAMESTOWN
81—Peter Anderson

JOHNS HOPKINS
65—Robert Smith

75—Andrew Schreiber
91—Andy Enfield
92—Jay Gangemi
KALAMAZOO
65—Thomas Nicolai
73—James Van Sweden
79—David Dame
82—John Schelske
96—Jeremy Cole
KANSAS
74—Thomas Kivisto
78—Kenneth Koenigs
KANSAS ST.
68—Earl Seyfert
KENT
94—Rodney Koch
KENTUCKY
75—Robert Guyette
96—Mark Pope
KENYON
95—Jamie Harless
KING'S (PA.)
81—James Shea
KNOX
65—James Jepson
LA SALLE
92—John Hurd
LAFAYETTE
72—Joseph Mottola
80—Robert Falconiero
91—Bruce Stankavage
94—Keith Brazzo
LAKE FOREST
68—Frederick Broda
LAMAR
70—James Nicholson
LEWIS
89—James Martin
LONG BEACH ST.
90—Tyrone Mitchell
LORAS
71—Patrick Lillis
72—John Buri
LOUISVILLE
77—Phillip Bond
LOYOLA MARYMOUNT
73—Stephen Smith
LOYOLA (MD.)
79—John Vogt
LUTHER
68—David Mueller
74—Timothy O'Neill
82—Douglas Kintzinger
86—Scott Sawyer
MAINE
90—Dean Smith
MARQUETTE
84—Marc Marotta
MARSHALL
73—Michael D'Antoni
MARYLAND
74—Tom McMillen
81—Gregory Manning
91—Matt Roe
MASS.-LOWELL
70—Alfred Spinell Jr.
MIT
66—John Mazola
67—Robert Hardt
68—David Jansson
71—Bruce Wheeler
91—David Tomlinson
MCNEESE ST.
78—John Rudd

MIAMI (OHIO)
82—George Sweigert
MICHIGAN
81—Martin Bodnar
93—Rob Pelinka
MICHIGAN TECH
78—Michael Trewhella
81—Russell Van Duine
MIDDLEBURY
75—David Pentkowski
82—Paul Righi
MINNESOTA
70—Michael Regenfuss
MISSISSIPPI ST.
76—Richard Knarr
MISSOURI
72—Gregory Flaker
MO.-ROLLA
77—Ross Klie
MO.-ST. LOUIS
77—Robert Bone
MONMOUTH (ILL.)
92—Steve Swanson
MONTANA
68—Gregory Hanson
81—Craig Zanon
86—Larry Krystkowiak
92—Daren Engellant
95—Jeremy Lake
MONTANA ST.
88—Ray Willis Jr.
96—Nico Harrison
MOORHEAD ST.
80—Kevin Mulder
96—Brett Beeson
MORNINGSIDE
86—John Kelzenberg
MT. ST. MARY'S (MD.)
76—Richard Kidwell
MUHLENBERG
76—Glenn Salo
MUSKINGUM
74—Gary Ferber
83—Myron Dulkoski Jr.
NAVY
79—Kevin Sinnett
84—Clifford Maurer
95—Wesley Cooper
NEBRASKA
72—Alan Nissen
86—John Matzke
87—William Jackman
91—Beau Reid
NEB.-OMAHA
81—James Gregory
NEB. WESLEYAN
95—Justin Wilkins
UNLV
84—Danny Tarkanian
NEW MEXICO
73—Breck Roberts
NEW YORK POLY
68—Charles Privalsky
NEW YORK U.
96—Greg Belinfanti
NORTH CARO.
66—Robert Bennett Jr.
74—John O'Donnell
77—Bruce Buckley
86—Steve Hale
95—Pearce Landry
NORTH CARO. ST.
66—Peter Coker
85—Terrence Gannon

96—Todd Fuller
NORTH DAK. ST.
89—Joe Regnier
NORTHEASTERN
78—David Caligaris
NORTHERN ARIZ.
79—Troy Hudson
NORTHERN COLO.
68—Dennis Colson
90—Toby Moser
NORTHERN ILL.
84—Timothy Dillion
NORTHERN IOWA
79—Michael Kemp
NORTHWEST MO. ST.
89—Robert Sundell
NORTHWESTERN
73—Richard Sund
80—Michael Campbell
90—Walker Lambiotte
94—Kevin Rankin
NOTRE DAME
69—Robert Arnzen
74—Gary Novak
83—John Paxson
OAKLAND
90—Brian Gregory
OBERLIN
72—Victor Guerrieri
OCCIDENTAL
73—Douglas McAdam
81—Miles Glidden
96—John Pike
OGLETHORPE
92—David Fischer
OHIO
67—John Hamilton
68—Wayne Young
79—Steven Skaggs
OHIO ST.
68—Wilmer Hosket
OKLAHOMA
72—Scott Martin
75—Robert Pritchard
80—Terry Stotts
88—Dave Sieger
OKLAHOMA CITY
67—Gary Gray
OKLAHOMA ST.
65—Gary Hassmann
69—Joseph Smith
OLD DOMINION
75—Gray Eubank
OREGON
71—William Drozdiak
88—Keith Balderston
OREGON ST.
67—Edward Fredenburg
PACIFIC (CAL.)
67—Bruce Parsons Jr.
79—Terence Carney
86—Richard Anema
92—Delano Demps
PENNSYLVANIA
72—Robert Morse
PENN ST.
82—Michael Edelman
95—John Amaechi
PITTSBURGH
76—Thomas Richards
86—Joseph David
92—Darren Morningstar
POMONA-PITZER
66—Gordon Schloming

70—Douglas Covey
86—David Di Cesaris
PORTLAND ST.
66—John Nelson
PRINCETON
69—Christopher Thomforde
PRINCIPIA
79—William Kelsey
PUGET SOUND
74—Richard Brown
PURDUE
71—George Faerber
81—Brian Walker
REDLANDS
90—Robert Stone
REGIS (COLO.)
88—John Nilles
94—Pat Holloway
RENSSELAER
67—Kurt Hollasch
RHODES
94—Greg Gonda
96—Scott Brown
RICE
95—Adam Peakes
RICHMOND
86—John Davis Jr.
RIPON
78—Ludwig Wurtz
ROLLINS
93—David Wolf
RUTGERS
85—Stephen Perry
ST. ANSELM
80—Sean Canning
ST. JOHN'S (N.Y.)
81—Frank Gilroy
ST. JOSEPH'S (IND.)
75—James Thordsen
ST. JOSEPH'S (PA.)
66—Charles McKenna
ST. LAWRENCE
69—Philip McWhorter
ST. LEO
81—Kevin McDonald
ST. LOUIS
67—John Kilo
95—Scott Highmark
ST. MARY'S (CAL.)
80—Calvin Wood
ST. NORBERT
87—Andris Arians
ST. OLAF
66—Eric Grimsrud
71—David Finholt
ST. THOMAS (MINN.)
67—Daniel Hansard
95—John Tauer
SAN DIEGO
78—Michael Strode
SAN DIEGO ST.
76—Steven Copp
SAN FRANCISCO
90—Joel DeBortoli
SANTA CLARA
94—Peter Eisenrich
SCRANTON
74—Joseph Cantafio
84—Michael Banas
85—Daniel Polacheck

88—John Andrejko
93—Matt Cusano
SETON HALL
69—John Suminski
SEWANEE
67—Thomas Ward Jr.
76—Henry Hoffman Jr.
82—James Sherman
SIENA
92—Bruce Schroeder
SIMPSON
80—John Hines
95—David Otte
SLIPPERY ROCK
75—Clyde Long
SOUTH DAK.
76—Rick Nissen
SOUTH DAK. ST.
73—David Thomas
SOUTH FLA.
92—Radenko Dobras
SOUTHERN CAL
74—Daniel Anderson
75—John Lambert
SOUTHERN ILL.
77—Michael Glenn
SOUTHERN METHODIST
77—Peter Lodwick
SOUTHERN UTAH
91—Peter Johnson
93—Richard Barton
SOUTHWEST MO. ST.
71—Tillman Williams
STANFORD
76—Edward Schweitzer
80—Kimberly Belton
SUSQUEHANNA
86—Donald Harnum
94—Lloyd Wolf
SWARTHMORE
65—Cavin Wright
87—Michael Dell
SYRACUSE
81—Dan Schayes
TENNESSEE
93—Lang Wiseman
TENN.-MARTIN
76—Michael Baker
TEXAS
74—Harry Larrabee
79—Jim Krivacs
TEXAS A&M
70—James Heitmann
TEXAS-ARLINGTON
80—Paul Renfor
TEXAS CHRISTIAN
70—Jeffrey Harp
81—Larry Frevert
TEX.-PAN AMERICAN
76—Jesus Guerra Jr.
TEXAS TECH
85—Brooks Jennings Jr.
86—Tobin Doda

TOLEDO
67—William Backensto
80—Timothy Selgo
TRANSYLVANIA
72—Robert Jobe Jr.
80—Lawrence Kopczyk
TRINITY (CONN.)
71—Howard Greenblatt
96—Keith Wolff
TRINITY (TEX.)
75—Phillip Miller
TUFTS
81—Scott Brown
UCLA
69—Kenneth Heitz
71—George Schofield
80—Kiki Vandeweghe
95—George Zidek
UTAH
68—Lyndon MacKay
71—Michael Newlin
77—Jeffrey Jonas
UTAH ST.
96—Eric Franson
VANDERBILT
76—Jeffrey Fosnes
VILLANOVA
83—John Pinone
VIRGINIA
73—James Hobgood
VMI
69—John Mitchell
71—Jan Essenburg
77—William Bynum III
81—Andrew Kolesar
87—Gay Elmore Jr.
96—Bobby Prince
VIRGINIA TECH
72—Robert McNeer
WABASH
76—Len Fulkerson
WAKE FOREST
69—Jerry Montgomery
94—Marcus Blucas
96—Rusty LaRue
WARTBURG
72—David Platte
74—Fred Waldstein
91—Dan Nettleton
WASHINGTON
70—Vincent Stone
74—Raymond Price
87—Rodney Ripley
WASHINGTON (MD.)
79—Joseph Wilson
90—Mike Keehan
WASHINGTON (MO.)
91—Jed Bargen
WASH. & JEFF.
70—Terry Evans
81—David Damico
WASH. & LEE
83—Brian Hanson
84—John Graves

Rusty LaRue was a 1996 NCAA postgraduate scholarship recipient. LaRue is the third Wake Forest player to be awarded a postgraduate scholarship.

Photo from Wake Forest sports information

WEBER ST.
80—Mark Mattos
85—Kent Hagan
WESLEYAN (CONN.)
73—Brad Rogers
74—Richard Fairbrother
77—Steve Malinowski
82—Steven Maizes
85—Gregory Porydzy
WESTERN CARO.
82—Gregory Dennis
87—Richard Rogers
WESTERN ILL.
84—Todd Hutcheson
WESTERN MD.
83—Douglas Pinto
WESTMINSTER (PA.)
67—John Fontanella
WHEATON (ILL.)
95—Nathan Frank
WHITTIER
77—Rodney Snook
WICHITA ST.
69—Ronald Mendell
91—Paul Guffrovich
WIDENER
83—Louis DeRogatis

WILLIAM & MARY
85—Keith Cieplicki
WILLIAMS
65—Edgar Coolidge III
86—Timothy Walsh
WISCONSIN
87—Rodney Ripley
WIS.-PLATTEVILLE
93—T. J. Van Wie
WIS.-STEVENS POINT
83—John Mack
WITTENBERG
84—Jay Ferguson
96—Scott Schwartz
WOOSTER
95—Scott Meech
WRIGHT ST.
78—Alan McGee
XAVIER (OHIO)
75—Peter Accetta
81—Gary Massa
YALE
67—Richard Johnson
68—Robert McCallum Jr.

Coaching Records

All-Division Coaching Records

Coaches With At Least 500 Career Wins

The following list includes all coaches who have won at least 500 games regardless of classification with a minimum 10 head coaching seasons at NCAA schools.

Coach (Alma Mater) Teams Coached, Tenure	Yrs.	Won	Lost	Pct.
1. Adolph Rupp (Kansas '23) Kentucky 1931-52, 54-72	41	876	190	.822
2. Dean Smith (Kansas '53) North Caro. 1962-96*	35	851	247	.775
3. Clarence "Big House" Gaines (Morgan St. '45) Winston-Salem 1947-93	47	828	447	.649
4. Henry Iba (Northwest Mo. St. '28) Northwest Mo. St. 1930-33, Colorado 34, Oklahoma St. 35-70	41	767	338	.694
5. Ed Diddle (Centre '21) Western Ky. 1923-64	42	759	302	.715
6. Jim Phelan (La Salle '51) Mt. St. Mary's (Md.) 1955-96*	42	758	400	.655
7. F. C. "Phog" Allen (Kansas '06) Baker 1906-08, Kansas 08-09, Haskell 09, Central Mo. St. 13-19, Kansas 20-56	48	746	264	.739
8. Ray Meyer (Notre Dame '38) DePaul 1943-84	42	724	354	.672
9. Jerry Johnson (Fayetteville St. '51) LeMoyne-Owen 1959-96*	38	697	326	.681
10. Dick Sauers (Slippery Rock '51) Albany St. (N.Y.) 1956-87, 89-96*	40	685	320	.682
11. Bob Knight (Ohio St. '62) Army 1966-71, Indiana 72-96*	31	678	247	.733
11. Don Haskins (Oklahoma St. '53) UTEP 1962-96*	35	678	313	.684
11. Norm Stewart (Missouri '56) Northern Iowa 1962-67, Missouri 68-96*	35	678	334	.670
14. Charles "Lefty" Driesell (Duke '54) Davidson 1961-69, Maryland 70-86, James Madison 89-96*	34	667	322	.674
15. John Wooden (Purdue '32) Indiana St. 1947-48, UCLA 49-75	29	664	162	.804
16. Lou Henson (New Mexico St. '56) Hardin-Simmons 1963-66, New Mexico St. 67-75, Illinois 76-96	34	663	331	.667
17. Ralph Miller (Kansas '42) Wichita St. 1952-64, Iowa 65-70, Oregon St. 71-89@+	38	657	382	.632
18. Marv Harshman (Pacific Lutheran '42) Pacific Lutheran 1946-58, Washington St. 59-71, Washington 72-85%	40	654	449	.593
19. Ed Messbarger (Northwest Mo. St. '56) Benedictine Heights 1957-60, Dallas 61-63, St. Mary's (Tex.) 63-78, Angelo St. 79-96*	39	649	479	.575
20. Jerry Tarkanian (Fresno St. '56) Long Beach St. 1969-73, UNLV 74-92, Fresno St. 96*	25	647	133	.829
20. Gene Bartow (Truman St. '53) Central Mo. St. 1962-64, Valparaiso 65-70, Memphis 71-74, Illinois 75, UCLA 76-77, UAB 79-96	34	647	353	.647
22. Ed Adams (Tuskegee '33) N.C. Central 1935-36, Tuskegee 37-49, Texas Southern 50-58	24	645	153	.808
23. John Lance (Pittsburg St. '18) Southwestern Okla. 1919-22, Pittsburg St. 23-63	45	643	345	.651
24. Ken Anderson (Wis.-Eau Claire '55) Wis.-Eau Claire 1969-95	27	631	152	.806
25. Cam Henderson [Salem (W.Va.) '17] Muskingum 1920-23, Davis & Elkins 24-35, Marshall 36-55	35	630	243	.722
26. Norm Sloan (North Caro. St. '51) Presbyterian 1952-55, Citadel 57-60, Florida 61-66, North Caro. St. 67-80, Florida 81-89+	37	624	393	.614
27. Herb Magee (Phila. Textile '63) Phila. Textile 1968-96*	29	618	221	.737
28. Dean Nicholson (Central Wash. '50) Central Wash. 1965-90	26	609	219	.736
29. Amory "Slats" Gill (Oregon St. '25) Oregon St. 1929-64	36	599	392	.604
30. Abe Lemons (Oklahoma City '49) Oklahoma City 1956-73, Tex.-Pan American 74-76, Texas 77-82, Oklahoma City 84-90	34	597	344	.634
31. Guy Lewis (Houston '47) Houston 1957-86	30	592	279	.680
32. Dom Rosselli (Geneva '59) Youngstown St. 1941-42 & 47-82	38	591	384	.606
33. Joe Hutton (Carleton '24) Hamline 1931-65	35	590	208	.739
34. Denny Crum (UCLA '58) Louisville 1972-96*	25	587	224	.724
35. Fred Hobdy (Grambling '49) Grambling 1957-86	30	571	287	.666
36. Eddie Sutton (Oklahoma St. '58) Creighton 1970-74, Arkansas 75-85, Kentucky 86-89, Oklahoma St. 91-96*	26	570	219	.722
37. Gary Colson (David Lipscomb '56) Valdosta St. 1959-68, Pepperdine 69-79, New Mexico 81-88, Fresno St. 91-95	34	563	385	.594
38. Dennis Bridges (Ill. Wesleyan '61) Ill. Wesleyan 1966-96*	31	557	289	.658

Coach (Alma Mater) Teams Coached, Tenure	Yrs.	Won	Lost	Pct.
38. Paul "Tony" Hinkle (Chicago '21) Butler 1927-42 & 46-70	41	557	393	.586
40. John Thompson (Providence '64) Georgetown 1973-96*	24	553	208	.727
41. Glenn Wilkes (Mercer '50) Stetson 1958-93	36	551	436	.558
42. Frank McGuire [St. John's (N.Y.) '36] St. John's (N.Y.) 1948-52, North Caro. 53-61, South Caro. 65-80	30	549	236	.699
43. Bill Knapton (Wis.-La Crosse '52) Beloit 1958-96*	39	548	329	.625
44. Jim Gudger (Western Caro. '42) Western Caro. 1951-69, Tex. A&M-Commerce 70-83	33	547	365	.600
45. Eldon Miller (Wittenberg '61) Wittenberg 1963-70, Western Mich. 71-76, Ohio St. 77-86, Northern Iowa 87-96*	34	542	390	.582
46. John Chaney (Bethune-Cookman '55) Cheyney 1973-82, Temple 1983-96*	24	540	188	.742
47. Bruce Webster (Rutgers '59) Bridgeport 1966-96*	31	539	335	.617
48. Harry Miller (Eastern N.M. '51) Western St. (Colo.) 1953-58, Fresno St. 61-65, Eastern N.M. 66-70, North Tex. St. 71, Wichita St. 72-78, Stephen F. Austin 79-88	34	534	374	.588
49. Hugh Durham (Florida St. '59) Florida St. 67-78, Georgia 79-95	29	527	310	.630
50. Lou Carnesecca [St. John's (N.Y.) '46] St. John's (N.Y.) 1966-70, 74-92	24	526	200	.725
51. Pete Carril (Lafayette '52) Lehigh 1967, Princeton 68-96	30	525	273	.658
52. Tom Young (Maryland '58) Catholic 1959-67, American 70-73, Rutgers 74-85, Old Dominion 86-91	31	524	328	.615
53. John McLendon Jr. (Kansas '36) N.C. Central 1941-52, Hampton 53-54, Tennessee St. 55-59, Kentucky St. 64-66, Cleveland St. 67-69	25	523	165	.760
54. Fred Enke (Minnesota '21) Louisville 1924-25, Arizona 26-61	38	522	344	.603
55. Bill C. Foster (Carson-Newman '58) Shorter 1963-67, N.C.-Charlotte 71-75, Clemson 76-84, Miami (Fla.) 86-90, Virginia Tech 92-96*	29	517	309	.626
56. Arad McCutchan (Evansville '34) Evansville 1947-77	31	514	314	.621
57. Jim Smith (Marquette '56) St. John's (Minn.) 1965-96*	32	512	340	.601
58. Paul Webb (William & Mary '51) Randolph-Macon 1957-75, Old Dominion 76-85	29	511	257	.665
59. Lewis Levick (Drake '50) Wartburg 1966-93	28	510	225	.694
59. Aubrey Bonham (Northern Iowa '27) Whittier 1938-43 & 46-68	29	510	285	.642
61. Glenn Robinson (West Chester '67) Frank. & Marsh. 1972-96*	25	509	178	.741
62. Clarence "Hec" Edmundson (Idaho '09) Idaho 1917-18, Washington 21-47	29	508	204	.713
63. Lute Olson (Augsburg '56) Long Beach St. 1974, Iowa 75-83, Arizona 85-96*	23	507	194	.723
64. Leo Nicholson (Washington '25) Central Wash. 1930-43 & 46-64	33	505	281	.642
65. Harold Anderson (Otterbein '24) Toledo 1935-42, Bowling Green 43-63	29	504	226	.690
65. C. Alan Rowe (Villanova '53) Widener 1966-96*	31	504	303	.625
67. Jerry Welsh (Ithaca '58) Potsdam St. 1969-91, Iona 92-95	26	502	205	.710
68. Ed Martin (North Caro. A&T '51) South Caro. 1956-68, Tennessee St. 69-85	30	501	253	.664
68. Robert Vaughan (Virginia St. '48) Elizabeth City St. 1952-86	34	501	363	.580
70. Gene Mehaffey (Southern Methodist '54) Carson-Newman 1968-78, Ohio Wesleyan 80-96*	28	500	334	.600

*Active. %Includes one forfeit over Oregon State. @Miller lost 15 wins by action of NCAA Council (see footnote for coaches all-time wins). +Tournament participation voided by NCAA Executive Committee (see footnote for coaches all-time wins).

Division I Coaching Records

Winningest Active Coaches

(Minimum five years as a Division I head coach; includes record at four-year U.S. colleges only.)

BY PERCENTAGE

Coach, Team	Years	Won	Lost	Pct.
1. Jerry Tarkanian, Fresno St.	25	647	133	.829
2. Roy Williams, Kansas	8	213	56	.792
3. John Kresse, Charleston (S.C.)	17	412	109	.791
4. Dean Smith, North Caro.	35	851	247	.775
5. Jim Boeheim, Syracuse	20	483	159	.752
6. Nolan Richardson, Arkansas	16	391	132	.748
7. Bill Herrion, Drexel	5	112	38	.747

Coach, Team	Years	Won	Lost	Pct.
8. John Chaney, Temple	24	540	188	.742
9. Bob Knight, Indiana	31	678	247	.733
10. Larry Hunter, Ohio	20	430	159	.730
11. Bill Musselman, South Ala.	11	209	78	.728
12. Rick Pitino, Kentucky	14	317	119	.727
13. John Thompson, Georgetown	24	553	208	.727
14. Denny Crum, Louisville	25	587	224	.724
15. Lute Olson, Arizona	23	507	194	.723
16. Eddie Sutton, Oklahoma St.	26	570	219	.722
17. Blaine Taylor, Montana	5	104	41	.717
18. Bob Huggins, Cincinnati	15	334	135	.712
19. Rick Majerus, Utah	12	250	103	.708
20. Pete Gillen, Providence	11	237	100	.703
21. Gene Keady, Purdue	18	386	167	.698
22. Mike Krzyzewski, Duke	21	449	199	.693
23. Steve Fisher, Michigan	8	160	71	.693
24. Jim Harrick, UCLA	17	358	160	.691
25. Wimp Sanderson, Ark.-Little Rock	14	305	137	.690
26. Ralph Underhill, Wright St.	18	356	162	.687
27. Ron Abegglen, Weber St.	10	206	95	.684
28. Don Haskins, UTEP	35	678	313	.684
29. Charlie Spoonhour, St. Louis	13	271	126	.683
30. Roger Reid, Brigham Young	7	151	71	.680
31. Lefty Driesell, James Madison	34	667	322	.674
32. Billy Tubbs, Texas Christian	22	470	228	.673
33. James Dickey, Texas Tech	5	100	49	.671
34. Norm Stewart, Missouri	35	678	334	.670
35. Tim Floyd, Iowa St.	10	209	103	.670
36. Neil McCarthy, New Mexico St.	21	429	212	.669
37. Ron Shumate, Southeast Mo. St.	22	433	214	.669
38. Jim Calhoun, Connecticut	24	470	236	.666
39. Mack McCarthy, Tenn.-Chatt.	11	219	111	.664
40. Pat Foster, Nevada	16	321	163	.663
41. Gale Catlett, West Va.	24	471	241	.662
42. Kevin Bannon, Rider	14	262	137	.657
43. Mike Deane, Marquette	12	234	123	.655
44. James Phelan, Mt. St. Mary's (Md.)	42	758	400	.655
45. Fran Dunphy, Pennsylvania	7	123	65	.654
46. Tubby Smith, Georgia	5	100	53	.654
47. Dick Bennett, Wisconsin	20	378	203	.651
48. Tom Davis, Iowa	25	481	259	.650
49. Mike Jarvis, Geo. Washington	11	214	118	.645
50. Tom Asbury, Kansas St.	8	154	86	.642
51. Joey Meyer, DePaul	12	222	125	.640
52. Larry Finch, Memphis	10	204	115	.639
53. Bill Frieder, Arizona St.	16	310	178	.635
54. Davey L. Whitney, Alcorn St.	25	450	263	.631
55. Pat Kennedy, Florida St.	16	306	179	.631
56. Mike Montgomery, Stanford	18	336	197	.630
57. Jim Wooldridge, Louisiana Tech	11	201	119	.628
58. Bill C. Foster, Virginia Tech	29	517	309	.626
59. Mike Vining, Northeast La.	15	279	167	.626
60. Jim Crews, Evansville	11	200	121	.623
61. Larry Eustachy, Utah St.	6	114	69	.623
62. Ron Mitchell, Coppin St.	10	183	111	.622
63. Bobby Cremins, Georgia Tech	21	398	242	.622
64. Jeff Jones, Virginia	6	117	72	.619
65. Cliff Ellis, Auburn	21	383	238	.617
66. Kevin Eastman, Washington St.	9	159	99	.616
67. Dave Bliss, New Mexico	21	391	246	.614
68. Dave Odom, Wake Forest	10	180	114	.612
69. Dale Brown, LSU	24	438	281	.609
70. Tom Penders, Texas	25	446	290	.606
71. Speedy Morris, La Salle	10	183	119	.606
72. Rollie Massimino, Cleveland St.	23	425	278	.605
73. Jim Molinari, Bradley	7	125	82	.604
74. Scott Edgar, Duquesne	5	88	58	.603
75. Gary Williams, Maryland	18	329	218	.601
76. Seth Greenberg, South Fla.	6	105	70	.600

(Coaches with less than five years as a Division I head coach; includes record at four-year U.S. colleges only.)

Coach, Team	Years	Won	Lost	Pct.
1. John Giannini, Maine	7	168	38	.816
2. Jim Boone, Robert Morris	10	227	71	.762
3. Mike Heideman, Wis.-Green Bay	5	91	29	.758
4. George Scholz, Jacksonville	10	222	84	.725
5. Bill Jones, Jacksonville St.	24	455	195	.700
6. Steve Alford, Southwest Mo. St.	5	94	41	.696
7. Dan Peters, Youngstown St.	11	195	99	.663
8. Kurt Kanaskie, Drake	11	207	107	.659
9. Dan Hipsher, Akron	7	129	68	.655
10. Pat Flannery, Bucknell	7	124	68	.646
11. Mark Adams, Tex.-Pan American	13	249	144	.634

Coach, Team	Years	Won	Lost	Pct.
12. John Beilein, Canisius	14	255	150	.630
13. Ron Bradley, Radford	10	181	109	.624
14. Don Maestri, Troy St.	14	245	153	.616

BY VICTORIES

Coach, Team	Wins
1. Dean Smith, North Caro.	851
2. James Phelan, Mt. St. Mary's (Md.)	758
3. Bob Knight, Indiana	678
3. Don Haskins, UTEP	678
3. Norm Stewart, Missouri	678
6. Lefty Driesell, James Madison	667
7. Jerry Tarkanian, Fresno St.	647
8. Denny Crum, Louisville	587
9. Eddie Sutton, Oklahoma St.	570
10. John Thompson, Georgetown	553
11. Eldon Miller, Northern Iowa	542
12. John Chaney, Temple	540
13. Bill C. Foster, Virginia Tech	517
14. Lute Olson, Arizona	507
15. Jim Boeheim, Syracuse	483
16. Tom Davis, Iowa	481
17. Gale Catlett, West Va.	471
18. Billy Tubbs, Texas Christian	470
18. Jim Calhoun, Connecticut	470
20. Calvin C. Luther, Tenn.-Martin	468
21. Davey L. Whitney, Alcorn St.	450
22. Mike Krzyzewski, Duke	449
22. George Blaney, Seton Hall	449
24. Tom Penders, Texas	446
25. Dale Brown, LSU	438
26. Ron Shumate, Southeast Mo. St.	433
27. Larry Hunter, Ohio	430
28. Neil McCarthy, New Mexico St.	429
29. Rollie Massimino, Cleveland St.	425
30. John Kresse, Charleston (S.C.)	412
31. Bobby Cremins, Georgia Tech	398
32. Nolan Richardson, Arkansas	391
32. Dave Bliss, New Mexico	391
34. Don DeVoe, Navy	388
35. Gene Keady, Purdue	386
36. Cliff Ellis, Auburn	383
37. Dick Bennett, Wisconsin	378
38. Jerry Pimm, UC Santa Barb.	376
39. Homer Drew, Valparaiso	366
40. Jim Harrick, UCLA	358
41. Ralph Underhill, Wright St.	356
42. Robert Moreland, Texas Southern	340
43. Mike Montgomery, Stanford	336
43. Charlie Woollum, William & Mary	336
45. Bob Huggins, Cincinnati	334
46. Ben Braun, California	333
47. Gary Williams, Maryland	329
48. Pat Foster, Nevada	321
49. Rick Pitino, Kentucky	317
50. Sonny Smith, Va. Commonwealth	316
51. Bill Frieder, Arizona St.	310
52. J. D. Barnett, Northwestern St.	308
53. Pat Kennedy, Florida St.	306

Coach, Team	Wins
54. Wimp Sanderson, Ark.-Little Rock	305
55. Bob Donewald, Western Mich.	302
56. Rees Johnson, Northeastern Ill.	298
57. Danny Nee, Nebraska	292
58. Nick Macarchuk, Fordham	286
59. Mike Vining, Northeast La.	279
60. Paul Westhead, George Mason	275
60. Billy Lee, Campbell	275
62. Elwood Plummer, Prairie View	274
63. Charlie Spoonhour, St. Louis	271
63. Clem Haskins, Minnesota	271
65. Kevin Bannon, Rider	262
66. Stan Morrison, San Jose St.	259
67. Rick Majerus, Utah	250
68. Pete Gillen, Providence	237
68. Lon Kruger, Illinois	237
70. Dan Fitzgerald, Gonzaga	236
70. Bill Hodges, Mercer	236
70. Jeff Meyer, Liberty	236
73. Mike Deane, Marquette	234
73. Rick Samuels, Eastern Ill.	234
75. Joey Meyer, DePaul	222
76. Mack McCarthy, Tenn.-Chatt.	219
76. Tom Green, Fairleigh Dickinson	219
78. Kelvin Sampson, Oklahoma	216
79. Mike Jarvis, Geo. Washington	214
80. Jim O'Brien, Boston College	213
80. Roy Williams, Kansas	213
82. Dave Magarity, Marist	211
83. Bill Musselman, South Ala.	209
83. Tim Floyd, Iowa St.	209
85. Ron Abegglen, Weber St.	206
86. Jerry Green, Oregon	205
86. Bob Wenzel, Rutgers	205
86. Dick Kuchen, Yale	205
89. Larry Finch, Memphis	204
89. Jack Bruen, Colgate	204
91. Jim Wooldridge, Louisiana Tech	201
91. Marty Fletcher, Southwestern La.	201
93. Jim Crews, Evansville	200

(Coaches with less than five years as a Division I head coach; includes record at four-year U.S. colleges only.)

Coach, Team	Wins
1. Bill Jones, Jacksonville St.	455
2. John Beilein, Canisius	255
3. Mark Adams, Tex.-Pan American	249
4. Don Maestri, Troy St.	245
5. Jim Boone, Robert Morris	227
6. George Scholz, Jacksonville	222
7. Kurt Kanaskie, Drake	207

Winningest Coaches All-Time

(Minimum 10 head coaching seasons in Division I)

BY PERCENTAGE

Coach (Team coached, tenure)	Years	Won	Lost	Pct.
1. Jerry Tarkanian (Long Beach St. 1969-73, UNLV 74-92, Fresno St. 96)*	25	+647	133	.829
2. Clair Bee (Rider 1929-31, LIU-Brooklyn 32-45 and 46-51)	21	412	87	.826
3. Adolph Rupp (Kentucky 1931-72)	41	$876	190	.822
4. John Wooden (Indiana St. 1947-48, UCLA 49-75)	29	664	162	.804

Coach (Team coached, tenure)	Years	Won	Lost	Pct.
5. Dean Smith (North Caro. 1962-96)*	35	851	247	.775
6. Harry Fisher (Columbia 1907-16, Army 22-23, 25)	13	147	44	.770
7. Frank Keaney (Rhode Island 1921-48)	27	387	117	.768
8. George Keogan (St. Louis 1916, Allegheny 19, Valparaiso 20-21, Notre Dame 24-43)	24	385	117	.767
9. Jack Ramsay [St. Joseph's (Pa.) 1956-66]	11	+231	71	.765
10. Vic Bubas (Duke 1960-69)	10	213	67	.761
11. Jim Boeheim (Syracuse 1977-96)*	20	483	159	.752
12. Charles "Chick" Davies (Duquesne 1925-43 and 47-48)	21	314	106	.748
13. Nolan Richardson (Tulsa 1981-85, Arkansas 86-96)*	16	391	132	.748
14. Ray Mears (Wittenberg 1957-62, Tennessee 63-77)	21	399	135	.747
15. John Chaney (Cheyney 1973-82, Temple 83-96)*	24	540	188	.742
16. Al McGuire (Belmont Abbey 1958-64, Marquette 65-77)	20	#405	143	.739
17. Everett Case (North Caro. St. 1947-64)	18	376	133	.739
18. F. C. "Phog" Allen (Baker 1906-08, Kansas 08-09, Haskell 09, Central Mo. St. 13-19, Kansas 20-56)	48	746	264	.739
19. Walter Meanwell (Wisconsin 1912-17 and 21-34, Missouri 18, 20)	22	280	101	.735
20. Bob Knight (Army 1966-71, Indiana 72-96)*	31	##678	247	.733
21. Rick Pitino (Boston U. 1979-83, Providence 1986-87, Kentucky 90-96)*	14	317	119	.727
22. John Thompson (Georgetown 1973-96)*	24	553	208	.727
23. Lew Andreas (Syracuse 1925-43 and 45-50)	25	355	134	.726
24. Lou Carnesecca [St. John's (N.Y.) 1966-70 and 74-92]	24	526	200	.725
25. Denny Crum (Louisville 1972-96)*	25	587	224	.724
26. Fred Schaus (West Va. 1955-60, Purdue 73-78)	12	#251	96	.723
27. Lute Olson (Long Beach St. 1974, Iowa 75-83, Arizona 84-96)*	23	##507	194	.723
28. Eddie Sutton (Creighton 1970-74, Arkansas 75-85, Kentucky 86-89, Oklahoma St. 91-96)*	26	570	219	.722
29. Cam Henderson (Muskingum 1920-23, Davis & Elkins 24-35, Marshall 36-55)	35	630	243	.722
30. Hugh Greer (Connecticut 1947-63)	17	290	112	.721
31. Joe Lapchick [St. John's (N.Y.) 1937-47 and 57-65]	20	335	130	.720
32. Donald "Dudey" Moore (Duquesne 1949-58, La Salle 59-63)	15	270	107	.716
33. Ed Diddle (Western Ky. 1923-64)	42	759	302	.715
34. Tom Blackburn (Dayton 1948-64)	17	352	141	.714
35. John Lawther (Westminster 1927-36, Penn St. 37-49)	23	317	127	.714
35. Clarence "Hec" Edmundson (Idaho 1917-18, Washington 21-47)	29	508	204	.713
37. Bob Huggins (Walsh 1981-83, Akron 85-89, Cincinnati 90-96)*	15	334	135	.712
38. Harlan "Pat" Page (Chicago 1913-20, Butler 21-26)	14	242	99	.710
39. Ward "Piggy" Lambert (Purdue 1917 and 19-45)	29	371	152	.709
40. Rick Majerus (Marquette 1984-86, Ball St. 88-89, Utah 90-96)*	12	250	103	.708
41. Peck Hickman (Louisville 1945-67)	23	443	183	.708
42. Lee Rose (Transylvania 1965-75, N.C.-Charlotte 76-78, Purdue 79-80, South Fla. 81-86)	19	388	162	.705
43. Joe Hall [Regis (Colo.) 1960-64, Central Mo. St. 65, Kentucky 73-85]	19	373	156	.705
44. Pete Gillen [Xavier (Ohio) 1986-94, Providence 96]*	11	237	100	.703
45. Frank McGuire [St. John's (N.Y.) 1948-52, North Caro. 53-61, South Caro. 65-80]	30	549	236	.699
46. Gene Keady (Western Ky. 1979-80, Purdue 81-96)*	18	386	167	.698
47. Boyd Grant (Fresno St. 1978-86, Colorado St. 88-91)	13	275	120	.696
48. Doug Mills (Illinois 1937-47)	11	151	66	.696
49. Henry Iba (Northwest Mo. St. 1930-33, Colorado 34, Oklahoma St. 35-70)	41	767	338	.694
50. Mike Krzyzewski (Army 1976-80, Duke 81-96)*	21	449	199	.693
51. John "Honey" Russell (Seton Hall 1937-43 & 50-60, Manhattan 46)	19	308	137	.692
52. Larry Weise (St. Bonaventure 1962-73)	12	202	90	.692
53. Jim Harrick (Pepperdine 1980-88, UCLA 1989-96)*	17	358	160	.691
54. Gene Smithson (Illinois St. 1976-78, Wichita St. 79-86)	11	221	99	.691
55. Harold Anderson (Toledo 1935-42, Bowling Green 42-63)	29	504	226	.690
56. Nat Holman (CCNY 1920-52 and 55-56 and 59-60)	37	423	190	.690

Coach (Team coached, tenure)	Years	Won	Lost	Pct.
57. Wimp Sanderson (Alabama 1981-92, Ark.-Little Rock 95-96)*	14	305	137	.690
58. Don Haskins (UTEP 1962-96)*	35	678	313	.684
59. Charlie Spoonhour (Southwest Mo. St. 1984-92, St. Louis 93-96)*	13	271	126	.683
60. Dana Kirk (Tampa 1967-71, Va. Commonwealth 77-79, Memphis 80-86)	15	+281	131	.682
61. Ozzie Cowles (Carleton 1925-30, Wis.-River Falls 34-36, Dartmouth 37-43 and 45-46, Michigan 47-48, Minnesota 49-59)	31	421	198	.680
62. Guy Lewis (Houston 1957-86)	30	592	279	.680
63. Johnny Oldham (Tennessee Tech 1956-64, Western Ky. 65-71)	16	+260	123	.679
64. Harry Combes (Illinois 1948-67)	20	316	150	.678
65. Richard "Digger" Phelps (Fordham 1971, Notre Dame 72-91)	21	419	200	.677
66. Bob King (New Mexico 1963-72, Indiana St. 76-78)	13	236	113	.676
67. Charles "Lefty" Driesell (Davidson 1961-69, Maryland 70-86, James Madison 89-96)*	34	667	322	.674
68. Jack Gardner (Kansas St. 1940-42 and 47-53, Utah 54-71)	28	486	235	.674
69. Billy Tubbs [Southwestern (Tex.) 1972-73, Lamar 77-80, Oklahoma 81-94, Texas Christian 95-96]*	22	470	228	.673
70. Roy Skinner (Vanderbilt 1959 and 62-76)	16	278	135	.673
71. Alex Severance (Villanova 1937-61)	25	413	201	.673
72. Ben Jobe (Talladega 1965-73, Alabama St. 68, South Caro. St. 69-73, Denver 79-80, Alabama A&M 83-86, Southern U. 87-96, Tuskegee)*	25	468	228	.672
73. Ray Meyer (DePaul 1943-84)	42	724	354	.672
74. Herbert Read (Western Mich. 1923-49)	27	351	172	.671
75. Norm Stewart (Northern Iowa 1962-67, Missouri 68-96)*	35	678	334	.670
76. Tim Floyd (Idaho 1987-88, New Orleans 89-94, Iowa St. 95-96)*	10	209	103	.670
77. Don Corbett [Lincoln (Mo.) 1972-79, North Caro. A&T 80-93]	22	413	204	.669
78. Neil McCarthy (Weber St. 1976-85, New Mexico St. 86-96)*	21	429	212	.669
79. Lou Henson (Hardin-Simmons 1963-66, New Mexico St. 67-75, Illinois 76-96)	34	##663	331	.667
80. Charles Moir (Roanoke 1968-73, Tulane 74-76, Virginia Tech 77-87)	20	392	196	.667
80. Joel Eaves (Auburn 50-64)	15	224	112	.667
80. Jack Gray (Texas 1937-42 and 46-51)	12	194	97	.667
80. Burke "Dutch" Hermann (Penn St. 1916-17 and 20-32)	15	148	74	.667
84. Harold Bradley (Hartwick 1948-50, Duke 51-59, Texas 60-67)	20	337	169	.666
85. Jim Calhoun (Northeastern 1973-86, Connecticut 87-96)*	24	470	236	.666
86. Mack McCarthy (Tenn.-Chatt. 1986-96)*	11	219	111	.664
87. Pat Foster (Lamar 1981-86, Houston 87-93, Nevada 94-96)*	16	321	163	.663
88. Gale Catlett (Cincinnati 1973-78, West Va. 79-96)*	24	471	241	.662
89. Branch McCracken (Ball St. 1930-37, Indiana 39-43 and 47-65)	32	450	231	.661
90. Dave Gavitt (Dartmouth 1968-69, Providence 70-79)	12	227	117	.660
91. Terry Holland (Davidson 1970-74, Virginia 75-90)	21	418	216	.659
92. Harry Litwack (Temple 1953-73)	21	373	193	.659
93. Pete Carril (Lehigh 1967, Princeton 68-96)	30	525	273	.658
94. Pete Newell (San Francisco 1947-50, Michigan St. 51-54, California 55-60)	14	234	123	.655
94. Mike Deane (Oswego St. 1981-82, Siena 87-94, Marquette 95-96)*	12	234	123	.655
96. Dick Tarrant (Richmond 1982-93)	12	239	126	.655
97. Jack Kraft (Villanova 1962-73, Rhode Island 74-81)	20	+361	191	.654
98. Paul Evans (St. Lawrence 1974-80, Navy 81-86, Pittsburgh 87-94)	21	392	208	.653
99. Jack Hartman (Southern Ill. 1963-70, Kansas St. 71-86)	24	#439	233	.653
100. Eddie Hickey (Creighton 1936-43 and 47, St. Louis 48-58, Marquette 59-64)	26	435	231	.653
101. Fred Taylor (Ohio St. 1959-76)	18	297	158	.653
102. George King [Charleston (S.C.) 1957, West Va. 61-65, Purdue 66-72]	13	223	119	.652
103. Dick Bennett (Wis.-Stevens Point 1981-85, Wis. Green Bay 86-95, Wisconsin 96)*	20	378	203	.651
104. Tom Davis (Lafayette 1972-77, Boston College 78-82, Stanford 83-86, Iowa 87-96)*	25	481	259	.650

BY VICTORIES

	Coach, Team	Wins
1.	Adolph Rupp	876
2.	Dean Smith*	851
3.	Henry Iba	767
4.	Ed Diddle	759
5.	Phog Allen	746
6.	Ray Meyer	724
7.	Bob Knight*	##678
7.	Don Haskins*	678
7.	Norm Stewart*	678
10.	Lefty Driesell*	667
11.	John Wooden	664
12.	Lou Henson	##663
13.	Ralph Miller (Wichita St. 1952-64, Iowa 65-70, Oregon St. 71-89)	+**657
14.	Marv Harshman (Pacific Lutheran 1946-58, Washington St. 59-71, Washington 72-85)	%654
15.	Jerry Tarkanian*	+647
15.	Gene Bartow (Central Mo. St. 1962-64, Valparaiso 65-70, Memphis 71-74, Illinois 75, UCLA 76-77, UAB 79-96)	%647
17.	Cam Henderson	630
18.	Norm Sloan (Presbyterian 1952-55, Citadel 57-60, North Caro. St. 67-80, Florida 61-66, 81-89)	627
19.	Amory "Slats" Gill (Oregon St. 1929-64)	599
20.	Abe Lemons (Oklahoma City 1956-73, 84-90, Tex.-Pan American 74-76, Texas 77-82)	597
21.	Guy Lewis	592
22.	Denny Crum*	587
23.	Eddie Sutton*	570
24.	Gary Colson (Valdosta St. 1959-68, Pepperdine 69-79, New Mexico 81-88, Fresno St. 91-95)	563
25.	Paul "Tony" Hinkle (Butler 1927-43, 46-70)	557
26.	John Thompson*	553
27.	Glenn Wilkes (Stetson 1958-93)	551
28.	Frank McGuire	549
29.	Eldon Miller (Wittenberg 1963-70, Western Mich. 71-76, Ohio St. 77-86, Northern Iowa 87-95)*	##542
30.	John Chaney*	540
31.	Harry Miller (Western St. 1953-58, Fresno St. 61-65, Eastern N.M. 66-70, North Texas 71, Wichita St. 72-78, Stephen F. Austin 79-88)	534
32.	Hugh Durham (Florida St. 1967-78, Georgia 79-95)	527
33.	Lou Carnesecca	526
34.	Pete Carril	525
35.	Tom Young (Catholic 1959-67, American 70-73, Rutgers 74-85, Old Dominion 86-91)	524
36.	Fred Enke (Louisville 1924-25, Arizona 27-61)	522
37.	Bill C. Foster [Shorter 1963-67, N.C.-Charlotte 71-75, Clemson 76-84, Miami (Fla.) 86-90, Virginia Tech 92-96]*	517
38.	C. M. Newton (Transylvania 1956-68, Alabama 69-80, Vanderbilt 82-89)	509
39.	Hec Edmundson	508
40.	Lute Olson*	507
41.	Harold Anderson	504
42.	Ned Wulk [Xavier (Ohio) 1952-57, Arizona St. 58-82]	495
43.	Jack Friel (Washington St. 1929-58)	494
43.	Everett Shelton (Phillips 1924-26, Wyoming 40-59, Cal St. Sacramento 60-68)	494
45.	Jack Gardner	486
46.	Bob Hallberg [St. Xavier (Ill.) 1972-77, Chicago St. 78-87, Ill.-Chicago 88-96]	484
47.	Jim Boeheim*	483
48.	Butch van Breda Kolff (Lafayette 1952-55, 85-88, Hofstra 56-62, 89-94, Princeton 63-67, New Orleans 78-79)	482
49.	Tom Davis*	481
50.	Gale Catlett*	471
51.	Jim Calhoun*	470
51.	Billy Tubbs*	470
53.	Calvin Luther (DePauw 1955-58, Murray St. 59-73, Longwood 82-90, Tenn.-Martin 91-96)*	468
53.	Ben Jobe*	468
55.	Bill E. Foster (Bloomsburg 1961-63, Rutgers 64-71, Utah 72-74, Duke 75-80, South Caro. 81-86, Northwestern 87-93)	467
56.	Johnny Orr (Massachusetts 1964-66, Michigan 69-80, Iowa St. 81-94)	466
57.	John "Taps" Gallagher (Niagara 1932-65)	465
58.	Bill Reinhart (Oregon 1924-35, Geo. Washington 36-66)	464
59.	Clarence "Nibs" Price (California 1925-54)	463
60.	Tex Winter (Marquette 1952-53, Kansas St. 54-68, Washington 69-71, Northwestern 74-78, Long Beach St. 79-83)	##454
61.	Branch McCracken	450
61.	Davey Whitney (Texas Southern 1965-69, Alcorn St. 70-89)*	450
63.	Mike Krzyzewski*	449
63.	George Blaney (Stonehill 1968-69, Dartmouth 70-72, Holy Cross 73-96)*	449

Photo by Rich Clarkson/NCAA photos

COACHING RECORDS

North Carolina's Dean Smith needs 26 victories to surpass Kentucky's Adolph Rupp as the all-time winningest coach in Division I. Smith, who has guided the Tar Heels since 1962, has won at least 20 games in 29 of 35 seasons.

	Coach, Team	Wins
65.	Tom Penders (Tufts 1972-74, Columbia 75-78, Fordham 79-86, Rhode Island 87-88, Texas 89-96)*	446
66.	Peck Hickman	443
66.	Shelby Metcalf (Texas A&M 1964-90)	443
68.	Jack Hartman	#439
69.	Dale Brown (LSU 1973-96)*	438
70.	Don Donoher (Dayton 1965-89)	437
71.	Eddie Hickey	435
72.	Neil McCarthy*	429
73.	Rollie Massimino (Stony Brook 1970-71, Villanova 74-92, UNLV 93-94, Cleveland St.)*	425
74.	Nat Holman	423
75.	Ozzie Cowles	421
76.	Richard "Digger" Phelps	419
77.	Terry Holland	418
78.	Jud Heathcote (Montana 1972-76, Michigan St. 77-95)	417
79.	Don Corbett*	413
79.	Alex Severance	413
81.	Clair Bee	412
82.	Howard Cann (New York U. 1924-58)	409
83.	Al McGuire	405
84.	Howard Hobson (Southern Ore. 1933-35, Oregon 36-48, Yale 49-56)	401

*Active coaches. %Includes one forfeit over Oregon State. #One, ##two forfeits over Minnesota, both by action of NCAA Council under restitution provisions of Section 10, Official Procedure Governing NCAA Enforcement Program (adopted by NCAA membership at 69th annual Convention, January 1975). Restitution may be applied when a student-athlete has been permitted to participate while ineligible due to a court order against his institution or the NCAA, if the court order subsequently is overturned. **Miller lost 15 victories and Dutcher 24 in those cases; Miller 674-370, .646, and Dutcher 314-172, .646, without voids and forfeits. $Kentucky played no varsity schedule in 1953—under NCAA suspension. +NCAA tournament record voided: Alabama 2-1 from 1987, Memphis 9-5 from 1982-86, Georgia 1-1 in 1985, Long Beach St. 6-3 from 1971-73, Western Ky. 4-1 in 1971, Villanova 4-1 in 1971, St. Joseph's (Pa.) 3-1 in 1961, Austin Peay 1-2 in 1973, and Oregon State 2-3 from 1980-82. (Tarkanian was head coach at Long Beach State in 1971-73.)

Top 10 Best Career Starts By Percentage

(Head coaches with at least half their seasons at Division I)

1 SEASON

Coach, Team	Season	W	L	Pct.
Norman Shepard, North Caro.	1924	23	0	1.000
Bill Hodges, Indiana St.	1979	33	1	.970
Tom Gola, La Salle	1969	23	1	.958
Lou Rossini, Columbia	1951	21	1	.955
Earl Brown, Dartmouth	1944	19	2	.905
Phil Johnson, Weber St.	1969	27	3	.900
Gary Cunningham, UCLA	1978	25	3	.893
Bob Davies, Seton Hall	1947	24	3	.889
Jerry Tarkanian, Long Beach St.	1969	23	3	.885
John Castellani, Seattle	1957	22	3	.880

2 SEASONS

Coach, Team	Seasons	W	L	Pct.
Lew Andreas, Syracuse	1925-26	33	3	.917
Everett Case, North Caro. St.	1947-48	55	8	.873
Buck Freeman, St. John's (N.Y.)	1928-29	41	6	.872
Gary Cunningham, UCLA	1978-79	50	8	.862
Nibs Price, California	1925-26	25	4	.862
Denny Crum, Louisville	1972-73	49	8	.860
Adolph Rupp, Kentucky	1931-32	30	5	.857
Jerry Tarkanian, Long Beach St.	1969-70	47	8	.855
John Castellani, Seattle	1957-58	45	9	.833
Hugh Greer, Connecticut	1947-48	29	6	.829

3 SEASONS

Coach, Team	Seasons	W	L	Pct.
Nibs Price, California	1925-27	38	4	.905
Buck Freeman, St. John's (N.Y.)	1928-30	64	7	.901
Lew Andreas, Syracuse	1925-27	48	7	.873
Adolph Rupp, Kentucky	1931-33	51	8	.864
Jerry Tarkanian, Long Beach St.	1969-71	71	13	.845
Jim Boeheim, Syracuse	1977-79	74	14	.841
Everett Case, North Caro. St.	1947-49	80	16	.833
Ben Carnevale, North Caro. & Navy	1945-47	68	14	.829
Phil Johnson, Weber St.	1969-71	68	16	.810
Fred Taylor, Ohio St.	1959-61	63	15	.808

4 SEASONS

Coach, Team	Seasons	W	L	Pct.
Buck Freeman, St. John's (N.Y.)	1928-31	85	8	.914
Adolph Rupp, Kentucky	1931-34	67	9	.882
Jerry Tarkanian, Long Beach St.	1969-72	96	17	.850
Jim Boeheim, Syracuse	1977-80	100	18	.847
Fred Taylor, Ohio St.	1959-62	89	17	.840
Everett Case, North Caro. St.	1947-50	107	22	.829
Nibs Price, California	1925-28	47	10	.825
Nat Holman, CCNY	1920-23	46	10	.821
Denny Crum, Louisville	1972-75	98	22	.817
Lew Andreas, Syracuse	1925-28	58	13	.817

5 SEASONS

Coach, Team	Seasons	W	L	Pct.
Buck Freeman, St. John's (N.Y.)	1928-32	107	12	.899
Adolph Rupp, Kentucky	1931-35	86	11	.887
Jerry Tarkanian, Long Beach St. & UNLV	1969-73	122	20	.859
Nat Holman, CCNY	1920-24	58	11	.841
Fred Taylor, Ohio St.	1959-63	109	21	.838
Nibs Price, California	1925-29	64	13	.831
Everett Case, North Caro. St.	1947-51	137	29	.825
Buster Sheary, Holy Cross	1949-53	110	27	.803
Jim Boeheim, Syracuse	1977-81	122	30	.803
Lew Andreas, Syracuse	1925-29	69	17	.802

6 SEASONS

Coach, Team	Seasons	W	L	Pct.
Buck Freeman, St. John's (N.Y.)	1928-33	130	16	.890
Adolph Rupp, Kentucky	1931-36	101	17	.856
Jerry Tarkanian, Long Beach St. & UNLV	1969-74	142	26	.845
Nat Holman, CCNY	1920-25	70	13	.843
Buster Sheary, Holy Cross	1949-54	136	29	.824
Lew Andreas, Syracuse	1925-30	87	19	.821
Everett Dean, Carleton & Indiana	1922-27	82	18	.820
Clair Bee, Rider & LIU-Brooklyn	1929-34	101	23	.815
Fred Taylor, Ohio St.	1959-64	125	29	.812
Everett Case, North Caro. St.	1947-52	161	39	.805

7 SEASONS

Coach, Team	Seasons	W	L	Pct.
Buck Freeman, St. John's (N.Y.)	1928-34	146	19	.885
Jerry Tarkanian, Long Beach St. & UNLV	1969-75	166	31	.843
Adolph Rupp, Kentucky	1931-37	118	22	.843
Clair Bee, Rider & LIU-Brooklyn	1929-35	125	25	.833
Everett Dean, Carleton & Indiana	1922-28	97	20	.829
Lew Andreas, Syracuse	1925-31	103	23	.817
Nat Holman, CCNY	1920-26	79	18	.814
Buster Sheary, Holy Cross	1949-55	155	36	.812
Everett Case, North Caro. St.	1947-53	187	45	.806
Vic Bubas, Duke	1960-66	158	39	.802

8 SEASONS

Coach, Team	Seasons	W	L	Pct.
Clair Bee, Rider & LIU-Brooklyn	1929-36	150	25	.857
Buck Freeman, St. John's (N.Y.)	1928-35	159	27	.855
Jerry Tarkanian, Long Beach St. & UNLV	1969-76	195	33	.855
Adolph Rupp, Kentucky	1931-38	131	27	.829
Nat Holman, CCNY	1920-27	88	21	.807
Everett Case, North Caro. St.	1947-54	213	52	.804
Hugh Greer, Connecticut	1947-54	151	38	.799
Lew Andreas, Syracuse	1925-32	116	30	.795
Roy Williams, Kansas	1989-96	213	56	.792
Henry Iba, Northwest Mo. St., Colorado & Oklahoma St.	1930-37	157	42	.789

9 SEASONS

Coach, Team	Seasons	W	L	Pct.
Clair Bee, Rider & LIU-Brooklyn	1929-37	177	28	.863
Jerry Tarkanian, Long Beach St. & UNLV	1969-77	224	36	.862
Buck Freeman, St. John's (N.Y.)	1928-36	177	31	.851
Adolph Rupp, Kentucky	1931-39	147	31	.826
Everett Case, North Caro. St.	1947-55	241	56	.811
Lew Andreas, Syracuse	1925-33	130	32	.802
Henry Iba, Northwest Mo. St., Colorado & Oklahoma St.	1930-38	182	45	.802
Denny Crum, Louisville	1972-80	219	55	.799
Hugh Greer, Connecticut	1947-55	171	43	.799
Nat Holman, CCNY	1920-28	99	25	.798

10 SEASONS

Coach, Team	Seasons	W	L	Pct.
Clair Bee, Rider & LIU-Brooklyn	1929-38	200	32	.862
Jerry Tarkanian, Long Beach St. & UNLV	1969-78	244	44	.847
Everett Case, North Caro. St.	1947-56	265	60	.815
Adolph Rupp, Kentucky	1931-40	162	37	.814
Lew Andreas, Syracuse	1925-34	145	34	.810
Henry Iba, Northwest Mo. St., Colorado & Oklahoma St.	1930-39	201	53	.791
Denny Crum, Louisville	1972-81	240	64	.789
Harold Anderson, Toledo & Bowling Green	1935-44	182	50	.784
Nat Holman, CCNY	1920-29	108	30	.783
Joseph Lapchick, St. John's (N.Y.)	1937-46	165	47	.778

11 SEASONS

Coach, Team	Seasons	W	L	Pct.
Clair Bee, Rider & LIU-Brooklyn	1929-39	223	32	.875
Jerry Tarkanian, Long Beach St. & UNLV	1969-79	259	49	.841
Lew Andreas, Syracuse	1925-35	160	36	.816
Henry Iba, Northwest Mo. St., Colorado & Oklahoma St.	1930-40	227	56	.802
Adolph Rupp, Kentucky	1931-41	179	45	.799
Everett Case, North Caro. St.	1947-57	280	71	.798
Harold Anderson, Toledo & Bowling Green	1935-45	206	54	.792
Nat Holman, CCNY	1920-30	119	33	.783
Denny Crum, Louisville	1972-82	263	74	.780
Joe Mullaney, Norwich & Providence	1955-65	221	63	.778

12 SEASONS

Coach, Team	Seasons	W	L	Pct.
Clair Bee, Rider & LIU-Brooklyn	1929-40	242	36	.871
Jerry Tarkanian, Long Beach St. & UNLV	1969-80	282	58	.829
Lew Andreas, Syracuse	1925-36	172	41	.806
Harold Anderson, Toledo & Bowling Green	1935-46	233	59	.798
Henry Iba, Northwest Mo. St., Colorado & Oklahoma St.	1930-41	245	63	.795
Adolph Rupp, Kentucky	1931-42	198	51	.795
Everett Case, North Caro. St.	1947-58	298	77	.795
Denny Crum, Louisville	1972-83	295	78	.791
Joe Mullaney, Norwich & Providence	1955-66	243	68	.781
Nat Holman, CCNY	1920-31	131	37	.780

13 SEASONS

Coach, Team	Seasons	W	L	Pct.
Clair Bee, Rider & LIU-Brooklyn	1929-41	267	38	.875
Jerry Tarkanian, Long Beach St. & UNLV	1969-81	298	70	.810
Lew Andreas, Syracuse	1925-37	185	45	.804
Harold Anderson, Toledo & Bowling Green	1935-47	261	66	.798
Everett Case, North Caro. St.	1947-59	320	81	.798
Nat Holman, CCNY	1920-32	147	38	.795
Henry Iba, Northwest Mo. St., Colorado & Oklahoma St.	1930-42	265	69	.793
Adolph Rupp, Kentucky	1931-43	215	57	.790
Denny Crum, Louisville	1972-84	319	89	.782
Joe Mullaney, Norwich & Providence	1955-67	264	75	.779

14 SEASONS

Coach, Team	Seasons	W	L	Pct.
Clair Bee, Rider & LIU-Brooklyn	1929-42	291	41	.877
Nat Holman, CCNY	1920-33	160	39	.804
Harold Anderson, Toledo & Bowling Green	1935-48	288	72	.800
Jerry Tarkanian, Long Beach St. & UNLV	1969-82	318	80	.799
Adolph Rupp, Kentucky	1931-44	234	59	.799
Lew Andreas, Syracuse	1925-38	198	50	.798
Henry Iba, Northwest Mo. St., Colorado & Oklahoma St.	1930-43	279	79	.779
Everett Case, North Caro. St.	1947-60	331	96	.775
Jim Boeheim, Syracuse	1977-90	343	108	.761
Denny Crum, Louisville	1972-85	338	107	.760
Ray Mears, Wittenberg & Tennessee	1957-70	266	84	.760

15 SEASONS

Coach, Team	Seasons	W	L	Pct.
Clair Bee, Rider & LIU-Brooklyn	1929-43	304	47	.866
Nat Holman, CCNY	1920-34	174	40	.813
Jerry Tarkanian, Long Beach St. & UNLV	1969-83	346	83	.807
Adolph Rupp, Kentucky	1931-45	256	63	.803
Harold Anderson, Toledo & Bowling Green	1935-49	312	79	.798
Lew Andreas, Syracuse	1925-39	212	54	.797
Henry Iba, Northwest Mo. St., Colorado & Oklahoma St.	1930-44	306	85	.783
Everett Case, North Caro. St.	1947-61	347	105	.768
Denny Crum, Louisville	1972-86	370	114	.764
Jim Boeheim, Syracuse	1977-91	369	114	.764

16 SEASONS

Coach, Team	Seasons	W	L	Pct.
Clair Bee, Rider & LIU-Brooklyn	1929-43, 46	318	56	.850
Adolph Rupp, Kentucky	1931-46	284	65	.814
Jerry Tarkanian, Long Beach St. & UNLV	1969-84	375	89	.808
Nat Holman, CCNY	1920-35	184	46	.800
Henry Iba, Northwest Mo. St., Colorado & Oklahoma St.	1930-45	333	89	.789
Harold Anderson, Toledo & Bowling Green	1935-50	331	90	.786
Lew Andreas, Syracuse	1925-40	222	62	.782
Everett Case, North Caro. St.	1947-62	358	111	.763
Ray Mears, Wittenberg & Tennessee	1957-72	306	97	.759
Jim Boeheim, Syracuse	1977-92	391	124	.759

17 SEASONS

Coach, Team	Seasons	W	L	Pct.
Clair Bee, Rider & LIU-Brooklyn	1929-43, 46-47	335	61	.850
Adolph Rupp, Kentucky	1931-47	318	68	.824
Jerry Tarkanian, Long Beach St. & UNLV	1969-85	403	93	.813
Henry Iba, Northwest Mo. St., Colorado & Oklahoma St.	1930-46	364	91	.800
Nat Holman, CCNY	1920-36	194	50	.795
Harold Anderson, Toledo & Bowling Green	1935-51	341	94	.784
Lew Andreas, Syracuse	1925-41	236	67	.779
Jim Boeheim, Syracuse	1977-93	411	133	.756
Joseph Lapchick, St. John's (N.Y.)	1937-47, 57-62	291	95	.754
Ray Mears, Wittenberg & Tennessee	1957-73	321	106	.752

18 SEASONS

Coach, Team	Seasons	W	L	Pct.
Clair Bee, Rider & LIU-Brooklyn	1929-43, 46-48	352	65	.844
Adolph Rupp, Kentucky	1931-48	354	71	.833
Jerry Tarkanian, Long Beach St. & UNLV	1969-86	436	98	.816
Henry Iba, Northwest Mo. St., Colorado & Oklahoma St.	1930-47	388	99	.797
Nat Holman, CCNY	1920-37	204	56	.785
Harold Anderson, Toledo & Bowling Green	1935-52	358	104	.775
Lew Andreas, Syracuse	1925-42	251	73	.775
Jim Boeheim, Syracuse	1977-94	434	140	.756
Dean Smith, North Caro.	1962-79	386	127	.752
John Thompson, Georgetown	1973-90	423	142	.749

19 SEASONS

Coach, Team	Seasons	W	L	Pct.
Adolph Rupp, Kentucky	1931-49	386	73	.841
Clair Bee, Rider & LIU-Brooklyn	1929-43, 46-49	370	77	.828
Jerry Tarkanian, Long Beach St. & UNLV	1969-87	473	100	.825
Henry Iba, Northwest Mo. St., Colorado & Oklahoma St.	1930-48	415	103	.801
Nat Holman, CCNY	1920-38	217	59	.786
Lew Andreas, Syracuse	1925-43	259	83	.757
Harold Anderson, Toledo & Bowling Green	1935-53	370	119	.757
Jim Boeheim, Syracuse	1977-95	454	150	.752
Dean Smith, North Caro.	1962-80	407	135	.751
Frank Keaney, Rhode Island	1922-40	244	82	.748
Denny Crum, Louisville	1972-90	463	156	.748

20 SEASONS

Coach, Team	Seasons	W	L	Pct.
Adolph Rupp, Kentucky	1931-50	411	78	.840
Clair Bee, Rider & LIU-Brooklyn	1929-43, 46-50	390	82	.826
Jerry Tarkanian, Long Beach St. & UNLV	1969-88	501	106	.825
Henry Iba, Northwest Mo. St., Colorado & Oklahoma St.	1930-49	438	108	.802
Phog Allen, Baker, Kansas, Haskell, Central Mo. St. & Kansas	1906-09, 13-28	325	89	.785
Nat Holman, CCNY	1920-39	228	65	.778
John Chaney, Cheyney & Temple	1973-92	458	143	.762
Frank Keaney, Rhode Island	1922-41	265	86	.755
Harold Anderson, Toledo & Bowling Green	1935-54	387	126	.754
Dean Smith, North Caro.	1962-81	436	143	.753

21 SEASONS

Coach, Team	Seasons	W	L	Pct.
Adolph Rupp, Kentucky	1931-51	443	80	.847
Clair Bee, Rider & LIU-Brooklyn	1929-43, 46-51	410	86	.827
Jerry Tarkanian, Long Beach St. & UNLV	1969-89	530	114	.823
Henry Iba, Northwest Mo. St., Colorado & Oklahoma St.	1930-50	456	117	.796
Nat Holman, CCNY	1920-40	236	73	.764
Dean Smith, North Caro.	1962-82	468	145	.763
Phog Allen, Baker, Kansas, Haskell, Central Mo. St. & Kansas	1906-09, 13-29	328	104	.759
Frank Keaney, Rhode Island	1922-42	283	90	.759
John Chaney, Cheyney & Temple	1973-93	478	156	.754
Chick Davies, Duquesne	1925-40, 47-48	314	106	.748

22 SEASONS

Coach, Team	Seasons	W	L	Pct.
Adolph Rupp, Kentucky	1931-52	472	83	.850
Jerry Tarkanian, Long Beach St. & UNLV	1969-90	565	119	.826
Henry Iba, Northwest Mo. St., Colorado & Oklahoma St.	1930-51	485	123	.798
Nat Holman, CCNY	1920-41	253	78	.764
Dean Smith, North Caro.	1962-83	496	153	.764
Frank Keaney, Rhode Island	1922-43	299	93	.763
Phog Allen, Baker, Kansas, Haskell, Central Mo. St. & Kansas	1906-09, 13-30	342	108	.760
John Wooden, Indiana St. & UCLA	1947-68	464	151	.754
John Chaney, Cheyney & Temple	1973-94	501	164	.753
Lew Andreas, Syracuse	1925-47	308	105	.746

23 SEASONS

Coach, Team	Seasons	W	L	Pct.
Adolph Rupp, Kentucky	1931-52, 54	497	83	.857
Jerry Tarkanian, Long Beach St. & UNLV	1969-91	599	120	.833
Henry Iba, Northwest Mo. St., Colorado & Oklahoma St.	1930-52	504	131	.794
Dean Smith, North Caro.	1962-84	524	156	.771
Nat Holman, CCNY	1920-42	269	81	.769
John Wooden, Indiana St. & UCLA	1947-69	493	152	.764
Phog Allen, Baker, Kansas, Haskell, Central Mo. St. & Kansas	1906-09, 13-31	357	111	.763
Frank Keaney, Rhode Island	1922-44	313	99	.760
John Chaney, Cheyney & Temple	1973-95	520	175	.748
Ed Diddle, Western Ky.	1923-45	395	134	.747

24 SEASONS

Coach, Team	Seasons	W	L	Pct.
Adolph Rupp, Kentucky	1931-52, 54-55	520	86	.858
Jerry Tarkanian, Long Beach St. & UNLV	1969-92	625	122	.837
Henry Iba, Northwest Mo. St., Colorado & Oklahoma St.	1930-53	527	138	.792
John Wooden, Indiana St. & UCLA	1947-70	521	154	.772
Dean Smith, North Caro.	1962-85	551	165	.770
Frank Keaney, Rhode Island	1922-45	333	104	.762

COACHING RECORDS

Coach, Team	Seasons	W	L	Pct.
Phog Allen, Baker, Kansas, Haskell, Central Mo. St. & Kansas	1906-09, 13-32	370	116	.761
Nat Holman, CCNY	1920-43	277	91	.753
Bob Knight, Army & Indiana	1966-89	514	187	.733
Lew Andreas, Syracuse	1925-49	337	125	.729

25 SEASONS

Coach, Team	Seasons	W	L	Pct.
Adolph Rupp, Kentucky	1931-52, 54-56	540	92	.854
Jerry Tarkanian, Long Beach St., UNLV & Fresno St.	1969-92, 96	647	133	.829
Henry Iba, Northwest Mo. St., Colorado & Oklahoma St.	1930-54	551	143	.794
John Wooden, Indiana St. & UCLA	1947-71	550	155	.780
Dean Smith, North Caro.	1962-86	579	171	.772
Frank Keaney, Rhode Island	1922-46	354	107	.768
Phog Allen, Baker, Kansas, Haskell, Central Mo. St. & Kansas	1906-09, 13-33	383	120	.761
Nat Holman, CCNY	1920-44	283	102	.735
Ed Diddle, Western Ky.	1923-47	435	157	.735
Bob Knight, Army & Indiana	1966-90	532	198	.729

26 SEASONS

Coach, Team	Seasons	W	L	Pct.
Adolph Rupp, Kentucky	1931-52, 54-57	563	97	.853
John Wooden, Indiana St. & UCLA	1947-72	580	155	.789
Henry Iba, Northwest Mo. St., Colorado & Oklahoma St.	1930-55	563	156	.783
Dean Smith, North Caro.	1962-87	611	175	.777
Frank Keaney, Rhode Island	1922-47	371	110	.771
Phog Allen, Baker, Kansas, Haskell, Central Mo. St. & Kansas	1906-09, 13-34	399	121	.767
Ed Diddle, Western Ky.	1923-48	463	159	.744
Nat Holman, CCNY	1920-45	295	106	.736
Bob Knight, Army & Indiana	1966-91	561	203	.734
Eddie Sutton, Creighton, Arkansas, Kentucky & Oklahoma St.	1970-89, 91-96	570	219	.722

27 SEASONS

Coach, Team	Seasons	W	L	Pct.
Adolph Rupp, Kentucky	1931-52, 54-58	586	103	.851
John Wooden, Indiana St. & UCLA	1947-73	610	155	.797
Henry Iba, Northwest Mo. St., Colorado & Oklahoma St.	1930-56	581	165	.779
Dean Smith, North Caro.	1962-88	638	182	.778
Frank Keaney, Rhode Island	1922-48	387	117	.768
Phog Allen, Baker, Kansas, Haskell, Central Mo. St. & Kansas	1906-09, 13-35	414	126	.767
Ed Diddle, Western Ky.	1923-49	488	163	.750
Nat Holman, CCNY	1920-46	309	110	.737
Bob Knight, Army & Indiana	1966-92	588	210	.737
Frank McGuire, St. John's (N.Y.), North Caro. & South Caro.	1948-77	502	201	.714

28 SEASONS

Coach, Team	Seasons	W	L	Pct.
Adolph Rupp, Kentucky	1931-52, 54-59	610	106	.852
John Wooden, Indiana St. & UCLA	1947-74	636	159	.800
Dean Smith, North Caro.	1962-89	667	190	.778
Henry Iba, Northwest Mo. St., Colorado & Oklahoma St.	1930-57	598	174	.775
Phog Allen, Baker, Kansas, Haskell, Central Mo. St. & Kansas	1906-09, 13-36	435	128	.773
Ed Diddle, Western Ky.	1923-50	513	169	.752
Bob Knight, Army & Indiana	1966-93	619	214	.743
Nat Holman, CCNY	1920-47	326	116	.738
Frank McGuire, St. John's (N.Y.), North Caro. & South Caro.	1948-78	518	213	.709
Don Haskins, UTEP	1962-89	542	232	.700

29 SEASONS

Coach, Team	Seasons	W	L	Pct.
Adolph Rupp, Kentucky	1931-52, 54-60	628	113	.848
John Wooden, Indiana St. & UCLA	1947-75	664	162	.804
Phog Allen, Baker, Kansas, Haskell, Central Mo. St. & Kansas	1906-09, 13-37	450	132	.773
Henry Iba, Northwest Mo. St., Colorado & Oklahoma St.	1930-58	619	182	.773
Dean Smith, North Caro.	1962-90	688	203	.772
Ed Diddle, Western Ky.	1923-51	532	179	.748
Nat Holman, CCNY	1920-48	344	119	.743
Bob Knight, Army & Indiana	1966-94	640	223	.742
Frank McGuire, St. John's (N.Y.), North Caro. & South Caro.	1948-79	533	225	.703
Don Haskins, UTEP	1962-90	563	243	.699

30 SEASONS

Coach, Team	Seasons	W	L	Pct.
Adolph Rupp, Kentucky	1931-52, 54-61	647	122	.841
Phog Allen, Baker, Kansas, Haskell, Central Mo. St. & Kansas	1906-09, 13-38	468	134	.777
Dean Smith, North Caro.	1962-91	717	209	.774
Henry Iba, Northwest Mo. St., Colorado & Oklahoma St.	1930-59	630	196	.763
Ed Diddle, Western Ky.	1923-52	558	184	.752
Nat Holman, CCNY	1920-49	361	127	.740
Bob Knight, Army & Indiana	1966-95	659	235	.737
Frank McGuire, St. John's (N.Y.), North Caro. & South Caro.	1948-80	549	236	.699
Don Haskins, UTEP	1962-91	579	256	.693
Lefty Driesell, Davidson, Maryland & James Madison	1961-86, 89-92	600	270	.690

31 SEASONS

Coach, Team	Seasons	W	L	Pct.
Adolph Rupp, Kentucky	1931-52, 54-62	670	125	.843
Phog Allen, Baker, Kansas, Haskell, Central Mo. St. & Kansas	1906-09, 13-39	481	141	.773
Dean Smith, North Caro.	1962-92	740	219	.772
Ed Diddle, Western Ky.	1923-53	583	190	.754
Henry Iba, Northwest Mo. St., Colorado & Oklahoma St.	1930-60	640	211	.752
Nat Holman, CCNY	1920-50	385	132	.745
Bob Knight, Army & Indiana	1966-96	678	247	.733
Don Haskins, UTEP	1962-92	606	263	.697
Lefty Driesell, Davidson, Maryland & James Madison	1961-86, 89-93	621	279	.690
Lou Henson, Hardin-Simmons & Illinois	1963-93	609	295	.674

32 SEASONS

Coach, Team	Seasons	W	L	Pct.
Adolph Rupp, Kentucky	1931-52, 54-63	686	134	.837
Dean Smith, North Caro.	1962-93	774	223	.776
Phog Allen, Baker, Kansas, Haskell, Central Mo. St. & Kansas	1906-09, 13-40	500	147	.773
Ed Diddle, Western Ky.	1923-54	612	193	.760
Henry Iba, Northwest Mo. St., Colorado & Oklahoma St.	1930-61	655	221	.748
Nat Holman, CCNY	1920-51	397	139	.741
Don Haskins, UTEP	1962-93	627	276	.694
Lefty Driesell, Davidson, Maryland & James Madison	1961-86, 89-94	641	289	.689
Lou Henson, Hardin-Simmons & Illinois	1963-94	626	306	.672
Norm Stewart, Northern Iowa & Missouri	1962-93	612	306	.667

33 SEASONS

Coach, Team	Seasons	W	L	Pct.
Adolph Rupp, Kentucky	1931-52, 54-64	707	140	.835
Dean Smith, North Caro.	1962-94	802	230	.777
Phog Allen, Baker, Kansas, Haskell, Central Mo. St. & Kansas	1906-09, 13-41	512	153	.770
Ed Diddle, Western Ky.	1923-55	630	203	.756
Henry Iba, Northwest Mo. St., Colorado & Oklahoma St.	1930-62	669	232	.743
Nat Holman, CCNY	1920-52	405	150	.730
Don Haskins, UTEP	1962-94	645	288	.691
Lefty Driesell, Davidson, Maryland & James Madison	1961-86, 89-95	657	302	.685
Norm Stewart, Northern Iowa & Missouri	1962-94	640	310	.674
Fred Enke, Louisville & Arizona	1926-56	474	265	.641

34 SEASONS

Coach, Team	Seasons	W	L	Pct.
Adolph Rupp, Kentucky	1931-52, 54-65	722	150	.828
Dean Smith, North Caro.	1962-95	830	236	.779
Phog Allen, Baker, Kansas, Haskell, Central Mo. St. & Kansas	1906-09, 13-42	529	158	.770
Ed Diddle, Western Ky.	1923-56	646	215	.750
Henry Iba, Northwest Mo. St., Colorado & Oklahoma St.	1930-63	685	241	.740
Nat Holman, CCNY	1920-52, 55	413	160	.721
Don Haskins, UTEP	1962-95	665	298	.691
Lefty Driesell, Davidson, Maryland & James Madison	1961-86, 89-96	667	322	.674
Norm Stewart, Northern Iowa & Missouri	1962-95	660	319	.674
Fred Enke, Louisville & Arizona	1926-57	487	278	.637

35 SEASONS

Coach, Team	Seasons	W	L	Pct.
Adolph Rupp, Kentucky	1931-52, 54-66	749	152	.831
Dean Smith, North Caro.	1962-96	851	247	.775

Coach, Team	Seasons	W	L	Pct.
Phog Allen, Baker, Kansas, Haskell, Central Mo. St. & Kansas	1906-09, 13-43	551	164	.771
Ed Diddle, Western Ky.	1923-57	663	224	.747
Henry Iba, Northwest Mo. St., Colorado & Oklahoma St.	1930-64	700	251	.736
Nat Holman, CCNY	1920-52, 55-56	417	174	.706
Don Haskins, UTEP	1962-96	678	313	.684
Norm Stewart, Northern Iowa & Missouri	1962-96	678	334	.670
Fred Enke, Louisville & Arizona	1926-58	497	293	.629
Ralph Miller, Wichita St., Iowa & Oregon St.	1952-86	596	352	.629

36 SEASONS

Coach, Team	Seasons	W	L	Pct.
Adolph Rupp, Kentucky	1931-52, 54-67	762	165	.822
Phog Allen, Baker, Kansas, Haskell, Central Mo. St. & Kansas	1906-09, 13-44	568	173	.767
Ed Diddle, Western Ky.	1923-58	677	235	.742
Henry Iba, Northwest Mo. St., Colorado & Oklahoma St.	1930-65	720	258	.736
Nat Holman, CCNY	1920-52, 55-56, 59	423	186	.695
Ray Meyer, DePaul	1943-78	571	327	.636
Ralph Miller, Wichita St., Iowa & Oregon St.	1952-87	615	363	.629
Fred Enke, Louisville & Arizona	1926-59	501	315	.614
Norm Sloan, Presbyterian, Citadel, Florida, North Caro. St. & Florida	1952-55, 57-88	606	382	.613
Slats Gill, Oregon St.	1929-64	599	393	.604

37 SEASONS

Coach, Team	Seasons	W	L	Pct.
Adolph Rupp, Kentucky	1931-52, 54-68	784	170	.822
Phog Allen, Baker, Kansas, Haskell, Central Mo. St. & Kansas	1906-09, 13-45	580	178	.765
Ed Diddle, Western Ky.	1923-59	693	245	.739
Henry Iba, Northwest Mo. St., Colorado & Oklahoma St.	1930-66	724	279	.722
Nat Holman, CCNY	1920-52, 55-56, 59-60	423	190	.690
Ray Meyer, DePaul	1943-79	597	333	.642
Ralph Miller, Wichita St., Iowa & Oregon St.	1952-88	635	374	.629
Norm Sloan, Presbyterian, Citadel, Florida, North Caro. St. & Florida	1952-55, 57-89	627	395	.614
Fred Enke, Louisville & Arizona	1926-60	511	329	.608
Tony Hinkle, Butler	1927-42, 46-66	511	336	.603

38 SEASONS

Coach, Team	Seasons	W	L	Pct.
Adolph Rupp, Kentucky	1931-52, 54-69	807	175	.822
Phog Allen, Baker, Kansas, Haskell, Central Mo. St. & Kansas	1906-09, 13-46	599	180	.769
Ed Diddle, Western Ky.	1923-60	714	252	.739
Henry Iba, Northwest Mo. St., Colorado & Oklahoma St.	1930-67	731	297	.711
Ray Meyer, DePaul	1943-80	623	335	.650
Ralph Miller, Wichita St., Iowa & Oregon St.	1952-89	657	382	.632
Fred Enke, Louisville & Arizona	1926-61	522	344	.603
Tony Hinkle, Butler	1927-42, 46-67	520	353	.596
Marv Harshman, Pacific Lutheran, Washington St. & Washington	1946-83	608	432	.585

39 SEASONS

Coach, Team	Seasons	W	L	Pct.
Adolph Rupp, Kentucky	1931-52, 54-70	833	177	.825
Phog Allen, Baker, Kansas, Haskell, Central Mo. St. & Kansas	1906-09, 13-47	607	185	.766
Ed Diddle, Western Ky.	1923-61	732	260	.740
Henry Iba, Northwest Mo. St., Colorado & Oklahoma St.	1930-68	741	313	.703
Ray Meyer, DePaul	1943-81	650	337	.659
Tony Hinkle, Butler	1927-42, 46-68	531	367	.591
Marv Harshman, Pacific Lutheran, Washington St. & Washington	1946-84	632	439	.590

40 SEASONS

Coach, Team	Seasons	W	L	Pct.
Adolph Rupp, Kentucky	1931-52, 54-71	855	183	.824
Phog Allen, Baker, Kansas, Haskell, Central Mo. St. & Kansas	1906-09, 13-48	616	200	.755
Ed Diddle, Western Ky.	1923-62	749	270	.735
Henry Iba, Northwest Mo. St., Colorado & Oklahoma St.	1930-69	753	326	.698
Ray Meyer, DePaul	1943-82	676	339	.666
Marv Harshman, Pacific Lutheran, Washington St. & Washington	1946-85	654	449	.593
Tony Hinkle, Butler	1927-42, 46-69	542	382	.587

41 SEASONS

Coach, Team	Seasons	W	L	Pct.
Adolph Rupp, Kentucky	1931-52, 54-72	876	190	.822
Phog Allen, Baker, Kansas, Haskell, Central Mo. St. & Kansas	1906-09, 13-49	628	212	.748
Ed Diddle, Western Ky.	1923-63	754	286	.725
Henry Iba, Northwest Mo. St., Colorado & Oklahoma St.	1930-70	767	338	.694
Ray Meyer, DePaul	1943-83	697	351	.665
Tony Hinkle, Butler	1927-42, 46-70	557	393	.586

42 SEASONS

Coach, Team	Seasons	W	L	Pct.
Phog Allen, Baker, Kansas, Haskell, Central Mo. St. & Kansas	1906-09, 13-50	642	223	.742
Ed Diddle, Western Ky.	1923-64	759	302	.715
Ray Meyer, DePaul	1943-84	724	354	.672

Top 10 Best Career Starts By Wins

(Head coaches with at least half their seasons at Division I)

1 SEASON

Coach, Team	Season	W	L	Pct.
Bill Hodges, Indiana St.	1979	33	1	.970
John Warren, Oregon	1945	30	13	.698
Phil Johnson, Weber St.	1969	27	3	.900
Blaine Taylor, Montana	1992	27	4	.871
Jim Boeheim, Syracuse	1977	26	4	.867
Everett Case, North Caro. St.	1947	26	5	.839
Denny Crum, Louisville	1972	26	5	.839
Pete Herrmann, Navy	1987	26	6	.813
Nolan Richardson, Tulsa	1981	26	7	.788
Dick Hunsaker, Ball St.	1990	26	7	.788
Larry Finch, Memphis	1987	26	8	.765

2 SEASONS

Coach, Team	Seasons	W	L	Pct.
Everett Case, North Caro. St.	1947-48	55	8	.873
Ben Carnevale, North Caro.	1945-46	52	11	.825
Gary Cunningham, UCLA	1978-79	50	8	.862
Kermit Davis Jr., Idaho	1989-90	50	12	.806
Nolan Richardson, Tulsa	1981-82	50	13	.794
Stan Watts, Brigham Young	1950-51	50	21	.704
Denny Crum, Louisville	1972-73	49	8	.860
Bill Hodges, Indiana St.	1979-80	49	12	.803
Peter Barry, San Francisco	1981-82	49	13	.790
Roy Williams, Kansas	1989-90	49	17	.742

3 SEASONS

Coach, Team	Seasons	W	L	Pct.
Everett Case, North Caro. St.	1947-49	80	16	.833
Roy Williams, Kansas	1989-91	76	25	.752
Jim Boeheim, Syracuse	1977-79	74	14	.841
Jerry Tarkanian, Long Beach St.	1969-71	71	13	.845
Dick Hunsaker, Ball St.	1990-92	71	26	.732
Denny Crum, Louisville	1972-74	70	19	.787
Don Donoher, Dayton	1965-67	70	19	.787
Pat Foster, Lamar	1981-83	70	20	.777
Pete Gillen, Xavier (Ohio)	1986-88	70	22	.761
Randy Ayers, Ohio St.	1990-92	70	23	.753
Speedy Morris, La Salle	1987-89	70	29	.707

4 SEASONS

Coach, Team	Seasons	W	L	Pct.
Everett Case, North Caro. St.	1947-50	107	22	.829
Bruce Stewart, West Va. Wesleyan & Middle Tenn. St.	1983-86	104	34	.754
Roy Williams, Kansas	1989-92	103	30	.774
Jim Boeheim, Syracuse	1977-80	100	18	.847
Speedy Morris, La Salle	1987-90	100	31	.763
Denny Crum, Louisville	1972-75	98	22	.817
Dick Hunsaker, Ball St.	1990-93	97	34	.740
Jerry Tarkanian, Long Beach St.	1969-72	96	17	.850
Pat Foster, Lamar	1981-84	96	25	.793
Nolan Richardson, Tulsa	1981-84	96	29	.768

5 SEASONS

Coach, Team	Seasons	W	L	Pct.
Everett Case, North Caro. St.	1947-51	137	29	.825
Roy Williams, Kansas	1989-93	132	37	.781
Bruce Stewart, West Va. Wesleyan & Middle Tenn. St.	1983-87	126	41	.754

Coach, Team	Seasons	W	L	Pct.
Forddy Anderson, Drake & Bradley	1947-51	123	42	.745
Jerry Tarkanian, Long Beach St. & UNLV	1969-73	122	20	.859
Jim Boeheim, Syracuse	1977-81	122	30	.803
Fred Schaus, West Va.	1955-59	120	32	.789
Larry Brown, UCLA & Kansas	1980-81, 84-86	120	38	.759
Nolan Richardson, Tulsa	1981-85	119	37	.763
Speedy Morris, La Salle	1987-91	119	41	.744
Pete Gillen, Xavier (Ohio)	1986-90	119	39	.753

6 SEASONS

Coach, Team	Seasons	W	L	Pct.
Everett Case, North Caro. St.	1947-52	161	39	.805
Roy Williams, Kansas	1989-94	159	45	.779
Bruce Stewart, West Va. Wesleyan & Middle Tenn. St.	1983-88	149	52	.741
Fred Schaus, West Va.	1955-60	146	37	.798
Larry Brown, UCLA & Kansas	1980-81, 84-87	145	49	.747
Jerry Tarkanian, Long Beach St. & UNLV	1969-74	142	26	.845
Pete Gillen, Xavier (Ohio)	1986-91	141	49	.742
Forddy Anderson, Drake & Bradley	1947-52	140	54	.722
Denny Crum, Louisville	1972-77	139	37	.790
Speedy Morris, La Salle	1987-92	139	52	.728

7 SEASONS

Coach, Team	Seasons	W	L	Pct.
Everett Case, North Caro. St.	1947-53	187	45	.806
Roy Williams, Kansas	1989-95	184	51	.783
Larry Brown, UCLA & Kansas	1980-81, 84-88	172	60	.741
Bruce Stewart, West Va. Wesleyan & Middle Tenn. St.	1983-89	172	60	.741
Jerry Tarkanian, Long Beach St. & UNLV	1969-75	166	31	.843
Denny Crum, Louisville	1972-78	162	44	.786
Howard Hobson, Southern Ore. & Oregon	1933-39	162	48	.771
Fred Schaus, West Va. & Purdue	1955-60, 73	161	46	.778
Jim Boeheim, Syracuse	1977-83	159	53	.750
Vic Bubas, Duke	1960-66	158	39	.802

8 SEASONS

Coach, Team	Seasons	W	L	Pct.
Everett Case, North Caro. St.	1947-54	213	52	.804
Roy Williams, Kansas	1989-96	213	56	.792
Jerry Tarkanian, Long Beach St. & UNLV	1969-76	195	33	.855
Denny Crum, Louisville	1972-79	186	52	.782
Bruce Stewart, West Va. Wesleyan & Middle Tenn. St.	1983-90	184	75	.710

Roy Williams' 213 victories at Kansas are the most ever compiled by a Division I coach in his first eight seasons. Williams, who showcases a .792 winning percentage, shares the mark with North Carolina State's Everett Case (1947-54).

Photo from Kansas sports information

Coach, Team	Seasons	W	L	Pct.
Fred Schaus, West Va. & Purdue	1955-60, 73-74	182	55	.768
Jim Boeheim, Syracuse	1977-84	182	62	.745
Howard Hobson, Southern Ore. & Oregon	1933-40	181	60	.751
Pete Gillen, Xavier (Ohio)	1986-93	180	67	.729
Boyd Grant, Fresno St.	1978-85	179	59	.752

9 SEASONS

Coach, Team	Seasons	W	L	Pct.
Everett Case, North Caro. St.	1947-55	241	56	.811
Jerry Tarkanian, Long Beach St. & UNLV	1969-77	224	36	.862
Denny Crum, Louisville	1972-80	219	55	.799
Jim Boeheim, Syracuse	1977-85	204	71	.742
Fred Schaus, West Va. & Purdue	1955-60, 73-75	199	66	.751
Howard Hobson, Southern Ore. & Oregon	1933-41	199	78	.718
Vic Bubas, Duke	1960-68	198	54	.786
Tom Blackburn, Dayton	1948-56	198	74	.728
Charlie Spoonhour, Southwest Mo. St.	1984-92	197	81	.709
Nolan Richardson, Tulsa & Arkansas	1981-89	196	83	.703

10 SEASONS

Coach, Team	Seasons	W	L	Pct.
Everett Case, North Caro. St.	1947-56	265	60	.815
Jerry Tarkanian, Long Beach St. & UNLV	1969-78	244	44	.847
Denny Crum, Louisville	1972-81	240	64	.789
Jim Boeheim, Syracuse	1977-86	230	77	.749
Nolan Richardson, Tulsa & Arkansas	1981-90	226	88	.720
Pete Gillen, Xavier (Ohio) & Providence	1986-95	219	88	.713
Tom Blackburn, Dayton	1948-57	217	83	.723
Boyd Grant, Fresno St. & Colorado St.	1978-86, 88	216	87	.713
Gene Keady, Western Ky. & Purdue	1979-88	216	88	.711
Wimp Sanderson, Alabama	1981-90	216	99	.686

11 SEASONS

Coach, Team	Seasons	W	L	Pct.
Everett Case, North Caro. St.	1947-57	280	71	.798
Denny Crum, Louisville	1972-82	263	74	.780
Jim Boeheim, Syracuse	1977-87	261	84	.757
Nolan Richardson, Tulsa & Arkansas	1981-91	260	92	.739
Jerry Tarkanian, Long Beach St. & UNLV	1969-79	259	49	.841
Tom Blackburn, Dayton	1948-58	242	87	.736
Boyd Grant, Fresno St. & Colorado St.	1978-86, 88-89	239	97	.711
Wimp Sanderson, Alabama	1981-91	239	109	.687
Pete Gillen, Xavier (Ohio) & Providence	1986-96	237	100	.703
Fred Schaus, West Va. & Purdue	1955-60, 73-77	235	85	.734
Bob Huggins, Walsh, Akron & Cincinnati	1981-92	235	103	.695

12 SEASONS

Coach, Team	Seasons	W	L	Pct.
Everett Case, North Caro. St.	1947-58	298	77	.795
Denny Crum, Louisville	1972-83	295	78	.791
Jim Boeheim, Syracuse	1977-88	287	93	.755
Nolan Richardson, Tulsa & Arkansas	1981-92	286	100	.741
Jerry Tarkanian, Long Beach St. & UNLV	1969-80	282	58	.829
Wimp Sanderson, Alabama	1981-92	265	118	.692
John Thompson, Georgetown	1973-84	262	104	.716
Bob Huggins, Walsh, Akron & Cincinnati	1981-93	262	108	.708
Boyd Grant, Fresno St. & Colorado St.	1978-86, 88-90	260	106	.710
Peck Hickman, Louisville	1945-56	256	79	.764
Lou Carnesecca, St. John's (N.Y.)	1966-70, 74-80	256	90	.740
Tom Blackburn, Dayton	1948-59	256	99	.721

13 SEASONS

Coach, Team	Seasons	W	L	Pct.
Everett Case, North Caro. St.	1947-59	320	81	.798
Denny Crum, Louisville	1972-84	319	89	.782
Jim Boeheim, Syracuse	1977-89	317	101	.758
Nolan Richardson, Tulsa & Arkansas	1981-93	308	109	.739
Jerry Tarkanian, Long Beach St. & UNLV	1969-81	298	70	.810
John Thompson, Georgetown	1973-85	297	107	.735
Bob Huggins, Walsh, Akron & Cincinnati	1981-94	284	118	.706
Rick Pitino, Boston U., Providence & Kentucky	1979-83, 86-87, 90-95	283	117	.708
Wimp Sanderson, Alabama & Ark.-Little Rock	1981-92, 95	282	130	.684
Peck Hickman, Louisville	1945-57	277	84	.767
Tom Blackburn, Dayton	1948-60	277	106	.723

14 SEASONS

Coach, Team	Seasons	W	L	Pct.
Jim Boeheim, Syracuse	1977-90	343	108	.761
Nolan Richardson, Tulsa & Arkansas	1981-94	339	112	.752
Denny Crum, Louisville	1972-85	338	107	.760
Everett Case, North Caro. St.	1947-60	331	96	.775

Coach, Team	Seasons	W	L	Pct.
John Thompson, Georgetown	1973-86	321	115	.736
Jerry Tarkanian, Long Beach St. & UNLV	1969-82	318	80	.799
Rick Pitino, Boston U., Providence & Kentucky	1979-83, 86-87, 90-96	317	119	.727
Bob Huggins, Walsh, Akron & Cincinnati	1981-95	306	130	.702
Billy Tubbs, Southwest Tex. St., Lamar & Oklahoma	1972-73, 77-88	306	142	.683
Wimp Sanderson, Alabama & Ark.-Little Rock	1981-92, 95-96	305	137	.690

15 SEASONS

Coach, Team	Seasons	W	L	Pct.
Nolan Richardson, Tulsa & Arkansas	1981-95	371	119	.757
Denny Crum, Louisville	1972-86	370	114	.764
Jim Boeheim, Syracuse	1977-91	369	114	.764
John Thompson, Georgetown	1973-87	350	120	.745
Everett Case, North Caro. St.	1947-61	347	105	.768
Jerry Tarkanian, Long Beach St. & UNLV	1969-83	346	83	.807
Bob Huggins, Walsh, Akron & Cincinnati	1981-96	334	135	.712
Billy Tubbs, Southwest Tex. St., Lamar & Oklahoma	1972-73, 77-89	336	148	.694
Lou Carnesecca, St. John's (N.Y.)	1966-70, 74-83	322	115	.737
Tom Blackburn, Dayton	1948-62	321	121	.726

16 SEASONS

Coach, Team	Seasons	W	L	Pct.
Jim Boeheim, Syracuse	1977-92	391	124	.759
Nolan Richardson, Tulsa & Arkansas	1981-96	391	132	.748
Denny Crum, Louisville	1972-87	388	128	.752
Jerry Tarkanian, Long Beach St. & UNLV	1969-84	375	89	.808
John Thompson, Georgetown	1973-88	370	130	.740
Billy Tubbs, Southwest Tex. St., Lamar & Oklahoma	1972-73, 77-90	363	153	.703
Everett Case, North Caro. St.	1947-62	358	111	.763
Eddie Sutton, Creighton, Arkansas & Kentucky	1970-85	342	125	.732
Dean Smith, North Caro.	1962-77	340	113	.751
Lou Carnesecca, St. John's (N.Y.)	1966-70, 74-84	340	127	.728

17 SEASONS

Coach, Team	Seasons	W	L	Pct.
Denny Crum, Louisville	1972-88	412	139	.748
Jim Boeheim, Syracuse	1977-93	411	133	.756
Jerry Tarkanian, Long Beach St. & UNLV	1969-85	403	93	.813
John Thompson, Georgetown	1973-89	399	135	.747
Billy Tubbs, Southwest Tex. St., Lamar & Oklahoma	1972-73, 77-91	383	168	.695
Eddie Sutton, Creighton, Arkansas & Kentucky	1970-86	374	129	.744
Lou Carnesecca, St. John's (N.Y.)	1966-70, 74-85	371	131	.739
Mike Krzyzewski, Army & Duke	1976-92	370	169	.686
Everett Case, North Caro. St.	1947-63	368	122	.751
Henry Iba, Northwest Mo. St., Colorado & Oklahoma St.	1930-46	364	91	.800

18 SEASONS

Coach, Team	Seasons	W	L	Pct.
Jerry Tarkanian, Long Beach St. & UNLV	1969-86	436	98	.816
Denny Crum, Louisville	1972-89	436	148	.747
Jim Boeheim, Syracuse	1977-94	434	140	.756
John Thompson, Georgetown	1973-90	423	142	.749
Billy Tubbs, Southwest Tex. St., Lamar & Oklahoma	1972-73, 77-92	404	177	.695
Lou Carnesecca, St. John's (N.Y.)	1966-70, 74-86	402	136	.747
Mike Krzyzewski, Army & Duke	1976-93	394	177	.690
Eddie Sutton, Creighton, Arkansas & Kentucky	1970-87	392	140	.740
Henry Iba, Northwest Mo. St., Colorado & Oklahoma St.	1930-47	388	99	.797
Dean Smith, North Caro.	1962-79	386	127	.752
Gene Keady, Western Ky. & Purdue	1979-96	386	167	.698

19 SEASONS

Coach, Team	Seasons	W	L	Pct.
Jerry Tarkanian, Long Beach St. & UNLV	1969-87	473	100	.825
Denny Crum, Louisville	1972-90	463	156	.748
Jim Boeheim, Syracuse	1977-95	454	150	.752
John Thompson, Georgetown	1973-91	442	155	.740
Billy Tubbs, Southwest Tex. St., Lamar & Oklahoma	1972-73, 77-93	424	189	.692
Lou Carnesecca, St. John's (N.Y.)	1966-70, 74-87	423	145	.745
Mike Krzyzewski, Army & Duke	1976-94	422	183	.698
Eddie Sutton, Creighton, Arkansas & Kentucky	1970-88	417	145	.742
Henry Iba, Northwest Mo. St., Colorado & Oklahoma St.	1930-48	415	103	.801
Dean Smith, North Caro.	1962-80	407	135	.751

20 SEASONS

Coach, Team	Seasons	W	L	Pct.
Jerry Tarkanian, Long Beach St. & UNLV	1969-88	501	106	.825
Jim Boeheim, Syracuse	1977-96	483	159	.752
Denny Crum, Louisville	1972-91	477	172	.735
John Thompson, Georgetown	1973-92	464	165	.738
John Chaney, Cheyney & Temple	1973-92	458	143	.762
Lou Carnesecca, St. John's (N.Y.)	1966-70, 74-88	440	157	.737
Billy Tubbs, Southwest Tex. St., Lamar & Oklahoma	1972-73, 77-94	439	202	.685
Henry Iba, Northwest Mo. St., Colorado & Oklahoma St.	1930-49	438	108	.802
Dean Smith, North Caro.	1962-81	436	143	.753
Mike Krzyzewski, Army & Duke	1976-95	431	186	.699

21 SEASONS

Coach, Team	Seasons	W	L	Pct.
Jerry Tarkanian, Long Beach St. & UNLV	1969-89	530	114	.823
Denny Crum, Louisville	1972-92	496	183	.730
John Thompson, Georgetown	1973-93	484	178	.731
John Chaney, Cheyney & Temple	1973-93	478	156	.754
Dean Smith, North Caro.	1962-82	468	145	.763
Lou Carnesecca, St. John's (N.Y.)	1966-70, 74-89	460	170	.730
Lute Olson, Long Beach St., Iowa & Arizona	1974-94	458	179	.719
Henry Iba, Northwest Mo. St., Colorado & Oklahoma St.	1930-50	456	117	.796
Billy Tubbs, Southwest Tex. St., Lamar, Oklahoma & Texas Christian	1972-73, 77-95	455	213	.681
Eddie Sutton, Creighton, Arkansas, Kentucky & Oklahoma St.	1970-89, 91	454	172	.725

22 SEASONS

Coach, Team	Seasons	W	L	Pct.
Jerry Tarkanian, Long Beach St. & UNLV	1969-90	565	119	.826
Denny Crum, Louisville	1972-93	518	192	.730
John Thompson, Georgetown	1973-94	503	190	.726
John Chaney, Cheyney & Temple	1973-94	501	190	.726
Dean Smith, North Caro.	1962-83	496	153	.764
Henry Iba, Northwest Mo. St., Colorado & Oklahoma St.	1930-51	485	123	.798
Lou Carnesecca, St. John's (N.Y.)	1966-70, 74-90	484	180	.729
Eddie Sutton, Creighton, Arkansas, Kentucky & Oklahoma St.	1970-89, 91-92	482	180	.728
Lute Olson, Long Beach St., Iowa & Arizona	1974-95	481	187	.720
Adolph Rupp, Kentucky	1931-52	472	83	.850

23 SEASONS

Coach, Team	Seasons	W	L	Pct.
Jerry Tarkanian, Long Beach St. & UNLV	1969-91	599	120	.833
Denny Crum, Louisville	1972-94	546	198	.734
Dean Smith, North Caro.	1962-84	524	156	.771
John Thompson, Georgetown	1973-95	524	200	.724
John Chaney, Cheyney & Temple	1973-95	520	175	.748
Lou Carnesecca, St. John's (N.Y.)	1966-70, 74-91	507	189	.728
Lute Olson, Long Beach St., Iowa & Arizona	1974-96	507	194	.723
Henry Iba, Northwest Mo. St., Colorado & Oklahoma St.	1930-52	504	131	.794
Eddie Sutton, Creighton, Arkansas, Kentucky & Oklahoma St.	1970-89, 91-93	502	189	.726
Adolph Rupp, Kentucky	1931-52, 54	497	83	.857

24 SEASONS

Coach, Team	Seasons	W	L	Pct.
Jerry Tarkanian, Long Beach St. & UNLV	1969-92	625	122	.837
Denny Crum, Louisville	1972-95	565	212	.727
John Thompson, Georgetown	1973-96	553	208	.727
Dean Smith, North Caro.	1962-85	551	165	.770
John Chaney, Cheyney & Temple	1973-96	540	188	.742
Henry Iba, Northwest Mo. St., Colorado & Oklahoma St.	1930-53	527	138	.792
Eddie Sutton, Creighton, Arkansas, Kentucky & Oklahoma St.	1970-89, 91-94	526	199	.726
Lou Carnesecca, St. John's (N.Y.)	1966-70, 74-92	526	200	.725
John Wooden, Indiana St. & UCLA	1947-70	521	154	.772
Adolph Rupp, Kentucky	1931-52, 54-55	520	86	.858

25 SEASONS

Coach, Team	Seasons	W	L	Pct.
Jerry Tarkanian, Long Beach St., UNLV & Fresno St.	1969-92, 96	647	133	.829
Dean Smith, North Caro.	1962-86	579	171	.772
Eddie Sutton, Creighton, Arkansas, Kentucky & Oklahoma St.	1970-89, 91-95	553	209	.726
Henry Iba, Northwest Mo. St., Colorado & Oklahoma St.	1930-54	551	143	.794

Coach, Team	Seasons	W	L	Pct.
John Wooden, Indiana St. & UCLA	1947-71	550	155	.780
Adolph Rupp, Kentucky	1931-52, 54-56	540	92	.854
Bob Knight, Army & Indiana	1966-90	532	198	.729
Lefty Driesell, Davidson & Maryland	1961-85	505	220	.706
Lou Henson, Hardin-Simmons & Illinois	1963-87	481	234	.673
Gene Bartow, Central Mo. St., Valparaiso, Memphis, Illinois, UCLA, & UAB	1962-77, 78-87	476	243	.662

26 SEASONS

Coach, Team	Seasons	W	L	Pct.
Dean Smith, North Caro.	1962-87	611	175	.777
John Wooden, Indiana St. & UCLA	1947-72	580	155	.789
Eddie Sutton, Creighton, Arkansas, Kentucky & Oklahoma St.	1970-89, 91-96	570	219	.722
Henry Iba, Northwest Mo. St., Colorado & Oklahoma St.	1930-55	563	156	.783
Adolph Rupp, Kentucky	1931-52, 54-57	563	97	.853
Bob Knight, Army & Indiana	1966-91	561	203	.734
Lefty Driesell, Davidson & Maryland	1961-86	524	224	.701
Lou Henson, Hardin-Simmons & Illinois	1963-88	504	244	.674
Guy Lewis, Houston	1957-82	499	243	.673
Don Haskins, UTEP	1962-87	493	215	.696

27 SEASONS

Coach, Team	Seasons	W	L	Pct.
Dean Smith, North Caro.	1962-88	638	182	.778
John Wooden, Indiana St. & UCLA	1947-73	610	155	.797
Bob Knight, Army & Indiana	1966-92	588	210	.737
Adolph Rupp, Kentucky	1931-52, 54-58	586	103	.851
Henry Iba, Northwest Mo. St., Colorado & Oklahoma St.	1930-56	581	165	.779
Lefty Driesell, Davidson, Maryland & James Madison	1961-86, 89	540	238	.694
Lou Henson, Hardin-Simmons & Illinois	1963-89	535	249	.682
Guy Lewis, Houston	1957-83	530	246	.683
Don Haskins, UTEP	1962-88	516	225	.696
Gene Bartow, Central Mo. St., Valparaiso, Memphis, Illinois, UCLA, & UAB	1962-77, 78-89	514	270	.656

28 SEASONS

Coach, Team	Seasons	W	L	Pct.
Dean Smith, North Caro.	1962-89	667	190	.778
John Wooden, Indiana St. & UCLA	1947-74	636	159	.800
Bob Knight, Army & Indiana	1966-93	619	214	.743
Adolph Rupp, Kentucky	1931-52, 54-59	610	106	.852
Henry Iba, Northwest Mo. St., Colorado & Oklahoma St.	1930-57	598	174	.775
Guy Lewis, Houston	1957-84	562	251	.691
Lefty Driesell, Davidson, Maryland & James Madison	1961-86, 89-90	560	249	.692
Lou Henson, Hardin-Simmons & Illinois	1963-90	556	257	.684
Don Haskins, UTEP	1962-89	542	232	.700
Gene Bartow, Central Mo. St., Valparaiso, Memphis, Illinois, UCLA, & UAB	1962-77, 78-90	536	279	.658

29 SEASONS

Coach, Team	Seasons	W	L	Pct.
Dean Smith, North Caro.	1962-90	688	203	.772
John Wooden, Indiana St. & UCLA	1947-75	664	162	.804
Bob Knight, Army & Indiana	1966-94	640	223	.742
Adolph Rupp, Kentucky	1931-52, 54-60	628	113	.848
Henry Iba, Northwest Mo. St., Colorado & Oklahoma St.	1930-58	619	182	.773
Lefty Driesell, Davidson, Maryland & James Madison	1961-86, 89-91	579	259	.691
Guy Lewis, Houston	1957-85	578	265	.686
Lou Henson, Hardin-Simmons & Illinois	1963-91	577	267	.684
Don Haskins, UTEP	1962-90	563	243	.699
Gene Bartow, Central Mo. St., Valparaiso, Memphis, Illinois, UCLA, & UAB	1962-77, 78-91	554	292	.655

30 SEASONS

Coach, Team	Seasons	W	L	Pct.
Dean Smith, North Caro.	1962-91	717	209	.774
Bob Knight, Army & Indiana	1966-95	659	235	.737
Adolph Rupp, Kentucky	1931-52, 54-61	647	122	.841
Henry Iba, Northwest Mo. St., Colorado & Oklahoma St.	1930-59	630	196	.763
Lefty Driesell, Davidson, Maryland & James Madison	1961-86, 89-92	600	270	.690
Guy Lewis, Houston	1957-86	592	279	.680
Lou Henson, Hardin-Simmons & Illinois	1963-92	590	282	.677
Don Haskins, UTEP	1962-91	579	256	.693
Gene Bartow, Central Mo. St., Valparaiso, Memphis, Illinois, & UAB	1962-77, 78-92	574	301	.656
Norm Stewart, Northern Iowa & Missouri	1962-91	572	283	.669

31 SEASONS

Coach, Team	Seasons	W	L	Pct.
Dean Smith, North Caro.	1962-92	740	219	.772
Bob Knight, Army & Indiana	1966-96	678	247	.733
Adolph Rupp, Kentucky	1931-52, 54-62	670	125	.843
Henry Iba, Northwest Mo. St., Colorado & Oklahoma St.	1930-60	640	211	.752
Lefty Driesell, Davidson, Maryland & James Madison	1961-86, 89-93	621	279	.690
Lou Henson, Hardin-Simmons & Illinois	1963-93	609	295	.674
Don Haskins, UTEP	1962-92	606	263	.697
Gene Bartow, Central Mo. St., Valparaiso, Memphis, Illinois, UCLA, & UAB	962-77, 78-93	595	315	.654
Norm Stewart, Northern Iowa & Missouri	1962-92	593	292	.670
Ed Diddle, Western Ky.	1923-53	583	190	.754

32 SEASONS

Coach, Team	Seasons	W	L	Pct.
Dean Smith, North Caro.	1962-93	774	223	.776
Adolph Rupp, Kentucky	1931-52, 54-63	686	134	.837
Henry Iba, Northwest Mo. St., Colorado & Oklahoma St.	1930-61	655	221	.748
Lefty Driesell, Davidson, Maryland & James Madison	1961-86, 89-94	641	289	.689
Don Haskins, UTEP	1962-93	627	276	.694
Lou Henson, Hardin-Simmons & Illinois	1963-94	626	306	.672
Gene Bartow, Central Mo. St., Valparaiso, Memphis, Illinois, UCLA, & UAB	1962-77, 78-94	617	323	.656
Ed Diddle, Western Ky.	1923-54	612	193	.760
Norm Stewart, Northern Iowa & Missouri	1962-93	612	306	.667
Abe Lemons, Oklahoma City, Tex.-Pan American, Texas & Oklahoma City	1956-82, 84-88	567	317	.641

33 SEASONS

Coach, Team	Seasons	W	L	Pct.
Dean Smith, North Caro.	1962-94	802	230	.777
Adolph Rupp, Kentucky	1931-52, 54-64	707	140	.835
Henry Iba, Northwest Mo. St., Colorado & Oklahoma St.	1930-62	669	232	.743
Lefty Driesell, Davidson, Maryland & James Madison	1961-86, 89-95	657	302	.685
Don Haskins, UTEP	1962-94	645	288	.691
Lou Henson, Hardin-Simmons & Illinois	1963-95	645	318	.670
Norm Stewart, Northern Iowa & Missouri	1962-94	640	310	.674
Gene Bartow, Central Mo. St., Valparaiso, Memphis, Illinois, UCLA & UAB	1962-77, 78-95	631	339	.651
Ed Diddle, Western Ky.	1923-55	630	203	.756
Abe Lemons, Oklahoma City, Tex.-Pan American, Texas & Oklahoma City	1956-82, 84-89	579	331	.636

34 SEASONS

Coach, Team	Seasons	W	L	Pct.
Dean Smith, North Caro.	1962-95	830	236	.779
Adolph Rupp, Kentucky	1931-52, 54-65	722	150	.828
Henry Iba, Northwest Mo. St., Colorado & Oklahoma St.	1930-63	685	241	.740
Lefty Driesell, Davidson, Maryland & James Madison	1961-86, 89-96	667	322	.674
Don Haskins, UTEP	1962-95	665	298	.691
Norm Stewart, Northern Iowa & Missouri	1962-95	660	319	.674
Ed Diddle, Western Ky.	1923-56	646	215	.750
Abe Lemons, Oklahoma City, Tex.-Pan American, Texas & Oklahoma City	1956-82, 84-90	597	344	.634
Ralph Miller, Wichita St., Iowa & Oregon St.	1952-85	584	337	.634
Gary Colson, Valdosta St., Pepperdine, New Mexico & Fresno St.	1959-79, 81-88, 91-95	563	385	.594

35 SEASONS

Coach, Team	Seasons	W	L	Pct.
Dean Smith, North Caro.	1962-96	851	247	.775
Adolph Rupp, Kentucky	1931-52, 54-66	749	152	.831
Henry Iba, Northwest Mo. St., Colorado & Oklahoma St.	1930-64	700	251	.736
Don Haskins, UTEP	1962-96	678	313	.684
Norm Stewart, Northern Iowa & Missouri	1962-96	678	334	.670
Ed Diddle, Western Ky.	1923-57	663	224	.747
Ralph Miller, Wichita St., Iowa & Oregon St.	1952-86	596	352	.629
Norm Sloan, Presbyterian, Citadel, Florida, North Caro. St. & Florida	1952-55, 57-87	583	370	.612
Marv Harshman, Pacific Lutheran, Washington St. & Washington	1946-80	559	394	.587

Coach, Team	Seasons	W	L	Pct.
Phog Allen, Baker, Kansas, Haskell, Central Mo. St. & Kansas	1906-09, 13-43	551	164	.771

36 SEASONS

Coach, Team	Seasons	W	L	Pct.
Adolph Rupp, Kentucky	1931-52, 54-67	762	165	.822
Henry Iba, Northwest Mo. St., Colorado & Oklahoma St.	1930-65	720	258	.736
Ed Diddle, Western Ky.	1923-58	677	235	.742
Ralph Miller, Wichita St., Iowa & Oregon St.	1952-87	615	363	.629
Norm Sloan, Presbyterian, Citadel, Florida, North Caro. St. & Florida	1952-55, 57-88	606	382	.613
Slats Gill, Oregon St.	1929-64	599	393	.604
Marv Harshman, Pacific Lutheran, Washington St. & Washington	1946-81	573	407	.585
Ray Meyer, DePaul	1943-78	571	327	.636
Phog Allen, Baker, Kansas, Haskell, Central Mo. St. & Kansas	1906-09, 13-44	568	173	.767
Glenn Wilkes, Stetson	1958-93	551	436	.558

37 SEASONS

Coach, Team	Seasons	W	L	Pct.
Adolph Rupp, Kentucky	1931-52, 54-68	784	170	.822
Henry Iba, Northwest Mo. St., Colorado & Oklahoma St.	1930-66	724	279	.722
Ed Diddle, Western Ky.	1923-59	693	245	.739
Ralph Miller, Wichita St., Iowa & Oregon St.	1952-88	635	374	.629
Norm Sloan, Presbyterian, Citadel, Florida, North Caro. St. & Florida	1952-55, 57-89	627	395	.614
Ray Meyer, DePaul	1943-79	597	333	.642
Marv Harshman, Pacific Lutheran, Washington St. & Washington	1946-82	592	417	.587
Phog Allen, Baker, Kansas, Haskell, Central Mo. St. & Kansas	1906-09, 13-45	580	178	.765
Fred Enke, Louisville & Arizona	1926-60	511	329	.608
Tony Hinkle, Butler	1927-42, 46-66	511	336	.603

38 SEASONS

Coach, Team	Seasons	W	L	Pct.
Adolph Rupp, Kentucky	1931-52, 54-69	807	175	.822
Henry Iba, Northwest Mo. St., Colorado & Oklahoma St.	1930-67	731	297	.711
Ed Diddle, Western Ky.	1923-60	714	252	.739
Ralph Miller, Wichita St., Iowa & Oregon St.	1952-89	657	382	.632
Ray Meyer, DePaul	1943-80	623	335	.650
Marv Harshman, Pacific Lutheran, Washington St. & Washington	1946-83	608	432	.585
Phog Allen, Baker, Kansas, Haskell, Central Mo. St. & Kansas	1906-09, 13-46	599	180	.769
Fred Enke, Louisville & Arizona	1926-61	522	344	.603
Tony Hinkle, Butler	1927-42, 46-67	520	353	.596

39 SEASONS

Coach, Team	Seasons	W	L	Pct.
Adolph Rupp, Kentucky	1931-52, 54-70	833	177	.825
Henry Iba, Northwest Mo. St., Colorado & Oklahoma St.	1930-68	741	313	.703
Ed Diddle, Western Ky.	1923-61	732	260	.740
Ray Meyer, DePaul	1943-81	650	337	.659
Marv Harshman, Pacific Lutheran, Washington St. & Washington	1946-84	632	439	.590
Phog Allen, Baker, Kansas, Haskell, Central Mo. St. & Kansas	1906-09, 13-47	607	185	.766
Tony Hinkle, Butler	1927-42, 46-68	531	367	.591

40 SEASONS

Coach, Team	Seasons	W	L	Pct.
Adolph Rupp, Kentucky	1931-52, 54-71	855	183	.824
Henry Iba, Northwest Mo. St., Colorado & Oklahoma St.	1930-69	753	326	.698
Ed Diddle, Western Ky.	1923-62	749	270	.735
Ray Meyer, DePaul	1943-82	676	339	.666
Marv Harshman, Pacific Lutheran, Washington St. & Washington	1946-85	654	449	.593
Phog Allen, Baker, Kansas, Haskell, Central Mo. St. & Kansas	1906-09, 13-40	616	200	.755
Tony Hinkle, Butler	1927-42, 46-69	542	382	.587

41 SEASONS

Coach, Team	Seasons	W	L	Pct.
Adolph Rupp, Kentucky	1931-52, 54-72	876	190	.822
Henry Iba, Northwest Mo. St., Colorado & Oklahoma St.	1930-70	767	338	.694
Ed Diddle, Western Ky.	1923-63	754	286	.725
Ray Meyer, DePaul	1943-83	697	351	.665
Phog Allen, Baker, Kansas, Haskell, Central Mo. St. & Kansas	1906-09, 13-49	628	212	.748
Tony Hinkle, Butler	1927-42, 46-70	557	393	.586

42 SEASONS

Coach, Team	Seasons	W	L	Pct.
Ed Diddle, Western Ky.	1923-64	759	302	.715
Ray Meyer, DePaul	1943-84	724	354	.672
Phog Allen, Baker, Kansas, Haskell, Central Mo. St. & Kansas	1906-09, 13-50	642	223	.742

Active Coaching Longevity Records

(Minimum five years as a Division I head coach)

MOST GAMES

No.	Coach, Team and Seasons
1,158	James Phelan, Mt. St. Mary's (Md.) 1955-96
1,098	Dean Smith, North Caro. 1962-96
1,012	Norm Stewart, Northern Iowa 1962-67, Missouri 68-96
991	Don Haskins, UTEP 1962-96
989	Lefty Driesell, Davidson 1961-69, Maryland 70-86, James Madison 89-96
932	Eldon Miller, Wittenberg 1963-70, Western Mich. 71-76, Ohio St. 77-86, Northern Iowa 87-96
925	Bob Knight, Army 1966-71, Indiana 72-96
876	Calvin Luther, DePauw 1955-58, Murray St. 59-73, Longwood 82-90, Tenn.-Martin 91-96
826	Bill C. Foster, Shorter 1963-67, N.C.-Charlotte 71-75, Clemson 76-84, Miami (Fla.) 86-90, Virginia Tech 92-96
813	George Blaney, Stonehill 1968-69, Dartmouth 70-72, Holy Cross 73-94, Seton Hall 95-96
811	Denny Crum, Louisville 1972-96
789	Eddie Sutton, Creighton 1970-74, Arkansas 75-85, Kentucky 86-89, Oklahoma St. 91-96
780	Jerry Tarkanian, Long Beach St. 1969-73, UNLV 74-92, Fresno St. 96
761	John Thompson, Georgetown, 1973-96
740	Tom Davis, Lafayette 1972-77, Boston College 78-82, Stanford 83-86, Iowa 87-96
736	Tom Penders, Tufts, 1972-74, Columbia 75-78, Fordham 79-86, Rhode Island 87-88, Texas 89-96
728	John Chaney, Cheyney 1973-82, Temple 83-96
719	Dale Brown, LSU 1973-96
713	Davey Whitney, Texas Southern 1965-69, Alcorn St. 70-89
712	Gale Catlett, Cincinnati 1973-78, West Va. 79-96
706	Jim Calhoun, Northeastern 1973-86, Connecticut 87-96
703	Rollie Massimino, Stony Brook 1970-71, Villanova 74-92, UNLV 93-94, Cleveland St.
701	Lute Olson, Long Beach St. 1974, Iowa 75-83, Arizona 84-96
698	Billy Tubbs, Southwestern Tex. St. 1972-73, Lamar 77-80, Oklahoma 81-94, Texas Christian 95-96
696	Ben Jobe, Talladega 1965-67, Alabama St. 68, South Caro. St. 69-73, Denver 79-80, Alabama A&M 83-86, Southern U. 87-96, Tuskegee

MOST SEASONS

No.	Coach, Team and Seasons
42	James Phelan, Mt. St. Mary's (Md.) 1955-96
35	Don Haskins, UTEP 1962-96
35	Calvin Luther, DePauw 1955-58, Murray St. 59-73, Longwood 82-90, Tenn.-Martin 91-96
35	Dean Smith, North Caro. 1962-96
35	Norm Stewart, Northern Iowa 1962-67, Missouri 68-96
34	Lefty Driesell, Davidson 1961-69, Maryland 70-86, James Madison 89-96
34	Eldon Miller, Wittenberg 1963-70, Western Mich. 71-76, Ohio St. 77-86, Northern Iowa 87-96
31	Bob Knight, Army 1966-71, Indiana 72-96
29	George Blaney, Stonehill 1968-69, Dartmouth 70-72, Holy Cross 73-94, Seton Hall 95-96
29	Bill C. Foster, Shorter 1963-67, N.C.-Charlotte 71-75, Clemson 76-84, Miami (Fla.) 86-90, Virginia Tech 92-96
26	Eddie Sutton, Creighton 1970-74, Arkansas 75-85, Kentucky 86-89, Oklahoma St. 91-96
25	Denny Crum, Louisville 1972-96
25	Tom Davis, Lafayette 1972-77, Boston College 78-82, Stanford 83-86, Iowa 87-96
25	Ben Jobe, Talladega 1965-67, Alabama St. 68, South Caro. St. 69-73, Denver 79-80, Alabama A&M 83-86, Southern U. 87-96, Tuskegee
25	Tom Penders, Tufts, 1972-74, Columbia 75-78, Fordham 79-86, Rhode Island 87-88, Texas 89-96
25	Jerry Tarkanian, Long Beach St. 1969-73, UNLV 74-92, Fresno St. 96
25	Davey Whitney, Texas Southern 1965-69, Alcorn St. 70-89
24	Dale Brown, LSU 1973-96
24	Jim Calhoun, Northeastern 1973-86, Connecticut 87-96

COACHING RECORDS

No.	Coach, Team and Seasons
24	John Chaney, Cheyney 1973-82, Temple 83-96
24	John Thompson, Georgetown 1973-96
24	Gale Catlett, Cincinnati 1973-78, West Va. 79-96
23	Don DeVoe, Virginia Tech 1972-76, Wyoming 77-78, Tennessee 79-89, Florida 90, Navy 93-96
23	Rollie Massimino, Stony Brook 1970-71, Villanova 74-92, UNLV 93-94, Cleveland St.
23	Lute Olson, Long Beach St. 1974, Iowa 75-83, Arizona 84-96

MOST SEASONS WITH CURRENT TEAM

No.	Coach, Team and Seasons
42	James Phelan, #Mt. St. Mary's (Md.) 1955-96
35	Don Haskins, #UTEP 1962-96
35	Dean Smith, #North Caro. 1962-96
29	Norm Stewart, Missouri 1968-96
25	Denny Crum, #Louisville 1972-96
25	Bob Knight, Indiana 1972-96
24	Dale Brown, #LSU 1973-96
24	John Thompson, #Georgetown 1973-96
21	Robert Moreland, #Texas Southern 1976-96
20	Jim Boeheim, #Syracuse 1977-96

#Has coached only at this school.

MOST 20-WIN SEASONS

No.	Coach, Team and Seasons
29	Dean Smith, North Caro. 1962-96
24	Jerry Tarkanian, Long Beach St. 1969-73, UNLV 74-92, Fresno St. 96
20	Denny Crum, Louisville 1972-96
20	Charles "Lefty" Driesell, Davidson 1961-69, Maryland 70-86, James Madison 89-96
19	Jim Boeheim, Syracuse 1977-96
19	Bob Knight, Army 1966-71, Indiana 72-96
19	James Phelan, Mt. St. Mary's (Md.) 1955-96
18	John Chaney, Cheyney 1973-82, Temple 83-96
18	Lute Olson, Long Beach St. 1974, Iowa 75-83, Arizona 84-96
18	John Thompson, Georgetown 1973-96
17	Don Haskins, UTEP 1962-96
17	Norm Stewart, Northern Iowa 1962-67, Missouri 68-96
17	Eddie Sutton, Creighton 1970-74, Arkansas 75-85, Kentucky 86-89, Oklahoma St. 91-96
15	Billy Tubbs, Southwestern (Tex.) 1972-73, Lamar 77-80, Oklahoma 81-94, Texas Christian 95-96
14	Neil McCarthy, Weber St. 1976-85, New Mexico St. 86-96
13	Gale Catlett, Cincinnati 1973-78, West Va. 79-96
13	Tom Davis, Lafayette 1972-77, Boston College 78-82, Stanford 83-86, Iowa 87-96
13	Mike Krzyzewski, Army 1976-80, Duke 81-96
13	Nolan Richardson, Tulsa 1981-85, Arkansas 86-96
12	Jim Calhoun, Northeastern 1973-86, Connecticut 87-96
12	Jim Harrick, Pepperdine 1980-88, UCLA 1989-96
12	Bob Huggins, Walsh 1981-83, Akron 85-89, Cincinnati 90-96
12	Gene Keady, Western Ky. 1979-80, Purdue 81-96
12	John Kresse, Charleston (S.C.) 1980-96
11	Dave Bliss, Oklahoma 1976-80, Southern Methodist 81-88, New Mexico 89-96
11	Bill Foster, Shorter 1963-67, N.C.-Charlotte 71-75, Clemson 76-84, Miami (Fla.) 86-90, Virginia Tech 92-96
11	Tom Penders, Tufts 1972-74, Columbia 75-78, Fordham 79-86, Rhode Island 87-88, Texas 89-96

MOST TEAMS

No.	Coach, Team and Seasons
6	J. D. Barnett, Lenoir Rhyne 1970, High Point 71, Louisiana Tech 78-79, Va. Commonwealth 80-85, Tulsa 86-91, Northwestern St. 95-96
6	Ben Jobe, Talladega 1965-67, Alabama St. 68, South Caro. St. 69-73, Denver 79-80, Alabama A&M 83-86, Southern U. 87-96, Tuskegee
5	Don DeVoe, Virginia Tech 1972-76, Wyoming 77-78, Tennessee 79-89, Florida 90, Navy 93-96
5	Bill C. Foster, Shorter 1963-67, N.C.-Charlotte 71-75, Clemson 76-84, Miami (Fla.) 86-90, Virginia Tech 92-96
5	Tom Penders, Tufts 1972-74, Columbia 75-78, Fordham 79-86, Rhode Island 87-88, Texas 89-96
4	George Blaney, Stonehill 1968-69, Dartmouth 70-72, Holy Cross 73-94, Seton Hall 95
4	Tim Cohane, Manhattanville 1975-79, Dartmouth 80-83, Merchant Marine 89-94, Buffalo 94-96
4	Tom Davis, Lafayette 1972-77, Boston College 78-82, Stanford 83-86, Iowa 87-96
4	Rees Johnson, Carroll (Wis.) 1977-78, Augsburg 79-82, Wis.-Parkside 83-88, Northeastern Ill. 90-96
4	Calvin Luther, DePauw 1955-58, Murray St. 59-73, Longwood 82-90, Tenn.-Martin 91-96
4	Rollie Massimino, Stony Brook 1970-71, Villanova 74-92, UNLV 93-94, Cleveland St.

No.	Coach, Team and Seasons
4	Eldon Miller, Wittenberg 1963-70, Western Mich. 71-76, Ohio St. 77-86, Northern Iowa 87-96
4	Eddie Sutton, Creighton 1970-74, Arkansas 75-85, Kentucky 86-89, Oklahoma St. 91-96
4	Billy Tubbs, Southwestern (Tex.) 1972-73, Lamar 77-80, Oklahoma 81-94, Texas Christian 95-96
4	Gary Williams, American 1979-82, Boston College 83-86, Ohio St. 87-89, Maryland 91-96

All-Time Coaching Longevity Records

(Minimum 10 head coaching seasons in Division I)

MOST GAMES

No.	Coach, Team and Seasons
1,105	Henry Iba, Northwest Mo. St. 1930-33, Colorado 34, Oklahoma St. 35-70
1,098	Dean Smith, North Caro. 1962-96*
1,090	Marv Harshman, Pacific Lutheran 1946-58, Washington St. 59-71, Washington 72-85
1,078	Ray Meyer, DePaul 1943-84
1,066	Adolph Rupp, Kentucky 1931-72
1,061	Ed Diddle, Western Ky. 1923-64
1,039	Ralph Miller, Wichita St. 1952-64, Iowa 65-70, Oregon St. 71-89
1,017	Norm Sloan, Presbyterian 1952-55, Citadel 57-60, Florida 61-66, North Caro. St. 67-80, Florida 81-89
1,012	Norm Stewart, Northern Iowa 1962-67, Missouri 68-96*
1,010	Phog Allen, Baker 1906-08, Kansas 08-09, Haskell 09, Central Mo. St. 13-19, Kansas 20-56
1,000	Gene Bartow, Central Mo. St. 1962-64, Valparaiso 65-70, Memphis 71-74, Illinois 75, UCLA 76-77, UAB 79-96
994	Lou Henson, Hardin-Simmons 1963-66, New Mexico St. 67-75, Illinois 76-96
991	Slats Gill, Oregon St. 1929-64
991	Don Haskins, UTEP 1962-96*
989	Lefty Driesell, Davidson 1961-69, Maryland 70-86, James Madison 89-96*
987	Glenn Wilkes, Stetson 1958-93
950	Tony Hinkle, Butler 1927-42, 46-70
948	Gary Colson, Valdosta St. 1959-68, Pepperdine 69-79, New Mexico 81-88, Fresno St. 91-95
941	Abe Lemons, Oklahoma City 1956-73, Tex.-Pan American 74-76, Texas 77-82, Oklahoma City 84-90
932	Eldon Miller, Wittenberg 1963-70, Western Mich. 71-76, Ohio St. 77-86, Northern Iowa 87-96*
925	Bob Knight, Army 1966-71, Indiana 72-96*
908	Harry Miller, Western St. 1953-58, Fresno St. 61-65, Eastern N.M. 66-70, North Texas 71, Wichita St. 72-78, Stephen F. Austin 79-88
884	C. M. Newton, Transylvania 1956-64 and 66-68, Alabama 69-80, Vanderbilt 82-89
876	Bill E. Foster, Bloomsburg 1961-63, Rutgers 64-71, Utah 72-74, Duke 75-80, South Caro. 81-86, Northwestern 87-93
876	Calvin Luther, DePauw 1955-58, Murray St. 59-73, Longwood 82-90, Tenn.-Martin 91-96*

*Active.

MOST SEASONS

No.	Coach, Team and Seasons
48	Phog Allen, Baker 1906-08, Kansas 08-09, Haskell 09, Central Mo. St. 13-19, Kansas 20-56
42	Ed Diddle, Western Ky. 23-64
42	Ray Meyer, DePaul 1943-84
41	Tony Hinkle, Butler 1927-42, 46-70
41	Henry Iba, Northwest Mo. St. 1930-33, Colorado 34, Oklahoma St. 35-70
41	Adolph Rupp, Kentucky 1931-72
40	Marv Harshman, Pacific Lutheran 1946-58, Washington St. 59-71, Washington 72-85
38	Fred Enke, Louisville 1924-25, Arizona 26-61
38	Ralph Miller, Wichita St. 1952-64, Iowa 65-70, Oregon St. 71-89
37	Nat Holman, CCNY 1920-52 and 55-56 and 59-60
37	Norm Sloan, Presbyterian 1952-55, Citadel 57-60, Florida 61-66, North Caro. St. 67-80, Florida 81-89
36	Slats Gill, Oregon St. 1929-64
36	William Reinhart, Oregon 1924-35, Geo. Washington 36-42 and 50-66
36	Glenn Wilkes, Stetson 1958-93
35	Don Haskins, UTEP 1962-96*
35	Cam Henderson, Muskingum 1921-23, Davis & Elkins 24-35, Marshall 36-55
35	Abe Lemons, Oklahoma City 1956-73, Tex.-Pan American 74-76, Texas 77-82, Oklahoma City 84-90
35	Calvin Luther, DePauw 1955-58, Murray St. 59-73, Longwood 82-90, Tenn.-Martin 91-96*
35	Dean Smith, North Caro. 1962-96*
35	Norm Stewart, Northern Iowa 1962-67, Missouri 68-96*
34	Gene Bartow, Central Mo. St. 1962-64, Valparaiso 65-70, Memphis 71-74, Illinois 75, UCLA 76-77, UAB 79-96

No.	Coach, Team and Seasons
34	Gary Colson, Valdosta St. 1959-68, Pepperdine 69-79, New Mexico 81-88, Fresno St. 91-95
34	Lefty Driesell, Davidson 1961-69, Maryland 70-86, James Madison 89-96*
34	Lou Henson, Hardin-Simmons 1963-66, New Mexico St. 67-75, Illinois 76-96
34	Eldon Miller, Wittenberg 1963-70, Western Mich. 71-76, Ohio St. 77-86, Northern Iowa 87-96*
34	Harry Miller, Western St. 1953-58, Fresno St. 61-65, Eastern N. M. 66-70, North Texas 71, Wichita St. 72-78, Stephen F. Austin 79-88

*Active.

MOST SEASONS WITH ONE TEAM

No.	Coach, Team and Seasons
42	Ed Diddle, #Western Ky. 1923-64
42	Ray Meyer, #DePaul 1943-84
41	Tony Hinkle, #Butler 1927-42, 46-70
41	Adolph Rupp, #Kentucky 1931-72
39	Phog Allen, Kansas 1908-09 and 20-56
37	Nat Holman, #CCNY 1920-52 and 55-56 and 59-60
36	Fred Enke, Arizona 1926-61
36	Slats Gill, #Oregon St. 1929-64
36	Henry Iba, Oklahoma St. 1935-70
36	Glenn Wilkes, #Stetson 1958-93
35	Don Haskins, #UTEP 1962-96*
35	Dean Smith, #North Caro. 1962-96*
31	Taps Gallagher, #Niagara 1932-43 and 47-65
31	Cy McClairen, #Bethune-Cookman 1962-66 and 68-93
30	Jack Friel, #Washington St. 1929-58
30	Guy Lewis, #Houston 1957-86
30	Nibs Price, #California 1925-54
29	Pete Carril, Princeton 1968-96
29	Piggy Lambert, #Purdue 1917 and 19-46
29	Harry Rabenhorst, #LSU 1926-42 and 46-57
29	Norm Stewart, Missouri 1968-96*
28	Frank Keaney, #Rhode Island 1921-48
27	Hec Edmundson, Washington 1921-47
27	Frank Keaney, Rhode Island 1922-48
27	Shelby Metcalf, #Texas A&M 1964-90
27	Herbert Read, #Western Mich. 1923-49
27	John Wooden, UCLA 1949-75

*Active. #Has coached only at this school.

MOST 20-WIN SEASONS

No.	Coach, Team and Seasons
29	Dean Smith, North Caro. 1962-96*
24	Jerry Tarkanian, Long Beach St. 1969-73, UNLV 74-92, Fresno St. 96*
23	Adolph Rupp, Kentucky 1931-72
20	Denny Crum, Louisville 1972-96*
20	Lefty Driesell, Davidson 1961-69, Maryland 70-86, James Madison 89-96*
19	Jim Boeheim, Syracuse 1977-96*
19	Bob Knight, Army 1966-71, Indiana 72-96*
18	Lou Carnesecca, St. John's (N.Y.) 1966-70 and 74-92
18	John Chaney, Cheyney 1973-82, Temple 83-96*
18	Ed Diddle, Western Ky. 1923-64
18	Henry Iba, Northwest Mo. St. 1930-33, Colorado 34, Oklahoma St. 35-70
18	Lute Olson, Long Beach St. 1974, Iowa 75-83, Arizona 84-96*
18	John Thompson, Georgetown 1973-96*
18	John Wooden, Indiana St. 1947-48, UCLA 49-75
17	Don Haskins, UTEP 1962-96*
17	Lou Henson, Hardin-Simmons 1963-66, New Mexico St. 67-75, Illinois 76-96
17	Norm Stewart, Northern Iowa 1962-67, Missouri 68-96*
17	Eddie Sutton, Creighton 1970-74, Arkansas 75-85, Kentucky 86-89, Oklahoma St. 1991-96*
16	Gene Bartow, Central Mo. St. 1962-64, Valparaiso 65-70, Memphis 71-74, Illinois 1975, UCLA 76-77, UAB 79-96
15	Cam Henderson, Muskingum 1921-23, Davis & Elkins 24-35, Marshall 36-55
15	Billy Tubbs, Southwestern (Tex.) 1972-73, Lamar 77-80, Oklahoma 81-94, Texas Christian 95-96*
14	Guy Lewis, Houston 1957-86
14	Neil McCarthy, Weber St. 1976-85, New Mexico St. 86-96*
14	Richard "Digger" Phelps, Fordham 1971, Notre Dame 72-91
13	eight tied

*Active.

MOST TEAMS

No.	Coach, Team and Seasons
7	Elmer Ripley, Wagner 1923-25, Georgetown 28-29, 39-43 and 47-49, Yale 30-35, Columbia 44-45, Notre Dame 46, John Carroll 50-51, Army 52-53
7	Bob Vanatta, Central Mo. St. 1943 and 48-50, Southwest Mo. St. 51-53, Army 54, Bradley 55-56, Memphis 57-62, Missouri 63-67, Delta St. 73
6	J. D. Barnett, Lenoir Rhyne 1970, High Point 71, Louisiana Tech 78-79, Va. Commonwealth 80-85, Tulsa 86-91, Northwestern St. 95-96*
6	Gene Bartow, Central Mo. St. 1962-64, Valparaiso 65-70, Memphis 71-74, Illinois 75, UCLA 76-77, UAB 79-96

No.	Coach, Team and Seasons
6	Bill E. Foster, Bloomsburg 1961-63, Rutgers 64-71, Utah 72-74, Duke 75-80, South Caro. 81-83, Northwestern 87-93
6	Robert Hopkins, Prairie View 1965, Alcorn St. 67-69, Xavier (La.) 70-74, Southern U. 85-86, Grambling 87-89, Md.-East. Shore 91-92
6	Ben Jobe, Talladega 1965-67, Alabama St. 68, South Caro. St. 69-73, Denver 79-80, Alabama A&M 83-86, Southern U. 87-96, Tuskegee*
6	Press Maravich, West Va. Wesleyan 1950, Davis & Elkins 51-52; Clemson 57-62, North Caro. St. 65-66, LSU 1967-72, Appalachian St. 73-75
6	Harry Miller, Western St. 1953-58, Fresno St. 61-65, Eastern N. M. 66-70, North Texas 71, Wichita St. 72-78, Stephen F. Austin 79-88
6	Hal Wissel, Trenton St. 1965-67, Lafayette 68-71, Fordham 72-76, Fla. Southern 78-82, N.C.-Charlotte 83-85, Springfield 87-90
5	Ozzie Cowles, Carleton 1925-30, Wis.-River Falls 34-36, Dartmouth 37-43 and 45-46, Michigan 47-48, Minnesota 49-59
5	Don DeVoe, Virginia Tech 1972-76, Wyoming 77-78, Tennessee 79-89, Florida 90, Navy 93-96*
5	Bill C. Foster, Shorter 1963-67, N.C.-Charlotte 71-75, Clemson 76-84, Miami (Fla.) 86-90, Virginia Tech 92-96*
5	Ron Greene, Loyola (La.) 1968-69, New Orleans 70-77, Mississippi St. 78, Murray St. 79-85, Indiana St. 86-89
5	Blair Gullion, Earlham 1928-35, Tennessee 36-38, Cornell 39-42, Connecticut 46-47, Washington (Mo.) 48-59
5	Tates Locke, Army 1964-65, Miami (Ohio) 67-70, Clemson 71-75, Jacksonville 79-81, Indiana St. 91-94
5	John Mauer, Kentucky 1928-30, Miami (Ohio) 31-38, Tennessee 39-47, Army 48-51, Florida 52-60
5	Tom Penders, Tufts 1972-74, Columbia 75-78, Fordham 79-86, Rhode Island 87-88, Texas 89-96*
5	Gordon Stauffer, Washburn 1967, Indiana St. 68-75, IU/PU-Ft. Wayne 76-79, Geneva 80-81, Nicholls St. 82-90
5	Tex Winter, Marquette 1952-53, Kansas St. 54-68, Washington 69-71, Northwestern 74-78, Long Beach St. 79-83

*Active.

Division I Coach of the Year

Season	United Press International	The Associated Press	U.S. Basketball Writers Assn.	National Assn. of Basketball Coaches
1955	Phil Woolpert San Francisco			
1956	Phil Woolpert San Francisco			
1957	Frank McGuire North Caro.			
1958	Tex Winter Kansas St.			
1959	Adolph Rupp Kentucky			Eddie Hickey Marquette
1960	Pete Newell California			Pete Newell California
1961	Fred Taylor Ohio St.			Fred Taylor Ohio St.
1962	Fred Taylor Ohio St.			Fred Taylor Ohio St.

Photo from UTEP sports information

Don Haskins has been at the helm of the UTEP program for 35 years, the second-longest tenure among active Division I coaches. Haskins, who guided UTEP to the 1966 national championship, has won at least 20 games in a season on 17 occasions.

Season	United Press International	The Associated Press	U.S. Basketball Writers Assn.	National Assn. of Basketball Coaches
1963	Ed Jucker Cincinnati		Ed Jucker Cincinnati	
1964	John Wooden UCLA		John Wooden UCLA	
1965	Dave Strack Michigan		Bill van Breda Kolff Princeton	
1966	Adolph Rupp Kentucky		Adolph Rupp Kentucky	
1967	John Wooden UCLA	John Wooden UCLA	John Wooden UCLA	
1968	Guy Lewis Houston	Guy Lewis Houston	Guy Lewis Houston	
1969	John Wooden UCLA	John Wooden UCLA	Maury John Drake	John Wooden UCLA
1970	John Wooden UCLA	John Wooden UCLA	John Wooden UCLA	John Wooden UCLA
1971	Al McGuire Marquette	Al McGuire Marquette	Al McGuire Marquette	Jack Kraft Villanova
1972	John Wooden UCLA	John Wooden UCLA	John Wooden UCLA	John Wooden UCLA
1973	John Wooden UCLA	John Wooden UCLA	John Wooden UCLA	Gene Bartow Memphis
1974	Digger Phelps Notre Dame	Norm Sloan North Caro. St.	Norm Sloan North Caro. St.	Al McGuire Marquette
1975	Bob Knight Indiana	Bob Knight Indiana	Bob Knight Indiana	Bob Knight Indiana
1976	Tom Young Rutgers	Bob Knight Indiana	Bob Knight Indiana	Johnny Orr Michigan
1977	Bob Gaillard San Francisco	Bob Gaillard San Francisco	Eddie Sutton Arkansas	Dean Smith North Caro.
1978	Eddie Sutton Arkansas	Eddie Sutton Arkansas	Ray Meyer DePaul	Bill Foster Duke; Abe Lemons Texas
1979	Bill Hodges Indiana St.	Bill Hodges Indiana St.	Dean Smith North Caro.	Ray Meyer DePaul
1980	Ray Meyer DePaul	Ray Meyer DePaul	Ray Meyer DePaul	Lute Olson Iowa
1981	Ralph Miller Oregon St.	Ralph Miller Oregon St.	Ralph Miller Oregon St.	Ralph Miller Oregon St.; Jack Hartman Kansas St.
1982	Norm Stewart Missouri	Ralph Miller Oregon St.	John Thompson Georgetown	Don Monson Idaho
1983	Jerry Tarkanian UNLV	Guy Lewis Houston	Lou Carnesecca St. John's (N.Y.)	Lou Carnesecca St. John's (N.Y.)
1984	Ray Meyer DePaul	Ray Meyer DePaul	Gene Keady Purdue	Marv Harshman Washington
1985	Lou Carnesecca St. John's (N.Y.)	Bill Frieder Michigan	Lou Carnesecca St. John's (N.Y.)	John Thompson Georgetown
1986	Mike Krzyzewski Duke	Eddie Sutton Kentucky	Dick Versace Bradley	Eddie Sutton Kentucky
1987	John Thompson Georgetown	Tom Davis Iowa	John Chaney Temple	Rick Pitino Providence
1988	John Chaney Temple	John Chaney Temple	John Chaney Temple	John Chaney Temple
1989	Bob Knight Indiana	Bob Knight Indiana	Bob Knight Indiana	P. J. Carlesimo Seton Hall
1990	Jim Calhoun Connecticut	Jim Calhoun Connecticut	Roy Williams Kansas	Jud Heathcote Michigan St.
1991	Rick Majerus Utah	Randy Ayers Ohio St.	Randy Ayers Ohio St.	Mike Krzyzewski Duke
1992	Perry Clark Tulane	Roy Williams Kansas	Perry Clark Tulane	George Raveling Southern Cal
1993	Eddie Fogler Vanderbilt	Eddie Fogler Vanderbilt	Eddie Fogler Vanderbilt	Eddie Fogler Vanderbilt
1994	Norm Stewart Missouri	Norm Stewart Missouri	Charlie Spoonhour St. Louis	Nolan Richardson Arkansas; Gene Keady Purdue
1995	Leonard Hamilton Miami (Fla.)	Kelvin Sampson Oklahoma	Kelvin Sampson Oklahoma	Jim Harrick UCLA
1996	Gene Keady Purdue	Gene Keady Purdue	Gene Keady Purdue	John Calipari Massachusetts

Note: The Naismith Coach of the Year: 1987—Bob Knight, Indiana; 1988—Larry Brown, Kansas; 1989—Mike Krzyzewski, Duke; 1990—Bobby Cremins, Georgia Tech; 1991—Randy Ayers, Ohio St; 1992—Mike Krzyzewski, Duke; 1993—Dean Smith, North Caro.; 1994—Nolan Richardson, Arkansas; 1995—Jim Harrick, UCLA; 1996—John Calipari, Massachusetts.

Division I Head Coaching Changes

Year	Teams	Chngs.	Pct.	1st Yr.	Year	Teams	Chngs.	Pct.	1st Yr.
1950	154	22	14.3	11	1974	234	41	17.5	23
1951	156	28	17.9	15	1975	235	44	18.7	30
1952	159	23	14.5	18	1976	235	34	14.5	20
1953	165	20	12.1	13	1977	245	39	15.9	21
1954	165	12	7.3	7	1978	254	39	15.4	24
1955	165	21	12.7	9	1979	257	53	20.6	28
1956	169	18	10.7	12	1980	261	43	16.5	23
1957	170	18	10.6	9	1981	264	42	15.9	21
1958	174	14	8.0	8	1982	272	37	13.6	20
1959	177	20	11.3	10	1983	274	37	13.5	18
1960	177	23	13.0	15	1984	276	38	13.8	21
1961	176	15	8.5	11	1985	282	26	9.2	15
1962	179	15	8.4	14	1986	283	56	19.8	21
1963	180	24	13.3	15	1987	290	66	22.8	35
1964	180	23	12.8	17	1988	290	39	13.4	16
1965	185	15	8.1	8	1989	293	42	14.3	24
1966	185	24	13.0	20	1990	292	54	18.5	29
1967	186	33	17.7	18	1991	295	41	13.9	16
1968	192	26	13.5	16	1992	298	39	13.1	15
1969	196	29	14.8	19	1993	298	34	11.4	15
1970	197	29	14.7	17	1994	301	33	11.0	17
1971	203	30	14.8	17	1995	302	58	19.2	28
1972	210	37	17.6	21	1996	305	42	13.8	31
1973	217	38	17.5	24					

Division II Coaching Records

Winningest Active Coaches

(Minimum five years as a head coach; includes record at four-year U.S. colleges only.)

BY PERCENTAGE

	Coach, Team	Years	Won	Lost	Pct.
1.	Dave Robbins, Virginia Union	18	451	101	.817
2.	L. Vann Pettaway, Alabama A&M	10	239	68	.779
3.	Gordon Gibbons, Fla. Southern	6	138	41	.771
4.	Pat Douglass, Cal St. Bakersfield	15	347	115	.751
5.	John Kochan, Millersville	13	285	96	.748
6.	Bob Chipman, Washburn	17	398	138	.743
7.	Herb Magee, Phila. Textile	29	618	221	.737
8.	Brian Beaury, St. Rose	10	227	82	.735
9.	Stanley Spirou, New Hamp. Col.	11	250	91	.733
10.	Rick Cooper, West Tex. A&M	9	207	78	.726
11.	John Masi, UC Riverside	17	354	138	.720
12.	Michael Bernard, Norfolk St.	11	233	92	.717
13.	Richard Schmidt, Tampa	15	321	129	.713
14.	Jerry Waters, S.C.-Spartanburg	18	366	151	.708
15.	Greg Jackson, N.C. Central	5	102	42	.708
16.	Tom Galeazzi, LIU-C. W. Post	15	311	129	.707
17.	Gary Stanfield, Drury	5	103	44	.701
18.	Mike Jones, Mississippi Col.	8	152	68	.691
19.	Dale Race, Minn.-Duluth	16	332	154	.683
20.	Richard Sauers, Albany (N.Y.)	40	685	320	.682
21.	Jerry Johnson, LeMoyne-Owen	38	697	326	.681
22.	Dave Boots, South Dak.	14	267	125	.681
23.	Arthur Luptowski, Franklin Pierce	7	140	66	.680
24.	Bob Olson, Northern St.	11	233	111	.677
25.	Ben Jobe, Tuskegee	25	468	228	.672
26.	Greg Walcavich, Edinboro	15	283	138	.672
27.	Jerry Hueser, Neb.-Kearney	26	519	256	.670
28.	Royce Waltman, Indianapolis	9	165	82	.668
29.	Charles Chronister, Bloomsburg	25	450	229	.663
30.	Jerry Schmutte, Morningside	15	277	146	.655
31.	Craig Carse, Mont. St-Billings	5	98	52	.653
32.	Dick Peth, Denver	11	207	111	.651
33.	Leighton McCrary, Grand Canyon	6	114	61	.651
34.	Keith Dickson, St. Anselm	10	195	106	.648
35.	Michael Carey, Salem-Teikyo	8	148	81	.646
36.	Dave Gunther, Bemidji St.	24	431	238	.644
37.	Lonn Reisman, Tarleton St.	8	155	86	.643
38.	Rich Glas, North Dak.	18	323	183	.638
39.	Ron Spry, Paine	16	326	186	.637
40.	Perry Ford, Southwest St.	11	201	116	.634

Coach, Team	Years	Won	Lost	Pct.
41. Ken Bone, Seattle Pacific	7	126	73	.633
42. Jerry Slocum, Gannon	21	401	235	.631
43. Tom Marshall, Cal Poly Pomona	13	214	127	.628
44. Dan McCarrell, Mankato St.	29	495	295	.627
45. Dave Bike, Sacred Heart	18	336	201	.626
46. Herbert Greene, Columbus	17	296	181	.621
47. Greg Kampe, Oakland	12	212	130	.620
48. Dale Layer, Queens (N.C.)	7	122	75	.619
49. Bruce Webster, Bridgeport	31	539	335	.617
50. Lonnie Porter, Regis (Colo.)	19	330	206	.616
51. Gary Elliott, North Ala.	11	190	119	.615
52. Steve Cox, Concord	7	128	80	.615
53. Tom Klusman, Rollins	16	272	172	.613
54. Al Sokaitis, Alas. Fairbanks	9	143	91	.611
55. Rick Scruggs, Gardner-Webb	10	193	124	.609
56. Steve Rives, Delta St.	11	186	120	.608
57. Dick DeLaney, West Chester	9	148	96	.607
58. William Jones, Dist. Columbia	12	199	130	.605
59. Dan Schmotzer, Coker	9	144	95	.603
60. Bill Carter, Tex. A&M-Kingsville	11	185	123	.601
61. Bob Williams, UC Davis	8	134	90	.598
62. Jay Lawson, Bentley	5	83	56	.597
63. Earl Diddle, Eastern N.M.	12	206	140	.595
64. Butch Raymond, St. Cloud St.	26	428	294	.593
65. Steve Hawkins, Quincy	5	83	57	.593

BY VICTORIES

Coach, Team	Wins
1. Jerry Johnson, LeMoyne-Owen	697
2. Richard Sauers, Albany (N.Y.)	685
3. Ed Messbarger, Angelo St.	649
4. Herb Magee, Phila. Textile	618
5. Bruce Webster, Bridgeport	539
6. Jerry Steele, High Point	532
7. Jerry Hueser, Neb.-Kearney	519
8. Dan McCarrell, Mankato St.	495
9. Ben Jobe, Tuskegee	468
10. Arthur McAfee, Morehouse	459
11. Dave Robbins, Virginia Union	451
12. Charles Chronister, Bloomsburg	450
13. Paul Peak, Tex. A&M-Commerce	443
14. Ron Slaymaker, Emporia St	441
15. Richard Meckfessel, Mo.-St. Louis	440
16. Lewis Hill, Francis Marion	434
17. Dave Gunther, Bemidji St.	431
18. Butch Raymond, St. Cloud St.	428
19. Jerry Slocum, Gannon	401
20. Bob Chipman, Washburn	398
21. James Dominey, Valdosta St.	387
22. Robert Pratt, Saginaw Valley	375
23. Jerry Waters, S.C.-Spartanburg	366
24. Oliver Jones, Albany St. (Ga.)	357
25. Jim Seward, Central Okla.	356
26. John Masi, UC Riverside	354
27. Pat Douglass, Cal St. Bakersfield	347
28. Tom Smith, Mo. Western St.	341
29. Dave Bike, Sacred Heart	336
30. Dale Race, Minn.-Duluth	332
31. Lonnie Porter, Regis (Colo.)	330
32. Pat Sullivan, St. Francis (Ill.)	329
33. Ron Spry, Pace	326
34. Rich Glas, North Dak.	323
35. Richard Schmidt, Tampa	321
36. Tom Galeazzi, LIU-C. W. Post	311
37. Dave Schellhase, Moorhead St.	310

Coach, Team	Wins
37. Rodger Goodling, Shippensburg	310
39. Mike Sandifar, Oakland City.	300
40. Herbert Greene, Columbus St.	296
41. Les Wothke, Winona St.	291
42. Dave Yanai, Cal St. Dom. Hills	287
43. John Kochan, Millersville	285
44. Greg Walcavich, Edinboro	283
45. Jerry Schmutte, Morningside	277
46. Terry Brown, Bluefield St.	273
47. Tom Klusman, Rollins	272
48. Lynn Nance, Southwest Baptist	269
48. Ed Murphy, West Ga.	269
50. Jack Margenthaler, SIU-Edwardsville	268
51. Dave Boots, South Dak.	267
52. Denny Alexander, Shepherd.	251
53. Stanley Spirou, New Hamp. Col.	250
54. Gene Iba, Pittsburg St.	240
55. L. Vann Pettaway, Alabama A&M	239
56. Andy Russo, Florida Tech	237
57. Ajac Triplett, Morris Brown	235
57. Arthur Leary, Southern Conn. St.	235
59. Michael Bernard, Norfolk St.	233
59. Bob Olson, Northern St.	233
61. Bert Hammel, Merrimack	232
62. Serge Debari, Assumption	230
63. Brian Beaury, St. Rose	227
64. John Lentz, Lenoir-Rhyne	219
65. Gary Garner, Fort Hays St.	218
66. Tom Marshall, Cal Poly Pomona	214
67. Greg Kampe, Oakland	212
68. Darrell Halloran, Pace	207
69. Rick Cooper, West Tex. A&M	207
69. Dick Peth, Denver	207
71. Earl Diddle, Eastern N.M.	206
72. Tom Wood, Humboldt St.	205
73. Joe Folda, Southern Colo.	204
74. Perry Ford, Southwest St.	201

Winningest Coaches All-Time

(Minimum 10 head coaching seasons in Division II.)

BY PERCENTAGE

Coach (Team coached, tenure)	Years	Won	Lost	Pct.
1. Dave Robbins (Virginia Union 1979-96)*	18	451	101	.817
2. Walter Harris (Phila. Textile 1954-65, 67)	13	240	56	.811
3. Dolph Stanley (Beloit 1946-57)	12	238	56	.810
4. Ed Adams (N.C. Central 1935-36, Tuskegee 37-49, Texas Southern 50-58)	24	645	153	.808
5. Harry Good (Indianapolis 1929-43)	15	194	53	.785
6. L. Vann Pettaway (Alabama A&M 1987-96)*	10	239	68	.779
7. Charles Christian (Norfolk St. 1974-90)	14	318	95	.770
8. John McLendon Jr. (N.C. Central 1941-52, Hampton 53-54, Tennessee St. 55-59, Kentucky St. 64-66, Cleveland St. 67-69)	25	523	165	.760
9. Lucias Mitchell (Alabama St. 1964-67, Kentucky St. 68-75, Norfolk St. 79-81)	15	325	103	.759
10. Pat Douglass (Mont. St.-Billings 1982-87, Cal St. Bakersfield 88-96)*	15	347	115	.751
11. John Kochan (Millersville 1984-96)*	13	285	96	.748
12. Rock Oglesby (Florida A&M 1950-70, 72)	22	386	132	.745
13. Joe Hutton (Hamline 1931-65)	35	590	208	.739
14. Herb Magee (Phila. Textile 1968-96)*	29	618	221	.737
15. Dean Nicholson (Central Wash. 1965-90)	26	609	219	.736
16. Calvin Irvin (Johnson C. Smith 1948-51, North Caro. A&T 55-72)	22	397	144	.734
17. Stanley Spirou (New Hamp. Col. 1986-96)*	11	250	91	.733
18. Garland Pinholster (Oglethorpe 1957-66)	10	180	68	.726
19. John Masi (UC Riverside 1980-96)*	17	354	138	.720
20. Michael Bernard (N.C. Central 1986-91, Norfolk St. 92-96)*	11	233	92	.717
21. Richard Schmidt (Vanderbilt 1980-81, Tampa 84-96)*	15	321	129	.713
22. Ed Jucker (Merchant Marine 1946-47, RPI 49-53, Cincinnati 61-65, Rollins 73-77)	17	266	109	.709
23. Tom Galeazzi (LIU-C.W. Post 1982-96)*	15	311	129	.707
24. Al Shields (Bentley 1964-78)	15	257	107	.706
25. Lou D'Allesandro (New Hamp. Col. 1964-75)	10	183	77	.704
26. Bill Boylan (Monmouth (N.J.) 1957-77)	21	368	155	.704
27. Beryl Shipley (Southwestern La. 1958-73)	16	296	129	.696
28. Ernest Hole (Wooster 1927-58)	32	412	181	.695
29. Sam Cozen (Drexel 1953-68)	16	213	94	.694
30. Barney Steen (Calvin 1954-66)	13	189	84	.692
31. Robert Rainey (Albany St. (Ga.) 1961-72)	12	243	112	.685
32. Dale Race (Milton 1975-79, Minn.-Duluth 85-96)*	16	332	154	.683
33. Danny Rose (Central Mich. 1938-53)	13	163	76	.682
34. Russell Beichly (Akron 1941-59)	19	288	141	.671
35. Jim McDonald (Edinboro 1963-71, 73-75)	12	179	89	.668
36. William Lucas (Central St. 1961-74)	14	241	120	.668
37. Roger Kaiser (West Ga. 1971-90)	20	379	189	.667
38. Fred Hobdy (Grambling 1957-86)	30	571	287	.666
39. Paul Webb (Randolph-Macon 1957-75, Old Dominion 76-85)	29	511	257	.665
40. Ed Martin (South Caro. St. 1956-68, Tennessee St. 69-85)	30	501	253	.664
41. Marlowe Severson (St. Cloud 1959-69, Mankato St. 70-73)	15	250	127	.663
42. Charles Chronister (Bloomsburg 1972-96)*	25	450	229	.663
43. Don Zech (Puget Sound 1969-89)	21	386	197	.662
44. Malcolm Eiken (Buffalo 1947-56)	10	141	72	.662
45. Dave Buss (Wis.-Green Bay 1970-82, Long Beach St. 84, St. Olaf 88-94)	21	381	195	.661
46. Donald Feeley (Sacred Heart 1966-78, Fairleigh Dickinson 81-83)	16	285	148	.658
47. Jim Phelan [Mt. St. Mary's (Md.) 1955-96]*	42	758	400	.655
48. Boyd King (Truman St. 1947-71)	25	377	199	.655
49. Ernie Wheeler (Cal Poly SLO 1973-86, Mont. St.-Billings 89-91)	17	314	166	.654
50. Scotty Robertson (Louisiana Tech 1965-74)	10	162	86	.653
51. Jim Wink (Ferris St. 1960-81)	21	337	179	.653
52. Joseph O'Brien (Assumption 1968-85)	18	322	172	.652
53. Dick Peth (Denver 1986-96)*	11	207	111	.651
54. John Lance (Southwestern Okla. 1919-22, Pittsburg St. 23-63)	45	643	345	.651
55. Ed Steitz (Springfield 1957-66)	10	160	86	.650
56. LeRoy Moore (Prairie View 1954-66)	13	191	103	.650

BY VICTORIES

Coach	Wins
1. Clarence "Big House" Gaines (Winston-Salem 1947-93)	828
2. Jim Phelan*	758
3. Ed Messbarger [Benedictine Heights 1957-60, Dallas 61-63, St. Mary's (Tex.) 63-78, Angelo St. 79-96]*	649
4. Ed Adams	645
5. John Lance	643
6. Herb Magee*	618
7. Dean Nicholson	609
8. Dom Rosselli (Youngstown St. 1941-42 & 47-82)	591
9. Joe Hutton	590
10. Fred Hobdy	571

Coach	Wins
11. Jim Gudger (Western Caro. 1951-69, Tex. A&M-Commerce 70-83)	547
12. Bruce Webster (Bridgeport 1966-96)*	539
13. Harry Miller [Western St. (Colo.) 1953-58, Fresno St. 61-65, Eastern N.M. 66-70, North Tex. St. 71, Wichita St. 72-78, Stephen F. Austin 79-88]	534
14. John McLendon Jr.	523
15. Arad McCutchan (Evansville 1947-77)	514
16. Paul Webb	511
17. Aubrey Bonham (Whittier 1938-43 & 46-68)	510
18. Leo Nicholson (Central Wash. 1930-43 & 46-64)	505
19. Ed Martin	501
19. Robert Vaughan (Elizabeth City St. 1952-86)	501
21. Dan McCarrell (North Park 1968-84, Mankato St. 85-96)*	495
22. Angus Nicoson (Indianapolis 1948-77)	483
23. Bill Detrick (Central Conn. St. 1960-88, Coast Guard 90)	476
24. Hamlet Peterson (Luther 1923-65)	465
25. Arthur McAfee [Lane 1961, Mississippi Val. 62, Lincoln (Mo.) 63, Bishop 64-65, Morehouse 66-96]*	459
25. Burt Kahn (Quinnipiac 1962-91)	459
27. Dave Robbins*	451
28. Charles Chronister*	450
29. J. B. Scearce (North Ga. 1942-43, Cumberland 47, Ga. Southern 48-80)	445
30. Richard Meckfessel [Charleston (S.C.) 1966-79, Mo.-St. Louis 83-96]*	440
31. Tom Villemure (Detroit Business 1967, Grand Valley St. 73-96)	437
32. Dave Gunther [Wayne St. (Neb.) 1968-70, North Dak. 1971-88, Buena Vista 94-95, Bemidji St. 1996*]	431
32. Leonidas Epps (Clark Atlanta 1950-78)	431
34. Butch Raymond (Augsburg 1971-73, Mankato St. 74-84, St. Cloud St. 85-96)*	428
35. Jim Harley (Eckerd 1956-96)	420
36. Irvin Peterson (Neb. Wesleyan 1949-80)	419
37. Tom Feely (St. Thomas 1955-80)	417
38. Ernest Hole	412

Active coaches.

Division III Coaching Records

Winningest Active Coaches

(Minimum five years as a head coach; includes record at four-year U.S. colleges only.)

BY PERCENTAGE

	Coach, Team	Years	Won	Lost	Pct.
1.	Bo Ryan, Wis.-Platteville	12	269	71	.791
2.	Bob Campbell, Western Conn. St.	12	251	76	.768
3.	James Catalano, N.J. Inst. of Tech.	17	355	115	.755
4.	Glenn Van Wieren, Hope	19	358	120	.749
5.	Gerry Mathews, Richard Stockton	10	207	72	.742
6.	Brian Baptiste, Mass.-Dartmouth	13	266	93	.741
7.	Glenn Robinson, Frank. & Marsh.	25	509	178	.741
8.	Joe Nesci, New York U.	8	149	53	.738
9.	Joe Campoli, Ohio Northern	5	81	29	.736
10.	Richard Bihr, Buffalo St.	17	334	122	.732
11.	Harry Sheehy, Williams	13	231	87	.726
12.	Rick Simonds, St. Joseph's (Me.)	16	329	125	.725
13.	Dave Vander Meulen, Wis.-Whitewater	18	357	139	.720
14.	Bosko Djurickovic, Carthage	9	180	70	.720
15.	Charles Brown, Jersey City St.	14	280	115	.709
16.	John Dzik, Cabrini	16	323	133	.708
17.	Bob Gillespie, Ripon	16	266	111	.706
18.	Tom Murphy, Hamilton	26	459	192	.705
19.	Page Moir, Roanoke	7	132	58	.695
20.	Stan Ogrodnik, Trinity (Conn.)	15	247	109	.694
21.	Bob Bessoir, Scranton	24	472	210	.692
22.	Dick Whitmore, Colby	26	439	195	.692
23.	Todd Raridon, Neb. Wesleyan	7	128	57	.692
24.	Jim Todd, Salem St.	11	207	93	.690
25.	Steve Moore, Wooster	15	275	124	.689
26.	Steve Yount, Augustana (Ill.)	6	107	50	.682
27.	Nick Lambros, Hartwick	19	336	159	.679
28.	Bob Ward, St. John Fisher	9	160	76	.678
29.	Tony Shaver, Hampden-Sydney	10	184	88	.676
30.	Terry Glasgow, Monmouth (Ill.)	24	364	176	.674
31.	Marvin Hohenberger, Defiance	31	573	278	.673
32.	Bill Harris, Wheaton (Ill.)	11	213	104	.672
33.	C. J. Woollum, Chris. Newport	12	227	113	.668
34.	Mark Hanson, Gust. Adolphus	6	105	53	.665
35.	Dennis Bridges, Ill. Wesleyan	31	557	289	.658

	Coach, Team	Years	Won	Lost	Pct.
36.	Dick Reynolds, Otterbein	24	427	226	.654
37.	Rudy Marisa, Waynesburg	27	447	238	.653
38.	Steve Fritz, St. Thomas (Minn.)	16	278	151	.648
39.	Steve Larson, Edgewood	10	202	110	.647
40.	Hal Nunnally, Randolph-Macon	21	374	207	.644
41.	Joe Haklin, Kalamazoo	9	150	83	.644
42.	David Hixon, Amherst	19	295	166	.640
43.	John McCloskey, Alvernia	5	88	50	.638
44.	John Stroud, Millsaps	6	100	57	.637
45.	Herb Hilgeman, Rhodes	20	310	178	.635
46.	Randy Lambert, Maryville (Tenn.)	16	259	155	.626
47.	Chuck Mancuso, Mt. St. Vincent	15	239	143	.626
48.	Paul Phillips, Clark (Mass.)	10	166	99	.626
49.	Bill Knapton, Beloit	39	548	329	.625
50.	C. Alan Rowe, Widener	31	504	303	.625
51.	Peter Barry, Coast Guard	14	250	150	.625
52.	Robert Sheldon, Tufts	8	123	74	.624
53.	Bill Fenlon, DePauw	11	175	106	.623
54.	Paul Hogan, Plymouth St.	6	100	62	.617
55.	Bill Nelson, Johns Hopkins	16	255	160	.614
56.	Tom Baker, Ithaca	19	303	192	.612
57.	Lionel Sinn, Central (Iowa)	20	346	223	.608
58.	Mark Edwards, Washington (Mo.)	15	237	154	.606
59.	Cliff Garrison, Hendrix	24	403	264	.604
60.	Jim Smith, St. John's (Minn.)	32	512	340	.601
61.	Larry Robinson, Stillman	15	196	130	.601
62.	Gene Mehaffey, Ohio Wesleyan	28	500	334	.600

BY VICTORIES

	Coach, Team	Wins
1.	Marvin Hohenberger, Defiance	573
2.	Dennis Bridges, Ill. Wesleyan	557
3.	Bill Knapton, Beloit	548
4.	Jim Smith, St. John's (Minn.)	512
5.	Glenn Robinson, Frank. & Marsh.	509
6.	C. Alan Rowe, Widener	504
7.	Gene Mehaffey, Ohio Wesleyan	500
8.	Bob Bessoir, Scranton	472
9.	Tom Murphy, Hamilton	459
10.	Rudy Marisa, Waynesburg	447
11.	Dick Whitmore, Colby	439
12.	Dick Reynolds, Otterbein	427
13.	Jim Burson, Muskingum	423
14.	Cliff Garrison, Hendrix	403
15.	Leon Richardson, William Penn	400
16.	Hal Nunnally, Randolph-Macon	374
17.	Jack Jensen, Guilford	369
18.	Ward Lambert, Salisbury St.	367
19.	Terry Glasgow, Monmouth (Ill.)	364
20.	Glenn Van Wieren, Hope	358
21.	Dave Vander Meulen, Wis.-Whitewater	357
22.	James Catalano, N.J. Inst. of Tech.	355
23.	Lionel Sinn, Central (Iowa)	346
24.	Nick Lambros, Hartwick	336
25.	Richard Bihr, Buffalo St.	334
26.	Rick Simonds, St. Joseph's (Me.)	329
27.	Gary Smith, Redlands	326
28.	John Dzik, Cabrini	323
29.	Tom Finnegan, Washington (Md.)	318
30.	Mike Turner, Albion	313
30.	Lee McKinney, Fontbonne	313
32.	Herb Hilgeman, Rhodes	310
33.	Mike Neer, Rochester	305
34.	Tom Baker, Ithaca	303
35.	John Barr, Grove City	299
36.	John Hill, Heidelberg	296
36.	Mac Petty, Wabash	296
38.	David Hixon, Amherst	295
38.	David Wells, Claremont-M-S.	295

	Coach, Team	Wins
40.	Jack Berkshire, Oglethorpe	287
41.	Gary Morrison, Olivet	284
42.	Charles Brown, Jersey City St.	280
42.	William Sudeck, Case Reserve	280
44.	Steve Fritz, St. Thomas (Minn.)	278
45.	Steve Moore, Wooster	275
46.	Bo Ryan, Wis.-Platteville	269
47.	Mike Beitzel, Hanover	267
48.	Brian Baptiste, Mass.-Dartmouth	266
48.	Bob Gillespie, Ripon	266
50.	Ken Kaufman, Worcester Tech	262
51.	Randy Lambert, Maryville (Tenn.)	259
52.	Bill Nelson, Johns Hopkins	255
53.	Bob Campbell, Western Conn. St.	251
54.	Peter Barry, Coast Guard	250
55.	Stan Ogrodnik, Trinity (Conn.)	247
56.	Jim Walker, Moravian	245
57.	Jeff Gamber, York (Pa.)	244
58.	Bob McVean, Rochester Inst.	242
58.	Bob Gay, MacMurray	242
60.	Chuck Mancuso, Mt. St. Vincent	239
61.	Bob Johnson, Emory & Henry	238
62.	Mark Edwards, Washington (Mo.)	237
63.	Steve Bankson, Baldwin-Wallace	233
64.	Gregory Prechtl, Fredonia St.	232
65.	Harry Sheehy, Williams	231
66.	C. J. Woollum, Chris. Newport	227
67.	Charlie Titus, Mass.-Boston	225
68.	Roger Kindel, FDU-Madison	223
69.	George Palke, Bethel (Minn.)	214
70.	Bill Harris, Wheaton (Ill.)	213
71.	Mike Griffin, Rensselaer	211
72.	James Adams, Rhode Island Col.	208
72.	Jonathon Halpert, Yeshiva	208
74.	Gerry Mathews, Richard Stockton	207
74.	Jim Todd, Salem St.	207
76.	Michael Raffa, Salve Regina	206
77.	Steve Larson, Edgewood	202
77.	Joe Davis, Lynchburg	202

Winningest Coaches All-Time

(Minimum 10 head coaching seasons in Division III.)

BY PERCENTAGE

Coach (Team coached, tenure)	Years	Won	Lost	Pct.
1. Ken Anderson (Wis.-Eau Claire 1969-95)	27	631	152	.806
2. Bo Ryan (Wis.-Platteville 1985-96)*	12	269	71	.791
3. Bob Campbell (Western Conn. St. 1985-96)*	12	251	76	.768
4. Jim Borcherding [Augustana (Ill.) 1970-84]	15	313	100	.758
5. James Catalano (N.J. Inst. of Tech 1980-96)*	17	355	115	.755
6. Glenn Van Wieren (Hope 1978-96)*	19	358	120	.749
7. Gerry Mathews (Richard Stockton 1987-96)*	10	207	72	.742
8. Brian Baptiste (Mass.-Dartmouth 1984-96)*	13	266	93	.741
9. Glenn Robinson (Frank. & Marsh. 1972-96)*	25	509	178	.741
10. Richard Bihr (Buffalo St. 1980-96)*	17	334	122	.732
11. Harry Sheehy (Williams 1984-96)*	13	231	87	.726
12. Rick Simonds [St. Joseph's (Me.) 1980-96]*	16	329	125	.725
13. Dave Vander Meulen (Wis.-Whitewater 1981-96)*18	357	139	.720	
14. Dave Darnall (Eureka 1975-94)	20	383	150	.719
15. Jerry Welsh (Potsdam St. 1969-91, Iona 92-95)	26	502	205	.710
16. Charles Brown (Jersey City St. 1983-96)*	14	280	115	.709
17. John Dzik (Cabrini 1981-96)*	16	323	133	.708
18. Jerry Waters (Sewanee 1979-89, S.C.-Spartanburg 90-96)*	18	366	151	.708
19. Bob Gillespie (Ripon 1981-96)*	16	266	111	.706
20. Tom Murphy (Hamilton 1971-96)*	26	459	192	.705
21. John Reynders (Allegheny 1980-89)	10	180	78	.698
22. Lewis Levick (Wartburg 1966-93)	28	510	225	.694
23. Stan Ogrodnik [Trinity (Conn.) 1982-96]*	15	247	109	.694
24. Dick Whitmore (Colby 1971-96)*	26	439	195	.692
25. Bob Bessoir (Scranton 1973-96)*	24	472	210	.692
26. Jim Todd (Fitchburg St. 1978-79, Salem St. 88-96)*	11	207	93	.690
27. Steve Moore (Muhlenberg 1982-87, Wooster 88-96)*	15	275	124	.689
28. Ed Douma (Alma 1974, Lake Superior St. 75-78, Kent 79-82, N.C.-Greensboro 83-85, Calvin 85-96)	23	419	189	.689
29. Dick Sauers [Albany St. (N.Y.) 1956-87, 89-96]*	40	685	320	.682
30. Jerry Johnson (LeMoyne-Owen 1959-96)*	38	697	326	.681
31. Nick Lambros (Hartwick 1978-96)*	19	336	159	.679
32. Tony Shaver (Hampden-Sydney 1987-96)*	10	184	88	.676
33. Terry Glasgow [Monmouth (Ill.) 1973-96]*	24	364	176	.674
34. C. J. Woollum (Chris. Newport 85-96)*	12	227	113	.668
35. Naylond Hayes (Rust 1970-88)	18	338	169	.667
36. Dennis Bridges (Ill. Wesleyan 1966-96)*	31	557	289	.658
37. Dick Reynolds (Otterbein 1973-96)*	24	427	226	.654

BY VICTORIES

Coach	Wins
1. Jerry Johnson*	697
2. Dick Sauers*	685
3. Ken Anderson (Wis.-Eau Claire 1969-95)	631
4. Dennis Bridges (Ill. Wesleyan 1966-96)*	557
5. Bill Knapton (Beloit 1958-96)*	548
6. Jim Smith [St. John's (Minn.) 1965-96]*	512
7. Lewis Levick	510
8. Glenn Robinson*	509
9. C. Alan Rowe (Widener 1966-96)*	504
10. Jerry Welsh	502
11. Gene Mehaffey (Carson Newman 1968-78, Ohio Wesleyan 80-96)*	500
12. Will Renken (Bloomfield 1948-52, Albright 56-88)	497
13. Bob Bessoir*	472
14. Verne Canfield (Wash. & Lee 1965-95)	460
15. Tom Murphy*	459
16. Dick Whitmore*	439
17. Ollie Gelston (Jersey City St. 1960-67, Montclair St. 1968-91)	429
18. Dick Reynolds*	427
19. Jim Burson (Muskingum 1968-96)*	423
20. Ed Douma (Alma 194, Lake Superior St. 75-78, Kent 79-82, N.C.-Greensboro 83-85, Calvin 85-96)	419
20. Don Smith (Elizabethtown 1955-64 & 73-88, Bucknell 65-72)	413
22. Leon Richardson (Ozarks 1956, Dubuque 58-59, Drury 60-65, William Penn 75-96)*	400

*Active coaches.

COACHING RECORDS

Championships

Division I Championship

1996 Results

FIRST ROUND

Connecticut 68, Colgate 59
Eastern Mich. 75, Duke 60
Mississippi St. 58, Va. Commonwealth 51
Princeton 43, UCLA 41
Boston College 64, Indiana 51
Georgia Tech 90, Austin Peay 79
Temple 61, Oklahoma 43
Cincinnati 66, N.C.-Greensboro 61
Purdue 73, Western Caro. 71
Georgia 81, Clemson 74
Drexel 75, Memphis 63
Syracuse 88, Montana St. 55
Iowa 81, Geo. Washington 79
Arizona 90, Valparaiso 51
Santa Clara 91, Maryland 79
Kansas 92, South Caro. St. 54
Massachusetts 92, Central Fla. 70
Stanford 66, Bradley 58
Arkansas 86, Penn St. 80
Marquette 68, Monmouth (N.J.) 44
North Caro. 83, New Orleans 62
Texas Tech 74, Northern Ill. 73
New Mexico 69, Kansas St. 48
Georgetown 93, Mississippi Val. 56
Kentucky 110, San Jose St. 72
Virginia Tech 61, Wis.-Green Bay 48
Iowa St. 74, California 64
Utah 72, Canisius 43
Louisville 82, Tulsa 80 (ot)
Villanova 92, Portland 58

Texas 80, Michigan 76
Wake Forest 62, Northeast La. 50

SECOND ROUND

Connecticut 95, Eastern Mich. 81
Mississippi St. 63, Princeton 41
Georgia Tech 103, Boston College 89
Cincinnati 78, Temple 65
Georgia 76, Purdue 69
Syracuse 69, Drexel 58
Arizona 87, Iowa 73
Kansas 76, Santa Clara 51
Massachusetts 79, Stanford 74
Arkansas 65, Marquette 56
Texas Tech 92, North Caro. 73
Georgetown 73, New Mexico 62
Kentucky 84, Virginia Tech 60
Utah 73, Iowa St. 67
Louisville 68, Villanova 64
Wake Forest 65, Texas 62

REGIONAL SEMIFINALS

Mississippi St. 60, Connecticut 55
Cincinnati 87, Georgia Tech 70
Syracuse 83, Georgia 81 (ot)
Kansas 83, Arizona 80
Massachusetts 79, Arkansas 63
Georgetown 98, Texas Tech 90
Kentucky 101, Utah 70
Wake Forest 60, Louisville 59

REGIONAL CHAMPIONSHIPS

Mississippi St. 73, Cincinnati 63
Syracuse 60, Kansas 57
Massachusetts 86, Georgetown 62
Kentucky 83, Wake Forest 63

SEMIFINALS

Syracuse 77, Mississippi St. 69
Kentucky 81, Massachusetts 74

CHAMPIONSHIP

Kentucky 76, Syracuse 67

Final Four Box Scores

SEMIFINALS

AT EAST RUTHERFORD, NEW JERSEY
March 30, 1996
Syracuse 77, Mississippi St. 69

Mississippi St.	FG-FGA	FT-FTA	RB	PF	TP
Russell Walters	5- 9	0- 0	6	5	10
Dontaé Jones	6-16	2- 2	6	4	16
Erick Dampier	4- 6	4- 4	14	1	12
Marcus Bullard	4- 9	0- 0	5	2	11
Darryl Wilson	7-16	0- 0	2	4	20
Whit Hughes	0- 0	0- 0	5	0	0
Tyrone Washington	0- 0	0- 0	1	1	0
Bart Hyche	0- 0	0- 0	1	1	0
Team			1		
TOTALS	26-56	6- 6	41	18	69

Syracuse	FG-FGA	FT-FTA	RB	PF	TP
Todd Burgan	6-11	5- 6	7	1	19
John Wallace	6-14	8-10	4	2	21
Otis Hill	7-11	1- 2	2	4	15
Lazarus Sims	3- 5	4- 4	5	2	11
Jason Cipolla	3- 9	2- 2	1	0	9
J. B. Reafsnyder	1- 3	0- 0	2	1	2
Marius Janulis	0- 2	0- 0	0	1	0
Team			0		
TOTALS	26-55	20-24	21	11	77

Half time: Tied at 36. Three-point field goals: Mississippi St. 11-28 (Jones 2-8, Bullard 3-7, Wilson 6-13); Syracuse 5-12 (Burgan 2-4, Wallace 1-1, Sims 1-3, Cipolla 1-3, Janulis 0-1). Officials: Andre Pattillo, Frank Scagliotta, Mike Sanzere. Attendance: 19,229.

Kentucky 81, Massachusetts 74

Kentucky	FG-FGA	FT-FTA	RB	PF	TP
Derek Anderson	1- 3	4- 5	5	4	6
Antoine Walker	5-10	4- 5	6	2	14
Walter McCarty	4- 8	0- 0	10	1	8
Tony Delk	7-16	5- 9	2	2	20
Anthony Epps	3- 6	0- 0	4	1	7
Mark Pope	1- 2	6- 6	3	4	8
Jeff Sheppard	2- 2	3- 4	2	3	7
Wayne Turner	1- 2	0- 0	1	0	2
Ron Mercer	4- 6	0- 1	0	1	9
Allen Edwards	0- 0	0- 0	0	2	0
Team			5		
TOTALS	28-55	22-30	38	20	81

Massachusetts	FG-FGA	FT-FTA	RB	PF	TP
Dana Dingle	4- 6	0- 0	4	3	8
Donta Bright	7-14	1- 2	9	5	15
Marcus Camby	9-18	7- 9	8	4	25
Edgar Padilla	2-10	1- 2	2	5	6
Carmelo Travieso	3- 7	2- 2	4	4	10
Tyrone Weeks	0- 2	1- 2	2	0	1
Charlton Clarke	1- 2	1- 2	1	1	3
Inus Norville	1- 1	0- 0	0	0	2
Rigoberto Nunez	0- 0	0- 0	0	0	0
Giddel Padilla	2- 4	0- 0	1	2	4
Team			4		
TOTALS	29-64	13-19	35	24	74

Half time: Kentucky 36, Massachusetts 28. Three-point field goals: Kentucky 3-9 (Anderson 0-1, McCarty 0-1, Delk 1-4, Epps 1-2, Mercer 1-1); Massachusetts 3-9 (Bright 0-1, Camby 0-1, E. Padilla 1-3, Travieso 2-4). Officials: Ed Hightower, Tom Rucker, Michael Kitts. Attendance: 19,229.

CHAMPIONSHIP

AT EAST RUTHERFORD, NEW JERSEY
April 1, 1996
Kentucky 76, Syracuse 67

Syracuse	FG-FGA	FT-FTA	RB	PF	TP
Todd Burgan	7-10	2- 5	8	5	19
John Wallace	11-19	5- 5	10	5	29
Otis Hill	3- 9	1- 1	10	2	7
Lazarus Sims	2- 5	1- 2	2	2	6
Jason Cipolla	3- 8	0- 0	1	1	6
J. B. Reafsnyder	0- 1	0- 0	4	0	0
Marius Janulis	0- 0	0- 0	2	2	0
Elimu Nelson	0- 0	0- 0	0	0	0
Team			1		
TOTALS	26-52	9-13	38	17	67

Kentucky	FG-FGA	FT-FTA	RB	PF	TP
Derek Anderson	4- 8	1- 1	4	2	11
Antoine Walker	4-12	3- 6	9	2	11
Walter McCarty	2- 6	0- 0	7	3	4
Tony Delk	8-20	1- 2	7	2	24
Anthony Epps	0- 6	0- 0	4	1	0
Mark Pope	1- 6	2- 2	3	3	4
Ron Mercer	8-12	1- 1	2	3	20
Jeff Sheppard	1- 2	0- 1	2	3	2
Allen Edwards	0- 1	0- 0	0	0	0
Team			2		
TOTALS	28-73	8-13	40	19	76

Half time: Kentucky 42, Syracuse 33. Three-point field goals: Syracuse 6-15 (Burgan 3-5, Wallace 2-3, Sims 1-4, Cipolla 0-3); Kentucky 12-27 (Anderson 2-3, Walker 0-1, Delk 7-12, Epps 0-3, Pope 0-2, Mercer 3-4, Sheppard 0-1, Edwards 0-1). Officials: John Clougherty, Scott Thornley, David Libbey. Attendance: 19,229.

Kentucky's Rick Pitino celebrates the Wildcats' national championship title by cutting a piece of the net. Pitino, who guided Kentucky to a third-place finish in 1993, won his first national title.

Photo by Brian Gadbery/NCAA photos

Year-by-Year Results

Season	Champion	Score	Runner-Up	Third Place	Fourth Place
1939	Oregon	46-33	Ohio St.	+ Oklahoma	+ Villanova
1940	Indiana	60-42	Kansas	+ Duquesne	+ Southern Cal
1941	Wisconsin	39-34	Washington St.	+ Pittsburgh	+ Arkansas
1942	Stanford	53-38	Dartmouth	+ Colorado	+ Kentucky
1943	Wyoming	46-34	Georgetown	+ Texas	+ DePaul
1944	Utah	42-40(ot)	Dartmouth	+ Iowa St.	+ Ohio St.
1945	Oklahoma St.	49-45	New York U.	+ Arkansas	+ Ohio St.
1946	Oklahoma St.	43-40	North Caro.	Ohio St.	California
1947	Holy Cross	58-47	Oklahoma	Texas	CCNY
1948	Kentucky	58-42	Baylor	Holy Cross	Kansas St.
1949	Kentucky	46-36	Oklahoma St.	Illinois	Oregon St.
1950	CCNY	71-68	Bradley	North Caro. St.	Baylor
1951	Kentucky	68-58	Kansas St.	Illinois	Oklahoma St.
1952	Kansas	80-63	St. John's (N.Y.)	Illinois	Santa Clara
1953	Indiana	69-68	Kansas	Washington	LSU
1954	La Salle	92-76	Bradley	Penn St.	Southern Cal
1955	San Francisco	77-63	La Salle	Colorado	Iowa
1956	San Francisco	83-71	Iowa	Temple	Southern Meth.
1957	North Caro.	54-53(3ot)	Kansas	San Francisco	Michigan St.
1958	Kentucky	84-72	Seattle	Temple	Kansas St.
1959	California	71-70	West Va.	Cincinnati	Louisville
1960	Ohio St.	75-55	California	Cincinnati	New York U.
1961	Cincinnati	70-65(ot)	Ohio St.	* St. Joseph's (Pa.)	Utah
1962	Cincinnati	71-59	Ohio St.	Wake Forest	UCLA
1963	Loyola (Ill.)	60-58(ot)	Cincinnati	Duke	Oregon St.
1964	UCLA	98-83	Duke	Michigan	Kansas St.
1965	UCLA	91-80	Michigan	Princeton	Wichita St.
1966	UTEP	72-65	Kentucky	Duke	Utah
1967	UCLA	79-64	Dayton	Houston	North Caro.
1968	UCLA	78-55	North Caro.	Ohio St.	Houston
1969	UCLA	92-72	Purdue	Drake	North Caro.
1970	UCLA	80-69	Jacksonville	New Mexico St.	St. Bonaventure
1971	UCLA	68-62	* Villanova	* Western Ky.	Kansas
1972	UCLA	81-76	Florida St.	North Caro.	Louisville
1973	UCLA	87-66	Memphis	Indiana	Providence
1974	North Caro. St.	76-64	Marquette	UCLA	Kansas
1975	UCLA	92-85	Kentucky	Louisville	Syracuse
1976	Indiana	86-68	Michigan	UCLA	Rutgers
1977	Marquette	67-59	North Caro.	UNLV	N.C.-Charlotte
1978	Kentucky	94-88	Duke	Arkansas	Notre Dame
1979	Michigan St.	75-64	Indiana St.	DePaul	Penn
1980	Louisville	59-54	* UCLA	Purdue	Iowa
1981	Indiana	63-50	North Caro.	Virginia	LSU
1982	North Caro.	63-62	Georgetown	+ Houston	+ Louisville
1983	North Caro. St.	54-52	Houston	+ Georgia	+ Louisville
1984	Georgetown	84-75	Houston	+ Kentucky	+ Virginia
1985	Villanova	66-64	Georgetown	+ St. John's (N.Y.)	+* Memphis
1986	Louisville	72-69	Duke	+ Kansas	+ LSU
1987	Indiana	74-73	Syracuse	+UNLV	+ Providence
1988	Kansas	83-79	Oklahoma	+ Arizona	+ Duke
1989	Michigan	80-79(ot)	Seton Hall	+ Duke	+ Illinois
1990	UNLV	103-73	Duke	+ Arkansas	+ Georgia Tech
1991	Duke	72-65	Kansas	+UNLV	+ North Caro.
1992	Duke	71-51	Michigan	+ Cincinnati	+ Indiana
1993	North Caro.	77-71	Michigan	+ Kansas	+ Kentucky
1994	Arkansas	76-72	Duke	+ Arizona	+ Florida
1995	UCLA	89-78	Arkansas	+ North Caro.	+ Oklahoma St.
1996	Kentucky	76-67	Syracuse	+ Massachusetts	+ Mississippi St.

+Tied for third place. *Record later vacated.

Sophomore Ron Mercer was instrumental to Kentucky's national title victory, scoring 29 points in two Final Four appearances, including 20 in the championship game.

Photo by Rich Clarkson/NCAA photos

Season	Site of Finals	Coach of Champion	Outstanding Player Award
1939	Evanston, Ill.	Howard Hobson, Oregon	None Selected
1940	Kansas City, Mo.	Branch McCracken, Indiana	Marvin Huffman, Indiana
1941	Kansas City, Mo.	Harold Foster, Wisconsin	John Kotz, Wisconsin
1942	Kansas City, Mo.	Everett Dean, Stanford	Howard Dallmar, Stanford
1943	New York City	Everett Shelton, Wyoming	Ken Sailors, Wyoming
1944	New York City	Vadal Peterson, Utah	Arnold Ferrin, Utah
1945	New York City	Henry Iba, Oklahoma St.	Bob Kurland, Oklahoma St.
1946	New York City	Henry Iba, Oklahoma St.	Bob Kurland, Oklahoma St.
1947	New York City	Alvin Julian, Holy Cross	George Kaftan, Holy Cross
1948	New York City	Adolph Rupp, Kentucky	Alex Groza, Kentucky
1949	Seattle, Wash.	Adolph Rupp, Kentucky	Alex Groza, Kentucky
1950	New York City	Nat Holman, CCNY	Irwin Dambrot, CCNY
1951	Minneapolis, Minn.	Adolph Rupp, Kentucky	None Selected
1952	Seattle, Wash.	Forrest Allen, Kansas	Clyde Lovellette, Kansas
1953	Kansas City, Mo.	Branch McCracken, Indiana	B. H. Born, Kansas
1954	Kansas City, Mo.	Kenneth Loeffler, La Salle	Tom Gola, La Salle
1955	Kansas City, Mo.	Phil Woolpert, San Francisco	Bill Russell, San Francisco
1956	Evanston, Ill.	Phil Woolpert, San Francisco	Hal Lear, Temple
1957	Kansas City, Mo.	Frank McGuire, North Caro.	Wilt Chamberlain, Kansas

CHAMPIONSHIPS

Photo by Rich Clarkson/NCAA photos

Syracuse's John Wallace scored a tournament-leading 131 points in six games to finish as the championship's leading scorer.

Season	Site of Finals	Coach of Champion	Outstanding Player Award
1958	Louisville, Ky.	Adolph Rupp, Kentucky	Elgin Baylor, Seattle
1959	Louisville, Ky.	Pete Newell, California	Jerry West, West Va.
1960	San Francisco, Calif.	Fred Taylor, Ohio St.	Jerry Lucas, Ohio St.
1961	Kansas City, Mo.	Edwin Jucker, Cincinnati	Jerry Lucas, Ohio St.
1962	Louisville, Ky.	Edwin Jucker, Cincinnati	Paul Hogue, Cincinnati
1963	Louisville, Ky.	George Ireland, Loyola (Ill.)	Art Heyman, Duke
1964	Kansas City, Mo.	John Wooden, UCLA	Walt Hazzard, UCLA
1965	Portland, Ore.	John Wooden, UCLA	Bill Bradley, Princeton
1966	College Park, Md.	Don Haskins, UTEP	Jerry Chambers, Utah
1967	Louisville, Ky.	John Wooden, UCLA	Lew Alcindor, UCLA
1968	Los Angeles, Calif.	John Wooden, UCLA	Lew Alcindor, UCLA
1969	Louisville, Ky.	John Wooden, UCLA	Lew Alcindor, UCLA
1970	College Park, Md.	John Wooden, UCLA	Sidney Wicks, UCLA
1971	Houston, Texas	John Wooden, UCLA	*Howard Porter, Villanova
1972	Los Angeles, Calif.	John Wooden, UCLA	Bill Walton, UCLA
1973	St. Louis, Mo.	John Wooden, UCLA	Bill Walton, UCLA
1974	Greensboro, N.C.	Norm Sloan, North Caro. St.	David Thompson, North Caro. St.
1975	San Diego, Calif.	John Wooden, UCLA	Richard Washington, UCLA
1976	Philadelphia, Pa.	Bob Knight, Indiana	Kent Benson, Indiana
1977	Atlanta, Ga.	Al McGuire, Marquette	Butch Lee, Marquette
1978	St. Louis, Mo.	Joe Hall, Kentucky	Jack Givens, Kentucky
1979	Salt Lake City, Utah	Jud Heathcote, Michigan St.	Earvin Johnson, Michigan St.
1980	Indianapolis, Ind.	Denny Crum, Louisville	Darrell Griffith, Louisville
1981	Philadelphia, Pa.	Bob Knight, Indiana	Isiah Thomas, Indiana
1982	New Orleans, La.	Dean Smith, North Caro.	James Worthy, North Caro.
1983	Albuquerque, N.M.	Jim Valvano, North Caro. St.	Akeem Olajuwon, Houston
1984	Seattle, Wash.	John Thompson, Georgetown	Patrick Ewing, Georgetown
1985	Lexington, Ky.	Rollie Massimino, Villanova	Ed Pinckney, Villanova
1986	Dallas, Texas	Denny Crum, Louisville	Pervis Ellison, Louisville
1987	New Orleans, La.	Bob Knight, Indiana	Keith Smart, Indiana
1988	Kansas City, Mo.	Larry Brown, Kansas	Danny Manning, Kansas
1989	Seattle, Wash.	Steve Fisher, Michigan	Glen Rice, Michigan
1990	Denver, Colo.	Jerry Tarkanian, UNLV	Anderson Hunt, UNLV
1991	Indianapolis, Ind.	Mike Krzyzewski, Duke	Christian Laettner, Duke
1992	Minneapolis, Minn.	Mike Krzyzewski, Duke	Bobby Hurley, Duke
1993	New Orleans, La.	Dean Smith, North Caro.	Donald Williams, North Caro.
1994	Charlotte, N.C.	Nolan Richardson, Arkansas	Corliss Williamson, Arkansas
1995	Seattle, Wash.	Jim Harrick, UCLA	Ed O'Bannon, UCLA
1996	East Rutherford, N.J.	Rick Pitino, Kentucky	Tony Delk, Kentucky

*Later vacated.

LEADING SCORER

Season	Player, Team	G	FG	FT	Pts.	Avg.
1939	Jim Hull, Ohio St.	3	22	14	58	19.3
1940	Howard Engleman, Kansas	3	18	3	39	13.0
1941	John Adams, Arkansas	2	21	6	48	24.0
1942	Jim Pollard, Stanford	2	19	5	43	21.5
	Chet Palmer, Rice	2	20	3	43	21.5
1943	John Hargis, Texas	2	21	17	59	29.5
1944	Aud Brindley, Dartmouth	3	24	4	52	17.3
1945	Bob Kurland, Oklahoma St.	3	30	5	65	21.7
1946	Bob Kurland, Oklahoma St.	3	28	16	72	24.0
1947	George Kaftan, Holy Cross	3	25	13	63	21.0
1948	Alex Groza, Kentucky	3	23	8	54	18.0
1949	Alex Groza, Kentucky	3	31	20	82	27.3
1950	Sam Ranzino, North Caro. St.	3	25	25	75	25.0
1951	Don Sunderlage, Illinois	4	28	27	83	20.8
1952	Clyde Lovellette, Kansas	4	53	35	141	35.3
1953	Bob Houbregs, Washington	4	57	25	139	34.8
1954	Tom Gola, La Salle	5	38	38	114	22.8
1955	Bill Russell, San Francisco	5	49	20	118	23.6
1956	Hal Lear, Temple	5	63	34	160	32.0
1957	Len Rosenbluth, North Caro.	5	53	34	140	28.0
1958	Elgin Baylor, Seattle	5	48	39	135	27.0
1959	Jerry West, West Va.	5	57	46	160	32.0
1960	Oscar Robertson, Cincinnati	4	47	28	122	30.5
1961	Billy McGill, Utah	4	49	21	119	29.8
1962	Len Chappell, Wake Forest	5	45	44	134	26.8
1963	Mel Counts, Oregon St.	5	50	23	123	24.6
1964	Jeff Mullins, Duke	4	50	16	116	29.0
1965	Bill Bradley, Princeton	5	65	47	177	35.4
1966	Jerry Chambers, Utah	4	55	33	143	35.8
1967	Elvin Hayes, Houston	5	57	14	128	25.6
1968	Elvin Hayes, Houston	5	70	27	167	33.4
1969	Rick Mount, Purdue	4	49	24	122	30.5
1970	Austin Carr, Notre Dame	3	68	22	158	52.7
1971	*Jim McDaniels, Western Ky.	5	61	25	147	29.4
	Austin Carr, Notre Dame	3	48	29	125	41.7

Season	Player, Team	G	FG	FT	Pts.	Avg.
1972	Jim Price, Louisville	4	41	21	103	25.8
1973	Ernie DiGregorio, Providence	5	59	10	128	25.6
1974	David Thompson, North Caro. St.	4	38	21	97	24.3
1975	Jim Lee, Syracuse	5	51	17	119	23.8
1976	Scott May, Indiana	5	45	23	113	22.6
1977	Cedric Maxwell, N.C.-Charlotte	5	39	45	123	24.6
1978	Mike Gminski, Duke	5	45	19	109	21.8
1979	Tony Price, Pennsylvania	6	58	26	142	23.7
1980	Joe Barry Carroll, Purdue	6	63	32	158	26.3
1981	Al Wood, North Caro.	5	44	21	109	21.8
1982	Rob Williams, Houston	5	30	28	88	17.6
1983	Dereck Whittenburg, North Caro. St.	6	47	26	120	20.0
1984	Roosevelt Chapman, Dayton	4	35	35	105	26.3
1985	Chris Mullin, St. John's (N.Y.)	5	39	32	110	22.0
1986	Johnny Dawkins, Duke	6	66	21	153	25.5

Season	Player, Team	G	FG	3FG	FT	Pts.	Avg.
1987	Steve Alford, Indiana	6	42	21	33	138	23.0
	Rony Seikaly, Syracuse	6	87	0	32	138	23.0
1988	Danny Manning, Kansas	6	69	2	23	163	27.2
1989	Glen Rice, Michigan	6	75	27	7	184	30.7
1990	Dennis Scott, Georgia Tech	5	51	24	27	153	30.6
1991	Christian Laettner, Duke	6	37	2	49	125	20.8
1992	Christian Laettner, Duke	6	39	7	30	115	19.2
1993	Donald Williams, North Caro.	6	40	22	16	118	19.7
1994	Khalid Reeves, Arizona	5	45	8	39	137	27.4
1995	Corliss Williamson, Arkansas	6	49	0	27	125	20.8
1996	John Wallace, Syracuse	6	47	7	30	131	21.8

*Record later vacated.

HIGHEST SCORING AVERAGE
(Minimum: 50% of maximum tournament games)

Season	Player, Team	G	FG	FT	Pts.	Avg.
1939	Jim Hull, Ohio St.	3	22	14	58	19.3
1940.	Howard Engleman, Kansas	3	18	3	39	13.0
	Bob Kinney, Rice	2	12	2	26	13.0

Season	Player, Team	G	FG	FT	Pts.	Avg.
1941	John Adams, Arkansas	2	21	6	48	24.0
1942	Chet Palmer, Rice	2	19	5	43	21.5
	Jim Pollard, Stanford	2	20	3	43	21.5
1943	John Hargis, Texas	2	21	17	59	29.5
1944	Nick Bozolich, Pepperdine	2	17	11	45	22.5
1945	Dick Wilkins, Oregon	2	19	6	44	22.0
1946	Bob Kurland, Oklahoma St.	3	28	16	72	24.0
1947	George Kaftan, Holy Cross	3	25	13	63	21.0
1948	Jack Nichols, Washington	2	13	13	39	19.5
1949	Alex Groza, Kentucky	3	31	20	82	27.3
1950	Sam Ranzino, North Caro. St.	3	25	25	75	25.0
1951	William Kukoy, North Caro. St.	3	25	19	69	23.0
1952	Clyde Lovellette, Kansas	4	53	35	141	35.3
1953	Bob Houbregs, Washington	4	57	25	139	34.8
1954	John Clune, Navy	3	30	19	79	26.3
1955	Terry Rand, Marquette	3	31	11	73	24.3
1956	Hal Lear, Temple	5	63	34	160	32.0
1957	Wilt Chamberlain, Kansas	4	40	41	121	30.3
1958	Wayne Embry, Miami (Ohio)	3	32	19	83	27.7
1959	Jerry West, West Va.	5	57	46	160	32.0
1960	Jerry West, West Va.	3	35	35	105	35.0
1961	Billy McGill, Utah	4	49	21	119	29.8
1962	Len Chappell, Wake Forest	5	45	44	134	26.8
1963	Barry Kramer, New York U.	3	31	28	100	33.3
1964	Jeff Mullins, Duke	4	50	16	116	29.0
1965	Bill Bradley, Princeton	5	65	47	147	35.4
1966	Jerry Chambers, Utah	4	55	33	143	35.8
1967	Lew Alcindor, UCLA	3	39	28	106	26.5
1968	Elvin Hayes, Houston	5	70	27	167	33.4
1969	Rick Mount, Purdue	4	49	24	122	30.5
1970	Austin Carr, Notre Dame	3	68	22	158	52.7
1971	Austin Carr, Notre Dame	3	48	29	125	41.7
1972	*Dwight Lamar, Southwestern La.	4	41	18	100	33.3
	Jim Price, Louisville	4	41	21	103	25.8
1973	Larry Finch, Memphis	4	34	39	107	26.8
1974	John Shumate, Notre Dame	3	35	16	86	28.7
1975	Adrian Dantley, Notre Dame	3	29	34	92	30.7
1976	Willie Smith, Missouri	3	38	18	94	31.3
1977	Cedric Maxwell, N.C.-Charlotte	5	39	45	123	24.6
1978	Dave Corzine, DePaul	3	33	16	82	27.3
1979	Larry Bird, Indiana St.	5	52	32	136	27.2
1980	Joe Barry Carroll, Purdue	6	63	32	158	26.3
1981	Al Wood, North Caro.	5	44	21	109	21.8
1982	Oliver Robinson, UAB	3	27	12	66	22.0
1983	Greg Stokes, Iowa	3	24	13	61	20.3
1984	Roosevelt Chapman, Dayton	4	35	35	105	26.3
1985	Kenny Walker, Kentucky	3	28	19	75	25.0
1986	David Robinson, Navy	4	35	40	110	27.5

Season	Player, Team	G	FG	3FG	FT	Pts.	Avg.
1987	Fennis Dembo, Wyoming	3	25	11	23	84	28.0
1988	Danny Manning, Kansas	6	69	2	23	163	27.2
1989	Glen Rice, Michigan	6	75	27	7	184	30.7
1990	Bo Kimble, Loyola Marymount	4	51	15	26	143	35.8
1991	Terry Dehere, Seton Hall	4	34	12	17	97	24.3
1992	Jamal Mashburn, Kentucky	4	34	6	22	96	24.0
1993	Calbert Cheaney, Indiana	4	40	3	23	106	26.5
1994	Gary Collier, Tulsa	3	30	13	21	94	31.3
1995	Darryl Wilson, Mississippi St.	3	21	9	22	73	24.3
1996	Allen Iverson, Georgetown	4	38	12	23	111	27.8

*Record later vacated.

CAREER SCORING

Player, Team (Seasons Competed)	G	FG	3FG	FT	Pts.	Avg.
Christian Laettner, Duke (1989-90-91-92)	23	128	9	142	407	17.7
Elvin Hayes, Houston (1966-67-68)	13	152	–	54	358	27.5
Danny Manning, Kansas (1985-86-87-88)	16	140	2	46	328	20.5
Oscar Robertson, Cincinnati (1958-59-60)	10	117	–	90	324	32.4
Glen Rice, Michigan (1986-87-88-89)	13	128	35	17	308	23.7
Lew Alcindor, UCLA (1967-68-69)	12	115	–	74	304	25.3
Bill Bradley, Princeton (1963-64-65)	9	108	–	87	303	33.7
Corliss Williamson, Arkansas (1993-94-95)	15	123	0	57	303	20.2
Austin Carr, Notre Dame (1969-70-71)	7	117	–	55	289	41.3
Juwan Howard, Michigan (1992-93-94)	16	109	1	61	280	17.5

BEST SINGLE-GAME SCORING PERFORMANCES

Player, Team vs. Opponent, Season	Round	FG	3FG	FT	Pts.
Austin Carr, Notre Dame vs. Ohio, 1970	1st	25	–	11	61
Bill Bradley, Princeton vs. Wichita St., 1965	N3d	22	–	14	58
Oscar Robertson, Cincinnati vs. Arkansas, 1958	R3d	21	–	14	56
Austin Carr, Notre Dame vs. Kentucky, 1970	RSF	22	–	8	52
Austin Carr, Notre Dame vs. Texas Christian, 1971	1st	20	–	12	52
David Robinson, Navy vs. Michigan, 1987	1st	22	0	6	50
Elvin Hayes, Houston vs. Loyola (Ill.), 1968	1st	20	–	9	49

Player, Team vs. Opponent, Season	Round	FG	3FG	FT	Pts.
Hal Lear, Temple vs. Southern Methodist, 1956	N3d	17	–	14	48
Austin Carr, Notre Dame vs. Houston, 1971	R3d	17	–	13	47
Dave Corzine, DePaul vs. Louisville, 1978	RSF	18	–	10	46

[Key: 1st–first round; 2nd–second round; RSF–regional semifinal; RF–regional final; R3d--regional third place; N3d–national third place; CH–national championship.]

LEADING REBOUNDER

Season	Player, Team	G	Reb.	Avg.
1951	Bill Spivey, Kentucky	4	65	16.3
1957	John Green, Michigan St.	4	77	19.3
1958	Elgin Baylor, Seattle	5	91	18.2
1959	Jerry West, West Va.	5	73	14.6
1960	Tom Sanders, New York U.	5	83	16.6
1961	Jerry Lucas, Ohio St.	4	73	18.3
1962	Len Chappell, Wake Forest	5	86	17.2
1963	Nate Thurmond, Bowling Green	3	70	23.3
	Vic Rouse, Loyola (Ill.)	5	70	14.0
1964	Paul Silas, Creighton	3	57	19.0
1965	Bill Bradley, Princeton	5	57	11.4
1966	Jerry Chambers, Utah	4	56	14.0
1967	Don May, Dayton	5	82	16.4
1968	Elvin Hayes, Houston	5	97	19.4
1969	Lew Alcindor, UCLA	4	64	16.0
1970	Artis Gilmore, Jacksonville	5	93	18.6
1971	*Clarence Glover, Western Ky.	5	89	17.8
	Sidney Wicks, UCLA	4	52	13.0
1972	Bill Walton, UCLA	4	64	16.0
1973	Bill Walton, UCLA	4	58	14.5
1974	Tom Burleson, North Caro. St.	4	61	15.3
1975	Richard Washington, UCLA	5	60	12.0
1976	Phil Hubbard, Michigan	5	61	12.2
1977	Cedric Maxwell, N.C.-Charlotte	5	64	12.8
1978	Eugene Banks, Duke	5	50	10.0
1979	Larry Bird, Indiana St.	5	67	13.4
1980	Mike Sanders, UCLA	6	60	10.0
1981	Cliff Levingston, Wichita St.	4	53	13.3
1982	Clyde Drexler, Houston	5	42	8.4
1983	Akeem Olajuwon, Houston	5	65	13.0
1984	Akeem Olajuwon, Houston	5	57	11.4
1985	Ed Pinckney, Villanova	6	48	8.0
1986	Pervis Ellison, Louisville	6	57	9.5
1987	Derrick Coleman, Syracuse	6	73	12.2
1988	Danny Manning, Kansas	6	56	9.3
1989	Daryll Walker, Seton Hall	6	58	9.7
1990	Larry Johnson, UNLV	6	75	12.5
1991	Larry Johnson, UNLV	5	51	10.2
1992	Chris Webber, Michigan	6	58	9.7
1993	Chris Webber, Michigan	6	68	11.3
1994	Cherokee Parks, Duke	6	55	9.2
1995	Ed O'Bannon, UCLA	6	54	9.0
1996	Tim Duncan, Wake Forest	4	52	13.0

*Record later vacated.

HIGHEST REBOUNDING AVERAGE

Season	Player, Team	G	Reb.	Avg.
1951	Bill Spivey, Kentucky	4	65	16.3
1957	John Green, Michigan St.	4	77	19.3
1958	Elgin Baylor, Seattle	5	91	18.2
1959	Oscar Robertson, Cincinnati	4	63	15.8
1960	Howard Jolliff, Ohio	3	64	21.3
1961	Jerry Lucas, Ohio St.	4	73	18.3
1962	Mel Counts, Oregon St.	3	53	17.7
1963	Nate Thurmond, Bowling Green	3	70	23.3
1964	Paul Silas, Creighton	3	57	19.0
1965	James Ware, Oklahoma City	3	55	18.3
1966	Elvin Hayes, Houston	3	50	16.7
1967	Don May, Dayton	5	82	16.4
1968	Elvin Hayes, Houston	5	97	19.4
1969	Lew Alcindor, UCLA	4	64	16.0
1970	Artis Gilmore, Jacksonville	5	93	18.6
1971	*Clarence Glover, Western Ky.	5	89	17.8
	Collis Jones, Notre Dame	3	49	16.3
1972	Bill Walton, UCLA	4	64	16.0
1973	Bill Walton, UCLA	4	58	14.5
1974	Marvin Barnes, Providence	3	51	17.0
1975	Mike Franklin, Cincinnati	3	49	16.3
1976	Al Fleming, Arizona	3	39	13.0
1977	Phil Hubbard, Michigan	3	45	15.0
1978	Greg Kelser, Michigan St.	3	37	12.3
1979	Larry Bird, Indiana St.	5	67	13.4
1980	Durand Macklin, LSU	3	31	10.3
1981	Cliff Levingston, Wichita St.	4	53	13.3
1982	Ed Pinckney, Villanova	3	30	10.0

Season	Player, Team	G	Reb.	Avg.
1983	Akeem Olajuwon, Houston	5	65	13.0
1984	*Keith Lee, Memphis	3	37	12.3
	Akeem Olajuwon, Houston	5	57	11.4
1985	Karl Malone, Louisiana Tech	3	40	13.3
1986	David Robinson, Navy	4	47	11.8
1987	Derrick Coleman, Syracuse	6	73	12.2
1988	Pervis Ellison, Louisville	3	33	11.0
1989	Pervis Ellison, Louisville	3	31	10.3
	Stacey King, Oklahoma	3	31	10.3
1990	Dale Davis, Clemson	3	44	14.7
1991	Byron Houston, Oklahoma St.	3	36	12.0
1992	Doug Edwards, Florida St.	3	32	10.7
1993	Chris Webber, Michigan	6	68	11.3
1994	Juwan Howard, Michigan	6	51	12.8
1995	Tim Duncan, Wake Forest	3	43	14.3
1996	Tim Duncan, Wake Forest	4	52	13.0

*Record later vacated.

CAREER REBOUNDING

Player, Team (Seasons Competed)	G	Reb.	Avg.
Elvin Hayes, Houston (1966-67-68)	13	222	17.1
Lew Alcindor, UCLA (1967-68-69)	12	201	16.8
Jerry Lucas, Ohio St. (1960-61-62)	12	197	16.4

Player, Team (Seasons Competed)	G	Reb.	Avg.
Bill Walton, UCLA (1972-73-74)	12	176	14.7
Christian Laettner, Duke (1989-90-91-92)	23	169	7.3
Paul Hogue, Cincinnati (1960-61-62)	12	160	13.3
Sam Lacey, New Mexico St. (1968-69-70)	11	157	14.3
Derrick Coleman, Syracuse (1987-88-89-90)	14	155	11.1
Akeem Olajuwon, Houston (1982-83-84)	15	153	10.2
Patrick Ewing, Georgetown (1982-83-84-85)	18	144	8.0

BEST SINGLE-GAME REBOUNDING PERFORMANCES

Player, Team vs. Opponent, Season	Round	Reb.
Fred Cohen, Temple vs. Connecticut, 1956	RSF	34
Nate Thurmond, Bowling Green vs. Mississippi St., 1963	R3d	31
Jerry Lucas, Ohio St. vs. Kentucky, 1961	RF	30
Toby Kimball, Connecticut vs. St. Joseph's (Pa.), 1965	1st	29
Elvin Hayes, Houston vs. Pacific (Cal.), 1966	R3d	28
Bill Russell, San Francisco vs. Iowa, 1956	CH	27
John Green, Michigan St. vs. Notre Dame, 1957	2nd	27
Paul Silas, Creighton vs. Oklahoma City, 1964	1st	27
Elvin Hayes, Houston vs. Loyola (Ill.), 1968	1st	27
Howard Jolliff, Ohio vs. Georgia Tech, 1960	RSF	26
Phil Hubbard, Michigan vs. Detroit, 1977	RSF	26

[Key: 1st—first round; 2nd—second round; RSF—regional semifinal; RF—regional final; R3d—regional third place; NSF—national semifinal; CH—national championship.]

INDIVIDUAL RECORDS

Single Game

MOST POINTS
61—Austin Carr, Notre Dame vs. Ohio, SE 1st, 1970

MOST POINTS BY TWO TEAMMATES
85—Austin Carr (61) and Collis Jones (24), Notre Dame vs. Ohio, SE 1st, 1970

MOST POINTS BY TWO OPPOSING PLAYERS
96—Austin Carr (52), Notre Dame, and Dan Issel (44), Kentucky, SE RSF, 1970

MOST FIELD GOALS
25—Austin Carr, Notre Dame vs. Ohio, SE 1st, 1970

MOST FIELD GOALS ATTEMPTED
44—Austin Carr, Notre Dame vs. Ohio, SE 1st, 1970

HIGHEST FIELD-GOAL PERCENTAGE (Minimum 11 Made)
100% (11-11)—Kenny Walker, Kentucky vs. Western Ky., SE 2nd, 1986

MOST THREE-POINT FIELD GOALS
11—Jeff Fryer, Loyola Marymount vs. Michigan, West 2nd, 1990

MOST THREE-POINT FIELD GOALS ATTEMPTED
22—Jeff Fryer, Loyola Marymount vs. Arkansas, MW 1st, 1989

HIGHEST THREE-POINT FIELD-GOAL PERCENTAGE (Minimum 7 Made)
100% (7-7)—Sam Cassell, Florida St. vs. Tulane, SE 2nd, 1993

MOST FREE THROWS
23—Bob Carney, Bradley vs. Colorado, MW RSF, 1954; Travis Mays, Texas vs. Georgia, MW 1st, 1990

MOST FREE THROWS ATTEMPTED
27—David Robinson, Navy vs. Syracuse, East 2nd, 1986; Travis Mays, Texas vs. Georgia, MW 1st, 1990

HIGHEST FREE-THROW PERCENTAGE (Minimum 16 Made)
100% (16-16)—Bill Bradley, Princeton vs. St. Joseph's (Pa.), East 1st, 1963; Fennis Dembo, Wyoming vs. UCLA, West 2nd, 1987

MOST REBOUNDS
34—Fred Cohen, Temple vs. Connecticut, East RSF, 1956

MOST ASSISTS
18—Mark Wade, UNLV vs. Indiana, NSF, 1987

MOST BLOCKED SHOTS
11—Shaquille O'Neal, LSU vs. Brigham Young, West 1st, 1992

MOST STEALS
8—Darrell Hawkins, Arkansas vs. Holy Cross, East 1st, 1993; Grant Hill, Duke vs. California, MW 2nd, 1993

Series

(Three-game minimum for averages and percentages)

MOST POINTS
184—Glen Rice, Michigan, 1989 (6 games)

HIGHEST SCORING AVERAGE
52.7—Austin Carr, Notre Dame, 1970 (158 points in 3 games)

MOST FIELD GOALS
75—Glen Rice, Michigan, 1989 (6 games)

MOST FIELD GOALS ATTEMPTED
138—*Jim McDaniels, Western Ky., 1971 (5 games)
137—Elvin Hayes, Houston, 1968 (5 games)

HIGHEST FIELD-GOAL PERCENTAGE (Minimum 5 Made Per Game)
78.8% (26-33)—Christian Laettner, Duke, 1989 (5 games)

MOST THREE-POINT FIELD GOALS
27—Glen Rice, Michigan, 1989 (6 games)

MOST THREE-POINT FIELD GOALS ATTEMPTED
65—Freddie Banks, UNLV, 1987 (5 games)

HIGHEST THREE-POINT FIELD-GOAL PERCENTAGE (Minimum 1.5 Made Per Game)
100% (6-6)—Ranzino Smith, North Caro., 1987 (4 games)

MOST FREE THROWS
55—Bob Carney, Bradley, 1954 (5 games)

MOST FREE THROWS ATTEMPTED
71—Jerry West, West Va., 1959 (5 games)

HIGHEST PERFECT FREE-THROW PERCENTAGE (Minimum 2.5 Made Per Game)
100% (23-23)—Richard Morgan, Virginia, 1989 (4 games)

MOST REBOUNDS
97—Elvin Hayes, Houston, 1968 (5 games)

HIGHEST REBOUND AVERAGE
23.3—Nate Thurmond, Bowling Green, 1963 (70 rebounds in 3 games)

MOST ASSISTS
61—Mark Wade, UNLV, 1987 (5 games)

MOST BLOCKED SHOTS
23—David Robinson, Navy, 1986 (4 games)

MOST STEALS
23—Mookie Blaylock, Oklahoma, 1988 (6 games)

Career

(Two-year minimum for averages and percentages)

MOST POINTS
407—Christian Laettner, Duke, 1989-90-91-92 (23 games)

HIGHEST SCORING AVERAGE (Minimum 6 Games)
41.3—Austin Carr, Notre Dame, 1969-70-71 (289 points in 7 games)

MOST FIELD GOALS
152—Elvin Hayes, Houston, 1966-67-68

MOST FIELD GOALS ATTEMPTED
310—Elvin Hayes, Houston, 1966-67-68

HIGHEST FIELD-GOAL PERCENTAGE (Minimum 70 Made)
68.6% (109-159)—Bill Walton, UCLA, 1972-74

MOST THREE-POINT FIELD GOALS
42—Bobby Hurley, Duke, 1990-91-92-93 (20 games)

MOST THREE-POINT FIELD GOALS ATTEMPTED
103—Anderson Hunt, UNLV, 1989-90-91 (15 games)

HIGHEST THREE-POINT FIELD-GOAL PERCENTAGE
(Minimum 30 made)
56.5% (35-62)—Glen Rice, Michigan, 1986-87-88-89 (13 games)
(Minimum 20 made)
65.0% (26-40)—William Scott, Kansas St., 1987-88 (5 games)

MOST FREE THROWS
142—Christian Laettner, Duke, 1989-90-91-92 (23 games)

MOST FREE THROWS ATTEMPTED
167—Christian Laettner, Duke, 1989-90-91-92 (23 games)

HIGHEST FREE-THROW PERCENTAGE
(Minimum 50 made)
90.6% (87-96)—Bill Bradley, Princeton, 1963-64-65 (9 games)
(Minimum 30 made)
95.7% (45-47), LaBradford Smith, Louisville, 1988-89-90 (8 games)

MOST REBOUNDS
222—Elvin Hayes, Houston, 1966-67-68 (13 games)

HIGHEST REBOUNDING AVERAGE (Minimum 6 Games)
19.7—John Green, Michigan St., 1957-59 (118 rebounds in 6 games)

MOST ASSISTS
145—Bobby Hurley, Duke, 1990-91-92-93 (20 games)

MOST BLOCKED SHOTS
43—Marcus Camby, Massachusetts, 1994-95-96 (11 games)

MOST STEALS
39—Grant Hill, Duke, 1991-92-93-94 (20 games)

MOST GAMES PLAYED
23—Christian Laettner, Duke, 1989-90-91-92

TEAM RECORDS

Single Game

MOST POINTS
149—Loyola Marymount vs. Michigan, West 2nd, 1990

FEWEST POINTS
20—North Caro. vs. Pittsburgh (26), East RF, 1941

LARGEST WINNING MARGIN
69—Loyola (Ill.) (111) vs. Tennessee Tech (42), SE 1st, 1963

SMALLEST WINNING MARGIN
1—120 tied (most recent: two in 1996)

MOST POINTS SCORED BY LOSING TEAM
120—Utah vs. *St. Joseph's (Pa.) (127), N3d, 1961 (4 ot)

MOST FIELD GOALS
52—Iowa vs. Notre Dame, SE R3d, 1970

FEWEST FIELD GOALS
8—Springfield vs. Indiana, East 1st, 1940

MOST FIELD GOALS ATTEMPTED
112—Marshall vs. Southwestern La., MW 1st, 1972

HIGHEST FIELD-GOAL PERCENTAGE
80.0% (28-35)—Oklahoma St. vs. Tulane, SE 2nd, 1992

LOWEST FIELD-GOAL PERCENTAGE
12.7% (8-63)—Springfield vs. Indiana, East RSF, 1940

MOST THREE-POINT FIELD GOALS
21—Loyola Marymount vs. Michigan, West 2nd, 1990

MOST THREE-POINT FIELD GOALS ATTEMPTED
41—Loyola Marymount vs. UNLV, West RF, 1990

HIGHEST THREE-POINT FIELD-GOAL PERCENTAGE (Minimum 7 Made)
88.9% (8-9)—Kansas St. vs. Georgia, West 1st, 1987

MOST FREE THROWS
41—Utah vs. Santa Clara, West R3d, 1960; Navy vs. Syracuse, East 2nd, 1986

MOST FREE THROWS ATTEMPTED
55—UTEP vs. Tulsa, West 1st, 1985

HIGHEST FREE-THROW PERCENTAGE (Minimum 22 Made)
100% (22-22)—Fordham vs. South Caro., East R3d, 1971

MOST REBOUNDS
86—Notre Dame vs. Tennessee Tech, SE 1st, 1958

LARGEST REBOUND MARGIN
42—Notre Dame (86) vs. Tennessee Tech (44), SE 1st, 1958

MOST ASSISTS
36—North Caro. vs. Loyola Marymount, West 2nd, 1988

MOST BLOCKED SHOTS
13—Louisville vs. Illinois, MW RSF, 1989; Brigham Young vs. Virginia, West 1st, 1991

MOST STEALS
19—Providence vs. Austin Peay, SE 2nd, 1987; Connecticut vs. Boston U., East 1st, 1990

MOST PERSONAL FOULS
41—Dayton vs. Illinois, East RSF, 1952

MOST PLAYERS DISQUALIFIED
6—Kansas vs. Notre Dame, MW 1st, 1975

Single Game, Both Teams

MOST POINTS
264—Loyola Marymount (149) vs. Michigan (115), West 2nd, 1990

MOST FIELD GOALS
97—Iowa (52) vs. Notre Dame (45), SE R3d, 1970

MOST FIELD GOALS ATTEMPTED
204—Utah (103) vs. *St. Joseph's (Pa.) (101), N3d, 1961 (4 ot)

MOST THREE-POINT FIELD GOALS
27—Wisconsin (15) vs. Missouri (12), West 2nd, 1994

MOST THREE-POINT FIELD GOALS ATTEMPTED
59—Loyola Marymount (41) vs. UNLV (18), West RF, 1990; North Caro. A&T (31) vs. Arkansas (28), MW 1st, 1994

MOST FREE THROWS
69—Morehead St. (37) vs. Pittsburgh (32), SE 1st, 1957

MOST FREE THROWS ATTEMPTED
105—Iowa (52) vs. Morehead St. (53), MW RSF, 1956

MOST REBOUNDS
134—Marshall (68) vs. *Southwestern La. (66), MW 1st, 1972

MOST ASSISTS
58—UNLV (35) vs. Loyola Marymount (23), West RF, 1990

MOST BLOCKED SHOTS
18—Iowa (10) vs. Duke (8), East 2nd, 1992

MOST STEALS
28—North Caro. A&T (16) vs. Arkansas (12), MW 1st, 1994

MOST PERSONAL FOULS
61—West Va. (32) vs. Manhattan (29), East 1st, 1958; Kentucky (31) vs. Syracuse (30), NSF, 1975

Series

(Three-game minimum for averages and percentages)

MOST POINTS
571—UNLV, 1990 (6 games)

HIGHEST SCORING AVERAGE
105.8—Loyola Marymount, 1990 (423 points in 4 games)

MOST FIELD GOALS
218—UNLV, 1977 (5 games)

MOST FIELD GOALS ATTEMPTED
442—*Western Ky., 1971 (5 games) 441—UNLV, 1977 (6 games)

HIGHEST FIELD-GOAL PERCENTAGE
60.4% (113-187)—North Caro., 1975 (3 games)

MOST THREE-POINT FIELD GOALS
60—Arkansas, 1995 (6 games)

MOST THREE-POINT FIELD GOALS ATTEMPTED
165—Arkansas, 1995 (6 games)

HIGHEST THREE-POINT FIELD-GOAL PERCENTAGE
(Minimum 30 made)
51.9% (40-77)—Kansas, 1993 (5 games)
(Minimum 12 made)
60.9% (14-23)—Indiana, 1995 (3 games)

MOST FREE THROWS
146—Bradley, 1954 (5 games)

MOST FREE THROWS ATTEMPTED
194—Bradley, 1954 (5 games)

HIGHEST FREE-THROW PERCENTAGE
87.0% (47-54)—St. John's (N.Y.), 1969 (3 games)

MOST REBOUNDS
306—Houston, 1968 (5 games)

MOST ASSISTS
143—Kentucky, 1996 (6 games)

MOST BLOCKED SHOTS
37—Massachusetts, 1995 (4 games)

MOST STEALS
72—Oklahoma, 1988 (6 games)

MOST PERSONAL FOULS
150—Pennsylvania, 1979 (6 games)

CH-National championship game
NSF-National semifinal game
N3d-National third-place game
RF-Regional final game
RSF-Regional semifinal game
R3d-Regional third-place game
2nd-Second-round game
1st-First-round game
Op-Opening-round game
East-East region
SE-Southeast/Mideast region
MW-Midwest region
West-West/Far West region

Record later vacated.

Photo by Brian Gadbery/NCAA photos

Massachusetts' Marcus Camby set the career standard for blocked shots in Division I tournament play, amassing a record 43 in 11 games.

CHAMPIONSHIPS

All-Time Division I Tournament Records

RECORD OF EACH TEAM COACH BY COACH
(261 Teams)

	Yrs.	Won	Lost	CH	2D	3d%	4th	RR
AIR FORCE								
Bob Spear (DePauw '41) 60, 62	2	0	2	0	0	0	0	0
TOTAL	2	0	2	0	0	0	0	0
AKRON								
Bob Huggins (West Va. '77) 86	1	0	1	0	0	0	0	0
TOTAL	1	0	1	0	0	0	0	0
ALABAMA*								
C. M. Newton (Kentucky '52) 75, 76	2	1	2	0	0	0	0	0
Wimp Sanderson (North Ala. '59) 82, 83, 84, 85, 86, 87, 89, 90, 91, 92	10	12	10	0	0	0	0	0
David Hobbs (Va. Commonwealth '71) 94, 95	2	2	2	0	0	0	0	0
TOTAL	14	15	14	0	0	0	0	0
UAB								
Gene Bartow (Truman St. '53) 81, 82RR 83, 84, 85, 86, 87, 90, 94	9	6	9	0	0	0	0	1
TOTAL	9	6	9	0	0	0	0	1
ALCORN ST.								
Davey Whitney (Kentucky St. '53) 80, 82, 83, 84	4	3	4	0	0	0	0	0
TOTAL	4	3	4	0	0	0	0	0
APPALACHIAN ST.								
Bobby Cremins (South Caro. '70) 79	1	0	1	0	0	0	0	0
TOTAL	1	0	1	0	0	0	0	0
ARIZONA								
Fred Enke (Minnesota '21) 51	1	0	1	0	0	0	0	0
Fred Snowden [Wayne St. (Mich.) '58] 76RR, 77	2	2	2	0	0	0	0	1
Robert "Lute" Olson (Augsburg '57) 85, 86, 87, 88-T3d, 89, 90, 91, 92, 93, 94-T3d, 95, 96	12	15	12	0	0	2	0	0
TOTAL	15	17	15	0	0	2	0	1
ARIZONA ST.								
Ned Wulk (Wis.-La Crosse '42) 58, 61RR, 62, 63RR, 64, 73, 75RR, 80, 81	9	8	10	0	0	0	0	3
Bill Frieder (Michigan '64) 91, 95	2	3	2	0	0	0	0	0
TOTAL	11	11	12	0	0	0	0	3
ARKANSAS								
Eugene Lambert (Arkansas '29) 45-T3d, 49RR	2	2	2	0	0	1	0	1
Glen Rose (Arkansas '28) 41-T3d, 58	2	1	3	0	0	1	0	0
Eddie Sutton (Oklahoma St. '58) 77, 78-3d, 79RR, 80, 81, 82, 83, 84, 85	9	10	9	0	0	1	0	1
Nolan Richardson (UTEP '65) 88, 89, 90-T3d, 91RR, 92, 93, 94-CH, 95-2d, 96	9	24	8	1	1	1	0	1
TOTAL	22	37	22	1	1	4	0	3
ARK.-LITTLE ROCK								
Mike Newell (Sam Houston St. '73) 86, 89, 90	3	1	3	0	0	0	0	0
TOTAL	3	1	3	0	0	0	0	0
AUBURN								
Sonny Smith (Milligan '58) 84, 85, 86RR, 87, 88	5	7	5	0	0	0	0	1
TOTAL	5	7	5	0	0	0	0	1
AUSTIN PEAY*								
Lake Kelly (Georgia Tech '56) 73, 74, 87	3	2	4	0	0	0	0	0
Dave Loos (Memphis '70) 96	1	0	1	0	0	0	0	0
TOTAL	4	2	5	0	0	0	0	0
BALL ST.								
Steve Yoder (Ill. Wesleyan '62) 81	1	0	1	0	0	0	0	0
Al Brown (Purdue '64) 86	1	0	1	0	0	0	0	0
Rick Majerus (Marquette '70) 89	1	1	1	0	0	0	0	0
Dick Hunsaker (Weber St. '77) 90, 93	2	2	2	0	0	0	0	0
Ray McCallum (Ball St. '83) 95	1	0	1	0	0	0	0	0
TOTAL	6	3	6	0	0	0	0	0
BAYLOR								
R. E. "Bill" Henderson (Howard Payne '25) 46RR, 48-2d, 50-4th	3	3	5	0	1	0	1	1
Gene Iba (Tulsa '63) 88	1	0	1	0	0	0	0	0
TOTAL	4	3	6	0	1	0	1	1

	Yrs.	Won	Lost	CH	2D	3d%	4th	RR
BOISE ST.								
Doran "Bus" Connor (Idaho St. '55) 76	1	0	1	0	0	0	0	0
Bob Dye (Idaho St. '62) 88, 93, 94	3	0	3	0	0	0	0	0
TOTAL	4	0	4	0	0	0	0	0
BOSTON COLLEGE								
Donald Martin (Georgetown '41) 58	1	0	1	0	0	0	0	0
Bob Cousy (Holy Cross '48) 67RR, 68	2	2	2	0	0	0	0	1
Bob Zuffelato (Central Conn. St. '59) 75	1	1	2	0	0	0	0	0
Tom Davis (Wis.-Platteville '60) 81, 82RR	2	5	2	0	0	0	0	1
Gary Williams (Maryland '67) 83, 85	2	3	2	0	0	0	0	0
Jim O'Brien (Boston College '71) 94RR, 96	2	4	2	0	0	0	0	1
TOTAL	10	15	11	0	0	0	0	3
BOSTON U.								
Matt Zunic (Geo. Washington '42) 59RR	1	2	1	0	0	0	0	1
Rick Pitino (Massachusetts '74) 83	1	0	1	0	0	0	0	0
Mike Jarvis (Northeastern '68) 88, 90	2	0	2	0	0	0	0	0
TOTAL	4	2	4	0	0	0	0	1
BOWLING GREEN								
Harold Anderson (Otterbein '24) 59, 62, 63	3	1	4	0	0	0	0	0
Bill Fitch (Coe '54) 68	1	0	1	0	0	0	0	0
TOTAL	4	1	5	0	0	0	0	0
BRADLEY								
Forrest "Forddy" Anderson (Stanford '42) 50-2d, 54-2d	2	6	2	0	2	0	0	0
Bob Vanatta (Central Methodist '45) 55RR	1	2	1	0	0	0	0	1
Dick Versace (Wisconsin '64) 80, 86	2	1	2	0	0	0	0	0
Stan Albeck (Bradley '55) 88	1	0	1	0	0	0	0	0
Jim Molinari (Ill. Wesleyan '77) 96	1	0	1	0	0	0	0	0
TOTAL	7	9	7	0	2	0	0	1
BRIGHAM YOUNG								
Stan Watts (Brigham Young '38) 50RR, 51RR, 57, 65, 69, 71, 72	7	4	10	0	0	0	0	2
Frank Arnold (Idaho St. '56) 79, 80, 81RR	3	3	3	0	0	0	0	1
Ladell Andersen (Utah St. '51) 84, 87, 88	3	2	3	0	0	0	0	0
Roger Reid (Weber St. '67) 90, 91, 92, 93, 95	5	2	5	0	0	0	0	0
TOTAL	18	11	21	0	0	0	0	3
BROWN								
George Allen (West Va. '35) 39RR	1	0	1	0	0	0	0	1
Mike Cingiser (Brown '62) 86	1	0	1	0	0	0	0	0
TOTAL	2	0	2	0	0	0	0	1
BUCKNELL								
Charles Woollum (William & Mary '62) 87, 89	2	0	2	0	0	0	0	0
TOTAL	2	0	2	0	0	0	0	0
BUTLER								
Paul "Tony" Hinkle (Chicago '21) 62	1	2	1	0	0	0	0	0
TOTAL	1	2	1	0	0	0	0	0
CALIFORNIA								
Clarence "Nibs" Price (California '14) 46-4th	1	1	2	0	0	0	1	0
Pete Newell (Loyola Marymount '40) 57RR, 58RR, 59-CH, 60-2d	4	10	3	1	1	0	0	2
Lou Campanelli (Montclair St. '60) 90	1	1	1	0	0	0	0	0
Todd Bozeman (Rhode Island '86) 93, 94, 96	3	2	3	0	0	0	0	0
TOTAL	9	14	9	1	1	0	1	2
UC SANTA BARB.								
Jerry Pimm (Southern Cal '61) 88, 90	2	1	2	0	0	0	0	0
TOTAL	2	1	2	0	0	0	0	0
CAL ST. FULLERTON								
Bob Dye (Idaho St. '62) 78RR	1	2	1	0	0	0	0	1
TOTAL	1	2	1	0	0	0	0	1
CAL ST. LOS ANGELES								
Bob Miller (Occidental '53) 74	1	0	1	0	0	0	0	0
TOTAL	1	0	1	0	0	0	0	0
CAMPBELL								
Billy Lee (Barton '71) 92	1	0	1	0	0	0	0	0
TOTAL	1	0	1	0	0	0	0	0
CANISIUS								
Joseph Curran (Canisius '43) 55RR, 56RR, 57	3	6	3	0	0	0	0	2
John Beilein (Wheeling Jesuit '75) 96	1	0	1	0	0	0	0	0
TOTAL	4	6	4	0	0	0	0	2
CATHOLIC								
John Long (Catholic '28) 44RR	1	0	2	0	0	0	0	1
TOTAL	1	0	2	0	0	0	0	1

	Yrs.	Won	Lost	CH	2D	3d%	4th	RR
CENTRAL FLA.								
Kirk Speraw (Iowa '80) 94, 96	2	0	2	0	0	0	0	0
TOTAL	2	0	2	0	0	0	0	0
CENTRAL MICH.								
Dick Parfitt (Central Mich. '53) 75, 77	2	2	2	0	0	0	0	0
Charlie Coles [Miami (Ohio) '65] 87	1	0	1	0	0	0	0	0
TOTAL	3	2	3	0	0	0	0	0
CHARLESTON (S.C.)								
John Kresse [St. John's (N.Y.) '64] 94	1	0	1	0	0	0	0	0
TOTAL	1	0	1	0	0	0	0	0
CINCINNATI								
George Smith (Cincinnati '35) 58, 59-3d, 60-3d	3	7	3	0	0	2	0	0
Ed Jucker (Cincinnati '40) 61-CH, 62-CH, 63-2d	3	11	1	2	1	0	0	0
Tay Baker (Cincinnati '50) 66	1	0	2	0	0	0	0	0
Gale Catlett (West Va. '63) 75, 76, 77	3	2	3	0	0	0	0	0
Bob Huggins (West Va. '77) 92-T3d, 93RR, 94, 95, 96RR	5	11	5	0	0	1	0	2
TOTAL	15	31	14	2	1	3	0	2
CCNY								
Nat Holman (Savage School of Phys. Ed. '17) 47-4th, 50-CH	2	4	2	1	0	0	1	0
TOTAL	2	4	2	1	0	0	1	0
CLEMSON								
William C. "Bill" Foster (Carson-Newman '58) 80RR	1	3	1	0	0	0	0	1
Cliff Ellis (Florida St. '68) 87, 89, 90	3	3	3	0	0	0	0	0
Rick Barnes (Lenoir Rhyne '77) 96	1	0	1	0	0	0	0	0
TOTAL	5	6	5	0	0	0	0	1
CLEVELAND ST.								
Kevin Mackey (St. Anselm '67) 86	1	2	1	0	0	0	0	0
TOTAL	1	2	1	0	0	0	0	0
COASTAL CARO.								
Russ Bergman (LSU '70) 91, 93	2	0	2	0	0	0	0	0
TOTAL	2	0	2	0	0	0	0	0
COLGATE								
Jack Bruen (Catholic '72) 95, 96	2	0	2	0	0	0	0	0
TOTAL	2	0	2	0	0	0	0	0
COLORADO								
Forrest "Frosty" Cox (Kansas '30) 40RR, 42-T3d, 46RR	3	2	4	0	0	1	0	2
Horace "Bebe" Lee (Stanford '38) 54, 55-3d	2	3	3	0	0	1	0	0
Russell "Sox" Walseth (Colorado '48) 62RR, 63RR, 69	3	3	3	0	0	0	0	2
TOTAL	8	8	10	0	0	2	0	4
COLORADO ST.								
Bill Strannigan (Wyoming '41) 54	1	0	2	0	0	0	0	0
Jim Williams (Utah St. '47) 63, 65, 66, 69RR	4	2	4	0	0	0	0	1
Boyd Grant (Colorado St. '57) 89, 90	2	1	2	0	0	0	0	0
TOTAL	7	3	8	0	0	0	0	1
COLUMBIA								
Gordon Ridings (Oregon '29) 48RR	1	0	2	0	0	0	0	1
Lou Rossini (Columbia '48) 51	1	0	1	0	0	0	0	0
John "Jack" Rohan (Columbia '53) 68	1	2	1	0	0	0	0	0
TOTAL	3	2	4	0	0	0	0	1
CONNECTICUT								
Hugh Greer (Connecticut '26) 51, 54, 56, 57, 58, 59, 60	7	1	8	0	0	0	0	0
George Wigton (Ohio St. '56) 63	1	0	1	0	0	0	0	0
Fred Shabel (Duke '54) 64RR, 65, 67	3	2	3	0	0	0	0	1
Donald "Dee" Rowe (Middlebury '52) 76	1	1	1	0	0	0	0	0
Dom Perno (Connecticut '64) 79	1	0	1	0	0	0	0	0
Jim Calhoun (American Int'l '68) 90RR, 91, 92, 94, 95RR, 96	6	13	6	0	0	0	0	2
TOTAL	19	17	20	0	0	0	0	3
COPPIN ST.								
Ron Mitchell (Edison '84) 90, 93	2	0	2	0	0	0	0	0
TOTAL	2	0	2	0	0	0	0	0
CORNELL								
Royner Greene (Illinois '29) 54	1	0	2	0	0	0	0	0
Mike Dement (East Caro. '76) 88	1	0	1	0	0	0	0	0
TOTAL	2	0	3	0	0	0	0	0
CREIGHTON								
Eddie Hickey (Creighton '27) 41RR	1	1	1	0	0	0	0	1
John "Red" McManus (St. Ambrose '49) 62, 64	2	3	3	0	0	0	0	0
Eddie Sutton (Oklahoma St. '58) 74	1	2	1	0	0	0	0	0
Tom Apke (Creighton '65) 75, 78, 81	3	0	3	0	0	0	0	0
Tony Barone (Duke '68) 89, 91	2	1	2	0	0	0	0	0
TOTAL	9	7	10	0	0	0	0	1
DARTMOUTH								
Osborne "Ozzie" Cowles (Carleton '22) 41RR, 42-2d, 43RR	3	4	3	0	1	0	0	2
Earl Brown (Notre Dame '39) 44-2d	1	2	1	0	1	0	0	0
Alvin "Doggie" Julian (Bucknell '23) 56, 58RR, 59	3	4	3	0	0	0	0	1
TOTAL	7	10	7	0	2	0	0	3
DAVIDSON								
Charles "Lefty" Driesell (Duke '54) 66, 68RR, 69RR	3	5	4	0	0	0	0	2
Terry Holland (Davidson '64) 70	1	0	1	0	0	0	0	0
Bobby Hussey (Appalachian St. '62) 86	1	0	1	0	0	0	0	0
TOTAL	5	5	6	0	0	0	0	2
DAYTON								
Tom Blackburn [Wilmington (Ohio) '31] 52	1	1	1	0	0	0	0	0
Don Donoher (Dayton '54) 65, 66, 67-2d, 69, 70, 74, 84RR, 85	8	11	10	0	1	0	0	1
Jim O'Brien [St. Joseph's (Pa.) '74] 90	1	1	1	0	0	0	0	0
TOTAL	10	13	12	0	1	0	0	1
DELAWARE								
Steve Steinwedel (Mississippi St. '75) 92, 93	2	0	2	0	0	0	0	0
TOTAL	2	0	2	0	0	0	0	0
DEPAUL*								
Ray Meyer (Notre Dame '38) 43-T3d, 53, 56, 59, 60, 65, 76, 78RR, 79-3d, 80, 81, 82, 84	13	14	16	0	0	2	0	1
Joey Meyer (DePaul '71) 85, 86, 87, 88, 89, 91, 92	7	6	7	0	0	0	0	0
TOTAL	20	20	23	0	0	2	0	1
DETROIT								
Robert Calihan (Detroit '40) 62	1	0	1	0	0	0	0	0
Dick Vitale (Seton Hall '62) 77	1	1	1	0	0	0	0	0
Dave "Smokey" Gaines (LeMoyne-Owen '63) 79	1	0	1	0	0	0	0	0
TOTAL	3	1	3	0	0	0	0	0
DRAKE								
Maurice John (Central Mo. St. '41) 69-3d, 70RR, 71RR	3	5	3	0	0	1	0	2
TOTAL	3	5	3	0	0	1	0	2
DREXEL								
Eddie Burke (La Salle '67) 86	1	0	1	0	0	0	0	0
Bill Herrion (Merrimack '81) 94, 95, 96	3	1	3	0	0	0	0	0
TOTAL	4	1	4	0	0	0	0	0
DUKE								
Harold Bradley (Hartwick '34) 55	1	0	1	0	0	0	0	0
Vic Bubas (North Caro. St. '51) 60RR, 63-3d, 64-2d, 66-3d	4	11	4	0	1	2	0	1
William E. "Bill" Foster (Elizabethtown '54) 78-2d, 79, 80RR	3	6	3	0	1	0	0	1
Mike Krzyzewski (Army '69) 84, 85, 86-2d, 87, 88-T3d, 89-T3d, 90-2d, 91-CH, 92-CH, 93, 94-2d, 96	12	39	10	2	3	2	0	0
TOTAL	20	56	18	2	5	4	0	2
DUQUESNE								
Charles "Chick" Davies (Duquesne '34) 40-T3d	1	1	1	0	0	1	0	0
Donald "Dudey" Moore (Duquesne '34) 52RR	1	1	1	0	0	0	0	1
John "Red" Manning (Duquesne '51) 69, 71	2	2	2	0	0	0	0	0
John Cinicola (Duquesne '55) 77	1	0	1	0	0	0	0	0
TOTAL	5	4	5	0	0	1	0	1
EAST CARO.								
Tom Quinn (Marshall '54) 72	1	0	1	0	0	0	0	0
Eddie Payne (Wake Forest '73) 93	1	0	1	0	0	0	0	0
TOTAL	2	0	2	0	0	0	0	0
EAST TENN. ST.								
J. Madison Brooks (Louisiana Tech '37) 68	1	1	2	0	0	0	0	0
Les Robinson (North Caro. St. '64) 89, 90	2	0	2	0	0	0	0	0
Alan LeForce (Cumberland '57) 91, 92	2	1	2	0	0	0	0	0
TOTAL	5	2	6	0	0	0	0	0

	Yrs.	Won	Lost	CH	2D	3d%	4th	RR
EASTERN ILL.								
Rick Samuels (Chadron St. '71) 92	1	0	1	0	0	0	0	0
TOTAL	1	0	1	0	0	0	0	0
EASTERN KY.								
Paul McBrayer (Kentucky '30) 53, 59	2	0	2	0	0	0	0	0
Jim Baechtold (Eastern Ky. '52) 65	1	0	1	0	0	0	0	0
Guy Strong (Eastern Ky. '55) 72	1	0	1	0	0	0	0	0
Ed Byhre [Augustana (S.D.) '66] 79	1	0	1	0	0	0	0	0
TOTAL	5	0	5	0	0	0	0	0
EASTERN MICH.								
Ben Braun (Wisconsin '75) 88, 91, 96	3	3	3	0	0	0	0	0
TOTAL	3	3	3	0	0	0	0	0
EVANSVILLE								
Dick Walters (Illinois St. '69) 82	1	0	1	0	0	0	0	0
Jim Crews (Indiana '76) 89, 92, 93	3	1	3	0	0	0	0	0
TOTAL	4	1	4	0	0	0	0	0
FAIRFIELD								
Mitch Buonaguro (Boston College '75) 86, 87	2	0	2	0	0	0	0	0
TOTAL	2	0	2	0	0	0	0	0
FAIRLEIGH DICKINSON								
Tom Green (Syracuse '71) 85, 88	2	0	2	0	0	0	0	0
TOTAL	2	0	2	0	0	0	0	0
FLORIDA*								
Norm Sloan (North Caro. St. '51) 87, 88, 89	3	3	3	0	0	0	0	0
Lon Kruger (Kansas St. '74) 94-T3d, 95	2	4	2	0	0	1	0	0
TOTAL	5	7	5	0	0	1	0	0
FLORIDA INT'L								
Bob Weltlich (Ohio St. '67) 95	1	0	1	0	0	0	0	0
TOTAL	1	0	1	0	0	0	0	0
FLORIDA ST.								
Hugh Durham (Florida St. '59) 68, 72-2d, 78	3	4	3	0	1	0	0	0
Joe Williams (Southern Methodist '56) 80	1	1	1	0	0	0	0	0
Pat Kennedy (King's (Pa.) '76) 88, 89, 91, 92, 93RR	5	6	5	0	0	0	0	1
TOTAL	9	11	9	0	1	0	0	1
FORDHAM								
John Bach (Fordham '48) 53, 54	2	0	2	0	0	0	0	0
Richard "Digger" Phelps (Rider '63) 71	1	2	1	0	0	0	0	0
Nick Macarchuk (Fairfield '63) 92	1	0	1	0	0	0	0	0
TOTAL	4	2	4	0	0	0	0	0
FRESNO ST.								
Boyd Grant (Colorado St. '61) 81, 82, 84	3	1	3	0	0	0	0	0
TOTAL	3	1	3	0	0	0	0	0
FURMAN								
Joe Williams (Southern Methodist '56) 71, 73, 74, 75, 78	5	1	6	0	0	0	0	0
Eddie Holbrook (Lenoir-Rhyne '62) 80	1	0	1	0	0	0	0	0
TOTAL	6	1	7	0	0	0	0	0
GEORGE MASON								
Ernie Nestor (Alderson-Broaddus '68) 89	1	0	1	0	0	0	0	0
TOTAL	1	0	1	0	0	0	0	0
GEO. WASHINGTON								
Bill Reinhart (Oregon '23) 54, 61	2	0	2	0	0	0	0	0
Mike Jarvis (Northeastern '68) 93, 94, 96	3	3	3	0	0	0	0	0
TOTAL	5	3	5	0	0	0	0	0
GEORGETOWN								
Elmer Ripley (No college) 43-2d	1	2	1	0	1	0	0	0
John Thompson (Providence '64) 75, 76, 79, 80RR, 81, 82-2d, 83, 84-CH, 85-2d, 86, 87RR, 88, 89RR, 90, 91, 92, 94, 95, 96RR	19	34	18	1	2	0	0	4
TOTAL	20	36	19	1	3	0	0	4
GEORGIA*								
Hugh Durham (Florida St. '59) 83-T3d, 85, 87, 90, 91	5	4	5	0	0	1	0	0
Tubby Smith (High Point '73) 96	1	2	1	0	0	0	0	0
TOTAL	6	6	6	0	0	1	0	0
GA. SOUTHERN								
Frank Kerns (Alabama '57) 83, 87, 92	3	0	3	0	0	0	0	0
TOTAL	3	0	3	0	0	0	0	0
GEORGIA ST.								
Bob Reinhart (Indiana '61) 91	1	0	1	0	0	0	0	0
TOTAL	1	0	1	0	0	0	0	0

	Yrs.	Won	Lost	CH	2D	3d%	4th	RR
GEORGIA TECH								
John "Whack" Hyder (Georgia Tech '37) 60RR	1	1	1	0	0	0	0	1
Bobby Cremins (South Caro. '70) 85RR, 86, 87, 88, 89, 90-T3d, 91, 92, 93, 96	10	15	10	0	0	1	0	1
TOTAL	11	16	11	0	0	1	0	2
GONZAGA								
Dan Fitzgerald (Cal St. Los Angeles '65) 95	1	0	1	0	0	0	0	0
TOTAL	1	0	1	0	0	0	0	0
HARDIN-SIMMONS								
Bill Scott (Hardin-Simmons '47) 53, 57	2	0	2	0	0	0	0	0
TOTAL	2	0	2	0	0	0	0	0
HARVARD								
Floyd Stahl (Illinois '26) 46RR	1	0	2	0	0	0	0	1
TOTAL	1	0	2	0	0	0	0	1
HAWAII								
Ephraim "Red" Rocha (Oregon St. '50) 72	1	0	1	0	0	0	0	0
Riley Wallace [Centenary (La.) '64] 94	1	0	1	0	0	0	0	0
TOTAL	2	0	2	0	0	0	0	0
HOFSTRA								
Roger Gaeckler (Gettysburg '65) 76, 77	2	0	2	0	0	0	0	0
TOTAL	2	0	2	0	0	0	0	0
HOLY CROSS								
Alvin "Doggie" Julian (Bucknell '23) 47-CH, 48-3d	2	5	1	1	0	1	0	0
Lester "Buster" Sheary (Catholic '33) 50RR, 53RR	2	2	3	0	0	0	0	2
Roy Leenig [Trinity (Conn.) '42] 56	1	0	1	0	0	0	0	0
George Blaney (Holy Cross '61) 77, 80, 93	3	0	3	0	0	0	0	0
TOTAL	8	7	8	1	0	1	0	2
HOUSTON								
Alden Pasche (Rice '32) 56	1	0	2	0	0	0	0	0
Guy Lewis (Houston '47) 61, 65, 66, 67-3d, 68-4th, 70, 71, 72, 73, 78, 81, 82-T3d, 83-2d, 84-2d	14	26	18	0	2	2	1	0
Pat Foster (Arkansas '61) 87, 90, 92	3	0	3	0	0	0	0	0
TOTAL	18	26	23	0	2	2	1	0
HOUSTON BAPTIST								
Gene Iba (Tulsa '63) 84	1	0	1	0	0	0	0	0
TOTAL	1	0	1	0	0	0	0	0
HOWARD								
A. B. Williamson (North Caro. A&T '68) 81	1	0	1	0	0	0	0	0
Alfred "Butch" Beard (Louisville '72) 92	1	0	1	0	0	0	0	0
TOTAL	2	0	2	0	0	0	0	0
IDAHO								
Don Monson (Idaho '55) 81, 82	2	1	2	0	0	0	0	0
Kermit Davis Jr. (Mississippi St. '82) 89, 90	2	0	2	0	0	0	0	0
TOTAL	4	1	4	0	0	0	0	0
IDAHO ST.								
Steve Belko (Idaho '39) 53, 54, 55, 56	4	2	4	0	0	0	0	0
John Grayson (Oklahoma '38) 57, 58, 59	3	4	5	0	0	0	0	0
John Evans (Idaho '48) 60	1	0	1	0	0	0	0	0
Jim Killingsworth (Northeastern Okla. '48) 74, 77RR	2	2	2	0	0	0	0	1
Jim Boutin (Lewis & Clark '64) 87	1	0	1	0	0	0	0	0
TOTAL	11	8	13	0	0	0	0	1
ILLINOIS								
Doug Mills (Illinois '30) 42RR	1	0	2	0	0	0	0	1
Harry Combes (Illinois '37) 49-3d, 51-3d, 52-3d, 63RR	4	9	4	0	0	3	0	1
Lou Henson (New Mexico St. '55) 81, 83, 84RR, 85, 86, 87, 88, 89-T3d, 90, 93, 94, 95	12	12	12	0	0	1	0	1
TOTAL	17	21	18	0	0	4	0	3
ILLINOIS ST.								
Bob Donewald (Hanover '64) 83, 84, 85	3	2	3	0	0	0	0	0
Bob Bender (Duke '80) 90	1	0	1	0	0	0	0	0
TOTAL	4	2	4	0	0	0	0	0
INDIANA								
Branch McCracken (Indiana '30) 40-CH, 53-CH, 54, 58	4	9	2	2	0	0	0	0
Lou Watson (Indiana '50) 67	1	1	1	0	0	0	0	0
Bob Knight (Ohio St. '62) 73-3d, 75RR, 76-CH, 78, 80, 81-CH, 82, 83, 84RR, 86, 87-CH, 88, 89, 90, 91, 92-T3d, 93RR, 94, 95, 96	20	40	17	3	0	2	0	3
TOTAL	25	50	20	5	0	2	0	3

INDIANA ST.

	Yrs.	Won	Lost	CH	2D	3d%	4th	RR
Bill Hodges (Marian '70) 79-2d	1	4	1	0	1	0	0	0
TOTAL	1	4	1	0	1	0	0	0

IONA*

	Yrs.	Won	Lost	CH	2D	3d%	4th	RR
Jim Valvano (Rutgers '67) 79, 80	2	1	2	0	0	0	0	0
Pat Kennedy [King's (Pa.) '76] 84, 85	2	0	2	0	0	0	0	0
TOTAL	4	1	4	0	0	0	0	0

IOWA

	Yrs.	Won	Lost	CH	2D	3d%	4th	RR
Frank "Bucky" O'Connor (Drake '38) 55-4th, 56-2d	2	5	3	0	1	0	1	0
Ralph Miller (Kansas '42) 70	1	1	1	0	0	0	0	0
Robert "Lute" Olson (Augsburg '57) 79, 80-4th, 81, 82, 83	5	7	6	0	0	0	1	0
George Raveling (Villanova '60) 85, 86	2	0	2	0	0	0	0	0
Tom Davis (Wis.-Platteville '60) 87RR, 88, 89, 91, 92, 93, 96	7	10	7	0	0	0	0	1
TOTAL	17	23	19	0	1	0	2	1

IOWA ST.

	Yrs.	Won	Lost	CH	2D	3d%	4th	RR
Louis Menze (Central Mo. St. '28) 44-T3d	1	1	1	0	0	1	0	0
Johnny Orr (Beloit '49) 85, 86, 88, 89, 92, 93	6	3	6	0	0	0	0	0
Tim Floyd (Louisiana Tech '77) 95, 96	2	2	2	0	0	0	0	0
TOTAL	9	6	9	0	0	1	0	0

JACKSONVILLE

	Yrs.	Won	Lost	CH	2D	3d%	4th	RR
Joe Williams (Southern Methodist '56) 70-2d	1	4	1	0	1	0	0	0
Tom Wasdin (Florida '57) 71, 73	2	0	2	0	0	0	0	0
Tates Locke (Ohio Wesleyan '59) 79	1	0	1	0	0	0	0	0
Bob Wenzel (Rutgers '71) 86	1	0	1	0	0	0	0	0
TOTAL	5	4	5	0	1	0	0	0

JAMES MADISON

	Yrs.	Won	Lost	CH	2D	3d%	4th	RR
Lou Campanelli (Montclair St. '60) 81, 82, 83	3	3	3	0	0	0	0	0
Charles "Lefty" Driesell (Duke '54) 94	1	0	1	0	0	0	0	0
TOTAL	4	3	4	0	0	0	0	0

KANSAS

	Yrs.	Won	Lost	CH	2D	3d%	4th	RR
Forrest C. "Phog" Allen (Kansas '06) 40-2d, 42RR, 52-CH, 53-2d	4	10	3	1	2	0	0	1
Dick Harp (Kansas '40) 57-2d, 60RR	2	4	2	0	1	0	0	1
Ted Owens (Oklahoma '51) 66RR, 67, 71-4th, 74-4th, 75, 78, 81	7	8	9	0	0	0	2	1
Larry Brown (North Caro. '63) 84, 85, 86-T3d, 87, 88-CH	5	14	4	1	0	1	0	0
Roy Williams (North Caro. '72) 90, 91-2d, 92, 93-T3d, 94, 95, 96RR	7	18	7	0	1	1	0	1
TOTAL	25	54	25	2	4	2	2	4

KANSAS ST.

	Yrs.	Won	Lost	CH	2D	3d%	4th	RR
Jack Gardner (Southern Cal '32) 48-4th, 51-2d	2	4	3	0	1	0	1	0
Fred "Tex" Winter (Southern Cal '47) 56, 58-4th, 59RR, 61RR, 64-4th, 68	6	7	9	0	0	0	2	2
Lowell "Cotton" Fitzsimmons (Midwestern St. '55) 70	1	1	1	0	0	0	0	0
Jack Hartman (Oklahoma St. '49) 72RR, 73RR, 75RR, 77, 80, 81RR, 82	7	11	7	0	0	0	0	4
Lon Kruger (Kansas St. '74) 87, 88RR, 89, 90	4	4	4	0	0	0	0	1
Dana Altman (Eastern N.M. '80) 93	1	0	1	0	0	0	0	0
Tom Asbury (Wyoming '67) 96	1	0	1	0	0	0	0	0
TOTAL	22	27	26	0	1	0	3	7

KENTUCKY*

	Yrs.	Won	Lost	CH	2D	3d%	4th	RR
Adolph Rupp (Kansas '23) 42-T3d, 45RR, 48-CH, 49-CH, 51-CH, 52RR, 55, 56RR, 57, 58-CH, 59, 61RR, 62RR, 64, 66-2d, 68RR, 69, 70RR, 71, 72RR	20	30	18	4	1	1	0	9
Joe Hall (Sewanee '51) 73RR, 75-2d, 77RR, 78-CH, 80, 81, 82, 83RR, 84-T3d, 85	10	20	9	1	1	1	0	3
Eddie Sutton (Oklahoma St. '58) 86RR, 87, 88	3	5	3	0	0	0	0	1
Rick Pitino (Massachusetts '74) 92RR, 93-T3d, 94, 95RR, 96-CH	5	17	4	1	0	1	0	2
TOTAL	38	72	34	6	2	3	0	15

LA SALLE

	Yrs.	Won	Lost	CH	2D	3d%	4th	RR
Ken Loeffler (Penn St. '24) 54-CH, 55-2d	2	9	1	1	1	0	0	0
Jim Harding (Iowa '49) 68	1	0	1	0	0	0	0	0
Paul Westhead [St. Joseph's (Pa.) '61] 75, 78	2	0	2	0	0	0	0	0
Dave "Lefty" Ervin (La Salle '68) 80, 83	2	1	2	0	0	0	0	0
Bill "Speedy" Morris [St. Joseph's (Pa.) '73] 88, 89, 90, 92	4	1	4	0	0	0	0	0
TOTAL	11	11	10	1	1	0	0	0

LAFAYETTE

	Yrs.	Won	Lost	CH	2D	3d%	4th	RR
George Davidson (Lafayette '51) 57	1	0	2	0	0	0	0	0
TOTAL	1	0	2	0	0	0	0	0

LAMAR

	Yrs.	Won	Lost	CH	2D	3d%	4th	RR
Billy Tubbs (Lamar '58) 79, 80	2	3	2	0	0	0	0	0
Pat Foster (Arkansas '61) 81, 83	2	2	2	0	0	0	0	0
TOTAL	4	5	4	0	0	0	0	0

LEBANON VALLEY

	Yrs.	Won	Lost	CH	2D	3d%	4th	RR
George "Rinso" Marquette (Lebanon Valley '48) 53	1	1	2	0	0	0	0	0
TOTAL	1	1	2	0	0	0	0	0

LEHIGH

	Yrs.	Won	Lost	CH	2D	3d%	4th	RR
Tom Schneider (Bucknell '69) 85	1	0	1	0	0	0	0	0
Fran McCaffery (Pennsylvania '82) 88	1	0	1	0	0	0	0	0
TOTAL	2	0	2	0	0	0	0	0

LIBERTY

	Yrs.	Won	Lost	CH	2D	3d%	4th	RR
Jeff Meyer (Taylor '76) 94	1	0	1	0	0	0	0	0
TOTAL	1	0	1	0	0	0	0	0

LONG BEACH ST.*

	Yrs.	Won	Lost	CH	2D	3d%	4th	RR
Jerry Tarkanian (Fresno St. '56) 70, 71RR, 72RR, 73	4	7	5	0	0	0	0	2
Dwight Jones (Pepperdine '65) 77	1	0	1	0	0	0	0	0
Seth Greenberg (Fairleigh Dickinson '78) 93, 95	2	0	2	0	0	0	0	0
TOTAL	7	7	8	0	0	0	0	2

LIU-BROOKLYN

	Yrs.	Won	Lost	CH	2D	3d%	4th	RR
Paul Lizzo (Northwest Mo. St. '63) 81, 84	2	0	2	0	0	0	0	0
TOTAL	2	0	2	0	0	0	0	0

LSU

	Yrs.	Won	Lost	CH	2D	3d%	4th	RR
Harry Rabenhorst (Wake Forest '21) 53-4th, 54	2	2	4	0	0	0	1	0
Dale Brown (Minot St. '57) 79, 80RR, 81-4th, 84, 85, 86-T3d, 87RR, 88, 89, 90, 91, 92, 93	13	15	14	0	0	1	1	2
TOTAL	15	17	18	0	0	1	2	2

LOUISIANA TECH

	Yrs.	Won	Lost	CH	2D	3d%	4th	RR
Andy Russo (Lake Forest '70) 84, 85	2	3	2	0	0	0	0	0
Tommy Eagles (Louisiana Tech '71) 87, 89	2	1	2	0	0	0	0	0
Jerry Loyd (LeTourneau '76) 91	1	0	1	0	0	0	0	0
TOTAL	5	4	5	0	0	0	0	0

LOUISVILLE

	Yrs.	Won	Lost	CH	2D	3d%	4th	RR
Bernard "Peck" Hickman (Western Ky. '35) 51, 59-4th, 61, 64, 67	5	5	7	0	0	0	1	0
John Dromo (John Carroll '39) 68	1	1	1	0	0	0	0	0
Denny Crum (UCLA '59) 72-4th, 74, 75-3d, 77, 78, 79, 80-CH, 81, 82-T3d, 83-T3d 84, 86-CH, 88, 89, 90, 92, 93, 94, 95, 96	20	39	20	2	0	3	1	0
TOTAL	26	45	28	2	0	3	2	0

LOYOLA (ILL.)

	Yrs.	Won	Lost	CH	2D	3d%	4th	RR
George Ireland (Notre Dame '36) 63-CH, 64, 66, 68	4	7	3	1	0	0	0	0
Gene Sullivan (Notre Dame '53) 85	1	2	1	0	0	0	0	0
TOTAL	5	9	4	1	0	0	0	0

LOYOLA (LA.)

	Yrs.	Won	Lost	CH	2D	3d%	4th	RR
Jim McCafferty [Loyola (La.) '42] 54, 57	2	0	2	0	0	0	0	0
Jim Harding (Iowa '49) 58	1	0	1	0	0	0	0	0
TOTAL	3	0	3	0	0	0	0	0

LOYOLA (MD.)

	Yrs.	Won	Lost	CH	2D	3d%	4th	RR
Skip Prosser (Merchant Marine '72) 94	1	0	1	0	0	0	0	0
TOTAL	1	0	1	0	0	0	0	0

LOYOLA MARYMOUNT*

	Yrs.	Won	Lost	CH	2D	3d%	4th	RR
William Donovan (Loyola Marymount '50) 61	1	1	1	0	0	0	0	0
Ron Jacobs (Southern Cal '64) 80	1	0	1	0	0	0	0	0
Paul Westhead [St. Joseph's (Pa.) '61] 88, 89, 90RR	3	4	3	0	0	0	0	1
TOTAL	5	5	5	0	0	0	0	1

MANHATTAN

	Yrs.	Won	Lost	CH	2D	3d%	4th	RR
Ken Norton (LIU-Brooklyn '39) 56, 58	2	1	3	0	0	0	0	0
Fran Fraschilla (Brooklyn Col. '80) 93, 95	2	1	2	0	0	0	0	0
TOTAL	4	2	5	0	0	0	0	0

MARIST

	Yrs.	Won	Lost	CH	2D	3d%	4th	RR
Matt Furjanic (Point Park '73) 86	1	0	1	0	0	0	0	0
Dave Magarity [St. Francis (Pa.) '74] 87	1	0	1	0	0	0	0	0
TOTAL	2	0	2	0	0	0	0	0

CHAMPIONSHIPS

	Yrs.	Won	Lost	CH	2D	3d%	4th	RR
MARQUETTE								
Jack Nagle (Marquette '40) 55RR	1	2	1	0	0	0	0	1
Eddie Hickey (Creighton '27) 59, 61	2	1	3	0	0	0	0	0
Al McGuire (St. John's (N.Y.) '51) 68, 69RR, 71, 72, 73, 74-2d, 75, 76RR, 77-CH	9	20	9	1	1	0	0	2
Hank Raymonds (St. Louis '48) 78, 79, 80, 82, 83	5	2	5	0	0	0	0	0
Kevin O'Neill (McGill '79) 93, 94	2	2	2	0	0	0	0	0
Mike Deane (Potsdam St. '74) 96	1	1	1	0	0	0	0	0
TOTAL	20	28	21	1	1	0	0	3
MARSHALL*								
Jule Rivlin (Marshall '40) 56	1	0	1	0	0	0	0	0
Carl Tacy (Davis & Elkins '56) 72	1	0	1	0	0	0	0	0
Rick Huckabay (Louisiana Tech '67) 84, 85, 87	3	0	3	0	0	0	0	0
TOTAL	5	0	5	0	0	0	0	0
MARYLAND*								
H. A. "Bud" Millikan (Oklahoma St. '42) 58	1	2	1	0	0	0	0	0
Charles "Lefty" Driesell (Duke '54) 73RR, 75RR, 80, 81, 83, 84, 85, 86	8	10	8	0	0	0	0	2
Bob Wade (Morgan St. '67) 88	1	1	1	0	0	0	0	0
Gary Williams (Maryland '67) 94, 95, 96	3	4	3	0	0	0	0	0
TOTAL	13	17	13	0	0	0	0	2
MASSACHUSETTS								
Matt Zunic (Geo. Washington '42) 62	1	0	1	0	0	0	0	0
John Calipari (Clarion St. '82) 92, 93, 94, 95RR, 96-T3d	5	11	5	0	0	1	0	1
TOTAL	6	11	6	0	0	1	0	1
MCNEESE ST.								
Steve Welch (Southeastern La. '71) 89	1	0	1	0	0	0	0	0
TOTAL	1	0	1	0	0	0	0	0
MEMPHIS*								
Eugene Lambert (Arkansas '29) 55, 56	2	0	2	0	0	0	0	0
Bob Vanatta (Central Methodist '45) 62	1	0	1	0	0	0	0	0
Gene Bartow (Truman St. '53) 73-2d	1	3	1	0	1	0	0	0
Wayne Yates (Memphis '61) 76	1	0	1	0	0	0	0	0
Dana Kirk (Marshall '60) 82, 83, 84, 85-T3d, 86	5	9	5	0	0	1	0	0
Larry Finch (Memphis '73) 88, 89, 92RR, 93, 95, 96	6	6	6	0	0	0	0	1
TOTAL	16	18	16	0	1	1	0	1
MERCER								
Bill Bibb (Ky. Wesleyan '57) 81, 85	2	0	2	0	0	0	0	0
TOTAL	2	0	2	0	0	0	0	0
MIAMI (FLA.)								
Bruce Hale (Santa Clara '41) 60	1	0	1	0	0	0	0	0
TOTAL	1	0	1	0	0	0	0	0
MIAMI (OHIO)								
Bill Rohr (Ohio Wesleyan '40) 53, 55, 57	3	0	3	0	0	0	0	0
Dick Shrider (Ohio '48) 58, 66	2	1	3	0	0	0	0	0
Tates Locke (Ohio Wesleyan '59) 69	1	1	2	0	0	0	0	0
Darrell Hedric [Miami (Ohio) '55] 71, 73, 78, 84	4	1	4	0	0	0	0	0
Jerry Peirson [Miami (Ohio) '66] 85, 86	2	0	2	0	0	0	0	0
Joby Wright (Indiana '72) 92	1	0	1	0	0	0	0	0
Herb Sendek (Carnegie Mellon '85) 95	1	1	1	0	0	0	0	0
TOTAL	14	4	16	0	0	0	0	0
MICHIGAN#								
Osborne "Ozzie" Cowles (Carleton '22) 48RR	1	1	1	0	0	0	0	1
Dave Strack (Michigan '46) 64-3d, 65-2d, 66RR	3	7	3	0	1	1	0	1
Johnny Orr (Beloit '49) 74RR, 75, 76-2d, 77RR	4	7	4	0	1	0	0	2
Bill Frieder (Michigan '64) 85, 86, 87, 88	4	5	4	0	0	0	0	0
Steve Fisher (Illinois St. '67) 89-CH, 90, 92-2d, 93-2d, 94RR, 95, 96	7	20	6	1	2	0	0	1
TOTAL	19	40	18	1	4	1	0	5
MICHIGAN ST.								
Forrest "Forddy" Anderson (Stanford '42) 57-4th, 59RR	2	3	3	0	0	0	1	1
George "Jud" Heathcote (Washington St. '50) 78RR, 79-CH, 85, 86, 90, 91, 92, 94, 95	9	14	8	1	0	0	0	1
TOTAL	11	17	11	1	0	0	1	2
MIDDLE TENN. ST.								
Jimmy Earle (Middle Tenn. St. '59) 75, 77	2	0	2	0	0	0	0	1
Stan Simpson (Ga. Southern '61) 82	1	1	1	0	0	0	0	0
Bruce Stewart (Jacksonville St. '75) 85, 87, 89	3	1	3	0	0	0	0	0
TOTAL	6	2	6	0	0	0	0	0

	Yrs.	Won	Lost	CH	2D	3d%	4th	RR
MINNESOTA*								
Bill Musselman (Wittenberg '61) 72	1	1	1	0	0	0	0	0
Jim Dutcher (Michigan '55) 82	1	1	1	0	0	0	0	0
Clem Haskins (Western Ky. '67) 89, 90RR, 94, 95	4	6	4	0	0	0	0	1
TOTAL	6	8	6	0	0	0	0	1
MISSISSIPPI								
Bob Weltlich (Ohio St. '67) 81	1	0	1	0	0	0	0	0
TOTAL	1	0	1	0	0	0	0	0
MISSISSIPPI ST.								
James "Babe" McCarthy (Mississippi St. '49) 63	1	1	1	0	0	0	0	0
Richard Williams (Mississippi St. '67) 91, 95, 96-T3d	3	6	3	0	0	1	0	0
TOTAL	4	7	4	0	0	1	0	0
MISSISSIPPI VAL.								
Lafayette Stribling (Mississippi Industrial '57) 86, 92, 96	3	0	3	0	0	0	0	0
TOTAL	3	0	3	0	0	0	0	0
MISSOURI#*								
George Edwards (Missouri '13) 44RR	1	1	1	0	0	0	0	1
Norm Stewart (Missouri '56) 76RR, 78, 80, 81, 82, 83, 86, 87, 88, 89, 90, 92, 93, 94RR, 95	15	12	15	0	0	0	0	2
TOTAL	16	13	16	0	0	0	0	3
MONMOUTH (N.J.)								
Wayne Szoke (Maryland '63) 96	1	0	1	0	0	0	0	0
TOTAL	1	0	1	0	0	0	0	0
MONTANA								
George "Jud" Heathcote (Washington St. '50) 75	1	1	2	0	0	0	0	0
Stew Morrill (Gonzaga '74) 91	1	0	1	0	0	0	0	0
Blaine Taylor (Montana '82) 92	1	0	1	0	0	0	0	0
TOTAL	3	1	4	0	0	0	0	0
MONTANA ST.								
John Breeden (Montana St. '29) 51	1	0	1	0	0	0	0	0
Stu Starner (Minn.-Morris '65) 86	1	0	1	0	0	0	0	0
Mike Durham (Montana St. '79) 96	1	0	1	0	0	0	0	0
TOTAL	3	0	3	0	0	0	0	0
MOREHEAD ST.								
Robert Laughlin (Morehead St. '37) 56, 57, 61	3	3	4	0	0	0	0	0
Wayne Martin (Morehead St. '68) 83, 84	2	1	2	0	0	0	0	0
TOTAL	5	4	6	0	0	0	0	0
MT. ST. MARY'S (MD.)								
Jim Phelan (La Salle '51) 95	1	0	1	0	0	0	0	0
TOTAL	1	0	1	0	0	0	0	0
MURRAY ST.								
Cal Luther (Valparaiso '51) 64, 69	2	0	2	0	0	0	0	0
Steve Newton (Indiana St. '63) 88, 90, 91	3	1	3	0	0	0	0	0
Scott Edgar (Pitt.-Johnstown '78) 92, 95	2	0	2	0	0	0	0	0
TOTAL	7	1	7	0	0	0	0	0
NAVY								
Ben Carnevale (New York U. '38) 47RR, 53, 54RR, 59, 60	5	4	6	0	0	0	0	2
Paul Evans (Ithaca '67) 85, 86RR	2	4	2	0	0	0	0	1
Pete Herrmann (Geneseo St. '70) 87	1	0	1	0	0	0	0	0
Don DeVoe (Ohio St. '64) 94	1	0	1	0	0	0	0	0
TOTAL	9	8	10	0	0	0	0	3
NEBRASKA								
Moe Iba (Oklahoma St. '62) 86	1	0	1	0	0	0	0	0
Danny Nee (St. Mary of the Plains '71) 91, 92, 93, 94	4	0	4	0	0	0	0	0
TOTAL	5	0	5	0	0	0	0	0
NEVADA								
Sonny Allen (Marshall '59) 84, 85	2	0	2	0	0	0	0	0
TOTAL	2	0	2	0	0	0	0	0
UNLV								
Jerry Tarkanian (Fresno St. '56) 75, 76, 77-3d, 83, 84, 85, 86, 87-T3d, 88, 89RR, 90-CH, 91-T3d	12	30	11	1	0	3	0	1
TOTAL	12	30	11	1	0	3	0	1
NEW MEXICO								
Bob King (Iowa '47) 68	1	0	2	0	0	0	0	0
Norm Ellenberger (Butler '55) 74, 78	2	2	2	0	0	0	0	0
Dave Bliss (Cornell '65) 91, 93, 94, 96	4	1	4	0	0	0	0	0
TOTAL	7	3	8	0	0	0	0	0

NEW MEXICO ST.

	Yrs.	Won	Lost	CH	2D	3d%	4th	RR
George McCarty (New Mexico St. '50) 52	1	0	2	0	0	0	0	0
Presley Askew (Southeastern Okla. '30) 59, 60	2	0	2	0	0	0	0	0
Lou Henson (New Mexico St. '55) 67, 68, 69, 70-3d, 71, 75	6	7	7	0	0	1	0	0
Ken Hayes (Northeastern St. '56) 79	1	0	1	0	0	0	0	0
Neil McCarthy (Sacramento St. '65) 90, 91, 92, 93, 94	5	3	5	0	0	0	0	0
TOTAL	15	10	17	0	0	1	0	0

NEW ORLEANS

	Yrs.	Won	Lost	CH	2D	3d%	4th	RR
Benny Dees (Wyoming '58) 87	1	1	1	0	0	0	0	0
Tim Floyd (Louisiana Tech '77) 91, 93	2	0	2	0	0	0	0	0
Tic Price (Virginia Tech '79) 96	1	0	1	0	0	0	0	0
TOTAL	4	1	4	0	0	0	0	0

NEW YORK U.

	Yrs.	Won	Lost	CH	2D	3d%	4th	RR
Howard Cann (New York U. '20) 43RR, 45-2d, 46RR	3	3	4	0	1	0	0	2
Lou Rossini (Columbia '48) 60-4th, 62, 63	3	6	5	0	0	0	1	0
TOTAL	6	9	9	0	1	0	1	2

NIAGARA

	Yrs.	Won	Lost	CH	2D	3d%	4th	RR
Frank Layden (Niagara '55) 70	1	1	2	0	0	0	0	0
TOTAL	1	1	2	0	0	0	0	0

NICHOLLS ST.

	Yrs.	Won	Lost	CH	2D	3d%	4th	RR
Rickey Broussard (Southwestern La. '70) 95	1	0	1	0	0	0	0	0
TOTAL	1	0	1	0	0	0	0	0

NORTH CARO.

	Yrs.	Won	Lost	CH	2D	3d%	4th	RR
Bill Lange (Wittenberg '21) 41RR	1	0	2	0	0	0	0	1
Ben Carnevale (New York U. '38) 46-2d	1	2	1	0	1	0	0	0
Frank McGuire [St. John's (N.Y.) '36] 57-CH, 59	2	5	1	1	0	0	0	0
Dean Smith (Kansas '53) 67-4th, 68-2d, 69-4th, 72-3d, 75, 76, 77-2d, 78, 79, 80, 81-2d, 82-CH, 83RR, 84, 85RR, 86, 87RR, 88RR, 89, 90, 91-T3d, 92, 93-CH, 94, 95-T3d, 96	26	61	26	2	3	3	2	4
TOTAL	30	68	30	3	4	3	2	5

NORTH CARO. A&T

	Yrs.	Won	Lost	CH	2D	3d%	4th	RR
Don Corbett [Lincoln (Mo.) '65] 82, 83, 84, 85, 86, 87, 88	7	0	7	0	0	0	0	0
Jeff Capel (Fayetteville St. '77) 94	1	0	1	0	0	0	0	0
Roy Thomas (Baylor '74) 95	1	0	1	0	0	0	0	0
TOTAL	9	0	9	0	0	0	0	0

N.C.-CHARLOTTE

	Yrs.	Won	Lost	CH	2D	3d%	4th	RR
Lee Rose (Transylvania '58) 77-4th	1	3	2	0	0	0	1	0
Jeff Mullins (Duke '64) 88, 92, 95	3	0	3	0	0	0	0	0
TOTAL	4	3	5	0	0	0	1	0

N.C.-GREENSBORO

	Yrs.	Won	Lost	CH	2D	3d%	4th	RR
Randy Peele (Va. Wesleyan '80) 96	1	0	1	0	0	0	0	0
TOTAL	1	0	1	0	0	0	0	0

NORTH CARO. ST.*

	Yrs.	Won	Lost	CH	2D	3d%	4th	RR
Everett Case (Canterbury 16-18, Wisconsin '23) 50-3d, 51RR, 52, 54, 56	5	6	6	0	0	1	0	1
Press Maravich (Davis & Elkins '41) 65	1	1	1	0	0	0	0	0
Norm Sloan (North Caro. St. '51) 70, 74-CH, 80	3	5	2	1	0	0	0	0
Jim Valvano (Rutgers '67) 82, 83-CH, 85RR, 86RR, 87, 88, 89	7	14	6	1	0	0	0	2
Les Robinson (North Caro. St. '64) 91	1	1	1	0	0	0	0	0
TOTAL	17	27	16	2	0	1	0	3

NORTH TEXAS

	Yrs.	Won	Lost	CH	2D	3d%	4th	RR
Jimmy Gales (Alcorn St. '63) 88	1	0	1	0	0	0	0	0
TOTAL	1	0	1	0	0	0	0	0

NORTHEAST LA.

	Yrs.	Won	Lost	CH	2D	3d%	4th	RR
Mike Vining (Northeast La. '67) 82, 86, 90, 91, 92, 93, 96	7	0	7	0	0	0	0	0
TOTAL	7	0	7	0	0	0	0	0

NORTHEASTERN

	Yrs.	Won	Lost	CH	2D	3d%	4th	RR
Jim Calhoun (American Int'l '66) 81, 82, 84, 85, 86	5	3	5	0	0	0	0	0
Karl Fogel (Colby '68) 87, 91	2	0	2	0	0	0	0	0
TOTAL	7	3	7	0	0	0	0	0

NORTHERN ILL.

	Yrs.	Won	Lost	CH	2D	3d%	4th	RR
John McDougal (Evansville '50) 82	1	0	1	0	0	0	0	0
Jim Molinari (Ill. Wesleyan '77) 91	1	0	1	0	0	0	0	0
Brian Hammel (Bentley '75) 96	1	0	1	0	0	0	0	0
TOTAL	3	0	3	0	0	0	0	0

NORTHERN IOWA

	Yrs.	Won	Lost	CH	2D	3d%	4th	RR
Eldon Miller (Wittenberg '61) 90	1	1	1	0	0	0	0	0
TOTAL	1	1	1	0	0	0	0	0

NOTRE DAME

	Yrs.	Won	Lost	CH	2D	3d%	4th	RR
John Jordan (Notre Dame '35) 53RR, 54RR, 57, 58RR, 60, 63	6	8	6	0	0	0	0	3
Johnny Dee (Notre Dame '46) 65, 69, 70, 71	4	2	6	0	0	0	0	0
Richard "Digger" Phelps (Rider '63) 74, 75, 76, 77, 78-4th, 79RR, 80, 81, 85, 86, 87, 88, 89, 90	14	15	16	0	0	0	1	1
TOTAL	24	25	28	0	0	0	1	4

OHIO

	Yrs.	Won	Lost	CH	2D	3d%	4th	RR
James Snyder (Ohio '41) 60, 61, 64RR, 65, 70, 72, 74	7	3	8	0	0	0	0	1
Danny Nee (St. Mary of the Plains '71) 83, 85	2	1	2	0	0	0	0	0
Larry Hunter (Ohio '71) 94	1	0	1	0	0	0	0	0
TOTAL	10	4	11	0	0	0	0	1

OHIO ST.

	Yrs.	Won	Lost	CH	2D	3d%	4th	RR
Harold Olsen (Wisconsin '17) 39-2d, 44-T3d, 45-T3d, 46-3d	4	6	4	0	1	3	0	0
William H. H. "Tippy" Dye (Ohio St. '37) 50RR	1	1	1	0	0	0	0	0
Fred Taylor (Ohio St. '50) 60-CH, 61-2d, 62-2d, 68-3d, 71RR	5	14	4	1	2	1	0	1
Eldon Miller (Wittenberg '61) 80, 82, 83, 85	4	3	4	0	0	0	0	0
Gary Williams (Maryland '67) 87	1	1	1	0	0	0	0	0
Randy Ayers [Miami (Ohio) '78] 90, 91, 92RR	3	6	3	0	0	0	0	0
TOTAL	18	31	17	1	3	4	0	3

OKLAHOMA

	Yrs.	Won	Lost	CH	2D	3d%	4th	RR
Bruce Drake (Oklahoma '29) 39-T3d, 43RR, 47-2d	3	4	3	0	1	1	0	1
Dave Bliss (Cornell '65) 79	1	1	1	0	0	0	0	0
Billy Tubbs (Lamar '58) 83, 84, 85RR, 86, 87, 88-2d, 89, 90, 92	9	15	9	0	1	0	0	1
Kelvin Sampson (N.C.-Pembroke '78) 95, 96	2	0	2	0	0	0	0	0
TOTAL	15	20	15	0	2	1	0	2

OKLAHOMA CITY

	Yrs.	Won	Lost	CH	2D	3d%	4th	RR
Doyle Parrack (Oklahoma St. '45) 52, 53, 54, 55	4	1	5	0	0	0	0	0
A. E. "Abe" Lemons (Oklahoma City '49) 56RR, 57RR 63, 64, 65, 66, 73	7	7	8	0	0	0	0	2
TOTAL	11	8	13	0	0	0	0	2

OKLAHOMA ST.

	Yrs.	Won	Lost	CH	2D	3d%	4th	RR
Henry Iba [Westminster (Mo.) '28] 45-CH, 46-CH, 49-2d, 51-4th, 53RR, 54RR, 58RR, 65RR	8	15	7	2	1	0	1	4
Paul Hansen (Oklahoma City '50) 83	1	0	1	0	0	0	0	0
Eddie Sutton (Oklahoma St. '58) 91, 92, 93, 94, 95-T3d	5	10	5	0	0	1	0	0
TOTAL	14	25	13	2	1	1	1	4

OLD DOMINION

	Yrs.	Won	Lost	CH	2D	3d%	4th	RR
Paul Webb (William & Mary '51) 80, 82, 85	3	0	3	0	0	0	0	0
Tom Young (Maryland '58) 86	1	1	1	0	0	0	0	0
Oliver Purnell (Old Dominion '75) 92	1	0	1	0	0	0	0	0
Jeff Capel (Fayetteville St. '77) 95	1	1	1	0	0	0	0	0
TOTAL	6	2	6	0	0	0	0	0

ORAL ROBERTS

	Yrs.	Won	Lost	CH	2D	3d%	4th	RR
Ken Trickey (Middle Tenn. St. '54) 74RR	1	2	1	0	0	0	0	1
Dick Acres (UC Santa Barb.) 84	1	0	1	0	0	0	0	0
TOTAL	2	2	2	0	0	0	0	1

OREGON

	Yrs.	Won	Lost	CH	2D	3d%	4th	RR
Howard Hobson (Oregon '26) 39-CH	1	3	0	1	0	0	0	0
John Warren (Oregon '28) 45RR	1	1	1	0	0	0	0	1
Steve Belko (Idaho '39) 60RR, 61	2	2	2	0	0	0	0	1
Jerry Green (Appalachian St. '68) 95	1	0	1	0	0	0	0	0
TOTAL	5	6	4	1	0	0	0	2

OREGON ST.*

	Yrs.	Won	Lost	CH	2D	3d%	4th	RR
Amory "Slats" Gill (Oregon St. '25) 47RR, 49-4th, 55RR, 62RR, 63-4th, 64	6	8	8	0	0	0	2	3
Paul Valenti (Oregon St. '42) 66RR	1	1	1	0	0	0	0	1
Ralph Miller (Kansas '42) 75, 80, 81, 82RR, 84, 85, 88, 89	8	3	9	0	0	0	0	1
Jim Anderson (Oregon St. '59) 90	1	0	1	0	0	0	0	0
TOTAL	16	12	19	0	0	0	2	5

PACIFIC (CAL.)

	Yrs.	Won	Lost	CH	2D	3d%	4th	RR
Dick Edwards (Culver-Stockton '52) 66, 67RR, 71	3	2	4	0	0	0	0	1
Stan Morrison (California '62) 79	1	0	1	0	0	0	0	0
TOTAL	4	2	5	0	0	0	0	1

CHAMPIONSHIPS

PENNSYLVANIA

	Yrs.	Won	Lost	CH	2D	3d%	4th	RR
Howie Dallmar (Stanford '48) 53	1	1	1	0	0	0	0	0
Dick Harter (Pennsylvania '53) 70, 71RR	2	2	2	0	0	0	0	1
Chuck Daly (Bloomsburg '53) 72RR, 73, 74, 75	4	3	5	0	0	0	0	1
Bob Weinhauer (Cortland St. '61) 78, 79-4th, 80, 82	4	6	5	0	0	0	1	0
Craig Littlepage (Pennsylvania '73) 85	1	0	1	0	0	0	0	0
Tom Schneider (Bucknell '69) 87	1	0	1	0	0	0	0	0
Fran Dunphy (La Salle '70) 93, 94, 95	3	1	3	0	0	0	0	0
TOTAL	16	13	18	0	0	0	1	2

PENN ST.

	Yrs.	Won	Lost	CH	2D	3d%	4th	RR
John Lawther [Westminster (Pa.) '19] 42RR	1	1	1	0	0	0	0	1
Elmer Gross (Penn St. '42) 52, 54-3d	2	4	3	0	0	1	0	0
John Egli (Penn St. '47) 55, 65	2	1	3	0	0	0	0	0
Bruce Parkhill (Lock Haven '71) 91	1	1	1	0	0	0	0	0
Jerry Dunn (George Mason '80) 96	1	0	1	0	0	0	0	0
TOTAL	7	7	9	0	0	1	0	1

PEPPERDINE

	Yrs.	Won	Lost	CH	2D	3d%	4th	RR
Al Duer (Emporia St. '29) 44RR	1	0	2	0	0	0	0	1
R. L. "Duck" Dowell (Northwest Mo. St. '33) 62	1	1	1	0	0	0	0	0
Gary Colson (David Lipscomb '56) 76, 79	2	2	2	0	0	0	0	0
Jim Harrick [Charleston (W. Va.) '60] 82, 83, 85, 86	4	1	4	0	0	0	0	0
Tom Asbury (Wyoming '67) 91, 92, 94	3	0	3	0	0	0	0	0
TOTAL	11	4	12	0	0	0	0	1

PITTSBURGH

	Yrs.	Won	Lost	CH	2D	3d%	4th	RR
Henry Carlson (Pittsburgh '17) 41-T3d	1	1	1	0	0	1	0	0
Bob Timmons (Pittsburgh '33) 57, 58, 63	3	1	4	0	0	0	0	0
Charles "Buzz" Ridl [Westminster (Pa.) '42] 74RR	1	2	1	0	0	0	0	1
Roy Chipman (Maine '61) 81, 82, 85	3	1	3	0	0	0	0	0
Paul Evans (Ithaca '67) 87, 88, 89, 91, 93	5	3	5	0	0	0	0	0
TOTAL	13	8	14	0	0	1	0	1

PORTLAND

	Yrs.	Won	Lost	CH	2D	3d%	4th	RR
Al Negratti (Seton Hall '43) 59	1	0	1	0	0	0	0	0
Rob Chavez (Mesa St. '80) 96	1	0	1	0	0	0	0	0
TOTAL	2	0	2	0	0	0	0	0

PRINCETON#

	Yrs.	Won	Lost	CH	2D	3d%	4th	RR
Franklin Cappon (Michigan '24) 52, 55, 60	3	0	5	0	0	0	0	0
J. L. "Jake" McCandless (Princeton '51) 61	1	1	2	0	0	0	0	0
Bill van Breda Kolff (Princeton '47) 63, 64, 65-3d, 67	4	7	5	0	0	1	0	0
Pete Carril (Lafayette '52) 69, 76, 77, 81, 83, 84, 89, 90, 91, 92	10	3	10	0	0	0	0	0
TOTAL	18	11	22	0	0	1	0	0

PROVIDENCE

	Yrs.	Won	Lost	CH	2D	3d%	4th	RR
Joe Mullaney (Holy Cross '49) 64, 65RR, 66	3	2	3	0	0	0	0	1
Dave Gavitt (Dartmouth '59) 72, 73-4th, 74, 77, 78	5	5	6	0	0	0	1	0
Rick Pitino (Massachusetts '74) 87-T3d	1	4	1	0	0	1	0	0
Rick Barnes (Lenoir-Rhyne '77) 89, 90, 94	3	0	3	0	0	0	0	0
TOTAL	12	11	13	0	0	1	1	1

PURDUE

	Yrs.	Won	Lost	CH	2D	3d%	4th	RR
George King [Charleston (W. Va.) '50] 69-2d	1	3	1	0	1	0	0	0
Fred Schaus (West Va. '49) 77	1	0	1	0	0	0	0	0
Lee Rose (Transylvania '58) 80-3d	1	5	1	0	0	1	0	0
Gene Keady (Kansas St. '58) 83, 84, 85, 86, 87, 88, 90, 91, 93, 94RR, 95, 96	12	10	12	0	0	0	0	1
TOTAL	15	18	15	0	1	1	0	1

RHODE ISLAND

	Yrs.	Won	Lost	CH	2D	3d%	4th	RR
Ernie Calverley (Rhode Island '46) 61, 66	2	0	2	0	0	0	0	0
Jack Kraft [St. Joseph's (Pa.) '42] 78	1	0	1	0	0	0	0	0
Tom Penders (Connecticut '67) 88	1	2	1	0	0	0	0	0
Al Skinner (Massachusetts '74) 93	1	1	1	0	0	0	0	0
TOTAL	5	3	5	0	0	0	0	0

RICE

	Yrs.	Won	Lost	CH	2D	3d%	4th	RR
Byron "Buster" Brannon (Texas Christian '33) 40RR, 42RR	2	1	3	0	0	0	0	2
Don Suman (Rice '44) 54	1	1	1	0	0	0	0	0
Don Knodel [Miami (Ohio) '53] 70	1	0	1	0	0	0	0	0
TOTAL	4	2	5	0	0	0	0	2

RICHMOND

	Yrs.	Won	Lost	CH	2D	3d%	4th	RR
Dick Tarrant (Fordham '51) 84, 86, 88, 90, 91	5	5	5	0	0	0	0	0
TOTAL	5	5	5	0	0	0	0	0

RIDER

	Yrs.	Won	Lost	CH	2D	3d%	4th	RR
John Carpenter (Penn St. '58) 84	1	0	1	0	0	0	0	0
Kevin Bannon (St. Peter's '79) 93, 94	2	0	2	0	0	0	0	0
TOTAL	3	0	3	0	0	0	0	0

ROBERT MORRIS

	Yrs.	Won	Lost	CH	2D	3d%	4th	RR
Matt Furjanic (Point Park '73) 82, 83	2	1	2	0	0	0	0	0
Jarrett Durham (Duquesne '71) 89, 90, 92	3	0	3	0	0	0	0	0
TOTAL	5	1	5	0	0	0	0	0

RUTGERS

	Yrs.	Won	Lost	CH	2D	3d%	4th	RR
Tom Young (Maryland '58) 75, 76-4th, 79, 83	4	5	5	0	0	0	1	0
Bob Wenzel (Rutgers '71) 89, 91	2	0	2	0	0	0	0	0
TOTAL	6	5	7	0	0	0	1	0

ST. BONAVENTURE

	Yrs.	Won	Lost	CH	2D	3d%	4th	RR
Eddie Donovan (St. Bonaventure '50) 61	1	2	1	0	0	0	0	0
Larry Weise (St. Bonaventure '58) 68, 70-4th	2	4	4	0	0	0	1	0
Jim Satalin (St. Bonaventure '69) 78	1	0	1	0	0	0	0	0
TOTAL	4	6	6	0	0	0	1	0

ST. FRANCIS (PA.)

	Yrs.	Won	Lost	CH	2D	3d%	4th	RR
Jim Baron (St. Bonaventure '77) 91	1	0	1	0	0	0	0	0
TOTAL	1	0	1	0	0	0	0	0

ST. JOHN'S (N.Y.)

	Yrs.	Won	Lost	CH	2D	3d%	4th	RR
Frank McGuire [St. John's (N.Y.) '36] 51RR, 52-2d	2	5	2	0	1	0	0	1
Joe Lapchick (No college) 61	1	0	1	0	0	0	0	0
Frank Mulzoff [St. John's (N.Y.) '51] 73	1	0	1	0	0	0	0	0
Lou Carnesecca [St. John's (N.Y.) '46] 67, 68, 69, 76, 77, 78, 79RR, 80, 82, 83, 84, 85-T3d, 86, 87, 88, 90, 91RR, 92	18	17	20	0	0	1	0	2
Brian Mahoney (Manhattan '71) 93	1	1	1	0	0	0	0	0
TOTAL	23	23	25	0	1	1	0	3

ST. JOSEPH'S (PA.)*

	Yrs.	Won	Lost	CH	2D	3d%	4th	RR
John "Jack" Ramsay [St. Joseph's (Pa.) '49] 59, 60, 61-3d, 62, 63RR, 65, 66	7	8	11	0	0	1	0	1
John "Jack" McKinney [St. Joseph's (Pa.) '57] 69, 71, 73, 74	4	0	4	0	0	0	0	0
Jim Lynam [St. Joseph's (Pa.) '64] 81RR	1	3	1	0	0	0	0	1
Jim Boyle [St. Joseph's (Pa.) '64] 82, 86	2	1	2	0	0	0	0	0
TOTAL	14	12	18	0	0	1	0	2

ST. LOUIS

	Yrs.	Won	Lost	CH	2D	3d%	4th	RR
Eddie Hickey (Creighton '27) 52RR, 57	2	1	3	0	0	0	0	1
Charlie Spoonhour (School of Ozarks '61) 94, 95	2	1	2	0	0	0	0	0
TOTAL	4	2	5	0	0	0	0	1

ST. MARY'S (CAL.)

	Yrs.	Won	Lost	CH	2D	3d%	4th	RR
James Weaver (DePaul '47) 59RR	1	1	1	0	0	0	0	1
Lynn Nance (Washington '65) 89	1	0	1	0	0	0	0	0
TOTAL	2	1	2	0	0	0	0	1

ST. PETER'S

	Yrs.	Won	Lost	CH	2D	3d%	4th	RR
Ted Fiore (Seton Hall '62) 91, 95	2	0	2	0	0	0	0	0
TOTAL	2	0	2	0	0	0	0	0

SAN DIEGO

	Yrs.	Won	Lost	CH	2D	3d%	4th	RR
Jim Brovelli (San Francisco '64) 84	1	0	1	0	0	0	0	0
Hank Egan (Navy '60) 87	1	0	1	0	0	0	0	0
TOTAL	2	0	2	0	0	0	0	0

SAN DIEGO ST.

	Yrs.	Won	Lost	CH	2D	3d%	4th	RR
Tim Vezie (Denver '67) 75, 76	2	0	2	0	0	0	0	0
Dave "Smokey" Gaines (LeMoyne-Owen '63) 85	1	0	1	0	0	0	0	0
TOTAL	3	0	3	0	0	0	0	0

SAN FRANCISCO

	Yrs.	Won	Lost	CH	2D	3d%	4th	RR
Phil Woolpert (Loyola Marymount '40) 55-CH, 56-CH, 57-3d, 58	4	13	2	2	0	1	0	0
Peter Peletta (Cal St. Sacramento '50) 63, 64RR, 65RR	3	3	3	0	0	0	0	2
Bob Gaillard (San Francisco '62) 72, 73RR, 74RR, 77, 78	5	4	5	0	0	0	0	2
Dan Belluomini (San Francisco '64) 79	1	1	1	0	0	0	0	0
Peter Barry (San Francisco '70) 81, 82	2	0	2	0	0	0	0	0
TOTAL	15	21	13	2	0	1	0	4

SAN JOSE ST.

	Yrs.	Won	Lost	CH	2D	3d%	4th	RR
Walter McPherson (San Jose St. '40) 51	1	0	1	0	0	0	0	0
Bill Berry (Michigan St. '65) 80	1	0	1	0	0	0	0	0
Stan Morrison (California '62) 96	1	0	1	0	0	0	0	0
TOTAL	3	0	3	0	0	0	0	0

SANTA CLARA

	Yrs.	Won	Lost	CH	2D	3d%	4th	RR
Bob Feerick (Santa Clara '41) 52-4th, 53RR, 54RR, 60	4	6	6	0	0	0	1	2
Dick Garibaldi (Santa Clara '57) 68RR, 69RR, 70	3	3	3	0	0	0	0	2
Carroll Williams (San Jose St. '55) 87	1	0	1	0	0	0	0	0
Dick Davey [Pacific (Cal.) '64] 93, 95, 96	3	2	3	0	0	0	0	0
TOTAL	11	11	13	0	0	0	1	4

SEATTLE#

	Yrs.	Won	Lost	CH	2D	3d%	4th	RR
Al Brightman [Charleston (W.Va.)] 53, 54, 55, 56	4	4	6	0	0	0	0	0
John Castellani (Notre Dame '52) 58-2d	1	4	1	0	1	0	0	0
Vince Cazzetta (Arnold '50) 61, 62	2	0	2	0	0	0	0	0
Clair Markey (Seattle '63) 63	1	0	1	0	0	0	0	0
Bob Boyd (Southern Cal '53) 64	1	2	1	0	0	0	0	0
Lionel Purcell (UC Santa Barb. '52) 67	1	0	1	0	0	0	0	0
Morris Buckwalter (Utah '56) 69	1	0	1	0	0	0	0	0
TOTAL	11	10	13	0	1	0	0	0

SETON HALL

	Yrs.	Won	Lost	CH	2D	3d%	4th	RR
P. J. Carlesimo (Fordham '71) 88, 89-2d, 91RR, 92, 93, 94	6	12	6	0	1	0	0	1
TOTAL	6	12	6	0	1	0	0	1

SIENA

	Yrs.	Won	Lost	CH	2D	3d%	4th	RR
Mike Deane (Potsdam St. '74) 89	1	1	1	0	0	0	0	0
TOTAL	1	1	1	0	0	0	0	0

SOUTH ALA.

	Yrs.	Won	Lost	CH	2D	3d%	4th	RR
Cliff Ellis (Florida St. '68) 79, 80	2	0	2	0	0	0	0	0
Ronnie Arrow (Southwest Tex. St. '69) 89, 91	2	1	2	0	0	0	0	0
TOTAL	4	1	4	0	0	0	0	0

SOUTH CARO.

	Yrs.	Won	Lost	CH	2D	3d%	4th	RR
Frank McGuire [St. John's (N.Y.) '36] 71, 72, 73, 74	4	4	5	0	0	0	0	0
George Felton (South Caro. '75) 89	1	0	1	0	0	0	0	0
TOTAL	5	4	6	0	0	0	0	0

SOUTH CARO. ST.

	Yrs.	Won	Lost	CH	2D	3d%	4th	RR
Cy Alexander (Catawba '75) 89, 96	2	0	2	0	0	0	0	0
TOTAL	2	0	2	0	0	0	0	0

SOUTH FLA.

	Yrs.	Won	Lost	CH	2D	3d%	4th	RR
Bobby Paschal (Stetson '64) 90, 92	2	0	2	0	0	0	0	0
TOTAL	2	0	2	0	0	0	0	0

SOUTHERN U.

	Yrs.	Won	Lost	CH	2D	3d%	4th	RR
Carl Stewart (Grambling '54) 81	1	0	1	0	0	0	0	0
Robert Hopkins (Grambling '56) 85	1	0	1	0	0	0	0	0
Ben Jobe (Fisk '56) 87, 88, 89, 93	4	1	4	0	0	0	0	0
TOTAL	6	1	6	0	0	0	0	0

SOUTHERN CAL

	Yrs.	Won	Lost	CH	2D	3d%	4th	RR
Justin "Sam" Barry (Lawrence '13) 40-T3d	1	1	1	0	0	1	0	0
Forrest Twogood (Iowa '29) 54-4th, 60, 61	3	3	5	0	0	0	1	0
Bob Boyd (Southern Cal '53) 79	1	1	1	0	0	0	0	0
Stan Morrison (California '62) 82, 85	2	0	2	0	0	0	0	0
George Raveling (Villanova '60) 91, 92	2	1	2	0	0	0	0	0
TOTAL	9	6	11	0	0	1	1	0

SOUTHERN ILL.

	Yrs.	Won	Lost	CH	2D	3d%	4th	RR
Paul Lambert (William Jewell '56) 77	1	1	1	0	0	0	0	0
Rich Herrin (McKendree '56) 93, 94, 95	3	0	3	0	0	0	0	0
TOTAL	4	1	4	0	0	0	0	0

SOUTHERN METHODIST

	Yrs.	Won	Lost	CH	2D	3d%	4th	RR
E. O. "Doc" Hayes (North Texas '27) 55, 56-4th, 57, 65, 66, 67RR	6	7	8	0	0	0	1	1
Dave Bliss (Cornell '65) 84, 85, 88	3	3	3	0	0	0	0	0
John Shumate (Notre Dame '74) 93	1	0	1	0	0	0	0	0
TOTAL	10	10	12	0	0	0	1	1

SOUTHERN MISS.

	Yrs.	Won	Lost	CH	2D	3d%	4th	RR
M. K. Turk (West Ala. '64) 90, 91	2	0	2	0	0	0	0	0
TOTAL	2	0	2	0	0	0	0	0

SOUTHWEST MO. ST.

	Yrs.	Won	Lost	CH	2D	3d%	4th	RR
Charlie Spoonhour (School of Ozarks '61) 87, 88, 89, 90, 92	5	1	5	0	0	0	0	0
TOTAL	5	1	5	0	0	0	0	0

SOUTHWEST TEX. ST.

	Yrs.	Won	Lost	CH	2D	3d%	4th	RR
Jim Wooldridge (Louisiana Tech '77) 94	1	0	1	0	0	0	0	0
TOTAL	1	0	1	0	0	0	0	0

SOUTHWESTERN LA.*

	Yrs.	Won	Lost	CH	2D	3d%	4th	RR
Beryl Shipley (Delta St. '51) 72, 73	2	3	3	0	0	0	0	0
Bobby Paschal (Stetson '64) 82, 83	2	0	2	0	0	0	0	0
Marty Fletcher (Maryland '73) 92, 94	2	1	2	0	0	0	0	0
TOTAL	6	4	7	0	0	0	0	0

In 1996, Jim Boeheim led Syracuse to the national championship game for the second time in his career. Boeheim, who has guided the Orangemen program since 1977, has earned 17 tournament appearances.

Photo by Rich Clarkson/NCAA photos

SPRINGFIELD

	Yrs.	Won	Lost	CH	2D	3d%	4th	RR
Ed Hickox (Ohio Wesleyan '05) 40RR	1	0	1	0	0	0	0	1
TOTAL	1	0	1	0	0	0	0	1

STANFORD

	Yrs.	Won	Lost	CH	2D	3d%	4th	RR
Everett Dean (Indiana '21) 42-CH	1	3	0	1	0	0	0	0
Mike Montgomery (Long Beach St. '68) 89, 92, 95, 96	4	2	4	0	0	0	0	0
TOTAL	5	5	4	1	0	0	0	0

SYRACUSE

	Yrs.	Won	Lost	CH	2D	3d%	4th	RR
Marc Guley (Syracuse '36) 57RR	1	2	1	0	0	0	0	1
Fred Lewis (Eastern Ky. '46) 66RR	1	1	1	0	0	0	0	1
Roy Danforth (Southern Miss. '62) 73, 74, 75-4th, 76	4	5	5	0	0	0	1	0
Jim Boeheim (Syracuse '66) 77, 78, 79, 80, 83, 84, 85, 86, 87-2d, 88, 89RR, 90, 91, 92, 94, 95, 96-2d	17	27	17	0	2	0	0	1
TOTAL	23	35	24	0	2	0	1	3

TEMPLE

	Yrs.	Won	Lost	CH	2D	3d%	4th	RR
Josh Cody (Vanderbilt '20) 44RR	1	1	1	0	0	0	0	1
Harry Litwack (Temple '30) 56-3d, 58-3d, 64, 67, 70, 72	6	7	6	0	0	2	0	0
Don Casey (Temple '70) 79	1	0	1	0	0	0	0	0
John Chaney (Bethune-Cookman '55) 84, 85, 86, 87, 88RR, 90, 91RR, 92, 93RR, 94, 95, 96	12	15	12	0	0	0	0	3
TOTAL	20	23	20	0	0	2	0	4

TENNESSEE

	Yrs.	Won	Lost	CH	2D	3d%	4th	RR
Ramon "Ray" Mears [Miami (Ohio) '49] 67, 76, 77	3	0	4	0	0	0	0	0
Don DeVoe (Ohio St. '64) 79, 80, 81, 82, 83, 89	6	5	6	0	0	0	0	0
TOTAL	9	5	10	0	0	0	0	0

TENN.-CHATT.

	Yrs.	Won	Lost	CH	2D	3d%	4th	RR
Murray Arnold (American '60) 81, 82, 83	3	1	3	0	0	0	0	0
Mack McCarthy (Virginia Tech '74) 88, 93, 94, 95	4	0	4	0	0	0	0	0
TOTAL	7	1	7	0	0	0	0	0

TENNESSEE ST.

	Yrs.	Won	Lost	CH	2D	3d%	4th	RR
Frankie Allen (Roanoke '71) 93, 94	2	0	2	0	0	0	0	0
TOTAL	2	0	2	0	0	0	0	0

CHAMPIONSHIPS

	Yrs.	Won	Lost	CH	2D	3d%	4th	RR
TENNESSEE TECH								
Johnny Oldham (Western Ky. '48) 58, 63 ..	2	0	2	0	0	0	0	0
TOTAL	2	0	2	0	0	0	0	0
TEXAS								
H. C. "Bully" Gilstrap (Texas '22) 43-T3d	1	1	1	0	0	1	0	0
Jack Gray (Texas '35) 39RR, 47-3d	2	2	3	0	0	1	0	1
Harold Bradley (Hartwick '34) 60, 63	2	2	3	0	0	0	0	0
Leon Black (Texas '53) 72, 74	2	1	3	0	0	0	0	0
A. E. "Abe" Lemons (Oklahoma City '49) 79	1	0	1	0	0	0	0	0
Tom Penders (Connecticut '67) 89, 90RR, 91, 92, 94, 95, 96	7	8	7	0	0	0	0	1
TOTAL	15	14	18	0	0	2	0	2
TEXAS A&M								
John Floyd (Oklahoma St. '41) 51	1	0	1	0	0	0	0	0
Shelby Metcalf (Tex. A&M-Commerce '53) 64, 69, 75, 80, 87	5	3	6	0	0	0	0	0
TOTAL	6	3	7	0	0	0	0	0
TEXAS CHRISTIAN								
Byron "Buster" Brannon (Texas Christian '33) 52, 53, 59	3	3	3	0	0	0	0	0
Johnny Swaim (Texas Christian '53) 68RR, 71	2	1	2	0	0	0	0	1
Jim Killingsworth (Northeastern St. '48) 87	1	1	1	0	0	0	0	0
TOTAL	6	5	6	0	0	0	0	1
TEXAS-SAN ANTONIO								
Ken Burmeister [St. Mary's (Tex.) '71] 88	1	0	1	0	0	0	0	0
TOTAL	1	0	1	0	0	0	0	0
TEXAS SOUTHERN								
Robert Moreland (Tougaloo '62) 90, 94, 95	3	0	3	0	0	0	0	0
TOTAL	3	0	3	0	0	0	0	0
TEXAS TECH								
Polk Robison (Texas Tech '35) 54, 56, 61	3	1	3	0	0	0	0	0
Gene Gibson (Texas Tech '50) 62	1	1	2	0	0	0	0	0
Gerald Myers (Texas Tech '59) 73, 76, 85, 86	4	1	4	0	0	0	0	0
James Dickey (Central Ark. '76) 93, 96	2	2	2	0	0	0	0	0
TOTAL	10	5	11	0	0	0	0	0
TOLEDO								
Jerry Bush [St. John's (N.Y.) '38] 54	1	0	1	0	0	0	0	0
Bob Nichols (Toledo '53) 67, 79, 80	3	1	3	0	0	0	0	0
TOTAL	4	1	4	0	0	0	0	0
TOWSON ST.								
Terry Truax (Maryland '68) 90, 91	2	0	2	0	0	0	0	0
TOTAL	2	0	2	0	0	0	0	0
TRINITY (TEX.)								
Bob Polk (Evansville '39) 69	1	0	1	0	0	0	0	0
TOTAL	1	0	1	0	0	0	0	0
TUFTS								
Richard Cochran (Tufts '34) 45RR	1	0	2	0	0	0	0	1
TOTAL	1	0	2	0	0	0	0	1
TULANE								
Perry Clark (Gettysburg '74) 92, 93, 95	3	3	3	0	0	0	0	0
TOTAL	3	3	3	0	0	0	0	0
TULSA								
Clarence Iba (Panhandle St. '36) 55	1	1	1	0	0	0	0	0
Nolan Richardson (UTEP '65) 82, 84, 85	3	0	3	0	0	0	0	0
J. D. Barnett (Winona St. '66) 86, 87	2	0	2	0	0	0	0	0
Tubby Smith (High Point '73) 94, 95	2	4	2	0	0	0	0	0
Steve Robinson (Radford '81) 96	1	0	1	0	0	0	0	0
TOTAL	9	5	9	0	0	0	0	0
UCLA*								
John Wooden (Purdue '32) 50RR, 52, 56, 62-4th, 63, 64-CH, 65-CH, 67-CH, 68-CH, 69-CH, 70-CH, 71-CH, 72-CH, 73-CH, 74-3d, 75-CH	16	47	10	10	0	1	1	1
Gene Bartow (Truman St. '53) 76-3d, 77	2	5	2	0	0	1	0	0
Gary Cunningham (UCLA '62) 78, 79RR	2	3	2	0	0	0	0	1
Larry Brown (North Caro. '63) 80-2d, 81	2	5	2	0	1	0	0	0
Larry Farmer (UCLA '73) 83	1	0	1	0	0	0	0	0
Walt Hazzard (UCLA '64) 87	1	1	1	0	0	0	0	0
Jim Harrick [Charleston (W. Va.) '60] 89, 90, 91, 92RR, 93, 94, 95-CH, 96	8	13	7	1	0	0	0	1
TOTAL	32	74	25	11	1	2	1	3
UTAH								
Vadal Peterson (Utah '20) 44-CH, 45RR	2	3	2	1	0	0	0	1
Jack Gardner (Southern Cal '32) 55, 56RR, 59, 60, 61-4th, 66-4th	6	8	9	0	0	0	2	1
Jerry Pimm (Southern Cal '61) 77, 78, 79, 81, 83	5	5	5	0	0	0	0	0
Lynn Archibald (Fresno St. '68) 86	1	0	1	0	0	0	0	0
Rick Majerus (Marquette '70) 91, 93, 95, 96	4	6	4	0	0	0	0	0
TOTAL	18	22	21	1	0	0	2	2
UTAH ST.								
E. L. "Dick" Romney (Utah '17) 39RR	1	1	1	0	0	0	0	1
Ladell Andersen (Utah St. '51) 62, 63, 64, 70RR, 71	5	4	7	0	0	0	0	1
Gordon "Dutch" Belnap (Utah St. '58) 75, 79	2	0	2	0	0	0	0	0
Rod Tueller (Utah St. '59) 80, 83, 88	3	0	3	0	0	0	0	0
TOTAL	11	5	13	0	0	0	0	2
UTEP								
Don Haskins (Oklahoma St. '53) 63, 64, 66-CH, 67, 70, 75, 84, 85, 86, 87, 88, 89, 90, 92	14	14	13	1	0	0	0	0
TOTAL	14	14	13	1	0	0	0	0
VALPARAISO								
Homer Drew (William Jewell '66) 96	1	0	1	0	0	0	0	0
TOTAL	1	0	1	0	0	0	0	0
VANDERBILT								
Roy Skinner (Presbyterian '52) 65RR, 74	2	1	3	0	0	0	0	1
C. M. Newton (Kentucky '52) 88, 89	2	2	2	0	0	0	0	0
Eddie Fogler (North Caro. '70) 91, 93	2	2	2	0	0	0	0	0
TOTAL	6	5	7	0	0	0	0	1
VILLANOVA*								
Alex Severance (Villanova '29) 39-T3d, 49RR, 51, 55	4	4	4	0	0	1	0	1
Jack Kraft [St. Joseph's (Pa.) '42] 62RR, 64, 69, 70RR, 71-2d, 72	6	11	7	0	1	0	0	2
Rollie Massimino (Vermont '56) 78RR, 80, 81, 82RR, 83RR, 84, 85-CH, 86, 88RR, 90, 91	11	20	10	1	0	0	0	4
Steve Lappas (CCNY '77) 95, 96	2	1	2	0	0	0	0	0
TOTAL	23	36	23	1	1	1	0	7
VIRGINIA								
Terry Holland (Davidson '64) 76, 81-3d, 82, 83RR, 84-T3d, 86, 87, 89RR, 90	9	15	9	0	0	2	0	2
Jeff Jones (Virginia '82) 91, 93, 94, 95RR	4	6	4	0	0	0	0	1
TOTAL	13	21	13	0	0	2	0	3
VA. COMMONWEALTH								
J. D. Barnett (Winona St. '66) 80, 81, 83, 84, 85	5	4	5	0	0	0	0	0
Sonny Smith (Milligan '58) 96	1	0	1	0	0	0	0	0
TOTAL	6	4	6	0	0	0	0	0
VMI								
Louis "Weenie" Miller (Richmond '47) 64	1	0	1	0	0	0	0	0
Bill Blair (VMI '64) 76RR	1	2	1	0	0	0	0	1
Charlie Schmaus (VMI '66) 77	1	1	1	0	0	0	0	0
TOTAL	3	3	3	0	0	0	0	1
VIRGINIA TECH								
Howard Shannon (Kansas St. '48) 67RR	1	2	1	0	0	0	0	1
Don DeVoe (Ohio St. '64) 76	1	0	1	0	0	0	0	0
Charles Moir (Appalachian St. '52) 79, 80, 85, 86	4	2	4	0	0	0	0	0
Bill C. Foster (Carson-Newman '58) 96	1	1	1	0	0	0	0	0
TOTAL	7	5	7	0	0	0	0	1
WAKE FOREST								
Murray Greason (Wake Forest '26) 39RR, 53	2	1	2	0	0	0	0	1
Horace "Bones" McKinney (North Caro. '46) 61RR, 62-3d	2	6	2	0	0	1	0	1
Carl Tacy (Davis & Elkins '56) 77RR, 81, 82, 84RR	4	5	4	0	0	0	0	2
Dave Odom (Guilford '65) 91, 92, 93, 94, 95, 96RR	6	9	6	0	0	0	0	1
TOTAL	14	21	14	0	0	1	0	5
WASHINGTON								
Clarence "Hec" Edmundson (Idaho '09) 43RR	1	0	2	0	0	0	0	1
Art McLarney (Washington St. '32) 48RR	1	1	1	0	0	0	0	1
William H. H. "Tippy" Dye (Ohio St. '37) 51RR, 53-3d	2	5	2	0	0	1	0	1
Marv Harshman (Pacific Lutheran '42) 76, 84, 85	3	2	3	0	0	0	0	0
Andy Russo (Lake Forest '70) 86	1	0	1	0	0	0	0	0
TOTAL	8	8	9	0	0	1	0	3

	Yrs.	Won	Lost	CH	2D	3d%	4th	RR
WASHINGTON ST.								
Jack Friel (Washington St. '23) 41-2d.......	1	2	1	0	1	0	0	0
George Raveling (Villanova '60) 80, 83	2	1	2	0	0	0	0	0
Kelvin Sampson (N.C.-Pembroke '78) 94 ...	1	0	1	0	0	0	0	0
TOTAL	4	3	4	0	1	0	0	0
WAYNE ST. (MICH.)								
Joel Mason (Western Mich. '36) 56	1	1	2	0	0	0	0	0
TOTAL	1	1	2	0	0	0	0	0
WEBER ST.								
Dick Motta (Utah St. '53) 68	1	0	1	0	0	0	0	0
Phil Johnson (Utah St. '53) 69, 70, 71......	3	2	3	0	0	0	0	0
Gene Visscher (Weber St. '66) 72, 73	2	1	3	0	0	0	0	0
Neil McCarthy (Cal St. Sacramento '65) 78, 79, 80, 83	4	1	4	0	0	0	0	0
Ron Abegglen (Brigham Young '62) 95	1	1	1	0	0	0	0	0
TOTAL	11	5	12	0	0	0	0	0
WEST TEX. A&M								
W. A. "Gus" Miller (West Tex. A&M '27) 55	1	0	1	0	0	0	0	0
TOTAL	1	0	1	0	0	0	0	0
WEST VA.								
Fred Schaus (West Va. '49) 55, 56, 57, 58, 59-2d, 60	6	6	6	0	1	0	0	0
George King [Charleston (W. Va.) '50] 62, 63, 65	3	2	3	0	0	0	0	0
Raymond "Bucky" Waters (North Caro. St. '57) 67	1	0	1	0	0	0	0	0
Gale Catlett (West Va. '63) 82, 83, 84, 86, 87, 89, 92	7	3	7	0	0	0	0	0
TOTAL	17	11	17	0	1	0	0	0
WESTERN CARO.								
Phil Hopkins (Gardner-Webb '72) 96	1	0	1	0	0	0	0	0
TOTAL	1	0	1	0	0	0	0	0
WESTERN KY.*								
Ed Diddle (Centre '21) 40RR, 60, 62	3	3	4	0	0	0	0	1
Johnny Oldham (Western Ky. '48) 66, 67, 70, 71-3d	4	6	4	0	0	1	0	0
Jim Richards (Western Ky. '59) 76, 78	2	1	2	0	0	0	0	0
Gene Keady (Kansas St. '58) 80	1	0	1	0	0	0	0	0
Clem Haskins (Western Ky. '67) 81, 86	2	1	2	0	0	0	0	0
Murray Arnold (American '60) 87	1	1	1	0	0	0	0	0
Ralph Willard (Holy Cross '67) 93, 94	2	2	2	0	0	0	0	0
Matt Kilcullen (Lehman '76) 95	1	1	1	0	0	0	0	0
TOTAL	16	15	17	0	0	1	0	1
WESTERN MICH.								
Eldon Miller (Wittenberg '61) 76..............	1	1	1	0	0	0	0	0
TOTAL	1	1	1	0	0	0	0	0
WICHITA ST.								
Ralph Miller (Kansas '42) 64RR.................	1	1	1	0	0	0	0	1
Gary Thompson (Wichita St. '54) 65-4th ...	1	2	2	0	0	0	1	0
Harry Miller (Eastern N.M. '51) 76	1	0	1	0	0	0	0	0
Gene Smithson (North Central '61) 81RR, 85	2	3	2	0	0	0	0	1
Eddie Fogler (North Caro. '70) 87, 88	2	0	2	0	0	0	0	0
TOTAL	7	6	8	0	0	0	1	2
WILLIAMS								
Alex Shaw (Michigan '32) 55....................	1	0	1	0	0	0	0	0
TOTAL	1	0	1	0	0	0	0	0
WISCONSIN								
Harold "Bud" Foster (Wisconsin '30) 41-CH, 47RR.......................................	2	4	1	1	0	0	0	1
Stu Jackson (Seattle '78) 94	1	1	1	0	0	0	0	0
TOTAL	3	5	2	1	0	0	0	1
WIS.-GREEN BAY								
Dick Bennett (Ripon '65) 91, 94, 95	3	1	3	0	0	0	0	0
Mike Heideman (Wis.-La Crosse '71) 96 ...	1	0	1	0	0	0	0	0
TOTAL	4	1	4	0	0	0	0	0
WRIGHT ST.								
Ralph Underhill (Tennessee Tech '64) 93....	1	0	1	0	0	0	0	0
TOTAL	1	0	1	0	0	0	0	0
WYOMING								
Everett Shelton (Phillips '23) 41RR, 43-CH, 47RR, 48RR, 49RR, 52RR, 53, 58	8	4	12	1	0	0	0	5
Bill Strannigan (Wyoming '41) 67	1	0	2	0	0	0	0	0
Jim Brandenburg (Colorado St. '58) 81, 82, 87	3	4	3	0	0	0	0	0
Benny Dees (Wyoming '58) 88	1	0	1	0	0	0	0	0
TOTAL	13	8	18	1	0	0	0	5

	Yrs.	Won	Lost	CH	2D	3d%	4th	RR
XAVIER (OHIO)								
Jim McCafferty [Loyola (La.) '42] 61	1	0	1	0	0	0	0	0
Bob Staak (Connecticut '71) 83	1	0	1	0	0	0	0	0
Pete Gillen (Fairfield '68) 86, 87, 88, 89, 90, 91, 93	7	5	7	0	0	0	0	0
Skip Prosser (Merchant Marine '72) 95......	1	0	1	0	0	0	0	0
TOTAL	10	5	10	0	0	0	0	0
YALE								
Howard Hobson (Oregon '26) 49RR	1	0	2	0	0	0	0	1
Joe Vancisin (Dartmouth '44) 57, 62	2	0	2	0	0	0	0	0
TOTAL	3	0	4	0	0	0	0	1

%National third-place games did not start until 1946 and ended in 1981; in other years, two teams tied for third and both are listed in this column. RR Regional runner-up, or one victory from Final Four, thus in top eight.

#NOTES ON TEAMS AND COACHES:

MICHIGAN: Steve Fisher coached Michigan in the 1989 tournament; Bill Frieder was the coach during the regular season.

MISSOURI: Rich Daly coached Missouri in the 1989 tournament due to Norm Stewart's illness; Missouri credits the entire 1989 season and tournament to Stewart.

PRINCETON: J. L. McCandless coached Princeton in the 1961 tournament; Franklin Cappon suffered a heart attack 11 games into the season; Princeton credits the 1961 regular season to Cappon and the postseason to McCandless.

SEATTLE: Clair Markey coached Seattle in the 1963 tournament due to Vince Cazetta's resignation.

*TEAMS VACATING NCAA TOURNAMENT ACTION:

Teams	Seasons	Rec.	Place	Conference
Alabama	1987	2-1		Southeastern
Austin Peay	1973	1-2		Ohio Valley
Clemson...............	1990	2-1		Atlantic Coast
DePaul..................	1986-87-88-89	6-4		Independent
Florida	1987-88	3-2		Southeastern
Georgia	1985	1-1		Southeastern
Iona	1980	1-1		Metro Atlantic
Kentucky	1988	2-1		Southeastern
Long Beach St.	1971-72-73	6-3	2RR	Big West
Loyola Marymount ..	1980	0-1		West Coast
Marshall	1987	0-1		Southern
Maryland	1988	1-1		Atlantic Coast
Memphis...............	1982-83-84-85-86	9-5	3d	Metro
Minnesota	1972	1-1		Big Ten
New Mexico St.	1992-93-94	3-3		Big West
North Caro. St.	1987-88	0-2		Atlantic Coast
Oregon St..............	1980-81-82	2-3		Pacific-10
St. Joseph's (Pa.).....	1961	3-1	3d	Atlantic 10
Southwestern La......	1972-73	3-3		Independent
UCLA	1980	5-1	2d	Pacific-10
Villanova	1971	4-1	2d	Big East
Western Ky.	1971	4-1	3d	Ohio Valley
22 teams	38 years	59-40	2 2d, 3 3d, 2RR	

Official NCAA Records:	Yrs.	Won	Lost	CH	2d	3d	4th	RR
Alabama	13	13	13	0	0	0	0	0
Austin Peay	3	1	3	0	0	0	0	0
Clemson...............................	4	4	4	0	0	0	0	1
DePaul.................................	16	14	19	0	0	2	0	1
Florida	3	4	3	0	0	0	0	0
Georgia	5	5	5	0	0	1	0	0
Iona	3	0	3	0	0	0	0	0
Kentucky	37	70	33	6	2	3	0	15
Long Beach St.	4	1	5	0	0	0	0	0
Loyola Marymount	4	5	4	0	0	0	0	0
Marshall	4	0	4	0	0	0	0	0
Maryland	11	16	11	0	0	0	0	2
Memphis...............................	11	6	11	0	0	0	0	1
Minnesota	5	7	5	0	0	0	0	1
New Mexico St.	12	7	14	0	0	1	0	0
North Caro. St.	15	27	14	2	0	1	0	2
Oregon St..............................	13	10	16	0	0	2	0	3
St. Joseph's (Pa.).....................	13	9	17	0	0	0	0	2
Southwestern La......................	4	1	4	0	0	0	0	0
UCLA	31	69	24	11	0	2	1	2
Villanova..............................	22	32	22	1	0	1	0	6
Western Ky.	15	11	16	0	0	0	0	0

Final Four All-Tournament Teams

(First player listed on each team was the outstanding player in the Final Four)

1939—Not chosen.

1940—Marvin Huffman, Indiana
Howard Engleman, Kansas
Bob Allen, Kansas
Jay McCreary, Indiana
William Menke, Indiana

1941-51—Not chosen.

1952—Clyde Lovellette, Kansas
Bob Zawoluk, St. John's (N.Y.)
John Kerr, Illinois
Ron MacGilvray, St. John's (N.Y.)
Dean Kelley, Kansas

1953—B. H. Born, Kansas
Bob Houbregs, Washington
Bob Leonard, Indiana
Dean Kelley, Kansas
Don Schlundt, Indiana

1954—Tom Gola, La Salle
Chuck Singley, La Salle
Jesse Arnelle, Penn St.
Roy Irvin, Southern Cal
Bob Carney, Bradley

1955—Bill Russell, San Francisco
Tom Gola, La Salle
K. C. Jones, San Francisco
Jim Ranglos, Colorado
Carl Cain, Iowa

1956—Hal Lear, Temple
Bill Russell, San Francisco
Carl Cain, Iowa
Hal Perry, San Francisco
Bill Logan, Iowa

1957—Wilt Chamberlain, Kansas
Len Rosenbluth, North Caro.
John Green, Michigan St.
Gene Brown, San Francisco
Pete Brennan, North Caro.

1958—Elgin Baylor, Seattle
John Cox, Kentucky
Guy Rodgers, Temple
Charley Brown, Seattle
Vern Hatton, Kentucky

1959—Jerry West, West Va.
Oscar Robertson, Cincinnati
Darrall Imhoff, California
Don Goldstein, Louisville
Denny Fitzpatrick, California

1960—Jerry Lucas, Ohio St.
Oscar Robertson, Cincinnati
Mel Nowell, Ohio St.
Darrall Imhoff, California
Tom Sanders, New York U.

1961—Jerry Lucas, Ohio St.
Bob Wiesenhahn, Cincinnati
Larry Siegfried, Ohio St.
Carl Bouldin, Cincinnati
Vacated†

1962—Paul Hogue, Cincinnati
Jerry Lucas, Ohio St.
Tom Thacker, Cincinnati
John Havlicek, Ohio St.
Len Chappell, Wake Forest

1963—Art Heyman, Duke
Tom Thacker, Cincinnati
Les Hunter, Loyola (Ill.)
George Wilson, Cincinnati
Ron Bonham, Cincinnati

1964—Walt Hazzard, UCLA
Jeff Mullins, Duke
Bill Buntin, Michigan
Willie Murrell, Kansas St.
Gail Goodrich, UCLA

1965—Bill Bradley, Princeton
Gail Goodrich, UCLA
Cazzie Russell, Michigan

Edgar Lacey, UCLA
Kenny Washington, UCLA

1966—Jerry Chambers, Utah
Pat Riley, Kentucky
Jack Marin, Duke
Louie Dampier, Kentucky
Bobby Joe Hill, UTEP

1967—Lew Alcindor, UCLA
Don May, Dayton
Mike Warren, UCLA
Elvin Hayes, Houston
Lucius Allen, UCLA

1968—Lew Alcindor, UCLA
Lynn Shackelford, UCLA
Mike Warren, UCLA
Lucius Allen, UCLA
Larry Miller, North Caro.

1969—Lew Alcindor, UCLA
Rick Mount, Purdue
Charlie Scott, North Caro.
Willie McCarter, Drake
John Vallely, UCLA

1970—Sidney Wicks, UCLA
Jimmy Collins, New Mexico St.
John Vallely, UCLA
Artis Gilmore, Jacksonville
Curtis Rowe, UCLA

1971—Vacated†
Vacated†
Vacated†
Steve Patterson, UCLA
Sidney Wicks, UCLA

1972—Bill Walton, UCLA
Keith Wilkes, UCLA
Robert McAdoo, North Caro.
Jim Price, Louisville
Ron King, Florida St.

1973—Bill Walton, UCLA
Steve Downing, Indiana
Ernie DiGregorio, Providence
Larry Finch, Memphis
Larry Kenon, Memphis

1974—David Thompson, North Caro. St.
Bill Walton, UCLA
Tom Burleson, North Caro. St.
Monte Towe, North Caro. St.
Maurice Lucas, Marquette

1975—Richard Washington, UCLA
Kevin Grevey, Kentucky
Dave Myers, UCLA
Allen Murphy, Louisville
Jim Lee, Syracuse

1976—Kent Benson, Indiana
Scott May, Indiana
Rickey Green, Michigan
Marques Johnson, UCLA
Tom Abernethy, Indiana

1977—Butch Lee, Marquette
Mike O'Koren, North Caro.
Cedric Maxwell, N.C.-Charlotte
Bo Ellis, Marquette
Walter Davis, North Caro.
Jerome Whitehead, Marquette

1978—Jack Givens, Kentucky
Ron Brewer, Arkansas
Mike Gminski, Duke
Rick Robey, Kentucky
Jim Spanarkel, Duke

1979—Earvin Johnson, Michigan St.
Greg Kelser, Michigan St.
Larry Bird, Indiana St.
Mark Aguirre, DePaul
Gary Garland, DePaul

1980—Darrell Griffith, Louisville
Vacated†
Joe Barry Carroll, Purdue
Vacated†
Rodney McCray, Louisville

1981—Isiah Thomas, Indiana
Jeff Lamp, Virginia
Jim Thomas, Indiana
Landon Turner, Indiana
Al Wood, North Caro.

1982—James Worthy, North Caro.
Patrick Ewing, Georgetown
Eric Floyd, Georgetown
Michael Jordan, North Caro.
Sam Perkins, North Caro.

1983—Akeem Olajuwon, Houston
Thurl Bailey, North Caro. St.
Sidney Lowe, North Caro. St.
Milt Wagner, Louisville
Dereck Whittenburg, North Caro. St.

1984—Patrick Ewing, Georgetown
Michael Graham, Georgetown
Akeem Olajuwon, Houston
Michael Young, Houston
Alvin Franklin, Houston

1985—Patrick Ewing, Georgetown
Ed Pinckney, Villanova
Dwayne McClain, Villanova
Harold Jensen, Villanova
Gary McLain, Villanova

1986—Pervis Ellison, Louisville
Billy Thompson, Louisville
Johnny Dawkins, Duke
Mark Alarie, Duke
Tommy Amaker, Duke

1987—Keith Smart, Indiana
Sherman Douglas, Syracuse
Derrick Coleman, Syracuse
Armon Gilliam, UNLV
Steve Alford, Indiana

1988—Danny Manning, Kansas
Milt Newton, Kansas
Stacey King, Oklahoma
Dave Sieger, Oklahoma
Sean Elliott, Arizona

1989—Glen Rice, Michigan
Rumeal Robinson, Michigan
Danny Ferry, Duke
Gerald Greene, Seton Hall
John Morton, Seton Hall

1990—Anderson Hunt, UNLV
Stacey Augmon, UNLV
Larry Johnson, UNLV
Phil Henderson, Duke
Dennis Scott, Georgia Tech

1991—Christian Laettner, Duke
Bobby Hurley, Duke
Bill McCaffrey, Duke
Mark Randall, Kansas
Anderson Hunt, UNLV

1992—Bobby Hurley, Duke
Grant Hill, Duke
Christian Laettner, Duke
Jalen Rose, Michigan
Chris Webber, Michigan

1993—Donald Williams, North Caro.
Eric Montross, North Caro.
George Lynch, North Caro.
Chris Webber, Michigan
Jamal Mashburn, Kentucky

1994—Corliss Williamson, Arkansas
Corey Beck, Arkansas
Scotty Thurman, Arkansas
Grant Hill, Duke
Antonio Lang, Duke

1995—Ed O'Bannon, UCLA
Toby Bailey, UCLA
Corliss Williamson, Arkansas
Clint McDaniel, Arkansas
Bryant Reeves, Oklahoma St.

1996—Tony Delk, Kentucky
Ron Mercer, Kentucky
Marcus Camby, Massachusetts
Todd Burgan, Syracuse
John Wallace, Syracuse

†The following student-athletes and the teams they represented were declared ineligible subsequent to the tournament. Under NCAA rules, the teams' and student-athletes' records were deleted and the teams' places in the final standings were vacated: 1961–John Egan, St. Joseph's (Pa.); 1971–Howard Porter, Villanova; Hank Siemiontkowski, Villanova; Jim McDaniels, Western Kentucky; 1980–Kiki Vandeweghe, UCLA; Rod Foster, UCLA.

National Invitation Tournament Year-by-Year Results

Season	Champion	Score	Runner-Up	Third Place	Fourth Place
1938	Temple	60-36	Colorado	Oklahoma St.	New York U.
1939	LIU-Brooklyn	44-32	Loyola (Ill.)	Bradley	St. John's (N.Y.)
1940	Colorado	51-40	Duquesne	Oklahoma St.	DePaul
1941	LIU-Brooklyn	56-42	Ohio	CCNY	Seton Hall
1942	West Va.	47-45	Western Ky.	Creighton	Toledo
1943	St. John's (N.Y.)	48-27	Toledo	Wash. & Jeff.	Fordham
1944	St. John's (N.Y.)	47-39	DePaul	Kentucky	Oklahoma St.
1945	DePaul	71-54	Bowling Green	St. John's (N.Y.)	Rhode Island
1946	Kentucky	46-45	Rhode Island	West Va.	Muhlenberg
1947	Utah	49-45	Kentucky	North Caro. St.	West Va.
1948	St. Louis	65-52	New York U.	Western Ky.	DePaul
1949	San Francisco	48-47	Loyola (Ill.)	Bowling Green	Bradley
1950	CCNY	69-61	Bradley	St. John's (N.Y.)	Duquesne
1951	Brigham Young	62-43	Dayton	St. John's (N.Y.)	Seton Hall
1952	La Salle	75-64	Dayton	St. Bonaventure	Duquesne
1953	Seton Hall	58-46	St. John's (N.Y.)	Duquesne	Manhattan
1954	Holy Cross	71-62	Duquesne	Niagara	Western Ky.
1955	Duquesne	70-58	Dayton	Cincinnati	St. Francis (Pa.)
1956	Louisville	93-80	Dayton	St. Joseph's (Pa.)	St. Francis (N.Y.)
1957	Bradley	84-83	Memphis	Tampa	St. Bonaventure
1958	Xavier (Ohio)	78-74(ot)	Dayton	St. Bonaventure	St. John's (N.Y.)
1959	St. John's (N.Y.)	76-71(ot)	Bradley	New York U.	Providence
1960	Bradley	88-72	Providence	Utah St.	St. Bonaventure
1961	Providence	62-59	St. Louis	Holy Cross	Dayton
1962	Dayton	73-67	St. John's (N.Y.)	Loyola (Ill.)	Duquesne
1963	Providence	81-66	Canisius	Marquette	Villanova
1964	Bradley	86-54	New Mexico	Army	New York U.
1965	St. John's (N.Y.)	55-51	Villanova	Army	New York U.
1966	Brigham Young	97-84	New York U.	Villanova	Army
1967	Southern Ill.	71-56	Marquette	Rutgers	Marshall
1968	Dayton	61-48	Kansas	Notre Dame	St. Peter's
1969	Temple	89-76	Boston College	Tennessee	Army
1970	Marquette	65-53	St. John's (N.Y.)	Army	LSU
1971	North Caro.	84-66	Georgia Tech	St. Bonaventure	Duke
1972	Maryland	100-69	Niagara	Jacksonville	St. John's (N.Y.)
1973	Virginia Tech	92-91(ot)	Notre Dame	North Caro.	Alabama
1974	Purdue	87-81	Utah	Boston College	Jacksonville
1975	Princeton	80-69	Providence	Oregon	St. John's (N.Y.)
1976	Kentucky	81-76	N.C.-Charlotte	North Caro. St.	Providence
1977	St. Bonaventure	94-91	Houston	Villanova	Alabama
1978	Texas	101-93	North Caro. St.	Rutgers	Georgetown
1979	Indiana	53-52	Purdue	Alabama	Ohio St.
1980	Virginia	58-55	Minnesota	Illinois	UNLV
1981	Tulsa	86-84(ot)	Syracuse	Purdue	West Va.
1982	Bradley	67-58	Purdue	+Georgia	+Oklahoma
1983	Fresno St.	69-60	DePaul	+Nebraska	+Wake Forest
1984	Michigan	83-63	Notre Dame	Virginia Tech	Southwestern La.
1985	UCLA	65-62	Indiana	Tennessee	Louisville
1986	Ohio St.	73-63	Wyoming	Louisiana Tech	Florida
1987	Southern Miss.	84-80	La Salle	Nebraska	Ark.-Little Rock
1988	Connecticut	72-67	Ohio St.	Colorado St.	Boston College
1989	St. John's (N.Y.)	73-65	St. Louis	UAB	Michigan St.
1990	Vanderbilt	74-72	St. Louis	Penn St.	New Mexico
1991	Stanford	78-72	Oklahoma	Colorado	Massachusetts
1992	Virginia	81-76	Notre Dame	Utah	Florida
1993	Minnesota	92-61	Georgetown	UAB	Providence
1994	Villanova	80-73	Vanderbilt	Siena	Kansas St.
1995	Virginia Tech	65-64(ot)	Marquette	Penn St.	Canisius
1996	Nebraska	60-56	St. Joseph's (Pa.)	Tulane	Alabama

+Tied for third place.

Nebraska freshman Tyronn Lue attempts a shot in the championship game of the 1996 National Invitation Tournament. The Cornhuskers defeated St. Joseph's (Pennsylvania) to win their first NIT title.

Photo from Nebraska sports information

CHAMPIONSHIPS

POSTSEASON CHARITY GAME

During World War II, the Red Cross sponsored a basketball game to raise money for the war effort. The game featured that year's NCAA champion versus the NIT champion.

Season	Winner	Score	Loser	Site
1943	Wyoming (NCAA champion)	52-47(ot)	St. John's (N.Y.) (NIT champion)	New York
1944	Utah (NCAA champion)	43-36	St. John's (N.Y.) (NIT champion)	New York
1945	Oklahoma St. (NCAA champion)	52-44	DePaul (NIT champion)	New York

NABC All-Star Game Results

Season	Winner	Score	Attendance	Most Valuable Player	Winning Coach	Losing Coach
1963	East	77-70	9,000	Art Heyman, Duke	Harold Anderson	Cliff Wells
1964	West	79-78	9,700	Willie Murrell, Kansas St.	Slats Gill	Jack Gardner
1965	West	87-74	7,000	Gail Goodrich, UCLA	Doggie Julian	Joe Lapchick
1966	East	126-99	8,000	Cazzie Russell, Michigan	Taps Gallagher	Forrest Twogood
1967	East	102-93	7,300	Sonny Dove, St. John's (N.Y.)	Ben Carnevale	Everest Shelton
1968	West	95-88	14,500	Pete Maravich, LSU	Phog Allen & Tex Winter	Art Schabinger & John Bach
1969	East	104-80	6,100	Neal Walk, Florida	Tony Hinkle	Branch McCracken
1970	East	116-102	14,756	Charlie Scott, North Caro.	Nat Holman	Bud Foster
1971	East	106-104(ot)	13,178	Jim McDaniels, Western Ky.	Dutch Lonborg	Vadal Peterson
1972	East	96-91(ot)	7,856	Billy Shepard, Butler	Howard Hobson	Henry Iba
1973	West	98-94	8,609	Jim Brewer, Minnesota	Stan Warts	Adolph Rupp
1974	East	105-85	8,396	Marvin Barnes, Providence	Harry Litwack	John Hyder
1975	West	110-89	NA	Gus Williams, Southern Cal	Bruce Drake	Eddie Hickey
1976	West	101-98	5,951	Chuckie Williams, Kansas St.	Marv Harshman	Dean Smith
1977	East	114-93	6,537	Ernie Grunfeld, Tennessee	Bob Knight	Johnny Orr
1978	East	93-87	4,275	Butch Lee, Marquette	Frank McGuire	Al McGuire
1979	East	114-109	7,472	Greg Deane Utah	Joe B. Hall	Bill Foster
1980	East	88-79	7,600	Mike O'Koren, North Caro.	Bill Hodges	Jud Heathcote
1981	West	99-97	3,116	Danny Ainge, Brigham Young	Larry Brown	Denny Crum
1982	West	102-68	3,965	Ricky Frazier, Missouri	Dale Brown	Bob Knight
1983	West	99-94	4,178	Darrell Walker, Arkansas	John Thompson	Dean Smith
1984	West	111-77	4,126	Fred Reynolds, UTEP	Marv Harshman	Jim Valvano
1985	West	97-90	10,464	Lorenzo Charles, North Caro. St.	Guy Lewis	Joe B. Hall
1986	West	94-92	7,009	David Wingate, Georgetown	Rollie Massimino	Lou Carnesecca
1987	West	92-91	8,041	David Robinson, Navy	Denny Crum	Mike Krzyzewski
1988	East	97-91	8,528	David Rivers, Notre Dame	Jim Boeheim	Jerry Tarkanian
1989	West	150-111	7,541	Tim Hardaway, UTEP	Lute Olson	Billy Tubbs
1990	East	127-126	7,161	Travis Mays, Texas	P. J. Carlesimo	Steve Fisher
1991	West	122-113	8,000	Jimy Oliver, Purdue	Nolan Richardson	Bobby Cremins
1992	West	117-93	10,344	Doug Christie, Pepperdine	Roy Williams	Clem Haskins
1993	West	104-95	6,604	Ervin Johnson, New Orleans	Bob Huggins	Mike Krzyzewski
1994	East	77-73	6,500	Charlie Ward, Florida St.	Clarence "Bighouse" Gaines	Guy Lewis
1995	West	117-88	7,900	Fred Hoiberg, Iowa St.	Lute Olson	Lon Kruger
1996	East	99-92	5,500	Dametri Hill, Florida	Eddie Sutton	Jim Harrick

Game Sites: 1963-67—Lexington, Kentucky; 1968-70—Indianapolis, Indiana; 1971-74—Dayton, Ohio; 1975-77—Tulsa, Oklahoma; 1978-present—same city as the Final Four.

Division II Championship

1996 Results

FIRST ROUND
Edinboro 90, Bloomsburg 82
Fairmont St. 78, Bluefield St. 66
S.C.-Spartanburg 91, Clark Atlanta 71
Columbus St. 88, Rollins 80
Regis (Colo.) 73, Neb.-Kearney 70
North Dak. St. 71, Denver 70
Central Mo. St. 89, Tex. A&M-Commerce 86 (ot)
North Ala. 78, Delta St. 69
Franklin Pierce 83, Le Moyne 53
New Hamp. Col. 68, Adelphi 52
Pfeiffer 71, N.C. Central 62
High Point 76, Presbyterian 67
Grand Canyon 105, Alas. Anchorage 96 (ot)
UC Davis 89, Mont. St.-Billings 80
Indianapolis 105, Lake Superior St. 81
Northern St. 98, Oakland 92

REGIONAL SEMIFINALS
Calif. (Pa.) 84, Edinboro 76
Indiana (Pa.) 84, Fairmont St. 83
Alabama A&M 106, S.C.-Spartanburg 91
Columbus St. 83, Fla. Southern 77
Fort Hays St. 97, Regis (Colo.) 69
South Dak. St. 94, North Dak. St. 88
Mo.-Rolla 72, Central Mo. St. 67
North Ala. 85, Tex. A&M-Kingsville 80
St. Anselm 78, Franklin Pierce 70
St. Rose 83, New Hamp. Col. 82
Virginia Union 49, Pfeiffer 47

Queens (N.C.) 81, High Point 70
Cal St. Bakersfield 71, Grand Canyon 66
Seattle Pacific 79, UC Davis 65
Southern Ind. 75, Indianapolis 71
Northern Ky. 82, Northern St. 71

REGIONAL CHAMPIONSHIPS
Calif. (Pa.) 78, Indiana (Pa.) 68
Alabama A&M 98, Columbus St. 82
Fort Hays St. 99, South Dak. St. 90
North Ala. 92, Mo.-Rolla 80
St. Rose 87, St. Anselm 76
Virginia Union 81, Queens (N.C.) 58
Cal St. Bakersfield 78, Seattle Pacific 65
Northern Ky. 99, Southern Ind. 87

QUARTERFINALS
Calif. (Pa.) 95, Alabama A&M 85
Fort Hays St. 71, North Ala. 68
Virginia Union 99, St. Rose 72
Northern Ky. 56, Cal St. Bakersfield 55

SEMIFINALS
Fort Hays St. 76, Calif. (Pa.) 56
Northern Ky. 68, Virginia Union 66

CHAMPIONSHIP
Fort Hays St. 70, Northern Ky. 63

Box Scores

SEMIFINALS

Fort Hays St. 76, Calif. (Pa.) 56

Fort Hays St.	FG-FGA	FT-FTA	RB	PF	TP
Sherick Simpson	5- 8	3- 5	6	4	15
Anthony Pope	6-10	2- 2	7	3	17
Alonzo Goldston	5-12	2- 3	10	5	12
Chad Creamer	1- 6	0- 0	5	2	3
Geoff Eck	6-13	4- 6	4	0	19
Mark Eck	2- 4	1- 2	1	3	5
Earl Tyson	1- 1	2- 2	3	1	5
Jeremie Kester	0- 1	0- 0	1	0	0
Lance Hammond	0- 1	0- 0	0	0	0
Matt Starkey	0- 0	0- 0	0	1	0
Brooke Thompson	0- 1	0- 0	1	0	0
Team			1		
TOTALS	26-57	14-20	39	20	76

Calif. (Pa.)	FG-FGA	FT-FTA	RB	PF	TP
Shea Fleenor	0- 1	0- 0	2	5	0
Robert Jones	7-15	6- 7	7	2	20
Derrick Scott	5-13	2- 3	5	1	12
Candice Pickens	0- 6	5- 8	12	4	5
Brent Kincaid	4-13	0- 2	1	2	12
Stewart Davis	2- 2	0- 0	1	0	4
Reon Nesmith	0- 5	0- 2	1	3	0
Eric Watson	0- 2	0- 2	5	0	0
Lavon Kincaid	0- 0	0- 0	0	0	0
Matt Kerns	0- 0	0- 0	0	0	0
Jimmy Arnold	0- 0	0- 0	0	0	0
Niall Phelan	1- 1	0- 0	0	0	3
Team			4		
TOTALS	19-58	13-24	38	17	56

Half time: Fort Hays St. 30, Calif. (Pa.) 25. Three-point field goals: Fort Hays St. 10-23 (Simpson 2-3, Pope 3-7, Creamer 1-5, G. Eck 3-6, Tyson 1-1, Hammond 0-1); Calif. (Pa.) 5-14 (Kincaid 4-11, Nesmith 0-2, Phelan 1-1). Officials: William Cheek, Sean Hull, Jamie Luckie. Attendance: 2,596.

Northern Ky. 68, Virginia Union 66

Virginia Union	FG-FGA	FT-FTA	RB	PF	TP
Thomas Meredith	4-14	2- 3	3	3	11
Luther Bates	8-11	4- 4	8	2	20
Ben Wallace	3-11	2- 4	14	1	8
Maurice Greene	5-12	0- 0	7	4	11
Jay Butler	1- 4	5- 5	3	1	8

	FG-FGA	FT-FTA	RB	PF	TP
Marquise Newbie	3- 6	0- 3	3	1	6
James Marshall	0- 2	0- 0	1	0	0
Perry Morris	1- 1	0- 0	1	1	2
Ihsan Scott	0- 0	0- 0	0	0	0
Team			3		
TOTALS	25-61	13-19	43	13	66

Northern Ky.	FG-FGA	FT-FTA	RB	PF	TP
Paul Cluxton	7-14	0- 1	1	3	20
LaRon Moore	8-19	4- 4	11	4	20
Reggie Talbert	2- 5	0- 0	3	0	4
Andy Listerman	4- 7	0- 0	3	2	11
Kevin Listerman	0- 2	0- 0	3	2	0
Andre McClendon	2- 3	0- 0	2	1	4
Shannon Minor	2- 8	0- 0	2	3	5
John Gibson	1- 2	0- 0	2	0	2
Chuck Perry	1- 1	0- 0	1	2	2
Team			2		
TOTALS	27-61	4- 5	30	17	68

Half time: Northern Ky. 37, Virginia Union 25. Three-point field goals: Virginia Union 3-13 (Meredith 1-5, Bates 0-1, Greene 1-6, Butler 1-1); Northern Ky. 10-25 (Cluxton 6-12, Moore 0-1, A. Listerman 3-5, K. Listerman 0-1, Minor 1-6). Officials: Bruce Bolivar, Joe Lindsay, Steve Quinn. Attendance: 2,596.

CHAMPIONSHIP

Fort Hays St. 70, Northern Ky. 63

Northern Ky.	FG-FGA	FT-FTA	RB	PF	TP
Paul Cluxton	5- 8	4- 4	3	2	17
LaRon Moore	4-11	6- 7	7	5	14
Reggie Talbert	0- 5	0- 0	2	4	0
Andy Listerman	5-15	2- 2	9	4	15
Kevin Listerman	1- 4	0- 0	3	3	3
Andre McClendon	2- 6	7-11	5	2	11
Shannon Minor	0- 9	3- 5	4	3	3
John Gibson	0- 0	0- 0	1	1	0
Chuck Perry	0- 0	0- 0	0	0	0
Team			3		
TOTALS	17-58	22-29	36	25	63

Fort Hays St.	FG-FGA	FT-FTA	RB	PF	TP
Sherick Simpson	8-10	6- 6	10	3	24
Anthony Pope	6- 8	1- 4	5	3	19
Alonzo Goldston	4-10	4- 4	9	5	12
Chad Creamer	0- 0	0- 0	1	0	0
Geoff Eck	3-10	2- 2	6	2	9
Mark Eck	0- 4	0- 0	4	0	0
Earl Tyson	0- 7	4- 7	2	4	4
Jeremie Kester	1- 1	0- 0	2	1	2
Team			2		
TOTALS	22-50	17-23	41	18	70

Half time: Fort Hays St. 32, Northern Ky. 24. Three-point field goals: Northern Ky. 7-21 (Cluxton 3-3, Moore 0-1, A. Listerman 3-7, K. Listerman 1-3, Minor 0-7); Fort Hays St. 9-19 (Simpson 2-3, Pope 6-7, G. Eck 1-5, M. Eck 0-1, Tyson 0-3). Officials: William Cheek, Sean Hull, Jamie Luckie. Attendance: 3,707.

Year-by-Year Results

Season	Champion	Score	Runner-Up	Third Place	Fourth Place
1957	Wheaton (Ill.)	89-65	Ky. Wesleyan	Mt. St. Mary's (Md.)	Cal St. Los Angeles
1958	South Dak.	75-53	St. Michael's	Evansville	Wheaton (Ill.)
1959	Evansville	83-67	Southwest Mo. St.	North Caro. A&T	Cal St. Los Angeles
1960	Evansville	90-69	Chapman	Ky. Wesleyan	Cornell College
1961	Wittenberg	42-38	Southeast Mo. St.	South Dak. St.	Mt. St. Mary's (Md.)
1962	Mt. St. Mary's (Md.)	58-57(ot)	Cal St. Sacramento	Southern Ill.	Neb. Wesleyan
1963	South Dak. St.	44-42	Wittenberg	Oglethorpe	Southern Ill.
1964	Evansville	72-59	Akron	North Caro. A&T	Northern Iowa
1965	Evansville	85-82(ot)	Southern Ill.	North Dak.	St. Michael's
1966	Ky. Wesleyan	54-51	Southern Ill.	Akron	North Dak.
1967	Winston-Salem	77-74	Southwest Mo. St.	Ky. Wesleyan	Illinois St.
1968	Ky. Wesleyan	63-52	Indiana St.	Trinity (Tex.)	Ashland
1969	Ky. Wesleyan	75-71	Southwest Mo. St.	**American Int'l	Ashland
1970	Phila. Textile	76-65	Tennessee St.	UC Riverside	Buffalo St.
1971	Evansville	97-82	Old Dominion	**Southwestern La.	Ky. Wesleyan
1972	Roanoke	84-72	Akron	Tennessee St.	Eastern Mich.
1973	Ky. Wesleyan	78-76(ot)	Tennessee St.	Assumption	Brockport St.
1974	Morgan St.	67-52	Southwest Mo. St.	Assumption	New Orleans
1975	Old Dominion	76-74	New Orleans	Assumption	Tenn.-Chatt.
1976	Puget Sound	83-74	Tenn.-Chatt.	Eastern Ill.	Old Dominion
1977	Tenn.-Chatt.	71-62	Randolph-Macon	North Ala.	Sacred Heart
1978	Cheyney	47-40	Wis.-Green Bay	Eastern Ill.	Central Fla.
1979	North Ala.	64-50	Wis.-Green Bay	Cheyney	Bridgeport
1980	Virginia Union	80-74	New York Tech	Fla. Southern	North Ala.
1981	Fla. Southern	73-68	Mt. St. Mary's (Md.)	Cal Poly SLO	Wis.-Green Bay
1982	Dist. Columbia	73-63	Fla. Southern	Ky. Wesleyan	Cal St. Bakersfield
1983	Wright St.	92-73	Dist. Columbia	*Cal St. Bakersfield	*Morningside
1984	Central Mo. St.	81-77	St. Augustine's	*Ky. Wesleyan	*North Ala.
1985	Jacksonville St.	74-73	South Dak. St.	*Ky. Wesleyan	*Mt. St. Mary's (Md.)
1986	Sacred Heart	93-87	Southeast Mo. St.	*Cheyney	*Fla. Southern
1987	Ky. Wesleyan	92-74	Gannon	*Delta St.	*Mont. St.-Billings
1988	Mass.-Lowell	75-72	Alas. Anchorage	Fla. Southern	Troy St.
1989	N.C. Central	73-46	Southeast Mo. St.	UC Riverside	Jacksonville St.
1990	Ky. Wesleyan	93-79	Cal St. Bakersfield	North Dak.	Morehouse
1991	North Ala.	79-72	Bridgeport	*Cal St. Bakersfield	*Virginia Union
1992	Virginia Union	100-75	Bridgeport	*Cal St. Bakersfield	*Calif. (Pa.)
1993	Cal St. Bakersfield	85-72	Troy St.	*Wayne St. (Mich.)	*New Hamp. Col.
1994	Cal St. Bakersfield	92-86	Southern Ind.	*Washburn	*New Hamp. Col.
1995	Southern Ind.	71-63	UC Riverside	*Norfolk St.	*Indiana (Pa.)
1996	Fort Hays St.	70-63	Northern Ky.	*Virginia Union	*Calif. (Pa.)

*Indicates tied for third. **Student-athletes representing American International in 1969 and Southwestern Louisiana in 1971 were declared ineligible after the tournament. Under NCAA rules, the teams' and ineligible student-athletes' records were deleted, and the teams' places in the final standings were vacated.

Season	Site of Finals	Coach of Champion	Outstanding Player Award
1957	Evansville, Ind.	Lee Pfund, Wheaton (Ill.)	Mel Peterson, Wheaton (Ill.)
1958	Evansville, Ind.	Duane Clodfelter, South Dak.	Ed Smallwood, Evansville
1959	Evansville, Ind.	Arad McCutchan, Evansville	Hugh Ahlering, Evansville
1960	Evansville, Ind.	Arad McCutchan, Evansville	Ed Smallwood, Evansville
1961	Evansville, Ind.	Ray Mears, Wittenberg	Don Jacobsen, South Dak. St.
1962	Evansville, Ind.	Jim Phelan, Mt. St. Mary's (Md.)	Ron Rohrer, Cal. St. Sacramento
1963	Evansville, Ind.	Jim Iverson, South Dak. St.	Wayne Rasmussen, South Dak. St.
1964	Evansville, Ind.	Arad McCutchan, Evansville	Jerry Sloan, Evansville
1965	Evansville, Ind.	Arad McCutchan, Evansville	Jerry Sloan, Evansville
1966	Evansville, Ind.	Guy Strong, Ky. Wesleyan	Sam Smith, Ky. Wesleyan
1967	Evansville, Ind.	C. E. Gaines, Winston-Salem	Earl Monroe, Winston-Salem

Photo by Chris Hall/NCAA photos

CHAMPIONSHIPS

Chad Creamer of Fort Hays State celebrates the Tigers' first national title. The Tigers defeated Northern Kentucky, 70-63, in the Division II championship game.

Photo by Chris Hall/NCAA photos

Sherick Simpson (32) and Chad Creamer congratulate each other after Fort Hays State's victory over Northern Kentucky in the Division II championship game. Simpson was named the championship's most outstanding player.

Season	Site of Finals	Coach of Champion	Outstanding Player Award
1968	Evansville, Ind.	Bob Daniels, Ky. Wesleyan	Jerry Newsom, Indiana St.
1969	Evansville, Ind.	Bob Daniels, Ky. Wesleyan	George Tinsley, Ky. Wesleyan
1970	Evansville, Ind.	Herb Magee, Phila. Textile	Ted McClain, Tennessee St.
1971	Evansville, Ind.	Arad McCutchan, Evansville	Don Buse, Evansville
1972	Evansville, Ind.	Charles Moir, Roanoke	Hal Johnston, Roanoke
1973	Evansville, Ind.	Bob Jones, Ky. Wesleyan	Mike Williams, Ky. Wesleyan
1974	Evansville, Ind.	Nathaniel Frazier, Morgan St.	Marvin Webster, Morgan St.
1975	Evansville, Ind.	Sonny Allen, Old Dominion	Wilson Washington, Old Dominion
1976	Evansville, Ind.	Don Zech, Puget Sound	Curt Peterson, Puget Sound
1977	Springfield, Mass.	Ron Shumate, Tenn.-Chatt.	Wayne Golden, Tenn.-Chatt.
1978	Springfield, Mo.	John Chaney, Cheyney	Andrew Fields, Cheyney
1979	Springfield, Mo.	Bill Jones, North Ala.	Perry Oden, North Ala.
1980	Springfield, Mass.	Dave Robbins, Virginia Union	Keith Valentine, Virginia Union
1981	Springfield, Mass.	Hal Wissel, Fla. Southern	John Ebeling, Fla. Southern
1982	Springfield, Mass.	Wil Jones, Dist. Columbia	Michael Britt, Dist. Columbia
1983	Springfield, Mass.	Ralph Underhill, Wright St.	Gary Monroe, Wright St.
1984	Springfield, Mass.	Lynn Nance, Central Mo. St.	Ron Nunnelly, Central Mo. St.
1985	Springfield, Mass.	Bill Jones, Jacksonville St.	Mark Tetzlaff, South Dak. St.
1986	Springfield, Mass.	Dave Bike, Sacred Heart	Roger Younger, Sacred Heart
1987	Springfield, Mass.	Wayne Chapman, Ky. Wesleyan	Sam Smith, Ky. Wesleyan
1988	Springfield, Mass.	Don Doucette, Mass.-Lowell	Leo Parent, Mass.-Lowell
1989	Springfield, Mass.	Michael Bernard, N.C. Central	Miles Clarke, N.C. Central
1990	Springfield, Mass.	Wayne Chapman, Ky. Wesleyan	Wade Green, Cal St. Bakersfield
1991	Springfield, Mass.	Gary Elliott, North Ala.	Lambert Shell, Bridgeport
1992	Springfield, Mass.	Dave Robbins, Virginia Union	Derrick Johnson, Virginia Union
1993	Springfield, Mass.	Pat Douglass, Cal St. Bakersfield	Tyrone Davis, Cal St. Bakersfield
1994	Springfield, Mass.	Pat Douglass, Cal St. Bakersfield	Stan Gourad, Southern Ind.
1995	Louisville, Ky.	Bruce Pearl, Southern Ind.	William Wilson, UC Riverside
1996	Louisville, Ky.	Gary Garner, Fort Hays St.	Sherick Simpson, Fort Hays St.

Individual Records

MOST POINTS, ONE GAME
54—Willie Jones, American (91) vs. Evansville (101), 1960; Bill Fennelly, Central Mo. St. (112) vs. Jacksonville St. (91), 1980.

MOST POINTS, SERIES
185—Jack Sullivan, Mt. St. Mary's (Md.), 1957 (36 vs. CCNY, 48 vs. N.C. Central, 39 vs. Rider, 19 vs. Ky. Wesleyan, 43 vs. Cal St. Los Angeles).

MOST FIELD GOALS, ONE GAME
22—Phil Jackson, North Dak. (107) vs. Parsons (56), 1967.

MOST FIELD GOALS, SERIES
71—Jack Sullivan, Mt. St. Mary's (Md.), 1957 (14 vs. CCNY, 19 vs. N.C. Central, 16 vs. Rider, 8 vs. Ky. Wesleyan, 14 vs. Cal St. Los Angeles).

MOST THREE-POINT FIELD GOALS, ONE GAME
11—Kenny Warren, Cal St. Bakersfield (98) vs. Grand Canyon (68), 1993.

MOST THREE-POINT FIELD GOALS, SERIES
22—Kenny Warren, Cal St. Bakersfield, 1993 [11 vs. Grand Canyon, 3 vs. Alas. Anchorage, 5 vs. N.C. Central, 1 vs. Wayne St. (Mich.), 2 vs. Troy St.].

MOST FREE THROWS, ONE GAME
24—Dave Twardzik, Old Dominion (102) vs. Norfolk St. (97), 1971.

MOST FREE THROWS, SERIES
55—Don Jacobsen, South Dak. St., 1961 [9 vs. Cornell College, 22 vs. Prairie View, 9 vs. UC Santa Barb., 11 vs. Southeast Mo. St., 4 vs. Mt. St. Mary's (Md.)].

HIGHEST FREE-THROW PERCENTAGE, ONE GAME (Minimum 18 Made)
100%—Ralph Talley, Norfolk St. (70) vs. Virginia Union (60), 1986 (18-18).

MOST ASSISTS, ONE GAME
20—Steve Ray, Bridgeport (132) vs. Stonehill (127) (ot), 1989.

MOST ASSISTS, SERIES
49—Tyrone Tate, Southern Ind., 1994 [8 vs. Ky. Wesleyan, 3 vs. Wayne St. (Mich.), 16 vs. South Dak., 16 vs. New Hamp. Col., 6 vs. Cal St. Bakersfield].

Team Records

MOST POINTS, ONE GAME
132—Bridgeport vs. Stonehill (127) (ot), 1989; Central Okla. vs. Washburn (114), 1992.

MOST POINTS, SERIES
567—Southern Ind., 1995 (95 vs. Hillsdale, 102 vs. Ky. Wesleyan, 102 vs. Northern Ky., 108 vs. New Hamp. Col., 89 vs. Norfolk St., 71 vs. UC Riverside).

MOST FIELD GOALS, ONE GAME
54—Bentley (129) vs. Stonehill (118), 1989.

MOST FIELD GOALS, SERIES
198—Southern Ind., 1995 (37 vs. Hillsdale, 37 vs. Ky. Wesleyan, 34 vs. Northern Ky., 40 vs. New Hamp. Col., 26 vs. Norfolk St., 24 vs. UC Riverside).

MOST THREE-POINT FIELD GOALS, ONE GAME
23—Troy St. (126) vs. New Hamp. Col. (123), 1993.

MOST THREE-POINT FIELD GOALS, SERIES
57—Troy St., 1993 (9 vs. Fla. Southern, 14 vs. Delta St., 6 vs. Washburn, 23 vs. New Hamp. Col., 5 vs. Cal St. Bakersfield).

MOST FREE THROWS, ONE GAME
46—Evansville (110) vs. North Caro. A&T (92), 1959.

MOST FREE THROWS, SERIES
142—Mt. St. Mary's (Md.), 1957.

MOST ASSISTS, ONE GAME
36—Troy St. (126) vs. New Hamp. Col. (123), 1993.

MOST ASSISTS, SERIES
120—North Dak., 1990.

All-Tournament Teams

(First player listed on each team was the outstanding player of the championship)

1957—Mel Peterson, Wheaton (Ill.)
Jack Sullivan, Mt. St. Mary's (Md.)
Mason Cope, Ky. Wesleyan
Bob Whitehead, Wheaton (Ill.)
Jim Daniels, South Dak.

1958—Ed Smallwood, Evansville
Jim Browne, St. Michael's
Jim Daniels, South Dak.
Mel Peterson, Wheaton (Ill.)
Dick Zeitler, St. Michael's

1959—Hugh Ahlering, Evansville
Joe Cotton, North Caro. A&T
Jack Israel, Southwest Mo. St.
Paul Benes, Hope
Leo Hill, Cal St. Los Angeles

1960—Ed Smallwood, Evansville
Dale Wise, Evansville
Tom Cooke, Chapman
Gary Auten, Ky. Wesleyan
William Jones, American

1961—Don Jacobsen, South Dak. St.
John O'Reilly, Mt. St. Mary's (Md.)
George Fisher, Wittenberg
Vivan Reed, Southeast Mo. St.
Carl Ritter, Southeast Mo. St.

1962—Ron Rohrer, Cal St. Sacramento
Jim Mumford, Neb. Wesleyan
Ed Spila, Southern Ill.
John O'Reilly, Mt. St. Mary's (Md.)
Ed Pfeiffer, Mt. St. Mary's (Md.)

1963—Wayne Rasmussen, South Dak. St.
Tom Black, South Dak. St.
Bob Cherry, Wittenberg

Bill Fisher, Wittenberg
Al Thrasher, Wittenberg
1964—Jerry Sloan, Evansville
Maurice McHartley, North Caro. A&T
Larry Humes, Evansville
Bill Stevens, Akron
Buster Briley, Evansville
1965—Jerry Sloan, Evansville
Richard Tarrant, St. Michael's
Walt Frazier, Southern Ill.
George McNeil, Southern Ill.
Larry Humes, Evansville
1966—Sam Smith, Ky. Wesleyan
Clarence Smith, Southern Ill.
George McNeil, Southern Ill.
David Lee, Southern Ill.
Phil Jackson, North Dak.
1967—Earl Monroe, Winston-Salem
Lou Shepherd, Southwest Mo. St.
Sam Smith, Ky. Wesleyan
Danny Bolden, Southwest Mo. St.
Dallas Thornton, Ky. Wesleyan
1968—Jerry Newsom, Indiana St.
Larry Jeffries, Trinity (Tex.)
George Tinsley, Ky. Wesleyan
Fred Hardman, Indiana St.
Dallas Thornton, Ky. Wesleyan
1969—George Tinsley, Ky. Wesleyan
Curtis Perry, Southwest Mo. St.
Tommy Hobgood, Ky. Wesleyan
Mert Bancroft, Southwest Mo. St.
Bob Rutherford, American Int'l
1970—Ted McClain, Tennessee St.
Randy Smith, Buffalo St.
Carl Poole, Phila. Textile
Howard Lee, UC Riverside
John Pierantozzi, Phila. Textile
1971—Don Buse, Evansville
Dwight Lamar*, Southwestern La.
Rick Coffey, Evansville
John Duncan, Ky. Wesleyan
Skip Noble, Old Dominion
1972—Hal Johnston, Roanoke
Leonard Robinson, Tennessee St.
Lloyd Neal, Tennessee St.
Jay Piccola, Roanoke
Len Paul, Akron
1973—Mike Williams, Ky. Wesleyan
Ron Gilliam, Brockport St.
Mike Boylan, Assumption
Leonard Robinson, Tennessee St.
Roger Zornes, Ky. Wesleyan
1974—Marvin Webster, Morgan St.
John Grochowalski, Assumption
Randy Magers, Southwest Mo. St.
William Doolittle, Southwest Mo. St.
Alvin O'Neal, Morgan St.
1975—Wilson Washington, Old Dominion
Wilbur Holland, New Orleans
John Grochowalski, Assumption
Joey Caruthers, Old Dominion
Paul Brennan, Assumption
1976—Curt Peterson, Puget Sound
Wayne Golden, Tenn.-Chatt.
Jeff Fuhrmann, Old Dominion
Jeff Furry, Eastern Ill.
Brant Gibler, Puget Sound
1977—Wayne Golden, Tenn.-Chatt.
Joe Allen, Randolph-Macon
Otis Boddie, North Ala.
William Gordon, Tenn.-Chatt.
Hector Olivencia, Sacred Heart
1978—Andrew Fields, Cheyney
Kenneth Hynson, Cheyney
Tom Anderson, Wis.-Green Bay
Charlie Thomas, Eastern Ill.
Jerry Prather, Central Fla.
1979—Perry Oden, North Ala.
Carlton Hurdle, Bridgeport
Ron Ripley, Wis.-Green Bay
Ron Darby, North Ala.
Rory Lindgren, Wis.-Green Bay
1980—Keith Valentine, Virginia Union
Larry Holmes, Virginia Union
Bobby Jones, New York Tech

John Ebeling, Fla. Southern
Johnny Buckmon, North Ala.
1981—John Ebeling, Fla. Southern
Mike Hayes, Fla. Southern
Durelle Lewis, Mt. St. Mary's (Md.)
Jim Rowe, Mt. St. Mary's (Md.)
Jay Bruchak, Mt. St. Mary's (Md.)
1982—Michael Britt, Dist. Columbia
John Ebeling, Fla. Southern
Dwight Higgs, Ky. Wesleyan
Earl Jones, Dist. Columbia
Wayne McDaniel, Cal St. Bakersfield
1983—Gary Monroe, Wright St.
Anthony Bias, Wright St.
Fred Moore, Wright St.
Earl Jones, Dist. Columbia
Michael Britt, Dist. Columbia
1984—Ron Nunnelly, Central Mo. St.
Brian Pesko, Central Mo. St.
Kenneth Bannister, St. Augustine's
Rod Drake, Ky. Wesleyan
Robert Harris, North Ala.
1985—Mark Tetzlaff, South Dak. St.
Dave Bennett, Ky. Wesleyan
Melvin Allen, Jacksonville St.
Robert Spurgeon, Jacksonville St.
Darryle Edwards, Mt. St. Mary's (Md.)
1986—Roger Younger, Sacred Heart
Kevin Stevens, Sacred Heart
Keith Johnson, Sacred Heart
Riley Ellis, Southeast Mo. St.
Ronny Rankin, Southeast Mo. St.
1987—Sam Smith, Ky. Wesleyan
Andra Whitlow, Ky. Wesleyan
John Worth, Ky. Wesleyan
Mike Runski, Gannon
Jerome Johnson, Mont. St.-Billings
1988—Leo Parent, Mass.-Lowell
Bobby Licare, Mass.-Lowell
Averian Parrish, Alas. Anchorage
Jerry Johnson, Fla. Southern
Darryl Thomas, Troy St.
1989—Miles Clarke, N.C. Central
Dominique Stephens, N.C. Central
Antoine Sifford, N.C. Central
Earnest Taylor, Southeast Mo. St.
Maurice Pullum, UC Riverside
1990—Wade Green, Cal St. Bakersfield
LeRoy Ellis, Ky. Wesleyan
Corey Crowder, Ky. Wesleyan
Dave Vonesh, North Dak.
Vincent Mitchell, Ky. Wesleyan
1991—Lambert Shell, Bridgeport
Pat Morris, Bridgeport
Fred Stafford, North Ala.
Allen Williams, North Ala.
Carl Wilmer, North Ala.
1992—Derrick Johnson, Virginia Union
Reggie Jones, Virginia Union
Winston Jones, Bridgeport
Steve Wills, Bridgeport
Kenney Toomer, Calif. (Pa.)
1993—Tyrone Davis, Cal St. Bakersfield
Roheen Oats, Cal St. Bakersfield
Terry McCord, Troy St.
Wayne Robertson, New Hamp. Col.
Danny Lewis, Wayne St. (Mich.)
1994—Stan Gouard, Southern Ind.
Kenny Warren, Cal St. Bakersfield
Reggie Phillips, Cal St. Bakersfield
Roheen Oats, Cal St. Bakersfield
Tyrone Tate, Southern Ind.
1995—William Wilson, UC Riverside
Brian Huebner, Southern Ind.
Chad Gilbert, Southern Ind.
Boo Purdom, UC Riverside
Corey Williams, Norfolk St.
1996—Sherick Simpson, Fort Hays St.
Paul Cluxton, Northern Ky.
LaRon Moore, Northern Ky.
Alonzo Goldston, Fort Hays St.
Kebu Stewart, Cal St. Bakersfield

The participation of Dwight Lamar (Southwestern Louisiana) in the 1971 tournament was voided by action of the NCAA Council.

Division III Championship

1996 Results

FIRST ROUND
Geneseo St. 73, Rochester Inst. 51
Buffalo St. 74, St. John Fisher 65
Wilkes 87, Allentown 72
Cabrini 85, Catholic 65
St. Lawrence 85, Hamilton 78
Rensselaer 68, Hartwick 55
Lycoming 103, Gettysburg 75
Frank. & Marsh. 118, Salisbury St. 69
Wis.-Whitewater 85, Wis.-Platteville 77
Claremont-M-S 70, Upper Iowa 58
Hope 65, Kalamazoo 62
John Carroll 86, Wooster 72
Wis.-Oshkosh 79, Simpson 74
Gust. Adolphus 72, Concordia-M'head 61
Capital 68, Ohio Northern 57
Wittenberg 70, Baldwin-Wallace 61
Williams 78, Plymouth St. 62
Bowdoin 62, Springfield 56
Rowan 130, York (N.Y.) 66
Jersey City St. 73, Staten Island 63
Anna Maria 111, Babson 90
Salem St. 76, Western Conn. St. 60
New York. U. 105, N.J. Inst. of Tech. 88
Richard Stockton 80, Mt. St. Vincent 54
Wheaton (Ill.) 131, Grinnell 117
Washington (Mo.) 76, Rose-Hulman 74
Chris. Newport 66, Randolph-Macon 57
Millsaps 83, Bridgewater (Va.) 72
Hanover 85, Fontbonne 43
Ill. Wesleyan 77, Ripon 66
Hendrix 97, Stillman 85
Roanoke 128, Shenandoah 110

SECOND ROUND
Buffalo St. 71, Geneseo St. 61
Wilkes 96, Cabrini 91 (ot)
Rensselaer 78, St. Lawrence 70
Frank. & Marsh. 72, Lycoming 61
Wis.-Whitewater 63, Claremont-M-S 62
Hope 80, John Carroll 61
Gust. Adolphus 61, Wis.-Oshkosh 60 (2 ot)
Wittenberg 65, Capital 60
Williams 91, Bowdoin 64
Rowan 102, Jersey City St. 83
Anna Maria 74, Salem St. 67
Richard Stockton 81, New York U. 77 (ot)
Washington (Mo.) 93, Wheaton (Ill.) 75
Chris. Newport 73, Millsaps 69
Ill. Wesleyan 73, Hanover 67
Roanoke 80, Hendrix 64

SECTIONAL SEMIFINALS
Wilkes 64, Buffalo St. 59
Frank. & Marsh. 74, Rensselaer 58
Hope 88, Wis.-Whitewater 66
Wittenberg 76, Gust. Adolphus 68
Rowan 85, Williams 77
Richard Stockton 95, Anna Maria 88
Washington (Mo.) 87, Chris. Newport 71
Ill. Wesleyan 116, Roanoke 88

SECTIONAL CHAMPIONSHIPS
Frank. & Marsh. 107, Wilkes 70
Hope 69, Wittenberg 60
Rowan 98, Richard Stockton 70
Ill. Wesleyan 73, Washington (Mo.) 61

SEMIFINALS
Hope 76, Frank. & Marsh. 57
Rowan 79, Ill. Wesleyan 77

THIRD PLACE
Ill. Wesleyan 89, Frank. & Marsh. 57

CHAMPIONSHIP
Rowan 100, Hope 93

CHAMPIONSHIPS

Box Scores

SEMIFINALS

Hope 76, Frank. & Marsh. 57

Frank. & Marsh.	FG-FGA	FT-FTA	RB	PF	TP
Jeremiah Henry	5-10	11-12	3	3	23
Mike Mehaffey	4-8	0-1	11	2	8
Darren Sanborn	1-5	1-3	4	1	3
Chris Kelliher	2-5	0-2	3	4	4
Chris Loftus	3-6	3-4	4	2	11
Mike Keslosky	1-4	0-0	1	1	2
Matt Leddy	0-1	0-0	0	0	0
Tom Deitzler	0-0	0-0	3	1	0
Jeff Lerner	0-2	0-0	0	0	0
Rich Davis	3-9	0-0	5	4	6
Josh Fabian	0-0	0-0	1	0	0
Team			2		
TOTALS	19-50	15-22	37	18	57

Hope	FG-FGA	FT-FTA	RB	PF	TP
Dan VanHekken	3-5	0-0	2	4	7
Kris Merritt	4-10	0-1	11	4	8
Duane Bosma	8-14	4-5	8	3	20
Joel Holstege	5-11	4-4	5	3	17
Kevin Brintnell	3-12	2-2	0	1	9
Jason VanderWoude	0-1	0-0	1	0	0
Joe Davelaar	0-0	0-0	0	0	0
Marc Whitford	0-5	1-2	3	1	1
Matt Brown	1-1	0-0	0	0	2
Pat Stegeman	0-1	2-2	2	1	2
Matt Spencer	0-2	0-0	3	0	0
Jeff VanFossan	2-5	6-7	4	1	10
Jon Vertalka	0-0	0-0	0	0	0
Tom Gortsema	0-0	0-0	1	0	0
Team			2		
TOTALS:	26-67	19-23	42	16	76

Half time: Hope 31, Frank. & Marsh. 24. Three-point field goals: Frank. & Marsh. 4-9 (Henry 2-4, Loftus 2-4, Keslosky 0-1); Hope 5-19 (VanHekken 1-3, Bosma 0-1, Holstege 3-4, Brintnell 1-6, Whitford 0-3, Spencer 0-2). Attendance: 3,812.

Rowan 79, Ill. Wesleyan 77

Rowan	FG-FGA	FT-FTA	RB	PF	TP
Terrence Stewart	12-18	1-1	8	3	30
Lamonte Harvin	3-7	3-4	5	3	9
Demetrius Poles	2-7	0-0	6	1	4
Osco Williams	1-5	0-0	2	2	2
Antwan Dasher	7-16	4-6	3	2	19
Ryan Cochrane	1-2	0-0	0	1	2
Chris McShane	2-4	0-0	2	3	5
Robert Scott	0-1	0-0	2	1	0
Roscoe Harris	4-13	0-0	5	2	8
Team			2		
TOTALS	32-73	8-11	35	18	79

Ill. Wesleyan	FG-FGA	FT-FTA	RB	PF	TP
Bryan Crabtree	7-13	5-7	4	5	21
Jon Litwiller	3-5	0-0	4	3	6
Chris Simich	8-17	11-12	13	1	27
Brady Knight	3-6	1-1	4	4	7
T. J. Posey	4-8	0-0	2	2	12
Kyle Tudeen	0-0	0-0	0	0	0
Nathan Hubbard	0-0	0-0	0	0	0
Andrew Boyden	0-1	0-0	0	0	0
Scott Peterson	0-2	0-3	1	1	0
Matt Swingler	1-1	2-2	2	0	4
Team			7		
TOTALS	26-53	19-25	37	16	77

Half time: Rowan 47, Ill. Wesleyan 45. Three-point field goals: Rowan 7-25 (Stewart 5-9, Williams 0-1, Dasher 1-6, McShane 1-2, Harris 0-7); Ill. Wesleyan 6-12 (Crabtree 2-4, Litwiller 0-1, Posey 4-7). Attendance: 3,872.

THIRD PLACE

Ill. Wesleyan 89, Frank. & Marsh. 57

Frank. & Marsh.	FG-FGA	FT-FTA	RB	PF	TP
Mike Mehaffey	9-13	3-3	7	2	21
Darren Sanborn	3-7	4-6	6	3	10
Jeremiah Henry	2-9	0-0	0	2	6
Chris Kelliher	3-5	1-2	3	3	7
Chris Loftus	0-4	0-0	3	1	0
Mike Keslosky	0-1	0-0	1	1	0
Matt Leddy	2-3	1-1	0	2	5
Erik Mahland	1-1	0-0	0	0	2
Matt McKelvey	0-2	0-0	2	0	0
Tom Deitzler	0-3	0-0	1	2	0
Adam Sorce	0-1	0-0	0	2	0
Jeff Lerner	0-0	3-4	1	0	3
Rich Davis	0-2	1-2	1	4	1
Josh Fabian	1-2	0-2	2	2	2
Team			2		
TOTALS	21-53	13-20	26	24	57

Ill. Wesleyan	FG-FGA	FT-FTA	RB	PF	TP
Bryan Crabtree	6-15	7-8	5	2	21
Jon Litwiller	0-4	0-0	4	1	0
Chris Simich	9-13	1-2	11	2	19
Brady Knight	4-5	2-2	1	3	10
T. J. Posey	2-2	1-2	2	3	7
Tony Pacetti	0-0	2-2	0	2	2
Kyle Tudeen	2-3	0-0	1	0	5
Brian Green	0-1	1-4	3	0	1
Nathan Hubbard	1-1	0-1	2	0	2
Brent Niebrugge	1-3	0-1	2	0	2
Andrew Boyden	2-3	0-0	3	3	4
John Baines	1-4	0-0	3	1	2
Scott Peterson	4-5	0-2	5	2	9
Chris Senica	0-0	0-0	1	1	0
Matt Swingler	2-6	1-2	2	0	5
Team			3		
TOTALS	34-65	15-26	48	20	89

Half time: Ill. Wesleyan 40, Frank. & Marsh. 25. Three-point field goals: Frank. & Marsh. 2-16 (Henry 2-9, Loftus 0-3, Leddy 0-1, Deitzler 0-2, Sorce 0-1); Ill. Wesleyan 6-10 (Crabtree 2-5, Posey 2-2, Tudeen 1-1, Peterson 1-1, Swingler 0-1). Attendance: 2,895.

CHAMPIONSHIP

Rowan 100, Hope 93

Hope	FG-FGA	FT-FTA	RB	PF	TP
Dan VanHekken	0-1	2-2	1	3	2
Kris Merritt	1-6	2-2	5	3	4
Duane Bosma	11-18	6-9	8	4	28
Joel Holstege	13-19	6-6	4	5	39
Kevin Brintnell	2-9	1-2	2	3	6
Jason VanderWoude	0-0	0-0	0	0	0
Marc Whitford	6-9	0-0	3	2	14
Pat Stegeman	0-0	0-0	1	0	0
Matt Spencer	0-0	0-0	2	0	0
Jeff VanFossan	0-1	0-0	0	1	0
Tom Gortsema	0-0	0-0	1	2	0
Team			2		
TOTALS	33-63	17-21	27	25	93

Rowan	FG-FGA	FT-FTA	RB	PF	TP
Osco Williams	1-5	0-0	1	1	2
Demetrius Poles	2-3	0-1	2	4	4
Lamonte Harvin	6-11	0-0	9	3	12
Terrence Stewart	6-12	1-2	7	4	17
Antwan Dasher	5-10	9-9	4	2	19
Ryan Cochrane	2-5	3-4	2	0	7
Darius Taraila	1-1	0-0	0	0	2
Chris McShane	7-9	1-2	8	1	16
Robert Scott	1-4	2-2	3	2	4
Roscoe Harris	3-5	9-11	2	1	17
Team			2		
TOTALS	34-65	25-33	40	18	100

Half time: Rowan 46, Hope 43. Three-point field goals: Hope 10-25 (VanHekken 0-1, Holstege 7-12, Brintnell 1-8, Whitford 2-4); Rowan 7-18 (Williams 0-2, Stewart 4-6, Dasher 0-4, Cochrane 0-1, McShane 1-2, Harris 2-3). Attendance: 3,944.

Photo by Andy Alonso/NCAA photos

A balanced offensive attack and the three-point shooting of Terrence Stewart helped Rowan outlast Hope and claim its first Division III national title.

Year-by-Year Results

Season	Champion	Score	Runner-Up	Third Place	Fourth Place
1975	LeMoyne-Owen	57-54	Rowan	Augustana (Ill.)	Brockport St.
1976	Scranton	60-57	Wittenberg	Augustana (Ill.)	Plattsburgh St.
1977	Wittenberg	79-66	Oneonta St.	Scranton	Hamline
1978	North Park	69-57	Widener	Albion	Stony Brook
1979	North Park	66-62	Potsdam St.	Frank. & Marsh.	Centre
1980	North Park	83-76	Upsala	Wittenberg	Longwood
1981	Potsdam St.	67-65(ot)	Augustana (Ill.)	Ursinus	Otterbein
1982	Wabash	83-62	Potsdam St.	Brooklyn	Cal St. Stanislaus
1983	Scranton	64-63	Wittenberg	Roanoke	Wis.-Whitewater
1984	Wis.-Whitewater	103-86	Clark (Mass.)	DePauw	Upsala
1985	North Park	72-71	Potsdam St.	Neb. Wesleyan	Widener
1986	Potsdam St.	76-73	LeMoyne-Owen	Neb. Wesleyan	Jersey City St.
1987	North Park	106-100	Clark (Mass.)	Wittenberg	Richard Stockton
1988	Ohio Wesleyan	92-70	Scranton	Neb. Wesleyan	Hartwick
1989	Wis.-Whitewater	94-86	Trenton St.	Southern Me.	Centre
1990	Rochester	43-42	DePauw	Washington (Md.)	Calvin
1991	Wis.-Platteville	81-74	Frank. & Marsh.	Otterbein	Ramapo
1992	Calvin	62-49	Rochester	Wis.-Platteville	Jersey City St.
1993	Ohio Northern	71-68	Augustana (Ill.)	Rowan	Mass.-Dartmouth
1994	Lebanon Valley	66-59†	New York U.	Wittenberg	St. Thomas (Minn.)
1995	Wis.-Platteville	69-55	Manchester	Rowan	Trinity (Conn.)
1996	Rowan	100-93	Hope	Ill. Wesleyan	Frank. & Marsh.

Season	Site of Finals	Coach of Champion	Outstanding Player Award
1975	Reading, Pa.	Jerry Johnson, LeMoyne-Owen	Bob Newman, LeMoyne-Owen
1976	Reading, Pa.	Bob Bessoir, Scranton	Jack Maher, Scranton
1977	Rock Island, Ill.	Larry Hunter, Wittenberg	Rick White, Wittenberg
1978	Rock Island, Ill.	Dan McCarrell, North Park	Michael Harper, North Park
1979	Rock Island, Ill.	Dan McCarrell, North Park	Michael Harper, North Park
1980	Rock Island, Ill.	Dan McCarrell, North Park	Michael Thomas, North Park
1981	Rock Island, Ill.	Jerry Welsh, Potsdam St.	Maxwell Artis, Augustana (Ill.)
1982	Grand Rapids, Mich.	Mac Petty, Wabash	Pete Metzelaars, Wabash
1983	Grand Rapids, Mich.	Bob Bessoir, Scranton	Bill Bessoir, Scranton
1984	Grand Rapids, Mich.	Dave Vander Meulen, Wis.-Whitewater	Andre McKoy, Wis.-Whitewater
1985	Grand Rapids, Mich.	Bosco Djurickovic, North Park	Earnest Hubbard, North Park
1986	Grand Rapids, Mich.	Jerry Welsh, Potsdam St.	Roosevelt Bullock, Potsdam St.
1987	Grand Rapids, Mich.	Bosco Djurickovic, North Park	Michael Starks, North Park
1988	Grand Rapids, Mich.	Gene Mehaffey, Ohio Wesleyan	Scott Tedder, Ohio Wesleyan
1989	Springfield, Ohio	Dave Vander Meulen, Wis.-Whitewater	Greg Grant, Trenton St.
1990	Springfield, Ohio	Mike Neer, Rochester	Chris Fite, Rochester
1991	Springfield, Ohio	Bo Ryan, Wis.-Platteville	Shawn Frison, Wis.-Platteville
1992	Springfield, Ohio	Ed Douma, Calvin	Steve Honderd, Calvin
1993	Buffalo, New York	Joe Campoli, Ohio Northern	Kirk Anderson, Augustana (Ill.)
1994	Buffalo, New York	Pat Flannery, Lebanon Valley	Mike Rhoades, Lebanon Valley Adam Crawford, New York U.
1995	Buffalo, New York	Bo Ryan, Wis.-Platteville	Ernie Peavy, Wis.-Platteville
1996	Salem, Virginia	John Giannini, Rowan	Terrence Stewart, Rowan

Photo by Andy Alonso/NCAA photos

Rowan coach John Giannini shouts instruction to his squad during the Division III championship game. Giannini guided Rowan to its first national title.

Individual Records

MOST POINTS, ONE GAME
49—Gerald Reece, William Penn (85) vs. North Park (81), 1981.

MOST POINTS, SERIES
167—Greg Grant, Trenton St., 1989 (30 vs. Shenandoah, 28 vs. Jersey City St., 38 vs. Potsdam St., 36 vs. Southern Me., 35 vs. Wis.-Whitewater).

MOST FIELD GOALS, ONE GAME
21—Gerald Reece, William Penn (85) vs. North Park (81), 1981.

MOST FIELD GOALS, SERIES
68—Greg Grant, Trenton St., 1989 (11 vs. Shenandoah, 11 vs. Jersey City St., 16 vs. Potsdam St., 16 vs. Southern Me., 14 vs. Wis.-Whitewater).

MOST THREE-POINT FIELD GOALS, ONE GAME
12—Kirk Anderson, Augustana (Ill.) (100) vs. Wis.-Platteville (86), 1993.

MOST THREE-POINT FIELD GOALS, SERIES
35—Kirk Anderson, Augustana (Ill.), 1993 (4 vs. DePauw, 5 vs. Beloit, 4 vs. La Verne, 12 vs. Wis.-Platteville, 6 vs. Rowan, 4 vs. Ohio Northern).

MOST FREE THROWS, ONE GAME
21—Tom Montsma, Calvin (88) vs. Wabash (76), 1980.

MOST FREE THROWS, SERIES
50—Mike Rhoades, Lebanon Valley, 1994 (9 vs. Johns Hopkins, 10 vs. Mass.-Dartmouth, 10 vs. Amherst, 14 vs. Wittenberg, 7 vs. New York U.).

MOST ASSISTS, ONE GAME
20—Matt Nadelhoffer, Wheaton (Ill.) (131) vs. Grinnell (117), 1996

MOST ASSISTS, SERIES
62—Ricky Spicer, Wis.-Whitewater, 1989.

Team Records

MOST POINTS, ONE GAME
131—Wheaton (Ill.) vs. Grinnell (117), 1996

MOST POINTS, SERIES
594—Rowan, 1996 (130 vs. York [N.Y.], 102 vs. Jersey City St., 85 vs. Williams, 98 vs. Richard Stockton, 79 vs. Ill. Wesleyan, 100 vs. Hope).

MOST FIELD GOALS, ONE GAME
52—Wheaton (Ill.) (131) vs. Grinnell (117), 1996.

MOST FIELD GOALS, SERIES
206—Rowan, 1996 (45 vs. York [N.Y.], 31 vs. Jersey City St., 29 vs. Williams, 35 vs. Richard Stockton, 32 vs. Ill. Wesleyan, 34 vs. Hope).

MOST THREE-POINT FIELD GOALS, ONE GAME
22—Grinnell (117) vs. Wheaton (Ill.) (131), 1996.

MOST THREE-POINT FIELD GOALS, SERIES
59—Augustana (Ill.), 1993 (6 vs. DePauw, 11 vs. Beloit, 11 vs. La Verne, 14 vs. Wis.-Platteville, 9 vs. Rowan, 8 vs. Ohio Northern).

MOST FREE THROWS, ONE GAME
43—Capital (103) vs. Va. Wesleyan (93), 1982; Potsdam St. (91) vs. Jersey City St. (89), 1986.

MOST FREE THROWS, SERIES
130—North Park, 1987 [28 vs. Ripon, 26 vs. Ill. Wesleyan, 28 vs. Wartburg, 17 vs. Wittenberg, 31 vs. Clark (Mass.)]; Rowan, 1996 (22 vs. York [N.Y.], 33 vs. Jersey City St., 21 vs. Williams, 21 vs. Richard Stockton, 8 vs. Ill. Wesleyan, 25 vs. Hope).

MOST ASSISTS, ONE GAME
34—Hampden-Sydney (105) vs. Greensboro (79), 1995.

MOST ASSISTS, SERIES
122—Rowan, 1996 (31 vs. York [N.Y.], 21 vs. Jersey City St., 15 vs. Williams, 21 vs. Richard Stockton, 14 vs. Ill. Wesleyan, 20 vs. Hope).

All-Tournament Teams

(First player listed on each team was the outstanding player of the championship)

1975—Robert Newman, LeMoyne-Owen
Clint Jackson, LeMoyne-Owen
Dan Panaggio, Brockport St.
Bruce Hamming, Augustana (Ill.)
Greg Ackles, Rowan

1976—Jack Maher, Scranton
Tom Dunn, Wittenberg
Bob Heubner, Wittenberg
Ronnie Wright, Plattsburgh St.
Terry Lawrence, Augustana (Ill.)

1977—Rick White, Wittenberg
Phil Smyczek, Hamline
Paul Miernicki, Scranton
Clyde Eberhardt, Wittenberg
Ralph Christian, Oneonta St.

1978—Michael Harper, North Park
Dennis James, Widener
John Nibert, Albion
Earl Keith, Stony Brook
Tom Florentine, North Park

1979—Michael Harper, North Park
Don Marsh, Frank. & Marsh.
Derrick Rowland, Potsdam St.
Michael Thomas, North Park
Modzel Greer, North Park

1980—Michael Thomas, North Park
Ellonya Green, Upsala
Steve Keenan, Upsala
Tyronne Curtis, Wittenberg
Keith French, North Park

1981—Max Artis, Augustana (Ill.)
Bill Rapier, Augustana (Ill.)
Ed Jachim, Potsdam St.
Derrick Rowland, Potsdam St.
Ron Stewart, Otterbein

1982—Pete Metzelaars, Wabash
Doug Cornfoot, Cal St. Stanislaus
Rick Davis, Brooklyn
Merlin Nice, Wabash
Leroy Witherspoon, Potsdam St.
Maurice Woods, Potsdam St.

1983—Bill Bessoir, Scranton
Mickey Banas, Scranton
Jay Ferguson, Wittenberg
Mark Linde, Wis.-Whitewater
Gerald Holmes, Roanoke

1984—Andre McKoy, Wis.-Whitewater
Mark Linde, Wis.-Whitewater
James Gist, Upsala
Dan Trant, Clark (Mass.)
David Hathaway, DePauw

1985—Earnest Hubbard, North Park
Justyne Monegain, North Park

CHAMPIONSHIPS

Dana Janssen, Neb. Wesleyan
Brendan Mitchell, Potsdam St.
Lou Stevens, Widener
1986—Roosevelt Bullock, Potsdam St.
Barry Stanton, Potsdam St.
Johnny Mayers, Jersey City St.
Michael Neal, LeMoyne-Owen
Dana Janssen, Neb. Wesleyan
1987—Michael Starks, North Park
Mike Barach, North Park
Steve Iannarino, Wittenberg
Kermit Sharp, Clark (Mass.)
Donald Ellison, Richard Stockton
1988—Scott Tedder, Ohio Wesleyan
Lee Rowlinson, Ohio Wesleyan
J. P. Andrejko, Scranton
Charlie Burt, Neb. Wesleyan
Tim McGraw, Hartwick
1989—Greg Grant, Trenton St.
Danny Johnson, Centre

Jeff Bowers, Southern Me.
Ricky Spicer, Wis.-Whitewater
Elbert Gordon, Wis.-Whitewater
Jeff Seifriz, Wis.-Whitewater
1990—Chris Fite, Rochester
Brett Crist, DePauw
Chris Brandt, Washington (Md.)
Brett Hecko, DePauw
Steve Honderd, Calvin
1991—Shawn Frison, Wis.-Platteville
James Bradley, Otterbein
Robby Jeter, Wis.-Platteville
Will Lasky, Frank. & Marsh.
David Wilding, Frank. & Marsh.
1992—Steve Honderd, Calvin
Matt Harrison, Calvin
Mike LeFebre, Calvin
Chris Fite, Rochester
Kyle Meeker, Rochester
1993—Kirk Anderson, Augustana (Ill.)

Mark Gooden, Ohio Northern
Aaron Madry, Ohio Northern
Steven Haynes, Mass.-Dartmouth
Keith Wood, Rowan
1994—Mike Rhoades,* Lebanon Valley
Adam Crawford,* New York U.
Jonathan Gabriel, New York U.
John Harper, Lebanon Valley
Matt Croci, Wittenberg
1995—Ernie Peavy, Wis.-Platteville
Brad Knoy, Manchester
Kyle Hupfer, Manchester
Aaron Lancaster, Wis.-Platteville
Charles Grasty, Rowan
1996—Terrence Stewart, Rowan
Antwan Dasher, Rowan
Joel Holstege, Hope
Duane Bosma, Hope
Chris Simich, Ill. Wesleyan

*Rhoades and Crawford shared most outstanding player honors in 1994.

Statistical Leaders

1996 Division I Individual Leaders

Scoring

	Cl.	Ht.	G	TFG	FGA	Pct.	3FG	FGA	Pct.	FT	FTA	Pct.	Reb.	Avg.	Pts.	Avg.
1. Kevin Granger, Texas Southern	Sr	6-3	24	194	392	49.5	30	86	34.9	230	290	79.3	168	7.0	648	27.0
2. Marcus Brown, Murray St.	Sr	6-3	29	254	536	47.4	74	175	42.3	185	220	84.1	139	4.8	767	26.4
3. Bubba Wells, Austin Peay	Jr	6-5	30	312	568	54.9	34	78	43.6	131	173	75.7	219	7.3	789	26.3
4. Jafonde Williams, Hampton	Sr	6-2	26	220	534	41.2	83	228	36.4	146	183	79.8	103	4.0	669	25.7
5. Bonzi Wells, Ball St.	So	6-5	28	269	544	49.4	31	92	33.7	143	202	70.8	246	8.8	712	25.4
6. Anquell McCollum, Western Caro.	Sr	6-1	30	257	566	45.4	99	241	41.1	138	166	83.1	159	5.3	751	25.0
#7. Allen Iverson, Georgetown	So	6-0	37	312	650	48.0	87	238	36.6	215	317	67.8	141	3.8	926	25.0
8. Eddie Benton, Vermont	Sr	5-11	26	187	500	37.4	69	201	34.3	193	229	84.3	86	3.3	636	24.5
9. Matt Alosa, New Hampshire	Sr	6-2	26	199	476	41.8	76	220	34.5	150	180	83.3	79	3.0	624	24.0
#10. Ray Allen, Connecticut	Jr	6-5	35	292	618	47.2	115	247	46.6	119	147	81.0	228	6.5	818	23.4
11. Michael Hart, Tenn.-Martin	Sr	6-7	27	246	436	56.4	1	1	100.0	123	172	71.5	248	9.2	616	22.8
12. Tunji Awojobi, Boston U.	Jr	6-7	29	253	435	58.2	3	23	13.0	149	211	70.6	314	10.8	658	22.7
13. Darren McLinton, James Madison	Sr	5-11	30	213	501	42.5	122	294	41.5	132	154	85.7	65	2.2	680	22.7
14. Reggie Elliott, Mercer	Sr	6-5	29	226	555	40.7	54	190	28.4	150	188	79.8	186	6.4	656	22.6
15. Jeff Nordgaard, Wis.-Green Bay	Sr	6-7	29	277	500	55.4	8	25	32.0	93	131	71.0	183	6.3	655	22.6
16. Reggie Freeman, Texas	Jr	6-6	31	237	630	37.6	87	270	32.2	134	183	73.2	208	6.7	695	22.4
17. Anthony Harris, Hawaii	Sr	6-2	28	219	443	49.4	24	73	32.9	164	197	83.2	82	2.9	626	22.4
18. Jason Daisy, Northern Iowa	Jr	6-3	27	208	425	48.9	68	162	42.0	119	163	73.0	107	4.0	603	22.3
19. Chris McGuthrie, Mt. St Mary's (Md.)	Sr	5-9	29	229	524	43.7	102	261	39.1	87	108	80.6	70	2.4	647	22.3
20. John Wallace, Syracuse	Sr	6-8	38	293	599	48.9	37	88	42.0	222	291	76.3	329	8.7	845	22.2
21. Curtis McCants, George Mason	Jr	6-0	27	200	453	44.2	39	125	31.2	155	186	83.3	109	4.0	594	22.0
22. Sam Bowie, Southeastern La.	Sr	6-5	27	208	458	45.4	59	183	32.2	115	165	69.7	144	5.3	590	21.9
23. Craig Thames, Toledo	Sr	5-11	32	216	441	49.0	59	146	40.4	208	245	84.9	196	6.1	699	21.8
#24. Ronnie Henderson, LSU	Jr	6-4	23	183	397	46.1	49	146	33.6	87	127	68.5	107	4.7	502	21.8
25. Marcus Mann, Mississippi Val.	Sr	6-8	29	251	415	60.5	1	2	50.0	126	197	64.0	394	13.6	629	21.7
26. Keith Van Horn, Utah	Jr	6-9	32	236	439	53.8	54	132	40.9	160	188	85.1	283	8.8	686	21.4
27. Paul Marshall, Northeast La.	Sr	6-2	30	214	494	43.3	115	281	40.9	97	125	77.6	107	3.6	640	21.3
28. Troy Hudson, Southern Ill.	So	6-1	25	179	459	39.0	93	247	37.7	82	103	79.6	110	4.4	533	21.3
29. Ryan Minor, Oklahoma	Sr	6-7	30	217	521	41.7	62	191	32.5	143	174	82.2	229	7.6	639	21.3
30. Jimmy Degraffenried, Weber St.	Sr	6-6	30	214	374	57.2	47	100	47.0	162	188	86.2	199	6.6	637	21.2
31. Brian Evans, Indiana	Sr	6-8	31	212	474	44.7	62	158	39.2	172	203	84.7	221	7.1	658	21.2
32. Charles Smith, Rider	Jr	6-6	29	235	465	50.5	41	104	39.4	102	134	76.1	199	6.9	613	21.1
33. Andrell Hoard, Northeastern Ill.	Jr	6-3	27	223	552	40.4	26	98	26.5	97	161	60.2	115	4.3	569	21.1
#34. Shareef Abdur-Rahim, California	Fr	6-10	28	206	398	51.8	8	21	38.1	170	249	68.3	236	8.4	590	21.1
35. Todd Fuller, North Caro. St.	Sr	6-11	31	225	445	50.6	16	43	37.2	183	229	79.9	308	9.9	649	20.9
36. Zendon Hamilton, St. John's(N.Y.)	So	6-11	27	179	368	48.6	0	4	0.0	204	256	79.7	277	10.3	562	20.8
37. Terrence Brandon, Georgia St.	Jr	6-7	24	195	420	46.4	5	27	18.5	104	154	67.5	249	10.4	499	20.8
#38. Vitaly Potapenko, Wright St.	Jr	6-10	26	198	328	60.4	1	6	16.7	141	197	71.6	193	7.4	538	20.7
39. Tommy McGhee, Rice	Sr	6-2	28	197	432	45.6	76	169	45.0	105	128	82.0	109	3.9	575	20.5
40. Damion Walker, Texas Christian	Fr	6-8	30	230	457	50.3	0	1	0.0	156	162	96.3	264	8.8	616	20.5
41. Dedric Willoughby, Iowa St.	Jr	6-3	33	204	492	41.5	88	261	33.7	180	227	79.3	137	4.2	676	20.5
42. Brian Tolbert, Eastern Mich.	Sr	6-2	31	221	464	47.6	74	191	38.7	119	140	85.0	133	4.3	635	20.5
#43. Marcus Camby, Massachusetts	Jr	6-11	33	256	537	47.7	0	8	0.0	163	233	70.0	271	8.2	675	20.5
44. Kerry Kittles, Villanova	Sr	6-5	30	216	475	45.5	78	193	40.4	103	145	71.0	213	7.1	613	20.4
45. Marlon Anderson, Texas-San Antonio	Sr	6-4	28	189	425	44.5	96	236	40.7	95	121	78.5	167	6.0	569	20.3
46. Carlo Williams, UAB	Jr	6-7	30	223	525	42.5	49	151	32.5	112	158	70.9	253	8.4	607	20.2
47. Malik Rose, Drexel	Sr	6-7	31	219	368	59.5	7	21	33.3	182	255	71.4	409	13.2	627	20.2
48. Adonal Foyle, Colgate	So	6-10	29	228	441	51.7	0	3	0.0	129	264	48.9	364	12.6	585	20.2
49. Danny Fortson, Cincinnati	So	6-7	33	222	413	53.8	0	1	0.0	220	292	75.3	316	9.6	664	20.1
50. Ron Riley, Arizona St.	Sr	6-5	27	186	478	38.9	58	198	29.3	113	157	72.0	166	6.1	543	20.1
51. Decarlos Anders, Alcorn St.	Sr	6-6	25	199	435	45.7	14	58	24.1	89	130	68.5	180	7.2	501	20.0
52. Jonathan Pixley, Samford	Jr	6-5	27	160	365	43.8	81	198	40.9	138	159	86.8	107	4.0	539	20.0
53. Mike Powell, Loyola (Md.)	So	6-2	27	187	446	41.9	40	121	33.1	124	164	75.6	132	4.9	538	19.9
54. Monte O'Quinn, Northeastern Ill.	Sr	6-8	27	199	385	51.7	1	6	16.7	138	229	60.3	285	10.6	537	19.9
54. Jason Alexander, Stetson	Sr	5-10	27	175	422	41.5	64	166	38.6	123	140	87.9	134	5.0	537	19.9
56. Geno Carlisle, Northwestern	So	6-2	27	170	433	39.3	73	197	37.1	119	154	77.3	71	2.6	532	19.7
57. Keith Veney, Marshall	Jr	6-1	28	169	381	44.4	111	244	45.5	101	134	75.4	64	2.3	550	19.6
58. Monty Wilson, Tennessee St.	Jr	6-5	27	189	451	41.9	62	198	31.3	89	115	77.4	190	7.0	529	19.6
59. Danya Abrams, Boston College	Jr	6-7	30	190	403	47.1	9	28	32.1	198	281	70.5	287	9.6	587	19.6
60. James Cotton, Long Beach St.	So	6-5	26	153	353	43.3	66	166	39.8	136	174	78.2	106	4.1	508	19.5
61. Jason Sasser, Texas Tech	Sr	6-7	31	202	441	45.8	31	101	30.7	170	234	72.6	242	7.8	605	19.5
62. Darrell Barley, Canisius	Sr	6-5	24	167	326	51.2	23	57	40.4	111	163	68.1	183	7.6	468	19.5
63. Adrian Griffin, Seton Hall	Sr	6-5	28	213	438	48.6	12	44	27.3	107	161	66.5	231	8.3	545	19.5
64. Charles Smith, New Mexico	Jr	6-4	33	233	506	46.0	69	188	36.7	107	132	81.1	153	4.6	642	19.5
65. Vincent Rainey, Murray St.	Jr	6-4	29	217	461	47.1	24	65	36.9	106	143	74.1	174	6.0	564	19.4
66. Kendric Brooks, Fresno St.	Jr	6-5	33	192	461	41.6	96	243	39.5	160	215	74.4	126	3.8	640	19.4
67. Mark Lueking, Army	Sr	5-10	27	166	434	38.2	99	262	37.8	91	114	79.8	53	2.0	522	19.3
68. Chucky Atkins, South Fla.	Sr	5-11	28	175	405	43.2	82	220	37.3	109	141	77.3	85	3.0	541	19.3
69. Kenneth Roberts, Brigham Young	Sr	6-8	28	170	316	53.8	12	27	44.4	187	230	81.3	198	7.1	539	19.3
70. Tim Duncan, Wake Forest	Jr	6-10	32	228	411	55.5	7	23	30.4	149	217	68.7	395	12.3	612	19.1
71. Terquin Mott, Coppin St.	Jr	6-8	28	208	326	63.8	1	8	12.5	115	182	63.2	206	7.4	532	19.0

#Entered NBA draft.

Field-Goal Percentage

(Min. 5 FG Made Per Game)	Cl.	Ht.	G	FG	FGA	Pct.
1. Quadre Lollis, Montana St.	Sr	6-7	30	212	314	67.5
2. Daniel Watts, Nevada	Sr	6-8	29	145	221	65.6
3. Lincoln Abrams, Centenary (La.)	Sr	6-7	27	187	286	65.4
4. Alexander Koul, Geo. Washington	So	7-1	29	163	254	64.2
5. Terquin Mott, Coppin St.	Jr	6-8	28	208	326	63.8
6. Antawn Jamison, North Caro.	Fr	6-8	32	201	322	62.4
7. Stanley Caldwell, Tennessee St.	Fr	6-6	22	110	178	61.8
8. Greg Smith, Delaware	Jr	6-7	27	173	282	61.3
9. Marcus Mann, Mississippi Val.	Sr	6-8	29	251	415	60.5
10. Curtis Fincher, Eastern Ky.	Sr	6-7	27	148	245	60.4
#11. Vitaly Potapenko, Wright St.	Jr	6-10	26	198	328	60.4
12. Brian Skinner, Baylor	So	6-10	27	187	311	60.1
13. Ben Handlogten, Western Mich.	Sr	6-10	27	154	257	59.9
14. Carl Parker, William & Mary	Sr	6-6	26	164	274	59.9
15. Justice Sueing, Hawaii	Sr	6-6	24	150	252	59.5
16. Malik Rose, Drexel	Sr	6-7	31	219	368	59.5
17. Kenwan Alford, George Mason	Sr	6-6	27	191	323	59.1
18. Rashon Turner, Fairleigh Dickinson	So	6-6	27	147	251	58.6
19. Nate Huffman, Central Mich.	Jr	7-1	20	113	193	58.5
20. Howard Porter, Central Fla.	Sr	6-6	30	159	273	58.2
21. Tunji Awojobi, Boston U.	Jr	6-7	29	253	435	58.2
22. Kenny Thomas, New Mexico	Fr	6-9	33	170	294	57.8
23. Paul Rogers, Gonzaga	Jr	7-0	30	163	282	57.8
23. Sam Allen, San Jose St.	Sr	6-7	30	163	282	57.8
25. Steve Hamer, Tennessee	Sr	7-0	29	187	325	57.5
26. Jimmy Degraffenried, Weber St.	Sr	6-6	30	214	374	57.2
27. Mark Hendrickson, Washington St	Sr	6-9	23	127	222	57.2
28. J. R. Henderson, UCLA	So	6-9	29	159	278	57.2
29. Otis Hill, Syracuse	Jr	6-8	38	193	338	57.1
30. Patrick Evans, Delaware	Sr	6-5	27	140	246	56.9

#Entered NBA draft.

Three-Point Field Goals Made Per Game

	Cl.	Ht.	G	3FG	Avg.
1. Dominick Young, Fresno St.	Jr	5-10	29	120	4.1
2. Darren McLinton, James Madison	Sr	5-11	30	122	4.1
3. Keith Veney, Marshall	Jr	6-1	28	111	4.0
4. Paul Marshall, Northeast La.	Sr	6-2	30	115	3.8
5. Troy Hudson, Southern Ill.	So	6-1	25	93	3.7
6. Mark Lueking, Army	Sr	5-10	27	99	3.7
7. Troy Green, Southeastern La.	Fr	6-2	27	98	3.6
8. James Hannah, Grambling	Jr	5-11	28	101	3.6
9. David Sivulich, St. Mary's (Cal.)	So	5-10	27	96	3.6
10. Eric Washington, Alabama	Jr	6-4	32	113	3.5
11. Chris McGuthrie, Mt. St Mary's (Md.)	Sr	5-9	29	102	3.5
12. Mike Martinho, Buffalo	So	5-11	27	94	3.5
13. Marlon Anderson, Texas-San Antonio	Sr	6-4	28	96	3.4
14. Lance Weems, Auburn	Sr	6-2	32	108	3.4
15. Bernie Cieplicki, Vermont	Sr	6-3	27	91	3.4
15. DeWayne Powell, Tenn.-Martin	Sr	6-2	27	91	3.4
15. Rhodney Donaldson, Troy St.	Jr	6-0	27	91	3.4
18. Anquell McCollum, Western Caro.	Sr	6-1	30	99	3.3
19. Pete Lisicky, Penn St.	So	6-4	27	89	3.3
#20. Ray Allen, Connecticut	Jr	6-5	35	115	3.3
20. Conley Verdun, Southwestern La.	Jr	5-10	28	92	3.3
22. Ben Larson, Cal Poly SLO	Fr	6-0	29	94	3.2
23. Tim Gill, Oral Roberts	So	6-2	27	87	3.2
24. Frank Seckar, Vanderbilt	Sr	6-1	32	103	3.2
25. Jafonde Williams, Hampton	Sr	6-2	26	83	3.2
26. Dedric Taylor, Florida Int'l	Jr	5-10	28	89	3.2
26. Josh Kohn, N.C.-Asheville	Sr	5-10	28	89	3.2
28. Harry Kennedy, Central Fla.	Jr	6-5	30	94	3.1
29. Tim Roberts, Southern U.	Sr	6-5	28	87	3.1
30. Brandt Schuckman, Cornell	Sr	6-2	26	79	3.0

#Entered NBA draft.

Three-Point Field-Goal Percentage

(Min. 1.5 3FG Made Per Game and 40%)	Cl.	Ht.	G	FG	FGA	Pct.
1. Joe Stafford, Western Caro.	Jr	6-5	30	58	110	52.7
2. Ricky Peral, Wake Forest	Jr	6-10	32	51	100	51.0
3. Justyn Tebbs, Weber St.	Sr	6-4	30	50	100	50.0
4. Aaron Brown, Central Mich.	Fr	6-8	26	51	104	49.0
5. Isaac Fontaine, Washington St.	Jr	6-3	29	66	136	48.5
6. Mike Derocckis, Drexel	Fr	6-2	31	85	178	47.8
7. Mike Frensley, St. Peter's	Sr	5-10	27	58	123	47.2
8. Pete Lisicky, Penn St.	So	6-4	27	89	189	47.1

	Cl.	Ht.	G	FG	FGA	Pct.
9. Jimmy Degraffenried, Weber St.	Sr	6-6	30	47	100	47.0
10. Justin Jones, Utah St.	So	6-3	33	77	165	46.7
10. Shane Miller, Fairfield	So	6-5	25	49	105	46.7
12. Jason Sutherland, Missouri	Jr	6-1	33	69	148	46.6
#13. Ray Allen, Connecticut	Jr	6-5	35	115	247	46.6
14. Damon Watlington, Virginia Tech	Sr	6-2	29	60	129	46.5
15. Rusty LaRue, Wake Forest	Sr	6-2	32	65	140	46.4
16. Stuart Sullivan, Samford	Jr	6-0	27	42	92	45.7
17. Tige Darner, Appalachian St.	So	6-5	28	46	101	45.5
18. John Giraldo, Monmouth (N.J.)	Sr	5-11	30	61	134	45.5
19. Keith Veney, Marshall	Jr	6-1	28	111	244	45.5
20. Neil Reed, Indiana	So	6-3	31	60	132	45.5
21. George King, North Texas	Sr	6-5	28	68	150	45.3
22. Tim Gill, Oral Roberts	So	6-2	27	87	193	45.1
23. Duane Simpkins, Maryland	Sr	6-0	27	45	100	45.0
24. Tommy McGhee, Rice	Sr	6-2	28	76	169	45.0
25. Michael Brown, Providence	Sr	6-1	30	53	118	44.9
26. Landon Hackim, Miami (Ohio)	Sr	5-10	29	69	154	44.8
27. Ben Berlowski, Wis.-Green Bay	Sr	6-3	29	64	143	44.8
28. Mark Ingles, UTEP	Sr	6-2	27	80	179	44.7
29. Garrick Thomas, Pittsburgh	Sr	6-5	26	42	94	44.7
30. Jason Lansdown, Radford	Sr	6-3	27	53	119	44.5

#Entered NBA draft.

Free-Throw Percentage

(Min. 2.5 Made Per Game)	Cl.	Ht.	G	FT	FTA	Pct.
1. Mike Dillard, Sam Houston St.	Jr	6-6	25	63	68	92.6
2. Dion Cross, Stanford	Sr	6-2	29	81	88	92.0
3. Roderick Howard, N.C.-Charlotte	Jr	5-10	29	93	103	90.3
4. Geoff Billet, Rutgers	Fr	6-0	26	72	80	90.0
5. Steve Nash, Santa Clara	Sr	6-3	29	101	113	89.4
6. Derek Grimm, Missouri	Jr	6-10	33	100	113	88.5
7. Marcus Wilson, Evansville	Fr	6-3	25	75	85	88.2
8. Nod Carter, Middle Tenn. St.	Jr	6-6	27	104	118	88.1
9. Alhamisi Simms, Md.-Balt. County	Fr	6-1	27	74	84	88.1
10. Jason Alexander, Stetson	Sr	5-10	27	123	140	87.9
11. Jason Sutherland, Missouri	Jr	6-1	33	114	130	87.7
12. Terrence Martin, St. Francis (Pa.)	Jr	6-6	24	84	96	87.5
13. Landon Hackim, Miami (Ohio)	Sr	5-10	29	82	94	87.2
14. Jonathan Pixley, Samford	Jr	6-5	27	138	159	86.8
15. Bryce Drew, Valparaiso	So	6-3	32	103	119	86.6
16. Darian Devries, Northern Iowa	So	6-3	27	90	104	86.5
17. Jim Williamson, Loyola Marymount	Jr	5-10	29	95	110	86.4
17. Mark Ingles, UTEP	Sr	6-2	27	76	88	86.4
19. Jimmy Degraffenried, Weber St.	Sr	6-6	30	162	188	86.2
20. Kiwane Garris, Illinois	Jr	6-2	25	112	130	86.2
21. Chauncey Billups, Colorado	Fr	6-3	26	130	151	86.1
22. Mike Richardson, Hartford	Jr	6-4	23	67	78	85.9
23. Darren McLinton, James Madison	Sr	5-11	30	132	154	85.7
24. Austin Croshere, Providence	Jr	6-9	30	109	128	85.2
25. Keith Van Horn, Utah	Jr	6-9	32	160	188	85.1
26. Brian Tolbert, Eastern Mich.	Sr	6-2	31	119	140	85.0
27. Aaron Hutchins, Marquette	So	5-9	31	90	106	84.9
28. Craig Thames, Toledo	Sr	5-11	32	208	245	84.9
29. Doron Sheffer, Connecticut	Sr	6-5	35	101	119	84.9
30. Brevin Knight, Stanford	Jr	5-10	29	151	178	84.8

Rebounds

	Cl.	Ht.	G	Reb.	Avg.
1. Marcus Mann, Mississippi Val.	Sr	6-8	29	394	13.6
2. Malik Rose, Drexel	Sr	6-7	31	409	13.2
3. Adonal Foyle, Colgate	So	6-10	29	364	12.6
4. Tim Duncan, Wake Forest	Jr	6-10	32	395	12.3
5. Scott Farley, Mercer	Sr	6-10	29	349	12.0
6. Chris Ensminger, Valparaiso	Sr	6-11	32	368	11.5
7. Thaddeous Delaney, Charleston (S.C.)	Jr	6-8	29	330	11.4
8. Alan Tomidy, Marist	Sr	6-11	29	329	11.3
9. Quadre Lollis, Montana St.	Sr	6-7	30	340	11.3
10. Kyle Snowden, Harvard	Jr	6-6	26	289	11.1
11. Tim Moore, Houston	Sr	6-8	21	228	10.9
12. Tunji Awojobi, Boston U.	Jr	6-7	29	314	10.8
13. Curtis Fincher, Eastern Ky.	Sr	6-7	27	292	10.8
14. Greg Logan, Maine	Sr	6-6	28	300	10.7
15. Monte O'Quinn, Northeastern Ill.	Sr	6-8	27	285	10.6
#16. Lorenzen Wright, Memphis	So	6-11	30	313	10.4
17. James Harper, South Fla.	Jr	6-7	28	291	10.4
18. H. L. Coleman, Wyoming	Jr	6-7	29	301	10.4
19. Terrence Brandon, Georgia St.	Sr	6-7	24	249	10.4
20. Stanley Caldwell, Tennessee St.	Sr	6-6	22	228	10.4

	Cl.	Ht.	G	Reb.	Avg.
21. Harry Harrison, Idaho	Sr	6-7	25	258	10.3
22. Zendon Hamilton, St. John's (N.Y.)	So	6-11	27	277	10.3
23. Jason Winningham, Southeastern La.	Sr	6-9	27	276	10.2
24. Will Johnson, St. Joseph's (Pa.)	Sr	6-8	32	326	10.2
25. Ernie Abercrombie, Oklahoma	Sr	6-4	30	304	10.1
26. Bernard Hopkins, Va. Commonwealth	Sr	6-7	33	333	10.1
27. Artemus McClary, Jacksonville	Sr	6-5	28	279	10.0
28. Michael Tardy, Grambling	Sr	6-6	26	259	10.0
29. Todd Fuller, North Caro. St.	Sr	6-11	31	308	9.9
30. Devin Davis, Miami (Ohio)	Jr	6-7	29	287	9.9

#Entered NBA draft.

Assists

	Cl.	Ht.	G	Ast.	Avg.
1. Raimonds Miglinieks, UC Irvine	Sr	6-3	27	230	8.5
2. Curtis McCants, George Mason	Jr	6-0	27	223	8.3
3. Dan Pogue, Campbell	Sr	6-1	23	183	8.0
4. Pointer Williams, McNeese St.	Sr	6-1	27	200	7.4
5. Lazarus Sims, Syracuse	Sr	6-4	38	281	7.4
6. Brevin Knight, Stanford	Jr	5-10	29	212	7.3
7. Phillip Turner, UC Santa Barb.	Sr	6-3	26	190	7.3
8. Reggie Geary, Arizona	Sr	6-2	33	231	7.0
9. David Fizdale, San Diego	Sr	6-2	28	195	7.0
10. Aaron Hutchins, Marquette	So	5-9	31	215	6.9
11. Colby Pierce, Austin Peay	Jr	6-2	30	205	6.8
12. Kyle Kessel, Texas A&M	So	6-0	27	183	6.8
13. Jamar Smiley, Illinois St.	So	5-11	34	229	6.7
14. Wes Flanigan, Auburn	Jr	6-1	32	214	6.7
15. Edgar Padilla, Massachusetts	Jr	6-2	37	247	6.7
16. Anthony Johnson, Charleston (S.C.)	Jr	6-3	29	193	6.7
17. Kareem Reid, Arkansas	Fr	5-10	33	219	6.6
18. Drew Barry, Georgia Tech	Sr	6-5	36	238	6.6
19. Shane Belnap, Montana	Sr	6-0	28	185	6.6
20. Jacque Vaughn, Kansas	Jr	6-1	34	223	6.6
21. Dominick Young, Fresno St.	Jr	5-10	29	190	6.6
22. Shawnta Rogers, Geo. Washington	Fr	5-3	23	150	6.5
23. God Shammgod, Providence	Fr	6-0	29	189	6.5
24. Allen Watson, Coppin St.	Sr	5-10	29	186	6.4
25. Deon Hames, Rider	Sr	5-10	30	192	6.4
26. Jason Williams, Marshall	Fr	6-1	28	178	6.4
27. Darius Burton, Hofstra	Jr	5-9	27	169	6.3
28. Casey Arena, Maine	Sr	6-1	28	172	6.1
29. Javone Moore, Canisius	Jr	5-11	27	165	6.1
30. Doron Sheffer, Connecticut	Sr	6-5	35	212	6.1

Blocked Shots

	Cl.	Ht.	G	Blk.	Avg.
1. Keith Closs, Central Conn. St.	So	7-2	28	178	6.4
2. Adonal Foyle, Colgate	So	6-10	29	165	5.7
3. Roy Rogers, Alabama	Sr	6-10	32	156	4.9
4. Jerome James, Florida A&M	So	7-1	27	119	4.4
4. Alan Tomidy, Marist	Sr	6-11	29	113	3.9
5. Peter Aluma, Liberty	Jr	6-10	29	113	3.9
#7. Marcus Camby, Massachusetts	Jr	6-11	33	128	3.9
8. Tim Duncan, Wake Forest	Jr	6-10	32	120	3.8
9. Calvin Booth, Penn St.	Fr	6-11	28	101	3.6
10. Lorenzo Coleman, Tennessee Tech	Jr	7-1	28	96	3.4
11. David Cully, William & Mary	Sr	6-9	25	84	3.4
12. Jelani McCoy, UCLA	Fr	6-10	31	102	3.3
#13. Erick Dampier, Mississippi St.	Jr	6-11	34	106	3.1
14. Brian Skinner, Baylor	So	6-10	27	82	3.0
15. Jason Lawson, Villanova	Jr	6-11	32	95	3.0
16. Jason Terry, Ohio	Sr	7-2	30	89	3.0
17. Avondre Jones, Southern Cal	Jr	6-11	25	72	2.9
18. Theron Wilson, Eastern Mich.	Sr	6-9	28	78	2.8
19. Terrell Bell, Georgia	Sr	6-10	31	83	2.7
20. Erik Nelson, Vermont	So	6-7	27 •	71	2.6
20. Kelvin Cato, Iowa St.	Jr	6-11	27	71	2.6
22. Mikkel Larsen, Iona	Sr	6-10	29	76	2.6
23. Kirill Misyuchenko, Citadel	So	7-0	25	65	2.6
24. Gerben Van Dorpe, Mt. St. Mary's (Md.)	So	6-11	29	72	2.5
24. Scott Farley, Mercer	Sr	6-10	29	72	2.5
26. Scot Pollard, Kansas	Jr	6-10	34	84	2.5
27. Dennis Newton, Northeast La.	So	6-9	30	74	2.5
28. Charles Smith, Rider	Jr	6-6	29	68	2.3
29. Nate Huffman, Central Mich.	Jr	7-1	20	46	2.3
30. Joe Vogel, Colorado St.	Sr	6-10	27	62	2.3

#Entered NBA draft.

Steals

	Cl.	Ht.	G	Stl.	Avg.
1. Pointer Williams, McNeese St.	Sr	6-1	27	118	4.4
2. Johnny Rhodes, Maryland	Sr	6-5	30	110	3.7
3. Roderick Taylor, Jackson St.	Sr	5-9	29	106	3.7
4. Rasul Salahuddin, Long Beach St.	Sr	6-3	28	101	3.6
5. Andrell Hoard, Northeastern Ill.	Jr	6-3	27	97	3.6
6. Ben Larson, Cal Poly SLO	Fr	6-0	29	100	3.4
#7. Allen Iverson, Georgetown	So	6-0	37	124	3.4
8. Bonzi Wells, Ball St.	So	6-5	28	87	3.1
9. Jerry McCullough, Pittsburgh	Sr	5-11	25	76	3.0
10. Edgar Padilla, Massachusetts	Jr	6-2	37	108	2.9
11. Charles Thomas, Northern Ariz.	Jr	6-0	26	72	2.8
12. Riley Inge, Mt. St. Mary's (Md.)	Sr	6-3	29	79	2.7
13. Sidney Coles, Marshall	Jr	6-5	26	70	2.7
14. Darius Burton, Hofstra	Jr	5-9	27	71	2.6
15. Ted Bettencourt, Holy Cross	Sr	5-11	29	76	2.6
16. Kevin Batiste, Alcorn St.	Jr	6-1	21	55	2.6
17. Chris Robinson, Western Ky.	Sr	6-5	26	68	2.6
17. Gerald Walker, San Francisco	Sr	6-1	26	68	2.6
19. Jermaine Watts, DePaul	So	6-1	29	75	2.6
20. Craig Thames, Toledo	Sr	5-11	32	82	2.6
21. Dominick Young, Fresno St.	Jr	5-10	29	74	2.6
22. Shandue McNeill, St. Bonaventure	Jr	5-7	28	71	2.5
23. Adrian Griffin, Seton Hall	Jr	6-5	28	70	2.5
24. Alvin Sims, Louisville	Jr	6-4	34	84	2.5
25. Lemont Daniels, Portland	Sr	6-4	30	74	2.5
25. Eric Fernandez, South Caro. St.	Sr	6-1	30	74	2.5
27. Dan Knuckey, Drake	Sr	6-2	27	66	2.4
27. Bernard Wheeler, Buffalo	Fr	5-10	27	66	2.4
29. Ladrell Whitehead, Wyoming	So	5-8	29	70	2.4
30. Elliott Hatcher, Kansas St.	Sr	6-0	27	65	2.4
30. Warren Anderson, Wagner	Jr	5-11	27	65	2.4

#Entered NBA draft.

1996 Division I Game Highs

Individual Highs

SCORING

Pts.	Player, Team vs. Opponent	Date
45	Marcus Brown, Murray St. vs. Washington (Mo.)	Dec. 16
45	Eddie Benton, Vermont vs. Hartford	Feb. 2
43	Shanta Cotright, Cal Poly SLO vs. George Mason	Jan. 13
43	JaFonde Williams, Hampton vs. Maine	Jan. 29
43	Tunji Awojobi, Boston U. vs. Vermont	Feb. 10
43	Steve Rich, Miami (Fla.) vs. St. John's (N.Y.)	Feb. 20
42	Eddie Benton, Vermont vs. Hofstra	Dec. 9
42	Bubba Wells, Austin Peay vs. Air Force	Dec. 29
42	Eddie Benton, Vermont vs. Hartford	Jan. 14
42	David McMahan, Winthrop vs. Coastal Caro.	Jan. 15

FIELD-GOAL PERCENTAGE
(Min. 10 FG Made)

Pct.	Player, Team vs. Opponent	Date
100.0 (13-13)	Ben Handlogten, Western Mich. vs. Toledo	Jan. 27
100.0 (10-10)	Kirk King, Connecticut vs. Providence	Jan. 12
100.0 (10-10)	Paul Morris, Ohio vs. Coppin St.	Dec. 30
100.0 (10-10)	Todd MacCulloch, Washington vs. Arizona St.	Feb. 29
94.4 (17-18)	Silas Mills, Utah St. vs. Hawaii-Hilo	Nov. 26
93.3 (14-15)	Tony Lane, UNLV vs. San Jose St.	Feb. 1
92.3 (12-13)	Bernard Hopkins, Va. Commonwealth vs. James Madison	Nov. 26
92.3 (12-13)	Chad Lambert, Stetson vs. Florida Int'l	Jan. 25
92.3 (12-13)	Charlie Nelson, Air Force vs. San Diego St.	Feb. 10
92.3 (12-13)	Steve Hamer, Tennessee vs. Vanderbilt	Feb. 24
92.3 (12-13)	Quadre Lollis, Montana St. vs. Syracuse	Mar. 14

THREE-POINT FIELD GOALS

3FG	Player, Team vs. Opponent	Date
12	David McMahan, Winthrop vs. Coastal Caro.	Jan. 15
11	Troy Hudson, Southern Ill. vs. Hawaii-Hilo	Dec. 29
10	Lance Weems, Auburn vs. Arkansas	Jan. 6
10	Keith Veney, Marshall vs. Hampton	Jan. 6
10	John Gordon, Maine vs. New Hampshire	Jan. 19
10	Mike Martinbo, Buffalo vs. Troy St.	Feb. 22
9	12 tied	

FREE-THROW PERCENTAGE
(Min. 10 FT Made)

Pct.	Player, Team vs. Opponent	Date
100.0 (18-18)	Anquell McCollum, Western Caro. vs. Marshall	Feb. 6
100.0 (16-16)	Chauncey Billups, Colorado vs. Oklahoma	Feb. 17
100.0 (16-16)	Keith Van Horn, Utah vs. Brigham Young	Mar. 2
100.0 (15-15)	Jimmy DeGraffenried, Weber St. vs. Alas. Anchorage	Jan. 6
100.0 (15-15)	Jason Wright, New Orleans vs. Western Ky.	Feb. 1
100.0 (14-14)	Vincent Rainey, Murray St. vs. Western Mich.	Nov. 28
100.0 (14-14)	Daryl Oliver, Richmond vs. Radford	Dec. 4
100.0 (14-14)	Donta Bright, Massachusetts vs. Rhode Island	Jan. 17
100.0 (14-14)	Brian Evans, Indiana vs. Minnesota	Feb. 6
100.0 (14-14)	Jason Sutherland, Missouri vs. Nebraska	Feb. 7
100.0 (14-14)	Jason Alexander, Stetson vs. Florida Int'l	Feb. 24

REBOUNDS

Reb.	Player, Team vs. Opponent	Date
28	Marcus Mann, Mississippi Val. vs. Jackson St.	Mar. 9
26	Larry Callis, Wichita St. vs. Drake	Jan. 13
26	David Cully, William & Mary vs. VMI	Jan. 17
24	Chris Ensminger, Valparaiso vs. Northeastern Ill.	Jan. 4
22	Scott Farley, Mercer vs. Alabama	Dec. 16
22	Frantz Pierre-Louis, Wagner vs. LIU-Brooklyn	Jan. 17
22	Alan Tomidy, Marist vs. LIU-Brooklyn	Feb. 8
22	Ernie Abercrombie, Oklahoma vs. Mississippi St.	Feb. 10
22	Greg Logan, Maine vs. Vermont	Feb. 18
22	Tim Duncan, Wake Forest vs. Georgia Tech	Mar. 10

ASSISTS

Ast.	Player, Team vs. Opponent	Date
15	Steve Nash, Santa Clara vs. Southern U.	Dec. 9
15	Raimonds Miglinieks, UC Irvine vs. Cal St. Fullerton	Feb. 10
15	Colby Pierce, Austin Peay vs. Tennessee Tech	Feb. 12
15	Kyle Kessel, Texas A&M vs. Texas Christian	Feb. 26
15	Andre Owens, Oklahoma St. vs. Oklahoma	Feb. 29
14	Shane Belnap, Montana vs. Simon Fraser	Nov. 11
14	Dionn Holton, Portland vs. Southern Ore.	Dec. 9
14	Stais Boseman, Southern Cal vs. George Mason	Dec. 21
14	Randy Reid, Brigham Young vs. Texas Tech	Dec. 22
14	Curtis McCants, George Mason vs. Hampton	Dec. 28
14	Raimonds Miglinieks, UC Irvine vs. San Jose St.	Jan. 2
14	Rodney Hamilton, Georgia St. vs. Florida Int'l	Jan. 11
14	Gary Grzisk, Wis.-Green Bay vs. Ill.-Chicago	Feb. 22
14	Ryan Owens, Tenn.-Martin vs. Middle Tenn. St.	Feb. 26

BLOCKED SHOTS

Blk.	Player, Team vs. Opponent	Date
14	Roy Rogers, Alabama vs. Georgia	Feb. 10
12	Keith Closs, Central Conn. St. vs. Troy St.	Jan. 20
11	Jelani McCoy, UCLA vs. Maryland	Dec. 9
11	Keith Closs, Central Conn. St. vs. Northeastern Ill.	Jan. 8
11	Keith Closs, Central Conn. St. vs. Eastern Ill.	Jan. 15
11	Alan Tomidy, Marist vs. LIU-Brooklyn	Feb. 8
10	Keith Closs, Central Conn. St. vs. Delaware St.	Dec. 2
10	Lorenzo Coleman, Tennessee Tech vs. Lambuth	Dec. 16
10	Keith Closs, Central Conn. St. vs. St. Francis (Pa.)	Dec. 29
10	Gerben Van Dorpe, Mt. St. Mary's (Md.) vs. Rider	Jan. 11
10	Tim Duncan, Wake Forest vs. Maryland	Jan. 13
10	Roy Rogers, Alabama vs. LSU	Feb. 17
10	David Cully, William & Mary vs. George Mason	Feb. 26
10	Adonal Foyle, Colgate vs. Holy Cross	Mar. 5

STEALS

Stl.	Player, Team vs. Opponent	Date
10	Bonzi Wells, Ball St. vs. Ohio U.	Jan. 3
10	Allen Iverson, Georgetown vs. Miami (Fla.)	Jan. 13
9	Alvin Sims, Louisville vs. Va. Commonwealth	Nov. 25
9	Jason Hamilton, Washington vs. Eastern Wash.	Nov. 28
9	Johnny Rhodes, Maryland vs. North Caro.	Feb. 6
8	Andrell Hoard, Northeastern Ill. vs. Miami (Ohio)	Nov. 24
8	Mark Miller, Ill.-Chicago vs. Olivet Nazarene	Nov. 28
8	Ben Larson, Cal Poly SLO vs. UC Santa Cruz	Dec. 9
8	Pointer Williams, McNeese St. vs. Prairie View	Dec. 10
8	Nate Langley, George Mason vs. West Va. Tech	Dec. 16
8	Andrell Hoard, Northeastern Ill. vs. Central Conn. St.	Jan. 8
8	Rasul Salahuddin, Long Beach St. vs. New Mexico St.	Feb. 10
8	Allen Iverson, Georgetown vs. Connecticut	Feb. 19

Santa Clara's Steve Nash enjoyed a standout senior campaign in 1996, amassing 174 assists, including a Division I-best 15 vs. Southern University on December 9, 1995.

Photo from Santa Clara sports information

Team Highs

SCORING

Pts.	Team vs. Opponent	Date
142	Prairie View vs. Bay Ridge Christian	Nov. 27
142	George Mason vs. Troy St.	Nov. 28
141	Tulsa vs. Prairie View	Dec. 1
139	George Mason vs. Delaware St.	Nov. 25
132	Colorado vs. George Mason	Dec. 2
129	Kentucky vs. LSU	Jan. 16
128	Chicago St. vs. Troy St.	Jan. 8
127	Troy St. vs. George Mason	Nov. 28
125	Western Caro. vs. Marshall	Feb. 5
124	Marshall vs. Milligan	Nov. 25
124	Texas Christian vs. Alas. Anchorage	Jan. 3
124	Kentucky vs. Mississippi St.	Jan. 20

FIELD-GOAL PERCENTAGE

Pct.	Team vs. Opponent	Date
73.1 (38-52)	UCLA vs. Southern Cal	Jan. 24
72.3 (34-47)	Evansville vs. Southern Ill.	Feb. 24
71.8 (28-39)	Gonzaga vs. St. Mary's (Cal.)	Jan. 13
70.9 (39-55)	Weber St. vs. Eastern Wash.	Jan. 27
69.8 (30-43)	Tulsa vs. North Caro. A&T	Dec. 2
69.4 (43-62)	Utah St. vs. Hawaii-Hilo	Nov. 26
68.8 (33-48)	Jacksonville St. vs. Alabama St.	Nov. 28
68.3 (28-41)	Fla. Atlantic vs. Florida Int'l	Feb. 1
68.3 (41-60)	Weber St. vs. Northern Ariz.	Mar. 2
68.2 (45-66)	Central Conn. St. vs. Troy St.	Feb. 17

THREE-POINT FIELD GOALS

3FG	Team vs. Opponent	Date
23	Troy St. vs. George Mason	Nov. 28
18	Florida Int'l vs. Palm Beach Atlantic	Nov. 25
18	Morehead St. vs. Centre	Dec. 2
18	Florida A&M vs. Palm Beach Atlantic	Dec. 4
18	Southern Ill. vs. Hawaii-Hilo	Dec. 29
18	Marshall vs. Hampton	Jan. 6
18	Pacific (Cal.) vs. Nevada	Feb. 8
18	LIU-Brooklyn vs. St. Francis (N.Y.)	Feb. 19

STATISTICAL LEADERS

3FG	Team vs. Opponent	Date
17	Cal Poly SLO vs. George Mason	Jan. 13
17	Pacific (Cal.) vs. New Mexico St.	Feb. 1
17	Ill.-Chicago vs. Northern Ill.	Feb. 8
17	VMI vs. Western Caro.	Mar. 2

FREE-THROW PERCENTAGE
(Min. 15 FT Made)

Pct.	Team vs. Opponent	Date
100.0 (17-17)	Cincinnati vs. Temple	Dec. 16

Pct.	Team vs. Opponent	Date
100.0 (16-16)	Wis.-Green Bay vs. Butler	Feb. 24
97.0 (32-33)	Toledo vs. Old Dominion	Dec. 9
97.0 (32-33)	Hawaii vs. New Mexico	Feb. 24
96.6 (28-29)	Boston College vs. Providence	Feb. 1
96.4 (27-28)	Rutgers vs. Pacific (Cal.)	Dec. 28
96.2 (25-26)	Colorado vs. Oklahoma	Feb. 17
96.0 (24-25)	James Madison vs. Hampton	Dec. 8
95.7 (22-23)	Md.-Balt. County vs. Morgan St.	Dec. 7
95.4 (21-22)	Vermont vs. New Hampshire	Feb. 16

1996 Division I Team Leaders

Scoring Offense

		G	W-L	Pts.	Avg.
1.	Troy St.	27	11-16	2,551	94.5
2.	Kentucky	36	34-2	3,292	91.4
3.	Marshall	28	17-11	2,560	91.4
4.	George Mason	27	11-16	2,443	90.5
5.	Southern U.	28	17-11	2,521	90.0
6.	Mississippi Val.	29	22-7	2,486	85.7
7.	Southeastern La.	27	15-12	2,296	85.0
8.	Davidson	30	25-5	2,528	84.3
9.	VMI	28	18-10	2,358	84.2
10.	Weber St.	30	20-10	2,524	84.1
11.	Texas Christian	30	15-15	2,519	84.0
12.	Eastern Mich.	31	25-6	2,594	83.7
13.	Georgetown	37	29-8	3,082	83.3
14.	Drexel	31	27-4	2,560	82.6
15.	Connecticut	35	32-3	2,890	82.6
16.	Brigham Young	28	15-13	2,303	82.3
17.	Texas Tech	32	30-2	2,629	82.2
18.	Prairie View	27	4-23	2,214	82.0
19.	Texas	31	21-10	2,535	81.8
20.	Arizona	33	26-7	2,693	81.6
21.	Jacksonville St.	27	10-17	2,203	81.6
22.	Maryland	30	17-13	2,440	81.3
23.	North Caro. St.	31	15-16	2,517	81.2
24.	Western Caro.	30	17-13	2,431	81.0
25.	Montana St.	30	21-9	2,425	80.8
26.	Kansas	34	29-5	2,741	80.6
27.	Fresno St.	33	22-11	2,652	80.4
28.	Cal Poly SLO	29	16-13	2,328	80.3
29.	Nebraska	35	21-14	2,808	80.2
30.	Georgia Tech	36	24-12	2,888	80.2

Scoring Defense

		G	W-L	Pts.	Avg.
1.	Princeton	29	22-7	1,498	51.7
2.	Wis.-Green Bay	29	25-4	1,620	55.9
3.	South Ala.	27	12-15	1,571	58.2
4.	Temple	33	20-13	1,922	58.2
5.	N.C.-Wilmington	29	13-16	1,694	58.4
6.	Harvard	26	15-11	1,581	60.8
7.	Wake Forest	32	26-6	1,963	61.3
8.	Manhattan	29	17-12	1,802	62.1
9.	Charleston (S.C.)	29	25-4	1,806	62.3
10.	Massachusetts	37	35-2	2,307	62.4
11.	Virginia Tech	29	23-6	1,825	62.9
12.	Clemson	29	18-11	1,826	63.0
13.	Tennessee	29	14-15	1,827	63.0
14.	Canisius	30	19-11	1,891	63.0
15.	St. Peter's	27	15-12	1,702	63.0
16.	Pennsylvania	27	17-10	1,704	63.1
17.	Marquette	31	23-8	1,964	63.4
18.	Iowa St.	33	24-9	2,091	63.4
19.	Utah	34	27-7	2,171	63.9
20.	Oklahoma St.	27	17-10	1,725	63.9
21.	Tex.-Pan American	28	9-19	1,789	63.9
22.	Miami (Ohio)	29	21-8	1,854	63.9
23.	San Francisco	27	15-12	1,727	64.0
24.	Penn St.	28	21-7	1,794	64.1
25.	St. Louis	30	16-14	1,924	64.1
26.	Michigan St.	32	16-16	2,053	64.2
27.	Detroit	29	18-11	1,862	64.2
28.	South Caro. St.	30	22-8	1,927	64.2
29.	Purdue	32	26-6	2,058	64.3
30.	Campbell	28	17-11	1,802	64.4

Scoring Margin

		Off.	Def.	Mar.
1.	Kentucky	91.4	69.4	22.1
2.	Connecticut	82.6	64.7	17.9
3.	Drexel	82.6	66.3	16.3
4.	Davidson	84.3	68.2	16.0
5.	Kansas	80.6	65.3	15.4
6.	Georgetown	83.3	68.8	14.5
7.	Cincinnati	79.6	65.2	14.4
8.	Utah	76.7	63.9	12.9
9.	Texas Tech	82.2	69.4	12.8
10.	Massachusetts	74.8	62.4	12.5
11.	Charleston (S.C.)	74.6	62.3	12.3
12.	Iowa	79.6	67.9	11.8
13.	Tulsa	76.4	65.0	11.4
14.	Georgia	79.2	68.1	11.2
15.	Montana St.	80.8	69.9	10.9
16.	Miami (Ohio)	74.8	63.9	10.9
17.	Penn St.	74.8	64.1	10.8
18.	Arizona	81.6	71.9	9.7
19.	Marquette	72.9	63.4	9.5
20.	Eastern Mich.	83.7	74.3	9.4
21.	Mississippi Val.	85.7	76.5	9.2
22.	Northern Ill.	75.0	66.0	9.0
23.	Wis.-Green Bay	64.8	55.9	8.9
24.	Villanova	75.5	66.6	8.9
25.	Purdue	73.1	64.3	8.8
26.	Ark.-Little Rock	76.5	67.8	8.7
27.	Stanford	75.2	66.7	8.5
28.	New Mexico	77.8	69.5	8.3
29.	Gonzaga	72.6	64.6	8.1
30.	Memphis	73.5	65.7	7.8
30.	South Caro. St.	72.0	64.2	7.8

Won-Lost Percentage

		W-L	Pct.
1.	Massachusetts	35-2	.946
2.	Kentucky	34-2	.944
3.	Texas Tech	30-2	.938
4.	Connecticut	32-3	.914
5.	Drexel	27-4	.871
6.	Wis.-Green Bay	25-4	.862
6.	Charleston (S.C.)	25-4	.862
8.	Kansas	29-5	.853
9.	Cincinnati	28-5	.848
9.	New Mexico	28-5	.848
11.	Davidson	25-5	.833
12.	Purdue	26-6	.813
12.	Wake Forest	26-6	.813
14.	Eastern Mich.	25-6	.806
15.	Utah	27-7	.794
16.	Virginia Tech	23-6	.793
17.	Arizona	26-7	.788
17.	Villanova	26-7	.788
19.	Georgetown	29-8	.784
20.	Ark.-Little Rock	23-7	.767
21.	Mississippi St.	26-8	.765
22.	Syracuse	29-9	.763
23.	Marist	22-7	.759
23.	Mississippi Val.	22-7	.759
23.	Princeton	22-7	.759
26.	Penn St.	21-7	.750
27.	UCLA	23-8	.742
27.	Marquette	23-8	.742

Field-Goal Percentage

		FG	FGA	Pct.
1.	UCLA	897	1,698	52.8
2.	Colorado St.	851	1,683	50.6
3.	Coppin St.	828	1,650	50.2
4.	Montana St.	898	1,800	49.9
5.	Weber St.	880	1,766	49.8
6.	Marshall	927	1,874	49.5
7.	New Mexico	889	1,802	49.3
8.	Toledo	822	1,670	49.2
9.	North Caro.	919	1,869	49.2
10.	Arizona	973	1,981	49.1
11.	Oral Roberts	757	1,542	49.1
12.	Hawaii	747	1,530	48.8
13.	Montana	740	1,518	48.7
14.	Kentucky	1,198	2,461	48.7
15.	Louisville	925	1,906	48.5
16.	Charleston (S.C.)	811	1,681	48.2
17.	Nebraska	1,007	2,089	48.2
18.	Gonzaga	769	1,597	48.2
19.	Utah	887	1,845	48.1
20.	Austin Peay	888	1,848	48.1
21.	Delaware	727	1,513	48.1
22.	Iowa	898	1,871	48.0
23.	Eastern Mich.	943	1,967	47.9
24.	Valparaiso	915	1,910	47.9
25.	Davidson	890	1,859	47.9
26.	South Caro.	856	1,788	47.9
27.	Mississippi St.	881	1,842	47.8
28.	Georgia Tech	1,031	2,161	47.7
29.	Tenn.-Martin	737	1,545	47.7
30.	Georgetown	1,121	2,356	47.6

Field-Goal Percentage Defense

		FG	FGA	Pct.
1.	Temple	670	1,741	38.5
2.	Marquette	682	1,772	38.5
3.	Mississippi St.	803	2,084	38.5
4.	Connecticut	840	2,175	38.6
5.	Kansas	777	2,008	38.7
6.	Massachusetts	812	2,098	38.7
7.	Cincinnati	723	1,860	38.9
8.	Tulsa	677	1,728	39.2
9.	Wake Forest	725	1,846	39.3
10.	Virginia	642	1,628	39.4
11.	Marist	717	1,817	39.5
12.	Iona	711	1,800	39.5
13.	Detroit	623	1,570	39.7
14.	Utah	786	1,966	40.0
15.	Liberty	661	1,652	40.0
16.	Kansas St.	681	1,699	40.1
17.	Drexel	782	1,950	40.1
18.	Arkansas	832	2,074	40.1
19.	Charleston (S.C.)	643	1,600	40.2
20.	Wis.-Green Bay	566	1,403	40.3
21.	Villanova	795	1,968	40.4
22.	Colgate	765	1,893	40.4
23.	Minnesota	727	1,797	40.5
24.	Tennessee	632	1,562	40.5
25.	Pennsylvania	603	1,488	40.5
26.	South Caro. St.	703	1,733	40.6

	FG	FGA	Pct.
27. Rhode Island	838	2,063	40.6
28. Bucknell	659	1,619	40.7
29. Northern Ill.	717	1,758	40.8
30. Syracuse	942	2,307	40.8

Three-Point Field Goals Made Per Game

	G	3FG	Avg.
1. Troy St.	27	300	11.1
2. Marshall	28	284	10.1
3. North Caro. St.	31	292	9.4
4. Southern Ill.	29	268	9.2
5. Samford	27	243	9.0
5. Southern U.	28	252	9.0
7. Auburn	32	287	9.0
8. Pacific (Cal.)	27	241	8.9
9. Mt. St. Mary's (Md.)	29	255	8.8
10. St. Mary's (Cal.)	27	233	8.6
11. Florida Int'l	28	240	8.6
12. Fresno St.	33	279	8.5
13. Morehead St.	27	227	8.4
14. Georgia Tech	36	296	8.2
15. Weber St.	30	245	8.2
16. Wake Forest	32	260	8.1
17. Ill.-Chicago	28	224	8.0
18. Alabama	32	255	8.0
19. VMI	28	223	8.0
20. Southeastern La.	27	213	7.9
21. La Salle	30	236	7.9
22. Vermont	27	212	7.9
23. Texas Tech	32	251	7.8
24. Southwestern La.	28	219	7.8
25. Drexel	31	241	7.8
26. Texas	31	239	7.7
27. Cal Poly SLO	29	223	7.7
28. Northern Iowa	27	204	7.6
28. Pittsburgh	27	204	7.6
30. Northeast La.	30	225	7.5
30. Southern Utah	28	210	7.5
30. Duke	31	231	7.5

Three-Point Field-Goal Percentage

(Min. 3.0 3FG Per Game)	G	3FG	3FGA	Pct.
1. Weber St.	30	245	577	42.5
2. Wake Forest	32	260	618	42.1
3. Penn St.	28	197	482	40.9
4. Connecticut	35	258	633	40.8
5. N.C.-Greensboro	30	205	503	40.8
6. Western Caro.	30	204	503	40.6
7. Evansville	27	180	444	40.5
8. St. Peter's	27	123	305	40.3
9. Miami (Ohio)	29	188	471	39.9
10. Marshall	28	284	712	39.9
11. Western Mich.	27	140	352	39.8
12. Kentucky	36	266	670	39.7
13. North Caro.	32	235	593	39.6
14. Virginia Tech	29	155	392	39.5
15. Colorado St.	30	182	461	39.5
16. Missouri	33	154	391	39.4
17. Drexel	31	241	612	39.4
18. Central Mich.	26	150	383	39.2
19. Indiana	31	184	470	39.1
20. UTEP	28	182	465	39.1
21. Radford	27	158	404	39.1
22. Southern Utah	28	210	538	39.0
23. Washington St.	29	181	464	39.0
24. Oral Roberts	27	173	447	38.7
25. North Texas	28	162	420	38.6
26. N.C.-Asheville	28	183	475	38.5
27. Tennessee	29	171	444	38.5
28. Jacksonville	28	167	434	38.5
29. Samford	27	243	632	38.4
30. Pacific (Cal.)	27	241	628	38.4

Free-Throw Percentage

	FT	FTA	Pct.
1. Utah	649	828	78.4
2. Weber St.	519	675	76.9
3. Brigham Young	587	767	76.5
4. Stanford	558	736	75.8
5. VMI	469	623	75.3
6. Hawaii	550	732	75.1
7. Stetson	347	464	74.8
8. Samford	499	669	74.6
9. Toledo	563	755	74.6
10. Wis.-Green Bay	428	574	74.6
11. Kent	447	603	74.1
12. Delaware	409	552	74.1
13. Harvard	383	518	73.9
14. North Caro. St.	457	622	73.5
15. Radford	340	463	73.4
16. Wagner	446	610	73.1
17. Connecticut	510	698	73.1
18. Rider	481	661	72.8
19. Eastern Wash.	323	444	72.7
20. Wyoming	541	745	72.6
21. Washington St.	461	637	72.4
22. Murray St.	474	655	72.4
23. Mt. St. Mary's (Md.)	324	448	72.3
24. Rutgers	431	597	72.2
25. Vermont	438	607	72.2
26. Jacksonville St.	521	723	72.1
27. Bucknell	509	707	72.0
28. San Diego St.	457	635	72.0
29. Iowa	557	777	71.7
30. Fairfield	486	678	71.7

Rebound Margin

	Off.	Def.	Mar.
1. Mississippi Val.	48.3	36.8	11.6
2. Utah St.	39.5	29.5	10.0
3. Utah	39.6	30.0	9.6
4. Iowa	40.5	31.4	9.1
5. Connecticut	43.4	34.4	9.0
6. Tulsa	43.2	34.8	8.3
7. Va. Commonwealth	40.2	32.0	8.3
8. Cincinnati	41.2	33.4	7.8
9. Dayton	39.8	32.1	7.6
10. Navy	40.4	32.9	7.5
11. Georgetown	43.4	35.9	7.5
12. Michigan St.	37.6	30.6	7.1
13. South Caro. St.	40.2	33.3	6.8
14. Northern Ill.	40.5	33.8	6.7
15. Ohio	40.2	33.8	6.4
16. Mississippi St.	39.0	32.6	6.3
17. North Caro.	38.8	32.6	6.3
18. Manhattan	37.9	31.6	6.2
19. Texas Tech	42.4	36.3	6.2
20. Penn St.	38.5	32.4	6.1
21. Drexel	41.3	35.3	6.0
22. UCLA	37.3	31.3	6.0
23. Harvard	37.8	31.9	5.9
24. Kentucky	41.7	35.8	5.9
25. Providence	38.8	33.0	5.8
26. Kansas	42.5	36.7	5.8
27. Houston	41.6	36.0	5.7
28. Massachusetts	40.1	34.4	5.6
29. Valparaiso	36.8	31.4	5.4
30. St. Peter's	36.0	30.7	5.4

1997 Division I Top Returnees

Career Totals

SCORING AVERAGE

Seniors (Min. 1,200 Pts.)

	Ht.	Yrs.	G	FG	3FG	FT	Pts.	Avg.
1. Tunji Awojobi, Boston U.	6-5	3	87	682	10	409	1,783	20.5
2. Keith Van Horn, Utah	6-9	3	90	643	148	403	1,837	20.4
3. Bubba Wells, Austin Peay	6-2	3	86	652	47	313	1,664	19.3
4. Charles Smith, Rider	6-6	3	88	681	69	262	1,693	19.2
5. Shea Seals, Tulsa	6-5	3	90	496	214	377	1,583	17.6
6. Curtis McCants, George Mason	6-0	3	81	478	91	351	1,398	17.3
7. Danya Abrams, Boston College	6-7	3	92	532	9	488	1,561	17.0
8. Jerald Honeycutt, Tulane	6-9	3	94	579	125	308	1,591	16.9
9. Monty Wilson, Tennessee St.	6-5	4	86	501	199	244	1,445	16.8
10. Jonathan Pixley, Samford	6-5	3	80	412	207	300	1,331	16.6

Juniors (Min. 800 Pts.)

	Ht.	Yrs.	G	FG	3FG	FT	Pts.	Avg.
1. Bonzi Wells, Ball St.	6-5	2	58	446	64	230	1,186	20.4
2. Adonal Foyle, Colgate	6-10	2	59	435	0	224	1,094	18.5
3. Danny Fortson, Cincinnati	6-7	2	67	412	0	354	1,178	17.6
4. Felipe Lopez, St. John's (N.Y.)	6-6	2	65	322	61	230	935	17.0
5. Tim Gill, Oral Roberts	6-2	2	53	305	155	132	897	16.9
6. LaDrell Whitehead, Wyoming	5-8	2	57	266	118	281	931	16.3
7. Ronnell Williams, Southern U.	6-7	2	52	351	0	136	838	16.1

Photo from Ball State sports information

Bonzi Wells of Ball State enters the 1997 campaign as the highest-scoring junior in Division I. Wells, who had the nation's fifth-highest scoring average (25.4) in 1996, has compiled 1,186 points in two seasons at Ball State.

	Ht.	Yrs.	G	FG	3FG	FT	Pts.	Avg.
8. Zendon Hamilton, St. John's (N.Y.)	6-11	2	55	291	0	299	881	16.0
9. Geno Carlisle, Northwestern	6-2	2	53	273	103	187	836	15.8
10. Matt Harpring, Georgia Tech	6-7	2	65	354	94	219	1,021	15.7

MOST POINTS

Seniors	Ht.	Yrs.	G	FG	3FG	FT	Pts.	Avg.
1. Keith Van Horn, Utah	6-9	3	90	643	148	403	1,837	20.4
2. Tunji Awojobi, Boston U.	6-5	3	87	682	10	409	1,783	20.5
3. Charles Smith, Rider	6-6	3	88	681	69	262	1,693	19.2
4. Bubba Wells, Austin Peay	6-2	3	86	652	47	313	1,664	19.3
5. Jerald Honeycutt, Tulane	6-9	3	94	579	125	308	1,591	16.9
6. Shea Seals, Tulsa	6-5	3	90	496	214	377	1,583	17.6
7. DeJuan Wheat, Louisville	6-0	3	101	532	226	286	1,576	15.6
8. Danya Abrams, Boston College	6-7	3	92	532	9	488	1,561	17.0
9. Odell Hodge, Old Dominion	6-9	4	95	625	0	271	1,521	16.0
10. Tim Duncan, Wake Forest	6-10	3	97	556	11	349	1,472	15.2

Juniors	Ht.	Yrs.	G	FG	3FG	FT	Pts.	Avg.
1. Bonzi Wells, Ball St.	6-5	2	58	446	64	230	1,186	20.4
2. Danny Fortson, Cincinnati	6-7	2	67	412	0	354	1,178	17.6
3. Adonal Foyle, Colgate	6-10	2	59	435	0	224	1,094	18.5
4. Matt Harpring, Georgia Tech	6-7	2	65	354	94	219	1,021	15.7
5. Felipe Lopez, St. John's (N.Y.)	6-6	2	55	322	61	230	935	17.0
6. LaDrell Whitehead, Wyoming	5-8	2	57	266	118	281	931	16.3
7. Tyson Wheeler, Rhode Island	5-10	2	61	297	129	195	918	15.0
8. Bryce Drew, Valparaiso	6-3	2	59	295	170	152	912	15.5
9. Tim Gill, Oral Roberts	6-2	2	53	305	155	132	897	16.9
10. Joe Bunn, Old Dominion	6-6	2	60	288	0	309	885	14.8

HIGHEST FIELD-GOAL PERCENTAGE

Seniors (Min. 300 FGM)	Ht.	Yrs.	G	FG	FGA	Pct.
1. Greg Smith, Delaware	6-7	3	78	394	654	60.2
2. Darnell McCulloch, Fresno St.	6-5	2	61	304	506	60.1
3. Rayshard Allen, Tulane	6-7	3	92	477	817	58.4
4. Jason Lawson, Villanova	6-11	3	97	395	681	58.0
5. Lorenzo Coleman, Tennessee Tech	7-1	3	85	360	622	57.9
6. Tim Duncan, Wake Forest	6-10	3	97	556	983	56.6
7. Shannon Bowman, Fairfield	6-4	3	84	439	788	55.7
8. Odell Hodge, Old Dominion	6-9	4	95	625	1,122	55.7
9. Scot Pollard, Kansas	6-10	3	100	331	596	55.5
10. Otis Hill, Syracuse	6-8	3	98	369	669	55.2

Juniors (Min. 240 FGM)	Ht.	Yrs.	G	FG	FGA	Pct.
1. Alexander Koul, Geo. Washington	7-1	2	61	323	507	63.7
2. Brian Skinner, Baylor	6-10	2	45	285	475	60.0
3. Rashon Turner, Fairleigh Dickinson	6-6	2	55	262	464	56.5
4. Kareem Livingston, Appalachian St.	6-7	2	57	247	438	56.4
5. J. R. Henderson, UCLA	6-9	2	62	282	503	56.1
6. Ronnell Williams, Southern U.	6-7	2	52	351	629	55.8
7. Raef LaFrentz, Kansas	6-11	2	65	332	616	53.9
8. Danny Fortson, Cincinnati	6-7	2	67	412	768	53.6
9. Adonal Foyle, Colgate	6-10	2	59	435	811	53.6
10. Joe Bunn, Old Dominion	6-6	2	60	288	538	53.5

MOST THREE-POINT FIELD GOALS MADE PER GAME

Seniors (Min. 120 3FGM)	Ht.	Yrs.	G	3FG	Avg.
1. Keith Veney, Marshall	6-3	3	82	279	3.40
2. Dominick Young, Fresno St.	5-10	2	57	177	3.11
3. Adam Jacobsen, Pacific (Cal.)	6-2	3	85	234	2.75
4. Cedric Foster, Alcorn St.	5-9	2	48	126	2.63
5. Jonathan Pixley, Samford	6-5	3	80	207	2.59
6. Tom Pipkins, Duquesne	6-2	3	85	212	2.49
7. Rhodney Donaldson, Troy St.	6-0	3	81	199	2.46
8. Shea Seals, Tulsa	6-5	3	90	214	2.38
9. Monty Wilson, Tennessee St.	6-5	4	86	199	2.31
10. Seth Chadwick, Wofford	6-4	3	75	173	2.31

Juniors (Min. 90 3FGM)	Ht.	Yrs.	G	3FG	Avg.
1. Troy Hudson, Southern Ill.	6-1	1	25	93	3.72
2. David Sivulich, St. Mary's (Cal.)	5-10	1	27	96	3.56
3. Curtis Staples, Virginia	6-3	2	61	185	3.03
4. Tim Gill, Oral Roberts	6-2	2	53	155	2.92
5. Bryce Drew, Valparaiso	6-3	2	59	170	2.88
6. Mike Martinho, Buffalo	5-11	2	55	157	2.85
7. Pete Lisicky, Penn St.	6-4	2	59	157	2.66
8. Shane Hawkins, Southern Ill.	6-2	2	60	148	2.47
9. Joe Sibbitt, Austin Peay	6-0	2	59	141	2.39
10. Johnny Miller, Temple	6-1	2	46	104	2.26

HIGHEST THREE-POINT FIELD-GOAL PERCENTAGE

Seniors (Min. 120 3FGM)	Ht.	Yrs.	G	3FG	3FGA	Pct.
1. Isaac Fontaine, Washington St.	6-3	3	90	133	285	46.7
2. Brad Divine, Western Ky.	6-0	3	81	128	295	43.4
3. Aaron Zobrist, Bradley	6-1	3	82	143	332	43.1
4. Jonathan Pixley, Samford	6-5	3	80	207	493	42.0
5. Keith Van Horn, Utah	6-9	3	90	148	364	40.7
6. Joel Burns, Western Mich.	6-1	3	82	141	350	40.3
7. Keith Veney, Marshall	6-3	3	82	279	694	40.2
8. Anthony Parker, Bradley	6-5	3	91	166	415	40.0
9. Brett Larrick, Charleston So.	6-4	3	84	174	440	39.5
10. Darnell Burton, Cincinnati	6-2	3	97	212	541	39.2

Juniors (Min. 90 3FGM)	Ht.	Yrs.	G	3FG	3FGA	Pct.
1. Justin Jones, Utah St.	6-3	2	61	112	255	43.9
2. Pete Lisicky, Penn St.	6-4	2	59	157	362	43.4
3. Bryce Drew, Valparaiso	6-3	2	59	170	401	42.4
4. Tim Gill, Oral Roberts	6-2	2	53	155	368	42.1
5. Matt Harpring, Georgia Tech	6-7	2	65	94	227	41.4
6. Jim Secretarski, Siena	5-10	2	54	119	288	41.3
7. Joe Sibbitt, Austin Peay	6-0	2	59	141	354	39.8
8. Shane Hawkins, Southern Ill.	6-2	2	60	148	373	39.7
9. Clayton Shields, New Mexico	6-8	2	63	99	252	39.3
10. Mike Martinho, Buffalo	5-11	2	55	157	410	38.3

HIGHEST FREE-THROW PERCENTAGE

Seniors (Min. 180 FTM)	Ht.	Yrs.	G	FG	FGA	Pct.
1. Roderick Howard, N.C.-Charlotte	5-10	3	81	204	233	87.6
2. Jason Sutherland, Missouri	6-1	3	92	191	225	84.9
3. Keith Van Horn, Utah	6-9	3	90	403	484	83.3
4. Jonathan Pixley, Samford	6-5	3	80	300	362	82.9
5. Kiwane Garris, Illinois	6-2	3	84	411	496	82.9
6. Derek Grimm, Missouri	6-10	3	84	180	219	82.2
7. Nod Carter, Middle Tenn. St.	6-6	3	82	219	267	82.0
8. Austin Croshere, Providence	6-9	3	85	204	253	80.6
9. Anthony Walker, Radford	6-0	3	82	227	282	80.5
10. Curtis McCants, George Mason	6-0	3	81	351	437	80.3

Juniors (Min. 110 FTM)	Ht.	Yrs.	G	FG	FGA	Pct.
1. Darian Devries, Northern Iowa	6-3	2	53	134	157	85.4
2. Bryce Drew, Valparaiso	6-3	2	59	152	184	82.6
3. Jeremy Veal, Arizona St.	6-3	2	60	110	134	82.1
4. Juan Bragg, Texas Christian	6-1	2	38	111	137	81.0
5. Tim Gill, Oral Roberts	6-2	2	53	132	163	81.0
6. Michael Heary, Navy	6-5	2	55	157	195	80.5
7. Aaron Hutchins, Marquette	5-9	2	64	134	167	80.2
8. James Cotton, Long Beach St.	6-5	2	53	217	280	77.5
9. LaDrell Whitehead, Wyoming	5-8	2	57	281	363	77.4
10. Thomas Kilgore, Central Mich.	6-2	2	36	140	182	76.9

MOST REBOUNDS PER GAME

Seniors (Min. 500 Rebs.)	Ht.	Yrs.	G	Reb.	Avg.
1. Tim Duncan, Wake Forest	6-10	3	97	1,113	11.47
2. Tunji Awojobi, Boston U.	6-5	3	87	962	11.06
3. Ace Custis, Virginia Tech	6-7	3	92	899	9.77
4. Thaddeous Delaney, Charleston (S.C.)	6-8	3	84	816	9.71
5. Kyle Snowden, Harvard	6-6	3	74	655	8.85
6. Keith Van Horn, Utah	6-9	3	90	771	8.57
7. Danya Abrams, Boston College	6-7	3	92	784	8.52
8. Odell Hodge, Old Dominion	6-9	4	95	803	8.45
9. Jamie Arnold, Wichita St.	6-7	3	65	548	8.43
10. Devin Davis, Miami (Ohio)	6-7	3	89	744	8.36

Juniors (Min. 300 Rebs.)	Ht.	Yrs.	G	Reb.	Avg.
1. Adonal Foyle, Colgate	6-10	2	59	735	12.46
2. Danny Fortson, Cincinnati	6-7	2	67	574	8.57
3. Keith Closs, Central Conn. St.	7-2	2	54	452	8.37
4. Gerald Jordan, Pittsburgh	6-11	2	56	458	8.18
5. Ronnell Williams, Southern U.	6-7	2	52	425	8.17
6. Joe Bunn, Old Dominion	6-6	2	60	480	8.00
7. Raef LaFrentz, Kansas	6-11	2	65	509	7.83
8. Zendon Hamilton, St. John's (N.Y.)	6-11	2	55	418	7.60
9. Kevin Simmons, UC Irvine	6-8	2	55	410	7.45
10. Bonzi Wells, Ball St.	6-5	2	58	429	7.40

MOST REBOUNDS

Seniors	Ht.	Yrs.	G	Reb.
1. Tim Duncan, Wake Forest	6-10	3	97	1,113
2. Tunji Awojobi, Boston U.	6-5	3	87	962
3. Ace Custis, Virginia Tech	6-7	3	92	899
4. Thaddeous Delaney, Charleston (S.C.)	6-8	3	84	816
5. Odell Hodge, Old Dominion	6-9	4	95	803
6. Danya Abrams, Boston College	6-7	3	92	784
7. Keith Van Horn, Utah	6-9	3	90	771
8. Devin Davis, Miami (Ohio)	6-7	3	89	744
9. Jerald Honeycutt, Tulane	6-9	3	94	669
10. Lorenzo Coleman, Tennessee Tech	7-1	3	85	668

Juniors	Ht.	Yrs.	G	Reb.
1. Adonal Foyle, Colgate	6-10	2	59	735
2. Danny Fortson, Cincinnati	6-7	2	67	574
3. Raef LaFrentz, Kansas	6-11	2	65	509
4. Joe Bunn, Old Dominion	6-6	2	60	480
5. Matt Harpring, Georgia Tech	6-7	2	65	473
6. Gerald Jordan, Pittsburgh	6-11	2	56	458

	Ht.	Yrs.	G	Reb.
7. Keith Closs, Central Conn. St.	7-2	2	54	452
8. Alexander Koul, Geo. Washington	7-1	2	61	439
9. Bonzi Wells, Ball St.	6-5	2	58	429
10. Ronnell Williams, Southern U.	6-7	2	52	425

MOST ASSISTS PER GAME

Seniors (Min. 300 Asts.)

	Ht.	Yrs.	G	Ast.	Avg.
1. Curtis McCants, George Mason	6-0	3	81	598	7.38
2. Dominick Young, Fresno St.	5-10	2	57	387	6.79
3. Brevin Knight, Stanford	5-10	3	85	546	6.42
4. Jacque Vaughn, Kansas	6-1	3	100	642	6.42
5. Chris Garner, Memphis	5-10	3	92	512	5.57
6. Darius Burton, Hofstra	5-9	3	84	463	5.51
7. Shandue McNeill, St. Bonaventure	5-7	3	86	457	5.31
8. Donminic Ellison, Washington St.	5-10	3	84	441	5.25
9. Wes Flanigan, Auburn	6-1	3	89	435	4.89
10. Andre Woolridge, Iowa	6-1	3	95	444	4.67

Juniors (Min. 200 Asts.)

	Ht.	Yrs.	G	Ast.	Avg.
1. Kyle Kessel, Texas A&M	6-0	2	57	344	6.04
2. Tyson Wheeler, Rhode Island	5-10	2	61	338	5.54
3. Bryce Drew, Valparaiso	6-3	2	59	326	5.53
4. Jamar Smiley, Illinois St.	5-11	2	67	335	5.00
5. Aaron Hutchins, Marquette	5-9	2	64	274	4.28
6. LaDrell Whitehead, Wyoming	5-8	2	57	213	3.74
7. Jermaine Watts, DePaul	6-1	2	56	200	3.57

MOST BLOCKED SHOTS PER GAME

Seniors (Min. 100 Blks.)

	Ht.	Yrs.	G	Blk.	Avg.
1. Tim Duncan, Wake Forest	6-10	3	97	379	3.91
2. Lorenzo Coleman, Tennessee Tech	7-1	3	85	305	3.59
3. Peter Aluma, Liberty	6-10	3	87	269	3.09
4. Kelvin Cato, Iowa St.	6-11	2	51	156	3.06
5. Jason Lawson, Villanova	6-11	3	97	270	2.78
6. Tunji Awojobi, Boston U.	6-5	3	87	228	2.62
7. Charles Smith, Rider	6-6	3	88	220	2.50
8. Brian Gilpin, Dartmouth	7-0	3	78	182	2.33
9. Odell Hodge, Old Dominion	6-9	4	95	202	2.13
10. Avondre Jones, Southern Cal	6-11	2	50	101	2.02

Juniors (Min. 80 Blks.)

	Ht.	Yrs.	G	Blk.	Avg.
1. Keith Closs, Central Conn. St.	7-2	2	54	317	5.87
2. Adonal Foyle, Colgate	6-10	2	59	312	5.29
3. Jerome Mason, Florida A&M	7-1	1	27	119	4.41
4. Brian Skinner, Baylor	6-10	2	45	151	3.36
5. Erik Nelson, Vermont	6-7	2	54	133	2.46
6. Corey Louis, Florida St.	6-10	2	50	117	2.34
7. Alexander Koul, Geo. Washington	7-1	2	61	106	1.74
8. Gerben Van Dorpe, Mt. St. Mary's (Md.)	6-11	2	49	80	1.63
9. Dennis Newton, Northeast La.	6-9	2	62	100	1.61
10. Tony Battie, Texas Tech	6-11	2	59	91	1.54

MOST STEALS PER GAME

Seniors (Min. 150 Stls.)

	Ht.	Yrs.	G	Stl.	Avg.
1. Dominick Young, Fresno St.	5-10	2	57	155	2.72
2. Chris Garner, Memphis	5-10	3	92	236	2.57
3. Brevin Knight, Stanford	5-10	3	85	215	2.53
4. Darius Burton, Hofstra	5-9	3	84	210	2.50
5. Shandue McNeill, St. Bonaventure	5-7	3	86	213	2.48
6. Dave Masciale, LIU-Brooklyn	5-10	3	82	187	2.28
7. Jeff Myers, Drexel	6-1	3	87	174	2.00
8. Warren Anderson, Wagner	5-11	3	82	160	1.95
9. Shea Seals, Tulsa	6-5	3	90	158	1.76
10. Edgar Padilla, Massachusetts	6-2	3	105	184	1.75

Juniors (Min. 80 Stls.)

	Ht.	Yrs.	G	Stl.	Avg.
1. Bonzi Wells, Ball St.	6-5	2	58	171	2.95
2. LaDrell Whitehead, Wyoming	5-8	2	57	122	2.14
3. Jermaine Watts, DePaul	6-1	2	56	102	1.82
4. Tyson Wheeler, Rhode Island	5-10	2	61	103	1.69
5. Matt Harpring, Georgia Tech	6-7	2	65	102	1.57
6. Tim Gill, Oral Roberts	6-2	2	53	82	1.55
7. Bryce Drew, Valparaiso	6-3	2	59	83	1.41

1996 Division II Individual Leaders

Scoring

	Cl.	G	TFG	3FG	FT	Pts.	Avg.
1. Brett Beeson, Moorhead St.	Sr	27	305	58	232	900	33.3
2. Carlos Knox, IU/PU-Indianapolis	Jr	29	301	70	255	927	32.0
3. Tyrone Mason, Edinboro	Sr	29	307	33	153	800	27.6
4. Shawn Harvey, West Va. St.	Sr	26	256	69	135	716	27.5
5. Dan Buie, Washburn	So	27	242	2	193	679	25.1
6. Dathon Brown, Fort Valley St.	Sr	22	181	45	145	552	25.1
7. Raul Varela, Colorado Mines	Sr	27	202	86	179	669	24.8
8. Alan Rainge, Northwood	Sr	26	236	14	156	642	24.7
9. Tim Jones, Georgia Col.	Jr	27	234	62	123	653	24.2
10. Tyrone Hopkins, Central Okla.	Jr	29	234	37	175	680	23.4
11. Pat Coleman, Mankato St.	Sr	27	265	24	77	631	23.4
12. Wil Pierce, Western St.	Sr	31	226	109	160	721	23.3
13. Marshall Dibble, Lander	Jr	27	223	0	178	624	23.1
14. Reece Gliko, Mont. St.-Billings	Jr	28	207	96	133	643	23.0
15. Derrick Henry, Mercy	Jr	24	201	53	94	549	22.9
15. Travis Tuttle, North Dak.	Jr	24	183	81	102	549	22.9
17. Rosendo Bryden, N.C.-Pembroke	Sr	27	190	70	166	616	22.8
18. Robbie Turner, Gardner-Webb	Sr	26	206	29	146	587	22.6
19. Derrick Pickens, West Ala.	Jr	26	208	70	99	585	22.5
20. Maurice Blanding, So. Colo.	Jr	28	235	0	159	629	22.5
21. Derron Jones, Adams St.	Sr	26	206	40	131	583	22.4
22. Andre Wheeler, Salem-Teikyo	Jr	28	195	96	137	623	22.3
23. Melvin Abrams, Johnson Smith	Sr	27	181	58	180	600	22.2
24. Steve Mercer, Bellarmine	Jr	27	226	2	144	598	22.1
25. David Clark, Bluefield St.	Sr	31	214	28	227	683	22.0
26. Cederick Wilbon, West Tex. A&M	Sr	28	201	72	138	612	21.9
27. Daniel Parke, Rollins	Jr	28	194	79	139	606	21.6
28. Brad Barron, Morningside	Sr	27	247	1	84	579	21.4
29. Deron Rutledge, Tex. A&M-Kingsville	Sr	29	231	0	157	619	21.3
30. Cedric Matthews, Delta St.	Sr	27	184	89	118	575	21.3
31. Chris Givens, Tarleton St.	Sr	26	189	74	101	553	21.3
32. Levelle Moton, N.C. Central	Sr	27	191	76	116	574	21.3
33. Kevin Vulin, Sacred Heart	Sr	27	239	2	93	573	21.2
34. Jerome Goforth, New Haven	Sr	26	214	53	70	551	21.2
35. Ashley Day, Denver	Sr	28	212	46	121	591	21.1
35. Jason Hall, Tex. A&M-Commerce	Sr	28	217	70	87	591	21.1
37. Adam Stockwell, Le Moyne	Sr	30	229	81	94	633	21.1
38. James Barber, Mars Hill	Jr	29	192	66	159	609	21.0
39. Deartrus Goodmon, Alabama A&M	Sr	31	219	80	130	648	20.9
40. Ryan Samelson, Neb.-Kearney	Sr	33	254	45	132	685	20.8
41. Perry Herbert, Adelphi	Sr	30	231	44	113	619	20.6
42. Kerwin Thompson, Eckerd	Sr	27	196	0	165	557	20.6
43. Robert Misenko, Indiana (Pa.)	Sr	30	202	13	199	616	20.5
44. Mike Shue, Lock Haven	Jr	24	147	84	112	490	20.4
45. Troy Anderson, Eastern N.M.	Jr	27	192	76	90	550	20.4
46. Alonzo Goldston, Fort Hays St.	Jr	34	282	0	128	692	20.4
47. Roger Powers, St. Rose	Jr	32	243	96	69	651	20.3
48. Kevin Rowe, Millersville	Sr	27	201	38	109	549	20.3
49. Jim Coyle, Shepherd	So	27	191	78	88	548	20.3
50. Mike Ellzy, Bloomsburg	Jr	28	192	58	126	568	20.3
51. Douglas Hines, Virginia St.	Sr	27	196	5	139	536	19.9
52. Nathan Norman, S.C.-Spartanburg	Jr	30	195	93	112	595	19.8
53. Mike Kuhens, Queens (N.Y.)	So	26	163	90	98	514	19.8
54. Joe Jones, Longwood	Sr	28	235	2	80	552	19.7
55. Daren Alix, Merrimack	Jr	28	172	114	92	550	19.6
56. Perrell Lucas, Indianapolis	Sr	24	171	53	76	471	19.6
57. Khyl Horton, Gannon	Sr	25	174	66	76	490	19.6
58. John Hemenway, South Dak.	Sr	27	154	42	179	529	19.6
59. Darren Clough, St. Anselm	Sr	31	222	1	158	603	19.5
60. Brent Montague, Mont. St.-Billings	Sr	28	197	78	72	544	19.4
61. Brian Sand, North Dak. St.	Sr	29	218	13	114	563	19.4
62. Kebu Stewart, Cal St. Bakersfield	Jr	30	201	0	180	582	19.4
63. Shewn Winfree, Fairmont St.	Sr	29	216	18	112	562	19.4
64. Ryan Williams, Alas. Anchorage	Jr	28	208	5	121	542	19.4
65. Brian Basich, Truman St.	Sr	26	173	83	73	502	19.3
66. Marcus Harris, Regis (Colo.)	So	30	196	33	154	579	19.3
67. Marc Eddington, Pittsburg St.	So	28	204	53	78	539	19.3
68. Kevin Lee, Shippensburg	Jr	25	172	0	135	479	19.2
69. Eddie Reece, Mo. Southern St.	Sr	26	178	54	88	498	19.2
70. Ervin Josey, Albany St. (Ga.)	Jr	27	192	53	80	517	19.1

Field-Goal Percentage

(Min. 5 FG Made Per Game)	Cl.	G	FG	FGA	Pct.
1. Kyle Kirby, IU/PU-Ft. Wayne	So	26	133	195	68.2
2. Garth Joseph, St. Rose	So	24	147	223	65.9
3. John Dixon, Dist. Columbia	Sr	22	116	180	64.4
4. Alex Falcon, American (P.R.)	Sr	26	179	280	63.9
5. James Morris, Cameron	Jr	22	134	210	63.8
6. J. J. Sims, West Ga.	Sr	28	181	285	63.5
7. Ed Madec, Sonoma St.	Sr	28	159	252	63.1
8. Demetris Montgomery, Lynn	Jr	25	147	233	63.1
9. Robert Misenko, Indiana (Pa.)	Sr	30	202	321	62.9
10. Pat Grabner, Minn.-Duluth	So	25	164	261	62.8

	Cl.	G	FG	FGA	Pct.
11. Eric Harris, St. Augustine's	Jr	25	148	236	62.7
12. Maurice Profit, Mercyhurst	So	27	135	216	62.5
13. Dewayne Rogers, Central Okla.	Sr	29	178	285	62.5
14. Marshall Dibble, Lander	Jr	27	223	358	62.3
15. Deron Rutledge, Tex. A&M-Kingsville	Sr	29	231	371	62.3
16. Mark Davis, Mass. Lowell	Jr	24	185	298	62.1
17. J. D. Asselta, Bentley	Sr	27	204	329	62.0
18. Alonzo Goldston, Fort Hays St.	Jr	34	282	455	62.0
19. Robert Jones, Calif. (Pa.)	Jr	33	189	305	62.0
20. Scott Smith, New Hamp. Col.	Jr	27	175	285	61.4
21. Levi Bradley, Wis.-Parkside	Jr	25	173	283	61.1
22. Quincy Baker, Henderson St.	Jr	27	154	252	61.1
23. Jeremy Vliem, Northern St.	Jr	29	182	299	60.9
24. Eric Powers, South Dak.	Sr	27	159	262	60.7
25. Derrick Scott, Calif. (Pa.)	Jr	33	205	338	60.7
26. Sherick Simpson, Fort Hays St.	Jr	34	188	310	60.6
27. Doug Price, Denver	Jr	28	152	251	60.6
28. Chris Morris, Alderson-Broaddus	Sr	28	191	316	60.4
29. Broderick Bobb, Abilene Christian	So	27	153	254	60.2
30. Otis Key, Lincoln (Mo.)	Sr	25	171	284	60.2

Three-Point Field Goals Made Per Game

	Cl.	G	3FG	Avg.
1. Daren Alix, Merrimack	Jr	28	114	4.1
2. Chris Brown, Tuskegee	Sr	26	104	4.0
3. Kelly Dorenkamp, Southern Colo.	Sr	28	107	3.8
4. Tony Sanders, Cal St. San B'dino	Sr	27	96	3.6
5. William Burr, Clark Atlanta	Jr	29	103	3.6
6. Shane Karlon, St. Andrews	Jr	27	95	3.5
7. Wil Pierce, Western St.	Sr	31	109	3.5
8. Mike Shue, Lock Haven	Jr	24	84	3.5
9. Mike Kuhens, Queens (N.Y.)	So	26	90	3.5
9. Lafonte Moses, St. Augustine's	Fr	26	90	3.5
11. Reece Gliko, Mont. St.-Billings	Jr	28	96	3.4
11. Andre Wheeler, Salem-Teikyo	Jr	28	96	3.4
13. Travis Tuttle, North Dak.	Jr	24	81	3.4
14. Stephen Hamrick, Eastern N.M.	Sr	26	87	3.3
15. Paul Cluxton, Northern Ky.	Jr	32	106	3.3
16. Cedric Matthews, Delta St.	Sr	27	89	3.3
16. Jesse Ogden, Edinboro	So	27	89	3.3
18. Primoz Samardzija, Ala.-Huntsville	So	26	85	3.3

Paul Cluxton of Northern Kentucky was at his best "behind the lines" when it came to shooting the basketball in 1996. Cluxton posted the best free-throw percentage and the fourth-best three-point field-goal percentage among Division II competitors.

Photo from Northern Kentucky sports information

	Cl.	G	3FG	Avg.
19. Shae Johnson, Bowie St.	So	27	88	3.3
20. Geoff Eck, Fort Hays St.	Sr	34	109	3.2
21. Brendan McCarthy, St. Anselm	Sr	31	99	3.2
22. Brian Basich, Truman St.	Sr	26	83	3.2
23. Charles Jackson, Abilene Christian	Fr	27	86	3.2
23. Raul Varela, Colorado Mines	Sr	27	86	3.2
25. Geoff Ping, Seattle Pacific	Jr	29	91	3.1
26. Nathaniel Allen, Western St.	Jr	30	94	3.1
27. Mark Mulvey, St. Michael's	Jr	27	84	3.1
28. Lance Luitjens, Northern St.	Sr	29	90	3.1
29. Nathan Norman, S.C.-Spartanburg	Jr	30	93	3.1
30. Jay Harrie, Cal St. Chico	Sr	25	77	3.1
30. Jeremy Ward, Metro St.	Fr	25	77	3.1

Three-Point Field-Goal Percentage

(Min. 1.5 3FG Made Per Game)	Cl.	G	FG	FGA	Pct.
1. Matt Hopson, Oakland City	Jr	31	84	145	57.9
2. Jon Bryant, St. Cloud St.	Fr	27	54	94	57.4
3. Kris Kidwell, Oakland City	Jr	28	44	78	56.4
4. Paul Cluxton, Northern Ky.	Jr	32	106	198	53.5
5. Jermaine Henderson, St. Rose	So	29	55	103	53.4
6. Charles Ballmer, Ferris St.	Jr	24	54	106	50.9
7. Kris Matuszewski, Oakland	So	25	46	91	50.5
8. Todd Woelfle, Oakland City	So	28	43	86	50.0
8. Russ Nichols, Mesa St.	So	25	52	104	50.0
10. Geoff Ping, Seattle Pacific	Jr	29	91	183	49.7
11. Jason Sempsrott, South Dak. St.	Jr	29	57	115	49.6
12. Perrell Lucas, Indianapolis	Sr	24	53	108	49.1
13. Jon Cummins, West Liberty St.	Jr	26	44	90	48.9
14. Marc Hostetter, Southern Ind.	Jr	29	53	109	48.6
15. Michael Brooks, Indianapolis	Sr	29	72	149	48.3
16. Nick Smith, Ferris St.	Jr	26	43	89	48.3
17. Matt Kaminski, Neb.-Kearney	So	29	52	110	47.3
18. Anthony Pope, Fort Hays St.	Jr	34	83	177	46.9
19. Tony Sanders, Cal St. San B'dino	Sr	27	96	205	46.8
20. Stephen Hamrick, Eastern N.M.	Sr	26	87	186	46.8
21. Brendan McCarthy, St. Anselm	Sr	31	99	212	46.7
22. Dustin Jones, Lake Superior St.	Fr	28	47	101	46.5
23. Geoff Eck, Fort Hays St.	Sr	34	109	235	46.4
24. Sean Ryan, St. Anselm	Sr	31	79	171	46.2
25. Chad Bultynck, Michigan Tech	So	29	54	117	46.2
26. Raul Varela, Colorado Mines	Sr	27	86	187	46.0
27. Mark Mulvey, St. Michael's	Jr	27	84	183	45.9
28. Brad Schick, Northern Colo.	Fr	25	61	133	45.9
29. Derek Lewis, Queens (N.Y.)	Sr	25	43	94	45.7
30. Ofir Kuchly, Lynn	Sr	27	62	136	45.6

Free-Throw Percentage

(Min. 2.5 FT Made Per Game)	Cl.	G	FT	FTA	Pct.
1. Paul Cluxton, Northern Ky.	Jr	32	100	108	92.6
2. Roger Suchy, Lewis	Sr	27	83	92	90.2
3. Rosendo Bryden, N.C.-Pembroke	Sr	27	166	185	89.7
4. Mike Brown, Georgia Col.	Sr	28	85	95	89.5
5. Ryan McCarty, Wis.-Parkside	Sr	24	92	103	89.3
6. John Hemenway, South Dak.	Sr	27	179	201	89.1
7. Mike Shue, Lock Haven	Jr	24	112	126	88.9
8. Lance Luitjens, Northern St.	Sr	29	117	132	88.6
9. Dan Shanks, Coker	Jr	26	128	145	88.3
10. David Thompson, West Va. Tech	Sr	29	109	125	87.2
11. Chris Daley, Lock Haven	So	25	88	101	87.1
12. Brendan McCarthy, St. Anselm	Sr	31	81	93	87.1
13. Mark Mulvey, St. Michael's	Jr	27	100	115	87.0
14. Tyrone Mason, Edinboro	Sr	29	153	176	86.9
15. Nathan Norman, S.C.-Spartanburg	Jr	30	112	129	86.8
16. Carlos Knox, IU/PU-Indianapolis	Jr	29	255	294	86.7
17. John Wadsworth, Lenoir-Rhyne	Sr	26	65	75	86.7
18. Jason Holmes, SIU-Edwardsville	Jr	25	89	103	86.4
19. Jim Borodawica, Mass.-Lowell	Sr	26	81	94	86.2
20. Ervin Josey, Albany St. (Ga.)	Jr	27	80	93	86.0
21. Brian Basich, Truman St.	Sr	26	73	85	85.9
22. Jason Sempsrott, South Dak. St.	Jr	29	114	133	85.7
23. Tim Holloway, Mo.-Rolla	Jr	31	94	110	85.5
24. Desmond Greer, North Ala.	Jr	32	129	151	85.4
25. Joel Weyand, Morningside	Jr	27	70	82	85.4
26. Jake Biddle, Francis Marion	So	23	64	75	85.3
27. Adrian Machado, Stonehill	Sr	26	81	95	85.3
28. Andy Waggoner, Quincy	Sr	27	69	81	85.2
29. Mike Feller, Catawba	Sr	24	120	141	85.1
30. John Miller, Cal Poly Pomona	Jr	27	102	120	85.0

Rebounding

	Cl.	G	Reb.	Avg.
1. J. J. Sims, West Ga.	Sr	28	374	13.4
2. Tommie Foster, Morris Brown	Sr	25	329	13.2
3. John Burke, LIU-Southampton	Sr	28	344	12.3
4. Andrew Betts, LIU-C. W. Post	So	29	349	12.0
5. Garth Joseph, St. Rose	So	24	284	11.8
6. Kevin Vulin, Sacred Heart	Sr	27	316	11.7
7. Otis Key, Lincoln (Mo.)	Sr	25	282	11.3
8. Kino Outlaw, Mount Olive	Sr	27	295	10.9
9. Kenisy Adair, Kennesaw St.	Jr	26	282	10.8
10. Kebu Stewart, Cal St. Bakersfield	Jr	30	324	10.8
11. Deron Rutledge, Tex. A&M-Kingsville	Sr	29	311	10.7
12. Chris McKelvey, Tuskegee	Jr	25	267	10.7
13. Josh Chapin, Tampa	Jr	26	276	10.6
14. Kevin Lee, Shippensburg	Jr	25	264	10.6
15. Pat Coleman, Mankato St.	Sr	27	284	10.5
16. Ben Wallace, Virginia Union	Sr	31	324	10.5
17. Rob Layton, Emporia St.	Sr	26	270	10.4
18. Linzy Bennett, Northwood	Jr	26	266	10.2
19. John Skokan, Neb.-Omaha	Sr	27	276	10.2
20. Earl Tabor, Fort Lewis	Jr	26	265	10.2
21. Billy Layne, Wingate	Jr	27	273	10.1
22. Charles Ward, Tex. A&M-Commerce	Jr	22	221	10.0
23. Derrick Bryant, Norfolk St.	Sr	27	269	10.0
24. Brandon Heckroth, N.M. Highlands	Jr	26	259	10.0
25. Shawn Harvey, West Va. St.	Sr	26	256	9.8
26. Douglas Hines, Virginia St.	Sr	27	263	9.7
27. Alonzo Goldston, Fort Hays St.	Jr	34	331	9.7
28. Bryant Tyler, Cal St. Chico	Sr	26	253	9.7
29. Dashawn Harris, West Tex. A&M	Jr	28	269	9.6
30. Adrian Machado, Stonehill	Sr	26	248	9.5

Assists

	Cl.	G	Ast.	Avg.
1. Bobby Banks, Metro St.	Sr	27	244	9.0
2. Danny Gimpel, Adelphi	Jr	30	243	8.1
3. Joe Jessen, St. Andrews	Fr	27	217	8.0
4. Alex Mavroukas, Bentley	So	23	175	7.6
5. Candice Pickens, Calif. (Pa.)	Sr	33	249	7.5
6. Jamie Stevens, Mont. St.-Billings	So	28	210	7.5
7. Michael McClain, Mo.-Rolla	Sr	31	231	7.5
8. Jay Driscoll, Quincy	So	27	196	7.3
9. Matt Stone, Keene St.	Sr	22	159	7.2
10. Warren King, Seattle Pacific	Sr	29	204	7.0
11. Don Carlson, Lake Superior St.	Sr	28	196	7.0
12. Oronn Brown, Clarion	Jr	25	173	6.9
13. Troy McGee, Tuskegee	Sr	26	179	6.9
14. Derrick Henry, Mercy	Jr	24	161	6.7
15. Mike Sheppard, Tampa	Jr	22	147	6.7
16. Usani Phillips, Adams St.	Sr	27	179	6.6
17. Matt Hurst, Mars Hill	Sr	29	192	6.6
18. Rick Stafford, Alas. Anchorage	Jr	28	182	6.5
19. David Terrell, Albany St. (Ga.)	Jr	27	175	6.5
20. Kevin Kovach, Oakland	Sr	29	185	6.4
21. Rob Atene, Le Moyne	Jr	30	191	6.4
22. Ed Buecker, St. Anselm	Jr	31	195	6.3
23. Orlando Ranson, New Hamp. Col.	Fr	29	181	6.2
24. Jay Butler, Virginia Union	Sr	30	187	6.2
25. Adrian Bell, Elizabeth City St.	Jr	26	162	6.2
26. Kenya Crandell, Neb.-Kearney	Sr	27	166	6.1
27. John Hemenway, South Dak.	Sr	27	165	6.1
28. Shun Stargell, Valdosta St.	Sr	27	162	6.0
29. Chris Jackson, Lander	Jr	27	161	6.0
30. Curtis Green, Fort Valley St.	Jr	27	157	5.8

Blocked Shots

	Cl.	G	Blk.	Avg.
1. John Burke, LIU-Southampton	Sr	28	142	5.1
2. Kino Outlaw, Mount Olive	Sr	27	117	4.3
3. Derek Moore, S.C.-Aiken	Fr	26	97	3.7
4. Ben Wallace, Virginia Union	Sr	31	114	3.7
5. Horacio Llamas, Grand Canyon	Sr	29	106	3.7
6. Garth Joseph, St. Rose	So	24	78	3.3
7. James Doyle, Concord	So	28	87	3.1
8. Shawn Harvey, West Va. St.	Sr	26	80	3.1

	Cl.	G	Blk.	Avg.
9. Kerwin Thompson, Eckerd	Sr	27	83	3.1
10. Eliecer Ellis, American (P.R.)	Jr	26	75	2.9
11. Coata Malone, Alabama A&M	Sr	31	89	2.9
12. Antwain Smith, St. Paul's	Fr	28	78	2.8
13. Adrian Machado, Stonehill	Sr	26	72	2.8
14. John Tomsich, Le Moyne	Fr	30	78	2.6
15. Alonzo Goldston, Fort Hays St.	Jr	34	88	2.6
16. Zach Bush, Phila. Textile	Fr	27	69	2.6
17. Emile Shephard, Seattle Pacific	Sr	28	70	2.5
18. Steve McCorkle, St. Andrews	Fr	27	67	2.5
19. Kelvin Richardson, Central Mo. St.	Jr	31	76	2.5
20. Francisco Wilson, Mississippi Col.	So	25	61	2.4
21. John Skokan, Neb.-Omaha	Sr	27	64	2.4
22. Antwine Moore, Millersville	Jr	27	63	2.3
23. Antatius Clark, Fla. Southern	Jr	30	67	2.2
24. Otis Key, Lincoln (Mo.)	Sr	25	52	2.1
25. Chris Blanton, Cal St. Hayward	Jr	25	49	2.0
26. Yogi Leo, Queens (N.C.)	Sr	31	60	1.9
27. Joel Sargent, Elon	Jr	28	53	1.9
28. Frank Duru, Adams St.	So	27	51	1.9
28. Anthony Smith, Gardner-Webb	Jr	27	51	1.9
30. Chris McKelvey, Tuskegee	Jr	25	47	1.9

Steals

	Cl.	G	Stl.	Avg.
1. David Clark, Bluefield St.	Sr	31	118	3.8
2. Bob Cunningham, New York Tech	Sr	25	85	3.4
3. Craig Furgeson, Columbus St.	Sr	32	107	3.3
4. Oronn Brown, Clarion	Jr	25	80	3.2
5. Jimai Springfield, Cheyney	Jr	27	86	3.2
6. Paul Cannon, West Va. St.	Jr	26	81	3.1
7. Ray Carter, Rollins	Sr	28	86	3.1
8. Derrick Henry, Mercy	Jr	24	73	3.0
9. Malcolm Turner, Sonoma St.	Sr	28	85	3.0
10. Johnny Estelle, Tex. A&M-Kingsville	Sr	29	88	3.0
11. Wallace Corker, Morehouse	Sr	27	78	2.9
12. Jason Hall, Tex. A&M-Commerce	Sr	28	80	2.9
13. Shannon Holmes, New York Tech	Sr	25	71	2.8
14. Tim Jones, Georgia Col.	Jr	27	76	2.8
15. Monte Reese, Pace	Sr	26	73	2.8
16. Deartrus Goodmon, Alabama A&M	Sr	31	86	2.8
17. Kwane Thomas, LIU-Southampton	Sr	29	80	2.8
18. James Robinson, Chadron St.	So	27	74	2.7
19. Dean Doss, Edinboro	Jr	29	79	2.7
20. Mike Hancock, Neb.-Kearney	So	33	89	2.7
21. Brett Beeson, Moorhead St.	Sr	27	72	2.7
21. Orlando Santiago, Dowling	Jr	27	72	2.7
23. Terrance Gist, S.C.-Spartanburg	So	30	78	2.6
24. Khyl Horton, Gannon	Sr	25	64	2.6
25. John Miller, Cal Poly Pomona	Jr	27	69	2.6
26. Shewn Winfree, Fairmont St.	Sr	29	74	2.6
27. Devlin Herring, Pitt.-Johnstown	So	25	63	2.5
28. Rahsaah Roland, Mercyhurst	Sr	27	68	2.5
29. Ricky Thompson, Drury	Jr	24	60	2.5
30. Keith Linson, Central Mo. St.	Jr	31	77	2.5

1996 Division II Game Highs

Individual Highs

SCORING

Pts.	Player, Team vs. Opponent	Date
54	Brett Beeson, Moorhead St. vs. Minn.-Morris	Feb. 26
52	Derrick Henry, Mercy vs. Assumption	Nov. 27
50	Carlos Knox, IU/PU-Indianapolis vs. Indiana Tech	Jan. 10
48	Brett Beeson, Moorhead St. vs. North Dak. St.	Dec. 2
47	Joel Curbelo, American (P.R.) vs. Louisville	Nov. 25
46	Carlos Knox, IU/PU-Indianapolis vs. Central St.	Feb. 21
45	Dan Buie, Washburn vs. Mo.-Rolla	Feb. 27
44	Travis Tuttle, North Dak. vs. Morningside	Mar. 1
44	Tyrone Mason, Edinboro vs. Clarion	Feb. 7
44	Kevin Lee, Shippensburg vs. Pitt.-Johnstown	Nov. 27

STATISTICAL LEADERS

THREE-POINT FIELD GOALS

3FG	Player, Team vs. Opponent	Date
12	Tony Sanders, Cal St. San B'dino vs. Grand Canyon	Feb. 22
11	Orlando Santiago, Dowling vs. Mercy	Jan. 29
10	Nick Karageorgos, New Hamp. Col. vs. Keene St.	Feb. 7
10	Chris Brown, Tuskegee vs. Kentucky St.	Jan. 15
10	Kevin Towns, Millersville vs. Kutztown	Jan. 13
10	Martin Lattibeaudiere, West Tex. A&M vs. LeTourneau	Nov. 24
10	Jay Harrie, Cal St. Chico vs. Biola	Nov. 18

FIELD-GOAL PERCENTAGE

(Min. 10 FG Made)

Pct.	Player, Team vs. Opponent	Date
100.0 (14-14)	Derrick Scott, Calif. (Pa.) vs. Columbia Union	Dec. 6
100.0 (13-13)	Derrick Freeman, Indiana (Pa.) vs. Clarion	Feb. 17
100.0 (13-13)	Ralfs Jansons, St. Rose vs. Concordia (N.Y.)	Jan. 13
100.0 (12-12)	J. J. Sims, West Ga. vs. Gardner-Webb	Dec. 2
100.0 (11-11)	DeWayne Rogers, Central Okla. vs. Eastern N.M.	Feb. 3
100.0 (11-11)	Brian Ehrp, North Dak. vs. Augustana (S.D.)	Jan. 13
100.0 (10-10)	Ralfs Jansons, St. Rose vs. New York Tech	Feb. 17
100.0 (10-10)	Marc Tompkins, Mo.-Rolla vs. Northwest Mo. St.	Jan. 6
92.9 (13-14)	J. D. Asselta, Bentley vs. Quinnipiac	Dec. 9
92.9 (13-14)	John Hemenway, South Dak. vs. Minn.-Crookston	Dec. 2
92.9 (13-14)	Kyle Kirby, IU/PU-Ft. Wayne vs. Northern Ky.	Nov. 25

FREE-THROW PERCENTAGE

(Min. 10 FT Made)

Pct.	Player, Team vs. Opponent	Date
100.0 (18-18)	Carlos Knox, IU/PU-Indianapolis vs. Hawaii-Hilo	Dec. 16
100.0 (14-14)	Marc Eddington, Pittsburg St. vs. Northwest Mo. St.	Feb. 27
100.0 (14-14)	Kebu Stewart, Cal St. Bakersfield vs. Cal St. Hayward	Nov. 21
100.0 (12-12)	Michael Brooks, Indianapolis vs. Quincy	Feb. 22
100.0 (12-12)	Matt Hurst, Mars Hill vs. Wingate	Feb. 10
100.0 (12-12)	Chris Daley, Lock Haven vs. Kutztown	Jan. 29
100.0 (12-12)	Tyrone Hopkins, Central Okla. vs. West Tex. A&M	Feb. 1
100.0 (12-12)	Rosendo Bryden, N.C.-Pembroke vs. St. Andrews	Jan. 20
100.0 (12-12)	Nathan Norman, S.C.-Spartanburg vs. Southern Wesleyan	Jan. 22
100.0 (12-12)	Doug Peters, Bemidji St. vs. Moorhead St.	Jan. 20
100.0 (12-12)	John Hemenway, South Dak. vs. St. Cloud St.	Jan. 12
100.0 (12-12)	Desmond Greer, North Ala. vs. Delta St.	Dec. 4
100.0 (12-12)	James Moore, Shepherd vs. Shenandoah	Nov. 21

REBOUNDS

Reb.	Player, Team vs. Opponent	Date
27	Tommie Foster, Morris Brown vs. Kentucky St.	Feb. 24
26	Otis Key, Lincoln (Mo.) vs. Mo. Western St.	Feb. 24
25	Elbert Jones, West Fla. vs. La Grange	Nov. 27
23	John Skokan, Neb.-Omaha vs. St. Cloud St.	Mar. 1
23	John Burke, LIU-Southampton vs. Mercy	Feb. 12
23	Kino Outlaw, Mount Olive vs. Lenoir-Rhyne	Dec. 2
21	Linzy Bennett, Northwood vs. Saginaw Valley St.	Feb. 24
21	James Clark, Gannon vs. Mercyhurst	Feb. 8
21	Claudia Copeland, Franklin Pierce vs. Le Moyne	Feb. 3
21	Andrew Betts, LIU-C.W.-Post vs. Dowling	Jan. 28
21	Matt Stuck, Oakland vs. Mercyhurst	Jan. 26
21	Coata Malone, Alabama A&M vs. Alabama St.	Jan. 10
21	Kevin Lee, Shippensburg vs. Shepherd	Nov. 18

ASSISTS

Ast.	Player, Team vs. Opponent	Date
17	Bobby Banks, Metro St. vs. Denver	Feb. 17
17	Joe Jessen, St. Andrews vs. N.C.-Pembroke	Jan. 20
16	Moochie Norris, West Fla. vs. Valdosta St.	Feb. 24
16	Mike Sheppard, Tampa vs. Otterbein	Nov. 25
15	Several times	

BLOCKED SHOTS

Blk.	Player, Team vs. Opponent	Date
14	Victorlus Payne, Lane vs. Talladega	Jan. 26
12	John Burke, LIU-Southampton vs. New York Tech	Feb. 27
12	Kino Outlaw, Mount Olive vs. Newport News	Dec. 5

Blk.	Player, Team vs. Opponent	Date
12	John Burke, LIU-Southampton vs. Molloy	Dec. 13
10	Derrick Moore, S.C.-Aiken vs. Augusta St.	Feb. 17
10	Shawn Harvey, West Va. St. vs. Shepherd	Jan. 15
10	Horacio Llamas, Grand Canyon vs. Clarke	Dec. 16
10	Mike Johnson, Edinboro vs. Point Park	Nov. 22
10	Derek Moore, S.C.-Aiken vs. Southern Wesleyan	Nov. 17

STEALS

Stl.	Player, Team vs. Opponent	Date
10	Deartus Goodman, Alabama A&M vs. Morehouse	Nov. 22
9	Dave McKenzie, Alderson-Broaddus vs. Glenville St.	Jan. 20
9	Mike Hancock, Neb.-Kearney vs. Neb.-Omaha	Dec. 16
8	Bobby Cunningham, New York Tech vs. LIU-C.W. Post	Dec. 16
8	Pancho Conley, Pittsburg St. vs. Tabor	Dec. 9
8	Terrance Gist, S.C.-Spartanburg vs. North Greenville	Dec. 5
8	Matt Hopson, Oakland City vs. Central Okla.	Dec. 1
8	Monti Carr, Coker vs. Morris	Nov. 21
8	Terrance Gist, S.C.-Spartanburg vs. Voorhees	Nov. 20
8	Von Hilliard, Livingstone vs. Knoxville	Nov. 19

Team Highs

SCORING

Pts.	Team vs. Opponent	Date
158	Central Okla. vs. Ark. Baptist	Dec. 9
144	Fort Lewis vs. American Indian Col.	Jan. 29
140	Mont. St.-Billings vs. Alas. Anchorage	Feb. 1
135	Morningside vs. Westmar	Nov. 18
133	New York Tech vs. Mercy	Dec. 13
130	Western St. vs. Neb.-Kearney	Feb. 24

FIELD-GOAL PERCENTAGE

Pct.	Team vs. Opponent	Date
78.0 (32-41)	Coker vs. Morris	Nov. 21
75.5 (40-53)	Fort Hays St. vs. Hastings	Dec. 30
72.1 (31-43)	Presbyterian vs. Augusta	Nov. 20
71.2 (37-52)	South Dak. St. vs. South Dak.	Jan. 20
70.3 (45-64)	Lynn vs. Webber	Feb. 5
70.2 (40-57)	New York Tech vs. Queens (N.Y.)	Jan. 13
69.0 (40-58)	Lynn vs. St. Thomas (Fla.)	Nov. 24
68.6 (24-35)	Michigan Tech vs. Wayne St. (Mich.)	Jan. 11
68.3 (41-60)	Fort Hays St. vs. Adams St.	Dec. 2

FREE-THROW PERCENTAGE

(Min. 15 FT Made)

Pct.	Team vs. Opponent	Date
100.0 (27-27)	Cal St. Hayward vs. Notre Dame (Cal.)	Feb. 16
100.0 (20-20)	Dowling vs. Molloy	Feb. 17
100.0 (17-17)	Lenoir-Rhyne vs. Carson-Newman	Feb. 8
100.0 (15-15)	St. Augustine's vs. Fayetteville St.	Jan. 18
94.7 (18-19)	Quinnipiac vs. Stonehill	Jan. 27
94.4 (17-18)	Moorhead St. vs. Bemidji St.	Feb. 1
94.4 (17-18)	American (P.R.) vs. Ponce	Feb. 13
94.4 (34-36)	Lewis vs. Southern Ind.	Jan. 20
93.1 (27-29)	Indiana (Pa.) vs. Ky. Wesleyan	Nov. 20
92.6 (25-27)	Cal St. Chico vs. Sonoma St.	Jan. 6

THREE-POINT FIELD GOALS

3FG	Team vs. Opponent	Date
21	Cal St. San B'dino vs. Grand Canyon	Feb. 22
19	Fort Hays St. vs. McPherson	Feb. 14
19	Bentley vs. Assumption	Jan. 10
18	Mont. St.-Billings vs. Chaminade	Feb. 29
18	Western St. vs. Adams St.	Feb. 2
18	Western St. vs. Fort Lewis	Feb. 1
18	Oakland vs. Aquinas	Dec. 29
18	Southwest St. vs. Washburn	Nov. 25

1996 Division II Team Leaders

Scoring Offense

	G	W-L	Pts.	Avg.
1. Central Okla.	29	19-10	2,933	101.1
2. Southern Ind.	29	25-4	2,761	95.2
3. Mont. St.-Billings	28	19-9	2,664	95.1
4. New York Tech	27	19-8	2,543	94.2
5. Neb.-Kearney	33	24-9	3,071	93.1
6. Alas. Anchorage	28	19-9	2,590	92.5
7. Fort Hays St.	34	34-0	3,130	92.1
8. St. Rose	32	28-4	2,929	91.5
9. Alabama A&M	31	28-3	2,809	90.6
10. Fort Lewis	26	8-18	2,337	89.9
11. Moorhead St.	27	19-8	2,424	89.8
12. Morningside	27	18-9	2,422	89.7
13. Oakland	29	21-8	2,575	88.8
14. South Dak. St.	29	24-5	2,569	88.6
15. Northern St.	29	23-6	2,560	88.3
16. St. Anselm	31	28-3	2,736	88.3
17. Edinboro	29	21-8	2,559	88.2
18. Quincy	27	17-10	2,374	87.9
19. Alas. Fairbanks	27	10-17	2,358	87.3
20. LeMoyne-Owen	27	14-13	2,342	86.7
21. Tex. A&M-Kingsville	29	23-6	2,515	86.7
22. Gardner-Webb	27	15-12	2,341	86.7
23. Miles	27	14-13	2,340	86.7
24. West Va. Tech	29	19-10	2,505	86.4
25. Eastern N.M.	27	17-10	2,330	86.3
26. Bentley	27	18-9	2,325	86.1
27. IU/PU-Indianapolis	29	22-7	2,494	86.0
28. Abilene Christian	27	13-14	2,318	85.9
29. Clark Atlanta	29	21-8	2,477	85.4
30. South Dak.	27	20-7	2,301	85.2

Scoring Defense

	G	W-L	Pts.	Avg.
1. Coker	26	16-10	1,592	61.2
2. UC Davis	30	24-6	1,861	62.0
3. Virginia Union	31	28-3	1,974	63.7
4. Seattle Pacific	29	23-6	1,861	64.2
5. Cal St. Dom. Hills	27	17-10	1,736	64.3
6. Pfeiffer	29	21-8	1,869	64.4
7. North Fla.	29	14-15	1,880	64.8
8. Cal St. Bakersfield	30	26-4	1,954	65.1
9. Phila. Textile	28	19-9	1,837	65.6
10. Pace	26	11-15	1,720	66.2
11. Presbyterian	30	19-11	1,988	66.3
12. Glenville St.	25	13-12	1,660	66.4
13. Francis Marion	27	8-19	1,798	66.6
14. St. Francis (Ill.)	29	19-10	1,940	66.9
15. Cal Poly Pomona	27	17-10	1,813	67.1
16. Franklin Pierce	29	23-6	1,956	67.4
17. Ala.-Huntsville	26	12-14	1,756	67.5
18. Regis (Colo.)	30	25-5	2,029	67.6
19. Fla. Southern	30	26-4	2,034	67.8
20. Armstrong Atlantic	26	12-14	1,764	67.8
21. UC Riverside	27	18-9	1,834	67.9
22. Queens (N.C.)	31	25-6	2,113	68.2
23. Bloomsburg	28	21-7	1,915	68.4
24. Le Moyne	30	24-6	2,055	68.5
25. Eckerd	27	17-10	1,850	68.5
26. Minn.-Duluth	25	15-10	1,714	68.6
27. Mississippi Col.	25	17-8	1,717	68.7
28. Michigan Tech	29	18-11	1,992	68.7
29. Norfolk St.	27	23-4	1,855	68.7
30. Florida Tech	26	12-14	1,798	69.2

Scoring Margin

	Off.	Def.	Mar.
1. Fort Hays St.	92.1	70.2	21.9
2. Southern Ind.	95.2	77.7	17.6
3. Virginia Union	80.8	63.7	17.1
4. Cal St. Bakersfield	80.5	65.1	15.3
5. Alabama A&M	90.6	76.2	14.4
6. St. Rose	91.5	77.2	14.3
7. St. Anselm	88.3	74.2	14.0
8. Oakland	88.8	75.2	13.6
9. Edinboro	88.2	74.8	13.5
10. Alas. Anchorage	92.5	79.6	12.9
11. Norfolk St.	81.3	68.7	12.6
12. South Dak.	85.2	72.6	12.6
13. South Dak. St.	88.6	76.3	12.3
14. Seattle Pacific	76.4	64.2	12.2
15. Calif. (Pa.)	83.2	71.1	12.1
16. Fairmont St.	84.8	72.9	11.9
17. New York Tech	94.2	82.5	11.7
18. Grand Canyon	85.0	73.8	11.2
19. Oakland City	84.5	73.5	11.0
20. Franklin Pierce	78.4	67.4	11.0
21. Indiana (Pa.)	83.0	72.2	10.7
22. Northern St.	88.3	77.7	10.6
23. UC Riverside	78.4	67.9	10.5
24. Eastern N.M.	86.3	76.1	10.2
25. UC Davis	72.0	62.0	10.0
26. Neb.-Kearney	93.1	83.2	9.9
27. IU/PU-Indianapolis	86.0	76.2	9.8
28. Northern Ky.	82.0	72.7	9.3
29. Fla. Southern	77.1	67.8	9.3
30. Bloomsburg	77.5	68.4	9.1

Won-Lost Percentage

	W-L	Pct.
1. Fort Hays St.	34-0	1.000
2. Alabama A&M	28-3	.903
2. St. Anselm	28-3	.903
2. Virginia Union	28-3	.903
5. St. Rose	28-4	.875
6. Cal St. Bakersfield	26-4	.867
6. Fla. Southern	26-4	.867
8. Southern Ind.	25-4	.862
9. Norfolk St.	23-4	.852
10. Regis (Colo.)	25-5	.833
11. South Dak. St.	24-5	.828
11. Fairmont St.	24-5	.828
13. Calif. (Pa.)	27-6	.818
14. Columbus St.	26-6	.813
15. Mo.-Rolla	25-6	.806
15. Queens (N.C.)	25-6	.806
17. UC Davis	24-6	.800
17. Le Moyne	24-6	.800
19. Franklin Pierce	23-6	.793
19. Seattle Pacific	23-6	.793
19. Tex. A&M-Kingsville	23-6	.793
19. Grand Canyon	23-6	.793
19. Northern St.	23-6	.793
24. Northern Ky.	25-7	.781
25. Indiana (Pa.)	24-7	.774
25. High Point	24-7	.774
27. Adelphi	23-7	.767
28. Denver	22-7	.759
28. IU/PU-Indianapolis	22-7	.759
30. North Ala.	24-8	.750
30. Bloomsburg	21-7	.750

Field-Goal Percentage

	FG	FGA	Pct.
1. Fort Hays St.	1,158	2,145	54.0
2. Southern Ind.	964	1,809	53.3
3. St. Rose	1,022	1,941	52.7
4. Calif. (Pa.)	960	1,843	52.1
5. South Dak. St.	947	1,829	51.8
6. Lynn	789	1,526	51.7
7. Edinboro	978	1,913	51.1
8. Queens (N.C.)	889	1,761	50.5
9. High Point	899	1,786	50.3
10. Oakland City	947	1,885	50.2
11. Northern St.	899	1,796	50.1
12. SIU-Edwardsville	718	1,435	50.0
13. Cal St. Bakersfield	847	1,693	50.0
14. Lewis	763	1,533	49.8
14. Johnson Smith	742	1,491	49.8
16. Presbyterian	741	1,489	49.8
17. Charleston (W.Va.)	748	1,507	49.6
18. Henderson St.	794	1,603	49.5
19. Oakland	891	1,802	49.4
20. Minn.-Duluth	699	1,418	49.3
21. IU/PU-Ft. Wayne	741	1,507	49.2
22. Indiana (Pa.)	919	1,873	49.1
23. UC Davis	770	1,574	48.9
24. Northern Ky.	914	1,869	48.9
25. Wis.-Parkside	651	1,332	48.9
26. Cameron	773	1,582	48.9
27. Denver	828	1,696	48.8
28. St. Michael's	830	1,702	48.8
29. New Hamp. Col.	817	1,676	48.7
30. Georgia Col.	850	1,745	48.7
31. Southwest St.	752	1,546	48.6

Field-Goal Percentage Defense

	FG	FGA	Pct.
1. Virginia Union	718	1,944	36.9
2. Seattle Pacific	656	1,672	39.2
3. St. Rose	894	2,252	39.7
4. UC Davis	640	1,603	39.9
5. Franklin Pierce	692	1,718	40.3
6. Cal St. Dom. Hills	616	1,529	40.3
7. Fla. Southern	703	1,743	40.3
8. Calif. (Pa.)	864	2,142	40.3
9. Bloomsburg	704	1,740	40.5
10. Millersville	684	1,683	40.6
11. Grand Canyon	736	1,810	40.7
12. Salem-Teikyo	766	1,882	40.7
13. Alabama A&M	849	2,083	40.8
14. Pace	594	1,453	40.9
15. Norfolk St.	657	1,606	40.9
16. UC Riverside	667	1,617	41.2
17. Eckerd	638	1,542	41.4
18. Delta St.	756	1,827	41.4
19. Presbyterian	696	1,681	41.4
20. West Liberty St.	705	1,699	41.5
21. Armstrong Atlantic	607	1,462	41.5
22. Cal Poly Pomona	628	1,510	41.6
23. Southern Conn. St.	686	1,649	41.6
24. Clark Atlanta	813	1,953	41.6
25. Glenville St.	566	1,357	41.7
26. Cal St. Bakersfield	708	1,694	41.8
27. Coker	546	1,306	41.8
28. Regis (Colo.)	685	1,638	41.8
29. Fort Hays St.	879	2,096	41.9
30. Stonehill	688	1,636	42.1

Three-Point Field Goals Made Per Game

	G	3FG	Avg.
1. Mont. St.-Billings	28	304	10.9
2. Oakland	29	299	10.3
3. Western St.	31	318	10.3
4. Lake Superior St.	28	279	10.0
5. Bellarmine	27	266	9.9
6. Eastern N.M.	27	259	9.6
7. Alas. Anchorage	28	268	9.6
8. West Va. Tech	29	277	9.6
9. Bentley	27	257	9.5
10. Wayne St. (Mich.)	27	256	9.5
11. Southwest St.	27	255	9.4
12. Alderson-Broaddus	28	259	9.3
13. St. Anselm	31	284	9.2
14. Cal St. San B'dino	27	246	9.1
15. North Dak. St.	29	264	9.1
16. Hillsdale	26	229	8.8
17. Southern Colo.	28	246	8.8
18. St. Andrews	27	237	8.8
19. Central Okla.	29	252	8.7
20. Fort Hays St.	34	293	8.6
21. Merrimack	28	241	8.6
22. Adelphi	30	256	8.5
23. Abilene Christian	27	228	8.4
24. Northern Mich.	28	236	8.4
25. Oakland City	31	260	8.4
26. Tex. A&M-Commerce	28	233	8.3
27. New Hamp. Col.	29	240	8.3

STATISTICAL LEADERS

	G	3FG	Avg.
28. Neb.-Kearney	33	273	8.3
29. St. Augustine's	26	215	8.3
30. Keene St.	24	198	8.3

	G	FG	FGA	Pct.
28. Pittsburg St.	28	160	410	39.0
29. Henderson St.	27	174	446	39.0
30. North Dak.	27	167	429	38.9

	FT	FTA	Pct.
29. Minn.-Duluth	337	466	72.3
30. Clarion	410	567	72.3

Three-Point Field-Goal Percentage

(Min. 3.0 3FG Per Game)

	G	FG	FGA	Pct.
1. Oakland City	31	260	537	48.4
2. Indianapolis	29	193	424	45.5
3. Southern Ind.	29	175	406	43.1
4. Northern Ky.	32	250	582	43.0
5. St. Rose	32	181	422	42.9
6. New Hamp. Col.	29	240	564	42.6
7. Fort Hays St.	34	293	693	42.3
8. IU/PU-Ft. Wayne	27	197	468	42.1
9. Northern Mich.	28	236	563	41.9
10. St. Anselm	31	284	687	41.3
11. Western St.	31	318	778	40.9
12. South Dak. St.	29	148	363	40.8
13. Colorado Mines	28	185	457	40.5
14. Neb.-Kearney	33	273	679	40.2
15. Bentley	27	257	640	40.2
16. Seattle Pacific	29	220	548	40.1
17. St. Augustine's	26	215	536	40.1
18. Franklin Pierce	29	171	429	39.9
19. Southern Colo.	28	246	619	39.7
20. Oakland	29	299	753	39.7
21. Millersville	27	207	522	39.7
22. West Liberty St.	27	190	480	39.6
23. Queens (N.Y.)	26	188	475	39.6
24. Michigan Tech	29	228	578	39.4
25. North Dak. St.	29	264	671	39.3
26. LeMoyne-Owen	27	193	491	39.3
27. West Fla.	30	183	468	39.1

Free-Throw Percentage

	FT	FTA	Pct.
1. South Dak.	501	648	77.3
2. Lewis	487	630	77.3
3. Indianapolis	480	621	77.3
4. Moorhead St.	565	739	76.5
5. Oakland	494	649	76.1
6. Dowling	527	694	75.9
7. Northern St.	572	754	75.9
8. Western St.	545	725	75.2
9. Denver	571	760	75.1
10. Neb.-Kearney	594	793	74.9
11. Mont. St.-Billings	572	766	74.7
12. Northern Mich.	373	501	74.5
13. IU/PU-Indianapolis	600	808	74.3
14. Mars Hill	640	862	74.2
15. Quinnipiac	468	632	74.1
16. North Dak. St.	440	599	73.5
17. West Chester	427	582	73.4
18. Mansfield	415	566	73.3
19. Catawba	412	562	73.3
20. Abilene Christian	492	672	73.2
21. Seattle Pacific	407	556	73.2
22. Merrimack	458	626	73.2
23. Michigan Tech	477	652	73.2
24. Lake Superior St.	482	659	73.1
25. Lock Haven	431	590	73.1
26. UC Riverside	398	547	72.8
27. Western N.M.	307	422	72.7
28. Wis.-Parkside	377	520	72.5

Rebound Margin

	Off.	Def.	Mar.
1. Virginia Union	48.0	36.1	11.9
2. Alabama A&M	50.7	39.2	11.5
3. Fort Hays St.	40.6	31.6	9.0
4. Fairmont St.	43.4	34.6	8.9
5. Lynn	38.8	30.1	8.7
6. Cal St. Dom. Hills	42.3	33.7	8.7
7. Cal St. Bakersfield	39.5	31.0	8.5
8. Calif. (Pa.)	41.1	32.8	8.2
9. West Ga.	42.4	34.7	7.7
10. Lake Superior St.	41.4	33.8	7.5
11. St. Rose	43.5	36.1	7.4
12. Tarleton St.	39.7	33.1	6.6
13. Southern Ind.	39.3	32.9	6.4
14. Presbyterian	37.0	30.6	6.4
15. Grand Canyon	41.9	35.6	6.3
16. Seattle Pacific	37.9	31.7	6.2
17. Northern St.	39.7	33.7	6.0
18. Kennesaw St.	39.1	33.1	6.0
19. Oakland	39.8	33.9	5.9
20. LIU-C. W. Post	40.4	34.9	5.6
21. Bloomsburg	42.9	37.4	5.5
22. LIU-Southampton	48.3	42.8	5.5
23. Southwest Baptist	38.3	32.8	5.5
24. Wingate	38.9	33.7	5.2
25. Delta St.	42.1	36.9	5.2
26. Lewis	34.5	29.3	5.2
27. Franklin Pierce	40.1	35.0	5.1
28. Stonehill	41.7	36.7	5.0
29. Millersville	40.8	35.9	4.9
30. Moorhead St.	40.8	35.9	4.9

1996 Division III Individual Leaders

Scoring

	Cl.	G	TFG	3FG	FT	Pts.	Avg.
1. Ed Brands, Grinnell	Sr	24	260	158	136	814	33.9
2. Rick Hughes, Thomas More	Sr	25	253	8	146	660	26.4
3. Alex Butler, Rhode Island Col.	Jr	27	243	65	126	677	25.1
4. David Stephens, Colby	Sr	27	217	38	197	669	24.8
5. Jon D'orlando, Endicott	So	22	196	47	103	542	24.6
6. Craig Jones, Rochester Inst.	Jr	26	243	0	154	640	24.6
7. Antoine Harden, Eastern	Sr	25	250	16	99	615	24.6
8. Ben Virges, Rust	Sr	24	204	0	168	576	24.0
9. J. R. Shumate, Ohio Wesleyan	Sr	25	204	95	96	599	24.0
10. John Wassenbergh, St. Joseph's (Me.)	Sr	28	246	6	167	665	23.8
11. Jim McGilvery, Colby-Sawyer	Sr	25	211	48	119	589	23.6
12. Kevin Kozup, Bethany (W.Va.)	Jr	25	183	90	111	567	22.7
13. Phil Dixon, Shenandoah	Sr	27	214	57	108	611	22.6
14. Keith Wolff, Trinity (Conn.)	Sr	22	169	54	105	497	22.6
15. James Gomes, Mass-Boston	Sr	24	189	22	142	542	22.6
16. David Benter, Hanover	Sr	27	246	34	82	608	22.5
17. Bryant Butler, Plattsburgh St.	So	24	198	59	84	539	22.5
18. Purvis Presha, Stillman	Sr	25	200	50	111	561	22.4
19. Carl Cochran, Richard Stockton	Jr	30	212	100	147	671	22.4
20. Mike Raimon, Fitchburg St.	Sr	25	193	79	93	558	22.3
21. Daimen Hunter, Alvernia	So	25	203	48	103	557	22.3
22. Ron Sanchez, Oneonta St.	Sr	28	242	16	121	621	22.2
23. Cam Dyer, Wash. & Lee	Sr	24	198	0	136	532	22.2
24. Clarence Pierce, N.J. Inst. of Tech.	Sr	27	191	59	157	598	22.1
25. Craig Brunnemer, Anderson	Sr	25	208	28	108	552	22.1
26. John Patraitis, Anna Maria	So	30	273	0	115	661	22.0
27. Greg Crider, Eureka	Sr	24	175	45	130	525	21.9
28. Matt George, Colby-Sawyer	So	26	180	75	133	568	21.8
29. Karnell James, St. Thomas (Minn.)	Jr	23	182	42	96	502	21.8
30. Ivo Moyano, Polytechnic (N.Y.)	Jr	22	170	43	97	480	21.8
31. Scott Clarke, Utica	Sr	26	193	69	110	565	21.7
32. Peter Lark, Concordia (Ill.)	So	25	198	0	145	541	21.6
32. Henry Shannon, Maryville (Mo.)	Fr	25	204	34	99	541	21.6
34. Jason Cook, Carroll (Wis.)	Sr	23	191	27	88	497	21.6
35. Jay Longino, Colorado Col.	Sr	25	184	67	105	540	21.6
36. Jason Evers, Buena Vista	Sr	25	195	10	139	539	21.6
37. Mark Specht, Neb. Wesleyan	Sr	25	175	49	139	538	21.5
38. Mike Hunter, Ferrum	Fr	24	183	70	80	516	21.5
38. Jamar Milsap, Rochester	Jr	24	197	1	121	516	21.5
40. Burt Paddock, Manchester	Jr	27	184	95	117	580	21.5
41. Caleb Wilkinson, Vassar	Jr	24	185	54	91	515	21.5
41. Jim Naughton, Worcester Tech	Sr	24	167	22	159	515	21.5
43. Kelly Matthews, Villa Julie	So	22	160	17	134	471	21.4
44. Nick Bertke, Ohio Northern	Sr	27	229	2	118	578	21.4
45. Michael Kingsley, Babson	Jr	28	198	74	128	598	21.4
46. Jason Light, Emory & Henry	So	25	207	0	116	530	21.2
47. Eric Burdette, Wis.-Whitewater	Sr	28	184	130	93	591	21.1
48. Jason White, Westminster (Mo.)	Sr	26	196	31	125	548	21.1
49. Al White, Shenandoah	Sr	27	219	7	122	567	21.0
49. Scott Macdonald, Menlo	Sr	25	223	2	77	525	21.0
51. Akil Screen, Skidmore	Sr	25	201	0	122	524	21.0
52. Mike Nogelo, Williams	So	27	196	77	95	564	20.9
53. Keith Born, North Park	Sr	24	160	54	123	497	20.7
54. Jason Rhodes, Hendrix	Sr	27	202	20	134	558	20.7
55. Morgan Bell, Occidental	Fr	25	198	2	118	516	20.6
56. Marcus Toney, Ferrum	So	23	145	76	108	474	20.6
57. Jay Adams, Brockport St.	Jr	27	174	75	133	556	20.6
58. Eric Smith, Millikin	Jr	23	191	0	91	473	20.6
59. Luke Schmidt, Carleton	Fr	23	182	1	107	471	20.5
60. Shuron Woodyard, Villa Julie	Jr	25	211	22	67	511	20.4
61. Darnell Hickman, Utica/Rome	Sr	24	165	9	151	490	20.4
62. Tommy Doyle, Salem St.	Sr	28	167	124	112	570	20.4
63. Irie Humphrey, CCNY	So	25	191	3	123	508	20.3
63. Chad Onofrio, Tufts	Jr	25	181	52	94	508	20.3
65. Artie Challenor, York (N.Y.)	Sr	25	175	58	98	506	20.2
66. Matt Garvey, Bates	Jr	24	146	91	102	485	20.2
67. Mike Bockenstedt, Luther	Sr	25	210	0	83	503	20.1
68. Casey Musick, Salisbury St.	Sr	28	208	53	93	560	20.1
69. Chris Weih, Coe	Jr	22	150	17	123	440	20.0
70. David Masciola, Allegheny	Sr	27	182	75	99	538	19.9

Field-Goal Percentage

(Min. 5 FG Made Per Game)

	Cl.	G	FG	FGA	Pct.
1. Jason Light, Emory & Henry	So	25	207	294	70.4
2. John Patraitis, Anna Maria	So	30	273	393	69.5
3. James Christopher, Webster	Sr	25	131	192	68.2

(Min. 5 FG Made Per Game)	Cl.	G	FG	FGA	Pct.
4. Kipp Christianson, St. John's (Minn.)	Jr	23	179	268	66.8
5. Nate Thomas, Neb. Wesleyan	So	24	122	185	65.9
6. Jason Hayes, Marietta	Jr	28	187	285	65.6
7. Adam Doll, Simpson	Fr	26	136	208	65.4
8. Frank Hodge, Cortland St.	Jr	22	115	176	65.3
9. Jim South, Augsburg	Sr	24	177	272	65.1
10. Scott Macdonald, Menlo	Sr	25	223	346	64.5
11. Matt Chitwood, Wis.-River Falls	So	24	155	241	64.3
12. Rick Hughes, Thomas More	Sr	25	253	394	64.2
13. Jason Jahnel, Potsdam St.	Sr	24	121	190	63.7
14. Derek Archer, Monmouth (Ill.)	Jr	21	111	176	63.1
15. Tim Schilling, St. Olaf	Jr	24	177	281	63.0
16. John Wassenbergh, St. Joseph's (Me.)	Sr	28	246	398	61.8
17. Ryan Harrigan, Sewanee	So	25	173	281	61.6
18. Scott Lauinger, Gust. Adolphus	Sr	29	218	355	61.4
19. Andy Rutherford, Lycoming	So	27	204	333	61.3
20. Kevin Folkl, Washington (Mo.)	Sr	27	170	280	60.7
20. Ed Kearney, Allentown	Sr	26	136	224	60.7
20. Greg Liebrecht, Bluffton	Sr	26	153	252	60.7
23. Cory Kulig, Wis.-Eau Claire	Jr	24	145	239	60.7
24. Jay Taylor, East. Mennonite	Jr	25	147	244	60.2
25. Mike Mehaffey, Frank. & Marsh.	Sr	29	156	261	59.8
26. Woody Anderson, Gordon	Sr	24	171	289	59.2
27. Akida Ellerbee, N.J. Inst. of Tech.	Jr	27	220	372	59.1
28. Imants Katlaps, Lakeland	Sr	26	161	273	59.0
29. Jason Rhodes, Hendrix	Sr	27	202	343	58.9
30. Mike Paynter, Wis.-Stevens Point	Jr	25	148	252	58.7

Three-Point Field Goals Made Per Game

	Cl.	G	3FG	Avg.
1. Ed Brands, Grinnell	Sr	24	158	6.6
2. Eric Burdette, Wis.-Whitewater	Jr	28	130	4.6
3. Luke Madsen, Wis.-River Falls	Sr	22	98	4.5
4. Tommy Doyle, Salem St.	Sr	28	124	4.4
5. Chris Payne, Elmhurst	Sr	25	105	4.2
6. Greg Bonczkowski, Hartwick	Sr	26	103	4.0
7. John Hebert, Colby	Jr	27	106	3.9
8. J. R. Shumate, Ohio Wesleyan	Sr	25	95	3.8
8. Jamie Haver, Union (N.Y.)	Jr	25	95	3.8
10. Matt Garvey, Bates	Jr	24	91	3.8
11. Marty Keithline, King's (Pa.)	Sr	24	90	3.8
12. Kevin Kozup, Bethany (W.Va.)	Jr	25	90	3.6
13. Brian Zimliki, Stevens Tech	Fr	25	89	3.6
14. Mike Van Helvoirt, Carroll (Wis.)	So	21	74	3.5
15. Burt Paddock, Manchester	Jr	27	95	3.5
16. Gene Nolan, Washington (Mo.)	Sr	29	102	3.5
17. Jason Sorenson, Concordia-M'head	Sr	27	94	3.5
18. Mark Heerema, Cal Lutheran	Sr	25	84	3.4
19. Carl Cochran, Richard Stockton	Jr	30	100	3.3
20. Kevin Richardson, Hardin-Simmons	Sr	25	83	3.3
20. Turner Emery, Sewanee	So	25	83	3.3
22. Marcus Toney, Ferrum	So	23	76	3.3
23. Erik Quamme, Beloit	Sr	22	72	3.3
24. Dan Pierce, Drew	Sr	27	88	3.3
25. Kipp Kissinger, Neb. Wesleyan	So	25	81	3.2
26. Dontay Hardneh, Kenyon	So	25	80	3.2
27. Jason Malott, Fontbonne	Jr	27	86	3.2
28. Matt Labuda, Wilkes	Sr	30	95	3.2
29. Mike Raimon, Fitchburg St.	Sr	25	79	3.2
30. Ryan Odom, Hampden-Sydney	Sr	22	69	3.1

Three-Point Field-Goal Percentage

(Min. 1.5 3FG Made Per Game)	Cl.	G	FG	FGA	Pct.
1. Joey Bigler, John Carroll	Jr	27	54	111	48.6
2. John Hebert, Colby	Jr	27	106	219	48.4
3. Carl Cochran, Richard Stockton	Jr	30	100	208	48.1
4. Kris Schantz, Maritime (N.Y.)	So	24	36	75	48.0
5. Kenny Stockhaus, Nichols	Jr	24	44	92	47.8
6. Scott Ruthsatz, Heidelberg	Jr	24	43	90	47.8
7. Ryan Vickers, Oglethorpe	Sr	24	47	99	47.5
8. Brian Fleming, Roger Williams	Jr	25	70	148	47.3
9. Paul Howard, Gettysburg	Jr	27	64	136	47.1
9. Andy Bardeschewski, St. Lawrence	So	27	64	136	47.1
11. Kevin Richardson, Hardin-Simmons	Sr	25	83	178	46.6
12. Mark Heerema, Cal Lutheran	Sr	25	84	181	46.4
13. Jerry Ambooken, Allegheny	So	27	70	151	46.4
14. Brad Brown, Augsburg	Jr	24	38	82	46.3
15. Mark Giovino, Babson	So	28	48	104	46.2
16. Chuck Guest, Rensselaer	Sr	28	64	139	46.0
17. David Powell, Chris. Newport	So	30	46	100	46.0

	Cl.	G	FG	FGA	Pct.
18. Nick Elisano, Trenton St.	Sr	22	53	116	45.7
19. Gerard Wilson, Wm. Paterson	Jr	24	46	101	45.5
20. Martins Bondars, Lakeland	Jr	26	61	134	45.5
21. Steve Reed, Redlands	Jr	25	75	165	45.5
22. Eric Shaner, St. John Fisher	Jr	26	39	86	45.3
23. Jon Miller, Hanover	Jr	27	53	117	45.3
24. J. J. Richardson, John Carroll	Jr	27	77	170	45.3
25. Jason Quam, Gust. Adolphus	Jr	29	74	164	45.1
26. David Parker, Rhodes	Sr	25	64	142	45.1
27. Paul Morrissey, Cortland St.	Sr	28	52	116	44.8
28. Mike Dillion, Mt. St. Mary's (N.Y.)	Sr	24	43	96	44.8
29. Hans Koppenhoefer, Buffalo St.	Sr	30	64	143	44.8
30. Sebastian Payton, Gordon	Sr	23	42	94	44.7

Free-Throw Percentage

(Min. 2.5 FT Made Per Game)	Cl.	G	FT	FTA	Pct.
1. Charlie Nanick, Scranton	Jr	25	96	103	93.2
2. Dan Trippler, Wis.-Superior	Jr	25	63	68	92.6
3. Matt Labuda, Wilkes	Sr	30	90	98	91.8
4. Keith Wolff, Trinity (Conn.)	Sr	22	105	117	89.7
5. Josh Murphy, Heidelberg	Jr	25	87	97	89.7
6. Chad Onofrio, Tufts	Sr	25	94	105	89.5
7. Marcus Buckley, Wis.-Eau Claire	Sr	19	56	63	88.9
8. Eric Burdette, Wis.-Whitewater	Jr	28	93	105	88.6
9. Matt Grieser, Anderson	Sr	25	69	78	88.5
10. Ryan Odom, Hampden-Sydney	Sr	22	60	68	88.2
11. Gerald Ross, Susquehanna	Jr	20	59	67	88.1
12. Donnie Gohmann, Franklin	Jr	24	71	81	87.7
13. J. J. Richardson, John Carroll	Jr	27	106	121	87.6
14. Jon D'orlando, Endicott	So	22	103	118	87.3
15. Kent Seemann, Defiance	Sr	24	77	89	86.5
16. Matt Garvey, Bates	Jr	24	102	118	86.4
17. Kevin Spainhour, Guilford	Jr	24	63	73	86.3
18. Steve Reed, Redlands	Jr	25	87	101	86.1
19. Rich Kuc, Utica	Jr	25	78	91	85.7
20. Bernie Rogers, Ursinus	Sr	24	101	118	85.6
21. Mike Nogelo, Williams	So	27	95	111	85.6
22. Adam Dechristopher, Plymouth St.	Fr	28	124	145	85.5
23. Burt Paddock, Manchester	Jr	27	117	137	85.4
24. Ray Cullinan, Potsdam St.	Sr	22	76	89	85.4
25. Kyle Werve, Aurora	So	25	110	129	85.3
26. Kurt Axe, Randolph-Macon	Sr	27	102	120	85.0
27. Jonathon Denney, Webster	Jr	24	106	125	84.8
28. Mark Specht, Neb. Wesleyan	Sr	25	139	164	84.8
29. Phil Yontz, Wooster	Fr	26	72	85	84.7
30. Dennis Ruedinger, Wis.-Oshkosh	Jr	27	110	130	84.6
30. Jay Roberts, Illinois Col.	Sr	20	55	65	84.6

Rebounding

	Cl.	G	Reb.	Avg.
1. Craig Jones, Rochester Inst.	Jr	26	363	14.0
2. Kevin Braaten, Baldwin-Wallace	Sr	28	372	13.3
3. Mark Harris, Coast Guard	Sr	25	317	12.7
4. Greg Belinfanti, New York U.	Sr	27	334	12.4
5. Antoine Harden, Eastern	Sr	25	308	12.3
6. Ira Nicholson, Mt. St. Vincent	Jr	27	331	12.3
7. Chris Kelly, Staten Island	Jr	28	329	11.8
7. Mike Nukk, Maritime (N.Y.)	Fr	24	282	11.8
9. Justin Hackley, Salve Regina	Sr	23	270	11.7
10. David Stephens, Colby	Sr	27	312	11.6
11. Jason Turner, Wilkes	Sr	30	337	11.2
12. Joe Mrozienski, Hamilton	Sr	25	278	11.1
13. Chris Beeler, Maine Maritime	So	18	200	11.1
14. Akil Screen, Skidmore	Sr	25	277	11.1
15. Jason Hayes, Marietta	Jr	28	309	11.0
16. Mike Bockenstedt, Luther	Sr	25	274	11.0
17. Jim Naughton, Worcester Tech	Sr	24	263	11.0
18. Jim White, Westminster (Mo.)	Sr	26	282	10.8
19. Sean McGee, Baruch	Sr	26	281	10.8
20. Ari Kriegsman, Middlebury	Sr	23	247	10.7
21. Lenny Smith, Elmira	Jr	26	279	10.7
22. Andris Upitis, Grinnell	Sr	24	252	10.5
23. Clarence Pierce, N.J. Inst. of Tech.	Sr	27	283	10.5
24. James Wilson, Utica/Rome	Sr	24	250	10.4
25. Antoine Hyman, Keuka	Jr	25	259	10.4
26. Bill Jones, Martime (N.Y.)	Sr	24	247	10.3
27. Terry Thomas, Chris. Newport	Sr	30	307	10.2
28. Chris Jones, Parks	Jr	23	235	10.2
29. Ben Virges, Rust	Sr	24	245	10.2
30. Eric Smith, Millikin	Jr	23	233	10.1

STATISTICAL LEADERS

Assists

	Cl.	G	Ast.	Avg.
1. Andre Bolton, Chris. Newport	Sr	30	289	9.6
2. Phil Dixon, Shenandoah	Sr	27	258	9.6
3. Dax Kajiwara, Vassar	Sr	24	213	8.9
4. Chris Perrin, Simpson	Jr	26	223	8.6
5. Adam Piandes, Bates	Sr	24	200	8.3
6. Zach Goring, St. Olaf	Fr	24	197	8.2
7. Matt Nadelhoffer, Wheaton (Ill.)	Jr	27	221	8.2
8. J. J. Siepierski, Washington (Mo.)	Jr	29	236	8.1
9. Matt Grieser, Anderson	Sr	25	193	7.7
10. Jamal Elliott, Haverford	Sr	23	168	7.3
11. Jeff Boyle, Grinnell	Sr	24	173	7.2
12. Kevin Clipperton, Upper Iowa	Jr	25	176	7.0
13. Joel Heckendorf, Martin Luther	Jr	17	118	6.9
14. Greg Dean, Concordia-M'head	Jr	27	185	6.9
15. Kevin Alexander, Emory & Henry	Sr	24	162	6.8
16. Stefan Bergan, Gallaudet	So	25	166	6.6
17. Jason Malott, Fontbonne	Jr	27	176	6.5
18. Nathan Reeves, York (N.Y.)	Jr	28	180	6.4
19. Sammy Briggs, Catholic	Sr	27	166	6.1
20. Mike Smith, Knox	Sr	23	140	6.1
21. Nathan Hungate, Roanoke	So	25	152	6.1
22. Danny Mannix, Mt. St. Vincent	Sr	27	163	6.0
23. Jeff Scott, Salem St.	Sr	28	168	6.0
23. Deron Black, Allegheny	Sr	27	162	6.0
25. Marvin Patterson, Hunter	Sr	22	131	6.0
25. Joe Harvey, Misericordia	Jr	22	131	6.0
27. Gary Pymm, Keuka	Jr	25	148	5.9
28. Clarence Pierce, N.J. Inst. of Tech.	Sr	27	159	5.9
29. Eric Prenderville, Salisbury St.	Fr	26	151	5.8
30. Michael Kingsley, Babson	Jr	28	162	5.8

Blocked Shots

	Cl.	G	Blk.	Avg.
1. Ira Nicholson, Mt. St. Vincent	Jr	27	163	6.0
2. Antoine Hyman, Keuka	Jr	25	131	5.2
3. Damon Avinger, CCNY	Sr	25	106	4.2
4. Mike Mientus, Allentown	Jr	24	86	3.6

Photo from Keuka sports information

Antoine Hyman of Keuka had few peers when it came to blocking shots in 1996. Hyman registered 11 or more blocks in a game on three occasions, including a Division III record-tying 15 against Hobart on February 21, 1996.

	Cl.	G	Blk.	Avg.
5. Jason White, Westminster (Mo.)	Sr	26	92	3.5
6. Mark Awantang, Washington (Md.)	Jr	23	77	3.3
7. Terry Thomas, Chris. Newport	Sr	30	90	3.0
7. Aljumar Earl, Montclair St.	Jr	19	57	3.0
9. John Garber, Millsaps	Jr	27	80	3.0
10. Ken Laflamme, Emerson-MCA	Jr	27	79	2.9
11. Jeremy Putman, Dubuque	Sr	25	71	2.8
12. Joe Slotnick, Vassar	Fr	23	64	2.8
13. Rich Berry, Stevens Tech	Fr	26	72	2.8
14. David Kline, Widener	Jr	23	60	2.6
15. Joel Dorsett, Albertus Magnus	Jr	24	62	2.6
16. Chris Vreeland, Delaware Valley	Fr	23	59	2.6
17. Mike Paynter, Wis.-Stevens Point	Jr	25	64	2.6
18. Mike Nukk, Maritime (N.Y.)	Fr	24	60	2.5
19. Jason Alexander, Catholic	So	27	67	2.5
20. Brett Durham, Rensselaer	Jr	28	69	2.5
21. Tyronne Bennett, Methodist	Jr	25	60	2.4
22. Tory Black, N.J. Inst. of Tech.	Fr	27	63	2.3
22. Khris Silveria, Salem St.	So	27	63	2.3
22. Cory Kulig, Wis.-Eau Claire	Jr	24	56	2.3
25. Keith Silzer, Elmhurst	Sr	25	58	2.3
26. James Wilson, Utica/Rome	Sr	24	54	2.3
27. Ryan Stumpf, Capital	Sr	26	55	2.1
28. Kenny Nelson, Concordia-M'head	Sr	27	57	2.1
29. Orick Smith, Beaver	Jr	25	51	2.0
30. Kenneth Newton, York (N.Y.)	So	28	56	2.0

Steals

	Cl.	G	Stl.	Avg.
1. Purvis Presha, Stillman	Sr	25	144	5.8
2. Joel Heckendorf, Martin Luther	Jr	17	84	4.9
3. Deron Black, Allegheny	Sr	27	123	4.6
4. Scott Clarke, Utica	Sr	26	118	4.5
5. Ivo Moyano, Polytechnic (N.Y.)	Jr	22	93	4.2
6. Chris Heller, Bethany (W.Va.)	So	25	102	4.1
7. Greg Dean, Concordia-M'head	Jr	27	108	4.0
8. Keith Poopor, Amherst	Sr	27	103	3.8
9. John Gallogly, Salve Regina	So	23	86	3.7
10. Duke McCabe, Maritime (N.Y.)	Fr	24	89	3.7
11. Clarence Pierce, N.J. Inst. of Tech.	Sr	27	94	3.5
12. Joel Depagter, Lawrence	So	22	75	3.4
13. Jamal Elliott, Haverford	Sr	23	78	3.4
14. Nathan Reeves, York (N.Y.)	Jr	28	91	3.3
15. Kelly Matthews, Villa Julie	So	22	69	3.1
16. Ben Arcuri, Ramapo	Jr	24	75	3.1
17. Shuron Woodyard, Villa Julie	Jr	25	78	3.1
18. Richie Cole, Mt. St. Vincent	Sr	27	84	3.1
19. Donta Johnson, Springfield	So	28	87	3.1
20. Michael Kingsley, Babson	Jr	28	86	3.1
21. Darnell Hickman, Utica/Rome	Sr	24	73	3.0
22. Marvin Patterson, Hunter	Sr	22	66	3.0
23. Mike Raimon, Fitchburg St.	Sr	25	74	3.0
24. Chad Rowley, Bowdoin	Jr	25	73	2.9
25. Jeff Boyle, Grinnell	Sr	24	70	2.9
26. Mike Gruetzmacher, St. Norbert	Sr	22	64	2.9
27. Nigel Hucey, Oneonta St.	So	27	78	2.9
28. John Botti, Williams	Sr	25	71	2.8
29. Andre Bolton, Chris. Newport	Sr	30	84	2.8
29. Damon Stevenson, Frostburg St.	Sr	25	70	2.8
29. Antoine Harden, Eastern	Sr	25	70	2.8

1996 Division III Game Highs

Individual Highs

SCORING

Pts.	Player, Team vs. Opponent	Date
60	Ed Brands, Grinnell vs.Ripon	Feb. 24
59	Ed Brands, Grinnell vs.Chicago	Nov. 18
52	Jason Cook, Carroll (Wis.) vs. Grinnell	Feb. 23
51	Burt Paddock, Manchester vs. Rose-Hulman	Jan. 20

Pts.	Player, Team vs. Opponent	Date
47	Kurt Axe, Randolph-Macon vs. Emory & Henry	Feb. 11
47	Jeff Branson, Fontbonne vs. Harris-Stowe	Dec. 4
46	Ed Brands, Grinnell vs. Carroll (Wis.)	Feb. 23
46	Morgan Bell, Occidental vs. Whittier	Feb. 23
46	Dave Stephens, Colby vs. Trinity (Conn.)	Feb. 4
46	Shane Buck, Hardin-Simmons vs. Austin	Feb. 3
46	Greg Crider, Eureka vs. Clarke	Nov. 28

THREE-POINT FIELD GOALS

3FG	Player, Team vs. Opponent	Date
#14	Ed Brands, Grinnell vs. Ripon	Feb. 24
12	Eric Burdette, Wis.-Whitewater vs. Wis.-Eau Claire	Feb. 24
11	Ed Brands, Grinnell vs. Carroll (Wis.)	Feb. 23
11	Dan Pierce, Drew vs. Delaware Valley	Feb. 17
11	Ed Brands, Grinnell vs. Ripon	Jan. 21
10	Casey Craig, Juniata vs. Misericordia	Feb. 7
10	Ed Brands, Grinnell vs. Iowa Wesleyan	Jan. 8
10	Matt Garvey, Bates vs. Colby-Sawyer	Jan. 7
10	Jamie Harer, Union (N.Y.) vs. Skidmore	Dec. 9
10	Chris Planer, Bard vs. Mt. St. Vincent	Dec. 7
10	Ed Brands, Grinnell vs. Chicago	Nov. 18

#Tied Division III record.

FIELD-GOAL PERCENTAGE
(Min. 10 FG Made)

Pct.	Player, Team vs. Opponent	Date
*100.0 (18-18)	Jason Light, Emory & Henry vs. King (Tenn.)	Dec. 2
100.0 (11-11)	Brad Shanfelt, Randolph-Macon vs. St. Mary's (Md.)	Dec. 29
100.0 (11-11)	Rohan Sutherland, Montclair St. vs. Jersey City St.	Dec. 6
100.0 (10-10)	Ed Kearney, Allentown vs. Cabrini	Feb. 14
92.9 (13-14)	Pete Craig, Frostburg St. vs. Western Md.	Jan. 31
92.3 (12-13)	Imants Katlaps, Lakeland vs. Edgewood	Feb. 25
92.3 (12-13)	Jason Hayes, Marietta vs. Ohio Northern	Feb. 23
92.3 (12-13)	Levar Barrino, New England Col. vs. Nichols	Feb. 7
92.3 (12-13)	Jason Hayes, Marietta vs. Baldwin-Wallace	Dec. 16

*Division III record.

FREE-THROW PERCENTAGE
(Min. 10 FT Made)

Pct.	Player, Team vs. Opponent	Date
100.0 (18-18)	Donnie Gohmann, Franklin vs. Manchester	Feb. 7
100.0 (16-16)	Burt Paddock, Manchester vs. Rose-Hulman	Jan. 20
100.0 (16-16)	Kelly Matthews, Villa Julie vs. Phila. Pharmacy	Jan. 15
100.0 (15-15)	Matt George, Colby-Sawyer vs. Norwich	Nov. 18
100.0 (14-14)	Jeff Scott, Salem St. vs. Westfield St.	Feb. 8
100.0 (14-14)	Sean Covington, Trenton St. vs. Kean	Feb. 7
100.0 (14-14)	Ludger Bain, Wentworth Inst. vs. Eastern Nazarene	Jan. 24
100.0 (14-14)	Christian Toombs, Muskingum vs. Heidelberg	Jan. 20
100.0 (14-14)	Casey Craig, Juniata vs. Widener	Dec. 2
100.0 (14-14)	Chad Comerford, Franklin vs. North Central	Nov. 18
100.0 (14-14)	T. J. McNulty, Scranton vs. Marywood	Nov. 17

REBOUNDS

Reb.	Player, Team vs. Opponent	Date
26	Ryan Zolner, FDU-Madison vs. Delaware Valley	Feb. 7
26	Ari Kriegsman, Middlebury vs. Western Md.	Jan. 7
25	Mike Bockenstedt, Luther vs. Grinnell	Nov. 28
25	Gilberto Parker, Medgar Evers vs. Purchase St.	Dec. 2
22	Craig Jones, Rochester Inst. vs. Geneseo St.	Feb. 29
22	Jason White, Westminster (Mo.) vs. Fontbonne	Feb. 23
22	Eric Smith, Millikin vs. Augustana (Ill.)	Jan. 17
22	Mark Harris, Coast Guard vs. Norwich	Jan. 12
22	Mike Nukk, Maritime (N.Y.) vs. Casenovia	Dec. 3
22	Ryan Vickers, Oglethorpe vs. Ferrum	Nov. 18

ASSISTS

Ast.	Player, Team vs. Opponent	Date
20	Matt Nadelhoffer, Wheaton (Ill.) vs. Grinnell	Feb. 29
20	Dax Kajiwara, Vassar vs. Bard	Feb. 14
18	Clarence Pierce, N.J. Inst. of Tech vs. Centenary (N.J.)	Jan. 18
18	Zach Goring, St. Olaf vs. Hamline	Jan. 15
18	Matt Nadelhoffer, Wheaton (Ill.) vs. Calvin	Dec. 7
17	Jeff Boyle, Grinnell vs. Chicago	Nov. 18
17	Chris Perrin, Simpson vs. Grinnell	Nov. 25
16	Matt Nadelhoffer, Wheaton (Ill.) vs. Greenville	Dec. 9

BLOCKED SHOTS

Blk.	Player, Team vs. Opponent	Date
#15	Antoine Hyman, Keuka vs. Hobart	Feb. 21
13	Damon Avinger, CCNY vs. St. Joseph's (N.Y.)	Jan. 7
11	Antoine Hyman, Keuka vs. Nazareth	Feb. 19
11	Antoine Hyman, Keuka vs. Elmira	Jan. 10
11	Ira Nicholson, Mt. St. Vincent vs. Bard	Dec. 7
10	Jason White, Westminster (Mo.) vs. Principia	Jan. 30
10	John Garber, Millsaps vs. Centre	Jan. 19
10	Damon Avinger, CCNY vs. John Jay	Dec. 6

#Tied Division III record.

STEALS

Stl.	Player, Team vs. Opponent	Date
12	Deron Black, Allegheny vs. Case Reserve	Jan. 17
12	Jamal Elliott, Haverford vs. Gwynedd Mercy	Jan. 15
11	Greg Dean, Concordia-M'head vs. St. John's (Minn.)	Feb. 3
11	Richie Cole, Mt. St. Vincent vs. Bard	Jan. 24
11	Ivo Moyano, Polytechnic (N.Y.) vs. N.J. Inst. of Tech.	Dec. 9
10	Adam Poe, Washington (Md.) vs. Wesley	Jan. 31
10	Kelly McClure, Otterbein vs. MacMurray	Dec. 28
10	Jeff Boyle, Grinnell vs. Mt. Mercy	Nov. 21

Team Highs

SCORING

Pts.	Team vs. Opponent	Date
157	Simpson vs. Grinnell	Nov. 25
152	Grinnell vs. Chicago	Nov. 18
140	Franklin vs. Indiana-East	Dec. 8
139	Salisbury St. vs. Marywood	Jan. 7
137	Grinnell vs. Simpson	Nov. 25
137	Chicago vs. Grinnell	Nov. 28
132	Grinnell vs. Colorado Col.	Nov. 17
131	Wheaton (Ill.) vs. Grinnell	Feb. 29
130	Rowan vs. Lebanon Valley	Jan. 6
129	Howard Payne vs. Wayland Baptist	Nov. 30

FIELD-GOAL PERCENTAGE

Pct.	Team vs. Opponent	Date
77.1 (37-48)	Capital vs. Defiance	Nov. 17
76.9 (70-91)	Simpson vs. Grinnell	Nov. 25
72.3 (34-47)	Menlo vs. UC Santa Cruz	Jan. 12
71.9 (46-64)	Manchester vs. Ind.-Northwest	Nov. 25
70.5 (31-44)	Wabash vs. Emory & Henry	Nov. 17
70.2 (40-57)	Bluffton vs. Bethany (W. Va.)	Feb. 7
68.9 (31-45)	Upper Iowa vs. Mt. Mercy	Dec. 2
68.8 (33-48)	Frank. & Marsh. vs. Swarthmore	Dec. 9
68.6 (35-51)	Millsaps vs. Sewanee	Jan. 21
68.3 (41-60)	Thomas More vs. Cornell College	Jan. 2

FREE-THROW PERCENTAGE
(Min. 15 FT Made)

Pct.	Team vs. Opponent	Date
100.0 (20-20)	Juniata vs. Widener	Dec. 2
100.0 (16-16)	Anderson vs. Wabash	Jan. 9
100.0 (15-15)	Roger Williams vs. Curry	Feb. 17
95.7 (22-23)	Neb. Wesleyan vs. Dana	Jan. 4
95.2 (20-21)	Wabash vs. Franklin	Jan. 20
95.2 (20-21)	Lycoming vs. Gwynedd-Mercy	Nov. 17
95.0 (19-20)	Roger Williams vs. Salve Regina	Jan. 24
95.0 (19-20)	Wentworth Inst. vs. Curry	Jan. 16
94.4 (17-18)	Western Md. vs. Haverford	Jan. 27
94.1 (16-17)	Merchant Marine vs. Vassar	Jan. 22

THREE-POINT FIELD GOALS

3FG	Team vs. Opponent	Date
*30	Grinnell vs. Colorado Col.	Nov. 17
23	Grinnell vs. Carroll (Wis.)	Feb. 23
22	Grinnell vs. Wheaton (Ill.)	Feb. 29
22	UC San Diego vs. Menlo	Jan. 27
22	Grinnell vs. Chicago	Nov. 18
21	Grinnell vs. Ripon	Feb. 24
21	Grinnell vs. Iowa Wesleyan	Feb. 8
21	Grinnell vs. Simpson	Nov. 25
20	Carroll (Wis.) vs. Beloit	Feb. 3
19	Grinnell vs. Ripon	Jan. 21
19	Grinnell vs. Iowa Wesleyan	Jan. 8
19	Grinnell vs. Knox	Dec. 2
18	Grinnell vs. Coe	Feb. 3

*Division III record.

1996 Division III Team Leaders

Scoring Offense

		G	W-L	Pts.	Avg.
1.	Grinnell	25	17-8	2,587	103.5
2.	Salisbury St.	28	19-9	2,755	98.4
3.	Simpson	26	20-6	2,483	95.5
4.	Babson	28	21-7	2,625	93.8
5.	Shenandoah	27	18-9	2,506	92.8
6.	Rowan	32	28-4	2,967	92.7
7.	St. Joseph's (Me.)	28	24-4	2,557	91.3
8.	Howard Payne	27	14-13	2,423	89.7
9.	Cabrini	27	24-3	2,414	89.4
10.	Anna Maria	30	25-5	2,681	89.4
11.	Stillman	25	21-4	2,225	89.0
12.	Tufts	25	15-10	2,220	88.8
13.	Colby-Sawyer	26	18-8	2,298	88.4
14.	Roanoke	29	24-5	2,529	87.2
15.	Salem St.	28	25-3	2,433	86.9
16.	UC San Diego	25	11-14	2,171	86.8
17.	Emory & Henry	25	14-11	2,167	86.7
18.	Hardin-Simmons	25	20-5	2,164	86.6
19.	Mt. St. Mary's (N.Y.)	25	15-10	2,163	86.5
20.	Wilkes	30	28-2	2,592	86.4
21.	Lycoming	27	21-6	2,330	86.3
22.	Hendrix	27	21-6	2,325	86.1
23.	Wheaton (Ill.)	27	25-2	2,314	85.7
24.	Goucher	25	15-10	2,141	85.6
25.	Williams	27	24-3	2,312	85.6
26.	Curry	24	11-13	2,035	84.8
27.	Worcester St.	26	10-16	2,204	84.8
28.	N.J. Inst. of Tech.	27	17-10	2,288	84.7
29.	Amherst	27	21-6	2,283	84.6
30.	Augustana (Ill.)	24	16-8	2,029	84.5

Scoring Defense

		G	W-L	Pts.	Avg.
1.	Upper Iowa	26	21-5	1,500	57.7
2.	Wis.-Platteville	26	23-3	1,505	57.9
3.	Hanover	27	21-6	1,593	59.0
4.	Wooster	26	19-7	1,537	59.1
5.	St. Norbert	22	8-14	1,323	60.1
6.	Frank. & Marsh.	32	29-3	1,945	60.8
7.	Buffalo St.	30	22-8	1,824	60.8
8.	Grove City	26	16-10	1,592	61.2
9.	Gust. Adolphus	29	24-5	1,778	61.3
10.	Wis.-Oshkosh	27	23-4	1,657	61.4
11.	Wittenberg	31	26-5	1,910	61.6
12.	DePauw	26	17-9	1,612	62.0
13.	Marietta	28	15-13	1,787	63.8
14.	Martin Luther	17	11-6	1,088	64.0
15.	Williams	27	24-3	1,734	64.2
16.	Richard Stockton	30	26-4	1,929	64.3
17.	Rose-Hulman	28	19-9	1,801	64.3
18.	Hartwick	26	17-9	1,687	64.9
19.	Cal Tech	23	4-19	1,493	64.9
20.	Ithaca	26	16-10	1,695	65.2
21.	Springfield	28	21-7	1,834	65.5
22.	Binghamton	25	10-15	1,641	65.6
23.	Moravian	25	17-8	1,643	65.7
24.	St. John Fisher	26	20-6	1,711	65.8
25.	Widener	23	10-13	1,514	65.8
26.	Manchester	27	19-8	1,783	66.0
27.	Ramapo	24	11-13	1,586	66.1
28.	Muskingum	27	10-17	1,787	66.2
29.	Claremont-M-S	27	19-8	1,791	66.3
29.	Ohio Northern	27	18-9	1,791	66.3

Scoring Margin

		Off.	Def.	Mar.
1.	Cabrini	89.4	67.6	21.8
2.	Williams	85.6	64.2	21.4
3.	Rowan	92.7	71.4	21.3
4.	St. Joseph's (Me.)	91.3	71.5	19.9
5.	Wilkes	86.4	68.5	17.9

		Off.	Def.	Mar.
6.	St. John Fisher	82.7	65.8	16.9
7.	Salem St.	86.9	70.5	16.4
8.	Wis.-Platteville	74.0	57.9	16.2
9.	Hanover	74.4	59.0	15.4
10.	Ill. Wesleyan	84.5	69.3	15.2
11.	Alvernia	82.5	67.5	15.0
12.	Frank. & Marsh.	75.6	60.8	14.8
13.	Hope	83.4	69.4	14.0
13.	Ripon	84.0	70.0	14.0
15.	Hardin-Simmons	86.6	72.8	13.7
16.	Anna Maria	89.4	76.1	13.3
17.	Wheaton (Ill.)	85.7	73.1	12.6
18.	Wittenberg	74.1	61.6	12.5
19.	Lycoming	86.3	74.1	12.2
20.	Cal Lutheran	79.2	67.0	12.1
21.	Millsaps	82.7	70.6	12.1
22.	Upper Iowa	69.6	57.7	11.9
23.	Manchester	77.7	66.0	11.7
24.	Rose-Hulman	75.9	64.3	11.6
25.	Hendrix	86.1	74.7	11.4
26.	Mt. St. Vincent	80.7	69.8	10.9
27.	Simpson	95.5	84.8	10.7
28.	Amherst	84.6	73.9	10.6
29.	Wis.-Oshkosh	72.0	61.4	10.6
30.	Stillman	89.0	78.5	10.5

Won-Lost Percentage

		W-L	Pct.
1.	Wilkes	28-2	.933
2.	Wheaton (Ill.)	25-2	.926
3.	Frank. & Marsh.	29-3	.906
4.	Ill. Wesleyan	28-3	.903
5.	Salem St.	25-3	.893
6.	Cabrini	24-3	.889
7.	Williams	24-3	.889
8.	Wis.-Platteville	23-3	.885
9.	Rowan	28-4	.875
10.	Richard Stockton	26-4	.867
11.	St. Joseph's (Me.)	24-4	.857
12.	Wis.-Oshkosh	23-4	.852
13.	Rochester Inst.	22-4	.846
14.	Hope	27-5	.844
15.	Ripon	21-4	.840
15.	Stillman	21-4	.840
17.	Wittenberg	26-5	.839
18.	Anna Maria	25-5	.833
19.	Gust. Adolphus	24-5	.828
19.	Roanoke	24-5	.828
21.	Millsaps	22-5	.815
22.	Upper Iowa	21-5	.808
23.	Chris. Newport	24-6	.800
23.	Hardin-Simmons	20-5	.800
25.	Washington (Mo.)	23-6	.793
26.	Staten Island	22-6	.786
27.	Amherst	21-6	.778
27.	Concordia-M'head	21-6	.778
27.	Lycoming	21-6	.778
27.	Hanover	21-6	.778
27.	Hendrix	21-6	.778

Field-Goal Percentage

		FG	FGA	Pct.
1.	Simpson	946	1,749	54.1
2.	Ill. Wesleyan	941	1,812	51.9
3.	Neb. Wesleyan	738	1,429	51.6
4.	St. Joseph's (Me.)	972	1,886	51.5
5.	Augustana (Ill.)	727	1,415	51.4
6.	Hardin-Simmons	750	1,472	51.0
7.	Hendrix	849	1,676	50.7
8.	Ripon	775	1,531	50.6
9.	Menlo	709	1,401	50.6
10.	Hanover	750	1,485	50.5
11.	Bluffton	702	1,394	50.4
12.	Wis.-Stevens Point	699	1,390	50.3
13.	Wheaton (Ill.)	820	1,634	50.2
14.	Frank. & Marsh.	853	1,708	49.9
15.	Shenandoah	963	1,930	49.9
16.	Carroll (Wis.)	634	1,280	49.5
17.	Defiance	623	1,258	49.5
18.	Rose-Hulman	783	1,585	49.4

		FG	FGA	Pct.
19.	Babson	972	1,968	49.4
20.	Anna Maria	932	1,890	49.3
21.	Thomas More	747	1,517	49.2
22.	Lakeland	710	1,442	49.2
23.	Chapman	753	1,531	49.2
24.	Western Conn. St.	817	1,662	49.2
25.	Emory & Henry	771	1,575	49.0
26.	Manchester	758	1,549	48.9
27.	Wis.-Oshkosh	662	1,353	48.9
28.	Alvernia	759	1,552	48.9
29.	Salem St.	834	1,706	48.9
30.	Rhodes	745	1,525	48.9

Field-Goal Percentage Defense

		FG	FGA	Pct.
1.	Bowdoin	569	1,482	38.4
2.	Wooster	541	1,406	38.5
3.	Maine Maritime	504	1,297	38.9
4.	Elmira	642	1,639	39.2
5.	Williams	640	1,627	39.3
6.	Colby	661	1,670	39.6
7.	Upper Iowa	553	1,396	39.6
8.	Staten Island	654	1,649	39.7
9.	Binghamton	593	1,490	39.8
10.	Lakeland	636	1,596	39.8
11.	Springfield	673	1,681	40.0
12.	Merchant Marine	686	1,711	40.1
13.	Gust. Adolphus	623	1,552	40.1
14.	Keuka	626	1,559	40.2
15.	Wis.-Eau Claire	587	1,461	40.2
16.	Manchester	618	1,535	40.3
17.	Calvin	596	1,480	40.3
18.	Trinity (Conn.)	581	1,437	40.4
19.	Cabrini	659	1,626	40.5
20.	Hartwick	626	1,544	40.5
21.	St. John Fisher	621	1,531	40.6
22.	Rochester Inst.	677	1,668	40.6
23.	Edgewood	614	1,510	40.7
24.	Wilkes	765	1,876	40.8
25.	Vassar	646	1,581	40.9
26.	Muhlenberg	608	1,487	40.9
27.	Grove City	569	1,390	40.9
28.	Connecticut Col.	654	1,597	41.0
29.	Endicott	555	1,355	41.0
30.	Wittenberg	710	1,733	41.0

Three-Point Field Goals Made Per Game

		G	3FG	Avg.
1.	Grinnell	25	415	16.6
2.	UC San Diego	25	276	11.0
3.	Beloit	22	209	9.5
4.	Stillman	25	235	9.4
5.	Anna Maria	30	281	9.4
6.	Carroll (Wis.)	23	206	9.0
7.	Tufts	25	222	8.9
8.	Fontbonne	27	234	8.7
9.	Claremont-M-S	27	231	8.6
10.	Wis.-Whitewater	28	239	8.5
11.	Ferrum	24	204	8.5
12.	Hamilton	25	212	8.5
13.	Sewanee	25	205	8.2
14.	Lawrence	22	180	8.2
15.	Gust. Adolphus	29	236	8.1
16.	Emory & Henry	25	202	8.1
17.	Alma	25	200	8.0
17.	Cal Lutheran	25	200	8.0
17.	Hartwick	26	208	8.0
20.	Wilkes	30	239	8.0
21.	Wesleyan (Conn.)	23	182	7.9
22.	Bates	24	189	7.9
22.	Swarthmore	24	189	7.9
24.	Colorado Col.	25	196	7.8
24.	Loras	25	196	7.8
26.	Rowan	32	250	7.8
27.	Elmhurst	25	195	7.8
28.	Thiel	25	194	7.8
29.	Aurora	25	193	7.7
30.	Southern Me.	25	191	7.6

Three-Point Field-Goal Percentage

(Min. 3.0 3FG Per Game)	G	FG	FGA	Pct.
1. John Carroll	27	169	388	43.6
2. Augustana (Ill.)	24	132	312	42.3
3. Neb. Wesleyan	25	160	379	42.2
4. Wis.-Oshkosh	27	161	382	42.1
5. Babson	28	206	489	42.1
6. Goucher	25	125	301	41.5
7. Hardin-Simmons	25	163	396	41.2
8. Carroll (Wis.)	23	206	503	41.0
9. Bridgewater (Va.)	28	155	379	40.9
10. Nichols	25	154	377	40.8
11. Franklin	24	147	361	40.7
12. Gust. Adolphus	29	236	581	40.6
13. East. Mennonite	25	155	385	40.3
14. Richard Stockton	30	219	544	40.3
15. Manchester	27	158	393	40.2
16. Carleton	25	190	474	40.1
17. Wheaton (Ill.)	27	181	452	40.0
18. Roanoke	29	211	527	40.0
19. Colby	27	177	445	39.8
20. Hanover	27	155	390	39.7
21. Rutgers-Newark	27	184	463	39.7
22. Lakeland	26	145	365	39.7
22. Johnson St.	22	116	292	39.7
24. Hartwick	26	208	524	39.7
25. Staten Island	28	147	371	39.6
26. Elmhurst	25	195	493	39.6
27. Alvernia	25	138	349	39.5
28. Alfred	25	190	483	39.3
29. Rensselaer	28	211	539	39.1
30. Wentworth Inst.	27	114	292	39.0

Free-Throw Percentage

	FT	FTA	Pct.
1. Anderson	454	592	76.7
2. Aurora	416	550	75.6
3. Hope	584	773	75.5
4. Wis.-Platteville	528	699	75.5
5. Kalamazoo	482	641	75.2
6. Hendrix	468	623	75.1
7. Trinity (Conn.)	338	451	74.9
8. Roger Williams	287	385	74.5
9. Nazareth	402	540	74.4
10. Ursinus	351	472	74.4
11. Hartwick	276	372	74.2
12. Heidelberg	310	418	74.2
13. Utica	395	534	74.0
14. Salem St.	610	826	73.8
15. Wis.-Whitewater	379	514	73.7
16. Baldwin-Wallace	439	597	73.5
17. Elizabethtown	394	536	73.5
18. Allentown	506	689	73.4
19. Defiance	376	512	73.4
20. Lakeland	389	531	73.3
21. Frank. & Marsh.	573	783	73.2
22. Beloit	302	413	73.1
23. Rochester	347	475	73.1
24. Chris. Newport	513	703	73.0
25. Bates	340	466	73.0
26. Wis.-Oshkosh	458	628	72.9
27. Franklin	493	676	72.9
28. Upper Iowa	371	509	72.9
29. Colby-Sawyer	449	619	72.5
30. Carleton	453	625	72.5

Rebound Margin

	Off.	Def.	Mar.
1. Cabrini	47.9	34.7	13.1
2. Rowan	44.7	33.3	11.3
3. Savannah A&D	37.4	27.1	10.3
4. Wilkes	44.9	35.0	9.9
5. Wooster	39.5	30.5	9.0
6. St. Joseph's (Me.)	41.0	32.1	8.8
7. Wittenberg	38.3	29.8	8.5
8. Williams	41.3	33.2	8.1
9. Hope	41.0	33.0	8.0
10. Rochester Inst.	42.5	34.7	7.9
11. Chapman	41.6	33.9	7.7
12. Denison	37.7	30.1	7.6
13. St. John's (Minn.)	38.0	30.5	7.5
14. Baruch	42.4	35.0	7.4
15. Carnegie Mellon	44.9	37.6	7.3
16. Neb. Wesleyan	39.5	32.3	7.2
17. Trinity (Conn.)	43.2	36.1	7.1
18. Maritime (N.Y.)	45.6	38.5	7.1
19. Wis.-Platteville	35.5	28.4	7.1
20. Hanover	35.1	28.1	7.0
21. St. John Fisher	42.0	35.1	6.9
22. Hampden-Sydney	41.3	34.4	6.9
23. Rose-Hulman	37.4	30.5	6.9
24. Chris. Newport	42.7	35.9	6.8
25. Salem St.	38.9	32.1	6.8
26. Utica/Rome	42.3	35.8	6.5
27. Daniel Webster	45.7	39.3	6.4
28. Colby	40.6	34.3	6.3
29. Bridgewater (Va.)	38.4	32.1	6.3
30. Rhode Island Col.	40.9	34.7	6.1

Conferences

1996 Division I Conference Standings

#Won conference tournament.

AMERICAN WEST CONFERENCE

Team	Conference			Full Season		
	W	L	Pct.	W	L	Pct.
Cal Poly SLO	5	1	.833	16	13	.552
Southern Utah#	3	3	.500	15	13	.536
Cal St. Northridge	2	4	.333	7	20	.259
Cal St. Sacramento	2	4	.333	7	20	.259

ATLANTIC COAST CONFERENCE

Team	Conference			Full Season		
	W	L	Pct.	W	L	Pct.
Georgia Tech	13	3	.813	24	12	.667
Wake Forest#	12	4	.750	26	6	.813
North Caro.	10	6	.625	21	11	.656
Duke	8	8	.500	18	13	.581
Maryland	8	8	.500	17	13	.567
Clemson	7	9	.438	18	11	.621
Virginia	6	10	.375	12	15	.444
Florida St.	5	11	.313	13	14	.481
North Caro. St.	3	13	.188	15	16	.484

ATLANTIC 10 CONFERENCE

Team	Conference			Full Season		
East Division	W	L	Pct.	W	L	Pct.
Massachusetts#	15	1	.938	35	2	.946
Temple	12	4	.750	20	13	.606
St. Joseph's (Pa.)	9	7	.563	19	13	.594
Rhode Island	8	8	.500	20	14	.588
St. Bonaventure	4	12	.250	10	18	.357
Fordham	2	14	.125	4	23	.148
West Division						
Virginia Tech	13	3	.813	23	6	.793
Geo. Washington	13	3	.813	21	8	.724
Xavier (Ohio)	8	8	.500	13	15	.464
Dayton	6	10	.375	15	14	.517
La Salle	3	13	.188	6	24	.200
Duquesne	3	13	.188	9	18	.333

BIG EAST CONFERENCE

Team	Conference			Full Season		
Big East 7	W	L	Pct.	W	L	Pct.
Georgetown	13	5	.722	29	8	.784
Syracuse	12	6	.667	29	9	.763
Providence	9	9	.500	18	12	.600
Miami (Fla.)	8	10	.444	15	13	.536
Seton Hall	7	11	.389	12	16	.429
Rutgers	6	12	.333	9	18	.333
Pittsburgh	5	13	.278	10	17	.370
Big East 6						
Connecticut#	17	1	.944	32	3	.914
Villanova	14	4	.778	26	7	.788
Boston College	10	8	.556	19	11	.633
West Va.	7	11	.389	12	15	.444
St. John's (N.Y.)	5	13	.278	11	16	.407
Notre Dame	4	14	.222	9	18	.333

BIG EIGHT CONFERENCE

Team	Conference			Full Season		
	W	L	Pct.	W	L	Pct.
Kansas	12	2	.857	29	5	.853
Iowa St.#	9	5	.643	24	9	.727
Oklahoma	8	6	.571	17	13	.567
Oklahoma St.	7	7	.500	17	10	.630
Kansas St.	7	7	.500	17	12	.586
Missouri	6	8	.429	18	15	.545
Nebraska	4	10	.286	21	14	.600
Colorado	3	11	.214	9	18	.333

BIG SKY CONFERENCE

Team	Conference			Full Season		
	W	L	Pct.	W	L	Pct.
Montana St.#	11	3	.786	21	9	.700
Weber St.	10	4	.714	20	10	.667
Montana	10	4	.714	20	8	.714
Boise St.	10	4	.714	15	13	.536
Idaho St.	7	7	.500	11	15	.423
Idaho	5	9	.357	12	16	.429
Northern Ariz.	3	11	.214	6	20	.231
Eastern Wash.	0	14	.000	3	23	.115

BIG SOUTH CONFERENCE

Team	Conference			Full Season		
	W	L	Pct.	W	L	Pct.
N.C.-Greensboro#	11	3	.786	20	10	.667
N.C.-Asheville	9	5	.643	18	10	.643
Liberty	9	5	.643	17	12	.586
Charleston So.	9	5	.643	15	13	.536
Radford	8	6	.571	14	13	.519
Winthrop	6	8	.429	7	19	.269
Md.-Balt. County	3	11	.214	5	22	.185
Coastal Caro.	1	13	.071	5	21	.192

BIG TEN CONFERENCE

Team	Conference			Full Season		
	W	L	Pct.	W	L	Pct.
Purdue	15	3	.833	26	6	.813
Penn St.	12	6	.667	21	7	.750
Indiana	12	6	.667	19	12	.613
Iowa	11	7	.611	23	9	.719
Michigan	10	8	.556	20	12	.625
Minnesota	10	8	.556	19	13	.594
Michigan St.	9	9	.500	16	16	.500
Wisconsin	8	10	.444	17	15	.531
Illinois	7	11	.389	18	13	.581
Ohio St.	3	18	.143	10	17	.370
Northwestern	2	16	.111	7	20	.259

BIG WEST CONFERENCE

Team	Conference			Full Season		
	W	L	Pct.	W	L	Pct.
Long Beach St.	12	6	.667	17	11	.607
UC Irvine	11	7	.611	15	12	.556
Pacific (Cal.)	11	7	.611	15	12	.556
Utah St.	10	8	.556	18	15	.545
Nevada	9	9	.500	16	13	.552
San Jose St.#	9	9	.500	13	17	.433
New Mexico St.	8	10	.444	11	15	.423
UC Santa Barb.	8	10	.444	11	15	.423
UNLV	7	11	.389	10	16	.385
Cal St. Fullerton	5	13	.278	6	20	.231

COLONIAL ATHLETIC ASSOCIATION

Team	Conference			Full Season		
	W	L	Pct.	W	L	Pct.
Va. Commonwealth#	14	2	.875	24	9	.727
Old Dominion	12	4	.750	18	13	.581
N.C.-Wilmington	9	7	.563	13	16	.448
East Caro.	8	8	.500	17	11	.607
American	8	8	.500	12	15	.444
George Mason	6	10	.375	11	16	.407
William & Mary	6	10	.375	10	16	.385
James Madison	6	10	.375	10	20	.333
Richmond	3	13	.188	8	20	.286

CONFERENCE USA

Team	Conference			Full Season		
Red Division	W	L	Pct.	W	L	Pct.
Tulane	9	5	.643	22	10	.688
UAB	6	8	.429	16	14	.533
Southern Miss.	6	8	.429	12	15	.444
South Fla.	2	12	.143	12	16	.429
White Division						
Memphis	11	3	.786	22	8	.733
Louisville	10	4	.714	22	12	.647
N.C.-Charlotte	6	8	.429	14	15	.483
Blue Division						
Cincinnati#	11	3	.786	28	5	.848
Marquette	10	4	.714	23	8	.742
St. Louis	4	10	.286	16	14	.533
DePaul	2	12	.143	11	18	.379

IVY GROUP

Team	Conference			Full Season		
	W	L	Pct.	W	L	Pct.
Princeton	13	2	.867	22	7	.759
Pennsylvania	12	3	.800	17	10	.630
Dartmouth	9	5	.643	16	10	.615
Harvard	7	7	.500	15	11	.577
Brown	5	9	.357	10	16	.385
Cornell	5	9	.357	10	16	.385
Yale	3	11	.214	8	18	.308
Columbia	3	11	.214	7	19	.269

METRO ATLANTIC ATHLETIC CONFERENCE

Team	Conference			Full Season		
	W	L	Pct.	W	L	Pct.
Iona	10	4	.714	21	8	.724
Fairfield	10	4	.714	20	10	.667
Manhattan	9	5	.643	17	12	.586
Loyola (Md.)	8	6	.571	12	15	.444
Canisius#	7	7	.500	19	11	.633
Niagara	6	8	.429	13	15	.464
St. Peter's	5	9	.357	15	12	.556
Siena	1	13	.071	5	22	.185

MID-AMERICAN ATHLETIC CONFERENCE

Team	Conference			Full Season		
	W	L	Pct.	W	L	Pct.
Eastern Mich.#	14	4	.778	25	6	.806
Western Mich.	13	5	.722	15	12	.556
Miami (Ohio)	12	6	.667	21	8	.724
Ohio	11	7	.611	14	13	.533
Ball St.	11	7	.611	16	12	.571
Bowling Green	9	9	.500	14	13	.519
Toledo	9	9	.500	18	14	.563
Kent	8	10	.444	14	13	.519
Central Mich.	3	15	.167	6	20	.231
Akron	0	18	.000	3	23	.115

MID-CONTINENT CONFERENCE

Team	Conference			Full Season		
	W	L	Pct.	W	L	Pct.
Valparaiso#	13	5	.722	21	11	.656
Western Ill.	12	6	.667	17	12	.586
Northeastern Ill.	10	8	.556	14	13	.519
Buffalo	10	8	.556	13	14	.481
Mo.-Kansas City	10	8	.556	12	15	.444
Central Conn. St.	9	9	.500	13	15	.464
Eastern Ill.	9	9	.500	13	15	.464
Troy St.	8	10	.444	11	16	.407
Youngstown St.	7	11	.389	12	15	.444
Chicago St.	2	16	.111	2	25	.074

MID-EASTERN ATHLETIC CONFERENCE

Team	Conference			Full Season		
	W	L	Pct.	W	L	Pct.
South Caro. St.#	14	2	.875	22	8	.733
Coppin St.	14	2	.875	19	10	.655
Bethune-Cookman	8	8	.500	12	15	.444
Delaware St.	8	8	.500	11	17	.393
North Caro. A&T	7	9	.438	10	17	.370
Md.-East. Shore	6	10	.375	11	16	.407
Howard	6	10	.375	7	20	.259
Morgan St.	6	10	.375	7	20	.259
Florida A&M	3	13	.188	8	19	.296
Hampton	—	—	—	9	17	.346

MIDWESTERN COLLEGIATE CONFERENCE

Team	Conference			Full Season		
	W	L	Pct.	W	L	Pct.
Wis.-Green Bay	16	0	1.000	25	4	.862
Butler	12	4	.750	19	8	.704
Northern Ill.#	10	6	.625	20	10	.667
Wright St.	8	8	.500	14	13	.519
Detroit	8	8	.500	18	11	.621
Wis.-Milwaukee	5	11	.313	9	18	.333
Ill.-Chicago	5	11	.313	10	18	.357
Loyola (Ill.)	5	11	.313	8	19	.296
Cleveland St.	3	13	.188	5	21	.192

MISSOURI VALLEY CONFERENCE

Team	Conference			Full Season		
	W	L	Pct.	W	L	Pct.
Bradley	15	3	.833	22	8	.733
Illinois St.	13	5	.722	22	12	.647
Tulsa#	12	6	.667	22	8	.733
Southwest Mo. St.	11	7	.611	16	12	.571
Creighton	9	9	.500	14	15	.483
Evansville	9	9	.500	13	14	.481
Northern Iowa	8	10	.444	14	13	.519
Drake	8	10	.444	14	13	.444
Indiana St.	6	12	.333	10	16	.385
Southern Ill.	4	14	.222	11	18	.379
Wichita St.	4	14	.222	8	21	.276

NORTH ATLANTIC CONFERENCE

Team	Conference			Full Season		
	W	L	Pct.	W	L	Pct.
Drexel#	17	1	.944	27	4	.871
Boston U.	13	5	.722	18	11	.621
Maine	11	7	.611	15	13	.536
Delaware	11	7	.611	15	12	.556
Towson St.	11	7	.611	16	12	.571
Vermont	10	8	.556	12	15	.444
Hofstra	5	13	.278	9	18	.333
New Hampshire	5	13	.278	6	21	.222
Hartford	5	13	.278	6	22	.214
Northeastern	2	16	.111	4	24	.143

NORTHEAST CONFERENCE

Team	Conference			Full Season		
	W	L	Pct.	W	L	Pct.
Mt. St. Mary's (Md.)	16	2	.889	21	8	.724
Marist	14	4	.778	22	7	.759
Monmouth (N.J.)#	14	4	.778	20	10	.667
Rider	12	6	.667	19	11	.633
St. Francis (Pa.)	11	7	.611	13	14	.481
Wagner	7	11	.389	10	17	.370
Fairleigh Dickinson	6	12	.333	7	20	.259
LIU-Brooklyn	5	13	.278	9	19	.321
St. Francis (N.Y.)	3	15	.167	9	18	.333
Robert Morris	2	16	.111	5	23	.179

OHIO VALLEY CONFERENCE

Team	Conference			Full Season		
	W	L	Pct.	W	L	Pct.
Murray St.	12	4	.750	19	10	.655
Tennessee St.	11	5	.688	15	13	.536
Austin Peay#	10	6	.625	19	11	.633
Middle Tenn. St.	9	7	.563	15	12	.556
Tenn.-Martin	9	7	.563	13	14	.481
Eastern Ky.	7	9	.438	13	14	.481
Tennessee Tech	7	9	.438	13	15	.464
Southeast Mo. St.	5	11	.313	8	19	.296
Morehead St.	2	14	.125	7	20	.259

PACIFIC-10 CONFERENCE

Team	Conference			Full Season		
	W	L	Pct.	W	L	Pct.
UCLA	16	2	.889	23	8	.742
Arizona	13	5	.722	26	7	.788
Stanford	12	6	.667	20	9	.690
California	11	7	.611	17	11	.607
Washington	9	9	.500	16	12	.571
Oregon	9	9	.500	16	13	.552
Washington St.	8	10	.444	17	12	.586
Arizona St.	6	12	.333	11	16	.407
Southern Cal	4	14	.222	11	19	.367
Oregon St.	2	16	.111	4	23	.148

PATRIOT LEAGUE

Team	Conference			Full Season		
	W	L	Pct.	W	L	Pct.
Navy	9	3	.750	15	12	.556
Colgate#	9	3	.750	15	15	.500
Bucknell	8	4	.667	17	11	.607
Holy Cross	8	4	.667	16	13	.552
Lafayette	4	8	.333	7	20	.259
Army	2	10	.167	7	20	.259
Lehigh	2	10	.167	4	23	.148

SOUTHEASTERN CONFERENCE

Team	Conference			Full Season		
Eastern Division	W	L	Pct.	W	L	Pct.
Kentucky	16	0	1.000	34	2	.944
Georgia	9	7	.563	21	10	.677
South Caro.	8	8	.500	19	12	.613
Vanderbilt	7	9	.438	18	14	.563
Florida	6	10	.375	12	16	.429
Tennessee	6	10	.375	14	15	.483
Western Division						
Mississippi St. #	10	6	.625	26	8	.765
Arkansas	9	7	.563	20	13	.606
Alabama	9	7	.563	19	13	.594
Mississippi	6	10	.375	12	15	.444
Auburn	6	10	.375	19	13	.594
LSU	4	12	.250	12	17	.414

SOUTHERN CONFERENCE

Team	Conference			Full Season		
Northern Division	W	L	Pct.	W	L	Pct.
Davidson	14	0	1.000	25	5	.833
VMI	10	4	.714	18	10	.643
Marshall	8	6	.571	17	11	.607
East Tenn. St.	3	11	.214	7	20	.259
Appalachian St.	3	11	.214	8	20	.286
Southern Division						
Western Caro.#	10	4	.714	17	13	.567
Tenn.-Chatt.	9	5	.643	15	12	.556
Furman	6	8	.429	10	17	.370
Citadel	5	9	.357	10	16	.385
Ga. Southern	2	12	.143	3	23	.115

SOUTHLAND CONFERENCE

Team	Conference			Full Season		
	W	L	Pct.	W	L	Pct.
Northeast La.#	13	5	.722	16	14	.533
North Texas	12	6	.667	15	13	.536
Texas-San Antonio	12	6	.667	14	14	.500
Stephen F. Austin	11	7	.611	17	11	.607
McNeese St.	11	7	.611	15	12	.556
Sam Houston St.	9	9	.500	11	16	.407
Southwest Tex. St.	7	11	.389	11	15	.423
Texas-Arlington	7	11	.389	11	15	.423
Nicholls St.	5	13	.278	5	21	.192
Northwestern St.	3	15	.167	5	21	.192

SOUTHWEST CONFERENCE

Team	Conference			Full Season		
	W	L	Pct.	W	L	Pct.
Texas Tech#	14	0	1.000	30	2	.938
Houston	11	3	.786	17	10	.630
Texas	10	4	.714	21	10	.677
Texas Christian	6	8	.429	15	15	.500
Rice	5	9	.357	14	14	.500
Baylor	4	10	.286	9	18	.333
Southern Methodist	3	11	.214	8	20	.286
Texas A&M	3	11	.214	11	16	.407

SOUTHWESTERN ATHLETIC CONFERENCE

Team	Conference			Full Season		
	W	L	Pct.	W	L	Pct.
Mississippi Val.#	11	3	.786	22	7	.759
Jackson St.	11	3	.786	16	13	.552
Southern U.	8	5	.615	17	11	.607
Texas Southern	7	7	.500	11	15	.423
Alcorn St.	7	7	.500	10	15	.400
Grambling	6	7	.462	12	16	.429
Alabama St.	5	9	.357	9	18	.333
Prairie View	0	14	.000	4	23	.148

SUN BELT CONFERENCE

Team	Conference			Full Season		
	W	L	Pct.	W	L	Pct.
Ark.-Little Rock	14	4	.778	23	7	.767
New Orleans#	14	4	.778	21	9	.700
Jacksonville	10	8	.556	15	13	.536
Western Ky.	10	8	.556	13	14	.481
Southwestern La.	9	9	.500	16	12	.571
Lamar	7	11	.389	12	15	.444
South Ala.	7	11	.389	12	15	.444
Arkansas St.	7	11	.389	9	18	.333
Louisiana Tech	6	12	.333	11	17	.393
Tex.-Pan American	6	12	.333	9	19	.321

TRANS AMERICA ATHLETIC CONFERENCE

Team	Conference			Full Season		
East Division	W	L	Pct.	W	L	Pct.
Charleston (S.C.)	15	1	.938	25	4	.862
Campbell	11	5	.688	17	11	.607
Central Fla.#	6	10	.375	11	19	.367
Stetson	6	10	.375	10	17	.370
Florida Int'l	6	11	.353	13	15	.464
Fla. Atlantic	5	11	.313	9	18	.333
West Division						
Samford	11	5	.688	16	11	.593
Southeastern La.	11	5	.688	15	12	.556

Team	Conference			Full Season		
	W	L	Pct.	W	L	Pct.
Centenary (La.)	8	8	.500	11	16	.407
Mercer	8	9	.471	15	14	.517
Georgia St.	6	10	.375	10	16	.385
Jacksonville St.	4	12	.250	10	17	.370

WEST COAST CONFERENCE

Team	Conference			Full Season		
	W	L	Pct.	W	L	Pct.
Santa Clara	10	4	.714	20	9	.690
Gonzaga	10	4	.714	21	9	.700
Loyola Marymount	8	6	.571	18	11	.621
San Francisco	8	6	.571	15	12	.556
Portland#	7	7	.500	19	11	.633
San Diego	6	8	.429	14	14	.500
St. Mary's (Cal.)	5	9	.357	12	15	.444
Pepperdine	2	12	.143	10	18	.357

WESTERN ATHLETIC CONFERENCE

Team	Conference			Full Season		
	W	L	Pct.	W	L	Pct.
Utah	15	3	.833	27	7	.794
New Mexico#	14	4	.778	28	5	.848
Fresno St.	13	5	.722	22	11	.667
Colorado St.	11	7	.611	18	12	.600
Brigham Young	9	9	.500	15	13	.536
San Diego St.	8	10	.444	15	14	.517
Wyoming	8	10	.444	14	15	.483
Hawaii	7	11	.389	10	18	.357
UTEP	4	14	.222	13	15	.464
Air Force	1	17	.056	5	23	.179

DIVISION I INDEPENDENTS

Team	Full Season		
	W	L	Pct.
Oral Roberts	18	9	.667
Wofford	4	22	.154

Division I Conference Champions Season By Season

Regular-season and conference tournament champions; No. refers to the number of teams in the conference or tournament.

AMERICA EAST CONFERENCE

Season	No.	Regular Season
1980	10	Boston U./Northeastern
1981	9	Northeastern
1982	9	Northeastern
1983	9	Boston U./New Hampshire
1984	8	Northeastern
1985	9	Northeastern/Canisius
1986	10	Northeastern
1987	10	Northeastern
1988	10	Siena
1989	10	Siena
1990	7	Northeastern
1991	6	Northeastern
1992	8	Delaware
1993	8	Drexel/Northeastern
1994	9	Drexel
1995	9	Drexel
1996	10	Drexel

Season	No.	Conference Tournament
1980	8	Holy Cross
1981	6	Northeastern
1982	6	Northeastern

Season	No.	Conference Tournament
1983	9	Boston U.
1984	8	Northeastern
1985	9	Northeastern
1986	10	Northeastern
1987	10	Northeastern
1988	10	Boston U.
1989	10	Siena
1990	7	Boston U.
1991	6	Northeastern
1992	8	Delaware
1993	8	Delaware
1994	8	Drexel
1995	9	Drexel
1996	10	Drexel

AMERICAN SOUTH CONFERENCE

Season	No.	Regular Season
1988	6	Louisiana Tech/New Orleans
1989	6	New Orleans
1990	6	Louisiana Tech/New Orleans
1991	7	New Orleans/Arkansas St.

Season	No.	Conference Tournament
1988	6	Louisiana Tech
1989	6	Louisiana Tech
1990	6	New Orleans
1991	7	Louisiana Tech

AMERICAN WEST CONFERENCE

Season	No.	Regular Season
1995	4	Southern Utah
1996	4	Cal Poly SLO

Season	No.	Conference Tournament
1995	4	Southern Utah
1996	4	Southern Utah

ATLANTIC COAST CONFERENCE

Season	No.	Regular Season
1954	8	Duke
1955	8	North Caro. St.
1956	8	North Caro. St./North Caro.
1957	8	North Caro.
1958	8	Duke
1959	8	North Caro. St./North Caro.
1960	8	North Caro.
1961	8	North Caro.
1962	8	Wake Forest
1963	8	Duke
1964	8	Duke
1965	8	Duke
1966	8	Duke
1967	8	North Caro.
1968	8	North Caro.
1969	8	North Caro.
1970	8	South Caro.
1971	8	North Caro.
1972	7	North Caro.
1973	7	North Caro. St.
1974	7	North Caro. St.
1975	7	Maryland
1976	7	North Caro.
1977	7	North Caro.
1978	7	North Caro.
1979	7	Duke/North Caro.
1980	8	Maryland
1981	8	Virginia
1982	8	North Caro./Virginia
1983	8	North Caro./Virginia
1984	8	North Caro.
1985	8	Georgia Tech/North Caro./North Caro. St.
1986	8	Duke
1987	8	North Caro.
1988	8	North Caro.
1989	8	North Caro. St.
1990	8	Clemson
1991	8	Duke
1992	9	Duke
1993	9	North Caro.
1994	9	Duke
1995	9	Maryland/North Caro./Virginia/Wake Forest
1996	9	Georgia Tech

Season	No.	Conference Tournament
1954	8	North Caro. St.
1955	8	North Caro. St.
1956	8	North Caro. St.
1957	8	North Caro.
1958	8	Maryland
1959	8	North Caro. St.
1960	8	Duke
1961	7	Wake Forest
1962	8	Wake Forest
1963	8	Duke
1964	8	Duke
1965	8	North Caro. St.
1966	8	Duke
1967	8	North Caro.
1968	8	North Caro.
1969	8	North Caro.
1970	8	North Caro. St.
1971	8	South Caro.
1972	7	North Caro.
1973	7	North Caro. St.
1974	7	North Caro. St.
1975	7	North Caro.
1976	7	Virginia
1977	7	North Caro.
1978	7	Duke
1979	7	North Caro.
1980	8	Duke
1981	8	North Caro.
1982	8	North Caro.
1983	8	North Caro. St.
1984	8	Maryland
1985	8	Georgia Tech
1986	8	Duke
1987	8	North Caro. St.
1988	8	Duke
1989	8	North Caro.
1990	8	Georgia Tech
1991	7	North Caro.
1992	9	Duke
1993	9	Georgia Tech
1994	9	North Caro.
1995	9	Wake Forest
1996	9	Wake Forest

ATLANTIC 10 CONFERENCE

Season	No.	Regular Season
1977	8	Rutgers (Eastern)/West Va. (Western)/Penn St. (Western)
1978	8	Rutgers/Villanova
1979	8	Villanova
1980	8	Villanova/Duquesne/Rutgers
1981	8	Rhode Island/Duquesne
1982	8	West Va.
1983	10	Rutgers (Eastern)/St. Bonaventure (Western)/West Va. (Western)
1984	10	Temple
1985	10	West Va.
1986	10	St. Joseph's (Pa.)
1987	10	Temple
1988	10	Temple
1989	10	West Va.
1990	10	Temple
1991	10	Rutgers
1992	9	Massachusetts
1993	8	Massachusetts
1994	9	Massachusetts
1995	9	Massachusetts
1996	12	Massachusetts (East)/Geo. Washington (West)/Virginia Tech (West)

Season	No.	Conference Tournament
1977	8	Duquesne
1978	8	Villanova
1979	8	Rutgers
1980	8	Villanova
1981	8	Pittsburgh
1982	8	Pittsburgh
1983	10	West Va.
1984	10	West Va.
1985	10	Temple
1986	10	St. Joseph's (Pa.)
1987	10	Temple
1988	10	Temple
1989	10	Rutgers
1990	10	Temple
1991	10	Penn St.
1992	9	Massachusetts
1993	8	Massachusetts
1994	9	Massachusetts
1995	9	Massachusetts
1996	12	Massachusetts

BIG EAST CONFERENCE

Season	No.	Regular Season
1980	7	Syracuse/Georgetown/St. John's (N.Y.)
1981	8	Boston College
1982	8	Villanova
1983	9	Boston College/Villanova/St. John's (N.Y.)
1984	9	Georgetown
1985	9	St. John's (N.Y.)
1986	9	St. John's (N.Y.)/Syracuse
1987	9	Syracuse/Georgetown/Pittsburgh
1988	9	Pittsburgh
1989	9	Georgetown
1990	9	Connecticut/Syracuse
1991	9	Syracuse
1992	10	Seton Hall/Georgetown/St. John's (N.Y.)
1993	10	Seton Hall
1994	10	Connecticut
1995	10	Connecticut
1996	13	Georgetown (Big East 7)/Connecticut (Big East 6)

Season	No.	Conference Tournament
1980	7	Georgetown
1981	8	Syracuse
1982	8	Georgetown
1983	9	St. John's (N.Y.)
1984	9	Georgetown
1985	9	Georgetown
1986	9	St. John's (N.Y.)
1987	9	Georgetown
1988	9	Syracuse
1989	9	Georgetown
1990	9	Connecticut
1991	9	Seton Hall
1992	10	Syracuse
1993	10	Seton Hall
1994	10	Providence
1995	10	Villanova
1996	13	Connecticut

BIG EIGHT CONFERENCE

(Note: The Big Eight and Missouri Valley conferences share the same history from 1908-28.)

Season	No.	Regular Season
1908	6	Kansas
1909	6	Kansas
1910	6	Kansas
1911	5	Kansas
1912	6	Nebraska/Kansas
1913	6	Nebraska
1914	7	Kansas/Nebraska
1915	7	Kansas
1916	7	Nebraska
1917	7	Kansas St.
1918	7	Missouri
1919	8	Kansas St.
1920	8	Missouri
1921	9	Missouri
1922	9	Missouri/Kansas
1923	9	Kansas
1924	9	Kansas
1925	9	Kansas
1926	10	Kansas
1927	10	Kansas
1928	10	Oklahoma
1929	6	Oklahoma
1930	6	Missouri
1931	6	Kansas
1932	6	Kansas
1933	6	Kansas
1934	6	Kansas
1935	6	Iowa St.
1936	6	Kansas
1937	6	Kansas/Nebraska
1938	6	Kansas
1939	6	Missouri/Oklahoma
1940	6	Kansas/Missouri/Oklahoma
1941	6	Iowa St./Kansas
1942	6	Kansas/Oklahoma
1943	6	Kansas
1944	6	Iowa St./Oklahoma
1945	6	Iowa St.
1946	6	Kansas
1947	6	Oklahoma
1948	7	Kansas St.
1949	7	Nebraska/Oklahoma

Season	No.	Regular Season
1950	7	Kansas/Kansas St./Nebraska
1951	7	Kansas St.
1952	7	Kansas
1953	7	Kansas
1954	7	Kansas/Colorado
1955	7	Colorado
1956	7	Kansas St.
1957	7	Kansas
1958	7	Kansas St.
1959	8	Kansas St.
1960	8	Kansas/Kansas St.
1961	8	Kansas St.
1962	8	Colorado
1963	8	Colorado/Kansas St.
1964	8	Kansas St.
1965	8	Oklahoma St.
1966	8	Kansas
1967	8	Kansas
1968	8	Kansas St.
1969	8	Colorado
1970	8	Kansas St.
1971	8	Kansas
1972	8	Kansas St.
1973	8	Kansas St.
1974	8	Kansas
1975	8	Kansas
1976	8	Missouri
1977	8	Kansas St.
1978	8	Kansas
1979	8	Oklahoma
1980	8	Missouri
1981	8	Missouri
1982	8	Missouri
1983	8	Missouri
1984	8	Oklahoma
1985	8	Oklahoma
1986	8	Kansas
1987	8	Missouri
1988	8	Oklahoma
1989	8	Oklahoma
1990	8	Missouri
1991	8	Oklahoma St./Kansas
1992	8	Kansas
1993	8	Kansas
1994	8	Missouri
1995	8	Kansas
1996	8	Kansas

Season	No.	Conference Tournament
1977	8	Kansas St.
1978	8	Missouri
1979	8	Oklahoma
1980	8	Kansas St.
1981	8	Kansas
1982	8	Missouri
1983	8	Oklahoma St.
1984	8	Kansas
1985	8	Oklahoma
1986	8	Kansas
1987	8	Missouri
1988	8	Oklahoma
1989	8	Missouri
1990	8	Oklahoma
1991	8	Missouri
1992	8	Kansas
1993	8	Missouri
1994	8	Nebraska
1995	8	Oklahoma St.
1996	8	Iowa St.

BIG SKY CONFERENCE

Season	No.	Regular Season
1964	6	Montana St.
1965	6	Weber St.
1966	6	Weber St./Gonzaga
1967	6	Gonzaga/Montana St.
1968	6	Weber St.
1969	6	Weber St.
1970	6	Weber St.
1971	6	Weber St.
1972	8	Weber St.
1973	8	Weber St.
1974	8	Idaho St./Montana
1975	8	Montana
1976	8	Boise St./Weber St./Idaho St.
1977	8	Idaho St.
1978	8	Montana
1979	8	Weber St.
1980	8	Weber St.
1981	8	Idaho
1982	8	Weber St./Nevada
1983	8	Weber St./Nevada
1984	8	Weber St.
1985	8	Nevada
1986	8	Northern Ariz./Montana
1987	8	Montana St.
1988	9	Boise St.
1989	9	Boise St./Idaho
1990	9	Idaho
1991	9	Montana
1992	9	Montana
1993	8	Idaho
1994	8	Weber St./Idaho St.
1995	8	Montana/Weber St.
1996	8	Montana St.

Season	No.	Conference Tournament
1976	8	Boise St.
1977	8	Idaho St.
1978	8	Weber St.
1979	8	Weber St.
1980	8	Weber St.
1981	8	Idaho
1982	8	Idaho
1983	8	Weber St.
1984	8	Nevada
1985	8	Nevada
1986	7	Montana St.
1987	8	Idaho St.
1988	9	Boise St.
1989	9	Idaho
1990	9	Idaho
1991	9	Montana
1992	6	Montana
1993	6	Boise St.
1994	6	Boise St.
1995	6	Weber St.
1996	6	Montana St.

BIG SOUTH CONFERENCE

Season	No.	Regular Season
1986	8	Charleston So.
1987	8	Charleston So.
1988	7	Coastal Caro.
1989	7	Coastal Caro.
1990	7	Coastal Caro.
1991	8	Coastal Caro.
1992	8	Radford
1993	9	Towson St.
1994	10	Towson St.
1995	9	N.C.-Greensboro
1996	9	N.C.-Greensboro

Season	No.	Conference Tournament
1986	8	Charleston So.
1987	8	Charleston So.
1988	7	Winthrop
1989	7	N.C.-Asheville
1990	7	Coastal Caro.
1991	8	Coastal Caro.
1992	8	Campbell
1993	9	Coastal Caro.
1994	8	Liberty
1995	8	Charleston So.
1996	8	N.C.-Greensboro

BIG TEN CONFERENCE

Season	No.	Regular Season
1906	6	Minnesota
1907	5	Chicago/Minnesota/Wisconsin
1908	5	Chicago/Wisconsin
1909	8	Chicago
1910	8	Chicago
1911	8	Purdue/Minnesota
1912	8	Purdue/Wisconsin
1913	9	Wisconsin
1914	9	Wisconsin
1915	9	Illinois
1916	9	Wisconsin
1917	9	Minnesota/Illinois
1918	10	Wisconsin
1919	10	Minnesota
1920	10	Chicago
1921	10	Michigan/Wisconsin/Purdue
1922	10	Purdue
1923	10	Iowa/Wisconsin
1924	10	Wisconsin/Illinois/Chicago
1925	10	Ohio St.
1926	10	Purdue/Indiana/Michigan/Iowa
1927	10	Michigan
1928	10	Indiana/Purdue
1929	10	Wisconsin/Michigan
1930	10	Purdue
1931	10	Northwestern
1932	10	Purdue
1933	10	Northwestern/Ohio St.
1934	10	Purdue
1935	10	Purdue/Illinois/Wisconsin
1936	10	Indiana/Purdue
1937	10	Minnesota/Illinois
1938	10	Purdue
1939	10	Ohio St.
1940	10	Purdue
1941	10	Wisconsin
1942	10	Illinois
1943	10	Illinois
1944	10	Ohio St.
1945	10	Iowa
1946	10	Ohio St.
1947	9	Wisconsin
1948	9	Michigan
1949	9	Illinois
1950	9	Ohio St.
1951	10	Illinois
1952	10	Illinois
1953	10	Indiana
1954	10	Indiana
1955	10	Iowa
1956	10	Iowa
1957	10	Indiana/Michigan St.
1958	10	Indiana
1959	10	Michigan St.
1960	10	Ohio St.
1961	10	Ohio St.
1962	10	Ohio St.
1963	10	Ohio St./Illinois
1964	10	Michigan/Ohio St.
1965	10	Michigan
1966	10	Michigan
1967	10	Indiana/Michigan St.
1968	10	Ohio St./Iowa
1969	10	Purdue
1970	10	Iowa
1971	10	Ohio St.
1972	10	Minnesota
1973	10	Indiana
1974	10	Indiana/Michigan
1975	10	Indiana
1976	10	Indiana
1977	10	Michigan
1978	10	Michigan St.
1979	10	Michigan St./Purdue/Iowa
1980	10	Indiana
1981	10	Indiana
1982	10	Minnesota
1983	10	Indiana
1984	10	Illinois/Purdue
1985	10	Michigan
1986	10	Michigan
1987	10	Indiana/Purdue
1988	10	Purdue
1989	10	Indiana
1990	10	Michigan St.
1991	10	Ohio St./Indiana
1992	10	Ohio St.
1993	11	Indiana
1994	11	Purdue
1995	11	Purdue
1996	11	Purdue

BIG WEST CONFERENCE

Season	No.	Regular Season
1970	6	Long Beach St.
1971	6	Long Beach St.
1972	7	Long Beach St.
1973	7	Long Beach St.
1974	7	Long Beach St.
1975	6	Long Beach St.
1976	6	Long Beach St./Cal St. Fullerton
1977	7	Long Beach St./San Diego St.
1978	8	Fresno St./San Diego St.
1979	8	Pacific (Cal.)
1980	8	Utah St.
1981	8	Fresno St.
1982	8	Fresno St.
1983	9	UNLV
1984	10	UNLV
1985	10	UNLV

Season	No.	Regular Season
1986	10	UNLV
1987	10	UNLV
1988	10	UNLV
1989	10	UNLV
1990	10	UNLV
1991	10	UNLV
1992	10	UNLV
1993	10	New Mexico St.
1994	10	New Mexico St.
1995	10	Utah St.
1996	10	Long Beach St.

Season	No.	Conference Tournament
1976	4	San Diego St.
1977	7	Long Beach St.
1978	7	Cal St. Fullerton
1979	8	Pacific (Cal.)
1980	7	San Jose St.
1981	7	Fresno St.
1982	7	Fresno St.
1983	8	UNLV
1984	8	Fresno St.
1985	8	UNLV
1986	8	UNLV
1987	8	UNLV
1988	10	Utah St.
1989	10	UNLV
1990	10	UNLV
1991	8	UNLV
1992	8	New Mexico St.
1993	8	Long Beach St.
1994	10	New Mexico St.
1995	10	Long Beach St.
1996	6	San Jose St.

BORDER CONFERENCE

Season	No.	Regular Season
1932	5	Arizona
1933	6	Texas Tech
1934	6	Texas Tech
1935	6	Texas Tech
1936	7	Arizona
1937	7	New Mexico St.
1938	7	New Mexico St.
1939	7	New Mexico St.
1940	7	New Mexico St.
1941		DNP
1942	9	West Tex. A&M
1943	8	West Tex. A&M
1944	4	Northern Ariz.
1945	9	New Mexico
1946	9	Arizona
1947	9	Arizona
1948	9	Arizona
1949	9	Arizona
1950	9	Arizona
1951	9	Arizona
1952	8	New Mexico St./West Tex. A&M
1953	8	Arizona/Hardin-Simmons
1954	7	Texas Tech
1955	7	Texas Tech/West Tex. A&M
1956	7	Texas Tech
1957	6	UTEP
1958	6	Arizona St.
1959	6	Arizona St./New Mexico St./UTEP
1960	6	New Mexico St.
1961	6	Arizona St./New Mexico St.
1962	5	Arizona St.

COLONIAL ATHLETIC ASSOCIATION

Season	No.	Regular Season
1983	6	William & Mary
1984	6	Richmond
1985	8	Navy/Richmond
1986	8	Navy
1987	8	Navy
1988	8	Richmond
1989	8	Richmond
1990	8	James Madison
1991	8	James Madison
1992	8	Richmond/James Madison
1993	8	James Madison/Old Dominion
1994	8	James Madison/Old Dominion
1995	8	Old Dominion
1996	9	Va. Commonwealth

Season	No.	Conference Tournament
1983	6	James Madison
1984	6	Richmond
1985	8	Navy
1986	8	Navy
1987	8	Navy
1988	8	Richmond
1989	8	George Mason
1990	8	Richmond
1991	8	Richmond
1992	8	Old Dominion
1993	8	East Caro.
1994	8	James Madison
1995	8	Old Dominion
1996	9	Va. Commonwealth

CONFERENCE USA

Season	No.	Regular Season
1996	11	Tulane (Red)/Memphis (White)/Cincinnati (Blue)

Season	No.	Conference Tournament
1996	11	Cincinnati

EAST COAST CONFERENCE

Season	No.	Regular Season
1959	10	St. Joseph's (Pa.)
1960	10	St. Joseph's (Pa.)
1961	10	St. Joseph's (Pa.)
1962	10	St. Joseph's (Pa.)
1963	9	St. Joseph's (Pa.)
1964	8	Temple
1965	8	St. Joseph's (Pa.)
1966	10	St. Joseph's (Pa.)
1967	12	Temple
1968	11	La Salle
1969	12	Temple
1970	12	St. Joseph's (Pa.) (East)/Rider (West)/Lehigh (West)/Lafayette (West)
1971	13	St. Joseph's (Pa.) (East)/Lafayette (West)
1972	13	Temple (East)/Rider (West)
1973	13	St. Joseph's (Pa.) (East)/Lafayette (West)
1974	13	St. Joseph's (Pa.) (East)/La Salle (East)/Rider (West)
1975	12	American (East)/La Salle (East)/Lafayette (West)
1976	12	St. Joseph's (Pa.) (East)/Lafayette (West)
1977	12	Temple (East)/Hofstra (East)/Lafayette (West)
1978	12	La Salle (East)/Lafayette (West)
1979	12	Temple (East)/Bucknell (West)
1980	12	St. Joseph's (Pa.) (East)/Lafayette (West)
1981	12	American (East)/Lafayette (West)/Rider (West)
1982	12	Temple (East)/West Chester (East)
1983	10	American (East)/La Salle (East)/Hofstra (East)/Rider (West)
1984	9	Bucknell
1985	8	Bucknell
1986	8	Drexel
1987	8	Bucknell
1988	8	Lafayette
1989	8	Bucknell
1990	8	Towson St./Hofstra/Lehigh
1991	7	Towson St.
1992	7	Hofstra
1993		DNP
1994	6	Troy St.

Season	No.	Conference Tournament
1975	12	La Salle
1976	12	Hofstra
1977	12	Hofstra
1978	12	La Salle
1979	12	Temple
1980	12	La Salle
1981	12	St. Joseph's (Pa.)
1982	12	St. Joseph's (Pa.)
1983	10	La Salle
1984	9	Rider
1985	8	Lehigh
1986	8	Drexel
1987	8	Bucknell
1988	8	Lehigh
1989	8	Bucknell
1990	8	Towson St.

Season	No.	Conference Tournament
1991	7	Towson St.
1992	7	Towson St.
1993		DNP
1994	6	Hofstra

GREAT MIDWEST CONFERENCE

Season	No.	Regular Season
1992	6	DePaul/Cincinnati
1993	6	Cincinnati
1994	7	Marquette
1995	7	Memphis

Season	No.	Conference Tournament
1992	6	Cincinnati
1993	6	Cincinnati
1994	7	Cincinnati
1995	7	Cincinnati

GULF STAR CONFERENCE

Season	No.	Regular Season
1985	6	Southeast La.
1986	6	Sam Houston St.
1987	6	Stephen F. Austin

IVY GROUP

Season	No.	Regular Season
1902	5	Yale
1903	5	Yale
1904	6	Columbia
1905	5	Columbia
1906	6	Pennsylvania
1907	6	Yale
1908	5	Pennsylvania
1909-10		DNP
1911	5	Columbia
1912	6	Columbia
1913	5	Cornell
1914	6	Cornell/Columbia
1915	6	Yale
1916	6	Pennsylvania
1917	6	Yale
1918	6	Pennsylvania
1919	5	Pennsylvania
1920	6	Pennsylvania
1921	6	Pennsylvania
1922	6	Princeton
1923	6	Yale
1924	6	Cornell
1925	6	Princeton
1926	6	Columbia
1927	6	Dartmouth
1928	6	Pennsylvania
1929	6	Pennsylvania
1930	6	Columbia
1931	6	Columbia
1932	6	Princeton
1933	6	Yale
1934	7	Pennsylvania
1935	7	Pennsylvania
1936	7	Columbia
1937	7	Pennsylvania
1938	7	Dartmouth
1939	7	Dartmouth
1940	7	Dartmouth
1941	7	Dartmouth
1942	7	Dartmouth
1943	7	Dartmouth
1944	5	Dartmouth
1945	4	Pennsylvania
1946	5	Dartmouth
1947	7	Columbia
1948	7	Columbia
1949	7	Yale
1950	7	Princeton
1951	7	Columbia
1952	7	Princeton
1953	7	Pennsylvania
1954	8	Cornell
1955	8	Princeton
1956	8	Dartmouth
1957	8	Yale
1958	8	Dartmouth
1959	8	Dartmouth
1960	8	Princeton
1961	8	Princeton
1962	8	Yale
1963	8	Princeton
1964	8	Princeton

Season	No.	Regular Season
1965	8	Princeton
1966	8	Pennsylvania
1967	8	Princeton
1968	8	Columbia
1969	8	Princeton
1970	8	Pennsylvania
1971	8	Pennsylvania
1972	8	Pennsylvania
1973	8	Pennsylvania
1974	8	Pennsylvania
1975	8	Pennsylvania
1976	8	Princeton
1977	8	Princeton
1978	8	Pennsylvania
1979	8	Pennsylvania
1980	8	Pennsylvania
1981	8	Princeton
1982	8	Pennsylvania
1983	8	Princeton
1984	8	Princeton
1985	8	Pennsylvania
1986	8	Brown
1987	8	Pennsylvania
1988	8	Cornell
1989	8	Princeton
1990	8	Princeton
1991	8	Princeton
1992	8	Princeton
1993	8	Pennsylvania
1994	8	Pennsylvania
1995	8	Pennsylvania
1996	8	Princeton

METRO ATLANTIC ATHLETIC CONFERENCE

Season	No.	Regular Season
1982	6	St. Peter's
1983	6	Iona
1984	8	La Salle/St. Peter's/Iona
1985	8	Iona
1986	8	Fairfield
1987	8	St. Peter's
1988	8	La Salle
1989	8	La Salle
1990	12	Holy Cross (North)/La Salle (South)
1991	9	Siena
1992	9	Manhattan
1993	8	Manhattan
1994	8	Canisius
1995	8	Manhattan
1996	8	Fairfield/Iona

Season	No.	Conference Tournament
1982	6	Fordham
1983	6	Fordham
1984	8	Iona
1985	8	Iona
1986	8	Fairfield
1987	8	Fairfield
1988	8	La Salle
1989	8	La Salle
1990	12	La Salle
1991	9	St. Peter's
1992	9	La Salle
1993	8	Manhattan
1994	8	Loyola (Md.)
1995	8	St. Peter's
1996	8	Canisius

METROPOLITAN COLLEGIATE ATHLETIC CONFERENCE

Season	No.	Regular Season
1976	6	Tulane
1977	7	Louisville
1978	7	Florida St.
1979	7	Louisville
1980	7	Louisville
1981	7	Louisville
1982	7	Memphis
1983	7	Louisville
1984	8	Memphis/Louisville
1985	8	Memphis
1986	7	Louisville
1987	7	Louisville
1988	7	Louisville
1989	7	Florida St.
1990	8	Louisville

Season	No.	Regular Season
1991	8	Southern Miss.
1992	7	Tulane
1993	7	Louisville
1994	7	Louisville
1995	7	N.C.-Charlotte

Season	No.	Conference Tournament
1976	6	Cincinnati
1977	7	Cincinnati
1978	7	Louisville
1979	7	Virginia Tech
1980	7	Louisville
1981	7	Louisville
1982	7	Memphis
1983	7	Louisville
1984	8	Memphis
1985	8	Memphis
1986	7	Louisville
1987	7	Memphis
1988	7	Louisville
1989	5	Louisville
1990	8	Louisville
1991	8	Florida St.
1992	7	N.C.-Charlotte
1993	7	Louisville
1994	7	Louisville
1995	7	Louisville

METROPOLITAN NEW YORK CONFERENCE

Season	No.	Regular Season
1943	8	St. John's (N.Y.)
1944-45		DNP
1946	7	New York U./St. John's (N.Y.)
1947	7	St. John's (N.Y.)
1948	7	New York U.
1949	7	Manhattan/St. John's (N.Y.)
1950	7	CCNY
1951	7	St. John's (N.Y.)
1952	7	St. John's (N.Y.)
1953	7	Manhattan
1954	7	St. Francis (N.Y.)
1955	7	Manhattan
1956	7	St. Francis (N.Y.)
1957	7	New York U.
1958	7	St. John's (N.Y.)
1959	7	Manhattan
1960	7	New York U.
1961	7	St. John's (N.Y.)
1962	7	St. John's (N.Y.)
1963	7	Fordham

MID-AMERICAN ATHLETIC CONFERENCE

Season	No.	Regular Season
1947	5	Butler/Cincinnati
1948	6	Cincinnati
1949	6	Cincinnati
1950	6	Cincinnati
1951	5	Cincinnati
1952	7	Miami (Ohio)/Western Mich.
1953	7	Miami (Ohio)
1954	8	Toledo
1955	8	Miami (Ohio)
1956	7	Marshall
1957	7	Miami (Ohio)
1958	7	Miami (Ohio)
1959	7	Bowling Green
1960	7	Ohio
1961	7	Ohio
1962	7	Bowling Green
1963	7	Bowling Green
1964	7	Ohio
1965	7	Ohio
1966	7	Miami (Ohio)
1967	7	Toledo
1968	7	Bowling Green
1969	7	Miami (Ohio)
1970	6	Ohio
1971	6	Miami (Ohio)
1972	6	Ohio
1973	7	Miami (Ohio)
1974	7	Ohio
1975	8	Central Mich.
1976	10	Western Mich.
1977	10	Central Mich.
1978	10	Miami (Ohio)
1979	10	Toledo

Season	No.	Regular Season
1980	10	Toledo
1981	10	Ball St./Northern Ill./Toledo/Western Mich./Bowling Green
1982	10	Ball St.
1983	10	Bowling Green
1984	10	Miami (Ohio)
1985	10	Ohio
1986	10	Miami (Ohio)
1987	9	Central Mich.
1988	9	Eastern Mich.
1989	9	Ball St.
1990	9	Ball St.
1991	9	Eastern Mich.
1992	8	Miami (Ohio)
1993	10	Ball St./Miami (Ohio)
1994	10	Ohio
1995	10	Miami (Ohio)
1996	10	Eastern Mich.

Season	No.	Conference Tournament
1980	7	Toledo
1981	7	Ball St.
1982	7	Northern Ill.
1983	7	Ohio
1984	7	Miami (Ohio)
1985	7	Ohio
1986	7	Ball St.
1987	7	Central Mich.
1988	7	Eastern Mich.
1989	8	Ball St.
1990	8	Ball St.
1991	8	Eastern Mich.
1992	8	Miami (Ohio)
1993	10	Ball St.
1994	8	Ohio
1995	8	Ball St.
1996	8	Eastern Mich.

MID-CONTINENT CONFERENCE

Season	No.	Regular Season
1983	8	Western Ill.
1984	8	Ill.-Chicago
1985	8	Cleveland St.
1986	8	Cleveland St.
1987	8	Southwest Mo. St.
1988	8	Southwest Mo. St.
1989	8	Southwest Mo. St.
1990	7	Southwest Mo. St.
1991	9	Northern Ill.
1992	9	Wis.-Green Bay
1993	9	Cleveland St.
1994	10	Wis.-Green Bay
1995	10	Valparaiso
1996	10	Valparaiso

Season	No.	Conference Tournament
1984	8	Western Ill.
1985	8	Eastern Ill.
1986	8	Cleveland St.
1987	8	Southwest Mo. St.
1988		DNP
1989	7	Southwest Mo. St.
1990	7	Northern Iowa
1991	8	Wis.-Green Bay
1992	8	Eastern Ill.
1993	8	Wright St.
1994	8	Wis.-Green Bay
1995	8	Valparaiso
1996	8	Valparaiso

MID-EASTERN ATHLETIC CONFERENCE

Season	No.	Regular Season
1972	7	North Caro. A&T
1973	7	Md.-East. Shore
1974	7	Md.-East. Shore/Morgan St.
1975	7	North Caro. A&T
1976	7	North Caro. A&T/Morgan St.
1977	7	South Caro. St.
1978	7	North Caro. A&T
1979	7	North Caro. A&T
1980	7	Howard
1981	6	North Caro. A&T
1982	7	North Caro. A&T
1983	7	Howard
1984	6	North Caro. A&T
1985	7	North Caro. A&T
1986	8	North Caro. A&T
1987	8	Howard

Season	No.	Regular Season
1988	9	North Caro. A&T
1989	9	South Caro. St.
1990	9	Coppin St.
1991	9	Coppin St.
1992	9	North Caro. A&T/Howard
1993	9	Coppin St.
1994	9	Coppin St.
1995	9	Coppin St.
1996	10	Coppin St./South Caro. St.

Season	No.	Conference Tournament
1972	7	North Caro. A&T
1973	7	North Caro. A&T
1974	7	Md.-East. Shore
1975	7	North Caro. A&T
1976	7	North Caro. A&T
1977	7	Morgan St.
1978	7	North Caro. A&T
1979	7	North Caro. A&T
1980	7	Howard
1981	6	Howard
1982	7	North Caro. A&T
1983	7	North Caro. A&T
1984	6	North Caro. A&T
1985	6	North Caro. A&T
1986	6	North Caro. A&T
1987	7	North Caro. A&T
1988	7	North Caro. A&T
1989	8	South Caro. St.
1990	8	Coppin St.
1991	9	Florida A&M
1992	9	Howard
1993	9	Coppin St.
1994	9	North Caro. A&T
1995	9	North Caro. A&T
1996	8	South Caro. St.

MIDWESTERN COLLEGIATE CONFERENCE

Season	No.	Regular Season
1980	6	Loyola (Ill.)
1981	7	Xavier (Ohio)
1982	7	Evansville
1983	8	Loyola (Ill.)
1984	8	Oral Roberts
1985	8	Loyola (Ill.)
1986	7	Xavier (Ohio)
1987	7	Evansville/Loyola (Ill.)
1988	6	Xavier (Ohio)
1989	7	Evansville
1990	8	Xavier (Ohio)
1991	8	Xavier (Ohio)
1992	6	Evansville
1993	8	Evansville/Xavier (Ohio)
1994	6	Xavier (Ohio)
1995	11	Xavier (Ohio)
1996	9	Wis.-Green Bay

Season	No.	Conference Tournament
1980	6	Oral Roberts
1981	7	Oklahoma City
1982	7	Evansville
1983	8	Xavier (Ohio)
1984	8	Oral Roberts
1985	8	Loyola (Ill.)
1986	7	Xavier (Ohio)
1987	7	Xavier (Ohio)
1988	6	Xavier (Ohio)
1989	7	Evansville
1990	8	Dayton
1991	8	Xavier (Ohio)
1992	6	Evansville
1993	8	Evansville
1994	6	Detroit
1995	10	Wis.-Green Bay
1996	8	Northern Ill.

MISSOURI VALLEY CONFERENCE

(Note: The Big Eight and Missouri Valley conferences share the same history from 1908-28.)

Season	No.	Regular Season
1908	6	Kansas
1909	6	Kansas
1910	6	Kansas
1911	5	Kansas
1912	6	Nebraska/Kansas
1913	6	Nebraska
1914	7	Kansas/Nebraska
1915	7	Kansas

Season	No.	Regular Season
1916	7	Nebraska
1917	7	Kansas St.
1918	7	Missouri
1919	8	Kansas St.
1920	8	Missouri
1921	9	Missouri
1922	9	Missouri/Kansas
1923	9	Kansas
1924	9	Kansas
1925	9	Kansas
1926	10	Kansas
1927	10	Kansas
1928	10	Oklahoma
1929	5	Washington (Mo.)
1930	5	Creighton/Washington (Mo.)
1931	5	Creighton/Oklahoma St.
1932	5	Creighton
1933	6	Butler
1934	6	Butler
1935	7	Creighton/Drake
1936	7	Creighton/Oklahoma St./Drake
1937	7	Oklahoma St.
1938	7	Oklahoma St.
1939	8	Oklahoma St./Drake
1940	7	Oklahoma St.
1941	7	Creighton
1942	6	Oklahoma St./Creighton
1943	6	Creighton
1944	4	Oklahoma St.
1945	5	Oklahoma St.
1946	7	Oklahoma St.
1947	7	St. Louis
1948	6	Oklahoma St.
1949	6	Oklahoma St.
1950	7	Bradley
1951	8	Oklahoma St.
1952	8	St. Louis
1953	6	Oklahoma St.
1954	6	Oklahoma St.
1955	6	Tulsa/St. Louis
1956	7	Houston
1957	8	St. Louis
1958	8	Cincinnati
1959	8	Cincinnati
1960	8	Cincinnati
1961	7	Cincinnati
1962	7	Cincinnati
1963	7	Cincinnati
1964	7	Wichita St.
1965	8	Wichita St.
1966	8	Cincinnati
1967	8	Louisville
1968	9	Louisville
1969	9	Louisville
1970	9	Drake
1971	8	Drake
1972	8	Louisville
1973	10	Memphis
1974	9	Louisville
1975	8	Louisville
1976	7	Wichita St.
1977	7	Southern Ill./New Mexico St.
1978	9	Creighton
1979	9	Indiana St.
1980	9	Bradley
1981	9	Wichita St.
1982	10	Bradley
1983	10	Wichita St.
1984	9	Tulsa/Illinois St.
1985	9	Tulsa
1986	9	Bradley
1987	8	Tulsa
1988	8	Bradley
1989	8	Creighton
1990	8	Southern Ill.
1991	9	Creighton
1992	10	Southern Ill./Illinois St.
1993	10	Illinois St.
1994	10	Southern Ill./Tulsa
1995	11	Tulsa
1996	11	Bradley

Season	No.	Conference Tournament
1977	8	Southern Ill.
1978	9	Creighton
1979	8	Indiana St.
1980	8	Bradley
1981	8	Creighton
1982	8	Tulsa
1983	8	Illinois St.

Season	No.	Conference Tournament
1984	8	Tulsa
1985	8	Wichita St.
1986	8	Tulsa
1987	7	Wichita St.
1988	8	Bradley
1989	8	Creighton
1990	8	Illinois St.
1991	9	Creighton
1992	8	Southwest Mo. St.
1993	8	Southern Ill.
1994	8	Southern Ill.
1995	8	Southern Ill.
1996	8	Tulsa

MOUNTAIN STATES CONFERENCE

Season	No.	Regular Season
1938	7	Colorado/Utah
1939	7	Colorado
1940	7	Colorado
1941	7	Wyoming
1942	7	Colorado
1943	5	Wyoming
1944	7	Utah
1945	7	Utah
1946	7	Wyoming
1947	7	Wyoming
1948	6	Brigham Young
1949	6	Wyoming
1950	6	Brigham Young
1951	6	Brigham Young
1952	8	Wyoming
1953	8	Wyoming
1954	8	Colorado
1955	8	Utah
1956	8	Utah
1957	8	Brigham Young
1958	8	Wyoming
1959	8	Utah
1960	8	Utah
1961	8	Colorado St./Utah
1962	8	Utah

NEW ENGLAND CONFERENCE

Season	No.	Regular Season
1938	5	Rhode Island
1939	5	Rhode Island
1940	5	Rhode Island
1941	5	Rhode Island
1942	5	Rhode Island
1943	5	Rhode Island
1944	4	Rhode Island
1945		DNP
1946	5	Rhode Island

NEW JERSEY-NEW YORK 7 CONFERENCE

Season	No.	Regular Season
1977	7	Columbia/Seton Hall
1978	7	Rutgers/St. John's (N.Y.)
1979	7	Rutgers

NORTHEAST CONFERENCE

Season	No.	Regular Season
1982	11	Fairleigh Dickinson (North)/Robert Morris (South)
1983	10	LIU-Brooklyn (North)/Robert Morris (South)
1984	9	LIU-Brooklyn/Robert Morris
1985	8	Marist
1986	9	Fairleigh Dickinson
1987	9	Marist
1988	9	Fairleigh Dickinson/Marist
1989	9	Robert Morris
1990	9	Robert Morris
1991	9	St. Francis (Pa.)/Fairleigh Dickinson
1992	9	Robert Morris
1993	10	Rider
1994	10	Rider
1995	10	Rider
1996	10	Mt. St. Mary's (Md.)

Season	No.	Conference Tournament
1982	8	Robert Morris
1983	8	Robert Morris
1984	8	LIU-Brooklyn
1985	8	Fairleigh Dickinson

Season	No.	Conference Tournament
1986	8	Marist
1987	6	Marist
1988	6	Fairleigh Dickinson
1989	6	Robert Morris
1990	6	Robert Morris
1991	7	St. Francis (Pa.)
1992	9	Robert Morris
1993	10	Rider
1994	10	Rider
1995	10	Mt. St. Mary's (Md.)
1996	10	Monmouth (N.J.)

OHIO VALLEY CONFERENCE

Season	No.	Regular Season
1949	8	Western Ky.
1950	7	Western Ky.
1951	7	Murray St.
1952	7	Morehead St.
1953	6	Eastern Ky.
1954	6	Western Ky.
1955	6	Western Ky.
1956	6	Morehead St./Tennessee Tech/ Western Ky.
1957	6	Morehead St./Western Ky.
1958	7	Tennessee Tech
1959	7	Eastern Ky.
1960	7	Western Ky.
1961	7	Morehead St./Western Ky./ Eastern Ky.
1962	6	Western Ky.
1963	7	Tennessee Tech/Morehead St.
1964	8	Murray St.
1965	8	Eastern Ky.
1966	8	Western Ky.
1967	8	Western Ky.
1968	8	East Tenn. St./Murray St.
1969	8	Murray St./Morehead St.
1970	8	Western Ky.
1971	8	Western Ky.
1972	8	Eastern Ky./Morehead St./ Western Ky.
1973	8	Austin Peay
1974	8	Austin Peay/Morehead St.
1975	8	Middle Tenn. St.
1976	8	Western Ky.
1977	8	Austin Peay
1978	8	Middle Tenn. St./Eastern Ky.
1979	7	Eastern Ky.
1980	7	Western Ky./Murray St.
1981	8	Western Ky.
1982	8	Murray St./Western Ky.
1983	8	Murray St.
1984	8	Morehead St.
1985	8	Tennessee Tech
1986	8	Akron/Middle Tenn. St.
1987	8	Middle Tenn. St.
1988	8	Murray St.
1989	7	Middle Tenn. St./Murray St.
1990	7	Murray St.
1991	7	Murray St.
1992	8	Murray St.
1993	9	Tennessee St.
1994	9	Tennessee St.
1995	9	Murray St./Tennessee St.
1996	9	Murray St.

Season	No.	Conference Tournament
1949	8	Western Ky.
1950	7	Eastern Ky.
1951	7	Murray St.
1952	7	Western Ky.
1953	6	Western Ky.
1954	6	Western Ky.
1955	6	Eastern Ky.
1956-63		DNP
1964	8	Murray St.
1965	8	Western Ky.
1966	8	Western Ky.
1967	8	Tennessee Tech
1968-74		DNP
1975	4	Middle Tenn. St.
1976	8	Western Ky.
1977	4	Middle Tenn. St.
1978	4	Western Ky.
1979	4	Eastern Ky.
1980	4	Western Ky.
1981	4	Western Ky.
1982	4	Middle Tenn. St.
1983	4	Morehead St.

Season	No.	Conference Tournament
1984	4	Morehead St.
1985	7	Middle Tenn. St.
1986	7	Akron
1987	7	Austin Peay
1988	7	Murray St.
1989	7	Middle Tenn. St.
1990	7	Murray St.
1991	7	Murray St.
1992	7	Murray St.
1993	6	Tennessee St.
1994	7	Tennessee St.
1995	7	Murray St.
1996	7	Austin Peay

PACIFIC-10 CONFERENCE

Season	No.	Regular Season
1916	3	California/Oregon St.
1917	6	Washington St.
1918		DNP
1919	6	Oregon
1920	6	Stanford
1921	6	Stanford
1922	8	Idaho
1923	8	Idaho
1924	9	California
1925	8	California
1926	9	California
1927	9	California
1928	10	Southern Cal
1929	10	California
1930	9	Southern Cal
1931	9	Washington
1932	9	California
1933	9	Oregon St.
1934	9	Washington
1935	9	Southern Cal
1936	9	Stanford
1937	9	Stanford
1938	10	Stanford
1939	9	Oregon
1940	9	Southern Cal
1941	9	Washington St.
1942	9	Stanford
1943	9	Washington
1944	8	Washington (North)/ California (South)
1945	8	Oregon (North)/UCLA (South)
1946	9	California
1947	9	Oregon St.
1948	9	Washington
1949	9	Oregon St.
1950	9	UCLA
1951	9	Washington
1952	9	UCLA
1953	9	Washington
1954	9	Southern Cal
1955	9	Oregon St.
1956	9	UCLA
1957	9	California
1958	9	Oregon St./California
1959	9	California
1960	5	California
1961	5	Southern Cal
1962	5	UCLA
1963	5	UCLA/Stanford
1964	6	UCLA
1965	8	UCLA
1966	8	Oregon St.
1967	8	UCLA
1968	8	UCLA
1969	8	UCLA
1970	8	UCLA
1971	8	UCLA
1972	8	UCLA
1973	8	UCLA
1974	8	UCLA
1975	8	UCLA
1976	8	UCLA
1977	8	UCLA
1978	8	UCLA
1979	10	UCLA
1980	10	Oregon St.
1981	10	Oregon St.
1982	10	Oregon St.
1983	10	UCLA
1984	10	Washington/Oregon St.
1985	10	Washington/Southern Cal
1986	10	Arizona
1987	10	UCLA

Season	No.	Regular Season
1988	10	Arizona
1989	10	Arizona
1990	10	Oregon St./Arizona
1991	10	Arizona
1992	10	UCLA
1993	10	Arizona
1994	10	Arizona
1995	10	UCLA
1996	10	UCLA

Season	No.	Conference Tournament
1987	10	UCLA
1988	10	Arizona
1989	10	Arizona
1990	10	Arizona

PATRIOT LEAGUE

Season	No.	Regular Season
1990	7	Fordham
1991	7	Fordham
1992	8	Bucknell/Fordham
1993	8	Bucknell
1994	8	Navy/Fordham/Colgate/ Holy Cross
1995	8	Bucknell/Colgate
1996	7	Colgate/Navy

Season	No.	Conference Tournament
1990	7	Fordham
1991	7	Fordham
1992	8	Fordham
1993	8	Holy Cross
1994	8	Navy
1995	8	Colgate
1996	7	Colgate

ROCKY MOUNTAIN CONFERENCE

Season	No.	Regular Season
1922	6	Colorado Col.
1923	5	Colorado Col.
1924	6	Colorado Col.
1925	12	Colorado Col. (East)/ Brigham Young (West)
1926	12	Colorado St. (East)/Utah (West)
1927	12	Colorado Col. (East)/ Montana St. (West)
1928	12	Wyoming (East)/ Montana St. (West)
1929	12	Colorado (East)/ Montana St. (West)
1930	12	Colorado (East)/ Montana St. (West)/Utah St. (West)
1931	12	Wyoming (East)/Utah (West)
1932	12	Wyoming (East)/ Brigham Young (West)/Utah (West)
1933	12	Wyoming (East)/ Colorado St. (East)/Brigham Young (West)/ Utah (West)
1934	12	Wyoming (East)/ Brigham Young (West)
1935	12	Northern Colo. (East)/ Utah St. (West)
1936	12	Wyoming (East)/Utah (West)
1937	12	Denver (East)/Colorado (East)/ Montana St. (West)/Utah (West)
1938	5	Montana St.
1939	5	Northern Colo.
1940	5	Northern Colo.
1941	5	Northern Colo.
1942	5	Northern Colo.
1943	3	Northern Colo.
1944	3	Colorado Col.
1945	3	Colorado Col.
1946	5	Colorado St.
1947	5	Montana St.
1948	4	Colorado St.
1949	5	Colorado St.
1950	6	Montana St.
1951	6	Montana St.
1952	6	Colorado St./Montana St.
1953	6	Idaho St.
1954	6	Idaho St.
1955	6	Idaho St.
1956	6	Idaho St.
1957	6	Idaho St.
1958	6	Idaho St.
1959	6	Idaho St.
1960	6	Idaho St.

SOUTHEASTERN CONFERENCE

Season	No.	Regular Season
1933	13	Kentucky
1934	13	Alabama
1935	13	LSU/Kentucky
1936	13	Tennessee
1937	13	Kentucky
1938	13	Georgia Tech
1939	13	Kentucky
1940	13	Kentucky
1941	12	Tennessee
1942	12	Kentucky
1943	12	Tennessee
1944	6	Kentucky
1945	12	Kentucky
1946	12	Kentucky
1947	12	Kentucky
1948	12	Kentucky
1949	12	Kentucky
1950	12	Kentucky
1951	12	Kentucky
1952	12	Kentucky
1953	11	LSU
1954	12	Kentucky/LSU
1955	12	Kentucky
1956	12	Alabama
1957	12	Kentucky
1958	12	Kentucky
1959	12	Mississippi St.
1960	12	Auburn
1961	12	Mississippi St.
1962	12	Mississippi St./Kentucky
1963	12	Mississippi St.
1964	12	Kentucky
1965	11	Vanderbilt
1966	11	Kentucky
1967	10	Tennessee
1968	10	Kentucky
1969	10	Kentucky
1970	10	Kentucky
1971	10	Kentucky
1972	10	Tennessee/Kentucky
1973	10	Kentucky
1974	10	Vanderbilt/Alabama
1975	10	Kentucky/Alabama
1976	10	Alabama
1977	10	Kentucky/Tennessee
1978	10	Kentucky
1979	10	LSU
1980	10	Kentucky
1981	10	LSU
1982	10	Kentucky/Tennessee
1983	10	Kentucky
1984	10	Kentucky
1985	10	LSU
1986	10	Kentucky
1987	10	Alabama
1988	10	Kentucky*
1989	10	Florida
1990	10	Georgia
1991	10	Mississippi St./LSU
1992	12	Kentucky (Eastern)/Arkansas (Western)
1993	12	Vanderbilt (Eastern)/Arkansas (Western)
1994	12	Florida (Eastern)/Kentucky (Eastern)/Arkansas (Western)
1995	12	Kentucky (Eastern)/Arkansas (Western)/Mississippi St. (Western)
1996	12	Kentucky (Eastern)/Mississippi St. (Western)

Season	No.	Conference Tournament
1933	13	Kentucky
1934	10	Alabama
1935		DNP
1936	9	Tennessee
1937	8	Kentucky
1938	11	Georgia Tech
1939	12	Kentucky
1940	12	Kentucky
1941	12	Tennessee
1942	12	Kentucky
1943	11	Tennessee
1944	6	Kentucky
1945	11	Kentucky
1946	12	Kentucky
1947	12	Kentucky
1948	12	Kentucky
1949	12	Kentucky
1950	12	Kentucky
1951	12	Vanderbilt
1952	12	Kentucky
1953-78		DNP
1979	10	Tennessee
1980	10	LSU
1981	10	Mississippi
1982	10	Alabama
1983	10	Georgia
1984	10	Kentucky
1985	10	Auburn
1986	10	Kentucky
1987	10	Alabama
1988	10	Kentucky*
1989	10	Alabama
1990	9	Alabama
1991	9	Alabama
1992	11	Kentucky
1993	12	Kentucky
1994	12	Kentucky
1995	12	Kentucky
1996	12	Mississippi St.

*Later vacated.

SOUTHERN CONFERENCE

Season	No.	Regular Season
1922	13	Virginia
1923	19	North Caro.
1924	21	Tulane
1925	21	North Caro.
1926	22	Kentucky
1927	22	South Caro.
1928	22	Auburn
1929	23	Wash. & Lee
1930	23	Alabama
1931	22	Georgia
1932	23	Kentucky/Maryland
1933	10	South Caro.
1934	10	South Caro.
1935	10	North Caro.
1936	10	Wash. & Lee
1937	16	Wash. & Lee
1938	15	North Caro.
1939	15	Wake Forest
1940	15	Duke
1941	15	North Caro.
1942	16	Duke
1943	15	Duke
1944	12	North Caro.
1945	14	South Caro.
1946	16	North Caro.
1947	16	North Caro. St.
1948	16	North Caro. St.
1949	16	North Caro. St.
1950	16	North Caro. St.
1951	17	North Caro. St.
1952	17	West Va.
1953	17	North Caro. St.
1954	10	Geo. Washington
1955	10	West Va.
1956	10	Geo. Washington/West Va.
1957	10	West Va.
1958	10	West Va.
1959	9	West Va.
1960	9	Virginia Tech
1961	9	West Va.
1962	9	West Va.
1963	9	West Va.
1964	9	Davidson
1965	10	Davidson
1966	9	Davidson
1967	9	West Va.
1968	9	Davidson
1969	8	Davidson
1970	8	Davidson
1971	7	Davidson
1972	8	Davidson
1973	8	Davidson
1974	8	Furman
1975	8	Furman
1976	8	VMI
1977	10	Furman/VMI
1978	8	Appalachian St.
1979	9	Appalachian St.
1980	9	Furman
1981	9	Appalachian St./Davidson/Tenn.-Chatt.
1982	9	Tenn.-Chatt.
1983	9	Tenn.-Chatt.
1984	9	Marshall
1985	9	Tenn.-Chatt.
1986	9	Tenn.-Chatt.
1987	9	Marshall
1988	9	Marshall
1989	8	Tenn.-Chatt.
1990	8	East Tenn. St.
1991	8	East Tenn. St./Furman/Tenn.-Chatt.
1992	8	East Tenn. St./Tenn.-Chatt.
1993	10	Tenn.-Chatt.
1994	10	Tenn.-Chatt.
1995	10	Marshall (Northern)/Tenn.-Chatt. (Southern)
1996	10	Davidson (Northern)/Western Caro. (Southern)

Season	No.	Conference Tournament
1921		Kentucky
1922	23	North Caro.
1923	22	Mississippi St.
1924	16	North Caro.
1925	17	North Caro.
1926	16	North Caro.
1927	14	Vanderbilt
1928	16	Mississippi
1929	16	North Caro. St.
1930	16	Alabama
1931	16	Maryland
1932	16	Georgia
1933	8	South Caro.
1934	8	Wash. & Lee
1935	8	North Caro.
1936	8	Wash. & Lee
1937	8	Wash. & Lee
1938	8	Duke
1939	11	Clemson
1940	8	North Caro.
1941	8	Duke
1942	8	Duke
1943	8	Geo. Washington
1944	8	Duke
1945	8	North Caro.
1946	8	Duke
1947	8	North Caro. St.
1948	10	North Caro. St.
1949	8	North Caro. St.
1950	8	North Caro. St.
1951	8	North Caro. St.
1952	8	North Caro. St.
1953	8	Wake Forest
1954	8	Geo. Washington
1955	8	West Va.
1956	8	West Va.
1957	8	West Va.
1958	8	West Va.
1959	8	West Va.
1960	8	West Va.
1961	8	Geo. Washington
1962	8	West Va.
1963	8	West Va.
1964	8	VMI
1965	8	West Va.
1966	8	Davidson
1967	8	West Va.
1968	8	Davidson
1969	8	Davidson
1970	8	Davidson
1971	7	Furman
1972	8	East Caro.
1973	8	Furman
1974	8	Furman
1975	8	Furman
1976	8	VMI
1977	7	VMI
1978	8	Furman
1979	8	Appalachian St.
1980	8	Furman
1981	8	Tenn.-Chatt.
1982	8	Tenn.-Chatt.
1983	8	Tenn.-Chatt.
1984	8	Marshall
1985	8	Marshall
1986	8	Davidson
1987	8	Marshall
1988	8	Tenn.-Chatt.
1989	8	East Tenn. St.
1990	8	East Tenn. St.
1991	8	East Tenn. St.
1992	8	East Tenn. St.
1993	10	Tenn.-Chatt.

CONFERENCES

Season	No.	Conference Tournament
1994	10	Tenn.-Chatt.
1995	10	Tenn.-Chatt.
1996	9	Western Caro.

SOUTHLAND CONFERENCE

Season	No.	Regular Season
1964	5	Lamar
1965	5	Abilene Christian/Arkansas St.
1966	5	Abilene Christian
1967	5	Arkansas St.
1968	5	Abilene Christian
1969	5	Trinity (Tex.)
1970	5	Lamar
1971	5	Arkansas St.
1972	7	Louisiana Tech
1973	7	Louisiana Tech
1974	3	Arkansas St.
1975	5	McNeese St.
1976	6	Louisiana Tech
1977	6	Southwestern La.
1978	6	McNeese St./Lamar
1979	6	Lamar
1980	6	Lamar
1981	6	Lamar
1982	6	Southwestern La.
1983	7	Lamar
1984	7	Lamar
1985	7	Louisiana Tech
1986	7	Northeast La.
1987	6	Louisiana Tech
1988	8	North Texas
1989	8	North Texas
1990	8	Northeast La.
1991	8	Northeast La.
1992	10	Texas-San Antonio
1993	10	Northeast La.
1994	10	Northeast La.
1995	10	Nicholls St.
1996	10	Northeast La.

Season	No.	Conference Tournament
1981	6	Lamar
1982	5	Southwestern La.
1983	7	Lamar
1984	7	Louisiana Tech
1985	7	Louisiana Tech
1986	7	Northeast La.
1987	6	Louisiana Tech
1988	6	North Texas
1989	6	McNeese St.
1990	7	Northeast La.
1991	4	Northeast La.
1992	6	Northeast La.
1993	6	Northeast La.
1994	8	Southwest Tex. St.
1995	8	Nicholls St.
1996	6	Northeast La.

SOUTHWEST CONFERENCE

Season	No.	Regular Season
1915	5	Texas
1916	5	Texas
1917	3	Texas
1918	5	Rice
1919	5	Texas
1920	5	Texas A&M
1921	5	Texas A&M
1922	6	Texas A&M
1923	6	Texas A&M
1924	8	Texas
1925	8	Oklahoma St.
1926	7	Arkansas
1927	7	Arkansas
1928	7	Arkansas
1929	7	Arkansas
1930	7	Arkansas
1931	7	Texas Christian
1932	7	Baylor
1933	7	Texas
1934	7	Texas Christian
1935	7	Arkansas/Rice/Southern Methodist
1936	7	Arkansas
1937	7	Southern Methodist
1938	7	Arkansas
1939	7	Texas
1940	7	Rice
1941	7	Arkansas
1942	7	Rice/Arkansas

Season	No.	Regular Season
1943	7	Texas/Rice
1944	7	Arkansas/Rice
1945	7	Rice
1946	7	Baylor
1947	7	Texas
1948	7	Baylor
1949	7	Arkansas/Baylor/Rice
1950	7	Baylor/Arkansas
1951	7	Texas A&M/Texas Christian/Texas
1952	7	Texas Christian
1953	7	Texas Christian
1954	7	Rice/Texas
1955	7	Southern Methodist
1956	7	Southern Methodist
1957	7	Southern Methodist
1958	8	Arkansas/Southern Methodist
1959	8	Texas Christian
1960	8	Texas
1961	8	Texas Tech
1962	8	Southern Methodist/Texas
1963	8	Texas
1964	8	Texas A&M
1965	8	Southern Methodist/Texas
1966	8	Southern Methodist
1967	8	Southern Methodist
1968	8	Texas Christian
1969	8	Texas A&M
1970	8	Rice
1971	8	Texas Christian
1972	8	Texas/Southern Methodist
1973	8	Texas Tech
1974	8	Texas
1975	8	Texas A&M
1976	9	Texas A&M
1977	9	Arkansas
1978	9	Texas/Arkansas
1979	9	Texas/Arkansas
1980	9	Texas A&M
1981	9	Arkansas
1982	9	Arkansas
1983	9	Houston
1984	9	Houston
1985	9	Texas Tech
1986	9	Texas Christian/Texas/Texas A&M
1987	9	Texas Christian
1988	9	Southern Methodist
1989	9	Arkansas
1990	9	Arkansas
1991	9	Arkansas
1992	8	Houston/Texas
1993	8	Southern Methodist
1994	8	Texas
1995	8	Texas/Texas Tech
1996	8	Texas Tech

Season	No.	Conference Tournament
1976	9	Texas Tech
1977	9	Arkansas
1978	9	Houston
1979	9	Arkansas
1980	9	Texas A&M
1981	9	Houston
1982	9	Arkansas
1983	9	Houston
1984	9	Houston
1985	8	Texas Tech
1986	8	Texas Tech
1987	8	Texas A&M
1988	8	Southern Methodist
1989	8	Arkansas
1990	8	Arkansas
1991	9	Arkansas
1992	8	Houston
1993	8	Texas Tech
1994	8	Texas
1995	7	Texas
1996	8	Texas Tech

SOUTHWESTERN ATHLETIC CONFERENCE

Season	No.	Regular Season
1957	6	Texas Southern
1958	6	Texas Southern
1959	8	Grambling
1960	8	Grambling
1961	8	Prairie View
1962	7	Prairie View

Season	No.	Regular Season
1963	8	Grambling
1964	8	Grambling/Jackson St.
1965	8	Southern U.
1966	8	Alcorn St./Grambling
1967	8	Alcorn St./Arkansas AM&N/Grambling
1968	8	Alcorn St./Jackson St.
1969	8	Alcorn St.
1970	8	Jackson St.
1971	7	Grambling
1972	7	Grambling
1973	7	Alcorn St.
1974	7	Jackson St.
1975	7	Jackson St.
1976	7	Alcorn St.
1977	7	Texas Southern
1978	7	Jackson St./Southern U.
1979	7	Alcorn St.
1980	7	Alcorn St.
1981	7	Alcorn St./Southern U.
1982	7	Alcorn St./Jackson St.
1983	8	Texas Southern
1984	8	Alcorn St.
1985	8	Alcorn St.
1986	8	Alcorn St./Southern U.
1987	8	Grambling
1988	8	Southern U.
1989	8	Grambling/Southern U./Texas Southern
1990	8	Southern U.
1991	8	Jackson St.
1992	8	Mississippi Val./Texas Southern
1993	8	Jackson St.
1994	8	Texas Southern
1995	8	Texas Southern
1996	8	Jackson St./Mississippi Val.

Season	No.	Conference Tournament
1980	7	Alcorn St.
1981	7	Southern U.
1982	7	Alcorn St.
1983	7	Alcorn St.
1984	8	Alcorn St.
1985	4	Southern U.
1986	8	Mississippi Val.
1987	8	Southern U.
1988	8	Southern U.
1989	8	Southern U.
1990	8	Texas Southern
1991	8	Jackson St.
1992	8	Mississippi Val.
1993	8	Southern U.
1994	8	Texas Southern
1995	6	Texas Southern
1996	6	Mississippi Val.

SUN BELT CONFERENCE

Season	No.	Regular Season
1977	6	N.C.-Charlotte
1978	6	N.C.-Charlotte
1979	6	South Ala.
1980	8	South Ala.
1981	7	Va. Commonwealth/South Ala./UAB
1982	6	UAB
1983	8	Va. Commonwealth/Old Dominion
1984	8	Va. Commonwealth
1985	8	Va. Commonwealth
1986	8	Old Dominion
1987	8	Western Ky.
1988	8	N.C.-Charlotte
1989	8	South Ala.
1990	8	UAB
1991	8	South Ala.
1992	11	Louisiana Tech/Southwestern La.
1993	10	New Orleans
1994	10	Western Ky.
1995	10	Western Ky.
1996	10	Ark.-Little Rock/New Orleans

Season	No.	Conference Tournament
1977	6	N.C.-Charlotte
1978	6	New Orleans
1979	6	Jacksonville
1980	8	Va. Commonwealth
1981	7	Va. Commonwealth
1982	6	UAB
1983	8	UAB
1984	8	UAB
1985	8	Va. Commonwealth

Season	No.	Conference Tournament
1986	8	Jacksonville
1987	8	UAB
1988	8	N.C.-Charlotte
1989	8	South Ala.
1990	8	South Fla.
1991	8	South Ala.
1992	11	Southwestern La.
1993	9	Western Ky.
1994	10	Southwestern La.
1995	10	Western Ky.
1996	10	New Orleans

TRANS AMERICA ATHLETIC CONFERENCE

Season	No.	Regular Season
1979	8	Northeast La.
1980	7	Northeast La.
1981	9	Houston Baptist
1982	9	Ark.-Little Rock
1983	8	Ark.-Little Rock
1984	8	Houston Baptist
1985	8	Ga. Southern
1986	8	Ark.-Little Rock
1987	10	Ark.-Little Rock
1988	10	Ark.-Little Rock/Ga. Southern
1989	10	Ga. Southern
1990	9	Centenary (La.)
1991	8	Texas-San Antonio
1992	8	Ga. Southern
1993	7	Florida Int'l
1994	10	Charleston (S.C.)
1995	11	Charleston (S.C.)
1996	12	Charleston (S.C.) (East)/Samford (West)/Southeastern La. (West)

Season	No.	Conference Tournament
1979	6	Northeast La.
1980	7	Centenary (La.)
1981	9	Mercer
1982	7	Northeast La.
1983	8	Ga. Southern
1984	8	Houston Baptist
1985	8	Mercer
1986	8	Ark.-Little Rock
1987	8	Ga. Southern
1988	8	Texas-San Antonio
1989	8	Ark.-Little Rock
1990	8	Ark.-Little Rock
1991	8	Georgia St.
1992	8	Ga. Southern
1993		DNP
1994	8	Central Fla.
1995	8	Florida Int'l
1996	8	Central Fla.

WEST COAST CONFERENCE

Season	No.	Regular Season
1953	5	Santa Clara
1954	5	Santa Clara
1955	5	San Francisco
1956	8	San Francisco
1957	8	San Francisco
1958	7	San Francisco
1959	7	St. Mary's (Cal.)
1960	7	Santa Clara
1961	7	Loyola Marymount
1962	7	Pepperdine
1963	7	San Francisco
1964	7	San Francisco
1965	8	San Francisco
1966	8	Pacific (Cal.)
1967	8	Pacific (Cal.)
1968	8	Santa Clara
1969	8	Santa Clara
1970	8	Santa Clara
1971	8	Pacific (Cal.)
1972	8	San Francisco
1973	8	San Francisco
1974	8	San Francisco
1975	8	UNLV
1976	7	Pepperdine
1977	8	San Francisco
1978	8	San Francisco
1979	8	San Francisco
1980	9	San Francisco/St. Mary's (Cal.)
1981	8	San Francisco/Pepperdine
1982	8	Pepperdine
1983	7	Pepperdine
1984	7	San Diego
1985	7	Pepperdine

Season	No.	Regular Season
1986	8	Pepperdine
1987	8	San Diego
1988	8	Loyola Marymount
1989	8	St. Mary's (Cal.)
1990	8	Loyola Marymount
1991	8	Pepperdine
1992	8	Pepperdine
1993	8	Pepperdine
1994	8	Gonzaga
1995	8	Santa Clara
1996	8	Gonzaga/Santa Clara

Season	No.	Conference Tournament
1987	8	Santa Clara
1988	8	Loyola Marymount
1989	8	Loyola Marymount
1990		DNP
1991	8	Pepperdine
1992	8	Pepperdine
1993	8	Santa Clara
1994	8	Pepperdine
1995	8	Gonzaga
1996	8	Portland

WESTERN ATHLETIC CONFERENCE

Season	No.	Regular Season
1963	6	Arizona St.
1964	6	New Mexico/Arizona St.
1965	6	Brigham Young
1966	6	Utah
1967	6	Wyoming/Brigham Young
1968	6	New Mexico
1969	6	Brigham Young/Wyoming
1970	8	UTEP
1971	8	Brigham Young
1972	8	Brigham Young
1973	8	Arizona St.
1974	8	New Mexico
1975	8	Arizona St.
1976	8	Arizona
1977	8	Utah
1978	8	New Mexico
1979	7	Brigham Young
1980	8	Brigham Young
1981	9	Utah/Wyoming
1982	9	Wyoming
1983	9	UTEP/Utah
1984	9	UTEP
1985	9	UTEP
1986	9	Wyoming/UTEP/Utah
1987	9	UTEP
1988	9	Brigham Young
1989	9	Colorado St.
1990	9	Colorado St./Brigham Young
1991	9	Utah
1992	9	UTEP/Brigham Young
1993	10	Brigham Young/Utah
1994	10	New Mexico
1995	10	Utah
1996	10	Utah

Season	No.	Conference Tournament
1984	9	UTEP
1985	9	San Diego St.
1986	9	UTEP
1987	9	Wyoming
1988	9	Wyoming
1989	9	UTEP
1990	9	UTEP
1991	9	Brigham Young
1992	8	Brigham Young
1993	10	New Mexico
1994	10	Hawaii
1995	10	Utah
1996	10	New Mexico

WESTERN NEW YORK LITTLE THREE CONFERENCE

Season	No.	Regular Season
1947	3	Canisius
1948	3	Niagara
1949	3	Niagara
1950	3	Canisius/Niagara/St. Bonaventure
1951	3	St. Bonaventure
1952		DNP
1953	3	Niagara
1954	3	Niagara
1955	3	Niagara
1956	3	Canisius

Season	No.	Regular Season
1957	3	Canisius/St. Bonaventure
1958	3	St. Bonaventure

YANKEE CONFERENCE

Season	No.	Regular Season
1947	6	Vermont
1948	6	Connecticut
1949	6	Connecticut
1950	6	Rhode Island
1951	6	Connecticut
1952	6	Connecticut
1953	6	Connecticut
1954	6	Connecticut
1955	6	Connecticut
1956	6	Connecticut
1957	6	Connecticut
1958	6	Connecticut
1959	6	Connecticut
1960	6	Connecticut
1961	6	Rhode Island
1962	6	Massachusetts
1963	6	Connecticut
1964	6	Connecticut/Rhode Island
1965	6	Connecticut
1966	6	Connecticut/Rhode Island
1967	6	Connecticut
1968	6	Massachusetts/Rhode Island
1969	6	Massachusetts
1970	6	Connecticut/Massachusetts
1971	6	Massachusetts
1972	6	Rhode Island
1973	7	Massachusetts
1974	7	Massachusetts
1975	7	Massachusetts

INDEPENDENTS
(Best Record)

Season	No.	Regular Season
1946	30	Yale
1947	32	Duquesne
1948	40	Bradley
1949	34	Villanova
1950	36	Toledo
1951	37	Dayton
1952	42	Seton Hall
1953	42	Seattle
1954	39	Holy Cross/Seattle
1955	41	Marquette
1956	35	Temple
1957	32	Seattle
1958	29	Temple
1959	32	St. Bonaventure
1960	34	Providence
1961	35	Memphis
1962	34	Loyola (Ill.)
1963	47	Loyola (Ill.)
1964	51	UTEP
1965	45	Providence
1966	44	UTEP
1967	47	Boston College
1968	47	Houston
1969	47	Boston College
1970	52	Jacksonville
1971	55	Marquette
1972	59	Oral Roberts
1973	68	Providence
1974	73	Notre Dame
1975	79	Tex.-Pan American
1976	79	Rutgers
1977	73	UNLV
1978	70	DePaul
1979	68	Syracuse
1980	55	DePaul
1981	54	DePaul
1982	52	DePaul
1983	19	New Orleans
1984	19	DePaul
1985	22	Notre Dame
1986	17	Notre Dame
1987	18	DePaul
1988	18	Akron
1989	22	Akron
1990	19	Wright St.
1991	17	DePaul
1992	12	Penn St.
1993	14	Wis.-Milwaukee
1994	6	Southern Utah
1995	2	Notre Dame
1996	2	Oral Roberts

CONSECUTIVE REGULAR-SEASON WINNER

No.	Team	Conference	Seasons
13	UCLA	Pacific-10	1967-79
10	Connecticut	Yankee	1951-60
10	UNLV	Big West	1983-92
9	Kentucky	Southeastern	1944-52
8	Idaho St.	Rocky Mountain	1953-60
8	Long Beach St.	Big West	1970-77
7	Dartmouth	Ivy	1938-44
7	Rhode Island	New England	1938-44
6	Arizona	Border	1946-51
6	Cincinnati	Missouri Valley	1958-63
6	Davidson	Southern	1968-73
6	Kansas	Missouri Valley	1922-27
6	Kentucky	Southeastern	1968-73
6	Pennsylvania	Ivy	1970-75
6	Weber St.	Big Sky	1968-73

CONSECUTIVE CONFERENCE TOURNAMENT WINNER

No.	Team	Conference	Seasons
7	Kentucky	Southeastern	1944-50
7	North Caro. A&T	Mid-Eastern	1982-88
6	North Caro. St.	Southern	1947-52
6	West Va.	Southern	1955-60
5	Massachusetts	Atlantic 10	1992-96
4	Cincinnati	Great Midwest	1992-95
4	East Tenn. St.	Southern	1989-92
4	Kentucky	Southeastern	1992-95
4	Northeast La.	Southland	1990-93
4	Northeastern	America East	1984-87
3	23 tied		

Division I Conference Alignment History

AMERICA EAST CONFERENCE (1980-present)
ECAC North (1980-82)
ECAC North Atlantic (1983-89)
North Atlantic (1990-96)
America East (1997-present)

Boston U.	1980-present
Canisius	1980-89
Colgate	1980-90
Delaware	1992-present
Drexel	1992-present
Hartford	1986-present
Hofstra	1995-present
Holy Cross	1980-83
Maine	1980-present
New Hampshire	1980-present
Niagara	1980-89
Northeastern	1980-present
Rhode Island	1980
Siena	1985-89
Towson St.	1996-present
Vermont	1980-present

AMERICAN SOUTH CONFERENCE (1988-91)

Arkansas St.	1988-91
Central Fla.	1991
Lamar	1988-91
Louisiana Tech	1988-91
New Orleans	1988-91
Southwestern La.	1988-91
Tex.-Pan American	1988-91

AMERICAN WEST CONFERENCE (1995-96)

Cal Poly SLO	1995-96
Cal St. Northridge	1995-96
Cal St. Sacramento	1995-96
Southern Utah	1995-96

ATLANTIC COAST CONFERENCE (1954-present)

Clemson	1954-present
Duke	1954-present
Florida St.	1992-present
Georgia Tech	1980-present
Maryland	1954-present
North Caro.	1954-present
North Caro. St.	1954-present
South Caro.	1954-71
Virginia	1954-present
Wake Forest	1954-present

ATLANTIC 10 CONFERENCE (1977-present)
Eastern Collegiate Basketball League (1977-78)
Eastern AA (1979-82)
Eastern 8
Atlantic 10 (1983-present)

Dayton	1996-present
Duquesne	1977-92, 94-present
Fordham	1996-present
Geo. Washington	1977-present
La Salle	1996-present
Massachusetts	1977-present
Penn St.	1977-79, 83-91
Pittsburgh	1977-82
Rhode Island	1981-present
Rutgers	1977-95
St. Bonaventure	1980-present
St. Joseph's (Pa.)	1983-present
Temple	1983-present
Villanova	1977-80
Virginia Tech	1996-present
West Va.	1977-95
Xavier (Ohio)	1996-present

BIG EAST CONFERENCE (1980-present)

Boston College	1980-present
Connecticut	1980-present
Georgetown	1980-present
Miami (Fla.)	1992-present
Notre Dame	1996-present
Pittsburgh	1983-present
Providence	1980-present
Rutgers	1996-present
St. John's (N.Y.)	1980-present
Seton Hall	1980-present
Syracuse	1980-present
Villanova	1980-present
West Va.	1996-present

BIG EIGHT CONFERENCE (1908-96)
Missouri Valley (1908-28)
Big Six (1929-47)
Big Seven (1948-58)
Big Eight (1959-96)

Colorado	1948-96
Drake	1908-28
Grinnell	1919-28
Iowa St.	1908-96
Kansas	1908-96
Kansas St.	1914-96
Missouri	1908-96
Nebraska	1908-19, 21-96
Oklahoma	1920-96
Oklahoma St.	1926-28, 59-96
Washington (Mo.)	1908-10, 12-28

BIG SKY CONFERENCE (1964-present)

Boise St.	1971-96
Cal St. Northridge	1997-present
Cal St. Sacramento	1997-present
Eastern Wash.	1988-present
Gonzaga	1964-79
Idaho	1964-96
Idaho St.	1964-present
Montana	1964-present
Montana St.	1964-present
Nevada	1980-92
Northern Ariz.	1971-present
Weber St.	1964-present

BIG SOUTH CONFERENCE (1986-present)

Armstrong Atlantic	1986-87
Augusta St.	1986-91
Campbell	1986-94
Charleston So.	1986-present
Coastal Caro.	1986-present
Davidson	1991-92
Liberty	1992-present
Md.-Balt. County	1993-present
N.C.-Asheville	1986-present
N.C.-Greensboro	1993-present
Radford	1986-present
Towson St.	1993-95
Winthrop	1986-present

BIG TEN CONFERENCE (1895-present)
Intercollegiate Conference of Faculty Representatives
Western Intercollegiate
Big Nine (1947-48)
Big Ten (1912-46, 49-present)

Chicago	1895-46
Illinois	1895-present
Indiana	1899-present
Iowa	1899-present
Michigan	1895-present
Michigan St.	1949-present
Minnesota	1895-present
Northwestern	1895-present
Ohio St.	1912-present
Penn St.	1993-present
Purdue	1895-present
Wisconsin	1895-present

BIG TWELVE CONFERENCE (1997-present)

Baylor	1997-present
Colorado	1997-present
Iowa St.	1997-present
Kansas	1997-present
Kansas St.	1997-present
Missouri	1997-present
Nebraska	1997-present
Oklahoma	1997-present
Oklahoma St.	1997-present
Texas	1997-present
Texas A&M	1997-present
Texas Tech	1997-present

BIG WEST CONFERENCE (1970-present)
Pacific Coast (1970-88)
Big West (1989-present)

Boise St.	1997-present
UC Irvine	1978-present
UC Santa Barb.	1970-74, 77-present
Cal Poly SLO	1997-present
Cal St. Fullerton	1975-present
Cal St. Los Angeles	1970-74
Fresno St.	1970-92
Idaho	1997-present
Long Beach St.	1970-present
Nevada	1993-present
UNLV	1983-96
New Mexico St.	1984-present
North Texas	1997-present
Pacific (Cal.)	1972-present
San Diego St.	1970-78
San Jose St.	1970-96
Utah St.	1979-present

BORDER CONFERENCE (1932-40, 42-62)

Arizona	1932-40, 42-61
Arizona St.	1932-40, 42-43, 44-62
Hardin-Simmons	1942-43, 45-62
New Mexico	1932-40, 42, 45-51
New Mexico St.	1932-40, 42-62
Northern Ariz.	1932-40, 42-53
Texas Tech	1933-40, 42-56
UTEP	1936-40, 42-43, 44-62
West Texas	1942-43, 45-62

COLONIAL ATHLETIC ASSOCIATION (1983-present)

American	1985-present
East Caro.	1983-present
George Mason	1983-present
James Madison	1983-present
Navy	1983-91
N.C.-Wilmington	1985-present
Old Dominion	1992-present
Richmond	1983-present
Va. Commonwealth	1996-present
William & Mary	1983-present

CONFERENCE USA (1996-present)

UAB	1996-present
Cincinnati	1996-present
DePaul	1996-present
Houston	1997-present
Louisville	1996-present
Marquette	1996-present
Memphis	1996-present
N.C.-Charlotte	1996-present
St. Louis	1996-present
South Fla.	1996-present
Southern Miss.	1996-present
Tulane	1996-present

EAST COAST CONFERENCE (1959-92, 94)
Middle Atlantic (1959-74)
East Coast (1975-92, 94)

American	1967-84
Brooklyn	1992
Bucknell	1959-90
Buffalo	1992, 94
Central Conn. St.	1991-92, 94
Chicago St.	1994
Delaware	1959-91
Drexel	1959-91
Gettysburg	1959-74
Hofstra	1966-92, 94
Lafayette	1959-90
La Salle	1959-83
Lehigh	1959-90
Md.-Balt. County	1991-92
Muhlenberg	1959-64
Northeastern Ill.	1994
Rider	1967-92
Rutgers	1959-62
St. Joseph's (Pa.)	1959-82
Temple	1959-82
Towson St.	1983-92
Troy St.	1994
West Chester	1966-67, 69-74

GREAT MIDWEST CONFERENCE (1992-95)

UAB	1992-95
Cincinnati	1992-95
Dayton	1994-95
DePaul	1992-95
Marquette	1992-95
Memphis	1992-95
St. Louis	1992-95

GULF STAR CONFERENCE (1985-87)

Nicholls St.	1985-87
Northwestern St.	1985-87
Sam Houston St.	1985-87
Southeastern La.	1985-87
Southwest Texas	1985-87
Stephen F. Austin	1985-87

IVY GROUP (1902-08, 11-18, 20-present)
Eastern Intercollegiate League

Brown	1954-present
Columbia	1902-08, 11-18, 20-present
Cornell	1902-08, 11-18, 20-present
Dartmouth	1912-18, 20-present
Harvard	1902-04, 06-07, 34-present
Pennsylvania	1904-08, 11-18, 20-present
Princeton	1902-08, 11-18, 20-present
Yale	1902-08, 11-18, 20-present

METRO ATLANTIC ATHLETIC CONFERENCE (1982-present)

Army	1982-90
Canisius	1990-present
Fairfield	1982-present
Fordham	1982-90
Holy Cross	1984-90
Iona	1982-present
La Salle	1984-92
Loyola (Md.)	1990-present
Manhattan	1982-present
Niagara	1990-present
St. Peter's	1982-present
Siena	1990-present

METROPOLITAN COLLEGIATE ATHLETIC CONFERENCE (1976-95)

Cincinnati	1976-91
Florida St.	1977-91
Georgia Tech	1976-78
Louisville	1976-95
Memphis	1976-91
N.C.-Charlotte	1992-95
St. Louis	1976-82
South Caro.	1984-91
South Fla.	1992-95
Southern Miss.	1983-95
Tulane	1976-85, 90-95
Va. Commonwealth	1992-95
Virginia Tech	1979-95

METROPOLITAN COLLEGIATE CONFERENCE (1966-69)

Fairleigh Dickinson	1966-69
Hofstra	1966-69
Iona	1966-69
LIU-Brooklyn	1966-69
Manhattan	1966-69
New York U.	1966-67
St. Peter's	1966-69
St. Francis (N.Y.)	1966-68
Seton Hall	1966-69
Wagner	1966-69

METROPOLITAN NEW YORK CONFERENCE (1943, 46-63)

CCNY	1943, 46-63
Brooklyn	1943, 46-63
Fordham	1943, 46-63
Hofstra	1943
Manhattan	1943, 46-63
New York U.	1943, 46-63
St. Francis (N.Y.)	1943, 46-63
St. John's (N.Y.)	1943, 46-63

MID-AMERICAN ATHLETIC CONFERENCE (1947-present)

Akron	1993-present
Ball St.	1976-present
Bowling Green	1954-present
Butler	1947-50
Central Mich.	1973-present
Cincinnati	1947-53
Eastern Mich.	1975-present
Kent	1952-present
Marshall	1954-69
Miami (Ohio)	1948-present
Northern Ill.	1976-86
Ohio	1947-present
Toledo	1952-present
Wayne St. (Mich.)	1947
Western Mich.	1948-present
Case Reserve	1947-55

MID-CONTINENT CONFERENCE (1983-present)

Akron	1991-92
Buffalo	1995-present
Central Conn. St.	1995-present
Chicago St.	1995-present
Cleveland St.	1983-94
Eastern Ill.	1983-96
Ill.-Chicago	1983-94
Mo.-Kansas City	1995-present
Northeastern Ill.	1995-present
Northern Ill.	1991-94
Northern Iowa	1983-91
Southwest Mo. St.	1983-90
Troy St.	1995-present
Valparaiso	1983-present
Western Ill.	1983-present
Wis.-Green Bay	1983-94
Wis.-Milwaukee	1994
Wright St.	1992-94
Youngstown St.	1993-present

MID-EASTERN ATHLETIC CONFERENCE (1972-present)

Bethune-Cookman	1981-present
Coppin St.	1986-present
Delaware St.	1972-87, 89-present
Florida A&M	1981-83, 88-present
Hampton	1996-present
Howard	1972-present
Md.-East. Shore	1972-79, 83-present
Morgan St.	1972-80, 85-present
North Caro. A&T	1972-present
North Caro. Central	1972-80
South Caro. St.	1972-present

MIDWESTERN COLLEGIATE CONFERENCE (1980-present)

Butler	1980-present
Cleveland St.	1995-present
Dayton	1989-93
Detroit	1981-present
Duquesne	1993
Evansville	1980-94
La Salle	1993-95
Loyola (Ill.)	1980-present
Marquette	1990-91
Northern Ill.	1995-present
Oklahoma City	1980-85
Oral Roberts	1980-87
St. Louis	1983-91
Wis.-Green Bay	1995-present
Wis.-Milwaukee	1995-present
Wright St.	1995-present
Xavier (Ohio)	1980-95

MISSOURI VALLEY CONFERENCE (1908-present)

Bradley	1949-51, 56-present
Butler	1933-34
Cincinnati	1958-70
Creighton	1928-43, 46-48, 78-present
Detroit	1950-57
Drake	1908-51, 57-present
Grinnell	1919-39
Houston	1951-60
Illinois St.	1982-present
Indiana St.	1978-present
Iowa St.	1908-28
Kansas	1908-28
Kansas St.	1914-28
Louisville	1965-75
Memphis	1968-73
Missouri	1908-28
Nebraska	1908-19, 21-28
New Mexico St.	1973-83
Northern Iowa	1992-present
North Texas	1958-75
Oklahoma	1920-28
Oklahoma St.	1926-57
St. Louis	1938-43, 45-74
Southern Ill.	1976-present
Southwest Mo. St.	1991-present
Tulsa	1935-96
Washburn	1935-41
Washington (Mo.)	1908-10, 12-47
West Tex. A&M	1973-86
Wichita St.	1946-present

MOUNTAIN STATES CONFERENCE (1911-43, 46-62)

Rocky Mountain (1911-37)
Big Seven (1938-43, 46-47)
Skyline Six (1948-51)
Skyline Eight (1952-62)
Mountain States (1938-43, 46-62)

Brigham Young	1924-42, 46-62
Colorado	1911-42, 46-47
Colorado Col.	1911-37
Colorado Mines	1911-37
Colorado St.	1911-22, 24-42, 46-62
Denver	1911-42, 46-62
Montana	1952-62
Montana St.	1925-37
New Mexico	1952-62
Northern Colo.	1925-37
Utah	1924-42, 46-62
Utah St.	1924-42, 46-62
Western St.	1925-37
Wyoming	1923-43, 46-62

NEW JERSEY-NEW YORK 7 CONFERENCE (1977-79)

Columbia	1977-79
Fordham	1977-79
Manhattan	1977-79
Princeton	1977-79
Rutgers	1977-79
St. John's (N.Y.)	1977-79
Seton Hall	1977-79

NORTHEAST CONFERENCE (1982-present)

ECAC Metro (1982-88)
Northeast (1989-present)

Baltimore	1982-83
Fairleigh Dickinson	1982-present
LIU-Brooklyn	1982-present
Loyola (Md.)	1982-89
Marist	1982-present
Monmouth (N.J.)	1986-present
Mt. St. Mary's (Md.)	1990-present
Rider	1993-present
Robert Morris	1982-present
St. Francis (N.Y.)	1982-present
St. Francis (Pa.)	1982-present
Siena	1982-84
Towson St.	1982
Wagner	1982-present

OHIO VALLEY CONFERENCE (1949-present)

Akron	1981-87
Austin Peay	1964-present
Eastern Ill.	1997-present
Eastern Ky.	1949-present
East Tenn. St.	1958-78
Evansville	1949-52
Louisville	1949
Marshall	1949-52
Middle Tenn.	1953-present
Morehead St.	1949-present
Murray St.	1949-present
Southeast Mo. St.	1992-present
Tenn.-Martin	1993-present
Tennessee St.	1988-present
Tennessee Tech	1949-present
Western Ky.	1949-82
Youngstown St.	1982-88

PACIFIC-10 CONFERENCE (1916-17, 19-present)

Pacific Coast (1916-59)
Big Five (1960-62)
Big Six (1963)
**Athletic Association of Western Universities—
   AAWU (1963-68)**
Pacific 8 (1969-78)
Pacific-10 (1979-present)

Arizona	1979-present
Arizona St.	1979-present
California	1916-17, 19-present
Idaho	1922-59

Montana	1924-29
Oregon	1917, 19-59, 65-present
Oregon St.	1916-17, 19-59, 65-present
Southern Cal	1922-24, 26-present
Stanford	1917, 19-43, 46-present
UCLA	1928-present
Washington	1916-17, 19-present
Washington St.	1917, 19-59, 64-present

PATRIOT LEAGUE (1991-present)

Army	1991-present
Bucknell	1991-present
Colgate	1991-present
Fordham	1991-95
Holy Cross	1991-present
Lafayette	1991-present
Lehigh	1991-present
Navy	1992-present

SOUTHEASTERN CONFERENCE (1933-present)

Alabama	1933-43, 45-present
Arkansas	1992-present
Auburn	1933-43, 45-present
Florida	1933-43, 45-present
Georgia	1933-present
Georgia Tech	1933-64
Kentucky	1933-52, 54-present
LSU	1933-present
Mississippi	1933-43, 45-present
Mississippi St.	1933-43, 45-present
Sewanee	1933-40
South Caro.	1992-present
Tennessee	1933-43, 45-present
Tulane	1933-66
Vanderbilt	1933-present

SOUTHERN CONFERENCE (1922-present)

**Southern Intercollegiate Athletic Association—
   SIAA (1895-1921)**

Appalachian St.	1973-present
Alabama	1922-32
Auburn	1922-32
Citadel	1937-present
Clemson	1922-53
Davidson	1937-88, 93-present
Duke	1929-53
East Caro.	1966-77
East Tenn. St.	1979-present
Florida	1923-32
Furman	1937-42, 45-present
Geo. Washington	1942-43, 46-70
Georgia	1922-32
Ga. Southern	1993-present
Ga. Tech	1922-32
Kentucky	1922-32
LSU	1923-32
Marshall	1977-present
Maryland	1924-53
Mississippi	1923-32
Mississippi St.	1922-30, 32
North Caro.	1922-53
North Caro. St.	1922-53
Richmond	1937-76
South Caro.	1923-53
Sewanee	1924-32
Tennessee	1922-32
Tenn.-Chatt.	1977-present
Tulane	1923-32
Vanderbilt	1923-32
Virginia	1922-37
VMI	1926-present
Virginia Tech	1922-65
Wake Forest	1937-43, 45-53
Wash. & Lee	1922-43, 46-58
West Va.	1951-68
Western Caro.	1977-present
William & Mary	1937-77

SOUTHLAND CONFERENCE (1964-present)

Abilene Christian	1964-73
Arkansas St.	1964-87
Lamar	1964-87

Louisiana Tech	1972-87
McNeese St.	1973-present
Nicholls St.	1992-present
North Texas	1983-96
Northeast La.	1983-present
Northwestern St.	1988-present
Sam Houston St.	1988-present
Southwest Tex. St.	1988-present
Southwestern La.	1972-82
Stephen F. Austin	1988-present
Texas-Arlington	1964-86, 88-present
Texas-San Antonio	1992-present
Trinity (Tex.)	1964-72

SOUTHWEST CONFERENCE (1915-96)

Arkansas	1924-91
Baylor	1915-96
Houston	1976-96
Oklahoma St.	1918, 22-25
Phillips	1920
Rice	1915-16, 18-96
Southern Methodist	1919-96
Southwestern (Tex.)	1915-16
Texas	1915-96
Texas A&M	1915-96
Texas Christian	1924-96
Texas Tech	1958-96

SOUTHWESTERN ATHLETIC CONFERENCE (1978-present)

Alabama St.	1983-present
Alcorn St.	1978-present
Grambling	1978-present
Jackson St.	1978-present
Mississippi Val.	1978-present
Prairie View	1978-present
Southern U.	1978-present
Texas Southern	1978-present

SUN BELT CONFERENCE (1977-present)

UAB	1980-91
Ark.-Little Rock	1992-present
Arkansas St.	1992-present
Central Fla.	1992
Georgia St.	1977-81
Jacksonville	1977-present
Lamar	1992-present
Louisiana Tech	1992-present
New Orleans	1977-80, 92-present
N.C.-Charlotte	1977-91
Old Dominion	1983-91
South Ala.	1977-present
South Fla.	1977-91
Southwestern La.	1992-present
Tex.-Pan American	1992-present
Va. Commonwealth	1980-91
Western Ky.	1983-present

TRANS AMERICA ATHLETIC CONFERENCE (1979-present)

Ark.-Little Rock	1981-91
Campbell	1995-present
Centenary (La.)	1979-present
Central Fla.	1993-present
Charleston (S.C.)	1993-present
Fla. Atlantic	1994-present
Florida Int'l	1992-present
Georgia Southern	1981-92
Georgia St.	1985-present
Hardin-Simmons	1979-89
Houston Bapt.	1979-89
Jacksonville St.	1996-present
Mercer	1979-present
Nicholls St.	1983-84
Northeast La.	1979-82
Northwestern St.	1981-84
Oklahoma City	1979
Samford	1979-present
Southeastern La.	1992-present
Stetson	1987-present
Tex.-Pan American	1979-80

WEST COAST CONFERENCE
(1953-present)

UC Santa Barb.	1965-69
Fresno St.	1956-57
Gonzaga	1980-present
Loyola Marymount	1956-present
Nevada	1970-79
UNLV	1970-75
Pacific (Cal.)	1953-71
Pepperdine	1956-present
Portland	1977-present
St. Mary's (Cal.)	1953-present
San Diego	1980-present
San Francisco	1953-82, 86-present
San Jose St.	1953-69
Santa Clara	1953-present
Seattle	1972-80

WESTERN ATHLETIC CONFERENCE
(1963-present)

Air Force	1981-present
Arizona	1963-78
Arizona St.	1963-78
Brigham Young	1963-present
Colorado St.	1970-present
Fresno St.	1993-present
Hawaii	1980-present
UNLV	1997-present
New Mexico	1963-present
Rice	1997-present
San Diego St.	1979-present
San Jose St.	1997-present
Southern Methodist	1997-present
Texas Christian	1997-present
Tulsa	1997-present
UTEP	1970-present
Utah	1963-present
Wyoming	1963-present

WESTERN NEW YORK LITTLE THREE CONFERENCE
(1947-51, 53-58)

Canisius	1947-51, 53-58
Niagara	1947-51, 53-58
St. Bonaventure	1947-51, 53-58

YANKEE CONFERENCE
(1938-43, 46-76)

Boston U.	1973-76
Connecticut	1938-43, 46-76
Maine	1938-43, 46-76
Massachusetts	1947-76
New Hampshire	1938-43, 46-76
Northeastern	1938-43, 46
Rhode Island	1938-43, 46-76
Vermont	1947-76

1996 Division II Conference Standings

#Won conference tournament.

CALIFORNIA COLLEGIATE ATHLETIC ASSOCIATION

	Conference			Full Season		
Team	W	L	Pct.	W	L	Pct.
Cal St. Bakersfield	10	2	.833	26	4	.867
Grand Canyon	8	4	.667	23	6	.793
UC Riverside	7	5	.583	18	9	.667
Cal Poly Pomona	7	5	.583	17	10	.630
Cal St. Dom. Hills	5	7	.417	17	10	.630
Cal St. San B'dino	4	8	.333	15	12	.556
Cal St. Los Angeles	1	11	.083	9	18	.333

CAROLINAS INTERCOLLEGIATE ATHLETIC CONFERENCE

	Conference			Full Season		
Team	W	L	Pct.	W	L	Pct.
High Point	16	2	.889	24	7	.774
Queens (N.C.)#	14	4	.778	25	6	.806
Pfeiffer	14	4	.778	20	8	.714
Coker	11	7	.611	16	10	.615
Mount Olive	8	10	.444	16	12	.571
Barton	7	11	.389	13	14	.481
Lees-McRae	7	11	.389	13	15	.464
Longwood	7	11	.389	11	17	.393
Erskine	6	12	.333	11	17	.393
Belmont Abbey	5	13	.278	9	18	.333
St. Andrews	4	14	.222	6	21	.222

CENTRAL INTERCOLLEGIATE ATHLETIC ASSOCIATION

	Conference			Full Season		
Northern Division	W	L	Pct.	W	L	Pct.
Virginia Union	9	1	.900	28	3	.903
Norfolk St.#	8	2	.800	23	4	.852
Elizabeth City St.	6	4	.600	15	11	.577
St. Paul's	3	7	.300	12	16	.429
Bowie St.	3	7	.300	8	19	.296
Virginia St.	1	9	.100	10	17	.370
Southern Division						
N.C. Central	11	1	.917	20	7	.741
Shaw	7	5	.583	15	13	.536
Livingstone	6	6	.500	10	17	.370
St. Augustine's	6	6	.500	13	13	.500
Johnson Smith	4	8	.333	11	16	.407
Fayetteville St.	4	8	.333	10	17	.370
Winston-Salem	4	8	.333	7	18	.280

CHICAGOLAND COLLEGIATE ATHLETIC CONFERENCE

	Conference			Full Season		
Team	W	L	Pct.	W	L	Pct.
St. Xavier	10	2	.833	28	7	.800
St. Francis (Ill.)	10	2	.833	19	10	.655
Olivet Nazarene	8	4	.667	20	14	.588
Rosary	5	7	.417	16	17	.485
Ind.-South Bend	5	7	.417	10	23	.303
Purdue-Calumet	3	9	.250	6	25	.194
Illinois Tech	1	11	.083	7	20	.259

COLORADO ATHLETIC CONFERENCE

	Conference			Full Season		
Team	W	L	Pct.	W	L	Pct.
Regis (Colo.)	7	3	.700	25	5	.833
Denver	7	3	.700	22	7	.759
Southern Colo.	7	3	.700	17	11	.607
Metro St.	6	4	.600	18	9	.667
UC-Colo. Spgs.	2	8	.200	5	20	.200
Colo. Christian	1	9	.100	5	21	.192

GREAT LAKES INTERCOLLEGIATE ATHLETIC CONFERENCE

	Conference			Full Season		
Team	W	L	Pct.	W	L	Pct.
Oakland	13	5	.722	21	8	.724
Lake Superior St.	13	5	.722	19	9	.679
Michigan Tech	12	6	.667	18	11	.621
Saginaw Valley	11	7	.611	18	11	.621
Northern Mich.	11	7	.611	17	11	.607
Mercyhurst	11	7	.611	15	12	.556
Wayne St. (Mich.)	10	8	.556	16	10	.615
Ashland	9	9	.500	14	12	.538
Grand Valley St.	9	9	.500	11	15	.423
Northwood	7	11	.389	15	11	.577
Gannon	5	13	.278	10	16	.385
Ferris St.	3	15	.167	6	20	.231
Hillsdale	3	15	.167	4	22	.154

GREAT LAKES VALLEY CONFERENCE

	Conference			Full Season		
Team	W	L	Pct.	W	L	Pct.
Southern Ind.	18	2	.900	25	4	.862
Northern Ky.	15	5	.750	25	7	.781
Indianapolis	14	6	.700	20	9	.690
Ky. Wesleyan	13	7	.650	17	10	.630
Lewis	11	9	.550	18	9	.667
Quincy	11	9	.550	17	10	.630
St. Joseph's (Ind.)	8	12	.400	12	15	.444
SIU-Edwardsville	7	13	.350	10	15	.400
Bellarmine	5	15	.250	11	16	.407
IU/PU-Ft. Wayne	4	16	.200	8	19	.296
Wis.-Parkside	4	16	.200	6	20	.231

GULF SOUTH CONFERENCE

	Conference			Full Season		
East Division	W	L	Pct.	W	L	Pct.
North Ala.#	10	4	.714	24	8	.750
West Ga.	10	4	.714	19	9	.679
Valdosta St.	9	5	.643	17	10	.630
West Fla.	8	6	.571	15	15	.500
Lincoln Memorial	6	8	.429	13	13	.500
Ala.-Huntsville	6	8	.429	12	14	.462
Montevallo	4	10	.286	5	21	.192
West Ala.	3	11	.214	9	17	.346
West Division						
Delta St.	9	3	.750	18	11	.621
Mississippi Col.	8	4	.667	17	8	.680
Arkansas Tech	7	5	.583	19	10	.655
Henderson St.	7	5	.583	11	16	.407
Central Ark.	6	6	.500	12	13	.480
Southern Ark.	4	8	.333	11	13	.458
Ark.-Monticello	1	11	.083	4	20	.167

LONE STAR CONFERENCE

	Conference			Full Season		
Team	W	L	Pct.	W	L	Pct.
Tex. A&M-Kingsville#	11	3	.786	23	6	.793
Tex. A&M-Commerce	11	3	.786	20	8	.714
West Tex. A&M	8	6	.571	18	10	.643
Central Okla.	8	6	.571	19	10	.655
Eastern N.M.	7	7	.500	17	10	.630
Abilene Christian	6	8	.429	13	14	.481
Tarleton St.	3	11	.214	11	16	.407
Angelo St.	2	12	.143	6	19	.240

MID-AMERICA INTERCOLLEGIATE ATHLETICS ASSOCIATION

	Conference			Full Season		
Team	W	L	Pct.	W	L	Pct.
Northwest Mo. St.	12	4	.750	19	7	.731
Mo.-Rolla#	12	4	.750	25	6	.806
Mo.-St. Louis	9	7	.563	15	13	.536
Central Mo. St.	9	7	.563	22	9	.710
Emporia St.	9	7	.563	12	15	.444
Mo. Western St.	9	7	.563	17	10	.630
Washburn	9	7	.563	16	11	.593
Pittsburg St.	9	7	.563	14	14	.500
Mo. Southern St.	7	9	.438	12	14	.462
Lincoln (Mo.)	4	12	.250	9	16	.360
Southwest Baptist	4	12	.250	7	19	.269
Truman St.	3	13	.188	6	20	.231

NEW ENGLAND COLLEGIATE CONFERENCE

	Conference			Full Season		
Team	W	L	Pct.	W	L	Pct.
Franklin Pierce	18	2	.900	23	6	.793
New Hamp. Col.	16	4	.800	21	8	.724
Le Moyne#	16	4	.800	24	6	.800
Southern Conn. St.	13	7	.650	17	12	.586
Sacred Heart	11	9	.550	13	14	.481
Albany (N.Y.)	9	11	.450	12	15	.444
Mass.-Lowell	8	12	.400	9	17	.346
New Haven	7	13	.350	10	16	.385
Stony Brook	6	14	.300	9	17	.346
Bridgeport	6	14	.300	9	17	.346
Keene St.	0	20	.000	2	22	.083

NEW YORK COLLEGIATE ATHLETIC CONFERENCE

	Conference			Full Season		
Team	W	L	Pct.	W	L	Pct.
St. Rose	20	2	.909	28	4	.875
Adelphi#	17	5	.773	23	7	.767
Phila. Textile	16	6	.727	19	9	.679
New York Tech	16	6	.727	19	8	.704
LIU-Southampton	12	10	.545	16	13	.552
LIU-C. W. Post	11	11	.500	13	16	.448
Dowling	11	11	.500	15	14	.517
Queens (N.Y.)	10	12	.455	11	15	.423
Pace	10	12	.455	11	15	.423
Mercy	4	18	.182	4	20	.167
Concordia (N.Y.)	3	19	.136	5	21	.192
Molloy	2	20	.091	3	23	.115

NORTH CENTRAL INTERCOLLEGIATE ATHLETIC CONFERENCE

Team	Conference			Full Season		
	W	L	Pct.	W	L	Pct.
South Dak. St.	15	3	.833	24	5	.828
South Dak.	12	6	.667	20	7	.741
North Dak. St.	12	6	.667	20	9	.690
Morningside	10	8	.556	18	9	.667
St. Cloud St.	10	8	.556	18	9	.667
North Dak.	9	9	.500	15	12	.556
Mankato St.	8	10	.444	16	11	.593
Augustana (S.D.)	7	11	.389	14	13	.519
Northern Colo.	6	12	.333	11	16	.407
Neb.-Omaha	1	17	.056	6	21	.222

NORTHEAST-10 CONFERENCE

Team	Conference			Full Season		
	W	L	Pct.	W	L	Pct.
St. Anselm#	16	0	1.000	28	3	.903
St. Michael's	11	5	.688	19	8	.704
Bentley	11	5	.688	18	9	.667
Stonehill	8	8	.500	16	10	.615
Bryant	8	8	.500	13	14	.481
Merrimack	7	9	.438	12	16	.429
American Int'l	7	9	.438	11	18	.379
Assumption	3	13	.188	6	19	.240
Quinnipiac	1	15	.063	5	22	.185

NORTHERN CALIFORNIA ATHLETIC CONFERENCE

Team	Conference			Full Season		
	W	L	Pct.	W	L	Pct.
UC Davis	14	0	1.000	24	6	.800
Sonoma St.	10	4	.714	15	13	.536
Humboldt St.	8	6	.571	14	13	.519
Cal St. Chico	7	7	.500	14	13	.519
Cal St. Stanislaus	6	8	.429	8	18	.308
Cal St. Hayward	5	9	.357	8	18	.308
San Fran. St.	5	9	.357	8	18	.308
Notre Dame (Cal.)	1	13	.071	4	22	.154

NORTHERN SUN INTERCOLLEGIATE CONFERENCE

Team	Conference			Full Season		
	W	L	Pct.	W	L	Pct.
Northern St.	10	2	.833	23	6	.793
Moorhead St.	8	4	.667	19	8	.704
Southwest St.	8	4	.667	18	9	.667
Minn.-Duluth	8	4	.667	15	10	.600
Minn.-Morris	5	7	.417	13	14	.481
Winona St.	3	9	.250	8	18	.308
Bemidji St.	0	12	.000	4	23	.148

PACIFIC WEST CONFERENCE

Team	Conference			Full Season		
	W	L	Pct.	W	L	Pct.
Seattle Pacific	9	3	.750	23	6	.793
Mont. St.-Billings	9	3	.750	19	9	.679
Alas. Anchorage	9	3	.750	19	9	.679
Hawaii-Hilo	6	6	.500	8	19	.296
Western N.M.	4	8	.333	8	18	.308
Alas. Fairbanks	3	9	.250	10	17	.370
Chaminade	2	10	.167	4	22	.154

PEACH BELT ATHLETIC CONFERENCE

Team	Conference			Full Season		
	W	L	Pct.	W	L	Pct.
Columbus St.	15	3	.833	26	6	.813
Georgia Col.	14	4	.778	21	7	.750
S.C.-Spartanburg	13	5	.722	23	8	.742
Lander	11	7	.611	19	8	.704
N.C.-Pembroke	8	10	.444	15	13	.536
Kennesaw St.	8	10	.444	12	15	.444
Augusta St.	6	12	.333	11	16	.407
Armstrong Atlantic	5	13	.278	12	14	.462
S.C.-Aiken	5	13	.278	9	17	.346
Francis Marion	5	13	.278	8	19	.296

PENNSYLVANIA STATE ATHLETIC CONFERENCE

Eastern Division	Conference			Full Season		
	W	L	Pct.	W	L	Pct.
Bloomsburg	9	3	.750	21	7	.750
Cheyney	9	3	.750	17	11	.607
East Stroudsburg	7	5	.583	14	13	.519
Millersville	6	6	.500	17	10	.630
West Chester	5	7	.417	15	11	.577
Kutztown	5	7	.417	8	17	.320
Mansfield	1	11	.083	10	16	.385
Western Division						
Calif. (Pa.)#	11	1	.917	27	6	.818
Indiana (Pa.)	9	3	.750	24	7	.774
Edinboro	8	4	.667	21	8	.724
Lock Haven	5	7	.417	13	13	.500
Clarion	4	8	.333	12	13	.480
Shippensburg	4	8	.333	12	13	.480
Slippery Rock	1	11	.083	2	24	.077

ROCKY MOUNTAIN ATHLETIC CONFERENCE

Team	Conference			Full Season		
	W	L	Pct.	W	L	Pct.
Fort Hays St.	16	0	1.000	34	0	1.000
Neb.-Kearney	12	4	.750	24	9	.727
Western St.	11	5	.688	18	13	.581
Adams St.	8	8	.500	12	15	.444
Colorado Mines	7	9	.438	13	15	.464
Mesa St.	6	10	.375	12	13	.480
Chadron St.	5	11	.313	10	17	.370
Fort Lewis	5	11	.313	8	18	.308
N.M. Highlands	2	14	.125	4	22	.154

SOUTH ATLANTIC CONFERENCE

Team	Conference			Full Season		
	W	L	Pct.	W	L	Pct.
Catawba	10	4	.714	16	10	.630
Presbyterian#	8	6	.571	19	11	.633
Gardner-Webb	7	7	.500	15	12	.556
Lenoir-Rhyne	7	7	.500	14	12	.538
Mars Hill	7	7	.500	16	13	.552
Carson-Newman	7	7	.500	13	15	.464
Elon	5	9	.357	14	14	.500
Wingate	5	9	.357	11	16	.407

SOUTHERN INTERCOLLEGIATE ATHLETIC CONFERENCE

Eastern Region	Conference			Full Season		
	W	L	Pct.	W	L	Pct.
Albany St. (Ga.)	12	4	.750	17	10	.630
Clark Atlanta	10	6	.625	21	8	.724
Savannah St.	8	8	.500	13	14	.481
Morris Brown	7	9	.438	11	15	.423
Fort Valley St.	7	9	.438	11	16	.407
Paine	2	14	.125	6	18	.250
Western Region						
Alabama A&M	15	1	.938	28	3	.903
Morehouse	10	6	.625	18	9	.667
Miles	9	7	.563	14	13	.519
LeMoyne-Owen	9	7	.563	14	13	.519
Tuskegee	4	12	.250	9	17	.346
Kentucky St.	3	13	.188	7	20	.259

SUNSHINE STATE CONFERENCE

Team	Conference			Full Season		
	W	L	Pct.	W	L	Pct.
Fla. Southern#	13	1	.929	26	4	.867
Rollins	8	6	.571	20	8	.714
Barry	8	6	.571	18	10	.643
Eckerd	8	6	.571	17	10	.630
Tampa	6	8	.429	14	13	.519
North Fla.	5	9	.357	14	15	.483
St. Leo	4	10	.286	8	19	.296
Florida Tech	4	10	.286	12	14	.462

WEST VIRGINIA INTERCOLLEGIATE ATHLETIC CONFERENCE

Team	Conference			Full Season		
	W	L	Pct.	W	L	Pct.
Fairmont St.	16	3	.842	24	5	.828
West Liberty St.	13	6	.684	17	10	.630
West Va. Tech	12	7	.632	19	10	.655
Salem-Teikyo	12	7	.632	20	9	.690
West Va.	12	7	.632	17	10	.630
Alderson-Broaddus	12	7	.632	16	12	.571
Glenville St.	11	8	.579	13	12	.520
Charleston (W.Va.)	11	8	.579	12	14	.462
Bluefield St.#	7	12	.368	15	16	.484
West Va. Wesleyan	7	12	.368	9	17	.346
Wheeling Jesuit	7	12	.368	11	16	.407
Concord	6	13	.316	12	17	.414
Shepherd	6	13	.316	8	19	.296
Davis & Elkins	1	18	.053	2	25	.074

DIVISION II INDEPENDENTS

Team	Full Season		
	W	L	Pct.
American (P.R.)	18	8	.692
Cameron	12	14	.462
Dist. Columbia	9	18	.333
Drury	16	11	.593
IU/PU-Indianapolis	22	7	.759
Lane	14	11	.560
Lynn	16	11	.593
Newberry	11	10	.524
Oakland City	18	13	.581
Pitt.-Johnstown	13	12	.520
Wayne St. (Neb.)	12	15	.444

1996 Division III Conference Standings

#Won conference tournament.

ASSOCIATION OF MIDEAST COLLEGES

Team	Conference			Full Season		
	W	L	Pct.	W	L	Pct.
Thomas More	4	0	1.000	13	12	.520
Bluffton	2	2	.500	14	12	.538
Wilmington (Ohio)	0	4	.000	9	16	.360

CAPITAL ATHLETIC CONFERENCE

Team	Conference			Full Season		
	W	L	Pct.	W	L	Pct.
Catholic	12	2	.857	19	8	.704
Salisbury St.#	12	2	.857	19	9	.679
Goucher	9	5	.643	15	10	.600
Marymount (Va.)	5	9	.357	12	15	.444
York (Pa.)	5	9	.357	9	16	.360
St. Mary's (Md.)	5	9	.357	8	18	.308
Gallaudet	4	10	.286	6	19	.240
Mary Washington	4	10	.286	6	19	.240

CENTENNIAL CONFERENCE

East Division	Conference			Full Season		
	W	L	Pct.	W	L	Pct.
Haverford	8	5	.615	14	10	.583
Muhlenberg	8	5	.615	13	12	.520
Ursinus	6	7	.462	11	13	.458
Swarthmore	5	8	.385	9	15	.375
Washington (Md.)	4	9	.308	9	15	.375
West Division						
Frank. & Marsh.	12	1	.923	29	3	.906
Gettysburg	9	4	.692	18	9	.667
Johns Hopkins	6	7	.462	13	11	.542
Dickinson	5	8	.385	9	15	.375
Western Md.	2	11	.154	4	20	.167

CITY UNIVERSITY OF NEW YORK ATHLETIC CONFERENCE

North Division	Conference			Full Season		
	W	L	Pct.	W	L	Pct.
John Jay	5	5	.500	12	14	.462
Baruch	5	5	.500	17	10	.630
CCNY	3	7	.300	11	14	.440
Lehman	3	7	.300	8	16	.333
South Division						
Staten Island	9	1	.900	22	6	.786
York (N.Y.)	8	2	.800	18	10	.643
Hunter	6	4	.600	7	18	.280
Medgar Evers	1	9	.100	7	16	.304

COLLEGE CONFERENCE OF ILLINOIS AND WISCONSIN

Team	Conference			Full Season		
	W	L	Pct.	W	L	Pct.
Wheaton (Ill.)	13	1	.929	25	2	.926
Ill. Wesleyan	12	2	.857	28	3	.903
Elmhurst	10	4	.714	16	9	.640
Augustana (Ill.)	8	6	.571	16	8	.667
North Park	4	10	.286	6	18	.250
Millikin	3	11	.214	8	17	.320
Carthage	3	11	.214	5	20	.200
North Central	3	11	.214	5	20	.200

COMMONWEALTH COAST CONFERENCE

Team	Conference			Full Season		
North Division	W	L	Pct.	W	L	Pct.
Anna Maria	7	1	.875	25	5	.833
Colby-Sawyer	6	2	.750	18	8	.692
Gordon	4	4	.500	9	15	.375
Nichols	3	5	.375	12	13	.480
New England Col.	0	8	.000	0	22	.000
South Division						
Wentworth Inst.	6	2	.750	19	8	.704
Eastern Nazarene	6	2	.750	19	8	.704
Roger Williams	4	4	.500	8	17	.320
Salve Regina	2	6	.250	6	17	.261
Curry	2	6	.250	11	13	.458

CONSTITUTION ATHLETIC CONFERENCE

Team	Conference			Full Season		
	W	L	Pct.	W	L	Pct.
Babson	12	2	.857	21	7	.750
Springfield#	12	2	.857	21	7	.750
Coast Guard	7	7	.500	15	10	.600
Norwich	7	7	.500	15	11	.577
Clark (Mass.)	7	7	.500	12	13	.480
Worcester Tech	6	8	.429	12	12	.500
Western New Eng.	3	11	.214	5	20	.200
MIT	2	12	.143	4	21	.160

DIXIE INTERCOLLEGIATE ATHLETIC CONFERENCE

Team	Conference			Full Season		
	W	L	Pct.	W	L	Pct.
Shenandoah	9	3	.750	18	9	.667
Chris. Newport#	9	3	.750	24	6	.800
Ferrum	8	4	.667	11	13	.458
Methodist	7	5	.583	14	11	.560
N.C. Wesleyan	5	7	.417	11	14	.440
Greensboro	3	9	.250	9	16	.360
Averett	1	11	.083	2	23	.080

EMPIRE ATHLETIC ASSOCIATION

Team	Conference			Full Season		
	W	L	Pct.	W	L	Pct.
Rochester Inst.	5	0	1.000	22	4	.846
Ithaca	3	2	.600	16	10	.615
Nazareth	3	2	.600	12	13	.480
Hartwick	2	3	.400	17	9	.654
Utica	1	4	.200	16	10	.615
Alfred	1	4	.200	4	21	.160

INDEPENDENT ATHLETIC CONFERENCE

Team	Conference			Full Season		
North Division	W	L	Pct.	W	L	Pct.
Mt. St. Vincent	7	1	.875	18	9	.667
Maritime (N.Y.)	3	5	.375	9	15	.375
Bard	0	8	.000	0	21	.000
St. Joseph (N.Y.)*				7	19	.269
South Division						
N.J. Inst. of Tech#	8	1	.889	17	10	.630
Stevens Tech	6	3	.667	16	11	.593
Yeshiva	4	5	.444	13	12	.520
Polytechnic (N.Y.)	2	7	.222	10	13	.435

Ineligible for conference championship

INDIANA COLLEGIATE ATHLETIC CONFERENCE

Team	Conference			Full Season		
	W	L	Pct.	W	L	Pct.
Hanover	11	1	.917	21	6	.778
Manchester	8	4	.667	18	8	.692
Rose-Hulman	6	6	.500	19	9	.679
DePauw	6	6	.500	17	9	.654
Franklin	4	8	.333	13	11	.542
Wabash	4	8	.333	12	12	.500
Anderson	3	9	.250	14	11	.560

IOWA INTERCOLLEGIATE ATHLETIC CONFERENCE

Team	Conference			Full Season		
	W	L	Pct.	W	L	Pct.
Upper Iowa	14	2	.875	20	5	.808
Simpson	13	3	.813	20	6	.769
Dubuque	12	4	.750	13	12	.520
Luther	9	7	.563	15	10	.600
Loras	7	9	.438	13	12	.520
Central (Iowa)	7	9	.438	11	14	.440
Buena Vista	4	12	.250	7	18	.280
Wartburg	4	12	.250	10	15	.400
William Penn	2	14	.125	5	20	.200

LAKE MICHIGAN CONFERENCE

Team	Conference			Full Season		
	W	L	Pct.	W	L	Pct.
Wis. Lutheran	13	1	.929	22	7	.759
Lakeland#	11	3	.786	18	8	.692
Edgewood	9	5	.643	14	12	.538
Cardinal Stritch	7	7	.500	10	15	.400
Concordia (Wis.)	6	8	.429	8	17	.320
Marian (Wis.)	5	9	.357	9	17	.346
Maranatha Baptist	3	11	.214	9	16	.360
Milwaukee Engr.	2	12	.143	3	22	.120

LITTLE EAST CONFERENCE

Team	Conference			Full Season		
	W	L	Pct.	W	L	Pct.
Mass.-Dartmouth	10	2	.833	19	8	.704
Plymouth St.	9	3	.750	19	9	.679
Rhode Island Col.	9	3	.750	18	9	.667
Western Conn. St.	7	5	.583	19	8	.704
Southern Me.	4	8	.333	10	15	.400
Eastern Conn. St.	2	10	.167	8	17	.320
Mass.-Boston	1	11	.083	4	21	.160

MASSACHUSETTS STATE COLLEGE ATHLETIC CONFERENCE

Team	Conference			Full Season		
	W	L	Pct.	W	L	Pct.
Salem St. #	12	0	1.000	25	3	.893
Bri'water (Mass.)	9	3	.750	18	10	.643
Westfield St.	8	4	.667	14	12	.538
Worcester St.	6	6	.500	10	16	.385
Fitchburg St.	4	8	.333	9	16	.360
Framingham St.	2	10	.167	5	20	.200
North Adams St.	1	11	.083	5	20	.200

MICHIGAN INTERCOLLEGIATE ATHLETIC ASSOCIATION

Team	Conference			Full Season		
	W	L	Pct.	W	L	Pct.
Hope	11	1	.917	27	5	.844
Kalamazoo	8	4	.667	17	11	.607
Albion	7	5	.583	16	9	.640
Calvin	7	5	.583	16	10	.615
Adrian	4	8	.333	11	13	.458
Olivet	3	9	.250	9	16	.360
Alma	2	10	.167	4	21	.160

MIDDLE ATLANTIC STATES CONFERENCE

Commonwealth League	Conference			Full Season		
	W	L	Pct.	W	L	Pct.
Susquehanna	10	4	.714	14	12	.538

	Conference			Full Season		
	W	L	Pct.	W	L	Pct.
Moravian	10	4	.714	17	8	.680
Elizabethtown	9	5	.643	15	10	.600
Lebanon Valley	9	5	.643	12	13	.480
Widener	7	7	.500	10	13	.435
Albright	6	8	.429	10	13	.435
Juniata	3	11	.214	7	17	.292
Messiah	2	12	.143	4	20	.167
Freedom League						
Wilkes#	12	0	1.000	28	2	.933
Lycoming	10	2	.833	21	6	.778
Drew	7	5	.583	14	13	.519
Scranton	6	6	.500	10	15	.400
King's (Pa.)	4	8	.333	5	19	.208
FDU-Madison	3	9	.250	8	16	.333
Delaware Valley	0	12	.000	0	23	.000

MIDWEST CONFERENCE

Team	Conference			Full Season		
North Division	W	L	Pct.	W	L	Pct.
Ripon	13	1	.929	21	4	.840
Carroll (Wis.)	11	3	.786	16	7	.696
Beloit	8	6	.571	13	9	.591
Lawrence	7	7	.500	14	8	.636
Lake Forest	4	10	.286	7	15	.318
St. Norbert	2	12	.143	8	14	.364
South Division						
Grinnell#	11	3	.786	17	8	.680
Knox	9	5	.643	15	8	.652
Coe	9	5	.643	10	12	.455
Monmouth (Ill.)	4	10	.286	8	13	.381
Illinois Col.	3	10	.231	7	14	.333
Cornell College	2	11	.154	4	17	.190

MINNESOTA INTERCOLLEGIATE ATHLETIC CONFERENCE

Team	Conference			Full Season		
	W	L	Pct.	W	L	Pct.
Gust. Adolphus	18	2	.900	24	5	.828
Concordia-M'head	16	4	.800	21	6	.778
Carleton	15	5	.750	17	8	.680
St. Thomas (Minn.)	12	8	.600	15	10	.600
St. Olaf	11	9	.550	15	9	.625
Augsburg	11	9	.550	15	9	.625
St. John's (Minn.)	10	10	.500	12	12	.500
Bethel (Minn.)	7	13	.350	8	16	.333
Hamline	5	15	.250	6	18	.250
St. Mary's (Minn.)	4	16	.200	6	18	.250
Macalester	1	19	.050	3	21	.125

NEBRASKA-IOWA ATHLETIC CONFERENCE

Team	Conference			Full Season		
	W	L	Pct.	W	L	Pct.
Concordia (Neb.)	10	2	.833	24	4	.857
Neb. Wesleyan	8	4	.667	16	9	.640
Doane	8	4	.667	17	15	.531
Hastings	6	6	.500	16	12	.571
N'western (Iowa)	6	6	.500	15	12	.556
Dana	4	8	.333	16	13	.552
Midland Lutheran	0	12	.000	8	18	.308

NEW ENGLAND SMALL COLLEGE ATHLETIC CONFERENCE

(Did not compete for a regular-season conference title)

Team	Full Season		
	W	L	Pct.
Williams	24	3	.889
Amherst	21	6	.778
Bowdoin	19	6	.760
Connecticut Col.	18	8	.692
Trinity (Conn.)	14	8	.636
Tufts	15	10	.600
Colby	16	11	.593
Middlebury	11	12	.478
Bates	10	14	.417
Wesleyan (Conn.)	5	18	.217

NEW JERSEY ATHLETIC CONFERENCE

Team	Conference			Full Season		
	W	L	Pct.	W	L	Pct.
Richard Stockton#	16	2	.889	26	4	.867
Rowan	16	2	.889	28	4	.875
Jersey City St.	12	6	.667	16	11	.593
Rutgers-Newark	9	9	.500	16	11	.593
Col. of New Jersey	9	9	.500	12	10	.545
Wm. Paterson	8	10	.444	12	12	.500
Kean	7	11	.389	9	14	.391
Ramapo	7	11	.389	11	13	.458
Montclair St.	6	12	.333	9	15	.375
Rutgers-Camden	0	18	.000	0	24	.000

NORTH COAST ATHLETIC CONFERENCE

Team	Conference			Full Season		
	W	L	Pct.	W	L	Pct.
Wittenberg	15	1	.938	26	5	.839
Wooster	12	4	.750	19	7	.731
Allegheny	10	6	.625	17	10	.630
Case Reserve	10	6	.625	13	13	.500
Denison	9	7	.563	13	12	.520
Kenyon	6	10	.375	9	16	.360
Earlham	5	11	.313	8	17	.320
Ohio Wesleyan	5	11	.313	8	17	.320
Oberlin	0	16	.000	2	22	.083

NORTHERN ILLINOIS INTERCOLLEGIATE CONFERENCE

Team	Conference			Full Season		
	W	L	Pct.	W	L	Pct.
Trinity Int'l	8	2	.800	25	6	.806
Benedictine (Ill.)	7	3	.700	11	14	.440
Aurora	5	5	.500	12	13	.480
Concordia (Ill.)	5	5	.500	9	16	.360
Judson	3	7	.300	6	25	.194
Rockford	2	8	.200	2	23	.080

OHIO ATHLETIC CONFERENCE

Team	Conference			Full Season		
	W	L	Pct.	W	L	Pct.
John Carroll	14	4	.778	19	8	.704
Capital	13	5	.722	19	8	.704
Ohio Northern	12	6	.667	18	9	.667
Baldwin-Wallace#	10	8	.556	16	12	.571
Mount Union	9	9	.500	13	12	.520
Otterbein	9	9	.500	12	13	.480
Marietta	8	10	.444	15	13	.536
Hiram	6	12	.333	9	16	.360
Muskingum	5	13	.278	10	17	.370
Heidelberg	4	14	.222	8	17	.320

OLD DOMINION ATHLETIC CONFERENCE

Team	Conference			Full Season		
	W	L	Pct.	W	L	Pct.
Roanoke#	14	4	.778	24	5	.828
Randolph-Macon	13	5	.722	18	9	.667
Bridgewater (Va.)	12	6	.667	18	10	.643
Hampden-Sydney	11	7	.611	17	9	.654
Va. Wesleyan	11	7	.611	15	10	.600
Emory & Henry	10	8	.556	14	11	.560
Lynchburg	7	11	.389	10	15	.400
East. Mennonite	6	12	.333	10	15	.400
Wash. & Lee	3	15	.167	3	21	.125
Guilford	3	15	.167	7	17	.292

PENNSYLVANIA ATHLETIC CONFERENCE

Team	Conference			Full Season		
	W	L	Pct.	W	L	Pct.
Cabrini	16	0	1.000	24	3	.889
Alvernia	12	4	.750	15	10	.600
Allentown	11	5	.688	17	10	.630
Misericordia	9	7	.563	16	12	.571
Beaver	8	8	.500	14	11	.560
Eastern	8	8	.500	8	17	.320
Marywood	4	12	.250	7	17	.292
Gwynedd-Mercy	2	14	.125	4	19	.174
Neumann	2	14	.125	3	21	.125

PRESIDENT'S ATHLETIC CONFERENCE

Team	Conference			Full Season		
	W	L	Pct.	W	L	Pct.
Waynesburg	8	1	.889	19	7	.731
Grove City	7	2	.778	16	10	.615
Wash. & Jeff.	2	6	.250	8	17	.320
Bethany (W.Va.)	2	6	.250	8	17	.320
Thiel	2	6	.250	6	19	.240

ST. LOUIS INTERCOLLEGIATE ATHLETIC CONFERENCE

Team	Conference			Full Season		
	W	L	Pct.	W	L	Pct.
Greenville	13	3	.813	21	8	.724
Fontbonne#	12	4	.750	17	10	.630
MacMurray	12	4	.750	14	13	.519
Westminster (Mo.)	10	6	.625	14	12	.538
Maryville (Mo.)	8	8	.500	11	14	.440
Blackburn	8	8	.500	10	16	.385
Webster	5	11	.313	8	17	.320
Parks	3	13	.188	8	16	.333
Principia	1	15	.063	1	23	.042

SKYLINE CONFERENCE

Team	Conference			Full Season		
	W	L	Pct.	W	L	Pct.
Staten Island	9	1	.900	22	6	.786
Hunter	6	4	.600	7	18	.280
N.J. Inst. of Tech.	5	5	.500	17	10	.630
Merchant Marine	5	5	.500	16	12	.571
Mt. St. Mary (N.Y.)	4	6	.400	15	10	.600
Manhattanville	4	6	.400	10	14	.417

SOUTHERN CALIFORNIA INTERCOLLEGIATE ATHLETIC CONFERENCE

Team	Conference			Full Season		
	W	L	Pct.	W	L	Pct.
Claremont-M-S	12	2	.857	19	8	.704
Cal Lutheran	11	3	.786	19	6	.760
Pomona-Pitzer	10	4	.714	15	9	.625
Occidental	7	7	.500	15	10	.600
La Verne	7	7	.500	10	15	.400
Redlands	5	9	.357	8	17	.320
Whittier	4	10	.286	9	16	.360
Cal Tech	0	14	.000	4	19	.174

SOUTHERN COLLEGIATE ATHLETIC CONFERENCE

Team	Conference			Full Season		
	W	L	Pct.	W	L	Pct.
Millsaps#	11	3	.786	22	5	.815
Hendrix	10	4	.714	21	6	.778
Sewanee	9	5	.643	18	7	.720
Rhodes	8	6	.571	18	7	.720
Trinity (Tex.)	7	7	.500	17	8	.680
Centre	6	8	.429	8	17	.320
Oglethorpe	3	11	.214	7	17	.292
Southwestern (Tex.)	2	12	.143	6	18	.250

STATE UNIVERSITY OF NEW YORK ATHLETIC CONFERENCE

Team	Conference			Full Season		
East Division	W	L	Pct.	W	L	Pct.
Cortland St.	11	5	.688	16	12	.571
Oneonta St.	10	6	.625	17	11	.607
Binghamton	8	8	.500	10	15	.400
New Paltz St.	8	8	.500	13	14	.481
Plattsburgh St.	7	9	.438	11	13	.458
Potsdam St.	4	12	.250	7	17	.292
West Division						
Geneseo St.	11	5	.688	17	10	.630
Buffalo St.#	11	5	.688	22	8	.733
Brockport St.	10	6	.625	14	13	.519
Fredonia St.	8	8	.500	14	13	.519
Utica/Rome	6	10	.375	11	13	.458
Oswego St.	2	14	.125	3	21	.125

TEXAS INTERCOLLEGIATE ATHLETIC ASSOCIATION

Team	Conference			Full Season		
	W	L	Pct.	W	L	Pct.
McMurry	8	2	.800	16	8	.667
Howard Payne	8	2	.800	14	13	.519
Hardin-Simmons	7	3	.700	20	5	.800
Sul Ross St.	4	6	.400	9	14	.391
Austin	3	7	.300	6	18	.250
Dallas	0	10	.000	4	20	.167

UNIVERSITY ATHLETIC ASSOCIATION

Team	Conference			Full Season		
	W	L	Pct.	W	L	Pct.
Washington (Mo.)	13	1	.929	23	6	.793
Chicago	11	3	.786	18	7	.720
New York U.	10	4	.714	19	8	.704
Carnegie Mellon	6	8	.429	13	12	.520
Rochester	5	9	.357	13	13	.500
Brandeis	4	10	.286	9	16	.360
Emory	1	13	.071	6	18	.250
*Johns Hopkins	5	3	.625	13	11	.542
*Case Reserve	2	6	.250	13	13	.500

*Ineligible for conference championship.

UPSTATE COLLEGIATE ATHLETIC ASSOCIATION

Team	Conference			Full Season		
	W	L	Pct.	W	L	Pct.
Rensselaer	10	2	.833	20	8	.714
Hamilton	10	2	.833	16	9	.640
St. Lawrence	8	4	.667	18	9	.667
Hobart	6	6	.500	7	18	.280
Skidmore	5	7	.417	12	13	.480
Union (N.Y.)	2	10	.167	6	19	.240
Clarkson	1	11	.083	5	20	.200

WISCONSIN STATE UNIVERSITY CONFERENCE

Team	Conference			Full Season		
	W	L	Pct.	W	L	Pct.
Wis.-Platteville	15	1	.938	23	3	.885
Wis.-Oshkosh	13	3	.813	23	4	.852
Wis.-Whitewater	10	6	.625	19	9	.679
Wis.-Eau Claire	9	7	.563	17	7	.708
Wis.-Stevens Point	9	7	.563	17	8	.680
Wis.-River Falls	5	11	.313	13	12	.520
Wis.-Stout	4	12	.250	10	13	.435
Wis.-Superior	4	12	.250	9	16	.360
Wis.-La Crosse	3	13	.188	10	14	.417

DIVISION III INDEPENDENTS

Team	Full Season		
	W	L	Pct.
Stillman	19	4	.826
St. John Fisher	20	6	.769
Martin Luther	11	6	.647
Old Westbury	18	11	.621
Defiance	14	10	.583
Vassar	14	10	.583
Chapman	14	11	.560
Colorado Col.	14	11	.560
Rust	13	11	.542
Lincoln (Pa.)	14	12	.538
Frostburg St.	13	12	.520
Menlo	13	12	.520
Penn St.-Behrend	13	12	.520
Elmira	14	13	.519
Savannah A&D	11	13	.458
UC San Diego	11	14	.440
Eureka	9	16	.360
Keuka	9	16	.360
UC Santa Cruz	7	17	.292
Maine Maritime	5	13	.278
Wesley	6	18	.250
Villa Julie	6	19	.240
Wheaton (Mass.)	6	19	.240
Johnson St.	4	18	.182
Fisk	1	24	.040

Attendance Records

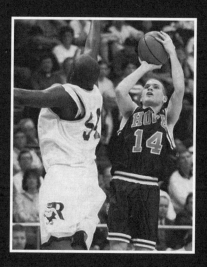

Attendance

1996 Attendance Summary

(For All NCAA Varsity Teams)

	Total Teams	Games or Sessions	1996 Attendance	Avg. PG or Sess.	Change@ in Total		Change@ in Avg.	
Home Attendance, NCAA Division I	*305	3,998	21,204,735	5,304	Down	339,384	Down	34
NCAA Championship Tournament		34	643,290	18,920	Up	103,850	Up	2,062
Other Division I Neutral-Site Attendance		181	1,694,627	9,363	Up	217,691	Down	1,187
NCAA DIVISION I TOTALS	***305**	**4,213**	**23,542,652**	**5,588**	**Down**	**17,843**	**Down**	**53**
Home Attendance, NCAA Division II	242	3,111	2,918,802	938	Down	207,172	Down	54
Home Attendance, NCAA Division III	319	3,663	1,730,357	472	Down	71,944	Down	15
Neutral-Site Attendance for Divisions II & III		12	8,570	714	Down	10,574	Down	243
NCAA Division II Tournament Neutral Sites		12	16,420	1,368	–		–	
NCAA Division III Tournament Neutral Sites		3	8,551	2,850	–		–	
NATIONAL TOTALS FOR 1996	**866**	**11,014**	**28,225,352**	**2,563**	**Down**	**322,806**	**Down**	**18**

*Record high. Notes: The neutral-site attendance for Divisions II and III does not include any tournaments. The total attendance for the Division II tournament was 65,882 for a 2,353 average over 28 sessions and the Division III tournament was 87,437 for a 1,508 average over 58 sessions.

All Division I Conferences

	Total Teams	Games or Sessions	1996 Attendance	Avg. PG or Sess.	Change in Total		Change in Avg.	
1. Big Ten	11	165	2,106,810	12,769	Up	48,047	Up	60
2. Atlantic Coast	9	132	*1,496,076	*11,334	Down	52,513	Up	428
3. Southeastern	12	187	*2,119,158	11,332	Up	116,397	Down	178
4. Big East#	13	198	*2,023,380	10,219	Up	344,068	Down	976
5. Conference USA#	11	160	1,601,901	10,012	–		–	
6. Big Eight	8	125	1,238,413	9,907	Down	28,770	Down	565
7. Western Athletic	10	167	*1,570,529	9,404	Up	127,379	Up	551
8. Pacific-10	10	137	1,097,013	8,007	Down	50,658	Up	200
9. Missouri Valley	11	155	969,164	6,253	Up	44,895	Up	132
10. Atlantic 10#	12	146	*862,209	*5,906	Up	239,047	Up	798
11. Southwest	8	108	580,815	5,378	Up	24,071	Up	126
12. Big West	10	137	651,825	4,758	Down	27,735	Down	313
13. Big Sky	8	105	465,189	4,430	Down	60,053	Down	259
14. Colonial#	9	117	481,020	4,111	Down	1,476	Down	573
15. Mid-American	10	137	561,551	4,099	Up	970	Up	66
16. Midwestern#	9	119	431,394	3,625	Down	214,569	Down	739
17. Sun Belt	10	136	452,810	3,329	Down	53,060	Down	418
18. Ohio Valley	9	115	364,960	3,174	Down	4,915	Up	91
19. Southern	10	131	402,524	3,073	Down	23,620	Down	231
20. West Coast	8	107	270,212	2,525	Down	8,647	Down	57
21. Metro Atlantic	8	100	213,443	2,134	Down	18,628	Down	186
22. Southwestern	8	91	188,975	2,077	Down	68,103	Down	718
23. Mid-Eastern	10	115	213,570	1,857	Down	5,027	Down	265
24. Big South	8	99	176,324	*1,781	Down	8,911	Up	112
25. American West	4	55	*92,932	*1,690	Up	19,891	Up	67
26. Southland	10	122	199,944	1,639	Down	42,043	Down	223
27. Mid-Continent	10	125	202,120	1,617	Down	41,743	Down	382
28. Ivy	8	89	143,097	1,608	Down	37,053	Down	416
29. America East	10	120	191,300	1,594	Up	10,066	Down	53
30. Patriot	7	83	129,368	1,559	Down	60,319	Down	283
31. Trans America#	12	159	233,760	1,470	Up	16,869	Down	79
32. Northeast	10	123	176,634	1,436	Up	9,077	Up	137
Division I Independents#	2	25	86,652	3,466	–		–	

*Record high for that conference. #Different lineups in 1995. Note: Includes conference tournaments.

Leading Division II Conferences

	Total Teams	G or Sess.	1996 Attendance	Avg. PG or Sess.	Change@ in Avg.	
1. North Central	10	146	341,119	2,336	Down	161
2. SIAC	12	150	247,231	1,648	Down	207
3. CIAA	13	141	225,924	1,602	Down	101
4. Mid-America	12	164	219,002	1,335	Down	43
5. Rocky Mountain	9	119	150,611	1,266	Up	2
6. Great Lakes Valley	11	155	194,259	1,253	Down	29
7. Northern Sun	7	94	115,665	1,230	Down	225
8. California	7	101	95,894	949	Up	158
9. Pennsylvania	14	182	171,448	942	Up	88
10. South Atlantic	8	95	89,481	942	Up	16

Leading Division III Conferences

	Total Teams	G or Sess.	1996 Attendance	Avg. PG or Sess.	Change@ in Avg.	
1. Michigan	7	76	80,376	1,058	Down	125
2. Illinois & Wisconsin	8	100	99,045	990	Up	6
3. Iowa	9	110	93,008	846	Up	38
4. Wisconsin State	9	111	88,732	799	Down	160
5. Indiana	7	87	68,697	790	Up	107
6. North Coast	9	110	83,484	759	Down	4
7. Ohio	10	119	88,653	745	Down	78
8. Middle Atlantic	15	173	94,551	547	Up	44
9. New England	11	129	70,198	544	Up	55
10. Old Dominion	10	115	60,636	527	Down	65

@1995 figures used in this compilation reflect 1996 changes in conference lineups (i.e., 1996 lineups vs. same teams in 1995, whether members or not in 1995).

Leading Teams

DIVISION I

	G/S	1996 Attendance	Avg.	Change in Avg.	
1. Kentucky	13	310,633	23,895	Up	89
2. Syracuse	16	363,653	22,728	Down	1,517
3. North Caro.	12	250,949	20,912	Down	319
4. Louisville	14	273,754	19,554	Up	897
5. Arkansas	18	346,698	19,261	Down	820
6. Brigham Young	15	269,422	17,961	Down	877
7. St. Louis	16	271,771	16,986	Down	728
8. Indiana	13	217,716	16,747	Down	205
9. New Mexico	20	320,517	16,026	Down	59
10. Kansas	13	204,500	15,731	Up	138
11. Iowa	15	231,244	15,416	Up	258
12. Illinois	16	236,674	14,792	Down	1,049
13. Tennessee	17	244,410	14,377	Down	505
14. Utah	15	214,216	14,281	Down	834
15. Arizona	16	228,064	14,254	Down	3
16. Memphis	17	241,996	14,235	Up	4,470
17. Minnesota	17	240,378	14,140	Up	93
18. Purdue	14	197,157	14,083	Down	40
19. Maryland	14	186,533	13,324	Down	490
20. Michigan St.	15	199,659	13,311	Down	1,431
21. Michigan	15	199,207	13,280	Down	282
22. Connecticut	15	193,672	12,911	Down	85
23. Wake Forest	14	179,109	12,794	Up	835
24. Marquette	16	204,061	12,754	Down	60
25. Missouri	16	204,023	12,751	Down	549

1996 DIVISION I TEAM-BY-TEAM ATTENDANCE

Team	G	Total Att.	Avg.
Air Force	15	22,834	1,522
Akron	13	29,761	2,289
Alabama	14	109,216	7,801
Alabama St.	13	21,113	1,624
UAB	14	72,700	5,193
Alcorn St.	11	19,865	1,806
American	13	23,626	1,817
Appalachian St.	13	26,211	2,016
Arizona	16	228,064	14,254
Arizona St.	16	152,218	9,514
Arkansas	18	346,698	19,261
Arkansas St.	13	64,067	4,928
Ark.-Little Rock	16	73,162	4,573
Army	12	12,175	1,015
Auburn	14	96,206	6,872
Austin Peay	12	32,082	2,674
Ball St.	13	84,469	6,498
Baylor	14	50,586	3,613
Bethune-Cookman	11	19,491	1,772
Boise St.	13	88,396	6,800
Boston College	15	98,144	6,543
Boston U.	12	11,645	970
Bowling Green	12	33,219	2,768
Bradley	13	125,733	9,672
Brigham Young	15	269,422	17,961
Brown	10	9,034	903
Bucknell	10	19,175	1,918
Buffalo	12	22,010	1,834
Butler	12	43,120	3,593
California	13	115,885	8,914
UC Irvine	12	34,467	2,872
UC Santa Barb.	13	46,707	3,593
Cal Poly SLO	14	31,540	2,253
Cal St. Fullerton	12	13,450	1,121
Cal St. Northridge	13	5,570	428
Cal St. Sacramento	14	14,722	1,052
Campbell	13	7,928	610
Canisius	10	21,858	2,186
Centenary (La.)	12	21,640	1,803
Central Conn. St.	12	8,245	687
Central Fla.	13	13,914	1,070
Central Mich.	13	34,242	2,634
Charleston (S.C.)	16	52,783	3,299
Charleston So.	12	10,397	866
Chicago St.	11	4,187	381
Cincinnati	14	178,065	12,719
Citadel	12	24,258	2,022
Clemson	16	149,850	9,366
Cleveland St.	13	23,013	1,770
Coastal Caro.	11	8,108	737
Colgate	10	23,949	2,395
Colorado	16	69,668	4,354
Colorado St.	16	107,270	6,704
Columbia	9	9,380	1,042
Connecticut	15	193,672	12,911
Coppin St.	11	21,296	1,936
Cornell	12	15,075	1,256
Creighton	14	64,755	4,625
Dartmouth	12	17,831	1,486
Davidson	14	28,492	2,035
Dayton	16	181,468	11,342
Delaware	14	48,982	3,499
Delaware St.	12	14,976	1,248
DePaul	14	101,434	7,245
Detroit	14	44,340	3,167
Drake	13	50,031	3,849
Drexel	10	17,527	1,753
Duke	15	139,710	9,314
Duquesne	12	46,499	3,875
East Caro.	14	61,556	4,397
East Tenn. St.	13	55,651	4,281
Eastern Ill.	12	20,098	1,675
Eastern Ky.	13	32,900	2,531
Eastern Mich.	14	42,019	3,001
Eastern Wash.	12	16,194	1,350
Evansville	14	146,400	10,457
Fairfield	13	25,388	1,953
Fairleigh Dickinson	13	16,960	1,305
Florida	12	94,757	7,896
Florida A&M	12	22,434	1,870
Fla. Atlantic	14	12,106	865
Florida Int'l	13	8,267	636
Florida St.	15	87,769	5,851
Fordham	12	17,621	1,468
Fresno St.	20	198,955	9,948
Furman	12	19,876	1,656
George Mason	13	45,360	3,489
Georgetown	16	201,659	12,604
Georgia	13	104,732	8,056
Ga. Southern	10	12,483	1,248
Georgia St.	12	11,863	989
Georgia Tech	13	134,498	10,346
Geo. Washington	11	46,378	4,216
Gonzaga	13	41,514	3,193
Grambling	12	13,077	1,090
Hampton	9	15,377	1,709
Hartford	12	10,412	868
Harvard	13	11,629	895
Hawaii	16	110,594	6,912
Hofstra	12	13,088	1,091
Holy Cross	14	20,600	1,471
Houston	13	61,069	4,698
Howard	11	26,022	2,366
Idaho	12	33,157	2,763
Idaho St.	11	37,786	3,435
Illinois	16	236,674	14,792
Illinois St.	14	108,454	7,747
Ill.-Chicago	12	35,622	2,969
Indiana	13	217,716	16,747
Indiana St.	13	65,407	5,031
Iona	14	31,570	2,255
Iowa	15	231,244	15,416
Iowa St.	16	192,174	12,011
Jackson St.	9	31,293	3,477
Jacksonville	13	23,026	1,771
Jacksonville St.	12	12,362	1,030
James Madison	13	59,400	4,569
Kansas	13	204,500	15,731
Kansas St.	14	100,937	7,210
Kent	14	28,507	2,036
Kentucky	13	310,633	23,895
La Salle	10	16,244	1,624
Lafayette	11	14,903	1,355
Lamar	15	42,330	2,822
Lehigh	12	12,335	1,028
Liberty	15	75,883	5,059
Long Beach St.	13	46,571	3,582
LIU-Brooklyn	11	4,800	436
LSU	18	165,710	9,206
Louisiana Tech	12	24,005	2,000
Louisville	14	273,754	19,554
Loyola Marymount	14	27,735	1,981
Loyola (Ill.)	12	33,658	2,805
Loyola (Md.)	12	15,943	1,329

ATTENDANCE RECORDS

Team	G	Total Att.	Avg.
Maine	12	15,659	1,305
Manhattan	12	30,979	2,582
Marist	15	44,043	2,936
Marquette	16	204,061	12,754
Marshall	13	72,106	5,547
Maryland	14	186,533	13,324
Md.-Balt. County	11	11,768	1,070
Md.-East. Shore	11	14,620	1,329
Massachusetts	10	94,930	9,493
McNeese St.	13	30,600	2,354
Memphis	17	241,996	14,235
Mercer	12	7,508	626
Miami (Fla.)	16	46,150	2,884
Miami (Ohio)	14	79,463	5,676
Michigan	15	199,207	13,280
Michigan St.	15	199,659	13,311
Middle Tenn. St.	14	34,101	2,436
Minnesota	17	240,378	14,140
Mississippi	13	51,521	3,963
Mississippi St.	13	97,996	7,538
Mississippi Val.	10	27,150	2,715
Missouri	16	204,023	12,751
Mo.-Kansas City	13	39,894	3,069
Monmouth (N.J.)	14	25,133	1,795
Montana	16	85,229	5,327
Montana St.	17	100,162	5,892
Morehead St.	14	23,950	1,711
Morgan St.	10	10,118	1,012
Mt. St. Mary's (Md.)	13	35,341	2,719
Murray St.	13	50,320	3,871
Navy	14	26,231	1,874
Nebraska	16	168,225	10,514
Nevada	13	81,973	6,306
UNLV	15	142,690	9,513
New Hampshire	12	21,442	1,787
New Mexico	20	320,517	16,026
New Mexico St.	14	85,997	6,143
New Orleans	13	28,677	2,206
Niagara	10	20,355	2,036
Nicholls St.	9	7,759	862
North Caro.	12	250,949	20,912
North Caro. A&T	11	38,790	3,526
North Caro. St.	14	148,160	10,583
N.C.-Asheville	13	18,685	1,437
N.C.-Charlotte	11	38,931	3,539
N.C.-Greensboro	11	13,625	1,239
N.C.-Wilmington	12	42,765	3,564
North Texas	12	27,767	2,314
Northeast La.	11	23,997	2,182
Northeastern	11	12,230	1,112
Northeastern Ill.	12	3,739	312
Northern Ariz.	12	16,896	1,408
Northern Ill.	13	35,346	2,719
Northern Iowa	14	37,270	2,662
Northwestern	14	65,578	4,684
Northwestern St.	12	16,568	1,381
Notre Dame	13	136,869	10,528
Ohio	13	93,166	7,167
Ohio St.	14	163,980	11,713
Oklahoma	15	139,236	9,282
Oklahoma St.	15	88,979	5,932
Old Dominion	12	72,422	6,035
Oral Roberts	15	70,457	4,697
Oregon	13	100,061	7,697
Oregon St.	12	59,028	4,919
Pacific (Cal.)	13	45,235	3,480
Penn St.	14	152,836	10,917
Pennsylvania	11	47,187	4,290
Pepperdine	10	18,256	1,826
Pittsburgh	15	123,957	8,264
Portland	13	26,167	2,013
Prairie View	11	26,381	2,398
Princeton	11	24,839	2,258
Providence	16	168,554	10,535
Purdue	14	197,157	14,083
Radford	13	19,950	1,535
Rhode Island	15	84,513	5,634
Rice	12	37,414	3,118
Richmond	11	58,886	5,353
Rider	13	18,907	1,454
Robert Morris	12	11,509	959
Rutgers	14	79,186	5,656
St. Bonaventure	11	55,292	5,027

Team	G	Total Att.	Avg.
St. Francis (N.Y.)	11	3,189	290
St. Francis (Pa.)	11	10,370	943
St. John's (N.Y.)	13	110,300	8,485
St. Joseph's (Pa.)	8	23,948	2,994
St. Louis	16	271,771	16,986
St. Mary's (Cal.)	13	23,257	1,789
St. Peter's	12	17,568	1,464
Sam Houston St.	13	14,022	1,079
Samford	12	24,746	2,062
San Diego	14	23,142	1,653
San Diego St.	15	40,161	2,677
San Francisco	16	56,742	3,546
San Jose St.	14	25,330	1,809
Santa Clara	11	45,552	4,141
Seton Hall	15	146,831	9,789
Siena	13	32,958	2,535
South Ala.	14	37,130	2,652
South Caro.	18	160,776	8,932
South Caro. St.	13	21,845	1,680
South Fla.	13	73,318	5,640
Southeast Mo. St.	13	59,897	4,607
Southeastern La.	13	24,425	1,879
Southern Cal	14	42,329	3,024
Southern Ill.	13	51,968	3,998
Southern Methodist	12	25,892	2,158
Southern Miss.	14	64,067	4,576
Southern Utah	13	40,572	3,121
Southern U.	12	29,038	2,420
Southwest Mo. St.	14	101,858	7,276
Southwest Tex. St.	12	19,269	1,606
Southwestern La.	14	65,423	4,673
Stanford	13	70,642	5,434
Stephen F. Austin	12	24,557	2,046
Stetson	14	27,666	1,976
Syracuse	16	363,653	22,728
Temple	10	32,609	3,261
Tennessee	17	244,410	14,377
Tennessee St.	9	39,530	4,392
Tennessee Tech	12	41,572	3,464
Tenn.-Chatt.	15	92,138	6,143
Tenn.-Martin	12	35,934	2,995
Texas	14	174,067	12,433
Texas A&M	11	34,636	3,149
Texas Christian	15	65,820	4,388
Texas Southern	11	15,179	1,380
Texas Tech	13	99,189	7,630
Texas-Arlington	12	9,021	752
UTEP	16	135,167	8,448
Texas-San Antonio	13	17,819	1,371
Tex.-Pan American	12	19,702	1,642
Toledo	15	94,545	6,303
Towson St.	11	14,659	1,333
Troy St.	12	5,682	474
Tulane	14	54,717	3,908
Tulsa	14	94,369	6,741
UCLA	13	154,331	11,872
Utah	15	214,216	14,281
Utah St.	15	113,067	7,538
Valparaiso	12	46,628	3,886
Vanderbilt	18	226,354	12,575
Vermont	11	15,404	1,400
Villanova	14	130,392	9,314
Virginia	14	108,293	7,735
Va. Commonwealth	13	63,345	4,873
VMI	13	28,025	2,156
Virginia Tech	11	91,933	8,358
Wagner	10	6,382	638
Wake Forest	14	179,109	12,794
Washington	15	77,171	5,145
Washington St.	12	97,284	8,107
Weber St.	11	81,542	7,413
West Va.	14	106,749	7,625
Western Caro.	11	22,507	2,046
Western Ill.	12	19,936	1,661
Western Ky.	12	71,500	5,958
Western Mich.	14	30,957	2,211
Wichita St.	15	82,915	5,528
William & Mary	14	41,560	2,969
Winthrop	12	16,386	1,366
Wisconsin	18	202,381	11,243
Wis.-Green Bay	13	71,186	5,476
Wis.-Milwaukee	12	23,880	1,990
Wofford	10	16,195	1,620

Team	G	Total Att.	Avg.
Wright St.	15	102,110	6,807
Wyoming	14	100,459	7,176
Xavier (Ohio)	14	124,191	8,871
Yale	11	8,122	738
Youngstown St.	13	19,799	1,523

DIVISION I ALL GAMES ATTENDANCE (HOME, ROAD, NEUTRAL)

1. Kentucky		725,884
2. Syracuse		672,172
3. Arkansas		576,494
4. Georgetown		532,972
5. Louisville		521,124
6. Connecticut		503,272
7. North Caro.		491,767
8. Indiana		481,429
9. Wake Forest		479,553
10. Kansas		476,852
11. Georgia Tech		473,157
12. Utah		453,273
13. New Mexico		445,837
14. Massachusetts		437,849
15. Mississippi St.		436,877
16. Cincinnati		434,003
17. Iowa		431,697
18. Illinois		430,627
19. Arizona		410,218
20. Michigan		409,537

DIVISION II

	G/S	1996 Attendance	Avg.	Change in Avg.	
1. South Dak. St.	14	69,229	4,945	Up	1,708
2. Alabama A&M	14	61,386	4,385	Down	756
3. Norfolk St.	11	41,385	3,762	Down	618
4. Northern St.	16	55,800	3,488	Down	146
5. North Dak. St.	15	48,978	3,265	Down	888
6. South Dak.	16	46,752	2,922	Down	626
7. Southern Ind.	17	49,200	2,894	Up	121
8. Fort Hays St.	19	53,609	2,822	Up	651
9. Augustana (S.D.)	16	41,163	2,573	Down	310
10. Cal St. Bakersfield	19	48,810	2,569	Up	552
11. Elizabeth City St.	10	24,765	2,477	Up	901
12. Southern Colo.	14	32,387	2,313	Down	431
13. Ky. Wesleyan	15	34,000	2,267	Down	693
14. Mo.-Rolla	19	42,066	2,214	Up	1,089
15. North Dak.	14	30,806	2,200	Down	358

DIVISION III

	G/S	1996 Attendance	Avg.	Change in Avg.	
1. Hope	11	26,500	2,409	Down	95
2. Calvin	13	29,857	2,297	Down	495
3. Ill. Wesleyan	17	35,350	2,079	Down	434
4. Wis.-Platteville	11	21,180	1,925	Down	135
5. Wheaton (Ill.)	15	27,750	1,850	Down	21
6. Wittenberg	19	31,738	1,670	Up	210
7. Gust. Adolphus	15	21,806	1,454	Up	579
8. Loras	14	19,931	1,424	Up	104
9. Wis.-Eau Claire	14	18,200	1,300	Down	644
10. Wilkes	15	19,350	1,290	Up	432
11. Hardin-Simmons	12	15,268	1,272	Up	522
12. Otterbein	11	13,414	1,219	Down	703
13. Simpson	13	15,684	1,206	Up	103
14. Rose-Hulman	12	14,340	1,195	Up	313
15. Frank. & Marsh.	19	21,175	1,114	Up	44

Annual NCAA Attendance

ALL DIVISIONS

Season	Teams	Attendance	Per Game Average	Change in Avg.	
1977	717	23,324,040	2,710	—	
1978	726	23,590,952	2,678	Down	32
1979	718	24,482,516	2,757	Up	79
1980	715	24,861,722	2,765	Up	8
1981	730	25,159,358	2,737	Down	28
1982	741	25,416,017	2,727	Down	10
1983	755	26,122,785	2,706	Down	21
1984	750	26,271,613	2,728	Up	22
1985	753	26,584,426	2,712	Down	16
1986	760	26,368,815	2,654	Down	58
1987	760	26,797,644	2,698	Up	44
1988	761	27,452,948	2,777	Up	79
1989	772	28,270,260	2,814	Up	37
1990	767	28,740,819	*2,860	Up	46
1991	796	29,249,583	2,796	Down	64
1992	813	*29,378,161	2,747	Down	49
1993	831	28,527,348	2,703	Down	44
1994	858	28,390,491	2,604	Down	99
1995	*868	28,548,158	2,581	Down	23
1996	866	28,225,352	2,563	Down	18

DIVISION I

Season	Teams	Attendance	Per Game Average	Change in Avg.	
1976	238	15,059,892	4,759	—	
1977	245	16,469,250	5,021	Up	262
1978	254	17,669,080	5,124	Up	103
1979	257	18,649,383	5,271	Up	147
1980	261	19,052,743	5,217	Down	54
1981	264	19,355,690	5,131	Down	86
1982	273	19,789,706	5,191	Up	60
1983	274	20,488,437	5,212	Up	21
1984	275	20,715,426	5,243	Up	31
1985	282	21,394,261	5,258	Up	15
1986	283	21,244,519	5,175	Down	83
1987	290	21,756,709	5,205	Up	30
1988	290	22,463,476	5,443	Up	238
1989	293	23,059,429	5,565	Up	122
1990	292	23,581,823	5,721	Up	156
1991	295	23,777,437	*5,735	Up	14
1992	298	*23,893,993	5,643	Down	92
1993	298	23,321,655	5,635	Down	8
1994	301	23,275,158	5,571	Down	64
1995	302	23,560,495	5,641	Up	70
1996	*305	23,542,652	5,588	Down	53

DIVISION II

Season	Teams	Attendance	Per Game Average	Change in Avg.	
1977	177	*3,846,907	*1,811	—	
1978	173	3,168,419	1,515	Down	296
1979	172	3,295,149	1,535	Up	20
1980	177	3,324,670	1,479	Down	56
1981	190	3,543,766	1,486	Up	7
1982	190	3,329,518	1,391	Down	95
1983	195	3,364,184	1,324	Down	67
1984	189	3,199,307	1,306	Down	18
1985	181	2,988,083	1,255	Down	51
1986	184	2,946,020	1,204	Down	51
1987	179	2,893,392	1,220	Up	16
1988	175	2,902,400	1,242	Up	22
1989	189	3,157,464	1,273	Up	31
1990	189	3,104,462	1,223	Down	50
1991	204	3,388,278	1,221	Down	2
1992	214	3,395,684	1,188	Down	33
1993	220	3,201,765	1,145	Down	43
1994	243	3,219,979	1,036	Down	109
1995	*244	3,125,974	992	Down	44
1996	242	2,918,802	938	Down	54

DIVISION III

Season	Teams	Attendance	Per Game Average	Change in Avg.	
1977	295	*2,881,400	*912	—	
1978	299	2,632,678	816	Down	96
1979	289	2,427,688	770	Down	46
1980	277	2,387,142	783	Up	13
1981	276	2,132,000	693	Down	90
1982	278	2,183,895	711	Up	18
1983	286	2,148,736	685	Down	26
1984	286	2,233,340	701	Up	16
1985	290	2,081,452	629	Down	72
1986	293	2,053,693	615	Down	14
1987	291	2,021,459	606	Down	9
1988	296	1,970,823	583	Down	23
1989	290	1,935,058	573	Down	10
1990	286	1,939,795	581	Up	8
1991	297	1,967,087	564	Down	17
1992	301	1,962,598	553	Down	11
1993	313	1,883,283	531	Down	22
1994	314	1,741,867	493	Down	38
1995	*322	1,802,301	487	Down	6
1996	319	1,730,357	472	Down	15

*Record.

Kevin Britnell and the Flying Dutchmen of Hope College were the biggest home draw in Division III, playing before average home crowds of 2,409 fans in 1996. Hope has led Division III in attendance three times since 1984.

Photo by Andy Alonso/NCAA photos

DIVISION III

Season	Conference	Teams	Attendance	P/G Avg.
1990	Wisconsin State University	9	*170,276	*1,362
1991	Wisconsin State University	7	84,615	1,128
1992	Michigan Intercollegiate	7	89,549	1,163
1993	Michigan Intercollegiate	7	97,624	1,236
1994	Michigan Intercollegiate	7	97,418	1,203
1995	Michigan Intercollegiate	7	86,353	1,183
1996	Michigan Intercollegiate	7	80,376	1,058

*Record.

Annual Team Attendance Champions

DIVISION I

Season	Champion	Games	Attendance	Avg.
1970	Illinois	11	157,206	14,291
1971	Illinois	11	177,408	16,128
1972	Brigham Young	12	261,815	21,818
1973	Brigham Young	14	260,102	18,579
1974	Brigham Young	10	162,510	16,251
1975	Minnesota	13	219,047	16,850
1976	Indiana	12	202,700	16,892
1977	Kentucky	14	312,527	22,323
1978	Kentucky	16	373,367	23,335
1979	Kentucky	15	351,042	23,403
1980	Kentucky	15	352,511	23,501
1981	Kentucky	15	354,996	23,666
1982	Kentucky	16	371,093	23,193
1983	Kentucky	15	356,776	23,785
1984	Kentucky	16	380,453	23,778
1985	Syracuse	15	388,049	25,870
1986	Syracuse	19	498,850	26,255
1987	Syracuse	19	474,214	24,959
1988	Syracuse	16	461,223	28,826
1989	Syracuse	19	*537,949	28,313
1990	Syracuse	16	478,686	*29,918
1991	Syracuse	17	497,179	29,246
1992	Syracuse	17	460,752	27,103
1993	Syracuse	16	405,620	25,351
1994	Syracuse	17	419,039	24,649
1995	Syracuse	16	387,925	24,245
1996	Kentucky	13	310,633	23,895

DIVISION II

Season	Champion	Avg.
1977	Evansville	4,576
1978	Norfolk St.	4,226
1979	Norfolk St.	4,984
1980	Norfolk St.	4,917
1981	North Dak. St.	5,300
1982	North Dak. St.	4,385
1983	North Dak. St.	6,057
1984	Norfolk St.	*6,663
1985	Norfolk St.	6,116
1986	St. Cloud St.	4,539
1987	North Dak. St.	4,820
1988	Southeast Mo. St.	5,227
1989	Southeast Mo. St.	5,052
1990	Southeast Mo. St.	5,287
1991	Southeast Mo. St.	5,370
1992	North Dak.	4,943
1993	Alabama A&M	4,748
1994	South Dak.	4,852
1995	Alabama A&M	5,141
1996	South Dak. St.	4,945

*Record.

DIVISION III

Season	Champion	Avg.
1977	Scranton	2,707
1978	Calvin	*3,630
1979	Savannah St.	2,870
1980	Savannah St.	2,917
1981	Potsdam St.	2,873
1982	Wis.-Stevens Point	2,929
1983	Augustana (Ill.)	3,033
1984	Hope	2,144
1985	Wis.-Stevens Point	2,313
1986	Calvin	2,570
1987	Concordia-M'head	2,869
1988	Calvin	2,627
1989	Calvin	2,544
1990	Calvin	2,622
1991	Hope	2,480
1992	Calvin	2,757
1993	Calvin	4,018
1994	Calvin	2,734
1995	Calvin	2,792
1996	Hope	2,409

Annual Conference Attendance Champions

DIVISION I

Season	Conference	Teams	Attendance	P/G Avg.
1976	Atlantic Coast	7	863,082	9,590
1977	Big Ten	10	1,346,889	9,977
1978	Big Ten	10	1,539,589	11,238
1979	Big Ten	10	1,713,380	12,238
1980	Big Ten	10	1,877,048	12,189
1981	Big Ten	10	1,779,892	12,026
1982	Big Ten	10	1,688,834	11,810
1983	Big Ten	10	1,747,910	11,499
1984	Big Ten	10	1,774,140	12,069
1985	Big Ten	10	1,911,325	12,097
1986	Big Ten	10	1,908,629	11,929
1987	Big Ten	10	1,805,263	11,877
1988	Big Ten	10	1,925,617	12,423
1989	Big Ten	10	1,971,110	12,635
1990	Big Ten	10	2,017,407	*13,449
1991	Big Ten	10	2,042,836	13,095
1992	Big Ten	10	1,994,144	12,865
1993	Big Ten	11	*2,163,693	12,728
1994	Big Ten	11	2,107,600	12,696
1995	Big Ten	11	2,058,763	12,708
1996	Big Ten	11	2,106,810	12,769

DIVISION II

Season	Conference	Teams	Attendance	P/G Avg.
1979	Central Intercollegiate	12	375,370	2,760
1980	Mid-Continent	5	189,193	2,782
1981	North Central Intercollegiate	8	312,410	2,840
1982	North Central Intercollegiate	8	290,995	2,622
1983	North Central Intercollegiate	8	356,777	2,567
1984	North Central Intercollegiate	10	392,154	2,801
1985	North Central Intercollegiate	10	380,087	2,639
1986	North Central Intercollegiate	10	379,701	2,601
1987	North Central Intercollegiate	10	393,940	2,626
1988	North Central Intercollegiate	10	413,956	2,797
1989	North Central Intercollegiate	10	438,403	2,923
1990	North Central Intercollegiate	10	436,292	2,889
1991	North Central Intercollegiate	10	438,746	2,868
1992	North Central Intercollegiate	10	*482,213	*3,014
1993	North Central Intercollegiate	10	408,624	2,919
1994	North Central Intercollegiate	10	362,572	2,627
1995	North Central Intercollegiate	10	382,042	2,497
1996	North Central Intercollegiate	10	341,119	2,336

Annual NCAA Tournament Attendance

DIVISION I

Season	Sess.	Attend.	P/G Avg.
1939	5	15,025	3,005
1940	5	36,880	7,376
1941	5	48,055	9,611
1942	5	24,372	4,874
1943	5	56,876	11,375
1944	5	59,369	11,874
1945	5	67,780	13,556

Season	Sess.	Attend.	P/G Avg.
1946	5	73,116	14,623
1947	5	72,959	14,592
1948	5	72,523	14,505
1949	5	66,077	13,215
1950	5	75,464	15,093
1951	9	110,645	12,294
1952	10	115,712	11,571
1953	14	127,149	9,082
1954	15	115,391	7,693
1955	15	116,983	7,799
1956	15	132,513	8,834
1957	14	108,891	7,778
1958	14	176,878	12,634
1959	14	161,809	11,558
1960	16	155,491	9,718
1961	14	169,520	12,109
1962	14	177,469	12,676
1963	14	153,065	10,933
1964	14	140,790	10,056
1965	13	140,673	10,821
1966	13	140,925	10,840
1967	14	159,570	11,398
1968	14	160,888	11,492
1969	15	165,712	11,047
1970	16	146,794	9,175
1971	16	207,200	12,950
1972	16	147,304	9,207
1973	16	163,160	10,198
1974	16	154,112	9,632
1975	18	183,857	10,214
1976	18	202,502	11,250
1977	18	241,610	13,423
1978	18	227,149	12,619
1979	22	262,101	11,914
1980	26	321,260	12,356
1981	26	347,414	13,362
1982	26	427,251	16,433
1983	28	364,356	13,013
1984	28	397,481	14,196
1985	34	422,519	12,427
1986	34	499,704	14,697
1987	34	654,744	19,257
1988	34	558,998	16,441
1989	34	613,242	18,037
1990	34	537,138	15,798
1991	34	665,707	19,580
1992	34	580,462	17,072
1993	34	*707,719	*20,815
1994	34	578,007	17,000
1995	34	539,440	15,866
1996	34	643,290	18,920

DIVISION II

Season	Sess.	Attend.	P/G Avg.
1977	22	*87,602	*3,982
1978	22	83,058	3,775
1979	22	66,446	3,020
1980	22	50,649	2,302
1981	22	69,470	3,158
1982	22	67,925	3,088
1983	22	70,335	3,197
1984	22	81,388	3,699
1985	22	81,476	3,703
1986	22	71,083	3,231
1987	22	77,934	3,542
1988	22	72,462	3,294
1989	20	69,008	3,450
1990	20	64,212	3,211
1991	20	59,839	2,992
1992	20	60,629	3,031
1993	20	56,125	2,806
1994	20	60,511	3,026
1995	36	86,767	2,410
1996	28	65,882	2,353

DIVISION III

Season	Sess.	Attend.	P/G Avg.
1977	21	38,881	1,851
1978	21	37,717	1,796
1979	22	43,850	1,993
1980	22	46,518	2,114
1981	22	58,432	*2,656
1982	22	44,973	2,044
1983	22	51,093	2,322
1984	22	42,152	1,916
1985	22	39,154	1,780
1986	22	53,500	2,432
1987	22	48,150	2,189
1988	22	43,787	1,990
1989	28	49,301	1,761
1990	26	50,527	1,943
1991	34	56,942	1,675
1992	34	65,257	1,919
1993	34	49,675	1,461
1994	34	54,848	1,613
1995	59	*88,684	1,503
1996	58	87,437	1,508

*Record.

ATTENDANCE RECORDS

Division I Attendance Records

SINGLE GAME (PAID)
68,112—LSU (87) vs. Notre Dame (64), January 20, 1990, at Louisiana Superdome, New Orleans, La. (regular-season game)

SINGLE GAME (TURNSTILE)
58,903—North Caro. (78) vs. Kansas (68) and Michigan (81) vs. Kentucky (78 (ot)), April 3, 1993, at Louisiana Superdome, New Orleans, La. (NCAA semifinals)

HOME COURT, SINGLE GAME
33,048—Syracuse (62) vs. Georgetown (58), March 3, 1991, at Carrier Dome, Syracuse, N.Y.

HOME-COURT AVERAGE, SEASON
29,918—Syracuse, 1990 (478,686 in 16 games at Carrier Dome)

HOME-COURT TOTAL, SEASON
537,949—Syracuse, 1989 (19 games)

FULL-SEASON AVERAGE, ALL GAMES
(home, road, neutral, tournaments)
22,501—Syracuse, 1989 (855,053 in 38 games)

FULL-SEASON TOTAL, ALL GAMES
(home, road, neutral, tournaments)
855,053—Syracuse, 1989 (38 games)

TOP 10 ATTENDANCE GAMES (PAID)*
68,112—LSU (87) vs. Notre Dame (64), January 20, 1990, at Louisiana Superdome, New Orleans, La.

66,144—LSU (82) vs. Georgetown (80), January 28, 1989, at Louisiana Superdome, New Orleans, La.

64,959—Indiana (74) vs. Syracuse (73), March 30, 1987, at Louisiana Superdome, New Orleans, La. (NCAA final); Indiana (97) vs. UNLV (93) and Syracuse (77) vs. Providence (63), March 28, 1987, at Louisiana Superdome, New Orleans, La. (NCAA semifinals)

64,151—North Caro. (77) vs. Michigan (71), April 5, 1993, at Louisiana Superdome, New Orleans, La. (NCAA final); North Caro. (78) vs. Kansas (68) and Michigan (81) vs. Kentucky (78) (ot), April 3, 1993, at Louisiana Superdome, New Orleans, La. (NCAA semifinals)

61,612—North Caro. (63) vs. Georgetown (62), March 29, 1982, at Louisiana Superdome, New Orleans, La. (NCAA final); North Caro. (68) vs. Houston (63) and Georgetown (50) vs. Louisville (46), March 27,

1982, at Louisiana Superdome, New Orleans, La. (NCAA semifinals)

61,304—LSU (84) vs. Texas (83), January 3, 1992, at Louisiana Superdome, New Orleans, La.

52,693—Houston (71) vs. UCLA (69), January 20, 1968, at The Astrodome, Houston, Texas.

50,379—Duke (71) vs. Michigan (51), April 6, 1992, at Hubert H. Humphrey Metrodome, Minneapolis, Minn. (NCAA final); Duke (81) vs. Indiana (78) and Michigan (76) vs. Cincinnati (72), April 4, 1992, at Hubert H. Humphrey Metrodome, Minneapolis, Minn. (NCAA semifinals)

47,100—Duke (72) vs. Kansas (65), April 1, 1991, at RCA Dome, Indianapolis, Ind. (NCAA final); Kansas (79) vs. North Caro. (73) and Duke (79) vs. UNLV (77), March 30, 1991, at RCA Dome, Indianapolis, Ind. (NCAA semifinals)

45,214—Louisville (101) vs. Indiana (79) and Notre Dame (81) vs. Kentucky (65), December 3, 1988, at RCA Dome, Indianapolis, Ind.

*Note: Figures for games at the Final Four also include the media.

TOP FIVE ATTENDANCE GAMES (TURNSTILE)
58,903—North Caro. (78) vs. Kansas (68) and Michigan (81) vs. Kentucky (78) (ot), April 3, 1993, at Louisiana Superdome, New

Orleans, La. (NCAA semifinals)

56,707—Indiana (74) vs. Syracuse (73), March 30, 1987, at Louisiana Superdome, New Orleans, La. (NCAA final)

56,264—North Caro. (77) vs. Michigan (71), April 5, 1993, at Louisiana Superdome, New Orleans, La. (NCAA final)

55,841—Indiana (97) vs. UNLV (93) and Syracuse (77) vs. Providence (63), March 28, 1987, at Louisiana Superdome, New Orleans, La. (NCAA semifinals)

54,321—LSU (82) vs. Georgetown (80), January 28, 1989, at Louisiana Superdome, New Orleans, La. (regular-season game)

TOP 10 REGULAR-SEASON GAMES (PAID)

68,112—LSU (87) vs. Notre Dame (64), January 20, 1990, at Louisiana Superdome, New Orleans, La.

66,144—LSU (82) vs. Georgetown (80), January 28, 1989, at Louisiana Superdome, New Orleans, La.

61,304—LSU (84) vs. Texas (83), January 3, 1992, at Louisiana Superdome, New Orleans, La.

52,693—Houston (71) vs. UCLA (69), January 20, 1968, at The Astrodome, Houston, Texas.

45,214—Louisville (101) vs. Indiana (79) and Notre Dame (81) vs. Kentucky (65), December 3, 1988, at RCA Dome, Indianapolis, Ind.

43,601—Notre Dame (69) vs. Louisville (54) and Kentucky (82) vs. Indiana (76), December 5, 1987, at RCA Dome, Indianapolis, Ind.

41,071—Kentucky (89) vs. Indiana (82), December 2, 1995, at RCA Dome, Indianapolis, Ind.

40,128—Louisville (84) vs. Notre Dame (73) and Indiana (71) vs. Kentucky (69), December 2, 1989, at RCA Dome, Indianapolis, Ind.

38,194—Indiana (96) vs. Kentucky (84), December 4, 1993, at RCA Dome, Indianapolis, Ind.

38,043—Kentucky (98) vs. Notre Dame (90) and Indiana (72) vs. Louisville (52), December 1, 1990, at RCA Dome, Indianapolis, Ind.

Playing Rules History

Photo from NCAA archives

More than 100 years have passed since Dr. James Naismith invented the game of basketball. While the game has undergone numerous changes since its inception in Springfield, Massachusetts, some of the original principles developed by Dr. Naismith still apply today.

Dr. James Naismith's 13 Original Rules Of Basketball

1. The ball may be thrown in any direction with one or both hands.

2. The ball may be batted in any direction with one or both hands (never with the fist).

3. A player cannot run with the ball. The player must throw it from the spot on which he catches it, allowance to be made for a man who catches the ball when running at a good speed if he tries to stop.

4. The ball must be held in or between the hands; the arms or body must not be used for holding it.

5. No shouldering, holding, pushing, tripping, or striking in any way the person of an opponent shall be allowed; the first infringement of this rule by any player shall count as a foul, the second shall disqualify him until the next goal is made, or, if there was evident intent to injure the person, for the whole of the game, no substitute allowed.

6. A foul is striking at the ball with the fist, violation of Rules 3, 4, and such as described in Rule 5.

7. If either side makes three consecutive fouls, it shall count a goal for the opponents (consecutive means without the opponents in the mean time making a foul).

8. A goal shall be made when the ball is thrown or batted from the grounds into the basket and stays there, providing those defending the goal do not touch or disturb the goal. If the ball rests on the edges, and the opponent moves the basket, it shall count as a goal.

9. When the ball goes out of bounds, it shall be thrown into the field of play by the person first touching it. In case of a dispute, the umpire shall throw it straight into the field. The thrower-in is allowed five seconds; if he holds it longer, it shall go to the opponent. If any side persists in delaying the game, the umpire shall call a foul on that side.

10. The umpire shall be judge of the men and shall note the fouls and notify the referee when three consecutive fouls have been made. He shall have power to disqualify men according to Rule 5.

11. The referee shall be judge of the ball and shall decide when the ball is in play, in bounds, to which side it belongs, and shall keep the time. He shall decide when a goal has been made, and keep account of the goals with any other duties that are usually performed by a referee.

12. The time shall be two 15-minute halves, with five minutes' rest between.

13. The side making the most goals in that time shall be declared the winner. In case of a draw, the game may, by agreement of the captains, be continued until another goal is made.

Note: These first published rules appeared in January 1892 in the Springfield College school newspaper, The Triangle.

Important Rules Changes

1891-92
• The 13 original rules of basketball are written by Dr. James Naismith in December 1891 in Springfield, Massachusetts.

1894-95
• The free-throw line is moved from 20 to 15 feet.

1895-96
• A field goal changes from three to two points, and free throws from three points to one point.

1896-97
• Backboards first are installed.

1900-01
• A dribbler may not shoot for a field goal and may dribble only once, and then with two hands.

1908-09
• A dribbler is permitted to shoot. The dribble is defined as the "continuous passage of the ball," making the double dribble illegal.
• A second referee is added for games in an effort to curb the rough play.

1910-11
• Players are disqualified upon committing their fourth personal foul.
• No coaching is allowed during the progress of the game by anybody connected with either team. A warning is given for the first violation and a free throw is awarded after that.

1913-14
• The bottom of the net is left open.

1914-15
• College, YMCA and AAU rules are made the same for the first time.

1920-21
• A player can reenter the game once. Before this rule, if a player left the game, he could not reenter for the rest of the game.
• The backboards are moved two feet from the wall of the court. Before this rule, players would "climb" up the padded wall to sink baskets.

1921-22
• Running with the ball changes from a foul to a violation.

1923-24
• The player fouled must shoot his own free throws. Before this rule, one person usually shot all his team's free throws.

1928-29
• The charging foul by the dribbler is introduced.

1930-31
• A "held ball" may be called when a closely guarded player is withholding the ball from play for five seconds. The result will be a jump ball.
• The maximum circumference of the ball is reduced from 32 to 31 inches, and the maximum weight from 23 to 22 ounces.

1932-33
• The 10-second center line is introduced to cut down on stalling.
• No player can stand in the free-throw lane with the ball more than three seconds.

1933-34
- A player may reenter the game twice.

1934-35
- The circumference of the ball again is reduced to between 29½ and 30¼ inches.

1935-36
- No offensive player can remain in the free-throw lane, with or without the ball, for more than three seconds.
- After a made free throw, the team scored upon shall put the ball in play at the end of the court where the goal had been scored.

1937-38
- The center jump after every goal scored is eliminated.

1938-39
- The ball will be thrown in from out of bounds at midcourt by the team shooting a free throw after a technical foul. Before, the ball was put into play with a center jump after a technical foul free throw.
- The circumference of the ball is established as 30 inches.

1939-40
- Teams have the choice of whether to take a free throw or take the ball out of bounds at midcourt. If two or more free throws are awarded, this option applies to the last throw.
- The backboards are moved from two to four feet from the end line to permit freer movement under the basket.

1940-41
- Fan-shaped backboards are made legal.

1942-43
- Any player who is eligible to start an overtime period will be allowed an extra personal foul, upping the total so disqualification is on the fifth foul.

1944-45
- Defensive goaltending is banned.
- Five personal fouls now disqualify a player. An extra foul is not permitted in overtime games.
- Unlimited substitution is introduced.
- It becomes a violation for an offensive player to remain in the free-throw lane more than three seconds.

1946-47
- Transparent backboards are authorized.

1947-48
- The clock is stopped on every dead ball the last three minutes of the second half and of every overtime period. This includes every time a goal is scored because the ball is considered dead until put into play again. (This rule was abolished in 1951.)

1948-49
- Coaches are allowed to speak to players during a timeout.

1951-52
- Games are to be played in four 10-minute quarters. Before this, games were played in two 20-minute halves.

1952-53
- Teams can no longer waive free throws in favor of taking the ball out of bounds.
- The one-and-one free-throw rule is introduced, although the bonus is used only if the first shot is missed. The rule will be in effect the entire game except the last three minutes, when every foul is two shots.

1954-55
- The one-and-one free throw is changed so that the bonus shot is given only if the first shot is made.
- Games are changed back to being played in two 20-minute halves.

1955-56
- The two-shot penalty in the last three minutes of the game is eliminated. The one-and-one is now in effect the entire game.

1956-57
- The free-throw lane is increased from six feet to 12 feet. On the lineup for a free throw, the two spaces adjacent to the end line must be occupied by opponents of the free thrower. In the past, one space was marked "H" for a home team player to occupy, and across the lane the first space was marked "V" for a visiting team player to stand in.
- Grasping the basket is now classified as a technical foul under unsportsmanlike tactics.

1957-58
- Offensive goaltending is now banned, as an addition to the original 1945 rule.
- One free throw for each common foul is taken for the first six personal fouls by one team in each half, and the one-and-one is used thereafter.
- On uniforms, the use of the single digit numbers one and two and any digit greater than five is prohibited.
- A ball that passes over the backboard—either front to back or back to front—is considered out of bounds.

1964-65
- Coaches must remain seated on the bench except while the clock is stopped or to direct or encourage players on the court. This rule is to help keep coaches from inciting undesirable crowd reactions toward the officials.

1967-68
- The dunk is made illegal during the game and pregame warm-up.

1970-71
- During a jump ball, a nonjumper may not change his position from the time the official is ready to make the toss until after the ball has been touched.

1972-73
- The free throw on the first six common fouls each half by a team is eliminated.
- Players cannot attempt to create the false impression that they have been fouled in charging-guarding situations or while screening when the contact was only incidental. An official can charge the "actor" with a technical foul for unsportsmanlike conduct if, in the official's opinion, the actor is making a travesty of the game.
- Freshmen are eligible to play varsity basketball. This was the result of a change in the NCAA bylaws, not the basketball playing rules.

1973-74
- Officials may now penalize players for fouls occurring away from the ball, such as grabbing, holding and setting illegal screens.

1974-75
- During a jump ball, a nonjumper on the restraining circle may move around it after the ball has left the official's hands.
- A player charged with a foul is no longer required to raise his hand. (In 1978, however, it was strongly recommended that a player start raising his hand again.)

1976-77
- The dunk is made legal again.

1981-82
- The jump ball is used only at the beginning of the game and the start of each overtime. An alternating arrow will indicate possession in jump-ball situations during the game.
- All fouls charged to bench personnel shall be assessed to the head coach.

1982-83
- When the closely guarded five-second count is reached, it is no longer a jump-ball situation. It is a violation, and the ball is awarded to the defensive team out of bounds.

1983-84
- Two free throws are taken for each common foul committed within the last two minutes of the second half and the entire overtime period, if the bonus rule is in effect. (This rule was rescinded one month into the season.)

1984-85
- The coaching box is introduced, whereby a coach and all bench personnel must remain in the 28-foot-long coaching box unless seeking information from the scorer's table.

1985-86
- The 45-second clock is introduced. The team in control of the ball must now shoot for a goal within 45 seconds after it attains team control.
- If a shooter is fouled intentionally and the shot is missed, the penalty will be two shots and possession of the ball out of bounds to the team that was fouled.
- The head coach may stand throughout the game, while all other bench personnel must remain seated.

1986-87
- The three-point field goal is introduced and set at 19 feet 9 inches from the center of the basket.
- A coach may leave the confines of the bench at any time without penalty to correct a scorer's or timer's mistake. A technical foul is assessed if there is no mistake. (This was changed the next year to a timeout.) Also, a television replay may be used to prevent or rectify a scorer's or timer's mistake or a malfunction of the clock.

1987-88
- Each intentional personal foul carries a two-shot penalty plus possession of the ball.

1988-89
- Any squad member who participates in a fight will be ejected from the game and will be placed on probation. If that player participates in a second fight during the season, he will be suspended for one game. A third fight involving the same person results in suspension for the rest of the season including championship competition.

1990-91
- Beginning with the team's 10th personal foul in a half, two free throws are awarded for each common foul, except player-control fouls.
- Three free throws are awarded when a shooter is fouled during an unsuccessful three-point try.
- The fighting rule is amended. The first time any squad member or bench personnel participates in a fight he will be suspended for the team's next game. If that same person participates in a second fight, he will be suspended for the rest of the season including championship competition.

1991-92
- Contact technical fouls count toward the five fouls for player disqualification and toward the team fouls in reaching bonus free-throw situations.
- The shot clock is reset when the ball strikes the basket ring, not when a shot leaves the shooter's hands as it had been ever since the rule was introduced in 1986.

1992-93
- Unsporting technical fouls, in addition to contact technical fouls, count toward the five fouls for player disqualification and toward the team fouls in reaching bonus free-throw situations.

1993-94
- The shot clock is reduced to 35 seconds from 45. The team in control of the ball must now shoot for a goal within 35 seconds after it gains team control.
- A foul shall be ruled intentional if, while playing the ball, a player causes excessive contact with an opponent.
- The game clock will be stopped after successful field goals in the last minute of the game and the last minute of any overtime period with no substitution allowed.
- The five-second dribbling violation when closely guarded is eliminated.
- The rule concerning the use of profanity is expanded to include abusive and obscene language in an effort to curtail verbal misconduct by players and coaches.

1994-95
- The inner circle at midcourt is eliminated.
- Scoring is restricted to a tap-in when three-tenths (.3) of a second or less remain on the game clock or shot clock.
- The fighting and suspension rules are expanded to include coaches and team personnel.

1995-96
- All unsporting technical fouls charged to anyone on the bench count toward the team foul total.
- Teams are allowed one 20-second timeout per half. This was an experimental rule in the 1994-95 season.

1996-97
- Teams shall warm up and shoot at the end of the court farthest from their own bench for the first half. Previously, teams had the choice of baskets in the first half.
- In games not involving commercial electronic media, teams are entitled to four full-length timeouts and two 20-second timeouts per game. In games involving commercial electronic media, teams are entitled to two full-length timeouts and three 20-second timeouts per game.

Division I Basketball Firsts

The First Time...

Playing rules were published:
January 1892 in the Springfield College school newspaper, The Triangle.

A game was played:
January 20, 1892, at the Training School of the International YMCA College, now known as Springfield College in Massachusetts

A game was played in public:
March 11, 1892, at Springfield College. A crowd of 200 saw the students defeat the teachers, 5-1.

A full schedule of games was played by a college:
1894 when the University of Chicago compiled a 6-1 season record.

A game between two colleges was played:
February 9, 1895, when the Minnesota School of Agriculture defeated Hamline, 9-3. Nine players were allowed on the court at the same time for both teams.

A game between two colleges was played with five players on each team:
January 16, 1896, when Chicago defeated Iowa, 15-12, in Iowa City. Iowa's starting lineup was composed of a YMCA team that just happened to be university students.

A game between two true college teams with five players on a team was played:
1897 when Yale defeated Pennsylvania, 32-10.

A conference season was played:
1901-02 by the East League, known today as the Ivy Group.

A conference tournament was played:
1921 by the Southern Conference. Kentucky was the winner.

A consensus all-America team was selected:
1929. Members were Charley Hyatt, Pittsburgh; Joe Schaaf, Pennsylvania; Charles Murphy, Purdue; Vern Corbin, California; Thomas Churchill, Oklahoma; and John Thompson, Montana State.

An Associated Press poll was published:
1949 when Kentucky was declared No. 1.

The National Invitation Tournament was played:
1938 when Temple was the winner.

A college game was televised:
February 28, 1940, when Pittsburgh defeated Fordham, 50-37, at Madison Square Garden in New York City.

NCAA Tournament Firsts

The first game:
March 17, 1939, when Villanova defeated Brown, 42-30, in Philadelphia.

The first championship game:
March 27, 1939, when Oregon defeated Ohio State, 46-33, in Evanston, Illinois.

The first time two teams from the same conference played in the NCAA tournament:
1944 when Iowa State and Missouri, both of the Big Six, played in the Western regional.

The first time four teams advanced to the final site:
1946 (North Carolina, Ohio State, Oklahoma State and California).

The first championship game televised:
1946 locally in New York City by WCBS-TV. Oklahoma State defeated North Carolina, 43-40. An estimated 500,000 watched the game on television.

The first repeat champion:
Oklahoma State followed its 1945 championship with a title in 1946.

First NCAA championship team to have an integrated roster of white and black players:
CCNY's 1950 squad is believed to be the first integrated championship team.

The first time conference champions qualified automatically:
1951.

The first time a conference champion qualified automatically for the NCAA tournament instead of the regular-season champion:
1952, North Carolina State finished second in the Southern Conference but won the conference postseason tournament.

The first time there were four regional sites:
1952.

The first time games were televised regionally:
1952.

The first time a Final Four was played on Friday and Saturday:
1954.

The first tournament championship game televised nationally:
1954 for a broadcast rights fee of $7,500.

The first time an undefeated team won the NCAA championship:
1956 when San Francisco went 29-0.

The first time two teams from the same state played in the NCAA title game:
1961 when Cincinnati defeated Ohio State, 70-65, in overtime.

The first championship team to start five African-Americans:
UTEP in 1966—Harry Flournoy, David Lattin, Bobby Joe Hill, Orsten Artis, Willie Cager.

The first time the Final Four was played on Thursday and Saturday:
1969.

The first time the Final Four was played on Saturday and Monday:
1973.

The first NCAA title game televised during prime time:
UCLA's win over Memphis in1973 was televised by NBC.

The first time television rights totaled more than $1 million:
1973.

The first public draw for Final Four tickets:
1973 for the 1974 championship.

The first time teams other than the conference champion could be chosen at large from the same conference:
1975.

The first reference to the term "Final Four":
1975 Official Collegiate Basketball Guide, page 5 in national preview-review section written by Ed Chay of the Cleveland Plain Dealer. Chay wrote, "Outspoken Al McGuire of Marquette, whose team was one of the final four in Greensboro, was among several coaches who said it was good for college basketball that UCLA was finally beaten."

The first time two teams from the same conference played in the Final Four title game:
1976 when Indiana defeated Michigan, 86-68. Both teams were Big Ten members.

The first time the seeding process was used to align teams in the bracket:
1978.

The first reference to term "Final Four" is capitalized:
1978 Official Collegiate Basketball Guide (page 7, first line).

The first time all teams were seeded in the bracket:
1979.

The first public lottery for Final Four tickets:
1979.

The first time more than two teams from the same conference were allowed in the NCAA tournament:
1980.

The first time none of the No. 1 seeds in the NCAA tournament advanced to the Final Four:
1980.

The first time the Ratings Percentage Index (RPI), a computer ranking system, was used as an aid in evaluating teams for at-large selections and seeding:
1981.

The first time two No. 1 seeds in the NCAA tournament advanced to the Final Four:
1981.

The first live television broadcast of the selection show announcing the NCAA tournament bracket:
1982.

The first time CBS was awarded the television rights for the NCAA tournament:
1982.

The first time a men's and women's team from the same school advanced to the Final Four in the same year:
1983, when both Georgia teams lost in the national semifinals.

The first time awards were presented to all participating teams in the NCAA championship tournament:
1984.

The first time 64 teams participated in the NCAA tournament:
1985.

The first time three teams from the same conference advanced to the Final Four:
1985, when Georgetown, St. John's (New York) and Villanova represented the Big East.

The first time all 64 NCAA tournament teams were subject to drug testing:
1987.

The first time neutral courts were used in all rounds of the NCAA tournament:
1989.

The first time all the Nos. 1 and 2 seeds in the NCAA tournament advanced to the Sweet Sixteen:
1989.

The first time a minimum facility seating capacity of 12,000 for first and second rounds and regionals was established:
1993.

The first time three No. 1 seeds in the NCAA tournament advanced to the Final Four:
1993.

The first time two former Final Four most outstanding players returned to the Final Four:
1995, when North Carolina's Donald Williams (1993) and Arkansas' Corliss Williamson (1994) returned to the Final Four.

The first NCAA tournament MOP:
Marv Huffman of Indiana in 1940.

The first freshman named NCAA tournament MOP:
Arnie Ferrin of Utah in 1944.

The first two-time NCAA tournament MOP:
Bob Kurland of Oklahoma State in 1945 and 1946.

The first NCAA tournament MOP not to play on the national championship team:
B. H. Born of Kansas in 1953.

The first football Heisman Trophy winner to play in the Final Four:
Terry Baker of Oregon State in 1963.

The first three-time NCAA tournament MOP:
Lew Alcindor of UCLA in 1967, 1968 and 1969.

The first player to play for two teams in the Final Four championship game:
Bob Bender with Indiana 1976 and Duke 1978.

The first coach to win the NCAA title in his first year as a head coach:
Steve Fisher of Michigan in 1989.

The First Team(s)...

To win 30 games in a season:
Wyoming went 31-2 in1943.

To win a football bowl game and the NCAA tournament title in the same academic year:
Oklahoma State won the Cotton Bowl and the NCAA championship in 1944-45.

To be ranked No. 1 in the final regular-season poll and go on to win the NCAA championship:
Kentucky ended the 1949 regular season ranked No. 1 and proceeded to win its second NCAA title.

To win the NCAA tournament and the NIT in the same year:
CCNY won both tournaments in 1950.

To play for the national championship in both football and basketball in the same academic year:
Oklahoma lost in both the Orange Bowl and the Final Four title game in 1987-88.

Representing the same school to be ranked No. 1 in the men's and women's polls:
Connecticut's men's and women's basketball programs were ranked No. 1 in their respective top 25 polls February 13, 1995.

The First Coach...

Who also happened to be the inventor of the game:
Dr. James Naismith invented the game in December 1891 at Springfield College in Massachusetts.

To lead his team to a finish among the final four teams in the nation in his first season as a head coach:
Ray Meyer of DePaul in 1943.

To be recognized as coach of the year:
Phil Woolpert of San Francisco was named the 1955 coach of the year by United Press International.

To take two different schools to the NCAA championship game:
Frank McGuire in 1957 with North Carolina after St. John's (New York) in 1952.

To win the NCAA championship after playing for an NCAA championship team:
Bob Knight coached Indiana to the championship in 1976 after playing for the 1960 Ohio State champs.

Arkansas' Corliss Williamson is one of only two players to return to the Final Four after being named the tournament's most outstanding player.

PLAYING RULES HISTORY

To take two different teams to the Final Four:
Forddy Anderson and Frank McGuire. Anderson—Bradley in 1950 (first year) and Michigan State in 1957; McGuire—St. John's (N.Y.) (first year) in 1952 and North Carolina in 1957.

To take two different teams to the NCAA tournament:
Ben Carnevale—North Carolina in 1946 (first year) and Navy in 1947.

To take three different teams to the NCAA tournament:
Eddie Hickey—Creighton in 1941 (first year), St. Louis in 1952 and Marquette in 1959.

To take four different teams to the NCAA tournament:
Eddie Sutton—Creighton in 1974 (first year), Arkansas in 1977, Kentucky in 1986 and Oklahoma State in 1991.

The First Player...

To be named consensus all-American three times:
John Wooden of Purdue from 1930-32.

To score 1,000 points in his career:
Christian Steinmetz of Wisconsin from 1903-05.

To score 50 points in one game:
Hank Luisetti of Stanford, who scored 50 in a win over Duquesne, January 1, 1938.

To popularize the jump shot:
Hank Luisetti of Stanford in 1936-38.

African-American to be named to the consensus all-America team:
Don Barksdale of UCLA in 1947.

To score 2,000 points in his career:
Jim Lacy of Loyola (Md.) scored 2,154 points in 1946-49.

To lead the nation in scoring during the regular season and play for the NCAA championship team in the same year:
Clyde Lovellette of Kansas in 1952.

To grab 50 rebounds in one game:
Bill Chambers of William & Mary brought down 51 boards against Virginia on February 14, 1953.

To grab 700 rebounds in a season:
Walt Dukes of Seton Hall brought down 734 boards during the 1953 season.

To score 100 points in a game:
Frank Selvy of Furman scored 100 points in a 149-95 victory over Newberry on February 13, 1954, in Greenville, S.C.

To score 1,000 points in a single season:
Frank Selvy of Furman scored 1,209 during the 1954 season.

To average 40 points a game for a season:
Frank Selvy of Furman averaged 41.7 points a game during the 1954 season.

To average 30 points a game for a career:
Frank Selvy of Furman averaged 32.5 points a game from 1952-54.

Recognized as the player of the year:
Tom Gola of La Salle was named the 1955 player of the year by United Press International.

To score 3,000 points in his career:
Pete Maravich of LSU scored 3,667 points from 1968-70.

To average 40 points a game for a career:
Pete Maravich of LSU averaged 44.2 points a game from 1968-70.

To lead the nation in scoring and rebounding in the same season:
Xavier McDaniel of Wichita State in 1985.

To make 400 three-point field goals in his career:
Doug Day of Radford hit 401 three-pointers from 1990-93.

Schedules/Results

198 SCHEDULES AND RESULTS

1997 Schedules/ 1996 Results—All Divisions

Following is an alphabetical listing of the 1996-97 schedules and 1995-96 season's game-by-game scores for the men's teams of the member colleges and universities of the National Collegiate Athletic Association. Below each team's name and location appear the name of its head coach, his alma mater and his complete won-lost record as a college head coach. Divisional designation for each team is indicated in the upper right-hand corner of each listing.

Squares (■) indicate home games, daggers (†) indicate neutral-site games and section symbols (§) indicate forfeits. Games played and subsequently forfeited do not alter records.

All records are restricted to varsity games between four-year college institutions.

ABILENE CHRISTIAN
Abilene, TX 79699 II

Coach: Shanon Hays
Alma Mater: Lubbock Christian '91
(First year as head coach)

1996-97 SCHEDULE
Abilene Christian Cl	Nov. 15-16
Schreiner ■	Nov. 21
South Ala.	Nov. 23
Texas-San Antonio	Nov. 26
Western N.M. Tr.	Nov. 29-30
National Christian	Dec. 5
West Tex. A&M ■	Dec. 14
Eastern N.M. ■	Dec. 16
Angelo St. Cl.	Dec. 27-28
Midwestern St.	Jan. 2
Central Okla.	Jan. 4
Tarleton St. ■	Jan. 7
Texas A&M-Commerce ■	Jan. 9
Tex. A&M-Kingsville	Jan. 13
Angelo St. ■	Jan. 18
Central Okla. ■	Jan. 23
Midwestern St. ■	Jan. 25
Texas A&M-Commerce	Jan. 30
Tarleton St.	Feb. 1
Tex. A&M-Kingsville ■	Feb. 6
Angelo St.	Feb. 15
Eastern N.M.	Feb. 20
West Tex. A&M	Feb. 22

1995-96 RESULTS (13-14)
102	Adams St. ■	70
90	Cameron ■	81
116	Schreiner ■	68
78	Arkansas St.	82
64	South Ala.	74
113	Huston-Tillotson ■	88
128	National Christian ■	47
69	West Tex. A&M	92
83	Eastern N.M.	111
124	Ouachita Baptist †	94
78	Lubbock Chrst. †	66
83	Midwestern St. ■	86
97	Central Okla. ■	102
66	Tarleton St.	73
63	Texas A&M-Commerce	79
65	Tex. A&M-Kingsville ■	67
81	Angelo St. ■	78
92	Central Okla.	106
106	Midwestern St.	111
72	Texas A&M-Commerce ■	65
81	Tarleton St. ■	78
88	Tex. A&M-Kingsville	95
74	Cameron	77
78	Angelo St.	70
80	Eastern N.M. ■	68
74	West Tex. A&M ■	69
73	West Tex. A&M	79

Nickname: Wildcats
Colors: Purple & White
Arena: Moody Coliseum
  Capacity: 4,600; Year Built: 1968

AD: Stan Lambert
SID: Garner Roberts

ADAMS ST.
Alamosa, CO 81102 II

Coach: Larry Mortensen
Alma Mater: Adams St. '88
(First year as head coach)

1996-97 SCHEDULE
Abilene Christian Cl	Nov. 15-16
Colorado St.	Nov. 22
Denver Cl.	Nov. 29-30
Colo. Christian	Dec. 6
Regis (Colo.) ■	Dec. 7
Air Force	Dec. 10
Colorado Mines	Dec. 13
Metro St.	Dec. 14
Chadron St. ■	Jan. 4
Fort Hays St.	Jan. 10
Neb.-Kearney	Jan. 11
Fort Lewis ■	Jan. 15
N.M. Highlands	Jan. 18
UC-Colo. Spgs. ■	Jan. 24
Southern Colo. ■	Jan. 25
Western St.	Jan. 31
Mesa St.	Feb. 1
UC-Colo. Spgs.	Feb. 7
Southern Colo.	Feb. 8
Fort Lewis	Feb. 11
Denver ■	Feb. 14
N.M. Highlands ■	Feb. 15
Western St. ■	Feb. 21
Mesa St. ■	Feb. 22

1995-96 RESULTS (12-15)
70	Abilene Christian	102
79	Angelo St. †	81
91	Colo. Christian	68
81	Air Force	94
81	Neb.-Kearney	90
80	Fort Hays St.	109
79	Mesa St. ■	73
69	Western St. ■	74
91	Denver ■	104
87	Southern Colo.	86
75	West Tex. A&M ■	77
114	Colorado Col.	95
106	Fort Lewis ■	100
77	Colo. Christian ■	62
65	N.M. Highlands	60
99	Chadron St.	89
75	Colorado Mines	68
73	Neb.-Kearney ■	91
71	Fort Hays St. ■	81
81	Mesa St.	95
85	Western St.	98
64	N.M. Highlands ■	59
88	Fort Lewis	93
93	Denver	96
92	Chadron St. ■	66
76	Colorado Mines ■	64
82	Colorado Mines ■	83

Nickname: Grizzlies
Colors: Green & White
Arena: Plachy Hall
  Capacity: 3,200; Year Built: 1960
AD: Rodger Jehlicka
SID: Lloyd Engen

ADELPHI
Garden City, NY 11530 II

Coach: Steve Clifford
Alma Mater: Me.-Farmington '83
Record: 1 Year, W-23, L-7

1996-97 SCHEDULE
Bentley Tr.	Nov. 15-16
Molloy	Nov. 23
Stony Brook	Nov. 26
St. Michael's ■	Nov. 30
New York Tech ■	Dec. 4
LIU-C. W. Post ■	Dec. 11
Dowling	Dec. 14
Concordia (N.Y.) ■	Dec. 21
Mercy ■	Jan. 4
LIU-Southampton ■	Jan. 8
St. Rose	Jan. 11
Queens (N.Y.) ■	Jan. 13
Phila. Textile	Jan. 15
Pace ■	Jan. 18
New York Tech	Jan. 20
Concordia (N.Y.) ■	Jan. 22
LIU-C. W. Post	Jan. 25
Dowling ■	Jan. 29
Mercy	Feb. 1
Molloy ■	Feb. 5
LIU-Southampton	Feb. 8
St. Rose ■	Feb. 12
Queens (N.Y.)	Feb. 15
Phila. Textile ■	Feb. 19
Pace	Feb. 22

1995-96 RESULTS (23-7)
78	St. Michael's	73
63	Pace	57
94	Shepherd †	82
86	Millersville	92
95	Molloy	73
75	Dowling ■	72
93	LIU-C. W. Post ■	75
73	Concordia (N.Y.) ■	55
87	St. Rose	95
93	LIU-Southampton ■	84
83	Queens (N.Y.)	91
76	Phila. Textile ■	73
91	New York Tech ■	87
84	Mercy	80
67	Pace ■	78
84	Concordia (N.Y.)	64
99	Molloy ■	73
65	Stony Brook †	52
71	Dowling	75
85	LIU-C. W. Post	72
93	St. Rose ■	96
80	LIU-Southampton	77
83	Queens (N.Y.) ■	68
74	Phila. Textile	62
106	New York Tech	98
90	Mercy ■	77
84	Dowling ■	80
76	Phila. Textile †	69
77	St. Rose	76
52	New Hamp. Col. †	68

Nickname: Panthers
Colors: Brown & Gold
Arena: Woodruff Hall
  Capacity: 800; Year Built: 1929
AD: Robert Hartwell
SID: Joe DiBari

ADRIAN
Adrian, MI 49221 III

Coach: Buck Riley
Alma Mater: Southwest Okla. '67
Record: 14 Years, W-127, L-211

1996-97 SCHEDULE
Thiel Cl.	Nov. 22-23
Bluffton ■	Nov. 27
Wilmington Tr.	Dec. 6-7
Marian Tr.	Dec. 20-21
Thomas More ■	Dec. 28
Oberlin	Dec. 30
Bluffton	Jan. 4
Albion	Jan. 8
Olivet ■	Jan. 11
Kalamazoo ■	Jan. 15
Defiance ■	Jan. 18
Calvin	Jan. 22
Hope	Jan. 25
Alma ■	Jan. 29
Albion ■	Feb. 1
Olivet	Feb. 5
Kalamazoo	Feb. 8
Siena Heights ■	Feb. 10
Calvin ■	Feb. 15
Hope ■	Feb. 19
Alma	Feb. 22

1995-96 RESULTS (11-13)
76	Oberlin ■	48
96	Bluffton	99
73	Pitt.-Bradford †	82
77	Bethany (W.Va.) †	56
75	Concordia (Mich.) ■	68
75	Grace Bible (Mich.) ■	73
92	Bluffton ■	67
65	Albion ■	69
68	Olivet	80
60	Concordia (Mich.)	57
46	Kalamazoo	45
61	Calvin ■	92
53	Hope ■	73
76	Alma	67
81	Albion	86
73	Michigan Christian ■	74
74	Olivet ■	67
68	Kalamazoo ■	74
78	Grace Bible (Mich.)	55
52	Calvin	82
78	Siena Heights	88
74	Hope	92
81	Alma ■	72
51	Albion	54

Nickname: Bulldogs
Colors: Gold & Black
Arena: Merillat Center
  Capacity: 1,350; Year Built: 1990
AD: Henry Mensing
SID: Darcy Gifford

AIR FORCE
USAF Academy, CO 80840 I

Coach: Reggie Minton
Alma Mater: Wooster '63
Record: 13 Years, W-126, L-240

1996-97 SCHEDULE
Regis (Colo.) ■	Nov. 23
Bucknell ■	Nov. 28
Navy ■	Nov. 30
Doane ■	Dec. 3
Cal Poly SLO ■	Dec. 7
Adams St. ■	Dec. 10
UC-Colo. Spgs. ■	Dec. 21
Montana St. Cl.	Dec. 28-29
Southern Methodist	Jan. 4
Hawaii ■	Jan. 9
San Diego St. ■	Jan. 11
San Jose St.	Jan. 16
Fresno St.	Jan. 18
Southern Methodist ■	Jan. 22
UNLV ■	Jan. 25
Wyoming ■	Jan. 30
Colorado St. ■	Feb. 1
San Diego St.	Feb. 6
Hawaii	Feb. 8
San Jose St. ■	Feb. 13
Fresno St. ■	Feb. 15
UNLV	Feb. 20

Wofford ■ ....Feb. 22
Colorado St. ....Feb. 27
Wyoming ....Mar. 1
Western Ath. Conf. Tr. ....Mar. 4-8

1995-96 RESULTS (5-23)

87	Navy	.89
94	Adams St. ■	.81
71	Doane	.58
65	Regis (Colo.) ■	.76
75	Navy	.69
84	UC-Colo. Spgs. ■	.52
63	Northern Ill. ■	.70
72	Austin Peay †	.91
60	William & Mary †	.64
48	UTEP ■	.53
49	New Mexico ■	.61
64	Brigham Young	.68
45	Utah	.69
67	Fresno St. ■	.73
92	Hawaii ■	.83
69	San Diego St. ■	.77
67	Wyoming	.84
71	Colorado St. ■	.94
65	Wyoming ■	.72
89	Colorado St.	.91
62	Hawaii	.81
72	San Diego St.	.81
50	Fresno St.	.82
66	Brigham Young ■	.80
50	Utah ■	.74
55	New Mexico	.67
59	UTEP	.69
69	San Diego St. †	.80

Nickname: Falcons
Colors: Blue & Silver
Arena: Cadet Field House
  Capacity: 6,002; Year Built: 1968
AD: Col. Randall W. Spetman
SID: Dave Kellogg

AKRON
Akron, OH 44325 I

Coach: Dan Hipsher
Alma Mater: Bowling Green '77
Record: 7 Years, W-129, L-68

1996-97 SCHEDULE

Cleveland St. ■ ....Nov. 25
Duquesne ....Nov. 30
Wooster ■ ....Dec. 3
UC Santa Barbara Cl. ....Dec. 5-7
Canisius ....Dec. 15
Xavier (Ohio) ■ ....Dec. 21
George Mason ■ ....Dec. 29
Miami (Ohio) ....Jan. 4
Toledo ■ ....Jan. 8
Ohio ....Jan. 11
Bowling Green ■ ....Jan. 13
Western Mich. ....Jan. 15
Ball St. ■ ....Jan. 18
Central Mich. ....Jan. 22
Kent ....Jan. 25
Eastern Mich. ....Jan. 29
Toledo ....Feb. 1
Ohio ■ ....Feb. 5
Bowling Green ....Feb. 8
Western Mich. ■ ....Feb. 12
Ball St. ....Feb. 15
Central Mich. ■ ....Feb. 19
Kent ■ ....Feb. 22
Eastern Mich. ....Feb. 26
Miami (Ohio) ■ ....Mar. 1
Mid-American Conf. Tr. ....Mar. 4-8

1995-96 RESULTS (3-23)

54	Notre Dame	.65
72	Canisius	.68
77	Cleveland St.	.52
82	Slippery Rock ■	.58
82	Fairfield ■	.83
61	Northern Ill.	.81
57	N.C.-Greensboro	.82
75	Duquesne ■	.76
63	Central Mich.	.69

73	Eastern Mich. ■	.82
61	Ball St.	.83
70	Miami (Ohio) ■	.83
68	Kent	.89
60	Ohio ■	.81
61	Toledo	.67
51	Bowling Green	.70
46	Western Mich. ■	.51
53	Eastern Mich.	.62
64	Ball St. ■	.89
50	Miami (Ohio)	.99
63	Kent ■	.86
59	Ohio	.73
62	Toledo ■	.74
50	Bowling Green ■	.68
49	Western Mich.	.89
68	Central Mich. ■	.69

Nickname: Zips
Colors: Blue & Gold
Arena: James A. Rhodes Arena
  Capacity: 5,500; Year Built: 1983
AD: Mike Bobinski
SID: Jeff Brewer

ALABAMA
Tuscaloosa, AL 34587 I

Coach: David Hobbs
Alma Mater: Va. Commonwealth '71
Record: 4 Years, W-78, L-46

1996-97 SCHEDULE

Top of the World Cl. ....Nov. 22-24
Northeastern Ill. ■ ....Nov. 30
Ark.-Pine Bluff ■ ....Dec. 2
Minnesota ....Dec. 5
Florida Int'l ....Dec. 7
Western Caro. ■ ....Dec. 14
North Texas ■ ....Dec. 18
Va. Commonwealth
  [Birmingham] ....Dec. 21
Santa Clara Cl. ....Dec. 27-28
Vanderbilt ....Jan. 4
Mississippi ....Jan. 8
Syracuse ■ ....Jan. 11
Arkansas ■ ....Jan. 15
Florida ....Jan. 18
South Caro. ....Jan. 22
LSU ....Jan. 25
Auburn ....Jan. 28
Mississippi St. ....Feb. 1
Georgia ■ ....Feb. 5
Tennessee ....Feb. 8
Mississippi ■ ....Feb. 12
LSU ....Feb. 15
Kentucky ■ ....Feb. 19
Auburn ■ ....Feb. 22
Arkansas ....Feb. 26
Mississippi St. ■ ....Mar. 1
Southeastern Conf. Tr. ....Mar. 6-9

1995-96 RESULTS (19-13)

84	Winthrop ■	.69
74	North Texas ■	.72
90	Tennessee Tech ■	.78
100	Mercer ■	.73
80	Florida A&M ■	.39
80	Tulane ■	.79
49	St. Peter's †	.59
64	Bucknell †	.72
80	Vanderbilt ■	.71
77	LSU	.99
72	Auburn ■	.65
56	Mississippi St.	.55
62	Tennessee ■	.53
67	South Caro.	.90
63	Arkansas ■	.71
63	Mississippi	.70
68	Florida ■	.65
68	Syracuse	.81
83	Southern Miss.	.69
55	Georgia	.68
75	Auburn	.72
76	LSU ■	.73
65	Kentucky	.84
65	Mississippi St. ■	.73

98	Arkansas	.89
67	Mississippi ■	.63
65	Tennessee †	.77
72	Illinois	.69
72	Missouri ■	.49
68	South Caro.	.67
69	St. Joseph's (Pa.) †	.74
76	Tulane †	.87

Nickname: Crimson Tide
Colors: Crimson & White
Arena: Coleman Coliseum
  Capacity: 15,043; Year Built: 1968
AD: Bob Bockrath
SID: Barbara Butler

ALABAMA A&M
Normal, AL 35762 II

Coach: L. Vann Pettaway
Alma Mater: Alabama A&M '80
Record: 10 Years, W-239, L-68

1996-97 SCHEDULE

Central St. ....Nov. 21
Morehouse ....Nov. 26
Miles ....Dec. 3
Albany St. (Ga.) ■ ....Dec. 7
LeMoyne-Owen ....Dec. 9
Alabama St. ....Dec. 14
Virginia St. [Indianapolis] ......Dec. 28
Paine ....Jan. 4
Albany St. (Ga.) ....Jan. 6
Kentucky St. ....Jan. 11
Clark Atlanta ....Jan. 13
LeMoyne-Owen ■ ....Jan. 15
Tuskegee ■ ....Jan. 18
Morris Brown ■ ....Jan. 20
Morehouse ■ ....Jan. 23
Tuskegee ....Jan. 25
Fort Valley St. † ....Jan. 27
Miles ■ ....Jan. 29
Fort Valley St. ....Feb. 3
Clark Atlanta ■ ....Feb. 6
Savannah St. ■ ....Feb. 8
Morris Brown ....Feb. 12
Paine ■ ....Feb. 15
Kentucky St. ■ ....Feb. 17
Ala.-Huntsville ■ ....Feb. 20
Lane ■ ....Feb. 22

1995-96 RESULTS (28-3)

77	Morehouse	.63
81	Miles	.77
99	Albany St. (Ga.) ■	.71
85	Morris Brown	.78
109	LeMoyne-Owen ■	.90
74	Paine	.60
93	Savannah St.	.79
83	Albany St. (Ga.)	.90
80	Alabama St.	.79
99	Kentucky St.	.75
63	Clark Atlanta	.66
99	LeMoyne-Owen ■	.94
97	Tuskegee	.82
82	Morris Brown ■	.62
82	Ala.-Huntsville	.69
126	Tuskegee ■	.82
95	Fort Valley St.	.78
103	Miles ■	.84
89	Central St. †	.69
83	Clark Atlanta ■	.71
92	Savannah St. ■	.84
83	Morehouse	.76
89	Alabama St. ■	.83
86	Paine ■	.63
110	Kentucky St. ■	.80
90	Fort Valley St. ■	.50
79	Clark Atlanta	.70
92	Morehouse	.70
106	S.C.-Spartanburg †	.91
98	Columbus St. †	.82
85	Calif. (Pa.) †	.95

Nickname: Bulldogs
Colors: Maroon & White
Arena: Elmore Health Science Building

Capacity: 6,000; Year Built: 1973
AD: Jerome Fitch
SID: To be named

ALABAMA ST.
Montgomery, AL 36101 I

Coach: Rob Spivery
Alma Mater: Ashland '72
Record: 11 Years, W-174, L-145

1996-97 SCHEDULE

George Mason ....Nov. 23
Georgetown ....Nov. 26
Jacksonville St. ....Nov. 30
Troy St. ■ ....Dec. 3
Hawaii Inv. ....Dec. 6-7
Alabama A&M ■ ....Dec. 14
Ohio St. ....Dec. 18
Dayton ....Dec. 20
Minnesota ....Dec. 23
Texas Southern ....Jan. 4
Prairie View ....Jan. 6
Southern U. ■ ....Jan. 11
Alcorn St. ■ ....Jan. 13
Mississippi Val. ....Jan. 18
Grambling ■ ....Jan. 20
Jackson St. ■ ....Jan. 25
Troy St. ....Jan. 28
Texas Southern ■ ....Feb. 1
Prairie View ■ ....Feb. 3
Southern U. ....Feb. 8
Alcorn St. ....Feb. 10
George Mason ■ ....Feb. 12
Mississippi Val. ....Feb. 15
Grambling ....Feb. 17
Florida St. ....Feb. 19
Jackson St. ....Feb. 22
Jacksonville St. ■ ....Feb. 26
Southwestern Conf. Tr. ....Mar. 5-8

1995-96 RESULTS (9-18)

106	Selma ■	.81
65	Jacksonville St. ■	.92
69	Tenn.-Chatt. ■	.66
65	Wagner †	.72
56	N.C.-Wilmington †	.85
93	Troy St. ■	.110
68	Jacksonville St. †	.82
47	Texas-Arlington †	.51
71	Prairie View ■	.70
83	Texas Southern ■	.81
79	Alabama A&M ■	.80
86	Southern U.	.113
61	Alcorn St.	.85
82	Troy St.	.80
83	Grambling	.72
75	Mississippi Val. ■	.83
81	Jackson St.	.85
92	Prairie View	.87
75	Texas Southern	.73
66	Southern U. ■	.96
80	Alcorn St.	.77
83	Alabama A&M ■	.89
68	Grambling ■	.78
69	Mississippi Val.	.83
68	Jackson St. ■	.80
65	Jacksonville St.	.105
59	Grambling ■	.71

Nickname: Hornets
Colors: Black & Gold
Arena: Joe L. Reed Acadome
  Capacity: 8,000; Year Built: 1992
AD: W. Curtis Williams
SID: Peter Forest

UAB
Birmingham, AL 35294 I

Coach: Murry Bartow
Alma Mater: UAB '85
(First year as head coach)

1996-97 SCHEDULE

Auburn ■ ....Nov. 22

Florida A&M ■ ....Nov. 27
Grambling ■ ....Dec. 1
Vanderbilt ....Dec. 4
Md.-East. Shore ■ ....Dec. 7
South Ala. ....Dec. 10
Hawaii Festival ....Dec. 14-15
Tenn.-Chatt. ■ ....Dec. 18
UAB Tr. ....Dec. 20-21
Arizona St. Cl. ....Dec. 27-28
Louisville ■ ....Jan. 3
Tulane ■ ....Jan. 5
Cincinnati ....Jan. 8
Houston ....Jan. 11
Southern Miss. ....Jan. 18
Memphis ■ ....Jan. 25
St. Louis ....Jan. 29
South Fla. ....Feb. 1
Tenn.-Chatt. ....Feb. 6
DePaul ■ ....Feb. 8
Tulane ....Feb. 13
Southern Miss. ■ ....Feb. 15
Marquette ■ ....Feb. 17
N.C.-Charlotte ....Feb. 23
South Fla. ....Mar. 1
Conference USA ....Mar. 5-8

1995-96 RESULTS (16-14)

66	Auburn	54
60	Portland	69
105	Prairie View ■	52
41	South Ala. ■	39
61	Jacksonville ■	56
65	Western Ky. ■	77
73	Tenn.-Chatt. ■	69
67	Jacksonville	64
70	Texas-Arlington ■	65
83	Jacksonville St. ■	72
81	Southern Ill. †	87
87	Neb.-Kearney †	80
87	Hawaii-Hilo ■	74
61	Southern Miss. ■	78
71	Tulane ■	70
55	Tulsa ■	70
64	St. Louis ■	55
70	Louisville ■	78
70	Cincinnati ■	68
77	Memphis ■	86
64	Marquette ■	73
69	DePaul ■	50
66	Louisville	81
64	Southern Miss. ■	67
72	Duquesne ■	92
79	South Fla. ■	63
63	N.C.-Charlotte ■	56
58	Tulane	60
64	South Fla.	73
57	South Fla. †	73

Nickname: Blazers
Colors: Green & Gold
Arena: UAB Arena
   Capacity: 8,500; Year Built: 1987
AD: Gene Bartow
SID: Grant Shingleton

ALA.-HUNTSVILLE
Huntsville, AL 35899 II

Coach: Bill Peterson
Alma Mater: Eckerd '80
Record: 6 Years, W-96, L-81

1996-97 SCHEDULE

Athens St. ■ ....Nov. 19
Mississippi Col. ■ ....Nov. 25
Florida Tech Cl. ....Nov. 29-30
Christian Bros. ....Dec. 3
Athens St. ....Dec. 14
Mississippi Col. ....Dec. 16
Vanderbilt ....Dec. 19
Johnson Smith ■ ....Dec. 30
Oakland City ....Jan. 2
Valdosta St. ■ ....Jan. 4
West Fla. ■ ....Jan. 6
West Ala. ....Jan. 11
Montevallo ■ ....Jan. 13

West Ga. ■ ....Jan. 18
Lincoln Memorial ■ ....Jan. 20
North Ala. ....Jan. 25
Oakland City ■ ....Jan. 27
Christian Bros. ■ ....Jan. 30
Montevallo ....Feb. 1
West Ala. ■ ....Feb. 3
West Fla. ....Feb. 8
Valdosta St. ....Feb. 10
West Ga. ....Feb. 15
Lincoln Memorial ■ ....Feb. 17
Alabama A&M ■ ....Feb. 20
North Ala. ■ ....Feb. 22

1995-96 RESULTS (12-14)

75	Ark.-Monticello	74
103	Sanford Brown †	48
85	Oakland City	82
70	Faulkner ■	84
59	Athens St. ■	63
72	Campbellsville †	81
58	Madonna †	53
57	Athens St.	65
73	Faulkner	60
67	Johnson Smith	74
82	Ark.-Monticello ■	59
54	Valdosta St.	60
51	West Fla. ■	56
57	West Ala. ■	56
66	Montevallo	63
56	West Ga.	84
80	Lincoln Memorial ■	77
69	Alabama A&M ■	82
61	North Ala. ■	70
91	Montevallo ■	55
63	West Fla. ■	58
72	Valdosta St. ■	77
59	West Ga. ■	78
52	Lincoln Memorial	69
58	North Ala.	71
58	West Ala.	57

Nickname: Chargers
Colors: Blue & White
Arena: Spragins Hall
   Capacity: 2,000; Year Built: 1977
AD: Jim Harris
SID: Julie Woltjen

ALAS. ANCHORAGE
Anchorage, AK 99508 II

Coach: Charlie Bruns
Alma Mater: Eastern Wash. '68
Record: 3 Years, W-56, L-30

1996-97 SCHEDULE

Alas. Anchorage Tr. ....Nov. 8-12
Aquinas ■ ....Nov. 15
Aquinas ■ ....Nov. 19
Great Alas. Shootout ....Nov. 27-30
Texas Col. ■ ....Dec. 6
Texas Col. ■ ....Dec. 7
Shaw ■ ....Dec. 13
Shaw ■ ....Dec. 14
Stanford ....Dec. 18
St. Mary's (Cal.) ....Dec. 20
Seton Hall Tr. ....Dec. 29-30
Seattle Pacific ....Jan. 9
Alas. Fairbanks ■ ....Jan. 18
Chaminade ....Jan. 23
Hawaii-Hilo ....Jan. 25
Seattle Pacific ■ ....Feb. 1
Mont. St.-Billings ■ ....Feb. 6
Western N.M. ■ ....Feb. 8
Chaminade ■ ....Feb. 15
Hawaii-Hilo ■ ....Feb. 17
Western N.M. ....Feb. 20
Mont. St.-Billings ....Feb. 22
Alas. Fairbanks ....Mar. 1

1995-96 RESULTS (19-9)

106	Mt. Senario ■	97
90	Langston ■	57
119	Crown ■	50
107	Crown ■	42
79	Indiana ■	84

77	Old Dominion ■	78
89	Texas Christian ■	78
99	Cardinal Stritch ■	76
94	Cardinal Stritch ■	69
93	Western St. ■	69
96	Western St. ■	62
72	Charleston (S.C.)	93
82	Lafayette †	75
78	Texas Christian	124
101	Weber St.	108
98	Alas. Fairbanks	94
83	Seattle Pacific ■	54
91	Western N.M. ■	49
78	Hawaii-Hilo	83
90	Chaminade	82
114	Mont. St.-Billings	141
100	Mont. St.-Billings	84
88	Chaminade ■	63
112	Hawaii-Hilo ■	77
72	Western N.M.	67
74	Seattle Pacific	90
112	Alas. Fairbanks ■	78
96	Grand Canyon †	105

Nickname: Seawolves
Colors: Green & Gold
Arena: UAA Sports Center
   Capacity: 2,000; Year Built: 1978
AD: Timothy J. Dillon
SID: To be named

ALAS. FAIRBANKS
Fairbanks, AK 99775 II

Coach: Al Sokaitis
Alma Mater: North Adams St. '76
Record: 9 Years, W-143, L-91

1996-97 SCHEDULE

Alas. Anchorage ....Jan. 18
Northwest Col. ■ ....Nov. 8
Northwest Col. ■ ....Nov. 9
Aquinas ■ ....Nov. 15
Aquinas ■ ....Nov. 16
Top of the World Cl. ....Nov. 22-24
Texas Col. ■ ....Dec. 9
Texas Col. ■ ....Dec. 10
Chico St. Tr. ....Dec. 28-30
Mary Hardin-Baylor ....Jan. 3
Seattle Pacific ....Jan. 11
Hawaii-Hilo ....Jan. 23
Chaminade ....Jan. 25
Seattle Pacific ■ ....Jan. 30
Western N.M. ■ ....Feb. 6
Mont. St.-Billings ■ ....Feb. 8
Chaminade ■ ....Feb. 13
Hawaii-Hilo ■ ....Feb. 15
Mont. St.-Billings ....Feb. 20
Western N.M. ....Feb. 22
Alas. Anchorage ■ ....Mar. 1

1995-96 RESULTS (10-17)

91	Ind.-South Bend ■	94
90	Ind.-South Bend ■	83
74	Wis.-Platteville ■	78
101	Oklahoma City ■	106
110	Crown ■	64
97	Crown ■	72
74	Concordia (Ore.) ■	93
63	Oregon	105
93	Warner Pacific ■	61
79	Western St. ■	104
94	Western St. ■	79
99	Cal Poly Pomona †	98
89	Cal St. Chico	98
69	UC Riverside †	99
86	Cal St. Chico	80
94	Alas. Anchorage ■	112
94	Western N.M. ■	68
76	Seattle Pacific ■	88
65	Chaminade	86
97	Hawaii-Hilo	111
88	Mont. St.-Billings ■	106
103	Mont. St.-Billings ■	109
118	Hawaii-Hilo ■	95
95	Chaminade	77

67	Seattle Pacific	84
74	Western N.M.	84
78	Alas. Anchorage	112

Nickname: Nanooks
Colors: Blue & Gold
Arena: Patty Center
   Capacity: 2,000; Year Built: 1962
AD: Kelly Higgins
SID: Scott Roselius

ALBANY (N.Y.)
Albany, NY 12222 II

Coach: Richard Sauers
Alma Mater: Slippery Rock '51
Record: 40 Years, W-685, L-320

1996-97 SCHEDULE

Me.-Presque Isle ■ ....Nov. 17
Le Moyne ....Nov. 20
Old Westbury ■ ....Nov. 26
East Stroudsburg ■ ....Dec. 1
Bridgeport ....Dec. 7
Mass.-Lowell ....Dec. 11
Keene St. ■ ....Dec. 14
Albany (N.Y.) Tr. ....Dec. 30-31
Skidmore ....Jan. 6
Teikyo Post ....Jan. 9
Sacred Heart ■ ....Jan. 11
Keene St. ....Jan. 14
Southern Conn. St. ....Jan. 16
New Haven ■ ....Jan. 18
Franklin Pierce ....Jan. 20
New Hamp. Col. ....Jan. 22
New Haven ....Jan. 25
Stony Brook ■ ....Jan. 29
Sacred Heart ....Feb. 1
New Hamp. Col. ■ ....Feb. 4
Bridgeport ■ ....Feb. 8
Franklin Pierce ■ ....Feb. 15
Stony Brook ....Feb. 18
Southern Conn. St. ■ ....Feb. 20
Mass.-Lowell ■ ....Feb. 22

1995-96 RESULTS (12-15)

89	Keuka ■	75
71	Plattsburgh St. ■	60
74	New Haven ■	62
81	Southern Conn. St. ■	75
69	Mass.-Lowell	79
66	New Hamp. Col.	87
101	Hilbert ■	49
62	Stonehill ■	69
78	Bridgeport ■	73
78	Sacred Heart ■	80
62	Southern Conn. St.	86
54	Franklin Pierce	76
95	Keene St.	78
76	Stony Brook	67
59	New Hamp. Col. ■	71
68	Mass.-Lowell ■	66
64	Le Moyne ■	70
63	Old Westbury ■	67
95	Keene St. ■	72
61	Franklin Pierce ■	59
66	Le Moyne ■	67
68	Sacred Heart ■	70
89	Bridgeport ■	97
61	Southern Vt. ■	68
63	New Haven	65
79	Stony Brook ■	65
73	Le Moyne	76

Nickname: Great Danes
Colors: Purple & Gold
Arena: Rec. & Convocation Center
   Capacity: 5,000; Year Built: 1992
AD: Milt Richards
SID: Brian DePasquale

ALBANY ST. (GA.)
Albany, GA 31705 II

Coach: Oliver Jones
Alma Mater: Albany St. (Ga.) '71

Record: 24 Years, W-357, L-302

1996-97 SCHEDULE

Schedule unavailable

1995-96 RESULTS (17-10)

88	Columbus St.	96
80	Ga. Southwestern	92
102	Tuskegee ■	96
108	Georgia Col. ■	106
71	Alabama A&M	99
82	Kentucky St.	68
89	Columbus St.	84
65	Georgia Col.	87
93	Ga. Southwestern ■	78
68	Morehouse	70
90	Alabama A&M ■	83
69	Savannah St.	76
79	Fort Valley St.	77
94	Miles	98
79	Paine	64
100	LeMoyne-Owen ■	82
103	Clark Atlanta	88
94	Valdosta St.	79
72	Fort Valley St. ■	75
64	Morris Brown	62
100	Savannah St. ■	95
93	Clark Atlanta ■	74
85	Valdosta St.	77
70	Morris Brown ■	58
85	Miles ■	86
76	Paine ■	69
64	Tuskegee †	69

Nickname: Golden Rams
Colors: Blue & Gold
Arena: Sanford Gymnasium
 Capacity: 1,400; Year Built: 1954
AD: Shirley Reese
SID: To be named

ALBERTUS MAGNUS
New Haven, CT 06511 III

Coach: Mike Papale
Alma Mater: Assumption '83
Record: 2 Years, W-23, L-28

1996-97 SCHEDULE

Western New Eng. ■	Nov. 23
John Jay	Nov. 26
Western Conn. St.	Nov. 30
Anna Maria Inv.	Dec. 7-8
Roger Williams	Dec. 10
Wesleyan (Conn.)	Dec. 12
Mt. St. Mary (N.Y.) ■	Jan. 6
Connecticut Col. ■	Jan. 8
Westfield St.	Jan. 11
Southern Vt.	Jan. 14
Eastern Conn. St. ■	Jan. 16
Trinity (Conn.) ■	Jan. 18
Daniel Webster	Jan. 23
Emerson-MCA ■	Jan. 25
Endicott ■	Jan. 29
Rivier	Feb. 1
Johnson & Wales ■	Feb. 4
Daniel Webster ■	Feb. 8
Johnson & Wales	Feb. 12
Endicott	Feb. 15
Emerson-MCA ■	Feb. 18
Rivier	Feb. 22

1995-96 RESULTS (14-12)

Results unavailable

Nickname: Falcons
Colors: Royal Blue & White
Arena: Cosgrove Marcus Messer Center
 Capacity: 700; Year Built: 1989
AD: Joe Tonelli
SID: Eva Esposito

ALBION
Albion, MI 49224 III

Coach: Mike Turner
Alma Mater: Albion '69

Record: 22 Years, W-313, L-216

1996-97 SCHEDULE

Albion Tr.	Nov. 22-23
DePauw	Nov. 26
Lake Superior St. ■	Dec. 3
Rose-Hulman Inv.	Dec. 6-8
Bluffton	Dec. 10
Tri-State	Dec. 19
Muskingham Tr.	Dec. 21-22
Nova Southeastern	Jan. 4
Palm Beach Atl.	Jan. 6
Adrian ■	Jan. 8
Calvin	Jan. 11
Hope	Jan. 15
Alma ■	Jan. 18
Olivet ■	Jan. 25
Kalamazoo ■	Jan. 29
Adrian	Feb. 1
Calvin ■	Feb. 5
Hope ■	Feb. 8
Alma	Feb. 12
Olivet ■	Feb. 19
Kalamazoo	Feb. 22

1995-96 RESULTS (16-9)

91	North Central	76
78	Wittenberg †	76
73	Cornerstone	83
82	Saginaw Valley †	96
75	Ind.-South Bend †	68
88	Bluffton ■	83
55	DePauw	74
88	Tri-State	62
101	Spring Arbor	87
81	Concordia (Mich.) †	65
83	Capital †	77
69	Adrian	65
82	Calvin ■	71
70	Hope ■	88
88	Alma	80
86	Olivet ■	52
73	Kalamazoo	77
86	Adrian ■	81
44	Calvin	85
80	Hope	94
83	Alma ■	58
84	Olivet	66
67	Kalamazoo ■	85
54	Adrian	51
62	Hope	75

Nickname: Britons
Colors: Purple & Gold
Arena: Kresge Gymnasium
 Capacity: 1,380; Year Built: 1925
AD: Pete Schmidt
SID: Robin Hartman

ALBRIGHT
Reading, PA 19612 III

Coach: Ken Tyler
Alma Mater: William & Mary '87
Record: 1 Year, W-10, L-13

1996-97 SCHEDULE

VMI	Nov. 22
Roanoke Tr.	Nov. 23-24
Widener	Dec. 3
Frank. & Marsh. ■	Dec. 5
Messiah	Dec. 7
Moravian ■	Dec. 12
Albright Tr.	Jan. 3-4
FDU-Madison	Jan. 11
Juniata	Jan. 15
Elizabethtown ■	Jan. 18
Susquehanna ■	Jan. 22
Lebanon Valley	Jan. 25
East Stroudsburg ■	Jan. 27
Widener ■	Jan. 29
Messiah	Feb. 1
Moravian	Feb. 5
Juniata	Feb. 8
Phila. Pharmacy ■	Feb. 10
Drew	Feb. 12
Elizabethtown	Feb. 15

Susquehanna ....Feb. 19
Lebanon Valley ■ ....Feb. 22

1995-96 RESULTS (9-14)

74	Kenyon †	81
85	Wash. & Lee	77
83	Muhlenberg ■	89
60	Widener ■	75
51	Frank. & Marsh.	75
84	Messiah	67
59	Moravian ■	79
75	Alvernia ■	79
57	Elizabethtown ■	65
99	Susquehanna	97
54	Lebanon Valley ■	64
62	East Stroudsburg	72
70	Widener	59
77	Messiah ■	94
90	Moravian ■	82
64	King's (Pa.) ■	61
83	Juniata ■	72
68	Juniata	59
62	Drew ■	77
70	Elizabethtown	91
76	Susquehanna ■	79
70	Lebanon Valley	88
74	Scranton	70

Nickname: Lions
Colors: Cardinal & White
Arena: Bollman Center
 Capacity: 1,800; Year Built: 1952
AD: Sally A. Miller
SID: Stan Hyman

ALCORN ST.
Lorman, MS 39096 I

Coach: Davey L. Whitney
Alma Mater: Kentucky St. '53
Record: 25 Years, W-450, L-263

1996-97 SCHEDULE

Iowa St.	Nov. 26
Ark.-Pine Bluff ■	Nov. 30
Murray St.	Dec. 5
Tougaloo ■	Dec. 7
St. Louis	Dec. 9
IU/PU-Indianapolis ■	Dec. 14
Oklahoma St.	Dec. 16
Ark.-Little Rock	Dec. 21
Murray St.	Dec. 28
Mississippi Val. ■	Jan. 4
Grambling ■	Jan. 6
Jackson St.	Jan. 11
Alabama St.	Jan. 13
Prairie View	Jan. 18
Texas Southern	Jan. 20
Southern U.	Jan. 25
Ark.-Pine Bluff	Jan. 29
Mississippi Val.	Feb. 1
Grambling	Feb. 3
Oral Roberts ■	Feb. 5
Jackson St. ■	Feb. 8
Alabama St. ■	Feb. 10
Prairie View ■	Feb. 15
Texas Southern ■	Feb. 17
Southern U. ■	Feb. 22
Oral Roberts	Feb. 26
Southwestern Conf. Tr.	Mar. 5-8

1995-96 RESULTS (10-15)

81	Belhaven ■	70
76	Cleveland St. ■	62
79	Montana St. ■	87
75	Arkansas	116
60	Ball St.	103
60	St. Louis	63
69	Montana St.	121
64	Wyoming †	87
76	Eastern Ky. †	82
110	Faith Bapt. Bible ■	60
78	Mississippi Val.	113
76	Grambling	92
69	Jackson St. ■	68
85	Alabama St. ■	61
105	Prairie View ■	84

75	Texas Southern ■	85
87	Southern U. ■	95
56	Cleveland St.	58
77	Mississippi Val. ■	74
65	Grambling ■	77
59	Jackson St.	75
77	Alabama St.	80
84	Prairie View	83
102	Texas Southern	98
97	Southern U.	94

Nickname: Braves
Colors: Purple & Gold
Arena: Davey L. Whitney Complex
 Capacity: 7,000; Year Built: 1974
AD: Lloyd N. Hill
SID: Derick S. Hackett

ALDERSON-BROADDUS
Philippi, WV 26416 II

Coach: Brett Vincent
Alma Mater: Marshall '91
(First year as head coach)

1996-97 SCHEDULE

Fairmont St. Cl.	Nov. 15-16
Central St. ■	Nov. 18
Geneva	Nov. 26
Mercyhurst Cl.	Nov. 29-30
Davis & Elkins ■	Dec. 4
Fairmont St.	Dec. 7
Bluefield St. ■	Jan. 8
West Va. St.	Jan. 11
Concord ■	Jan. 13
Charleston (W.Va.) ■	Jan. 15
Glenville St.	Jan. 18
Wheeling Jesuit ■	Jan. 22
West Liberty St. ■	Jan. 25
Shepherd	Jan. 27
West Va. Wesleyan ■	Jan. 29
Charleston (W.Va.)	Feb. 1
Central St.	Feb. 3
Salem-Teikyo ■	Feb. 5
West Va. Tech	Feb. 8
Davis & Elkins	Feb. 12
Wheeling Jesuit ■	Feb. 15
West Liberty St.	Feb. 17
Shepherd ■	Feb. 19
West Va. Wesleyan	Feb. 22

1995-96 RESULTS (16-12)

74	Wayne St. (Mich.) †	77
79	Cheyney †	98
95	Geneva	90
81	West Va. Tech †	96
105	Ohio Valley †	104
73	Southern Tech †	46
88	Lipscomb †	96
83	Davis & Elkins	56
82	Fairmont St.	90
103	Bluefield St.	88
61	West Va. St. ■	87
79	Concord	66
90	Charleston (W.Va.)	98
89	Glenville St.	68
86	Wheeling Jesuit ■	80
62	West Liberty St.	80
108	Shepherd ■	88
70	West Va. Wesleyan	51
89	Salem-Teikyo	80
82	West Va. Tech	90
83	Charleston (W.Va.) ■	72
91	Davis & Elkins ■	58
66	Wheeling Jesuit	72
99	West Liberty St. ■	94
85	Shepherd	73
63	West Va. Wesleyan ■	65
85	Shepherd ■	70
74	Salem-Teikyo †	87

Nickname: Battlers
Colors: Blue, Gray & Gold
Arena: Rex Pyles Arena
 Capacity: 3,000; Year Built: 1970
AD: Steve Dodd
SID: Dave Stingo

ALFRED

Alfred, NY 14802 III

Coach: Jay Murphy
Alma Mater: Brockport St. '81
Record: 13 Years, W-78, L-243

1996-97 SCHEDULE

Ithaca	Nov. 23
Hilbert ■	Nov. 26
Nazareth Tr.	Nov. 30-Dec. 1
Cazenovia	Dec. 3
Pitt.-Bradford ■	Dec. 7
Cortland St.	Dec. 10
Clarkson	Dec. 13
St. Lawrence	Dec. 14
Hamilton Inv.	Jan. 11-12
Grove City ■	Jan. 18
Thiel ■	Jan. 22
Grove City	Jan. 25
Nazareth ■	Jan. 28
Bethany (W.Va.) ■	Jan. 29
Waynesburg	Feb. 1
Wash. & Jeff. ■	Feb. 5
Thiel	Feb. 8
Rochester Inst.	Feb. 11
Bethany (W.Va.)	Feb. 15
Elmira ■	Feb. 18
Waynesburg ■	Feb. 19
Wash. & Jeff.	Feb. 22
Hilbert	Feb. 28

1995-96 RESULTS (4-21)

51	Fredonia St. †	83
65	WPI †	79
66	Nazareth ■	74
57	Keuka ■	66
64	Wash. & Jeff.	80
88	Thiel	82
74	Houghton	82
75	Union (N.Y.)	77
68	Clarkson †	83
64	Clarkson ■	57
74	St. Lawrence ■	90
78	Pitt.-Bradford	93
70	Rochester Inst.	84
56	Ithaca	77
82	Utica ■	75
66	Geneseo St. ■	77
67	Utica	77
58	Hartwick	72
69	Nazareth	85
59	Ithaca ■	78
74	Elmira	83
60	Rochester Inst. ■	90
70	Penn St.-Behrend ■	65
92	Roberts Wesleyan	95
70	St. John Fisher	82

Nickname: Saxons
Colors: Purple & Gold
Arena: James A. McLane P.E. Center
    Capacity: 2,800; Year Built: 1971
AD: Hank Ford
SID: To be named

ALLEGHENY

Meadville, PA 16335 III

Coach: Phil Ness
Alma Mater: Lafayette '78
Record: 7 Years, W-98, L-85

1996-97 SCHEDULE

Wash. & Jeff.	Nov. 22
Grove City ■	Nov. 23
Juniata ■	Nov. 26
Allegheny Cl.	Nov. 29-30
Case Reserve	Dec. 4
Denison	Dec. 7
Earlham	Jan. 3
Wittenberg	Jan. 4
Westminster (Pa.)	Jan. 8
Ohio Wesleyan	Jan. 11
Wooster	Jan. 15
Denison ■	Jan. 18

Case Reserve ■	Jan. 22
Kenyon	Jan. 25
Penn St.-Behrend	Jan. 28
Wittenberg ■	Jan. 31
Earlham ■	Feb. 1
Oberlin ■	Feb. 5
Ohio Wesleyan ■	Feb. 8
Wooster	Feb. 12
St. John Fisher ■	Feb. 16
Oberlin	Feb. 19
Kenyon ■	Feb. 22

1995-96 RESULTS (17-10)

91	Grove City †	86
67	Wash. & Jeff. †	53
87	Nazareth ■	62
53	Ramapo ■	55
102	Oberlin ■	61
76	Denison	83
61	Wooster ■	79
66	Kenyon ■	59
94	Juniata ■	86
54	Wittenberg ■	76
71	Earlham ■	60
51	Westminster (Pa.)	65
70	Ohio Wesleyan ■	64
71	Case Reserve	53
64	Denison	62
57	Wooster	82
87	Kenyon ■	59
78	Penn St.-Behrend ■	65
79	Earlham	85
64	Wittenberg ■	72
81	Oberlin ■	60
94	Ohio Wesleyan	87
83	St. John Fisher	98
76	Case Reserve ■	70
58	Kenyon ■	53
81	Ohio Wesleyan †	67
55	Wittenberg ■	65

Nickname: Gators
Colors: Blue & Gold
Arena: David Mead Field House
    Capacity: 2,000; Year Built: 1954
AD: Rick Creehan
SID: Steve Mest

ALLENTOWN

Center Valley, PA 18034 III

Coach: Scott Coval
Alma Mater: William & Mary '86
Record: 3 Years, W-47, L-31

1996-97 SCHEDULE

Muhlenberg Tr.	Nov. 22-23
Moravian	Nov. 26
Misericordia ■	Dec. 4
Drew ■	Dec. 7
Neumann ■	Dec. 14
Roanoke Cl.	Jan. 4-5
Muhlenberg ■	Jan. 8
Marywood	Jan. 11
Gwynedd-Mercy ■	Jan. 13
Eastern	Jan. 15
Cabrini	Jan. 18
Beaver ■	Jan. 20
Alvernia	Jan. 22
Neumann	Jan. 29
Misericordia	Feb. 1
Marywood ■	Feb. 5
Gwynedd-Mercy ■	Feb. 8
Lebanon Valley	Feb. 10
Eastern ■	Feb. 12
Cabrini ■	Feb. 15
Beaver	Feb. 19
Alvernia ■	Feb. 22

1995-96 RESULTS (17-10)

64	Moravian ■	75
78	Catholic	77
95	Marywood ■	66
69	Beaver	62
81	Misericordia ■	57
77	Gwynedd-Mercy ■	60
80	Olivet †	72

82	Randolph-Macon	100
55	Muhlenberg ■	52
73	Alvernia	83
64	Neumann ■	57
73	Eastern ■	63
91	Marywood	73
78	Cabrini	89
56	Gwynedd-Mercy	53
63	Drew	71
64	Misericordia ■	68
92	Beaver ■	88
80	Alvernia ■	73
61	Eastern	62
72	Lebanon Valley ■	69
95	Cabrini	105
112	Neumann ■	74
92	Eastern ■	61
93	Alvernia	85
67	Cabrini	85
72	Wilkes	87

Nickname: Centaurs
Colors: Red & Blue
Arena: Billera Hall
    Capacity: 1,000; Year Built: 1964
AD: Joy Richman
SID: John Gump

ALMA

Alma, MI 48801 III

Coach: Kevin Skaggs
Alma Mater: Western Mich. '80
Record: 1 Year, W-4, L-21

1996-97 SCHEDULE

Penn St.-Behrend Tr.	Nov. 23-24
Elmhurst ■	Nov. 30
Concordia (Mich.)	Dec. 7
Ind.-South Bend	Dec. 17
Alma Tr.	Dec. 30-31
Thomas More Cl.	Jan. 4-5
Calvin ■	Jan. 8
Hope	Jan. 11
Grace Bible (Mich.) ■	Jan. 13
Bluffton ■	Jan. 15
Albion	Jan. 18
Olivet ■	Jan. 22
Kalamazoo ■	Jan. 25
Adrian	Jan. 29
Calvin	Feb. 1
Grace Bible (Mich.)	Feb. 3
Hope ■	Feb. 5
Albion ■	Feb. 12
Olivet	Feb. 15
Kalamazoo	Feb. 19
Adrian ■	Feb. 22

1995-96 RESULTS (4-21)
Results unavailable

Nickname: Scots
Colors: Maroon & Cream
Arena: Cappaert Gymnasium
    Capacity: 3,000; Year Built: 1969
AD: Dennis Griffin
SID: Greg Baadte

ALVERNIA

Reading, PA 19607 III

Coach: John McCloskey
Alma Mater: Kutztown '64
Record: 5 Years, W-88, L-50

1996-97 SCHEDULE

Frank. & Marsh. Cl.	Nov. 22-23
Holy Family ■	Dec. 5
West Chester ■	Dec. 7
Neumann ■	Dec. 11
Marywood	Dec. 14
Albright Tr.	Jan. 3-4
Eastern ■	Jan. 8
Beaver	Jan. 11
Misericordia ■	Jan. 15
Gwynedd-Mercy	Jan. 18

Cabrini ■	Jan. 20
Allentown ■	Jan. 22
Neumann ■	Jan. 25
Gettysburg ■	Jan. 27
Marywood ■	Jan. 29
Eastern ■	Feb. 1
Beaver ■	Feb. 3
Elizabethtown ■	Feb. 6
Misericordia	Feb. 12
Gwynedd-Mercy ■	Feb. 15
Cabrini	Feb. 19
Allentown	Feb. 22

1995-96 RESULTS (15-10)

80	Gallaudet †	65
96	Susquehanna	85
102	Misericordia ■	76
76	Cabrini	86
78	Gwynedd-Mercy	69
101	Marywood	74
93	Lycoming †	103
82	Elizabethtown	98
79	Albright	75
83	Allentown ■	73
75	Eastern	57
91	Neumann ■	67
71	Gettysburg	73
62	Misericordia	69
84	Beaver	69
56	Frank. & Marsh.	67
75	Eastern ■	68
72	Cabrini	89
73	Allentown	80
105	Marywood ■	80
76	Neumann	68
95	Beaver ■	69
97	Gwynedd-Mercy ■	58
67	Frank. & Marsh. †	77
85	Allentown ■	93

Nickname: Crusaders
Colors: Maroon & Gold
Arena: Physical Education Center
    Capacity: 1,000; Year Built: 1987
AD: Sandra Slabik
SID: To be named

AMERICAN

Washington, DC 20016 I

Coach: Chris Knoche
Alma Mater: American '80
Record: 6 Years, W-66, L-102

1996-97 SCHEDULE

Catholic ■	Nov. 23
Iona	Nov. 30
Geo. Washington ■	Dec. 2
Loyola (Md.)	Dec. 4
Montana Cl.	Dec. 6-7
La Salle	Dec. 10
Howard	Dec. 14
Maryland	Dec. 21
Richmond ■	Jan. 2
East Caro.	Jan. 4
N.C.-Wilmington	Jan. 6
James Madison ■	Jan. 11
Old Dominion ■	Jan. 15
George Mason ■	Jan. 18
Va. Commonwealth ■	Jan. 22
James Madison	Jan. 29
N.C.-Wilmington ■	Feb. 1
East Caro. ■	Feb. 3
Va. Commonwealth ■	Feb. 8
William & Mary	Feb. 10
Richmond	Feb. 12
Manhattan ■	Feb. 17
Old Dominion	Feb. 19
William & Mary ■	Feb. 22
George Mason	Feb. 24
Colonial Conf. Tr.	Feb. 28-Mar. 3

1995-96 RESULTS (12-15)

65	Loyola (Md.) ■	58
69	Wagner †	71
60	Iona	71
66	Rider	74

123	Marymount (Va.) ■	62
62	La Salle ■	64
89	Howard ■	49
79	Maryland	104
52	Stanford	80
80	Richmond ■	76
58	N.C.-Wilmington ■	61
91	William & Mary	80
85	East Caro. ■	75
84	James Madison ■	71
68	Va. Commonwealth	73
85	George Mason	96
47	Old Dominion ■	67
89	East Caro.	73
58	N.C.-Wilmington	73
100	William & Mary ■	66
57	Va. Commonwealth ■	65
73	Iona	83
88	George Mason ■	100
76	Richmond	68
83	Old Dominion ■	74
72	James Madison	75
60	East Caro. †	76

Nickname: Eagles
Colors: Red, White & Blue
Arena: Bender Arena
  Capacity: 5,000; Year Built: 1988
AD: Lee McElroy
SID: Matt Winkler

AMERICAN (P.R.)
Bayamon, PR 00621 II

Coach: William Colon
Alma Mater: Puerto Rico '81
Record: 2 Years, W-28, L-20

1996-97 SCHEDULE
Puerto Rico Shootout	Nov. 29-Dec. 1
St. Leo	Dec. 4
Tampa	Dec. 5
Rollins	Dec. 6
Florida Tech	Dec. 7
Fla. Southern	Dec. 10
American (P.R.) Tr.	Dec. 17-19
Southwest Baptist	Dec. 28
Missouri So. Tr.	Dec. 30-31
Virgin Islands	Jan. 25
Virgin Islands ■	Feb. 8
P.R.-Mayaguez	Feb. 11
Int. Am.-San German ■	Feb. 13
P.R.-Arecibo ■	Feb. 18
P.R.-Cayey ■	Feb. 20
Turabo ■	Feb. 25
P.R.-Ponce	Feb. 27
P.R.-Bayamon Tech ■	Mar. 6
P.R.-Rio Piedras ■	Mar. 11
Humacao ■	Mar. 13
Sacred Heart (P.R.)	Mar. 18
Bayamon Central	Mar. 20

1995-96 RESULTS (18-8)
86	Louisville ■	90
86	Western Ky. ■	85
77	Illinois St. ■	79
79	Valdosta St. ■	93
68	Rollins	75
68	Fla. Southern	80
81	Lynn	91
75	Eckerd ■	93
87	LIU-C. W. Post ■	73
80	Mo. Southern St. ■	76
85	Tampa	73
80	Minn.-Duluth †	73
76	Barry	68
63	Florida Tech	60
81	Eckerd	85
97	P.R.-Ponce ■	80
111	P.R.-Rio Piedras ■	83
69	Sacred Heart (P.R.) ■	52
88	P.R.-Cayey	62
123	Bayamon Central ■	73
107	Humacao	68
93	P.R.-Bayamon Tech	78
90	P.R.-Mayaguez ■	64
83	Int. Am.-San German	80
87	P.R.-Arecibo ■	78
71	Turabo ■	63

Nickname: Pirates
Colors: Navy & Gold
Arena: Eugenio Guerra Sports Complex
  Capacity: 3,000; Year Built: 1989
AD: Carlos Morales
SID: Doris Roura

AMERICAN INT'L
Springfield, MA 01109 II

Coach: Andy Johnston
Alma Mater: New Hampshire '87
Record: 1 Year, W-11, L-18

1996-97 SCHEDULE
So. Conn. St. Cl.	Nov. 22-23
Sacred Heart	Dec. 1
Franklin Pierce	Dec. 4
Le Moyne ■	Dec. 8
St. Michael's ■	Dec. 14
Dowling	Dec. 21
Albany (N.Y.) Tr.	Dec. 30-31
New Haven ■	Jan. 4
Quinnipiac	Jan. 7
Bryant ■	Jan. 10
Assumption	Jan. 13
Bentley	Jan. 16
Stonehill ■	Jan. 18
St. Anselm	Jan. 21
Merrimack ■	Jan. 25
Quinnipiac ■	Jan. 28
St. Michael's	Feb. 1
Assumption ■	Feb. 4
Stonehill	Feb. 8
Bentley ■	Feb. 11
Bryant	Feb. 13
St. Anselm ■	Feb. 15
Le Moyne	Feb. 19
Merrimack	Feb. 22

1995-96 RESULTS (11-18)
62	Endicott ■	50
48	Southern Conn. St. ■	78
70	Salem-Teikyo †	83
55	St. Michael's †	64
67	Franklin Pierce ■	78
69	Merrimack	58
70	Sacred Heart ■	86
76	St. Leo	86
45	Fla. Southern	66
68	Quinnipiac	61
70	St. Michael's ■	72
75	Bentley	72
61	Bryant ■	57
57	New Haven	79
68	Assumption	75
72	St. Anselm ■	81
89	Stonehill ■	80
78	St. Michael's	82
58	Bryant	72
78	Bentley ■	87
64	Merrimack ■	73
74	Stonehill	83
76	Springfield	70
77	Quinnipiac ■	61
87	Assumption ■	77
58	St. Anselm	83
87	Bentley †	85
76	Merrimack †	65
65	St. Anselm	80

Nickname: Yellow Jackets
Colors: Gold & White
Arena: Henry A. Butova Gymnasium
  Capacity: 2,500; Year Built: 1965
AD: Bob Burke
SID: Frank Polera

AMHERST
Amherst, MA 01002 III

Coach: David Hixon
Alma Mater: Amherst '75

Record: 19 Years, W-295, L-166

1996-97 SCHEDULE
Plattsburgh Cl.	Nov. 22-23
Clark (Mass.) ■	Dec. 5
Middlebury	Dec. 7
Western New Eng. ■	Dec. 10
Johnson & Wales ■	Jan. 7
Westfield St. ■	Jan. 9
Wheaton (Mass.)	Jan. 11
Colby ■	Jan. 15
Williams ■	Jan. 18
Connecticut Col.	Jan. 21
Bowdoin ■	Jan. 24
Babson	Jan. 28
Hamilton ■	Feb. 1
Framingham St. ■	Feb. 4
Williams	Feb. 8
Emerson-MCA ■	Feb. 10
Brandeis ■	Feb. 13
Wesleyan (Conn.) ■	Feb. 15
Trinity (Conn.)	Feb. 19
Wesleyan (Conn.) ■	Feb. 22
Tufts ■	Feb. 25
Skidmore	Mar. 1

1995-96 RESULTS (21-6)
77	Haverford	58
74	Swarthmore	69
88	Nichols ■	74
102	Framingham St.	66
102	Middlebury	72
86	Western New Eng.	81
91	Clark (Mass.)	62
120	Westfield St.	89
104	Johnson & Wales	66
81	Savannah A&D	71
84	Babson	89
68	Williams	87
107	Connecticut Col. ■	82
65	Bowdoin	80
70	Colby	75
92	Southern Vt. ■	72
86	Hamilton	77
67	Williams	79
84	Brandeis	93
81	Wesleyan (Conn.) ■	76
83	Trinity (Conn.) ■	72
51	Wesleyan (Conn.)	40
89	Tufts	86
97	Skidmore	85
95	Rhode Island Col. ■	72
73	Connecticut Col.	59
66	Colby	64

Nickname: Lord Jeffs
Colors: Purple & White
Arena: LeFrak Gymnasium
  Capacity: 2,000; Year Built: 1986
AD: Peter Gooding
SID: To be named

ANDERSON (IND.)
Anderson, IN 46012 III

Coach: Denny Lehnus
Alma Mater: Anderson '65
Record: 3 Years, W-34, L-41

1996-97 SCHEDULE
Anderson/Hanover Cl.	Nov. 22-23
Anderson Cl.	Nov. 29-30
Butler	Dec. 4
Anderson Inv.	Dec. 6-7
Earlham	Dec. 11
Bluffton ■	Dec. 14
Grand Canyon	Dec. 31
Manchester ■	Jan. 8
DePauw	Jan. 11
Wabash	Jan. 15
Franklin ■	Jan. 18
Rose-Hulman	Jan. 22
Ind.-East ■	Jan. 25
Hanover	Jan. 29
Wabash ■	Feb. 1
Manchester	Feb. 5
DePauw	Feb. 8
Rose-Hulman ■	Feb. 11
Franklin	Feb. 15
Hanover ■	Feb. 18
Lincoln Chrst.	Feb. 21

1995-96 RESULTS (14-11)
Results unavailable

Nickname: Ravens
Colors: Orange & Black
Arena: O. C. Lewis Gym
  Capacity: 3,000
AD: Barrett Bates
SID: Jim Hazen

ANGELO ST.
San Angelo, TX 76909 II

Coach: Ed Messbarger
Alma Mater: Northwest Mo. St. '56
Record: 39 Years, W-649, L-479

1996-97 SCHEDULE
Abilene Christian Cl	Nov. 15-16
Texas-San Antonio	Nov. 23
Lamar	Nov. 25
McMurry ■	Nov. 27
Texas Col. ■	Nov. 30
Tex.-Pan American	Dec. 7
Eastern N.M. ■	Dec. 14
West Tex. A&M ■	Dec. 16
Angelo St. Cl.	Dec. 27-28
Central Okla.	Jan. 2
Midwestern St.	Jan. 4
Texas A&M-Commerce ■	Jan. 7
Tarleton St.	Jan. 9
Tex. A&M-Kingsville	Jan. 11
Abilene Christian	Jan. 18
Midwestern St. ■	Jan. 23
Central Okla. ■	Jan. 25
Tarleton St. ■	Jan. 30
Texas A&M-Commerce	Feb. 1
Howard Payne ■	Feb. 4
Tex. A&M-Kingsville ■	Feb. 8
Abilene Christian ■	Feb. 15
West Tex. A&M	Feb. 20
Eastern N.M.	Feb. 22

1995-96 RESULTS (6-19)
79	Cameron †	88
81	Adams St. †	79
96	Mary Hardin-Baylor ■	99
88	McMurry ■	84
91	Texas-San Antonio	93
86	Eastern N.M.	88
72	Eastern N.M.	76
60	West Tex. A&M	106
71	Lubbock Chrst.	48
73	Ouachita Baptist ■	82
84	Central Okla.	92
63	Midwestern St.	83
64	Texas A&M-Commerce	74
72	Tarleton St.	96
76	Tex. A&M-Kingsville ■	85
2	National Christian §	0
69	Abilene Christian	81
93	Midwestern St.	107
77	Central Okla.	107
67	Tarleton St.	66
62	Texas A&M-Commerce ■	73
79	Tex. A&M-Kingsville	83
70	Abilene Christian ■	78
87	West Tex. A&M ■	83
69	Eastern N.M.	96

Nickname: Rams
Colors: Blue & Gold
Arena: Asu P.E. Building
  Capacity: 4,224; Year Built: 1973
AD: Jerry Vandergriff
SID: M. L. Stark Hinkle

ANNA MARIA
Paxton, MA 01612 III

Coach: David Shea
Alma Mater: Anna Maria '93

(First year as head coach)
1996-97 SCHEDULE

Skidmore Inv.	Nov. 22-23
Tufts ■	Nov. 26
Worcester St. ■	Dec. 1
Anna Maria Inv.	Dec. 7-8
WPI ■	Dec. 10
Salem St. Tr.	Dec. 29-30
Fitchburg St.	Jan. 11
Roger Williams	Jan. 16
Wentworth Inst.	Jan. 18
Nichols	Jan. 21
New England Col.	Jan. 23
Curry ■	Jan. 25
Colby-Sawyer ■	Jan. 29
Eastern Nazarene	Feb. 1
Nichols ■	Feb. 4
Gordon ■	Feb. 6
Colby-Sawyer	Feb. 10
Salve Regina	Feb. 15
New England Col. ■	Feb. 20
Gordon	Feb. 22

1995-96 RESULTS (25-5)

94	Framingham St. †	73
87	Babson	107
96	Tufts	91
95	Worcester St.	84
108	Mass. Pharmacy ■	73
90	Worcester St. ■	66
76	WPI	73
115	Fitchburg St. ■	78
97	Eastern Conn. St. †	76
66	Salem St.	83
86	Roger Williams ■	70
76	Wentworth Inst.	73
84	Nichols ■	76
108	New England Col. ■	84
93	Curry	82
57	Bowdoin ■	78
90	Colby-Sawyer	84
75	Eastern Nazarene ■	69
103	Nichols	94
67	Gordon	87
75	Colby-Sawyer ■	74
91	Salve Regina ■	80
121	New England Col.	68
98	Gordon ■	85
90	Salve Regina ■	78
76	Eastern Nazarene ■	72
94	Wentworth Inst. ■	63
111	Babson ■	90
74	Salem St.	67
88	Richard Stockton †	95

Nickname: AMCATS
Colors: Royal Blue & White
Arena: Fuller Activities Center
  Capacity: 500; Year Built: 1986
AD: Stephen Washkevich
SID: To be named

APPALACHIAN ST.
Boone, NC 28608 I

Coach: Buzz Peterson
Alma Mater: North Caro. '86
(First year as head coach)

1996-97 SCHEDULE

Wingate ■	Nov. 22
East Caro. ■	Nov. 26
Milligan ■	Nov. 30
N.C.-Charlotte	Dec. 2
N.C.-Greensboro ■	Dec. 5
Georgia	Dec. 7
Marquette	Dec. 19
Montana St.	Dec. 21
New Mexico Inv.	Dec. 27-28
Niagara	Jan. 4
VMI ■	Jan. 6
N.C.-Greensboro	Jan. 8
Western Caro.	Jan. 11
Furman	Jan. 14
Ga. Southern ■	Jan. 18
Davidson ■	Jan. 20

Marshall	Jan. 25
East Tenn. St. ■	Jan. 27
Tenn.-Chatt.	Feb. 1
VMI	Feb. 3
Western Caro.	Feb. 8
Marshall ■	Feb. 10
East Tenn. St.	Feb. 15
Citadel ■	Feb. 17
Davidson	Feb. 22
Southern Conf. Tr.	Feb. 27-Mar. 2

1995-96 RESULTS (8-20)

90	Catawba ■	87
55	Clemson	91
65	Georgia Tech ■	89
81	N.C.-Charlotte ■	85
112	Mars Hill ■	77
64	N.C.-Greensboro	80
50	Wake Forest	91
78	Loyola (Ill.) ■	70
59	Indiana †	103
62	Kent †	63
61	St. Bonaventure ■	58
39	East Caro.	63
89	Marshall ■	87
75	Citadel	84
68	Davidson	90
64	VMI	84
83	Western Caro. ■	93
68	East Tenn. St.	100
72	Ga. Southern	74
93	Furman	78
66	Davidson	84
64	Marshall	95
95	East Tenn. St. ■	79
66	Tenn.-Chatt.	80
75	VMI ■	85
72	Western Caro.	91
75	Citadel †	73
66	Western Caro. †	74

Nickname: Mountaineers
Colors: Black & Gold
Arena: Varsity Gymnasium
  Capacity: 8,000; Year Built: 1968
AD: Roachel Laney
SID: Rick Covington

ARIZONA
Tucson, AZ 85721 I

Coach: Lute Olson
Alma Mater: Augsburg '56
Record: 23 Years, W-507, L-194

1996-97 SCHEDULE

North Caro. [Springfield]	Nov. 22
Northern Ariz. ■	Nov. 26
New Mexico	Nov. 30
Utah [Anaheim]	Dec. 7
Texas ■	Dec. 9
Jackson St. ■	Dec. 14
Michigan [Auburn Hills]	Dec. 21
Arizona Cl.	Dec. 28-30
California ■	Jan. 2
Stanford ■	Jan. 4
Arizona St.	Jan. 11
Southern Cal	Jan. 16
UCLA	Jan. 18
Oregon St. ■	Jan. 23
Oregon ■	Jan. 25
Washington St. ■	Jan. 30
Washington	Feb. 2
Arizona St. ■	Feb. 5
Tulane [Phoenix]	Feb. 9
UCLA ■	Feb. 13
Southern Cal ■	Feb. 15
Oregon	Feb. 20
Oregon St.	Feb. 22
Washington St. ■	Feb. 27
Washington ■	Mar. 1
Stanford	Mar. 6
California [San Francisco]	Mar. 8

1995-96 RESULTS (26-7)

91	Long Beach St. ■	57
83	Arkansas	73

86	Michigan †	79
91	Georgetown †	81
73	Houston	69
84	Montana ■	66
90	Towson St.	84
90	UTEP ■	70
70	Syracuse ■	79
88	Texas A&M ■	44
79	Rutgers ■	70
75	California	99
71	Stanford	80
108	Arizona St. ■	76
93	Southern Cal ■	81
88	UCLA ■	79
66	Oregon St. ■	59
70	Oregon	65
79	Washington ■	80
96	Washington St. ■	78
71	Arizona St.	69
79	Cincinnati †	76
75	UCLA	76
86	Southern Cal	72
81	Oregon ■	63
84	Oregon St. ■	60
72	Washington St.	62
67	Washington	65
79	Stanford ■	85
71	California ■	68
90	Valparaiso †	51
87	Iowa †	73
80	Kansas †	83

Nickname: Wildcats
Colors: Cardinal & Navy
Arena: McKale Center
  Capacity: 14,428; Year Built: 1973
AD: Jim Livengood
SID: Brett Hansen

ARIZONA ST.
Tempe, AZ 85287 I

Coach: Bill Frieder
Alma Mater: Michigan '64
Record: 16 Years, W-310, L-178

1996-97 SCHEDULE

Jacksonville ■	Nov. 22
Great Alas. Shootout	Nov. 27-30
Sam Houston St. ■	Dec. 2
Oklahoma St. ■	Dec. 7
Houston Baptist	Dec. 10
Jackson St. ■	Dec. 20
Northeastern Ill. ■	Dec. 22
Arizona St. Cl.	Dec. 27-28
Stanford ■	Jan. 2
California ■	Jan. 4
Chaminade	Jan. 6
Arizona ■	Jan. 11
UCLA	Jan. 16
Southern Cal	Jan. 18
Oregon	Jan. 23
Oregon St. ■	Jan. 25
Washington	Jan. 30
Washington St.	Feb. 1
Arizona	Feb. 5
Southern Cal ■	Feb. 13
UCLA ■	Feb. 15
Oregon St.	Feb. 20
Oregon	Feb. 22
Washington ■	Feb. 27
Washington St. ■	Mar. 1
California	Mar. 6
Stanford	Mar. 8

1995-96 RESULTS (11-16)

103	Texas Southern ■	77
82	Southern Utah ■	76
85	Oklahoma St.	90
79	New Mexico	86
85	Cal St. Sacramento ■	73
76	Northern Ariz. ■	62
62	Southern Methodist ■	58
66	Detroit ■	72
70	Stanford	83
82	California	97

76	Arizona	108
73	UCLA ■	87
67	Southern Cal ■	80
74	Oregon	73
93	Oregon St.	75
58	Washington St. ■	72
88	Washington ■	79
69	Arizona ■	71
69	North Caro. St. †	89
69	Southern Cal	66
70	UCLA	87
63	Oregon St. ■	58
70	Oregon ■	81
64	Washington	75
78	Washington St.	103
56	California ■	53
53	Stanford ■	67

Nickname: Sun Devils
Colors: Maroon & Gold
Arena: University Activity Center
  Capacity: 14,198; Year Built: 1974
AD: Kevin White
SID: Doug Tammaro

ARKANSAS
Fayetteville, AR 72701 I

Coach: Nolan Richardson
Alma Mater: UTEP '65
Record: 16 Years, W-391, L-132

1996-97 SCHEDULE

Jackson St. ■	Nov. 22
Oral Roberts ■	Nov. 27
San Francisco ■	Nov. 30
Missouri	Dec. 7
Troy St. ■	Dec. 10
McNeese St. ■	Dec. 19
Louisville ■	Dec. 21
Southern Utah ■	Dec. 28
Mississippi ■	Jan. 2
Florida	Jan. 5
Auburn	Jan. 8
LSU ■	Jan. 11
Alabama	Jan. 15
Cincinnati	Jan. 18
Mississippi St. ■	Jan. 21
Kentucky ■	Jan. 26
Mississippi	Jan. 29
Memphis ■	Feb. 1
Tennessee ■	Feb. 5
Vanderbilt	Feb. 8
Auburn ■	Feb. 11
Georgia ■	Feb. 15
South Caro.	Feb. 18
Mississippi St.	Feb. 23
Alabama ■	Feb. 26
LSU	Mar. 1
Southeastern Conf. Tr.	Mar. 6-9

1995-96 RESULTS (20-13)

75	Northeast La. ■	67
73	Arizona ■	83
72	Michigan St. †	75
103	North Caro. A&T ■	49
116	Alcorn St. ■	75
104	Missouri ■	93
67	Cincinnati ■	82
73	Southern Methodist ■	46
86	Tennessee St. ■	67
86	Jackson St. ■	77
75	Florida ■	60
76	Auburn	101
63	Mississippi	62
73	Vanderbilt ■	80
72	Memphis	94
80	Mississippi St. ■	68
71	Alabama	63
66	Oral Roberts ■	65
76	LSU ■	68
81	South Caro. ■	69
63	Mississippi St.	78
73	Kentucky ■	88
79	Mississippi ■	73
87	Auburn ■	77

59	Tennessee	66
59	Georgia	71
89	Alabama ■	98
94	LSU	79
80	South Caro. †	58
75	Kentucky †	95
86	Penn St. †	80
65	Marquette †	56
63	Massachusetts †	79

Nickname: Razorbacks
Colors: Cardinal & White
Arena: Bud Walton Arena
Capacity: 19,200; Year Built: 1993
AD: Frank Broyles
SID: Rick Schaeffer

ARKANSAS ST.
State University, AR 72467........I

Coach: Dickey Nutt
Alma Mater: Oklahoma St. '82
Record: 1 Year, W-9, L-18

1996-97 SCHEDULE

Mississippi Val.	Nov. 25
Southwestern (Kan.) ■	Nov. 27
Jacksonville	Nov. 30
Missouri	Dec. 4
West Ala. ■	Dec. 7
Murray St. ■	Dec. 14
Tennessee Tech	Dec. 17
Mississippi Val. ■	Dec. 19
Oklahoma St. ■	Dec. 23
Southwestern La.	Jan. 2
South Ala.	Jan. 4
Jacksonville ■	Jan. 9
Louisiana Tech ■	Jan. 11
Tex.-Pan American	Jan. 16
New Orleans	Jan. 18
Southwestern La. ■	Jan. 23
South Ala. ■	Jan. 25
New Orleans ■	Jan. 27
Lamar	Jan. 30
Ark.-Little Rock	Feb. 1
Western Ky. ■	Feb. 6
Louisiana Tech	Feb. 8
Western Ky.	Feb. 13
Ark.-Little Rock ■	Feb. 15
Tex.-Pan American ■	Feb. 20
Lamar ■	Feb. 22
Sun Belt Conf. Tr.	Feb. 28-Mar. 4

1995-96 RESULTS (9-18)

82	Abilene Christian ■	78
67	Colorado St.	91
82	Murray St.	94
57	Georgia St. ■	72
63	Missouri ■	73
74	Georgia St.	67
87	Tennessee Tech	89
62	Oklahoma St.	97
68	Ark.-Little Rock	95
80	Western Ky. ■	68
62	Louisiana Tech ■	50
82	Southwestern La.	96
70	New Orleans	79
52	South Ala.	55
93	Jacksonville	101
75	Lamar ■	58
77	Southwestern La. ■	71
69	Louisiana Tech	64
63	Ark.-Little Rock ■	84
64	Western Ky.	91
46	Tex.-Pan American ■	38
66	New Orleans ■	69
62	South Ala. ■	54
75	Jacksonville ■	77
60	Tex.-Pan American	74
63	Lamar	75
65	Louisiana Tech †	70

Nickname: Indians
Colors: Scarlet & Black
Arena: Convocation Center
Capacity: 10,563; Year Built: 1987
AD: Barry Dowd
SID: Gina Bowman

ARK.-LITTLE ROCK
Little Rock, AR 72204................I

Coach: Wimp Sanderson
Alma Mater: North Ala. '59
Record: 14 Years, W-305, L-137

1996-97 SCHEDULE

NIT	Nov. 20-29
Faulkner ■	Nov. 30
Texas Tech	Dec. 2
Auburn	Dec. 5
Sam Houston St. ■	Dec. 7
Ark.-Pine Bluff	Dec. 12
Truman ■	Dec. 19
Alcorn St. ■	Dec. 21
Lamar ■	Dec. 28
South Ala.	Jan. 2
New Orleans ■	Jan. 4
Louisiana Tech ■	Jan. 9
Jacksonville ■	Jan. 11
Ark.-Pine Bluff ■	Jan. 13
Southwestern La.	Jan. 16
Louisiana Tech	Jan. 18
South Ala. ■	Jan. 23
Southwestern La. ■	Jan. 25
Western Ky. ■	Jan. 27
Tex.-Pan American	Jan. 30
Arkansas St. ■	Feb. 1
Lamar	Feb. 5
Western Ky.	Feb. 9
Arkansas St.	Feb. 15
Jacksonville	Feb. 17
New Orleans ■	Feb. 20
Tex.-Pan American ■	Feb. 22
Sun Belt Conf. Tr.	Feb. 28-Mar. 4

1995-96 RESULTS (23-7)

83	West Ala. ■	61
93	Sam Houston St.	89
62	Texas Tech ■	71
70	Mississippi St.	68
72	Southwest Tex. St. ■	63
62	Grambling	57
112	William Carey ■	77
95	Arkansas St.	68
66	Louisiana Tech ■	60
84	Western Ky. ■	76
65	New Orleans	78
64	Lamar	73
91	Grambling ■	67
65	Western Ky.	83
80	Louisiana Tech	63
65	Lamar ■	63
72	South Ala. ■	60
84	Arkansas St. ■	63
89	Jacksonville	57
69	New Orleans ■	66
76	Tex.-Pan American ■	72
78	Southwestern La.	79
55	Tex.-Pan American	52
87	Southwestern La. ■	67
61	South Ala.	49
103	Jacksonville ■	77
89	Tex.-Pan American ■	71
67	Jacksonville ■	60
56	New Orleans	57
80	Vanderbilt	86

Nickname: Trojans
Colors: Maroon & White
Arena: Barton Coliseum
Capacity: 8,303; Year Built: 1952
AD: Rick Mello
SID: Mike Garrity

ARMSTRONG ATLANTIC
Savannah, GA 31419 II

Coach: Griff Mills
Alma Mater: DePauw '88
Record: 5 Years, W-69, L-64

1996-97 SCHEDULE

Southern Wesleyan ■	Nov. 18
Savannah St. ■	Nov. 23
Fla. Memorial ■	Nov. 25
Lenoir-Rhyne Cl.	Nov. 29-30
Clayton St.	Dec. 10
Clayton St. ■	Dec. 17
East Caro.	Dec. 28
S.C.-Aiken	Jan. 2
Kennesaw St. ■	Jan. 4
Augusta St. ■	Jan. 8
Francis Marion ■	Jan. 11
Georgia Col.	Jan. 13
Columbus St.	Jan. 15
S.C.-Spartanburg ■	Jan. 18
N.C.-Pembroke ■	Jan. 22
Lander ■	Jan. 25
S.C.-Aiken ■	Jan. 29
Kennesaw St.	Feb. 1
Augusta St.	Feb. 5
Francis Marion	Feb. 8
Georgia Col.	Feb. 10
Columbus St. ■	Feb. 12
S.C.-Spartanburg	Feb. 15
N.C.-Pembroke	Feb. 19
Lander	Feb. 22

1995-96 RESULTS (12-14)

70	Fla. Memorial ■	64
59	Savannah St. †	49
60	Southern Wesleyan ■	55
57	Claflin	63
76	Warner Southern ■	54
74	Clayton St. ■	57
60	Clayton St.	59
80	Tampa ■	66
68	S.C.-Aiken ■	61
49	Kennesaw St.	55
60	Augusta St.	78
51	Francis Marion ■	59
72	Georgia Col.	92
70	Columbus St.	67
73	S.C.-Spartanburg	82
53	N.C.-Pembroke ■	56
66	Lander	83
58	S.C.-Aiken	72
72	Kennesaw St. ■	77
64	Augusta St. ■	61
52	Francis Marion	59
83	Georgia Col. ■	77
61	Columbus St. ■	79
72	S.C.-Spartanburg ■	84
75	N.C.-Pembroke ■	84
74	Lander ■	71

Nickname: Pirates
Colors: Maroon & Gold
Arena: Armstrong St. Sports Center
Capacity: 3,088; Year Built: 1995
AD: Roger Counsil
SID: Darrell Stephens

ARMY
West Point, NY 10996 I

Coach: Dino Gaudio
Alma Mater: Ohio '81
Record: 3 Years, W-26, L-56

1996-97 SCHEDULE

Vassar ■	Nov. 26
Bethany (W.Va.) ■	Nov. 30
Harvard ■	Dec. 4
Yale ■	Dec. 10
Duke	Dec. 22
Indiana Hoosier Cl.	Dec. 27-28
Marist	Jan. 2
Brown ■	Jan. 4
Navy	Jan. 8
Holy Cross ■	Jan. 11
Cornell ■	Jan. 14
Colgate	Jan. 18
Columbia ■	Jan. 20
Lehigh ■	Jan. 22
Lafayette	Jan. 25
Dartmouth ■	Jan. 27
Bucknell ■	Jan. 29
Navy	Feb. 1
Holy Cross	Feb. 5
Wofford	Feb. 8
Colgate ■	Feb. 12
Lehigh	Feb. 15
Lafayette ■	Feb. 18
Bucknell ■	Feb. 22
Patriot Conf. Tr.	Mar. 1-5

1995-96 RESULTS (7-20)

88	Hobart ■	67
60	Harvard	89
57	Monmouth (N.J.)	78
59	Columbia ■	73
68	Bethany (W.Va.) ■	37
72	Dartmouth	73
62	Northwestern	84
52	St. Francis (N.Y.) ■	69
58	Hofstra	82
74	Wofford	71
70	Lehigh	84
37	Bucknell ■	75
75	Cornell	78
83	Lafayette ■	79
66	Holy Cross	81
44	Navy	75
72	Colgate ■	81
81	Wesley ■	59
91	Lehigh ■	75
64	Yale	65
65	Bucknell	82
72	Lafayette	77
69	Holy Cross ■	81
51	Navy ■	54
73	Colgate	88
64	Navy †	58
65	Holy Cross	68

Nickname: Cadets/Black Knights
Colors: Black, Gold & Gray
Arena: Christl Arena
Capacity: 5,043; Year Built: 1985
AD: Al Vanderbush
SID: Bob Beretta

ASHLAND
Ashland, OH 44805 II

Coach: To be named

1996-97 SCHEDULE

West Va. Tech ■	Nov. 16
Northern Ky.	Nov. 23
Cedarville	Nov. 26
Hiram ■	Nov. 30
Edinboro	Dec. 3
Saginaw Valley ■	Dec. 7
Northwood	Dec. 19
Lake Superior St.	Dec. 21
Lake Erie ■	Dec. 28
Wayne St. (Mich.)	Jan. 2
Oakland	Jan. 4
Central St. ■	Jan. 9
Hillsdale ■	Jan. 11
Gannon ■	Jan. 16
Mercyhurst ■	Jan. 18
Grand Valley St.	Jan. 23
Ferris St.	Jan. 25
Northern Mich.	Jan. 30
Michigan Tech ■	Feb. 1
Lake Erie	Feb. 3
Wayne St. (Mich.) ■	Feb. 6
Oakland ■	Feb. 8
Hillsdale	Feb. 15
Gannon	Feb. 20
Mercyhurst	Feb. 22

1995-96 RESULTS (14-12)

60	Walsh †	71
73	Lake Erie †	57
56	Fairmont St. ■	74
73	Glenville St.	63
93	Cedarville ■	78
76	Edinboro ■	74
93	Hillsdale	77
78	Ohio Dominican	60
58	Murray St.	81
76	Gannon	85
62	Ferris St.	65
79	Saginaw Valley ■	78
75	Michigan Tech ■	58

SCHEDULES/RESULTS

78	Wayne St. (Mich.)	86
66	Lake Superior St.	76
58	Northern Mich.	80
68	Mercyhurst ■	70
58	Northwood ■	56
69	Grand Valley St. ■	79
87	Oakland	103
84	Hillsdale	64
83	Gannon ■	90
72	Oakland ■	70
76	Ferris St. ■	74
86	Grand Valley St.	79
84	Mercyhurst	67

Nickname: Eagles
Colors: Purple & Gold
Arena: Charles Kates Gymnasium
  Capacity: 3,200; Year Built: 1967
AD: William Weidner
SID: Al King

ASSUMPTION

Worcester, MA 01615..............II

Coach: Serge Debari
Alma Mater: Assumption '71
Record: 16 Years, W-230, L-169

1996-97 SCHEDULE

New Hamp. Col. Cl.	Nov. 15-16
So. Conn. St. Cl.	Nov. 22-23
St. Anselm	Dec. 3
Bentley ■	Dec. 8
St. Rose Cl.	Dec. 27-29
Le Moyne	Jan. 7
St. Michael's ■	Jan. 11
American Int'l ■	Jan. 13
Quinnipiac	Jan. 16
Merrimack	Jan. 18
Stonehill ■	Jan. 21
Bryant ■	Jan. 23
Le Moyne ■	Jan. 26
Bentley	Feb. 1
American Int'l	Feb. 4
Merrimack ■	Feb. 6
Quinnipiac ■	Feb. 11
St. Michael's	Feb. 13
Stonehill	Feb. 16
St. Anselm ■	Feb. 19
Bryant	Feb. 22

1995-96 RESULTS (6-19)

87	St. Rose	116
107	Queens (N.Y.) †	101
96	Clark (Mass.) ■	103
127	Mercy	115
96	Husson ■	66
88	LIU-Southampton	89
64	St. Anselm	99
69	Rollins	88
75	Flagler	78
89	Merrimack	122
74	Bentley	106
78	Bryant ■	84
80	Quinnipiac	70
99	Merrimack ■	107
79	Stonehill	82
75	American Int'l ■	68
64	St. Michael's	84
92	Bentley	110
95	Quinnipiac ■	88
59	Bryant	73
78	St. Anselm ■	102
83	St. Michael's	105
71	Stonehill ■	75
77	American Int'l	87
78	Quinnipiac	101

Nickname: Greyhounds
Colors: Royal Blue & White
Arena: Andrew Laska Gymnasium
  Capacity: 3,000; Year Built: 1962
AD: Rita Castagna
SID: Steve Morris

AUBURN

Auburn University, AL 36831......I

Coach: Cliff Ellis
Alma Mater: Florida St. '68
Record: 21 Years, W-383, L-238

1996-97 SCHEDULE

UAB	Nov. 22
Ark.-Pine Bluff ■	Nov. 25
Hawaii-Hilo Inv.	Nov. 29-Dec. 1
Ark.-Little Rock ■	Dec. 5
Georgia St. ■	Dec. 7
Baylor ■	Dec. 14
Western Caro. ■	Dec. 15
South Ala. ■	Dec. 18
Murray St. [Birmingham]	Dec. 21
Florida A&M	Dec. 28
Winthrop ■	Dec. 30
South Caro.	Jan. 4
Arkansas ■	Jan. 8
Florida ■	Jan. 11
Tennessee ■	Jan. 15
Kentucky	Jan. 18
LSU	Jan. 22
Georgia	Jan. 25
Alabama ■	Jan. 28
Mississippi	Feb. 1
Mississippi St. ■	Feb. 5
LSU ■	Feb. 8
Arkansas	Feb. 11
Vanderbilt ■	Feb. 15
Alabama	Feb. 22
Mississippi St.	Feb. 26
Mississippi ■	Mar. 1
Southeastern Conf. Tr.	Mar. 6-9

1995-96 RESULTS (19-13)

70	La Salle †	60
82	James Madison †	71
82	Louisville †	78
91	Jacksonville St. ■	74
54	UAB	66
63	Liberty †	58
83	Baylor	64
59	South Ala.	50
80	Northeast La. ■	71
82	Coastal Caro. ■	66
73	Wofford ■	56
92	Norfolk St. †	56
84	Florida A&M	54
62	Tennessee	66
101	Arkansas ■	76
65	Alabama	72
89	Georgia	86
95	LSU ■	87
69	Mississippi	82
62	Vanderbilt	76
75	Mississippi St. ■	78
84	South Caro. ■	73
73	Florida	70
72	Alabama ■	75
77	Arkansas	87
69	Mississippi ■	62
67	LSU	93
73	Kentucky ■	88
51	Mississippi St.	67
68	Vanderbilt †	65
58	Mississippi St. †	69
73	Tulane	87

Nickname: Tigers
Colors: Orange & Blue
Arena: Beard-Eaves-Memorial
  Capacity: 10,108; Year Built: 1969
AD: David Housel
SID: Chuck Gallina

AUGSBURG

Minneapolis, MN 55454..........III

Coach: Brian Ammann
Alma Mater: Augsburg '85
Record: 8 Years, W-87, L-109

1996-97 SCHEDULE

Minn.-Crookston ■	Nov. 24
Concordia-St. Paul ■	Nov. 26
Wartburg ■	Dec. 2
St. Scholastica	Dec. 5
St. Olaf	Dec. 9
Macalester ■	Dec. 11
Bethel (Minn.) ■	Dec. 14
Gust. Adolphus ■	Jan. 4
St. Thomas (Minn.)	Jan. 6
St. John's (Minn.)	Jan. 8
Carleton ■	Jan. 11
Hamline	Jan. 13
St. Mary's (Minn.) ■	Jan. 15
Concordia-M'head ■	Jan. 18
St. Olaf ■	Jan. 25
Macalester	Jan. 29
Bethel (Minn.)	Feb. 1
Gust. Adolphus	Feb. 3
St. Thomas (Minn.) ■	Feb. 5
St. John's (Minn.) ■	Feb. 8
Carleton	Feb. 12
Hamline ■	Feb. 15
St. Mary's (Minn.) ■	Feb. 17
Concordia-M'head	Feb. 19

1995-96 RESULTS (15-9)

88	Minn.-Crookston	85
107	St. Scholastica	84
72	Wartburg	62
70	Concordia-St. Paul	61
89	Bethel (Minn.)	100
90	Hamline	82
75	St. Olaf ■	90
50	St. Mary's (Minn.) ■ ■	45
84	Carleton	82
60	St. Thomas (Minn.) ■	62
73	Concordia-M'head	84
58	Gust. Adolphus ■	68
73	Macalester	56
97	Bethel (Minn.) ■	68
73	Hamline ■	57
61	St. Olaf	63
80	St. John's (Minn.) ■	79
66	St. Mary's (Minn.)	35
66	Carleton ■	73
73	St. Thomas (Minn.) ■	64
66	Concordia-M'head	68
74	Gust. Adolphus	80
83	Macalester	65
63	St. John's (Minn.)	60

Nickname: Auggies
Colors: Maroon & Gray
Arena: Si Melby Hall
  Capacity: 2,800; Year Built: 1961
AD: Paul Grauer
SID: Chris Brown

AUGUSTA ST.

Augusta, GA 30904 II

Coach: Clint Bryant
Alma Mater: Belmont Abbey '77
Record: 8 Years, W-98, L-128

1996-97 SCHEDULE

Paine Cl.	Nov. 15-16
Shorter ■	Nov. 18
North Greenville ■	Nov. 23
Presbyterian	Nov. 25
N.C.-Pembroke	Dec. 11
Francis Marion	Dec. 15
S.C.-Aiken ■	Dec. 18
Georgia Col. ■	Jan. 2
Lander	Jan. 4
Armstrong Atlantic	Jan. 8
Kennesaw St. ■	Jan. 11
N.C.-Pembroke	Jan. 12
S.C.-Spartanburg ■	Jan. 15
Columbus St. ■	Jan. 18
Clayton St.	Jan. 22
Paine [Augusta]	Jan. 25
Georgia Col.	Jan. 29
Lander ■	Feb. 1
Morehouse	Feb. 3
Armstrong Atlantic ■	Feb. 5
Kennesaw St.	Feb. 8
S.C.-Spartanburg ■	Feb. 12
S.C.-Aiken ■	Feb. 15
Francis Marion ■	Feb. 19
Columbus St.	Feb. 22

1995-96 RESULTS (11-16)
Results unavailable

Nickname: Jaguars
Colors: Blue & White
Arena: AC P.E./Athletic Complex
  Capacity: 3,500; Year Built: 1990
AD: Clint Bryant
SID: Frank Mercogliano

AUGUSTANA (ILL.)

Rock Island, IL 61201 III

Coach: Steve Yount
Alma Mater: Augustana (Ill.) '80
Record: 6 Years, W-107, L-50

1996-97 SCHEDULE

Wis.-Whitewater	Nov. 23
St. Ambrose	Nov. 26
Beloit ■	Nov. 30
Aurora ■	Dec. 3
Augustana (Ill.) Inv	Dec. 6-7
North Park ■	Dec. 11
Teikyo Marycrest ■	Dec. 18
Grand View	Dec. 30
Roanoke Cl.	Jan. 4-5
North Central ■	Jan. 8
Elmhurst ■	Jan. 11
Ill. Wesleyan ■	Jan. 15
Carthage	Jan. 18
Mt. Mercy ■	Jan. 22
North Park	Jan. 25
Millikin ■	Jan. 29
Elmhurst	Feb. 1
Ill. Wesleyan ■	Feb. 5
Wheaton (Ill.)	Feb. 8
Millikin	Feb. 11
Carthage ■	Feb. 15
North Central	Feb. 22
Wheaton (Ill.) ■	Feb. 26

1995-96 RESULTS (16-8)

90	Olivet Nazarene	97
100	Trinity Christian †	91
84	Mt. Mercy	92
99	Eureka ■	85
73	Teikyo Marycrest ■	57
96	Aurora	85
96	Beloit	93
89	Carthage ■	70
114	Rockford ■	69
94	St. Ambrose	72
71	Teikyo Marycrest	60
72	Ill. Wesleyan	98
96	North Central ■	71
77	Millikin	65
67	Wheaton (Ill.) ■	81
82	North Park ■	67
79	Carthage	65
80	Elmhurst	74
66	Ill. Wesleyan ■	76
84	Millikin ■	77
90	North Central	69
62	Wheaton (Ill.)	72
104	North Park	106
64	Elmhurst	74

Nickname: Vikings
Colors: Gold & Blue
Arena: Carver P.E. Center
  Capacity: 3,200; Year Built: 1971
AD: John Farwell
SID: Dave Wrath

AUGUSTANA (S.D.)

Sioux Falls, SD 57102..............II

Coach: Gary Thomas

Armstrong Atlantic ■ ....Feb. 5
Kennesaw St. ....Feb. 8
S.C.-Spartanburg ■ ....Feb. 12
S.C.-Aiken ■ ....Feb. 15
Francis Marion ■ ....Feb. 19
Columbus St. ....Feb. 22

Alma Mater: Augustana (S.D.) '79
Record: 4 Years, W-45, L-61

1996-97 SCHEDULE

Valley City St. ■		Nov. 22
Northern St. ■		Nov. 26
Sioux Falls ■		Nov. 30
Wayne St. (Neb.)		Dec. 3
Dak. Wesleyan		Dec. 7
Dakota St.		Dec. 12
Presentation ■		Dec. 14
Mt. Marty		Dec. 18
Briar Cliff ■		Dec. 20
Mankato St.		Dec. 28
St. Cloud St.		Dec. 29
South Dak. St. ■		Jan. 4
Northern Colo. ■		Jan. 10
Neb.-Omaha ■		Jan. 11
North Dak. St.		Jan. 17
North Dak.		Jan. 18
South Dak. ■		Jan. 24
Morningside ■		Jan. 25
South Dak. St.		Feb. 1
Neb.-Omaha		Feb. 7
Northern Colo.		Feb. 8
North Dak. St. ■		Feb. 14
North Dak. St. ■		Feb. 15
Morningside		Feb. 21
South Dak.		Feb. 22
St. Cloud St. ■		Feb. 28
Mankato St. ■		Mar. 1

1995-96 RESULTS (14-13)

76	Moorhead St. ■	82
79	Southwest St.	67
65	Sioux Falls ■	62
97	Bellevue ■	63
88	Mayville St. ■	57
85	Wayne St. (Neb.) ■	77
84	Dak. Wesleyan ■	86
86	Mt. Marty	69
74	Briar Cliff	70
68	South Dak. St.	83
55	Northern Colo.	57
75	Neb.-Omaha ■	58
74	North Dak. St. ■	70
77	North Dak. ■	85
85	South Dak.	100
86	Morningside	85
94	Mankato St. ■	85
83	St. Cloud St. ■	80
79	Neb.-Omaha ■	58
83	Northern Colo. ■	74
99	North Dak.	108
61	North Dak. St.	86
77	Morningside ■	90
67	South Dak. ■	82
68	St. Cloud St.	75
82	Mankato St. ■	87
83	South Dak. St. ■	86

Nickname: Vikings
Colors: Navy & Yellow
Arena: Elmen Center
   Capacity: 4,000; Year Built: 1989
AD: Bill Gross
SID: Karen Madsen

AURORA
Aurora, IL 60506 III

Coach: James Lancaster
Alma Mater: Aurora '86
Record: 2 Years, W-26, L-24

1996-97 SCHEDULE

North Central Cl.		Nov. 22-23
Northern Ill.		Nov. 25
Augustana (Ill.)		Dec. 3
Loras		Dec. 6
Dubuque		Dec. 7
Beloit		Dec. 12
Ill. Wesleyan ■		Dec. 14
Millikin ■		Dec. 20
Defiance Tr.		Dec. 27-28
Monmouth (Ill.) ■		Jan. 8
Clarke ■		Jan. 15

Concordia (Ill.) ....Jan. 18
Benedictine (Ill.) ■ ....Jan. 22
Eureka ....Jan. 25
Trinity Int'l ....Jan. 29
Rockford ....Feb. 1
Judson (Ill.) ....Feb. 5
Clarke ....Feb. 8
Concordia (Ill.) ■ ....Feb. 12
Benedictine (Ill.) ....Feb. 15
Eureka ....Feb. 19
Judson (Ill.) ■ ....Feb. 22
Rockford ....Feb. 26

1995-96 RESULTS (12-13)

73	Millikin	79
77	Beloit ■	93
77	Northern Ill.	116
87	North Central	77
83	Savannah A&D †	75
75	Carroll (Wis.) †	74
85	Augustana (Ill.) ■	96
79	Aquinas †	95
80	Hope	113
77	Blackburn	69
78	Monmouth (Ill.)	73
89	Ill. Wesleyan	105
88	Loras ■	80
86	Lake Forest ■	78
84	Dubuque ■	87
84	Concordia (Ill.)	72
60	Judson (Ill.)	62
85	Rockford	73
102	Trinity Int'l	101
84	Benedictine (Ill.) ■	89
100	Concordia (Ill.) ■	81
95	Judson (Ill.) ■	97
109	Rockford	88
101	Trinity Int'l ■	111
75	Benedictine (Ill.)	78

Nickname: Spartans
Colors: Royal Blue & White
Arena: Thornton Gymnasium
   Capacity: 2,200; Year Built: 1970
AD: Rita Yerkes
SID: Dave Beyer

AUSTIN PEAY
Clarksville, TN 37044 I

Coach: Dave Loos
Alma Mater: Memphis '70
Record: 10 Years, W-158, L-147

1996-97 SCHEDULE

Cumberland (Tenn.) ■		Nov. 23
Thomas ■		Nov. 25
Hawaii Tip-Off		Nov. 29-Dec. 1
Eastern Ky.		Dec. 7
Southern Ill.		Dec. 14
Northern Ill.		Dec. 18
Western Caro. ■		Dec. 22
Iowa		Dec. 27
Wis.-Green Bay Cl.		Dec. 30-31
Eastern Ill. ■		Jan. 2
Southeast Mo. St. ■		Jan. 4
Tennessee Tech		Jan. 9
Murray St.		Jan. 11
Tenn.-Martin		Jan. 13
Tennessee St.		Jan. 18
Middle Tenn. St. ■		Jan. 23
Eastern Ky. ■		Jan. 25
Morehead St. ■		Jan. 27
Eastern Ill.		Feb. 1
Southeast Mo. St.		Feb. 3
Middle Tenn. St.		Feb. 6
Tenn.-Martin ■		Feb. 8
Murray St. ■		Feb. 10
Tennessee St. ■		Feb. 15
Tennessee Tech ■		Feb. 20
Morehead St.		Feb. 22
Ohio Valley Conf. Tr.		Feb. 25-Mar. 1

1995-96 RESULTS (19-11)

68	Northern Ill. ■	65
98	Martin Methodist ■	81
63	Samford ■	67

70	Tennessee	80
100	Cumberland (Tenn.) ■	70
58	Missouri	81
78	Southern Ill.	65
91	Air Force †	72
74	Toledo	88
69	Middle Tenn. St.	88
76	Tennessee St.	81
86	Tennessee Tech	83
82	Southeast Mo. St. ■	69
72	Eastern Ky.	71
71	Morehead St.	65
64	Murray St. ■	71
83	Tenn.-Martin	91
66	Middle Tenn. St. ■	75
85	Samford	69
84	Southeast Mo. St.	71
93	Tennessee Tech	74
102	Tennessee St. ■	75
89	Morehead St. ■	78
90	Eastern Ky. ■	75
64	Tenn.-Martin	67
80	Murray St.	65
89	Eastern Ky. †	67
83	Tennessee St.	62
70	Murray St. †	68
79	Georgia Tech †	90

Nickname: Governors
Colors: Red & White
Arena: Winfield Dunn Center
   Capacity: 9,092; Year Built: 1975
AD: Kaye Hart
SID: Brad Kirtley

AVERETT
Danville, VA 24541 III

Coach: Kirk Chandler
Alma Mater: Elon '81
Record: 4 Years, W-21, L-78

1996-97 SCHEDULE

Lynchburg Inv.		Nov. 22-23
Guilford ■		Nov. 26
Hampden-Sydney		Dec. 2
Elon		Dec. 5
Newport News App. ■		Dec. 8
Bluefield Col. ■		Dec. 14
Clinch Valley		Dec. 19
Maryville (Tenn.) ■		Jan. 11
Warren Wilson		Jan. 12
Ferrum		Jan. 15
Greensboro		Jan. 18
Methodist		Jan. 22
Chris. Newport		Jan. 25
Newport News App.		Jan. 26
N.C. Wesleyan ■		Jan. 29
Shenandoah		Feb. 1
Ferrum		Feb. 5
Greensboro ■		Feb. 8
Methodist		Feb. 10
Chris. Newport ■		Feb. 14
N.C. Wesleyan		Feb. 19
Shenandoah ■		Feb. 22

1995-96 RESULTS (2-23)
Results unavailable

Nickname: Cougars
Colors: Navy & Gold
Arena: Cougar Gym
   Capacity: 500
AD: Vesa Hiltunen
SID: Danny Miller

BABSON
Babson Park, MA 02157 III

Coach: Steve Brennan
Alma Mater: Bates '87
Record: 1 Year, W-21, L-7

1996-97 SCHEDULE

Babson Inv.		Nov. 22-23
MIT		Nov. 26

Harvard ....Dec. 2
WPI ■ ....Dec. 4
Springfield ■ ....Dec. 9
Western New Eng. ....Dec. 12
Marietta Tr. ....Dec. 28-29
Salem St. ....Jan. 11
Brandeis ....Jan. 14
Clark (Mass.) ■ ....Jan. 18
Coast Guard ....Jan. 22
Norwich ■ ....Jan. 25
Amherst ■ ....Jan. 28
Clark (Mass.) ....Feb. 1
Tufts ....Feb. 4
Springfield ....Feb. 6
Norwich ....Feb. 8
Suffolk ....Feb. 11
Western New Eng. ■ ....Feb. 13
WPI ....Feb. 15
Coast Guard ■ ....Feb. 19
MIT ■ ....Feb. 22

1995-96 RESULTS (21-7)

109	Suffolk ■	69
107	Anna Maria ■	87
98	MIT ■	69
60	Harvard	108
96	WPI	83
84	Springfield	88
119	Western New Eng. ■	81
101	Brandeis ■	80
88	Whittier	95
82	Chapman †	81
89	Amherst	84
99	Clark (Mass.)	79
102	Norwich	91
92	Coast Guard ■	83
118	Eastern Conn. St.	111
101	Clark (Mass.)	88
91	Tufts ■	100
79	Springfield ■	67
106	Norwich ■	110
100	Suffolk ■	50
99	Western New Eng.	81
104	WPI ■	80
87	Coast Guard	64
77	MIT	65
81	MIT ■	65
96	Norwich ■	85
70	Springfield ■	78
90	Anna Maria	111

Nickname: Beavers
Colors: Green & White
Arena: Staake Gymnasium
   Capacity: 750; Year Built: 1989
AD: Steve Stirling
SID: Andy Dutton

BALDWIN-WALLACE
Berea, OH 44017 III

Coach: Steve Bankson
Alma Mater: Graceland '63
Record: 16 Years, W-233, L-194

1996-97 SCHEDULE

Dickinson Tr.		Nov. 22-23
Wilmington (Ohio)		Nov. 26
Mount Union		Dec. 4
Marietta		Dec. 7
Bethany (W.Va.) ■		Dec. 11
Capital ■		Dec. 14
Muskingum		Dec. 18
Wooster Tr.		Dec. 27-28
Hiram ■		Jan. 8
Otterbein ■		Jan. 11
Ohio Northern ■		Jan. 15
Heidelberg ■		Jan. 18
John Carroll ■		Jan. 22
Otterbein		Jan. 25
Ohio Northern ■		Jan. 29
Heidelberg		Feb. 1
John Carroll		Feb. 5
Marietta		Feb. 8
Mount Union ■		Feb. 12
Capital		Feb. 15

Hiram .... Feb. 19
Muskingum ■ .... Feb. 22

1995-96 RESULTS (16-12)
93 Greensboro † 83
76 York (N.Y.) † 48
56 Bethany (W.Va.) 63
66 Heidelberg ■ 71
80 Hiram 76
97 Capital ■ 86
52 Toledo 89
56 Marietta 71
62 Northwood † 85
87 Alma 77
70 Muskingum ■ 60
66 Ohio Northern 76
61 Mount Union 58
69 Otterbein ■ 58
61 John Carroll 77
63 Ohio Northern ■ 67
67 Mount Union ■ 77
70 Capital 71
80 Hiram ■ 67
76 Marietta ■ 59
77 Muskingum 63
71 Heidelberg 59
71 John Carroll ■ 75
80 Otterbein 52
81 Mount Union ■ 74
73 Muskingum † 48
60 Marietta † 59
61 Wittenberg 70

Nickname: Yellow Jackets
Colors: Brown & Gold
Arena: Ursprung Gymnasium
   Capacity: 2,800; Year Built: 1949
AD: Steve Bankson
SID: Kevin Ruple

BALL ST.
Muncie, IN 47306 I

Coach: Ray McCallum
Alma Mater: Ball St. '83
Record: 3 Years, W-51, L-35

1996-97 SCHEDULE
Grand Valley St. ■ .... Nov. 23
Michigan .... Nov. 26
Ball St. Cl. .... Nov. 29-30
Western Mich. ■ .... Dec. 5
Butler .... Dec. 7
Hawaii Festival .... Dec. 14-15
Northeast La. .... Dec. 21
Wisconsin ■ .... Dec. 26
Indiana St. ■ .... Dec. 30
Toledo .... Jan. 4
Ohio ■ .... Jan. 8
Bowling Green .... Jan. 11
Central Mich. .... Jan. 15
Akron .... Jan. 18
Kent ■ .... Jan. 22
Eastern Mich. .... Jan. 25
Miami (Ohio) ■ .... Jan. 29
Ohio .... Feb. 1
Bowling Green ■ .... Feb. 5
Western Mich. .... Feb. 8
Central Mich. ■ .... Feb. 12
Akron ■ .... Feb. 15
Kent .... Feb. 19
Eastern Mich. ■ .... Feb. 22
Miami (Ohio) .... Feb. 26
Toledo ■ .... Mar. 1
Mid-American Conf. Tr. .... Mar. 4-8

1995-96 RESULTS (16-12)
52 Michigan ■ 80
57 Butler ■ 67
103 Alcorn St. ■ 60
80 San Jose St. † 64
53 Illinois 97
60 UNLV 51
78 Coppin St. ■ 55
66 Indiana St. 78
57 Ohio 54
69 Toledo 92

83 Akron ■ 61
71 Western Mich. 75
82 Central Mich. ■ 69
102 Eastern Mich. 109
54 Bowling Green 50
82 Miami (Ohio) ■ 70
85 Kent 95
88 Toledo ■ 68
89 Akron 64
78 Western Mich. ■ 67
82 Central Mich. ■ 75
75 Eastern Mich. ■ 91
73 Bowling Green ■ 60
57 Miami (Ohio) 76
66 Kent ■ 52
67 Ohio 87
86 Ohio 80
71 Eastern Mich. † 87

Nickname: Cardinals
Colors: Cardinal & White
Arena: University Arena
   Capacity: 11,500; Year Built: 1992
AD: Andrea Seger
SID: Joe Hernandez

BARD
Annadale-on-Hudson, NY 12504 .. III

Coach: Glenn Bell
Alma Mater: Southern Ill.
Record: 1 Year, W-0, L-21

1996-97 SCHEDULE
Schedule unavailable

1995-96 RESULTS (0-21)
44 Vassar 108
26 Mt. St. Mary (N.Y.) † 102
40 N.J. Inst. of Tech. 127
24 Yeshiva 70
27 Marywood ■ 71
35 Lehman ■ 70
17 Wentworth Inst. ■ 59
34 Merchant Marine ■ 82
65 Mt. St. Vincent 111
38 Maritime (N.Y.) ■ 101
41 Pratt 86
50 Mt. St. Vincent ■ 115
24 Albany Pharmacy 76
34 Polytechnic (N.Y.) ■ 82
45 St. Joseph's (L.I.) ■ 83
36 Stevens Tech ■ 103
33 St. Joe's-Brooklyn 94
48 Maritime (N.Y.) 100
41 Vassar ■ 83
35 Southern Vt. ■ 104
48 Albany Pharmacy 84

Nickname: Blazers
Colors: Red, White & Black
Arena: Stevenson Gym
   Capacity: 675; Year Built: 1988
AD: Kristen Hall
SID: Kristen Hall

BARRY
Miami Shores, FL 33161 II

Coach: Cesar Odio
Alma Mater: Fla. Southern '81
Record: 2 Years, W-34, L-21

1996-97 SCHEDULE
St. Thomas (Fla.) ■ .... Nov. 16
Fla. Memorial .... Nov. 21
Nova Southeastern ■ .... Nov. 23
Barry Cl. .... Nov. 29-30
Southern Ind. Tr. .... Dec. 6-7
Lynn .... Dec. 14
Simon Fraser ■ .... Dec. 30
Tri-State ■ .... Jan. 2
Rhode Island Col. ■ .... Jan. 3
Lynn ■ .... Jan. 4
Tampa ■ .... Jan. 8
North Fla. .... Jan. 11

Fla. Southern .... Jan. 15
Rollins ■ .... Jan. 18
Florida Tech .... Jan. 22
St. Leo ■ .... Jan. 25
Eckerd .... Jan. 29
Fla. Southern ■ .... Feb. 1
Rollins .... Feb. 5
North Fla. ■ .... Feb. 8
Florida Tech ■ .... Feb. 12
St. Leo .... Feb. 15
Eckerd ■ .... Feb. 19
Tampa .... Feb. 22

1995-96 RESULTS (18-10)
104 St. Thomas (Fla.) ■ 77
75 Nova Southeastern 60
65 West Fla. ■ 55
74 Nova Southeastern 53
85 Fla. Memorial 73
101 Fla. Memorial ■ 72
69 Florida Int'l 72
81 Lynn ■ 69
91 Shippensburg ■ 72
68 American (P.R.) ■ 76
81 Lenoir-Rhyne ■ 70
87 St. Leo 92
69 Florida Tech 59
75 Tampa ■ 70
63 Rollins 72
83 North Fla. 64
63 Fla. Southern 77
76 Eckerd ■ 81
70 Lynn 88
67 St. Leo 64
76 Florida Tech ■ 55
63 Tampa 62
82 Rollins ■ 71
80 North Fla. 68
66 Fla. Southern ■ 76
56 Eckerd 66
84 Tampa † 67
56 Fla. Southern † 59

Nickname: Buccaneers
Colors: Red, Black & Silver
Arena: Health & Sports Center
   Capacity: 1,500; Year Built: 1990
AD: Dr. G. Jean Cerra
SID: Fred Battenfield

BARTON
Wilson, NC 27893 II

Coach: Ron Lievense
Alma Mater: St. Thomas (Minn.) '83
Record: 8 Years, W-60, L-147

1996-97 SCHEDULE
Queens (N.C.) ■ .... Nov. 25
Methodist ■ .... Nov. 26
Pfeiffer ■ .... Dec. 4
N.C. Wesleyan ■ .... Dec. 7
Columbia Union ■ .... Dec. 8
Newport News App. ■ .... Dec. 13
Longwood .... Jan. 4
High Point .... Jan. 8
St. Andrews .... Jan. 11
Mount Olive ■ .... Jan. 13
Erskine .... Jan. 16
Belmont Abbey .... Jan. 18
Coker ■ .... Jan. 23
Longwood ■ .... Jan. 25
Lees-McRae .... Jan. 27
St. Andrews ■ .... Feb. 1
Coker .... Feb. 3
Mount Olive .... Feb. 5
Lees-McRae ■ .... Feb. 8
High Point ■ .... Feb. 10
Queens (N.C.) .... Feb. 13
Pfeiffer .... Feb. 15
Savannah A&D ■ .... Feb. 17
Erskine ■ .... Feb. 19
Belmont Abbey ■ .... Feb. 22

1995-96 RESULTS (13-14)
83 Brewton Parker ■ 78
73 Chowan ■ 65

98 Embry-Riddle 78
70 Newport News App. 67
68 Pfeiffer 86
81 Methodist 59
71 Mount Olive ■ 76
81 Columbia Union 77
82 Elizabeth City St. ■ 86
69 Erskine ■ 53
61 Longwood 74
70 Queens (N.C.) 78
70 High Point 83
65 Coker ■ 49
75 St. Andrews 63
96 Belmont Abbey ■ 98
90 Lees-McRae ■ 69
75 Pfeiffer ■ 84
82 Longwood ■ 74
76 Hampton 88
72 Queens (N.C.) ■ 77
63 Lees-McRae 71
83 Erskine 89
81 Mount Olive 61
70 High Point ■ 84
49 Coker 47
65 Queens (N.C.) † 77

Nickname: Bulldogs
Colors: Royal Blue & White
Arena: Wilson Gym
   Capacity: 2,500; Year Built: 1965
AD: Gary Hall
SID: John Hackney

BARUCH
New York, NY 10010 III

Coach: Ray Rankis
Alma Mater: Lehman '75
Record: 13 Years, W-140, L-196

1996-97 SCHEDULE
Purchase St. ■ .... Nov. 22
Molloy Tr. .... Nov. 29-30
Polytechnic (N.Y.) .... Dec. 2
Merchant Marine ■ .... Dec. 4
Emerson Cl. .... Dec. 6-7
Yeshiva ■ .... Dec. 9
CCNY .... Jan. 3
John Jay .... Jan. 8
Lehman .... Jan. 14
St. Joseph's Tr. .... Jan. 17-18
CCNY ■ .... Jan. 21
Stevens Tech .... Jan. 23
Lehman ■ .... Jan. 30
Mt. St. Vincent .... Feb. 1
Brooklyn ■ .... Feb. 3
John Jay ■ .... Feb. 7
Hunter .... Feb. 12
Staten Island .... Feb. 15
Old Westbury ■ .... Feb. 17
Medgar Evers ■ .... Feb. 17
York (N.Y.) ■ .... Feb. 19

1995-96 RESULTS (17-10)
Results unavailable

Nickname: Statesmen
Colors: Azure Blue & White
Arena: Xavier High School
   Capacity: 1,200; Year Built: 1966
AD: William Eng
SID: Burt Beagle

BATES
Lewiston, ME 04240 III

Coach: Jeffrey C. Brown
Alma Mater: Vermont '82
Record: 2 Years, W-22, L-25

1996-97 SCHEDULE
New England .... Dec. 2
Bowdoin .... Dec. 4
Thomas .... Dec. 7
Western Conn St. Tr. .... Dec. 28-29
Colby .... Jan. 8

Colby-Sawyer ....Jan. 11
Suffolk ■ ....Jan. 14
Hamilton ■ ....Jan. 18
Skidmore ■ ....Jan. 19
Southern Me. ....Jan. 22
Western New Eng. ■ ....Jan. 24
Williams ....Jan. 25
Emerson-MCA ....Jan. 30
Me.-Farmington ....Feb. 3
St. Joseph's (Me.) ■ ....Feb. 5
Trinity (Conn.) ■ ....Feb. 8
Bowdoin ■ ....Feb. 11
Norwich ■ ....Feb. 14
Middlebury ■ ....Feb. 15
Maine Maritime ■ ....Feb. 17
Tufts ■ ....Feb. 19
Connecticut Col. ....Feb. 22
Colby ....Feb. 24

1995-96 RESULTS (10-14)

81	Potsdam St. †	63
69	Plattsburgh St.	85
86	Bowdoin ■	66
87	Maine Maritime	60
93	New England ■	89
92	Suffolk	75
98	Colby-Sawyer ■	107
80	Thomas ■	74
74	Skidmore	88
69	Union (N.Y.)	79
79	Southern Me. ■	85
104	Western New Eng. ■	94
70	Williams ■	98
72	Colby ■	86
103	Emerson-MCA ■	90
73	Me.-Farmington	81
75	St. Joseph's (Me.) ■	90
72	Trinity (Conn.) ■	93
75	Bowdoin	82
86	Norwich	80
62	Middlebury	85
88	Tufts ■	106
78	Connecticut Col. ■	99
89	Colby	84

Nickname: Bobcats
Colors: Garnet
Arena: Alumni Gymnasium
   Capacity: 750; Year Built: 1925
AD: Suzanne Coffey
SID: Adam Levin

BAYLOR

Waco, TX 76711 I

Coach: Harry Miller
Alma Mater: Texas Lutheran '74
Record: 2 Years, W-18, L-37

1996-97 SCHEDULE

Top of the World Cl. ....Nov. 22-24
Lamar ....Nov. 30
Mo.-Kansas City ■ ....Dec. 3
Baylor Tr. ....Dec. 6-7
Auburn ....Dec. 14
Prairie View ■ ....Dec. 18
Tex.-Pan American ■ ....Dec. 21
Northwestern St. ■ ....Dec. 28
Drake ■ ....Dec. 31
Texas Tech ....Jan. 4
Texas A&M ■ ....Jan. 8
Kansas ....Jan. 11
Missouri ....Jan. 14
Oklahoma ....Jan. 18
Colorado ■ ....Jan. 21
Oklahoma St. ....Jan. 25
Texas ■ ....Jan. 29
Oklahoma St. ■ ....Feb. 1
Iowa St. ....Feb. 5
Texas ....Feb. 12
Texas Tech ■ ....Feb. 15
Nebraska ■ ....Feb. 19
Texas A&M ....Feb. 22
Kansas St. ■ ....Feb. 26
Oklahoma ■ ....Mar. 1
Big 12 Conf. Tr. ....Mar. 6-9

1995-96 RESULTS (9-18)

79	Sam Houston St. ■	82
55	Mo.-Kansas City	70
80	Nevada ■	88
111	Prairie View ■	85
80	Centenary (La.) ■	77
64	Auburn ■	83
78	Drake	75
54	Pacific (Cal.)	77
66	Northwestern Okla.	73
71	Oklahoma †	84
74	Louisiana Tech †	55
93	Hardin-Simmons ■	47
74	Texas A&M ■	67
63	Southern Methodist	68
69	Texas Tech ■	75
81	Texas	90
84	Houston ■	91
64	Rice	79
64	Texas A&M	67
78	Southern Methodist ■	74
72	Texas Tech	78
72	Texas Christian ■	70
72	Texas	80
69	Houston	79
101	Rice ■	88
75	Texas Christian	77
65	Texas †	86

Nickname: Bears
Colors: Green & Gold
Arena: Ferrell Center
   Capacity: 10,084; Year Built: 1988
AD: Richard Ellis
SID: Tommy Newsom

BEAVER

Glenside, PA 19038 III

Coach: Michael G. Holland
Alma Mater: West Chester '71
Record: 3 Years, W-45, L-31

1996-97 SCHEDULE

Cabrini ....Dec. 4
Misericordia ....Dec. 7
Phila. Pharmacy ■ ....Dec. 11
Widener Cl. ....Dec. 13-14
Gwynedd-Mercy ■ ....Dec. 16
Frank. & Marsh. Tr. ....Jan. 4-5
Alvernia ■ ....Jan. 11
Neumann ■ ....Jan. 13
Marywood ■ ....Jan. 15
Eastern ....Jan. 18
Allentown ....Jan. 20
Misericordia ■ ....Jan. 25
Gwynedd-Mercy ....Jan. 29
Cabrini ■ ....Feb. 1
Alvernia ....Feb. 3
Neumann ....Feb. 8
Marywood ....Feb. 12
Eastern ■ ....Feb. 15
Allentown ■ ....Feb. 19

1995-96 RESULTS (14-11)

95	Montclair St. †	89
76	Dickinson	70
94	Gwynedd-Mercy ■	62
83	Marywood	57
62	Allentown ■	69
57	Neumann	72
97	FDU-Madison ■	94
71	Haverford ■	70
54	Elizabethtown †	67
65	Eastern †	57
83	Misericordia	89
74	Cabrini ■	92
81	Marywood ■	66
70	Gwynedd-Mercy	65
76	Eastern	68
69	Alvernia ■	84
52	Cabrini	80
87	Neumann ■	71
88	Allentown	92
67	Phila. Pharmacy ■	91
103	Western Md. ■	87

78	Alvernia	95
61	Misericordia ■	58
61	Eastern ■	60
59	Misericordia	64

Nickname: Knights
Colors: Scarlet & Gray
Arena: Kuch Center
   Capacity: 2,000; Year Built: 1993
AD: Shirley M. Liddle
SID: Lisa Brackbill

BELLARMINE

Louisville, KY 40205 II

Coach: Bob Valvano
Alma Mater: Va. Wesleyan '79
Record: 13 Years, W-145, L-205

1996-97 SCHEDULE

Knoxville ....Nov. 23
Ind.-Southeast ■ ....Nov. 30
St. Joseph's (Ind.) ....Dec. 2
Spalding ■ ....Dec. 5
IU/PU-Ft. Wayne ....Dec. 30
Indianapolis ....Jan. 2
Northern Ky. ■ ....Jan. 4
Knoxville ....Jan. 7
Ky. Wesleyan ■ ....Jan. 9
Lewis ....Jan. 11
Southern Ind. ....Jan. 16
SIU-Edwardsville ....Jan. 18
Quincy ■ ....Jan. 23
Mo.-St. Louis ■ ....Jan. 25
IU/PU-Ft. Wayne ■ ....Jan. 30
St. Joseph's (Ind.) ■ ....Feb. 1
Northern Ky. ....Feb. 6
Indianapolis ■ ....Feb. 8
Ky. Wesleyan ....Feb. 13
Wis.-Parkside ■ ....Feb. 15
Ind.-Southeast ....Feb. 18
Southern Ind. ■ ....Feb. 20
SIU-Edwardsville ■ ....Feb. 22
Mo.-St. Louis ....Feb. 27
Quincy ....Mar. 1

1995-96 RESULTS (11-16)

107	Knoxville ■	64
90	Spalding	77
87	Kentucky St. ■	58
75	Ky. Wesleyan	90
74	IU/PU-Ft. Wayne	79
63	St. Joseph's (Ind.)	76
75	Quincy	78
95	Lewis ■	79
86	Marymount (Va.) †	75
62	Holy Family †	57
69	Indianapolis	81
71	Northern Ky.	84
74	Wis.-Parkside ■	57
68	St. Joseph's (Ind.) ■	71
97	Ind.-Southeast	79
68	SIU-Edwardsville	74
72	Quincy	90
76	Kentucky St.	84
73	Ky. Wesleyan	84
69	Southern Ind.	84
71	IU/PU-Ft. Wayne ■	68
63	Indianapolis ■	82
68	Lewis	70
73	Wis.-Parkside	69
64	Southern Ind. ■	88
101	SIU-Edwardsville ■	93
79	Northern Ky.	84

Nickname: Knights
Colors: Scarlet & Silver
Arena: Knights Hall
   Capacity: 3,000; Year Built: 1960
AD: Jay Gardiner
SID: Mark Mulloy

BELMONT ABBEY

Belmont, NC 28012 II

Coach: Tim Jaeger

Alma Mater: Middlebury '86
Record: 3 Years, W-30, L-50

1996-97 SCHEDULE

Limestone ....Nov. 16
N.C.-Pembroke ■ ....Nov. 19
S.C.-Spartanburg Tr. ....Nov. 22-23
Mount Olive ■ ....Nov. 26
Lees-McRae ....Dec. 5
N.C.-Pembroke ....Dec. 7
Limestone ■ ....Dec. 16
Coker ....Jan. 8
High Point ■ ....Jan. 11
Pfeiffer ■ ....Jan. 13
Longwood ■ ....Jan. 16
Barton ■ ....Jan. 18
St. Andrews ....Jan. 20
Queens (N.C.) ....Jan. 23
St. Andrews ■ ....Jan. 25
Erskine ....Jan. 27
Mount Olive ....Jan. 29
High Point ....Feb. 1
Queens (N.C.) ■ ....Feb. 3
Pfeiffer ....Feb. 6
Erskine ■ ....Feb. 8
Coker ....Feb. 10
Lees-McRae ■ ....Feb. 15
Longwood ....Feb. 19
Barton ....Feb. 22

1995-96 RESULTS (9-18)

80	Elon	90
68	Lenoir-Rhyne †	74
75	Methodist ■	79
119	Johnson & Wales ■	55
86	Limestone	72
54	Methodist	56
57	Coker	74
104	Johnson & Wales ■	45
108	Limestone ■	80
68	Pfeiffer ■	76
71	Mount Olive	86
58	St. Andrews ■	67
85	Longwood	71
79	Queens (N.C.) ■	92
98	Barton	96
80	High Point	82
68	Erskine	72
83	Erskine ■	68
77	High Point ■	81
66	Pfeiffer	79
66	Coker ■	69
94	Mount Olive ■	90
66	Lees-McRae	68
60	Lees-McRae ■	62
71	St. Andrews	65
66	Longwood ■	80
48	Erskine †	74

Nickname: Crusaders
Colors: Red & White
Arena: Wheeler Center
   Capacity: 1,500; Year Built: 1968
AD: Julie LeVeck
SID: Phil Hess

BELOIT

Beloit, WI 53511 III

Coach: Bill Knapton
Alma Mater: Wis.-La Crosse '52
Record: 39 Years, W-548, L-329

1996-97 SCHEDULE

Carthage ....Nov. 23
Augustana (Ill.) ....Nov. 30
Concordia (Ill.) ....Dec. 9
Aurora ■ ....Dec. 12
Elmhurst Cl. ....Dec. 28-29
Hawaii-Hilo ....Jan. 4
Rockford ■ ....Jan. 8
St. Norbert ■ ....Jan. 11
Lawrence ....Jan. 14
Cornell College ■ ....Jan. 17
Monmouth (Ill.) ■ ....Jan. 18
Illinois Col. ....Jan. 24
Knox ....Jan. 25

SCHEDULES/RESULTS

Carroll (Wis.) ■ ...Jan. 29
Ripon ...Feb. 1
Lake Forest ...Feb. 4
St. Norbert ...Feb. 8
Lawrence ...Feb. 12
Carroll (Wis.) ...Feb. 15
Ripon ■ ...Feb. 19
Lake Forest ■ ...Feb. 22

1995-96 RESULTS (13-9)
Results unavailable

Nickname: Buccaneers
Colors: Navy Blue & Gold
Arena: Flood Arena
  Capacity: 2,250; Year Built: 1987
AD: Ed DeGeorge
SID: Paul Erickson

BEMIDJI ST.
Bemidji, MN 56601 ...II

Coach: Dave Gunther
Alma Mater: Iowa '59
Record: 24 Years, W-431, L-238

1996-97 SCHEDULE
Northern Mich. ...Nov. 16
Valley City St. ...Nov. 26
Mayville St. ■ ...Nov. 29
Minn.-Crookston ...Dec. 3
St. Cloud St. ■ ...Dec. 7
St. Scholastica ...Dec. 10
North Dak. ...Dec. 13
Minn.-Crookston ■ ...Dec. 17
N'western (Minn.) ■ ...Dec. 19
Mankato St. ...Dec. 21
Black Hills St. Cl. ...Dec. 28-30
Presentation ■ ...Jan. 7
Southwest St. ...Jan. 11
Winona St. ...Jan. 15
Moorhead St. ■ ...Jan. 18
Minn.-Duluth ■ ...Jan. 22
Northern St. ...Jan. 25
Minn.-Morris ...Jan. 29
Wayne St. (Neb.) ■ ...Feb. 1
Winona St. ■ ...Feb. 5
Southwest St. ■ ...Feb. 8
Minn.-Duluth ...Feb. 12
Moorhead St. ...Feb. 15
Minn.-Morris ...Feb. 19
Northern St. ■ ...Feb. 22
Wayne St. (Neb.) ...Mar. 1

1995-96 RESULTS (4-23)
77 Mayville St. ■ ...69
83 Minn.-Crookston ■ ...58
80 Valley City St. ■ ...82
57 Mankato St. ■ ...66
58 North Dak. ■ ...76
74 Wis.-Stevens Point ■ ...84
58 St. Cloud St. ...103
69 St. Scholastica ...68
88 Minn.-Crookston ...80
69 North Dak. St. ...95
64 Emporia St. † ...79
54 Drury ...66
54 Mayville St. ...79
66 Southwest St. ...81
70 Winona St. ■ ...90
65 Moorhead St. ■ ...85
36 Minn.-Duluth ■ ...88
67 Northern St. ■ ...85
63 Minn.-Morris ...90
91 Wayne St. (Neb.) ■ ...100
66 Winona St. ...75
52 Southwest St. ...76
60 Minn.-Duluth ...79
81 Moorhead St. ■ ...92
83 Minn.-Morris ■ ...92
67 Northern St. ...98
78 Wayne St. (Neb.) ...88

Nickname: Beavers
Colors: Green & White
Arena: BSU Gymnasium
  Capacity: 2,200; Year Built: 1959

AD: Bob Peters
SID: To be named

BENEDICTINE (ILL.)
Lisle, IL 60532 ...III

Coach: Keith Bunkenburg
Alma Mater: Benedictine (Ill.) '89
Record: 1 Year, W-11, L-14

1996-97 SCHEDULE
St. Vincent's Inv. ...Nov. 23-24
North Park ■ ...Nov. 26
Carroll (Wis.) ...Dec. 3
Augustana (Ill.) Inv ...Dec. 6-7
Concordia (Ill.) ...Dec. 18
North Central ■ ...Dec. 21
St. Mary's (Minn.) ...Dec. 30
Loras Catholic Tr. ...Jan. 1-5
Eureka ...Jan. 11
Rockford ■ ...Jan. 15
Clarke ...Jan. 18
Aurora ...Jan. 22
Trinity Int'l ...Jan. 25
Judson (Ill.) ...Jan. 29
Concordia (Ill.) ■ ...Feb. 1
Eureka ■ ...Feb. 5
Rockford ...Feb. 8
Clarke ■ ...Feb. 12
Aurora ■ ...Feb. 15
Trinity Int'l ...Feb. 19
Ill. Wesleyan ■ ...Mar. 1

1995-96 RESULTS (11-14)
53 Trinity Christian † ...87
61 Olivet Nazarene ...79
64 St. Mary's (Minn.) ■ ...71
96 Carleton ...100
85 North Park ...77
72 DePauw † ...80
79 Franklin ...82
71 Carroll (Wis.) ■ ...77
63 Ill. Wesleyan ...82
88 North Central ...63
58 Illinois Tech ...67
52 St. Thomas Aquinas † ...42
58 Carroll (Mont.) † ...59
63 Mt. Mercy † ...75
81 Beloit ■ ...68
62 Concordia (Ill.) ■ ...64
78 Trinity Int'l ...88
91 Judson (Ill.) ...78
105 Rockford ■ ...81
89 Aurora ...84
99 Trinity Int'l ■ ...78
78 Concordia (Ill.) ...91
94 Judson (Ill.) ...60
104 Rockford ...81
78 Aurora ...75

Nickname: Eagles
Colors: Cardinal & White
Arena: Dan & Ada Rice Center
  Capacity: 2,000; Year Built: 1976
AD: Tony Lascala
SID: Keith Bunkenburg

BENTLEY
Waltham, MA 02154 ...II

Coach: Jay Lawson
Alma Mater: New Hampshire '79
Record: 5 Years, W-83, L-56

1996-97 SCHEDULE
Bentley Tr. ...Nov. 15-16
Mass.-Lowell ...Nov. 26
Merrimack ■ ...Dec. 3
Assumption ...Dec. 8
Sacred Heart ...Dec. 22
Bentley Festival ...Dec. 28-29
St. Leo ...Jan. 2
Florida Tech ...Jan. 4
St. Anselm ■ ...Jan. 8
Quinnipiac ■ ...Jan. 11
Stonehill ...Jan. 14
American Int'l ■ ...Jan. 16
St. Michael's ...Jan. 18
Bryant ...Jan. 21
Le Moyne ...Jan. 25
St. Anselm ...Jan. 28
Assumption ■ ...Feb. 1
Stonehill ■ ...Feb. 5
St. Michael's ■ ...Feb. 8
American Int'l ...Feb. 11
Quinnipiac ...Feb. 13
Bryant ■ ...Feb. 16
Merrimack ■ ...Feb. 19
Le Moyne ...Feb. 22

1995-96 RESULTS (18-9)
71 New Hamp. Col. ...83
91 Franklin Pierce † ...96
95 Sacred Heart ■ ...62
88 Mass.-Lowell ...80
103 Southern Conn. St. ...96
97 Quinnipiac ■ ...82
105 Brandeis ...65
95 Stonehill ...81
72 East Stroudsburg ■ ...64
77 Fla. Southern ■ ...66
66 Lynn ...63
71 St. Anselm † ...88
106 Assumption ...74
72 American Int'l ■ ...75
86 St. Anselm ■ ...90
87 Quinnipiac ...62
100 Merrimack ...83
97 St. Michael's ■ ...89
59 Bryant ...57
110 Assumption ■ ...92
74 St. Anselm ...89
87 American Int'l ...78
87 Bryant ■ ...67
86 Stonehill ■ ...63
76 Merrimack ...81
82 St. Michael's ...96
85 American Int'l † ...87

Nickname: Falcons
Colors: Royal Blue & Gold
Arena: Charles Dana P.E. Center
  Capacity: 2,600; Year Built: 1973
AD: Bob DeFelice
SID: Dick Lipe

BETHANY (W.VA.)
Bethany, WV 26032 ...III

Coach: Rob Clune
Alma Mater: Albany St. (Ga.) '81
Record: 1 Year, W-8, L-17

1996-97 SCHEDULE
Earlham Cl. ...Nov. 22-23
Army ...Nov. 30
Savannah A&D ■ ...Dec. 5
Frostburg St. ...Dec. 7
Baldwin-Wallace ...Dec. 11
Denison ...Dec. 14
Fairmont St. ...Dec. 16
Pitt.-Bradford ...Jan. 4
Geneva ...Jan. 7
Bluffton ■ ...Jan. 10
Oberlin ...Jan. 11
Frostburg St. ...Jan. 15
Penn St.-Behrend ■ ...Jan. 18
Grove City ...Jan. 22
Waynesburg ■ ...Jan. 25
Alfred ...Jan. 29
Wash. & Jeff. ■ ...Feb. 1
Thiel ...Feb. 5
Grove City ■ ...Feb. 8
Penn St.-Behrend ...Feb. 10
Waynesburg ...Feb. 12
Alfred ■ ...Feb. 15
Wash. & Jeff. ...Feb. 19
Thiel ■ ...Feb. 22

1995-96 RESULTS (8-17)
65 Earlham ■ ...69
78 Denison ...91
83 La Roche ■ ...78
63 Baldwin-Wallace ■ ...56
66 Penn St.-Behrend ...73
56 Adrian † ...77
37 Army ...68
84 Valley Forge Chrst. ...56
76 Wilmington (Ohio) ■ ...65
77 Pitt.-Bradford ■ ...81
90 CCNY ...70
86 York (N.Y.) ■ ...88
88 Houghton ...85
75 Waynesburg ...88
84 Penn St.-Behrend ■ ...86
81 La Roche ...98
71 Thiel ■ ...85
48 Grove City ■ ...59
59 Oberlin ...64
83 Wash. & Jeff. ■ ...81
65 Waynesburg ...90
79 Bluffton ...97
75 Thiel ...88
46 Grove City ...74
79 Wash. & Jeff. ■ ...76

Nickname: Bison
Colors: Green & White
Arena: Hummel Field House
  Capacity: 1,400; Year Built: 1948
AD: Wally Neel
SID: John Strom

BETHEL (MINN.)
St. Paul, MN 55112 ...III

Coach: George Palke
Alma Mater: Bethel (Minn.) '66
Record: 17 Years, W-214, L-221

1996-97 SCHEDULE
Bethel (Minn.) Tr. ...Nov. 22-23
Viterbo Tr. ...Nov. 29-30
Gust. Adolphus ■ ...Dec. 7
St. Olaf ...Dec. 11
Augsburg ...Dec. 14
Carleton ...Jan. 6
Macalester ...Jan. 8
St. Thomas (Minn.) ■ ...Jan. 11
St. Mary's (Minn.) ■ ...Jan. 13
St. John's (Minn.) ■ ...Jan. 15
Hamline ...Jan. 18
Concordia-M'head ...Jan. 22
Gust. Adolphus ...Jan. 25
St. Olaf ...Jan. 29
Augsburg ■ ...Feb. 1
Carleton ■ ...Feb. 5
Macalester ■ ...Feb. 8
St. Thomas (Minn.) ...Feb. 12
St. Mary's (Minn.) ...Feb. 15
St. John's (Minn.) ■ ...Feb. 19
Hamline ...Feb. 19
Concordia-M'head ■ ...Feb. 22

1995-96 RESULTS (8-16)
97 N'western (Minn.) ■ ...95
95 Northland ...102
68 BYU-Hawaii † ...96
80 Hawaii Pacific † ...96
100 Augsburg ■ ...89
83 Macalester ...67
68 Gust. Adolphus ...64
93 St. Olaf ...99
60 St. Mary's (Minn.) ...70
71 St. John's (Minn.) ■ ...67
85 Hamline ...76
71 Carleton ...87
57 St. Thomas (Minn.) ...68
78 Concordia-M'head ...104
68 Augsburg ...97
79 Macalester ■ ...75
54 Gust. Adolphus ■ ...71
89 St. Olaf ...87
77 St. Mary's (Minn.) ■ ...76
91 St. John's (Minn.) ...98
76 Hamline ...82
104 Carleton ■ ...111
63 St. Thomas (Minn.) ■ ...65
90 Concordia-M'head ■ ...93

Nickname: Royals
Colors: Royal Blue & Gold
Arena: Robertson P.E. Center
Capacity: 2,000
AD: Dave Klostreich
SID: Leland Christenson

BETHUNE-COOKMAN
Daytona Beach, FL 32015.........I

Coach: Tony Sheals
Alma Mater: Bethune-Cookman '80
Record: 3 Years, W-33, L-49

1996-97 SCHEDULE
Florida	Nov. 25
North Caro.	Dec. 2
Central Fla.	Dec. 7
Morris Brown ■	Dec. 10
Kansas St.	Dec. 14
Creighton	Dec. 16
Long Beach St.	Dec. 30
Hampton	Jan. 2
St. Peter's ■	Jan. 6
Delaware St. ■	Jan. 11
Md.-East. Shore ■	Jan. 13
South Caro. St.	Jan. 18
North Caro. A&T ■	Jan. 20
Morgan St. ■	Jan. 23
Howard	Jan. 25
Coppin St.	Jan. 27
North Caro. A&T	Feb. 1
South Caro. St.	Feb. 3
Florida A&M ■	Feb. 8
Morgan St. ■	Feb. 13
Howard ■	Feb. 15
Coppin St. ■	Feb. 17
Delaware St.	Feb. 22
Md.-East. Shore	Feb. 24
Hampton ■	Feb. 26
Florida A&M	Mar. 1
Mid-Eastern Conf. Tr.	Mar. 5-8

1995-96 RESULTS (12-15)
69	Siena	74
53	Minnesota	93
77	Shaw ■	67
67	Morris Brown ■	61
85	Edward Waters ■	81
91	Elizabeth City St. ■	76
61	Northern Iowa	79
50	Texas A&M	69
83	Delaware St.	92
78	Md.-East. Shore	84
61	South Caro. St.	76
56	North Caro. A&T	59
55	Coppin St. ■	71
65	Howard ■	53
68	Morgan St. ■	58
64	North Caro. A&T ■	63
56	South Caro. St. ■	51
60	Florida A&M †	45
59	Dayton	60
79	Coppin St.	93
58	Howard	72
78	Morgan St.	70
62	South Fla.	80
78	Delaware St. ■	83
63	Md.-East. Shore ■	55
75	Florida A&M	62
74	North Caro. A&T †	75

Nickname: Wildcats
Colors: Maroon & Gold
Arena: Moore Gymnasium
Capacity: 3,000; Year Built: 1958
AD: Lynn W. Thompson
SID: W. Earl Kitchings

BINGHAMTON
Binghamton, NY 13902.........III

Coach: Jim Norris
Alma Mater: Rochester '47
(First year as head coach)

1996-97 SCHEDULE
Binghamton Cl.	Nov. 22-23
Scranton	Nov. 26
New Paltz St.	Dec. 3
Geneseo St. ■	Dec. 6
Buffalo St. ■	Dec. 7
Ithaca ■	Dec. 13
Elmira Tr.	Jan. 3-4
Hartwick	Jan. 9
Elmira	Jan. 12
Oneonta St. ■	Jan. 14
Oswego St.	Jan. 18
Cortland St. ■	Jan. 21
Cortland St. ■	Jan. 25
Utica/Rome ■	Jan. 28
Fredonia St.	Feb. 1
Potsdam St. ■	Feb. 7
Plattsburgh St.	Feb. 8
New Paltz St. ■	Feb. 11
Brockport St.	Feb. 15
Oneonta St.	Feb. 18
Plattsburgh St. ■	Feb. 21
Potsdam St. ■	Feb. 22

1995-96 RESULTS (10-15)
47	Castleton St. ■	73
87	Hilbert ■	58
56	Scranton	63
63	Brockport St. ■	71
53	Fredonia St. ■	51
68	New Paltz St.	64
60	Keuka †	73
65	Hilbert †	45
66	Hartwick ■	76
69	Haverford ■	77
67	Utica/Rome ■	58
86	Oswego St. ■	75
61	Cortland St. ■	64
47	Oneonta St.	62
53	Buffalo St.	80
57	New Paltz St. ■	56
55	Potsdam St. ■	74
80	Plattsburgh St. ■	61
65	Cortland St.	72
59	Ithaca	64
60	Geneseo St.	63
69	Oneonta St. ■	49
91	Potsdam St.	70
60	Plattsburgh St.	74
48	Buffalo St. †	68

Nickname: Colonials
Colors: Green & White
Arena: East Gym
Capacity: 2,800; Year Built: 1958
AD: Joel Thirer
SID: John Hartrick

BLACKBURN
Carlinville, IL 62626.........III

Coach: Ira Zeff
Alma Mater: Blackburn
Record: 6 Years, W-89, L-77

1996-97 SCHEDULE
Illinois Col. ■	Nov. 22
Grace ■	Nov. 23
Lincoln Chrst. ■	Nov. 26
Sanford Brown ■	Nov. 30
Rose-Hulman	Dec. 1
Logan Chiropractic	Dec. 4
Millikin	Dec. 7
Knox ■	Dec. 10
Wooster Tr.	Dec. 27-28
Principia	Jan. 9
Webster ■	Jan. 11
Greenville	Jan. 16
Maryville (Mo.)	Jan. 18
Westminster (Mo.) ■	Jan. 23
Fontbonne	Jan. 25
MacMurray	Jan. 30
Principia ■	Feb. 1
Webster	Feb. 6
Greenville ■	Feb. 8
Maryville (Mo.) ■	Feb. 13
Westminster (Mo.)	Feb. 15
Fontbonne	Feb. 20
MacMurray ■	Feb. 22

1995-96 RESULTS (10-16)
39	Illinois Col.	71
94	Lincoln Chrst.	78
54	Rose-Hulman ■	70
69	Sanford Brown ■	78
81	Millikin ■	84
59	Wabash	88
58	Defiance †	70
69	Aurora ■	77
70	Webster	63
99	Parks ■	74
92	Fontbonne	104
79	Maryville (Mo.) ■	81
63	Greenville ■	79
72	Westminster (Mo.)	76
62	Principia ■	58
78	MacMurray ■	84
80	Webster ■	55
96	Parks	92
85	Fontbonne ■	74
85	Maryville (Mo.)	75
70	Greenville	74
78	Westminster (Mo.) ■	82
69	Principia	53
50	MacMurray	62
78	Maryville (Mo.)	69
68	MacMurray	72

Nickname: Beavers
Colors: Scarlet & Black
Arena: Dawes Gymnasium
Capacity: 500; Year Built: 1938
AD: Ira Zeff
SID: Tom Emery

BLOOMSBURG
Bloomsburg, PA 17815.........II

Coach: Charles Chronister
Alma Mater: East Stroudsburg '63
Record: 25 Years, W-450, L-229

1996-97 SCHEDULE
Virginia St. ■	Nov. 15
Wheeling Jesuit Tr.	Nov. 22-23
Caldwell	Nov. 26
Lock Haven	Dec. 2
Shippensburg Tr.	Dec. 6-7
Bloomsburg Inv.	Jan. 4-5
Millersville	Jan. 8
West Chester ■	Jan. 11
Mansfield	Jan. 15
East Stroudsburg	Jan. 18
Susquehanna ■	Jan. 20
Kutztown ■	Jan. 22
Indiana (Pa.) ■	Jan. 25
Cheyney	Jan. 29
West Chester	Feb. 1
Millersville	Feb. 5
East Stroudsburg ■	Feb. 8
Mansfield ■	Feb. 12
Kutztown	Feb. 15
Houghton ■	Feb. 17
Cheyney ■	Feb. 19
Indiana (Pa.)	Feb. 22

1995-96 RESULTS (21-7)
103	Queens (N.Y.) †	91
77	St. Rose	81
64	St. Thomas Aquinas ■	56
78	Caldwell ■	54
76	Shippensburg ■	66
82	Lock Haven ■	69
76	Clarion ■	75
93	Shippensburg	75
105	Phila. Bible ■	49
83	Lycoming ■	68
71	Cheyney ■	56
73	Scranton	43
73	Kutztown	69
77	East Stroudsburg	72
86	York (Pa.)	63
72	Mansfield ■	65
82	West Chester ■	55
89	Millersville	82
65	Indiana (Pa.)	81
61	Cheyney	75
87	Kutztown ■	68
72	Mansfield	88
64	East Stroudsburg ■	50
55	Millersville ■	50
75	West Chester	79
79	Lock Haven	68
70	Indiana (Pa.) †	77
82	Edinboro †	90

Nickname: Huskies
Colors: Maroon & Gold
Arena: E. H. Nelson Fieldhouse
Capacity: 3,000; Year Built: 1972
AD: Mary Gardner
SID: Scott Leightman

BLUEFIELD ST.
Bluefield, WV 24701.........II

Coach: Terry Brown
Alma Mater: Bluefield St. '75
Record: 17 Years, W-273, L-231

1996-97 SCHEDULE
Fla. Southern	Nov. 15
Rollins	Nov. 16
Gardner-Webb Cl.	Nov. 22-23
Bluefield St. Cl.	Nov. 29-30
West Va. Tech ■	Dec. 7
Glenville St. ■	Dec. 14
Concord	Dec. 16
Lincoln Memorial	Jan. 2
Alderson-Broaddus	Jan. 8
Salem-Teikyo ■	Jan. 11
Fairmont St.	Jan. 13
Wheeling Jesuit ■	Jan. 15
West Liberty St. ■	Jan. 18
West Va. Wesleyan	Jan. 22
Glenville St.	Jan. 25
West Va. St.	Jan. 27
Charleston (W.Va.) ■	Jan. 29
Shepherd	Feb. 1
Davis & Elkins ■	Feb. 8
West Va. Tech	Feb. 10
Concord ■	Feb. 12
West Va. Wesleyan ■	Feb. 15
West Va. St. ■	Feb. 19
Charleston (W.Va.)	Feb. 22

1995-96 RESULTS (15-16)
100	Va. Intermont	101
88	Warren Wilson	62
101	Ohio Valley ■	77
76	West Va. Tech ■	78
97	Lincoln Memorial ■	90
100	Va. Intermont	118
95	King (Tenn.)	79
89	Concord	80
87	West Va. Tech	94
70	Glenville St.	67
88	Alderson-Broaddus ■	103
83	Salem-Teikyo	89
79	Fairmont St. ■	86
78	Wheeling Jesuit	76
88	West Liberty St.	93
97	West Va. Wesleyan ■	75
62	Glenville St. ■	55
75	West Va. St.	73
89	Charleston (W.Va.)	93
94	Davis & Elkins	75
101	West Va. Tech ■	103
92	Concord	103
82	Shepherd ■	94
80	West Va. Wesleyan	87
80	West Va. St.	83
74	Charleston (W.Va.) ■	76
77	Fairmont St. †	74
83	West Va. Wesleyan ■	60
91	Salem-Teikyo †	81
61	West Va. Tech †	58
66	Fairmont St. †	78

Nickname: Big Blues

Colors: Blue & Gold
Arena: Ned Shott Gymnasium
   Capacity: 1,500; Year Built: 1969
AD: Terry Brown
SID: Terry Brown

BLUFFTON

Bluffton, OH 45817 III

Coach: Guy Neal
Alma Mater: Bowling Green '82
Record: 7 Years, W-72, L-110

1996-97 SCHEDULE

Lake Erie	Nov. 23
Adrian	Nov. 27
Franklin Cl.	Dec. 6-7
Albion ■	Dec. 10
Anderson (Ind.) ■	Dec. 14
Olivet ■	Dec. 18
Hanover ■	Dec. 21
Kalamazoo Cl.	Dec. 27-28
Denison ■	Jan. 2
Adrian ■	Jan. 4
Defiance	Jan. 8
Bethany (W.Va.)	Jan. 10
Alma	Jan. 15
Thomas More ■	Jan. 18
Wilmington (Ohio) ■	Jan. 25
Goshen	Jan. 30
Thomas More	Feb. 1
Defiance ■	Feb. 5
Wilmington (Ohio)	Feb. 8
Lake Erie ■	Feb. 12
Goshen ■	Feb. 20

1995-96 RESULTS (14-12)

91	Alma ■	73
99	Adrian ■	96
60	Ohio Northern ■	73
97	Concordia (Mich.) ■	72
83	Albion	88
65	Lake Erie	60
72	Olivet	80
53	Hanover	86
73	Kalamazoo ■	60
67	Adrian	92
82	Lake Erie †	51
74	Marietta	69
65	Denison	83
68	Concordia (Mich.)	50
83	Defiance ■	85
91	Wilmington (Ohio)	74
89	Thomas More ■	93
60	Defiance	88
86	Goshen ■	89
64	Thomas More	75
97	Bethany (W.Va.) ■	79
68	Wilmington (Ohio)	50
94	Goshen	76
96	Lake Erie ■	91
77	Wilmington (Ohio) †	69
67	Thomas More	90

Nickname: Beavers
Colors: Northwestern Purple & White
Arena: Founders Hall
   Capacity: 1,500; Year Built: 1952
AD: Carlin Carpenter
SID: Ron Geiser

BOISE ST.

Boise, ID 83725 I

Coach: Rod Jensen
Alma Mater: Redlands '75
Record: 1 Year, W-15, L-13

1996-97 SCHEDULE

Washington St.	Nov. 23
Pepperdine ■	Nov. 30
Idaho St.	Dec. 2
Weber St.	Dec. 7
Brigham Young Cl.	Dec. 13-14
Oregon ■	Dec. 20
Boise St. Cl.	Dec. 27-28

Long Beach St.	Jan. 6
Utah St. ■	Jan. 9
Nevada ■	Jan. 11
Eastern Mich. ■	Jan. 16
Idaho	Jan. 18
North Texas	Jan. 23
New Mexico St. ■	Jan. 25
UC Irvine ■	Jan. 30
Cal St. Fullerton ■	Feb. 1
Cal Poly SLO ■	Feb. 6
UC Santa Barb. ■	Feb. 8
New Mexico St. ■	Feb. 13
North Texas ■	Feb. 15
Nevada	Feb. 20
Utah St.	Feb. 22
Pacific (Cal.) ■	Feb. 27
Idaho ■	Mar. 1
Big West Conf. Tr.	Mar. 7-9

1995-96 RESULTS (15-13)

71	Brigham Young	86
41	Princeton †	61
45	Maine †	62
78	UC-Colo. Spgs. ■	64
81	Nevada	76
64	Southern Utah ■	71
54	Oregon	65
53	Lewis-Clark St.	67
66	Tennessee Tech ■	65
49	Portland	70
68	Gonzaga	83
61	Pepperdine	58
73	Eastern Wash. ■	49
76	Idaho ■	72
67	Weber St.	75
65	Northern Ariz.	60
69	Montana	59
69	Montana St.	61
71	Idaho St.	51
57	Idaho	53
70	Eastern Wash.	65
68	Northern Ariz. ■	45
62	Weber St. ■	64
65	Montana St.	76
61	Montana	76
65	Idaho St. ■	62
66	Idaho St. †	54
70	Weber St. †	77

Nickname: Broncos
Colors: Orange & Blue
Arena: Pavilion
   Capacity: 12,200; Year Built: 1982
AD: Gene Bleymaier
SID: Brad Larrondo

BOSTON COLLEGE

Chestnut Hill, MA 02167 I

Coach: Jim O'Brien
Alma Mater: Boston College '71
Record: 14 Years, W-213, L-208

1996-97 SCHEDULE

Brown ■	Nov. 22
New Hampshire ■	Nov. 25
Rutgers ■	Dec. 4
Connecticut	Dec. 7
Vanderbilt ■	Dec. 9
Holy Cross	Dec. 21
Central Conn. St. ■	Dec. 27
Louisville	Dec. 29
Miami (Fla.) ■	Jan. 2
Seton Hall	Jan. 4
Syracuse	Jan. 7
Notre Dame	Jan. 11
Georgetown ■	Jan. 13
Fairfield	Jan. 15
Massachusetts [Boston]	Jan. 18
Pittsburgh ■	Jan. 21
Villanova ■	Jan. 25
West Va.	Jan. 29
Providence	Feb. 1
Syracuse ■	Feb. 4
St. John's (N.Y.)	Feb. 9
Connecticut ■	Feb. 12

Seton Hall ■	Feb. 16
Miami (Fla.)	Feb. 19
Pittsburgh	Feb. 23
Notre Dame ■	Mar. 1
Big East Conf. Tr.	Mar. 5-8

1995-96 RESULTS (19-11)

89	Buffalo ■	49
97	Holy Cross ■	60
81	Louisville	67
62	Connecticut	63
55	Pittsburgh ■	53
57	Massachusetts †	65
78	Md.-Balt. County	56
106	Hartford	67
116	LIU-Brooklyn ■	81
90	Vanderbilt	74
95	Rutgers	67
77	Villanova	94
72	Notre Dame ■	57
83	Seton Hall ■	80
91	St. John's (N.Y.) ■	78
73	Syracuse	88
75	Providence ■	76
84	West Va.	63
89	St. John's (N.Y.)	73
62	Miami (Fla.)	58
63	Georgetown ■	66
70	Providence	68
89	West Va. ■	108
64	Georgetown	67
71	Villanova ■	76
73	Rutgers ■	72
70	Pittsburgh †	66
61	Syracuse †	69
64	Indiana †	51
89	Georgia Tech †	103

Nickname: Eagles
Colors: Maroon & Gold
Arena: Silvio O. Conte Forum
   Capacity: 8,606; Year Built: 1988
AD: Chet S. Gladchuk Jr.
SID: Reid Oslin

BOSTON U.

Boston, MA 02215 I

Coach: Dennis Wolff
Alma Mater: Connecticut '78
Record: 4 Years, W-63, L-45

1996-97 SCHEDULE

Geo. Washington Cl.	Nov. 22-23
East Caro. [Halifax]	Nov. 30
Towson St.	Dec. 6
Delaware	Dec. 8
Harvard	Dec. 10
Texas Christian	Dec. 12
Rhode Island	Dec. 23
South Fla. Tr.	Dec. 27-28
New Hampshire	Jan. 2
Maine	Jan. 4
Hofstra ■	Jan. 10
Drexel ■	Jan. 12
Hartford	Jan. 16
Vermont	Jan. 18
Northeastern ■	Jan. 21
Delaware ■	Jan. 24
Towson St. ■	Jan. 26
Northeastern	Feb. 1
Hofstra	Feb. 7
Drexel	Feb. 9
Vermont ■	Feb. 13
Hartford ■	Feb. 15
New Hampshire ■	Feb. 20
Maine	Feb. 23
America East Conf. Tr.	Feb. 28-Mar. 2

1995-96 RESULTS (18-11)

62	Rider	64
54	Holy Cross ■	57
60	Maine	62
70	New Hampshire ■	67
70	Md.-Balt. County ■	56
72	Harvard	60
74	Providence	80

75	Pepperdine †	61
83	New Mexico	95
75	Hartford	68
69	Vermont ■	55
68	North Caro. St.	78
50	Delaware	62
71	Towson St.	93
73	Hofstra ■	61
47	Drexel ■	67
63	Northeastern ■	59
76	Drexel	74
86	Hofstra	71
82	Delaware ■	75
68	Towson St. ■	56
79	Hartford ■	65
72	Vermont	75
77	Northeastern	56
79	Maine ■	62
80	New Hampshire	69
69	Northeastern †	54
66	Maine †	64
67	Drexel	76

Nickname: Terriers
Colors: Scarlet & White
Arena: Case Gym
   Capacity: 2,500; Year Built: 1971
AD: Gary Strickler
SID: Edward Carpenter

BOWDOIN

Brunswick, ME 04011 III

Coach: Timothy Gilbride
Alma Mater: Providence '74
Record: 11 Years, W-136, L-125

1996-97 SCHEDULE

New England	Nov. 26
Southern Maine Tr.	Nov. 29-Dec. 1
Bates ■	Dec. 4
Tufts	Dec. 7
Plymouth St.	Jan. 8
Thomas ■	Jan. 13
Colby-Sawyer	Jan. 15
Skidmore ■	Jan. 18
Union (N.Y.) ■	Jan. 19
Maine Maritime ■	Jan. 21
Amherst	Jan. 24
Western New Eng.	Jan. 25
Norwich	Jan. 31
Middlebury	Feb. 1
Colby	Feb. 5
Wesleyan (Conn.) ■	Feb. 7
Bates	Feb. 11
Connecticut Col. ■	Feb. 14
Wheaton (Mass.) ■	Feb. 15
Me.-Farmington	Feb. 19
Colby	Mar. 1

1995-96 RESULTS (19-6)

77	New England ■	62
66	Bates	86
87	Tufts ■	78
71	Thomas	59
78	Maine Maritime	58
62	Mt. St. Mary (N.Y.) †	63
70	Plymouth St.	67
71	Union (N.Y.)	62
72	Hamilton	77
80	Amherst ■	65
77	Western New Eng. ■	56
78	Anna Maria	57
81	Norwich ■	88
79	Middlebury ■	65
66	Colby ■	58
61	Wesleyan (Conn.)	53
93	Me.-Augusta	42
82	Bates	75
59	Connecticut Col.	76
91	Wheaton (Mass.)	64
77	Me.-Farmington	60
84	Colby-Sawyer ■	69
72	Colby	71
62	Springfield ■	56
64	Williams	91

Nickname: Polar Bears
Colors: White
Arena: Morrell Gymnasium
   Capacity: 2,000; Year Built: 1965
AD: Sidney Watson
SID: Jac Coyne

BOWIE ST.
Bowie, MD 20715 II

Coach: Taft Hickman
Alma Mater: Northeast Okla. '70
Record: 4 Years, W-29, L-74

1996-97 SCHEDULE
Pitt.-Johnstown Tr.	Nov. 15-16
Cheyney	Nov. 23
Livingstone	Nov. 29
Winston-Salem	Dec. 1
Shaw	Dec. 2
Kutztown	Dec. 4
St. Augustine's ■	Dec. 6
Fayetteville St.	Dec. 14
Cheyney ■	Jan. 7
Virginia St.	Jan. 8
N.C. Central ■	Jan. 9
Johnson Smith ■	Jan. 11
Dist. Columbia ■	Jan. 17
Columbia Union	Jan. 19
Elizabeth City St. ■	Jan. 21
Virginia Union ■	Jan. 25
St. Paul's ■	Jan. 27
Norfolk St. ■	Jan. 30
Elizabeth City St.	Feb. 1
Norfolk St.	Feb. 3
Lynn ■	Feb. 7
Virginia Union	Feb. 8
Virginia St. ■	Feb. 12
Dist. Columbia	Feb. 13
St. Paul's	Feb. 19

1995-96 RESULTS (8-19)
75	Slippery Rock †	38
70	West Chester	74
78	Shaw ■	83
88	Livingstone ■	68
94	Kutztown ■	84
78	Winston-Salem ■	85
83	St. Augustine's	77
79	Fayetteville St.	108
63	Florida Tech	95
80	St. Anselm †	103
70	Lynn	81
66	N.C. Central	98
66	Johnson Smith	77
77	Virginia St. ■	75
57	Norfolk St.	116
86	Elizabeth City St.	99
71	Virginia Union	93
75	St. Paul's	80
71	Dist. Columbia	55
72	Elizabeth City St. ■	74
81	Norfolk St. ■	69
51	Virginia Union ■	82
84	Virginia St.	71
70	Dist. Columbia ■	72
81	St. Paul's ■	93
92	Delaware St.	93
81	St. Augustine's †	92

Nickname: Bulldogs
Colors: Black & Gold.
Arena: A. C. Jordan Basketball Arena
   Capacity: 4,000; Year Built: 1973
AD: Charles A. Guilford
SID: Scott A. Rouch

BOWLING GREEN
Bowling Green, OH 43403 I

Coach: Jim Larranaga
Alma Mater: Providence '71
Record: 12 Years, W-175, L-160

1996-97 SCHEDULE
James Madison	Nov. 23
Detroit ■	Nov. 26
Purdue	Nov. 30
Northern Ill. ■	Dec. 4
Nebraska Cl.	Dec. 6-7
Wright St. ■	Dec. 11
Tiffin ■	Dec. 14
Puerto Rico Tr.	Dec. 30-Jan. 1
Central Mich.	Jan. 4
Western Mich.	Jan. 8
Ball St. ■	Jan. 11
Akron	Jan. 13
Kent ■	Jan. 15
Eastern Mich.	Jan. 19
Miami (Ohio) ■	Jan. 22
Toledo	Jan. 25
Ohio ■	Jan. 29
Western Mich. ■	Feb. 1
Ball St.	Feb. 5
Akron ■	Feb. 8
Kent	Feb. 12
Eastern Mich. ■	Feb. 15
Miami (Ohio)	Feb. 19
Toledo ■	Feb. 22
Ohio	Feb. 26
Central Mich. ■	Mar. 1
Mid-American Conf. Tr.	Mar. 4-8

1995-96 RESULTS (14-13)
90	Heidelberg ■	59
64	Detroit	67
53	Northern Ill.	49
91	Defiance ■	60
79	Citadel †	56
67	Indiana	78
64	Syracuse	75
88	James Madison ■	72
63	Western Mich.	66
83	Kent ■	68
81	Central Mich. ■	70
84	Ohio ■	69
58	Eastern Mich.	77
76	Toledo ■	75
50	Ball St.	54
70	Akron ■	51
64	Miami (Ohio)	80
58	Kent	59
74	Central Mich. ■	63
67	Ohio	83
72	Eastern Mich. ■	70
65	Toledo	53
60	Ball St. ■	73
68	Akron	50
56	Miami (Ohio) ■	58
44	Western Mich. ■	62
53	Miami (Ohio)	81

Nickname: Falcons
Colors: Orange & Brown
Arena: Anderson Arena
   Capacity: 5,000; Year Built: 1960
AD: Ron Zwierlein
SID: Steve Barr

BRADLEY
Peoria, IL 61625 I

Coach: Jim Molinari
Alma Mater: Ill. Wesleyan '77
Record: 7 Years, W-125, L-82

1996-97 SCHEDULE
Chicago St. ■	Nov. 30
Michigan	Dec. 2
Kansas St. ■	Dec. 7
Butler ■	Dec. 10
Penn St.	Dec. 18
Western Ill. ■	Dec. 23
Oregon Cl.	Dec. 27-28
Southern Ill. ■	Dec. 31
Southwest Mo. St.	Jan. 5
Wichita St.	Jan. 7
Evansville ■	Jan. 11
Indiana St. ■	Jan. 13
Creighton	Jan. 18
Northern Iowa	Jan. 20
Southwest Mo. St. ■	Jan. 25
Wichita St. ■	Jan. 27
Illinois St.	Feb. 1
Evansville	Feb. 5
Creighton ■	Feb. 8
Southern Ill.	Feb. 10
Drake ■	Feb. 13
Indiana St.	Feb. 15
Northern Iowa ■	Feb. 17
Illinois St. ■	Feb. 22
Drake	Feb. 24
Missouri Val. Conf. Tr.	Feb. 28-Mar. 3

1995-96 RESULTS (22-8)
72	Kansas St.	75
63	Villanova	70
87	New Orleans ■	72
78	St. Louis	68
71	Western Ill. ■	54
110	Chicago St. ■	80
84	Georgia Tech †	82
72	Penn St. †	75
75	Creighton	62
60	Northern Iowa	51
68	Creighton	54
58	Southwest Mo. St. ■	61
73	Southern Ill. ■	57
72	Illinois St.	77
71	Evansville	60
68	Indiana St.	58
68	Wichita St. ■	49
77	Drake ■	60
85	Tulsa	72
68	Southwest Mo. St.	57
73	Northern Iowa ■	71
60	Wichita St.	76
74	Tulsa	73
73	Evansville ■	58
65	Illinois St. ■	64
79	Southern Ill.	76
64	Drake †	51
64	Southwest Mo. St. †	62
46	Tulsa †	60
58	Stanford †	66

Nickname: Braves
Colors: Red & White
Arena: Carver Arena
   Capacity: 10,470; Year Built: 1982
AD: Ken Kavanagh
SID: Joseph S. Dalfonso

BRANDEIS
Waltham, MA 02254 III

Coach: Ken Still
Alma Mater: Brandeis '72
Record: 5 Years, W-61, L-67

1996-97 SCHEDULE
Case Reserve ■	Nov. 23
Middlebury	Nov. 26
MIT ■	Dec. 3
Suffolk ■	Dec. 5
Johns Hopkins	Dec. 8
Mass.-Dartmouth ■	Dec. 10
New York U.	Jan. 11
Babson ■	Jan. 14
Washington (Mo.)	Jan. 17
Chicago	Jan. 19
WPI ■	Jan. 22
Emory ■	Jan. 24
Carnegie Mellon ■	Jan. 26
Rochester ■	Jan. 31
Wesleyan (Conn.)	Feb. 4
Carnegie Mellon	Feb. 7
Emory	Feb. 9
Wheaton (Mass.)	Feb. 11
Amherst	Feb. 13
Rochester	Feb. 16
Chicago ■	Feb. 21
Washington (Mo.) ■	Feb. 23
Tufts ■	Feb. 27
New York U. ■	Mar. 1

1995-96 RESULTS (9-16)
84	Case Reserve	102
69	Middlebury ■	79
76	MIT	65
65	Johns Hopkins ■	67
84	Mass.-Dartmouth	86
82	Suffolk	77
65	Bentley ■	105
81	New York U. ■	80
80	Babson	101
73	Washington (Mo.) ■	93
60	Chicago ■	68
66	WPI	69
77	Emory	68
76	Carnegie Mellon	85
68	Rochester	82
72	Wesleyan (Conn.) ■	65
82	Carnegie Mellon ■	87
65	Emory ■	58
91	Wheaton (Mass.) ■	75
93	Amherst	84
70	Rochester ■	55
74	Chicago	79
70	Washington (Mo.)	93
91	Tufts	105
66	New York U.	78

Nickname: Judges
Colors: Blue & White
Arena: Red Auerbach Arena
   Capacity: 2,500; Year Built: 1991
AD: Jeff Cohen
SID: Jack Molloy

BRIDGEPORT
Bridgeport, CT 06601 II

Coach: Bruce Webster
Alma Mater: Rutgers '59
Record: 31 Years, W-539, L-335

1996-97 SCHEDULE
Bridgeport Cl.	Nov. 16-17
So. Conn. St. Cl.	Nov. 22-23
Albany (N.Y.) ■	Dec. 7
Teikyo Post	Dec. 12
St. Rose Cl.	Dec. 27-29
Keene St.	Jan. 8
Mass.-Lowell ■	Jan. 11
New Hamp. Col.	Jan. 14
New Haven	Jan. 16
Franklin Pierce ■	Jan. 18
Stony Brook ■	Jan. 22
Franklin Pierce	Jan. 25
Southern Conn. St. ■	Jan. 29
Mass.-Lowell	Feb. 1
Stony Brook	Feb. 4
New Hamp. Col. ■	Feb. 6
Albany (N.Y.) ■	Feb. 8
Sacred Heart ■	Feb. 12
Keene St. ■	Feb. 15
Southern Conn. St.	Feb. 18
New Haven ■	Feb. 20
Sacred Heart	Feb. 22

1995-96 RESULTS (9-17)
80	Merrimack †	59
79	Quinnipiac †	65
99	New York Tech	107
80	LIU-C. W. Post	83
100	Keene St.	93
71	Franklin Pierce	74
57	Bryant	69
70	Southern Conn. St. ■	79
87	New Haven	78
76	Teikyo Post ■	68
73	Albany (N.Y.)	78
71	Le Moyne	87
87	Stony Brook	84
79	Franklin Pierce ■	95
96	Keene St. ■	89
67	Southern Conn. St.	83
78	New Hamp. Col.	85
64	Mass.-Lowell	88
74	New Haven ■	82
69	Sacred Heart ■	72
57	Stony Brook ■	60
62	Le Moyne ■	80
97	Albany (N.Y.) ■	89

79 Sacred Heart ... 84
81 Mass.-Lowell ■ ... 73
70 New Hamp. Col. ■ ... 95

Nickname: Purple Knights
Colors: Purple & White
Arena: Harvey Hubbell Gymnasium
Capacity: 1,607; Year Built: 1955
AD: Bob Baird
SID: Bob Baird

BRIDGEWATER (VA.)

Bridgewater, VA 22812 ... III

Coach: Bill Leatherman
Alma Mater: Milligan '66
Record: 11 Years, W-165, L-121

1996-97 SCHEDULE

Juniata Tr. ... Nov. 23-24
Villa Julie ■ ... Dec. 2
Bridgewater (Va.) Tr ... Dec. 6-7
Hampden-Sydney ... Dec. 11
Randolph-Macon ■ ... Dec. 14
Marymount (Va.) ■ ... Dec. 17
East. Mennonite ■ ... Jan. 7
Guilford ■ ... Jan. 9
Va. Wesleyan ■ ... Jan. 11
Emory & Henry ■ ... Jan. 12
Roanoke ... Jan. 15
Guilford ... Jan. 18
Hampden-Sydney ■ ... Jan. 20
Va. Wesleyan ... Jan. 22
Wash. & Lee ... Jan. 24
East. Mennonite ... Jan. 27
Lynchburg ■ ... Feb. 1
Roanoke ■ ... Feb. 6
Emory & Henry ... Feb. 8
Randolph-Macon ... Feb. 12
Lynchburg ... Feb. 15
Wash. & Lee ■ ... Feb. 17

1995-96 RESULTS (18-10)

64 N.C. Wesleyan † ... 59
81 Shenandoah ... 82
69 Guilford ... 67
82 Villa Julie ... 73
78 Newport News App. ■ ... 71
86 East. Mennonite ■ ... 68
77 Wash. & Lee ... 65
67 Hampden-Sydney ■ ... 60
88 East. Mennonite ... 80
81 Marymount (Va.) ... 91
64 Randolph-Macon ■ ... 67
63 Va. Wesleyan ... 72
79 Emory & Henry ■ ... 83
85 Roanoke ■ ... 81
70 Guilford ■ ... 65
74 Hampden-Sydney ... 70
59 Va. Wesleyan ■ ... 58
90 Wash. & Lee ■ ... 65
79 East. Mennonite ■ ... 65
72 Lynchburg ... 63
67 Roanoke ... 97
112 Emory & Henry ... 114
62 Randolph-Macon ... 67
77 Lynchburg ■ ... 70
91 Emory & Henry † ... 86
72 Randolph-Macon † ... 68
72 Roanoke † ... 74
72 Millsaps ... 83

Nickname: Eagles
Colors: Crimson & Gold
Arena: Nininger Hall
Capacity: 2,000; Year Built: 1957
AD: Tom Kinder
SID: Douglas Barton

BRI'WATER (MASS.)

Bridgewater, MA 02324 ... III

Coach: Joe Farroba
Alma Mater: Boston St. '76
Record: 3 Years, W-44, L-35

1996-97 SCHEDULE

Wesleyan (Conn.) ... Nov. 23
Suffolk ■ ... Nov. 25
Mass.-Dartmouth ■ ... Dec. 3
Bri'water (Mass.) Cl ... Dec. 6-7
Wentworth Inst. ■ ... Dec. 10
Surf 'n Slam Inv. ... Dec. 26-Jan. 1
Westfield St. ■ ... Jan. 14
Framingham St. ... Jan. 18
North Adams St. ■ ... Jan. 20
Mass.-Boston ... Jan. 23
Rhode Island Col. ... Jan. 25
Worcester St. ■ ... Jan. 28
Salem St. ... Feb. 1
Fitchburg St. ■ ... Feb. 4
Plymouth St. ■ ... Feb. 6
Westfield St. ... Feb. 8
Framingham St. ■ ... Feb. 11
North Adams St. ... Feb. 13
Worcester St. ... Feb. 18
Salem St. ■ ... Feb. 20
Fitchburg St. ... Feb. 22

1995-96 RESULTS (18-10)

62 Richard Stockton † ... 73
84 Thomas † ... 71
73 Suffolk ... 76
73 Stonehill † ... 81
85 Mass.-Dartmouth † ... 64
79 Wentworth Inst. ... 59
77 Wesleyan (Conn.) ■ ... 90
77 Clarkson † ... 55
72 Union (N.Y.) ... 57
77 Westfield St. ... 85
83 Framingham St. ■ ... 73
77 North Adams St. ... 63
67 Mass.-Boston ■ ... 54
85 Rhode Island Col. ■ ... 75
91 Worcester St. ... 75
64 Salem St. ■ ... 90
86 Fitchburg St. ... 62
69 Plymouth St. ... 73
94 Westfield St. ■ ... 81
85 Framingham St. ... 60
90 North Adams St. ■ ... 72
85 Worcester St. ■ ... 61
71 Salem St. ... 77
82 Fitchburg St. ■ ... 79
82 North Adams St. ■ ... 64
89 Westfield St. † ... 84
56 Salem St. ... 77
72 Connecticut Col. ■ ... 81

Nickname: Bears
Colors: Crimson & White
Arena: Kelly Gym
Capacity: 800; Year Built: 1960
AD: John C. Harper
SID: Mike Storey

BRIGHAM YOUNG

Provo, UT 84602 ... I

Coach: Roger Reid
Alma Mater: Weber St. '68
Record: 7 Years, W-151, L-71

1996-97 SCHEDULE

Cal St. Fullerton ■ ... Nov. 22
Washington ... Nov. 26
Pacific (Cal.) ■ ... Nov. 30
Weber St. ... Dec. 4
Utah St. ■ ... Dec. 10
Brigham Young Cl. ... Dec. 13-14
Georgia [Atlanta] ... Dec. 21
Penn St. ... Dec. 27
San Diego St. ■ ... Dec. 31
Wyoming ... Jan. 4
Utah ■ ... Jan. 11
Texas Christian ... Jan. 16
Southern Methodist ... Jan. 18
Rice ■ ... Jan. 23
Tulsa ■ ... Jan. 25
UTEP ... Feb. 1
New Mexico ... Feb. 3
Utah ... Feb. 6
Wyoming ■ ... Feb. 8
Texas Christian ■ ... Feb. 13
Southern Methodist ■ ... Feb. 15
Tulsa ... Feb. 20
Rice ... Feb. 22
New Mexico ■ ... Feb. 27
UTEP ■ ... Mar. 1
Western Ath. Conf. Tr. ... Mar. 4-8

1995-96 RESULTS (15-13)

86 Boise St. ■ ... 71
77 Nevada ... 79
74 Mississippi St. ... 79
76 Utah St. ■ ... 52
99 Cal St. Northridge ■ ... 74
74 Louisiana Tech ■ ... 64
91 Weber St. ■ ... 86
71 Texas Tech ... 81
110 Morgan St. ■ ... 69
77 Utah ... 83
68 Air Force ■ ... 64
97 Fresno St. ■ ... 84
76 San Diego St. ... 83
78 Hawaii ... 77
84 Wyoming ■ ... 75
76 Colorado St. ■ ... 78
77 New Mexico ... 83
90 UTEP ... 82
81 New Mexico ■ ... 88
82 UTEP ■ ... 71
76 Colorado St. ... 81
81 Wyoming ... 71
81 San Diego St. ■ ... 68
89 Hawaii ■ ... 94
80 Air Force ... 66
83 Fresno St. ... 95
85 Utah ■ ... 96
84 Colorado St. † ... 100

Nickname: Cougars
Colors: Royal Blue & White
Arena: Marriott Center
Capacity: 22,700; Year Built: 1971
AD: Rondo Fehlberg
SID: Ralph Zobell

BROCKPORT ST.

Brockport, NY 14420 ... III

Coach: Bill Bowe
Alma Mater: Cortland St. '86
Record: 4 Years, W-52, L-53

1996-97 SCHEDULE

Skidmore Inv. ... Nov. 22-23
Cortland St. ... Dec. 6
Buffalo St. ■ ... Dec. 10
Roberts Wesleyan ■ ... Dec. 13
Rensselaer ... Jan. 10
Chase Rochester Tr. ... Jan. 15-18
Oswego St. ... Jan. 21
Geneseo St. ... Jan. 24
Utica/Rome ■ ... Jan. 25
Fredonia St. ... Jan. 28
Plattsburgh St. ■ ... Jan. 31
Potsdam St. ■ ... Feb. 1
Buffalo St. ... Feb. 4
Oneonta St. ... Feb. 7
New Paltz St. ... Feb. 8
Fredonia St. ■ ... Feb. 11
St. John Fisher ... Feb. 13
Binghamton ■ ... Feb. 15
Oswego St. ■ ... Feb. 18
Utica/Rome ... Feb. 21
Geneseo St. ■ ... Feb. 22

1995-96 RESULTS (14-13)

66 Muhlenberg ... 71
63 Moravian † ... 66
71 Binghamton ... 63
79 Geneseo St. ■ ... 104
62 Buffalo St. ... 68
81 Oneonta St. ■ ... 86
87 New Paltz St. ■ ... 75
80 Daemen ■ ... 83
57 Rochester † ... 69
63 Hobart † ... 68
87 Roberts Wesleyan † ... 67
80 Oswego St. ■ ... 66
72 Utica/Rome ... 80
82 Fredonia St. ■ ... 70
85 Plattsburgh St. ... 79
86 Potsdam St. ... 66
36 Buffalo St. ■ ... 59
82 Fredonia St. ... 94
79 St. John Fisher ■ ... 73
91 Roberts Wesleyan ... 80
73 Cortland St. ■ ... 66
101 Oswego St. ... 85
80 Utica/Rome ■ ... 71
73 Geneseo St. ... 66
62 Oneonta St. † ... 60
71 New Paltz St. † ... 79
89 Cortland St. ■ ... 92

Nickname: Golden Eagles
Colors: Green & Gold
Arena: Tuttle North Gym
Capacity: 3,000; Year Built: 1973
AD: Linda Case
SID: Mike Andriatch

BROWN

Providence, RI 02912 ... I

Coach: Frank Dobbs
Alma Mater: Villanova '84
Record: 5 Years, W-53, L-77

1996-97 SCHEDULE

Boston College ... Nov. 22
St. Francis (N.Y.) ... Nov. 30
Lafayette ... Dec. 1
Rhode Island ... Dec. 4
Wisconsin ... Dec. 7
Holy Cross ■ ... Dec. 10
Providence ... Dec. 21
Cal St. Fullerton ... Dec. 28
Loyola Marymount ... Dec. 30
Kansas ... Jan. 2
Army ... Jan. 4
Princeton ■ ... Jan. 10
Pennsylvania ■ ... Jan. 11
Yale ■ ... Jan. 18
Bucknell ... Jan. 20
Yale ... Jan. 25
Harvard ... Jan. 31
Dartmouth ... Feb. 1
Cornell ■ ... Feb. 7
Columbia ■ ... Feb. 8
Pennsylvania ... Feb. 14
Princeton ... Feb. 15
Columbia ... Feb. 21
Cornell ... Feb. 22
Dartmouth ■ ... Feb. 28
Harvard ■ ... Mar. 1

1995-96 RESULTS (10-16)

71 Rhode Island ■ ... 89
67 Providence ... 100
56 Niagara † ... 54
56 Marist ... 59
53 St. Francis (N.Y.) † ... 56
47 Md.-East. Shore † ... 48
47 Pittsburgh ... 95
60 Maine † ... 47
60 Northwestern ... 56
97 Holy Cross ... 89
81 Lafayette ■ ... 73
71 Pennsylvania ... 74
36 Princeton ... 64
69 Bucknell ■ ... 75
56 Yale ... 62
73 Yale ■ ... 56
60 Dartmouth ■ ... 64
73 Harvard ■ ... 70
74 Columbia ... 62
53 Cornell ... 67
56 Princeton ■ ... 58
53 Pennsylvania ■ ... 83
79 Cornell ■ ... 75
55 Columbia ■ ... 61

75	Harvard	62
54	Dartmouth	64

Nickname: Bears
Colors: Cardinal Red & White
Arena: Pizzitola Sports Center
  Capacity: 3,100; Year Built: 1989
AD: David Roach
SID: Chris Humm

BRYANT
Smithfield, RI 02917 II

Coach: Edward Reilly
Alma Mater: Holy Cross '76
Record: 8 Years, W-59, L-128

1996-97 SCHEDULE

Franklin Pierce	Nov. 19
Bryant Cl.	Nov. 23-24
New Haven	Nov. 26
Mass.-Lowell ■	Dec. 1
St. Michael's ■	Dec. 3
St. Anselm ■	Dec. 7
Sacred Heart	Dec. 20
New Hamp. Col.	Jan. 5
Merrimack	Jan. 7
American Int'l	Jan. 10
Le Moyne ■	Jan. 12
Stonehill	Jan. 16
Quinnipiac	Jan. 18
Bentley ■	Jan. 21
Assumption	Jan. 23
Merrimack ■	Jan. 27
St. Anselm	Feb. 1
Le Moyne	Feb. 4
Quinnipiac ■	Feb. 8
Stonehill ■	Feb. 11
American Int'l ■	Feb. 13
Bentley	Feb. 16
St. Michael's	Feb. 19
Assumption ■	Feb. 22

1995-96 RESULTS (13-14)

92	Franklin Pierce ■	89
88	Mass.-Lowell	75
103	New Hamp. Col. ■	110
90	Quinnipiac ■	66
69	Bridgeport ■	57
80	St. Anselm	82
73	Dowling	76
59	Cal St. Dom. Hills	64
66	Cal St. Los Angeles	79
81	Cal St. Bakersfield	88
74	Stonehill	73
84	Assumption	78
57	American Int'l	61
76	St. Anselm ■	101
73	St. Michael's	87
81	Merrimack ■	75
57	Bentley ■	59
63	Stonehill	66
72	American Int'l ■	58
73	Assumption ■	59
72	Quinnipiac	67
67	Bentley	87
73	New Haven ■	70
99	St. Michael's ■	96
63	Merrimack	65
68	Stonehill †	66
81	St. Anselm	100

Nickname: Bulldogs
Colors: Black & Gold
Arena: Bryant Gymnasium
  Capacity: 2,700; Year Built: 1971
AD: Linda Hackett
SID: John White

BUCKNELL
Lewisburg, PA 17837 I

Coach: Pat Flannery
Alma Mater: Bucknell '80
Record: 7 Years, W-124, L-68

1996-97 SCHEDULE

Robert Morris ■	Nov. 23
Niagara ■	Nov. 25
Air Force	Nov. 28
Colorado St.	Nov. 30
Delaware ■	Dec. 4
St. Francis (Pa.) ■	Dec. 7
Princeton	Dec. 10
Penn St.	Dec. 22
New Mexico Inv.	Dec. 27-28
Cornell	Jan. 3
Colgate	Jan. 8
Lehigh ■	Jan. 11
Lafayette	Jan. 15
Brown ■	Jan. 20
Navy ■	Jan. 22
Holy Cross	Jan. 25
Army ■	Jan. 29
Colgate ■	Feb. 1
Western Md. ■	Feb. 3
Lehigh	Feb. 5
Lafayette ■	Feb. 8
Md.-Balt. County	Feb. 12
Navy	Feb. 15
Holy Cross ■	Feb. 18
Army	Feb. 22
Patriot Conf. Tr.	Mar. 1-5

1995-96 RESULTS (17-11)

68	San Francisco	65
66	St. Mary's (Cal.)	84
64	Delaware	73
80	Hartford ■	70
91	Dickinson ■	40
54	St. Joseph's (Pa.)	74
77	St. Francis (Pa.)	50
70	Widener ■	46
54	Penn St.	85
69	Wichita St.	85
72	Alabama †	64
80	Cornell ■	59
57	Navy	60
75	Army	37
75	Brown	69
78	Lehigh ■	65
83	Colgate	75
79	Lafayette ■	71
90	Holy Cross	83
72	Navy ■	65
82	Army ■	65
55	St. Bonaventure	60
83	Lehigh	63
68	Colgate ■	73
52	Lafayette	73
73	Holy Cross ■	93
56	Lafayette †	55
61	Colgate †	67

Nickname: Bison
Colors: Orange & Blue
Arena: Davis Gymnasium
  Capacity: 2,300; Year Built: 1938
AD: Rick Hartzell
SID: Pat Farabaugh

BUENA VISTA
Storm Lake, IA 50588 III

Coach: Brian Van Haaften
Alma Mater: Central (Iowa) '85
(First year as head coach)

1996-97 SCHEDULE

Teikyo Westmar	Nov. 22
Valley City St. ■	Nov. 23
Midland Lutheran	Nov. 26
Dana	Dec. 3
N'western (Minn.) ■	Dec. 6
Morningside	Dec. 9
Martin Luther ■	Dec. 14
Embry-Riddle Tr.	Dec. 30-31
Wartburg	Jan. 10
William Penn	Jan. 11
Dubuque ■	Jan. 17
Upper Iowa ■	Jan. 18
Luther	Jan. 24
Central (Iowa)	Jan. 25

Simpson ■	Jan. 31
Loras	Feb. 1
Dubuque	Feb. 4
Wartburg ■	Feb. 14
Upper Iowa	Feb. 15
William Penn ■	Feb. 21
Loras ■	Feb. 22
Simpson	Feb. 25
Central (Iowa) ■	Feb. 28
Luther ■	Mar. 1

1995-96 RESULTS (7-18)

74	Jamestown	82
87	Valley City St.	81
80	Dana	84
80	Teikyo Westmar ■	86
66	Mt. Marty	92
84	N'western (Minn.) ■	67
75	Gust. Adolphus ■	62
68	Midland Lutheran ■	76
52	Upper Iowa	75
69	Central (Iowa)	83
76	Wartburg ■	70
71	Loras	72
61	Luther ■	64
71	Dubuque ■	72
65	William Penn	69
65	Central (Iowa) ■	60
61	Dubuque	65
52	Luther	55
79	Simpson	90
56	Upper Iowa ■	68
93	William Penn ■	57
72	Martin Luther	84
77	Wartburg	73
112	Simpson ■	120
90	Loras	95

Nickname: Beavers
Colors: Blue & Gold
Arena: Siebens Fieldhouse
  Capacity: 4,000; Year Built: 1969
AD: Roger Egland
SID: Paul Misner

BUFFALO
Buffalo, NY 14260 I

Coach: Tim Cohane
Alma Mater: Navy '67
Record: 14 Years, W-185, L-187

1996-97 SCHEDULE

Miami (Fla.)	Nov. 22
Cornell	Nov. 26
Niagara ■	Nov. 30
Canisius ■	Dec. 3
St. Bonaventure ■	Dec. 7
Syracuse ■	Dec. 10
Morgan St. ■	Dec. 13
Niagara	Dec. 18
Toledo Tr.	Dec. 29-30
Central Conn. St. ■	Jan. 4
Valparaiso	Jan. 8
Mo.-Kansas City ■	Jan. 11
Troy St. ■	Jan. 13
Western Ill.	Jan. 18
Youngstown St. ■	Jan. 22
Chicago St.	Jan. 25
Northeastern Ill.	Jan. 27
Valparaiso ■	Feb. 1
Western Ill. ■	Feb. 3
Troy St.	Feb. 6
Mo.-Kansas City	Feb. 8
Youngstown St.	Feb. 12
Northeastern Ill. ■	Feb. 15
Chicago St. ■	Feb. 17
Central Conn. St.	Feb. 22
Mid-Continent Conf. Tr.	Mar. 2-4

1995-96 RESULTS (13-14)

78	Rutgers	74
75	Canisius	82
64	St. Bonaventure	74
68	Niagara ■	58
71	Southern Miss. †	77

74	Mississippi Val. †	73
60	Youngstown St. ■	56
48	Mo.-Kansas City	43
74	Western Ill.	93
69	Chicago St. ■	62
80	Northeastern Ill. ■	66
65	Valparaiso	86
49	Boston College	89
52	Eastern Ill.	60
84	Central Conn. St. ■	68
76	Troy St. ■	61
53	Youngstown St.	51
63	Western Ill. ■	58
63	Mo.-Kansas City ■	72
85	Northeastern Ill.	77
78	Chicago St.	68
61	Eastern Ill. ■	64
64	Valparaiso ■	73
86	Troy St.	88
62	Central Conn. St.	75
60	Cornell ■	62
55	Eastern Ill. †	59

Nickname: Bulls
Colors: Royal Blue & White
Arena: Alumni Arena
  Capacity: 8,464; Year Built: 1982
AD: Nelson Townsend
SID: Paul Vecchio

BUFFALO ST.
Buffalo, NY 14222 III

Coach: Richard Bihr
Alma Mater: Buffalo St. '69
Record: 17 Years, W-334, L-122

1996-97 SCHEDULE

Buffalo St. Cl.	Nov. 22-23
Fredonia St. ■	Dec. 6
Binghamton	Dec. 7
Brockport St.	Dec. 10
Utica/Rome ■	Dec. 14
Buffalo St. Inv.	Jan. 3-4
Lebanon Valley Tr.	Jan. 10-11
Plattsburgh St.	Jan. 17
Potsdam St.	Jan. 18
Oswego St. ■	Jan. 24
Geneseo St.	Jan. 25
St. John Fisher	Jan. 29
Cortland St. ■	Feb. 1
Brockport St. ■	Feb. 4
Utica/Rome	Feb. 8
Pitt.-Bradford	Feb. 12
Oneonta St. ■	Feb. 14
New Paltz St. ■	Feb. 15
Fredonia St.	Feb. 18
Geneseo St. ■	Feb. 21
Oswego St.	Feb. 22

1995-96 RESULTS (22-8)

90	Lehman ■	63
82	Daemen ■	73
59	Fredonia St.	53
61	Cortland St.	77
68	Brockport St. ■	62
55	Utica/Rome	44
71	Mass.-Dartmouth †	64
42	Wis.-Eau Claire	59
64	Madonna	59
57	Geneva ■	72
75	Plattsburgh St. ■	54
81	Potsdam St. ■	70
73	Geneseo St. ■	80
61	Oswego St.	52
81	St. John Fisher ■	74
80	Binghamton ■	53
72	Pitt.-Bradford ■	65
59	Brockport St.	36
74	Utica/Rome ■	51
60	Oneonta St.	72
48	New Paltz St.	58
64	Fredonia St. ■	52
63	Geneseo St.	75
88	Oswego St. ■	72
68	Binghamton †	48

64	Fredonia St. †	43
75	New Paltz St. †	53
74	St. John Fisher ■	65
71	Geneseo St. ■	61
59	Wilkes †	64

Nickname: Bengals
Colors: Orange & Black
Arena: Sports Arena
  Capacity: 4,000; Year Built: 1991
AD: Gail Maloney (Interim)
SID: Keith Bullion

BUTLER
Indianapolis, IN 46208.............I

Coach: Barry Collier
Alma Mater: Butler '76
Record: 7 Years, W-106, L-93

1996-97 SCHEDULE

Indiana St.	Nov. 26
Puerto Rico Shootout	Nov. 29-Dec. 1
Anderson (Ind.) ■	Dec. 4
Ball St. ■	Dec. 7
Bradley	Dec. 10
Evansville	Dec. 14
Indiana	Dec. 23
Florida Int'l	Dec. 28
Florida St.	Dec. 30
Cleveland St.	Jan. 2
Western Ky. ■	Jan. 5
Ill.-Chicago	Jan. 9
Loyola (Ill.)	Jan. 11
Wis.-Milwaukee ■	Jan. 16
Wis.-Green Bay ■	Jan. 18
Detroit	Jan. 20
Northern Ill.	Jan. 23
Wright St.	Jan. 25
Cleveland St. ■	Jan. 30
Detroit ■	Feb. 1
Marshall	Feb. 5
Loyola (Ill.) ■	Feb. 8
Ill.-Chicago ■	Feb. 12
Wis.-Milwaukee	Feb. 15
Wis.-Green Bay	Feb. 18
Northern Ill. ■	Feb. 20
Wright St. ■	Feb. 22
Midwestern Conf. Tr.	Feb. 28-Mar. 4

1995-96 RESULTS (19-8)

75	Md.-East. Shore ■	44
56	Hanover ■	53
67	Ball St.	57
50	Western Ky.	56
81	Indiana St. ■	61
102	Marshall	92
65	James Madison	63
59	Montana	84
65	James Madison †	75
78	Ill.-Chicago ■	58
87	Portland ■	80
71	Wis.-Milwaukee	67
71	Wright St. ■	68
61	Wis.-Green Bay ■	64
67	Loyola (Ill.)	59
57	Northern Ill.	84
71	Cleveland St. ■	56
70	Detroit ■	62
78	Loyola (Ill.) ■	66
65	Wis.-Milwaukee ■	45
76	Cleveland St.	68
61	Wright St. ■	67
85	Ill.-Chicago	82
73	Northern Ill. ■	58
69	Detroit	61
66	Wis.-Green Bay ■	73
97	Ill.-Chicago †	107

Nickname: Bulldogs
Colors: Blue & White
Arena: Hinkle Fieldhouse
  Capacity: 11,043; Year Built: 1928
AD: John Parry
SID: Jim McGrath

CABRINI
Radnor, PA 19087.................III

Coach: John Dzik
Alma Mater: West Chester '72
Record: 16 Years, W-323, L-133

1996-97 SCHEDULE

Ursinus Tr.	Nov. 22-23
Beaver ■	Dec. 4
Eastern	Dec. 7
Marywood ■	Dec. 10
Loras Catholic Tr.	Jan. 1-5
Elizabethtown Cl.	Jan. 10-11
Misericordia	Jan. 13
Gwynedd-Mercy	Jan. 15
Allentown ■	Jan. 18
Alvernia	Jan. 20
Neumann ■	Jan. 22
Marywood	Jan. 25
Centenary (N.J.) ■	Jan. 27
Eastern ■	Jan. 29
Beaver	Feb. 1
Misericordia ■	Feb. 8
Gwynedd-Mercy ■	Feb. 12
Allentown	Feb. 15
Alvernia ■	Feb. 19
Neumann	Feb. 22

1995-96 RESULTS (24-3)

86	Ursinus †	62
74	Phila. Pharmacy	81
77	Neumann	43
86	Alvernia	76
103	Dickinson ■	56
71	Hunter	57
83	St. Scholastica †	64
79	Mt. St. Clare †	78
65	Loras	66
73	Eastern	57
92	Beaver	74
98	Misericordia	64
92	Neumann ■	65
107	Gwynedd-Mercy	56
89	Allentown	78
115	Marywood	75
80	Beaver ■	52
89	Alvernia ■	72
91	Eastern ■	58
102	Gwynedd-Mercy ■	82
96	Misericordia	70
105	Allentown ■	95
110	Marywood	62
90	Misericordia	55
85	Allentown	67
85	Catholic ■	65
91	Wilkes	96

Nickname: Cavaliers
Colors: Royal Blue & White
Arena: Sacred Heart Gymnasium
  Capacity: 750; Year Built: 1958
AD: John Dzik
SID: Rich Schepis

CALIFORNIA
Berkeley, CA 94720.................I

Coach: Ben Braun
Alma Mater: Wisconsin '75
Record: 19 Years, W-333, L-235

1996-97 SCHEDULE

Maui Inv.	Nov. 25-27
Texas Southern ■	Nov. 30
Illinois ■	Dec. 3
Maryland Tr.	Dec. 8-9
Penn St. [East Rutherford]	Dec. 20
San Francisco	Dec. 23
California Cl.	Dec. 28-29
Arizona	Jan. 2
Arizona St.	Jan. 4
Southern Cal [San Francisco]	Jan. 9
UCLA [San Francisco]	Jan. 11
Oregon St.	Jan. 16

Oregon	Jan. 18
Washington St. ■	Jan. 23
Washington ■	Jan. 25
Stanford ■	Jan. 29
UCLA	Feb. 6
Southern Cal	Feb. 8
Oregon ■	Feb. 13
Oregon St. ■	Feb. 15
Washington	Feb. 20
Washington St.	Feb. 22
Stanford	Mar. 1
Arizona St. ■	Mar. 6
Arizona [San Francisco]	Mar. 8

1995-96 RESULTS (17-11)

111	Northern Ariz. ■	83
112	Texas Southern	73
83	San Francisco †	70
70	Minnesota	67
70	Cincinnati ■	77
69	Illinois †	83
75	Holy Cross ■	64
58	Kansas St.	65
99	Arizona	75
97	Arizona St.	82
63	Southern Cal	60
73	UCLA	93
70	Oregon St. ■	52
97	Oregon ■	72
87	Washington St.	79
69	Washington	71
79	Stanford	93
62	DePaul †	59
65	UCLA ■	73
85	Southern Cal ■	69
58	Oregon	60
57	Oregon St.	51
67	Washington ■	56
71	Washington St. ■	67
85	Stanford ■	69
53	Arizona St.	56
68	Arizona	71
64	Iowa St. †	74

Nickname: Golden Bears
Colors: Blue & Gold
Arena: Harmon Gym
  Capacity: 6,578; Year Built: 1933
AD: John Kasser
SID: Herb Benenson

CALIF. (PA.)
California, PA 15419.................II

Coach: Bill Brown
Alma Mater: Ohio '74
Record: 10 Years, W-125, L-127

1996-97 SCHEDULE

Charleston (W.Va.) ■	Nov. 19
Salem-Teikyo ■	Nov. 25
Wheeling Jesuit	Nov. 30
Columbia Union ■	Dec. 3
California (Pa.) Tr.	Dec. 6-7
Thiel ■	Dec. 13
Ohio Valley ■	Dec. 14
Charleston (W.Va.)	Dec. 16
Gannon Tr.	Dec. 29-30
Washington (Md.) ■	Jan. 4
Clarion ■	Jan. 8
Indiana (Pa.)	Jan. 11
Pitt.-Johnstown	Jan. 15
Lock Haven ■	Jan. 18
Shippensburg	Jan. 22
Edinboro ■	Jan. 25
Slippery Rock ■	Jan. 29
Indiana (Pa.) ■	Feb. 1
Clarion	Feb. 5
Lock Haven	Feb. 8
Hilbert ■	Feb. 12
Shippensburg ■	Feb. 15
Slippery Rock	Feb. 19
Edinboro	Feb. 22

1995-96 RESULTS (27-6)

88	Davis & Elkins	49

67	Mansfield	58
85	Ohio Valley ■	69
112	Wheeling Jesuit ■	91
69	Virginia Union	71
102	Columbia Union	82
72	West Chester	82
86	Mansfield ■	62
74	Salem-Teikyo	88
86	Denver †	88
108	Minn.-Crookston †	56
70	Phila. Textile	58
66	Slippery Rock	48
71	Edinboro	59
92	Shippensburg ■	67
78	Lock Haven	75
97	Hilbert	48
76	Indiana (Pa.) ■	73
89	Clarion	77
79	Edinboro ■	64
90	Slippery Rock	62
73	Shippensburg	63
99	Pitt.-Johnstown	83
83	Lock Haven ■	64
79	Clarion	72
81	Indiana (Pa.)	99
80	Millersville ■	68
92	Cheyney ■	81
87	Indiana (Pa.) ■	84
84	Edinboro	76
78	Indiana (Pa.) ■	68
95	Alabama A&M †	85
56	Fort Hays St. †	76

Nickname: Vulcans
Colors: Red & Black
Arena: Hamer Hall
  Capacity: 3,800; Year Built: 1966
AD: Tom Pucci
SID: Bruce Wald

CAL LUTHERAN
Thousand Oaks, CA 91360......III

Coach: Rich Rider
Alma Mater: Truman St. '68
Record: 11 Years, W-172, L-118

1996-97 SCHEDULE

Menlo Cl.	Nov. 22-23
Chapman ■	Nov. 26
Westmont	Dec. 7
Pacific Christian ■	Dec. 14
UC San Diego	Dec. 22
Cal Lutheran Tr.	Dec. 29-30
UC Santa Cruz Tr.	Jan. 3-4
UC Santa Cruz ■	Jan. 9
Cal Tech	Jan. 11
Pomona-Pitzer	Jan. 15
Claremont-M-S	Jan. 18
Whittier	Jan. 22
Redlands	Jan. 25
Occidental ■	Jan. 29
La Verne	Feb. 1
Cal Tech ■	Feb. 5
Pomona-Pitzer	Feb. 8
Claremont-M-S ■	Feb. 12
Whittier	Feb. 15
Redlands ■	Feb. 19
Occidental	Feb. 22
La Verne	Feb. 26

1995-96 RESULTS (19-6)

74	Col. of Idaho †	79
76	Menlo	63
77	Christian Heritage ■	60
98	Pacific Christian ■	63
87	Chapman	71
83	Westmont ■	81
79	Azusa-Pacific	92
101	UC San Diego ■	66
82	Luther	70
82	Concordia (Ill.) ■	63
73	Holy Names	78
66	Claremont-M-S	75
79	La Verne	73

92	Whittier ■	58
73	Cal Tech	51
73	Pomona-Pitzer ■	66
81	Occidental	69
90	Redlands	67
70	Claremont-M-S ■	72
82	La Verne ■	48
69	Whittier	63
84	Cal Tech ■	40
56	Pomona-Pitzer	63
69	Occidental	65
83	Redlands ■	80

Nickname: Kingsmen
Colors: Purple & Gold
Arena: CLU Gymnasium
 Capacity: 500; Year Built: 1962
AD: Bruce Bryde
SID: John Czimbal

CAL POLY POMONA
Pomona, CA 91768 II

Coach: Tom Marshall
Alma Mater: San Diego St. '77
Record: 13 Years, W-214, L-127

1996-97 SCHEDULE
Cal Poly Pomona Cl.	Nov. 22-23
Grand Junction Tr.	Nov. 29-30
Concordia (Cal.)	Dec. 7
San Jose St.	Dec. 9
Christian Heritage ■	Dec. 14
Cal Poly Pomona Tr.	Dec. 19-21
Chico St. Tr.	Dec. 28-30
Pacific Christian ■	Jan. 6
Azusa-Pacific	Jan. 10
Cal St. Los Angeles	Jan. 16
Cal St. Bakersfield ■	Jan. 18
Cal St. San B'dino	Jan. 23
UC Riverside	Jan. 25
Grand Canyon ■	Jan. 30
Cal St. Dom. Hills	Feb. 6
Cal St. Bakersfield	Feb. 8
Cal St. San B'dino ■	Feb. 13
UC Riverside ■	Feb. 15
Grand Canyon	Feb. 20
Cal St. Los Angeles ■	Feb. 27
Cal St. Dom. Hills ■	Mar. 1

1995-96 RESULTS (17-10)
60	Biola ■	79
68	Concordia (Cal.) ■	65
67	Pt. Loma Nazarene †	76
101	UC San Diego	75
70	UC-Colo. Spgs.	48
64	Colorado Mines	59
48	San Diego St. ■	67
76	Cal St. Hayward	57
73	Sonoma St.	60
34	UC Davis	60
98	Alas. Fairbanks †	99
73	Lewis & Clark †	71
83	Sonoma St. †	61
81	Azusa-Pacific	77
64	St. Thomas Aquinas ■	54
54	Cal St. San B'dino ■	53
77	UC Riverside	64
76	Grand Canyon	78
65	Cal St. Los Angeles	42
69	Cal St. Bakersfield ■	75
78	Cal St. Dom. Hills ■	57
53	UC Riverside ■	70
85	Grand Canyon	73
71	Cal St. Bakersfield	78
74	Cal St. Los Angeles ■	70
66	Cal St. San B'dino	83
64	Cal St. Dom. Hills ■	62

Nickname: Broncos
Colors: Green & Gold
Arena: Kellogg Gym
 Capacity: 5,000; Year Built: 1966
AD: Karen Miller
SID: Ron Fremont

CAL POLY SLO
San Luis Obispo, CA 93407 I

Coach: Jeff Schneider
Alma Mater: Virginia Tech '82
Record: 1 Year, W-16, L-13

1996-97 SCHEDULE
Simon Fraser ■	Nov. 22
Cal St. Hayward ■	Nov. 23
Loyola Marymount ■	Nov. 26
Fresno St. Cl.	Nov. 29-30
UC Santa Cruz ■	Dec. 3
Air Force	Dec. 7
Hawaii Festival	Dec. 14-15
George Mason	Dec. 22
California Cl.	Dec. 28-29
Portland ■	Jan. 4
New Mexico St. ■	Jan. 9
UC Santa Barb. ■	Jan. 11
UC Irvine ■	Jan. 16
Cal St. Fullerton ■	Jan. 18
Pacific (Cal.) ■	Jan. 23
Long Beach St.	Jan. 25
Utah St.	Jan. 30
Nevada	Feb. 1
Boise St. ■	Feb. 6
Idaho ■	Feb. 8
Long Beach St. ■	Feb. 13
Pacific (Cal.) ■	Feb. 15
Idaho St. ■	Feb. 18
North Texas	Feb. 20
UC Santa Barb.	Feb. 22
Cal St. Fullerton	Feb. 27
UC Irvine	Mar. 1
Big West Conf. Tr.	Mar. 7-9

1995-96 RESULTS (16-13)
94	Notre Dame (Cal.) ■	51
71	Northern Ariz.	83
68	Montana	87
64	Western Ill. †	69
118	UC Santa Cruz ■	61
82	Eastern Wash. ■	66
70	Portland	91
83	North Caro. St. ■	102
73	Harvard ■	64
78	Northern Ariz. ■	75
74	Simon Fraser ■	69
82	Oral Roberts ■	74
86	Idaho ■	84
68	St. Mary's (Cal.) ■	88
106	George Mason ■	110
78	Idaho	94
102	Cal St. Sacramento	86
64	Loyola Marymount	76
77	Idaho St.	88
79	Cal St. Sacramento	63
66	Cal St. Northridge ■	59
91	Southern Utah	78
90	Chapman ■	54
97	Cal St. Northridge	84
84	Cleveland St.	67
84	Southern Utah ■	85
73	San Diego	77
73	Cal St. Sacramento †	66
53	Southern Utah †	55

Nickname: Mustangs
Colors: Green & Gold
Arena: Robert A. Mott Gymnasium
 Capacity: 3,500; Year Built: 1960
AD: John McCutcheon
SID: Eric McDowell

CAL ST. BAKERSFIELD
Bakersfield, CA 93311 II

Coach: Pat Douglass
Alma Mater: Pacific (Cal.) '72
Record: 15 Years, W-347, L-115

1996-97 SCHEDULE
Va. Union Tr.	Nov. 8-10
UC Davis ■	Nov. 16
Concordia (Cal.) ■	Nov. 21
Quincy ■	Nov. 26
Cal St. Bakersfield Cl.	Nov. 29-30
Pt. Loma Nazarene ■	Dec. 6
Cal St. Stanislaus	Dec. 12
Sonoma St.	Dec. 14
BYU-Hawaii	Dec. 20
Hawaii Pacific	Dec. 22
Cal St. Bakersfield Tr.	Dec. 27-28
Cal Baptist ■	Jan. 4
Master's	Jan. 11
Cal St. Dom. Hills ■	Jan. 16
Cal Poly Pomona ■	Jan. 18
Grand Canyon	Jan. 25
UC Riverside ■	Jan. 30
Cal St. San B'dino ■	Feb. 1
Cal St. Los Angeles ■	Feb. 6
Cal Poly Pomona	Feb. 8
Grand Canyon ■	Feb. 15
Cal St. San B'dino	Feb. 20
UC Riverside	Feb. 22
Cal St. Dom. Hills	Feb. 27
Cal St. Los Angeles	Mar. 1

1995-96 RESULTS (26-4)
105	San Fran. St. ■	44
115	Cal St. Hayward	68
93	Tex. A&M-Kingsville ■	68
90	Azusa-Pacific	71
98	Cal St. Stanislaus ■	71
75	UC Davis	61
67	Sonoma St.	62
83	Northern Ky. ■	71
118	La Verne ■	68
89	Colorado Mines	66
76	UC Davis ■	71
88	Bryant	81
91	UC-Colo. Spgs.	67
67	Master's	78
81	Lynn ■	65
66	Grand Canyon	68
74	UC Riverside ■	63
86	Cal St. San B'dino ■	81
61	Cal St. Dom. Hills ■	46
75	Cal Poly Pomona ■	69
74	Cal St. Los Angeles ■	61
57	Grand Canyon ■	59
69	UC Riverside	62
81	Cal St. San B'dino ■	55
78	Cal Poly Pomona ■	71
72	Cal St. Dom. Hills ■	64
81	Cal St. Los Angeles ■	57
71	Grand Canyon	65
78	Seattle Pacific ■	65
55	Northern Ky. †	56

Nickname: Roadrunners
Colors: Blue & Gold
Arena: CSUB Activities Center
 Capacity: 3,764; Year Built: 1989
AD: Rudy Carvajal
SID: Bill Macriss

CAL ST. CHICO
Chico, CA 95929 II

Coach: Prescott Smith
Alma Mater: Southwestern Okla. '65
Record: 9 Years, W-145, L-114

1996-97 SCHEDULE
Southern Ore. St.	Nov. 19
Grand Canyon Inv.	Nov. 22-23
Oregon Tech	Nov. 26
UC Davis Shootout	Dec. 6-7
Seattle Pacific	Dec. 13
Pacific (Cal.)	Dec. 14
Holy Names ■	Dec. 22
Chico St. Tr.	Dec. 28-30
Humboldt St.	Jan. 3
Sonoma St.	Jan. 4
Cal St. Stanislaus ■	Jan. 10
Cal St. Hayward	Jan. 11
San Fran. St. ■	Jan. 17
Notre Dame (Cal.)	Jan. 18
UC Davis ■	Jan. 25
San Fran. St.	Jan. 31

CAL ST. HAYWARD

Notre Dame (Cal.) ■	Feb. 1
Cal St. Hayward ■	Feb. 7
Cal St. Stanislaus	Feb. 8
Sonoma St. ■	Feb. 14
Humboldt St. ■	Feb. 15
UC Davis	Feb. 20

1995-96 RESULTS (14-13)
73	Concordia (Cal.) †	70
77	Biola †	76
71	UC Riverside	85
94	Southern Ore. St. ■	90
88	Puget Sound	83
60	Seattle Pacific	61
94	Oregon Tech	99
118	San Jose Christian ■	90
99	Lewis & Clark ■	91
98	Alas. Fairbanks ■	89
79	Master's	84
80	Alas. Fairbanks ■	86
78	Humboldt St. ■	80
94	Sonoma St. ■	89
85	Cal St. Stanislaus ■	83
83	Cal St. Hayward ■	89
68	San Fran. St.	69
100	Notre Dame (Cal.) ■	79
75	UC Davis	90
75	San Fran. St. ■	62
66	Notre Dame (Cal.)	62
75	Cal St. Hayward	74
78	Cal St. Stanislaus	73
78	Sonoma St.	85
59	Humboldt St.	90
62	UC Davis ■	70
79	UC Davis	94

Nickname: Wildcats
Colors: Cardinal & White
Arena: Art Acker Gym
 Capacity: 2,500; Year Built: 1962
AD: Don W. Batie
SID: Teresa Clements

CAL ST. DOM. HILLS
Carson, CA 90747 II

Coach: To be named

1996-97 SCHEDULE
Westmont	Nov. 19
Biola	Nov. 22
Cal St. Northridge	Nov. 27
Quincy ■	Nov. 29
UC Davis Shootout	Dec. 6-7
Azusa-Pacific	Dec. 13
San Fran. St. ■	Dec. 14
Notre Dame (Cal.) ■	Dec. 21
Seattle Pacific Cl.	Dec. 27-28
Redlands ■	Dec. 31
Master's	Jan. 8
Pt. Loma Nazarene ■	Jan. 11
Cal St. Bakersfield	Jan. 16
Cal St. Los Angeles ■	Jan. 18
UC Riverside	Jan. 23
Cal St. San B'dino ■	Jan. 25
Christian Heritage ■	Jan. 29
Grand Canyon ■	Feb. 1
Cal Poly Pomona ■	Feb. 6
Cal St. Los Angeles ■	Feb. 8
UC Riverside ■	Feb. 13
Cal St. San B'dino ■	Feb. 15
Grand Canyon	Feb. 22
Cal St. Bakersfield ■	Feb. 27
Cal Poly Pomona	Mar. 1

1995-96 RESULTS (17-10)
70	Pt. Loma Nazarene ■	67
68	Tex. A&M-Kingsville ■	63
63	Southern Colo.	66
59	Colo. Christian †	54
84	Redlands	64
82	Azusa-Pacific ■	65
82	Notre Dame (Cal.)	62
71	Cal St. Hayward	45
64	Bryant	59
79	Cal Baptist ■	63
69	Westmont ■	64

63 Biola ■ 74
76 Lynn ■ 57
66 UC Riverside ■ 63
55 Cal St. San B'dino 68
62 Master's ■ 68
74 Grand Canyon ■ 84
46 Cal St. Bakersfield ■ 61
78 Cal St. Los Angeles 65
57 Cal Poly Pomona ■ 78
78 Cal St. San B'dino ■ 61
59 Christian Heritage ■ 49
86 Grand Canyon ■ 80
62 Cal St. Los Angeles ■ 50
64 Cal St. Bakersfield 72
51 UC Riverside 70
62 Cal Poly Pomona 64

Nickname: Toros
Colors: Cardinal & Gold
Arena: Torodome
 Capacity: 4,200; Year Built: 1978
AD: Ron Prettyman
SID: Patrick Guillen

CAL ST. FULLERTON
Fullerton, CA 92634 I

Coach: Bob Hawking
Alma Mater: Cal St. Northridge '71
Record: 2 Years, W-13, L-40

1996-97 SCHEDULE
Brigham Young .....Nov. 22
Utah ■ .....Nov. 30
Montana .....Dec. 3
Loyola Marymount .....Dec. 7
San Diego .....Dec. 10
Loyola (Ill.) ■ .....Dec. 14
Pepperdine ■ .....Dec. 21
Brown ■ .....Dec. 28
Columbia ■ .....Dec. 30
Gonzaga .....Jan. 4
Pacific (Cal.) ■ .....Jan. 11
Long Beach St. ■ .....Jan. 13
UC Santa Barb. .....Jan. 16
Cal Poly SLO .....Jan. 18
Utah St. ■ .....Jan. 23
UC Irvine .....Jan. 25
Idaho .....Jan. 30
Boise St. .....Feb. 1
New Mexico St. ■ .....Feb. 6
North Texas ■ .....Feb. 8
UC Irvine ■ .....Feb. 13
Nevada .....Feb. 15
Pacific (Cal.) .....Feb. 20
Long Beach St. .....Feb. 22
Cal Poly SLO ■ .....Feb. 27
UC Santa Barb. ■ .....Mar. 1
Big West Conf. Tr. .....Mar. 7-9

1995-96 RESULTS (6-20)
63 UCLA 79
76 Cal St. Northridge 77
85 San Diego St. 83
57 Gonzaga ■ 83
63 Loyola Marymount ■ 67
53 San Francisco 72
58 Utah 108
62 Montana ■ 70
77 San Jose St. ■ 88
79 Pacific (Cal.) ■ 69
62 UC Santa Barb. 65
66 Long Beach St. 79
81 UC Irvine ■ 73
64 UNLV ■ 61
85 New Mexico St. ■ 72
49 Utah St. 73
70 Nevada 89
56 Long Beach St. ■ 73
72 UC Santa Barb. ■ 85
75 UC Irvine 85
68 New Mexico St. 63
59 UNLV 68
66 Nevada ■ 71
53 Utah St. ■ 66
63 Pacific (Cal.) 87
80 San Jose St. 90

Nickname: Titans
Colors: Blue, Orange & White
Arena: Titan Gym
 Capacity: 4,000; Year Built: 1964
AD: John Easterbrook
SID: Mel Franks

CAL ST. HAYWARD
Hayward, CA 94542 II

Coach: Gary Stewart
Alma Mater: La Verne '84
Record: 9 Years, W-124, L-109

1996-97 SCHEDULE
Cal Poly SLO .....Nov. 23
Holy Names ■ .....Nov. 26
Southern Utah .....Nov. 30
Bethany (Cal.) .....Dec. 3
Patten ■ .....Dec. 7
Cal St. San B'dino ■ .....Dec. 16
Cal Poly Pomona Tr. .....Dec. 19-21
Pepperdine .....Dec. 27
Cal St. Los Angeles .....Dec. 28
Patten .....Dec. 30
St. Mary's (Cal.) .....Jan. 2
Notre Dame (Cal.) ■ .....Jan. 3
San Fran. St. .....Jan. 4
Sonoma St. .....Jan. 8
UC Davis .....Jan. 10
Cal St. Chico ■ .....Jan. 11
Humboldt St. .....Jan. 17
Cal St. Stanislaus ■ .....Jan. 25
Sonoma St. ■ .....Jan. 31
Humboldt St. ■ .....Feb. 1
Cal St. Chico .....Feb. 7
UC Davis ■ .....Feb. 8
Notre Dame (Cal.) .....Feb. 14
San Fran. St. ■ .....Feb. 15
Cal St. Stanislaus .....Feb. 20

1995-96 RESULTS (8-18)
72 Holy Names ■ 68
68 Cal St. Bakersfield ■ 115
86 Bethany (Cal.) 53
52 Long Beach St. 101
81 Occidental † 71
76 Azusa-Pacific † 98
57 Cal Poly Pomona 76
66 UC Riverside ■ 83
40 San Francisco 66
45 Cal St. Dom. Hills ■ 71
51 Cal St. Los Angeles 59
62 Fresno Pacific 77
63 Notre Dame (Cal.) 54
84 San Fran. St. ■ 64
58 UC Davis ■ 73
89 Cal St. Chico 83
69 Humboldt St. ■ 75
72 Sonoma St. ■ 81
85 Cal St. Stanislaus 89
64 Sonoma St. 74
73 Humboldt St. 61
74 Cal St. Chico ■ 75
55 UC Davis 70
91 Notre Dame (Cal.) ■ 83
81 San Fran. St. ■ 91
77 Cal St. Stanislaus 78

Nickname: Pioneers
Colors: Red & White
Arena: Pioneer Gym
 Capacity: 5,000; Year Built: 1967
AD: Doug Weiss
SID: Marty Valdez

CAL ST. LOS ANGELES
Los Angeles, CA 90032 II

Coach: David Yanai
Alma Mater: Long Beach St. '66
Record: 19 Years, W-287, L-223

1996-97 SCHEDULE
Westmont ■ .....Nov. 15
Biola ■ .....Nov. 19
Cal Baptist .....Nov. 26
UC Davis Shootout .....Dec. 6-7
San Fran. St. .....Dec. 13
Concordia (Cal.) ■ .....Dec. 14
Notre Dame (Cal.) ■ .....Dec. 19
Cal St. Stanislaus .....Dec. 21
Sonoma St. .....Dec. 23
Cal St. Hayward ■ .....Dec. 28
Master's .....Dec. 30
Christian Heritage .....Jan. 3
Pacific Christian .....Jan. 13
Cal Poly Pomona ■ .....Jan. 16
Cal St. Dom. Hills .....Jan. 18
Grand Canyon ■ .....Jan. 23
Master's ■ .....Jan. 25
Cal St. San B'dino .....Jan. 30
UC Riverside ■ .....Feb. 1
Cal St. Bakersfield ■ .....Feb. 6
Cal St. Dom. Hills ■ .....Feb. 8
Grand Canyon .....Feb. 13
UC Riverside .....Feb. 20
Cal St. San B'dino ■ .....Feb. 22
Cal Poly Pomona .....Feb. 27
Cal St. Bakersfield ■ .....Mar. 1

1995-96 RESULTS (9-18)
76 Hawaii Pacific † 74
81 Master's 68
73 Westmont ■ 86
77 Biola ■ 79
88 Cal St. Stanislaus ■ 67
68 Metro St. 76
67 Regis (Colo.) 73
63 Northern Ky. ■ 76
51 UC Davis ■ 53
72 Notre Dame (Cal.) 61
59 Cal St. Hayward 51
79 Bryant ■ 66
100 Pacific Christian ■ 59
80 Christian Heritage ■ 67
55 Grand Canyon 77
70 Cal St. San B'dino ■ 66
50 UC Riverside 63
42 Cal Poly Pomona ■ 65
65 Cal St. Dom. Hills ■ 78
61 Cal St. Bakersfield 74
79 Master's ■ 95
51 Cal St. San B'dino 54
65 UC Riverside ■ 86
50 Cal St. Dom. Hills 62
70 Cal Poly Pomona 74
57 Cal St. Bakersfield 81
71 Grand Canyon 79

Nickname: Golden Eagles
Colors: Black & Gold
Arena: Eagles' Nest
 Capacity: 5,000; Year Built: 1947
AD: Carol Dunn
SID: Kevin Glimore

CAL ST. NORTHRIDGE
Northridge, CA 91330 I

Coach: Bobby Braswell
Alma Mater: Cal St. Northridge '84
(First year as head coach)

1996-97 SCHEDULE
UNLV .....Nov. 23
Cal St. Dom. Hills ■ .....Nov. 27
Loyola Marymount .....Nov. 30
UCLA ■ .....Dec. 3
Ohio ■ .....Dec. 12
St. Mary's (Cal.) ■ .....Dec. 16
Pepperdine .....Dec. 19
UC Irvine ■ .....Dec. 21
UC Santa Barb. ■ .....Dec. 23
Iowa .....Dec. 29
Portland St. ■ .....Jan. 2
Eastern Wash. ■ .....Jan. 4
Montana St. .....Jan. 9
Montana .....Jan. 11
Cal St. Sacramento ■ .....Jan. 15
Weber St. ■ .....Jan. 16
Idaho St. .....Jan. 24

Northern Ariz. ■ .....Feb. 1
Montana ■ .....Feb. 6
Montana St. ■ .....Feb. 8
Eastern Wash. .....Feb. 13
Portland St. .....Feb. 15
Weber St. .....Feb. 20
Cal St. Sacramento .....Feb. 22
Northern Ariz. .....Feb. 27
Idaho St. ■ .....Mar. 1
Big Sky Conf. Tr. .....Mar. 6-8

1995-96 RESULTS (7-20)
56 UNLV 80
77 Fresno St. 97
77 Cal St. Fullerton ■ 76
81 Pepperdine ■ 90
74 Brigham Young 99
90 Stephen F. Austin † 95
74 Northeastern Ill. ■ 73
67 UC Santa Barb. 94
64 St. Mary's (Cal.) 67
55 Samford † 70
64 South Caro. St. † 59
59 Colorado Mines ■ 63
73 UC-Colo. Spgs. ■ 54
67 Grand Canyon 78
53 Oral Roberts 88
58 Oklahoma St. 91
56 San Diego ■ 72
65 Southern Utah 72
47 San Diego St. 80
71 Cal St. Sacramento 62
59 Cal Poly SLO 66
59 Oral Roberts ■ 77
96 Southern Utah ■ 75
84 Cal Poly SLO ■ 97
66 Cal St. Sacramento 83
81 Loyola Marymount ■ 75
54 Cal St. Sacramento 57

Nickname: Matadors
Colors: Red, White & Black
Arena: The Matadome
 Capacity: 3,000; Year Built: 1962
AD: Paul Bubb
SID: Ryan Finney

CAL ST. SACRAMENTO
Sacramento, CA 95819 I

Coach: Don Newman
Alma Mater: Idaho '80
Record: 3 Years, W-10, L-71

1996-97 SCHEDULE
Northern Ariz. .....Nov. 22
St. Mary's (Cal.) ■ .....Nov. 26
Montana .....Nov. 30
UC Davis .....Dec. 4
Colorado St. Cl. .....Dec. 6-7
Creighton .....Dec. 14
Pacific (Cal.) .....Dec. 23
Pacific (Cal.) ■ .....Jan. 4
Portland St. ■ .....Jan. 7
Eastern Wash. .....Jan. 9
Cal St. Northridge .....Jan. 15
Idaho St. .....Jan. 18
Montana St. ■ .....Jan. 22
Montana ■ .....Jan. 24
Oral Roberts ■ .....Jan. 26
Montana St. .....Jan. 30
Weber St. ■ .....Feb. 1
Portland St. .....Feb. 6
Eastern Wash. ■ .....Feb. 8
Montana .....Feb. 13
Idaho St. ■ .....Feb. 15
Northern Ariz. ■ .....Feb. 20
Cal St. Northridge ■ .....Feb. 22
Weber St. .....Feb. 27
Northern Ariz. .....Mar. 1
Big Sky Conf. Tr. .....Mar. 6-8

1995-96 RESULTS (7-20)
80 San Diego ■ 84
70 Montana 75
51 UC Davis ■ 50
69 Notre Dame (Cal.) ■ 59

60	Fairfield	.75
58	Georgetown	113
82	Idaho St.	.77
73	Arizona St.	.85
63	Minnesota	.86
91	Geo. Washington ■	.98
62	Old Dominion ■	.69
77	Idaho St.	.74
47	Montana St.	.90
44	Gonzaga	.66
67	Creighton ■	.74
75	St. Mary's (Cal.)	.87
86	Cal Poly SLO ■	102
55	San Diego St.	.85
62	Cal St. Northridge ■	.71
63	Cal Poly SLO	.79
66	Oral Roberts	.78
65	Eastern Wash. ■	.73
59	Southern Utah	.87
82	Southern Utah ■	.70
83	Cal St. Northridge ■	.66
71	Northern Ariz. ■	.66
66	Cal Poly SLO †	.73

Nickname: Hornets
Colors: Green & Gold
Arena: Memorial Auditorium
  Capacity: 4,500
AD: Judith Davidson
SID: To be named

CAL ST. SAN B'DINO
San Bernardino, CA 92407 II

Coach: Denny Aye
Alma Mater: St. Ambrose '73
Record: 2 Years, W-32, L-21

1996-97 SCHEDULE

San Fran. St.	Nov. 15
Sonoma St.	Nov. 16
Christian Heritage ■	Nov. 26
Pacific Christian ■	Dec. 3
Pt. Loma Nazarene ■	Dec. 5
Cal St. Stanislaus	Dec. 14
Cal St. Hayward ■	Dec. 16
Las Vegas Cl.	Dec. 18-19
Chico St. Tr.	Dec. 28-30
Azusa-Pacific ■	Jan. 8
Wis. Lutheran ■	Jan. 11
Grand Canyon	Jan. 16
Cal Poly Pomona ■	Jan. 23
Cal St. Dom. Hills	Jan. 25
Cal St. Los Angeles ■	Jan. 30
Cal St. Bakersfield ■	Feb. 1
UC Riverside	Feb. 6
Cal Poly Pomona	Feb. 13
Cal St. Dom. Hills ■	Feb. 15
Cal St. Bakersfield	Feb. 20
Cal St. Los Angeles	Feb. 22
UC Riverside ■	Feb. 27
Grand Canyon ■	Mar. 1

1995-96 RESULTS (15-12)

101	Southern Ore. St. †	.86
85	Humboldt St.	.93
79	San Fran. St. ■	.65
106	Pacific Christian ■	.54
63	Sonoma St. ■	.66
88	Colo. Christian	.74
73	Denver	.76
84	Westmont ■	.67
100	Notre Dame (Cal.)	.87
75	Cal St. Stanislaus	.60
70	Azusa-Pacific ■	.82
79	Humboldt St. ■	.59
78	MidAmerica Naz. ■	.58
61	St. Thomas Aquinas ■	.51
87	Lynn ■	.72
53	Cal Poly Pomona	.54
68	Cal St. Dom. Hills ■	.55
66	Cal St. Los Angeles	.70
81	Cal St. Bakersfield	.86
88	Grand Canyon ■	.93
67	UC Riverside	.73
61	Cal St. Dom. Hills	.78

54	Cal St. Los Angeles ■	.51
55	Cal St. Bakersfield ■	.81
99	Grand Canyon ■	.97
83	Cal Poly Pomona ■	.66
72	UC Riverside ■	.76

Nickname: Coyotes
Colors: Light Blue & Brown
Arena: Coussoulis Arena
  Capacity: 5,000; Year Built: 1994
AD: Nancy P. Simpson
SID: Bill Gray

CAL ST. STANISLAUS
Turlock, CA 95380 II

Coach: John Jones
Alma Mater: Humboldt St.
Record: 8 Years, W-114, L-106

1996-97 SCHEDULE

Pacific (Cal.)	Nov. 23
Fresno Pacific Tr.	Nov. 29-30
Cal St. Stanislaus Tr.	Dec. 6-7
Cal St. Bakersfield ■	Dec. 12
Cal St. San B'dino ■	Dec. 14
Fresno Pacific	Dec. 18
Cal St. Los Angeles ■	Dec. 21
Cal St. Bakersfield Tr.	Dec. 27-28
San Fran. St. ■	Jan. 3
Notre Dame (Cal.)	Jan. 4
Cal St. Chico	Jan. 10
UC Davis ■	Jan. 11
Sonoma St.	Jan. 17
Humboldt St.	Jan. 18
Cal St. Hayward	Jan. 25
Humboldt St. ■	Jan. 31
Sonoma St. ■	Feb. 1
UC Davis	Feb. 7
Cal St. Chico ■	Feb. 8
San Fran. St.	Feb. 14
Notre Dame (Cal.) ■	Feb. 15
Cal St. Hayward ■	Feb. 20

1995-96 RESULTS (8-18)

67	Fresno Pacific ■	.76
49	Southern Utah	.84
73	San Jose Christian ■	.71
47	Fresno Pacific ■	.69
71	Cal St. Bakersfield ■	.98
67	Cal St. Los Angeles ■	.88
67	Grand Canyon	.87
87	Southwest Adventist	.73
60	Cal St. San B'dino ■	.75
50	UC Davis †	.74
85	Colorado Mines †	.88
70	San Fran. St.	.85
68	San Fran. St. ■	.67
63	Notre Dame (Cal.) ■	.79
83	Cal St. Chico ■	.85
54	UC Davis	.86
70	Sonoma St. ■	.79
79	Humboldt St. ■	.57
89	Cal St. Hayward ■	.85
74	Humboldt St.	.97
65	Sonoma St.	.82
73	UC Davis ■	.84
73	Cal St. Chico	.78
84	San Fran. St. ■	.73
92	Notre Dame (Cal.) ■	.83
78	Cal St. Hayward	.77

Nickname: Warriors
Colors: Red & Gold
Arena: Warrior Gym
  Capacity: 2,000; Year Built: 1978
AD: Joe Donahue
SID: Will Keener

CAL TECH
Pasadena, CA 91125 III

Coach: Gene Victor
Alma Mater: Cal St. Los Angeles
Record: 9 Years, W-46, L-159

1996-97 SCHEDULE

LIFE Bible ■	Nov. 15
Pacific Christian ■	Nov. 20
Simpson (Cal.) ■	Nov. 22
Cal Tech Tr. #1	Nov. 29-30
S'western (Ariz.) ■	Dec. 6
Cal Tech Tr. #2	Jan. 3-4
Cal Lutheran	Jan. 11
La Verne	Jan. 15
Redlands ■	Jan. 18
Occidental ■	Jan. 22
Pomona-Pitzer	Jan. 25
Claremont-M-S	Jan. 29
Whittier ■	Feb. 1
Cal Lutheran ■	Feb. 5
La Verne ■	Feb. 8
Redlands	Feb. 12
Occidental	Feb. 15
Pomona-Pitzer ■	Feb. 19
Claremont-M-S ■	Feb. 22
Whittier	Feb. 26

1995-96 RESULTS (4-19)

62	LIFE Bible ■	.67
64	Cal Maritime ■	.48
66	La Sierra	.69
33	Washington (Mo.)	.65
40	MIT †	.46
53	Principia ■	.50
44	La Sierra ■	.54
76	Arizona Bible ■	.55
71	S'western (Ariz.) ■	.61
59	Occidental	.71
37	Whittier	.70
59	Redlands ■	.58
51	Cal Lutheran ■	.73
39	Claremont-M-S	.72
41	Pomona-Pitzer	.92
55	La Verne ■	.59
44	Occidental ■	.68
47	Whittier ■	.62
68	Redlands	.71
40	Cal Lutheran	.84
33	Claremont-M-S ■	.70
39	Pomona-Pitzer ■	.65
36	La Verne	.63

Nickname: Beavers
Colors: Orange & White
Arena: Braun Athletic Center
  Capacity: 1,500; Year Built: 1992
AD: Dan Bridges
SID: Denise Gabaldon

UC DAVIS
Davis, CA 95616 II

Coach: Bob Williams
Alma Mater: San Jose St. '75
Record: 8 Years, W-134, L-90

1996-97 SCHEDULE

Cal St. Bakersfield	Nov. 16
Patten ■	Nov. 26
UC Santa Cruz ■	Nov. 30
Cal St. Sacramento ■	Dec. 4
UC Davis Shootout	Dec. 6-7
San Jose Christian ■	Dec. 14
Seattle Pacific ■	Dec. 18
Dominican (Cal.) ■	Dec. 21
Grand Canyon Cl.	Dec. 27-28
Sonoma St.	Jan. 3
Humboldt St.	Jan. 4
Cal St. Hayward ■	Jan. 10
Cal St. Stanislaus	Jan. 11
Notre Dame (Cal.) ■	Jan. 17
San Fran. St.	Jan. 18
Cal St. Chico	Jan. 25
Notre Dame (Cal.)	Jan. 31
San Fran. St. ■	Feb. 1
Cal St. Stanislaus ■	Feb. 7
Cal St. Hayward	Feb. 8
Humboldt St. ■	Feb. 14
Sonoma St. ■	Feb. 15
Cal St. Chico	Feb. 20

1995-96 RESULTS (24-6)

71	Dominican (Cal.) ■	.60
82	Bethany (Cal.)	.42
50	Cal St. Sacramento	.51
62	Colorado Mines	.68
76	UC-Colo. Spgs. †	.61
83	Patten ■	.67
61	Cal St. Bakersfield ■	.75
62	Pacific (Cal.)	.76
60	Cal Poly Pomona	.34
53	Cal St. Los Angeles	.51
74	Cal St. Stanislaus †	.50
71	Cal St. Bakersfield	.76
67	Sonoma St. ■	.66
82	Humboldt St. ■	.61
73	Cal St. Hayward	.58
86	Cal St. Stanislaus ■	.54
55	Notre Dame (Cal.) ■	.52
70	San Fran. St. ■	.51
90	Cal St. Chico	.75
67	Notre Dame (Cal.) ■	.50
61	San Fran. St.	.59
84	Cal St. Stanislaus	.73
70	Cal St. Hayward ■	.55
78	Humboldt St.	.63
80	Sonoma St.	.68
70	Cal St. Chico	.62
94	Cal St. Chico ■	.79
75	Sonoma St. ■	.67
89	Mont. St.-Billings †	.80
65	Seattle Pacific †	.79

Nickname: Aggies
Colors: Yale Blue & Gold
Arena: Recreation Hall
  Capacity: 7,600; Year Built: 1977
AD: Greg Warzecka
SID: Mike Robles

UC IRVINE
Irvine, CA 92697 I

Coach: Rod Baker
Alma Mater: Holy Cross '74
Record: 10 Years, W-123, L-143

1996-97 SCHEDULE

San Diego St.	Nov. 22
Washington St.	Dec. 2
Eastern Wash.	Dec. 4
UNLV ■	Dec. 7
Southern Cal ■	Dec. 15
Cal St. Northridge ■	Dec. 21
San Diego	Dec. 23
Utah ■	Dec. 28
San Francisco	Jan. 5
Pacific (Cal.) ■	Jan. 9
Long Beach St. ■	Jan. 11
Cal Poly SLO	Jan. 16
UC Santa Barb.	Jan. 18
Nevada ■	Jan. 23
Cal St. Fullerton	Jan. 25
Boise St.	Jan. 30
Idaho	Feb. 1
North Texas ■	Feb. 6
New Mexico St. ■	Feb. 8
Cal St. Fullerton	Feb. 13
Utah St.	Feb. 15
Long Beach St.	Feb. 20
Pacific (Cal.)	Feb. 22
Southern Utah	Feb. 25
UC Santa Barb. ■	Feb. 27
Cal Poly SLO ■	Mar. 1
Big West Conf. Tr.	Mar. 7-9

1995-96 RESULTS (15-12)

87	Siena †	.70
83	St. John's (N.Y.)	.77
57	Oregon St.	.64
86	Eastern Wash. ■	.66
79	Southern Cal	.82
78	San Diego	.81
81	Washington St. ■	.88
72	Pacific (Cal.) ■	.54
78	San Jose St. ■	.70
66	UC Santa Barb.	.84

73	Cal St. Fullerton	.81
74	New Mexico St. ■	.66
66	UNLV ■	.61
72	Nevada	.70
78	Utah St.	.72
74	UC Santa Barb. ■	.62
65	Long Beach St. ■	.69
85	Southern Utah ■	.75
85	Cal St. Fullerton ■	.75
84	Long Beach St.	.81
77	New Mexico St.	.83
60	UNLV	.63
74	Nevada ■	.68
81	Utah St. ■	.76
70	San Jose St.	.81
74	Pacific (Cal.)	.80
67	San Jose St. †	.71

Nickname: Anteaters
Colors: Blue & Gold
Arena: Bren Events Center
  Capacity: 5,000; Year Built: 1987
AD: Dan Guerrero
SID: Bob Olson

UC RIVERSIDE
Riverside, CA 92521 II

Coach: John Masi
Alma Mater: UC Riverside '70
Record: 17 Years, W-354, L-138

1996-97 SCHEDULE
Seattle ■	Nov. 22
Cal Baptist ■	Nov. 23
Notre Dame (Cal.)	Dec. 6
Sonoma St.	Dec. 7
Point Loma Tr.	Dec. 13-14
Las Vegas Cl.	Dec. 18-19
Chico St. Tr.	Dec. 28-30
UC Santa Cruz ■	Jan. 10
Grand Canyon	Jan. 18
Cal St. Dom. Hills ■	Jan. 23
Cal Poly Pomona	Jan. 25
Cal St. Bakersfield	Jan. 30
Cal St. Los Angeles	Feb. 1
Cal St. San B'dino ■	Feb. 6
Grand Canyon ■	Feb. 8
Cal St. Dom. Hills	Feb. 13
Cal Poly Pomona ■	Feb. 15
Cal St. Los Angeles ■	Feb. 20
Cal St. Bakersfield ■	Feb. 22
Cal St. San B'dino	Feb. 27
Master's	Mar. 1

1995-96 RESULTS (18-9)
95	Cal Baptist	.71
85	Cal St. Chico ■	.71
85	Master's ■	.88
84	Sonoma St. ■	.69
95	Pacific Christian ■	.62
83	Cal St. Hayward	.66
78	Notre Dame (Cal.)	.52
87	Mo. Western St. †	.89
81	Central Mo. St. †	.82
72	Western N.M. †	.50
72	Master's †	.81
99	Alas. Fairbanks †	.69
79	Olivet Nazarene	.65
103	UC San Diego ■	.64
75	St. Thomas Aquinas ■	.56
63	Cal St. Dom. Hills	.66
64	Cal Poly Pomona ■	.77
63	Cal St. Bakersfield	.74
63	Cal St. Los Angeles ■	.50
77	Grand Canyon ■	.69
73	Cal St. San B'dino ■	.67
70	Cal Poly Pomona	.53
62	Cal St. Bakersfield ■	.69
86	Cal St. Los Angeles	.65
78	Grand Canyon	.86
70	Cal St. Dom. Hills ■	.51
76	Cal St. San B'dino	.72

Nickname: Highlanders
Colors: Blue & Gold
Arena: UCR Student Rec Center

Capacity: 2,800; Year Built: 1994
AD: John Masi
SID: Tom Phillips

UC SAN DIEGO
La Jolla, CA 92093 III

Coach: Greg Lanthier
Alma Mater: Point Loma '87
Record: 2 Years, W-23, L-27

1996-97 SCHEDULE
Claremont-M-S ■	Nov. 22
Whittier	Nov. 23
Occidental	Nov. 26
UC San Diego Tr.	Nov. 29-30
Pomona-Pitzer ■	Dec. 3
Redlands Tr.	Dec. 5-7
Wooster ■	Dec. 18
Cal Lutheran ■	Dec. 22
Clark (Mass.)	Dec. 27
Gust. Adolphus	Dec. 31
La Jolla Cl.	Jan. 3-4
Redlands	Jan. 8
Chapman ■	Jan. 24
Menlo ■	Jan. 31
UC Santa Cruz ■	Feb. 1
Master's	Feb. 8
Chapman	Feb. 14
Menlo	Feb. 21
UC Santa Cruz	Feb. 22
Christian Heritage ■	Feb. 25

1995-96 RESULTS (11-14)
92	Redlands	.91
105	Occidental ■	.111
92	Christian Heritage ■	.95
75	Cal Poly Pomona ■	.101
67	Concordia (Cal.) †	.87
87	Menlo †	.73
94	Hamline †	.80
89	Pomona-Pitzer	.81
100	Whittier ■	.90
88	Claremont-M-S	.96
66	Cal Lutheran	.101
88	Azusa-Pacific	.90
83	Sewanee ■	.71
104	Ripon ■	.97
64	UC Riverside	.103
78	Chapman	.90
94	Master's ■	.110
117	Menlo ■	.65
86	Chapman ■	.93
85	Pt. Loma Nazarene	.89
69	Menlo	.65
83	UC Santa Cruz	.82
78	Southern Cal Col.	.99
88	Christian Heritage	.103
99	UC Santa Cruz	.76

Nickname: Tritons
Colors: Blue & Gold
Arena: RIMAC Arena
  Capacity: 5,000; Year Built: 1995
AD: Judith Sweet
SID: Bill Gannon

UC SANTA BARB.
Santa Barbara, CA 93106 I

Coach: Jerry Pimm
Alma Mater: Southern Cal '60
Record: 22 Years, W-376, L-254

1996-97 SCHEDULE
Westmont ■	Nov. 22
Pepperdine	Nov. 25
St. Mary's (Cal.)	Dec. 1
UC Santa Barbara Cl.	Dec. 5-7
San Francisco ■	Dec. 14
Colorado	Dec. 21
Cal St. Northridge ■	Dec. 23
San Diego ■	Dec. 30
Loyola Marymount ■	Jan. 4
North Texas ■	Jan. 9

Cal Poly SLO	Jan. 11
Cal St. Fullerton ■	Jan. 16
UC Irvine ■	Jan. 18
Long Beach St.	Jan. 23
Pacific (Cal.)	Jan. 25
Nevada	Jan. 30
Utah St.	Feb. 1
Idaho ■	Feb. 6
Boise St. ■	Feb. 8
Pacific (Cal.) ■	Feb. 13
Long Beach St. ■	Feb. 15
New Mexico St. ■	Feb. 20
Cal Poly SLO ■	Feb. 22
UC Irvine ■	Feb. 27
Cal St. Fullerton	Mar. 1
Big West Conf. Tr.	Mar. 7-9

1995-96 RESULTS (11-15)
71	Colorado ■	.47
71	DePaul	.91
76	San Diego	.73
73	Loyola Marymount	.83
67	Pepperdine ■	.68
94	Cal St. Northridge ■	.67
66	St. Joseph's (Pa.)	.84
78	St. Mary's (Cal.)	.80
54	Long Beach St.	.76
65	Cal St. Fullerton ■	.62
84	UC Irvine ■	.66
60	New Mexico St.	.56
55	UNLV	.64
64	Nevada ■	.72
85	Utah St. ■	.80
66	Pacific (Cal.)	.64
80	San Jose St.	.77
62	UC Irvine	.74
85	Cal St. Fullerton	.72
59	New Mexico St. ■	.60
65	UNLV ■	.57
63	Utah St.	.78
61	Nevada	.65
66	San Jose St. ■	.69
72	Pacific (Cal.) ■	.79
69	Long Beach St. ■	.74

Nickname: Gauchos
Colors: Blue & Gold
Arena: The Thunderdome
  Capacity: 6,000; Year Built: 1979
AD: Gary Cunningham
SID: Bill Mahoney

UC SANTA CRUZ
Santa Cruz, CA 95064 III

Coach: Duane Garner
Alma Mater: Kalamazoo '76
Record: 5 Years, W-42, L-79

1996-97 SCHEDULE
Menlo Cl.	Nov. 22-23
Bethany (Cal.)	Nov. 26
UC Davis	Nov. 30
Cal Poly SLO	Dec. 3
Redlands Tr.	Dec. 5-7
Humboldt St. ■	Dec. 13
UC Santa Cruz Tr.	Jan. 3-4
UC Riverside	Jan. 10
Cal Maritime ■	Jan. 18
San Jose Christian ■	Jan. 24
Chapman	Jan. 31
UC San Diego	Feb. 1
San Jose Christian	Feb. 14
Chapman ■	Feb. 21
UC San Diego ■	Feb. 22

1995-96 RESULTS (7-17)
98	Menlo	.87
31	Col. of Idaho	.111
77	Whitman ■	.80
73	Redlands	.85
78	Hamline †	.90
55	Menlo †	.69
68	Whittier ■	.81
51	Southern Cal Col.	.74

61	Cal Poly SLO	.118
72	Western Ore. ■	.87
69	Dominican (Cal.) ■	.82
71	Simpson (Cal.) ■	.62
68	Menlo	.79
83	Chapman ■	.82
73	Dominican (Cal.)	.69
67	Bethany (Cal.) ■	.56
92	San Jose Christian	.89
37	Southern Utah	.94
67	San Jose Christian ■	.63
82	UC San Diego ■	.83
73	Bethany (Cal.)	.86
75	Menlo ■	.84
61	Chapman	.96
76	UC San Diego	.99

Nickname: Banana Slugs
Colors: Blue & Gold
Arena: West Field House
  Capacity: 300
AD: Mark Majeski
SID: To be named

CALVIN
Grand Rapids, MI 49546 III

Coach: Kevin van de Streek
Alma Mater: Dordt '81
Record: 6 Years, W-93, L-80

1996-97 SCHEDULE
Wheaton (Ill.) Cl.	Nov. 22-23
Calvin Shootout	Nov. 29-30
Wayne St. (Mich.)	Dec. 10
Oakland (Mich.) Cl.	Dec. 27-28
Aquinas	Jan. 4
Alma	Jan. 8
Albion ■	Jan. 11
Olivet	Jan. 15
Kalamazoo	Jan. 18
Adrian ■	Jan. 22
St. Mary's (Mich.)	Jan. 25
Hope ■	Jan. 29
Alma ■	Feb. 1
Albion	Feb. 5
Olivet ■	Feb. 8
Kalamazoo ■	Feb. 12
Adrian	Feb. 15
St. Mary's (Mich.) ■	Feb. 18
Hope	Feb. 22

1995-96 RESULTS (16-10)
80	Point Park †	.86
75	Defiance †	.67
78	Michigan Christian ■	.61
85	Aquinas ■	.53
67	Ferris St. ■	.53
61	Wabash	.57
77	Wheaton (Ill.)	.92
61	Wayne St. (Mich.) ■	.64
66	Kenyon †	.67
75	MacMurray †	.53
73	Alma	.75
71	Albion	.82
81	Olivet ■	.60
59	Kalamazoo ■	.65
92	Adrian	.61
82	Madonna ■	.73
70	Hope	.93
94	Alma	.85
85	Albion ■	.44
72	Olivet	.61
76	Kalamazoo	.73
82	Adrian ■	.83
104	Grace Bible (Mich.) ■	.37
66	Hope	.67
87	Olivet ■	.68
68	Kalamazoo †	.83

Nickname: Knights
Colors: Maroon & Gold
Arena: Calvin Fieldhouse
  Capacity: 4,200; Year Built: 1965
AD: Ralph Honderd
SID: Jeff Febus

CAMERON
Lawton, OK 73501 II

Coach: Jerry Stone
Alma Mater: McMurry '63
Record: 11 Years, W-110, L-179

1996-97 SCHEDULE
Mid-America Bible ■	Nov. 15
Mary Hardin-Baylor ■	Nov. 19
Midwestern St. Cl.	Nov. 22-23
Western N.M. Tr.	Nov. 29-30
Drury	Dec. 3
Ambassador ■	Dec. 4
Midwestern St. ■	Dec. 7
East Central	Dec. 11
McMurry ■	Dec. 14
Western N.M. ■	Jan. 6
Bartlesville Wesl. ■	Jan. 8
Northeastern Okla. ■	Jan. 11
Southeastern Okla.	Jan. 13
East Central ■	Jan. 15
Langston	Jan. 18
Tarleton St. ■	Jan. 25
Mary Hardin-Baylor	Jan. 29
Okla. Sci. & Arts ■	Feb. 1
Northeastern Okla.	Feb. 5
Southeastern Okla. ■	Feb. 8
Langston ■	Feb. 12
Tarleton St.	Feb. 17
Midwestern St.	Feb. 22
Okla. Sci. & Arts	Feb. 24
Drury ■	Feb. 26

1995-96 RESULTS (12-14)
88	Angelo St. †	79
81	Abilene Christian	90
71	Stephen F. Austin	90
83	Tarleton St. ■	80
81	West Tex. A&M ■	71
88	Midwestern St.	82
88	Okla. Sci. & Arts ■	72
114	Central Okla. ■	97
71	Mo. Southern St.	80
76	Central Mo. St. †	83
87	Chaminade †	68
77	East Central ■	86
86	Midwestern St.	101
70	East Central	77
66	Southeastern Okla. ■	92
57	Texas A&M-Commerce ■	65
60	West Tex. A&M	69
72	Tarleton St.	66
68	Southwestern Okla. ■	63
76	Southwestern Okla.	69
88	Central Okla.	100
77	Abilene Christian ■	74
57	Southeastern Okla. ■	66
67	Okla. Sci. & Arts	71
54	Texas A&M-Commerce	66
80	Drury ■	61

Nickname: Aggies
Colors: Gold & Black
Arena: Aggie Gymnasium
 Capacity: 1,800; Year Built: 1958
AD: Sam Carrol
SID: Bob Beumer

CAMPBELL
Buies Creek, NC 27506 I

Coach: Billy Lee
Alma Mater: Barton '71
Record: 18 Years, W-275, L-245

1996-97 SCHEDULE
Clinch Valley ■	Nov. 27
East Caro. ■	Dec. 2
Tusculum ■	Dec. 12
N.C.-Wilmington	Dec. 14
Richmond	Dec. 19
Wake Forest	Dec. 21
Boise St. Cl.	Dec. 27-28
Georgia St.	Jan. 2
Mercer	Jan. 4

Samford ■	Jan. 9
Jacksonville St.	Jan. 11
Duke	Jan. 13
Florida Int'l ■	Jan. 16
Fla. Atlantic ■	Jan. 18
Wofford	Jan. 20
Charleston (S.C.)	Jan. 25
Stetson	Jan. 30
Central Fla.	Feb. 1
Charleston (S.C.) ■	Feb. 3
Stetson ■	Feb. 6
Central Fla. ■	Feb. 8
Fla. Atlantic	Feb. 13
Florida Int'l	Feb. 15
Centenary (La.) ■	Feb. 20
Southeastern La.	Feb. 22
Trans America Conf. Tr.	Feb. 27-Mar. 1

1995-96 RESULTS (17-11)
62	Richmond ■	69
76	Georgia Tech	87
60	N.C.-Greensboro	69
88	St. Andrews ■	57
68	Methodist ■	50
74	N.C.-Wilmington	52
57	East Caro.	62
43	Clemson	67
60	Georgia St.	57
60	Mercer ■	57
63	Hampton ■	62
58	Samford	62
73	Jacksonville St. ■	62
69	Florida Int'l	66
75	Fla. Atlantic	69
78	Wofford ■	62
74	Charleston (S.C.) ■	76
62	Stetson ■	75
58	Central Fla. ■	79
45	Charleston (S.C.)	58
53	Stetson	50
70	Central Fla.	69
68	Fla. Atlantic ■	66
64	Florida Int'l ■	57
75	Centenary (La.)	58
69	Southeastern La.	65
67	Stetson	59
71	Central Fla. †	80

Nickname: Fighting Camels
Colors: Orange & Black
Arena: Carter Gymnasium
 Capacity: 945; Year Built: 1953
AD: Tom Collins
SID: Stan Cole

CANISIUS
Buffalo, NY 14208 I

Coach: John Beilein
Alma Mater: Wheeling Jesuit '75
Record: 14 Years, W-255, L-150

1996-97 SCHEDULE
Western Mich. ■	Nov. 23
Valparaiso ■	Nov. 25
St. Bonaventure ■	Nov. 30
Buffalo	Dec. 3
Niagara ■	Dec. 7
Akron ■	Dec. 15
Toledo	Dec. 18
N.C.-Charlotte ■	Dec. 21
Tenn.-Chatt. Cl.	Dec. 28-29
Colgate ■	Jan. 2
Fairfield	Jan. 6
Kentucky	Jan. 9
Manhattan ■	Jan. 14
Loyola (Md.) ■	Jan. 20
Providence	Jan. 22
St. Peter's	Jan. 26
Iona ■	Jan. 31
Siena ■	Feb. 2
Niagara	Feb. 5
Fairfield ■	Feb. 8
St. Peter's ■	Feb. 10
Loyola (Md.)	Feb. 13
Siena	Feb. 15

Iona	Feb. 21
Manhattan	Feb. 23
Metro Atlantic Conf. Tr.	Mar. 1-3

1995-96 RESULTS (19-11)
73	Western Mich.	53
68	Akron	72
77	St. Bonaventure ■	64
82	Buffalo	75
62	Washington St. †	73
64	Columbia †	42
65	Colgate	63
75	Toledo	67
72	Valparaiso	68
62	Colgate ■	51
63	Fairfield	56
63	Providence	91
71	Niagara	74
53	St. Bonaventure	38
64	St. Peter's	68
72	Iona	75
82	Fairfield ■	72
62	Manhattan ■	57
76	Iona ■	54
60	Siena	55
72	Loyola (Md.)	67
56	Niagara ■	58
66	Siena ■	49
63	Loyola (Md.) ■	64
57	St. Peter's ■	60
61	Manhattan	78
74	Loyola (Md.) †	67
63	Iona †	62
52	Fairfield †	46
43	Utah †	72

Nickname: Golden Griffins
Colors: Blue & Gold
Arena: Marine Midland Arena
 Capacity: 20,000; Year Built: 1996
AD: Daniel P. Starr
SID: John Maddock

CAPITAL
Columbus, OH 43209..............III

Coach: Damon Goodwin
Alma Mater: Dayton '86
Record: 2 Years, W-33, L-19

1996-97 SCHEDULE
Capital Cl.	Nov. 22-23
Ohio Wesleyan ■	Nov. 30
Marietta ■	Dec. 4
Hiram ■	Dec. 7
Baldwin-Wallace	Dec. 14
Ohio Northern ■	Dec. 18
Wis.-Platteville Tr.	Dec. 27-28
Wilmington (Ohio) ■	Jan. 6
Otterbein	Jan. 8
Mount Union	Jan. 11
John Carroll ■	Jan. 15
Muskingum	Jan. 18
Heidelberg ■	Jan. 22
Mount Union ■	Jan. 25
John Carroll	Jan. 29
Muskingum ■	Feb. 1
Heidelberg ■	Feb. 5
Hiram	Feb. 8
Marietta	Feb. 12
Baldwin-Wallace ■	Feb. 15
Otterbein ■	Feb. 19
Ohio Northern	Feb. 22

1995-96 RESULTS (19-8)
93	Defiance ■	61
102	Point Park ■	87
70	Wittenberg ■	65
78	Mount Union	82
86	Ohio Northern ■	77
86	Baldwin-Wallace	97
85	John Carroll	89
71	Wilmington (Ohio)	63
69	Tri-State †	64
77	Albion †	83
71	Heidelberg ■	66
69	Otterbein ■	68

78	Marietta	75
85	Muskingum ■	84
97	Hiram ■	73
84	Otterbein ■	75
57	Marietta ■	60
71	Baldwin-Wallace ■	70
63	Ohio Northern	78
84	John Carroll ■	74
81	Heidelberg ■	78
89	Mount Union ■	66
79	Hiram	73
75	Muskingum	61
58	Marietta ■	69
68	Ohio Northern	57
60	Wittenberg	65

Nickname: Crusaders
Colors: Purple & White
Arena: Alumni Gymnasium
 Capacity: 2,300; Year Built: 1951
AD: Roger Welsh
SID: Barry Katz

CARLETON
Northfield, MN 55057 III

Coach: Guy Kalland
Alma Mater: Concordia (Minn.) '74
Record: 12 Years, W-155, L-147

1996-97 SCHEDULE
BYU-Hawaii Tr.	Nov. 29-30
Chaminade	Dec. 3
St. Thomas (Minn.)	Dec. 7
St. John's (Minn.)	Dec. 11
Concordia-M'head	Dec. 14
Macalester	Jan. 4
Bethel (Minn.) ■	Jan. 6
Hamline ■	Jan. 8
Augsburg	Jan. 11
Gust. Adolphus ■	Jan. 13
St. Olaf	Jan. 15
St. Mary's (Minn.)	Jan. 22
St. Thomas (Minn.) ■	Jan. 25
St. John's (Minn.) ■	Jan. 29
Concordia-M'head	Feb. 1
Macalester ■	Feb. 3
Bethel (Minn.)	Feb. 5
Hamline	Feb. 8
Augsburg ■	Feb. 12
Gust. Adolphus	Feb. 15
St. Olaf ■	Feb. 17
St. Mary's (Minn.)	Feb. 22

1995-96 RESULTS (17-8)
78	Illinois Tech	59
80	Chicago	82
100	Benedictine (Ill.)	96
62	St. Cloud St.	82
58	Gust. Adolphus	65
78	St. John's (Minn.) ■	65
57	St. Mary's (Minn.)	59
78	St. Olaf	72
82	Augsburg ■	84
77	Concordia-M'head	84
84	Macalester	50
87	Bethel (Minn.) ■	71
91	Hamline	78
84	St. Thomas (Minn.) ■	72
57	Gust. Adolphus ■	73
81	St. John's (Minn.)	73
61	St. Mary's (Minn.) ■	43
84	St. Olaf ■	64
73	Augsburg	66
100	Concordia-M'head ■	78
87	Macalester ■	71
111	Bethel (Minn.)	104
76	Hamline ■	58
92	St. Thomas (Minn.)	71
71	Concordia-M'head	83

Nickname: Knights
Colors: Maize & Blue
Arena: West Gymnasium
 Capacity: 1,850; Year Built: 1964
AD: Leon Lunder
SID: Ryan Beckers

CARNEGIE MELLON
Pittsburgh, PA 15213 ... III

Coach: Tony Wingen
Alma Mater: Springfield '82
Record: 8 Years, W-90, L-102

1996-97 SCHEDULE
Grove City [Washington] ... Nov. 22
Wash. & Jeff. ... Nov. 23
Case Reserve ... Nov. 26
Carnegie Mellon Inv. ... Nov. 30-Dec. 1
Emory ■ ... Dec. 8
Pittsburgh ... Dec. 16
Wabash-DePauw Cl. ... Dec. 21-22
Dickinson ... Jan. 7
Rochester ... Jan. 11
Thiel ... Jan. 14
Johns Hopkins ■ ... Jan. 17
La Roche ■ ... Jan. 21
New York U. ... Jan. 24
Brandeis ... Jan. 26
Washington (Mo.) ■ ... Jan. 31
Chicago ■ ... Feb. 2
Brandeis ■ ... Feb. 7
New York U. ■ ... Feb. 9
Chicago ... Feb. 14
Washington (Mo.) ... Feb. 16
Emory ... Feb. 21
Thiel ■ ... Feb. 27
Rochester ■ ... Mar. 1

1995-96 RESULTS (13-12)
70 Wash. & Jeff. ■ ... 62
68 Grove City ... 64
73 Case Reserve ■ ... 63
89 Keuka ■ ... 83
61 John Carroll ■ ... 66
60 Robert Morris ... 94
61 Emory ... 62
66 Juniata ■ ... 70
75 Trinity (Tex.) † ... 55
57 Springfield ... 66
67 Rochester ■ ... 63
101 Thiel ... 70
73 Johns Hopkins ... 82
55 New York U. ■ ... 71
85 Brandeis ■ ... 76
74 Washington (Mo.) ... 93
68 Chicago ... 70
87 Brandeis ... 82
59 New York U. ... 83
68 Chicago ■ ... 71
67 Washington (Mo.) ■ ... 78
69 Emory ■ ... 63
78 La Roche ... 73
57 Thiel ■ ... 55
58 Rochester ... 52

Nickname: Tartans
Colors: Cardinal, White & Grey
Arena: Skibo Gymnasium
Capacity: 1,500; Year Built: 1924
AD: John Harvey
SID: E. J. Borghetti

CARROLL (WIS.)
Waukesha, WI 53186 ... III

Coach: Gary Richert
Alma Mater: Lakeland '66
(First year as head coach)

1996-97 SCHEDULE
Barat ■ ... Nov. 23
Benedictine (Ill.) ■ ... Dec. 3
Maranatha Bapt. ... Dec. 5
Wis.-Whitewater ■ ... Dec. 7
Elmhurst ... Dec. 14
Flager Inv. ... Jan. 3-4
Milwaukee Engr. ... Jan. 8
Ripon ■ ... Jan. 11
St. Norbert ... Jan. 14
Monmouth (Ill.) ■ ... Jan. 17
Cornell College ■ ... Jan. 18
Knox ... Jan. 24
Illinois Col. ... Jan. 25
Beloit ... Jan. 29
Lake Forest ■ ... Feb. 1
Lawrence ■ ... Feb. 5
Ripon ... Feb. 8
St. Norbert ■ ... Feb. 12
Beloit ■ ... Feb. 15
Lake Forest ... Feb. 18
Lawrence ... Feb. 22

1995-96 RESULTS (16-7)
58 Milwaukee Engr. ■ ... 43
70 Wis.-Whitewater ... 73
81 Chicago ... 59
74 Aurora † ... 75
77 Benedictine (Ill.) ... 71
77 Maranatha Bapt. ■ ... 63
77 Embry-Riddle † ... 85
76 Skidmore † ... 66
72 Lawrence ■ ... 49
58 Ripon ... 90
57 St. Norbert ■ ... 54
75 Cornell College ... 62
82 Monmouth (Ill.) ... 61
77 Beloit ... 64
99 Illinois Col. ■ ... 81
58 Knox ■ ... 60
77 Lake Forest ■ ... 66
104 Beloit ■ ... 66
91 Lawrence ... 80
82 Ripon ■ ... 85
59 St. Norbert ... 57
63 Lake Forest ... 60
106 Grinnell ... 109

Nickname: Pioneers
Colors: Orange & White
Arena: Van Male Fieldhouse
Capacity: 2,000; Year Built: 1965
AD: Merle Masonholder
SID: Shawn Ama

CARSON-NEWMAN
Jefferson City, TN 37760 ... II

Coach: Dale Clayton
Alma Mater: Milligan '73
Record: 8 Years, W-108, L-120

1996-97 SCHEDULE
Lees-McRae ■ ... Nov. 16
Tusculum ... Nov. 18
Knoxville ■ ... Nov. 20
IU/PU-Indianapolis ... Nov. 23
Lincoln Memorial ■ ... Nov. 26
Elon ... Dec. 3
Tusculum ■ ... Dec. 7
Lincoln Memorial ... Dec. 14
Rollins Tr. ... Jan. 3-4
Gardner-Webb ■ ... Jan. 8
Catawba ■ ... Jan. 11
Mars Hill ... Jan. 15
Wingate ■ ... Jan. 18
Lenoir-Rhyne ■ ... Jan. 22
Presbyterian ... Jan. 25
Newberry ... Jan. 27
Elon ■ ... Feb. 1
Gardner-Webb ... Feb. 5
Catawba ... Feb. 8
Newberry ■ ... Feb. 10
Mars Hill ■ ... Feb. 12
Wingate ... Feb. 15
Lenoir-Rhyne ... Feb. 19
Presbyterian ■ ... Feb. 22

1995-96 RESULTS (13-15)
60 Indianapolis ... 80
52 Oakland City † ... 55
67 Lincoln Memorial ... 68
68 Francis Marion † ... 65
88 Emmanuel † ... 66
63 East Tenn. St. ... 86
71 Lees-McRae ... 79
66 Newberry ■ ... 53
66 Lincoln Memorial ■ ... 48
106 Knoxville ■ ... 60
60 Lees-McRae ■ ... 65
58 Presbyterian ... 73
77 Lenoir-Rhyne ... 72
67 Elon ■ ... 73
82 Gardner-Webb ... 91
70 Catawba ■ ... 68
80 Mars Hill ■ ... 75
63 Wingate ... 61
69 Newberry ... 80
69 Lenoir-Rhyne ■ ... 79
71 Elon ... 70
85 Gardner-Webb ■ ... 79
61 Catawba ... 66
60 Presbyterian ■ ... 67
80 Mars Hill ... 95
78 Wingate ■ ... 64
89 Gardner-Webb † ... 74
60 Presbyterian † ... 71

Nickname: Eagles
Colors: Orange & Blue
Arena: Holt Fieldhouse
Capacity: 2,000; Year Built: 1961
AD: David Barger
SID: Eric Trainer

CARTHAGE
Kenosha, WI 53140 ... III

Coach: Bosko Djurickovic
Alma Mater: Loyola Marymount '70
Record: 9 Years, W-180, L-70

1996-97 SCHEDULE
Beloit ■ ... Nov. 23
Lake Forest ■ ... Nov. 24
Wis.-Parkside ■ ... Nov. 26
Lakeland ■ ... Nov. 30
Wis.-Oshkosh ... Dec. 3
Ill. Wesleyan ... Dec. 7
Mt. Senario ■ ... Dec. 9
Edgewood ... Dec. 14
Tampa ... Dec. 28
Rollins ... Dec. 30
St. Norbert ■ ... Jan. 4
North Park ■ ... Jan. 8
Millikin ■ ... Jan. 11
North Central ... Jan. 15
Augustana (Ill.) ■ ... Jan. 18
Elmhurst ... Jan. 22
Millikin ... Jan. 25
Wheaton (Ill.) ■ ... Jan. 29
Ill. Wesleyan ■ ... Feb. 1
North Central ■ ... Feb. 5
North Park ... Feb. 8
Augustana (Ill.) ... Feb. 15
Wheaton (Ill.) ... Feb. 20
Elmhurst ■ ... Feb. 22
Trinity Int'l ■ ... Feb. 25

1995-96 RESULTS (5-20)
103 Cardinal Stritch ■ ... 94
85 Wis.-Stevens Point ... 99
68 St. Xavier † ... 81
46 Wis.-Oshkosh ■ ... 76
72 Beloit ... 74
63 Edgewood ■ ... 64
70 Augustana (Ill.) ... 89
77 Lake Forest ... 82
75 Teikyo Marycrest ■ ... 63
86 Mankato St. ... 108
52 Marian (Wis.) ■ ... 66
59 Ill. Wesleyan ■ ... 72
72 North Park ■ ... 61
94 Millikin ■ ... 80
58 Elmhurst ... 60
79 North Central ... 82
65 Lakeland ... 96
65 Augustana (Ill.) ■ ... 79
74 Wheaton (Ill.) ■ ... 91
78 North Park ... 88
65 Elmhurst ■ ... 66
74 Millikin ... 60
57 North Central ■ ... 63
64 Ill. Wesleyan ... 94
74 Wheaton (Ill.) ... 100

Nickname: Redmen
Colors: Red, White & Black
Arena: Physical Education Center
Capacity: 3,500; Year Built: 1964
AD: Robert Bonn
SID: Steve Marovich

CASE RESERVE
Cleveland, OH 44106 ... III

Coach: William C. Sudeck
Alma Mater: Kent '48
Record: 33 Years, W-280, L-431

1996-97 SCHEDULE
Brandeis ... Nov. 23
Carnegie Mellon ■ ... Nov. 26
New York U. ■ ... Dec. 1
Allegheny ■ ... Dec. 4
Emory ■ ... Dec. 6
Rochester ... Dec. 10
Ohio Wesleyan ■ ... Dec. 30
Wittenberg ... Jan. 3
Earlham ... Jan. 4
Oberlin ■ ... Jan. 8
Wooster ... Jan. 11
Kenyon ■ ... Jan. 15
Ohio Wesleyan ... Jan. 18
Allegheny ... Jan. 22
Washington (Mo.) ... Jan. 24
Chicago ... Jan. 26
Earlham ■ ... Jan. 31
Wittenberg ■ ... Feb. 1
Johns Hopkins ■ ... Feb. 3
Wooster ■ ... Feb. 5
Denison ■ ... Feb. 8
Oberlin ... Feb. 12
Kenyon ... Feb. 15
Denison ... Feb. 22

1995-96 RESULTS (13-13)
102 Brandeis ■ ... 84
63 Carnegie Mellon ... 73
87 New York U. ... 96
54 Wooster ... 66
86 Emory ... 80
82 Rochester ■ ... 87
91 Oberlin ■ ... 70
79 Kenyon ■ ... 89
70 Earlham ■ ... 54
69 Wittenberg ■ ... 66
72 Ohio Wesleyan ... 70
73 Denison ... 71
53 Allegheny ■ ... 71
67 Washington (Mo.) ■ ... 77
64 Chicago ■ ... 70
82 Kenyon ... 72
75 Ohio Wesleyan ■ ... 71
64 Johns Hopkins ... 72
76 Wittenberg ... 101
96 Earlham ... 91
80 Denison ■ ... 77
63 Wooster ■ ... 79
93 Oberlin ... 85
70 Allegheny ... 76
75 Denison ■ ... 73
70 Wittenberg ... 104

Nickname: Spartans
Colors: Blue, Gray & White
Arena: Emerson P.E. Center
Capacity: 3,000; Year Built: 1958
AD: Dave Hutter
SID: Sue Herdle Penicka

CATAWBA
Salisbury, NC 28144 ... II

Coach: Jim Baker
Alma Mater: Catawba '78
Record: 2 Years, W-33, L-21

1996-97 SCHEDULE
Anderson (S.C.) ■ ... Nov. 19
Allen ■ ... Nov. 21
Longwood Inv. ... Nov. 23-24
Voorhees ■ ... Nov. 27

Southern Wesleyan ■ ....Nov. 30
Catawba Cl. ....Dec. 6-7
Newport News App. ■...........Dec. 14
Barbados Tr..............Dec. 28-Jan. 1
Presbyterian ....Jan. 8
Carson-Newman ....Jan. 11
Elon ■...................................Jan. 15
Lenoir-Rhyne ■ ....Jan. 18
Wingate ....Jan. 22
Mars Hill ....Jan. 25
Gardner-Webb ■....................Jan. 29
Gardner-Webb ....Feb. 1
Presbyterian ....Feb. 5
Carson-Newman ....Feb. 8
Elon ....Feb. 12
Lenoir-Rhyne ....Feb. 15
Wingate ■ ....Feb. 19
Mars Hill ■ ....Feb. 22

1995-96 RESULTS (16-10)

82	Lees-McRae	92
71	Elizabeth City St. ■	67
87	Appalachian St.	90
73	Livingstone	65
87	Concord ■	75
60	Pfeiffer ■	75
64	Lees-McRae ■	59
77	St. Paul's	66
85	Ohio Valley †	93
61	Furman	76
84	Wingate	74
86	Gardner-Webb ■	84
84	Presbyterian	75
68	Carson-Newman	70
78	Elon ■	72
71	Lenoir-Rhyne ■	63
74	Mars Hill	81
85	Anderson (Ind.) ■	53
51	Wingate	45
86	Gardner-Webb	89
63	Presbyterian ■	57
66	Carson-Newman ■	61
76	Mars Hill ■	61
87	Elon	84
56	Lenoir-Rhyne ■	78
65	Elon †	71

Nickname: Indians
Colors: Blue & White
Arena: Goodman Gym
 Capacity: 3,500; Year Built: 1970
AD: Dennis Davidson
SID: Jim Lewis

CATHOLIC
Washington, DC 20064 III

Coach: Mike Lonergan
Alma Mater: Catholic '88
Record: 4 Years, W-65, L-40

1996-97 SCHEDULE

American ....Nov. 23
Haverford.............................Nov. 26
William & Mary ....Dec. 2
Salisbury St. ....Dec. 4
Scranton ....Dec. 7
Whittier Cl. ....Jan. 3-4
Western Md. ....Jan. 8
Catholic Cl. ....Jan. 11-12
Mary Washington ....Jan. 15
St. Mary's (Md.) ■ ....Jan. 18
Marymount (Va.) ■ ....Jan. 20
York (Pa.) ■ ....Jan. 22
Goucher ....Jan. 25
Salisbury St. ■ ....Jan. 29
Gallaudet ....Feb. 1
Mary Washington ■ ....Feb. 4
Marymount (Va.) ....Feb. 8
St. Mary's (Md.) ....Feb. 11
Goucher ■ ....Feb. 15
Villa Julie ....Feb. 17
York (Pa.) ....Feb. 19
Gallaudet ■ ....Feb. 22

1995-96 RESULTS (19-8)

81	Tufts †	94

82	Drew †	64
77	Allentown ■	78
59	Davidson	101
115	Salisbury St.	112
81	Western Md.	79
74	Scranton ■	65
59	Radford	87
97	King's (Pa.) ■	90
85	Mt. St. Mary (N.Y.) ■	83
73	Gallaudet ■	76
67	York (Pa.) ■	38
92	Rowan ■	88
76	St. Mary's (Md.) ■	62
77	Marymount (Va.)	70
96	Salisbury St. ■	100
80	Goucher ■	66
77	Mary Washington ■	64
100	Goucher	96
98	Marymount (Va.) ■	87
83	Gallaudet ■	70
98	York (Pa.)	63
76	Mary Washington	58
92	St. Mary's (Md.)	86
56	Mary Washington ■	53
82	Marymount (Va.) ■	87
65	Cabrini	85

Nickname: Cardinals
Colors: Cardinal Red & Black
Arena: Dufour Center
 Capacity: 2,000; Year Built: 1985
AD: Bob Talbot
SID: Mike Graber

CENTENARY (LA.)
Shreveport, LA 71104 I

Coach: Tommy Vardeman
Alma Mater: Stephen F. Austin '65
Record: 7 Years, W-95, L-101

1996-97 SCHEDULE

Lamar ....Nov. 23
Texas Christian ....Nov. 25
New Mexico ....Nov. 27
Wiley ■ ....Nov. 30
Northwestern St. ....Dec. 2
East Tex. Bapt. ■.....................Dec. 4
Southwest Tex. St. ■ ....Dec. 7
Oklahoma.............................Dec. 14
Southern Methodist ....Dec. 16
Tulane ....Dec. 19
Fla. Atlantic ....Jan. 2
Florida Int'l ■ ....Jan. 4
Central Fla. ....Jan. 9
Stetson ....Jan. 11
Jacksonville St. ....Jan. 16
Samford ....Jan. 18
Southeastern La. ■ ....Jan. 25
Mercer ■ ....Jan. 30
Georgia St. ■..........................Feb. 1
Southeastern La. ....Feb. 3
Mercer ....Feb. 6
Georgia St. ....Feb. 8
Samford ....Feb. 13
Jacksonville St. ■ ....Feb. 15
Campbell ....Feb. 20
Charleston (S.C.) ....Feb. 22
Trans America Conf. Tr....Feb. 27-Mar. 1

1995-96 RESULTS (11-16)

89	East Tex. Bapt. ■	85
75	Tulane ■	88
108	Wiley ■	71
65	Louisiana Tech ■	58
81	Texas Christian	93
77	Louisiana Tech	90
63	LSU	65
77	Baylor	80
71	Liberty †	73
76	Fla. Atlantic ■	75
108	Florida Int'l	95
84	Central Fla.	60
83	Stetson	96
94	Jacksonville St. ■	85
57	Samford ■	61

70	Lamar	88
77	Southeastern La.	89
66	Mercer	89
92	Southeastern La.	90
87	Mercer ■	77
79	Georgia St. ■	76
58	Georgia St.	74
63	Samford	74
95	Jacksonville St.	79
58	Campbell ■	75
54	Charleston (S.C.) ■	75
61	Mercer †	72

Nickname: Gentlemen
Colors: Maroon & White
Arena: Gold Dome
 Capacity: 4,000; Year Built: 1971
AD: Russ Sharp
SID: Charlie Cavell

CENTRAL (IOWA)
Pella, IA 50219 III

Coach: Lionel Sinn
Alma Mater: Indiana '63
Record: 20 Years, W-346, L-223

1996-97 SCHEDULE

Coe ....Nov. 22
Teikyo Marycrest ■ ....Nov. 26
Central (Iowa) Tr. ....Dec. 6-7
Wheaton (Ill.) ■.....................Dec. 14
Greenville ....Jan. 4
Maryville (Mo.) ....Jan. 6
Sanford Brown ....Jan. 7
Upper Iowa ....Jan. 10
Dubuque ....Jan. 11
Colorado Col. ■ ....Jan. 18
Simpson ....Jan. 24
Buena Vista ■ ....Jan. 25
Loras ■ ....Jan. 31
Wartburg ....Feb. 1
William Penn ....Feb. 4
Luther ....Feb. 7
Upper Iowa ■ ....Feb. 8
Loras ....Feb. 14
Wartburg ■ ....Feb. 15
Simpson ....Feb. 21
Luther ....Feb. 22
William Penn ■ ....Feb. 25
Buena Vista ....Feb. 28
Dubuque ....Mar. 1

1995-96 RESULTS (11-14)

62	Truman St.	66
48	Regis (Colo.)	61
58	Colorado Col.	78
76	Sterling	58
71	N'western (Iowa) ■	69
67	Dordt ■	77
65	Teikyo Marycrest	54
73	Coe ■	65
77	Simpson	88
83	Buena Vista ■	69
71	Dubuque ■	64
67	Luther	75
89	William Penn	64
68	Wartburg	72
75	Luther ■	78
60	Buena Vista	65
92	Loras ■	67
70	Wartburg ■	65
40	Upper Iowa ■	51
90	Simpson	87
82	Loras	83
59	Neb. Wesleyan ■	78
77	William Penn	71
64	Dubuque ■	73
67	Upper Iowa	72

Nickname: Flying Dutchmen
Colors: Red & White
Arena: Kuyper Gymnasium
 Capacity: 3,000; Year Built: 1970
AD: Sam Bedrosian
SID: Larry Happel

CENTRAL ARK.
Conway, AR 72032 II

Coach: Arch Jones
Alma Mater: Arkansas Tech '64
Record: 3 Years, W-46, L-32

1996-97 SCHEDULE

North Ala. Tr. ....Nov. 15-16
John Brown ....Nov. 19
Ouachita Baptist ■.................Nov. 21
Mo. Southern St. ....Nov. 23
Southwest Baptist ■ ....Nov. 26
Florida Tech Cl. ....Nov. 29-30
Harding ....Dec. 3
John Brown ....Dec. 5
Ouachita Baptist. ....Dec. 14
Delta St. ....Jan. 4
Christian Bros. ....Jan. 6
Lyon ....Jan. 9
Southern Ark. ....Jan. 13
Ark.-Monticello ■ ....Jan. 16
Henderson St. ....Jan. 20
Arkansas Tech ....Jan. 25
Lyon ■ ....Jan. 27
Delta St. ....Feb. 1
Christian Bros. ■ ....Feb. 3
Harding ....Feb. 8
Southern Ark. ■ ....Feb. 10
Ark.-Monticello ....Feb. 13
Henderson St. ■ ....Feb. 17
Arkansas Tech ■ ....Feb. 22

1995-96 RESULTS (12-13)

69	John Brown	80
64	Ouachita Baptist	76
87	Grand Canyon	95
71	Harding	76
83	Mo. Southern St. ■	79
76	Southwest Baptist	80
80	John Brown ■	79
80	Ouachita Baptist ■	51
75	Texas Col.	71
63	Harding	75
63	Delta St.	94
71	Mississippi Col. ■	68
68	Lyon ■	73
68	Southern Ark. ■	67
97	Ark.-Monticello	91
69	Henderson St.	73
91	Texas Col. ■	79
52	Arkansas Tech ■	59
74	Lyon	64
61	Mississippi Col.	79
62	Southern Ark.	60
67	Ark.-Monticello ■	64
80	Henderson St. ■	79
75	Arkansas Tech	82
67	Delta St. ■	75

Nickname: Bears
Colors: Purple & Gray
Arena: Jeff Farris Center
 Capacity: 6,300; Year Built: 1973
AD: Bill Stephens
SID: Steve East

CENTRAL CONN. ST.
New Britain, CT 06050 I

Coach: Howie Dickenman
Alma Mater: Central Conn. St. '70
(First year as head coach)

1996-97 SCHEDULE

St. Francis (Pa.) ■ ....Nov. 23
St. Peter's ■ ....Dec. 4
Md.-Balt. County ....Dec. 6
Vermont ■ ....Dec. 9
St. Francis (N.Y.) ....Dec. 14
South Fla. Cl. ....Dec. 20-21
Boston College ....Dec. 27
St. Francis (Pa.) ....Dec. 30
Youngstown St. ....Jan. 2
Buffalo ....Jan. 4
Northeastern Ill. ■ ....Jan. 6

Chicago St. ■ ....Jan. 8
Fairfield ....Jan. 11
Valparaiso ....Jan. 18
Western Ill. ....Jan. 20
Troy St. ■ ....Jan. 25
Mo.-Kansas City ■ ....Jan. 27
Chicago St. ■ ....Feb. 1
Northeastern Ill. ....Feb. 3
Western Ill. ■ ....Feb. 10
Valparaiso ■ ....Feb. 12
Mo.-Kansas City ....Feb. 15
Troy St. ....Feb. 17
Buffalo ■ ....Feb. 22
Youngstown St. ■ ....Feb. 24
Mid-Continent Conf. Tr. ....Mar. 2-4

1995-96 RESULTS (13-15)
45 Iowa St. 70
52 Ohio St. 79
98 Delaware St. ■ 77
96 North Adams St. ■ 58
80 Dartmouth 83
63 Md.-Balt. County ■ 62
60 St. Francis (Pa.) 79
59 Mo.-Kansas City ■ 66
97 Western Ill. ■ 69
60 Chicago St. 42
99 Northeastern Ill. 100
76 Valparaiso ■ 79
86 Eastern Ill. ■ 80
106 Troy St. ■ 90
46 Connecticut 116
68 Buffalo 84
79 Youngstown St. 65
66 Northeastern Ill. ■ 85
123 Chicago St. ■ 72
84 Eastern Ill. 87
82 Valparaiso 97
119 Troy St. 118
66 Youngstown St. ■ 57
75 Buffalo 62
63 Western Ill. 82
69 Mo.-Kansas City † 76
89 Mo.-Kansas City † 83
66 Western Ill. † 68

Nickname: Blue Devils
Colors: Blue & White
Arena: Detrick Gymnasium
 Capacity: 4,500; Year Built: 1965
AD: Charles "C. J." Jones
SID: Brent Rutkowski

CENTRAL FLA.
Orlando, FL 32816 I

Coach: Kirk Speraw
Alma Mater: Iowa '80
Record: 3 Years, W-43, L-44

1996-97 SCHEDULE
Florida ....Nov. 22
Winthrop ■ ....Nov. 27
Tenn. Temple ■ ....Nov. 30
Nova Southeastern ■ ....Dec. 3
Bethune-Cookman ■ ....Dec. 7
South Fla. ....Dec. 14
North Caro. St. ....Dec. 19
Youngstown St. ■ ....Dec. 23
Tenn.-Chatt. Cl. ....Dec. 28-29
Jacksonville St. ■ ....Jan. 2
Samford ■ ....Jan. 4
Centenary (La.) ....Jan. 9
Southeastern La. ....Jan. 11
Mercer ....Jan. 16
Georgia St. ■ ....Jan. 18
Fla. Atlantic ....Jan. 23
Florida Int'l ....Jan. 26
Charleston (S.C.) ■ ....Jan. 30
Campbell ■ ....Feb. 1
Stetson ....Feb. 3
Charleston (S.C.) ....Feb. 6
Campbell ....Feb. 8
Stetson ....Feb. 15
Florida Int'l ■ ....Feb. 20
Fla. Atlantic ■ ....Feb. 22
Trans America Conf. Tr. ....Feb. 27-Mar. 1

1995-96 RESULTS (11-19)
101 Palm Beach Atl. ■ 74
77 Winthrop 65
78 Northern Iowa ■ 95
82 South Fla. 92
72 Eastern Ky. ■ 79
54 Georgia 103
71 Northern Iowa 76
51 Davidson † 90
53 UNLV 74
93 Jacksonville St. 73
78 Samford 92
60 Centenary (La.) ■ 84
84 Southeastern La. ■ 95
74 North Caro. St. ■ 81
65 Mercer ■ 67
95 Georgia St. 75
79 Fla. Atlantic ■ 68
78 Florida Int'l ■ 83
61 Charleston (S.C.) 103
79 Campbell 58
75 Stetson 66
65 Charleston (S.C.) ■ 69
69 Campbell ■ 70
73 Stetson ■ 62
86 Florida Int'l 93
71 Fla. Atlantic 88
83 Southeastern La. † 80
80 Campbell † 71
86 Mercer † 77
70 Massachusetts † 92

Nickname: Golden Knights
Colors: Black & Gold
Arena: UCF Arena
 Capacity: 5,100; Year Built: 1991
AD: Steve Sloan
SID: Cory Rogers

CENTRAL MICH.
Mt. Pleasant, MI 48859 I

Coach: Leonard Drake
Alma Mater: Central Mich. '77
Record: 3 Years, W-14, L-64

1996-97 SCHEDULE
Mich.-Dearborn ■ ....Nov. 22
Northwestern ....Nov. 26
Fairfield ....Nov. 30
Illinois Cl. ....Dec. 6-7
Detroit ■ ....Dec. 17
South Fla. Cl. ....Dec. 20-21
Bowling Green ■ ....Jan. 4
Eastern Mich. ....Jan. 8
Western Mich. ■ ....Jan. 11
Miami (Ohio) ....Jan. 13
Ball St. ■ ....Jan. 15
Toledo ....Jan. 18
Akron ■ ....Jan. 22
Ohio ....Jan. 25
Kent ■ ....Jan. 29
Eastern Mich. ■ ....Feb. 1
Western Mich. ....Feb. 5
Miami (Ohio) ■ ....Feb. 8
Ball St. ....Feb. 12
Toledo ■ ....Feb. 15
Akron ....Feb. 19
Ohio ■ ....Feb. 22
Kent ....Feb. 26
Bowling Green ....Mar. 1
Mid-American Conf. Tr. ....Mar. 4-8

1995-96 RESULTS (6-20)
80 Tri-State ■ 66
76 Purdue ■ 78
54 Detroit 57
69 Mich.-Dearborn ■ 49
63 Northwestern ■ 64
51 Wichita St. 58
69 Michigan St. 62
57 Rice † 65
69 Akron ■ 63
74 Western Mich. 81
70 Bowling Green 81
76 Eastern Mich. ■ 81
69 Ball St. 82

72 Miami (Ohio) ■ 88
85 Kent 82
65 Ohio ■ 72
59 Toledo 65
51 Western Mich. ■ 73
63 Bowling Green 74
79 Eastern Mich. 91
75 Ball St. 82
54 Miami (Ohio) ■ 78
53 Kent ■ 74
73 Ohio 76
102 Toledo ■ 103
69 Akron 68

Nickname: Chippewas
Colors: Maroon & Gold
Arena: Rose Arena
 Capacity: 5,200; Year Built: 1973
AD: Herb Deromedi
SID: Fred Stabley Jr

CENTRAL MO. ST.
Warrensburg, MO 64093 II

Coach: Don Doucette
Alma Mater: Boston St. '76
Record: 19 Years, W-183, L-212

1996-97 SCHEDULE
Rockhurst ■ ....Nov. 21
Monmouth (Ill.) ■ ....Nov. 23
Drury ■ ....Nov. 26
Washburn ....Nov. 30
Graceland (Iowa) ■ ....Dec. 2
Lincoln (Mo.) ....Dec. 4
Las Vegas Cl. ....Dec. 18-19
Doane ■ ....Dec. 28
Harris-Stowe ■ ....Dec. 30
Emporia St. ■ ....Jan. 2
Mo. Western St. ....Jan. 4
Southwest Baptist ■ ....Jan. 8
Mo. Southern St. ....Jan. 11
Pittsburg St. ....Jan. 13
Northwest Mo. St. ■ ....Jan. 15
Mo.-Rolla ....Jan. 18
Truman St. ....Jan. 22
Pittsburg St. ■ ....Jan. 25
Mo. Southern St. ■ ....Jan. 27
Southwest Baptist ....Feb. 1
Lincoln (Mo.) ....Feb. 5
Washburn ■ ....Feb. 8
Emporia St. ....Feb. 12
Northwest Mo. St. ....Feb. 15
Truman St. ■ ....Feb. 19

1995-96 RESULTS (22-9)
107 Monmouth (Ill.) ■ 71
91 Ark.-Monticello ■ 77
101 Doane ■ 71
77 Drury 65
90 Rockhurst 69
114 IU/PU-Indianapolis ■ 108
95 Missouri Baptist ■ 69
83 Cameron † 76
82 UC Riverside † 81
110 Central Meth. ■ 78
86 Southwest Baptist 98
69 Emporia St. ■ 74
77 Lincoln (Mo.) 68
98 Mo. Southern St. 90
91 Mo. Western St. ■ 72
83 Washburn 71
66 Northwest Mo. St. 74
67 Mo.-Rolla 74
68 Pittsburg St. ■ 56
88 Truman St. ■ 67
86 Mo.-St. Louis 89
81 Emporia St. 77
88 Lincoln (Mo.) ■ 78
72 Mo. Southern St. ■ 75
78 Mo. Western St. 75
65 Washburn 66
64 Emporia St. ■ 63
66 Pittsburg St. ■ 62
65 Mo.-Rolla 67
89 Texas A&M-Commerce † 86
67 Mo.-Rolla 72

Nickname: Mules
Colors: Cardinal & Black
Arena: CMSU Multipurpose Building
 Capacity: 8,500; Year Built: 1976
AD: Jerry Hughes
SID: Bill Turnage

CENTRAL OKLA.
Edmond, OK 73034 II

Coach: Jim Seward
Alma Mater: Hiram Scott '69
Record: 22 Years, W-356, L-258

1996-97 SCHEDULE
Texas Col. ■ ....Nov. 21
Paul Quinn ■ ....Nov. 26
Ky. Wesleyan Cl. ....Nov. 29-30
Mo. Western St. Cl. ....Dec. 6-7
Southwestern Okla. ■ ....Dec. 10
Tex. A&M-Kingsville ....Dec. 14
Las Vegas Cl. ....Dec. 18-19
Angelo St. ....Jan. 2
Abilene Christian ■ ....Jan. 4
Eastern N.M. ■ ....Jan. 7
West Tex. A&M ....Jan. 9
Midwestern St. ....Jan. 13
Texas A&M-Commerce ■ ....Jan. 16
Tarleton St. ■ ....Jan. 18
Abilene Christian ....Jan. 23
Angelo St. ■ ....Jan. 25
West Tex. A&M ■ ....Jan. 30
Eastern N.M. ....Feb. 1
Southwestern Okla. ....Feb. 5
Midwestern St. ■ ....Feb. 8
Tarleton St. ....Feb. 13
Texas A&M-Commerce ....Feb. 15
Tex. A&M-Kingsville ■ ....Feb. 22

1995-96 RESULTS (19-10)
117 Texas Col. ■ 87
112 Paul Quinn ■ 95
106 Benedictine ■ 72
94 Oakland City † 87
116 Southern Ind. 114
97 Cameron 114
158 Ark. Baptist ■ 54
99 Tex. A&M-Kingsville ■ 107
76 Grand Canyon † 102
98 Drury † 88
92 Angelo St. 84
102 Abilene Christian 97
93 Eastern N.M. ■ 105
85 West Tex. A&M ■ 88
113 Midwestern St. 117
91 Texas A&M-Commerce 97
100 Tarleton St. 93
106 Abilene Christian ■ 92
107 Angelo St. ■ 77
83 West Tex. A&M 111
92 Eastern N.M. 85
100 Cameron ■ 88
124 Midwestern St. ■ 105
111 Tarleton St. ■ 93
89 Texas A&M-Commerce ■ 83
86 Tex. A&M-Kingsville 109
100 Eastern N.M. ■ 94
91 Texas A&M-Commerce 86
95 Tex. A&M-Kingsville † 112

Nickname: Bronchos
Colors: Bronze & Blue
Arena: Hamilton Field House
 Capacity: 3,000; Year Built: 1965
AD: John "Skip" Wagnon
SID: Mike Kirk

CENTRE
Danville, KY 40422 III

Coach: Mike DeWitt
Alma Mater: Ohio Wesleyan '87
Record: 2 Years, W-15, L-35

1996-97 SCHEDULE
Trinity (Tex.) Inv. ....Nov. 22-23

Asbury ....Nov. 26
Hanover...................................Dec. 3
Rose-Hulman ....Dec. 16
Centre Tr. ....Dec. 28-29
Transylvania ....Jan. 7
Oglethorpe ■ ....Jan. 10
Millsaps ■ ....Jan. 12
Southwestern (Tex.) ■ ....Jan. 17
Trinity (Tex.) ■ ....Jan. 19
Maryville (Tenn.) ■ ....Jan. 21
Hendrix ....Jan. 24
Rhodes ....Jan. 26
Transylvania ■ ....Jan. 28
Southwestern (Tex.) ....Jan. 31
Trinity (Tex.) ....Feb. 2
Hendrix ■ ....Feb. 7
Rhodes ■ ....Feb. 9
Sewanee ....Feb. 16
Oglethorpe ....Feb. 21
Millsaps ....Feb. 23
Maryville (Tenn.) ■ ....Feb. 26
Sewanee ■ ....Mar. 1

1995-96 RESULTS (8-17)

53	Maryville (Tenn.)	68
65	Transylvania	81
88	Asbury ■	66
68	Morehead St.	115
51	Hanover ■	57
61	Rose-Hulman	82
69	Rose-Hulman ■	92
68	Hiram	84
78	Earlham ■	72
93	Sewanee ■	75
82	Trinity (Tex.) ■	63
83	Southwestern (Tex.) ■	69
62	Millsaps	80
78	Oglethorpe	76
70	Transylvania ■	90
77	Rhodes	89
68	Hendrix	86
60	Millsaps ■	67
83	Oglethorpe ■	74
76	Rhodes ■	75
62	Hendrix ■	72
69	Trinity (Tex.)	93
74	Southwestern (Tex.)	77
64	Maryville (Tenn.) ■	70
72	Sewanee	91

Nickname: Colonels
Colors: Gold & White
Arena: Alumni Memorial Gymnasium
    Capacity: 1,800; Year Built: 1950
AD: Ray Hammond
SID: To be named

CHADRON ST.
Chadron, NE 69337 II

Coach: Bob Wood
Alma Mater: Chadron St. '80
Record: 9 Years, W-100, L-154

1996-97 SCHEDULE

South Dak. Tech ■ ....Nov. 23
Black Hills St. ■ ....Nov. 25
Northern St. Tr. ....Nov. 29-30
South Dak. Tech ....Dec. 3
N.M. Highlands ....Dec. 7
Denver.....................................Dec. 9
Southern Colo. ■ ....Dec. 13
UC-Colo. Spgs. ■ ....Dec. 14
Black Hills St. ....Dec. 21
Fort Lewis ....Jan. 3
Adams St. ....Jan. 4
Mesa St. ....Jan. 9
Western St. ■ ....Jan. 11
Regis (Colo.) ■ ....Jan. 16
Colo. Christian ■ ....Jan. 18
Neb.-Kearney ....Jan. 24
Fort Hays St. ....Jan. 25
Metro St. ■ ....Jan. 30
Colorado Mines ■ ....Feb. 1
Neb.-Kearney ■ ....Feb. 7

Fort Hays St. ■ ....Feb. 8
Regis (Colo.) ....Feb. 14
Colo. Christian ....Feb. 15
Metro St. ....Feb. 21
Colorado Mines ....Feb. 25

1995-96 RESULTS (10-17)

89	Rocky Mountain †	83
107	Trinity Bible †	72
113	Black Hills St. ■	98
85	Northern St.	103
96	Moorhead St. †	77
81	Colorado Mines	89
71	Regis (Colo.) ■	73
77	South Dak. Tech ■	78
95	Neb.-Kearney ■	110
86	Fort Hays St. ■	93
97	South Dak. Tech	80
72	Black Hills St.	87
70	Regis (Colo.)	82
88	N.M. Highlands ■	80
68	Mesa St.	89
85	Western St.	111
89	Adams St. ■	99
118	Fort Lewis ■	97
84	Colorado Mines ■	100
75	N.M. Highlands	70
73	Neb.-Kearney	96
61	Fort Hays St.	98
72	Mesa St. ■	69
84	Western St. ■	85
66	Adams St.	92
112	Fort Lewis	111
81	Neb.-Kearney	95

Nickname: Eagles
Colors: Cardinal & White
Arena: Armstrong
    Capacity: 3,200; Year Built: 1965
AD: Brad Smith
SID: Con Marshall

CHAMINADE
Honolulu, HI 96816 II

Coach: Al Walker
Alma Mater: Brockport St. '81
Record: 8 Years, W-96, L-111

1996-97 SCHEDULE

Maui Inv. ....Nov. 25-27
Oakland City ■ ....Nov. 29
Carleton ■ ....Dec. 3
Chico St. Tr. ....Dec. 28-30
Neb. Wesleyan ■ ....Jan. 2
Arizona St. ■ ....Jan. 6
Western N.M. ....Jan. 9
Mont. St.-Billings ....Jan. 11
Chapman ■ ....Jan. 16
Seattle Pacific ■ ....Jan. 18
BYU-Hawaii ■ ....Jan. 20
Alas. Anchorage ■ ....Jan. 23
Alas. Fairbanks ■ ....Jan. 25
Hawaii Pacific ....Jan. 27
Western N.M. ■ ....Jan. 30
Mont. St.-Billings ■ ....Feb. 1
Belmont ■ ....Feb. 5
Hawaii-Hilo ....Feb. 8
Alas. Fairbanks ....Feb. 13
Alas. Anchorage ....Feb. 15
Seattle Pacific ....Feb. 17
Hawaii Pacific ■ ....Feb. 21
BYU-Hawaii ....Feb. 25
Hawaii-Hilo ■ ....Mar. 1

1995-96 RESULTS (4-22)

66	Michigan St. †	69
71	Vanderbilt †	96
66	Wisconsin †	104
96	Hawaii Pacific	98
84	Hawaii-Hilo ■	88
52	Utah St.	98
65	Washburn †	71
68	Cameron †	87
80	Willamette ■	78
40	Seattle Pacific	85

80	Mont. St.-Billings	115
40	Western N.M.	68
81	Hawaii-Hilo	87
88	Christian Heritage ■	81
86	Alas. Fairbanks	65
82	Alas. Anchorage ■	90
49	Hawaii Pacific ■	79
48	Seattle Pacific ■	75
53	Western N.M. ■	52
63	BYU-Hawaii	88
74	Hawaii-Hilo ■	84
63	Alas. Anchorage	88
77	Alas. Fairbanks	95
60	Hawaii Pacific	80
65	BYU-Hawaii ■	92
68	Mont. St.-Billings ■	96

Nickname: Silverswords
Colors: Royal Blue & White
Arena: McCabe Gym
    Capacity: 2,500
AD: Al Walker
SID: Aaron Griess

CHAPMAN
Orange, CA 92666 III

Coach: Mike Bokosky
Alma Mater: Fort Lewis '78
Record: 4 Years, W-56, L-45

1996-97 SCHEDULE

Chapman Inv. ....Nov. 22-23
Cal Lutheran ....Nov. 26
Pacific Christian Tr ....Nov. 29-30
Redlands Tr. ....Dec. 5-7
Claremont-M-S ....Dec. 14
Whittier ■ ....Dec. 17
Occidental Tr. ....Dec. 27-28
UC Santa Cruz Tr. ....Jan. 3-4
Pomona-Pitzer ....Jan. 8
BYU-Hawaii ....Jan. 14
Chaminade ....Jan. 16
UC San Diego ■ ....Jan. 24
La Sierra ....Jan. 29
UC Santa Cruz ■ ....Jan. 31
Menlo ■ ....Feb. 1
Pacific Christian ■ ....Feb. 6
UC San Diego ■ ....Feb. 14
UC Santa Cruz ■ ....Feb. 21
Menlo ....Feb. 22

1995-96 RESULTS (14-11)

75	Pomona-Pitzer ■	72
99	LIFE Bible ■	75
101	S'western (Ariz.) ■	47
70	Hamline †	67
84	Redlands	81
58	Concordia (Cal.) †	68
71	Cal Lutheran ■	87
84	Claremont-M-S ■	69
68	Cal Baptist	76
82	Hartwick †	85
81	Babson †	82
64	Claremont-M-S	70
111	Cal Maritime ■	62
90	UC San Diego ■	78
82	UC Santa Cruz	83
72	Holy Names	84
100	LIFE Bible ■	60
60	Menlo ■	69
93	UC San Diego	86
72	Menlo	63
90	Patten	68
87	La Sierra ■	58
54	Cal Poly SLO	90
65	Christian Heritage ■	67
96	UC Santa Cruz ■	61

Nickname: Panthers
Colors: Cardinal & Gray
Arena: Hutton Sports Center
    Capacity: 2,400; Year Built: 1978
AD: Dave Currey
SID: Jim Moore

CHARLESTON (S.C.)
Charleston, SC 29424 I

Coach: John Kresse
Alma Mater: St. John's (N.Y.) '64
Record: 17 Years, W-412, L-109

1996-97 SCHEDULE

Charleston So. ....Nov. 22
Great Alas. Shootout ....Nov. 27-30
Citadel ■ ....Dec. 7
Presbyterian ■ ....Dec. 14
Elon ■ ....Dec. 16
Oklahoma St. ....Dec. 18
Charleston (S.C.) Cl ....Dec. 28-29
Mercer.....................................Jan. 2
Georgia St. ....Jan. 4
Jacksonville St. ....Jan. 9
Samford ....Jan. 11
Wofford ....Jan. 13
Fla. Atlantic ■ ....Jan. 16
Florida Int'l ■ ....Jan. 18
Campbell ■ ....Jan. 25
Central Fla. ■ ....Jan. 30
Stetson ....Feb. 1
Campbell ....Feb. 3
Central Fla. ■ ....Feb. 6
Stetson ■ ....Feb. 8
Florida Int'l ....Feb. 13
Fla. Atlantic ....Feb. 15
Southeastern La. ■ ....Feb. 20
Centenary (La.) ■ ....Feb. 22
Trans America Conf. Tr. ....Feb. 27-Mar. 1

1995-96 RESULTS (25-4)

84	Southern Wesleyan ■	49
68	Charleston So. ■	64
61	Syracuse	72
60	Connecticut ■	77
93	Alas. Anchorage ■	72
72	Coastal Caro.	52
67	Richmond ■	58
98	Mercer ■	65
91	Georgia St. ■	78
92	Charleston So.	71
89	Jacksonville St. ■	80
58	Samford ■	50
79	Wofford	68
61	Fla. Atlantic ■	58
72	Florida Int'l	59
76	Citadel	69
76	Campbell	74
103	Central Fla. ■	61
63	Stetson	50
58	Campbell ■	45
69	Central Fla.	65
68	Stetson	58
80	Florida Int'l ■	56
72	Fla. Atlantic ■	50
83	Southeastern La.	93
75	Centenary (La.)	54
83	Wofford ■	47
55	Tennessee	49
58	Rhode Island	62

Nickname: Cougars
Colors: Maroon & White
Arena: F. Mitchell Johnson Center
    Capacity: 3,052; Year Built: 1983
AD: Jerry Baker
SID: Tony Ciuffo

CHARLESTON (W.VA.)
Charleston, WV 25304 II

Coach: Jayson Gee
Alma Mater: Charleston (W.Va.) '88
(First year as head coach)

1996-97 SCHEDULE

Central St. ■ ....Nov. 16
Calif. (Pa.) ....Nov. 19
Ky. Christian ■ ....Nov. 22
Bluefield St. Cl. ....Nov. 29-30
West Va. St. ....Dec. 2
Glenville St. ....Dec. 7

Calif. (Pa.) ■		Dec. 16
Shepherd ■		Jan. 9
West Liberty St. ■		Jan. 11
Davis & Elkins		Jan. 13
Alderson-Broaddus ■		Jan. 15
Fairmont St. ■		Jan. 18
Concord ■		Jan. 22
West Va. Tech		Jan. 25
Salem-Teikyo ■		Jan. 27
Bluefield St.		Jan. 29
Alderson-Broaddus ■		Feb. 1
West Va. Wesleyan		Feb. 5
Wheeling Jesuit		Feb. 8
Central St.		Feb. 10
West Va. St. ■		Feb. 12
Concord		Feb. 15
West Va. Tech ■		Feb. 17
Salem-Teikyo		Feb. 19
Bluefield St. ■		Feb. 22

1995-96 RESULTS (12-14)

71	Cumberland (Ky.) †	80
109	Urbana	100
69	Georgetown (Ky.)	105
83	Oakland City †	85
78	Southern Ind.	101
90	West Va. St. ■	85
50	Glenville St. ■	65
69	West Liberty St.	65
96	Davis & Elkins ■	69
98	Alderson-Broaddus ■	90
82	Fairmont St.	94
94	Shepherd ■	84
82	Concord	80
71	West Va. Tech ■	75
80	Salem-Teikyo	89
93	Bluefield St. ■	89
81	Georgetown (Ky.) ■	101
101	West Va. Wesleyan ■	93
74	Wheeling Jesuit	73
72	Alderson-Broaddus ■	83
97	West Va. St.	96
84	Concord ■	88
72	West Va. Tech ■	80
79	Salem-Teikyo ■	87
76	Bluefield St.	74
73	Concord ■	76

Nickname: Golden Eagles
Colors: Maroon & Gold
Arena: Eddie King Gym
  Capacity: 2,100
AD: Linda Bennett
SID: Joe Tewkesbury

CHARLESTON SO.
Charleston, SC 29406 I

Coach: Tom Conrad
Alma Mater: Old Dominion '79
(First year as head coach)

1996-97 SCHEDULE

Charleston (S.C.) ■		Nov. 22
Anderson (S.C.) ■		Nov. 26
Toledo		Nov. 30
Centenary (N.J.) ■		Dec. 2
Marist Cl.		Dec. 6-7
Clemson		Dec. 14
Furman		Dec. 16
South Caro. St. ■		Dec. 18
Citadel		Dec. 21
South Caro.		Dec. 28
Citadel ■		Jan. 2
Coastal Caro. ■		Jan. 9
N.C.-Greensboro		Jan. 11
Md.-Balt. County ■		Jan. 16
N.C.-Asheville		Jan. 18
Liberty		Jan. 25
Radford		Jan. 27
Winthrop ■		Jan. 30
N.C.-Asheville ■		Feb. 1
Coastal Caro.		Feb. 3
N.C.-Greensboro ■		Feb. 8
Winthrop		Feb. 13
Radford ■		Feb. 15

Liberty ■		Feb. 17
Md.-Balt. County		Feb. 22
Big South Conf. Tr.		Feb. 26-Mar. 1

1995-96 RESULTS (15-13)

65	Florida	83
67	Minnesota	82
90	Citadel	96
110	Webber ■	45
60	Clemson	79
64	Charleston (S.C.)	68
57	South Caro. St.	61
63	UNLV	55
89	Furman	81
86	Clinch Valley ■	60
82	Citadel	74
81	N.C.-Asheville	67
71	Charleston (S.C.) ■	92
54	Md.-Balt. County	38
86	Winthrop	69
75	Liberty	81
80	Radford	75
91	Coastal Caro.	78
64	N.C.-Greensboro	90
82	Winthrop	73
63	N.C.-Asheville ■	64
68	Md.-Balt. County ■	46
74	Coastal Caro.	64
61	Liberty	77
87	Radford	85
59	N.C.-Greensboro	70
55	Radford †	52
60	N.C.-Greensboro †	69

Nickname: Buccaneers
Colors: Blue & Gold
Arena: CSU Fieldhouse
  Capacity: 1,500; Year Built: 1965
AD: Howard Bagwell
SID: Mike Hoffman

CHEYNEY
Cheyney, PA 19319 II

Coach: Alonzo Lewis
Alma Mater: La Salle '57
Record: 1 Year, W-17, L-11

1996-97 SCHEDULE

West Va. Wesleyan		Nov. 15
West Va. St.		Nov. 16
Dist. Columbia		Nov. 19
Bowie St. ■		Nov. 23
Columbia Union		Nov. 26
Lincoln (Pa.) [Philadelphia]		Nov. 30
Virginia St.		Dec. 2
Holy Family		Dec. 7
Le Moyne		Dec. 14
Elizabeth City St. ■		Jan. 3
Bowie St.		Jan. 7
Kutztown		Jan. 11
Wilmington (Del.) ■		Jan. 13
Millersville ■		Jan. 15
Mansfield		Jan. 18
West Chester ■		Jan. 22
East Stroudsburg ■		Jan. 25
Bloomsburg		Jan. 29
Kutztown ■		Feb. 1
Dist. Columbia ■		Feb. 4
Mansfield ■		Feb. 8
Millersville		Feb. 12
West Chester		Feb. 15
Bloomsburg ■		Feb. 19
East Stroudsburg		Feb. 22

1995-96 RESULTS (17-11)

73	Fairmont St.	91
98	Alderson-Broaddus †	79
84	Virginia St.	92
77	Lincoln (Pa.) †	63
80	Dist. Columbia	95
67	West Va. St.	73
68	Benedict	76
87	Virginia St.	82
82	New York Tech	94
56	Bloomsburg	71
72	Shaw	76

79	Wilberforce	74
88	East Stroudsburg ■	63
71	West Chester ■	57
71	Mansfield	60
75	Millersville	85
100	Kutztown ■	64
83	Dist. Columbia ■	80
70	East Stroudsburg	99
75	Bloomsburg	61
69	West Chester	64
70	Wilmington (Del.)	58
78	Millersville ■	60
92	Mansfield ■	89
92	Columbia Union ■	77
90	Kutztown	89
85	Edinboro ■	78
81	Calif. (Pa.)	92

Nickname: Wolves
Colors: Blue & White
Arena: Cope Hall
  Capacity: 3,200; Year Built: 1961
AD: Andy Hinson
SID: To be named

CHICAGO
Chicago, IL 60637 III

Coach: Pat Cunningham
Alma Mater: Kalamazoo '74
Record: 8 Years, W-88, L-147

1996-97 SCHEDULE

North Central Cl.		Nov. 22-23
Wheaton (Ill.) ■		Nov. 26
Kalamazoo		Nov. 30
DePauw ■		Dec. 3
Illinois Tech		Dec. 7
North Park		Dec. 14
Wabash		Dec. 30
Washington (Mo.)		Jan. 4
Lake Forest		Jan. 7
St. Mary's (Md.)		Jan. 10
Johns Hopkins		Jan. 12
New York U.		Jan. 17
Brandeis		Jan. 19
Rochester ■		Jan. 24
Case Reserve ■		Jan. 26
Emory		Jan. 31
Carnegie Mellon		Feb. 2
Rochester		Feb. 9
Carnegie Mellon ■		Feb. 14
Emory ■		Feb. 16
Brandeis		Feb. 21
New York U.		Feb. 23
Washington (Mo.) ■		Mar. 1

1995-96 RESULTS (18-7)

100	William Penn †	81
137	Grinnell	152
82	Carleton ■	80
100	Oberlin ■	58
68	Wheaton (Ill.)	84
59	Carroll (Wis.)	81
69	Savannah A&D ■	56
88	Lake Forest	66
78	Kalamazoo ■	69
74	Washington (Mo.)	85
72	Johns Hopkins	53
79	Moody Bible	52
67	New York U.	93
68	Brandeis	60
65	Rochester	58
70	Case Reserve	64
69	Emory ■	57
70	Carnegie Mellon	68
81	Robert Morris (Ill.) ■	89
74	Rochester	65
71	Carnegie Mellon	68
72	Emory	66
79	Brandeis	74
98	New York U. ■	68
73	Washington (Mo.)	83

Nickname: Maroons
Colors: White & Maroon
Arena: Henry Crown Field House

  Capacity: 1,500; Year Built: 1931
AD: Tom Weingartner
SID: Dave Hilbert

CHICAGO ST.
Chicago, IL 60628 I

Coach: Craig Hodges
Alma Mater: Long Beach St. '82
Record: 2 Years, W-8, L-45

1996-97 SCHEDULE

Missouri		Nov. 23
Bradley		Nov. 30
Maryland		Dec. 2
Loyola (Ill.) ■		Dec. 4
Ill.-Chicago ■		Dec. 7
Illinois		Dec. 11
Western Mich. ■		Dec. 18
Colorado St.		Dec. 21
Northern Ill.		Dec. 23
Indiana St.		Dec. 27
Northeastern Ill.		Jan. 2
Central Conn. St.		Jan. 8
Western Ill. ■		Jan. 11
Valparaiso ■		Jan. 14
Mo.-Kansas City ■		Jan. 18
Troy St.		Jan. 20
Buffalo ■		Jan. 25
Youngstown St.		Jan. 27
Central Conn. St. ■		Feb. 1
Valparaiso		Feb. 6
Western Ill.		Feb. 8
Troy St. ■		Feb. 10
Mo.-Kansas City		Feb. 12
Youngstown St. ■		Feb. 15
Buffalo		Feb. 17
Northeastern Ill. ■		Feb. 22
Mid-Continent Conf. Tr.		Mar. 2-4

1995-96 RESULTS (2-25)

79	Ill.-Chicago ■	96
69	Evansville	111
45	Missouri	117
75	Northern Ill. ■	115
76	Dayton	110
80	Bradley	110
56	St. Louis	96
74	Western Mich.	99
62	Valparaiso	80
66	Eastern Ill.	89
42	Central Conn. St. ■	60
128	Troy St. ■	94
62	Buffalo	69
59	Youngstown St.	89
77	Mo.-Kansas City ■	66
87	Western Ill.	96
68	Northeastern Ill. ■	81
72	Central Conn. St.	123
75	Youngstown St. ■	87
108	Troy St.	117
68	Buffalo	78
73	Western Ill.	93
73	Mo.-Kansas City	99
69	Northeastern Ill.	97
73	Eastern Ill. ■	90
73	Valparaiso ■	87
83	Valparaiso †	118

Nickname: Cougars
Colors: Green & White
Arena: P.E. & Athletic Building
  Capacity: 2,000; Year Built: 1971
AD: Charles N. Smith
SID: Terrence Jackson

CHRIS. NEWPORT
Newport News, VA 23606 III

Coach: C. J. Woollum
Alma Mater: Ky. Wesleyan '71
Record: 12 Years, W-227, L-113

1996-97 SCHEDULE

Mary Washington		Nov. 23
Va. Wesleyan ■		Nov. 26

Christ. Newport Inv. ....Nov. 29-30
Goucher ....Dec. 8
Salisbury St. ■ ....Dec. 14
Newport News App. ....Dec. 16
Chowan ■ ....Dec. 20
Virginia St. ....Jan. 2
Clinch Valley ■ ....Jan. 4
N.C. Wesleyan ....Jan. 15
Shenandoah ....Jan. 18
Ferrum ■ ....Jan. 22
Averett ■ ....Jan. 25
Methodist ....Jan. 31
Greensboro ....Feb. 1
N.C. Wesleyan ■ ....Feb. 5
Shenandoah ■ ....Feb. 8
Chowan ....Feb. 10
Averett ....Feb. 14
Ferrum ....Feb. 15
Greensboro ■ ....Feb. 21
Methodist ■ ....Feb. 22

1995-96 RESULTS (24-6)

84	Mary Washington ■	64
83	Va. Wesleyan ■	76
72	Newport News App. ■	50
69	Elmira ■	64
95	Salisbury St.	79
89	Goucher ■	92
101	Wilmington (Del.) †	97
101	Washington (Md.)	88
69	Chowan ■	54
70	Newport News App.	63
83	Virginia St. ■	85
82	N.C. Wesleyan ■	72
90	Shenandoah ■	81
87	Ferrum	92
97	Averett	69
75	Methodist ■	62
77	Greensboro ■	58
85	N.C. Wesleyan	83
94	Shenandoah	97
88	Ferrum ■	70
101	Averett ■	59
72	Chowan	68
63	Greensboro	59
69	Methodist	71
106	Averett †	62
74	Greensboro †	67
103	Shenandoah	93
66	Randolph-Macon ■	57
73	Millsaps ■	69
71	Washington (Mo.) †	87

Nickname: Captains
Colors: Blue & Silver
Arena: Ratcliffe Gym
   Capacity: 1,000; Year Built: 1967
AD: C. J. Woollum
SID: Wayne Block

CINCINNATI
Cincinnati, OH 45221 I

Coach: Bob Huggins
Alma Mater: West Va. '77
Record: 15 Years, W-334, L-135

1996-97 SCHEDULE

Western Caro. ■ ....Nov. 23
Xavier (Ohio) ■ ....Nov. 26
Rutgers ■ ....Nov. 30
Kansas [Chicago] ....Dec. 4
Howard ■ ....Dec. 17
Eastern Mich. ■ ....Dec. 19
Western Ky. [Cleveland] ....Dec. 28
Puerto Rico Tr. ....Dec. 30-Jan. 1
St. Louis ....Jan. 5
UAB ....Jan. 8
Miami (Ohio) ■ ....Jan. 10
Temple ■ ....Jan. 16
Arkansas ■ ....Jan. 18
N.C.-Charlotte ....Jan. 21
Southern Cal ....Jan. 26
Louisville ....Jan. 30
DePaul ■ ....Feb. 1
Tulane ■ ....Feb. 6

Marquette ■ ....Feb. 8
Washington ....Feb. 10
St. Louis ■ ....Feb. 13
South Caro. ■ ....Feb. 15
Houston ■ ....Feb. 18
South Fla. ■ ....Feb. 20
DePaul ....Feb. 22
Southern Miss. ■ ....Feb. 25
Marquette ....Feb. 27
Memphis ....Mar. 1
Conference USA ....Mar. 5-8

1995-96 RESULTS (28-5)

101	Wyoming ■	51
82	N.C.-Wilmington ■ ■	47
100	Wagner ■	64
82	Arkansas ■	67
84	Minnesota ■	50
70	Temple †	49
77	California	70
103	McNeese St. ■ ■	69
71	South Fla. ■	69
75	Southern Miss. ■	70
91	Marquette ■	70
99	Xavier (Ohio)	90
68	UAB ■	70
71	DePaul ■	61
85	Southern Cal ■	53
78	N.C.-Charlotte ■ ■	64
91	Illinois St. ■	57
79	South Fla. ■	60
81	St. Louis ■	49
76	Arizona †	79
87	DePaul	60
69	St. Louis	64
66	Louisville ■	72
65	Tulane	63
71	Memphis ■	66
72	Marquette	74
62	St. Louis †	59
92	Louisville †	81
85	Marquette †	84
66	N.C.-Greensboro †	61
78	Temple †	65
87	Georgia Tech †	70
63	Mississippi St. †	73

Nickname: Bearcats
Colors: Red & Black
Arena: Myrl Shoemaker Center
   Capacity: 13,172; Year Built: 1989
AD: Gerald O'Dell
SID: Tom Hathaway

CITADEL
Charleston, SC 29409 I

Coach: Pat Dennis
Alma Mater: Wash. & Lee '78
Record: 4 Years, W-42, L-65

1996-97 SCHEDULE

Limestone ■ ....Nov. 22
Wake Forest ■ ....Nov. 25
Greensboro ■ ....Nov. 27
William & Mary ....Nov. 30
Anderson (S.C.) ■ ....Dec. 3
Charleston (S.C.) ....Dec. 7
Winthrop ■ ....Dec. 12
Wingate ■ ....Dec. 14
Charleston So. ■ ....Dec. 21
Stetson ....Dec. 30
Charleston So. ....Jan. 2
Western Caro. ■ ....Jan. 6
East Tenn. St. ....Jan. 11
Marshall ■ ....Jan. 13
VMI ■ ....Jan. 18
Western Caro. ....Jan. 20
Ga. Southern ....Jan. 25
Davidson ■ ....Jan. 27
Furman ■ ....Feb. 1
Tenn.-Chatt. ■ ....Feb. 3
VMI ....Feb. 8
Tenn.-Chatt. ....Feb. 10
Ga. Southern ■ ....Feb. 15

Appalachian St. ....Feb. 17
South Caro. ■ ....Feb. 20
Furman ....Feb. 22
Southern Conf. Tr. ....Feb. 27-Mar. 2

1995-96 RESULTS (10-16)

94	Newberry ■	65
96	Charleston So. ■	90
65	Randolph-Macon ■	58
66	Hampton ■	83
56	Bowling Green †	79
46	Delaware †	68
102	St. Mary's (Md.) ■	53
61	South Caro.	112
74	Charleston So.	62
68	Winthrop	62
73	Tenn.-Chatt. ■	64
63	Ga. Southern	56
84	Appalachian St. ■	75
88	Furman ■	77
69	Charleston (S.C.) ■	76
74	Western Caro.	88
49	East Tenn. St. ■	64
54	Marshall	98
52	VMI	91
73	Western Caro. ■	74
67	Ga. Southern ■	63
54	Davidson	82
67	Furman	68
44	Tenn.-Chatt.	70
83	VMI ■	85
73	Appalachian St. †	75

Nickname: Bulldogs
Colors: Blue & White
Arena: McAlister Field House
   Capacity: 6,000; Year Built: 1939
AD: Walt Nadzak
SID: To be named

CCNY
New York, NY 10031 III

Coach: Gary Smith
Alma Mater: Lehman '72
Record: 8 Years, W-68, L-133

1996-97 SCHEDULE

Juniata Tr. ....Nov. 23-24
New York U. ■ ....Nov. 26
Yeshiva ....Dec. 2
John Jay ....Dec. 4
Pratt ■ ....Dec. 9
Mt. St. Vincent Tr. ....Dec. 28-29
Baruch ....Jan. 3
Lehman ....Jan. 7
St. Joe's-Brooklyn ■ ....Jan. 9
St. Joseph's (L.I.) ....Jan. 14
John Jay ■ ....Jan. 16
Baruch ....Jan. 21
York (N.Y.) ....Jan. 24
Hunter ....Jan. 27
Bard ■ ....Jan. 29
Brooklyn ....Jan. 30
Old Westbury ....Feb. 1
Staten Island ■ ....Feb. 3
Lehman ....Feb. 11
Medgar Evers ■ ....Feb. 14
Yeshiva ■ ....Feb. 17
Vassar ■ ....Feb. 21

1995-96 RESULTS (11-14)

52	Yeshiva ■	49
60	Gallaudet ■	72
66	King's (Pa.) †	84
84	Pratt	63
78	John Jay	74
67	Old Westbury †	87
66	St. Joe's-Brooklyn †	64
73	Baruch ■	80
70	Bethany (W.Va.) ■	90
45	Lehman	72
73	St. Joseph's (L.I.) ■	58
66	York (N.Y.) ■	93
71	Mt. St. Vincent ■	82
48	Hunter ■	67

73	Baruch ■	82
72	Purchase St. ■	70
87	John Jay ■	88
62	Old Westbury ■	76
55	Staten Island	68
74	Yeshiva	68
95	Medgar Evers	87
76	Lehman	73
90	Mass. Pharmacy †	52
85	St. Joe's-Brooklyn	77
66	York (N.Y.) †	69

Nickname: Beavers
Colors: Lavender & Black
Arena: Nat Holman Gymnasium
   Capacity: 3,500; Year Built: 1972
AD: Richard Zerneck
SID: Charles DeCicco

CLAREMONT-M-S
Claremont, CA 91711 III

Coach: David Wells
Alma Mater: Claremont-M-S '72
Record: 22 Years, W-295, L-265

1996-97 SCHEDULE

UC San Diego ....Nov. 22
Azusa-Pacific ....Nov. 26
Pomona-Pitzer Cl. ....Nov. 29-30
Washington (Mo.) Cl. ....Dec. 6-7
Cal Baptist ■ ....Dec. 10
Chapman ■ ....Dec. 14
La Jolla Cl. ....Jan. 3-4
Concordia (Cal.) ■ ....Jan. 8
Whittier ■ ....Jan. 11
Redlands ■ ....Jan. 15
Cal Lutheran ■ ....Jan. 18
La Verne ■ ....Jan. 22
Occidental ■ ....Jan. 25
Cal Tech ■ ....Jan. 29
Pomona-Pitzer ....Feb. 1
Whittier ....Feb. 5
Redlands ■ ....Feb. 8
Cal Lutheran ....Feb. 12
La Verne ....Feb. 15
Occidental ■ ....Feb. 19
Cal Tech ....Feb. 22
Pomona-Pitzer ■ ....Feb. 26

1995-96 RESULTS (19-8)

62	Concordia (Cal.)	79
62	Washington (Mo.) †	78
78	Colby ■	71
70	Azusa-Pacific ■	86
88	Principia ■	41
58	Cal Baptist ■	80
69	Chapman ■	84
96	UC San Diego ■	88
75	Elmhurst	73
75	Beloit †	65
70	Chapman	64
75	Cal Lutheran ■	66
89	Occidental	77
60	La Verne ■	68
87	Redlands ■	63
72	Cal Tech ■	39
76	Whittier	63
66	Pomona-Pitzer ■	61
72	Cal Lutheran	70
74	Occidental	57
66	La Verne ■	69
75	Redlands	69
70	Cal Tech	33
93	Whittier ■	70
71	Pomona-Pitzer	56
70	Upper Iowa	58
62	Wis.-Whitewater ■	63

Nickname: Stags
Colors: Maroon, Gold & White
Arena: Ducey Gymnasium
   Capacity: 1,200; Year Built: 1959
AD: David Wells
SID: Kelly Beck

CLARION
Clarion, PA 16214 II

Coach: Ron Righter
Alma Mater: St. Joseph's (Pa.) '75
Record: 10 Years, W-139, L-117

1996-97 SCHEDULE
Gannon ....Nov. 21
Phila. Bible ■ ....Nov. 23
Mansfield ....Nov. 26
Clarion Cl............................Nov. 29-30
St. Vincent ■ ....Dec. 4
Mansfield ....Dec. 7
Elizabethtown ....Dec. 18
Clarion Tr...........................Jan. 3-4
Calif. (Pa.) ■ ....Jan. 8
La Roche ■ ....Jan. 11
Slippery Rock ■ ....Jan. 15
Indiana (Pa.) ■ ....Jan. 18
Pitt.-Johnstown ■ ....Jan. 20
Lock Haven ....Jan. 22
Shippensburg ■ ....Jan. 25
Edinboro ■ ....Jan. 29
Calif. (Pa.) ■ ....Feb. 5
Indiana (Pa.) ■ ....Feb. 8
Slippery Rock ....Feb. 12
Lock Haven ■ ....Feb. 15
Daemen ....Feb. 17
Edinboro ....Feb. 19
Shippensburg ....Feb. 22

1995-96 RESULTS (12-13)
112	Teikyo Post ■	73
59	Gannon ■	62
95	Point Park ■	94
67	Westminster (Pa.) ■	88
75	Bloomsburg	76
90	Kutztown	77
94	Kutztown ■	67
104	Teikyo Post	102
94	Bapt. Bible (Pa.) ■	92
92	St. Vincent ■	77
71	Edinboro	93
77	Shippensburg ■	97
98	Phila. Bible	40
81	Lock Haven ■	74
92	Indiana (Pa.)	90
88	Slippery Rock	70
83	Pitt.-Johnstown	89
77	Calif. (Pa.) ■	89
79	Shippensburg	84
95	Edinboro ■	103
64	Lock Haven	84
75	Slippery Rock ■	61
92	Indiana (Pa.) ■	104
86	St. Vincent	88
72	Calif. (Pa.)	79

Nickname: Golden Eagles
Colors: Blue & Gold
Arena: W. S. Tippin Gymnasium
  Capacity: 4,000; Year Built: 1968
AD: Bob Carlson
SID: Rich Herman

CLARK (MASS.)
Worcester, MA 01610 III

Coach: Paul Phillips
Alma Mater: Assumption '76
Record: 10 Years, W-166, L-99

1996-97 SCHEDULE
New York U. Tr.....................Nov. 22-23
Western New Eng. ■ ....Dec. 3
Amherst ....Dec. 5
Norwich ....Dec. 8
UC San Diego ....Dec. 27
La Verne ....Dec. 30
Eastern Conn. St. ■ ....Jan. 4
Springfield ■ ....Jan. 7
Norwich ■ ....Jan. 11
MIT ....Jan. 14
Mass.-Dartmouth ■ ....Jan. 16
Babson ....Jan. 18
Coast Guard ■ ....Jan. 20
Wesleyan (Conn.) ....Jan. 23
WPI..Jan. 25
Suffolk ....Jan. 30
Babson ■ ....Feb. 1
Trinity (Conn.) ■ ....Feb. 4
WPI ■ ....Feb. 8
MIT ■ ....Feb. 13
Coast Guard ....Feb. 15
Western New Eng. ....Feb. 18
Springfield ....Feb. 20

1995-96 RESULTS (12-13)
78	North Adams St. †	62
64	Wheaton (Mass.)	72
103	Assumption	96
92	Western New Eng. ■	60
88	Norwich ■	91
62	Amherst ■	91
58	Coast Guard	82
66	Springfield	68
64	Montclair St. ■	67
93	Eastern Conn. St.	81
92	Norwich	100
75	MIT ■	53
93	Mass.-Dartmouth	87
79	Babson	99
78	Wesleyan (Conn.) ■	82
105	WPI ■	92
95	Western New Eng.	79
78	Suffolk ■	58
88	Babson	101
75	Trinity (Conn.)	89
65	WPI	86
61	MIT	54
86	Coast Guard ■	78
70	Springfield ■	67
72	Norwich	76

Nickname: Cougars
Colors: Scarlet & White
Arena: Kneller Athletic Center
  Capacity: 2,000; Year Built: 1977
AD: Linda Moulton
SID: Kathryn Smith

CLARK ATLANTA
Atlanta, GA 30314..................II

Coach: Anthony Witherspoon
Alma Mater: Clark Atlanta '77
Record: 9 Years, W-99, L-150

1996-97 SCHEDULE
Schedule unavailable

1995-96 RESULTS (21-8)
85	Clayton St. ■	69
94	Xavier (La.)	91
82	Dillard	69
81	Miles	75
83	Winston-Salem ■	77
78	Xavier (La.) ■	71
85	Miles	80
107	Kentucky St. ■	92
78	Paine ■	72
87	Morris Brown	68
66	Alabama A&M ■ †	63
97	Tuskegee ■	83
85	Savannah St.	73
100	Clayton St.	77
79	Paine	77
67	Savannah St. ■	78
88	Albany St. (Ga.) ■	103
93	Morehouse	100
89	Morris Brown ■	78
71	Alabama A&M	83
87	Fort Valley St. ■	63
74	Albany St. (Ga.)	93
81	Tuskegee	71
84	Fort Valley St.	83
85	LeMoyne-Owen ■	89
135	Fisk ■	67
95	LeMoyne-Owen †	84
70	Alabama A&M ■	79
71	S.C.-Spartanburg †	91

Nickname: Panthers

Colors: Red, Black & Grey
Arena: V. W. Henderson Gymnasium
  Capacity: 1,500
AD: Richard Cosby
SID: Roger Caruth

CLARKSON
Potsdam, NY 13699 III

Coach: Walter Townes
Alma Mater: Clark (Mass.) '84
Record: 1 Year, W-5, L-20

1996-97 SCHEDULE
Elmira Cl. ....Nov. 23-24
Utica.....................................Nov. 26
Hartwick ....Dec. 3
St. John Fisher ....Dec. 5
Union (N.Y.) ....Dec. 7
St. Lawrence ....Dec. 11
Alfred ■ ....Dec. 13
Rochester Inst. ....Jan. 10
Nazareth ....Jan. 11
Potsdam St. ....Jan. 14
St. Lawrence ■ ....Jan. 18
Hobart ■ ....Jan. 24
Hamilton ■ ....Jan. 25
Potsdam St. ■ ....Jan. 28
Rensselaer ....Jan. 31
Skidmore ....Feb. 1
Union (N.Y.) ■ ....Feb. 7
Ithaca ■ ....Feb. 8
Plattsburgh St. ....Feb. 11
Skidmore ■ ....Feb. 14
Rensselaer ■ ....Feb. 15
Hamilton ....Feb. 21
Hobart ....Feb. 22
Middlebury.............................Feb. 27

1995-96 RESULTS (5-20)
43	John Carroll †	98
69	Lincoln (Pa.) †	74
60	Utica	65
56	Skidmore ■	64
53	Rensselaer	75
60	St. Lawrence ■	68
57	Hamilton	69
55	Bri'water (Mass.) †	77
83	Alfred †	68
57	Alfred	64
62	Ithaca	76
62	Hobart ■	74
61	Union (N.Y.) ■	66
65	Potsdam St. ■	67
60	Rensselaer ■	85
66	Skidmore ■	77
64	Rochester Inst. ■	68
73	Nazareth ■	60
80	Plattsburgh St. ■	68
68	Union (N.Y.)	59
55	Hobart	81
59	St. Lawrence	69
66	Hamilton ■	88
75	Hartwick ■	64
48	St. John Fisher	71

Nickname: Golden Knights
Colors: Green & Gold
Arena: Alumni Gymnasium
  Capacity: 2,000; Year Built: 1952
AD: Bill O'Flaherty
SID: Gary Mikel

CLEMSON
Clemson, SC 29631 I

Coach: Rick Barnes
Alma Mater: Lenoir-Rhyne '77
Record: 9 Years, W-161, L-110

1996-97 SCHEDULE
Kentucky [Indianapolis]..............Nov. 15
Coastal Caro. ■ ....Nov. 23
San Juan Shootout ....Nov. 29-Dec. 1
Furman ■ ....Dec. 4
Virginia..................................Dec. 7
Charleston So. ■ ....Dec. 14
South Caro. ■ ....Dec. 17
Wofford ■ ....Dec. 20
Texas A&M ....Dec. 22
Marshall ■ ....Dec. 28
South Caro. St. ....Dec. 30
Duke ■ ....Jan. 7
Florida St. ....Jan. 11
Maryland ....Jan. 15
North Caro. St. ■ ....Jan. 18
Wake Forest ■ ....Jan. 23
North Caro. ....Jan. 26
Georgia Tech ■ ....Jan. 30
North Caro. St. ....Feb. 1
Western Ky. ■ ....Feb. 4
Maryland ■ ....Feb. 8
Wake Forest ....Feb. 12
Virginia ■ ....Feb. 15
Duke ....Feb. 18
Florida St. ■ ....Feb. 23
North Caro. ■ ....Feb. 26
Georgia Tech..........................Mar. 1
Atlantic Coast Conf. Tr............Mar. 6-9

1995-96 RESULTS (18-11)
83	N.C.-Asheville ■	64
91	Appalachian St. ■	55
79	Winthrop	63
79	Charleston So. ■	60
72	South Caro. ■	58
76	Furman ■	61
79	Minnesota	66
66	Miami (Fla.)	52
67	Campbell ■	43
51	Duke ■	48
89	Virginia ■	79
53	North Caro.	86
62	Florida St.	75
55	Wake Forest ■	41
60	Maryland	65
61	North Caro. St. ■	64
73	Georgia Tech ■	70
53	Duke	83
77	Wofford ■	28
51	Virginia	62
48	North Caro.	53
67	Florida St. ■	59
48	Wake Forest	68
68	Maryland ■	61
80	North Caro. St.	76
74	Georgia Tech	87
75	North Caro. †	73
60	Wake Forest †	68
74	Georgia †	81

Nickname: Tigers
Colors: Purple & Orange
Arena: Littlejohn Coliseum
  Capacity: 11,020; Year Built: 1968
AD: Bobby Robinson
SID: Tim Bourret

CLEVELAND ST.
Cleveland, OH 44115 I

Coach: Rollie Massimino
Alma Mater: Vermont '56
Record: 23 Years, W-425, L-278

1996-97 SCHEDULE
Georgetown ■ ....Nov. 23
Akron ....Nov. 25
Michigan ■ ....Nov. 30
Michigan St. ....Dec. 3
Wichita St. ....Dec. 7
Oregon...................................Dec. 14
Youngstown St. ■ ....Dec. 16
Toledo ....Dec. 23
Colorado St. ■ ....Dec. 30
Butler ....Jan. 2
Wright St. ■ ....Jan. 4
Wis.-Green Bay ....Jan. 9
Wis.-Milwaukee ....Jan. 11
Iona ....Jan. 15
Loyola (Ill.) ■ ....Jan. 18
Northern Ill. ■ ....Jan. 20

Detroit ■ ....Jan. 23
Ill.-Chicago ....Jan. 25
Butler ....Jan. 30
Wright St. ....Feb. 1
Wis.-Green Bay ■ ....Feb. 6
Wis.-Milwaukee ■ ....Feb. 8
Northern Ill. ....Feb. 13
Loyola (Ill.) ....Feb. 15
Detroit ....Feb. 20
Ill.-Chicago ■ ....Feb. 22
Midwestern Conf. Tr. .....Feb. 28-Mar. 4

1995-96 RESULTS (5-21)

65	Iona ■	.62
62	Alcorn St.	.76
52	Ohio St.	.75
52	Akron ■	.77
49	Youngstown St.	.59
60	Dayton ■	.68
55	Michigan	.84
44	Toledo ■	.71
55	Wis.-Milwaukee ■	.73
57	Wis.-Green Bay	.71
83	Ill.-Chicago ■	.69
83	Wright St. ■	.68
62	Northern Ill.	.76
48	Detroit ■	.47
56	Butler	.71
71	Loyola (Ill.) ■	.81
58	Alcorn St. ■	.56
48	Wis.-Green Bay ■	.74
74	Detroit	.103
84	Wis.-Milwaukee ■	.97
82	Butler ■	.76
54	Wright St. ■	.65
58	Loyola (Ill.) ■	.100
67	Cal Poly SLO ■	.84
53	Northern Ill. ■	.61
69	Ill.-Chicago	.73

Nickname: Vikings
Colors: Green & White
Arena: Henry J. Goodman Arena
　Capacity: 13,610; Year Built: 1991
AD: John Konstantinos
SID: Rick Love

COAST GUARD
New London, CT 06320 III

Coach: Peter Barry
Alma Mater: San Francisco '70
Record: 14 Years, W-250, L-150

1996-97 SCHEDULE

Navy ....Nov. 22
Trinity (Conn.) ....Nov. 26
Wentworth Inst. ....Dec. 3
Connecticut Col. Tr. ....Dec. 6-7
MIT ....Dec. 9
Springfield ■ ....Dec. 11
Catholic Cl. ....Jan. 11-12
Norwich ....Jan. 17
Norwich ....Jan. 18
Clark (Mass.) ....Jan. 20
Babson ■ ....Jan. 22
MIT ■ ....Jan. 25
Connecticut Col. ■ ....Jan. 27
Western New Eng. ....Jan. 30
WPI ■ ....Feb. 1
Springfield ....Feb. 3
Merchant Marine ....Feb. 5
Western New Eng. ■ ....Feb. 8
Wesleyan (Conn.) ■ ....Feb. 11
Clark (Mass.) ■ ....Feb. 15
Babson ....Feb. 19
WPI ....Feb. 22

1995-96 RESULTS (15-10)

81	Roger Williams ■	.59
75	Wentworth Inst. ■	.51
93	Trinity (Conn.) ■	.88
81	Ithaca †	.92
84	Daniel Webster †	.83
64	MIT ■	.67
62	Springfield	.82
82	Clark (Mass.)	.58

82	Albertus Magnus	.65
81	Norwich ■	.58
73	Norwich ■	.60
83	Babson	.92
75	MIT	.69
76	Connecticut Col.	.84
74	Western New Eng. ■	.40
67	WPI ■	.64
75	Springfield ■	.78
64	Merchant Marine ■	.58
94	Western New Eng.	.97
67	Wesleyan (Conn.)	.57
78	Clark (Mass.)	.86
64	Babson ■	.87
77	WPI ■	.73
76	WPI ■	.74
64	Springfield	.75

Nickname: Cadets, Bears
Colors: Blue, White & Orange
Arena: John Merriman Gymnasium
　Capacity: 2,400; Year Built: 1964
AD: Chuck Mills
SID: Jason Southard

COASTAL CARO.
Conway, SC 29526 I

Coach: Michael Hopkins
Alma Mater: Coastal Caro. '83
Record: 2 Years, W-11, L-41

1996-97 SCHEDULE

Clemson ....Nov. 23
Wingate ■ ....Nov. 26
Ball St. Cl. ....Nov. 29-30
Mount Olive ■ ....Dec. 4
Virginia Tech ....Dec. 7
Lees-McRae ■ ....Dec. 14
Marquette ....Dec. 16
Furman ....Dec. 21
Tenn.-Chatt. Cl. ....Dec. 28-29
Ga. Southern ■ ....Jan. 2
Charleston So. ....Jan. 9
Winthrop ....Jan. 11
Md.-Balt. County ■ ....Jan. 18
N.C.-Asheville ....Jan. 20
Radford ....Jan. 25
Liberty ....Jan. 27
N.C.-Asheville ■ ....Jan. 30
N.C.-Greensboro ■ ....Feb. 1
Charleston So. ■ ....Feb. 3
Md.-Balt. County ....Feb. 8
Liberty ■ ....Feb. 15
Radford ■ ....Feb. 17
Winthrop ■ ....Feb. 20
N.C.-Greensboro ....Feb. 22
Big South Conf. Tr. ....Feb. 26-Mar. 1

1995-96 RESULTS (5-21)

78	Montreat ■	.59
49	Virginia Tech	.93
62	Dayton	.80
91	Allen ■	.64
62	East Caro. ■	.74
66	Auburn	.82
61	Ga. Southern	.59
87	Hampton ■	.80
52	Charleston (S.C.)	.72
50	Furman	.72
66	N.C.-Asheville ■	.77
60	N.C.-Greensboro	.85
78	Winthrop	.84
55	Radford	.64
62	Liberty ■	.67
78	Charleston So. ■	.91
67	Md.-Balt. County	.73
71	Winthrop ■	.63
86	N.C.-Asheville	.93
62	N.C.-Greensboro ■	.75
64	Charleston So.	.74
68	Radford	.87
57	Liberty	.71
66	Hampton	.95
75	Md.-Balt. County ■	.80
67	N.C.-Greensboro †	.78

Nickname: Chanticleers
Colors: Coastal Green, Bronze & Black
Arena: Myrtle Beach Convention Center
　Capacity: 5,000; Year Built: 1993
AD: George F. "Buddy" Sasser
SID: Wayne White

COE
Cedar Rapids, IA 52402 III

Coach: Brent Brase
Alma Mater: Cornell College '90
Record: 2 Years, W-22, L-23

1996-97 SCHEDULE

Central (Iowa) ■ ....Nov. 22
Loras ....Nov. 23
Wis.-Platteville ....Nov. 26
Rockford Cl. ....Nov. 29-30
Luther ■ ....Dec. 2
Illinois Col. ■ ....Dec. 6
Knox ....Dec. 7
Mt. Mercy ■ ....Jan. 6
Illinois Col. ....Jan. 10
Knox ....Jan. 11
Ripon ....Jan. 17
Lake Forest ....Jan. 18
St. Norbert ■ ....Jan. 24
Lawrence ....Jan. 25
Grinnell ■ ....Feb. 1
Monmouth (Ill.) ....Feb. 5
Cornell College ■ ....Feb. 8
Mt. Mercy ....Feb. 10
Grinnell ....Feb. 15
Monmouth (Ill.) ■ ....Feb. 19
Cornell College ....Feb. 22

1995-96 RESULTS (10-12)

54	South Dak. St.	.85
63	Upper Iowa	.81
68	Loras ■	.54
71	Knox ■	.80
89	Illinois Col. ■	.79
68	Mt. St. Joseph	.90
56	Luther	.74
67	Wartburg ■	.79
65	Central (Iowa)	.73
74	Cornell College ■	.71
57	Knox	.72
71	Illinois Col.	.61
87	Ripon ■	.80
80	Lake Forest ■	.78
65	Lawrence	.87
56	St. Norbert ■	.45
68	Monmouth (Ill.)	.66
85	Grinnell	.92
84	Mt. St. Joseph ■	.106
78	Cornell College	.65
86	Monmouth (Ill.)	.85
73	Grinnell ■	.75

Nickname: Kohawks
Colors: Crimson & Gold
Arena: Moray L. Eby Fieldhouse
　Capacity: 2,600; Year Built: 1931
AD: Barron Bremner
SID: Alice Davidson

COKER
Hartsville, SC 29550 II

Coach: Dan Schmotzer
Alma Mater: St. Edwards '74
Record: 9 Years, W-144, L-95

1996-97 SCHEDULE

N.C.-Pembroke ■ ....Nov. 16
Morris ....Nov. 19
Morris ....Nov. 23
Longwood ■ ....Nov. 26
St. Andrews ....Dec. 2
High Point ....Dec. 4
Francis Marion ....Dec. 10
Rollins Tr. ....Jan. 3-4
Belmont Abbey ....Jan. 8
Erskine ■ ....Jan. 11

Lees-McRae ....Jan. 16
Pfeiffer ■ ....Jan. 18
Mount Olive ....Jan. 20
Barton ....Jan. 23
Mount Olive ■ ....Jan. 25
Queens (N.C.) ■ ....Jan. 27
Longwood ....Jan. 30
Erskine ....Feb. 1
Barton ■ ....Feb. 3
Queens (N.C.) ....Feb. 8
Belmont Abbey ■ ....Feb. 10
St. Andrews ■ ....Feb. 13
High Point ■ ....Feb. 15
Lees-McRae ■ ....Feb. 19
Pfeiffer ....Feb. 22

1995-96 RESULTS (16-10)

80	North Ga. †	.63
56	Life (Ga.) †	.73
95	Morris ■	.80
78	N.C.-Pembroke	.74
60	Western Caro.	.58
63	Morris	.60
74	Belmont Abbey ■	.57
77	Mount Olive ■	.68
62	Life (Ga.)	.66
56	High Point	.69
50	Queens (N.C.)	.61
52	St. Andrews ■	.61
68	Lees-McRae	.64
49	Barton	.65
63	Erskine	.48
52	Pfeiffer ■	.49
48	Longwood	.53
40	High Point ■	.55
65	Queens (N.C.) ■	.58
65	St. Andrews	.59
63	Longwood ■	.60
69	Belmont Abbey	.66
76	Mount Olive	.66
58	Lees-McRae ■	.53
47	Barton ■	.49
54	Mount Olive †	.57

Nickname: Cobras
Colors: Navy Blue & Gold
Arena: Timberlake-Lawnon Gym
　Capacity: 750
AD: Tim Griggs
SID: David Shulimson

COLBY
Waterville, ME 04901 III

Coach: Dick Whitmore
Alma Mater: Bowdoin '65
Record: 26 Years, W-439, L-195

1996-97 SCHEDULE

Colby Inv. ....Nov. 22-23
Southern Maine Tr. ....Nov. 29-Dec. 1
Tufts ....Dec. 6
Southern Me. ■ ....Dec. 11
Embry-Riddle Tr. ....Dec. 28-29
Bates ■ ....Jan. 8
Mass.-Boston ■ ....Jan. 11
Amherst ....Jan. 15
Union (N.Y.) ■ ....Jan. 18
Hamilton ■ ....Jan. 19
Williams ....Jan. 24
Middlebury ....Jan. 31
Norwich ....Feb. 1
Bowdoin ■ ....Feb. 5
Trinity (Conn.) ■ ....Feb. 7
Wesleyan (Conn.) ■ ....Feb. 8
Wheaton (Mass.) ■ ....Feb. 14
Connecticut Col. ■ ....Feb. 15
Bates ....Feb. 24
Bowdoin ....Mar. 1

1995-96 RESULTS (16-11)

81	Daniel Webster ■	.56
92	Western Conn. St. ■	.86
63	Pomona-Pitzer	.68
71	Claremont-M-S	.78
97	Tufts ■	.88
70	Southern Me.	.64

59	Me.-Presque Isle ■	52
87	Southern Me. ■	68
59	St. Joseph's (Me.) †	66
68	Hamilton	83
54	Skidmore	57
76	Colby-Sawyer	83
75	Williams	76
75	Amherst ■	70
86	Bates	72
87	Middlebury ■	67
87	Norwich ■	62
58	Bowdoin ■	66
62	Wesleyan (Conn.)	46
88	Trinity (Conn.)	75
70	Wheaton (Mass.)	66
63	Connecticut Col.	56
84	Bates ■	89
69	Bowdoin	72
62	Eastern Nazarene	43
64	Mass.-Dartmouth †	59
64	Amherst	66

Nickname: White Mules
Colors: Blue & Gray
Arena: Wadsworth Gymnasium
Capacity: 2,480; Year Built: 1966
AD: Dick Whitmore
SID: Marc Glass

COLBY-SAWYER
New London, NH 03257 III

Coach: Bill Foti
Alma Mater: New Hampshire '86
Record: 4 Years, W-73, L-31

1996-97 SCHEDULE
Norwich	Nov. 23
Lyndon St. ■	Dec. 1
New England Col.	Dec. 3
Emerson Cl.	Dec. 6-7
Colby-Sawyer Tr.	Dec. 11-12
Embry-Riddle Tr.	Dec. 29-30
Bates ■	Jan. 11
Bowdoin ■	Jan. 15
Curry	Jan. 18
Middlebury	Jan. 23
Salve Regina ■	Jan. 25
Gordon ■	Jan. 27
Anna Maria	Jan. 29
Roger Williams	Feb. 1
New England Col. ■	Feb. 4
Nichols	Feb. 6
Wentworth Inst. ■	Feb. 8
Anna Maria ■	Feb. 10
Gordon	Feb. 12
Eastern Nazarene	Feb. 15
Nichols	Feb. 22

1995-96 RESULTS (18-8)
86	Norwich ■	93
93	Albertus Magnus ■	67
90	Lyndon St.	77
101	New England Col. ■	63
62	Wesleyan (Conn.)	56
87	Rivier †	89
105	New England Col.	73
107	Bates	98
119	Curry ■	88
83	Colby ■	76
84	Middlebury ■	81
80	Salve Regina	72
91	Gordon	79
84	Anna Maria ■	90
102	Roger Williams ■	75
80	New England Col.	57
100	Nichols ■	81
68	Wentworth Inst.	87
74	Anna Maria	75
84	Gordon ■	65
102	Eastern Nazarene ■	82
78	Rivier	90
71	Bowdoin	84
84	Nichols	82
115	Roger Williams ■	80
68	Wentworth Inst.	71

Nickname: Chargers
Colors: Blue & White
Arena: Hogan Sports Center
Capacity: 650; Year Built: 1991
AD: Debi McGrath
SID: Adam S. Kamras

COLGATE
Hamilton, NY 13346 I

Coach: Jack Bruen
Alma Mater: Catholic '72
Record: 14 Years, W-204, L-180

1996-97 SCHEDULE
Dartmouth	Nov. 22
Fairfield ■	Nov. 26
Nebraska Cl.	Dec. 6-7
Harvard ■	Dec. 20
Syracuse	Dec. 22
Indiana Hoosier Cl.	Dec. 27-28
Canisius	Jan. 2
Siena	Jan. 4
Manhattan ■	Jan. 6
Bucknell ■	Jan. 8
Navy ■	Jan. 11
Holy Cross	Jan. 15
Army	Jan. 18
Cornell	Jan. 21
Iona ■	Jan. 23
Lehigh	Jan. 25
Lafayette ■	Jan. 29
Bucknell	Feb. 1
Navy	Feb. 5
Holy Cross ■	Feb. 8
Army	Feb. 12
St. Bonaventure [Buffalo]	Feb. 17
Lehigh ■	Feb. 19
Lafayette	Feb. 22
Patriot Conf. Tr.	Mar. 1-5

1995-96 RESULTS (15-15)
57	Georgetown	106
55	Syracuse	89
53	Mississippi †	51
59	Iowa	79
68	Niagara †	72
75	Cornell	70
63	Canisius	65
77	Providence	83
51	Canisius	62
66	Yale	56
60	Manhattan	73
54	Harvard	63
82	Fairfield	92
85	Holy Cross ■	67
77	Lehigh	60
89	Navy	67
75	Bucknell ■	83
81	Army	72
74	Iona	97
91	Lafayette ■	76
101	Siena ■	84
89	Holy Cross	94
79	Lehigh	67
57	Navy ■	60
73	Bucknell	68
88	Army ■	73
85	Lafayette	72
67	Bucknell †	61
74	Holy Cross ■	65
59	Connecticut †	68

Nickname: Red Raiders
Colors: Maroon, Gray & White
Arena: Cotterell Court
Capacity: 3,091; Year Built: 1966
AD: Mark Murphy
SID: Bob Cornell

COLORADO
Boulder, CO 80309 I

Coach: Ricardo Patton
Alma Mater: Belmont '80
Record: 1 Year, W-4, L-9

1996-97 SCHEDULE
Drake	Nov. 24
Hawaii-Hilo Inv.	Nov. 29-Dec. 1
Texas-Arlington ■	Dec. 5
George Mason	Dec. 7
Wyoming	Dec. 10
Colorado St. ■	Dec. 12
UC Santa Barb. ■	Dec. 21
Georgia	Dec. 23
Mo.-Kansas City	Dec. 28
Northwestern St.	Dec. 30
Nebraska ■	Jan. 4
Missouri ■	Jan. 7
Texas Tech	Jan. 11
Oklahoma St. ■	Jan. 15
Iowa St. ■	Jan. 18
Baylor	Jan. 21
Kansas ■	Jan. 26
Kansas St.	Jan. 29
Nebraska	Feb. 5
Texas A&M ■	Feb. 8
Oklahoma	Feb. 12
Kansas	Feb. 15
Kansas St. ■	Feb. 19
Missouri ■	Feb. 22
Wofford ■	Feb. 24
Iowa St.	Feb. 26
Texas ■	Mar. 1
Big 12 Conf. Tr.	Mar. 6-9

1995-96 RESULTS (9-18)
47	UC Santa Barb.	71
85	Northwestern St. ■	82
86	Tennessee St.	72
132	George Mason ■	117
71	Colorado St.	91
77	Houston ■	74
81	Wyoming ■	83
92	Texas-San Antonio ■	77
85	Iowa ■	100
68	Washington	76
66	Missouri	77
74	Nebraska	79
57	Kansas St.	70
80	Southern Utah ■	82
78	Kansas ■	80
63	Iowa St. ■	75
106	Missouri ■	94
73	Oklahoma St.	96
64	Kansas St.	63
84	Mo.-Kansas City ■	55
70	Kansas	85
88	Oklahoma ■	119
59	Oklahoma	81
64	Oklahoma St. ■	66
78	Nebraska ■	64
65	Iowa St.	74
55	Kansas †	88

Nickname: Golden Buffaloes
Colors: Silver, Gold & Black
Arena: Coors Events/Conference Center
Capacity: 11,198; Year Built: 1979
AD: Dick Tharp
SID: Matt Finnigan

COLO. CHRISTIAN
Lakewood, CO 80226 II

Coach: Craig Ross
Alma Mater: Minn.-Morris '89
Record: 1 Year, W-5, L-22

1996-97 SCHEDULE
Southwest St. Cl.	Nov. 22-23
Baker	Nov. 30
Southwest St.	Dec. 2
Adams St.	Dec. 6
Fort Lewis	Dec. 7
Western St.	Dec. 13
Mesa St. ■	Dec. 14
Colorado Col. ■	Dec. 30
N.M. Highlands	Jan. 4
UC-Colo. Spgs. ■	Jan. 10
Southern Colo.	Jan. 11
Regis (Colo.)	Jan. 14
Denver	Jan. 16
Chadron St.	Jan. 18
Colorado Mines ■	Jan. 24
Metro St. ■	Jan. 25
Fort Hays St.	Jan. 31
Neb.-Kearney	Feb. 1
Colorado Mines	Feb. 7
Metro St.	Feb. 8
Regis (Colo.) ■	Feb. 12
Chadron St. ■	Feb. 15
Fort Hays St. ■	Feb. 21
Neb.-Kearney ■	Feb. 22

1995-96 RESULTS (5-21)
Results unavailable

Nickname: Cougars
Colors: Blue & Gold
Arena: CCU Gymnasium
Capacity: 1,500; Year Built: 1990
AD: Michael Sumpter
SID: Kevin Hudson

COLORADO COL.
Colorado Springs, CO 80903 ..III

Coach: Brett Zuver
Alma Mater: Lake Superior St. '91
Record: 2 Years, W-25, L-25

1996-97 SCHEDULE
Menlo Cl.	Nov. 22-23
Regis (Colo.) ■	Nov. 26
Colorado Col. Tr.	Nov. 29-30
Panhandle St. ■	Dec. 2
McMurry Tr.	Dec. 5-6
Fort Lewis	Dec. 10
Metro St.	Dec. 28
Colo. Christian	Dec. 30
Wis.-Eau Claire Cl.	Jan. 2-3
Fort Lewis ■	Jan. 8
Bellevue ■	Jan. 10
Bethany (Kan.)	Jan. 13
McPherson	Jan. 14
Central (Iowa)	Jan. 18
Denver	Jan. 30
Metro St. ■	Feb. 1
Southern Colo. ■	Feb. 10
Panhandle St.	Feb. 15
Bellevue	Feb. 21
Neb. Wesleyan	Mar. 1

1995-96 RESULTS (14-11)
110	Grinnell	132
79	William Penn †	59
78	Central (Iowa) ■	58
78	Lakeland ■	72
90	Alma	73
76	Defiance †	71
68	UC-Colo. Spgs.	81
63	Northern Ariz.	81
99	Bethany (Kan.) ■	81
99	Oglethorpe	68
72	DePauw †	85
91	Fort Lewis	80
95	Adams St. ■	114
84	Northwestern Okla. ■	77
85	Bellevue	77
73	Denver ■	77
81	Metro St.	92
87	Panhandle St.	97
60	Regis (Colo.)	82
93	UC-Colo. Spgs.	77
74	Southwestern (Kan.)	80
60	Mesa St.	97
100	Bellevue ■	83
71	Panhandle St.	66
76	Neb. Wesleyan ■	74

Nickname: Tigers
Colors: Black & Gold
Arena: J. Juan Reid Gymnasium
Capacity: 1,000; Year Built: 1970
AD: Marty Scarano
SID: Dave Moross

COLORADO MINES
Golden, CO 80401 II

Coach: Keith Brown
Alma Mater: Pacific (Cal.) '78
Record: 4 Years, W-33, L-80

1996-97 SCHEDULE
Bay Ridge Christian ■	Nov. 21
Montana Tech	Nov. 22-23
Rice	Nov. 26
UC-Colo. Spgs.	Dec. 6
Southern Colo.	Dec. 7
Adams St. ■	Dec. 13
Fort Lewis ■	Dec. 14
Las Vegas Cl.	Dec. 18-19
Western St.	Jan. 3
Mesa St.	Jan. 4
N.M. Highlands ■	Jan. 11
Fort Hays St. ■	Jan. 17
Neb.-Kearney ■	Jan. 18
Colo. Christian	Jan. 24
Regis (Colo.)	Jan. 25
Metro St.	Jan. 28
Chadron St.	Feb. 1
Colo. Christian ■	Feb. 7
Regis (Colo.) ■	Feb. 8
Fort Hays St.	Feb. 14
Neb.-Kearney	Feb. 15
Metro St. ■	Feb. 19
Denver ■	Feb. 21
Chadron St. ■	Feb. 25

1995-96 RESULTS (13-15)
69	Metro St.	67
60	Northern Colo. †	68
74	Panhandle St.	81
89	Chadron St. ■	81
68	UC Davis ■	62
59	Cal Poly Pomona ■	64
61	Fort Hays St. ■	80
91	Neb.-Kearney ■	104
98	Bethany (Kan.) ■	67
66	Cal St. Bakersfield	89
88	Cal St. Stanislaus †	85
63	Cal St. Northridge	59
72	N.M. Highlands	74
76	Western St.	71
67	Mesa St.	66
81	Fort Lewis ■	100
68	Adams St. ■	75
100	Chadron St.	84
69	Denver ■	79
75	N.M. Highlands ■	60
69	Fort Hays St.	86
78	Neb.-Kearney	99
92	Western St. ■	82
85	Mesa St. ■	98
104	Fort Lewis	84
64	Adams St.	76
83	Adams St.	82
61	Fort Hays St. †	81

Nickname: Orediggers
Colors: Silver & Blue
Arena: Volk Gymnasium
    Capacity: 1,000; Year Built: 1959
AD: Marv Kay
SID: Steve Smith

COLORADO ST.
Fort Collins, CO 80523 I

Coach: Stew Morrill
Alma Mater: Gonzaga '74
Record: 10 Years, W-178, L-120

1996-97 SCHEDULE
Simon Fraser ■	Nov. 15
Adams St. ■	Nov. 22
Texas A&M ■	Nov. 26
Bucknell ■	Nov. 30
Nevada ■	Dec. 3
Colorado St. Cl.	Dec. 6-7
Colorado	Dec. 12
Utah St.	Dec. 14

Chicago St. ■	Dec. 21
Denver ■	Dec. 28
Cleveland St.	Dec. 30
Utah	Jan. 4
Wyoming ■	Jan. 11
Hawaii	Jan. 16
San Diego St.	Jan. 18
Fresno St. ■	Jan. 23
San Jose St. ■	Jan. 25
UNLV	Jan. 30
Air Force	Feb. 1
Wyoming	Feb. 6
Utah ■	Feb. 8
San Diego St. ■	Feb. 13
Hawaii ■	Feb. 15
San Jose St.	Feb. 20
Fresno St.	Feb. 22
Air Force ■	Feb. 27
UNLV ■	Mar. 1
Western Ath. Conf. Tr.	Mar. 4-8

1995-96 RESULTS (18-12)
89	Montana Tech ■	55
91	Arkansas St. ■	67
78	Northeast La. ■	60
58	Weber St. ■	66
91	Colorado ■	71
75	Nevada	76
72	East Caro.	80
78	Western Mich.	77
94	West Tex. A&M ■	64
67	San Diego St.	87
74	Hawaii	69
68	Wyoming	63
66	UTEP ■	62
65	New Mexico	67
82	Utah	86
78	Brigham Young	76
91	Fresno St. ■	83
94	Air Force ■	71
72	Fresno St.	86
91	Air Force	89
81	Brigham Young ■	76
73	Utah ■	78
77	UTEP	76
66	New Mexico ■	78
80	Wyoming ■	66
87	San Diego St. ■	74
65	Hawaii ■	75
100	Brigham Young †	84
69	Utah †	71
83	Nebraska ■	91

Nickname: Rams
Colors: Green & Gold
Arena: Moby Arena
    Capacity: 10,000; Year Built: 1966
AD: Tom Jurich
SID: Gary Ozzello

UC-COLO. SPGS.
Colorado Springs, CO 80933 ...II

Coach: Ed Pipes
Alma Mater: Okla. Christian '78
(First year as head coach)

1996-97 SCHEDULE
Panhandle St.	Nov. 22
Eastern N.M.	Nov. 24
UC-Colo. Springs Cl.	Nov. 29-30
West Tex. A&M ■	Dec. 2
Colorado Mines ■	Dec. 6
Metro St. ■	Dec. 7
Chadron St.	Dec. 14
Air Force	Dec. 21
Fort Hays St. ■	Jan. 3
Neb.-Kearney ■	Jan. 4
Colo. Christian	Jan. 10
Regis (Colo.)	Jan. 11
Western St. ■	Jan. 17
Mesa St. ■	Jan. 18
Adams St.	Jan. 24
Fort Lewis	Jan. 25
Southern Colo. ■	Jan. 29
N.M. Highlands	Feb. 2

Adams St. ■	Feb. 7
Fort Lewis ■	Feb. 8
Denver	Feb. 11
Western St.	Feb. 14
Mesa St.	Feb. 15
Southern Colo.	Feb. 19
N.M. Highlands ■	Feb. 22

1995-96 RESULTS (5-20)
Results unavailable

Nickname: Gold
Colors: Gold & Colorado Blue
Arena: Gold Pit
    Capacity: 500; Year Built: 1989
AD: Theophilus Gregory
SID: Jerry Cross

COLUMBIA
New York, NY 10027 I

Coach: Armond Hill
Alma Mater: Princeton '85
Record: 1 Year, W-7, L-19

1996-97 SCHEDULE
New Mexico Cl.	Nov. 22-23
Fordham ■	Nov. 26
Providence	Nov. 30
Illinois Cl.	Dec. 6-7
St. Francis (N.Y.) ■	Dec. 10
Cal St. Fullerton	Dec. 30
San Diego	Jan. 2
Lehigh	Jan. 6
Harvard	Jan. 10
Dartmouth	Jan. 11
Ursinus ■	Jan. 14
Cornell	Jan. 18
Army ■	Jan. 20
Cornell ■	Jan. 25
Pennsylvania ■	Jan. 31
Princeton ■	Feb. 1
Yale	Feb. 7
Brown	Feb. 8
Dartmouth ■	Feb. 14
Harvard ■	Feb. 15
Brown ■	Feb. 21
Yale ■	Feb. 22
Princeton	Feb. 28
Pennsylvania	Mar. 1

1995-96 RESULTS (7-19)
77	Ursinus ■	35
60	Fordham	48
45	Marquette	72
39	Texas A&M †	65
73	Army	59
60	Syracuse	83
42	Canisius †	64
51	Lafayette	64
67	Florida Int'l	82
62	Miami (Fla.)	69
58	Fla. Atlantic	70
76	Lehigh ■	69
57	Dartmouth	59
48	Harvard	72
71	Cornell ■	75
63	Cornell	76
45	Princeton	66
50	Pennsylvania	74
62	Brown ■	74
74	Yale	58
44	Harvard ■	71
54	Dartmouth ■	71
63	Yale	62
61	Brown	55
62	Pennsylvania ■	82
55	Princeton ■	57

Nickname: Lions
Colors: Columbia Blue & White
Arena: Levien Gym
    Capacity: 3,408; Year Built: 1974
AD: John Reeves
SID: Todd Kennedy

COLUMBUS ST.
Columbus, GA 31907 II

Coach: Herbert Greene
Alma Mater: Auburn '66
Record: 17 Years, W-296, L-181

1996-97 SCHEDULE
Edward Waters ■	Nov. 23
Ga. Southwestern	Nov. 26
Albany St. (Ga.) ■	Nov. 30
Lander	Dec. 7
Ga. Southwestern ■	Dec. 10
Lander ■	Dec. 12
Albany St. (Ga.)	Dec. 16
Francis Marion ■	Jan. 4
Kennesaw St.	Jan. 6
Georgia Col. ■	Jan. 8
S.C.-Spartanburg	Jan. 11
Armstrong Atlantic	Jan. 15
Augusta St.	Jan. 18
S.C.-Aiken	Jan. 22
N.C.-Pembroke ■	Jan. 26
Kennesaw St. ■	Jan. 29
Francis Marion	Feb. 1
N.C.-Pembroke	Feb. 2
Georgia Col.	Feb. 5
S.C.-Spartanburg ■	Feb. 8
Armstrong Atlantic ■	Feb. 12
Clayton St. ■	Feb. 15
S.C.-Aiken ■	Feb. 19
Augusta St. ■	Feb. 22

1995-96 RESULTS (26-6)
96	Albany St. (Ga.) ■	88
75	Piedmont ■	59
66	West Ga.	81
88	Fort Valley St.	72
73	Lander	67
84	Albany St. (Ga.)	89
86	Talladega	81
82	Lander ■	67
101	Fort Valley St.	90
66	Kennesaw St. ■	50
78	Francis Marion	69
81	N.C.-Pembroke	72
74	Georgia Col.	85
101	S.C.-Spartanburg ■	91
67	Armstrong Atlantic	70
80	S.C.-Aiken	73
87	Augusta St. ■	74
79	N.C.-Pembroke ■	74
84	Kennesaw St.	77
74	Francis Marion ■	48
82	Georgia Col. ■	79
77	S.C.-Spartanburg	80
79	Armstrong Atlantic ■	61
92	Clayton St. ■	61
95	S.C.-Aiken ■	71
100	Augusta St.	98
49	Francis Marion †	30
93	N.C.-Pembroke †	66
95	S.C.-Spartanburg †	83
88	Rollins †	80
83	Fla. Southern †	77
82	Alabama A&M †	98

Nickname: Cougars
Colors: Red, White & Blue
Arena: Woodruff Gym
    Capacity: 1,700; Year Built: 1963
AD: Herbert Greene
SID: Mike Peacock

CONCORD
Athens, WV 24712 II

Coach: Steve Cox
Alma Mater: Salem-Teikyo '74
Record: 7 Years, W-128, L-80

1996-97 SCHEDULE
Salem-Teikyo Tr.	Nov. 15-16
Ohio Valley	Nov. 25
Ohio Valley ■	Dec. 3
Catawba Cl.	Dec. 6-7

Radford ....Dec. 12
West Va. Tech ....Dec. 14
Bluefield St. ■ ....Dec. 16
Davis & Elkins ■ ....Jan. 8
Fairmont St. ■ ....Jan. 11
Alderson-Broaddus ....Jan. 13
West Liberty St. ■ ....Jan. 17
Wheeling Jesuit ■ ....Jan. 18
Charleston (W.Va.) ....Jan. 22
West Va. Wesleyan ■ ....Jan. 25
Glenville St. ....Jan. 27
West Va. St. ....Jan. 29
Salem-Teikyo ....Feb. 1
West Va. Tech ■ ....Feb. 5
Shepherd ■ ....Feb. 8
Bluefield St. ....Feb. 12
Charleston (W.Va.) ....Feb. 15
West Va. Wesleyan ■ ....Feb. 17
Glenville St. ■ ....Feb. 19
West Va. St. ....Feb. 22

1995-96 RESULTS (12-17)
93	Ohio Valley †	66
76	Salem-Teikyo	95
91	Bluefield Col.	101
82	Anderson (S.C.) †	58
75	Catawba	87
80	Bluefield St.	89
93	West Va. Tech ■	103
90	Bluefield Col.	62
77	Ohio Valley	65
61	Davis & Elkins ■	81
74	Fairmont St.	83
66	Alderson-Broaddus ■	79
77	West Liberty St.	70
68	Wheeling Jesuit	76
80	Charleston (W.Va.) ■	82
54	West Va. Wesleyan	71
67	Glenville St.	66
72	West Va. St.	94
66	Salem-Teikyo ■	81
84	West Va. Tech	79
73	Shepherd	71
103	Bluefield St.	92
88	Charleston (W.Va.)	84
79	West Va. Wesleyan ■	87
70	Glenville St. ■	75
81	West Va. St.	87
76	Charleston (W.Va.)	73
70	West Liberty St. †	67
81	West Va. Tech †	86

Nickname: Mountain Lions
Colors: Maroon & Gray
Arena: Centennial Hall
 Capacity: 2,500; Year Built: 1972
AD: Don Christie
SID: Don Christie

CONCORDIA (ILL.)
River Forest, IL 60305 III

Coach: Gary Gutenkunst
Alma Mater: Concordia (Neb.) '81
Record: 2 Years, W-18, L-32
1996-97 SCHEDULE
Albion Tr. ....Nov. 22-23
Lawrence ....Nov. 26
Elmhurst ■ ....Dec. 3
Rose-Hulman Inv ....Dec. 6-8
Beloit ■ ....Dec. 9
North Central ....Dec. 13
Benedictine (Ill.) ■ ....Dec. 18
Lipscomb ....Jan. 4
Rockford ■ ....Jan. 6
Trinity Int'l ....Jan. 11
Judson (Ill.) ■ ....Jan. 15
Aurora ■ ....Jan. 18
Eureka ....Jan. 22
Concordia (Ill.) Inv ....Jan. 24-25
Clarke ....Jan. 29
Benedictine (Ill.) ....Feb. 1
Trinity Int'l ■ ....Feb. 5
Judson (Ill.) ....Feb. 8
Aurora ....Feb. 12

Eureka ■ ....Feb. 15
Rockford ....Feb. 19
Clarke ■ ....Feb. 22

1995-96 RESULTS (9-16)
63	Ripon	94
69	North Park †	87
60	Elmhurst	63
53	Hope	107
58	Anderson (Ind.)	83
72	Concordia (Mich.) ■	69
65	Beloit	84
68	St. Joseph's (Ind.)	94
65	Concordia (Cal.) †	84
63	Cal Lutheran	82
65	Concordia (Cal.)	85
46	St. Norbert ■	43
92	Rockford	65
96	Marian (Wis.) ■	92
64	Benedictine (Ill.)	62
72	Aurora ■	84
67	Concordia (Wis.) †	75
78	Concordia-St. Paul †	67
88	Judson (Ill.)	58
60	Rockford	63
86	Judson (Ill.)	81
85	Trinity Int'l	95
81	Aurora	100
91	Benedictine (Ill.) ■	78
86	Trinity Int'l	91

Nickname: Cougars
Colors: Maroon & Gold
Arena: Geisman Gymnasium
 Capacity: 2,200; Year Built: 1964
AD: Jan Fisher
SID: Jim Egan

CONCORDIA (N.Y.)
Bronxville, NY 10708 II

Coach: Lou DeMello
Alma Mater: Manhattan '84
Record: 2 Years, W-13, L-41
1996-97 SCHEDULE
Dominican (N.Y.) ■ ....Nov. 27
Nova Southeastern ■ ....Nov. 29
Pace ....Dec. 4
Lynn Cl. ....Dec. 6-7
Dowling ....Dec. 11
Molloy ■ ....Dec. 14
Adelphi ■ ....Dec. 21
St. Rose ....Jan. 4
Phila. Textile ■ ....Jan. 6
New York Tech ....Jan. 8
LIU-C. W. Post ....Jan. 11
Mercy ■ ....Jan. 13
LIU-Southampton ....Jan. 15
Queens (N.Y.) ■ ....Jan. 18
Pace ....Jan. 20
Adelphi ....Jan. 22
Dowling ■ ....Jan. 25
Molloy ....Jan. 29
St. Rose ■ ....Feb. 1
Phila. Textile ....Feb. 5
New York Tech ■ ....Feb. 8
LIU-C. W. Post ■ ....Feb. 12
Mercy ....Feb. 15
LIU-Southampton ■ ....Feb. 19
Queens (N.Y.) ....Feb. 22

1995-96 RESULTS (5-21)
80	Bloomfield	59
65	Dominican (N.Y.)	73
71	LIU-Southampton	66
56	Mount Olive	60
78	Dist. Columbia †	62
70	LIU-C. W. Post ■	73
74	Molloy	66
51	Phila. Textile	56
55	Adelphi	73
75	Dowling ■	78
46	Pace	70
66	St. Rose	98
68	Queens (N.Y.) ■	73
53	New York Tech	95
79	LIU-Southampton	83
64	Adelphi ■	84
82	Mercy	78
52	LIU-C. W. Post	61
60	Molloy	71
40	Phila. Textile	69
89	Mercy ■	92
69	Dowling	86
51	Pace	69
40	St. Rose ■	85
51	Queens (N.Y.)	65
61	New York Tech ■	110

Nickname: Clippers
Colors: Blue & Gold
Arena: Meyer Athletic Center
 Capacity: 1,000; Year Built: 1963
AD: Ivan Marquez
SID: Ivan Marquez

CONCORDIA-M'HEAD
Moorhead, MN 56560 III

Coach: Duane Siverson
Alma Mater: Yankton '78
Record: 5 Years, W-67, L-58
1996-97 SCHEDULE
New Jersey Tech Tr. ....Nov. 22-23
Moorhead St. ....Nov. 26
St. John's (Minn.) ....Dec. 7
Gust. Adolphus ■ ....Dec. 11
Carleton ....Dec. 14
St. Mary's (Minn.) ■ ....Jan. 4
Macalester ....Jan. 6
St. Olaf ■ ....Jan. 8
St. Thomas (Minn.) ....Jan. 13
Hamline ■ ....Jan. 15
Augsburg ....Jan. 18
Bethel (Minn.) ■ ....Jan. 22
St. John's (Minn.) ■ ....Jan. 25
Gust. Adolphus ....Jan. 29
Carleton ■ ....Feb. 1
Macalester ■ ....Feb. 5
St. Olaf ....Feb. 8
St. Mary's (Minn.) ■ ....Feb. 10
St. Thomas (Minn.) ■ ....Feb. 15
Hamline ....Feb. 17
Augsburg ■ ....Feb. 19
Bethel (Minn.) ....Feb. 22

1995-96 RESULTS (21-6)
73	Jamestown ■	70
87	Minn.-Crookston	63
90	Hamline	77
76	St. Thomas (Minn.) ■	53
62	Gust. Adolphus	74
83	Moorhead St. ■	89
87	Jamestown	83
67	St. John's (Minn.) ■	66
84	Carleton ■	77
84	Augsburg	73
81	Macalester ■	72
75	St. Mary's (Minn.)	59
71	St. Olaf	70
104	Bethel (Minn.) ■	78
95	Hamline	75
70	St. Thomas (Minn.)	53
62	Gust. Adolphus ■	69
77	St. John's (Minn.)	86
78	Carleton	100
68	Augsburg ■	66
83	Macalester	65
68	St. Mary's (Minn.) ■	49
86	St. Olaf	77
93	Bethel (Minn.)	90
83	Carleton	71
47	Gust. Adolphus	43
61	Gust. Adolphus	72

Nickname: Cobbers
Colors: Maroon & Gold
Arena: Memorial Auditorium
 Capacity: 3,500; Year Built: 1951
AD: Armin Pipho
SID: Jerry Pyle

CONNECTICUT
Storrs, CT 06269 I

Coach: Jim Calhoun
Alma Mater: American Int'l '68
Record: 24 Years, W-470, L-236
1996-97 SCHEDULE
Indiana [Indianapolis] ....Nov. 15
Northeastern ■ ....Nov. 25
Yale ■ ....Nov. 29
Southwest Tex. St. ■ ....Dec. 2
Pittsburgh ....Dec. 4
Boston College ■ ....Dec. 7
Fairfield ■ ....Dec. 21
Virginia ■ ....Dec. 23
Massachusetts ■ ....Dec. 27
Hartford ■ ....Dec. 29
Rutgers ■ ....Jan. 2
West Va. ■ ....Jan. 4
St. John's (N.Y.) ■ ....Jan. 8
Georgetown ....Jan. 11
Kansas ....Jan. 19
Miami (Fla.) ....Jan. 22
Syracuse ■ ....Jan. 26
Providence ■ ....Jan. 29
Seton Hall ....Feb. 1
Georgetown ■■ ....Feb. 3
Notre Dame ....Feb. 8
Boston College ....Feb. 12
Miami (Fla.) ■ ....Feb. 15
Syracuse ....Feb. 17
Villanova ....Feb. 23
Pittsburgh ■ ....Feb. 25
Seton Hall ....Mar. 1
Big East Conf. Tr. ....Mar. 5-8

1995-96 RESULTS (32-3)
102	Texas Christian †	76
95	Iowa †	101
86	Indiana †	52
86	Northeastern ■	39
63	Boston College ■	62
85	Notre Dame	65
93	Yale ■	66
79	Florida St.	61
86	Fairfield ■	52
77	Charleston (S.C.)	60
102	Hartford ■	63
89	West Va.	79
73	Miami (Fla.) ■	52
81	Villanova ■	73
83	Providence	74
88	St. John's (N.Y.) ■	73
79	Syracuse	59
116	Central Conn. St. ■	46
69	Pittsburgh	63
76	Virginia ■	46
77	Rutgers	59
77	St. John's (N.Y.)	63
99	Providence ■	77
87	West Va. ■	69
85	Notre Dame ■	77
65	Georgetown	77
70	Villanova	59
78	Rutgers ■	66
79	Pittsburgh	58
79	Seton Hall	58
79	Seton Hall †	58
85	Syracuse †	67
75	Georgetown †	74
68	Colgate †	59
95	Eastern Mich. †	81
55	Mississippi St. †	60

Nickname: Huskies
Colors: Blue & White
Arena: Harry A. Gampel Pavilion
 Capacity: 8,241; Year Built: 1990
AD: Lew Perkins
SID: Tim Tolokan

CONNECTICUT COL
New London, CT 06320 III

Coach: Glen Miller

Alma Mater: Northeastern
Record: 3 Years, W-28, L-46

1996-97 SCHEDULE

Babson Inv.	Nov. 22-23
Manhattanville	Nov. 26
Roger Williams ■	Dec. 3
Connecticut Col. Tr.	Dec. 6-7
Salve Regina	Dec. 11
Davidson	Jan. 5
Albertus Magnus	Jan. 8
Williams ■	Jan. 11
Curry ■	Jan. 14
Suffolk	Jan. 18
Amherst ■	Jan. 21
Middlebury ■	Jan. 25
Coast Guard	Jan. 27
Trinity (Conn.)	Feb. 1
Wheaton (Mass.) ■	Feb. 4
MIT	Feb. 6
Nichols ■	Feb. 10
Bowdoin	Feb. 14
Colby	Feb. 15
Wesleyan (Conn.) ■	Feb. 18
Bates ■	Feb. 22
Tufts ■	Mar. 1

1995-96 RESULTS (18-8)

72	Gettysburg	98
72	Heidelberg †	93
74	Manhattanville ■	72
80	Roger Williams	60
92	Daniel Webster ■	73
87	Ithaca	82
82	Salve Regina ■	75
102	Curry	78
84	Albertus Magnus ■	70
97	Suffolk ■	65
82	Amherst	107
50	Middlebury	64
84	Coast Guard ■	76
67	Endicott	57
68	Trinity (Conn.) ■	74
82	Wheaton (Mass.)	66
47	MIT ■	44
105	Nichols	54
76	Bowdoin ■	59
56	Colby ■	63
71	Wesleyan (Conn.)	68
99	Bates	78
68	Williams	86
83	Tufts	79
81	Bri'water (Mass.)	72
59	Amherst	73

Nickname: Camels
Colors: Royal Blue & White
Arena: Luce Fieldhouse/Gymnasium
 Capacity: 800; Year Built: 1992
AD: Robert Malekoff
SID: Michael King

COPPIN ST.

Baltimore, MD 21216 I

Coach: Ron Mitchell
Alma Mater: Edison St. '84
Record: 10 Years, W-183, L-111

1996-97 SCHEDULE

Oklahoma	Nov. 30
Nebraska Cl.	Dec. 6-7
Duquesne ■	Dec. 10
Kansas St.	Dec. 12
Illinois	Dec. 14
Michigan St. Cl.	Dec. 27-28
South Caro. St.	Jan. 9
Hampton	Jan. 11
North Caro. A&T ■	Jan. 15
Hampton ■	Jan. 18
Md.-East. Shore	Jan. 20
Florida A&M ■	Jan. 25
Bethune-Cookman ■	Jan. 27
Howard	Jan. 30
Morgan St.	Feb. 1
Delaware St.	Feb. 5
Morgan St. ■	Feb. 8

Howard ■	Feb. 10
Delaware St. ■	Feb. 12
Florida A&M	Feb. 15
Bethune-Cookman	Feb. 17
South Caro. St. ■	Feb. 20
North Caro. A&T ■	Feb. 26
Md.-East. Shore ■	Mar. 1
Mid-Eastern Conf. Tr.	Mar. 5-8

1995-96 RESULTS (19-10)

119	Lincoln (Pa.) ■	73
98	West Va. St. ■	63
69	Marquette	95
76	Duquesne	77
86	Ill.-Chicago ■	73
86	Texas Christian	89
55	Ball St.	78
57	Wis.-Green Bay	66
92	Ohio †	94
59	Iowa St.	77
82	North Caro. A&T ■	71
72	Md.-East. Shore ■	69
92	Delaware St.	77
71	Bethune-Cookman	55
81	Florida A&M	65
69	Md.-East. Shore	60
78	Morgan St. ■	77
62	Howard	63
91	Morgan St. ■	68
93	Bethune-Cookman ■	79
78	Florida A&M ■	68
90	Delaware St. ■	77
78	North Caro. A&T	60
69	South Caro. St.	81
73	South Caro. St.	70
87	Howard ■	54
83	Howard †	63
78	Delaware St. †	64
56	South Caro. St. †	69

Nickname: Eagles
Colors: Royal Blue & Gold
Arena: Coppin Center
 Capacity: 3,000; Year Built: 1987
AD: Ron Mitchell
SID: David Popham

CORNELL

Ithaca, NY 14853 I

Coach: Scott Thompson
Alma Mater: Iowa '76
Record: 9 Years, W-105, L-149

1996-97 SCHEDULE

Buffalo ■	Nov. 26
Lehigh	Nov. 30
Haverford ■	Dec. 2
Purdue Inv.	Dec. 6-7
Iona	Dec. 14
Montana St. Cl.	Dec. 28-29
Bucknell ■	Jan. 3
Lafayette ■	Jan. 6
Dartmouth	Jan. 10
Harvard	Jan. 11
Army	Jan. 14
Columbia ■	Jan. 18
Colgate ■	Jan. 21
Columbia	Jan. 25
Princeton ■	Jan. 31
Pennsylvania ■	Feb. 1
Brown	Feb. 7
Yale	Feb. 8
Harvard ■	Feb. 14
Dartmouth ■	Feb. 15
Yale ■	Feb. 21
Brown ■	Feb. 22
Pennsylvania	Feb. 28
Princeton	Mar. 1

1995-96 RESULTS (10-16)

69	Lafayette	78
64	Iona	70
74	Wagner †	69
82	Lehigh ■	61
70	Colgate ■	75
60	LSU	70

46	Kansas	100
59	Bucknell	80
90	Elmira ■	52
47	Harvard	65
57	Dartmouth	68
78	Army ■	75
75	Columbia	71
61	Holy Cross	68
76	Columbia ■	63
63	Pennsylvania	77
54	Princeton	57
49	Yale ■	53
67	Brown ■	53
61	Dartmouth ■	57
60	Harvard ■	65
75	Brown	79
71	Yale	65
62	Buffalo	60
49	Princeton ■	65
55	Pennsylvania ■	70

Nickname: Big Red
Colors: Carnelian & White
Arena: Newman Arena
 Capacity: 4,750; Year Built: 1989
AD: Charles H. Moore
SID: Patrick Gillespie

CORNELL COLLEGE

Mt. Vernon, IA 52314 III

Coach: Ed Timm
Alma Mater: Central (Iowa) '85
Record: 3 Years, W-25, L-44

1996-97 SCHEDULE

Lawrence Tr.	Nov. 22-23
Clarke ■	Nov. 26
Monmouth (Ill.)	Dec. 7
Franklin Tr.	Dec. 13-14
Wartburg ■	Dec. 21
Cornell College Tr.	Jan. 3-4
Monmouth (Ill.)	Jan. 11
Beloit	Jan. 17
Carroll (Wis.)	Jan. 18
Lake Forest ■	Jan. 24
Ripon ■	Jan. 25
Knox	Jan. 29
Illinois Col. ■	Feb. 1
Grinnell	Feb. 5
Coe	Feb. 8
Knox ■	Feb. 12
Illinois Col.	Feb. 15
Grinnell ■	Feb. 19
Coe ■	Feb. 22

1995-96 RESULTS (4-17)

69	Mt. St. Joseph	90
87	Pillsbury †	77
111	Rockford ■	99
55	Luther ■	69
59	Loras	75
91	Simpson	105
76	Monmouth (Ill.)	82
77	Thomas More	97
76	St. Ambrose †	114
71	Coe	74
88	Monmouth (Ill.) ■	62
107	Grinnell ■	104
62	Carroll (Wis.) ■	75
63	Beloit	68
44	Lake Forest	78
67	Ripon	104
46	Knox	83
65	Coe ■	78
64	Grinnell	88
83	Illinois Col. ■	87
55	Knox ■	58

Nickname: Rams
Colors: Purple & White
Arena: Cornell Fieldhouse
 Capacity: 2,500; Year Built: 1926
AD: Charles Moore
SID: Greg Suckow

CORTLAND ST.

Cortland, NY 13045 III

Coach: Tom Spanbauer
Alma Mater: Cortland St. '83
Record: 2 Years, W-28, L-25

1996-97 SCHEDULE

Hartwick Cl.	Nov. 22-23
Cazenovia	Nov. 26
Ithaca	Dec. 3
Brockport St. ■	Dec. 6
Fredonia St. ■	Dec. 7
Alfred ■	Dec. 10
Ithaca ■	Jan. 8
Utica	Jan. 14
Utica/Rome	Jan. 16
New Paltz St. ■	Jan. 18
Binghamton ■	Jan. 21
Binghamton	Jan. 25
Oswego St. ■	Jan. 28
Buffalo St.	Feb. 1
Oneonta St.	Feb. 4
Plattsburgh St. ■	Feb. 7
Potsdam St. ■	Feb. 8
Oneonta St. ■	Feb. 11
Cazenovia ■	Feb. 13
Geneseo St.	Feb. 15
New Paltz St.	Feb. 18
Potsdam St. ■	Feb. 21
Plattsburgh St. ■	Feb. 22

1995-96 RESULTS (16-12)

68	Rochester	75
62	St. Lawrence †	75
83	Cazenovia	44
66	Geneseo St. ■	55
77	Buffalo St. ■	61
65	Oneonta St. ■	68
57	Ithaca	62
57	Oswego St. ■	56
72	Utica/Rome ■	65
64	Binghamton	61
85	Utica ■	81
60	Ithaca	87
83	New Paltz St.	74
62	Cazenovia	58
55	Fredonia St.	74
75	Oneonta St. ■	69
80	Plattsburgh St. ■	72
67	Potsdam St. ■	60
72	Binghamton ■	65
74	Rochester Inst.	89
66	Brockport St.	73
56	New Paltz St. ■	80
65	Plattsburgh St.	73
77	Potsdam St.	72
61	Fredonia St. †	70
92	Brockport St.	89
83	Utica	78
66	Oneonta St.	80

Nickname: Red Dragons
Colors: Red & White
Arena: Whitney Corey Gym
 Capacity: 3,500; Year Built: 1973
AD: Lee Roberts
SID: Fran Elia

CREIGHTON

Omaha, NE 68178 I

Coach: Dana Altman
Alma Mater: Eastern N.M. '80
Record: 7 Years, W-104, L-101

1996-97 SCHEDULE

Wyoming	Nov. 22
Mo.-Kansas City ■	Nov. 25
San Juan Shootout	Nov. 29-Dec. 1
Northern Iowa ■	Dec. 7
Cal St. Sacramento ■	Dec. 14
Bethune-Cookman ■	Dec. 16
Houston	Dec. 21
Illinois St. ■	Dec. 29
Northern Iowa	Jan. 2

Houston ■	Jan. 4
Nebraska	Jan. 8
Wichita St.	Jan. 11
Southern Ill. ■	Jan. 16
Bradley ■	Jan. 18
Southern Utah ■	Jan. 20
Evansville	Jan. 25
Southern Ill.	Jan. 27
Southwest Mo. St.	Jan. 30
Evansville ■	Feb. 2
Drake ■	Feb. 6
Bradley	Feb. 8
Indiana St. ■	Feb. 10
Southwest Mo. St. ■	Feb. 15
Drake	Feb. 17
Wichita St. ■	Feb. 20
Indiana St.	Feb. 22
Illinois St.	Feb. 24
Missouri Val. Conf. Tr.	Feb. 28-Mar. 3

1995-96 RESULTS (14-15)

63	Southern Methodist	59
74	Neb.-Omaha ■	71
67	Nebraska ■	88
80	Oral Roberts ■	64
63	Morgan St. ■	56
58	Nevada †	61
58	Hawaii	84
70	Mo.-Kansas City	72
72	Evansville	60
62	Bradley ■	75
66	Wichita St. ■	57
56	Drake	59
54	Bradley	68
74	Cal St. Sacramento	67
72	Tulsa ■	59
57	Indiana St. ■	61
52	Tulsa	55
81	Southwest Mo. St. ■	75
79	Southern Ill. ■	77
68	Wichita St.	56
72	Illinois St. ■	74
68	Southern Ill.	63
78	Indiana St.	72
57	Marquette ■	63
57	Northern Iowa ■	58
73	Northern Iowa	87
66	Southwest Mo. St.	67
76	Drake ■	62
58	Southwest Mo. St. †	65

Nickname: Bluejays
Colors: Blue & White
Arena: Omaha Civic Auditorium
Capacity: 9,481; Year Built: 1954
AD: Bruce Rasmussen
SID: Bobby Parker

CURRY

Milton, MA 02186 III

Coach: Patrick Skerry
Alma Mater: Tufts '92
(First year as head coach)

1996-97 SCHEDULE

Johnson & Wales	Nov. 22
Emerson-MCA ■	Nov. 23
Notre Dame (N.H.)	Nov. 26
Suffolk	Dec. 3
Endicott ■	Dec. 5
Framingham St. ■	Dec. 7
Maine Maritime ■	Jan. 12
Connecticut Col.	Jan. 14
Gordon	Jan. 16
Colby-Sawyer ■	Jan. 18
Wentworth Inst.	Jan. 21
Salve Regina	Jan. 23
Anna Maria	Jan. 25
MIT	Jan. 30
New England Col.	Feb. 1
Wentworth Inst. ■	Feb. 4
Roger Williams ■	Feb. 6
Mass. Pharmacy ■	Feb. 8
Eastern Nazarene ■	Feb. 12
Nichols ■	Feb. 15
Eastern Nazarene	Feb. 18
Salve Regina ■	Feb. 20
Roger Williams	Feb. 22

1995-96 RESULTS (11-13)

101	Atlantic Union	67
106	Emerson-MCA	95
102	Suffolk ■	103
92	Endicott	83
92	Thomas	79
128	Unity	92
106	Notre Dame (N.H.) ■	76
80	Trinity (Conn.)	122
85	Atlantic Union ■	81
78	Connecticut Col. ■	102
67	Gordon ■	94
88	Colby-Sawyer	119
54	Wentworth Inst. ■	67
91	Salve Regina ■	88
82	Anna Maria ■	93
76	MIT ■	70
82	New England Col. ■	67
76	Wentworth Inst.	73
69	Roger Williams	99
62	Eastern Nazarene	82
76	Nichols	91
69	Eastern Nazarene ■	99
67	Salve Regina	69
84	Roger Williams ■	89

Nickname: Colonels
Colors: Purple & White
Arena: Miller Gymnasium
Capacity: 300; Year Built: 1952
AD: Pam Samuelson
SID: Adam Polgreen

DANIEL WEBSTER

Nashua, NH 03063 III

Coach: To be named

1996-97 SCHEDULE

Lyndon St. ■	Nov. 23
Keene St.	Nov. 25
Embry-Riddle ■	Nov. 27
Gordon	Dec. 3
Atlantic Union ■	Dec. 5
New England Col. ■	Dec. 7
Nichols	Dec. 10
Plymouth St.	Dec. 12
Framingham St.	Jan. 16
Fitchburg St. ■	Jan. 21
Albertus Magnus	Jan. 23
Endicott	Jan. 25
Mass. Pharmacy ■	Jan. 27
Johnson & Wales	Jan. 29
Emerson-MCA	Feb. 1
Rivier ■	Feb. 4
Mass. Pharmacy	Feb. 6
Albertus Magnus ■	Feb. 8
Rivier	Feb. 12
Johnson & Wales ■	Feb. 15
New England Col.	Feb. 16
Endicott ■	Feb. 18
Notre Dame (N.H.) ■	Feb. 20
Emerson-MCA ■	Feb. 22

1995-96 RESULTS (10-15)

56	Colby	81
72	Me.-Presque Isle †	90
91	Keene St. ■	76
91	Gordon ■	85
73	Connecticut Col.	92
83	Coast Guard †	84
87	New England Col. ■	60
74	Rivier	82
91	Nichols ■	85
84	Emerson-MCA ■	73
72	Albertus Magnus ■	83
80	Endicott	86
59	Fitchburg St.	61
79	Johnson & Wales ■	77
96	Mass. Pharmacy †	72
61	Rivier	71
65	Emerson-MCA	82
83	Albertus Magnus	101
66	Plymouth St. ■	85
61	Endicott ■	80
84	Notre Dame (N.H.)	76
74	Rivier ■	75
89	Johnson & Wales	85
87	Mass. Pharmacy ■	71
53	Emerson-MCA †	56

Nickname: Eagles
Colors: Blue, White & Gold
Arena: Mario Vagge Gymnasium
Capacity: 1,000; Year Built: 1979
AD: To be named
SID: To be named

DARTMOUTH

Hanover, NH 03755 I

Coach: Dave Faucher
Alma Mater: New Hampshire '73
Record: 5 Years, W-60, L-70

1996-97 SCHEDULE

Colgate ■	Nov. 22
Lafayette ■	Nov. 24
St. Peter's Tr.	Nov. 30-Dec. 1
Holy Cross	Dec. 4
New Hampshire ■	Dec. 14
Harvard	Dec. 17
Navy	Dec. 21
Toledo Tr.	Dec. 29-30
Middlebury ■	Jan. 3
Harvard ■	Jan. 6
Cornell ■	Jan. 10
Columbia ■	Jan. 11
Vermont	Jan. 21
Army	Jan. 27
Yale ■	Jan. 31
Brown ■	Feb. 1
Princeton	Feb. 7
Pennsylvania	Feb. 8
Columbia	Feb. 14
Cornell	Feb. 15
Pennsylvania ■	Feb. 21
Princeton ■	Feb. 22
Brown	Feb. 28
Yale	Mar. 1

1995-96 RESULTS (16-10)

82	Holy Cross ■	75
81	Middlebury	49
82	Vermont ■	66
73	Army ■	72
70	Harvard	61
83	Central Conn. St. ■	80
66	North Caro.	96
54	Rice	62
66	New Mexico	91
66	Pepperdine †	69
40	Harvard ■	59
59	Columbia ■	57
68	Cornell ■	57
69	New Hampshire	72
72	Lafayette	71
59	Navy ■	48
64	Brown	60
66	Yale	49
54	Pennsylvania ■	53
41	Princeton ■	52
57	Cornell	61
71	Columbia	54
39	Princeton	65
51	Pennsylvania	80
65	Yale ■	63
64	Brown ■	54

Nickname: Big Green
Colors: Green & White
Arena: Leede Arena
Capacity: 2,100; Year Built: 1986
AD: Dick Jaeger
SID: Kathy Slattery

DAVIDSON

Davidson, NC 28036 I

Coach: Bob McKillop
Alma Mater: Hofstra '72
Record: 7 Years, W-100, L-100

1996-97 SCHEDULE

Fairleigh Dickinson	Nov. 23
Lynchburg ■	Nov. 27
Wake Forest	Nov. 29
Mississippi ■	Dec. 2
Southern Methodist ■	Dec. 5
Sewanee ■	Dec. 7
Duke	Dec. 11
N.C.-Charlotte ■	Dec. 14
New Hampshire	Dec. 21
Massachusetts [Puerto Rico]	Jan. 2
Connecticut Col. ■	Jan. 5
Marshall ■	Jan. 8
Ga. Southern	Jan. 11
Western Caro. ■	Jan. 13
Tenn.-Chatt. ■	Jan. 18
Appalachian St.	Jan. 20
East Tenn. St.	Jan. 22
Citadel	Jan. 27
VMI ■	Feb. 1
Marshall	Feb. 3
Siena ■	Feb. 6
Furman ■	Feb. 8
East Tenn. St. ■	Feb. 10
Furman	Feb. 15
VMI	Feb. 17
Appalachian St. ■	Feb. 22
Southern Conf. Tr.	Feb. 27-Mar. 2

1995-96 RESULTS (25-5)

91	Rhodes ■	46
84	Mississippi	83
101	Catholic ■	59
56	N.C.-Wilmington	73
80	North Caro. St. ■	84
96	Fairleigh Dickinson ■	56
93	Williams ■	87
90	Central Fla. †	51
70	Michigan †	82
93	Lafayette ■	68
87	Navy ■	58
88	East Tenn. St. ■	56
102	Furman ■	97
56	N.C.-Charlotte	47
90	Appalachian St.	68
106	Marshall	57
71	Ga. Southern ■	46
86	VMI ■	79
98	Western Caro.	85
70	Tenn.-Chatt.	58
84	Appalachian St. ■	66
96	East Tenn. St.	66
82	Citadel ■	54
95	VMI	76
83	Marshall ■	77
88	Furman	79
67	East Tenn. St. †	43
92	Marshall †	77
60	Western Caro. †	69
73	South Caro.	100

Nickname: Wildcats
Colors: Red & Black
Arena: Belk Arena
Capacity: 5,700; Year Built: 1989
AD: Jim Murphy
SID: Emil Parker

DAVIS & ELKINS

Elkins, WV 26241 II

Coach: Russell Shepherd
Alma Mater: Glenville St. '62
Record: 1 Year, W-2, L-25

1996-97 SCHEDULE

Schedule unavailable

1995-96 RESULTS (2-25)

70	St. Vincent	85
59	Malone †	110
49	Calif. (Pa.) ■	88
49	Radford	94
89	Waynesburg	84
56	Alderson-Broaddus ■	83
69	Salem-Teikyo ■	98
65	St. Vincent †	96
98	Bapt. Bible (Pa.) †	106
81	Concord	61
59	West Va. Wesleyan ■	90
69	Charleston (W.Va.)	96
65	West Va. St.	96
83	West Va. Tech ■	101
53	Glenville St. ■	62
87	Wheeling Jesuit	105
84	West Liberty St. ■	88
84	Shepherd	113
69	West Va. St. ■	77
69	Fairmont St.	109
75	Bluefield St. ■	94
58	Alderson-Broaddus	91
48	Glenville St.	82
47	Wheeling Jesuit ■	94
70	West Liberty St.	113
72	Shepherd ■	73
68	Salem-Teikyo	78

Nickname: Senators
Colors: Scarlet & White
Arena: Memorial Gymnasium
  Capacity: 1,875; Year Built: 1950
AD: Will Shaw
SID: Rick Wiese

DAYTON
Dayton, OH 45469 I

Coach: Oliver Purnell
Alma Mater: Old Dominion '75
Record: 8 Years, W-123, L-109

1996-97 SCHEDULE

Florida A&M ■	Nov. 30
Miami (Ohio)	Dec. 4
Delaware St. ■	Dec. 7
Louisville	Dec. 11
Alabama St. ■	Dec. 20
Morehead St. ■	Dec. 22
Marquette ■	Dec. 27
DePaul ■	Dec. 30
Rhode Island	Jan. 4
Xavier (Ohio) ■	Jan. 7
Wright St.	Jan. 9
La Salle	Jan. 11
Temple ■	Jan. 13
Geo. Washington ■	Jan. 18
Fordham ■	Jan. 25
Southern U. ■	Jan. 27
Duquesne	Jan. 30
Virginia Tech	Feb. 1
St. Joseph's (Pa.) ■	Feb. 4
St. Bonaventure	Feb. 8
Xavier (Ohio)	Feb. 12
Virginia Tech ■	Feb. 15
La Salle ■	Feb. 20
Massachusetts ■	Feb. 23
Duquesne ■	Feb. 26
Geo. Washington	Mar. 1
Atlantic 10 Conf. Tr.	Mar. 5-8

1995-96 RESULTS (15-14)

72	Hawaii	78
86	LSU †	73
80	Coastal Caro. ■	62
65	Eastern Ky.	71
98	Wright St. ■	80
68	Cleveland St.	60
110	Chicago St. ■	76
85	Eastern Ill.	65
86	McNeese St. ■	76
56	Miami (Ohio) ■	79
91	Hampton ■	65
58	Massachusetts	78
46	Temple ■	62

84	Rhode Island ■	77
62	Virginia Tech	63
58	Geo. Washington ■	77
61	Xavier (Ohio) ■	55
56	Duquesne	59
65	Geo. Washington	77
60	St. Joseph's (Pa.)	73
60	Bethune-Cookman ■	59
58	Fordham	68
66	St. Bonaventure ■	58
95	Xavier (Ohio)	102
67	La Salle	60
72	Duquesne ■	69
66	La Salle ■	64
54	Virginia Tech †	73
60	St. Bonaventure †	72

Nickname: Flyers
Colors: Red & Blue
Arena: Univ. of Dayton Arena
  Capacity: 13,455; Year Built: 1969
AD: Ted Kissell
SID: Doug Hauschild

DEPAUL
Chicago, IL 60614 I

Coach: Joey Meyer
Alma Mater: DePaul '71
Record: 12 Years, W-222, L-125

1996-97 SCHEDULE

Eastern Ill. ■	Nov. 23
Georgetown	Nov. 30
Illinois St. [St. Louis]	Dec. 4
Northwestern ■	Dec. 7
Indiana	Dec. 10
St. Joseph's (Pa.)	Dec. 15
Louisiana Tech ■	Dec. 18
Niagara	Dec. 21
Montana St. [Ontario]	Dec. 23
Miami (Fla.)	Dec. 28
Dayton	Dec. 30
Temple ■	Jan. 4
Marquette	Jan. 9
South Fla. ■	Jan. 11
Memphis ■	Jan. 15
Houston	Jan. 18
Southern Miss.	Jan. 21
Marquette ■	Jan. 26
Louisville	Jan. 28
Cincinnati	Feb. 1
N.C.-Charlotte ■	Feb. 4
UAB	Feb. 8
St. Louis	Feb. 16
Tulane	Feb. 19
Cincinnati ■	Feb. 22
St. Louis ■	Mar. 1
Conference USA	Mar. 5-8

1995-96 RESULTS (11-18)

65	Michigan	73
91	UC Santa Barb. ■	71
90	Stetson ■	57
84	Texas ■	88
77	Eastern Ill.	50
80	Florida St. †	85
72	Maine ■	58
71	Northwestern	61
84	Western Ky.	69
84	Indiana	82
61	Georgetown ■	81
71	Louisville ■	81
55	Memphis	74
67	Southern Miss. ■	82
60	Marquette ■	73
59	St. Louis	60
61	Cincinnati	71
74	Tulane	84
82	Memphis ■	83
59	California †	62
50	UAB ■	69
65	Marquette	75
60	Cincinnati ■	87
79	Loyola (Ill.) ■	65
65	South Fla.	61

69	N.C.-Charlotte	81
66	St. Louis ■	51
66	N.C.-Charlotte †	60
69	Memphis	92

Nickname: Blue Demons
Colors: Scarlet & Blue
Arena: Rosemont Horizon
  Capacity: 17,500; Year Built: 1980
AD: Bill Bradshaw
SID: John Lanctot

DEPAUW
Greencastle, IN 46135 III

Coach: Bill Fenlon
Alma Mater: Northwestern '79
Record: 11 Years, W-175, L-106

1996-97 SCHEDULE

Washington (Mo.) Tr.	Nov. 22-23
Albion	Nov. 26
Millikin ■	Dec. 1
Chicago	Dec. 3
Franklin Cl.	Dec. 6-7
Thomas More ■	Dec. 14
Wabash-DePauw Cl.	Dec. 21-22
North Park ■	Jan. 4
Purdue-North Cent. ■	Jan. 5
Rose-Hulman ■	Jan. 8
Anderson (Ind.)	Jan. 11
Manchester	Jan. 18
Wabash	Jan. 22
Hanover	Jan. 25
Franklin	Jan. 29
Rose-Hulman	Feb. 5
Anderson (Ind.) ■	Feb. 8
Wabash	Feb. 12
Manchester ■	Feb. 15
Franklin	Feb. 19
Hanover ■	Feb. 22

1995-96 RESULTS (17-9)

73	Washington (Mo.) †	76
61	Neb. Wesleyan †	65
75	Thomas More	65
69	Millikin	65
63	Webster	46
80	Benedictine (Ill.) †	72
99	Rockford †	49
74	Albion ■	55
90	Ind.-Northwest ■	30
65	Marian (Ind.) †	48
81	Ohio Northern †	77
85	Colorado Col. †	72
57	Rose-Hulman	65
66	Anderson (Ind.)	64
66	Manchester ■	42
67	Wabash	73
53	Hanover ■	60
65	Franklin	82
60	Rose-Hulman ■	45
81	Anderson (Ind.)	64
62	Wabash ■	61
58	Manchester	72
79	Franklin ■	74
49	Hanover	75
67	Franklin ■	57
53	Manchester †	58

Nickname: Tigers
Colors: Old Gold & Black
Arena: Neal Fieldhouse
  Capacity: 3,200; Year Built: 1982
AD: Page Cotton
SID: Bill Wagner

DEFIANCE
Defiance, OH 43512 III

Coach: Marvin Hohenberger
Alma Mater: MacMurray '62
Record: 31 Years, W-573, L-278

1996-97 SCHEDULE

North Central Cl.	Nov. 22-23

Carnegie Mellon Inv.	Nov. 30-Dec. 1
Mt. Vernon Tr.	Dec. 6-7
Ohio Northern ■	Dec. 11
Olivet	Dec. 20
Defiance Tr.	Dec. 27-28
Huntington	Jan. 4
Bluffton ■	Jan. 8
Tri-State ■	Jan. 15
Adrian	Jan. 18
Goshen	Jan. 23
Thomas More ■	Jan. 25
Wittenberg	Jan. 28
Lake Erie	Feb. 1
Bluffton	Feb. 5
Thomas More	Feb. 15
Tri-State	Feb. 17
Ohio Wesleyan ■	Feb. 19
Olivet ■	Feb. 22

1995-96 RESULTS (14-10)

61	Capital	93
67	Calvin †	75
49	Ohio Northern	61
80	Heidelberg	85
93	Tri-State †	80
71	Colorado Col. †	76
60	Bowling Green	91
69	Knox †	74
70	Blackburn †	58
90	Lake Erie ■	61
81	North Central ■	55
65	Manchester ■	81
81	Ohio Wesleyan	59
82	Huntington ■	67
85	Bluffton	83
83	Thomas More	68
49	Wittenberg ■	64
88	Bluffton ■	60
72	Lake Erie ■	58
76	Findlay ■	62
77	Thomas More ■	70
62	Tri-State ■	72
81	Knoxville	80
71	Maryville (Tenn.)	69

Nickname: Yellow Jackets
Colors: Purple & Gold
Arena: College Community Center
  Capacity: 2,000; Year Built: 1964
AD: Marvin Hohenberger
SID: Tom Palombo

DELAWARE
Newark, DE 19716 I

Coach: Mike Brey
Alma Mater: Geo. Washington '82
Record: 1 Year, W-15, L-12

1996-97 SCHEDULE

Delaware St. ■	Nov. 22
Rider	Nov. 26
San Juan Shootout	Nov. 29-Dec. 1
Bucknell	Dec. 4
Northeastern ■	Dec. 6
Boston U. ■	Dec. 8
Washington (Md.) ■	Dec. 20
Widener ■	Dec. 22
Virginia	Dec. 30
Marshall	Jan. 3
Towson St. ■	Jan. 5
Hofstra	Jan. 7
Hartford ■	Jan. 10
Vermont ■	Jan. 12
New Hampshire	Jan. 16
Maine	Jan. 18
Drexel ■	Jan. 21
Boston U. ■	Jan. 24
Northeastern	Jan. 26
Drexel	Jan. 31
Hofstra ■	Feb. 2
Hartford	Feb. 6
Vermont	Feb. 8
Maine ■	Feb. 13
New Hampshire ■	Feb. 15
St. Joseph's (Pa.)	Feb. 18

Towson St. ....Feb. 22
America East Conf. Tr. ....Feb. 28-Mar. 2

1995-96 RESULTS (15-12)

100	Washington (Md.) ■	58
73	Bucknell ■	64
56	St. Joseph's (Pa.) ■	64
68	Indiana	85
68	Citadel †	46
73	Duke	79
81	Widener ■	38
58	Villanova	71
62	Maine	64
57	New Hampshire	52
62	Boston U. ■	50
99	Northeastern ■	69
75	Drexel †	91
77	Hartford	79
66	Vermont	67
90	Hartford ■	66
77	Vermont ■	59
75	Boston U.	82
60	Northeastern	59
93	Hofstra ■	65
65	Maine ■	77
93	New Hampshire ■	75
67	Hofstra	57
78	Drexel	82
81	Towson St. ■	73
71	Towson St. ■	70
78	Towson St. ■	85

Nickname: Fightin' Blue Hens
Colors: Blue & Gold
Arena: Bob Carpenter Center
   Capacity: 5,000; Year Built: 1992
AD: Edgar Johnson
SID: Scott Selheimer

DELAWARE ST.

Dover, DE 19901 I

Coach: Art Perry
(First year as head coach)
1996-97 SCHEDULE

Delaware		Nov. 22
Illinois		Nov. 25
Tulsa		Dec. 2
Oklahoma		Dec. 4
Dayton		Dec. 7
Georgetown		Dec. 10
Houston		Dec. 19
Wagner		Dec. 21
Wyoming		Dec. 23
Md.-East. Shore ■		Jan. 7
Bethune-Cookman		Jan. 11
Florida A&M ■		Jan. 13
Morgan St.		Jan. 18
Howard		Jan. 20
Hampton ■		Jan. 22
North Caro. A&T ■		Jan. 25
South Caro. St. ■		Jan. 27
Coppin St. ■		Feb. 5
North Caro. A&T		Feb. 8
South Caro. St.		Feb. 10
Coppin St.		Feb. 12
Md.-East. Shore		Feb. 15
Howard ■		Feb. 17
Morgan St. ■		Feb. 20
Bethune-Cookman ■		Feb. 22
Florida A&M ■		Feb. 24
Hampton		Mar. 1
Mid-Eastern Conf. Tr.		Mar. 5-8

1995-96 RESULTS (11-17)

73	George Mason	139
68	St. Francis (N.Y.) ■	73
64	James Madison	88
77	Central Conn. St.	98
64	Wagner	59
64	St. Francis (Pa.) ■	82
57	Xavier (Ohio)	87
41	Nebraska	88
66	Md.-East. Shore ■	72
92	Bethune-Cookman ■	83
79	Florida A&M ■	68

77	Coppin St. ■	92
73	Howard ■	71
55	Maryland	118
66	North Caro. A&T	68
71	South Caro. St.	87
75	Morgan St.	66
87	North Caro. A&T ■	78
67	South Caro. St. ■	99
75	Morgan St. ■	68
67	Md.-East. Shore †	70
65	Howard	63
77	Coppin St.	90
83	Bethune-Cookman ■	78
80	Florida A&M ■	86
93	Bowie St. ■	92
59	Md.-East. Shore †	56
64	Coppin St. †	78

Nickname: Hornets
Colors: Red & Coumbia Blue
Arena: Memorial Hall
   Capacity: 3,000; Year Built: 1982
AD: Bill Collick
SID: Craig Cotton

DELAWARE VALLEY

Doylestown, PA 18901 III

Coach: David Duda
Alma Mater: Spring Garden
(First year as head coach)
1996-97 SCHEDULE

Ursinus Tr.		Nov. 23-24
Elizabethtown ■		Nov. 26
Phila. Pharmacy		Dec. 2
Scranton ■		Dec. 4
Lycoming		Dec. 7
King's (Pa.) ■		Dec. 10
Widener Cl.		Dec. 13-14
Elmira Tr.		Jan. 3-4
Moravian		Jan. 11
FDU-Madison		Jan. 15
Wilkes ■		Jan. 21
Drew		Jan. 25
Scranton		Jan. 29
Lycoming ■		Feb. 1
King's (Pa.)		Feb. 4
Gwynedd-Mercy ■		Feb. 8
FDU-Madison ■		Feb. 12
Misericordia		Feb. 17
Wilkes		Feb. 19
Drew ■		Feb. 22

1995-96 RESULTS (0-23)

41	Phila. Pharmacy	88
49	Ursinus †	74
39	Elizabethtown	92
54	Phila. Pharmacy ■	76
63	Lycoming ■	104
59	Scranton	90
67	Misericordia ■	79
58	King's (Pa.)	94
59	Widener	93
59	Lincoln (Pa.) †	100
31	Kean	62
64	Vassar ■	72
58	Caldwell ■	85
50	Wilkes	110
72	Drew ■	81
57	Scranton ■	64
51	FDU-Madison ■	65
37	Lycoming	91
64	King's (Pa.) ■	69
66	Moravian	93
60	FDU-Madison	73
59	Wilkes ■	95
66	Drew	109

Nickname: Aggies
Colors: Green & Gold
Arena: James Work Gymnasium
   Capacity: 1,800; Year Built: 1969
AD: Frank Wolfgang
SID: Matthew Levy

DELTA ST.

Cleveland, MS 38733 II

Coach: Steve Rives
Alma Mater: Mississippi Col. '72
Record: 11 Years, W-186, L-120
1996-97 SCHEDULE

Ky. Wesleyan		Nov. 16
Drury		Nov. 18
John Brown Inv.		Nov. 22-23
Belhaven ■		Nov. 26
Lane ■		Dec. 3
Ky. Wesleyan ■		Dec. 5
Aub.-Montgomery		Dec. 14
Central Ark.		Jan. 4
Arkansas Tech ■		Jan. 7
Ark.-Monticello		Jan. 11
Henderson St.		Jan. 13
Aub.-Montgomery ■		Jan. 18
Southern Ark. ■		Jan. 20
Selma ■		Jan. 23
Christian Bros.		Jan. 25
Lane		Jan. 28
La. Christian		Jan. 30
Central Ark. ■		Feb. 1
Arkansas Tech		Feb. 4
Ark.-Monticello ■		Feb. 8
Henderson St. ■		Feb. 10
Drury ■		Feb. 15
Southern Ark.		Feb. 17
Christian Bros. ■		Feb. 22

1995-96 RESULTS (18-11)

80	Belhaven ■	65
77	North Ala. ■	82
77	Montevallo †	58
71	Lane †	74
80	Mississippi Val. ■	87
72	Belhaven	56
75	North Ala.	84
76	Mississippi Val.	78
80	Christian Bros. ■	69
82	Tougaloo	73
94	Central Ark. ■	63
62	Arkansas Tech	70
101	Ark.-Monticello ■	94
107	Henderson St. ■	95
95	Lane	80
67	Southern Ark.	75
70	Mississippi Col. ■	63
99	Bapt. Christian ■	65
81	Arkansas Tech ■	60
104	Ark.-Monticello	84
100	Henderson St.	89
85	Southern Ark. ■	62
79	Lane	82
49	Mississippi Col.	50
75	Central Ark.	67
95	West Ga. ■	93
65	North Ala. ■	80
69	North Ala. †	78

Nickname: Statesmen
Colors: Green & White
Arena: Walter Sillers Coliseum
   Capacity: 4,000; Year Built: 1961
AD: Jim Jordan
SID: Bryan Roller

DENISON

Granville, OH 43023 III

Coach: Michael Sheridan
Alma Mater: Wooster '85
Record: 5 Years, W-55, L-71
1996-97 SCHEDULE

Gettysburg Tr.		Nov. 22-23
Earlham		Dec. 4
Allegheny ■		Dec. 7
Kenyon		Dec. 11
Bethany (W.Va.)		Dec. 14
Ohio Dominican		Dec. 21
Hiram ■		Dec. 28

Bluffton		Jan. 2
Ohio Wesleyan ■		Jan. 4
Wooster ■		Jan. 8
Wittenberg		Jan. 11
Oberlin		Jan. 15
Allegheny		Jan. 18
Wilmington (Ohio) ■		Jan. 22
Earlham ■		Jan. 25
Kenyon ■		Jan. 31
Wooster		Feb. 1
Ohio Wesleyan		Feb. 5
Case Reserve ■		Feb. 8
Wittenberg ■		Feb. 12
Oberlin ■		Feb. 15
Case Reserve ■		Feb. 22

1995-96 RESULTS (13-12)

71	Hiram	48
91	Bethany (W.Va.) ■	78
48	Kenyon	53
83	Allegheny ■	76
84	Ohio Wesleyan ■	62
74	Earlham ■	71
70	Kent	100
57	Ohio Dominican ■	73
75	Heidelberg	80
73	Wilmington (Ohio) †	43
83	Bluffton ■	65
77	Oberlin	51
47	Wittenberg	73
71	Case Reserve ■	73
74	Wooster	70
62	Allegheny	64
74	Oberlin	67
78	Earlham	46
61	Kenyon	59
85	Ohio Wesleyan ■	70
77	Case Reserve	80
63	Wittenberg ■	70
64	Wilmington (Ohio)	66
51	Wooster	63
73	Case Reserve	75

Nickname: Big Red
Colors: Red & White
Arena: Livingston Gymnasium
   Capacity: 3,000; Year Built: 1949
AD: Larry Scheiderer
SID: Jack Hire

DENVER

Denver, CO 80208 II

Coach: Dick Peth
Alma Mater: Iowa '81
Record: 11 Years, W-207, L-111
1996-97 SCHEDULE

Holy Names ■		Nov. 17
Denver Cl.		Nov. 29-30
N.M. Highlands		Dec. 3
Bethel (Kan.) Cl.		Dec. 6-7
Chadron St. ■		Dec. 9
Las Vegas Cl.		Dec. 18-19
Colorado St.		Dec. 28
Wyoming		Dec. 31
Mt. Senario ■		Jan. 4
Western St. ■		Jan. 9
Mesa St. ■		Jan. 11
Colo. Christian ■		Jan. 16
Regis (Colo.) ■		Jan. 18
Fort Hays St.		Jan. 24
Neb.-Kearney		Jan. 25
Colorado Col.		Jan. 30
Southern Colo.		Feb. 4
Wayne St. (Neb.) ■		Feb. 8
UC-Colo. Spgs. ■		Feb. 11
Adams St.		Feb. 14
Fort Lewis		Feb. 15
Colorado Mines		Feb. 21
Metro St.		Feb. 22

1995-96 RESULTS (22-7)

94	Langston	68
101	Humboldt St. ■	82
94	Western St. ■	83
83	Wyoming	97

106	Arizona Bible ■	44
77	Doane ■	54
76	Cal St. San B'dino ■	73
77	Fort Lewis	78
104	Adams St.	91
88	Calif. (Pa.) †	86
93	North Dak.	87
95	Fort Lewis ■	78
59	Weber St.	95
86	Colorado Col.	73
80	Colo. Christian	53
93	Southern Colo.	96
67	UC-Colo. Spgs.	65
85	Metro St. ■	77
79	Colorado Mines	69
83	Regis (Colo.)	74
69	Colo. Christian ■	64
90	Southern Colo. ■	75
85	UC-Colo. Spgs. ■	68
88	Metro St.	91
96	Adams St. ■	93
62	Regis (Colo.) ■	77
77	Southern Colo. ■	66
84	Regis (Colo.) ■	67
70	North Dak. St. †	71

Nickname: Pioneers
Colors: Crimson & Gold
Arena: Denver Fieldhouse
  Capacity: 1,800; Year Built: 1972
AD: Paul Hogue
SID: Dave Mellin

DETROIT
Detroit, MI 48221 I

Coach: Perry Watson
Alma Mater: Eastern Mich. '72
Record: 3 Years, W-47, L-39

1996-97 SCHEDULE

Wayne St. (Mich.) ■	Nov. 23
Bowling Green	Nov. 26
Hawaii Tip-Off	Nov. 29-Dec. 1
Michigan	Dec. 5
Michigan St. ■	Dec. 14
Central Mich.	Dec. 17
Iona ■	Dec. 21
Western Mich.	Dec. 23
Santa Clara Cl.	Dec. 27-28
Wright St. ■	Jan. 2
Memphis	Jan. 4
Wis.-Milwaukee	Jan. 9
Wis.-Green Bay	Jan. 11
Loyola (Ill.) ■	Jan. 16
Ill.-Chicago ■	Jan. 18
Butler ■	Jan. 20
Cleveland St.	Jan. 23
Northern Ill.	Jan. 25
Wright St.	Jan. 30
Butler	Feb. 1
Wis.-Milwaukee ■	Feb. 6
Ill.-Chicago ■	Feb. 8
Loyola (Ill.)	Feb. 13
Wis.-Green Bay ■	Feb. 16
Cleveland St. ■	Feb. 20
Northern Ill. ■	Feb. 22
Midwestern Conf. Tr.	Feb. 28-Mar. 4

1995-96 RESULTS (18-11)

52	Long Beach St. ■	45
67	Bowling Green ■	64
48	Michigan ■	68
57	Central Mich. ■	54
63	Michigan St.	61
65	Western Mich. ■	50
86	Wayne St. (Mich.) ■	69
76	Iona	79
77	Pennsylvania †	65
72	Arizona St.	66
60	Northern Ill.	80
78	Loyola (Ill.)	63
76	Wis.-Milwaukee ■	59
69	Wis.-Green Bay	71
47	Cleveland St.	48

57	Wright St. ■	59
89	Ill.-Chicago ■	78
62	Butler	70
103	Cleveland St. ■	74
69	Wis.-Milwaukee	65
90	Ill.-Chicago	71
44	Wis.-Green Bay ■	46
63	Wright St.	70
61	Butler ■	69
62	Loyola (Ill.) ■	48
77	Northern Ill. ■	75
67	Wright St.	61
56	Wis.-Green Bay †	50
63	Northern Ill. †	84

Nickname: Titans
Colors: Red, White & Blue
Arena: Calihan Hall
  Capacity: 8,837; Year Built: 1952
AD: Brad Kinsman
SID: Mark Engel

DICKINSON
Carlisle, PA 17013 III

Coach: David Frohman
Alma Mater: Indiana '72
Record: 7 Years, W-90, L-89

1996-97 SCHEDULE

Dickinson Tr.	Nov. 22-23
Lebanon Valley	Nov. 26
Ursinus ■	Dec. 4
Washington (Md.)	Dec. 7
Randolph-Macon Tr.	Dec. 29-30
Carnegie Mellon ■	Jan. 7
Dickinson Tr.	Jan. 10-11
Western Md.	Jan. 15
Gettysburg ■	Jan. 18
York (Pa.) ■	Jan. 20
Frank. & Marsh.	Jan. 22
Haverford ■	Jan. 25
King's (Pa.) ■	Jan. 27
Messiah ■	Jan. 30
Muhlenberg	Feb. 1
Johns Hopkins	Feb. 5
Gettysburg	Feb. 8
Western Md. ■	Feb. 12
Swarthmore	Feb. 15
Frank. & Marsh. ■	Feb. 19
Johns Hopkins ■	Feb. 22

1995-96 RESULTS (9-15)

78	King's (Pa.) ■	66
70	Beaver ■	76
94	Lebanon Valley ■	74
65	Ursinus	83
89	Washington (Md.) ■	78
40	Bucknell	91
83	Messiah	76
56	Cabrini	103
31	Wooster	86
43	Grove City †	63
68	Messiah ■	66
72	Shippensburg ■	94
84	Western Md. ■	75
74	Gettysburg	88
68	York (Pa.)	84
51	Frank. & Marsh. ■	90
67	Haverford	82
69	Muhlenberg ■	77
50	Johns Hopkins ■	71
94	Gettysburg ■	74
67	Western Md.	62
66	Swarthmore	63
61	Frank. & Marsh. ■	93
76	Johns Hopkins	80

Nickname: Red Devils
Colors: Red & White
Arena: Kline Life/Sports Center
  Capacity: 2,000; Year Built: 1980
AD: Les J. Poolman
SID: Matt Howell

DIST. COLUMBIA
Washington, DC 20005 II

Coach: William S. Jones
Alma Mater: American '60
Record: 12 Years, W-199, L-130

1996-97 SCHEDULE

Cheyney ■	Nov. 19
Mt. Olive Tr.	Nov. 21-22
East Stroudsburg	Nov. 26
Kutztown	Dec. 6
St. Augustine's ■	Dec. 8
West Chester ■	Dec. 19
Fairmount Cl.	Jan. 3-4
East Stroudsburg ■	Jan. 11
West Chester	Jan. 15
Bowie St.	Jan. 17
St. Paul's	Jan. 18
Millersville	Jan. 20
Lincoln (Pa.) ■	Jan. 23
St. Paul's ■	Jan. 28
Columbia Union	Jan. 30
Cheyney	Feb. 4
Lynn ■	Feb. 8
Millersville ■	Feb. 10
Bowie St. ■	Feb. 13
Columbia Union ■	Feb. 20
Pitt.-Johnstown ■	Feb. 24

1995-96 RESULTS (9-18)

68	Lock Haven †	63
90	West Va. Wesleyan †	78
93	Pitt.-Johnstown ■	82
86	East Stroudsburg ■	83
95	Cheyney ■	80
80	Lenoir-Rhyne †	85
62	Concordia (N.Y.) †	78
80	Millersville	92
82	West Chester ■	70
63	East Stroudsburg	68
96	Morehouse †	107
89	Clayton St. †	73
79	St. Paul's	88
80	Millersville	94
82	Mount Olive ■	86
78	Columbia Union	82
80	Cheyney	83
55	Bowie St. ■	71
77	Kutztown ■	72
68	St. Paul's ■	74
82	Lincoln (Pa.)	83
72	Bowie St.	70
50	Kutztown	60
56	West Chester	76
60	Columbia Union ■	64
75	Pitt.-Johnstown	94
70	St. Augustine's	94

Nickname: Firebirds
Colors: Red & Yellow
Arena: Physical Activities Center
  Capacity: 3,000; Year Built: 1976
AD: Dwight Datcher
SID: Donald Huff

DOWLING
Oakdale, NY 11769 II

Coach: Joseph Pellicane
Alma Mater: Dowling '70
Record: 10 Years, W-156, L-126

1996-97 SCHEDULE

Bryant Cl.	Nov. 23-24
Queens (N.Y.) ■	Dec. 4
Pace	Dec. 7
Concordia (N.Y.) ■	Dec. 11
Adelphi ■	Dec. 14
American Int'l	Dec. 21
Franklin Pierce	Dec. 30
Molloy	Jan. 4
St. Rose	Jan. 6
Phila. Textile ■	Jan. 8
New York Tech ■	Jan. 11
LIU-C. W. Post	Jan. 13
Mercy	Jan. 15
LIU-Southampton ■	Jan. 18
Queens (N.Y.)	Jan. 20
Pace ■	Jan. 22
Concordia (N.Y.)	Jan. 25
Adelphi	Jan. 29
Molloy ■	Feb. 1
St. Rose ■	Feb. 5
Phila. Textile ■	Feb. 8
New York Tech	Feb. 12
LIU-C. W. Post ■	Feb. 15
Mercy ■	Feb. 19
LIU-Southampton	Feb. 22

1995-96 RESULTS (15-14)

89	Johnson Smith	86
93	Benedict †	87
85	St. Rose ■	104
91	Mercy	74
64	Pace ■	47
72	Adelphi	75
76	Bryant ■	73
82	Queens (N.Y.) ■	71
95	New York Tech ■	92
78	Franklin Pierce	85
78	Concordia (N.Y.) ■	75
73	Molloy	60
84	LIU-C. W. Post ■	86
95	LIU-Southampton	103
85	Phila. Textile ■	95
63	St. Rose	85
117	Mercy ■	89
85	LIU-C. W. Post	93
67	Pace	82
75	Adelphi ■	71
55	Queens (N.Y.)	85
82	New York Tech	99
86	Concordia (N.Y.) ■	69
89	Molloy ■	64
94	LIU-Southampton ■	81
66	Phila. Textile	67
80	Adelphi	84
91	LIU-Southampton	87
81	St. Michael's	96

Nickname: Golden Lions
Colors: Blue & Gold
Arena: Lasalle Center
  Capacity: 1,500
AD: Robert Dranoff
SID: Norma Jean Coleman

DRAKE
Des Moines, IA 50311 I

Coach: Kurt Kanaskie
Alma Mater: La Salle '80
Record: 11 Years, W-207, L-107

1996-97 SCHEDULE

Colorado	Nov. 24
Eastern Mich. ■	Nov. 30
Iowa ■	Dec. 3
Liberty	Dec. 5
Samford	Dec. 7
Iowa St.	Dec. 11
Southwest Mo. St.	Dec. 21
Baylor	Dec. 31
Loyola (Ill.) ■	Jan. 4
Indiana St. ■	Jan. 8
Southwest Mo. St. ■	Jan. 12
Evansville	Jan. 16
Indiana St.	Jan. 18
Wichita St.	Jan. 22
Northern Iowa ■	Jan. 25
Evansville ■	Jan. 30
Southern Ill.	Feb. 1
Illinois St. ■	Feb. 3
Creighton	Feb. 6
Southern Ill. ■	Feb. 8
Wichita St. ■	Feb. 10
Bradley	Feb. 13
Illinois St.	Feb. 15
Creighton ■	Feb. 17
Northern Iowa	Feb. 22
Bradley ■	Feb. 24

Missouri Val. Conf. Tr......Feb. 28-Mar. 3

1995-96 RESULTS (12-15)

80	Liberty ■	59
66	Iowa	98
70	Loyola (Ill.)	62
50	Utah	86
62	Iowa St. ■	65
77	Samford ■	64
75	Baylor ■	78
94	Texas-San Antonio	86
66	Wichita St. ■	62
59	Creighton ■	56
64	Tulsa	86
64	Wichita St.	55
81	Indiana St. ■	65
76	Northern Iowa	82
87	Southern Ill. ■	67
72	Illinois St. ■	68
73	Tulsa ■	79
60	Bradley	77
65	Evansville ■	61
83	Indiana St.	85
69	Evansville	80
52	Illinois St. ■	74
71	Southern Ill.	68
81	Southwest Mo. St. ■	84
66	Northern Iowa ■	83
62	Creighton	76
51	Bradley †	64

Nickname: Bulldogs
Colors: Blue & White
Arena: Knapp Center
 Capacity: 7,002; Year Built: 1992
AD: Lynn King
SID: Mike Mahon

DREW
Madison, NJ 07940...III

Coach: Mark Coleman
Alma Mater: St. Lawrence '83
Record: 1 Year, W-14, L-13

1996-97 SCHEDULE

Drew Cl....Nov. 22-23
Stevens Tech...Nov. 26
King's (Pa.) ■...Dec. 4
Allentown ■...Dec. 7
Moravian...Dec. 10
Gettysburg ■...Jan. 6
Elizabethtown Cl....Jan. 10-11
Swarthmore...Jan. 14
Wilkes...Jan. 18
Lycoming ■...Jan. 20
FDU-Madison ■...Jan. 22
Delaware Valley ■...Jan. 25
Misericordia ■...Jan. 27
King's (Pa.)...Jan. 29
Scranton ■...Feb. 1
Lycoming...Feb. 5
Lebanon Valley...Feb. 8
Albright ■...Feb. 12
Wilkes ■...Feb. 15
Scranton...Feb. 17
FDU-Madison...Feb. 19
Delaware Valley...Feb. 22

1995-96 RESULTS (14-13)

58	New York U.	71
64	Catholic †	82
63	Scranton ■	60
54	King's (Pa.)	67
64	Stevens Tech ■	69
77	Lycoming	102
78	Moravian ■	74
89	Stevens Tech	92
79	Rensselaer †	91
63	Gettysburg	89
77	FDU-Madison	69
81	Delaware Valley	72
90	Misericordia	85
73	King's (Pa.) ■	66
69	Scranton	66
71	Allentown ■	63
72	Lycoming ■	75
64	Lebanon Valley ■	62
71	Wilkes ■	75
77	Albright	62
73	Wilkes	95
75	Swarthmore ■	68
93	FDU-Madison ■	73
109	Delaware Valley ■	66
77	Moravian	59
70	Wilkes	72
60	Rutgers-Newark	75

Nickname: Rangers
Colors: Lincoln Green & Oxford Blue
Arena: Simon Forum & Athletic Center
 Capacity: 1,000; Year Built: 1992
AD: Connee Zotos
SID: Jennifer Dougher Brauner

DREXEL
Philadelphia, PA 19104...I

Coach: Bill Herrion
Alma Mater: Merrimack '81
Record: 5 Years, W-112, L-38

1996-97 SCHEDULE

NIT...Nov. 20-29
Monmouth (N.J.) ■...Dec. 3
New Hampshire...Dec. 6
Maine...Dec. 8
Massachusetts...Dec. 12
La Salle...Dec. 14
Lehigh ■...Dec. 21
Charleston (S.C.) Cl...Dec. 28-29
Hartford ■...Jan. 2
Vermont ■...Jan. 4
Towson St. ■...Jan. 7
Northeastern...Jan. 10
Boston U. ■...Jan. 12
Pennsylvania...Jan. 15
Hofstra...Jan. 18
Delaware...Jan. 21
Maine ■...Jan. 24
New Hampshire ■...Jan. 26
Delaware ■...Jan. 31
Towson St....Feb. 2
Northeastern ■...Feb. 7
Boston U. ■...Feb. 9
St. Joseph's (Pa.)...Feb. 11
Hofstra ■...Feb. 16
Hartford...Feb. 20
Vermont...Feb. 22
America East Conf. Tr. ....Feb. 28-Mar. 2

1995-96 RESULTS (27-4)

82	St. Anselm ■	59
75	Murray St. †	76
83	Ill.-Chicago †	72
97	Vermont ■	58
79	Hartford	72
78	Oklahoma	85
75	James Madison †	55
68	Montana St.	62
100	Hofstra	71
110	New Hampshire ■	68
88	Maine ■	70
91	Delaware †	75
87	Northeastern	65
67	Boston U. ■	47
74	Boston U. ■	76
84	Northeastern ■	47
87	New Hampshire	75
73	Maine	52
96	Towson St. ■	87
93	Hofstra ■	63
93	Lehigh	73
75	Towson St.	56
82	Delaware	78
87	Md.-Balt. County	55
86	Vermont ■	59
74	Hartford ■	56
83	Hartford †	71
84	Towson St. †	74
76	Boston U. ■	67
75	Memphis †	63
58	Syracuse †	69

Nickname: Dragons
Colors: Navy Blue & Gold
Arena: P.E. Athletic Center
 Capacity: 2,300; Year Built: 1975
AD: Louis Marciani
SID: Jan Giel

DRURY
Springfield, MO 65802...II

Coach: Gary Stanfield
Alma Mater: John Brown '69
Record: 5 Years, W-103, L-44

1996-97 SCHEDULE

Mo.-Rolla...Nov. 16
Delta St. ■...Nov. 18
Mankato St. Cl....Nov. 22-23
Central Mo. St....Nov. 26
Missouri Baptist ■...Nov. 29
Northern Mich....Nov. 30
Cameron...Dec. 3
Drury Tr....Dec. 6-7
Pittsburg St....Dec. 9
Truman St....Dec. 21
BYU-Hawaii [Honolulu]...Jan. 4
Hawaii Pacific...Jan. 5
Lyon ■...Jan. 11
IU/PU-Indianapolis...Jan. 18
Harding...Jan. 20
Rockhurst ■...Jan. 22
Arkansas Tech ■...Jan. 29
Lyon...Feb. 1
IU/PU-Indianapolis ■...Feb. 8
Arkansas Tech...Feb. 13
Delta St....Feb. 15
Harding ■...Feb. 17
Rockhurst...Feb. 22
Cameron...Feb. 26
Mississippi Col. ■...Mar. 1

1995-96 RESULTS (16-11)

78	Lincoln (Mo.)	69
81	Tabor ■	59
87	Wayne St. (Neb.) ■	76
65	Central Mo. St. ■	77
76	Sterling †	64
73	Emporia St.	42
68	Lincoln (Mo.)	62
86	Southwest Baptist	60
73	Mo.-Rolla ■	59
63	Morningside †	85
88	Central Okla. †	98
67	Lincoln Memorial ■	72
66	Bemidji St. ■	54
68	Lyon	62
55	Pittsburg St.	62
77	Oakland City	97
60	IU/PU-Indianapolis	72
76	Rockhurst	93
59	Arkansas Tech	57
100	Lyon ■	85
89	Harding	97
81	Oakland City ■	73
63	IU/PU-Indianapolis	83
71	Arkansas Tech ■	60
76	Harding	65
77	Rockhurst ■	55
61	Cameron	80

Nickname: Panthers
Colors: Scarlet & Gray
Arena: Weiser Gymnasium
 Capacity: 2,250; Year Built: 1948
AD: Bruce Harger
SID: Dan Cashel

DUBUQUE
Dubuque, IA 52001...III

Coach: Grayling Gordon
Alma Mater: Dubuque '89
Record: 3 Years, W-33, L-42

1996-97 SCHEDULE

Viterbo...Nov. 26
Dubuque Cl....Nov. 29-30
St. Ambrose...Dec. 6
Aurora ■...Dec. 7
Wis.-La Crosse...Dec. 11
Rosary...Dec. 14
Wis.-Whitewater...Dec. 20
Luther ■...Jan. 10
Central (Iowa) ■...Jan. 11
Buena Vista...Jan. 17
Simpson...Jan. 18
Wartburg ■...Jan. 24
Loras...Jan. 25
Upper Iowa...Jan. 31
Simpson ■...Feb. 1
Buena Vista ■...Feb. 4
William Penn...Feb. 8
Wartburg...Feb. 8
Mt. Mercy ■...Feb. 15
Luther...Feb. 21
William Penn ■...Feb. 22
Loras...Feb. 25
Upper Iowa ■...Feb. 28
Central (Iowa)...Mar. 1

1995-96 RESULTS (13-12)

72	Viterbo ■	74
79	St. Ambrose ■	95
70	Teikyo Marycrest ■	75
56	Mt. Mercy	91
60	Wis.-Whitewater ■	91
62	St. Ambrose ■	85
46	Wis.-La Crosse ■	62
71	Purdue-Calumet	95
67	William Penn	61
65	Wartburg	61
87	Aurora	84
64	Central (Iowa) ■	71
50	Upper Iowa ■	74
59	Loras	57
72	Buena Vista	71
79	Simpson	106
65	Buena Vista ■	61
72	William Penn ■	70
68	Luther	65
80	Wartburg ■	60
55	Upper Iowa	53
86	Loras ■	78
73	Central (Iowa)	64
69	Luther	60
78	Simpson ■	96

Nickname: Spartans
Colors: Blue & White
Arena: McCormick Gym
 Capacity: 1,500; Year Built: 1916
AD: Connie Bandy Hodge
SID: Greg Yoko

DUKE
Durham, NC 27708...I

Coach: Mike Krzyzewski
Alma Mater: Army '69
Record: 21 Years, W-449, L-199

1996-97 SCHEDULE

NIT...Nov. 20-29
Lehigh ■...Dec. 2
Florida St. ■...Dec. 5
Michigan...Dec. 8
Davidson ■...Dec. 11
Villanova...Dec. 14
Army ■...Dec. 22
Western Caro. ■...Dec. 30
South Caro. St. ■...Jan. 2
Georgia Tech...Jan. 5
Clemson...Jan. 7
Wake Forest ■...Jan. 11
Campbell ■...Jan. 13
N.C.-Greensboro ■...Jan. 15
Virginia ■...Jan. 18
North Caro. St....Jan. 21
Maryland...Jan. 26
North Caro. ■...Jan. 29
Georgia Tech ■...Feb. 2
Wake Forest...Feb. 5

North Caro. St. ■ ....Feb. 8
Virginia ....Feb. 11
Florida St. ....Feb. 15
Clemson ■ ....Feb. 18
UCLA ■ ....Feb. 23
Maryland ■ ....Feb. 27
North Caro. ....Mar. 2
Atlantic Coast Conf. Tr. ......Mar. 6-9

1995-96 RESULTS (18-13)

75	Old Dominion †	55
70	Indiana †	64
88	Iowa †	81
71	N.C.-Greensboro ■	57
65	Illinois ■	75
84	South Caro. St. ■	64
84	Michigan	88
79	Delaware ■	73
107	Western Caro. ■	67
69	Monmouth (N.J.) ■	53
87	Northeastern	56
48	Clemson	51
81	Georgia Tech	86
54	Wake Forest ■	57
66	Virginia	77
71	North Caro. St.	70
85	Florida St. ■	65
58	Temple †	59
83	Maryland ■	73
72	North Caro.	73
83	Clemson ■	53
71	Georgia Tech ■	73
65	Wake Forest	79
79	Virginia ■	69
79	North Caro. St. ■	76
93	Florida St.	87
85	UCLA ■	66
77	Maryland	75
78	North Caro. ■	84
69	Maryland †	82
60	Eastern Mich. †	75

Nickname: Blue Devils
Colors: Royal Blue & White
Arena: Cameron Indoor Stadium
   Capacity: 9,314; Year Built: 1939
AD: Tom Butters
SID: Mike Cragg

DUQUESNE
Pittsburgh, PA 15282 I

Coach: Scott Edgar
Alma Mater: Pitt.-Johnstown '78
Record: 5 Years, W-88, L-58

1996-97 SCHEDULE

St. Francis (Pa.) ■ ....Nov. 27
Akron ■ ....Nov. 30
Western Ky. ....Dec. 4
Florida ■ ....Dec. 7
Coppin St. ....Dec. 10
Illinois St. ■ ....Dec. 14
Pittsburgh ■ ....Dec. 21
Ohio ....Dec. 28
West Va. ■ ....Dec. 30
Radford ■ ....Jan. 4
Virginia Tech ■ ....Jan. 6
Geo. Washington ■ ....Jan. 11
Rhode Island ■ ....Jan. 16
La Salle ....Jan. 18
St. Joseph's (Pa.) ....Jan. 21
Xavier (Ohio) ....Jan. 25
Dayton ■ ....Jan. 30
Fordham ....Feb. 1
Massachusetts ■ ....Feb. 6
Temple ■ ....Feb. 9
La Salle ■ ....Feb. 13
Geo. Washington ....Feb. 17
Xavier (Ohio) ■ ....Feb. 20
Virginia Tech ....Feb. 23
Dayton ....Feb. 26
St. Bonaventure ■ ....Mar. 1
Atlantic 10 Conf. Tr. ....Mar. 5-8

1995-96 RESULTS (9-18)

73	Pittsburgh	84
77	Illinois St.	65
77	West Va.	93
77	Coppin St. ■	76
79	Robert Morris ■	72
93	Ohio ■	80
86	Georgetown †	88
76	Akron ■	75
64	Radford	65
59	Geo. Washington ■	87
69	Virginia Tech ■	88
40	Temple ■	72
69	La Salle	73
89	Massachusetts ■	93
68	Rhode Island ■	87
59	Dayton ■	56
85	La Salle ■	75
87	Fordham ■	75
63	Virginia Tech	69
72	St. Bonaventure	74
92	UAB ■	72
70	St. Joseph's (Pa.) ■	76
72	Geo. Washington	84
105	Xavier (Ohio)	116
69	Dayton	72
75	Xavier (Ohio) ■	76
72	St. Joseph's (Pa.) †	80

Nickname: Dukes
Colors: Red & Blue
Arena: A. J. Palumbo Center
   Capacity: 6,200; Year Built: 1988
AD: Brian Colleary
SID: Sue Ryan

EARLHAM
Richmond, IN 47374 III

Coach: Tony Gary
Alma Mater: Tri-State '85
Record: 4 Years, W-20, L-80

1996-97 SCHEDULE

Earlham Cl. ....Nov. 22-23
Denison ■ ....Dec. 4
Wooster ■ ....Dec. 7
Anderson (Ind.) ■ ....Dec. 11
Thomas More ....Dec. 16
Marietta Tr. ....Dec. 28-29
Allegheny ■ ....Jan. 3
Case Reserve ■ ....Jan. 4
Ohio Wesleyan ....Jan. 8
Kenyon ....Jan. 11
Wilmington (Ohio) ■ ....Jan. 15
Oberlin ....Jan. 18
Wittenberg ■ ....Jan. 22
Denison ....Jan. 25
Case Reserve ....Jan. 31
Allegheny ....Feb. 1
Kenyon ■ ....Feb. 8
Ohio Wesleyan ■ ....Feb. 12
Wooster ....Feb. 15
Wittenberg ....Feb. 19
Oberlin ■ ....Feb. 22

1995-96 RESULTS (8-17)

69	Bethany (W.Va.)	65
86	Cincinnati Bible	84
66	Ohio Wesleyan ■	69
64	Wooster	73
91	Taylor-Ft. Wayne ■	67
71	Denison	74
86	Wittenberg ■	93
67	Anderson (Ind.)	90
77	John Carroll †	97
72	Centre	78
54	Case Reserve	70
60	Allegheny	71
55	Kenyon	86
78	Oberlin ■	69
52	St. Francis (Ind.)	75
54	Wooster	91
74	Ohio Wesleyan	64
46	Denison ■	78
85	Allegheny ■	79
91	Case Reserve ■	96

72	Wittenberg	95
91	Oberlin ■	76
71	Taylor-Ft. Wayne	73
72	Kenyon ■	60
68	Wittenberg	95

Nickname: Quakers
Colors: Maroon & White
Arena: Trueblood Fieldhouse
   Capacity: 2,200; Year Built: 1923
AD: Porter Miller
SID: David Knight

EAST CARO.
Greenville, NC 27858 I

Coach: Joe Dooley
Alma Mater: Geo. Washington '88
Record: 1 Year, W-17, L-11

1996-97 SCHEDULE

Fairfield ....Nov. 23
Appalachian St. ....Nov. 26
Boston U. [Halifax] ....Nov. 30
Campbell ....Dec. 2
Jacksonville St. ■ ....Dec. 4
Southwestern La. ■ ....Dec. 14
Georgia ....Dec. 17
St. Joseph's (Pa.) ■ ....Dec. 19
Armstrong Atlantic ■ ....Dec. 28
William & Mary ■ ....Jan. 2
American ■ ....Jan. 4
George Mason ■ ....Jan. 6
Old Dominion ....Jan. 11
Va. Commonwealth ■ ....Jan. 15
Richmond ■ ....Jan. 18
James Madison ■ ....Jan. 21
N.C.-Wilmington ....Jan. 25
Old Dominion ■ ....Jan. 29
George Mason ....Feb. 1
American ....Feb. 3
Jacksonville St. ....Feb. 10
Va. Commonwealth ■ ....Feb. 12
James Madison ■ ....Feb. 15
Richmond ....Feb. 17
N.C.-Wilmington ■ ....Feb. 22
William & Mary ....Feb. 24
Colonial Conf. Tr. ....Feb. 28-Mar. 3

1995-96 RESULTS (17-11)

89	Elon ■	74
65	N.C.-Charlotte	80
68	Wofford	58
74	Coastal Caro.	62
62	Campbell ■	57
80	Colorado St. ■	72
62	Southwest Mo. St. ■	59
52	Illinois St.	64
62	James Madison	56
76	George Mason	80
63	Appalachian St. ■	39
73	Va. Commonwealth ■	72
75	American	85
72	Old Dominion ■	67
81	Richmond ■	65
45	N.C.-Wilmington ■	44
71	William & Mary	65
66	Richmond	58
73	American ■	89
78	George Mason	92
71	Va. Commonwealth	80
88	William & Mary ■	78
79	Wofford ■	60
70	James Madison ■	72
45	N.C.-Wilmington	67
57	Old Dominion	81
76	American †	60
60	Va. Commonwealth †	75

Nickname: Pirates
Colors: Purple & Gold
Arena: Williams Arena at Minges
   Capacity: 7,500; Year Built: 1968
AD: Mike Hamrick
SID: Norm Reilly

EAST STROUDSBURG
East Stroudsburg, PA 18301 II

Coach: To be named

1996-97 SCHEDULE

Bryant Cl. ....Nov. 23-24
Dist. Columbia ■ ....Nov. 26
Albany (N.Y.) ....Dec. 1
East Stroudsburg Cl. ....Dec. 6-7
Columbia Union ■ ....Dec. 12
Bloomfield ....Dec. 14
St. Michael's Cl. ....Dec. 28-29
Fairmont Cl. ....Jan. 3-4
West Chester ....Jan. 8
Dist. Columbia ....Jan. 11
Kutztown ■ ....Jan. 15
Bloomsburg ■ ....Jan. 18
Millersville ....Jan. 22
Cheyney ....Jan. 25
Albright ....Jan. 27
Mansfield ■ ....Jan. 29
West Chester ■ ....Feb. 5
Bloomsburg ....Feb. 8
Kutztown ....Feb. 12
Millersville ■ ....Feb. 15
Mansfield ....Feb. 19
Cheyney ■ ....Feb. 22

1995-96 RESULTS (14-13)

72	LIU-Southampton	83
83	Dist. Columbia	86
83	St. Michael's ■	78
64	Salem-Teikyo ■	80
66	West Va. Wesleyan ■	61
65	Columbia Union	71
68	Dist. Columbia	63
64	Bentley	72
60	LIU-C. W. Post †	71
105	Palm Beach Atl.	88
73	Nova Southeastern	72
91	Webber	95
84	Mansfield ■	78
63	Cheyney	88
79	Millersville ■	78
72	Bloomsburg ■	77
72	Albright ■	62
89	Kutztown	98
76	West Chester	62
99	Cheyney ■	70
71	Bloomfield ■	54
86	Mansfield ■	73
77	Millersville	88
94	Kutztown ■	71
50	Bloomsburg	64
89	West Chester ■	82
67	Indiana (Pa.)	86

Nickname: Warriors
Colors: Red & Black
Arena: Leroy Koehler Fieldhouse
   Capacity: 2,650; Year Built: 1967
AD: Earl W. Edwards
SID: Peter Nevins

EAST TENN. ST.
Johnson City, TN 37614 I

Coach: Ed DeChellis
Alma Mater: Penn St. '82
(First year as head coach)

1996-97 SCHEDULE

N.C.-Asheville ■ ....Nov. 23
Michigan St. ....Nov. 25
Lees-McRae ■ ....Nov. 30
Virginia Tech ....Dec. 5
West Va. ....Dec. 14
Wofford ■ ....Dec. 17
Bluefield Col. ■ ....Dec. 19
Iowa St. Cl. ....Dec. 21-22
Radford ■ ....Dec. 30
Tennessee ....Jan. 4
Ga. Southern ....Jan. 6
Citadel ■ ....Jan. 11
Furman ■ ....Jan. 18

VMI ■ ....Jan. 20
Davidson ■.........Jan. 22
Wofford ....Jan. 25
Appalachian St. ....Jan. 27
Tenn.-Chatt. ....Jan. 29
Marshall ■.........Feb. 1
Western Caro. ....Feb. 3
Tenn.-Chatt. ■.........Feb. 8
Davidson ....Feb. 10
Appalachian St. ■.........Feb. 15
Marshall ....Feb. 17
VMI ....Feb. 22
Southern Conf. Tr. ....Feb. 27-Mar. 2

1995-96 RESULTS (7-20)
84 Lees-McRae ■ 70
86 Carson-Newman ■ 63
58 Iowa 104
50 Mississippi † 65
77 Radford 88
57 Michigan St. 63
68 Radford ■.........64
73 Kansas 108
81 Texas Tech ■.........99
56 Davidson 88
70 Tennessee St. ■.........73
93 Wofford 86
82 Marshall ■ 76
86 VMI 96
68 Ga. Southern ■.........70
64 Citadel 49
100 Appalachian St. ■ 68
73 Tenn.-Chatt. ■.........75
79 VMI 82
66 Davidson ■.........96
88 Furman 89
79 Appalachian St. 95
84 Marshall 111
76 Wofford ■ 81
91 Western Caro. ■.........93
60 Tenn.-Chatt. † 93
43 Davidson † 67

Nickname: Buccaneers
Colors: Blue & Gold
Arena: Memorial Center
  Capacity: 12,000; Year Built: 1977
AD: Keener Fry Jr
SID: Annabelle Vaughan

EASTERN
St. Davids, PA 19087 III

Coach: Dennis Hunt
Alma Mater: Manchester '82
(First year as head coach)

1996-97 SCHEDULE
Widener Tr. ....Nov. 22-23
Phila. Textile ■ ....Dec. 2
Gwynedd-Mercy ....Dec. 4
Cabrini ■ ....Dec. 7
Rollins ....Dec. 28
Albright Tr. ....Jan. 3-4
Alvernia ■.........Jan. 8
Neumann ....Jan. 11
Marywood ....Jan. 13
Allentown ■.........Jan. 15
Beaver ■ ....Jan. 18
Misericordia ....Jan. 22
Gwynedd-Mercy ■.........Jan. 25
Phila. Pharmacy ■.........Jan. 27
Cabrini ....Jan. 29
Alvernia ....Feb. 1
Neumann ■.........Feb. 5
Marywood ■.........Feb. 8
Allentown ....Feb. 12
Beaver ....Feb. 15
West Chester ....Feb. 17
Misericordia ■.........Feb. 22

1995-96 RESULTS (8-17)
77 Rowan 100
67 Phila. Textile 71
100 Bapt. Bible (Pa.) ■.........104
73 Gwynedd-Mercy 59
78 Misericordia 73

59 Phila. Pharmacy 76
48 West Chester ■ 65
104 Marywood ■.........73
47 Frank. & Marsh. 94
57 Beaver † 65
57 Cabrini 73
76 East. Mennonite 81
73 Neumann ■.........61
57 Alvernia 75
63 Allentown 73
68 Beaver ■.........76
81 Misericordia ■ 75
68 Alvernia 75
58 Cabrini 91
90 Neumann 62
62 Allentown ■.........61
82 Gwynedd-Mercy ■ 64
76 Marywood 86
60 Beaver 61
61 Allentown 92

Nickname: Eagles
Colors: Maroon & White
Arena: Eastern College Gym
  Capacity: 1,200
AD: Wayne Rasmussen
SID: To be named

EASTERN CONN. ST.
Willimantic, CT 06226 III

Coach: Barry Davis
Alma Mater: St. Lawrence '82
Record: 11 Years, W-63, L-233

1996-97 SCHEDULE
Eastern Conn. St. Tr. ....Nov. 22-23
Westfield St. ■.........Dec. 5
Worcester St. ....Dec. 10
North Adams St. ■.........Dec. 12
Southern Me. ■.........Dec. 14
Salem St. Tr. ....Dec. 29-30
Clark (Mass.) ....Jan. 4
Wesleyan (Conn.) ....Jan. 11
Rhode Island Col. ■ ....Jan. 14
Albertus Magnus ....Jan. 16
Plymouth St. ....Jan. 18
Western Conn. St. ■ ....Jan. 21
Wheaton (Mass.) ■ ....Jan. 23
Mass.-Boston ....Jan. 25
Mass.-Dartmouth ....Jan. 28
Rhode Island Col. ....Feb. 4
Southern Me. ....Feb. 8
Western Conn. St. ....Feb. 11
Plymouth St. ■.........Feb. 15
Mass.-Dartmouth ....Feb. 18
Mass.-Boston ■.........Feb. 22

1995-96 RESULTS (8-17)
68 Thomas ■ 62
75 Richard Stockton ■ 78
88 Trinity (Conn.) † 89
101 Framingham St. † 89
81 North Adams St. 61
84 Worcester St. ■ 77
71 Wesleyan (Conn.) ■ 65
73 Southern Me. 78
76 Anna Maria † 97
79 Suffolk † 59
81 Clark (Mass.) 93
67 Plymouth St. ■ 69
66 Western Conn. St. 82
57 Wheaton (Mass.) 65
73 Mass.-Boston ■ 55
61 Mass.-Dartmouth 78
111 Babson 118
62 Rhode Island Col. ■ 73
84 Southern Me. ■ 78
72 Western Conn. St. ■ 82
71 Rhode Island Col. 83
56 Plymouth St. 81
66 Mass.-Dartmouth ■.........85
73 Mass.-Boston 80
74 Rhode Island Col. 81

Nickname: Warriors
Colors: Blue & White

Arena: Geissler Gymnasium
  Capacity: 3,000; Year Built: 1974
AD: Sharlene Peter
SID: Bob Molta

EASTERN ILL.
Charleston, IL 61920 I

Coach: Rick Samuels
Alma Mater: Chadron St. '71
Record: 16 Years, W-234, L-228

1996-97 SCHEDULE
DePaul ....Nov. 23
Wash. & Jeff. ....Nov. 30
Western Ill. ■.........Dec. 2
Indiana St. ■ ....Dec. 4
Indiana Cl. ....Dec. 13-14
Elmhurst ■.........Dec. 16
St. Louis ....Dec. 21
Austin Peay ....Jan. 2
Tennessee St. ....Jan. 4
Murray St. ■.........Jan. 9
Morehead St. ■ ....Jan. 11
Eastern Ky. ■.........Jan. 13
Tennessee Tech ....Jan. 18
Middle Tenn. ....Jan. 20
Southeast Mo. St. ....Jan. 25
Tenn.-Martin ■ ....Jan. 30
Austin Peay ■.........Feb. 1
Tennessee St. ■.........Feb. 3
Eastern Ky. ....Feb. 8
Morehead St. ....Feb. 10
Tenn.-Martin ....Feb. 13
Middle Tenn. ■.........Feb. 15
Tennessee Tech ■.........Feb. 17
Murray St. ....Feb. 20
Southeast Mo. St. ■.........Feb. 22
Ohio Valley Conf. Tr. ....Feb. 25-Mar. 1

1995-96 RESULTS (13-15)
68 Oral Roberts 57
57 Illinois 89
72 Millikin ■ 65
50 DePaul ■ 77
54 Indiana St. 70
65 Dayton 85
70 Wisconsin 105
89 Chicago St. ■ 66
66 Valparaiso 83
85 Troy St. 96
80 Central Conn. St. 86
74 Youngstown St. ■ 68
60 Buffalo ■ 52
48 Northeastern Ill. ■ 73
83 Western Ill. 68
56 Mo.-Kansas City 54
61 Oral Roberts ■ 58
59 Valparaiso 63
87 Central Conn. St. ■ 84
84 Troy St. ■ 95
64 Buffalo 61
65 Youngstown St. 74
73 Mo.-Kansas City ■ 82
77 Western Ill. 53
90 Chicago St. 73
72 Northeastern Ill. 83
59 Buffalo † 55
65 Valparaiso † 78

Nickname: Panthers
Colors: Blue & Gray
Arena: Lantz Gym
  Capacity: 6,500; Year Built: 1966
AD: Lou Hencken
SID: Dave Kidwell

EASTERN KY.
Richmond, KY 40475 I

Coach: Mike Calhoun
Alma Mater: Georgetown (Ky.) '72
Record: 4 Years, W-50, L-59

1996-97 SCHEDULE
Loyola (Ill.) ....Nov. 23

Ohio Valley ■ ....Nov. 26
Illinois St. ....Nov. 30
Austin Peay ■ ....Dec. 7
Miami (Ohio) ....Dec. 10
Florida Int'l ■ ....Dec. 14
Samford ■ ....Dec. 21
Iona Tr. ....Dec. 27-28
Middle Tenn. St. ■ ....Jan. 4
Tennessee Tech ■ ....Jan. 6
Southeast Mo. St. ....Jan. 11
Eastern Ill. ....Jan. 13
Morehead St. ....Jan. 16
Murray St. ■ ....Jan. 18
Tenn.-Martin ■ ....Jan. 20
Austin Peay ....Jan. 25
Tennessee St. ....Jan. 27
Tennessee Tech ....Feb. 1
Middle Tenn. St. ....Feb. 3
Eastern Ill. ■ ....Feb. 8
Southeast Mo. St. ■ ....Feb. 10
Morehead St. ■ ....Feb. 13
Tenn.-Martin ....Feb. 15
Murray St. ....Feb. 17
Tennessee St. ■ ....Feb. 22
Ohio Valley Conf. Tr. ....Feb. 25-Mar. 1

1995-96 RESULTS (13-14)
68 Miami (Ohio) ■ 89
101 West Va. St. 88
64 Wright St. 76
71 Dayton ■ 65
68 Loyola (Ill.) ■ 61
70 Louisville 87
79 Central Fla. 72
95 Oakland City ■ 69
88 Ohio St. † 92
82 Alcorn St. † 76
64 Morehead St. 68
89 Southeast Mo. St. ■ 73
76 Morehead St. ■ 64
64 Murray St. 73
60 Tenn.-Martin 59
71 Austin Peay ■ 72
70 Middle Tenn. St. ■ 64
69 Tennessee St. 72
80 Tennessee Tech 86
79 Southeast Mo. St. 76
77 Tenn.-Martin ■ 74
62 Murray St. 85
70 Middle Tenn. St. 74
75 Austin Peay 90
87 Tennessee Tech ■ 83
67 Tennessee St. ■ 82
67 Austin Peay † 89

Nickname: Colonels
Colors: Maroon & White
Arena: McBrayer Arena
  Capacity: 6,500; Year Built: 1963
AD: Robert Baugh
SID: Karl Park

EAST. MENNONITE
Harrisonburg, VA 22801 III

Coach: Tom Baker
Alma Mater: East. Mennonite '81
Record: 4 Years, W-24, L-74

1996-97 SCHEDULE
Gordon Tr. ....Nov. 22-23
Va. Wesleyan ■ ....Dec. 2
Bridgewater (Va.) Tr ....Dec. 6-7
Randolph-Macon ■ ....Dec. 16
VMI ....Dec. 18
Bridgewater (Va.) ....Jan. 7
Emory & Henry ■ ....Jan. 11
Roanoke ....Jan. 13
Guilford ....Jan. 17
Lynchburg ....Jan. 23
Guilford ■ ....Jan. 25
Bridgewater (Va.) ■ ....Jan. 27
Lynchburg ■ ....Jan. 30
Hampden-Sydney ....Feb. 1
Randolph-Macon ....Feb. 5
Wash. & Lee ....Feb. 8

Emory & Henry ....Feb. 9
Roanoke ■ ....Feb. 12
Hampden-Sydney ■ ....Feb. 15
Va. Wesleyan ■ ....Feb. 17
Wash. & Lee ■ ....Feb. 19

1995-96 RESULTS (10-15)

99	Gordon †	78
78	Eastern Nazarene †	67
63	Randolph-Macon ■	93
87	Averett †	60
68	Bridgewater (Va.) ■	86
61	Va. Wesleyan	71
68	Roanoke	90
80	Bridgewater (Va.) ■	88
62	VMI	91
101	Emory & Henry ■	88
83	Guilford ■	70
81	Eastern ■	76
75	Lynchburg	92
65	Guilford	62
65	Bridgewater (Va.)	79
83	Lynchburg ■	78
76	Hampden-Sydney ■	88
82	Randolph-Macon	83
79	Wash. & Lee	100
98	Emory & Henry	108
93	Roanoke ■	100
75	Hampden-Sydney	98
68	Va. Wesleyan ■	62
96	Wash. & Lee ■	77
82	Roanoke †	84

Nickname: Royals
Colors: Royal Blue & White
Arena: EMU Gymnasium
    Capacity: 900; Year Built: 1957
AD: Lester Zook
SID: Larry Guengerich

EASTERN MICH.

Ypsilanti, MI 48197 I

Coach: Milton Barnes
Alma Mater: Albion '79
(First year as head coach)

1996-97 SCHEDULE

Oakland ■ ....Nov. 23
St. Joseph's (Ind.) ■ ....Nov. 26
Drake......................................Nov. 30
Jackson St. ....Dec. 7
Syracuse Cl. ....Dec. 13-14
Cincinnati ....Dec. 19
Hilo Holiday Tr. ....Dec. 28-30
Kent ....Jan. 4
Central Mich. ■ ....Jan. 8
Toledo ■ ....Jan. 13
Boise St. ....Jan. 16
Bowling Green ■ ....Jan. 19
Western Mich. ....Jan. 22
Ball St. ■ ....Jan. 25
Akron ....Jan. 29
Central Mich. ■ ....Feb. 1
Ohio ....Feb. 3
Miami (Ohio) ■ ....Feb. 6
Toledo ....Feb. 8
Ohio ■ ....Feb. 12
Bowling Green ....Feb. 15
Western Mich. ■ ....Feb. 19
Ball St. ....Feb. 22
Miami (Ohio)...........................Feb. 24
Akron ■ ....Feb. 26
Kent ....Mar. 1
Mid-American Conf. Tr.............Mar. 4-8

1995-96 RESULTS (25-6)

83	St. Francis (Ind.) ■	70
83	St. Bonaventure †	63
95	Montana St. ■	71
111	San Fran. St. ■	61
74	Rutgers	71
88	Manhattan ■	76
93	Texas Tech †	77
73	UTEP	80
91	Toledo ■	87
82	Akron	73

88	Western Mich. ■	65
81	Central Mich.	76
77	Bowling Green ■	58
109	Ball St. ■	102
73	Miami (Ohio)	60
96	Kent ■	81
73	Ohio	82
62	Akron	53
89	Western Mich.	83
91	Central Mich. ■	79
70	Bowling Green	72
91	Ball St.	75
68	Miami (Ohio) ■	75
73	Kent	91
81	Ohio ■	77
95	Toledo	85
84	Kent ■	72
87	Ball St. †	71
77	Toledo †	63
75	Duke †	60
81	Connecticut †	95

Nickname: Eagles
Colors: Green & White
Arena: Bowen Field House
    Capacity: 5,600; Year Built: 1955
AD: Tim Weiser
SID: Jim Streeter

EASTERN NAZARENE

Quincy, MA 02170 III

Coach: Mark E. Fleming
Alma Mater: Olivet Nazarene '82
Record: 9 Years, W-99, L-131

1996-97 SCHEDULE

Gordon Tr. ....Nov. 22-23
Rhode Island Col. ....Dec. 3
Worcester St. ■........................Dec. 7
Atlantic Union ■ ....Dec. 10
Notre Dame (N.H.) ....Dec. 13
MIT ....Jan. 8
Suffolk ....Jan. 11
Trinity (Conn.) ....Jan. 14
Salem St. ■ ....Jan. 18
New England Col. ■ ....Jan. 21
Roger Williams ■ ....Jan. 25
Gordon ....Jan. 25
Wentworth Inst. ....Jan. 29
Anna Maria ■ ....Feb. 1
Roger Williams ....Feb. 4
Salve Regina ■ ....Feb. 6
Nichols ....Feb. 8
Wentworth Inst. ....Feb. 10
Curry ....Feb. 12
Colby-Sawyer ■ ....Feb. 15
Curry ■ ....Feb. 18
Salve Regina ....Feb. 22

1995-96 RESULTS (19-8)

85	Messiah	77
67	East. Mennonite †	78
81	Worcester St.	72
53	Rhode Island Col. ■	52
84	Notre Dame (N.H.) ■	43
94	Endicott ■	63
62	Nova Southeastern ■	65
75	MIT	36
82	Suffolk ■	74
80	Trinity (Conn.) ■	73
84	Salem St.	78
97	New England Col.	54
68	Roger Williams	44
79	Gordon ■	69
77	Wentworth Inst. ■	82
69	Anna Maria	75
85	Roger Williams ■	61
73	Salve Regina	64
88	Nichols ■	67
75	Wentworth Inst.	93
82	Curry ■	62
82	Colby-Sawyer	102
99	Curry	69
84	Salve Regina ■	64
88	Gordon ■	76

72	Anna Maria	76
43	Colby ■	62

Nickname: Crusaders
Colors: Red & White
Arena: Lahue Center
    Capacity: 1,600; Year Built: 1973
AD: Mark Fleming
SID: To be named

EASTERN N.M.

Portales, NM 88130 II

Coach: Earl Diddle
Alma Mater: Ashland '72
Record: 12 Years, W-206, L-140

1996-97 SCHEDULE

N.M. Highlands.......................Nov. 18
UC-Colo. Spgs. ■ ....Nov. 24
Wayland Baptist ....Nov. 26
UC-Colo. Springs Cl. ....Nov. 29-30
Wayland Baptist ■ ....Dec. 3
Eastern N.M. Cl. ....Dec. 6-7
Angelo St. ....Dec. 14
Abilene Christian ....Dec. 16
Central Okla. ■ ....Jan. 7
Midwestern St. ■ ....Jan. 9
Texas A&M-Commerce ....Jan. 11
Tarleton St. ....Jan. 13
Tex. A&M-Kingsville ■ ....Jan. 16
West Tex. A&M ■ ....Jan. 25
Midwestern St. ....Jan. 30
Central Okla. ....Feb. 1
N.M. Highlands ■ ....Feb. 4
Tarleton St. ■ ....Feb. 6
Texas A&M-Commerce ■ ....Feb. 8
West Tex. A&M ....Feb. 10
Tex. A&M-Kingsville ....Feb. 15
Abilene Christian ■ ....Feb. 20
Angelo St. ■ ....Feb. 22

1995-96 RESULTS (17-10)

77	N.M. Highlands ■	61
116	National Christian ■	61
117	Wiley †	66
112	LeTourneau †	66
74	UC-Colo. Spgs.	81
85	Western N.M. †	62
76	St. Edward's †	70
76	Angelo St. ■	72
111	Abilene Christian ■	83
78	N.M. Highlands	65
105	Central Okla.	93
90	Midwestern St.	92
73	Texas A&M-Commerce ■	80
101	Tarleton St. ■	63
65	West Tex. A&M	79
91	Tex. A&M-Kingsville	87
81	West Tex. A&M	90
76	Lubbock Chrst.	63
68	Midwestern St. ■	66
85	Central Okla. ■	92
73	Tarleton St.	70
63	Texas A&M-Commerce	66
93	Lubbock Chrst.	79
86	Tex. A&M-Kingsville ■	98
68	Abilene Christian	80
96	Angelo St.	69
94	Central Okla.	100

Nickname: Greyhounds
Colors: Green & Silver
Arena: Greyhound Arena
    Capacity: 4,800; Year Built: 1967
AD: B. B. Lees (Interim)
SID: Judy Willson

EASTERN WASH.

Cheney, WA 99004 I

Coach: Steve Aggers
Alma Mater: Chadron St. '71
Record: 12 Years, W-191, L-163

1996-97 SCHEDULE

New Mexico Cl. ....Nov. 22-23
Western Mont. ■ ....Nov. 26
San Diego St. ....Nov. 30
UC Irvine ■ ....Dec. 4
Washington St. [Spokane]......Dec. 7
Sam Houston St. ....Dec. 14
Santa Clara ■ ....Dec. 17
Gonzaga ■ ....Dec. 21
Washington ....Dec. 28
Northern Ariz. ....Jan. 2
Cal St. Northridge ....Jan. 4
Cal St. Sacramento ■ ....Jan. 9
Weber St. ■ ....Jan. 11
Montana St. ■ ....Jan. 16
Montana ■ ....Jan. 18
Weber St. ....Jan. 22
Portland St. ....Jan. 25
Portland St. ■ ....Jan. 31
Idaho St. ....Feb. 6
Cal St. Sacramento ....Feb. 8
Cal St. Northridge ■ ....Feb. 13
Northern Ariz. ■ ....Feb. 15
Montana St. ....Feb. 20
Montana ....Feb. 22
Idaho St. ■ ....Feb. 27
Big Sky Conf. Tr. ....Mar. 6-8

1995-96 RESULTS (3-23)

58	Washington St.	90
55	Washington ■	74
48	San Francisco	66
68	Hofstra †	78
72	Portland ■	87
66	UC Irvine	86
66	Cal Poly SLO	82
72	Carroll (Mont.) ■	64
55	Gonzaga	68
93	Whitman ■	59
53	Gonzaga ■	63
49	Boise St.	73
78	Idaho St. ■	81
53	Idaho ■	75
58	Northern Ariz. ■	60
88	Weber St. ■	119
66	Montana St.	85
70	Montana	71
55	Idaho St.	56
65	Boise St. ■	70
73	Cal St. Sacramento	65
63	Idaho	76
83	Weber St.	106
57	Northern Ariz.	71
69	Montana	76
64	Montana St. ■	92

Nickname: Eagles
Colors: Red & White
Arena: Reese Court
    Capacity: 5,000; Year Built: 1975
AD: John Johnson
SID: Dave Cook

ECKERD

St. Petersburg, FL 33733 II

Coach: Tom Ryan
Alma Mater: Eckerd '87
(First year as head coach)

1996-97 SCHEDULE

Warner Southern ■ ....Nov. 19
Morehouse ....Nov. 23
Franklin ■ ....Nov. 26
Eckerd Cl. ....Nov. 29-30
St. Thomas (Fla.) ■ ....Dec. 9
Nova Southeastern ....Dec. 14
Queens (N.C.) Cl. ....Jan. 3-5
Fla. Southern ....Jan. 8
Florida Tech ....Jan. 11
North Fla. ....Jan. 15
St. Leo ■ ....Jan. 18
Rollins ....Jan. 22
Tampa ■ ....Jan. 25
Barry ■ ....Jan. 29
North Fla.................................Feb. 1

St. Leo....Feb. 5
Florida Tech ■....Feb. 8
Rollins ■....Feb. 12
Tampa....Feb. 15
Barry....Feb. 19
Fla. Southern ■....Feb. 22

1995-96 RESULTS (17-10)

73 Otterbein ■....87
79 Washburn †....67
60 Mo.-Rolla....76
94 Nova Southeastern ■....56
93 American (P.R.)....75
84 Mo. Southern St. †....75
69 LIU-C. W. Post †....50
77 Ill. Wesleyan ■....82
86 Morehouse....76
85 American (P.R.) ■....81
72 Central Meth. ■....58
88 Fla. Southern ■....80
72 Florida Tech ■....75
68 Tampa....73
92 Rollins ■....77
61 St. Leo....63
81 Barry....76
58 North Fla.....64
56 North Fla. ■....51
69 Fla. Southern....79
69 Florida Tech....60
67 Tampa ■....59
68 Rollins....70
78 St. Leo ■....68
66 Barry ■....56
58 St. Leo †....55
52 North Fla. †....61

Nickname: Tritons
Colors: Red, White & Black
Arena: McArthur Center
Capacity: 1,300; Year Built: 1970
AD: James R. Harley
SID: Jack Heupel

EDGEWOOD

Madison, WI 53711....III

Coach: Steve Larson
Alma Mater: Wis.-Oshkosh '74
Record: 10 Years, W-202, L-110

1996-97 SCHEDULE

St. Norbert ■....Nov. 23
Wis.-Stout....Nov. 26
St. Thomas Aquinas....Nov. 30
Lakeland....Dec. 4
Edgewood Cl.....Dec. 6-7
Carthage ■....Dec. 14
Wis.-Whitewater....Dec. 29
St. Thomas Aquinas ■....Dec. 31
Wis.-Stevens Point ■....Jan. 2
Wis.-Oshkosh....Jan. 4
Concordia (Wis.)....Jan. 11
Cardinal Stritch ■....Jan. 15
Marian (Wis.) ■....Jan. 18
North Park....Jan. 22
Milwaukee Engr.....Jan. 25
Wis. Lutheran....Jan. 28
Lakeland ■....Jan. 30
Maranatha Bapt.....Feb. 1
Wis. Lutheran ■....Feb. 6
Cardinal Stritch....Feb. 8
Concordia (Wis.) ■....Feb. 13
Marian (Wis.)....Feb. 15
Maranatha Bapt.....Feb. 17

1995-96 RESULTS (14-12)

68 Dak. Wesleyan †....71
63 Mt. St. Clare †....66
78 Wis.-Stout ■....60
85 Lawrence....95
75 Illinois Tech....62
54 Milwaukee Engr. ■....47
57 Mt. St. Clare ■....60
64 Carthage....63
74 Cardinal Stritch....88
67 Maranatha Bapt.....60
42 Wis.-Oshkosh ■....61
63 Wis.-La Crosse †....58
56 St. Norbert....58
73 Lakeland ■....67
74 Wis. Lutheran ■....89
50 Concordia (Wis.)....52
77 Marian (Wis.)....51
77 Milwaukee Engr.....51
66 Lakeland....79
70 Maranatha Bapt. ■....61
83 Wis. Lutheran....85
88 Cardinal Stritch ■....65
64 Concordia (Wis.)....61
74 Marian (Wis.) ■....62
64 Concordia (Wis.) ■....59
73 Lakeland....80

Nickname: Eagles
Colors: Black, White & Red
Arena: Todd Weh Edgedome
Capacity: 1,000; Year Built: 1961
AD: G. Steven Larson
SID: David E. Smith

EDINBORO

Edinboro, PA 16444....II

Coach: Greg Walcavich
Alma Mater: Rutgers '73
Record: 15 Years, W-283, L-138

1996-97 SCHEDULE

Columbia Union ■....Nov. 19
Point Park ■....Nov. 21
Gannon....Nov. 26
Salem-Teikyo....Nov. 30
Ashland ■....Dec. 3
West Va. Wesleyan....Dec. 6
Lake Erie ■....Dec. 14
Mercyhurst....Dec. 18
Daemen ■....Jan. 4
Slippery Rock....Jan. 8
Lock Haven ■....Jan. 11
Indiana (Pa.) ■....Jan. 15
Shippensburg ■....Jan. 18
Mercyhurst ■....Jan. 22
Calif. (Pa.)....Jan. 25
Clarion....Jan. 29
Lock Haven....Feb. 1
Gannon ■....Feb. 3
Slippery Rock ■....Feb. 5
Shippensburg....Feb. 8
Indiana (Pa.)....Feb. 12
Pitt.-Johnstown....Feb. 15
Pitt.-Bradford ■....Feb. 17
Clarion ■....Feb. 19
Calif. (Pa.) ■....Feb. 22

1995-96 RESULTS (21-8)

92 Columbia Union ■....76
81 Point Park ■....79
91 Mercyhurst ■....69
74 Ashland....76
78 Gannon ■....51
116 Thiel ■....67
106 Lake Erie ■....64
90 Hillsdale †....70
85 Gannon....92
103 Daemen ■....54
75 Salem-Teikyo ■....67
93 Clarion ■....71
59 Calif. (Pa.) ■....71
99 Mercyhurst....90
117 Ohio Valley ■....69
94 Shippensburg....83
73 Indiana (Pa.) ■....74
96 Lock Haven....87
89 Pitt.-Johnstown ■....84
91 Slippery Rock ■....40
64 Calif. (Pa.)....79
103 Clarion....95
86 Indiana (Pa.)....96
96 Shippensburg ■....69
89 Slippery Rock....82
75 Lock Haven ■....62
78 Cheyney....85
90 Bloomsburg †....82
76 Calif. (Pa.)....84

Nickname: Fighting Scots
Colors: Red & White
Arena: McComb Fieldhouse
Capacity: 4,000; Year Built: 1970
AD: Jody Mooradian
SID: Shawn Ahearn

ELIZABETHTOWN

Elizabethtown, PA 17022....III

Coach: Robert Schlosser
Alma Mater: East Stoudsburg '77
Record: 6 Years, W-81, L-71

1996-97 SCHEDULE

Binghamton Cl.....Nov. 22-23
Delaware Valley....Nov. 26
King's (Pa.) ■....Dec. 2
Messiah....Dec. 5
Susquehanna ■....Dec. 7
Widener....Dec. 10
Clarion ■....Dec. 18
Elizabethtown Cl.....Jan. 10-11
Lebanon Valley ■....Jan. 15
Albright....Jan. 18
Juniata....Jan. 21
Moravian....Jan. 25
Messiah ■....Jan. 28
Muhlenberg ■....Jan. 30
Susquehanna....Feb. 1
Widener ■....Feb. 4
Alvernia....Feb. 6
Scranton....Feb. 8
Lebanon Valley....Feb. 12
Albright ■....Feb. 15
Juniata ■....Feb. 18
Moravian ■....Feb. 22

1995-96 RESULTS (15-10)

69 Roanoke....95
80 Ferrum †....76
92 Delaware Valley ■....39
63 King's (Pa.)....61
83 Messiah ■....75
62 Susquehanna....67
61 Widener ■....50
79 Holy Family ■....90
98 Alvernia ■....82
67 Beaver †....54
61 Frank. & Marsh.....73
89 Lebanon Valley....68
65 Albright....57
94 Juniata ■....73
62 Moravian ■....76
83 Messiah....66
75 Muhlenberg....68
75 Susquehanna ■....80
65 Widener....60
80 Scranton ■....92
62 Lebanon Valley ■....76
91 Albright ■....70
102 Juniata....62
60 Moravian....61
60 Lycoming....61

Nickname: Blue Jays
Colors: Blue & Grey
Arena: Thompson Gymnasium
Capacity: 2,400; Year Built: 1969
AD: Nancy Latimore
SID: Matt Mackowski

ELMHURST

Elmhurst, IL 60126....III

Coach: Mark Scherer
Alma Mater: Eureka '83
(First year as head coach)

1996-97 SCHEDULE

Loras ■....Nov. 26
Alma....Nov. 30
Concordia (Ill.)....Dec. 3
Carroll (Wis.) ■....Dec. 14
Eastern Ill.....Dec. 16
Schreiner....Dec. 19
Trinity (Tex.)....Dec. 21
Elmhurst Cl.....Dec. 28-29
Rose-Hulman....Jan. 4
Teikyo Marycrest ■....Jan. 7
Augustana (Ill.)....Jan. 11
Millikin....Jan. 14
North Central ■....Jan. 18
Carthage ■....Jan. 22
Ill. Wesleyan ■....Jan. 25
North Park....Jan. 29
Augustana (Ill.) ■....Feb. 1
Ill. Wesleyan....Feb. 8
North Central....Feb. 11
Millikin ■....Feb. 15
Wheaton (Ill.) ■....Feb. 18
Carthage....Feb. 22
North Park ■....Feb. 26
Wheaton (Ill.)....Mar. 1

1995-96 RESULTS (16-9)

69 MacMurray....63
63 Concordia (Ill.) ■....60
62 Western Ill.....89
87 Ind.-Southeast †....98
75 Purdue-Calumet †....60
101 Alma ■....85
70 La Verne....61
55 Southern Cal Col.....56
73 Claremont-M-S ■....75
71 Wis.-River Falls ■....83
61 Teikyo Marycrest....51
55 Wheaton (Ill.) ■....56
94 North Park ■....87
60 Carthage ■....58
47 Ill. Wesleyan....84
73 North Central....58
88 Millikin ■....69
74 Augustana (Ill.) ■....80
66 Wheaton (Ill.)....84
66 Carthage....65
98 North Park....73
86 Ill. Wesleyan ■....72
85 North Central ■....50
74 Millikin....59
74 Augustana (Ill.)....64

Nickname: Bluejays
Colors: Blue & White
Arena: Physical Education Center
Capacity: 1,800; Year Built: 1983
AD: Chris Ragdale
SID: John Quigley

ELMIRA

Elmira, NY 14901....III

Coach: Terry Zeh
Alma Mater: St. Bonaventure '90
Record: 1 Year, W-14, L-13

1996-97 SCHEDULE

Elmira Cl.....Nov. 23-24
Pitt.-Bradford....Nov. 26
Rochester Inv.....Nov. 30-Dec. 1
Ithaca ■....Dec. 7
Elmira Tr.....Jan. 3-4
Binghamton ■....Jan. 12
Oswego St. ■....Jan. 14
Hartwick....Jan. 17
Utica....Jan. 18
Nazareth ■....Jan. 24
Rochester Inst. ■....Jan. 25
Keuka....Jan. 28
Utica ■....Jan. 31
Hartwick ■....Feb. 1
Ithaca....Feb. 4
St. John Fisher ■....Feb. 8
Geneseo St. ■....Feb. 12
Rochester Inst.....Feb. 14
Nazareth....Feb. 15
Alfred....Feb. 18
Penn St.-Behrend ■....Feb. 22
Cazenovia....Feb. 27

1995-96 RESULTS (14-13)

78	Westfield St. †	68
53	Hartwick	69
83	Pitt.-Bradford ■	60
81	Daemen †	67
64	Chris. Newport	69
76	Wesley ■	58
48	Southern Vt. ■	62
70	Hartwick ■	74
71	Oswego St.	68
63	Mansfield	87
57	Oneonta St. ■	60
71	Point Park ■	81
52	Cornell	90
77	Keuka ■	49
69	Houghton ■	76
61	Roberts Wesleyan ■	59
72	Cazenovia	51
80	Nazareth ■	67
81	St. John Fisher	96
77	Keuka	62
90	Geneseo St.	75
83	Alfred ■	74
68	Penn St.-Behrend	81
74	Pitt.-Bradford	83
83	Utica	79
71	Fredonia St.	69
59	Oneonta St. ■	76

Nickname: Soaring Eagles
Colors: Purple & Gold
Arena: Speidel Gymnasium
  Capacity: 1,000; Year Built: 1995
AD: Patricia Thompson
SID: Terry Zeh

ELON

Elon College, NC 27244 II

Coach: Mark Simons
Alma Mater: Aquinas '72
Record: 10 Years, W-117, L-161

1996-97 SCHEDULE

Longwood ■	Nov. 16
Davis & Elkins	Nov. 21
Newberry ■	Nov. 23
Gannon Cl.	Nov. 29-30
Carson-Newman ■	Dec. 3
Averett ■	Dec. 5
Warner-Southern Tr.	Dec. 13-14
Charleston (S.C.)	Dec. 16
Longwood	Jan. 2
Davis & Elkins ■	Jan. 4
Mars Hill ■	Jan. 8
Wingate	Jan. 11
Catawba	Jan. 15
Presbyterian ■	Jan. 18
Gardner-Webb ■	Jan. 22
Lenoir-Rhyne	Jan. 25
Newberry	Jan. 29
Carson-Newman	Feb. 1
Mars Hill	Feb. 5
Wingate ■	Feb. 8
Catawba ■	Feb. 12
Presbyterian	Feb. 15
Gardner-Webb	Feb. 19
Lenoir-Rhyne ■	Feb. 22

1995-96 RESULTS (14-14)

90	Belmont Abbey ■	80
90	N.C.-Pembroke ■	85
67	Pfeiffer ■	80
74	East Caro.	89
71	Longwood ■	62
76	Limestone ■	71
82	Queens (N.C.)	87
88	Averett ■	76
87	Palm Beach Atl. †	81
71	Warner Southern †	63
72	Longwood	94
90	Gardner-Webb ■	84
73	Carson-Newman	67
83	Mars Hill	93
90	Wingate ■	61
72	Catawba	78

65	Presbyterian ■	71
82	Limestone ■	71
85	Gardner-Webb	90
70	Carson-Newman ■	71
73	Lenoir-Rhyne ■	56
79	Mars Hill ■	75
56	Wingate	63
75	Lenoir-Rhyne	77
84	Catawba ■	87
78	Presbyterian	87
71	Catawba †	65
81	Mars Hill †	90

Nickname: Fightin' Christians
Colors: Maroon & Gold
Arena: Koury Center/Alumni Gym
  Capacity: 2,500; Year Built: 1949
AD: Alan J. White
SID: David Hibbard

EMERSON-MCA

Boston, MA 02116 III

Coach: Hank Smith
Alma Mater: Quincy '95
Record: 2 Years, W-25, L-26

1996-97 SCHEDULE

Curry	Nov. 23
Yeshiva ■	Nov. 24
Mass.-Boston ■	Dec. 4
Emerson Cl.	Dec. 6-7
Mass. Pharmacy	Dec. 11
Roger Williams	Dec. 12
Mass. Pharmacy	Jan. 18
Wheaton (Mass.) ■	Jan. 20
Johnson & Wales	Jan. 23
Albertus Magnus	Jan. 25
Westfield St.	Jan. 27
Rivier	Jan. 29
Bates ■	Jan. 30
Daniel Webster ■	Feb. 1
Endicott	Feb. 4
Johnson & Wales ■	Feb. 6
Southern Vt.	Feb. 9
Amherst	Feb. 10
Endicott	Feb. 12
Rivier ■	Feb. 15
Albertus Magnus ■	Feb. 18
Daniel Webster	Feb. 22

1995-96 RESULTS (8-19)

76	Wentworth Inst.	85
54	Yeshiva	77
95	Curry ■	106
76	Baruch ■	78
88	Salve Regina ■	93
95	Salem St. ■	105
73	Roger Williams ■	79
70	Southern Vt. ■	77
87	Mass. Pharmacy ■	54
72	Wheaton (Mass.)	73
73	Daniel Webster	84
66	Rivier	88
71	Johnson & Wales ■	62
90	Bates	103
84	Albertus Magnus ■	106
85	Mass. Pharmacy	73
86	Endicott ■	88
82	Daniel Webster ■	65
87	Rivier	83
73	New England	103
79	Johnson & Wales	77
59	Westfield St. ■	78
78	Endicott	86
61	Albertus Magnus ■	71
56	Daniel Webster †	53
76	Endicott	69
81	Albertus Magnus	103

Nickname: Lions
Colors: Purple & Gold
Arena: MCA Gymnasium
  Capacity: 1,200
AD: Joseph T. Walsh
SID: Chris Elias

EMORY

Atlanta, GA 30322 III

Coach: Pete Manuel
Alma Mater: Eastern Ill. '79
Record: 4 Years, W-29, L-70

1996-97 SCHEDULE

Sewanee Cl.	Nov. 22-23
Oglethorpe ■	Nov. 26
Pomona-Pitzer Cl.	Nov. 29-30
Case Reserve	Dec. 6
Carnegie Mellon	Dec. 8
Haverford	Jan. 3
Sewanee ■	Jan. 6
Rochester	Jan. 9
Oakwood ■	Jan. 11
Johns Hopkins ■	Jan. 19
Atlanta Christian	Jan. 21
Brandeis	Jan. 24
New York U.	Jan. 26
Chicago	Jan. 31
Washington (Mo.) ■	Feb. 2
New York U. ■	Feb. 7
Brandeis ■	Feb. 9
Oglethorpe	Feb. 12
Washington (Mo.)	Feb. 14
Chicago	Feb. 16
Carnegie Mellon ■	Feb. 21
Rochester ■	Feb. 23
Oakwood	Mar. 1

1995-96 RESULTS (6-18)

89	Wash. & Lee	86
62	Kenyon †	46
75	Savannah A&D ■	59
73	Oglethorpe	76
80	Case Reserve ■	86
62	Carnegie Mellon ■	61
58	Oglethorpe ■	37
48	Dallas ■	47
55	Rochester ■	75
60	Millsaps ■	84
48	Johns Hopkins	59
65	Sewanee	83
68	Brandeis ■	77
68	New York U. ■	73
57	Chicago	69
60	Washington (Mo.)	91
69	New York U.	77
58	Brandeis	65
67	Washington (Mo.) ■	74
66	Chicago ■	72
63	Carnegie Mellon	69
70	Rochester	78
70	Sewanee ■	93
62	Savannah A&D	81

Nickname: Eagles
Colors: Blue & Gold
Arena: Woodruff P.E. Center
  Capacity: 2,000; Year Built: 1983
AD: Chuck Gordon
SID: John Arenberg

EMORY & HENRY

Emory, VA 24327 III

Coach: Bob Johnson
Alma Mater: Dickinson '68
Record: 16 Years, W-238, L-184

1996-97 SCHEDULE

Sewanee Cl.	Nov. 22-23
King (Tenn.)	Nov. 26
Roanoke	Dec. 4
Wash. & Lee	Dec. 11
Guilford	Dec. 14
Va. Intermont ■	Jan. 11
East. Mennonite	Jan. 11
Bridgewater (Va.)	Jan. 12
Maryville (Tenn.)	Jan. 15
Hampden-Sydney	Jan. 18
Lynchburg	Jan. 19
Wash. & Lee ■	Jan. 22
Hampden-Sydney ■	Jan. 25

Maryville (Tenn.)	Jan. 27
Roanoke ■	Jan. 29
Va. Wesleyan	Feb. 1
Randolph-Macon ■	Feb. 2
Lynchburg ■	Feb. 5
Bridgewater (Va.) ■	Feb. 8
East. Mennonite ■	Feb. 9
Guilford	Feb. 12
Va. Wesleyan ■	Feb. 15
Randolph-Macon ■	Feb. 16

1995-96 RESULTS (14-11)

85	Wabash †	89
75	Savannah A&D †	63
80	Roanoke	94
99	King (Tenn.) †	92
101	Va. Intermont †	82
84	Maryville (Tenn.) ■	64
86	Wash. & Lee	92
100	Guilford	78
88	East. Mennonite	101
83	Bridgewater (Va.)	79
72	Hampden-Sydney	98
92	Lynchburg	75
84	Wash. & Lee	73
94	Hampden-Sydney ■	81
76	Roanoke	96
80	Va. Wesleyan ■	76
61	Randolph-Macon ■	65
91	Lynchburg ■	62
114	Bridgewater (Va.) ■	112
108	East. Mennonite ■	98
86	Guilford ■	64
81	Va. Wesleyan	82
86	Randolph-Macon	95
75	Maryville (Tenn.)	85
86	Bridgewater (Va.) †	91

Nickname: Wasps
Colors: Blue & Gold
Arena: King Health & P.E. Center
  Capacity: 2,200; Year Built: 1970
AD: Lou Wacker
SID: Nathan Graybeal

EMPORIA ST.

Emporia, KS 66801 II

Coach: Ron Slaymaker
Alma Mater: Emporia St. '60
Record: 26 Years, W-441, L-333

1996-97 SCHEDULE

Friends ■	Nov. 23
Ottawa ■	Nov. 25
Northwest Mo. St.	Dec. 3
St. Mary-Plains	Dec. 4
Emporia St. Cl.	Dec. 6-7
Fort Hays St. ■	Dec. 21
Grand Canyon Cl.	Dec. 27-28
Central Mo. St.	Jan. 2
Mo.-Rolla	Jan. 4
Mo. Southern St.	Jan. 8
Lincoln (Mo.) ■	Jan. 11
Southwest Baptist	Jan. 14
Pittsburg St.	Jan. 18
Mo. Western St.	Jan. 22
Truman St. ■	Jan. 25
Washburn ■	Jan. 29
Mo. Southern St.	Feb. 1
Mo.-Rolla	Feb. 3
Northwest Mo. St. ■	Feb. 5
Truman St.	Feb. 10
Central Mo. St. ■	Feb. 12
Southwest Baptist ■	Feb. 15
Mo. Western St. ■	Feb. 19
Washburn	Feb. 22

1995-96 RESULTS (12-15)

96	Friends ■	80
61	S.C.-Spartanburg †	87
78	Florida Tech	87
57	Kansas St.	63
80	Baker ■	57
42	Drury ■	73
79	Fort Hays St.	102
48	Fort Hays St. ■	78

79	Bemidji St. †	64
66	Lincoln Memorial †	68
79	Truman St. ■	55
74	Central Mo. St.	69
72	Washburn	66
87	Mo. Western St. ■	73
73	Lincoln (Mo.)	59
69	Mo. Southern St.	79
56	Southwest Baptist	52
47	Northwest Mo. St. ■	42
63	Mo.-Rolla	73
62	Mo.-St. Louis	64
88	Pittsburg St. ■	80
77	Central Mo. St. ■	81
72	Washburn	86
60	Mo. Western St.	74
80	Lincoln (Mo.) ■	86
70	Mo. Southern St. ■	56
63	Central Mo. St.	64

Nickname: Hornets
Colors: Black & Gold
Arena: White Auditorium
    Capacity: 3,700; Year Built: 1945
AD: Bill Quayle
SID: J. D. Campbell

ENDICOTT
Beverly, MA 01915 III

Coach: Al Delucia
Alma Mater: Boston St.
(First year as head coach)
1996-97 SCHEDULE

Endicott Tr.	Nov. 23-24
Framingham St.	Nov. 26
Rochester Inv.	Nov. 30-Dec. 1
Salve Regina ■	Dec. 3
Curry	Dec. 5
Westbrook Tr.	Dec. 7-8
Lyndon St. ■	Dec. 10
Gordon	Dec. 14
Wheaton (Mass.)	Jan. 15
Maine Maritime	Jan. 18
Keene St. ■	Jan. 20
Rivier	Jan. 23
Daniel Webster	Jan. 25
Roger Williams ■	Jan. 27
Albertus Magnus	Jan. 29
Johnson & Wales	Feb. 1
Emerson-MCA	Feb. 4
Rivier ■	Feb. 7
Johnson St.	Feb. 10
Emerson-MCA ■	Feb. 12
Albertus Magnus ■	Feb. 15
Daniel Webster	Feb. 18
Johnson & Wales ■	Feb. 22
Williams	Feb. 24

1995-96 RESULTS (13-9)
Results unavailable

Nickname: Powergulls
Colors: Royal Blue & Kelly Green
Arena: Bierkoe Gym
    Capacity: 600
AD: Larry Hiser
SID: Lauren Lavigne

ERSKINE
Due West, SC 29639 II

Coach: Ralph Patterson
Alma Mater: Colorado '81
Record: 4 Years, W-33, L-76
1996-97 SCHEDULE

Lander	Nov. 16
Newberry ■	Nov. 18
High Point ■	Nov. 20
Lees-McRae ■	Nov. 23
Presbyterian	Dec. 2
St. Andrews ■	Dec. 4
Furman	Dec. 7
Mount Olive	Dec. 14

Pfeiffer	Jan. 8
Coker	Jan. 11
Longwood ■	Jan. 13
Barton ■	Jan. 16
Queens (N.C.)	Jan. 18
Anderson (S.C.)	Jan. 20
Lees-McRae	Jan. 25
Belmont Abbey ■	Jan. 27
High Point	Jan. 29
Coker ■	Feb. 1
Lander ■	Feb. 3
Belmont Abbey	Feb. 8
Pfeiffer ■	Feb. 10
Mount Olive ■	Feb. 13
St. Andrews	Feb. 15
Longwood	Feb. 17
Barton	Feb. 19
Queens (N.C.) ■	Feb. 22

1995-96 RESULTS (11-17)

87	Limestone †	62
84	Gardner-Webb	98
75	Lander ■	79
72	Furman	80
64	High Point	68
63	Presbyterian ■	55
80	Longwood ■	79
53	Barton	69
80	St. Andrews	78
71	Mount Olive	81
47	Pfeiffer ■	77
66	Lees-McRae	57
65	Lander	66
48	Coker ■	63
56	Queens (N.C.)	77
83	Anderson (S.C.) ■	37
72	Belmont Abbey ■	68
68	Belmont Abbey	83
62	Mount Olive ■	66
80	Newberry	83
89	Barton ■	83
49	Longwood	64
71	High Point ■	88
56	Pfeiffer	79
53	St. Andrews ■	54
72	Lees-McRae ■	65
74	Belmont Abbey †	48
64	High Point †	68

Nickname: The Flying Fleet
Colors: Maroon & Gold
Arena: Galloway P.E. Center
    Capacity: 2,000; Year Built: 1980
AD: Chip Sherer
SID: Tom Lewis

EUREKA
Eureka, IL 61530 III

Coach: Dennis Dighton
Alma Mater: Eureka '75
Record: 2 Years, W-25, L-28
1996-97 SCHEDULE

North Central Cl.	Nov. 22-23
McKendree	Nov. 27
Ripon ■	Nov. 30
McKendree ■	Dec. 3
St. Joseph's (Ind.)	Dec. 5
Upper Iowa	Dec. 7
Franklin Tr.	Dec. 13-14
Rose-Hulman ■	Dec. 20
Brescia	Jan. 4
Benedictine (Ill.) ■	Jan. 11
Trinity Int'l	Jan. 15
Concordia (Ill.) ■	Jan. 22
Aurora ■	Jan. 25
Robert Morris (Ill.) ■	Jan. 27
Rockford	Jan. 29
Clarke ■	Feb. 1
Benedictine (Ill.)	Feb. 5
Trinity Int'l ■	Feb. 8
Judson (Ill.)	Feb. 12
Concordia (Ill.)	Feb. 15
Aurora	Feb. 19
Rockford ■	Feb. 22
Clarke	Feb. 26

1995-96 RESULTS (9-16)

68	SIU-Edwardsville	76
98	McKendree ■	96
64	Olivet Nazarene †	79
82	Ind. Wesleyan †	79
93	Clarke	95
85	Augustana (Ill.)	99
74	Trinity Christian †	93
73	Judson (Ill.) ■	62
73	Westminster (Mo.) ■	64
72	Ripon	90
42	Rose-Hulman ■	64
40	McKendree	104
79	Manchester †	103
85	North Central †	72
88	Judson (Ill.)	89
72	Brescia	74
92	Rockford ■	71
69	Lindenwood	83
80	Rosary	57
58	Upper Iowa ■	81
48	Trinity Christian	62
84	Robert Morris (Ill.)	91
71	Lindenwood ■	79
76	Brescia ■	66
80	St. Joseph's (Ind.) ■	67

Nickname: Red Devils
Colors: Maroon & Gold
Arena: Reagan Gym
    Capacity: 2,200; Year Built: 1970
AD: Martin Stromberger
SID: Becky Duffield

EVANSVILLE
Evansville, IN 47722 I

Coach: Jim Crews
Alma Mater: Indiana '76
Record: 11 Years, W-200, L-121
1996-97 SCHEDULE

NIT	Nov. 20-29
Radford ■	Nov. 24
Tenn.-Martin	Dec. 1
Robert Morris ■	Dec. 3
Western Mich.	Dec. 7
Butler ■	Dec. 14
Michigan St. ■	Dec. 17
Indiana [Indianapolis]	Dec. 21
Vanderbilt ■	Dec. 29
Wichita St. ■	Jan. 2
Illinois St.	Jan. 4
Southern Ill.	Jan. 7
Bradley	Jan. 11
Drake ■	Jan. 16
Illinois St. ■	Jan. 19
Indiana St.	Jan. 22
Creighton ■	Jan. 25
Northern Iowa ■	Jan. 27
Drake	Jan. 30
Creighton	Feb. 2
Bradley ■	Feb. 5
Southwest Mo. St. ■	Feb. 8
Northern Iowa	Feb. 11
Wichita St.	Feb. 15
Southwest Mo. St.	Feb. 17
Southern Ill. ■	Feb. 22
Indiana St. ■	Feb. 24
Missouri Val. Conf. Tr.	Feb. 28-Mar. 3

1995-96 RESULTS (13-14)

111	Chicago St. ■	69
81	Western Mich. ■	61
63	Michigan St.	67
91	Wichita St. ■	74
58	North Texas ■	54
48	Indiana ■	76
91	Kent	96
60	Creighton ■	72
82	Florida Int'l ■	75
57	Tulsa ■	67
71	Indiana St.	67
77	Northern Iowa ■	64
84	Southwest Mo. St.	82
61	Vanderbilt	75

60	Bradley ■	71
80	Southern Ill.	68
69	Illinois St. ■	73
61	Drake	65
82	Northern Iowa	91
80	Drake ■	69
53	Tulsa	74
73	Indiana St. ■	52
69	Illinois St.	70
58	Bradley	73
96	Southern Ill. ■	64
72	Southwest Mo. St. ■	63
55	Tulsa †	65

Nickname: Aces
Colors: Purple & White
Arena: Roberts Stadium
    Capacity: 12,300; Year Built: 1956
AD: Jim Byers
SID: Bob Boxell

FAIRFIELD
Fairfield, CT 06430 I

Coach: Paul Cormier
Alma Mater: New Hampshire '73
Record: 12 Years, W-150, L-172
1996-97 SCHEDULE

East Caro. ■	Nov. 23
Colgate	Nov. 26
Central Mich. ■	Nov. 30
Wagner	Dec. 3
San Francisco Cl.	Dec. 6-7
Connecticut	Dec. 21
Southern Utah	Dec. 31
Canisius ■	Jan. 6
Fordham	Jan. 7
Central Conn. St. ■	Jan. 11
Boston College ■	Jan. 15
Iona	Jan. 18
Siena	Jan. 20
St. Peter's ■	Jan. 24
Siena ■	Jan. 26
Manhattan	Jan. 29
Loyola (Md.) ■	Jan. 31
St. Peter's	Feb. 5
Canisius	Feb. 8
Niagara	Feb. 10
Manhattan ■	Feb. 15
Iona ■	Feb. 18
Niagara ■	Feb. 21
Loyola (Md.)	Feb. 23
Metro Atlantic Conf. Tr.	Mar. 1-3

1995-96 RESULTS (20-10)

81	Monmouth (N.J.)	79
79	Hartford	71
62	Western Ill. †	59
62	Montana	92
73	Southeast Mo. St. ■	65
75	Cal St. Sacramento ■	60
83	Akron	86
52	Connecticut	86
95	Wagner ■	86
56	Canisius ■	63
62	Fordham ■	76
92	Colgate ■	82
75	Manhattan ■	65
60	Siena	47
71	Niagara	69
72	Canisius	82
73	Manhattan	81
69	Marist †	80
75	St. Peter's	63
72	Niagara ■	73
71	Loyola (Md.) ■	68
74	St. Peter's ■	65
61	Iona	67
70	Loyola (Md.)	59
66	Siena	60
82	Iona ■	67
69	St. Peter's †	64
70	Niagara †	47
46	Canisius †	52
79	Providence ■	91

Nickname: Stags
Colors: Cardinal Red
Arena: Alumni Hall
  Capacity: 2,479; Year Built: 1959
AD: To be named
SID: Victor D'Ascenzo

FDU-MADISON
Madison, NJ 07940 III

Coach: Roger Kindel
Alma Mater: Seton Hall '72
Record: 19 Years, W-223, L-239

1996-97 SCHEDULE
Wheaton (Mass.) Cl.	....	Nov. 23-24
Bapt. Bible (Pa.) ■	....	Dec. 3
Wilkes	....	Dec. 7
Scranton	....	Dec. 11
Staten Island	....	Dec. 14
John Jay ■	....	Dec. 16
Jersey City St. ■	....	Dec. 21
Kean Cl.	....	Jan. 4-5
Col. of New Jersey	....	Jan. 8
Albright ■	....	Jan. 11
Delaware Valley ■	....	Jan. 15
Lycoming	....	Jan. 18
Drew	....	Jan. 22
King's (Pa.) ■	....	Jan. 25
Caldwell	....	Jan. 27
Wilkes ■	....	Feb. 1
Stevens Tech ■	....	Feb. 3
Scranton ■	....	Feb. 5
Delaware Valley ■	....	Feb. 12
Lycoming ■	....	Feb. 15
Drew ■	....	Feb. 19
King's (Pa.)	....	Feb. 22

1995-96 RESULTS (8-16)
64	Utica †	78
72	Albertus Magnus †	64
66	Wheaton (Mass.) ■	42
52	Frank. & Marsh. ■	63
71	Wilkes	99
42	Scranton ■	51
61	Staten Island ■	63
73	John Jay	63
94	Beaver	97
61	Jersey City St.	90
63	Rowan †	99
90	Hunter †	74
67	Lycoming ■	78
69	Drew ■	77
57	Caldwell	67
65	Delaware Valley	51
56	Wilkes ■	72
88	Stevens Tech	81
74	Scranton	77
69	King's (Pa.)	76
73	Delaware Valley ■	60
66	Lycoming	84
73	Drew	93
82	King's (Pa.) ■	74

Nickname: Devils
Colors: Black, Blue & White
Arena: Ferguson Rec Center
  Capacity: 2,500; Year Built: 1995
AD: Bill Klika
SID: Allan Wickstrom

FAIRLEIGH DICKINSON
Teaneck, NJ 07666 I

Coach: Tom Green
Alma Mater: Syracuse '71
Record: 13 Years, W-219, L-157

1996-97 SCHEDULE
Davidson ■	....	Nov. 23
Hartford	....	Nov. 26
Rhode Island	....	Nov. 30
Indiana St. ■	....	Dec. 7
Iona	....	Dec. 11
St. John's (N.Y.)	....	Dec. 21
St. Peter's ■	....	Dec. 28

Manhattan	....	Dec. 31
Mt. St. Mary's (Md.) ■	....	Jan. 4
Rider ■	....	Jan. 6
St. Francis (Pa.)	....	Jan. 9
Robert Morris	....	Jan. 11
Marist ■	....	Jan. 15
St. Francis (N.Y.)	....	Jan. 18
LIU-Brooklyn	....	Jan. 20
Wagner ■	....	Jan. 23
Monmouth (N.J.) ■	....	Jan. 25
Mt. St. Mary's (Md.)	....	Feb. 1
Rider	....	Feb. 3
St. Francis (Pa.) ■	....	Feb. 6
Robert Morris ■	....	Feb. 8
Marist	....	Feb. 12
St. Francis (N.Y.) ■	....	Feb. 14
LIU-Brooklyn ■	....	Feb. 17
Wagner	....	Feb. 20
Monmouth (N.J.)	....	Feb. 22
Northeast Conf. Tr.	....	Feb. 25-Mar. 6

1995-96 RESULTS (7-20)
65	Rhode Island ■	90
67	Md.-East. Shore	74
85	Florida Int'l ■	60
58	Illinois St.	79
56	Davidson ■	96
43	St. Peter's	70
59	Indiana St.	68
66	Iona ■	82
61	St. Francis (Pa.) ■	64
73	Robert Morris ■	59
79	St. Francis (N.Y.)	69
77	LIU-Brooklyn	72
57	Marist	70
68	Wagner ■	56
52	Monmouth (N.J.) ■	59
73	Mt. St. Mary's (Md.) ■	76
71	Rider ■	76
69	St. Francis (Pa.)	94
65	Robert Morris	64
67	St. Francis (N.Y.) ■	70
95	LIU-Brooklyn ■	77
69	Marist ■	79
57	Wagner	81
75	Monmouth (N.J.) ■	86
72	Rider	88
66	Mt. St. Mary's (Md.)	85
66	Robert Morris ■	68

Nickname: Knights
Colors: Blue & Black
Arena: Rothman Center
  Capacity: 5,000; Year Built: 1987
AD: Gerry Oswald
SID: Tom Bonerbo

FAIRMONT ST.
Fairmont, WV 26554 II

Coach: Butch Haswell
Alma Mater: Fairmont St. '73
Record: 3 Years, W-55, L-28

1996-97 SCHEDULE
Va. Union Tr.	....	Nov. 8-10
Fairmont St. Cl.	....	Nov. 15-16
Point Park ■	....	Nov. 19
Wilberforce ■	....	Nov. 26
Salem-Teikyo ■	....	Dec. 2
Alderson-Broaddus ■	....	Dec. 7
Bethany (W.Va.) ■	....	Dec. 16
Fairmount Cl.	....	Jan. 3-4
Glenville St. ■	....	Jan. 8
Concord	....	Jan. 11
Bluefield St. ■	....	Jan. 13
West Va. Wesleyan	....	Jan. 15
Charleston (W.Va.)	....	Jan. 18
Shepherd	....	Jan. 22
West Va. St. ■	....	Jan. 25
Wheeling Jesuit	....	Jan. 27
West Liberty St. ■	....	Jan. 29
West Va. Tech	....	Feb. 1
Davis & Elkins	....	Feb. 5
West Va. Wesleyan ■	....	Feb. 8
Salem-Teikyo	....	Feb. 12

Shepherd ■	....	Feb. 15
Wheeling Jesuit ■	....	Feb. 19
West Liberty St.	....	Feb. 22

1995-96 RESULTS (24-5)
91	Cheyney ■	73
82	Wayne St. (Mich.) ■	65
74	Ashland	56
116	Point Park ■	65
87	Phila. Bible ■	50
90	Salem-Teikyo	81
78	St. Vincent	77
90	Alderson-Broaddus ■	82
75	Westminster (Pa.)	64
58	Glenville St.	60
83	Concord	74
86	Bluefield St.	79
83	West Va. Wesleyan ■	76
94	Charleston (W.Va.) ■	82
90	Shepherd	61
82	West Va. St.	77
89	Wheeling Jesuit ■	80
83	West Liberty St.	77
95	West Va. Tech ■	71
109	Davis & Elkins ■	69
81	West Va. Wesleyan	73
85	Salem-Teikyo ■	79
71	Shepherd	72
90	West Va. St. ■	80
84	Wheeling Jesuit	75
79	West Liberty St. ■	89
74	Bluefield St. †	77
78	Bluefield St. †	66
83	Indiana (Pa.) †	84

Nickname: Falcons
Colors: Maroon & White
Arena: Feaster Center
  Capacity: 4,000; Year Built: 1978
AD: Colin Cameron
SID: Jim Brinkman

FAYETTEVILLE ST.
Fayetteville, NC 28301 II

Coach: Ricky Duckett
Alma Mater: North Caro. '79
Record: 3 Years, W-43, L-38

1996-97 SCHEDULE
Johnson C. Smith Cl.	....	Nov. 15-16
Claflin ■	....	Nov. 19
Elizabeth City St. ■	....	Nov. 25
Claflin	....	Nov. 30
Francis Marion	....	Dec. 2
Clark Atlanta Cl.	....	Dec. 6-7
Bowie St.	....	Dec. 14
St. Paul's ■	....	Dec. 17
Virginia Union	....	Jan. 2
N.C. Central ■	....	Jan. 4
Norfolk St.	....	Jan. 8
Livingstone ■	....	Jan. 11
Winston-Salem ■	....	Jan. 14
St. Augustine's	....	Jan. 16
Shaw ■	....	Jan. 18
Johnson Smith	....	Jan. 23
N.C. Central	....	Jan. 25
Livingstone	....	Jan. 30
Shaw	....	Feb. 1
Francis Marion ■	....	Feb. 3
Johnson Smith ■	....	Feb. 8
Winston-Salem	....	Feb. 13
St. Augustine's ■	....	Feb. 15
Virginia St. ■	....	Feb. 20

1995-96 RESULTS (10-17)
95	Claflin	97
55	Newberry ■	49
69	Elizabeth City St.	57
65	Francis Marion	74
68	N.C.-Pembroke	72
72	Southern Wesleyan ■	75
88	St. Paul's ■	72
108	Bowie St.	79
61	Francis Marion	72
65	N.C. Central	70
59	Norfolk St. ■	82

83	Livingstone	89
99	Winston-Salem	76
69	St. Augustine's ■	70
63	Shaw	75
72	Johnson Smith ■	61
54	N.C. Central	62
80	Livingstone ■	85
56	Johnson Smith	58
91	Shaw ■	88
78	Claflin	65
68	Winston-Salem ■	63
67	St. Augustine's	71
68	Virginia Union ■	77
78	Virginia St. ■	85
81	Newberry	64
79	St. Paul's †	89

Nickname: Broncos
Colors: White & Royal Blue
Arena: FSU P.E. Complex, Capel Arena
  Capacity: 4,000; Year Built: 1995
AD: Horace Small
SID: Marion Crowe Jr

FERRIS ST.
Big Rapids, MI 49307 II

Coach: Edgar Wilson
Alma Mater: Michigan St. '78
(First year as head coach)

1996-97 SCHEDULE
Cornerstone ■	....	Nov. 19
Kent	....	Nov. 23
St. Francis (Ill.) ■	....	Nov. 26
Calvin Shootout	....	Nov. 29-30
Gannon	....	Dec. 5
Mercyhurst	....	Dec. 7
St. Joseph's (Ind.) ■	....	Dec. 14
Wayne St. (Mich.) ■	....	Dec. 19
Hillsdale ■	....	Dec. 21
Oakland (Mich.) Cl.	....	Dec. 27-28
Michigan Tech	....	Jan. 4
Northern Mich.	....	Jan. 6
Lake Superior St. ■	....	Jan. 9
Grand Valley St. ■	....	Jan. 13
Northwood ■	....	Jan. 16
Saginaw Valley ■	....	Jan. 18
Ashland ■	....	Jan. 25
Oakland	....	Jan. 30
St. Mary's (Mich.) ■	....	Feb. 1
Northern Mich. ■	....	Feb. 6
Michigan Tech ■	....	Feb. 8
Grand Valley St.	....	Feb. 10
Lake Superior St.	....	Feb. 13
Northwood	....	Feb. 20
Saginaw Valley	....	Feb. 22

1995-96 RESULTS (6-20)
80	Manchester †	66
82	Ohio Wesleyan	84
60	St. Joseph's (Ind.)	71
53	Calvin	67
73	Cornerstone ■	68
82	Michigan Christian ■	66
53	Mercyhurst	66
82	Gannon	59
59	Wayne St. (Mich.)	82
66	St. Francis (Ill.)	75
59	Wayne St. (Mich.) ■	68
65	Ashland ■	62
65	Grand Valley St.	74
72	Hillsdale ■	77
63	Saginaw Valley	79
75	Oakland	93
69	Lake Superior St. ■	66
48	Northern Mich. ■	64
67	Michigan Tech.	83
72	Northwood	74
79	Grand Valley St. ■	94
78	Mercyhurst ■	109
51	Michigan Tech ■	70
74	Ashland	76
61	Northern Mich.	83
77	Oakland	104

Nickname: Bulldogs

Colors: Crimson & Gold
Arena: Jim Wink Arena
Capacity: 4,175; Year Built: 1963
AD: Larry Marfise
SID: Sarah Stinson

FERRUM

Ferrum, VA 24085 III

Coach: Larry Mangino
Alma Mater: Montclair St. '83
Record: 5 Years, W-52, L-74

1996-97 SCHEDULE

Roanoke Tr.	Nov. 23-24
Gallaudet Tr.	Nov. 29-30
Guilford ■	Dec. 2
Maryville (Tenn.)	Dec. 7
Chowan	Dec. 10
Newport News App.	Jan. 8
Maryville (Tenn.) ■	Jan. 12
Averett	Jan. 15
Methodist ■	Jan. 18
Newport News App. ■	Jan. 19
Chris. Newport	Jan. 22
N.C. Wesleyan ■	Jan. 25
Chowan ■	Jan. 27
Shenandoah	Jan. 30
Greensboro ■	Feb. 3
Averett ■	Feb. 5
Methodist	Feb. 8
N.C. Wesleyan	Feb. 12
Chris. Newport ■	Feb. 15
Greensboro	Feb. 18
Shenandoah ■	Feb. 21

1995-96 RESULTS (11-13)

83	Oglethorpe †	97
76	Elizabethtown †	80
77	Roanoke ■	101
82	Chowan	85
94	Guilford	73
63	Newport News App. ■	57
76	Maryville (Tenn.) ■	81
51	Newport News App.	63
63	Averett	59
79	Methodist	75
89	N.C. Wesleyan	100
92	Chris. Newport ■	87
63	Frostburg St. ■	89
78	Greensboro	76
97	Shenandoah ■	106
71	Chowan ■	61
95	Averett ■	81
70	Chris. Newport	88
85	N.C. Wesleyan ■	73
75	Greensboro ■	70
93	Shenandoah	95
68	Maryville (Tenn.)	89
90	Methodist ■	79
67	Greensboro †	86

Nickname: Panthers
Colors: Black & Gold
Arena: Swartz Gymnasium
Capacity: 1,200; Year Built: 1960
AD: T. Michael Kinder
SID: Gary Holden

FISK

Nashville, TN 37203 III

Coach: To be named

1996-97 SCHEDULE

American Bapt. ■	Nov. 23
Millsaps	Nov. 25
Sewanee ■	Nov. 26
Stillman Tr.	Nov. 29-30
Rhodes ■	Dec. 3
Belmont	Dec. 5
Lane ■	Jan. 8
Rust Tr.	Jan. 9-10
Rust ■	Jan. 17
Free Will Baptist	Jan. 21
Tenn. Temple ■	Jan. 25
Rust	Jan. 28
Oakwood	Feb. 1
Maryville (Tenn.) ■	Feb. 2
Millsaps ■	Feb. 4
Tenn. Temple	Feb. 7
Stillman	Feb. 8
Free Will Baptist ■	Feb. 11
Lane	Feb. 12
Stillman ■	Feb. 14
Rhodes	Feb. 17
Morehouse	Feb. 22
Sewanee	Feb. 26

1995-96 RESULTS (1-24)

80	Miles ■	120
67	Millsaps ■	100
67	Sewanee ■	109
52	Rust ■	107
88	Allen	84
59	Rhodes ■	84
71	Sewanee	101
74	Rhodes	84
60	Stillman ■	107
63	Rust	95
81	Rust ■	96
94	Lane	107
75	Stillman ■	101
87	Morehouse ■	125
63	Free Will Baptist ■	66
66	Rust	98
85	Savannah A&D ■	90
73	Millsaps	101
55	Savannah A&D	95
77	Free Will Baptist	85
68	Lane ■	92
74	Stillman	124
85	Miles	145
67	Clark Atlanta	135
73	Morehouse	121

Nickname: Bulldogs
Colors: Blue & Gold
Arena: Johnson Memorial Gym
Capacity: 2,500; Year Built: 1950
AD: To be named
SID: To be named

FITCHBURG ST.

Fitchburg, MA 01420.............. III

Coach: Robert Bonci
Alma Mater: Worcester St. '77
Record: 7 Years, W-53, L-117

1996-97 SCHEDULE

Mass.-Boston ■	Nov. 23
Mass. Pharmacy	Nov. 24
Wentworth Inst. ■	Nov. 26
Western New Eng. ■	Dec. 5
Embry-Riddle Tr.	Dec. 28-29
Anna Maria ■	Jan. 11
Worcester St.	Jan. 14
Rivier ■	Jan. 16
Salem St. ■	Jan. 18
Daniel Webster	Jan. 21
Suffolk	Jan. 23
Westfield St.	Jan. 25
Framingham St. ■	Jan. 28
Nichols	Jan. 30
North Adams St. ■	Feb. 1
Bri'water (Mass.)	Feb. 4
Worcester St. ■	Feb. 8
Salem St.	Feb. 11
Roger Williams	Feb. 13
Westfield St. ■	Feb. 15
Framingham St.	Feb. 18
North Adams St.	Feb. 20
Bri'water (Mass.) ■	Feb. 22

1995-96 RESULTS (9-16)

62	Teikyo Post †	89
88	Notre Dame (N.H.) †	68
75	Mass.-Boston	69
58	Wentworth Inst.	89
73	Western New Eng.	90
81	Endicott ■	92
79	Nichols ■	88
78	Anna Maria	115
76	Worcester St. ■	109
79	Rivier	104
81	Salem St.	92
84	Suffolk ■	80
57	Westfield St. ■	84
93	Framingham St.	83
61	Daniel Webster ■	59
48	North Adams St.	78
62	Bri'water (Mass.) ■	86
84	Worcester St.	72
49	Salem St. ■	71
80	Roger Williams ■	55
67	Westfield St.	76
75	Framingham St. ■	73
74	North Adams St. ■	70
79	Bri'water (Mass.)	82
70	Worcester St.	89

Nickname: Falcons
Colors: Green, Gold & White
Arena: Parkinson Gymnasium
Capacity: 420; Year Built: 1957
AD: Sue Lauder
SID: Dave Marsh

FLORIDA

Gainesville, FL 32604 I

Coach: Billy Donovan
Alma Mater: Providence '87
Record: 2 Years, W-35, L-20

1996-97 SCHEDULE

Central Fla. ■	Nov. 22
Bethune-Cookman ■	Nov. 25
San Juan Shootout	Nov. 29-Dec. 1
Texas ■	Dec. 4
Duquesne	Dec. 7
South Fla. ■	Dec. 10
Stetson ■	Dec. 14
Florida St. [Orlando]	Dec. 21
Arizona Cl.	Dec. 28-30
Arkansas ■	Jan. 5
LSU	Jan. 8
Auburn	Jan. 11
South Caro. ■	Jan. 15
Alabama ■	Jan. 18
Georgia	Jan. 22
Tennessee	Jan. 25
Kentucky ■	Jan. 29
Vanderbilt ■	Feb. 1
Jacksonville ■	Feb. 3
South Caro.	Feb. 8
Mississippi St.	Feb. 12
Kentucky	Feb. 15
Tennessee ■	Feb. 19
Mississippi ■	Feb. 23
Georgia ■	Feb. 26
Vanderbilt	Mar. 1
Southeastern Conf. Tr.	Mar. 6-9

1995-96 RESULTS (12-16)

83	Charleston So. ■	65
58	South Fla.	73
75	Geo. Washington †	66
58	Massachusetts †	80
53	Wake Forest ■	77
52	Florida St. †	74
78	Stetson ■	46
71	Louisiana Tech †	56
76	Oklahoma †	72
60	Arkansas	75
66	Mississippi St. ■	69
54	Kansas ■	69
81	South Caro. ■	69
46	Georgia	71
59	Mississippi	55
77	Vanderbilt ■	55
73	LSU ■	70
65	Alabama	68
63	Kentucky	77
63	Tennessee ■	51
70	Auburn ■	73
56	Vanderbilt	70
75	South Caro.	80
63	Kentucky ■	94
70	Georgia ■	86
73	Tennessee	71
75	Mississippi †	62
76	Kentucky †	100

Nickname: Gators
Colors: Orange & Blue
Arena: Stephen C. O'Connell Center
Capacity: 12,000; Year Built: 1980
AD: Jeremy Foley
SID: Steve McClain

FLORIDA A&M

Tallahassee, FL 32307 I

Coach: Mickey Clayton
Alma Mater: Florida A&M '75
Record: 1 Year, W-2, L-6

1996-97 SCHEDULE

Geo. Washington Cl.	Nov. 22-23
UAB	Nov. 27
Dayton	Nov. 30
Xavier (Ohio)	Dec. 2
South Ala.	Dec. 7
Ga. Southern	Dec. 19
Auburn ■	Dec. 28
Hampton	Jan. 4
Md.-East. Shore ■	Jan. 11
Delaware St. ■	Jan. 13
North Caro. A&T ■	Jan. 18
South Caro. St. ■	Jan. 20
Howard	Jan. 23
Coppin St.	Jan. 25
Morgan St.	Jan. 27
South Caro. St.	Feb. 1
North Caro. A&T	Feb. 3
Hampton ■	Feb. 5
Bethune-Cookman	Feb. 8
Howard ■	Feb. 13
Coppin St. ■	Feb. 15
Morgan St. ■	Feb. 17
Md.-East. Shore	Feb. 22
Delaware St.	Feb. 24
Bethune-Cookman ■	Mar. 1
Mid-Eastern Conf. Tr.	Mar. 5-8

1995-96 RESULTS (8-19)

39	West Va.	80
79	Warner Southern ■	61
50	Memphis	80
103	Palm Beach Atl. ■	69
47	Ga. Southern ■	43
39	Alabama	80
72	West Fla. ■	53
54	Auburn ■	84
71	Bryan ■	68
66	Md.-East. Shore	71
68	Delaware St.	79
67	North Caro. A&T	74
54	South Caro. St.	71
74	Howard ■	65
54	Morgan St. ■	57
53	Miami (Fla.)	77
65	Coppin St. ■	81
47	South Caro. St. ■	56
59	North Caro. A&T ■	81
45	Bethune-Cookman †	60
55	Howard	85
74	Morgan St.	81
68	Coppin St.	78
62	Md.-East. Shore ■	46
86	Delaware St. ■	80
62	Bethune-Cookman ■	75
58	South Caro. St. ■	79

Nickname: Rattlers
Colors: Orange & Green
Arena: Gaither Athletic Center
Capacity: 3,365; Year Built: 1963
AD: Walter Reed
SID: Alvin Hollins

FLA. ATLANTIC
Boca Raton, FL 33431 I

Coach: Kevin Billerman
Alma Mater: Duke '75
Record: 1 Year, W-9, L-18

1996-97 SCHEDULE

North Caro. St.	Nov. 22
Miami (Fla.)	Nov. 24
Hofstra ■	Nov. 27
Thomas ■	Nov. 30
Florida St.	Dec. 2
South Fla.	Dec. 4
Robert Morris	Dec. 14
Lehigh ■	Dec. 28
Fordham ■	Dec. 30
Centenary (La.) ■	Jan. 2
Southeastern La.	Jan. 4
Winthrop	Jan. 6
Mercer	Jan. 9
Georgia St. ■	Jan. 11
Charleston (S.C.)	Jan. 16
Campbell	Jan. 18
Central Fla. ■	Jan. 23
Stetson ■	Jan. 25
Florida Int'l ■	Jan. 30
Jacksonville St.	Feb. 1
Samford	Feb. 3
Florida Int'l	Feb. 8
Campbell ■	Feb. 13
Charleston (S.C.) ■	Feb. 15
Nova Southeastern ■	Feb. 17
Stetson	Feb. 20
Central Fla.	Feb. 22
Trans America Conf. Tr.	Feb. 27-Mar. 1

1995-96 RESULTS (9-18)

56	Miami (Fla.) ■	76
70	Jacksonville	88
71	Robert Morris ■	68
64	Southern Ill.	66
55	South Fla.	56
95	Winthrop ■	73
51	Miami (Fla.) ■	61
70	Columbia ■	58
80	Nova Southeastern ■	47
75	Centenary (La.)	76
69	Southeastern La. ■	72
67	Mercer	59
60	Georgia St. ■	62
58	Charleston (S.C.) ■	61
69	Campbell	75
68	Central Fla.	79
76	Stetson	84
84	Florida Int'l ■	61
91	Jacksonville St. ■	72
66	Samford	70
64	Florida Int'l	76
55	St. Louis	65
66	Campbell	68
50	Charleston (S.C.)	72
64	Tulane ■	79
83	Stetson ■	72
88	Central Fla. ■	71

Nickname: Owls
Colors: Blue & Gray
Arena: Fau Gymnasium
  Capacity: 5,000; Year Built: 1984
AD: Tom Cargill
SID: Katrina McCormick

FLORIDA INT'L
Miami, FL 33199 I

Coach: Shakey Rodriquez
Alma Mater: Florida Int'l '75
Record: 1 Year, W-13, L-15

1996-97 SCHEDULE

Liberty	Nov. 22
Hofstra ■	Nov. 25
St. Peter's Tr.	Nov. 30-Dec. 1
Fordham	Dec. 3
Alabama ■	Dec. 7

Eastern Ky.	Dec. 14
Mississippi	Dec. 20
Butler ■	Dec. 28
VMI	Dec. 30
Southeastern La. ■	Jan. 2
Centenary (La.)	Jan. 4
Georgia St. ■	Jan. 9
Mercer ■	Jan. 11
Campbell	Jan. 16
Charleston (S.C.)	Jan. 18
Stetson ■	Jan. 23
Central Fla. ■	Jan. 26
Fla. Atlantic	Jan. 30
Samford ■	Feb. 1
Jacksonville St.	Feb. 3
Fla. Atlantic ■	Feb. 8
Charleston (S.C.) ■	Feb. 13
Campbell ■	Feb. 15
Central Fla.	Feb. 20
Stetson	Feb. 22
Trans America Conf. Tr.	Feb. 27-Mar. 1

1995-96 RESULTS (13-15)

123	Palm Beach Atl. ■	81
44	Florida St.	92
60	Fairleigh Dickinson	85
61	Va. Commonwealth	82
72	Barry ■	69
92	Liberty ■	89
80	Northeastern ■	66
82	Columbia ■	67
73	Fordham ■	72
75	Evansville	82
71	Southeastern La.	91
95	Centenary (La.) ■	108
68	Georgia St.	75
74	Mercer	73
66	Campbell ■	69
59	Charleston (S.C.) ■	72
68	Stetson	87
83	Central Fla.	78
61	Fla. Atlantic ■	84
68	Samford ■	63
90	Jacksonville St. ■	88
76	Fla. Atlantic	64
56	Charleston (S.C.)	80
57	Campbell	64
93	Central Fla. ■	86
73	Stetson ■	82
58	Samford †	55
76	Mercer †	101

Nickname: Golden Panthers
Colors: Blue & Yellow
Arena: Golden Panther Arena
  Capacity: 5,000; Year Built: 1986
AD: Ted Aceto
SID: Rich Kelch

FLA. SOUTHERN
Lakeland, FL 33802 II

Coach: Gordon Gibbons
Alma Mater: Springfield '68
Record: 6 Years, W-138, L-41

1996-97 SCHEDULE

Va. Union Tr.	Nov. 8-10
Bluefield St. ■	Nov. 15
Embry-Riddle ■	Nov. 20
Northern Ky. ■	Nov. 25
Virgin Islands ■	Dec. 4
North Central ■	Dec. 7
American (P.R.) ■	Dec. 10
Webber ■	Dec. 21
West Florida Cl.	Dec. 28-29
Merrimack ■	Jan. 2
Franklin Pierce ■	Jan. 4
Mass.-Dartmouth ■	Jan. 5
Eckerd ■	Jan. 8
Rollins	Jan. 11
Barry ■	Jan. 15
North Fla. ■	Jan. 18
St. Leo	Jan. 22
Florida Tech ■	Jan. 25
Tampa	Jan. 29

Barry	Feb. 1
North Fla.	Feb. 5
Rollins ■	Feb. 8
St. Leo ■	Feb. 12
Florida Tech	Feb. 15
Tampa ■	Feb. 19
Eckerd	Feb. 22

1995-96 RESULTS (26-4)

72	Lynn	85
86	Quincy ■	73
72	Lake Superior St. ■	65
80	American (P.R.) ■	68
101	Webber ■	79
91	Kennesaw St. ■	57
88	Elizabeth City St. ■	63
63	Mankato St. ■	46
87	LIU-C. W. Post †	70
66	Bentley	77
88	St. Joseph's (Me.) ■	66
66	American Int'l ■	45
71	Florida Tech ■	68
80	Eckerd	88
84	North Fla. ■	64
75	St. Leo	68
72	Tampa	69
77	Barry ■	63
77	Rollins ■	75
90	Florida Tech	86
79	Eckerd ■	69
84	North Fla.	81
74	St. Leo ■	72
70	Tampa ■	52
76	Barry	66
79	Rollins	64
75	Florida Tech †	68
59	Barry †	56
53	North Fla. †	49
77	Columbus St. †	83

Nickname: Moccasins
Colors: Scarlet & White
Arena: Jenkins Field House
  Capacity: 2,500; Year Built: 1966
AD: Hal Smeltzly
SID: Tracy Walkiewicz

FLORIDA ST.
Tallahassee, FL 32316 I

Coach: Pat Kennedy
Alma Mater: King's (Pa.) '75
Record: 16 Years, W-306, L-179

1996-97 SCHEDULE

Southwestern La. ■	Nov. 22
Rice ■	Nov. 29
Fla. Atlantic ■	Dec. 2
Duke	Dec. 5
Jacksonville ■	Dec. 14
Tennessee St. ■	Dec. 17
Florida [Orlando]	Dec. 21
Marist ■	Dec. 28
Butler ■	Dec. 30
North Caro. St. ■	Jan. 4
Virginia ■	Jan. 8
Clemson ■	Jan. 11
Georgia Tech	Jan. 15
Seton Hall ■	Jan. 18
North Caro.	Jan. 22
Wake Forest	Jan. 25
Maryland ■	Jan. 29
Virginia	Feb. 1
North Caro.	Feb. 6
Georgia Tech ■	Feb. 9
Maryland	Feb. 13
Duke ■	Feb. 15
Alabama St. ■	Feb. 19
Clemson	Feb. 23
North Caro. St.	Feb. 26
Wake Forest ■	Mar. 1
Atlantic Coast Conf. Tr.	Mar. 6-9

1995-96 RESULTS (13-14)

97	Howard ■	81
92	Florida Int'l ■	44
87	Jacksonville ■	80

77	Tulane	78
85	DePaul †	80
61	Connecticut ■	79
74	Florida †	52
79	Radford	59
80	Md.-Balt. County ■	56
79	Md.-East. Shore ■	66
69	Virginia	64
73	Wake Forest ■	75
65	North Caro. St.	71
75	Clemson ■	62
65	Duke	85
71	North Caro.	82
58	Georgia Tech	79
59	Virginia ■	64
67	Wake Forest	81
100	Maryland ■	78
79	North Caro. St. ■	66
59	Clemson	67
87	Duke ■	93
84	North Caro.	80
68	Georgia Tech ■	83
78	Maryland	88
65	North Caro. St. †	80

Nickname: Seminoles
Colors: Garnet & Gold
Arena: Leon County Civic Center
  Capacity: 12,500; Year Built: 1981
AD: Dave Hart Jr.
SID: Chris Walker

FLORIDA TECH
Melbourne, FL 32901 II

Coach: Andy Russo
Alma Mater: Lake Forest '70
Record: 14 Years, W-237, L-169

1996-97 SCHEDULE

Edward Waters ■	Nov. 20
Northwest Mo. St. Cl.	Nov. 22-23
Lynn	Nov. 25
Florida Tech Cl.	Nov. 29-30
Lynn ■	Dec. 2
American (P.R.) ■	Dec. 7
American (P.R.) Tr.	Dec. 17-19
Mass.-Dartmouth ■	Jan. 1
Bentley ■	Jan. 4
Rollins ■	Jan. 8
Eckerd ■	Jan. 11
St. Leo ■	Jan. 15
Tampa	Jan. 18
Barry ■	Jan. 22
Fla. Southern	Jan. 25
North Fla. ■	Jan. 29
St. Leo	Feb. 1
Tampa ■	Feb. 5
Eckerd	Feb. 8
Barry	Feb. 12
Fla. Southern ■	Feb. 15
North Fla.	Feb. 19
Rollins ■	Feb. 22

1995-96 RESULTS (12-14)

67	Caldwell ■	65
63	Lake Superior St. ■	76
87	Emporia St. ■	78
81	SIU-Edwardsville ■	55
68	Lynn	60
57	Lynn ■	56
71	Webber ■	53
71	Ill. Wesleyan ■	81
79	St. Joseph's (Me.) ■	62
60	American (P.R.)	63
95	Bowie St. ■	63
68	Fla. Southern	71
59	Barry ■	69
75	Eckerd	72
40	North Fla.	56
87	St. Leo ■	75
65	Rollins	94
71	Tampa ■	79
86	Fla. Southern ■	90
55	Barry	76
60	Eckerd ■	69

65 North Fla. ■ ... 48
68 St. Leo ... 73
67 Rollins ■ ... 73
61 Tampa ... 59
68 Fla. Southern † ... 75

Nickname: Panthers
Colors: Crimson & Gray
Arena: Percy Hedgecock Gymnasium
Capacity: 1,000; Year Built: 1964
AD: Bill Jurgens
SID: Dean Watson

FONTBONNE

St. Louis, MO 63105 ... III

Coach: Lee McKinney
Alma Mater: Southeast Mo. St. '60
Record: 18 Years, W-313, L-221

1996-97 SCHEDULE

Moody Bible Inv. ... Nov. 22-23
Rhodes ■ ... Nov. 26
Sanford Brown ■ ... Dec. 5
St. Louis Christian ■ ... Dec. 10
Webster ■ ... Dec. 14
Ind.-Northwest ... Dec. 16
Lincoln Chrst. ■ ... Jan. 6
MacMurray ■ ... Jan. 9
Maryville (Mo.) ... Jan. 11
Principia ... Jan. 16
Westminster (Mo.) ■ ... Jan. 18
Blackburn ... Jan. 25
Greenville ■ ... Jan. 30
MacMurray ... Feb. 1
Maryville (Mo.) ■ ... Feb. 6
Principia ■ ... Feb. 8
Washington (Mo.) ■ ... Feb. 10
Westminster (Mo.) ... Feb. 13
Webster ... Feb. 15
Blackburn ■ ... Feb. 20
Greenville ... Feb. 22

1995-96 RESULTS (17-10)

100 Sanford Brown ■ ... 86
79 Lincoln (Mo.) ■ ... 105
103 Harris-Stowe ■ ... 111
116 St. Louis Christian ■ ... 79
72 Anderson (Ind.) ■ ... 82
82 Webster ... 77
75 Illinois Col. ... 92
92 Webster ■ ... 84
104 Blackburn ■ ... 92
93 Parks ... 82
72 Westminster (Mo.) ■ ... 85
66 Maryville (Mo.) ... 54
88 Principia ... 64
88 MacMurray ■ ... 65
74 Blackburn ... 85
62 Washington (Mo.) ... 91
96 Parks ■ ... 79
84 Maryville (Mo.) ■ ... 80
75 Greenville ... 72
118 Westminster (Mo.) ... 104
65 MacMurray ... 85
85 Greenville ■ ... 91
83 Principia ■ ... 57
107 Parks ■ ... 91
84 Westminster (Mo.) ■ ... 76
72 MacMurray ... 67
43 Hanover ... 85

Nickname: Griffins
Colors: Purple & Gold
Arena: Dunham Student Act. Center
Capacity: 1,800; Year Built: 1993
AD: Lee McKinney
SID: Darin Hendrickson

FORDHAM

Bronx, NY 10458 ... I

Coach: Nick Macarchuk
Alma Mater: Fairfield '63
Record: 19 Years, W-286, L-263

1996-97 SCHEDULE

Columbia ... Nov. 26
Holy Cross ■ ... Nov. 30
Florida Int'l ■ ... Dec. 3
Seton Hall ... Dec. 6
Manhattan ... Dec. 15
Iona ■ ... Dec. 18
Hofstra ■ ... Dec. 22
Jacksonville ... Dec. 28
Fla. Atlantic ... Dec. 30
Geo. Washington ... Jan. 4
Fairfield ■ ... Jan. 7
Xavier (Ohio) ■ ... Jan. 11
St. Bonaventure ... Jan. 18
Temple ■ ... Jan. 23
Dayton ... Jan. 25
St. Bonaventure ■ ... Jan. 29
Duquesne ■ ... Feb. 1
Massachusetts ■ ... Feb. 3
St. Joseph's (Pa.) ... Feb. 6
Virginia Tech ■ ... Feb. 8
Rhode Island ... Feb. 11
St. Joseph's (Pa.) ■ ... Feb. 16
Massachusetts ... Feb. 20
Temple ... Feb. 24
La Salle ... Feb. 27
Rhode Island ■ ... Mar. 1
Atlantic 10 Conf. Tr. ... Mar. 5-8

1995-96 RESULTS (4-23)

48 Columbia ■ ... 60
95 St. Francis (N.Y.) ■ ... 98
66 Iona ... 80
58 Manhattan ■ ... 61
75 LIU-Brooklyn ■ ... 67
47 St. John's (N.Y.) ■ ... 66
72 Florida Int'l ... 73
60 Rhode Island ... 93
76 Fairfield ... 62
50 St. Bonaventure ■ ... 57
61 Xavier (Ohio) ... 74
48 Temple ■ ... 69
53 Rhode Island ■ ... 68
64 St. Joseph's (Pa.) ■ ... 68
64 Holy Cross ... 77
57 Virginia Tech ... 81
50 Massachusetts ... 80
75 Duquesne ... 87
47 Massachusetts † ... 73
68 Dayton ■ ... 58
62 Geo. Washington ■ ... 77
56 Temple ... 77
57 Hofstra ... 69
47 St. Bonaventure ... 73
58 St. Joseph's (Pa.) ... 69
60 La Salle ■ ... 57
54 Xavier (Ohio) † ... 61

Nickname: Rams
Colors: Maroon & White
Arena: Rose Hill Gym
Capacity: 3,470; Year Built: 1926
AD: Frank McLaughlin
SID: Bill Holtz

FORT HAYS ST.

Hays, KS 67601 ... II

Coach: Gary Garner
Alma Mater: Missouri '65
Record: 13 Years, W-218, L-162

1996-97 SCHEDULE

Mont. St.-Billings ■ ... Nov. 15
Washburn ■ ... Nov. 19
Northwestern Okla. ■ ... Nov. 23
Tabor ■ ... Nov. 25
Ottawa ■ ... Nov. 30
Western St. ... Dec. 6
Mesa St. ... Dec. 7
N.M. Highlands ■ ... Dec. 14
Emporia St. ... Dec. 21
UC-Colo. Spgs. ... Jan. 3
Southern Colo. ... Jan. 4
Adams St. ■ ... Jan. 10
Fort Lewis ■ ... Jan. 11
Colorado Mines ... Jan. 17
Metro St. ... Jan. 18
Neb.-Kearney ... Jan. 22
Denver ■ ... Jan. 24
Chadron St. ■ ... Jan. 25
Colo. Christian ■ ... Jan. 31
Regis (Colo.) ■ ... Feb. 1
Neb.-Kearney ■ ... Feb. 5
Chadron St. ... Feb. 8
Colorado Mines ■ ... Feb. 14
Metro St. ■ ... Feb. 15
Colo. Christian ... Feb. 21
Regis (Colo.) ... Feb. 22

1995-96 RESULTS (34-0)

107 Okla. Sci. & Arts ■ ... 81
94 Pittsburg St. ■ ... 74
107 Ottawa ■ ... 70
91 Washburn ... 74
92 Friends ■ ... 67
122 Fort Lewis ■ ... 86
109 Adams St. ■ ... 80
102 Emporia St. ■ ... 79
80 Colorado Mines ... 61
93 Chadron St. ... 86
78 Emporia St. ... 48
105 Hastings ■ ... 63
94 Western St. ■ ... 83
80 Mesa St. ■ ... 57
82 Neb.-Kearney ... 79
78 N.M. Highlands ■ ... 50
89 Fort Lewis ... 75
81 Adams St. ... 71
97 Neb.-Kearney ■ ... 84
86 Colorado Mines ■ ... 69
98 Chadron St. ■ ... 61
114 Kan. Wesleyan ■ ... 71
104 McPherson ■ ... 71
88 N.M. Highlands ... 68
99 Western St. ... 59
69 Mesa St. ... 62
112 Fort Lewis ■ ... 72
81 Colorado Mines † ... 61
85 Neb.-Kearney † ... 79
97 Regis (Colo.) ■ ... 69
99 South Dak. St. ■ ... 90
71 North Ala. † ... 68
76 Calif. (Pa.) † ... 56
70 Northern Ky. † ... 63

Nickname: Tigers
Colors: Black & Gold
Arena: Gross Memorial Coliseum
Capacity: 6,814; Year Built: 1973
AD: Tom Spicer
SID: Jack Kuestermeyer

FORT LEWIS

Durango, CO 81301 ... II

Coach: Jim Cross
Alma Mater: Springfield '74
Record: 13 Years, W-141, L-204

1996-97 SCHEDULE

Arizona Bible ■ ... Nov. 23
Southern Colo. Cl. ... Nov. 29-30
Regis (Colo.) ■ ... Dec. 6
Colo. Christian ■ ... Dec. 7
Colorado Col. ■ ... Dec. 10
Metro St. ... Dec. 13
Colorado Mines ... Dec. 14
Chadron St. ■ ... Jan. 3
Colorado Col. ... Jan. 8
Neb.-Kearney ... Jan. 10
Fort Hays St. ... Jan. 11
Adams St. ... Jan. 15
N.M. Highlands ... Jan. 16
Southern Colo. ■ ... Jan. 24
UC-Colo. Spgs. ■ ... Jan. 25
Mesa St. ... Jan. 31
Western St. ... Feb. 1
Southern Colo. ... Feb. 7
UC-Colo. Spgs. ... Feb. 8
Adams St. ■ ... Feb. 11
N.M. Highlands ■ ... Feb. 14
Denver ■ ... Feb. 15
Mesa St. ■ ... Feb. 21
Western St. ■ ... Feb. 22

1995-96 RESULTS (8-18)

117 Arizona Bible ■ ... 49
74 Seattle Pacific ... 92
90 Western Wash. † ... 102
86 Fort Hays St. ... 122
101 Neb.-Kearney ... 119
87 Western St. ■ ... 102
57 Mesa St. ■ ... 70
78 Denver ■ ... 77
78 Denver ... 95
80 Colorado Col. ... 91
98 Southern Colo. ... 117
100 Adams St. ... 106
66 Southern Colo. ■ ... 69
83 N.M. Highlands ... 77
100 Colorado Mines ... 81
97 Chadron St. ... 118
75 Fort Hays St. ■ ... 89
100 Neb.-Kearney ■ ... 93
144 Amer. Indian Bib. † ... 48
102 Western St. ... 105
82 Mesa St. ... 81
82 N.M. Highlands ■ ... 89
93 Adams St. ■ ... 88
84 Colorado Mines ■ ... 104
111 Chadron St. ■ ... 112
72 Fort Hays St. ... 112

Nickname: Skyhawks
Colors: Blue & Gold
Arena: FLC Fieldhouse
Capacity: 3,000
AD: To be named
SID: Chris Aaland

FORT VALLEY ST.

Ft. Valley, GA 31030 ... II

Coach: Michael D. Moore
Alma Mater: Albany St. (Ga.)
Record: 3 Years, W-27, L-50

1996-97 SCHEDULE

Morris Brown Tr. ... Nov. 15-16
Fla. Memorial ■ ... Nov. 18
Tuskegee ■ ... Nov. 21
Kennesaw St. ■ ... Nov. 23
Kennesaw St. ... Dec. 10
Clayton St. ... Dec. 30
Savannah St. ■ ... Jan. 4
Kentucky St. ■ ... Jan. 6
Morehouse ... Jan. 9
Albany St. (Ga.) ■ ... Jan. 11
Paine ■ ... Jan. 13
Savannah St. ... Jan. 15
Miles ... Jan. 18
Clayton St. ■ ... Jan. 20
LeMoyne-Owen ... Jan. 25
Alabama A&M ... Jan. 27
Albany St. (Ga.) ... Feb. 1
Alabama A&M ■ ... Feb. 3
Miles ■ ... Feb. 6
Clark Atlanta ■ ... Feb. 8
Morris Brown ■ ... Feb. 10
Paine ... Feb. 12
Clark Atlanta ... Feb. 15
Tuskegee ... Feb. 17
Morris Brown ... Feb. 19

1995-96 RESULTS (11-16)

64 Claflin † ... 72
67 Talladega † ... 77
72 Columbus St. ■ ... 88
87 Tuskegee ... 117
79 Fla. Memorial ... 60
90 Columbus St. ... 101
80 Savannah St. ... 88
76 Clayton St. ... 69
91 Morehouse ■ ... 85
77 Albany St. (Ga.) ■ ... 79
82 Paine ... 81
66 Savannah St. ■ ... 57
62 Miles ■ ... 80

60	Morris Brown	66
73	LeMoyne-Owen ■	78
78	Alabama A&M ■	95
75	Albany St. (Ga.)	72
68	Clayton St. ■	64
63	Clark Atlanta	87
86	Kentucky St.	75
78	Paine ■	75
83	Clark Atlanta ■	84
80	Tuskegee ■	65
87	Morris Brown ■	93
60	Lynn ■	91
72	Morris Brown ■	67
50	Alabama A&M	90

Nickname: Wildcats
Colors: Old Gold & Blue
Arena: George Woodward Gymnasium
  Capacity: 1,345; Year Built: 1959
AD: Douglas Porter
SID: Russell Boone Jr

FRAMINGHAM ST.
Framingham, MA 01701 III

Coach: Togo Palazzi
Alma Mater: Holy Cross '54
Record: 5 Years, W-48, L-74

1996-97 SCHEDULE
Williams Cl. ....Nov. 22-23
Endicott ■ ....Nov. 26
Rhode Island Col. Tr ....Nov. 29-30
Tufts ■ ....Dec. 3
Curry ....Dec. 7
Mass. Pharmacy ....Dec. 10
Wheaton (Mass.) ....Dec. 14
North Adams St. ....Jan. 14
Daniel Webster ■ ....Jan. 16
Bri'water (Mass.) ■ ....Jan. 18
Worcester St. ....Jan. 21
Salem St. ■ ....Jan. 25
Fitchburg St. ....Jan. 28
Mass.-Dartmouth ■ ....Jan. 30
Westfield St. ....Feb. 1
Amherst ....Feb. 4
North Adams St. ■ ....Feb. 8
Bri'water (Mass.) ....Feb. 11
Worcester St. ■ ....Feb. 13
Salem St. ....Feb. 15
Fitchburg St. ■ ....Feb. 18
Westfield St. ■ ....Feb. 20

1995-96 RESULTS (5-20)
73	Anna Maria †	94
78	Suffolk †	73
87	Endicott	88
67	Mass.-Boston	85
89	Eastern Conn. St. †	101
66	Amherst	102
77	Salve Regina †	76
67	Baruch †	85
63	Rhode Island Col.	106
87	Tufts	93
83	Wheaton (Mass.) ■	69
74	North Adams St. ■	68
73	Bri'water (Mass.)	83
97	Worcester St. ■	102
65	Salem St.	109
83	Fitchburg St. ■	93
47	Mass.-Dartmouth ■	93
67	Westfield St. ■	71
75	North Adams St.	60
60	Bri'water (Mass.) ■	85
68	Worcester St.	83
56	Salem St. ■	73
73	Fitchburg St.	75
68	Westfield St. ■	95
76	Westfield St.	85

Nickname: Rams
Colors: Black & Gold
Arena: Dwight Gymnasium
  Capacity: 450
AD: Thomas Kelly
SID: Elizabeth Rieb

FRANCIS MARION
Florence, SC 29501 II

Coach: Lewis Hill
Alma Mater: Mars Hill '65
Record: 26 Years, W-434, L-302

1996-97 SCHEDULE
Shaw ■ ....Nov. 16
Longwood Inv. ....Nov. 23-24
Fayetteville St. ■ ....Dec. 2
Shaw ....Dec. 4
Coker ■ ....Dec. 10
Augusta St. ■ ....Dec. 15
N.C.-Pembroke ....Jan. 2
Columbus St. ....Jan. 4
S.C.-Aiken ....Jan. 9
Armstrong Atlantic ■ ....Jan. 11
S.C.-Spartanburg ....Jan. 13
Lander ■ ....Jan. 15
Kennesaw St. ....Jan. 18
Benedict ■ ....Jan. 22
Georgia Col. ....Jan. 25
N.C.-Pembroke ■ ....Jan. 29
Columbus St. ■ ....Feb. 1
Fayetteville St. ....Feb. 3
S.C.-Aiken ....Feb. 5
Armstrong Atlantic ....Feb. 8
S.C.-Spartanburg ■ ....Feb. 10
Lander ....Feb. 12
Kennesaw St. ■ ....Feb. 15
Augusta St. ....Feb. 19
Georgia Col. ■ ....Feb. 22

1995-96 RESULTS (8-19)
77	Col. of West Va. †	81
63	Wingate †	48
65	Carson-Newman †	68
74	Lenoir-Rhyne	78
74	Fayetteville St. ■	65
73	Gardner-Webb	93
70	S.C.-Aiken †	84
62	Augusta St. ■	69
72	Fayetteville St.	61
71	N.C.-Pembroke ■	54
69	Columbus St. ■	78
74	S.C.-Aiken	64
59	Armstrong Atlantic	51
56	S.C.-Spartanburg ■	69
39	Lander	68
56	Kennesaw St. ■	77
62	Georgia Col.	68
58	N.C.-Pembroke	64
48	Columbus St.	74
69	S.C.-Aiken ■	63
59	Armstrong Atlantic †	52
43	S.C.-Spartanburg	52
55	Lander	57
60	Kennesaw St.	64
60	Augusta St.	64
72	Georgia Col.	83
30	Columbus St. †	49

Nickname: Patriots
Colors: Red, White & Blue
Arena: Smith University Center
  Capacity: 3,027; Year Built: 1974
AD: Gerald Griffin
SID: Michael G. Hawkins

FRANKLIN
Franklin, IN 46131 III

Coach: Kerry Prather
Alma Mater: Indiana '77
Record: 13 Years, W-197, L-152

1996-97 SCHEDULE
Warner Southern ....Nov. 25
Eckerd ....Nov. 26
Franklin Cl. ....Dec. 6-7
Franklin Tr. ....Dec. 13-14
Millikin ....Dec. 17
Sewanee ■ ....Dec. 19
Ind.-Southeast ....Jan. 4
Hanover ....Jan. 8

Kalamazoo ....Jan. 11
Rose-Hulman ....Jan. 15
Anderson (Ind.) ....Jan. 18
Manchester ■ ....Jan. 22
Wabash ■ ....Jan. 25
DePauw ....Jan. 29
Rose-Hulman ....Feb. 1
Hanover ■ ....Feb. 5
Thomas More ■ ....Feb. 8
Manchester ....Feb. 12
Anderson (Ind.) ■ ....Feb. 15
DePauw ■ ....Feb. 19
Wabash ....Feb. 22

1995-96 RESULTS (13-11)
68	Wittenberg †	79
98	North Central	86
91	Rockford	80
67	Kalamazoo ■	78
71	Thomas More	69
93	Rockford ■	78
82	Benedictine (Ill.) ■	79
140	Ind.-East ■	79
69	Union (Ky.) ■	68
101	Millikin ■	87
88	Hanover ■	97
75	Knox	69
66	Rose-Hulman ■	77
79	Anderson (Ind.) ■	62
70	Manchester	77
93	Wabash ■	73
82	DePauw ■	65
74	Rose-Hulman ■	73
63	Hanover	91
80	Manchester ■	87
74	Anderson (Ind.)	79
74	DePauw	79
71	Wabash ■	73
57	DePauw	67

Nickname: Grizzlies
Colors: Blue & Gold
Arena: Spurlock Center
  Capacity: 2,000; Year Built: 1975
AD: Kerry Prather
SID: Kevin Elixman

FRANKLIN PIERCE
Rindge, NH 03461 II

Coach: Arthur Luptowski
Alma Mater: Bloomsburg '73
Record: 7 Years, W-140, L-66

1996-97 SCHEDULE
New Hamp. Col. Cl. ....Nov. 15-16
Bryant ■ ....Nov. 19
St. Michael's ....Nov. 23
American Int'l ■ ....Dec. 4
Stony Brook ....Dec. 8
New Haven ....Dec. 10
Dowling ■ ....Dec. 30
Tampa ....Jan. 3
Fla. Southern ....Jan. 4
Keene St. ■ ....Jan. 11
Mass.-Lowell ■ ....Jan. 14
New Hamp. Col. ....Jan. 16
Bridgeport ....Jan. 18
Albany (N.Y.) ■ ....Jan. 20
Southern Conn. St. ....Jan. 22
Bridgeport ■ ....Jan. 25
Sacred Heart ....Jan. 29
Keene St. ....Feb. 1
Southern Conn. St. ■ ....Feb. 4
Mass.-Lowell ....Feb. 6
Stony Brook ■ ....Feb. 8
New Haven ....Feb. 12
Albany (N.Y.) ....Feb. 15
Sacred Heart ■ ....Feb. 18
New Hamp. Col. ■ ....Feb. 22

1995-96 RESULTS (23-6)
Results unavailable

Nickname: Ravens
Colors: Crimson & Gray
Arena: Field House

Capacity: 1,000; Year Built: 1967
AD: Bruce Kirsh
SID: Chris O'Donnell

FRANK. & MARSH.
Lancaster, PA 17604 III

Coach: Glenn Robinson
Alma Mater: West Chester '67
Record: 25 Years, W-509, L-178

1996-97 SCHEDULE
Frank. & Marsh. Cl. ....Nov. 22-23
Roanoke ■ ....Dec. 1
Albright ....Dec. 5
Haverford ■ ....Dec. 7
Frank. & Marsh. Tr. ....Jan. 4-5
Swarthmore ....Jan. 11
Western Md. ■ ....Jan. 18
Lebanon Valley ■ ....Jan. 20
Dickinson ....Jan. 22
Ursinus ■ ....Jan. 25
York (Pa.) ....Jan. 27
Washington (Md.) ■ ....Jan. 29
Johns Hopkins ....Feb. 1
Gettysburg ■ ....Feb. 5
Western Md. ....Feb. 8
Muhlenberg ■ ....Feb. 12
Johns Hopkins ■ ....Feb. 15
Dickinson ....Feb. 19
Gettysburg ....Feb. 22

1995-96 RESULTS (29-3)
81	York (Pa.) ■	77
79	Goucher ■	63
63	FDU-Madison	52
75	Albright ■	51
65	Haverford	60
79	York (Pa.) ■	45
86	Swarthmore ■	67
94	Eastern ■	47
73	Elizabethtown ■	61
75	Scranton †	62
69	Western Md.	54
90	Dickinson	51
67	Ursinus ■	58
61	Lebanon Valley	46
88	Washington (Md.) ■	55
71	Johns Hopkins	66
67	Alvernia	56
69	Gettysburg	62
74	Western Md. ■	58
49	Muhlenberg	66
72	Johns Hopkins	62
93	Dickinson ■	61
66	Gettysburg ■	49
77	Alvernia †	67
72	Muhlenberg ■	59
79	Gettysburg ■	67
118	Salisbury St. ■	69
72	Lycoming ■	61
74	Rensselaer ■	58
107	Wilkes ■	70
57	Hope †	76
57	Ill. Wesleyan †	89

Nickname: Diplomats
Colors: Blue & White
Arena: Mayser Center
  Capacity: 3,000; Year Built: 1960
AD: William A. Marshall
SID: Tom Byrnes

FREDONIA ST.
Fredonia, NY 14063 III

Coach: Gregory Prechtl
Alma Mater: Fredonia St. '69
Record: 19 Years, W-232, L-246

1996-97 SCHEDULE
Rochester Tip-Off ....Nov. 22-23
Lake Erie ....Nov. 30
Geneseo St. ■ ....Dec. 3
Buffalo St. ....Dec. 6
Cortland St. ....Dec. 7

Roberts Wesleyan ■ ...Dec. 13
Penn St.-Behrend ...Jan. 9
Hilbert ■ ...Jan. 13
Potsdam St. ■ ...Jan. 17
Plattsburgh St. ...Jan. 18
St. John Fisher ■ ...Jan. 21
Utica/Rome ...Jan. 24
Oswego St. ■ ...Jan. 25
Brockport St. ■ ...Jan. 28
Penn St.-Behrend ■ ...Jan. 30
Binghamton ■ ...Feb. 1
Geneseo St. ...Feb. 4
Brockport St. ■ ...Feb. 11
New Paltz St. ■ ...Feb. 14
Oneonta St. ■ ...Feb. 15
Buffalo St. ■ ...Feb. 18
Oswego St. ...Feb. 21
Utica/Rome ■ ...Feb. 22

1995-96 RESULTS (14-13)

83 Alfred † ...51
58 Johns Hopkins ...44
67 Penn St.-Behrend ...55
53 Buffalo St. ■ ...59
51 Binghamton ...53
51 Geneseo St. ■ ...63
81 Thiel ...90
62 Penn St.-Behrend ■ ...65
86 Potsdam St. ■ ...83
81 Plattsburgh St. ■ ...75
66 St. John Fisher ...77
47 Oswego St. ...66
66 Utica/Rome ...71
70 Brockport St. ...82
84 Roberts Wesleyan ■ ...69
74 Cortland St. ■ ...55
81 Nazareth ...60
80 Geneseo St. ■ ...77
94 Brockport St. ■ ...82
66 New Paltz St. ...76
67 Oneonta St. ...61
52 Buffalo St. ...64
76 Oswego St. ■ ...60
78 Utica/Rome ■ ...75
70 Cortland St. † ...61
43 Buffalo St. † ...64
69 Elmira ■ ...71

Nickname: Blue Devils
Colors: Blue & White
Arena: Steele Hall
   Capacity: 3,500; Year Built: 1983
AD: Tom Prevet
SID: Donna Valone

FRESNO ST.
Fresno, CA 93740 ...I

Coach: Jerry Tarkanian
Alma Mater: Fresno St. '55
Record: 25 Years, W-647, L-133

1996-97 SCHEDULE

Pacific (Cal.) ■ ...Nov. 22
Santa Clara ...Nov. 26
Fresno St. Cl. ...Nov. 29-30
Western St. ■ ...Dec. 3
Oregon ...Dec. 7
Massachusetts ...Dec. 10
Texas ...Dec. 14
Texas Tech [Las Vegas] ...Dec. 21
St. Mary's (Cal.) ...Dec. 23
LSU ...Dec. 28
Puerto Rico Tr. ...Dec. 30-Jan. 1
Rice ...Jan. 6
San Jose St. ■ ...Jan. 11
Air Force ■ ...Jan. 18
UNLV ■ ...Jan. 20
Colorado St. ...Jan. 23
Wyoming ...Jan. 25
San Diego St. ■ ...Jan. 30
Hawaii ...Feb. 1
San Jose St. ...Feb. 6
Rice ■ ...Feb. 8
Air Force ...Feb. 15
UNLV ...Feb. 17
Wyoming ■ ...Feb. 20
Colorado St. ■ ...Feb. 22
Hawaii ■ ...Feb. 27
San Diego St. ...Mar. 1
Western Ath. Conf. Tr. ...Mar. 4-8

1995-96 RESULTS (22-11)

86 Weber St. ■ ...102
97 Cal St. Northridge ■ ...77
66 Maine ...49
54 Princeton ■ ...59
92 San Jose St. ■ ...68
70 Pacific (Cal.) ...73
58 Santa Clara ...66
83 Oregon ...82
109 Southern Colo. ■ ...88
75 St. Mary's (Cal.) ■ ...74
76 New Mexico ...75
83 UTEP ■ ...74
65 Utah ...64
84 Brigham Young ...97
73 Air Force ...67
79 San Diego St. ■ ...67
84 Hawaii ■ ...80
83 Colorado St. ...91
81 Wyoming ...96
86 Colorado St. ■ ...72
74 Wyoming ■ ...70
99 San Diego St. ...89
76 Hawaii ...97
82 Air Force ■ ...50
71 Utah ■ ...68
95 Brigham Young ■ ...83
88 UTEP ...87
84 New Mexico ...86
91 Wyoming † ...82
99 New Mexico ...104
58 Miami (Ohio) ■ ...57
80 Michigan St. ■ ...70
71 Nebraska ...83

Nickname: Bulldogs
Colors: Cardinal & Blue
Arena: Selland Arena
   Capacity: 10,132; Year Built: 1966
AD: Allen Bohl
SID: Dave Haglund

FROSTBURG ST.
Frostburg, MD 21532 ...III

Coach: Oscar Lewis
Alma Mater: Frostburg St. '72
Record: 11 Years, W-143, L-125

1996-97 SCHEDULE

Frostburg St. Cl. ...Nov. 22-23
Gallaudet ...Nov. 26
Shenandoah ■ ...Dec. 2
Wash. & Jeff. ■ ...Dec. 5
Bethany (W.Va.) ...Dec. 7
St. Mary's (Md.) ...Dec. 11
Shenandoah ...Dec. 15
Gettysburg ...Jan. 8
Frostburg St. Inv. ...Jan. 10-11
Bethany (W.Va.) ■ ...Jan. 15
Villa Julie ...Jan. 18
Chowan ■ ...Jan. 20
La Roche ■ ...Jan. 23
Western Md. ...Jan. 27
Lincoln (Pa.) ...Feb. 1
Waynesburg ...Feb. 3
Mary Washington ■ ...Feb. 8
Villa Julie ■ ...Feb. 9
La Roche ...Feb. 12
Chowan ...Feb. 15
Wesley ■ ...Feb. 17
Pitt.-Greensburg ...Feb. 19
Lincoln (Pa.) ■ ...Feb. 22

1995-96 RESULTS (13-12)

78 York (N.Y.) ■ ...82
74 Greensboro ...80
64 Washington (Md.) ...65
73 Mary Washington ■ ...57
105 Shenandoah ■ ...101
68 Shenandoah ...81
54 Muskingum ...77
64 Malone † ...65
91 Waynesburg ■ ...74
58 Grove City ■ ...67
64 Wash. & Jeff. ...68
73 Lincoln (Pa.) ...72
89 Ferrum ...63
71 Wesley ...69
109 Salisbury St. ■ ...83
79 Villa Julie ■ ...62
103 Western Md. ■ ...82
75 Chowan ...65
53 Waynesburg ...55
64 Gettysburg ...80
103 Villa Julie ...77
83 Wesley ■ ...61
102 Lincoln (Pa.) ■ ...106
62 Hilbert ...52
63 Chowan ...77

Nickname: Bobcats
Colors: Red, White & Black
Arena: Bobcat Arena
   Capacity: 3,600; Year Built: 1977
AD: Loyal Park
SID: Jeff Krone

FURMAN
Greenville, SC 29613 ...I

Coach: Joe Cantafio
Alma Mater: Scranton '74
Record: 10 Years, W-99, L-181

1996-97 SCHEDULE

Georgia ...Nov. 22
Stetson ...Nov. 25
N.C. Wesleyan ■ ...Nov. 30
Clemson ...Dec. 4
Erskine ■ ...Dec. 7
St. Louis ...Dec. 14
Charleston So. ■ ...Dec. 16
Coastal Caro. ...Dec. 21
South Caro. St. ■ ...Dec. 28
South Caro. ...Dec. 30
Tenn.-Chatt. ■ ...Jan. 9
Marshall ...Jan. 11
Appalachian St. ■ ...Jan. 14
East Tenn. St. ...Jan. 18
Tenn.-Chatt. ...Jan. 20
Wofford ■ ...Jan. 22
VMI ■ ...Jan. 25
Western Caro. ...Jan. 27
Citadel ...Feb. 1
Ga. Southern ■ ...Feb. 3
Davidson ...Feb. 8
Ga. Southern ...Feb. 10
Wofford ...Feb. 13
Davidson ■ ...Feb. 15
Western Caro. ■ ...Feb. 17
Citadel ■ ...Feb. 22
Southern Conf. Tr. ...Feb. 27-Mar. 2

1995-96 RESULTS (10-17)

80 Erskine ■ ...72
71 N.C.-Asheville ■ ...73
63 Vanderbilt ...87
81 South Caro. ...99
77 Lynchburg ■ ...56
61 Clemson ...76
66 South Caro. St. ...82
81 Charleston So. ...89
53 Stetson ...66
49 Wake Forest ...81
72 Coastal Caro. ■ ...50
76 Catawba ■ ...61
62 Ga. Southern ■ ...55
97 Davidson ...102
97 Western Caro. ...86
77 Citadel ...88
69 Tenn.-Chatt. ...59
71 Marshall ■ ...95
80 Ga. Southern ...38
78 Appalachian St. ...93
56 Tenn.-Chatt. ...86
57 VMI ...83
89 East Tenn. St. ■ ...88
85 Western Caro. ...97
68 Citadel ...67
79 Davidson ■ ...88
89 VMI † ...91

Nickname: Paladins
Colors: Purple & White
Arena: Greenville Auditorium
   Capacity: 6,000; Year Built: 1958
AD: John Block
SID: Hunter Reid

GALLAUDET
Washington, DC 20002 ...III

Coach: James DeStefano
Alma Mater: Gallaudet '85
Record: 8 Years, W-78, L-125

1996-97 SCHEDULE

Roanoke Tr. ...Nov. 23-24
Frostburg St. ...Nov. 26
Gallaudet Tr. ...Nov. 29-30
York (Pa.) ...Dec. 4
Goucher ■ ...Dec. 7
Washington (Md.) ...Jan. 8
Mt. St. Vincent ...Jan. 10
Haverford ■ ...Jan. 12
Salisbury St. ■ ...Jan. 15
Mary Washington ...Jan. 18
St. Mary's (Md.) ...Jan. 22
Marymount (Va.) ...Jan. 25
Ursinus ...Jan. 28
York (Pa.) ■ ...Jan. 30
Catholic ...Feb. 1
Salisbury St. ...Feb. 5
Goucher ...Feb. 8
Villa Julie ...Feb. 11
Mary Washington ...Feb. 13
Marymount (Va.) ■ ...Feb. 15
St. Mary's (Md.) ■ ...Feb. 19
Catholic ...Feb. 22

1995-96 RESULTS (6-19)

65 Alvernia † ...80
72 Wm. Paterson † ...85
115 Washington Bible ...64
70 Haverford ...89
72 CCNY ■ ...60
71 Phila. Pharmacy ■ ...80
57 York (Pa.) ...72
73 Goucher ...79
68 Flagler ...75
67 Rhode Island Col. † ...92
76 Catholic ...73
85 Marymount (Va.) ...92
58 Mary Washington ■ ...61
89 Salisbury St. ...99
72 Mary Washington ...68
69 York (Pa.) ■ ...60
68 St. Mary's (Md.) ■ ...80
76 Villa Julie ■ ...78
78 Salisbury St. ■ ...118
70 Catholic ...83
94 Goucher ...95
75 Washington (Md.) ■ ...77
76 St. Mary's (Md.) ...84
83 Marymount (Va.) ■ ...79
74 Salisbury St. ...97

Nickname: Bison
Colors: Buff & Blue
Arena: Fieldhouse
   Capacity: 1,500; Year Built: 1984
AD: Richard Pelletier
SID: Brett Marhanka

GANNON
Erie, PA 16541 ...II

Coach: Jerry Slocum
Alma Mater: King's (N.Y.) '75
Record: 21 Years, W-401, L-235

1996-97 SCHEDULE

Columbia Union ■	Nov. 18
Clarion ■	Nov. 21
Edinboro ■	Nov. 26
Gannon Cl.	Nov. 29-30
Ferris St.	Dec. 5
Grand Valley St.	Dec. 7
Michigan Tech	Dec. 12
Northern Mich.	Dec. 14
Hilbert ■	Dec. 21
Gannon Tr.	Dec. 29-30
Mercyhurst	Jan. 4
Oakland ■	Jan. 9
Wayne St. (Mich.) ■	Jan. 11
Ashland	Jan. 16
Hillsdale	Jan. 18
Saginaw Valley	Jan. 23
Northwood ■	Jan. 30
Lake Superior St. ■	Feb. 1
Edinboro	Feb. 3
Mercyhurst ■	Feb. 8
Oakland	Feb. 13
Wayne St. (Mich.) ■	Feb. 15
Ashland	Feb. 20
Hillsdale ■	Feb. 22

1995-96 RESULTS (10-16)

99	Pitt.-Johnstown ■	103
79	Slippery Rock ■	67
62	Clarion	59
68	West Va. Wesleyan ■	81
51	Edinboro	78
65	Mercyhurst	70
59	Ferris St. ■	82
60	Slippery Rock ■	44
82	Saginaw Valley ■	76
92	Edinboro	85
85	Ashland ■	76
75	Hillsdale	65
65	Saginaw Valley	69
57	Lake Superior St. ■	78
72	Northern Mich.	77
61	Michigan Tech	82
78	Northwood	68
77	Oakland ■	90
60	Wayne St. (Mich.) ■	65
79	Grand Valley St.	74
68	Mercyhurst ■	77
90	Ashland	83
65	Northwood ■	67
83	Hillsdale ■	89
63	Oakland	105
83	Wayne St. (Mich.)	115

Nickname: Golden Knights
Colors: Maroon & Gold
Arena: Hammermill Center
  Capacity: 2,800; Year Built: 1949
AD: Richard Dunford
SID: Bob Shreve

GARDNER-WEBB
Boiling Springs, NC 28017 II

Coach: Rick Scruggs
Alma Mater: Georgia '79
Record: 10 Years, W-193, L-124

1996-97 SCHEDULE

Gardner-Webb Cl.	Nov. 22-23
Marshall	Nov. 25
N.C.-Pembroke	Nov. 26
Southern Tech Tr.	Nov. 29-30
North Greenville ■	Dec. 5
Johnson & Wales	Dec. 14
North Fla.	Jan. 3
Carson-Newman	Jan. 8
Presbyterian ■	Jan. 11
Lenoir-Rhyne	Jan. 15
Mars Hill ■	Jan. 18
Lynn	Jan. 20
Elon	Jan. 22
Wingate	Jan. 25
Catawba	Jan. 29

Catawba ■	Feb. 1
Limestone ■	Feb. 3
Carson-Newman ■	Feb. 5
Presbyterian	Feb. 8
Lenoir-Rhyne ■	Feb. 12
Johnson & Wales ■	Feb. 14
Mars Hill ■	Feb. 15
Elon ■	Feb. 19
Wingate ■	Feb. 22

1995-96 RESULTS
Results unavailable

Nickname: Bulldogs
Colors: Scarlet, White & Black
Arena: Paul Porter Arena
  Capacity: 5,000; Year Built: 1982
AD: Woody Fish
SID: Mark Wilson

GENESEO ST.
Geneseo, NY 14454 III

Coach: Steve Holmes
Alma Mater: Plattsburgh St. '83
Record: 2 Years, W-37, L-18

1996-97 SCHEDULE

Heidelberg Cl.	Nov. 22-23
Fredonia St.	Dec. 3
Binghamton	Dec. 6
Oswego St. ■	Dec. 7
St. John Fisher	Jan. 11
Chase Rochester Tr.	Jan. 15-18
Utica/Rome	Jan. 21
Brockport St. ■	Jan. 24
Buffalo St. ■	Jan. 25
Pitt.-Bradford ■	Jan. 28
Potsdam St. ■	Jan. 31
Plattsburgh St. ■	Feb. 1
Fredonia St. ■	Feb. 4
New Paltz St.	Feb. 7
Oneonta St.	Feb. 8
Oswego St. ■	Feb. 11
Elmira	Feb. 12
Cortland St. ■	Feb. 15
Utica/Rome ■	Feb. 18
Buffalo St.	Feb. 21
Brockport St.	Feb. 22

1995-96 RESULTS (17-10)

62	Keuka †	79
68	Oswego St. †	58
55	Cortland St.	66
104	Brockport St.	79
63	Fredonia St.	51
67	New Paltz St. ■	57
75	Oneonta St.	78
104	Nazareth ■	112
77	Roberts Wesleyan †	70
68	Hobart †	57
78	Utica/Rome ■	67
80	Buffalo St.	73
91	Oswego St. ■	76
69	Potsdam St.	60
65	Plattsburgh St. ■	64
77	Alfred	66
77	Fredonia St. ■	80
80	Oswego St.	75
75	Elmira ■	90
71	St. John Fisher ■	68
63	Binghamton ■	60
75	Utica/Rome	85
75	Buffalo St. ■	63
66	Brockport St. ■	73
65	New Paltz St. ■	76
73	Rochester Inst.	51
61	Buffalo St.	71

Nickname: Blue Knights
Colors: Blue & White
Arena: Louise Kuhl Gymnasium
  Capacity: 3,000; Year Built: 1973
AD: John Spring
SID: George Gagnier

GEORGE MASON
Fairfax, VA 22030 I

Coach: Paul Westhead
Alma Mater: St. Joseph's (Pa.) '61
Record: 17 Years, W-275, L-206

1996-97 SCHEDULE

Alabama St. ■	Nov. 23
Virginia ■	Nov. 30
Morehead St. ■	Dec. 3
Colorado ■	Dec. 7
Long Beach St. ■	Dec. 10
Ohio St.	Dec. 14
St. Francis (Pa.) ■	Dec. 20
Cal Poly SLO ■	Dec. 22
Akron	Dec. 29
Va. Commonwealth	Jan. 2
N.C.-Wilmington	Jan. 4
East Caro.	Jan. 6
Old Dominion ■	Jan. 8
James Madison	Jan. 13
Richmond ■	Jan. 15
American	Jan. 18
William & Mary ■	Jan. 25
Va. Commonwealth ■	Jan. 29
East Caro. ■	Feb. 1
N.C.-Wilmington ■	Feb. 3
Richmond	Feb. 5
James Madison ■	Feb. 8
Alabama St.	Feb. 12
William & Mary	Feb. 15
Old Dominion	Feb. 22
American ■	Feb. 24
Colonial Conf. Tr.	Feb. 28-Mar. 3

1995-96 RESULTS (11-16)

139	Delaware St. ■	73
142	Troy St. ■	127
117	Colorado	132
87	Ohio St. ■	92
113	West Va. Tech ■	110
97	Southern Cal	118
84	Long Beach St.	98
84	Hampton ■	74
74	Morehead St.	83
44	N.C.-Wilmington ■	68
80	East Caro.	76
74	Va. Commonwealth	86
110	Cal Poly SLO	106
86	Old Dominion	103
72	James Madison	80
95	William & Mary ■	92
96	American ■	85
91	Richmond	105
81	Va. Commonwealth ■	94
46	N.C.-Wilmington	54
92	East Caro.	78
98	Richmond ■	91
92	Old Dominion ■	93
100	American	88
80	James Madison ■	81
92	William & Mary	96
77	Richmond	93

Nickname: Patriots
Colors: Green & Gold
Arena: Patriot Center
  Capacity: 10,000; Year Built: 1985
AD: Tom O'Connor
SID: Jim Engelhardt

GEO. WASHINGTON
Washington, DC 20052 I

Coach: Mike Jarvis
Alma Mater: Northeastern '68
Record: 11 Years, W-214, L-118

1996-97 SCHEDULE

Geo. Washington Cl.	Nov. 22-23
South Fla. ■	Nov. 26
Texas Tech ■	Nov. 30
American	Dec. 2
Maryland Tr.	Dec. 8-9
Kansas	Dec. 11

N.C.-Charlotte	Dec. 30
Fordham ■	Jan. 4
St. Bonaventure	Jan. 6
Duquesne	Jan. 11
St. Joseph's (Pa.) ■	Jan. 15
Dayton	Jan. 18
Xavier (Ohio) ■	Jan. 23
La Salle ■	Jan. 25
Massachusetts ■	Jan. 30
La Salle	Feb. 1
Virginia Tech ■	Feb. 4
Old Dominion ■	Feb. 11
Xavier (Ohio) ■	Feb. 15
Duquesne ■	Feb. 17
Virginia Tech ■	Feb. 20
Temple ■	Feb. 22
Rhode Island ■	Feb. 26
Dayton ■	Mar. 1
Atlantic 10 Conf. Tr.	Mar. 5-8

1995-96 RESULTS (21-8)

81	Hartford ■	69
80	Hampton ■	73
66	Florida †	75
81	Maryland †	98
76	James Madison	68
71	South Fla. †	69
98	Cal St. Sacramento	91
84	Idaho †	83
87	Duquesne	59
87	St. Bonaventure ■	78
77	Missouri	92
71	Virginia Tech †	79
77	Dayton ■	58
64	Virginia Tech ■	47
77	Dayton	65
64	Temple ■	47
72	N.C.-Charlotte ■	67
77	Xavier (Ohio) ■	69
92	La Salle ■	83
77	Fordham	62
70	La Salle	76
84	Duquesne ■	72
86	Massachusetts ■	76
81	Xavier (Ohio)	77
76	Rhode Island ■	72
82	St. Joseph's (Pa.)	86
81	St. Joseph's (Pa.) †	71
65	Massachusetts †	74
79	Iowa †	81

Nickname: Colonials
Colors: Buff & Blue
Arena: Charles E. Smith Center
  Capacity: 5,000; Year Built: 1975
AD: Jack Kvancz
SID: Brad Bower

GEORGETOWN
Washington, DC 20057 I

Coach: John Thompson
Alma Mater: Providence '64
Record: 24 Years, W-553, L-208

1996-97 SCHEDULE

Cleveland St.	Nov. 23
Alabama St. ■	Nov. 26
DePaul ■	Nov. 30
Seton Hall ■	Dec. 2
Massachusetts [Chicago]	Dec. 4
Rutgers ■	Dec. 7
Delaware St. ■	Dec. 10
St. Leo ■	Dec. 18
Morgan St. ■	Dec. 21
Pacific (Cal.) [Halifax]	Dec. 28
West Va.	Jan. 2
Miami (Fla.) ■	Jan. 4
Notre Dame ■	Jan. 7
Connecticut ■	Jan. 11
Boston College	Jan. 13
Miami (Fla.)	Jan. 18
St. John's (N.Y.) ■	Jan. 21
Pittsburgh ■	Jan. 25
Villanova ■	Jan. 27
St. John's (N.Y.)	Feb. 1

Connecticut ....Feb. 3
Syracuse ....Feb. 8
Providence ■ ....Feb. 12
Pittsburgh ....Feb. 20
Memphis ....Feb. 22
Rutgers ■ ....Feb. 26
Providence ....Mar. 2
Big East Conf. Tr. ....Mar. 5-8

1995-96 RESULTS (29-8)

106	Colgate ■	57
74	Temple ■	49
94	Georgia Tech †	72
81	Arizona †	91
96	Southern-N.O. ■	65
86	West Va.	83
83	Rutgers ■	52
113	Cal St. Sacramento ■	58
88	St. Francis (Pa.) ■	55
104	Morgan St. ■	60
88	Duquesne †	86
123	St. Leo †	65
81	DePaul	61
85	Seton Hall ■	76
56	Pittsburgh	75
72	Miami (Fla.) ■	67
74	Notre Dame	69
82	Seton Hall	62
83	Syracuse ■	64
72	St. John's (N.Y.)	83
91	West Va. ■	67
70	Notre Dame ■	53
66	Villanova	79
64	Syracuse ■	85
66	Boston College	63
81	Memphis ■	60
77	Connecticut ■	65
67	Boston College ■	64
77	Providence	84
106	Villanova ■	68
92	Miami (Fla.) †	62
84	Villanova †	76
74	Connecticut †	75
93	Mississippi Val. †	56
73	New Mexico †	62
98	Texas Tech †	90
62	Massachusetts †	86

Nickname: Hoyas
Colors: Blue & Gray
Arena: USAir Arena
  Capacity: 19,035; Year Built: 1980
AD: Joseph Lang
SID: Bill Shapland

GEORGIA
Athens, GA 30613 I

Coach: Tubby Smith
Alma Mater: High Point '73
Record: 5 Years, W-100, L-53

1996-97 SCHEDULE

Furman ■ ....Nov. 22
Georgia St. ■ ....Nov. 26
Ga. Southern ■ ....Nov. 29
Georgia Tech ....Dec. 3
Appalachian St. ■ ....Dec. 7
Virginia Tech ....Dec. 14
East Caro. ■ ....Dec. 17
Brigham Young [Atlanta] ....Dec. 21
Colorado ■ ....Dec. 23
Hawaii Rainbow Cl. ....Dec. 27-30
Mississippi ....Jan. 5
Vanderbilt ....Jan. 8
Kentucky ■ ....Jan. 14
South Caro. ....Jan. 18
Florida ■ ....Jan. 22
Auburn ■ ....Jan. 25
Tennessee ....Jan. 29
Kentucky ....Feb. 1
Alabama ....Feb. 5
Mississippi St. ■ ....Feb. 8
South Caro. ■ ....Feb. 12
Arkansas ....Feb. 15
Vanderbilt ■ ....Feb. 19

LSU ■ ....Feb. 22
Florida ....Feb. 26
Tennessee ■ ....Mar. 1
Southeastern Conf. Tr. ....Mar. 6-9

1995-96 RESULTS (21-10)

88	Ga. Southern †	44
91	Western Caro. ■	71
85	Pittsburgh	66
74	North Caro.	85
81	Winthrop	55
94	Georgia Tech ■	70
85	Virginia Tech †	72
103	Central Fla. ■	54
95	Mercer ■	68
86	Jacksonville ■	59
74	Mississippi ■	38
73	South Caro.	85
86	Auburn	89
71	Florida ■	46
62	Tennessee	67
77	Kentucky ■	82
62	Vanderbilt	66
73	Mississippi St.	76
68	Tennessee ■	49
85	LSU	82
68	Alabama ■	55
73	Kentucky	86
77	Vanderbilt ■	68
71	Arkansas ■	59
86	Florida	70
88	South Caro. ■	73
74	Tennessee †	63
68	Mississippi St. †	86
81	Clemson †	74
76	Purdue †	69
81	Syracuse †	83

Nickname: Bulldogs
Colors: Red & Black
Arena: Georgia Coliseum
  Capacity: 10,523; Year Built: 1963
AD: Vince Dooley
SID: Norm Reilly

GEORGIA COL.
Milledgeville, GA 31061 II

Coach: Terry Sellers
Alma Mater: Aub.-Montgomery
Record: 3 Years, W-45, L-37

1996-97 SCHEDULE

Brewton Parker ■ ....Nov. 16
North Ga. ....Nov. 19
Albany St. (Ga.) ....Nov. 21
North Ga. ■ ....Nov. 30
Albany St. (Ga.) ■ ....Dec. 11
Valdosta St. Inv. ....Dec. 13-14
Brewton Parker ....Dec. 30
Augusta St. ....Jan. 2
S.C.-Aiken ■ ....Jan. 4
Columbus St. ....Jan. 8
N.C.-Pembroke ■ ....Jan. 11
Armstrong Atlantic ....Jan. 13
Kennesaw St. ■ ....Jan. 15
Lander ....Jan. 18
S.C.-Spartanburg ■ ....Jan. 22
Francis Marion ■ ....Jan. 25
Augusta St. ■ ....Jan. 29
S.C.-Aiken ....Feb. 1
Columbus St. ■ ....Feb. 5
N.C.-Pembroke ....Feb. 8
Armstrong Atlantic ■ ....Feb. 10
Kennesaw St. ....Feb. 12
Lander ■ ....Feb. 15
S.C.-Spartanburg ....Feb. 19
Francis Marion ....Feb. 22

1995-96 RESULTS (21-7)

97	North Ga. ■	78
86	Clayton St. ■	89
106	Albany St. (Ga.) ■	108
97	Savannah St. ■	79
90	North Ga. ■	64
87	Albany St. (Ga.) ■	65
95	Clayton St.	83

80	Savannah St.	76
75	Augusta St. ■	68
83	S.C.-Aiken	59
85	Columbus St. ■	74
91	N.C.-Pembroke	78
92	Armstrong Atlantic ■	72
78	Kennesaw St.	73
65	Lander	60
72	S.C.-Spartanburg	82
68	Francis Marion	62
97	Augusta St.	87
89	S.C.-Aiken ■	72
79	Columbus St.	82
93	N.C.-Pembroke ■	86
77	Armstrong Atlantic	83
86	Kennesaw St. ■	77
77	Lander	80
98	S.C.-Spartanburg ■	76
83	Francis Marion ■	72
91	Augusta St. ■	65
67	S.C.-Spartanburg ■	85

Nickname: Colonials
Colors: Brown & Gold
Arena: Centennial Center
  Capacity: 4,100; Year Built: 1990
AD: Stan Aldridge
SID: Michael Martin

GA. SOUTHERN
Statesboro, GA 30460 I

Coach: Gregg Polinsky
Alma Mater: Northern Ariz. '82
Record: 1 Year, W-3, L-23

1996-97 SCHEDULE

Indiana St. ....Nov. 23
Georgia ....Nov. 29
Texas A&M ....Dec. 10
Mercer ■ ....Dec. 14
Florida A&M ■ ....Dec. 19
Georgia St. ■ ....Dec. 21
Toledo Tr. ....Dec. 29-30
Coastal Caro. ....Jan. 2
East Tenn. St. ■ ....Jan. 6
Davidson ■ ....Jan. 11
VMI ....Jan. 13
Virginia Tech ....Jan. 15
Appalachian St. ....Jan. 18
Marshall ■ ....Jan. 20
Citadel ■ ....Jan. 25
Tenn.-Chatt. ....Jan. 27
Western Caro. ■ ....Feb. 1
Furman ....Feb. 3
Marshall ....Feb. 8
Furman ■ ....Feb. 10
Citadel ....Feb. 15
Tenn.-Chatt. ■ ....Feb. 17
Western Caro. ....Feb. 22
Southern Conf. Tr. ....Feb. 27-Mar. 2

1995-96 RESULTS (3-23)

44	Georgia †	88
59	Nebraska	82
59	Pepperdine †	69
83	Shorter †	48
58	Georgia St.	60
43	Florida A&M	47
59	Coastal Caro. ■	61
60	Indiana St. ■	69
48	South Fla.	78
57	Yale †	62
63	Texas A&M †	67
55	Furman	62
56	Citadel ■	63
55	Tenn.-Chatt.	81
71	Western Caro.	81
70	East Tenn. St.	68
46	Davidson	71
38	Furman	80
74	Appalachian St. ■	72
48	VMI ■	71
52	Marshall ■	71
63	Citadel	67
45	South Caro.	57

50	Tenn.-Chatt. ■	71
64	Western Caro.	83
50	Marshall	96

Nickname: Eagles
Colors: Blue & White
Arena: Hanner Fieldhouse
  Capacity: 5,500; Year Built: 1969
AD: Sam Baker
SID: Jim Stephan

GEORGIA ST.
Atlanta, GA 30303 I

Coach: Carter Wilson
Alma Mater: Clark Atlanta '76
Record: 2 Years, W-21, L-33

1996-97 SCHEDULE

Southern Wesleyan ■ ....Nov. 7
Georgia ....Nov. 26
Tennessee ....Dec. 1
Auburn ....Dec. 7
Covenant ■ ....Dec. 14
Troy St. ....Dec. 14
Winthrop ....Dec. 16
Ga. Southern ....Dec. 21
Troy St. ■ ....Dec. 30
Campbell ■ ....Jan. 2
Charleston (S.C.) ■ ....Jan. 4
Florida Int'l ....Jan. 9
Fla. Atlantic ....Jan. 11
N.C.-Asheville ■ ....Jan. 13
Stetson ■ ....Jan. 16
Central Fla. ....Jan. 18
Samford ■ ....Jan. 23
Jacksonville St. ■ ....Jan. 25
Southeastern La. ....Jan. 30
Centenary (La.) ■ ....Feb. 1
Mercer ■ ....Feb. 3
Southeastern La. ■ ....Feb. 6
Centenary (La.) ■ ....Feb. 8
Mercer ■ ....Feb. 15
Jacksonville St. ....Feb. 20
Samford ....Feb. 22
Trans America Conf. Tr. ......Feb. 27-Mar. 1

1995-96 RESULTS (10-16)

78	Morris Brown ■	80
59	Tennessee	74
69	Memphis	89
68	Tenn.-Martin	90
72	Arkansas St.	57
60	Ga. Southern ■	58
67	Arkansas St. ■	74
76	Grambling	62
55	Tulane	62
87	Winthrop ■	76
57	Campbell	60
78	Charleston (S.C.)	91
75	Florida Int'l ■	68
62	Fla. Atlantic ■	60
61	Stetson	73
75	Central Fla.	95
73	Samford	76
65	Jacksonville St.	83
86	Southeastern La. ■	81
90	Mercer ■	96
86	Southeastern La.	91
76	Centenary (La.)	79
74	Centenary (La.) ■	58
74	Mercer	66
82	Jacksonville St. ■	76
72	Samford ■	93

Nickname: Panthers
Colors: Royal Blue, Crimson & White
Arena: GSU Sports Arena
  Capacity: 4,200; Year Built: 1972
AD: Orby Moss Jr
SID: Martin Harmon

GEORGIA TECH
Atlanta, GA 30332 I

Coach: Bobby Cremins

Alma Mater: South Caro. '70
Record: 21 Years, W-398, L-242

1996-97 SCHEDULE

Wofford ■ ....Nov. 22
Morgan St. ■ ....Nov. 26
Radford ■ ....Nov. 29
Georgia ■ ....Dec. 3
Temple [Atlantic City] ....Dec. 7
Maryland ■ ....Dec. 12
Kentucky ■ ....Dec. 21
ECAC Holiday Tr. ....Dec. 26-28
N.C.-Greensboro ■ ....Dec. 31
Duke ....Jan. 5
Wake Forest ■ ....Jan. 8
Louisville ....Jan. 11
Florida St. ■ ....Jan. 15
North Caro. ....Jan. 18
Virginia ....Jan. 22
North Caro. St. ■ ....Jan. 25
Clemson ....Jan. 30
Duke ■ ....Feb. 2
Virginia ■ ....Feb. 6
Florida St. ....Feb. 9
North Caro. ■ ....Feb. 15
Maryland ■ ....Feb. 19
North Caro. St. ....Feb. 22
Wake Forest ....Feb. 25
Clemson ■ ....Mar. 1
Atlantic Coast Conf. Tr. ....Mar. 6-9

1995-96 RESULTS (24-12)

87 Manhattan ■ 67
83 Oklahoma ■ 72
72 Georgetown † 94
77 Michigan † 61
87 Campbell ■ 76
89 Appalachian St. 65
60 Kentucky 83
70 Georgia 94
88 Louisville ■ 77
69 Mt. St. Mary's (Md.) ■ ..71
67 Massachusetts † 75
82 Bradley † 84
66 Santa Clara † 71
98 Maryland ■ 84
86 Duke 81
80 North Caro. ■ 77
91 Western Caro. ■ 78
63 Wake Forest 66
90 Virginia 70
76 North Caro. St. 71
79 Florida St. ■ 58
70 Clemson 73
74 Maryland 88
73 Duke ■ 71
92 North Caro. 83
64 Wake Forest ■ 63
84 Virginia 75
92 North Caro. St. ■ 83
83 Florida St. 68
87 Clemson ■ 74
88 North Caro. St. † 73
84 Maryland † 79
74 Wake Forest † 75
90 Austin Peay † 79
103 Boston College † 89
70 Cincinnati † 87

Nickname: Yellow Jackets
Colors: Old Gold & White
Arena: Alexander Memorial Coliseum
   Capacity: 9,800; Year Built: 1957
AD: Homer Rice
SID: Mike Finn

GETTYSBURG
Gettysburg, PA 17325.............III

Coach: George Petrie
Alma Mater: Lebanon Valley '72
Record: 7 Years, W-80, L-91

1996-97 SCHEDULE

Gettysburg Tr. ....Nov. 22-23
Messiah ....Nov. 25
York (Pa.) ■ ....Dec. 2

Haverford ....Dec. 4
Muhlenberg ■ ....Dec. 7
Navy ....Dec. 9
Goucher ■ ....Dec. 12
Drew ....Jan. 6
Frostburg St. ....Jan. 8
Lebanon Valley Tr. ....Jan. 10-11
Johns Hopkins ....Jan. 15
Dickinson ....Jan. 18
Western Md. ■ ....Jan. 22
Washington (Md.) ■ ....Jan. 25
Alvernia ....Jan. 27
Swarthmore ■ ....Feb. 1
Frank. & Marsh. ....Feb. 5
Dickinson ■ ....Feb. 8
Johns Hopkins ■ ....Feb. 12
Western Md. ....Feb. 15
Ursinus ....Feb. 19
Frank. & Marsh. ■ ....Feb. 22

1995-96 RESULTS (18-9)

98 Connecticut Col. ■ 72
85 Rensselaer ■ 71
85 Messiah ■ 53
88 York (Pa.) 71
66 Muhlenberg 75
72 Goucher 89
85 Haverford ■ 69
62 Navy 93
65 Roanoke 89
96 Jersey City St. † 75
88 Dickinson ■ 74
89 Drew ■ 63
88 Western Md. 80
77 Washington (Md.) 64
73 Alvernia ■ 71
81 Johns Hopkins 73
88 Swarthmore 81
62 Frank. & Marsh. ■ 69
74 Dickinson 94
80 Frostburg St. ■ 64
79 Johns Hopkins ■ 69
97 Western Md. ■ 65
86 Ursinus 78
49 Frank. & Marsh. 66
69 Haverford 68
67 Frank. & Marsh. ■ 79
75 Lycoming 103

Nickname: Bullets
Colors: Orange & Blue
Arena: Bream Gymnasium
   Capacity: 3,200; Year Built: 1962
AD: Charles Winters
SID: Robert Kenworthy

GLENVILLE ST.
Glenville, WV 26351.............II

Coach: Gary Nottingham
Alma Mater: Glenville St. '79
Record: 14 Years, W-196, L-170

1996-97 SCHEDULE

Slippery Rock ....Nov. 19
Winston-Salem ....Nov. 21
Ohio Valley ....Nov. 23
Pitt.-Johnstown ....Nov. 26
St. Vincent ....Nov. 30
West Va. Wesleyan ■ ....Dec. 2
Charleston (W.Va.) ■ ....Dec. 7
Ohio Valley ■ ....Dec. 9
Bluefield St. ....Dec. 14
Fairmont St. ....Jan. 8
Shepherd ■ ....Jan. 11
West Liberty St. ....Jan. 13
Salem-Teikyo ....Jan. 15
Alderson-Broaddus ■ ....Jan. 18
Davis & Elkins ....Jan. 22
Bluefield St. ■ ....Jan. 25
Concord ■ ....Jan. 27
West Va. Tech ....Jan. 29
Wheeling Jesuit ....Feb. 1
West Va. St. ■ ....Feb. 5
Salem-Teikyo ■ ....Feb. 8
West Va. Wesleyan ....Feb. 11
Davis & Elkins ....Feb. 15

Concord ....Feb. 19
West Va. Tech ■ ....Feb. 22

1995-96 RESULTS (13-12)

63 Findlay † 108
63 St. Vincent ■ 65
63 Ashland 73
62 Pitt.-Johnstown ■ 47
67 West Va. Wesleyan 68
65 Charleston (W.Va.) 50
67 Bluefield St. ■ 70
60 Fairmont St. ■ 58
50 West Liberty St. ■ 59
79 Salem-Teikyo ■ 55
68 Alderson-Broaddus 89
62 Davis & Elkins 53
55 Bluefield St. 62
66 Concord ■ 67
74 West Va. Tech 70
77 Wheeling Jesuit ■ 62
62 Shepherd 51
67 West Va. St. 86
77 Salem-Teikyo 70
77 West Va. Wesleyan ■ 62
82 Davis & Elkins ■ 48
75 Concord 70
78 West Va. Tech ■ 82
73 Wheeling Jesuit ■ 62
62 West Va. Tech † 73

Nickname: Pioneers
Colors: Royal Blue & White
Arena: Pioneer Gym
   Capacity: 1,600; Year Built: 1951
AD: Rich Rodriguez
SID: Rick Conklin

GONZAGA
Spokane, WA 99258.............I

Coach: Dan Fitzgerald
Alma Mater: Cal St. Los Angeles '65
Record: 14 Years, W-236, L-159

1996-97 SCHEDULE

Southern Utah ....Nov. 23
St. Martin's ■ ....Nov. 26
Washington St. ■ ....Nov. 30
Central Wash. ....Dec. 3
Colorado St. Cl. ....Dec. 6-7
Montana St. ■ ....Dec. 11
Montana ■ ....Dec. 14
Eastern Wash. ....Dec. 21
Boise St. Cl. ....Dec. 27-28
Cal St. Fullerton ■ ....Jan. 4
Santa Clara ■ ....Jan. 9
St. Mary's (Cal.) ....Jan. 11
San Diego ....Jan. 16
San Francisco ....Jan. 18
Loyola Marymount ■ ....Jan. 23
Pepperdine ■ ....Jan. 25
Pepperdine ....Jan. 31
Loyola Marymount ....Feb. 1
Portland ■ ....Feb. 5
Portland ....Feb. 8
San Francisco ■ ....Feb. 13
San Diego ■ ....Feb. 15
St. Mary's (Cal.) ....Feb. 21
Santa Clara ....Feb. 22
West Coast Conf. Tr. ....Mar. 1-3

1995-96 RESULTS (21-9)

67 Washington St. ■ 72
86 Central Wash. ■ 66
77 Southern Utah ■ 60
56 Montana St. 58
83 Cal St. Fullerton 57
90 Western Mont. ■ 65
68 Eastern Wash. ■ 55
60 South Ala. † 43
58 Washington 62
83 Boise St. ■ 68
63 Eastern Wash. 53
66 Cal St. Sacramento ■ 44
61 Santa Clara 72
81 St. Mary's (Cal.) 71
60 San Diego 53

60 San Francisco ■ 55
95 Portland ■ 72
66 Portland 67
69 Loyola Marymount 83
78 Pepperdine 66
94 Pepperdine ■ 80
81 Loyola Marymount ■ 68
73 San Francisco 59
69 San Diego 59
83 St. Mary's (Cal.) ■ 82
71 Santa Clara ■ 77
64 St. Mary's (Cal.) † 54
76 Pepperdine † 48
68 Portland † 76
73 Washington St. 92

Nickname: Bulldogs, Zags
Colors: Blue, White & Red
Arena: Charlotte Y. Martin Center
   Capacity: 4,000; Year Built: 1965
AD: Dan Fitzgerald
SID: Oliver Pierce

GORDON
Wenham, MA 01984.............III

Coach: Jerry Gilsdorf
Alma Mater: Judson '86
(First year as head coach)

1996-97 SCHEDULE

Gordon Tr. ....Nov. 22-23
Mass. Pharmacy ....Nov. 26
Daniel Webster ....Dec. 3
North Adams St. ....Dec. 5
Salem St. ■ ....Dec. 10
Endicott ■ ....Dec. 14
Buffalo St. Inv. ....Jan. 3-4
New England ....Jan. 8
St. Joseph's (Me.) ....Jan. 11
Curry ■ ....Jan. 16
Notre Dame (N.H.) ....Jan. 18
Nichols ■ ....Jan. 23
Eastern Nazarene ■ ....Jan. 25
Colby-Sawyer ....Jan. 27
New England Col. ■ ....Jan. 29
Salve Regina ....Feb. 1
Anna Maria ....Feb. 6
Roger Williams ■ ....Feb. 8
New England Col. ....Feb. 10
Colby-Sawyer ....Feb. 12
Wentworth Inst. ....Feb. 15
Nichols ....Feb. 20
Anna Maria ■ ....Feb. 22

1995-96 RESULTS (9-15)

78 East. Mennonite † 99
80 Messiah 101
66 St. Joseph's (Me.) 86
85 Daniel Webster 91
71 Plymouth St. 86
78 MIT 59
75 New England ■ 70
73 St. Lawrence † 78
47 Williams 73
84 Salem St. 107
94 Curry 67
64 Nichols 76
69 Eastern Nazarene 79
79 Colby-Sawyer ■ 91
82 New England Col. 58
87 Salve Regina ■ 75
87 Anna Maria ■ 67
70 Roger Williams 61
78 New England Col. ■ 67
65 Colby-Sawyer 84
74 Wentworth Inst. ■ 78
93 Nichols ■ 79
85 Anna Maria 98
76 Eastern Nazarene 88

Nickname: The Fighting Scots
Colors: Blue & White
Arena: Bennett Athletic Center
   Capacity: 1,800; Year Built: 1996
AD: Walter Bowman
SID: Amy Reiter

GOUCHER
Baltimore, MD 21204 III

Coach: Leonard Trevino
Alma Mater: Texas Tech '87
Record: 6 Years, W-70, L-81

1996-97 SCHEDULE
Hampden-Sydney Cl.	Nov. 22-23
Johns Hopkins	Nov. 26
St. Mary's (Md.) ■	Dec. 4
Gallaudet	Dec. 7
Chris. Newport ■	Dec. 8
Villa Julie	Dec. 9
Gettysburg	Dec. 12
Susquehanna Cl.	Dec. 20-21
Roanoke Cl.	Jan. 4-5
York (Pa.)	Jan. 15
Salisbury St.	Jan. 18
Mary Washington ■	Jan. 22
Catholic	Jan. 25
St. Mary's (Md.)	Jan. 29
Marymount (Va.)	Feb. 1
York (Pa.) ■	Feb. 5
Gallaudet ■	Feb. 8
Salisbury St. ■	Feb. 12
Catholic	Feb. 15
Mary Washington	Feb. 20
Marymount (Va.) ■	Feb. 22

1995-96 RESULTS (15-10)
83	Lebanon Valley †	80
63	Frank. & Marsh.	79
64	Johns Hopkins ■	66
110	Villa Julie ■	83
92	Chris. Newport	89
90	Wesley ■	57
89	Gettysburg ■	72
79	Gallaudet	73
79	N.C. Wesleyan	75
78	Millikin †	95
75	York (Pa.)	64
69	St. Mary's (Md.) ■	70
99	Salisbury St. ■	86
69	Mary Washington	85
66	Catholic	80
116	Marymount (Va.) ■	111
64	Savannah A&D ■	65
96	Catholic ■	100
88	St. Mary's (Md.)	84
89	York (Pa.) ■	86
109	Mary Washington ■	83
95	Gallaudet ■	94
98	Marymount (Va.)	93
102	Salisbury St.	121
79	St. Mary's (Md.) ■	87

Nickname: Gophers
Colors: Blue & Gold
Arena: Goucher Recreation Center
  Capacity: 1,200; Year Built: 1991
AD: Geoff Miller
SID: Kevin Fillman

GRAMBLING
Grambling, LA 71245..............I

Coach: Lacey Reynolds
Alma Mater: Miss. Industrial '74
Record: 1 Year, W-12, L-16

1996-97 SCHEDULE
New Mexico Cl.	Nov. 22-23
Texas-Arlington ■	Nov. 26
South Ala.	Nov. 29
UAB	Dec. 1
Tougaloo ■	Dec. 3
Iowa Shootout	Dec. 6-7
Wiley ■	Dec. 14
Southeastern La.	Dec. 16
Northwestern St. ■	Dec. 19
Ill.-Chicago	Dec. 21
Southern U.	Jan. 4
Alcorn St.	Jan. 6
Prairie View ■	Jan. 11
Texas Southern ■	Jan. 13

Jackson St.	Jan. 18
Alabama St.	Jan. 20
Mississippi Val. ■	Jan. 25
Southern U. [Monroe]	Feb. 1
Alcorn St. ■	Feb. 3
Prairie View	Feb. 8
Texas Southern	Feb. 10
Jackson St. [Monroe]	Feb. 15
Alabama St. ■	Feb. 17
Mississippi Val.	Feb. 22
Southwestern Conf. Tr.	Mar. 5-8

1995-96 RESULTS (12-16)
61	Hampton †	71
62	Hartford †	59
86	Texas-Arlington	82
69	Pepperdine †	62
80	Nebraska	96
91	Bapt. Christian ■	65
100	Wiley ■	86
57	Ark.-Little Rock ■	62
66	Georgia St. ■	76
68	Southeastern La. ■	74
69	Northwestern St.	89
89	Southern U. †	92
92	Alcorn St. ■	76
75	Texas Southern	87
110	Prairie View	75
67	Ark.-Little Rock	91
72	Alabama St. ■	83
54	Jackson St. †	56
70	Mississippi Val.	76
77	Alcorn St.	65
69	Southern U.	72
77	Texas Southern †	61
96	Prairie View ■	92
78	Alabama St.	68
68	Jackson St.	70
72	Mississippi Val. ■	78
71	Alabama St.	59
57	Jackson St. †	60

Nickname: Tigers
Colors: Black & Gold
Arena: Tiger Memorial Gym
  Capacity: 4,500; Year Built: 1954
AD: Wilbert Ellis
SID: Vernon Cheek

GRAND CANYON
Phoenix, AZ 85017 II

Coach: Leighton McCrary
Alma Mater: Philander Smith '74
Record: 6 Years, W-114, L-61

1996-97 SCHEDULE
Grand Canyon Inv.	Nov. 22-23
Southern Colo. Cl.	Nov. 29-30
St. Thomas (Minn.) ■	Dec. 3
North Dakota Cl.	Dec. 21-22
Grand Canyon Cl.	Dec. 27-28
Anderson (Ind.) ■	Dec. 31
St. Ambrose ■	Jan. 4
St. Thomas Aquinas ■	Jan. 7
Christian Heritage ■	Jan. 10
Cal St. San B'dino ■	Jan. 16
UC Riverside	Jan. 18
Cal St. Los Angeles	Jan. 23
Cal St. Bakersfield ■	Jan. 25
Cal Poly Pomona ■	Jan. 30
Cal St. Dom. Hills ■	Feb. 1
UC Riverside	Feb. 8
Cal St. Los Angeles ■	Feb. 13
Cal St. Bakersfield ■	Feb. 15
Cal Poly Pomona ■	Feb. 20
Cal St. Dom. Hills ■	Feb. 22
Master's ■	Feb. 25
Cal St. San B'dino	Mar. 1

1995-96 RESULTS (23-6)
89	Tarleton St. ■	71
85	North Dak. ■	71
106	Colo. Christian ■	68
95	Central Ark. ■	87
76	Concordia (Cal.) ■	69
69	Black Hills St. ■	67

87	Cal St. Stanislaus ■	67
106	Clarke ■	59
102	Central Okla. †	76
79	Washburn †	80
104	Southwestern (Kan.) ■	73
78	Master's ■	69
78	Cal St. Northridge	67
106	Pacific Christian ■	54
92	IU/PU-Indianapolis ■	83
77	Cal St. Los Angeles ■	55
68	Cal St. Bakersfield ■	66
78	Cal Poly Pomona ■	76
84	Cal St. Dom. Hills ■	74
93	Cal St. San B'dino ■	88
69	UC Riverside	77
59	Cal St. Bakersfield ■	57
73	Cal Poly Pomona ■	85
80	Cal St. Dom. Hills ■	86
97	Cal St. San B'dino ■	99
86	UC Riverside ■	78
79	Cal St. Los Angeles	71
105	Alas. Anchorage †	96
65	Cal St. Bakersfield	71

Nickname: Antelopes
Colors: Purple & White
Arena: Antelope Gym
  Capacity: 2,000; Year Built: 1994
AD: B. Keith Baker
SID: Deron Filip

GRAND VALLEY ST.
Allendale, MI 49401 II

Coach: Jay Smith
Alma Mater: Saginaw Valley '84
(First year as head coach)

1996-97 SCHEDULE
Madonna ■	Nov. 16
Wayne St. (Mich.)	Nov. 18
Michigan Christian ■	Nov. 20
Ball St.	Nov. 23
St. Mary's (Mich.) ■	Nov. 26
Grand Rapids Cl.	Nov. 29-30
Mercyhurst	Dec. 5
Gannon	Dec. 7
Wayne St. (Mich.) ■	Dec. 21
Hillsdale ■	Dec. 23
Michigan Tech	Jan. 2
Northern Mich.	Jan. 4
Lake Superior St. ■	Jan. 11
Ferris St.	Jan. 13
Saginaw Valley ■	Jan. 16
Northwood ■	Jan. 18
Ashland ■	Jan. 23
IU/PU-Indianapolis	Jan. 25
Oakland	Feb. 1
Michigan Tech ■	Feb. 6
Northern Mich. ■	Feb. 8
Ferris St. ■	Feb. 10
Lake Superior St.	Feb. 15
Saginaw Valley	Feb. 20
Northwood	Feb. 22

1995-96 RESULTS (11-15)
63	Union (Ky.) †	75
60	Bethel (Tenn.) †	76
70	West Fla. †	84
76	Nova Southeastern †	60
89	Aquinas	63
65	Lewis ■	74
64	Northern Mich. ■	71
93	Lake Superior St. ■	75
75	Geneva †	85
89	Spring Arbor †	94
79	Saginaw Valley	84
64	Michigan Tech	73
74	Ferris St. ■	65
73	Oakland ■	93
95	Hillsdale	65
98	Northwood	80
78	Wayne St. (Mich.) ■	90
79	Ashland	69
87	Mercyhurst ■	72
74	Gannon ■	79

94	Ferris St.	79
94	Lake Superior St.	100
95	Mercyhurst	89
52	Michigan Tech ■	67
79	Ashland ■	86
68	Hillsdale ■	57

Nickname: Lakers
Colors: Blue, Black & White
Arena: Grand Valley Field House
  Capacity: 4,010; Year Built: 1982
AD: Tim Selgo
SID: Robert McKinney

GREENSBORO
Greensboro, NC 27420..........III

Coach: Bill Chambers
Alma Mater: North Caro. '76
Record: 10 Years, W-149, L-115

1996-97 SCHEDULE
Dickinson Tr.	Nov. 22-23
Citadel	Nov. 27
Warren Wilson	Dec. 3
Newport News App. ■	Dec. 7
Guilford [Greensboro]	Dec. 10
Winston-Salem	Dec. 13
Wittenberg Cl.	Dec. 27-28
Catholic Cl.	Jan. 11-12
Methodist	Jan. 15
Averett	Jan. 18
N.C. Wesleyan ■	Jan. 22
Shenandoah ■	Jan. 26
Chris. Newport ■	Feb. 1
Ferrum	Feb. 3
Methodist ■	Feb. 5
Averett	Feb. 8
Maryville (Tenn.) ■	Feb. 10
Shenandoah	Feb. 15
Ferrum ■	Feb. 18
Chris. Newport	Feb. 21
N.C. Wesleyan	Feb. 22

1995-96 RESULTS (9-16)
83	Baldwin-Wallace †	93
80	Frostburg St.	74
85	Barber-Scotia	101
100	Warren Wilson ■	70
80	Maryville (Tenn.)	86
63	Guilford †	78
73	Newport News App. ■	70
79	Illinois Tech †	69
87	Warner Southern	84
59	Life (Ga.) †	90
69	Methodist ■	51
99	Averett	76
81	Shenandoah	86
74	Newport News App.	89
76	Ferrum ■	78
78	N.C. Wesleyan	86
58	Chris. Newport	77
85	Methodist	88
65	Averett ■	66
66	N.C. Wesleyan ■	55
81	Shenandoah	94
70	Ferrum	75
59	Chris. Newport ■	63
86	Ferrum †	67
67	Chris. Newport †	74

Nickname: The Pride
Colors: Green & White
Arena: Hanes Gymnasium
  Capacity: 850; Year Built: 1964
AD: Kim Stroble
SID: Scott Rash

GRINNELL
Grinnell, IA 50112..............III

Coach: David Arseneault
Alma Mater: Colby '76
Record: 7 Years, W-75, L-80

1996-97 SCHEDULE

Grinnell Tr.	Nov. 22-23
Simpson	Nov. 26
Luther	Nov. 30
Knox ■	Dec. 6
Illinois Col. ■	Dec. 7
Teikyo Marycrest ■	Dec. 11
Mt. Mercy	Dec. 14
Martin Luther ■	Jan. 8
Knox	Jan. 10
Illinois Col.	Jan. 11
Lake Forest	Jan. 17
Ripon	Jan. 18
Lawrence ■	Jan. 24
St. Norbert ■	Jan. 25
Coe	Feb. 1
Cornell College ■	Feb. 5
Monmouth (Ill.) ■	Feb. 8
Iowa Wesleyan	Feb. 13
Coe ■	Feb. 15
Cornell College	Feb. 19
Monmouth (Ill.)	Feb. 22

1995-96 RESULTS (17-8)

132	Colorado Col. ■	110
152	Chicago ■	137
103	Mt. Mercy	127
137	Simpson	157
79	Luther ■	114
124	Illinois Col. ■	112
123	Knox ■	96
98	Monmouth (Ill.) ■	88
95	Mt. Mercy ■	103
110	Iowa Wesleyan ■	101
107	Illinois Col.	94
86	Knox	73
104	Cornell College	107
95	Lake Forest ■	74
113	Ripon ■	119
81	St. Norbert	62
70	Lawrence	95
92	Coe ■	85
86	Monmouth (Ill.)	72
97	Iowa Wesleyan	77
88	Cornell College ■	64
75	Coe	73
109	Carroll (Wis.) ■	106
114	Ripon ■	92
117	Wheaton (Ill.)	131

Nickname: Pioneers
Colors: Scarlet & Black
Arena: Darby Gym
Capacity: 1,250; Year Built: 1942
AD: Dee Fairchild
SID: Andy Hamilton

GROVE CITY

Grove City, PA 16127 III

Coach: John Barr
Alma Mater: Ohio St. '60
Record: 24 Years, W-299, L-269

1996-97 SCHEDULE

Carnegie Mellon [Washington]	Nov. 22
Allegheny	Nov. 23
Wooster ■	Nov. 26
La Roche	Dec. 3
Hilbert ■	Dec. 7
Hiram	Dec. 11
Pitt.-Greensburg ■	Dec. 14
Defiance Tr.	Dec. 27-28
Penn St.-Behrend	Jan. 4
La Roche ■	Jan. 7
Pitt.-Bradford ■	Jan. 9
Geneva ■	Jan. 11
Penn St.-Behrend ■	Jan. 15
Alfred	Jan. 18
Bethany (W.Va.) ■	Jan. 22
Alfred ■	Jan. 25
Wash. & Jeff.	Jan. 29
Thiel	Feb. 1
Waynesburg ■	Feb. 5
Bethany (W.Va.)	Feb. 8
Wash. & Jeff. ■	Feb. 15
Thiel ■	Feb. 19
Waynesburg	Feb. 22

1995-96 RESULTS (16-10)

86	Allegheny †	91
64	Carnegie Mellon ■	68
61	La Roche	68
68	Hilbert	50
56	Geneva ■	82
70	Westminster (Pa.)	57
63	Hiram ■	50
53	Mount Union †	59
63	Dickinson †	43
66	Lincoln (Pa.) †	59
67	Frostburg St.	58
78	La Roche ■	64
66	Pitt.-Bradford	71
52	Geneva	72
56	Penn St.-Behrend ■	55
87	Thiel ■	56
78	Wash. & Jeff. ■	64
59	Bethany (W.Va.)	48
53	Waynesburg	56
74	Penn St.-Behrend	60
95	Thiel	58
78	Wash. & Jeff.	63
74	Bethany (W.Va.) ■	46
71	Waynesburg ■	59
50	Waynesburg †	59
70	Misericordia †	76

Nickname: Wolverines
Colors: Crimson & White
Arena: College Arena
Capacity: 1,800; Year Built: 1953
AD: Chris Smith
SID: Joe Klimchak

GUILFORD

Greensboro, NC 27410...........III

Coach: Jack Jensen
Alma Mater: Wake Forest '61
Record: 26 Years, W-369, L-336

1996-97 SCHEDULE

Guilford Inv.	Nov. 22-23
Averett	Nov. 26
Va. Wesleyan ■	Nov. 30
Ferrum	Dec. 2
Lynchburg ■	Dec. 4
Wash. & Lee	Dec. 6
Greensboro [Greensboro]	Dec. 10
Emory & Henry	Dec. 14
Bridgewater (Va.)	Jan. 9
Hampden-Sydney	Jan. 11
Randolph-Macon	Jan. 15
East. Mennonite ■	Jan. 17
Bridgewater (Va.) ■	Jan. 18
Roanoke ■	Jan. 22
East. Mennonite	Jan. 25
Lynchburg	Jan. 26
Randolph-Macon ■	Jan. 31
Wash. & Lee ■	Feb. 1
Hampden-Sydney ■	Feb. 5
Newport News App.	Feb. 7
Va. Wesleyan	Feb. 8
Emory & Henry ■	Feb. 12
Roanoke	Feb. 17

1995-96 RESULTS (7-17)

57	Warren Wilson ■	44
75	Va. Intermont ■	62
67	Bridgewater (Va.) ■	69
61	Va. Wesleyan	68
65	Averett ■	53
56	Lynchburg	80
87	Wash. & Lee ■	72
78	Greensboro †	63
73	Ferrum ■	94
78	Emory & Henry ■	100
56	Hampden-Sydney ■	83
76	Randolph-Macon ■	65
70	East. Mennonite	83
65	Bridgewater (Va.)	70
70	Roanoke	112
62	East. Mennonite ■	65
61	Lynchburg ■	74
54	Randolph-Macon	87
84	Wash. & Lee	76
72	Hampden-Sydney	84
70	Va. Wesleyan ■	75
64	Emory & Henry	86
68	Chowan	82
72	Roanoke ■	76

Nickname: Quakers
Colors: Crimson & Gray
Arena: Ragan-Brown Field House
Capacity: 2,500; Year Built: 1980
AD: Mike Ketchum (Interim)
SID: Dave Walters

GUST. ADOLPHUS

St. Peter, MN 56082..............III

Coach: Mark Hanson
Alma Mater: Gust. Adolphus '83
Record: 6 Years, W-105, L-53

1996-97 SCHEDULE

Luther	Nov. 25
Concordia-St. Paul	Dec. 2
Bethel (Minn.)	Dec. 7
Concordia-M'head	Dec. 11
Concordia (Cal.)	Dec. 28
UC San Diego	Dec. 31
Augsburg	Jan. 4
St. Olaf ■	Jan. 6
St. Mary's (Minn.) ■	Jan. 8
Hamline	Jan. 11
Carleton	Jan. 13
St. Thomas (Minn.) ■	Jan. 15
Macalester ■	Jan. 18
St. John's (Minn.)	Jan. 22
Bethel (Minn.) ■	Jan. 25
Concordia-M'head ■	Jan. 29
Augsburg ■	Feb. 3
St. Olaf	Feb. 5
St. Mary's (Minn.)	Feb. 8
Hamline ■	Feb. 12
Carleton ■	Feb. 15
St. Thomas (Minn.)	Feb. 17
Macalester	Feb. 19
St. John's (Minn.) ■	Feb. 22

1995-96 RESULTS (24-5)

61	Luther ■	51
71	N'western (Minn.)	64
65	Carleton ■	58
66	St. Mary's (Minn.) ■	47
74	Concordia-M'head ■	62
62	Buena Vista	75
84	N'western (Minn.) †	76
64	Bethel (Minn.) ■	63
48	Macalester	36
85	Hamline ■	48
78	St. Olaf	74
68	Augsburg	58
73	St. Thomas (Minn.) ■	77
84	St. John's (Minn.) ■	66
73	Carleton	57
54	St. Mary's (Minn.)	52
69	Concordia-M'head	62
71	Bethel (Minn.)	54
69	Macalester ■	48
77	Hamline	68
64	St. Olaf ■	75
80	Augsburg ■	74
77	St. Thomas (Minn.)	63
80	St. John's (Minn.)	64
76	St. Thomas (Minn.) ■	62
43	Concordia-M'head ■	47
72	Concordia-M'head ■	61
61	Wis.-Oshkosh ■	60
68	Wittenberg	76

Nickname: Golden Gusties
Colors: Black & Gold
Arena: Gus Young Court
Capacity: 3,000; Year Built: 1984
AD: James Malmquist
SID: Tim Kennedy

HAMILTON

Clinton, NY 13323 III

Coach: Tom Murphy
Alma Mater: Springfield '60
Record: 26 Years, W-459, L-192

1996-97 SCHEDULE

Utica/Rome ■	Dec. 3
Rensselaer ■	Dec. 6
Skidmore ■	Dec. 7
Hobart ■	Dec. 10
Oneonta St.	Jan. 8
Hamilton Inv.	Jan. 11-12
Bates	Jan. 18
Colby	Jan. 19
St. Lawrence	Jan. 24
Clarkson	Jan. 25
Williams ■	Jan. 29
Union (N.Y.)	Jan. 31
Amherst	Feb. 1
Utica ■	Feb. 4
Rensselaer	Feb. 7
Tufts	Feb. 8
Skidmore	Feb. 11
Union (N.Y.) ■	Feb. 14
Clarkson ■	Feb. 21
St. Lawrence ■	Feb. 22
Rochester ■	Feb. 26
Hobart	Feb. 28

1995-96 RESULTS (16-9)

90	Hobart ■	75
83	MIT †	65
69	Washington (Mo.)	91
81	Union (N.Y.)	77
95	St. Lawrence ■	83
69	Clarkson ■	57
75	Thomas More †	81
87	Hobart †	70
83	Colby ■	68
77	Bowdoin ■	72
79	Rensselaer ■	86
92	Skidmore	76
65	Williams	83
89	Union (N.Y.) ■	68
77	Amherst ■	86
85	Utica	82
89	Rensselaer ■	79
90	Tufts ■	91
73	Rochester	77
66	Skidmore ■	68
88	Clarkson	66
85	St. Lawrence	71
72	Utica/Rome	66
75	Hobart	73
78	St. Lawrence ■	85

Nickname: Continentals
Colors: Buff & Blue
Arena: Scott Field House
Capacity: 2,500; Year Built: 1978
AD: Thomas Murphy
SID: Marc Simon

HAMLINE

St. Paul, MN 55104................III

Coach: Tom Gilles
Alma Mater: Iowa '86
Record: 1 Year, W-6, L-18

1996-97 SCHEDULE

St. Scholastica	Nov. 26
Concordia-St. Paul	Dec. 4
Macalester ■	Dec. 7
Wis.-River Falls	Dec. 11
St. Thomas (Minn.)	Dec. 14
St. John's (Minn.)	Jan. 4
St. Mary's (Minn.) ■	Jan. 6
Carleton	Jan. 8
Gust. Adolphus ■	Jan. 11
Augsburg ■	Jan. 13
Concordia-M'head	Jan. 15
Bethel (Minn.)	Jan. 18
St. Olaf ■	Jan. 22

Macalester	Jan. 25
N'western (Minn.) ■	Jan. 28
St. Thomas (Minn.) ■	Feb. 1
St. John's (Minn.) ■	Feb. 3
St. Mary's (Minn.)	Feb. 5
Carleton ■	Feb. 8
Gust. Adolphus	Feb. 12
Augsburg	Feb. 15
Concordia-M'head ■	Feb. 17
Bethel (Minn.) ■	Feb. 19
St. Olaf	Feb. 22

1995-96 RESULTS (6-18)

77	Concordia-M'head ■	90
67	Chapman †	70
90	UC Santa Cruz †	78
80	UC San Diego †	94
82	Augsburg ■	90
46	St. Thomas (Minn.) ■	59
81	St. John's (Minn.) ■	86
72	N'western (Minn.)	79
48	Gust. Adolphus	85
74	St. Mary's (Minn.) ■	62
76	Bethel (Minn.)	85
64	St. Olaf	92
78	Carleton ■	91
71	Macalester	67
75	Concordia-M'head	95
57	Augsburg	73
60	St. Thomas (Minn.)	64
64	St. John's (Minn.)	75
68	Gust. Adolphus ■	77
73	St. Mary's (Minn.)	66
82	Bethel (Minn.) ■	76
81	St. Olaf ■	85
58	Carleton	76
100	Macalester ■	82

Nickname: Pipers
Colors: Red & Grey
Arena: Hutton Fieldhouse
Capacity: 2,000; Year Built: 1940
AD: Dick Tressel
SID: Tom Gilles

HAMPDEN-SYDNEY

Hampden-Sydney, VA 23943 ... III

Coach: Tony Shaver
Alma Mater: North Caro. '76
Record: 10 Years, W-184, L-88

1996-97 SCHEDULE

Hampden-Sydney Cl.	Nov. 22-23
Newport News App. ■	Nov. 26
Averett ■	Dec. 2
Wash. & Lee	Dec. 4
Lynchburg	Dec. 7
Bridgewater (Va.) ■	Dec. 11
Oglethorpe Cl.	Dec. 29-30
Randolph-Macon	Jan. 8
Guilford ■	Jan. 11
Va. Wesleyan ■	Jan. 15
Emory & Henry ■	Jan. 18
Bridgewater (Va.)	Jan. 20
Randolph-Macon ■	Jan. 22
Emory & Henry	Jan. 25
Wash. & Lee ■	Jan. 29
Roanoke	Feb. 1
East. Mennonite ■	Feb. 3
Guilford	Feb. 5
Roanoke ■	Feb. 8
Va. Wesleyan	Feb. 12
East. Mennonite	Feb. 15
Lynchburg ■	Feb. 17

1995-96 RESULTS (17-9)

104	Wesley ■	74
87	Staten Island ■	73
87	St. Mary's (Md.) †	72
65	Wash. & Lee ■	60
61	Lynchburg	66
67	Mary Washington	60
60	Bridgewater (Va.)	67
78	Randolph-Macon ■	81
77	P.R.-Arecibo	75
59	P.R.-Mayaguez	62
72	Va. Wesleyan	66
98	Emory & Henry ■	72
70	Bridgewater (Va.) ■	74
70	Randolph-Macon	77
81	Emory & Henry	94
97	Wash. & Lee	75
82	Roanoke ■	68
88	East. Mennonite	76
84	Guilford ■	72
78	Roanoke	85
83	Guilford	56
70	Va. Wesleyan ■	61
98	East. Mennonite ■	75
87	Lynchburg ■	49
80	Va. Wesleyan †	68
73	Roanoke †	77

Nickname: Tigers
Colors: Garnet & Grey
Arena: Douglass Fleet Gymnasium
Capacity: 2,700; Year Built: 1979
AD: Joe Bush
SID: Dean Hybl

HAMPTON

Hampton, VA 23668 ... I

Coach: Byron Samuels
Alma Mater: N.C.-Asheville '86
Record: 1 Year, W-9, L-17

1996-97 SCHEDULE

William & Mary ■	Nov. 25
Manhattan	Dec. 1
Iona	Dec. 4
Liberty ■	Dec. 16
James Madison	Dec. 18
N.C.-Greensboro	Dec. 21
New Orleans Cl.	Dec. 27-28
Bethune-Cookman ■	Jan. 2
Florida A&M ■	Jan. 4
South Caro. St.	Jan. 7
Coppin St. ■	Jan. 11
Coppin St.	Jan. 18
Delaware St.	Jan. 22
Morgan St. ■	Jan. 25
Howard	Jan. 27
North Caro. A&T ■	Jan. 30
Md.-East. Shore ■	Feb. 3
Florida A&M	Feb. 5
Howard ■	Feb. 8
Morgan St.	Feb. 10
South Caro. St. ■	Feb. 13
Md.-East. Shore	Feb. 18
North Caro. A&T	Feb. 20
Bethune-Cookman	Feb. 26
Delaware St. ■	Mar. 1
Mid-Eastern Conf. Tr.	Mar. 5-8

1995-96 RESULTS (9-17)

71	Grambling †	61
73	Geo. Washington	80
67	Old Dominion	75
69	Marist	87
62	Niagara †	64
83	Citadel	66
86	James Madison †	88
78	N.C.-Greensboro ■	86
84	William & Mary	76
80	Coastal Caro.	87
74	George Mason	84
88	Va. Wesleyan	73
65	Dayton	91
95	Marshall	123
62	Campbell	63
69	Iona ■	91
64	Manhattan ■	98
65	South Caro. St.	83
81	Maine ■	84
77	Liberty	72
88	Barton ■	76
71	South Caro. St. ■	61
67	Maine	66
68	Oral Roberts ■	72
95	Coastal Caro. ■	66
54	Oral Roberts	96

Nickname: Pirates
Colors: Royal Blue & White
Arena: Convocation Center
Capacity: 7,200; Year Built: 1993
AD: Dr. Dennis Thomas
SID: LeCounte Conaway

HANOVER

Hanover, IN 47243 ... III

Coach: Mike Beitzel
Alma Mater: Wooster '68
Record: 16 Years, W-267, L-186

1996-97 SCHEDULE

Anderson/Hanover Cl.	Nov. 22-23
Ind.-Southeast ■	Nov. 25
Wittenberg ■	Nov. 30
Centre ■	Dec. 3
Hanover Tr.	Dec. 6-7
Wilmington (Ohio) ■	Dec. 16
Bluffton	Dec. 21
Oglethorpe Cl.	Dec. 29-30
Franklin ■	Jan. 8
Rose-Hulman	Jan. 11
Manchester	Jan. 15
Wabash	Jan. 18
Thomas More	Jan. 22
DePauw ■	Jan. 25
Anderson (Ind.) ■	Jan. 29
Manchester ■	Feb. 1
Franklin	Feb. 5
Rose-Hulman ■	Feb. 8
Wabash ■	Feb. 15
Anderson (Ind.)	Feb. 18
DePauw	Feb. 22

1995-96 RESULTS (21-6)

97	Cincinnati Bible ■	31
51	Purdue-Calumet ■	48
63	Thomas More ■	58
53	Butler	56
91	Goshen ■	55
73	Union (Ky.) ■	66
57	Centre	51
83	Wilmington (Ohio)	43
86	Bluffton ■	53
78	Rollins	81
97	Franklin	88
59	Rose-Hulman ■	55
82	Manchester ■	56
80	Wabash ■	83
78	Ind.-Southeast	84
60	DePauw	53
74	Anderson (Ind.)	55
63	Manchester	60
91	Franklin ■	63
58	Rose-Hulman	57
102	Asbury ■	56
74	Wabash	47
59	Anderson (Ind.) ■	54
75	DePauw ■	49
74	Rose-Hulman ■	75
85	Fontbonne ■	43
67	Ill. Wesleyan	73

Nickname: Panthers
Colors: Red & Blue
Arena: John Collier Arena
Capacity: 2,000; Year Built: 1995
AD: Dick Naylor
SID: Carter Cloyd

HARDIN-SIMMONS

Abilene, TX 79698 ... III

Coach: Dennis Harp
Alma Mater: Mt. Marty '78
Record: 8 Years, W-122, L-88

1996-97 SCHEDULE

Mid-America Bible ■	Nov. 22
Southern Methodist	Nov. 23
Dallas Christian ■	Nov. 25
Bay Ridge Christian ■	Nov. 26
Mid-America Bible	Dec. 3
Hillsdale Free Will ■	Dec. 5
SW'ern of Christ.Min	Dec. 7
Southwest Tex. St.	Dec. 14
Sul Ross St.	Jan. 2
Bay Ridge Christian ■	Jan. 6
McMurry ■	Jan. 11
Howard Payne ■	Jan. 16
Sul Ross St. ■	Jan. 18
Dallas	Jan. 23
Austin	Jan. 25
SW'ern of Christ. Min ■	Jan. 28
Dallas Christian ■	Jan. 30
Ozarks (Ark.)	Feb. 1
McMurry	Feb. 8
Howard Payne	Feb. 13
Sul Ross St.	Feb. 15
Dallas ■	Feb. 20
Austin ■	Feb. 22
Ozarks (Ark.) ■	Mar. 1

1995-96 RESULTS (19-5)

92	Mid-America Bible ■	78
109	Southwest Adventist ■	71
45	Southern Methodist	74
109	Mid-America Bible	85
102	Southwestern Aly God	76
105	Hillsdale Free Will	76
84	Hillsdale Free Will ■	76
110	Southwest Adventist †	51
79	Sul Ross St. †	61
47	Baylor	93
74	National Christian ■	49
105	Southwestern Aly God ■	75
87	Faith Bapt. Bible ■	63
89	Howard Payne	93
109	Sul Ross St. ■	76
88	Dallas ■	71
103	McMurry	91
119	Austin ■	113
88	Howard Payne ■	101
67	Sul Ross St.	53
79	Southwest Adventist	66
89	McMurry ■	94
98	Dallas	85
85	Austin	80

Nickname: Cowboys
Colors: Purple & Gold
Arena: Mabee Complex
Capacity: 3,003; Year Built: 1979
AD: Jimmie Keeling
SID: John Neese

HARTFORD

West Hartford, CT 06117 ... I

Coach: Paul Brazeau
Alma Mater: Boston College '81
Record: 4 Years, W-47, L-64

1996-97 SCHEDULE

Yale	Nov. 22
Fairleigh Dickinson ■	Nov. 26
St. Francis (N.Y.) ■	Dec. 3
Vermont ■	Dec. 7
Siena	Dec. 10
Miami (Fla.)	Dec. 13
St. Peter's ■	Dec. 21
Connecticut	Dec. 29
Holy Cross	Dec. 31
Drexel	Jan. 2
Hofstra	Jan. 4
Maine ■	Jan. 7
Delaware	Jan. 10
Towson St.	Jan. 12
Boston U. ■	Jan. 16
Northeastern ■	Jan. 19
New Hampshire ■	Jan. 21
Vermont	Jan. 25
New Hampshire	Jan. 30
Maine	Feb. 1
Delaware ■	Feb. 6
Towson St. ■	Feb. 8
Northeastern	Feb. 13
Boston U.	Feb. 15
Drexel ■	Feb. 20

Hofstra ■ ...Feb. 22
America East Conf. Tr. ....Feb. 28-Mar. 2

1995-96 RESULTS (6-22)

69	Geo. Washington	81
59	Grambling †	62
71	Fairfield ■	79
70	Bucknell	80
77	Hofstra ■	58
72	Drexel ■	79
70	Siena ■	76
67	Boston College	106
63	Connecticut	102
68	Boston U. ■	75
83	Northeastern	74
68	New Hampshire	89
80	Vermont	107
79	Delaware ■	77
73	Towson St. ■	88
66	Maine	79
66	Delaware	90
73	Towson St.	81
95	Vermont ■	98
92	Holy Cross ■	95
65	Boston U.	79
82	Northeastern ■	79
67	Maine	92
87	New Hampshire ■	66
56	Drexel	74
77	Hofstra	83
76	New Hampshire †	73
71	Drexel †	83

Nickname: Hawks
Colors: Scarlet & White
Arena: The Sports Center
   Capacity: 4,475; Year Built: 1990
AD: Pat Meiser-McKnett
SID: James R. Keener Jr

HARTWICK
Oneonta, NY 13820 ...III

Coach: Nick Lambros
Alma Mater: Hartwick '61
Record: 19 Years, W-336, L-159

1996-97 SCHEDULE

Hartwick Cl. ...Nov. 22-23
Skidmore ...Nov. 26
Clarkson ■ ...Dec. 3
Cazenovia ...Dec. 6
Binghamton ■ ...Jan. 9
Springfield ...Jan. 11
Oswego St. ■ ...Jan. 17
Elmira ■ ...Jan. 17
Ithaca ■ ...Jan. 18
Oneonta St. ...Jan. 21
Utica ■ ...Jan. 25
Union (N.Y.) ■ ...Jan. 28
Ithaca ...Jan. 31
Elmira ...Feb. 1
Rensselaer ■ ...Feb. 4
Rochester Inst. ...Feb. 7
Nazareth ...Feb. 8
Keuka ■ ...Feb. 10
Utica ...Feb. 12
St. John Fisher ...Feb. 15
St. Lawrence ...Feb. 18
Nazareth ■ ...Feb. 21
Rochester Inst. ■ ...Feb. 22

1995-96 RESULTS (17-9)

76	Manhattanville ■	45
69	Elmira	53
69	Oswego St.	67
70	Wooster †	75
55	Rochester	50
79	Skidmore ■	72
80	Nazareth	84
74	Elmira	70
85	Chapman †	82
57	Whittier	67
76	Binghamton	66
65	Rensselaer	71
94	Oneonta St. ■	68
72	Keuka	72
57	Springfield ■	54
90	Union (N.Y.)	81
69	St. John Fisher ■	49
78	Hilbert ■	44
72	Alfred ■	58
79	Utica ■	69
61	Rochester Inst. ■	73
46	Ithaca	55
68	St. Lawrence	75
64	Clarkson	75
65	Ithaca ■	44
55	Rensselaer	68

Nickname: Hawks
Colors: Royal Blue & White
Arena: Binder P.E. Center
   Capacity: 1,800; Year Built: 1968
AD: Ken Kutler
SID: Dave Caspole

HARVARD
Cambridge, MA 02138 ...I

Coach: Frank Sullivan
Alma Mater: Westfield St. '73
Record: 12 Years, W-156, L-174

1996-97 SCHEDULE

Lafayette ...Nov. 26
New Hampshire ■ ...Nov. 30
Babson ■ ...Dec. 2
Army ...Dec. 4
Holy Cross ■ ...Dec. 7
Boston U. ■ ...Dec. 10
Dartmouth ■ ...Dec. 17
Colgate ...Dec. 20
Vermont ■ ...Dec. 22
New Orleans Cl. ...Dec. 27-28
Navy ...Jan. 2
Dartmouth ...Jan. 6
Columbia ■ ...Jan. 10
Cornell ■ ...Jan. 11
Lehigh ■ ...Jan. 28
Brown ■ ...Jan. 31
Yale ■ ...Feb. 1
Pennsylvania ...Feb. 7
Princeton ...Feb. 8
Cornell ...Feb. 14
Columbia ...Feb. 15
Princeton ■ ...Feb. 21
Pennsylvania ■ ...Feb. 22
Yale ...Feb. 28
Brown ...Mar. 1

1995-96 RESULTS (15-11)

108	Babson ■	60
89	Army ■	60
64	Lafayette ■	44
92	Holy Cross	64
70	Lehigh	80
61	Dartmouth ■	70
81	Vermont ■	72
60	Boston U.	72
64	Cal Poly SLO	65
59	Stanford	65
49	Navy ■	48
59	Dartmouth	40
63	Colgate ■	54
65	Cornell ■	47
72	Columbia ■	48
66	New Hampshire	61
62	Yale	47
70	Brown	73
44	Princeton ■	49
63	Pennsylvania ■	77
71	Columbia	44
65	Cornell	60
64	Pennsylvania	66
58	Princeton	65
62	Brown	75
87	Yale ■	67

Nickname: Crimson
Colors: Crimson, Black & White
Arena: Lavietes Pavilion
   Capacity: 2,195; Year Built: 1926
AD: William Cleary
SID: John Veneziano

HAVERFORD
Haverford, PA 19041 ...III

Coach: Mike Mucci
Alma Mater: Villanova '77
Record: 1 Year, W-14, L-10

1996-97 SCHEDULE

Swarthmore Cl. ...Nov. 22-23
Catholic ■ ...Nov. 26
Cornell ...Dec. 2
Gettysburg ■ ...Dec. 4
Frank. & Marsh. ...Dec. 7
Ursinus ...Dec. 11
Lafayette ...Dec. 20
Emory ...Jan. 3
Sewanee ...Jan. 4
Wash. & Lee ...Jan. 6
Gallaudet ...Jan. 12
Phila. Pharmacy ...Jan. 14
Wesleyan (Conn.) ...Jan. 18
Washington (Md.) ...Jan. 22
Dickinson ...Jan. 25
Muhlenberg ■ ...Jan. 28
Western Md. ...Feb. 1
Swarthmore ...Feb. 5
Johns Hopkins ...Feb. 8
Ursinus ■ ...Feb. 12
Muhlenberg ...Feb. 15
Washington (Md.) ■ ...Feb. 19
Swarthmore ■ ...Feb. 22

1995-96 RESULTS (14-10)

58	Amherst ■	77
71	Macalester †	65
65	Phila. Pharmacy ■	78
89	Gallaudet	70
60	Frank. & Marsh. ■	65
70	Ursinus ■	73
69	Gettysburg	85
70	Beaver	71
49	Methodist †	45
77	Binghamton	69
97	Gwynedd-Mercy	69
81	Washington (Md.) ■	78
82	Dickinson ■	67
74	Muhlenberg	68
69	King's (Pa.)	67
87	Western Md.	71
46	Princeton	75
58	Swarthmore ■	44
73	Johns Hopkins ■	68
80	Ursinus	56
76	Muhlenberg ■	66
69	Washington (Md.)	78
55	Swarthmore	56
68	Gettysburg	69

Nickname: Fords
Colors: Scarlet & Black
Arena: Alumni Fieldhouse
   Capacity: 1,200; Year Built: 1957
AD: Greg Kannerstein
SID: Mike Wilhelm

HAWAII
Honolulu, HI 96822 ...I

Coach: Riley Wallace
Alma Mater: Centenary (La.) '64
Record: 11 Years, W-149, L-162

1996-97 SCHEDULE

Tex.-Pan American ■ ...Nov. 26
Hawaii Tip-Off ...Nov. 29-Dec. 1
Hawaii Inv. ...Dec. 6-7
Hawaii Festival ...Dec. 14-15
Hawaii Rainbow Cl. ...Dec. 27-30
New Mexico ■ ...Jan. 4
Air Force ...Jan. 9
UNLV ...Jan. 11
Colorado St. ■ ...Jan. 16
Wyoming ■ ...Jan. 18
San Diego St. ...Jan. 25
San Jose St. ...Jan. 30
Fresno St. ...Feb. 1
UNLV ■ ...Feb. 6
Air Force ■ ...Feb. 8
Wyoming ...Feb. 13
Colorado St. ...Feb. 15
San Diego St. ■ ...Feb. 19
New Mexico ...Feb. 22
Fresno St. ■ ...Feb. 27
San Jose St. ■ ...Mar. 1
Western Ath. Conf. Tr. ...Mar. 4-8

1995-96 RESULTS (10-18)

78	Dayton ■	72
72	St. Louis ■	66
66	Long Beach St.	71
80	Loyola Marymount	82
84	Creighton ■	58
74	Rhode Island ■	89
81	Illinois ■	82
89	Missouri ■	95
63	Wyoming ■	53
69	Colorado St. ■	74
75	UTEP	85
72	New Mexico	78
46	Utah	82
77	Brigham Young ■	78
83	Air Force	92
80	Fresno St.	84
88	San Diego St. ■	79
94	San Diego St.	103
81	Air Force ■	62
97	Fresno St. ■	76
59	Utah	69
94	Brigham Young	89
83	UTEP ■	75
79	New Mexico ■	88
78	Wyoming	95
75	Colorado St.	65
69	UTEP †	77
63	Utah †	76

Nickname: Rainbows
Colors: Green & White
Arena: Special Events Arena
   Capacity: 10,225; Year Built: 1994
AD: Hugh Yoshida
SID: Lois Manin

HAWAII-HILO
Hilo, HI 96720 ...II

Coach: Jim Forkum
Alma Mater: California Bapt. '69
Record: 1 Year, W-8, L-19

1996-97 SCHEDULE

Hawaii-Hilo Inv. ...Nov. 29-Dec. 1
Hawaii Pacific ...Dec. 7
Hawaii-Hilo Cl. ...Dec. 17-19
Hilo Holiday Tr. ...Dec. 28-30
Beloit ■ ...Jan. 4
Mont. St.-Billings ...Jan. 9
Western N.M. ...Jan. 11
Seattle Pacific ■ ...Jan. 16
Alas. Fairbanks ■ ...Jan. 23
Alas. Anchorage ■ ...Jan. 25
St. Martin's ■ ...Jan. 28
Mont. St.-Billings ■ ...Jan. 30
Western N.M. ■ ...Feb. 1
BYU-Hawaii ...Feb. 4
Chaminade ■ ...Feb. 8
Seattle Pacific ...Feb. 13
Alas. Fairbanks ...Feb. 15
Alas. Anchorage ...Feb. 17
BYU-Hawaii ■ ...Feb. 22
Hawaii Pacific ■ ...Feb. 25
Chaminade ...Mar. 1

1995-96 RESULTS (8-19)

86	Utah St. ■	103
81	Oregon ■	115
75	Toledo ■	104
84	BYU-Hawaii ■	97
88	Chaminade	84
93	IU/PU-Indianapolis ■	106
83	Northern Mich. ■	86
114	Susquehanna ■	110
87	Neb.-Kearney ■	110
86	Southern Ill.	98
74	UAB ■	87

88	Hawaii Pacific	112
97	Mont. St.-Billings	114
95	Western N.M.	73
49	Seattle Pacific	99
87	Chaminade ■	81
83	Alas. Anchorage ■	78
111	Alas. Fairbanks ■	97
73	Western N.M. ■	58
45	Seattle Pacific ■	59
79	BYU-Hawaii ■	85
84	Chaminade	74
95	Alas. Fairbanks	118
77	Alas. Anchorage	112
64	BYU-Hawaii	84
71	Hawaii Pacific ■	89
110	Mont. St.-Billings ■	111

Nickname: Vulcans
Colors: Red, White & Blue
Arena: Afook-Chinen Civic Center
Capacity: 3,000
AD: William Trumbo
SID: Kelly Leong

HEIDELBERG

Tiffin, OH 44883 III

Coach: John Hill
Alma Mater: Heidelberg '70
Record: 20 Years, W-296, L-243

1996-97 SCHEDULE

Heidelberg Cl.	Nov. 22-23
Wilmington (Ohio)	Nov. 30
Toledo	Dec. 2
Ohio Northern	Dec. 4
Muskingum	Dec. 7
Otterbein ■	Dec. 14
Mount Union	Dec. 18
Otterbein Tr.	Dec. 28-29
John Carroll ■	Jan. 8
Marietta	Jan. 11
Hiram ■	Jan. 15
Baldwin-Wallace	Jan. 18
Capital ■	Jan. 22
Marietta ■	Jan. 25
Hiram	Jan. 29
Baldwin-Wallace ■	Feb. 1
Capital	Feb. 5
Muskingum ■	Feb. 8
Ohio Northern ■	Feb. 12
Otterbein	Feb. 15
John Carroll	Feb. 19
Mount Union ■	Feb. 22

1995-96 RESULTS (8-17)

71	Rensselaer †	82
93	Connecticut Col. †	72
85	Defiance ■	80
59	Bowling Green	90
71	Baldwin-Wallace	66
68	Otterbein ■	71
62	Marietta	78
65	Hiram	70
80	Denison ■	75
76	Westminster (Pa.) ■	75
66	Capital	71
59	Muskingum ■	56
66	John Carroll	81
62	Mount Union	70
54	Ohio Northern ■	67
75	Muskingum	92
73	John Carroll ■	82
78	Marietta ■	60
69	Otterbein	71
74	Hiram ■	67
78	Capital ■	81
59	Baldwin-Wallace ■	71
62	Ohio Northern	65
68	Mount Union ■	74
58	Marietta	61

Nickname: Student Princes
Colors: Red, Orange & Black
Arena: Seiberling Gymnasium
Capacity: 2,200; Year Built: 1952
AD: John Hill
SID: Dick Edmond

HENDERSON ST.

Arkadelphia, AR 71923 II

Coach: Eric Bozeman
Alma Mater: Arkansas Tech '81
Record: 3 Years, W-31, L-50

1996-97 SCHEDULE

Jarvis Christian ■	Nov. 19
Ark. Baptist ■	Nov. 21
Texas A&M-Commerce	Nov. 26
Texas Col. ■	Dec. 4
Drury Tr.	Dec. 6-7
Ouachita Baptist ■	Dec. 12
Lyon	Dec. 14
Missouri So. Tr.	Dec. 30-31
Southern Ark.	Jan. 6
Harding ■	Jan. 9
Christian Bros. ■	Jan. 11
Delta St. ■	Jan. 13
Arkansas Tech ■	Jan. 18
Central Ark.	Jan. 20
Ark.-Monticello	Jan. 23
Lyon ■	Jan. 25
Ouachita Baptist	Jan. 30
Southern Ark. ■	Feb. 3
Harding	Feb. 6
Christian Bros.	Feb. 8
Delta St.	Feb. 10
Arkansas Tech	Feb. 15
Central Ark. ■	Feb. 17
Ark.-Monticello ■	Feb. 20

1995-96 RESULTS (11-16)

76	LeMoyne-Owen †	77
82	Morehouse †	90
87	East Tex. Bapt.	91
87	Lyon †	81
54	Harding	68
62	Louisiana Tech	70
72	Mo. Southern St. ■	67
78	Texas A&M-Commerce ■	89
61	Harding ■	75
85	Jarvis Christian	77
72	Southern Ark. ■	69
105	East Tex. Bapt. ■	72
74	Mississippi Col.	79
95	Delta St.	107
70	Arkansas Tech	66
73	Central Ark. ■	69
107	Ark.-Monticello ■	98
81	Ouachita Baptist ■	92
88	Southern Ark.	83
74	Mississippi Col. ■	82
89	Delta St. ■	100
80	Arkansas Tech ■	73
79	Lyon	85
79	Central Ark.	80
109	Ark.-Monticello	96
91	Ouachita Baptist	113
90	West Ga. †	99

Nickname: Reddies
Colors: Red & Gray
Arena: Duke Wells Center
Capacity: 2,100; Year Built: 1972
AD: Ken Turner
SID: David Worlock

HENDRIX

Conway, AR 72032 III

Coach: Cliff Garrison
Alma Mater: Central Ark. '62
Record: 24 Years, W-403, L-264

1996-97 SCHEDULE

Dallas ■	Nov. 22
Ozarks (Ark.) ■	Nov. 23
Austin	Nov. 27
Dallas Cl.	Nov. 29-30
Ozarks (Ark.)	Dec. 5
Austin ■	Dec. 7
Westminster (Mo.) Cl	Dec. 13-14
Hendrix Cl.	Jan. 3-4
Southwestern (Tex.)	Jan. 10
Trinity (Tex.)	Jan. 12
Millsaps	Jan. 17
Oglethorpe	Jan. 19
Centre ■	Jan. 24
Sewanee ■	Jan. 26
Millsaps ■	Jan. 31
Oglethorpe ■	Feb. 2
Centre	Feb. 7
Sewanee	Feb. 9
Rhodes ■	Feb. 15
Southwestern (Tex.) ■	Feb. 21
Trinity (Tex.) ■	Feb. 23
Rhodes	Mar. 1

1995-96 RESULTS (21-6)

99	Austin ■	72
85	Dallas ■	62
99	LSU-Shreveport	74
83	Austin †	70
117	Dallas	73
81	Williams Baptist ■	80
72	Ozarks (Ark.)	90
79	Williams Baptist	75
95	LSU-Shreveport ■	60
104	Ozarks (Ark.) ■	73
86	Rhodes	74
83	Oglethorpe	69
75	Millsaps	86
75	Trinity (Tex.) ■	71
105	Southwestern (Tex.) ■	89
101	Messenger ■	71
70	Sewanee ■	78
86	Centre ■	68
71	Trinity (Tex.)	78
96	Southwestern (Tex.)	81
76	Sewanee	87
72	Centre	62
90	Oglethorpe ■	71
82	Millsaps ■	66
82	Rhodes ■	78
97	Stillman ■	85
64	Roanoke	80

Nickname: Warriors
Colors: Orange & Black
Arena: Ivan H. Grove
Capacity: 1,200; Year Built: 1961
AD: Cliff Garrison
SID: James Eaton

HIGH POINT

High Point, NC 27262 II

Coach: Jerry Steele
Alma Mater: Wake Forest '61
Record: 32 Years, W-532, L-369

1996-97 SCHEDULE

Anderson (S.C.)	Nov. 16
Erskine	Nov. 20
Lees-McRae ■	Dec. 2
Coker ■	Dec. 4
Winston-Salem ■	Dec. 7
Bahamas Shootout	Jan. 1-6
Barton ■	Jan. 8
Belmont Abbey ■	Jan. 11
Queens (N.C.) ■	Jan. 13
St. Andrews	Jan. 16
Longwood	Jan. 18
Pfeiffer ■	Jan. 22
Queens (N.C.)	Jan. 25
Mount Olive	Jan. 27
Erskine ■	Jan. 29
Belmont Abbey	Feb. 1
Pfeiffer	Feb. 3
Mount Olive ■	Feb. 8
Barton	Feb. 10
Lees-McRae	Feb. 12
Coker	Feb. 15
St. Andrews ■	Feb. 19
Longwood ■	Feb. 22

1995-96 RESULTS (24-7)

69	Winston-Salem	71
85	Col. of West Va.	95
59	Pfeiffer ■	53
68	Erskine ■	64
100	Col. of West Va. ■	87
76	Queens (N.C.) ■	68
75	Winston-Salem ■	62
68	Life (Ga.) †	86
72	St. Thomas (Fla.) †	59
73	Illinois Tech †	63
69	Coker ■	56
81	St. Andrews	78
78	Lees-McRae	51
83	Barton ■	70
78	Mount Olive	93
69	Pfeiffer	84
68	Longwood ■	61
82	Belmont Abbey ■	80
55	Coker	40
80	Lees-McRae ■	62
81	Belmont Abbey	77
89	St. Andrews ■	72
79	Queens (N.C.)	76
88	Erskine	71
84	Barton	70
91	Mount Olive ■	71
68	Erskine †	64
85	Mount Olive ■	80
73	Queens (N.C.) ■	86
76	Presbyterian †	67
70	Queens (N.C.) †	81

Nickname: Panthers
Colors: Purple & White
Arena: Millis Athletic Center
Capacity: 1,850; Year Built: 1992
AD: Jerry Steele
SID: Mike Tuttle

HILLSDALE

Hillsdale, MI 49242 II

Coach: Bernie Balikian
Alma Mater: Point Loma '78
Record: 11 Years, W-148, L-173

1996-97 SCHEDULE

Indianapolis Cl.	Nov. 22-23
IU/PU-Ft. Wayne	Nov. 26
Tri-State ■	Nov. 30
Michigan Tech ■	Dec. 5
Northern Mich. ■	Dec. 7
Ind.-South Bend ■	Dec. 10
Siena Heights ■	Dec. 14
Ferris St.	Dec. 21
Grand Valley St.	Dec. 23
Wittenberg Cl.	Dec. 27-28
Oakland	Jan. 2
Wayne St. (Mich.)	Jan. 4
Ashland	Jan. 11
Mercyhurst ■	Jan. 16
Gannon ■	Jan. 18
Lake Superior St.	Jan. 23
Northwood	Jan. 25
Saginaw Valley ■	Feb. 1
Oakland ■	Feb. 6
Wayne St. (Mich.) ■	Feb. 8
Indiana Tech	Feb. 12
Ashland ■	Feb. 15
Mercyhurst	Feb. 20
Gannon	Feb. 22

1995-96 RESULTS (4-22)

95	Siena Heights	90
61	Manchester	80
54	Ky. Wesleyan	103
74	North Ala. †	91
89	IU/PU-Ft. Wayne ■	95
68	Wayne St. (Mich.)	88
77	Ashland	93
74	Tri-State	84
70	Edinboro †	90
56	Saginaw Valley †	83
70	Mercyhurst ■	75
65	Gannon ■	75
75	Saginaw Valley ■	84
65	Grand Valley St. ■	95
77	Ferris St.	72
42	Lake Superior St.	78
69	Northern Mich.	77
60	Michigan Tech ■	77
77	Northwood ■	91
77	Oakland	87

68	Wayne St. (Mich.) ■	76
64	Ashland ■	84
59	Northern Mich. ■	63
89	Gannon ■	83
84	Northwood ■	70
57	Grand Valley St.	68

Nickname: Chargers
Colors: Royal Blue & White
Arena: Jesse Philips Arena
Capacity: 2,500; Year Built: 1989
AD: Mike Kovalchik
SID: Greg Younger

HIRAM
Hiram, OH 44234 III

Coach: Steve Minton
Alma Mater: Heidelberg '86
(First year as head coach)

1996-97 SCHEDULE
Wooster Cl. ....Nov. 22-23
Ashland ....Nov. 30
John Carroll ....Dec. 4
Capital ....Dec. 7
Grove City ■ ....Dec. 11
Muskingum ■ ....Dec. 14
Otterbein ....Dec. 18
Denison ....Dec. 28
Thiel ....Jan. 6
Baldwin-Wallace ....Jan. 8
Ohio Northern ■ ....Jan. 11
Heidelberg ....Jan. 15
Marietta ■ ....Jan. 18
Mount Union ■ ....Jan. 22
Ohio Northern ....Jan. 25
Heidelberg ■ ....Jan. 29
Marietta ....Feb. 1
Mount Union ....Feb. 5
Capital ■ ....Feb. 8
John Carroll ■ ....Feb. 12
Muskingum ....Feb. 15
Baldwin-Wallace ■ ....Feb. 19
Otterbein ....Feb. 22

1995-96 RESULTS (9-16)
Results unavailable

Nickname: Terriers
Colors: Red & Blue
Arena: Price Gymnasium
Capacity: 2,000; Year Built: 1959
AD: Cindy McKnight
SID: Tom Cammett

HOBART
Geneva, NY 14456 III

Coach: Brian Streeter
Alma Mater: Texas A&M '79
Record: 13 Years, W-131, L-190

1996-97 SCHEDULE
Rochester Inst. ....Dec. 3
Skidmore ■ ....Dec. 6
Rensselaer ■ ....Dec. 7
Hamilton ....Dec. 10
Sprinfield Cl. ....Jan. 4-5
Keuka ■ ....Jan. 8
Chase Rochester Tr. ....Jan. 15-18
Roberts Wesleyan ■ ....Jan. 21
Clarkson ....Jan. 24
St. Lawrence ....Jan. 25
Le Moyne ■ ....Jan. 28
Union (N.Y.) ....Feb. 1
Skidmore ....Feb. 7
Rensselaer ■ ....Feb. 8
Ithaca ....Feb. 11
Union (N.Y.) ■ ....Feb. 15
Rochester ■ ....Feb. 19
St. Lawrence ■ ....Feb. 21
Clarkson ■ ....Feb. 22
Keuka ....Feb. 26
Hamilton ■ ....Feb. 28

1995-96 RESULTS (7-18)

67	Army	88
75	Hamilton	90
88	Union (N.Y.) ■	75
76	Skidmore	83
66	Rensselaer ■	69
81	Embry-Riddle	91
70	Hamilton †	87
71	Rochester Inst.	77
68	Brockport St. †	63
57	Geneseo St. †	68
84	Rochester Inst. ■	86
74	Clarkson	62
72	St. Lawrence	91
64	Roberts Wesleyan	72
63	Union (N.Y.) ■	60
56	Ithaca	79
70	Le Moyne ■	84
68	Keuka	81
76	St. Lawrence ■	68
81	Clarkson ■	55
67	Rochester	75
72	Rensselaer	80
74	Skidmore	72
66	Keuka ■	77
73	Hamilton ■	75

Nickname: Statesmen
Colors: Orange & Purple
Arena: Bristol Gym
Capacity: 2,200; Year Built: 1965
AD: Michael Hanna
SID: Eric Reuscher

HOFSTRA
Hempstead, NY 11550 I

Coach: Jay Wright
Alma Mater: Bucknell '83
Record: 2 Years, W-19, L-36

1996-97 SCHEDULE
Stony Brook ■ ....Nov. 22
Florida Int'l ....Nov. 25
Fla. Atlantic ....Nov. 27
St. John's (N.Y.) ....Nov. 30
Maine ....Dec. 6
New Hampshire ....Dec. 8
Xavier (Ohio) ....Dec. 14
Fordham ....Dec. 22
ECAC Holiday Tr. ....Dec. 26-28
Vermont ■ ....Jan. 2
Hartford ■ ....Jan. 4
Delaware ....Jan. 7
Boston U. ....Jan. 10
Northeastern ....Jan. 12
Drexel ■ ....Jan. 18
Towson St. ....Jan. 21
New Hampshire ■ ....Jan. 24
Maine ■ ....Jan. 26
Towson St. ■ ....Jan. 31
Delaware ....Feb. 2
Boston U. ■ ....Feb. 7
Northeastern ■ ....Feb. 9
Drexel ....Feb. 16
Vermont ....Feb. 20
Hartford ....Feb. 22
America East Conf. Tr. ....Feb. 28-Mar. 2

1995-96 RESULTS (9-18)

91	Stony Brook ■	72
66	Southwest Tex. St. †	68
78	Eastern Wash. †	68
58	Hartford	77
83	Vermont	103
51	Manhattan	74
57	Villanova	91
82	Army ■	58
71	Drexel ■	100
64	Maine ■	51
75	New Hampshire ■	56
70	Northeastern	65
61	Boston U.	73
83	Towson St.	63
68	Northeastern ■	71
71	Boston U. ■	86
55	Pennsylvania ■	83
57	Maine ■	75
65	New Hampshire ■	77
65	Delaware	93
63	Drexel	93
57	Delaware ■	67
56	Towson St. ■	74
69	Fordham ■	57
83	Vermont ■	96
83	Hartford ■	77
61	Northeastern †	71

Nickname: Flying Dutchmen
Colors: Blue, White & Gold
Arena: Physical Fitness Center
Capacity: 3,500; Year Built: 1970
AD: Jim Garvey
SID: Jim Sheehan

HOLY CROSS
Worcester, MA 01610 I

Coach: Bill Raynor
Alma Mater: Dartmouth '74
Record: 2 Years, W-31, L-25

1996-97 SCHEDULE
Geo. Washington Cl. ....Nov. 22-23
Yale ■ ....Nov. 26
Fordham ....Nov. 30
Dartmouth ■ ....Dec. 4
Harvard ....Dec. 7
Brown ....Dec. 10
Boston College ■ ....Dec. 21
New Orleans Cl. ....Dec. 27-28
Hartford ■ ....Dec. 31
La Salle ....Jan. 4
Siena ....Jan. 8
Army ....Jan. 11
Colgate ■ ....Jan. 15
Lehigh ....Jan. 18
Lafayette ....Jan. 22
Bucknell ■ ....Jan. 25
Navy ....Jan. 29
Army ■ ....Feb. 5
Colgate ....Feb. 8
New Hampshire ....Feb. 10
Lehigh ■ ....Feb. 12
Lafayette ■ ....Feb. 15
Bucknell ....Feb. 18
Navy ■ ....Feb. 22
Patriot Conf. Tr. ....Mar. 1-5

1995-96 RESULTS (16-13)

75	Dartmouth	82
60	Boston College	97
57	Boston U.	54
75	La Salle ■	72
64	Harvard ■	92
75	Yale	78
101	New Hampshire ■	79
64	California	75
55	Loyola (Md.) †	73
89	Brown	97
78	Siena	83
85	Lafayette ■	82
67	Colgate	85
63	Navy	67
81	Army ■	66
68	Cornell ■	61
77	Fordham ■	64
100	Lehigh	81
83	Bucknell ■	90
85	Lafayette	92
95	Hartford	92
94	Colgate ■	89
77	Navy ■	67
81	Army	69
84	Lehigh ■	77
93	Bucknell	73
81	Lehigh ■	66
68	Army †	65
65	Colgate	74

Nickname: Crusaders
Colors: Royal Purple
Arena: Hart Recreation Center
Capacity: 3,600; Year Built: 1975
AD: Ron Perry
SID: Frank Mastrandrea

HOPE
Holland, MI 49423 III

Coach: Glenn Van Wieren
Alma Mater: Hope '64
Record: 19 Years, W-358, L-120

1996-97 SCHEDULE
Cornerstone Cl. ....Nov. 22-23
Concordia (Mich.) ....Nov. 26
Grand Rapids Cl. ....Nov. 29-30
North Park ■ ....Dec. 4
Trinity Christian ....Dec. 7
Hope Cl. ....Dec. 20-21
Embry-Riddle Tr. ....Jan. 3-4
Lipscomb ....Jan. 6
Alma ■ ....Jan. 11
Albion ■ ....Jan. 15
Olivet ....Jan. 18
Kalamazoo ■ ....Jan. 22
Adrian ■ ....Jan. 25
Calvin ....Jan. 29
Alma ....Feb. 5
Albion ....Feb. 8
Olivet ■ ....Feb. 12
Kalamazoo ....Feb. 15
Adrian ....Feb. 19
Calvin ■ ....Feb. 22

1995-96 RESULTS (28-4)

80	Bethel (Ind.) †	94
90	Ind.-South Bend †	65
76	Concordia (Mich.) ■	61
76	Trinity Christian	63
107	Concordia (Ill.) ■	53
85	North Park	72
72	Cornerstone ■	83
113	Aurora	80
97	Aquinas	58
74	Widener †	45
69	Ramapo	56
94	Rensselaer ■	88
74	Alma	60
88	Albion	70
97	Olivet ■	75
73	Kalamazoo ■	68
73	Adrian	53
93	Calvin ■	70
89	Alma	67
94	Albion ■	80
97	Olivet	68
65	Kalamazoo	67
92	Adrian ■	74
67	Calvin	66
75	Albion ■	62
89	Kalamazoo ■	78
65	Kalamazoo ■	62
80	John Carroll	61
88	Wis.-Whitewater †	66
69	Wittenberg	60
76	Frank. & Marsh. †	57
93	Rowan †	100

Nickname: Flying Dutchmen
Colors: Blue & Orange
Arena: Holland Civic Center
Capacity: 2,500; Year Built: 1954
AD: Ray Smith
SID: Tom Renner

HOUSTON
Houston, TX 77204 I

Coach: Alvin Brooks
Alma Mater: Lamar '80
Record: 3 Years, W-34, L-48

1996-97 SCHEDULE
Ark.-Pine Bluff ■ ....Nov. 23
Houston Baptist ■ ....Nov. 27
Texas-San Antonio ■ ......Nov. 30
Tulsa ■ ....Dec. 4

Mississippi ....Dec. 7
Brigham Young Cl. ....Dec. 13-14
Delaware St. ■ ....Dec. 19
Creighton ■ ....Dec. 21
Northeast La. ....Dec. 28
McNeese St. ■ ....Dec. 30
Creighton ....Jan. 4
UAB ■ ....Jan. 11
Louisville ....Jan. 15
DePaul ■ ....Jan. 18
South Fla. ■ ....Jan. 22
St. Louis ....Jan. 25
N.C.-Charlotte ....Jan. 29
Southern Miss. ....Feb. 6
N.C.-Charlotte ■ ....Feb. 9
Memphis ■ ....Feb. 12
Louisville ■ ....Feb. 15
Cincinnati ....Feb. 18
Tulane ■ ....Feb. 23
Memphis ....Feb. 26
Marquette ....Mar. 2
Conference USA ....Mar. 5-8

1995-96 RESULTS (17-10)
91	Houston Baptist ■	.59
81	McNeese St.	.83
94	Texas-San Antonio	.90
69	Arizona ■	.73
73	Southern Cal	.96
74	Colorado	.77
49	Tennessee	.69
67	Mississippi ■	.76
98	Northeast La. ■	.64
88	Texas Lutheran ■	.66
69	Memphis ■	.67
63	Southern Methodist	.62
76	Rice	.74
89	Texas Christian ■	.86
76	Texas Tech	.95
78	Texas A&M ■	.67
91	Baylor	.84
63	Texas	.80
97	James Madison	.72
63	Rice ■	.59
86	Texas Christian	.82
84	Texas Tech ■	.93
79	Texas A&M	.75
79	Baylor ■	.69
62	Southern Methodist	.59
86	Texas ■	.76
57	Southern Methodist	.62

Nickname: Cougars
Colors: Scarlet & White
Arena: Hofheinz Pavilion
  Capacity: 10,132; Year Built: 1969
AD: Bill Carr
SID: Donna Turner

HOWARD
Washington, DC 20059 I

Coach: Mike McLeese
Alma Mater: Elizabeth City '74
Record: 2 Years, W-16, L-38

1996-97 SCHEDULE
Maryland ....Nov. 26
Morehouse ■ ....Nov. 30
Mt. St. Mary's (Md.) ■ ....Dec. 3
Liberty ....Dec. 7
American ■ ....Dec. 14
Cincinnati ....Dec. 17
California Cl. ....Dec. 28-29
South Caro. St. ....Jan. 11
North Caro. A&T ....Jan. 13
Md.-East. Shore ■ ....Jan. 18
Delaware St. ■ ....Jan. 20
Florida A&M ■ ....Jan. 22
Bethune-Cookman ■ ....Jan. 25
Hampton ■ ....Jan. 27
Coppin St. ■ ....Jan. 30
Md.-East. Shore ....Feb. 1
Morgan St. ....Feb. 3
Hampton ....Feb. 8
Coppin St. ....Feb. 10
Florida A&M ....Feb. 13

Bethune-Cookman ....Feb. 15
Delaware St. ....Feb. 17
South Caro. St. ■ ....Feb. 22
North Caro. A&T ■ ....Feb. 24
Morgan St. ■ ....Mar. 1
Mid-Eastern Conf. Tr. ....Mar. 5-8

1995-96 RESULTS (7-20)
62	Morehouse	.65
81	Florida St.	.97
74	Texas Christian ■	.103
58	Liberty ■	.61
71	Maryland	.88
57	Mt. St. Mary's (Md.)	.74
49	American	.89
81	Northeastern ■	.86
65	St. Peter's	.82
58	South Caro. St. ■	.67
65	Md.-East. Shore	.71
71	Delaware St.	.73
65	Florida A&M	.74
53	Bethune-Cookman	.65
64	Morgan St.	.73
58	Md.-East. Shore ■	.55
63	Coppin St. ■	.62
81	Loyola (Md.) ■	.69
92	Morgan St. ■	.90
85	Florida A&M ■	.55
72	Bethune-Cookman ■	.58
63	Delaware St. ■	.65
63	South Caro. St.	.77
68	North Caro. A&T	.70
87	North Caro. A&T ■	.76
54	Coppin St.	.87
63	Coppin St. †	.83

Nickname: Bison
Colors: Blue, White & Red
Arena: Burr Gymnasium
  Capacity: 2,700; Year Built: 1963
AD: David C. Simmons
SID: Edward Hill Jr

HOWARD PAYNE
Brownwood, TX 76801 III

Coach: Charles Pattillo
Alma Mater: Howard Payne '65
Record: 3 Years, W-37, L-40

1996-97 SCHEDULE
Texas Lutheran ....Nov. 23
Southwestern (Tex.) ■ ....Nov. 30
Tarleton St. ....Dec. 2
Texas Lutheran ■ ....Dec. 4
Wayland Bapt. Cl. ....Dec. 6-7
Trinity (Tex.) ■ ....Dec. 10
Ambassador ....Dec. 12
Ambassador ■ ....Jan. 7
Sul Ross St. ■ ....Jan. 11
Southwestern (Tex.) ....Jan. 14
Hardin-Simmons ....Jan. 16
McMurry ....Jan. 18
Ozarks (Ark.) ■ ....Jan. 25
Dallas ....Jan. 30
Austin ....Feb. 1
Angelo St. ■ ....Feb. 4
Sul Ross St. ....Feb. 8
Trinity (Tex.) ....Feb. 11
Hardin-Simmons ■ ....Feb. 13
McMurry ■ ....Feb. 15
Ozarks (Ark.) ....Feb. 22
Dallas ■ ....Feb. 27
Austin ■ ....Mar. 1

1995-96 RESULTS (14-13)
96	Mary Hardin-Baylor ■	.101
67	Incarnate Word ■	.72
120	Texas Lutheran ■	.117
81	Trinity (Tex.)	.82
129	Wayland Baptist	.133
77	Northwestern Okla. †	.85
105	Schreiner †	.85
82	Trinity (Tex.) ■	.86
79	Texas Lutheran	.118
103	Ambassador	.115
56	Lubbock Chrst.	.93

78	Wayland Baptist ■	.72
67	Incarnate Word	.73
98	Ambassador ■	.86
93	Hardin-Simmons ■	.89
86	Austin	.68
110	McMurry ■	.80
72	Sul Ross St.	.74
101	Hardin-Simmons	.88
108	Austin ■	.92
91	Dallas	.65
81	McMurry	.88
99	Sul Ross St. ■	.77
79	Southwestern (Tex.)	.59
110	Dallas ■	.82
82	McMurry †	.75
73	Whitworth †	.103

Nickname: Yellow Jackets
Colors: Gold & Blue
Arena: Brownwood Coliseum
  Capacity: 5,000; Year Built: 1968
AD: Larry Nickell
SID: Mike Blackwell

HUMBOLDT ST.
Arcata, CA 95521 II

Coach: Tom Wood
Alma Mater: UC Davis '71
Record: 15 Years, W-205, L-210

1996-97 SCHEDULE
Southern Ore. St. ■ ....Nov. 16
Western Ore. ■ ....Nov. 23
Seattle ....Nov. 29
Central Wash. ....Nov. 30
Utah St. ....Dec. 7
UC Santa Cruz ....Dec. 13
Holy Names ....Dec. 14
Bethany (Cal.) ■ ....Dec. 17
Minn.-Duluth ■ ....Dec. 20
Concordia (Cal.) ■ ....Dec. 28
Oregon Tech ■ ....Dec. 30
Cal St. Chico ....Jan. 3
UC Davis ■ ....Jan. 4
San Fran. St. ....Jan. 10
Notre Dame (Cal.) ....Jan. 11
Cal St. Hayward ....Jan. 17
Cal St. Stanislaus ....Jan. 18
Sonoma St. ....Jan. 25
Cal St. Stanislaus ■ ....Jan. 31
Cal St. Hayward ■ ....Feb. 1
Notre Dame (Cal.) ■ ....Feb. 7
San Fran. St. ■ ....Feb. 8
UC Davis ....Feb. 14
Cal St. Chico ....Feb. 15
Sonoma St. ■ ....Feb. 20

1995-96 RESULTS (14-13)
67	Eastern Ore. ■	.52
93	Cal St. San B'dino ■	.85
82	Denver	.101
74	Westmont	.89
73	Western Ore.	.68
74	Central Wash. †	.87
56	Oregon Tech	.73
78	Southern Ore. St.	.69
74	Seattle Pacific ■	.88
91	Holy Names ■	.75
59	Cal St. San B'dino	.79
86	Mary Hardin-Baylor †	.65
80	Cal St. Chico	.78
61	UC Davis	.82
61	San Fran. St. ■	.50
90	Notre Dame (Cal.) ■	.57
75	Cal St. Hayward	.69
57	Cal St. Stanislaus	.79
71	Sonoma St. ■	.74
97	Cal St. Stanislaus ■	.74
61	Cal St. Hayward ■	.73
76	Notre Dame (Cal.)	.64
99	San Fran. St.	.91
63	UC Davis ■	.78
90	Cal St. Chico ■	.59
53	Sonoma St.	.67
58	Sonoma St.	.74

Nickname: Lumberjacks
Colors: Green & Gold
Arena: HSU East Gym
  Capacity: 1,400; Year Built: 1956
AD: Scott Nelson
SID: Dan Pambianco

HUNTER
New York, NY 10021 III

Coach: Bill Savarese
Alma Mater: Staten Island '75
Record: 2 Years, W-24, L-29

1996-97 SCHEDULE
New Jersey Inv. ....Nov. 22-23
Manhattanville ....Dec. 2
York (N.Y.) ....Dec. 4
Medgar Evers ■ ....Dec. 6
Western Conn. St. ■ ....Dec. 11
York (Pa.) Cl. ....Dec. 28-29
St. Joseph's (Me.) ■ ....Jan. 7
Ramapo ■ ....Jan. 9
New Paltz St. ....Jan. 14
Staten Island ■ ....Jan. 16
Brooklyn ....Jan. 20
Merchant Marine ■ ....Jan. 22
Lehman ....Jan. 25
CCNY ■ ....Jan. 27
Staten Island ....Jan. 29
N.J. Inst. of Tech. ....Jan. 31
Medgar Evers ....Feb. 5
Baruch ....Feb. 7
York (N.Y.) ....Feb. 10
Mt. St. Mary (N.Y.) ■ ....Feb. 15
Brooklyn ■ ....Feb. 17
John Jay ....Feb. 19

1995-96 RESULTS (7-18)
71	Salem St. †	.83
61	Old Westbury †	.70
80	Manhattanville ■	.83
66	York (N.Y.)	.73
79	Teikyo Post ■	.89
73	Merchant Marine	.75
68	Old Westbury	.86
68	Rowan ■	.104
57	Cabrini	.71
51	Lebanon Valley	.60
74	FDU-Madison †	.90
84	New Paltz St. ■	.68
59	Teikyo Post	.62
51	Staten Island	.65
78	Lehman ■	.65
67	CCNY	.48
78	N.J. Inst. of Tech. ■	.81
71	Staten Island	.74
77	Medgar Evers	.72
81	Baruch	.76
70	York (N.Y.) ■	.112
80	Mt. St. Mary (N.Y.) ■	.85
80	Medgar Evers ■	.77
77	John Jay ■	.69
50	Baruch †	.61

Nickname: Hawks
Colors: Purple, White & Gold
Arena: Hunter College Sportsplex
  Capacity: 1,700; Year Built: 1985
AD: Terry Wansart
SID: Ron Ratner

IDAHO
Moscow, ID 83843 I

Coach: Kermit Davis
Alma Mater: Mississippi St. '82
Record: 3 Years, W-58, L-33

1996-97 SCHEDULE
Purdue ....Nov. 24
Idaho St. ■ ....Nov. 27
Southwest Mo. St. ....Nov. 30
Washington ....Dec. 3
Idaho St. ....Dec. 5
St. Martin's ■ ....Dec. 8

Lewis-Clark St. ■ ....Dec. 11
Washington St. ....Dec. 14
Western Baptist ....Dec. 23
Hilo Holiday Tr. ....Dec. 28-30
Lewis-Clark St. ■ ....Jan. 3
Nevada ■ ....Jan. 9
Utah St. ■ ....Jan. 11
Pacific (Cal.) ■ ....Jan. 16
Boise St. ■ ....Jan. 18
New Mexico St. ....Jan. 23
North Texas ....Jan. 25
Cal St. Fullerton ■ ....Jan. 30
UC Irvine ■ ....Feb. 1
Southern Utah ■ ....Feb. 3
UC Santa Barb. ....Feb. 6
Cal Poly SLO ....Feb. 8
Washington St. ■ ....Feb. 11
North Texas ■ ....Feb. 13
New Mexico St. ■ ....Feb. 15
Utah St. ....Feb. 20
Nevada ....Feb. 22
Long Beach St. ■ ....Feb. 27
Boise St. ....Mar. 1
Big West Conf. Tr. ....Mar. 7-9

1995-96 RESULTS (12-16)

86	St. Martin's ■	64
61	Mississippi Val. †	63
95	Troy St. †	86
64	Washington	61
56	Southern Utah	71
54	Washington St.	66
100	Rocky Mountain ■	68
65	Old Dominion †	54
83	Geo. Washington †	84
84	Cal Poly SLO	86
57	Idaho St.	74
72	Boise St.	76
94	Cal Poly SLO ■	78
75	Eastern Wash.	53
86	Weber St. ■	83
66	Northern Ariz. ■	64
68	Montana	94
70	Montana St.	78
53	Boise St.	57
62	Idaho St. ■	66
59	Washington St. ■	68
76	Eastern Wash. ■	63
69	Northern Ariz.	79
75	Weber St.	86
78	Montana St.	81
84	Montana	75
72	Montana †	67
66	Montana St.	91

Nickname: Vandals
Colors: Silver & Gold
Arena: Kibbie Dome
   Capacity: 10,000; Year Built: 1975
AD: Kathy Clark
SID: Sean Johnson

IDAHO ST.
Pocatello, ID 83209 I

Coach: Herb Williams
Alma Mater: Evansville '68
Record: 6 Years, W-77, L-91

1996-97 SCHEDULE

Idaho ....Nov. 27
Pacific (Ore.) ■ ....Nov. 30
Boise St. ■ ....Dec. 2
Idaho ■ ....Dec. 5
Texas-San Antonio ....Dec. 10
Texas-San Antonio ■ ....Dec. 21
Boise St. Cl. ....Dec. 27-28
Montana ■ ....Jan. 2
Montana St. ■ ....Jan. 4
Weber St. ....Jan. 9
Portland St. ....Jan. 11
Northern Ariz. ....Jan. 16
Cal St. Sacramento ■ ....Jan. 18
Cal St. Northridge ■ ....Jan. 24
Northern Ariz. ■ ....Jan. 25
Montana ....Jan. 31
Montana St. ....Feb. 1

Eastern Wash. ■ ....Feb. 6
Portland St. ■ ....Feb. 8
Weber St. ■ ....Feb. 12
Cal St. Sacramento ....Feb. 15
Cal Poly SLO ....Feb. 18
Southern Utah ■ ....Feb. 22
Eastern Wash. ....Feb. 27
Cal St. Northridge ....Mar. 1
Big Sky Conf. Tr. ....Mar. 6-8

1995-96 RESULTS (11-15)

89	Western Mont. ■	56
84	Stephen F. Austin †	88
89	Tenn.-Martin †	72
86	Rocky Mountain ■	61
56	Wis.-Green Bay	73
77	Cal St. Sacramento	82
49	Southern Utah	72
56	Rice †	73
55	Michigan St.	68
74	Cal St. Sacramento ■	77
74	Idaho	57
81	Eastern Wash. ■	78
73	Northern Ariz.	59
67	Weber St.	93
65	Montana St. ■	89
75	Montana ■	94
88	Cal Poly SLO ■	77
51	Boise St. ■	71
56	Eastern Wash.	55
66	Idaho	62
77	Weber St. ■	70
85	Northern Ariz. ■	75
69	Montana	80
52	Montana St.	78
62	Boise St.	65
54	Boise St. †	66

Nickname: Bengals
Colors: Orange & Black
Arena: Holt Arena
   Capacity: 8,721; Year Built: 1970
AD: Irv Cross
SID: Glenn Alford

ILLINOIS
Champaign, IL 61820 I

Coach: Lon Kruger
Alma Mater: Kansas St. '74
Record: 14 Years, W-237, L-185

1996-97 SCHEDULE

Ill.-Chicago ....Nov. 22
Delaware St. ■ ....Nov. 25
Hawaii-Hilo Inv. ....Nov. 29-Dec. 1
California ....Dec. 3
Illinois Cl. ....Dec. 6-7
Chicago St. ■ ....Dec. 11
Coppin St. ■ ....Dec. 14
UCLA [Chicago] ....Dec. 21
Missouri [St. Louis] ....Dec. 28
Purdue ■ ....Jan. 2
Ohio St. ....Jan. 4
Michigan ....Jan. 9
Penn St. ■ ....Jan. 11
Minnesota ■ ....Jan. 14
Michigan St. ■ ....Jan. 22
Wisconsin ....Jan. 25
Iowa ....Jan. 29
Indiana ....Feb. 2
Northwestern ■ ....Feb. 5
Iowa ■ ....Feb. 9
Wisconsin ....Feb. 12
Michigan St. ■ ....Feb. 15
Minnesota ....Feb. 22
Penn St. ....Feb. 25
Michigan ■ ....Mar. 1
Ohio St. ■ ....Mar. 5
Purdue ....Mar. 8

1995-96 RESULTS (18-13)

83	Texas-San Antonio ■	80
89	Eastern Ill.	57
75	Duke	65
82	Kansas St. ■	56
89	Southeast Mo. St. ■	70

97	Ball St. ■	53
81	Ill.-Chicago ■	73
96	Missouri †	85
83	California †	69
64	Syracuse †	75
82	Hawaii	81
85	North Caro. St. †	76
64	Minnesota	69
58	Michigan St. ■	68
68	Michigan	83
71	Indiana ■	85
79	Iowa	82
71	Purdue	67
77	Ohio St. ■	46
74	Northwestern	62
56	Wisconsin ■	57
58	Penn St.	61
93	Northwestern ■	62
76	Ohio St.	67
71	Purdue ■	74
91	Iowa ■	86
64	Indiana	76
73	Michigan	62
67	Michigan St.	77
66	Minnesota	67
69	Alabama ■	72

Nickname: Fighting Illini
Colors: Orange & Blue
Arena: Assembly Hall
   Capacity: 16,450; Year Built: 1963
AD: Ron Guenther
SID: Dave Johnson

ILLINOIS COL.
Jacksonville, IL 62650 III

Coach: Mike Worrell
Alma Mater: Urbana '86
(First year as head coach)

1996-97 SCHEDULE

Blackburn ....Nov. 22
Maryville (Mo.) Cl. ....Nov. 29-30
Greenville ■ ....Dec. 4
Coe ....Dec. 6
Grinnell ....Dec. 7
Webster ....Dec. 11
Coe ■ ....Jan. 10
Grinnell ■ ....Jan. 11
Principia ■ ....Jan. 14
Lawrence ....Jan. 17
St. Norbert. ....Jan. 18
Beloit ■ ....Jan. 24
Carroll (Wis.) ....Jan. 25
Monmouth (Ill.) ■ ....Jan. 29
Cornell College ....Feb. 1
Millikin ■ ....Feb. 6
Knox ....Feb. 8
Monmouth (Ill.) ....Feb. 12
Cornell College ■ ....Feb. 15
MacMurray ....Feb. 18
Knox ■ ....Feb. 22

1995-96 RESULTS (7-14)

71	Blackburn ■	39
77	Principia ■	63
92	Fontbonne ■	75
112	Grinnell	124
79	Coe	89
91	Greenville ■	104
67	Millikin	87
92	Webster ■	94
78	Knox ■	77
94	Grinnell ■	107
61	Coe ■	71
54	St. Norbert ■	51
54	Lawrence ■	71
67	Ill. Wesleyan ■	82
81	Carroll (Wis.) ■	99
80	Beloit ■	86
64	Monmouth (Ill.) ■	72
82	MacMurray ■	94
68	Knox	75
87	Cornell College ■	83
75	Monmouth (Ill.)	83

Nickname: Blueboys
Colors: Blue & White
Arena: Memorial Gymnasium
   Capacity: 2,000; Year Built: 1951
AD: Richard Johanningmeier
SID: James Murphy

ILLINOIS ST.
Normal, IL 61761 I

Coach: Kevin Stallings
Alma Mater: Purdue '82
Record: 3 Years, W-58, L-36

1996-97 SCHEDULE

Pittsburgh ....Nov. 24
Eastern Ky. ■ ....Nov. 30
DePaul [St. Louis] ....Dec. 4
Ohio ■ ....Dec. 7
Duquesne ....Dec. 14
Northwestern ....Dec. 18
Wis.-Green Bay ....Dec. 21
Ill.-Chicago ■ ....Dec. 23
Creighton ....Dec. 29
Evansville ■ ....Jan. 4
Northern Iowa ■ ....Jan. 9
Southern Ill. ....Jan. 12
Indiana St. ■ ....Jan. 16
Evansville ....Jan. 19
Northern Iowa ....Jan. 22
Wichita St. ■ ....Jan. 25
Southwest Mo. St. ■ ....Jan. 27
Bradley ■ ....Feb. 1
Drake ....Feb. 3
Wichita St. ....Feb. 8
Southwest Mo. St. ....Feb. 10
Southern Ill. ■ ....Feb. 13
Drake ■ ....Feb. 15
Indiana St. ....Feb. 18
Bradley ....Feb. 22
Creighton ■ ....Feb. 24
Missouri Val. Conf. Tr. ......Feb. 28-Mar. 3

1995-96 RESULTS (22-12)

85	James Madison †	86
72	La Salle †	65
79	American (P.R.)	77
65	Duquesne ■	77
66	Ohio	65
79	Fairleigh Dickinson ■	58
78	Santa Clara ■	80
69	N.C.-Wilmington	57
72	Va. Commonwealth	74
64	East Caro. ■	52
78	Indiana St. ■	68
75	Southern Ill.	97
86	Southwest Mo. St. ■	79
74	Tulsa	71
61	Wichita St.	59
77	Bradley ■	72
76	Southwest Mo. St.	69
68	Drake ■	72
74	Wichita St. ■	57
73	Evansville	69
57	Cincinnati	91
74	Creighton	72
97	Northern Iowa ■	80
71	Southern Ill. ■	74
74	Drake	52
70	Evansville ■	69
69	Tulsa ■	64
64	Bradley	65
60	Indiana St.	64
64	Northern Iowa †	58
52	Tulsa †	69
73	Mt. St. Mary's (Md.) ■	49
77	Wisconsin	62
72	Tulane	83

Nickname: Redbirds
Colors: Red & White
Arena: Redbird Arena
   Capacity: 10,600; Year Built: 1989
AD: Rick Greenspan
SID: Kenny Mossman

ILL. WESLEYAN

Bloomington, IL 61701 III

Coach: Dennis Bridges
Alma Mater: Ill. Wesleyan '61
Record: 31 Years, W-557, L-289

1996-97 SCHEDULE

Washington (Mo.) Tr.	Nov. 22-23
Rockford ■	Dec. 4
Carthage ■	Dec. 7
Olivet Nazarene ■	Dec. 10
Aurora	Dec. 14
Rose-Hulman ■	Dec. 22
Concordia (Cal.)	Dec. 31
Westmont Tr.	Jan. 3-4
Millikin ■	Jan. 8
North Park ■	Jan. 11
Augustana (Ill.) ■	Jan. 15
Wheaton (Ill.)	Jan. 18
North Central	Jan. 22
Elmhurst	Jan. 25
Carthage	Feb. 1
Augustana (Ill.)	Feb. 5
Elmhurst ■	Feb. 8
Wheaton (Ill.) ■	Feb. 12
North Park	Feb. 15
North Central ■	Feb. 19
Millikin	Feb. 22
Benedictine (Ill.)	Mar. 1

1995-96 RESULTS (28-3)

80	Neb. Wesleyan ■	65
83	Washington (Mo.) ■	74
72	Rose-Hulman ■	67
110	Rockford ■	39
62	Olivet Nazarene	57
82	Benedictine (Ill.) ■	63
103	Teikyo Marycrest ■	64
105	Aurora ■	89
81	Florida Tech	71
82	Eckerd	77
72	Carthage	59
98	Augustana (Ill.) ■	72
68	Wheaton (Ill.) ■	67
85	North Central	60
84	Elmhurst ■	47
82	Illinois Col. ■	67
86	North Park	76
86	Millikin	71
76	Augustana (Ill.)	66
84	North Central ■	68
71	Wheaton (Ill.)	83
72	Elmhurst	86
94	Carthage ■	64
96	North Park ■	89
100	Millikin ■	90
77	Ripon ■	66
73	Hanover ■	67
116	Roanoke	88
73	Washington (Mo.) †	61
77	Rowan †	79
89	Frank. & Marsh. †	57

Nickname: Titans
Colors: Green & White
Arena: Shirk Center
Capacity: 2,680; Year Built: 1994
AD: Dennis Bridges
SID: Stew Salowitz

ILL.-CHICAGO

Chicago, IL 60608 I

Coach: Jimmy Collins
Alma Mater: New Mexico St. '70
(First year as head coach)

1996-97 SCHEDULE

Illinois ■	Nov. 22
Texas A&M	Dec. 1
Michigan St.	Dec. 5
Chicago St. ■	Dec. 7
Valparaiso	Dec. 14
Northeastern Ill.	Dec. 17
Grambling ■	Dec. 21
Illinois St.	Dec. 23
Oral Roberts	Dec. 28
Northern Ill. ■	Jan. 2
Wis.-Green Bay	Jan. 4
Butler ■	Jan. 9
Wright St.	Jan. 16
Detroit	Jan. 18
Wis.-Milwaukee ■	Jan. 23
Cleveland St. ■	Jan. 25
Northern Ill.	Jan. 30
Wis.-Green Bay ■	Feb. 1
Loyola (Ill.)	Feb. 3
Wright St. ■	Feb. 6
Detroit ■	Feb. 8
Butler	Feb. 12
Wis.-Milwaukee	Feb. 17
Loyola (Ill.) ■	Feb. 19
Cleveland St.	Feb. 22
Oral Roberts ■	Feb. 24
Midwestern Conf. Tr.	Feb. 28-Mar. 4

1995-96 RESULTS (10-18)

96	Chicago St.	79
99	Olivet Nazarene ■	78
67	Purdue	78
72	Drexel †	83
84	Northeastern Ill. ■	68
73	Illinois	81
73	Coppin St.	86
84	Valparaiso ■	72
62	Texas A&M ■	79
58	Butler	78
91	Wright St. ■	79
69	Cleveland St.	83
70	Northern Ill. ■	67
81	Marquette	103
67	Wis.-Green Bay	73
95	Loyola (Ill.) ■	64
78	Detroit ■	89
87	Wis.-Milwaukee ■	76
74	Wright St.	91
90	Northern Ill.	98
71	Detroit	90
82	Butler ■	85
48	Wis.-Milwaukee	79
85	Loyola (Ill.)	89
56	Wis.-Green Bay ■	90
73	Cleveland St. ■	69
107	Butler †	97
60	Northern Ill. †	95

Nickname: Flames
Colors: Navy Blue & Fire Engine Red
Arena: UIC Pavilion
Capacity: 9,200; Year Built: 1982
AD: Jim Schmidt
SID: Anne Schoenherr

INDIANA

Bloomington, IN 47405 I

Coach: Bob Knight
Alma Mater: Ohio St. '62
Record: 31 Years, W-678, L-247

1996-97 SCHEDULE

Connecticut [Indianapolis]	Nov. 15
NIT	Nov. 20-29
Notre Dame	Dec. 2
Kentucky [Louisville]	Dec. 7
DePaul	Dec. 10
Indiana Cl.	Dec. 13-14
Evansville [Indianapolis]	Dec. 21
Butler ■	Dec. 23
Indiana Hoosier Cl.	Dec. 27-28
Michigan St. ■	Jan. 2
Wisconsin	Jan. 4
Minnesota ■	Jan. 8
Northwestern	Jan. 15
Purdue	Jan. 18
Michigan ■	Jan. 21
Penn St.	Jan. 26
Ohio St.	Jan. 30
Illinois ■	Feb. 2
Iowa	Feb. 4
Ohio St. ■	Feb. 8
Penn St. ■	Feb. 11
Michigan	Feb. 16
Purdue ■	Feb. 18
Northwestern ■	Feb. 22
Minnesota	Mar. 1
Wisconsin ■	Mar. 5
Michigan St.	Mar. 8

1995-96 RESULTS (19-12)

84	Alas. Anchorage	79
64	Duke †	70
52	Connecticut †	86
73	Notre Dame ■	53
82	Kentucky †	89
85	Delaware ■	68
78	Bowling Green ■	67
83	Kansas †	91
76	Evansville	48
82	DePaul ■	84
103	Appalachian St. †	59
82	Weber St. †	62
60	Michigan St.	65
89	Ohio St. ■	67
81	Wisconsin ■	55
85	Illinois	71
69	Purdue	74
99	Michigan ■	83
68	Penn St.	82
76	Iowa ■	73
95	Northwestern ■	61
81	Minnesota	66
50	Iowa	76
72	Penn St. ■	54
75	Michigan	80
72	Purdue ■	74
76	Illinois ■	64
76	Wisconsin	68
73	Ohio St.	56
57	Michigan St. ■	53
51	Boston College †	64

Nickname: Hoosiers
Colors: Cream & Crimson
Arena: Assembly Hall
Capacity: 17,357; Year Built: 1971
AD: Clarence Doninger
SID: Kit Klingelhoffer

INDIANA (PA.)

Indiana, PA 15705 II

Coach: Gary Edwards
Alma Mater: Va. Wesleyan '79
Record: 12 Years, W-177, L-174

1996-97 SCHEDULE

Point Park ■	Nov. 30
Pitt.-Johnstown ■	Dec. 4
Millersville Cl.	Dec. 6-7
Indiana (Pa.) Cl.	Jan. 4-5
Lock Haven	Jan. 8
Calif. (Pa.) ■	Jan. 11
Edinboro	Jan. 15
Clarion	Jan. 18
Slippery Rock ■	Jan. 22
Bloomsburg	Jan. 25
Shippensburg ■	Jan. 29
Calif. (Pa.)	Feb. 1
Lock Haven ■	Feb. 5
Clarion ■	Feb. 8
Edinboro ■	Feb. 12
Slippery Rock	Feb. 15
Shippensburg	Feb. 19
Bloomsburg ■	Feb. 22

1995-96 RESULTS (24-7)

93	Oakland City †	77
80	Indianapolis	66
115	Point Park ■	89
95	La Roche ■	65
82	North Ala. †	68
75	Ky. Wesleyan	71
93	Pitt.-Johnstown	69
90	Millersville	77
71	Lake Erie ■	60
80	Dominican (N.Y.) ■	56
69	Columbia Union ■	44
63	West Chester ■	67
64	Millersville ■	68
90	Shippensburg	82
91	Slippery Rock	55
90	Clarion ■	92
74	Edinboro	73
73	Calif. (Pa.)	76
69	Lock Haven ■	77
81	Bloomsburg ■	65
81	Shippensburg ■	80
80	Slippery Rock ■	51
96	Edinboro ■	86
104	Clarion	92
75	Lock Haven	67
99	Calif. (Pa.) ■	81
86	East Stroudsburg ■	67
77	Bloomsburg †	70
84	Calif. (Pa.)	87
84	Fairmont St. †	83
68	Calif. (Pa.)	78

Nickname: Indians
Colors: Crimson & Gray
Arena: Memorial Field House
Capacity: 2,365; Year Built: 1966
AD: Frank Cignetti
SID: John Gworek

INDIANA ST.

Terre Haute, IN 47809 I

Coach: Sherman Dillard
Alma Mater: James Madison '78
Record: 2 Years, W-17, L-35

1996-97 SCHEDULE

Ga. Southern ■	Nov. 23
Butler ■	Nov. 26
Eastern Ill.	Dec. 4
Fairleigh Dickinson	Dec. 7
Middle Tenn. St. ■	Dec. 19
Loyola (Ill.)	Dec. 22
Chicago St. ■	Dec. 27
Ball St.	Dec. 30
Wichita St. ■	Jan. 4
Drake	Jan. 8
Northern Iowa ■	Jan. 11
Bradley	Jan. 13
Illinois St.	Jan. 16
Drake ■	Jan. 18
Evansville ■	Jan. 22
Southern Ill.	Jan. 25
Wichita St.	Jan. 30
Southwest Mo. St.	Feb. 1
Southern Ill. ■	Feb. 3
Northern Iowa	Feb. 8
Creighton	Feb. 10
Southwest Mo. St. ■	Feb. 13
Bradley ■	Feb. 15
Illinois St. ■	Feb. 18
Creighton ■	Feb. 22
Evansville	Feb. 24
Missouri Val. Conf. Tr.	Feb. 28-Mar. 3

1995-96 RESULTS (10-16)

78	Middle Tenn. St.	81
73	Loyola (Ill.) ■	77
61	Butler	81
70	Eastern Ill. ■	54
64	Mercer	71
69	Ga. Southern	60
68	Fairleigh Dickinson ■	59
78	Ball St. ■	66
68	Illinois St.	78
78	Southwest Mo. St. ■	89
60	Wichita St.	78
67	Evansville ■	71
65	Drake	81
61	Creighton	57
66	Wichita St. ■	51
58	Bradley ■	68
78	Northern Iowa ■	67
65	Southern Ill.	78
72	Northern Iowa	87
85	Drake ■	83
72	Creighton ■	78

52	Evansville	73
62	Southwest Mo. St.	94
75	Tulsa	111
94	Southern Ill. ■	80
64	Illinois St. ■	60

Nickname: Sycamores
Colors: Blue & White
Arena: Hulman Center
 Capacity: 10,200; Year Built: 1972
AD: Larry Gallo
SID: Jennifer Little

IU/PU-FT. WAYNE
Ft. Wayne, IN 46805 II

Coach: John Williams
Alma Mater: Ball St.
Record: 9 Years, W-85, L-144

1996-97 SCHEDULE
IUPU-Ft. Wayne Tr.	Nov. 22-23
Hillsdale ■	Nov. 26
Tri-State ■	Dec. 10
Grace ■	Dec. 12
Purdue-Calumet ■	Dec. 14
Kent	Dec. 23
Ky. Wesleyan ■	Dec. 28
Bellarmine ■	Dec. 30
Mo.-St. Louis	Jan. 2
Quincy	Jan. 4
St. Joseph's (Ind.)	Jan. 9
SIU-Edwardsville ■	Jan. 11
Northern Ky. ■	Jan. 16
Indianapolis ■	Jan. 18
Lewis	Jan. 23
Wis.-Parkside	Jan. 25
Bellarmine	Jan. 30
Ky. Wesleyan	Feb. 1
Quincy ■	Feb. 6
Mo.-St. Louis ■	Feb. 8
St. Joseph's (Ind.) ■	Feb. 13
Southern Ind.	Feb. 15
Indianapolis	Feb. 20
Northern Ky.	Feb. 22
Wis.-Parkside ■	Feb. 27
Lewis ■	Mar. 1

1995-96 RESULTS (8-19)
Results unavailable

Nickname: Mastodons
Colors: Blue & White
Arena: Gates Sports Center
 Capacity: 2,700; Year Built: 1981
AD: Butch Perchan
SID: Matt Delong

IU/PU-INDIANAPOLIS
Indianapolis, IN 46260 II

Coach: Ron Hunter
Alma Mater: Miami (Ohio) '86
Record: 2 Years, W-38, L-20

1996-97 SCHEDULE
Walsh ■	Nov. 16
Carson-Newman ■	Nov. 23
Murray St.	Nov. 25
West Texas A&M Tr.	Nov. 29-30
Lynn Cl.	Dec. 6-7
Alcorn St.	Dec. 14
St. Ambrose ■	Dec. 16
Las Vegas Cl.	Dec. 18-19
Grand Canyon Cl.	Dec. 27-28
West Va. St. ■	Jan. 4
Central St.	Jan. 7
Drury ■	Jan. 18
Indiana Tech	Jan. 21
Grand Valley St. ■	Jan. 25
Ind.-Southeast	Jan. 28
St. Francis (Ill.)	Feb. 4
Drury	Feb. 8
Central St. ■	Feb. 12
Wilberforce	Feb. 15
Indiana Tech ■	Feb. 19

	Kentucky St. ■	Feb. 22
	Wilberforce ■	Feb. 24
	Greenville ■	Mar. 1

1995-96 RESULTS (22-7)
90	Huron †	54
82	Mankato St.	91
105	Southwest Baptist ■	77
87	Indianapolis	86
80	Ky. Wesleyan ■	58
91	Virginia Union †	103
94	Wheeling Jesuit †	66
108	Central Mo. St.	114
71	Truman St. ■	48
106	Hawaii-Hilo	93
71	Susquehanna †	62
80	Northern Mich. †	61
81	St. Francis (Ind.) ■	69
85	Southwest Baptist	84
94	McKendree ■	86
84	Ky. Wesleyan ■	95
75	McKendree	76
99	Indiana Tech	77
83	Grand Canyon	92
72	Truman St.	54
61	Indianapolis	70
72	Drury ■	60
88	Central St.	83
95	Kentucky St.	77
74	St. Francis (Ill.) ■	59
83	Drury	63
98	Indiana Tech	97
83	Winona St.	82
102	Central St. ■	72

Nickname: Metros
Colors: Red & Gold
Arena: IUPUI Gymnasium
 Capacity: 1,800; Year Built: 1982
AD: Mike Moore
SID: Greg Seiter

INDIANAPOLIS
Indianapolis, IN 46227 II

Coach: Royce Waltman
Alma Mater: Slippery Rock '64
Record: 9 Years, W-165, L-82

1996-97 SCHEDULE
P.R.-Mayaguez ■	Nov. 20
Indianapolis Cl.	Nov. 22-23
Madonna ■	Nov. 30
Central St.	Dec. 4
Oakland City ■	Dec. 7
St. Francis (Ill.)	Dec. 14
Lewis ■	Dec. 21
Wis.-Parkside ■	Dec. 23
Bellarmine	Jan. 2
Ky. Wesleyan	Jan. 4
Northern Ky. ■	Jan. 9
Mo.-St. Louis ■	Jan. 11
St. Joseph's (Ind.)	Jan. 16
IU/PU-Ft. Wayne	Jan. 18
SIU-Edwardsville ■	Jan. 23
Southern Ind. ■	Jan. 25
Lewis	Jan. 30
Wis.-Parkside	Feb. 1
Ky. Wesleyan ■	Feb. 6
Bellarmine ■	Feb. 8
Northern Ky.	Feb. 13
Quincy	Feb. 15
IU/PU-Ft. Wayne ■	Feb. 20
St. Joseph's (Ind.) ■	Feb. 22
Southern Ind.	Feb. 27
SIU-Edwardsville	Mar. 1

1995-96 RESULTS (20-9)
80	Carson-Newman ■	60
66	Indiana (Pa.) ■	80
86	IU/PU-Indianapolis	87
93	North Ala.	86
89	Northern Ky. ■	73
72	Oakland City	63
60	St. Francis (Ill.) ■	47
71	Wis.-Parkside ■	65
63	St. Joseph's (Ind.) ■	60

80	SIU-Edwardsville	81
84	Quincy	90
81	Bellarmine ■	69
78	Ky. Wesleyan ■	73
77	IU/PU-Ft. Wayne ■	56
70	IU/PU-Indianapolis ■	61
77	Lewis	74
66	Wis.-Parkside ■	53
86	Southern Ind. ■	83
98	SIU-Edwardsville ■	73
67	Northern Ky.	70
82	Bellarmine	63
56	St. Joseph's (Ind.)	55
76	IU/PU-Ft. Wayne	66
95	Quincy ■	78
68	Lewis ■	78
65	Ky. Wesleyan	69
73	Southern Ind.	96
105	Lake Superior St. †	81
71	Southern Ind.	75

Nickname: Greyhounds
Colors: Crimson & Grey
Arena: Nicoson Hall
 Capacity: 4,200; Year Built: 1960
AD: Dave Huffman
SID: Joe Gentry

IONA
New Rochelle, NY 10801 I

Coach: Tim Welsh
Alma Mater: Potsdam St. '84
Record: 1 Year, W-21, L-8

1996-97 SCHEDULE
NIT	Nov. 20-29
American ■	Nov. 30
Hampton ■	Dec. 4
Wagner ■	Dec. 7
Fairleigh Dickinson ■	Dec. 11
Cornell	Dec. 14
Fordham	Dec. 18
Detroit	Dec. 21
Iona Tr.	Dec. 27-28
Rhode Island	Jan. 2
Loyola (Md.)	Jan. 8
Siena	Jan. 12
Cleveland St. ■	Jan. 15
Fairfield ■	Jan. 18
St. Peter's ■	Jan. 21
Colgate	Jan. 23
Niagara ■	Jan. 26
Canisius	Jan. 31
Niagara	Feb. 2
Manhattan ■	Feb. 6
Loyola (Md.) ■	Feb. 9
Manhattan	Feb. 12
St. Peter's	Feb. 15
Fairfield	Feb. 18
Canisius ■	Feb. 21
Siena ■	Feb. 23
Metro Atlantic Conf. Tr.	Mar. 1-3

1995-96 RESULTS (21-8)
62	Cleveland St.	65
70	Cornell ■	64
71	American ■	60
80	Fordham ■	66
87	Rhode Island ■	78
79	Detroit ■	76
70	St. John's (N.Y.)	57
79	Kentucky †	106
82	Fairleigh Dickinson ■	66
91	Hampton	69
87	Loyola (Md.) ■	62
75	Canisius ■	72
67	Manhattan	49
65	St. Peter's ■	60
97	Colgate ■	74
70	Siena ■	59
78	Niagara	59
54	Canisius	76
77	Niagara ■	69
50	Manhattan ■	63
57	St. Peter's	86

83	American	73
67	Fairfield ■	61
66	Siena	62
61	Loyola (Md.) ■	57
67	Fairfield	82
71	Siena †	59
62	Canisius †	63
78	St. Joseph's (Pa.) ■	82

Nickname: Gaels
Colors: Maroon & Gold
Arena: John Mulcahy Campus Centr
 Capacity: 3,200; Year Built: 1975
AD: Rich Petriccione
SID: Shawn Brennan

IOWA
Iowa City, IA 52242 I

Coach: Tom Davis
Alma Mater: Wis.-Platteville '60
Record: 25 Years, W-481, L-259

1996-97 SCHEDULE
Western Ill. [Moline]	Nov. 22
Maui Inv.	Nov. 25-27
Drake	Dec. 3
Iowa Shootout	Dec. 6-7
Northern Iowa ■	Dec. 10
Iowa St. ■	Dec. 14
Missouri ■	Dec. 21
Austin Peay ■	Dec. 27
Cal St. Northridge ■	Dec. 29
Northwestern ■	Jan. 2
Penn St.	Jan. 4
Purdue	Jan. 7
Wisconsin ■	Jan. 11
Ohio St. ■	Jan. 15
Michigan	Jan. 19
Minnesota ■	Jan. 23
Illinois ■	Jan. 29
Indiana ■	Feb. 4
Illinois	Feb. 9
Michigan St. ■	Feb. 12
Minnesota ■	Feb. 15
Michigan ■	Feb. 20
Ohio St.	Feb. 22
Wisconsin	Feb. 26
Purdue ■	Mar. 1
Penn St. ■	Mar. 5
Northwestern	Mar. 8

1995-96 RESULTS (23-9)
78	Ohio †	51
101	Connecticut †	95
81	Duke †	88
98	Drake ■	66
104	East Tenn. St. ■	58
79	Colgate ■	59
78	Northern Iowa	73
56	Iowa St.	50
110	Texas Southern ■	67
93	Western Ill. ■	41
82	Morehead St.	57
100	Colorado	85
61	Purdue	85
92	Minnesota	63
81	Ohio St. ■	53
71	Wisconsin	80
82	Illinois ■	79
60	Michigan St.	62
70	Michigan	61
73	Indiana	76
87	Penn St. ■	95
88	Northwestern	77
76	Indiana ■	50
60	Michigan	55
83	Michigan St. ■	47
86	Illinois	91
69	Wisconsin ■	54
73	Ohio St.	64
64	Minnesota	72
56	Purdue ■	52
81	Geo. Washington †	79
73	Arizona †	87

Nickname: Hawkeyes
Colors: Old Gold & Black
Arena: Carver-Hawkeye Arena
Capacity: 15,500; Year Built: 1983
AD: Bob Bowlsby
SID: Phil Haddy

IOWA ST.

Ames, IA 50011 I

Coach: Tim Floyd
Alma Mater: Louisiana Tech '77
Record: 10 Years, W-209, L-103

1996-97 SCHEDULE

Alcorn St. ■	Nov. 26
Md.-East. Shore ■	Dec. 1
Iowa St. Challenge	Dec. 5-6
Drake ■	Dec. 11
Iowa	Dec. 14
Iowa St. Cl.	Dec. 21-22
Tex.-Pan American ■	Dec. 30
Missouri	Jan. 4
Marquette ■	Jan. 7
Oklahoma ■	Jan. 11
Kansas	Jan. 13
Colorado	Jan. 18
Kansas St. ■	Jan. 22
Texas Tech ■	Jan. 25
Nebraska	Jan. 29
Texas A&M	Feb. 1
Baylor ■	Feb. 5
Kansas ■	Feb. 9
Missouri ■	Feb. 12
Kansas St.	Feb. 15
Texas	Feb. 19
Nebraska ■	Feb. 22
Colorado ■	Feb. 26
Oklahoma St.	Mar. 1
Big 12 Conf. Tr.	Mar. 6-9

1995-96 RESULTS (24-9)

70	Central Conn. St. ■	45
63	Wis.-Milwaukee ■	52
75	Tennessee St. ■	67
82	Richmond ■	64
65	Drake	62
50	Iowa ■	56
70	Wyoming	66
76	Mo.-St. Louis ■	63
50	Princeton ■	47
71	Samford ■	59
60	Purdue †	79
69	N.C.-Charlotte †	61
77	Coppin St. ■	59
55	Kansas St.	72
56	Marquette	58
79	Oklahoma St. ■	71
73	Missouri ■	62
75	Colorado	63
67	Oklahoma ■	61
75	Nebraska	65
70	Kansas	89
74	Nebraska ■	59
70	Oklahoma	58
50	Kansas ■	61
46	Oklahoma St.	58
78	Missouri	74
87	Kansas St. ■	92
74	Colorado ■	65
62	Nebraska †	60
57	Missouri †	53
56	Kansas †	55
74	California †	64
67	Utah †	73

Nickname: Cyclones
Colors: Cardinal & Gold
Arena: James H. Hilton Coliseum
Capacity: 14,020; Year Built: 1971
AD: Gene Smith
SID: Beth Haag

ITHACA

Ithaca, NY 14850 III

Coach: Tom Baker
Alma Mater: Ithaca '63
Record: 19 Years, W-303, L-192

1996-97 SCHEDULE

Alfred ■	Nov. 23
Cortland St. ■	Dec. 3
Elmira	Dec. 7
New Paltz St.	Dec. 10
Binghamton	Dec. 13
Cortland St.	Jan. 8
Union (N.Y.) Inv.	Jan. 10-11
Plattsburgh St. ■	Jan. 13
Utica	Jan. 17
Hartwick	Jan. 18
Cazenovia	Jan. 21
Rochester Inst. ■	Jan. 24
Nazareth ■	Jan. 25
Hartwick ■	Jan. 31
Utica ■	Feb. 1
Elmira ■	Feb. 4
St. Lawrence	Feb. 7
Clarkson	Feb. 8
Hobart ■	Feb. 11
Nazareth	Feb. 14
Rochester Inst.	Feb. 15
Cazenovia ■	Feb. 18
St. John Fisher	Feb. 20
Keuka	Feb. 22

1995-96 RESULTS (16-10)

63	New Paltz St. ■	45
92	Coast Guard †	81
82	Connecticut Col.	87
62	Cortland St.	57
66	Utica ■	87
60	Plattsburgh St.	62
72	St. Lawrence ■	41
76	Clarkson ■	62
58	Daemen	62
75	St. John Fisher ■	87
87	Cortland St. ■	60
77	Alfred ■	56
55	Nazareth	50
62	Rochester Inst. ■	72
79	Hobart	56
75	Cazenovia ■	65
83	Southern Vt. ■	75
73	Rochester Inst.	78
64	Binghamton ■	59
78	Alfred	59
55	Hartwick ■	46
80	Keuka ■	61
87	Cazenovia	54
92	Roberts Wesleyan	93
44	Hartwick	65
63	Oneonta St.	75

Nickname: Bombers
Colors: Blue & Gold
Arena: Ben Light Gymnasium
Capacity: 2,500; Year Built: 1964
AD: Robert Deming
SID: Pete Moore

JACKSON ST.

Jackson, MS 39217 I

Coach: Andy Stoglin
Alma Mater: UTEP '65
Record: 9 Years, W-142, L-125

1996-97 SCHEDULE

Arkansas	Nov. 22
Southern Miss.	Nov. 26
Southeastern La. ■	Nov. 30
Memphis	Dec. 2
Tougaloo ■	Dec. 4
Eastern Mich. ■	Dec. 7
Arizona	Dec. 14
UCLA	Dec. 17
Arizona St.	Dec. 20
New Mexico	Dec. 23
McNeese St.	Dec. 28
Tennessee St. ■	Jan. 2
Prairie View	Jan. 4
Texas Southern	Jan. 6
Alcorn St. ■	Jan. 11
Southern U. ■	Jan. 13
Grambling ■	Jan. 18
Mississippi Val. ■	Jan. 20
Alabama St.	Jan. 25
Prairie View ■	Feb. 1
Texas Southern ■	Feb. 3
Alcorn St.	Feb. 8
Southern U.	Feb. 10
Grambling [Monroe]	Feb. 15
Mississippi Val.	Feb. 17
Alabama St. ■	Feb. 22
Southwestern Conf. Tr.	Mar. 5-8

1995-96 RESULTS (16-13)

68	Oklahoma	99
67	Memphis	90
61	Southern Miss.	68
76	Washington	92
90	Southeastern La.	79
87	Tougaloo ■	72
63	Missouri	86
71	Oklahoma St.	81
87	LSU	76
48	Va. Commonwealth †	66
62	San Francisco †	71
77	Arkansas	86
72	Belhaven ■	57
63	Texas Southern ■	67
102	Prairie View ■	84
68	Alcorn St.	69
85	Southern U.	74
93	Mississippi Val. ■	94
56	Grambling †	54
85	Alabama St. ■	81
80	Texas Southern	77
92	Prairie View	78
75	Alcorn St. ■	59
85	Southern U. ■	84
81	Mississippi Val.	79
70	Grambling ■	68
80	Alabama St.	68
60	Grambling †	57
94	Mississippi Val. †	111

Nickname: Tigers
Colors: Blue & White
Arena: Williams Athletics Center
Capacity: 8,000; Year Built: 1981
AD: Paul Covington
SID: Sam Jefferson

JACKSONVILLE

Jacksonville, FL 32211 I

Coach: George Scholz
Alma Mater: Jacksonville '74
Record: 10 Years, W-222, L-84

1996-97 SCHEDULE

Arizona St.	Nov. 22
UNLV	Nov. 26
Arkansas St. ■	Nov. 30
South Fla.	Dec. 7
Florida St. ■	Dec. 14
Miami (Fla.)	Dec. 18
Western Ky. ■	Dec. 21
Fordham ■	Dec. 28
Monmouth (N.J.) ■	Dec. 30
New Orleans ■	Jan. 2
Southwestern La. ■	Jan. 4
Arkansas St.	Jan. 9
Ark.-Little Rock	Jan. 11
South Ala. ■	Jan. 13
Louisiana Tech	Jan. 16
Lamar	Jan. 18
Tex.-Pan American	Jan. 25
Western Ky.	Jan. 30
Lamar ■	Feb. 1
Florida	Feb. 3
Southwestern La.	Feb. 6
Tex.-Pan American ■	Feb. 8
New Orleans	Feb. 13
South Ala.	Feb. 15
Ark.-Little Rock ■	Feb. 17
Louisiana Tech ■	Feb. 22
Sun Belt Conf. Tr.	Feb. 28-Mar. 4

1995-96 RESULTS (15-13)

88	Fla. Atlantic ■	70
80	Florida St.	87
74	Stetson ■	66
56	UAB	61
65	South Ala. ■	53
64	UAB ■	67
84	South Fla. ■	75
89	Siena	76
59	Georgia	86
85	Lamar ■	75
80	Southwestern La. ■	69
87	Western Ky.	85
75	Louisiana Tech	76
101	Arkansas St. ■	93
69	New Orleans	73
76	South Ala.	80
61	Tex.-Pan American	75
92	Western Ky. ■	78
57	Ark.-Little Rock ■	89
70	Louisiana Tech ■	68
80	Lamar	70
88	New Orleans ■	97
77	Arkansas St.	75
81	Tex.-Pan American ■	73
84	Southwestern La.	86
77	Ark.-Little Rock	103
63	Lamar †	62
60	Ark.-Little Rock	67

Nickname: Dolphins
Colors: Green & White
Arena: Jacksonville Coliseum
Capacity: 9,150; Year Built: 1960
AD: Tom Seitz
SID: Richard Paige

JACKSONVILLE ST.

Jacksonville, AL 36265 I

Coach: Bill Jones
Alma Mater: Jacksonville St. '66
Record: 24 Years, W-455, L-195

1996-97 SCHEDULE

Mississippi Val. ■	Nov. 23
Alabama St. ■	Nov. 30
Marshall ■	Dec. 2
East Caro.	Dec. 4
Jacksonville Cl.	Dec. 6-7
Mississippi Val.	Dec. 14
UAB Tr.	Dec. 20-21
Central Fla.	Jan. 2
Stetson	Jan. 4
Charleston (S.C.)	Jan. 9
Campbell ■	Jan. 11
Centenary (La.) ■	Jan. 16
Southeastern La. ■	Jan. 18
Mercer	Jan. 23
Georgia St.	Jan. 25
Samford ■	Jan. 30
Fla. Atlantic ■	Feb. 1
Florida Int'l ■	Feb. 3
Samford	Feb. 8
East Caro. ■	Feb. 10
Southeastern La.	Feb. 13
Centenary (La.)	Feb. 15
Georgia St. ■	Feb. 20

Mercer ■ ....Feb. 22
Alabama St. ....Feb. 26
Trans America Conf. Tr....Feb. 27-Mar. 1

1995-96 RESULTS (10-17)

68	Mississippi Val.	93
92	Alabama St.	65
74	Auburn	91
93	Bapt. Christian ■	72
102	Mississippi Val. ■	94
53	UTEP	76
91	Freed-Hardeman ■	65
82	Alabama St. †	68
72	UAB	83
73	Central Fla. ■	93
96	Stetson ■	67
80	Charleston (S.C.) ■	89
62	Campbell	73
85	Centenary (La.)	94
90	Southeastern La.	93
95	Mercer ■	99
83	Georgia St. ■	65
63	Samford	79
72	Fla. Atlantic	91
88	Florida Int'l	90
78	Samford ■	65
90	Marshall	111
92	Southeastern La. ■	84
79	Centenary (La.) ■	95
76	Georgia St.	82
69	Mercer	78
105	Alabama St. ■	65

Nickname: Gamecocks
Colors: Red & White
Arena: Pete Mathews Coliseum
  Capacity: 5,500; Year Built: 1974
AD: Jerry Cole
SID: Mike Galloway

JAMES MADISON
Harrisonburg, VA 22807 I

Coach: Lefty Driesell
Alma Mater: Duke '54
Record: 34 Years, W-667, L-322

1996-97 SCHEDULE

Bowling Green ■ ....Nov. 23
Shippensburg ■ ....Nov. 25
Mississippi St. ....Nov. 30
Washington ■ ....Dec. 7
Montana St. ■ ....Dec. 14
Hampton ■ ....Dec. 18
Southern Ill. ....Dec. 21
Towson St. ....Dec. 28
Md.-Balt. County ■ .....Dec. 30
William & Mary ....Jan. 4
Va. Commonwealth ■ .....Jan. 8
American ....Jan. 11
George Mason ■ ....Jan. 13
N.C.-Wilmington ■ ......Jan. 18
East Caro. ....Jan. 21
Old Dominion ■ ....Jan. 25
Richmond ....Jan. 27
American ■ ....Jan. 29
N.C.-Charlotte ■ ....Feb. 1
Va. Commonwealth ....Feb. 5
George Mason ....Feb. 8
N.C.-Wilmington ....Feb. 12
East Caro. ■ ....Feb. 15
William & Mary ■ ....Feb. 19
Richmond ■ ....Feb. 22
Old Dominion ....Feb. 24
Colonial Conf. Tr. ....Feb. 28-Mar. 3

1995-96 RESULTS (10-20)

86	Illinois St. †	85
71	Auburn †	82
60	Va. Commonwealth †	66
88	Delaware St. ■	64
68	Geo. Washington ■	76
88	Hampton †	86
72	Bowling Green	88
63	Butler ■	65
64	Towson St. ■	67
55	Drexel †	75
75	Butler †	65
56	East Caro. ■	62
70	William & Mary ■	81
48	N.C.-Wilmington	57
70	Va. Commonwealth	81
80	George Mason ■	72
71	American	84
45	Old Dominion ■	58
71	Richmond	78
51	William & Mary	68
41	N.C.-Charlotte	55
72	Houston	97
80	Richmond ■	84
72	Old Dominion	76
59	N.C.-Wilmington ■	58
76	Va. Commonwealth ■	75
72	East Caro.	70
81	George Mason	80
75	American ■	72
72	Old Dominion †	75

Nickname: Dukes
Colors: Purple & Gold
Arena: JMU Convocation Center
  Capacity: 7,612; Year Built: 1982
AD: Donald L. Lemish
SID: Gary Michael

JERSEY CITY ST.
Jersey City, NJ 07305 III

Coach: Charles Brown
Alma Mater: Jersey City St. '65
Record: 14 Years, W-280, L-115

1996-97 SCHEDULE

Binghamton Cl. ....Nov. 22-23
Richard Stockton ....Nov. 26
Kean ■ ....Nov. 30
Rutgers-Camden ....Dec. 4
Col. of New Jersey .....Dec. 7
Wm. Paterson ■ ....Dec. 11
Montclair St. ....Dec. 14
FDU-Madison ■ ....Dec. 21
Western Conn St. Tr. ...Dec. 28-29
John Jay ■ ....Jan. 11
Rutgers-Newark ....Jan. 15
Rowan ■ ....Jan. 18
Ramapo ....Jan. 22
Rutgers-Camden ■ ....Jan. 25
Richard Stockton ■ .....Jan. 29
Kean ....Feb. 1
Rutgers-Newark ■ ....Feb. 5
Col. of New Jersey ■ ...Feb. 8
Wm. Paterson ....Feb. 12
Montclair St. ■ ....Feb. 15
Ramapo ■ ....Feb. 19
Rowan ....Feb. 22

1995-96 RESULTS (16-11)

76	Old Westbury ■	67
73	Salem St. ■	86
78	Rutgers-Camden	61
76	Col. of New Jersey	74
70	Kean	74
84	Rutgers-Newark ■	83
79	Montclair St. ■	80
64	Richard Stockton	69
90	FDU-Madison ■	61
70	Menlo †	73
75	Gettysburg †	96
75	Bloomfield	66
63	Wm. Paterson ■	59
81	Rowan ■	68
86	Ramapo ■	78
89	Kean ■	65
90	Rutgers-Camden	68
61	Col. of New Jersey ■	53
68	Wm. Paterson	73
93	Montclair St.	85
58	Richard Stockton ■	60
84	Rutgers-Newark	68
78	Ramapo	55
69	Rowan	99
96	Rowan	102
73	Staten Island	63
83	Rowan	102

Nickname: Gothic Knights
Colors: Green & Gold
Arena: Athletic & Fitness Center
  Capacity: 2,000; Year Built: 1994
AD: Larry Schiner
SID: John Stallings

JOHN CARROLL
Cleveland, OH 44118 III

Coach: Mike Moran
Alma Mater: Xavier (Ohio) '73
Record: 4 Years, W-62, L-42

1996-97 SCHEDULE
Schedule unavailable

1995-96 RESULTS (19-8)

98	Clarkson †	43
87	St. John Fisher	90
90	Wash. & Lee †	61
66	Carnegie Mellon	61
78	Muskingum	66
75	Mount Union	68
68	Otterbein	62
89	Capital ■	85
97	Earlham †	77
70	Hiram †	71
75	Hiram	74
62	Marietta ■	64
81	Heidelberg ■	66
64	Ohio Northern	66
77	Baldwin-Wallace ■	61
56	Marietta	78
82	Heidelberg	73
103	Otterbein ■	87
61	Mount Union	58
74	Capital	84
92	Hiram ■	70
66	Muskingum	65
75	Baldwin-Wallace	71
85	Ohio Northern ■	80
89	Muskingum	93
86	Wooster ■	72
61	Hope	80

Nickname: Blue Streaks
Colors: Blue & Gold
Arena: Don Shula Sports Center
  Capacity: 2,448; Year Built: 1957
AD: Tony DeCarlo
SID: Chris Wenzler

JOHN JAY
New York, NY 10019 III

Coach: Ted Gustus
Alma Mater: John Jay '79
Record: 1 Year, W-12, L-14

1996-97 SCHEDULE

Potsdam Tr. ....Nov. 22-23
Albertus Magnus ■ ......Nov. 26
CCNY ■ ....Dec. 4
Emerson Cl. ....Dec. 6-7
Medgar Evers ■ ....Dec. 13
FDU-Madison ....Dec. 16
Kean ■ ....Dec. 28
Staten Island ....Jan. 4
St. Joseph's (Me.) ■ ...Jan. 6
Baruch ....Jan. 8
Jersey City St. ....Jan. 11
York (N.Y.) ....Jan. 13
CCNY ....Jan. 16
Brooklyn ....Jan. 23
Yeshiva ....Jan. 26
Lehman ....Jan. 28
Old Westbury ....Feb. 1
Baruch ....Feb. 5
Lehman ....Feb. 7
Vassar ....Feb. 14
Mt. St. Mary (N.Y.) ■ ..Feb. 18
Hunter ....Feb. 19

1995-96 RESULTS (12-14)

63	Col. of New Jersey	84
69	Yeshiva ■	65
91	Pratt	62
81	Purchase St. ■	61
111	Cazenovia	72
92	Utica	94
74	CCNY ■	78
102	Medgar Evers ■	83
63	FDU-Madison ■	73
72	Lehman	70
88	Brooklyn ■	80
94	Worcester St. †	104
61	Baruch	64
66	Old Westbury ■	68
81	Albertus Magnus	83
75	Baruch	49
42	Staten Island	81
70	Lehman	74
88	CCNY	87
73	Baruch ■	68
88	Vassar ■	84
63	York (N.Y.) ■	75
82	Mt. St. Mary (N.Y.)	88
69	Hunter	77
72	Medgar Evers	62
47	York (N.Y.) †	51

Nickname: Bloodhounds
Colors: Blue & Gold
Arena: College Gym
  Capacity: 700; Year Built: 1989
AD: Susan Larkin
SID: Jeff Risener

JOHNS HOPKINS
Baltimore, MD 21218 III

Coach: Bill Nelson
Alma Mater: Brockport St. '65
Record: 16 Years, W-255, L-160

1996-97 SCHEDULE

Johns Hopkins Cl. ......Nov. 22-23
Goucher ■ ....Nov. 26
Swarthmore ....Dec. 3
New York U. ....Dec. 6
Brandeis ■ ....Dec. 8
Washington (Md.) ■ .....Dec. 10
Rochester ■ ....Jan. 6
Washington (Mo.) ■ .....Jan. 10
Chicago ■ ....Jan. 12
Gettysburg ....Jan. 15
Carnegie Mellon ....Jan. 17
Emory ....Jan. 19
Ursinus ....Jan. 22
Muhlenberg ■ ....Jan. 25
Western Md. ■ ....Jan. 29
Frank. & Marsh. ....Feb. 1
Case Reserve ....Feb. 3
Dickinson ■ ....Feb. 5
Haverford ■ ....Feb. 8
Gettysburg ■ ....Feb. 12
Frank. & Marsh. ■ ......Feb. 15
Western Md. ....Feb. 19
Dickinson ....Feb. 22

1995-96 RESULTS (13-11)

62	WPI	58
44	Fredonia St. ■	58
66	Goucher	64
65	Swarthmore ■	61
76	New York U. ■	78
67	Brandeis	65
78	Washington (Md.)	73
69	Rochester	53
88	Washington (Mo.)	91
53	Chicago	72
82	Carnegie Mellon ■	73
59	Emory ■	48
59	Ursinus ■	61
63	Muhlenberg	53
94	Western Md.	98
73	Gettysburg ■	81
66	Frank. & Marsh.	71
72	Case Reserve ■	64
71	Dickinson	50
68	Haverford ■	73
69	Gettysburg	79

SCHEDULES/RESULTS

62	Frank. & Marsh. ■	72
65	Western Md. ■	53
80	Dickinson ■	76

Nickname: Blue Jays
Colors: Columbia Blue & Black
Arena: White Athletic Center
Capacity: 1,200; Year Built: 1965
AD: Tom Calder
SID: Jennifer Hoover

JOHNSON SMITH

Charlotte, NC 28216 II

Coach: Steve Joyner
Alma Mater: Johnson Smith '73
Record: 9 Years, W-151, L-105

1996-97 SCHEDULE

Johnson C. Smith Cl.	Nov. 15-16
St. Paul's	Nov. 19
Virginia St.	Nov. 23
Montevallo	Dec. 6
Montevallo	Dec. 7
Queens (N.C.)	Dec. 10
Ala.-Huntsville	Dec. 30
N.C. Central	Jan. 2
Virginia Union	Jan. 4
Elizabeth City St. ■	Jan. 6
St. Augustine's	Jan. 9
Bowie St.	Jan. 11
Morehouse	Jan. 15
Winston-Salem	Jan. 18
Fayetteville St. ■	Jan. 23
Shaw ■	Jan. 25
N.C. Central ■	Jan. 30
Winston-Salem ■	Feb. 1
St. Augustine's ■	Feb. 6
Fayetteville St.	Feb. 8
Shaw	Feb. 11
Livingstone ■	Feb. 15
Norfolk St. ■	Feb. 18
Livingstone	Feb. 22

1995-96 RESULTS (11-16)

86	Dowling ■	89
79	Concordia (Tex.) ■	80
85	St. Paul's ■	65
95	Virginia St. ■	82
98	Montevallo	81
93	Aub.-Montgomery	101
66	Virginia Union	96
74	Ala.-Huntsville ■	67
75	N.C. Central ■	93
60	Norfolk St.	74
74	Elizabeth City St.	83
77	Bowie St. ■	66
71	Winston-Salem ■	74
82	St. Augustine's ■	90
61	Fayetteville St.	72
82	Shaw	71
78	N.C. Central	94
71	Queens (N.C.) ■	68
86	St. Augustine's	83
58	Fayetteville St. ■	56
70	Shaw ■	71
86	Livingstone	88
71	Winston-Salem	80
72	Savannah St.	75
83	Livingstone ■	61
94	Elizabeth City St. †	83
67	Shaw †	72

Nickname: Golden Bulls
Colors: Blue & Gold
Arena: Brayboy Gymnasium
Capacity: 3,200; Year Built: 1961
AD: Stephen Joyner
SID: Kelli Gilmore

JOHNSON ST.

Johnson, VT 05656 III

Coach: Charles Mason
Alma Mater: Concordia-Montreal '91
Record: 1 Year, W-4, L-18

1996-97 SCHEDULE

Endicott Tr.	Nov. 23-24
St. Joseph (Vt.)	Nov. 26
Plymouth St.	Dec. 3
Castleton St.	Dec. 5
North Adams St. ■	Dec. 10
Atlantic Union	Dec. 12
Plattsburgh St. ■	Jan. 8
St. Joseph (Vt.)	Jan. 10
Potsdam St.	Jan. 12
Lyndon St. ■	Jan. 15
Green Mountain ■	Jan. 18
Castleton St. ■	Jan. 22
Manhattanville Cl.	Jan. 25-26
Lyndon St.	Jan. 29
Westbrook	Feb. 1
Notre Dame (N.H.)	Feb. 2
Atlantic Union ■	Feb. 8
Notre Dame (N.H.) ■	Feb. 9
Endicott ■	Feb. 10
Westbrook ■	Feb. 15
New England Col.	Feb. 18
St. Joseph (Vt.) ■	Feb. 20
Green Mountain	Feb. 22

1995-96 RESULTS (4-18)

53	Plattsburgh St.	89
52	Potsdam St. †	74
51	Plymouth St. ■	89
50	Seattle ■	75
49	Atlantic Union ■	48
57	Norwich	87
53	Plattsburgh St.	75
53	North Adams St.	65
41	Westbrook	76
59	St. Joseph's (Me.) ■	78
77	Notre Dame (N.H.)	67
64	Castleton St. ■	84
52	Atlantic Union	55
80	Lyndon St. ■	57
53	Green Mountain	94
53	Seattle	81
87	Notre Dame (N.H.) ■	55
53	Lyndon St.	59
38	Green Mountain ■	68
55	Castleton St.	85
60	Westbrook ■	80
55	Westbrook	91

Nickname: Badgers
Colors: Green, Blue & White
Arena: Carter Gymnasium
Capacity: 700; Year Built: 1965
AD: Barbara Lougee
SID: To be named

JUNIATA

Huntingdon, PA 16652 III

Coach: Rick Ferry
Alma Mater: Susquehanna '85
(First year as head coach)

1996-97 SCHEDULE

Juniata Tr.	Nov. 23-24
Allegheny	Nov. 26
Carnegie Mellon Inv.	Nov. 30-Dec. 1
Lebanon Valley	Dec. 4
Widener ■	Dec. 7
Messiah	Dec. 10
Thomas More Cl.	Jan. 4-5
Lycoming	Jan. 8
Thiel ■	Jan. 11
Albright	Jan. 15
Moravian ■	Jan. 18
Elizabethtown ■	Jan. 21
Susquehanna	Jan. 25
Lebanon Valley ■	Jan. 29
Widener	Feb. 1
Messiah ■	Feb. 5
Albright ■	Feb. 8
Misericordia	Feb. 10
Moravian	Feb. 15
Elizabethtown	Feb. 18
Susquehanna ■	Feb. 22

1995-96 RESULTS (7-17)

63	Mount Union	72
58	Wilmington (Ohio) †	74
92	Thiel	77
51	Lebanon Valley ■	69
61	Widener	71
82	Messiah ■	78
70	Carnegie Mellon	66
76	York (Pa.) ■	59
86	Allegheny ■	94
60	Wis.-Eau Claire	87
53	Mass.-Dartmouth †	90
67	Moravian	91
73	Elizabethtown	94
76	Susquehanna ■	88
55	Lebanon Valley	71
56	Widener ■	73
62	Lycoming ■	112
76	Messiah	65
72	Albright	83
59	Albright ■	68
72	Misericordia ■	70
73	Moravian ■	66
62	Elizabethtown ■	102
74	Susquehanna	103

Nickname: Eagles
Colors: Yale Blue & Old Gold
Arena: Kennedy Sports & Recreation Center
Capacity: 1,500; Year Built: 1982
AD: Larry Bock
SID: Michael Emery

KALAMAZOO

Kalamazoo, MI 49006 III

Coach: Joe Haklin
Alma Mater: Wabash '73
Record: 9 Years, W-150, L-83

1996-97 SCHEDULE

Cornerstone	Nov. 26
Chicago ■	Nov. 30
Goshen	Dec. 7
Lake Forest	Dec. 10
Spring Arbor	Dec. 14
Purdue-Calumet	Dec. 17
Wabash-DePauw Cl.	Dec. 21-22
Kalamazoo Cl.	Dec. 27-28
Concordia (Mich.)	Jan. 4
Olivet ■	Jan. 8
Franklin ■	Jan. 11
Adrian	Jan. 15
Calvin ■	Jan. 18
Hope ■	Jan. 22
Alma	Jan. 25
Albion	Jan. 29
Olivet	Feb. 1
Adrian ■	Feb. 8
Calvin	Feb. 12
Hope	Feb. 15
Alma ■	Feb. 19
Albion ■	Feb. 22

1995-96 RESULTS (17-11)

79	Concordia (Mich.) ■	80
72	Cornerstone ■	86
78	Franklin	67
100	Goshen ■	57
80	North Park ■	64
69	Chicago	78
69	Grace	59
60	Bluffton	73
63	Huntington ■	60
73	Lake Forest ■	61
77	Olivet	84
87	Spring Arbor	92
45	Adrian ■	46
65	Calvin	59
68	Hope	73
78	Alma ■	61
77	Albion ■	73
73	Olivet ■	43
68	Aquinas	67
74	Adrian	68
73	Calvin ■	76
67	Hope ■	65
77	Alma	72
85	Albion	67
75	Alma ■	59
83	Calvin †	68
78	Hope	89
62	Hope	65

Nickname: Hornets
Colors: Orange & Black
Arena: Anderson Athletic Center
Capacity: 2,000; Year Built: 1980
AD: Bob Kent
SID: Michael Molde

KANSAS

Lawrence, KS 66045 I

Coach: Roy Williams
Alma Mater: North Caro. '72
Record: 8 Years, W-203, L-56

1996-97 SCHEDULE

Santa Clara	Nov. 22
Maui Inv.	Nov. 25-27
San Diego ■	Dec. 1
Cincinnati [Chicago]	Dec. 4
UCLA	Dec. 7
Geo. Washington ■	Dec. 11
N.C.-Asheville ■	Dec. 15
North Caro. St. ■	Dec. 21
Washburn ■	Dec. 30
Brown ■	Jan. 2
Kansas St.	Jan. 4
Texas ■	Jan. 6
Niagara ■	Jan. 9
Baylor	Jan. 11
Iowa St. ■	Jan. 13
Connecticut	Jan. 19
Texas A&M ■	Jan. 22
Colorado	Jan. 26
Texas Tech	Jan. 29
Nebraska ■	Feb. 1
Missouri	Feb. 4
Iowa St.	Feb. 9
Oklahoma St. ■	Feb. 12
Colorado ■	Feb. 15
Missouri ■	Feb. 17
Kansas St. ■	Feb. 22
Oklahoma	Feb. 24
Nebraska	Mar. 2
Big 12 Conf. Tr.	Mar. 6-9

1995-96 RESULTS (29-5)

79	Utah †	68
72	Virginia †	66
85	UCLA ■	70
83	Rice	63
101	San Diego	71
91	Indiana †	83
103	Pittsburg St. ■	48
66	Temple †	74
100	Cornell ■	46
108	East Tenn. St. ■	73
83	Southern Methodist ■	61
76	Oklahoma St.	61
69	Florida	54
85	St. Peter's ■	71
80	Colorado	78
72	Oklahoma ■	66
88	Nebraska	73
84	Oklahoma St. ■	66
72	Kansas St. ■	62
89	Iowa St. ■	70
73	Missouri	77
85	Colorado ■	70
61	Iowa St.	50
81	Nebraska ■	71
77	Kansas St.	66
87	Missouri ■	65
79	Oklahoma	85
88	Colorado †	55
61	Kansas St. †	55
55	Iowa St. †	56
92	South Caro. St. †	54
76	Santa Clara †	51

83	Arizona †	80
57	Syracuse †	60

Nickname: Jayhawks
Colors: Crimson & Blue
Arena: Allen Fieldhouse
  Capacity: 16,300; Year Built: 1955
AD: Bob Frederick
SID: Dean Buchan

KANSAS ST.
Manhattan, KS 66506 I

Coach: Tom Asbury
Alma Mater: Wyoming '68
Record: 8 Years, W-154, L-86

1996-97 SCHEDULE
Mo.-Kansas City ■	Nov. 22
N.C.-Asheville ■	Nov. 26
Morgan St. ■	Nov. 30
Wichita St. ■	Dec. 3
Bradley	Dec. 7
Coppin St. ■	Dec. 12
Bethune-Cookman ■	Dec. 14
Michigan St.	Dec. 21
Ark.-Pine Bluff ■	Dec. 23
Xavier (Ohio)	Dec. 29
Kansas ■	Jan. 4
Texas	Jan. 12
Nebraska	Jan. 15
Texas Tech ■	Jan. 18
Iowa St.	Jan. 22
Texas A&M ■	Jan. 25
Colorado ■	Jan. 29
Missouri	Feb. 1
Oklahoma St.	Feb. 5
Oklahoma ■	Feb. 8
Nebraska ■	Feb. 10
Iowa St. ■	Feb. 15
Colorado	Feb. 19
Kansas	Feb. 22
Baylor ■	Feb. 26
Missouri ■	Mar. 1
Big 12 Conf. Tr.	Mar. 6-9

1995-96 RESULTS (17-12)
75	Bradley ■	72
63	Emporia St. ■	57
106	Marshall ■	88
56	Illinois	82
60	Washington	74
54	Michigan St. ■	67
69	Morgan St. ■	60
73	Xavier (Ohio)	67
69	Mo.-Kansas City	54
76	Loyola (Md.) †	69
65	California	58
70	Wichita St. ■	64
72	Iowa St.	55
59	Oklahoma ■	64
70	Colorado	57
75	Oklahoma	60
62	Oklahoma St. ■	59
80	Missouri	86
77	Nebraska ■	68
62	Kansas	72
63	Colorado ■	64
60	Oklahoma St.	83
69	Missouri ■	64
66	Kansas ■	77
92	Iowa St.	87
66	Nebraska	70
58	Oklahoma St. †	55
55	Kansas †	61
48	New Mexico †	69

Nickname: Wildcats
Colors: Purple & White
Arena: Bramlage Coliseum
  Capacity: 13,500; Year Built: 1988
AD: Max Urick
SID: Kent Brown

KEAN
Union, NJ 07083 III

Coach: Bruce Hamburger
Alma Mater: Kean '81
Record: 1 Year, W-9, L-14

1996-97 SCHEDULE
Drew Cl.	Nov. 22-23
Rutgers-Newark ■	Nov. 26
Jersey City St.	Nov. 30
Wm. Paterson	Dec. 3
Richard Stockton ■	Dec. 11
Rowan	Dec. 14
John Jay	Dec. 28
Kean Cl.	Jan. 4-5
York (N.Y.) ■	Jan. 8
Montclair St.	Jan. 11
Col. of New Jersey ■	Jan. 15
Ramapo ■	Jan. 18
Rutgers-Camden ■	Jan. 22
Wm. Paterson ■	Jan. 25
Rutgers-Newark	Jan. 29
Jersey City St. ■	Feb. 1
Col. of New Jersey	Feb. 5
Montclair St. ■	Feb. 8
Richard Stockton	Feb. 12
Rowan ■	Feb. 15
Rutgers-Camden	Feb. 19
Ramapo	Feb. 22

1995-96 RESULTS (9-14)
79	Neumann †	61
67	Western Md.	73
62	Rowan	90
83	Montclair St. ■	70
74	Jersey City St. ■	70
67	Wm. Paterson	57
71	Col. of New Jersey	74
65	Rutgers-Newark ■	75
61	Caldwell	63
62	Delaware Valley ■	31
72	Ramapo	59
55	Richard Stockton ■	71
75	Jersey City St.	89
79	Rutgers-Camden ■	48
82	Rowan ■	113
70	Montclair St.	80
53	Centenary (N.J.) ■	66
67	Rutgers-Camden	63
64	Wm. Paterson ■	73
61	Col. of New Jersey ■	75
72	Rutgers-Newark	60
50	Richard Stockton	59
68	Ramapo	79

Nickname: Cougars
Colors: Royal Blue & Silver
Arena: D'angola Gymnasium
  Capacity: 700; Year Built: 1963
AD: Glenn Hedden
SID: Adam Fenton

KEENE ST.
Keene, NH 03431 II

Coach: Phil Rowe
Alma Mater: Plymouth St. '74
Record: 10 Years, W-129, L-119

1996-97 SCHEDULE
Rhode Island Col.	Nov. 23
Daniel Webster ■	Nov. 25
Williams	Nov. 30
New Hamp. Col. ■	Dec. 4
Southern Conn. St.	Dec. 7
Albany (N.Y.)	Dec. 14
Western Conn St. Tr.	Dec. 28-29
Bridgeport	Jan. 8
Franklin Pierce	Jan. 11
Albany (N.Y.) ■	Jan. 14
Mass.-Lowell	Jan. 16

Stony Brook ■	Jan. 18
Endicott	Jan. 20
Sacred Heart ■	Jan. 22
Stony Brook	Jan. 25
New Haven ■	Jan. 29
Franklin Pierce ■	Feb. 1
Sacred Heart	Feb. 4
Southern Conn. St. ■	Feb. 8
Johnson & Wales ■	Feb. 10
New Hamp. Col.	Feb. 12
Bridgeport	Feb. 15
New Haven ■	Feb. 17
Mass.-Lowell ■	Feb. 20

1995-96 RESULTS (2-22)
76	Daniel Webster	91
92	Rivier	91
93	Bridgeport ■	100
71	Sacred Heart ■	85
87	Stony Brook ■	93
76	Old Westbury †	88
71	Southern Me. †	69
53	Southern Conn. St.	83
80	New Haven	108
67	New Hamp. Col.	92
77	Le Moyne	100
78	Albany (N.Y.) ■	95
68	Sacred Heart	92
89	Bridgeport	96
80	Mass.-Lowell ■	108
71	Stony Brook	98
55	Franklin Pierce ■	97
72	Albany (N.Y.)	95
72	Le Moyne	111
75	New Hamp. Col. ■	111
77	New Haven ■	98
81	Southern Conn. St. ■	110
79	Mass.-Lowell	102
72	Franklin Pierce	109

Nickname: Owls
Colors: Red & White
Arena: Spaulding Gym
  Capacity: 2,100; Year Built: 1968
AD: John Ratliff
SID: Stuart Kaufman

KENNESAW ST.
Marietta, GA 30061 II

Coach: Greg Yarlett
Alma Mater: Jacksonville St. '81
(First year as head coach)

1996-97 SCHEDULE
Shorter ■	Nov. 20
Fort Valley St.	Nov. 23
North Ga.	Nov. 26
Kennesaw St. Inv.	Nov. 29-30
Fort Valley St. ■	Dec. 10
S.C.-Aiken	Dec. 14
Tusculum	Dec. 16
Shorter	Dec. 31
Armstrong Atlantic ■	Jan. 4
Columbus St. ■	Jan. 6
S.C.-Spartanburg ■	Jan. 8
Augusta St.	Jan. 11
Georgia Col.	Jan. 15
Francis Marion	Jan. 18
Lander	Jan. 22
N.C.-Pembroke ■	Jan. 25
Columbus St.	Jan. 29
Armstrong Atlantic	Feb. 1
S.C.-Spartanburg	Feb. 5
Augusta St. ■	Feb. 8
S.C.-Aiken ■	Feb. 10
Georgia Col. ■	Feb. 12
Francis Marion	Feb. 15
Lander ■	Feb. 19
N.C.-Pembroke	Feb. 22

1995-96 RESULTS (12-15)
90	Clayton St.	109

68	North Ga. ■	64
68	Southern Tech ■	61
68	West Ga. ■	66
69	Life (Ga.) ■	84
62	S.C.-Aiken	64
80	St. Leo	72
57	Fla. Southern	91
79	La Grange	82
50	Columbus St.	66
55	Armstrong Atlantic ■	49
98	S.C.-Spartanburg	92
82	Augusta St. ■	65
73	Georgia Col. ■	78
77	Francis Marion	56
63	Lander ■	76
72	N.C.-Pembroke ■	81
77	Columbus St.	84
77	Armstrong Atlantic	72
59	S.C.-Spartanburg ■	60
59	Augusta St.	61
74	S.C.-Aiken ■	60
77	Georgia Col.	86
64	Francis Marion	60
63	Lander	76
69	N.C.-Pembroke	65
51	S.C.-Spartanburg †	59

Nickname: Fighting Owls
Colors: Black & Gold
Arena: Owls Nest
  Capacity: 2,307; Year Built: 1963
AD: Dave Waples
SID: To be named

KENT
Kent, OH 44242 I

Coach: Gary Waters
Alma Mater: Ferris St. '75
(First year as head coach)

1996-97 SCHEDULE
Ferris St. ■	Nov. 23
N.C.-Charlotte ■	Nov. 26
Loyola (Ill.)	Nov. 30
Ohio St.	Dec. 3
Southern Methodist ■	Dec. 7
IU/PU-Ft. Wayne ■	Dec. 23
Michigan St. Cl.	Dec. 27-28
Eastern Mich.	Jan. 4
Miami (Ohio) ■	Jan. 8
Toledo ■	Jan. 11
Ohio ■	Jan. 13
Bowling Green	Jan. 15
Western Mich.	Jan. 18
Ball St.	Jan. 22
Akron ■	Jan. 25
Central Mich. ■	Jan. 29
Miami (Ohio)	Feb. 1
Toledo	Feb. 5
Ohio	Feb. 8
Bowling Green ■	Feb. 12
Western Mich.	Feb. 15
Ball St. ■	Feb. 19
Akron	Feb. 22
Central Mich. ■	Feb. 26
Eastern Mich. ■	Mar. 1
Mid-American Conf. Tr.	Mar. 4-8

1995-96 RESULTS (14-13)
90	Loyola (Ill.) ■	73
108	Morehead St. ■	84
86	Rice ■	76
59	Siena	69
100	Denison ■	70
96	Evansville ■	91
66	Weber St. †	79
63	Appalachian St. †	62
59	Miami (Ohio)	71
68	Bowling Green	83
69	Ohio ■	68
70	Toledo	80

89	Akron ■	68
71	Western Mich.	69
82	Central Mich. ■	85
81	Eastern Mich.	96
95	Ball St. ■	85
59	Bowling Green ■	58
61	Ohio	69
70	Toledo ■	86
86	Akron	63
70	Western Mich. ■	84
74	Central Mich.	53
91	Eastern Mich. ■	73
52	Ball St.	66
63	Miami (Ohio) ■	77
72	Eastern Mich.	84

Nickname: Golden Flashes
Colors: Navy Blue & Gold
Arena: Memorial Athletic & Convocation Center
  Capacity: 6,327; Year Built: 1950
AD: Laing Kennedy
SID: Dale Gallagher

KENTUCKY
Lexington, KY 40506 I

Coach: Rick Pitino
Alma Mater: Massachusetts '74
Record: 14 Years, W-317, L-119

1996-97 SCHEDULE
Clemson [Indianapolis]	Nov. 15
Great Alas. Shootout	Nov. 27-30
Purdue [Chicago]	Dec. 3
Indiana [Louisville]	Dec. 7
Wright St. ■	Dec. 9
Notre Dame	Dec. 14
Georgia Tech	Dec. 21
N.C.-Asheville ■	Dec. 23
Ohio St. [Cleveland]	Dec. 28
Louisville	Dec. 31
Tennessee ■	Jan. 4
Mississippi St. ■	Jan. 7
Canisius ■	Jan. 9
Mississippi	Jan. 11
Georgia	Jan. 14
Auburn ■	Jan. 18
Vanderbilt [Cincinnati]	Jan. 22
Arkansas	Jan. 26
Florida	Jan. 29
Georgia ■	Feb. 1
South Caro.	Feb. 4
Western Caro. ■	Feb. 6
Villanova	Feb. 9
LSU ■	Feb. 12
Florida ■	Feb. 15
Alabama	Feb. 19
Vanderbilt	Feb. 22
Tennessee	Feb. 25
South Caro. ■	Mar. 2
Southeastern Conf. Tr.	Mar. 6-9

1995-96 RESULTS (34-2)
96	Maryland †	84
82	Massachusetts †	92
89	Indiana †	82
74	Wis.-Green Bay ■	62
83	Georgia Tech ■	60
96	Morehead St. ■	32
118	Marshall †	99
89	Louisville ■	66
90	Rider †	65
106	Iona †	79
89	South Caro.	60
90	Mississippi ■	60
74	Mississippi St.	56
61	Tennessee ■	44
129	LSU	97
124	Texas Christian ■	80
82	Georgia	77
89	South Caro. ■	57
77	Florida	63
120	Vanderbilt	81
88	Arkansas ■	73
86	Georgia ■	73

90	Tennessee	50
84	Alabama ■	65
94	Florida	63
88	Auburn	73
101	Vanderbilt ■	63
100	Florida †	76
95	Arkansas †	75
73	Mississippi St. †	84
110	San Jose St. †	72
84	Virginia Tech †	60
101	Utah †	70
83	Wake Forest †	63
81	Massachusetts †	74
76	Syracuse †	67

Nickname: Wildcats
Colors: Blue & White
Arena: Rupp Arena
  Capacity: 23,000; Year Built: 1976
AD: C. M. Newton
SID: Brooks Downing

KENTUCKY ST.
Frankfort, KY 40601 II

Coach: Thomas Snowden
Alma Mater: Alabama St. '75
Record: 2 Years, W-20, L-35

1996-97 SCHEDULE
Wilberforce ■	Nov. 23
Spalding	Nov. 30
Union (Ky.)	Dec. 4
Savannah St.	Dec. 7
Morehouse	Dec. 21
Albany St. (Ga.)	Jan. 4
Fort Valley St.	Jan. 6
Miles	Jan. 9
Alabama A&M	Jan. 11
Tuskegee	Jan. 13
Central St.	Jan. 15
Morris Brown	Jan. 18
Tuskegee ■	Jan. 20
Wilberforce	Jan. 23
Morehouse ■	Jan. 25
Paine	Jan. 27
Georgetown (Ky.) ■	Jan. 30
LeMoyne-Owen	Feb. 1
Clark Atlanta	Feb. 3
Oakland City	Feb. 5
Central St. ■	Feb. 8
LeMoyne-Owen ■	Feb. 10
Miles ■	Feb. 15
Alabama A&M	Feb. 17
Oakland City ■	Feb. 19
IU/PU-Indianapolis	Feb. 22

1995-96 RESULTS (7-20)
96	Wilberforce ■	67
56	Paine ■	75
77	Spalding ■	62
68	Albany St. (Ga.) ■	82
58	Bellarmine	87
73	Morehouse	91
75	Savannah St.	88
69	LeMoyne-Owen	70
92	Clark Atlanta	107
85	Miles ■	89
75	Alabama A&M ■	99
97	Tuskegee ■	96
82	Wilberforce	85
37	Central St. ■	75
63	Tuskegee	62
68	Morehouse ■	66
84	Bellarmine ■	76
60	LeMoyne-Owen ■	72
59	Union (Ky.) ■	56
77	IU/PU-Indianapolis ■	95
77	Central St.	81
75	Fort Valley St. ■	86
91	Spalding	95
76	Miles	94
80	Alabama A&M	110
65	Morris Brown	81
87	LeMoyne-Owen	105

Nickname: Thorobreds
Colors: Green & Gold
Arena: William Exum HPER Center
  Capacity: 4,500; Year Built: 1994
AD: Don Lyons
SID: Ron Braden

KY. WESLEYAN
Owensboro, KY 42301 II

Coach: Ray Harper
Alma Mater: Ky. Wesleyan '85
(First year as head coach)

1996-97 SCHEDULE
Delta St. ■	Nov. 16
Oakland City ■	Nov. 21
Ky. Wesleyan Cl.	Nov. 29-30
Delta St.	Dec. 5
Spalding ■	Dec. 7
Oakland City	Dec. 14
Hawaii-Hilo Cl.	Dec. 17-19
IU/PU-Ft. Wayne	Dec. 28
St. Joseph's (Ind.)	Dec. 30
Northern Ky. ■	Jan. 2
Indianapolis ■	Jan. 4
Bellarmine	Jan. 9
Wis.-Parkside	Jan. 11
SIU-Edwardsville	Jan. 16
Southern Ind.	Jan. 18
Mo.-St. Louis	Jan. 23
Quincy ■	Jan. 25
St. Joseph's (Ind.) ■	Jan. 30
IU/PU-Ft. Wayne ■	Feb. 1
Indianapolis	Feb. 6
Northern Ky.	Feb. 8
Bellarmine ■	Feb. 13
Lewis ■	Feb. 15
SIU-Edwardsville ■	Feb. 20
Southern Ind. ■	Feb. 22
Quincy	Feb. 27
Mo.-St. Louis	Mar. 1

1995-96 RESULTS (17-10)
58	IU/PU-Indianapolis	80
103	Hillsdale	54
71	Indiana (Pa.) ■	75
92	Oakland City	84
90	Bellarmine ■	75
98	Ind.-Southeast ■	75
80	Wis.-Parkside	72
91	St. Joseph's (Ind.)	90
74	SIU-Edwardsville ■	64
79	Quincy	77
95	IU/PU-Indianapolis ■	84
85	IU/PU-Ft. Wayne	87
73	Indianapolis	78
75	Lewis	76
73	Wis.-Parkside ■	57
73	Southern Ind.	90
95	SIU-Edwardsville	91
79	Northern Ky.	81
74	Bellarmine	73
79	St. Joseph's (Ind.) ■	70
79	IU/PU-Ft. Wayne ■	67
97	Quincy	86
77	Lewis	84
86	Oakland City ■	91
65	Southern Ind. ■	81
69	Indianapolis ■	65
80	Northern Ky. ■	74

Nickname: Panthers
Colors: Purple & White
Arena: Owensboro Sportscenter
  Capacity: 5,450; Year Built: 1949
AD: William Meadors
SID: Roy Pickerill

KENYON
Gambier, OH 43022 III

Coach: Richard Whitmore
Alma Mater: Brown '90
Record: 3 Years, W-30, L-41

1996-97 SCHEDULE
Albion Tr.	Nov. 22-23
Olivet	Nov. 26
Ohio Wesleyan	Dec. 4
Thiel ■	Dec. 7
Denison ■	Dec. 11
Oglethorpe Cl.	Dec. 29-30
Wooster ■	Jan. 3
Oberlin	Jan. 4
Wittenberg ■	Jan. 8
Earlham ■	Jan. 11
Case Reserve	Jan. 15
Wash. & Jeff. ■	Jan. 18
Wooster	Jan. 22
Allegheny ■	Jan. 25
Oberlin ■	Jan. 28
Denison	Jan. 31
Ohio Wesleyan ■	Feb. 1
Wittenberg	Feb. 5
Earlham	Feb. 8
Mt. Vernon Naz.	Feb. 11
Case Reserve ■	Feb. 15
Allegheny	Feb. 22

1995-96 RESULTS (9-16)
81	Albright †	74
46	Emory †	62
53	Denison	48
64	Ohio Wesleyan	67
67	Wittenberg	70
59	Allegheny ■	66
58	Youngstown St.	84
67	Calvin †	66
76	Otterbein	78
89	Case Reserve	79
56	Wooster	62
103	Thiel ■	64
86	Earlham ■	55
52	Wittenberg ■	57
72	Oberlin	66
81	Ohio Wesleyan ■	68
72	Case Reserve ■	82
59	Allegheny	87
59	Wash. & Jeff.	63
59	Denison	61
92	Oberlin ■	69
64	Mt. Vernon Naz. ■	70
43	Wooster	48
60	Earlham	72
53	Allegheny	58

Nickname: Lords
Colors: Purple & White
Arena: Tomsich Arena
  Capacity: 2,000; Year Built: 1981
AD: Robert Bunnell
SID: Joe Wasiluk

KEUKA
Keuka Park, NY 14478 III

Coach: David Sweet
Alma Mater: Cleary '78
Record: 11 Years, W-140, L-137

1996-97 SCHEDULE
St. John Fisher Inv.	Nov. 23-24
Penn St.-Behrend ■	Nov. 26
Nazareth Tr.	Nov. 30-Dec. 1
Potsdam St. ■	Dec. 3
Cazenovia ■	Dec. 3
Hobart	Jan. 8
Hamilton Inv.	Jan. 11-12
Cazenovia	Jan. 14
Hilbert ■	Jan. 18
Rochester Inst.	Jan. 20
Medaille	Jan. 22
Elmira ■	Jan. 28
St. John Fisher	Jan. 31
Centenary (N.J.) ■	Feb. 3
St. John Fisher ■	Feb. 6
Penn St.-Behrend	Feb. 8
Hartwick	Feb. 10
Hilbert	Feb. 18
Medaille ■	Feb. 21
Ithaca ■	Feb. 22

Nazareth ....Feb. 24
Hobart ■ ....Feb. 26

1995-96 RESULTS (9-16)

79	Geneseo St. †	62
60	Skidmore	61
75	Albany (N.Y.) ■	89
83	Carnegie Mellon	89
93	Wash. & Lee †	79
66	Alfred	57
84	Rochester Inst.	91
86	Utica ■	87
73	Binghamton †	60
65	Nazareth	69
82	Penn St.-Behrend ■	68
49	Elmira	77
63	Pitt-Bradford	64
72	Hartwick ■	73
61	Hilbert	49
68	Pitt-Bradford ■	78
55	Rochester Inst. ■	56
62	St. John Fisher	72
62	Elmira	77
81	Hobart ■	68
59	Penn St.-Behrend ■	57
61	Ithaca	80
58	Utica	72
65	Nazareth ■	82
77	Hobart	66

Nickname: Warriors
Colors: Green & Gold
Arena: Weed Physical Arts Center
  Capacity: 1,800; Year Built: 1973
AD: David Sweet
SID: Wendy Caraher

KING'S (PA.)
Wilkes-Barre, PA 18702 III

Coach: Jim Casciano
Alma Mater: Drexel '75
(First year as head coach)

1996-97 SCHEDULE

Gettysburg Tr. ....Nov. 22-23
Muhlenberg ■ ....Nov. 26
Elizabethtown ....Dec. 2
Drew ....Dec. 4
Delaware Valley ....Dec. 10
Susquehanna ....Dec. 12
King's (Pa.) Cl. ....Dec. 28-29
Union (N.Y.) Inv. ....Jan. 10-11
Wilkes ■ ....Jan. 15
Scranton ■ ....Jan. 18
Lycoming ....Jan. 22
FDU-Madison ■ ....Jan. 25
Dickinson ■ ....Jan. 27
Drew ■ ....Jan. 29
Delaware Valley ■ ....Feb. 4
Centenary (N.J.) ■ ....Feb. 8
Wilkes ....Feb. 11
Scranton ....Feb. 15
Lycoming ■ ....Feb. 19
FDU-Madison ■ ....Feb. 22

1995-96 RESULTS (5-19)

66	Dickinson	78
70	Montclair St. †	74
78	Teikyo Post ■	84
61	Elizabethtown ■	63
67	Drew ■	54
53	Phila. Pharmacy †	68
84	CCNY †	66
94	Delaware Valley ■	58
57	Penn St.-Behrend ■	71
51	Wilmington (Del.) ■	77
90	Catholic	97
76	Wilkes	97
66	Scranton ■	84
69	Nova Southeastern ■	82
54	Lycoming ■	80
66	Drew	73
67	Haverford	69
69	Delaware Valley ■	64
61	Albright	64
76	FDU-Madison ■	69

65	Wilkes ■	79
61	Scranton ■	80
76	Lycoming ■	86
74	FDU-Madison ■	82

Nickname: Monarchs
Colors: Red & Gold
Arena: Scandlon Gym
  Capacity: 3,450; Year Built: 1968
AD: John Dorish
SID: Bob Ziadie

KNOX
Galesburg, IL 61401 III

Coach: Tim Heimann
Alma Mater: Knox '70
Record: 12 Years, W-143, L-122

1996-97 SCHEDULE

Principia ■ ....Nov. 27
Knox Cl. ....Nov. 30-Dec. 1
MacMurray ....Dec. 2
Grinnell ....Dec. 6
Coe ....Dec. 7
Blackburn ....Dec. 10
Savannah A&D ....Dec. 12
Flagler ....Dec. 14
Mt. St. Clare ■ ....Jan. 7
Grinnell ■ ....Jan. 10
Coe ■ ....Jan. 11
St. Norbert ....Jan. 17
Lawrence ....Jan. 18
Carroll (Wis.) ■ ....Jan. 24
Beloit ■ ....Jan. 25
Cornell College ■ ....Jan. 29
Monmouth (Ill.) ....Feb. 1
Illinois Col. ■ ....Feb. 8
Cornell College ....Feb. 12
Monmouth (Ill.) ■ ....Feb. 15
Illinois Col. ....Feb. 22

1995-96 RESULTS (15-8)

88	Principia	63
82	Iowa Wesleyan ■	70
67	Webster ■	52
80	Coe	71
96	Grinnell	123
87	MacMurray ■	80
74	Defiance †	69
59	Wabash	67
72	Mt. St. Clare	65
77	Illinois Col.	78
69	Franklin ■	75
72	Coe ■	57
73	Grinnell ■	86
67	Lawrence ■	61
69	St. Norbert ■	73
79	Beloit	71
60	Carroll (Wis.)	58
72	Monmouth (Ill.) ■	66
83	Cornell College ■	46
75	Illinois Col. ■	68
92	Monmouth (Ill.)	95
58	Cornell College	55
78	Ripon †	83

Nickname: Prairie Fire
Colors: Purple & Gold
Arena: Memorial Gym
  Capacity: 3,000; Year Built: 1951
AD: Harlan Knosher
SID: Andy Gibbons

KUTZTOWN
Kutztown, PA 19530 II

Coach: Jeff Jones
Alma Mater: Illinois St. '75
Record: 10 Years, W-111, L-160

1996-97 SCHEDULE

North Caro. Cent. Cl............Nov. 16-17
Phila. Bible ■ ....Nov. 19
Shippensburg ■ ....Nov. 23
Phila. Textile ....Nov. 30

Bowie St. ■ ....Dec. 4
Dist. Columbia ■ ....Dec. 6
Columbia Union ....Dec. 18
Barbados Tr. ....Dec. 28-Jan. 1
Shippensburg ....Jan. 4
Mansfield ■ ....Jan. 8
Cheyney ■ ....Jan. 11
East Stroudsburg ....Jan. 15
Bloomsburg ....Jan. 22
Millersville ....Jan. 25
West Chester ■ ....Jan. 29
Cheyney ....Feb. 1
Columbia Union ■ ....Feb. 3
Mansfield ....Feb. 5
East Stroudsburg ■ ....Feb. 12
Bloomsburg ■ ....Feb. 15
West Chester ....Feb. 19
Millersville ■ ....Feb. 22

1995-96 RESULTS (8-17)

63	Shippensburg	83
84	Bowie St.	94
77	Clarion ■	90
67	Clarion	94
74	Pitt-Johnstown ■	92
62	West Chester	65
74	Millersville	97
52	Lock Haven	83
69	Bloomsburg ■	73
79	Phila. Bible	55
80	Columbia Union ■	68
98	East Stroudsburg	89
64	Cheyney	100
75	Lock Haven ■	80
87	Mansfield	83
69	Millersville ■	65
72	Dist. Columbia	77
81	West Chester ■	63
68	Bloomsburg	87
50	Columbia Union	53
71	East Stroudsburg	94
60	Dist. Columbia ■	50
59	Pitt-Johnstown	91
75	Mansfield ■	63
89	Cheyney ■	90

Nickname: Golden Bears
Colors: Maroon & Gold
Arena: Keystone Hall
  Capacity: 4,000; Year Built: 1971
AD: Clark Yeager
SID: Matt Santos

LA SALLE
Philadelphia, PA 19141 I

Coach: Speedy Morris
Alma Mater: St. Joseph's (Pa.) '73
Record: 10 Years, W-183, L-119

1996-97 SCHEDULE

Mt. St. Mary's (Md.)................Nov. 30
Iowa Shootout ....Dec. 6-7
American ■ ....Dec. 10
Drexel ■ ....Dec. 14
Marquette ....Dec. 22
California Cl. ....Dec. 28-29
Holy Cross ■ ....Jan. 4
Massachusetts ■ ....Jan. 8
Dayton ■ ....Jan. 11
Duquesne ■ ....Jan. 18
Virginia Tech ■ ....Jan. 20
Pennsylvania ■ ....Jan. 23
Geo. Washington ■ ....Jan. 25
Temple ....Jan. 28
Geo. Washington ■ ....Feb. 1
Xavier (Ohio) ■ ....Feb. 4
Rhode Island ■ ....Feb. 6
Virginia Tech ■ ....Feb. 10
Duquesne ■ ....Feb. 13
St. Bonaventure ■ ....Feb. 15
Dayton ....Feb. 20
Xavier (Ohio) ....Feb. 22
Fordham ■ ....Feb. 27
St. Joseph's (Pa.) ■ ....Mar. 1
Atlantic 10 Conf. Tr. ....Mar. 5-8

1995-96 RESULTS (6-24)

60	Auburn †	70
65	Illinois St. †	72
63	Western Ky. †	71
53	Miami (Ohio) †	74
72	Holy Cross	75
66	Mt. St. Mary's (Md.) ■	81
68	Marquette †	65
64	American	62
62	UTEP	69
58	Texas Tech †	62
52	Princeton ■	49
60	Xavier (Ohio) ■	69
55	Virginia Tech †	71
73	Duquesne ■	69
65	St. Joseph's (Pa.) †	67
48	Temple ■	68
59	Xavier (Ohio)	60
66	Pennsylvania †	68
75	Duquesne	85
96	St. Bonaventure ■	79
65	Rhode Island ■	74
83	Geo. Washington	92
50	Villanova	90
53	Massachusetts	70
76	Geo. Washington ■	70
56	Virginia Tech	61
60	Dayton ■	67
64	Dayton	66
57	Fordham	60
59	Rhode Island †	85

Nickname: Explorers
Colors: Blue & Gold
Arena: Core States Spectrum
  Capacity: 18,168; Year Built: 1967
AD: Bob Mullen
SID: Maureen Coyle

LA VERNE
La Verne, CA 91750 III

Coach: Terry Boesel
Alma Mater: Oregon St. '86
Record: 1 Year, W-10, L-15

1996-97 SCHEDULE

LIFE Bible ■ ....Nov. 26
Pacific Christian Tr ....Nov. 29-30
Cal St. Stanislaus Tr. ....Dec. 6-7
La Sierra ■ ....Dec. 10
Southern Cal Col. ....Dec. 18
Clark (Mass.) ■ ....Dec. 30
Occidental Cl. ....Jan. 3-4
Redlands ■ ....Jan. 11
Cal Tech ■ ....Jan. 15
Occidental ....Jan. 18
Claremont-M-S ■ ....Jan. 22
Whittier ■ ....Jan. 25
Pomona-Pitzer ■ ....Jan. 29
Cal Lutheran ....Feb. 1
Redlands ■ ....Feb. 5
Cal Tech ....Feb. 8
Occidental ■ ....Feb. 12
Claremont-M-S ■ ....Feb. 15
Whittier ....Feb. 19
Pomona-Pitzer ....Feb. 22
Cal Lutheran ■ ....Feb. 26

1995-96 RESULTS (10-15)

56	Trinity (Tex.)	93
50	Rose-Hulman †	87
58	Biola	102
82	LIFE Bible ■	42
69	Pt. Loma Nazarene	90
62	Dominican (Cal.) †	71
61	Elmhurst ■	70
68	Cal St. Bakersfield	118
87	Wartburg †	97
88	N.J. Inst. of Tech. †	80
84	La Sierra	67
45	Pomona-Pitzer	85
73	Cal Lutheran ■	79
68	Claremont-M-S ■	60
88	Occidental	94
65	Whittier	66

100	Redlands ■	81
59	Cal Tech	55
70	Pomona-Pitzer ■	81
48	Cal Lutheran	82
69	Claremont-M-S	66
75	Occidental ■	72
83	Whittier ■	68
94	Redlands	95
63	Cal Tech ■	36

Nickname: Leopards, Leos
Colors: Orange & Green
Arena: Student Center Gym
 Capacity: 900; Year Built: 1973
AD: Jim Paschal
SID: Mark Bagley

LAFAYETTE
Easton, PA 18042 I

Coach: Fran O'Hanlon
Alma Mater: Villanova '70
Record: 1 Year, W-7, L-20

1996-97 SCHEDULE

Dartmouth	Nov. 24
Harvard ■	Nov. 26
Brown ■	Dec. 1
Princeton ■	Dec. 3
Marist Cl.	Dec. 6-7
Swarthmore ■	Dec. 10
Haverford ■	Dec. 20
Maryland	Dec. 23
Tulane	Dec. 28
LSU	Dec. 30
Cornell	Jan. 6
Lehigh	Jan. 8
Yale	Jan. 13
Bucknell ■	Jan. 15
Navy	Jan. 18
Holy Cross ■	Jan. 22
Army ■	Jan. 25
Pennsylvania ■	Jan. 27
Colgate	Jan. 29
Lehigh ■	Feb. 1
Bucknell	Feb. 8
Navy ■	Feb. 12
Holy Cross	Feb. 15
Army	Feb. 18
Colgate ■	Feb. 22
Patriot Conf. Tr.	Mar. 1-5

1995-96 RESULTS (7-20)

63	Syracuse	87
78	Cornell ■	69
47	Princeton	62
44	Harvard	64
69	Swarthmore ■	70
64	Columbia ■	51
47	Richmond †	63
75	Alas. Anchorage †	82
68	Davidson	93
58	N.C.-Charlotte	88
73	Brown	81
82	Holy Cross	85
64	Navy ■	73
79	Army	83
71	Dartmouth ■	72
57	Pennsylvania	74
84	Lehigh ■	64
71	Bucknell	79
76	Colgate	91
92	Holy Cross ■	85
59	Navy	61
77	Army ■	72
67	Yale ■	58
67	Lehigh	70
73	Bucknell ■	52
72	Colgate ■	85
55	Bucknell †	56

Nickname: Leopards
Colors: Maroon & White
Arena: Allan Kirby Field House
 Capacity: 3,500; Year Built: 1973
AD: Eve Atkinson
SID: Scott Morse

LAKE FOREST
Lake Forest, IL 60045 III

Coach: Chris Conger
Alma Mater: Wisconsin '95
(First year as head coach)

1996-97 SCHEDULE

Carthage	Nov. 24
Milwaukee Engr. ■	Nov. 26
Viterbo Tr.	Nov. 29-30
Wis.-Whitewater ■	Dec. 4
Cardinal Stritch	Dec. 7
Kalamazoo ■	Dec. 10
Chicago	Jan. 7
Lawrence ■	Jan. 11
Ripon	Jan. 14
Grinnell ■	Jan. 17
Coe ■	Jan. 18
Cornell College	Jan. 24
Monmouth (Ill.)	Jan. 25
St. Norbert	Jan. 29
Carroll (Wis.)	Feb. 1
Beloit ■	Feb. 4
Lawrence	Feb. 8
Ripon ■	Feb. 12
St. Norbert ■	Feb. 15
Carroll (Wis.) ■	Feb. 18
Beloit	Feb. 22

1995-96 RESULTS (7-15)

68	Loras	74
69	Wheaton (Ill.) ■	70
66	Chicago	88
63	Viterbo ■	36
82	Carthage	77
78	Purdue-Calumet †	65
61	Kalamazoo	73
78	Aurora	86
66	Beloit	79
71	Lawrence ■	78
74	Ripon	95
74	Grinnell	95
78	Coe	80
51	St. Norbert ■	33
66	Monmouth (Ill.)	57
78	Cornell College ■	44
66	Carroll (Wis.)	77
48	St. Norbert	43
55	Beloit ■	60
66	Lawrence	72
56	Ripon ■	73
60	Carroll (Wis.)	63

Nickname: Foresters
Colors: Red & Black
Arena: Sports Center
 Capacity: 1,200; Year Built: 1968
AD: Jackie Slaats
SID: To be named

LAKE SUPERIOR ST.
Sault Ste. Marie, MI 49783 II

Coach: Terry Smith
Alma Mater: Michigan St. '84
Record: 5 Years, W-62, L-69

1996-97 SCHEDULE

North Ala. Tr.	Nov. 15-16
Lake Superior St. Tr	Nov. 22-23
Albion	Dec. 3
Oakland	Dec. 7
Great Lake Christian ■	Dec. 10
Cornerstone	Dec. 14
Ashland ■	Dec. 21
Northwood	Jan. 4
Ferris St.	Jan. 9
Grand Valley St.	Jan. 11
Saginaw Valley ■	Jan. 13
Northern Mich.	Jan. 16
Michigan Tech ■	Jan. 18
Hillsdale ■	Jan. 23
Wayne St. (Mich.) ■	Jan. 25
Mercyhurst	Jan. 30
Gannon	Feb. 1

Northwood ■	Feb. 8
Saginaw Valley	Feb. 10
Ferris St. ■	Feb. 13
Grand Valley St.	Feb. 15
Northern Mich. ■	Feb. 20
Michigan Tech ■	Feb. 22

1995-96 RESULTS (19-9)

101	Northland Bapt. ■	61
79	Tri-State	61
76	Florida Tech	63
95	S.C.-Spartanburg †	99
65	Fla. Southern	72
116	St. Mary's (Mich.) ■	66
83	Northwood	85
75	Grand Valley St.	93
101	Cornerstone ■	91
81	Oakland	90
85	Wayne St. (Mich.) ■	78
64	Mercyhurst	73
78	Gannon	57
76	Ashland	66
78	Hillsdale ■	42
66	Ferris St.	69
80	Northern Mich. ■	57
107	Saginaw Valley	100
64	Michigan Tech	70
91	Northwood ■	84
100	Grand Valley St. ■	94
72	Saginaw Valley	68
85	Wayne St. (Mich.)	82
93	Michigan Tech ■	78
80	Northern Mich.	78
75	Michigan Tech †	72
106	Oakland	102
81	Indianapolis †	105

Nickname: Lakers
Colors: Royal Blue & Gold
Arena: James Norris Gym
 Capacity: 2,800; Year Built: 1976
AD: Jeff Jackson
SID: Scott Monaghan

LAKELAND
Sheboygan, WI 53082 III

Coach: Brian Miller
Alma Mater: Wis.-Milwaukee '87
Record: 2 Years, W-39, L-14

1996-97 SCHEDULE

Viterbo ■	Nov. 22
Wis.-Platteville ■	Nov. 23
Rockford	Nov. 26
Carthage	Nov. 30
Edgewood ■	Dec. 4
Lakeland Inv.	Dec. 6-7
Wheaton (Ill.) ■	Dec. 12
Wis. Lutheran	Dec. 14
Webber Inv.	Dec. 28-29
Milwaukee Engr.	Jan. 7
Concordia (Wis.) ■	Jan. 9
Northland	Jan. 11
Marian (Wis.) ■	Jan. 15
Maranatha Bapt.	Jan. 18
Cardinal Stritch	Jan. 25
Edgewood	Jan. 30
Milwaukee Engr. ■	Feb. 1
Marian (Wis.)	Feb. 5
Wis. Lutheran ■	Feb. 12
Maranatha Bapt. ■	Feb. 15
Cardinal Stritch ■	Feb. 18

1995-96 RESULTS (18-8)

86	Rockford ■	70
64	Viterbo †	62
94	Sterling †	77
72	Colorado Col.	78
46	Wis.-Platteville	79
74	Wheaton (Ill.)	81
69	Concordia (Wis.)	56
65	Wis.-Oshkosh	81
75	St. Scholastica †	63
82	Wis.-Stevens Point	89
82	Milwaukee Engr. ■	66
67	Edgewood	73

83	Marian (Wis.)	59
81	Wis. Lutheran ■	68
96	Carthage	65
90	Maranatha Bapt.	66
90	Cardinal Stritch	77
79	Edgewood ■	66
78	Milwaukee Engr.	62
64	Marian (Wis.)	50
60	Concordia (Wis.) ■	55
55	Wis. Lutheran	72
66	Maranatha Bapt.	75
89	Cardinal Stritch	79
68	Marian (Wis.)	58
80	Edgewood ■	73

Nickname: Muskies
Colors: Navy & Gold
Arena: Todd Wehr Center
 Capacity: 1,500
AD: Jane Bouche
SID: David Moyer

LAMAR
Beaumont, TX 77710 I

Coach: Grey Giovanine
Alma Mater: Central Mo. St. '81
Record: 3 Years, W-33, L-48

1996-97 SCHEDULE

Centenary (La.)	Nov. 23
Angelo St. ■	Nov. 25
North Caro. St.	Nov. 27
Baylor	Nov. 30
Nicholls St.	Dec. 7
McNeese St. ■	Dec. 14
Mary Hardin-Baylor	Dec. 18
Southwest Tex. St. ■	Dec. 21
Ark.-Little Rock	Dec. 28
Western Ky. ■	Jan. 2
Louisiana Tech	Jan. 4
Southwestern La.	Jan. 9
South Ala. ■	Jan. 11
Western Ky.	Jan. 16
Jacksonville ■	Jan. 18
Tex.-Pan American	Jan. 23
Louisiana Tech ■	Jan. 25
Arkansas St. ■	Jan. 30
Jacksonville	Feb. 1
Tex.-Pan American ■	Feb. 3
Ark.-Little Rock ■	Feb. 5
New Orleans ■	Feb. 8
South Ala.	Feb. 13
New Orleans	Feb. 15
Southwestern La. ■	Feb. 20
Arkansas St.	Feb. 22
Sun Belt Conf. Tr.	Feb. 28-Mar. 4

1995-96 RESULTS (12-15)

72	Southern Cal	76
106	Sam Houston St. ■	79
108	Concordia (Tex.) ■	81
86	Mississippi ■	81
72	McNeese St.	74
101	Schreiner ■	45
82	Texas ■	96
79	Tex.-Pan American ■	68
75	Jacksonville	85
76	New Orleans ■	70
59	South Ala.	51
73	Ark.-Little Rock ■	64
69	Southwestern La.	82
56	Tex.-Pan American	64
88	Centenary (La.) ■	70
58	Arkansas St.	75
63	Ark.-Little Rock	65
69	Southwestern La. ■	82
57	Louisiana Tech	56
73	Western Ky.	92
70	Jacksonville	80
68	South Ala.	70
67	Louisiana Tech ■	55
69	Western Ky.	90
48	New Orleans	84
75	Arkansas St. ■	63
62	Jacksonville †	63

Nickname: Cardinals
Colors: Red & White
Arena: Montagne Center
Capacity: 10,080; Year Built: 1984
AD: Mike O'Brien
SID: Daucy Crizer

LANDER
Greenwood, SC 29649 II

Coach: Roger Bagwell
Alma Mater: Western Ky. '68
(First year as head coach)

1996-97 SCHEDULE
Erskine ■	Nov. 16
Anderson (S.C.)	Nov. 22
North Greenville	Nov. 26
Newberry ■	Dec. 2
Columbus St. ■	Dec. 7
Columbus St.	Dec. 12
Nassau Tr.	Dec. 18-23
S.C.-Spartanburg ■	Jan. 2
Augusta St. ■	Jan. 4
N.C.-Pembroke ■	Jan. 8
S.C.-Aiken	Jan. 11
Anderson (S.C.) ■	Jan. 13
Francis Marion	Jan. 15
Georgia Col. ■	Jan. 18
North Greenville ■	Jan. 20
Kennesaw St. ■	Jan. 22
Armstrong Atlantic	Jan. 25
S.C.-Spartanburg	Jan. 29
Augusta St.	Feb. 1
Erskine	Feb. 3
N.C.-Pembroke ■	Feb. 5
S.C.-Aiken ■	Feb. 8
Francis Marion ■	Feb. 12
Georgia Col.	Feb. 15
Newberry ■	Feb. 17
Kennesaw St.	Feb. 19
Armstrong Atlantic ■	Feb. 22

1995-96 RESULTS (19-8)
105	Anderson (S.C.) ■	64
64	Southern Wesleyan ■	60
79	Erskine	75
79	North Greenville ■	64
67	Columbus St. ■	73
91	Newberry ■	71
67	Columbus St.	82
88	S.C.-Spartanburg	96
85	Augusta St.	67
77	N.C.-Pembroke ■	80
81	S.C.-Aiken ■	84
68	Francis Marion ■	39
60	Georgia Col. ■	65
66	Erskine ■	65
76	Kennesaw St. ■	63
83	Armstrong Atlantic ■	66
94	S.C.-Spartanburg ■	71
65	Augusta St. ■	63
91	North Greenville	77
80	N.C.-Pembroke ■	73
79	S.C.-Aiken	70
68	Newberry	66
57	Francis Marion	55
80	Georgia Col. ■	77
76	Kennesaw St.	63
71	Armstrong Atlantic	74
65	N.C.-Pembroke †	67

Nickname: Senators
Colors: Blue & Gold
Arena: Finis Horne Arena
Capacity: 2,500; Year Built: 1993
AD: Finis Horne
SID: Bob Stoner

LANE
Jackson, TN 38301..........II

Coach: J. L. Perry
Alma Mater: Lane '71
Record: 3 Years, W-33, L-40

1996-97 SCHEDULE
LeMoyne-Owen	Nov. 19
North Ala.	Nov. 21
Tougaloo ■	Nov. 25
West Ala. ■	Nov. 26
Mississippi Col. Cl.	Nov. 29-30
Delta St.	Dec. 3
Fisk	Jan. 8
LeMoyne-Owen ■	Jan. 9
Ark.-Pine Bluff ■	Jan. 11
Rust	Jan. 16
Ark.-Pine Bluff ■	Jan. 18
West Ala. ■	Jan. 23
Talladega ■	Jan. 24
Delta St. ■	Jan. 28
Rust ■	Feb. 1
Lambuth ■	Feb. 3
North Ala. ■	Feb. 6
Tougaloo	Feb. 10
Fisk ■	Feb. 12
Lynn ■	Feb. 15
Talladega ■	Feb. 17
Lambuth	Feb. 20
Alabama A&M ■	Feb. 22

1995-96 RESULTS (14-11)
79	North Ala.	97
69	St. Leo †	65
67	West Ala. ■	71
65	Mississippi Col.	71
74	Delta St. †	71
54	Mississippi Col. ■	62
98	Miles ■	74
105	Lambuth ■	95
82	Ark.-Pine Bluff †	96
86	Langston †	81
88	Lambuth	92
87	LeMoyne-Owen ■	82
79	Ark.-Pine Bluff	67
80	Delta St.	95
107	Fisk ■	94
85	Rust ■	72
69	West Ala.	73
99	Talladega	89
71	Miles	96
98	LeMoyne-Owen	103
89	Mississippi Col.	82
95	Ark.-Pine Bluff ■	86
92	Fisk	68
82	Delta St. ■	79
69	Talladega ■	80

Nickname: Dragons
Colors: Blue & Red
Arena: J. F. Lane Center
Capacity: 2,500; Year Built: 1974
AD: J. L. Perry
SID: John P. Gore

LAWRENCE
Appleton, WI 54911..........III

Coach: John Tharp
Alma Mater: Beloit '91
Record: 2 Years, W-21, L-22

1996-97 SCHEDULE
Lawrence Tr.	Nov. 22-23
Concordia (Ill.) ■	Nov. 26
Concordia (Wis.)	Dec. 3
Lakeland Inv.	Dec. 6-7
Occidental Cl.	Jan. 3-4
Lake Forest	Jan. 11
Beloit ■	Jan. 14
Illinois Col. ■	Jan. 17
Knox ■	Jan. 18
Grinnell	Jan. 24
Coe	Jan. 25
Ripon ■	Jan. 29
St. Norbert	Feb. 1
Carroll (Wis.)	Feb. 5
Lake Forest ■	Feb. 8
Beloit	Feb. 12
Ripon	Feb. 15
St. Norbert ■	Feb. 19
Carroll (Wis.) ■	Feb. 22

1995-96 RESULTS (14-8)
78	Marian (Wis.)	81
85	Wis. Lutheran ■	83
95	Edgewood ■	85
69	Ripon ■	102
75	Concordia (Wis.) ■	55
80	Nova Southeastern	74
82	Webber	81
78	Milwaukee Engr.	73
49	Carroll (Wis.) ■	72
78	Lake Forest	71
61	Beloit ■	72
61	Knox	67
71	Illinois Col.	54
87	Coe ■	65
95	Grinnell	70
74	St. Norbert ■	58
60	Ripon	77
80	Carroll (Wis.) ■	91
72	Lake Forest ■	66
65	Beloit	83
80	St. Norbert	77
75	Northland Bapt. ■	48

Nickname: Vikings
Colors: Navy & White
Arena: Alexander Gym
Capacity: 1,000; Year Built: 1929
AD: Amy Proctor
SID: Jeff School

LE MOYNE
Syracuse, NY 13214 II

Coach: Scott Hicks
Alma Mater: Le Moyne '88
Record: 4 Years, W-74, L-39

1996-97 SCHEDULE
Phila. Textile	Nov. 16
Albany (N.Y.) ■	Nov. 20
Roberts Wesleyan ■	Nov. 26
New York Tech	Dec. 1
Quinnipiac	Dec. 7
American Int'l	Dec. 8
Cheyney	Dec. 14
Stony Brook Inv.	Dec. 28-29
Assumption ■	Jan. 7
Stonehill	Jan. 11
Bryant	Jan. 12
Merrimack ■	Jan. 16
St. Anselm ■	Jan. 18
St. Michael's	Jan. 20
Bentley	Jan. 25
Assumption	Jan. 26
Hobart	Jan. 28
Quinnipiac ■	Feb. 1
Bryant ■	Feb. 4
St. Anselm	Feb. 8
Merrimack	Feb. 9
Stonehill ■	Feb. 13
St. Michael's ■	Feb. 15
American Int'l ■	Feb. 19
Bentley ■	Feb. 22

1995-96 RESULTS (24-6)
78	Molloy ■	41
75	Daemen	69
120	Mercy ■	92
71	St. Michael's	73
73	Southern Conn. St. ■	70
72	New Haven ■	69
64	New Hamp. Col. ■	65
75	Mass.-Lowell	71
74	Stony Brook	62
87	Sacred Heart ■	62
87	Bridgeport ■	71
100	Keene St.	77
61	Franklin Pierce	65
76	Mass.-Lowell ■	68
77	New Hamp. Col.	69
70	Albany (N.Y.) ■	64
60	New Haven	57
63	Southern Conn. St.	58
84	Hobart	70
72	Franklin Pierce ■	77
111	Keene St. ■	72
67	Albany (N.Y.)	66
80	Bridgeport	62
81	Sacred Heart	92
62	Stony Brook ■	50
86	St. Lawrence	66
76	Albany (N.Y.) ■ †	73
81	New Hamp. Col. †	68
77	Southern Conn. St. †	73
53	Franklin Pierce †	83

Nickname: Dolphins
Colors: Green & Gold
Arena: Henninger Athletic Center
Capacity: 2,500; Year Built: 1962
AD: Richard Rockwell
SID: Mike Tuberosa

LEMOYNE-OWEN
Memphis, TN 38126 II

Coach: Jerry Johnson
Alma Mater: Fayetteville St. '51
Record: 38 Years, W-697, L-326

1996-97 SCHEDULE
Christian Bros.	Nov. 16
Lane ■	Nov. 19
Miles ■	Nov. 25
Dillard Cl.	Nov. 27-28
Paine	Nov. 30
Morris Brown	Dec. 2
Morehouse	Dec. 7
Alabama A&M ■	Dec. 9
Clark Atlanta	Dec. 14
Christian Bros. ■	Dec. 21
Ark.-Pine Bluff [Memphis]	Dec. 28
Savannah St.	Jan. 6
Lane	Jan. 9
Alabama A&M	Jan. 15
Rust ■	Jan. 21
Albany St. (Ga.) ■	Jan. 23
Fort Valley St. ■	Jan. 25
Miles	Jan. 27
Tuskegee	Jan. 28
Kentucky St. ■	Feb. 1
Tuskegee ■	Feb. 8
Kentucky St.	Feb. 10
Rust	Feb. 15
Morehouse	Feb. 18

1995-96 RESULTS (14-13)
77	Henderson St. †	76
70	Mississippi Col.	76
94	Christian Bros.	118
63	Paine ■	84
85	Christian Bros.	94
90	Miles ■	104
78	Morehouse ■	73
70	Kentucky St. ■	69
90	Alabama A&M	109
82	Lane	87
94	Alabama A&M ■	99
87	Morris Brown ■	72
77	Rust ■	71
82	Albany St. (Ga.) ■	100
78	Fort Valley St.	73
88	Miles	74
80	Tuskegee	90
72	Kentucky St.	60
103	Lane ■	98
99	Tuskegee ■	96
107	Savannah St. ■	106
92	Rust	84
89	Clark Atlanta	85
78	Morehouse	90
80	Ark.-Pine Bluff	83
105	Kentucky St. ■	87
84	Clark Atlanta ■	95

Nickname: Magicians
Colors: Purple & Old Gold
Arena: Bruce Hall
Capacity: 2,500; Year Built: 1954
AD: E. D. Wilkens
SID: Eddie Cook

LEBANON VALLEY
Annville, PA 17003 III

Coach: Brad McAlester
Alma Mater: LIU-Southampton '53
Record: 2 Years, W-34, L-19

1996-97 SCHEDULE
New Jersey Inv. ....Nov. 22-23
Dickinson ■...........................Nov. 26
Ursinus ■ ....Dec. 2
Juniata ■ ....Dec. 4
Moravian ....Dec. 7
Wilkes ....Dec. 17
Susquehanna ....Jan. 7
Lebanon Valley Tr. ....Jan. 10-11
Elizabethtown.......................Jan. 15
Messiah ■ ....Jan. 18
Frank. & Marsh. ....Jan. 20
Widener ....Jan. 22
Albright ■ ....Jan. 25
Juniata ....Jan. 29
Moravian ■ ....Feb. 1
Susquehanna ■ ....Feb. 4
Drew ■ ....Feb. 8
Allentown ....Feb. 10
Elizabethtown ■ ....Feb. 12
Messiah ....Feb. 15
Widener ■ ....Feb. 18
Albright ....Feb. 22

1995-96 RESULTS (12-13)
80	Goucher †	83
92	York (Pa.) ■	78
74	Dickinson	94
69	Juniata	51
65	Moravian ■	68
57	Susquehanna ■	75
71	Ursinus	75
91	Wesley ■	64
60	Hunter ■	51
77	Rowan ■	130
68	Elizabethtown ■	89
85	Messiah	76
76	Widener ■	73
64	Albright	54
46	Frank. & Marsh. ■	61
71	Juniata ■	55
62	Moravian	79
79	Susquehanna	81
62	Drew	64
76	Elizabethtown	62
79	Messiah ■	73
69	Allentown	72
48	Widener	47
88	Albright ■	70
68	Wilkes	78

Nickname: Flying Dutchmen
Colors: Royal Blue & White
Arena: Lynch Memorial Gymnasium
    Capacity: 2,500; Year Built: 1950
AD: Louis Sorrentino
SID: John Deamer

LEES-McRAE
Banner Elk, NC 28604 II

Coach: David Noles
Alma Mater: Appalachian St. '64
Record: 11 Years, W-128, L-125

1996-97 SCHEDULE
Carson-Newman ....Nov. 16
S.C.-Aiken ■ ....Nov. 21
Erskine ....Nov. 23
Pfeiffer ■ ....Nov. 26
East Tenn. St. ....Nov. 30
High Point ....Dec. 2
Belmont Abbey ■ ....Dec. 5
Coastal Caro. ....Dec. 14
Clarion Tr. ....Jan. 3-4
Queens (N.C.) ....Jan. 9
Longwood ....Jan. 11
St. Andrews ■ ....Jan. 13
Coker ■ ....Jan. 16

Mount Olive...........................Jan. 22
Erskine ■ ....Jan. 25
Barton ■ ....Jan. 27
Pfeiffer ....Jan. 29
Longwood ■ ....Feb. 1
Mount Olive ■ ....Feb. 3
St. Andrews ....Feb. 6
Barton ■ ....Feb. 8
Queens (N.C.) ■ ....Feb. 10
High Point ■ ....Feb. 12
Belmont Abbey ....Feb. 15
Coker ....Feb. 19

1995-96 RESULTS (13-15)
92	Catawba ■	82
70	East Tenn. St. ■	84
79	Carson-Newman ■	71
94	Mars Hill ■	79
73	St. Andrews	65
73	Queens (N.C.) ■	84
59	Catawba	64
65	Carson-Newman	60
50	Queens (N.C.)	78
66	Pfeiffer ■	62
51	High Point ■	78
64	Coker ■	68
57	Erskine ■	66
89	Mount Olive ■	86
79	Longwood	81
69	Barton	90
94	Gardner-Webb ■	78
62	High Point	80
71	Barton ■	63
85	Mars Hill ■	92
83	St. Andrews ■	72
68	Belmont Abbey ■	66
62	Belmont Abbey	60
53	Coker	58
65	Erskine	72
67	Pfeiffer	70
91	Lee	86
78	LIFE Bible	103

Nickname: Bobcats
Colors: Forest Green & Gold
Arena: Williams Gym
    Capacity: 1,200; Year Built: 1975
AD: Ried Estus
SID: Chad Esposito

LEHIGH
Bethlehem, PA 18015 I

Coach: Sal Mentesana
Alma Mater: Providence '69
Record: 9 Years, W-133, L-117

1996-97 SCHEDULE
Vermont ■ ....Nov. 22
St. Francis (N.Y.) ....Nov. 26
Cornell ■ ....Nov. 30
Duke ....Dec. 2
Yale....................................Dec. 4
Pennsylvania ■ ....Dec. 7
Princeton ....Dec. 10
Drexel ....Dec. 21
Fla. Atlantic ....Dec. 28
Miami (Fla.) ....Dec. 30
Niagara ....Jan. 2
Columbia ....Jan. 6
Lafayette ■ ....Jan. 8
Bucknell ....Jan. 11
Navy ■ ....Jan. 15
Holy Cross ■ ....Jan. 18
Army ....Jan. 22
Colgate ■ ....Jan. 25
Harvard ....Jan. 28
Lafayette ....Feb. 1
Bucknell ■ ....Feb. 5
Navy ....Feb. 8
Holy Cross ....Feb. 12
Army ■ ....Feb. 15
Md.-Balt. County ■ ....Feb. 17
Colgate ....Feb. 19
Patriot Conf. Tr. ....Mar. 1-5

1995-96 RESULTS (4-23)
78	St. Francis (N.Y.)	92
45	Princeton ■	62
72	Yale ■	89
53	Wake Forest	68
61	Cornell	82
80	Harvard	70
76	Muhlenberg ■	58
66	Washington	82
55	South Ala. †	67
75	Niagara ■	83
69	Columbia	76
84	Army ■	70
67	Md.-Balt. County	72
60	Colgate ■	77
65	Bucknell	78
64	Lafayette	84
81	Holy Cross ■	100
63	Navy ■	69
75	Army	91
73	Pennsylvania	90
67	Colgate	79
73	Drexel	93
63	Bucknell ■	83
70	Lafayette ■	67
77	Holy Cross	84
59	Navy	73
66	Holy Cross	81

Nickname: Mountain Hawks
Colors: Brown & White
Arena: Stabler Center
    Capacity: 5,600; Year Built: 1979
AD: Joseph Sterrett
SID: Glenn Hofmann

LEHMAN
Bronx, NY 10468 III

Coach: Joe Meade
Alma Mater: St. Thomas Aquinas '79
Record: 2 Years, W-24, L-27

1996-97 SCHEDULE
Frostburg St. Cl. ....Nov. 22-23
Utica/Rome ■ ....Nov. 26
Vassar ....Dec. 2
Caldwell ■ ....Dec. 4
Montclair St. ■ ....Dec. 7
Mt. St. Mary (N.Y.) ....Dec. 10
CCNY ....Jan. 7
Stevens Tech ....Jan. 9
Western Conn. St. ....Jan. 11
Baruch ....Jan. 14
St. Joseph's (L.I.) ■ ....Jan. 16
Brooklyn ....Jan. 18
Mt. St. Vincent ■ ....Jan. 23
Hunter ■ ....Jan. 25
John Jay ■ ....Jan. 28
Baruch ....Jan. 30
Medgar Evers ....Feb. 3
Staten Island ....Feb. 5
John Jay ....Feb. 7
CCNY ....Feb. 11
York (N.Y.) ■ ....Feb. 14
Old Westbury ■ ....Feb. 19

1995-96 RESULTS (8-16)
63	Buffalo St.	90
83	N.J. Inst. of Tech. †	93
77	Stevens Tech ■	94
87	St. Joseph's (L.I.)	74
59	Caldwell	73
70	Bard	35
81	Mt. St. Mary (N.Y.) ■	72
73	St. Joe's-Brooklyn ■	58
66	Wilkes ■	105
70	John Jay	72
62	Western Conn. St. ■	70
72	CCNY	45
59	Baruch	61
46	St. Thomas Aquinas ■	62
65	Hunter	78
74	John Jay ■	70
67	York (N.Y.)	88
51	Baruch	74

69	Medgar Evers ■	61
48	Staten Island ■	69
62	Old Westbury	87
73	CCNY ■	76
82	Pratt	36
57	Staten Island	71

Nickname: Lightning
Colors: Blue, Green & White
Arena: Lehman College APEX
    Capacity: 1,000; Year Built: 1994
AD: Martin Zwiren
SID: John Balkam

LENOIR-RHYNE
Hickory, NC 28603 II

Coach: John Lentz
Alma Mater: Lenoir-Rhyne '74
Record: 14 Years, W-219, L-151

1996-97 SCHEDULE
North Caro. Cent. Cl. ....Nov. 16-17
S.C.-Spartanburg Tr. ....Nov. 22-23
Lenoir-Rhyne Cl. ....Nov. 29-30
Newberry ■ ....Dec. 4
Jacksonville Cl. ....Dec. 6-7
Presbyterian ....Jan. 4
Newberry ....Jan. 6
Wingate ....Jan. 8
Mars Hill ■ ....Jan. 11
Gardner-Webb ■ ....Jan. 15
Catawba ....Jan. 18
Carson-Newman ....Jan. 22
Elon ■ ....Jan. 25
Presbyterian ■ ....Feb. 1
Wingate ■ ....Feb. 5
Mars Hill ....Feb. 8
Gardner-Webb ....Feb. 12
Catawba ■ ....Feb. 15
Carson-Newman ■ ....Feb. 19
Elon ....Feb. 22

1995-96 RESULTS (14-12)
59	N.C.-Pembroke †	77
74	Belmont Abbey †	68
83	Newberry ■	73
111	Emmanuel ■	66
78	Francis Marion ■	74
85	Dist. Columbia †	80
73	Mount Olive	83
66	Lynn	77
71	St. Thomas (Fla.)	66
70	Barry	81
72	Carson-Newman ■	77
65	Presbyterian	75
49	Wingate	60
91	Mars Hill ■	76
98	Gardner-Webb ■	87
63	Catawba	71
85	Newberry	76
79	Carson-Newman	69
57	Presbyterian ■	48
56	Elon	73
70	Wingate ■	64
76	Mars Hill	82
77	Elon ■	75
64	Gardner-Webb	77
78	Catawba ■	56
79	Mars Hill †	87

Nickname: Bears
Colors: Red & Black
Arena: Shuford Memorial Gym
    Capacity: 3,200; Year Built: 1957
AD: Keith Ochs
SID: Dom Donnelly

LEWIS
Romeoville, IL 60441 II

Coach: Jim Whitesell
Alma Mater: Luther '82
Record: 9 Years, W-120, L-120

1996-97 SCHEDULE

P.R.-Mayaguez ■	Nov. 19
Judson (Ill.) ■	Nov. 23
St. Mary's (Minn.) ■	Nov. 30
St. Francis (Ill.)	Dec. 3
Trinity Christian ■	Dec. 14
Northern Ky.	Dec. 19
Indianapolis	Dec. 21
Mt. St. Clare ■	Dec. 30
Southern Ind. ■	Jan. 2
SIU-Edwardsville ■	Jan. 4
Wis.-Parkside ■	Jan. 9
Bellarmine ■	Jan. 11
Mo.-St. Louis	Jan. 16
Quincy	Jan. 18
IU/PU-Ft. Wayne ■	Jan. 23
St. Joseph's (Ind.) ■	Jan. 25
Indianapolis ■	Jan. 30
Northern Ky. ■	Feb. 1
SIU-Edwardsville	Feb. 6
Southern Ind.	Feb. 8
Wis.-Parkside ■	Feb. 13
Ky. Wesleyan	Feb. 15
Quincy ■	Feb. 20
Mo.-St. Louis ■	Feb. 22
St. Joseph's (Ind.)	Feb. 27
IU/PU-Ft. Wayne	Mar. 1

1995-96 RESULTS (18-9)

74	St. Mary's (Minn.) ■	62
97	Trinity Christian ■	44
80	Teikyo Marycrest ■	51
74	Grand Valley St.	65
74	St. Francis (Ill.) ■	70
57	St. Joseph's (Ind.) ■	69
97	Rockford	53
78	SIU-Edwardsville ■	49
103	Southern Ind. ■	109
70	Northern Ky.	80
79	Bellarmine	95
79	IU/PU-Ft. Wayne ■	72
91	Quincy	65
87	Judson (Ill.) ■	61
76	Ky. Wesleyan	75
79	Southern Ind.	105
74	Indianapolis ■	77
68	Northern Ky. ■	64
70	Wis.-Parkside	82
71	St. Joseph's (Ind.)	58
80	SIU-Edwardsville	89
92	Quincy	100
70	Bellarmine ■	68
84	Ky. Wesleyan ■	77
75	IU/PU-Ft. Wayne ■	69
78	Indianapolis	68
83	Wis.-Parkside ■	59

Nickname: Flyers
Colors: Red & White
Arena: J. F. K. Sports Center
  Capacity: 1,250; Year Built: 1961
AD: Paul Ruddy
SID: Mickey Smith

LIBERTY
Lynchburg, VA 24506 I

Coach: Jeff Meyer
Alma Mater: Taylor '76
Record: 15 Years, W-236, L-197

1996-97 SCHEDULE

Florida Int'l ■	Nov. 22
Maine	Nov. 25
Fresno St. Cl.	Nov. 29-30
Randolph-Macon ■	Dec. 3
Drake ■	Dec. 5
Howard ■	Dec. 7
Hampton	Dec. 16
Virginia	Dec. 18
Hilo Holiday Tr.	Dec. 28-30
Texas Christian	Jan. 2
Montreat ■	Jan. 7
N.C.-Asheville	Jan. 11
Md.-Balt. County	Jan. 13
Winthrop ■	Jan. 18

N.C.-Greensboro ■	Jan. 20
Virginia Tech ■	Jan. 23
Charleston So. ■	Jan. 25
Coastal Caro. ■	Jan. 27
Radford ■	Feb. 1
N.C.-Greensboro	Feb. 6
Winthrop	Feb. 8
N.C.-Asheville ■	Feb. 10
Coastal Caro.	Feb. 15
Charleston So.	Feb. 17
Md.-Balt. County ■	Feb. 20
Radford	Feb. 22
Big South Conf. Tr.	Feb. 26-Mar. 1

1995-96 RESULTS (17-12)

59	Drake	80
87	Mt. St. Mary's (Md.) ■	72
86	Va. Commonwealth ■	71
61	Howard	58
58	Auburn †	63
73	Centenary (La.) †	71
89	Florida Int'l	92
48	Virginia	76
84	King (Tenn.) ■	55
78	Montreat ■	66
79	Md.-Balt. County	63
48	N.C.-Asheville	66
65	Radford	71
81	Charleston So. ■	75
67	Coastal Caro.	62
76	Winthrop	77
56	N.C.-Greensboro	63
72	Hampton ■	77
53	Radford ■	50
51	Md.-Balt. County ■	48
65	N.C.-Asheville ■	43
53	Virginia Tech	56
67	N.C.-Greensboro ■	47
77	Charleston So.	61
71	Coastal Caro. ■	57
77	Winthrop	78
74	Md.-Balt. County ■	52
73	N.C.-Asheville ■	60
53	N.C.-Greensboro ■	79

Nickname: Flames
Colors: Red, White & Blue
Arena: Vines Center
  Capacity: 9,000; Year Built: 1990
AD: Chuck Burch
SID: Mike Montoro

LIMESTONE
Gaffney, SC 29340 II

Coach: Ralph Pim
Alma Mater: Northwestern St. '81
Record: 5 Years, W-65, L-60

1996-97 SCHEDULE

Belmont Abbey ■	Nov. 16
Warren Wilson ■	Nov. 18
Citadel	Nov. 22
Johnson & Wales	Nov. 23
Western Caro.	Dec. 2
Wingate ■	Dec. 4
Allen ■	Dec. 14
Belmont Abbey	Dec. 16
St. Andrews	Jan. 8
Tusculum	Jan. 11
Newberry ■	Jan. 16
Anderson (S.C.) ■	Jan. 18
North Greenville	Jan. 23
Allen ■	Jan. 25
Wingate ■	Jan. 27
Clayton St.	Jan. 29
Tusculum ■	Feb. 1
Gardner-Webb	Feb. 3
Col. of West Va.	Feb. 6
Newberry	Feb. 8
Montreat ■	Feb. 13
Johnson & Wales	Feb. 15
Anderson (S.C.)	Feb. 17
Clayton St. ■	Feb. 19
North Greenville ■	Feb. 22
Col. of West Va. ■	Feb. 25

1995-96 RESULTS
Results unavailable

Nickname: Saints
Colors: Royal Blue & Gold
Arena: Timken Center
  Capacity: 1,500; Year Built: 1973
AD: Dennis Bloomer
SID: Dennis Bloomer

LINCOLN (MO.)
Jefferson City, MO 65102 II

Coach: Gene Jones
Alma Mater: Missouri '68
Record: 5 Years, W-38, L-91

1996-97 SCHEDULE

Harris-Stowe	Nov. 16
Rockhurst ■	Nov. 18
Columbia (Mo.)	Nov. 23
Park	Nov. 26
Columbia (Mo.) ■	Dec. 2
Central Mo. St. ■	Dec. 4
Park ■	Dec. 7
Quincy ■	Dec. 12
Mo.-Rolla	Dec. 14
Southwest Baptist ■	Dec. 21
Mo. Southern St. ■	Jan. 4
Northwest Mo. St.	Jan. 8
Emporia St.	Jan. 11
Pittsburg St. ■	Jan. 15
Mo. Western St. ■	Jan. 18
Washburn	Jan. 25
Truman St.	Jan. 29
Northwest Mo. St. ■	Feb. 1
Central Mo. St.	Feb. 5
Southwest Baptist	Feb. 8
Washburn ■	Feb. 10
Mo.-Rolla	Feb. 12
Pittsburg St.	Feb. 15
Mo. Western St.	Feb. 17
Truman St. ■	Feb. 22

1995-96 RESULTS (9-16)

89	Quincy	96
69	Drury ■	78
77	Columbia (Mo.) ■	81
87	Harris-Stowe ■	84
105	Fontbonne	79
62	Drury	68
53	Columbia (Mo.)	49
66	Langston †	60
77	Ark.-Pine Bluff †	63
59	Mo.-Rolla	68
108	Mo. Southern St.	105
68	Central Mo. St. ■	77
73	Washburn	83
59	Emporia St. ■	73
66	Mo. Western St.	76
75	Truman St.	67
76	Mo.-St. Louis ■	78
60	Southwest Baptist ■	77
72	Pittsburg St.	74
87	Northwest Mo. St.	90
100	Mo. Southern St. ■	91
78	Central Mo. St.	88
75	Washburn ■	84
86	Emporia St.	80
61	Mo. Western St. ■	74

Nickname: Blue Tigers
Colors: Navy Blue & White
Arena: Jason Gym
  Capacity: 2,500; Year Built: 1958
AD: Ron Coleman
SID: Walt Klein

LINCOLN (PA.)
Lincoln University, PA 19352 III

Coach: Robert Byars
Alma Mater: Cheyney '78
Record: 9 Years, W-97, L-127

1996-97 SCHEDULE

Pitt.-Bradford Cl.	Nov. 22-23
Millersville	Nov. 25
Cheyney [Philadelphia]	Nov. 30
Wilmington (Del.) ■	Dec. 3
Salisbury Cl.	Dec. 6-7
Widener Cl.	Dec. 13-14
Md.-East. Shore	Dec. 17
Frank. & Marsh. Tr.	Jan. 4-5
Holy Family	Jan. 8
Frostburg St. Inv.	Jan. 10-11
Rutgers-Camden ■	Jan. 13
Centenary (N.J.) ■	Jan. 16
Dist. Columbia	Jan. 23
Col. of New Jersey ■	Jan. 30
Frostburg St. ■	Feb. 1
Holy Family ■	Feb. 5
Neumann	Feb. 10
Wilmington (Del.)	Feb. 18
Shaw ■	Feb. 20
Frostburg St.	Feb. 22

1995-96 RESULTS (14-12)

69	St. John Fisher	103
74	Clarkson †	69
63	Cheyney †	77
73	Coppin St.	119
92	Old Westbury †	83
95	Salisbury St.	108
67	Misericordia †	87
100	Delaware Valley †	59
77	Millersville	98
59	Grove City †	66
61	Waynesburg †	56
84	Columbia Union	99
72	Frostburg St. ■	73
110	Wesley	63
97	Neumann ■	80
78	Richard Stockton	89
86	Holy Family ■	83
101	Columbia Union ■	95
100	Rutgers-Camden	96
89	Wilmington (Del.)	86
77	Holy Family	82
83	Dist. Columbia ■	82
95	Phila. Pharmacy	97
106	Frostburg St.	102
85	Waynesburg	75
92	Misericordia †	77

Nickname: Lions
Colors: Orange & Blue
Arena: Manuel Rivero Hall
  Capacity: 3,000; Year Built: 1973
AD: Cyrus Jones
SID: To be named

LINCOLN MEMORIAL
Harrogate, TN 37752 II

Coach: Craig Rasmuson
Alma Mater: Ashland '90
Record: 2 Years, W-21, L-31

1996-97 SCHEDULE

Clinch Valley ■	Nov. 16
Oakland City	Nov. 18
Gardner-Webb Cl.	Nov. 22-23
Carson-Newman	Nov. 26
Milligan ■	Dec. 2
Lincoln Memorial Tr.	Dec. 6-7
Carson-Newman ■	Dec. 14
Bluefield St. ■	Jan. 2
Montevallo ■	Jan. 4
West Ala. ■	Jan. 6
Valdosta St.	Jan. 11
West Fla.	Jan. 13
North Ala. ■	Jan. 18
Ala.-Huntsville ■	Jan. 20
West Ga.	Jan. 25
Tusculum ■	Jan. 29
West Fla. ■	Feb. 1
Valdosta St. ■	Feb. 3
West Ala.	Feb. 8
Montevallo	Feb. 10
Asbury ■	Feb. 12

North Ala. ....Feb. 15
Ala.-Huntsville ....Feb. 17
West Ga. ■ ....Feb. 22

1995-96 RESULTS (13-13)

68	Carson-Newman ■	.67
90	Bluefield St.	.97
72	Knoxville ■	.82
48	Carson-Newman	.66
83	Trevecca Nazarene ■	.91
83	Tusculum ■	.80
71	King (Tenn.) ■	.49
72	Drury	.67
68	Emporia St. †	.66
49	Montevallo	.50
95	West Ala.	.91
47	Western Caro.	.94
69	Valdosta St. ■	.72
86	West Fla. ■	.71
75	North Ala.	.92
77	Ala.-Huntsville	.80
92	West Ga. ■	.90
59	West Fla.	.76
80	Valdosta St.	.84
89	Asbury ■	.83
72	West Ala. ■	.62
60	Montevallo ■	.68
72	North Ala. ■	.70
69	Ala.-Huntsville ■	.52
59	West Ga.	.60
86	North Greenville ■	.74

Nickname: Railsplitters
Colors: Blue & Gray
Arena: Turner Arena
   Capacity: 5,009; Year Built: 1990
AD: Jack Bondurant
SID: Tom Amis

LIVINGSTONE

Salisbury, NC 28114 II

Coach: Charles McCullough
Alma Mater: N.C. Central
Record: 2 Years, W-13, L-41

1996-97 SCHEDULE
Schedule unavailable

1995-96 RESULTS (10-17)

73	West Ga. †	.84
82	Knoxville †	.59
68	Bowie St.	.88
77	St. Paul's	.74
65	Catawba	.73
94	Anderson (Ind.) †	.49
68	Virginia Union	.97
100	Barber-Scotia †	.66
60	North Caro. A&T	.83
71	Norfolk St. ■	.80
95	St. Augustine's ■	.90
87	Shaw ■	.92
89	Fayetteville St. ■	.83
78	Elizabeth City St. ■	.93
52	Shaw	.61
100	Morris	.103
88	N.C. Central ■	.92
81	St. Augustine's	.77
85	Fayetteville St.	.80
76	Barber-Scotia	.81
71	Winston-Salem ■	.80
86	N.C. Central	.73
88	Johnson Smith ■	.86
74	Virginia St. ■	.78
52	Winston-Salem	.60
71	Virginia St. †	.87
61	Johnson Smith	.83

Nickname: Fighting Bears
Colors: Columbia Blue & Black
Arena: Trent Gymnasium
AD: H. R. Doub
SID: Clifton Huff

LOCK HAVEN

Lock Haven, PA 17745 II

Coach: Dave Blank
Alma Mater: South Caro. '82
Record: 8 Years, W-118, L-98

1996-97 SCHEDULE

Fairmont St. Cl. ....Nov. 15-16
Bapt. Bible (Pa.) ....Nov. 19
Indianapolis Cl. ....Nov. 22-23
Gannon Cl. ....Nov. 29-30
Bloomsburg ■ ....Dec. 2
Millersville ....Dec. 4
Phila. Bible ■ ....Dec. 10
Mansfield ....Dec. 13
Mansfield ■ ....Jan. 4
Pitt.-Bradford ....Jan. 6
Indiana (Pa.) ■ ....Jan. 8
Edinboro ....Jan. 11
Shippensburg ....Jan. 15
Calif. (Pa.) ....Jan. 18
Clarion ....Jan. 22
Slippery Rock ■ ....Jan. 25
Pitt.-Johnstown ....Jan. 27
Edinboro ■ ....Feb. 1
Indiana (Pa.) ....Feb. 5
Calif. (Pa.) ■ ....Feb. 8
Shippensburg ■ ....Feb. 12
Clarion ....Feb. 15
Pitt.-Johnstown ■ ....Feb. 19
Slippery Rock ....Feb. 22

1995-96 RESULTS (13-13)

63	Dist. Columbia †	.68
80	Pitt.-Johnstown	.76
45	Virginia Union	.80
59	Longwood †	.63
98	Millersville ■	.86
69	Bloomsburg	.82
81	Mansfield	.99
75	Mansfield ■	.71
96	Bapt. Bible (Pa.)	.81
83	Kutztown ■	.52
78	Slippery Rock ■	.74
74	Clarion	.81
75	Calif. (Pa.) ■	.78
81	Pitt.-Johnstown ■	.72
88	Shippensburg ■	.83
87	Edinboro ■	.96
80	Kutztown	.75
77	Indiana (Pa.)	.69
78	Slippery Rock ■	.69
84	Clarion ■	.64
72	Shippensburg	.85
64	Calif. (Pa.)	.83
89	Pitt.-Bradford ■	.87
67	Indiana (Pa.) ■	.75
62	Edinboro	.75
68	Bloomsburg	.79

Nickname: Bald Eagles
Colors: Crimson & White
Arena: Thomas Field House
   Capacity: 2,000; Year Built: 1928
AD: Sharon Taylor
SID: Pat Donghia

LONG BEACH ST.

Long Beach, CA 90840 I

Coach: Wayne Morgan
Alma Mater: St. Lawrence '73
(First year as head coach)

1996-97 SCHEDULE

Wyoming ■ ....Nov. 25
Southern Cal ....Nov. 30
Oregon St. ■ ....Dec. 3
Purdue Inv. ....Dec. 6-7
George Mason ....Dec. 10
Montana ....Dec. 21

Bethune-Cookman ■ ....Dec. 30
St. Mary's (Cal.) ....Jan. 4
Boise St. ■ ....Jan. 6
Southwest Mo. St. ■ ....Jan. 9
UC Irvine ■ ....Jan. 11
Cal St. Fullerton ....Jan. 13
Pacific (Cal.) ....Jan. 18
UC Santa Barb. ■ ....Jan. 23
Cal Poly SLO ....Jan. 25
New Mexico St. ....Jan. 30
North Texas ....Feb. 1
Nevada ■ ....Feb. 6
Utah St. ■ ....Feb. 8
Cal Poly SLO ....Feb. 13
UC Santa Barb. ....Feb. 15
UC Irvine ■ ....Feb. 20
Cal St. Fullerton ■ ....Feb. 22
Idaho ....Feb. 27
Pacific (Cal.) ■ ....Mar. 1
Big West Conf. Tr. ....Mar. 7-9

1995-96 RESULTS (17-11)

57	Arizona	.91
45	Detroit	.52
101	Cal St. Hayward ■	.52
71	Hawaii ■	.66
65	Oregon St.	.54
62	Miami (Ohio) †	.69
86	St. Mary's (Cal.) ■	.69
98	George Mason ■	.84
76	UC Santa Barb. ■	.54
68	Nebraska	.69
79	Cal St. Fullerton ■	.66
72	UNLV	.85
80	Utah St. ■	.73
75	Nevada ■	.79
63	New Mexico St.	.76
76	San Jose St.	.63
83	Pacific (Cal.)	.77
73	Cal St. Fullerton	.56
69	UC Irvine	.65
84	UNLV ■	.65
73	New Mexico St. ■	.57
81	UC Irvine ■	.84
73	Nevada	.76
71	Utah St.	.50
61	Pacific (Cal.) ■	.71
105	San Jose St. ■	.86
74	UC Santa Barb.	.69
73	Utah St. †	.86

Nickname: Forty Niners
Colors: Black & Gold
Arena: The Pyramid
   Capacity: 5,000; Year Built: 1994
AD: Bill Shumard
SID: Tony Gervase

LIU-BROOKLYN

Brooklyn, NY 11201 I

Coach: Ray Haskins
Alma Mater: Shaw '72
Record: 2 Years, W-18, L-36

1996-97 SCHEDULE

St. John's (N.Y.) ....Nov. 23
Providence ....Nov. 27
Ohio St. ....Dec. 7
Xavier (Ohio) ■ ....Dec. 10
Niagara ....Dec. 14
UAB Tr. ....Dec. 20-21
Minnesota ....Dec. 28
St. Francis (Pa.) ■ ....Jan. 4
Robert Morris ■ ....Jan. 6
Mt. St. Mary's (Md.) ....Jan. 9
Rider ■ ....Jan. 11
Wagner ■ ....Jan. 15
Marist ....Jan. 18
Fairleigh Dickinson ■ ....Jan. 20
Monmouth (N.J.) ■ ....Jan. 23
St. Francis (N.Y.) ....Jan. 25

St. Francis (Pa.) ....Feb. 1
Robert Morris ....Feb. 3
Mt. St. Mary's (Md.) ■ ....Feb. 6
Rider ....Feb. 8
Wagner ....Feb. 12
Marist ■ ....Feb. 15
Fairleigh Dickinson ....Feb. 17
Monmouth (N.J.) ....Feb. 20
St. Francis (N.Y.) ■ ....Feb. 22
Northeast Conf. Tr. ....Feb. 25-Mar. 6

1995-96 RESULTS (9-19)

105	Medgar Evers ■	.83
78	Xavier (Ohio)	.109
76	Md.-East. Shore ■	.66
67	Pittsburgh	.108
67	Fordham	.75
81	Boston College	.116
87	Yale †	.74
60	South Fla.	.86
74	Mt. St. Mary's (Md.)	.92
69	Marist ■	.86
72	Fairleigh Dickinson	.77
79	Wagner	.78
55	Monmouth (N.J.) ■	.71
80	St. Francis (N.Y.)	.78
65	St. Francis (Pa.)	.76
87	Robert Morris	.73
80	Rider	.112
77	Mt. St. Mary's (Md.) ■	.99
75	Rider ■	.96
74	Marist	.104
77	Fairleigh Dickinson ■	.95
94	Wagner ■	.99
68	Monmouth (N.J.)	.85
105	St. Francis (N.Y.) ■	.77
87	Robert Morris ■	.75
80	St. Francis (Pa.) ■	.94
82	St. Francis (N.Y.) ■	.63
58	Mt. St. Mary's (Md.)	.93

Nickname: Blackbirds
Colors: Blue & White
Arena: Schwartz Athletic Center
   Capacity: 1,700; Year Built: 1963
AD: James A. Martin Sr
SID: Greg Fox

LIU-C. W. POST

Greenvale, NY 11548 II

Coach: Tom Galeazzi
Alma Mater: Cortland St. '61
Record: 15 Years, W-311, L-129

1996-97 SCHEDULE

Phila. Textile ■ ....Dec. 4
New York Tech ....Dec. 7
Adelphi ....Dec. 11
Mercy ....Dec. 14
Sacred Heart ■ ....Dec. 17
Southern Conn. St. ■ ....Dec. 21
Queens (N.Y.) ■ ....Jan. 6
Pace ....Jan. 8
Concordia (N.Y.) ■ ....Jan. 11
Dowling ....Jan. 13
Molloy ....Jan. 15
St. Rose ■ ....Jan. 18
Phila. Textile ....Jan. 20
New York Tech ■ ....Jan. 22
Adelphi ■ ....Jan. 25
Mercy ■ ....Jan. 29
LIU-Southampton ■ ....Feb. 1
Queens (N.Y.) ....Feb. 5
Pace ■ ....Feb. 8
Concordia (N.Y.) ....Feb. 12
Dowling ....Feb. 15
Molloy ■ ....Feb. 19
St. Rose ....Feb. 22

1995-96 RESULTS (13-16)

83	Bridgeport ■	.80

65	Molloy ■	54
77	Queens (N.Y.)	71
73	Concordia (N.Y.)	70
75	Adelphi	93
71	New York Tech ■	93
72	Mo. Southern St. †	86
73	American (P.R.)	87
50	Eckerd †	69
70	Fla. Southern †	87
71	East Stroudsburg †	60
70	LIU-Southampton	73
65	Phila. Textile ■	79
113	Mercy ■	78
86	Dowling	84
49	Pace ■	47
52	St. Rose ■	89
72	Molloy	69
72	Queens (N.Y.) ■	63
93	Dowling	85
61	Concordia (N.Y.) ■	52
67	New York Tech	81
72	Adelphi ■	85
64	LIU-Southampton ■	68
78	Phila. Textile	87
53	Mercy	52
67	Pace	72
62	St. Rose	91
61	Phila. Textile	72

Nickname: Pioneers
Colors: Green & Gold
Arena: Conolly Gym
   Capacity: 600; Year Built: 1960
AD: Vin Salamone
SID: Jeremy Kniffin

LIU-SOUTHAMPTON
Southampton, NY 11968 II

Coach: Sidney Green
Alma Mater: UNLV '83
Record: 1 Year, W-16, L-13

1996-97 SCHEDULE
So. Conn. St. Cl. ....Nov. 22-23
Molloy ....Dec. 4
St. Rose ■ ....Dec. 7
Mercy ....Dec. 9
New York Tech ....Dec. 14
Bloomsburg Inv. ....Jan. 4-5
Adelphi ....Jan. 8
Phila. Textile ■ ....Jan. 10
Queens (N.Y.) ■ ....Jan. 11
Pace ....Jan. 13
Concordia (N.Y.) ■ ....Jan. 15
Dowling ....Jan. 18
Molloy ■ ....Jan. 20
St. Rose ....Jan. 22
Phila. Textile ....Jan. 25
New York Tech ■ ....Jan. 29
LIU-C. W. Post ....Feb. 1
Mercy ■ ....Feb. 5
Adelphi ■ ....Feb. 8
Queens (N.Y.) ....Feb. 12
Pace ■ ....Feb. 15
Concordia (N.Y.) ....Feb. 19
Dowling ....Feb. 22

1995-96 RESULTS (16-13)
83	East Stroudsburg ■	72
66	Concordia (N.Y.)	71
89	Assumption	88
89	New York Tech	105
79	Queens (N.Y.) ■	83
92	York (N.Y.)	86
96	Molloy ■	70
112	St. Rose ■	104
73	LIU-C. W. Post ■	70
84	Adelphi	93
55	Phila. Textile ■	64
103	Dowling	95
88	Pace	85
83	Concordia (N.Y.) ■	79
75	St. Rose	94
89	New York Tech ■	100
96	Queens (N.Y.)	85

58	Stony Brook	74
73	Molloy	70
68	LIU-C. W. Post ■	64
118	Mercy	92
77	Adelphi ■	80
69	Phila. Textile ■	102
121	Mercy	103
81	Dowling	94
78	Pace ■	53
82	New York Tech	74
77	St. Rose	80
87	Dowling	91

Nickname: Colonials
Colors: Blue & Gold
Arena: Southampton Gym
   Capacity: 1,500; Year Built: 1964
AD: Mary Topping
SID: Cindy Corwith

LONGWOOD
Farmville, VA 23901 II

Coach: Ron Carr
Alma Mater: Wofford '82
Record: 6 Years, W-95, L-73

1996-97 SCHEDULE
Elon ....Nov. 16
Longwood Inv. ....Nov. 23-24
Coker ....Nov. 26
Pfeiffer ■ ....Dec. 2
Queens (N.C.) ■ ....Dec. 6
Va. Wesleyan ■ ....Dec. 16
Elon ■ ....Jan. 2
Barton ....Jan. 4
Mount Olive ■ ....Jan. 9
Lees-McRae ■ ....Jan. 11
Erskine ....Jan. 13
Belmont Abbey ■ ....Jan. 16
High Point ■ ....Jan. 18
St. Andrews ....Jan. 23
Barton ....Jan. 25
Coker ....Jan. 30
Lees-McRae ....Feb. 1
St. Andrews ■ ....Feb. 3
Virginia St. ■ ....Feb. 5
Mount Olive ....Feb. 10
Pfeiffer ....Feb. 13
Queens (N.C.) ....Feb. 15
Erskine ■ ....Feb. 17
Belmont Abbey ....Feb. 19
High Point ....Feb. 22

1995-96 RESULTS (11-17)
73	Queens (N.C.) ■	75
64	Mars Hill †	72
63	Lock Haven †	59
62	Elon	71
86	Southern Wesleyan ■	73
53	N.C.-Pembroke ■	55
63	Virginia St.	69
82	Va. Wesleyan ■	90
79	Erskine	80
94	Elon ■	72
64	Mount Olive	61
74	Barton ■	61
75	Pfeiffer	80
71	Belmont Abbey ■	85
81	Lees-McRae ■	79
61	High Point	68
53	Coker ■	48
70	St. Andrews	88
50	Pfeiffer ■	65
60	Coker	63
72	Mount Olive ■	80
64	Erskine ■	49
74	Barton	82
59	Queens (N.C.)	74
86	St. Andrews ■	71
80	Belmont Abbey	66
75	St. Andrews †	54
71	Pfeiffer †	81

Nickname: Lancers
Colors: Blue & White
Arena: Lancer Hall

   Capacity: 2,500; Year Built: 1980
AD: Jack E. Williams
SID: Hoke Currie

LORAS
Dubuque, IA 52001 III

Coach: John Lembezeder
Alma Mater: Wisconsin '78
Record: 3 Years, W-44, L-31

1996-97 SCHEDULE
Coe ....Nov. 23
Elmhurst ....Nov. 26
Aurora ■ ....Dec. 6
Ripon ■ ....Dec. 7
Milwaukee Engr. ....Dec. 21
Loras Catholic Tr. ....Jan. 1-5
William Penn ■ ....Jan. 17
Wartburg ■ ....Jan. 18
Upper Iowa ■ ....Jan. 24
Dubuque ....Jan. 25
Central (Iowa) ....Jan. 31
Buena Vista ■ ....Feb. 1
Luther ....Feb. 4
Simpson ■ ....Feb. 7
William Penn ....Feb. 8
Central (Iowa) ....Feb. 14
Simpson ....Feb. 15
Upper Iowa ....Feb. 21
Buena Vista ....Feb. 22
Dubuque ■ ....Feb. 25
Luther ■ ....Feb. 28
Wartburg ....Mar. 1

1995-96 RESULTS (13-12)
74	Lake Forest ■	68
54	Coe	68
75	Ripon	59
75	Cornell College ■	59
80	Aurora	88
72	Cardinal Stritch	61
53	Viterbo ■	47
66	Cabrini ■	65
52	St. Xavier ■	53
69	Simpson	79
72	Buena Vista	71
57	Dubuque ■	59
64	Luther ■	61
60	Upper Iowa ■	78
63	Wartburg ■	60
67	Central (Iowa)	92
81	Simpson ■	90
67	William Penn	57
83	William Penn ■	67
83	Central (Iowa) ■	82
78	Dubuque	86
51	Upper Iowa ■	54
53	Luther	75
79	Wartburg	85
95	Buena Vista ■	90

Nickname: Duhawks
Colors: Purple & Gold
Arena: Loras Fieldhouse
   Capacity: 1,200; Year Built: 1923
AD: Bob Bierie
SID: Howard Thomas

LSU
Baton Rouge, LA 70894 I

Coach: Dale Brown
Alma Mater: Minot St. '57
Record: 24 Years, W-438, L-281

1996-97 SCHEDULE
Troy St. ■ ....Nov. 22
Maui Inv. ....Nov. 25-27
North Caro. A&T ■ ....Nov. 30
Samford ■ ....Dec. 2
Louisville [Anaheim] ....Dec. 7
Michigan [Auburn Hills] ....Dec. 15
North Caro. [Greensboro] .....Dec. 18
Oral Roberts ■ ....Dec. 21
Prairie View ■ ....Dec. 23

Fresno St. ■ ....Dec. 28
Lafayette ■ ....Dec. 30
Mississippi St. ....Jan. 4
Florida ■ ....Jan. 8
Arkansas ....Jan. 11
Vanderbilt ■ ....Jan. 15
Tennessee ....Jan. 19
Auburn ■ ....Jan. 22
Alabama ....Jan. 25
Mississippi St. ■ ....Jan. 29
South Caro. ■ ....Feb. 1
Mississippi ....Feb. 5
Auburn ....Feb. 8
Kentucky ■ ....Feb. 12
Alabama ■ ....Feb. 15
Georgia ....Feb. 22
Mississippi ....Feb. 26
Arkansas ■ ....Mar. 1
Southeastern Conf. Tr. ....Mar. 6-9

1995-96 RESULTS (12-17)
70	St. Louis †	79
73	Dayton †	86
109	Southern U. ■	100
83	McNeese St. ■	73
68	Michigan ■	69
93	Tenn.-Martin ■	74
65	Centenary (La.) ■	63
76	Jackson St. ■	87
104	Louisiana Col. ■	65
80	Marist ■	65
70	Cornell ■	60
64	Mississippi St. ■	77
99	Alabama ■	77
71	Vanderbilt ■	68
97	Kentucky ■	129
87	Auburn	95
86	Nicholls St. ■	69
70	Florida	73
68	Arkansas	76
71	Mississippi ■	66
82	Georgia ■	85
68	South Caro. ■	106
65	Tennessee ■	73
73	Alabama	76
77	Mississippi St.	88
93	Auburn ■	67
48	Mississippi	75
79	Arkansas ■	94
76	South Caro. †	85

Nickname: Fighting Tigers
Colors: Purple & Gold
Arena: Maravich Assembly Center
   Capacity: 14,164; Year Built: 1972
AD: Joe Dean
SID: Herb Vincent

LOUISIANA TECH
Ruston, LA 71272 I

Coach: Jim Wooldridge
Alma Mater: Louisiana Tech '77
Record: 11 Years, W-201, L-119

1996-97 SCHEDULE
Tarleton St. ■ ....Nov. 26
Ohio Northern ■ ....Nov. 30
Northwestern St. ....Dec. 5
Texas Christian ....Dec. 7
Southeast Mo. St. ■ ....Dec. 9
Indiana Cl. ....Dec. 13-14
Tarleton St. ■ ....Dec. 17
DePaul ....Dec. 18
New Orleans ■ ....Dec. 22
Tex.-Pan American ....Jan. 2
Lamar ....Jan. 4
Ark.-Little Rock ....Jan. 9
Arkansas St. ....Jan. 11
Jacksonville ■ ....Jan. 16
Ark.-Little Rock ■ ....Jan. 18
New Orleans ....Jan. 22
Lamar ■ ....Jan. 25
Tex.-Pan American ■ ....Jan. 27
Southwestern La. ....Jan. 30
Western Ky. ■ ....Feb. 1

South Ala. ...Feb. 3
Arkansas St. ■ ...Feb. 8
Western Ky. ...Feb. 15
Southwestern La. ■ ...Feb. 17
South Ala. ■ ...Feb. 20
Jacksonville ...Feb. 22
Sun Belt Conf. Tr. ...Feb. 28-Mar. 4

1995-96 RESULTS (11-17)
70 Henderson St. ■ ...62
58 Centenary (La.) ...65
68 Stephen F. Austin † ...58
64 Brigham Young ...74
90 Centenary (La.) ■ ...77
91 Northwestern St. ■ ...61
77 Southwestern La. ■ ...80
56 Florida † ...71
55 Baylor † ...74
60 Ark.-Little Rock ...66
50 Arkansas St. ...62
56 Tex.-Pan American ■ ...55
76 Jacksonville ■ ...75
45 New Orleans ...70
46 South Ala. ■ ...45
63 Ark.-Little Rock ■ ...80
57 Western Ky. ...59
64 Arkansas St. ■ ...69
56 Lamar ■ ...57
68 Jacksonville ...70
47 South Ala. ■ ...41
61 Southwestern La. ...54
55 Lamar ...67
61 New Orleans ■ ...70
72 Western Ky. ■ ...66
45 Tex.-Pan American ...47
70 Arkansas St. † ...65
57 New Orleans † ...67

Nickname: Bulldogs
Colors: Red & Blue
Arena: Thomas Assembly Center
Capacity: 8,000; Year Built: 1982
AD: Jim Oakes
SID: Byron Avery

LOUISVILLE
Louisville, KY 40292 ...I

Coach: Denny Crum
Alma Mater: UCLA '58
Record: 25 Years, W-587, L-224

1996-97 SCHEDULE
Hawaii-Hilo Inv. ...Nov. 29-Dec. 1
LSU [Anaheim] ...Dec. 7
Dayton ...Dec. 11
Purdue [Indianapolis] ...Dec. 14
Wright St. ■ ...Dec. 16
Arkansas ...Dec. 21
Tennessee St. ■ ...Dec. 23
Boston College ■ ...Dec. 29
Kentucky ■ ...Dec. 31
UAB ...Jan. 3
N.C.-Charlotte ...Jan. 6
Georgia Tech ■ ...Jan. 11
Houston ...Jan. 15
Texas ...Jan. 19
Memphis ■ ...Jan. 23
UCLA ■ ...Jan. 25
DePaul ■ ...Jan. 28
Cincinnati ■ ...Jan. 30
Temple ...Feb. 2
St. Louis ...Feb. 6
Memphis ...Feb. 9
Houston ...Feb. 15
South Fla. ■ ...Feb. 17
Marquette ...Feb. 20
Southern Miss. ...Feb. 22
N.C.-Charlotte ■ ...Feb. 26
Tulane ...Mar. 1
Conference USA ...Mar. 5-8

1995-96 RESULTS (22-12)
78 Auburn † ...82
90 American (P.R.) ...86
83 Va. Commonwealth † ...74

67 Boston College ...81
79 Michigan St. ■ ...59
119 Morehead St. ■ ...61
101 Texas ...78
87 Eastern Ky. ■ ...70
77 Georgia Tech ...88
81 Murray St. ■ ...72
66 Kentucky ...89
96 Towson St. ■ ...72
81 DePaul ...71
66 N.C.-Charlotte ■ ...78
64 St. John's (N.Y.) ...86
78 UAB ...70
87 Southern Miss. ■ ...61
67 St. Louis ...63
61 St. Louis ■ ...57
78 UCLA ...76
57 South Fla. ...54
74 Memphis ■ ...56
65 Tulane ...68
81 UAB ■ ...66
67 N.C.-Charlotte ■ ...64
72 Cincinnati ...66
54 Memphis ...57
79 Marquette ■ ...80
59 Massachusetts ■ ...62
98 Tulane † ...79
81 Cincinnati † ...92
82 Tulsa † ...80
68 Villanova † ...64
59 Wake Forest † ...60

Nickname: Cardinals
Colors: Red, Black, White
Arena: Freedom Hall
Capacity: 18,865; Year Built: 1956
AD: William Olsen
SID: Kenny Klein

LOYOLA (ILL.)
Chicago, IL 60626 ...I

Coach: Ken Burmeister
Alma Mater: Loyola (Tex.) '71
Record: 6 Years, W-85, L-85

1996-97 SCHEDULE
Eastern Ky. ■ ...Nov. 23
St. Peter's ...Nov. 26
Kent ...Nov. 30
Chicago St. ...Dec. 4
Robert Morris (Ill.) ■ ...Dec. 7
Cal St. Fullerton ...Dec. 14
Northwestern ...Dec. 21
Indiana St. ■ ...Dec. 22
Notre Dame ■ ...Dec. 30
Drake ...Jan. 4
Northern Ill. ■ ...Jan. 8
Butler ...Jan. 11
Detroit ...Jan. 16
Cleveland St. ...Jan. 18
Wright St. ■ ...Jan. 23
Wis.-Green Bay ...Jan. 25
Wis.-Green Bay ■ ...Jan. 30
Wis.-Milwaukee ...Feb. 1
Ill.-Chicago ■ ...Feb. 3
Northern Ill. ...Feb. 6
Butler ■ ...Feb. 8
Detroit ■ ...Feb. 13
Cleveland St. ■ ...Feb. 15
Ill.-Chicago ...Feb. 19
Wis.-Milwaukee ■ ...Feb. 22
Wright St. ...Feb. 26
Midwestern Conf. Tr. ...Feb. 28-Mar. 4

1995-96 RESULTS (8-19)
73 Kent ...90
102 Trinity Christian ■ ...81
62 Drake ■ ...70
77 Indiana St. ...73
61 Eastern Ky. ...68
72 Northern Iowa ...82
70 Appalachian St. ...78
66 Loyola Marymount ■ ...65
78 Northwestern ■ ...81

62 Northern Ill. ...65
63 Detroit ...78
51 Wis.-Green Bay ■ ...64
73 Wright St. ...87
59 Butler ■ ...67
64 Ill.-Chicago ...95
70 Wis.-Milwaukee ■ ...76
81 Cleveland St. ...71
66 Butler ...78
72 Northern Ill. ■ ...68
85 Wright St. ■ ...67
39 Wis.-Green Bay ...56
100 Cleveland St. ■ ...58
89 Ill.-Chicago ■ ...85
65 DePaul ...79
48 Detroit ...62
58 Wis.-Milwaukee ...61
48 Wis.-Green Bay † ...58

Nickname: Ramblers
Colors: Maroon & Gold
Arena: Loyola Events Center
Capacity: 5,200; Year Built: 1996
AD: Chuck Schwarz
SID: Ian Solomon

LOYOLA (MD.)
Baltimore, MD 21210 ...I

Coach: Brian Ellerbe
Alma Mater: Rutgers '85
Record: 2 Years, W-21, L-33

1996-97 SCHEDULE
Md.-Balt. County ...Nov. 23
Penn St. ...Nov. 30
American ■ ...Dec. 4
Mt. St. Mary's (Md.) ■ ...Dec. 7
Towson St. ...Dec. 10
Notre Dame ...Dec. 21
South Fla. Tr. ...Dec. 27-28
Virginia ...Jan. 2
N.C.-Greensboro ...Jan. 4
Iona ...Jan. 8
St. Peter's ...Jan. 12
Siena ■ ...Jan. 15
Niagara ...Jan. 18
Canisius ...Jan. 20
N.C.-Greensboro ■ ...Jan. 22
Manhattan ...Jan. 26
Fairfield ...Jan. 31
Manhattan ...Feb. 2
Iona ...Feb. 9
Rutgers ...Feb. 11
Canisius ■ ...Feb. 13
Niagara ■ ...Feb. 16
Siena ...Feb. 18
St. Peter's ■ ...Feb. 21
Fairfield ■ ...Feb. 23
Metro Atlantic Conf. Tr. ...Mar. 1-3

1995-96 RESULTS (12-15)
76 William & Mary ...72
58 American ...65
53 Md.-Balt. County ■ ...56
62 Towson St. ■ ...66
62 Notre Dame ■ ...70
73 Mt. St. Mary's (Md.) ...83
59 Monmouth (N.J.) ■ ...73
69 Kansas St. † ...76
73 Holy Cross † ...55
80 St. Joseph's (Pa.) ■ ...78
62 Siena ...77
59 Manhattan ...54
62 Iona ■ ...87
71 Niagara ...65
64 St. Peter's ...63
58 Manhattan ■ ...50
69 Howard ...81
70 St. Peter's ■ ...60
67 Canisius ■ ...72
68 Fairfield ...71
80 Niagara ...68
64 Canisius ...63
59 Fairfield ■ ...70

57 Iona ...61
67 Siena ...53
98 St. Mary's (Md.) ■ ...52
67 Canisius † ...74

Nickname: Greyhounds
Colors: Green & Grey
Arena: Reitz Arena
Capacity: 3,000; Year Built: 1984
AD: Joseph Boylan
SID: Steve Jones

LOYOLA MARYMOUNT
Los Angeles, CA 90045 ...I

Coach: John Olive
Alma Mater: Villanova '77
Record: 4 Years, W-44, L-67

1996-97 SCHEDULE
Seattle ■ ...Nov. 23
Cal Poly SLO ...Nov. 26
Cal St. Northridge ...Nov. 30
Southern Cal ...Dec. 2
Xavier (Ohio) ■ ...Dec. 5
Cal St. Fullerton ■ ...Dec. 7
San Diego St. ...Dec. 14
Northern Ariz. ...Dec. 18
Washington ...Dec. 23
Providence ■ ...Dec. 28
Brown ...Dec. 30
UC Santa Barb. ...Jan. 4
San Francisco ■ ...Jan. 10
San Diego ...Jan. 11
Pepperdine ■ ...Jan. 15
Pepperdine ...Jan. 18
Gonzaga ...Jan. 23
Portland ■ ...Jan. 25
Portland ...Jan. 31
Gonzaga ■ ...Feb. 1
Santa Clara ...Feb. 7
St. Mary's (Cal.) ...Feb. 8
St. Mary's (Cal.) ■ ...Feb. 14
Santa Clara ■ ...Feb. 15
San Diego ...Feb. 20
San Francisco ...Feb. 22
West Coast Conf. Tr. ...Mar. 1-3

1995-96 RESULTS (18-11)
85 Sonoma St. ■ ...66
70 Seattle ...55
61 San Diego St. ■ ...62
70 UNLV ■ ...67
86 Southern Cal ■ ...83
83 UC Santa Barb. ■ ...73
67 Cal St. Fullerton ...63
82 Hawaii ...80
75 Nevada † ...67
65 Loyola (Ill.) ...66
51 Notre Dame ...84
67 Northern Ariz. ...61
57 San Francisco ...61
63 San Diego ...56
71 Santa Clara ...62
64 St. Mary's (Cal.) ■ ...76
76 Cal Poly SLO ■ ...64
66 St. Mary's (Cal.) ...60
60 Santa Clara ...78
83 Gonzaga ■ ...62
70 Portland ■ ...69
77 Portland ...97
68 Gonzaga ...81
74 Pepperdine ...64
75 Pepperdine ■ ...62
59 San Diego ■ ...65
71 San Francisco ■ ...51
75 Cal St. Northridge ...81
51 San Diego † ...75

Nickname: Lions
Colors: Crimson & Blue
Arena: Albert Gersten Pavilion
Capacity: 4,156; Year Built: 1982
AD: Brian Quinn
SID: Bruce Meyers

LUTHER

Decorah, IA 52101 III

Coach: Jeff Olinger
Alma Mater: Luther '85
Record: 5 Years, W-55, L-71

1996-97 SCHEDULE

Gust. Adolphus ■ ....Nov. 25
Grinnell ■ ....Nov. 30
Coe ....Dec. 2
N'western (Minn.) ....Dec. 7
Clarke ....Dec. 10
Mt. Mercy ■ ....Dec. 29
N'western (Iowa) Tr. ....Jan. 3-4
Dubuque ....Jan. 10
Upper Iowa ....Jan. 11
Wartburg ■ ....Jan. 17
William Penn ■ ....Jan. 18
Buena Vista ■ ....Jan. 24
Simpson ....Jan. 25
Martin Luther ■ ....Feb. 1
Loras ■ ....Feb. 4
Central (Iowa) ....Feb. 7
Simpson ■ ....Feb. 8
Upper Iowa ■ ....Feb. 14
William Penn ....Feb. 15
Wartburg ....Feb. 18
Dubuque ■ ....Feb. 21
Central (Iowa) ....Feb. 22
Loras ....Feb. 28
Buena Vista ....Mar. 1

1995-96 RESULTS (15-10)

51	Gust. Adolphus	61
81	Clarke ■	61
114	Grinnell	79
69	Cornell College	55
79	Mt. Mercy	77
74	Coe ■	56
78	N'western (Minn.) ■	65
70	Cal Lutheran	82
45	Concordia (Cal.) †	73
60	Wartburg	63
82	William Penn ■	66
52	Upper Iowa ■	62
75	Central (Iowa) ■	67
64	Buena Vista	61
61	Loras	64
78	Central (Iowa)	75
72	Upper Iowa	68
87	Simpson ■	98
55	Buena Vista ■	52
65	Dubuque ■	68
73	Wartburg ■	66
82	Simpson	97
75	Loras ■	53
60	Dubuque	69
92	William Penn ■	77

Nickname: Norse
Colors: Blue & White
Arena: Luther Field House
Capacity: 3,500; Year Built: 1964
AD: Joe Thompson
SID: Dave Blanchard

LYCOMING

Williamsport, PA 17701 III

Coach: Joe Bressi
Alma Mater: East Stroudsburg '71
Record: 2 Years, W-32, L-19

1996-97 SCHEDULE

Gettysburg Tr. ....Nov. 22-23
Misericordia ....Nov. 26
Delaware Valley ■ ....Dec. 7
Susquehanna Cl. ....Dec. 20-21
York (Pa.) Cl. ....Dec. 28-29
Waynesburg ....Jan. 4
Juniata ■ ....Jan. 8
Pitt.-Greensburg ....Jan. 11
Scranton ....Jan. 15
FDU-Madison ■ ....Jan. 18
Drew ....Jan. 20
King's (Pa.) ■ ....Jan. 22
Wilkes ■ ....Jan. 28
Bapt. Bible (Pa.) ■ ....Jan. 30
Delaware Valley ....Feb. 1
Drew ■ ....Feb. 5
Susquehanna ....Feb. 8
Scranton ■ ....Feb. 12
FDU-Madison ....Feb. 15
Wilkes ....Feb. 17
King's (Pa.) ....Feb. 19

1995-96 RESULTS (21-6)

108	Gwynedd-Mercy ■	70
73	Centenary (N.J.) ■	68
100	Misericordia	94
110	Bloomfield ■	89
104	Delaware Valley	63
102	Drew ■	77
103	Alvernia †	93
83	Holy Family †	98
77	Pitt.-Johnstown †	74
68	Bloomsburg	83
88	Scranton ■	81
78	FDU-Madison ■	67
80	King's (Pa.)	54
65	Wilkes	66
91	Delaware Valley ■	37
112	Juniata	62
75	Drew	72
87	Susquehanna ■	77
85	Scranton	76
84	FDU-Madison ■	66
82	Wilkes ■	85
86	King's (Pa.) ■	76
98	Bapt. Bible (Pa.)	93
61	Elizabethtown ■	60
66	Susquehanna	73
103	Gettysburg ■	75
61	Frank. & Marsh.	72

Nickname: Warriors
Colors: Blue & Gold
Arena: Lamade Gymnasium
Capacity: 2,300; Year Built: 1979
AD: Frank Girardi
SID: Jeff Michaels

LYNCHBURG

Lynchburg, VA 24501 III

Coach: Joe Davis
Alma Mater: Va. Commonwealth '66
Record: 15 Years, W-202, L-199

1996-97 SCHEDULE

Lynchburg Inv. ....Nov. 22-23
Mary Washington ■ ....Nov. 25
Davidson ....Nov. 27
Guilford ....Dec. 4
Hampden-Sydney ■ ....Dec. 7
Frank. & Marsh. Tr. ....Jan. 4-5
Va. Wesleyan ....Jan. 8
Randolph-Macon ....Jan. 11
Wash. & Lee ....Jan. 15
Emory & Henry ■ ....Jan. 19
East. Mennonite ■ ....Jan. 23
Va. Wesleyan ■ ....Jan. 25
Guilford ■ ....Jan. 26
East. Mennonite ....Jan. 30
Bridgewater (Va.) ....Feb. 1
Roanoke ■ ....Feb. 3
Emory & Henry ....Feb. 5
Randolph-Macon ■ ....Feb. 8
Roanoke ....Feb. 10
Wash. & Lee ■ ....Feb. 12
Bridgewater (Va.) ■ ....Feb. 15
Hampden-Sydney ....Feb. 17

1995-96 RESULTS (10-15)

92	Marymount (Va.) ■	72
73	Chowan	64
84	Mary Washington	74
80	Guilford	56
66	Hampden-Sydney ■	61
74	VMI	107
79	Shenandoah	90
56	Furman	77
66	Randolph-Macon	88
71	Wash. & Lee	74
75	Emory & Henry ■	92
92	East. Mennonite ■	75
74	Va. Wesleyan ■	71
74	Guilford	61
78	East. Mennonite	83
63	Bridgewater (Va.) ■	72
63	Roanoke	83
62	Emory & Henry ■	91
58	Va. Wesleyan ■	81
70	Roanoke	73
68	Wash. & Lee ■	65
70	Bridgewater (Va.)	77
49	Hampden-Sydney	87
72	Randolph-Macon ■	45
65	Randolph-Macon †	72

Nickname: Hornets
Colors: Crimson & Gray
Arena: Turner Gym
Capacity: 2,500; Year Built: 1970
AD: Jack Toms
SID: Greg Prouty

LYNN

Boca Raton, FL 33431 II

Coach: Jeff Price
Alma Mater: Pikeville '88
Record: 3 Years, W-59, L-28

1996-97 SCHEDULE

Fla. Memorial ■ ....Nov. 20
Florida Tech ■ ....Nov. 25
Florida Tech ....Dec. 2
Lynn Cl. ....Dec. 6-7
Barry ....Dec. 14
Transylvania ■ ....Dec. 28
Tri-State ■ ....Dec. 30
Barry ....Jan. 4
St. Augustine's ....Jan. 11
Winston-Salem ....Jan. 13
St. Thomas (Fla.) ■ ....Jan. 16
Paine ....Jan. 18
Gardner-Webb ....Jan. 20
Fla. Memorial ....Jan. 27
Montevallo ■ ....Jan. 28
St. Augustine's ■ ....Feb. 1
St. Thomas (Fla.) ■ ....Feb. 3
Bowie St. ....Feb. 7
Dist. Columbia ....Feb. 8
Columbia Union ....Feb. 10
Lane ....Feb. 15
Lambuth ....Feb. 17
Virgin Islands ....Feb. 22
Virgin Islands ....Feb. 23

1995-96 RESULTS (16-11)

85	Fla. Southern ■	72
102	St. Thomas (Fla.) †	89
79	North Fla.	63
60	Florida Tech ■	68
91	American (P.R.) ■	81
56	Florida Tech	57
69	Barry	81
77	Lenoir-Rhyne ■	66
83	Shippensburg ■	80
84	Wheaton (Mass.) ■	36
63	Bentley ■	66
81	Bowie St. ■	70
72	Cal St. San B'dino	87
57	Cal St. Dom. Hills	76
65	Cal St. Bakersfield	81
76	Molloy	59
79	St. Thomas (Fla.)	72
88	Barry ■	70
107	Webber ■	69
76	Fla. Memorial	72
68	Georgetown (Ky.)	94
65	Transylvania	77
79	St. Thomas (Fla.) ■	71
77	Fla. Memorial	64
87	Valdosta St.	89
91	Fort Valley St.	60
65	Columbia Union ■	76

Nickname: Knights
Colors: Royal Blue & White
Arena: de Hoernle Center
Capacity: 1,500; Year Built: 1993
AD: Dick Young
SID: Dave Geringer

MACMURRAY

Jacksonville, IL 62650 III

Coach: Bob Gay
Alma Mater: MacMurray '67
Record: 21 Years, W-242, L-295

1996-97 SCHEDULE

Albion Tr. ....Nov. 22-23
Goshen ....Nov. 25
Knox ....Dec. 2
Monmouth (Ill.) ■ ....Dec. 5
Wheaton (Ill.) ....Dec. 7
Lincoln Chrst. ■ ....Dec. 13
Fontbonne ....Jan. 9
Principia ■ ....Jan. 11
Washington (Mo.) ....Jan. 14
Webster ....Jan. 16
Greenville ■ ....Jan. 18
Maryville (Mo.) ■ ....Jan. 23
Westminster (Mo.) ....Jan. 25
Blackburn ■ ....Jan. 30
Fontbonne ■ ....Feb. 1
Millikin ....Feb. 4
Principia ....Feb. 6
Webster ■ ....Feb. 8
Greenville ....Feb. 13
Maryville (Mo.) ....Feb. 15
Illinois Col. ■ ....Feb. 18
Westminster (Mo.) ■ ....Feb. 20
Blackburn ....Feb. 22

1995-96 RESULTS (14-13)

63	Elmhurst ■	69
66	Wheaton (Ill.)	69
64	Washington (Mo.) ■	78
65	Monmouth (Ill.)	84
80	Knox	87
66	Otterbein	79
65	Calvin †	75
85	Fontbonne ■	65
57	Maryville (Mo.) ■	53
64	Greenville	60
69	Westminster (Mo.)	65
69	Principia ■	57
87	Parks ■	58
77	Webster ■	67
84	Blackburn	78
65	Fontbonne	88
65	Maryville (Mo.) ■	80
76	Greenville	83
79	Westminster (Mo.) ■	68
65	Principia	59
64	Illinois Col.	82
71	Parks	85
61	Webster	53
62	Blackburn ■	50
56	Principia ■	52
72	Blackburn ■	68
67	Fontbonne ■	72

Nickname: Highlanders
Colors: Scarlet & Navy
Arena: Education Complex Gym
Capacity: 1,500; Year Built: 1975
AD: Bob Gay
SID: To be named

MACALESTER

St. Paul, MN 55105 III

Coach: Andy Manning
Alma Mater: Slippery Rock '74
Record: 2 Years, W-5, L-43

1996-97 SCHEDULE

North Central ■ ....Nov. 26
Hamline ....Dec. 7
St. Mary's (Minn.) ■ ....Dec. 9

Augsburg ....Dec. 11
Wis.-River Falls Tr. ....Dec. 29-30
Carleton ■ ....Jan. 4
Concordia-M'head ■ ....Jan. 6
Bethel (Minn.) ■ ....Jan. 8
St. Olaf ....Jan. 11
St. John's (Minn.) ■ ....Jan. 13
Gust. Adolphus ....Jan. 18
N'western (Minn.) ■ ....Jan. 20
St. Thomas (Minn.) ■ ....Jan. 22
Hamline ■ ....Jan. 25
Augsburg ■ ....Jan. 29
St. Mary's (Minn.) ....Feb. 1
Carleton ....Feb. 3
Concordia-M'head ....Feb. 5
Bethel (Minn.) ....Feb. 8
St. Olaf ■ ....Feb. 12
St. John's (Minn.) ■ ....Feb. 15
Gust. Adolphus ■ ....Feb. 19
St. Thomas (Minn.) ■ ....Feb. 22

1995-96 RESULTS (3-21)

88	Swarthmore †	82
65	Haverford †	71
83	North Cent. Bible †	60
65	St. Olaf ■	76
67	Bethel (Minn.) ■	83
51	St. John's (Minn.)	86
63	St. Thomas (Minn.)	72
36	Gust. Adolphus ■	48
62	Presentation ■	73
50	Carleton	84
72	Concordia-M'head	81
56	Augsburg ■	73
67	Hamline ■	71
58	St. Olaf	74
75	Bethel (Minn.)	79
64	St. John's (Minn.) ■	67
41	St. Mary's (Minn.) ■	49
62	St. Thomas (Minn.) ■	61
48	Gust. Adolphus	69
71	Carleton	87
65	Concordia-M'head ■	83
65	Augsburg	83
53	St. Mary's (Minn.) ■	74
82	Hamline	100

Nickname: Scots
Colors: Orange & Blue
Arena: Macalester Gymnasium
Capacity: 850; Year Built: 1927
AD: Ken Andrews
SID: Andy Johnson

MAINE
Orono, ME 04469 I

Coach: John Giannini
Alma Mater: North Central '84
Record: 7 Years, W-168, L-38

1996-97 SCHEDULE

Southern Me. ■ ....Nov. 23
Liberty ■ ....Nov. 25
Great Alas. Shootout ....Nov. 27-30
Husson ■ ....Dec. 3
Hofstra ■ ....Dec. 6
Drexel ■ ....Dec. 8
Youngstown St. ....Dec. 13
Mt. St. Mary's Cl. ....Dec. 27-28
Northeastern ■ ....Jan. 2
Boston U. ■ ....Jan. 4
Hartford ....Jan. 7
New Hampshire ....Jan. 11
Towson St. ■ ....Jan. 16
Delaware ■ ....Jan. 18
St. Louis ....Jan. 20
Drexel ....Jan. 24
Hofstra ....Jan. 26
Vermont ■ ....Jan. 30
Hartford ■ ....Feb. 1
Marquette ....Feb. 5
New Hampshire ....Feb. 8
Delaware ....Feb. 13
Towson St. ....Feb. 15
Vermont ....Feb. 17

Northeastern ■ ....Feb. 20
Boston U. ■ ....Feb. 23
America East Conf. Tr. ....Feb. 28-Mar. 2

1995-96 RESULTS (15-13)

49	Fresno St.	66
62	Boise St. †	45
62	Boston U. ■	60
76	Northeastern	62
58	DePaul	72
70	Youngstown St. ■	54
47	Brown †	60
54	Northern Ill.	57
64	Delaware	62
85	Towson St. ■	72
77	Vermont ■	48
51	Hofstra	64
70	Drexel	88
103	New Hampshire ■	106
79	Hartford ■	66
82	New Hampshire	73
84	Hampton	81
75	Hofstra ■	57
52	Drexel ■	73
77	Delaware	65
56	Towson St.	65
66	Hampton ■	67
92	Hartford	67
61	Vermont	60
62	Boston U.	79
59	Northeastern ■	75
84	Vermont †	75
64	Boston U. †	66

Nickname: Black Bears
Colors: Blue & White
Arena: Alfond Arena
Capacity: 6,000; Year Built: 1977
AD: Suzanne Tyler
SID: Matt Bourque

MAINE MARITIME
Castine, ME 04420 III

Coach: Chris Murphy
Alma Mater: Maine '73
Record: 4 Years, W-25, L-51

1996-97 SCHEDULE

N.Y. Maritime Tr. ....Nov. 23-24
Unity ■ ....Dec. 4
Westbrook Tr. ....Dec. 7-8
Me.-Machias ■ ....Dec. 10
Me.-Augusta ■ ....Dec. 12
Johnson & Wales ....Jan. 11
Curry ....Jan. 12
Thomas ■ ....Jan. 16
Endicott ■ ....Jan. 18
Bowdoin ....Jan. 21
Me.-Augusta ■ ....Jan. 23
New England ■ ....Jan. 26
Unity ....Jan. 28
Me.-Presque Isle ■ ....Feb. 2
New England ....Feb. 5
Suffolk ....Feb. 8
Mass. Pharmacy ....Feb. 9
Me.-Farmington ■ ....Feb. 11
Thomas ....Feb. 13
Bates ....Feb. 17

1995-96 RESULTS (5-13)

57	Merchant Marine	78
71	Brooklyn †	60
70	Unity	63
60	Bates ■	87
31	St. Joseph's (Me.) ■	106
74	Me.-Augusta	44
58	Bowdoin ■	78
58	Southern Me.	98
69	Me.-Farmington	83
95	Thomas ■	106
65	New England ■	72
69	Westbrook ■	95
59	New England	75
78	Unity ■	46
68	Me.-Augusta ■	47
64	Thomas	78

53	Me.-Presque Isle	86
78	Me.-Machias	96

Nickname: Mariners
Colors: Royal Blue & Gold
Arena: Margaret Chase Smith Gym
Capacity: 1,000; Year Built: 1965
AD: Bill Mottola
SID: Holly Daste

MANCHESTER
North Manchester, IN 46962....III

Coach: Dick Hunsaker
Alma Mater: Weber St. '77
Record: 4 Years, W-97, L-34

1996-97 SCHEDULE

Manchester Tr. ....Nov. 22-23
Purdue-North Cent. ■ ....Nov. 29
Ind.-Northwest ....Nov. 30
Huntington ....Dec. 3
Ind.-Northwest ■ ....Dec. 12
Grace [Ft. Wayne] ....Dec. 14
Goshen ....Dec. 20
Embry-Riddle Tr. ....Dec. 29-30
Anderson (Ind.) ....Jan. 8
Wabash ■ ....Jan. 11
Hanover ■ ....Jan. 15
DePauw ■ ....Jan. 18
Franklin ....Jan. 22
Rose-Hulman ■ ....Jan. 25
Hanover ....Feb. 1
Anderson (Ind.) ■ ....Feb. 5
Wabash ....Feb. 8
Franklin ■ ....Feb. 12
DePauw ....Feb. 15
Rose-Hulman ■ ....Feb. 22

1995-96 RESULTS (18-8)

66	Ferris St. †	80
62	Huntington	65
112	Ind.-Northwest	51
80	Hillsdale	61
78	Purdue-Calumet ■	72
86	Ind.-Southeast ■	70
80	Grace	49
57	Ind. Wesleyan	65
103	Eureka †	79
81	Defiance	65
87	Anderson (Ind.) ■	59
82	Wabash	80
56	Hanover	82
42	DePauw	66
77	Franklin ■	70
94	Rose-Hulman ■	74
116	Ind.-Northwest ■	43
60	Hanover ■	63
68	Anderson (Ind.)	55
71	Wabash ■	59
87	Franklin	80
72	DePauw ■	58
78	Rose-Hulman	88
90	Anderson (Ind.) ■	79
58	DePauw †	53
60	Rose-Hulman †	70

Nickname: Spartans
Colors: Black & Gold
Arena: PERC Arena
Capacity: 1,700; Year Built: 1983
AD: Tom Jarman
SID: Rob Nichols

MANHATTAN
Riverdale, NY 10471 I

Coach: John Leonard
Alma Mater: Manhattan '82
Record: 3 Years, W-21, L-49

1996-97 SCHEDULE

Marist [Albany] ....Nov. 23
Hampton ....Dec. 1
Stanford [Sacramento] ....Dec. 7
Fordham ■ ....Dec. 15

N.C.-Wilmington ....Dec. 19
Monmouth (N.J.) ....Dec. 23
ECAC Holiday Tr. ....Dec. 26-28
Fairleigh Dickinson ■ ....Dec. 31
Princeton ■ ....Jan. 3
Colgate ■ ....Jan. 6
Niagara ....Jan. 12
Canisius ....Jan. 14
St. Peter's ....Jan. 19
Niagara ■ ....Jan. 24
Loyola (Md.) ■ ....Jan. 26
Fairfield ....Jan. 29
St. Peter's ■ ....Jan. 31
Loyola (Md.) ■ ....Feb. 2
Iona ....Feb. 6
Siena ....Feb. 10
Iona ■ ....Feb. 12
Fairfield ....Feb. 15
American ....Feb. 17
Siena ■ ....Feb. 21
Canisius ■ ....Feb. 23
Metro Atlantic Conf. Tr. ....Mar. 1-3

1995-96 RESULTS (17-12)

67	Georgia Tech	87
68	St. John's (N.Y.) ■	71
74	Hofstra	51
74	Monmouth (N.J.) ■	46
61	Fordham	58
76	Eastern Mich.	88
76	Wright St.	85
69	N.C.-Wilmington ■	62
65	Marist	68
73	Colgate ■	60
81	Rutgers	76
71	St. Peter's ■	52
54	Loyola (Md.) ■	59
65	Fairfield	75
98	Hampton	64
49	Iona ■	67
61	Siena ■	40
50	Loyola (Md.)	58
81	Fairfield ■	73
57	Canisius	61
74	Niagara	53
65	Notre Dame ■	44
63	Iona	50
66	Siena	64
68	St. Peter's	50
73	Niagara ■	61
78	Canisius ■	61
60	Niagara †	62
42	Wisconsin	55

Nickname: Jaspers
Colors: Kelly Green & White
Arena: Draddy Gymnasium
Capacity: 3,000; Year Built: 1979
AD: Robert Byrnes
SID: Jeff Bernstein

MANHATTANVILLE
Purchase, NY 10577 III

Coach: Brian Curtin
Alma Mater: St. Michael's '87
Record: 2 Years, W-14, L-35

1996-97 SCHEDULE

Wheaton (Mass.) Cl. ....Nov. 23-24
Connecticut Col. ■ ....Nov. 26
Hunter ■ ....Dec. 2
New York U. ....Dec. 8
St. Joe's-Brooklyn ....Dec. 11
Mt. St. Vincent ■ ....Dec. 14
Marymount (Va.) Tr. ....Jan. 4-5
Wm. Paterson ....Jan. 10
Merchant Marine ....Jan. 15
N.J. Inst. of Tech. ■ ....Jan. 19
Maritime (N.Y.) ....Jan. 21
Manhattanville Cl. ....Jan. 25-26
Mt. St. Mary (N.Y.) ....Jan. 29
Staten Island ....Feb. 1
Maritime (N.Y.) ■ ....Feb. 3
Stevens Tech ....Feb. 5
Mt. St. Mary (N.Y.) ■ ....Feb. 8

Mt. St. Vincent ....Feb. 11
Merchant Marine ■ ....Feb. 15
N.J. Inst. of Tech. ■ ....Feb. 18
Purchase St. ■ ....Feb. 21
Vassar ....Feb. 26

1995-96 RESULTS (10-14)

45	Hartwick	76
59	Westfield St. †	82
72	Connecticut Col.	74
83	Hunter	80
59	Staten Island	82
81	Mt. St. Vincent	98
83	Purchase St. †	58
80	St. Joseph's (L.I.) ■	66
73	New York U. ■	81
65	Centenary (N.J.) †	74
58	St. Mary's (Md.) †	72
57	Merchant Marine ■	59
72	Brooklyn	66
75	Mt. St. Mary (N.Y.)	68
79	Villa Julie ■	76
53	Southern Vt. ■	69
86	N.J. Inst. of Tech. ■	82
68	Mt. St. Mary (N.Y.) ■	80
61	Centenary (N.J.)	74
66	Mt. St. Vincent ■	63
72	Merchant Marine	67
62	N.J. Inst. of Tech.	85
89	Purchase St. ■	56
70	Vassar ■	77

Nickname: Valiants
Colors: Red & White
Arena: Kennedy Gymnasium
Capacity: 800; Year Built: 1957
AD: Karen Peterson
SID: Chris Gonzales

MANKATO ST.
Mankato, MN 56002 II

Coach: Dan McCarrell
Alma Mater: North Park '61
Record: 29 Years, W-495, L-295

1996-97 SCHEDULE

Mankato St. Cl. ....Nov. 22-23
Seattle Pacific Cl. ....Nov. 29-30
Southwest St. ■ ....Dec. 6
Minn.-Crookston ■ ....Dec. 9
Minn.-Duluth ....Dec. 14
Minn.-Morris ....Dec. 19
Bemidji St. ■ ....Dec. 21
Augustana (S.D.) ■ ....Dec. 28
South Dak. St. ■ ....Dec. 29
Neb.-Omaha ....Jan. 3
Northern Colo. ....Jan. 4
North Dak. St. ■ ....Jan. 10
North Dak. ■ ....Jan. 11
Morningside ....Jan. 17
South Dak. ■ ....Jan. 18
St. Cloud St. ■ ....Jan. 25
Northern Colo. ■ ....Jan. 31
Neb.-Omaha ■ ....Feb. 1
North Dak. ....Feb. 7
North Dak. St. ....Feb. 8
South Dak. ....Feb. 14
Morningside ■ ....Feb. 15
St. Cloud St. ....Feb. 22
South Dak. St. ....Feb. 28
Augustana (S.D.) ....Mar. 1

1995-96 RESULTS (16-11)

86	Mo.-St. Louis ■	85
91	IU/PU-Indianapolis ■	82
87	Mt. Senario ■	76
66	Bemidji St.	57
83	Minn.-Duluth ■	77
74	Southwest St.	72
87	Minn.-Morris ■	75
46	Fla. Southern	63
108	Carthage ■	86
107	Neb.-Omaha ■	105
71	Northern Colo. ■	76
83	North Dak. St.	79
86	North Dak. ■	70
72	Morningside ■	83

64	South Dak. ■	68
72	St. Cloud St.	85
85	Augustana (S.D.) ■	94
83	South Dak. St.	89
70	North Dak. ■	71
94	North Dak. St. ■	85
94	South Dak.	84
83	Morningside	93
63	St. Cloud St. ■	65
82	South Dak. St. ■	81
87	Augustana (S.D.) ■	82
72	Northern Colo.	82
67	Neb.-Omaha	54

Nickname: Mavericks
Colors: Purple & Gold
Arena: Otto Arena
Capacity: 5,500; Year Built: 1965
AD: Don Amiot
SID: Paul Allan

MANSFIELD
Mansfield, PA 16933 II

Coach: Tom Ackerman
Alma Mater: St. Vincent '79
Record: 11 Years, W-116, L-181

1996-97 SCHEDULE

Shippensburg ....Nov. 20
Clarion ■ ....Nov. 26
Pitt.-Johnstown ■ ....Nov. 30
Pitt.-Bradford ■ ....Dec. 2
Daemen ....Dec. 5
Clarion ....Dec. 7
Lock Haven ■ ....Dec. 13
Westminster (Pa.) ■ ....Dec. 18
Slippery Rock ■ ....Dec. 21
Gannon Tr. ....Dec. 29-30
Lock Haven ....Jan. 4
Shippensburg ■ ....Jan. 6
Kutztown ....Jan. 8
Millersville ■ ....Jan. 11
Bloomsburg ■ ....Jan. 15
Cheyney ■ ....Jan. 18
Daemen ■ ....Jan. 22
West Chester ....Jan. 25
East Stroudsburg ....Jan. 29
Millersville ....Feb. 1
Kutztown ■ ....Feb. 5
Cheyney ....Feb. 8
Bloomsburg ....Feb. 12
East Stroudsburg ■ ....Feb. 19
West Chester ■ ....Feb. 22

1995-96 RESULTS (10-16)

97	Roberts Wesleyan ■	72
58	Calif. (Pa.) ■	67
69	Pitt.-Bradford ■	60
89	Wilmington (Ohio) †	56
69	Shippensburg	83
83	Daemen	78
99	Lock Haven ■	81
62	Calif. (Pa.)	86
86	Daemen ■	59
87	Elmira ■	63
66	Slippery Rock	63
71	Lock Haven	75
78	East Stroudsburg ■	84
70	West Chester ■	87
86	Slippery Rock ■	68
60	Cheyney	71
65	Bloomsburg	72
64	Millersville ■	80
83	Kutztown ■	87
74	West Chester	104
73	East Stroudsburg	86
77	Pitt.-Johnstown ■	85
88	Bloomsburg ■	72
89	Cheyney ■	92
63	Kutztown	75
64	Millersville	68

Nickname: Mountaineers
Colors: Red & Black
Arena: Decker Gymnasium
Capacity: 2,500; Year Built: 1970

AD: Roger Maisner
SID: Steve McCloskey

MARIETTA
Marietta, OH 45750 III

Coach: Doug Foote
Alma Mater: Xavier (Ohio) '87
Record: 4 Years, W-34, L-70

1996-97 SCHEDULE

Hampden-Sydney Cl. ....Nov. 22-23
Thomas More ....Nov. 27
Capital ....Dec. 4
Baldwin-Wallace ■ ....Dec. 7
John Carroll ■ ....Dec. 11
Ohio Northern ■ ....Dec. 14
Wilmington (Ohio) ■ ....Dec. 21
Marietta Tr. ....Dec. 28-29
Mount Union ■ ....Jan. 8
Heidelberg ■ ....Jan. 11
Otterbein ■ ....Jan. 15
Hiram ....Jan. 18
Muskingum ■ ....Jan. 22
Heidelberg ....Jan. 25
Otterbein ....Jan. 29
Hiram ■ ....Feb. 1
Muskingum ....Feb. 5
Baldwin-Wallace ....Feb. 8
Capital ■ ....Feb. 12
Ohio Northern ....Feb. 15
Mount Union ....Feb. 19
John Carroll ■ ....Feb. 22

1995-96 RESULTS (15-13)

86	Thomas More ■	79
67	Wilmington (Ohio)	70
90	Tusculum †	63
76	Maryville (Tenn.)	66
47	Ohio Northern	66
65	Muskingum ■	61
78	Heidelberg ■	62
71	Baldwin-Wallace ■	56
75	Oberlin ■	35
69	Bluffton ■	74
64	Otterbein	74
64	John Carroll	62
75	Capital ■	78
71	Hiram	69
48	Mount Union ■	59
78	John Carroll ■	56
60	Capital	57
60	Heidelberg	78
50	Muskingum	52
59	Baldwin-Wallace ■	76
63	Otterbein ■	65
60	Ohio Northern ■	71
62	Mount Union	66
75	Hiram ■	65
61	Heidelberg ■	58
69	Capital	58
73	Ohio Northern	56
59	Baldwin-Wallace †	60

Nickname: Pioneers
Colors: Navy Blue & White
Arena: Ban Johnson Fieldhouse
Capacity: 3,000; Year Built: 1929
AD: Debora Lazorik
SID: Jeff Schaly

MARIST
Poughkeepsie, NY 12601 I

Coach: Dave Magarity
Alma Mater: St. Francis (Pa.) '74
Record: 15 Years, W-211, L-210

1996-97 SCHEDULE

Manhattan [Albany] ....Nov. 23
Vermont ■ ....Nov. 30
Marist Cl. ....Dec. 6-7
Siena [Albany] ....Dec. 22
Florida St. ....Dec. 28
Army ■ ....Jan. 2
Monmouth (N.J.) ....Jan. 4
Mt. St. Mary's (Md.) ■ ....Jan. 6

Robert Morris ....Jan. 9
St. Francis (Pa.) ....Jan. 11
Fairleigh Dickinson ....Jan. 15
LIU-Brooklyn ■ ....Jan. 18
Rider ....Jan. 20
St. Francis (N.Y.) ■ ....Jan. 23
Wagner ....Jan. 25
Monmouth (N.J.) ■ ....Feb. 1
Mt. St. Mary's (Md.) ....Feb. 3
Robert Morris ■ ....Feb. 6
St. Francis (Pa.) ■ ....Feb. 8
Fairleigh Dickinson ■ ....Feb. 12
LIU-Brooklyn ....Feb. 15
Rider ■ ....Feb. 17
St. Francis (N.Y.) ....Feb. 20
Wagner ■ ....Feb. 22
Northeast Conf. Tr. ....Feb. 25-Mar. 6

1995-96 RESULTS (22-7)

73	Northeastern	55
87	Hampton	69
59	Brown ■	56
49	Siena	47
86	Northeastern ■	65
65	LSU	80
68	Manhattan ■	65
65	Robert Morris	55
67	St. Francis (Pa.) ■	50
86	LIU-Brooklyn	69
89	Rider ■	73
70	Fairleigh Dickinson	57
72	St. Francis (N.Y.)	57
100	Wagner ■	85
81	Monmouth (N.J.)	75
55	Mt. St. Mary's (Md.) ■	61
77	Robert Morris	70
80	Fairfield †	69
65	St. Francis (Pa.)	67
104	LIU-Brooklyn ■	74
67	Rider	80
79	Fairleigh Dickinson ■	69
52	St. Francis (N.Y.)	43
75	Wagner	70
64	Mt. St. Mary's (Md.)	74
56	Monmouth (N.J.) ■	49
70	Robert Morris ■	51
56	Monmouth (N.J.) ■	57
77	Rhode Island	82

Nickname: Red Foxes
Colors: Red & White
Arena: McCann Recreation Center
Capacity: 3,944; Year Built: 1977
AD: Tim Murray
SID: Sean Morrison

MARITIME (N.Y.)
New York, NY 10465 III

Coach: John Owinell
Alma Mater: Springfield '81
Record: 7 Years, W-79, L-99

1996-97 SCHEDULE

N.Y. Maritime Tr. ....Nov. 23-24
Mt. St. Vincent ■ ....Dec. 5
N.J. Inst. of Tech. ....Dec. 7
Yeshiva ....Dec. 12
Union (N.Y.) Inv. ....Jan. 10-11
Polytechnic (N.Y.) ■ ....Jan. 13
New York U. ■ ....Jan. 14
Manhattanville ■ ....Jan. 21
Vassar ■ ....Jan. 23
Merchant Marine ....Jan. 25
Mt. St. Mary (N.Y.) ■ ....Jan. 27
Medgar Evers ....Jan. 30
Yeshiva ■ ....Feb. 1
Manhattanville ....Feb. 3
Mt. St. Mary (N.Y.) ....Feb. 6
Mt. St. Vincent ....Feb. 8
Vassar ....Feb. 10
Merchant Marine ■ ....Feb. 12
Utica ■ ....Feb. 15
Purchase St. ■ ....Feb. 18
Brooklyn ....Feb. 20
N.J. Inst. of Tech. ■ ....Feb. 22

1995-96 RESULTS (9-15)
Results unavailable

Nickname: Privateers
Colors: Cardinal Red, Blue & White
Arena: Riesenberg Gymnasium
  Capacity: 2,000; Year Built: 1964
AD: James Migli
SID: To be named

MARQUETTE
Milwaukee, WI 53233 I

Coach: Mike Deane
Alma Mater: Potsdam St. '74
Record: 12 Years, W-234, L-123

1996-97 SCHEDULE

Wis.-Milwaukee ■	Nov. 24
Santa Clara ■	Nov. 29
Marquette Tr.	Dec. 6-7
Wis.-Green Bay ■	Dec. 14
Coastal Caro. ■	Dec. 16
Appalachian St. ■	Dec. 19
La Salle ■	Dec. 22
Dayton	Dec. 27
Wisconsin	Dec. 31
Southern Miss. ■	Jan. 4
Iowa St.	Jan. 7
DePaul ■	Jan. 9
Memphis	Jan. 12
St. Louis ■	Jan. 18
DePaul	Jan. 26
South Fla.	Jan. 30
Tulane ■	Feb. 1
Maine ■	Feb. 5
Cincinnati	Feb. 8
N.C.-Charlotte	Feb. 15
UAB	Feb. 17
Louisville ■	Feb. 20
St. Louis	Feb. 25
Cincinnati ■	Feb. 27
Houston ■	Mar. 2
Conference USA	Mar. 5-8

1995-96 RESULTS (23-8)

91	Wis.-Milwaukee ■	74
72	Columbia	45
64	Wis.-Green Bay ■	44
95	Coppin St. ■	69
65	La Salle †	68
78	Santa Clara ■	49
89	Vermont ■	58
46	Wisconsin	55
98	Morgan St. ■	58
69	St. Louis ■	47
58	Iowa St. ■	56
70	Cincinnati	91
103	Ill.-Chicago ■	81
73	DePaul	60
59	Memphis ■	55
69	N.C.-Charlotte	79
73	UAB ■	64
74	Tulane	75
82	South Fla. ■	61
75	DePaul ■	65
63	Creighton	57
58	Southern Miss.	55
78	N.C.-Charlotte ■	68
58	St. Louis	56
80	Louisville	79
74	Cincinnati ■	72
65	South Fla. †	56
72	Memphis	60
84	Cincinnati †	85
68	Monmouth (N.J.) †	44
56	Arkansas †	65

Nickname: Golden Eagles
Colors: Blue & Gold
Arena: Bradley Center
  Capacity: 18,592; Year Built: 1988
AD: Bill Cords
SID: Kathleen Hohl

MARS HILL
Mars Hill, NC 28754.............II

Coach: David Riggins
Alma Mater: South Caro. '74
Record: 10 Years, W-147, L-135

1996-97 SCHEDULE

Tusculum	Nov. 20
Montreat ■	Nov. 23
Newberry ■	Nov. 25
Tusculum ■	Dec. 4
Wingate ■	Dec. 7
Newberry ■	Dec. 14
Queens (N.C.) Cl.	Jan. 3-5
Elon	Jan. 8
Lenoir-Rhyne	Jan. 11
Carson-Newman ■	Jan. 15
Gardner-Webb	Jan. 18
Presbyterian	Jan. 22
Catawba	Jan. 25
Anderson (S.C.) ■	Jan. 29
Wingate	Feb. 1
Anderson (S.C.)	Feb. 3
Elon ■	Feb. 5
Lenoir-Rhyne	Feb. 8
Carson-Newman	Feb. 12
Gardner-Webb ■	Feb. 15
Presbyterian ■	Feb. 19
Catawba	Feb. 22

1995-96 RESULTS (16-13)

68	Montreat	79
72	Longwood †	64
67	Virginia Union	82
79	Lees-McRae ■	94
117	Newberry	103
77	Appalachian St.	112
97	St. Andrews †	85
57	North Fla. †	68
73	Newberry †	65
72	Presbyterian ■	73
91	Wingate	85
79	Newberry ■	64
93	Elon	83
76	Lenoir-Rhyne	91
108	Anderson (S.C.) ■	61
75	Carson-Newman	80
116	Gardner-Webb	104
81	Catawba ■	74
62	Presbyterian	75
86	Wingate ■	77
92	Lees-McRae	85
75	Elon	79
82	Lenoir-Rhyne ■	76
61	Catawba	76
95	Carson-Newman ■	80
91	Gardner-Webb	95
87	Lenoir-Rhyne †	79
90	Elon †	81
77	Presbyterian †	82

Nickname: Lions
Colors: Blue & Gold
Arena: Chambers Gymnasium
  Capacity: 3,500; Year Built: 1967
AD: Ed Hoffmeyer
SID: Rick Baker

MARSHALL
Huntington, WV 25701 I

Coach: Greg White
Alma Mater: Marshall '82
Record: 10 Years, W-119, L-153

1996-97 SCHEDULE

Gardner-Webb ■	Nov. 25
Southwestern La.	Nov. 29
Jacksonville St.	Dec. 2
Radford	Dec. 7
Morehead St. ■	Dec. 14
West Va. [Charleston]	Dec. 17
N.C.-Asheville	Dec. 21
Tenn.-Chatt. ■	Dec. 23
Clemson	Dec. 28
Delaware ■	Jan. 3
N.C.-Asheville	Jan. 6
Davidson	Jan. 8
Furman ■	Jan. 11
Citadel	Jan. 13
Western Caro. ■	Jan. 18
Ga. Southern	Jan. 20
Appalachian St. ■	Jan. 25
VMI ■	Jan. 27
East Tenn. St.	Feb. 1
Davidson ■	Feb. 3
Butler	Feb. 5
Ga. Southern ■	Feb. 8
Appalachian St.	Feb. 10
VMI ■	Feb. 15
East Tenn. St. ■	Feb. 17
Tenn.-Chatt.	Feb. 22
Southern Conf. Tr.	Feb. 27-Mar. 2

1995-96 RESULTS (17-11)

124	Milligan ■	71
95	Tenn.-Chatt.	86
88	Kansas St.	106
92	Morehead St.	85
92	Butler ■	102
77	Southwestern La. ■	70
99	Kentucky †	118
101	Radford ■	73
83	Nevada	92
123	Hampton	95
87	Appalachian St.	89
78	VMI ■	71
91	West Va.	87
76	East Tenn. St.	82
86	Tenn.-Chatt.	69
57	Davidson ■	106
95	Furman	71
98	Citadel ■	54
104	Western Caro.	125
71	Ga. Southern	52
111	Jacksonville St. ■	90
95	Appalachian St. ■	64
94	VMI	103
111	East Tenn. St. ■	84
77	Davidson	83
96	Ga. Southern ■	50
82	Tenn.-Chatt. †	81
77	Davidson †	92

Nickname: Thundering Herd
Colors: Green & White
Arena: Henderson Center
  Capacity: 10,250; Year Built: 1981
AD: Lance West
SID: Clark Haptonstall

MARTIN LUTHER
Watertown, WI 53094.............III

Coach: Jerome Kruse
Alma Mater: Wis.-Oshkosh '57
Record: 12 Years, W-101, L-149

1996-97 SCHEDULE

Lawrence Tr.	Nov. 22-23
Wis.-La Crosse	Nov. 26
Edgewood Cl.	Dec. 6-7
Pillsbury	Dec. 10
Buena Vista	Dec. 14
Grinnell	Jan. 8
N'western (Minn.)	Jan. 14
Crown ■	Jan. 16
Concordia-St. Paul ■	Jan. 23
St. Scholastica	Jan. 25
Pillsbury ■	Jan. 28
Luther	Feb. 1
Sioux Falls	Feb. 4
St. Scholastica ■	Feb. 8
N'western (Minn.) ■	Feb. 11
Concordia-St. Paul	Feb. 15
Wis.-Superior	Feb. 17

1995-96 RESULTS (11-6)

52	Wis.-Superior	74
70	Concordia-St. Paul †	44
54	Wis.-La Crosse ■	81
69	Mt. St. Clare †	78
55	Milwaukee Engr. †	49
74	Concordia-St. Paul ■	48
51	Wis.-River Falls	70
71	Wis.-Stout	91
61	N'western (Minn.)	71
86	North Cent. Bible	62
85	Crichton	53
78	Pillsbury	65
71	N'western (Minn.)	62
73	North Cent. Bible ■	63
84	Buena Vista	72
78	Concordia-St. Paul	54
81	Pillsbury ■	61

Nickname: Knights
Colors: Black, Red & White
Arena: Martin Luther
  Capacity: 2,500
AD: Barb Leopold
SID: Dave Wietzke

MARY WASHINGTON
Fredericksburg, VA 22401........III

Coach: Tom Davies
Alma Mater: Brigham Young '64
Record: 18 Years, W-180, L-292

1996-97 SCHEDULE

Chris. Newport ■	Nov. 23
Lynchburg	Nov. 25
Western Md.	Dec. 3
Marymount (Va.) ■	Dec. 4
St. Mary's (Md.) ■	Dec. 6
Shenandoah	Jan. 13
Catholic ■	Jan. 15
Villa Julie	Jan. 16
Gallaudet	Jan. 18
Va. Wesleyan	Jan. 20
Goucher	Jan. 22
Salisbury St. ■	Jan. 25
Marymount (Va.)	Jan. 28
Newport News App. ■	Jan. 30
York (Pa.)	Feb. 1
Catholic	Feb. 4
St. Mary's (Md.) ■	Feb. 7
Frostburg St.	Feb. 8
Newport News App.	Feb. 11
Gallaudet ■	Feb. 13
Salisbury St.	Feb. 15
Shenandoah ■	Feb. 18
Goucher ■	Feb. 20
York (Pa.)	Feb. 22

1995-96 RESULTS (6-19)

74	Va. Wesleyan ■	80
64	Chris. Newport	84
74	Lynchburg ■	84
57	Frostburg St.	73
79	St. Mary's (Md.) ■	81
60	Hampden-Sydney ■	67
86	Western Md.	78
57	Newport News App.	64
80	St. Mary's (Md.) ■	68
76	Salisbury St.	94
59	Marymount (Va.) ■	57
61	Gallaudet	58
85	Goucher ■	69
68	Gallaudet ■	72
94	Shenandoah	98
70	York (Pa.) ■	75
64	Catholic	77
74	Marymount (Va.)	95
73	Shenandoah ■	93
83	Goucher	109
114	Salisbury St. ■	122
67	Newport News App. ■	76
58	Catholic ■	74
59	York (Pa.)	62
53	Catholic	56

Nickname: Eagles
Colors: Navy, Gray & White
Arena: Goolrick Gymnasium
  Capacity: 800; Year Built: 1967
AD: Ed Hegmann
SID: Vince Benigni

MARYLAND
College Park, MD 20740 I

Coach: Gary Williams
Alma Mater: Maryland '68
Record: 18 Years, W-329, L-218

1996-97 SCHEDULE
Howard ■...................................Nov. 26
Towson St. ■.............................Nov. 30
Chicago St. ■.............................Dec. 2
Md.-Balt. County ■....................Dec. 4
Maryland Tr. ....Dec. 8-9
Georgia Tech ■........................Dec. 12
American ■..............................Dec. 21
Lafayette ■...............................Dec. 23
Hawaii Rainbow Cl. ....Dec. 27-30
Virginia ■..................................Jan. 4
North Caro. ....Jan. 8
North Caro. St. ....Jan. 12
Clemson ■................................Jan. 15
Wake Forest ....Jan. 19
Pennsylvania ■.........................Jan. 21
Duke ■......................................Jan. 26
Florida St. ....Jan. 29
Wake Forest ■............................Feb. 1
North Caro. St. ■........................Feb. 5
Clemson ....Feb. 8
Florida St. ■.............................Feb. 13
Massachusetts [Worcester].......Feb. 15
Georgia Tech ....Feb. 19
North Caro. ■...........................Feb. 20
Duke ....Feb. 27
Virginia ....Mar. 2
Atlantic Coast Conf. Tr. ....Mar. 6-9

1995-96 RESULTS (17-13)
84	Kentucky †	96
70	Towson St. †	67
47	Massachusetts †	50
98	Geo. Washington †	81
88	Howard ■	71
63	UCLA †	73
83	Rider ■	67
104	American ■	79
104	Md.-East. Shore ■	66
84	Georgia Tech	98
86	North Caro. ■	88
64	Wake Forest	77
118	Delaware St. ■	55
77	North Caro. St. ■	74
65	Clemson	60
73	Duke	83
80	Virginia	72
88	Georgia Tech ■	74
84	North Caro.	78
78	Florida St.	100
78	Wake Forest ■	85
91	Missouri ■	72
86	North Caro. St.	84
61	Clemson	68
75	Duke ■	77
83	Virginia ■	71
88	Florida St. ■	78
82	Duke †	69
79	Georgia Tech †	84
79	Santa Clara †	91

Nickname: Terps
Colors: Red, White, Black & Gold
Arena: Cole Field House
 Capacity: 14,500; Year Built: 1955
AD: Deborah A. Yow
SID: Chuck Walsh

MD.-BALT. COUNTY
Baltimore, MD 21228 I

Coach: Tom Sullivan
Alma Mater: Fordham '72
Record: 11 Years, W-158, L-147

1996-97 SCHEDULE
Loyola (Md.) ■...........................Nov. 23
Towson St. ■.............................Nov. 26
Maryland...................................Dec. 4
Central Conn. St. ■.....................Dec. 6
Rutgers....................................Dec. 11
Rider ....Dec. 14
Virginia ....Dec. 21
St. Mary's (Md.) ■.....................Dec. 28
James Madison ■......................Dec. 30
N.C.-Asheville ....Jan. 4
N.C.-Greensboro ....Jan. 6
St. Peter's ....Jan. 9
Radford ■................................Jan. 11
Liberty ■..................................Jan. 13
Charleston So. ■.......................Jan. 16
Coastal Caro. ■........................Jan. 18
Winthrop ■...............................Jan. 25
N.C.-Greensboro ■....................Jan. 29
Winthrop ....Feb. 1
Radford ....Feb. 3
Coastal Caro. ■..........................Feb. 8
Bucknell ■................................Feb. 12
N.C.-Asheville ■........................Feb. 15
Lehigh ....Feb. 17
Liberty ....Feb. 20
Charleston So. ■.......................Feb. 22
Big South Conf. Tr. ......Feb. 26-Mar. 1

1995-96 RESULTS (5-22)
67	North Texas	82
47	Texas A&M	75
56	Loyola (Md.) ■	53
68	Rider	69
56	Morgan St.	57
56	Boston College	78
56	Boston U.	70
58	St. Peter's ■	79
62	Central Conn. St.	63
56	Florida St.	80
63	Winthrop ■	69
63	Liberty ■	79
38	Charleston So.	54
72	Lehigh	67
48	Radford	66
73	N.C.-Asheville	76
65	N.C.-Greensboro	77
73	Coastal Caro. ■	67
63	Radford ■	73
48	Liberty	51
46	Charleston So.	68
63	Winthrop	73
62	N.C.-Asheville ■	61
55	Drexel ■	87
49	N.C.-Greensboro ■	68
80	Coastal Caro.	75
52	Liberty	74

Nickname: Retrievers
Colors: Black, Gold & Red
Arena: UMBC Fieldhouse
 Capacity: 4,024; Year Built: 1973
AD: Charles Brown
SID: Steve Levy

MD.-EAST. SHORE
Princess Anne, MD 21853 I

Coach: Lonnie Williams
(First year as head coach)

1996-97 SCHEDULE
St. Peter's ■.............................Nov. 22
New Mexico St..........................Nov. 25
Iowa St. ....Dec. 1
Centenary (N.J.) ■......................Dec. 3
UAB...Dec. 7
Wilmington (Del.) ■..................Dec. 10
Lincoln (Pa.) ■.........................Dec. 17
Syracuse..................................Dec. 30
Delaware St. ....Jan. 7
Florida A&M ....Jan. 11
Bethune-Cookman ....Jan. 13
Morgan St. ■............................Jan. 16
Howard.....................................Jan. 18
Coppin St. ■............................Jan. 20
South Caro. St. ■......................Jan. 25
North Caro. A&T ■....................Jan. 27
Morgan St. ....Jan. 30
Howard ■....................................Feb. 1

Hampton ....Feb. 3
South Caro. St. ....Feb. 8
North Caro. A&T ....Feb. 10
Delaware St. ■..........................Feb. 15
Hampton ■................................Feb. 18
Florida A&M ■..........................Feb. 22
Bethune-Cookman ■.................Feb. 24
Coppin St. ....Mar. 1
Mid-Eastern Conf. Tr. ....Mar. 5-8

1995-96 RESULTS (11-16)
44	Butler	75
74	Fairleigh Dickinson	67
109	Wilmington (Del.) ■	62
66	LIU-Brooklyn	76
54	St. Peter's	81
48	Brown †	47
63	St. Francis (N.Y.) ■	61
78	Centenary (N.J.) ■	63
66	Maryland	104
66	Florida St.	79
72	Delaware St.	66
71	Florida A&M ■	66
84	Bethune-Cookman ■	78
69	Coppin St.	72
71	Howard ■	65
66	Morgan St.	79
50	South Caro. St.	67
61	North Caro. A&T	62
60	Coppin St. ■	69
55	Howard	58
56	South Caro. St. ■	69
56	North Caro. A&T ■	65
70	Delaware St. †	67
46	Florida A&M	62
55	Bethune-Cookman	63
92	Morgan St. ■	90
56	Delaware St. †	59

Nickname: Hawks
Colors: Maroon & Gray
Arena: Millard Tawes Gymnasium
 Capacity: 1,000; Year Built: 1964
AD: Hallie Gregory
SID: Erika L. Forsythe

MARYMOUNT (VA.)
Arlington, VA 22207 III

Coach: Webb Hatch
Alma Mater: VMI '69
Record: 9 Years, W-98, L-133

1996-97 SCHEDULE
Dickinson Tr. ....Nov. 22-23
Villa Julie ■.............................Nov. 26
Wesley ■....................................Dec. 2
Mary Washington ....Dec. 4
Shenandoah..............................Dec. 14
Bridgewater (Va.) ■..................Dec. 17
Rowan ■...................................Dec. 21
Marymount (Va.) Tr. ....Jan. 4-5
Villa Julie ....Jan. 9
St. Mary's (Md.) ■....................Jan. 15
York (Pa.) ■..............................Jan. 18
Catholic....................................Jan. 20
Salisbury St. ....Jan. 22
Gallaudet ■..............................Jan. 25
Mary Washington ■..................Jan. 28
Goucher ■..................................Feb. 1
St. Mary's (Md.) ■......................Feb. 5
Catholic ■..................................Feb. 8
York (Pa.) ....Feb. 12
Gallaudet ....Feb. 15
Salisbury St. ■..........................Feb. 18
Goucher ....Feb. 22

1995-96 RESULTS (12-15)
72	Lynchburg	92
93	Averett †	75
102	Villa Julie ■	77
67	William & Mary	100
72	Wesley ■	70
62	American	123
91	Bridgewater (Va.) ■	81
88	North Park †	82
75	Bellarmine †	86

65	Tufts †	71
92	Gallaudet ■	85
57	Mary Washington	59
77	York (Pa.) ■	73
70	Catholic ■	77
93	Salisbury St.	114
101	St. Mary's (Md.)	105
111	Goucher	116
82	Salisbury St. ■	112
95	Mary Washington ■	74
87	Catholic	98
73	St. Mary's (Md.) ■	67
93	Goucher ■	98
84	York (Pa.)	76
79	Gallaudet	83
83	York (Pa.) ■	75
87	Catholic	82
81	Salisbury St.	93

Nickname: Saints
Colors: Royal Blue, White & Green
Arena: Butler Hall
 Capacity: 800; Year Built: 1962
AD: Bill Finney
SID: Webb Hatch

MARYVILLE (MO.)
Creve Coeur, MO 63141 III

Coach: Dennis Kruse
Alma Mater: Quincy '66
Record: 1 Year, W-11, L-14

1996-97 SCHEDULE
Anderson/Hanover Cl. ....Nov. 22-23
Mo.-Rolla................................Nov. 25
Maryville (Mo.) Cl. ....Nov. 29-30
Central (Iowa) Tr. ....Dec. 6-7
Central (Iowa) ■........................Jan. 6
Greenville ■...............................Jan. 9
Fontbonne ....Jan. 11
Westminster (Mo.) ■................Jan. 16
Blackburn ■.............................Jan. 18
MacMurray ....Jan. 23
Principia ....Jan. 25
Webster ■.................................Jan. 30
Greenville ....Feb. 1
Fontbonne ....Feb. 6
Westminster (Mo.) ....Feb. 8
Blackburn ....Feb. 13
MacMurray ■............................Feb. 15
Principia ■................................Feb. 20
Webster ....Feb. 22

1995-96 RESULTS (11-14)
71	Rhodes	72
86	St. Louis Pharmacy	59
58	Millsaps †	76
84	Rhodes	100
68	Mo.-Rolla	91
69	Anderson (Ind.) ■	43
70	William Penn ■	72
53	MacMurray ■	57
81	Webster	68
81	Blackburn	79
54	Fontbonne ■	66
75	Greenville	93
83	Westminster (Mo.)	70
82	Principia	76
85	St. Louis Pharmacy ■	54
80	MacMurray	65
56	Webster ■	73
75	Blackburn ■	85
80	Fontbonne	84
88	Parks ■	71
64	Greenville ■	66
93	Parks	72
67	Westminster (Mo.)	70
84	Principia ■	48
69	Blackburn ■	78

Nickname: Saints
Colors: Red & White
Arena: Moloney Arena
 Capacity: 3,000; Year Built: 1980
AD: Dave Pierce
SID: Lonnie Folks

MARYVILLE (TENN.)
Maryville, TN 37801 III

Coach: Randy Lambert
Alma Mater: Maryville (Tenn.) '76
Record: 16 Years, W-259, L-155

1996-97 SCHEDULE
Millsaps Cl.	Nov. 23-24
Maryville (Tenn.) Tr	Nov. 30-Dec. 1
King (Tenn.)	Dec. 4
Ferrum ■	Dec. 7
Savannah A&D	Dec. 14
Methodist	Dec. 16
Methodist ■	Jan. 8
Averett	Jan. 11
Ferrum	Jan. 12
Emory & Henry	Jan. 15
Centre	Jan. 21
Covenant ■	Jan. 23
Emory & Henry ■	Jan. 27
Belmont	Feb. 1
Fisk	Feb. 2
Savannah A&D ■	Feb. 6
Rust ■	Feb. 8
Greensboro	Feb. 10
Sewanee ■	Feb. 13
Rust	Feb. 22
Centre ■	Feb. 26

1995-96 RESULTS (18-7)
Results unavailable

Nickname: Scots
Colors: Orange & Garnet
Arena: P.E. Building
    Capacity: 1,800; Year Built: 1971
AD: Randy Lambert
SID: Eric S. Etchison

MARYWOOD
Scranton, PA 18509 III

Coach: Ed Gosgrove
Alma Mater: Marywood '93
Record: 3 Years, W-8, L-59

1996-97 SCHEDULE
Misericordia Tr	Nov. 22-23
Bard ■	Nov. 26
Pracitical Bible	Dec. 3
Holy Family Tr.	Dec. 7-8
Cabrini	Dec. 10
Alvernia ■	Dec. 14
Wilkes Cl.	Jan. 4-5
Neumann	Jan. 8
Allentown ■	Jan. 11
Eastern ■	Jan. 13
Beaver	Jan. 15
Misericordia	Jan. 20
Gwynedd-Mercy ■	Jan. 22
Cabrini	Jan. 25
Alvernia	Jan. 29
Neumann ■	Feb. 1
Allentown	Feb. 5
Eastern	Feb. 8
Beaver ■	Feb. 12
Misericordia ■	Feb. 19
Gwynedd-Mercy	Feb. 22

1995-96 RESULTS (7-17)
71	Scranton	93
77	Bapt. Bible (Pa.) †	98
71	Bard	27
66	Allentown	95
57	Beaver ■	83
96	Pracitical Bible	89
74	Alvernia ■	101
73	Eastern	104
67	Wilkes ■	116
90	Salisbury St. †	139
72	Misericordia	81
101	Gwynedd-Mercy ■	89
66	Beaver	81
96	Pracitical Bible ■	74
73	Allentown ■	91

75	Cabrini ■	115
90	Neumann ■	85
78	Misericordia ■	83
80	Alvernia	105
82	Gwynedd-Mercy	85
60	Phila. Pharmacy	91
86	Eastern ■	76
89	Neumann	80
62	Cabrini	110

Nickname: Pacers
Colors: Green & White
Arena: Health & P.E. Center
AD: Mary Jo Gunning
SID: John Seitzinger

MASSACHUSETTS
Amherst, MA 01003 I

Coach: James "Bruiser" Flint
Alma Mater: St. Joseph's (Pa.) '87
(First year as head coach)

1996-97 SCHEDULE
Maui Inv.	Nov. 25-27
Georgetown [Chicago]	Dec. 4
Wyoming ■	Dec. 7
Fresno St.	Dec. 10
Drexel	Dec. 12
Wake Forest	Dec. 14
North Caro. [East Rutherford]	Dec. 20
N.C.-Wilmington	Dec. 22
Connecticut	Dec. 27
Davidson [Puerto Rico]	Jan. 2
St. Joseph's (Pa.) ■	Jan. 5
La Salle	Jan. 8
Virginia Tech	Jan. 12
St. Bonaventure	Jan. 14
Boston College [Boston]	Jan. 18
Rhode Island ■	Jan. 21
Temple	Jan. 25
Geo. Washington	Jan. 30
Xavier (Ohio) ■	Feb. 1
Fordham	Feb. 3
Duquesne ■	Feb. 6
Rhode Island	Feb. 8
St. Bonaventure ■	Feb. 11
Maryland [Worcester]	Feb. 15
Fordham ■	Feb. 20
Dayton	Feb. 23
St. Joseph's (Pa.)	Feb. 25
Temple ■	Mar. 1
Atlantic 10 Conf. Tr.	Mar. 5-8

1995-96 RESULTS (35-2)
92	Kentucky †	82
50	Maryland †	47
80	Florida †	58
60	Wake Forest ■	46
65	Boston College †	57
77	N.C.-Wilmington ■	51
75	Georgia Tech †	67
78	North Caro. St. †	67
78	Southern Cal †	63
65	Syracuse †	47
64	Memphis †	61
78	Dayton ■	58
94	St. Joseph's (Pa.)	89
65	St. Bonaventure	52
77	Rhode Island ■	71
93	Duquesne	89
79	Pittsburgh	71
72	St. Bonaventure ■	47
80	Fordham ■	50
59	Temple	35
78	Xavier (Ohio)	74
73	Fordham †	47
84	Temple ■	55
70	La Salle ■	53
74	Virginia Tech	58
74	Rhode Island	69
76	Geo. Washington ■	86
68	St. Joseph's (Pa.) ■	66
62	Louisville	59
69	St. Bonaventure †	56
74	Geo. Washington †	65

75	Temple †	61
92	Central Fla. †	70
79	Stanford †	74
79	Arkansas †	63
86	Georgetown †	62
74	Kentucky †	81

Nickname: Minutemen
Colors: Maroon & White
Arena: Mullins Center
    Capacity: 9,493; Year Built: 1992
AD: Bob Marcum
SID: Bill Strickland

MIT
Cambridge, MA 02139 III

Coach: Larry Anderson
Alma Mater: Rust '87
Record: 1 Year, W-4, L-21

1996-97 SCHEDULE
New York U. Tr.	Nov. 22-23
Babson ■	Nov. 26
WPI	Nov. 30
Brandeis ■	Dec. 3
Wentworth Inst. ■	Dec. 7
Coast Guard	Dec. 9
Eastern Nazarene	Jan. 8
Clark (Mass.) ■	Jan. 14
Suffolk	Jan. 16
Springfield	Jan. 18
Western New Eng.	Jan. 21
Savannah A&D ■	Jan. 23
Coast Guard	Jan. 25
Norwich	Jan. 28
Curry ■	Jan. 30
Connecticut Col. ■	Feb. 6
Springfield ■	Feb. 8
Tufts ■	Feb. 11
Clark (Mass.)	Feb. 13
Western New Eng. ■	Feb. 15
Norwich ■	Feb. 18
WPI ■	Feb. 20
Babson	Feb. 22

1995-96 RESULTS (4-21)
Results unavailable

Nickname: Engineers
Colors: Cardinal & Gray
Arena: Rockwell Cage
    Capacity: 600
AD: Richard Hill
SID: Roger Crosley

MASS.-BOSTON
Boston, MA 02125 III

Coach: Charlie Titus
Alma Mater: St. Michael's '72
Record: 21 Years, W-225, L-267

1996-97 SCHEDULE
Fitchburg St.	Nov. 23
Mass.-Boston Inv.	Nov. 29-30
Emerson-MCA	Dec. 4
Western Conn. St. ■	Dec. 7
Westfield St.	Dec. 12
North Adams St.	Dec. 14
St. Michael's Cl.	Dec. 28-29
Colby ■	Jan. 11
Mass.-Dartmouth	Jan. 14
Rhode Island Col.	Jan. 18
Plymouth St. ■	Jan. 21
Bri'water (Mass.) ■	Jan. 23
Eastern Conn. St. ■	Jan. 25
Southern Me. ■	Jan. 28
Western Conn. St.	Feb. 1
Mass.-Dartmouth ■	Feb. 4
Salem St.	Feb. 6
Tufts	Feb. 13
Rhode Island Col. ■	Feb. 15
Southern Me.	Feb. 18
Eastern Conn. St.	Feb. 22

1995-96 RESULTS (4-21)
69	Fitchburg St.	75
85	Framingham St. ■	67
64	Trinity (Conn.) ■	82
77	Western Conn. St. ■	87
64	Westfield St.	72
71	North Adams St. ■	89
78	Salem St.	89
67	Warner Southern	68
63	Illinois Tech †	70
88	St. Thomas (Fla.) †	80
65	Mass.-Dartmouth ■	81
68	Rhode Island Col. ■	94
79	Plymouth St.	92
54	Bri'water (Mass.)	67
55	Eastern Conn. St.	73
61	Southern Me.	86
62	Western Conn. St.	89
56	Mass.-Dartmouth	68
86	Suffolk	64
63	Plymouth St. ■	78
72	Tufts ■	99
77	Rhode Island Col.	87
60	Southern Me. ■	68
80	Eastern Conn. St. ■	73
60	Plymouth St.	91

Nickname: Beacons
Colors: Blue & White
Arena: Clark Athletic Center
    Capacity: 3,500; Year Built: 1981
AD: Charlie Titus
SID: Chuck Sullivan

MASS.-DARTMOUTH
North Dartmouth, MA 02747 III

Coach: Brian Baptiste
Alma Mater: American Int'l '76
Record: 13 Years, W-266, L-93

1996-97 SCHEDULE
Worcester St. ■	Nov. 26
Bri'water (Mass.)	Dec. 3
Bri'water (Mass.) Cl.	Dec. 6-7
Brandeis	Dec. 10
Western Conn. St.	Dec. 14
Florida Tech	Jan. 2
Fla. Southern	Jan. 5
Plymouth St. ■	Jan. 11
Mass.-Boston ■	Jan. 14
Clark (Mass.)	Jan. 16
Wheaton (Mass.)	Jan. 18
Rhode Island Col. ■	Jan. 21
Southern Me. ■	Jan. 25
Eastern Conn. St.	Jan. 28
Framingham St.	Jan. 30
Plymouth St.	Feb. 1
Mass.-Boston	Feb. 4
Salem St. ■	Feb. 6
Western Conn. St. ■	Feb. 8
Rhode Island Col.	Feb. 11
Trinity (Conn.) ■	Feb. 15
Eastern Conn. St. ■	Feb. 18
Southern Me.	Feb. 22

1995-96 RESULTS (19-8)
98	Albertus Magnus	58
96	Wheaton (Mass.)	59
64	Bri'water (Mass.) †	85
86	Brandeis ■	84
89	Worcester St.	80
81	Western Conn. St. ■	68
64	Buffalo St. †	71
90	Juniata †	53
93	Plymouth St. ■	91
81	Mass.-Boston	65
87	Clark (Mass.) ■	93
80	Wheaton (Mass.) ■	59
61	Rhode Island Col.	84
68	Southern Me.	56
78	Eastern Conn. St. ■	61
93	Framingham St. ■	47
68	Plymouth St. ■	74
68	Mass.-Boston ■	56

75	Salem St.	84
79	Western Conn. St.	78
72	Rhode Island Col. ■	60
75	Trinity (Conn.)	53
85	Eastern Conn. St.	66
78	Southern Me. ■	55
63	Western Conn. St. ■	66
88	Tufts ■	85
59	Colby †	64

Nickname: Corsairs
Colors: Blue, Gold & White
Arena: Tripp Athletic Center
  Capacity: 3,000; Year Built: 1972
AD: Robert Dowd
SID: William Gathright

MASS.-LOWELL
Lowell, MA 01854 II

Coach: Gary Manchel
Alma Mater: Vermont '85
Record: 4 Years, W-47, L-62

1996-97 SCHEDULE
Quinnipiac	Nov. 16
St. Anselm ■	Nov. 20
Merrimack	Nov. 23
Bentley ■	Nov. 26
Bryant	Dec. 1
Sacred Heart ■	Dec. 7
Albany (N.Y.) ■	Dec. 11
St. Michael's Cl.	Dec. 28-29
Stonehill	Jan. 5
Stony Brook ■	Jan. 8
Bridgeport	Jan. 11
Franklin Pierce	Jan. 14
Keene St. ■	Jan. 16
Southern Conn. St. ■	Jan. 18
New Haven	Jan. 20
Southern Conn. St.	Jan. 25
New Hamp. Col.	Jan. 28
Bridgeport ■	Feb. 1
New Haven	Feb. 4
Franklin Pierce ■	Feb. 6
Sacred Heart	Feb. 8
Stony Brook	Feb. 15
New Hamp. Col. ■	Feb. 18
Keene St.	Feb. 20
Albany (N.Y.)	Feb. 22

1995-96 RESULTS (9-17)
85	St. Anselm	87
75	Bryant ■	88
80	Bentley	88
74	Stony Brook	82
79	Albany (N.Y.) ■	69
71	Le Moyne ■	75
73	Stonehill ■	83
64	Franklin Pierce ■	66
64	New Haven	61
51	Southern Conn. St.	66
61	Merrimack ■	75
68	Le Moyne	76
66	Albany (N.Y.) ■	68
108	Keene St.	80
88	Sacred Heart ■	80
88	Bridgeport ■	64
75	New Hamp. Col. ■	61
72	Southern Conn. St.	86
73	New Haven	76
48	Franklin Pierce	78
54	Stony Brook ■	63
83	Quinnipiac ■	62
102	Keene St. ■	79
73	Bridgeport	81
88	Sacred Heart	68
66	New Hamp. Col.	82

Nickname: River Hawks
Colors: Red, White & Blue
Arena: Costello Gymnasium
  Capacity: 2,100; Year Built: 1965
AD: Dana Skinner
SID: Jim Seavey

MCNEESE ST
Lake Charles, LA 70601 I

Coach: Ron Everhart
Alma Mater: Virginia Tech '85
Record: 2 Years, W-26, L-28

1996-97 SCHEDULE
Texas Christian	Nov. 23
Mobile ■	Nov. 26
Louisiana Col. ■	Nov. 30
Northern Ariz.	Dec. 3
Hawaii Inv.	Dec. 6-7
Lamar	Dec. 14
Prairie View ■	Dec. 16
Arkansas	Dec. 19
Jackson St. ■	Dec. 28
Houston	Dec. 30
Southwest Tex. St.	Jan. 2
Texas-San Antonio	Jan. 4
Texas-Arlington	Jan. 9
Nicholls St.	Jan. 13
Northeast La. ■	Jan. 16
Northwestern St. ■	Jan. 18
Stephen F. Austin	Jan. 23
Sam Houston St.	Jan. 25
Texas-Arlington ■	Jan. 30
Texas-San Antonio ■	Feb. 6
Southwest Tex. St. ■	Feb. 8
Northeast La.	Feb. 13
Northwestern St.	Feb. 15
Sam Houston St. ■	Feb. 20
Stephen F. Austin ■	Feb. 22
Southern U.	Feb. 25
Nicholls St. ■	Mar. 1
Southland Conf. Tr.	Mar. 5-8

1995-96 RESULTS (15-12)
83	Houston ■	81
73	LSU	83
101	Prairie View ■	62
74	Lamar ■	72
83	Texas A&M ■	68
76	Dayton	86
69	Cincinnati	103
94	Northwestern St.	75
81	Northeast La. ■	65
76	Texas-San Antonio	80
66	Southwest Tex. St.	67
72	Texas-Arlington	65
75	North Texas ■	63
72	Sam Houston St.	65
73	Stephen F. Austin	94
75	Northeast La.	78
80	Northwestern St.	57
69	Southwest Tex. St. ■	49
89	Texas-San Antonio ■	83
90	Nicholls St.	71
65	North Texas	67
86	Texas-Arlington	73
66	Stephen F. Austin ■	69
66	Sam Houston St. ■	70
82	Southern U.	94
92	Nicholls St. ■	80
91	Stephen F. Austin †	94

Nickname: Cowboys
Colors: Blue & Gold
Arena: Burton Coliseum
  Capacity: 8,000; Year Built: 1986
AD: Bobby Keasler
SID: Louis Bonnette

MEMPHIS
Memphis, TN 38152 I

Coach: Larry Finch
Alma Mater: Memphis '73
Record: 10 Years, W-204, L-115

1996-97 SCHEDULE
Wisconsin [Ottawa]	Nov. 23
North Caro. ■	Nov. 30
Jackson St. ■	Dec. 2
Vanderbilt ■	Dec. 7
Tennessee	Dec. 15
Northeast La. ■	Dec. 18
Texas Southern ■	Dec. 21
Oklahoma ■	Dec. 23
Hawaii Rainbow Cl.	Dec. 27-30
Detroit ■	Jan. 4
South Fla. ■	Jan. 7
N.C.-Charlotte ■	Jan. 9
Marquette ■	Jan. 12
DePaul	Jan. 15
N.C.-Charlotte ■	Jan. 19
Louisville	Jan. 23
UAB	Jan. 25
Southern Miss. ■	Jan. 30
Arkansas	Feb. 1
Vanderbilt	Feb. 5
Louisville ■	Feb. 9
Houston	Feb. 12
Tulane	Feb. 16
St. Louis	Feb. 19
Georgetown ■	Feb. 22
Houston ■	Feb. 26
Cincinnati ■	Mar. 1
Conference USA	Mar. 5-8

1995-96 RESULTS (22-8)
91	Purdue †	76
90	Jackson St.	67
80	Florida A&M ■	50
89	Georgia St. ■	69
57	Tennessee ■	55
74	Sam Houston St.	51
96	Northeast La.	76
68	Temple ■	58
61	Massachusetts †	64
67	Houston	69
57	N.C.-Charlotte ■	55
74	DePaul	55
60	South Fla.	59
94	Arkansas ■	72
55	Marquette	59
86	UAB ■	77
81	Southern Miss.	68
80	St. Louis ■	63
83	DePaul	82
56	Louisville	74
68	N.C.-Charlotte	55
60	Georgetown	81
91	Southern Miss. ■	66
63	Tenn.-Chatt.	55
57	Louisville ■	54
66	Cincinnati	71
86	Tulane ■	75
92	DePaul ■	69
60	Marquette ■	72
63	Drexel †	75

Nickname: Tigers
Colors: Blue & Gray
Arena: The Pyramid
  Capacity: 20,142; Year Built: 1991
AD: R. C. Johnson
SID: Mark Owens

MENLO
Menlo Park, CA 94025 III

Coach: E. J. Chavez
Alma Mater: Santa Clara '78
(First year as head coach)

1996-97 SCHEDULE
Menlo Cl.	Nov. 22-23
Redlands Tr.	Dec. 5-7
Whitman Tr.	Dec. 13-14
San Fran. St.	Dec. 20
Holy Names ■	Jan. 10
Patten	Jan. 11
Dominican (Cal.)	Jan. 17
San Jose Christian	Jan. 18
Cal Maritime	Jan. 21
Simpson (Cal.)	Jan. 25
Pacific Union	Jan. 26
UC San Diego	Jan. 31
Chapman	Feb. 1
Holy Names	Feb. 7
Patten ■	Feb. 8
Dominican (Cal.)	Feb. 13
Cal Maritime ■	Feb. 15
Pacific Union	Feb. 18
UC San Diego ■	Feb. 21
Chapman ■	Feb. 22

1995-96 RESULTS (13-12)
87	UC Santa Cruz ■	98
63	Cal Lutheran ■	76
68	Holy Names ■	76
79	Whitman ■	74
71	Cal Baptist †	77
73	UC San Diego †	87
69	UC Santa Cruz ■	55
75	San Jose Christian ■	59
68	Notre Dame (Cal.)	72
65	San Fran. St.	64
73	Jersey City St. †	70
54	Roanoke	78
96	Washington (Md.)	83
79	UC Santa Cruz ■	68
82	BYU-Hawaii	75
72	Hawaii Pacific ■	91
69	Dominican (Cal.)	72
69	Chapman	60
65	UC San Diego	117
63	Chapman ■	72
91	Pacific Union	89
65	UC San Diego	69
99	Simpson (Cal.) ■	55
84	UC Santa Cruz ■	75
88	Dominican (Cal.)	67

Nickname: Oaks
Colors: Navy Blue & White
Arena: Haynes-Prim Pavilion
  Capacity: 700; Year Built: 1981
AD: Doug Cosbie
SID: Matt Monroe

MERCER
Macon, GA 31207 I

Coach: Bill Hodges
Alma Mater: Marian '70
Record: 14 Years, W-236, L-185

1996-97 SCHEDULE
Brewton Parker ■	Nov. 23
North Ga. ■	Dec. 2
Purdue Inv.	Dec. 6-7
Ga. Southern	Dec. 14
Western Caro. ■	Dec. 17
Missouri	Dec. 19
Minnesota	Dec. 31
Charleston (S.C.) ■	Jan. 2
Campbell ■	Jan. 4
Fla. Atlantic	Jan. 9
Florida Int'l.	Jan. 11
Central Fla. ■	Jan. 16
Stetson	Jan. 18
Jacksonville St. ■	Jan. 23
Samford ■	Jan. 25
Centenary (La.)	Jan. 30
Southeastern La.	Feb. 1
Georgia St. ■	Feb. 3
Centenary (La.) ■	Feb. 6
Southeastern La. ■	Feb. 8
Wofford ■	Feb. 10
Georgia St.	Feb. 15
Wofford	Feb. 17
Samford	Feb. 20
Jacksonville St.	Feb. 22
Trans America Conf. Tr.	Feb. 27-Mar. 1

1995-96 RESULTS (15-14)
87	Western Caro. †	83
72	New Mexico	107
97	North Ga. ■	78
76	Wofford ■	58
68	Wofford	56
91	Augusta St. ■	67
73	Alabama	100
71	Indiana St. ■	64
68	Georgia	95
56	Minnesota	92
65	Charleston (S.C.)	98

57	Campbell	60
59	Fla. Atlantic ■	67
73	Florida Int'l ■	74
67	Central Fla.	65
77	Stetson ■	67
99	Jacksonville St.	95
63	Samford	58
89	Centenary (La.) ■	66
62	Southeastern La. ■	78
96	Georgia St.	90
77	Centenary (La.)	87
88	Southeastern La.	94
66	Georgia St. ■	74
71	Samford ■	78
78	Jacksonville St. ■	69
72	Centenary (La.) †	61
101	Florida Int'l †	76
77	Central Fla. †	86

Nickname: Bears
Colors: Orange & Black
Arena: Macon Coliseum
  Capacity: 8,500; Year Built: 1968
AD: Bobby Pope
SID: Kevin Coulombe

MERCHANT MARINE
Kings Point, NY 11024 III

Coach: Andrew Greer
Alma Mater: Brockport St. '84
Record: 3 Years, W-32, L-45

1996-97 SCHEDULE
N.Y. Maritime Tr.		Nov. 23-24
Mt. St. Vincent ■		Nov. 26
Baruch		Dec. 4
Vassar ■		Dec. 8
New York U.		Dec. 11
Moravian Cl.		Jan. 4-5
Ursinus ■		Jan. 8
Mt. St. Vincent		Jan. 13
Manhattanville ■		Jan. 15
N.J. Inst. of Tech. ■		Jan. 18
Hunter		Jan. 22
Maritime (N.Y.) ■		Jan. 25
Stevens Tech		Jan. 28
Mt. St. Mary (N.Y.)		Feb. 1
Coast Guard ■		Feb. 5
N.J. Inst. of Tech.		Feb. 8
Maritime (N.Y.)		Feb. 12
Manhattanville		Feb. 15
Staten Island ■		Feb. 19
York (N.Y.) ■		Feb. 21
Mt. St. Mary (N.Y.) ■		Feb. 25
Union (N.Y.) ■		Feb. 28
Rensselaer		Mar. 1

1995-96 RESULTS (16-12)
78	Maine Maritime ■	57
87	Maritime (N.Y.) ■	59
65	Mt. St. Vincent	69
66	Rochester	60
55	Wooster †	75
78	New York U. ■	88
96	Stevens Tech ■	81
82	Bard	34
75	Hunter ■	73
77	Purchase St.	57
76	Mt. St. Vincent ■	72
59	Manhattanville	57
84	N.J. Inst. of Tech. ■	68
76	Vassar	74
66	Centenary (N.J.) ■	53
66	Mt. St. Mary (N.Y.) ■	62
58	Coast Guard	64
60	Union (N.Y.) ■	57
73	Maritime (N.Y.) ■	76
68	N.J. Inst. of Tech.	72
64	Staten Island	68
67	Manhattanville ■	72
74	Mt. St. Mary (N.Y.)	90
66	Centenary (N.J.)	81
59	Rensselaer ■	73
54	Baruch ■	53
73	Old Westbury ■	54
53	Rutgers-Newark	72

Nickname: Mariners
Colors: Blue & Gray
Arena: O'Hara Hall
  Capacity: 1,200; Year Built: 1943
AD: Susan Petersen Lubow
SID: Kim Robinson

MERCY
Dobbs Ferry, NY 10522 II

Coach: Steve Kelly
Alma Mater: Fordham '69
Record: 9 Years, W-123, L-121

1996-97 SCHEDULE
Bridgeport Cl.		Nov. 16-17
St. Rose ■		Dec. 4
Phila. Textile ■		Dec. 7
LIU-Southampton ■		Dec. 9
New York Tech ■		Dec. 11
LIU-C. W. Post ■		Dec. 14
Adelphi		Jan. 4
Queens (N.Y.)		Jan. 8
Pace ■		Jan. 11
Concordia (N.Y.)		Jan. 13
Dowling ■		Jan. 15
Molloy ■		Jan. 18
St. Rose		Jan. 20
Phila. Textile		Jan. 22
New York Tech		Jan. 25
LIU-C. W. Post ■		Jan. 29
Adelphi ■		Feb. 1
LIU-Southampton		Feb. 5
Queens (N.Y.) ■		Feb. 8
Pace		Feb. 12
Concordia (N.Y.) ■		Feb. 15
Dowling		Feb. 19
Molloy		Feb. 22

1995-96 RESULTS (4-20)
92	Le Moyne	120
115	Assumption ■	127
93	Queens (N.Y.) ■	89
74	Dowling ■	91
97	St. Rose	116
81	Pace ■	74
105	New York Tech	133
76	Molloy ■	75
78	LIU-C. W. Post	113
62	Phila. Textile	80
80	Adelphi ■	84
74	Queens (N.Y.)	85
89	Dowling	117
78	Concordia (N.Y.) ■	82
89	St. Rose ■	128
67	Pace	82
94	New York Tech ■	104
92	Concordia (N.Y.) ■	89
92	LIU-Southampton ■	118
74	Molloy	81
52	LIU-C. W. Post ■	53
103	LIU-Southampton	121
71	Phila. Textile ■	87
77	Adelphi	90

Nickname: Flyers
Colors: Blue & White
Arena: Westchester Community College
  Capacity: 2,000
AD: Neil Judge
SID: Steve Balsan

MERCYHURST
Erie, PA 16546 II

Coach: Karl Fogel
Alma Mater: Colby '68
Record: 12 Years, W-179, L-155

1996-97 SCHEDULE
Roberts Wesleyan		Nov. 19
Westminster Cl.		Nov. 22-23
Daemen		Nov. 26
Mercyhurst Cl.		Nov. 29-30
Grand Valley St. ■		Dec. 5
Ferris St. ■		Dec. 7
Northern Mich.		Dec. 13
Michigan Tech		Dec. 14
Edinboro		Dec. 18
Daemen ■		Jan. 2
Gannon ■		Jan. 4
Wayne St. (Mich.) ■		Jan. 9
Oakland ■		Jan. 11
Hillsdale		Jan. 16
Ashland		Jan. 18
Edinboro		Jan. 22
Saginaw Valley		Jan. 25
Lake Superior St. ■		Jan. 30
Northwood ■		Feb. 1
Gannon		Feb. 8
Wayne St. (Mich.) ■		Feb. 13
Oakland		Feb. 15
Hillsdale ■		Feb. 20
Ashland ■		Feb. 22

1995-96 RESULTS (15-12)
Results unavailable

Nickname: Lakers
Colors: Blue & Green
Arena: Mercyhurst Athletic Centr
  Capacity: 2,000; Year Built: 1970
AD: Pete Russo
SID: Ed Hess

MERRIMACK
North Andover, MA 01845 II

Coach: Bert Hammel
Alma Mater: Bentley '73
Record: 16 Years, W-232, L-222

1996-97 SCHEDULE
Bentley Tr.		Nov. 15-16
Mass.-Lowell ■		Nov. 23
New Hamp. Col. ■		Nov. 26
Bentley		Dec. 3
Stonehill		Dec. 22
Merrimack Inv.		Dec. 27-28
St. Leo		Dec. 31
Fla. Southern		Jan. 2
Bryant ■		Jan. 7
St. Anselm		Jan. 11
St. Michael's ■		Jan. 14
Le Moyne		Jan. 16
Assumption ■		Jan. 18
Quinnipiac ■		Jan. 21
American Int'l		Jan. 25
Bryant		Jan. 27
Stonehill ■		Feb. 1
St. Michael's		Feb. 4
Assumption		Feb. 6
Le Moyne ■		Feb. 9
St. Anselm ■		Feb. 13
Quinnipiac		Feb. 16
Bentley ■		Feb. 19
American Int'l		Feb. 22

1995-96 RESULTS (12-16)
59	Bridgeport †	80
70	Southern Conn. St.	79
79	Sacred Heart ■	74
71	New Hamp. Col.	83
58	American Int'l	69
107	New England Col. ■	51
95	Westbrook ■	72
75	Tampa	84
74	Embry-Riddle †	89
83	Gardner-Webb †	96
122	Assumption	89
90	St. Anselm	99
82	Stonehill	88
93	St. Michael's	86
75	Mass.-Lowell	61
107	Assumption	99
83	Bentley	100
86	Quinnipiac ■	63
75	Bryant	81
76	St. Anselm ■	93
81	St. Michael's	100
57	Stonehill	76
73	American Int'l	64
81	Bentley ■	76

65	Quinnipiac	72
65	Bryant ■	63
84	St. Michael's †	78
65	American Int'l †	76

Nickname: Warriors
Colors: Navy Blue & Gold
Arena: Volpe Complex
  Capacity: 1,600; Year Built: 1972
AD: Robert DeGregorio Jr
SID: Tom Caraccioli

MESA ST.
Grand Junction, CO 81501 II

Coach: Jim Heaps
Alma Mater: Mesa St. '82
(First year as head coach)

1996-97 SCHEDULE
Northern Colo.		Nov. 21
Mesa St. Tr.		Nov. 29-30
Neb.-Kearney ■		Dec. 6
Fort Hays St. ■		Dec. 7
Regis (Colo.)		Dec. 13
Colo. Christian		Dec. 14
Mesa St. Cl.		Dec. 28-30
Metro St. ■		Jan. 3
Colorado Mines ■		Jan. 4
Chadron St.		Jan. 9
Denver		Jan. 11
Southern Colo.		Jan. 17
UC-Colo. Spgs.		Jan. 18
Western St.		Jan. 21
N.M. Highlands ■		Jan. 23
Fort Lewis		Jan. 31
Adams St. ■		Feb. 1
Western St. ■		Feb. 4
N.M. Highlands		Feb. 7
Southern Colo. ■		Feb. 14
UC-Colo. Spgs. ■		Feb. 15
Fort Lewis		Feb. 21
Adams St.		Feb. 22

1995-96 RESULTS (12-13)
73	Western St. †	70
65	Southern Colo.	69
77	Evangel ■	71
67	Southern Colo. ■	63
73	N.M. Highlands ■	56
73	Adams St.	79
70	Fort Lewis	57
50	Metro St.	73
78	Linfield ■	74
82	Pacific Lutheran ■	81
81	Neb.-Kearney	96
57	Fort Hays St.	80
89	Chadron St. ■ †	68
66	Colorado Mines ■	67
59	Western St. ■	62
70	N.M. Highlands	61
95	Adams St. ■	81
81	Fort Lewis	82
74	Western St.	80
97	Colorado Col. ■	60
69	Chadron St.	72
98	Colorado Mines	85
74	Neb.-Kearney ■	87
62	Fort Hays St. ■	73
69	Western St.	73

Nickname: Mavericks
Colors: Maroon, White & Gold
Arena: Saunders
  Capacity: 3,800
AD: James Paronto
SID: Tish Elliott

MESSIAH
Grantham, PA 17027 III

Coach: Jack Cole
Alma Mater: Ashland '84
Record: 3 Years, W-6, L-66

1996-97 SCHEDULE
Gordon Tr.		Nov. 22-23

Gettysburg ■ ....Nov. 25
Elizabethtown ■ ....Dec. 5
Albright............................Dec. 7
Juniata...........................Dec. 10
Elmira Tr. ....Jan. 3-4
Dickinson Tr. ....Jan. 10-11
Susquehanna ....Jan. 16
Lebanon Valley ....Jan. 18
Moravian..........................Jan. 21
Widener ■ ....Jan. 25
Elizabethtown ■ ....Jan. 28
Dickinson ....Jan. 30
Albright ■ ....Feb. 1
Juniata ....Feb. 5
Susquehanna ■ ....Feb. 12
Lebanon Valley ■ ....Feb. 15
Moravian..........................Feb. 19
Widener ....Feb. 22

1995-96 RESULTS (4-20)
77	Eastern Nazarene ■	85
101	Gordon ■	80
53	Gettysburg ■	85
78	Western Md. ■	75
75	Elizabethtown	83
67	Albright ■	84
78	Juniata	82
76	Dickinson ■	83
38	Wis.-Platteville †	80
63	Col. of New Jersey †	92
72	Muhlenberg †	76
66	Dickinson	68
59	Susquehanna †	79
76	Susquehanna ■	84
76	Lebanon Valley ■	85
55	Moravian	68
53	Widener ■	65
66	Elizabethtown ■	83
94	Albright	77
65	Juniata ■	76
96	Susquehanna	93
73	Lebanon Valley	79
60	Moravian ■	69
63	Widener	74

Nickname: Falcons
Colors: Blue & White
Arena: Brubaker Auditorium
    Capacity: 1,450; Year Built: 1972
AD: Lori Braa
SID: To be named

METHODIST
Fayetteville, NC 28301 III

Coach: Bob McEvoy
Alma Mater: Kent '73
Record: 11 Years, W-134, L-154
1996-97 SCHEDULE
Schedule unavailable
1995-96 RESULTS (14-11)
79	Belmont Abbey	75
77	Chowan	58
81	Savannah A&D	57
56	Belmont Abbey ■	54
59	Barton ■	81
50	Campbell	68
75	Savannah A&D	70
45	Haverford †	49
51	Greensboro	69
75	Ferrum ■	79
88	Averett ■	73
107	Shenandoah	92
83	N.C. Wesleyan ■	59
73	Chowan ■	80
62	Chris. Newport	75
63	Newport News App.	60
88	Greensboro ■	85
93	Averett	67
69	Newport News App. ■	72
86	Shenandoah ■	67
63	N.C. Wesleyan	69
71	Chris. Newport ■	69
79	Ferrum	90
72	N.C. Wesleyan †	67

66   Shenandoah 81

Nickname: Monarchs
Colors: Green & Gold
Arena: March F. Riddle Center
    Capacity: 1,200; Year Built: 1990
AD: Bob McEvoy
SID: Matt Eviston

METRO ST.
Denver, CO 80204 II

Coach: Charles Bradley
Alma Mater: Wyoming '81
Record: 2 Years, W-24, L-30
1996-97 SCHEDULE
Holy Names ■ ....Nov. 15
Bay Ridge Christian ■ ....Nov. 20
Colo. Mines Tr. ....Nov. 22-23
Southern Colo. ....Dec. 6
UC-Colo. Spgs. ....Dec. 7
Fort Lewis ■ ....Dec. 13
Adams St. ■ ....Dec. 14
Colorado Col. ....Dec. 28
Mesa St. ....Jan. 3
Western St. ....Jan. 4
N.M. Highlands ■ ....Jan. 9
Neb.-Kearney ....Jan. 17
Fort Hays St. ....Jan. 18
Regis (Colo.) ....Jan. 24
Colo. Christian ....Jan. 25
Colorado Mines ■ ....Jan. 28
Chadron St. ....Jan. 30
Colorado Col. ....Feb. 1
Regis (Colo.) ■ ....Feb. 7
Colo. Christian ■ ....Feb. 8
Neb.-Kearney ....Feb. 14
Fort Hays St. ....Feb. 15
Colorado Mines ....Feb. 19
Chadron St. ■ ....Feb. 21
Denver ■ ....Feb. 22
1995-96 RESULTS (18-9)
67	Colorado Mines ■	69
74	Northern Colo.	71
64	Westmont ■	75
108	Cal Baptist ■	82
108	Arizona Bible ■	50
87	North Central ■	65
80	Mont. St.-Billings	105
76	Cal St. Los Angeles ■	68
73	Mesa St. ■	50
64	Northern Colo.	59
109	Mont. St.-Billings	100
107	Ursinus ■	84
89	Winona St. ■	72
75	Neb.-Kearney	93
67	UC-Colo. Spgs.	65
70	Regis (Colo.) ■	73
92	Colorado Col. ■	81
77	Denver	85
85	Southern Colo.	83
66	Colo. Christian ■	54
101	UC-Colo. Spgs. ■	70
75	Regis (Colo.)	77
91	Denver ■	88
89	Southern Colo.	90
87	Colo. Christian	82
74	UC-Colo. Spgs. ■	73
80	Regis (Colo.) †	84

Nickname: Roadrunners
Colors: Navy Blue & Columbia Blue
Arena: Auraria Events Center
    Capacity: 3,000; Year Built: 1970
AD: William Helman
SID: Daniel R. Smith

MIAMI (FLA.)
Coral Gables, FL 33124 I

Coach: Leonard Hamilton
Alma Mater: Tenn.-Martin '71
Record: 10 Years, W-120, L-169

1996-97 SCHEDULE
Buffalo ■ ....Nov. 22
Fla. Atlantic ■ ....Nov. 24
UNLV ....Nov. 29
St. John's (N.Y.) ■ ....Dec. 3
Syracuse ....Dec. 7
Hartford ■ ....Dec. 13
Jacksonville ■ ....Dec. 18
Tennessee ■ ....Dec. 22
DePaul ■ ....Dec. 28
Lehigh ■ ....Dec. 30
Boston College ....Jan. 2
Georgetown ....Jan. 4
Pittsburgh ■ ....Jan. 8
Villanova ....Jan. 11
Providence ....Jan. 15
Georgetown ■ ....Jan. 18
Connecticut ■ ....Jan. 22
Rutgers ....Feb. 2
Pittsburgh ■ ....Feb. 5
Rutgers ■ ....Feb. 8
Seton Hall ....Feb. 10
Connecticut ....Feb. 15
Boston College ■ ....Feb. 19
St. John's (N.Y.) ....Feb. 22
Notre Dame ....Feb. 25
West Va. ■ ....Mar. 1
Big East Conf. Tr. ....Mar. 5-8
1995-96 RESULTS (15-13)
81	Northeastern Ill. ■	58
76	Fla. Atlantic	56
80	Seton Hall ■	70
68	Villanova ■	70
77	Florida A&M ■	53
81	Winthrop ■	56
61	Fla. Atlantic ■	51
52	Clemson ■	66
54	Tennessee ■	56
69	Columbia ■	62
75	Syracuse ■	66
52	Connecticut	73
63	Seton Hall	66
67	Georgetown	72
66	Pittsburgh ■	57
72	Notre Dame ■	64
62	Villanova	90
51	Syracuse	72
68	West Va. ■	65
58	Boston College ■	62
54	Providence	77
69	West Va.	72
96	St. John's (N.Y.) ■	91
55	Rutgers	71
71	Notre Dame	59
66	Providence ■	59
77	Rutgers †	67
62	Georgetown †	92

Nickname: Hurricanes
Colors: Orange, Green & White
Arena: Miami Arena
    Capacity: 15,508; Year Built: 1988
AD: Paul Dee
SID: Rob Wilson

MIAMI (OHIO)
Oxford, OH 45056 I

Coach: Charlie Coles
Alma Mater: Miami (Ohio) '65
Record: 6 Years, W-92, L-84

1996-97 SCHEDULE
Va. Commonwealth ....Nov. 23
Xavier (Ohio) ....Nov. 30
Dayton ■ ....Dec. 4
Baylor Tr. ....Dec. 6-7
Eastern Ky. ■ ....Dec. 10
Wright St. ....Dec. 14
Akron ■ ....Jan. 4
Kent ....Jan. 8
Cincinnati ....Jan. 11
Central Mich. ■ ....Jan. 13
Toledo ....Jan. 15
Ohio ■ ....Jan. 18

Bowling Green ....Jan. 22
Western Mich. ■ ....Jan. 25
Ball St. ....Jan. 29
Kent ■ ....Feb. 1
Eastern Mich. ■ ....Feb. 6
Central Mich. ....Feb. 8
Toledo ■ ....Feb. 12
Ohio ....Feb. 15
Bowling Green ■ ....Feb. 19
Western Mich. ....Feb. 22
Eastern Mich. ■ ....Feb. 24
Ball St. ■ ....Feb. 26
Akron ....Mar. 1
Mid-American Conf. Tr. ....Mar. 4-8
1995-96 RESULTS (21-8)
89	Eastern Ky.	68
90	New Hampshire ■	64
74	La Salle †	53
85	Xavier (Ohio) ■	71
99	Hiram	58
69	Long Beach St. †	62
105	Wright St. ■	86
79	Dayton	56
71	Kent ■	59
56	Ohio	65
42	Toledo ■	43
83	Akron	70
62	Western Mich. ■	61
88	Central Mich.	72
60	Eastern Mich. ■	73
70	Ball St.	82
80	Bowling Green ■	64
76	Ohio	61
70	Toledo	76
99	Akron ■	50
65	Western Mich.	76
78	Central Mich. ■	54
75	Eastern Mich.	68
76	Ball St. ■	57
58	Bowling Green	56
77	Kent	63
81	Bowling Green ■	53
55	Toledo	75
57	Fresno St.	58

Nickname: Redskins
Colors: Red & White
Arena: Millett Hall
    Capacity: 9,200; Year Built: 1968
AD: Eric Hyman
SID: John Estes

MICHIGAN
Ann Arbor, MI 48109 I

Coach: Steve Fisher
Alma Mater: Illinois St. '67
Record: 8 Years, W-160, L-71

1996-97 SCHEDULE
Ball St. ....Nov. 26
Cleveland St. ....Nov. 30
Bradley ■ ....Dec. 2
Detroit ■ ....Dec. 5
Duke ....Dec. 8
St. John's (N.Y.) ■ ....Dec. 11
LSU [Auburn Hills] ....Dec. 15
Arizona [Auburn Hills] ....Dec. 21
Hawaii Rainbow Cl. ....Dec. 27-30
Ohio St. ....Jan. 2
Northwestern ....Jan. 4
Illinois ■ ....Jan. 9
Minnesota ....Jan. 11
Purdue ■ ....Jan. 16
Iowa ....Jan. 19
Indiana ....Jan. 21
Michigan St. ....Jan. 25
Penn St. ....Jan. 28
Michigan St. ■ ....Feb. 1
St. John's (N.Y.) ....Feb. 3
Wisconsin ....Feb. 6
Penn St. ■ ....Feb. 8
Indiana ■ ....Feb. 16
Iowa ....Feb. 20
Purdue ....Feb. 23

Minnesota ■ ... Feb. 26
Illinois ... Mar. 1
Northwestern ■ ... Mar. 5
Ohio St. ... Mar. 8

1995-96 RESULTS (20-12)
73	DePaul ■	65
80	Weber St. ■	62
79	Arizona †	86
61	Georgia Tech †	77
84	St. Francis (Pa.) ■	52
80	Ball St.	52
68	Detroit	48
69	LSU	68
88	Duke ■	84
60	Washington ■	59
84	Cleveland St. ■	55
64	UNLV	66
82	Davidson †	70
46	Wisconsin	51
83	Northwestern ■	51
83	Illinois ■	68
76	Michigan St.	54
67	Penn St. ■	66
83	Indiana	99
61	Iowa	70
59	Purdue ■	80
77	Ohio St. ■	58
64	Purdue	69
55	Iowa ■	62
80	Indiana ■	75
57	Penn St.	67
65	Minnesota ■	62
75	Michigan St. ■	46
62	Illinois	73
77	Northwestern	50
65	Wisconsin ■	51
76	Texas †	80

Nickname: Wolverines
Colors: Maize & Blue
Arena: Crisler Arena
 Capacity: 13,562; Year Built: 1967
AD: Joe Roberson
SID: Bruce Madej

MICHIGAN ST.
East Lansing, MI 48824 ... I

Coach: Tom Izzo
Alma Mater: Northern Mich. '77
Record: 1 Year, W-16, L-16

1996-97 SCHEDULE
East Tenn. St. ■ ... Nov. 25
Cleveland St. ■ ... Dec. 3
Ill.-Chicago ■ ... Dec. 5
Detroit ... Dec. 14
Evansville ... Dec. 17
Kansas St. ... Dec. 21
Michigan St. Cl. ... Dec. 27-28
Indiana ... Jan. 2
Minnesota ■ ... Jan. 4
Wisconsin ... Jan. 9
Ohio St. ■ ... Jan. 11
Penn St. ... Jan. 15
Northwestern ■ ... Jan. 18
Illinois ■ ... Jan. 22
Michigan ■ ... Jan. 25
Purdue ... Jan. 29
Michigan ... Feb. 1
Purdue ■ ... Feb. 8
Iowa ■ ... Feb. 12
Illinois ... Feb. 15
Northwestern ... Feb. 19
Penn St. ■ ... Feb. 22
Ohio St. ... Feb. 26
Wisconsin ■ ... Mar. 1
Minnesota ... Mar. 6
Indiana ■ ... Mar. 8

1995-96 RESULTS (16-16)
69	Chaminade †	66
70	North Caro. †	92
71	Santa Clara †	77
75	Arkansas †	72
59	Louisville	79
67	Evansville ■	63
61	Detroit ■	63
67	Kansas St.	54
57	Oklahoma St.	68
63	East Tenn. St. ■	57
62	Central Mich. ■	69
68	Idaho St. ■	55
65	Indiana ■	60
68	Illinois	58
54	Michigan ■	76
48	Wisconsin	61
62	Iowa ■	60
68	Northwestern ■	54
68	Minnesota	54
61	Penn St. ■	58
51	Purdue	56
55	Ohio St. ■	41
50	Penn St.	54
63	Minnesota ■	64
75	Northwestern	57
47	Iowa	83
52	Wisconsin ■	73
46	Michigan	75
77	Illinois ■	67
53	Indiana	57
64	Washington ■	50
70	Fresno St.	80

Nickname: Spartans
Colors: Green & White
Arena: Breslin Events Center
 Capacity: 15,138; Year Built: 1989
AD: Merritt Norvell
SID: John Farina

MICHIGAN TECH
Houghton, MI 49931 ... II

Coach: Kevin Luke
Alma Mater: Northern Mich. '82
Record: 2 Years, W-34, L-23

1996-97 SCHEDULE
Northland ■ ... Nov. 16
Mankato St. Cl. ... Nov. 22-23
Minn.-Duluth ■ ... Nov. 26
Northern St. Tr. ... Nov. 29-30
Hillsdale ... Dec. 5
Wayne St. (Mich.) ... Dec. 7
Gannon ■ ... Dec. 12
Mercyhurst ■ ... Dec. 14
Northland Bapt. ■ ... Dec. 17
Minn.-Duluth ... Dec. 29
Grand Valley St. ■ ... Jan. 2
Ferris St. ■ ... Jan. 4
Saginaw Valley ... Jan. 9
Northwood ... Jan. 11
Lake Superior St. ■ ... Jan. 18
Northern Mich. ... Jan. 20
Oakland ■ ... Jan. 25
Ashland ... Feb. 1
Grand Valley St. ... Feb. 6
Ferris St. ... Feb. 8
Saginaw Valley ■ ... Feb. 13
Northwood ■ ... Feb. 15
Northern Mich. ■ ... Feb. 17
Lake Superior St. ... Feb. 22

1995-96 RESULTS (18-11)
70	Wis.-Parkside ■	50
71	Moorhead St. †	63
65	Northern St.	99
96	Minn.-Duluth ■	74
81	Minn.-Morris	89
64	Northern Mich. ■	70
63	Oakland	61
60	Minn.-Duluth	67
52	Wis.-Green Bay	60
87	Northwood	70
73	Grand Valley St. ■	64
87	Wayne St. (Mich.)	83
58	Ashland	75
80	Mercyhurst ■	45
82	Gannon ■	61
99	Northland ■	60
77	Hillsdale	60
76	Saginaw Valley	78
83	Ferris St. ■	67
70	Lake Superior St. ■	64
66	Northern Mich.	56
78	Oakland ■	87
70	Ferris St.	51
67	Grand Valley St.	52
78	Lake Superior St.	93
53	Saginaw Valley ■	79
75	Northern Mich. †	67
72	Lake Superior St. †	75
90	Saginaw Valley †	72

Nickname: Huskies
Colors: Silver & Gold
Arena: SDC Gymnasium
 Capacity: 3,200; Year Built: 1981
AD: Rick Yeo
SID: Dave Fischer

MIDDLE TENN. ST.
Murfreesboro, TN 37132 ... I

Coach: Randy Wiel
Alma Mater: North Caro. '79
Record: 3 Years, W-32, L-50

1996-97 SCHEDULE
Top of the World Cl. ... Nov. 22-24
Montreat ■ ... Nov. 27
New Orleans ... Nov. 30
Murray St. ■ ... Dec. 2
Southern U. ... Dec. 7
Tenn.-Chatt. ■ ... Dec. 14
Belmont ■ ... Dec. 16
Indiana St. ... Dec. 19
Sue Bennett ■ ... Dec. 29
Eastern Ky. ... Jan. 4
Morehead St. ... Jan. 6
Tennessee St. ■ ... Jan. 9
Tennessee Tech ... Jan. 11
Southeast Mo. St. ■ ... Jan. 18
Eastern Ill. ■ ... Jan. 20
Austin Peay ... Jan. 23
Murray St. ... Jan. 25
Tenn.-Martin ■ ... Jan. 27
Morehead St. ■ ... Jan. 30
North Caro. ... Feb. 1
Eastern Ky. ■ ... Feb. 3
Austin Peay ■ ... Feb. 6
Tennessee Tech ... Feb. 8
Tennessee St. ... Feb. 13
Eastern Ill. ... Feb. 15
Southeast Mo. St. ... Feb. 17
Tenn.-Martin ■ ... Feb. 22
Ohio Valley Conf. Tr. ... Feb. 25-Mar. 1

1995-96 RESULTS (15-12)
81	Indiana St. ■	78
91	Oral Roberts	74
83	Texas Christian	86
66	Truman St. ■	51
77	Radford	92
67	New Orleans ■	69
64	North Caro. A&T ■	53
56	Vanderbilt	70
65	Wis.-Parkside ■	64
88	Austin Peay ■	69
78	Tennessee Tech	68
63	Southeast Mo. St. ■	65
86	Tennessee St. ■	74
59	Morehead St.	68
64	Eastern Ky.	70
88	Southern U. ■	73
81	Tenn.-Martin ■	68
72	Murray St. ■	73
75	Austin Peay	66
79	Tennessee St.	74
78	Southeast Mo. St.	75
71	Tennessee Tech ■	77
74	Eastern Ky. ■	70
73	Morehead St. ■	71
67	Murray St.	80
83	Tenn.-Martin	91
69	Tennessee Tech †	89

Nickname: Blue Raiders
Colors: Blue & White
Arena: Murphy Athletic Center
 Capacity: 11,520; Year Built: 1972
AD: Lee Fowler
SID: Ed Given

MIDDLEBURY
Middlebury, VT 05753 ... III

Coach: Russell Reilly
Alma Mater: Bates '66
Record: 18 Years, W-166, L-243

1996-97 SCHEDULE
Colby Inv. ... Nov. 22-23
Brandeis ■ ... Nov. 26
Tufts ■ ... Nov. 30
Skidmore ■ ... Dec. 3
Amherst ■ ... Dec. 7
Dartmouth ... Jan. 3
Springfield ... Jan. 9
Rensselaer ■ ... Jan. 12
Castleton St. ■ ... Jan. 14
Wesleyan (Conn.) ■ ... Jan. 16
Tufts ... Jan. 18
Williams ... Jan. 21
Colby-Sawyer ■ ... Jan. 23
Connecticut Col. ... Jan. 25
Colby ... Jan. 31
Bowdoin ■ ... Feb. 1
Norwich ... Feb. 11
Me.-Farmington ... Feb. 14
Bates ... Feb. 15
Williams ... Feb. 19
Union (N.Y.) ■ ... Feb. 25
Clarkson ■ ... Feb. 28
Trinity (Conn.) ... Mar. 1

1995-96 RESULTS (11-12)
72	Springfield ■	60
79	Brandeis ■	69
49	Dartmouth	81
72	Amherst ■	102
69	Trinity (Conn.) ■	67
52	Swarthmore †	71
83	Western Md. †	67
77	Wesleyan (Conn.) ■	71
69	Tufts	77
57	Williams	84
81	Colby-Sawyer	84
64	Connecticut Col. ■	50
63	Rensselaer	68
67	Colby	87
68	Bowdoin	79
74	Skidmore	80
68	Castleton St.	90
65	Norwich ■	62
89	Me.-Farmington ■	56
85	Bates	62
58	Williams ■	54
69	Tufts	106
82	Union (N.Y.) ■	65

Nickname: Panthers
Colors: Blue & White
Arena: Pepin Gymnasium
 Capacity: 1,200; Year Built: 1949
AD: G. Thomas Lawson
SID: Brad Nadeau

MILES
Birmingham, AL 35208 ... II

Coach: Kirk Patrick
Alma Mater: Texas College
Record: 1 Year, W-14, L-13

1996-97 SCHEDULE
Schedule unavailable

1995-96 RESULTS (14-13)
120	Fisk	80
72	Stillman	85
77	Alabama A&M ■	81
75	Clark Atlanta ■	81
104	LeMoyne-Owen	90

74	Lane	98
96	Morehouse ■	90
74	Paine ■	86
101	Stillman ■	95
80	Clark Atlanta	85
89	Kentucky St.	85
98	Albany St. (Ga.) ■	94
62	Morris Brown ■	73
80	Fort Valley St.	62
70	Savannah St.	74
85	Tuskegee ■	78
96	Lane	71
74	LeMoyne-Owen ■	88
84	Alabama A&M	103
74	Tuskegee	90
75	Paine	63
99	Savannah St. ■	74
77	Morehouse	78
94	Kentucky St. ■	76
145	Fisk ■	85
86	Albany St. (Ga.) ■	85
79	Tuskegee ■	89

Nickname: Golden Bears
Colors: Purple & Gold
Arena: Knox-Windham
　　Capacity: 2,500; Year Built: 1949
AD: Augustus James
SID: Willie K. Patterson Jr

MILLERSVILLE
Millersville, PA 17551 II

Coach: John Kochan
Alma Mater: Lehman '72
Record: 13 Years, W-285, L-96

1996-97 SCHEDULE
Lincoln (Pa.) ■	Nov. 25
Columbia Union	Nov. 30
Lock Haven ■	Dec. 4
Millersville Cl.	Dec. 6-7
St. Rose Cl.	Dec. 27-29
Neumann ■	Jan. 4
Bloomsburg ■	Jan. 8
Mansfield	Jan. 11
Cheyney	Jan. 15
West Chester	Jan. 18
Dist. Columbia ■	Jan. 20
East Stroudsburg ■	Jan. 22
Kutztown ■	Jan. 25
Columbia Union ■	Jan. 27
Wilmington (Del.) ■	Jan. 29
Mansfield ■	Feb. 1
Bloomsburg ■	Feb. 5
West Chester ■	Feb. 8
Dist. Columbia	Feb. 10
Cheyney ■	Feb. 12
East Stroudsburg	Feb. 15
Centenary (N.J.) ■	Feb. 17
Kutztown	Feb. 22

1995-96 RESULTS (17-10)
113	Nova Southeastern ■	98
84	Slippery Rock †	50
97	Pitt.-Johnstown †	88
86	Lock Haven	98
101	Slippery Rock ■	68
92	Adelphi ■	86
92	Dist. Columbia	80
77	Indiana (Pa.) ■	90
98	Lincoln (Pa.)	77
68	Indiana (Pa.)	64
97	Kutztown ■	74
69	Columbia Union	71
78	East Stroudsburg	79
62	West Chester	63
94	Dist. Columbia ■	80
85	Cheyney	75
80	Mansfield	64
82	Bloomsburg ■	89
65	Kutztown	69
76	Columbia Union ■	65
77	Centenary (N.J.) ■	69
88	East Stroudsburg ■	77
60	Cheyney	78

72	West Chester ■	58
50	Bloomsburg	55
68	Mansfield ■	64
68	Calif. (Pa.)	80

Nickname: Marauders
Colors: Black & Gold
Arena: Pucillo Gymnasium
　　Capacity: 3,000; Year Built: 1970
AD: Gene Carpenter
SID: Greg Wright

MILLIKIN
Decatur, IL 62522 III

Coach: Tim Littrell
Alma Mater: Millikin '77
(First year as head coach)

1996-97 SCHEDULE
Washington (Mo.)	Nov. 26
DePauw	Dec. 1
Wabash	Dec. 4
Blackburn ■	Dec. 7
Rose-Hulman ■	Dec. 14
Franklin ■	Dec. 17
Aurora	Dec. 20
Whittier Cl.	Jan. 3-4
Ill. Wesleyan	Jan. 8
Carthage	Jan. 11
Elmhurst ■	Jan. 14
North Park ■	Jan. 18
Wheaton (Ill.)	Jan. 21
Carthage ■	Jan. 25
Augustana (Ill.)	Jan. 29
Wheaton (Ill.) ■	Feb. 1
MacMurray	Feb. 4
Illinois Col.	Feb. 6
North Central	Feb. 8
Augustana (Ill.) ■	Feb. 11
Elmhurst	Feb. 15
North Park	Feb. 19
Ill. Wesleyan ■	Feb. 22
North Central	Feb. 26

1995-96 RESULTS (8-17)
79	Aurora ■	73
65	DePauw ■	69
67	Wabash	79
65	Eastern Ill.	72
84	Blackburn	81
76	Washington (Mo.) ■	90
87	Illinois Col. ■	67
87	Franklin	101
91	Rose-Hulman	105
80	Chowan †	69
95	Goucher †	78
61	North Central	59
80	Carthage	94
65	Augustana (Ill.) ■	77
78	North Park	81
63	Wheaton (Ill.)	78
69	Elmhurst	88
71	Ill. Wesleyan ■	86
81	North Central	63
77	Augustana (Ill.)	84
60	Carthage ■	74
90	North Park	78
85	Wheaton (Ill.) ■	87
59	Elmhurst ■	74
90	Ill. Wesleyan	100

Nickname: Big Blue
Colors: Royal & White
Arena: Griswold P.E. Center
　　Capacity: 4,000; Year Built: 1970
AD: Lori Kerans
SID: To be named

MILLSAPS
Jackson, MS 39210 III

Coach: John Stroud
Alma Mater: Mississippi '80
Record: 6 Years, W-100, L-57

1996-97 SCHEDULE
Millsaps Cl.	Nov. 23-24
Fisk	Nov. 25
Loyola (La.)	Nov. 26
Maryville (Tenn.) Tr	Nov. 30-Dec. 1
Loyola (La.) ■	Dec. 3
Rhodes Tr.	Dec. 6-7
Rust	Dec. 10
Pensacola Christian ■	Jan. 4
Rust ■	Jan. 7
Sewanee	Jan. 10
Centre	Jan. 12
Hendrix	Jan. 17
Rhodes ■	Jan. 19
Trinity (Tex.) ■	Jan. 24
Southwestern (Tex.)	Jan. 26
Hendrix	Jan. 31
Rhodes	Feb. 2
Fisk	Feb. 4
Trinity (Tex.)	Feb. 7
Southwestern (Tex.)	Feb. 9
Oglethorpe	Feb. 15
Sewanee ■	Feb. 21
Centre ■	Feb. 23
Oglethorpe ■	Mar. 1

1995-96 RESULTS (22-5)
90	Loyola (La.)	70
100	Fisk	67
78	LSU-Shreveport ■	70
76	Maryville (Mo.) †	58
81	Westminster (Mo.) †	69
69	Rust ■	71
78	Loyola (La.)	65
85	Pensacola Christian	71
83	Pensacola Christian	56
84	Emory	60
88	Rhodes ■	72
86	Hendrix ■	75
80	Centre ■	62
102	Sewanee ■	85
92	Southwestern (Tex.)	73
79	Trinity (Tex.)	92
67	Centre	60
85	Sewanee	67
101	Fisk ■	73
92	Southwestern (Tex.) ■	80
83	Trinity (Tex.) ■	64
75	Oglethorpe	63
88	Rhodes	82
66	Hendrix	82
72	Oglethorpe	74
83	Bridgewater (Va.) ■	72
69	Chris. Newport	73

Nickname: Majors
Colors: Purple & White
Arena: Physical Activities Center
　　Capacity: 3,000; Year Built: 1974
AD: Ron Jurney
SID: Trey Porter

MILWAUKEE ENGR.
Milwaukee, WI 53201 III

Coach: Brian Good
Alma Mater: Wisconsin '91
Record: 1 Year, W-3, L-22

1996-97 SCHEDULE
Wis.-Stout Cl.	Nov. 22-23
Lake Forest	Nov. 26
St. Norbert ■	Nov. 30
Maranatha Bapt.	Dec. 3
Edgewood Cl.	Dec. 6-7
Northland Bapt.	Dec. 10
Marian (Wis.) ■	Dec. 14
Loras ■	Dec. 21
Purdue-Calumet	Jan. 4
Lakeland ■	Jan. 7
Carroll (Wis.) ■	Jan. 8
Wis. Lutheran ■	Jan. 15
Concordia (Wis.) ■	Jan. 18
Cardinal Stritch	Jan. 22
Edgewood ■	Jan. 25
Maranatha Bapt. ■	Jan. 28

Barat ■	Jan. 30
Lakeland	Feb. 1
Cardinal Stritch ■	Feb. 6
Wis. Lutheran	Feb. 8
Marian (Wis.)	Feb. 13
Concordia (Wis.) ■	Feb. 15

1995-96 RESULTS (3-22)
43	Carroll (Wis.)	58
60	St. Norbert	86
75	Northland	77
47	Edgewood	54
49	Martin Luther †	55
48	Maranatha Bapt.	69
71	Trinity Int'l.	88
87	Dr. Wm. Scholl	60
57	Rollins	86
64	Warner Southern	92
73	Lawrence ■	78
66	Lakeland	82
52	Barat	86
80	Cardinal Stritch ■	102
38	Marian (Wis.)	63
62	Wis. Lutheran	91
64	Concordia (Wis.)	70
51	Edgewood	77
49	Maranatha Bapt.	68
62	Lakeland ■	78
57	Cardinal Stritch	65
63	Wis. Lutheran ■	76
61	Marian (Wis.) ■	60
79	Concordia (Wis.) ■	73
53	Marian (Wis.)	68

Nickname: Raiders
Colors: Cardinal & White
Arena: MSOE Sports Center
　　Capacity: 700
AD: Dan Harris
SID: Fiona Husband

MINNESOTA
Minneapolis, MN 55455 I

Coach: Clem Haskins
Alma Mater: Western Ky. '67
Record: 16 Years, W-271, L-210

1996-97 SCHEDULE
Stephen F. Austin ■	Nov. 23
West Va.	Nov. 26
San Juan Shootout	Nov. 29-Dec. 1
Alabama	Dec. 5
St. John's (N.Y.) ■	Dec. 15
Rhode Island	Dec. 17
Nebraska	Dec. 21
Alabama St. ■	Dec. 23
LIU-Brooklyn ■	Dec. 28
Mercer ■	Dec. 31
Wisconsin ■	Jan. 2
Michigan St.	Jan. 4
Indiana	Jan. 8
Michigan ■	Jan. 11
Illinois	Jan. 14
Ohio St.	Jan. 18
Iowa ■	Jan. 23
Purdue ■	Jan. 25
Northwestern	Feb. 1
Penn St. ■	Feb. 5
Purdue	Feb. 12
Iowa	Feb. 15
Ohio St. ■	Feb. 19
Illinois ■	Feb. 22
Michigan	Feb. 26
Indiana ■	Mar. 1
Michigan St. ■	Mar. 6
Wisconsin	Mar. 8

1995-96 RESULTS (19-13)
70	Valparaiso †	66
64	Wichita St. †	55
85	Nebraska †	96
82	Charleston So.	67
93	Bethune-Cookman ■	53
91	Nebraska	80
50	Cincinnati	84
67	California ■	70

66	Clemson	.79
86	Cal St. Sacramento	.63
87	Mt. St. Mary's (Md.) ■	.62
92	Mercer ■	.56
69	Illinois ■	.64
63	Iowa	.92
61	Penn St. ■	.76
62	Purdue ■	.76
56	Ohio St. ■	.50
65	Wisconsin	.73
54	Michigan St. ■	.68
77	Northwestern ■	.68
66	Indiana ■	.81
66	Northwestern	.47
64	Michigan St.	.63
70	Wisconsin ■	.66
60	Ohio St. ■	.57
62	Michigan	.65
61	Purdue	.67
65	Penn St. ■	.60
72	Iowa ■	.64
67	Illinois	.66
68	St. Louis ■	.52
65	Tulane	.84

Nickname: Golden Gophers
Colors: Maroon & Gold
Arena: Williams Arena
   Capacity: 14,300; Year Built: 1928
AD: Mark Dienhart
SID: Bill Crumley

MINN.-DULUTH
Duluth, MN 55812 II

Coach: Dale Race
Alma Mater: Wis.-Oshkosh '70
Record: 16 Years, W-332, L-154

1996-97 SCHEDULE

Northern Mich.	Nov. 25
Michigan Tech	Nov. 26
Minn.-Duluth Cl.	Nov. 29-30
Wis.-Superior	Dec. 4
St. Cloud St.	Dec. 10
Mankato St. ■	Dec. 14
Northland ■	Dec. 16
Humboldt St.	Dec. 20
San Fran. St.	Dec. 22
Michigan Tech ■	Dec. 29
Northern Mich. ■	Dec. 30
St. Scholastica	Jan. 8
Mt. Senario ■	Jan. 11
Minn.-Morris ■	Jan. 15
Northern St. ■	Jan. 18
Bemidji St.	Jan. 22
Southwest St.	Jan. 25
Winona St. ■	Jan. 29
Moorhead St.	Feb. 1
Minn.-Morris	Feb. 5
Crown ■	Feb. 8
Bemidji St. ■	Feb. 12
Northern St.	Feb. 15
Winona St.	Feb. 19
Southwest St. ■	Feb. 22
Moorhead St. ■	Feb. 26

1995-96 RESULTS (15-10)

86	Wis.-Superior ■	.74
74	Michigan Tech	.96
68	Northern Mich. ■	.61
79	Northland	.58
77	Mankato St.	.83
67	Michigan Tech ■	.60
67	St. Cloud St. ■	.68
73	American (P.R.) †	.80
76	Tampa	.79
76	St. Leo	.60
57	Northern Mich.	.70
89	St. Scholastica ■	.73
56	Northern St.	.57
88	Bemidji St. ■	.36
70	Southwest St. ■	.78
67	Winona St.	.52
89	Moorhead St. ■	.100
77	Minn.-Morris	.65
78	Mt. Senario ■	.67

79	Bemidji St.	.60
81	Northern St. ■	.66
78	Winona St.	.56
61	Southwest St.	.71
67	Minn.-Morris	.65
82	Moorhead St.	.79

Nickname: Bulldogs
Colors: Maroon & Gold
Arena: Romano Gymnasium
   Capacity: 2,759; Year Built: 1953
AD: Pat Merrier
SID: Bob Nygaard

MINN.-MORRIS
Morris, MN 56267 II

Coach: Jim Severson
Alma Mater: Minn.-Morris '77
Record: 1 Year, W-13, L-14

1996-97 SCHEDULE

South Dak. St. ■	Nov. 16
Wis.-Milwaukee	Nov. 22
Mt. Marty	Nov. 26
Mary	Nov. 30
St. Scholastica ■	Dec. 3
South Dak. ■	Dec. 7
North Dak.	Dec. 14
St. Cloud St.	Dec. 17
Mankato St. ■	Dec. 19
Valley City St. ■	Dec. 21
Minn.-Crookston	Jan. 4
Moorhead St.	Jan. 11
Minn.-Duluth	Jan. 15
Southwest St. ■	Jan. 18
Winona St. ■	Jan. 22
Wayne St. (Neb.) ■	Jan. 25
Bemidji St.	Jan. 29
Northern St. ■	Feb. 1
Mt. Senario	Feb. 3
Minn.-Duluth ■	Feb. 5
Moorhead St. ■	Feb. 8
Winona St.	Feb. 12
Southwest St.	Feb. 15
Bemidji St. ■	Feb. 19
N'western (Minn.)	Feb. 20
Wayne St. (Neb.)	Feb. 22
Northern St.	Feb. 26

1995-96 RESULTS (13-14)
Results unavailable

Nickname: Cougars
Colors: Maroon & Gold
Arena: P.E. Center
   Capacity: 3,500; Year Built: 1971
AD: Mark Fohl
SID: Broderick Powell

MISERICORDIA
Dallas, PA 18612 III

Coach: David Martin
Alma Mater: Wilkes '90
Record: 6 Years, W-61, L-90

1996-97 SCHEDULE

Misericordia Tr.	Nov. 22-23
Lycoming ■	Nov. 26
Allentown	Dec. 4
Beaver ■	Dec. 7
King's (Pa.) Cl.	Dec. 28-29
Gwynedd-Mercy ■	Jan. 11
Cabrini	Jan. 13
Alvernia	Jan. 15
Neumann	Jan. 18
Marywood ■	Jan. 20
Eastern ■	Jan. 22
Beaver	Jan. 25
Drew	Jan. 27
Allentown ■	Feb. 1
Gwynedd-Mercy	Feb. 5
Cabrini ■	Feb. 8
Juniata ■	Feb. 10
Alvernia ■	Feb. 12

Neumann ■		Feb. 15
Delaware Valley ■		Feb. 17
Marywood		Feb. 19
Eastern		Feb. 22

1995-96 RESULTS (16-12)

102	Bapt. Bible (Pa.) †	.99
73	Scranton	.69
94	Lycoming	.100
76	Alvernia	.102
73	Eastern ■	.78
79	Delaware Valley	.67
57	Allentown	.81
87	Lincoln (Pa.) †	.67
80	Widener	.73
89	Beaver ■	.83
81	Marywood ■	.72
64	Cabrini ■	.98
85	Drew ■	.90
69	Alvernia ■	.62
75	Eastern	.81
88	Gwynedd-Mercy	.82
68	Allentown ■	.64
79	Neumann ■	.59
83	Marywood	.78
70	Juniata	.72
70	Cabrini	.96
85	Neumann	.76
58	Beaver	.61
83	Gwynedd-Mercy ■	.62
64	Beaver	.59
55	Cabrini	.90
76	Grove City †	.70
77	Lincoln (Pa.) †	.92

Nickname: Cougars
Colors: Royal Blue & Gold
Arena: Anderson Sports-Health Center
   Capacity: 1,500; Year Built: 1992
AD: Michael Mould
SID: Scott Crispell

MISSISSIPPI
University, MS 38677 I

Coach: Rob Evans
Alma Mater: New Mexico St. '68
Record: 4 Years, W-44, L-65

1996-97 SCHEDULE

Portland St. ■	Nov. 23
Prairie View ■	Nov. 26
Davidson	Dec. 2
Houston ■	Dec. 7
Wichita St. ■	Dec. 14
Stetson ■	Dec. 17
Florida Int'l ■	Dec. 20
New Mexico Inv.	Dec. 27-28
Morgan St. ■	Dec. 31
Arkansas	Jan. 2
Georgia ■	Jan. 5
Alabama ■	Jan. 8
Kentucky ■	Jan. 11
Mississippi St.	Jan. 15
Vanderbilt	Jan. 18
Tennessee ■	Jan. 22
South Caro.	Jan. 25
Arkansas ■	Jan. 29
Auburn ■	Feb. 1
LSU	Feb. 5
Alabama	Feb. 12
Mississippi St. ■	Feb. 19
Florida	Feb. 23
LSU ■	Feb. 26
Auburn	Mar. 1
Southeastern Conf. Tr.	Mar. 6-9

1995-96 RESULTS (12-15)

83	Davidson ■	.84
51	Colgate †	.53
65	East Tenn. St. †	.50
81	Lamar	.86
59	Wichita St.	.72
113	Southern Miss. ■	.107
76	Houston	.67
66	Nicholls St. ■	.54
96	Prairie View ■	.51

38	Georgia	.74
60	Kentucky	.90
62	Arkansas ■	.63
47	Mississippi St.	.53
55	Florida ■	.59
82	Auburn ■	.69
70	Alabama ■	.63
52	Tennessee	.67
66	LSU	.71
106	Houston Baptist ■	.63
78	Vanderbilt ■	.55
73	Arkansas	.79
71	Mississippi St. ■	.64
62	Auburn	.69
75	South Caro. ■	.65
75	LSU ■	.48
63	Alabama	.67
62	Florida †	.75

Nickname: Rebels
Colors: Red & Blue
Arena: C. M. "Tad" Smith Coliseum
   Capacity: 8,135; Year Built: 1966
AD: Pete Boone
SID: Jeff Romero

MISSISSIPPI COL.
Clinton, MS 39058 II

Coach: Mike Jones
Alma Mater: Mississippi Col. '75
Record: 8 Years, W-152, L-68

1996-97 SCHEDULE

Mississippi Col. Tr.	Nov. 22-23
Ala.-Huntsville	Nov. 25
Mississippi Col. Cl.	Nov. 29-30
Rust	Dec. 3
Southern Ark. ■	Dec. 12
Ala.-Huntsville ■	Dec. 16
Southern Ark.	Dec. 30
Morehouse ■	Jan. 6
Ark.-Monticello ■	Jan. 9
Ouachita Baptist ■	Jan. 11
West Ala. ■	Jan. 16
Lyon	Jan. 18
Sul Ross St.	Jan. 25
McMurry	Jan. 27
McMurry ■	Feb. 1
Ouachita Baptist	Feb. 3
Ark.-Monticello	Feb. 6
West Ala.	Feb. 12
Lyon ■	Feb. 15
La. Christian ■	Feb. 17
Sul Ross St. ■	Feb. 22
Rust ■	Feb. 24
Drury	Mar. 1

1995-96 RESULTS (17-8)

63	Morehouse ■	.65
76	LeMoyne-Owen ■	.70
71	Lane ■	.65
77	Montevallo ■	.63
62	Lane	.54
76	Athens St. ■	.66
89	Talladega	.81
61	Arkansas Tech ■	.45
68	Central Ark.	.71
79	Henderson St. ■	.74
89	Ark.-Monticello ■	.77
63	Southern Ark.	.74
74	La. Christian	.65
63	Delta St.	.70
79	Central Ark. ■	.61
82	Lane ■	.89
82	Henderson St.	.74
88	Ark.-Monticello	.96
62	Southern Ark. ■	.51
102	La. Christian ■	.60
79	Talladega ■	.82
50	Delta St. ■	.49
63	Arkansas Tech	.54
70	Valdosta St. †	.69
75	North Ala. †	.92

Nickname: Choctaws
Colors: Blue & Gold

Arena: A. E. Wood Coliseum
  Capacity: 3,500; Year Built: 1979
AD: Terry McMillan
SID: Pete Smith

MISSISSIPPI ST.
Mississippi State, MS 39762 I

Coach: Richard Williams
Alma Mater: Mississippi St. '67
Record: 10 Years, W-164, L-130

1996-97 SCHEDULE
Northwestern St. ■	Nov. 23
Southeastern La. ■	Nov. 26
James Madison ■	Nov. 30
Wake Forest [Chicago]	Dec. 3
Maryland Tr.	Dec. 8-9
Loyola (La.) ■	Dec. 14
Texas Southern ■	Dec. 17
Old Dominion ■	Dec. 19
N.C.-Wilmington	Dec. 21
Puerto Rico Tr.	Dec. 30-Jan. 1
LSU ■	Jan. 4
Kentucky	Jan. 7
South Caro. ■	Jan. 11
Mississippi ■	Jan. 15
Arkansas	Jan. 21
Vanderbilt ■	Jan. 25
LSU	Jan. 29
Alabama ■	Feb. 1
Auburn	Feb. 5
Georgia	Feb. 8
Florida ■	Feb. 12
Tennessee	Feb. 15
Mississippi	Feb. 19
Arkansas ■	Feb. 23
Auburn ■	Feb. 26
Alabama	Mar. 1
Southeastern Conf. Tr.	Mar. 6-9

1995-96 RESULTS (26-8)
121	Southeastern La. ■	78
77	N.C.-Wilmington ■	54
79	Brigham Young ■	74
123	Troy St. ■	73
68	Ark.-Little Rock ■	70
72	Southern Miss.	69
66	Northeast La. ■	60
76	Oregon St. †	62
69	Nebraska †	66
77	LSU	64
69	Florida	66
56	Kentucky ■	74
55	Alabama ■	56
53	Mississippi ■	47
68	Arkansas	80
69	South Caro.	77
60	Tennessee ■	59
76	Georgia ■	73
78	Auburn	75
78	Arkansas ■	63
76	Oklahoma	71
64	Mississippi	71
67	Auburn ■	51
69	Auburn †	58
86	Georgia †	68
84	Kentucky †	73
58	Va. Commonwealth †	51
63	Princeton †	41
60	Connecticut †	55
73	Cincinnati †	63
69	Syracuse †	77

Nickname: Bulldogs
Colors: Maroon & White
Arena: Humphrey Coliseum
  Capacity: 10,000; Year Built: 1975
AD: Larry Templeton
SID: David Rosinski

MISSISSIPPI VAL.
Itta Bena, MS 38941 I

Coach: Lafayette Stribling
Alma Mater: Miss. Industrial '57
Record: 13 Years, W-180, L-191

1996-97 SCHEDULE
Jacksonville St.	Nov. 23
Arkansas St. ■	Nov. 25
Oklahoma St.	Dec. 4
Southwest Mo. St. Cl.	Dec. 6-7
Jacksonville St. ■	Dec. 14
Ark.-Pine Bluff	Dec. 16
Arkansas St.	Dec. 19
Vanderbilt	Dec. 23
Tennessee St. [Memphis]	Dec. 28
Alcorn St.	Jan. 4
Southern U.	Jan. 6
Texas Southern ■	Jan. 11
Prairie View ■	Jan. 13
Alabama St. ■	Jan. 18
Jackson St.	Jan. 20
Grambling	Jan. 25
Ark.-Pine Bluff ■	Jan. 27
Alcorn St. ■	Feb. 1
Southern U. ■	Feb. 3
Texas Southern	Feb. 8
Prairie View	Feb. 10
Alabama St.	Feb. 15
Jackson St. ■	Feb. 17
Southern Miss.	Feb. 19
Grambling ■	Feb. 22
Southwestern Conf. Tr.	Mar. 5-8

1995-96 RESULTS (22-7)
93	Jacksonville St. ■	68
87	Delta St.	80
63	Idaho †	61
84	Southeast Mo. St.	80
78	Delta St. ■	76
86	Tennessee St. †	70
93	Ark.-Pine Bluff ■	62
94	Jacksonville St.	102
81	Stetson	61
63	Utah St.	80
73	Buffalo †	74
113	Ark.-Pine Bluff	44
113	Alcorn St. ■	78
94	Southern U. ■	92
95	Prairie View	88
97	Texas Southern	74
94	Jackson St.	93
83	Alabama St.	75
76	Grambling ■	70
74	Alcorn St.	77
87	Southern U.	93
96	Prairie View ■	76
79	Texas Southern ■	59
79	Jackson St. ■	81
83	Alabama St. ■	69
78	Grambling	72
83	Southern U. †	76
111	Jackson St. †	94
56	Georgetown †	93

Nickname: Delta Devils
Colors: Green & White
Arena: Harrison HPER Complex
  Capacity: 6,000; Year Built: 1970
AD: Charles Prophet
SID: Charles Prophet

MISSOURI
Columbia, MO 65211 I

Coach: Norm Stewart
Alma Mater: Missouri '56
Record: 35 Years, W-678, L-334

1996-97 SCHEDULE
Chicago St. ■	Nov. 23
San Juan Shootout	Nov. 29-Dec. 1
Arkansas St. ■	Dec. 4
Arkansas ■	Dec. 7
Southeast Mo. St. ■	Dec. 15
Northwest Mo. St. ■	Dec. 17
Mercer ■	Dec. 19
Iowa	Dec. 21
Illinois [St. Louis]	Dec. 28
Southern U. ■	Dec. 30
Iowa St. ■	Jan. 4
Colorado	Jan. 7
Oklahoma St.	Jan. 11
Baylor ■	Jan. 14
Nebraska	Jan. 18
Nebraska ■	Jan. 22
Texas	Jan. 26
Texas A&M	Jan. 28
Kansas St. ■	Feb. 1
Kansas ■	Feb. 4
Wake Forest ■	Feb. 9
Iowa St.	Feb. 12
Oklahoma ■	Feb. 15
Kansas	Feb. 17
Colorado	Feb. 22
Texas Tech ■	Feb. 25
Kansas St.	Mar. 1
Big 12 Conf. Tr.	Mar. 6-9

1995-96 RESULTS (18-15)
86	Wofford ■	60
89	Tennessee St. ■	75
66	Southern Methodist ■	51
117	Chicago St. ■	45
93	Arkansas	104
86	Jackson St. ■	63
73	Arkansas St.	63
81	Austin Peay ■	58
85	Illinois †	96
64	Southern Cal †	75
68	North Caro. St. †	87
95	Hawaii	89
102	Southeast Mo. St. ■	65
77	Colorado ■	66
92	Geo. Washington ■	77
75	Oklahoma ■	73
62	Iowa St.	73
58	Nebraska	76
86	Kansas St. ■	80
94	Colorado	106
68	Oklahoma	104
99	Nebraska ■	98
77	Kansas ■	73
63	Oklahoma St.	59
72	Maryland	91
64	Kansas St.	69
74	Iowa St. ■	78
65	Kansas	87
49	Oklahoma St. ■	51
92	Oklahoma †	88
53	Iowa St. †	57
89	Murray St. ■	85
49	Alabama	72

Nickname: Tigers
Colors: Old Gold & Black
Arena: Hearnes Arena
  Capacity: 13,349; Year Built: 1972
AD: Joe Castiglione
SID: Bob Brendel

MO. SOUTHERN ST.
Joplin, MO 64801 II

Coach: Robert Corn
Alma Mater: Mo. Southern St. '78
Record: 7 Years, W-100, L-93

1996-97 SCHEDULE
Ozark Christian ■	Nov. 15
Central Ark. ■	Nov. 23
SIU-Edwardsville	Nov. 26
Missouri So. Cl.	Nov. 29-30
Southwest Baptist	Dec. 3
Rockhurst	Dec. 14
Missouri So. Tr.	Dec. 30-31
Lincoln (Mo.)	Jan. 4
Emporia St.	Jan. 8
Central Mo. St. ■	Jan. 11
Mo. Western St. ■	Jan. 13
Truman St. ■	Jan. 15
Washburn ■	Jan. 18
Mo.-Rolla	Jan. 22
Central Mo. St.	Jan. 27
Pittsburg St.	Jan. 29
Emporia St. ■	Feb. 1
Northwest Mo. St. ■	Feb. 3
Southwest Baptist ■	Feb. 5
Northwest Mo. St.	Feb. 8
Mo. Western St. ■	Feb. 12
Truman St.	Feb. 15
Mo.-Rolla ■	Feb. 19
Pittsburg St. ■	Feb. 22

1995-96 RESULTS (12-14)
83	Pittsburg St. ■	73
78	Christian Bros. ■	67
69	Arkansas Tech ■	77
79	Central Ark.	83
67	Henderson St.	72
80	Cameron ■	71
85	Missouri Valley ■	71
86	LIU-C. W. Post †	72
75	Eckerd †	84
76	American (P.R.)	80
69	Pittsburg St.	66
105	Lincoln (Mo.) ■	108
78	Mo. Western St.	77
90	Central Mo. St. ■	98
89	Washburn	95
79	Emporia St. ■	69
78	Mo.-St. Louis	76
107	Truman St.	97
71	Northwest Mo. St.	89
81	Mo.-Rolla ■	91
84	Southwest Baptist ■	79
91	Lincoln (Mo.)	100
60	Mo. Western St. ■	69
75	Central Mo. St.	72
80	Washburn	94
56	Emporia St.	70

Nickname: Lions
Colors: Green & Gold
Arena: Robert Ellis Young Gym
  Capacity: 1,700; Year Built: 1968
AD: Jim Frazier
SID: Dennis Slusher

MO. WESTERN ST.
St. Joseph, MO 64507 II

Coach: Tom Smith
Alma Mater: Valparaiso '67
Record: 21 Years, W-341, L-255

1996-97 SCHEDULE
Northwest Mo. St. Cl.	Nov. 22-23
Rockhurst	Dec. 2
Washburn	Dec. 4
Mo. Western St. Cl.	Dec. 6-7
Angelo St. Cl.	Dec. 27-28
Benedictine ■	Jan. 2
Central Mo. St. ■	Jan. 4
Truman St.	Jan. 8
Mo.-Rolla ■	Jan. 11
Mo. Southern St. ■	Jan. 13
Lincoln (Mo.)	Jan. 18
Emporia St. ■	Jan. 22
Southwest Baptist ■	Jan. 25
Pittsburg St. ■	Jan. 27
Northwest Mo. St.	Jan. 29
Truman St. ■	Feb. 1
Washburn ■	Feb. 5
Pittsburg St.	Feb. 8
Southwest Baptist	Feb. 10
Mo. Southern St.	Feb. 12
Lincoln (Mo.) ■	Feb. 17

Emporia St. ....Feb. 19
Northwest Mo. St. ■ ....Feb. 22

1995-96 RESULTS (17-10)

87	Benedictine ■	74
80	Western Wash. †	77
71	Seattle Pacific	89
114	Ark.-Monticello ■	90
87	Northwest Mo. St. ■	70
83	Rockhurst ■	59
92	Evangel ■	79
106	Doane ■	82
89	UC Riverside †	87
91	Rollins †	95
71	Mo.-St. Louis ■	73
59	Washburn	56
77	Mo. Southern St. ■	78
73	Emporia St.	87
72	Central Mo. St.	91
76	Lincoln (Mo.) ■	66
73	Pittsburg St.	71
85	Southwest Baptist ■	73
87	Truman St.	73
72	Northwest Mo. St.	87
63	Mo.-Rolla ■	78
72	Washburn ■	65
69	Mo. Southern St.	60
74	Emporia St. ■	60
75	Central Mo. St. ■	78
74	Lincoln (Mo.)	61
59	Mo.-St. Louis	62

Nickname: Griffons
Colors: Black & Gold
Arena: MWSC Fieldhouse
  Capacity: 4,000; Year Built: 1981
AD: Don Kaverman
SID: To be named

MO.-KANSAS CITY
Kansas City, MO 64110............I

Coach: Bob Sundvold
Alma Mater: South Dak. St. '77
Record: 4 Years, W-81, L-39

1996-97 SCHEDULE

Kansas St. ....Nov. 22
Creighton ....Nov. 25
Southwest St. ■ ....Nov. 27
Baylor.....................................Dec. 3
St. Louis ....Dec. 7
Nebraska.................................Dec. 11
Monmouth (Ill.) ■ ....Dec. 14
Texas A&M ■ ....Dec. 20
Colorado ■ ....Dec. 28
Northern Iowa ....Dec. 30
Western Ill. ....Jan. 2
Valparaiso ■ ....Jan. 4
Troy St. ....Jan. 6
Buffalo ....Jan. 11
Youngstown St. ....Jan. 13
Chicago St. ....Jan. 18
Northeastern Ill. ....Jan. 20
Central Conn. St. ....Jan. 27
Troy St. ■ ....Feb. 1
Youngstown St. ■ ....Feb. 6
Buffalo ■ ....Feb. 8
Northeastern Ill. ■ ....Feb. 10
Chicago St. ■ ....Feb. 12
Central Conn. St. ■ ....Feb. 15
Valparaiso ....Feb. 22
Western Ill. ....Feb. 24
Mid-Continent Conf. Tr............Mar. 2-4

1995-96 RESULTS (12-15)

60	Montana	70
70	Baylor ■	55
74	St. Louis ■	82
54	Kansas St. ■	69
72	Creighton ■	70
66	Central Conn. St.	59
89	Troy St.	90
43	Buffalo ■	48
55	Youngstown St. ■	66
80	Western Ill. ■	60
69	Nebraska	87

66	Chicago St. ■	77
83	Northeastern Ill.	79
57	Valparaiso ■	65
54	Eastern Ill. ■	56
69	Youngstown St.	59
72	Buffalo	63
55	Colorado	84
67	Western Ill.	72
59	Oral Roberts	70
57	Northeastern Ill. ■	55
99	Chicago St. ■	73
82	Eastern Ill.	73
57	Valparaiso	69
120	Troy St. ■	95
76	Central Conn. St. ■	69
83	Central Conn. St. †	89

Nickname: Kangaroos
Colors: Blue & Gold
Arena: Municipal Auditorium
  Capacity: 11,126; Year Built: 1936
AD: Lee Hunt
SID: Chad Harberts

MO.-ROLLA
Rolla, MO 65401 II

Coach: Dale Martin
Alma Mater: Central Mo. St. '76
Record: 9 Years, W-123, L-116

1996-97 SCHEDULE

Drury ■ ....Nov. 16
Harris-Stowe ■ ....Nov. 23
Maryville (Mo.) ■ ■ ....Nov. 25
Eckerd Cl. ....Nov. 29-30
Pittsburg St. ....Dec. 4
Mo.-Rolla Shootout.................Dec. 6-7
Westminster (Mo.) ■ ....Dec. 11
Lincoln (Mo.) ■ ....Dec. 14
Truman St. ....Dec. 30
Emporia St. ....Jan. 4
Northwest Mo. St. ....Jan. 6
Mo. Western St. ■ ....Jan. 11
Washburn.................................Jan. 15
Central Mo. St. ....Jan. 18
Mo. Southern St. ■ ....Jan. 22
Northwest Mo. St. ■ ....Jan. 25
Southwest Baptist ....Jan. 28
Emporia St. ■ ....Feb. 3
Pittsburg St. ■ ....Feb. 5
Truman St. ....Feb. 8
Lincoln (Mo.)..........................Feb. 12
Washburn ■ ....Feb. 15
Mo. Southern St. ....Feb. 19
Southwest Baptist ■ ....Feb. 22

1995-96 RESULTS (25-6)

90	Lyon	75
87	Lindenwood ■	82
83	Missouri Baptist ■	74
76	Eckerd ■	60
91	Maryville (Mo.) ■	68
96	Westminster (Mo.) ■	72
59	Drury	73
86	Lyon ■	63
75	Central Wash. †	69
81	Seattle Pacific	68
68	Lincoln (Mo.)	59
66	Northwest Mo. St.	71
82	Mo.-St. Louis ■	83
81	Southwest Baptist ■	66
81	Truman St.	77
79	Pittsburg St.	82
75	Washburn ■	62
74	Central Mo. St. ■	67
73	Emporia St.	63
91	Mo. Southern St.	81
78	Mo. Western St.	63
63	Northwest Mo. St. ■	72
60	Mo.-St. Louis	59
79	Southwest Baptist	73
69	Truman St. ■	62
84	Pittsburg St. ■	76
112	Washburn ■	104
74	Mo.-St. Louis ■	69
67	Central Mo. St. ■	65

| 72 | Central Mo. St. ■ | 67 |
| 80 | North Ala. ■ | 92 |

Nickname: Miners
Colors: Silver & Gold
Arena: Bullman Multi-Purpose
  Capacity: 5,000; Year Built: 1969
AD: Mark Mullin
SID: John Kean

MO.-ST. LOUIS
St. Louis, MO 63121 II

Coach: Richard Meckfessel
Alma Mater: Washington (Mo.) '61
Record: 28 Years, W-440, L-360

1996-97 SCHEDULE

Southern Ind. ....Nov. 23
Cal St. Bakersfield Cl.............Nov. 29-30
Missouri Baptist ....Dec. 3
Drury Tr..................................Dec. 6-7
Washington (Mo.) ....Dec. 14
SIU-Edwardsville ....Dec. 21
IU/PU-Ft. Wayne ■ ....Jan. 2
St. Joseph's (Ind.) ■ ....Jan. 4
Quincy ....Jan. 9
Indianapolis ....Jan. 11
Lewis ■ ....Jan. 16
Wis.-Parkside ■ ....Jan. 18
Ky. Wesleyan ....Jan. 23
Bellarmine ■ ....Jan. 25
SIU-Edwardsville ....Jan. 30
Southern Ind. ■ ....Feb. 1
St. Joseph's (Ind.) ....Feb. 6
IU/PU-Ft. Wayne ....Feb. 8
Quincy ■ ....Feb. 13
Northern Ky. ■ ....Feb. 15
Wis.-Parkside ....Feb. 20
Lewis ....Feb. 22
Bellarmine ■ ....Feb. 27
Ky. Wesleyan ■ ....Mar. 1

1995-96 RESULTS (15-13)

85	Mankato St.	86
68	Huron †	98
85	Missouri Baptist ■	69
76	Quincy ■	90
93	Harris-Stowe ■	84
102	Parks ■	91
72	Washington (Mo.) ■	69
72	SIU-Edwardsville	79
63	Iowa St.	76
123	Sanford Brown	58
73	Mo. Western St.	71
84	Southwest Baptist	75
83	Mo.-Rolla	82
74	Truman St.	93
79	Pittsburg St. ■	58
68	Northwest Mo. St.	76
76	Mo. Southern St.	78
78	Lincoln (Mo.)	76
65	Washburn ■	74
64	Emporia St. ■	62
89	Central Mo. St.	86
94	Southwest Baptist	88
59	Mo.-Rolla ■	60
80	Truman St. ■	63
66	Pittsburg St.	87
67	Northwest Mo. St. ■	83
62	Mo. Western St. ■	59
69	Mo.-Rolla	74

Nickname: Rivermen
Colors: Red & Gold
Arena: Mark Twain Building
  Capacity: 4,736; Year Built: 1971
AD: Patricia Dolan
SID: Chuck Yahng

MOLLOY
Rockville Centre, NY 11570 II

Coach: Charles Marquardt III
Alma Mater: St. Joseph's (Me.) '86
Record: 2 Years, W-6, L-47

1996-97 SCHEDULE

St. Thomas Aquinas ....Nov. 19
Adelphi ....Nov. 23
Molloy Tr................................Nov. 29-30
Stony Brook ■ ....Dec. 2
LIU-Southampton ■ ....Dec. 4
Queens (N.Y.) ■ ....Dec. 7
Pace ■ ....Dec. 11
Concordia (N.Y.) ■ ....Dec. 14
Phila. Textile ....Jan. 2
Dowling ■ ....Jan. 4
St. Rose ....Jan. 8
New York Tech ■ ....Jan. 13
LIU-C. W. Post ■ ....Jan. 15
Mercy ....Jan. 18
LIU-Southampton ....Jan. 20
Queens (N.Y.) ■ ....Jan. 22
Pace ....Jan. 25
Concordia (N.Y.) ■ ....Jan. 29
Dowling ....Feb. 1
Adelphi ....Feb. 5
St. Rose ■ ....Feb. 8
Phila. Textile ■ ....Feb. 12
New York Tech ■ ....Feb. 15
LIU-C. W. Post ....Feb. 19
Mercy ■ ....Feb. 22

1995-96 RESULTS (3-23)

41	Le Moyne	78
52	Phila. Textile	73
59	Yeshiva ■	61
66	St. Joseph's (L.I.) ■	59
54	LIU-C. W. Post	65
60	New York Tech	109
53	St. Rose	84
73	Adelphi ■	95
66	Concordia (N.Y.)	74
70	LIU-Southampton	96
65	Queens (N.Y.) ■	73
75	Mercy	76
65	Pace ■	76
89	St. Rose	105
59	Lynn	76
69	LIU-C. W. Post ■	72
81	New York Tech	86
73	Adelphi	99
71	Concordia (N.Y.) ■	60
60	Dowling ■	73
70	LIU-Southampton ■	73
77	Phila. Textile ■	93
81	Mercy ■	74
64	Dowling	89
42	Pace	67
68	Queens (N.Y.)	77

Nickname: Lions
Colors: Maroon & White
Arena: Quealy Hall
  Capacity: 350; Year Built: 1955
AD: Bob Houlihan
SID: Bob Houlihan

MONMOUTH (ILL.)
Monmouth, IL 61462 III

Coach: Terry Glasgow
Alma Mater: Parsons '66
Record: 24 Years, W-364, L-176

1996-97 SCHEDULE

Central Mo. St. ....Nov. 23
Clarke ■ ....Nov. 30
Teikyo Marycrest ■ ....Dec. 1
MacMurray ■ ....Dec. 5
Cornell College ■ ....Dec. 7
Truman St. ....Dec. 13
Mo.-Kansas City ....Dec. 14
Teikyo Marycrest ....Dec. 21
Aurora ....Jan. 8
Cornell College ....Jan. 11
Carroll (Wis.) ■ ....Jan. 17
Beloit ....Jan. 18
Ripon ■ ....Jan. 24
Lake Forest ■ ....Jan. 25
Illinois Col. ....Jan. 29
Knox ■ ....Feb. 1
Coe ■ ....Feb. 5

Grinnell ... Feb. 8
Illinois Col. ■ ... Feb. 12
Knox ... Feb. 15
Coe ... Feb. 19
Grinnell ■ ... Feb. 22

1995-96 RESULTS (8-13)

71	Central Mo. St.	107
67	Truman St.	76
78	Webster	61
84	Iowa Wesleyan ■	81
84	MacMurray ■	65
76	Iowa Wesleyan	60
88	Grinnell	98
82	Cornell College ■	76
73	Aurora ■	78
62	Cornell College	88
80	Beloit ■	87
61	Carroll (Wis.) ■	82
57	Lake Forest	66
62	Ripon	90
66	Coe ■	68
72	Illinois Col.	64
66	Knox	72
72	Grinnell ■	86
85	Coe	86
95	Knox ■	92
83	Illinois Col. ■	75

Nickname: Fighting Scots
Colors: Crimson & White
Arena: Glennie Gymnasium
Capacity: 2,200; Year Built: 1982
AD: Terry Glasgow
SID: Chris Pio

MONMOUTH (N.J.)
West Long Branch, NJ 07764 I

Coach: Wayne Szoke
Alma Mater: Maryland '63
Record: 12 Years, W-186, L-150

1996-97 SCHEDULE
Notre Dame ... Nov. 24
Drexel ... Dec. 3
St. Peter's ■ ... Dec. 7
Princeton ■ ... Dec. 14
Manhattan ■ ... Dec. 23
South Fla. Tr. ... Dec. 27-28
Jacksonville ... Dec. 30
Marist ■ ... Jan. 4
Wagner ... Jan. 6
Rider ... Jan. 9
St. Francis (N.Y.) ... Jan. 11
Mt. St. Mary's (Md.) ■ ... Jan. 15
St. Francis (Pa.) ■ ... Jan. 18
Robert Morris ■ ... Jan. 20
LIU-Brooklyn ... Jan. 23
Fairleigh Dickinson ... Jan. 25
Marist ... Feb. 1
Wagner ■ ... Feb. 3
Rider ... Feb. 6
St. Francis (N.Y.) ... Feb. 8
Mt. St. Mary's (Md.) ■ ... Feb. 11
St. Francis (Pa.) ... Feb. 15
Robert Morris ... Feb. 17
LIU-Brooklyn ■ ... Feb. 20
Fairleigh Dickinson ■ ... Feb. 22
Northeast Conf. Tr. ... Feb. 25-Mar. 6

1995-96 RESULTS (20-10)

79	Fairfield ■	81
67	Seton Hall	83
55	Rutgers	57
78	Army ■	57
46	Manhattan	74
65	Princeton	56
73	Loyola (Md.) ■	59
53	Duke	69
79	Rider ■	54
74	St. Francis (N.Y.) ■	65
71	St. Francis (Pa.)	59
73	Robert Morris	62
82	Mt. St. Mary's (Md.) ■	77
71	LIU-Brooklyn	55
59	Fairleigh Dickinson	52
75	Marist ■	81
78	Wagner ■	68
70	Rider	66
82	St. Francis (N.Y.)	63
72	St. Francis (Pa.) ■	85
75	Robert Morris ■	54
63	Mt. St. Mary's (Md.)	73
85	LIU-Brooklyn ■	68
86	Fairleigh Dickinson ■	75
77	Wagner	68
49	Marist	56
64	Wagner ■	55
57	Marist	56
60	Rider ■	59
44	Marquette †	68

Nickname: Hawks
Colors: Royal Blue & White
Arena: Boylan Gymnasium
Capacity: 2,500; Year Built: 1965
AD: Marilyn McNeil
SID: Brian Ierardi

MONTANA
Missoula, MT 59812 I

Coach: Blaine Taylor
Alma Mater: Montana '82
Record: 5 Years, W-104, L-41

1996-97 SCHEDULE
Top of the World Cl. ... Nov. 22-24
Cal St. Sacramento ... Nov. 30
Cal St. Fullerton ■ ... Dec. 3
Montana Cl. ... Dec. 6-7
Washington St. ... Dec. 10
Gonzaga ... Dec. 14
Western Mont. ■ ... Dec. 18
Long Beach St. ■ ... Dec. 21
Texas-Arlington ... Dec. 28
Idaho St. ... Jan. 2
Weber St. ... Jan. 3
Northern Ariz. ■ ... Jan. 9
Cal St. Northridge ■ ... Jan. 11
Portland St. ... Jan. 16
Eastern Wash. ... Jan. 18
Cal St. Sacramento ■ ... Jan. 23
Montana St. ■ ... Jan. 25
Weber St. ■ ... Jan. 29
Idaho St. ■ ... Jan. 31
Cal St. Northridge ... Feb. 6
Northern Ariz. ... Feb. 8
Cal St. Sacramento ■ ... Feb. 13
Oral Roberts ... Feb. 15
Portland St. ■ ... Feb. 21
Eastern Wash. ■ ... Feb. 22
Montana St. ... Mar. 1
Big Sky Conf. Tr. ... Mar. 6-8

1995-96 RESULTS (20-8)

83	Simon Fraser ■	57
70	Mo.-Kansas City ■	60
75	Cal St. Sacramento	70
87	Cal Poly SLO ■	68
92	Fairfield ■	62
66	Arizona	84
74	Nevada ■	56
87	Washington St.	98
77	Lewis-Clark St.	59
64	Oregon ■	66
70	Cal St. Fullerton	62
74	Black Hills St. ■	72
70	St. Mary's (Cal.) ■	63
66	Northern Ariz. ■	64
84	Weber St. ■	77
65	Montana St.	72
59	Boise St. ■	69
94	Idaho St.	75
94	Idaho ■	68
71	Eastern Wash. ■	70
80	Weber St.	97
77	Northern Ariz.	46
73	Montana St. ■	64
80	Idaho St. ■	69
76	Boise St.	61
76	Eastern Wash.	69
75	Idaho	84
67	Idaho †	72

Nickname: Grizzlies
Colors: Copper, Silver & Gold
Arena: Dahlberg Arena
Capacity: 9,029; Year Built: 1953
AD: Wayne Hogan
SID: Dave Guffey

MONTANA ST.
Bozeman, MT 59717 I

Coach: Mick Durham
Alma Mater: Montana St. '79
Record: 6 Years, W-93, L-76

1996-97 SCHEDULE
Simon Fraser ■ ... Nov. 24
Hawaii-Hilo Inv. ... Nov. 29-Dec. 1
Rocky Mountain ■ ... Dec. 5
Nevada ■ ... Dec. 7
Gonzaga ... Dec. 11
James Madison ... Dec. 14
Wyoming [Billings] ... Dec. 19
Appalachian St. ■ ... Dec. 21
DePaul [Ontario] ... Dec. 23
Montana St. Cl. ... Dec. 28-29
Weber St. ... Jan. 2
Idaho St. ... Jan. 4
Cal St. Northridge ■ ... Jan. 9
Northern Ariz. ■ ... Jan. 11
Eastern Wash. ... Jan. 16
Portland St. ... Jan. 18
Cal St. Sacramento ... Jan. 22
Montana ... Jan. 25
Cal St. Sacramento ■ ... Jan. 30
Idaho St. ■ ... Feb. 1
Northern Ariz. ... Feb. 6
Cal St. Northridge ■ ... Feb. 8
Weber St. ■ ... Feb. 14
Southern Utah ... Feb. 17
Eastern Wash. ■ ... Feb. 20
Portland St. ■ ... Feb. 21
Montana ■ ... Mar. 1
Big Sky Conf. Tr. ... Mar. 6-8

1995-96 RESULTS (21-9)

79	Simon Fraser ■	65
99	Minn.-Morris ■	64
87	Alcorn St.	79
71	Eastern Mich.	95
58	Gonzaga ■	56
84	Nevada	86
81	Southern Utah ■	51
121	Alcorn St. ■	69
84	Butler ■	59
62	Drexel ■	68
67	Texas Tech	86
90	Cal St. Sacramento ■	47
96	Texas Christian	98
90	Weber St. ■	71
87	Northern Ariz. ■	58
72	Montana ■	65
89	Idaho St.	65
61	Boise St.	69
85	Eastern Wash. ■	66
78	Idaho ■	70
76	Northern Ariz.	61
90	Weber St.	94
64	Montana	73
76	Boise St. ■	65
78	Idaho St. ■	52
81	Idaho	78
92	Eastern Wash.	64
91	Idaho ■	66
81	Weber St. ■	70
55	Syracuse †	88

Nickname: Bobcats
Colors: Blue & Gold
Arena: Worthington Arena
Capacity: 7,848; Year Built: 1956
AD: Chuck Lindemann
SID: Bill Lamberty

MONT. ST.-BILLINGS
Billings, MT 59101 II

Coach: Craig Carse
Alma Mater: West Va.
Record: 5 Years, W-98, L-52

1996-97 SCHEDULE
Fort Hays St. ... Nov. 15
Carroll (Mont.) ■ ... Nov. 17
Southwest St. Cl. ... Nov. 22-23
Mont.St.-Billings Tr ... Nov. 29-30
Rocky Mountain ■ ... Dec. 4
Northern Colo. ... Dec. 7
South Dak. ... Dec. 15
Northern Colo. ■ ... Dec. 18
Northwest Nazarene ■ ... Dec. 21
Southern Ore. St. ■ ... Dec. 28
Northern Mont. ■ ... Dec. 30
Hawaii-Hilo ■ ... Jan. 9
Chaminade ■ ... Jan. 11
Western Mont. ■ ... Jan. 15
Western N.M. ■ ... Jan. 18
Rocky Mountain ... Jan. 22
Seattle Pacific ■ ... Jan. 25
Hawaii-Hilo ... Jan. 30
Chaminade ... Feb. 1
Alas. Anchorage ... Feb. 6
Alas. Fairbanks ... Feb. 8
Western N.M. ... Feb. 15
Alas. Fairbanks ■ ... Feb. 20
Alas. Anchorage ■ ... Feb. 22
Seattle Pacific ... Feb. 27

1995-96 RESULTS (19-9)

111	Western Mont. ■	72
85	Northern Mont. ■	97
77	South Dak. ■	76
92	Montana Tech	104
86	South Dak. St.	117
104	Western Mont.	69
105	Metro St. ■	80
78	Rocky Mountain ■	69
103	Colo. Christian	87
100	Metro St.	109
95	Southern Ore. St.	84
79	Oregon St.	74
90	Montana Tech ■	72
114	Hawaii-Hilo	97
115	Chaminade ■	80
94	Northern Mont.	91
100	Rocky Mountain	105
92	Western N.M. ■	70
141	Alas. Anchorage ■	114
106	Alas. Fairbanks ■	88
109	Alas. Fairbanks	103
84	Alas. Anchorage	100
66	Seattle Pacific	81
91	Seattle Pacific ■	86
60	Western N.M.	78
96	Chaminade	68
111	Hawaii-Hilo	110
80	UC Davis †	89

Nickname: Yellowjackets
Colors: Blue & Gold
Arena: Alterowitz Gymnasium
Capacity: 4,000; Year Built: 1967
AD: Gary Gray
SID: Eric Schoh

MONTCLAIR ST.
Upper Montclair, NJ 07043 III

Coach: Nick DelTufo
Alma Mater: Upsala '81
Record: 6 Years, W-49, L-58

1996-97 SCHEDULE
Western Md. Tr. ... Nov. 22-23
Wm. Paterson ... Nov. 26
Richard Stockton ... Nov. 30
Ramapo ... Dec. 4
Lehman ... Dec. 7
Rutgers-Camden ... Dec. 11
Jersey City St. ■ ... Dec. 14

Caldwell ■ ....Dec. 29
Stevens Tech ■ ....Jan. 6
Kean ■ ....Jan. 11
Staten Island ■ ....Jan. 13
Rowan ■ ....Jan. 15
Col. of New Jersey ....Jan. 18
Rutgers-Newark ■ ....Jan. 22
Ramapo ■ ....Jan. 25
Wm. Paterson ■ ....Jan. 29
Richard Stockton ....Feb. 1
Rowan ■ ....Feb. 5
Kean ....Feb. 8
Rutgers-Camden ■ ....Feb. 12
Jersey City St. ....Feb. 15
Rutgers-Newark ....Feb. 19
Col. of New Jersey ■ ....Feb. 22

1995-96 RESULTS (9-15)

89	Beaver †	.95
74	King's (Pa.) †	.70
53	Col. of New Jersey ■	.76
70	Kean	.83
67	Ramapo	.59
80	Jersey City St.	.79
61	Pitt.-Bradford †	.74
74	Potsdam St. †	.65
67	Richard Stockton ■	.88
74	Staten Island	.88
74	Rowan ■	.108
67	Clark (Mass.)	.64
71	Rutgers-Newark ■	.85
85	Rutgers-Camden ■	.49
77	Wm. Paterson	.75
45	Ramapo ■	.64
51	Col. of New Jersey	.62
80	Kean	.70
67	Rutgers-Newark ■	.83
52	Richard Stockton	.68
85	Jersey City St. ■	.93
81	Rowan	.110
72	Wm. Paterson ■	.87
79	Rutgers-Camden	.76

Nickname: Red Hawks
Colors: Scarlet & White
Arena: Panzer Gymnasium
Capacity: 1,200; Year Built: 1956
AD: Gregory Lockard
SID: Al Langer

MOORHEAD ST.
Moorhead, MN 56560 II

Coach: Dave Schellhase
Alma Mater: Purdue '66
Record: 18 Years, W-310, L-229

1996-97 SCHEDULE

Wis.-Stevens Pt. Cl. ....Nov. 22-23
Concordia-M'head ■ ....Nov. 26
Northern St. Tr. ....Nov. 29-30
St. Cloud St. ....Dec. 3
Minn.-Crookston ■ ....Dec. 5
North Dak. ■ ....Dec. 7
Valley City St. ....Dec. 10
Mayville St. ■ ....Dec. 12
North Dak. St. ....Dec. 14
North Dakota Cl. ....Dec. 21-22
Jamestown ....Jan. 4
Minn.-Morris ■ ....Jan. 11
Northern St. ■ ....Jan. 15
Bemidji St. ....Jan. 18
Winona St. ■ ....Jan. 25
Mayville St. ■ ....Jan. 27
Southwest St. ....Jan. 29
Minn.-Duluth ....Feb. 1
Northern St. ....Feb. 5
Minn.-Morris ....Feb. 8
Bemidji St. ■ ....Feb. 15
Southwest St. ■ ....Feb. 19
Winona St. ....Feb. 22
Minn.-Duluth ....Feb. 26

1995-96 RESULTS (19-8)

82	Augustana (S.D.)	.76
84	Northwest Mo. St. †	.74
79	Mayville St. ■	.77
63	Michigan Tech †	.71

77	Chadron St. †	.96
83	Jamestown	.88
96	North Dak. St. ■	.95
102	Minn.-Crookston	.83
116	Valley City St. ■	.68
101	St. Cloud St. ■	.90
89	Concordia-M'head	.83
100	Mayville St.	.90
73	North Dak.	.94
102	Wayne St. (Neb.)	.98
66	Minn.-Morris	.63
85	Bemidji St. ■	.65
87	Wayne St. (Neb.) ■	.70
87	Winona St.	.63
97	Southwest St. ■	.98
100	Minn.-Duluth	.89
76	Northern St.	.90
92	Bemidji St.	.81
101	Southwest St.	.98
113	Winona St. ■	.81
106	Minn.-Morris ■	.98
88	Northern St.	.98
79	Minn.-Duluth ■	.82

Nickname: Dragons
Colors: Scarlet & White
Arena: Alex Nemzek Hall
Capacity: 3,400; Year Built: 1960
AD: Katy Wilson
SID: Larry Scott

MORAVIAN
Bethlehem, PA 18018 III

Coach: Jim Walker
Alma Mater: Gettysburg '65
Record: 16 Years, W-245, L-186

1996-97 SCHEDULE

Trinity (Tex.) Inv. ....Nov. 22-23
Allentown ■ ....Nov. 26
Susquehanna ....Dec. 3
Lebanon Valley ■ ....Dec. 7
Drew ■ ....Dec. 10
Albright ....Dec. 12
Moravian Cl. ....Jan. 4-5
Scranton ....Jan. 8
Delaware Valley ■ ....Jan. 11
Muhlenberg ....Jan. 14
Widener ■ ....Jan. 16
Juniata ....Jan. 18
Messiah ....Jan. 21
Elizabethtown ■ ....Jan. 25
Susquehanna ■ ....Jan. 29
Lebanon Valley ....Feb. 1
Albright ■ ....Feb. 5
Wilkes ■ ....Feb. 8
Widener ....Feb. 12
Juniata ■ ....Feb. 15
Messiah ■ ....Feb. 19
Elizabethtown ....Feb. 22

1995-96 RESULTS (17-8)

54	Randolph-Macon †	.68
66	Brockport St. †	.63
75	Allentown	.64
81	Susquehanna ■	.71
68	Lebanon Valley	.65
79	Albright ■	.59
73	Muhlenberg	.66
74	Drew	.78
105	Western Md. ■	.54
61	Swarthmore	.45
57	Widener	.72
91	Juniata ■	.67
68	Messiah ■	.55
76	Elizabethtown	.62
72	Scranton ■	.58
71	Susquehanna	.80
79	Lebanon Valley ■	.62
82	Albright	.90
93	Delaware Valley ■	.66
58	Wilkes	.64
67	Widener ■	.64
66	Juniata	.73
69	Messiah	.60
61	Elizabethtown ■	.60

59	Drew ■	.77

Nickname: Greyhounds
Colors: Blue & Grey
Arena: Johnston Hall
Capacity: 1,600; Year Built: 1952
AD: John Makuvek
SID: Mike Warwick

MOREHEAD ST.
Morehead, KY 40351 I

Coach: Dick Fick
Alma Mater: Lewis '75
Record: 5 Years, W-56, L-82

1996-97 SCHEDULE

Tennessee ....Nov. 24
Asbury ■ ....Nov. 30
George Mason ....Dec. 3
Southwest Mo. St. Cl. ....Dec. 6-7
Marshall ....Dec. 14
Dayton ....Dec. 22
Marion ....Dec. 23
Tennessee Tech ■ ....Jan. 4
Middle Tenn. St. ■ ....Jan. 6
Eastern Ill. ....Jan. 11
Southeast Mo. St. ....Jan. 13
Eastern Ky. ■ ....Jan. 16
Tenn.-Martin ■ ....Jan. 18
Murray St. ■ ....Jan. 20
Tennessee St. ....Jan. 25
Austin Peay ....Jan. 27
Middle Tenn. St. ....Jan. 30
Tennessee Tech ....Feb. 3
Southeast Mo. St. ■ ....Feb. 8
Eastern Ill. ■ ....Feb. 10
Eastern Ky. ....Feb. 13
Murray St. ....Feb. 15
Tenn.-Martin ....Feb. 17
Tennessee St. ■ ....Feb. 20
Austin Peay ■ ....Feb. 22
Ohio Valley Conf. Tr. ......Feb. 25-Mar. 1

1995-96 RESULTS (7-20)

113	Berea ■	.92
84	Kent	.108
115	Centre ■	.68
110	Spalding ■	.97
61	Louisville	.119
85	Marshall ■	.92
32	Kentucky	.96
89	Thomas More ■	.85
57	Iowa	.82
83	George Mason ■	.74
68	Eastern Ky. ■	.64
64	Southeast Mo. St. ■	.81
64	Eastern Ky.	.76
62	Tenn.-Martin ■	.74
70	Murray St.	.98
68	Middle Tenn. St. ■	.59
65	Austin Peay ■	.71
72	Tennessee Tech	.85
76	Tennessee St.	.86
74	Southeast Mo. St.	.76
66	Murray St. ■	.81
67	Tenn.-Martin ■	.77
78	Austin Peay	.89
71	Middle Tenn. St.	.73
60	Tennessee St.	.65
78	Tennessee Tech ■	.88
60	Tennessee St.	.71

Nickname: Eagles
Colors: Blue & Gold
Arena: Ellis T. Johnson Arena
Capacity: 6,500; Year Built: 1981
AD: Steve Hamilton
SID: Randy Stacy

MOREHOUSE
Atlanta, GA 30314 II

Coach: Arthur McAfee
Alma Mater: Wichita St. '51
Record: 36 Years, W-459, L-459

1996-97 SCHEDULE

Savannah St. ■ ....Nov. 16
Paine ....Nov. 19
Eckerd ■ ....Nov. 23
Alabama A&M ■ ....Nov. 26
Howard ....Nov. 30
Miles ....Dec. 5
LeMoyne-Owen ■ ....Dec. 7
Rollins ■ ....Dec. 14
Kentucky St. ■ ....Dec. 21
Dillard ....Jan. 4
Mississippi Col. ....Jan. 6
Fort Valley St. ■ ....Jan. 9
Tuskegee ....Jan. 11
Johnson Smith ■ ....Jan. 15
Albany St. (Ga.) ■ ....Jan. 18
Alabama A&M. ....Jan. 23
Kentucky St. ....Jan. 25
Clark Atlanta ■ ....Jan. 29
Tuskegee ■ ....Feb. 1
Augusta St. ■ ....Feb. 3
Morris Brown ....Feb. 8
Miles ■ ....Feb. 11
LeMoyne-Owen ....Feb. 18
Fisk ....Feb. 22

1995-96 RESULTS (18-9)

65	Mississippi Col.	.63
90	Henderson St. †	.82
63	Alabama A&M ■	.77
65	Howard ■	.62
73	LeMoyne-Owen	.78
90	Miles	.96
91	Kentucky St. ■	.73
107	Dist. Columbia †	.96
75	Augusta St.	.86
76	Eckerd	.86
70	Albany St. (Ga.)	.68
85	Fort Valley St.	.91
86	Tuskegee ■	.82
74	Savannah St.	.69
76	Paine	.73
125	Fisk	.87
66	Kentucky St.	.66
100	Clark Atlanta ■	.93
80	Morris Brown ■	.70
76	Alabama A&M ■	.83
78	Miles ■	.77
90	LeMoyne-Owen ■	.78
84	Tuskegee	.66
121	Fisk ■	.73
77	Paine †	.66
81	Tuskegee †	.69
70	Alabama A&M †	.92

Nickname: Maroon Tigers
Colors: Maroon & White
Arena: To be named
Capacity: 6,000; Year Built: 1996
AD: Arthur McAfee
SID: James Nix

MORGAN ST.
Baltimore, MD 21239 I

Coach: Chris Fuller
Alma Mater: Buffalo '73
Record: 1 Year, W-7, L-20

1996-97 SCHEDULE

Georgia Tech ....Nov. 26
Kansas St. ....Nov. 30
St. Francis (N.Y.) ■ ....Dec. 7
St. Bonaventure ....Dec. 11
Buffalo ....Dec. 13
Georgetown ....Dec. 21
UCLA ....Dec. 28
Mississippi ....Dec. 31
North Caro. A&T ....Jan. 11
South Caro. St. ....Jan. 13
Md.-East. Shore ....Jan. 16
Delaware St. ■ ....Jan. 18
Bethune-Cookman ■ ....Jan. 23
Hampton ....Jan. 25
Florida A&M ■ ....Jan. 27
Md.-East. Shore ....Jan. 30
Coppin St. ■ ....Feb. 1

Howard ■		Feb. 3
Coppin St. ■		Feb. 8
Hampton ■		Feb. 10
Bethune-Cookman ■		Feb. 13
Florida A&M ■		Feb. 17
Delaware St. ■		Feb. 20
North Caro. A&T ■		Feb. 22
South Caro. St. ■		Feb. 24
Howard		Mar. 1
Mid-Eastern Conf. Tr.		Mar. 5-8

1995-96 RESULTS (7-20)

65	Penn St.	90
54	Wis.-Green Bay	76
69	St. Francis (N.Y.)	87
57	Md.-Balt. County ■	56
56	Creighton	63
60	Kansas St.	69
60	Georgetown	104
80	West Va.	108
69	Brigham Young	110
59	Xavier (Ohio)	78
58	Marquette	98
56	South Caro. St. ■	72
79	Md.-East. Shore ■	66
57	Florida A&M	54
58	Bethune-Cookman	68
73	Howard ■	64
77	Coppin St.	78
66	Delaware St. ■	75
68	Coppin St. ■	91
90	Howard	92
68	Delaware St.	75
81	Florida A&M ■	74
70	Bethune-Cookman ■	78
77	North Caro. A&T	74
78	South Caro. St.	92
78	North Caro. A&T ■	74
90	Md.-East. Shore	92

Nickname: Bears
Colors: Blue & Orange
Arena: Hill Field House
   Capacity: 6,500; Year Built: 1975
AD: Garnett Purnell
SID: Joseph McIver

MORNINGSIDE

Sioux City, IA 51106 II

Coach: Jerry Schmutte
Alma Mater: Neb. Wesleyan '67
Record: 15 Years, W-277, L-146

1996-97 SCHEDULE

Rocky Mountain ■		Nov. 23
St. Leo		Nov. 27
Florida Tech Cl.		Nov. 29-30
Sioux Falls ■		Dec. 7
Buena Vista		Dec. 9
Briar Cliff ■		Dec. 13
Dana ■		Dec. 15
Doane ■		Dec. 21
Briar Cliff ■		Dec. 23
Neb.-Omaha ■		Dec. 28
Northern Colo. ■		Dec. 29
North Dak. St.		Jan. 3
North Dak.		Jan. 4
South Dak. ■		Jan. 11
Mankato St. ■		Jan. 17
St. Cloud St. ■		Jan. 18
South Dak. St.		Jan. 24
Augustana (S.D.)		Jan. 25
North Dak. ■		Jan. 31
North Dak. St. ■		Feb. 1
South Dak. ■		Feb. 8
St. Cloud St.		Feb. 14
Mankato St.		Feb. 15
Augustana (S.D.) ■		Feb. 21
South Dak. St. ■		Feb. 22
Northern Colo.		Feb. 28
Neb.-Omaha		Mar. 1

1995-96 RESULTS (18-9)

135	Teikyo Westmar ■	74
91	Wayne St. (Neb.)	97
107	Hastings ■	87

113	Midland Lutheran ■	76
93	Briar Cliff ■	79
118	Grand View ■	64
85	Drury †	63
80	Southwest Baptist †	71
94	Briar Cliff †	80
79	North Dak. St. ■	69
88	North Dak. ■	74
75	South Dak. ■	96
83	Mankato St. ■	72
82	St. Cloud St. ■	80
83	South Dak. St. ■	99
85	Augustana (S.D.) ■	86
82	Neb.-Omaha ■	75
69	Northern Colo. ■	84
57	South Dak.	86
98	St. Cloud St.	82
93	Mankato St.	83
90	Augustana (S.D.)	77
78	South Dak. St.	94
91	Northern Colo. ■	62
89	Neb.-Omaha ■	79
98	North Dak.	107
85	North Dak. St.	107

Nickname: Chiefs
Colors: Maroon & White
Arena: Allee Gymnasium
   Capacity: 3,000; Year Built: 1949
AD: Bill Goldring
SID: Ron Christian

MORRIS BROWN

Atlanta, GA 30314 II

Coach: Ajac Triplett
Alma Mater: Western Mich. '68
Record: 18 Years, W-235, L-249

1996-97 SCHEDULE

Morris Brown Tr.		Nov. 15-16
Tuskegee		Nov. 19
LeMoyne-Owen ■		Dec. 2
Clark Atlanta Cl.		Dec. 6-7
Bethune-Cookman		Dec. 10
Albany St. (Ga.)		Dec. 14
Barbados Tr.		Dec. 28-Jan. 2
Clark Atlanta		Jan. 11
Miles		Jan. 15
Kentucky St.		Jan. 18
Alabama A&M		Jan. 20
Paine		Jan. 22
Albany St. (Ga.) ■		Jan. 25
Savannah St. ■		Jan. 27
Paine		Jan. 29
Clark Atlanta ■		Feb. 1
Morehouse ■		Feb. 8
Fort Valley St. ■		Feb. 10
Alabama A&M ■		Feb. 12
Savannah St. ■		Feb. 15
Fort Valley St.		Feb. 19

1995-96 RESULTS (11-15)

88	Talladega ■	83
77	Claflin ■	68
80	Georgia St.	78
60	Paine	65
86	Xavier (La.) †	83
68	Winston-Salem †	57
61	Bethune-Cookman	67
78	Alabama A&M ■	85
64	Virginia Union	105
62	Virginia St. †	74
68	Clark Atlanta ■	87
73	Miles	62
72	LeMoyne-Owen ■	87
62	Alabama A&M ■	82
66	Fort Valley St. ■	60
65	Paine	60
70	Savannah St. ■	78
65	Tuskegee ■	72
78	Clark Atlanta	89
62	Albany St. (Ga.) ■	64
70	Morehouse	80
70	Savannah St.	62
58	Albany St. (Ga.)	70
93	Fort Valley St.	87

81	Kentucky St. ■	65
67	Fort Valley St. ■	72

Nickname: Wolverines
Colors: Purple & Black
Arena: John H. Lewis Gym
   Capacity: 4,500; Year Built: 1970
AD: Gene Bright
SID: Antoine Bell

MOUNT OLIVE

Mount Olive, NC 28365 II

Coach: Bill Cligan
Alma Mater: Northeastern St.
Record: 6 Years, W-97, L-75

1996-97 SCHEDULE

Mt. Olive Tr.		Nov. 22-23
Belmont Abbey		Nov. 26
Coastal Caro.		Dec. 4
N.C.-Pembroke ■		Dec. 9
Erskine ■		Dec. 14
Newport News App.		Jan. 6
Longwood		Jan. 9
Pfeiffer ■		Jan. 11
Barton		Jan. 13
Queens (N.C.)		Jan. 16
St. Andrews		Jan. 18
Coker ■		Jan. 20
Lees-McRae ■		Jan. 22
Coker		Jan. 25
High Point ■		Jan. 27
Belmont Abbey ■		Jan. 29
Pfeiffer		Feb. 1
Lees-McRae ■		Feb. 3
Barton ■		Feb. 5
High Point		Feb. 8
Longwood ■		Feb. 10
Erskine		Feb. 13
Queens (N.C.) ■		Feb. 19
St. Andrews ■		Feb. 22

1995-96 RESULTS (16-12)

80	Brewton Parker ■	71
69	N.C.-Pembroke	70
91	Averett	62
60	Concordia (N.Y.) ■	56
83	Lenoir-Rhyne ■	73
90	Newport News App. ■	73
76	Barton	71
68	Coker	77
79	Newport News App.	64
61	Longwood ■	64
86	Belmont Abbey ■	71
81	Erskine ■	71
68	Queens (N.C.) ■	74
93	High Point ■	78
86	Lees-McRae	89
86	Dist. Columbia	82
80	St. Andrews ■	72
60	Pfeiffer	76
66	Erskine	62
70	Pfeiffer ■	69
80	Longwood	72
61	Barton ■	81
90	Belmont Abbey	94
66	Coker ■	76
81	Queens (N.C.)	92
71	High Point	91
57	Coker †	54
80	High Point	85

Nickname: Trojans
Colors: Forest Green & White
Arena: College Hall
   Capacity: 2,000; Year Built: 1987
AD: Mac Cassell
SID: To be named

MT. ST. MARY (N.Y.)

Newburgh, NY 12550 III

Coach: Duane Davis
Alma Mater: Empire St. '69
Record: 1 Year, W-15, L-10

1996-97 SCHEDULE

Bard Tr.		Nov. 22-23
Purchase St.		Nov. 25
N.J. Inst. of Tech.		Dec. 3
Mt. St. Mary (NY) Tr		Dec. 7-8
Lehman ■		Dec. 10
Centenary (N.J.)		Dec. 12
Albertus Magnus		Jan. 6
Staten Island		Jan. 11
Rensselaer		Jan. 15
Mt. St. Vincent ■		Jan. 17
Medgar Evers ■		Jan. 21
St. Joseph's (L.I.)		Jan. 23
Maritime (N.Y.)		Jan. 27
Manhattanville ■		Jan. 29
Merchant Marine ■		Feb. 1
Mt. St. Vincent		Feb. 4
Maritime (N.Y.) ■		Feb. 6
Manhattanville		Feb. 8
N.J. Inst. of Tech. ■		Feb. 12
Hunter ■		Feb. 15
John Jay		Feb. 17
Centenary (N.J.) ■		Feb. 20
Merchant Marine		Feb. 25

1995-96 RESULTS (15-10)

60	New Paltz St.	63
102	Bard †	26
99	St. Joseph's (L.I.) ■	48
93	N.J. Inst. of Tech.	95
72	Lehman	81
95	Centenary (N.J.)	103
83	Mt. St. Vincent ■	86
102	Albertus Magnus ■	90
63	Bowdoin †	62
83	Catholic	85
79	Mt. St. Vincent	93
105	Medgar Evers	81
74	St. Joseph's (L.I.)	63
68	Manhattanville ■	75
62	Merchant Marine	66
96	Purchase St. ■	49
93	Staten Island ■	88
80	Manhattanville	68
93	N.J. Inst. of Tech. ■	82
85	Hunter	80
88	John Jay ■	82
94	Albany Pharmacy ■	87
90	Merchant Marine ■	74
91	Centenary (N.J.) ■	78
95	Old Westbury ■	97

Nickname: Knights
Colors: Royal Blue & Gold
Arena: Kaplan Recreation Center
   Capacity: 1,500; Year Built: 1992
AD: John Wright
SID: Richard Johnson

MT. ST. MARY'S (MD.)

Emmitsburg, MD 21727 I

Coach: James Phelan
Alma Mater: La Salle '51
Record: 42 Years, W-758, L-400

1996-97 SCHEDULE

Penn St.		Nov. 23
La Salle ■		Nov. 30
Howard		Dec. 3
Loyola (Md.)		Dec. 7
Villanova		Dec. 21
Pittsburgh		Dec. 23
Mt. St. Mary's Cl.		Dec. 27-28
Fairleigh Dickinson		Jan. 4
Marist		Jan. 6
LIU-Brooklyn ■		Jan. 9
Wagner		Jan. 11
Monmouth (N.J.) ■		Jan. 15
Rider		Jan. 18
St. Francis (N.Y.) ■		Jan. 20
Robert Morris		Jan. 23
St. Francis (Pa.)		Jan. 25
Fairleigh Dickinson ■		Feb. 1
Marist ■		Feb. 3
LIU-Brooklyn		Feb. 6

Wagner ■ ....Feb. 8
Monmouth (N.J.) ....Feb. 11
Rider ....Feb. 15
St. Francis (N.Y.) ....Feb. 17
Robert Morris ■ ....Feb. 20
St. Francis (Pa.) ■ ....Feb. 22
Northeast Conf. Tr. ....Feb. 25-Mar. 6

1995-96 RESULTS (21-8)
62	Wake Forest	75
72	Liberty	87
81	La Salle	66
74	Howard	57
83	Loyola (Md.) ■	73
71	Georgia Tech	69
62	Minnesota	87
75	Tulane	100
92	LIU-Brooklyn ■	74
78	Rider	56
50	St. Francis (N.Y.)	60
77	Monmouth (N.J.)	82
84	Robert Morris ■	76
73	St. Francis (Pa.) ■	44
76	Fairleigh Dickinson	73
61	Marist	55
73	Wagner	70
99	LIU-Brooklyn	77
89	Wagner ■	69
80	Rider ■	70
85	St. Francis (N.Y.) ■	56
73	Monmouth (N.J.) ■	63
80	Robert Morris	69
72	St. Francis (Pa.)	56
74	Marist ■	64
85	Fairleigh Dickinson ■	66
93	LIU-Brooklyn ■	58
70	Rider	74
49	Illinois St.	73

Nickname: Mountaineers
Colors: Blue & White
Arena: Knott ARCC
  Capacity: 3,196; Year Built: 1987
AD: Harold P. Menninger
SID: Eric Kloiber

MT. ST. VINCENT
Bronx, NY 10471 III

Coach: Chuck Mancuso
Alma Mater: Concordia (N.Y.) '81
Record: 15 Years, W-239, L-143

1996-97 SCHEDULE
Merchant Marine ....Nov. 26
Stevens Tech ....Dec. 2
Maritime (N.Y.) ....Dec. 5
Bard ....Dec. 10
Manhattanville ....Dec. 14
Yeshiva ....Dec. 18
Mt. St. Vincent Tr. ....Dec. 28-29
N.J. Inst. of Tech. ■ ....Jan. 4
St. Joe's-Brooklyn ....Jan. 7
Gallaudet ....Jan. 10
Merchant Marine ■ ....Jan. 13
Mt. St. Mary (N.Y.) ■ ....Jan. 17
Vassar ■ ....Jan. 20
Lehman ....Jan. 23
N.J. Inst. of Tech. ....Jan. 27
St. Joseph's (L.I.) ....Jan. 29
Baruch ....Feb. 1
Mt. St. Mary (N.Y.) ■ ....Feb. 4
Maritime (N.Y.) ■ ....Feb. 8
Manhattanville ■ ....Feb. 11
Polytechnic (N.Y.) ....Feb. 13
Bard ■ ....Feb. 17
St. Joe's-Brooklyn ■ ....Feb. 19

1995-96 RESULTS (18-9)
69	Merchant Marine ■	65
89	Stevens Tech	78
85	Maritime (N.Y.) ■	69
98	Manhattanville ■	81
83	Medgar Evers	84
111	Bard	65
86	Mt. St. Mary (N.Y.)	83
74	Yeshiva	62
73	N.J. Inst. of Tech.	78
84	St. Joe's-Brooklyn ■	54
72	Old Westbury ■	66
73	Centenary (N.J.)	83
93	Mt. St. Mary (N.Y.) ■	79
72	Merchant Marine	76
82	CCNY	71
81	N.J. Inst. of Tech.	80
115	Bard	50
65	Maritime (N.Y.) ■	76
89	Pratt	30
81	Vassar	89
105	St. Joseph's (L.I.) ■	51
63	Manhattanville	66
67	Polytechnic (N.Y.)	61
76	Centenary (N.J.) ■	58
73	Yeshiva †	57
64	N.J. Inst. of Tech. †	74
54	Richard Stockton	80

Nickname: Dolphins
Colors: Blue, White & Gold
Arena: Cardinal Hayes Gymnasium
  Capacity: 450; Year Built: 1910
AD: Chuck Mancuso
SID: Chuck Mancuso

MOUNT UNION
Alliance, OH 44601 III

Coach: Lee Hood
Alma Mater: Ohio Northern '82
Record: 5 Years, W-43, L-58

1996-97 SCHEDULE
Pitt.-Bradford Cl. ....Nov. 22-23
Rochester Inv. ....Nov. 30-Dec. 1
Baldwin-Wallace ■ ....Dec. 4
Ohio Northern ....Dec. 7
John Carroll ....Dec. 14
Heidelberg ....Dec. 18
Centre Tr. ....Dec. 28-29
Marietta ....Jan. 8
Capital ■ ....Jan. 11
Muskingum ....Jan. 15
Otterbein ....Jan. 18
Hiram ....Jan. 22
Capital ....Jan. 25
Muskingum ■ ....Jan. 29
Otterbein ....Feb. 1
Hiram ■ ....Feb. 5
Ohio Northern ■ ....Feb. 8
Baldwin-Wallace ....Feb. 12
John Carroll ■ ....Feb. 15
Marietta ■ ....Feb. 19
Heidelberg ....Feb. 22

1995-96 RESULTS (13-12)
72	Juniata ■	63
78	Olivet †	64
83	Southern Colo. †	95
81	Evangel	61
82	Capital ■	78
68	John Carroll	75
78	Muskingum	80
82	Otterbein ■	80
59	Grove City †	53
51	Wooster	56
76	Ohio Northern	71
64	Hiram	68
58	Baldwin-Wallace ■	61
70	Heidelberg ■	62
59	Marietta	48
54	Hiram	66
77	Baldwin-Wallace	67
51	Muskingum	47
58	John Carroll ■	61
68	Otterbein	79
68	Ohio Northern ■	70
66	Capital	89
66	Marietta ■	62
74	Heidelberg	68
74	Baldwin-Wallace	81

Nickname: Purple Raiders
Colors: Purple & White
Arena: Timken P. E. Building
Capacity: 3,200; Year Built: 1970
AD: Larry Kehres
SID: Michael De Matteis

MUHLENBERG
Allentown, PA 18104 III

Coach: Dave Madeira
Alma Mater: Concord '69
Record: 9 Years, W-133, L-95

1996-97 SCHEDULE
Muhlenberg Tr. ....Nov. 22-23
King's (Pa.) ....Nov. 26
Phila. Pharmacy ■ ....Dec. 4
Gettysburg ....Dec. 7
Susquehanna Cl. ....Dec. 20-21
Moravian Cl. ....Jan. 4-5
Allentown ....Jan. 8
Western Md. ■ ....Jan. 11
Moravian ....Jan. 14
Washington (Md.) ....Jan. 18
Swarthmore ....Jan. 22
Johns Hopkins ....Jan. 25
Haverford ....Jan. 28
Elizabethtown ....Jan. 30
Dickinson ■ ....Feb. 1
Ursinus ■ ....Feb. 5
Washington (Md.) ■ ....Feb. 8
Frank. & Marsh. ....Feb. 12
Haverford ■ ....Feb. 15
Swarthmore ■ ....Feb. 19
Ursinus ....Feb. 22

1995-96 RESULTS (13-12)
71	Brockport St. ■	66
65	Randolph-Macon	62
89	Albright	83
75	Gettysburg ■	66
66	Moravian	73
78	Western Md.	69
58	Lehigh	76
63	Col. of New Jersey †	79
46	Wis.-Platteville †	73
76	Messiah †	72
52	Allentown ■	55
81	Washington (Md.)	82
80	Gwynedd-Mercy ■	61
78	Swarthmore	65
53	Johns Hopkins ■	63
68	Haverford ■	74
68	Elizabethtown ■	75
77	Dickinson	69
71	Ursinus	80
77	Washington (Md.) ■	63
66	Frank. & Marsh. ■	49
66	Haverford	76
57	Swarthmore	53
67	Ursinus ■	65
59	Frank. & Marsh.	72

Nickname: Mules
Colors: Carinal & Grey
Arena: Memorial Hall
  Capacity: 3,529; Year Built: 1954
AD: Connie Kunda
SID: Mike Falk

MURRAY ST.
Murray, KY 42071 I

Coach: Mark Gottfried
Alma Mater: Alabama '87
Record: 1 Year, W-19, L-10

1996-97 SCHEDULE
Belmont ■ ....Nov. 23
IU/PU-Indianapolis ■ ....Nov. 26
Middle Tenn. St. ....Dec. 2
Alcorn St. ■ ....Dec. 5
Campbellsville ■ ....Dec. 7
Arkansas St. ....Dec. 14
St. Louis ....Dec. 18
Auburn [Birmingham] ....Dec. 21
Alcorn St. ....Dec. 28
Tenn.-Martin ....Jan. 6
Eastern Ill. ....Jan. 9
Austin Peay ■ ....Jan. 11
Tennessee St. ■ ....Jan. 13
Eastern Ky. ....Jan. 18
Morehead St. ....Jan. 20
Southeast Mo. St. ■ ....Jan. 23
Middle Tenn. St. ■ ....Jan. 25
Tennessee Tech ....Jan. 27
Tenn.-Martin ■ ....Feb. 1
Southeast Mo. St. ....Feb. 6
Tennessee St. ....Feb. 8
Austin Peay ....Feb. 10
Tennessee Tech ■ ....Feb. 13
Morehead St. ■ ....Feb. 15
Eastern Ky. ■ ....Feb. 17
Eastern Ill. ■ ....Feb. 20
Ohio Valley Conf. Tr. ....Feb. 25-Mar. 1

1995-96 RESULTS (19-10)
108	Berry ■	62
98	Western Mich. ■	88
76	Drexel †	75
76	Purdue	88
94	Arkansas St. ■	82
71	Western Mich.	83
108	Washington (Mo.) ■	87
72	Louisville	81
81	Ashland ■	58
63	Tennessee Tech	64
71	Tennessee St.	67
73	Eastern Ky.	64
98	Morehead St. ■	70
80	Tenn.-Martin ■	68
68	St. Louis	74
71	Austin Peay	64
73	Middle Tenn. St.	72
81	Southeast Mo. St. ■	77
72	Tennessee St. ■	78
81	Morehead St.	68
85	Eastern Ky.	62
87	Tenn.-Martin ■	81
76	Tennessee Tech	77
79	Southeast Mo. St.	61
80	Middle Tenn. St.	67
65	Austin Peay ■	80
85	Tennessee Tech †	71
68	Austin Peay †	70
85	Missouri	89

Nickname: Racers
Colors: Blue & Gold
Arena: Racer Arena
  Capacity: 5,550; Year Built: 1954
AD: Mike Strickland
SID: Brian Morgan

MUSKINGUM
New Concord, OH 43762 III

Coach: Jim Burson
Alma Mater: Muskingum '63
Record: 29 Years, W-423, L-308

1996-97 SCHEDULE
Muhlenberg Tr. ....Nov. 22-23
Wash. & Jeff. ■ ....Nov. 26
Otterbein ....Dec. 5
Heidelberg ■ ....Dec. 7
Hiram ....Dec. 14
Baldwin-Wallace ■ ....Dec. 18
Muskingum Tr. ....Dec. 21-22
Muskingham Tr. ....Dec. 21-22
Wilmington (Ohio) ....Jan. 4
Ohio Northern ....Jan. 8
John Carroll ....Jan. 11
Mount Union ■ ....Jan. 15
Capital ....Jan. 18
Marietta ....Jan. 22
John Carroll ■ ....Jan. 25
Mount Union ....Jan. 29
Capital ■ ....Feb. 1
Marietta ■ ....Feb. 5
Heidelberg ....Feb. 8
Otterbein ■ ....Feb. 12
Hiram ■ ....Feb. 15
Ohio Northern ■ ....Feb. 19
Baldwin-Wallace ....Feb. 22

1995-96 RESULTS (10-17)

62	Wilmington (Ohio) ■	58
58	Wash. & Jeff. ■	54
66	John Carroll ■	78
61	Marietta	65
80	Mount Union ■	78
63	Ohio Northern ■	70
77	Frostburg St. ■	54
57	Wooster ■	64
53	Wis.-Whitewater †	65
66	Wabash †	71
60	Baldwin-Wallace ■	70
56	Heidelberg	59
84	Hiram ■	61
84	Capital	85
59	Otterbein ■	43
92	Heidelberg ■	75
55	Hiram	56
47	Mount Union ■	51
52	Marietta ■	50
57	Ohio Northern ■	63
63	Baldwin-Wallace ■	77
65	John Carroll ■	66
63	Otterbein	92
61	Capital ■	75
69	Hiram	61
93	John Carroll	89
48	Baldwin-Wallace †	73

Nickname: Fighting Muskies
Colors: Black & Magenta
Arena: Muskingum Recreation Center
  Capacity: 3,000; Year Built: 1986
AD: Jeff Heacock
SID: Craig McKendry

NAVY
Annapolis, MD 21402 I

Coach: Don DeVoe
Alma Mater: Ohio St. '64
Record: 23 Years, W-388, L-281

1996-97 SCHEDULE

Coast Guard ■	Nov. 22
Towson St.	Nov. 24
Pittsburgh ■	Nov. 26
Air Force	Nov. 30
New Hampshire ■	Dec. 3
VMI	Dec. 5
Wofford	Dec. 7
Gettysburg ■	Dec. 9
Dartmouth ■	Dec. 21
St. Bonaventure	Dec. 23
Stanford	Dec. 28
Rice	Dec. 30
Harvard ■	Jan. 2
Army	Jan. 8
Colgate	Jan. 11
William & Mary ■	Jan. 13
Lehigh	Jan. 15
Lafayette ■	Jan. 18
Bucknell	Jan. 22
Holy Cross ■	Jan. 29
Army	Feb. 1
Colgate ■	Feb. 5
Lehigh ■	Feb. 8
Lafayette	Feb. 12
Bucknell ■	Feb. 15
Holy Cross	Feb. 22
Patriot Conf. Tr.	Mar. 1-5

1995-96 RESULTS (15-12)

89	Air Force ■	87
60	Towson St. ■	74
66	New Hampshire ■	63
84	St. Mary's (Md.) ■	59
69	Air Force	75
93	Gettysburg ■	62
62	Stanford ■	80
64	St. Bonaventure ■	68
48	Harvard	49
64	Rice ■	56
58	Davidson	87
60	Bucknell ■	57
73	Lafayette	64

48	William & Mary	69
67	Holy Cross ■	63
67	Colgate ■	89
75	Army ■	44
48	Dartmouth	59
69	Lehigh	63
60	Bucknell ■	72
61	Lafayette ■	59
67	Holy Cross	77
60	Colgate	57
54	Army	51
73	Lehigh ■	59
73	Wofford ■	55
58	Army †	64

Nickname: Midshipmen
Colors: Navy Blue & Gold
Arena: Alumni Hall
  Capacity: 5,710; Year Built: 1991
AD: Jack Lengyel
SID: Scott Strasemeier

NAZARETH
Rochester, NY 14610 III

Coach: Mike Daley
Alma Mater: St. Bonaventure '66
Record: 10 Years, W-134, L-125

1996-97 SCHEDULE

Oswego St.	Nov. 26
Nazareth Tr.	Nov. 30-Dec. 1
Rochester	Dec. 4
Roberts Wesleyan ■	Dec. 14
Rochester Inst.	Jan. 8
St. Lawrence ■	Jan. 10
Clarkson ■	Jan. 11
Chase Rochester Tr.	Jan. 15-18
Hilbert	Jan. 21
Elmira	Jan. 24
Ithaca	Jan. 25
Alfred	Jan. 28
Hilbert ■	Feb. 4
Utica ■	Feb. 7
Hartwick ■	Feb. 8
Ithaca ■	Feb. 14
Elmira ■	Feb. 15
Rochester Inst.	Feb. 18
Hartwick	Feb. 21
Utica	Feb. 22
Keuka ■	Feb. 24
St. John Fisher	Feb. 27

1995-96 RESULTS (12-13)

74	Alfred	66
62	Allegheny	87
56	Westminster (Pa.) †	60
61	Rochester ■	70
84	Hartwick ■	80
60	Hilbert ■	48
69	Keuka ■	65
112	Geneseo St.	104
85	St. John Fisher †	117
72	Rochester Inst. †	84
73	Roberts Wesleyan ■	84
68	Hilbert	63
67	Elmira	80
50	Ithaca ■	55
60	Fredonia St. ■	81
67	St. Lawrence	75
60	Clarkson	73
93	Oswego St. ■	87
85	Alfred ■	69
79	Hilbert	63
72	Rochester Inst.	91
54	St. John Fisher ■	65
82	Keuka	65
73	Utica ■	61
85	Union (N.Y.) ■	68

Nickname: Golden Flyers
Colors: Purple & Gold
Arena: Robert A. Kidera Gym
  Capacity: 1,200; Year Built: 1976
AD: Bill Carey
SID: Joe Seil

NEBRASKA
Lincoln, NE 68588 I

Coach: Danny Nee
Alma Mater: St. Mary of the Plains '71
Record: 16 Years, W-292, L-198

1996-97 SCHEDULE

Texas	Nov. 23
Weber St. ■	Nov. 26
Oregon St. ■	Nov. 30
Texas-San Antonio ■	Dec. 3
Nebraska Cl.	Dec. 6-7
Mo.-Kansas City	Dec. 11
Northern Iowa	Dec. 14
Minnesota ■	Dec. 21
Puerto Rico Tr.	Dec. 30-Jan. 1
Colorado ■	Jan. 4
Creighton ■	Jan. 8
Texas A&M ■	Jan. 11
Kansas St. ■	Jan. 15
Missouri ■	Jan. 18
Missouri	Jan. 22
Oklahoma	Jan. 25
Iowa St. ■	Jan. 29
Kansas	Feb. 1
Colorado ■	Feb. 5
Texas Tech ■	Feb. 8
Kansas St.	Feb. 10
Texas ■	Feb. 16
Baylor	Feb. 19
Iowa St.	Feb. 22
Oklahoma St. ■	Feb. 26
Kansas ■	Mar. 2
Big 12 Conf. Tr.	Mar. 6-9

1995-96 RESULTS (21-14)

72	Toledo †	59
114	Oregon †	106
96	Minnesota †	85
82	Ga. Southern ■	59
96	Grambling ■	80
88	Creighton	67
80	Minnesota	91
104	Northern Iowa ■	109
94	Northeastern Ill. ■	76
88	Delaware St. ■	41
99	Oregon †	76
66	Mississippi St. †	69
85	Texas	69
69	Long Beach St. ■	68
79	Colorado ■	74
100	Oklahoma	117
87	Mo.-Kansas City ■	69
66	Oklahoma St.	57
76	Missouri ■	58
73	Kansas ■	88
68	Kansas St.	77
65	Iowa St. ■	75
98	Missouri	99
59	Iowa St.	74
57	Oklahoma St. ■	72
71	Kansas	81
76	Oklahoma ■	80
64	Colorado	78
70	Kansas St. ■	66
60	Iowa St. †	62
91	Colorado St. ■	83
82	Washington St. ■	73
83	Fresno St.	71
90	Tulane †	78
60	St. Joseph's (Pa.) †	56

Nickname: Cornhuskers
Colors: Scarlet & Cream
Arena: Bob Devaney Sports Center
  Capacity: 14,302; Year Built: 1976
AD: Bill Byrne
SID: Chris Anderson

NEB. WESLEYAN
Lincoln, NE 68504 III

Coach: Todd Raridon
Alma Mater: Hastings '80
Record: 7 Years, W-128, L-57

1996-97 SCHEDULE

Park ■	Nov. 12
Mt. St. Clare ■	Nov. 26
Neb. Wesleyan Cl.	Nov. 29-30
Park ■	Dec. 4
Simpson ■	Dec. 7
Mt. Marty ■	Dec. 14
Hawaii Pacific	Dec. 30
Chaminade	Jan. 2
Dana ■	Jan. 8
Concordia (Neb.) ■	Jan. 11
Midland Lutheran	Jan. 15
N'western (Iowa) ■	Jan. 18
Peru St.	Jan. 21
Hastings	Jan. 25
Doane ■	Jan. 29
Dana	Feb. 1
Concordia (Neb.)	Feb. 5
Midland Lutheran ■	Feb. 8
N'western (Iowa)	Feb. 12
Briar Cliff ■	Feb. 15
Hastings ■	Feb. 19
Doane	Feb. 22
Grand View	Feb. 24
Colorado Col. ■	Mar. 1

1995-96 RESULTS (16-9)

65	Ill. Wesleyan	80
65	DePauw †	61
83	Simpson	97
89	Lindenwood ■	67
78	St. John's (Minn.) ■	49
103	Grand View	60
98	York (Neb.)	86
89	Iowa Wesleyan	93
63	Fresno Pacific	64
98	Dana	86
65	Concordia (Neb.)	72
80	Midland Lutheran ■	71
114	York (Neb.) ■	62
88	N'western (Iowa) ■	70
89	Peru St. ■	62
76	Hastings ■	69
64	Doane	81
69	Dana ■	72
62	Concordia (Neb.) ■	70
79	Midland Lutheran	68
105	N'western (Iowa) ■	92
90	Hastings	81
78	Central (Iowa) ■	59
76	Doane ■	67
74	Colorado Col.	76

Nickname: Plainsmen
Colors: Yellow & Brown
Arena: Snyder Arena
  Capacity: 2,350; Year Built: 1995
AD: Mary Beth Kennedy
SID: Jim Angele

NEB.-KEARNEY
Kearney, NE 68849 II

Coach: Jerry Hueser
Alma Mater: Wayne St. (Neb.) '59
Record: 26 Years, W-519, L-256

1996-97 SCHEDULE

Hastings ■	Nov. 22
Briar Cliff	Nov. 26
Mesa St.	Dec. 6
Western St.	Dec. 7
Hastings	Dec. 10
N.M. Highlands ■	Dec. 13
Neb.-Omaha	Dec. 21
Southern Colo.	Jan. 3
UC-Colo. Spgs.	Jan. 4
Fort Lewis ■	Jan. 10
Adams St. ■	Jan. 11
Metro St.	Jan. 17
Colorado Mines	Jan. 18
Fort Hays St. ■	Jan. 22
Chadron St. ■	Jan. 24
Denver ■	Jan. 25
Wayne St. (Neb.)	Jan. 27
Regis (Colo.) ■	Jan. 31

Colo. Christian ■ ....Feb. 1
Fort Hays St. ....Feb. 5
Chadron St. ....Feb. 7
Wayne St. (Neb.) ■ ....Feb. 11
Metro St. ■ ....Feb. 14
Colorado Mines ■ ....Feb. 15
Regis (Colo.) ....Feb. 21
Colo. Christian ■ ....Feb. 22

1995-96 RESULTS (24-9)

85	South Dak. St. ■	73
87	North Dak. St. ■	81
83	Neb.-Omaha	74
79	Hastings	76
90	Adams St. ■	81
119	Fort Lewis ■	101
110	Chadron St.	95
104	Colorado Mines	91
106	Neb.-Omaha	78
110	Hawaii-Hilo	87
80	UAB †	87
94	Southern Ill. †	81
96	Mesa St. ■	81
99	Western St. ■	79
101	Northern St.	84
93	Metro St.	75
79	Fort Hays St. ■	82
105	N.M. Highlands ■	86
91	Wayne St. (Neb.)	103
91	Adams St.	73
93	Fort Lewis	100
75	Hastings ■	78
84	Fort Hays St.	97
96	Chadron St. ■	73
99	Colorado Mines	78
83	Wayne St. (Neb.) ■	75
88	N.M. Highlands	62
87	Mesa St.	74
126	Western St.	130
95	Chadron St. ■	81
94	Western St. †	70
79	Fort Hays St. †	85
70	Regis (Colo.) †	73

Nickname: Antelopes, Lopers
Colors: Royal Blue & Light Old Gold
Arena: Health & Sports Center
   Capacity: 6,000; Year Built: 1990
AD: Dick Dull
SID: Aaron Babcock

NEB.-OMAHA
Omaha, NE 68182 II

Coach: Kevin Lehman
Alma Mater: Wartburg '77
Record: 1 Year, W-6, L-21

1996-97 SCHEDULE

Midland Lutheran ■ ....Nov. 18
Wayne St. (Neb.) ■ ....Nov. 22
Iowa Wesleyan ■ ....Nov. 25
Huron Tr. ....Nov. 29-30
Presentation ....Dec. 7
St. Mary-Plains ■ ....Dec. 9
Dakota St. ■ ....Dec. 14
Neb.-Kearney ....Dec. 21
Morningside ....Dec. 28
South Dak. ....Dec. 29
Mankato St. ■ ....Jan. 3
St. Cloud St. ■ ....Jan. 4
South Dak. St. ....Jan. 10
Augustana (S.D.) ■ ....Jan. 11
Northern Colo. ■ ....Jan. 18
North Dak. St. ■ ....Jan. 24
North Dak. ■ ....Jan. 25
St. Cloud St. ....Jan. 31
Mankato St. ....Feb. 1
Augustana (S.D.) ■ ....Feb. 7
South Dak. St. ■ ....Feb. 8
Northern Colo. ....Feb. 15
North Dak. ....Feb. 21
North Dak. St. ....Feb. 22
South Dak. ■ ....Feb. 28
Morningside ■ ....Mar. 1

1995-96 RESULTS (6-21)

72	Wayne St. (Neb.)	63
68	Doane ■	75
74	Neb.-Kearney ■	83
71	Creighton ■	74
82	Dana ■	78
78	Dakota St. ■	71
114	St. Mary-Plains ■	73
78	Neb.-Kearney	106
71	Mary ■	53
105	Mankato St.	107
58	St. Cloud St.	73
85	South Dak. St. ■	96
58	Augustana (S.D.) ■	75
72	Northern Colo.	71
67	North Dak. St.	71
85	North Dak. ■	88
75	Morningside ■	82
79	South Dak. ■	86
58	Augustana (S.D.)	79
63	South Dak. St.	85
56	Northern Colo. ■	67
52	North Dak. ■	63
52	North Dak. St. ■	72
67	South Dak.	85
79	Morningside	89
70	St. Cloud St. ■	76
54	Mankato St. ■	67

Nickname: Mavericks
Colors: Black & Crimson
Arena: UNO Fieldhouse
   Capacity: 3,500; Year Built: 1950
AD: Robert Gibson
SID: Gary Anderson

NEUMANN
Aston, PA 19014 III

Coach: George Wallace
Alma Mater: Neumann '89
Record: 4 Years, W-23, L-74

1996-97 SCHEDULE

Western Md. Tr. ....Nov. 22-23
Wesley ....Dec. 4
Washington Bible ■ ....Dec. 6
Alvernia ....Dec. 11
Allentown ....Dec. 14
Phila. Pharmacy Tr. ....Dec. 28-29
Millersville ....Jan. 4
Marywood ■ ....Jan. 8
Eastern ■ ....Jan. 11
Beaver ....Jan. 13
Misericordia ■ ....Jan. 18
Gwynedd-Mercy ■ ....Jan. 20
Cabrini ....Jan. 22
Alvernia ■ ....Jan. 25
Allentown ■ ....Jan. 29
Marywood ....Feb. 1
Eastern ....Feb. 5
Beaver ■ ....Feb. 8
Lincoln (Pa.) ■ ....Feb. 10
Misericordia ....Feb. 15
Phila. Pharmacy ....Feb. 17
Gwynedd-Mercy ....Feb. 19
Cabrini ■ ....Feb. 22

1995-96 RESULTS (3-21)

61	Kean †	79
73	Villa Julie †	75
65	Wesley ■	84
43	Cabrini ■	77
77	Agnes Scott	80
72	Beaver ■	57
80	Maritime (N.Y.) ■	79
49	Gwynedd-Mercy ■	51
87	Gwynedd-Mercy ■	66
61	Eastern	73
57	Allentown ■	64
67	Alvernia	91
65	Cabrini	92
80	Lincoln (Pa.)	97
85	Marywood	90
71	Beaver	87
59	Misericordia ■	79

62	Eastern ■	90
68	Alvernia ■	76
65	Holy Family	97
76	Misericordia ■	85
80	Marywood ■	89
74	Allentown	112
78	Phila. Pharmacy ■	86

Nickname: Knights
Colors: Blue, Gold & White
Arena: Bruder Gym
   Capacity: 400; Year Built: 1985
AD: Len Schuler
SID: Len Schuler

NEVADA
Reno, NV 89557 I

Coach: Pat Foster
Alma Mater: Arkansas '61
Record: 16 Years, W-321, L-163

1996-97 SCHEDULE

Weber St. ■ ....Nov. 30
Colorado St. ....Dec. 3
Montana St. ....Dec. 7
UNLV ■ ....Dec. 14
Oregon ....Dec. 16
Portland ■ ....Dec. 18
Iowa St. Cl. ....Dec. 21-22
Oklahoma St. [Tulsa] ....Dec. 30
Utah St. ....Jan. 2
St. Mary's (Tex.) ■ ....Jan. 6
Idaho ....Jan. 9
Boise St. ....Jan. 11
New Mexico St. ■ ....Jan. 16
North Texas ■ ....Jan. 19
UC Irvine ....Jan. 23
Utah St. ■ ....Jan. 25
UC Santa Barb. ■ ....Jan. 30
Cal Poly SLO ■ ....Feb. 1
Long Beach St. ....Feb. 6
Pacific (Cal.) ■ ....Feb. 8
Cal St. Fullerton ■ ....Feb. 15
Boise St. ■ ....Feb. 20
Idaho ■ ....Feb. 22
North Texas ....Feb. 27
New Mexico St. ....Mar. 1
Big West Conf. Tr. ....Mar. 7-9

1995-96 RESULTS (16-13)

79	Brigham Young	77
88	Baylor	80
56	Montana	74
76	Boise St.	81
86	Montana St. ■	84
76	Colorado St. ■	75
61	Creighton †	58
67	Loyola Marymount †	75
83	San Diego	66
92	Marshall ■	83
68	New Mexico St.	83
71	Utah St. ■	75
83	San Jose St. ■	64
75	Pacific (Cal.) ■	55
72	UC Santa Barb.	64
79	Long Beach St.	75
70	UC Irvine ■	72
89	Cal St. Fullerton ■	70
71	UNLV	64
62	Utah St.	72
56	Pacific (Cal.)	90
91	San Jose St. ■	96
76	Long Beach St. ■	73
65	UC Santa Barb. ■	61
71	Cal St. Fullerton	66
68	UC Irvine	74
61	UNLV ■	64
62	New Mexico St. ■	66
65	Utah St. ■	70

Nickname: Wolf Pack
Colors: Silver & Blue
Arena: Lawlor Events Center
   Capacity: 11,200; Year Built: 1983
AD: Chris Ault
SID: Paul Stuart

UNLV
Las Vegas, NV 89154 I

Coach: Bill Bayno
Alma Mater: Sacred Heart '85
Record: 1 Year, W-10, L-16

1996-97 SCHEDULE

Cal St. Northridge ■ ....Nov. 23
Jacksonville ■ ....Nov. 26
Miami (Fla.) ■ ....Nov. 29
UC Irvine ....Dec. 7
Nevada ....Dec. 14
Syracuse ....Dec. 18
Tulane ■ ....Dec. 21
Southern Utah ■ ....Dec. 23
Southern Cal ■ ....Dec. 28
Northern Ariz. ■ ....Dec. 30
San Jose St. ....Jan. 2
Texas Christian ■ ....Jan. 6
San Diego St. ■ ....Jan. 9
Hawaii ....Jan. 11
Oklahoma St. ....Jan. 18
Fresno St. ....Jan. 20
Air Force ....Jan. 25
Colorado St. ■ ....Jan. 30
Wyoming ■ ....Feb. 1
Hawaii ....Feb. 6
San Diego St. ....Feb. 8
San Jose St. ■ ....Feb. 15
Fresno St. ■ ....Feb. 17
Air Force ■ ....Feb. 20
Texas Christian ■ ....Feb. 22
Wyoming ....Feb. 27
Colorado St. ....Mar. 1
Western Ath. Conf. Tr. ....Mar. 4-8

1995-96 RESULTS (10-16)

80	Cal St. Northridge ■	56
67	Loyola Marymount	70
72	Southern Cal	82
51	Ball St. ■	60
55	Charleston So. ■	63
82	UCLA ■	89
66	Michigan	64
74	Central Fla. ■	53
66	Utah St. ■	57
68	Pacific (Cal.) ■	88
64	San Jose St. ■	66
85	Long Beach St. ■	72
64	UC Santa Barb. ■	55
61	Cal St. Fullerton	64
61	UC Irvine	66
66	New Mexico St.	68
64	Nevada ■	71
84	San Jose St. ■	75
65	Long Beach St.	84
57	UC Santa Barb.	65
55	Pacific (Cal.)	80
68	Cal St. Fullerton ■	59
63	UC Irvine ■	60
72	New Mexico St. ■	81
64	Nevada	61
69	Utah St.	82

Nickname: Runnin' Rebels
Colors: Scarlet & Gray
Arena: Thomas & Mack Center
   Capacity: 18,500; Year Built: 1983
AD: Charles Cavagnaro
SID: Jim Gemma

NEW ENGLAND COL.
Henniker, NH 03242 III

Coach: John Scheinman
Alma Mater: Marist '84
Record: 1 Year, W-22, L-7

1996-97 SCHEDULE

Endicott Tr. ....Nov. 23-24
Colby-Sawyer ■ ....Dec. 3
Lyndon St. ....Dec. 5
Daniel Webster ....Dec. 7
Colby-Sawyer Tr. ....Dec. 11-12
Notre Dame (N.H.) ....Jan. 14

Wentworth Inst. ■		Jan. 16
Eastern Nazarene		Jan. 18
Mass. Pharmacy ■		Jan. 21
Anna Maria ■		Jan. 23
Roger Williams ■		Jan. 25
Nichols		Jan. 27
Gordon		Jan. 29
Curry ■		Feb. 1
Colby-Sawyer		Feb. 4
Salve Regina ■		Feb. 8
Gordon ■		Feb. 10
Nichols ■		Feb. 12
Daniel Webster ■		Feb. 16
Johnson St. ■		Feb. 18
Anna Maria		Feb. 20

1995-96 RESULTS (0-22)

66	Wheaton (Mass.)	83
58	North Adams St.	85
62	Notre Dame (N.H.) ■	74
84	Lyndon St. ■	90
63	Colby-Sawyer	101
60	Daniel Webster	87
73	Colby-Sawyer ■	105
78	Norwich	94
51	Merrimack	107
72	Rensselaer	117
56	Wentworth Inst.	67
54	Eastern Nazarene ■	97
84	Anna Maria	108
68	Roger Williams ■	98
74	Nichols ■	96
58	Gordon ■	82
67	Curry	82
57	Colby-Sawyer ■	80
59	Salve Regina ■	85
67	Gordon	78
83	Nichols	100
68	Anna Maria ■	121

Nickname: Pilgrims
Colors: Scarlet & Royal Blue
Arena: Bridges Gym
    Capacity: 300; Year Built: 1965
AD: Mary Ellen Alger
SID: Jason Shaffer

NEW HAMPSHIRE
Durham, NH 03824 I

Coach: Jeff Jackson
Alma Mater: Cornell '84
(First year as head coach)

1996-97 SCHEDULE

Rider ■		Nov. 23
Boston College		Nov. 25
Harvard		Nov. 30
Navy		Dec. 3
Drexel ■		Dec. 6
Hofstra ■		Dec. 8
Notre Dame		Dec. 10
Dartmouth		Dec. 14
Davidson		Dec. 21
Boston U. ■		Jan. 2
Northeastern		Jan. 4
Vermont		Jan. 7
Maine		Jan. 11
Delaware ■		Jan. 16
Towson St. ■		Jan. 18
Hartford		Jan. 21
Hofstra		Jan. 24
Drexel		Jan. 26
Hartford ■		Jan. 30
Vermont ■		Feb. 2
Maine ■		Feb. 8
Holy Cross ■		Feb. 10
Towson St.		Feb. 13
Delaware		Feb. 15
Boston U.		Feb. 20
Northeastern ■		Feb. 22
America East Conf. Tr.		Feb. 28-Mar. 2

1995-96 RESULTS (6-21)

78	Providence	92
64	Miami (Ohio)	90
63	Navy ■	66

98	Northeastern ■	90
67	Boston U.	70
79	Holy Cross	101
80	Seton Hall	93
74	Texas Christian †	93
68	Towson St.	79
52	Delaware	57
89	Hartford ■	68
68	Drexel	110
56	Hofstra	75
72	Dartmouth ■	69
106	Maine	103
90	Vermont	92
73	Maine ■	82
61	Harvard ■	66
75	Drexel ■	87
77	Hofstra ■	65
70	Towson St.	79
75	Delaware	93
79	Vermont ■	88
66	Hartford	87
78	Northeastern	72
69	Boston U. ■	80
73	Hartford †	76

Nickname: Wildcats
Colors: Blue & White
Arena: Whittemore Center
    Capacity: 7,200; Year Built: 1995
AD: Judith Ray
SID: Scott Stapin

NEW HAMP. COL.
Manchester, NH 03104 II

Coach: Stanley Spirou
Alma Mater: Keene St. '74
Record: 11 Years, W-250, L-91

1996-97 SCHEDULE

New Hamp. Col. Cl.		Nov. 15-16
Merrimack		Nov. 26
Keene St.		Dec. 4
New Haven ■		Dec. 7
Stonehill ■		Dec. 19
St. Rose Cl.		Dec. 27-29
Bryant		Jan. 5
Southern Conn. St.		Jan. 8
Stony Brook		Jan. 11
Bridgeport ■		Jan. 14
Franklin Pierce ■		Jan. 16
Sacred Heart		Jan. 18
Albany (N.Y.)		Jan. 22
Sacred Heart ■		Jan. 25
Mass.-Lowell ■		Jan. 28
St. Anselm		Jan. 30
Stony Brook ■		Feb. 1
Albany (N.Y.) ■		Feb. 4
Bridgeport		Feb. 6
New Haven		Feb. 8
Keene St. ■		Feb. 12
Southern Conn. St. ■		Feb. 15
Mass.-Lowell		Feb. 18
Franklin Pierce		Feb. 22

1995-96 RESULTS (21-8)

83	Bentley ■	71
79	St. Anselm ■	95
82	Stonehill	68
110	Bryant	103
75	Stony Brook	68
83	Merrimack ■	71
65	Le Moyne ■	64
87	Albany (N.Y.) ■	66
92	Keene St. ■	67
79	Southern Conn. St. ■	70
85	New Haven ■	75
81	St. Anselm	101
71	Albany (N.Y.)	59
69	Le Moyne	77
77	Franklin Pierce	57
85	Bridgeport ■	78
85	Sacred Heart ■	67
61	Mass.-Lowell	75
72	New Haven	63

64	Southern Conn. St.	78
111	Keene St.	75
87	Stony Brook ■	73
68	Franklin Pierce ■	82
89	Sacred Heart	64
95	Bridgeport	70
82	Mass.-Lowell	66
68	Le Moyne †	81
68	Adelphi †	52
82	St. Rose †	83

Nickname: Penmen
Colors: Blue & Gold
Arena: NHC Fieldhouse
    Capacity: 2,500; Year Built: 1980
AD: Joseph Polak
SID: Tom McDermott

NEW HAVEN
West Haven, CT 06516 II

Coach: Jim O'Connor
Alma Mater: Cortland St. '84
Record: 8 Years, W-121, L-107

1996-97 SCHEDULE

Quinnipiac ■		Nov. 20
So. Conn. St. Cl.		Nov. 22-23
Bryant ■		Nov. 26
Teikyo Post ■		Nov. 30
New Hamp. Col.		Dec. 7
Franklin Pierce ■		Dec. 10
Bentley Festival		Dec. 28-29
American Int'l		Jan. 4
Stony Brook ■		Jan. 6
Sacred Heart ■		Jan. 8
Southern Conn. St. ■		Jan. 11
Stony Brook		Jan. 14
Bridgeport		Jan. 16
Albany (N.Y.)		Jan. 18
Mass.-Lowell		Jan. 20
Albany (N.Y.) ■		Jan. 25
Keene St.		Jan. 29
Southern Conn. St.		Feb. 1
Mass.-Lowell ■		Feb. 4
New Hamp. Col. ■		Feb. 8
Franklin Pierce		Feb. 12
Sacred Heart ■		Feb. 15
Keene St. ■		Feb. 17
Bridgeport ■		Feb. 20

1995-96 RESULTS (10-16)

71	Stonehill ■	81
78	St. Michael's ■	95
78	Teikyo Post	73
92	Quinnipiac	69
62	Albany (N.Y.)	74
69	Le Moyne	72
68	Sacred Heart	74
78	Bridgeport	87
69	Franklin Pierce ■	73
108	Keene St. ■	80
66	Stony Brook ■	58
61	Mass.-Lowell	64
75	New Hamp. Col.	85
79	American Int'l ■	57
82	Stony Brook	71
82	Sacred Heart ■	88
57	Le Moyne ■	60
82	Bridgeport	74
63	New Hamp. Col. ■	72
76	Mass.-Lowell ■	73
76	Southern Conn. St. ■	78
98	Keene St.	77
65	Franklin Pierce	83
70	Bryant	73
65	Albany (N.Y.) ■	63
65	Southern Conn. St.	69

Nickname: Chargers
Colors: Blue & Gold
Arena: North Campus Gymnasium
    Capacity: 1,500; Year Built: 1963
AD: Deborah Chin
SID: Jack Jones

COL. OF NEW JERSEY
Ewing, NJ 08650 III

Coach: John Castaldo
Alma Mater: Col. of New Jersey
Record: 3 Years, W-39, L-32

1996-97 SCHEDULE

New Jersey Inv.		Nov. 22-Dec. 23
Rutgers-Camden ■		Nov. 26
Savannah A&D Tr.		Nov. 29-30
Rutgers-Newark		Dec. 4
Jersey City St. ■		Dec. 7
Rowan ■		Dec. 11
Wm. Paterson		Dec. 14
FDU-Madison ■		Jan. 8
Ramapo		Jan. 11
Kean		Jan. 15
Montclair St. ■		Jan. 18
Richard Stockton		Jan. 22
Rutgers-Newark ■		Jan. 25
Rutgers-Camden		Jan. 29
Lincoln (Pa.)		Jan. 30
Ramapo ■		Feb. 1
Kean ■		Feb. 5
Jersey City St.		Feb. 8
Rowan		Feb. 11
Wm. Paterson ■		Feb. 15
Richard Stockton ■		Feb. 19
Montclair St.		Feb. 22

1995-96 RESULTS (12-10)

84	John Jay ■	63
76	Montclair St.	53
74	Jersey City St. ■	76
62	Richard Stockton	66
81	Rowan	101
74	Kean ■	71
99	Rutgers-Camden	73
79	Muhlenberg †	63
92	Messiah †	63
64	Wis.-Platteville †	75
65	Ramapo	69
57	Wm. Paterson ■	75
63	Rutgers-Newark	66
70	Richard Stockton ■	60
62	Montclair St. ■	51
53	Jersey City St.	61
60	Ramapo ■	54
72	Rowan ■	82
75	Kean	61
97	Rutgers-Camden ■	51
60	Rutgers-Newark ■	74
82	Wm. Paterson	72

Nickname: Lions
Colors: Blue & Gold
Arena: Packer Hall
    Capacity: 1,200; Year Built: 1962
AD: Kevin McHugh
SID: Ann Bready

N.J. INST. OF TECH.
Newark, NJ 07102 III

Coach: James Catalano
Alma Mater: Jersey City St. '73
Record: 17 Years, W-355, L-115

1996-97 SCHEDULE

New Jersey Tech Tr.		Nov. 22-23
Yeshiva ■		Nov. 26
Mt. St. Mary (N.Y.) ■		Dec. 3
Staten Island		Dec. 5
Maritime (N.Y.) ■		Dec. 7
Patten		Dec. 29
Holy Names		Dec. 30
Mt. St. Vincent		Jan. 4
St. Joseph's (L.I.) ■		Jan. 13
Stevens Tech		Jan. 15
Merchant Marine		Jan. 18
Manhattanville		Jan. 19
Polytechnic (N.Y.) ■		Jan. 23
Mt. St. Vincent ■		Jan. 27
Hunter ■		Jan. 31
Stevens Tech ■		Feb. 1

Yeshiva ...Feb. 3
Polytechnic (N.Y.) ...Feb. 5
Merchant Marine ■ ...Feb. 8
Bard ■ ...Feb. 10
Mt. St. Mary (N.Y.) ...Feb. 12
Manhattanville ...Feb. 18
Maritime (N.Y.) ...Feb. 22

1995-96 RESULTS (17-10)
96 Daemen † ...108
93 Lehman † ...83
127 Bard ■ ...40
95 Mt. St. Mary (N.Y.) ■ ...93
91 Centenary (N.J.) ...101
75 Staten Island ■ ...86
71 Yeshiva ...57
77 Polytechnic (N.Y.) ...55
73 Occidental ...88
80 La Verne † ...88
78 Mt. St. Vincent ■ ...73
78 Stevens Tech ■ ...67
91 Centenary (N.J.) ■ ...52
68 Merchant Marine ...84
80 Mt. St. Vincent ...81
81 Hunter ...78
91 Yeshiva ■ ...64
82 Manhattanville ...86
94 Stevens Tech ...90
98 Polytechnic (N.Y.) ■ ...70
82 Mt. St. Mary (N.Y.) ...93
72 Merchant Marine ■ ...68
81 Maritime (N.Y.) ■ ...69
85 Manhattanville ■ ...62
87 Stevens Tech ...76
74 Mt. St. Vincent † ...64
88 New York U. ...105

Nickname: Highlanders
Colors: Red & White
Arena: Entwistle Gym
  Capacity: 1,500; Year Built: 1960
AD: Malcolm Simon
SID: Mike Ruane

NEW MEXICO
Albuquerque, NM 87131 ...I

Coach: Dave Bliss
Alma Mater: Cornell '65
Record: 21 Years, W-391, L-246

1996-97 SCHEDULE
Simon Fraser ■ ...Nov. 18
New Mexico Cl. ...Nov. 22-23
Centenary (La.) ■ ...Nov. 27
Arizona ...Nov. 30
Texas Tech ...Dec. 4
New Mexico St. ...Dec. 7
New Mexico St. ■ ...Dec. 13
Sam Houston St. ■ ...Dec. 21
Jackson St. ■ ...Dec. 23
New Mexico Inv. ...Dec. 27-28
Hawaii ...Jan. 4
Texas Christian ■ ...Jan. 9
Southern Methodist ■ ...Jan. 11
Tulsa ...Jan. 16
Rice ...Jan. 18
UTEP ■ ...Jan. 25
Utah ■ ...Feb. 1
Brigham Young ■ ...Feb. 3
Southern Methodist ...Feb. 6
Texas Christian ...Feb. 8
Rice ■ ...Feb. 13
Tulsa ■ ...Feb. 16
UTEP ...Feb. 20
Hawaii ■ ...Feb. 22
Brigham Young ...Feb. 27
Utah ...Mar. 1
Western Ath. Conf. Tr. ...Mar. 4-8

1995-96 RESULTS (28-5)
81 Simon Fraser ■ ...67
76 Texas-Arlington ■ ...56
107 Mercer ■ ...72
80 Tex.-Pan American ■ ...56
86 Arizona St. ...79
91 New Mexico St. ■ ...75

69 New Mexico St. ...68
72 Southwest Tex. St. ■ ...62
91 Dartmouth ■ ...66
95 Boston U. ■ ...83
75 Fresno St. ...76
61 Air Force ...49
77 San Diego St. ■ ...74
78 Hawaii ■ ...72
58 Wyoming ...61
67 Colorado St. ...65
64 UTEP ...60
83 Brigham Young ■ ...77
64 Utah ■ ...82
88 Brigham Young ...81
58 Utah ...74
81 UTEP ■ ...52
70 Wyoming ■ ...69
78 Colorado St. ■ ...66
83 San Diego St. ...78
88 Hawaii ...79
67 Air Force ■ ...55
86 Fresno St. ■ ...84
94 San Diego St. ■ ...75
104 Fresno St. ■ ...99
64 Utah ■ ...60
69 Kansas St. † ...48
62 Georgetown † ...73

Nickname: Lobos
Colors: Cherry & Silver
Arena: University Arena; The Pit
  Capacity: 18,018; Year Built: 1966
AD: Rudy Davalos
SID: Greg Remington

N.M. HIGHLANDS
Las Vegas, NM 87701 ...II

Coach: John McCullough
Alma Mater: Oklahoma St.
(First year as head coach)

1996-97 SCHEDULE
Eastern N.M. ■ ...Nov. 18
West Tex. A&M ...Nov. 22
Western N.M. Tr. ...Nov. 29-30
Denver ■ ...Dec. 3
Chadron St. ■ ...Dec. 7
Neb.-Kearney ■ ...Dec. 13
Fort Hays St. ...Dec. 14
Regis (Colo.) ...Jan. 3
Colo. Christian ■ ...Jan. 4
Metro St. ...Jan. 9
Colorado Mines ...Jan. 11
Western N.M. ...Jan. 14
Fort Lewis ■ ...Jan. 16
Adams St. ■ ...Jan. 18
Mesa St. ...Jan. 23
Western St. ...Jan. 25
Southern Colo. ■ ...Jan. 31
UC-Colo. Spgs. ■ ...Feb. 2
Eastern N.M. ...Feb. 4
Mesa St. ■ ...Feb. 7
Western St. ■ ...Feb. 9
Fort Lewis ...Feb. 14
Adams St. ...Feb. 15
Southern Colo. ...Feb. 20
UC-Colo. Spgs. ...Feb. 22

1995-96 RESULTS (4-22)
61 Eastern N.M. ...77
69 Western N.M. ■ ...67
73 Southern Colo. ■ ...77
81 Western N.M. ■ ...74
56 Mesa St. ...73
81 Western St. ■ ...93
58 Regis (Colo.) ■ ...70
65 Eastern N.M. ■ ...78
80 Chadron St. ■ ...88
74 Colorado Mines ...72
75 Colo. Baptist ■ ...83
60 Adams St. ■ ...65
77 Fort Lewis ■ ...83
86 Neb.-Kearney ...105
50 Fort Hays St. ...78
61 Mesa St. ■ ...70

68 Western St. ■ ...71
70 Chadron St. ...75
60 Colorado Mines ...75
62 Regis (Colo.) ...69
59 Adams St. ...64
89 Fort Lewis ...82
62 Neb.-Kearney ■ ...88
68 Fort Hays St. ■ ...88
77 Colo. Baptist ■ ...100
77 Southern Colo. ...100

Nickname: Cowboys
Colors: Purple & White
Arena: Wilson Complex
  Capacity: 4,241; Year Built: 1985
AD: To be named
SID: Jesse Gallegos

NEW MEXICO ST.
Las Cruces, NM 88003 ...I

Coach: Neil McCarthy
Alma Mater: Cal St. Sacramento '65
Record: 21 Years, W-429, L-212

1996-97 SCHEDULE
Western N.M. ■ ...Nov. 22
Md.-East. Shore ■ ...Nov. 25
UTEP ■ ...Nov. 30
UTEP ...Dec. 4
New Mexico ■ ...Dec. 7
New Mexico ...Dec. 13
Southern-N.O. ■ ...Dec. 21
Wyoming Shootout ...Dec. 27-28
N.C.-Asheville ■ ...Dec. 30
Cal Poly SLO ■ ...Jan. 9
North Texas ...Jan. 11
Nevada ...Jan. 16
Utah St. ...Jan. 18
Idaho ...Jan. 23
Boise St. ■ ...Jan. 25
Long Beach St. ■ ...Jan. 30
Pacific (Cal.) ■ ...Feb. 1
Cal St. Fullerton ...Feb. 6
UC Irvine ...Feb. 8
Boise St. ...Feb. 13
Idaho ...Feb. 15
UC Santa Barb. ■ ...Feb. 20
North Texas ■ ...Feb. 22
Utah St. ...Feb. 27
Nevada ■ ...Mar. 1
Big West Conf. Tr. ...Mar. 7-9

1995-96 RESULTS (11-15)
67 UTEP ■ ...73
70 UTEP ...77
80 Western N.M. ■ ...56
50 Northwestern St. ■ ...46
75 New Mexico ...91
68 New Mexico ■ ...69
57 Tulsa ...73
81 Southern Utah ■ ...75
83 Nevada ■ ...68
60 San Jose St. ...74
66 Pacific (Cal.) ...78
56 UC Santa Barb. ■ ...60
66 UC Irvine ...74
72 Cal St. Fullerton ...85
76 Long Beach St. ■ ...63
68 UNLV ■ ...66
60 Utah St. ■ ...70
59 Pacific (Cal.) ...75
74 San Jose St. ■ ...73
60 UC Santa Barb. ...59
57 Long Beach St. ...73
63 Cal St. Fullerton ■ ...68
83 UC Irvine ■ ...77
69 Utah St. ...76
81 UNLV ...72
66 Nevada ...62

Nickname: Aggies
Colors: Crimson & White
Arena: Pan American Center
  Capacity: 13,071; Year Built: 1968
AD: Al Gonzales
SID: Steve Shutt

NEW ORLEANS
New Orleans, LA 70148 ...I

Coach: Tic Price
Alma Mater: Virginia Tech '79
Record: 2 Years, W-41, L-20

1996-97 SCHEDULE
Middle Tenn. St. ■ ...Nov. 30
San Francisco Cl. ...Dec. 6-7
Southern Miss. ■ ...Dec. 14
Va. Commonwealth ...Dec. 18
Louisiana Tech ...Dec. 22
New Orleans Cl. ...Dec. 27-28
Jacksonville ...Jan. 2
Ark.-Little Rock ■ ...Jan. 4
Western Ky. ■ ...Jan. 9
Tex.-Pan American ■ ...Jan. 11
Tulane [New Orleans] ...Jan. 13
Arkansas St. ■ ...Jan. 18
South Ala. ...Jan. 20
Louisiana Tech ■ ...Jan. 22
Western Ky. ...Jan. 25
Arkansas St. ...Jan. 27
South Ala. ■ ...Jan. 30
Southwestern La. ■ ...Feb. 1
Tex.-Pan American ...Feb. 6
Lamar ...Feb. 8
Jacksonville ■ ...Feb. 13
Lamar ■ ...Feb. 15
Ark.-Little Rock ...Feb. 20
Southwestern La. ...Feb. 22
Sun Belt Conf. Tr. ...Feb. 28-Mar. 4

1995-96 RESULTS (21-9)
72 Bradley ...87
68 Southern Miss. ...66
69 Middle Tenn. St. ...67
61 Oregon St. ■ ...68
72 Villanova ...80
94 San Francisco ■ ...84
92 Va. Commonwealth ■ ...75
80 Western Ky. ...94
69 Tex.-Pan American ...50
70 Lamar ...76
78 Ark.-Little Rock ■ ...65
79 Arkansas St. ■ ...70
77 Tulane † ...86
70 Louisiana Tech ■ ...45
67 Southwestern La. ...59
73 Jacksonville ■ ...69
58 Tex.-Pan American ■ ...54
90 Western Ky. ■ ...82
54 South Ala. ...55
66 Ark.-Little Rock. ...69
69 Arkansas St. ...66
97 Jacksonville ...88
72 South Ala. ■ ...50
70 Louisiana Tech ...61
84 Lamar ■ ...48
66 Southwestern La. ...62
67 Louisiana Tech † ...57
75 Southwestern La. † ...71
57 Ark.-Little Rock. ...56
62 North Caro. † ...83

Nickname: Privateers
Colors: Royal Blue & Silver
Arena: Kiefer Lakefront Arena
  Capacity: 10,000; Year Built: 1983
AD: Ron Maestri
SID: Ed Cassiere

NEW PALTZ ST.
New Paltz, NY 12561 ...III

Coach: Paul Clune
Alma Mater: Rochester Inst. '84
Record: 7 Years, W-81, L-96

1996-97 SCHEDULE
Bard Tr. ...Nov. 22-23
Green Mountain ■ ...Nov. 26
Binghamton ■ ...Dec. 3
Plattsburgh St. ...Dec. 6
Potsdam St. ...Dec. 7

Ithaca ■ ...Dec. 10
Wilkes ■ ...Jan. 7
New Paltz Inv. ...Jan. 11-12
Hunter ...Jan. 14
Cortland St. ...Jan. 18
Potsdam St. ■ ...Jan. 24
Plattsburgh St. ■ ...Jan. 25
Oneonta St. ...Jan. 28
Oswego St. ■ ...Jan. 31
Utica/Rome ...Feb. 1
Geneseo ■ ...Feb. 7
Brockport St. ■ ...Feb. 8
Binghamton ...Feb. 11
Fredonia St. ...Feb. 14
Buffalo St. ■ ...Feb. 15
Cortland St. ■ ...Feb. 18
Oneonta St. ■ ...Feb. 22

1995-96 RESULTS (13-14)
63 Mt. St. Mary (N.Y.) ■ ...60
79 Vassar ■ ...55
69 Wilkes ...84
45 Ithaca ...63
69 Plattsburgh St. ■ ...81
74 Potsdam St. ■ ...84
64 Binghamton ...68
57 Geneseo St. ...67
75 Brockport St. ...87
74 Rutgers-Newark ■ ...78
68 Hunter ...84
64 Green Mountain ...67
79 Plattsburgh St. ...70
73 Potsdam St. ...64
74 Cortland St. ■ ...83
75 Utica/Rome ■ ...66
71 Oswego St. ...59
56 Binghamton ...57
64 Oneonta St. ...57
66 Rutgers-Newark ...61
76 Fredonia St. ■ ...66
58 Buffalo St. ■ ...48
80 Cortland St. ...56
69 Oneonta St. ...78
76 Geneseo St. ...65
79 Brockport St. † ...71
53 Buffalo St. † ...75

Nickname: Hawks
Colors: Orange & Blue
Arena: Elting Gymnasium
 Capacity: 2,000; Year Built: 1964
AD: Jim Zalacca
SID: Dave Hines

NEW YORK TECH
Old Westbury, NY 11568...II

Coach: Bob Holford
Alma Mater: Roger Williams
(First year as head coach)
1996-97 SCHEDULE
Roberts Wesleyan ...Nov. 30
Le Moyne ■ ...Dec. 1
Adelphi ...Dec. 4
LIU-C. W. Post ■ ...Dec. 7
Mercy ...Dec. 11
LIU-Southampton ■ ...Dec. 14
Stony Brook Inv. ...Dec. 28-29
Queens (N.Y.) ...Jan. 4
Pace ...Jan. 6
Concordia (N.Y.) ■ ...Jan. 8
Dowling ...Jan. 11
Molloy ■ ...Jan. 13
St. Rose ...Jan. 15
Phila. Textile ■ ...Jan. 18
Adelphi ■ ...Jan. 20
LIU-C. W. Post ...Jan. 22
Mercy ■ ...Jan. 25
LIU-Southampton ...Jan. 29
Queens (N.Y.) ■ ...Feb. 1
Pace ■ ...Feb. 5
Concordia (N.Y.) ...Feb. 8
Dowling ■ ...Feb. 12
Molloy ...Feb. 15
St. Rose ■ ...Feb. 19

Phila. Textile ...Feb. 22
1995-96 RESULTS (19-8)
Results unavailable

Nickname: Bears
Colors: Navy Blue & Gold
Arena: NYIT Field House
 Capacity: 500; Year Built: 1970
AD: Clyde Doughty Jr
SID: Tom Riordan

NEW YORK U.
New York, NY 10012...III

Coach: Joe Nesci
Alma Mater: Brooklyn '79
Record: 8 Years, W-149, L-53
1996-97 SCHEDULE
New York U. Tr. ...Nov. 22-23
CCNY ...Nov. 26
Case Reserve ...Dec. 1
Johns Hopkins ■ ...Dec. 6
Manhattanville ■ ...Dec. 8
Merchant Marine ■ ...Dec. 11
Stevens Tech Tr. ...Jan. 3-4
Wm. Paterson ■ ...Jan. 8
Brandeis ■ ...Jan. 11
Maritime (N.Y.) ...Jan. 14
Chicago ...Jan. 17
Washington (Mo.) ...Jan. 19
Carnegie Mellon ■ ...Jan. 24
Emory ■ ...Jan. 26
Polytechnic (N.Y.) ■ ...Jan. 28
Vassar ...Jan. 29
Rochester ■ ...Feb. 2
Emory ...Feb. 7
Carnegie Mellon ...Feb. 9
Rochester ...Feb. 14
Washington (Mo.) ...Feb. 21
Chicago ■ ...Feb. 23
Brandeis ...Mar. 1

1995-96 RESULTS (19-8)
71 Drew ■ ...58
78 Tufts ■ ...81
69 Ursinus ■ ...73
96 Case Reserve ■ ...87
88 Merchant Marine ...78
78 Johns Hopkins ...76
65 Staten Island ■ ...71
81 Manhattanville ...73
85 Maritime (N.Y.) ■ ...74
101 Medgar Evers ■ ...74
80 Brandeis ...81
93 Chicago ■ ...67
90 Washington (Mo.) ■ ...78
71 Carnegie Mellon ...55
73 Emory ...68
75 York (N.Y.) ■ ...70
77 Rochester ...78
110 Pratt ...61
77 Emory ...69
83 Carnegie Mellon ■ ...59
89 Rochester ■ ...69
84 Old Westbury ■ ...80
74 Washington (Mo.) ...94
68 Chicago ...98
78 Brandeis ■ ...66
105 N.J. Inst. of Tech. ■ ...88
77 Richard Stockton ...81

Nickname: Violets
Colors: Purple & White
Arena: Coles Sports Center
 Capacity: 1,900; Year Built: 1981
AD: Barnett Hamberger (Interim)
SID: Sean Dillon

NEWBERRY
Newberry, SC 29108 ...II

Coach: Grafton Young
Alma Mater: Warren Wilson '79
Record: 3 Years, W-30, L-51

1996-97 SCHEDULE
Erskine ...Nov. 18
Presbyterian ■ ...Nov. 20
Elon ...Nov. 23
Mars Hill ■ ...Nov. 25
Presbyterian ...Nov. 27
Lenoir-Rhyne Cl. ...Nov. 29-30
Lander ...Dec. 2
Lenoir-Rhyne ...Dec. 4
Mars Hill ...Dec. 14
Queens (N.C.) Cl. ...Jan. 3-5
Lenoir-Rhyne ■ ...Jan. 6
Anderson (S.C.) ...Jan. 11
Limestone ...Jan. 16
Wingate ...Jan. 20
Allen ■ ...Jan. 22
Carson-Newman ■ ...Jan. 27
Elon ...Jan. 29
Wingate ■ ...Feb. 3
Limestone ...Feb. 8
Carson-Newman ...Feb. 10
Allen ...Feb. 15
Lander ...Feb. 17
Anderson (S.C.) ■ ...Feb. 22

1995-96 RESULTS (11-16)
87 Gardner-Webb ...96
84 Limestone † ...65
73 Lenoir-Rhyne ...83
49 Fayetteville St. ...55
65 Citadel ...94
69 Presbyterian ■ ...65
53 Carson-Newman ...66
103 Mars Hill ■ ...117
71 Lander ...91
79 S.C.-Aiken ...82
72 Wingate † ...59
69 Queens (N.C.) ...97
65 Mars Hill † ...73
71 S.C.-Aiken ...70
89 Allen ■ ...64
64 Mars Hill ...79
73 Limestone ...71
65 Presbyterian ...72
80 Carson-Newman ■ ...69
76 Lenoir-Rhyne ■ ...85
71 Limestone ■ ...69
91 Anderson (S.C.) ...79
69 Erskine ■ ...80
66 Lander ■ ...68
86 Allen † ...73
114 Anderson (S.C.) ■ ...76
64 Fayetteville St. ...81

Nickname: Indians
Colors: Scarlet & Gray
Arena: Eleazer Arena
 Capacity: 1,800; Year Built: 1981
AD: William Young
SID: Darrell Orand

NIAGARA
Niagara University, NY 14109...I

Coach: Jack Armstrong
Alma Mater: Fordham '85
Record: 7 Years, W-75, L-124
1996-97 SCHEDULE
Northeastern ...Nov. 23
Bucknell ...Nov. 25
Buffalo ...Nov. 30
Robert Morris ...Dec. 5
Canisius ...Dec. 7
LIU-Brooklyn ■ ...Dec. 14
Buffalo ■ ...Dec. 18
DePaul ■ ...Dec. 21
Lehigh ...Jan. 2
Appalachian St. ■ ...Jan. 4
Kansas ...Jan. 9
Manhattan ■ ...Jan. 12
St. John's (N.Y.) ■ ...Jan. 14
Loyola (Md.) ■ ...Jan. 18
St. Bonaventure ...Jan. 21
Manhattan ...Jan. 24
Iona ...Jan. 26

Siena ■ ...Jan. 31
Iona ■ ...Feb. 2
Canisius ■ ...Feb. 5
St. Peter's ■ ...Feb. 8
Fairfield ■ ...Feb. 10
Siena ...Feb. 13
Loyola (Md.) ...Feb. 16
Fairfield ...Feb. 21
St. Peter's ...Feb. 23
Metro Atlantic Conf. Tr. ...Mar. 1-3

1995-96 RESULTS (13-15)
72 St. John's (N.Y.) ...88
68 Siena † ...51
54 Brown † ...56
64 Hampton † ...62
55 St. Bonaventure ■ ...77
68 Robert Morris ■ ...57
72 Colgate † ...68
58 Buffalo ...68
54 Northern Ill. ...69
60 Youngstown St. ...69
83 Lehigh ...75
53 St. Peter's ...50
74 Canisius ■ ...71
52 Siena ...50
65 Loyola (Md.) ...71
69 Fairfield ...71
81 Northeastern ...62
59 Iona ■ ...78
53 Manhattan ...74
69 Iona ...77
64 Fairfield ...72
58 Canisius ...56
68 Loyola (Md.) ■ ...80
79 Siena ...77
61 Manhattan ...73
58 St. Peter's ■ ...55
62 Manhattan † ...60
47 Fairfield † ...70

Nickname: Purple Eagles
Colors: Purple, White & Gold
Arena: Marine Midland Arena
 Capacity: 21,000
AD: Michael Jankowski
SID: Mark Vandergrift

NICHOLLS ST.
Thibodaux, LA 70301 ...I

Coach: Rickey Broussard
Alma Mater: Southwestern La. '70
Record: 6 Years, W-80, L-86
1996-97 SCHEDULE
Texas Tech ■ ...Nov. 25
Loyola (La.) ■ ...Nov. 27
Missouri Valley ■ ...Nov. 30
Lamar ...Dec. 7
Southern Miss. ...Dec. 11
Vanderbilt ...Dec. 15
Southeastern La. ■ ...Dec. 18
South Ala. ...Dec. 21
Notre Dame ...Dec. 23
Texas-San Antonio ...Jan. 2
Southwest Tex. St. ...Jan. 4
Tulane ...Jan. 8
Texas-Arlington ...Jan. 11
McNeese St. ■ ...Jan. 13
Northwestern St. ■ ...Jan. 16
Northeast La. ...Jan. 18
Sam Houston St. ...Jan. 23
Stephen F. Austin ...Jan. 25
Texas-Arlington ...Feb. 1
Southwest Tex. St. ■ ...Feb. 6
Texas-San Antonio ■ ...Feb. 8
Northwestern St. ...Feb. 13
Northeast La. ...Feb. 15
Stephen F. Austin ■ ...Feb. 20
Sam Houston St. ■ ...Feb. 22
McNeese St. ...Mar. 1
Southland Conf. Tr. ...Mar. 5-8

1995-96 RESULTS (5-21)
65 Southeastern La. ...89
62 Tulane ...82

56	Texas Tech	.95
47	Oklahoma	.87
53	Samford †	.69
51	Princeton †	.86
54	Mississippi	.66
72	Northeast La. ■	.75
75	Northwestern St. ■	.67
53	Southwest Tex. St.	.61
66	Texas-San Antonio	.83
67	North Texas ■	.62
80	Texas-Arlington ■	.64
69	LSU	.86
71	Stephen F. Austin	.54
71	Sam Houston St.	.78
63	Northwestern St.	.59
85	Northeast La.	.125
60	Texas-San Antonio ■	.64
61	Southwest Tex. St. ■	.67
71	McNeese St. ■	.90
82	Texas-Arlington	.83
67	North Texas	.81
85	Sam Houston St. ■	.94
58	Stephen F. Austin ■	.76
80	McNeese St. ■	.92

Nickname: Colonels
Colors: Red & Gray
Arena: David Stopher Gymnasium
Capacity: 3,800; Year Built: 1967
AD: Mike Knight
SID: Ron Mears

NICHOLS
Dudley, MA 01571 III

Coach: Rich Lengieza
Alma Mater: Nichols '83
Record: 5 Years, W-53, L-66

1996-97 SCHEDULE

WPI	.Nov. 23
Suffolk ■	.Nov. 27
Mass. Pharmacy ■	.Dec. 2
Worcester St.	.Dec. 4
Daniel Webster ■	.Dec. 10
Johnson & Wales	.Dec. 12
Salve Regina ■	.Jan. 16
Roger Williams ■	.Jan. 18
Anna Maria ■	.Jan. 21
Gordon	.Jan. 23
Wheaton (Mass.)	.Jan. 25
New England Col. ■	.Jan. 27
Fitchburg St. ■	.Jan. 30
Wentworth Inst.	.Feb. 1
Anna Maria	.Feb. 4
Colby-Sawyer ■	.Feb. 6
Eastern Nazarene ■	.Feb. 8
Connecticut Col.	.Feb. 10
New England Col.	.Feb. 12
Curry	.Feb. 15
Gordon ■	.Feb. 20
Colby-Sawyer	.Feb. 22

1995-96 RESULTS (12-13)

98	Western New Eng. ■	.95
74	Amherst	.88
82	Rivier	.95
87	Worcester St. ■	.81
94	WPI ■	.88
76	Suffolk	.73
88	Fitchburg St.	.79
93	Johnson & Wales ■	.64
85	Daniel Webster	.91
90	Roger Williams ■	.70
76	Anna Maria	.84
76	Gordon ■	.64
80	Wheaton (Mass.) ■	.93
96	New England Col.	.74
80	Wentworth Inst. ■	.83
94	Anna Maria ■	.103
81	Colby-Sawyer	.100
67	Eastern Nazarene	.88
54	Connecticut Col. ■	.105
100	New England Col. ■	.83
91	Curry ■	.76
78	Salve Regina	.72

79	Gordon	.93
82	Colby-Sawyer ■	.84
71	Wentworth Inst.	.83

Nickname: Bison
Colors: Black & Green
Arena: Chalmers Field House
Capacity: 650; Year Built: 1965
AD: Tom Cafaro
SID: Scott Gibbons

NORFOLK ST.
Norfolk, VA 23504 II

Coach: Michael Bernard
Alma Mater: Kentucky St. '70
Record: 11 Years, W-233, L-92

1996-97 SCHEDULE

Columbia Union ■	.Nov. 24
Southeast Mo. St. Cl.	.Nov. 29-30
Central St. ■	.Dec. 14
St. Rose Cl.	.Dec. 27-29
West Va. Wesleyan ■	.Jan. 4
Fayetteville St. ■	.Jan. 8
St. Paul's ■	.Jan. 11
Livingstone ■	.Jan. 13
Virginia Union ■	.Jan. 16
Elizabeth City St. ■	.Jan. 18
Shaw ■	.Jan. 23
Virginia St. ■	.Jan. 25
Winston-Salem ■	.Jan. 27
Bowie St.	.Jan. 30
Virginia Union	.Feb. 1
Bowie St. ■	.Feb. 3
Virginia St.	.Feb. 8
St. Augustine's	.Feb. 13
Elizabeth City St.	.Feb. 15
Johnson Smith	.Feb. 18
N.C. Central	.Feb. 22

1995-96 RESULTS (23-4)

85	Augusta St. ■	.60
69	West Va. Wesleyan	.60
84	Knoxville	.75
56	Auburn †	.92
71	West Fla. †	.52
80	Livingstone	.71
75	Winston-Salem ■	.62
74	Johnson Smith ■	.60
82	Fayetteville St.	.59
80	St. Paul's ■	.65
60	Virginia Union	.76
88	Elizabeth City St.	.83
116	Bowie St. ■	.57
65	Shaw	.52
87	Virginia St.	.63
115	Knoxville ■	.65
69	Bowie St.	.81
77	Virginia Union ■	.74
97	St. Paul's	.77
101	Virginia St. ■	.83
80	St. Augustine's ■	.87
76	Columbia Union	.55
88	Elizabeth City St. ■	.74
84	N.C. Central ■	.66
85	Virginia St. †	.69
80	N.C. Central †	.67
72	Virginia Union †	.70

Nickname: Spartans
Colors: Green & Gold
Arena: Echols Arena
Capacity: 7,600; Year Built: 1982
AD: Dick Price
SID: John Holley

NORTH ADAMS ST.
North Adams, MA 01247 III

Coach: Matt Capeless
Alma Mater: Massachusetts '80
Record: 3 Years, W-18, L-59

1996-97 SCHEDULE

Potsdam Tr.	.Nov. 22-23

Western New Eng. ■	.Nov. 26
Gordon ■	.Dec. 5
Johnson St.	.Dec. 10
Eastern Conn. St.	.Dec. 12
Mass.-Boston ■	.Dec. 14
Tufts ■	.Jan. 6
Williams	.Jan. 8
New Paltz Inv.	.Jan. 11-12
Framingham St. ■	.Jan. 14
Bri'water (Mass.) ■	.Jan. 20
Worcester St.	.Jan. 25
Salem St. ■	.Jan. 28
Trinity (Conn.) ■	.Jan. 30
Fitchburg St.	.Feb. 1
Westfield St. ■	.Feb. 4
Framingham St.	.Feb. 8
Bri'water (Mass.)	.Feb. 13
Worcester St. ■	.Feb. 15
Salem St.	.Feb. 17
Fitchburg St. ■	.Feb. 20
Westfield St.	.Feb. 22

1995-96 RESULTS (5-20)

62	Clark (Mass.) †	.78
85	New England Col. ■	.58
82	Western New Eng.	.74
61	Eastern Conn. St. ■	.81
70	Castleton St.	.85
58	Central Conn. St.	.96
53	Williams ■	.85
89	Mass.-Boston	.71
70	Southern Vt.	.89
65	Johnson St. ■	.53
68	Framingham St.	.74
63	Bri'water (Mass.) ■	.77
80	Worcester St.	.92
60	Salem St.	.79
57	Trinity (Conn.)	.89
78	Fitchburg St. ■	.48
64	Westfield St.	.66
60	Framingham St. ■	.75
79	Endicott ■	.91
72	Bri'water (Mass.)	.90
67	Worcester St.	.98
54	Salem St. ■	.90
70	Fitchburg St.	.74
86	Westfield St. ■	.89
64	Bri'water (Mass.)	.82

Nickname: Mohawks
Colors: Navy & Gold
Arena: Campus Center Gymnasium
Capacity: 3,500; Year Built: 1975
AD: Scott Nichols
SID: Matt Capeless

NORTH ALA.
Florence, AL 35631 II

Coach: Gary Elliott
Alma Mater: Alabama '70
Record: 11 Years, W-190, L-119

1996-97 SCHEDULE

North Ala. Tr.	.Nov. 15-16
Lane ■	.Nov. 21
Athens St. ■	.Nov. 26
Mississippi Col. Cl.	.Nov. 29-30
Voorhees ■	.Dec. 6
Athens St.	.Dec. 11
Missouri So. Tr.	.Dec. 30-31
West Fla. ■	.Jan. 4
Valdosta St. ■	.Jan. 6
Montevallo	.Jan. 11
West Ala. ■	.Jan. 13
Lincoln Memorial	.Jan. 18
West Ga. ■	.Jan. 20
Knoxville	.Jan. 23
Ala.-Huntsville ■	.Jan. 25
West Ala.	.Feb. 1
Montevallo ■	.Feb. 3
Lane	.Feb. 6
Valdosta St.	.Feb. 8
West Fla.	.Feb. 10
Lincoln Memorial ■	.Feb. 15
West Ga.	.Feb. 17

Ala.-Huntsville	.Feb. 22

1995-96 RESULTS (24-8)

97	Lane ■	.79
83	Tex. A&M-Kingsville ■	.85
82	Delta St.	.77
93	Faulkner ■	.86
86	Indianapolis	.93
68	Indiana (Pa.) †	.82
91	Hillsdale †	.74
84	Delta St.	.75
84	Athens St. ■	.81
71	Martin Methodist ■	.56
88	Bapt. Christian	.63
100	West Fla.	.71
83	Valdosta St.	.93
118	Montevallo ■	.84
60	West Ala.	.44
92	Lincoln Memorial ■	.75
87	West Ga. ■	.75
70	Ala.-Huntsville	.61
78	Athens St. ■	.78
76	Valdosta St. ■	.72
86	West Fla. ■	.74
79	West Ala.	.64
70	Lincoln Memorial	.72
81	West Ga.	.96
88	Montevallo	.100
71	Ala.-Huntsville ■	.58
92	Mississippi Col. †	.75
80	Delta St.	.65
78	Delta St. †	.69
85	Tex. A&M-Kingsville †	.80
92	Mo.-Rolla	.80
68	Fort Hays St. †	.71

Nickname: Lions
Colors: Purple & Gold
Arena: Flowers Hall
Capacity: 3,800; Year Built: 1972
AD: Dan Summy
SID: Jeff Hodges

NORTH CARO.
Chapel Hill, NC 27514 I

Coach: Dean Smith
Alma Mater: Kansas '53
Record: 35 Years, W-851, L-247

1996-97 SCHEDULE

Arizona [Springfield]	.Nov. 22
Richmond ■	.Nov. 25
Pittsburgh ■	.Nov. 29
Bethune-Cookman ■	.Dec. 2
Charlotte Inv.	.Dec. 6-7
VMI	.Dec. 15
LSU [Greensboro]	.Dec. 18
Massachusetts [East Rutherford]	.Dec. 20
Princeton	.Dec. 22
Wake Forest	.Jan. 4
Maryland ■	.Jan. 8
Virginia	.Jan. 11
North Caro. St.	.Jan. 15
Georgia Tech ■	.Jan. 18
Florida St.	.Jan. 22
Clemson ■	.Jan. 26
Duke	.Jan. 29
Middle Tenn. St. ■	.Feb. 1
Florida St. ■	.Feb. 6
Virginia ■	.Feb. 8
North Caro. St.	.Feb. 12
Georgia Tech	.Feb. 15
Wake Forest ■	.Feb. 19
Maryland	.Feb. 22
Clemson	.Feb. 26
Duke ■	.Mar. 2
Atlantic Coast Conf. Tr.	.Mar. 6-9

1995-96 RESULTS (21-11)

71	Vanderbilt †	.63
92	Michigan St. †	.70
75	Villanova †	.77
83	Richmond ■	.76
89	Tulane †	.71
87	Stanford †	.63
85	Georgia ■	.74

96	Dartmouth ■	66
66	Pittsburgh	49
66	N.C.-Asheville	49
72	Texas	74
96	North Caro. St. ■	72
88	Maryland	86
77	Georgia Tech	80
86	Clemson ■	53
67	Virginia	53
56	Villanova	76
82	Florida St.	71
65	Wake Forest ■	59
73	Duke	72
75	North Caro. St.	78
78	Maryland ■	84
83	Georgia Tech ■	92
53	Clemson	48
71	Virginia ■	66
99	VMI ■	76
80	Florida St.	84
60	Wake Forest	84
84	Duke	78
73	Clemson †	75
83	New Orleans †	62
73	Texas Tech †	92

Nickname: Tar Heels
Colors: Carolina Blue & White
Arena: Smith Center
   Capacity: 21,572; Year Built: 1985
AD: John Swofford
SID: Steve Kirschner

NORTH CARO. A&T
Greensboro, NC 27411 I

Coach: Roy Thomas
Alma Mater: Baylor '74
Record: 2 Years, W-25, L-32
1996-97 SCHEDULE
Texas A&M	Nov. 23
LSU	Nov. 30
Oklahoma St.	Dec. 2
N.C.-Greensboro [Greensboro]	Dec. 7
N.C. Central [Greensboro]	Dec. 14
Livingstone ■	Dec. 30
Winston-Salem	Jan. 9
Morgan St. ■	Jan. 11
Howard ■	Jan. 13
Coppin St.	Jan. 15
Florida A&M	Jan. 18
Bethune-Cookman	Jan. 20
Delaware St.	Jan. 25
Md.-East. Shore	Jan. 27
Hampton	Jan. 30
Bethune-Cookman ■	Feb. 1
Florida A&M ■	Feb. 3
Delaware St. ■	Feb. 8
Md.-East. Shore ■	Feb. 10
South Caro. St. ■	Feb. 15
Hampton ■	Feb. 20
Morgan St.	Feb. 22
Howard	Feb. 24
Coppin St. ■	Feb. 26
South Caro. St.	Mar. 1
Mid-Eastern Conf. Tr.	Mar. 5-8

1995-96 RESULTS (10-17)
69	Winston-Salem ■	61
49	Arkansas	103
51	Tulsa	100
59	St. Peter's ■	76
76	N.C.-Greensboro †	82
81	Vanderbilt	96
53	Middle Tenn. St.	64
83	Livingstone ■	60
71	Coppin St.	82
74	Florida A&M ■	67
59	Bethune-Cookman ■	56
70	N.C. Central †	76
68	Delaware St. ■	66
62	Md.-East. Shore ■	61
63	Bethune-Cookman	64
81	Florida A&M	59
78	Delaware St.	87

65	Md.-East. Shore	56
53	South Caro. St.	74
74	Morgan St. ■	77
60	Coppin St. ■	78
70	Howard ■	68
74	Morgan St.	78
76	Howard	87
59	South Caro. St. ■	88
75	Bethune-Cookman †	74
46	South Caro. St. †	69

Nickname: Aggies
Colors: Blue & Gold
Arena: Ellis Corbett Sports Center
   Capacity: 6,500; Year Built: 1978
AD: Dr. Willie J. Burden
SID: Bradford I. Evans Jr

N.C. CENTRAL
Durham, NC 27707 II

Coach: Greg Jackson
Alma Mater: St. Paul's '81
Record: 5 Years, W-102, L-42
1996-97 SCHEDULE
North Caro. Cent. Cl.	Nov. 16-17
Paine	Nov. 25
Virginia St.	Dec. 4
Clark Atlanta Cl.	Dec. 6-7
North Caro. A&T [Greensboro]	Dec. 14
Johnson Smith ■	Jan. 2
Fayetteville St. ■	Jan. 4
Shaw	Jan. 7
Bowie St.	Jan. 9
Winston-Salem ■	Jan. 11
St. Paul's	Jan. 13
St. Augustine's ■	Jan. 18
Livingstone ■	Jan. 23
Fayetteville St.	Jan. 25
Johnson Smith	Jan. 30
Livingstone	Feb. 1
Shaw ■	Feb. 3
Winston-Salem	Feb. 6
Elizabeth City St. ■	Feb. 8
St. Augustine's	Feb. 11
Virginia Union ■	Feb. 15
Pfeiffer ■	Feb. 20
Norfolk St. ■	Feb. 22

1995-96 RESULTS (20-7)
78	Knoxville ■	57
83	West Ga. ■	61
79	South Caro. St.	84
93	N.C. Wesleyan ■	69
74	Virginia St. ■	69
93	Johnson Smith	75
70	Fayetteville St. ■	65
79	Shaw ■	73
98	Bowie St. ■	66
95	St. Paul's ■	79
76	North Caro. A&T †	70
72	St. Augustine's	67
65	Winston-Salem ■	51
92	Livingstone	88
62	Fayetteville St.	54
70	Paine	65
94	Johnson Smith ■	78
77	Shaw	73
74	Winston-Salem	73
80	Elizabeth City St.	83
85	St. Augustine's ■	82
73	Livingstone	86
59	Virginia Union	73
66	Norfolk St.	84
86	St. Paul's †	73
67	Norfolk St. †	80
62	Pfeiffer †	71

Nickname: Eagles
Colors: Maroon & Gray
Arena: McLendon-McDougald Gym
   Capacity: 4,500; Year Built: 1955
AD: William E. Lide
SID: Kyle Serba

NORTH CARO. ST.
Raleigh, NC 27695 I

Coach: Herb Sendek
Alma Mater: Carnegie Mellon '85
Record: 3 Years, W-63, L-26
1996-97 SCHEDULE
Fla. Atlantic ■	Nov. 22
Penn St. ■	Nov. 25
Lamar ■	Nov. 27
Memphis	Nov. 30
Winthrop ■	Dec. 3
Wake Forest ■	Dec. 7
Central Fla. ■	Dec. 19
Kansas	Dec. 21
Ark.-Pine Bluff ■	Dec. 31
Florida St.	Jan. 4
Tex.-Pan American ■	Jan. 7
Maryland ■	Jan. 12
North Caro.	Jan. 15
Clemson ■	Jan. 18
Duke ■	Jan. 21
Georgia Tech	Jan. 25
Virginia	Jan. 28
Clemson ■	Feb. 1
Maryland	Feb. 5
Duke	Feb. 8
North Caro. ■	Feb. 12
Wake Forest	Feb. 16
Virginia ■	Feb. 19
Georgia Tech ■	Feb. 22
Florida St. ■	Feb. 26
Wofford ■	Mar. 1
Atlantic Coast Conf. Tr.	Mar. 6-9

1995-96 RESULTS (15-16)
104	VMI ■	78
97	Winthrop ■	48
99	Wofford ■	60
84	Davidson	80
120	N.C.-Asheville ■	71
102	Cal Poly SLO ■	83
67	Massachusetts †	78
87	Missouri †	68
76	Illinois †	85
102	Western Caro. ■	71
72	North Caro.	96
69	Virginia	73
78	Boston U. ■	62
71	Florida St. ■	65
81	Central Fla.	74
70	Duke ■	71
74	Maryland	76
71	Georgia Tech ■	76
64	Clemson	61
62	Wake Forest ■	66
78	North Caro. ■	75
82	Virginia ■	84
89	Arizona St. †	69
66	Florida St.	79
76	Duke	79
84	Maryland ■	86
83	Georgia Tech	92
76	Clemson ■	80
70	Wake Forest	72
80	Florida St. †	65
73	Georgia Tech †	88

Nickname: Wolfpack
Colors: Red & White
Arena: Reynolds Coliseum
   Capacity: 12,400; Year Built: 1949
AD: Les Robinson
SID: Mark Bockelman

N.C. WESLEYAN
Rocky Mount, NC 27801 III

Coach: John Thompson
Alma Mater: N.C.-Greensboro '84
Record: 1 Year, W-11, L-14
1996-97 SCHEDULE
Western Md. Tr.	Nov. 22-23
Chowan	Nov. 25

Furman	Nov. 30
Warren Wilson	Dec. 1
Barton	Dec. 7
Warren Wilson ■	Dec. 14
N.C. Wesleyan Tr.	Jan. 10-11
Chris. Newport ■	Jan. 15
Shenandoah	Jan. 19
Greensboro	Jan. 22
Ferrum	Jan. 25
Methodist ■	Jan. 27
Averett	Jan. 29
Savannah A&D [Hilton Head]	Feb. 1
Chris. Newport	Feb. 5
Chowan ■	Feb. 7
Shenandoah ■	Feb. 9
Ferrum ■	Feb. 12
Newport News App.	Feb. 15
Methodist	Feb. 17
Averett ■	Feb. 19
Greensboro ■	Feb. 22

1995-96 RESULTS (11-14)
59	Bridgewater (Va.) †	64
109	Salisbury St. †	107
92	Newport News App. ■	88
69	N.C. Central	93
85	Salisbury St.	106
69	Old Westbury †	76
67	Chowan	86
119	Columbia (S.C.) ■	63
75	Goucher ■	79
72	Chowan ■	67
72	Chris. Newport	82
65	Shenandoah ■	105
100	Ferrum ■	89
79	Chowan	65
59	Methodist	83
91	Averett ■	71
86	Greensboro ■	78
83	Chris. Newport ■	85
84	Shenandoah	103
55	Greensboro	66
73	Ferrum	85
69	Methodist ■	63
72	Averett	64
62	Newport News App.	61
67	Methodist †	72

Nickname: Battling Bishops
Colors: Royal Blue & Gold
Arena: Everett Gymnasium
   Capacity: 800; Year Built: 1960
AD: Mike Fox
SID: Rob Donnenwirth

N.C.-ASHEVILLE
Asheville, NC 28804 I

Coach: Eddie Biedenbach
Alma Mater: North Caro. St. '68
Record: 3 Years, W-29, L-51
1996-97 SCHEDULE
East Tenn. St.	Nov. 23
Kansas St.	Nov. 26
Montreat ■	Dec. 2
Kansas	Dec. 15
South Caro.	Dec. 19
Marshall	Dec. 21
Kentucky	Dec. 23
Mt. St. Mary's Cl.	Dec. 27-28
New Mexico St.	Dec. 30
Md.-Balt. County ■	Jan. 4
Marshall ■	Jan. 6
Radford	Jan. 9
Liberty ■	Jan. 11
Georgia St. ■	Jan. 13
Winthrop ■	Jan. 15
Charleston So. ■	Jan. 18
Coastal Caro. ■	Jan. 20
N.C.-Greensboro	Jan. 25
Coastal Caro.	Jan. 30
Charleston So.	Feb. 1
Radford ■	Feb. 8
Liberty	Feb. 10
Md.-Balt. County	Feb. 15

N.C.-Greensboro ■ ....Feb. 20
Winthrop ....Feb. 22
Big South Conf. Tr. ....Feb. 26-Mar. 1

1995-96 RESULTS (18-10)

97	Bryan ■	70
64	Clemson	83
73	Furman	71
105	Montreat ■	71
66	Vanderbilt	80
68	Samford	60
71	North Caro. St.	120
49	North Caro.	66
84	Milligan ■	76
98	Tusculum ■	51
67	Charleston So. ■	81
77	Coastal Caro.	66
66	Liberty ■	48
64	N.C.-Greensboro ■	65
76	Md.-Balt. County ■	73
83	Winthrop	65
74	Radford ■	56
82	Wofford ■	53
64	Charleston So.	63
93	Coastal Caro. ■	86
43	Liberty	65
65	N.C.-Greensboro	56
76	Wofford	67
61	Md.-Balt. County	62
89	Winthrop ■	70
74	Radford	77
69	Winthrop †	61
60	Liberty	73

Nickname: Bulldogs
Colors: Royal Blue & White
Arena: Charlie Justice Center
　Capacity: 2,500; Year Built: 1963
AD: Tom Hunnicutt
SID: Mike Gore

N.C.-CHARLOTTE

Charlotte, NC 28223 I

Coach: Melvin Watkins
Alma Mater: N.C.-Charlotte '77
(First year as head coach)

1996-97 SCHEDULE

Kent ....Nov. 26
Old Dominion ....Nov. 30
Appalachian St. ■ ....Dec. 2
Charlotte Inv. ....Dec. 6-7
Davidson ■ ....Dec. 14
Southern Ill. ■ ....Dec. 18
Canisius ....Dec. 21
Tennessee ■ ....Dec. 28
Geo. Washington ■ ....Dec. 30
VMI ■ ....Jan. 4
Louisville ■ ....Jan. 6
Memphis ■ ....Jan. 9
St. Louis ■ ....Jan. 11
South Fla. ....Jan. 14
Memphis ....Jan. 19
Cincinnati ■ ....Jan. 21
Tulane ....Jan. 25
Houston ■ ....Jan. 29
James Madison ....Feb. 1
DePaul ....Feb. 4
Houston ....Feb. 9
Marquette ■ ....Feb. 15
UAB ■ ....Feb. 23
Louisville ....Feb. 26
Southern Miss. ....Mar. 2
Conference USA ....Mar. 5-8

1995-96 RESULTS (14-15)

79	Tennessee	76
80	East Caro. ■	65
63	N.C.-Wilmington	60
85	Appalachian St.	81
74	Va. Commonwealth	85
81	Southern Ill.	73
61	Iowa St. †	69
67	Purdue †	73
60	Virginia Tech †	76
88	Lafayette ■	58
55	Memphis	57
78	Louisville	66
60	Tulane	58
47	Davidson ■	56
89	South Fla. ■	56
79	Marquette ■	69
58	St. Louis	72
64	Cincinnati	78
55	James Madison ■	41
67	Geo. Washington ■	72
55	Memphis ■	68
77	Tulane	95
64	Louisville ■	67
62	N.C.-Greensboro ■	58
68	Marquette	78
56	UAB	63
81	DePaul ■	69
77	Southern Miss. ■	66
60	DePaul †	66

Nickname: 49ers
Colors: Green & White
Arena: Dale F. Halton Arena
　Capacity: 9,105; Year Built: 1996
AD: Judy W. Rose
SID: Mark Colone

N.C.-GREENSBORO

Greensboro, NC 27412 I

Coach: Randy Peele
Alma Mater: Va. Wesleyan '80
Record: 1 Year, W-20, L-10

1996-97 SCHEDULE

William & Mary ....Nov. 23
Great Alas. Shootout ....Nov. 27-30
Appalachian St. ....Dec. 5
North Caro. A&T [Greensboro] ....Dec. 7
Virginia Tech ■ ....Dec. 9
Hampton ■ ....Dec. 21
Charleston (S.C.) Cl ....Dec. 28-29
Georgia Tech ....Dec. 31
Loyola (Md.) ■ ....Jan. 4
Md.-Balt. County ■ ....Jan. 6
Appalachian St. ■ ....Jan. 8
Charleston So. ....Jan. 11
Duke ■ ....Jan. 15
Radford ....Jan. 18
Liberty ....Jan. 20
Loyola (Md.) ....Jan. 22
N.C.-Asheville ■ ....Jan. 25
Md.-Balt. County ....Jan. 29
Coastal Caro. ....Feb. 1
Winthrop ■ ....Feb. 3
Liberty ■ ....Feb. 6
Charleston So. ■ ....Feb. 8
Radford ■ ....Feb. 13
Winthrop ....Feb. 15
N.C.-Asheville ....Feb. 20
Coastal Caro. ■ ....Feb. 22
Big South Conf. Tr. ....Feb. 26-Mar. 1

1995-96 RESULTS (20-10)

64	South Caro.	82
57	Duke	71
69	Campbell ■	60
80	Appalachian St. ■	64
82	North Caro. A&T †	76
86	Hampton	78
82	Akron ■	57
78	Southern U.	96
64	Southwestern La.	77
67	St. Francis (Pa.) ■	47
85	Coastal Caro.	60
65	N.C.-Asheville	64
82	Winthrop ■	60
77	Md.-Balt. County ■	65
73	Radford	81
90	Charleston So. ■	64
63	Liberty ■	56
48	Virginia Tech	74
67	Radford	81
75	Coastal Caro.	62
56	N.C.-Asheville ■	65
47	Liberty	67
89	Winthrop ■	60
58	N.C.-Charlotte	62
68	Md.-Balt. County	49
70	Charleston So.	59
78	Coastal Caro. †	67
69	Charleston So. †	60
79	Liberty ■	53
61	Cincinnati †	66

Nickname: Spartans
Colors: Gold, White & Navy
Arena: Fleming Gym
　Capacity: 2,320; Year Built: 1989
AD: Nelson Bobb
SID: Chris Militello

N.C.-PEMBROKE

Pembroke, NC 28372 II

Coach: John Haskins
Alma Mater: N.C.-Wilmington '80
Record: 4 Years, W-49, L-58

1996-97 SCHEDULE

Coker ....Nov. 16
Belmont Abbey ....Nov. 19
Gardner-Webb ■ ....Nov. 26
North Fla. Cl. ....Nov. 29-30
Belmont Abbey ■ ....Dec. 7
Mount Olive ....Dec. 9
Augusta St. ■ ....Dec. 11
Francis Marion ....Jan. 2
S.C.-Spartanburg ....Jan. 4
Lander ■ ....Jan. 8
Georgia Col. ....Jan. 11
Augusta St. ....Jan. 12
S.C.-Aiken ....Jan. 15
Armstrong Atlantic ■ ....Jan. 22
Kennesaw St. ....Jan. 25
Columbus St. ....Jan. 26
Francis Marion ....Jan. 29
S.C.-Spartanburg ■ ....Feb. 1
Columbus St. ■ ....Feb. 2
Lander ....Feb. 5
Georgia Col. ■ ....Feb. 8
St. Andrews ■ ....Feb. 10
S.C.-Aiken ■ ....Feb. 12
Armstrong Atlantic ....Feb. 19
Kennesaw St. ■ ....Feb. 22

1995-96 RESULTS (15-13)

77	Lenoir-Rhyne †	59
85	Elon	90
70	Mount Olive ■	69
74	Coker ■	78
72	Fayetteville St.	68
55	Longwood	53
73	Augusta St. ■	57
77	Gardner-Webb	75
54	Francis Marion	71
82	S.C.-Spartanburg ■	85
72	Columbus St. ■	81
80	Lander	77
78	Georgia Col. ■	91
60	Augusta St.	68
85	S.C.-Aiken ■	70
89	St. Andrews	81
56	Armstrong Atlantic	53
81	Kennesaw St.	72
74	Columbus St.	79
64	Francis Marion ■	58
96	S.C.-Spartanburg	86
73	Lander ■	80
86	Georgia Col.	93
70	S.C.-Aiken	74
84	Armstrong Atlantic ■	75
65	Kennesaw St. ■	69
67	Lander †	65
66	Columbus St. †	93

Nickname: Braves
Colors: Black & Gold
Arena: Jones P.E. Center
　Capacity: 3,000; Year Built: 1972
AD: Raymond Pennington
SID: To be named

N.C.-WILMINGTON

Wilmington, NC 28403 I

Coach: Jerry Wainwright
Alma Mater: Colorado Col. '68
Record: 2 Years, W-29, L-27

1996-97 SCHEDULE

Top of the World Cl. ....Nov. 22-24
Wisconsin ....Nov. 30
Southwest Mo. St. ....Dec. 2
Campbell ■ ....Dec. 14
Manhattan ■ ....Dec. 19
Mississippi St. ....Dec. 21
Massachusetts ■ ....Dec. 22
Mt. St. Mary's Cl. ....Dec. 27-28
Villanova ....Dec. 30
George Mason ■ ....Jan. 4
American ■ ....Jan. 6
Va. Commonwealth ....Jan. 11
Old Dominion ....Jan. 13
William & Mary ....Jan. 16
James Madison ....Jan. 18
Richmond ■ ....Jan. 20
East Caro. ■ ....Jan. 25
William & Mary ■ ....Jan. 29
American ....Feb. 1
George Mason ....Feb. 3
Old Dominion ■ ....Feb. 8
James Madison ■ ....Feb. 12
Richmond ....Feb. 15
Va. Commonwealth ■ ....Feb. 19
East Caro. ....Feb. 22
Colonial Conf. Tr. ....Feb. 28-Mar. 3

1995-96 RESULTS (13-16)

60	N.C.-Charlotte	63
54	Mississippi St.	77
51	Southwestern La.	67
73	Davidson ■	56
47	Cincinnati	82
85	Alabama St. †	56
51	Massachusetts	77
52	Campbell ■	74
57	Illinois St.	69
62	Manhattan	69
68	George Mason	44
61	American	58
48	Old Dominion	61
57	James Madison ■	48
64	Richmond	47
67	William & Mary ■	54
44	East Caro.	45
45	Va. Commonwealth ■	63
50	Old Dominion	51
54	George Mason ■	46
73	American	58
58	James Madison	59
46	William & Mary	63
44	Va. Commonwealth	63
67	East Caro. ■	45
63	Richmond	59
63	William & Mary †	55
59	Old Dominion †	39
43	Va. Commonwealth †	46

Nickname: Seahawks
Colors: Green, Gold & Navy Blue
Arena: Trask Coliseum
　Capacity: 6,100; Year Built: 1978
AD: Paul A. Miller
SID: Joe Browning

NORTH CENTRAL

Naperville, IL 60566 III

Coach: Bill Warden
Alma Mater: North Central '55
Record: 15 Years, W-191, L-200

1996-97 SCHEDULE

North Central Cl. ....Nov. 22-23
Macalester ....Nov. 26
Tampa ....Dec. 3
Rollins ....Dec. 5
Fla. Southern ....Dec. 7

Winona St. ....Dec. 9
Concordia (Ill.) ■ ....Dec. 13
Olivet Nazarene ■ ....Dec. 17
Benedictine (Ill.) ....Dec. 21
Kalamazoo Cl. ....Dec. 27-28
Illinois Tech ■ ....Jan. 4
Augustana (Ill.) ■ ....Jan. 8
Carthage ■ ....Jan. 15
Elmhurst ....Jan. 18
Ill. Wesleyan ■ ....Jan. 22
Wheaton (Ill.) ■ ....Jan. 25
North Park ■ ....Feb. 1
Carthage ....Feb. 5
Millikin ■ ....Feb. 8
Elmhurst ■ ....Feb. 11
Wheaton (Ill.) ....Feb. 15
Ill. Wesleyan ....Feb. 19
Augustana (Ill.) ■ ....Feb. 22
Millikin ■ ....Feb. 26
North Park ....Feb. 29

1995-96 RESULTS (5-20)
76	Albion ■	91
86	Franklin ■	98
77	Aurora	87
59	Regis (Colo.)	61
65	Metro St.	87
58	Colo. Christian	57
79	Olivet Nazarene	92
63	Benedictine (Ill.) ■	88
55	Defiance	81
72	Eureka †	85
79	Rockford ■	70
59	Millikin	61
71	Augustana (Ill.)	96
60	Ill. Wesleyan ■	85
82	Carthage ■	79
58	Elmhurst ■	73
49	Wheaton (Ill.)	76
83	North Park	97
63	Millikin ■	81
68	Ill. Wesleyan	84
69	Augustana (Ill.)	90
63	Carthage	57
50	Elmhurst	85
77	Wheaton (Ill.) ■	86
90	North Park ■	82

Nickname: Cardinals
Colors: Cardinal & White
Arena: Gregory Arena
  Capacity: 3,000; Year Built: 1931
AD: Walter Johnson
SID: Mike Koon

NORTH DAK.
Grand Forks, ND 58202 II

Coach: Rich Glas
Alma Mater: Bemidji St. '70
Record: 18 Years, W-323, L-183

1996-97 SCHEDULE
Sioux Falls ■ ....Nov. 23
Denver Cl. ....Nov. 29-30
Minot St. ■ ....Dec. 4
Moorhead St. ....Dec. 7
Bemidji St. ■ ....Dec. 13
Minn.-Morris ■ ....Dec. 14
North Dakota Cl. ....Dec. 21-22
North Dak. St. ....Dec. 28
South Dak. ■ ....Jan. 3
Morningside ■ ....Jan. 4
St. Cloud St. ....Jan. 10
Mankato St. ....Jan. 11
South Dak. St. ■ ....Jan. 17
Augustana (S.D.) ■ ....Jan. 18
Northern Colo. ....Jan. 24
Neb.-Omaha ....Jan. 25
Morningside ....Jan. 31
South Dak. ....Feb. 1
Mankato St. ■ ....Feb. 7
St. Cloud St. ■ ....Feb. 8
Augustana (S.D.) ....Feb. 14
South Dak. St. ....Feb. 15
Neb.-Omaha ■ ....Feb. 21

Northern Colo. ■ ....Feb. 22
North Dak. St. ■ ....Mar. 1

1995-96 RESULTS (15-12)
95	Colo. Christian †	67
71	Grand Canyon	85
51	Wis.-Platteville ■	59
83	Dak. Wesleyan ■	64
111	Minot St.	86
76	Bemidji St. ■	58
94	Moorhead St. ■	73
95	Minn.-Crookston ■	72
87	Denver	93
82	South Dak.	93
74	Morningside	88
58	St. Cloud St. ■	63
70	Mankato St. ■	86
79	South Dak. St.	85
85	Augustana (S.D.)	77
62	Northern Colo. ■	59
88	Neb.-Omaha	85
76	North Dak. St. ■	89
71	Mankato St.	70
70	St. Cloud St.	90
108	Augustana (S.D.) ■	99
96	South Dak. St. ■	71
63	Neb.-Omaha ■	52
82	Northern Colo.	62
73	North Dak. St.	85
107	Morningside ■	98
66	South Dak.	86

Nickname: Sioux
Colors: Green & White
Arena: Hyslop Sports Center
  Capacity: 6,800; Year Built: 1951
AD: Terry Wanless
SID: Mike Cohen

NORTH DAK. ST.
Fargo, ND 58105 II

Coach: Tom Billeter
Alma Mater: Illinois '83
Record: 4 Years, W-75, L-43

1996-97 SCHEDULE
Mt. Senario ■ ....Nov. 23
Mayville St. ■ ....Nov. 25
Florida Tech Cl. ....Nov. 29-30
Valley City St. ■ ....Dec. 5
Jamestown ■ ....Dec. 11
Moorhead St. ■ ....Dec. 14
Minn.-Crookston ■ ....Dec. 19
Presentation ■ ....Dec. 21
North Dak. ■ ....Dec. 28
Morningside ■ ....Jan. 3
South Dak. ■ ....Jan. 4
Mankato St. ....Jan. 10
St. Cloud St. ....Jan. 11
Augustana (S.D.) ■ ....Jan. 17
South Dak. St. ■ ....Jan. 18
Neb.-Omaha ....Jan. 24
Northern Colo. ....Jan. 25
South Dak. ....Jan. 31
Morningside ....Feb. 1
St. Cloud St. ■ ....Feb. 7
Mankato St. ■ ....Feb. 8
South Dak. St. ....Feb. 14
Augustana (S.D.) ....Feb. 15
Northern Colo. ■ ....Feb. 21
Neb.-Omaha ■ ....Feb. 22
North Dak. ....Mar. 1

1995-96 RESULTS (20-9)
92	Mayville St. ■	58
81	Neb.-Kearney	87
79	Valley City St.	73
92	MidAmerica Naz.	75
95	Moorhead St.	96
71	Mt. Senario ■	61
97	Minn.-Crookston ■	60
69	Jamestown	66
95	Bemidji St. ■	69
69	Morningside	79
80	South Dak.	78
79	Mankato St. ■	83

79	St. Cloud St. ■	73
70	Augustana (S.D.)	74
101	South Dak. St.	96
71	Neb.-Omaha ■	67
57	Northern Colo. ■	62
89	North Dak.	76
79	St. Cloud St.	64
85	Mankato St.	94
81	South Dak. St. ■	82
86	Augustana (S.D.) ■	61
86	Northern Colo.	84
72	Neb.-Omaha	52
85	North Dak. ■	73
78	South Dak.	68
107	Morningside ■	85
71	Denver †	70
88	South Dak. St. †	94

Nickname: Bison
Colors: Yellow & Green
Arena: Bison Sports Arena
  Capacity: 8,000; Year Built: 1970
AD: Robert Entzion
SID: George Ellis

NORTH FLA.
Jacksonville, FL 32216 II

Coach: Rich Zvosec
Alma Mater: Defiance '83
Record: 7 Years, W-81, L-113

1996-97 SCHEDULE
Mt. Olive Tr. ....Nov. 22-23
Edward Waters ■ ....Nov. 26
North Fla. Cl. ....Nov. 29-30
Savannah St. ....Dec. 2
Valdosta St. ....Dec. 17
Wis.-Superior ■ ....Dec. 21
Gardner-Webb ■ ....Jan. 3
St. Leo ■ ....Jan. 8
Barry ■ ....Jan. 11
Eckerd ....Jan. 15
Fla. Southern ....Jan. 18
Tampa ■ ....Jan. 22
Rollins ■ ....Jan. 25
Florida Tech ....Jan. 29
Eckerd ■ ....Feb. 1
Fla. Southern ■ ....Feb. 5
Barry ....Feb. 8
Savannah St. ■ ....Feb. 10
Tampa ....Feb. 12
Rollins ....Feb. 15
Florida Tech ■ ....Feb. 19
St. Leo ....Feb. 22

1995-96 RESULTS (14-15)
55	Pfeiffer ■	71
81	Wingate ■	69
63	Lynn	79
77	Edward Waters	73
67	Flagler ■	51
75	Savannah St. ■	63
64	Elizabeth City St.	71
76	Valdosta St. ■	71
60	Spring Hill †	53
68	Mars Hill †	57
51	Queens (N.C.)	70
73	Rollins	74
64	Fla. Southern	84
56	Florida Tech ■	40
64	Barry	83
79	Tampa ■	61
67	St. Leo	58
64	Eckerd ■	58
51	Eckerd	56
65	Rollins	57
81	Fla. Southern	84
48	Florida Tech	65
68	Barry ■	80
50	Tampa	53
63	Savannah St.	65
69	St. Leo ■	78
56	Rollins †	51
61	Eckerd †	52
49	Fla. Southern †	53

Nickname: Ospreys
Colors: Navy Blue & Gray
Arena: UNF Arena
  Capacity: 5,800; Year Built: 1993
AD: Richard Gropper
SID: Bonnie Senappe

NORTH PARK
Chicago, IL 60625 III

Coach: Keith Peterson
Alma Mater: Concordia (Ill.) '75
Record: 8 Years, W-82, L-121

1996-97 SCHEDULE
Bethel (Minn.) Tr. ....Nov. 22-23
Benedictine (Ill.) ....Nov. 26
Hope ....Dec. 4
Concordia (Wis.) ■ ....Dec. 7
Augustana (Ill.) ....Dec. 11
Chicago ....Dec. 14
Surf 'n Slam Inv. ....Dec. 26-Jan. 1
DePauw ....Jan. 4
Carthage ....Jan. 8
Ill. Wesleyan ....Jan. 11
Millikin ....Jan. 18
Edgewood ■ ....Jan. 22
Augustana (Ill.) ■ ....Jan. 25
Elmhurst ■ ....Jan. 29
North Central ....Feb. 1
Wheaton (Ill.) ....Feb. 4
Carthage ■ ....Feb. 8
Ill. Wesleyan ....Feb. 15
Millikin ....Feb. 19
Wheaton (Ill.) ....Feb. 22
Elmhurst ....Feb. 26
North Central ■ ....Feb. 29

1995-96 RESULTS (6-18)
80	Wis. Lutheran †	98
87	Concordia (Ill.) †	69
75	Olivet Nazarene	90
77	Benedictine (Ill.) ■	85
64	Kalamazoo	80
72	Hope ■	85
77	Illinois Tech	85
69	St. John's (Minn.) ■	77
82	Marymount (Va.) †	88
72	Grace †	64
61	Carthage	72
87	Elmhurst	94
72	Wheaton (Ill.) ■	91
81	Millikin	78
67	Augustana (Ill.)	82
76	Ill. Wesleyan ■	86
97	North Central ■	83
88	Carthage ■	78
65	Wheaton (Ill.)	76
73	Elmhurst ■	98
78	Millikin	90
106	Augustana (Ill.) ■	104
89	Ill. Wesleyan	96
82	North Central	90

Nickname: Vikings
Colors: Blue & Gold
Arena: North Park Gymnasium
  Capacity: 1,800; Year Built: 1958
AD: Jerry Chaplin
SID: Steve Vanden Branden

NORTH TEXAS
Denton, TX 76203 I

Coach: Tim Jankovich
Alma Mater: Kansas St. '82
Record: 3 Years, W-43, L-41

1996-97 SCHEDULE
Sam Houston St. ....Nov. 23
Mary Hardin-Baylor ■ ....Nov. 25
Southeast Mo. St. Cl. ....Nov. 29-30
Southern Methodist ....Dec. 2
Texas A&M ■ ....Dec. 5
Texas ....Dec. 7
Alabama ....Dec. 18

Rice ■ ....Dec. 22
Phillips (Okla.) ■ ....Jan. 4
UC Santa Barb. ....Jan. 9
New Mexico St. ....Jan. 11
Utah St. ....Jan. 16
Nevada ....Jan. 19
Boise St. ■ ....Jan. 23
Idaho ■ ....Jan. 25
Pacific (Cal.) ■ ....Jan. 30
Long Beach St. ■ ....Feb. 1
UC Irvine ....Feb. 6
Cal St. Fullerton ....Feb. 8
Idaho ....Feb. 13
Boise St. ....Feb. 15
Cal Poly SLO ■ ....Feb. 20
New Mexico St. ■ ....Feb. 22
Nevada ■ ....Feb. 27
Utah St. ■ ....Mar. 1
Big West Conf. Tr. ....Mar. 7-9

1995-96 RESULTS (15-13)
67	Texas	88
82	Md.-Balt. County ■	67
56	Rice	58
72	Alabama ■	74
50	Texas A&M	68
54	Evansville	58
67	Texas Christian	77
63	Texas-Arlington ■	66
71	Sam Houston St. ■	59
75	Stephen F. Austin ■	66
62	Nicholls St.	67
63	McNeese St.	75
62	Texas-San Antonio	59
68	Northwestern St. ■	62
65	Northeast La.	74
62	Southern Methodist ■	55
67	Texas-Arlington	70
72	Stephen F. Austin	65
64	Sam Houston St.	62
67	McNeese St. ■	65
81	Nicholls St. ■	67
67	Southwest Tex. St.	55
67	Northeast La.	95
78	Northwestern St.	53
67	Southwest Tex. St. ■	60
75	Texas-San Antonio ■	55
80	Texas-San Antonio †	71
60	Northeast La. †	71

Nickname: Mean Green Eagles
Colors: Green & White
Arena: Super Pit
   Capacity: 10,032; Year Built: 1973
AD: Craig Helwig
SID: To be named

NORTHEAST LA.
Monroe, LA 71209 I

Coach: Mike Vining
Alma Mater: Northeast La. '67
Record: 15 Years, W-279, L-167

1996-97 SCHEDULE
Oklahoma ....Nov. 23
Oral Roberts ....Nov. 25
Southern Miss. ■ ....Nov. 30
Ark.-Monticello ■ ....Dec. 3
Baylor Tr. ....Dec. 6-7
Memphis ....Dec. 18
Ball St. ....Dec. 21
Houston ....Dec. 28
Stephen F. Austin ....Jan. 4
Southwest Tex. St. ■ ....Jan. 9
Texas-San Antonio ■ ....Jan. 11
McNeese St. ....Jan. 16
Nicholls St. ....Jan. 18
Texas-Arlington ■ ....Jan. 23
Northwestern St. ....Jan. 27
Texas-San Antonio ....Jan. 30
Southwest Tex. St. ....Feb. 1
Stephen F. Austin ■ ....Feb. 6
Sam Houston St. ■ ....Feb. 8
McNeese St. ■ ....Feb. 13
Nicholls St. ■ ....Feb. 15

Sam Houston St. ....Feb. 18
Northwestern St. ■ ....Feb. 22
Texas-Arlington ....Feb. 27
Oral Roberts ■ ....Mar. 1
Southland Conf. Tr. ....Mar. 5-8

1995-96 RESULTS (16-14)
67	Arkansas	75
113	Ark.-Monticello ■	83
60	Colorado St.	78
73	Texas Southern †	76
71	Auburn	80
60	Mississippi St. ■	66
76	Memphis	96
64	Houston	98
75	Nicholls St.	72
65	McNeese St. ■	81
58	Southern Miss.	89
94	Northwestern St. ■	74
56	Southwest Tex. St. ■	61
61	Texas-San Antonio ■	75
70	Sam Houston St. ■	67
82	Texas-Arlington	64
74	North Texas ■	65
78	McNeese St. ■	75
125	Nicholls St. ■	85
80	Northwestern St.	70
71	Texas-San Antonio	73
75	Southwest Tex. St.	60
97	Stephen F. Austin ■	90
95	North Texas	67
87	Texas-Arlington ■	67
92	Stephen F. Austin	82
86	Sam Houston St. ■	92
92	Stephen F. Austin †	73
71	North Texas †	60
50	Wake Forest †	62

Nickname: Indians
Colors: Maroon & Gold
Arena: Ewing Coliseum
   Capacity: 8,000; Year Built: 1971
AD: Richard Giannini
SID: Robby Edwards

NORTHEASTERN
Boston, MA 02115 I

Coach: Rudy Keeling
Alma Mater: Quincy '70
Record: 8 Years, W-106, L-122

1996-97 SCHEDULE
Niagara ■ ....Nov. 23
Connecticut ....Nov. 25
Fresno St. Cl. ....Nov. 29-30
Delaware ....Dec. 6
Towson St. ....Dec. 8
Rider ....Dec. 21
Iona Tr. ....Dec. 27-28
Rutgers ....Dec. 30
Maine ■ ....Jan. 2
New Hampshire ■ ....Jan. 4
Drexel ■ ....Jan. 10
Hofstra ■ ....Jan. 12
Vermont ....Jan. 16
Hartford ....Jan. 19
Boston U. ....Jan. 21
Towson St. ■ ....Jan. 24
Delaware ■ ....Jan. 26
Boston U. ■ ....Feb. 1
Drexel ....Feb. 7
Hofstra ....Feb. 9
Hartford ■ ....Feb. 13
Vermont ■ ....Feb. 15
Maine ....Feb. 20
New Hampshire ....Feb. 22
America East Conf. Tr. ....Feb. 28-Mar. 2

1995-96 RESULTS (4-24)
55	Marist ■	73
39	Connecticut	86
61	Rhode Island	78
90	New Hampshire	98
62	Maine ■	76
65	Marist	86
66	Florida Int'l	80

86	Howard	81
56	Duke ■	87
69	Vermont ■	73
74	Hartford ■	83
65	Towson St.	78
69	Delaware	99
65	Hofstra ■	70
65	Drexel ■	87
62	Niagara ■	81
59	Boston U.	63
71	Hofstra	68
47	Drexel	84
67	Towson St. ■	73
59	Delaware ■	60
64	Vermont	77
79	Hartford	82
56	Boston U. ■	77
72	New Hampshire ■	78
75	Maine	59
71	Hofstra †	61
54	Boston U. †	69

Nickname: Huskies
Colors: Red & Black
Arena: Matthews Arena
   Capacity: 6,000; Year Built: 1909
AD: Barry Gallup
SID: Jack Grinold

NORTHEASTERN ILL.
Chicago, IL 60625 I

Coach: Rees Johnson
Alma Mater: Winona St. '71
Record: 20 Years, W-298, L-268

1996-97 SCHEDULE
Trinity Bible ■ ....Nov. 26
Alabama ....Nov. 30
Wis.-Green Bay ....Dec. 3
Wis. Lutheran ■ ....Dec. 7
Wis.-Milwaukee ....Dec. 12
Oral Roberts ■ ....Dec. 14
Ill.-Chicago ■ ....Dec. 17
Oregon St. ....Dec. 20
Arizona St. ....Dec. 22
Chicago St. ■ ....Jan. 2
Central Conn. St. ....Jan. 6
Valparaiso ■ ....Jan. 11
Western Ill. ■ ....Jan. 13
Troy St. ....Jan. 18
Mo.-Kansas City ■ ....Jan. 20
Youngstown St. ■ ....Jan. 25
Buffalo ■ ....Jan. 27
Oral Roberts ....Feb. 1
Central Conn. St. ■ ....Feb. 3
Western Ill. ....Feb. 6
Valparaiso ....Feb. 8
Mo.-Kansas City ....Feb. 10
Troy St. ■ ....Feb. 12
Buffalo ....Feb. 15
Youngstown St. ....Feb. 17
Chicago St. ....Feb. 22
Mid-Continent Conf. Tr. ....Mar. 2-4

1995-96 RESULTS (14-13)
58	Miami (Fla.)	81
98	Cardinal Stritch ■	63
55	Wisconsin	89
69	Wis.-Milwaukee ■	52
68	Ill.-Chicago	84
74	Wis.-Milwaukee ■	72
73	Cal St. Northridge	74
76	Nebraska	94
92	Viterbo ■	68
79	Valparaiso	91
96	Troy St. ■	92
100	Central Conn. St.	99
56	Youngstown St.	54
66	Buffalo	80
72	Western Ill. ■	80
79	Mo.-Kansas City ■	83
73	Eastern Ill.	48
81	Chicago St.	68
85	Central Conn. St.	66
86	Troy St.	90

77	Buffalo ■	85
76	Youngstown St. ■	62
55	Mo.-Kansas City ■	57
86	Western Ill.	105
97	Chicago St. ■	69
100	Valparaiso ■	96
83	Eastern Ill. ■	72

Nickname: Golden Eagles
Colors: Royal Blue & Gold
Arena: P.E. Complex
   Capacity: 2,000; Year Built: 1988
AD: Vivian Fuller
SID: Damion Jones

NORTHERN ARIZ.
Flagstaff, AZ 86011 I

Coach: Ben Howland
Alma Mater: Weber St. '80
Record: 2 Years, W-14, L-38

1996-97 SCHEDULE
Cal St. Sacramento ■ ....Nov. 22
Arizona ....Nov. 26
Sam Houston St. ■ ....Nov. 30
McNeese St. ■ ....Dec. 3
Texas-Arlington ■ ....Dec. 7
Southern Utah ....Dec. 16
Loyola Marymount ....Dec. 18
Occidental ■ ....Dec. 21
UNLV ....Dec. 30
Eastern Wash. ■ ....Jan. 2
Portland St. ■ ....Jan. 4
Montana ....Jan. 9
Montana St. ....Jan. 11
Idaho St. ■ ....Jan. 16
Weber St. ■ ....Jan. 18
Idaho St. ....Jan. 25
Southern Utah ■ ....Jan. 28
Cal St. Northridge ....Feb. 1
Montana St. ■ ....Feb. 6
Montana ■ ....Feb. 8
Portland St. ....Feb. 13
Eastern Wash. ....Feb. 15
Cal St. Sacramento ....Feb. 20
Weber St. ....Feb. 22
Cal St. Northridge ■ ....Feb. 27
Cal St. Sacramento ....Mar. 1
Big Sky Conf. Tr. ....Mar. 6-8

1995-96 RESULTS (6-20)
83	California	111
83	Cal Poly SLO ■	71
77	Texas-Arlington	88
74	Sam Houston St.	85
81	Colorado Col.	63
66	Montana Tech ■	50
66	Oral Roberts ■	70
62	Arizona St.	76
75	Cal Poly SLO	78
60	San Diego	67
61	Loyola Marymount ■	67
64	Montana	66
58	Montana St.	87
59	Idaho St. ■	73
60	Boise St. ■	65
60	Eastern Wash.	58
64	Idaho	66
67	Weber St.	89
61	Montana St. ■	76
46	Montana ■	77
45	Boise St.	68
75	Idaho St.	85
79	Idaho ■	69
71	Eastern Wash. ■	57
66	Cal St. Sacramento	71
64	Weber St.	101

Nickname: Lumberjacks
Colors: Blue & Gold
Arena: Walkup Skydome
   Capacity: 9,500; Year Built: 1977
AD: Steve Holton
SID: Kevin Klintworth

NORTHERN COLO.

Greeley, CO 80639 II

Coach: Ken Smith
Alma Mater: San Diego '77
Record: 4 Years, W-44, L-65

1996-97 SCHEDULE

Western St. ■	Nov. 16
Mesa St. ■	Nov. 21
Bay Ridge Christian ■	Nov. 23
Colo. Christian Tr.	Nov. 29-30
Mont. St.-Billings ■	Dec. 7
Mont. St.-Billings	Dec. 18
South Dak.	Dec. 28
Morningside	Dec. 29
St. Cloud St. ■	Jan. 3
Mankato St. ■	Jan. 4
Mt. Senario ■	Jan. 6
Augustana (S.D.)	Jan. 10
South Dak. St.	Jan. 11
Neb.-Omaha	Jan. 18
North Dak. ■	Jan. 24
North Dak. St. ■	Jan. 25
Mankato St.	Jan. 31
St. Cloud St.	Feb. 1
South Dak. St. ■	Feb. 7
Augustana (S.D.) ■	Feb. 8
Neb.-Omaha ■	Feb. 15
North Dak. St.	Feb. 21
North Dak.	Feb. 22
Morningside ■	Feb. 28
South Dak. ■	Mar. 1

1995-96 RESULTS (11-16)

71	Metro St.	74
68	Colorado Mines †	60
63	UC-Colo. Spgs.	78
97	Arizona Bible ■	46
91	Colo. Christian †	69
67	Southern Colo.	58
63	Wyoming	92
69	UC-Colo. Spgs. ■	54
59	Metro St. ■	64
63	St. Cloud St.	78
76	Mankato St.	71
57	Augustana (S.D.) ■	55
54	South Dak. St. ■	63
71	Neb.-Omaha ■	72
59	North Dak.	62
62	North Dak. St.	57
69	South Dak. ■	76
84	Morningside ■	69
64	South Dak. St.	90
74	Augustana (S.D.)	83
67	Neb.-Omaha	56
84	North Dak. St. ■	86
62	North Dak. ■	82
62	Morningside	91
72	South Dak.	93
82	Mankato St. ■	72
64	St. Cloud St. ■	70

Nickname: Bears
Colors: Navy & Gold
Arena: Butler Hancock Hall
Capacity: 4,500; Year Built: 1975
AD: Jim Fallis
SID: Scott Leisinger

NORTHERN ILL.

De Kalb, IL 60115 I

Coach: Brian Hammel
Alma Mater: Bentley '75
Record: 11 Years, W-166, L-136

1996-97 SCHEDULE

Aurora ■	Nov. 25
Valparaiso ■	Nov. 27
Southern Ill.	Nov. 30
Western Mich. ■	Dec. 2
Bowling Green	Dec. 4
Austin Peay ■	Dec. 18
Western Mich.	Dec. 21
Chicago St. ■	Dec. 23
Charleston (S.C.) Cl	Dec. 28-29
Ill.-Chicago	Jan. 2
Wis.-Milwaukee ■	Jan. 4
Loyola (Ill.)	Jan. 8
Wright St.	Jan. 11
Wis.-Green Bay ■	Jan. 16
Cleveland St.	Jan. 20
Butler ■	Jan. 23
Detroit ■	Jan. 25
Ill.-Chicago ■	Jan. 30
Wis.-Milwaukee	Feb. 3
Loyola (Ill.) ■	Feb. 6
Wright St. ■	Feb. 8
Wis.-Green Bay	Feb. 10
Cleveland St. ■	Feb. 13
Butler	Feb. 20
Detroit	Feb. 22
Midwestern Conf. Tr.	Feb. 28-Mar. 4

1995-96 RESULTS (20-10)

116	Aurora ■	77
65	Austin Peay	68
63	Southern Ill. ■	65
49	Bowling Green ■	53
77	Wichita St.	52
115	Chicago St.	75
81	Akron ■	61
70	Air Force	63
69	Niagara ■	54
57	Maine	54
65	Loyola (Ill.) ■	62
80	Detroit ■	60
67	Wis.-Milwaukee ■	64
67	Ill.-Chicago	70
76	Cleveland St. ■	62
84	Butler ■	57
53	Wis.-Green Bay	61
71	Wright St.	63
68	Loyola (Ill.)	72
98	Ill.-Chicago ■	90
51	Wis.-Green Bay ■	57
100	Wis.-Milwaukee	90
58	Butler	73
61	Cleveland St.	53
81	Wright St. ■	71
75	Detroit	77
80	Wis.-Milwaukee †	78
95	Ill.-Chicago †	60
84	Detroit †	63
73	Texas Tech †	74

Nickname: Huskies
Colors: Cardinal & Black
Arena: Chick Evans Field House
Capacity: 6,044; Year Built: 1957
AD: Cary Groth
SID: Steve Nemeth

NORTHERN IOWA

Cedar Falls, IA 50613 I

Coach: Eldon Miller
Alma Mater: Wittenberg '61
Record: 34 Years, W-542, L-390

1996-97 SCHEDULE

Wis.-Green Bay ■	Nov. 25
Oral Roberts ■	Dec. 2
Creighton	Dec. 7
Iowa	Dec. 10
Nebraska ■	Dec. 14
UTEP Tr.	Dec. 27-28
Mo.-Kansas City	Dec. 30
Creighton ■	Jan. 2
Oral Roberts	Jan. 4
Illinois St.	Jan. 9
Indiana St.	Jan. 11
Southwest Mo. St.	Jan. 15
Southern Ill. ■	Jan. 18
Bradley ■	Jan. 20
Illinois St. ■	Jan. 22
Drake	Jan. 25
Evansville	Jan. 27
Wichita St. ■	Feb. 1
Southwest Mo. St. ■	Feb. 4
Indiana St. ■	Feb. 8
Evansville ■	Feb. 11
Southern Ill.	Feb. 15
Bradley	Feb. 17
Drake ■	Feb. 22
Wichita St.	Feb. 24
Missouri Val. Conf. Tr.	Feb. 28-Mar. 3

1995-96 RESULTS (14-13)

77	Southern Utah ■	64
95	Central Fla.	78
73	Iowa ■	78
109	Nebraska	104
82	Loyola (Ill.) ■	72
76	Central Fla. ■	71
79	Bethune-Cookman ■	61
87	Southwest Mo. St.	95
51	Bradley ■	60
66	Southern Ill.	64
70	Southern Utah	81
64	Evansville	77
82	Drake ■	76
91	Southern Ill. ■	65
67	Indiana St.	78
79	Tulsa ■	89
87	Indiana St. ■	72
91	Evansville ■	82
80	Illinois St.	97
71	Bradley	73
64	Southwest Mo. St. ■	67
58	Creighton	57
68	Wichita St. ■	80
87	Creighton ■	73
83	Drake	66
88	Tulsa	95
58	Illinois St. †	64

Nickname: Panthers
Colors: Purple & Old Gold
Arena: Uni-Dome
Capacity: 10,000; Year Built: 1976
AD: Christopher Ritrievi
SID: Nancy Justis

NORTHERN KY.

Highland Heights, KY 41076.....II

Coach: Ken Shields
Alma Mater: Dayton '64
Record: 8 Years, W-124, L-103

1996-97 SCHEDULE

Va. Union Tr.	Nov. 8-10
Pikeville ■	Nov. 21
Ashland ■	Nov. 23
Fla. Southern	Nov. 25
Tampa	Nov. 27
Ind.-Southeast ■	Dec. 3
California (Pa.) Tr.	Dec. 6-7
Lewis ■	Dec. 19
Wis.-Parkside ■	Dec. 21
Ky. Wesleyan	Jan. 2
Bellarmine	Jan. 4
Indianapolis	Jan. 9
Quincy ■	Jan. 11
IU/PU-Ft. Wayne	Jan. 16
St. Joseph's (Ind.)	Jan. 18
Southern Ind. ■	Jan. 23
SIU-Edwardsville ■	Jan. 25
Wis.-Parkside	Jan. 30
Lewis	Feb. 1
Bellarmine ■	Feb. 6
Ky. Wesleyan ■	Feb. 8
Indianapolis ■	Feb. 13
Mo.-St. Louis	Feb. 15
St. Joseph's (Ind.) ■	Feb. 20
IU/PU-Ft. Wayne ■	Feb. 22
SIU-Edwardsville	Feb. 27
Southern Ind.	Mar. 1

1995-96 RESULTS (25-7)

100	Bethel (Tenn.) ■	67
93	Union (Ky.) ■	77
94	Oakland City ■	58
98	IU/PU-Ft. Wayne	73
95	Ind.-Southeast ■	74
73	Indianapolis	89
71	Cal St. Bakersfield	83
76	Cal St. Los Angeles	63
80	Lewis ■	70
82	Wis.-Parkside ■	68
66	Southern Ind.	99
79	SIU-Edwardsville	67
91	Oakland City	59
84	Bellarmine ■	71
83	St. Joseph's (Ind.) ■	60
78	IU/PU-Ft. Wayne ■	70
85	Quincy	73
64	Lewis	68
81	Ky. Wesleyan ■	79
102	Southern Ind. ■	103
70	Indianapolis ■	67
94	Wis.-Parkside	60
67	St. Joseph's (Ind.)	64
96	SIU-Edwardsville ■	73
96	Quincy ■	84
84	Bellarmine	79
74	Ky. Wesleyan	80
82	Northern St. †	71
99	Southern Ind.	87
56	Cal St. Bakersfield †	55
68	Virginia Union †	66
63	Fort Hays St. †	70

Nickname: Norse
Colors: Gold, Black & White
Arena: Regents Hall
Capacity: 1,800; Year Built: 1972
AD: Jane Meier
SID: Don Owen

NORTHERN MICH.

Marquette, MI 49855................II

Coach: Dean Ellis
Alma Mater: Northern Mich. '83
Record: 10 Years, W-160, L-122

1996-97 SCHEDULE

Bemidji St. ■	Nov. 16
Northland Bapt. ■	Nov. 19
Wis.-Green Bay	Nov. 22
Minn.-Duluth ■	Nov. 25
Drury Tr.	Nov. 29-30
Drury	Nov. 30
Wayne St. (Mich.)	Dec. 5
Hillsdale	Dec. 7
Mercyhurst ■	Dec. 13
Gannon ■	Dec. 14
Minn.-Duluth	Dec. 30
Grand Valley St. ■	Jan. 4
Ferris St. ■	Jan. 6
Northwood	Jan. 9
Saginaw Valley	Jan. 11
Lake Superior St. ■	Jan. 16
Northland ■	Jan. 18
Michigan Tech ■	Jan. 20
Oakland ■	Jan. 23
Ashland	Jan. 30
Ferris St.	Feb. 6
Grand Valley St.	Feb. 8
Northwood ■	Feb. 13
Saginaw Valley ■	Feb. 15
Michigan Tech	Feb. 17
Lake Superior St.	Feb. 20

1995-96 RESULTS (17-11)

58	Tri-State †	59
96	Northland Bapt. †	74
61	Minn.-Duluth	68
70	Michigan Tech	64
71	Grand Valley St.	64
65	Northwood	61
86	Hawaii-Hilo	83
61	IU/PU-Indianapolis †	80
67	Oakland ■	89
82	Wayne St. (Mich.) ■	75
70	Minn.-Duluth ■	57
51	Mercyhurst	56
77	Gannon	72
80	Ashland ■	58
77	Hillsdale ■	69
64	Ferris St.	48
57	Lake Superior St.	80

92	Northland Bapt. ■	76
72	Saginaw Valley ■	74
56	Michigan Tech ■	66
78	Northwood ■	75
90	Northland	79
63	Hillsdale	59
56	Oakland	59
83	Ferris St. ■	61
78	Lake Superior St. ■	80
85	Mt. Senario ■	79
67	Michigan Tech †	75

Nickname: Wildcats
Colors: Old Gold & Olive Green
Arena: Hedgcock Fieldhouse
  Capacity: 5,000; Year Built: 1948
AD: Rick Comley
SID: Jim Pinar

NORTHERN ST.
Aberdeen, SD 57401 II

Coach: Bob Olson
Alma Mater: Northern St. '77
Record: 11 Years, W-233, L-111

1996-97 SCHEDULE

Dak. Wesleyan ■	Nov. 16
Mayville St. ■	Nov. 20
Augustana (S.D.)	Nov. 26
Northern St. Tr.	Nov. 29-30
Huron	Dec. 3
South Dak. St. ■	Dec. 7
Sioux Falls	Dec. 10
Huron ■	Dec. 12
St. Cloud St. ■	Dec. 14
Valley City St. ■	Jan. 2
Briar Cliff	Jan. 4
Mt. Senario ■	Jan. 8
Winona St.	Jan. 11
Moorhead St.	Jan. 15
Minn.-Duluth	Jan. 18
Southwest St. ■	Jan. 22
Bemidji St. ■	Jan. 25
Wayne St. (Neb.) ■	Jan. 29
Minn.-Morris	Feb. 1
Moorhead St. ■	Feb. 5
Winona St. ■	Feb. 8
Southwest St.	Feb. 12
Minn.-Duluth	Feb. 15
Wayne St. (Neb.)	Feb. 19
Bemidji St.	Feb. 22
Minn.-Morris ■	Feb. 26

1995-96 RESULTS (23-6)

99	Mt. Senario ■	76
101	Valley City St.	65
103	Chadron St. ■	85
99	Michigan Tech ■	65
75	Huron	71
101	MidAmerica Naz. ■	78
81	Dak. Wesleyan ■	64
78	South Dak. St. ■	82
97	Sioux Falls ■	79
92	Huron ■	72
118	Graceland (Iowa) ■	91
89	Briar Cliff	68
84	Neb.-Kearney ■	101
77	Winona St.	59
57	Minn.-Duluth ■	56
84	Southwest St.	83
85	Bemidji St.	67
93	Wayne St. (Neb.)	100
95	Minn.-Morris	69
90	Moorhead St.	76
68	Winona St.	65
96	Southwest St. ■	93
66	Minn.-Duluth	81
80	Wayne St. (Neb.) ■	77
98	Bemidji St. ■	67
98	Moorhead St. ■	88
92	Minn.-Morris ■	100
98	Oakland †	92
71	Northern Ky. †	82

Nickname: Wolves
Colors: Maroon & Gold

Arena: Barnett Center
  Capacity: 8,057; Year Built: 1987
AD: Jim Kretchman
SID: Deb Smith

NORTHWEST MO. ST.
Maryville, MO 64468 II

Coach: Steve Tappmeyer
Alma Mater: Southeast Mo. St. '79
Record: 8 Years, W-127, L-93

1996-97 SCHEDULE

Park ■	Nov. 16
Bethany (Kan.) ■	Nov. 19
Northwest Mo. St. Cl.	Nov. 22-23
MidAmerica Naz. ■	Nov. 26
Emporia St. ■	Dec. 3
Pittsburg St. ■	Dec. 7
Lindenwood ■	Dec. 10
Wayne St. (Neb.) ■	Dec. 14
Missouri	Dec. 17
Mo.-Rolla ■	Jan. 6
Lincoln (Mo.) ■	Jan. 8
Southwest Baptist	Jan. 11
Park	Jan. 13
Central Mo. St.	Jan. 15
Truman St. ■	Jan. 18
Washburn	Jan. 22
Mo.-Rolla	Jan. 25
Mo. Western St. ■	Jan. 29
Lincoln (Mo.)	Feb. 1
Mo. Southern St.	Feb. 3
Emporia St.	Feb. 5
Mo. Southern St. ■	Feb. 8
Pittsburg St.	Feb. 12
Central Mo. St. ■	Feb. 15
Washburn ■	Feb. 19
Mo. Western St.	Feb. 22

1995-96 RESULTS (19-7)

76	Southwest St.	74
74	Moorhead St. †	84
91	Hannibal-La Grange ■	66
68	Rockhurst ■	56
75	William Jewell ■	66
70	Mo. Western St. ■	87
83	MidAmerica Naz. ■	73
63	Wayne St. (Neb.) ■	60
106	Graceland (Iowa) ■	94
83	Washburn	68
71	Mo.-Rolla ■	66
60	Truman St.	55
65	Pittsburg St.	69
80	Southwest Baptist ■	74
76	Mo.-St. Louis ■	68
77	Central Mo. St.	66
42	Emporia St.	47
89	Mo. Southern St. ■	71
87	Mo. Western St. ■	72
90	Lincoln (Mo.) ■	87
72	Mo.-Rolla	63
58	Truman St. ■	66
82	Pittsburg St. ■	86
86	Southwest Baptist	81
83	Mo.-St. Louis	67
98	Pittsburg St. †	101

Nickname: Bearcats
Colors: Green & White
Arena: Bearcat Arena
  Capacity: 2,500; Year Built: 1955
AD: James Redd
SID: To be named

NORTHWESTERN
Evanston, IL 60208 I

Coach: Ricky Byrdsong
Alma Mater: Iowa St. '78
Record: 8 Years, W-80, L-143

1996-97 SCHEDULE

Tenn.-Martin ■	Nov. 22
Central Mich. ■	Nov. 26
Tennessee Tech ■	Nov. 30

San Diego St. ■	Dec. 3
DePaul	Dec. 7
Seton Hall ■	Dec. 14
Illinois St. ■	Dec. 18
Loyola (Ill.) ■	Dec. 21
Hawaii Rainbow Cl.	Dec. 27-30
Iowa	Jan. 2
Michigan ■	Jan. 4
Purdue ■	Jan. 11
Indiana ■	Jan. 15
Michigan St.	Jan. 18
Penn St. ■	Jan. 22
Ohio St. ■	Jan. 25
Wisconsin	Jan. 29
Minnesota ■	Feb. 1
Illinois	Feb. 5
Wisconsin ■	Feb. 8
Ohio St.	Feb. 13
Penn St.	Feb. 15
Michigan St. ■	Feb. 19
Indiana	Feb. 22
Purdue ■	Feb. 26
Michigan	Mar. 5
Iowa ■	Mar. 8

1995-96 RESULTS (7-20)

63	San Diego St.	83
67	Youngstown St. ■	61
66	Robert Morris ■	46
70	Seton Hall	85
84	Army ■	62
61	DePaul ■	71
64	Central Mich.	63
81	Loyola (Ill.)	78
56	Brown ■	60
51	Michigan	83
51	Purdue ■	67
74	Penn St. ■	83
71	Ohio St.	72
62	Wisconsin ■	52
54	Michigan St.	68
62	Illinois ■	74
68	Minnesota	77
63	Indiana ■	95
77	Iowa ■	88
47	Minnesota ■	66
62	Illinois	93
57	Michigan St. ■	75
82	Wisconsin	71
60	Ohio St. ■	82
62	Penn St.	78
56	Purdue	79
50	Michigan ■	77

Nickname: Wildcats
Colors: Purple & White
Arena: Welsh-Ryan Arena
  Capacity: 8,117; Year Built: 1952
AD: Rick Taylor
SID: Brad Hurlbut

NORTHWESTERN ST.
Natchitoches, LA 71497 I

Coach: J. D. Barnett
Alma Mater: Winona St. '70
Record: 18 Years, W-308, L-210

1996-97 SCHEDULE

Mississippi St.	Nov. 23
Ark.-Monticello ■	Nov. 25
Centenary (La.)	Dec. 2
Louisiana Tech ■	Dec. 5
Southwest Mo. St. ■	Dec. 10
Samford ■	Dec. 14
Grambling	Dec. 19
Southeastern La.	Dec. 21
Baylor	Dec. 28
Colorado	Dec. 30
Sam Houston St.	Jan. 4
Stephen F. Austin	Jan. 6
Texas-San Antonio ■	Jan. 9
Southwest Tex. St. ■	Jan. 11
Nicholls St.	Jan. 16
McNeese St. ■	Jan. 18
Texas-Arlington ■	Jan. 25
Northeast La. ■	Jan. 27

Southwest Tex. St.	Jan. 30
Texas-San Antonio.	Feb. 1
Sam Houston St. ■	Feb. 6
Stephen F. Austin ■	Feb. 8
Nicholls St. ■	Feb. 13
McNeese St. ■	Feb. 15
Northeast La.	Feb. 22
Texas-Arlington	Mar. 1
Southland Conf. Tr.	Mar. 5-8

1995-96 RESULTS (5-21)

73	La. Christian ■	81
82	Colorado	85
67	UTEP	88
46	New Mexico St.	50
90	Southeastern La. ■	75
68	Southwest Mo. St.	79
61	Louisiana Tech	91
89	Grambling	69
75	McNeese St.	94
67	Nicholls St.	75
74	Northeast La.	94
56	Texas-San Antonio ■	62
72	Southwest Tex. St. ■	61
68	Stephen F. Austin ■	83
62	North Texas	68
63	Texas-Arlington	61
59	Nicholls St. ■	63
57	McNeese St. ■	80
70	Northeast La. ■	80
57	Southwest Tex. St.	41
84	Texas-San Antonio	95
64	Texas-Arlington ■	73
53	North Texas ■	78
69	Sam Houston St. ■	70
70	Stephen F. Austin ■	76
64	Sam Houston St.	85

Nickname: Demons
Colors: Purple, White & Burnt Orange
Arena: Prather Coliseum
  Capacity: 3,900; Year Built: 1964
AD: Greg Burke
SID: Doug Ireland

NORTHWOOD
Midland, MI 48640 II

Coach: Dean Lockwood
Alma Mater: Spring Arbor '82
Record: 5 Years, W-49, L-87

1996-97 SCHEDULE

Aquinas	Nov. 23
Mich.-Dearborn	Nov. 26
Oakland ■	Dec. 5
Cornerstone ■	Dec. 7
Michigan Christian ■	Dec. 12
Concordia (Mich.) ■	Dec. 14
Madonna	Dec. 16
Ashland ■	Dec. 19
Alma Tr.	Dec. 30-31
Saginaw Valley	Jan. 2
Lake Superior St. ■	Jan. 4
Northern Mich. ■	Jan. 9
Michigan Tech ■	Jan. 11
Ferris St.	Jan. 16
Grand Valley St.	Jan. 18
Wayne St. (Mich.) ■	Jan. 23
Hillsdale ■	Jan. 25
Gannon	Jan. 30
Mercyhurst	Feb. 1
Saginaw Valley ■	Feb. 6
Lake Superior St.	Feb. 8
Northern Mich.	Feb. 13
Michigan Tech	Feb. 15
Ferris St. ■	Feb. 20
Grand Valley St. ■	Feb. 22

1995-96 RESULTS (15-11)

73	Mich.-Dearborn ■	65
105	Spring Arbor ■	77
95	Cornerstone	87
85	Lake Superior St. ■	83
61	Northern Mich. ■	65
89	Aquinas ■	81
65	Concordia (Mich.)	60

76	Madonna ■	71
85	Baldwin-Wallace †	62
84	Concordia (Mich.) †	87
70	Michigan Tech	87
53	Oakland	89
78	Wayne St. (Mich.)	77
71	Saginaw Valley	88
80	Grand Valley St. ■	98
75	Mercyhurst ■	64
68	Gannon ■	78
56	Ashland	58
91	Hillsdale	77
74	Ferris St. ■	72
84	Lake Superior St.	91
75	Northern Mich.	78
67	Gannon	65
86	Wayne St. (Mich.) ■	82
70	Hillsdale	84
79	Saginaw Valley ■	73

Nickname: Northmen
Colors: Columbia Blue & White
Arena: E. W. Bennett Sports Center
  Capacity: 1,260; Year Built: 1979
AD: Dave Coffey
SID: Fritz Reznor

NORWICH
Northfield, VT 05663 III

Coach: Paul Booth
Alma Mater: St. Joseph's (Vt.)
Record: 7 Years, W-85, L-105

1996-97 SCHEDULE
Colby-Sawyer ■	Nov. 23
Castleton St.	Nov. 26
Carnegie Mellon Inv.	Nov. 30-Dec. 1
Springfield ■	Dec. 4
Clark (Mass.) ■	Dec. 8
WPI ■	Dec. 13
Clark (Mass.)	Jan. 11
Coast Guard ■	Jan. 17
Coast Guard ■	Jan. 18
Springfield	Jan. 21
Lyndon St. ■	Jan. 23
Babson	Jan. 25
MIT ■	Jan. 28
Bowdoin ■	Jan. 31
Colby ■	Feb. 1
WPI	Feb. 4
Western New Eng.	Feb. 6
Babson ■	Feb. 8
Middlebury ■	Feb. 11
Bates	Feb. 14
Me.-Farmington ■	Feb. 15
MIT	Feb. 18
Western New Eng.	Feb. 22

1995-96 RESULTS (15-11)
93	Colby-Sawyer	86
89	Castleton St. ■	68
66	Springfield	79
91	Clark (Mass.) ■	88
87	Johnson St. ■	57
94	New England Col.	78
100	Clark (Mass.) ■	92
60	Coast Guard	73
58	Coast Guard	81
59	Springfield ■	75
98	Lyndon St.	64
91	Babson ■	102
98	MIT	66
88	Bowdoin	81
62	Colby	87
77	WPI	82
78	Western New Eng. ■	83
110	Babson	106
62	Middlebury	65
80	Bates ■	86
69	Me.-Farmington ■	58
78	MIT	46
79	Western New Eng.	71
80	WPI ■	62
76	Clark (Mass.) ■	72
85	Babson	96

Nickname: Cadets
Colors: Maroon & Gold
Arena: Andrews Hall
  Capacity: 1,500; Year Built: 1980
AD: Tony Mariano
SID: Todd Bamford

NOTRE DAME
Notre Dame, IN 46556 I

Coach: John MacLeod
Alma Mater: Bellarmine '59
Record: 11 Years, W-153, L-149

1996-97 SCHEDULE
Monmouth (N.J.) ■	Nov. 24
Youngstown St. ■	Nov. 26
Indiana ■	Dec. 2
Providence	Dec. 7
New Hampshire ■	Dec. 10
Kentucky	Dec. 14
Loyola (Md.) ■	Dec. 21
Nicholls St. ■	Dec. 23
Loyola (Ill.)	Dec. 30
Syracuse ■	Jan. 2
Rutgers ■	Jan. 4
Georgetown	Jan. 7
Boston College ■	Jan. 11
Villanova ■	Jan. 14
Syracuse	Jan. 18
Seton Hall ■	Jan. 22
West Va.	Jan. 25
Pittsburgh ■	Jan. 29
St. John's (N.Y.) ■	Feb. 5
Connecticut ■	Feb. 8
West Va.	Feb. 11
Villanova	Feb. 16
Seton Hall	Feb. 18
Providence ■	Feb. 22
Miami (Fla.) ■	Feb. 25
Boston College	Mar. 1
Big East Conf. Tr.	Mar. 5-8

1995-96 RESULTS (9-18)
65	Akron ■	54
53	Indiana	73
80	Rutgers	86
65	Connecticut ■	85
70	Loyola (Md.)	62
58	UCLA	83
72	Xavier (Ohio)	70
90	San Diego ■	63
84	Loyola Marymount ■	51
57	Villanova	76
57	Boston College	72
65	Pittsburgh	75
69	Georgetown ■	74
79	Rutgers ■	67
64	Miami (Fla.)	72
59	West Va. ■	69
86	St. John's (N.Y.)	83
53	Georgetown	70
44	Manhattan	65
66	St. John's (N.Y.) ■	74
77	Pittsburgh ■	69
65	Connecticut	85
72	Providence ■	73
72	Seton Hall ■	60
59	Miami (Fla.) ■	71
67	Syracuse	71
55	Syracuse †	76

Nickname: Fighting Irish
Colors: Gold & Blue
Arena: Joyce Center
  Capacity: 11,418; Year Built: 1968
AD: Mike Wadsworth
SID: John Heisler

OAKLAND
Rochester, MI 48063 II

Coach: Greg Kampe
Alma Mater: Bowling Green '78
Record: 12 Years, W-212, L-130

1996-97 SCHEDULE
Concordia (Mich.)	Nov. 19
Eastern Mich.	Nov. 23
Madonna	Nov. 26
Northwood ■	Dec. 5
Lake Superior St. ■	Dec. 7
Mich.-Dearborn	Dec. 10
Saginaw Valley ■	Dec. 14
Las Vegas Cl.	Dec. 18-19
Oakland (Mich.) Cl.	Dec. 27-28
Hillsdale ■	Jan. 2
Ashland ■	Jan. 4
Gannon	Jan. 9
Mercyhurst	Jan. 11
Wayne St. (Mich.) ■	Jan. 18
Northern Mich.	Jan. 23
Michigan Tech	Jan. 25
Ferris St. ■	Jan. 30
Grand Valley St. ■	Feb. 1
Hillsdale	Feb. 6
Ashland	Feb. 8
Gannon ■	Feb. 13
Mercyhurst ■	Feb. 15
Michigan Christian ■	Feb. 17
Wayne St. (Mich.) ■	Feb. 20

1995-96 RESULTS (21-8)
104	Madonna	74
72	Aquinas †	83
82	Michigan Christian †	65
108	Mich.-Dearborn ■	80
78	Saginaw Valley ■	65
61	Michigan Tech ■	63
69	Michigan Christian ■	55
100	Aquinas ■	66
86	Mich.-Dearborn ■	61
90	Lake Superior St.	81
89	Northern Mich.	67
89	Northwood ■	53
93	Grand Valley St.	73
78	Wayne St. (Mich.) ■	80
93	Ferris St.	75
93	Mercyhurst ■	100
90	Gannon	77
103	Ashland ■	87
87	Hillsdale ■	77
118	Michigan Christian ■	74
73	Saginaw Valley	86
87	Michigan Tech	78
70	Ashland	72
59	Northern Mich. ■	56
105	Gannon ■	63
104	Ferris St. ■	77
100	Saginaw Valley ■	90
102	Lake Superior St. ■	106
92	Northern St. †	98

Nickname: Pioneers
Colors: Gold, Black & White
Arena: The Bubble
  Capacity: 477; Year Built: 1996
AD: Jack Mehl
SID: Andy Glantzman

OAKLAND CITY
Oakland City, IN 47660 II

Coach: Mike Sandifar
Alma Mater: Panhandle St. '71
Record: 18 Years, W-300, L-209

1996-97 SCHEDULE
Oakland City Cl.	Nov. 15-16
Lincoln Memorial ■	Nov. 18
Ky. Wesleyan	Nov. 21
BYU-Hawaii	Nov. 26
Chaminade	Nov. 29
Lindenwood ■	Dec. 3
Indianapolis	Dec. 7
Ky. Wesleyan ■	Dec. 14
Southeast Mo. St.	Dec. 18
Cincinnati Bible ■	Dec. 21
Ind.-East ■	Dec. 30
Ala.-Huntsville ■	Jan. 2
Ohio St.-Lima ■	Jan. 4
St. Francis (Ill.) ■	Jan. 11

Montevallo ■		Jan. 15
Tusculum		Jan. 22
Ind.-Northwest ■		Jan. 25
Ala.-Huntsville		Jan. 27
Kentucky St. ■		Feb. 5
St. Louis Christian ■		Feb. 8
Tusculum ■		Feb. 10
Montevallo		Feb. 15
Kentucky St.		Feb. 19
Ind.-East ■		Mar. 1

1995-96 RESULTS (18-13)
77	Indiana (Pa.) †	93
55	Carson-Newman †	52
58	Northern Ky.	94
83	Robert Morris (Ill.) ■	60
82	Ala.-Huntsville ■	85
78	Southeast Mo. St.	82
87	Central Okla. †	94
85	Charleston (W.Va.) †	83
84	Ky. Wesleyan ■	92
63	Indianapolis ■	72
95	St. Louis Christian	53
93	Martin Methodist ■	71
69	Eastern Ky.	95
129	Ind.-East ■	60
83	St. Francis (Ill.) ■	86
59	Northern Ky. ■	91
114	Purdue-North Cent. ■	47
102	Robert Morris (Ill.) ■	71
97	Drury ■	77
83	Montevallo	91
105	Ind.-Northwest ■	60
87	St. Meinrad ■	57
73	Drury	81
104	Oakwood ■	68
91	Ky. Wesleyan ■	86
88	Montevallo ■	86
96	Ind.-East ■	57
79	Grace †	52
67	Ind. Wesleyan	69
67	Greenville †	50
88	Western Baptist †	69

Nickname: Mighty Oaks
Colors: Navy & White
Arena: Johnson Center
  Capacity: 1,600; Year Built: 1987
AD: Mike Sandifar
SID: Denise Sandifar

OBERLIN
Oberlin, OH 44074 III

Coach: Gene DeLorenzo
Alma Mater: Colby '75
Record: 5 Years, W-25, L-92

1996-97 SCHEDULE
Capital Cl.	Nov. 22-23
Thiel	Nov. 26
Wooster ■	Dec. 5
Wittenberg ■	Dec. 7
Adrian ■	Dec. 30
Ohio Wesleyan	Jan. 3
Kenyon ■	Jan. 4
Case Reserve	Jan. 8
Bethany (W.Va.) ■	Jan. 11
Wash. & Jeff.	Jan. 13
Denison	Jan. 15
Earlham ■	Jan. 18
Ohio Wesleyan ■	Jan. 22
Wittenberg	Jan. 25
Kenyon	Jan. 28
Wooster ■	Jan. 31
Penn St.-Behrend ■	Feb. 1
Allegheny	Feb. 5
Case Reserve ■	Feb. 12
Denison	Feb. 15
Allegheny ■	Feb. 19
Earlham	Feb. 22

1995-96 RESULTS (2-22)
48	Adrian	76
59	Thiel ■	86
58	Chicago	100
61	Allegheny ■	102

44	Wittenberg ■	.71
70	Case Reserve	.91
67	Wash. & Jeff. ■	.63
35	Marietta	.75
67	Lake Erie †	.71
66	Ohio Wesleyan	.71
51	Denison ■	.77
47	Wooster	.88
69	Earlham	.78
66	Kenyon ■	.72
41	Wittenberg	.85
67	Denison	.74
57	Penn St.-Behrend ■	.83
64	Bethany (W.Va.) ■	.59
62	Wooster ■	.65
69	Kenyon	.92
60	Allegheny	.81
76	Earlham ■	.91
85	Case Reserve ■	.93
70	Ohio Wesleyan ■	.80

Nickname: Yeomen
Colors: Crimson & Gold
Arena: Philips Gymnasium
　Capacity: 1,800; Year Built: 1971
AD: Don Hunsinger
SID: Scott Wargo

OCCIDENTAL

Los Angeles, CA 90041 III

Coach: Brian Newhall
Alma Mater: Occidental '83
Record: 8 Years, W-110, L-90

1996-97 SCHEDULE

Chapman Inv.	Nov. 22-23
UC San Diego ■	Nov. 26
La Sierra	Nov. 30
Northern Ariz.	Dec. 21
Occidental Tr.	Dec. 27-28
Occidental Cl.	Jan. 3-4
Swarthmore ■	Jan. 7
La Sierra ■	Jan. 9
Pomona-Pitzer ■	Jan. 11
Whittier	Jan. 15
La Verne ■	Jan. 18
Cal Tech ■	Jan. 22
Claremont-M-S ■	Jan. 25
Cal Lutheran ■	Jan. 29
Redlands	Feb. 1
Pomona-Pitzer ■	Feb. 5
Whittier ■	Feb. 8
La Verne	Feb. 12
Cal Tech ■	Feb. 15
Claremont-M-S ■	Feb. 19
Cal Lutheran	Feb. 22
Redlands ■	Feb. 26

1995-96 RESULTS (15-10)

111	UC San Diego	.105
92	S'western (Ariz.) †	.74
97	LIFE Bible †	.48
71	Cal St. Hayward †	.81
73	Holy Names †	.77
91	Clarke ■	.73
83	Simpson ■	.77
88	N.J. Inst. of Tech. ■	.73
70	Wartburg ■	.54
81	Concordia (Ore.)	.94
83	Multnomah Bible	.70
71	Cal Tech ■	.59
77	Claremont-M-S ■	.89
63	Pomona-Pitzer	.75
94	La Verne ■	.88
79	Redlands ■	.86
69	Cal Lutheran	.81
61	Whittier ■	.58
68	Cal Tech	.44
57	Claremont-M-S	.74
74	Pomona-Pitzer ■	.73
72	La Verne	.75
95	Redlands ■	.78
65	Cal Lutheran ■	.69
86	Whittier	.77

Nickname: Tigers

Colors: Orange & Black
Arena: Rush Gymnasium
　Capacity: 1,800; Year Built: 1967
AD: Dale Widolff
SID: James Kerman

OGLETHORPE

Atlanta, GA 30319 III

Coach: Jack Berkshire
Alma Mater: Mississippi St. '62
Record: 20 Years, W-287, L-236

1996-97 SCHEDULE

Guilford Inv.	Nov. 22-23
Emory	Nov. 26
Warren Wilson ■	Dec. 7
Toccoa Falls Inst.	Dec. 9
Oglethorpe Cl.	Dec. 29-30
Ursinus ■	Jan. 5
Centre	Jan. 10
Sewanee	Jan. 12
Rhodes ■	Jan. 17
Hendrix ■	Jan. 19
Toccoa Falls Inst.	Jan. 21
Southwestern (Tex.) ■	Jan. 24
Trinity (Tex.) ■	Jan. 26
Atlanta Christian ■	Jan. 28
Rhodes	Jan. 31
Hendrix	Feb. 2
Southwestern (Tex.)	Feb. 7
Trinity (Tex.)	Feb. 9
Emory ■	Feb. 12
Millsaps ■	Feb. 15
Centre ■	Feb. 21
Sewanee ■	Feb. 23
Millsaps	Mar. 1

1995-96 RESULTS (7-17)

97	Ferrum †	.83
67	Roanoke	.93
76	Emory ■	.73
107	Atlanta Christian ■	.74
64	Savannah A&D ■	.76
37	Emory	.58
68	Colorado Col. ■	.99
64	Ohio Northern ■	.87
89	Dallas ■	.57
78	Savannah A&D	.91
69	Hendrix ■	.83
77	Rhodes ■	.95
58	Sewanee ■	.67
76	Centre	.78
77	Trinity (Tex.)	.83
69	Southwestern (Tex.)	.87
67	Sewanee	.85
74	Centre	.83
84	Trinity (Tex.) ■	.75
85	Southwestern (Tex.) ■	.81
63	Millsaps	.75
71	Hendrix	.90
68	Rhodes ■	.89
74	Millsaps ■	.72

Nickname: Stormy Petrels
Colors: Black & Gold
Arena: Dorough Fieldhouse
　Capacity: 2,000; Year Built: 1962
AD: Jack Berkshire
SID: Dunn Neugebauer

OHIO

Athens, OH 45701 I

Coach: Larry Hunter
Alma Mater: Ohio '71
Record: 20 Years, W-430, L-159

1996-97 SCHEDULE

Wilmington (Ohio) ■	Nov. 27
West Va.	Nov. 30
Illinois St.	Dec. 7
Cal St. Northridge	Dec. 12
UCLA	Dec. 14
Wright St. ■	Dec. 18
Radford ■	Dec. 21

Duquesne ■	Dec. 28
Western Mich. ■	Jan. 4
Ball St. ■	Jan. 8
Akron ■	Jan. 11
Kent	Jan. 13
Miami (Ohio)	Jan. 18
Toledo ■	Jan. 22
Central Mich. ■	Jan. 25
Bowling Green	Jan. 29
Ball St.	Feb. 1
Eastern Mich. ■	Feb. 3
Akron	Feb. 5
Kent ■	Feb. 8
Eastern Mich. ■	Feb. 12
Miami (Ohio) ■	Feb. 15
Toledo	Feb. 19
Central Mich.	Feb. 22
Bowling Green ■	Feb. 26
Western Mich.	Mar. 1
Mid-American Conf. Tr.	Mar. 4-8

1995-96 RESULTS (16-14)

51	Iowa †	.78
86	Texas Christian †	.68
90	Old Dominion †	.89
65	Illinois St. ■	.66
103	Xavier (Ohio) ■	.72
77	Wright St.	.88
69	West Va.	.94
97	Rio Grande ■	.74
80	Duquesne	.93
60	Princeton †	.65
94	Coppin St. †	.92
54	Ball St.	.57
65	Miami (Ohio) ■	.56
68	Kent	.69
69	Bowling Green	.84
70	Toledo ■	.57
81	Akron	.60
59	Western Mich. ■	.66
72	Central Mich.	.65
82	Eastern Mich. ■	.73
61	Miami (Ohio)	.76
69	Kent ■	.61
83	Bowling Green ■	.67
72	Toledo	.60
73	Akron ■	.59
51	Western Mich.	.54
76	Central Mich. ■	.73
77	Eastern Mich.	.81
87	Ball St. ■	.67
80	Ball St. ■	.86

Nickname: Bobcats
Colors: Ohio Green & White
Arena: Convocation Center
　Capacity: 13,000; Year Built: 1968
AD: Tom Boeh
SID: George E. Mauzy Jr

OHIO NORTHERN

Ada, OH 45810 III

Coach: Joe Campoli
Alma Mater: Rhode Island '64
Record: 5 Years, W-81, L-29

1996-97 SCHEDULE

Louisiana Tech	Nov. 30
Heidelberg ■	Dec. 4
Mount Union ■	Dec. 7
Defiance	Dec. 11
Marietta	Dec. 14
Capital	Dec. 18
Wilmington (Ohio) ■	Dec. 23
Wittenberg Cl.	Dec. 27-28
Muskingum ■	Jan. 8
Hiram	Jan. 11
Baldwin-Wallace ■	Jan. 15
John Carroll	Jan. 18
Otterbein ■	Jan. 22
Hiram ■	Jan. 25
Baldwin-Wallace	Jan. 29
John Carroll ■	Feb. 1
Otterbein	Feb. 5
Mount Union	Feb. 8

Heidelberg	Feb. 12
Marietta ■	Feb. 15
Muskingum	Feb. 19
Capital ■	Feb. 22

1995-96 RESULTS (18-9)

61	Defiance ■	.49
85	Ohio Wesleyan	.71
73	Bluffton	.60
66	Marietta ■	.47
77	Capital	.86
66	Hiram ■	.71
84	Lake Erie ■	.69
70	Muskingum	.63
77	DePauw †	.81
87	Oglethorpe	.64
71	Mount Union ■	.76
76	Baldwin-Wallace ■	.66
72	Otterbein	.79
66	John Carroll ■	.64
67	Heidelberg	.54
67	Baldwin-Wallace ■	.63
67	Otterbein ■	.59
63	Hiram	.65
78	Capital ■	.63
63	Muskingum ■	.57
70	Mount Union	.68
71	Marietta	.60
65	Heidelberg ■	.62
80	John Carroll	.85
70	Otterbein ■	.68
56	Marietta ■	.73
57	Capital ■	.68

Nickname: Polar Bears
Colors: Burnt Orange & Black
Arena: ONU Sports Center
　Capacity: 3,400; Year Built: 1975
AD: Gale Daugherty
SID: Tim Glon

OHIO ST.

Columbus, OH 43210 I

Coach: Randy Ayers
Alma Mater: Miami (Ohio) '78
Record: 7 Years, W-114, L-91

1996-97 SCHEDULE

South Fla.	Nov. 23
Southwestern La. ■	Dec. 1
Kent	Dec. 3
LIU-Brooklyn ■	Dec. 7
George Mason ■	Dec. 14
Alabama St. ■	Dec. 18
Southern Cal	Dec. 21
San Diego St.	Dec. 23
Kentucky [Cleveland]	Dec. 28
Michigan	Jan. 2
Illinois ■	Jan. 4
Penn St. ■	Jan. 8
Michigan St.	Jan. 11
Iowa	Jan. 15
Minnesota ■	Jan. 18
Northwestern	Jan. 25
Indiana ■	Jan. 30
Wisconsin ■	Feb. 1
Purdue	Feb. 5
Indiana	Feb. 8
Northwestern ■	Feb. 13
Minnesota	Feb. 19
Iowa ■	Feb. 22
Michigan St. ■	Feb. 26
Penn St.	Mar. 1
Illinois	Mar. 5
Michigan ■	Mar. 8

1995-96 RESULTS (10-17)

79	Central Conn. St. ■	.52
77	West Va. ■	.52
75	Cleveland St. ■	.52
92	George Mason	.87
105	Seton Hall ■	.96
70	Tenn.-Chatt.	.83
72	San Diego St. ■	.56
92	Eastern Ky. †	.88
67	Wyoming †	.73

69	Penn St. ■	72
67	Indiana ■	89
53	Iowa	81
72	Northwestern ■	71
50	Minnesota ■	56
46	Illinois	77
53	Purdue	70
66	Wisconsin ■	53
58	Michigan ■	77
41	Michigan St.	55
56	Wisconsin	62
55	Purdue ■	63
67	Illinois ■	76
57	Minnesota	60
82	Northwestern	60
64	Iowa ■	73
56	Indiana ■	73
70	Penn St.	86

Nickname: Buckeyes
Colors: Scarlet & Gray
Arena: St. John Arena
  Capacity: 13,276; Year Built: 1956
AD: Andy Geiger
SID: Gerry Emig

OHIO WESLEYAN
Delaware, OH 43015 III

Coach: Gene Mehaffey
Alma Mater: Southern Methodist '54
Record: 28 Years, W-500, L-334

1996-97 SCHEDULE

Frank. & Marsh. Cl.	Nov. 22-23
Ohio Dominican ■	Nov. 27
Capital ■	Nov. 30
Kenyon ■	Dec. 4
Thomas More	Dec. 12
Findlay ■	Dec. 21
Case Reserve	Dec. 30
Oberlin ■	Jan. 3
Denison	Jan. 4
Earlham ■	Jan. 8
Allegheny	Jan. 11
Wittenberg	Jan. 15
Case Reserve ■	Jan. 18
Oberlin	Jan. 22
Wooster ■	Jan. 25
Wilmington (Ohio) ■	Jan. 29
Kenyon	Feb. 1
Denison ■	Feb. 5
Allegheny ■	Feb. 8
Earlham	Feb. 12
Wittenberg ■	Feb. 15
Defiance	Feb. 19
Wooster	Feb. 22

1995-96 RESULTS (8-17)

84	Ferris St. ■	82
62	Ohio Dominican ■	66
71	Ohio Northern ■	85
69	Earlham	66
67	Kenyon ■	64
62	Denison	84
60	Findlay	88
83	Thomas More ■	79
59	Defiance ■	81
71	Oberlin ■	66
49	Wooster	68
70	Case Reserve ■	72
64	Allegheny	70
55	Wittenberg ■	74
68	Kenyon	81
64	Earlham ■	74
71	Case Reserve	75
66	Wilmington (Ohio) ■	74
70	Denison ■	85
73	Wooster ■	61
87	Allegheny ■	94
55	Wittenberg	82
80	Oberlin	70
71	Wooster	62
67	Allegheny †	81

Nickname: Battling Bishops
Colors: Red & Black

Arena: Branch Rickey Arena
  Capacity: 2,300; Year Built: 1976
AD: Jay Martin
SID: Mark Beckenbach

OKLAHOMA
Norman, OK 73019 I

Coach: Kelvin Sampson
Alma Mater: N.C.-Pembroke '78
Record: 13 Years, W-216, L-170

1996-97 SCHEDULE

Northeast La. ■	Nov. 23
Sam Houston St. ■	Nov. 27
Coppin St. ■	Nov. 30
Delaware St. ■	Dec. 4
Southeast Mo. St. ■	Dec. 7
Centenary (La.) ■	Dec. 14
Purdue ■	Dec. 21
Memphis	Dec. 23
Oklahoma Tr.	Dec. 27-28
Texas A&M	Jan. 5
Iowa St.	Jan. 11
Texas Tech	Jan. 15
Baylor ■	Jan. 18
Texas ■	Jan. 22
Nebraska ■	Jan. 25
Oklahoma St.	Jan. 27
Texas	Feb. 1
Texas A&M	Feb. 4
Kansas St.	Feb. 8
Colorado ■	Feb. 12
Missouri	Feb. 15
Texas Tech	Feb. 19
Oklahoma St. ■	Feb. 22
Kansas ■	Feb. 24
Baylor	Mar. 1
Big 12 Conf. Tr.	Mar. 6-9

1995-96 RESULTS (17-13)

99	Jackson St. ■	68
72	Georgia Tech	83
69	Texas Tech ■	81
63	Purdue	77
107	Texas-San Antonio ■	75
87	Nicholls St. ■	47
77	Texas Southern ■	63
87	Oral Roberts	53
85	Drexel ■	78
84	Baylor †	71
72	Florida †	76
84	Southern Methodist ■	74
64	Kansas St.	59
117	Nebraska ■	100
73	Missouri	75
60	Kansas St. ■	75
66	Kansas	72
61	Iowa St.	67
67	Texas	65
104	Missouri ■	68
81	Oklahoma St.	75
71	Mississippi St. ■	76
58	Iowa St. ■	70
119	Colorado	88
81	Colorado ■	59
80	Nebraska	76
67	Oklahoma St. ■	89
85	Kansas ■	79
88	Missouri †	92
43	Temple †	61

Nickname: Sooners
Colors: Crimson & Cream
Arena: Lloyd Noble Center
  Capacity: 11,100; Year Built: 1975
AD: Steve Owens
SID: Mike Prusinski

OKLAHOMA ST.
Stillwater, OK 74078 I

Coach: Eddie Sutton
Alma Mater: Oklahoma St. '58
Record: 26 Years, W-570, L-219

1996-97 SCHEDULE

NIT	Nov. 20-29
North Caro. A&T ■	Dec. 2
Mississippi Val. ■	Dec. 4
Arizona St.	Dec. 7
Alcorn St. ■	Dec. 16
Charleston (S.C.) ■	Dec. 18
Southern Methodist ■	Dec. 21
Arkansas St.	Dec. 23
Nevada [Tulsa]	Dec. 30
Texas	Jan. 4
Texas Tech ■	Jan. 8
Missouri ■	Jan. 11
Colorado	Jan. 15
UNLV ■	Jan. 18
Texas Tech	Jan. 20
Baylor ■	Jan. 25
Oklahoma ■	Jan. 27
Oral Roberts	Jan. 29
Baylor	Feb. 1
Kansas St. ■	Feb. 5
Texas ■	Feb. 8
Kansas	Feb. 12
Texas A&M	Feb. 15
Texas A&M ■	Feb. 19
Oklahoma	Feb. 22
Nebraska	Feb. 26
Iowa St.	Mar. 1
Big 12 Conf. Tr.	Mar. 6-9

1995-96 RESULTS (17-10)

76	St. Mary's (Tex.) ■	61
53	Wake Forest †	69
90	Arizona St. ■	85
80	Texas-Arlington ■	63
67	Southern Methodist	60
68	Michigan St.	57
81	Jackson St. ■	71
97	Arkansas St. ■	62
49	Temple †	41
53	Tulsa	57
61	Kansas ■	76
73	Oral Roberts ■	56
71	Iowa St.	79
91	Cal St. Northridge ■	58
57	Nebraska ■	66
59	Kansas St.	62
66	Kansas	84
96	Colorado ■	73
75	Oklahoma	81
83	Kansas St. ■	60
59	Missouri ■	63
72	Nebraska	57
58	Iowa St. ■	46
66	Colorado	64
89	Oklahoma ■	67
51	Missouri	49
55	Kansas St. †	58

Nickname: Cowboys
Colors: Orange & Black
Arena: Gallagher-Iba Arena
  Capacity: 6,381; Year Built: 1938
AD: Terry Don Phillips
SID: Mike Strauss

OLD DOMINION
Norfolk, VA 23529 I

Coach: Jeff Capel
Alma Mater: Fayetteville St. '77
Record: 7 Years, W-118, L-89

1996-97 SCHEDULE

Towson St.	Nov. 22
Toledo ■	Nov. 25
N.C.-Charlotte ■	Nov. 30
Tennessee St. ■	Dec. 2
Washington ■	Dec. 5
Syracuse Cl.	Dec. 13-14
Mississippi St.	Dec. 19
Puerto Rico Tr.	Dec. 30-Jan. 1
Richmond ■	Jan. 4
George Mason	Jan. 8
East Caro. ■	Jan. 11
N.C.-Wilmington ■	Jan. 13

American	Jan. 15
Va. Commonwealth	Jan. 18
William & Mary ■	Jan. 22
James Madison ■	Jan. 25
East Caro.	Jan. 29
Richmond ■	Feb. 1
William & Mary	Feb. 5
N.C.-Wilmington	Feb. 8
Geo. Washington	Feb. 11
Va. Commonwealth ■	Feb. 15
American ■	Feb. 19
George Mason ■	Feb. 22
James Madison ■	Feb. 24
Colonial Conf. Tr.	Feb. 28-Mar. 3

1995-96 RESULTS (18-13)

55	Duke †	75
78	Alas. Anchorage	77
89	Ohio †	90
75	Hampton	67
65	Southern Ill. ■	73
61	South Fla. ■	67
80	Toledo	92
84	Texas Tech	89
66	Wyoming	52
54	Idaho †	65
69	Cal St. Sacramento	62
62	St. Joseph's (Pa.) ■	60
70	Va. Commonwealth ■	85
61	N.C.-Wilmington	48
84	Richmond	69
103	George Mason ■	86
67	East Caro.	72
58	James Madison	45
86	William & Mary	82
67	American ■	47
51	N.C.-Wilmington ■	50
76	Va. Commonwealth	85
49	Virginia	87
76	James Madison ■	72
93	George Mason	92
70	Richmond ■	63
91	William & Mary ■	86
74	American	83
81	East Caro. ■	57
75	James Madison †	72
39	N.C.-Wilmington †	59

Nickname: Monarchs
Colors: Slate Blue & Silver
Arena: Norfolk Scope
  Capacity: 10,253; Year Built: 1971
AD: Jim Jarrett
SID: Carol Hudson

OLD WESTBURY
Long Island, NY 11568 III

Coach: Ron Jackson
Alma Mater: North Caro. Col. '64
Record: 5 Years, W-58, L-64

1996-97 SCHEDULE

Pace	Nov. 19
Eastern Conn. St. Tr.	Nov. 22-23
Albany (N.Y.)	Nov. 26
Purchase St.	Dec. 3
Mt. St. Mary (NY) Tr	Dec. 7-8
York (N.Y.)	Dec. 13
Kean Cl.	Jan. 4-5
Centenary (N.J.) ■	Jan. 18
Teikyo Post	Jan. 21
Old Westbury Tr.	Jan. 24-25
Stony Brook ■	Jan. 27
CCNY ■	Feb. 1
John Jay ■	Feb. 3
St. Joe's-Brooklyn	Feb. 5
Staten Island	Feb. 7
Pratt	Feb. 13
Baruch	Feb. 15
Lehman	Feb. 19
St. Joseph's (L.I.) ■	Feb. 24

1995-96 RESULTS (18-11)

67	Jersey City St.	76
70	Hunter †	61
93	Teikyo Post ■	83

109	Webb Inst.	49
83	Lincoln (Pa.) †	92
76	N.C. Wesleyan †	69
86	Hunter ■	68
73	York (N.Y.) ■	84
76	Utica/Rome ■	83
88	Keene St. †	76
70	Stony Brook	87
71	Baruch ■	83
87	CCNY †	67
68	John Jay	66
78	Staten Island	84
66	Mt. St. Vincent	72
67	Albany (N.Y.)	63
76	CCNY	62
95	Pratt ■	75
91	Purchase St. ■	55
87	Lehman ■	62
80	New York U.	84
75	Dominican (N.Y.)	86
84	St. Joseph's (L.I.)	46
86	St. Joe's-Brooklyn	51
82	St. Joseph's (L.I.) ■	45
78	St. Joe's-Brooklyn ■	69
97	Mt. St. Mary (N.Y.)	95
54	Merchant Marine	73

Nickname: Panthers
Colors: Green & White
Arena: Clark Center
  Capacity: 2,500; Year Built: 1981
AD: Dora Ierides
SID: To be named

OLIVET
Olivet, MI 49076 III

Coach: Gary Morrison
Alma Mater: Kalamazoo '57
Record: 29 Years, W-284, L-380

1996-97 SCHEDULE
Marian Tr.	Nov. 22-23
Kenyon ■	Nov. 26
Spring Arbor ■	Dec. 3
Hanover Tr.	Dec. 6-7
Aquinas ■	Dec. 11
Cornerstone	Dec. 16
Bluffton	Dec. 18
Defiance ■	Dec. 20
Kalamazoo	Jan. 8
Adrian	Jan. 11
Calvin ■	Jan. 15
Hope ■	Jan. 18
Alma ■	Jan. 22
Albion ■	Jan. 25
Concordia (Mich.) ■	Jan. 28
Kalamazoo ■	Feb. 1
Adrian ■	Feb. 5
Calvin	Feb. 8
Hope	Feb. 12
Alma ■	Feb. 15
Albion	Feb. 19
Defiance	Feb. 22

1995-96 RESULTS (9-16)
52	Wilmington (Ohio) †	44
64	Mount Union †	78
77	Spring Arbor	92
51	Aquinas †	71
88	Grace Bible (Mich.) †	65
82	Concordia (Mich.)	77
80	Bluffton ■	72
84	Cornerstone	91
82	Concordia (Mich.)	54
72	Allentown †	80
71	St. Mary's (Md.) †	67
84	Kalamazoo ■	77
80	Adrian ■	68
60	Calvin	81
75	Hope ■	97
71	Cornerstone ■	84
85	Alma ■	82
52	Albion	86
43	Kalamazoo	73
67	Adrian	74
61	Calvin ■	72

68	Hope ■	97
86	Alma	99
66	Albion ■	84
68	Calvin	87

Nickname: Comets
Colors: Red & White
Arena: Upton Gymnasium
  Capacity: 1,500; Year Built: 1981
AD: Richard A. Kaiser
SID: Tom Shaw

ONEONTA ST.
Oneonta, NY 13820 III

Coach: Jeri Mirabito
Alma Mater: Potsdam St. '83
Record: 5 Years, W-44, L-82

1996-97 SCHEDULE
Hartwick Cl.	Nov. 22-23
Pracitical Bible ■	Nov. 25
Potsdam St.	Dec. 6
Plattsburgh St.	Dec. 7
Southern Vt.	Dec. 11
Hamilton	Jan. 8
Utica ■	Jan. 10
Binghamton	Jan. 14
Hartwick ■	Jan. 21
Plattsburgh St. ■	Jan. 24
Potsdam St. ■	Jan. 25
New Paltz St. ■	Jan. 28
Utica/Rome ■	Jan. 31
Oswego St.	Feb. 1
Cortland St. ■	Feb. 4
Brockport St. ■	Feb. 7
Geneseo St. ■	Feb. 8
Cortland St.	Feb. 11
Buffalo St.	Feb. 14
Fredonia St.	Feb. 15
Binghamton ■	Feb. 18
New Paltz St.	Feb. 22

1995-96 RESULTS (17-11)
75	Hilbert †	64
64	Castleton St. †	74
70	Potsdam St. ■	68
86	Plattsburgh St. ■	89
68	Cortland St. ■	65
86	Brockport St.	81
78	Geneseo St.	75
60	Elmira	57
90	Potsdam St. †	77
65	Utica	69
68	Hartwick	94
62	Potsdam St.	72
80	Plattsburgh St.	69
62	Binghamton ■	47
79	Oswego St. ■	73
79	Utica/Rome ■	65
69	Cortland St.	75
57	New Paltz St. ■	64
72	Buffalo St. ■	60
61	Fredonia St. ■	67
49	Binghamton	69
78	New Paltz St.	69
52	Southern Vt. ■	82
97	Pracitical Bible	79
60	Brockport St. †	62
75	Ithaca ■	63
76	Elmira	59
80	Cortland St. ■	66

Nickname: Red Dragons
Colors: Red & White
Arena: Red Dragon Gymnasium
  Capacity: 1,200; Year Built: 1962
AD: Steve Garner
SID: Barbara Blodgett

ORAL ROBERTS
Tulsa, OK 74171 I

Coach: Bill Self
Alma Mater: Oklahoma St. '85
Record: 3 Years, W-34, L-47

1996-97 SCHEDULE
Rockhurst ■	Nov. 22
Northeast La. ■	Nov. 25
Arkansas ■	Nov. 27
Stephen F. Austin ■	Nov. 30
Northern Iowa	Dec. 2
Montana Cl.	Dec. 6-7
Northeastern Ill. ■	Dec. 14
LSU	Dec. 21
Ill.-Chicago ■	Dec. 28
Southern Miss. ■	Dec. 30
Northern Iowa ■	Jan. 4
Villanova ■	Jan. 8
Tulsa	Jan. 11
Montevallo ■	Jan. 15
Valparaiso ■	Jan. 20
Cal St. Sacramento ■	Jan. 26
Oklahoma St. ■	Jan. 29
Northeastern Ill.	Feb. 1
Alcorn St.	Feb. 5
Stephen F. Austin	Feb. 11
Montana ■	Feb. 15
Southern Utah ■	Feb. 19
Ill.-Chicago	Feb. 24
Alcorn St. ■	Feb. 26
Northeast La.	Mar. 1
Southern Utah	Mar. 4

1995-96 RESULTS (18-9)
57	Eastern Ill. ■	68
74	Middle Tenn. St. ■	91
81	Tennessee Tech ■	62
64	Creighton	80
74	Southeast Mo. St.	58
70	Northern Ariz.	66
53	Oklahoma	87
90	Tulsa ■	78
74	Cal Poly SLO	82
77	Southern Utah	74
56	Oklahoma St.	73
88	Cal St. Northridge ■	53
69	Southern Utah ■	67
105	John Brown ■	56
65	Arkansas	66
74	Texas Tech ■	78
58	Eastern Ill.	61
78	Cal St. Sacramento ■	66
89	Tennessee Tech	74
77	Cal St. Northridge	59
70	Mo.-Kansas City ■	59
72	Hampton	68
102	Huston-Tillotson	66
85	Southeast Mo. St. ■	69
61	Wichita St.	60
85	Tenn.-Martin ■	69
96	Hampton ■	54

Nickname: Golden Eagles
Colors: Navy Blue, White & Vegas Gold
Arena: Mabee Center
  Capacity: 10,575; Year Built: 1972
AD: Mike Carter
SID: Allison Starke

OREGON
Eugene, OR 97401 I

Coach: Jerry Green
Alma Mater: Appalachian St. '68
Record: 13 Years, W-205, L-167

1996-97 SCHEDULE
San Diego St. ■	Nov. 26
Wis.-Green Bay	Nov. 30
Portland St.	Dec. 4
Fresno St. ■	Dec. 7
Cleveland St. ■	Dec. 14
Nevada	Dec. 16
Boise St.	Dec. 20
Oregon Cl.	Dec. 27-28
Oregon St.	Jan. 4
Washington St. [Spokane]	Jan. 9
Washington	Jan. 11
Stanford ■	Jan. 16
California	Jan. 18
Arizona St.	Jan. 23
Arizona	Jan. 25

UCLA ■	Jan. 30
Southern Cal ■	Feb. 1
Washington ■	Feb. 6
Washington St. ■	Feb. 8
California	Feb. 13
Stanford	Feb. 15
Arizona ■	Feb. 20
Arizona St. ■	Feb. 22
Southern Cal	Feb. 27
UCLA	Mar. 1
Oregon St. ■	Mar. 8

1995-96 RESULTS (16-13)
115	Hawaii-Hilo	81
106	Nebraska †	114
74	Wichita St. †	64
106	West Fla. ■	66
105	Alas. Fairbanks ■	63
71	Wis.-Green Bay ■	81
82	Fresno St. ■	83
65	Boise St. ■	54
66	Montana	64
76	Nebraska †	99
75	Oregon St. †	50
70	Oregon St. ■	59
70	Washington St. ■	63
69	Washington ■	72
74	Stanford	94
72	California	97
73	Arizona St. ■	74
65	Arizona ■	70
78	UCLA	85
99	Southern Cal	78
55	Washington	52
65	Washington St.	70
60	California ■	58
64	Stanford ■	62
63	Arizona	81
81	Arizona St.	70
80	Southern Cal ■	60
71	UCLA ■	77
62	Oregon St.	46

Nickname: Ducks
Colors: Green & Yellow
Arena: McArthur Court
  Capacity: 10,063; Year Built: 1927
AD: Bill Moos
SID: Jamie Klund

OREGON ST.
Corvallis, OR 97331 I

Coach: Eddie Payne
Alma Mater: Wake Forest '73
Record: 10 Years, W-163, L-132

1996-97 SCHEDULE
Portland ■	Nov. 26
Nebraska	Nov. 30
Long Beach St.	Dec. 3
Azusa-Pacific ■	Dec. 7
Portland St. ■	Dec. 14
Texas ■	Dec. 18
Northeastern Ill. ■	Dec. 20
Oregon Cl.	Dec. 27-28
Oregon ■	Jan. 4
Washington	Jan. 9
Washington St. [Spokane]	Jan. 11
California ■	Jan. 16
Stanford ■	Jan. 18
Arizona	Jan. 23
Arizona St.	Jan. 25
Southern Cal ■	Jan. 30
UCLA ■	Feb. 1
Washington St. ■	Feb. 6
Washington ■	Feb. 8
Stanford	Feb. 13
California	Feb. 15
Arizona St. ■	Feb. 20
Arizona ■	Feb. 22
UCLA	Feb. 27
Southern Cal	Mar. 1
Oregon	Mar. 8

1995-96 RESULTS (4-23)
45	Santa Clara †	50

50	Portland	61
64	UC Irvine ■	57
54	Long Beach St. ■	65
54	Texas	83
68	New Orleans	61
62	Mississippi St. †	76
50	Oregon †	75
74	Mont. St.-Billings ■	79
59	Oregon	70
63	Washington ■	55
62	Washington St. ■	76
52	California	70
51	Stanford	84
59	Arizona ■	66
75	Arizona St. ■	93
47	Southern Cal	64
60	UCLA	69
42	Washington St.	61
40	Washington	50
50	Stanford ■	65
51	California ■	57
58	Arizona St.	63
60	Arizona	84
66	UCLA ■	68
56	Southern Cal ■	54
46	Oregon ■	62

Nickname: Beavers
Colors: Orange & Black
Arena: Gill Coliseum
　Capacity: 10,400; Year Built: 1949
AD: Dutch Baughman
SID: Hal Cowan

OSWEGO ST.
Oswego, NY 13126 III

Coach: Kevin Broderick
Alma Mater: Nazareth '89
(First year as head coach)

1996-97 SCHEDULE
Thiel Cl.		Nov. 22-23
Nazareth ■		Nov. 26
St. Lawrence		Dec. 3
Utica/Rome ■		Dec. 6
Geneseo St.		Dec. 7
Rochester Inst. ■		Dec. 10
Utica		Dec. 12
Hartwick		Jan. 12
Elmira		Jan. 14
Binghamton ■		Jan. 18
Brockport St. ■		Jan. 21
Buffalo St.		Jan. 24
Fredonia St.		Jan. 25
Cortland St.		Jan. 28
New Paltz St.		Jan. 31
Oneonta St. ■		Feb. 1
Utica/Rome		Feb. 4
Geneseo St. ■		Feb. 11
Potsdam St. ■		Feb. 14
Plattsburgh St. ■		Feb. 15
Brockport St.		Feb. 18
Fredonia St. ■		Feb. 21
Buffalo St. ■		Feb. 22

1995-96 RESULTS (3-21)
60	Skidmore	81
58	Geneseo St. †	68
67	Hartwick	69
69	St. Lawrence ■	66
77	Utica/Rome ■	76
68	Elmira ■	71
71	Utica	75
56	Cortland St. ■	57
75	Binghamton	86
66	Brockport St.	80
66	Fredonia St. ■	47
52	Buffalo St. ■	61
76	Geneseo St.	91
73	Oneonta St.	79
59	New Paltz St.	71
50	Rochester Inst.	77
64	Utica/Rome	66
75	Geneseo St. ■	80
87	Nazareth	93

90	Potsdam St. ■	100
66	Plattsburgh St.	89
85	Brockport St. ■	101
60	Fredonia St.	76
72	Buffalo St.	88

Nickname: Lakers
Colors: Green, Gold & White
Arena: Max Ziel Gymnasium
　Capacity: 4,200; Year Built: 1968
AD: Sandra Moore
SID: Danielle Drews

OTTERBEIN
Westerville, OH 43081 III

Coach: Dick Reynolds
Alma Mater: Otterbein '65
Record: 24 Years, W-427, L-226

1996-97 SCHEDULE
Cumberland (Tenn.)		Nov. 30
Lipscomb		Dec. 2
Sewanee		Dec. 3
Muskingum		Dec. 5
John Carroll ■		Dec. 7
Wittenberg ■		Dec. 11
Heidelberg		Dec. 14
Hiram		Dec. 18
Otterbein Tr.		Dec. 28-29
Capital ■		Jan. 8
Baldwin-Wallace		Jan. 11
Marietta		Jan. 15
Mount Union		Jan. 18
Ohio Northern ■		Jan. 22
Baldwin-Wallace ■		Jan. 25
Marietta		Jan. 29
Mount Union ■		Feb. 1
Ohio Northern		Feb. 5
John Carroll		Feb. 8
Muskingum ■		Feb. 12
Heidelberg ■		Feb. 15
Capital		Feb. 19
Hiram		Feb. 22

1995-96 RESULTS (12-13)
93	Tampa	101
87	Eckerd	73
60	Embry-Riddle	76
72	Hiram ■	51
71	Heidelberg	68
62	John Carroll ■	68
63	Wittenberg	84
80	Mount Union ■	82
79	MacMurray ■	66
78	Kenyon ■	76
74	Marietta ■	64
68	Capital	69
79	Ohio Northern ■	72
58	Baldwin-Wallace	69
43	Muskingum	59
75	Capital ■	84
59	Ohio Northern	67
87	John Carroll	103
71	Heidelberg ■	69
79	Mount Union	68
65	Marietta	63
68	Hiram	62
92	Muskingum ■	63
52	Baldwin-Wallace ■	80
68	Ohio Northern	70

Nickname: Cardinals
Colors: Tan & Cardinal
Arena: The Rike Center
　Capacity: 3,100; Year Built: 1974
AD: Dick Reynolds
SID: Ed Syguda

PACE
New York, NY 10038 II

Coach: Darrell Halloran
Alma Mater: Rice '72
Record: 13 Years, W-210, L-160

1996-97 SCHEDULE
Old Westbury ■		Nov. 19
Stonehill ■		Nov. 26
Concordia (N.Y.)		Dec. 4
Dowling ■		Dec. 7
Molloy		Dec. 11
St. Rose		Dec. 14
Merrimack Inv.		Dec. 27-28
Phila. Textile		Jan. 4
New York Tech ■		Jan. 6
LIU-C. W. Post ■		Jan. 8
Mercy		Jan. 11
LIU-Southampton ■		Jan. 13
Queens (N.Y.)		Jan. 15
Adelphi		Jan. 18
Concordia (N.Y.) ■		Jan. 20
Dowling		Jan. 22
Molloy ■		Jan. 25
St. Rose		Jan. 29
Phila. Textile ■		Feb. 1
New York Tech		Feb. 5
LIU-C. W. Post		Feb. 8
Mercy ■		Feb. 12
LIU-Southampton		Feb. 15
Queens (N.Y.) ■		Feb. 19
Adelphi ■		Feb. 22

1995-96 RESULTS (11-15)
Results unavailable

Nickname: Setters
Colors: Blue & Gold
Arena: Civic Center Gym
　Capacity: 1,650; Year Built: 1947
AD: Christopher Bledsoe
SID: Nicholas Renda

PACIFIC (CAL.)
Stockton, CA 95211 I

Coach: Bob Thomason
Alma Mater: Pacific (Cal.) '71
Record: 11 Years, W-164, L-143

1996-97 SCHEDULE
Fresno St.		Nov. 22
Cal St. Stanislaus ■		Nov. 23
Brigham Young		Nov. 30
San Diego		Dec. 5
Pepperdine		Dec. 7
Cal St. Chico ■		Dec. 14
Santa Clara ■		Dec. 21
Cal St. Sacramento ■		Dec. 23
Georgetown [Halifax]		Dec. 28
Cal St. Sacramento		Jan. 4
UC Irvine		Jan. 9
Cal St. Fullerton		Jan. 11
Idaho		Jan. 16
Long Beach St. ■		Jan. 23
Cal Poly SLO ■		Jan. 23
UC Santa Barb. ■		Jan. 25
North Texas		Jan. 30
New Mexico St.		Feb. 1
Utah St. ■		Feb. 6
Nevada ■		Feb. 8
UC Santa Barb.		Feb. 13
Cal Poly SLO		Feb. 15
Cal St. Fullerton ■		Feb. 20
UC Irvine ■		Feb. 22
Boise St.		Feb. 27
Long Beach St.		Mar. 1
Big West Conf. Tr.		Mar. 7-9

1995-96 RESULTS (15-12)
80	San Diego ■	78
46	St. Mary's (Cal.)	53
73	Fresno St. ■	70
76	UC Davis ■	62
77	Baylor ■	54
70	Santa Clara	75
68	Rutgers †	69
72	Texas A&M †	77
54	UC Irvine	72
69	Cal St. Fullerton	79
88	UNLV	68
78	New Mexico St. ■	66

71	Utah St.	73
55	Nevada	75
81	San Jose St. ■	60
64	UC Santa Barb. ■	66
77	Long Beach St. ■	83
75	New Mexico St.	59
90	Nevada ■	56
74	Utah St. ■	57
80	UNLV ■	55
73	San Jose St.	79
71	Long Beach St.	61
79	UC Santa Barb.	72
87	Cal St. Fullerton ■	63
80	UC Irvine ■	74
57	San Jose St. †	77

Nickname: Tigers
Colors: Orange & Black
Arena: A. C. Spanos Center
　Capacity: 6,000; Year Built: 1981
AD: Bob Lee
SID: Kevin Messenger

PARKS
Cahokia, IL 62206 III

Coach: Steve Jarvis
Alma Mater: Maryville (Mo.) '88
Record: 6 Years, W-34, L-100

1996-97 SCHEDULE
Schedule unavailable

1995-96 RESULTS (8-16)
75	St. Louis Pharmacy ■	70
77	Sanford Brown	75
83	Westminster (Mo.)	96
95	Sanford Brown	76
64	Wheaton (Ill.)	113
91	Mo.-St. Louis	102
117	Logan Chiropractic ■	108
74	Blackburn	99
60	Principia	63
82	Fontbonne ■	93
80	St. Louis Pharmacy	77
58	MacMurray	87
72	Greenville ■	76
78	Webster	88
67	Westminster (Mo.) ■	77
92	Blackburn ■	96
78	Principia ■	57
79	Fontbonne	96
71	Maryville (Mo.)	88
85	MacMurray ■	71
72	Maryville (Mo.) ■	93
73	Greenville	114
69	Webster ■	64
91	Fontbonne	107

Nickname: Falcons
Colors: Blue & White
Arena: Alumni Student Center
　Capacity: 1,000; Year Built: 1986
AD: Jerry Kurfman
SID: To be named

PENN ST.
University Park, PA 16802..........I

Coach: Jerry Dunn
Alma Mater: George Mason '80
Record: 1 Year, W-21, L-7

1996-97 SCHEDULE
Mt. St. Mary's (Md.) ■		Nov. 23
North Caro. St.		Nov. 25
Loyola (Md.) ■		Nov. 30
Tenn.-Chatt.		Dec. 3
Tennessee		Dec. 7
Bradley ■		Dec. 18
California [East Rutherford]		Dec. 20
Bucknell ■		Dec. 22
Brigham Young ■		Dec. 27
Iowa ■		Jan. 4
Ohio St.		Jan. 8
Illinois		Jan. 11

Michigan St. ■.................Jan. 15
Wisconsin.....................Jan. 18
Northwestern ■...............Jan. 22
Indiana ■......................Jan. 26
Michigan ■....................Jan. 28
Purdue ■.......................Feb. 1
Minnesota.....................Feb. 5
Michigan......................Feb. 8
Indiana.......................Feb. 11
Northwestern ■...............Feb. 15
Wisconsin ■...................Feb. 19
Michigan St. ■................Feb. 22
Illinois ■.....................Feb. 25
Ohio St. ■.....................Mar. 1
Iowa..........................Mar. 5

1995-96 RESULTS (21-7)
90	Morgan St. ■	65
99	Vermont ■	61
99	VMI ■	73
69	Tennessee	57
88	Pennsylvania †	61
81	Tenn.-Chatt. ■	48
85	Bucknell ■	54
70	Santa Clara †	49
75	Bradley †	72
72	Ohio St.	69
79	Wisconsin ■	50
76	Minnesota ■	61
83	Northwestern	74
66	Michigan ■	67
87	Purdue ■	77
82	Indiana ■	68
58	Michigan St.	61
95	Iowa ■	87
61	Illinois ■	58
54	Michigan St. ■	50
54	Indiana	72
49	Purdue	66
67	Michigan ■	57
78	Northwestern ■	62
60	Minnesota	65
52	Wisconsin	54
86	Ohio St. ■	70
80	Arkansas †	86

Nickname: Nittany Lions
Colors: Blue & White
Arena: Bryce Jordan Center
    Capacity: 15,300; Year Built: 1996
AD: Tim Curley
SID: Jeff Nelson

PENN ST.-BEHREND
Erie, PA 16563 III

Coach: Dave Niland
Alma Mater: Le Moyne '89
Record: 2 Years, W-26, L-24
1996-97 SCHEDULE
Penn St.-Behrend Tr. ....Nov. 23-24
Keuka ....Nov. 26
Thiel ■........................Dec. 3
Wash. & Jeff. ■................Dec. 7
Otterbein Tr...................Dec. 28-29
Grove City ■...................Jan. 4
Wash. & Jeff. ■................Jan. 6
Fredonia St. ■.................Jan. 9
Waynesburg ■...................Jan. 13
Grove City.....................Jan. 15
Bethany (W.Va.) ■..............Jan. 18
Pitt.-Bradford ■...............Jan. 25
Allegheny ■....................Jan. 28
Fredonia St....................Jan. 30
Oberlin........................Feb. 1
La Roche.......................Feb. 5
Keuka ■........................Feb. 8
Bethany (W.Va.) ■..............Feb. 10
Waynesburg.....................Feb. 17
La Roche ■.....................Feb. 19
Elmira.........................Feb. 22
Pitt.-Bradford ■...............Feb. 26
Thiel..........................Mar. 1

1995-96 RESULTS (13-12)
90	Thiel	66
58	Hilbert	64
55	Fredonia St. ■	67
73	Bethany (W.Va.)	66
76	Pitt.-Bradford ■	74
62	Wash. & Jeff. ■	59
71	King's (Pa.)	57
63	Wm. Paterson †	65
82	Waynesburg ■	69
68	Keuka	82
65	Fredonia St.	62
55	Grove City	56
86	Bethany (W.Va.)	84
72	Waynesburg	85
83	Oberlin ■	57
65	Allegheny	78
83	Thiel ■	60
60	Grove City ■	74
72	La Roche	61
57	Keuka ■	59
63	Wash. & Jeff.	68
60	Lake Erie	68
81	Elmira ■	68
65	Alfred	70
70	La Roche ■	55

Nickname: Lions
Colors: Blue, White & Red
Arena: Erie Hall
    Capacity: 700; Year Built: 1952
AD: Herb Lauffer
SID: Paul Benim

PENNSYLVANIA
Philadelphia, PA 19104 I

Coach: Fran Dunphy
Alma Mater: La Salle '70
Record: 7 Years, W-123, L-65
1996-97 SCHEDULE
Towson St. ■...................Dec. 3
Lehigh.........................Dec. 7
Villanova ■....................Dec. 10
Temple.........................Dec. 21
Arizona Cl.....................Dec. 28-30
Rice...........................Jan. 4
Yale...........................Jan. 10
Brown..........................Jan. 11
Drexel ■.......................Jan. 15
St. Joseph's (Pa.) ■...........Jan. 18
Maryland.......................Jan. 21
La Salle.......................Jan. 23
Lafayette......................Jan. 27
Columbia.......................Jan. 31
Cornell........................Feb. 1
Harvard ■......................Feb. 7
Dartmouth ■....................Feb. 8
Princeton ■....................Feb. 11
Brown ■........................Feb. 14
Yale ■.........................Feb. 15
Dartmouth......................Feb. 21
Harvard........................Feb. 22
Cornell ■......................Feb. 28
Columbia ■.....................Mar. 1
Princeton......................Mar. 4

1995-96 RESULTS (17-10)
78	Southern Cal ■	80
51	St. Louis	58
67	Towson St.	61
61	Penn St. †	88
65	Detroit †	77
67	Southern Methodist †	79
57	Princeton	55
74	Brown ■	71
66	Yale ■	56
70	St. Joseph's (Pa.) †	86
74	Lafayette ■	57
68	La Salle †	66
83	Hofstra	55
77	Cornell ■	63
74	Columbia ■	50
90	Lehigh ■	73
53	Dartmouth	54
77	Harvard	63
60	Yale	62
83	Brown	53
42	Temple ■	53
66	Harvard ■	64
80	Dartmouth ■	51
82	Columbia	62
70	Cornell	55
63	Princeton ■	49
56	Princeton †	63

Nickname: Quakers
Colors: Red & Blue
Arena: The Palestra
    Capacity: 8,700; Year Built: 1927
AD: Steve Bilsky
SID: Shaun May

PEPPERDINE
Malibu, CA 90263 I

Coach: Lorenzo Romar
Alma Mater: Washington '80
(First year as head coach)
1996-97 SCHEDULE
Weber St.......................Nov. 22
UC Santa Barb. ■...............Nov. 25
Boise St.......................Nov. 30
San Jose St. ■.................Dec. 3
Pacific (Cal.) ■...............Dec. 7
Syracuse Cl....................Dec. 13-14
Cal St. Northridge ■...........Dec. 19
Cal St. Fullerton..............Dec. 21
Cal St. Hayward................Dec. 27
Wis.-Green Bay Cl..............Dec. 30-31
San Diego ■....................Jan. 10
San Francisco ■................Jan. 11
Loyola Marymount...............Jan. 15
Loyola Marymount...............Jan. 18
Portland.......................Jan. 23
Gonzaga........................Jan. 25
Gonzaga ■......................Jan. 31
Portland ■.....................Feb. 1
St. Mary's (Cal.)..............Feb. 7
Santa Clara....................Feb. 9
Santa Clara ■..................Feb. 14
St. Mary's (Cal.) ■............Feb. 15
San Francisco..................Feb. 20
San Diego......................Feb. 22
West Coast Conf. Tr. ....Mar. 1-3

1995-96 RESULTS (10-18)
58	South Fla.	65
76	Seattle ■	62
62	Grambling †	69
69	Ga. Southern †	59
90	Cal St. Northridge ■	81
99	Weber St. ■	88
68	UC Santa Barb.	67
80	Southern Utah	97
80	San Jose St.	76
61	Boston U. †	75
69	Dartmouth †	66
58	Boise St. ■	61
70	San Diego	81
54	San Francisco	56
79	St. Mary's (Cal.) ■	89
76	Santa Clara	87
72	Santa Clara	69
88	St. Mary's (Cal.)	78
72	Portland ■	78
66	Gonzaga ■	78
80	Gonzaga	94
76	Portland	89
64	Loyola Marymount ■	74
62	Loyola Marymount	75
51	San Francisco ■	63
61	San Diego ■	80
63	Santa Clara	60
48	Gonzaga †	76

Nickname: Waves
Colors: Blue & Orange
Arena: Firestone Fieldhouse
    Capacity: 3,104; Year Built: 1973
AD: Wayne Wright
SID: Michael Zapolski

PFEIFFER
Misenheimer, NC 28109 II

Coach: Kirk Earlywine
Alma Mater: Campbell '87
(First year as head coach)
1996-97 SCHEDULE
Barber-Scotia ■................Nov. 16
Queens (N.C.)..................Nov. 19
Claflin ■......................Nov. 23
Lees-McRae ■...................Nov. 26
North Fla. Cl..................Nov. 29-30
Longwood.......................Dec. 2
Barton ■.......................Dec. 4
Barber-Scotia..................Dec. 7
Erskine........................Jan. 8
Mount Olive....................Jan. 11
Belmont Abbey..................Jan. 13
Claflin........................Jan. 15
Coker..........................Jan. 18
High Point.....................Jan. 22
St. Andrews....................Jan. 27
Lees-McRae ■...................Jan. 29
Mount Olive ■..................Feb. 1
High Point ■...................Feb. 3
Belmont Abbey ■................Feb. 6
St. Andrews ■..................Feb. 8
Erskine........................Feb. 10
Longwood ■.....................Feb. 13
Barton.........................Feb. 15
Queens (N.C.) ■................Feb. 17
N.C. Central...................Feb. 20
Coker..........................Feb. 22

1995-96 RESULTS (20-8)
71	North Fla.	55
80	Elon	67
101	Barber-Scotia ■	68
91	St. Augustine's ■	96
53	High Point	59
86	Barton ■	68
75	Catawba	60
77	St. Andrews ■	65
76	Belmont Abbey	68
62	Lees-McRae	66
80	Longwood ■	75
77	Erskine	47
63	Queens (N.C.)	72
84	High Point ■	69
49	Coker	52
76	Mount Olive ■	60
84	Barton	75
65	Longwood	50
69	Mount Olive	70
79	Belmont Abbey ■	66
73	St. Andrews	54
79	Erskine ■	56
65	Queens (N.C.) ■	64
70	Lees-McRae ■	67
81	Longwood †	71
64	Queens (N.C.) †	65
71	N.C. Central †	62
47	Virginia Union	49

Nickname: Falcons
Colors: Black & Gold
Arena: Merner Gymnasium
    Capacity: 2,200; Year Built: 1973
AD: T. J. Kostecky
SID: Seph Hatley

PHILA. TEXTILE
Philadelphia, PA 19144 II

Coach: Herb Magee
Alma Mater: Phila. Textile '63
Record: 29 Years, W-618, L-221
1996-97 SCHEDULE
Le Moyne ■.....................Nov. 16
West Chester...................Nov. 26
Kutztown ■.....................Nov. 30
Eastern........................Dec. 2
LIU-C. W. Post.................Dec. 4
Mercy..........................Dec. 7

Queens (N.Y.) ....Dec. 14
St. Rose ■ ....Dec. 22
Molloy ■ ....Jan. 2
Pace ■ ....Jan. 4
Concordia (N.Y.) ....Jan. 6
Dowling ■ ....Jan. 8
LIU-Southampton ....Jan. 10
Adelphi ■ ....Jan. 15
New York Tech ....Jan. 18
LIU-C. W. Post ■ ....Jan. 20
Mercy ■ ....Jan. 22
LIU-Southampton ■ ....Jan. 25
Queens (N.Y.) ■ ....Jan. 29
Pace ....Feb. 1
Concordia (N.Y.) ■ ....Feb. 5
Dowling ....Feb. 8
Molloy ....Feb. 12
St. Rose ....Feb. 15
Adelphi ....Feb. 19
New York Tech ■ ....Feb. 22

1995-96 RESULTS (19-9)

71	Eastern ■	67
73	Molloy ■	52
65	West Chester ■	68
86	New York Tech ■	81
64	Pace	46
60	Queens (N.Y.) ■	43
62	St. Rose	82
56	Concordia (N.Y.)	51
68	Holy Family	58
58	Calif. (Pa.)	70
79	LIU-C. W. Post	65
64	LIU-Southampton	55
73	Adelphi	76
80	Mercy ■	62
95	Dowling	85
68	New York Tech	70
49	Pace ■	67
75	Queens (N.Y.)	49
58	St. Rose ■	77
69	Concordia (N.Y.)	40
93	Molloy	77
87	LIU-C. W. Post ■	78
102	LIU-Southampton ■	69
62	Adelphi ■	74
87	Mercy	71
67	Dowling ■	66
72	LIU-C. W. Post ■	61
69	Adelphi †	76

Nickname: Rams
Colors: Maroon & White
Arena: Buckey Harris Gymnasium
  Capacity: 1,200; Year Built: 1960
AD: Tom Shirley
SID: Shannon Wasson

PITTSBURG ST.
Pittsburg, KS 66762 II

Coach: Gene Iba
Alma Mater: Tulsa '63
Record: 16 Years, W-240, L-216

1996-97 SCHEDULE

Southwestern Okla. ■ ....Nov. 16
Park ....Nov. 20
Bethel (Kan.) ■ ....Nov. 26
Missouri So. Cl. ....Nov. 29-30
Mo.-Rolla ■ ....Dec. 4
Northwest Mo. St. ....Dec. 7
Drury ■ ....Dec. 9
Ottawa ■ ....Dec. 19
Truman St. ....Jan. 4
Washburn ■ ....Jan. 8
Park ■ ....Jan. 10
Central Mo. St. ■ ....Jan. 13
Lincoln (Mo.) ....Jan. 15
Emporia St. ■ ....Jan. 18
Southwest Baptist ■ ....Jan. 22
Central Mo. St. ....Jan. 25
Mo. Western St. ....Jan. 27
Mo. Southern St. ■ ....Jan. 29
Washburn ....Feb. 1
Mo.-Rolla ....Feb. 5
Mo. Western St. ■ ....Feb. 8

Northwest Mo. St. ■ ....Feb. 12
Lincoln (Mo.) ....Feb. 15
Southwest Baptist ....Feb. 18
Mo. Southern St. ....Feb. 22

1995-96 RESULTS (14-14)
Results unavailable

Nickname: Gorillas
Colors: Crimson & Gold
Arena: John Lance Arena
  Capacity: 6,500; Year Built: 1971
AD: Bill Samuels
SID: Dan Wilkes

PITTSBURGH
Pittsburgh, PA 15213 I

Coach: Ralph Willard
Alma Mater: Holy Cross '67
Record: 6 Years, W-101, L-77

1996-97 SCHEDULE

Illinois St. ■ ....Nov. 24
Navy ....Nov. 26
North Caro. ....Nov. 29
Connecticut ■ ....Dec. 4
Seton Hall ....Dec. 8
Va. Commonwealth ■ ....Dec. 14
Carnegie Mellon ■ ....Dec. 16
St. Francis (Pa.) ■ ....Dec. 18
Duquesne ....Dec. 21
Mt. St. Mary's (Md.) ■ ....Dec. 23
Hawaii Rainbow Cl. ....Dec. 27-30
St. John's (N.Y.) ....Jan. 4
Miami (Fla.) ■ ....Jan. 8
Rutgers ■ ....Jan. 11
St. John's (N.Y.) ■ ....Jan. 18
Boston College ....Jan. 21
Georgetown ....Jan. 25
Notre Dame ■ ....Jan. 29
West Va. ....Feb. 1
Miami (Fla.) ....Feb. 5
Seton Hall ■ ....Feb. 8
Villanova ■ ....Feb. 12
Providence ....Feb. 15
Georgetown ■ ....Feb. 20
Boston College ■ ....Feb. 23
Connecticut ....Feb. 25
Syracuse ....Mar. 2
Big East Conf. Tr. ....Mar. 5-8

1995-96 RESULTS (10-17)

84	Duquesne ■	73
66	Georgia ■	85
53	Boston College	55
72	Va. Commonwealth ■	69
108	LIU-Brooklyn ■	67
49	North Caro.	66
101	Prairie View ■	59
95	Brown ■	47
84	West Va.	83
75	Georgetown ■	56
75	Notre Dame ■	65
77	Rutgers	78
57	Miami (Fla.)	66
71	Massachusetts ■	79
63	Connecticut ■	69
70	Providence	85
75	Seton Hall ■	69
55	Villanova	88
67	Syracuse ■	73
71	Providence ■	80
69	Notre Dame	77
64	Villanova ■	67
70	Rutgers ■	71
60	Syracuse	77
83	West Va. ■	63
68	St. John's (N.Y.)	74
66	Boston College †	70

Nickname: Panthers
Colors: Gold & Blue
Arena: Fitzgerald Field House
  Capacity: 6,798; Year Built: 1951
AD: L. Oval Jaynes
SID: Ron Wahl

PITT.-JOHNSTOWN
Johnstown, PA 15904 II

Coach: Bob Rukavina
Alma Mater: Indiana (Pa.) '85
Record: 7 Years, W-83, L-100

1996-97 SCHEDULE

Pitt.-Johnstown Tr. ....Nov. 16-17
West Va. Wesleyan ....Nov. 19
Shepherd ■ ....Nov. 23
Glenville St. ■ ....Nov. 26
Mansfield ■ ....Nov. 30
Lake Erie ■ ....Dec. 2
Indiana (Pa.) ■ ....Dec. 4
Shippensburg Tr. ....Dec. 6-7
La Roche ■ ....Dec. 14
Shepherd ....Jan. 4
Shippensburg ■ ....Jan. 8
Columbia Union ....Jan. 13
Calif. (Pa.) ■ ....Jan. 15
Slippery Rock ■ ....Jan. 18
Clarion ■ ....Jan. 20
Lake Erie ....Jan. 22
Lock Haven ■ ....Jan. 27
Central St. ....Jan. 29
St. Vincent ....Feb. 1
Westminster (Pa.) ■ ....Feb. 4
Slippery Rock ....Feb. 8
West Chester ■ ....Feb. 11
Edinboro ■ ....Feb. 15
Columbia Union ■ ....Feb. 17
Lock Haven ....Feb. 19
Dist. Columbia ....Feb. 24

1995-96 RESULTS (13-12)

90	West Va. Wesleyan ■	102
76	Lock Haven ■	80
82	Dist. Columbia	93
103	Gannon	99
88	Millersville †	97
97	Shippensburg	93
47	Glenville St.	62
69	Indiana (Pa.) ■	93
92	Kutztown	74
74	Lycoming †	77
101	Phila. Bible †	71
59	Columbia Union ■	50
74	Slippery Rock	69
72	Lock Haven	81
89	Clarion ■	83
84	Edinboro ■	89
63	Columbia Union	74
85	Mansfield ■	77
81	West Chester	87
83	Calif. (Pa.) ■	99
85	Slippery Rock ■	78
91	Kutztown ■	59
81	St. Vincent ■	79
97	Point Park	86
94	Dist. Columbia ■	75

Nickname: Mountain Cats
Colors: Gold & Blue
Arena: Sports Center
  Capacity: 2,400; Year Built: 1976
AD: Ed Sherlock
SID: To be named

PLATTSBURGH ST.
Plattsburgh, NY 12901 III

Coach: Larry Cowan
Alma Mater: Ithaca '81
Record: 9 Years, W-111, L-115

1996-97 SCHEDULE

Plattsburgh Cl. ....Nov. 22-23
New Paltz St. ■ ....Dec. 6
Oneonta St. ■ ....Dec. 7
Potsdam St. ....Dec. 10
Southern Vt. ■ ....Dec. 13
Johnson St. ....Jan. 8
Ithaca ....Jan. 13
Buffalo St. ■ ....Jan. 17
Fredonia St. ■ ....Jan. 18

St. Lawrence ■ ....Jan. 21
Oneonta St. ....Jan. 24
New Paltz St. ■ ....Jan. 25
Brockport St. ■ ....Jan. 31
Geneseo St. ....Feb. 1
Cortland St. ■ ....Feb. 7
Binghamton ■ ....Feb. 8
Clarkson ■ ....Feb. 11
Utica/Rome ■ ....Feb. 14
Oswego St. ....Feb. 15
Potsdam St. ■ ....Feb. 18
Binghamton ....Feb. 21
Cortland St. ....Feb. 22

1995-96 RESULTS (11-13)

89	Johnson St. ■	53
85	Bates ■	69
60	Albany (N.Y.) ■	71
81	New Paltz St.	69
89	Oneonta St.	86
76	Potsdam St.	75
75	Johnson St. ■	53
62	Ithaca	60
54	Buffalo St.	75
75	Fredonia St.	81
49	St. Lawrence ■	83
70	New Paltz St. ■	79
69	Oneonta St.	80
79	Brockport St. ■	85
64	Geneseo St. ■	65
61	Vermont	88
72	Cortland St. ■	80
61	Binghamton	80
68	Clarkson	80
60	Utica/Rome	75
89	Oswego St. ■	66
82	Potsdam St. ■	71
73	Cortland St. ■	65
74	Binghamton ■	60

Nickname: Cardinals
Colors: Cardinal Red & White
Arena: Memorial Hall Gymnasium
  Capacity: 1,500; Year Built: 1961
AD: Peter Luguri
SID: Brian Micheels

PLYMOUTH ST.
Plymouth, NH 03264 III

Coach: Paul Hogan
Alma Mater: Plymouth St. '79
Record: 6 Years, W-100, L-62

1996-97 SCHEDULE

Plattsburgh Cl. ....Nov. 22-23
Johnson St. ■ ....Dec. 3
Salem St. ....Dec. 5
Rivier ■ ....Dec. 7
Daniel Webster ■ ....Dec. 12
Rhode Island Col. ....Dec. 14
Merrimack Tr. ....Dec. 27-28
Bowdoin ■ ....Jan. 8
Mass.-Dartmouth ....Jan. 11
Southern Me. ....Jan. 15
Eastern Conn. St. ■ ....Jan. 18
Mass.-Boston ....Jan. 21
Me.-Farmington ■ ....Jan. 23
Western Conn. St. ....Jan. 25
Mass.-Dartmouth ■ ....Feb. 1
Southern Me. ....Feb. 4
Bri'water (Mass.) ■ ....Feb. 6
Rhode Island Col. ■ ....Feb. 8
Mass.-Boston ■ ....Feb. 11
Eastern Conn. St. ....Feb. 15
New England ....Feb. 19
Western Conn. St. ■ ....Feb. 22

1995-96 RESULTS (19-9)

124	Notre Dame (N.H.) ■	63
81	Teikyo Post	85
75	Southern Me.	94
89	Johnson St.	51
73	Salem St. ■	66
98	Rivier	83
86	Gordon ■	71
88	Rhode Island Col. ■	77

91	Mass.-Dartmouth ■	93
67	Bowdoin ■	70
69	Eastern Conn. St.	67
92	Mass.-Boston	79
89	Me.-Farmington	101
85	Western Conn. St. ■	94
83	Castleton St. ■	98
74	Mass.-Dartmouth	68
95	Southern Me. ■	77
73	Bri'water (Mass.) ■	69
68	Rhode Island Col.	56
78	Mass.-Boston	63
85	Daniel Webster ■	66
81	Eastern Conn. St. ■	56
96	New England ■	67
75	Western Conn. St.	70
91	Mass.-Boston ■	60
77	Rhode Island Col. †	68
64	Western Conn. St. †	80
62	Williams	78

Nickname: Panthers
Colors: Green & White
Arena: Foley Gymnasium
 Capacity: 2,000; Year Built: 1969
AD: Steve Bamford
SID: Kent Cherrington

POLYTECHNIC (N.Y.)
Brooklyn, NY 11201 III

Coach: Laddy Baldwin
Alma Mater: LIU-Brooklyn '74
Record: 9 Years, W-46, L-158

1996-97 SCHEDULE
Webb Inst. ....Nov. 19
New York U. Tr. ....Nov. 22-23
Baruch ■ ....Dec. 2
Polytechnic Tr. ....Dec. 6-7
St. Joseph's (L.I.) ■ ....Dec. 9
Yeshiva ■ ....Dec. 14
St. Joseph's (L.I.) ....Jan. 9
Brooklyn ■ ....Jan. 11
Maritime (N.Y.) ....Jan. 13
Vassar ....Jan. 15
Savannah Tr. ....Jan. 18-19
N.J. Inst. of Tech. ....Jan. 23
New York U. ....Jan. 28
Stevens Tech ....Jan. 30
Pratt ■ ....Feb. 1
N.J. Inst. of Tech. ■ ....Feb. 5
St. Joe's-Brooklyn ■ ....Feb. 8
Yeshiva ....Feb. 11
Mt. St. Vincent ■ ....Feb. 13
Vassar ....Feb. 15
Stevens Tech ....Feb. 18
Bard ....Feb. 22

1995-96 RESULTS (10-13)
68	Brooklyn	75
87	Cooper Union ■	61
78	Webb Inst. ■	36
64	Baruch	78
74	Webb Inst.	41
55	N.J. Inst. of Tech. ■	77
61	St. Joseph's (L.I.)	59
60	Yeshiva ■	71
49	Stevens Tech	85
69	Rutgers-Newark	78
66	Vassar ■	60
93	Cooper Union ■	49
76	Maritime (N.Y.) ■	87
63	Stevens Tech ■	69
82	Bard	34
68	Warren Wilson	67
70	N.J. Inst. of Tech.	98
54	Yeshiva	58
70	Vassar	88
72	Pratt	54
61	Mt. St. Vincent ■	67
59	Maritime (N.Y.)	50
68	Stevens Tech	89

Nickname: Blue Jays
Colors: Blue & Gray
AD: Joseph Martini
SID: Onofrio Russo

POMONA-PITZER
Claremont, CA 91711 III

Coach: Charles Katsiaficas
Alma Mater: Tufts '84
Record: 8 Years, W-133, L-99

1996-97 SCHEDULE
Swarthmore Cl. ....Nov. 22-23
Pomona-Pitzer Cl. ....Nov. 29-30
UC San Diego ....Dec. 3
Southern Cal Col. ....Dec. 7
Biola ■ ....Dec. 14
Wooster ■ ....Dec. 21
La Sierra ....Jan. 4
Swarthmore ■ ....Jan. 6
Chapman ■ ....Jan. 8
Occidental ■ ....Jan. 11
Cal Lutheran ■ ....Jan. 15
Whittier ....Jan. 18
Redlands ■ ....Jan. 22
Cal Tech ■ ....Jan. 25
La Verne ....Jan. 29
Claremont-M-S ■ ....Feb. 1
Occidental ....Feb. 5
Cal Lutheran ■ ....Feb. 8
Whittier ■ ....Feb. 12
Redlands ....Feb. 15
Cal Tech ....Feb. 19
La Verne ■ ....Feb. 22
Claremont-M-S ....Feb. 26

1995-96 RESULTS (15-9)
72	Chapman	75
68	Colby ■	63
78	Washington (Mo.) †	70
63	San Diego	82
94	La Sierra ■	67
69	Concordia (Cal.) ■	67
81	UC San Diego	89
71	Southern Cal Col.	68
65	Biola	70
85	Cal Baptist	104
85	La Verne ■	45
86	Redlands	63
75	Occidental ■	63
75	Whittier ■	63
66	Cal Lutheran	73
92	Cal Tech ■	41
61	Claremont-M-S	66
81	La Verne	70
102	Redlands ■	77
73	Occidental	74
95	Whittier	78
63	Cal Lutheran ■	56
65	Cal Tech	39
56	Claremont-M-S ■	71

Nickname: Sagehens
Colors: Blue, Orange & White
Arena: Voelkel Gymnasium
 Capacity: 1,500; Year Built: 1989
AD: Curt Tong
SID: Kirk Reynolds

PORTLAND
Portland, OR 97203 I

Coach: Rob Chavez
Alma Mater: Mesa St. '80
Record: 4 Years, W-68, L-46

1996-97 SCHEDULE
Pacific Lutheran ■ ....Nov. 22
Oregon St. ....Nov. 26
Hawaii Tip-Off ....Nov. 29-Dec. 1
Portland St. ■ ....Dec. 7
San Jose St. ■ ....Dec. 14
Nevada ....Dec. 18
Washington ■ ....Dec. 21
Utah St. Tr. ....Dec. 27-28
Southern Utah ....Jan. 2
Cal Poly SLO ....Jan. 4
St. Mary's (Cal.) ■ ....Jan. 9
Santa Clara ■ ....Jan. 11
San Francisco ....Jan. 16
San Diego ....Jan. 18

Pepperdine ■		Jan. 23
Loyola Marymount ■		Jan. 25
Loyola Marymount		Jan. 31
Pepperdine		Feb. 1
Gonzaga		Feb. 5
Gonzaga ■		Feb. 8
San Diego ■		Feb. 13
San Francisco ■		Feb. 15
Santa Clara		Feb. 21
St. Mary's (Cal.)		Feb. 22
West Coast Conf. Tr.		Mar. 1-3

1995-96 RESULTS (19-11)
69	UAB	60
61	Oregon St. ■	50
84	Pacific Lutheran ■	64
87	Eastern Wash.	72
113	Southern Ore. St. ■	65
91	Cal Poly SLO ■	70
79	San Jose St.	87
59	Washington	71
92	Texas Southern †	64
70	Boise St.	49
88	Southern Utah ■	83
80	Butler	87
97	St. Mary's (Cal.)	86
66	Santa Clara	86
57	San Francisco ■	63
78	San Diego ■	64
72	Gonzaga	95
67	Gonzaga ■	66
78	Pepperdine	72
62	Loyola Marymount	70
97	Loyola Marymount ■	77
89	Pepperdine ■	76
68	San Diego	76
43	San Francisco	66
80	Santa Clara ■	71
83	St. Mary's (Cal.) ■	91
78	San Francisco †	72
65	San Diego †	52
76	Gonzaga †	68
58	Villanova †	92

Nickname: Pilots
Colors: Purple & White
Arena: Chiles Center
 Capacity: 5,000; Year Built: 1984
AD: Joe Etzel
SID: Steve Walker

POTSDAM ST.
Potsdam, NY 13676 III

Coach: Bill Mitchell
Alma Mater: Michigan '83
Record: 5 Years, W-46, L-77

1996-97 SCHEDULE
Schedule unavailable

1995-96 RESULTS (7-17)
63	Bates †	81
74	Johnson St. †	52
68	Oneonta St.	70
84	New Paltz St.	74
75	Plattsburgh St. ■	76
61	Rochester Inst.	79
65	Montclair St. †	74
84	Point Park †	83
77	Oneonta St. †	90
83	Fredonia St.	86
70	Buffalo St.	81
72	Oneonta St. ■	62
64	New Paltz St. ■	73
67	Clarkson	65
60	Geneseo St. ■	69
66	Brockport St. ■	86
74	Binghamton	55
60	Cortland St.	67
74	St. Lawrence ■	76
100	Oswego St.	90
69	Utica/Rome ■	76
71	Plattsburgh St.	82
70	Binghamton ■	91
72	Cortland St.	77

Nickname: Bears

Colors: Maroon & Gray
Arena: Maxcy Hall
 Capacity: 3,600; Year Built: 1972
AD: William Donohue
SID: Mark Mende

PRAIRIE VIEW
Prairie View, TX 77445 I

Coach: Elwood Plummer
Alma Mater: Jackson St. '66
Record: 22 Years, W-274, L-331

1996-97 SCHEDULE
Mississippi ....Nov. 26
Tulane ....Dec. 4
Marquette Tr. ....Dec. 6-7
McNeese St. ....Dec. 16
Baylor ....Dec. 18
Wichita St. ....Dec. 21
LSU ....Dec. 23
Southern Methodist ■ ....Dec. 30
Jackson St. ....Jan. 4
Alabama St. ■ ....Jan. 6
Grambling ....Jan. 11
Mississippi Val. ....Jan. 13
Alcorn St. ■ ....Jan. 18
Southern U. ■ ....Jan. 20
Texas Southern ....Jan. 25
Jackson St. ■ ....Feb. 1
Alabama St. ....Feb. 3
Grambling ■ ....Feb. 8
Mississippi Val. ■ ....Feb. 10
Alcorn St. ....Feb. 15
Southern U. ....Feb. 17
Texas Southern ■ ....Feb. 22
Southwestern Conf. Tr. ....Mar. 5-8

1995-96 RESULTS (4-23)
72	Tulane	113
54	Texas Tech	101
142	Bay Ridge Christian ■	75
52	UAB	105
109	Faith Bapt. Bible ■	81
85	Baylor	111
125	Huston-Tillotson ■	123
62	McNeese St.	101
50	Tulsa	141
59	Pittsburgh	101
51	Mississippi	96
70	Alabama St. ■	71
84	Jackson St.	102
88	Mississippi Val. ■	95
75	Grambling ■	110
84	Alcorn St.	105
89	Southern U.	108
115	National Christian ■	97
69	Texas Southern	77
87	Alabama St. ■	92
78	Jackson St. ■	92
76	Mississippi Val.	96
92	Grambling	96
83	Alcorn St. ■	84
103	Southern U. ■	125
79	Texas Southern	91
81	Southern U. †	107

Nickname: Panthers
Colors: Purple & Gold
Arena: Baby Dome
 Capacity: 5,000; Year Built: 1968
AD: Hensley Sapenter
SID: Harlan Robinson

PRESBYTERIAN
Clinton, SC 29325 II

Coach: Gregg Nibert
Alma Mater: Marietta '79
Record: 6 Years, W-103, L-74

1996-97 SCHEDULE
Anderson (S.C.) ■ ....Nov. 15
Newberry ....Nov. 20
Augusta St. ■ ....Nov. 25
Newberry ■ ....Nov. 27
Erskine ■ ....Dec. 2

Anderson (S.C.)		Dec. 7
Charleston (S.C.)		Dec. 14
Lenoir-Rhyne ■		Jan. 4
Catawba ■		Jan. 8
Gardner-Webb		Jan. 11
Wingate ■		Jan. 15
Elon		Jan. 18
Mars Hill ■		Jan. 22
Carson-Newman ■		Jan. 25
Lenoir-Rhyne		Feb. 1
Catawba		Feb. 5
Gardner-Webb ■		Feb. 8
Wingate		Feb. 12
Elon ■		Feb. 15
Mars Hill		Feb. 19
Carson-Newman		Feb. 22

1995-96 RESULTS (19-11)

91	Augusta St.	57
103	Allen ■	55
65	Newberry	69
55	Erskine	63
100	Voorhees ■	62
64	Western Caro.	68
87	Elizabeth City St. ■	60
73	S.C.-Aiken ■	57
73	Carson-Newman ■	58
73	Mars Hill	72
75	Lenoir-Rhyne ■	65
90	Anderson (S.C.)	54
75	Catawba ■	84
82	Gardner-Webb	93
72	Newberry ■	65
74	Wingate ■	65
71	Elon	65
74	Voorhees	87
75	Mars Hill ■	62
48	Lenoir-Rhyne	57
74	Anderson (S.C.) ■	44
57	Catawba	63
81	Gardner-Webb ■	88
67	Carson-Newman	60
60	Wingate	62
87	Elon ■	78
83	Wingate	62
71	Carson-Newman †	60
82	Mars Hill †	77
67	High Point †	76

Nickname: Blue Hose
Colors: Garnet & Blue
Arena: Templeton Center
   Capacity: 2,500; Year Built: 1975
AD: Allen Morris
SID: Art Chase

PRINCETON
Princeton, NJ 08544 I

Coach: Bill Carmody
Alma Mater: Union '75
(First year as head coach)

1996-97 SCHEDULE

NIT	Nov. 20-29
Lafayette	Dec. 3
Marquette Tr.	Dec. 6-7
Bucknell ■	Dec. 10
Monmouth (N.J.)	Dec. 14
Lehigh ■	Dec. 19
North Caro. ■	Dec. 22
UTEP Tr.	Dec. 27-28
Manhattan	Jan. 3
Rutgers ■	Jan. 6
Brown	Jan. 10
Yale	Jan. 11
Cornell	Jan. 31
Columbia	Feb. 1
Dartmouth ■	Feb. 7
Harvard ■	Feb. 8
Pennsylvania	Feb. 11
Yale ■	Feb. 14
Brown ■	Feb. 15
Harvard	Feb. 21
Dartmouth	Feb. 22
Columbia ■	Feb. 28

Cornell ■		Mar. 1
Pennsylvania ■		Mar. 4

1995-96 RESULTS (22-7)

62	Lehigh	45
62	Lafayette	47
61	Boise St. †	41
59	Fresno St.	54
56	Monmouth (N.J.) ■	65
88	St. Joseph's (Pa.) ■	78
47	Iowa St.	50
86	Nicholls St. †	51
65	Ohio †	60
35	Wis.-Green Bay	55
49	La Salle	52
55	Pennsylvania ■	57
56	Yale ■	55
64	Brown	36
75	Haverford ■	46
66	Columbia ■	45
57	Cornell ■	54
49	Harvard	44
52	Dartmouth	41
58	Brown	56
64	Yale	42
65	Dartmouth ■	39
65	Harvard ■	58
65	Cornell	49
57	Columbia	55
49	Pennsylvania	63
63	Pennsylvania †	56
43	UCLA †	41
41	Mississippi St. †	63

Nickname: Tigers
Colors: Orange & Black
Arena: Jadwin Gymnasium
   Capacity: 7,500; Year Built: 1969
AD: Gary D. Walters
SID: Jerry Price

PROVIDENCE
Providence, RI 02918 I

Coach: Pete Gillen
Alma Mater: Fairfield '68
Record: 11 Years, W-237, L-100

1996-97 SCHEDULE

Top of the World Cl.	Nov. 22-24
LIU-Brooklyn ■	Nov. 27
Columbia ■	Nov. 30
Villanova	Dec. 4
Notre Dame ■	Dec. 7
Rhode Island ■	Dec. 10
Brown	Dec. 21
Wisconsin	Dec. 23
Loyola Marymount	Dec. 28
Texas ■	Dec. 31
St. John's (N.Y.) ■	Jan. 2
Villanova ■	Jan. 6
Seton Hall	Jan. 11
Miami (Fla.)	Jan. 15
West Va.	Jan. 19
Canisius ■	Jan. 22
St. John's (N.Y.)	Jan. 25
Connecticut	Jan. 29
Boston College ■	Feb. 1
Rutgers ■	Feb. 5
West Va. ■	Feb. 8
Georgetown	Feb. 12
Pittsburgh ■	Feb. 15
Rutgers	Feb. 18
Notre Dame ■	Feb. 22
Syracuse ■	Feb. 24
Georgetown ■	Mar. 2
Big East Conf. Tr.	Mar. 5-8

1995-96 RESULTS (18-12)

92	New Hampshire ■	78
100	Brown	67
78	Syracuse ■	82
72	Seton Hall	79
83	Rhode Island ■	76
58	Wisconsin ■	57
83	Texas	92
80	Boston U. ■	74

83	Colgate ■	77
77	Seton Hall ■	82
82	St. John's (N.Y.)	78
91	Canisius ■	63
75	Syracuse	77
74	Connecticut ■	83
95	West Va. ■	78
65	Villanova	69
85	Pittsburgh ■	70
76	Boston College	75
79	Rutgers ■	68
77	Connecticut	99
80	Pittsburgh ■	71
77	Miami (Fla.) ■	54
68	Boston College ■	70
73	Notre Dame ■	72
84	Georgetown ■	77
59	Miami (Fla.)	66
80	St. John's (N.Y.) †	72
68	Villanova †	78
91	Fairfield ■	79
62	St. Joseph's (Pa.) ■	82

Nickname: Friars
Colors: Black & White
Arena: Providence Civic Center
   Capacity: 13,106; Year Built: 1972
AD: John Marinatto
SID: Tim Connor

PURDUE
West Lafayette, IN 47907 I

Coach: Gene Keady
Alma Mater: Kansas St. '58
Record: 18 Years, W-386, L-167

1996-97 SCHEDULE

Idaho ■	Nov. 24
Western Mich.	Nov. 26
Bowling Green ■	Nov. 30
Kentucky [Chicago]	Dec. 3
Purdue Inv.	Dec. 6-7
Louisville [Indianapolis]	Dec. 14
Tenn.-Martin ■	Dec. 16
Oklahoma	Dec. 21
Texas Christian	Dec. 30
Illinois	Jan. 2
Iowa ■	Jan. 7
Northwestern	Jan. 11
Michigan	Jan. 16
Indiana ■	Jan. 18
Wisconsin ■	Jan. 22
Minnesota	Jan. 25
Michigan St. ■	Jan. 29
Penn St. ■	Feb. 1
Ohio St. ■	Feb. 5
Michigan St.	Feb. 8
Minnesota ■	Feb. 12
Wisconsin	Feb. 15
Indiana	Feb. 18
Michigan ■	Feb. 23
Northwestern	Feb. 26
Iowa	Mar. 1
Illinois ■	Mar. 8

1995-96 RESULTS (26-6)

76	Memphis †	91
78	Central Mich.	76
78	Ill.-Chicago ■	67
88	Murray St. ■	76
77	Oklahoma	63
50	Villanova †	67
88	Texas Christian †	69
86	Western Mich. ■	56
74	Valparaiso	53
78	Seton Hall	76
79	Iowa St. †	60
73	N.C.-Charlotte †	67
85	Iowa	61
67	Northwestern	51
76	Minnesota	62
74	Indiana ■	69
67	Illinois ■	71
77	Penn St.	87
70	Ohio St. ■	53
80	Michigan	59

56	Michigan St. ■	51
75	Wisconsin ■	42
69	Michigan ■	64
63	Ohio St. ■	55
66	Penn St. ■	49
74	Illinois	71
74	Indiana	72
67	Minnesota ■	61
79	Northwestern ■	56
52	Iowa	56
73	Western Caro. †	71
69	Georgia †	76

Nickname: Boilermakers
Colors: Old Gold & Black
Arena: Mackey Arena
   Capacity: 14,123; Year Built: 1967
AD: Morgan Burke
SID: Mark Adams

QUEENS (N.Y.)
Flushing, NY 11367 II

Coach: Kyrk Peponakis
Alma Mater: St. John's (N.Y.) '88
Record: 1 Year, W-11, L-15

1996-97 SCHEDULE

Southern Conn. St.	Nov. 30
Dowling	Dec. 4
Molloy ■	Dec. 7
St. Rose	Dec. 11
Phila. Textile ■	Dec. 14
Bentley Festival	Dec. 28-29
New York Tech ■	Jan. 4
LIU-C. W. Post	Jan. 6
Mercy ■	Jan. 8
LIU-Southampton	Jan. 11
Adelphi	Jan. 13
Pace ■	Jan. 15
Concordia (N.Y.)	Jan. 18
Dowling ■	Jan. 20
Molloy	Jan. 22
St. Rose ■	Jan. 25
Phila. Textile	Jan. 29
New York Tech	Feb. 1
LIU-C. W. Post ■	Feb. 5
Mercy	Feb. 8
LIU-Southampton ■	Feb. 12
Adelphi ■	Feb. 15
Pace	Feb. 19
Concordia (N.Y.) ■	Feb. 22

1995-96 RESULTS (11-15)

91	Bloomsburg †	103
101	Assumption †	107
72	New York Tech ■	89
89	Mercy	93
71	LIU-C. W. Post ■	77
43	Phila. Textile	60
83	LIU-Southampton	79
71	Dowling	82
73	Molloy	65
61	Pace ■	49
70	St. Rose	96
91	Adelphi †	83
85	New York Tech	106
73	Concordia (N.Y.)	68
85	Mercy ■	74
63	LIU-C. W. Post	72
49	Phila. Textile ■	75
85	LIU-Southampton ■	96
85	Baruch	74
85	Dowling ■	55
54	Pace	77
83	St. Rose ■	75
68	Adelphi	83
65	Concordia (N.Y.) ■	51
77	Molloy ■	68
76	St. Rose	87

Nickname: Knights
Colors: Blue & Silver
Arena: Fitzgerald Gymnasium
   Capacity: 3,000; Year Built: 1958
AD: Richard Wettan
SID: Neal Kaufer

QUEENS (N.C.)
Charlotte, NC 28274 II

Coach: Dale Layer
Alma Mater: Eckerd '80
Record: 7 Years, W-122, L-75

1996-97 SCHEDULE
Pfeiffer ■ .... Nov. 19
St. Andrews ■ .... Nov. 21
Col. of West Va. .... Nov. 23
Barton .... Nov. 25
Longwood .... Dec. 6
Johnson Smith ■ .... Dec. 10
Queens (N.C.) Cl. .... Jan. 3-5
Lees-McRae ■ .... Jan. 9
High Point .... Jan. 13
Mount Olive .... Jan. 16
Erskine ■ .... Jan. 18
Belmont Abbey ■ .... Jan. 23
High Point ■ .... Jan. 25
Coker .... Jan. 27
St. Andrews .... Jan. 30
Belmont Abbey .... Feb. 3
Coker ■ .... Feb. 8
Lees-McRae .... Feb. 10
Barton ■ .... Feb. 13
Longwood .... Feb. 15
Pfeiffer .... Feb. 17
Mount Olive ■ .... Feb. 19
Erskine .... Feb. 22

1995-96 RESULTS (25-6)
75	Longwood	73
89	Wingate ■	76
76	Gardner-Webb ■	72
87	Elon ■	82
68	High Point	76
84	Lees-McRae ■	73
91	Col. of West Va. ■	69
87	Limestone ■	75
97	Newberry ■	69
70	North Fla. ■	51
78	Lees-McRae ■	50
61	Coker ■	50
78	Barton ■	70
74	Mount Olive ■	68
72	Pfeiffer ■	63
92	Belmont Abbey	79
77	Erskine ■	56
76	St. Andrews ■	60
58	Coker	65
68	Johnson Smith	71
77	Barton	72
67	St. Andrews	56
76	High Point ■	79
74	Longwood ■	59
92	Mount Olive ■	81
64	Pfeiffer	65
77	Barton †	65
65	Pfeiffer †	64
86	High Point	73
81	High Point †	70
58	Virginia Union	81

Nickname: Royals
Colors: Royal & Light Blue, & White
Arena: Ovens Athletic Center
    Capacity: 900; Year Built: 1989
AD: Dale Layer
SID: Jeff Aumend

QUINCY
Quincy, IL 62301 II

Coach: Steve Hawkins
Alma Mater: South Ala. '85
Record: 5 Years, W-83, L-57

1996-97 SCHEDULE
Truman St. .... Nov. 20
Cal St. Bakersfield .... Nov. 26
Cal St. Dom. Hills .... Nov. 29
Harris-Stowe ■ .... Dec. 7
Lincoln (Mo.) .... Dec. 12
Truman St. ■ .... Dec. 14

SIU-Edwardsville .... Dec. 19
Southern Ind. .... Dec. 22
St. Joseph's (Ind.) ■ .... Jan. 2
IU/PU-Ft. Wayne .... Jan. 4
Mo.-St. Louis .... Jan. 9
Northern Ky. .... Jan. 11
Wis.-Parkside ■ .... Jan. 16
Lewis ■ .... Jan. 18
Bellarmine .... Jan. 23
Ky. Wesleyan ■ .... Jan. 25
Southern Ind. .... Jan. 30
SIU-Edwardsville ■ .... Feb. 1
Hannibal-La Grange ■ .... Feb. 3
IU/PU-Ft. Wayne ■ .... Feb. 6
St. Joseph's (Ind.) .... Feb. 8
Mo.-St. Louis .... Feb. 13
Indianapolis .... Feb. 15
Lewis .... Feb. 20
Wis.-Parkside .... Feb. 22
Ky. Wesleyan ■ .... Feb. 27
Bellarmine ■ .... Mar. 1

1995-96 RESULTS (17-10)
96	Lincoln (Mo.) ■	89
73	Fla. Southern	86
75	Truman St.	70
90	Mo.-St. Louis	76
99	Hannibal-La Grange ■	89
109	Culver-Stockton	78
110	Truman St. ■	104
71	SIU-Edwardsville ■	73
78	Bellarmine	75
77	Ky. Wesleyan ■	79
92	IU/PU-Ft. Wayne ■	80
90	Indianapolis ■	84
65	Lewis	91
81	Wis.-Parkside ■	79
87	Southern Ind.	116
112	SIU-Edwardsville ■	110
73	Northern Ky. ■	85
90	Bellarmine ■	72
83	St. Joseph's (Ind.)	72
85	IU/PU-Ft. Wayne ■	77
100	Lewis ■	92
86	Ky. Wesleyan ■	97
84	Southern Ind. ■	98
74	Indianapolis	95
84	Northern Ky.	96
94	Wis.-Parkside ■	54
116	St. Joseph's (Ind.) ■	93

Nickname: Hawks
Colors: Brown, White & Gold
Arena: Quincy Memorial Gymnasium
    Capacity: 2,500; Year Built: 1950
AD: Jim Naumovich
SID: J. D. Hamilton

QUINNIPIAC
Hamden, CT 06518 II

Coach: Joe DeSantis
Alma Mater: Fairfield '79
(First year as head coach)

1996-97 SCHEDULE
Mass.-Lowell ■ .... Nov. 16
New Haven .... Nov. 20
Barry Cl. .... Nov. 29-30
Stonehill ■ .... Dec. 3
Le Moyne ■ .... Dec. 7
Southern Conn. St. .... Dec. 10
St. Anselm .... Dec. 21
Albany (N.Y.) Tr. .... Dec. 30-31
American Int'l .... Jan. 7
Bentley .... Jan. 11
Assumption ■ .... Jan. 16
Bryant ■ .... Jan. 18
Merrimack .... Jan. 21
St. Michael's ■ .... Jan. 25
American Int'l .... Jan. 28
Le Moyne .... Feb. 1
St. Anselm ■ .... Feb. 4
Bryant .... Feb. 8
Assumption .... Feb. 11
Bentley ■ .... Feb. 13

Merrimack ■ .... Feb. 16
Stonehill .... Feb. 19
St. Michael's .... Feb. 22

1995-96 RESULTS (5-22)
68	Sacred Heart †	82
65	Bridgeport †	79
86	Southern Conn. St. ■	75
69	New Haven ■	92
71	Franklin Pierce ■	90
66	Bryant	90
82	Bentley	97
73	Mercyhurst †	89
72	Pace †	66
75	St. Francis (Ill.) †	61
61	American Int'l ■	68
74	St. Michael's	80
70	Assumption ■	80
62	Bentley ■	87
63	Merrimack ■	86
77	Stonehill ■	88
75	St. Anselm	116
88	Assumption	95
74	St. Michael's ■	104
67	Bryant ■	72
66	St. Anselm ■	87
62	Mass.-Lowell ■	83
61	American Int'l	77
72	Merrimack ■	65
65	Stonehill	72
101	Assumption	78
62	St. Anselm	99

Nickname: Braves
Colors: Blue & Gold
Arena: Burt Kahn Court-Athletic Center
    Capacity: 1,500; Year Built: 1969
AD: Jack McDonald
SID: Bill Berger

RADFORD
Radford, VA 24142 I

Coach: Ron Bradley
Alma Mater: Eastern Nazarene '74
Record: 10 Years, W-181, L-109

1996-97 SCHEDULE
Evansville .... Nov. 24
Tenn.-Martin .... Nov. 26
Georgia Tech .... Nov. 29
Va. Commonwealth ■ .... Dec. 2
Richmond .... Dec. 5
Marshall ■ .... Dec. 7
VMI ■ .... Dec. 10
Concord .... Dec. 12
Ohio .... Dec. 21
Virginia .... Dec. 28
East Tenn. St. .... Dec. 30
Duquesne .... Jan. 4
N.C.-Asheville ■ .... Jan. 9
Md.-Balt. County .... Jan. 11
N.C.-Greensboro ■ .... Jan. 18
Winthrop .... Jan. 21
Coastal Caro. ■ .... Jan. 25
Charleston So. ■ .... Jan. 27
Liberty .... Feb. 1
Md.-Balt. County ■ .... Feb. 3
N.C.-Asheville .... Feb. 8
Winthrop ■ .... Feb. 10
N.C.-Greensboro .... Feb. 13
Charleston So. .... Feb. 15
Coastal Caro. .... Feb. 17
Liberty ■ .... Feb. 22
Big South Conf. Tr. .... Feb. 26-Mar. 1

1995-96 RESULTS (14-13)
92	Tenn.-Martin ■	77
94	Davis & Elkins ■	49
103	VMI	110
67	Richmond	73
88	East Tenn. St. ■	77
92	Middle Tenn. St. ■	77
87	Catholic	59
59	Florida St.	79
73	Marshall	101
64	East Tenn. St.	68

69	South Caro.	90
65	Duquesne ■	64
66	Winthrop ■	70
71	Liberty ■	65
66	Md.-Balt. County ■	48
64	Coastal Caro. ■	55
75	Charleston So.	80
68	N.C.-Greensboro ■	73
56	N.C.-Asheville ■	74
73	Md.-Balt. County	63
50	Liberty	53
81	N.C.-Greensboro ■	67
92	Winthrop	82
87	Coastal Caro. ■	68
85	Charleston So. ■	87
77	N.C.-Asheville	74
52	Charleston So. †	55

Nickname: Highlanders
Colors: Blue, Red, Green & White
Arena: Donald N. Dedmon Center
    Capacity: 5,000; Year Built: 1981
AD: Greig Denny
SID: Mike Ashley

RAMAPO
Mahwah, NJ 07430 III

Coach: Neil Rosa
Alma Mater: Bentley
Record: 1 Year, W-11, L-13

1996-97 SCHEDULE
Wheaton (Mass.) Cl. .... Nov. 23-24
Rowan .... Nov. 26
Montclair St. ■ .... Dec. 4
Richard Stockton ■ .... Dec. 7
Rutgers-Newark ■ .... Dec. 11
Rutgers-Camden .... Dec. 14
Sprinfield Cl. .... Jan. 4-5
Hunter .... Jan. 9
Col. of New Jersey ■ .... Jan. 11
Wm. Paterson ■ .... Jan. 15
Kean .... Jan. 18
Jersey City St. ■ .... Jan. 22
Montclair St. .... Jan. 25
Rowan ■ .... Jan. 29
Col. of New Jersey .... Feb. 1
Wm. Paterson .... Feb. 5
Richard Stockton .... Feb. 7
Rutgers-Newark .... Feb. 12
Rutgers-Camden ■ .... Feb. 15
Jersey City St. .... Feb. 19
Kean ■ .... Feb. 22

1995-96 RESULTS (11-13)
61	Rutgers-Newark	58
63	Westminster (Pa.) †	58
55	Allegheny	53
51	Richard Stockton	53
59	Montclair St. ■	67
86	Rutgers-Camden ■	77
79	York (N.Y.) ■	59
46	Rowan ■	62
61	Wm. Paterson ■	48
77	Staten Island	71
56	Hope ■	69
69	Col. of New Jersey ■	65
59	Kean ■	72
78	Jersey City St.	86
64	Montclair St.	45
63	Rutgers-Newark ■	69
65	Richard Stockton ■	79
56	Caldwell	64
54	Col. of New Jersey	60
77	Rutgers-Camden	64
55	Rowan	86
46	Wm. Paterson	75
55	Jersey City St. ■	78
79	Kean	68

Nickname: Roadrunners
Colors: Red & Gold
Arena: Ramapo Athletic Center
    Capacity: 1,800; Year Built: 1974
AD: Catherine Collins
SID: Michael Rastelli

RANDOLPH-MACON
Ashland, VA 23005 III

Coach: Hal Nunnally
Alma Mater: Randolph-Macon '62
Record: 21 Years, W-374, L-207

1996-97 SCHEDULE
Schedule unavailable

1995-96 RESULTS (18-9)

68	Moravian †	54
62	Muhlenberg	65
93	East. Mennonite ■	63
58	Citadel	65
80	Roanoke ■	86
81	Hampden-Sydney	78
83	St. Mary's (Md.) ■	61
100	Allentown †	82
67	Bridgewater (Va.)	64
88	Lynchburg ■	66
65	Guilford	76
81	Wash. & Lee ■	66
70	Va. Wesleyan	82
77	Hampden-Sydney ■	70
83	Roanoke	85
66	Va. Wesleyan ■	57
87	Guilford ■	54
65	Emory & Henry	61
83	East. Mennonite ■	82
88	Wash. & Lee	71
67	Bridgewater (Va.) ■	62
66	Wesley	63
95	Emory & Henry ■	86
45	Lynchburg	72
72	Lynchburg †	65
68	Bridgewater (Va.) ■ †	72
57	Chris. Newport ■	66

Nickname: Yellow Jackets
Colors: Lemon & Black
Arena: Crenshaw Gymnasium
  Capacity: 2,500; Year Built: 1965
AD: Ted Keller
SID: Todd Hilder

REDLANDS
Redlands, CA 92373 III

Coach: Gary Smith
Alma Mater: Redlands '64
Record: 25 Years, W-326, L-319

1996-97 SCHEDULE

Trinity (Tex.) Inv.	Nov. 22-23
La Sierra	Nov. 26
Redlands Tr.	Dec. 5-7
LIFE Bible	Dec. 16
Cal St. Dom. Hills	Dec. 31
Pacific (Ore.) ■	Jan. 4
UC San Diego ■	Jan. 8
La Verne ■	Jan. 11
Claremont-M-S ■	Jan. 15
Cal Tech	Jan. 18
Pomona-Pitzer	Jan. 22
Cal Lutheran ■	Jan. 25
Whittier	Jan. 29
Occidental ■	Feb. 1
La Verne	Feb. 5
Claremont-M-S	Feb. 8
Cal Tech ■	Feb. 12
Pomona-Pitzer ■	Feb. 15
Cal Lutheran	Feb. 19
Whittier ■	Feb. 22
Occidental	Feb. 26

1995-96 RESULTS (8-17)

91	UC San Diego ■	92
101	La Sierra ■	75
85	UC Santa Cruz ■	73
81	Chapman ■	84
93	Cal Baptist ■	96
111	LIFE Bible ■	52
64	Cal St. Dom. Hills	84
65	Christian Heritage	90
86	Biola	95

51	Ripon †	90
68	Sewanee †	90
71	Whittier ■	76
63	Pomona-Pitzer ■	86
62	Cal Tech	59
63	Claremont-M-S	87
86	Occidental ■	79
81	La Verne ■	100
67	Cal Lutheran ■	90
96	Whittier	93
77	Pomona-Pitzer ■	102
71	Cal Tech	68
69	Claremont-M-S ■	75
78	Occidental	95
95	La Verne ■	94
80	Cal Lutheran	83

Nickname: Bulldogs
Colors: Maroon & Gray
Arena: Currier Gym
  Capacity: 1,200; Year Built: 1929
AD: Carl Clapp
SID: Chuck Sadowski

REGIS (COLO.)
Denver, CO 80221 II

Coach: Lonnie Porter
Alma Mater: Adams St. '65
Record: 19 Years, W-330, L-206

1996-97 SCHEDULE

Holy Names ■	Nov. 16
Air Force	Nov. 23
Colorado Col.	Nov. 26
William Penn ■	Dec. 1
Fort Lewis	Dec. 6
Adams St.	Dec. 7
Mesa St. ■	Dec. 13
Western St. ■	Dec. 14
N.M. Highlands	Jan. 3
Mt. Senario ■	Jan. 5
Southern Colo. ■	Jan. 10
UC-Colo. Spgs. ■	Jan. 11
Colo. Christian ■	Jan. 14
Chadron St.	Jan. 16
Denver	Jan. 18
Metro St. ■	Jan. 24
Colorado Mines ■	Jan. 25
Neb.-Kearney	Jan. 31
Fort Hays St.	Feb. 1
Metro St.	Feb. 7
Colorado Mines	Feb. 8
Colo. Christian	Feb. 12
Chadron St. ■	Feb. 14
Neb.-Kearney ■	Feb. 21
Fort Hays St. ■	Feb. 22

1995-96 RESULTS (25-5)

68	Langston ■	53
61	Central (Iowa) ■	48
72	Cal Baptist ■	69
76	Evangel ■	62
91	Western St. ■	77
73	Chadron St. ■	71
61	North Central ■	59
76	Air Force	65
70	N.M. Highlands ■	58
73	Cal St. Los Angeles ■	67
87	Ursinus ■	71
87	Western St.	77
82	Chadron St. ■	70
60	Winona St. ■	48
78	Southern Colo.	85
73	Metro St.	70
80	Grand Rapids B&M ■	57
82	Colorado Col. ■	60
63	UC-Colo. Spgs. ■	60
74	Denver ■	83
69	N.M. Highlands ■	62
74	Southern Colo. ■	71
77	Metro St. ■	75
87	Grand Rapids B&M	59
53	UC-Colo. Spgs.	59
77	Denver	62
84	Metro St. †	80

67	Denver	84
73	Neb.-Kearney †	70
69	Fort Hays St.	97

Nickname: Rangers
Colors: Navy Blue & Gold
Arena: Regis Univ. Fieldhouse
  Capacity: 2,500; Year Built: 1959
AD: Barbara Schroeder
SID: Doug Montgomery

RENSSELAER
Troy, NY 12180 III

Coach: Mike Griffin
Alma Mater: Columbia '65
Record: 19 Years, W-211, L-261

1996-97 SCHEDULE

Muhlenberg Tr.	Nov. 22-23
Williams ■	Dec. 3
Hamilton	Dec. 6
Hobart	Dec. 7
Stevens Tech Tr.	Jan. 3-4
Brockport St. ■	Jan. 10
Middlebury	Jan. 12
Mt. St. Mary (N.Y.) ■	Jan. 15
Stevens Tech	Jan. 18
Southern Vt.	Jan. 21
Union (N.Y.) ■	Jan. 24
Skidmore	Jan. 28
Clarkson ■	Jan. 31
St. Lawrence	Feb. 1
Hartwick	Feb. 4
Hamilton ■	Feb. 7
Hobart ■	Feb. 8
St. Lawrence ■	Feb. 14
Clarkson	Feb. 15
Union (N.Y.)	Feb. 22
Skidmore ■	Feb. 25
Merchant Marine ■	Mar. 1

1995-96 RESULTS (20-8)
Results unavailable

Nickname: Engineers
Colors: Cherry & White
Arena: Robison Gymnasium
  Capacity: 1,500; Year Built: 1920
AD: Bob Ducatte
SID: Leigh Jackman

RHODE ISLAND
Kingston, RI 02881 I

Coach: Al Skinner
Alma Mater: Massachusetts '74
Record: 8 Years, W-118, L-116

1996-97 SCHEDULE

Siena	Nov. 23
Texas	Nov. 27
Fairleigh Dickinson ■	Nov. 30
Brown ■	Dec. 4
Providence	Dec. 10
Minnesota ■	Dec. 14
Boston U. ■	Dec. 23
Seton Hall Tr.	Dec. 29-30
Iona ■	Jan. 2
Dayton ■	Jan. 4
Temple	Jan. 7
St. Joseph's (Pa.) ■	Jan. 11
Duquesne	Jan. 16
Virginia Tech	Jan. 18
Massachusetts	Jan. 21
St. Bonaventure ■	Jan. 25
Xavier (Ohio)	Jan. 28
St. Joseph's (Pa.)	Feb. 2
La Salle	Feb. 6
Massachusetts ■	Feb. 8
Fordham ■	Feb. 11
Temple ■	Feb. 16
St. Bonaventure	Feb. 20
Geo. Washington ■	Feb. 26
Fordham	Mar. 1
Atlantic 10 Conf. Tr.	Mar. 5-8

89	Brown	71
90	Fairleigh Dickinson	65
98	Siena	58
78	Northeastern ■	61
76	Providence	83
78	Iona	87
68	Va. Commonwealth †	63
89	Hawaii	74
66	Syracuse †	92
87	Southern Cal †	74
81	St. Mary's (Cal.) †	74
93	Fordham ■	60
77	Dayton	84
71	Massachusetts	77
68	Fordham	53
86	St. Joseph's (Pa.) ■	83
87	Duquesne ■	68
69	St. Bonaventure	72
66	Virginia Tech ■	72
74	La Salle	65
64	St. Joseph's (Pa.)	69
67	Temple	63
87	Xavier (Ohio) ■	70
69	Massachusetts ■	74
62	Temple ■	73
77	Texas ■	81
72	Geo. Washington	76
93	St. Bonaventure ■	71
85	La Salle †	59
77	Virginia Tech †	71
52	Temple †	64
82	Marist ■	77
62	Charleston (S.C.) ■	58
59	St. Joseph's (Pa.)	76

Nickname: Rams
Colors: Dark Blue, Light Blue & White
Arena: Keaney Gymnasium
  Capacity: 4,000; Year Built: 1953
AD: Ron Petro
SID: Mike Ballweg

RHODE ISLAND COL.
Providence, RI 02908 III

Coach: James Adams
Alma Mater: Rhode Island '58
Record: 17 Years, W-208, L-224

1996-97 SCHEDULE

Keene St. ■	Nov. 23
Rhode Island Col. Tr.	Nov. 29-30
Eastern Nazarene ■	Dec. 3
Roger Williams ■	Dec. 5
Southern Me.	Dec. 7
Salve Regina	Dec. 9
Plymouth St. ■	Dec. 14
Barry	Jan. 3
St. Thomas (Fla.)	Jan. 4
Nova Southeastern	Jan. 7
Eastern Conn. St.	Jan. 14
Mass.-Boston ■	Jan. 18
Mass.-Dartmouth	Jan. 21
Bri'water (Mass.) ■	Jan. 25
Western Conn. St.	Jan. 28
Mass. Pharmacy ■	Jan. 30
Southern Me. ■	Feb. 1
Eastern Conn. St. ■	Feb. 4
Plymouth St.	Feb. 8
Mass.-Dartmouth ■	Feb. 11
Mass.-Boston	Feb. 15
Western Conn. St. ■	Feb. 18
Wheaton (Mass.)	Feb. 20

1995-96 RESULTS (18-9)

83	Johnson & Wales ■	49
61	Williams	87
52	Eastern Nazarene	53
72	Roger Williams	70
81	Southern Me. ■	72
106	Framingham St. ■	63
89	Salve Regina ■	72
77	Plymouth St.	88
77	Nova Southeastern †	81
92	Gallaudet †	67

101	Mass. Pharmacy ■	.62
94	Mass.-Boston	.68
84	Mass.-Dartmouth ■	.61
82	Westfield St.	.76
75	Bri'water (Mass.)	.85
81	Western Conn. St. ■	.69
74	Southern Me.	.73
73	Eastern Conn. St.	.62
56	Plymouth St. ■	.68
60	Mass.-Dartmouth	.72
83	Eastern Conn. St. ■	.71
87	Mass.-Boston ■	.77
76	Western Conn. St.	.75
94	Wheaton (Mass.) ■	.50
81	Eastern Conn. St. ■	.74
68	Plymouth St. †	.77
72	Amherst	.95

Nickname: Anchormen
Colors: White & Gold
Arena: New Building
   Capacity: 8,000; Year Built: 1995
AD: Donald E. Tencher
SID: To be named

RHODES
Memphis, TN 38112 III

Coach: Herb Hilgeman
Alma Mater: Miami (Ohio) '72
Record: 20 Years, W-310, L-178

1996-97 SCHEDULE
Millsaps Cl.	Nov. 23-24
Fontbonne	Nov. 26
Principia ■	Nov. 30
Fisk	Dec. 3
Rhodes Tr.	Dec. 6-7
Ozarks (Ark.)	Dec. 9
Ozarks (Ark.) ■	Jan. 6
Trinity (Tex.)	Jan. 10
Southwestern (Tex.)	Jan. 12
Oglethorpe	Jan. 17
Millsaps	Jan. 19
Sewanee ■	Jan. 24
Centre ■	Jan. 26
Oglethorpe ■	Jan. 31
Millsaps ■	Feb. 2
Sewanee	Feb. 7
Centre	Feb. 9
Hendrix	Feb. 15
Fisk ■	Feb. 17
Trinity (Tex.) ■	Feb. 21
Southwestern (Tex.) ■	Feb. 23
Hendrix ■	Mar. 1

1995-96 RESULTS (18-7)
81	Webster	.56
106	Principia	.61
72	Maryville (Mo.) ■	.71
46	Davidson	.91
84	Fisk	.59
89	Westminster (Mo.) ■	.72
100	Maryville (Mo.)	.84
84	Fisk ■	.74
89	LSU-Shreveport ■	.65
83	Savannah A&D ■	.65
74	Hendrix ■	.86
72	Millsaps	.88
95	Oglethorpe	.77
78	Southwestern (Tex.) ■	.71
98	Trinity (Tex.) ■	.91
72	Yeshiva ■	.41
89	Centre ■	.77
82	Sewanee ■	.69
73	Southwestern (Tex.)	.64
71	Trinity (Tex.)	.69
75	Centre	.76
77	Sewanee	.81
82	Millsaps ■	.88
89	Oglethorpe ■	.68
78	Hendrix	.82

Nickname: Lynx
Colors: Red, Black & White
Arena: Mallory Gym
   Capacity: 2,000

AD: Mike Clary
SID: Matt Dean

RICE
Houston, TX 77005 I

Coach: Willis Wilson
Alma Mater: Rice '82
Record: 4 Years, W-62, L-51

1996-97 SCHEDULE
Houston Baptist ■	Nov. 22
Colorado Mines ■	Nov. 26
Florida St.	Nov. 29
St. Bonaventure	Dec. 3
Marquette Tr.	Dec. 6-7
North Texas	Dec. 22
Southern U.	Dec. 28
Navy ■	Dec. 30
Pennsylvania ■	Jan. 4
Fresno St. ■	Jan. 6
Tulsa	Jan. 13
UTEP ■	Jan. 16
New Mexico ■	Jan. 18
Brigham Young ■	Jan. 23
Utah ■	Jan. 25
Texas Christian ■	Jan. 30
Southern Methodist ■	Feb. 1
Tulsa ■	Feb. 6
Fresno St.	Feb. 8
New Mexico	Feb. 13
UTEP	Feb. 15
Brigham Young	Feb. 22
Utah ■	Feb. 24
Southern Methodist	Feb. 27
Texas Christian	Mar. 1
Western Ath. Conf. Tr.	Mar. 4-8

1995-96 RESULTS (14-14)
80	Yale †	.58
64	Stanford	.75
58	North Texas ■	.56
76	Kent	.86
63	Kansas ■	.83
78	Vanderbilt	.77
62	Dartmouth ■	.54
62	St. Bonaventure ■	.49
73	Idaho St. †	.56
65	Central Mich. †	.57
56	Navy	.64
80	Texas	.69
74	Houston ■	.76
69	Southern Methodist ■	.51
56	Texas A&M	.78
71	Texas Christian	.80
78	Southern U. ■	.70
79	Baylor ■	.64
57	Texas Tech ■	.79
64	Texas ■	.79
59	Houston	.63
71	Southern Methodist	.70
60	Texas A&M ■	.55
67	Texas Christian ■	.70
88	Baylor	101
70	Texas Tech	.84
78	Texas Christian †	.67
53	Texas Tech †	.68

Nickname: Owls
Colors: Blue & Gray
Arena: Autry Court
   Capacity: 5,000; Year Built: 1950
AD: Bobby May
SID: Bill Cousins

RICHARD STOCKTON
Pomona, NJ 08240 III

Coach: Gerry Mathews
Alma Mater: Newark St. '65
Record: 10 Years, W-207, L-72

1996-97 SCHEDULE
Lynchburg Inv.	Nov. 22-23
Jersey City St. ■	Nov. 26
Montclair St.	Nov. 30

Rowan	Dec. 3
Ramapo ■	Dec. 7
Kean	Dec. 11
Rutgers-Newark	Dec. 14
St. Rose Tr.	Dec. 27-29
Rutgers-Camden	Jan. 15
Wm. Paterson	Jan. 18
Col. of New Jersey ■	Jan. 22
Rowan ■	Jan. 25
Jersey City St.	Jan. 29
Montclair St. ■	Feb. 1
Rutgers-Camden ■	Feb. 5
Ramapo	Feb. 7
Kean ■	Feb. 12
Rutgers-Newark ■	Feb. 15
Col. of New Jersey	Feb. 19
Wm. Paterson ■	Feb. 21

1995-96 RESULTS (26-4)
73	Bri'water (Mass.) †	.62
78	Eastern Conn. St.	.75
70	Wm. Paterson	.62
53	Ramapo ■	.51
66	Col. of New Jersey ■	.62
50	Nova Southeastern	.62
89	Rutgers-Camden ■	.59
69	Jersey City St. ■	.64
88	Montclair St.	.67
69	York (N.Y.)	.65
80	Rutgers-Newark ■	.69
92	Bapt. Bible (Pa.) ■	.77
71	Kean	.55
60	Col. of New Jersey	.70
58	Rowan	.57
60	Wm. Paterson ■	.47
79	Ramapo	.65
89	Lincoln (Pa.) ■	.78
53	Rowan ■	.72
68	Montclair St. ■	.52
93	Rutgers-Camden	.54
60	Jersey City St.	.58
59	Kean ■	.50
65	Rutgers-Newark	.60
61	Rutgers-Newark ■	.57
75	Rowan ■	.62
80	Mt. St. Vincent ■	.54
81	New York U. ■	.77
95	Anna Maria †	.88
70	Rowan	.98

Nickname: Ospreys
Colors: Black & White
Arena: Campus Gymnasium
   Capacity: 800; Year Built: 1976
AD: Larry James
SID: Susan Newcomb

RICHMOND
Richmond, VA 23173 I

Coach: Bill Dooley
Alma Mater: Richmond '83
Record: 3 Years, W-30, L-54

1996-97 SCHEDULE
North Caro.	Nov. 25
Wofford ■	Nov. 27
Wake Forest ■	Dec. 1
Radford	Dec. 5
Campbell ■	Dec. 19
Iona Tr.	Dec. 27-28
American	Jan. 2
Old Dominion	Jan. 4
VMI ■	Jan. 8
William & Mary ■	Jan. 11
George Mason	Jan. 15
East Caro.	Jan. 18
N.C.-Wilmington	Jan. 20
Va. Commonwealth ■	Jan. 25
James Madison ■	Jan. 27
Virginia	Jan. 30
Old Dominion	Feb. 1
George Mason ■	Feb. 5
William & Mary	Feb. 8
American ■	Feb. 12
N.C.-Wilmington ■	Feb. 15

East Caro. ■	Feb. 17
Wofford	Feb. 19
James Madison	Feb. 22
Va. Commonwealth	Feb. 24
Colonial Conf. Tr.	Feb. 28-Mar. 3

1995-96 RESULTS (8-20)
69	Campbell	.62
76	North Caro.	.83
74	Tex.-Pan American †	.71
64	Iowa St.	.82
73	Radford ■	.67
52	Virginia	.67
63	Lafayette †	.47
58	Charleston (S.C.)	.67
76	American	.80
65	VMI ■	.77
78	William & Mary	.79
69	Old Dominion ■	.84
60	Wake Forest	.71
47	N.C.-Wilmington ■	.64
51	Va. Commonwealth	.79
65	East Caro.	.81
78	James Madison ■	.71
105	George Mason ■	.91
58	East Caro. ■	.66
64	William & Mary	.81
84	James Madison	.80
91	George Mason	.98
63	Old Dominion	.70
68	American ■	.70
67	Va. Commonwealth ■	.69
59	N.C.-Wilmington	.63
93	George Mason ■	.77
55	Va. Commonwealth ■	.89

Nickname: Spiders
Colors: Red & Blue
Arena: Robins Center
   Capacity: 9,171; Year Built: 1972
AD: Chuck Boone
SID: Phil Stanton

RIDER
Lawrenceville, NJ 08648 I

Coach: Kevin Bannon
Alma Mater: St. Peter's '79
Record: 14 Years, W-262, L-137

1996-97 SCHEDULE
New Hampshire	Nov. 23
Delaware	Nov. 26
Siena ■	Nov. 30
UC Santa Barbara Cl.	Dec. 5-7
Md.-Balt. County ■	Dec. 14
Northeastern	Dec. 28
Villanova	Dec. 28
Wagner ■	Jan. 4
Fairleigh Dickinson	Jan. 6
Monmouth (N.J.)	Jan. 9
LIU-Brooklyn	Jan. 11
St. Francis (N.Y.) ■	Jan. 15
Mt. St. Mary's (Md.)	Jan. 18
Marist	Jan. 23
St. Francis (Pa.) ■	Jan. 23
Robert Morris	Jan. 25
Wagner	Feb. 1
Fairleigh Dickinson ■	Feb. 3
Monmouth (N.J.) ■	Feb. 6
LIU-Brooklyn ■	Feb. 8
St. Francis (N.Y.)	Feb. 12
Mt. St. Mary's (Md.) ■	Feb. 15
Marist	Feb. 17
St. Francis (Pa.) ■	Feb. 20
Robert Morris ■	Feb. 22
Northeast Conf. Tr.	Feb. 25-Mar. 6

1995-96 RESULTS (19-11)
62	Temple	.75
64	Boston U. ■	.62
89	St. Peter's ■	.81
69	Md.-Balt. County	.68
74	American ■	.66
67	Maryland	.83
65	Kentucky †	.90
69	St. John's (N.Y.)	.79

73	Siena	53
54	Monmouth (N.J.)	79
56	Mt. St. Mary's (Md.) ■	78
73	Marist	89
70	St. Francis (N.Y.)	51
88	St. Francis (Pa.) ■	70
79	Robert Morris ■	59
67	Wagner	76
76	Fairleigh Dickinson	71
112	LIU-Brooklyn ■	80
66	Monmouth (N.J.) ■	70
96	LIU-Brooklyn	80
70	Mt. St. Mary's (Md.)	80
80	Marist ■	67
56	St. Francis (N.Y.) ■	50
81	St. Francis (Pa.)	49
94	Robert Morris	67
88	Fairleigh Dickinson	72
88	Wagner ■	67
84	St. Francis (Pa.) ■	70
74	Mt. St. Mary's (Md.)	70
59	Monmouth (N.J.)	60

Nickname: Broncs
Colors: Cranberry & White
Arena: Alumni Gymnasium
Capacity: 1,650; Year Built: 1959
AD: Curtis Blake
SID: Bud Focht

RIPON
Ripon, WI 54971 III

Coach: Bob Gillespie
Alma Mater: Lewis '71
Record: 16 Years, W-266, L-111

1996-97 SCHEDULE
Ripon Cl. .... Nov. 22-24
Eureka .... Nov. 30
Marian (Wis.) ■ .... Dec. 2
Loras .... Dec. 7
Maranatha Bapt. ■ .... Dec. 12
Marymount (Va.) Tr. .... Jan. 4-5
Carroll (Wis.) .... Jan. 11
Lake Forest ■ .... Jan. 14
Coe ■ .... Jan. 17
Grinnell ■ .... Jan. 18
Monmouth (Ill.) .... Jan. 24
Cornell College .... Jan. 25
Lawrence .... Jan. 29
Beloit ■ .... Feb. 1
St. Norbert .... Feb. 5
Carroll (Wis.) ■ .... Feb. 8
Lake Forest .... Feb. 12
Lawrence ■ .... Feb. 15
Beloit .... Feb. 19
St. Norbert ■ .... Feb. 22

1995-96 RESULTS (21-4)
Results unavailable

Nickname: Red Hawks
Colors: Red & White
Arena: Storzer Center
Capacity: 2,500; Year Built: 1967
AD: Robert Gillespie
SID: Chris Graham

ROANOKE
Salem, VA 24153 III

Coach: Page Moir
Alma Mater: Virginia Tech '84
Record: 7 Years, W-132, L-58

1996-97 SCHEDULE
Roanoke Tr. .... Nov. 23-24
Frank. & Marsh. .... Dec. 1
Emory & Henry ■ .... Dec. 4
Va. Wesleyan ■ .... Dec. 7
Roanoke Cl. .... Jan. 4-5
Washington (Mo.) .... Jan. 8
Wash. & Lee .... Jan. 11
East. Mennonite ■ .... Jan. 13
Bridgewater (Va.) ■ .... Jan. 15
Va. Wesleyan .... Jan. 18
Randolph-Macon .... Jan. 20
Guilford .... Jan. 22
Randolph-Macon .... Jan. 25
Emory & Henry .... Jan. 29
Hampden-Sydney ■ .... Feb. 1
Lynchburg .... Feb. 3
Bridgewater (Va.) .... Feb. 6
Hampden-Sydney .... Feb. 8
Lynchburg ■ .... Feb. 10
East. Mennonite .... Feb. 12
Wash. & Lee ■ .... Feb. 15
Guilford ■ .... Feb. 17

1995-96 RESULTS (24-5)

95	Elizabethtown ■	69
93	Oglethorpe ■	67
101	Ferrum	77
94	Emory & Henry	80
73	Va. Wesleyan ■	76
86	Randolph-Macon	80
90	East. Mennonite ■	68
89	Gettysburg	65
78	Menlo ■	54
81	Bridgewater (Va.)	85
56	Va. Wesleyan	82
90	Wash. & Lee	83
112	Guilford ■	70
85	Randolph-Macon ■	83
96	Emory & Henry ■	76
68	Hampden-Sydney	82
83	Lynchburg ■	63
97	Bridgewater (Va.) ■	67
85	Hampden-Sydney ■	78
73	Lynchburg	70
100	East. Mennonite	93
97	Wash. & Lee ■	79
76	Guilford	72
84	East. Mennonite †	82
77	Hampden-Sydney †	73
74	Bridgewater (Va.) †	72
128	Shenandoah ■	110
80	Hendrix ■	64
88	Ill. Wesleyan ■	116

Nickname: Maroons
Colors: Maroon & Gray
Arena: Bast Center
Capacity: 2,000; Year Built: 1982
AD: Scott Allison
SID: Howard Wimmer

ROBERT MORRIS
Coraopolis, PA 15108 I

Coach: Jim Boone
Alma Mater: West Va. St. '81
Record: 10 Years, W-227, L-71

1996-97 SCHEDULE
Bucknell .... Nov. 23
Vermont .... Nov. 27
Evansville .... Dec. 3
Niagara ■ .... Dec. 5
Fla. Atlantic ■ .... Dec. 14
West Va. .... Dec. 19
Arizona Cl. .... Dec. 28-30
St. Francis (N.Y.) .... Jan. 4
LIU-Brooklyn .... Jan. 6
Marist ■ .... Jan. 9
Fairleigh Dickinson ■ .... Jan. 11
St. Francis (Pa.) .... Jan. 15
Wagner .... Jan. 18
Monmouth (N.J.) .... Jan. 20
Mt. St. Mary's (Md.) ■ .... Jan. 23
Rider .... Jan. 25
St. Francis (N.Y.) ■ .... Feb. 1
LIU-Brooklyn ■ .... Feb. 3
Marist .... Feb. 6
Fairleigh Dickinson .... Feb. 8
St. Francis (Pa.) ■ .... Feb. 12
Wagner ■ .... Feb. 15
Monmouth (N.J.) ■ .... Feb. 17
Mt. St. Mary's (Md.) .... Feb. 20

Rider .... Feb. 22
Northeast Conf. Tr. .... Feb. 25-Mar. 6

1995-96 RESULTS (5-23)

75	Vermont	73
94	Carnegie Mellon ■	60
46	Northwestern	66
68	Fla. Atlantic	71
57	Niagara	68
72	Duquesne	79
59	Youngstown St. ■	66
69	West Va.	97
55	Marist	65
59	Fairleigh Dickinson	73
76	Wagner ■	80
62	Monmouth (N.J.)	73
45	St. Francis (Pa.) ■	57
76	Mt. St. Mary's (Md.)	84
59	Rider	79
82	St. Francis (N.Y.) ■	78
73	LIU-Brooklyn ■	87
70	Marist ■	77
64	Fairleigh Dickinson	65
66	Wagner	63
54	Monmouth (N.J.)	75
53	St. Francis (Pa.)	68
69	Mt. St. Mary's (Md.) ■	80
67	Rider ■	94
75	LIU-Brooklyn	87
47	St. Francis (N.Y.)	63
68	Fairleigh Dickinson ■	66
51	Marist	70

Nickname: Colonials
Colors: Blue & White
Arena: Charles L. Sewall Center
Capacity: 3,056; Year Built: 1985
AD: Bruce Corrie
SID: Marty Galosi

ROCHESTER
Rochester, NY 14627 III

Coach: Mike Neer
Alma Mater: Wash. & Lee '70
Record: 20 Years, W-305, L-214

1996-97 SCHEDULE
Rochester Tip-Off .... Nov. 22-23
Rochester Inv. .... Nov. 30-Dec. 1
Nazareth ■ .... Dec. 4
Rochester Inst. ■ .... Dec. 7
Case Reserve ■ .... Dec. 10
Johns Hopkins .... Jan. 6
Emory .... Jan. 9
Carnegie Mellon ■ .... Jan. 11
Chase Rochester Tr. .... Jan. 15-18
Chicago ■ .... Jan. 24
Washington (Mo.) ■ .... Jan. 26
Brandeis .... Jan. 31
New York U. .... Feb. 2
Washington (Mo.) ■ .... Feb. 7
Chicago .... Feb. 9
New York U. ■ .... Feb. 14
Brandeis ■ .... Feb. 16
Hobart .... Feb. 19
Emory .... Feb. 23
Hamilton .... Feb. 26
Carnegie Mellon .... Mar. 1

1995-96 RESULTS (13-13)

82	St. Lawrence ■	76
75	Cortland St. ■	68
60	Merchant Marine ■	66
50	Hartwick ■	55
70	Nazareth	61
87	Case Reserve ■	82
53	Johns Hopkins	69
47	Rochester Inst.	61
75	Emory	55
63	Carnegie Mellon	67
69	Brockport St. †	57
66	Rochester Inst.	55
63	St. John Fisher ■	62
58	Chicago ■	65
63	Washington (Mo.) ■	87
82	Brandeis ■	68
78	New York U. ■	77
74	Washington (Mo.)	82
65	Chicago	74
77	Hamilton ■	73
69	New York U.	89
55	Brandeis	70
75	Hobart ■	67
78	Emory ■	70
52	Carnegie Mellon ■	58
64	Utica ■	75

Nickname: Yellowjackets
Colors: Yellow & Blue
Arena: Louis Alexander Palestra
Capacity: 2,250; Year Built: 1930
AD: Jeff Vennell
SID: Dennis O'Donnell

ROCHESTER INST.
Rochester, NY 14623 III

Coach: Bob McVean
Alma Mater: Brockport St. '69
Record: 18 Years, W-242, L-204

1996-97 SCHEDULE
Hobart ■ .... Dec. 3
Rochester .... Dec. 7
Oswego St. .... Dec. 10
Houghton ■ .... Dec. 12
Nazareth ■ .... Jan. 8
Clarkson ■ .... Jan. 10
St. Lawrence ■ .... Jan. 11
Chase Rochester Tr. .... Jan. 15-18
Keuka ■ .... Jan. 20
Ithaca .... Jan. 24
Elmira .... Jan. 25
Roberts Wesleyan ■ .... Jan. 28
Rochestern Tech Cl. .... Jan. 31-Feb. 1
St. John Fisher .... Feb. 4
Hartwick ■ .... Feb. 7
Utica ■ .... Feb. 8
Alfred .... Feb. 11
Elmira ■ .... Feb. 14
Ithaca ■ .... Feb. 15
Nazareth .... Feb. 18
Utica .... Feb. 21
Hartwick .... Feb. 22

1995-96 RESULTS (22-4)

91	Keuka	84
90	Roberts Wesleyan	60
79	Potsdam St. ■	61
76	Pitt.-Bradford ■	66
61	Rochester ■	47
75	Rensselaer †	73
76	Stevens Tech	67
77	Hobart ■	71
55	Rochester	66
84	Nazareth †	72
86	Hobart	84
92	Houghton	83
84	Alfred ■	70
72	Ithaca	62
72	Oswego St. ■	50
56	Keuka	55
68	Clarkson	64
65	St. Lawrence	68
78	Ithaca ■	73
89	Cortland St. ■	74
73	Hartwick	61
91	Nazareth ■	72
85	Utica ■	74
90	Alfred	60
73	St. John Fisher ■	78
51	Geneseo St. ■	73

Nickname: Tigers
Colors: Burnt Umber, Orange & White
Arena: Clark Memorial Gymnasium
Capacity: 2,200; Year Built: 1968
AD: Lou Spiotti
SID: J. Roger Dykes

ROCKFORD

Rockford, IL 61101 ... III

Coach: Mike Duenser
Alma Mater: Loras '88
Record: 1 Year, W-2, L-23

1996-97 SCHEDULE

Wartburg Tr.	Nov. 22-23
Lakeland ■	Nov. 26
Rockford Cl.	Nov. 29-30
Ill. Wesleyan	Dec. 4
Upper Iowa	Dec. 11
Elmhurst Cl.	Dec. 28-29
Concordia (Ill.)	Jan. 6
Beloit	Jan. 8
Clarke ■	Jan. 11
Benedictine (Ill.)	Jan. 15
Trinity Int'l ■	Jan. 18
Judson (Ill.) ■	Jan. 22
Eureka ■	Jan. 29
Aurora ■	Feb. 1
Clarke	Feb. 5
Benedictine (Ill.) ■	Feb. 8
Trinity Int'l	Feb. 12
Judson (Ill.)	Feb. 15
Concordia (Ill.) ■	Feb. 19
Eureka	Feb. 22
Aurora	Feb. 26
Wis.-Oshkosh ■	Mar. 1

1995-96 RESULTS (2-23)

Results unavailable

Nickname: Regent Lions
Colors: Purple & White
Arena: Seaver Gym
Capacity: 1,700; Year Built: 1964
AD: William Langston
SID: Gary Lewis

ROGER WILLIAMS

Bristol, RI 02809 ... III

Coach: Thomas Sienkiewicz
Alma Mater: Villanova '81
Record: 1 Year, W-8, L-17

1996-97 SCHEDULE

Johnson & Wales	Nov. 26
Stevens Tech	Nov. 30
Connecticut Col.	Dec. 3
Rhode Island Col.	Dec. 5
Suffolk ■	Dec. 7
Albertus Magnus ■	Dec. 10
Emerson-MCA ■	Dec. 12
Worcester St.	Dec. 14
Rivier	Jan. 14
Anna Maria ■	Jan. 16
Nichols ■	Jan. 18
Eastern Nazarene	Jan. 21
Wentworth Inst. ■	Jan. 23
New England Col.	Jan. 25
Endicott	Jan. 27
Salve Regina ■	Jan. 29
Colby-Sawyer ■	Feb. 1
Eastern Nazarene ■	Feb. 4
Curry	Feb. 6
Gordon	Feb. 8
Salve Regina	Feb. 10
Fitchburg St. ■	Feb. 13
Wentworth Inst.	Feb. 20
Curry ■	Feb. 22

1995-96 RESULTS (8-17)

59	Coast Guard	81
60	Connecticut Col. ■	80
70	Rhode Island Col. ■	72
66	Suffolk	59
70	Johnson & Wales ■	60
79	Emerson-MCA	73
57	Endicott ■	62
75	Albertus Magnus	86
82	Worcester St. ■	91
71	Rivier ■	75
70	Anna Maria	86
70	Nichols	90
44	Eastern Nazarene ■	68
56	Wentworth Inst.	68
98	New England Col. ■	68
89	Salve Regina	81
75	Colby-Sawyer	102
61	Eastern Nazarene	85
99	Curry ■	69
61	Gordon ■	70
60	Salve Regina ■	59
55	Fitchburg St.	80
72	Wentworth Inst. ■	83
89	Curry	84
80	Colby-Sawyer	115

Nickname: Hawks
Colors: Blue & Gold
Arena: Paolino Recreation Center
Capacity: 3,000; Year Built: 1983
AD: William M. Baird
SID: David Kemmy

ROLLINS

Winter Park, FL 32789 ... II

Coach: Tom Klusman
Alma Mater: Rollins '76
Record: 16 Years, W-272, L-172

1996-97 SCHEDULE

Bluefield St. ■	Nov. 16
Webber ■	Nov. 19
Bryant Cl.	Nov. 23-24
Flagler ■	Nov. 26
North Central ■	Dec. 5
American (P.R.) ■	Dec. 6
Morehouse	Dec. 14
Eastern ■	Dec. 28
Carthage ■	Dec. 30
Rollins Tr.	Jan. 3-4
Florida Tech ■	Jan. 8
Fla. Southern ■	Jan. 11
Tampa	Jan. 15
Barry	Jan. 18
Eckerd ■	Jan. 22
North Fla.	Jan. 25
St. Leo	Jan. 29
Tampa ■	Feb. 1
Barry ■	Feb. 5
Fla. Southern	Feb. 8
Eckerd	Feb. 12
North Fla. ■	Feb. 15
St. Leo ■	Feb. 19
Florida Tech	Feb. 22

1995-96 RESULTS (20-8)

75	American (P.R.) ■	68
87	St. Thomas (Fla.) ■	72
92	SIU-Edwardsville ■	76
92	Warner Southern ■	57
81	Flagler	46
73	Southwest Baptist †	55
95	Mo. Western St. †	91
86	Milwaukee Engr. ■	57
81	Hanover ■	78
88	Assumption ■	69
79	Gardner-Webb ■	78
89	Embry-Riddle ■	74
96	Tampa ■	89
74	North Fla.	73
84	St. Leo ■	69
72	Barry ■	63
77	Eckerd	92
94	Florida Tech ■	65
75	Fla. Southern	77
62	Tampa	81
57	North Fla. ■	65
76	St. Leo	75
71	Barry	82
70	Eckerd ■	68
73	Florida Tech	67
64	Fla. Southern ■	79
51	North Fla. †	56
80	Columbus St. †	88

Nickname: Tars
Colors: Royal Blue & Gold
Arena: Enyart-Alumni Fieldhouse
Capacity: 2,500; Year Built: 1968
AD: Phil Roach
SID: Dean Hybl

ROSE-HULMAN

Terre Haute, IN 47803 ... III

Coach: Jim Shaw
Alma Mater: Indiana '82
Record: 2 Years, W-34, L-19

1996-97 SCHEDULE

Sewanee Cl.	Nov. 22-23
Ind. Wesleyan ■	Nov. 26
Blackburn ■	Dec. 1
Brescia	Dec. 3
Rose-Hulman Inv.	Dec. 6-8
Millikin	Dec. 14
Centre ■	Dec. 16
Eureka	Dec. 20
Ill. Wesleyan	Dec. 22
Elmhurst ■	Jan. 4
DePauw	Jan. 8
Hanover ■	Jan. 11
Franklin	Jan. 15
Anderson (Ind.) ■	Jan. 22
Manchester ■	Jan. 25
Wabash	Jan. 29
Franklin ■	Feb. 1
DePauw ■	Feb. 5
Hanover	Feb. 8
Anderson (Ind.)	Feb. 11
Wabash ■	Feb. 19
Manchester	Feb. 22

1995-96 RESULTS (19-9)

59	St. Thomas (Minn.) †	61
87	La Verne †	50
75	Southwestern (Tex.)	68
70	Blackburn	54
67	Ill. Wesleyan	72
104	Ind.-Northwest ■	32
87	Sewanee ■	70
82	Centre ■	61
64	Eureka ■	42
92	Centre	69
87	Ind. Wesleyan	54
105	Millikin ■	91
65	DePauw ■	57
55	Hanover	59
77	Franklin ■	66
91	Anderson (Ind.)	73
74	Manchester	94
67	Wabash ■	52
73	Franklin	74
45	DePauw	60
57	Hanover ■	58
85	Anderson (Ind.) ■	54
73	Wabash	82
88	Manchester ■	78
78	Wabash ■	60
75	Hanover	74
70	Manchester †	60
74	Washington (Mo.)	76

Nickname: Fightin' Engineers
Colors: Old Rose & White
Arena: Shook Memorial Fieldhouse
Capacity: 2,000; Year Built: 1948
AD: Scott Duncan
SID: Darin Bryan

ROWAN

Glassboro, NJ 08028 ... III

Coach: Joe Cassidy
Alma Mater: North Central '84
(First year as head coach)

1996-97 SCHEDULE

Ramapo ■	Nov. 26
Rutgers-Newark	Nov. 30
Richard Stockton ■	Dec. 3
Rutgers-Camden ■	Dec. 7
Col. of New Jersey	Dec. 11
Kean ■	Dec. 14
Marymount (Va.)	Dec. 21
Staten Island Tr.	Dec. 27-28
Elizabethtown Cl.	Jan. 10-11
Montclair St. ■	Jan. 15
Ursinus ■	Jan. 16
Jersey City St.	Jan. 18
Wm. Paterson ■	Jan. 21
Richard Stockton	Jan. 25
Ramapo	Jan. 29
Rutgers-Newark ■	Feb. 1
Montclair St.	Feb. 5
Rutgers-Camden	Feb. 8
Col. of New Jersey ■	Feb. 11
Kean	Feb. 15
Wm. Paterson	Feb. 19
Jersey City St. ■	Feb. 22

1995-96 RESULTS (28-4)

100	Eastern ■	77
90	Kean ■	62
72	Rutgers-Newark	66
94	Wm. Paterson	62
101	Col. of New Jersey ■	81
62	Ramapo	46
104	Hunter	68
108	Montclair St.	74
99	FDU-Madison †	63
130	Lebanon Valley	77
90	Ursinus	77
68	Jersey City St.	81
88	Catholic	92
120	Rutgers-Camden ■	54
83	Wm. Paterson ■	62
57	Richard Stockton ■	58
113	Kean	82
81	Rutgers-Newark ■	70
72	Richard Stockton	53
82	Col. of New Jersey	72
86	Ramapo ■	55
110	Montclair St. ■	81
100	Rutgers-Camden	65
99	Jersey City St. ■	69
102	Jersey City St. ■	96
62	Richard Stockton	75
130	York (N.Y.) ■	66
102	Jersey City St. ■	83
85	Williams ■	77
98	Richard Stockton ■	70
79	Ill. Wesleyan †	77
100	Hope †	93

Nickname: Profs
Colors: Brown & Gold
Arena: Esby Gym
Capacity: 1,500; Year Built: 1963
AD: Joy Reighn
SID: Sheila Stevenson

RUST

Holly Springs, MS 38635 ... III

Coach: Rodney Stennis
Alma Mater: Rust '69
Record: 9 Years, W-125, L-99

1996-97 SCHEDULE

Ark. Baptist	Jan. 13
Philander Smith	Nov. 25
Stillman Tr.	Nov. 29-30
Mississippi Col. ■	Dec. 3
Millsaps ■	Dec. 10
Ark. Baptist ■	Dec. 11
Millsaps	Jan. 7
Rust Tr.	Jan. 9-10
Lane ■	Jan. 16
Fisk	Jan. 17
Knoxville ■	Jan. 20
LeMoyne-Owen	Jan. 21
Selma	Jan. 25
Philander Smith ■	Jan. 27
Fisk ■	Jan. 28
Fisk ■	Jan. 28
Stillman	Jan. 30
Lane	Feb. 1
Knoxville	Feb. 7

Maryville (Tenn.)		Feb. 8
LeMoyne-Owen ■		Feb. 15
Stillman ■		Feb. 20
Maryville (Tenn.) ■		Feb. 22
Mississippi Col.		Feb. 24

1995-96 RESULTS (13-11)

74	Loyola (La.) ■		64
88	Tougaloo		87
87	Philander Smith ■		50
107	Fisk		52
78	Stillman		80
84	Union (Tenn.)		70
80	Tougaloo		84
63	Loyola (La.)		77
71	Millsaps		69
55	Lipscomb		89
92	LSU-Shreveport ■		69
78	Maryville (Tenn.) ■		58
95	Fisk ■		63
96	Fisk		81
72	Lane		85
71	LeMoyne-Owen ■		77
75	Stillman ■		76
73	LSU-Shreveport		80
98	Fisk		66
94	Knoxville		100
63	Maryville (Tenn.)		61
84	LeMoyne-Owen ■		92
72	Stillman		95
91	Philander Smith ■		65

Nickname: Bearcats
Colors: Blue & White
Arena: McMillan Multipurpose Center
Capacity: 2,000; Year Built: 1971
AD: Ishmell Edwards
SID: Paula Clark

RUTGERS

New Brunswick, NJ 08903 I

Coach: Bob Wenzel
Alma Mater: Rutgers '71
Record: 14 Years, W-205, L-205

1996-97 SCHEDULE

Wagner ■	Nov. 26
Cincinnati	Nov. 30
Boston College	Dec. 4
Georgetown ■	Dec. 7
Md.-Balt. County ■	Dec. 11
St. Peter's ■	Dec. 14
Northeastern ■	Dec. 30
Connecticut ■	Jan. 2
Notre Dame ■	Jan. 4
Princeton	Jan. 6
Pittsburgh	Jan. 11
West Va.	Jan. 15
Villanova	Jan. 18
West Va. ■	Jan. 22
Seton Hall ■	Jan. 26
St. John's (N.Y.)	Jan. 29
Miami (Fla.)	Feb. 2
Providence	Feb. 5
Miami (Fla.)	Feb. 8
Loyola (Md.) ■	Feb. 11
South Fla. ■	Feb. 13
St. John's (N.Y.) ■	Feb. 15
Providence ■	Feb. 18
Syracuse	Feb. 22
Georgetown	Feb. 26
Villanova ■	Mar. 1
Big East Conf. Tr.	Mar. 5-8

1995-96 RESULTS (9-18)

74	Buffalo		78
57	Monmouth (N.J.) ■		55
86	Notre Dame ■		80
52	Georgetown		83
71	Eastern Mich. ■		74
78	Wagner ■		80
108	Southern Conn. St. ■		56
69	Pacific (Cal.) †		68
70	Arizona		79
67	Boston College ■		95
76	Manhattan ■		81
80	Syracuse		81

78	Pittsburgh ■	77
67	Notre Dame	79
71	West Va.	86
78	Seton Hall	81
59	Connecticut	77
68	Providence	79
70	Seton Hall ■	61
64	Villanova	76
54	Syracuse ■	63
82	St. John's (N.Y.) ■	70
71	Pittsburgh	70
71	Miami (Fla.) ■	55
66	Connecticut	78
72	Boston College	73
67	Miami (Fla.) †	77

Nickname: Scarlet Knights
Colors: Scarlet
Arena: Louis Brown Center
Capacity: 9,000; Year Built: 1978
AD: Fred E. Gruninger
SID: Pete Kowalski

RUTGERS-CAMDEN

Camden, NJ 08102 III

Coach: Ray Pace
Alma Mater: Rutgers-Camden '76
Record: 1 Year, W-0, L-10

1996-97 SCHEDULE

Widener Tr.	Nov. 22-23
Col. of New Jersey	Nov. 26
Wm. Paterson	Nov. 30
Jersey City St. ■	Dec. 4
Rowan	Dec. 7
Montclair St. ■	Dec. 11
Ramapo ■	Dec. 14
Holy Family ■	Jan. 3
Bloomfield ■	Jan. 7
Lincoln (Pa.)	Jan. 13
Richard Stockton	Jan. 15
Rutgers-Newark ■	Jan. 18
Phila. Pharmacy ■	Jan. 20
Kean	Jan. 22
Jersey City St.	Jan. 25
Col. of New Jersey ■	Jan. 29
Wm. Paterson	Feb. 1
Richard Stockton	Feb. 5
Rowan ■	Feb. 8
Montclair St.	Feb. 12
Ramapo	Feb. 15
Kean ■	Feb. 19
Rutgers-Newark	Feb. 22

1995-96 RESULTS (0-24)

53	Widener		87
58	Washington (Md.) †		83
61	Jersey City St.		78
56	Wm. Paterson ■		65
52	Rutgers-Newark ■		75
70	Virginia St. ■		83
77	Ramapo		86
59	Richard Stockton		89
73	Col. of New Jersey ■		99
53	York (N.Y.) ■		75
49	Montclair St.		85
54	Rowan		120
73	Rutgers-Newark		103
48	Kean		79
68	Jersey City St. ■		90
53	Wm. Paterson		84
74	Phila. Pharmacy		87
63	Kean ■		67
64	Ramapo ■		77
96	Lincoln (Pa.) ■		100
54	Richard Stockton		93
51	Col. of New Jersey		97
65	Rowan ■		100
76	Montclair St. ■		79

Nickname: Pioneers
Colors: Scarlet & Black
Arena: Rutgers Camden Gymnasium
Capacity: 2,100; Year Built: 1973
AD: Wilbur Wilson
SID: Jack Carty

RUTGERS-NEWARK

Newark, NJ 07102 III

Coach: Jim Hill
Alma Mater: Upsala '70
Record: 6 Years, W-54, L-92

1996-97 SCHEDULE

Thiel Cl.	Nov. 22-23
Kean	Nov. 26
Rowan ■	Nov. 30
Col. of New Jersey ■	Dec. 4
Wm. Paterson	Dec. 6
Staten Island	Dec. 9
Ramapo	Dec. 11
Richard Stockton	Dec. 14
Green Mountain ■	Jan. 8
York (N.Y.) ■	Jan. 10
Jersey City St. ■	Jan. 15
Rutgers-Camden ■	Jan. 18
Montclair St.	Jan. 22
Col. of New Jersey	Jan. 25
Bloomfield ■	Jan. 27
Kean ■	Jan. 29
Rowan	Feb. 1
Jersey City St.	Feb. 5
Wm. Paterson ■	Feb. 8
Ramapo ■	Feb. 12
Richard Stockton	Feb. 15
Montclair St. ■	Feb. 19
Rutgers-Camden	Feb. 22

1995-96 RESULTS (16-11)

58	Ramapo ■		61
66	Rowan ■		72
75	Rutgers-Camden		52
83	Jersey City St.		84
76	Staten Island		72
81	Wm. Paterson ■		61
75	Kean		65
78	New Paltz St.		74
85	Montclair St. ■		71
69	Richard Stockton		80
66	Col. of New Jersey ■		63
78	Polytechnic (N.Y.) ■		69
103	Rutgers-Camden ■		73
75	Bloomfield ■		66
69	Ramapo		63
70	Rowan		81
83	Montclair St.		67
61	New Paltz St. ■		66
58	Wm. Paterson		63
60	Kean ■		72
68	Jersey City St. ■		84
74	Col. of New Jersey		60
60	Richard Stockton ■		65
57	Richard Stockton		61
75	Drew		60
90	Stevens Tech †		79
72	Merchant Marine ■		53

Nickname: Raiders
Colors: Scarlet
Arena: The Golden Dome
Capacity: 2,000; Year Built: 1977
AD: John K. Adams
SID: Howard J. Pachasa

SACRED HEART

Fairfield, CT 06432 II

Coach: Dave Bike
Alma Mater: Sacred Heart '69
Record: 18 Years, W-336, L-201

1996-97 SCHEDULE

So. Conn. St. Cl.	Nov. 22-23
American Int'l ■	Dec. 1
Mass.-Lowell ■	Dec. 7
LIU-C. W. Post	Dec. 17
Bryant	Dec. 20
Bentley ■	Dec. 22
Bloomsburg Inv.	Jan. 4-5
New Haven	Jan. 8
Albany (N.Y.)	Jan. 11
Southern Conn. St. ■	Jan. 14
Stony Brook	Jan. 16

New Hamp. Col.	Jan. 18
Keene St.	Jan. 22
New Hamp. Col. ■	Jan. 25
Franklin Pierce	Jan. 29
Albany (N.Y.) ■	Feb. 1
Keene St. ■	Feb. 4
Southern Conn. St.	Feb. 6
Mass.-Lowell ■	Feb. 8
Bridgeport ■	Feb. 12
New Haven ■	Feb. 15
Franklin Pierce ■	Feb. 18
Stony Brook ■	Feb. 20
Bridgeport	Feb. 22

1995-96 RESULTS (13-14)

82	Quinnipiac †		68
61	Stonehill †		76
74	Merrimack		79
62	Bentley		95
69	St. Anselm ■		87
62	Franklin Pierce		84
85	Keene St.		71
74	New Haven ■		68
73	Southern Conn. St.		68
86	American Int'l		70
62	Le Moyne		87
80	Albany (N.Y.)		78
69	Southern Conn. St. ■		70
92	Keene St.		68
67	Franklin Pierce ■		78
88	New Haven		82
80	Mass.-Lowell ■		88
67	New Hamp. Col.		85
72	Bridgeport		69
74	Stony Brook ■		70
70	Albany (N.Y.) ■		68
92	Le Moyne ■		81
84	Bridgeport ■		79
64	New Hamp. Col. ■		89
68	Mass.-Lowell		88
55	Stony Brook		58
69	Southern Conn. St.		82

Nickname: Pioneers
Colors: Scarlet & White
Arena: SHU Gymnasium
Capacity: 1,200; Year Built: 1960
AD: Don Cook
SID: Mike Guastelle

SAGINAW VALLEY

University Center, MI 48710......II

Coach: Robert Pratt
Alma Mater: Aquinas College '70
Record: 23 Years, W-375, L-285

1996-97 SCHEDULE

Siena Heights	Nov. 26
Calvin Shootout	Nov. 29-30
Aquinas	Dec. 3
Ashland	Dec. 7
Oakland ■	Dec. 14
Michigan Christian ■	Dec. 16
Cal St. Bakersfield Tr.	Dec. 27-28
Northwood ■	Jan. 2
Mich.-Dearborn	Jan. 4
Michigan Tech ■	Jan. 9
Northern Mich. ■	Jan. 11
Lake Superior St.	Jan. 13
Grand Valley St.	Jan. 16
Ferris St.	Jan. 18
Gannon ■	Jan. 23
Mercyhurst ■	Jan. 25
Wayne St. (Mich.)	Jan. 30
Hillsdale	Feb. 1
Northwood	Feb. 6
Lake Superior St. ■	Feb. 10
Michigan Tech	Feb. 13
Northern Mich.	Feb. 15
Grand Valley St. ■	Feb. 20
Ferris St. ■	Feb. 22

1995-96 RESULTS (18-11)

85	Aquinas ■		58
94	Siena Heights ■		52
64	St. Francis (Ill.)		73
96	Albion †		82

82	Spring Arbor	78
65	Oakland	78
93	Wayne St. (Mich.)	80
79	Michigan Christian ■	49
76	Gannon	82
83	Hillsdale †	56
84	Grand Valley St. ■	79
75	Mercyhurst ■	56
69	Gannon ■	65
78	Ashland	79
84	Hillsdale ■	75
88	Northwood ■	71
79	Ferris St. ■	63
78	Michigan Tech ■	76
100	Lake Superior St.	107
74	Northern Mich.	72
86	Oakland ■	73
66	Wayne St. (Mich.) ■	69
68	Lake Superior St. ■	72
64	Mercyhurst	82
79	Michigan Tech	53
73	Northwood	79
75	Mercyhurst †	73
90	Oakland	100
72	Michigan Tech †	90

Nickname: Cardinals
Colors: Red, White & Blue
Arena: James O'Neill Jr. Arena
 Capacity: 4,000; Year Built: 1989
AD: Bob Becker
SID: Tom Waske

ST. ANDREWS
Laurinburg, NC 28352 II

Coach: Mark Peeler
Alma Mater: St. Thomas '81
(First year as head coach)

1996-97 SCHEDULE
Queens (N.C.)	Nov. 21
Coker ■	Dec. 2
Erskine	Dec. 4
Johnson & Wales	Dec. 13
Queens (N.C.) Cl.	Jan. 3-5
Limestone ■	Jan. 8
Barton ■	Jan. 11
Lees-McRae	Jan. 13
High Point ■	Jan. 16
Mount Olive ■	Jan. 18
Belmont Abbey ■	Jan. 20
Longwood ■	Jan. 23
Belmont Abbey	Jan. 25
Pfeiffer ■	Jan. 27
Queens (N.C.) ■	Jan. 30
Barton	Feb. 1
Longwood	Feb. 3
Lees-McRae ■	Feb. 6
Pfeiffer	Feb. 8
N.C.-Pembroke ■	Feb. 10
Coker	Feb. 13
Erskine ■	Feb. 15
High Point	Feb. 19
Mount Olive	Feb. 22

1995-96 RESULTS (6-21)
68	Limestone	73
63	Wingate	65
57	Campbell	88
65	Lees-McRae ■	73
65	Pfeiffer	77
85	Mars Hill †	97
88	Spring Hill †	79
60	Wingate †	67
78	High Point ■	81
78	Erskine ■	80
61	Coker	52
67	Belmont Abbey	58
81	N.C.-Pembroke ■	89
63	Barton	75
72	Mount Olive	80
60	Queens (N.C.)	76
88	Longwood ■	70
93	Wingate ■	81
59	Coker ■	65

56	Queens (N.C.) ■	67
72	High Point	89
72	Lees-McRae ■	83
54	Pfeiffer ■	73
71	Longwood	86
65	Belmont Abbey ■	71
54	Erskine	53
54	Longwood †	75

Nickname: Knights
Colors: Royal Blue & White
Arena: Harris/Courts
 Capacity: 1,200; Year Built: 1967
AD: Carl Ullrich
SID: Mark Peeler

ST. ANSELM
Manchester, NH 03102 II

Coach: Keith Dickson
Alma Mater: New Hampshire '79
Record: 10 Years, W-195, L-106

1996-97 SCHEDULE
New Hamp. Col. Cl.	Nov. 15-16
Mass.-Lowell	Nov. 20
St. Vincent's Inv.	Nov. 23-24
Assumption ■	Dec. 3
Bryant	Dec. 7
Quinnipiac ■	Dec. 21
Clarion Tr.	Jan. 3-4
Bentley	Jan. 8
Merrimack ■	Jan. 11
St. Michael's	Jan. 16
Le Moyne	Jan. 18
American Int'l ■	Jan. 21
Stonehill	Jan. 25
Bentley ■	Jan. 28
New Hamp. Col.	Jan. 30
Bryant ■	Feb. 1
Quinnipiac	Feb. 4
Le Moyne ■	Feb. 8
St. Michael's ■	Feb. 11
Merrimack	Feb. 13
American Int'l	Feb. 15
Assumption	Feb. 19
Stonehill ■	Feb. 22

1995-96 RESULTS (28-3)
75	Franklin Pierce †	67
95	New Hamp. Col.	79
87	Mass.-Lowell ■	85
59	Drexel	82
87	Sacred Heart	69
99	Assumption ■	64
82	Bryant ■	80
58	St. Francis (Ill.) †	56
79	St. Rose †	80
103	Bowie St. †	80
88	Bentley †	71
99	Merrimack ■	90
101	New Hamp. Col. ■	81
101	Bryant	76
88	St. Michael's ■	75
89	Stonehill	78
81	American Int'l	72
116	Quinnipiac ■	75
93	Merrimack	76
89	Bentley ■	74
102	Assumption	78
87	Quinnipiac	66
86	St. Michael's	75
86	Stonehill ■	63
99	Quinnipiac ■	62
100	Bryant ■	81
83	American Int'l ■	58
80	American Int'l ■	65
78	Franklin Pierce †	70
76	St. Rose †	87
90	Bentley	86

Nickname: Hawks
Colors: Blue & White
Arena: Stoutenburgh Gymnasium
 Capacity: 1,600; Year Built: 1961
AD: Ted Paulauskas
SID: Ken Belbin

ST. AUGUSTINE'S
Raleigh, NC 27611 II

Coach: Novell Lee
Alma Mater: St. Augustine's '58
Record: 3 Years, W-23, L-29

1996-97 SCHEDULE
S.C.-Spartanburg	Nov. 18
Virginia Union ■	Nov. 20
St. Paul's	Nov. 25
Bowie St.	Dec. 6
Dist. Columbia	Dec. 8
Shawnee St.	Dec. 12
Paine ■	Dec. 14
Livingstone ■	Jan. 4
Winston-Salem ■	Jan. 7
Johnson Smith ■	Jan. 9
Lynn ■	Jan. 11
Virginia St. ■	Jan. 14
Fayetteville St. ■	Jan. 16
N.C. Central ■	Jan. 18
Barber-Scotia ■	Jan. 22
Southern-N.O.	Jan. 25
Livingstone	Jan. 27
Lynn	Feb. 1
Winston-Salem ■	Feb. 4
Johnson Smith	Feb. 6
Shawnee St. ■	Feb. 8
N.C. Central ■	Feb. 11
Norfolk St. ■	Feb. 13
Fayetteville St.	Feb. 15
Elizabeth City St.	Feb. 22

1995-96 RESULTS (13-13)
77	Paine	84
96	Pfeiffer	91
95	St. Paul's ■	86
96	Shaw	92
77	Bowie St. ■	83
93	St. Paul's †	101
79	Winston-Salem †	73
90	Livingstone	95
116	Elizabeth City St. ■	93
70	Fayetteville St.	69
67	N.C. Central ■	72
90	Johnson Smith	82
76	Winston-Salem	75
77	Livingstone ■	81
76	Virginia St.	84
71	Virginia Union	95
83	Johnson Smith ■	86
77	Shaw ■	97
82	N.C. Central	85
87	Norfolk St.	80
100	Gardner-Webb †	106
71	Fayetteville St. ■	67
80	Winston-Salem ■	74
94	Dist. Columbia	70
92	Bowie St. †	81
67	Virginia Union †	80

Nickname: Falcons
Colors: Blue & White
Arena: Emery Gymnasium
 Capacity: 1,000; Year Built: 1962
AD: Harvey Heartley
SID: Leon Carrington

ST. BONAVENTURE
St. Bonaventure, NY 14778 I

Coach: Jim Baron
Alma Mater: St. Bonaventure '77
Record: 9 Years, W-122, L-136

1996-97 SCHEDULE
Canisius	Nov. 30
Rice ■	Dec. 3
Buffalo ■	Dec. 7
Morgan St. ■	Dec. 11
Wisconsin ■	Dec. 14
Navy ■	Dec. 23
Arizona St. Cl.	Dec. 27-28
Virginia Tech	Jan. 2
Geo. Washington ■	Jan. 6
St. Joseph's (Pa.)	Jan. 9
Temple ■	Jan. 11
Massachusetts ■	Jan. 14
Fordham	Jan. 18
Niagara ■	Jan. 21
Rhode Island ■	Jan. 25
Fordham ■	Jan. 29
Temple ■	Feb. 4
Dayton ■	Feb. 8
Massachusetts ■	Feb. 11
La Salle ■	Feb. 15
Colgate [Buffalo]	Feb. 17
Rhode Island ■	Feb. 20
St. Joseph's (Pa.) ■	Feb. 22
Xavier (Ohio) ■	Feb. 27
Duquesne	Mar. 1
Atlantic 10 Conf. Tr.	Mar. 5-8

1995-96 RESULTS (10-18)
63	Eastern Mich. †	83
64	Canisius	77
77	Niagara	55
76	Wisconsin	62
74	Buffalo ■	64
49	Rice	62
68	Navy	64
56	Temple	58
58	Appalachian St.	61
78	Geo. Washington	87
57	Fordham	50
52	Massachusetts ■	65
38	Canisius	53
62	Xavier (Ohio) ■	76
58	Virginia Tech ■	65
47	Massachusetts	72
72	Rhode Island ■	69
79	La Salle	96
72	St. Joseph's (Pa.)	55
60	Bucknell ■	55
74	Duquesne ■	72
58	Dayton	66
56	St. Joseph's (Pa.) ■	47
73	Fordham ■	64
54	Temple ■	57
71	Rhode Island	93
72	Dayton †	60
56	Massachusetts †	69

Nickname: Bonnies
Colors: Brown & White
Arena: Reilly Center
 Capacity: 6,000; Year Built: 1966
AD: David L. Diles
SID: Mike Hardisky

ST. CLOUD ST.
St. Cloud, MN 56301 II

Coach: Butch Raymond
Alma Mater: Augsburg '63
Record: 26 Years, W-428, L-294

1996-97 SCHEDULE
Minn.-Crookston ■	Nov. 16
Winona St. ■	Nov. 26
Mayville St. ■	Nov. 30
Moorhead St. ■	Dec. 3
Bemidji St.	Dec. 7
Minn.-Duluth ■	Dec. 10
Northern St.	Dec. 14
Minn.-Morris ■	Dec. 17
Mt. Senario	Dec. 19
South Dak. St. ■	Dec. 28
Augustana (S.D.) ■	Dec. 29
Northern Colo.	Jan. 3
Neb.-Omaha	Jan. 4
North Dak. ■	Jan. 10
North Dak. St. ■	Jan. 11
South Dak.	Jan. 17
Morningside	Jan. 18
Mankato St. ■	Jan. 25
Neb.-Omaha ■	Jan. 31
Northern Colo. ■	Feb. 1
North Dak. St.	Feb. 7
North Dak.	Feb. 8
Morningside ■	Feb. 14

South Dak. ■..........................Feb. 15
Mankato St. ■.......................Feb. 22
Augustana (S.D.)..................Feb. 28
South Dak. St..........................Mar. 1

1995-96 RESULTS (18-9)

108	Mayville St. ■	69
86	Winona St. ■	65
82	Carleton ■	62
84	Mt. Senario ■	64
92	Minn.-Morris	89
90	Moorhead St. ■	101
103	Bemidji St. ■	58
100	Minn.-Crookston ■	68
68	Minn.-Duluth	67
78	Northern Colo. ■	63
73	Neb.-Omaha ■	58
63	North Dak.	58
73	North Dak. St.	79
93	South Dak. ■	79
80	Morningside ■	82
85	Mankato St. ■	72
89	South Dak. St.	106
80	Augustana (S.D.)	83
64	North Dak. St. ■	79
90	North Dak. ■	70
82	Morningside	98
79	South Dak.	83
65	Mankato St.	63
75	Augustana (S.D.) ■	68
84	South Dak. St. ■	91
76	Neb.-Omaha	70
70	Northern Colo.	64

Nickname: Huskies
Colors: Red & Black
Arena: Halenbeck Hall
   Capacity: 7,500; Year Built: 1965
AD: Morris Kurtz
SID: Anne Abicht

ST. FRANCIS (ILL.)
Joliet, IL 60435 II

Coach: Pat Sullivan
Alma Mater: Lewis '65
Record: 20 Years, W-329, L-268

1996-97 SCHEDULE

Wayne St. (Neb.) ....Nov. 16
Wis.-Parkside ■......................Nov. 20
Ferris St...............................Nov. 26
Winona St. ■.........................Nov. 30
Lewis ■..................................Dec. 3
California (Pa.) Tr..................Dec. 6-7
St. Joseph's (Ind.)..................Dec. 10
Indianapolis ■........................Dec. 14
Wayne St. (Mich.) ....Dec. 23
Winona St. ....Jan. 4
Rosary ■...................................Jan. 8
Oakland City ■........................Jan. 11
St. Xavier ....Jan. 15
Olivet Nazarene ....Jan. 18
Illinois Tech ....Jan. 22
Purdue-Calumet ....Jan. 25
Ind.-South Bend ■...................Jan. 29
Rosary......................................Feb. 1
IU/PU-Indianapolis ■................Feb. 4
St. Xavier ....Feb. 8
Olivet Nazarene ■...................Feb. 11
Illinois Tech ■..........................Feb. 15
Purdue-Calumet ■...................Feb. 19
Ind.-South Bend ....Feb. 22

1995-96 RESULTS (19-10)

82	Winona St. ■	83
80	Wis.-Parkside	63
73	Saginaw Valley ■	64
77	St. Joseph's (Ind.) ■	65
75	Wayne St. (Neb.) ■	73
70	Lewis	74
53	UTEP	89
47	Indianapolis	60
75	Ferris St.	66
69	Pace †	61
56	St. Anselm †	58
61	Quinnipiac †	75
86	Oakland City	83

64	St. Xavier ■	50
49	Olivet Nazarene †	61
64	Purdue-Calumet	50
85	Ind.-South Bend	67
87	Rosary ■	62
62	Illinois Tech ■	60
61	St. Xavier	44
74	Olivet Nazarene ■	68
59	IU/PU-Indianapolis	74
63	Purdue-Calumet ■	57
56	Ind.-South Bend	57
86	Rosary	69
76	Illinois Tech.	65
78	Rosary ■	67
100	Olivet Nazarene ■	92
68	BYU-Hawaii †	83

Nickname: Fighting Saints
Colors: Brown & Gold
Arena: CSF Recreation Center
   Capacity: 1,200; Year Built: 1986
AD: Pat Sullivan
SID: Dave Laketa

ST. FRANCIS (N.Y.)
Brooklyn Heights, NY 11201......I

Coach: Ron Ganulin
Alma Mater: LIU-Brooklyn '68
Record: 7 Years, W-70, L-117

1996-97 SCHEDULE

Lehigh ....Nov. 26
Brown ■.................................Nov. 30
Hartford ....Dec. 3
Morgan St................................Dec. 7
Columbia ....Dec. 10
Central Conn. St. ■.................Dec. 14
South Fla. Cl. ....Dec. 20-21
Robert Morris ■.......................Jan. 4
St. Francis (Pa.) ■....................Jan. 6
Wagner ....Jan. 9
Monmouth (N.J.) ....Jan. 11
Rider ....Jan. 15
Fairleigh Dickinson ■..............Jan. 18
Mt. St. Mary's (Md.) ....Jan. 20
Marist ....Jan. 23
LIU-Brooklyn ■.......................Jan. 25
Robert Morris ....Feb. 1
St. Francis (Pa.) ....Feb. 3
Wagner ■..................................Feb. 6
Monmouth (N.J.) ■...................Feb. 8
Rider ■....................................Feb. 12
Fairleigh Dickinson ....Feb. 14
Mt. St. Mary's (Md.) ■.............Feb. 17
Marist ■..................................Feb. 20
LIU-Brooklyn ....Feb. 22
Northeast Conf. Tr. ....Feb. 25-Mar. 6

1995-96 RESULTS (9-18)

92	Lehigh ■	78
73	Delaware St.	68
98	Fordham	95
87	Morgan St. ■	69
56	Brown †	53
69	St. Peter's	80
61	Md.-East. Shore	63
69	Army	52
69	Wagner	93
65	Monmouth (N.J.)	74
69	Fairleigh Dickinson ■	79
60	Mt. St. Mary's (Md.) ■	50
51	Rider ■	70
57	Marist	72
78	LIU-Brooklyn ■	80
78	Robert Morris	82
60	St. Francis (Pa.)	75
70	Wagner ■	100
63	Monmouth (N.J.) ■	82
70	Fairleigh Dickinson	67
56	Mt. St. Mary's (Md.)	85
50	Rider	56
43	Marist ■	52
77	LIU-Brooklyn	105
60	St. Francis (Pa.) ■	62
63	Robert Morris ■	47
63	LIU-Brooklyn	82

Nickname: Terriers
Colors: Red & Blue
Arena: Physical Education Center
   Capacity: 3,000; Year Built: 1971
AD: Tom Thompson
SID: Jim Hoffman

ST. FRANCIS (PA.)
Loretto, PA 15940 I

Coach: Tom McConnell
Alma Mater: Point Park '84
Record: 4 Years, W-47, L-63

1996-97 SCHEDULE

Central Conn. St. ....Nov. 23
Duquesne ....Nov. 27
Youngstown St. ....Nov. 30
Youngstown St. ■.....................Dec. 3
Bucknell ....Dec. 7
Pittsburgh ....Dec. 18
George Mason ....Dec. 20
Central Conn. St. ....Dec. 30
LIU-Brooklyn ....Jan. 4
St. Francis (N.Y.) ....Jan. 6
Fairleigh Dickinson ■................Jan. 9
Marist ■..................................Jan. 11
Robert Morris ■.......................Jan. 15
Monmouth (N.J.) ....Jan. 18
Wagner ....Jan. 20
Rider ■....................................Jan. 23
Mt. St. Mary's (Md.) ■.............Jan. 25
LIU-Brooklyn ....Feb. 1
St. Francis (N.Y.) ■....................Feb. 3
Fairleigh Dickinson ....Feb. 6
Marist ....Feb. 8
Robert Morris ....Feb. 12
Monmouth (N.J.) ■..................Feb. 15
Wagner ■................................Feb. 17
Rider ....Feb. 20
Mt. St. Mary's (Md.) ....Feb. 22
Northeast Conf. Tr. ......Feb. 25-Mar. 6

1995-96 RESULTS (13-14)

61	Xavier (Ohio)	88
52	Michigan	84
82	Delaware St.	64
50	Bucknell ■	77
55	Georgetown	88
79	Central Conn. St. ■	60
47	N.C.-Greensboro	67
64	Fairleigh Dickinson	61
50	Marist	67
59	Monmouth (N.J.) ■	74
73	Wagner ■	61
57	Robert Morris	45
70	Rider	88
44	Mt. St. Mary's (Md.)	73
76	LIU-Brooklyn ■	65
75	St. Francis (N.Y.) ■	60
54	St. Peter's	86
94	Fairleigh Dickinson ■	69
67	Marist ■	65
85	Monmouth (N.J.)	72
80	Wagner	81
68	Robert Morris ■	53
49	Rider ■	81
56	Mt. St. Mary's (Md.)	72
62	St. Francis (N.Y.)	60
94	LIU-Brooklyn	80
70	Rider	84

Nickname: Red Flash
Colors: Red & White
Arena: Maurice Stokes Athletic Center
   Capacity: 3,500; Year Built: 1972
AD: Frank Pergolizzi
SID: Kevin Southard

ST. JOHN FISHER
Rochester, NY 14618..............III

Coach: Bob Ward
Alma Mater: Rochester '69
Record: 9 Years, W-160, L-76

1996-97 SCHEDULE

St. John Fisher Inv................Nov. 23-24
Lake Erie ....Nov. 26
Hilbert ■..................................Dec. 3
Clarkson ■................................Dec. 5
Utica ■.....................................Dec. 7
Bapt. Bible (Pa.) ....Jan. 9
Geneseo St. ■..........................Jan. 11
Chase Rochester Tr. ....Jan. 15-18
Fredonia St. ....Jan. 21
Cazenovia ■.............................Jan. 25
Houghton.................................Jan. 27
Buffalo St. ■............................Jan. 29
Keuka ■...................................Jan. 31
Rochester Inst. ■......................Feb. 4
Keuka ....Feb. 6
Elmira ....Feb. 8
Brockport St. ■.......................Feb. 13
Hartwick ■..............................Feb. 15
Allegheny ....Feb. 16
Roberts Wesleyan ■................Feb. 18
Ithaca ■...................................Feb. 20
Nazareth ■..............................Feb. 27

1995-96 RESULTS (20-6)

103	Lincoln (Pa.) ■	69
90	John Carroll ■	87
104	Houghton ■	85
71	Hilbert ■	55
91	Roberts Wesleyan	72
92	Salisbury St. †	74
97	Wilkes	91
87	Roberts Wesleyan ■	76
117	Nazareth †	85
62	Rochester	63
77	Fredonia St. ■	66
87	Ithaca	75
102	Lake Erie ■	54
74	Buffalo St.	81
49	Hartwick	69
96	Elmira ■	81
72	Keuka ■	62
73	Brockport St.	79
68	Geneseo St.	71
75	Utica ■	73
98	Allegheny ■	83
65	Nazareth	54
78	Rochester Inst.	73
71	Clarkson ■	48
82	Alfred ■	70
65	Buffalo St.	74

Nickname: Cardinals
Colors: Cardinal Red & Gold
Arena: Athletic Center
   Capacity: 1,200; Year Built: 1963
AD: Bob Ward
SID: Chuck Mitrano

ST. JOHN'S (MINN.)
Collegeville, MN 56321...........III

Coach: Jim Smith
Alma Mater: Marquette '56
Record: 32 Years, W-512, L-340

1996-97 SCHEDULE

St. Vincent's Inv................Nov. 23-24
Concordia-St. Paul ....Nov. 30
Wis.-River Falls ■......................Dec. 4
Concordia-M'head ....Dec. 7
Carleton ■...............................Dec. 11
St. Olaf ■................................Dec. 14
Hamline ....Jan. 4
Augsburg ■................................Jan. 8
St. Mary's (Minn.) ....Jan. 11
Macalester ....Jan. 13
Bethel (Minn.) ■......................Jan. 15
St. Thomas (Minn.) ....Jan. 18
Gust. Adolphus ■.....................Jan. 22
Concordia-M'head ....Jan. 25
Carleton ....Jan. 29
St. Olaf ....Feb. 1
Hamline ....Feb. 3
Augsburg ....Feb. 8
St. Mary's (Minn.) ■................Feb. 12
Macalester ■............................Feb. 15

Bethel (Minn.) ....Feb. 17
St. Thomas (Minn.) ■ ....Feb. 19
Gust. Adolphus ....Feb. 22

1995-96 RESULTS (12-12)

82 Concordia-St. Paul ■ 53
78 Hastings † 100
49 Neb. Wesleyan 78
62 St. Thomas (Minn.) 66
65 Carleton 78
86 Macalester ■ 51
77 North Park 69
86 Hamline 81
66 Concordia-M'head 67
75 St. Olaf ■ 72
67 Bethel (Minn.) 71
64 St. Mary's (Minn.) 49
66 Gust. Adolphus 84
70 St. Thomas (Minn.) ■ 56
73 Carleton ■ 81
67 Macalester 64
79 Augsburg ■ 80
75 Hamline ■ 64
86 Concordia-M'head ■ 77
71 St. Olaf 76
98 Bethel (Minn.) ■ 91
66 St. Mary's (Minn.) ■ 65
60 Augsburg 63
64 Gust. Adolphus ■ 80

Nickname: Johnnies
Colors: Red & White
Arena: Warner Palestra
Capacity: 3,600; Year Built: 1974
AD: Jim Smith
SID: Tom Nelson

ST. JOHN'S (N.Y.)

Jamaica, NY 11439 I

Coach: Fran Fraschilla
Alma Mater: LIU-Brooklyn '80
Record: 4 Years, W-85, L-35

1996-97 SCHEDULE

LIU-Brooklyn ■ ....Nov. 23
Hofstra ■ ....Nov. 30
Miami (Fla.) ....Dec. 3
Villanova ■ ....Dec. 7
Michigan ....Dec. 11
Minnesota ....Dec. 15
Fairleigh Dickinson ■ ....Dec. 21
ECAC Holiday Tr. ....Dec. 26-28
Providence ....Jan. 2
Pittsburgh ■ ....Jan. 4
Connecticut ....Jan. 8
West Va. ■ ....Jan. 12
Niagara ....Jan. 14
Pittsburgh ....Jan. 18
Georgetown ....Jan. 21
Providence ■ ....Jan. 25
Rutgers ■ ....Jan. 29
Georgetown ■ ....Feb. 1
Michigan ■ ....Feb. 3
Notre Dame ....Feb. 5
Boston College ■ ....Feb. 9
Syracuse ■ ....Feb. 12
Rutgers ....Feb. 15
Villanova ....Feb. 19
Miami (Fla.) ■ ....Feb. 22
Seton Hall ....Feb. 26
Big East Conf. Tr. ....Mar. 5-8

1995-96 RESULTS (11-16)

88 Niagara ■ 72
77 UC Irvine ■ 83
71 Manhattan ■ 68
68 Villanova 83
72 Syracuse 97
80 San Francisco 78
66 Fordham 47
57 Iona ■ 70
79 Rider ■ 69
78 Providence ■ 82
89 West Va. ■ 74
86 Louisville ■ 64
73 Connecticut 88
78 Boston College 91
76 Seton Hall 82
83 Georgetown ■ 72
83 Notre Dame ■ 86
63 Connecticut ■ 77
73 Boston College ■ 89
74 Notre Dame 66
70 Rutgers 82
78 Seton Hall ■ 73
91 Miami (Fla.) 96
77 West Va. 92
79 Syracuse ■ 92
74 Pittsburgh ■ 68
72 Providence † 80

Nickname: Red Storm
Colors: Red & White
Arena: Alumni Hall
Capacity: 6,008; Year Built: 1961
AD: Edward J. Manetta Jr
SID: Dominic Scianna

ST. JOSEPH'S (IND.)

Rensselaer, IN 47978 II

Coach: Bill Bland
Alma Mater: North Park '82
Record: 3 Years, W-44, L-38

1996-97 SCHEDULE

P.R.-Mayaguez ■ ....Nov. 18
Eastern Mich. ....Nov. 26
Bellarmine ■ ....Dec. 2
Eureka ■ ....Dec. 5
St. Francis (Ill.) ■ ....Dec. 10
Ferris St. ....Dec. 14
Purdue-Calumet ....Dec. 21
St. Thomas Aquinas ■ ....Dec. 28
Ky. Wesleyan ■ ....Dec. 30
Quincy ....Jan. 2
Mo.-St. Louis ....Jan. 4
IU/PU-Ft. Wayne ■ ....Jan. 9
Southern Ind. ■ ....Jan. 11
Indianapolis ■ ....Jan. 16
Northern Ky. ■ ....Jan. 18
Wis.-Parkside ....Jan. 23
Lewis ....Jan. 25
Ky. Wesleyan ....Jan. 30
Bellarmine ....Feb. 1
Mo.-St. Louis ■ ....Feb. 6
Quincy ■ ....Feb. 8
IU/PU-Ft. Wayne ....Feb. 13
SIU-Edwardsville ....Feb. 15
Northern Ky. ....Feb. 20
Indianapolis ....Feb. 22
Lewis ■ ....Feb. 27
Wis.-Parkside ■ ....Mar. 1

1995-96 RESULTS (12-15)

71 Ferris St. ■ 60
65 St. Francis (Ill.) 77
64 St. Francis (Ind.) ■ 65
65 Ind. Wesleyan ■ 63
76 Purdue-Calumet ■ 57
69 Lewis 57
94 Concordia (Ill.) ■ 68
76 Bellarmine ■ 63
90 Ky. Wesleyan ■ 91
76 IU/PU-Ft. Wayne 75
60 Indianapolis 63
73 Wis.-Parkside 78
82 Southern Ind. ■ 80
82 SIU-Edwardsville ■ 70
60 Northern Ky. 83
71 Bellarmine 68
78 IU/PU-Ft. Wayne ■ 73
72 Quincy ■ 83
58 Lewis ■ 71
70 Ky. Wesleyan 79
67 Southern Ind. 75
55 Indianapolis ■ 56
64 Northern Ky. ■ 67
81 Wis.-Parkside ■ 69
67 Eureka 80
60 SIU-Edwardsville 75
93 Quincy 116

Nickname: Pumas
Colors: Cardinal & Purple
Arena: Richard F. Schapf Fldhous
Capacity: 2,000; Year Built: 1941
AD: Lynn Plett
SID: Joe Danahey

ST. JOSEPH'S (ME.)

North Windham, ME 04062 III

Coach: Rick Simonds
Alma Mater: Southern Me. '72
Record: 16 Years, W-329, L-125

1996-97 SCHEDULE

Me.-Farmington ■ ....Nov. 26
Southern Maine Tr. ....Nov. 29-Dec. 1
Me.-Presque Isle ....Dec. 7
Me.-Machias ....Dec. 8
New England ....Dec. 11
Thomas ■ ....Dec. 14
John Jay ....Jan. 6
Hunter ....Jan. 7
Gordon ....Jan. 11
New England ■ ....Jan. 15
Lyndon St. ■ ....Jan. 19
Thomas ....Jan. 21
Me.-Farmington ....Jan. 25
Atlantic Union ■ ....Jan. 28
Husson ■ ....Jan. 30
Worcester St. ....Feb. 1
Bates ■ ....Feb. 5
St. Joseph (Vt.) ....Feb. 8
Green Mountain ....Feb. 9
Southern Me. [Portland] ....Feb. 12
Me.-Presque Isle ■ ....Feb. 15
Husson ....Feb. 17
Me.-Machias ■ ....Feb. 21

1995-96 RESULTS (24-4)

86 Gordon ■ 66
90 Me.-Farmington ■ 76
112 Westbrook ■ 72
106 Maine Maritime 31
97 New England 63
111 Thomas ■ 65
62 Florida Tech 79
66 Fla. Southern 88
100 Westbrook † 95
98 Husson † 91
66 Colby † 59
73 Husson ■ 70
78 Johnson St. 59
128 Lyndon St. 72
93 New England ■ 77
89 Me.-Farmington 83
85 Thomas 57
104 Worcester St. ■ 85
90 Bates 75
109 St. Joseph (Vt.) ■ 58
97 Green Mountain ■ 53
94 Southern Me. † 77
109 Atlantic Union 84
73 Husson 75
97 Me.-Machias 71
88 New England † 62
82 Me.-Presque Isle † 68
74 Wis. Lutheran † 90

Nickname: Monks
Colors: Royal Blue, Red & White
Arena: Bernard Currier Gymnasium
Capacity: 500; Year Built: 1972
AD: Rick Simonds
SID: Rick Simonds

ST. JOSEPH'S (PA.)

Philadelphia, PA 19131 I

Coach: Phil Martelli
Alma Mater: Widener '76
Record: 1 Year, W-19, L-13

1996-97 SCHEDULE

NIT ....Nov. 20-29
Wyoming ■ ....Dec. 3
Tulsa [Atlantic City] ....Dec. 7
DePaul ■ ....Dec. 16
East Caro. ....Dec. 19
Villanova ■ ....Dec. 23
Wis.-Green Bay Cl. ....Dec. 30-31
Massachusetts ....Jan. 5
St. Bonaventure ■ ....Jan. 9
Rhode Island ....Jan. 11
Geo. Washington ....Jan. 15
Pennsylvania ....Jan. 18
Duquesne ■ ....Jan. 21
Virginia Tech ■ ....Jan. 25
Temple ■ ....Jan. 30
Rhode Island ■ ....Feb. 2
Dayton ....Feb. 4
Fordham ■ ....Feb. 6
Xavier (Ohio) ■ ....Feb. 8
Drexel ■ ....Feb. 11
Temple ....Feb. 13
Fordham ....Feb. 16
Delaware ■ ....Feb. 18
St. Bonaventure ....Feb. 22
Massachusetts ■ ....Feb. 25
La Salle ....Mar. 1
Atlantic 10 Conf. Tr. ....Mar. 5-8

1995-96 RESULTS (19-13)

64 Delaware 56
74 Bucknell ■ 54
78 Princeton 88
84 UC Santa Barb. ■ 66
93 Texas Christian † 92
74 Seton Hall 81
60 Old Dominion 62
78 Loyola (Md.) 80
89 Massachusetts ■ 94
86 Pennsylvania † 70
67 La Salle † 65
68 Fordham 64
83 Rhode Island 86
52 Temple † 54
76 Virginia Tech 85
71 Xavier (Ohio) 84
73 Dayton ■ 60
76 St. Bonaventure ■ 72
58 Temple 60
69 Rhode Island ■ 64
76 Duquesne 70
64 St. Bonaventure 56
69 Fordham ■ 58
66 Massachusetts 68
86 Geo. Washington ■ 82
80 Duquesne † 72
71 Geo. Washington † 81
82 Iona 78
82 Providence 62
76 Rhode Island ■ 59
74 Alabama † 69
56 Nebraska † 60

Nickname: Hawks
Colors: Crimson & Gray
Arena: Alumni Memorial Fieldhouse
Capacity: 3,200; Year Built: 1949
AD: Don DiJulia
SID: Larry Dougherty

ST. LAWRENCE

Canton, NY 13617 III

Coach: David Paulsen
Alma Mater: Williams '87
Record: 2 Years, W-28, L-24

1996-97 SCHEDULE

Rochester Tip-Off ....Nov. 22-23
Oswego St. ■ ....Dec. 3
Williams Cl. ....Dec. 6-7
Clarkson ■ ....Dec. 11
Alfred ■ ....Dec. 14
Potsdam St. ■ ....Jan. 7
Nazareth ....Jan. 10
Rochester Inst. ....Jan. 11
Union (N.Y.) ....Jan. 15
Clarkson ....Jan. 18
Plattsburgh St. ■ ....Jan. 21

Hamilton ■ ... Jan. 24
Hobart ■ ... Jan. 25
Skidmore ... Jan. 31
Rensselaer ... Feb. 1
Ithaca ■ ... Feb. 7
Union (N.Y.) ■ ... Feb. 8
Potsdam St. ■ ... Feb. 11
Rensselaer ■ ... Feb. 14
Skidmore ■ ... Feb. 15
Hartwick ... Feb. 18
Hobart ... Feb. 21
Hamilton ... Feb. 22

1995-96 RESULTS (18-9)
76 Rochester ... 82
75 Cortland St. † ... 62
66 Oswego St. ... 69
57 Rensselaer ... 62
65 Skidmore ... 58
68 Clarkson ... 60
83 Hamilton ... 95
78 Gordon † ... 73
97 Rivier † ... 58
41 Ithaca ... 72
90 Alfred ... 74
83 Plattsburgh St. ... 49
79 Union (N.Y.) ■ ... 61
91 Hobart ■ ... 72
79 Skidmore ■ ... 71
85 Rensselaer ■ ... 66
75 Nazareth ■ ... 67
68 Rochester Inst. ■ ... 65
76 Potsdam St. ... 74
68 Hobart ... 76
101 Union (N.Y.) ... 74
69 Clarkson ■ ... 59
75 Hartwick ■ ... 68
71 Hamilton ■ ... 85
66 Le Moyne ■ ... 86
85 Hamilton ... 78
70 Rensselaer † ... 78

Nickname: Saints
Colors: Scarlet & Brown
Arena: Burkman Gymnasium
Capacity: 1,500; Year Built: 1970
AD: John Clark
SID: Wally Johnson

ST. LEO
St. Leo, FL 33574 ... II

Coach: Mike Hanks
Alma Mater: Southern Methodist '75
Record: 6 Years, W-91, L-81

1996-97 SCHEDULE
Palm Beach Atl. ■ ... Nov. 18
Webber ■ ... Nov. 20
Morningside ■ ... Nov. 27
Shorter ■ ... Nov. 29
Fla. Memorial ■ ... Dec. 2
American (P.R.) ■ ... Dec. 4
Georgetown ... Dec. 18
St. Thomas (Fla.) ■ ... Dec. 20
Husson ■ ... Dec. 29
Merrimack ■ ... Dec. 31
Bentley ■ ... Jan. 2
North Fla. ... Jan. 8
Crown ■ ... Jan. 9
Tampa ■ ... Jan. 11
Florida Tech ... Jan. 15
Eckerd ... Jan. 18
Fla. Southern ■ ... Jan. 22
Barry ... Jan. 25
Rollins ■ ... Jan. 29
Florida Tech ■ ... Feb. 1
Eckerd ■ ... Feb. 5
Tampa ... Feb. 8
Fla. Southern ... Feb. 12
Barry ■ ... Feb. 15
Rollins ... Feb. 19
North Fla. ■ ... Feb. 22

1995-96 RESULTS (8-19)
84 Tex. A&M-Kingsville † ... 99
65 Lane † ... 69
70 Palm Beach Atl. ■ ... 59
86 Fla. Memorial ■ ... 71
76 Edward Waters ■ ... 60
73 Fla. Memorial ... 75
85 St. Thomas (Fla.) ... 87
72 Kennesaw St. ■ ... 80
67 Webber ■ ... 68
65 Georgetown † ... 123
86 American Int'l ■ ... 76
60 Minn.-Duluth ■ ... 76
92 Barry ■ ... 87
72 Tampa ... 75
69 Rollins ... 84
68 Fla. Southern ■ ... 75
75 Florida Tech ... 87
63 Eckerd ■ ... 61
58 North Fla. ■ ... 67
64 Barry ... 67
82 Tampa ■ ... 92
75 Rollins ■ ... 76
72 Fla. Southern ... 74
73 Florida Tech ■ ... 68
68 Eckerd ... 78
78 North Fla. ... 69
55 Eckerd † ... 58

Nickname: Monarchs
Colors: Forest Green & Old Gold
Arena: Marion Bowman Center
Capacity: 2,700; Year Built: 1970
AD: Ted Owens
SID: Tom O'Brien

ST. LOUIS
St. Louis, MO 63108 ... I

Coach: Charlie Spoonhour
Alma Mater: School of Ozarks '61
Record: 13 Years, W-271, L-126

1996-97 SCHEDULE
NIT ... Nov. 20-29
Southern Ill. ■ ... Dec. 4
Mo.-Kansas City ■ ... Dec. 7
Alcorn St. ■ ... Dec. 9
Furman ■ ... Dec. 14
Southwest Mo. St. ... Dec. 15
Murray St. ■ ... Dec. 18
Eastern Ill. ■ ... Dec. 21
UCLA ■ ... Dec. 23
Vanderbilt ... Dec. 31
Cincinnati ■ ... Jan. 5
N.C.-Charlotte ... Jan. 11
Southern Utah ■ ... Jan. 13
Marquette ... Jan. 18
Maine ■ ... Jan. 20
Tulane ... Jan. 22
Houston ■ ... Jan. 25
UAB ■ ... Jan. 29
Southern Miss. ■ ... Feb. 2
Louisville ... Feb. 6
Cincinnati ... Feb. 13
DePaul ■ ... Feb. 16
Memphis ■ ... Feb. 19
South Fla. ... Feb. 23
Marquette ■ ... Feb. 25
DePaul ... Mar. 1
Conference USA ... Mar. 5-8

1995-96 RESULTS (16-14)
79 LSU † ... 70
66 Hawaii ... 72
58 Pennsylvania ■ ... 51
68 Bradley ... 78
82 Mo.-Kansas City ... 74
63 Alcorn St. ■ ... 60
67 Southern Ill. ■ ... 63
65 Sam Houston St. ■ ... 48
96 Chicago St. ■ ... 56
75 Southwest Mo. St. ■ ... 65
47 Marquette ... 69
55 UAB ... 64
60 DePaul ■ ... 59
69 South Fla. ■ ... 56
63 Louisville ■ ... 67
74 Murray St. ■ ... 68
57 Louisville ... 61
72 N.C.-Charlotte ■ ... 58
63 Memphis ... 80
49 Cincinnati ... 81
65 Fla. Atlantic ■ ... 55
51 Tulane ■ ... 77
64 Cincinnati ■ ... 69
91 Tenn.-Martin ■ ... 65
69 Marquette ■ ... 58
46 Southern Miss. ... 62
51 DePaul ... 66
61 Southern Miss. † ... 44
59 Cincinnati † ... 62
52 Minnesota ... 68

Nickname: Billikens
Colors: Blue & White
Arena: The Kiel Center
Capacity: 20,000; Year Built: 1994
AD: Doug Woolard
SID: Doug McIlhagga

ST. MARY'S (CAL.)
Moraga, CA 94575 ... I

Coach: Ernie Kent
Alma Mater: Oregon '77
Record: 5 Years, W-67, L-72

1996-97 SCHEDULE
NIT ... Nov. 20-29
San Jose St. ■ ... Nov. 24
Cal St. Sacramento ... Nov. 26
UC Santa Barb. ■ ... Dec. 1
Hawaii Inv. ... Dec. 6-7
Brigham Young Cl. ... Dec. 13-14
Cal St. Northridge ... Dec. 16
Alas. Anchorage ■ ... Dec. 20
Fresno St. ■ ... Dec. 23
Cal St. Hayward ■ ... Jan. 2
Long Beach St. ■ ... Jan. 4
Portland ... Jan. 9
Gonzaga ... Jan. 11
Santa Clara ... Jan. 15
Santa Clara ■ ... Jan. 18
San Diego ■ ... Jan. 24
San Francisco ■ ... Jan. 25
San Francisco ... Jan. 30
San Diego ... Feb. 1
Pepperdine ■ ... Feb. 7
Loyola Marymount ■ ... Feb. 8
Loyola Marymount ... Feb. 14
Pepperdine ... Feb. 15
Gonzaga ■ ... Feb. 21
Portland ■ ... Feb. 22
West Coast Conf. Tr. ... Mar. 1-3

1995-96 RESULTS (12-15)
84 Bucknell ■ ... 66
61 San Jose St. ... 60
53 Pacific (Cal.) ■ ... 46
55 Texas A&M ... 83
69 Long Beach St. ... 86
67 Cal St. Northridge ■ ... 64
74 Fresno St. ... 75
80 UC Santa Barb. ... 78
74 Rhode Island ■ ... 81
63 Montana ... 70
88 Cal Poly SLO ■ ... 68
86 Portland ■ ... 97
71 Gonzaga ■ ... 81
87 Cal St. Sacramento ■ ... 75
89 Pepperdine ... 79
76 Loyola Marymount ... 64
60 Loyola Marymount ■ ... 66
78 Pepperdine ■ ... 88
66 San Diego ... 62
67 San Francisco ... 73
75 San Francisco ■ ... 79
62 San Diego ■ ... 58
64 Santa Clara ■ ... 79
61 Santa Clara ... 64
82 Gonzaga ... 83
91 Portland ... 83
54 Gonzaga † ... 64

Nickname: Gaels
Colors: Red & Blue
Arena: McKeon Pavilion
Capacity: 3,500; Year Built: 1978
AD: Rick Mazzuto
SID: Steve Janisch

ST. MARY'S (MD.)
St. Mary's City, MD 20686 ... III

Coach: Robert Flynn
Alma Mater: Mt. St. Mary's (Md.)
Record: 2 Years, W-16, L-35

1996-97 SCHEDULE
Johns Hopkins Cl. ... Nov. 22-23
Western Md. ... Nov. 26
Washington (Md.) ■ ... Dec. 2
Goucher ... Dec. 4
Mary Washington ■ ... Dec. 6
Frostburg St. ■ ... Dec. 11
Md.-Balt. County ... Dec. 28
Chicago ■ ... Jan. 10
Marymount (Va.) ... Jan. 15
Catholic ... Jan. 18
Wesley ... Jan. 20
Gallaudet ■ ... Jan. 22
York (Pa.) ... Jan. 25
Goucher ■ ... Jan. 29
Salisbury St. ... Feb. 1
Villa Julie [Baltimore] ... Feb. 3
Marymount (Va.) ■ ... Feb. 5
Mary Washington ... Feb. 7
Catholic ■ ... Feb. 11
Villa Julie ■ ... Feb. 13
York (Pa.) ■ ... Feb. 15
Gallaudet ... Feb. 19
Salisbury St. ■ ... Feb. 22

1995-96 RESULTS (8-18)
82 Western Md. ■ ... 75
72 Hampden-Sydney † ... 87
83 Washington (Md.) ... 88
81 Mary Washington ■ ... 79
59 Navy ... 84
53 Citadel ... 102
61 Randolph-Macon ... 83
67 Olivet † ... 71
72 Manhattanville † ... 58
68 Mary Washington ... 80
70 Goucher ... 69
62 Catholic ... 76
52 York (Pa.) ... 74
105 Marymount (Va.) ■ ... 101
97 Salisbury St. ... 102
80 Gallaudet ... 68
84 Goucher ■ ... 88
68 Villa Julie † ... 76
67 Marymount (Va.) ... 73
65 York (Pa.) ■ ... 66
70 Salisbury St. ■ ... 72
84 Gallaudet ■ ... 76
86 Catholic ■ ... 92
87 Goucher ... 79
81 Salisbury St. ... 124
52 Loyola (Md.) ... 98

Nickname: Seahawks
Colors: Navy Blue & Gold
Arena: Somerset
Capacity: 1,200; Year Built: 1969
AD: Paul Moyer
SID: To be named

ST. MARY'S (MINN.)
Winona, MN 55987 ... III

Coach: Will Rey
Alma Mater: Northeastern Ill. '75
Record: 7 Years, W-58, L-131

1996-97 SCHEDULE
Lewis ■ ... Nov. 30
Winona St. ■ ... Dec. 4
Viterbo ... Dec. 7
Macalester ... Dec. 9

St. Thomas (Minn.) ■ ....Dec. 11
Benedictine (Ill.) ■ ....Dec. 30
Concordia-M'head ■ ....Jan. 4
Hamline ....Jan. 6
Gust. Adolphus ....Jan. 8
St. John's (Minn.) ■ ....Jan. 11
Bethel (Minn.) ....Jan. 13
Augsburg ■ ....Jan. 15
St. Olaf ....Jan. 18
Carleton ■ ....Jan. 22
St. Thomas (Minn.) ....Jan. 29
Macalester ■ ....Feb. 1
Hamline ■ ....Feb. 5
Gust. Adolphus ■ ....Feb. 8
Concordia-M'head ....Feb. 10
St. John's (Minn.) ....Feb. 12
Bethel (Minn.) ■ ....Feb. 15
Augsburg ....Feb. 17
St. Olaf ■ ....Feb. 19
Carleton ....Feb. 22

1995-96 RESULTS (6-18)

62	Lewis	74
71	Benedictine (Ill.)	64
58	Winona St.	73
61	Viterbo ■	59
47	Gust. Adolphus	66
59	Carleton ■	57
45	Augsburg	50
69	St. Thomas (Minn.)	81
70	Bethel (Minn.) ■	60
62	Hamline	74
49	St. John's (Minn.) ■	64
59	Concordia-M'head ■	75
56	St. Olaf	67
52	Gust. Adolphus ■	54
43	Carleton	61
49	Macalester	41
35	Augsburg ■	66
50	St. Thomas (Minn.)	63
76	Bethel (Minn.)	77
66	Hamline ■	73
65	St. John's (Minn.)	66
49	Concordia-M'head	68
74	Macalester ■	53
66	St. Olaf ■	71

Nickname: Cardinals
Colors: Scarlet, Red & White
Arena: St. Mary's Fieldhouse
  Capacity: 3,500; Year Built: 1965
AD: Don Olson
SID: Donny Nadeau

ST. MICHAEL'S
Colchester, VT 05439 II

Coach: Tom Crowley
Alma Mater: Pennsylvania '78
Record: 6 Years, W-83, L-79

1996-97 SCHEDULE

Franklin Pierce ■ ....Nov. 23
Adelphi ....Nov. 30
Bryant ....Dec. 3
Vermont ....Dec. 11
American Int'l ....Dec. 14
St. Michael's Cl. ....Dec. 28-29
Bloomsburg Inv. ....Jan. 4-5
Stonehill ■ ....Jan. 8
Assumption ....Jan. 11
Merrimack ....Jan. 14
St. Anselm ■ ....Jan. 16
Bentley ■ ....Jan. 18
Le Moyne ■ ....Jan. 20
Quinnipiac ....Jan. 25
Stonehill ....Jan. 29
American Int'l ■ ....Feb. 1
Merrimack ■ ....Feb. 4
Bentley ....Feb. 8
St. Anselm ■ ....Feb. 11
Assumption ■ ....Feb. 13
Le Moyne ■ ....Feb. 15
Bryant ■ ....Feb. 19
Quinnipiac ■ ....Feb. 22

1995-96 RESULTS (19-8)

74	Southern Conn. St. †	72
95	New Haven	78
73	Adelphi ■	78
73	Le Moyne ■	71
78	East Stroudsburg	83
64	American Int'l †	55
103	Castleton St.	63
99	Green Mountain ■	82
80	Vermont	72
69	Stonehill	66
72	American Int'l	70
80	Quinnipiac ■	74
86	Merrimack	93
79	Stonehill ■	73
75	St. Anselm	88
87	Bryant ■	73
89	Bentley	97
84	Assumption	64
82	American Int'l ■	78
100	Merrimack ■	81
104	Quinnipiac	74
105	Assumption ■	83
75	St. Anselm ■	86
96	Bryant	99
96	Bentley ■	82
78	Merrimack †	84
96	Dowling	81

Nickname: Purple Knights
Colors: Purple & Gold
Arena: Ross Sports Center
  Capacity: 2,000; Year Built: 1974
AD: Edward Markey
SID: Chris Kenny

ST. NORBERT
De Pere, WI 54115 III

Coach: Paul De Noble
Alma Mater: Wis.-Oshkosh '73
Record: 7 Years, W-66, L-89

1996-97 SCHEDULE

Edgewood ....Nov. 23
Wis. Lutheran ■ ....Nov. 26
Milwaukee Engr. ....Nov. 30
Northland Bapt. ■ ....Dec. 2
Judson (Ill.) ■ ....Dec. 4
Wis.-Oshkosh ....Dec. 31
Carthage ....Jan. 4
Concordia (Wis.) ■ ....Jan. 7
Beloit ....Jan. 11
Carroll (Wis.) ■ ....Jan. 14
Knox ■ ....Jan. 17
Illinois Col. ■ ....Jan. 18
Coe ....Jan. 24
Grinnell ....Jan. 25
Lake Forest ....Jan. 29
Lawrence ■ ....Feb. 1
Ripon ■ ....Feb. 5
Beloit ■ ....Feb. 8
Carroll (Wis.) ....Feb. 12
Lake Forest ■ ....Feb. 15
Lawrence ....Feb. 19
Ripon ....Feb. 22

1995-96 RESULTS (8-14)

86	Milwaukee Engr. ■	60
52	Wis. Lutheran	72
62	Concordia (Wis.)	57
61	Northland Bapt. ■	53
61	Judson (Ill.)	42
47	Wis.-La Crosse ■	43
58	Edgewood ■	56
43	Concordia (Ill.)	46
44	Ripon ■	61
62	Beloit ■	66
54	Carroll (Wis.)	57
51	Illinois Col.	54
73	Knox	69
33	Lake Forest ■	51
62	Grinnell ■	81
45	Coe ■	56
58	Lawrence	74
43	Lake Forest	48

53	Ripon	72
72	Beloit	66
57	Carroll (Wis.) ■	59
77	Lawrence	80

Nickname: Green Knights
Colors: Green & Gold
Arena: Schuldes Sports Center
  Capacity: 2,000; Year Built: 1979
AD: Larry Van Alstine
SID: Len Wagner

ST. OLAF
Northfield, MN 55057 III

Coach: Dan Kosmoski
Alma Mater: Minnesota '80
Record: 2 Years, W-24, L-24

1996-97 SCHEDULE

Mt. Senario ■ ....Nov. 25
N'western (Minn.) ....Dec. 3
Augsburg ■ ....Dec. 9
Bethel (Minn.) ■ ....Dec. 11
St. John's (Minn.) ■ ....Dec. 14
Cal Lutheran Tr. ....Dec. 29-30
St. Thomas (Minn.) ■ ....Jan. 4
Gust. Adolphus ....Jan. 6
Concordia-M'head ■ ....Jan. 8
Macalester ■ ....Jan. 11
Carleton ....Jan. 15
St. Mary's (Minn.) ■ ....Jan. 18
Hamline ....Jan. 22
Augsburg ....Jan. 25
Bethel (Minn.) ....Jan. 29
St. John's (Minn.) ....Feb. 1
St. Thomas (Minn.) ....Feb. 3
Gust. Adolphus ■ ....Feb. 5
Concordia-M'head ....Feb. 8
Macalester ....Feb. 12
Carleton ....Feb. 17
St. Mary's (Minn.) ....Feb. 19
Hamline ■ ....Feb. 22

1995-96 RESULTS (15-9)

87	Morris	85
81	Dakota St. †	76
83	N'western (Minn.) ■	81
109	Concordia-St. Paul	59
76	Macalester	65
90	Augsburg	75
72	Carleton ■	78
99	Bethel (Minn.)	93
72	St. John's (Minn.)	75
74	Gust. Adolphus ■	78
70	St. Thomas (Minn.)	81
92	Hamline ■	64
70	Concordia-M'head ■	71
67	St. Mary's (Minn.) ■	56
74	Macalester ■	58
63	Augsburg ■	61
64	Carleton	84
87	Bethel (Minn.) ■	89
76	St. John's (Minn.) ■	71
75	Gust. Adolphus	64
67	St. Thomas (Minn.)	78
85	Hamline	81
77	Concordia-M'head	86
71	St. Mary's (Minn.)	66

Nickname: Oles
Colors: Black & Gold
Arena: Skoglund Athletic Center
  Capacity: 3,000; Year Built: 1968
AD: Lee Swan
SID: Nancy Moe

ST. PAUL'S
Lawrenceville, VA 23868 II

Coach: Edward Joyner
Alma Mater: Fla. Memorial '74
Record: 3 Years, W-26, L-54

1996-97 SCHEDULE

Johnson Smith ■ ....Nov. 19

St. Augustine's ■ ....Nov. 25
Livingstone ....Nov. 30
Shaw ....Dec. 10
Fayetteville St. ....Dec. 17
Smoke on the River ....Dec. 27-28
Virginia Union ....Jan. 7
Norfolk St. ....Jan. 11
N.C. Central ■ ....Jan. 13
Virginia St. ■ ....Jan. 16
Dist. Columbia ■ ....Jan. 18
Virginia Union ....Jan. 22
Elizabeth City St. ....Jan. 25
Bowie St. ....Jan. 27
Dist. Columbia ....Jan. 28
Col. of West Va. ■ ....Feb. 1
Winston-Salem ■ ....Feb. 10
Virginia St. ....Feb. 15
Elizabeth City St. ■ ....Feb. 17
Bowie St. ■ ....Feb. 19
Col. of West Va. ....Feb. 22

1995-96 RESULTS (12-16)

104	Barber-Scotia ■	73
65	Johnson Smith	85
74	Livingstone ■	77
72	Shaw ■	102
86	St. Augustine's	95
72	Fayetteville St.	88
66	Catawba	77
101	St. Augustine's †	93
102	Elizabeth City St. †	85
88	Dist. Columbia ■	79
79	Virginia Union ■	93
65	Norfolk St.	80
79	N.C. Central ■	95
94	Col. of West Va.	82
71	Virginia St.	61
65	Virginia Union	74
63	Elizabeth City St. ■	76
80	Bowie St. ■	75
75	Barber-Scotia	86
77	Norfolk St. ■	97
114	Col. of West Va. ■	97
74	Dist. Columbia	68
70	Winston-Salem	67
95	Virginia St. ■	101
93	Bowie St.	81
86	Elizabeth City St.	104
89	Fayetteville St. †	79
73	N.C. Central †	86

Nickname: Tigers
Colors: Black & Orange
Arena: Taylor-Whitehead Gym
  Capacity: 1,500; Year Built: 1965
AD: To be named
SID: Monique A. J. Morgan

ST. PETER'S
Jersey City, NJ 07306 I

Coach: Rodger Blind
Alma Mater: Ursinus '73
Record: 1 Year, W-15, L-12

1996-97 SCHEDULE

Md.-East. Shore ....Nov. 22
Loyola (Ill.) ■ ....Nov. 26
St. Peter's Tr. ....Nov. 30-Dec. 1
Central Conn. St. ....Dec. 4
Monmouth (N.J.) ....Dec. 7
Seton Hall ....Dec. 10
Rutgers ....Dec. 14
Hartford ....Dec. 21
Fairleigh Dickinson ....Dec. 28
Siena ....Jan. 2
Bethune-Cookman ....Jan. 6-00
Md.-Balt. County ■ ....Jan. 9
Loyola (Md.) ■ ....Jan. 12
Manhattan ■ ....Jan. 19
Iona ....Jan. 21
Fairfield ....Jan. 24
Canisius ■ ....Jan. 26
Siena ....Jan. 29
Manhattan ....Jan. 31
Fairfield ■ ....Feb. 5

Niagara.....Feb. 8
Canisius.....Feb. 10
Iona.....Feb. 15
Loyola (Md.).....Feb. 21
Niagara ■.....Feb. 23
Metro Atlantic Conf. Tr......Mar. 1-3

1995-96 RESULTS (15-12)

81	Rider	89
76	North Caro. A&T	59
81	Md.-East. Shore ■	54
80	St. Francis (N.Y.) ■	69
61	Seton Hall	59
79	Md.-Balt. County	58
70	Fairleigh Dickinson ■	43
59	Alabama †	49
56	Wichita St.	48
82	Howard ■	65
50	Niagara ■	53
52	Manhattan	71
71	Kansas	85
68	Canisius ■	64
63	Loyola (Md.) ■	64
60	Iona	65
68	Siena	51
86	St. Francis (Pa.) ■	54
60	Loyola (Md.)	70
63	Fairfield ■	75
88	Siena ■	74
86	Iona	57
65	Fairfield	74
50	Manhattan ■	68
60	Canisius	57
55	Niagara	58
64	Fairfield †	69

Nickname: Peacocks
Colors: Blue & White
Arena: Yanitelli Center
  Capacity: 3,200; Year Built: 1975
AD: William Stein
SID: Tim Camp

ST. ROSE
Albany, NY 12203.....II

Coach: Brian Beaury
Alma Mater: St. Rose '82
Record: 10 Years, W-227, L-82

1996-97 SCHEDULE
Va. Union Tr......Nov. 8-10
Mercy.....Dec. 4
LIU-Southampton.....Dec. 7
Queens (N.Y.) ■.....Dec. 11
Pace.....Dec. 14
Phila. Textile.....Dec. 22
St. Rose Cl......Dec. 27-29
Concordia (N.Y.) ■.....Jan. 4
Dowling.....Jan. 6
Molloy ■.....Jan. 8
Adelphi ■.....Jan. 11
New York Tech ■.....Jan. 15
LIU-C. W. Post.....Jan. 18
Mercy ■.....Jan. 20
LIU-Southampton ■.....Jan. 22
Queens (N.Y.).....Jan. 29
Pace ■.....Jan. 29
Concordia (N.Y.).....Feb. 1
Dowling ■.....Feb. 5
Molloy.....Feb. 8
Adelphi.....Feb. 12
Phila. Textile ■.....Feb. 15
New York Tech.....Feb. 19
LIU-C. W. Post ■.....Feb. 22

1995-96 RESULTS (28-4)

116	Assumption ■	87
81	Bloomsburg ■	77
104	Dowling	85
84	Molloy ■	53
116	Mercy ■	97
82	Phila. Textile ■	62
104	LIU-Southampton	112
94	Mercyhurst †	83
80	St. Anselm †	79
95	Adelphi	87
96	Queens (N.Y.) ■	70
105	New York Tech	94
98	Concordia (N.Y.) ■	66
80	Pace	70
105	Molloy	89
89	LIU-C. W. Post ■	52
85	Dowling ■	63
94	LIU-Southampton ■	75
128	Mercy ■	89
77	Phila. Textile	58
77	Pace ■	65
96	Adelphi	93
75	Queens (N.Y.)	83
107	New York Tech ■	93
85	Concordia (N.Y.)	40
91	LIU-C. W. Post	62
87	Queens (N.Y.) ■	76
80	LIU-Southampton ■	77
76	Adelphi ■	77
83	New Hamp. Col. †	82
87	St. Anselm †	76
72	Virginia Union †	99

Nickname: Golden Knights
Colors: Gold, White & Black
Arena: Activities Center
  Capacity: 500; Year Built: 1977
AD: Catherine Cummings Haker
SID: David Alexander

ST. SCHOLASTICA
Duluth, MN 55811.....III

Coach: Jim Datka
Alma Mater: Wis.-Lutheran '87
Record: 2 Years, W-10, L-40

1996-97 SCHEDULE
Wartburg Tr......Nov. 22-23
Hamline ■.....Nov. 26
Wis.-Stout ■.....Nov. 30
Minn.-Morris ■.....Dec. 3
Augsburg ■.....Dec. 5
Bemidji St......Dec. 10
Taylor Tr......Dec. 13-14
Presentation.....Dec. 18
Wis.-Oshkosh.....Dec. 21
Loras Catholic Tr......Jan. 1-5
Minn.-Duluth.....Jan. 8
Concordia-St. Paul.....Jan. 15
N'western (Minn.) ■.....Jan. 18
Northland.....Jan. 21
Martin Luther ■.....Jan. 25
Martin Luther.....Feb. 8
Wis.-Superior.....Feb. 12
N'western (Minn.).....Feb. 15
Northland ■.....Feb. 19
Concordia-St. Paul ■.....Feb. 22

1995-96 RESULTS
Results unavailable

Nickname: Saints
Colors: Blue & Gold
Arena: Reif Center
  Capacity: 1,200
AD: Kevin Snyder
SID: John Baggs

ST. THOMAS (MINN.)
St. Paul, MN 55105.....III

Coach: Steve Fritz
Alma Mater: St. Thomas (Minn.) '71
Record: 16 Years, W-278, L-151

1996-97 SCHEDULE
N'western (Minn.).....Nov. 25
Concordia (Cal.).....Nov. 30
Grand Canyon.....Dec. 3
Carleton.....Dec. 7
St. Mary's (Minn.).....Dec. 11
Hamline ■.....Dec. 14
Concordia-St. Paul ■.....Dec. 21
St. Olaf.....Jan. 4
Augsburg ■.....Jan. 6
Bethel (Minn.).....Jan. 11
Concordia-M'head ■.....Jan. 13
Gust. Adolphus ■.....Jan. 15
St. John's (Minn.) ■.....Jan. 18
Macalester ■.....Jan. 22
Carleton ■.....Jan. 25
St. Mary's (Minn.) ■.....Jan. 29
Hamline.....Feb. 1
St. Olaf ■.....Feb. 3
Augsburg.....Feb. 5
Bethel (Minn.) ■.....Feb. 12
Concordia-M'head.....Feb. 15
Gust. Adolphus ■.....Feb. 17
St. John's (Minn.).....Feb. 19
Macalester.....Feb. 22

1995-96 RESULTS (15-10)

61	Rose-Hulman †	59
71	Trinity (Tex.)	73
73	N'western (Minn.) ■	71
66	St. John's (Minn.) ■	62
53	Concordia-M'head ■	76
59	Hamline	46
72	Macalester ■	63
81	St. Mary's (Minn.) ■	69
62	Augsburg	73
85	Concordia-St. Paul	56
81	St. Olaf ■	70
77	Gust. Adolphus	73
68	Bethel (Minn.) ■	57
72	Carleton	84
56	St. John's (Minn.)	70
53	Concordia-M'head ■	70
64	Hamline	60
61	Macalester	62
63	St. Mary's (Minn.) ■	50
64	Augsburg ■	73
78	St. Olaf	67
63	Gust. Adolphus ■	77
65	Bethel (Minn.)	63
71	Carleton ■	92
62	Gust. Adolphus	76

Nickname: Tommies
Colors: Purple & Gray
Arena: Schoenecker Arena
  Capacity: 2,250; Year Built: 1982
AD: Steve Fritz
SID: Gene McGivern

SALEM ST.
Salem, MA 01970.....III

Coach: Jim Todd
Alma Mater: Fitchburg St. '76
Record: 11 Years, W-207, L-93

1996-97 SCHEDULE
Eastern Conn. St. Tr......Nov. 22-23
Plymouth St......Dec. 5
Gordon ■.....Dec. 10
Wheaton (Mass.).....Dec. 12
Salem St. Tr......Dec. 29-30
Babson ■.....Jan. 11
Eastern Nazarene.....Jan. 16
Fitchburg St......Jan. 18
Westfield St. ■.....Jan. 21
Tufts.....Jan. 23
Framingham St......Jan. 25
North Adams St......Jan. 28
Bri'water (Mass.) ■.....Feb. 1
Worcester St......Feb. 4
Mass.-Dartmouth.....Feb. 6
Mass.-Boston ■.....Feb. 8
Fitchburg St. ■.....Feb. 11
Westfield St......Feb. 13
Framingham St. ■.....Feb. 15
North Adams St. ■.....Feb. 17
Bri'water (Mass.).....Feb. 20
Worcester St. ■.....Feb. 22

1995-96 RESULTS (25-3)

83	Hunter †	71
86	Jersey City St.	73
66	Plymouth St.	73
105	Emerson-MCA	95
88	Wheaton (Mass.) ■	65
89	Mass.-Boston	78
83	Suffolk ■	59
83	Anna Maria ■	66
107	Gordon ■	84
78	Eastern Nazarene ■	84
92	Fitchburg St. ■	81
82	Westfield St.	66
89	Tufts	69
109	Framingham St. ■	65
79	North Adams St. ■	60
90	Bri'water (Mass.)	64
109	Worcester St. ■	83
84	Mass.-Dartmouth	75
71	Fitchburg St.	49
99	Westfield St. ■	92
73	Framingham St.	56
90	North Adams St.	54
77	Bri'water (Mass.) ■	71
94	Worcester St.	71
99	Worcester St. ■	79
77	Bri'water (Mass.) ■	56
76	Western Conn. St. ■	60
67	Anna Maria ■	74

Nickname: Vikings
Colors: Orange & Blue
Arena: O'Keefe Sports Center
  Capacity: 2,200; Year Built: 1976
AD: John Galaris
SID: Thomas Roundy

SALEM-TEIKYO
Salem, WV 26426.....II

Coach: Michael A. Carey
Alma Mater: Salem '80
Record: 8 Years, W-148, L-81

1996-97 SCHEDULE
Salem-Teikyo Tr......Nov. 15-16
Pikeville.....Nov. 21
Calif. (Pa.).....Nov. 25
Edinboro ■.....Nov. 30
Fairmont St......Dec. 2
Davis & Elkins ■.....Dec. 7
Elizabeth City St. ■.....Dec. 14
Pikeville ■.....Dec. 18
West Va. Wesleyan ■.....Jan. 8
Bluefield St......Jan. 11
West Va. Tech.....Jan. 13
Glenville St. ■.....Jan. 15
West Va. St......Jan. 18
West Liberty St. ■.....Jan. 22
Shepherd ■.....Jan. 25
Charleston (W.Va.).....Jan. 27
Wheeling Jesuit ■.....Jan. 29
Concord.....Feb. 1
Alderson-Broaddus ■.....Feb. 5
Glenville St......Feb. 8
Fairmont St. ■.....Feb. 12
West Liberty St......Feb. 15
Shepherd.....Feb. 17
Charleston (W.Va.) ■.....Feb. 19
Wheeling Jesuit.....Feb. 22

1995-96 RESULTS (20-9)

96	Spalding ■	80
95	Concord	76
83	American Int'l †	70
80	East Stroudsburg	64
81	Fairmont St. ■	90
91	Ohio Valley	90
98	Davis & Elkins	69
88	Calif. (Pa.) ■	74
67	Edinboro	75
88	West Va. Wesleyan	73
89	Bluefield St.	83
90	West Va. Tech ■	74
55	Glenville St.	79
85	West Va. St.	83
60	West Liberty St. ■	75
61	Shepherd	47
89	Charleston (W.Va.) ■	80
84	Wheeling Jesuit	73
81	Concord	66

80	Alderson-Broaddus ■	89
70	Glenville St. ■	77
79	Fairmont St.	85
83	West Liberty St. ■	88
82	Shepherd ■	56
87	Charleston (W.Va.)	79
77	Wheeling Jesuit ■	67
78	Davis & Elkins ■	68
87	Alderson-Broaddus †	74
81	Bluefield St. †	91

Nickname: Tigers
Colors: Green & White
Arena: T. Edward Davis Gymnasium
   Capacity: 1,500; Year Built: 1974
AD: Michael A. Carey
SID: Don Bordner

SALISBURY ST.
Salisbury, MD 21801 III

Coach: Ward Lambert
Alma Mater: Virginia '62
Record: 26 Years, W-367, L-317

1996-97 SCHEDULE
Lynchburg Inv.	Nov. 22-23
Washington (Md.) ■	Nov. 26
Catholic ■	Dec. 4
Salisbury Cl.	Dec. 6-7
York (Pa.) ■	Dec. 10
Chris. Newport	Dec. 14
Lebanon Valley Tr.	Jan. 10-11
Va. Wesleyan	Jan. 13
Gallaudet	Jan. 15
Goucher ■	Jan. 18
Marymount (Va.) ■	Jan. 22
Mary Washington	Jan. 25
Catholic	Jan. 29
St. Mary's (Md.) ■	Feb. 1
Gallaudet	Feb. 5
York (Pa.)	Feb. 8
Wesley	Feb. 10
Goucher	Feb. 12
Mary Washington ■	Feb. 15
Marymount (Va.)	Feb. 18
St. Mary's (Md.)	Feb. 22

1995-96 RESULTS (19-9)
83	Shenandoah	100
107	N.C. Wesleyan †	109
77	Va. Wesleyan ■	78
79	Chris. Newport ■	95
106	N.C. Wesleyan ■	85
108	Lincoln (Pa.) ■	95
112	Catholic ■	115
82	York (Pa.) ■	76
74	St. John Fisher †	92
139	Marywood †	90
94	Mary Washington ■	76
86	Goucher	99
99	Gallaudet ■	89
114	Marymount (Va.) ■	93
100	Catholic	96
83	Frostburg St.	109
102	St. Mary's (Md.) ■	97
112	Marymount (Va.)	82
80	York (Pa.)	72
118	Gallaudet	78
102	Wesley	88
122	Mary Washington	114
72	St. Mary's (Md.)	70
121	Goucher ■	102
97	Gallaudet ■	74
124	St. Mary's (Md.) ■	81
93	Marymount (Va.) ■	81
69	Frank. & Marsh.	118

Nickname: Sea Gulls
Colors: Maroon & Gold
Arena: Maggs Activities Center
   Capacity: 2,000; Year Built: 1977
AD: Michael Vienna
SID: Paul Ohanian

SALVE REGINA
Newport, RI 02904 III

Coach: Michael Raffa
Alma Mater: Barrington '68
Record: 17 Years, W-206, L-218

1996-97 SCHEDULE
Rivier Tr.	Nov. 23-24
WPI ■	Nov. 26
Endicott	Dec. 3
Rhode Island Col. ■	Dec. 9
Connecticut Col. ■	Dec. 11
Johnson & Wales ■	Dec. 14
Nichols	Jan. 16
Suffolk	Jan. 21
Curry ■	Jan. 23
Colby-Sawyer	Jan. 25
Wentworth Inst. ■	Jan. 27
Roger Williams	Jan. 29
Gordon ■	Feb. 1
Eastern Nazarene	Feb. 6
New England Col. ■	Feb. 8
Roger Williams ■	Feb. 10
Wentworth Inst.	Feb. 12
Anna Maria ■	Feb. 15
Curry	Feb. 20
Eastern Nazarene ■	Feb. 22

1995-96 RESULTS (6-17)
78	New England †	83
71	Rivier	80
59	WPI	84
71	Suffolk ■	57
76	Framingham St. †	77
93	Emerson-MCA	88
75	Connecticut Col.	82
72	Rhode Island Col.	89
79	Johnson & Wales	62
88	Curry	91
72	Colby-Sawyer ■	80
62	Wentworth Inst.	77
81	Roger Williams ■	89
75	Gordon	87
64	Eastern Nazarene ■	73
85	New England Col.	59
59	Roger Williams	60
73	Wentworth Inst. ■	62
80	Anna Maria	91
72	Nichols ■	78
69	Curry ■	67
64	Eastern Nazarene	84
78	Anna Maria	90

Nickname: Newporters
Colors: Blue, Green & White
Arena: Rogers Gymnasium
   Capacity: 4,000
AD: Lynn Sheedy
SID: Ed Habershaw

SAM HOUSTON ST.
Huntsville, TX 77341 I

Coach: Jerry Hopkins
Alma Mater: Tex. A&M-Kingsville '82
Record: 13 Years, W-151, L-207

1996-97 SCHEDULE
North Texas ■	Nov. 23
Oklahoma	Nov. 27
Northern Ariz.	Nov. 30
Arizona ■	Dec. 2
Ark.-Little Rock	Dec. 7
Eastern Wash. ■	Dec. 14
UTEP	Dec. 19
New Mexico	Dec. 21
Wichita St. Tr.	Dec. 27-28
Northwestern St. ■	Jan. 4
Texas-Arlington	Jan. 6
Stephen F. Austin ■	Jan. 11
Texas-San Antonio ■	Jan. 16
Southwest Tex. St.	Jan. 18
Nicholls St. ■	Jan. 23
McNeese St. ■	Jan. 25
Stephen F. Austin ■	Jan. 30

Northwestern St.	Feb. 6
Northeast La.	Feb. 8
Texas-Arlington ■	Feb. 13
Northeast La. ■	Feb. 18
McNeese St.	Feb. 20
Nicholls St.	Feb. 22
Texas-San Antonio	Feb. 27
Southwest Tex. St. ■	Mar. 1
Southland Conf. Tr.	Mar. 5-8

1995-96 RESULTS (11-16)
82	Baylor	79
89	Ark.-Little Rock ■	93
77	Concordia (Tex.) ■	80
79	Lamar	106
85	Northern Ariz. ■	74
73	East Tex. Bapt. ■	78
48	St. Louis	65
51	Memphis	74
75	Southwest Tex. St. ■	66
78	Texas-San Antonio ■	81
59	North Texas	71
81	Texas-Arlington	66
72	Stephen F. Austin ■	87
67	Northeast La.	70
65	McNeese St.	72
78	Nicholls St. ■	71
57	Southwest Tex. St.	64
88	Texas-Arlington ■	74
62	North Texas ■	64
77	Texas-San Antonio	88
65	Stephen F. Austin	74
70	Northwestern St.	69
94	Nicholls St. ■	85
70	McNeese St.	66
85	Northwestern St. ■	64
92	Northeast La. ■	86
58	Texas-San Antonio †	60

Nickname: Bearkats
Colors: Orange & White
Arena: Johnson Coliseum
   Capacity: 6,110; Year Built: 1976
AD: Ronnie Choate
SID: Paul Ridings

SAMFORD
Birmingham, AL 35229 I

Coach: John Brady
Alma Mater: Belhaven '76
Record: 5 Years, W-70, L-68

1996-97 SCHEDULE
Belhaven ■	Nov. 25
Southeast Mo. St. Cl.	Nov. 29-30
LSU	Dec. 2
Drake ■	Dec. 7
Northwestern St.	Dec. 14
Bethel (Tenn.) ■	Dec. 16
Eastern Ky.	Dec. 21
Utah St. Tr.	Dec. 27-28
Stetson	Jan. 2
Central Fla.	Jan. 4
Campbell	Jan. 9
Charleston (S.C.) ■	Jan. 11
Southeastern La. ■	Jan. 16
Centenary (La.) ■	Jan. 18
Georgia St.	Jan. 23
Mercer	Jan. 25
Jacksonville St.	Jan. 30
Florida Int'l ■	Feb. 1
Fla. Atlantic ■	Feb. 3
Jacksonville St. ■	Feb. 8
Centenary (La.)	Feb. 13
Southeastern La.	Feb. 15
Mercer ■	Feb. 20
Georgia St. ■	Feb. 22
Trans America Conf. Tr.	Feb. 27-Mar. 1

1995-96 RESULTS (16-11)
66	Tenn. Temple ■	47
78	Shorter	41
67	Austin Peay	63
64	Drake	77
60	N.C.-Asheville ■	68
70	Cal St. Northridge †	55

69	Nicholls St. †	53
59	Iowa St.	71
59	Tenn.-Chatt.	74
56	Stetson ■	54
92	Central Fla. ■	78
62	Campbell ■	58
50	Charleston (S.C.)	58
70	Southeastern La.	76
61	Centenary (La.) ■	57
76	Georgia St. ■	73
58	Mercer ■	63
79	Jacksonville St. ■	63
63	Florida Int'l	68
70	Fla. Atlantic	66
69	Austin Peay ■	85
65	Jacksonville St.	78
74	Centenary (La.) ■	63
91	Southeastern La. ■	80
78	Mercer	71
93	Georgia St.	72
55	Florida Int'l †	58

Nickname: Bulldogs
Colors: Red & Blue
Arena: Seibert Hall
   Capacity: 4,000; Year Built: 1957
AD: Steve Allgood
SID: Riley Adair

SAN DIEGO
San Diego, CA 92110 I

Coach: Brad Holland
Alma Mater: UCLA '79
Record: 4 Years, W-48, L-61

1996-97 SCHEDULE
Concordia (Cal.) ■	Nov. 24
San Jose St.	Nov. 26
Kansas	Dec. 1
Pacific (Cal.) ■	Dec. 5
San Diego St.	Dec. 8
Cal St. Fullerton ■	Dec. 10
Stanford ■	Dec. 14
Portland St. ■	Dec. 21
UC Irvine	Dec. 23
UC Santa Barb.	Dec. 30
Columbia ■	Jan. 2
Southern Utah	Jan. 4
Pepperdine	Jan. 10
Loyola Marymount	Jan. 11
Gonzaga ■	Jan. 16
Portland ■	Jan. 18
St. Mary's (Cal.)	Jan. 24
Santa Clara	Jan. 25
Santa Clara ■	Jan. 30
St. Mary's (Cal.) ■	Feb. 1
San Francisco	Feb. 5
San Francisco ■	Feb. 8
Portland	Feb. 13
Gonzaga	Feb. 15
Loyola Marymount ■	Feb. 20
Pepperdine ■	Feb. 22
West Coast Conf. Tr.	Mar. 1-3

1995-96 RESULTS (14-14)
84	Cal St. Sacramento	80
78	Pacific (Cal.)	80
82	Pomona-Pitzer ■	63
69	San Diego St.	65
73	UC Santa Barb. ■	76
71	Kansas ■	101
81	UC Irvine ■	78
66	Nevada	83
63	Notre Dame	90
67	Northern Ariz. ■	60
75	San Francisco ■	60
81	Pepperdine ■	70
56	Loyola Marymount ■	63
53	Gonzaga	60
64	Portland	78
72	Cal St. Northridge	56
41	San Francisco	52
62	St. Mary's (Cal.) ■	66
74	Santa Clara ■	64
52	Santa Clara	72

58	St. Mary's (Cal.)	62
76	Portland ■	68
59	Gonzaga ■	69
65	Loyola Marymount	59
80	Pepperdine	61
77	Cal Poly SLO ■	73
75	Loyola Marymount †	51
52	Portland †	65

Nickname: Toreros
Colors: Columbia Blue, Navy & White
Arena: USD Sports Center
 Capacity: 2,500; Year Built: 1963
AD: Tom Iannacone
SID: Ted Gosen

SAN DIEGO ST.
San Diego, CA 92182..............I

Coach: Fred Trenkle
Alma Mater: Idaho St. '70
Record: 2 Years, W-26, L-31

1996-97 SCHEDULE

UC Irvine ■	Nov. 22
Oregon	Nov. 26
Eastern Wash. ■	Nov. 30
Northwestern	Dec. 3
San Diego ■	Dec. 8
Southwest Tex. St.	Dec. 10
Loyola Marymount ■	Dec. 14
Southern Cal Col. ■	Dec. 20
Ohio St. ■	Dec. 23
Brigham Young	Dec. 31
UTEP ■	Jan. 4
UNLV	Jan. 9
Air Force ■	Jan. 11
Wyoming ■	Jan. 16
Colorado St. ■	Jan. 18
UTEP	Jan. 23
Hawaii ■	Jan. 25
Fresno St.	Jan. 30
San Jose St.	Feb. 1
Air Force	Feb. 6
UNLV ■	Feb. 8
Colorado St.	Feb. 13
Wyoming	Feb. 15
Hawaii	Feb. 19
Stanford	Feb. 24
San Jose St. ■	Feb. 27
Fresno St. ■	Mar. 1
Western Ath. Conf. Tr.	Mar. 4-8

1995-96 RESULTS (15-14)

83	Northwestern ■	63
62	Loyola Marymount	61
65	San Diego	69
83	Cal St. Fullerton ■	85
67	Cal Poly Pomona	48
79	Westmont ■	78
56	Ohio St.	72
87	Colorado St. ■	67
80	Wyoming ■	77
74	New Mexico	77
72	UTEP	71
83	Brigham Young ■	76
59	Utah ■	67
67	Fresno St.	79
77	Air Force	69
85	Cal St. Sacramento ■	55
79	Hawaii	88
80	Cal St. Northridge ■	47
103	Hawaii ■	94
89	Fresno St. ■	99
81	Air Force ■	72
68	Brigham Young	81
74	Utah	88
78	New Mexico ■	83
72	UTEP ■	69
74	Colorado St.	87
68	Wyoming	69
80	Air Force †	69
75	New Mexico	94

Nickname: Aztecs
Colors: Scarlet & Black
Arena: S.D. Sports Arena

Capacity: 13,741; Year Built: 1967
AD: Rick Bay
SID: John Rosenthal

SAN FRANCISCO
San Francisco, CA 94117..........I

Coach: Phil Mathews
Alma Mater: UC Irvine '72
Record: 1 Year, W-15, L-12

1996-97 SCHEDULE

Sonoma St. ■	Nov. 24
Arkansas	Nov. 30
Notre Dame (Cal.) ■ ■	Dec. 3
San Francisco Cl.	Dec. 6-7
San Jose St.	Dec. 11
UC Santa Barb.	Dec. 14
Southern U. ■	Dec. 20
California	Dec. 23
Seton Hall Tr.	Dec. 29-30
UC Irvine ■	Jan. 5
Loyola Marymount	Jan. 10
Pepperdine	Jan. 11
Portland ■	Jan. 16
Gonzaga ■	Jan. 18
Santa Clara	Jan. 24
St. Mary's (Cal.)	Jan. 25
St. Mary's (Cal.) ■	Jan. 30
Santa Clara	Feb. 1
San Diego ■	Feb. 5
San Diego	Feb. 8
Gonzaga	Feb. 13
Portland	Feb. 15
Pepperdine ■	Feb. 20
Loyola Marymount ■	Feb. 22
West Coast Conf. Tr.	Mar. 1-3

1995-96 RESULTS (15-12)

65	Bucknell ■	68
59	Stanford †	58
66	Eastern Wash. ■	48
70	Southwest Tex. St. ■	42
70	California †	83
78	St. John's (N.Y.)	80
66	Cal St. Hayward ■	40
72	Cal St. Fullerton ■	53
84	New Orleans	94
71	Jackson St. †	62
58	UCLA	92
85	Cal St. Stanislaus ■	70
66	San Diego	75
61	Loyola Marymount ■	57
56	Pepperdine ■	54
63	Portland	57
55	Gonzaga	60
52	San Diego ■	41
57	Santa Clara ■	70
73	St. Mary's (Cal.) ■	67
79	St. Mary's (Cal.)	75
41	Santa Clara	65
59	Gonzaga ■	73
66	Portland ■	43
63	Pepperdine	51
51	Loyola Marymount	71
72	Portland †	78

Nickname: Dons
Colors: Green & Gold
Arena: Memorial Gymnasium
 Capacity: 5,300; Year Built: 1958
AD: Bill Hogan
SID: Peter Simon

SAN FRAN. ST.
San Francisco, CA 94132........II

Coach: Charlie Thomas
Alma Mater: Virginia Tech '78
Record: 9 Years, W-111, L-139

1996-97 SCHEDULE

Cal St. San B'dino ■	Nov. 15
Bethany (Cal.) ■	Nov. 19
Patten ■	Nov. 23
Dominican (Cal.) ■	Nov. 25

Trevecca Nazarene ■	Nov. 27
Mary ■	Dec. 4
Holy Names ■	Dec. 10
Cal St. Los Angeles	Dec. 13
Cal St. Dom. Hills	Dec. 14
Westmont ■	Dec. 16
Menlo	Dec. 20
Minn.-Duluth ■	Dec. 22
Cal St. Stanislaus	Jan. 3
Cal St. Hayward ■	Jan. 4
Humboldt St. ■	Jan. 10
Sonoma St. ■	Jan. 11
Cal St. Chico	Jan. 17
UC Davis ■	Jan. 18
Notre Dame (Cal.) ■	Jan. 25
Cal St. Chico ■	Jan. 31
UC Davis	Feb. 1
Sonoma St.	Feb. 7
Humboldt St.	Feb. 8
Cal St. Stanislaus ■	Feb. 14
Cal St. Hayward	Feb. 15
Notre Dame (Cal.) ■	Feb. 20

1995-96 RESULTS (8-18)

44	Cal St. Bakersfield	105
65	Cal St. San B'dino ■	79
66	Biola	86
81	Patten ■	73
83	Dominican (Cal.) ■	86
61	Eastern Mich.	111
51	Toledo	67
97	Patten	74
70	Western Ore. ■	73
64	Menlo	65
64	Cal St. Stanislaus ■	68
64	Cal St. Hayward	84
50	Humboldt St.	61
79	Sonoma St.	78
88	Pacific Christian ■	52
69	Cal St. Chico	68
51	UC Davis	70
80	Notre Dame (Cal.) ■	71
62	Cal St. Chico	75
59	UC Davis	61
61	Sonoma St. ■	86
91	Humboldt St. ■	99
73	Cal St. Stanislaus	84
91	Cal St. Hayward ■	81
70	Master's ■	79
84	Notre Dame (Cal.)	83

Nickname: Gators
Colors: Purple & Gold
Arena: SFSU Main Gym
 Capacity: 2,000; Year Built: 1949
AD: Betsy Alden
SID: Kevin Gilmore

SAN JOSE ST.
San Jose, CA 95192 I

Coach: Stan Morrison
Alma Mater: California '62
Record: 21 Years, W-259, L-318

1996-97 SCHEDULE

St. Mary's (Cal.)	Nov. 24
San Diego ■	Nov. 26
Santa Clara [San Jose]	Dec. 1
Pepperdine	Dec. 3
Cal Poly Pomona ■	Dec. 9
San Francisco ■	Dec. 11
Portland	Dec. 14
Washington St.	Dec. 22
Santa Clara Cl.	Dec. 27-28
UNLV ■	Jan. 2
Tulsa ■	Jan. 4
Fresno St.	Jan. 11
Air Force ■	Jan. 16
Wyoming	Jan. 23
Colorado St.	Jan. 25
Hawaii ■	Jan. 30
San Diego St. ■	Feb. 1
Fresno St. ■	Feb. 6
Tulsa	Feb. 10
Air Force	Feb. 13

UNLV	Feb. 15
Colorado St. ■	Feb. 20
Wyoming ■	Feb. 22
San Diego St.	Feb. 27
Hawaii	Mar. 1
Western Ath. Conf. Tr.	Mar. 4-8

1995-96 RESULTS (13-17)

60	St. Mary's (Cal.) ■	61
51	Santa Clara ■	79
68	Fresno St.	92
64	Ball St. †	80
48	Southeast Mo. St. †	55
87	Portland ■	79
76	Pepperdine ■	80
74	Washington St. ■	90
88	Cal St. Fullerton ■	77
70	UC Irvine	78
74	New Mexico St. ■	60
66	UNLV ■	64
64	Nevada	83
58	Utah St.	60
60	Pacific (Cal.)	81
63	Long Beach St. ■	76
77	UC Santa Barb. ■	80
75	UNLV	84
73	New Mexico St.	74
68	Utah St. ■	65
96	Nevada ■	91
79	Pacific (Cal.) ■	73
69	UC Santa Barb.	66
86	Long Beach St.	105
81	UC Irvine ■	70
90	Cal St. Fullerton ■	80
77	Pacific (Cal.) †	57
71	UC Irvine †	67
76	Utah St. †	75
72	Kentucky †	110

Nickname: Spartans
Colors: Gold, White & Blue
Arena: The Event Center
 Capacity: 5,000; Year Built: 1989
AD: Thomas Brennan
SID: Lawrence Fan

SANTA CLARA
Santa Clara, CA 95053.............I

Coach: Dick Davey
Alma Mater: Pacific (Cal.) '64
Record: 4 Years, W-73, L-42

1996-97 SCHEDULE

Kansas ■	Nov. 22
Fresno St.	Nov. 26
Marquette ■	Nov. 29
San Jose St. [San Jose]	Dec. 1
San Francisco Cl.	Dec. 6-7
Indiana Cl.	Dec. 13-14
Eastern Wash.	Dec. 17
Pacific (Cal.)	Dec. 21
Santa Clara Cl.	Dec. 27-28
Gonzaga	Jan. 9
Portland	Jan. 11
St. Mary's (Cal.) ■	Jan. 15
St. Mary's (Cal.)	Jan. 18
San Francisco ■	Jan. 24
San Diego ■	Jan. 25
San Diego	Jan. 30
San Francisco	Feb. 1
Loyola Marymount ■	Feb. 7
Pepperdine ■	Feb. 9
Pepperdine	Feb. 14
Loyola Marymount	Feb. 15
Portland ■	Feb. 21
Gonzaga ■	Feb. 22
West Coast Conf. Tr.	Mar. 1-3

1995-96 RESULTS (20-9)

78	UCLA †	69
65	Villanova †	77
77	Michigan St. †	71
50	Oregon St. †	45
79	San Jose St.	51
98	Southern U. ■	59
66	Fresno St. ■	58

49	Marquette	78
80	Illinois St.	78
75	Pacific (Cal.) ■	70
49	Penn St. †	70
71	Georgia Tech †	66
72	Gonzaga ■	61
86	Portland ■	66
62	Loyola Marymount	71
87	Pepperdine	76
69	Pepperdine ■	72
78	Loyola Marymount ■	60
70	San Francisco	57
64	San Diego	74
72	San Diego ■	52
65	San Francisco ■	41
79	St. Mary's (Cal.)	64
64	St. Mary's (Cal.) ■	61
71	Portland	80
77	Gonzaga	71
60	Pepperdine ■	63
91	Maryland †	79
51	Kansas †	76

Nickname: Broncos
Colors: Bronco Red & White
Arena: Toso Pavilion
  Capacity: 5,000; Year Built: 1975
AD: Carroll Williams
SID: Jim Young

SAVANNAH A&D
Savannah, GA 31402 III

Coach: Ron Gerlufsen
Alma Mater: East Stroudsburg '72
Record: 13 Years, W-160, L-197

1996-97 SCHEDULE
Schedule unavailable

1995-96 RESULTS (11-13)

80	Sewanee	89
63	Emory & Henry †	75
72	Wash. & Lee ■	64
59	Emory	75
57	Methodist ■	81
75	Aurora †	83
56	Chicago	69
76	Oglethorpe	64
68	Swarthmore	63
65	Rhodes	83
70	Methodist ■	75
71	Amherst ■	81
91	Oglethorpe ■	78
71	Chowan ■	67
65	Rensselaer	71
90	Fisk ■	85
63	Maryville (Tenn.) ■	70
72	Warren Wilson ■	51
95	Fisk	55
55	Maryville (Tenn.)	79
81	Emory ■	62

Nickname: Bees
Colors: Black, White & Gold
Arena: Savannah Civic Center
  Capacity: 7,500; Year Built: 1974
AD: Karen A. Ryan
SID: To be named

SAVANNAH ST.
Savannah, GA 31404 II

Coach: Jimmie Westley
Alma Mater: Savannah St. '72
Record: 3 Years, W-42, L-37

1996-97 SCHEDULE

Morehouse	Nov. 16
Ga. Southwestern ■	Nov. 19
Armstrong Atlantic	Nov. 23
Fla. Memorial	Nov. 26
South Caro. St.	Nov. 30
North Fla. ■	Dec. 2

Kentucky St.	Dec. 7
Fort Valley St.	Jan. 4
LeMoyne-Owen ■	Jan. 6
Albany St. (Ga.) ■	Jan. 8
Claflin	Jan. 10
Fort Valley St. ■	Jan. 15
Clark Atlanta	Jan. 18
Miles	Jan. 20
Clark Atlanta ■	Jan. 25
Morris Brown	Jan. 27
Albany St. (Ga.)	Jan. 29
Paine	Jan. 31
Miles ■	Feb. 1
Edward Waters ■	Feb. 3
Paine	Feb. 5
Alabama A&M	Feb. 8
North Fla.	Feb. 10
Morris Brown ■	Feb. 15
Ga. Southwestern ■	Feb. 17
Tuskegee	Feb. 19
Edward Waters	Feb. 22

1995-96 RESULTS (13-14)

67	Fla. Memorial ■	64
49	Armstrong Atlantic †	59
79	Georgia Col.	97
63	North Fla.	75
88	Kentucky St. ■	75
76	Georgia Col. ■	80
88	Fort Valley St.	80
79	Alabama A&M ■	93
76	Albany St. (Ga.) ■	69
69	Morehouse	74
57	Fort Valley St.	66
73	Clark Atlanta ■	85
74	Miles ■	70
78	Clark Atlanta	67
78	Morris Brown	70
91	Paine	70
34	Paine ■	32
95	Albany St. (Ga.)	100
84	Alabama A&M	92
106	LeMoyne-Owen	107
74	Miles	99
62	Morris Brown ■	70
79	Tuskegee ■	76
75	Johnson Smith ■	72
65	North Fla. ■	63
96	Shaw ■	92
64	Paine †	67

Nickname: Tigers
Colors: Blue & Orange
Arena: Wiley Gym
  Capacity: 2,100; Year Built: 1964
AD: Hornsby Howell
SID: Lee Pearson

SCRANTON
Scranton, PA 18510 III

Coach: Bob Bessoir
Alma Mater: Scranton '55
Record: 24 Years, W-472, L-210

1996-97 SCHEDULE

Misericordia Tr.	Nov. 22-23
Binghamton ■	Nov. 26
Delaware Valley	Dec. 4
Catholic ■	Dec. 7
Susquehanna ■	Dec. 9
FDU-Madison ■	Dec. 11
Otterbein Tr.	Dec. 28-29
Albright Tr.	Jan. 3-4
Moravian ■	Jan. 8
Nova Southeastern	Jan. 13
Lycoming	Jan. 15
King's (Pa.) ■	Jan. 18
Wilkes	Jan. 25
Delaware Valley ■	Jan. 29
Drew	Feb. 1
FDU-Madison	Feb. 5
Elizabethtown ■	Feb. 8
Lycoming	Feb. 12
King's (Pa.)	Feb. 15
Drew ■	Feb. 17
Wilkes ■	Feb. 22

1995-96 RESULTS (10-15)

93	Marywood ■	71
69	Misericordia ■	73
60	Drew	63
75	Stony Brook ■	70
63	Binghamton ■	56
90	Delaware Valley ■	59
45	Westminster (Pa.) †	75
85	Point Park †	88
51	FDU-Madison	42
65	Catholic	74
62	Frank. & Marsh. †	75
81	Lycoming	88
84	King's (Pa.) ■	66
43	Bloomsburg	73
72	Wilkes ■	89
58	Moravian	72
64	Delaware Valley	57
66	Drew ■	69
77	FDU-Madison ■	74
92	Elizabethtown	80
76	Lycoming ■	85
80	King's (Pa.) ■	61
73	Wilkes	94
70	Albright	74
81	Susquehanna	92

Nickname: Royals
Colors: Purple & White
Arena: John Long Center
  Capacity: 2,800; Year Built: 1968
AD: Gary Wodder
SID: Kenneth Buntz

SEATTLE PACIFIC
Seattle, WA 98119 II

Coach: Ken Bone
Alma Mater: Seattle Pacific '83
Record: 7 Years, W-126, L-73

1996-97 SCHEDULE

Central Wash. ■	Nov. 16
Seattle ■	Nov. 19
Central Wash.	Nov. 23
Seattle Pacific Cl.	Nov. 29-30
Western Wash. ■	Dec. 7
Cal St. Chico	Dec. 13
UC Davis	Dec. 18
Seattle Pacific Cl.	Dec. 27-28
Western Wash.	Jan. 4
Alas. Anchorage	Jan. 9
Alas. Fairbanks ■	Jan. 11
Hawaii-Hilo	Jan. 16
Chaminade	Jan. 18
Western N.M.	Jan. 23
Mont. St.-Billings	Jan. 25
Puget Sound ■	Jan. 27
Alas. Fairbanks	Jan. 30
Alas. Anchorage	Feb. 1
Willamette ■	Feb. 8
Hawaii-Hilo ■	Feb. 13
Chaminade ■	Feb. 17
Seattle	Feb. 20
Northwest Col. ■	Feb. 24
Mont. St.-Billings ■	Feb. 27
Western N.M. ■	Mar. 1

1995-96 RESULTS (23-6)

72	Central Wash. ■	61
92	Fort Lewis ■	74
89	Mo. Western St. ■	71
63	Puget Sound	54
61	Cal St. Chico ■	60
52	Western Wash.	56
88	Humboldt St.	74
75	Sonoma St.	68
68	Seattle	53
70	Truman St. ■	60
68	Mo.-Rolla ■	81
60	Western Wash. ■	55
101	Whitman ■	45
85	Chaminade ■	40
99	Hawaii-Hilo ■	49
54	Alas. Anchorage	83
88	Alas. Fairbanks	76
76	Seattle ■	72

100	Western N.M. ■	57
75	Chaminade	48
59	Hawaii-Hilo	45
84	Northwest Col. ■	74
81	Mont. St.-Billings ■	66
51	Western N.M.	64
86	Mont. St.-Billings	91
84	Alas. Fairbanks ■	67
90	Alas. Anchorage ■	74
79	UC Davis †	65
65	Cal St. Bakersfield	78

Nickname: Falcons
Colors: Maroon & White
Arena: Royal Brougham Pavilion
  Capacity: 2,650; Year Built: 1953
AD: Alan Graham
SID: Frank MacDonald

SETON HALL
South Orange, NJ 07079 I

Coach: George Blaney
Alma Mater: Holy Cross '61
Record: 29 Years, W-449, L-364

1996-97 SCHEDULE

NIT	Nov. 20-29
Georgetown	Dec. 2
Fordham ■	Dec. 6
Pittsburgh ■	Dec. 8
St. Peter's ■	Dec. 10
Northwestern	Dec. 14
Stanford ■	Dec. 22
Wagner ■	Dec. 23
Seton Hall Tr.	Dec. 29-30
Villanova	Jan. 2
Boston College ■	Jan. 4
West Va.	Jan. 8
Providence ■	Jan. 11
Syracuse ■	Jan. 15
Florida St. ■	Jan. 18
Notre Dame ■	Jan. 22
Rutgers	Jan. 26
Syracuse	Jan. 29
Connecticut ■	Feb. 1
Pittsburgh	Feb. 8
Miami (Fla.)	Feb. 10
Boston College	Feb. 15
Notre Dame	Feb. 18
West Va. ■	Feb. 22
St. John's (N.Y.) ■	Feb. 26
Connecticut	Mar. 1
Big East Conf. Tr.	Mar. 5-8

1995-96 RESULTS (12-16)

83	Monmouth (N.J.) ■	67
70	Miami (Fla.)	80
79	Providence ■	72
85	Northwestern ■	70
59	St. Peter's ■	61
96	Ohio St.	105
76	Purdue ■	78
93	New Hampshire ■	74
81	St. Joseph's (Pa.) ■	74
82	Providence	77
76	Georgetown	85
66	Miami (Fla.) ■	63
80	Boston College	83
78	Villanova ■	73
62	Georgetown ■	82
82	St. John's (N.Y.)	76
81	Rutgers ■	75
69	Pittsburgh ■	75
60	Stanford †	83
61	Rutgers	70
59	West Va. ■	79
67	Villanova	79
73	St. John's (N.Y.) ■	78
80	Syracuse ■	79
60	Notre Dame	79
58	Connecticut	87
80	West Va. †	78
58	Connecticut †	79

Nickname: Pirates
Colors: Blue & White

Arena: Continental Airlines Arena
  Capacity: 20,029; Year Built: 1981
AD: Larry Keating
SID: John Wooding

SEWANEE
Sewanee, TN 37375..............III

Coach: Joe Thoni
Alma Mater: Sewanee '79
Record: 4 Years, W-60, L-40

1996-97 SCHEDULE
Sewanee Cl. ....Nov. 22-23
Fisk ....Nov. 26
Otterbein ■ ....Dec. 3
Davidson ....Dec. 7
Franklin...................................Dec. 19
Haverford ■ ....Jan. 4
Emory ....Jan. 6
Millsaps ■ ....Jan. 10
Oglethorpe ■ ....Jan. 12
Trinity (Tex.) ■ ....Jan. 17
Southwestern (Tex.) ■ ....Jan. 19
Rhodes ....Jan. 24
Hendrix ....Jan. 26
Trinity (Tex.) ....Jan. 31
Southwestern (Tex.) ....Feb. 2
Rhodes ■ ....Feb. 7
Hendrix ■ ....Feb. 9
Maryville (Tenn.) ....Feb. 13
Centre ■ ....Feb. 16
Millsaps ....Feb. 21
Oglethorpe ....Feb. 23
Fisk ■ ....Feb. 26
Centre ....Mar. 1

1995-96 RESULTS (18-7)
89	Savannah A&D ■	80
72	Wabash ■	66
109	Fisk	67
79	Marian (Ind.) †	65
70	Rose-Hulman	87
101	Fisk ■	71
71	UC San Diego	83
90	Redlands †	68
75	Centre	93
85	Southwestern (Tex.) ■	65
71	Trinity (Tex.) ■	84
83	Emory ■	65
67	Oglethorpe	58
85	Millsaps ■	102
78	Hendrix	70
69	Rhodes	82
69	Maryville (Tenn.) ■	62
85	Oglethorpe ■	67
67	Millsaps	85
87	Hendrix ■	76
81	Rhodes ■	77
81	Southwestern (Tex.)	63
62	Trinity (Tex.)	49
93	Emory	70
91	Centre ■	72

Nickname: Tigers
Colors: Purple & White
Arena: Juhan Gymnasium
  Capacity: 1,000; Year Built: 1955
AD: Mark Webb
SID: Larry Dagenhart

SHENANDOAH
Winchester, VA 22601 III

Coach: Dave Dutton
Alma Mater: James Madison '78
Record: 8 Years, W-117, L-97

1996-97 SCHEDULE
Shepherd ....Nov. 26
Frostburg St. ....Dec. 2
Bridgewater (Va.) Tr. ....Dec. 6-7
Marymount (Va.) ■ ....Dec. 14
Frostburg St. ....Dec. 15
Bahamas Shootout ....Dec. 19-22
Mary Washington ■ ....Jan. 13

Chris. Newport ■ ....Jan. 18
N.C. Wesleyan ■ ....Jan. 19
Chowan ■ ....Jan. 21
Methodist ■ ....Jan. 25
Greensboro ■ ....Jan. 26
Ferrum ■ ....Jan. 30
Averett ■ ....Feb. 1
Chris. Newport ....Feb. 8
N.C. Wesleyan ....Feb. 9
Methodist ....Feb. 12
Greensboro ■ ....Feb. 15
Mary Washington ....Feb. 18
Ferrum ....Feb. 21
Averett ....Feb. 22

1995-96 RESULTS (18-9)
100	Salisbury St. ■	83
82	Bridgewater (Va.) ■	81
102	Shepherd ■	120
107	Shepherd ■	104
101	Frostburg St.	105
90	Lynchburg ■	79
81	Frostburg St. ■	68
71	Newport News App. ■	70
90	Chowan	93
105	N.C. Wesleyan ■	65
81	Chris. Newport	90
86	Greensboro ■	81
92	Methodist ■	107
98	Mary Washington ■	94
106	Ferrum ■	97
84	Averett	73
81	Chowan ■	86
103	N.C. Wesleyan ■	84
97	Chris. Newport ■	94
93	Mary Washington	73
94	Greensboro	81
67	Methodist	86
95	Ferrum ■	93
116	Averett ■	90
81	Methodist ■	66
93	Chris. Newport ■	103
110	Roanoke	128

Nickname: Hornets
Colors: Red, White & Blue
Arena: Shingleton Gymnasium
  Capacity: 680; Year Built: 1969
AD: Dave Dutton
SID: Scott Musa

SHEPHERD
Shepherdstown, WV 25443 II

Coach: Denny Alexander
Alma Mater: Aquinas '67
Record: 15 Years, W-251, L-179

1996-97 SCHEDULE
Pitt.-Johnstown ....Nov. 23
Shenandoah ■ ....Nov. 26
West Liberty St. ■ ....Nov. 30
Wheeling Jesuit ■ ....Dec. 4
Shippensburg Tr. ....Dec. 6-7
Columbia Union ■ ....Dec. 16
Pitt.-Johnstown ■ ....Jan. 4
Charleston (W.Va.) ....Jan. 9
Glenville St. ....Jan. 11
West Va. St. ■ ....Jan. 13
West Va. Tech ....Jan. 15
West Va. Wesleyan ....Jan. 18
Fairmont St. ■ ....Jan. 22
Salem-Teikyo ■ ....Jan. 25
Alderson-Broaddus ■ ....Jan. 27
Davis & Elkins ■ ....Jan. 29
Bluefield St. ■ ....Feb. 1
West Liberty St. ....Feb. 3
Wheeling Jesuit ....Feb. 5
Concord ■ ....Feb. 8
Columbia Union ....Feb. 12
Fairmont St. ....Feb. 15
Salem-Teikyo ....Feb. 17
Alderson-Broaddus ....Feb. 19
Davis & Elkins ....Feb. 22

1995-96 RESULTS (8-19)
82	Shippensburg ■	83

120	Shenandoah ■	102
104	Shenandoah	107
82	Adelphi †	94
87	Slippery Rock †	79
78	Columbia Union ■	88
84	Wheeling Jesuit	90
73	West Liberty St.	76
77	West Va. St.	95
76	West Va. Tech	85
74	West Va. Wesleyan ■	64
84	Charleston (W.Va.) ■	94
61	Fairmont St.	90
47	Salem-Teikyo ■	61
88	Alderson-Broaddus ■	108
113	Davis & Elkins ■	84
51	Glenville St. ■	62
74	Wheeling Jesuit ■	81
71	Concord ■	73
63	West Liberty St. ■	62
49	Columbia Union	65
94	Bluefield St. ■	82
72	Fairmont St. ■	71
56	Salem-Teikyo	82
73	Alderson-Broaddus ■	85
73	Davis & Elkins	72
70	Alderson-Broaddus	85

Nickname: Rams
Colors: Blue & Gold
Arena: Butcher Athletic Center
  Capacity: 3,500; Year Built: 1989
AD: Monte Cater
SID: Ernie Larossa

SHIPPENSBURG
Shippensburg, PA 17257 II

Coach: Rodger Goodling
Alma Mater: Lock Haven '59
Record: 26 Years, W-310, L-359

1996-97 SCHEDULE
Fairmont St. Cl. ....Nov. 15-16
Mansfield ■ ....Nov. 20
Kutztown ....Nov. 23
James Madison ....Nov. 25
West Chester ....Dec. 3
Shippensburg Tr. ....Dec. 6-7
Bentley Festival ....Dec. 28-29
Kutztown ■ ....Jan. 4
Mansfield ....Jan. 6
Pitt.-Johnstown ....Jan. 8
Slippery Rock ....Jan. 11
Lock Haven ■ ....Jan. 15
Edinboro ....Jan. 18
Calif. (Pa.) ■ ....Jan. 22
Clarion ....Jan. 25
Indiana (Pa.) ■ ....Jan. 29
Slippery Rock ■ ....Feb. 1
Columbia Union ■ ....Feb. 5
Edinboro ■ ....Feb. 8
Lock Haven ....Feb. 12
Calif. (Pa.) ....Feb. 15
Indiana (Pa.) ■ ....Feb. 19
Clarion ■ ....Feb. 22

1995-96 RESULTS (12-13)
83	Shepherd	82
83	Kutztown ■	63
93	Pitt.-Johnstown ■	97
66	Bloomsburg	76
91	La Roche ■	77
83	Mansfield ■	69
83	West Chester ■	68
75	Bloomsburg ■	93
72	Barry	91
80	Lynn	83
81	St. Vincent ■	63
96	Susquehanna †	94
94	Dickinson	72
82	Indiana (Pa.) ■	90
97	Clarion	77
67	Calif. (Pa.)	92
83	Edinboro ■	94
83	Lock Haven	88

86	Slippery Rock ■	69
84	Clarion ■	79
80	Indiana (Pa.)	81
63	Calif. (Pa.)	73
85	Lock Haven ■	72
69	Edinboro	96
82	Slippery Rock	94

Nickname: Red Raiders
Colors: Red & Blue
Arena: Heiges Field House
  Capacity: 2,782; Year Built: 1970
AD: James Pribula
SID: John R. Alosi

SIENA
Loudonville, NY 12211 I

Coach: Bob Beyer
Alma Mater: Alfred '84
Record: 2 Years, W-13, L-41

1996-97 SCHEDULE
Rhode Island ■ ....Nov. 23
Rider ....Nov. 30
Iowa St. Challenge....................Dec. 5-6
Hartford ....Dec. 10
Marist [Albany] ....Dec. 22
Wagner ....Dec. 30
St. Peter's ....Jan. 2
Colgate ■ ....Jan. 4
Holy Cross ....Jan. 8
Iona ■ ....Jan. 12
Loyola (Md.) ....Jan. 15
Youngstown St. ....Jan. 18
Fairfield ■ ....Jan. 20
Yale ....Jan. 23
Fairfield ....Jan. 26
St. Peter's ■ ....Jan. 29
Niagara ....Jan. 31
Canisius ■ ....Feb. 2
Davidson ....Feb. 6
Manhattan ■ ....Feb. 10
Niagara ■ ....Feb. 13
Canisius ....Feb. 15
Loyola (Md.) ■ ....Feb. 18
Manhattan ....Feb. 21
Iona ....Feb. 23
Metro Atlantic Conf. Tr.............Mar. 1-3

1995-96 RESULTS (5-22)
70	UC Irvine †	87
51	Niagara †	68
74	Bethune-Cookman ■	69
58	Rhode Island	98
47	Marist ■	49
69	Kent ■	59
76	Hartford	70
76	Jacksonville ■	89
66	Wagner ■	80
53	Rider ■	73
83	Holy Cross ■	78
77	Loyola (Md.) ■	62
50	Niagara ■	52
47	Fairfield ■	60
40	Manhattan	61
51	St. Peter's ■	68
59	Iona	70
84	Colgate	101
55	Canisius ■	60
74	St. Peter's	88
64	Manhattan ■	66
49	Canisius	66
77	Niagara	79
62	Iona ■	66
57	Fairfield	66
53	Loyola (Md.)	67
59	Iona †	71

Nickname: Saints
Colors: Green & Gold
Arena: Knickerbocker Arena
  Capacity: 15,500; Year Built: 1974
AD: John D'Argenio
SID: Michael Hogan

SCHEDULES/RESULTS

SIMPSON
Indianola, IA 50125 III

Coach: Bruce Wilson
Alma Mater: Simpson '76
Record: 11 Years, W-157, L-128

1996-97 SCHEDULE
Grinnell ■	Nov. 26
Maryville (Mo.) Cl.	Nov. 29-30
Midland Lutheran	Dec. 3
Neb. Wesleyan ■	Dec. 7
Mt. Mercy	Dec. 13
Grand View ■	Dec. 14
Cornell College Tr.	Jan. 3-4
William Penn	Jan. 10
Wartburg	Jan. 11
Upper Iowa ■	Jan. 17
Dubuque ■	Jan. 18
Central (Iowa)	Jan. 24
Luther	Jan. 25
Buena Vista	Jan. 31
Dubuque	Feb. 1
Wartburg ■	Feb. 4
Loras	Feb. 7
Luther	Feb. 8
William Penn ■	Feb. 14
Loras ■	Feb. 15
Central (Iowa)	Feb. 21
Upper Iowa	Feb. 22
Buena Vista ■	Feb. 25

1995-96 RESULTS (20-6)
97	Neb. Wesleyan ■	83
157	Grinnell ■	137
65	Grand View	63
111	Midland Lutheran ■	88
105	Cornell College ■	91
85	Mt. Mercy ■	83
89	Whittier	91
77	Occidental	83
88	Central (Iowa)	77
67	Upper Iowa	78
79	Loras	69
87	Wartburg ■	86
104	Iowa Wesleyan	85
106	Dubuque ■	79
113	William Penn	82
98	Luther	87
90	Loras	81
90	Buena Vista ■	79
87	Central (Iowa) ■	90
107	Wartburg	93
72	Upper Iowa ■	73
97	Luther ■	82
122	William Penn ■	76
120	Buena Vista	112
96	Dubuque	78
74	Wis.-Oshkosh	79

Nickname: Storm
Colors: Red & Gold
Arena: Cowles Fieldhouse
 Capacity: 2,000; Year Built: 1976
AD: John Sirianni
SID: Vicki Klinge

SKIDMORE
Saratoga, NY 12866 III

Coach: John Quattrocchi
Alma Mater: Albany (N.Y.) '73
Record: 12 Years, W-144, L-156

1996-97 SCHEDULE
Skidmore Inv.	Nov. 22-23
Hartwick ■	Nov. 26
Middlebury	Dec. 3
Hobart	Dec. 6
Hamilton	Dec. 7
Trinity (Conn.) ■	Dec. 10
Green Mountain ■	Dec. 13
Albany (N.Y.)	Jan. 6
Williams	Jan. 15
Bowdoin	Jan. 18
Bates	Jan. 19

Union (N.Y.) ■	Jan. 25
Rensselaer	Jan. 28
St. Lawrence ■	Jan. 31
Clarkson ■	Feb. 1
Hobart ■	Feb. 7
Vassar ■	Feb. 8
Hamilton ■	Feb. 11
Clarkson	Feb. 14
St. Lawrence	Feb. 15
Utica ■	Feb. 18
Union (N.Y.)	Feb. 21
Rensselaer ■	Feb. 25
Amherst ■	Mar. 1

1995-96 RESULTS (12-13)
81	Oswego St. ■	60
61	Keuka ■	60
72	Hartwick	79
64	Clarkson ■	56
58	St. Lawrence ■	65
67	Trinity (Conn.)	72
83	Hobart	76
80	Union (N.Y.)	84
45	Wis.-Eau Claire †	78
66	Carroll (Wis.) †	76
72	Williams ■	114
88	Bates ■	74
57	Colby ■	54
76	Hamilton ■	92
71	St. Lawrence	79
77	Clarkson	66
80	Middlebury ■	74
93	Vassar	81
68	Hamilton	66
80	Rensselaer ■	86
65	Utica	56
78	Union (N.Y.) ■	49
72	Hobart ■	74
62	Rensselaer	84
85	Amherst ■	97

Nickname: Thoroughbreds
Colors: Green, White & Gold
Arena: Sports & Recreation Center
 Capacity: 1,500; Year Built: 1982
AD: Timothy Brown
SID: Bill Jones

SLIPPERY ROCK
Slippery Rock, PA 16057 II

Coach: Anthony Jones
Alma Mater: Illinois St. '81
Record: 1 Year, W-2, L-24

1996-97 SCHEDULE
Point Park ■	Nov. 16
Glenville St. ■	Nov. 19
Westminster Cl.	Nov. 22-23
St. Vincent ■	Nov. 26
Mercyhurst Cl.	Nov. 29-30
Westminster (Pa.)	Dec. 3
Pitt.-Greensburg ■	Dec. 7
Mansfield	Dec. 21
Lake Erie ■	Jan. 4
Edinboro ■	Jan. 8
Shippensburg ■	Jan. 11
Lake Erie	Jan. 13
Clarion	Jan. 15
Pitt.-Johnstown	Jan. 18
Indiana (Pa.)	Jan. 22
Lock Haven	Jan. 25
Calif. (Pa.) ■	Jan. 29
Shippensburg	Feb. 1
Edinboro	Feb. 5
Pitt.-Johnstown ■	Feb. 8
Clarion ■	Feb. 12
Indiana (Pa.) ■	Feb. 15
Calif. (Pa.)	Feb. 19
Lock Haven ■	Feb. 22

1995-96 RESULTS (2-24)
38	Bowie St. †	75
64	Wilmington (Del.)	71
61	Westminster (Pa.) ■	63
50	Millersville †	84

67	Gannon	79
74	St. Vincent	62
68	Millersville	101
79	Shepherd †	87
58	Akron	82
44	Gannon	60
63	Mansfield ■	66
48	Calif. (Pa.)	66
74	Lock Haven ■	78
68	Mansfield	86
55	Indiana (Pa.)	91
69	Pitt.-Johnstown ■	74
70	Clarion ■	88
69	Shippensburg	86
40	Edinboro	91
69	Lock Haven	78
62	Calif. (Pa.) ■	90
51	Indiana (Pa.)	80
61	Clarion	75
78	Pitt.-Johnstown	85
82	Edinboro ■	89
94	Shippensburg ■	82

Nickname: Rockets, The Rock
Colors: Green & White
Arena: Morrow Field House
 Capacity: 3,000; Year Built: 1962
AD: Paul Lueken
SID: John Carpenter

SONOMA ST.
Rohnert Park, CA 94928 II

Coach: Pat Fuscaldo
Alma Mater: San Fran. St. '83
Record: 5 Years, W-54, L-76

1996-97 SCHEDULE
Cal St. San B'dino ■	Nov. 16
Holy Names ■	Nov. 20
San Francisco	Nov. 24
Fresno Pacific	Nov. 27
Dominican (Cal.)	Dec. 2
UC Riverside	Dec. 7
Cal St. Bakersfield	Dec. 14
Cal St. Los Angeles ■	Dec. 23
Chico St. Tr.	Dec. 28-30
UC Davis	Jan. 3
Cal St. Chico ■	Jan. 4
Cal St. Hayward ■	Jan. 8
Notre Dame (Cal.)	Jan. 10
San Fran. St.	Jan. 11
Cal St. Stanislaus	Jan. 17
Humboldt St. ■	Jan. 25
Cal St. Hayward	Jan. 31
Cal St. Stanislaus	Feb. 1
San Fran. St. ■	Feb. 7
Notre Dame (Cal.) ■	Feb. 8
Cal St. Chico	Feb. 14
UC Davis ■	Feb. 15
Humboldt St.	Feb. 20

1995-96 RESULTS (15-13)
71	Westmont	74
84	Dominican (Cal.) ■	73
66	Loyola Marymount	85
66	Cal St. San B'dino	63
69	UC Riverside	84
62	Cal St. Bakersfield ■	67
60	Cal Poly Pomona ■	73
68	Seattle Pacific ■	75
76	Fresno Pacific ■	62
66	Master's †	87
79	Western N.M. †	63
61	Cal Poly Pomona †	83
66	UC Davis	67
89	Cal St. Chico	94
85	Notre Dame (Cal.) ■	67
78	San Fran. St. ■	79
79	Cal St. Stanislaus	70
81	Cal St. Hayward	72
74	Humboldt St.	71
74	Cal St. Hayward ■	64
82	Cal St. Stanislaus ■	65
86	San Fran. St.	61

99	Notre Dame (Cal.)	78
85	Cal St. Chico	78
68	UC Davis ■	80
67	Humboldt St. ■	53
74	Humboldt St. ■	58
67	UC Davis	75

Nickname: Cossacks
Colors: Columbian Blue, Navy & White
Arena: Cossack Gymnasium
 Capacity: 1,800; Year Built: 1968
AD: Ralph Barkey
SID: Mitch Cox

SOUTH ALA.
Mobile, AL 36688 I

Coach: Bill Musselman
Alma Mater: Wittenberg '62
Record: 11 Years, W-209, L-78

1996-97 SCHEDULE
Abilene Christian ■	Nov. 23
West Fla. ■	Nov. 26
Grambling ■	Nov. 29
Southern Miss. ■	Dec. 3
Florida A&M	Dec. 7
UAB ■	Dec. 10
Auburn	Dec. 18
Nicholls St. ■	Dec. 21
Southwestern La. ■	Dec. 28
Ark.-Little Rock ■	Jan. 2
Arkansas St. ■	Jan. 4
Tex.-Pan American ■	Jan. 9
Lamar	Jan. 11
Jacksonville	Jan. 18
Western Ky. ■	Jan. 18
New Orleans ■	Jan. 20
Ark.-Little Rock	Jan. 23
Arkansas St.	Jan. 25
New Orleans	Jan. 30
Tex.-Pan American ■	Feb. 1
Louisiana Tech ■	Feb. 3
Lamar ■	Feb. 13
Jacksonville ■	Feb. 15
Louisiana Tech	Feb. 20
Western Ky. ■	Feb. 22
Southwestern La.	Feb. 24
Sun Belt Conf. Tr.	Feb. 28-Mar. 4

1995-96 RESULTS (12-15)
74	Abilene Christian ■	64
72	Southern-N.O. ■	61
39	UAB	41
50	Auburn ■	59
53	Jacksonville	65
70	Troy St. ■	43
66	Southern Miss. ■	50
43	Gonzaga †	60
67	Lehigh †	55
63	Southwestern La. ■	43
62	Tex.-Pan American ■	35
51	Lamar	59
64	Western Ky.	75
55	Arkansas St. ■	52
45	Louisiana Tech ■	46
38	Tex.-Pan American	57
80	Jacksonville ■	76
60	Ark.-Little Rock	65
55	New Orleans ■	54
48	Southwestern La.	65
41	Louisiana Tech	47
70	Lamar ■	68
54	Arkansas St.	62
50	New Orleans	72
49	Ark.-Little Rock ■	61
92	Western Ky. ■	78
48	Tex.-Pan American †	61

Nickname: Jaguars
Colors: Red, White & Blue
Arena: Jaguar Gym
 Capacity: 3,138; Year Built: 1970
AD: Joe Gottfried
SID: Mike Nicholson

SOUTH CARO.

Columbia, SC 29208 I

Coach: Eddie Fogler
Alma Mater: North Caro. '70
Record: 10 Years, W-180, L-128

1996-97 SCHEDULE

Maui Inv.		Nov. 25-27
Wofford ■		Dec. 2
Charlotte Inv.		Dec. 6-7
Clemson ■		Dec. 17
N.C.-Asheville ■		Dec. 19
South Caro. St. ■		Dec. 21
Charleston So. ■		Dec. 28
Furman ■		Dec. 30
Auburn ■		Jan. 4
Tennessee ■		Jan. 8
Mississippi St.		Jan. 11
Florida		Jan. 15
Georgia ■		Jan. 18
Alabama ■		Jan. 22
Mississippi		Jan. 25
Vanderbilt		Jan. 29
LSU		Feb. 1
Kentucky ■		Feb. 4
Florida ■		Feb. 8
Georgia		Feb. 12
Cincinnati		Feb. 15
Arkansas ■		Feb. 18
Citadel		Feb. 20
Tennessee		Feb. 22
Vanderbilt ■		Feb. 26
Kentucky		Mar. 2
Southeastern Conf. Tr.		Mar. 6-9

1995-96 RESULTS (19-12)

82	N.C.-Greensboro ■	64
92	South Caro. St. ■	70
70	Stanford †	82
80	Tulane †	75
99	Furman ■	81
58	Clemson	72
112	Citadel ■	61
90	Radford ■	69
60	Kentucky ■	89
85	Georgia ■	73
62	Tennessee	58
69	Florida	81
87	Vanderbilt ■	83
90	Alabama ■	67
77	Mississippi St. ■	69
57	Kentucky	89
82	Wofford ■	55
69	Arkansas	81
73	Auburn	84
106	LSU ■	68
57	Ga. Southern ■	45
97	Vanderbilt	107
80	Florida ■	75
65	Mississippi	75
66	Tennessee ■	52
73	Georgia	88
85	LSU †	76
58	Arkansas †	80
100	Davidson ■	73
80	Vanderbilt ■	70
67	Alabama ■	68

Nickname: Fighting Gamecocks
Colors: Garnet & Black
Arena: Frank McGuire Arena
  Capacity: 12,401; Year Built: 1968
AD: Mike McGee
SID: Brian Binette

SOUTH CARO. ST.

Orangeburg, SC 29117 I

Coach: Cy Alexander
Alma Mater: Catawba '75
Record: 9 Years, W-150, L-114

1996-97 SCHEDULE

Savannah St. ■		Nov. 30
Benedict ■		Dec. 4

Claflin		Dec. 9
Charleston So.		Dec. 18
South Caro.		Dec. 21
Furman		Dec. 28
Clemson		Dec. 30
Duke		Jan. 2
Hampton ■		Jan. 7
Coppin St. ■		Jan. 9
Howard ■		Jan. 11
Morgan St. ■		Jan. 13
Bethune-Cookman		Jan. 18
Florida A&M		Jan. 20
Md.-East. Shore		Jan. 25
Delaware St.		Jan. 27
Florida A&M ■		Feb. 1
Bethune-Cookman ■		Feb. 3
Md.-East. Shore ■		Feb. 8
Delaware St. ■		Feb. 10
Hampton		Feb. 13
North Caro. A&T		Feb. 15
Coppin St.		Feb. 20
Howard		Feb. 22
Morgan St.		Feb. 24
North Caro. A&T ■		Mar. 1
Mid-Eastern Conf. Tr.		Mar. 5-8

1995-96 RESULTS (22-8)

84	N.C. Central ■	79
70	South Caro.	92
64	Duke	84
72	Claflin ■	63
61	Charleston So. ■	57
82	Furman ■	66
56	Tenn.-Chatt.	63
59	Cal St. Northridge †	64
72	Morgan St. ■	56
67	Howard	58
76	Bethune-Cookman ■	61
71	Florida A&M ■	54
67	Md.-East. Shore ■	50
87	Delaware St. ■	71
83	Hampton ■	65
56	Florida A&M	47
51	Bethune-Cookman	56
69	Md.-East. Shore	56
99	Delaware St.	67
61	Hampton	71
74	North Caro. A&T ■	53
92	Morgan St. ■	78
77	Howard ■	63
81	Coppin St. ■	69
70	Coppin St.	73
88	North Caro. A&T	59
79	Florida A&M	58
69	North Caro. A&T †	46
69	Coppin St. †	56
54	Kansas †	92

Nickname: Bulldogs
Colors: Garnet & Blue
Arena: SHM Memorial Center
  Capacity: 3,200; Year Built: 1968
AD: Tim Autry
SID: Bill Hamilton

S.C.-AIKEN

Aiken, SC 29801 II

Coach: Larry Epperly
Alma Mater: Emory & Henry '75
Record: 9 Years, W-117, L-139

1996-97 SCHEDULE

Morris ■		Nov. 18
Lees-McRae		Nov. 21
Tenn.-Chatt.		Nov. 23
Voorhees ■		Nov. 25
Anderson (S.C.)		Dec. 2
Clayton St.		Dec. 7
Kennesaw St. ■		Dec. 14
Augusta St.		Dec. 18
Armstrong Atlantic ■		Jan. 2
Georgia Col.		Jan. 4
Francis Marion		Jan. 9
Lander ■		Jan. 11
N.C.-Pembroke ■		Jan. 15

Clayton St.		Jan. 18
Columbus St.		Jan. 22
S.C.-Spartanburg ■		Jan. 25
Armstrong Atlantic		Jan. 29
Georgia Col. ■		Feb. 1
Francis Marion ■		Feb. 5
Lander		Feb. 8
Kennesaw St.		Feb. 10
N.C.-Pembroke		Feb. 12
Augusta St. ■		Feb. 15
Columbus St. ■		Feb. 19
S.C.-Spartanburg		Feb. 22
Anderson (S.C.) ■		Feb. 24

1995-96 RESULTS (9-17)

78	Southern Wesleyan †	64
61	Anderson (S.C.) †	50
61	Tenn.-Chatt.	86
66	West Ga. †	75
84	Francis Marion †	70
64	Kennesaw St. ■	62
82	Newberry ■	79
57	Presbyterian	73
61	Armstrong Atlantic	68
59	Georgia Col. ■	83
70	Newberry	71
64	Francis Marion ■	74
84	Lander	81
70	N.C.-Pembroke	85
63	Augusta St. †	76
73	Columbus St.	80
79	S.C.-Spartanburg	85
72	Armstrong Atlantic ■	58
72	Georgia Col.	89
63	Francis Marion	69
70	Lander ■	81
60	Kennesaw St.	74
74	N.C.-Pembroke ■	70
92	Augusta St. ■	78
71	Columbus St.	95
68	S.C.-Spartanburg	88

Nickname: Pacers
Colors: Cardinal & White
Arena: Student Activities Center
  Capacity: 3,000; Year Built: 1977
AD: Randy Warrick
SID: Lindy Brown

S.C.-SPARTANBURG

Spartanburg, SC 29303 II

Coach: Jerry Waters
Alma Mater: Belmont '67
Record: 18 Years, W-366, L-151

1996-97 SCHEDULE

St. Augustine's ■		Nov. 18
S.C.-Spartanburg Tr.		Nov. 22-23
Lenoir-Rhyne Cl.		Nov. 29-30
Southern Ind. Tr.		Dec. 6-7
Lander		Jan. 2
N.C.-Pembroke ■		Jan. 4
Kennesaw St.		Jan. 8
Columbus St. ■		Jan. 11
Francis Marion ■		Jan. 13
Augusta St. ■		Jan. 15
Armstrong Atlantic		Jan. 18
Georgia Col.		Jan. 22
S.C.-Aiken ■		Jan. 25
Anderson (S.C.) ■		Jan. 27
Lander ■		Jan. 29
N.C.-Pembroke		Feb. 1
Kennesaw St. ■		Feb. 5
Columbus St.		Feb. 8
Francis Marion		Feb. 10
Augusta St.		Feb. 12
Armstrong Atlantic ■		Feb. 15
Georgia Col. ■		Feb. 19
S.C.-Aiken ■		Feb. 22

1995-96 RESULTS (23-8)

96	Voorhees ■	81
87	Emporia St. †	61
99	Lake Superior St. †	95
108	Anderson (S.C.) ■	58
75	Southern Wesleyan ■	84

88	North Greenville ■	61
93	Anderson (S.C.)	47
96	Lander ■	88
85	N.C.-Pembroke ■	82
92	Kennesaw St. ■	98
91	Columbus St.	101
69	Francis Marion	56
77	Augusta St.	70
82	Armstrong Atlantic ■	73
88	Southern Wesleyan ■	84
82	Georgia Col. ■	72
85	S.C.-Aiken ■	79
71	Lander	94
86	N.C.-Pembroke ■	96
60	Kennesaw St.	59
80	Columbus St. ■	77
52	Francis Marion ■	43
76	Augusta St. ■	49
84	Armstrong Atlantic	72
76	Georgia Col.	98
88	S.C.-Aiken	68
59	Kennesaw St. †	51
85	Georgia Col.	67
83	Columbus St. †	95
91	Clark Atlanta †	71
91	Alabama A&M †	106

Nickname: Rifles
Colors: Kelly Green, White & Black
Arena: G. B. Hodge Center Gym
  Capacity: 1,535; Year Built: 1973
AD: Mike Hall
SID: Michael MacEachern

SOUTH DAK.

Vermillion, SD 57069 II

Coach: Dave Boots
Alma Mater: Augsburg '79
Record: 14 Years, W-267, L-125

1996-97 SCHEDULE

BYU-Hawaii		Nov. 19
Hawaii Pacific		Nov. 20
Rocky Mountain ■		Nov. 23
Dakota St. ■		Dec. 1
Bellevue ■		Dec. 3
Minn.-Morris		Dec. 7
Teikyo Westmar ■		Dec. 13
Mont. St.-Billings ■		Dec. 15
Midland Lutheran ■		Dec. 21
Northern Colo. ■		Dec. 28
Neb.-Omaha ■		Dec. 29
North Dak.		Jan. 3
North Dak. St.		Jan. 4
Morningside		Jan. 11
St. Cloud St. ■		Jan. 17
Mankato St. ■		Jan. 18
Augustana (S.D.)		Jan. 24
South Dak. St.		Jan. 25
North Dak. St. ■		Jan. 31
North Dak. ■		Feb. 1
Morningside ■		Feb. 8
Mankato St.		Feb. 14
St. Cloud St.		Feb. 15
South Dak. St. ■		Feb. 21
Augustana (S.D.) ■		Feb. 22
Neb.-Omaha		Feb. 28
Northern Colo.		Mar. 1

1995-96 RESULTS (20-7)

74	Mt. Senario ■	63
79	Rocky Mountain	69
76	Mont. St.-Billings	77
87	Mayville St. ■	68
113	Minn.-Crookston ■	71
108	Bellevue ■	57
104	Teikyo Westmar ■	56
90	Dakota St. ■	62
91	Doane	60
93	North Dak. ■	82
78	North Dak. St. ■	80
90	Morningside	75
79	St. Cloud St.	93
68	Mankato St.	64
100	Augustana (S.D.) ■	85

74	South Dak. St. ■	89
76	Northern Colo.	69
86	Neb.-Omaha ■	79
86	Morningside ■	57
84	Mankato St. ■	94
83	St. Cloud St. ■	79
62	South Dak. St.	82
82	Augustana (S.D.)	67
85	Neb.-Omaha ■	67
93	Northern Colo. ■	72
68	North Dak. St.	78
86	North Dak.	66

Nickname: Coyotes
Colors: Vermillion & White
Arena: Dakotadome
  Capacity: 10,000; Year Built: 1979
AD: Jack Doyle
SID: Kyle Johnson

SOUTH DAK. ST.
Brookings, SD 57007 II

Coach: Scott Nagy
Alma Mater: Delta St. '88
Record: 1 Year, W-24, L-5

1996-97 SCHEDULE
Minn.-Morris		Nov. 16
Mt. Senario ■		Nov. 22
Wayne St. (Neb.) ■		Nov. 26
Black Hills St. [Rapid City]		Nov. 29
South Dak. Tech [Rapid City]		Nov. 30
Dak. Wesleyan ■		Dec. 3
Northern St.		Dec. 7
Southwest St. ■		Dec. 10
Huron ■		Dec. 14
St. Cloud St.		Dec. 28
Mankato St.		Dec. 29
Augustana (S.D.)		Jan. 4
Neb.-Omaha ■		Jan. 10
Northern Colo. ■		Jan. 11
North Dak.		Jan. 17
North Dak. St.		Jan. 18
Morningside ■		Jan. 24
South Dak. ■		Jan. 25
Augustana (S.D.) ■		Feb. 1
Northern Colo.		Feb. 7
Neb.-Omaha		Feb. 8
North Dak. St. ■		Feb. 14
North Dak. ■		Feb. 15
South Dak.		Feb. 21
Morningside		Feb. 22
Mankato St. ■		Feb. 28
St. Cloud St. ■		Mar. 1

1995-96 RESULTS (24-5)
85	Coe ■	54
73	Neb.-Kearney	85
86	Wayne St. (Neb.)	64
118	Bellevue ■	64
117	Mont. St.-Billings ■	86
84	Dak. Wesleyan	71
82	Northern St.	78
76	Southwest St.	57
96	Mayville St. ■	57
83	Augustana (S.D.) ■	68
96	Neb.-Omaha	85
63	Northern Colo.	54
85	North Dak. ■	79
96	North Dak. St. ■	101
99	Morningside	83
89	South Dak.	74
106	St. Cloud St. ■	89
89	Mankato St. ■	83
90	Northern Colo. ■	64
85	Neb.-Omaha ■	63
82	North Dak. St.	81
71	North Dak.	96
82	South Dak. ■	62
94	Morningside ■	78
81	Mankato St.	82
91	St. Cloud St.	84
86	Augustana (S.D.)	83
94	North Dak. St. †	88
90	Fort Hays St.	99

Nickname: Jackrabbits
Colors: Yellow & Blue
Arena: Frost Arena
  Capacity: 9,000; Year Built: 1973
AD: Fred Oien
SID: Ron Lenz

SOUTH FLA.
Tampa, FL 33620 I

Coach: Seth Greenberg
Alma Mater: Fairleigh Dickinson '78
Record: 6 Years, W-105, L-70

1996-97 SCHEDULE
Ohio St. ■		Nov. 23
Geo. Washington		Nov. 26
Fla. Atlantic ■		Dec. 4
Jacksonville ■		Dec. 7
Florida		Dec. 10
Central Fla. ■		Dec. 14
South Fla. Cl.		Dec. 20-21
South Fla. Tr.		Dec. 27-28
Memphis		Jan. 7
DePaul		Jan. 11
N.C.-Charlotte ■		Jan. 14
Tulane		Jan. 18
Houston		Jan. 22
Southern Miss. ■		Jan. 25
Va. Commonwealth		Jan. 27
Marquette ■		Jan. 30
UAB		Feb. 1
Southern Miss.		Feb. 9
Rutgers		Feb. 13
Louisville ■		Feb. 17
Cincinnati ■		Feb. 20
St. Louis		Feb. 23
Tulane		Feb. 26
UAB ■		Mar. 1
Conference USA		Mar. 5-8

1995-96 RESULTS (12-16)
73	Florida	58
65	Pepperdine ■	58
67	Old Dominion	61
69	Geo. Washington †	71
92	Central Fla.	82
56	Fla. Atlantic ■	55
75	Jacksonville	84
43	Tennessee	54
86	LIU-Brooklyn	60
78	Ga. Southern ■	48
69	Cincinnati ■	71
63	Tulane	68
59	Memphis ■	60
56	N.C.-Charlotte	89
56	St. Louis	69
67	Southeast Mo. St.	41
54	Louisville ■	57
60	Cincinnati	79
61	Marquette ■	82
63	Southern Miss. ■	57
80	Bethune-Cookman ■	62
62	Tulane ■	70
63	UAB	79
51	Southern Miss.	59
61	DePaul ■	65
73	UAB ■	64
73	UAB †	57
56	Marquette †	65

Nickname: Bulls
Colors: Green & Gold
Arena: Sun Dome
  Capacity: 10,411; Year Built: 1980
AD: Paul Griffin
SID: John Gerdes

SOUTHEAST MO. ST.
Cape Girardeau, MO 63701 I

Coach: Ron Shumate
Alma Mater: Tenn. Tech '61
Record: 22 Years, W-433, L-214

1996-97 SCHEDULE
Southeast Mo. St. Cl		Nov. 29-30
McKendree ■		Dec. 5
Oklahoma		Dec. 7
Louisiana Tech		Dec. 9
Southern Ill. ■		Dec. 12
Missouri		Dec. 15
Oakland City ■		Dec. 18
Puerto Rico Tr.		Dec. 30-Jan. 1
Austin Peay		Jan. 4
Tennessee St.		Jan. 6
Tenn.-Martin ■		Jan. 9
Eastern Ky. ■		Jan. 11
Morehead St. ■		Jan. 13
Middle Tenn. St.		Jan. 18
Tennessee Tech		Jan. 20
Murray St.		Jan. 23
Eastern Ill. ■		Jan. 25
Tennessee St. ■		Feb. 1
Austin Peay ■		Feb. 3
Murray St. ■		Feb. 6
Morehead St.		Feb. 8
Eastern Ky.		Feb. 10
Tennessee Tech ■		Feb. 15
Middle Tenn. St. ■		Feb. 17
Tenn.-Martin		Feb. 20
Eastern Ill.		Feb. 22
Ohio Valley Conf. Tr.		Feb. 25-Mar. 1

1995-96 RESULTS (8-19)
82	Oakland City ■	78
109	Troy St. ■	91
80	Mississippi Val. ■	84
65	Fairfield	73
70	Illinois	89
55	San Jose St. †	48
64	Southern Ill.	70
58	Oral Roberts	74
65	Missouri	102
73	Eastern Ky.	89
81	Morehead St.	64
71	Tenn.-Martin ■	61
65	Middle Tenn. St.	63
69	Austin Peay	82
70	Tennessee St. ■	82
81	Tennessee Tech ■	78
41	South Fla. ■	67
77	Murray St.	81
76	Morehead St. ■	74
76	Eastern Ky. ■	79
59	Tenn.-Martin	79
71	Austin Peay ■	84
75	Middle Tenn. St. ■	78
69	Tennessee Tech	102
73	Tennessee St.	76
61	Murray St. ■	79
69	Oral Roberts	85

Nickname: Indians
Colors: Red & Black
Arena: Show Me Center
  Capacity: 7,000; Year Built: 1987
AD: Richard McDuffie
SID: Ron Hines

SOUTHEASTERN LA.
Hammond, LA 70402 I

Coach: John Lyles
Alma Mater: Louisiana College '77
Record: 2 Years, W-27, L-28

1996-97 SCHEDULE
Loyola (La.) ■		Nov. 23
Mississippi St.		Nov. 26
Jackson St.		Nov. 30
Ark.-Monticello ■		Dec. 5
Texas A&M		Dec. 7
Southern U. ■		Dec. 14
Grambling ■		Dec. 16
Nicholls St.		Dec. 18
Northwestern ■		Dec. 21
Stephen F. Austin ■		Dec. 28
Florida Int'l		Jan. 2
Fla. Atlantic ■		Jan. 4

Stetson ■		Jan. 9
Central Fla. ■		Jan. 11
Samford		Jan. 16
Jacksonville St.		Jan. 18
Centenary (La.) ■		Jan. 23
Georgia St. ■		Jan. 30
Mercer ■		Feb. 1
Centenary (La.) ■		Feb. 3
Georgia St.		Feb. 6
Mercer		Feb. 8
Jacksonville St. ■		Feb. 13
Samford ■		Feb. 15
Charleston (S.C.)		Feb. 20
Campbell		Feb. 22
Trans America Conf. Tr.		Feb. 27-Mar. 1

1995-96 RESULTS (15-12)
78	Mississippi St.	121
110	Texas Col. ■	75
89	Nicholls St. ■	65
86	Bapt. Christian ■	73
92	Texas Christian	95
75	Northwestern St.	90
79	Jackson St.	90
96	Southern U. ■	109
74	Grambling	68
71	Stephen F. Austin	91
91	Florida Int'l ■	71
72	Fla. Atlantic	69
94	Stetson	79
95	Central Fla.	84
76	Samford	70
93	Jacksonville St. ■	90
89	Centenary (La.) ■	77
81	Georgia St.	86
78	Mercer	62
90	Centenary (La.)	77
91	Georgia St. ■	86
94	Mercer ■	88
84	Jacksonville St.	92
80	Samford	91
93	Charleston (S.C.) ■	83
65	Campbell ■	69
80	Central Fla. †	83

Nickname: Lions
Colors: Green & Gold
Arena: University Center
  Capacity: 7,500; Year Built: 1982
AD: Tom Douple
SID: Barry Niemeyer

SOUTHERN CAL
Los Angeles, CA 90089 I

Coach: Henry Bibby
Alma Mater: UCLA '72
Record: 1 Year, W-0, L-9

1996-97 SCHEDULE
Long Beach St. ■		Nov. 30
Loyola Marymount ■		Dec. 2
Charlotte Inv.		Dec. 6-7
UC Irvine		Dec. 15
Tennessee		Dec. 18
Ohio St. ■		Dec. 21
UNLV		Dec. 28
Washington ■		Jan. 2
Washington St. ■		Jan. 4
California [San Francisco]		Jan. 9
Stanford		Jan. 11
Arizona		Jan. 16
Arizona St. ■		Jan. 18
UCLA ■		Jan. 23
Cincinnati		Jan. 26
Oregon St.		Jan. 30
Oregon		Feb. 1
Stanford ■		Feb. 6
California ■		Feb. 8
Arizona St.		Feb. 13
Arizona		Feb. 15
UCLA		Feb. 20
Oregon		Feb. 27
Oregon St. ■		Mar. 1
Washington St.		Mar. 6
Washington		Mar. 8

1995-96 RESULTS (11-19)
76	Lamar ■	72
80	Pennsylvania	78
83	Loyola Marymount	86
96	Houston ■	73
82	UNLV ■	72
82	UC Irvine ■	79
118	George Mason ■	97
49	Utah	84
75	Missouri †	64
63	Massachusetts †	78
74	Rhode Island †	87
72	Washington	94
83	Washington St.	81
60	California ■	63
84	Stanford ■	80
81	Arizona	93
80	Arizona St.	67
72	UCLA	99
53	Cincinnati	85
64	Oregon St. ■	47
78	Oregon ■	99
69	Stanford	99
69	California	85
66	Arizona St. ■	69
72	Arizona ■	86
59	UCLA ■	61
60	Oregon	80
54	Oregon St.	56
62	Washington St. ■	69
68	Washington ■	71

Nickname: Trojans
Colors: Cardinal & Gold
Arena: L.A. Sports Arena
  Capacity: 15,509; Year Built: 1959
AD: Mike Garrett
SID: Tim Tessalone

SOUTHERN COLO.
Pueblo, CO 81001 II

Coach: Joe Folda
Alma Mater: Northern Colo. '66
Record: 12 Years, W-204, L-141

1996-97 SCHEDULE
Grand Canyon Inv.	Nov. 22-23
West Tex. A&M ■	Nov. 25
Southern Colo. Cl.	Nov. 29-30
Metro St. ■	Dec. 6
Colorado Mines ■	Dec. 7
Chadron St.	Dec. 13
Neb.-Kearney ■	Jan. 3
Fort Hays St. ■	Jan. 4
Regis (Colo.)	Jan. 10
Colo. Christian	Jan. 11
Mesa St. ■	Jan. 17
Western St. ■	Jan. 18
Fort Lewis	Jan. 24
Adams St.	Jan. 25
UC-Colo. Spgs. †	Jan. 29
N.M. Highlands	Jan. 31
Denver	Feb. 4
Fort Lewis ■	Feb. 7
Adams St. ■	Feb. 8
Colorado Col.	Feb. 10
Mesa St.	Feb. 14
Western St.	Feb. 15
UC-Colo. Spgs. ■	Feb. 19
N.M. Highlands ■	Feb. 20

1995-96 RESULTS (17-11)
77	Western N.M. ■	70
69	Mesa St. ■	65
77	N.M. Highlands	73
95	Mount Union †	83
63	Mesa St.	67
77	Western St. ■	84
66	Cal St. Dom. Hills ■	63
58	Northern Colo. ■	67
80	West Tex. A&M	86
86	Adams St.	87
88	Fresno St.	109
117	Fort Lewis ■	98

85	Regis (Colo.) ■	78
96	Denver ■	93
82	Colo. Christian ■	64
75	UC-Colo. Spgs.	74
83	Metro St.	85
71	Regis (Colo.)	74
75	Denver	90
101	Colo. Christian	61
90	Metro St.	89
100	N.M. Highlands ■	77
90	Colo. Christian ■	72
66	Denver	77
78	Northwestern Okla. ■	67
57	Western St.	61
69	Fort Lewis ■	66
93	UC-Colo. Spgs. ■	74

Nickname: Thunderwolves
Colors: Red & Blue
Arena: Massari Arena
  Capacity: 5,000; Year Built: 1971
AD: Tony Taibi
SID: Todd Kelly

SOUTHERN CONN. ST.
New Haven, CT 06515 II

Coach: Arthur Leary
Alma Mater: Quinnipiac '71
Record: 18 Years, W-235, L-272

1996-97 SCHEDULE
So. Conn. St. Cl.	Nov. 22-23
Queens (N.Y.) ■	Nov. 30
Keene St. ■	Dec. 7
Quinnipiac ■	Dec. 10
Stonehill	Dec. 15
LIU-C. W. Post	Dec. 21
Merrimack Inv.	Dec. 27-28
New Hamp. Col. ■	Jan. 8
New Haven	Jan. 11
Sacred Heart	Jan. 14
Albany (N.Y.) ■	Jan. 16
Mass.-Lowell	Jan. 18
Franklin Pierce ■	Jan. 22
Mass.-Lowell ■	Jan. 25
Bridgeport	Jan. 29
New Haven ■	Feb. 1
Franklin Pierce	Feb. 4
Sacred Heart ■	Feb. 6
Keene St.	Feb. 8
Stony Brook	Feb. 12
New Hamp. Col.	Feb. 15
Bridgeport ■	Feb. 18
Albany (N.Y.)	Feb. 20
Stony Brook ■	Feb. 22

1995-96 RESULTS (17-12)
72	St. Michael's †	74
79	Merrimack ■	70
75	Quinnipiac	86
78	American Int'l	48
70	Le Moyne ■	73
75	Albany (N.Y.)	81
96	Bentley	103
79	Bridgeport	70
68	Sacred Heart ■	73
56	Rutgers	108
83	Keene St. ■	53
65	Franklin Pierce ■	85
86	Albany (N.Y.) ■	62
70	New Hamp. Col.	79
66	Mass.-Lowell	51
70	Sacred Heart	69
78	Stony Brook ■	57
83	Bridgeport ■	67
58	Le Moyne ■	63
86	Mass.-Lowell ■	72
78	New Hamp. Col. ■	64
78	New Haven	76
62	Franklin Pierce	68
110	Keene St.	81
61	Stony Brook	47
69	New Haven ■	65
82	Sacred Heart ■	69

90	Franklin Pierce	85
73	Le Moyne †	77

Nickname: Owls
Colors: Blue & White
Arena: James W. Moore Fieldhouse
  Capacity: 2,800; Year Built: 1973
AD: Darryl Rogers
SID: Richard Leddy

SOUTHERN ILL.
Carbondale, IL 62901 I

Coach: Rich Herrin
Alma Mater: McKendree '56
Record: 11 Years, W-198, L-141

1996-97 SCHEDULE
Top of the World Cl.	Nov. 22-24
Northern Ill. ■	Nov. 30
St. Louis	Dec. 4
Southeast Mo. St.	Dec. 12
Austin Peay ■	Dec. 14
N.C.-Charlotte	Dec. 18
James Madison ■	Dec. 21
Wyoming Shootout	Dec. 27-28
Bradley	Dec. 31
Utah St.	Jan. 4
Evansville ■	Jan. 7
Illinois St. ■	Jan. 12
Creighton	Jan. 16
Northern Iowa	Jan. 18
Southwest Mo. St.	Jan. 22
Indiana St. ■	Jan. 25
Creighton ■	Jan. 27
Drake ■	Feb. 1
Indiana St.	Feb. 3
Wichita St.	Feb. 5
Drake	Feb. 8
Bradley ■	Feb. 10
Illinois St.	Feb. 13
Northern Iowa ■	Feb. 15
Wichita St.	Feb. 17
Evansville	Feb. 22
Southwest Mo. St. ■	Feb. 24
Missouri Val. Conf. Tr.	Feb. 28-Mar. 3

1995-96 RESULTS (11-18)
65	Northern Ill.	63
73	Old Dominion	65
66	Fla. Atlantic ■	64
70	Southeast Mo. St. ■	64
63	St. Louis	67
73	N.C.-Charlotte ■	81
65	Austin Peay ■	78
87	UAB †	81
98	Hawaii-Hilo	86
81	Neb.-Kearney †	94
97	Illinois St. †	75
64	Northern Iowa ■	66
70	Utah St.	73
57	Bradley	73
76	Wichita St. ■	54
67	Drake	87
65	Northern Iowa	91
68	Evansville ■	80
77	Creighton	79
78	Indiana St. ■	65
65	Southwest Mo. St.	77
56	Wichita St.	59
63	Creighton ■	68
74	Illinois St.	71
75	Tulsa ■	84
68	Drake ■	71
80	Indiana St.	94
64	Evansville	96
76	Bradley ■	79

Nickname: Salukis
Colors: Maroon & White
Arena: The SIU Arena
  Capacity: 10,014; Year Built: 1964
AD: Jim Hart
SID: Fred Huff

SIU-EDWARDSVILLE
Edwardsville, IL 62026 II

Coach: Jack Margenthaler
Alma Mater: Houston '65
Record: 19 Years, W-268, L-258

1996-97 SCHEDULE
P.R.-Mayaguez ■	Nov. 15
Olivet Nazarene ■	Nov. 19
Truman St.	Nov. 23
Mo. Southern St. ■	Nov. 26
Winona St.	Dec. 7
Greenville ■	Dec. 14
Quincy ■	Dec. 19
Mo.-St. Louis ■	Dec. 21
Wis.-Parkside	Jan. 2
Lewis	Jan. 4
Southern Ind. ■	Jan. 9
IU/PU-Ft. Wayne	Jan. 11
Ky. Wesleyan ■	Jan. 16
Bellarmine ■	Jan. 18
Indianapolis	Jan. 23
Northern Ky.	Jan. 25
Mo.-St. Louis	Jan. 30
Quincy	Feb. 1
Lewis ■	Feb. 6
Wis.-Parkside ■	Feb. 8
Southern Ind.	Feb. 13
St. Joseph's (Ind.) ■	Feb. 15
Ky. Wesleyan	Feb. 20
Bellarmine	Feb. 22
Northern Ky. ■	Feb. 27
Indianapolis ■	Mar. 1

1995-96 RESULTS (10-15)
76	Eureka ■	68
78	Truman St. ■	63
55	Florida Tech	81
76	Rollins	92
79	Mo.-St. Louis ■	72
49	Lewis	78
73	Quincy	71
64	Ky. Wesleyan	74
83	Southern Ind.	109
81	Indianapolis ■	80
67	Northern Ky. ■	79
88	Wis.-Parkside	83
70	St. Joseph's (Ind.)	82
110	Quincy ■	112
74	Bellarmine ■	68
91	Ky. Wesleyan ■	95
92	IU/PU-Ft. Wayne	77
73	Indianapolis	98
89	Lewis ■	80
67	Wis.-Parkside ■	70
84	Southern Ind. ■	95
73	Northern Ky.	96
93	Bellarmine	101
75	St. Joseph's (Ind.) ■	60
88	IU/PU-Ft. Wayne ■	90

Nickname: Cougars
Colors: Red & White
Arena: Sam Vadalabene Center
  Capacity: 4,200; Year Built: 1984
AD: Cindy Jones
SID: Eric Hess

SOUTHERN IND.
Evansville, IN 47712 II

Coach: Bruce Pearl
Alma Mater: Boston College '82
Record: 4 Years, W-104, L-19

1996-97 SCHEDULE
P.R.-Mayaguez ■	Nov. 16
Mo.-St. Louis ■	Nov. 23
Southern Ind. Tr.	Dec. 6-7
Las Vegas Cl.	Dec. 18-19
Quincy ■	Dec. 22
Lewis	Jan. 2
Wis.-Parkside	Jan. 4
SIU-Edwardsville	Jan. 9
St. Joseph's (Ind.)	Jan. 11

Bellarmine ■ ....Jan. 16
Ky. Wesleyan ■ ....Jan. 18
Northern Ky. ....Jan. 23
Indianapolis ■ ....Jan. 25
Quincy ■ ....Jan. 30
Mo.-St. Louis ....Feb. 1
Wis.-Parkside ■ ....Feb. 6
Lewis ■ ....Feb. 8
SIU-Edwardsville ■ ....Feb. 13
IU/PU-Ft. Wayne ■ ....Feb. 15
Bellarmine ....Feb. 20
Ky. Wesleyan ....Feb. 22
Indianapolis ....Feb. 27
Northern Ky. ■ ....Mar. 1

1995-96 RESULTS (25-4)
117	Oklahoma City	98
85	Wis.-Platteville †	62
101	Charleston (W.Va.) ■	78
114	Central Okla. ■	116
99	Ind. Wesleyan ■	66
93	Grace ■	62
109	Lewis ■	103
84	Wis.-Parkside	62
109	SIU-Edwardsville ■	83
99	Northern Ky. ■	66
105	Ind.-South Bend ■	65
80	St. Joseph's (Ind.) ■	82
96	IU/PU-Ft. Wayne	60
116	Quincy ■	87
105	Lewis	79
90	Ky. Wesleyan ■	73
83	Indianapolis	86
103	Northern Ky.	102
84	Bellarmine ■	69
91	Wis.-Parkside ■	77
75	St. Joseph's (Ind.)	67
95	SIU-Edwardsville	84
98	Quincy	84
88	Bellarmine	64
81	Ky. Wesleyan	65
103	IU/PU-Ft. Wayne	69
96	Indianapolis ■	73
75	Indianapolis	71
87	Northern Ky.	99

Nickname: Screaming Eagles
Colors: Red, White & Blue
Arena: Physical Education Center
  Capacity: 3,500; Year Built: 1980
AD: Steve Newton
SID: Ray Simmons

SOUTHERN ME.
Gorham, ME 04038 III

Coach: Dan Costigan
Alma Mater: North Adams St. '76
(First year as head coach)
1996-97 SCHEDULE
Maine ....Nov. 23
Southern Maine Tr. ....Nov. 29-Dec. 1
New England ■ ....Dec. 5
Rhode Island Col. ■ ....Dec. 7
Colby ....Dec. 11
Eastern Conn. St. ■ ....Dec. 14
Kean Cl. ....Jan. 4-5
Wentworth Inst. ....Jan. 7
Plymouth St. ....Jan. 15
Western Conn. St. ■ ....Jan. 18
Bates ■ ....Jan. 22
Mass.-Dartmouth ....Jan. 25
Mass.-Boston ....Jan. 28
Rhode Island Col. ....Feb. 1
Plymouth St. ■ ....Feb. 4
Eastern Conn. St. ■ ....Feb. 8
St. Joseph's (Me.) [Portland] .....Feb. 12
Western Conn. St. ....Feb. 15
Mass.-Boston ■ ....Feb. 18
Mass.-Dartmouth ■ ....Feb. 22

1995-96 RESULTS (10-15)
69	Caldwell †	78
84	LSU-Shreveport †	74
94	Plymouth St. ■	75
79	New England	76
72	Rhode Island Col.	81
64	Colby	70
78	Eastern Conn. St. ■	73
98	Maine Maritime ■	58
57	Stony Brook	60
69	Keene St. †	71
71	Me.-Farmington †	58
68	Colby	87
86	Husson †	69
60	Western Conn. St.	82
85	Bates	79
61	Mass.-Dartmouth ■	68
86	Mass.-Boston	61
73	Rhode Island Col. ■	74
77	Plymouth St.	95
78	Eastern Conn. St.	84
77	St. Joseph's (Me.) †	94
64	Western Conn. St. ■	93
68	Mass.-Boston	60
55	Mass.-Dartmouth	78
77	Western Conn. St.	79

Nickname: Huskies
Colors: Crimson, Navy Blue & White
Arena: Warren G. Hill Gymnasium
  Capacity: 1,500; Year Built: 1963
AD: Al Bean
SID: B. L. Elfring

SOUTHERN METHODIST
Dallas, TX 75275 I

Coach: Mike Dement
Alma Mater: East Caro. '76
Record: 10 Years, W-130, L-143
1996-97 SCHEDULE
Hardin-Simmons ■ ....Nov. 23
Wichita St. ....Nov. 30
North Texas ■ ....Dec. 2
Davidson ....Dec. 5
Kent ....Dec. 7
Centenary (La.) ■ ....Dec. 16
Oklahoma St. ....Dec. 21
Stetson ....Dec. 28
Prairie View ■ ....Dec. 30
Air Force ■ ....Jan. 4
Yale ■ ....Jan. 6
UTEP ....Jan. 9
New Mexico ....Jan. 11
Utah ....Jan. 16
Brigham Young ■ ....Jan. 18
Air Force ....Jan. 22
Texas Christian ■ ....Jan. 25
Tulsa ....Jan. 30
Rice ....Feb. 1
New Mexico ■ ....Feb. 6
UTEP ■ ....Feb. 8
Utah ....Feb. 13
Brigham Young ....Feb. 15
Texas Christian ....Feb. 19
Rice ■ ....Feb. 27
Tulsa ■ ....Mar. 1
Western Ath. Conf. Tr. ....Mar. 4-8

1995-96 RESULTS (8-20)
59	Creighton ■	63
74	Hardin-Simmons ■	45
51	Missouri	66
65	Wichita St. ■	46
60	Oklahoma St. ■	67
84	McMurry ■	42
46	Arkansas	73
58	Arizona St.	62
79	Pennsylvania †	67
74	Oklahoma	84
61	Kansas	83
62	Houston	63
68	Baylor ■	63
51	Rice	69
63	Texas	81
60	Texas Tech ■	72
87	Texas Christian ■	83
55	North Texas	62
58	Texas A&M	62
74	Baylor	78
70	Rice ■	71
66	Texas ■	101
54	Texas Tech	75
79	Texas Christian	87
59	Houston ■	62
75	Texas A&M ■	72
62	Houston	57
67	Texas ■	89

Nickname: Mustangs
Colors: Red & Blue
Arena: Moody Coliseum
  Capacity: 8,998; Year Built: 1956
AD: Jim Copeland
SID: Jon Jackson

SOUTHERN MISS.
Hattiesburg, MS 39406 I

Coach: James Green
Alma Mater: Mississippi '83
(First year as head coach)
1996-97 SCHEDULE
Texas Tech ....Nov. 22
Jackson St. ■ ....Nov. 26
Northeast La. ....Nov. 30
South Ala. ■ ....Dec. 3
Iowa Shootout ....Dec. 6-7
Nicholls St. ■ ....Dec. 11
New Orleans ....Dec. 14
Southwestern La. ....Dec. 21
Texas Southern ■ ....Dec. 23
Oral Roberts ....Dec. 30
Marquette ....Jan. 4
Tulane ....Jan. 11
UAB ■ ....Jan. 18
DePaul ■ ....Jan. 21
South Fla. ....Jan. 25
Tulane ■ ....Jan. 27
Memphis ....Jan. 30
St. Louis ....Feb. 2
Houston ■ ....Feb. 6
South Fla. ■ ....Feb. 9
UAB ....Feb. 15
Mississippi Val. ■ ....Feb. 19
Louisville ■ ....Feb. 22
Cincinnati ....Feb. 25
N.C.-Charlotte ■ ....Mar. 2
Conference USA ....Mar. 5-8

1995-96 RESULTS (12-15)
68	Jackson St. ■	61
80	Southwestern La. ■	76
66	New Orleans ■	68
74	Tampa	60
69	Mississippi St. ■	72
107	Mississippi	113
74	Tenn.-Chatt.	57
50	South Ala.	66
77	Buffalo †	71
65	Utah St.	77
78	UAB ■	61
89	Northeast La. ■	58
70	Cincinnati ■	75
82	DePaul	67
61	Louisville	87
61	Tulane	76
68	Memphis ■	81
62	Tulane	61
69	Alabama ■	83
57	South Fla.	63
67	UAB	64
55	Marquette ■	58
66	Memphis	91
59	South Fla.	51
62	St. Louis ■	46
66	N.C.-Charlotte	77
44	St. Louis †	61

Nickname: Golden Eagles
Colors: Black & Gold
Arena: Reed Green Coliseum
  Capacity: 8,095; Year Built: 1965
AD: Bill McLellan
SID: M. R. Napier

SOUTHERN U.
Baton Rouge, LA 70813 I

Coach: Tommy Green
Alma Mater: Southern U. '78
Record: 25 Years, W-468, L-228
1996-97 SCHEDULE
Texas Col. ■ ....Nov. 26
Middle Tenn. St. ■ ....Dec. 7
Southeastern La. ....Dec. 14
Loyola (La.) ■ ....Dec. 16
Southwestern La. ....Dec. 18
San Francisco ....Dec. 20
Rice ■ ....Dec. 28
Missouri ....Dec. 30
Grambling ■ ....Jan. 4
Mississippi Val. ■ ....Jan. 6
Alabama St. ....Jan. 11
Jackson St. ....Jan. 13
Ark.-Pine Bluff ■ ....Jan. 15
Texas Southern ....Jan. 18
Prairie View ....Jan. 20
Alcorn St. ■ ....Jan. 25
Dayton ....Jan. 27
Grambling [Monroe] ....Feb. 1
Mississippi Val. ....Feb. 3
Alabama St. ■ ....Feb. 8
Jackson St. ■ ....Feb. 10
Texas Southern ■ ....Feb. 15
Prairie View ■ ....Feb. 17
Ark.-Pine Bluff ....Feb. 19
Alcorn St. ....Feb. 22
McNeese St. ■ ....Feb. 25
Southwestern Conf. Tr. ....Mar. 5-8

1995-96 RESULTS (17-11)
73	Texas Col. ■	68
100	LSU	109
93	Ark.-Pine Bluff ■	85
59	Santa Clara	98
109	Southeastern La.	96
96	N.C.-Greensboro ■	78
79	Tennessee St. †	84
81	West Ala. ■	63
92	Grambling †	89
92	Mississippi Val.	94
113	Alabama St. ■	86
74	Jackson St. ■	85
104	Ark.-Pine Bluff	85
85	Texas Southern ■	74
108	Prairie View ■	89
73	Middle Tenn. St.	88
95	Alcorn St.	87
70	Rice	78
93	Mississippi Val.	87
72	Grambling ■	69
96	Alabama St.	66
84	Jackson St.	85
81	Texas Southern	86
125	Prairie View	103
94	Alcorn St. ■	97
94	McNeese St. ■	82
107	Prairie View †	81
76	Mississippi Val. †	83

Nickname: Jaguars
Colors: Blue & Gold
Arena: Clark Activity Center
  Capacity: 7,500; Year Built: 1976
AD: Marino Casem
SID: Errol Domingue

SOUTHERN UTAH
Cedar City, UT 84720 I

Coach: Bill Evans
Alma Mater: Southern Utah '72
Record: 5 Years, W-68, L-50
1996-97 SCHEDULE
Gonzaga ■ ....Nov. 23
Va. Commonwealth ....Nov. 26
Cal St. Hayward ■ ....Nov. 30
Utah ....Dec. 4
Montana Cl. ....Dec. 6-7

Northern Ariz. ■ ...Dec. 16
UNLV ...Dec. 23
Arkansas ...Dec. 28
Fairfield ■ ...Dec. 31
Portland ■ ...Jan. 2
San Diego ...Jan. 4
Tulsa ...Jan. 8
Seattle ■ ...Jan. 11
St. Louis ...Jan. 13
Creighton ...Jan. 20
Western Ill. ...Jan. 22
Northern Ariz. ...Jan. 28
Idaho ...Feb. 3
Montana Tech ■ ...Feb. 5
Weber St. ...Feb. 7
Western Ore. ■ ...Feb. 10
Montana St. ...Feb. 17
Oral Roberts ■ ...Feb. 19
Idaho St. ...Feb. 22
UC Irvine ■ ...Feb. 25
Oral Roberts ...Mar. 4

1995-96 RESULTS (15-13)
84 Cal St. Stanislaus ■ ...49
64 Northern Iowa ...77
76 Arizona St. ...82
60 Gonzaga ...77
71 Idaho ■ ...56
71 Boise St. ...64
51 Montana St. ...81
97 Pepperdine ■ ...80
72 Idaho St. ...49
91 Western Ore. ■ ...63
75 New Mexico St. ...81
83 Portland ...88
74 Oral Roberts ■ ...77
68 UC-Colo. Spgs. ■ ...40
81 Northern Iowa ■ ...70
82 Colorado ...80
67 Oral Roberts ...69
72 Cal St. Northridge ■ ...65
73 Weber St. ■ ...78
94 UC Santa Cruz ■ ...37
75 UC Irvine ...85
78 Cal Poly SLO ■ ...91
75 Cal St. Northridge ...96
87 Cal St. Sacramento ■ ...59
70 Cal St. Sacramento ...82
85 Cal Poly SLO ...84
57 Cal St. Northridge ...54
55 Cal Poly SLO † ...53

Nickname: Thunderbirds
Colors: Scarlett & White
Arena: Centrum
  Capacity: 5,200; Year Built: 1985
AD: Jack Bishop
SID: Brett Jewkes

SOUTHWEST BAPTIST
Bolivar, MO 65613 ...II

Coach: Lynn Nance
Alma Mater: Washington '65
Record: 16 Years, W-269, L-188
1996-97 SCHEDULE
Harris-Stowe ■ ...Nov. 19
Central Ark. ...Nov. 26
Ga. Southwestern ■ ...Nov. 28
Mo. Southern St. ■ ...Dec. 3
Missouri Baptist ■ ...Dec. 11
Lincoln (Mo.) ...Dec. 21
American (P.R.) ■ ...Dec. 28
Washburn ...Jan. 4
Central Mo. St. ...Jan. 8
Northwest Mo. St. ■ ...Jan. 11
Emporia St. ...Jan. 14
Truman St. ...Jan. 20
Pittsburg St. ...Jan. 22
Mo. Western St. ...Jan. 25
Mo.-Rolla ...Jan. 28
Central Mo. St. ■ ...Feb. 1
Mo. Southern St. ...Feb. 5
Lincoln (Mo.) ■ ...Feb. 8
Mo. Western St. ■ ...Feb. 10

Truman St. ■ ...Feb. 13
Emporia St. ■ ...Feb. 15
Pittsburg St. ■ ...Feb. 18
Mo.-Rolla ...Feb. 22

1995-96 RESULTS (7-19)
72 Texas A&M-Commerce ■ ...66
77 IU/PU-Indianapolis ■ ...105
85 Wayne St. (Neb.) † ...95
66 Tabor † ...73
109 MidAmerica Naz. ■ ...95
80 Central Ark. ■ ...76
60 Drury ■ ...86
55 Rollins † ...73
71 Morningside † ...80
84 IU/PU-Indianapolis ■ ...85
98 Central Mo. St. ■ ...86
75 Mo.-St. Louis ...84
68 Pittsburg St. ■ ...71
66 Mo.-Rolla ...81
74 Northwest Mo. St. ...80
79 Truman St. ■ ...80
52 Emporia St. ■ ...56
73 Mo. Western St. ...85
77 Lincoln (Mo.) ...60
83 Washburn ■ ...77
79 Mo. Southern St. ...84
88 Mo.-St. Louis ■ ...94
76 Pittsburg St. ...81
73 Mo.-Rolla ■ ...79
81 Northwest Mo. St. ■ ...86
79 Truman St. ...91

Nickname: Bearcats
Colors: Purple & White
Arena: Davison Field House
  Capacity: 2,500; Year Built: 1963
AD: Rex Brown
SID: Christopher Johnson

SOUTHWEST MO. ST.
Springfield, MO 65804 ...I

Coach: Steve Alford
Alma Mater: Indiana '87
Record: 5 Years, W-94, L-41
1996-97 SCHEDULE
Southwestern La. ...Nov. 25
Idaho ■ ...Nov. 30
N.C.-Wilmington ■ ...Dec. 2
Southwest Mo. St. Cl ...Dec. 6-7
Northwestern St. ...Dec. 10
St. Louis ■ ...Dec. 15
Drake ■ ...Dec. 21
Puerto Rico Tr. ...Dec. 30-Jan. 1
Bradley ■ ...Jan. 5
Long Beach St. ...Jan. 9
Drake ...Jan. 12
Northern Iowa ■ ...Jan. 15
Wichita St. ...Jan. 18
Southern Ill. ■ ...Jan. 22
Bradley ...Jan. 25
Illinois St. ...Jan. 27
Creighton ■ ...Jan. 30
Indiana St. ■ ...Feb. 1
Northern Iowa ...Feb. 4
Evansville ■ ...Feb. 8
Illinois St. ■ ...Feb. 10
Indiana St. ...Feb. 13
Creighton ...Feb. 15
Evansville ...Feb. 17
Wichita St. ■ ...Feb. 22
Southern Ill. ...Feb. 24
Missouri Val. Conf. Tr. ...Feb. 28-Mar. 3

1995-96 RESULTS (16-12)
83 Tex.-Pan American ■ ...71
67 Southwestern La. ■ ...85
105 Tenn.-Martin ■ ...71
105 Stephen F. Austin ■ ...81
74 Texas Tech ...97
79 Northwestern St. ■ ...68
64 Wichita St. ■ ...52
59 East Caro. ...62
65 St. Louis ...75
95 Northern Iowa ■ ...87

89 Indiana St. ...78
79 Illinois St. ...86
61 Bradley ...58
82 Evansville ■ ...84
65 Tulsa ■ ...75
69 Illinois St. ■ ...76
75 Creighton ...81
66 Tulsa ...61
77 Southern Ill. ■ ...65
57 Bradley ■ ...68
67 Northern Iowa ...64
94 Indiana St. ■ ...62
84 Drake ...81
78 Wichita St. ...71
67 Creighton ■ ...66
63 Evansville ...72
65 Creighton † ...58
62 Bradley † ...64

Nickname: Bears
Colors: Maroon & White
Arena: Hammons Student Center
  Capacity: 8,858; Year Built: 1976
AD: Bill Rowe
SID: Mark Stillwell

SOUTHWEST ST.
Marshall, MN 56258 ...II

Coach: Perry Ford
Alma Mater: Jamestown '78
Record: 11 Years, W-201, L-118
1996-97 SCHEDULE
Southwest St. Cl. ...Nov. 22-23
Mo.-Kansas City ...Nov. 27
Southern Colo. Cl. ...Nov. 29-30
Colo. Christian ■ ...Dec. 2
Briar Cliff ■ ...Dec. 4
Mankato St. ...Dec. 6
South Dak. St. ...Dec. 10
Minn.-Crookston ■ ...Dec. 14
N'western (Iowa) Tr. ...Jan. 3-4
Briar Cliff ...Jan. 8
Bemidji St. ■ ...Jan. 11
Wayne St. (Neb.) ■ ...Jan. 15
Minn.-Morris ...Jan. 18
Northern St. ...Jan. 22
Minn.-Duluth ■ ...Jan. 25
Moorhead St. ■ ...Jan. 29
Winona St. ...Feb. 1
Wayne St. (Neb.) ...Feb. 5
Bemidji St. ...Feb. 8
Northern St. ■ ...Feb. 12
Minn.-Morris ■ ...Feb. 15
Moorhead St. ...Feb. 19
Minn.-Duluth ...Feb. 22
Winona St. ■ ...Feb. 26

1995-96 RESULTS
Results unavailable

Nickname: Golden Mustangs
Colors: Brown & Gold
Arena: SSU R/A Facility
  Capacity: 4,000; Year Built: 1996
AD: Ron Flowers
SID: Jennifer Peiffer

SOUTHWEST TEX. ST.
San Marcos, TX 78666 ...I

Coach: Mike Miller
Alma Mater: Tex. A&M-Commerce '87
Record: 2 Years, W-23, L-29
1996-97 SCHEDULE
Texas Southern ■ ...Nov. 25
Ball St. Cl. ...Nov. 29-30
Connecticut ...Dec. 2
Centenary (La.) ...Dec. 7
San Diego St. ■ ...Dec. 10
Hardin-Simmons ■ ...Dec. 14
Lamar ...Dec. 21
Oklahoma Tr. ...Dec. 27-28
McNeese St. ■ ...Jan. 2

Nicholls St. ■ ...Jan. 4
Northeast La. ...Jan. 9
Northwestern St. ...Jan. 11
Texas-Arlington ...Jan. 15
Sam Houston St. ■ ...Jan. 18
Stephen F. Austin ...Jan. 20
Texas-San Antonio ...Jan. 25
Northwestern St. ■ ...Jan. 30
Northeast La. ■ ...Feb. 1
Nicholls St. ...Feb. 6
McNeese St. ...Feb. 8
Texas-San Antonio ■ ...Feb. 15
Texas-Arlington ■ ...Feb. 20
Stephen F. Austin ■ ...Feb. 27
Sam Houston St. ...Mar. 1
Southland Conf. Tr. ...Mar. 5-8

1995-96 RESULTS (11-15)
86 Schreiner ■ ...51
68 Hofstra † ...66
42 San Francisco ...70
74 Tex.-Pan American ■ ...63
63 Ark.-Little Rock ...72
64 Loyola (La.) ■ ...45
62 New Mexico ...72
48 Tex.-Pan American ...58
66 Sam Houston St. ...75
62 Stephen F. Austin ...63
61 Nicholls St. ■ ...53
67 McNeese St. ■ ...66
61 Northeast La. ...56
61 Northwestern St. ...72
80 Texas-Arlington ■ ...72
42 Texas-San Antonio ...65
64 Stephen F. Austin ■ ...69
64 Sam Houston St. ■ ...57
49 McNeese St. ...69
67 Nicholls St. ...61
41 Northwestern St. ■ ...57
60 Northeast La. ■ ...75
55 North Texas ■ ...67
59 Texas-San Antonio ■ ...75
60 North Texas ...67
76 Texas-Arlington ...58

Nickname: Bobcats
Colors: Maroon & Gold
Arena: Strahan Coliseum
  Capacity: 7,200; Year Built: 1979
AD: Mike Alden
SID: Tony Brubaker

SOUTHWESTERN (TEX.)
Georgetown, TX 78626 ...III

Coach: Stephen W. Kenney
Alma Mater: Sewanee '89
Record: 1 Year, W-6, L-18
1996-97 SCHEDULE
McMurry ■ ...Nov. 22
Sul Ross St. ■ ...Nov. 26
Howard Payne ...Nov. 30
Dallas ...Dec. 3
Redlands Tr. ...Dec. 5-7
Dallas ...Jan. 8
Hendrix ■ ...Jan. 10
Rhodes ■ ...Jan. 12
Howard Payne ■ ...Jan. 14
Centre ...Jan. 17
Sewanee ...Jan. 19
Oglethorpe ...Jan. 24
Millsaps ...Jan. 26
Centre ■ ...Jan. 31
Sewanee ■ ...Feb. 2
Austin ...Feb. 5
Oglethorpe ■ ...Feb. 7
Millsaps ■ ...Feb. 9
Trinity (Tex.) ...Feb. 15
Austin ■ ...Feb. 17
Hendrix ...Feb. 21
Rhodes ...Feb. 23
Trinity (Tex.) ■ ...Mar. 1

1995-96 RESULTS (6-18)
76 Southwest Adventist † ...55
67 Mary Hardin-Baylor † ...88

68	Rose-Hulman ■	75
92	Dallas	84
71	Austin †	68
58	Houston Baptist	81
80	Austin	85
73	Austin ■	66
57	Dallas ■	59
65	Sewanee	85
69	Centre ■	83
71	Rhodes	78
89	Hendrix	105
73	Millsaps ■	92
87	Oglethorpe ■	69
64	Rhodes ■	73
81	Hendrix ■	96
80	Millsaps	92
81	Oglethorpe	85
66	Trinity (Tex.) ■	82
63	Sewanee ■	81
77	Centre ■	74
59	Howard Payne ■	79
52	Trinity (Tex.)	74

Nickname: Pirates
Colors: Black & Yellow
Arena: Corbin J. Robertson Center
 Capacity: 1,800; Year Built: 1995
AD: Colada Munt
SID: Jim Shelton

SOUTHWESTERN LA.

Lafayette, LA 70506 I

Coach: Marty Fletcher
Alma Mater: Maryland '73
Record: 14 Years, W-201, L-205

1996-97 SCHEDULE

Florida St.	Nov. 22
Southwest Mo. St. ■	Nov. 25
Marshall ■	Nov. 29
Ohio St.	Dec. 1
Va. Commonwealth	Dec. 11
East Caro.	Dec. 14
Southern U. ■	Dec. 18
Southern Miss. ■	Dec. 21
South Ala.	Dec. 28
Arkansas St. ■	Jan. 2
Jacksonville	Jan. 4
Lamar ■	Jan. 9
Western Ky. ■	Jan. 11
Ark.-Little Rock ■	Jan. 16
Tex.-Pan American	Jan. 18
Arkansas St.	Jan. 23
Ark.-Little Rock	Jan. 25
Louisiana Tech ■	Jan. 30
New Orleans	Feb. 1
Jacksonville ■	Feb. 6
Western Ky.	Feb. 11
Tex.-Pan American ■	Feb. 15
Louisiana Tech	Feb. 17
Lamar	Feb. 20
New Orleans ■	Feb. 22
South Ala. ■	Feb. 24
Sun Belt Conf. Tr.	Feb. 28-Mar. 4

1995-96 RESULTS (16-12)

121	Bapt. Christian ■	64
85	Southwest Mo. St.	67
67	N.C.-Wilmington ■	51
76	Southern Miss.	80
98	Louisiana Col. ■	67
70	Marshall	77
74	Texas A&M ■	69
80	Louisiana Tech	77
77	N.C.-Greensboro ■	64
43	South Ala.	63
69	Jacksonville	80
96	Arkansas St. ■	82
68	Tex.-Pan American ■	52
82	Lamar	69
59	New Orleans ■	67
71	Arkansas St.	77
82	Lamar	69
42	Tex.-Pan American	58
65	South Ala. ■	48

95	Western Ky. ■	85
54	Louisiana Tech ■	61
79	Ark.-Little Rock ■	78
78	Western Ky.	85
67	Ark.-Little Rock. ■	87
86	Jacksonville ■	84
62	New Orleans	66
98	Western Ky. †	94
71	New Orleans †	75

Nickname: Ragin' Cajuns
Colors: Vermilion & White
Arena: Cajundome
 Capacity: 12,000; Year Built: 1985
AD: Nelson Schexnayder
SID: Dan McDonald

SPRINGFIELD

Springfield, MA 01109 III

Coach: Mike Theulen
Alma Mater: Keene St. '80
Record: 6 Years, W-83, L-76

1996-97 SCHEDULE

Wesleyan (Conn.) ■	Nov. 26
Norwich	Dec. 4
Westfield St. ■	Dec. 7
Babson	Dec. 9
Coast Guard	Dec. 11
Sprinfield Cl.	Jan. 4-5
Clark (Mass.)	Jan. 7
Middlebury ■	Jan. 9
Hartwick ■	Jan. 11
Trinity (Conn.) ■	Jan. 16
MIT ■	Jan. 18
Norwich ■	Jan. 21
Wheaton (Mass.) ■	Jan. 28
WPI	Jan. 30
Western New Eng. ■	Feb. 1
Coast Guard ■	Feb. 3
Babson ■	Feb. 6
MIT	Feb. 8
Western New Eng.	Feb. 11
WPI ■	Feb. 13
Southern Vt.	Feb. 18
Clark (Mass.) ■	Feb. 20
Williams ■	Feb. 22

1995-96 RESULTS (21-7)

60	Middlebury	72
59	Wesleyan (Conn.)	53
79	Norwich	66
73	Westfield St.	66
88	Babson ■	84
82	Coast Guard	62
68	Clark (Mass.) ■	66
93	Western New Eng.	65
76	Whittier ■	60
66	Carnegie Mellon ■	57
86	Trinity (Conn.)	81
74	MIT	57
75	Norwich	59
54	Hartwick	57
85	Wheaton (Mass.)	60
86	WPI ■	71
88	Western New Eng.	46
78	Coast Guard	75
67	Babson	79
68	MIT ■	56
71	WPI	53
70	American Int'l ■	76
67	Clark (Mass.)	70
56	Williams	83
95	Western New Eng. ■	64
75	Coast Guard ■	64
78	Babson	70
56	Bowdoin	62

Nickname: Pride
Colors: Maroon & White
Arena: Blake Arena
 Capacity: 2,000; Year Built: 1981
AD: Edward Bilik
SID: Ken Cerino

STANFORD

Stanford, CA 94305 I

Coach: Mike Montgomery
Alma Mater: Long Beach St. '68
Record: 18 Years, W-336, L-197

1996-97 SCHEDULE

Great Alas. Shootout	Nov. 27-30
Manhattan [Sacramento]	Dec. 7
San Diego	Dec. 14
Alas. Anchorage ■	Dec. 18
Seton Hall	Dec. 22
Navy	Dec. 28
Arizona St.	Jan. 2
Arizona	Jan. 4
UCLA ■	Jan. 9
Southern Cal ■	Jan. 11
Oregon	Jan. 16
Oregon St.	Jan. 18
Washington ■	Jan. 23
Washington St. ■	Jan. 25
California	Jan. 29
Southern Cal	Feb. 6
UCLA	Feb. 8
Oregon St. ■	Feb. 13
Oregon ■	Feb. 15
Washington St.	Feb. 20
Washington	Feb. 22
San Diego St. ■	Feb. 24
California ■	Mar. 1
Arizona ■	Mar. 6
Arizona St. ■	Mar. 8

1995-96 RESULTS (20-9)

92	Stetson ■	60
75	Rice ■	64
58	San Francisco †	59
82	South Caro. †	70
63	North Caro. †	87
80	Navy	62
80	American ■	52
65	Harvard ■	59
83	Arizona St. ■	70
80	Arizona ■	71
56	UCLA	64
80	Southern Cal	84
94	Oregon ■	74
84	Oregon St. ■	51
71	Washington	74
78	Washington St.	67
93	California ■	79
83	Seton Hall †	60
99	Southern Cal ■	69
67	UCLA ■	66
65	Oregon St.	50
62	Oregon	64
59	Washington St. ■	68
71	Washington ■	56
69	California	85
85	Arizona	79
67	Arizona St.	53
66	Bradley †	58
74	Massachusetts †	79

Nickname: Cardinal
Colors: Cardinal & White
Arena: Maples Pavilion
 Capacity: 7,500; Year Built: 1968
AD: Ted Leland
SID: Bob Vazquez

STATEN ISLAND

Staten Island, NY 10301 III

Coach: Tony Petosa
Alma Mater: Staten Island '86
Record: 7 Years, W-102, L-85

1996-97 SCHEDULE

Widener Tr.	Nov. 22-23
York (N.Y.) ■	Nov. 25
N.J. Inst. of Tech. ■	Dec. 5
Rutgers-Newark ■	Dec. 9
Medgar Evers	Dec. 11
FDU-Madison ■	Dec. 14

Staten Island Tr.	Dec. 27-28
John Jay	Jan. 4
Medgar Evers ■	Jan. 8
Mt. St. Mary (N.Y.) ■	Jan. 11
Montclair St.	Jan. 13
Hunter	Jan. 16
Brooklyn ■	Jan. 25
Hunter ■	Jan. 29
Manhattanville	Feb. 1
CCNY	Feb. 3
Lehman ■	Feb. 5
Old Westbury ■	Feb. 7
Baruch ■	Feb. 12
Brooklyn ■	Feb. 15
York (N.Y.) ■	Feb. 17
Merchant Marine	Feb. 19

1995-96 RESULTS (22-6)

78	Newport News App. †	70
73	Hampden-Sydney	87
85	York (N.Y.)	76
82	Manhattanville ■	59
86	N.J. Inst. of Tech.	75
72	Rutgers-Newark ■	76
71	New York U.	65
63	FDU-Madison	61
80	Medgar Evers ■	60
88	Montclair St. ■	74
71	Ramapo ■	77
66	Widener ■	50
79	York (N.Y.) ■	67
76	Medgar Evers	85
84	Old Westbury ■	78
65	Hunter ■	51
81	John Jay ■	42
73	Brooklyn ■	53
74	Hunter	71
88	Mt. St. Mary (N.Y.)	93
68	CCNY ■	55
69	Lehman	48
68	Merchant Marine ■	64
74	Baruch	68
71	Lehman ■	57
72	Baruch †	67
66	York (N.Y.) †	62
63	Jersey City St. ■	73

Nickname: Dolphins
Colors: Maroon & Columbia Blue
Arena: Sports & Recreation Center
 Capacity: 1,200; Year Built: 1995
AD: Eugene Marshall
SID: Terry Small

STEPHEN F. AUSTIN

Nacogdoches, TX 75962 I

Coach: Derek Allister
Alma Mater: Cal St. Chico '76
(First year as head coach)

1996-97 SCHEDULE

Minnesota	Nov. 23
Schreiner ■	Nov. 27
Oral Roberts	Nov. 30
Iowa St. Challenge	Dec. 5-6
Houston Baptist ■	Dec. 16
UAB Tr.	Dec. 20-21
Southeastern La.	Dec. 28
Texas-Arlington ■	Jan. 2
Northeast La. ■	Jan. 4
Northwestern St. ■	Jan. 6
Sam Houston St.	Jan. 11
Texas-San Antonio ■	Jan. 18
Southwest Tex. St.	Jan. 20
McNeese St. ■	Jan. 23
Nicholls St. ■	Jan. 25
Sam Houston St. ■	Jan. 30
Northeast La.	Feb. 6
Northwestern St.	Feb. 8
Oral Roberts ■	Feb. 11
Texas-Arlington	Feb. 15
Nicholls St.	Feb. 20
McNeese St.	Feb. 22
Southwest Tex. St. ■	Feb. 27
Texas-San Antonio ■	Mar. 1

Southland Conf. Tr. ....Mar. 5-8

1995-96 RESULTS (17-11)
90	Cameron ■	71
99	St. Edward's ■	76
88	Idaho St. †	84
81	Southwest Mo. St.	105
58	Louisiana Tech ■	68
95	Cal St. Northridge †	90
88	UCLA	109
91	Southeastern La. ■	71
99	Texas-San Antonio ■	82
63	Southwest Tex. St. ■	62
78	Texas-Arlington	88
66	North Texas	75
87	Sam Houston St.	72
83	Northwestern St.	68
54	Nicholls St. ■	71
94	McNeese St. ■	73
69	Southwest Tex. St.	64
71	Texas-San Antonio	75
65	North Texas ■	72
78	Texas-Arlington ■	74
74	Sam Houston St. ■	65
90	Northeast La.	97
69	McNeese St.	66
76	Nicholls St.	58
76	Northwestern St. ■	70
82	Northeast La. ■	92
94	McNeese St. †	91
73	Northeast La. †	92

Nickname: Lumberjacks
Colors: Purple & White
Arena: William Johnson Coliseum
 Capacity: 7,200; Year Built: 1974
AD: Steve McCarty
SID: Bill Powers

STETSON
DeLand, FL 32720 I

Coach: Randy Brown
Alma Mater: Iowa '81
Record: 1 Year, W-10, L-17

1996-97 SCHEDULE
Palm Beach Atl. ■	Nov. 23
Furman	Nov. 25
William & Mary ■	Nov. 27
Wis.-Milwaukee	Nov. 30
Tenn. Temple ■	Dec. 2
Florida	Dec. 14
Mississippi	Dec. 17
Youngstown St. ■	Dec. 21
Southern Methodist ■	Dec. 28
Citadel ■	Dec. 30
Samford	Jan. 2
Jacksonville St. ■	Jan. 4
Southeastern La.	Jan. 9
Centenary (La.)	Jan. 11
Georgia St.	Jan. 16
Mercer ■	Jan. 18
Florida Int'l	Jan. 23
Fla. Atlantic	Jan. 25
Campbell ■	Jan. 30
Charleston (S.C.) ■	Feb. 1
Central Fla.	Feb. 3
Campbell	Feb. 6
Charleston (S.C.) ■	Feb. 8
Central Fla. ■	Feb. 15
Fla. Atlantic ■	Feb. 20
Florida Int'l ■	Feb. 22
Trans America Conf. Tr.	Feb. 27-Mar. 1

1995-96 RESULTS (10-17)
60	Stanford	92
78	Yale †	58
57	DePaul	90
66	Jacksonville	74
76	Embry-Riddle ■	53
85	West Fla.	65
61	Mississippi Val. ■	81
57	Wis.-Milwaukee ■	73
66	Furman ■	53
46	Florida	78
54	Samford	56
67	Jacksonville St.	96
79	Southeastern La. ■	94
96	Centenary (La.) ■	83
73	Georgia St. ■	61
67	Mercer	77
87	Florida Int'l ■	68
84	Fla. Atlantic ■	76
75	Campbell	62
50	Charleston (S.C.)	63
66	Central Fla. ■	75
50	Campbell	53
58	Charleston (S.C.) ■	68
62	Central Fla.	73
72	Fla. Atlantic	83
82	Florida Int'l	73
59	Campbell	67

Nickname: Hatters
Colors: Green & White
Arena: Edmunds Center
 Capacity: 5,000; Year Built: 1974
AD: Jeff Altier
SID: Tom McClellan

STEVENS TECH
Hoboken, NJ 07030 III

Coach: Charles Brown
Alma Mater: William Penn '76
Record: 4 Years, W-40, L-61

1996-97 SCHEDULE
Swarthmore Cl.	Nov. 22-23
Drew ■	Nov. 26
Roger Williams ■	Nov. 30
Mt. St. Vincent ■	Dec. 2
Yeshiva	Dec. 7
Stevens Tech Tr.	Jan. 3-4
Montclair St.	Jan. 6
Lehman ■	Jan. 9
Vassar ■	Jan. 13
N.J. Inst. of Tech. ■	Jan. 15
Rensselaer	Jan. 18
Baruch	Jan. 23
St. Joe's-Brooklyn ■	Jan. 25
Merchant Marine	Jan. 28
Polytechnic (N.Y.) ■	Jan. 30
N.J. Inst. of Tech.	Feb. 1
FDU-Madison	Feb. 3
Manhattanville ■	Feb. 5
Bard ■	Feb. 8
Yeshiva	Feb. 13
Wesley	Feb. 15
Polytechnic (N.Y.)	Feb. 18

1995-96 RESULTS (16-11)
64	Trinity (Conn.)	118
94	Lehman	77
78	Mt. St. Vincent	89
87	Maritime (N.Y.)	84
78	St. Joe's-Brooklyn ■	65
81	Merchant Marine	96
69	Drew	64
85	Baruch ■	87
81	Yeshiva ■	64
92	Drew	89
67	Rochester Inst. ■	76
85	Polytechnic (N.Y.) ■	49
67	N.J. Inst. of Tech.	78
85	Vassar	84
77	Maritime (N.Y.) ■	87
91	St. Joe's-Brooklyn	70
81	FDU-Madison ■	88
69	Polytechnic (N.Y.)	63
90	N.J. Inst. of Tech. ■	94
103	Bard	36
98	Wesley ■	90
98	Pratt	55
76	Yeshiva	70
89	Polytechnic (N.Y.) ■	68
76	N.J. Inst. of Tech. ■	87
90	Centenary (N.J.)	76
79	Rutgers-Newark †	90

Nickname: Ducks
Colors: Red & Gray
Arena: Schaeffer Center
 Capacity: 1,400; Year Built: 1994

AD: Frank Rotunda
SID: John Lyon

STILLMAN
Tuscaloosa, AL 35403 III

Coach: Larry Robinson
Alma Mater: Jackson St.
Record: 15 Years, W-196, L-130

1996-97 SCHEDULE
Philander Smith ■	Nov. 22
Talladega	Nov. 23
Stillman Tr.	Nov. 29-30
Talladega ■	Dec. 3
Oakwood	Dec. 5
Ark. Baptist ■	Dec. 7
Rust Tr.	Jan. 10-11
Philander Smith ■	Jan. 15
Ark. Baptist	Jan. 16
Oakwood ■	Jan. 18
Concordia (Ind.)	Jan. 25
Rust ■	Jan. 30
Selma	Feb. 1
Tenn. Temple ■	Feb. 4
Fisk ■	Feb. 8
Fisk	Feb. 14
Tenn. Temple	Feb. 15
Rust	Feb. 20
Concordia (Ind.)	Feb. 22

1995-96 RESULTS (19-4)
90	Talladega ■	103
85	Miles ■	72
100	Allen ■	63
80	Rust ■	78
77	Paul Quinn	73
97	Pensacola Christian	96
101	Talladega	95
95	Miles	101
56	Tenn. Temple	69
107	Fisk	60
77	Maryville (Tenn.)	72
96	Philander Smith	91
70	Ark. Baptist	63
101	Fisk	75
77	Concordia (Tex.) ■	75
76	Rust	75
70	Concordia (Tex.)	69
87	Tenn. Temple	85
92	La Grange ■	78
109	Philander Smith ■	95
124	Fisk	74
95	Rust ■	72
85	Hendrix	97

Nickname: Tigers
Colors: Old Gold & Navy Blue
Arena: Birthright
 Capacity: 1,500; Year Built: 1954
AD: Sharon Whittaker
SID: To be named

STONEHILL
North Easton, MA 02356 II

Coach: David DeCiantis
Alma Mater: Springfield '83
Record: 1 Year, W-16, L-10

1996-97 SCHEDULE
Pace	Nov. 26
Mercyhurst Cl.	Nov. 29-30
Quinnipiac	Dec. 3
Bridgewater (Va.) Tr.	Dec. 6-7
Southern Conn. St. ■	Dec. 15
New Hamp. Col.	Dec. 19
Merrimack ■	Dec. 22
Mass.-Lowell ■	Jan. 5
St. Michael's	Jan. 8
Le Moyne ■	Jan. 11
Bentley ■	Jan. 14
Bryant ■	Jan. 16
American Int'l	Jan. 18
Assumption	Jan. 21
St. Anselm ■	Jan. 25
St. Michael's ■	Jan. 29
Merrimack	Feb. 1
Bentley	Feb. 5
American Int'l ■	Feb. 8
Bryant	Feb. 11
Le Moyne	Feb. 13
Assumption ■	Feb. 16
Quinnipiac ■	Feb. 19
St. Anselm ■	Feb. 22

1995-96 RESULTS (16-10)
Results unavailable

Nickname: Chieftains
Colors: Purple & White
Arena: Merkert Gymnasium
 Capacity: 2,200; Year Built: 1973
AD: Paula Sullivan
SID: Bob Richards

STONY BROOK
Stony Brook, NY 11794 II

Coach: Bernard Tomlin
Alma Mater: Hofstra '76
Record: 7 Years, W-93, L-92

1996-97 SCHEDULE
Daeman Tr.	Nov. 14-15
Hofstra	Nov. 22
Adelphi ■	Nov. 26
Molloy	Dec. 2
Franklin Pierce ■	Dec. 8
Stony Brook Inv.	Dec. 28-29
New Haven ■	Jan. 6
Mass.-Lowell	Jan. 8
New Hamp. Col.	Jan. 11
New Haven	Jan. 14
Sacred Heart ■	Jan. 16
Keene St.	Jan. 18
Bridgeport	Jan. 22
Keene St. ■	Jan. 25
Old Westbury	Jan. 27
Albany (N.Y.)	Jan. 29
New Hamp. Col.	Feb. 1
Bridgeport ■	Feb. 4
Franklin Pierce	Feb. 8
Southern Conn. St. ■	Feb. 12
Mass.-Lowell ■	Feb. 15
Albany (N.Y.) ■	Feb. 18
Sacred Heart	Feb. 20
Southern Conn. St.	Feb. 22

1995-96 RESULTS (9-17)
70	Scranton	75
72	Hofstra	91
68	New Hamp. Col. ■	75
82	Mass.-Lowell ■	74
93	Keene St.	87
57	Franklin Pierce	77
60	Southern Me.	57
87	Old Westbury ■	70
62	Le Moyne ■	74
58	New Haven	66
84	Bridgeport	87
67	Albany (N.Y.) ■	76
71	New Haven ■	82
57	Southern Conn. St.	78
98	Keene St. ■	78
32	Franklin Pierce ■	50
52	Adelphi †	65
70	Sacred Heart	74
74	LIU-Southampton ■	58
60	Bridgeport	57
73	New Hamp. Col.	87
63	Mass.-Lowell	54
47	Southern Conn. St. ■	61
50	Le Moyne	62
65	Albany (N.Y.)	79
58	Sacred Heart ■	55

Nickname: Seawolves
Colors: Scarlet & Gray
Arena: Stony Brook Sports Complex
 Capacity: 5,226; Year Built: 1990
AD: Sandy Weeden
SID: To be named

SUFFOLK
Boston, MA 02114 III

Coach: Dennis McHugh
Alma Mater: Boston College '65
Record: 1 Year, W-3, L-21

1996-97 SCHEDULE
Babson Inv. ....Nov. 22-23
Bri'water (Mass.) ....Nov. 25
Nichols ....Nov. 27
Mass.-Boston Inv. ....Nov. 29-30
Curry ....Dec. 3
Brandeis ....Dec. 5
Roger Williams ....Dec. 7
Eastern Nazarene ■ ....Jan. 11
Bates ....Jan. 14
MIT ■ ....Jan. 16
Connecticut Col. ■ ....Jan. 18
Salve Regina ■ ....Jan. 21
Fitchburg St. ■ ....Jan. 23
Clark (Mass.) ■ ....Jan. 30
Tufts ....Feb. 1
WPI ....Feb. 6
Maine Maritime ■ ....Feb. 8
Babson ....Feb. 11
New England ....Feb. 15
Wentworth Inst. ■ ....Feb. 18
Wheaton (Mass.) ■ ....Feb. 25

1995-96 RESULTS (16-10)
Results unavailable

Nickname: Rams
Colors: Blue & Gold
AD: James Nelson
SID: Lou Connelly

SUSQUEHANNA
Selinsgrove, PA 17870 III

Coach: Frank Marcinek
Alma Mater: Penn St. '81
Record: 7 Years, W-108, L-73

1996-97 SCHEDULE
York (Pa.) ....Nov. 25
Moravian ■ ....Dec. 3
Elizabethtown ....Dec. 7
Scranton ....Dec. 9
King's (Pa.) ■ ....Dec. 12
Susquehanna Cl. ....Dec. 20-21
Lebanon Valley ■ ....Jan. 7
Dickinson Tr. ....Jan. 10-11
Wilkes ....Jan. 11
Messiah ■ ....Jan. 16
Widener ....Jan. 18
Bloomsburg ....Jan. 20
Albright ....Jan. 22
Juniata ■ ....Jan. 25
Moravian ....Jan. 29
Elizabethtown ■ ....Feb. 1
Lebanon Valley ....Feb. 4
Lycoming ■ ....Feb. 8
Messiah ....Feb. 12
Widener ■ ....Feb. 15
Albright ■ ....Feb. 19
Juniata ....Feb. 22

1995-96 RESULTS (14-12)
80	Wm. Paterson ■	66
85	Alvernia ■	96
77	York (Pa.) ■	82
71	Moravian	81
67	Elizabethtown ■	62
75	Lebanon Valley	57
64	Wilkes	94
62	IU/PU-Indianapolis †	71
110	Hawaii-Hilo	114
94	Shippensburg †	96
79	Messiah †	59
84	Messiah	76
97	Albright ■	99
88	Juniata	76
80	Moravian ■	71
80	Elizabethtown	75
81	Lebanon Valley ■	79

86	Widener ■	75
77	Lycoming	87
93	Messiah ■	96
64	Widener	67
79	Albright ■	76
103	Juniata ■	74
92	Scranton ■	81
73	Lycoming ■	66
49	Wilkes	71

Nickname: Crusaders
Colors: Orange & Maroon
Arena: O. W. Houts Gymnasium
  Capacity: 1,800; Year Built: 1976
AD: Donald Harnum
SID: Mike Ferlazzo

SWARTHMORE
Swarthmore, PA 19081 III

Coach: Lee Wimberly
Alma Mater: Stanford '68
Record: 10 Years, W-88, L-158

1996-97 SCHEDULE
Swarthmore Cl. ....Nov. 22-23
Gwynedd-Mercy ■ ....Nov. 26
Yale ....Dec. 1
Johns Hopkins ■ ....Dec. 3
Connecticut Col. Tr. ....Dec. 6-7
Lafayette ....Dec. 10
Pomona-Pitzer ....Jan. 6
Occidental ....Jan. 7
Frank. & Marsh. ■ ....Jan. 11
Drew ....Jan. 14
Washington (Md.) ....Jan. 16
Ursinus ■ ....Jan. 18
Muhlenberg ■ ....Jan. 22
Western Md. ....Jan. 25
Phila. Pharmacy ....Jan. 29
Gettysburg ....Feb. 1
Haverford ■ ....Feb. 5
Ursinus ....Feb. 8
Washington (Md.) ■ ....Feb. 12
Dickinson ■ ....Feb. 15
Muhlenberg ■ ....Feb. 19
Haverford ....Feb. 22

1995-96 RESULTS (9-15)
82	Macalester †	88
69	Amherst ■	74
83	Gwynedd-Mercy	66
61	Johns Hopkins	65
64	Williams	77
65	Yale	73
70	Lafayette	69
67	Frank. & Marsh.	86
63	Savannah A&D ■	68
71	Middlebury †	52
45	Moravian	61
55	Washington (Md.) ■	59
77	Ursinus	71
65	Muhlenberg	78
85	Western Md. ■	57
82	Phila. Pharmacy ■	65
81	Gettysburg ■	88
44	Haverford	58
74	Ursinus ■	65
61	Washington (Md.)	53
63	Dickinson	66
68	Drew	75
53	Muhlenberg ■	57
56	Haverford ■	55

Nickname: Garnet Tide
Colors: Garnet & White
Arena: Tarble Pavillion
  Capacity: 1,800; Year Built: 1978
AD: Robert Williams
SID: Mark Duzenski

SYRACUSE
Syracuse, NY 13244 I

Coach: Jim Boeheim
Alma Mater: Syracuse '66
Record: 20 Years, W-483, L-159

1996-97 SCHEDULE
Winthrop ■ ....Nov. 22
Great Alas. Shootout ....Nov. 27-30
West Va. ....Dec. 4
Miami (Fla.) ....Dec. 7
Buffalo ....Dec. 10
Syracuse Cl. ....Dec. 13-14
UNLV ....Dec. 18
Colgate ■ ....Dec. 22
Md.-East. Shore ■ ....Dec. 30
Notre Dame ....Jan. 2
Boston College ■ ....Jan. 7
Alabama ....Jan. 11
Seton Hall ....Jan. 15
Notre Dame ■ ....Jan. 18
Villanova ....Jan. 20
Connecticut ....Jan. 26
Seton Hall ■ ....Jan. 28
Villanova ....Feb. 1
Boston College ■ ....Feb. 4
Georgetown ■ ....Feb. 8
St. John's (N.Y.) ....Feb. 12
West Va. ■ ....Feb. 15
Connecticut ■ ....Feb. 17
Rutgers ■ ....Feb. 22
Providence ....Feb. 24
Pittsburgh ....Mar. 2
Big East Conf. Tr. ....Mar. 5-8

1995-96 RESULTS (29-9)
87	Lafayette	63
89	Colgate ■	55
82	Providence	78
97	St. John's (N.Y.) ■	72
83	Columbia	60
77	Washington St. ■	75
75	Bowling Green ■	64
72	Charleston (S.C.) ■	61
79	Arizona	70
75	Illinois †	64
92	Rhode Island †	66
47	Massachusetts †	65
66	Miami (Fla.)	75
77	Providence ■	75
81	Rutgers ■	80
78	West Va.	90
70	Connecticut	79
64	Georgetown	83
88	Boston College ■	73
69	Villanova ■	72
72	Miami (Fla.) ■	51
81	Alabama ■	68
73	Pittsburgh	67
85	Georgetown ■	64
63	Rutgers	54
79	Seton Hall	80
77	Pittsburgh ■	60
92	St. John's (N.Y.)	79
71	Notre Dame ■	67
76	Notre Dame †	55
69	Boston College †	61
67	Connecticut †	85
88	Montana St. †	55
69	Drexel †	58
83	Georgia †	81
60	Kansas †	57
77	Mississippi St. †	69
67	Kentucky †	76

Nickname: Orangemen
Colors: Orange
Arena: Carrier Dome
  Capacity: 33,000; Year Built: 1980
AD: Jake Crouthamel
SID: Larry Kimball

TAMPA
Tampa, FL 33606 II

Coach: Richard Schmidt
Alma Mater: Western Ky. '64
Record: 15 Years, W-321, L-129

1996-97 SCHEDULE
St. Thomas (Fla.) ■ ....Nov. 19
Webber ■ ....Nov. 26
Northern Ky. ■ ....Nov. 27
North Central ■ ....Dec. 3
American (P.R.) ■ ....Dec. 5
Embry-Riddle ■ ....Dec. 5
Valdosta St. Inv. ....Dec. 13-14
Carthage ■ ....Dec. 28
Husson ■ ....Dec. 30
Franklin Pierce ■ ....Jan. 3
Barry ....Jan. 8
St. Leo ....Jan. 11
Rollins ■ ....Jan. 15
Florida Tech ■ ....Jan. 18
North Fla. ....Jan. 25
Eckerd ■ ....Jan. 25
Fla. Southern ■ ....Jan. 29
Rollins ■ ....Feb. 1
Florida Tech ....Feb. 5
St. Leo ■ ....Feb. 8
North Fla. ■ ....Feb. 12
Eckerd ■ ....Feb. 15
Fla. Southern ....Feb. 19
Barry ■ ....Feb. 22

1995-96 RESULTS (14-13)
97	Webber ■	84
101	Otterbein ■	93
92	St. Thomas (Fla.) ■	83
93	Embry-Riddle ■	74
60	Southern Miss.	74
80	Valdosta St.	89
95	Judson (Ill.)	62
66	Armstrong Atlantic	80
73	American (P.R.) ■	85
84	Merrimack	75
79	Minn.-Duluth	76
100	Central Meth.	63
89	Rollins	96
75	St. Leo ■	72
70	Barry	75
73	Eckerd ■	68
69	Fla. Southern ■	72
61	North Fla.	79
79	Florida Tech	71
81	Rollins ■	62
92	St. Leo	82
62	Barry	63
59	Eckerd	67
52	Fla. Southern	70
53	North Fla. ■	50
59	Florida Tech ■	61
67	Barry †	84

Nickname: Spartans
Colors: Scarlet, Gold & Black
Arena: Martinez Sports Center
  Capacity: 3,432; Year Built: 1984
AD: Hindman Wall
SID: Gil Swalls

TARLETON ST.
Stephenville, TX 76401 II

Coach: Lonn Reisman
Alma Mater: Pittsburg St. '77
Record: 8 Years, W-155, L-86

1996-97 SCHEDULE
Ambassador ■ ....Nov. 16
LeTourneau ■ ....Nov. 23
Louisiana Tech ....Nov. 26
McMurry ■ ....Nov. 30
Howard Payne ■ ....Dec. 2
Okla. Sci. & Arts ■ ....Dec. 6
Mary Hardin-Baylor ■ ....Dec. 7
Texas A&M-Commerce ....Dec. 14
Louisiana Tech ....Dec. 17
Schreiner ■ ....Dec. 30
Tex. A&M-Kingsville ■ ....Jan. 4
Abilene Christian ■ ....Jan. 7
Angelo St. ....Jan. 9
West Tex. A&M ■ ....Jan. 11
Eastern N.M. ■ ....Jan. 13
Midwestern St. ....Jan. 18
Central Okla. ....Jan. 18
Tex. A&M-Kingsville ....Jan. 23
Cameron ■ ....Jan. 25
Angelo St. ■ ....Jan. 30
Abilene Christian ■ ....Feb. 1

(Texas A&M—Commerce, cont.)

	Eastern N.M.	Feb. 6
	West Tex. A&M	Feb. 8
	Central Okla. ■	Feb. 13
	Midwestern St. ■	Feb. 15
	Cameron ■	Feb. 17
	Texas A&M-Commerce ■	Feb. 22

1995-96 RESULTS (11-16)

Score	Opponent	Opp
71	Grand Canyon	89
82	Colo. Christian †	61
112	Southwest Adventist ■	46
80	Cameron	83
85	Sul Ross St. †	45
95	Austin †	58
83	Panhandle St. †	63
76	St. Edward's	68
46	Western N.M. ■	39
80	Texas A&M-Commerce ■	86
66	Tex. A&M-Kingsville	75
73	Abilene Christian ■	66
96	Angelo St. ■	72
74	West Tex. A&M	81
63	Eastern N.M.	101
88	Midwestern St. ■	100
93	Central Okla. ■	100
48	Tex. A&M-Kingsville ■	69
66	Cameron ■	72
66	Angelo St.	67
78	Abilene Christian ■	81
70	Eastern N.M. ■	73
66	West Tex. A&M ■	65
93	Central Okla.	111
81	Midwestern St.	89
110	Ambassador ■	61
63	Texas A&M-Commerce	75

Nickname: Texans
Colors: Purple & White
Arena: Wisdom Gymnasium
Capacity: 3,212; Year Built: 1970
AD: Lonn Reisman
SID: Reed Richmond

TEMPLE

Philadelphia, PA 19122 I

Coach: John Chaney
Alma Mater: Bethune-Cookman '55
Record: 24 Years, W-540, L-188

1996-97 SCHEDULE

Wisconsin ■	Dec. 4
Georgia Tech [Atlantic City]	Dec. 7
Tulane ■	Dec. 9
Tulsa ■	Dec. 14
Pennsylvania ■	Dec. 21
Oregon Cl.	Dec. 27-28
DePaul	Jan. 4
Rhode Island ■	Jan. 7
St. Bonaventure ■	Jan. 11
Dayton ■	Jan. 13
Cincinnati	Jan. 16
Xavier (Ohio) ■	Jan. 19
Fordham	Jan. 23
Massachusetts ■	Jan. 25
La Salle	Jan. 28
St. Joseph's (Pa.)	Jan. 30
Louisville ■	Feb. 2
St. Bonaventure	Feb. 4
Duquesne	Feb. 9
St. Joseph's (Pa.) ■	Feb. 13
Rhode Island	Feb. 16
Virginia Tech	Feb. 18
Geo. Washington ■	Feb. 22
Fordham ■	Feb. 24
Massachusetts	Mar. 1
Atlantic 10 Conf. Tr.	Mar. 5-8

1995-96 RESULTS (20-13)

Score	Opponent	Opp
65	Rider ■	62
49	Georgetown	74
54	Wisconsin	57
60	Tulsa ■	64
62	Villanova †	56
49	Cincinnati †	70
74	Kansas †	66
58	Memphis	68

41	Oklahoma St. †	49
58	St. Bonaventure ■	56
73	Xavier (Ohio) ■	56
62	Dayton	46
72	Duquesne ■	40
69	Fordham	48
59	Tulane	67
68	La Salle	48
59	Duke †	58
54	St. Joseph's (Pa.) †	52
35	Massachusetts ■	59
47	Geo. Washington	64
60	St. Joseph's (Pa.) ■	58
55	Massachusetts	84
63	Rhode Island ■	67
77	Fordham ■	56
53	Pennsylvania	42
73	Rhode Island	62
57	Virginia Tech	41
57	St. Bonaventure	54
67	Xavier (Ohio) †	50
64	Rhode Island ■	52
61	Massachusetts †	75
61	Oklahoma †	43
65	Cincinnati †	78

Nickname: Owls
Colors: Cherry & White
Arena: McGonigle Hall
Capacity: 3,900; Year Built: 1969
AD: Dave O'Brien
SID: Scott Cathcart

TENNESSEE

Knoxville, TN 37996 I

Coach: Kevin O'Neill
Alma Mater: McGill '79
Record: 8 Years, W-128, L-107

1996-97 SCHEDULE

Morehead St. ■	Nov. 24
Georgia ■	Dec. 1
Tennessee Tech ■	Dec. 4
Penn St.	Dec. 7
Memphis ■	Dec. 15
Southern Cal ■	Dec. 18
Miami (Fla.) ■	Dec. 22
N.C.-Charlotte	Dec. 28
East Tenn. St. ■	Dec. 31
Kentucky	Jan. 4
South Caro.	Jan. 8
Vanderbilt ■	Jan. 11
Auburn	Jan. 15
LSU ■	Jan. 19
Mississippi	Jan. 22
Florida ■	Jan. 25
Georgia ■	Jan. 29
Wofford ■	Feb. 1
Arkansas	Feb. 5
Alabama ■	Feb. 8
Vanderbilt	Feb. 12
Mississippi St. ■	Feb. 15
Florida	Feb. 19
South Caro. ■	Feb. 22
Kentucky ■	Feb. 25
Georgia	Mar. 1
Southeastern Conf. Tr.	Mar. 6-9

1995-96 RESULTS (14-15)

Score	Opponent	Opp
74	Georgia St. ■	59
76	N.C.-Charlotte ■	79
57	Penn St. ■	69
63	Western Caro. ■	51
80	Austin Peay ■	70
55	Memphis	57
69	Houston ■	49
54	South Fla. ■	43
56	Miami (Fla.)	54
66	Auburn ■	62
55	Vanderbilt	65
58	South Caro. ■	62
44	Kentucky	61
65	Tennessee Tech ■	53
53	Alabama	62
67	Georgia ■	62

59	Mississippi St.	60
67	Mississippi ■	52
49	Georgia	68
51	Florida	63
73	LSU	65
50	Kentucky ■	90
66	Arkansas ■	89
94	Vanderbilt ■	79
52	South Caro.	66
71	Florida ■	73
77	Alabama †	72
63	Georgia †	74
49	Charleston (S.C.) ■	55

Nickname: Volunteers
Colors: Orange & White
Arena: Thompson-Boling Arena
Capacity: 24,535; Year Built: 1987
AD: Doug Dickey
SID: David Grim

TENNESSEE ST.

Nashville, TN 37203 I

Coach: Frankie Allen
Alma Mater: Roanoke '71
Record: 9 Years, W-130, L-130

1996-97 SCHEDULE

Old Dominion	Dec. 2
Illinois Cl.	Dec. 6-7
Florida St.	Dec. 17
Tenn.-Chatt.	Dec. 21
Louisville	Dec. 23
Mississippi Val. [Memphis]	Dec. 28
Jackson St.	Jan. 2
Eastern Ill. ■	Jan. 4
Southeast Mo. St. ■	Jan. 6
Middle Tenn. St.	Jan. 9
Tenn.-Martin	Jan. 11
Murray St.	Jan. 13
Austin Peay ■	Jan. 18
Tennessee Tech	Jan. 23
Morehead St. ■	Jan. 25
Eastern Ky. ■	Jan. 27
Southeast Mo. St.	Feb. 1
Eastern Ill.	Feb. 3
Tennessee Tech ■	Feb. 6
Murray St. ■	Feb. 8
Tenn.-Martin ■	Feb. 10
Middle Tenn. St. ■	Feb. 13
Austin Peay	Feb. 15
Morehead St.	Feb. 20
Eastern Ky.	Feb. 22
Ohio Valley Conf. Tr.	Feb. 25-Mar. 1

1995-96 RESULTS (15-13)

Score	Opponent	Opp
75	Missouri	89
72	Colorado	86
67	Iowa St.	75
74	Tex.-Pan American †	68
70	Mississippi Val. †	86
74	Vanderbilt	93
67	Arkansas	86
84	Southern U. †	79
86	Wis.-Parkside	88
83	Tenn.-Martin ■	78
67	Murray St. ■	71
81	Austin Peay ■	76
73	East Tenn. St.	70
74	Middle Tenn. St.	86
82	Southeast Mo. St.	70
72	Eastern Ky. ■	69
86	Morehead St. ■	76
75	Tennessee Tech	71
67	Tenn.-Martin	71
78	Murray St.	72
74	Middle Tenn. St. ■	79
75	Austin Peay	102
76	Southeast Mo. St. ■	73
74	Tennessee Tech ■	65
65	Morehead St.	60
82	Eastern Ky.	76
71	Morehead St. ■	60
62	Austin Peay ■	83

Nickname: Tigers
Colors: Blue & White
Arena: Howard Gentry Complex
Capacity: 10,500; Year Built: 1980
AD: Howard Gentry Jr
SID: Johnny Franks

TENNESSEE TECH

Cookeville, TN 38505 I

Coach: Frank Harrell
Alma Mater: Ga. Southwestern '72
Record: 10 Years, W-117, L-169

1996-97 SCHEDULE

Clinch Valley	Nov. 23
Cumberland (Tenn.) ■	Nov. 25
Northwestern	Nov. 30
Tennessee	Dec. 4
Arkansas St. ■	Dec. 17
Vanderbilt	Dec. 21
Montana St. Cl.	Dec. 28-29
Morehead St.	Jan. 4
Eastern Ky.	Jan. 6
Austin Peay	Jan. 9
Middle Tenn. St.	Jan. 11
Tenn.-Martin ■	Jan. 16
Eastern Ill. ■	Jan. 18
Southeast Mo. St. ■	Jan. 20
Tennessee St. ■	Jan. 23
Tenn.-Martin	Jan. 25
Murray St.	Jan. 27
Eastern Ky. ■	Feb. 1
Morehead St. ■	Feb. 3
Tennessee St.	Feb. 6
Middle Tenn. St. ■	Feb. 8
Murray St. ■	Feb. 13
Southeast Mo. St.	Feb. 15
Eastern Ill.	Feb. 17
Austin Peay	Feb. 20
Ohio Valley Conf. Tr.	Feb. 25-Mar. 1

1995-96 RESULTS (13-15)

Score	Opponent	Opp
90	Cumberland (Tenn.) ■	55
62	Oral Roberts	81
78	Alabama	90
110	Bethel (Tenn.) ■	54
93	Lambuth ■	62
89	Arkansas St.	87
65	Boise St.	66
100	Texas Southern †	96
74	Tenn.-Martin ■	78
64	Murray St. ■	63
68	Middle Tenn. St. ■	78
83	Austin Peay	86
53	Tennessee	65
78	Southeast Mo. St.	81
85	Morehead St. ■	72
86	Eastern Ky. ■	80
71	Tennessee St. ■	75
71	Tenn.-Martin	75
74	Oral Roberts ■	89
74	Austin Peay ■	93
77	Middle Tenn. St.	71
102	Southeast Mo. St. ■	69
77	Murray St.	76
65	Tennessee St.	74
83	Eastern Ky.	87
88	Morehead St.	78
89	Middle Tenn. St. †	69
71	Murray St. †	85

Nickname: Golden Eagles
Colors: Purple & Gold
Arena: Eblen Center
Capacity: 10,150; Year Built: 1977
AD: Dr. David Larimore
SID: Rob Schabert

TENN.-CHATT.

Chattanooga, TN 37401 I

Coach: Mack McCarthy
Alma Mater: Virginia Tech '74
Record: 11 Years, W-219, L-111

1996-97 SCHEDULE
Tenn. Wesleyan ■ ...Nov. 22
S.C.-Aiken ■ ...Nov. 23
San Juan Shootout ...Nov. 29-Dec. 1
Penn St. ■ ...Dec. 3
Middle Tenn. St. ...Dec. 14
UAB ...Dec. 18
Tennessee St. ■ ...Dec. 21
Marshall ...Dec. 23
Tenn.-Chatt. Cl. ...Dec. 28-29
Wofford ■ ...Jan. 6
Furman ...Jan. 9
VMI ...Jan. 11
Davidson ...Jan. 18
Furman ■ ...Jan. 20
Western Caro. ...Jan. 25
Ga. Southern ■ ...Jan. 27
East Tenn. St. ■ ...Jan. 29
Appalachian St. ■ ...Feb. 1
Citadel ...Feb. 3
UAB ■ ...Feb. 6
East Tenn. St. ...Feb. 8
Citadel ■ ...Feb. 10
Western Caro. ...Feb. 15
Ga. Southern ...Feb. 17
Marshall ■ ...Feb. 22
Cumberland (Tenn.) ...Feb. 24
Southern Conf. Tr. ...Feb. 27-Mar. 2

1995-96 RESULTS (15-12)
86 S.C.-Aiken ■ ...61
86 Marshall ■ ...95
66 Alabama St. ...69
86 Cumberland (Tenn.) ■ ...52
69 UAB ...73
48 Penn St. ...81
83 Ohio St. ■ ...70
57 Southern Miss. ...74
63 South Caro. St. ■ ...56
74 Samford ■ ...59
86 Wofford ...60
64 Citadel ...73
84 Western Caro. ...70
81 Ga. Southern ■ ...55
69 Marshall ...86
59 Furman ...69
71 VMI ■ ...69
58 Davidson ■ ...70
75 East Tenn. St. ...73
86 Furman ■ ...56
76 Western Caro. ...81
71 Ga. Southern ...50
80 Appalachian St. ...66
55 Memphis ■ ...63
70 Citadel ■ ...44
93 East Tenn. St. ...60
81 Marshall † ...82

Nickname: Moccasins
Colors: Navy Blue & Gold
Arena: UTC Arena
  Capacity: 11,218; Year Built: 1982
AD: Ed Farrell
SID: Scott McKinney

TENN.-MARTIN
Martin, TN 38238 ...I

Coach: Calvin C. Luther
Alma Mater: Valparaiso '51
Record: 35 Years, W-468, L-408

1996-97 SCHEDULE
Northwestern ...Nov. 22
Cumberland (Tenn.) ■ ...Nov. 24
Radford ...Nov. 26
Western Ky. ...Nov. 29
Evansville ■ ...Dec. 1
Lyon ■ ...Dec. 3
Iowa St. Challenge ...Dec. 5-6
Purdue ...Dec. 16
Murray St. ■ ...Jan. 6
Southeast Mo. St. ...Jan. 9
Tennessee St. ■ ...Jan. 11
Austin Peay ■ ...Jan. 13
Tennessee Tech ...Jan. 16
Morehead St. ...Jan. 18
Eastern Ky. ...Jan. 20
Tennessee Tech ■ ...Jan. 25
Middle Tenn. St. ■ ...Jan. 27
Eastern Ill. ...Jan. 30
Murray St. ...Feb. 1
Austin Peay ...Feb. 8
Tennessee St. ...Feb. 10
Eastern Ill. ■ ...Feb. 13
Eastern Ky. ■ ...Feb. 15
Morehead St. ■ ...Feb. 17
Southeast Mo. St. ■ ...Feb. 20
Middle Tenn. St. ...Feb. 22
Ohio Valley Conf. Tr. ...Feb. 25-Mar. 1

1995-96 RESULTS (13-14)
65 Virginia ...84
77 Radford ...92
88 Covenant ■ ...65
71 Southwest Mo. St. ...105
72 Idaho St. † ...89
83 Lyon ■ ...65
90 Georgia St. ■ ...68
77 Tenn. Temple ■ ...48
74 LSU ...93
78 Tennessee Tech ...74
78 Tennessee St. ...83
61 Southeast Mo. St. ...71
74 Morehead St. ■ ...62
59 Eastern Ky. ■ ...60
68 Murray St. ■ ...80
68 Middle Tenn. St. ...81
91 Austin Peay ...83
71 Tennessee St. ■ ...67
75 Tennessee Tech ■ ...71
79 Southeast Mo. St. ■ ...59
74 Eastern Ky. ...77
77 Morehead St. ...67
81 Murray St. ...87
65 St. Louis ...91
67 Austin Peay ■ ...64
91 Middle Tenn. St. ■ ...83
69 Oral Roberts ...85

Nickname: Skyhawks
Colors: Orange, White & Royal Blue
Arena: Skyhawk Arena
  Capacity: 7,000; Year Built: 1978
AD: Benny Hollis
SID: Lee Wilmot

TEXAS
Austin, TX 78713 ...I

Coach: Tom Penders
Alma Mater: Connecticut '67
Record: 25 Years, W-446, L-290

1996-97 SCHEDULE
Nebraska ...Nov. 23
Rhode Island ■ ...Nov. 27
Florida ...Dec. 4
North Texas ■ ...Dec. 7
Arizona ...Dec. 9
Fresno St. ■ ...Dec. 14
Oregon St. ...Dec. 18
Utah ...Dec. 21
Providence ...Dec. 31
Oklahoma St. ■ ...Jan. 4
Kansas ...Jan. 6
Kansas St. ■ ...Jan. 12
Texas A&M ...Jan. 15
Louisville ...Jan. 19
Oklahoma ...Jan. 22
Missouri ■ ...Jan. 26
Baylor ...Jan. 29
Oklahoma ...Feb. 1
Texas Tech ■ ...Feb. 3
Oklahoma St. ...Feb. 8
Baylor ■ ...Feb. 12
Nebraska ...Feb. 16
Iowa St. ■ ...Feb. 19
Texas Tech ...Feb. 22
Texas A&M ■ ...Feb. 25
Colorado ...Mar. 1
Big 12 Conf. Tr. ...Mar. 6-9

1995-96 RESULTS (21-10)
88 North Texas ■ ...67
69 Utah ...70
88 DePaul ...84
110 Texas-San Antonio ■ ...98
78 Louisville ...101
83 Oregon St. ■ ...54
92 Providence ■ ...83
96 Lamar ...82
74 North Caro. ...72
69 Nebraska ...85
69 Rice ...80
103 Texas Christian ■ ...88
86 Texas A&M ...70
81 Southern Methodist ■ ...63
90 Baylor ■ ...81
78 Texas Tech ...79
65 Oklahoma ■ ...67
80 Houston ■ ...63
79 Rice ...64
102 Texas Christian ...81
69 Texas A&M ■ ...50
101 Southern Methodist ...66
80 Baylor ...72
58 Texas Tech ■ ...75
81 Rhode Island ...77
76 Houston ...86
86 Baylor † ...65
89 Southern Methodist ...67
73 Texas Tech † ...75
80 Michigan † ...76
62 Wake Forest † ...65

Nickname: Longhorns
Colors: Burnt Orange & White
Arena: Erwin Special Events Center
  Capacity: 16,042; Year Built: 1977
AD: DeLoss Dodds
SID: Dave Saba

TEXAS A&M
College Station, TX 77843 ...I

Coach: Tony Barone
Alma Mater: Duke '68
Record: 11 Years, W-162, L-164

1996-97 SCHEDULE
North Caro. A&T ■ ...Nov. 23
Colorado St. ...Nov. 26
Ill.-Chicago ■ ...Dec. 1
North Texas ...Dec. 5
Southeastern La. ■ ...Dec. 7
Ga. Southern ■ ...Dec. 10
Mo.-Kansas City ...Dec. 20
Clemson ■ ...Dec. 22
UTEP Tr. ...Dec. 27-28
Oklahoma ■ ...Jan. 5
Baylor ...Jan. 8
Nebraska ...Jan. 11
Texas ■ ...Jan. 15
Kansas ...Jan. 22
Kansas St. ■ ...Jan. 25
Missouri ■ ...Jan. 28
Iowa St. ■ ...Feb. 1
Oklahoma ...Feb. 4
Colorado ...Feb. 8
Texas Tech ■ ...Feb. 12
Oklahoma St. ■ ...Feb. 15
Oklahoma St. ...Feb. 19
Baylor ■ ...Feb. 22
Texas ...Feb. 25
Texas Tech ...Mar. 2
Big 12 Conf. Tr. ...Mar. 6-9

1995-96 RESULTS (11-16)
75 Md.-Balt. County ■ ...47
49 Wis.-Green Bay † ...60
65 Columbia † ...39
68 North Texas ■ ...50
83 St. Mary's (Cal.) ■ ...55
69 Southwestern La. ...74
68 McNeese St. ...83
44 Arizona ...88
77 Pacific (Cal.) † ...72
79 Ill.-Chicago ...62
69 Bethune-Cookman ■ ...50
67 Ga. Southern † ...63
67 Baylor ...74
54 Texas Tech ...82
70 Texas ■ ...86
78 Rice ...56
67 Houston ...78
76 Texas Christian ...80
62 Southern Methodist ■ ...58
67 Baylor ■ ...64
63 Texas Tech ■ ...66
50 Texas ...69
55 Rice ...60
75 Houston ■ ...79
89 Texas Christian ■ ...91
72 Southern Methodist ...75
57 Texas Tech † ...85

Nickname: Aggies
Colors: Maroon & White
Arena: G. Rollie White Coliseum
  Capacity: 7,500; Year Built: 1954
AD: Wally Groff
SID: Colin Killian

TEXAS A&M-COMMERCE
Commerce, TX 75428 ...II

Coach: Paul Peak
Alma Mater: Evangel '65
Record: 27 Years, W-443, L-334

1996-97 SCHEDULE
Schedule unavailable

1995-96 RESULTS (20-8)
66 Southwest Baptist ...72
112 LeTourneau ...82
89 Henderson St. ...78
68 Southern Ark. ...75
80 Jarvis Christian ■ ...67
108 National Christian ■ ...74
86 Tarleton St. ...80
109 Ambassador ■ ...69
73 Southern Ark. ■ ...58
62 Tex. A&M-Kingsville ...74
74 Angelo St. ■ ...64
79 Abilene Christian ...63
80 Eastern N.M. ...73
81 West Tex. A&M ■ ...80
97 Central Okla. ...91
91 Midwestern St. ■ ...79
65 Cameron ...57
75 Tex. A&M-Kingsville ■ ...64
65 Abilene Christian ...72
73 Angelo St. ...62
67 West Tex. A&M ■ ...61
66 Eastern N.M. ■ ...63
95 Midwestern St. ...108
83 Central Okla. ...89
66 Cameron ■ ...54
75 Tarleton St. ■ ...63
86 Central Okla. ...91
86 Central Mo. St. † ...89

Nickname: Lions
Colors: Blue & Gold
Arena: East Texas Field House
  Capacity: 5,000; Year Built: 1950
AD: Margo Harbison
SID: Bill Powers

TEX. A&M-KINGSVILLE
Kingsville, TX 78363 ...II

Coach: Bill Carter
Alma Mater: Dubuque '62
Record: 11 Years, W-185, L-123

1996-97 SCHEDULE
St. Edward's ■ ...Nov. 16
Schreiner ...Nov. 18
Incarnate Word [San Antonio] ...Nov. 22
St. Mary's (Tex.) [San Antonio] ...Nov. 23
Concordia (Tex.) ...Nov. 26
Texas Lutheran ...Dec. 2

St. Mary's (Tex.) ■ ....Dec. 4
Central Okla. ■ ....Dec. 14
Midwestern St. ■ ....Dec. 16
Texas A&M-Commerce ....Jan. 2
Tarleton St. ....Jan. 4
Angelo St. ■ ....Jan. 11
Abilene Christian ■ ....Jan. 13
Eastern N.M. ■ ....Jan. 16
West Tex. A&M ....Jan. 18
Tarleton St. ■ ....Jan. 23
Texas A&M-Commerce ■ ....Jan. 25
National Christian ■ ....Feb. 1
Abilene Christian ....Feb. 6
Angelo St. ....Feb. 8
West Tex. A&M ■ ....Feb. 13
Eastern N.M. ■ ....Feb. 15
Midwestern St. ....Feb. 20
Central Okla. ....Feb. 22

1995-96 RESULTS (23-6)

99	St. Leo †	84
85	North Ala.	83
83	St. Edward's	77
63	Cal St. Dom. Hills	68
68	Cal St. Bakersfield	93
85	Texas Lutheran ■	74
65	St. Mary's (Tex.) ■	55
114	Schreiner ■	67
107	Central Okla.	99
98	Midwestern St.	89
88	Texas-San Antonio	85
74	Texas A&M-Commerce ■	62
75	Tarleton St. ■	66
85	Angelo St.	76
67	Abilene Christian	65
87	Eastern N.M.	91
84	West Tex. A&M ■	73
69	Tarleton St.	48
64	Texas A&M-Commerce	75
108	National Christian ■	81
95	Abilene Christian ■	88
83	Angelo St.	79
79	West Tex. A&M	101
98	Eastern N.M.	86
97	Midwestern St. ■	94
109	Central Okla.	86
94	West Tex. A&M †	84
112	Central Okla. †	95
80	North Ala. †	85

Nickname: Javelinas
Colors: Blue & Gold
Arena: Steinke P.E. Center
  Capacity: 4,000; Year Built: 1970
AD: Ron Harms
SID: Fred Nuesch

TEXAS CHRISTIAN
Fort Worth, TX 76129 I

Coach: Billy Tubbs
Alma Mater: Lamar '58
Record: 22 Years, W-470, L-228

1996-97 SCHEDULE

McNeese St. ■ ....Nov. 23
Centenary (La.) ■ ....Nov. 25
Hawaii-Hilo Inv. ....Nov. 29-Dec. 1
Louisiana Tech ■ ....Dec. 7
Boston U. ■ ....Dec. 12
Texas Tech ■ ....Dec. 14
Texas-Arlington ■ ....Dec. 23
Wichita St. Tr. ....Dec. 27-28
Purdue ■ ....Dec. 30
Liberty ■ ....Jan. 2
UNLV ■ ....Jan. 6
New Mexico ....Jan. 9
UTEP ....Jan. 11
Brigham Young ■ ....Jan. 16
Utah ■ ....Jan. 18
Southern Methodist ....Jan. 25
Rice ....Jan. 30
Tulsa ....Feb. 1
UTEP ■ ....Feb. 6
New Mexico ■ ....Feb. 8
Brigham Young ....Feb. 13
Utah ....Feb. 15

Southern Methodist ■ ....Feb. 19
UNLV ....Feb. 22
Tulsa ■ ....Feb. 27
Rice ■ ....Mar. 1
Western Ath. Conf. Tr. ....Mar. 4-8

1995-96 RESULTS (15-15)

76	Connecticut †	102
68	Ohio †	86
78	Alas. Anchorage ■	89
86	Middle Tenn. St. ■	83
103	Howard ■	74
93	Centenary (La.) ■	81
95	Southeastern La. ■	92
69	Purdue †	88
77	North Texas	67
89	Coppin St. ■	86
92	St. Joseph's (Pa.) †	93
93	New Hampshire †	74
124	Alas. Anchorage ■	78
98	Montana St.	96
86	Texas Tech ■	90
88	Texas	103
86	Houston	89
80	Kentucky	124
80	Rice ■	71
83	Southern Methodist	87
80	Texas A&M ■	76
70	Texas Tech	85
81	Texas ■	102
82	Houston ■	86
70	Baylor ■	72
70	Rice	67
87	Southern Methodist ■	79
91	Texas A&M	89
77	Baylor ■	75
67	Rice †	78

Nickname: Horned Frogs
Colors: Purple & White
Arena: Daniel-Meyer Coliseum
  Capacity: 7,166; Year Built: 1961
AD: Frank Windegger
SID: Kent Johnson

TEXAS SOUTHERN
Houston, TX 77004 I

Coach: Robert Moreland
Alma Mater: Tougaloo '62
Record: 21 Years, W-340, L-266

1996-97 SCHEDULE

Tougaloo ■ ....Nov. 23
Southwest Tex. St. ....Nov. 25
California ....Nov. 30
Xavier (La.) ■ ....Dec. 3
Baylor Tr. ....Dec. 6-7
Tex.-Pan American ■ ....Dec. 14
Mississippi St. ....Dec. 17
Memphis ....Dec. 21
Southern Miss. ....Dec. 23
Utah St. Tr. ....Dec. 27-28
Alabama St. ■ ....Jan. 4
Jackson St. ■ ....Jan. 6
Mississippi Val. ....Jan. 11
Grambling ....Jan. 13
Southern U. ■ ....Jan. 18
Alcorn St. ■ ....Jan. 20
Prairie View ■ ....Jan. 25
Alabama St. ....Feb. 1
Jackson St. ....Feb. 3
Mississippi Val. ■ ....Feb. 8
Grambling ■ ....Feb. 10
Southern U. ....Feb. 15
Alcorn St. ....Feb. 17
Prairie View ....Feb. 22
Southwestern Conf. Tr. ....Mar. 5-8

1995-96 RESULTS (11-15)

77	Arizona St.	103
73	California	112
88	Weber St. †	100
76	Northeast La. †	73
108	Houston Baptist ■	100
93	Texas Col. ■	70
87	Tougaloo	73

67	Iowa	110
63	Oklahoma	77
69	Tex.-Pan American	61
64	Portland †	92
96	Tennessee Tech †	100
67	Jackson St.	63
81	Alabama St.	83
87	Grambling ■	75
74	Mississippi Val. ■	97
74	Southern U.	85
85	Alcorn St.	75
77	Prairie View	69
77	Jackson St. ■	80
73	Alabama St. ■	75
61	Grambling †	77
59	Mississippi Val.	79
86	Southern U. ■	81
98	Alcorn St. ■	102
91	Prairie View ■	79

Nickname: Tigers
Colors: Maroon & Gray
Arena: Health & P.E. Arena
  Capacity: 8,300; Year Built: 1988
AD: William A. Thomas
SID: Vincent K. Kannady

TEXAS TECH
Lubbock, TX 79409 I

Coach: James Dickey
Alma Mater: Central Ark. '76
Record: 5 Years, W-100, L-49

1996-97 SCHEDULE

Southern Miss. ■ ....Nov. 22
Nicholls St. ....Nov. 25
Geo. Washington ....Nov. 30
Ark.-Little Rock ■ ....Dec. 2
New Mexico ■ ....Dec. 4
Texas Christian ....Dec. 14
Texas-San Antonio ■ ....Dec. 17
Fresno St. [Las Vegas] ....Dec. 21
Wyoming Shootout ....Dec. 27-28
Baylor ■ ....Jan. 4
Oklahoma St. ....Jan. 8
Colorado ■ ....Jan. 11
Oklahoma ....Jan. 15
Kansas St. ....Jan. 18
Oklahoma St. ■ ....Jan. 20
Iowa St. ....Jan. 25
Kansas ■ ....Jan. 29
Texas ....Feb. 3
Nebraska ■ ....Feb. 8
Texas A&M ....Feb. 12
Baylor ....Feb. 15
Oklahoma ■ ....Feb. 19
Texas ■ ....Feb. 22
Missouri ....Feb. 25
Texas A&M ■ ....Mar. 2
Big 12 Conf. Tr. ....Mar. 6-9

1995-96 RESULTS (30-2)

101	Prairie View ■	54
81	Oklahoma	69
71	Ark.-Little Rock	62
97	Southwest Mo. St. ■	74
95	Nicholls St. ■	56
89	Old Dominion	84
81	Brigham Young ■	71
77	Eastern Mich. †	93
62	La Salle †	58
86	Montana St. ■	67
99	East Tenn. St.	81
90	Texas Christian	86
82	Texas A&M ■	54
75	Baylor	69
95	Houston ■	76
72	Southern Methodist ■	60
79	Texas ■	78
78	Oral Roberts	74
79	Rice	57
85	Texas Christian ■	70
66	Texas A&M	63
78	Baylor ■	72
93	Houston	84

75	Southern Methodist ■	54
75	Texas	58
84	Rice ■	70
85	Texas A&M †	57
68	Rice †	53
75	Texas †	73
74	Northern Ill. †	73
92	North Caro. †	73
90	Georgetown †	98

Nickname: Red Raiders
Colors: Scarlet & Black
Arena: Lubbock Mun. Coliseum
  Capacity: 8,174; Year Built: 1956
AD: Gerald Myers
SID: Richard Kilwien

TEXAS-ARLINGTON
Arlington, TX 76019 I

Coach: Eddie McCarter
Alma Mater: UAB '75
Record: 4 Years, W-44, L-66

1996-97 SCHEDULE

Tulane ....Nov. 22
Grambling ....Nov. 26
Tex.-Pan American ....Nov. 30
Jarvis Christian ■ ....Dec. 2
Colorado ....Dec. 5
Northern Ariz. ....Dec. 7
Texas Wesleyan ■ ....Dec. 17
Tex.-Pan American ■ ....Dec. 19
Texas Christian ....Dec. 23
Montana ....Dec. 28
Stephen F. Austin ....Jan. 2
Sam Houston St. ....Jan. 6
McNeese St. ....Jan. 9
Nicholls St. ....Jan. 11
Southwest Tex. St. ....Jan. 15
Texas-San Antonio ■ ....Jan. 21
Northeast La. ....Jan. 23
Northwestern St. ....Jan. 25
McNeese St. ■ ....Jan. 30
Nicholls St. ■ ....Feb. 1
Sam Houston St. ....Feb. 13
Stephen F. Austin ....Feb. 15
Southwest Tex. St. ....Feb. 20
Texas-San Antonio ....Feb. 27
Northeast La. ....Feb. 27
Northwestern St. ■ ....Mar. 1
Southland Conf. Tr. ....Mar. 5-8

1995-96 RESULTS (11-15)

56	New Mexico	76
92	Western Caro. †	83
82	Grambling ■	86
88	Northern Ariz. ■	77
63	Oklahoma St.	80
89	Texas Wesleyan ■	75
65	UAB	70
51	Alabama St. †	47
66	North Texas	63
88	Stephen F. Austin ■	78
66	Sam Houston St. ■	81
65	McNeese St.	72
64	Nicholls St.	80
72	Southwest Tex. St.	80
64	Northeast La. ■	82
61	Northwestern St. ■	63
70	North Texas ■	67
74	Sam Houston St.	88
74	Stephen F. Austin	78
83	Nicholls St. ■	82
73	McNeese St. ■	86
94	Texas-San Antonio	73
73	Northwestern St.	64
67	Northeast La.	87
70	Texas-San Antonio ■	68
58	Southwest Tex. St. ■	76

Nickname: Mavericks
Colors: Royal Blue & White
Arena: Texas Hall
  Capacity: 4,200; Year Built: 1965
AD: Pete Carlon
SID: Steve Weller

UTEP
El Paso, TX 79968 I

Coach: Don Haskins
Alma Mater: Oklahoma St. '52
Record: 35 Years, W-678, L-313

1996-97 SCHEDULE
Western Ore. ■ ....Nov. 23
New Mexico St. ....Nov. 30
New Mexico St. ■ ....Dec. 4
Sam Houston St. ■ ....Dec. 19
Iowa St. Cl. ....Dec. 21-22
UTEP Tr. ....Dec. 27-28
San Diego St. ....Jan. 4
Southern Methodist ■ ....Jan. 9
Texas Christian ....Jan. 11
Rice ....Jan. 16
Tulsa ....Jan. 18
San Diego St. ■ ....Jan. 23
New Mexico ....Jan. 25
Utah ■ ....Jan. 30
Brigham Young ■ ....Feb. 1
Texas Christian ....Feb. 6
Southern Methodist...............Feb. 8
Tulsa ■ ....Feb. 13
Rice ■ ....Feb. 15
New Mexico ■ ....Feb. 20
Montana Tech ■ ....Feb. 22
Utah ....Feb. 27
Brigham Young ....Mar. 1
Western Ath. Conf. Tr. ....Mar. 4-8

1995-96 RESULTS (13-15)
94	Southern Cal Col. ■	60
73	New Mexico St.	67
77	New Mexico St. ■	70
88	Northwestern St. ■	67
89	St. Francis (Ill.) ■	53
70	Arizona	90
76	Jacksonville St. ■	53
69	La Salle ■	62
80	Eastern Mich. ■	73
53	Air Force	48
74	Fresno St.	83
85	Hawaii ■	75
71	San Diego St. ■	72
62	Colorado St.	66
68	Wyoming	72
60	New Mexico ■	64
54	Utah ■	68
82	Brigham Young ■	90
62	Utah	77
71	Brigham Young	82
52	New Mexico	81
77	Wyoming ■	71
76	Colorado St. ■	77
75	Hawaii	83
69	San Diego St.	72
87	Fresno St. ■	88
69	Air Force ■	59
77	Hawaii †	69

Nickname: Miners
Colors: Orange, White & Blue
Arena: The Special Events Center
  Capacity: 12,222; Year Built: 1977
AD: John Thompson
SID: Gary Richter

TEX.-PAN AMERICAN
Edinburg, TX 78539 I

Coach: Mark Adams
Alma Mater: Texas Tech '79
Record: 13 Years, W-249, L-144

1996-97 SCHEDULE
McMurry ■ ....Nov. 23
Hawaii ....Nov. 26
Texas-Arlington ....Nov. 30
Angelo St. ■ ....Dec. 7
Texas Southern ....Dec. 14
Texas-Arlington ....Dec. 19
Baylor ....Dec. 21
Western Ky. ....Dec. 23

Iowa St. ....Dec. 30
Louisiana Tech ■ ....Jan. 2
North Caro. St. ....Jan. 7
South Ala. ....Jan. 9
New Orleans ....Jan. 11
Arkansas St. ■ ....Jan. 16
Southwestern La. ■ ....Jan. 18
Western Ky. ■ ....Jan. 20
Lamar ■ ....Jan. 23
Jacksonville ■ ....Jan. 25
Louisiana Tech ....Jan. 27
Ark.-Little Rock ■ ....Jan. 30
South Ala. ■ ....Feb. 1
Lamar ....Feb. 3
New Orleans ■ ....Feb. 6
Jacksonville ....Feb. 8
Southwestern La. ....Feb. 15
Arkansas St. ....Feb. 20
Ark.-Little Rock ....Feb. 22
Sun Belt Conf. Tr. ....Feb. 28-Mar. 4

1995-96 RESULTS (9-19)
71	Southwest Mo. St.	83
56	New Mexico	80
71	Richmond †	74
68	Tennessee St. †	74
63	Southwest Tex. St.	74
94	St. Edward's ■	67
61	Texas Southern ■	69
58	Southwest Tex. St. ■	48
68	Lamar	79
50	New Orleans	69
35	South Ala.	62
55	Louisiana Tech	56
52	Southwestern La.	68
50	Western Ky. ■	68
64	Lamar ■	56
57	South Ala. ■	38
54	New Orleans	58
75	Jacksonville ■	61
58	Southwestern La. ■	42
38	Arkansas St.	46
72	Ark.-Little Rock	76
51	Western Ky.	63
52	Ark.-Little Rock	55
73	Jacksonville	81
74	Arkansas St. ■	60
47	Louisiana Tech ■	45
61	South Ala. †	48
71	Ark.-Little Rock	89

Nickname: Broncs
Colors: Green & White
Arena: UT Pan Am Field House
  Capacity: 5,000; Year Built: 1969
AD: Gary Gallup
SID: Jim McKone

TEXAS-SAN ANTONIO
San Antonio, TX 78249 I

Coach: Tim Carter
Alma Mater: Kansas '79
Record: 2 Years, W-25, L-30

1996-97 SCHEDULE
Angelo St. ■ ....Nov. 23
Abilene Christian ■ ....Nov. 26
Houston ....Nov. 30
Nebraska ....Dec. 3
Colorado St. Cl. ....Dec. 6-7
Idaho St. ■ ....Dec. 10
Texas Tech ....Dec. 17
Idaho St. ....Dec. 21
Wis.-Milwaukee ■ ....Dec. 30
Nicholls St. ■ ....Jan. 2
McNeese St. ■ ....Jan. 4
Northwestern St. ....Jan. 9
Northeast La. ....Jan. 11
Sam Houston St. ■ ....Jan. 16
Stephen F. Austin ■ ....Jan. 18
Texas-Arlington ....Jan. 21
Southwest Tex. St. ■ ....Jan. 25
Northeast La. ■ ....Jan. 30
Northwestern St. ■ ....Feb. 1
McNeese St. ....Feb. 6

Nicholls St. ....Feb. 8
Southwest Tex. St. ....Feb. 15
Texas-Arlington ■ ....Feb. 22
Sam Houston St. ....Feb. 27
Stephen F. Austin ....Mar. 1
Southland Conf. Tr. ....Mar. 5-8

1995-96 RESULTS (14-14)
80	Illinois	83
90	Houston ■	94
93	Angelo St. ■	91
98	Texas	110
75	Oklahoma	107
85	Tex. A&M-Kingsville ■	88
77	Colorado	92
86	Drake ■	94
82	Stephen F. Austin	99
81	Sam Houston St.	78
80	McNeese St. ■	76
83	Nicholls St. ■	66
62	Northwestern St.	56
75	Northeast La.	61
59	North Texas ■	62
65	Southwest Tex. St. ■	42
75	Stephen F. Austin ■	71
64	Nicholls St.	60
83	McNeese St. ■	89
88	Sam Houston St. ■	77
73	Northeast La. ■	71
95	Northwestern St. ■	84
73	Texas-Arlington ■	94
75	Southwest Tex. St.	59
68	Texas-Arlington	70
55	North Texas	75
60	Sam Houston St. †	58
71	North Texas †	80

Nickname: Roadrunners
Colors: Orange, Navy Blue & White
Arena: Convocation Center
  Capacity: 5,100; Year Built: 1971
AD: Bobby Thompson
SID: Rick Nixon

THIEL
Greenville, PA 16125 III

Coach: Rich Marshall
Alma Mater: Marquette '80
Record: 4 Years, W-38, L-68

1996-97 SCHEDULE
Thiel Cl. ....Nov. 22-23
Oberlin ....Nov. 26
Penn St.-Behrend ....Dec. 3
La Roche ....Dec. 5
Kenyon ....Dec. 7
Calif. (Pa.) ....Dec. 13
Hiram ■ ....Jan. 6
Pitt.-Greensburg ....Jan. 9
Juniata ....Jan. 11
Carnegie Mellon ■ ....Jan. 14
Pitt.-Greensburg ■ ....Jan. 16
La Roche ■ ....Jan. 18
Alfred ....Jan. 22
Wash. & Jeff. ....Jan. 25
Waynesburg ....Jan. 29
Grove City ■ ....Feb. 1
Bethany (W.Va.) ■ ....Feb. 5
Alfred ■ ....Feb. 8
Wash. & Jeff. ■ ....Feb. 12
Waynesburg ■ ....Feb. 15
Grove City ....Feb. 19
Bethany (W.Va.) ....Feb. 22
Carnegie Mellon ....Feb. 27
Penn St.-Behrend ■ ....Mar. 1

1995-96 RESULTS (6-19)
66	Penn St.-Behrend ■	90
86	Oberlin	59
77	Juniata ■	92
74	Hiram	91
82	Alfred ■	88
79	Lake Erie	77
67	Edinboro	116
90	Fredonia St. ■	81
64	Kenyon ■	103

Carnegie Mellon ■ 101
Pitt.-Bradford ■ 91
Wash. & Jeff. ■ 71
Grove City ■ 87
Bethany (W.Va.) ■ 71
Waynesburg ■ 100
La Roche 89
Penn St.-Behrend 83
Wash. & Jeff. 97
Grove City ■ 95
Bethany (W.Va.) ■ 75
Waynesburg 88
Pitt.-Bradford ■ 106
Lake Erie ■ 78
Carnegie Mellon 57
La Roche ■ 76

Nickname: Tomcats
Colors: Navy Blue & Old Gold
Arena: Rissell-Beeghly Gymnasium
  Capacity: 1,000; Year Built: 1968
AD: John Dickason
SID: Michael Carpenter

THOMAS MORE
Crestview Hills, KY 41017 III

Coach: Larry Cox
Alma Mater: Hanover '81
Record: 6 Years, W-74, L-82

1996-97 SCHEDULE
Capital Cl. ....Nov. 22-23
Marietta ■ ....Nov. 27
Wright St. ....Nov. 30
Wabash ....Dec. 7
Ohio Wesleyan ■ ....Dec. 12
DePauw ....Dec. 14
Earlham ■ ....Dec. 16
Wittenberg ■ ....Dec. 21
Adrian ....Dec. 28
Thomas More Cl. ....Jan. 4-5
Wash. & Jeff. ■ ....Jan. 11
Asbury ....Jan. 14
Bluffton ■ ....Jan. 18
Hanover ■ ....Jan. 22
Defiance ....Jan. 25
Bluffton ....Feb. 1
Asbury ■ ....Feb. 4
Franklin ....Feb. 8
Wilmington (Ohio) ....Feb. 12
Defiance ■ ....Feb. 15
Cincinnati Bible ....Feb. 18
Wilmington (Ohio) ■ ....Feb. 22
Ind.-East ....Feb. 26

1995-96 RESULTS (13-12)
79	Marietta	86
65	DePauw ■	75
58	Hanover	63
69	Franklin ■	71
66	Lake Erie	67
110	Cincinnati Bible ■	51
79	Ohio Wesleyan	83
85	Morehead St.	89
60	Wittenberg ■	57
81	Hamilton †	75
80	Embry-Riddle	89
97	Cornell College ■	77
77	Berea	83
90	Lake Erie	85
68	Defiance ■	83
82	Asbury	68
93	Bluffton	89
87	Wilmington (Ohio) ■	70
85	Wash. & Jeff.	60
70	Wabash	81
75	Bluffton ■	64
72	Wilmington (Ohio)	69
70	Defiance	77
118	Asbury ■	65
90	Bluffton ■	67

Nickname: Saints
Colors: Royal Blue, White & Silver
Arena: Connor Convocation Center
  Capacity: 1,500; Year Built: 1989

AD: Vic Clark
SID: Ted Kiep

TOLEDO

Toledo, OH 43606 I

Coach: Stan Joplin
(First year as head coach)

1996-97 SCHEDULE

Old Dominion	Nov. 25
Charleston So. ■	Nov. 30
Heidelberg ■	Dec. 2
Canisius ■	Dec. 18
Wright St.	Dec. 21
Cleveland St. ■	Dec. 23
Toledo Tr.	Dec. 29-30
Ball St. ■	Jan. 4
Akron	Jan. 8
Kent ■	Jan. 11
Eastern Mich.	Jan. 13
Miami (Ohio) ■	Jan. 15
Central Mich. ■	Jan. 18
Ohio	Jan. 22
Bowling Green ■	Jan. 25
Western Mich.	Jan. 29
Akron ■	Feb. 1
Kent	Feb. 5
Eastern Mich. ■	Feb. 8
Miami (Ohio)	Feb. 12
Central Mich.	Feb. 15
Ohio ■	Feb. 19
Bowling Green	Feb. 22
Western Mich. ■	Feb. 26
Ball St.	Mar. 1
Mid-American Conf. Tr.	Mar. 4-8

1995-96 RESULTS (18-14)

59	Nebraska †	72
104	Hawaii-Hilo	75
65	Valparaiso †	84
67	San Fran. St. ■	51
92	Old Dominion ■	80
89	Baldwin-Wallace ■	52
57	Wright St. ■	62
67	Canisius	75
71	Cleveland St.	44
76	William & Mary ■	72
88	Austin Peay ■	74
87	Eastern Mich.	91
92	Ball St. ■	69
43	Miami (Ohio)	42
80	Kent ■	70
57	Ohio	70
75	Bowling Green	76
67	Akron ■	61
77	Western Mich.	81
65	Central Mich. ■	59
68	Ball St.	88
76	Miami (Ohio) ■	70
86	Kent	70
60	Ohio	72
53	Bowling Green ■	65
74	Akron	62
60	Western Mich. ■	68
103	Central Mich.	102
85	Eastern Mich.	95
71	Western Mich. ■	65
75	Miami (Ohio) ■	55
63	Eastern Mich.	77

Nickname: Rockets
Colors: Blue & Gold
Arena: John F. Savage Hall
   Capacity: 9,000; Year Built: 1976
AD: Pete Liske
SID: Rod Brandt

TOWSON ST.

Towson, MD 21204 I

Coach: Terry Truax
Alma Mater: Maryland '68
Record: 13 Years, W-193, L-184

1996-97 SCHEDULE

Old Dominion ■	Nov. 22
Navy ■	Nov. 24
Md.-Balt. County	Nov. 26
Maryland	Nov. 30
Pennsylvania	Dec. 3
Boston U. ■	Dec. 6
Northeastern ■	Dec. 8
Loyola (Md.) ■	Dec. 10
James Madison ■	Dec. 28
Delaware	Jan. 5
Drexel	Jan. 7
Vermont ■	Jan. 10
Hartford ■	Jan. 12
Maine	Jan. 16
New Hampshire	Jan. 18
Hofstra	Jan. 21
Northeastern	Jan. 24
Boston U. ■	Jan. 26
Hofstra	Jan. 31
Drexel ■	Feb. 2
Vermont	Feb. 6
Hartford	Feb. 8
New Hampshire ■	Feb. 13
Maine ■	Feb. 15
West Va.	Feb. 18
Delaware ■	Feb. 22
America East Conf. Tr.	Feb. 28-Mar. 2

1995-96 RESULTS (16-12)

67	Maryland †	70
74	Navy	60
66	Loyola (Md.)	62
61	Pennsylvania ■	67
84	Arizona	90
105	Washington (Md.) ■	86
67	James Madison	64
72	Louisville	96
79	New Hampshire	68
72	Maine	85
78	Northeastern	65
93	Boston U. ■	71
69	Vermont	67
88	Hartford	73
63	Hofstra	83
91	Vermont ■	83
81	Hartford ■	73
73	Northeastern	67
56	Boston U.	68
87	Drexel	96
79	New Hampshire ■	70
65	Maine ■	56
56	Drexel ■	75
74	Hofstra	56
73	Delaware	81
70	Delaware ■	71
85	Delaware	78
74	Drexel †	84

Nickname: Tigers
Colors: Gold, White & Black
Arena: Towson Center
   Capacity: 5,200; Year Built: 1976
AD: Wayne Edwards
SID: Peter Schlehr

TRINITY (CONN.)

Hartford, CT 06106 III

Coach: Stan Ogrodnik
Alma Mater: Providence '63
Record: 15 Years, W-247, L-109

1996-97 SCHEDULE

Skidmore Inv.	Nov. 22-23
Coast Guard ■	Nov. 26
Mass.-Boston Inv.	Nov. 29-30
Skidmore	Dec. 10
Eastern Nazarene ■	Jan. 14
Springfield	Jan. 16
Albertus Magnus ■	Jan. 18
Wesleyan (Conn.) ■	Jan. 21
Tufts ■	Jan. 25
North Adams St.	Jan. 30
Connecticut Col. ■	Feb. 1
Clark (Mass.)	Feb. 4
Colby	Feb. 7
Bates	Feb. 8
Williams ■	Feb. 12
Mass.-Dartmouth	Feb. 15
Amherst ■	Feb. 19
Wheaton (Mass.) ■	Feb. 22
Wesleyan (Conn.)	Feb. 25
Middlebury ■	Mar. 1

1995-96 RESULTS (14-8)

118	Stevens Tech ■	64
89	Eastern Conn. St. †	88
82	Mass.-Boston	64
88	Coast Guard	93
72	Skidmore ■	67
122	Curry ■	80
67	Middlebury	69
73	Eastern Nazarene	80
81	Springfield ■	86
77	Albertus Magnus ■	61
71	Wesleyan (Conn.)	67
105	Tufts	100
89	North Adams St. ■	57
74	Connecticut Col.	68
89	Clark (Mass.) ■	75
93	Bates	72
75	Colby ■	88
86	Williams	92
53	Mass.-Dartmouth ■	75
72	Amherst	83
85	Wheaton (Mass.)	63
86	Wesleyan (Conn.) ■	61

Nickname: Bantams
Colors: Blue & Gold
Arena: Oosting Gym
   Capacity: 2,000; Year Built: 1963
AD: Rick Hazleton
SID: Albert C. Carbone Jr

TRINITY (TEX.)

San Antonio, TX 78212 III

Coach: Charlie Brock
Alma Mater: Springfield '76
Record: 17 Years, W-198, L-211

1996-97 SCHEDULE

Trinity (Tex.) Inv.	Nov. 22-23
Dallas	Nov. 26
Austin	Dec. 3
Washington (Mo.) Cl.	Dec. 6-7
Howard Payne	Dec. 10
Elmhurst ■	Dec. 21
Dallas ■	Jan. 4
Austin	Jan. 7
Rhodes ■	Jan. 10
Hendrix ■	Jan. 12
Sewanee	Jan. 17
Centre	Jan. 19
Millsaps	Jan. 24
Oglethorpe	Jan. 26
Sewanee ■	Jan. 31
Centre	Feb. 2
Millsaps ■	Feb. 7
Oglethorpe ■	Feb. 9
Howard Payne ■	Feb. 11
Southwestern (Tex.) ■	Feb. 15
Rhodes	Feb. 21
Hendrix	Feb. 23
Southwestern (Tex.)	Mar. 1

1995-96 RESULTS (17-8)

93	La Verne ■	56
73	St. Thomas (Minn.) ■	71
84	Dallas	80
82	Howard Payne ■	81
83	Dallas ■	62
86	Howard Payne	82
80	Loyola (La.) ■	75
55	Carnegie Mellon †	75
78	Whittier †	62
81	Austin	73
63	Centre	82
84	Sewanee	71
71	Hendrix	75
91	Rhodes	98
83	Oglethorpe ■	77
92	Millsaps ■	79
78	Hendrix ■	71
69	Rhodes ■	71
75	Oglethorpe	84
64	Millsaps	83
82	Southwestern (Tex.)	66
93	Centre ■	69
49	Sewanee ■	62
82	Austin ■	67
74	Southwestern (Tex.) ■	52

Nickname: Tigers
Colors: Maroon & White
Arena: Earl C. Sams Gymnasium
   Capacity: 1,850; Year Built: 1992
AD: Bob King
SID: Tony Ziner

TROY ST.

Troy, AL 36081 I

Coach: Don Maestri
Alma Mater: Southern Miss. '68
Record: 14 Years, W-245, L-153

1996-97 SCHEDULE

LSU	Nov. 22
Ball St. Cl.	Nov. 29-30
Alabama St.	Dec. 3
Southwest Mo. St. Cl.	Dec. 6-7
Arkansas	Dec. 10
Loyola (La.) ■	Dec. 13
Georgia St. ■	Dec. 14
Georgia St.	Dec. 30
Valparaiso ■	Jan. 2
Western Ill. ■	Jan. 4
Mo.-Kansas City ■	Jan. 6
Youngstown St.	Jan. 11
Buffalo	Jan. 13
Northeastern Ill.	Jan. 18
Chicago St. ■	Jan. 20
Central Conn. St.	Jan. 25
Alabama St. ■	Jan. 28
Mo.-Kansas City	Feb. 1
Buffalo ■	Feb. 6
Youngstown St. ■	Feb. 8
Chicago St.	Feb. 10
Northeastern Ill. ■	Feb. 12
Central Conn. St. ■	Feb. 17
Western Ill.	Feb. 22
Valparaiso	Feb. 24
Mid-Continent Conf. Tr.	Mar. 2-4

1995-96 RESULTS (11-16)

119	North Greenville ■	56
127	George Mason	142
91	Southeast Mo. St.	109
86	Idaho †	95
73	Mississippi St.	123
119	Selma ■	64
110	Alabama St.	93
43	South Ala.	70
95	Western Ill. ■	98
90	Mo.-Kansas City ■	89
92	Northeastern Ill.	96
94	Chicago St.	128
96	Eastern Ill. ■	85
115	Valparaiso ■	104
80	Alabama St. ■	82
90	Central Conn. St.	106
80	Youngstown St.	90
61	Buffalo	76
90	Northeastern Ill. ■	86
92	Valparaiso	102
117	Chicago St. ■	108
95	Eastern Ill.	84
118	Central Conn. St. ■	119
88	Buffalo ■	86
93	Youngstown St. ■	88
95	Mo.-Kansas City	120
100	Western Ill.	120

Nickname: Trojans
Colors: Cardinal, Silver & Black
Arena: Sartain Hall
   Capacity: 3,000; Year Built: 1964

AD: John D. Williams
SID: Tom Ensey

TRUMAN ST.
Kirksville, MO 63501 II

Coach: Jack Schrader
Alma Mater: Arizona St. '75
Record: 1 Year, W-6, L-20

1996-97 SCHEDULE
Quincy ■	Nov. 20
SIU-Edwardsville ■	Nov. 23
Missouri Baptist ■	Nov. 27
Hannibal-La Grange ■	Dec. 2
Monmouth (Ill.) ■	Dec. 13
Quincy	Dec. 14
Ark.-Little Rock	Dec. 19
Drury	Dec. 21
Mo.-Rolla	Dec. 30
Pittsburg St. ■	Jan. 4
Mo. Western St. ■	Jan. 8
Washburn ■	Jan. 11
Mo. Southern St.	Jan. 15
Northwest Mo. St.	Jan. 18
Southwest Baptist	Jan. 20
Central Mo. St. ■	Jan. 22
Emporia St.	Jan. 25
Lincoln (Mo.) ■	Jan. 29
Mo. Western St.	Feb. 1
Washburn	Feb. 3
Mo.-Rolla ■	Feb. 8
Emporia St. ■	Feb. 10
Southwest Baptist	Feb. 13
Mo. Southern St. ■	Feb. 15
Central Mo. St.	Feb. 19
Lincoln (Mo.)	Feb. 22

1995-96 RESULTS (6-20)
66	Central (Iowa) ■	62
76	Monmouth (Ill.) ■	67
63	SIU-Edwardsville	78
70	Quincy ■	75
51	Middle Tenn. St.	66
48	IU/PU-Indianapolis	71
104	Quincy	110
60	Seattle Pacific	70
80	Central Wash.	70
55	Emporia St.	79
69	Pittsburg St.	74
55	Northwest Mo. St. ■	60
93	Mo.-St. Louis ■	74
54	IU/PU-Indianapolis ■	72
77	Mo.-Rolla	81
69	Southwest Baptist	79
67	Lincoln (Mo.) ■	75
97	Mo. Southern St. ■	107
73	Mo. Western St.	87
67	Central Mo. St.	88
66	Washburn	87
70	Pittsburg St. ■	80
66	Northwest Mo. St.	58
63	Mo.-St. Louis	80
62	Mo.-Rolla	69
91	Southwest Baptist ■	79

Nickname: Bulldogs
Colors: Purple & White
Arena: Pershing
  Capacity: 3,000; Year Built: 1959
AD: Walt Ryle
SID: Melissa Ware

TUFTS
Medford, MA 02155 III

Coach: Robert Sheldon
Alma Mater: St. Lawrence '77
Record: 8 Years, W-123, L-74

1996-97 SCHEDULE
Anna Maria	Nov. 26
Middlebury	Nov. 30
Framingham St.	Dec. 3
Colby ■	Dec. 6
Bowdoin ■	Dec. 7
Buffalo St. Inv.	Jan. 3-4
North Adams St.	Jan. 6
Middlebury ■	Jan. 18
Salem St.	Jan. 23
Trinity (Conn.)	Jan. 25
Wesleyan (Conn.)	Jan. 30
Suffolk ■	Feb. 1
Babson ■	Feb. 4
Wheaton (Mass.)	Feb. 6
Hamilton ■	Feb. 8
MIT	Feb. 11
Mass.-Boston	Feb. 15
Williams ■	Feb. 15
Bates	Feb. 19
Amherst	Feb. 25
Brandeis	Feb. 27
Connecticut Col.	Mar. 1

1995-96 RESULTS (15-10)
94	Catholic †	81
81	New York U.	78
91	Anna Maria ■	96
88	Colby	97
78	Bowdoin	87
93	Framingham St. ■	87
76	Holy Family †	79
71	Marymount (Va.) †	65
77	Middlebury	69
69	Salem St.	89
100	Trinity (Conn.) ■	105
94	Wesleyan (Conn.) ■	72
87	Suffolk	83
100	Babson	91
96	Wheaton (Mass.) ■	77
91	Hamilton	90
84	MIT	57
99	Mass.-Boston	72
84	Williams	97
106	Bates ■	88
106	Middlebury ■	69
86	Amherst ■	89
105	Brandeis ■	91
79	Connecticut Col. ■	83
85	Mass.-Dartmouth	88

Nickname: Jumbos
Colors: Brown & Blue
Arena: Cousens Gym
  Capacity: 2,000; Year Built: 1939
AD: Rocco Carzo
SID: Paul Sweeney

TULANE
New Orleans, LA 70118 I

Coach: Perry Clark
Alma Mater: Gettysburg '74
Record: 7 Years, W-126, L-86

1996-97 SCHEDULE
Texas-Arlington ■	Nov. 22
New Orleans [New Orleans]	Nov. 24
Portland St. ■	Nov. 26
Puerto Rico Shootout	Nov. 29-Dec. 1
Prairie View ■	Dec. 4
Temple	Dec. 9
Centenary (La.) ■	Dec. 19
UNLV	Dec. 21
Lafayette ■	Dec. 28
Tulsa ■	Dec. 31
UAB	Jan. 5
Nicholls St. ■	Jan. 8
Southern Miss. ■	Jan. 11
Xavier (Ohio) [Cincinnati]	Jan. 16
South Fla. ■	Jan. 18
St. Louis ■	Jan. 22
N.C.-Charlotte ■	Jan. 25
Southern Miss.	Jan. 27
Marquette	Feb. 1
Cincinnati	Feb. 6
Arizona [Phoenix]	Feb. 9
UAB ■	Feb. 13
Memphis ■	Feb. 16
DePaul	Feb. 19
Houston	Feb. 23
South Fla. ■	Feb. 26
Louisville ■	Mar. 1
Conference USA	Mar. 5-8

1995-96 RESULTS (22-10)
88	Centenary (La.)	75
113	Prairie View ■	72
71	North Caro. †	89
75	South Caro. †	80
78	Florida St. ■	77
82	Nicholls St. ■	62
79	Alabama	80
62	Georgia St. ■	55
100	Mt. St. Mary's (Md.) ■	75
70	UAB	71
68	South Fla. ■	63
58	N.C.-Charlotte	60
86	New Orleans †	77
67	Temple ■	59
76	Southern Miss.	61
84	DePaul ■	74
61	Southern Miss. ■	62
75	Marquette ■	74
68	Louisville	65
95	N.C.-Charlotte ■	77
77	St. Louis	51
70	South Fla.	62
79	Fla. Atlantic	64
63	Cincinnati ■	65
60	UAB ■	58
75	Memphis	86
79	Louisville †	98
87	Auburn	73
84	Minnesota	65
83	Illinois St. ■	72
78	Nebraska †	90
87	Alabama †	76

Nickname: Green Wave
Colors: Olive Green & Sky Blue
Arena: Avron B. Fogelman Arena
  Capacity: 3,600; Year Built: 1933
AD: Sandy Barbour
SID: Lenny Vangilder

TULSA
Tulsa, OK 74104 I

Coach: Steve Robinson
Alma Mater: Radford '81
Record: 1 Year, W-22, L-8

1996-97 SCHEDULE
NIT	Nov. 20-29
Delaware St. ■	Dec. 2
Houston	Dec. 4
St. Joseph's (Pa.) [Atlantic City]	Dec. 7
Temple ■	Dec. 14
Wichita St.	Dec. 19
Oklahoma Tr.	Dec. 27-28
Tulane	Dec. 31
San Jose St.	Jan. 4
Southern Utah ■	Jan. 8
Oral Roberts ■	Jan. 11
Rice	Jan. 13
New Mexico ■	Jan. 16
UTEP ■	Jan. 18
Brigham Young	Jan. 25
Utah	Jan. 27
Southern Methodist ■	Jan. 30
Texas Christian ■	Feb. 1
Rice	Feb. 6
San Jose St. ■	Feb. 10
UTEP	Feb. 13
New Mexico	Feb. 16
Brigham Young ■	Feb. 20
Utah ■	Feb. 22
Texas Christian	Feb. 27
Southern Methodist	Mar. 1
Western Ath. Conf. Tr.	Mar. 4-8

1995-96 RESULTS (22-8)
100	North Caro. A&T ■	51
73	Western Ky.	65
64	Temple	60
141	Prairie View ■	50
73	New Mexico St. ■	57
78	Oral Roberts	90

OKLAHOMA ST. / EVANSVILLE results (continuation column)
57	Oklahoma St. ■	53
67	Evansville	57
70	UAB ■	55
86	Drake ■	64
71	Illinois St. ■	74
59	Creighton	72
75	Southwest Mo. St.	65
55	Creighton ■	52
79	Drake	73
89	Northern Iowa	79
61	Southwest Mo. St. ■	66
72	Bradley	85
75	Wichita St.	47
74	Evansville ■	53
84	Southern Ill.	75
73	Bradley ■	74
111	Indiana St. ■	75
64	Illinois St.	69
72	Wichita St. ■	66
95	Northern Iowa ■	88
65	Evansville †	55
69	Illinois St. †	52
60	Bradley †	46
80	Louisville †	82

Nickname: Golden Hurricane
Colors: Blue, Red & Gold
Arena: Maxwell Convention Center
  Capacity: 8,659; Year Built: 1964
AD: Judy MacLeod
SID: Don Tomkalski

TUSKEGEE
Tuskegee, AL 36088 II

Coach: Ben Jobe
Alma Mater: Fisk '56
Record: 25 Years, W-468, L-228

1996-97 SCHEDULE
North Ala. Tr.	Nov. 15-16
Morris Brown ■	Nov. 19
Fort Valley St.	Nov. 21
Albany St. (Ga.) ■	Nov. 26
Voorhees ■	Nov. 29
Selma	Dec. 4
Valdosta St. ■	Dec. 19
Paine	Jan. 6
Valdosta St.	Jan. 9
Morehouse ■	Jan. 11
Kentucky St. ■	Jan. 13
Alabama A&M ■	Jan. 18
Kentucky St.	Jan. 20
Miles	Jan. 23
Alabama A&M ■	Jan. 25
LeMoyne-Owen ■	Jan. 28
Atlanta Christian ■	Jan. 30
Morehouse	Feb. 1
Miles ■	Feb. 5
LeMoyne-Owen	Feb. 8
Paine ■	Feb. 10
Clark Atlanta ■	Feb. 13
Fort Valley St. ■	Feb. 15
Savannah St. ■	Feb. 19

1995-96 RESULTS (9-17)
108	Selma ■	79
106	Edward Waters ■	116
106	Valdosta St. ■	103
96	Albany St. (Ga.) ■	102
87	Paine	78
117	Fort Valley St. ■	87
79	Valdosta St.	95
82	Morehouse	86
96	Kentucky St.	97
83	Clark Atlanta	97
82	Alabama A&M ■	97
62	Kentucky St. ■	63
78	Miles	85
82	Alabama A&M	126
90	LeMoyne-Owen ■	80
72	Morris Brown	65
90	Miles ■	74
96	LeMoyne-Owen	99
71	Clark Atlanta ■	81
76	Savannah St.	79

65	Fort Valley St.	80
78	Aub.-Montgomery	89
66	Morehouse ■	84
89	Miles	79
69	Albany St. (Ga.) †	64
69	Morehouse †	81

Nickname: Golden Tigers
Colors: Crimson & Gold
Arena: James Center Arena
Capacity: 5,000; Year Built: 1987
AD: Rick Comegy
SID: Arnold Houston

UCLA
Los Angeles, CA 90024 I

Coach: Jim Harrick
Alma Mater: Charleston (W.Va.) '60
Record: 17 Years, W-358, L-160

1996-97 SCHEDULE
NIT	Nov. 20-29
Cal St. Northridge ■	Dec. 3
Kansas ■	Dec. 7
Ohio ■	Dec. 14
Jackson St. ■	Dec. 17
Illinois [Chicago]	Dec. 21
St. Louis	Dec. 23
Morgan St. ■	Dec. 28
Washington St. ■	Jan. 2
Washington ■	Jan. 4
Stanford	Jan. 9
California [San Francisco]	Jan. 11
Arizona St.	Jan. 16
Arizona ■	Jan. 18
Southern Cal	Jan. 23
Louisville	Jan. 25
Oregon	Jan. 30
Oregon St.	Feb. 1
California ■	Feb. 6
Stanford ■	Feb. 8
Arizona	Feb. 13
Arizona St.	Feb. 15
Southern Cal ■	Feb. 20
Duke ■	Feb. 23
Oregon St. ■	Feb. 27
Oregon ■	Mar. 1
Washington	Mar. 6
Washington St.	Mar. 8

1995-96 RESULTS (23-8)
69	Santa Clara †	78
68	Wisconsin †	57
71	Vanderbilt †	75
79	Cal St. Fullerton ■	63
70	Kansas	85
73	Maryland †	63
109	Stephen F. Austin ■	88
83	Notre Dame	58
89	UNLV	82
92	San Francisco ■	58
78	Washington St.	73
78	Washington	70
64	Stanford ■	56
93	California ■	73
87	Arizona St.	73
79	Arizona	88
99	Southern Cal ■	72
76	Louisville ■	78
85	Oregon ■	78
69	Oregon St. ■	60
73	California	65
66	Stanford	67
76	Arizona ■	75
87	Arizona St. ■	70
61	Southern Cal	59
66	Duke	85
68	Oregon St. ■	66
77	Oregon	71
91	Washington ■	88
82	Washington St. ■	71
41	Princeton †	43

Nickname: Bruins
Colors: Navy Blue & Gold
Arena: Pauley Pavilion

Capacity: 12,819; Year Built: 1965
AD: Peter Dalis
SID: Marc Dellins

UNION (N.Y.)
Schenectady, NY 12308 III

Coach: Bob Montana
Alma Mater: Brockport St. '74
(First year as head coach)

1996-97 SCHEDULE
Wesleyan (Conn.)	Dec. 2
Vassar	Dec. 4
Clarkson ■	Dec. 7
Stevens Tech Tr.	Jan. 3-4
Union (N.Y.) Inv.	Jan. 10-11
St. Lawrence ■	Jan. 15
Colby	Jan. 18
Bowdoin	Jan. 19
Utica	Jan. 21
Rensselaer	Jan. 24
Skidmore	Jan. 25
Hartwick	Jan. 28
Hamilton ■	Jan. 31
Hobart ■	Feb. 1
Williams ■	Feb. 5
Clarkson	Feb. 7
St. Lawrence	Feb. 8
Hamilton	Feb. 14
Hobart	Feb. 15
Skidmore ■	Feb. 21
Rensselaer ■	Feb. 22
Middlebury ■	Feb. 25
Merchant Marine ■	Feb. 28

1995-96 RESULTS (6-19)
83	Wesleyan (Conn.) ■	75
92	Vassar ■	80
75	Hobart ■	88
77	Hamilton ■	81
88	Rensselaer ■	95
84	Skidmore ■	80
77	Alfred ■	75
57	Bri'water (Mass.) ■	72
62	Bowdoin ■	71
79	Bates ■	69
80	Utica ■	93
61	St. Lawrence	79
66	Clarkson	61
81	Hartwick ■	90
68	Hamilton	89
60	Hobart	63
51	Williams	89
57	Merchant Marine	60
67	Utica/Rome	74
59	Clarkson ■	68
74	St. Lawrence ■	101
49	Skidmore	78
61	Rensselaer	70
65	Middlebury	82
68	Nazareth	85

Nickname: Dutchmen
Colors: Garnet
Arena: Memorial Field House
Capacity: 3,000; Year Built: 1950
AD: Dick Sakala
SID: George Cuttita

UPPER IOWA
Fayette, IA 52142 III

Coach: Stu Engen
Alma Mater: Augsburg '86
Record: 4 Years, W-67, L-33

1996-97 SCHEDULE
Upper Iowa Tr.	Nov. 22-23
Mt. Mercy	Dec. 3
Eureka ■	Dec. 7
Rockford ■	Dec. 11
Iowa Wesleyan ■	Dec. 14
Viterbo ■	Dec. 16
Wis.-River Falls Tr.	Dec. 29-30
Central (Iowa) ■	Jan. 10

Luther ■	Jan. 11
Simpson	Jan. 17
Buena Vista ■	Jan. 18
Loras	Jan. 24
Wartburg ■	Jan. 25
Dubuque ■	Jan. 31
William Penn ■	Feb. 1
Wartburg	Feb. 7
Central (Iowa)	Feb. 8
Luther	Feb. 14
Buena Vista	Feb. 15
Loras ■	Feb. 21
Simpson ■	Feb. 22
Dubuque	Feb. 28
William Penn	Mar. 1

1995-96 RESULTS (20-5)
81	Coe ■	63
65	Viterbo ■	66
88	St. Scholastica †	85
87	Mt. Mercy ■	66
86	Wayne St. (Neb.) ■	58
63	Teikyo Marycrest	39
69	Malone †	74
75	Buena Vista ■	52
78	Simpson ■	67
62	Luther	52
74	Dubuque	50
79	Wartburg ■	53
79	William Penn ■	53
78	Loras ■	60
68	Luther ■	72
81	Eureka ■	58
51	Central (Iowa)	40
68	Buena Vista	56
53	Dubuque ■	55
73	Simpson	72
54	Loras	51
72	Central (Iowa) ■	67
67	William Penn	57
100	Wartburg	64
58	Claremont-M-S ■	70

Nickname: Peacocks
Colors: Blue & White
Arena: Dorman Memorial Gym
Capacity: 2,000; Year Built: 1963
AD: Paul Rudolph
SID: Julie Schroeder

URSINUS
Collegeville, PA 19426............III

Coach: George White
Alma Mater: Harvard '83
Record: 2 Years, W-17, L-31

1996-97 SCHEDULE
Ursinus Tr.	Nov. 22-23
Wheeling Jesuit ■	Nov. 26
Lebanon Valley	Dec. 2
Dickinson	Dec. 4
Western Md.	Dec. 7
Haverford ■	Dec. 11
Berry	Jan. 3
Oglethorpe	Jan. 5
Merchant Marine	Jan. 8
Phila. Pharmacy ■	Jan. 11
Columbia	Jan. 14
Rowan	Jan. 16
Swarthmore	Jan. 18
Johns Hopkins ■	Jan. 22
Frank. & Marsh.	Jan. 25
Gallaudet ■	Jan. 28
Washington (Md.)	Feb. 1
Muhlenberg ■	Feb. 5
Swarthmore ■	Feb. 8
Haverford	Feb. 12
Washington (Md.) ■	Feb. 15
Gettysburg ■	Feb. 19
Muhlenberg	Feb. 22

1995-96 RESULTS (11-13)
62	Cabrini †	86
74	Delaware Valley †	49
67	Wesley ■	55
73	New York U.	69

35	Columbia	77
83	Dickinson ■	65
73	Western Md. ■	85
73	Haverford	70
75	Lebanon Valley ■	71
71	Regis (Colo.)	87
84	Metro St.	107
74	Colo. Baptist	61
77	Rowan ■	90
71	Swarthmore ■	77
61	Johns Hopkins	59
58	Frank. & Marsh. ■	67
57	Phila. Pharmacy	59
71	Washington (Md.)	67
80	Muhlenberg ■	71
65	Swarthmore	74
56	Haverford ■	80
64	Washington (Md.) ■	62
78	Gettysburg	86
65	Muhlenberg	67

Nickname: Bears
Colors: Red, Old Gold & Black
Arena: Helfferich Hall
Capacity: 2,500; Year Built: 1972
AD: Robert Davidson
SID: Dave Sherman

UTAH
Salt Lake City, UT 84112 I

Coach: Rick Majerus
Alma Mater: Marquette '70
Record: 12 Years, W-250, L-103

1996-97 SCHEDULE
Azusa-Pacific ■	Nov. 23
Utah St.	Nov. 26
Cal St. Fullerton	Nov. 30
Southern Utah ■	Dec. 4
Arizona [Anaheim]	Dec. 7
Weber St. ■	Dec. 14
Texas	Dec. 21
Wis.-Milwaukee ■	Dec. 23
UC Irvine	Dec. 28
Wake Forest ■	Dec. 31
Colorado St. ■	Jan. 4
Brigham Young	Jan. 11
Southern Methodist	Jan. 16
Texas Christian	Jan. 18
Rice ■	Jan. 25
Tulsa ■	Jan. 27
UTEP	Jan. 30
New Mexico	Feb. 1
Brigham Young ■	Feb. 6
Colorado St.	Feb. 8
Southern Methodist ■	Feb. 13
Texas Christian ■	Feb. 15
Tulsa	Feb. 22
Rice	Feb. 24
UTEP ■	Feb. 27
New Mexico ■	Mar. 1
Western Ath. Conf. Tr.	Mar. 4-8

1995-96 RESULTS (27-7)
68	Kansas †	79
70	Texas	69
91	Lewis-Clark St. ■	64
86	Drake ■	50
89	Weber St.	60
59	Utah St. ■	43
87	St. Thomas (Fla.) ■	63
56	Wake Forest	60
84	Southern Cal ■	49
108	Cal St. Fullerton ■	58
83	Brigham Young ■	77
64	Fresno St. ■	65
69	Air Force ■	45
82	Hawaii	46
67	San Diego St. ■	59
86	Colorado St. ■	82
88	Wyoming ■	65
68	UTEP	54
82	New Mexico	64
77	UTEP ■	62
74	New Mexico ■	58

78 Colorado St. 73
76 Wyoming 80
69 Hawaii ■ 59
88 San Diego St. ■ 74
68 Fresno St. 71
74 Air Force 50
96 Brigham Young 85
76 Hawaii † 63
71 Colorado St. † 69
60 New Mexico 64
72 Canisius † 43
73 Iowa St. † 67
70 Kentucky † 101

Nickname: Utes
Colors: Crimson & White
Arena: Jon M. Huntsman Center
 Capacity: 15,000; Year Built: 1969
AD: Chris Hill
SID: Bruce Woodbury

UTAH ST.
Logan, UT 84322 I

Coach: Larry Eustachy
Alma Mater: Long Beach St.
Record: 6 Years, W-114, L-69

1996-97 SCHEDULE
Utah ■ .... Nov. 26
Humboldt St. ■ .... Dec. 7
Brigham Young ■ .... Dec. 10
Colorado St. ■ .... Dec. 14
Weber St. .... Dec. 19
Wyoming ■ .... Dec. 21
Utah St. Tr. .... Dec. 27-28
Nevada ■ .... Jan. 2
Southern Ill. ■ .... Jan. 4
Boise St. .... Jan. 9
Idaho .... Jan. 11
North Texas ■ .... Jan. 16
New Mexico St. ■ .... Jan. 18
Cal St. Fullerton .... Jan. 23
Nevada .... Jan. 25
Cal Poly SLO ■ .... Jan. 30
UC Santa Barb. ■ .... Feb. 1
Pacific (Cal.) .... Feb. 6
Long Beach St. .... Feb. 8
UC Irvine ■ .... Feb. 15
Idaho ■ .... Feb. 20
Boise St. ■ .... Feb. 22
New Mexico St. .... Feb. 27
North Texas .... Mar. 1
Big West Conf. Tr. .... Mar. 7-9

1995-96 RESULTS (18-15)
67 Simon Fraser ■ 52
61 Wichita St. † 63
70 Valparaiso † 79
103 Hawaii-Hilo 86
61 Lewis-Clark St. ■ 57
52 Brigham Young 76
43 Utah 59
79 Weber St. † 81
98 Chaminade ■ 52
80 Mississippi Val. ■ 63
77 Southern Miss. 65
57 UNLV 66
75 Nevada 71
69 Southern Ill. ■ 70
73 Pacific (Cal.) ■ 71
60 San Jose St. ■ 58
73 Long Beach St. 80
80 UC Santa Barb. 85
73 Cal St. Fullerton ■ 49
72 UC Irvine ■ 78
70 New Mexico St. 60
72 Nevada ■ 62
65 San Jose St. 68
57 Pacific (Cal.) 74
78 UC Santa Barb. ■ 63
50 Long Beach St. ■ 71
76 New Mexico St. ■ 69
66 Cal St. Fullerton 53
76 UC Irvine 81
82 UNLV ■ 69

70 Nevada 65
86 Long Beach St. † 73
75 San Jose St. † 76

Nickname: Aggies
Colors: Navy Blue & White
Arena: Spectrum
 Capacity: 10,270; Year Built: 1970
AD: Chuck Bell
SID: John Lewandowski

UTICA
Utica, NY 13502 III

Coach: Ed Jones
Alma Mater: Brockport St. '73
Record: 9 Years, W-122, L-106

1996-97 SCHEDULE
Potsdam Tr. .... Nov. 22-23
Clarkson ■ .... Nov. 26
St. John Fisher ■ .... Dec. 7
Oswego St. .... Dec. 12
Oneonta St. .... Jan. 10
Cortland St. ■ .... Jan. 14
Ithaca ■ .... Jan. 17
Elmira ■ .... Jan. 18
Union (N.Y.) ■ .... Jan. 21
Cazenovia .... Jan. 23
Hartwick .... Jan. 25
Elmira .... Jan. 31
Ithaca .... Feb. 1
Hamilton .... Feb. 4
Nazareth .... Feb. 7
Rochester Inst. .... Feb. 8
Utica/Rome ■ .... Feb. 10
Hartwick ■ .... Feb. 12
Maritime (N.Y.) .... Feb. 15
Skidmore .... Feb. 18
Rochester Inst. ■ .... Feb. 21
Nazareth ■ .... Feb. 22
Cazenovia ■ .... Feb. 25

1995-96 RESULTS (16-10)
78 FDU-Madison † 64
62 Southern Vt. 59
65 Clarkson 60
80 Utica/Rome ■ 61
85 Maritime (N.Y.) ■ 68
94 John Jay ■ 92
87 Keuka 86
75 Oswego St. ■ 71
87 Ithaca 66
69 Oneonta St. ■ 65
93 Union (N.Y.) 80
81 Cortland St. 85
86 Cazenovia 57
75 Alfred 82
82 Hamilton ■ 85
77 Alfred ■ 67
69 Hartwick 79
82 Cazenovia ■ 53
73 St. John Fisher 75
56 Skidmore ■ 65
74 Rochester Inst. 85
72 Keuka ■ 58
61 Nazareth 73
79 Elmira 83
75 Rochester 64
78 Cortland St. ■ 83

Nickname: Pioneers
Colors: Blue & Orange
Arena: Clark Athletic Center
 Capacity: 2,200; Year Built: 1970
AD: James Spartano
SID: Brian Welch

UTICA/ROME
Utica, NY 13502 III

Coach: Kevin Grimmer
Alma Mater: Hamilton '81
Record: 2 Years, W-14, L-34

1996-97 SCHEDULE
Lehman .... Nov. 26
Hamilton .... Dec. 3
Oswego St. .... Dec. 6
Cazenovia .... Dec. 8
Buffalo St. .... Dec. 14
Clearwater .... Jan. 10
Savannah A&D .... Jan. 12
Cortland St. ■ .... Jan. 16
Albany Pharmacy ■ .... Jan. 18
Geneseo St. ■ .... Jan. 21
Fredonia St. .... Jan. 24
Brockport St. .... Jan. 25
Binghamton .... Jan. 28
Oneonta St. .... Jan. 31
New Paltz St. ■ .... Feb. 1
Oswego St. ■ .... Feb. 4
Buffalo St. ■ .... Feb. 8
Utica ■ .... Feb. 10
Cazenovia .... Feb. 11
Plattsburgh St. .... Feb. 14
Potsdam St. ■ .... Feb. 15
Geneseo St. .... Feb. 18
Brockport St. ■ .... Feb. 21
Fredonia St. ■ .... Feb. 22

1995-96 RESULTS (11-13)
67 Cazenovia ■ 65
61 Utica 80
76 Oswego St. 77
71 Cazenovia 59
44 Buffalo St. ■ 55
83 Old Westbury 76
58 Binghamton 67
65 Cortland St. 72
67 Geneseo St. 78
80 Brockport St. ■ 72
71 Fredonia St. ■ 66
66 New Paltz St. ■ 8
65 Oneonta St. ■ 79
79 Southern Vt. ■ 87
66 Oswego St. ■ 64
51 Buffalo St. 74
74 Union (N.Y.) ■ 67
75 Plattsburgh St. ■ 60
76 Potsdam St. 69
85 Geneseo St. ■ 75
71 Brockport St. 80
75 Fredonia St. 78
66 Hamilton ■ 72
74 St. Joseph's (L.I.) 71

Nickname: Wildcats
Colors: Royal Blue & Grey
Arena: Campus Center Gym
 Capacity: 1,400; Year Built: 1987
AD: Jim Klein
SID: Jim Klein

VALDOSTA ST.
Valdosta, GA 31698 II

Coach: James Dominey
Alma Mater: Oglethorpe '66
Record: 25 Years, W-387, L-287

1996-97 SCHEDULE
Webber ■ .... Nov. 23
Albany St. (Ga.) ■ .... Dec. 2
Ga. Southwestern ■ .... Dec. 4
Valdosta St. Inv. .... Dec. 13-14
North Fla. ■ .... Dec. 17
Tuskegee .... Dec. 19
Thomas ■ .... Dec. 30
Ala.-Huntsville .... Jan. 4
North Ala. .... Jan. 6
Tuskegee .... Jan. 9
Lincoln Memorial ■ .... Jan. 11
West Ga. ■ .... Jan. 13
Clayton St. ■ .... Jan. 15
Montevallo .... Jan. 18
West Ala. ■ .... Jan. 20
West Fla. .... Jan. 25
Clayton St. ■ .... Jan. 27
Albany St. (Ga.) .... Jan. 29
West Ga. .... Feb. 1

Lincoln Memorial .... Feb. 3
North Ala. ■ .... Feb. 8
Ala.-Huntsville ■ .... Feb. 10
Montevallo ■ .... Feb. 15
West Ala. .... Feb. 17
West Fla. ■ .... Feb. 22

1995-96 RESULTS (17-10)
96 Clayton St. 87
103 Tuskegee 106
93 American (P.R.) ■ 79
104 Emmanuel ■ 68
94 Clayton St. ■ 93
89 Tampa ■ 80
71 North Fla. 76
107 Faulkner ■ 86
60 Ala.-Huntsville ■ 54
93 North Ala. ■ 83
95 Tuskegee ■ 79
72 Lincoln Memorial 69
98 West Ga. 87
83 Montevallo 80
63 West Ala. 65
79 West Fla. ■ 90
79 Albany St. (Ga.) 94
54 West Ga. 58
84 Lincoln Memorial ■ 80
72 North Ala. 76
77 Ala.-Huntsville 72
77 Albany St. (Ga.) ■ 85
68 Montevallo ■ 67
73 West Ala. ■ 71
89 Lynn 87
91 West Fla. 102
69 Mississippi Col. † 70

Nickname: Blazers
Colors: Red & Black
Arena: The Complex
 Capacity: 5,350; Year Built: 1982
AD: Herb Reinhard
SID: Steve Roberts

VALPARAISO
Valparaiso, IN 46383 I

Coach: Homer Drew
Alma Mater: William Jewell '66
Record: 20 Years, W-366, L-252

1996-97 SCHEDULE
NIT .... Nov. 20-29
Canisius .... Nov. 25
Northern Ill. .... Nov. 27
Ind. Wesleyan ■ .... Dec. 4
Wis.-Milwaukee ■ .... Dec. 7
Wis.-Green Bay ■ .... Dec. 10
Ill.-Chicago ■ .... Dec. 14
Indiana Hoosier Cl. .... Dec. 27-28
Troy St. .... Jan. 2
Mo.-Kansas City .... Jan. 4
Youngstown St. ■ .... Jan. 6
Buffalo .... Jan. 8
Northeastern Ill. .... Jan. 11
Chicago St. .... Jan. 14
Central Conn. St. ■ .... Jan. 18
Oral Roberts .... Jan. 20
Western Ill. ■ .... Jan. 25
Northland ■ .... Jan. 27
Buffalo .... Feb. 1
Youngstown St. ■ .... Feb. 3
Chicago St. ■ .... Feb. 6
Northeastern Ill. ■ .... Feb. 8
Central Conn. St. .... Feb. 12
Western Ill. .... Feb. 15
Mo.-Kansas City ■ .... Feb. 22
Troy St. ■ .... Feb. 24
Mid-Continent Conf. Tr. .... Mar. 2-4

1995-96 RESULTS (21-11)
66 Minnesota † 70
84 Toledo † 65
79 Utah St. † 70
75 Grace ■ 51
76 Marian (Ind.) ■ 65
82 Wis.-Milwaukee 77
73 Wisconsin 90

53	Purdue	.74
68	Canisius ■	.72
72	Ill.-Chicago	.84
80	Chicago St. ■	.62
91	Northeastern Ill. ■	.79
83	Eastern Ill. ■	.66
79	Central Conn. St.	.76
104	Troy St.	.115
86	Buffalo ■	.65
73	Youngstown St. ■	.63
65	Mo.-Kansas City	.57
73	Western Ill.	.79
63	Eastern Ill.	.59
102	Troy St. ■	.92
97	Central Conn. St. ■	.82
60	Youngstown St.	.75
73	Buffalo	.64
72	Western Ill. ■	.74
69	Mo.-Kansas City ■	.57
96	Northeastern Ill.	.100
87	Chicago St.	.73
118	Chicago St. †	.83
78	Eastern Ill. †	.65
75	Western Ill. †	.52
51	Arizona †	.90

Nickname: Crusaders
Colors: Brown & Gold
Arena: Athletics-Recreation Center
 Capacity: 4,500; Year Built: 1984
AD: William Steinbrecher
SID: Bill Rogers

VANDERBILT
Nashville, TN 37212 I

Coach: Jan van Breda Kolff
Alma Mater: Vanderbilt '74
Record: 5 Years, W-74, L-70

1996-97 SCHEDULE
NIT	Nov. 20-29
UAB ■	Dec. 4
Memphis	Dec. 7
Boston College	Dec. 9
Nicholls St. ■	Dec. 15
Ala.-Huntsville ■	Dec. 19
Tennessee Tech ■	Dec. 21
Mississippi Val. ■	Dec. 23
Evansville	Dec. 29
St. Louis ■	Dec. 31
Alabama ■	Jan. 4
Georgia ■	Jan. 8
Tennessee	Jan. 11
LSU	Jan. 15
Mississippi ■	Jan. 18
Kentucky [Cincinnati]	Jan. 22
Mississippi St. ■	Jan. 25
South Caro. ■	Jan. 29
Florida	Feb. 1
Memphis ■	Feb. 5
Arkansas ■	Feb. 8
Tennessee ■	Feb. 12
Auburn	Feb. 15
Georgia	Feb. 19
Kentucky ■	Feb. 22
South Caro.	Feb. 26
Florida ■	Mar. 1
Southeastern Conf. Tr.	Mar. 6-9

1995-96 RESULTS (18-14)
63	North Caro. †	.71
96	Chaminade †	.71
75	UCLA †	.71
97	Wofford ■	.59
87	Furman ■	.63
61	Virginia	.48
80	N.C.-Asheville ■	.66
72	Rice ■	.78
93	Tennessee St. ■	.74
96	North Caro. A&T ■	.81
70	Middle Tenn. St. ■	.56
74	Boston College ■	.90
71	Alabama	.80
65	Tennessee ■	.55
68	LSU ■	.71

80	Arkansas	.73
83	South Caro.	.87
75	Evansville ■	.61
55	Florida ■	.77
66	Georgia ■	.62
76	Auburn ■	.62
81	Kentucky ■	.120
55	Mississippi	.78
70	Florida ■	.56
107	South Caro. ■	.97
68	Georgia	.77
79	Tennessee	.94
69	Mississippi St. ■	.64
63	Kentucky	.101
65	Auburn †	.68
86	Ark.-Little Rock ■	.80
70	South Caro.	.80

Nickname: Commodores
Colors: Black & Gold
Arena: Memorial Gymnasium
 Capacity: 15,311; Year Built: 1952
AD: Todd Turner
SID: Andrew Maraniss

VASSAR
Poughkeepsie, NY 12601 III

Coach: Mike Dutton
Alma Mater: New Hampshire '81
Record: 2 Years, W-19, L-28

1996-97 SCHEDULE
Bard Tr.	Nov. 22-23
Army	Nov. 26
Lehman ■	Dec. 2
Union (N.Y.) ■	Dec. 4
Merchant Marine	Dec. 8
Dickinson Tr.	Jan. 10-11
Stevens Tech	Jan. 13
Polytechnic (N.Y.)	Jan. 15
Wesley ■	Jan. 18
Mt. St. Vincent	Jan. 20
Maritime (N.Y.)	Jan. 23
Wesleyan (Conn.) ■	Jan. 25
New York U	Jan. 29
St. Joe's-Brooklyn	Feb. 1
Centenary (N.J.) ■	Feb. 5
Skidmore	Feb. 8
Maritime (N.Y.) ■	Feb. 10
John Jay	Feb. 14
Polytechnic (N.Y.) ■	Feb. 15
Bard ■	Feb. 19
CCNY	Feb. 21
Albany Pharmacy	Feb. 23
Manhattanville ■	Feb. 26

1995-96 RESULTS (14-10)
108	Bard ■	.44
55	New Paltz St.	.79
80	Albany Pharmacy ■	.79
80	Union (N.Y.)	.92
59	Wentworth Inst. ■	.58
64	Maritime (N.Y.)	.79
73	St. Joe's-Brooklyn	.71
72	Delaware Valley	.64
57	Wesley	.95
84	Stevens Tech	.85
77	Maritime (N.Y.) ■	.66
52	Wesleyan (Conn.)	.77
74	Merchant Marine ■	.76
60	Polytechnic (N.Y.)	.66
80	St. Joe's-Brooklyn ■	.52
80	St. Joseph's (L.I.)	.64
81	Skidmore ■	.93
89	Mt. St. Vincent ■	.81
84	John Jay	.88
88	Polytechnic (N.Y.) ■	.70
83	Bard	.41
79	Purchase St. ■	.54
77	Manhattanville	.70
95	St. Joseph's (L.I.)	.38

Nickname: Brewers
Colors: Burgundy & Gray
Arena: Kenyon Gymnasium
 Capacity: 1,000; Year Built: 1934

AD: Andy Jennings
SID: Tony Brown

VERMONT
Burlington, VT 05405 I

Coach: Tom Brennan
Alma Mater: Georgia '71
Record: 15 Years, W-158, L-247

1996-97 SCHEDULE
Lehigh	Nov. 22
Robert Morris ■	Nov. 27
Marist	Nov. 30
Hartford	Dec. 7
Central Conn. St.	Dec. 9
St. Michael's ■	Dec. 11
Harvard ■	Dec. 22
Yale ■	Dec. 30
Hofstra	Jan. 2
Drexel	Jan. 4
New Hampshire ■	Jan. 7
Towson St.	Jan. 10
Delaware	Jan. 12
Northeastern ■	Jan. 16
Boston U. ■	Jan. 18
Dartmouth	Jan. 21
Hartford ■	Jan. 25
Maine	Jan. 30
New Hampshire	Feb. 2
Towson St. ■	Feb. 6
Delaware ■	Feb. 8
Boston U.	Feb. 13
Northeastern	Feb. 15
Maine ■	Feb. 17
Hofstra ■	Feb. 20
Drexel ■	Feb. 22
America East Conf. Tr.	Feb. 28-Mar. 2

1995-96 RESULTS (12-15)
73	Robert Morris	.75
61	Penn St.	.99
66	Dartmouth	.82
82	Yale	.64
58	Drexel	.97
103	Hofstra ■	.83
72	Harvard	.81
58	Marquette	.89
72	St. Michael's ■	.80
73	Northeastern	.69
55	Boston U.	.69
48	Maine	.77
107	Hartford ■	.80
67	Towson St. ■	.69
67	Delaware	.66
92	New Hampshire ■	.90
83	Towson St.	.91
59	Delaware	.77
88	Plattsburgh St. ■	.61
98	Hartford	.95
77	Northeastern ■	.64
75	Boston U. ■	.72
88	New Hampshire	.83
60	Maine	.61
59	Drexel	.86
96	Hofstra	.83
75	Maine †	.84

Nickname: Catamounts
Colors: Green & Gold
Arena: Roy L. Patrick Gymnasium
 Capacity: 3,200; Year Built: 1963
AD: Rick Farnham
SID: Gordon Woodworth

VILLA JULIE
Stevenson, MD 21153 III

Coach: Brett Adams
Alma Mater: York (Pa.) '89
Record: 1 Year, W-2, L-21

1996-97 SCHEDULE
Johns Hopkins Cl.	Nov. 22-23
Marymount (Va.)	Nov. 26
Bridgewater (Va.)	Dec. 2

Salisbury Cl.	Dec. 6-7
Goucher	Dec. 9
Washington (Md.) Cl.	Dec. 13-14
York (Pa.) Cl.	Dec. 28-29
Marymount (Va.)	Jan. 9
Washington (Md.)	Jan. 11
Mary Washington ■	Jan. 16
Frostburg St. ■	Jan. 18
Wesley	Jan. 22
Centenary (N.J.)	Jan. 26
Chowan ■	Feb. 1
St. Mary's (Md.) [Baltimore]	Feb. 3
Western Md. ■	Feb. 5
Frostburg St.	Feb. 9
Gallaudet ■	Feb. 11
St. Mary's (Md.)	Feb. 13
Catholic	Feb. 17
Chowan	Feb. 23

1995-96 RESULTS (6-19)
62	Western Md.	.89
75	Neumann †	.73
77	Marymount (Va.)	.102
73	Bridgewater (Va.) ■	.82
83	Goucher	.110
65	York (Pa.)	.66
77	York (N.Y.) †	.79
77	Holy Family	.100
61	Washington (Md.)	.97
94	Wilmington (Del.) †	.114
84	Phila. Pharmacy	.96
90	Wesley ■	.89
83	Centenary (N.J.) ■	.81
76	Manhattanville	.79
60	Cazenovia †	.75
62	Frostburg St.	.79
78	Gallaudet	.76
76	St. Mary's (Md.) †	.68
77	Frostburg St. ■	.103
65	Wilmington (Del.) ■	.75
89	Chowan	.114
91	Phila. Pharmacy ■	.108
75	Va. Wesleyan ■	.100
46	Chowan	.103
96	Capitol ■	.75

Nickname: Mustangs
Colors: Green & White
Arena: Maryvale Prep
AD: Brett Adams
SID: To be named

VILLANOVA
Villanova, PA 19085 I

Coach: Steve Lappas
Alma Mater: CCNY '77
Record: 8 Years, W-135, L-108

1996-97 SCHEDULE
Puerto Rico Shootout	Nov. 29-Dec. 1
Providence ■	Dec. 4
St. John's (N.Y.)	Dec. 7
Pennsylvania	Dec. 10
Duke ■	Dec. 14
Mt. St. Mary's (Md.) ■	Dec. 21
St. Joseph's (Pa.)	Dec. 23
Rider	Dec. 28
N.C.-Wilmington ■	Dec. 30
Seton Hall ■	Jan. 2
Providence	Jan. 6
Oral Roberts ■	Jan. 8
Miami (Fla.) ■	Jan. 11
Notre Dame	Jan. 14
Rutgers ■	Jan. 18
Syracuse ■	Jan. 20
Boston College ■	Jan. 25
Georgetown	Jan. 27
Syracuse	Feb. 1
West Va. ■	Feb. 5
Kentucky	Feb. 9
Pittsburgh	Feb. 12
Notre Dame ■	Feb. 16
St. John's (N.Y.) ■	Feb. 19
Connecticut ■	Feb. 23
West Va.	Feb. 26

Rutgers ... Mar. 1
Big East Conf. Tr. ... Mar. 5-8

1995-96 RESULTS (26-7)
66 Wisconsin † ... 58
77 Santa Clara † ... 65
77 North Caro. † ... 75
70 Bradley ■ ... 63
83 St. John's (N.Y.) ■ ... 68
70 Miami (Fla.) ... 68
67 Purdue † ... 50
56 Temple † ... 62
80 New Orleans ... 72
91 Hofstra ■ ... 57
71 Delaware ■ ... 58
76 Notre Dame ... 57
94 Boston College ■ ... 77
73 Connecticut ... 81
69 West Va. ... 67
73 Seton Hall ... 78
76 North Caro. ... 56
69 Providence ■ ... 65
90 Miami (Fla.) ■ ... 62
72 Syracuse ... 69
88 Pittsburgh ■ ... 55
79 Georgetown ■ ... 66
76 Rutgers ... 64
90 La Salle ... 50
79 Seton Hall ■ ... 67
67 Pittsburgh ■ ... 64
59 Connecticut ■ ... 70
76 Boston College ... 71
68 Georgetown ... 106
78 Providence † ... 68
76 Georgetown † ... 84
92 Portland † ... 58
64 Louisville † ... 68

Nickname: Wildcats
Colors: Blue & White
Arena: John E. Dupont Pavilion
  Capacity: 6,500; Year Built: 1986
AD: Gene DeFilippo
SID: Karen Frascona

VIRGINIA
Charlottesville, VA 22903 ... I

Coach: Jeff Jones
Alma Mater: Virginia '82
Record: 6 Years, W-117, L-72
1996-97 SCHEDULE
Maui Inv. ... Nov. 25-27
George Mason ... Nov. 30
William & Mary ... Dec. 4
Clemson ■ ... Dec. 7
Liberty ■ ... Dec. 18
Md.-Balt. County ■ ... Dec. 21
Connecticut ... Dec. 23
Radford ■ ... Dec. 28
Delaware ■ ... Dec. 30
Loyola (Md.) ■ ... Jan. 2
Maryland ... Jan. 4
Florida St. ... Jan. 8
North Caro. ... Jan. 11
Wake Forest ... Jan. 15
Duke ... Jan. 18
Georgia Tech ■ ... Jan. 22
North Caro. St. ... Jan. 28
Richmond ■ ... Jan. 30
Florida St. ■ ... Feb. 1
Georgia Tech ... Feb. 6
North Caro. ... Feb. 8
Duke ■ ... Feb. 11
Clemson ... Feb. 15
North Caro. St. ... Feb. 19
Wake Forest ■ ... Feb. 22
Virginia Tech [Richmond] ... Feb. 25
Maryland ■ ... Mar. 2
Atlantic Coast Conf. Tr. ... Mar. 6-9

1995-96 RESULTS (12-15)
84 Tenn.-Martin ■ ... 65
87 William & Mary ■ ... 58
66 Kansas † ... 72
48 Vanderbilt ■ ... 61

67 Richmond ... 52
80 Va. Commonwealth ■ ... 65
64 Virginia Tech † ... 72
76 Liberty ■ ... 48
64 Florida St. ... 69
73 North Caro. St. ■ ... 69
79 Clemson ... 89
77 Duke ■ ... 66
53 North Caro. ... 67
70 Georgia Tech ... 90
64 Wake Forest ■ ... 81
46 Connecticut ... 76
72 Maryland ■ ... 80
64 Florida St. ... 59
87 Old Dominion ■ ... 49
84 North Caro. St. ... 82
62 Clemson ■ ... 51
69 Duke ... 79
66 North Caro. ... 71
75 Georgia Tech ■ ... 84
67 Wake Forest ■ ... 49
71 Maryland ... 83
60 Wake Forest † ... 70

Nickname: Cavaliers
Colors: Orange & Blue
Arena: University Hall
  Capacity: 8,457; Year Built: 1965
AD: Terry Holland
SID: Rich Murray

VA. COMMONWEALTH
Richmond, VA 23284 ... I

Coach: Sonny Smith
Alma Mater: Milligan '58
Record: 20 Years, W-316, L-272
1996-97 SCHEDULE
Miami (Ohio) ■ ... Nov. 23
Southern Utah ■ ... Nov. 26
Radford ... Dec. 2
Southwestern La. ■ ... Dec. 11
Pittsburgh ... Dec. 14
New Orleans ■ ... Dec. 18
Alabama [Birmingham] ... Dec. 21
Wichita St. Tr. ... Dec. 27-28
George Mason ... Jan. 2
James Madison ... Jan. 8
N.C.-Wilmington ■ ... Jan. 11
East Caro. ■ ... Jan. 15
Old Dominion ■ ... Jan. 18
William & Mary ... Jan. 20
American ... Jan. 22
Richmond ... Jan. 25
South Fla. ... Jan. 27
George Mason ■ ... Jan. 29
William & Mary ■ ... Feb. 1
James Madison ■ ... Feb. 5
American ... Feb. 8
East Caro. ... Feb. 12
Old Dominion ... Feb. 15
N.C.-Wilmington ... Feb. 19
Richmond ■ ... Feb. 24
Colonial Conf. Tr. ... Feb. 28-Mar. 3

1995-96 RESULTS (24-9)
83 Western Ky. † ... 65
74 Louisville † ... 83
66 James Madison † ... 60
81 Xavier (Ohio) ■ ... 75
71 Liberty ... 86
82 Florida Int'l ■ ... 61
85 N.C.-Charlotte ■ ... 74
69 Pittsburgh ■ ... 72
63 Rhode Island † ... 68
65 Virginia ... 80
74 Illinois St. ■ ... 72
66 Jackson St. † ... 48
75 New Orleans ... 92
70 William & Mary ... 47
85 Old Dominion ... 70
86 George Mason ■ ... 74
72 East Caro. ... 73
81 James Madison ■ ... 70
79 Richmond ■ ... 51

73 American ■ ... 68
63 N.C.-Wilmington ... 45
94 George Mason ... 81
85 Old Dominion ■ ... 76
83 William & Mary ■ ... 68
80 East Caro. ... 71
65 American ... 57
75 James Madison ... 76
63 N.C.-Wilmington ... 44
69 Richmond ... 67
89 Richmond ... 55
75 East Caro. † ... 60
46 N.C.-Wilmington † ... 43
51 Mississippi St. † ... 58

Nickname: Rams
Colors: Black & Gold
Arena: Richmond Coliseum
  Capacity: 12,500; Year Built: 1971
AD: Richard Sander
SID: Mark Halstead

VMI
Lexington, VA 24450 ... I

Coach: Bart Bellairs
Alma Mater: Warren Wilson '79
Record: 4 Years, W-49, L-54
1996-97 SCHEDULE
Albright ■ ... Nov. 22
Wake Forest ... Nov. 24
Navy ■ ... Dec. 5
Wash. & Lee ■ ... Dec. 7
Radford ... Dec. 10
North Caro. ■ ... Dec. 15
East. Mennonite ■ ... Dec. 18
Winthrop ... Dec. 21
Florida Int'l ... Dec. 30
N.C.-Charlotte ... Jan. 4
Appalachian St. ... Jan. 6
Richmond ... Jan. 8
Tenn.-Chatt. ... Jan. 11
Ga. Southern ■ ... Jan. 13
Wofford ... Jan. 16
Citadel ... Jan. 18
East Tenn. St. ... Jan. 20
Furman ... Jan. 25
Marshall ■ ... Jan. 27
Davidson ... Feb. 1
Appalachian St. ■ ... Feb. 3
Citadel ■ ... Feb. 8
Western Caro. ... Feb. 10
Marshall ... Feb. 15
Davidson ... Feb. 17
East Tenn. St. ■ ... Feb. 22
Southern Conf. Tr. ... Feb. 27-Mar. 2

1995-96 RESULTS (18-10)
78 North Caro. St. ... 104
100 Wash. & Lee ■ ... 62
73 Penn St. ... 99
110 Radford ■ ... 103
107 Lynchburg ■ ... 74
67 Virginia Tech ... 99
71 Marshall ... 78
49 William & Mary ... 90
91 East. Mennonite ■ ... 62
101 Winthrop ... 78
77 Richmond ... 65
96 East Tenn. St. ... 86
84 Appalachian St. ■ ... 64
69 Tenn.-Chatt. ... 71
79 Davidson ... 86
80 Wofford ■ ... 66
91 Citadel ■ ... 52
71 Ga. Southern ... 48
82 East Tenn. St. ■ ... 79
83 Furman ■ ... 57
90 Western Caro. ... 73
103 Marshall ■ ... 94
76 Davidson ... 95
76 North Caro. ... 99
85 Appalachian St. ... 75
85 Citadel ... 83
91 Furman † ... 89

93 Western Caro. † ... 97
Nickname: Keydets
Colors: Red, White & Yellow
Arena: Cameron Hall
  Capacity: 5,000; Year Built: 1981
AD: Davis Babb
SID: Wade Branner

VIRGINIA ST.
Petersburg, VA 23806 ... II

Coach: Ralph Traynham
Alma Mater: Virginia St. '78
(First year as head coach)
1996-97 SCHEDULE
Bloomsburg ... Nov. 15
Johnson Smith ■ ... Nov. 23
Gannon Cl. ... Nov. 29-30
Cheyney ■ ... Dec. 2
N.C. Central ... Dec. 4
Benedict ... Dec. 6
Morris ... Dec. 7
Livingstone ■ ... Dec. 14
Alabama A&M [Indianapolis] ... Dec. 28
Chris. Newport ■ ... Jan. 2
Bowie St. ... Jan. 8
Elizabeth City St. ... Jan. 11
St. Augustine's ... Jan. 14
St. Paul's ... Jan. 16
Virginia Union ■ ... Jan. 19
Winston-Salem ... Jan. 22
Norfolk St. ... Jan. 25
Elizabeth City St. ■ ... Feb. 3
Longwood ... Feb. 5
Norfolk St. ■ ... Feb. 8
Bowie St. ... Feb. 12
St. Paul's ■ ... Feb. 15
Shaw ... Feb. 17
Fayetteville St. ... Feb. 20

1995-96 RESULTS (10-17)
92 Cheyney ... 84
82 Johnson Smith ... 95
83 Rutgers-Camden ... 70
69 Longwood ■ ... 63
69 N.C. Central ... 74
75 Barber-Scotia ■ ... 78
82 Cheyney ... 87
57 Benedict † ... 71
74 Morris Brown † ... 62
85 Chris. Newport ... 83
79 Elizabeth City St. ■ ... 82
55 Virginia Union ■ ... 85
75 Bowie St. ... 77
61 St. Paul's ■ ... 71
71 Winston-Salem ... 76
57 Virginia Union ... 84
63 Norfolk St. ... 87
84 St. Augustine's ■ ... 76
75 Elizabeth City St. ... 76
83 Norfolk St. ... 101
71 Bowie St. ■ ... 84
58 Shaw ■ ... 78
101 St. Paul's ... 95
78 Livingstone ... 74
85 Fayetteville St. ■ ... 78
87 Livingstone † ... 71
69 Norfolk St. † ... 85

Nickname: Trojans
Colors: Orange & Navy Blue
Arena: Daniel Gymnasium
  Capacity: 3,454; Year Built: 1965
AD: Alfreeda Goff
SID: Gregory Goings

VIRGINIA TECH
Blacksburg, VA 24061 ... I

Coach: Bill Foster
Alma Mater: Carson-Newman '58
Record: 29 Years, W-517, L-309

1996-97 SCHEDULE
Hawaii-Hilo Inv.	Nov. 29-Dec. 1
East Tenn. St. ■	Dec. 5
Coastal Caro. ■	Dec. 7
N.C.-Greensboro ■	Dec. 9
Georgia ■	Dec. 14
West Va.	Dec. 21
St. Bonaventure ■	Jan. 2
Xavier (Ohio) ■	Jan. 4
Duquesne ■	Jan. 6
William & Mary ■	Jan. 9
Massachusetts ■	Jan. 12
Ga. Southern ■	Jan. 15
Rhode Island ■	Jan. 18
La Salle ■	Jan. 20
Liberty	Jan. 23
St. Joseph's (Pa.) ■	Jan. 25
Wake Forest ■	Jan. 28
Dayton ■	Feb. 1
Geo. Washington ■	Feb. 4
Fordham ■	Feb. 8
La Salle	Feb. 10
Dayton	Feb. 15
Temple ■	Feb. 18
Geo. Washington	Feb. 20
Duquesne ■	Feb. 23
Virginia [Richmond]	Feb. 25
Xavier (Ohio) ■	Mar. 2
Atlantic 10 Conf. Tr.	Mar. 5-8

1995-96 RESULTS (23-6)
93	Coastal Caro. ■	49
71	William & Mary ■	66
99	VMI ■	67
72	Georgia †	85
68	West Va. ■	62
72	Virginia †	64
62	Wright St. †	46
76	N.C.-Charlotte †	60
88	Duquesne ■	69
71	La Salle †	55
79	Geo. Washington †	71
63	Dayton ■	62
65	St. Bonaventure	58
47	Geo. Washington ■	64
81	Fordham ■	57
85	St. Joseph's (Pa.) ■	76
74	N.C.-Greensboro ■	48
72	Rhode Island	66
69	Duquesne ■	63
78	Xavier (Ohio)	73
56	Liberty ■	53
58	Massachusetts ■	74
61	La Salle ■	56
41	Temple	57
70	Xavier (Ohio) ■	61
73	Dayton	54
71	Rhode Island †	77
61	Wis.-Green Bay †	48
60	Kentucky †	84

Nickname: Hokies, Gobblers
Colors: Orange & Maroon
Arena: Cassell Coliseum
 Capacity: 9,971; Year Built: 1962
AD: Dave Braine
SID: Dave Smith

VIRGINIA UNION
Richmond, VA 23220 II

Coach: Dave Robbins
Alma Mater: Catawba '66
Record: 18 Years, W-451, L-101

1996-97 SCHEDULE
Va. Union Tr.	Nov. 8-10
St. Augustine's	Nov. 20
Clark Atlanta	Nov. 26
Virginia Union Cl.	Nov. 29-30
Livingstone	Dec. 3
Mo. Western St. Cl.	Dec. 6-7
Gannon Tr.	Dec. 29-30
Fayetteville St. ■	Jan. 2
Johnson Smith ■	Jan. 4
St. Paul's ■	Jan. 7

Shaw ■	Jan. 14
Norfolk St.	Jan. 16
Virginia St.	Jan. 19
St. Paul's ■	Jan. 22
Bowie St.	Jan. 25
Elizabeth City St.	Jan. 28
Norfolk St. ■	Feb. 1
Bowie St. ■	Feb. 8
Elizabeth City St. ■	Feb. 11
N.C. Central	Feb. 15
Winston-Salem	Feb. 18
Clark Atlanta ■	Feb. 22

1995-96 RESULTS (28-3)
80	Lock Haven ■	45
82	Mars Hill ■	67
103	IU/PU-Indianapolis †	91
71	Calif. (Pa.) ■	69
97	Livingstone ■	68
96	Johnson Smith ■	66
105	Morris Brown ■	64
74	Benedict ■	51
93	St. Paul's ■	79
64	Benedict	54
85	Virginia St.	55
73	Shaw	62
76	Norfolk St. ■	60
74	St. Paul's ■	65
84	Virginia St. ■	57
93	Bowie St. ■	71
55	Elizabeth City St. ■	52
95	St. Augustine's ■	71
74	Norfolk St.	77
82	Bowie St. ■	51
80	Elizabeth City St.	74
73	N.C. Central	59
77	Fayetteville St. ■	68
89	Winston-Salem ■	58
80	St. Augustine's †	67
84	Shaw †	56
70	Norfolk St. †	72
49	Pfeiffer ■	47
81	Queens (N.C.) ■	58
99	St. Rose †	72
66	Northern Ky. †	68

Nickname: Panthers
Colors: Steel & Maroon
Arena: Arthur Ashe Athletic Center
 Capacity: 6,000; Year Built: 1982
AD: James Battle
SID: Paul Williams

VA. WESLEYAN
Norfolk, VA 23502 III

Coach: Terry Butterfield
Alma Mater: Eckerd '79
Record: 7 Years, W-97, L-86

1996-97 SCHEDULE
Babson Inv.	Nov. 22-23
Chris. Newport	Nov. 26
Guilford	Nov. 30
East. Mennonite	Dec. 2
Randolph-Macon ■	Dec. 4
Roanoke	Dec. 7
Longwood	Dec. 16
Wash. & Lee ■	Jan. 4
Lynchburg ■	Jan. 8
Bridgewater (Va.)	Jan. 11
Salisbury St. ■	Jan. 13
Hampden-Sydney	Jan. 15
Roanoke ■	Jan. 18
Mary Washington ■	Jan. 20
Bridgewater (Va.) ■	Jan. 22
Lynchburg	Jan. 25
Randolph-Macon ■	Jan. 29
Emory & Henry ■	Feb. 1
Wash. & Lee	Feb. 5
Guilford ■	Feb. 8
Hampden-Sydney ■	Feb. 12
Emory & Henry	Feb. 15
East. Mennonite ■	Feb. 17

1995-96 RESULTS (15-10)
80	Mary Washington	74

76	Chris. Newport ■	83
68	Guilford ■	61
78	Salisbury St.	77
76	Roanoke	73
71	East. Mennonite ■	61
90	Longwood	82
73	Hampton	88
103	Wash. & Lee	82
72	Bridgewater (Va.) ■	63
66	Hampden-Sydney ■	72
82	Roanoke ■	56
82	Randolph-Macon ■	70
58	Bridgewater (Va.)	59
71	Lynchburg ■	74
57	Randolph-Macon	66
76	Emory & Henry	80
78	Wash. & Lee ■	57
75	Guilford	70
81	Lynchburg	58
61	Hampden-Sydney	70
82	Emory & Henry ■	81
62	East. Mennonite	68
68	Hampden-Sydney †	80
100	Villa Julie ■	75

Nickname: Blue Marlins
Colors: Navy Blue & Silver
Arena: Van H. Cunningham Gym
AD: Donald Forsyth
SID: Don Birmingham

WABASH
Crawfordsville, IN 47933 III

Coach: Mac Petty
Alma Mater: Tennessee '68
Record: 23 Years, W-296, L-265

1996-97 SCHEDULE
Wheaton (Ill.) Cl.	Nov. 22-23
Webster	Nov. 26
Millikin	Dec. 1
Thomas More	Dec. 7
Wabash Inv.	Dec. 13-14
Wabash-DePauw Cl.	Dec. 21-22
Chicago	Dec. 30
Thomas More Cl.	Jan. 4-5
Manchester	Jan. 11
Anderson (Ind.) ■	Jan. 15
Hanover	Jan. 18
DePauw	Jan. 22
Franklin	Jan. 25
Rose-Hulman ■	Jan. 29
Anderson (Ind.)	Feb. 1
Manchester ■	Feb. 8
DePauw	Feb. 12
Hanover	Feb. 15
Rose-Hulman	Feb. 19
Franklin ■	Feb. 22

1995-96 RESULTS (12-12)
89	Emory & Henry †	85
66	Sewanee	72
79	Millikin	67
57	Calvin	61
88	Blackburn ■	59
67	Knox ■	59
87	Marian (Ind.) †	77
86	Ind.-Northwest ■	45
70	Wittenberg	71
71	Muskingum †	66
80	Manchester ■	82
78	Anderson (Ind.)	79
83	Hanover	80
73	DePauw ■	67
73	Franklin ■	93
52	Rose-Hulman	67
74	Anderson (Ind.) ■	84
81	Thomas More	70
59	Manchester	71
61	DePauw	62
47	Hanover	74
82	Rose-Hulman ■	73
73	Franklin	71
60	Rose-Hulman	78

Nickname: Little Giants

Colors: Scarlet & White
Arena: Chadwick Court
 Capacity: 2,500; Year Built: 1917
AD: Max Servies
SID: Jim Amidon

WAGNER
Staten Island, NY 10301 I

Coach: Tim Capstraw
Alma Mater: Wagner '82
Record: 7 Years, W-85, L-113

1996-97 SCHEDULE
Rutgers	Nov. 26
St. Peter's Tr.	Nov. 30-Dec. 1
Fairfield ■	Dec. 3
Iona ■	Dec. 7
Delaware St. ■	Dec. 21
Seton Hall	Dec. 23
Siena	Dec. 30
Rider	Jan. 4
Monmouth (N.J.) ■	Jan. 6
St. Francis (N.Y.) ■	Jan. 9
Mt. St. Mary's (Md.) ■	Jan. 11
LIU-Brooklyn	Jan. 15
Robert Morris	Jan. 18
St. Francis (Pa.) ■	Jan. 20
Fairleigh Dickinson	Jan. 23
Marist ■	Jan. 25
Rider ■	Feb. 1
Monmouth (N.J.)	Feb. 3
St. Francis (N.Y.)	Feb. 6
Mt. St. Mary's (Md.) ■	Feb. 8
LIU-Brooklyn ■	Feb. 12
Robert Morris ■	Feb. 15
St. Francis (Pa.) ■	Feb. 17
Fairleigh Dickinson ■	Feb. 20
Marist	Feb. 22
Northeast Conf. Tr.	Feb. 25-Mar. 6

1995-96 RESULTS (10-17)
64	American †	69
69	Cornell †	74
59	Delaware St.	64
72	Alabama St. †	65
64	Cincinnati	100
80	Rutgers	78
80	Siena ■	66
86	Fairfield	95
93	St. Francis (N.Y.) ■	69
80	Robert Morris	76
61	St. Francis (Pa.)	73
78	LIU-Brooklyn ■	79
56	Fairleigh Dickinson ■	68
85	Marist	100
76	Rider ■	67
68	Monmouth (N.J.)	78
70	Mt. St. Mary's (Md.) ■	73
100	St. Francis (N.Y.)	70
69	Mt. St. Mary's (Md.)	89
63	Robert Morris	66
81	St. Francis (Pa.) ■	80
99	LIU-Brooklyn	94
81	Fairleigh Dickinson	57
70	Marist ■	75
68	Monmouth (N.J.) ■	77
67	Rider	88
55	Monmouth (N.J.)	64

Nickname: Seahawks
Colors: Green & White
Arena: Sutter Gym
 Capacity: 1,650; Year Built: 1950
AD: Walt Hameline
SID: Tom Dowd

WAKE FOREST
Winston-Salem, NC 27109 I

Coach: Dave Odom
Alma Mater: Guilford '65
Record: 10 Years, W-180, L-114

1996-97 SCHEDULE
VMI ■	Nov. 24

Citadel....................................Nov. 25
Davidson ■..............................Nov. 29
Richmond..................................Dec. 1
Mississippi St. [Chicago].............Dec. 3
North Caro. St...........................Dec. 7
Massachusetts ■.......................Dec. 14
Campbell ■..............................Dec. 21
Utah ■....................................Dec. 31
North Caro. ■............................Jan. 4
Georgia Tech ■..........................Jan. 8
Duke.......................................Jan. 11
Virginia ■.................................Jan. 15
Maryland ■..............................Jan. 19
Clemson..................................Jan. 23
Florida St. ■.............................Jan. 25
Virginia Tech ■..........................Jan. 28
Wofford ■................................Jan. 29
Maryland..................................Feb. 1
Duke ■.....................................Feb. 5
Missouri...................................Feb. 9
Clemson ■...............................Feb. 12
North Caro. St. ■.......................Feb. 16
North Caro..............................Feb. 19
Virginia...................................Feb. 22
Georgia Tech ■.........................Feb. 25
Florida St..................................Mar. 1
Atlantic Coast Conf. Tr............Mar. 6-9

1995-96 RESULTS (26-6)

75	Mt. St. Mary's (Md.) ■	62
69	Oklahoma St. †	53
68	Lehigh ■	53
46	Massachusetts	60
77	Florida	53
91	Appalachian St. ■	50
60	Utah ■	56
81	Furman ■	49
75	Florida St.	73
57	Duke ■	54
77	Maryland ■	64
71	Richmond ■	60
66	Georgia Tech ■	63
41	Clemson	55
81	Virginia ■	64
59	North Caro.	65
66	North Caro. St. ■	62
81	Florida St. ■	67
79	Duke ■	65
85	Maryland	78
63	Georgia Tech	64
68	Clemson ■	48
49	Virginia	67
84	North Caro. ■	60
72	North Caro. St.	70
70	Virginia †	60
68	Clemson †	60
75	Georgia Tech †	74
62	Northeast La. †	50
65	Texas †	62
60	Louisville †	59
63	Kentucky †	83

Nickname: Demon Deacons
Colors: Old Gold & Black
Arena: Joel Memorial Coliseum
  Capacity: 14,407; Year Built: 1989
AD: Ron Wellman
SID: John Justus

WARTBURG
Waverly, IA 50677.................III

Coach: Marty Simmons
Alma Mater: Evansville '87
(First year as head coach)

1996-97 SCHEDULE

Wartburg Tr. ....Nov. 22-23
Augsburg.....................................Dec. 2
Clarke ■.....................................Dec. 12
Cornell College ....Dec. 21
Elmhurst Cl. ....Dec. 28-29
Mt. St. Clare...............................
Buena Vista ■.............................Jan. 10
Simpson ■..................................Jan. 11

Luther.......................................Jan. 17
Loras.......................................Jan. 18
Dubuque..................................Jan. 24
Upper Iowa...............................Jan. 25
William Penn............................Jan. 31
Central (Iowa) ■..........................Feb. 1
Simpson....................................Feb. 4
Upper Iowa ■.............................Feb. 7
Dubuque ■.................................Feb. 8
Buena Vista..............................Feb. 14
Central (Iowa)...........................Feb. 15
Luther ■...................................Feb. 18
William Penn............................Feb. 28
Loras..Mar. 1

1995-96 RESULTS (10-15)

93	Pillsbury ■	78
90	Mt. Mercy ■	88
64	Teikyo Marycrest	52
62	Augsburg ■	72
69	Clarke	55
79	Coe	67
72	Iowa Wesleyan ■	80
97	La Verne †	87
54	Occidental	70
63	Luther ■	60
61	Dubuque ■	65
70	Buena Vista	76
86	Simpson	87
53	Upper Iowa	79
72	Central (Iowa) ■	68
60	Loras	63
61	William Penn ■	62
65	Central (Iowa)	70
60	Dubuque	80
93	Simpson ■	107
66	Luther	73
63	William Penn	58
73	Buena Vista ■	77
85	Loras ■	79
64	Upper Iowa ■	100

Nickname: Knights
Colors: Orange & Black
Arena: Knights Gym
  Capacity: 1,800; Year Built: 1949
AD: Bob Nielson
SID: Duane Schroeder

WASHBURN
Topeka, KS 66621.................II

Coach: Bob Chipman
Alma Mater: Kansas St. '73
Record: 17 Years, W-398, L-138

1996-97 SCHEDULE

Va. Union Tr. ....Nov. 8-10
Fort Hays St.............................Nov. 19
Friends ■..................................Nov. 22
Central Mo. St. ■......................Nov. 30
Mo. Western St. ■.......................Dec. 4
Tabor...Dec. 7
MidAmerica Naz. ■....................Dec. 13
Las Vegas Cl. ....Dec. 18-19
Kansas......................................Dec. 30
Southwest Baptist ■...................Jan. 4
Pittsburg St................................Jan. 8
Truman St.................................Jan. 11
Mo.-Rolla ■...............................Jan. 15
Mo. Southern St........................Jan. 18
Northwest Mo. St. ■..................Jan. 22
Lincoln (Mo.)............................Jan. 25
Emporia St................................Jan. 29
Pittsburg St. ■............................Feb. 1
Truman St. ■..............................Feb. 3
Mo. Western St..........................Feb. 5
Central Mo. St...........................Feb. 8
Lincoln (Mo.) ■.........................Feb. 10
Rockhurst ■..............................Feb. 12
Mo.-Rolla.................................Feb. 15
Northwest Mo. St......................Feb. 19
Emporia St. ■............................Feb. 22

1995-96 RESULTS (16-11)

92	Friends ■	55

96	Doane ■	91
65	Southwest St. ■	90
74	Fort Hays St. ■	91
67	Eckerd †	79
79	Missouri Baptist †	75
94	Tabor	77
71	Chaminade †	65
80	Grand Canyon †	79
68	Northwest Mo. St. ■	83
56	Mo. Western St.	59
66	Emporia St.	72
83	Lincoln (Mo.) ■	73
95	Mo. Southern St.	89
71	Central Mo. St.	83
62	Mo.-Rolla	75
88	Pittsburg St. ■	66
106	Rockhurst	100
74	Mo.-St. Louis	65
77	Southwest Baptist	83
87	Truman St. ■	66
65	Mo. Western St.	72
86	Emporia St. ■	72
84	Lincoln (Mo.)	75
94	Mo. Southern St.	80
66	Central Mo. St. ■	65
104	Mo.-Rolla	112

Nickname: Ichabods
Colors: Yale Blue & White
Arena: Lee Arena
  Capacity: 4,298; Year Built: 1984
AD: Loren Ferre
SID: Robert Rodgers

WASHINGTON
Seattle, WA 98195.................I

Coach: Bob Bender
Alma Mater: Duke '80
Record: 7 Years, W-90, L-109

1996-97 SCHEDULE

Brigham Young ■.......................Nov. 26
Portland St. ■............................Nov. 30
Idaho...Dec. 3
Old Dominion............................Dec. 5
James Madison..........................Dec. 7
Portland...................................Dec. 21
Loyola Marymount ■.................Dec. 23
Eastern Wash............................Dec. 28
Southern Cal...............................Jan. 2
UCLA..Jan. 4
Oregon St. ■...............................Jan. 9
Oregon ■..................................Jan. 11
Washington St...........................Jan. 18
Stanford...................................Jan. 23
California..................................Jan. 25
Arizona St. ■.............................Jan. 30
Arizona ■...................................Feb. 2
Oregon.......................................Feb. 6
Oregon St...................................Feb. 8
Cincinnati ■...............................Feb. 10
Washington St. ■.......................Feb. 15
California ■...............................Feb. 20
Stanford ■.................................Feb. 22
Arizona St.................................Feb. 27
Arizona......................................Mar. 1
UCLA ■......................................Mar. 6
Southern Cal ■...........................Mar. 8

1995-96 RESULTS (16-12)

74	Eastern Wash.	55
92	Jackson St. ■	76
61	Idaho	64
74	Kansas St. ■	60
59	Michigan	60
71	Portland ■	59
82	Lehigh ■	66
62	Gonzaga ■	58
76	Colorado ■	68
94	Southern Cal ■	72
70	UCLA ■	78
55	Oregon St. ■	63
72	Oregon	69
85	Washington St. ■	71

74	Stanford ■	71
71	California ■	69
80	Arizona	79
79	Arizona St.	88
52	Oregon ■	55
50	Oregon St. ■	40
66	Washington St.	76
56	California	67
56	Stanford	67
75	Arizona St. ■	64
65	Arizona ■	67
88	UCLA	91
71	Southern Cal	68
50	Michigan	64

Nickname: Huskies
Colors: Purple & Gold
Arena: Hec Edmundson Pavilion
  Capacity: 7,900; Year Built: 1927
AD: Barbara Hedges
SID: Dan Lepse

WASHINGTON (MD.)
Chestertown, MD 21620.........III

Coach: Tom Finnegan
Alma Mater: Washington (Md.)
Record: 25 Years, W-318, L-280

1996-97 SCHEDULE

Johns Hopkins Cl.................Nov. 22-23
Salisbury St. ....Nov. 26
St. Mary's (Md.) ....Dec. 2
Dickinson ■................................Dec. 7
Johns Hopkins..........................Dec. 10
Washington (Md.) Cl. ....Dec. 13-14
Delaware..................................Dec. 20
Calif. (Pa.).................................Jan. 4
Gallaudet...................................Jan. 8
Villa Julie ■...............................Jan. 11
Swarthmore ■...........................Jan. 16
Muhlenberg..............................Jan. 18
Haverford ■..............................Jan. 22
Gettysburg................................Jan. 25
Frank. & Marsh. ■.....................Jan. 29
Ursinus ■....................................Feb. 1
Wesley ■.....................................Feb. 5
Muhlenberg ■.............................Feb. 8
Swarthmore...............................Feb. 12
Ursinus.....................................Feb. 15
Haverford.................................Feb. 19
Western Md. ■..........................Feb. 22

1995-96 RESULTS (9-15)

66	Wilkes †	92
83	Rutgers-Camden †	58
65	Frostburg St. ■	64
58	Delaware	100
88	St. Mary's (Md.) ■	83
78	Dickinson	89
73	Johns Hopkins ■	78
97	Villa Julie	61
88	Chris. Newport ■	101
86	Towson St.	105
83	Menlo ■	96
59	Swarthmore	55
82	Muhlenberg ■	81
78	Haverford	81
64	Gettysburg ■	77
55	Frank. & Marsh.	88
67	Ursinus ■	77
71	Wesley	77
63	Muhlenberg	77
53	Swarthmore ■	61
62	Ursinus	64
77	Gallaudet	75
78	Haverford ■	69
90	Western Md.	72

Nickname: Shoremen
Colors: Maroon & Black
Arena: Cain Athletic Center
  Capacity: 1,200; Year Built: 1957
AD: Bryan Matthews
SID: Dan Flynn

WASHINGTON (MO.)
St. Louis, MO 63130 III

Coach: Mark Edwards
Alma Mater: Washington (Mo.) '69
Record: 15 Years, W-237, L-154

1996-97 SCHEDULE
Washington (Mo.) Tr.	Nov. 22-23
Millikin ■	Nov. 26
Maryville (Mo.) Cl.	Nov. 29-30
Washington (Mo.) Cl.	Dec. 6-7
Mo.-St. Louis	Dec. 14
Chicago ■	Jan. 4
Roanoke ■	Jan. 8
Johns Hopkins	Jan. 10
MacMurray ■	Jan. 14
Brandeis ■	Jan. 17
New York U. ■	Jan. 19
Case Reserve ■	Jan. 24
Rochester	Jan. 26
Carnegie Mellon	Jan. 31
Emory	Feb. 2
Rochester	Feb. 7
Fontbonne	Feb. 10
Emory ■	Feb. 14
Carnegie Mellon ■	Feb. 16
New York U.	Feb. 21
Brandeis	Feb. 23
Chicago	Mar. 1

1995-96 RESULTS (23-6)
76	DePauw †	73
74	Ill. Wesleyan	83
78	MacMurray ■	64
78	Claremont-M-S †	62
70	Pomona-Pitzer †	78
65	Cal Tech ■	33
91	Hamilton ■	69
90	Millikin	76
69	Mo.-St. Louis	72
87	Murray St.	108
85	Chicago	74
91	Johns Hopkins ■	88
93	Brandeis	73
78	New York U.	90
77	Case Reserve	67
87	Rochester	63
93	Carnegie Mellon ■	74
91	Emory ■	60
91	Fontbonne ■	62
82	Rochester ■	74
74	Emory	67
78	Carnegie Mellon	67
94	New York U. ■	74
93	Brandeis ■	70
83	Chicago	73
76	Rose-Hulman ■	74
93	Wheaton (Ill.)	75
87	Chris. Newport †	71
61	Ill. Wesleyan †	73

Nickname: Bears
Colors: Red & Green
Arena: Washington Field House
  Capacity: 3,000; Year Built: 1928
AD: John Schael
SID: Mike Wolf

WASHINGTON ST.
Pullman, WA 99164 I

Coach: Kevin Eastman
Alma Mater: Richmond '77
Record: 9 Years, W-159, L-99

1996-97 SCHEDULE
Boise St. ■	Nov. 23
Gonzaga	Nov. 30
UC Irvine ■	Dec. 2
Eastern Wash. [Spokane]	Dec. 7
Montana	Dec. 10
Idaho ■	Dec. 14
San Jose St. ■	Dec. 22
Hawaii Rainbow Cl.	Dec. 27-30
UCLA	Jan. 2

Southern Cal	Jan. 4
Oregon [Spokane]	Jan. 9
Oregon St. [Spokane]	Jan. 11
Washington	Jan. 18
California	Jan. 23
Stanford	Jan. 25
Arizona ■	Jan. 30
Arizona St. ■	Feb. 1
Oregon St.	Feb. 6
Oregon	Feb. 8
Idaho	Feb. 11
Washington ■	Feb. 15
Stanford ■	Feb. 20
California ■	Feb. 22
Arizona	Feb. 27
Arizona St.	Mar. 1
Southern Cal ■	Mar. 6
UCLA ■	Mar. 8

1995-96 RESULTS (17-12)
72	Gonzaga	67
90	Eastern Wash. ■	58
73	Canisius †	62
75	Syracuse	77
98	Montana ■	87
66	Idaho ■	54
90	San Jose St.	74
88	UC Irvine	81
73	UCLA ■	78
81	Southern Cal ■	83
63	Oregon	70
76	Oregon St.	62
71	Washington	85
79	California ■	87
67	Stanford ■	78
72	Arizona St.	58
78	Arizona	96
61	Oregon St. ■	42
70	Oregon	65
68	Idaho	59
76	Washington ■	66
68	Stanford	59
67	California	71
62	Arizona	72
103	Arizona St. ■	78
69	Southern Cal	62
71	UCLA	82
92	Gonzaga	73
73	Nebraska	82

Nickname: Cougars
Colors: Crimson & Gray
Arena: Friel Court
  Capacity: 12,058; Year Built: 1973
AD: Rick Dickson
SID: Wes Werner

WASH. & JEFF.
Washington, PA 15301 III

Coach: Tom Reiter
Alma Mater: Wisconsin '75
Record: 3 Years, W-43, L-32

1996-97 SCHEDULE
Allegheny ■	Nov. 22
Carnegie Mellon ■	Nov. 23
Muskingum	Nov. 26
Eastern Ill.	Nov. 30
Savannah A&D ■	Dec. 3
Frostburg St.	Dec. 5
Penn St.-Behrend	Dec. 7
Penn St.-Behrend ■	Jan. 6
Wilmington (Ohio)	Jan. 10
Thomas More	Jan. 11
Oberlin ■	Jan. 13
La Roche	Jan. 15
Kenyon	Jan. 18
Waynesburg	Jan. 22
Thiel ■	Jan. 25
Grove City ■	Jan. 29
Bethany (W.Va.)	Feb. 1
La Roche ■	Feb. 5
Alfred	Feb. 6
Waynesburg ■	Feb. 8
Thiel	Feb. 12

Grove City	Feb. 15
Bethany (W.Va.) ■	Feb. 19
Alfred ■	Feb. 22

1995-96 RESULTS (8-17)
62	Carnegie Mellon	70
53	Allegheny †	67
44	Lake Erie	76
72	St. Vincent	79
54	Muskingum ■	58
80	Alfred ■	64
44	Youngstown St.	84
59	Penn St.-Behrend	62
63	Oberlin	67
67	Wilmington (Ohio) ■	83
68	Frostburg St. ■	64
71	Thiel	61
78	La Roche ■	66
56	Waynesburg	70
69	Savannah A&D ■	78
64	Grove City	78
60	Thomas More ■	85
63	Kenyon	59
81	Bethany (W.Va.) ■	83
97	Thiel ■	71
76	La Roche	59
66	Waynesburg	81
63	Grove City ■	78
68	Penn St.-Behrend ■	63
76	Bethany (W.Va.)	79

Nickname: Presidents
Colors: Red & Black
Arena: Henry Memorial Center
  Capacity: 2,800; Year Built: 1970
AD: John Luckhardt
SID: Susan Isola

WASH. & LEE
Lexington, VA 24450 III

Coach: Kevin Moore
Alma Mater: Brockport St. '83
Record: 9 Years, W-125, L-114

1996-97 SCHEDULE
Elmira Cl.	Nov. 23-24
Pomona-Pitzer Cl.	Nov. 29-30
Hampden-Sydney ■	Dec. 4
Guilford ■	Dec. 6
VMI	Dec. 7
Emory & Henry ■	Dec. 11
Va. Wesleyan	Jan. 4
Haverford ■	Jan. 6
Roanoke ■	Jan. 11
Lynchburg	Jan. 15
Randolph-Macon ■	Jan. 18
Emory & Henry	Jan. 22
Bridgewater (Va.) ■	Jan. 24
Hampden-Sydney	Jan. 29
Guilford	Feb. 1
Va. Wesleyan ■	Feb. 5
East. Mennonite ■	Feb. 8
Randolph-Macon	Feb. 10
Lynchburg ■	Feb. 12
Roanoke	Feb. 15
Bridgewater (Va.) ■	Feb. 17
East. Mennonite	Feb. 19

1995-96 RESULTS (3-21)
86	Emory ■	89
77	Albright ■	85
64	Savannah A&D	72
61	John Carroll †	90
79	Keuka †	93
62	VMI	100
60	Hampden-Sydney	65
72	Guilford	87
65	Bridgewater (Va.) ■	77
92	Emory & Henry ■	86
82	Va. Wesleyan ■	103
74	Lynchburg	71
66	Randolph-Macon	81
83	Roanoke ■	90
73	Emory & Henry	84
65	Bridgewater (Va.) ■	90
75	Hampden-Sydney ■	97

76	Guilford ■	84
57	Va. Wesleyan	78
100	East. Mennonite ■	79
71	Randolph-Macon ■	88
65	Lynchburg	68
79	Roanoke	97
77	East. Mennonite	96

Nickname: Generals
Colors: Royal Blue & White
Arena: Warner Center
  Capacity: 2,500; Year Built: 1972
AD: Mike Walsh
SID: Brian Logue

WAYNE ST. (MICH.)
Detroit, MI 48202 II

Coach: Ron Hammye
Alma Mater: Bowling Green '78
Record: 8 Years, W-131, L-97

1996-97 SCHEDULE
Concordia (Mich.) ■	Nov. 16
Grand Valley St. ■	Nov. 18
Siena Heights	Nov. 20
Detroit	Nov. 23
Northern Mich. ■	Dec. 5
Michigan Tech ■	Dec. 7
Calvin ■	Dec. 10
Madonna ■	Dec. 11
Ferris St.	Dec. 19
Grand Valley St.	Dec. 21
St. Francis (Ill.) ■	Dec. 23
Ashland ■	Jan. 2
Hillsdale ■	Jan. 4
Mercyhurst	Jan. 9
Gannon	Jan. 11
Oakland ■	Jan. 18
Northwood	Jan. 23
Lake Superior St.	Jan. 25
Saginaw Valley	Jan. 30
Michigan Christian ■	Feb. 1
Ashland	Feb. 6
Hillsdale	Feb. 8
Mercyhurst ■	Feb. 13
Gannon ■	Feb. 15
Oakland	Feb. 20

1995-96 RESULTS (16-10)
Results unavailable

Nickname: Tartars
Colors: Green & Gold
Arena: Matthaei Building
  Capacity: 2,000; Year Built: 1966
AD: Bob Brennan
SID: Richard Thompson Jr

WAYNE ST. (NEB.)
Wayne, NE 68787 II

Coach: Greg McDermott
Alma Mater: Northern Iowa
Record: 2 Years, W-26, L-28

1996-97 SCHEDULE
St. Francis (Ill.) ■	Nov. 16
Neb.-Omaha	Nov. 22
South Dak. St.	Nov. 26
Dakota St. ■	Nov. 30
Augustana (S.D.) ■	Dec. 3
Huron ■	Dec. 7
Northwest Mo. St.	Dec. 14
Hawaii-Hilo Cl.	Dec. 17-19
Neb. Christian ■	Jan. 7
Rockhurst ■	Jan. 13
Southwest St.	Jan. 15
Midland Lutheran	Jan. 20
Briar Cliff	Jan. 22
Minn.-Morris	Jan. 25
Neb.-Kearney	Jan. 27
Northern St.	Jan. 29
Bemidji St.	Feb. 1
Teikyo Westmar ■	Feb. 3
Southwest St. ■	Feb. 5

Denver ....Feb. 8
Neb.-Kearney ....Feb. 11
Presentation ■ ....Feb. 15
Briar Cliff ■ ....Feb. 17
Northern St. ■ ....Feb. 19
Minn.-Morris ■ ....Feb. 22
Rockhurst ....Feb. 26
Bemidji St. ■ ....Mar. 1

1995-96 RESULTS (12-15)
63	Neb.-Omaha ■	72
97	Morningside	91
95	Southwest Baptist †	85
76	Drury	87
64	South Dak. St. ■	86
73	St. Francis (Ill.)	75
58	Upper Iowa	86
77	Augustana (S.D.)	85
60	Northwest Mo. St.	63
93	Dakota St. ■	79
55	Huron	85
98	Moorhead St.	102
70	Rockhurst ■	65
74	Southwest St. ■	72
103	Neb.-Kearney	91
70	Moorhead St.	87
83	Minn.-Morris ■	74
100	Northern St. ■	93
100	Bemidji St.	91
80	Southwest St.	88
106	Briar Cliff ■	74
75	Neb.-Kearney	83
75	Teikyo Westmar ■	46
77	Northern St.	80
89	Minn.-Morris ■	101
66	Briar Cliff	73
88	Bemidji St. ■	78

Nickname: Wildcats
Colors: Black & Gold
Arena: Rice Auditorium
    Capacity: 2,000; Year Built: 1960
AD: Pete Chapman
SID: Jerry Rashid

WAYNESBURG
Waynesburg, PA 15370 III

Coach: Rudy Marisa
Alma Mater: Penn St. '56
Record: 27 Years, W-447, L-238

1996-97 SCHEDULE
Wooster Cl. ....Nov. 22-23
Phila. Bible ■ ....Dec. 7
Davis & Elkins ....Dec. 14
Lake Erie ■ ....Dec. 16
Lycoming ■ ....Jan. 4
Ohio-Eastern ....Jan. 6
Lake Erie ....Jan. 8
Frostburg St. Inv. ....Jan. 10-11
Penn St.-Behrend ....Jan. 13
Pitt.-Bradford ....Jan. 18
Wash. & Jeff. ■ ....Jan. 22
Bethany (W.Va.) ....Jan. 25
Pitt.-Greensburg ■ ....Jan. 27
Thiel ■ ....Jan. 29
Alfred ■ ....Feb. 1
Frostburg St. ■ ....Feb. 3
Grove City ....Feb. 5
Wash. & Jeff. ....Feb. 8
Bethany (W.Va.) ■ ....Feb. 12
Thiel ....Feb. 15
Penn St.-Behrend ■ ....Feb. 17
Alfred ....Feb. 19
Grove City ■ ....Feb. 22

1995-96 RESULTS (19-7)
71	Centenary (N.J.) †	73
86	Gwynedd-Mercy †	67
84	Davis & Elkins ■	89
98	Phila. Bible ■	60
91	Valley Forge Chrst.	61
83	La Roche ■	67
69	Penn St.-Behrend	82
116	Valley Forge Chrst.	66
74	Frostburg St.	91

56	Lincoln (Pa.) †	61
81	La Roche	70
90	Point Park ■	77
88	Bethany (W.Va.) ■	75
70	Wash. & Jeff.	56
85	Penn St.-Behrend ■	72
100	Thiel	83
89	Ohio-Eastern ■	54
56	Grove City ■	53
90	Bethany (W.Va.)	65
55	Frostburg St.	53
81	Wash. & Jeff. ■	66
102	Pitt.-Bradford ■	82
88	Thiel	58
59	Grove City	71
59	Grove City †	50
75	Lincoln (Pa.) ■	85

Nickname: Yellowjackets
Colors: Orange & Black
Arena: Recreation Center
    Capacity: 1,500; Year Built: 1985
AD: Rudy Marisa
SID: David Walkosky

WEBER ST.
Ogden, UT 84408 I

Coach: Ron Abegglen
Alma Mater: Brigham Young '62
Record: 10 Years, W-206, L-95

1996-97 SCHEDULE
Pepperdine ■ ....Nov. 22
Nebraska ....Nov. 26
Nevada ....Nov. 30
Brigham Young ■ ....Dec. 4
Boise St. ■ ....Dec. 7
Utah ....Dec. 14
Utah St. ■ ....Dec. 19
Michigan St. Cl. ....Dec. 27-28
Montana St. ■ ....Jan. 2
Montana ■ ....Jan. 3
Idaho St. ■ ....Jan. 9
Eastern Wash. ....Jan. 11
Cal St. Northridge ....Jan. 16
Northern Ariz. ....Jan. 18
Eastern Wash. ■ ....Jan. 22
Portland St. ....Jan. 23
Montana ....Jan. 29
Cal St. Sacramento ....Feb. 1
Portland St. ■ ....Feb. 3
Southern Utah ■ ....Feb. 7
Idaho St. ....Feb. 12
Montana St. ....Feb. 14
Cal St. Northridge ■ ....Feb. 20
Northern Ariz. ■ ....Feb. 22
Cal St. Sacramento ■ ....Feb. 27
Big Sky Conf. Tr. ....Mar. 6-8

1995-96 RESULTS (20-10)
102	Fresno St.	86
62	Michigan	80
100	Texas Southern †	88
66	Colorado St.	58
60	Utah ■	89
88	Pepperdine	99
86	Brigham Young	91
81	Utah St. †	79
85	Wyoming ■	68
79	Kent †	66
62	Indiana †	82
95	Denver ■	59
108	Alas. Anchorage ■	101
71	Montana St.	90
77	Montana	84
75	Boise St. ■	67
93	Idaho St. ■	67
83	Idaho	86
119	Eastern Wash.	88
78	Southern Utah	73
89	Northern Ariz. ■	67
97	Montana ■	80
94	Montana St.	90
70	Idaho St.	77
64	Boise St.	62

106	Eastern Wash. ■	83
86	Idaho ■	75
101	Northern Ariz.	64
77	Boise St. †	70
70	Montana St.	81

Nickname: Wildcats
Colors: Purple & White
Arena: Dee Events Center
    Capacity: 12,000; Year Built: 1977
AD: Dutch Belnap
SID: Brad Larsen

WEBSTER
Webster Groves, MO 63119....III

Coach: Tom Hart
Alma Mater: Niagara '83
Record: 5 Years, W-30, L-85

1996-97 SCHEDULE
Manchester Tr. ....Nov. 22-23
Wabash ....Nov. 26
St. Louis Pharmacy ....Dec. 3
William Penn ....Dec. 6
Illinois Col. ■ ....Dec. 11
Fontbonne ....Dec. 14
San Diego Tr. ....Dec. 27-29
Westminster (Mo.) ....Jan. 9
Blackburn ....Jan. 11
MacMurray ■ ....Jan. 16
Principia ■ ....Jan. 18
Sanford Brown ....Jan. 21
Greenville ....Jan. 25
Maryville (Mo.) ....Jan. 30
Westminster (Mo.) ■ ....Feb. 1
Blackburn ■ ....Feb. 6
MacMurray ....Feb. 8
Principia ....Feb. 13
Fontbonne ■ ....Feb. 15
Greenville ■ ....Feb. 20
Maryville (Mo.) ■ ....Feb. 22

1995-96 RESULTS (8-17)
56	Rhodes ■	81
61	Monmouth (Ill.)	78
52	Knox	67
46	DePauw ■	63
68	Sanford Brown ■	64
66	William Penn	67
81	St. Louis Pharmacy	69
94	Illinois Col.	92
84	Fontbonne	92
63	Blackburn ■	70
77	Fontbonne ■	82
68	Maryville (Mo.) ■	81
58	Greenville	78
71	Westminster (Mo.) ■	88
67	MacMurray	77
88	Parks ■	78
55	Blackburn	80
73	Maryville (Mo.)	56
60	Greenville ■	75
79	Westminster (Mo.)	73
69	Principia ■	68
59	Principia	55
53	MacMurray ■	61
64	Parks	69
71	Westminster (Mo.)	78

Nickname: Gorloks
Colors: Gold, Navy Blue & White
Arena: Grant Gym
    Capacity: 400; Year Built: 1992
AD: Tom Hart
SID: Jim Wilson

WENTWORTH INST.
Boston, MA 02115 III

Coach: Harry McShane
Alma Mater: Northeastern '83
Record: 2 Years, W-21, L-30

1996-97 SCHEDULE
Fitchburg St. ....Nov. 26

Coast Guard ■ ....Dec. 3
MIT ....Dec. 7
Bri'water (Mass.) ....Dec. 10
Embry-Riddle Tr. ....Dec. 28-29
Southern Me. ....Jan. 7
WPI ■ ....Jan. 11
New England Col. ....Jan. 16
Anna Maria ....Jan. 18
Curry ■ ....Jan. 21
Roger Williams ....Jan. 23
Salve Regina ....Jan. 27
Eastern Nazarene ■ ....Jan. 29
Nichols ■ ....Feb. 1
Curry ....Feb. 4
Colby-Sawyer ....Feb. 8
Eastern Nazarene ....Feb. 10
Salve Regina ■ ....Feb. 12
Gordon ■ ....Feb. 15
Suffolk ■ ....Feb. 18
Roger Williams ■ ....Feb. 20

1995-96 RESULTS (19-8)
85	Emerson-MCA ■	76
51	Coast Guard	75
89	Fitchburg St. ■	58
58	Vassar	59
59	Bard	17
60	WPI	82
59	Bri'water (Mass.) ■	79
83	Endicott	79
64	MIT ■	59
67	New England Col. ■	56
73	Anna Maria ■	76
67	Curry	54
68	Roger Williams ■	56
77	Salve Regina ■	62
82	Eastern Nazarene	77
83	Nichols	80
73	Curry ■	76
88	Mass. Pharmacy ■	70
87	Colby-Sawyer ■	68
93	Eastern Nazarene ■	75
62	Salve Regina	73
78	Gordon	74
87	Suffolk ■	65
83	Roger Williams	72
83	Nichols ■	71
71	Colby-Sawyer ■	68
63	Anna Maria	94

Nickname: Leopards
Colors: Black & Gold
Arena: Tansey Gymnasium
    Capacity: 700; Year Built: 1970
AD: Lee Conrad
SID: Bill Gorman

WESLEY
Dover, DE 19901 III

Coach: James Wentworth
Alma Mater: Pfeiffer '60
Record: 11 Years, W-77, L-176

1996-97 SCHEDULE
Penn St.-Behrend Tr. ....Nov. 23-24
Marymount (Va.) ■ ....Dec. 2
Neumann ■ ....Dec. 4
Bridgewater (Va.) Tr ....Dec. 6-7
Western Md. ■ ....Dec. 14
Palm Beach Atl. ....Jan. 3
Nova Southeastern ....Jan. 5
Embry-Riddle ....Jan. 7
Vassar ....Jan. 18
St. Mary's (Md.) ■ ....Jan. 20
Villa Julie ■ ....Jan. 22
Manhattanville Cl. ....Jan. 25-26
Valley Forge Chrst. ....Jan. 30
Washington (Md.) ....Feb. 5
Salisbury St. ....Feb. 10
Holy Family ■ ....Feb. 13
Stevens Tech ■ ....Feb. 15
Frostburg St. ....Feb. 17
Chowan ....Feb. 22

1995-96 RESULTS (6-18)
74	Hampden-Sydney	104

81	Newport News App. †	73
55	Ursinus	67
84	Neumann	65
95	Christendom ■	54
58	Elmira	76
82	Daemen †	105
57	Goucher	90
70	Marymount (Va.)	72
64	Lebanon Valley	91
95	Vassar ■	57
89	Villa Julie	90
84	Centenary (N.J.) ■	93
69	Frostburg St. ■	71
63	Lincoln (Pa.)	110
59	Army	81
77	Washington (Md.) ■	71
86	Valley Forge Chrst.	69
88	Salisbury St. ■	102
63	Randolph-Macon ■	66
90	Stevens Tech	98
61	Frostburg St.	83
56	Holy Family	87
68	Chowan ■	83

Nickname: Wolverines
Colors: Navy Blue & White
Arena: Wesley Field House
 Capacity: 1,000
AD: Steve Clark
SID: Jason Bowen

WESLEYAN (CONN.)
Middletown, CT 06457 III

Coach: Gerry McDowell
Alma Mater: Colby '76
(First year as head coach)
1996-97 SCHEDULE
Bri'water (Mass.) ■		Nov. 23
Springfield		Nov. 26
Union (N.Y.) ■		Dec. 2
Washington (Mo.) Cl.		Dec. 6-7
Albertus Magnus ■		Dec. 12
Eastern Conn. St. ■		Jan. 11
Middlebury		Jan. 16
Haverford ■		Jan. 18
Trinity (Conn.)		Jan. 21
Clark (Mass.) ■		Jan. 23
Vassar		Jan. 25
Tufts ■		Jan. 30
Williams		Feb. 1
Brandeis ■		Feb. 4
Bowdoin		Feb. 7
Colby		Feb. 8
Coast Guard ■		Feb. 11
Amherst ■		Feb. 15
Connecticut Col.		Feb. 18
Western New Eng.		Feb. 20
Amherst		Feb. 22
Trinity (Conn.) ■		Feb. 25
Williams ■		Mar. 1

1995-96 RESULTS (5-18)
53	Springfield	59
75	Union (N.Y.)	83
66	Western Conn. St.	71
56	Colby-Sawyer ■	62
65	Eastern Conn. St.	71
93	Albertus Magnus	78
90	Bri'water (Mass.)	77
71	Middlebury ■	77
67	Trinity (Conn.) ■	71
82	Clark (Mass.) ■	78
77	Vassar ■	52
72	Tufts	94
67	Williams ■	88
65	Brandeis	72
53	Bowdoin ■	61
46	Colby ■	62
57	Coast Guard ■	67
76	Amherst	81
68	Connecticut Col. ■	71
82	Western New Eng. ■	73
40	Amherst ■	51
61	Trinity (Conn.)	86
50	Williams	84

Nickname: Cardinals
Colors: Red & Black
Arena: Alumni Athletic Building
 Capacity: 1,500; Year Built: 1931
AD: John Biddiscombe
SID: Brian Katten

WEST ALA.
Livingston, AL 35470 II

Coach: Rick Reedy
Alma Mater: Flagler '77
Record: 12 Years, W-152, L-171
1996-97 SCHEDULE
Mississippi Col. Tr.		Nov. 22-23
Lane		Nov. 26
Athens St. ■		Nov. 28
Selma		Nov. 30
Arkansas St.		Dec. 7
West Ga. ■		Jan. 4
Lincoln Memorial		Jan. 6
Ala.-Huntsville ■		Jan. 11
North Ala. ■		Jan. 13
Mississippi Col.		Jan. 16
West Fla.		Jan. 18
Valdosta St. ■		Jan. 20
Lane ■		Jan. 23
Montevallo ■		Jan. 25
Selma ■		Jan. 28
North Ala.		Feb. 1
Ala.-Huntsville		Feb. 3
La. Christian		Feb. 5
Lincoln Memorial ■		Feb. 8
West Ga.		Feb. 10
Mississippi Col. ■		Feb. 12
West Fla. ■		Feb. 15
Valdosta St. ■		Feb. 17
Athens St. ■		Feb. 19
Montevallo		Feb. 22

1995-96 RESULTS (9-17)
71	Lane	67
61	Ark.-Little Rock	83
68	Athens St.	63
80	Talladega	84
91	Selma ■	60
63	Southern U.	81
47	West Ga. ■	64
91	Lincoln Memorial ■	95
73	Athens St. ■	81
56	Ala.-Huntsville	57
44	North Ala.	60
52	Faulkner	63
77	West Fla. ■	73
65	Valdosta St. ■	63
73	Lane ■	69
74	Montevallo	81
86	Selma	71
77	Talladega ■	82
62	Lincoln Memorial	72
56	West Ga.	67
64	North Ala. ■	79
61	West Fla.	73
71	Valdosta St.	73
68	Faulkner ■	58
94	Montevallo ■	77
57	Ala.-Huntsville ■	58

Nickname: Tigers
Colors: Red & White
Arena: Pruitt Hall
 Capacity: 1,500; Year Built: 1962
AD: Dee Outlaw
SID: To be named

WEST CHESTER
West Chester, PA 19380 II

Coach: Dick DeLaney
Alma Mater: West Chester '69
Record: 9 Years, W-148, L-96
1996-97 SCHEDULE
Bentley Tr.		Nov. 15-16
Wheeling Jesuit Tr.		Nov. 22-23
Phila. Textile ■		Nov. 26
Shippensburg ■		Dec. 3
Wilmington (Del.) ■		Dec. 5
Alvernia		Dec. 7
Dist. Columbia ■		Dec. 19
Albany (N.Y.) Tr.		Dec. 30-31
East Stroudsburg ■		Jan. 8
Bloomsburg		Jan. 11
Dist. Columbia ■		Jan. 15
Millersville ■		Jan. 18
Cheyney		Jan. 22
Mansfield ■		Jan. 25
Kutztown		Jan. 29
Bloomsburg ■		Feb. 1
East Stroudsburg ■		Feb. 5
Millersville		Feb. 8
Pitt.-Johnstown		Feb. 11
Cheyney ■		Feb. 15
Eastern ■		Feb. 17
Kutztown ■		Feb. 19
Mansfield		Feb. 22

1995-96 RESULTS (15-11)
79	Wilmington (Del.) ■	64
74	Bowie St. ■	70
68	Phila. Textile	65
65	Walsh †	82
68	West Liberty St. †	77
68	Shippensburg	83
82	Calif. (Pa.)	72
65	Eastern	48
70	Dist. Columbia	82
78	Central St. †	51
62	Indiana (Pa.)	63
79	Wheeling Jesuit ■	58
65	Kutztown ■	62
87	Mansfield	70
57	Cheyney	71
63	Millersville ■	62
55	Bloomsburg	82
62	East Stroudsburg ■	76
104	Mansfield ■	74
63	Kutztown	81
64	Cheyney ■	69
87	Pitt.-Johnstown ■	81
58	Millersville	72
76	Dist. Columbia ■	56
82	East Stroudsburg	89
79	Bloomsburg ■	75

Nickname: Golden Rams
Colors: Purple & Gold
Arena: Hollinger Field House
 Capacity: 2,500; Year Built: 1949
AD: Edward M. Matejkovic
SID: Tom Di Camillo

WEST FLA.
Pensacola, FL 32514 II

Coach: Don Hogan
Alma Mater: South Ala. '81
Record: 3 Years, W-42, L-43
1996-97 SCHEDULE
Selma ■		Nov. 20
William Carey ■		Nov. 23
South Ala.		Nov. 26
Eckerd Cl.		Nov. 29-30
La. Christian ■		Dec. 2
William Carey		Dec. 7
West Florida Cl.		Dec. 28-29
North Ala.		Jan. 4
Ala.-Huntsville ■		Jan. 6
West Ga. ■		Jan. 11
Lincoln Memorial ■		Jan. 13
West Ala. ■		Jan. 18
Montevallo		Jan. 20
Valdosta St. ■		Jan. 25
Lincoln Memorial		Feb. 1
West Ga. ■		Feb. 3
Ala.-Huntsville ■		Feb. 8
North Ala. ■		Feb. 10
West Ala.		Feb. 15
Montevallo ■		Feb. 17

WEST GA.
Carrollton, GA 30117 II

Coach: Ed Murphy
Alma Mater: Hardin-Simmons '64
Record: 17 Years, W-269, L-212
1996-97 SCHEDULE
Ga. Southwestern ■		Nov. 16
Voorhees ■		Nov. 18
North Ga.		Nov. 21
Central St. ■		Nov. 24
Voorhees		Dec. 3
Ga. Southwestern		Dec. 7
West Florida Cl.		Dec. 28-29
Clayton St.		Jan. 2
West Ala. ■		Jan. 4
Montevallo ■		Jan. 7
West Fla.		Jan. 11
Valdosta St.		Jan. 13
Ala.-Huntsville ■		Jan. 18
North Ala. ■		Jan. 20
Lincoln Memorial ■		Jan. 25
Valdosta St. ■		Feb. 1
West Fla. ■		Feb. 3
Clayton St. ■		Feb. 5
Montevallo		Feb. 8
West Ala.		Feb. 10
North Ga. ■		Feb. 12
Ala.-Huntsville		Feb. 15
North Ala.		Feb. 17
Knoxville ■		Feb. 19
Lincoln Memorial		Feb. 22

1995-96 RESULTS (19-9)
84	Livingstone †	73
61	N.C. Central	83
104	Talladega	95
99	Cumberland (Ky.) †	96
66	Kennesaw St.	68
81	Columbus St. ■	66
75	S.C.-Aiken †	66
78	Gardner-Webb †	94
98	Clayton St. ■	83

	Tenn. Temple ■	Feb. 20
	Valdosta St. ■	Feb. 22
	Thomas ■	Feb. 24

1995-96 RESULTS (15-15)
80	Selma ■	64
84	Grand Valley St. †	70
55	Barry	65
95	La Grange ■	58
66	Oregon	106
74	Concordia (Ore.) ■	76
75	William Carey	79
65	Stetson	85
53	Florida A&M	72
52	Norfolk St. †	71
90	Grace Bible (Mich.) ■	57
64	William Carey ■	82
71	North Ala. ■	100
56	Ala.-Huntsville ■	51
69	West Ga. ■	90
71	Lincoln Memorial	86
73	West Ala. ■	77
79	Montevallo ■	58
102	Selma	61
90	Valdosta St.	79
76	Lincoln Memorial ■	59
92	West Ga. ■	79
58	Ala.-Huntsville ■	63
74	North Ala.	86
73	West Ala. ■	61
77	Montevallo	71
102	Valdosta St. ■	91
99	Col. of West Va. ■	82
73	Columbia Union †	70
86	Life (Ga.)	91

Nickname: Argonauts
Colors: Blue & Green
Arena: UWF Field House
 Capacity: 3,000; Year Built: 1969
AD: Richard Berg
SID: Karen Harrell

83	Bapt. Christian ■	.73
64	West Ala.	.47
79	Montevallo	.71
90	West Fla. ■	.69
87	Valdosta St. ■	.98
84	Ala.-Huntsville	.56
75	North Ala.	.87
77	Clayton St.	.90
90	Lincoln Memorial	.92
58	Valdosta St.	.54
79	West Fla.	.92
70	Montevallo ■	.67
67	West Ala. ■	.56
78	Ala.-Huntsville	.59
96	North Ala. ■	.81
60	Lincoln Memorial ■	.59
78	Talladega ■	.73
99	Henderson St. †	.90
93	Delta St.	.95

Nickname: Braves
Colors: Red & Blue
Arena: HPE Building
 Capacity: 2,800; Year Built: 1965
AD: Ed Murphy
SID: Mitch Gray

WEST LIBERTY ST.
West Liberty, WV 26074 II

Coach: Dan Petri
Alma Mater: West Liberty St. '68
Record: 4 Years, W-60, L-45

1996-97 SCHEDULE

Davis & Elkins ■	Nov. 20
Wheeling Jesuit Tr.	Nov. 22-23
Shepherd	Nov. 30
Indiana (Pa.) Cl.	Jan. 4-5
West Va. Tech	Jan. 8
Charleston (W.Va.)	Jan. 11
Glenville St. ■	Jan. 13
Concord	Jan. 17
Bluefield St.	Jan. 18
Wheeling Jesuit	Jan. 20
Salem-Teikyo ■	Jan. 22
Alderson-Broaddus	Jan. 25
Fairmont St.	Jan. 29
West Va. Wesleyan ■	Feb. 1
Shepherd ■	Feb. 3
West Va. St.	Feb. 8
Wheeling Jesuit ■	Feb. 12
Salem-Teikyo	Feb. 15
Alderson-Broaddus ■	Feb. 17
Davis & Elkins	Feb. 19
Fairmont St. ■	Feb. 22

1995-96 RESULTS (17-10)

112	Ohio-Eastern †	.73
86	Wheeling Jesuit	.93
78	Col. of West Va.	.97
105	Point Park	.91
87	Mercyhurst	.90
77	West Chester †	.68
76	Shepherd ■	.73
89	West Va. Tech	.74
65	Charleston (W.Va.) ■	.69
59	Glenville St.	.50
70	Concord	.77
93	Bluefield St. ■	.88
98	Wheeling Jesuit ■	.87
75	Salem-Teikyo	.60
80	Alderson-Broaddus ■	.62
88	Davis & Elkins	.84
77	Fairmont St. ■	.83
74	West Va. Wesleyan	.68
86	Col. of West Va. ■	.82
91	West Va. St. ■	.92
62	Shepherd	.63
86	Wheeling Jesuit	.70
88	Salem-Teikyo ■	.83
113	Davis & Elkins ■	.70
94	Alderson-Broaddus	.99
89	Fairmont St.	.79
67	Concord †	.70

Nickname: Hilltoppers

Colors: Gold & Black
Arena: Bartell Fieldhouse
 Capacity: 1,800; Year Built: 1981
AD: James Watson
SID: Lynn Ullom

WEST TEX. A&M
Canyon, TX 79016 II

Coach: Rick Cooper
Alma Mater: Wayland Bapt. '81
Record: 9 Years, W-207, L-78

1996-97 SCHEDULE

N.M. Highlands ■	Nov. 22
Southern Colo.	Nov. 25
West Texas A&M Tr.	Nov. 29-30
UC-Colo. Spgs. ■	Dec. 2
Mo. Western St. Cl.	Dec. 6-7
Okla. Sci. & Arts ■	Dec. 11
Abilene Christian	Dec. 14
Angelo St.	Dec. 16
Southwestern Aly God ■	Jan. 3
Midwestern St.	Jan. 7
Central Okla. ■	Jan. 9
Tarleton St.	Jan. 11
Texas A&M-Commerce	Jan. 13
Tex. A&M-Kingsville ■	Jan. 18
Panhandle St. ■	Jan. 21
Eastern N.M.	Jan. 25
Central Okla.	Jan. 30
Midwestern St. ■	Feb. 1
Texas A&M-Commerce ■	Feb. 6
Tarleton St. ■	Feb. 8
Eastern N.M. ■	Feb. 10
Tex. A&M-Kingsville	Feb. 13
Angelo St. ■	Feb. 20
Abilene Christian ■	Feb. 22

1995-96 RESULTS (18-10)

68	McMurry ■	.65
80	UC-Colo. Spgs. ■	.69
88	National Christian ■	.69
111	LeTourneau ■	.63
120	Wiley ■	.77
71	Cameron	.81
86	Southern Colo. ■	.80
92	Abilene Christian ■	.69
106	Angelo St. ■	.60
77	Adams St.	.75
64	Colorado St.	.94
86	Midwestern St.	106
88	Central Okla.	.85
81	Tarleton St. ■	.74
80	Texas A&M-Commerce ■	.81
79	Eastern N.M.	.65
73	Tex. A&M-Kingsville	.84
69	Cameron	.60
90	Eastern N.M. ■	.81
111	Central Okla. ■	.83
92	Midwestern St. ■	.91
61	Texas A&M-Commerce	.67
65	Tarleton St.	.66
101	Tex. A&M-Kingsville ■	.79
83	Angelo St.	.87
69	Abilene Christian	.74
79	Abilene Christian ■	.73
84	Tex. A&M-Kingsville †	.94

Nickname: Buffaloes
Colors: Maroon & White
Arena: WTAMU Fieldhouse
 Capacity: 2,557; Year Built: 1951
AD: Ed Harris
SID: Bill Kauffman

WEST VA.
Morgantown, WV 26507 I

Coach: Gale Catlett
Alma Mater: West Va. '63
Record: 24 Years, W-471, L-241

1996-97 SCHEDULE

Minnesota	Nov. 26
Ohio	Nov. 30

Syracuse	Dec. 4
East Tenn. St. ■	Dec. 14
Marshall [Charleston]	Dec. 17
Robert Morris ■	Dec. 19
Virginia Tech	Dec. 21
Duquesne	Dec. 30
Georgetown ■	Jan. 2
Connecticut ■	Jan. 4
Seton Hall ■	Jan. 8
St. John's (N.Y.)	Jan. 12
Rutgers ■	Jan. 15
Providence ■	Jan. 19
Rutgers	Jan. 22
Notre Dame ■	Jan. 25
Boston College ■	Jan. 29
Pittsburgh ■	Feb. 1
Villanova ■	Feb. 4
Providence ■	Feb. 8
Notre Dame	Feb. 11
Syracuse ■	Feb. 15
Towson St. ■	Feb. 18
Seton Hall	Feb. 22
Villanova	Feb. 26
Miami (Fla.)	Mar. 1
Big East Conf. Tr.	Mar. 5-8

1995-96 RESULTS (12-15)

80	Florida A&M ■	.39
68	Ohio St.	.77
83	Georgetown	.86
93	Duquesne ■	.77
94	Ohio ■	.69
62	Virginia Tech	.68
108	Morgan St. ■	.80
97	Robert Morris ■	.69
79	Connecticut	.89
83	Pittsburgh ■	.84
74	St. John's (N.Y.)	.89
67	Villanova	.69
90	Syracuse ■	.78
87	Marshall ■	.91
78	Providence	.95
86	Rutgers ■	.71
69	Notre Dame	.59
67	Georgetown	.91
63	Boston College ■	.84
65	Miami (Fla.)	.68
77	Seton Hall	.59
69	Connecticut	.87
72	Miami (Fla.) ■	.77
108	Boston College	.89
92	St. John's (N.Y.) ■	.77
63	Pittsburgh	.83
78	Seton Hall †	.80

Nickname: Mountaineers
Colors: Old Gold & Blue
Arena: WVU Coliseum
 Capacity: 14,000; Year Built: 1970
AD: Ed Pastilong
SID: Shelly Poe

WEST VA. TECH
Montgomery, WV 25136 II

Coach: Jeff Kepreos
Alma Mater: Wheeling Jesuit '84
Record: 2 Years, W-27, L-29

1996-97 SCHEDULE

Ashland	Nov. 16
Ohio Valley	Nov. 21
Bluefield St. Cl.	Nov. 29-30
Col. of West Va. ■	Dec. 2
Bluefield St.	Dec. 7
Concord ■	Dec. 14
Clarion Tr.	Jan. 3-4
West Liberty St.	Jan. 8
Wheeling Jesuit ■	Jan. 11
Salem-Teikyo ■	Jan. 13
Shepherd	Jan. 15
Davis & Elkins ■	Jan. 18
West Va. St.	Jan. 22
Charleston (W.Va.)	Jan. 25
West Va. Wesleyan	Jan. 27
Glenville St. ■	Jan. 29
Fairmont St.	Feb. 1

Concord	Feb. 5
Alderson-Broaddus	Feb. 8
Bluefield St. ■	Feb. 10
West Va. St. ■	Feb. 15
Charleston (W.Va.) ■	Feb. 17
West Va. Wesleyan ■	Feb. 19
Glenville St.	Feb. 22

1995-96 RESULTS (19-10)

84	Wingate ■	.71
121	Col. of West Va. ■	104
84	Ohio Valley ■	.72
96	Alderson-Broaddus †	.81
78	Bluefield St.	.76
103	Concord	.93
94	Bluefield St. ■	.87
110	George Mason	113
104	Col. of West Va. ■	118
74	West Liberty St. ■	.89
78	Wheeling Jesuit	.93
74	Salem-Teikyo	.90
85	Shepherd ■	.76
101	Davis & Elkins ■	.83
94	West Va. St.	.90
75	Charleston (W.Va.)	.71
87	West Va. Wesleyan	.79
70	Glenville St. ■	.74
71	Fairmont St. ■	.95
79	Concord	.84
90	Alderson-Broaddus ■	.82
103	Bluefield St.	101
82	West Va. St.	.86
80	Charleston (W.Va.) ■	.72
85	West Va. Wesleyan	.72
82	Glenville St.	.78
73	Glenville St. †	.62
86	Concord †	.81
58	Bluefield St. †	.61

Nickname: Golden Bears
Colors: Royal Blue & Gold
Arena: Tech Fieldhouse
 Capacity: 3,000; Year Built: 1964
AD: Jeff Kepreos
SID: Frank Costa

WEST VA. WESLEYAN
Buckhannon, WV 26201 II

Coach: Charles Miller
Alma Mater: West Va. Wesleyan '66
Record: 15 Years, W-122, L-220

1996-97 SCHEDULE

Cheyney ■	Nov. 15
Pitt.-Johnstown ■	Nov. 19
Longwood Inv.	Nov. 23-24
Glenville St.	Dec. 2
West Va. St.	Dec. 4
Edinboro ■	Dec. 6
Norfolk St.	Jan. 4
Salem-Teikyo	Jan. 8
Davis & Elkins ■	Jan. 11
Wheeling Jesuit	Jan. 13
Fairmont St. ■	Jan. 15
Shepherd ■	Jan. 18
Bluefield St. ■	Jan. 22
Concord ■	Jan. 25
West Va. Tech ■	Jan. 27
Alderson-Broaddus	Jan. 29
West Liberty St.	Feb. 1
Charleston (W.Va.) ■	Feb. 5
Fairmont St.	Feb. 8
Glenville St. ■	Feb. 11
Bluefield St.	Feb. 15
Concord ■	Feb. 17
West Va. Tech	Feb. 19
Alderson-Broaddus ■	Feb. 22

1995-96 RESULTS (9-17)

102	Pitt.-Johnstown †	.90
78	Dist. Columbia †	.90
92	Rio Grande	.99
60	Norfolk St. ■	.69
81	Gannon	.68
68	Glenville St. ■	.67
61	East Stroudsburg	.66

78 West Va. St. ■ ...80
73 Salem-Teikyo ■ ...88
90 Davis & Elkins ■ ...59
64 Wheeling Jesuit ■ ...55
76 Fairmont St. ■ ...83
64 Shepherd ■ ...74
75 Bluefield St. ...97
71 Concord ...54
79 West Va. Tech ...87
51 Alderson-Broaddus ■ ...70
68 West Liberty St. ■ ...74
93 Charleston (W.Va.) ...101
73 Fairmont St. ■ ...81
62 Glenville St. ...77
87 Bluefield St. ■ ...80
87 Concord ...79
72 West Va. Tech ■ ...85
65 Alderson-Broaddus ...63
60 Bluefield St. ...83

Nickname: Bobcats
Colors: Orange & Black
Arena: Rockefeller Center
 Capacity: 4,000; Year Built: 1974
AD: George Klebez
SID: Matt Martin

WESTERN CARO.
Cullowhee, NC 28723 ...I

Coach: Phil Hopkins
Alma Mater: Gardner-Webb '72
Record: 1 Year, W-17, L-13
1996-97 SCHEDULE
Cincinnati ...Nov. 23
Bryan ...Nov. 26
Anderson (S.C.) ■ ...Nov. 30
Limestone ■ ...Dec. 2
Alabama ...Dec. 14
Auburn ...Dec. 15
Mercer ...Dec. 17
Austin Peay ...Dec. 22
Duke ...Dec. 30
Wofford ■ ...Jan. 4
Citadel ...Jan. 6
Wofford ...Jan. 9
Appalachian St. ■ ...Jan. 11
Davidson ...Jan. 13
Marshall ...Jan. 18
Citadel ■ ...Jan. 20
Tenn.-Chatt. ...Jan. 25
Furman ■ ...Jan. 27
Ga. Southern ■ ...Feb. 1
East Tenn. St. ■ ...Feb. 3
Kentucky ...Feb. 6
Appalachian St. ...Feb. 8
VMI ■ ...Feb. 10
Tenn.-Chatt. ■ ...Feb. 15
Furman ...Feb. 17
Ga. Southern ■ ...Feb. 22
Southern Conf. Tr. ...Feb. 27-Mar. 2

1995-96 RESULTS (17-13)
83 Mercer † ...87
83 Texas-Arlington † ...92
71 Georgia ...91
58 Coker ■ ...60
51 Tennessee ...63
68 Presbyterian ■ ...64
67 Duke ...107
71 North Caro. St. ...102
92 Wofford ...67
94 Lincoln Memorial ■ ...47
78 Georgia Tech ...91
70 Tenn.-Chatt. ...84
86 Furman ■ ...97
81 Ga. Southern ...71
88 Citadel ■ ...74
93 Appalachian St. ...83
85 Davidson ■ ...98
125 Marshall ■ ...104
84 Wofford ...72
74 Citadel ...73
81 Tenn.-Chatt. ■ ...76
73 VMI ...90
97 Furman ...85

83 Ga. Southern ■ ...64
93 East Tenn. St. ...91
91 Appalachian St. ■ ...72
74 Appalachian St. † ...66
97 VMI † ...93
69 Davidson † ...60
71 Purdue † ...73

Nickname: Catamounts
Colors: Purple & Gold
Arena: Ramsey Center
 Capacity: 7,826; Year Built: 1986
AD: Larry L. Travis
SID: Steve White

WESTERN CONN. ST.
Danbury, CT 06810 ...III

Coach: Bob Campbell
Alma Mater: Connecticut '72
Record: 12 Years, W-251, L-76
1996-97 SCHEDULE
Williams Cl. ...Nov. 22-23
Albertus Magnus ■ ...Nov. 30
Westfield St. ...Dec. 3
Mass.-Boston ...Dec. 7
Hunter ...Dec. 11
Mass.-Dartmouth ...Dec. 14
Western Conn St. Tr. ...Dec. 28-29
Lehman ...Jan. 11
Johnson & Wales ...Jan. 13
Southern Vt. ■ ...Jan. 15
Southern Me. ...Jan. 18
Eastern Conn. St. ...Jan. 21
Plymouth St. ■ ...Jan. 25
Rhode Island Col. ■ ...Jan. 28
Mass.-Boston ■ ...Feb. 1
Mass.-Dartmouth ...Feb. 8
Eastern Conn. St. ■ ...Feb. 11
Southern Me. ■ ...Feb. 15
Rhode Island Col. ...Feb. 18
Plymouth St. ...Feb. 22

1995-96 RESULTS (19-8)
86 Me.-Presque Isle † ...74
86 Colby ...92
70 Albertus Magnus ...96
85 Westfield St. ■ ...76
71 Wesleyan (Conn.) ■ ...66
87 Mass.-Boston ...77
80 Western New Eng. ...58
68 Mass.-Dartmouth ...81
66 Wm. Paterson ...63
86 Baruch ...74
89 Worcester St. ■ ...83
70 Lehman ...62
82 Southern Me. ■ ...60
82 Eastern Conn. St. ■ ...66
94 Plymouth St. ...85
69 Rhode Island Col. ...81
83 Johnson & Wales ■ ...50
89 Mass.-Boston ...62
78 Mass.-Dartmouth ...79
82 Eastern Conn. St. ...72
93 Southern Me. ...64
75 Rhode Island Col. ■ ...76
70 Plymouth St. ■ ...75
79 Southern Me. ■ ...77
66 Mass.-Dartmouth ...63
80 Plymouth St. † ...64
60 Salem St. ...76

Nickname: Colonials
Colors: Blue & White
Arena: Stephen Feldman Arena
 Capacity: 2,100; Year Built: 1994
AD: Ed Farrington
SID: Scott Ames

WESTERN ILL.
Macomb, IL 61455 ...I

Coach: Jim Kerwin
Alma Mater: Tulane '64
Record: 4 Years, W-51, L-60

1996-97 SCHEDULE
Iowa [Moline] ...Nov. 22
Wis.-Milwaukee ...Nov. 26
Eastern Ill. ...Dec. 2
Wis.-Milwaukee ■ ...Dec. 4
Cardinal Stritch ■ ...Dec. 14
Bradley ...Dec. 23
Oklahoma Tr. ...Dec. 27-28
Mo.-Kansas City ...Jan. 2
Troy St. ...Jan. 4
Youngstown St. ■ ...Jan. 8
Chicago St. ...Jan. 11
Northeastern Ill. ...Jan. 13
Buffalo ■ ...Jan. 18
Central Conn. St. ■ ...Jan. 20
Southern Utah ■ ...Jan. 22
Valparaiso ...Jan. 25
St. Ambrose ■ ...Jan. 27
Youngstown St. ...Feb. 1
Buffalo ...Feb. 3
Northeastern Ill. ■ ...Feb. 6
Chicago St. ■ ...Feb. 8
Central Conn. St. ...Feb. 10
Valparaiso ■ ...Feb. 15
Troy St. ■ ...Feb. 22
Mo.-Kansas City ...Feb. 24
Mid-Continent Conf. Tr. ...Mar. 2-4

1995-96 RESULTS (17-12)
89 Elmhurst ■ ...62
93 St. Ambrose ■ ...71
59 Fairfield † ...62
69 Cal Poly SLO † ...64
67 Wis.-Milwaukee ...69
54 Bradley ...71
41 Iowa ...93
98 Troy St. ...95
69 Central Conn. St. ...97
64 Youngstown St. ■ ...60
93 Buffalo ■ ...74
60 Mo.-Kansas City ...80
80 Northeastern Ill. ...72
96 Chicago St. ...87
68 Eastern Ill. ■ ...83
79 Valparaiso ■ ...73
75 Wis.-Milwaukee ■ ...83
58 Buffalo ...63
48 Youngstown St. ...73
72 Mo.-Kansas City ■ ...67
93 Chicago St. ■ ...73
105 Northeastern Ill. ■ ...86
74 Valparaiso ...72
53 Eastern Ill. ...77
82 Central Conn. St. ■ ...63
120 Troy St. ■ ...100
68 Youngstown St. † ...48
68 Central Conn. St. † ...66
52 Valparaiso † ...75

Nickname: Leathernecks
Colors: Purple & Gold
Arena: Western Hall
 Capacity: 5,139; Year Built: 1964
AD: Helen Smiley
SID: Greg Seiler

WESTERN KY.
Bowling Green, KY 42101 ...I

Coach: Matt Kilcullen
Alma Mater: Lehman '76
Record: 8 Years, W-102, L-115
1996-97 SCHEDULE
Xavier (Ohio) ...Nov. 23
Tenn.-Martin ■ ...Nov. 29
Belmont ■ ...Dec. 2
Duquesne ■ ...Dec. 4
Wis.-Green Bay ...Dec. 7
Jacksonville ...Dec. 21
Tex.-Pan American ...Dec. 23
Cincinnati [Cleveland] ...Dec. 28
Lamar ...Jan. 2
Butler ...Jan. 5
New Orleans ■ ...Jan. 9
Southwestern La. ...Jan. 11

Lamar ■ ...Jan. 16
South Ala. ■ ...Jan. 18
Tex.-Pan American ...Jan. 20
New Orleans ■ ...Jan. 25
Ark.-Little Rock ...Jan. 27
Jacksonville ■ ...Jan. 30
Louisiana Tech ■ ...Feb. 1
Clemson ...Feb. 4
Arkansas St. ...Feb. 6
Ark.-Little Rock ■ ...Feb. 9
Southwestern La. ■ ...Feb. 11
Arkansas St. ■ ...Feb. 13
Louisiana Tech ■ ...Feb. 15
South Ala. ...Feb. 22
Sun Belt Conf. Tr. ...Feb. 28-Mar. 4

1995-96 RESULTS (13-14)
65 Va. Commonwealth † ...83
85 American (P.R.) ...86
71 La Salle † ...63
65 Tulsa ...73
56 Butler ■ ...50
77 UAB ...65
69 DePaul ...84
56 Wis.-Green Bay ■ ...59
94 New Orleans ...80
68 Arkansas St. ...80
76 Ark.-Little Rock ...84
85 Jacksonville ...87
75 South Ala. ■ ...64
83 Ark.-Little Rock ■ ...65
68 Tex.-Pan American ...50
59 Louisiana Tech ...57
82 New Orleans ...90
78 Jacksonville ...92
91 Arkansas St. ■ ...64
92 Lamar ...73
85 Southwestern La. ...95
63 Tex.-Pan American ■ ...51
85 Southwestern La. ■ ...78
90 Lamar ■ ...69
66 Louisiana Tech ...72
78 South Ala. ...92
94 Southwestern La. † ...98

Nickname: Hilltoppers
Colors: Red & White
Arena: E.A. Diddle Arena
 Capacity: 11,300; Year Built: 1963
AD: Lewis Mills
SID: Paul Just

WESTERN MD.
Westminster, MD 21157 ...III

Coach: Nick Zoulias
Alma Mater: Keene St. '69
Record: 7 Years, W-54, L-115
1996-97 SCHEDULE
Western Md. Tr. ...Nov. 22-23
St. Mary's (Md.) ■ ...Nov. 26
Mary Washington ...Dec. 3
Ursinus ■ ...Dec. 7
Wesley ...Dec. 14
Wilkes Cl. ...Jan. 4-5
Catholic ...Jan. 8
Muhlenberg ...Jan. 11
Dickinson ■ ...Jan. 15
Frank. & Marsh. ...Jan. 18
Gettysburg ...Jan. 22
Swarthmore ■ ...Jan. 25
Frostburg St. ■ ...Jan. 27
Johns Hopkins ...Jan. 29
Haverford ...Feb. 1
Bucknell ...Feb. 3
Villa Julie ■ ...Feb. 5
Frank. & Marsh. ■ ...Feb. 8
Dickinson ...Feb. 12
Gettysburg ■ ...Feb. 15
Johns Hopkins ■ ...Feb. 19
Washington (Md.) ...Feb. 22

1995-96 RESULTS (4-20)
89 Villa Julie ■ ...62
73 Kean ■ ...67
75 St. Mary's (Md.) ...82

75	Messiah	78
85	Ursinus	73
78	Mary Washington ■	86
79	Catholic ■	81
69	Muhlenberg ■	78
88	Caldwell ■	89
54	Moravian ■	105
67	Middlebury †	83
75	Dickinson	84
54	Frank. & Marsh. ■	69
80	Gettysburg ■	88
57	Swarthmore	85
98	Johns Hopkins ■	94
71	Haverford	87
82	Frostburg St.	103
58	Frank. & Marsh. ■	74
62	Dickinson ■	67
87	Beaver	103
65	Gettysburg	97
53	Johns Hopkins	65
72	Washington (Md.) ■	90

Nickname: Green Terror
Colors: Green & Gold
Arena: Gill P.E. Learning Center
  Capacity: 3,000; Year Built: 1984
AD: Richard Carpenter
SID: Scott Deitch

WESTERN MICH.
Kalamazoo, MI 49008 I

Coach: Bob Donewald
Alma Mater: Hanover '64
Record: 18 Years, W-302, L-222

1996-97 SCHEDULE

Canisius	Nov. 23
Purdue ■	Nov. 26
Northern Ill.	Dec. 2
Ball St.	Dec. 5
Evansville ■	Dec. 7
Chicago St.	Dec. 18
Northern Ill. ■	Dec. 21
Detroit ■	Dec. 23
Wright St.	Dec. 28
Ohio	Jan. 4
Bowling Green ■	Jan. 8
Central Mich.	Jan. 11
Akron ■	Jan. 15
Kent	Jan. 18
Eastern Mich. ■	Jan. 22
Miami (Ohio)	Jan. 25
Toledo ■	Jan. 29
Bowling Green	Feb. 1
Central Mich. ■	Feb. 5
Ball St. ■	Feb. 8
Akron	Feb. 12
Kent ■	Feb. 15
Eastern Mich.	Feb. 19
Miami (Ohio) ■	Feb. 22
Toledo	Feb. 26
Ohio ■	Mar. 1
Mid-American Conf. Tr.	Mar. 4-8

1995-96 RESULTS (15-12)

53	Canisius ■	73
88	Murray St.	98
61	Evansville	81
83	Murray St. ■	71
50	Detroit	65
56	Purdue	86
77	Colorado St. ■	78
99	Chicago St. ■	74
66	Bowling Green ■	63
81	Central Mich. ■	74
65	Eastern Mich.	88
75	Ball St. ■	71
61	Miami (Ohio)	62
69	Kent ■	71
66	Ohio	59
81	Toledo ■	77
51	Akron	46
73	Central Mich.	51
83	Eastern Mich. ■	89
67	Ball St.	78
76	Miami (Ohio) ■	65

84	Kent	70
54	Ohio ■	51
68	Toledo	60
89	Akron ■	49
62	Bowling Green	44
65	Toledo ■	71

Nickname: Broncos
Colors: Brown & Gold
Arena: University Arena
  Capacity: 5,800; Year Built: 1957
AD: Jim Weaver
SID: John Beatty

WESTERN NEW ENG.
Springfield, MA 01119 III

Coach: Brett Bishop
Alma Mater: Springfield '87
Record: 3 Years, W-19, L-56

1996-97 SCHEDULE

Albertus Magnus	Nov. 23
North Adams St.	Nov. 26
Clark (Mass.)	Dec. 3
Fitchburg St.	Dec. 5
Anna Maria Inv.	Dec. 7-8
Amherst	Dec. 10
Babson ■	Dec. 12
Westfield St. ■	Jan. 16
WPI	Jan. 18
MIT ■	Jan. 21
Bates ■	Jan. 24
Bowdoin ■	Jan. 25
WPI ■	Jan. 28
Coast Guard ■	Jan. 30
Springfield	Feb. 1
Norwich ■	Feb. 6
Coast Guard	Feb. 8
Springfield ■	Feb. 11
Babson	Feb. 13
MIT	Feb. 15
Clark (Mass.) ■	Feb. 18
Wesleyan (Conn.) ■	Feb. 20
Norwich	Feb. 22

1995-96 RESULTS (5-20)

95	Nichols	98
74	North Adams St. ■	82
60	Clark (Mass.)	92
90	Fitchburg St. ■	73
81	Amherst ■	86
58	Western Conn. St. ■	80
81	Babson	119
84	Westfield St.	85
65	Springfield ■	93
74	WPI	95
63	MIT ■	56
94	Bates	104
56	Bowdoin	77
79	Clark (Mass.) ■	95
40	Coast Guard	74
46	Springfield	88
102	Albertus Magnus ■	82
83	Norwich	78
97	Coast Guard ■	94
81	Babson ■	99
51	MIT	67
77	WPI ■	83
73	Wesleyan (Conn.)	82
71	Norwich ■	79
64	Springfield	95

Nickname: Golden Bears
Colors: Royal Blue & Gold
Arena: Healthful Living Center
  Capacity: 2,000; Year Built: 1993
AD: Eric Geldart
SID: Gene Gumbs

WESTERN N.M.
Silver City, NM 88061 II

Coach: Troy Hudson
Alma Mater: Northern Ariz. '79
(First year as head coach)

1996-97 SCHEDULE

Abilene Christian Cl	Nov. 15-16
New Mexico St.	Nov. 22
Amer. Indian Bib. ■	Nov. 23
Western N.M. Tr.	Nov. 29-30
Eastern N.M. Cl.	Dec. 6-7
Arizona Bible ■	Dec. 14
Cal Poly Pomona Tr.	Dec. 19-21
Cameron	Jan. 6
Chaminade ■	Jan. 9
Hawaii-Hilo ■	Jan. 11
N.M. Highlands	Jan. 14
Mont. St.-Billings ■	Jan. 18
Seattle Pacific ■	Jan. 23
Chaminade	Jan. 30
Hawaii-Hilo	Feb. 1
Alas. Fairbanks ■	Feb. 6
Alas. Anchorage ■	Feb. 8
Mont. St.-Billings	Feb. 15
Alas. Anchorage ■	Feb. 20
Alas. Fairbanks ■	Feb. 22
Seattle Pacific	Mar. 1

1995-96 RESULTS (8-18)

70	Southern Colo.	77
80	Western St. †	94
67	N.M. Highlands ■	69
124	National Christian ■	92
74	N.M. Highlands ■	81
108	S'western (Ariz.) ■	41
56	New Mexico St.	80
62	Eastern N.M. †	85
39	Tarleton St.	46
50	UC Riverside †	72
63	Sonoma St. †	79
79	Lewis & Clark †	88
84	Pacific Christian	57
73	Hawaii-Hilo ■	95
68	Chaminade ■	40
68	Alas. Fairbanks	94
49	Alas. Anchorage	91
70	Mont. St.-Billings	92
57	Seattle Pacific	100
58	Hawaii-Hilo	73
52	Chaminade	53
101	Arizona Bible ■	39
64	Seattle Pacific ■	51
78	Mont. St.-Billings ■	60
67	Alas. Anchorage ■	72
84	Alas. Fairbanks ■	74

Nickname: Mustangs
Colors: Purple & Gold
Arena: Brancheau Gym
  Capacity: 2,200; Year Built: 1950
AD: Dick Drangmeister
SID: MarciBeth Phillips

WESTERN ST.
Gunnison, CO 81230 II

Coach: Bob Hofman
Alma Mater: Colorado '74
Record: 8 Years, W-117, L-114

1996-97 SCHEDULE

Northern Colo.	Nov. 16
Grand Canyon Inv.	Nov. 22-23
UC-Colo. Springs Cl.	Nov. 29-30
Fresno St.	Dec. 3
Fort Hays St. ■	Dec. 6
Neb.-Kearney ■	Dec. 7
Colo. Christian	Dec. 13
Regis (Colo.)	Dec. 14
Colorado Mines ■	Jan. 3
Metro St. ■	Jan. 4
Denver	Jan. 9
Chadron St.	Jan. 11
UC-Colo. Spgs.	Jan. 17
Southern Colo.	Jan. 18
Mesa St. ■	Jan. 21
N.M. Highlands ■	Jan. 25
Adams St. ■	Jan. 31
Fort Lewis ■	Feb. 1
Mesa St.	Feb. 4
N.M. Highlands	Feb. 9
UC-Colo. Spgs. ■	Feb. 14

Southern Colo. ■	Feb. 15
Adams St.	Feb. 21
Fort Lewis	Feb. 22

1995-96 RESULTS (18-13)

70	Mesa St.	73
94	Western N.M. †	80
77	Colo. Christian ■	76
89	Westmont †	80
83	Denver	94
84	Southern Colo.	77
77	Regis (Colo.)	91
93	N.M. Highlands ■	81
102	Fort Lewis	87
74	Adams St.	69
104	Alas. Fairbanks	79
79	Alas. Fairbanks	94
69	Alas. Anchorage	93
62	Alas. Anchorage	96
77	Regis (Colo.) ■	87
83	Fort Hays St.	94
79	Neb.-Kearney	99
61	Southern Colo. ■	57
71	Colorado Mines ■	76
111	Chadron St. ■	85
69	Mesa St.	59
71	N.M. Highlands	68
105	Fort Lewis ■	102
98	Adams St. ■	85
80	Mesa St. ■	74
82	Colorado Mines	92
85	Chadron St.	84
59	Fort Hays St. ■	99
130	Neb.-Kearney ■	126
73	Mesa St. ■	69
70	Neb.-Kearney †	94

Nickname: Mountaineers
Colors: Crimson & Slate
Arena: Paul Wright Gymnasium
  Capacity: 2,250; Year Built: 1951
AD: Greg Waggoner
SID: J. W. Campbell

WESTFIELD ST.
Westfield, MA 01085 III

Coach: Alan Wolejko
Alma Mater: North Adams St. '72
Record: 2 Years, W-25, L-27

1996-97 SCHEDULE

Hartwick Cl.	Nov. 22-23
Southern Vt. ■	Nov. 26
Western Conn. St. ■	Dec. 3
Eastern Conn. St.	Dec. 7
Springfield	Dec. 7
Mass.-Boston ■	Dec. 12
Amherst	Jan. 9
Albertus Magnus ■	Jan. 11
Bri'water (Mass.)	Jan. 14
Western New Eng.	Jan. 16
Worcester St. ■	Jan. 18
Salem St.	Jan. 21
Fitchburg St. ■	Jan. 25
Emerson-MCA	Jan. 27
Wheaton (Mass.) ■	Jan. 30
Framingham St. ■	Feb. 1
North Adams St.	Feb. 3
Bri'water (Mass.) ■	Feb. 8
Worcester St.	Feb. 11
Salem St. ■	Feb. 13
Fitchburg St.	Feb. 15
Framingham St.	Feb. 20
North Adams St. ■	Feb. 22

1995-96 RESULTS (14-12)

68	Elmira †	78
82	Manhattanville †	59
55	Southern Vt.	72
76	Western Conn. St.	85
66	Springfield	73
72	Mass.-Boston	64
89	Amherst ■	120
85	Western New Eng. ■	84
71	Albertus Magnus	93
85	Bri'water (Mass.) ■	77

107	Worcester St.	112
66	Salem St. ■	82
76	Rhode Island Col. ■	82
84	Fitchburg St.	57
79	Wheaton (Mass.)	61
71	Framingham St.	67
66	North Adams St. ■	64
81	Bri'water (Mass.)	94
83	Worcester St.	72
92	Salem St.	99
76	Fitchburg St. ■	67
78	Emerson-MCA	59
95	Framingham St. ■	68
89	North Adams St.	86
85	Framingham St. ■	76
84	Bri'water (Mass.) †	89

Nickname: Owls
Colors: Royal Blue & White
Arena: Parenzo Gym
 Capacity: 400; Year Built: 1956
AD: Ken Magarian
SID: Mickey Curtis

WESTMINSTER (MO.)
Fulton, MO 65251 III

Coach: Jim McEwen
Alma Mater: Central Mo. St. '64
Record: 12 Years, W-171, L-166

1996-97 SCHEDULE
Hendrix Tr.	Nov. 22-23
Culver-Stockton ■	Nov. 26
William Penn	Dec. 3
Rhodes Tr.	Dec. 6-7
Mo.-Rolla	Dec. 11
Westminster (Mo.) Cl	Dec. 13-14
Webster ■	Jan. 9
Greenville	Jan. 11
Maryville (Mo.) ■	Jan. 16
Fontbonne	Jan. 18
Blackburn	Jan. 23
MacMurray ■	Jan. 25
Principia	Jan. 30
Webster	Feb. 1
Greenville ■	Feb. 6
Maryville (Mo.)	Feb. 8
Fontbonne ■	Feb. 13
Blackburn ■	Feb. 15
MacMurray	Feb. 20
Principia ■	Feb. 22

1995-96 RESULTS (14-12)
96	Messenger ■	61
68	Missouri Valley ■	75
63	Culver-Stockton	61
96	Parks ■	83
58	William Penn	56
72	Rhodes	89
69	Millsaps †	81
64	Eureka ■	73
72	Mo.-Rolla	96
65	Principia ■	39
65	MacMurray ■	69
88	Webster	71
85	Fontbonne	72
70	Maryville (Mo.) ■	83
87	Greenville ■	75
77	Parks	67
79	Principia	62
68	MacMurray	79
73	Webster ■	79
82	Blackburn	78
104	Fontbonne ■	118
76	Blackburn ■	72
70	Maryville (Mo.)	67
83	Greenville	86
78	Webster ■	71
76	Fontbonne	84

Nickname: Blue Jays
Colors: Blue & White
Arena: Westminster Gym
 Capacity: 1,200; Year Built: 1928
AD: Jim McEwen
SID: Terry Logue

WHEATON (ILL.)
Wheaton, IL 60187 III

Coach: Bill Harris
Alma Mater: Gordon '70
Record: 11 Years, W-213, L-104

1996-97 SCHEDULE
Wheaton (Ill.) Cl.	Nov. 22-23
Chicago	Nov. 26
Illinois Tech ■	Dec. 5
MacMurray ■	Dec. 7
Mt. St. Clare ■	Dec. 10
Lakeland	Dec. 12
Central (Iowa)	Dec. 14
LeTourneau	Jan. 4
Dallas	Jan. 7
Austin	Jan. 9
Ill. Wesleyan	Jan. 18
Millikin ■	Jan. 21
North Central	Jan. 25
Carthage	Jan. 29
Millikin	Feb. 1
North Park ■	Feb. 4
Augustana (Ill.) ■	Feb. 8
Ill. Wesleyan	Feb. 12
North Central ■	Feb. 15
Elmhurst	Feb. 18
Carthage ■	Feb. 20
North Park	Feb. 22
Augustana (Ill.)	Feb. 26
Elmhurst ■	Mar. 1

1995-96 RESULTS (25-2)
69	MacMurray	66
108	Rockford ■	77
84	Chicago	68
70	Lake Forest	69
113	Parks ■	64
81	Lakeland ■	74
92	Calvin ■	77
105	Greenville ■	83
85	Warner Southern ■	77
91	St. Thomas (Fla.) †	81
82	Palm Beach Atl. †	79
56	Elmhurst	55
67	Ill. Wesleyan	68
91	North Park	72
81	Augustana (Ill.)	67
78	Millikin ■	63
76	North Central ■	49
91	Carthage	74
84	Elmhurst ■	66
76	North Park ■	65
83	Ill. Wesleyan ■	71
72	Augustana (Ill.) ■	62
87	Millikin	85
86	North Central	77
100	Carthage ■	74
131	Grinnell ■	117
75	Washington (Mo.) ■	93

Nickname: Crusaders
Colors: Orange & Blue
Arena: Centennial Gymnasium
 Capacity: 3,232; Year Built: 1960
AD: Tony Ladd
SID: Steve Schwepker

WHEATON (MASS.)
Norton, MA 02766 III

Coach: Tom Blake
Alma Mater: Connecticut '78
Record: 5 Years, W-48, L-76

1996-97 SCHEDULE
Wheaton (Mass.) Cl.	Nov. 23-24
Bri'water (Mass.) Cl.	Dec. 6-7
Salem St. ■	Dec. 12
Framingham St. ■	Dec. 14
Moravian Cl.	Jan. 4-5
Rivier	Jan. 9
Amherst ■	Jan. 11
Endicott ■	Jan. 15
Mass.-Dartmouth ■	Jan. 18

Emerson-MCA	Jan. 20
Eastern Conn. St.	Jan. 23
Nichols ■	Jan. 25
Springfield	Jan. 28
Westfield St.	Jan. 30
Connecticut Col.	Feb. 4
Tufts ■	Feb. 6
Brandeis ■	Feb. 11
Colby	Feb. 14
Bowdoin ■	Feb. 15
Rhode Island Col. ■	Feb. 20
Trinity (Conn.)	Feb. 22
Suffolk ■	Feb. 25

1995-96 RESULTS (6-19)
83	New England Col. ■	66
72	Clark (Mass.) ■	64
42	FDU-Madison	66
62	Endicott	74
59	Mass.-Dartmouth ■	96
59	Stonehill	90
65	Salem St.	88
69	Framingham St. ■	83
36	Lynn	84
68	Palm Beach Atl. ■	104
50	Nova Southeastern ■	94
59	Mass.-Dartmouth	80
73	Emerson-MCA ■	72
65	Eastern Conn. St. ■	57
93	Nichols	80
60	Springfield ■	85
61	Westfield St. ■	79
66	Connecticut Col. ■	82
77	Tufts	96
75	Brandeis	91
66	Colby ■	70
64	Bowdoin ■	91
50	Rhode Island Col.	94
63	Trinity (Conn.) ■	85
71	Suffolk	70

Nickname: Lyons
Colors: Royal & White
Arena: Haas Athletic Center
 Capacity: 850; Year Built: 1991
AD: Chad Yowell
SID: MaryKay Adams

WHEELING JESUIT
Wheeling, WV 26003 II

Coach: Jay DeFruscio
Alma Mater: Ursinus '82
Record: 8 Years, W-147, L-116

1996-97 SCHEDULE
Wheeling Jesuit Tr.	Nov. 22-23
Ursinus ■	Nov. 26
Calif. (Pa.) ■	Nov. 30
Shepherd	Dec. 4
Fairmount Cl.	Jan. 3-4
West Va. St. ■	Jan. 8
West Va. Tech	Jan. 11
West Va. Wesleyan ■	Jan. 13
Bluefield St.	Jan. 15
Concord	Jan. 18
West Liberty St. ■	Jan. 20
Alderson-Broaddus ■	Jan. 22
Davis & Elkins ■	Jan. 25
Fairmont St. ■	Jan. 27
Salem-Teikyo ■	Jan. 29
Glenville St. ■	Feb. 1
Shepherd ■	Feb. 5
Charleston (W.Va.) ■	Feb. 8
Davis & Elkins	Feb. 10
West Liberty St.	Feb. 12
Alderson-Broaddus	Feb. 15
Fairmont St.	Feb. 19
Salem-Teikyo ■	Feb. 22

1995-96 RESULTS (11-16)
96	La Roche ■	69
93	West Liberty St. ■	86
92	Geneva ■	86
91	Calif. (Pa.) ■	112
66	IU/PU-Indianapolis †	94
90	Shepherd ■	84

96	Ohio Valley ■	58
58	West Chester ■	79
90	West Va. St.	125
93	West Va. Tech ■	78
55	West Va. Wesleyan	64
76	Bluefield St. ■	78
76	Concord ■	68
87	West Liberty St.	98
80	Alderson-Broaddus ■	86
105	Davis & Elkins ■	87
80	Fairmont St.	89
73	Salem-Teikyo ■	84
62	Glenville St. ■	77
81	Shepherd	74
73	Charleston (W.Va.)	74
70	West Liberty St. ■	86
72	Alderson-Broaddus ■	66
94	Davis & Elkins ■	47
75	Fairmont St. ■	84
67	Salem-Teikyo	77
62	Glenville St.	73

Nickname: Cardinals
Colors: Crimson & Gold
Arena: Alma McDonough Center
 Capacity: 2,200; Year Built: 1994
AD: Jay DeFruscio
SID: Beth Gattuso

WHITTIER
Whittier, CA 90608 III

Coach: Rock Carter
Alma Mater: Whittier '89
Record: 2 Years, W-15, L-35

1996-97 SCHEDULE
UC San Diego ■	Nov. 23
La Sierra ■	Nov. 26
Colorado Col. Tr.	Nov. 29-30
LIFE Bible ■	Dec. 3
Biola	Dec. 7
Chapman	Dec. 17
Azusa-Pacific	Dec. 30
Whittier Cl.	Jan. 3-4
Claremont-M-S	Jan. 11
Occidental ■	Jan. 15
Pomona-Pitzer ■	Jan. 18
Cal Lutheran	Jan. 22
La Verne	Jan. 25
Redlands ■	Jan. 29
Cal Tech	Feb. 1
Claremont-M-S ■	Feb. 5
Occidental	Feb. 8
Pomona-Pitzer	Feb. 12
Cal Lutheran ■	Feb. 15
La Verne ■	Feb. 19
Redlands	Feb. 22
Cal Tech ■	Feb. 26

1995-96 RESULTS (9-16)
71	Pt. Loma Nazarene ■	91
64	Biola ■	69
78	La Sierra	63
81	UC Santa Cruz	68
57	Concordia (Cal.) ■	74
90	UC San Diego	100
91	Simpson ■	89
95	Babson ■	88
67	Hartwick ■	57
60	Springfield	76
62	Trinity (Tex.) †	78
76	Redlands	71
70	Cal Tech ■	37
58	Cal Lutheran	92
63	Pomona-Pitzer	75
66	La Verne ■	65
63	Claremont-M-S ■	76
58	Occidental	61
93	Redlands ■	96
62	Cal Tech	47
63	Cal Lutheran ■	69
78	Pomona-Pitzer ■	95
63	La Verne	83
70	Claremont-M-S	93
77	Occidental ■	86

Nickname: Poets
Colors: Purple & Gold
Arena: Graham Activity Center
   Capacity: 2,200; Year Built: 1979
AD: Dave Jacobs
SID: Rock Carter

WICHITA ST.
Wichita, KS 67260 I

Coach: Randy Smithson
(First year as head coach)

1996-97 SCHEDULE
Southern Methodist ■	Nov. 30
Kansas St.	Dec. 3
Cleveland St. ■	Dec. 7
Mississippi	Dec. 14
Tulsa ■	Dec. 19
Prairie View ■	Dec. 21
Wichita St. Tr.	Dec. 27-28
Evansville	Jan. 2
Indiana St.	Jan. 4
Bradley	Jan. 7
Creighton ■	Jan. 11
Southwest Mo. St. ■	Jan. 18
Drake	Jan. 22
Illinois St.	Jan. 25
Bradley ■	Jan. 27
Indiana St. ■	Jan. 30
Northern Iowa ■	Feb. 1
Southern Ill. ■	Feb. 5
Illinois St. ■	Feb. 8
Drake ■	Feb. 10
Evansville ■	Feb. 15
Southern Ill.	Feb. 17
Creighton	Feb. 20
Southwest Mo. St.	Feb. 22
Northern Iowa ■	Feb. 24
Missouri Val. Conf. Tr.	Feb. 28-Mar. 3

1995-96 RESULTS (8-21)
63	Utah St. †	61
55	Minnesota †	64
64	Oregon †	74
46	Southern Methodist	65
52	Northern Ill. ■	77
74	Evansville ■	91
72	Mississippi ■	59
52	Southwest Mo. St.	64
58	Central Mich. ■	51
85	Bucknell ■	69
48	St. Peter's ■	56
64	Kansas St.	70
62	Drake	66
57	Creighton	66
78	Indiana St. ■	60
55	Drake ■	64
59	Illinois St. ■	61
54	Southern Ill.	76
51	Indiana St.	66
57	Illinois St.	74
49	Bradley	68
56	Creighton ■	68
59	Southern Ill. ■	56
47	Tulsa ■	75
76	Bradley ■	60
80	Northern Iowa	68
71	Southwest Mo. St. ■	78
66	Tulsa	72
60	Oral Roberts ■	61

Nickname: Shockers
Colors: Yellow & Black
Arena: Levitt Arena
   Capacity: 10,656; Year Built: 1955
AD: Bill Belknap
SID: Larry Rankin

WIDENER
Chester, PA 19013 III

Coach: C. Alan Rowe
Alma Mater: Villanova '53
Record: 31 Years, W-504, L-303

1996-97 SCHEDULE
Widener Tr.	Nov. 22-23
Albright ■	Dec. 3
Juniata	Dec. 7
Elizabethtown ■	Dec. 10
Widener Cl.	Dec. 13-14
Delaware	Dec. 22
King's (Pa.) Cl.	Dec. 28-29
Catholic Cl.	Jan. 11-12
Moravian	Jan. 16
Susquehanna ■	Jan. 18
Lebanon Valley ■	Jan. 22
Messiah	Jan. 25
Albright	Jan. 29
Juniata ■	Feb. 1
Elizabethtown	Feb. 4
Moravian ■	Feb. 12
Susquehanna	Feb. 15
Lebanon Valley	Feb. 18
Messiah ■	Feb. 22

1995-96 RESULTS (10-13)
87	Rutgers-Camden ■	53
61	Wilkes	72
75	Albright	60
71	Juniata ■	61
50	Elizabethtown	61
93	Delaware Valley ■	59
73	Misericordia ■	80
46	Bucknell	70
38	Delaware	81
45	Hope †	74
50	Staten Island	66
83	Medgar Evers †	72
72	Moravian ■	57
73	Lebanon Valley	76
65	Messiah	53
59	Albright ■	70
73	Juniata	56
60	Elizabethtown ■	65
75	Susquehanna	86
64	Moravian	67
67	Susquehanna ■	64
47	Lebanon Valley ■	48
74	Messiah	63

Nickname: Pioneers
Colors: Widener Blue & Gold
Arena: Schwartz Center
   Capacity: 1,850; Year Built: 1971
AD: William J. Cubit
SID: Susan Fumagalli

WILKES
Wilkes-Barre, PA 18766 III

Coach: Jerry Rickrode
Alma Mater: Skidmore '85
Record: 4 Years, W-89, L-22

1996-97 SCHEDULE
Nyack Tr.	Nov. 22-23
Pracitical Bible	Dec. 3
Nova Southeastern ■	Dec. 5
FDU-Madison ■	Dec. 7
Lebanon Valley ■	Dec. 17
Wilkes Cl.	Jan. 4-5
New Paltz St.	Jan. 7
Susquehanna ■	Jan. 11
King's (Pa.)	Jan. 15
Drew	Jan. 18
Delaware Valley	Jan. 21
Scranton ■	Jan. 25
Lycoming	Jan. 28
FDU-Madison	Feb. 1
Caldwell ■	Feb. 5
Moravian	Feb. 8
King's (Pa.) ■	Feb. 11
Drew	Feb. 15
Lycoming ■	Feb. 17
Delaware Valley ■	Feb. 19
Scranton	Feb. 22

1995-96 RESULTS (28-2)
92	Washington (Md.) †	66
72	Widener	61
84	New Paltz St. ■	69
110	Pracitical Bible ■	69
99	FDU-Madison ■	71
94	Susquehanna	64
94	Purchase St. †	41
105	Lehman	66
116	Marywood	67
91	St. John Fisher ■	97
97	King's (Pa.) ■	76
110	Delaware Valley ■	50
66	Lycoming ■	65
72	FDU-Madison	56
89	Scranton	72
76	Caldwell	68
64	Moravian ■	58
75	Drew	71
79	King's (Pa.)	65
95	Drew ■	73
85	Lycoming	82
95	Delaware Valley	59
94	Scranton ■	73
78	Lebanon Valley ■	68
72	Drew	70
71	Susquehanna ■	49
87	Allentown ■	72
96	Cabrini	91
64	Buffalo St. †	59
70	Frank. & Marsh.	107

Nickname: Colonels
Colors: Navy & Gold
Arena: Arnaud Marts Sports Ctr
   Capacity: 3,500; Year Built: 1988
AD: Phil Wingert
SID: Tom McGuire

WM. PATERSON
Wayne, NJ 07470 III

Coach: Jose Rebimbas
Alma Mater: Seton Hall '90
Record: 2 Years, W-24, L-18

1996-97 SCHEDULE
Drew Cl.	Nov. 22-23
Montclair St. ■	Nov. 26
Rutgers-Camden	Nov. 30
Kean ■	Dec. 3
Rutgers-Newark ■	Dec. 6
Jersey City St.	Dec. 11
Col. of New Jersey ■	Dec. 14
King's (Pa.) Cl.	Dec. 28-29
New York U.	Jan. 8
Manhattanville ■	Jan. 10
Ramapo	Jan. 15
Richard Stockton ■	Jan. 18
Rowan	Jan. 21
Kean	Jan. 25
Montclair St.	Jan. 29
Rutgers-Camden ■	Feb. 1
Ramapo ■	Feb. 5
Rutgers-Newark	Feb. 8
Jersey City St. ■	Feb. 12
Col. of New Jersey	Feb. 15
Rowan ■	Feb. 19
Richard Stockton	Feb. 21

1995-96 RESULTS (12-12)
66	Susquehanna	80
85	Gallaudet †	72
62	Richard Stockton ■	70
65	Rutgers-Camden	56
62	Rowan ■	94
57	Kean	67
61	Rutgers-Newark	81
48	Ramapo	61
63	Western Conn. St. ■	66
80	Wilmington (Del.) †	66
65	Penn St.-Behrend †	63
93	Bloomfield	66
59	Jersey City St.	63
75	Col. of New Jersey	57
75	Montclair St.	77
62	Rowan	83
47	Richard Stockton	60
84	Rutgers-Camden ■	53
73	Jersey City St. ■	68
73	Kean	64
63	Rutgers-Newark ■	58
75	Ramapo	46
87	Montclair St.	72
72	Col. of New Jersey ■	82

Nickname: Pioneers
Colors: Orange & Black
Arena: Rec Center
   Capacity: 4,000; Year Built: 1984
AD: Arthur Eason
SID: Joe Martinelli

WILLIAM PENN
Oskaloosa, IA 52577 III

Coach: Leon Richardson
Alma Mater: Col. of Ozarks '53
Record: 31 Years, W-400, L-363

1996-97 SCHEDULE
Denver Cl.	Nov. 29-30
Regis (Colo.)	Dec. 1
Westminster (Mo.) ■	Dec. 3
Webster	Dec. 7
Mt. Mercy	Dec. 13-14
Westminster (Mo.) Cl	Dec. 13-14
Simpson ■	Jan. 10
Buena Vista ■	Jan. 11
Loras	Jan. 17
Luther	Jan. 18
St. Ambrose ■	Jan. 25
Wartburg	Jan. 31
Upper Iowa	Feb. 1
Central (Iowa) ■	Feb. 4
Dubuque ■	Feb. 7
Loras ■	Feb. 8
Simpson	Feb. 14
Luther ■	Feb. 15
Buena Vista	Feb. 21
Dubuque	Feb. 22
Central (Iowa)	Feb. 25
Wartburg ■	Feb. 28
Upper Iowa ■	Mar. 1

1995-96 RESULTS (5-20)
81	Chicago †	100
59	Colorado Col. †	79
56	Westminster (Mo.) ■	58
86	Mt. Mercy ■	91
92	St. Ambrose ■	102
67	Webster	66
72	Maryville (Mo.)	70
96	Grand View	76
61	Dubuque ■	67
66	Luther ■	82
54	Clarke	71
64	Central (Iowa) ■	89
53	Upper Iowa	79
69	Buena Vista ■	65
82	Simpson ■	113
62	Wartburg	61
70	Dubuque	72
57	Loras ■	67
67	Loras	83
57	Buena Vista	93
71	Central (Iowa) ■	77
58	Wartburg ■	63
76	Simpson	122
57	Upper Iowa ■	67
77	Luther	92

Nickname: The Statesmen
Colors: Navy Blue & Gold
Arena: Penn Gym
   Capacity: 2,000; Year Built: 1957
AD: Mike Laird
SID: John Eberline

WILLIAM & MARY
Williamsburg, VA 23187 I

Coach: Charlie Woollum
Alma Mater: William & Mary '62
Record: 21 Years, W-336, L-256

1996-97 SCHEDULE

N.C.-Greensboro ■	Nov. 23
Hampton	Nov. 25
Stetson	Nov. 27
Citadel ■	Nov. 30
Catholic ■	Dec. 2
Virginia ■	Dec. 4
Arizona St. Cl.	Dec. 27-28
East Caro.	Jan. 2
James Madison ■	Jan. 4
Virginia Tech	Jan. 9
Richmond	Jan. 11
Navy	Jan. 13
N.C.-Wilmington ■	Jan. 16
Va. Commonwealth ■	Jan. 20
Old Dominion ■	Jan. 22
George Mason	Jan. 25
N.C.-Wilmington	Jan. 29
Va. Commonwealth	Feb. 1
Old Dominion ■	Feb. 5
Richmond ■	Feb. 8
American ■	Feb. 10
George Mason ■	Feb. 15
James Madison	Feb. 19
American	Feb. 22
East Caro. ■	Feb. 24
Colonial Conf. Tr.	Feb. 28-Mar. 3

1995-96 RESULTS (10-16)

72	Loyola (Md.) ■	76
58	Virginia	87
100	Marymount (Va.) ■	67
66	Virginia Tech ■	71
76	Hampton ■	84
72	Toledo	76
64	Air Force †	60
47	Va. Commonwealth ■	70
81	James Madison ■	70
79	Richmond	78
80	American ■	91
69	Navy ■	48
90	VMI ■	49
54	N.C.-Wilmington	67
92	George Mason	95
82	Old Dominion ■	86
65	East Caro. ■	71
68	James Madison ■	51
81	Richmond ■	64
68	Va. Commonwealth	83
66	American	100
78	East Caro.	88
63	N.C.-Wilmington ■	46
86	Old Dominion	91
96	George Mason ■	92
55	N.C.-Wilmington †	63

Nickname: Tribe
Colors: Green, Gold & Silver
Arena: William & Mary Hall
 Capacity: 10,000; Year Built: 1969
AD: Edward C. Driscoll Jr
SID: Jean Elliott

WILLIAMS
Williamstown, MA 01267 III

Coach: Harry Sheehy
Alma Mater: Williams '75
Record: 13 Years, W-231, L-87

1996-97 SCHEDULE

Mass.-Boston Inv	Nov. 22-23
Keene St. ■	Nov. 30
Rensselaer	Dec. 3
Williams Cl.	Dec. 6-7
North Adams St. ■	Jan. 8
Connecticut Col.	Jan. 11
Skidmore ■	Jan. 15
Amherst	Jan. 18
Middlebury	Jan. 21
Colby ■	Jan. 24
Bates ■	Jan. 25
Hamilton	Jan. 29
Wesleyan (Conn.) ■	Feb. 1
Union (N.Y.) ■	Feb. 5
Amherst ■	Feb. 8
Trinity (Conn.)	Feb. 12
Tufts	Feb. 15
Middlebury ■	Feb. 19
Springfield	Feb. 22
Endicott ■	Feb. 24
Wesleyan (Conn.)	Mar. 1

1995-96 RESULTS (24-3)

105	Johnson & Wales ■	31
78	Green Mountain ■	64
87	Rhode Island Col. ■	61
94	Rensselaer ■	65
77	Swarthmore ■	64
85	North Adams St. ■	53
87	Davidson	93
86	Rivier ■	51
73	Gordon ■	47
114	Skidmore	72
87	Amherst ■	68
84	Middlebury ■	57
76	Colby	75
98	Bates ■	70
83	Hamilton ■	65
88	Wesleyan (Conn.) ■	67
89	Union (N.Y.) ■	51
79	Amherst	67
92	Trinity (Conn.) ■	86
97	Tufts ■	84
54	Middlebury	58
83	Springfield ■	56
86	Connecticut Col. ■	68
84	Wesleyan (Conn.) ■	50
78	Plymouth St. ■	62
91	Bowdoin ■	64
77	Rowan	85

Nickname: Ephs
Colors: Purple
Arena: Chandler Athletic Center
 Capacity: 2,400; Year Built: 1987
AD: Robert Peck
SID: Dick Quinn

WILMINGTON (OHIO)
Wilmington, OH 45177 III

Coach: Scott Stemple
Alma Mater: Ohio Northern '85
Record: 2 Years, W-16, L-34

1996-97 SCHEDULE

Wittenberg	Nov. 16
Wooster Cl.	Nov. 22-23
Baldwin-Wallace ■	Nov. 26
Ohio	Nov. 27
Heidelberg ■	Nov. 30
Wilmington Tr.	Dec. 6-7
Hanover	Dec. 16
Marietta	Dec. 21
Ohio Northern	Dec. 23
Muskingum ■	Jan. 4
Capital	Jan. 6
Wash. & Jeff. ■	Jan. 10
Earlham	Jan. 15
Circleville Bible ■	Jan. 18
Denison	Jan. 22
Bluffton	Jan. 25
Ohio Wesleyan	Jan. 29
Ind.-East	Feb. 1
Cincinnati Bible	Feb. 6
Bluffton ■	Feb. 8
Thomas More ■	Feb. 12
Shawnee St. ■	Feb. 18
Thomas More	Feb. 22

1995-96 RESULTS (9-16)

44	Olivet †	52
74	Juniata †	58
70	Marietta ■	67
53	Wright St.	102
58	Muskingum	62
56	Mansfield ■	89
80	La Roche †	75
43	Hanover	83
63	Capital ■	71
59	Westminster (Pa.) †	72
43	Denison †	73

65	Bethany (W.Va.)	76
83	Wash. & Jeff.	67
59	Lake Erie ■	56
74	Bluffton ■	91
125	Ind.-East ■	77
70	Thomas More	87
56	Lake Erie	72
74	Ohio Wesleyan ■	66
71	Shawnee St.	86
69	Thomas More ■	72
50	Bluffton	68
95	Cincinnati Bible ■	52
66	Denison ■	64
69	Bluffton †	77

Nickname: Quakers
Colors: Green & White
Arena: Hermann Court
 Capacity: 3,000; Year Built: 1966
AD: Terry Rupert
SID: Brian Neal

WINGATE
Wingate, NC 28174 II

Coach: John Thurston
Alma Mater: Seton Hall '70
Record: 14 Years, W-155, L-214

1996-97 SCHEDULE

Appalachian St.	Nov. 22
Coastal Caro.	Nov. 26
Kennesaw St. Inv.	Nov. 29-30
Limestone ■	Dec. 4
Mars Hill	Dec. 7
Citadel	Dec. 14
Queens (N.C.) Cl.	Jan. 3-5
Lenoir-Rhyne ■	Jan. 8
Elon ■	Jan. 11
Presbyterian	Jan. 15
Carson-Newman	Jan. 18
Newberry ■	Jan. 20
Catawba ■	Jan. 22
Gardner-Webb ■	Jan. 25
Limestone	Jan. 27
Mars Hill ■	Feb. 1
Newberry	Feb. 3
Lenoir-Rhyne	Feb. 5
Elon	Feb. 8
Presbyterian ■	Feb. 12
Carson-Newman ■	Feb. 15
Catawba	Feb. 19
Gardner-Webb	Feb. 22

1995-96 RESULTS (11-16)

71	West Va. Tech	84
48	Francis Marion †	63
76	Queens (N.C.) ■	89
69	North Fla.	81
95	St. Thomas (Fla.) †	89
65	St. Andrews ■	63
89	Limestone	78
59	Newberry †	72
84	Limestone †	62
67	St. Andrews †	60
74	Catawba	84
85	Mars Hill ■	91
60	Lenoir-Rhyne ■	49
61	Elon	90
84	Limestone ■	81
65	Presbyterian	74
61	Carson-Newman ■	63
81	Gardner-Webb	79
81	St. Andrews	93
45	Catawba ■	51
77	Mars Hill	86
64	Lenoir-Rhyne	70
63	Elon ■	56
74	Gardner-Webb ■	58
62	Presbyterian	60
64	Carson-Newman	78
62	Presbyterian ■	83

Nickname: Bulldogs
Colors: Navy Blue & Old Gold
Arena: Cuddy Arena
 Capacity: 2,300; Year Built: 1986

AD: Beth Lawrence
SID: David Sherwood

WINONA ST.
Winona, MN 55987 II

Coach: Les Wothke
Alma Mater: Greenville '61
Record: 20 Years, W-291, L-261

1996-97 SCHEDULE

Crown ■	Nov. 16
Mankato St. Cl.	Nov. 22-23
St. Cloud St.	Nov. 26
St. Francis (Ill.)	Nov. 30
Wis.-Parkside	Dec. 1
St. Mary's (Minn.)	Dec. 4
SIU-Edwardsville ■	Dec. 7
North Central ■	Dec. 9
Wis.-Eau Claire ■	Dec. 11
Wis.-Stevens Point ■	Dec. 14
St. Francis (Ill.) ■	Jan. 4
Wis.-La Crosse ■	Jan. 8
Northern St. ■	Jan. 11
Bemidji St. ■	Jan. 15
Concordia-St. Paul ■	Jan. 18
Minn.-Morris	Jan. 22
Moorhead St.	Jan. 25
Minn.-Duluth	Jan. 29
Southwest St. ■	Feb. 1
Bemidji St.	Feb. 5
Northern St.	Feb. 8
Minn.-Morris ■	Feb. 12
Mt. Senario ■	Feb. 15
Minn.-Duluth ■	Feb. 19
Moorhead St. ■	Feb. 22
Southwest St.	Feb. 26

1995-96 RESULTS (8-18)

83	St. Francis (Ill.)	82
65	St. Cloud St.	86
73	St. Mary's (Minn.) ■	58
72	Wis.-Parkside ■	82
99	Pillsbury ■	55
74	Wis.-Stevens Point ■	85
62	Wis.-Eau Claire	72
70	Wis.-La Crosse ■	78
48	Regis (Colo.)	60
72	Metro St.	89
63	Colo. Christian	66
59	Northern St.	77
90	Bemidji St.	70
94	Concordia-St. Paul ■	57
82	Minn.-Morris ■	62
63	Moorhead St. ■	87
52	Minn.-Duluth ■	67
75	Southwest St.	79
75	Bemidji St. ■	66
65	Northern St. ■	68
87	Mt. Senario ■	74
79	Minn.-Morris	88
82	IU/PU-Indianapolis	83
56	Minn.-Duluth	78
81	Moorhead St.	113
66	Southwest St. ■	75

Nickname: Warriors
Colors: Purple & White
Arena: McCown Gymnasium
 Capacity: 3,500; Year Built: 1973
AD: Fran Hummel
SID: Michael R. Herzberg

WINTHROP
Rock Hill, SC 29733 I

Coach: Dan Kenney
Alma Mater: East Caro. '75
Record: 11 Years, W-156, L-156

1996-97 SCHEDULE

Syracuse	Nov. 22
Va. Intermont ■	Nov. 25
Central Fla.	Nov. 27
North Caro. St.	Dec. 3
Johnson & Wales ■	Dec. 7

Citadel..................................Dec. 12
Georgia St. ■.......................Dec. 16
VMI ■...................................Dec. 21
Auburn ■..............................Dec. 30
Southern Wesleyan ■..........Jan. 2
Bryan ■.................................Jan. 4
Fla. Atlantic ■......................Jan. 6
Coastal Caro. ■...................Jan. 11
N.C.-Asheville ■..................Jan. 15
Liberty.................................Jan. 18
Radford ■.............................Jan. 21
Md.-Balt. County ■..............Jan. 25
Charleston So.....................Jan. 30
Md.-Balt. County ■..............Feb. 1
N.C.-Greensboro ■..............Feb. 3
Liberty ■...............................Feb. 8
Radford................................Feb. 10
Charleston So. ■.................Feb. 13
N.C.-Greensboro ■..............Feb. 15
Coastal Caro......................Feb. 20
N.C.-Asheville ■..................Feb. 22
Big South Conf. Tr........Feb. 26-Mar. 1

1995-96 RESULTS (7-19)

69	Alabama	84
48	North Caro. St.	97
65	Central Fla. ■	77
63	Clemson ■	79
55	Georgia ■	81
79	Montreat ■	65
56	Miami (Fla.)	81
73	Fla. Atlantic ■	95
76	Georgia St. ■	87
78	VMI ■	101
69	Md.-Balt. County ■	63
62	Citadel ■	68
70	Radford	66
84	Coastal Caro. ■	78
69	Charleston So.	86
60	N.C.-Greensboro ■	82
65	N.C.-Asheville ■	83
77	Liberty	76
73	Charleston So. ■	82
63	Coastal Caro.	71
82	Radford ■	92
73	Md.-Balt. County ■	63
60	N.C.-Greensboro	89
70	N.C.-Asheville	89
78	Liberty ■	77
61	N.C.-Asheville †	69

Nickname: Eagles
Colors: Garnet & Gold
Arena: Winthrop Coliseum
  Capacity: 6,100; Year Built: 1982
AD: Tom Hickman
SID: Jack Frost

WISCONSIN
Madison, WI 53711.................I

Coach: Dick Bennett
Alma Mater: Ripon '65
Record: 20 Years, W-378, L-203

1996-97 SCHEDULE

Memphis [Ottawa]....................Nov. 23
N.C.-Wilmington ■..................Nov. 30
Temple....................................Dec. 4
Brown ■..................................Dec. 7
Wis.-Milwaukee ■.................Dec. 10
St. Bonaventure ■.................Dec. 14
Providence ■..........................Dec. 23
Ball St. ■................................Dec. 26
Marquette...............................Dec. 31
Minnesota...............................Jan. 2
Indiana ■.................................Jan. 4
Michigan St. ■........................Jan. 9
Iowa..Jan. 11
Penn St. ■...............................Jan. 18
Purdue.....................................Jan. 22
Illinois.....................................Jan. 25
Northwestern ■.......................Jan. 29
Ohio St....................................Feb. 1
Michigan ■..............................Feb. 6
Northwestern...........................Feb. 8

Illinois ■...............................Feb. 12
Purdue ■...............................Feb. 15
Penn St................................Feb. 19
Iowa ■..................................Feb. 26
Michigan St..........................Mar. 1
Indiana.................................Mar. 5
Minnesota ■.........................Mar. 8

1995-96 RESULTS (17-15)

58	Villanova †	66
57	UCLA †	68
104	Chaminade †	66
89	Northeastern Ill.	55
57	Temple ■	54
94	Wright St.	91
62	St. Bonaventure ■	76
57	Providence	58
90	Valparaiso ■	73
94	Wis.-Milwaukee ■	63
105	Eastern Ill. ■	70
55	Marquette ■	46
51	Michigan ■	46
50	Penn St.	79
55	Indiana	81
80	Iowa ■	71
61	Michigan St. ■	48
52	Northwestern	62
73	Minnesota ■	65
53	Ohio St.	66
57	Illinois	56
42	Purdue ■	75
62	Ohio St. ■	56
66	Minnesota	70
71	Northwestern ■	82
73	Michigan St.	52
54	Iowa	69
68	Indiana ■	76
54	Penn St. ■	52
51	Michigan	65
55	Manhattan ■	42
62	Illinois St. ■	77

Nickname: Badgers
Colors: Cardinal & White
Arena: Wisconsin Field House
  Capacity: 11,500; Year Built: 1930
AD: Pat Richter
SID: Justin Doherty

WIS.-EAU CLAIRE
Eau Claire, WI 54702.............III

Coach: Terry Gibbons
Alma Mater: Wis.-Oshkosh '83
Record: 5 Years, W-65, L-73

1996-97 SCHEDULE

Wis.-Eau Claire Tr................Nov. 22-23
Colorado Col. Tr..................Nov. 29-30
Northland ■...........................Dec. 4
Wis.-River Falls....................Dec. 7
Winona St..............................Dec. 11
Wis.-Oshkosh ■....................Dec. 14
Wis.-Eau Claire Cl................Jan. 2-3
Wis.-Platteville......................Jan. 8
Wis.-Stevens Point ■............Jan. 15
Wis.-La Crosse......................Jan. 18
Wis.-Superior........................Jan. 22
Wis.-Whitewater ■.................Jan. 25
Wis.-Stout ■...........................Jan. 29
Wis.-River Falls ■..................Feb. 1
Wis.-Oshkosh........................Feb. 5
Mt. Senario ■.........................Feb. 8
Wis.-Stevens Point.................Feb. 12
Wis.-Platteville ■...................Feb. 15
Wis.-Superior ■......................Feb. 19
Wis.-La Crosse ■...................Feb. 22
Wis.-Stout..............................Feb. 26
Wis.-Whitewater.....................Mar. 1

1995-96 RESULTS (17-7)

78	Mt. St. Clare ■	51
86	Dak. Wesleyan ■	69
76	Northland ■	52
60	Wis.-River Falls ■	47
66	Wis.-Oshkosh ■	75
62	Wis.-Platteville ■	75

72	Winona St. ■	62
87	Juniata ■	60
59	Buffalo St. ■	42
78	Skidmore †	45
83	Embry-Riddle	75
78	Wis.-Stevens Point	90
80	Wis.-Superior ■	64
78	Wis.-Whitewater	96
71	Wis.-Stout	73
78	Wis.-River Falls	77
64	Wis.-Oshkosh ■	61
64	Mt. Senario ■	61
74	Wis.-Stevens Point ■	66
57	Wis.-Platteville	82
95	Wis.-Superior	82
76	Wis.-La Crosse	81
71	Wis.-Stout ■	70
75	Wis.-Whitewater ■	72

Nickname: Blugolds
Colors: Navy Blue & Old Gold
Arena: W. L. Zorn Arena
  Capacity: 2,550; Year Built: 1952
AD: Mel Lewis
SID: Tim Petermann

WIS.-GREEN BAY
Green Bay, WI 54311..............I

Coach: Mike Heideman
Alma Mater: Wis.-LaCrosse '71
Record: 5 Years, W-91, L-29

1996-97 SCHEDULE

Northern Mich. ■..................Nov. 22
Northern Iowa.......................Nov. 25
Oregon..................................Nov. 30
Northeastern Ill. ■.................Dec. 3
Western Ky. ■........................Dec. 7
Valparaiso..............................Dec. 10
Marquette...............................Dec. 14
Illinois St. ■............................Dec. 21
Wis.-Green Bay Cl................Dec. 30-31
Ill.-Chicago ■.........................Jan. 4
Wright St................................Jan. 6
Cleveland St. ■......................Jan. 9
Detroit ■.................................Jan. 11
Northern Ill............................Jan. 16
Butler......................................Jan. 18
Loyola (Ill.) ■.........................Jan. 25
Wis.-Milwaukee ■.................Jan. 27
Loyola (Ill.)............................Jan. 30
Ill.-Chicago............................Feb. 1
Cleveland St...........................Feb. 6
Northern Ill. ■.........................Feb. 10
Detroit.....................................Feb. 16
Butler ■...................................Feb. 18
Wright St. ■............................Feb. 20
Wis.-Milwaukee.....................Feb. 24
Midwestern Conf. Tr........Feb. 28-Mar. 4

1995-96 RESULTS (25-4)

76	Morgan St. ■	54
60	Texas A&M †	49
44	Marquette	64
62	Kentucky	74
73	Idaho St. ■	56
81	Oregon	71
60	Michigan Tech ■	52
59	Western Ky.	56
66	Coppin St. ■	57
55	Princeton	35
78	Wright St. ■	52
71	Cleveland St.	57
64	Loyola (Ill.)	51
64	Butler	61
71	Detroit	69
67	Wis.-Milwaukee	54
73	Ill.-Chicago ■	67
61	Northern Ill. ■	53
74	Cleveland St.	48
60	Wright St.	53
57	Northern Ill.	51
46	Detroit	44
56	Loyola (Ill.) ■	39
81	Wis.-Milwaukee ■	66

90	Ill.-Chicago	56
73	Butler ■	66
58	Loyola (Ill.) †	48
50	Detroit †	56
48	Virginia Tech †	61

Nickname: Phoenix
Colors: Red, Green & White
Arena: Brown County Arena
  Capacity: 5,600; Year Built: 1958
AD: Dennis "Otis" Chambers
SID: Sue Bodilly

WIS.-LA CROSSE
La Crosse, WI 54601..............III

Coach: Charlie Gross
Alma Mater: St. John's (Minn.) '86
Record: 7 Years, W-40, L-129

1996-97 SCHEDULE

Clarke ■..................................Nov. 23
Martin Luther ■......................Nov. 26
Viterbo ■.................................Dec. 4
Wis.-Stout ■............................Dec. 7
Dubuque ■..............................Dec. 11
Concordia-St. Paul.................Dec. 14
Occidental Tr..........................Dec. 27-28
Wis.-Platteville ■....................Jan. 4
Winona St. ■...........................Jan. 8
Wis.-Oshkosh ■......................Jan. 11
Wis.-Whitewater.....................Jan. 15
Wis.-Eau Claire ■...................Jan. 18
Wis.-River Falls......................Jan. 22
Wis.-Superior ■.......................Jan. 25
Wis.-Stevens Point..................Jan. 29
Wis.-Stout ■............................Feb. 1
Wis.-Platteville.......................Feb. 5
Wis.-Oshkosh ■......................Feb. 8
Wis.-Whitewater ■..................Feb. 12
Northland...............................Feb. 15
Wis.-River Falls ■...................Feb. 19
Wis.-Eau Claire......................Feb. 22
Wis.-Stevens Point ■..............Feb. 26
Wis.-Superior.........................Mar. 1

1995-96 RESULTS (10-14)

93	Clarke	57
81	Martin Luther	54
87	Northland ■	66
91	Viterbo †	63
58	Wis.-Stout ■	62
44	Wis.-Platteville	63
62	Dubuque	46
71	Concordia-St. Paul ■	49
78	Winona St.	70
43	St. Norbert	47
58	Edgewood †	63
63	Wis.-Oshkosh	65
75	Wis.-Whitewater ■	87
64	Wis.-River Falls ■	69
65	Wis.-Superior	84
57	Wis.-Stevens Point ■	93
69	Wis.-Stout.	70
56	Wis.-Platteville ■	65
79	Wis.-Oshkosh ■	73
92	Wis.-Whitewater	69
66	Wis.-River Falls	71
81	Wis.-Eau Claire	76
67	Wis.-Stevens Point	89
52	Wis.-Superior ■	54

Nickname: Eagles
Colors: Maroon & Gray
Arena: Mitchell Hall
  Capacity: 3,900; Year Built: 1964
AD: Bridget Belgiovine
SID: Todd Clark

WIS.-MILWAUKEE
Milwaukee, WI 53201.............I

Coach: Ric Cobb
Alma Mater: Marquette '70
Record: 1 Year, W-9, L-18

1996-97 SCHEDULE

Minn.-Morris ■	Nov. 22
Marquette ■	Nov. 24
Western Ill. ■	Nov. 26
Stetson ■	Nov. 30
Western Ill.	Dec. 4
Valparaiso	Dec. 7
Wisconsin	Dec. 10
Northeastern Ill. ■	Dec. 12
Utah	Dec. 23
Texas-San Antonio	Dec. 30
Northern Ill.	Jan. 4
Detroit ■	Jan. 9
Cleveland St. ■	Jan. 11
Butler	Jan. 16
Wright St. ■	Jan. 18
Ill.-Chicago	Jan. 23
Wis.-Green Bay	Jan. 27
Loyola (Ill.)	Feb. 1
Northern Ill. ■	Feb. 3
Detroit	Feb. 6
Cleveland St.	Feb. 8
Wright St.	Feb. 13
Butler ■	Feb. 15
Ill.-Chicago ■	Feb. 17
Loyola (Ill.)	Feb. 22
Wis.-Green Bay ■	Feb. 24
Midwestern Conf. Tr.	Feb. 28-Mar. 4

1995-96 RESULTS (9-18)

101	Illinois Tech ■	63
74	Marquette	91
52	Iowa St.	63
69	Western Ill. ■	67
52	Northeastern Ill. ■	69
77	Valparaiso ■	82
72	Northeastern Ill.	74
63	Wisconsin	94
73	Stetson	57
73	Cleveland St. ■	55
67	Butler ■	71
64	Northern Ill.	67
59	Detroit	76
54	Wis.-Green Bay ■	67
71	Wright St. ■	74
76	Loyola (Ill.)	70
76	Ill.-Chicago	87
83	Western Ill.	75
45	Butler	65
65	Detroit ■	69
97	Cleveland St.	84
90	Northern Ill. ■	100
79	Ill.-Chicago ■	48
66	Wis.-Green Bay	81
75	Wright St.	99
61	Loyola (Ill.) ■	58
78	Northern Ill. †	80

Nickname: Panthers
Colors: Black & Gold
Arena: MECCA Arena
 Capacity: 11,052; Year Built: 1950
AD: Bud Haidet
SID: Paul Helgren

WIS.-OSHKOSH
Oshkosh, WI 54901 III

Coach: Ted Van Dellen
Alma Mater: Wis.-Oshkosh '78
Record: 6 Years, W-88, L-66

1996-97 SCHEDULE

Marian (Wis.)	Nov. 26
Wis.-Oshkosh Cl.	Nov. 29-30
Carthage	Dec. 3
Wis.-Superior ■	Dec. 7
Wis.-Eau Claire	Dec. 14
St. Scholastica ■	Dec. 21
St. Norbert ■	Dec. 31
Edgewood ■	Jan. 4
Wis.-River Falls ■	Jan. 8
Wis.-La Crosse	Jan. 11
Wis.-Platteville ■	Jan. 15
Wis.-Stout ■	Jan. 18
Wis.-Stevens Point	Jan. 22

Northland ■	Jan. 25
Wis.-Whitewater	Jan. 29
Wis.-Superior	Feb. 1
Wis.-Eau Claire ■	Feb. 5
Wis.-La Crosse ■	Feb. 8
Wis.-Platteville	Feb. 12
Wis.-River Falls	Feb. 15
Wis.-Stevens Point ■	Feb. 19
Wis.-Stout	Feb. 22
Wis.-Whitewater ■	Feb. 26
Rockford	Mar. 1

1995-96 RESULTS (23-4)
Results unavailable

Nickname: Titans
Colors: Black, Gold & White
Arena: Kolf Sports Center
 Capacity: 5,800; Year Built: 1971
AD: Allen Ackerman
SID: Kennan Timm

WIS.-PARKSIDE
Kenosha, WI 53141 II

Coach: Jeff Rutter
Alma Mater: Winona St. '87
(First year as head coach)

1996-97 SCHEDULE

St. Francis (Ill.)	Nov. 20
Lake Superior St. Tr	Nov. 22-23
Carthage	Nov. 26
Winona St. ■	Dec. 1
Marian (Wis.)	Dec. 7
Mt. Senario	Dec. 14
Northern Ky.	Dec. 21
Indianapolis	Dec. 23
SIU-Edwardsville ■	Jan. 2
Southern Ind. ■	Jan. 4
Lewis ■	Jan. 9
Ky. Wesleyan ■	Jan. 11
Quincy	Jan. 16
Mo.-St. Louis	Jan. 18
St. Joseph's (Ind.) ■	Jan. 23
IU/PU-Ft. Wayne ■	Jan. 25
Northern Ky. ■	Jan. 30
Indianapolis ■	Feb. 1
Southern Ind.	Feb. 6
SIU-Edwardsville	Feb. 8
Lewis	Feb. 13
Bellarmine	Feb. 15
Mo.-St. Louis ■	Feb. 20
Quincy ■	Feb. 22
IU/PU-Ft. Wayne	Feb. 27
St. Joseph's (Ind.)	Mar. 1

1995-96 RESULTS (6-20)
Results unavailable

Nickname: Rangers
Colors: Green, White & Black
Arena: Physical Education Building
 Capacity: 2,000; Year Built: 1972
AD: Lenny Klaver
SID: Oscar Suman

WIS.-PLATTEVILLE
Platteville, WI 53818 III

Coach: Bo Ryan
Alma Mater: Wilkes '69
Record: 12 Years, W-269, L-71

1996-97 SCHEDULE

Lakeland	Nov. 23
Minn.-Crookston ■	Nov. 25
Coe	Nov. 26
Gordon Tr.	Nov. 29-30
Wis.-Stevens Point	Dec. 7
Wis.-Platteville Tr.	Dec. 27-28
Teikyo Marycrest ■	Jan. 2
Wis.-La Crosse	Jan. 4
Wis.-Eau Claire ■	Jan. 8
Wis.-Superior ■	Jan. 11
Wis.-Oshkosh	Jan. 15

Wis.-River Falls ■	Jan. 18
Wis.-Whitewater	Jan. 22
Wis.-Stout	Jan. 25
Mt. Senario ■	Jan. 29
Wis.-Stevens Point	Feb. 1
Wis.-La Crosse ■	Feb. 5
Wis.-Superior	Feb. 8
Wis.-Oshkosh ■	Feb. 12
Wis.-Eau Claire	Feb. 15
Wis.-Whitewater ■	Feb. 19
Wis.-River Falls	Feb. 22
Wis.-Stout ■	Mar. 1

1995-96 RESULTS (23-3)

78	Alas. Fairbanks	74
62	Southern Ind. †	85
59	North Dak.	51
80	Minn.-Crookston	56
79	Lakeland ■	46
74	Wis.-Stevens Point	60
63	Wis.-La Crosse ■	44
75	Wis.-Eau Claire	62
80	Messiah †	38
73	Muhlenberg †	46
75	Col. of New Jersey †	64
89	Wis.-Superior	84
63	Wis.-Oshkosh ■	50
60	Wis.-River Falls	32
86	Wis.-Whitewater ■	59
79	Wis.-Stout ■	65
74	Mt. Senario ■	40
63	Wis.-Stevens Point ■	56
65	Wis.-La Crosse	56
85	Wis.-Superior ■	56
58	Wis.-Oshkosh	59
82	Wis.-Eau Claire ■	57
84	Wis.-Whitewater	62
71	Wis.-River Falls ■	59
89	Wis.-Stout.	59
77	Wis.-Whitewater ■	85

Nickname: Pioneers
Colors: Blue & Orange
Arena: Williams Fieldhouse
 Capacity: 2,300; Year Built: 1962
AD: To be named
SID: Becky Bohm

WIS.-RIVER FALLS
River Falls, WI 54022 III

Coach: Rick Bowen
Alma Mater: Indiana '66
Record: 10 Years, W-136, L-124

1996-97 SCHEDULE

Bethel (Minn.) Tr.	Nov. 22-23
UC San Diego Tr.	Nov. 29-30
St. John's (Minn.)	Dec. 4
Wis.-Eau Claire ■	Dec. 7
Hamline ■	Dec. 11
Wis.-River Falls Tr.	Dec. 29-30
Wis.-Oshkosh	Jan. 8
Wis.-Whitewater	Jan. 11
Wis.-Stout ■	Jan. 15
Wis.-Platteville	Jan. 18
Wis.-La Crosse ■	Jan. 22
Wis.-Stevens Point ■	Jan. 25
Wis.-Superior	Jan. 29
Wis.-Eau Claire	Feb. 1
Wis.-Superior ■	Feb. 5
Wis.-Whitewater ■	Feb. 8
Wis.-Stout	Feb. 12
Wis.-Oshkosh ■	Feb. 15
Wis.-La Crosse	Feb. 19
Wis.-Platteville ■	Feb. 22
Wis.-Superior ■	Feb. 26
Wis.-Stevens Point	Mar. 1

1995-96 RESULTS (13-12)

91	Wis. Lutheran ■	82
66	Purdue-Calumet ■	61
80	Wis.-Parkside ■	62
47	Wis.-Eau Claire	60
94	North Cent. Bible	63
71	Wis.-Oshkosh	72
57	Wis.-Whitewater ■	75

70	Martin Luther ■	51
77	Beloit †	82
83	Elmhurst	71
81	Minn.-Morris	61
80	Wis.-Stout	67
32	Wis.-Platteville ■	60
69	Wis.-La Crosse	64
56	Wis.-Stevens Point	77
68	Wis.-Superior ■	69
77	Wis.-Eau Claire ■	78
87	St. Scholastica ■	73
81	Wis.-Whitewater ■	89
85	Wis.-Stout ■	72
53	Wis.-Oshkosh	71
71	Wis.-La Crosse ■	66
59	Wis.-Platteville	71
83	Wis.-Superior	72
74	Wis.-Stevens Point ■	80

Nickname: Falcons
Colors: Red & White
Arena: Karges Center
 Capacity: 2,000; Year Built: 1958
AD: Rick Bowen
SID: Jim Thies

WIS.-STEVENS POINT
Stevens Point, WI 54481 III

Coach: Jack Bennett
Alma Mater: Ripon '71
(First year as head coach)

1996-97 SCHEDULE

Wis.-Stevens Pt. Cl.	Nov. 22-23
Northland ■	Nov. 26
Mt. Senario ■	Dec. 4
Wis.-Platteville ■	Dec. 7
Wis.-Whitewater ■	Dec. 11
Winona St.	Dec. 14
Viterbo ■	Dec. 20
Wis.-Stevens Pt. Tr.	Dec. 28-29
Edgewood	Jan. 2
Wis.-Superior	Jan. 8
Wis.-Stout ■	Jan. 11
Wis.-Eau Claire	Jan. 15
Wis.-Oshkosh ■	Jan. 22
Wis.-River Falls	Jan. 25
Wis.-La Crosse ■	Jan. 29
Wis.-Platteville ■	Feb. 1
Wis.-Whitewater	Feb. 5
Wis.-Stout ■	Feb. 8
Wis.-Eau Claire ■	Feb. 12
Wis.-Superior ■	Feb. 15
Wis.-Oshkosh †	Feb. 19
Wis.-La Crosse ■	Feb. 26
Wis.-River Falls ■	Mar. 1

1995-96 RESULTS (17-8)

71	Teikyo Marycrest	82
80	Taylor †	71
99	Carthage ■	85
82	Mt. Senario ■	76
60	Wis.-Platteville ■	74
68	Wis.-Whitewater	76
85	Winona St. ■	74
82	Viterbo ■	61
89	Lakeland ■	82
89	Wis.-Stout ■	83
90	Wis.-Eau Claire ■	78
90	Northland ■	78
50	Wis.-Oshkosh	67
77	Wis.-River Falls ■	56
74	Wis.-Superior	66
93	Wis.-La Crosse	57
56	Wis.-Platteville	63
84	Wis.-Whitewater ■	85
80	Wis.-Stout	79
84	Bemidji St.	74
66	Wis.-Eau Claire	74
97	Wis.-Superior ■	91
66	Wis.-Oshkosh ■	74
89	Wis.-La Crosse ■	67
80	Wis.-River Falls	74

Nickname: Pointers
Colors: Purple & Gold

Arena: Quandt Fieldhouse
   Capacity: 3,281; Year Built: 1969
AD: Frank O'Brien
SID: Terry Owens

WIS.-STOUT
Menomonie, WI 54751............III

Coach: John Muraski
Alma Mater: Ripon '76
Record: 12 Years, W-151, L-158

1996-97 SCHEDULE
Wis.-Stout Cl.	Nov. 22-23
Edgewood ■	Nov. 26
St. Scholastica	Nov. 30
Wis.-La Crosse ■	Dec. 7
N'western (Minn.) ■	Dec. 16
Marian (Wis.) ■	Dec. 18
Surf 'n Slam Inv.	Dec. 26-Jan. 1
Wis.-Superior	Jan. 4
Wis.-Whitewater ■	Jan. 8
Wis.-Stevens Point ■	Jan. 11
Wis.-River Falls	Jan. 15
Wis.-Oshkosh	Jan. 18
Wis.-Platteville ■	Jan. 25
Wis.-Eau Claire	Jan. 29
Wis.-La Crosse	Feb. 1
Wis.-Superior ■	Feb. 5
Wis.-Stevens Point	Feb. 8
Wis.-River Falls ■	Feb. 12
Wis.-Whitewater	Feb. 15
Wis.-Oshkosh ■	Feb. 22
Wis.-Eau Claire	Feb. 26
Wis.-Platteville	Mar. 1

1995-96 RESULTS (10-15)
88	Northland †	103
82	N'western (Minn.) †	76
60	Edgewood	78
62	Marian (Wis.)	60
62	Wis.-La Crosse	58
73	Wis.-Superior ■	84
69	Wis.-Whitewater	78
89	St. Scholastica ■	58
89	South Dak. Tech †	78
69	Black Hills St.	71
82	N'western (Minn.)	80
83	Wis.-Stevens Point	89
67	Wis.-River Falls ■	80
63	Wis.-Oshkosh ■	66
91	Martin Luther ■	71
65	Wis.-Platteville	79
73	Wis.-Eau Claire ■	71
70	Wis.-La Crosse ■	69
81	Wis.-Superior	64
79	Wis.-Stevens Point ■	80
72	Wis.-River Falls	85
88	Wis.-Whitewater ■	94
73	Wis.-Oshkosh	87
70	Wis.-Eau Claire	71
59	Wis.-Platteville	89

Nickname: Blue Devils
Colors: Royal Blue & White
Arena: Johnson Fieldhouse
   Capacity: 1,500; Year Built: 1965
AD: Steve Terry
SID: Layne Pitt

WIS.-SUPERIOR
Superior, WI 54880...............III

Coach: Jeff Kaminsky
Alma Mater: Grand Valley St. '85
Record: 2 Years, W-14, L-36

1996-97 SCHEDULE
Schedule unavailable

1995-96 RESULTS (9-16)
74	Martin Luther ■	52
84	Concordia (Wis.) ■	82
74	Minn.-Duluth	86
84	Northland	92
62	Wis.-Oshkosh ■	70

84	Wis.-Stout	73
89	N'western (Minn.) ■	80
78	St. Scholastica ■	82
111	Pillsbury ■	66
84	Wis.-Platteville ■	89
73	Northland	59
66	Wis.-Whitewater	75
64	Wis.-Eau Claire	80
84	Wis.-La Crosse ■	65
66	Wis.-Stevens Point	74
69	Wis.-River Falls	68
57	Wis.-Oshkosh	70
64	Wis.-Stout ■	81
56	Wis.-Platteville	85
71	St. Scholastica	77
91	Wis.-Stevens Point	97
82	Wis.-Eau Claire ■	95
67	Wis.-Whitewater ■	72
72	Wis.-River Falls ■	83
54	Wis.-La Crosse	52

Nickname: Yellowjackets
Colors: Old Gold & Black
Arena: Gates Gym
   Capacity: 2,000; Year Built: 1966
AD: Patricia Dolan
SID: John Hack

WIS.-WHITEWATER
Whitewater, WI 53190............III

Coach: Dave Vander Meulen
Alma Mater: Wisconsin '62
Record: 18 Years, W-357, L-139

1996-97 SCHEDULE
Augustana (Ill.) ■	Nov. 23
Concordia (Wis.)	Nov. 26
Wis. Lutheran ■	Dec. 2
Lake Forest	Dec. 4
Carroll (Wis.)	Dec. 7
Wis.-Stevens Point	Dec. 11
Dubuque	Dec. 20
Teikyo Marycrest ■	Dec. 22
Edgewood	Dec. 29
Marian (Wis.) ■	Jan. 4
Wis.-Stout	Jan. 8
Wis.-River Falls ■	Jan. 11
Wis.-La Crosse ■	Jan. 15
Wis.-Superior	Jan. 18
Wis.-Platteville ■	Jan. 22
Wis.-Eau Claire	Jan. 25
Wis.-Oshkosh ■	Jan. 29
Wis.-Stevens Point ■	Feb. 5
Wis.-River Falls	Feb. 8
Wis.-La Crosse	Feb. 12
Wis.-Stout ■	Feb. 15
Wis.-Platteville	Feb. 19
Wis.-Superior ■	Feb. 22
Wis.-Oshkosh	Feb. 26
Wis.-Eau Claire ■	Mar. 1

1995-96 RESULTS (19-9)
84	Maranatha Bapt. ■	49
68	Concordia (Wis.) ■ ■	66
56	Ripon	64
73	Carroll (Wis.) ■	70
91	Dubuque	60
76	Wis.-Stevens Point ■	68
78	Wis.-Stout ■	69
75	Wis.-River Falls	57
70	Teikyo Marycrest	60
65	Muskingum †	53
66	Wittenberg	69
87	Wis.-La Crosse	75
75	Wis.-Superior	66
59	Wis.-Platteville	86
96	Wis.-Eau Claire ■	78
87	Maranatha Bapt.	57
59	Wis.-Oshkosh	72
85	Wis.-Stevens Point	84
89	Wis.-River Falls ■	81
69	Wis.-La Crosse ■	92
94	Wis.-Stout	88
62	Wis.-Platteville ■	84

72	Wis.-Superior	67
64	Wis.-Oshkosh ■	74
72	Wis.-Eau Claire	75
85	Wis.-Platteville	77
63	Claremont-M-S	62
66	Hope †	88

Nickname: Warhawks
Colors: Purple & White
Arena: Williams Center
   Capacity: 3,000; Year Built: 1967
AD: Willie Myers
SID: Tom Fick

WITTENBERG
Springfield, OH 45501 III

Coach: Bill L. Brown
Alma Mater: Wittenberg '73
Record: 7 Years, W-137, L-114

1996-97 SCHEDULE
Wilmington (Ohio) ■	Nov. 16
Washington (Mo.) Tr.	Nov. 22-23
Hanover	Nov. 30
Oberlin	Dec. 7
Otterbein	Dec. 11
Thomas More ■	Dec. 21
Wittenberg Cl.	Dec. 27-28
Case Reserve	Jan. 3
Allegheny ■	Jan. 4
Kenyon	Jan. 8
Denison ■	Jan. 11
Ohio Wesleyan ■	Jan. 15
Wooster	Jan. 18
Earlham	Jan. 22
Oberlin ■	Jan. 25
Defiance ■	Jan. 28
Allegheny	Jan. 31
Case Reserve ■	Feb. 1
Kenyon ■	Feb. 5
Wooster ■	Feb. 8
Denison	Feb. 12
Ohio Wesleyan	Feb. 15
Earlham ■	Feb. 19

1995-96 RESULTS (26-5)
79	Franklin †	68
76	Albion †	78
65	Capital	70
71	Oberlin	44
70	Kenyon ■	67
66	Wooster ■	47
84	Otterbein ■	63
93	Earlham	86
57	Thomas More ■	60
71	Wabash ■	70
69	Wis.-Whitewater ■	66
76	Allegheny	54
66	Case Reserve	69
73	Denison ■	47
57	Kenyon	52
74	Ohio Wesleyan	55
85	Oberlin ■	41
64	Defiance ■	49
46	Wooster	43
101	Case Reserve ■	76
72	Allegheny ■	64
95	Earlham ■	72
70	Denison	63
82	Ohio Wesleyan ■	55
95	Earlham ■	68
104	Case Reserve ■	70
65	Allegheny ■	55
70	Baldwin-Wallace ■	61
65	Capital ■	60
76	Gust. Adolphus ■	68
60	Hope †	69

Nickname: Tigers
Colors: Red & White
Arena: Health, P.E. & Recreation Center
   Capacity: 3,000; Year Built: 1982
AD: Carl Schraibman
SID: Alan Aldinger

WOFFORD
Spartanburg, SC 29301.............I

Coach: Richard Johnson
Alma Mater: Citadel '76
Record: 11 Years, W-172, L-126

1996-97 SCHEDULE
Georgia Tech	Nov. 22
Tusculum ■	Nov. 25
Richmond	Nov. 27
South Caro.	Dec. 2
Montreat ■	Dec. 5
Navy ■	Dec. 7
East Tenn. St.	Dec. 17
Clemson	Dec. 20
Western Caro.	Jan. 4
Tenn.-Chatt.	Jan. 6
Western Caro. ■	Jan. 9
Charleston (S.C.) ■	Jan. 13
VMI ■	Jan. 16
King (Tenn.) ■	Jan. 18
Campbell ■	Jan. 20
Furman	Jan. 22
East Tenn. St. ■	Jan. 25
Wake Forest	Jan. 29
Tennessee	Feb. 1
Army ■	Feb. 8
Mercer	Feb. 10
Furman ■	Feb. 13
Mercer ■	Feb. 17
Richmond ■	Feb. 19
Air Force	Feb. 22
Colorado	Feb. 24
North Caro. St.	Mar. 1

1995-96 RESULTS (4-22)
60	Missouri	86
59	Vanderbilt	97
60	North Caro. St.	99
58	Mercer	76
58	East Caro. ■	68
56	Mercer ■	68
56	Auburn	73
67	Western Caro.	92
71	Army	74
60	Tenn.-Chatt. ■	86
68	Charleston (S.C.) ■	79
86	East Tenn. St. ■	93
99	Tusculum ■	70
62	Campbell	78
53	N.C.-Asheville ■	82
55	South Caro.	82
66	VMI	80
28	Clemson	77
72	Western Caro. ■	84
100	Emmanuel ■	80
67	N.C.-Asheville ■	76
80	King (Tenn.) ■	55
60	East Caro.	79
81	East Tenn. St.	84
55	Navy	73
47	Charleston (S.C.)	83

Nickname: Terriers
Colors: Old Gold & Black
Arena: Benjamin Johnson Arena
   Capacity: 3,500; Year Built: 1981
AD: Danny Morrison
SID: Mark Cohen

WOOSTER
Wooster, OH 44691...............III

Coach: Steve Moore
Alma Mater: Wittenberg '74
Record: 15 Years, W-275, L-124

1996-97 SCHEDULE
Wooster Cl.	Nov. 22-23
Grove City	Nov. 26
Akron	Dec. 3
Oberlin ■	Dec. 5
Earlham	Dec. 7
UC San Diego	Dec. 18
Pomona-Pitzer	Dec. 21

Wooster Tr. ....Dec. 27-28
Kenyon ....Jan. 3
Denison ....Jan. 8
Case Reserve ■ ....Jan. 11
Allegheny ....Jan. 15
Wittenberg ■ ....Jan. 18
Kenyon ■ ....Jan. 22
Ohio Wesleyan ....Jan. 25
Oberlin ....Jan. 31
Denison ■ ....Feb. 1
Case Reserve ....Feb. 5
Wittenberg ....Feb. 8
Allegheny ■ ....Feb. 12
Earlham ■ ....Feb. 15
Ohio Wesleyan ....Feb. 22

1995-96 RESULTS (19-7)
68	Lake Erie ■	51
68	Walsh ■	79
75	Hartwick †	70
75	Merchant Marine †	55
66	Case Reserve ■	54
73	Earlham	64
79	Allegheny	61
47	Wittenberg	66
72	Malone †	66
64	Muskingum	57
86	Dickinson ■	31
56	Mount Union ■	51
62	Kenyon	56
68	Ohio Wesleyan ■	49
88	Oberlin ■	47
70	Denison	74
91	Earlham ■	54
82	Allegheny ■	57
43	Wittenberg ■	46
65	Oberlin	62
61	Ohio Wesleyan	73
79	Case Reserve	63
48	Kenyon ■	43
63	Denison ■	51
62	Ohio Wesleyan ■	71
72	John Carroll	86

Nickname: Fighting Scots
Colors: Black & Old Gold
Arena: Timken Gymnasium
 Capacity: 3,400; Year Built: 1968
AD: Robert Malekoff
SID: John Finn

WPI
Worcester, MA 01609 III

Coach: Ken Kaufman
Alma Mater: Bridgeport '68
Record: 21 Years, W-262, L-244

1996-97 SCHEDULE
Nichols ■ ....Nov. 23
Salve Regina ....Nov. 26
MIT ■ ....Nov. 30
Babson ....Dec. 4
Anna Maria ....Dec. 10
Norwich ....Dec. 13
Worcester St. ■ ....Jan. 9
Wentworth Inst. ....Jan. 11
Western New Eng. ■ ....Jan. 18
Brandeis ....Jan. 22
Clark (Mass.) ■ ....Jan. 25
Western New Eng. ....Jan. 28
Springfield ■ ....Jan. 30
Coast Guard ....Feb. 1
Norwich ■ ....Feb. 4
Suffolk ■ ....Feb. 6
Clark (Mass.) ....Feb. 8
Springfield ....Feb. 13
Babson ■ ....Feb. 15
MIT ....Feb. 20
Coast Guard ■ ....Feb. 22

1995-96 RESULTS (12-12)
58	Johns Hopkins	62
79	Alfred †	65
84	Salve Regina ■	59
61	MIT ■	53
83	Babson ■	96
88	Nichols	94
73	Anna Maria ■	76
82	Wentworth Inst. ■	60
88	Worcester St.	78
95	Western New Eng. ■	74
69	Brandeis ■	66
92	Clark (Mass.)	105
71	Springfield	86
64	Coast Guard ■	67
82	Norwich ■	77
65	Suffolk	61
86	Clark (Mass.) ■	65
53	Springfield ■	71
80	Babson	104
83	Western New Eng.	77
80	MIT ■	64
73	Coast Guard	77
62	Norwich	80
74	Coast Guard	76

Nickname: Engineers
Colors: Crimson & Gray
Arena: Harrington Auditorium
 Capacity: 3,200; Year Built: 1967
AD: Raymond Gilbert
SID: Geoff Hassard

WORCESTER ST.
Worcester, MA 01602 III

Coach: Dave Lindberg
Alma Mater: Worcester St. '91
Record: 2 Years, W-19, L-32

1996-97 SCHEDULE
Rochester Tip-Off ....Nov. 22-23
Mass.-Dartmouth ....Nov. 26
Anna Maria ....Dec. 1
Nichols ■ ....Dec. 4
Eastern Nazarene ....Dec. 7
Eastern Conn. St. ■ ....Dec. 10
Roger Williams ■ ....Dec. 14
Wis.-Eau Claire Cl. ....Jan. 2-3
WPI ....Jan. 9
Fitchburg St. ■ ....Jan. 14
Westfield St. ....Jan. 18
Framingham St. ■ ....Jan. 21
North Adams St. ■ ....Jan. 25
Bri'water (Mass.) ....Jan. 28
St. Joseph's (Me.) ■ ....Feb. 1
Salem St. ■ ....Feb. 4
Fitchburg St. ....Feb. 8
Westfield St. ■ ....Feb. 11
Framingham St. ....Feb. 13
North Adams St. ....Feb. 15
Bri'water (Mass.) ■ ....Feb. 18
Salem St. ....Feb. 22

1995-96 RESULTS (10-16)
72	Eastern Nazarene ■	81
84	Anna Maria	95
81	Nichols	87
110	Johnson & Wales †	61
66	Anna Maria	90
77	Eastern Conn. St.	84
80	Mass.-Dartmouth ■	89
91	Roger Williams	82
104	John Jay †	94
83	Western Conn. St.	89
109	Fitchburg St.	76
78	WPI	88
112	Westfield St. ■	107
102	Framingham St.	97
92	North Adams St.	80
75	Bri'water (Mass.) ■	91
85	St. Joseph's (Me.)	104
83	Salem St.	109
72	Fitchburg St. ■	84
72	Westfield St.	83
83	Framingham St. ■	68
98	North Adams St. ■	67
61	Bri'water (Mass.)	85
71	Salem St. ■	94
89	Fitchburg St.	70
79	Salem St.	99

Nickname: Lancers

Colors: Royal Blue & Gold
Arena: Lancer Gymnasium
 Capacity: 1,200; Year Built: 1953
AD: Susan Chapman
SID: Bruce Baker

WRIGHT ST.
Dayton, OH 45435 I

Coach: Ralph Underhill
Alma Mater: Tenn. Tech '64
Record: 18 Years, W-356, L-162

1996-97 SCHEDULE
Thomas More ■ ....Nov. 30
Kentucky ....Dec. 9
Bowling Green ■ ....Dec. 11
Miami (Ohio) ■ ....Dec. 14
Louisville ....Dec. 16
Ohio ....Dec. 18
Toledo ■ ....Dec. 21
Western Mich. ....Dec. 28
Youngstown St. ....Dec. 30
Detroit ....Jan. 2
Cleveland St. ....Jan. 4
Wis.-Green Bay ■ ....Jan. 6
Dayton ■ ....Jan. 9
Northern Ill. ■ ....Jan. 11
Ill.-Chicago ■ ....Jan. 16
Wis.-Milwaukee ....Jan. 18
Loyola (Ill.) ....Jan. 23
Butler ■ ....Jan. 25
Detroit ■ ....Jan. 30
Cleveland St. ■ ....Feb. 1
Ill.-Chicago ....Feb. 6
Northern Ill. ....Feb. 8
Wis.-Milwaukee ■ ....Feb. 13
Wis.-Green Bay ....Feb. 20
Butler ....Feb. 22
Loyola (Ill.) ■ ....Feb. 26
Midwestern Conf. Tr. ....Feb. 28-Mar. 4

1995-96 RESULTS (14-13)
102	Wilmington (Ohio) ■	53
76	Eastern Ky. ■	64
91	Wisconsin ■	94
80	Dayton	98
88	Ohio ■	77
62	Toledo	57
74	Youngstown St. ■	66
85	Manhattan ■	76
86	Miami (Ohio)	105
46	Virginia Tech †	62
52	Wis.-Green Bay	78
79	Ill.-Chicago	91
68	Butler ■	71
68	Cleveland St.	83
87	Loyola (Ill.) ■	73
74	Wis.-Milwaukee ■	71
59	Detroit	57
63	Northern Ill. ■	71
91	Ill.-Chicago ■	74
53	Wis.-Green Bay ■	60
67	Loyola (Ill.)	85
67	Butler	61
65	Cleveland St. ■	54
70	Detroit	63
99	Wis.-Milwaukee	75
71	Northern Ill.	81
61	Detroit ■	67

Nickname: Raiders
Colors: Green & Gold
Arena: Ervin J. Nutter Center
 Capacity: 10,632; Year Built: 1990
AD: Mike Cusack
SID: Robert J. Noss

WYOMING
Laramie, WY 82071 I

Coach: Joby Wright
Alma Mater: Indiana '72
Record: 6 Years, W-102, L-73

1996-97 SCHEDULE
Creighton ■ ....Nov. 22
Long Beach St. ■ ....Nov. 25
St. Joseph's (Pa.) ....Dec. 3
Massachusetts ....Dec. 7
Colorado ■ ....Dec. 10
Austin Peay ....Dec. 14
Montana St. [Billings] ....Dec. 19
Utah St. ....Dec. 21
Delaware St. ■ ....Dec. 23
Wyoming Shootout ....Dec. 27-28
Denver ....Dec. 31
Brigham Young ■ ....Jan. 4
Colorado St. ....Jan. 11
San Diego St. ■ ....Jan. 16
Hawaii ....Jan. 18
San Jose St. ■ ....Jan. 23
Fresno St. ■ ....Jan. 25
Air Force ....Jan. 30
UNLV ....Feb. 1
Colorado St. ■ ....Feb. 6
Brigham Young ....Feb. 8
Hawaii ■ ....Feb. 13
San Diego St. ■ ....Feb. 15
Fresno St. ....Feb. 20
San Jose St. ....Feb. 22
UNLV ■ ....Feb. 27
Air Force ■ ....Mar. 1
Western Ath. Conf. Tr. ....Mar. 4-8

1995-96 RESULTS (14-15)
86	Simon Fraser ■	71
97	Denver ■	83
51	Cincinnati	101
92	Northern Colo. ■	63
83	Colorado	81
66	Iowa St. ■	70
52	Old Dominion ■	66
68	Weber St.	85
87	Alcorn St. †	64
73	Ohio St. †	67
53	Hawaii	63
77	San Diego St.	80
63	Colorado St. ■	68
61	New Mexico ■	58
72	UTEP ■	68
75	Brigham Young	84
65	Utah	88
84	Air Force ■	67
96	Fresno St. ■	81
72	Air Force	65
70	Fresno St.	74
71	Brigham Young ■	81
80	Utah ■	76
71	UTEP	77
69	New Mexico	70
66	Colorado St.	80
95	Hawaii ■	78
69	San Diego St. ■	68
82	Fresno St. †	91

Nickname: Cowboys
Colors: Brown & Yellow
Arena: Arena-Auditorium
 Capacity: 15,028; Year Built: 1982
AD: Lee Moon
SID: Kevin McKinney

XAVIER (OHIO)
Cincinnati, OH 45207 I

Coach: Skip Prosser
Alma Mater: Merchant Marine '72
Record: 3 Years, W-53, L-33

1996-97 SCHEDULE
Western Ky. ■ ....Nov. 23
Cincinnati ....Nov. 26
Miami (Ohio) ■ ....Nov. 30
Florida A&M ■ ....Dec. 2
Loyola Marymount ....Dec. 5
LIU-Brooklyn ....Dec. 7
Hofstra ....Dec. 14
Akron ....Dec. 21
Kansas St. ■ ....Dec. 29
Virginia Tech ■ ....Jan. 4

SCHEDULES/RESULTS

Dayton.................................Jan. 7
Fordham..............................Jan. 11
Tulane [Cincinnati]..............Jan. 16
Temple ■............................Jan. 19
Geo. Washington.................Jan. 23
Duquesne ■.........................Jan. 25
Rhode Island ■....................Jan. 28
Massachusetts......................Feb. 1
La Salle...............................Feb. 3
St. Joseph's (Pa.)................Feb. 8
Dayton ■............................Feb. 12
Geo. Washington ■..............Feb. 15
Duquesne ■.........................Feb. 20
La Salle ■............................Feb. 22
St. Bonaventure ■................Feb. 27
Virginia Tech.......................Mar. 2
Atlantic 10 Conf. Tr. ....Mar. 5-8

1995-96 RESULTS (13-15)

88	St. Francis (Pa.) ■	61
75	Va. Commonwealth	81
109	LIU-Brooklyn ■	78
71	Miami (Ohio) ■	85
72	Ohio	103
87	Delaware St. ■	57
67	Kansas St.	73
70	Notre Dame ■	72
78	Morgan St. ■	59
69	La Salle	60
56	Temple	73
74	Fordham ■	61
90	Cincinnati ■	99
76	St. Bonaventure	62
60	La Salle ■	59
55	Dayton	61
84	St. Joseph's (Pa.) ■	71
74	Massachusetts ■	78
69	Geo. Washington	77
73	Virginia Tech ■	78
70	Rhode Island	87
102	Dayton ■	95
116	Duquesne ■	105
77	Geo. Washington ■	81
61	Virginia Tech	70
76	Duquesne	75
61	Fordham †	54
50	Temple †	67

Nickname: Musketeers
Colors: Navy Blue & White
Arena: Cincinnati Gardens
  Capacity: 10,400; Year Built: 1949
AD: Jeff Fogelson
SID: Tom Eiser

YALE
New Haven, CT 06520 I

Coach: Dick Kuchen
Alma Mater: Rider '66
Record: 17 Years, W-205, L-249

1996-97 SCHEDULE

Hartford ■............................Nov. 22
Holy Cross...........................Nov. 26
Connecticut..........................Nov. 29
Swarthmore ■.......................Dec. 1
Lehigh ■...............................Dec. 4
Marist Cl. ....Dec. 6-7
Army....................................Dec. 10
Vermont...............................Dec. 30
Southern Methodist...............Jan. 6
Pennsylvania ■......................Jan. 10
Princeton ■...........................Jan. 11
Lafayette ■...........................Jan. 13
Brown...................................Jan. 18
Siena ■.................................Jan. 23
Brown ■................................Jan. 25
Dartmouth.............................Jan. 31
Harvard................................Feb. 1
Columbia ■...........................Feb. 7
Cornell ■..............................Feb. 8
Princeton..............................Feb. 14
Pennsylvania.........................Feb. 15
Cornell.................................Feb. 21
Columbia..............................Feb. 22

Harvard ■.............................Feb. 28
Dartmouth ■..........................Mar. 1

1995-96 RESULTS (8-18)

58	Rice †	80
58	Stetson †	78
89	Lehigh	72
64	Vermont ■	82
73	Swarthmore ■	65
78	Holy Cross ■	75
66	Connecticut	93
74	LIU-Brooklyn †	87
62	Ga. Southern †	57
56	Colgate	66
55	Princeton	56
56	Pennsylvania	66
62	Brown ■	56
56	Brown	73
47	Harvard ■	62
49	Dartmouth ■	66
65	Army ■	64
53	Cornell	49
58	Columbia	74
58	Lafayette	67
62	Pennsylvania ■	60
42	Princeton	64
62	Columbia ■	63
65	Cornell ■	71
63	Dartmouth	65
67	Harvard	87

Nickname: Elis, Bulldogs
Colors: Yale Blue & White
Arena: John J. Lee Ampitheater
  Capacity: 3,100; Year Built: 1932
AD: Tom Beckett
SID: Tim Bennett

YESHIVA
New York, NY 10033.............III

Coach: Jonathan Halpert
Alma Mater: Yeshiva '66
Record: 24 Years, W-208, L-314

1996-97 SCHEDULE

Mass. Pharmacy.....................Nov. 23
Emerson-MCA........................Nov. 24
N.J. Inst. of Tech. ....Nov. 26
Molloy Tr..............................Nov. 29-30
CCNY ■................................Dec. 2
Bard....................................Dec. 5
Stevens Tech........................Dec. 7
Baruch.................................Dec. 9
Maritime (N.Y.) ■..................Dec. 12
Polytechnic (N.Y.) ■..............Dec. 14
Mt. St. Vincent.....................Dec. 18
St. Joseph's (L.I.) ■..............Dec. 22
John Jay...............................Jan. 26
Brooklyn ■............................Jan. 28
St. Joe's-Brooklyn.................Jan. 30
Maritime (N.Y.).....................Feb. 1
N.J. Inst. of Tech. ■..............Feb. 3
Polytechnic (N.Y.) ■..............Feb. 11
Stevens Tech ■.....................Feb. 13
CCNY...................................Feb. 17
St. Joseph's (L.I.)................Feb. 20

1995-96 RESULTS (13-12)
Results unavailable

Nickname: Maccabees
Colors: Blue & White
Arena: Max Stern Athletic Center
  Capacity: 1,100; Year Built: 1985
AD: Stephen Young
SID: To be named

YORK (N.Y.)
Jamaica, NY 11451.................III

Coach: Ronald St. John
Alma Mater: York (N.Y.) '80
Record: 8 Years, W-99, L-107

1996-97 SCHEDULE
Plattsburgh Cl.......................Nov. 22-23
Staten Island........................Nov. 25
Hunter.................................Dec. 4
St. Thomas Aquinas Tr..........Dec. 6-7
Brooklyn ■............................Dec. 11
Old Westbury ■.....................Dec. 13
St. Vincent Tr.......................Dec. 28-29
Kean....................................Jan. 8
Rutgers-Newark ■..................Jan. 10
John Jay ■............................Jan. 13
CCNY ■................................Jan. 24
Medgar Evers.......................Jan. 27
Bloomfield ■.........................Feb. 3
Medgar Evers ■....................Feb. 7
Hunter ■..............................Feb. 10
Brooklyn..............................Feb. 12
Lehman...............................Feb. 14
Staten Island ■.....................Feb. 17
Baruch.................................Feb. 19
Merchant Marine ■................Feb. 21

1995-96 RESULTS (18-10)

82	Frostburg St.	78
48	Baldwin-Wallace †	76
76	Staten Island ■	85
73	Hunter ■	66
75	St. Vincent	84
79	Villa Julie †	77
59	Ramapo	79
86	LIU-Southampton ■	92
84	Old Westbury	73
65	Richard Stockton ■	69
67	Staten Island	79
75	Rutgers-Camden	53
88	Bethany (W.Va.) ■	86
107	Pratt ■	48
93	CCNY	66
98	Medgar Evers ■	67
70	New York U.	75
88	Lehman ■	67
79	Baruch ■	69
108	Medgar Evers	67
112	Hunter	70
86	Bloomfield	72
75	John Jay	63
111	Brooklyn	77
69	CCNY †	66
51	John Jay †	47
62	Staten Island †	66
66	Rowan	130

Nickname: Cardinals
Colors: Red & White
Arena: Health & P.E. Complex
  Capacity: 1,200; Year Built: 1990
AD: Stu Bailin
SID: To be named

YORK (PA.)
York, PA 17405.....................III

Coach: Jeff Gamber
Alma Mater: Millersville '68
Record: 19 Years, W-244, L-246

1996-97 SCHEDULE
Frank. & Marsh. Cl..............Nov. 22-23
Susquehanna ■......................Nov. 25
Gettysburg ■.........................Dec. 2
Gallaudet ■...........................Dec. 4
Salisbury St...........................Dec. 10
York (Pa.) Cl........................Dec. 28-29
Buffalo St. Inv......................Jan. 3-4
Goucher ■.............................Jan. 15
Marymount (Va.)...................Jan. 18
Dickinson.............................Jan. 20
Catholic...............................Jan. 22
St. Mary's (Md.) ■................Jan. 25
Frank. & Marsh. ■................Jan. 27
Gallaudet.............................Jan. 30
Mary Washington ■...............Feb. 1
Goucher...............................Feb. 5
Salisbury St. ■......................Feb. 8
Marymount (Va.) ■................Feb. 12
St. Mary's (Md.)..................Feb. 15

Catholic ■............................Feb. 19
Mary Washington..................Feb. 22

1995-96 RESULTS (9-16)

77	Frank. & Marsh.	81
78	Lebanon Valley ■	92
82	Susquehanna	77
71	Gettysburg ■	88
66	Villa Julie ■	65
86	St. Vincent	77
45	Frank. & Marsh. ■	79
72	Gallaudet ■	57
76	Salisbury St.	82
59	Juniata	76
64	Goucher ■	75
38	Catholic	67
84	Dickinson	68
73	Marymount (Va.)	77
74	St. Mary's (Md.) ■	52
63	Bloomsburg ■	86
60	Gallaudet	69
75	Mary Washington	70
72	Salisbury St. ■	80
86	Goucher	89
63	Catholic ■	98
76	Marymount (Va.) ■	84
62	Mary Washington	59
75	Marymount (Va.)	83
66	St. Mary's (Md.)	65

Nickname: Spartans
Colors: Green & White
Arena: Wolf Gym
  Capacity: 1,200; Year Built: 1964
AD: Jeff Gamber
SID: Scott Guise

YOUNGSTOWN ST.
Youngstown, OH 44555 I

Coach: Dan Peters
Alma Mater: Kent '76
Record: 11 Years, W-195, L-99

1996-97 SCHEDULE
Notre Dame..........................Nov. 26
St. Francis (Pa.) ■.................Nov. 30
St. Francis (Pa.)...................Dec. 3
La Roche ■...........................Dec. 7
Maine ■................................Dec. 13
Cleveland St..........................Dec. 16
Stetson.................................Dec. 21
Central Fla............................Dec. 23
Wright St. ■..........................Dec. 30
Central Conn. St. ■...............Jan. 2
Valparaiso............................Jan. 6
Western Ill............................Jan. 8
Troy St. ■.............................Jan. 11
Mo.-Kansas City ■.................Jan. 13
Siena ■.................................Jan. 18
Buffalo.................................Jan. 22
Northeastern Ill.....................Jan. 25
Chicago St............................Jan. 27
Western Ill. ■........................Feb. 1
Valparaiso ■..........................Feb. 3
Mo.-Kansas City....................Feb. 6
Troy St. ....Feb. 8
Buffalo.................................Feb. 12
Chicago St. ■........................Feb. 15
Northeastern Ill. ■.................Feb. 17
Central Conn. St. ....Feb. 24
Mid-Continent Conf. Tr. ....Mar. 2-4

1995-96 RESULTS (12-15)

61	Northwestern	67
84	Wash. & Jeff. ■	44
84	Kenyon ■	58
59	Cleveland St. ■	49
54	Maine	70
66	Wright St.	74
66	Robert Morris	59
69	Niagara ■	60
56	Buffalo	60
60	Western Ill.	64
66	Mo.-Kansas City	55
54	Northeastern Ill. ■	56
89	Chicago St. ■	59

68	Eastern Ill. 74	59	Mo.-Kansas City ■.....69	74	Eastern Ill. ■.....65	Colors: Red & White
63	Valparaiso 73	73	Western Ill. ■.....48	57	Central Conn. St. 66	Arena: Beeghley Center
90	Troy St. ■.....80	87	Chicago St. 75	88	Troy St. 93	Capacity: 8,000; Year Built: 1972
65	Central Conn. St. ■.....79	62	Northeastern Ill. 76	48	Western Ill. †.....68	AD: Jim Tressel
51	Buffalo ■.....53	75	Valparaiso ■.....60		Nickname: Penguins	SID: Greg Gulas

Tournament Information

1997 NCAA Championship Dates and Sites

DIVISION I:
First and second rounds, March 13-16—Auburn Hills, Michigan; Charlotte, North Carolina; Kansas City, Missouri; Memphis, Tennessee; Pittsburgh; Salt Lake City; Tucson, Arizona; Winston-Salem, North Carolina. Regionals, March 20-23—Birmingham, Alabama; San Antonio, Texas; San Jose, California; Syracuse, New York. Semifinals and final, March 29-31—Indianapolis.

DIVISION II:
Regionals, March 6-9—On-campus sites to be determined. Quarterfinals, semifinals and final, March 19-22—Louisville, Kentucky.

DIVISION III:
First Round, March 6—On-campus sites to be determined. Second Round, March 8—On-campus sites to be determined. Sectionals, March 14-15—On-campus sites to be determined. Finals, March 21-22—Salem, Virginia.

Division I Men's Conference Tournaments

Dates	Conference	Site of Finals
February 28-March 2	America East	Campus Site
March 6-9	Atlantic Coast	Greensboro, NC
March 5-9	Atlantic 10	Philadelphia
March 5-8	Big East	New York
March 6-8	Big Sky	Campus Site
February 26-March 1	Big South	Lynchburg, VA
March 6-9	Big 12	Kansas City, MO
March 7-9	Big West	Reno, NV
February 28-March 3	Colonial	Richmond, VA
March 5-8	Conference USA	St. Louis
March 1-3	Metro Atlantic	Buffalo, NY
February 28-March 4	Midwestern	Dayton, OH
March 4-8	Mid-American	Toledo, OH
March 2-4	Mid-Continent	Moline, IL
March 5-8	Mid-Eastern	Tallahassee, FL
February 28-March 3	Missouri Valley	St. Louis
February 25-March 6	Northeast	Campus Site
February 25-March 1	Ohio Valley	Nashville, TN
March 1-5	Patriot	Campus Site
March 6-9	Southeastern	Memphis, TN
February 27-March 2	Southern	Greensboro, NC
March 5-8	Southland	Shreveport, LA
March 5-8	Southwestern	To be named
February 28-March 4	Sun Belt	Little Rock, AR
February 27-March 1	Trans America	Charleston, SC
March 1-3	West Coast	Los Angeles
March 4-8	Western Athletic	Las Vegas, NV

1996-97 Division I In-Season Tournaments

Date	Tournament, Site	Participating Teams
Nov. 20-29	Preseason NIT, New York, NY	Ark.-Little Rock, Drexel, Duke, Evansville, Indiana, Iona, Oklahoma St., Princeton, St. Joseph's (Pa.), St. Louis, St. Mary's (Cal.), Seton Hall, Tulsa, UCLA, Valparaiso, Vanderbilt
Nov. 22-23	Lobo Cl., Albuquerque, NM	Columbia, Eastern Wash., Grambling, New Mexico
Nov. 22-23	Red Auerbach Colonial Cl., Washington, D.C.	Boston U., Florida A&M, Geo. Washington, Holy Cross
Nov. 22-24	Top of the World Cl., Fairbanks, AK	Alabama, Alas.-Fairbanks, Baylor, Middle Tenn. St., Montana, N.C.-Wilmington, Providence, Southern Ill.
Nov. 25-27	Maui Inv., Lahaina, HI	California, Chaminade, Iowa, Kansas, LSU, Massachusetts, South Caro., Virginia
Nov. 27-30	Carrs Great Alaska Shootout, Anchorage, AK	Alas.-Anchorage, Arizona St., Charleston (S.C.), Kentucky, Maine, N.C.-Greensboro, Stanford, Syracuse
Nov. 29-30	Coors Light Cl., Fresno, CA	Cal Poly SLO, Fresno St., Liberty, Northeastern
Nov. 29-30	First Merchants Bank/CVC Cl., Muncie, IN	Ball St., Coastal Caro., Southwest Texas St., Troy St.
Nov. 29-30	Union Planters Cl., Cape Girardeau, MO	Norfolk St., North Texas, Samford, Southeast Mo. St.
Nov. 29-Dec. 1	Big Island Inv., Hilo, HI	Auburn, Colorado, Hawaii-Hilo, Illinois, Louisville, Montana St., Texas Christian, Virginia Tech
Nov. 29-Dec. 1	Puerto Rico Shootout, Bayamon, PR	American (P.R.), Butler, Tulane, Villanova
Nov. 29-Dec. 1	San Juan Shootout, San Juan, PR	Clemson, Creighton, Delaware, Florida, Minnesota, Missouri, Puerto Rico, Tenn.-Chatt.
Nov. 29-Dec. 1	United Airlines Tip-Off, Honolulu, HI	Austin Peay, Detroit, Hawaii, Portland
Nov. 30-Dec. 1	Summit Bank Cl., Jersey City, NJ	Dartmouth, Florida Int'l, St. Peter's, Wagner
Dec. 5-6	Cyclone Challenge, Ames, IA	Iowa St., Siena, Stephen F. Austin, Tenn.-Martin
Dec. 5-7	The Gaucho Cl., Santa Barbara, CA	Akron, UC Santa Barb., Rider, Westmont
Dec. 6-7	Ameritas Cl., Lincoln, NE	Bowling Green, Colgate, Coppin St., Nebraska
Dec. 6-7	Bank One-Foothills Dodge Ram Cl., Fort Collins, CO	Cal St.-Sacramento, Colorado St., Gonzaga, Tex.-San Antonio
Dec. 6-7	Boilermaker Inv., West Lafayette, IN	Cornell, Long Beach St., Mercer, Purdue
Dec. 6-7	Dr. Pepper Inv., Waco, TX	Baylor, Miami (Ohio), Northeast La., Texas Southern
Dec. 6-7	First Bank Cl., Milwaukee, WI	Marquette, Prairie View, Princeton, Rice
Dec. 6-7	Harris Teeter/Pepsi Challenge, Charlotte, NC	North Caro., N.C.-Charlotte, South Caro., Southern Cal
Dec. 6-7	Hawaii Invitation, Honolulu, HI	Alabama St., Hawaii, McNeese St., St. Mary's (Cal.)
Dec. 6-7	Illini Cl., Champaign, IL	Central Mich., Columbia, Illinois, Tennessee St.
Dec. 6-7	KYLT/Coca-Cola Cl., Missoula, MT	American, Montana, Oral Roberts, Southern Utah
Dec. 6-7	MetLife Cl., San Francisco, CA	Fairfield, New Orleans, San Francisco, Santa Clara
Dec. 6-7	Pepsi-Marist Cl., Poughkeepsie, NY	Charleston So., Lafayette, Marist, Yale
Dec. 6-7	Pizza Hut Cl., Springfield, MO	Mississippi Val., Morehead St., Southwest Mo. St., Troy St.
Dec. 6-7	Super Chevy Shootout, Iowa City, IA	Grambling, Iowa, La Salle, Southern Miss.
Dec. 6-7	Tom Roberson Cl., Jacksonville, AL	Baptist Christian, Jacksonville St., Lenoir-Rhyne, Piedmont
Dec. 8-9	Franklin National Bank Tr., Landover, MD	California, Geo. Washington, Maryland, Mississippi St.
Dec. 13-14	Carrier Cl., Syracuse, NY	Eastern Mich., Old Dominion, Pepperdine, Syracuse
Dec. 13-14	Cougar Cl., Provo, UT	Boise St., Brigham Young, Houston, St. Mary's (Cal.)
Dec. 13-14	Indiana Cl., Bloomington, IN	Eastern Ill., Indiana, Louisiana Tech, Santa Clara
Dec. 14-15	Hawaii-Nike Festival, Honolulu, HI	UAB, Ball St., Cal Poly SLO, Hawaii

Date	Tournament, Site	Participating Teams
Dec. 20-21	UAB Cl., Birmingham, AL	UAB, Jacksonville St., LIU-Brooklyn, Stephen F. Austin
Dec. 20-21	USF Holiday Inv., Tampa, FL	Central Conn. St., Central Mich., St. Francis (N.Y.), South Fla.
Dec. 21-22	Iowa St. Holiday Cl., Ames, IA	East Tenn. St., Iowa St., Nevada, UTEP
Dec. 26-28	Chemical Bank ECAC Holiday Festival, New York	Georgia Tech, Hofstra, Manhattan, St. John's (N.Y.)
Dec. 27-28	Albertsons Holiday Cl., Boise, ID	Boise St., Campbell, Gonzaga, Idaho St.
Dec. 27-28	All College Tr., Oklahoma City	Oklahoma, Southwest Mo. St., Tulsa, Western Ill.
Dec. 27-28	ASU Tribune Cl., Tempe, AZ	UAB, Arizona St., St. Bonaventure, William & Mary
Dec. 27-28	Bow Tie Cl., Emmitsburg, MD	Maine, Mt. St. Mary's (Md.), N.C.-Asheville, N.C.-Wilmington
Dec. 27-28	Cable Car Cl., Santa Clara, CA	Alabama, Detroit, San Jose St., Santa Clara
Dec. 27-28	Cessna Cl., Wichita, KS	Sam Houston St., Texas Christian, Va. Commonwealth, Wichita St.
Dec. 27-28	Cowboy Shootout, Casper, WY	New Mexico St., Southern Ill., Texas Tech, Wyoming
Dec. 27-28	Ford Far West Cl., Portland, OR	Bradley, Oregon, Oregon St., Temple
Dec. 27-28	Golden Bear Cl., Berkeley, CA	California, Cal Poly SLO, Howard, La Salle
Dec. 27-28	Hoosier Cl., Indianapolis	Army, Colgate, Indiana, Valparaiso
Dec. 27-28	Jones Intercable Lobo Inv., Albuquerque, NM	Appalachian St., Bucknell, Mississippi, New Mexico
Dec. 27-28	Oldsmobile Spartan Cl., East Lansing, MI	Coppin St., Kent, Michigan St., Weber St.
Dec. 27-28	USF Cl., Tampa, FL	Boston U., Loyola (Md.), Monmouth (N.J.), South Fla.
Dec. 27-28	Iona Pepsi Cl., New Rochelle, NY	Eastern Ky., Iona, Northeastern, Richmond
Dec. 27-28	Sun Carnival Tr., El Paso, TX	Northern Iowa, Princeton, Texas A&M, UTEP
Dec. 27-28	UNO Christmas Cl., New Orleans	Hampton, Harvard, Holy Cross, New Orleans
Dec. 27-28	Gossner Aggie Cl., Logan, UT	Portland, Samford, Texas Southern, Utah St.
Dec. 27-30	Outrigger Rainbow Cl., Honolulu, HI	Georgia, Hawaii, Maryland, Memphis, Michigan, Northwestern, Pittsburgh, Washington St.
Dec. 28-29	Bobcat Holiday Stores Cl., Bozeman, MT	Air Force, Cornell, Montana St., Tennessee Tech
Dec. 28-29	Dr. Pepper Cl., Chattanooga, TN	Canisius, Central Fla., Coastal Caro., Tenn.-Chatt.
Dec. 28-29	Franklin Life Cougar Cl., Charleston, SC	Charleston (S.C.), Drexel, N.C.-Greensboro, Northern Ill.
Dec. 28-30	Bank One Fiesta Bowl Cl., Tucson, AZ	Arizona, Florida, Pennsylvania, Robert Morris
Dec. 28-30	Hawaii-Hilo Shootout, Hilo, HI	Eastern Mich., Hawaii-Hilo, Idaho, Liberty
Dec. 29-30	Toledo MVP Cl., Toledo, OH	Buffalo, Dartmouth, Ga. Southern, Toledo
Dec. 29-30	Seton Hall/Meadowlands Tr., East Rutherford, NJ	Alas.-Anchorage, Rhode Island, San Francisco, Seton Hall
Dec. 30-31	Pepsi Oneida Bingo & Casino Cl., Green Bay, WI	Austin Peay, Pepperdine, St. Joseph's (Pa.), Wis.-Green Bay
Dec. 30-Jan. 1	Puerto Rico Tr., San Juan, PR	Bowling Green, Cincinnati, Fresno St., Mississippi St., Nebraska, Old Dominion, Southeast Mo. St., Southwest Mo. St.